NEW DICTIONARY OF THEOLOGY

HISTORICAL AND SYSTEMATIC

SECOND EDITION

NEW DICTIONARY OF
THEOLOGY

HISTORICAL AND SYSTEMATIC

SECOND EDITION

Editors:

Martin Davie
Tutor in Doctrine at Wycliffe Hall, Oxford

Tim Grass
Senior Research Fellow at Spurgeon's College, London

Stephen R. Holmes
Senior Lecturer in Theology at the University of St Andrews, Scotland

John McDowell
Director of Research, University of Divinity, Australia

T. A. Noble
Senior Research Fellow in Theology at the Nazarene Theological College, Manchester, and Research Professor of Theology at the Nazarene Theological Seminary, Kansas City, Missouri

Consulting editors:

Roland Chia
Chew Hock Hin Professor of Christian Doctrine and Dean of the School of Postgraduate Studies, Trinity Theological College, Singapore

David Emmanuel Singh
Research Tutor in Islamic Studies, Oxford Centre for Mission Studies

Kevin J. Vanhoozer
Research Professor of Systematic Theology at Trinity Evangelical Divinity School, Deerfield, Illinois

Inter-Varsity Press
London, England

InterVarsity Press
Downers Grove, Illinois, USA

INTER-VARSITY PRESS
36 Causton Street, London SW1P 4ST, England
Email: ivp@ivpbooks.com
Website: www.ivpbooks.com

© Inter-Varsity Press, 2016

All rights reserved. No part of this publication may be reproduced, stored in a retrieval system, or transmitted, in any form or by any means, electronic, mechanical, photocopying, recording or otherwise, without the prior permission of the publisher or the Copyright Licensing Agency.

Unless otherwise indicated, Scripture quotations are from the Holy Bible, New International Version. Copyright © 1973, 1978, 1984 by International Bible Society. Used by permission of Biblica, Inc.® All rights reserved worldwide. 'NIV' is a registered trademark of International Bible Society. UK trademark number 1448790.

Scripture quotations marked NRSV are from the New Revised Standard Version Bible, copyright © 1989 the Division of Christian Education of the National Council of Churches of Christ in the United States of America. Used by permission. All rights reserved.

Scripture quotations marked KJV are from the King James Version of the Bible.

First published 2016
Reprinted 2017

British Library Cataloguing-in-Publication Data
A catalogue record for this book is available from the British Library.

ISBN: 978-1-78359-396-5
eBook ISBN: 978-1-78359-457-3

Set in Sabon
Typeset in Great Britain by CRB Associates, Potterhanworth, Lincolnshire
Printed and bound by CPI Group (UK) Ltd, Croydon, CR0 4YY

Inter-Varsity Press publishes Christian books that are true to the Bible and that communicate the gospel, develop discipleship and strengthen the church for its mission in the world.

IVP originated within the Inter-Varsity Fellowship, now the Universities and Colleges Christian Fellowship, a student movement connecting Christian Unions in universities and colleges throughout Great Britain, and a member movement of the International Fellowship of Evangelical Students. Website: www.uccf.org.uk. That historic association is maintained, and all senior IVP staff and committee members subscribe to the UCCF Basis of Faith.

Contents

Preface to the first edition — vii

Preface to the second edition — ix

How to use this Dictionary — xi

Abbreviations — xiii

List of contributors — xvii

Dictionary articles — 1

Index of names — 987

Index of subjects — 997

Index of articles — 1011

Preface to the first edition

'Everything a theologian does in the church,' said Martin Luther, 'contributes to the spread of the knowledge of God and the salvation of men.' That may not sum up every Christian's attitude to theologians and theology, but it strikes the right note. The root meaning of 'theology' is 'speaking about God'. What Christian theology seeks to do is to spell out the significance of God's revelation, supremely in Jesus Christ, of himself and his provision and purposes for his world and the men and women he has made. Theology does this in different ways, some of which are suggested by qualifying epithets such as 'biblical', 'historical' and 'systematic'. Yet all the various methods and models of theology aim to set forth an ordered understanding of the revealed mind of God – about himself, about his creatures in this world, and about the way he plans us to live in fellowship with himself and one another. The Christian whose diet has no theological content is likely to suffer from stunted or unbalanced growth instead of developing maturity of mind and heart.

This Dictionary is intended to provide the enquiring reader with a basic introduction to the world of theology – its themes, both majestic and minor, its famous formulations and its important historical moments, its distinguished – and notorious – exponents, past as well as present, its sources, disciplines and styles, its technical vocabulary, its ebb and flow in movements, schools and traditions, and its interaction with other currents of thought and religion. While the common standpoint of the editors and contributors is allegiance to the supreme authority of the Scriptures, and their shared concern to set forth a biblical basis for theological knowledge and judgment, no attempt has been made to exclude or minimize diversity of interpretation within these boundary marks.

The production of a volume like this would never have been possible without the contributions of many individuals over many months. Special mention must be made of Richard Bauckham, who helped in the planning stages, and of successive theological editors of IVP, David Preston, Claire Evans and David Kingdon. The last-named has borne the heat and burden of the main part of the day. Their reward, and ours, in part will be the knowledge that this Dictionary fulfils its purpose – to promote an informed and biblically controlled approach to thinking and speaking about God and his works.

SINCLAIR B. FERGUSON
DAVID F. WRIGHT

Preface to the second edition

Many students and readers have expressed their appreciation for the *New Dictionary of Theology* (1988). As the second of the dictionaries produced by IVP (the first being the *New Bible Dictionary* in 1962), it has been a trustworthy and informative guide. After almost thirty years, however, there are many new writers, issues and themes on the agenda, for theology does not stand still, and this second edition therefore has over 400 new articles. Many of the existing articles have been expanded and amended, and almost all have additional bibliographical references.

The editors have tried to give more attention in this mainly British publication to theological writers and themes in North America and around the world. The excellent material on biblical theology has been (regretfully) deleted, since this subject is now covered at length in IVP's *New Dictionary of Biblical Theology* (2000). This book is therefore now more specifically a dictionary of systematic and historical theology, though we recognize that this cannot but take its rise from biblical theology.

Like the original editors, the revising editors share a commitment to the historic Christian faith and particularly to the evangelical tradition which acknowledges that our systematic theology is under the authority of Holy Scripture. This can be acknowledged without apology, since the false concept of objectivity as the stating of completely neutral facts, an activity incompatible with commitment to any position or viewpoint, is now regarded as an illusion. Nevertheless, the editors aspire to that degree of objectivity which begins with an acknowledgment of our own perspective, and therefore every care has been taken throughout the Dictionary to give a fair and accurate account not only of every tradition of evangelical theology, but of every Christian, and indeed every non-Christian, stance.

Thanks are due to all who have contributed, and particularly to the organizing editor, Steve Carter, whose work was completed by Dr Philip Duce. We acknowledge our debt to the original editors, Dr Sinclair Ferguson and Professor David Wright, and to the original consulting editor, Dr J. I. Packer. We dedicate this second edition to the late David F. Wright, Professor Emeritus of Patristic and Reformed Theology at the University of Edinburgh, in gratitude for his Christian witness and the painstaking scholarship which made him a guide and mentor to so many.

MARTIN DAVIE
TIM GRASS
STEPHEN HOLMES
JOHN MCDOWELL
T. A. NOBLE

How to use this Dictionary

Cross-references
It has been editorial policy in this Dictionary to group smaller topics together and treat them in a single longer article. For example, the various Reformation and post-Reformation 'Confessions of Faith' are collected under CONFESSIONS OF FAITH, and many matters are subsumed under EUCHARIST. Cross-referencing is therefore important. Four methods are in use:

1. Numerous one-line entries refer the user to the title of the article or articles where the topic is treated: e.g. COMMON GRACE, *see* GRACE.
2. An asterisk before a word or phrase indicates that further relevant information will be found in the article under that title. Readers should note:
   a. The form of the word asterisked will not always be precisely the same as that of the article to which the asterisk refers. For example, '*Trinitarianism' directs the reader to the article on TRINITY.
   b. The asterisk sometimes applies to two or three words rather than to the word asterisked. Thus, for example, '*covenant theology' directs you to the article COVENANT THEOLOGY.
3. A reference in brackets in the body of an article such as '(see *Angels)' speaks for itself.
4. A cross-reference at the end of an article is also self-explanatory: e.g. *See also:* ANABAPTIST THEOLOGY.

Abbreviations
A list of abbreviations used in the Dictionary is given on pp. xiii–xv.

Bibliographies
Guidance for further study has been provided for virtually every article, at the end. Writings by the subject of the article are placed first. The works listed in a Bibliography may include studies that take a different position from that of the contributor of the article.

Bible versions
Quotations from the Bible are from the New International Version (1984), unless otherwise indicated.

Abbreviations

1. Books and journals

ACW	*Ancient Christian Writers* (Westminster, MD, and London, etc., 1946–)
ANCL	*Ante-Nicene Christian Library*, 25 vols. (Edinburgh, 1866–97)
ANF	*Ante-Nicene Fathers* (re-edition of *ANCL* in 10 vols., Buffalo and New York, 1885–96, and Grand Rapids, MI, 1950–51)
AV(KJV)	Authorized Version (King James), 1611
BDE	*Biographical Dictionary of Evangelicals* (Leicester, 2003)
BJRL	*Bulletin of the John Rylands Library* (Manchester, 1903–)
BS	*Bibliotheca Sacra* (New York, etc., 1843–)
BZNW	Beiheft zur ZNW
CCCM	*Corpus Christianorum, Continuatio Medievalis* (Turnhout, 1966–)
CCET	*Cambridge Companion to Evangelical Theology*, ed. D. Treier and T. Larsen (Cambridge, 2007)
CCL	*Corpus Christianorum, Series Latina* (Turnhout, 1935–)
CD	*Church Dogmatics*, Karl Barth, 4 vols. in 13 + index vol. (ET, Edinburgh, 1936–81)
CG	*Christian Graduate* (London, etc., 1948–83)
CH	*Church History* (Scottdale, PA, etc., 1932–)
CHLGEMP	*Cambridge History of Later Greek and Early Medieval Philosophy*, ed. A. H. Armstrong (Cambridge, 1967)
CPG	*Clavis Patrum Graecorum*, ed. M. Geerard (Turnhout, 1983–)
CT	*Christianity Today* (Washington, 1956–)
CTJ	*Calvin Theological Journal* (Grand Rapids, MI, 1966–)
DBS	*Dictionnaire de la Bible*, Supplement, ed. L. Pirot *et al.* Paris, 1928–)
DCB	*Dictionary of Christian Biography*, ed. W. Smith and H. Wace, 4 vols. (London, 1877–87)
DEM	*Dictionary of the Ecumenical Movement* (Geneva, 1991)
DHT	*Dictionary of Historical Theology*, ed. T. A. Hart (Grand Rapids and Carlisle, 2000)
DLNTD	*Dictionary of the Later New Testament and Its Developments*, ed. R. P. Martin and P. H. Davids (Leicester, 1997)
DNB	*Dictionary of National Biography*, ed. L. Stephen and S. Lee *et al.* (London, 1885–)
DSp	*Dictionnaire de Spiritualité*, ed. M. Viller *et al.* (Paris, 1937–)
DTC	*Dictionnaire de théologie catholique*, ed. A. Vacant *et al.*, 15 vols. (Paris, 1903–50)
EC	*Encyclopedia of Christianity*, vols. 1–4 (no more published), eds. E. H. Palmer, G. G. Cohen and P. E. Hughes (Wilmington, DL, and Marshalton, DL, 1964–72)
EP	*Encyclopedia of Philosophy*, ed. P. Edwards, 8 vols. (New York, 1967)
EQ	*Evangelical Quarterly* (London, etc., 1929–)
ERE	*Encyclopaedia of Religion and Ethics*, ed. J. Hastings, 13 vols. (Edinburgh, 1908–26)
FC	*Fathers of the Church* (New York, etc., 1947–)
HR	*History of Religions* (Chicago, 1961–)
HTR	*Harvard Theological Review* (New York, etc., 1908–)
IJT	*Indian Journal of Theology* (Serampore, etc., 1952–)
Institutes	John Calvin, *Institutes of the Christian Religion*, tr. F. L. Battles, ed. J. T. McNeill, 2 vols. (London, 1961)
JAAR	*Journal of the American Academy of Religion* (Chambersburg, PA, 1967–)

Abbreviations

JEH	*Journal of Ecclesiastical History* (London, 1950–)
JETS	*Journal of the Evangelical Theological Society* (Wheaton, IL, 1969–)
JR	*Journal of Religion* (Chicago, 1921–)
JTS	*Journal of Theological Studies* (Oxford, 1899–)
LCC	*Library of Christian Classics*, 26 vols. (London and Philadelphia, 1953–70)
LCL	*Loeb Classical Library* (London and Cambridge, MA, 1912–)
LW	*Luther's Works* ('American edition'), ed. J. Pelikan and H. T. Lehmann (Philadelphia and St Louis, MO, 1955–)
MQR	*Mennonite Quarterly Review* (Goshen, IN, 1927–)
NCE	*New Catholic Encyclopedia*, ed. W. J. McDonald, 17 vols. (New York, 1967–79)
NIDNTT	*The New International Dictionary of New Testament Theology*, ed. C. Brown, 3 vols. (Exeter, 1975–8)
NPNF	*A Select Library of Nicene and Post-Nicene Fathers of the Christian Church*, First Series, ed. P. Schaff, 14 vols. (New York, 1886–90); Second Series, ed. H. Wace and P. Schaff, 14 vols. (New York, 1890–1900); new edition (Grand Rapids, MI, 1980)
NRT	*Nouvelle revue théologique* (Tournai, etc., 1879–)
NTS	*New Testament Studies* (Cambridge, 1954–)
PG	*Patrologia Graeca*, ed. J. P. Migne, 162 vols. (Paris, 1857–66)
PL	*Patrologia Latina*, ed. J. P. Migne, 221 vols. (Paris, 1844–64)
PTR	*Princeton Theological Review* (Philadelphia, 1903–29)
RB	*Revue Biblique* (Paris, 1892–)
RBén	*Revue Bénédictine* (Maredsous, 1884–)
RGG	*Die Religion in Geschichte und Gegenwart*, ed. K. Galling, 7 vols. (Tübingen, ^{3}1957–65)
SJT	*Scottish Journal of Theology* (Edinburgh, etc., 1948–)
SL	*Studia Liturgica* (Rotterdam, 1962–)
SM	*Sacramentum Mundi*, ed. K. Rahner et al., 5 vols. (New York, 1968–70)
SP	*Studia Patristica* (Berlin, etc., 1957–)
TDNT	*Theological Dictionary of the New Testament*, ed. G. W. Bromiley, 10 vols. (Grand Rapids, MI, 1964–76), ET of Theologisches Worterbuch zum Neuen Testament, ed. G. Kittell and G. Friedrich (Stuttgart, 1932–74)
Th	*Theology* (London, 1920–)
Them	*Themelios* (Lausanne, 1962–74; new series, London, etc., 1975–)
Tr	*Transformation* (Exeter, 1984–)
TRE	*Theologische Realenzyklopädie*, ed. G. Krause et al. (Berlin, NY, 1977–)
TS	*Theological Studies* (Woodstock, MD, 1940–)
TynB	*Tyndale Bulletin* (London, etc., 1956–)
VC	*Vigiliae Christianae* (Amsterdam, 1947–)
VT	*Vetus Testamentum* (Leiden, 1951–)
USQR	*Union Seminary Quarterly Review* (New York, 1945–)
WTJ	*Westminster Theological Journal* (Philadelphia, 1938–)
ZKG	*Zeitschrift für Kirchengeschichte* (Gotha, etc., 1877–)
ZTK	*Zeitschrift für Theologie und Kirche* (Tübingen, 1891–)

Editions are indicated by small superior figures: ^{2}2000.

2. Early Christian works

EH	Eusebius, *Ecclesiastical History*
Ep.	Polycarp, *Epistles to the Philippians*
Eph.	Ignatius, *Ephesians*
Strom.	Clement of Alexandria, *Stromateis*
Trall.	Ignatius, *Trallians*

Abbreviations

3. Biblical books

Books of the Old Testament
Gen., Exod., Lev., Num., Deut., Josh., Judg., Ruth, 1, 2 Sam., 1, 2 Kgs, 1, 2 Chr., Neh., Esth., Job, Ps. (Pss), Prov., Eccl., Song, Isa., Jer., Lam., Ezek., Dan., Hos., Joel, Amos, Obad., Jon., Mic., Nah., Hab., Zeph., Hag., Zech., Mal.

Books of the New Testament
Matt., Mark, Luke, John, Acts, Rom., 1, 2 Cor., Gal., Eph., Phil., Col., 1, 2 Thess., 1, 2 Tim., Titus, Phlm., Heb., Jas, 1, 2 Pet., 1, 2, 3 John, Rev.

4. General abbreviations

b.	born
c.	*circa*. (Lat.), about, approximately
cf.	*confer* (Lat.), compare
ch. (chs.)	chapter(s)
col. (cols.)	column(s)
d.	died
Ecclus.	Ecclesiasticus (Apocrypha)
ed. (eds.)	edited by, edition, editor(s)
Eng.	English
ET	English translation
et al.	*et alii* (Lat.), and others
EVV	English versions
f. (ff.)	and the following (verse(s), etc.)
fl.	*floruit* (Lat.), flourished
Ger.	German
Gk	Greek
Heb.	Hebrew
ibid.	ibidem (Lat.), the same work
idem	idem (Lat.), the same author
Lat.	Latin
lit.	literally
loc. cit.	*loco citato* (Lat.), in the place already quoted
Macc.	Maccabees (Apocrypha)
n.s.	new series
NT	New Testament
OT	Old Testament
par.	and parallel(s)
repr.	reprinted
tr.	translated, translation
v. (vv.)	verse(s)
viz.	*videlicit* (Lat.), namely
vol. (vols.)	volume(s)

List of contributors

Adams, N., Senior Lecturer in Theology and Philosophy, University of Edinburgh

Albin, T. R., Minister, United Methodist Church

Alsford, S. E., Senior Lecturer in Teaching and Learning, and Deputy Head of EDU, University of Greenwich

Althaus-Reid, M. (d. 2009), formerly Professor of Contextual Theology, New College, University of Edinburgh

Anderson, J. N., Associate Professor of Theology and Philosophy, Reformed Theological Seminary, Charlotte, USA

Armerding, C. E., formerly Academic Director, Schloss Mittersill Study Centre, Austria

Ashenden, G., Vicar, St Martin de Gouray, Jersey

Asprey, C. J. R., formerly doctoral candidate, University of Aberdeen

Atkinson, J. (d. 2011), Emeritus Professor of Biblical Studies, University of Sheffield

Avis, P. D. L., Chaplain to HRH Queen Elizabeth II, Director of Centre for the Study of the Christian Church, University of Exeter, and Editor in Chief, *Ecclesiology* magazine

Bacon, H. J., Senior Lecturer and Deputy Head, Department of Theology and Religious Studies, University of Chester

Badcock, G. D., Professor of Divinity and Chair of Graduate Programme, Faculty of Theology, Huron University College, Canada

Baker, J. P. (d.), formerly Rector of Newick, Lewes, East Sussex

Barclay, O. R. (d. 2013), formerly General Secretary of UCCF and Honorary Vice-President, IFES

Bartos, E., Dean of Theology, Emmanuel Bible Institute, Oradea, Romania

Bauckham, R. J., Emeritus Professor of New Testament Studies, University of St Andrews, and Senior Scholar, Ridley Hall, Cambridge

Baxter, C. A., formerly Principal, St John's College, Nottingham

Bebbington, D. W., Professor of History, University of Stirling

Bechtel, P. M. (d. 1998), formerly Chair, English Department, Wheaton College

Beck, W. D., formerly Professor of Philosophy, Liberty Baptist College, Virginia, USA

Beckwith, R. T., formerly Warden of Latimer House, Oxford

Bediako, K. (d. 2008), Founder of Krofi Christaller Memorial Centre for Mission Studies, Ghana

Beeke, J. R., President and Professor of Systematic Theology and Homiletics at Puritan Reformed Theological Seminary, and Pastor of the Heritage Netherlands Reformed Congregation in Grand Rapids, Michigan

Berry, R. J., Professor Emeritus of Genetics, University College London

Beyerhaus, P. P. J., formerly Professor of Missiology and Ecumenical Theology and Dean of the Theological Faculty, University of Tübingen, Germany

Bierma, L. D., P. J. Zondervan Professor of the History of Christianity, Calvin Theological Seminary, Michigan, USA

Billings, J. T., Gordon H. Girod Research Professor of Reformed Theology, Western Theological Seminary, Michigan, USA

Bingaman, B., Assistant Professor of Religious Studies, Wesleyan College, Georgia, USA

List of contributors

Blackham, P. R., Minister, Soul Church, Neath

Blocher, H. A. G., Gunther Knoedler Professor of Systematic Theology, Wheaton College Graduate School, Illinois, USA, and Professor of Systematic Theology, Faculté Libre de Théologie Évangélique, Vaux-sur-Seine, France

Bong, R. R., Academic Dean, Evangel Theological Seminary, Honolulu, USA

Bradshaw, T., Fellow and Tutor in Christian Doctrine, Senior Tutor and Tutor for Admissions, Regent's Park College, Oxford

Bray, G. L., Research Professor of Divinity, History and Doctrine, Beeson Divinity School, Samford, USA

Bretherton, L., Professor of Theological Ethics and Senior Fellow, Kenan Institute for Ethics, Duke Divinity School, North Carolina, USA

Breward, I., Emeritus Professor, Department of Church History, Catholic Theological College, Melbourne, Australia

Briggs, J., Professor Emeritus, University of Birmingham and sometime Director, Baptist History and Heritage Centre, Regent's Park College, University of Oxford

Bromiley, G. W. (d. 2009), formerly Professor Emeritus, Fuller Theological Seminary, California, USA

Brown, C., Senior Professor of Systematic Theology, Fuller Theological Seminary, California, USA

Brown, H. O. J. (d. 2007), formerly Professor and Mentor, Trinity Evangelical Divinity School and Reformed Theological Seminary, Illinois, USA

Brown, R., formerly Principal, Spurgeon's College, London

Bruce, F. F. (d. 1990), formerly Rylands Professor of Biblical Criticism and Exegesis, University of Manchester

Buchanan, C. O., formerly Bishop of Woolwich

Bunting, H., formerly Lecturer in Philosophy, University of Ulster, Northern Ireland

Burk, J. K., President, Interfaith CarePartners, Texas, USA

Cameron, N. M. de S., formerly Distinguished Professor of Theology and Culture, Trinity Evangelical Divinity School, and Provost, Trinity International University, Illinois, USA

Chaplin, J. P., Director of the Kirby Laing Institute for Christian Ethics, Tyndale House, Cambridge

Chestnutt, G. A., Minister, Church of Scotland, St John's Parish, Gourock

Chia, R., Chew Hock Hin Professor of Christian Doctrine, Trinity Theological College, Singapore

Chilcote, P. W., Academic Dean and Professor of Historical Theology and Wesleyan Studies, Ashland Theological Seminary, Ohio, USA

Chow, W. W., President Emeritus, China Graduate School of Theology, Hong Kong

Clark, A. C., Co-ordinator for the Philip Project, Friends International, Cambridge

Clark, D. K., formerly Associate Professor in Theology and Philosophy, Toccoa Falls College, Georgia, USA

Clark, K. J., Senior Research Fellow, Kaufman Interfaith Institute, Grand Valley State University, Michigan, USA

Clark, R. S., Professor of Church History and Historical Theology, Westminster Theological Seminary, California, USA

Clements, K., Co-ordinating Secretary for International Affairs, Council of Churches for Britain and Ireland

Clough, D. L., Professor of Theological Ethics, University of Chester

List of contributors

Clouse, R. G., Professor Emeritus, Department of History, Indiana State University, Indiana, USA

Clowney, D. W., Professor of Philosophy and Religious Studies, Rowan University, New Jersey, USA

Cole, G. A., Dean, Trinity Evangelical Divinity School, Illinois, USA

Colwell, J. E., Senior Research Fellow, Spurgeon's College, London

Colyer, E. M., Professor of Systematic Theology and Stanley Professor of Wesley Studies, University of Dubuque, Iowa, USA

Cook, E. D., Clinical Associate Professor of Marriage and Family Therapy, Wheaton College, Illinois, USA

Cortez, M., Adjunct Professor, Western Seminary and Associate Professor of Theology, Wheaton College, Illinois, USA

Cosden, D. T., Professor of Theological Studies, Judson University, Illinois, USA

Cotterell, F. P., formerly Associate Senior Lecturer, Islamic Studies, London School of Theology

Cowley, R. W. (d. 1986), formerly Course Leader of Non-Stipendiary Ministry Training Course, Oak Hill College, London

Crisp, O. D., Professor of Systematic Theology, Fuller Theological Seminary, California, USA

Croft, W. S., Priest in Charge, Diocese of Peterborough, UK

Cross, A. R., Member, Faculty of Theology and Religion, University of Oxford

Dallimore, A. (d. 1998), formerly Baptist Pastor and biographer

Daniel, C. D., Pastor, Faith Bible Church, Springfield, USA

Davie, M., Tutor of Doctrine, Wycliffe Hall, Oxford, and Theological Consultant, House of Bishops

Davis, D. C., formerly Chaplain and President, Redeemer Seminary, Texas, USA

De Graaff, G., Director of Studies and Tutor of Christian Doctrine and Ethics, South East Institute for Theological Education, Canterbury

Deboys, D. G., Associate Vicar, Tewkesbury Abbey

Demarest, B., formerly Senior Professor of Christian Theology and Spiritual Formation, Denver Seminary, Colorado, USA

Donner, T. G., Professor of Biblical History and Theology, Seminario Biblico de Colombia, Colombia

Douglas, J. D. (d. 2003), formerly Librarian, Tyndale House, Cambridge, and Editor of the *New Bible Dictionary*

Dowling, M., Visiting Lecturer, Old Testament and World Religions, Irish Baptist College

Dragas, G. D., Professor of Patristics, Hellenic College Holy Cross Greek Orthodox School of Theology, Massachusetts, USA

Drane, J., Affiliate Professor of New Testament and Practical Theology, Fuller Theological Seminary, California, USA, Fellow of St John's College, Durham, Trustee and Director of Fresh Expressions and Chair of the Mission Shaped Ministry Board

Draycott, A. J., Associate Professor of Biblical and Theological Studies, Biola University, California, USA

Duriez, C. P., writer of books and poetry

Elias, J. H. (d. 2011), formerly Senior Lecturer in Religious Studies, University of Glamorgan

Elliott, M. W., Professor of Historical and Biblical Theology, University of St Andrews

List of contributors

Ellis, B. E., Associate Publisher, Editorial for Lexham Press and Kirkdale Press

Ellis, K., Vicar of Holy Island, and Team Leader of the Bro Cybi Ministry Area

Escobar, S., Professor, Facultad Protestante de Teología UEBE, Madrid, Spain

Evans, E., Presbyterian Minister, Merthyr Tydfil

Faupel, D. W., Director of the Library and Professor of History of Christianity, Wesley Theological Seminary, Washington DC, USA

Feldmeth, N. P., Director of Faculty Development for Regional Campuses, and Assistant Professor of Church History, Fuller Theological Seminary, California, USA

Ferguson, E., Professor Emeritus of Church History, Abilene Christian University, Texas, USA

Ferguson, S. B., Professor of Systematic Theology, Redeemer Seminary, Texas, USA

Fields, B., Chair and Associate Professor of the Biblical and Systematic Theology Department, Trinity Evangelical Divinity School, South Chicago, USA

Flynn, G., Academic Leader for Research, Mater Dei Institute, Dublin

Forrester, D. B., Professor Emeritus, New College, University of Edinburgh

Forster, P. R., Bishop of Chester

Foster, B. E., formerly Pastor of Calvary Lutheran Church, Lemmon, South Dakota, USA

Frische, R. E., formerly Pastor at the Deaconesses' House, Bern, Switzerland, and Lecturer at the Preachers' College, St Crischona, Basel, Switzerland

Frost, R. N., Pastoral Care Consultant, Barnabas International, Illinois, USA

Gaffin, Jr, R. B., Emeritus Professor of Systematic Theology, Westminster Theological Seminary, Philadelphia, USA

Gasque, W. W., Executive Director, Pacific Association for Theological Studies, Canada

Gay, D., Lecturer in Theology and Religious Studies, University of Glasgow

Gazal, A. A., Member of the Religion Faculty, University of Northwestern Ohio, Ohio, USA

Geisler, N. L., Chancellor, Distinguished Professor of Theology and Apologetics and Occupant of the Norman L. Geisler Chair of Christian Apologetics, Veritas Evangelical Seminary, California, USA

Geivett, R. D., Professor of Philosophy, Talbot Department of Philosophy, Biola University, California, USA

Geldard, M. D., formerly Vicar of St John the Divine, Liverpool

Gerstner, J. H. (d. 1996), formerly Professor of Church History, Pittsburgh Theological Seminary, Pittsburgh, USA

Gilland, D. A., Senior Lecturer in Systematic Theology, University of Leuphana, Germany

Gladwin, J., formerly Bishop of Chelmsford and Chair of the Citizens Advice Bureau

Gleason, R., missionary, Nepal

Goddard, A., Senior Research Fellow, The Kirby Laing Institute for Christian Ethics, Cambridge

Goldingay, J., David Allan Hubbard Professor of Old Testament, Fuller Theological Seminary, California, USA

Goldsmith, M. F., international speaker, teacher and missiologist

Gordon, J., Principal, Scottish Baptist College, Scotland

Gordon, R. P., Emeritus Regius Professor of Hebrew, University of Cambridge

List of contributors

Gouldbourne, R., Minister, Bloomsbury Central Baptist Church, London

Graham, I., Parish Priest, The Greek Orthodox Community of the Holy Trinity, Oxford

Grass, T., Senior Research Fellow, Spurgeon's College, London, and Assistant Editor, Ecclesiastical History Society

Greaves, R. L. (d. 2004), formerly Robert O. Lawton Distinguished Professor of History, Florida State University, Florida, USA

Griffiths, M. C., formerly Principal, London Bible College

Hagner, D. A., George Eldon Ladd Professor Emeritus of New Testament and Senior Professor of New Testament, Fuller Theological Seminary, California, USA

Hancock, C. D., formerly Chaplain, Magdalene College, Cambridge

Hankins, Jr, J. D., formerly student at Trinity Evangelical Divinity School, PhD Theological Studies, Illinois, USA

Hardy, D. S., Professor of Spiritual Formation, Nazarene Theological Seminary, Missouri, USA

Harris, H., formerly Christian Scholar, Teversham, Cambridge

Harris, M. J., Professor Emeritus of New Testament Exegesis and Theology, Trinity Evangelical Divinity School, Illinois, USA

Harvey, T., Academic Dean, Oxford Centre for Mission Studies, Oxford

Haykin, M. A. G., Professor of Church History and Biblical Spirituality, The Southern Baptist Theological Seminary, Kentucky, USA

Heinze, R. W., Adjunct Professor, Wheaton College, Illinois, USA

Helm, P., Teaching Fellow of Philosophical Theology and John Calvin, Regent College, Vancouver, Canada

Hexham, I., Professor, Department of Religious Studies, University of Calgary, Alberta, Canada

Hicks, P. A. (d. 2013), formerly Baptist Pastor and Lecturer in Philosophy and Pastoral Care, London School of Theology

Higton, M., Professor, Department of Theology and Religion, University of Durham

Hilborn, D. H. K., Principal, St John's School of Mission, Nottingham

Hillyer, P. N., writer and editor

Hollingsworth, A., Assistant Professor of Theology, Boston University, Massachusetts, USA

Holmes, A. F. (d. 2011), formerly Professor of Philosophy, Wheaton College, Illinois, USA

Holmes, S. R., Senior Lecturer of Theology, University of St Andrews

Holtschneider, K. H., Senior Lecturer in Jewish Studies, School of Divinity, University of Edinburgh

Hordern, J. W. S., Lecturer in Theology, Jesus College, Oxford

Horrocks, D. G., Head of Public Affairs, Evangelical Alliance

Howard, T., formerly Professor of English, St John's Seminary, Massachusetts, USA

Hower, R. G., formerly Associate Professor of Church History, Evangelical Seminary, Myerstown, Pennsylvania, USA

Hughes, D. A., formerly Regional Coordinator, Tearfund, Wales

Ingersol, S., Denominational Archivist, Church of the Nazarene

Jason, N., formerly Pastor of Christ Church, Madras, India

Jensen, P. F., formerly Archbishop of Sydney, and Principal of Moore College, Sydney, Australia

List of contributors

Jenson, M., Associate Professor, Theology, Biola University, California, USA

Jones, D. G., Emeritus Professor of Anatomy, University of Otago, New Zealand

Jones, K., Senior Research Fellow, IBTS Centre, Amsterdam, the Netherlands

Jones, R. T., formerly Principal, Coleg Bala-Bangor, Bangor, Wales

Kanemoto, S. P., formerly Lecturer, Tokyo Christian College, Japan, and Lecturer, Kyoritsu Christian Institute, Japan

Kapic, K. M., Professor of Theological Studies, Covenant College, Georgia, USA

Kearsley, R., formerly Tutor, South Wales Baptist College

Kee, A. (d. 2011), formerly Professor of Religious Studies, University of Edinburgh

Keen, C. S., Professor, Department of Theology, Azusa Pacific University, California, USA

Keith, G. A., former school teacher, Ayr

Kelly, D. F., Richard Jordan Professor of Theology, Reformed Theological Seminary, Florida, USA

Kessler, E., Founder and Director, Woolf Institute, Cambridge

Kirby, G. W. (d. 2006), formerly Principal of London School of Theology

Kirk, J. A., Research Supervisor, London School of Theology

Klauber, M. I., Affiliate Professor of Church History, Trinity Evangelical Divinity School, Illinois, USA

Knight III, H. H., Donald and Pearl Wright Professor of Wesleyan Studies, Saint Paul School of Theology, Kansas, USA

Knight, J. A., Associate Professor of Religious Studies, Marist College, New York, USA

Knowles, S., Senior Lecturer in Religion and Popular Culture, University of Chester

Knudsen, R. D. (d. 2000), formerly Professor, Westminster Theological Seminary, Pennsylvania, USA

Krishna, P. M., formerly Professor of Oriental Studies, University of Durban, South Africa

Kristensen, B., formerly Lecturer, College of Social Work, Ede, the Netherlands

Lane, A. N. S., Professor of Historical Theology, London School of Theology

Letham, R. W. A., Professor of Systematic and Historical Theology, Union School of Theology, Bridgend

Lieu, S. N., Professorial Research Associate, Department of Languages and Cultures of Near and Middle East and Research Associate, Department of Religious Studies, SOAS University of London

Lillback, P. A., President and Professor of Historical Theology and Church History, Westminster Theological Seminary, Pennsylvania, USA

Loewen, H. J., Dean Emeritus and Senior Professor of Theology and Ethics, Fuller Theological Seminary, California, USA

Longman III, T., Robert H. Gundy Professor of Religious Studies, Westmont College, California, USA

Louth, A., Emeritus Professor of Patristic and Byzantine Studies, University of Durham

Lugioyo, B., Associate Professor, Department of Theology and Ethics, Azusa Pacific University, California, USA

Lund, E., Professor of Religion, St Olaf College, Minnesota, USA

Lundin, R., Arthur F. Holmes Professor of Faith and Learning, Wheaton College, Illinois, USA

Lyall, F., Professor of Public Law, University of Aberdeen

List of contributors

Macaskill, G., Senior Lecturer in New Testament, University of St Andrews

MacKay, D. M. (d. 1987), formerly Professor of Communication, University of Keele

Mackenzie, R., Postgraduate Research Programme Leader and Lecturer in Practical Theology and Buddhism, International Christian College, Glasgow

Macleod, D. (d.), formerly Professor of Systematic Theology, and Principal, Free Church College, Edinburgh

Maier, G., Professor of Institute of Evolutionary Ecology and Conservation Genomics, University of Ulm, Germany

Manetsch, S. M., Professor of Church History, Trinity Evangelical Divinity School, Illinois, USA

Mann, S., Senior Lecturer in Sociology, University of Greenwich

Marsden, G. M., Emeritus Professor of History, University of Notre Dame, Indiana, USA

Marshall, I. H. (d. 2015), formerly Professor Emeritus of New Testament Exegesis, University of Aberdeen

Matheson, P. C., Professor, Department of Systematic Theology, Catholic Theological College, Melbourne, Australia

McCall, T., Associate Professor of Biblical and Systematic Theology, and Director of the Carl F. H. Henry Centre for Theological Understanding, Trinity Evangelical Divinity School, Illinois, USA

McCormick, K. S., Professor of Historical Theology, Nazarene Theological Seminary, Missouri, USA

McDonald, H. D., formerly Vice-Principal and Senior Lecturer in Philosophy of Religion and Historical Theology, London Bible College

McFarlane, A., IT Professional and Theology Researcher, University of Edinburgh

McGowan, A. T. B., Minister, Inverness East Church of Scotland, and Lecturer in Systematic Theology, Highlands Theological College, Dingwall

McGuckin, J., Nielson Professor of Early Church History, Union Theological Seminary, Professor of Byzantine Studies, Columbia University, New York, USA, and Orthodox Archpriest

McIntosh, E., Lecturer in Religion, Philosophy and Ethics, Chair of Faculty Research Ethics Committee and Managing Editor, *International Journal of Public Theology*, York St John University

McNair, P. M. J., formerly Serena Professor and Head of the Department of Italian, University of Birmingham

McNutt, D. W., Associate Editor, IVP Academic, InterVarsity Press, Illinois, USA

McNutt, J. P., Associate Professor of Theology and History of Christianity, Wheaton College, Illinois, USA

McPake, J. L., Minister of Mossneuk Parish Church, East Kilbride

McPhee, I., formerly Editor, Trinity Press, Ontario, Canada

Meadows, P., Senior Research Fellow, Nazarene Theological College, Manchester

Merrick, J. R. A., Rector, St Mary's Church, Aberdeen

Miller, J. T., Overseer and Abbot of the Northumbria Community

Mills, A. R., formerly PhD candidate, Fuller Theological Seminary, California, USA

Mitchell, J. P., Professor of Communications, Arts and Religion, University of Edinburgh

Moore, A. J., Professor, Faculty of Theology and Religion, University of Oxford

List of contributors

Morden, P. J., Vice-Principal, Church History and Spirituality, Spurgeon's College, London

Morehead, J. W., Director, Western Institute for Intercultural Studies, Utah, USA

Morrow, T. W. J., Minister of Lucan Presbyterian Church, Co. Dublin, Republic of Ireland

Moseley, C. A. E., Tutor in Theology and Ethics, Sarum College, Salisbury

Mtukwa, G., Lecturer, Africa Nazarene University, Kenya

Murray, I. H., formerly Minister, St Giles Presbyterian Church, Sydney, USA

Murray Williams, S. W., Tutor in Mission and Director of the Centre for Anabaptist Studies, Bristol Baptist College

Mursell, G., formerly Bishop of Stafford

Nassif, B., Professor of Biblical and Theological Studies, North Park University, Illinois, USA

Nazir-Ali, M. J., formerly Bishop of Rochester, and Bishop of Raiwind, Pakistan and President, Oxford Centre for Training, Research, Advocacy and Dialogue

Needham, N. R., Lecturer Specialist in Church History, Highland Theological College, Dingwall

Nettles, T. J., formerly Professor of Historical Theology, Southern Baptist Theological Seminary, Kentucky, USA

Newman, D. J., Adjunct Professor, Washington Adventist University, Maryland, USA and former Editor of *Ministry* magazine

Nicholls, B. J., Senior Advisor, Asia Theological Institution

Nicole, R. (d. 2010), Founding Member of the International Council on Biblical Inerrancy and the Evangelical Theological Society

Nimmo, P. T., Chair, Systematic Theology, University of Aberdeen

Noble, T. A., Research Professor, Nazarene Theological Seminary, Missouri, and Senior Research Fellow, Nazarene Theological College, Manchester

Noll, M. A., Francis A. McAnaney Professor of History, University of Notre Dame, Indiana, USA

Noll, S. F., Professor Emeritus, Trinity School for Ministry, Pennsylvania, USA

Null, J. A., German Research Council Fellow, Humboldt University of Berlin, and Visiting Fellow, Faculty of Divinity, University of Cambridge and St John's College, Durham

O'Donovan, O. M. T., formerly Professor of Christian Ethics and Practical Theology, New College, Edinburgh

Oliver, S. A., Associate Professor of Theology, University of Nottingham

Ovey, M., Principal, Doctrine, Apologetics and Liturgy, Oak Hill College, London

Packer, J. I., Board of Governors' Professor of Theology, Regent College, Vancouver, Canada

Partridge, C., Professor, Department of Politics, Philosophy and Religion, University of Lancaster

Parushev, P. R., Vice-Principal and Director, IBTS Centre, Amsterdam, the Netherlands

Parvis, P., Honorary Fellow, School of Divinity, University of Edinburgh

Parvis, S., Senior Lecturer, Patristics, University of Edinburgh

Paul, I., Associate Minister, St Nic's, Nottingham, and Honorary Assistant Professor, University of Nottingham

Peacore, L., Adjunct Assistant Professor of Theology, Fuller Theological Seminary, California, USA

List of contributors

Penner, M. B., Professor, Philosophy, Dean, Faculty of Humanities and Social Sciences, Director, Master of Arts in Interdisciplinary Humanities, and Director, Anabaptist-Mennonite Centre for Faith and Learning, Trinity Western University, British Columbia, Canada

Percy, M., Principal of Ripon College, Cuddesdon and the Oxford Ministry Course, and Professor of Theological Education, King's College, London

Perrin, N., Franklin S. Dyrness Professor of Biblical Studies and Dean of the Graduate School, Wheaton College, Illinois, USA

Philip, J. (d. 2009), formerly Minister, Holyrood Abbey, Edinburgh

Pinnock, C. H. (d. 2010), formerly Professor Emeritus of Systematic Theology, McMaster Divinity College, Ontario, Canada

Pointer, S. R., Professor Emeritus in History, Trinity International University, Illinois, USA

Powell, S. M., Professor of Philosophy and Religion, Point Loma Nazarene University, California, USA

Preston, D. G., formerly Senior Lecturer in French, Ahmadu Bello University, Zaria, Nigeria

Price, R. M., formerly Instructor, Montclair State University, New Jersey, USA

Punshon, J. A., formerly Quaker Studies Tutor, Woodbrooke College, Birmingham

Quicke, M. J., Emeritus Professor of Preaching, Northern Seminary, Illinois, USA

Radner, E., Professor of Historical Theology, Wycliffe College, Toronto, Canada

Rae, M. A., Professor, Theology Programme, University of Otago, New Zealand

Rainey, D. L., Senior Lecturer in Theology, Nazarene Theological College, Manchester

Randall, I. M., Senior Research Fellow, IBTS Centre, Amsterdam, the Netherlands

Raser, H. E., Professor of History of Christianity, Nazarene Theological Seminary, Missouri, USA

Rauser, R., Professor of Historical Theology, Taylor Seminary, Alberta, Canada

Reichenbach, B. R., Professor Emeritus, Augsburg College, Minneapolis, USA

Rentel, A., Assistant Professor of Canon Law and Byzantine Studies and The John and Paraskeva Skvir Lecturer in Practical Theology, St Vladimir's Orthodox Theological Seminary, New York, USA

Rich, A. D., Director of In-Service Training and Tutor of Greek and Patristics, Spurgeon's College, London

Riddell, P. G., Academic Vice-Principal, Melbourne School of Theology, Australia

Rook, R., Founder and CEO, Chapel St, Surrey

Root, J. B., Reverend, St James Church Centre, London

Rosell, G. M., Senior Research Professor of Church History, Gordon Conwell Theological Seminary, Florida, USA

Rowdon, H. H., formerly Senior Lecturer in Church History, London Bible College

Roxborogh, W. J., formerly Lecturer in Church History and New Testament, Seminari Theoloji, Malaysia

Runia, K. (d. 2006), formerly Leader of the Protestant Church in the Netherlands

Russell, C. A. (d. 2013), formerly Emeritus Professor of History of Science and Technology, Open University, and Research Scholar, History and Philosophy of Science Department, University of Cambridge

Russell, S., formerly Lecturer in Theology, Northern College Congregational and United Reformed, Manchester

Sagovsky, N., Sub-Dean, Westminster Abbey, London

List of contributors

Samuel, V. K., formerly General Secretary, Evangelical Fellowship in the Anglican Communion

Sceats, D. D., formerly Rector of Colton, Staffordshire

Scorgie, G. G., Professor of Theology, Bethel Seminary, San Diego, USA

Sebastian, J. J., Dean of the Lutheran Theological Seminary, Philadelphia, USA

Sellers, I., formerly Senior Lecturer, North Cheshire College, Warrington

Severson, E., Associate Professor of Philosophy, Eastern Nazarene College, Massachusetts, USA

Sexton, J. S., Lecturer, California State University, California, USA

Shehata, S. F., Dean, Pro-Cathedral, St Mark, Alexandria, Egypt

Sheir-Jones, A. (d. 2011), formerly author and editor

Simuț, C. C., Professor of Historical and Systematic Theology, Emanuel University of Oradea, Romania

Sizer, S., Incumbent, Christ Church, Surrey

Smail, T. A. (d. 2012), formerly Team Rector, All Saints, Sanderstead

Smalley, S. J., formerly Lecturer in Historical and Contemporary Theology, University of Manchester

Smart, H. W., freelance writer, Montrose, Scotland

Smith, N. J. (d. 2010), formerly Lecturer in Missiology, University of South Africa, and Minister of the Dutch Reformed Church in Africa, Mamelodi, Pretoria

Spence, A. J., Minister, Sandwich United Reformed Church, Kent

So, D. W. K., Research Tutor, Trinity and Chapel Coordinator, Oxford Centre for Mission Studies, Oxford

Song, R. J., Professor, Department of Theology and Religion, University of Durham

Steven, J. H. S., Academic Dean and Programme Leader for Christian Liturgy, Sarum College, Salisbury

Stevenson, P. K., Principal, South Wales Baptist College, Cardiff, and Honorary Senior Tutor, University of Cardiff

Stiver, D. R., Professor, School of Theology, Harden-Simmons University, Texas, USA

Stobart, A. J., Presbyter, Methodist Church, Darlington

Storkey, A., formerly Director of Studies, Oak Hill College, London

Strange, D. S., Academic Vice-Principal and Lecturer in Culture, Religion and Public Theology, Oak Hill College, London

Stults, R., Online Workshop Coordinator, Voice of the Martyrs and Adjunct Professor, Religion and Philosophy, Oklahoma Wesleyan University, Oklahoma, USA

Sturch, R. L., formerly Rector of Islip, Oxfordshire

Sugden, C. M. N., Executive Secretary, Anglican Mainstream

Sung, E. Y., Associate Professor of Biblical and Systematic Theology, Trinity Evangelical Divinity School, Illinois, USA

Szurko, M. M., College Librarian, Oriel College, University of Oxford

Thacker, J., Lecturer, Practical and Public Theology, Cliff College, Sheffield

Thiselton, A. C., Emeritus Professor of Christian Theology, University of Nottingham, and Emeritus Canon Theologian of Leicester and of Southwell and Nottingham

List of contributors

Thomas, D. W. H., Robert Strong Professor of Systematic and Pastoral Theology, Reformed Theological Seminary, Atlanta, USA

Thompson, G. J., Co-ordinator of Studies: Systematic Theology, Pilgrim Theological College within the University of Divinity, Melbourne, Australia

Thompson, P. E., Professor of Systematic Theology and Christian Heritage, Sioux Falls Seminary, South Dakota, USA

Tidball, D. J., Visiting Scholar, Spurgeon's College, London

Tomlin, G., Principal, St Paul's Theological Centre and St Mellitus College, London

Toon, P. (d. 2009), formerly Priest-in-Charge of Biddulph Moor and Brown Edge, Staffordshire

Toth (Andronoviene), L., Lecturer in Practical Theology, Scottish Baptist College, Paisley

Treier, D. J., Blanchard Professor of Theology, Wheaton College, Illinois, USA

Truscott, J. A., Chaplain, Trinity Theological College, Singapore

Uchida, K., Professor Emeritus of New Testament, Japan Bible Seminary, Tokyo, Japan

Van Asselt, W. J. (d. 2014), formerly Professor of Historical Theology, Evangelical Theological Faculty, Leuven, Belgium

Vanhoozer, K. J., Research Professor of Systematic Theology, Trinity Evangelical Divinity School, Illinois, USA

Vermaat, J. A. E., Professor and Head of Earth Sciences and Economics, Amsterdam Global Change Institute, Amsterdam, the Netherlands

Vidu, A., Associate Professor of Theology, Gordon Conwell Theological Seminary, Massachusetts, USA

Vince, R. M., formerly Head Teacher, St Mark's Day School, Louisiana, USA

Vos, A., Emeritus Professor, Western Kentucky University, Kentucky, USA

Wallace, R. S. (d. 2006), formerly Professor Emeritus of Biblical Theology, Columbia Theological Seminary, Georgia, USA

Walls, A. F., Honorary Professor, University of Edinburgh, Professor of History of Mission, Liverpool Hope University, and Professor, Akrofi-Christaller Institute of Theology, Mission and Culture, Akropong, Ghana

Walters, P. M., formerly Research Director, Keston College (now the Keston Institute), York

Ward, J. W., former Director of Studies and Dean of Students, Regents Theological College, Nantwich (now at West Malvern)

Webster, J. B. (d. 2016), formerly Chair of Divinity, St Mary's College, University of St Andrews

Weinandy, T. G., Adjunct Professor of Systematic Theology, Dominican House of Studies, Washington DC, USA

Wellings, M., Superintendent Minister, Oxford Methodist Circuit

Wilkens, S., Professor, Department of Philosophy, Azusa Pacific University, California, USA

Williams, C. P., formerly Vice-Principal, Trinity College, Bristol

Williams, S. N., Professor of Systematic Theology and Church History, Union Theological College, Belfast

Wilson, J. R., Adjunct Instructor of Religious Studies, Virginia Commonwealth University, Virginia, USA

Wollaston, I., Senior Lecturer in Jewish and Holocaust Studies, University of Birmingham

List of contributors

Wood, A. S. (d. 1993), formerly Principal, Cliff College, Derbyshire

Wood, D. P. (d.), formerly Lecturer in History and Philosophy, School of Divinity, University of Aberdeen

Woods, J. D., Pastor, Lancing Tabernacle, West Sussex

Wright, D. F. (d. 2008), formerly Professor Emeritus of Patristic and Reformed Theology, University of Edinburgh

Wright, J. S. (d. 1985), formerly Principal, Tyndale Hall

Wright, M. J. (d. 2011), formerly Lecturer in Religious Studies, Open University

Wright, N. G., formerly Principal, Spurgeon's College, London

Wright, N. T., Research Professor of New Testament and Early Christianity, University of St Andrews

Yamauchi, E. M., Professor Emeritus, Department of History, Miami University, Ohio, USA

Yarnell III, M. B., Professor of Systematic Theology, Director of the Oxford Study Programme, Director of the Centre for Theological Research and Chair of the Systematic Theology Department, Southwestern Baptist Theological Seminary, Texas, USA

Yri, N., formerly Professor of New Testament Studies, Lutheran Theological College, Tanzania

Yu, C. T., Abundant Grace Distinguished Professor of Theological Studies and President Emeritus, China Graduate School of Theology, Hong Kong

Ziegler, P., Senior Lecturer in History and Philosophy, School of Divinity, University of Aberdeen

Zuidervaart, L., Professor of Philosophy, Institute for Christian Studies, Toronto, Canada

ABELARD, PETER (1079–1142)

Peter Abelard (or more accurately, Abailard) was born near Nantes, of Breton parents. He was probably the most brilliant thinker of the twelfth century, but his life was repeatedly marred by tragedy.

Abelard studied first under Roscelin (d. c. 1125), a thoroughgoing *nominalist, then under William of Champeaux (c. 1070–1121), an equally thoroughgoing *realist. While Roscelin was accused of regarding universals as mere words with no reality of their own, William maintained that the universal is more real than the individuals and in fact exists independently of them. Abelard took a mediating position, seeing universals as mental concepts. They have no existence independent of particular individuals, but they are not arbitrary names. A universal, like 'dog', is real, but it is not something that exists independently of individual dogs. It precedes individual dogs in that, when God planned the creation of dogs, the universal idea of 'dog' was in his mind; it exists in individual dogs; and it exists in our minds when we have the concept of 'dog'. This view came to be generally accepted and closed the debate until the time of *William of Ockham.

Abelard did not merely disagree with his teachers, he actively opposed them. He attacked Roscelin's doctrine of the *Trinity, which verged on *tritheism. He opposed William's realism and set himself up as a rival lecturer at Paris, forcing William to leave Paris and rethink his position on universals. Abelard later meted out the same treatment to Anselm of Laon (d. 1117), with whose exegetical methods he disagreed. After leaving Laon, Abelard returned to Paris where he committed his worst indiscretion. He lodged with Fulbert, a canon of Notre Dame, whose attractive and intelligent niece Héloise he tutored. Héloise gave birth to a baby boy. Fulbert later took revenge in a terrible incident in which Abelard was castrated.

In 1122 Abelard wrote Sic et Non (Yes and No). In this book he considers 158 different theological questions, juxtaposing apparently contradictory passages from the Bible, the Fathers and other authorities. His aim was not, as once was supposed, to discredit these authorities. He was rather commending reason as the arbiter to reconcile conflicting authorities and, if necessary, to choose between them. He did not invent this method. Gratian (died not later than 1179), an expert in *canon law, used this approach with great success in his Concord of Discordant Canons. Abelard's novelty lay in its application to theology and the documents of revelation.

Behind Sic et Non lay Abelard's basic approach to theology. *Anselm, like *Augustine, had followed the method of faith seeking understanding: 'I believe in order that I may understand' (see *Faith and reason). Abelard reversed this, introducing the method of doubt. The way to find the truth is to doubt, to ask questions. In the preface to Sic et Non Abelard stated that 'by doubting we come to enquire and by enquiring we reach truth'. *Doubt he sees not so much as sin (the traditional view) as the necessary beginning of all knowledge. Theology had become a science instead of a meditation, as in the tradition of *monastic theology.

In his commentary on Rom. 3:19–26, Abelard applied this method to the doctrine of the *atonement. He questioned the meaning of the statement that we are redeemed by Christ's death. He ridiculed the idea, already declining in popularity since Anselm, that the devil has any rights over mankind. If anything, Satan's seduction of the human race gives *us* the right of redress over *him*. The death of Christ was not offered to Satan as a ransom for mankind. The ransom was paid to God, not to Satan.

But Abelard goes on to question the need for any ransom at all. How could God demand the death of an innocent man, much less the death of his own Son? How could God be reconciled to the world by such a death? Abelard looks elsewhere for the significance of the *cross. He sees it as a supreme example of God's *love for us, which awakens a response of love in us. Abelard points here towards the 'moral influence theory' of the atonement, which sees its value in its effect upon us.

The idea that the cross awakens a loving response on our part is true as far as it goes, but manifestly fails to do full justice to Rom. 3:19–26. But was Abelard actually seeking to limit the atonement to merely an example of love? Elsewhere he continues to use traditional language of Christ bearing the punishment for our sins. Some hold that such passages cannot be taken seriously in the light of the commentary on Romans. Others see such passages as proof that Abelard did not wish to reduce the cross to merely an example of love. It may be significant that while he denies that a ransom was paid to Satan, he only asks *why it was necessary* for a ransom to be paid to God. Perhaps, as with *Sic et Non*, his aim is to stimulate rational enquiry rather than discredit scriptural teaching.

Abelard's innovative brilliance, combined with his contempt for those who were his elders but not his betters, launched him on a collision course with disaster. His *On the Divine Unity and Trinity* was condemned in his absence at the Council of Soissons in 1121 and burnt. This did not permanently affect his career. But he managed to incur the wrath of *Bernard of Clairvaux, who was appalled by his rationalistic approach and accused him of inventing a fifth gospel. Abelard was summoned before a council at Sens in 1140 and condemned. He appealed to Rome, but Bernard had already secured the ear of the pope with his treatise *The Errors of Peter* Abelard. Abelard became a monk at the abbey of Cluny and died in 1142.

Bibliography

Works: PL 178 and CCCM 11–12. *Sic et Non*, ed. B. B. Boyer and R. McKean (Chicago, 1976–77); *A Dialogue of a Philosopher . . .*, tr. P. J. Payer (Toronto, 1979); *Ethics*, tr. D. E. Luscombe (Oxford, 1971).

Studies: J. E. Brower and K. Guilfoy, *The Cambridge Companion to Abelard* (Cambridge, 2004); M. Clanchy, *Abelard: A Medieval Life* (Oxford, 1997); J. Marenbon, *The Philosophy of Peter Abelard* (Cambridge, 1997); R. E. Weingart, *The Logic of Divine Love: A Critical Analysis of the Soteriology of Peter Abailard* (Oxford, 1970).

A. N. S. LANE

ABSOLUTION, see GUILT AND FORGIVENESS

ACCOMMODATION

The theological importance of the question of accommodation is frequently overlooked. The term is normally used with reference to the way that *Scripture speaks of *God and his ways. God communicates with us not by directly describing himself as he is, but by 'accommodating' his speech to our understanding. To take a familiar example: God is represented in parts of Scripture as having eyes and hands, but this way of speaking is accommodated to our imaginative capacities. This is usually called 'anthropomorphism'; anthropomorphism is a form of accommodation.

Discussion of accommodation is complicated by at least two factors. The first is that while most commentators will agree that Scripture contains accommodated language, there is disagreement on the question of when it does so. When Scripture refers to God changing his mind, is that an accommodation to our ways of thinking and picturing God or a description of actual change? Or are the alternatives, as stated, too crude? The second is that in the history of theology 'accommodation' has not been used simply with reference to issues surrounding language. Thus, theologians have spoken of God's condescension to us in Jesus Christ as an 'accommodation', which refers more widely to God's activity and not simply to speech.

There was a wide and various use of the principle of accommodation amongst the Church Fathers, John *Chrysostom (*c*. 349–407) providing an outstanding example. They displayed exemplary sensitivity to the greatness of God and the limits of language, even if their approach was contentious at certain points (e.g. when the literal language of Scripture was read allegorically on the ground that the literal was an accommodation). But for Protestant theologians, 'accommodation' is particularly associated with the name of John *Calvin. He deploys it as a principle of biblical and theological interpretation both in the *Institutes* and, to a greater extent, in his commentaries. One indication of its complexity is Calvin's discussion of the accommodated nature of language that portrays the death of Christ as translating us from the sphere of divine wrath to the sphere of divine mercy (*Institutes* 2.16).

A theological grasp of the issue of accommodation is possible only when we are informed and sensitive about how the languages in which the Bible is written function. It may be that certain conventions in Hebrew narrative (in particular) will always remain unclear to us and to that extent we have an ongoing task. Quite generally, 'accommodation' is a reminder of our need to be humble in speech and thought, without weakening in our confidence that we can truly know and love God through Jesus Christ.

See also: HERMENEUTICS.

Bibliography

J. Balserak, *Divinity Compromised: A Study of Divine Accommodation in the Thought of John Calvin* (Dordrecht, 2006); F. L. Battles, 'God Was Accommodating Himself to Human Capacity', *Interpretation* 31, 1977, pp. 19–38; idem, 'God Was Accommodating Himself to Human Capacity', in R. Benedetto (ed.), *Interpreting John Calvin* (Grand Rapids, 1997); P. Helm, 'Divine Accommodation', in *John Calvin's Ideas* (New York/Oxford, 2004), pp. 184–208.

S. N. WILLIAMS

ADAM

The first Adam

A historical and systematic treatment of Adam must at least begin with the biblical figure first mentioned in the primeval history in Genesis. The Hebrew word '*adam* is a collective noun meaning 'humankind' which comes to refer in the narrative to the specific man Adam. Accordingly we are to understand references to Adam in the two creation accounts (Gen. 1:1 – 2:3 and 2:4–25) as referring to the representative of humanity in general. Hence Karl Barth could emphasize that being made in the *image of God is to be made male and female.

In the case of Gen. 1:26 – 2:3 the generic understanding of '*adam* has always been accepted in the tradition, although many different interpretations of the 'let us make' and 'in our image' have been offered. Augustine interpreted the 'us' and 'our' in trinitarian terms as the Father speaking to the Son. Thomas Aquinas also saw this as indicating the plurality of divine persons, rebuking those who interpreted it as referring to the angels. Luther took this a step further by saying that humans are distinct from animals primarily in being created by a unique counsel of God.

Humanity being made in the image of God, of course, has been of greater concern. Exegetically this simply means that we are to be God's representatives to the other creatures on earth, especially the animals. Only since the rise of modern biblical criticism has this been regained in theology. The Church Fathers needed to avoid the anthropomorphic notion that the image has to do with being like God physically. Thus the consensus among them was that the *imago Dei* referred primarily to rationality, an idea which they borrowed from Greek philosophy. Augustine exemplified this view, asserting even that the erect form of the human body testifies that our minds should be raised to things that are above.

Luther articulated the image somewhat differently. For him, it meant to live a godly life without fear of death and content with God's favour. Like Augustine, Luther's conception also had a physiological component. Before sin Adam was stronger, more intelligent, and sensationally superior to all other creatures. Like the Fathers, Thomas understood the image with reference to the mind, but, unlike Luther, he articulated the functional inferiority of certain human features relative to other creatures in terms of adaptability to the soul. In other words, humans' physical traits were proportionate to their use and necessity. Since our greatest asset is our soul or mind, it does not make sense for us to have large claws, for instance.

With regard to Gen. 2:4 – 3:24, however, the majority of theologians have held that Adam was a historical person. The reason that Luther asserted what he did about human physicality had to do with his conviction, following the tradition, that Adam originally lived in supreme bliss, in a state of innocence, without sin or death. Exegetically this conclusion is now questioned, although in Israel's post-exilic and apocalyptic literature Adam was considered to be immortal before he sinned. Most of the Fathers held this later interpretation, along with the idea that Adam was perfect while at first in paradise (Eden). Thomas agreed with this, including the notion that Adam had full understanding of all things that humans can naturally know. This was both a result of his emphasis on rationality and of his assertion that Adam was to be the father and teacher of humanity.

But it has been questioned whether there is a biblical basis for the idea of a primeval paradisiac perfection in which the first humans lived. Irenaeus did not see the world as created with a final perfection, but rather as unfinished and moving toward becoming perfect. When in the modern period the Genesis creation accounts were understood as saga adapted from Ancient Near Eastern texts, the idea of a perfect state of origin was abandoned in much Protestant theology by the nineteenth century.

Similarly, the understanding of Adam as a historical person is often regarded as no longer tenable in light of contemporary science and biblical scholarship. Even Augustine and many of his contemporaries read the creation accounts allegorically (a fact which Luther laments). Kierkegaard and Schleiermacher did not take them as historical, and even Barth denies that there ever was a golden age of original perfection. For him 'Adam' is meant as the name given to world history and all of humanity. Contemporary science suggests, moreover, that human populations never existed in less than several thousand individuals and that death and suffering happened before the emergence of human beings. Theologically, Adam is then understood as a type or representative of our shared humanity. A minority view (e.g. R. J. Berry) tries to find a place for a historic Adam within the scientific story (see *Creation; Creation and evolution).

The sin of Adam

What, then, are we to make of *sin? The idea that a historical Adam is necessary for a doctrine of original sin was formulated by Augustine, who developed an argument for infant *baptism in response to both the *Manicheans and the *Pelagians. Since baptism was understood as the washing away of sin, sense needed to be made of why babies were baptized if they had not yet sinned by their will. The answer was that the penalty for original guilt inherited from Adam had to be remitted (see *Fall). The corruption of original sinfulness, physically passed on to every human being since Adam through the lust of the father, remained however until death. The Eastern Church never explicitly adopted this view of inherited guilt, although they do maintain the original immortality of Adam and the universal sinfulness of humanity.

We are primarily concerned here, though, with Adam's sin. If, as the tradition has assumed, Adam was a historical person who lived in a paradise of perfection where he was fully satisfied, why would he sin? As LeRon Shults observes, if God created the first humans perfectly righteous and set them in a paradise that met all their needs, it is incomprehensible that they would choose evil. A perfectly good will would by definition will the good. This is precisely why many in the tradition have qualified Adam's perfection.

According to Thomas, Adam was not perfectly blissful. For Luther, similarly, Adam was completely perfect except for his will, which would be made perfect in the later spiritual life. The early Fathers, borrowing from *Stoicism, conceived of Adam as naturally free in his original innocence. These concessions were made not only in order to understand why Adam could possibly have sinned, but to exonerate God from any responsibility for the coming of sin into the world. It needed to be the case that Adam had the free *will to choose between good and evil.

If, on the other hand, we say that Adam was not a historical first person who passed sin on to us through a 'generative impulse' (Thomas), but rather that 'adam is all of humankind as such, what do we make of original sin? Certainly Pannenberg is right that sin is simply inherent to the human predicament as we know it. If we affirm the evolutionary origin of our species, then sin can be considered primarily as the broken relationality into which all creatures have emerged and into which all humans continue to be born. Even Augustine could say that sin is not found in things themselves (material creation is good), but in their illegitimate use, in that they are desired disproportionately against love of God and his commandments (i.e. wrongly related to). Theologically, then, Adam would be a type of the human person who suffers the brokenness and frailties of life common to all. Some have held that the problem with this perspective is that 'any distinction between God's creation and the entrance of sin into the world is collapsed and God is made directly responsible for sin, while human responsibility is diminished' (T. E. Fretheim, *God and the World*, p. 31).

The last Adam

The only other significant mention of Adam in the Bible comes in Paul's typological contrasts of Adam and *Christ in Rom. 5:12–21 and 1 Cor. 15:20–23. These, in connection with the statement in Col. 1:15 that Christ is the image of God, have led Christian theology to interpret the *imago Dei* primarily with reference to Christ. It is only in and through Christ that the image of God is realized for humanity.

Irenaeus, as we saw, understood the world as moving toward perfection. For him, human nature is a copy of the original which is the Word of God disclosed in the incarnation. A person fulfils his or her destiny by becoming a copy of Christ by the power of the Spirit. Similarly, Barth interpreted Paul to mean that Jesus takes the first place of the original and

Adam the second place. Paul knew Jesus first and then Adam. Barth can even say that as humanity is modelled on Jesus and Jesus is modelled on God, so humanity is made in the image of God.

Christ as the last Adam, then, can be seen as the human person in the fullness of eschatological glory. As the first fruits of *resurrection, Christ anticipates our true identity and destiny, our perfect 'adam. He is the revelation of God precisely because he is the true human and vice versa. In the context of his Hebrew tradition it only makes sense for Paul to use Adam as the first, or typological, human to demonstrate the universality of sin. Theologically, the point is that we are all in Adam, all sinners but made in the image of God as male and female, now eschatologically interpreted to mean becoming transformed by the Spirit (in)to the image who is Christ (Rom. 8:29). The Eastern tradition has preferred the term *theosis* for this.

Who is Adam? Whatever may be said about the historical Adam, it may be agreed that 'Adam' represents humanity as we are called out of relational patterns of sin and brokenness and toward ones of wholeness and peace by conforming to the image of God, the true and definitive human person which is Jesus Christ, by the power of the Spirit, to share perfect and immortal life with the Father.

Bibliography

Augustine, *On Genesis* (ET, Washington, 1991); K. Barth, *CD*; Henri Blocher, *Original Sin: Illuminating the Riddle* (Leicester, 1997); R. J. Berry and T. A. Noble (eds.), *Darwin, Creation and the Fall* (Nottingham, 2009); C. J. Collins, *Did Adam and Eve Really Exist?* (Wheaton, 2011); T. E. Fretheim, *God and the World in the Old Testament* (Nashville, 2005); R. Hess, 'Adam', in T. D. Alexander and D. W. Baker (eds.), *Dictionary of Old Testament: Pentateuch* (Leicester, 2003), pp. 18a–21b; L. J. Kreizer, 'Adam and Christ', in G. F. Hawthorne and R. P. Martin (eds.), *Dictionary of Paul and His Letters* (Leicester, 1993); M. Luther, *Lectures on Genesis* (ET, Saint Louis, 1958); E. Pagels, *Adam, Eve and the Serpent* (London, 1988); W. Pannenberg, *Human Nature, Election, and History* (Philadelphia, 1977); idem, *Anthropology in Theological Perspective* (ET, Philadelphia, 1985); idem, *Systematic Theology*, vol. 2 (ET, Grand Rapids, 1994); G. von Rad, *Genesis* (ET, Philadelphia, rev. edn 1973); R. Scroggs, *The Last Adam* (Philadelphia, 1966); F. L. Shults, *Reforming Theological Anthropology* (Grand Rapids, 2003); Thomas Aquinas, *Summa Theologiae* (ET, New York, 1964).

A. R. MILLS

ADIAPHORA

This concept (from the Gk for 'things indifferent') was explored controversially particularly by *Lutheran theologians in the mid-sixteenth century at a time when the Protestant movement was threatened by Catholic power in Germany. The basic question related to the status of certain ceremonies and rites, both public and private, which are neither commanded nor forbidden by the word of God in Scripture, and which have been introduced, it was claimed, into the church for the sake of good order, decorum and discipline. One party, led by Philipp *Melanchthon, held that in a period of persecution one may, with a clear conscience, at the insistence of the enemy, restore certain things such as the rite of *confirmation. The other party, led by Matthias Flacius (1520–75), contended that under no circumstances could this be done with a clear conscience. In the *Formula of Concord (1577), ch. X is entitled, 'The ecclesiastical rites that are called "Adiaphora" or things indifferent', where a middle way is proposed. In times of persecution, concessions are not to be offered, but at other times 'the community of God in every place and at every time has the right, authority and power to change, to reduce, or to increase ceremonies according to its circumstances, as long as it does so without frivolity and offence but in an orderly and appropriate way . . . for good order, evangelical decorum and the edification of the church'.

The issue of adiaphora was also contentious in England in the sixteenth century and in Lutheran *pietism in the seventeenth century, and in strong or weak forms has often arisen in churches which take the word of God as authoritative.

Bibliography

C. L. Manschreck, *Melanchthon, The Quiet Reformer* (New York and Nashville, 1958); B. J. Verkamp, *The Indifferent Mean: Adiaphorism in the English Reformation to 1554* (Athens, OH, 1977).

P. TOON

ADOPTION, see SONSHIP

ADOPTIONISM

The term is most commonly applied to the notion that Jesus was merely an ordinary man of unusual virtue or closeness to God whom God 'adopted' into divine sonship. This exceptional elevation, which in primitive adoptionism was usually associated with the event of Christ's baptism, involves nevertheless only a special divine activity upon or in Jesus, not the personal presence in him of a second member of the *Trinity bearing the proper name of Word (*Logos) or Son.

Although early material on adoptionism is scant, it seems clear that the movement first became prominent in the teachings of Theodotus, an erudite leather merchant active in Rome about 190. He taught that the 'Spirit' or 'Christ' descended upon Jesus at baptism, initiating miraculous powers in one who was, though supremely virtuous, just an ordinary man. Theodotus was an offence to his critics for defining Jesus as a 'mere man' (*psilos anthrōpos* – hence the label 'psilanthropism'), a term underlined by the adoptionist's own description of his previous lapse from faith as denial 'not of God but of a man'. According to *Hippolytus, Theodotus 'determined to deny the divinity of Christ'. Artemon, a convert in Rome to the teaching of Theodotus, sought to establish the historical pedigree of adoptionism; the significant response of one contemporary, held by some scholars to be Hippolytus, was to demonstrate that each of the early Christian *apologists 'proclaim Christ both God and man'.

The most famous heir to the early adoptionist tradition is Paul of *Samosata who, in most of the early witnesses, is firmly linked with the teaching of Artemon. Paul was finally condemned for his views at the Synod of Antioch (268). We have no contemporary record of his doctrine, but it is plain that he was understood to teach that Jesus was 'by nature an ordinary man' (*koinou tēn physin anthrōpou*). In the next century he was accused by the church historian *Eusebius of holding a demeaning view of Christ and thus denying both 'his God and his Lord'. It was his misdemeanour, alleged Eusebius, to draw back from acknowledging that the Son of God came down from heaven, confessing instead that Jesus was 'from below'.

Modern *Christologies sometimes defend themselves, with some justness, from the suspicion of adoptionism by consciously renouncing certain untenable features of the original movement, such as its impersonal interpretation of the divine presence with Jesus, its neglect of divine initiative over against human achievement and its blurring of the NT distinction between Christ's sonship and the adoptive counterpart in believers. These unsound traits, however, were, at least in the minds of the movement's critics, quite secondary to the inadequately expressed identity accorded in adoptionism to the Jesus borne by Mary. Its really characteristic error was to deny the divine origin and identity of Jesus, calling him a mere man, a failing combated by the later title *Theotokos* (God-bearer) for *Mary.

Adoptionism (or Adoptianism) is technically the title also for a less well-known movement in the Spanish church of the eighth century, condemned for making Christ's manhood participate in his dignity as Son only by adoption.

See also: MONARCHIANISM.

Bibliography

J. C. Cavadini, *The Last Christology of the West: Adoptionism in Spain and Gaul, 785–820* (Philadelphia, 1993); A. Grillmeier, *Christ in Christian Tradition, vol. 1: From the Apostolic Age to Chalcedon AD 451* (London, ²1975); J. N. D. Kelly, *Early Christian Doctrines* (London, ⁵1977); R. A. Norris, *The Christological Controversy: Sources of Early Christian Thought* (Philadelphia, 1980).

R. KEARSLEY

AESTHETICS

Aesthetics is the study of general features of the arts and aesthetic experience. 'The arts' include drama, music, painting, poetry and many other fields. Aesthetics has been a distinct branch of Western philosophy since the eighteenth century, when A. Baumgarten (1714–62) gave the subdiscipline its name. Important contributions have also come from other academic disciplines, as well as from artists, writers and cultural critics.

Modern philosophical aesthetics includes theory of the aesthetic dimension, philosophy of the arts and philosophy of arts criticism. For Christians in Western societies the most significant issues arising in these areas concern aesthetic responsibility, approaches to art, social frameworks and relationships between theology and philosophy. This article summarizes each of these issues, then suggests new directions for further work in aesthetics.

Aesthetic responsibility

To speak of 'aesthetic responsibility' is to challenge modern aesthetics. Since Immanuel *Kant's influential *Critique of Judgment* (1790), many philosophers have regarded aesthetic experience as a sanctuary from both natural necessity and moral obligation. Indeed, extreme positions have made the 'aesthetic experience' of 'beauty' or of 'fine art' a matter of enjoyment for enjoyment's sake. One of the first provocative Christian challenges came from Leo *Tolstoy in *What Is Art?* (Indianapolis, 1960 [1896]). When Tolstoy rejected 'beauty' as a defining feature of art, he also rejected 'aesthetic experience' as a poor excuse for irreligious and elitist hedonism.

N. Wolterstorff and C. Seerveld also challenge traditional notions of beauty, but without rejecting 'aesthetic experience' as such. These Christian philosophers in the Reformed tradition distinguish more carefully than Tolstoy did between *aesthetic* and *artistic* excellence. Both of them argue that all human beings have aesthetic responsibilities. Wolterstorff makes a case for aesthetic excellence in cities and churches. Seerveld urges Christians to lead an 'obedient aesthetic life' in their dwellings and social interactions. Although they have different definitions of aesthetic experience, both philosophers see the aesthetic dimension of life, culture and society as one in which human beings are created to give God praise and Christians are called to seek Christ's renewal of all creation.

Approaches to art

Authors who retain pre-modern notions of beauty tend to view recent art with suspicion. This tendency shows up in writings on modern art by H. R. Rookmaaker (1922–77) and F. A. *Schaeffer, and it continues in the approach their followers take to postmodern arts. Modern works by Picasso (1881–1974), Samuel Beckett (1906–89) and Ingmar Bergman (1918–2007) do not display the pleasurable proportion, integrity and brightness that *Thomas Aquinas associated with beauty. Nor do postmodern experiments in performance art and site-specific installations pursue the aims of traditional craftsmanship and moral uplift that many Protestants have inherited from the Victorian era. Christian cultural conservatives often regard such features as artistic defects that signal cultural decay. By contrast, other Christians praise modern art for its power to unsettle comfortable Christianity (e.g. N. A. Scott [ed.], *The New Orpheus*, New York, 1964) or point to postmodern arts as imaginative training grounds for a democratic culture (e.g. L. Zuidervaart, *Artistic Truth*).

Such divergent assessments imply different theologies of culture. How Christians practise and view the arts depends in part on how they relate to their culture and society. Isolationists wish to ward off contemporary art as a threat to their faith. Synthetic and accommodating Christians tend to use Christian teachings to justify contemporary art. Transformational Christians usually aim to promote renewal within contemporary art.

Here two philosophical issues arise: What are the characteristic features of art, and what are its proper roles within human life? Specific decisions about which artistic practices to promote, or how to use the arts in worship, already assume responses to these issues. For example, when Tolstoy rejected Shakespeare and commended Charles Dickens, he assumed that art's main task is to communicate feelings in a sincere fashion. We may distinguish three types of Western philosophies about the nature and purpose of art. *Instrumental* theories understand art as a means of improvement, indoctrination or emotional expression. *Referential* theories understand art as an imitation, reflection or projection of actual, ideal or imaginative realities. *Formalist* theories understand works of art as autonomous creations whose intrinsic worth lies in their formal and aesthetic qualities.

Each type of theory fails to do justice to wide ranges of artistic practice. A comprehensive Christian philosophy of the arts would try to correct and incorporate all three theories. It would note, for example, that instrumental theories underestimate the intrinsic worth of the arts; that referential theories ignore the non-cognitive functions of the arts; and that formalist theories treat works of art as if they were pure objects of secular devotion. One recent attempt at a comprehensive view proposes a new conception of artistic truth in which the production and use of art are just as

7

crucial to art's importance as are its allusive import and internal form (Zuidervaart, *Artistic Truth*).

Social frameworks

Many art lovers do in fact treat artworks as objects of secular devotion. This fact has led Christians like Tolstoy to repudiate the 'religion' of art spawned by nineteenth-century *Romanticism. It would be more fruitful, however, to analyse the social frameworks within which contemporary arts operate. Wolterstorff has described salient features of Western society's 'institution of high art'. He says that this social framework for making and using art contributes directly to the isolation of high art and the aesthetic impoverishment of everyday life. Although helpful, Wolterstorff's approach largely ignores the institution of low art, and it does not address sufficiently the *anti*-aesthetic turn in recent high art. Yet some of our aesthetic impoverishment is prompted by 'low art' – by popular music, film and advertising – as these operate within a 'culture industry' (T. W. Adorno) dedicated to commercial success. Even high art in museums and concert halls has become locked into an international culture industry where celebrity trumps quality and the sensational stands out. Christian criticisms of the arts, and our involvement in them, will make little difference if we do not address the political, economic and technological basis for social frameworks to contemporary art, both high and low. Important steps in this direction occur in the work of J. de Gruchy, W. Romanowski and B. Spackman.

Theology and philosophy

Christian artists and art critics often turn to theology for guidance. By itself, however, theology may prove insufficient. For example, in *Christian Letters to a Post-Christian World* (Grand Rapids, 1969) Dorothy Sayers notes the lack of a 'Christian philosophy of the arts' and tries to derive her own aesthetics from a lay theology of creation. But her use of this *theology* relies heavily on a *philosophy*, namely, R. G. Collingwood's *The Principles of Art* (Oxford, 1938).

To be sure, theology should provide touchstones for reflections about the arts and aesthetic experience. To become serviceable for art and life, however, such reflections need philosophical refinement. Protestants have long been hampered by their lack of a cogent philosophical aesthetics. The requisite philosophical aesthetics will be informed by Scripture, theology and Christian traditions, yet remain genuine philosophy, in conversation with other philosophies. When conjoined with theological reflections, work in aesthetics by Christian philosophers can help free us to serve God and our neighbours more fully in matters artistic and aesthetic.

New directions

Fortunately, there has been an upsurge in both philosophical and theological reflections among Christian scholars since the 1960s. Three traditions have contributed the most in this regard: the evangelical, the sacramental and the reformational traditions. Nourished by correlative traditions in *liturgy, doctrine and church governance, these traditions of aesthetic reflection spill across contemporary denominational alignments. Whereas the evangelical tradition emphasizes the detection and expression of worldviews in high art and popular culture (e.g. A. Chaplin *et al.* and H. R. Rookmaaker), the sacramental tradition stresses the incarnational character of artistic symbols (e.g. J. Begbie and R. Viladesau), and the reformational tradition gives priority to the transformation of art and society (e.g. de Gruchy, Seerveld and Wolterstorff). Of the three traditions, reformational scholarship has been the most overtly philosophical. Stemming from the revitalization of Dutch Calvinism led by Abraham *Kuyper, the reformational tradition regards Christians as agents of renewal in culture and society. With this comes the challenge to criticize and change cultural practices, social institutions, and the very structure of society where these dishonour God's intentions for creation, resist Christ's redemptive work in human history, or violate the biblical promise of a new heaven and new earth.

Recently this reformational vision has given rise to new directions in Christian aesthetics. It has prompted a turn away from evangelical worldview approaches to fresh explorations of complex interactions in the public spaces that artistic efforts help generate and maintain. The reformational vision has also led a younger generation of artists and scholars to emphasize the cultural institutions that make artistic practices possible, rather than simply the discrete artworks that sacramentalists see as sacred symbols.

Together these two developments call for an inner reformation of philosophical aesthetics itself. The new aesthetics will not restrict its attention to the aesthetic dimension, philosophy of the arts and philosophy of arts criticism. Without abandoning these topics, it will incorporate them into a social philosophy of the arts and culture where questions of cultural pluralism, new media, political power and economic exploitation have prominence. Bringing philosophy into direct conversation with cultural studies and the social sciences, this intrinsically interdisciplinary effort will seek new ways to address a globalizing world. For those who are called to be agents of healing and renewal, and who hear the cries of the oppressed, the wounds of God's world require an ongoing transformation of Christian aesthetics.

See also: CULTURAL THEORY AND THEOLOGY; CULTURE; WORSHIP.

Bibliography

J. Begbie, *Beholding the Glory: Incarnation through the Arts* (Grand Rapids, 2000); idem, *Sounding the Depths: Theology through the Arts* (London, 2002); idem, *Theology, Music, and Time* (Cambridge, 2000); idem, *Voicing Creation's Praise: Towards a Theology of the Arts* (Edinburgh, 1991); A. Chaplin and H. Brand, *Art and Soul: Signposts for Christians in the Arts* (Carlisle and Downers Grove, ²2001); J. W. de Gruchy, *Christianity, Art and Transformation: Theological Aesthetics in the Struggle for Justice* (Cambridge and New York, 2001); W. Dyrness, *Reformed Theology and Visual Culture: The Protestant Imagination from Calvin to Edwards* (Cambridge, 2004); idem, *Poetic Theology: God and the Poetics of Everyday Life* (Grand Rapids, 2011); idem, *Senses of the Soul: Art and the Visual in Christian Worship* (Eugene, 2008); idem, *Visual Faith: Art, Theology, and Worship in Dialogue* (Grand Rapids, 2001); P. Fiddes, *The Novel, Spirituality, and Modern Culture* (Cardiff, 2000); T. Gorringe, *Furthering Humanity: A Theology of Culture* (London, 2004); M. Hengelaar-Rookmaaker (ed.), *The Complete Works of Hans R. Rookmaaker* (Carlisle, 2002–2003); M. Kelly (ed.), *Encyclopedia of Aesthetics* (Oxford and New York, 1998); W. D. Romanowski, *Eyes Wide Open: Looking for God in Popular Culture* (Grand Rapids, 2001); B. Spackman, *A Profound Weakness: Christians and Kitsch* (Carlisle, 2005); D. J. Treier, M. Husbands and R. Lundin, *The Beauty of God: Theology and the Arts* (Downers Grove, 2007); R. Viladesau, *Theological Aesthetics: God in Imagination, Beauty, and Art* (Oxford and New York, 1999); N. Wolterstorff, *Art in Action: Toward a Christian Aesthetic* (Grand Rapids, 1980); L. Zuidervaart, *Artistic Truth: Aesthetics, Discourse, and Imaginative Disclosure* (Cambridge and New York, 2004); idem, 'Postmodern Arts and the Birth of a Democratic Culture', in L. Zuidervaart and H. Luttikhuizen (eds.), *The Arts, Community, and Cultural Democracy* (London and New York, 2000).

L. ZUIDERVAART

AFRICAN CHRISTIAN THEOLOGY

The rapid spread of Christianity in Africa in the twentieth century has been one of the notable features of modern Christian history. For some time now it has been acceptable even to speak of a shift in Christianity's geographical and cultural centre of gravity. The heartlands of the faith are no longer in the old Christendom of Western Europe and its extension in North America, but rather are to be found in the 'Southern' continents: Latin America, parts of Asia and the Pacific, and particularly tropical Africa.

This phenomenal rate of expansion of Christianity in Africa has led to an awareness that the Christian faith as professed by Africans ought to find expression in terms that arise out of African cultural values and life-experience. The effort to think through faith in Christ in terms which reflect authentically African perspectives has produced 'the quest for an African (Christian) theology' since the mid-1950s.

Admittedly, a certain amount of spontaneous 'theologizing' goes on in the life and witness of Africa's Christian communities, and this is probably most evident in the so-called *African Independent Churches. However, African theology in its academic and literary form has emerged largely from the Departments of Religion in the various universities on the continent. It is worth noting that the vast majority of Africa's theological academics are also ordained churchmen who maintain an active association with their churches. Already one can discern some positive achievements of this first flowering of African theological reflection.

The agenda of African theology is quite startling. The historical roots of African Christianity lie in the modern missionary enterprise from the West. Given the generally negative Western evaluation of indigenous African religions, it has come as a surprise that virtually all of Africa's leading theologians, though trained in theology according to Western models, have concentrated their research and writing on those very religious traditions of the African 'past' which were considered to be theologically insignificant. This concern with the African pre-Christian religious heritage assumed such proportions that one observer of the African theological scene ventured to suggest that an effect of this concentration of interest was that 'areas of traditional Christian doctrine which are not reflected in the African past disappear or are marginalized' (Adrian Hastings). The titles of significant publications by some of the leading theologians of the continent confirm this emphasis. An important question raised by African theological writing to date is how to account for this high level of interest that Africa's Christian theologians have manifested in the pre-Christian religious traditions of Africa, and often of the particular writer's own people.

To the extent that the Western missionary picture of pre-Christian Africa was that of a religious *tabula rasa*, the writings of African theologians may be said to have consisted in 'demonstrating that the African religious experience and heritage were not illusory and that they should have formed the vehicle for conveying the Gospel verities to Africa' (Desmond Tutu). The central theme of this African theological literature has been the nature of African pre-Christian religious life and values and their 'relationship of continuity rather than discontinuity with Christian belief' (Hastings). This attempt at rehabilitating the African pre-Christian religious consciousness has been carried out as a self-consciously Christian and theological effort, and can thus be said to have also been an attempt to define the nature of African Christian identity. This is so since the kind of study that the African theologian makes of traditional religion differs significantly in outlook from that made by the anthropologist. Neither can it be compared with 'a clinical observation of the sort one might make about Babylonian religion; he is handling dynamite, his own past, his people's present' (A. F. Walls).

The viewpoints of the major protagonists of this theological interpretation of the African pre-Christian religious heritage are by no means identical in all respects. E. Bolaji Idowu (Nigeria) is most noted for the position that the African experience of God in the pre-Christian tradition is essentially the same as in Christian belief. Idowu arrives at this conclusion by drastically reducing all 'lesser divinities' in the Yoruba pantheon, for example, to the status of manifestations or refractions of the Supreme God. The African world of divinity becomes, according to Idowu, one of 'diffused monotheism' (*Olódùmarè*, p. 204), so that, in the final analysis, 'in Africa, the real cohesive factor of religion is the living God' (*African Traditional Religion*, p. 104). Idowu, therefore, not only insists that Africa's 'old' religions are a proper (though by no means the sole) source for African Christian theology; his approach also tends towards the conclusion that African Christian experience does little more than bring into sharper focus the sense of God which African tradition had all along.

The writings of John Mbiti (a Kenyan who was Director of the Ecumenical Institute of the World Council of Churches from 1972 to 1980) reflect a more settled Christian self-consciousness, though they are equally concerned with the theological interpretation of Africa's pre-Christian heritage in religion. Mbiti has written of himself, 'It is with a deep Christian faith that I feel conscious of myself, that I respond to the universe and that I try to make something out of life' (Preface to his *Poems of Nature and Faith*, Nairobi, 1969).

For Mbiti it is important not only to recognize that 'historically Christianity is very much an African religion' (*African Religions and Philosophy*, pp. 229f.), but also to distinguish between the phenomenon of Christianity, in its cultural embodiment as the missionary religion brought to Africa, and the Christian faith, which as religious faith is capable of being apprehended by Africans in African terms without undue difficulty. This means that the task of constructing an African theology on the basis of an African experience of the Christian faith can proceed without anxiety or self-justification. This outlook stamps Mbiti's writings with a feeling of freedom, which, in the context of the quest by African theologians for an appropriate sense of identity, is quite remarkable.

Like Idowu, Mbiti also places positive value on the African pre-Christian heritage of religion, but only as *praeparatio evangelica*, as indicative of the African preparedness for the gospel, 'that final and completing element that crowns their traditional religiosity and brings its flickering light to full brilliance'. Mbiti, therefore, achieves a more profound integration of 'old' and 'new' than Idowu, and the vindication of an African theological point of view reflecting African cultural sensitivities, which Idowu affirms largely as a concomitant of African religious self-consciousness, is defended by Mbiti on the basis of African Christian experience itself. No other major African theologian uses the expression 'Christian Africa' in speaking of twentieth-century Africa as freely as Mbiti.

The generally sympathetic interpretation of the pre-Christian religious tradition and its integration into African Christian experience indicated in the writings of Idowu and Mbiti are echoed by the majority of Africa's theologians. The only notable exception is the late General Secretary of the Association of Evangelicals of Africa and Madagascar, Byang Kato. Kato postulated a radical discontinuity between the pre-Christian tradition and Christian belief. However, the prospects for fruitful dialogue with those on the 'other side' were ended with his sudden death in 1975. No other African theologian has espoused quite as extreme a view as Kato.

African theology has overturned virtually every negative verdict passed on African tradition by the ethnocentric perspective of the earlier Western missionary estimate of Africa. Now there are indications that African Christian theology is ready to take up themes and subjects which belong within the mainstream of Christian debate and reflection, like *Christology, soteriology and biblical *hermeneutics. It is likely that this development would not have been possible without an effective treatment in the first instance of the question of identity.

See also: BLACK THEOLOGY.

Bibliography

K. Bediako, 'Biblical Christologies in the Context of African Traditional Religion', in V. Samuel and C. Sugden (eds.), *Sharing Jesus in the Two-Thirds World* (Bangalore, 1983), pp. 115–175; idem, *Theology and Identity* (Oxford, 1992); idem, *Christianity in Africa* (Edinburgh, 1995); idem, *Jesus and the Gospel in Africa* (Maryknoll, 2004); K. Dickson and P. Ellingworth (eds.), *Biblical Revelation and African Beliefs* (London, 1969); A. Hastings, *African Christianity: An Essay in Interpretation* (London, 1976); S. de la Haye, *Bynag Kato: Ambassador for Christ* (Achimoto, Gahan, 1986); E. B. Idowu, *Olódùmarè: God in Yoruba Belief* (London, 1962); idem, *African Traditional Religion: A Definition* (London, 1973); B. H. Kato, *Theological Pitfalls in Africa* (Kisumu, 1975); J. H. O. Kombo, *The Doctrine of God in African Christian Thought* (Leiden, 2007); T. S. Maluleka, 'Half a Century of African Christian Theologies', *Journal of Theology for Southern Africa* 99, 1997, pp. 4–23; J. S. Mbiti, *African Religions and Philosophy* (London, 1969); idem, *Concepts of God in Africa* (London, 1970); idem, *Bible and Theology in African Christianity* (Nairobi, 1986); J. N. K. Mugambi and L. Magesa (eds.), *Jesus in African Christianity* (Nairobi, 1989); S. Ngewa, M. Shaw and T. Tiénou (eds.), *Issues in African Christian Theology* (Nairobi, 1998); C. Nyamiti, *African Tradition and the Christian God* (Eldoret, Kenya, n.d.); idem, *Christ as Our Ancestor: Christology from an African Perspective* (Gweru, 1984); L. Nyirongo, *Gods of Africa or the God of the Bible* (Potchefstroomse, 1997); J. S. Pobee, *Toward an African Theology* (Nashville, 1979); J. S. Pobee (ed.), *Exploring Afro-Christology* (Paris, 1992); T. Tiénou, 'Evangelical Theology in African Contexts', in *The Cambridge Companion to Evangelical Theology* (Cambridge, 2007); D. Tutu, 'Whither African Theology?', in E. W. Fashole-Luke et al. (eds.), *Christianity in Independent Africa* (London, 1978), pp. 364–369; A. F. Walls, 'Towards Understanding Africa's Place in Christian History', in J. S. Pobee, (ed.), *Religion in a Pluralistic Society* (Leiden, 1976), pp. 180–189.

K. BEDIAKO

AFRICAN INDEPENDENT CHURCHES, THEOLOGY OF

A notable feature of the phenomenal growth of Christianity in Africa in the twentieth century was the emergence of the so-called African Independent Churches. In 1968 a survey identified 6,000 such churches with a total membership of nearly 10 million spread over thirty-four countries on the continent and giving every indication that their numbers were still on the increase. A sign of their importance is the fact that these churches are now being considered as a fourth Christian strand alongside the Roman Catholic, Orthodox and Protestant traditions. They are in most cases the results of breakaways from mission churches. They testify to the vitality of an African genius in religion and a capacity to adapt a missionary faith to African needs and situations.

It is probably not the case that all the movements which are grouped under this general name qualify as genuinely Christian churches. It can be shown that some of them are non-Christian religious movements which use Christian symbols, or else teach heterodox forms of Christianity. However, it is undeniable that a large portion of them are properly Christian churches and reveal in their various ways an apprehension of the Christian faith in African terms.

When the 'quest for an African Christian theology' got under way in the mid-1960s, it was to the Independent Churches that some of Africa's academic theologians looked for signs of an authentically Africanized Christianity. Yet these churches have little, if any, explicit theology. Rather, they demonstrate the liveliness and power of Christian faith in which a theology is undoubtedly implicit.

While these churches display a tendency towards the use of ritual and symbolism reminiscent of the practice of African traditional religion, they also manifest a radical Bible-centredness which points to a consciousness of being in direct continuity with prophetic and apostolic times; hence their expectation that the power and *gifts of *prophets and *apostles must be available to them.

This radical biblicism needs to be distinguished from the *fundamentalism of other Christian groups. For the African Independents' approach does not stem from a rationally conceived 'doctrine' of the inspiration of Scripture; rather, the Bible in the vernacular is the living word of the living God who therefore is bound to demonstrate his *living* power in *living* experience. *Healing, prophetic guidance, protection against evil spirits, revelation through dreams – these are simply the demonstration that the God of Moses, of Elijah and of Paul is available today to all who call upon him. In this sense, the Independents have been compared to the *Radical Reformation in sixteenth-century Europe; they have been called modern Africa's *Anabaptists.

Since in these churches Christian faith is validated more in demonstration of power than in rational articulation of belief, some of them also tend to be imprecise on a doctrine such as the Trinity. A sense of the absolute lordship of Jesus may in one of them overshadow the Father, whereas in others, the intense awareness of the Spirit of power may appear to obscure the person of Christ. But even here it may be asked whether the 'distinction of persons' (see *Hypostasis) in Western Christian theology is closer to the biblical picture than the Independents' inclination to apprehend the activity of 'the three' in their unity and interchangeability.

The African Independent Churches may be said to be marked more by a *spirituality than by a theology, a spirituality which, though reflecting the sense of the spirituality of the whole of life in African traditional culture, yet transposes African life into a new 'key' by a radical faith in Christ.

One cannot assume that the Independents will remain content with an implicit theology. Some of them, like the important Kimbanguist Church in Zaire (a member of the World Council of Churches), have established their own theological faculties with curricula similar to those operated by the mission-related churches. Others welcome the assistance of the mission-related churches in the training of their leaders or participate in ecumenical training for the ministry. In the process, the peculiarly 'African' spirituality of these churches is already becoming their contribution to the emergence of an *African Christian theology which transcends denominational barriers.

Bibliography

A. Anderson, *Zion and Pentecost: The Spirituality and Experience of Pentecostal and Zionist/Apostolic Churches in South Africa* (Pretoria, 2000); D. B. Barrett, *Schism and Renewal in Africa: An Analysis of Six Thousand Contemporary Religious Movements* (Nairobi and London, 1968); M. L. Daneel, 'Towards a *theologia africana*? The Contribution of Independent Churches to African Theology', *Missionalia* 12 (1984), pp. 64–89; C. Pauw, 'African Independent Churches as a "People's Response" to the Christian Message', *Journal for the Study of Religion* 8 (1995), pp. 9–19; John S. Pobee and Gabriel Ositelu II, *African Initiatives in Christianity* (Geneva, 1998); G. M. Bengt Sundkler, *Bantu Prophets in South Africa*

(London, ²1961); idem, *Zulu Zion and Some Swazi Zionists* (Uppsala and London, 1976); H. W. Turner, *History of an African Independent Church*, 2 vols. (Oxford, 1967); D. Venter (ed.), *Engaging Modernity: Methods and Cases for Studying African Independent Churches in South Africa* (Westport, 2004); F. B. Welbourn and B. A. Ogot, *A Place to Feel at Home: A Study of Two Independent Churches in Western Kenya* (London, 1966).

K. Bediako

AFRICAN THEOLOGY: RECENT DEVELOPMENTS

Several years ago Dr Kwame Bediako saw 'indications that African Christian theology is ready to take themes and subjects which belong within the mainstream of Christian debate and reflection . . .' These indications have to a certain extent become reality, especially in the last twenty-five years. These developments are most articulated in the book *African Theology Comes of Age*, published by the Ecumenical Symposium of Eastern Africa Theologians (ESEAT) in 2010. Even though this book was written by mostly East African theologians, it captures the progress made in various parts of the continent. What is clear in this book and others is the fact that African theology has moved from a defence of the need for African theology to actual theologizing using African thought forms and idioms. 'African theology has come of age. The question whether or not there should be – or is – an African theology is now redundant, if not ludicrous' (Mugambi and Magesa, *Jesus in African Christianity*, p. 11). Areas of Christian theology that have seen developments include Christology, ecclesiology, *eschatology, Trinity, God, *sin and *salvation; and African theologians have also applied Christian theology to a myriad of problems that face Africa today, such as poverty, democracy, violence, HIV and AIDS.

The central theme of African Christian theology is *Christology. As a result, 'There is no doubt that Christology is the subject which has been most developed in today's African theology' (C. Nyamiti, in Mugambi and Magesa, *Jesus in African Christianity*, p. 70). Christology in Africa has sought to answer a key question, 'From the African Church, a clear and convincing answer is demanded to this question: Who is Jesus Christ for you, Africa? Who do you say that He is?' (Mugambi and Magesa, *Jesus in African Christianity*, p. xii). Diane Stinton has answered this question in her book *Jesus of Africa*, an extensive research of Christologies in Africa. She points out that key models from the African traditional setting have been used to talk about Jesus; these include Jesus as elder brother, traditional healer, head and master of initiation, healer, ancestor, the great ancestor, family friend, king/chief, etc. (pp. 72–240). It is understood these models will make Jesus palatable to the African. Christology is done with the understanding that, 'It cannot be separated from Africa's socio-political, religio-cultural and economical contexts – this is the real and concrete everyday experience within which we Christologize' (A. E. Akinade, *Asian Journal of Theology* 9, p. 184). Diane Stinton responds to those who would critique African Christologies when she says, '. . . the fact that the African christologies have not yet gained adequate acknowledgement beyond the continent is more reflective of enduring ethnocentrism within the wider theological community than of the value of the christologies *per se*' (*Jesus of Africa*, p. 251).

The results of developments in the doctrine of the *church are seen due to the fact that, 'Today, the Christian church on the continent is recognizably African, not only in song, dance, worship, colour, etc., but also in mission, identity, structure, and theology' (A. Orobator, *African Theology Comes of Age*, p. 37). Models that have been used to form African ecclesiologies are the clan system of J. M. Waliggo, Charles Nyamiti's ancestral-koinonia model and Benezet Bujo's model based on Christ as our proto-ancestor.

The doctrine of *God was the first to experience *contextualization, and Western missionaries were able to make a connection between Yahweh and African concepts of God. The result was that Yahweh got several names from various African communities. Recently contextualization has come in the doctrine of the *Trinity, where the African three-stone stove has been effectively used to communicate it to African people.

African Christian theology is certainly work in progress. Even as we focus on written theology, it is important to bear in mind excellent theologies being done orally by Africans both young and old. The task of African theology should include writing this theology, which is often expressed in song, sermons, drama, prayers, etc. Yet African theology has to rid itself of what J. D. Gwamna calls 'expedient theology', or the 'theology of the market place' which often is spread by quacks or freelance preachers (*Perspectives in African Theology*, p. 196). This is the major threat to African Christian theology. To be credible and of use to the African continent, African Christian theology will have to have its primary source as the Bible.

Andrew Walls' words could not be more correct today: '. . . Africa may be the theatre in which some of the determinative new directions in Christian thought and activity are being taken' (*The Cross-Cultural Process in Christian History*, p. 119).

See also: AFRICAN CHRISTIAN THEOLOGY; AFRICAN INDEPENDENT CHURCHES, THEOLOGY OF.

Bibliography

A. E. Akinade, 'Who Do You Say That I Am?', *Asia Journal of Theology* 9, no. 1, 1995; J. Gwamna, *Perspectives in African Theology* (Bukuru, 2008); J. N. K. Mugambi and L. Magesa (eds.), *Jesus in African Christianity: Experimentation and Diversity in African Christology* (Nairobi, ²1998); C. Nyamiti, 'African Christologies Today', in Mugambi and Magesa, *Jesus in African Christianity*, 1998); D. B. Stinton, *Jesus of Africa: Voices of Contemporary African Christology* (Maryknoll, 2004); idem, 'Africa's Contribution to Christology', in *African Theology Comes of Age: Revisiting Twenty Years of the Theology of the Ecumenical Symposium of Eastern Africa Theologians (ESEAT)* (Nairobi, 2010), pp. 13–34; A. F. Walls, *The Cross-Cultural Process in Christian History: Studies in the Transmission and Appropriation of Faith* (Maryknoll, 2002).

G. MTUKWA

AGAPE, see LOVE; NYGREN, ANDERS

AGNOSTICISM

A term coined by T. H. Huxley (1825–95) to express the view that since God's existence can neither be proved nor disproved the only rational position on the question is to suspend or withhold judgment or belief. Huxley added a negative prefix ('a') to the Greek term 'gnostic', referring to knowledge, to describe a person lacking knowledge. An agnostic refuses to make a judgment about God's non-existence. If an atheist holds the belief that God does not exist, then an agnostic, who neither affirms nor denies God's existence, is not an *atheist.

Agnosticism is often based on an *Enlightenment ethic of belief which requires that only those propositions should be believed for which there is sufficient evidence. However, William *James argued that it was rational to believe upon insufficient evidence when the choice involved was 'living, momentous and forced'. *Reformed epistemology holds that one can reasonably accept God's existence without the support of evidence or argument.

Bibliography

K. J. Clark, *Return to Reason* (Grand Rapids, 1990); T. H. Huxley, *Agnosticism and Christianity and Other Essays* (Loughton, 1992).

K. J. CLARK

ALBERTUS MAGNUS (*c*. 1193–1280)

A scholar, saint and bishop of the medieval church who was born in Bavaria sometime between 1193 and 1206. Albert entered the *Dominican order in 1223 and studied at the universities of Padua and Bologna. During 1228–40 he taught at convents in Germany where he composed a series of commentaries on the *Sentences* of Peter *Lombard. He attended the University of Paris, earning his doctorate there and becoming a master from 1245 to 1248. It was at this time that *Thomas Aquinas was one of his students and his assistant. In 1248 he was sent to Cologne to establish a new curriculum for his order. Later he became Bishop of Regensburg (1260–62). After leaving his administrative duties, he spent the remainder of his life in Cologne as a writer, teacher and controversialist.

Albert was one of the major leaders in the movement known as *scholasticism. Broadly defined, this is an intellectual product of the medieval universities that attempted to harmonize *faith and reason. There were mystical scholastics like *Bernard and *Bonaventura, empirical scholastics such as Robert Grosseteste (*c*. 1175–1253) and Roger Bacon (*c*. 1214–92), and there was the rational scholasticism of

Albert and Aquinas. The rational scholastics, like contemporary Jewish and Arab scholars, sought by means of reason to reconcile their faith with the philosophy of ancient pagan writers, especially *Aristotle.

Albert was attracted by the scientific works of Aristotle which were being translated and studied in the European universities for the first time. He mastered this material in a series of works which have been republished in twenty-eight volumes (1890–99). He is credited with establishing the study of *nature as a legitimate concern for Western Christian intellectuals. The encyclopaedic approach of the times led him to deal with a wide range of subjects in the natural sciences, including geography, psychology, physics, botany, zoology and mineralogy. His major books on religious thought are commentaries on Lombard's work, explanations of the major and minor prophets and a book of theology (*Summa Theologiae*). His work differs from that of many other scholastics because he does not comment on each line of the text, but instead paraphrases the work and adds his own observations. He was not as successful at developing a synthesis between Christianity and Aristotelian thought as was his student, Thomas Aquinas, but he did insist on the integrity of both the area of *revelation and the realm of reason. He taught the importance of secular learning, but affirmed that such knowledge cannot ultimately contradict divine revelation.

In a sense Albert was unique, living during the 'golden age of scholasticism' and, despite an enormously busy and varied life, mastering the most advanced knowledge of his day. Impatient with others who lacked his understanding, he combined his reading of scientific works with observations of nature, constantly trying to fit the details into coherent schemes. His achievements were recognized by his contemporaries, many of whom believed that they were due to magic. He was canonized in 1931 and became the patron of those who study the natural sciences.

Bibliography

S. M. Albert, *Albert the Great* (Oxford, 1948); T. M. Schwertner, *St Albert the Great* (Milwaukee, 1932); J. A. Weisheipl (ed.), *Albertus Magnus and the Sciences: Commemorative Essays* (Toronto, 1979).

R. G. CLOUSE

ALBIGENSES

The Albigenses were a medieval *dualistic sect, ultimately heir to *Manichaean teaching, that spread along the trade routes from the Middle East and became popular in northern Italy and southern France during the eleventh and twelfth centuries. At times called the Cathars, the followers of this group were known as Albigenses because their greatest strength centred in the town of Albi. They taught that there was a god of light (spirit) and a god of darkness (matter). The perfect life, one devoid of material things, could be approached by a rigorous *asceticism, including abstaining from meats and sex, and condemning the medieval church. They also objected to the orthodox teaching about Christ because they did not believe that the Son of God could be incarnate as a man.

Albigenses were divided into the 'perfect' who closely followed the teaching of the group and the 'believers' who could continue to live normal lives until their deathbeds, at which time, if they repented, they could be assured of salvation. At first, the papacy tried to bring them back into the church through peaceful means such as sending special preachers into southern France to convert them. However, in 1208 a papal representative was murdered in Toulouse, provoking Innocent III (1160–1216) to call a crusade which crushed the movement.

Bibliography

M. Barber, *The Cathars: Dualist Heretics in Languedoc in the High Middle Ages* (Harlow, 2000); M. Lambert, *The Cathars* (Oxford, 1998); S. O'Shea, *The Perfect Heresy* (London, 2000); S. Runciman, *The Medieval Manichee* (Cambridge, 1961 [1947]); W. Wakefield and A. P. Evans, *Heresies of the High Middle Ages* (New York, 1991).

R. G. CLOUSE

ALEXANDRIAN SCHOOL

The great city of Alexandria, on the Mediterranean coast of Egypt just west of the Nile delta, had, since its foundation by Alexander the Great, been one of the leading intellectual centres of the Hellenic world, prominent especially in philosophical, literary, mathematical and scientific studies. The beginnings of Christianity in Alexandria are murky, though associated in tradition (since at least the time of Eusebius of Caesarea at the very beginning of the fourth century) with the evangelist, Mark. But the first theologians to emerge with any clarity in Alexandria were *Gnostic or gnosticizing in their teaching: men like Basilides, Heracleon and Valentinus on the edges of, or beyond the pale of, what would become recognized 'orthodoxy'. With the work of *Clement in the 190s it becomes possible to speak for the first time of a more mainline or mainstream theological tradition in Alexandria.

To describe that tradition the phrase 'Alexandrian School' can be used in either a looser or in a narrower and more precise sense. Loosely, it is possible to point to certain lines of continuity other than merely geographical that run through the Alexandrian tradition from Clement to the end of the ancient world. They would include, first, a wide-ranging engagement with *Platonic thought; secondly and correlative with that, what we might term a 'noetic' spirituality in the sense of seeing the goal of the Christian life to be a rising up with the eyes of the mind from the material world of time and space (the world of coming to be and passing away), to the stable, unchanging, eternal realm beyond; and finally, ways of interpreting Scripture that see it above all as a storehouse of mysterious meanings that both reveal and veil the story of the soul's ascent to God. But it must be noted that, on the one hand, none of these three characteristics is unique to the Alexandrian tradition and, secondly, there are in all of them significant discontinuities to be observed as well, above all with the emergence of a radically new incarnational theology in the fourth century. It is to the latter, shaped above all by the thought of *Athanasius (bishop of Alexandria 328–73) and *Cyril (bishop 412–44) that the term 'Alexandrian School' can be applied in a narrower and more precise sense.

In the wider sense of the phrase, the pinnacle of the Alexandrian School is in many ways the work of *Origen. He was the most towering intellectual figure of third-century theology and a writer whose influence, above all on exegesis and spirituality, remained a formative factor on subsequent Christian tradition. Origen lived in a thoroughly Platonic intellectual world. He believed in the pre-existence of *souls – or, to be precise, in the creation of rational spirits – all alike and all engaged in the contemplation of God, before the creation of the material world. But for some (as Origen admits, inexplicable) reason these rational spirits became bored and looked down. All but the one that eventually became the human soul of Christ fell. They fell to varying degrees, some becoming angels, some human souls and others demons. And they fell into materiality – a material world that was in fact designed to be both a means of giving expression to this new diversity and a hard school in which they could eventually be taught to turn their gaze back to God. Scripture is a roadmap for this journey, or rather a complex set of clues and hints and puzzles meant to encourage us and train us and lead us on. Allegory (see *Hermeneutics) is the exegetical tool for unlocking this quarry of hidden meaning. What seem on the surface to be, for example, simple accounts of historical battles and kings in fact tell a timeless story of the soul's rational ascent in the contemplation of God. And occasionally, Origen thinks, the literal, surface meaning is actually either false or nonsensical, just to remind the reader that he always needs to look beneath that surface for the deeper meaning of Scripture.

In his thought about God, Origen developed the idea that the Son is eternally begotten of the Father: it is an act always, timelessly, in process, since God always and simply 'is'. The Son who is thus begotten is also the *Logos or Word of God, and he is the *Wisdom of God in whom there is a sort of cosmic blueprint of all the things that are to be made. What proved in the history of subsequent theology to be the downside of that idea is that the Word has for Origen a strongly cosmological function. He is the principle of order and harmony in the world, and that means that he is a bridge or a link between the One and the many, between God and his world. And so the Son was subordinate to the Father; he was God, but, in the end, less so.

For that and other reasons, Origen proved a controversial figure even in his own lifetime and was eventually to be condemned as a heretic by the Fifth Ecumenical *Council in 553, some three centuries after his death. But his influence continued to be felt, above all in Alexandria in the work of men like Dionysius the Great (bishop of Alexandria 248–c. 64) and the lay theologian Didymus the Blind (died 398).

By the time of Didymus, however, the theological landscape had been radically altered by the new thinking associated with the *Arian controversy. The thought of both Athanasius and Cyril is dominated by a pattern given expression in John 1:14, 'The Word became flesh and made his dwelling among us.' For Athanasius, everything in the transient world of coming to be and passing away is subject to change and so to decay – to corruption, as he says, by which he means not primarily moral corruption (though that is itself a symptom of the problem), but, quite simply, falling apart and rotting away. All things – including human beings – that have come into being will in and of themselves cease to exist. Life, true life, is made possible only when the Word or Son of God, who is, as the Council of *Nicaea affirmed in 325, 'one in being' (*homoousios*) with the Father, takes flesh and breaks into our world of time and space, living a human life, dying a human death and rising again. The flesh he takes is our flesh, and he transforms it, making it incorruptible and bestowing on us the gift of adoption as sons and daughters of God – giving us by grace a sonship which is his by nature.

This very physical emphasis on the bodily reality of the incarnation and of our salvation is taken up and developed by Cyril. Cyril was an implacable opponent of what he labelled as the heresy of *Nestorius, which gave expression in an uncompromising and provocative form to the theological traditions of Alexandria's great rival, *Antioch. That meant that, against the Antiochene tendency to hold the divinity and humanity in Christ apart and to make the 'man' in Christ a distinct moral agent, Cyril stressed the life-giving unity of Word and flesh. In the Incarnate there is only one subject, only one centre of action, only one 'he'. The person of Christ is not a sort of pantomime horse (as an extreme form of Antiochene theology could sometimes seem to imply) with two separate acting subjects, the Word and a man, agreeing to act in common. And thus, for example, for Cyril, it is necessary for our salvation to say that the Word of God died on the cross. He died not in and of his divinity, which is unchangeable and impassable, but in and through the flesh which is truly *his*. It has to be God who died (in the flesh) for the simple reason that there is no other 'he' in Christ who could have. Otherwise, Cyril would say, one ends up professing no more than a sort of moral cooperation between the Word and a good man who was no more than a sort of super-prophet. And a good man or a super-prophet, Cyril would say, cannot save.

The Alexandrian vision in that later and narrower sense came to dominate virtually the whole of *Eastern theology and Eastern spirituality and, especially from the thirteenth century on, was formative in the development of classical Western Christology as well. In particular, it is the vision to which the *Monophysite (or Miaphysite, since 'Monophysite' is a label imposed by their opponents) movement sought to give articulation. This was a theology of the one nature of the Word made flesh, of the inseparable life-giving union of divinity and humanity in Christ which has in principle transformed our world and *our* flesh, though the final victory will not be seen until the end of all things and the day of resurrection. That became the theology of the vast bulk of the people of Egypt and is still the Christology of the *Coptic Orthodox Church today.

See also: CHRISTOLOGY.

Bibliography

C. Bigg, *The Christian Platonists of Alexandria* (Oxford, ²1913); H. Chadwick, *Early Christian Thought and the Classical Tradition: Studies in Justin, Clement, and Origen* (Oxford, 1966); R. P. C. Hanson, *The Search for the Christian Doctrine of God: The Arian Controversy 318–381* (Edinburgh, 1988); J. R. Lyman, *Christology and Cosmology: Models of Divine Activity in Origen, Eusebius, and Athanasius* (Oxford, 1993); J. A. McGuckin, *St. Cyril of Alexandria, The Christological Controversy: Its History, Theology, and Texts* (Leiden and New York, 1994; repr. Crestwood, 2004); R. V. Sellers, *Two Ancient Christologies* (London, 1940).

P. PARVIS

ALIENATION

Alienation is the experience of being a stranger, 'away from home', estranged from others and from oneself. In the NT the verb *apallotrioō* (to estrange or alienate) is found only in Eph. 2:12; 4:18; and Col. 1:21, and always in the passive (see J. R. W. Stott, *The Message of Ephesians*, p. 90). Paul refers both to humankind's alienation from God and from his fellow human being. These fundamental estrangements are overcome in the cross of Christ (see *Atonement).

Alienation is also a theme of the Scriptures as a whole. Adam's eviction from Eden, Cain's wandering as a fugitive, Israel's servitude in

Egypt and later exile in Babylon, all symbolize an alienation that is the lot of mankind. In Luke 15 Jesus' parable of the prodigal son gives 'a microcosmic anatomy of estrangement' (G. V. Jones, *The Art and Truth of the Parables*, p. 176).

The word 'alienation' appears in English from 1388, and for centuries meant either transfer of ownership or insanity. Then, from the 1940s, the word was used increasingly to describe social and cultural estrangement. Influences include the vast disorientation caused by the Second World War, and the writings of *Weber, *Kierkegaard and *Tillich. A major source was the newly published *Economic and Philosophical Manuscripts* of *Marx.

*Hegel and *Feuerbach had seen alienation as part of man's developing self-consciousness, whereas Marx saw it as an urgent social and economic problem. For him, man was alienated in religion, under the state, but supremely in his labour. 'For Marx and Kierkegaard, the world in which Hegel felt "at home" had become alien' (K. Löwith, *From Hegel to Nietzsche*, p. 173). It would seem that we are inheritors of that world. Alienation, an important concept in social psychology, has its roots in a basic theological reality: that humankind is alienated from God, creation, fellow humans and self.

Bibliography

EB (1974 ed.), vol. 1, pp. 574–576; G. V. Jones, *The Art and Truth of the Parables* (London, 1964); K. Löwith, *From Hegel to Nietzsche: The Revolution in Nineteenth-Century Thought* (London, 1965); B. Ollman, *Alienation: Marx's Conception of Man in Capitalist Society* (Cambridge, 1976); J. R. W. Stott, *The Message of Ephesians: God's New Society* (Leicester, 1979); R. M. Vince, *Alienated Man: The Theme of Alienation in the Writings of Karl Marx and Søren Kierkegaard* (unpublished MTh dissertation, King's College, London, 1980).

R. M. VINCE

ALLEGORY, see HERMENEUTICS

ALLEN, ROLAND (1868–1947)

The mission theorist Roland Allen, son of a Bristol clergyman, studied at Oxford and Leeds Clergy School, and was ordained priest in 1893. In 1895 the Society for the Propagation of the Gospel appointed him to Beijing to teach catechists. The Boxer Rising of 1900 and the subsequent siege of the foreign embassies catalysed his thinking. His book about the siege (1901) highlights Western aggression in China and Chinese perceptions of missionary involvement in it. Transferred to pastoral work, Allen concluded that the Chinese should soon replace missionary supervision, and draw on Chinese customary lore. Ill health ended his missionary service in 1903. As an English parish priest, he caused controversy by refusing to baptize without evidence of Christian commitment from the child's sponsors. He resigned in 1907, and for the rest of his life writing was his principal work. The Survey Application Trust and World Dominion, founded for research that forwarded mission, provided a forum.

The titles of his best-known books, *Missionary Methods: St Paul's or Ours?* (^{2}1927 [1912]) and *The Spontaneous Expansion of the Church and the Causes That Hinder It* (1927) reflect his concerns. Allen argued that apostolic practice, trusting the Holy Spirit, passed church leadership to local converts; 'spontaneous' growth of the church along indigenous lines followed. Standard modern mission practice maintained foreign control and produced a culturally inappropriate professional ministry. In *Le Zoute* (1927) Allen accused Protestant mission policy in Africa of subordinating evangelization to the colonial agenda of education.

Relentlessly combative, Allen had limited impact on mainstream missionary thinking in his lifetime, but has since been seen as prophetic. Though a High Church Anglican treasuring the sacraments and episcopal governance, he found favour among evangelical non-denominational 'faith missions', the first leaders of the Three Self Patriotic Movement in China, and those seeking to free missions from colonial leftovers.

See also: MISSIOLOGY.

Bibliography

D. M. Paton, *Reform of the Ministry: A Study of the Work of Roland Allen* (London 1968); *idem* (ed.), *The Mission of the Spirit: Selected Writings of Roland Allen* (London 1960).

A. F. WALLS

ALTHAUS, PAUL (1888–1966)

One of the most significant twentieth-century *Lutheran theologians, Althaus had a long teaching career at the University of Erlangen. Most of his work is characterized by profound engagement with the thought of *Luther. Along with contemporaries such as Werner Elert (1885–1954), under the influence of his teachers *Holl and Carl Stange (1870–1959), Althaus represents a shift from a purely historical interest in Luther to a use of Luther as a fertile theological stimulus. His reinstatement of Luther as a theologian corrects earlier *Ritschlian accounts, notably over the centrality of Luther's doctrine of justification and his theology of the cross, though Althaus is critical of what he sees as Luther's excessive pessimism over sin and of his eucharistic theology. Althaus' own dogmatics, *Die christliche Wahrheit* (*Christian Truth*), represents a major alternative to *Barth's Christocentric understanding of *revelation. Among his other writings are an eschatology, an ethics and a much-used commentary on Romans.

Bibliography

Works in ET: *The Ethics of Martin Luther* (Philadelphia, 1972), see Foreword, 'The Theology of Martin Luther' (Philadelphia, 1966).

Studies: H. Grass, in *TRE* 2, pp. 329–337; W. Lohff, in L. Reinisch (ed.), *Theologians of Our Time* (Notre Dame, 1964), pp. 48–64.

J. B. WEBSTER

AMBROSE (c. 339–97)

Ambrose had a Christian upbringing in an aristocratic Roman family. He followed an administrative career, and at the age of thirty was appointed governor of Liguria-Aemilia, with his residence in Milan. In 374 this city was thrown into turmoil over an episcopal election. By popular acclamation Ambrose was designated the new bishop.

In office, Ambrose proved a resolute opponent of *Arianism. Being proficient in Greek, he could render the best of Eastern Nicene theology into clear Latin. The fruits of this work were his *On the Faith* and *On the Holy Spirit*. He was also involved politically in the demise of Arianism. He took initiatives to eliminate Arianism from Illyricum; while in the 380s he was pressurized in Milan itself by the mother of the boy emperor, Valentinian II, to hand over a church to Arian adherents in the city. Ambrose, whose own life was threatened, succeeded in his resistance only because of the support of the Milanese population. He based his stance on the argument that 'a temple of God could not be surrendered by a bishop'.

This was not the only occasion when Ambrose asserted the independence of the church from imperial control. In the reign of Theodosius I, who had been responsible for an indiscriminate massacre at Thessalonica, Ambrose effectively excommunicated the emperor until he did public penance for his crime. Theodosius accepted ecclesiastical discipline. But on other occasions Ambrose's assertion of ecclesiastical authority was not so felicitous. The bishop of Callinicum had inspired some monks to burn down the local synagogue. Theodosius wanted the synagogue rebuilt by the bishop, but was restrained by Ambrose on the ground that a Christian emperor ought not to show favour to unbelieving Jews. Ambrose took this position because he did not distinguish between personal duties and the duties of public office. But in general Ambrose's contribution to ecclesiastical authority in the West was good. He established that there were separate spheres of authority for church and *state. In some areas too, the emperor was bound by the instruction of the church.

Ambrose was keenly concerned with the practical duties of episcopacy, among which he gave pre-eminence to scriptural instruction. He acquired considerable repute as a preacher (in which capacity he contributed significantly to the conversion of *Augustine), while his writings were well-suited to help ordinary believers. Ambrose did not originate much new theological thought, though he did adumbrate the doctrine of original sin, and in *eucharistic theology he was the first in the West to speak of a change in the nature of the elements. This quasi-creative act was brought about by the priest, acting in Christ's stead, when he repeated the words used by Christ at the Last Supper. Ambrose was a prominent pioneer in the West of allegorical exegesis (see *Hermeneutics), Christian Neoplatonism (see *Platonism) and *ascetic theology.

A set of commentaries on the Pauline epistles was included among most manuscripts of Ambrose. Their real author, called Ambrosiaster by Erasmus, was a rough contemporary of Ambrose. This commentary exercised an important influence on the developing doctrine of original *sin by interpreting Rom. 5:12 as involving the whole human race in *Adam's sin and a consequent legacy of corruption for all Adam's descendants.

See also: STOICISM.

Bibliography

F. H. Dudden, *The Life and Times of St Ambrose*, 2 vols. (Oxford, 1935); H. von Campenhausen, *The Fathers of the Latin Church* (London, 1964); N. B. McLynn, *Ambrose of Milan: Church and Court in a Christian Capital* (Berkeley, CA, 1994); A. Paredi, *Saint Ambrose: His Life and Times* (Notre Dame, IN, 1964).

G. A. KEITH

AMBROSIASTER, see AMBROSE

AMES, WILLIAM (1576–1633)

William Ames (latinized as 'Amesius'), William *Perkins's most distinguished follower, was born in Ipswich, Suffolk, and reared by his maternal uncle, Robert Snelling. Snelling sent him in 1594 to Christ's College, Cambridge, known for its undiluted *Puritanism and *Ramist philosophy. Ames graduated with a Bachelor of Arts degree in 1598 and a master's degree in 1601. That same year he was elected to be a fellow at Christ's College and ordained to the ministry. While at Christ's College, he underwent a dramatic conversion experience under the rousing preaching of Perkins.

Ames quickly became the moral compass of the college, but left his position there in 1609 to avoid expulsion for his strong Puritan convictions. He escaped to the Netherlands, where he first spent time with John Robinson; he was then employed from 1611 to 1619 by Sir Horace Vere, commander of English forces in the Netherlands, to serve as military chaplain at The Hague. Here Ames presided over a small congregation, acted as spiritual counsellor to the Vere family, ministered to the troops during military campaigns, wrote four books against *Arminianism, and played a leading role in Calvinism's triumph over Arminianism at the *Synod of Dort.

To support his family, Ames gave lectures and tutored university students for three years. He then served as professor of theology at Franeker University in Friesland for eleven years (1622–33), where he became known as the 'Learned Doctor' who tried to 'Puritanize' the entire university. He maintained a strong anti-prelatical and anti-Arminian stance, but his greatest contribution was in theology and ethics, which he considered a unified system that promoted genuine piety. At Franeker, Ames wrote his two greatest works. *Medulla theologiae* (*The Marrow of Theology*, 1627) taught that theology was the science of living to God; it became known as the best succinct summary of Calvinistic theology (see *Reformed theology) ever written. He also wrote *De conscientia* (*Conscience with the Power and Cases Thereof*, 1630). Reprinted nearly twenty times in thirty years, *De conscientia* is a collection of five books explaining Puritan casuistry; it moves from a theoretical treatment of the nature of conscience to practical answers for 'cases of conscience'.

In 1633, Ames moved to Rotterdam to co-pastor a congregation of English refugees and to help the church develop a Puritan college in Rotterdam. Several months later, on 11 November, he died of pneumonia. Four years later, his wife and children went to live in the Puritan settlement of Salem, Massachusetts. They took Ames's library with them, which formed the nucleus of the original library for Harvard College.

Ames's influence proved to be greatest in New England (see *New England theology), where *Marrow* became the primary text at Harvard for a century. It was often read and quoted throughout the colonies. Ames's writings on church polity laid the groundwork for non-separating Congregationalism, which encouraged the Congregational churches of Massachusetts Bay Colony to support further reformation in the Church of England.

Bibliography

Works: *The Marrow of Theology* (Grand Rapids, 1997 [1627]); *Conscience, with the Power and Cases Thereof* (Norwood, 1975 [1630]); *Technometry* (Philadelphia, 1979 [1633]); *The Substance of Christian Religion: Or, a Plain and Easie Draught of the Christian Catechisme, in LII Lectures* (London, 1659); *An Analytical Exposition of Both the Epistles of the Apostle Peter* (London, 1641).

Studies: J. R. Beeke and J. Van Vliet, 'The Marrow of Theology by William Ames', in K. M. Kapic and R. C. Gleason (eds.), *The Devoted Life: An Invitation to the Puritan Classics* (Downers Grove, 2004); B. J. Boerkoel, Sr, *William Ames (1576–1633): Primogenitor of the Theologia-Pietatis in English-Dutch Puritanism*, ThM thesis (Calvin Theological Seminary, 1990); D. Horton (tr. and ed.), *William Ames by Matthew Nethenus, Hugo Visscher, and Karl Reuter* (Cambridge, 1965); K. L. Sprunger, *The Learned Doctor William Ames: Dutch Backgrounds of English and American Puritanism* (Chicago, 1972); J. Van Vliet, *William Ames: Marrow of the Theology and Piety of the Reformed Tradition*, PhD diss. (Westminster Theological Seminary, 2002).

J. R. BEEKE

AMYRALDISM

This word is derived from the Latin form of the name of Moise Amyraut (1596–1664), perhaps the most eminent and influential professor of the French Protestant Academy of Saumur. This was established in 1598 by a decision of the national synod of the French Reformed Churches. It enjoyed the special favour of Philippe Duplessis-Mornay (1549–1623), governor of Saumur and one of the noblest and most influential Protestant leaders at the turn of the century. Achieving wide acclaim in France and in foreign countries for the brilliance of its faculty, it attracted a very considerable number of students until it was abolished by order of King Louis XIV at the revocation of the Edict of Nantes in 1685.

The school was known also for its encouragement of progressive ideas and its special consideration to people of nobility or wealth. In philosophy this was made apparent by the vigorous advocacy of *Ramist over against *Aristotelian logic which remained the standard in more traditional institutions like Sedan, Geneva or Leiden. In theology, the influence of John Cameron (1579–1625) was a dominant feature, even though he taught there only between 1618 and 1621. During that time, however, he managed to exercise a very great influence on three of his students, Louis Cappel (1585–1658), Josué de la Place (Placaeus, 1596–1655) and Moise Amyraut mentioned above.

Each of these three was involved in controversy over teachings which tended to broaden the *Reformed orthodoxy represented for instance in the Synod of *Dort. Cappel was embroiled in a discussion relating to the presence of the vowel points in the original Hebrew text and contended against Johann Buxtorf of Basel that these were a later addition made by the Masoretes to facilitate the reading of Scripture by people who had little knowledge of Hebrew. Later scholarship has vindicated him in this, although it remains true that the text without vowel points constitutes a clear standard of truth. Placaeus promoted the theory of mediate imputation, according to which *Adam's descendants were not adjudged guilty of the first sin of Adam but were born corrupt as a result of that sin and incurred God's displeasure by virtue of this corruption. The National Synod of Charenton (1645) expressed reservations in this area, although theologians of Saumur insisted that it had not condemned Placaeus's view.

Moise Amyraut was undoubtedly the most celebrated theologian of this school and served from 1633 to the time of his death in 1664. He was involved in a severe controversy relating to the scope of divine grace, *predestination and the extent of Christ's *atonement. Amyraut intended to soften the edges of the traditional orthodox Reformed view and thus to relieve difficulties in the controversy with Roman Catholics and facilitate a reunion of Protestants in which Reformed and Lutheran could join ranks. In his *Traité de la Prédestination* (1634) he claimed that God, moved by his love for humankind, had appointed all human beings to salvation provided they repent and believe. He sent his Son, the Lord Jesus Christ, to die for the sins of all humankind in order to implement this purpose. However, since human beings would not on their own initiative repent and believe, God then chose to bestow a special measure of his Spirit to some only, who are the elect. Grace thus is seen as universal in the provision for salvation, but as particular in the application of it. In viewing matters in this fashion, Amyraut thought that he could continue to adhere to the Canons of Dort and at the same time provide a picture of God's benevolence that would be more faithful to Scripture and indeed to *Calvin than the thoroughly particularistic approach that characterized Reformed orthodoxy in the second quarter of the seventeenth century.

Amyraut's views were supported by his colleagues in Saumur and by the pastors of the influential Reformed Church of Charenton near Paris. He was strenuously opposed by Pierre du Moulin of Sedan (1568–1658), André Rivet of the Netherlands (1572–1651) and Friedrich Spanheim of Geneva and Leiden (1600–49). At the National Synod of Alençon (1637) he was admonished, but not condemned for heresy. The controversy raged until 1661, with three periods of special intensity: 1634–37, 1641–49 and 1655–61. In the last period Amyraut did not participate in the debates carried out by Jean Daillé (Dallaeus, 1594–1670) and Samuel Desmarets (Maresius, 1599–1673).

Various assessments of the impact of the Salmurian theology have been offered. It seems apparent that it tended to weaken the unity of Reformed thought and to open the door to increasing departures from Reformed orthodoxy. It may have influenced King Louis XIV and his counsellors into thinking that there was no intrinsic incompatibility between the Reformed faith and Roman Catholicism. He was thus led to believe erroneously that the revocation of the Edict of Nantes would not produce great turmoil in France. The three Saumur professors together produced the large work *Theses Theologicae Salmurienses* (4 parts in 2 vols., 1664 and again in 1665), which became a frequently used manual for the study of theology.

One of Amyraut's students and successors at Saumur, Claude Pajon (1625–85), carried the trend further by positing that the Spirit's work of *regeneration is merely an illumination of the mind which brings about, of necessity, a change in the direction of the human will (congruism; see *Merit). This stance, strenuously opposed by Pierre Jurieu (1637–1713), increased misgivings about Saumur's orthodoxy. In 1675 J. H. Heidegger, in concert with F. Turretin (1623–1687) and L. Gernler, issued the *Formula Consensus Helvetica* designed specifically as an anti-Salmurian document, but the influence of Saumur was felt in all the countries to which French Protestants fled after the revocation of the Edict of Nantes.

Bibliography

On Saumur the fullest treatment is still to be found in P. Daniel Bourchenin, *Etude sur les Académies protestantes en France au XVIIe et au XVIIIe Siècles* (Paris, 1882). The researches of Jean Paul Pittion at Trinity College, Dublin are very valuable but difficult to access.

Studies: B. Armstrong, *Calvinism and the Amyraut Heresy* (Madison, 1969); A. C. Clifford, *Amyraut Affirmed, or Owenism, a Caricature of Calvinism* (Norwich, 2004); François Laplanche, *Orthodoxie et Prédication* (Paris, 1965); J. Leith, *Creeds of the Churches* (Richmond, ^{3}1982); R. Nicole, *Moyse Amyraut: A Bibliography* (New York and London, 1981); P. Schaff, *Creeds of Christendom*, vol. 1 (London, 1877), pp. 477–489; B. B. Warfield, *The Plan of Salvation* (Grand Rapids, 1942). Note also the PhD theses by J. Moltmann (Göttingen, 1951) and L. Proctor (Leeds, 1952).

R. NICOLE

ANABAPTIST THEOLOGY

The Anabaptists, together with other groups known today as the revolutionaries, spiritualists and evangelical rationalists, belonged to the radical wing of the *Protestant Reformation. Contemporary scholarship makes a distinction between the 'revolutionary Anabaptists' who were associated with the Zwickau Prophets, Thomas *Müntzer and the later violent Münsterites, and the 'evangelical Anabaptists' who found their origin in Conrad Grebel (c. 1498–1526), Hans Hut (d. 1527), Pilgram Marpeck (d. 1556) and Menno *Simons. The latter had their beginnings in Zurich in Switzerland and spread to South Germany, Moravia and the Netherlands with considerable homogeneity between each region. More recent studies, however, have contended for the multiple origins and diversity of the Anabaptist movement in these various centres, rather than for the monogenesis of a normative movement in Switzerland. Accordingly, the theology of this movement cannot be characterized without allowing for exceptions and paradoxes. But its basic theological emphases are clearly discernible.

The Anabaptists did not consciously do theology in the classical sense, even though they accepted the substance of the Christian *creeds. Their theology was much more occasional in nature. It was largely an exposition of Bible doctrine as it applies to life. In this manner they developed a theological focus of their own alongside and in reaction to magisterial Protestantism.

One of the central points of difference between the Anabaptists and the mainline Reformers relates to the question of human nature and *salvation. Whereas the Reformers defined *sin as bondage of the *will, the Anabaptists, rejecting the *Augustinian interpretation of the sovereignty of God, viewed sin as a loss of capacity or a serious sickness. For them there is no real repentance and commitment without the freedom of the will. Consequently, Anabaptist theology is not regulated by the concept of sin as much as by the concept of wilful obedience. Salvation is not simply a certitude of being saved from damnation but a walking in newness of life. The emphasis is more on *regeneration of the new being in Christ than on *justification by faith (*Rechtfertigung*). God in effect makes us righteous (*Gerechtmachung*) in Christ and then accepts us on the basis of that *righteousness. In order to ensure a sinless Christ as a basis for a strong doctrine of salvation, Dutch and North German Anabaptism held to a questionable view of the celestial origin and nature of Christ's flesh. This view was later superseded by a more traditional *Christology.

The attendant theology of the *church as a visible fellowship of obedient disciples, exhibiting the way of suffering love, was another of the controlling features of Anabaptist theology which diverged from magisterial Protestantism most emphatically. Various concepts of the church prevailed among the Anabaptists: church as congregation, as inner spiritual reality, as intentional community and as *kingdom of God. However, at the centre was the idea of the church as a believers' fellowship (*Gemeinde*) versus the church as a state church (*Volkskirche*).

The practice of adult *baptism was essential to the Anabaptist view of the church. Their rejection of infant baptism was based on the lack of NT evidence for such a practice. For them believers' baptism was the consequence of understanding the church as a voluntary fellowship, consisting of those who had experienced conversion and who were baptized upon the confession of their faith. It was a distinguishing mark of separation from the world and of commitment to Christian discipleship.

The central aspects of Anabaptist ecclesiology were actual personal *conversion, holy living, suffering in the Spirit of Christ, practice of *love and non-resistance, separation from the *world, full community in the church, obedience to the great commission, maintenance of church *discipline, rejection of the use of power by Christians and of involvement in political office, and freedom of conscience. In contrast to the Reformers, the Anabaptists emphasized the fallenness of *Christendom and the restoration of the NT church.

The strong emphasis on separation from the world was balanced by a burning missionary zeal which took the Anabaptists into the world. Unbounded by national and racial lines, they were the first to make the great commission the responsibility of every church member. This represented a break with the territorial principle and with Protestant and Catholic doctrine. Moreover, the church's relationship to society was informed by a two-kingdom theology in which the conflict between the church and the *state was seen to be much greater in principle than for the other Reformers. The Anabaptists were emphatic about the fallenness of humanity and its potential for redemption, but not optimistic about changing the world system as such. Yet submission to governmental authority, ordered by God, was important, even though the state must not force the Christian community to compromise its allegiance to the way of the cross. For the most part Anabaptism was non-resistant in character. People who disagreed with the church should not be dealt with by the sword but by the process of church discipline governed by the way of Christ's suffering love. Thus, the non-resistance stance included more than a refusal to be involved in government, military service or war. It applied to personal, social and economic relationships.

Such a way of life reflected the empowering of the *Holy Spirit. The Anabaptists exhibited a frequent sense of reliance on the Spirit. Clearly the doctrine of the Spirit was central in relation to the walk of *faith. Moreover, the Spirit made the Bible a living word of God which must be obeyed and practised in daily life. The spiritual understanding of the *Scriptures was strongly linked to the believing community where one heard the word and discerned its meaning and will. The message of the Spirit was given in the community of believers gathered around the word. At times, however, subjectivistic and spiritualistic tendencies did emerge.

In their interpretation of Scripture the Anabaptists had much in common with their sixteenth-century contemporaries. However, some basic differences existed, especially on the relationship of the NT to the OT, the degree to which Scripture was the sole authority, and the extent to which biblical interpretation was dependent on obedience to Christ. For the Anabaptists a large part of interpreting the Bible was imitating it. Theirs was a *hermeneutic of obedience.

The centrality of the transformed life of discipleship resulted in severe persecutions. For many, suffering the way of the cross was essential to this kind of discipleship and profoundly shaped their *eschatology. *Suffering became a key to understanding the role of the believer in *history. The kingdom comes and is consummated through suffering for Christ. They generally agreed that they were living in the last days, in the tribulation preceding the second coming. Although chiliastic tendencies existed (see *Millennium) and eschatology was central to many Anabaptists, there was no agreement regarding the specific time of the end and their own stance towards it.

See also: MENNONITE THEOLOGY; REFORMATION, RADICAL.

Bibliography

H. S. Bender, 'The Anabaptist Vision', *CH* 13, 1944, pp. 3–24; H. S. Bender et al. (eds.), *The Mennonite Encyclopedia*, vols. I–IV (Scottdale, 1955–59); W. R. Estep, *The Anabaptist Story* (Grand Rapids, 1975); T. N. Finger, *A Contemporary Anabaptist Theology* (Downers Grove, 2004); R. Friedmann, *The Theology of Anabaptism* (Scottdale, 1973); H. Goertz, 'History and Theology: A Major Problem of Anabaptist Research Today', *MQR* 53, 1979, pp. 177–188; W. Klassen (ed.), *Anabaptism in Outline* (Scottdale, 1981); J. M. Stayer, W. O. Packull and K. Deppermann, 'From Monogenesis to Polygenesis: The Historical Discussion of Anabaptist Origins', *MQR* 49, 1975, pp. 83–121.

H. J. LOEWEN

ANALOGY

Analogy refers to the use of the same word to express a similarity of some sort between two different entities, without that word meaning either exactly the same thing in both cases (which would be univocity) or something completely different (which would be equivocity).

There are two principal types of analogy. The first type is the analogy of proportionality, in which the relation between one entity and one of its properties corresponds to the relation of a different entity to one of its properties, without any necessary connection being drawn. For example, both a pet and a design might be considered 'intelligent': a meaningful comparison is thereby offered, without any necessary relationship between the two entities being suggested. The second type is the analogy of attribution (or proportion), in which a word that applies most properly to one entity is, by derivative extension, applied to other entities. An example would be 'healthy', which is applied most properly to an individual and derivatively to things which contribute to health, for example, exercise and diet. The analogy of attribution can itself be used in two ways: first, extrinsically, where the property predicated is external to the second entity; and second, intrinsically, where the predication refers to an internal property of the second entity.

In the history of theology, these different types of analogy have figured prominently, if not without controversy, in the discussion of how human language can refer to *God. For *Thomas Aquinas, for example, if the statements 'God is wise' and 'that person is wise' were not only to be meaningful but also to preserve a sense of the difference between God and humanity, then analogous language alone was suitable. For *Duns Scotus, however, it was necessary to conceive of God in concepts that were not simply analogical but also (at least in part) univocal with reference to God and to the creature. This sort of debate about the necessity or otherwise of analogical language continues to the present day.

In the *Thomist tradition, a further debate arose over whether the more appropriate and useful type of analogy in theology was that of proportionality (e.g. Cajetan) or that of intrinsic attribution (e.g. Suárez). On both sides of this debate, however, there existed in Roman Catholic circles a fundamental presupposition that the use of analogy at all was only thinkable because God allowed the being of the creature to participate in some sense in the divine being. In other words, the use of analogy in language presupposed some sort of analogy of being, or *analogia entis*, between God and humanity. It was on this point that controversy arose in discussion between Protestant and Roman Catholic theologians in the twentieth century. While many significant Protestant theologians – such as Eberhard *Jüngel and Wolfhart *Pannenberg – advocated the importance of analogical language in speaking about God, there was greater reticence among Protestants to speak of an *analogia entis*. This reticence may, at least in part, have been influenced by Immanuel *Kant, who had previously undermined confidence in any concept of an analogous relation between God and humanity.

The strongest criticism of the *analogia entis* came from Karl *Barth, whose foremost concern was that the concept seemed to allow for a natural knowledge of God outside the event of divine revelation. By contrast, Barth saw the analogy between God and humanity not as a property possessed by the creature but as something which had always to be given and revealed and believed anew in an event of grace: the *analogia relationis* (analogy of relation) was given in the *analogia fidei* (analogy of faith). Roman Catholic responses to Barth from such figures as Hans Urs von *Balthasar made clear that Barth's criticism was directed at only one possible construal of the *analogia entis*, and that their own construal of the *analogia entis* was not beyond reconciliation with Barth's view. The question of the use of analogous language in theology remains a live one, and brings particularly into focus the relationships between nature and grace and between creation and reconciliation.

Bibliography

H. U. von Balthasar, *The Theology of Karl Barth: Exposition and Interpretation* (San Francisco, 1982); K. Barth, *CD*, vol. II/1 (Edinburgh, 1957); D. Bentley Hart, *The Beauty of the Infinite: The Aesthetics of Christian Truth* (Grand Rapids, 2003); J. Duns Scotus, 'Ordinatio' in *Philosophical Writings* (London, 1962); E. Jüngel, *God as the Mystery of the World* (Grand Rapids, 1983); W. Pannenberg, *Basic Questions in Theology*, vol. 1 (London, 1970); Thomas Aquinas, *Summa Theologiae*, vol. 3 (Cambridge, 2006).

P. T. NIMMO

ANALYTIC THEOLOGY

Analytic theology is a theological method that has its roots in twentieth-century analytic philosophy of religion. In the early 1980s, a number of those working in this field began to turn their attention to topics in philosophical theology. If questions in the *philosophy of religion are about generic philosophical issues raised by religious belief (e.g. the problem of evil, the justification of religious belief, etc.), philosophical theology concerns concrete matters pertaining to the theology of a particular religious tradition. The literature in philosophical theology gradually became more theologically informed, more sophisticated, and diversified to include a range of theological topics including central matters like the Trinity, incarnation, atonement, sin, eschatology, the nature of faith, and the like. It developed largely independently of contemporary *systematic theology, however, a matter that has been noted and lamented by people like R. R. Reno, who has written of 'theology's continental captivity', referring to the way in which theologians happily engage major continental philosophers as dialogue partners while ignoring analytics.

However, as this philosophical-theological literature matured into the 1990s, it became increasingly difficult for those outside the conversation to ignore. To all intents and purposes this was *theology being done by Christian philosophers independent of the theological schools and seminaries. By the early 2000s some rapprochement between the two sides was beginning to happen. Analytic theology was, as William Abraham has put it, 'an accident waiting to happen'. But what was new about it? In one respect, not very much. According to some pundits, it was merely *philosophical theology rebranded. Yet there were some important differences: theologians as well as philosophers were now working on theological topics using the sensibilities and literature of analytic philosophy to ask *dogmatic questions. Inevitably, this led to systematic theology done in the mode of analytic theology, as other theologians worked in the mode of *postliberalism, or *radical orthodoxy. Once there were practising theologians on board it became difficult to marginalize the movement within the study of *religion as the preserve of a few Christian philosophical trespassers. And, as the work of analytic theology has flourished since 2009, more collaboration has brought significant steps forward. Increasingly, this literature really engages with the theological tradition, with ancient and modern theologians, and with questions of theological method as well as constructive theology.

In many ways, analytic theology is a return to more classical analytical sensibilities that have governed Christian theology for much of its history in *scholasticism, as well as the work of key thinkers from St *Augustine and St

*Anselm of Canterbury to Jonathan *Edwards. Yet it is not just this; there is a real concern to engage in wider theological and religious discussion, and to foster dialogue between the Abrahamic faiths. There is also the beginnings of an awareness of the limits of analytic theology, and of worries it must take more seriously if it is to continue to flourish. These include concerns about ontotheology (roughly, the notion that the god of analytic theology is an *idol), criticisms from *feminist theology, the place of metaphor and tropes in *religious language (see also *Hermeneutics), and the relationship to other theological methodologies as well as allied disciplines such as biblical studies. There is much work to be done. But the fact that analytic theology has already made such headway indicates that it is meeting a theological need, and making a significant constructive contribution to twenty-first-century Christian theology.

Bibliography

The Journal of Analytic Theology, located at <http://journalofanalytictheology.com>; W. J. Abraham, *Analytic Theology: A Bibliography* (Dallas, 2012); O. D. Crisp, *A Reader in Contemporary Philosophical Theology* (London, 2009); idem, *God Incarnate: Explorations in Christology* (London, 2009); idem, 'Analytic Theology', *Expository Times* 122.10 (2011), pp. 1–9; idem, 'Reason, Style and Wisdom: More on Analytic Theology', *Journal of the American Academy of Religion* 81.3 (2013), pp. 609–613; O. D. Crisp and M. C. Rea, *Analytic Theology: New Essays in the Philosophy of Theology* (Oxford, 2009); K. Diller, *Theology's Epistemological Dilemma: How Karl Barth and Alvin Plantinga Provide a Unified Response* (Downers Grove, 2014); W. Hasker, *Metaphysics and the Tri-Personal God*, Oxford Studies in Analytic Theology (Oxford, 2013); P. A. Macdonald, 'Analytic Theology: A Summary, Evaluation, and Defence', *Modern Theology* 30.1 (2014), pp. 32–65; T. H. McCall, *Which Trinity? Whose Monotheism? Philosophical and Systematic Theologians on the Metaphysics of Trinitarian Theology* (Grand Rapids, 2010); T. H. McCall and M. C. Rea, *Philosophical and Theological Essays on the Trinity* (Oxford, 2010); R. Rauser, *Theology in Search of Foundations* (Oxford, 2009); M. C. Rea, *Oxford Readings in Philosophical Theology*, 2 vols. (Oxford, 2009); R. R. Reno, 'Theology's Continental Captivity', *First Things*, April 2006, located at: <http://www.firstthings.com/article/2006/04/theologys-continental-captivity>; W. Wood, 'Analytic Theology as a Way of Life', *Journal of Analytic Theology* 2 (2014), pp. 43–60.

O. D. CRISP

ANAMNESIS, see EUCHARIST

ANGELS

The term 'angel' (Heb. *mal'ak*, Gk *angelos*) refers to the particular function of 'messenger', whether divine or human. It is necessary, however, to narrow the category to divine or spiritual beings, and to expand it to include God's heavenly host, the so-called principalities and powers, and the evil spirits, including Satan.

Divine beings, the gods, are found in all religions. Biblical monotheism sought in various ways to emphasize the 'incomparability' of the God of Israel and hence to minimize the role of other divine beings. Nevertheless, the Bible itself and the Christian tradition have always made room for lesser spiritual beings, good and evil.

The classical tradition, from *Philo through *Thomas Aquinas, has seen angels as a particular kind of being, as 'minds without bodies'. In the so-called 'Celestial Hierarchy' of *Pseudo-Dionysius (sixth century), nine choirs of angels represents different ranks of angelic spirituality. The elaborate Thomistic speculation about angels led to a reaction by *William of Ockham, John *Calvin and later John *Locke. While quite different theologically, the latter emphasized the unknowability of angels, apart from the bare biblical attestations.

The rationalism of the Enlightenment went one step further in questioning the existence of angels altogether. *Schleiermacher relegated angels to the realm of the aesthetic, to be found only in hymnody and stained glass. 'Angelology' has dropped out of the theological syllabus as a topic, with the sole exception of Karl *Barth, who devoted a major portion of his *Church Dogmatics* to 'the representatives of Heaven'. Barth has been joined by some neo-classicists like Mortimer Adler, C. S. Lewis and Peter Kreeft, and by the postmodernist Walter Wink, who has tried to revitalize the idea of 'principalities and powers' as the 'actual spirituality of actual entities in the real world'. Among evangelicals, Wayne Grudem's dogmatic theology includes a major section on angels.

The other major sources of contemporary angelology today come from *Pentecostal writers, for whom the activity of angels and demons is considered real and present. Some missiologists like C. Peter Wagner see spiritual warfare among the principalities to be present in the mission field.

For those who accept the authority of the Bible, it seems clear that angels exist as distinct personalities, even if we can know very little about their essence. It is also clear that there are good and evil angels. It is possible that 'principalities and powers' are corrupted spiritual offices of God's governance of the fallen world.

All angels are creatures of God, but some have rebelled and are eternally damned. Other 'elect' angels serve God faithfully in heaven. Angels have a role to play in announcing salvation history, especially the coming of Jesus Christ. They also serve as a measure of the nature of Christ, who being in the form of God took on human nature, not angelic nature, and is now exalted above the angels (Hebrews 1 – 2).

Finally, angels remind us of the reality of heaven and hell. They represent the 'whence' of God's dwelling place and the 'whither' of God's final kingdom, where 'with angels and archangels and all the company of heaven' we cry 'Holy, holy, holy is the Lord of Hosts' (*Book of Common Prayer*).

See also: DEVILS AND DEMONS.

Bibliography

M. Adler, *The Angels and Us* (London, 1982); K. Barth, *CD*, vol. 3 (Edinburgh, 1960); *The Catechism of the Catholic Church* (London, 1994); W. Grudem, *Systematic Theology: An Introduction to Biblical Doctrine* (Leicester, 1994); P. Kreeft, *Angels and Demons: What Do We Really Know about Them?* (San Francisco, 1995); C. S. Lewis, *Perelandra* (London, 1944); S. F. Noll, *Angels of Light, Powers of Darkness: Thinking Biblically about Angels, Satan and Principalities* (Eugene, 1998); C. P. Wagner (ed.), *Engaging the Enemy: How to Fight and Defeat Territorial Spirits* (Ventura, 1991); W. Wink, *Unmasking the Powers: The Invisible Forces that Determine Human Existence* (Philadelphia, 1986).

S. F. NOLL

ANGLICANISM

The Church of England regards itself as catholic, part of the one universal *church, but reformed in the sixteenth century. Anglican Christians are committed to what they see in *Scripture as the interplay of many local churches and members on the one hand, and the universal church on the other. The local church is the universal church in a particular place. This can only be so when any particular local church is in communion with other local churches that make up the universal church. The Anglican Communion is that expression of the universal church to which local Anglican churches belong.

What is it to be an Anglican Christian?

Anglican theologians defended their reformation (see *Reformers, English) against the criticisms of the Roman Catholic Church, by affirming that Scripture could interpret itself, but not in the light of rational speculation about invisible realities. Rather, the observed realities of God's word in the Bible could be interpreted in the light of his observed handiwork in nature. This was the time of global exploration by sea, of founding new colonies in strange places such as America, and of discovering new species of plants and animals. So Anglican theologians argued that all truth was God's truth and that Scripture, while primary, should be listened to consistent with both the drama of redemption and God's work in the wider world.

The Reformers argued that all things necessary for salvation were clearly revealed in Scripture, and what was not clearly revealed was not necessary for salvation. How that salvation was to be proclaimed in different places and in different generations was to be decided appropriately by the people of that time and place, and not prescribed by Scripture. The Anglican distinctive is of doctrinal unity and acceptable diversity in how the Christian life is expressed.

For Anglicans the heart of Scripture was about salvation: saving truth is pastoral, and therefore has to be both conveyed in language that can be understood and in appropriate cultural forms. Anglican theology has therefore been engaged seriously with pastoral concerns and with culture.

As a result, the language of Scripture, worship, prayer and theology were to be in the mother tongue and culture of the people. So the Church of England produced Scripture in English and a book of prayer in the language of the common people. Liturgy has been very important for most Anglicans. The form of prayer book services teaches God's law, repentance, the basis of forgiveness, the need to hear God's word read and expounded, the creed, thanksgiving and intercessory prayer, the Lord's Prayer and the Lord's Supper or Eucharist (thanksgiving) focusing on the atoning death of Jesus. Evangelical Anglicans give priority to preaching as the principle medium for teaching the faith.

Anglicans also wished to demonstrate that in the Reformation they were not founding a new church, but were actually the legitimate continuation of the church that had been in the country through Augustine since the earliest times. They claimed to be restoring the relationship between the ancient biblical teaching and how the Fathers had been listening to that. So they were careful to demonstrate that their interpretations of Scripture were in line with the teaching of the early church and the Fathers of the church.

The focus on Scripture, interpreted in the light of culture and in conformity with the tradition of the church, has given rise to three particular emphases within the Anglican churches. The *Anglo-Catholic* tradition emphasizes continuity with the ancient apostolic church. Its key idea was that the Anglican Church was not just a *Protestant denomination but a branch of the Church Catholic. It points out that the historical succession of bishops and priests has been preserved in the Church of England since apostolic times; thus the validity of the sacraments that they celebrate is by people who have been validly ordained in an unbroken succession from the apostles. The *liberal* tradition developed a focus on reading Scripture in the light of culture. The Enlightenment made the rationality supreme in European thinking, and the liberal tradition refers to a way of reading the Bible as a collection of narratives of their time so as not to contradict current rational opinion, for example about miracles. The *evangelical* tradition seeks its roots in the Reformation itself, and in particular emphasizes that Scripture is fundamental and not just one among three co-equal ways of hearing the truth of God. Because of the Reformation emphasis on justification by faith, the evangelical tradition draws on the believer's personal experience of forgiveness and the presence of Christ. This was found in the emphasis on the transformation of the affections of the heart by *Cranmer, on personal faith in Christ which was developed by the *Wesleys and the subsequent *Methodist revival, and in the twentieth century on the reality of the presence of the Holy Spirit in the believer's life associated with the Pentecostal revival of the twentieth century.

These three strands co-exist in the Anglican Church. Some hold that their co-existence is the essential feature of Anglicanism as a bridge church between the Protestant and *Catholic traditions. Their co-existence is based on principled comprehensiveness, where each tradition respects the others and lives within the overall framework of submission to Scripture. The current difficulties in the Anglican Communion are related to unprincipled comprehensiveness, where all opinions are given equal value.

Expansion

When the Church of England began to expand beyond the boundaries of England, it did so in a variety of ways. It expanded to the Americas as the Society of the Propagation of the Gospel sent 300 clergy to North America between 1701 and 1776.

The Church of England, like other churches in Europe at the time, was not just a denomination but a folk and national church. Membership of the nation automatically involved membership of the national religion. But after the American Revolution, no religion was given special status, and all expressions of the Christian faith became denominations. How could the link with the Church of England therefore be maintained? The office of bishop was one way of securing this relationship, as all bishops were held to be part of one college. However, the bishops of the Anglican Church in North America could not, as Church of England bishops did, swear allegiance to the English crown. So after the American War of Independence their first bishops were ordained by Scottish bishops.

Two developments in the Anglican Church were very significant in its expansion. One was the insistence in the nineteenth century that every pastor in the Church of England had to live in the boundaries of his parish. This had not always been the case. Many had only visited their parishes very occasionally. As a result of this ruling, educated people now lived in even the most remote and poor areas. And these learned men, often with their wives, set up schools. By the end of the nineteenth century the whole of the education system in England was being run by the church. And where the Anglican Church spread throughout the world, the pattern of church and school was repeated.

A second development is linked with the foundation of the United States. After 1776, England at first grew tired of colonization and empire. It was occupied increasingly with defending its own shores against the armies of Napoleon. But some Anglican laymen were particularly exercised about the *slave trade and its horrendous effects on both slaves and slave owners. Reverend John Barclay, who was pastor on St Kitts in the Caribbean, observed the terrible conditions of the slaves working around his small church of St John's. He wrote to a friend in England, William Wilberforce. This was one of the factors that led eventually to the campaign led by Wilberforce and other Anglicans which succeeded in passing the law in 1807 outlawing the slave trade. The British navy was deployed around the world to intercept and stop slave ships. Then in 1832 the law was passed to free all slaves in British dominions.

The result for the Anglican Church was that there was a great concern to repay the debt to the African peoples for the horrors of the slave trade. So began the nineteenth-century missionary movement. In the West Indies the Anglican Church set up a diocese in 1825 to prepare the slaves for freedom. Missionaries went especially to Africa to bring Christian faith, education and commerce to replace the economy based on slavery. Treaties were drawn up with local rulers. Trading posts were established. These had to be protected on occasion, and gradually these areas were taken over. So the mission movement actually triggered the second phase of the British Empire.

The Anglican version of the Christian faith became very acceptable in many countries precisely because it emphasized the expression of the faith in the language, culture and traditions of the people. After all, the Church of England came into being because English Christians did not want to be ruled by Christian leaders outside England. However, these churches never became part of the Church of England in England. They were from the start regarded as free and independent churches. They were called the Church of England in the country where they were founded.

Questions therefore arose about what churches could be regarded as in fellowship with the Church of England. Inspired by the work of William Reed Huntingdon, a statement was drawn up at the General Convention of the Episcopal Church in Chicago in 1886, was subsequently adopted by the Lambeth Conference of 1888 and called therefore the Chicago/Lambeth Quadrilateral. It focused on four elements: the primacy of Scripture, the two dominical sacraments, the historic creeds and the episcopacy. If those four were in place, this could form the basis for fellowship between the Church of England and a sister church.

Later, questions were raised about what were legitimate interpretations of Scripture, by Bishop Colenso of South Africa, who founded the African National Congress. To resolve these questions, the Archbishop of Canterbury called the first conference of bishops of churches in fellowship with the Church of England in 1867. They met at Lambeth Palace, the archbishop's home in London.

This conference now meets every ten years to build fellowship and engage together on issues facing the worldwide communion of Anglican churches.

Recent growth

The Anglican Communion has never been so extensive as it is now. Since the 1960s it has grown with extraordinary vigour. The East African Revival of the 1920s and 1930s spread a desire for evangelism through lay people, as opposed to a church focused on the work of the clergy. And the independence of former British colonies in the 1960s brought to prominence many indigenous leaders who brought powerful and continuing renewal to a church growing tired towards the end of the colonial era. They also brought a deep concern to prove the contribution of the church to the well-being of the new nations.

At the time of writing, in Nigeria alone the Anglican Church has 18 million members. In Africa and Asia it has about 45 million members. In the USA it has 2 million and in the United Kingdom about 2 million regular church-going Anglicans.

The Anglican Communion is a fellowship of people across the barriers of race, colour, class and economics, most of whom are poor. The average Anglican is under thirty, black, female, lives on two dollars a day, walks three kilometres to get water and is orthodox in her faith. The gift of the Anglican Communion is that poor people are able to express their understanding of the Scripture in the one global church and that people of different cultures are able to correct each other's interpretation, thus preventing Christian faith and practice being subverted by elites.

In the view of many Anglicans in the Majority World, subordination to their prevailing culture characterizes the desire of many Anglican leaders in Western nations to dilute the biblical focus on the unique and exclusive lordship of Jesus, to compromise the biblical teaching on confining sex to marriage and, most specifically, to accept into the church's membership and leadership people who engage in same-sex practice without changing their behaviour. This latter contradicts the current teaching of the Anglican Church as set out in the 1998 Lambeth Conference resolution 1.10 that 'homosexual practice is incompatible with Scripture'. This resolution is being consistently disregarded by bishops in the US, Canada, New Zealand and in the British Isles. So the communion is seeking to address the issue of how they can live as a worldwide communion of autonomous (self-governing) churches and remain united and in partnership in the service of the gospel. Archbishop Drexel Gomez of the West Indies writes: 'Based on the 2004 Windsor Report from the Lambeth Commission on Communion and increasingly focused on that Report's proposed Anglican covenant, the shape of the answers to these challenges is gradually becoming clearer. They are answers which hold out the hope of developing a distinctively Anglican vision of national churches in an international communion that responds to the challenges of mission in the face of globalization while resisting the dangers of either captivity to our varied national cultures or a new form of ecclesial imperialism.'

In July 2007 all Anglican bishops, including those who had consecrated a partnered openly homosexual bishop in the USA, were invited to attend the Lambeth Conference in August 2008. Many bishops felt unable to have spiritual and table fellowship and decision-making with those who had consecrated such a bishop. But as they still needed to take counsel on vital matters of mission, over 1,000 Anglican bishops and leaders representing 35 million of the 60 million churchgoing Anglicans met in Jerusalem in June 2008 at the Global Anglican Future Conference 'to chart a way forward together that promotes and protects the biblical gospel and mission to the world'. They issued the Jerusalem Statement and Declaration and formed the Fellowship of Confessing Anglicans. While acknowledging Canterbury as an historic see, they did not accept that Anglican identity was determined necessarily through recognition by the Archbishop of Canterbury. They published the Jerusalem Declaration as the basis of their fellowship, and called on their Primates Council to assist in establishing the Anglican Church in North America. The Lambeth Conference will not meet in 2018.

See also: THIRTY-NINE ARTICLES; CHURCH GOVERNMENT.

Bibliography

D. Gomez, *On Being Anglican in the Twenty-First Century*, <http://www.anglican-mainstream.net/index.php/2007/03/30/anglicanism-one-of-the-most-vibrant-and-unstable-expressions-of-christianity-within-the-world-ab-drexel-gomez/>; Lambeth Commission, *The Windsor Report 2004* (London, 2004), <http://www.anglicancommunion.org/windsor2004/index.cfm>; H. R. McAdoo, *The Spirit of Anglicanism: A Survey of Anglican Theological Method in the 17th Century* (London, 1965); J. R. H. Moorman, *A History of the Church in England* (London, new edn, 1980); M. Nazir-Ali, *From Everywhere to Everywhere* (London, 1990); idem, *Shapes of the Church to Come* (Eastbourne, 2001); N. K. Okoh, V. Samuel and C. Sugden, *Being Faithful: The Shape of Historic Anglicanism Today* (Oxford, 2009); V. Samuel and C. Sugden, *Lambeth: A View from the Two-Thirds World* (London, 1989); A. Wingate, K. Ward, C. Pemberton and W. Sitshebo (eds.), *Anglicanism: A Global Communion* (London, 1998).

C. M. N. SUGDEN

ANGLO-CATHOLIC THEOLOGY

Anglo-Catholic theology is a style of theology within Anglicanism whose immediate historical origin is the Oxford Movement in the Church of England. Anglo-Catholic theologians would themselves understand their theology as a continuation of the broad stream of theological thinking stretching back behind the Reformation to the apostolic church and the patristic age.

The beginning of the Oxford Movement is traditionally seen in the preaching of the Assize Sermon by John *Keble in the University Church of St Mary's Oxford in 1833. This sermon was a riposte to the government of the day's decision to reduce the number of bishoprics in Ireland from twenty-two to twelve. Keble saw this as the state meddling with the things of God and, as such, a symbol of national apostasy. Keble's sermon can be seen as both conservative, in that it was a clarion call for the church to rouse itself against state-initiated reforms, but also as radical, in that it rooted the authority of the Church of England, not on the legal status given to it by the state, but on the spiritual authority given to it by God.

The leaders of the Oxford Movement promoted their thinking in a series of tracts, earning them the name Tractarians. The first of these tracts concerned the apostolicity of the church, and this was a declaration of what was to become a persistent theme in Anglo-Catholic theology: the doctrine of church. There were ninety tracts in all, which attempted to show that the doctrines of the Church of England were founded on its being directly related to the church of the apostles. The last tract, Tract 90, was written by John Henry *Newman and argued by a theological *tour de force* that there was nothing incompatible with Roman Catholic teaching in the *Thirty-Nine Articles of Religion, which articles had been born out of the controversies of the Reformation in England. For many, even those sympathetic to Newman, this was going too far. Indeed, Newman was by now persuading himself that he could no longer with integrity remain within the Church of England, and he was received into the Roman Catholic Church on 9 October 1845.

In some respects the Tractarians were inheritors of the earlier High Church tradition which, since the arrival of the Whig government in 1830, had waned in power, the influential Hackney Phalanx falling into disarray. The apostolic succession so dear to the hearts of Tractarians had been the subject of many works by high churchmen from 1760 to 1820. The Tractarians' theological views, however, set them apart from their immediate High Church predecessors, and historians still debate the origins of the Oxford Movement, seeing links with the Non-Jurors and, somewhat paradoxically, with the evangelical revival of the mid-eighteenth century. Several prominent members of the Oxford Movement had been evangelicals, including Newman. The Tractarians themselves, however, saw the eighteenth century as a period of decay for the Church of England. Somewhat artificially, they claimed a special relationship with the *Caroline Divines of the previous century. In Tract 90 Newman tried to ground his views in the thought of these men, but only by quoting them in a highly selective fashion.

The Oxford Movement was concerned with more than doctrine. Holiness of life was also of great concern, and this won admiration from those who were unconvinced by the movement's claims about the Church of England within the wider church. Edward Pusey, one of the movement's leaders, led a life of great austerity and was much sought after as a spiritual guide. Attention was given to how priests might best be trained, and the first independent theological college in England was set up by Charles Marriott at Chichester in 1839. Concern for establishing the apostolic credentials of the Church of England led to a revival of interest in the Church Fathers. Pusey, with others, started translating patristic works, beginning with the *Confessions* of St Augustine, in a series known as the *Library of the Fathers*.

The leaders of the movement taught the real presence of Christ in the *Eucharist, and, as the thought of the movement disseminated more widely in the church, changes in the style and setting of *worship manifested themselves. Candles on the altar, for example, began to make an appearance, and the surplice began to replace the customary black preaching gown. Some church architects were inspired to design churches whose interiors provided an elaborately beautiful setting for worship. Notable amongst their number was William Butterfield (1814–1900), a brilliant example of whose work can be seen at All Saints, Margaret Street, London. The style of worship flowing from the Oxford Movement is usually referred to as 'ritualism'. Great interest was shown in a court case (1889–90) brought by the Church Association against the saintly Bishop of Lincoln, Edward King, who was accused of a number of ritualistic offences. The liturgical and architectural changes introduced by the Oxford Movement were an attempt to make visible the continuity between the Church of England and the early and medieval church. These changes were controversial because they were seen as illegal departures from the *Book of Common Prayer* and as leading the Church of England towards the Roman Catholic Church.

In addition to these developments in worship, some priests saw the ideals of the Oxford Movement finding expression in social action. In the Anglo-Catholic tradition there are a number of priests whose memory is honoured for having devoted their lives to parish ministry in socially deprived contexts. Chief among these is Charles Lowder (1820–80), who worked in Wapping building a new parish church, St Peter's London Docks.

The influence and development of the Oxford Movement can be traced in a number of ways. Together with an increase in *liturgical scholarship it bore fruit in the Parish Communion movement. *Liturgy and Society* by A. G. Herbert was a seminal work, and British liturgical scholarship is forever indebted to the work of Gregory Dix, especially his work on the development of the Eucharist, *The Shape of the Liturgy*. In the face of German scholarship, Pusey had taken a conservative stance towards historical criticism as it applied to the Bible, but a shift towards the acceptance of modern biblical scholarship can be seen in the publication of *Lux Mundi* (1889) and *Essays Catholic and Critical* (1926).

The Oxford Movement thus found expression in a number of ways, including doctrine, personal holiness, the training of priests, scholarly research into the Fathers, worship and social action. Underlying these expressions are a number of theological concerns which motivated the leaders and thinkers of the Oxford Movement and continue to motivate those who would call themselves Anglo-Catholics today.

It is typical of Anglo-Catholic theology to reach for continuity rather than discontinuity, and integration rather than paradox. Searching for an underlying principle for the Anglo-Catholic doctrinal style, one might identify the *analogia entis,* associated particularly with the medieval theologian *Thomas Aquinas. This 'principle of *analogy' claims that there is continuity between God and the world, not because the world is identical in any sense with God, but because the world as God's creation can be a vehicle of divine expression. Anglo-Catholic theology therefore tends towards a sacramental view of the world as a whole, within which would be located a sacramental understanding of the church and its worship. The instinct for continuity also finds historical expression in the importance given to tradition. The tradition of the church is understood as that historical dynamic process, led by the Holy Spirit, which keeps the church faithful to its apostolic mission in each generation and guides the church through a process of development into the truth. A classic treatment of this dynamic concept of tradition is to be found in *An Essay on the Development of Christian Doctrine* by Newman.

The affirmation of the continuity between God and the created order undergirds the sacramentalism typical of Anglo-Catholicism. Anglo-Catholic theology has traditionally affirmed the seven *sacraments scheme of medieval Catholicism, but since the Second Vatican Council would now see the seven sacraments themselves as acts of the church, itself understood sacramentally. The claim of *Lumen Gentium*, Vatican II's *Dogmatic Constitution on the Church*, that the church 'is in the nature of sacrament – sign and instrument, that is, of communion with God and of unity among all men' (LG 1) would find ready acceptance in Anglo-Catholic circles. Seeing the whole church in sacramental terms lies behind the view that the church is integral to the mediation of grace. The mediatorial role is not seen as apart from Christ, let alone opposed to his unique mediatorial role, but as within Christ. The classic expression of this understanding of the church is found in the notion of the *totus Christus*, a favourite term of St Augustine of Hippo.

The sacramental understanding of the church is reflected in the Anglo-Catholic understanding of worship. The Eucharist is the supreme act of Christian worship and for that reason might well be celebrated not only every Sunday but also every day in some Anglo-Catholic parishes. Central to the understanding of the Eucharist is a strong belief in the presence of Christ in the consecrated elements, although not to the exclusion of Christ's presence in the whole of the eucharistic gathering. The environment and accoutrements of worship are typically ordered with great care, drawing on all the worshippers' senses to promote a sense of sacramental encounter with the living God in Christ. Vestments, coloured according to the sequence of the seasons of the church's year, are worn by the priest and other assistant ministers, incense is used and a bell or gong might be sounded at various points during the saying of the eucharistic prayer. Within such a setting, the ministry of the word is not ignored, but has its place within the Eucharist, interpreting what is enacted in the sacramental action.

The continuities typical of Anglo-Catholic theology in general are found in its theology of the church. The claim of the Church of England's canons that the 'the Church of England is part of the One, Holy, Catholic and Apostolic Church' (see Canon C15) is given full weight in Anglo-Catholic theology. On this view the Church in England exists in continuity with the ancient catholic church in England. It is not an invention of the Reformation nor a re-emergence of the church of the NT after centuries of error. The retention of the three-fold order of deacon, priest and bishop at the Reformation is seen as an important sign of the continuity of the Church in England during the upheavals of that period. An Anglo-Catholic theology of the church would demonstrate a strong sense of unity between the church militant and the church triumphant, and this would find a liturgical expression in the invocation of the saints, pre-eminent among whom would be the Virgin Mary.

The leaders of the Oxford Movement had developed a branch theory to account for the Church of England's apostolic origins in a divided church. Along with the Roman Catholic Church and the Orthodox Churches, according to this theory, Anglicanism was an authentic branch of the one true church. This historic account of the place of the Anglican Church within the one church is echoed in the *ecumenical movement of today in whose *faith and order agenda Anglo-Catholic concerns have a major role to play. For Anglo-Catholics the order of the church is not a matter of indifference, especially the ordering of the ministry. Typical of its concern for continuity, in this case historical continuity, the maintenance of the apostolic ministry in the church, including the historic episcopacy of the church, is of great importance. It was Michael Ramsay in *The Gospel and the Catholic Church* (1936), a classic statement of Anglo-Catholic ecclesiology, who argued for understanding church order as an integral part of the essential structure of the church. The church is an extension of the incarnation and as such has a visible structure which embodies the truth of the gospel of Jesus Christ. For Anglo-Catholics, ecumenical rapprochement with another church would be on the basis of a vision of a united church, including a ministry ordered in the apostolic succession. There is a natural sympathy with the work of the Anglican-Roman Catholic International Commission (ARCIC), including a largely positive reception of its work on authority in the church (*The Gift of Authority*, 1999) and the role of *Mary (*Mary: Grace and Hope in Christ*, 2004), work which has proved controversial in the wider Anglican Church.

For Anglo-Catholics, the ordination of women to the priesthood has proved controversial. For many within the Anglo-Catholic wing, this development is unacceptable without substantial ecumenical agreement. Typically, it is argued that the Church of England has no authority on its own to make this change since the priesthood belongs to the whole church, not merely to the Anglican Church. In practical terms, while the Roman Catholic Church remains unconvinced by the validity of this change, most Anglo-Catholics would find it unacceptable.

The concern for social action within Anglo-Catholicism can be understood within the sacramental perspective. The classic expression of this was by Frank Weston, Bishop of Zanzibar, who, presiding at the 1923 Anglo-Catholic Congress, said, 'You cannot claim to worship Jesus in the Tabernacle, if you do not pity Jesus in the slums . . . It is folly – it is madness – to suppose that you can worship Jesus in the Sacraments and Jesus on the throne of glory, when you are sweating him in the souls and bodies of his children.' Notable amongst contemporary Anglo-Catholic theologians who stand in this tradition is Kenneth Leech, author of several books, including *The Social God*. Kenneth Leech was a founder figure of the Jubilee Group which began in 1974 as a support group for politically left-wing priests, most of whom stood in the Catholic tradition of Anglicanism. It initiated the Jubilee 2000 campaign for the alleviation of Majority World debt.

Within all traditions in the church there are differences of emphasis and disagreements, and Anglo-Catholic theology is no exception. In the matter of the ordination of women to the priesthood, for example, there are those who would see themselves as Anglo-Catholic, or Anglican Catholics, who accept this development of ministry. The organization *Affirming Catholicism* provides a forum for such Anglicans to meet. On the other side of the debate, the organization *Forward in Faith* speaks for many Anglo-Catholics opposed to the ordination of women to the priesthood. Although there are some common deep-seated theological principles to be found in Anglo-Catholic theology it would be a mistake to think of this theology as monolithic.

See also: ANGLICANISM; CHURCH; LITURGY.

Bibliography

G. Dix, *The Shape of the Liturgy* (London, 1945); G. Guiver, *Faith in Momentum* (London, 1990); A. G. Herbert, *Liturgy and Society* (London, 1935); K. Leech, *The Social God* (London, 1981); J. H. Newman, *An Essay on the Development of Christian Doctrine* (Notre Dame, ^{6}1989 [1845]); P. B. Nockles, *The Oxford Movement in Context: Anglican High Churchmanship 1760–1857* (Cambridge, 1994); M. Ramsey, *The Gospel and the Catholic Church* (London, 1936).

W. S. CROFT

ANHYPOSTASIA, see HYPOSTASIS

ANIMISM

A term introduced into the discussion about the origin and nature of religion by the anthropologist E. B. Tylor (1832–1917). He used it as a synonym for religion which he defined as 'the belief in Spiritual Beings'. This belief arose when primitive humans, in attempting to explain phenomena such as sleep, death, dreams and visions, came to the conclusion that they possessed a detachable phantom or ghost soul. Their primitive imagination then led them to attribute a similar soul to animals, plants and even inanimate objects.

According to Tylor, from this primitive reasoning, by means of general cultural influence, all forms of religion developed. As a *positivist, he also believed that animism or 'the spiritualistic philosophy', based as it was on a false process of reasoning, was destined to disappear before the flood of 'materialistic philosophy'. But, though very influential for half a century, the theory was eventually superseded since it was based on the presupposition that so-called 'contemporary primitives' are 'survivals' of an actual primitive stage of human evolution. However, its influence is apparent in that, for example, the theories of primitive *monotheism of Lang (1844–1912) and Schmidt (1868–1954), the pre-animism of Marett (1866–1943) and the social theory of Durkheim were all presented as alternatives to it. Despite the fact that the theory has been superseded, the term can be usefully retained to describe a religion which is characterized by a belief in a multiplicity of spirits. It continues to be used as an umbrella term covering tribal or primal religions, in contrast with the major world faiths.

Bibliography

K. W. Bolle, 'Animism and Animatism', in M. Chade (ed.), *The Encyclopedia of Religion*, vol. 1 (New York, 1987); E. Durkheim, *The Elementary Forms of the Religious Life* (London, 1915); E. E. Evans-Pritchard, *Theories of Primitive Religion* (Oxford, 1965); G. Harvey, *Animism: Respecting the Living World* (London, 2005); A. Lang, *The Making of Religion* (London, 1898); R. R. Marett, *The Threshold of Religion* (London, ^{2}1914); W. Schmidt, *The Origin and Growth of Religion* (London, 1931); E. B. Tylor, *Primitive Culture* (London, 1871); E. B. Tylor, *Mind* 2, 1877, pp. 141–156.

D. A. HUGHES

ANNIHILATIONISM

Annihilationism holds that those who go to hell will suffer final destruction rather than eternal conscious punishment. As such, it diverges from the traditional teaching of the church that hell entails endless torment for the unsaved. Until quite recently the greatest challenge to this traditional view came from *universalism. However, since the 1980s support has grown for annihilationism, particularly among evangelical Christians who reject universalism, but who question the traditional view on exegetical, moral and pastoral grounds.

In common with traditionalists, annihilationists affirm a decisive division of saved and condemned persons at the last judgment. Yet they argue that the suffering of those condemned must eventually cease, since the perpetuation of that suffering, and of hell itself, would be inconsistent with God's plan to restore the cosmos to perfect peace and harmony (Eph. 1:9–10; Rev. 21:1–4). Whereas traditionalists characteristically stress that rejection of an eternal God deserves eternal reprobation, annihilationists highlight biblical indications that divine judgment might be graded in severity, and that this might correspond to varied lengths and degrees of finite punishment for the unsaved, rather than undifferentiated eternal punishment for them all (Luke 10:12; 12:47–48).

Annihilationsm was espoused in the early fourth century by Arnobius of Sicca, but it was more generally anathematized by the Second Council of Constantinople in 553 and again by the Lateran Council in 1513. It resurfaced among sectarian groups like *Socinians and Christadelphians, but by the later 1800s had gained the support of more mainstream Christian theologians like Edward White and Henry Constable.

While evangelicals remain largely opposed to annihilationism, certain evangelical scholars have sympathized with or propounded it in more recent times, including Edward Fudge, John Wenham, Clark *Pinnock, Stephen Travis, David Powys and John Stott. Stott tentatively identified himself with the annihilationist position in 1988, and in doing so prompted a debate which is ongoing, and which has featured firm restatements of the traditionalist case from J. I. *Packer, D. A. Carson, Kendall Harmon and others. In 2000, the UK Evangelical Alliance published a report on the matter, which concluded that annihilationism was a 'significant minority evangelical view' whose divergence from the traditional position should be regarded as a secondary rather than primary doctrinal issue.

Although annihilationism technically concerns the nature of hell as such, in practice it is closely linked to the doctrine of 'conditional immortality'. This posits that the concept of the 'immortality of the soul', which typically underpins the traditional view of hell, owes more to Platonist thought than to biblical teaching. Indeed, rather than viewing the human soul as inherently immortal, conditionalists argue that it acquires immortality as a condition of *justification by grace through faith (see Immortality; Soul, origin of). Those not justified will thereby cease to exist, so manifesting their mortality apart from Christ. Romans 6:23 is often adduced here: 'The wages of sin is death, but the gift of God is eternal life.' While Socinians and Christadelphians equate 'death' in this context with the end of earthly life, mainline conditionalists relate it to the annihilation of the impenitent only after they have been resurrected, judged, and punished in hell for some time.

Annihilationists emphasize images of destruction and extinction in biblical eschatology, and interpret divine retribution in this context. In particular, they argue that the term *apollumi* ('destroy') in the NT commonly implies the end of existence rather than the perpetuation of torment. So the plain sense of Jesus' warning that God 'can destroy both soul and body in hell' (Matt. 10:28) is set against Greek notions of innate immortality, and against traditionalist claims that *apollumi* and its synonyms can connote a process of endless 'perishing'. Similarly, whereas traditionalists relate the 'unquenchable fire' and 'undying worm' of Mark 9:48 to the eternal punishment of individuals, annihilationists argue that while the worm and the fire themselves may be everlasting, the effect they have on particular sinners may yet be terminal. Moreover, whereas Jesus in Matt. 25:46 appears to draw a straight parallel between 'eternal life' and 'eternal punishment' by applying the same adjective (*aionios*) to both states, annihilationists suggest that if the punishment in question is a punishment of destruction, it would again be eternal in its overall effect rather than in the existence of every condemned sinner. Here, as in Rev. 14:11 and 20:10, annihilationists also argue that *aionios* and its variants might well be read qualitatively rather than quantitatively – that is, as defining the intensity of punishment rather than its specific duration.

While some continue to insist that annihilationism is *heresy, it is at least clear that Scripture depicts the fate of the unsaved in terms normally associated with destruction, as well as in terms of protracted punishment and irrevocable separation from God. Indeed, on occasion all three concepts coalesce in a single verse (e.g. 2 Thess. 1:9). Given the serious challenges involved in the reconciliation of these concepts, it seems likely that having established itself as a prominent alternative to the traditional view of hell, annihilationism will remain a significant feature of theological discourse on the 'last things' for some time to come.

See also: ESCHATOLOGY, JUDGMENT OF GOD.

Bibliography

N. M. de S. Cameron (ed.), *Universalism and the Doctrine of Hell* (Carlisle, 1992); D. L.

Edwards and J. R. W. Stott, *Essentials: A Liberal-Evangelical Dialogue* (London, 1988); E. W. Fudge, *The Fire That Consumes: The Biblical Case for Conditional Immortality* (Carlisle, rev. edn, 1994); D. Hilborn (ed.), *The Nature of Hell: A Report by the Evangelical Alliance Commission on Unity and Truth among Evangelicals* (ACUTE) (Carlisle, 2001); C. W. Morgan and R. A. Peterson (eds.), *Hell under Fire: Modern Scholarship Reinvents Eternal Punishment* (Grand Rapids, 2004); C. H. Pinnock and R. C. Brow, *Unbounded Love: A Good News Theology for the 21st Century* (Carlisle, 1994); D. J. Powys, *'Hell': A Hard Look at a Hard Question* (Carlisle, 1997); G. Rowell, *Hell and the Victorians* (Oxford, 1974).

D. H. K. HILBORN

ANOMOEANS, see ARIANISM

ANONYMOUS CHRISTIANITY

A theological concept developed by Karl Rahner in order to explain the possibility of salvation without explicit Christian faith, which modern *Roman Catholic theology has widely acknowledged. As Rahner expounds it, the idea follows from some of the most basic themes of his theology. He holds that all human persons, in their pre-reflective experience, are orientated towards God, and that God gives himself in *grace to all humans, in the centre of their existence, as an offer which can be accepted or rejected. Thus God is always and everywhere present in human experience, and the possibility of a saving relationship with God is universal, corresponding to God's universal will for human salvation (see *Universalism). This universal revelation of God and the salvific experience of God which makes it possible are pre-reflective, implicit in human experience, before they are understood explicitly and conceptually. The religions of the world are more or less successful attempts to make this 'transcendental' experience of God explicit in reflective forms and social, historical embodiments. But salvation is possible not only within the non-Christian religions, but also for *atheists, who do not thematize their transcendental experience in religious terms at all.

For Rahner, the specifically Christian *revelation of God is his 'categorical' revelation: his revelation of himself in explicit, historical forms. It is the explicit form of his universal, transcendental revelation. Consequently, the salvation which is universally available is essentially the same as salvation within the Christian church. Explicit Christian faith is the explicit form of the implicit faith which is possible without any knowledge of the Christian revelation. Those who are saved through such implicit faith, Rahner calls 'anonymous Christians'. They are anonymous Christians because they do not have explicit Christian faith, but they are anonymous Christians, because Rahner retains the doctrine that there is no salvation apart from Christ. Their implicit faith must be related to Christ.

How is this possible? Jesus Christ is the complete and definitive expression of God's self-communication to humanity and the human acceptance of this. He is therefore the supreme and unique fulfilment of that possibility of salvific relationship with God which is everywhere present in the human spirit. As such, he is the goal towards which the faith even of the anonymous Christian is implicitly orientated. Rahner is able to claim that the anonymous Christian is saved because of Jesus Christ.

Rahner's concept of anonymous Christianity has been very influential in Roman Catholic thought, but it has also been strongly criticized by some other Roman Catholic theologians. Hans Urs von *Balthasar charged Rahner with relativizing the biblical revelation of God. Hans *Küng, while agreeing that non-Christians can be saved, thinks that the idea of 'anonymous Christianity' is offensive to non-Christians and evades the real challenge of the world religions by pre-empting the dialogue before it has begun.

A full appraisal of Rahner's proposal would need to examine the understanding of transcendental experience and Christian salvation on which it rests. It is arguable that Rahner's whole transcendental approach to theology gives insufficient weight to the historical nature of all human experience, and therefore to the historical character of the knowledge of God available through Jesus Christ.

See also: CHRISTIANITY AND OTHER RELIGIONS.

Bibliography

P. Conway and F. Ryan (eds.), *Karl Rahner: Theologian for the Twenty-First Century* (Oxford, 2010); K. Kilby, *The SPCK Introduction to Karl Rahner* (London, 2007); D. Marmian and M. E. Hines (eds.), *The Cambridge*

Companion to Karl Rahner (Cambridge, 2005); K. Rahner, *Theological Investigations* (London, 1961–81), vol. V, ch. 6; vol. VI, ch. 23; vol. IX, ch. 9; vol. XII, ch. 9; vol. XV1, chs. 4, 13; vol. XVII, ch. 5; vol. XVIII, ch. 17; idem, *Foundations of Christian Faith* (London, 1978).

R. J. Bauckham

ANSELM (*c.* 1033–1109)

Born in Aosta in Italy, at the age of twenty-six Anselm became a *Benedictine monk, entering the abbey of Bec in Normandy. In 1063 he was made prior, in succession to Lanfranc (*c.* 1005–89), and fifteen years later abbot, a post he held for a further fifteen years (1078–93). He then again succeeded Lanfranc, this time as Archbishop of Canterbury, for sixteen years, until his death in 1109. Anselm sought to uphold the pope's rights in England and to maintain the independence of the English church from the king. As a result, most of his time as archbishop was spent on the continent, in exile.

Anselm was the first truly great theologian of the medieval Western church and is seen by some as the founder of *scholasticism. He clearly held to the supreme authority of Scripture and was thoroughly *Augustinian in his theology. But whereas most theologians at that time relied heavily on citing traditional authorities (such as Augustine and the Bible), Anselm composed highly original works based on rational argument. It is in this respect that he was the forerunner of scholasticism. He allowed philosophy a significant, though limited, role in his theology, following Augustine's method of 'faith seeking understanding'. The content of the Christian faith is given by *revelation, not by philosophy. But believing theologians can then seek, by the use of reason, to understand more fully that which they believe. Reason can thus show the rationality and inner coherence of the Christian faith.

This method Anselm pursued in his three major works. In the *Monologion* (1077), originally called *An Example of Meditation on the Grounds of Faith*, he offers a 'proof' for the existence of God. The fact that we can discern degrees of goodness means that there is an absolute good, by which we measure it. This good is alone good of itself and is supremely good. Being supremely good, it is also supremely great. There is therefore a supremely good and supremely great being, the highest of all existing beings: God. Anselm's argument was not original, Augustine having argued similarly. It depends for its force on the 'realist' assumption that the universal is more real than particular manifestations of it (see *Nominalism). Thus the (*Platonic) idea of goodness is more real than the particular manifestation of it in the life of a good person. Anselm's apologetic would have had force in an age where Platonic realism was widely accepted, but carries little conviction today.

The following year Anselm broke new ground with the publication of his *Proslogion*, originally called *Faith Seeking Understanding*. Starting as a believer, he seeks to understand what he already believes. 'I am not seeking to understand in order to believe, but I believe in order to understand. For this too I believe: that unless I believe, I shall not understand.' In this work Anselm presents his famous ontological argument for the existence of God. God is defined as 'that, than which nothing greater can be conceived' or, to put it more simply, 'the greatest conceivable being'. This being must exist. Were he not to exist, he would be inferior to an identical being that did exist and thus would not be 'the greatest conceivable being'. Indeed, the 'greatest conceivable being' exists so certainly that it cannot even be *conceived* not to exist. For the mind can conceive of a being which cannot be conceived not to exist and such a being is greater than a being which *can* be conceived not to exist. Therefore there is a 'greatest conceivable being' that cannot even be conceived not to exist. Anselm identifies this being with the Christian God.

Anselm has, with some justice, been accused of attempting to define God into existence. His approach represents the supreme confidence of the eleventh-century West in the power of reason. Anselm considered that his argument should suffice to persuade even the 'fool' who denies God's existence (Ps. 14:1). But the validity of his argument was immediately questioned by a monk called Gaunilo, who wrote *On Behalf of the Fool*, to which Anselm wrote a *Reply*. The debate about the validity of the ontological argument continues to rage and shows no signs of abating.

Proslogion was of particular significance for one modern theologian: Karl *Barth. In his *Fides Quaerens Intellectum* (*Faith Seeking Understanding*, 1931), Barth analysed Anselm's method of 'faith seeking understanding' and found in it a precedent for his own approach to theology in the twentieth century.

Anselm's most ambitious work was his *Cur Deus Homo* (*Why God Became Man*), written in the 1090s. It is presented in the form of a dialogue between Anselm and Boso (one of his monks at Bec). Here Anselm, like the *apologists of the early church, faces the charge that it is unfitting and degrading for God to humble himself by becoming man and dying to save us. This charge was made by Jews and Muslims, and in Anselm's time there were regular debates between Jews and Christians. Anselm offers reasons why the *incarnation and *cross are in fact both necessary and fitting (see *Atonement). But this does not mean that he is offering a *natural theology, building theology purely on the basis of reason. Here, as in the *Proslogion*, his method is one of 'faith seeking understanding'. Having believed the doctrines of the incarnation and the cross, he uses reason to understand why they are true. He suspends not faith itself, but the appeal to faith. But this does not mean that Anselm is a *fideist, writing theology simply from the position of the believer and for believers. He does set out to convince the unbeliever, by arguing *remoto Christo*, as if we knew nothing about Christ. He starts, not with no presuppositions, but by assuming the existence of God as *Trinity, together with God's character, the nature of humanity and its sin against God. He then seeks to show, by necessary reasons, that given these presuppositions the incarnation and the cross are absolutely necessary, the only possible course of action open to God. Thus he seeks to show the unbeliever that the incarnation and the cross, far from being unfitting and degrading for God, are the only reasonable course of action open to him, granted a Christian view of God and humanity.

Anselm argues that *sin, understood as a failure to render due obedience to God, dishonours him. God, as the upholder of justice and law, cannot simply forgive, but must restore his lost honour. This can happen in one of only two ways: either a suitable satisfaction is offered to God, or he must restore his honour by punishing humanity. But the latter course is not open to God, as human beings are needed to replace the fallen angels. (This last point, taken from Augustine, does not carry much weight today, but there are other reasons why God cannot simply abandon the human race.) Therefore, sinful humanity must restore God's honour by offering him a suitable satisfaction. But here God faces a dilemma. It is man who owes the satisfaction, but only God is able to pay it (which Anselm argues by showing the seriousness of sin). The need is for a God-man, hence the incarnation. As man, Christ owes God the obedience of a perfect life. But as a perfect man, he need not die. His death earns him merit and serves as a suitable satisfaction for human sins, hence the cross.

Anselm's case is impressive, but not without its weaknesses. He has been criticized on a number of grounds, some of which amount to blaming him for addressing his own particular context, where, for instance, talk of honour and satisfaction was familiar both because of the *penitential system in the church and because of feudal concepts in society. He has with some justice been criticized for locating the salvific work of Christ exclusively in the cross, neglecting the life of Christ and his resurrection and ascension. But it must be remembered that his aim was precisely to give reasons why the cross, the great scandal to unbelievers, was necessary. Anselm also went beyond the usual Christian claim that the cross was necessary (i.e. God had to do something) to claim that it was absolutely necessary (i.e. God could not have done anything else, given the situation). Here again he reflects eleventh-century confidence in the power of reason. But the attractiveness of Anselm's case is that it is very flexible. His basic case, suitably modified, makes a powerful argument today that the incarnation and cross are indeed fitting and reasonable. A brief summary of his argument is found in his *Meditation on Human Redemption*.

Apart from these three, Anselm wrote a number of other significant works, including:

Truth: like the two following works, a dialogue written between 1080 and 1086. It explores the definition of truth, an unresolved issue from the *Monologion*, and defines it as 'a rectitude perceptible by mind alone'. Justice is 'rectitude of will preserved of its own sake'.

Freedom of Choice: a dialogue which explores how rational creatures are free to choose and defines freedom of choice as 'the power to preserve rectitude of will for its own sake'.

The Fall of the Devil: a dialogue concerning the origin of evil when Satan lost the righteousness in which he was created. Satan opted for his happiness above righteousness and so lost happiness; the good angels opted for righteousness above happiness and were rewarded with perfect happiness. Anselm follows Augustine in seeing evil as the absence of good, just as darkness is the absence of light.

The Procession of the Holy Spirit: a record of his contribution to the Council of Bari in 1098, where Latin and Greek theologians discussed the credal *filioque* clause. Anselm defended it on the ground of the symmetry in the relations of the three persons of the Trinity.

De Concordia: Anselm's last major work, in which he argues for the compatibility of God's foreknowledge, predestination and grace with human freedom. God's foreknowledge and predestination are not incompatible with human freedom when what he foreknows or predestines is that we shall *freely* will to do certain things.

Anselm's aim in his writings was to show how reasonable *faith is, rather than to offer a strict proof of it. The beauty of the inner harmony of the Christian faith gives joy to the believer, who sees the accord of faith and reason. Unbelievers' objections (e.g. that it is degrading for God to have become man) are met, and they are pointed to the truth of the Christian message. Anselm had considerable confidence in the power of reason to show the rationality of Christian beliefs, a confidence that was to be progressively eroded over the following four centuries.

See also: Apologetics; Faith and Reason.

Bibliography

Works: F. S. Schmitt (ed.), PL 158–59 and *Opera Omnia* (Edinburgh, 1946–61); ET J. Hopkins and H. Richardson (eds.), *Complete Works* (London and Toronto & New York, 1974–76); B. Davies and G. R. Evans (eds.), *Anselm of Canterbury: The Major Works* (Oxford, 1998).

Studies: G. R. Evans, *Anselm and Talking about God* (Oxford, 1978); G. R. Evans, *Anselm* (London, 2005 [1989]); D. S. Hogg, *Anselm of Canterbury: The Beauty of Theology* (Aldershot and Burlington, 2004); J. Hopkins, *A Companion to the Study of St Anselm* (Minneapolis, 1972); J. McIntyre, *St Anselm and his Critics: A Re-Interpretation of the* Cur Deus Homo (Edinburgh and London, 1954); R. W. Southern, *Saint Anselm: A Portrait in a Landscape* (Cambridge, 1990).

A. N. S. Lane

ANTHROPOLOGY

The word 'anthropology' means, by derivation, the study (*logos*) of humanity (*anthropos*), and usually refers to the related sciences of physical or biological anthropology (belonging to the natural sciences) and cultural or social anthropology (belonging to the social sciences). But the term is also used to refer to an area of Christian theology which may be more strictly designated as theological anthropology, often referred to in the past as the 'doctrine of man' and now, with recent developments in usage, as the 'doctrine of humanity'. This study is an integral part of theology, but it cannot neglect the question of how the Christian understanding of humanity relates to the view of humanity taken in the natural and social sciences.

Humanity in the OT

OT scholarship over the last century has helped us to shake off the longstanding tendency among Christians to read the Hebrew Scriptures through the interpretative framework of our Hellenistic heritage. Whereas traditional Christian theology has worked with a Greek *dualism differentiating soul and body as two different substances, and has often been highly individualistic, a more authentic understanding of the Hebrew view has been recovered in which each human being is understood to be a psychosomatic unity and humanity is viewed as corporate and not simply a collection of individuals.

The corporate solidarity of the race is to be seen in the use of the word 'flesh' (*basar*). It is frequently used to refer to the human race as a whole, as for example in Isa. 40: 'And the glory of the Lord shall be revealed, and all flesh shall see it together' (v. 5, RSV). The whole human race is of a common stock so that, quite contrary to the individualism of modern Western thought, the basic unit of humanity is not the individual, but the family or tribe or nation. All humanity is a corporate whole, sharing the same flesh. Moreover, 'flesh' means humanity in its weakness; we are transient and subject to decay and mortality, perishing like the plants: 'All flesh is grass, and all its beauty is like the flower of the field. The grass withers, the flower fades when the breath of the Lord blows upon it; surely the people is grass' (vv. 6–7, RSV).

The antithesis between 'flesh' and 'spirit' is subtly different then from that in Hellenistic thought in which the realm of the flesh is the realm of constant change and activity, while the realm of the spirit is the transcendent realm of unchanging eternal calm, so that to be 'spirit' is to be in some sense divine. In OT thinking, the flesh is weak and inert, while the Spirit (*ruach*) of God is the source of life and movement (see Isa. 31:3). This weak and mortal condition of human flesh is linked with the breakdown in humanity's relationship with God recounted in the narrative of Gen. 2 and 3 (esp. 3:3). But while humanity as 'flesh' is weak and mortal, and indeed inert, without the breathing 'Spirit' (*ruach*) of God, it is not evil as in the extreme *Gnostic versions of Hellenism.

Within that context of humanity as corporate, we may understand the OT view of each human being as a psychosomatic unity. The *adam* was formed by the Lord God out of the *adamah* (dust) according to Gen. 2:7, and it was when God breathed the breath of life into his nostrils that he became a living soul (*nephesh*). Clearly, then, the *nephesh* is not a pre-existing eternal divine substance, and the translation 'soul' is somewhat misleading if interpreted in that Hellenistic way. Rather, the implication is that the body formed from the mud came alive, that is, became a living being. The human being is therefore 'not so much an embodied soul as an ensouled body'. Hebrew psychology thinks of the 'heart' (*leb*) not just as the centre of the emotions, but as the seat of the intellect and will, and human motivation is physically based in the liver and bowels and blood. With no concept of the immortal soul, there is little or no hope in the early parts of the OT for life after death except as shadowy figures half-existing in the pit or *sheol* (see Job 10:2–21; Pss 6:5; 88; 89:48; Isa. 14: 9–11).

Humanity in the NT

The NT writers inherit the hope of resurrection which appeared in the later books of the OT and became widespread in Second Temple Judaism. But the difference for them originated in their belief that 'the Word became flesh' in Jesus, who raised our corporate mortal humanity immortal in his *resurrection as the 'firstfruits' (1 Cor. 15:20). Their thinking about the doctrine of Christ (*Christology) as the Son of God who became truly *human* therefore began to influence their understanding of what it is to be human. While they also inherited from the OT the view of the human being as a psychosomatic unity, they nevertheless were part of the Greco-Roman culture with its Hellenistic belief in the immortality of the soul. Also, in the light of the resurrection of their Lord, they had to account for the continuity between the mortal body and the resurrection body. Paul does not call that continuing reality a 'soul' in his discussion of this in 2 Cor. 5: 1–10, but clearly there is a continuity of personal identity. And yet the body (*soma*) is not an appendage to an eternal *soul: a human being does not have, but is, his or her body. Body (*soma*) and soul (*psyche*) are two ways of referring to the essential person, one referring to the physical dimension, and the other to the intellectual, relational, personal dimension. Paul rejects the idea of existing as a disembodied spirit: his clear expectation is the resurrection of the body and the life to come as a whole human being in the new creation. While NT anthropology is less monistic than that in the OT, it still assumes the psychosomatic unity of the human being.

Theological development

The Christian theologians of the first five or six centuries did not develop 'anthropology' as a distinct doctrine, but their understanding of what it means to be human can be seen in their debates about Christology. In the *Apollinarian debate, both sides assumed the generally *Platonist anthropology of their culture. *Docetism (that Christ only appeared to have a body) had already been ruled out, but assuming that the soul was a distinct entity, they differentiated the psyche (Lat. *anima*), a principle which gave movement (animation) and which was also found in 'animals', from the *nous* (Lat. *mens*), that is, the mind or rational soul. The teaching of Apollinarius that the Son of God did not assume a human mind was rejected as *heresy.

The phrase which appears in Gen. 1:26–27, '*image of God', is ignored in the rest of the OT and refers to Christ in the NT (2 Cor. 4:4; Col. 1:15, but see also 1 Cor. 11:7 and Col. 3:10). But it became significant for the Fathers (see *Patristic theology). *Irenaeus distinguished between the 'image' (*imago*) which we cannot lose without ceasing to be human and the 'likeness' (*similitudo*) into which we are called to grow. *Athanasius speaks of Christ as the image of God; but as images of the Image, who is the *Logos of God, we were created to be rational. Only in the *knowledge of God, therefore, restored through his incarnation, can we truly reflect him.

*Augustine wrestled with anthropological questions – the *fall and original *sin, *grace, *predestination and the freedom of the *will. He developed a fuller analysis of human psychology on the basis of the view that it was the rational human soul (not the body) which was the *imago dei*, and that therefore we could gain some grasp of the doctrine of the Trinity by contemplating the interaction of memory, understanding and will within the unity of the human mind. He developed the doctrine of human sinfulness already common to the Fathers of East and West, by teaching that 'original sin' (*peccatum originale*), which all human beings inherited, included both a share in Adam's original guilt (although that was washed away in baptism) and the 'disease' of original sin as a condition of sinful self-centred desire (*concupiscentia*) which remained in us as long as we were in the body.

Medieval theologians developed the notion derived from *Plato and *Aristotle that different 'faculties' could be differentiated within the soul; this survives today in popular speech which differentiates the activities of the mind or intellect, the will, the heart and the conscience. The *Reformers debated how far the *imago dei* had been destroyed by the fall. Calvin wrestled with the paradox that while in a wider sense, humanity mirrors the glory of God as all creation does, yet in a narrower sense, the *imago dei* is so totally perverted by sin that there is no true saving knowledge of God apart from the grace which has come to us in Christ. He emphasized that our only true knowledge of ourselves comes in the light of the knowledge of God which we have within the relationship which he has re-established in grace through Jesus Christ.

The modern era

The Catholic philosopher, René *Descartes, revitalized the ancient Platonist division between soul and body, making a fundamental distinction between the soul as *res cogitans* and the body as *res extensa*. Modern Christians have therefore tended to assume the Hellenistic distinction between the immortal soul and the mortal body, and often continued to think of the hereafter as the disembodied life of the soul in heaven. Some even debated whether one should think of a dichotomy (body and soul) or a trichotomy (spirit, soul and body; cf. 1 Thess. 5:23). But this whole dualistic anthropology was attacked by the philosopher Gilbert Ryle (1900–76) as 'the ghost in the machine' and seemed to be quite out of step with the development of modern psychology. At the same time, some biblical scholars took the view that dualism was not the anthropology of the OT nor even of the NT. Oscar *Cullmann, for example, put this starkly in *Immortality of the Soul or Resurrection of the Dead?* (1956).

Contemporary theological anthropology has to be aware of philosophical discussion, notably, for example, the highly individualistic approach of *existentialism with its suspicion of notions of a common human 'nature' as depersonalizing. But most of the challenges to develop new thinking come from the sciences (see *Science and theology). The establishing of some form of Darwinian evolution as the accepted position of biology and other life and earth sciences requires theologians and apologists to refute the popular notion that this invalidates the Christian understanding of the creation and nature of human beings (see *Adam). Current thinking among some biblical scholars and theologians tries to relate the biblical view of the human being with the psychosomatic view taken in modern experimental psychology and particularly with developments in neuroscience. There is still, however, a strong school of thought that the concept of the soul, and therefore some kind of dualism, is necessary (Richard Swinburne, John W. Cooper, William Hasker). In contrast, others argue for 'emergent monism' (Philip Clayton) or 'nonreductive physicalism' (Nancey Murphy and Warren Brown). Murphy and Brown accept that it is not necessary to postulate the existence of a distinct metaphysical entity such as the soul or spirit to account for human behaviour or to understand what it is to be human. But they oppose the 'reductive materialism' of scientists such as Francis Crick or B. F. Skinner, who allege that human life and personhood are 'nothing but' physical and chemical events.

Christian theology as a whole has vigorously opposed *racism. But the advent of *feminism prompted the question of whether theological anthropology is too male oriented, and led to more thought on the differentiation of the two sexes. At one level, this has prompted debate on the role of women in leadership in the church, but at a wider level the demand for equality has posed questions about the traditional understanding of the roles of men and women in marriage and society (see *Family). Theological anthropology today has to develop an understanding of what it is to be human which is not dominated by a merely male perspective.

The increasing cultural dominance of secular humanism in Western nations is a challenge to Christian theological anthropology today to show that the Christian faith is in fact the true *humanism. While the belief that the human race is merely the result of a fortuitous confluence of blind physical forces gives no strong basis for placing high value on humanity, the Christian belief that human beings were created in the image of God, and that the One who is the Image became human and shared in human death in order to bring us to the eternal life of the new creation, places the highest possible value on the human race.

Bibliography

K. Barth, *CD*, III, 2; J. Calvin, *Institutes*, 1, xv; II, i–v; W. S. Brown (ed.), *Whatever Happened to the Soul? Scientific and Theological Portraits of Human Nature* (Minneapolis, 1998); M. Cortez, *Embodied Souls: Ensouled Bodies* (London, 2008); M. Elliott (ed.), *The Dynamics of Human Life* (Carlisle, 2001); J. B. Green, *What about the Soul? Neuroscience and Christian Anthropology* (Nashville, 2004); idem, *Body, Soul and Human Life: The Nature of Humanity in the Bible* (Milton Keynes and Grand Rapids, 2008); W. Pannenberg, *Anthropology in Theological Perspective* (London, 1985); H. Schwarz, *The Human Being: A Theological Anthropology* (Grand Rapids, 2013); C. Sherlock, *The Doctrine of Humanity* (Downers Grove, 1996); H. W. Wolff, *The Anthropology of the Old Testament* (ET, Philadelphia, 1983).

T. A. Noble

ANTHROPOMORPHISM

Anthropomorphism refers to descriptions of *God's being, actions and emotions (more properly, anthropopathism) in human terms. God is invisible, infinite and without a body, but human characteristics are frequently ascribed to God in order to communicate information about his nature or acts.

Illustrations abound in Scripture. Though God is without a body, his acts are said to be the result of 'his mighty arm' (Exod. 15:16). Though God is without gender, he is characterized in masculine (father, shepherd, king), and occasionally feminine (compassionate mother) terms. Besides an arm, God is pictured as having a face (Ps. 27:8), hand (Pss 10:12; 88:5), finger (Deut. 9:10) and back (Exod. 33:23). God talks, walks, laughs, weeps; he is jealous, furious and caring.

Anthropomorphisms are poetic symbols or, more particularly, metaphors for divine attributes which would otherwise be indescribable. The Scriptures utilize anthropomorphic language, condescending to the limited abilities of men and women to understand God's nature and ways.

Danger enters when anthropomorphisms are taken literally rather than metaphorically, and people attribute a body to the invisible Creator (e.g. the Audians of the fourth and fifth centuries). On the other hand, rejection of anthropomorphic language leads to scepticism and *agnosticism, since God cannot be otherwise discussed. Other misconceptions stem from the belief that biblical anthropomorphisms are an expression of a primitive religion or that biblical religion conceived of God in man's image (so *Feuerbach).

The Bible provides divine justification for anthropomorphic language. It is full of such language, though it recognizes the limitations of anthropomorphisms (Isa. 40:18; 57:15; John 1:8). The propriety of anthropomorphic language is supported further by the recognition that man (see *Anthropology) is made in the *image of God and that God himself took on human form in the person of Jesus Christ.

See also (and for bibliography): Accommodation; Analogy; Religious Language.

T. Longman III

ANTICHRIST

The term (Gk *Anti-christos*) is found exclusively in the epistles of John in both singular and plural forms (1 John 2:18, 22; 4:3; 2 John 7) where he clearly assumes his readers will be familiar with the concept. Here it most likely refers to an opponent or opponents of Christ. The term can, however, also refer to one who falsely claims to be the Christ, and this view has become more popular, especially since the nineteenth century.

Within Jewish apocalyptic writings there is the anticipation of a personification of evil in a political ruler who would claim to be divine and lead the Gentile nations in opposition to God's people. Daniel's prophecy was most likely fulfilled by Antiochus Epiphanes in 168 BC who set up the 'abomination that causes desolation' in the temple and sparked the Maccabean Revolt (Dan. 8:9–12, 23–25; 11:21–45; cf. Mark 13:14). NT writers develop this apocalyptic expectation of an evil person under the control of Satan who will oppose Christ, deceive humanity and persecute Christians. He is seen as appearing in the final period of history, prior to the final defeat of evil and the establishment of God's universal *kingdom.

The concept of the Antichrist is multifaceted and has developed in three different if not mutually exclusive ways in Christian history.

In the patristic and medieval periods the idea of a personal and individual Antichrist was popular, and detailed accounts of his career emerged. Some saw this person as a political figure, while for others he would be a false religious leader. The Roman Emperor Nero was a popular candidate. After he committed suicide in AD 68, rumours developed that he had not died but escaped. *Chrysostom represented those who believed Nero would be resurrected (*redivivus*) and continue his evil reign. The *Didache*, on the other hand, predicted that the Deceiver would appear in the last days, performing miracles, persecuting believers and claiming to be the Son of God. Hippolytus, writing in the third century, combined both expectations, predicting the rise of a political tyrant who would also be the false Jewish Messiah.

While the Reformers rejected this idea, it nevertheless gained renewed popularity in the early nineteenth century, particularly through the writings of Edward *Irving and J. N. *Darby, and became an article of faith within *Dispensationalism. This view is known as 'futurist'. In the twentieth century, through the influence of the Scofield Reference Bible and apocalyptic writings of Hal Lindsey and Tim LaHaye especially, the idea of a personal Antichrist has become normative within *Pentecostalism and American Evangelicalism. Speculation as to the identity of the Antichrist has ranged from Napoleon III to Mussolini, Mikhail Gorbachev, Ronald Reagan and Saddam Hussein.

During the sixteenth century, Protestants developed the idea that the Antichrist represented a specific historical entity, not an individual. This is known as the 'ideal' or 'symbolic' view. Given its strong opposition to the Reformation, the Roman papacy came to be seen as the embodiment of the Antichrist by leaders like John *Wycliffe, Martin *Luther, John *Calvin, Thomas *Cranmer and John *Wesley, as well as the authors of the *Westminster Confession and 1689 Baptist Confession of Faith.

More generally, the Antichrist has been seen as an ageless principle of evil opposition to Christ existing throughout history which manifests itself in the form of individuals and movements which set themselves up against God and deceive or persecute his people. Polycarp, for example, in the second century, held that the Antichrist was the spirit of *heresy. He taught that those who denied the incarnation such as the *Docetists were of the Antichrist, as were those who denied the resurrection, whom he termed the firstborn of Satan. Irenaeus, also in the second century, instead equated the Antichrist with the Roman Empire (*Lateinos*). This view is not incompatible with a final embodiment or personification of evil in the future, but the emphasis is upon the spiritual reality of evil in the heavenly realms (Eph. 6:11–12).

See also: APOCALYPTIC; DEVILS AND DEMONS; EVIL.

Bibliography

C. Hill, *Antichrist in Seventeenth-Century England* (London, 1971); G. C. Jenks, *The Origins and Early Development of the Antichrist Myth*, BZNW 59 (Berlin, 1991); B. McGinn, *Antichrist: Two Thousand Years of the Human Fascination with Evil* (San Francisco, 1994); D. F. Watson, 'Antichrist', in *DLNTD*.

S. SIZER

ANTINOMIANISM

Martin *Luther used this term to criticize the teachings of Johannes Agricola, who was thought to have extended the doctrine of *justification by faith beyond the idea that good works do not contribute to salvation, to the notion that acts of disobedience cannot deprive one of salvation. It was feared that this changed legitimate Christian assurance of forgiveness to presumption. The word is often used

Antinomianism

pejoratively, and etymologically suggests an opposition ('anti') to law ('*nomos*'), so that an antinomian is one who opposes *law. However, since it is used in several contexts in relation to different theological topics, it is necessary to assess precisely what criticism is being made in a particular context. For this purpose, we may distinguish two ranges of question. An antinomian may be 'opposed' to 'law', but: what kind of opposition? and, what kind of law?

Kinds of opposition

One species of opposition argues against the idea that obeying biblical laws contributes to salvation. Legal obedience, the argument continues, is necessary as a matter of obedient discipleship (for a sovereign God has issued laws), but not for *salvation, which is by grace alone. This position is standard in *Reformed and other Protestant theologies. Since disobedience is not a matter of indifference in such systems, such Christians typically argue that if this position could be called antinomian, it is because Christian soteriology (salvation by grace alone) entails it, and is an innocent antinomianism. In fact, the argument runs, those castigating such antinomianism may be themselves in error in upholding synergistic accounts of salvation (such as *Semi-Pelagianism or even *Pelagianism).

A further issue in this specific area is what consequences are envisaged for disobedience. Traditional Reformed Christians would insist that true Christians persevere to final salvation in their calling (*perseverance of the saints), although they do commit sin after conversion (1 John 1:8). Disobedience may not therefore mean losing one's salvation, but may indeed signify one is not, and never has been, a true Christian. Other sanctions may continue to apply, such as church discipline, while the proper response to post-conversion sin is repentance (1 John 1:9). This would also be accepted by Christians who do not accept perseverance of the saints in the sense outlined above.

Other kinds of opposition to the Bible's laws may go further, suggesting that God applies no sanction or penalty to disobedience. Arguably, Henri Nouwen approaches this with his meditations on the prodigal son, to the effect that God does not punish sin, because disobedience carries its own punishment. Here, antinomianism relates to an issue in the doctrine of salvation, deliverance from God's penal *wrath.

Kinds of law

Different views are held over which laws currently bind Christians. Traditional distinctions have been drawn in the biblical material between moral, civil and ceremonial law (e.g. Article 7 of the *Thirty-Nine Articles), and most Christian theologies would hold that, for example, the OT laws of sacrifice (ceremonial) have been fulfilled in Christ (Heb. 10:12). Moral injunctions (e.g. do not bear false witness) continue to bind us, but differences arise over issues such as Sabbath observance. Different views of which biblical laws bind Christians today certainly can arise because one party is deeply antinomian, but may equally arise from different detailed interpretations within a framework where both parties accept that moral laws are binding. Antinomianism scarcely aptly describes this latter case.

Antinomianism may also pertain to laws of human origin, such as laws of state or church. For some, since state or church have a delegated authority from God (e.g. Rom. 13:1; 1 Thess. 5:12), they possess a general legislative competence and must be unconditionally obeyed, the alternative being antinomianism. Others maintain state and church possess only limited delegated authority, which certainly does not extend to, for example, forbidding prayer (see Dan. 6). This opposition to human law may be expressed in different ways. For instance, that no law may be passed which contradicts the Bible; that no law may be passed on which the Bible is silent; that a law with which one in conscience disagrees is not binding.

Antinomianism is theologically and culturally significant. Paul may have been accused of antinomianism in his teaching of salvation by grace (Rom. 6:1; Gal. 2:17); such antinomianism goes with being a Christian. However, the record of humanity from Gen. 3 speaks of a disposition which sets God's laws aside (see *Fall), and sin is called lawlessness (1 John 3:4). Intriguingly, humans may make void God's laws even while purporting to be observers of the law, as Jesus indicates of the Pharisees (Mark 7:8–13), so that we may be covertly antinomian while superficially looking like legalists. Moreover, our culture has a markedly antiauthoritarian strand which can include an antipathy to 'law', whether biblical or civil, and this makes it imperative to examine quite what content is being given to charges of antinomianism.

See also: LAW AND GOSPEL.

Bibliography

T. D. Bozeman, *The Precisionist Strain: Disciplinary Religion and Antinomian Backlash in Puritanism to 1638* (Chapel Hill, 2003); J. Calvin, *Institutes of the Christian Religion*, III.7; D. R. Como, *Blown by the Spirit: Puritanism and the Emergence of an Antinomian Underground in Pre-Civil-War England* (Stanford, 2004); J. Hogg, *The Private Memoirs and Confessions of a Justified Sinner* (1824); J. K. Jue, 'The Active Obedience of Christ and the Theology of the Westminster Standards: A Historical Investigation', in K. S. Oliphint (ed.), *Justified in Christ: God's Plan for Us in Justification* (Fearn, 2007), pp. 99–130; H. Nouwen, *The Return of the Prodigal Son* (London, 1992); F. Schaeffer, 'A Christian Manifesto', in *The Complete Works of Francis Schaeffer*, vol. 5 (Wheaton, 1982); F. Turretin, *Institutes of Elenctic Theology*, Topic 11, Q23, 'The Abrogation of the Moral Law' (ET, Phillipsburg, 1977).

M. OVEY

ANTIOCHENE SCHOOL

The Antiochene School is in its *Christology generally opposed to the *Alexandrian School, but it is worth remembering that originally both schools reflected differing responses to the *Arian threat. Countering the Arian attribution of suffering to the divine Word, the Antiochenes insisted on a rigid separation between the two natures in Christ. It was the human nature which experienced suffering, whereas the divine nature remained untouched by this. Central to Antiochene theology was the great gulf between the immortality, incorruptibility and impassibility of God and the mortality, corruptibility and passibility of humanity.

Diodore of Tarsus (*c.* 330–94), often regarded as the pioneer of this school, was content to use the Alexandrian terminology of the 'Word becoming flesh'. He departed, however, from the Alexandrian tradition when he challenged *Apollinarius' talk of one *hypostasis* (substance or person) in Christ. For Apollinarius this entailed a complete transfer of the properties (*communicatio idiomatum*; see *Christology) of the Word to the human side of Jesus' one nature; but for Diodore this inevitably involved the Word in suffering, and thereby compromised the divine nature. Diodore preferred to talk of two Sons and two natures, and to deny any sort of transfer of properties. Thus, it was only the human nature of Jesus which died on the cross, while the divine Word did not suffer. The denial of a transfer of properties remained the standard teaching of the Antiochene School.

It was Diodore's pupil, Theodore of Mopsuestia (*c.* 350–428), who first scrapped the Word-flesh framework in favour of the Word-man framework more commonly associated with the Antiochenes. He was motivated by a concern to do justice to Christ's human experiences. Since the weakness evident in these experiences could not be postulated of the divine nature, the divine Word must have assumed complete manhood, body and soul.

Theodore died shortly before the outbreak of the *Nestorian controversy, which focused on Nestorius, one of his pupils. Theodore may in some sense have paved the way for controversy, since his talk of Christ's humanity as 'the man assumed' did lead in the hands of more extreme exponents to the suspicion of *adoptionism. So clear was Theodore's differentiation between the two natures that he could treat Christ's humanity almost as a separate person, as at John 10:27–28, which he expounds as a conversation between Christ's two natures.

Theodore's opponents also pointed out that he failed to do justice to the interrelation of the two natures in Christ. He described this as a 'conjunction', a term which falls short of full union. He liked to illustrate this by the metaphor of indwelling. The human nature of Christ functions as a temple in which the Godhead dwells. But this indwelling, which is by God's own good pleasure, differs from God's indwelling in the prophets and other holy men by virtue of its permanence and completeness. Understandably, this theological construction was criticized as giving only the appearance of a union.

Though under fire in the Nestorian controversy, the Antiochene School was not completely identified with Nestorius, but produced more moderate exponents, of whom the monk-bishop, Theodoret of Cyrrhus (*c.* 393–458), was the most notable. In the aftermath of the Council of *Ephesus (431) they set forth a statement devoid of Nestorian excesses. In time, this document, which became known as the Formulary of Reunion, was accepted even by *Cyril of Alexandria, and brought fifteen years of relative peace in the Eastern church.

At the beginning of the Nestorian controversy, Theodoret had objected to Cyril's talk of a 'hypostatic' or natural union, because this signified to him a fusion of the deity and the humanity into a hybrid compound under the influence of some physical law of mechanical combination entirely opposed to any concept of the voluntary, gracious act which characterized the *incarnation. At this stage in his career Theodoret held that Christ had two natures and two hypostases, but later he was prepared to modify his terminology and distinguish between his one hypostasis and his two natures. In line with this, he saw orthodoxy as a middle path between the error of dividing Christ into two persons and the opposite error of confusing the two natures.

The Antiochenes held passionately by their Christology in order to safeguard their doctrine of *salvation. They would stress the perfection and distinctness of Christ's humanity, because sin and death which had been introduced into the world by a man could be undone only in human nature. Again, Christ had to demonstrate real moral progress because sin was essentially an act of wilful disobedience on the part of the soul and could be undone only by absolute obedience to the divine will. A divine initiative was required to secure human salvation. God had to intervene in human history by creating and uniting to himself a new Man if man was to be re-established in obedience to God's will. After its obedience on earth, Christ's human nature was elevated to heaven by virtue of its conjunction with the divine nature. By a parallel process, the believer, united to Christ at baptism, is granted intimacy with the divine nature – though it is never suggested that this intimacy is on the same scale as that enjoyed by Christ.

The moderate Antiochenes left their mark on the *Chalcedonian Definition (451; see also *Councils and *Creeds), which for many marked the dénouement of the Christological controversies of the fifth century. Its key phrase – one person 'made known in two natures' – reflects the Antiochene concern to preserve the integrity of the two natures in Christ. But the corresponding stress on the oneness of Christ represents a corrective to the Antiochene tendency not to give sufficient weight to the Word as the subject of the incarnation and to subordinate the concept of person to that of nature.

The Antiochenes gave biblical exegesis greater weight than systematic theology. Commentaries on Scripture were written by the leading members of the school, and the greatest expositor of the early church, John Chrysostom (c. 344/354–407), could be reckoned among them. The Antiochenes developed their own *hermeneutical principles in reaction to the unbridled allegorization of the Alexandrians. The Antiochenes insisted on the literal or historical interpretation, but were not averse to a further spiritual sense, provided this did not undermine the historicity of the passage and could form some reasonably obvious parallel to the literal sense. Insight (Gk *theoria*) was the name they gave to this additional sense. Diodore and Theodore, the theorists of the school, were also pioneers in a critical approach to the canon of *Scripture, but their work on this did not meet with much approval. Nor did it significantly undermine the school's excellent reputation in biblical exegesis.

Bibliography

A. Grillmeier, *Christ in Christian Tradition*, vol. 1 (London, ²1975); J. N. D. Kelly, *Golden Mouth: The Story of John Chrysostom – Ascetic, Preacher, Bishop* (Grand Rapids, 1995); R. V. Sellers, *Two Ancient Christologies* (London, 1940); D. S. Wallace-Hadrill, *Christian Antioch: A Study of Eastern Christian Thought* (Cambridge, 1982).

G. A. KEITH

ANTI-SEMITISM, see HOLOCAUST; JUDAISM AND CHRISTIANITY

APARTHEID, see DUTCH REFORMED THEOLOGY (SOUTH AFRICA); RACE

APOCALYPTIC

Apocalyptic is an adjective derived from the word 'apocalypse' (Gk *apokalypsis*), meaning 'revelation' or 'disclosure', and used primarily to describe a genre of literature. The word can also be used to define a type of *eschatology as well as religious movements associated with such revelations, as at Qumran and, more recently, millenarianism (see *Millennium).

Historically, biblical apocalyptic literature arose between the time of the Babylonian captivity (Ezekiel and Daniel) through the return of the exiles (Zechariah) to the Greek and Roman occupation of Palestine (Revelation), that is, from around 570 BC to AD 100. The writing of further apocalyptic literature continued within Judaism and Christianity until the late Middle Ages.

Extra-biblical Jewish apocalypses written between 200 BC and AD 200 include 1 Enoch, 2 Baruch, 4 Ezra (2 Edras), the *Apocalypse of Abraham* and the *Apocalypse of Zephaniah*. Early Christian apocalypses include the *Shepherd of Hermas*. More usually, Christian apocalypses were written anonymously, and under the names of OT figures or NT apostles.

Two main types of apocalyptic literature may be distinguished. *Cosmological* apocalyptic literature typically involves a heavenly journey with a celestial guide lifting the veil between heaven and earth. These revelations were communicated through visions, often using numerology, enigmatic symbolism and the vivid depictions of animals and of other living beings.

Historical-eschatological apocalypses reveal God's purposes in history between the 'now' and the 'not yet'. Predicting the future, and using symbolic language, they describe the rise and fall of empires as well as rulers who at various times tolerated or persecuted God's people. These visions end triumphantly with God intervening to bring *judgment on the wicked and vindicate the righteous and faithful remnant. They declare with certainty that the powers of the present evil age will finally be overthrown by God's *kingdom rule. Interpreters have differed on whether the imagery describing these 'Last Days' is intended to be understood figuratively, literally or symbolically. The Qumran *War Scroll*, for example, describes a series of seven battles that take place over a period of forty years between the Sons of Light and the Sons of Darkness. Only the decisive intervention of God in the final battle brings about the defeat of Belial and his army.

The Jewish apocalypses, including those written after the rise of Christianity, were largely preserved by Christian scribes and were influential in churches. 4 Ezra, for example, held almost canonical status during the Middle Ages. Christian apocalypses emulated both types of Jewish apocalypse. The cosmological type includes visionary descriptions of the torments of hell and the delights of paradise and were especially popular in the patristic and medieval periods. The most influential of these was the *Apocalypse of Paul*. Dante's *Divine Comedy* represents the literary culmination of this genre. The *Apocalypse of Thomas* is an example of the historical-eschatological type and was also influential in the Middle Ages.

During the patristic and medieval periods, apocalyptic speculation within Christianity gradually shifted from the writing of new apocalypses to the interpretation of the apocalyptic elements found in the canonical Scriptures, most notably Daniel and Revelation. The writings of *Joachim of Fiore (1135–1202), for example, became the basis of widespread eschatological expectations.

During the Reformation, both Catholic and Protestant commentators sought to interpret the social and political upheavals impacting Europe in apocalyptic terms. Thomas Brightman (1562–1607), for example, was the author of *Apocalypsis Apocalypseos,* meaning 'A Revelation of the Revelation'. He speculated that the seven vials or bowls of Rev. 16 began with Elizabeth's accession to the throne of England in 1558 and that the seventh trumpet of Rev. 10 had been sounded in 1588 with the destruction of the Spanish Armada. He argued that the Turkish Empire (the false prophet), having formed an unholy alliance with the Roman Church (the Antichrist), would be destroyed, followed by 'the calling of the Jews to be a Christian nation', leading to 'a most happy tranquillity from thence to the end of the world'.

The traumatic effects of the French Revolution (1789–99) and the Napoleonic Wars (1804–15) had a profound and lasting impact on the rise of apocalyptic movements right across Europe. George Stanley Faber (1773–1854) was one of the earliest to write speculative treaties on prophecy. In 1804, he wrote *A Dissertation on the Prophecies that have been fulfilled, are now fulfilling or will hereafter be fulfilled relative to the Great Period of 1260 years, the Papal and Mohammedan* (sic) *Apostasies, the Tyranical Reign of the Antichrist or the Infidel Power and the Restoration of the Jews*. Faber identified Napoleon, the head of the revived Roman Empire, as the *Antichrist. He predicted Napoleon would be destroyed in Palestine by an alliance of England and Russia. Faber's writings, along with those of Edward *Irving, Manuel Lacunza, John Nelson *Darby, and later, Cyrus Scofield, became the driving force behind the rise in popularity of futurist premillennialism and *Dispensationalism in the nineteenth century and Christian *Zionism in the twentieth.

Apocalyptic movements founded in the nineteenth century include the Catholic Apostolic Church, the Albury Circle, the Brethren, Millerites, Shakers, Adventists (see *Seventh-Day Adventism), Mormons and Jehovah Witnesses (see *New religions). Annual Bible prophecy conferences which began in Albury, Surrey in the 1820s, spread to Powerscourt in Ireland in the 1830s and then to the United States after the Civil War in the 1870s in locations such as Niagara and New York.

Through the writings of James Brookes, D. L. Moody, William Blackstone and Cyrus Scofield, apocalyptic speculation became mainstream in the USA, shaping and influencing fundamentalism, Pentecostalism and evangelicalism. The *Scofield Reference Bible* became the standard text for systematizing and legitimizing a futurist hermeneutic in which contemporary events were identified as the fulfilment of biblical prophecy. The founding of the state of Israel in 1948 and capture of Jerusalem in 1967 are two important examples. The Jewish people were increasingly seen as central to God's continuing purposes on earth separate from the church. American apocalyptic writings invariably have a polarized and dualistic worldview, in which God is blessing America because of its support for Israel. Communism and more recently Islam are identified with the enemies of God's people. Contemporary apocalypticism is also inherently mistrustful of institutions such as the European Community, the United Nations and with attempts to find a peaceful settlement of the Arab-Israeli conflict through international law.

Contemporary popular exponents of this tradition include John Hagee, Charles Dyer, Mike Evans, Hal Lindsey and Tim LaHaye. Lindsey, for example, in his book *Planet Earth 2000*, promises reassuringly: 'Hal will be your guide on a chilling tour of the world's future battlefields as the Great Tribulation, foretold more than two thousand years ago by Old and New Testament prophets, begins to unfold. You'll meet the world leaders who will bring man to the very edge of extinction and examine the causes of the current global situation – what it all means, what will shortly come to pass, and how it will all turn out.'

From the sixteenth century to the present day there has been an unbroken strand within evangelicalism that has interpreted Daniel and the book of Revelation in apocalyptic terms to explain contemporary events and link them to an imminent war of Armageddon, the return of Christ and climax of history. William Hendriksen warns: 'In emphasizing this basis of the Apocalyptic visions in the subsoil of the sacred Scriptures we must always bear in mind that it is wise to proceed from the clearer to the more obscure and never *vice versa*.' Christian history is littered with the wreckage of eccentric predictions uttered by those who have failed to heed that advice.

Bibliography

R. Bauckham, *Tudor Apocalypse* (Appleford, 1978); J. J. Collins, *The Apocalyptic Imagination* (Grand Rapids, 1998); W. Hendriksen, *More than Conquerors: An Interpretation of the Book of Revelation* (London, 1940); L. Morris, *Apocalyptic* (Leicester, 1972); C. Marvin Pate and C. B. Haines, Jr, *Doomsday Delusions* (Downers Grove, 1995); C. Rowland, *The Open Heaven: A Study of Apocalyptic in Judaism and Early Christianity* (London, 1982); D. S. Russell, *The Method and Message of Jewish Apocalyptic* (Philadelphia, 1964); S. Sizer, *Christian Zionism: Road-map to Armageddon?* (Leicester, 2004).

S. SIZER

APOCRYPHA, see SCRIPTURE

APOLLINARIANISM

The heresy which so stressed the unity of the person of Christ that it denied that he had a human mind, and spoke of the *Logos taking its place, was promoted by Apollinarius, Bishop of Laodicea in Syria (351–90). A friend of *Athanasius and a supporter of the *homoousion* (see *Trinity and Council of *Nicaea), Apollinarius wrote 'innumerable volumes on the holy Scriptures' (Jerome), and, on theological and apologetic subjects, 'filled the world with his books' (Basil). Most survive, however, only in fragments and quotations in other writers. Some appear under other names: a *Detailed Confession of Faith* attributed to Gregory Thaumaturgus; a sermon, *That Christ is One, On the Incarnation of the Word of God*, and a creed addressed to the emperor Jovian, attributed to Athanasius; *On the Union of Body and Deity in Christ, On Faith and*

Incarnation, and a letter to Dionysius of Rome, attributed to Pope Julius I.

The context of the Apollinarian *Christology is that of the *Alexandrian School of Athanasius and *Cyril, which was strong in declaring for the deity of Christ and the union of the two natures in his incarnate person. From these presuppositions Apollinarius attacked the *Antiochene *dualistic Christology. Throughout his concern was soteriological. A Christ less than totally divine cannot save. The death of a mere man has no redeeming efficacy. But if Christ is totally divine, his human nature must somehow be 'taken up' into his divinity and so become a right object of worship. Salvation consists in man partaking of Christ's apotheosized flesh in the *Eucharist. By the deifying of the human element through union with the divine Logos, Christ was rendered morally unchangeable.

Negatively, therefore, Apollinarius rejects any mere juxtaposing of the two natures in Christ. To Jovian he writes, 'There are not two natures (in Christ), one to be worshipped and one not to be worshipped. There is one nature (*mia physis*) in the Word of God incarnate.' The Scriptures present Christ as one being, the embodiment of the one active principle, the divine Logos. Positively, he credited to Christ a 'new nature', with the result that in the constitution of his person he is 'a new creation and a marvellous mixture, God and man have constituted one flesh'. But how have the human and divine so coalesced into such an absolute oneness?

A powerful motive in Apollinarius was to exempt Christ from the possibility of sinning. In current psychology the human mind was conceived as self-determining, being impelled by its own volition and so the seat of evil choices. Apollinarius thus eliminated this element from his structure of Christ's person. 'If with the Godhead which is itself mind, there was in Christ also a human mind, the first purpose of the incarnation which is the overthrow of sin is not accomplished in him' (*Apodeixis*, fragment, 74). Christ's person is then the 'co-mixture' of the Logos and 'abridged human nature': 'a mean between God and man, neither wholly man nor wholly God, but a combination of God and man' (*Syllogysmoi*, fragment, 113). The denudation of the human in the incarnation is counterbalanced from the divine end by a kenosis (see *Kenoticism). For the Logos who pervades all existence in his limitlessness must undergo self-limitation in human flesh.

Apollinarius was criticized by *Gregory of Nyssa for repudiating Christ's full human experiences of which the Gospels and the epistle to the Hebrews give ample proof. The full salvation of man requires Christ's full identification with him in all the elements of his make-up. Apollinarianism was successively condemned by *councils at Rome (377), Alexandria (378), Antioch (379) and finally at Constantinople (381).

Bibliography

J. N. D. Kelly, *Early Christian Doctrines* (London, ⁵1977); H. Lietzmann, *Apollinarius von Laodicea und seine Schule* (Tübingen, 1904); A. G. McGiffert, *A History of Christian Thought* (New York and London, 1932), vol. 1; J. Pelikan, *The Christian Tradition, vol. 1: The Emergence of the Catholic Tradition (100–600)* (Chicago, 1971); G. L. Prestige, *Fathers and Heretics* (London, 1940), pp. 193–246; C. E. Raven, *Apollinarianism* (Cambridge, 1923).

H. D. McDonald

APOLOGETICS

The word 'apologetics' derives from a Greek term, *apologia*, and was used for a defence that a person like Socrates might make of his views and actions. The apostle Peter tells every Christian to be ready to give a reason (*apologia*) for the hope that is in him (1 Pet. 3:15). Apologetics, then, is an activity of the Christian mind which attempts to show that the gospel message is true in what it affirms. An apologist is one who is prepared to defend the message against criticism and distortion, and to give evidences of its credibility.

Unfortunately, today the term apologetics has unpleasant connotations for many people. On a superficial level it sounds as if we are being asked to apologize for having faith. At a deeper level it may suggest an aggressive or opportunistic kind of person who resorts to fair means or foul in order to get people to accept his point of view. Such misunderstandings of apologetics are regrettable in view of the importance of the subject. A sound defence of the faith was important in the NT as it also is today.

The book of Acts presents the apostles engaging non-Christians in debates and arguments concerning the truth of the gospel (Acts 17:2–4; 19:8–10), and it is no exaggeration to say that most of the NT documents were written for specific apologetic reasons. They were written to commend the faith to one group or another, and to clear up questions that had arisen about the gospel.

Apologetic activities were vigorously pursued during the period of the early church and indeed throughout most of the church's history. In the beginning it was necessary both to define what the church believed in the face of heretical tendencies, and to offer an explication of its basis in rationality to enquirers and critics of different kinds. Since many of the *apologists were converts themselves – men such as *Justin, *Clement and *Augustine – they knew what was needed to commend the faith to outsiders. Believers also needed to be strengthened against the impact of hostile criticisms. It would be true to say that apologetics stood proudly alongside *dogmatics as two indispensable responses to the challenges of the age. It cannot be otherwise in a period of missionary expansion.

Early apologetics were generally either political or religious. The political apologies were designed to win acceptance, as well as a measure of toleration and legitimacy for Christianity in society, while the religious apologies were intended to win converts from both Judaism and paganism. Of necessity, such writings had to be flexible and respond to specific issues just as they do today. Among the practitioners of the art of apologetics we may number some of the finest minds and personalities: Augustine, *Anselm, *Thomas Aquinas, *Pascal, *Butler, *Newman and C. S. *Lewis. Their work contains a great variety of approaches and styles of argument, but what characterizes it all is boldness and confidence in the truth of the biblical message and its relevance to human history and philosophy.

In the modern period, however, apologetics has suffered a severe setback. It encountered in the European *Enlightenment a spirit of scepticism towards theology and metaphysics and a wholesale assault upon Christian beliefs. The apologetic arguments of earlier centuries were subjected to withering critique by men like *Hume, and many came to feel that the whole of Christianity needed to be revised and reworked. *Kant declared that the human mind was incapable of knowledge beyond the phenomenal realm. In future, he said, theology would have to be content to function within the limits of reason and reduce its claims to knowledge. A gauntlet was thrown down in the path of apologetics. Religion can be practised in the realm of existence or morality, but it cannot be advanced, as previously, on supposedly rational grounds.

The Enlightenment created a severe crisis for Christianity. In its wake, religious *liberalism sought to operate within the limits Kant had indicated, accepting the implications which this would have for Christian thinking. This led to the kind of revisionism which is familiar from the work of Paul *Tillich, Rudolf *Bultmann and John A. T. *Robinson. Even among classical Christians, the effect of the Enlightenment critique was clearly seen in a new hesitancy towards apologetics. In *Kierkegaard and *Barth one sees a kind of orthodoxy which does not rely upon apologetic arguments at all, but seeks to rest the claim of Christianity solely upon the faith-commitment.

But there has also been a resurgence of apologetics. Most widely read have been the writings of C. S. Lewis, but others such as Francis A. Schaeffer and Timothy Keller have stimulated popular interest in defending the faith. Others who have contributed at a more technical level include E. J. Carnell (1919–1967), Basil Mitchell (1917–2011), Alvin Plantinga (b. 1932), Richard Swinburne (b. 1934) and Keith Ward (b. 1938). John Polkinghorne (b. 1930), Francis Collins (b. 1950) and Alister McGrath (b. 1953) are among those who have taken up the specialist area of Christian apologetics in the light of modern science.

Bibliography

C. Brown, *Philosophy and the Christian Faith* (London, 1969); idem, *Miracles and the Critical Mind* (Grand Rapids and Exeter, 1984); E. J. Carnell, *An Introduction to Christian Apologetics* (Grand Rapids, 1952); F. Collins, *The Language of God: A Scientist Presents Evidence for Belief* (New York, 2006); A. Dulles, *A History of Apologetics* (Philadelphia, 1971); C. Campbell-Jack and G. J. McGrath (eds.), *New Dictionary of Christian Apologetics* (Leicester, 2006); N. L. Geisler, *Christian Apologetics* (Grand Rapids, 1988); idem, *Baker Encyclopedia of Christian Apologetics* (Grand Rapids, 1999); T. Keller, *The Reason for God* (New York, 2008); P. Kreeft, *Handbook of Christian Apologetics* (Downers Grove, 1994); G. R. Lewis, *Testing Christianity's Truth Claims: Approaches to Christian Apologetics*

(Chicago, 1976); A. McGrath, *The Twilight of Atheism* (New York, 2004); J. Polkinghorne, *Faith, Science and Understanding* (London, 2000); R. Swinburne, *The Existence of God*, 2nd edn (New York, 1991); C. van Til, *The Defense of the Faith* (Philadelphia, 1955); K. Ward, *God and the Philosophers* (Minneapolis, 2009).

C. H. PINNOCK

APOLOGISTS

A small group of Greek authors of the second century, who presented a defence of Christianity in the face of persecution, slander and intellectual attack (see *Apologetics). They sought to make Christianity understandable (and acceptable) to a Greco-Roman or Jewish audience, to bridge the gap between this 'barbarian' religion and the culture of their day. Yet they contain important insights into the development of Christian theology. In all of them we find a 'high' view of the transcendence of *God. God is the 'uncreated, eternal, invisible, impassible, incomprehensible, and infinite, who can be apprehended by mind and reason alone, who is encompassed by light, beauty, spirit, and indescribable power, and who created, adorned, and now rules the universe' (Athenagoras, *Supplication* 10:1). They expose the immorality and irrationality of pagan religion and they defend the truth of the *resurrection of the flesh. Because they also differ in their theology, we shall deal with each one separately.

Aristides wrote his *Apology* either *c.* 125 or *c.* 140. Textual problems make it difficult to be sure about the details of his thought (the less reliable text has the more explicit theological statements). God is understood as the 'prime mover', who created all things because of man. Jesus Christ is spoken of as Son of God and (perhaps) as God, who was incarnate through a virgin, died and rose again, and was preached by the twelve apostles in all the world. Christians live an exemplary life in the knowledge of a judgment after death. These doctrines can all be found in the Christian Scriptures.

*Justin Martyr, the most important of the apologists, wrote an *Apology* (I), some time after 151, to which he later added an *Appendix* (or *Apology II*). In his *Dialogue with Trypho* he seeks to persuade a Jew of the truth of Christianity. Unlike the other apologists, Justin focuses mainly on the nature and meaning of Christ. Christ was the *Logos who inspired the Greek philosophers and is present in all men as the Logos *spermatikos* (seminal reason or word; see *Stoicism). Through him, the best of the philosophers were able to grasp certain Christian truths (e.g. creation, the Trinity, final judgment, etc.). Those who lived according to the Logos, even before Christ, were Christians. In the OT theophanies it was the Logos who was revealed, because the transcendent God could not thus speak to men. Though Justin uses the trinitarian formula, his understanding of Christ is subordinationist (see *Trinity). The relation of the Son to the Father is compared to the relation of sunlight to the sun itself, but he also speaks of a fire kindled from a fire. At times the Logos and the Holy Spirit are apparently confused. Christ was incarnate for our salvation and healing, to teach us and to triumph over the demons (see *Devil) through the mystery of the cross. The demons were responsible for enslaving and deceiving men. They saw what was predicted in the OT about Christ and inspired the poets to say similar things about the Greek gods. They always instigate the persecution of just men. In order to be considered worthy of incorruption and of fellowship with God, it is necessary for men to believe these things and to do God's will.

The main evidence for Christianity consists in the fact that everything related to Christ's coming was foretold by the Hebrew prophets. Exegesis of the OT is important in the *Apology* and also in the *Dialogue*, where Justin argues that the Mosaic law has been abrogated, that the OT speaks of 'another besides God', who was manifest in the OT theophanies, and that the Christians are the true Israel. Justin is concerned to show the continuity between Greek philosophy and Christianity (see *Philosophy and theology; *Platonism), as well as the continuity between the OT and the NT. Christ is the culmination and completion of all the partial knowledge of truth in Greek philosophy and he is the culmination of the history of Israel. He himself is Israel and because of him the church now bears the name of Israel.

Tatian, a disciple of Justin, wrote a *Discourse to the Greeks* (*c.* 160). He maintains the divinity of the Logos (understood as 'light from light'). He speculates on the nature of man and on the nature and activity of the demons. He emphasizes free will and the necessity to obey God.

Athenagoras wrote a *Supplication* (*c.* 177). The treatise *On the Resurrection*, traditionally ascribed to him, may be the work of a later author. Athenagoras says that Father, Son and Holy Spirit are united in power, yet distinguished in rank. The Spirit is understood as an effluence, like light from a fire. Goodness is so much a part of God that, without it, he could not exist. *Evil exists because of the fall of (some of) the *angels, who had been entrusted with the administration of the world. Evil is associated with matter. The exemplary life of the Christians is strongly emphasized. The instructions for the Christian life, as well as all other knowledge about God, are found in the writings of the prophets.

The work *On the Resurrection* argues for the resurrection on almost purely rational grounds, showing that God is both able and willing to raise the dead and that this corresponds to the purpose of man's creation. The soul is *immortal. Both the righteous and the wicked are raised.

Theophilus of Antioch wrote three books *To Autolycus* (after 180), in which he speaks of God, the Logos and Sophia (*wisdom) as a 'triad'. The Logos was first innate (*endiathetos*) in God and was made external (*prophorikos*) before creation. Sometimes the distinction between Logos and Sophia (understood as the Holy Spirit) is blurred. God may be apprehended through his works in the universe, which he created out of nothing. Man was made to know God, with the capacity both for mortality and for immortality. Through disobedience he became mortal. Terms like faith, repentance, forgiveness and regeneration are used, and God is spoken of as healer. Yet man is to attain immortality primarily through obedience. All these doctrines may be found in the writings of the prophets, who were inspired by Sophia and whose authenticity is guaranteed by their antiquity and by the fact that their predictions have come true.

Bibliography

The Greek text of the Apologists may be found in E. J. Goodspeed, *Die ältesten Apologeten* (Göttingen, 1914); J. R. Harris, *The Apology of Aristides* (Cambridge, ²1893); J. C. Th. Otto, *Corpus Apologetarum Christianorum Saeculi Secundi* (Jena, 1847–72). English translations can be found in ANCL (repr. ANF); R. M. Grant (ed.), *Theophilus of Antioch: Ad Autolycum* (Oxford, 1970); C. C. Richardson (ed.), *The Early Christian Fathers* (Philadelphia, 1953); W. R. Schoedel (ed.), *Athenagoras: Legatio and De Resurrectione* (Oxford, 1972); A. Lukyn Williams (ed.), *Justin Martyr: The Dialogue with Trypho* (London, 1930).

T. G. DONNER

APOPHATIC THEOLOGY

Apophatic theology is a method of theological discourse that proceeds by way of negation (*via negativa*) using such language as 'God is incomprehensible' or 'God is non-material'. Unlike cataphatic theology (*via positiva*), which proceeds by way of affirmation ('God is good'), apophatic language reflects the utter limitations of human reason when it comes to describing the unknowable nature of *God.

Apophaticism became fully developed in the fourth century in the writings of the Cappadocian Fathers (see *Basil of Caesarea; *Gregory of Nazianzus; *Gregory of Nyssa) against Eunomius. Eunomius believed one could know the very essence of God and be fully united to it. The Cappadocians, however, corrected Eunomius by insisting upon the radical *un*knowability of the divine essence and thus moved apophaticism into the mainstream of the church. In the sixth century, apophaticism reached its classic expression through the work of *Pseudo-Dionysius the Aeropagite in his book *Mystical Theology*. Pseudo-Dionysius used the apophatic language of the Neoplatonists (see *Platonism) to articulate the mystery of God's being. In Neoplatonic thought, the negative way was an intellectual method of approaching the transcendence of God based on belief in an impersonal deity whose essence could be known and contemplated. Pseudo-Dionysius made massive use of apophatic theology throughout his writings and soon popularized the method throughout the Middle Ages in both the Eastern and Western halves of the church. It is still prominent in the *Eastern Orthodox Church today.

The apophatic emphasis on divine unknowability might at first seem to exclude any direct experience of God. But in fact, many who used the apophatic approach saw it not only as a tool for affirming God's transcendence, but also as a way to experience union with God through *prayer. By 'unknowing' God, the apophatic way did not lead to ignorance or the absence of knowledge. Rather, it was an active, positive experience of the living Lord. Negations became super-affirmations about God by saying and unsaying one's way into his presence, affirming and denying 'yes and no; this not that'. As one ascends to God, one discovers that God is beyond all human concepts. At that point, all speech, all thought and even all negations must be abandoned. Pseudo-Dionysius explains, 'And the more it climbs, the more language falters, and when it has passed up and beyond the ascent, it will turn silent completely, since it will finally be at one with him who is indescribable.'

Apophatic theology also shaped the doctrinal language of the church. The Church Fathers of the early ecumenical *councils (325–787) emphasized that doctrinal definitions are not ends in themselves, but are given chiefly in order to exclude wrong interpretations of the faith proposed by *heretics. The most important dogmatic definitions of the church were often couched in the language of apophaticism and antinomy in order to recognize the boundaries within which the mystery of God was to be understood. For example, the Chalcedonian Definition (451) (see *Creeds) – the church's classic statement of *Christology – used four negative adverbs to affirm the union of the human and divine natures in one person 'without confusion, without change, without division, without separation'. Vladimir *Lossky observes, 'Apophaticism teaches us to see above all a negative meaning in the dogmas of the Church: it forbids us to follow natural ways of thought and to form concepts which would usurp the place of spiritual realities. For Christianity is not a philosophical school for speculating about abstract concepts, but is essentially a communion with the living God.' To that end, apophatic theology underscores personal experience as an epistemological criterion of the faith. It tells us that we may apprehend God, but never comprehend him.

Bibliography

V. Lossky, *The Mystical Theology of the Eastern Church* (St Vladimir's, 1976); A. Louth, *The Origins of the Christian Mystical Tradition: From Plato to Denys* (Oxford, 1981); J. Pelikan, 'Who Do You Say That I Am – Not?: The Power of Negative Thinking in the Decrees of the Ecumenical Councils', in J. Cavadini (ed.), *Who Do You Say That I Am?: Confessing the Mystery of Christ* (University of Notre Dame, 2004); P. Rorem, *The Dionysian Mystical Theology* (Minneapolis, 2015); D. Turner, *The Darkness of God: Negativity in Christian Mysticism* (Cambridge, 1995); K. Ware, 'God Hidden and Revealed: The Apophatic Way and the Essence-Energies Distinction', *Eastern Churches Review* 7.2, 1975, pp. 125–136.

B. NASSIF

APOSTASY

Apostasy is a general falling away from religion or a denial of the faith by those who once held it. Paul prophesied serious apostasy before the end of the age (2 Thess. 2:3; see also *Antichrist). Erstwhile nominal believers can obviously cease from appearing even to profess *faith. But can a *regenerate believer cease to believe and so be finally lost? All agree that he may lapse temporarily from full faith and then repent. Calvinists hold that God's calling of the elect to faith prevents them from falling away; they point to texts which assert the eternal security of the believers: a faithful God will not allow any of his people to be overcome by unbelief and finally lost (see *Reformed theology; *Perseverance; *Predestination). Others point to the numerous warnings in the NT against the danger of apostasy and to specific references to apostate individuals. Calvinists insist that the warnings are hypothetical: their effect is to prevent people falling away (just as the sign 'Danger! Keep away from the edge!' prevents people from falling off a cliff). Those who fall away were never truly regenerate. The exegetical debate continues. While the Scriptures warn the deliberate sinner that he is in eternal danger, they also assure the worried believer that nothing can pluck him out of the Lord's hand.

In the early centuries of the church, the most famous (or infamous) apostate was Julian, who was Roman emperor from 355 to 263. He renounced his Christian faith, was influenced by Neoplatonism (see *Platonism) and attempted to restore the old religious practices of Rome, but his policies perished with his death in battle. Since the *Enlightenment, the church in Europe has seen a general movement of apostasy. Leading figures who renounced Christianity or at least gravitated towards unbelief include philosophers such as John Stuart Mill and Karl Marx, and scientists such as Charles Darwin. However, in very many cases, their previous religion was some form of *deism. The novelist Mary Anne Evans (George Eliot) was one of the few who renounced an evangelical faith.

Bibliography

G. C. Berkouwer, *Faith and Perseverance* (Grand Rapids, 1958); D. A. Carson, *Divine Sovereignty and Human Responsibility* (London, 1981); I. H. Marshall, *Kept by the Power of God* (Minneapolis, 1975); T. R. Schreiner and A. B. Caneday, *The Race Set before Us: A Biblical Theology of Perseverance and Assurance* (Downers Grove, 2001).

I. H. MARSHALL

APOSTLE

It is no exaggeration to say that different understandings of apostleship are of key significance for ecclesiology. To be 'apostolic' has frequently been seen as central to the nature of the universal church, as in the phrase 'one, holy, catholic and apostolic church' from the Nicene Creed. But in what sense or senses is the church apostolic? Because its leaders stand in a direct line of apostolic succession through the *laying on of hands? Because it is true to the gospel as proclaimed by the original apostles of Christ and now enshrined in the NT Scriptures? Or because local churches are established and receive guidance from apostles today who function with their teams to give guidance and equip churches for Spirit-empowered discipleship and mission?

The early church

The emphasis by Luke in Acts on the crucial significance of the Twelve as witnesses to Christ's resurrection and authoritative teachers, together with Paul's repeated insistence in his letters on his authority as an apostle of Christ, led to an acceptance of the Twelve and Paul as having special, non-repeatable offices. The wider NT use of the word 'apostle' for pioneer missionaries (e.g. Andronicus and Junia, Rom. 16:7), though reflected in the *Didache* (Syria, c. 95; the textual history is complex), was soon lost.

The need to combat growing *Gnostic influence in the latter part of the second century, with a stress on esoteric tradition secretly handed down, led to the compiling in the period 180–200 of 'succession lists' of bishops in the major cities. The main aim was to safeguard the apostolic message. The Apostles' *Creed, which in its full form stems from c. 700, is based on the Old Roman Creed of this period. Gradually in the third century the emphasis changed from a stress on an open succession of teachers to the significance of a personal succession of bishops going back to the apostles.

Apostolic succession

Churches today which emphasize the importance of a personal episcopal apostolic succession of bishops hold that Christ entrusted the obligation to transmit and preserve the 'deposit of faith' (the experience of Christ and his teachings contained in the doctrinal 'tradition' handed down from the time of the apostles, the written portion of which is *Scripture) to the apostles, who passed on this role by ordaining bishops after them. Paul's letters to Timothy and Titus are seen as his passing on of *authority to them, his personally appointed delegates. This understanding is seen as being developed by the *Apostolic Fathers. 1 Clement (written to the church at Corinth) defends the authority and prerogatives of a group of leaders in the church deposed and replaced by the congregation on its own initiative. The letter argues that the apostles appointed 'bishops and deacons' as successors, expecting them to appoint their own successors in turn (cf. 2 Tim. 2:2). So such church leaders were not to be removed without cause and due process. Tony Lane comments that this emphasis on the importance of due order in the church reflects 'traditional Roman values as well as biblical influence' (*A Concise History of Christian Thought*, p. 8). In the letters of Ignatius of Antioch at the beginning of the second century, the bishop is seen as a focus of unity against both schism and heresy. In the early third century *Tertullian, the father of Latin theology, writes as follows: 'Let them produce the original records of their churches; let them unfold the roll of their bishops, running down in due succession from the beginning in such a manner that [that first bishop of theirs] shall be able to show for his ordainer and predecessor some one of the apostles or of apostolic men' (*The Prescription against Heretics*, ch. 32). *Cyprian, Bishop of Carthage, developed further the significance of the apostolic succession, which protected the belief and inter-communion of the churches through the early centuries of persecution and international expansion.

Churches of the Catholic tradition hold that bishops form the necessary link in an unbroken chain of successors to the office of the apostles. The outward sign by which this connection is both symbolized and effected is the laying on of hands by the bishop at ordination. *Roman Catholic and Orthodox theologians hold that the power and authority to administer the *sacraments, with the exception of baptism and matrimony, is passed on only through the sacrament of Holy Orders, and that an unbroken line of ordination of bishops to the apostles is necessary for the valid celebration of the sacraments today.

Roman Catholics, of course, see the *pope as the successor to Peter, providing apostolic jurisdiction and leadership for the whole church, while for *Anglicans the bishop (who for *Anglo-Catholics and others shares in authority because of the link with apostolic succession) provides a focus of unity within a diocese. Apostolic succession is also claimed by the Anglican communion and some *Lutheran churches. However, in his papal bull of 1896, *Apostolicae Curae*, Pope Leo XIII denounced Anglican consecrations as 'absolutely invalid and utterly void' because of changes made to the rite of consecration under Edward VI. The theory of sacramental grace still stands as a barrier to greater organizational church unity.

While the Roman Catholic Church asserts that Christ gave Peter a unique primacy among the apostles, which has been passed on in the office of the papacy, in *Eastern Orthodox belief and practice all bishops are equal, with even the ecumenical patriarch seen as first among equals. Orthodox theologians see this as continuing the ancient practice of the church, which considered the Roman pontiff to be first but not superior to the rest of the bishops.

Apostolic teaching

In *Reformed understanding, Christ gave a special gift of remembrance, understanding and teaching to the original apostles (see John 14:26; 16:12–15). This gift enabled them to write or to oversee the NT Scriptures, which provide the doctrinal foundation for the whole church of subsequent history (see *Scripture, doctrine of). (Peter is seen, for example, as standing behind Mark's Gospel, and Paul behind Luke-Acts.) It is difficult to understate the importance of this stress on apostolic teaching for evangelical theology. Apostolic succession for them, as for most Protestants, is the faithful succession of apostolic teaching. There have, however, been different understandings of the apostolic authority 'to bind and to loose' (Matt. 16:19) or to forgive sins (John 20:23–23).

Most *Protestant churches would deny that the apostolicity of the church rests on an unbroken episcopacy.

Apostles today

The twentieth century saw the development of the idea of a continuing apostleship. The Apostolic Church, a *Pentecostal denomination tracing its origins to the Welsh Revival of 1904–5, now has over 6 million members in more than seventy nations. It is not a part of oneness Pentecostalism (denying the Trinity), which also terms itself apostolic. Many other churches of widely varying churchmanship also include the adjective 'apostolic' in their name, with varying significance. This is especially common with some Black majority church denominations. There is a sociological link here with the role of the leader or prophet in African traditional religion and life.

For Restorationism, a branch of the *charismatic movement, the fivefold ministries of apostle, prophet, evangelist, pastor and teacher (see Eph. 4:11) are of major significance. It is argued that there are apostles today in the sense of foundation-laying ministries, continuing *gifts of the ascended Christ. Often these are seen as being essential to the well-being of churches, providing links between local congregations and enabling them to benefit from the training and international links which apostolic ministries and teams provide. There is an emphasis on networking and building relationships, with church planting and social concern being seen as key activities. While in many Western countries such apostles with their teams may seem to be of marginal significance, in areas of the world where the church is growing rapidly they are frequently widely influential.

Since the Second *Vatican Council many in the Roman Catholic Church have placed greater emphasis on the apostolate of the whole church, including the laity. The 'one, holy, catholic and apostolic church' is a seen as a communion of churches whose validity is derived from the apostolic message it professes and the apostolic witness it lives out as much as through any personal apostolic succession of duly ordained bishops.

Sent on a mission

For many, the term 'apostolic' speaks primarily either of office and tradition, or of a body of doctrine to be defended. But the original meaning of 'apostle', based on the Jewish *shaliah* concept, is of one chosen and sent with a specific commission as the fully authorized delegate of the sender, to teach and act in his name and by his authority. Just as the original apostles were commissioned by the risen Lord to proclaim the *gospel to all nations, so today Christ continues to send his people into all the world to make disciples and establish churches (see *Evangelism, theology of). For the apostle Paul, as Jimmy Dunn has emphasized (*The Theology of the New Testament*, pp. 571–580), apostolic authority is always subservient to the gospel, exercised to build churches up rather than to dominate them, willing to contextualize, accepting of a particular sphere of ministry, and ready to suffer as Christ did. Such perspectives are greatly needed in cross-cultural mission today, so that empire building may give way to humble, Spirit-dependent ministry that truly builds up the church.

See also: CHURCH; CHURCH GOVERNMENT.

Bibliography

P. Brown, *The Rise of Western Christendom: Triumph and Diversity, AD 200–1000* (Cambridge, 1996); A. C. Clark, 'The Role of the Apostles', in I. H. Marshall and D. Petersen (eds.), *Witness to the Gospel: The Theology of Acts* (Cambridge, 1998); J. D. G. Dunn, *The Theology of the New Testament* (London, 1998); N. Geldenhuys, *Supreme Authority: The Authority of the Lord, His Apostles and the New Testament* (Grand Rapids, 1953); F. J. A. Hort, *The Christian Ecclesia* (London, 1902); W. K. Kay, *Apostolic Networks in Britain: New Ways of Being Church* (Milton Keynes, 2007); J. N. D. Kelly, *Early Christian Creeds* (London, 1952); idem, *Early Christian Doctrines* (London, [5]1978); K. E. Kirk (ed.), *The Apostolic Ministry* (London, 1946); H. Küng, *Structures of the Church* (London, 1965); A. N. S. Lane, *A Concise History of Christian Thought* (London, [3]2006); J. Orr, *Progress of Dogma* (Old Tappan, n.d.; preface, 1901); W. Pannenburg, *The Apostles' Creed in the Light of Today's Questions* (London, 1982); J. Pelikan, *The Christian Tradition: A History of the Development of Doctrine, Vol. 1. The Emergence of the Catholic Tradition (100–600)* (Chicago, 1971); C. H. Turner, 'Apostolic Succession', in H. B. Swete (ed.), *Essays on the Early History of the Church* (London, 1921); A. Walker, *Restoring the Kingdom: The Radical Christianity of the House Church Movement* (London, [3]1998).

A. C. CLARK

APOSTLES' CREED, see CREEDS

APOSTOLIC FATHERS

Although used in the seventh century by Anastasius of Sinai, modern use of this term to designate the collection of extant post-apostolic (*c*. 70–150) writings dates from 1672. By 1873, with addition of the *Didache*, the traditional (if rather arbitrary) corpus was established. The Apostolic Fathers sought to continue faithfully the teaching of the apostles, applying it to new situations, thus providing a crucial witness to the early development of Christianity.

The corpus is not a homogeneous collection. Although generally practical and pastoral in nature, the genres are varied: some letters (*1 Clement* to the Corinthian church, Polycarp to the Philippian church, and Ignatius' seven more personal letters); a manual of Christian conduct (the *Didache of the Twelve Apostles*); a pseudonymous sermon (*2 Clement*) and treatise (*Epistle of Barnabas*); a book of apocalyptic visions (the *Shepherd of Hermas*); an account of the martyrdom of Polycarp; fragments of exegesis of sayings of Jesus by Papias; and apologetic writing (the *Epistle to Diognetus* and a fragment of *Quadratus*).

The Apostolic Fathers wrote to settle disputes and establish doctrine and practice as different understandings of Christianity arose, clarifying the theological boundaries surrounding traditional central apostolic beliefs primarily to establish viable Christian communities free from division; in the process proto-orthodox Christianity began to emerge. In response to the challenge of *docetism, Ignatius insists on the two natures of Christ, and Polycarp anathematizes denial of Christ's humanity, the resurrection and the judgment. Ignatius also addresses pressures to Judaize Christianity (see *Ebionism), though it has been suggested that this may be an expression of docetism. It is partly in reaction to such challenges that *Christological orthodoxy became established as the church sought to establish its distinctive identity. The parousia, resurrection, judgment, end of the world and a belief that Christians were living in the last times dominate the theology of the second century (see *Eschatology), but the Apostolic Fathers also provide evidence of how the doctrine of the *Trinity was developing. Trinitarian language is used, and Christ is understood to be pre-existent, incarnate, human and divine, though the doctrine is not formally explored.

The practical orientation of these documents, which has sometimes given the mistaken impression that the doctrine of *grace was lost by the early second century, is a response to the changes and challenges of the period. As a result, attention is given to church governance and the theology of *martyrdom. The growing community called for more central administration in larger cities, and Ignatius promotes a hierarchical monepiscopal structure of bishop, presbyters and deacons (see *Church government). Martyrdom is seen as a work of supererogation rather than obligation in *Hermas*, and Ignatius, whose letters are shaped by reflection upon his impending death in Rome, sees it as a perfect *imitation of Christ, a means of freedom and a sacrifice that all believers should be ready to make. The *Martyrdom of Polycarp* is the earliest narrative of an individual martyrdom and evidence of the cult of martyrs.

The appeal of Clement of Rome (fl. c. 96) for the restoration of unity in the Corinthian church and submission to the authority of bishops and elders is based mainly on the OT and apostolic tradition. This is supported by a high Christology, emphasis on the resurrection of Christ and *atonement by his blood. Polycarp's letter to the Philippian church draws extensively on the Septuagint and NT epistles as he exhorts and instructs his readers in Christian behaviour and submission to church leaders. He stresses righteousness and salvation by *grace, and calls for imitation of Christ's endurance on the basis of his sacrificial death. Ignatius, in addition to the concerns already noted, makes use of early *confessions of faith and sees the *Eucharist as central to worship, closely associating the elements with the physical body of Christ. The *Didache* is primarily a practical manual of the Christian life, explaining the 'two ways' of life and death and providing instructions on such matters as pre-baptismal catechesis and baptismal practice (the earliest evidence of *baptism other than by immersion), the Eucharist (including the earliest eucharistic prayers), the proper treatment of missionaries, the role of bishops and deacons, fasting and hospitality. The *Epistle of Barnabas* explores the relationship between Christianity and *Judaism, which is viewed negatively, and, using allegorical exegesis of the OT, seeks to demonstrate that Christians are the true heirs of God's covenant. The *Shepherd of Hermas* relates and interprets a series of visions, thereby exploring the issues of post-baptismal sin and repentance, righteousness and forgiveness and the nature of the church and its members.

The Apostolic Fathers demonstrate how the early post-NT church addressed the problems of the day, using Scripture, the sayings of Jesus and the apostolic tradition in their attempt to consolidate the faith and practice of the church. Their writings are therefore significant for the study of the emerging canon of *Scripture as well as the early Christian understanding and use of it. Although their use of Scripture and tradition reflects the Jewish heritage of Christianity, the influence of *Hellenistic thought and philosophical language is also evident, not least because of the growing distance between Judaism and Christianity, the increasing number of converts with a Greco-Roman background and the search for a distinctive identity.

Although *Eusebius refers to the Apostolic Fathers, there is little use of them in the doctrinal controversies of the fourth and fifth centuries. Following the publication of the writings of the Apostolic Fathers in the seventeenth century, they were used in the doctrinal and largely denominational disputes of the period primarily to support existing positions. During the nineteenth century the date and authorship of the writings were debated and their authenticity finally established, since which they have made a significant contribution to the study of early Christian literature and history. The writings of the Apostolic Fathers bridge the gap between the NT and later Christian writers and allow the former to be read in a wider context.

Bibliography

P. Foster (ed.), *The Writings of the Apostolic Fathers* (London and New York, 2007); M. D. Goulder, 'Ignatius' "Docetists"', *Vigiliae Christianae* 53, 1999, pp. 16–30; R. M. Grant (ed.), *The Apostolic Fathers: A New Translation and Commentary*, 6 vols. (New York, 1964–8); M. W. Holmes (ed.), *The Apostolic Fathers: Greek Texts and English Translations* (Grand

Rapids, ³2007); J. B. Lightfoot, *The Apostolic Fathers*, 5 vols. (London, 1885–90).

A. D. RICH AND D. A. HAGNER

APOSTOLIC SUCCESSION, see MINISTRY

ARAB CHRISTIAN THOUGHT

Arab Christians offered a great contribution to Christianity in Syria, Iraq and the Arab peninsula before the rise of Islam, and to a later stage in the Islamic era. Arab culture was influenced by Arab Christians during the pre-Islamic era. Christian poets contributed to the development of the language through the tribes of Rabiea, Twghlub, abd-Al-Qis and Tamim who lived in Najd, north-east of the Arabian peninsula. The development of the Arabic script is credited to three poets from the Christian tribe of Tai.

The rise of Islam influenced Arab Christians, especially in the three Arab centres of Christianity: Hira, al-Jabia and Najran. Hira remained a Christian city for two centuries after the Islamic occupation of 633. Its inhabitants were from the tribe of al-ᶜIbad, and they continued to influence the new Islamic culture. Al-Jabia was the capital for the Ghassanids and continued as a political and military centre during the period of Ummayyad rule. Arab Muslim armies advanced to both Syria and Iraq, defeated the Byzantines and Persians, and brought to an end the Christian Arab Kingdoms of the Ghassanids and Montherits, Tadmur in Syria and the Nabatiens in Petra, Jordan.

The development of Arab Christian thought and its influence in the Arab cultures is represented by different Christian groups. The church of the *Jacobites* was persecuted in Syria under the Byzantine Empire and under the Persians. However, Jacobites translated Greek thought into Syriac and Arabic. Takrit was a great centre of learning, writing and translating. *Nestorians contributed to the Christian Arab literary heritage. The *Copts started the process of transformation by using Arabic instead of the Coptic language. During the time of the Fatimids, Christians used Arabic in writing, daily conversation and liturgy. Their contribution to Arab Christian literature began with the great figure of Bishop Severus Ibn Al-Muqaffa (d. 987).

Arab Christians lived under pressure during the different eras of Islamic rule: the Ummayyads (661–750), Abbasids (750–1258), Tulunids (868–905), Ikhshids (935–69), Fatimds (969–1171), Ayybids (1171–1250), Mamluks (1250–1517), and the Ottoman Empire from 1517. A new era for Arab Christians began with the end of the Ottoman Empire in 1920. Arab Christians called for independence from the Ottoman Empire and were pioneers in journalism; they translated much material in science, literature and philosophy.

The role of Christians in the early period of the spread of Islam was similar to modern times. Christians addressed the role of religion in their societies. Islamic *umma* (community of the faith) estranged Christians and made them feel like second-class citizens. They advocated an Arab identity based on language, history and destiny, and not on religion. The identity of Arab Christians is in full unity with Muslims and yet they are more reserved towards Arab Muslims in the identification between Arab and Islamic identity. When Christians feel accepted in society, they participate fully in any new movement and support it. But when they feel that they are not participating in the full sense, unity with Arabs or any other movement is seen as a threat of more marginalization. The question becomes: How far are Christians allowed to participate?

See also: ISLAM AND CHRISTIANITY; SYRIAN CHRISTIANITY.

Bibliography

T. Al-Bishry, *Muslims and Copts* (ET, Cairo, ⁴2004); A. Atiya, *A History of Eastern Christianity* (ET, Cairo, 2005); K. Cragg, *The Arab Christians: A History in the Middle East* (London, 1992); S. I. Saka, *Syrian Churches Heritage: History of Christianity in the East* (ET, Beirut ²2002); E. Shaheed, *Christian Arabic Heritage: History of Christianity in the East* (ET, Beirut ²2002); B. Suru, *Syrian (Assyrians) Churches Heritage, History of Christianity in the East* (ET, Beirut ²2002).

S. F. SHEHATA

ARIANISM

Arianism is, theologically speaking, the view that the Son is 'God but not true God': Christ is divine, God in an attenuated sense, but of a different nature and essence from God the Father. It derives its name from the Egyptian presbyter Arius of Alexandria, who expressed these views, and who was condemned by the Council of *Nicaea (the first Ecumenical Council) in 325.

Arius

The logic of Arius' position was that, as the only unbegotten being and origin of all that is, God the Father is completely different from everything else in existence, including the Son. Everything else, including the Son, belongs to the realm of coming to be and passing away, the realm of inherent instability; only God the Father simply is, and is eternally. The Son, since he is begotten by the Father, cannot be eternal, but must have come to be, whether in time or before time. The uniqueness of God the Father (Arius often simply calls him 'God') must be protected at all theological cost, because anything else is blasphemy.

Arius was not the only theologian to hold these views, in his own day or afterwards. It is now generally accepted that he was not the leader of a movement as such, merely the spark that ignited a theological disagreement that had been smouldering for some time, and the ill-favoured name that would best allow his opponents to attack his supporters in the wake of his theologically embarrassing death in a public lavatory in 336. Those of his contemporaries who shared his views felt that they were his guarantors rather than his followers, and later theologians who shared some of his views, which included the Gothic and Vandal churches of the fifth century and beyond, often claimed never to have heard of him. For this reason, most scholars in the field now prefer not to use the term 'Arianism' at all, except for the views of Arius himself and perhaps his immediate circle of Alexandrian associates. The controversy usually given Arius' name nonetheless remains one of the key disputes of doctrinal history.

One possible view of the controversy is that it was a debate within the Origenist tradition over different interpretations of *Origen's thought on the relationship between Father and Son, which came to draw in also theologians who were self-consciously opposed to this tradition. Origen had believed that the Son was eternal, but also that created things in general were eternal. There was agreement on both sides in the fourth century that created things were not eternal, but not on whether the Son, as 'first-born of all creation' was part of creation or not.

The initial dispute between Arius and Bishop Alexander of Alexandria over whether the Son was, in fact, eternal quickly spread beyond Egypt, not least because Arius was supported by some of the most powerful bishops of the day across the Eastern Roman Empire. These included the impeccably well-connected Eusebius, bishop of the then imperial capital of Nicomedia, to whom Arius appealed for help, and the renowned Scripture scholar and church historian *Eusebius of Caesarea. Alexander marshalled his allies in reply, and may even have planned a large council at Ancyra (Ankara) to solve the affair, but ecclesiastical councils were banned at around this time by Licinius, emperor of the Eastern empire. When *Constantine, emperor of the West, conquered Licinius near Nicomedia in late 324 and took over the East as well, the churches were in turmoil. Constantine set about trying to calm things down, moving the Ancyran synod to the imperial palace at Nicaea, and urging peace on all the bishops there.

The Council of Nicaea

The Council, which met in June 325, exonerated Eusebius of Caesarea (who had been provisionally excommunicated at an earlier synod), but condemned Arius, and Constantine sent Eusebius of Nicomedia into exile as well three months later, apparently for trying to plead Arius' cause after the Council ended. The Council also issued a *creed which makes some key theological moves. The creed, according to *Athanasius' later account in *On the Decrees of Nicaea*, was deliberately constructed by his own party to make it impossible for Arius or his allies to sign it, but most of the latter did so anyway, in the face of persuasion from Constantine, as Eusebius of Caesarea explains in an embarrassed and theologically somewhat tortuous letter to his church at home.

The key anti-Arian points of the creed of Nicaea and the anathemas (condemnations) attached to it are as follows. The Son is described as being 'begotten from the Father as Only-begotten, that is, from the Father's essence (*ousia*)', 'true God from true God' and 'begotten not made'. He is 'of the same essence (*homoousios*) with the Father'. 'And those who say "there was when he was not", and "Before he came to be he was not", and that he came to be out of nothing or from another hypostasis or essence, or that the Son of God is variable

Arianism

or changeable, these the catholic and apostolic church anathematizes.'

'Begotten from the Father as Only-begotten' is used to draw a distinction between the way in which created things are begotten and the way in which the Son is begotten. Arius and his allies had used Isa. 1:2, 'I reared children and brought them up, but they have rebelled against me', to show that 'begotten' did not necessarily imply anything special about the relationships between Father and Son, since it could also be used of human beings. But if John calls the Son 'only begotten' (John 1:18, KJV and NIV footnote), the creed implies that this must mean his mode of begetting is unique, and therefore different from that of the creatures. The same point is implied by 'Begotten not made': this demands that the two words mean different things (Arius had used them as equivalents).

'From the Father's essence' was a key and controversial statement: Athanasius shows how it was employed to rule out the possibility that the Son could be 'from the Father' in the way that all things are. It also rules out the possibility that the Son might be from nothing (as Arius had earlier asserted). 'True God from true God' echoes the form of two preceding phrases that had probably been borrowed from Eusebius of Caesarea's creed (God from God, Light from Light) but was meant to exclude the view (expressed by Eusebius himself) that the Son was God but not true God (in exegesis of John 17:3, 'That they know you, the only true God'). Arius had also expressed the view the Father was 'alone true'.

The expression '*homoousios* with the Father' (consubstantial/of the same essence) is the creed's most famous phrase. It spawned the analogous *homoiousios* (of like essence) as an attempted compromise in 358 (though the breadth of the appeal of this term should not be overestimated – it was on the table only for about three years, and only ever had a handful of supporters). The word was extremely controversial, not only because it was non-scriptural, but also because of its *Gnostic overtones (which Arius had already noted). It also worried a later generation of potential supporters of Nicaea, including Basil the Great, though they came to see Nicaea as the only chance of reuniting the church after so many decades of conflict. Whoever introduced it, its great defender was Athanasius, who saw it as guaranteeing the Son's true divinity.

The Nicene anathemas are also interesting, partly because they serve as a useful test of the intentions of those compiling their own creeds later in the controversy, who vary between exactly reproducing each Nicene anathema, using a subtly different version of it, or leaving it off altogether. The one which was most quickly agreed on was 'out of nothing' (*ex ouk ontôn*), which even Arius himself came to reject (though it was revived in the later stages of the controversy). The assertion that the Son of God is variable or changeable (the words could also mean 'varying' and 'changing') was also ruled out in the Second Creed of Antioch in 341, but this is less significant as it was widely agreed that the Son did not alter in fact: the question was whether he was alterable in principle. 'There was when he was not', and 'Before he came to be he was not', meanwhile, were never anathematized in this form again by any of the opponents of Nicaea, and, indeed, not even by the Council of Constantinople of 381.

From Nicaea to 357

The debates and the politics continued in the years after Nicaea. Eusebius of Caesarea and Eustathius, anti-Arian bishop of Antioch, debated the word *homoousios*; Eustathius was deposed in the late 320s for murky reasons, and Arius and Eusebius of Nicomedia were recalled by Constantine from exile, for reasons that are equally unclear. Athanasius, Marcellus of Ancyra and others were deposed in their turn in the mid-330s by some sharp political manoeuvring; they were allowed to return to their sees after the death of Constantine in 337, only to be deposed again two years later.

Athanasius and Marcellus fled to Rome at the invitation of Julius, the bishop there, who invited the Eastern bishops to an ecumenical council in Rome to discuss the cases. The Easterners declined and held their own large council, the Dedication Council of Antioch, in 341 instead, which ratified three creeds, all avoiding the characteristic language of Nicaea. The so-called Fourth Creed of Antioch, issued a few months later, became the basis for a series of creeds over the next fifteen years, with more and more detailed anathemas being added. Events of the 340s were partly shaped by the rivalry between Constantine's two surviving sons, Constantius and Constans, emperors of the Eastern and Western Empires respectively. Constans insisted on an ecumenical council, which was this time called to the frontier capital of Serdica (modern Sofia) in 343, but the leaders of the Eastern party used wrecking tactics to ensure the full council never met. Constans continued to insist that Athanasius and a further exiled bishop, Paul of Constantinople, be restored to their sees, finally threatening war. This was achieved in 345–6, but at a price: Paul was executed on Constans' death in 350, and Athanasius, who, having played his hand with greater skill, managed to hold on until 356, then had to flee for his life.

By 357, the defeat of the pro-Nicene party seemed secure. Athanasius was in hiding, Marcellus, who had become a lightning-rod for anti-Nicene sentiment, had withdrawn from the controversy, and his pupil and deacon Photinus of Sirmium was finally condemned in 351. A number of sympathetic Westerners had also been deposed. Meanwhile, the aged Ossius of Corduba, who had presided at Nicaea, had been kidnapped, held under house arrest and finally persuaded to sign a creed (the so-called 'blasphemy of Sirmium') which forbade the use of any *ousia* language as unscriptural, and particularly the expression *homoousios*. It was the symbolic death of Nicaea.

From Sirmium to Constantinople 381

It was also, however, the beginning of a new stage in the controversy. The opposing party, which like the pro-Nicene party had been in considerable tension ever since Serdica, at this point broke into open disagreement. Three parties are traditionally described as being formed at this point: the 'Semi-Arians' (as older treatments called them), or homoiousians, who held the Son to be *homoiousios* (like in substance) to the Father; the homoians (those using the formula that the Son is 'like', *homoios*, the Father); and the anomoians (or anhomoians), also sometimes called Neo-Arians or, more properly, heterousians, who held that the Son is unlike, or of a different substance than, the Father.

In practice, matters are not quite so neat. The 'homoiousians' were in reality a small coterie around Basil of Ancyra, Marcellus' replacement, who dropped out of the picture fairly quickly after Basil's deposition at Constantinople in 360. Nonetheless, they attracted some fairly widespread support at the Council of Seleucia in 359 from bishops who were unhappy with the room the 'homoian' position left for heterousian theology. *Homoios*, meanwhile, was something of a flag of convenience based on insistence on not going beyond the Scriptures for those whose positions were themselves fairly heterousian, such as Ursacius of Singidunum and Valens of Mursa in the West and Acacius of Caesarea in the East. But the heterousians nonetheless differed from the homoians in important ways, as much political as theological. They were a small band of intellectual rigorists, led by the scholars Aetius and Eunomius, who were more interested in pursuing the truth than in compromising their views to make them more generally palatable. But they had some success at the very end of Constantius' reign: Eunomius was appointed bishop of Cyzicus, near Constantinople, in 360, to replace one of the deposed homoiousians, while the sees of Constantinople and Antioch ended the reign in the hands of Eudoxius and Euzoius, intermittent supporters of Aetius.

Constantius died in 361, to be replaced by his co-emperor Julian, who quickly declared himself a pagan and caused chaos by allowing all the exiled bishops of every theological hue to return to their sees. Julian himself died in 363, to be replaced briefly by Jovian and then by the brothers Valentinian and Valens in West and East respectively; Valens continued to favour the homoians, but with less vigour than Constantius had done. Aetius, Eunomius and their associates set up a series of what became parallel churches – joining the three churches many cities now already had since the days of Julian: homoian, Nicene and 'homoiousian'.

The homoians in this period sent a highly successful missionary to the Goths, Wulfila, who converted them to homoian Christianity, more or less at the same time as homoianism was losing ground in the East to a new pro-Nicene tradition. In 378, when Valens died fighting the Goths in one of the most disastrous military campaigns in centuries, the homoians lost their Eastern imperial support for good. Theodosius, the new emperor, proclaimed that orthodoxy lay with those who were in communion with Damasus of Rome and Peter of Alexandria, Athanasius' pro-Nicene successor. A council, called to *Constantinople in 381, while almost entirely Eastern and dominated by internal squabbles, ratified the Nicene creed, though it also composed one of its own, the one most often described today as the 'Nicene Creed'. The Eastern homoians and heterousians retired for good to small churches outside the walls of the major cities, and to monastic communities on their country estates.

But the Gothic and Vandal kingdoms in the West would continue to be homoian for centuries to come.

See also: COUNCILS; CHRISTOLOGY; GOD; TRINITY.

Bibliography

L. Ayres, *Nicaea and Its Legacy: An Approach to Fourth-Century Trinitarian Theology* (Oxford and New York, 2004); R. C. Gregg and D. E. Groh, *Early Arianism: A View of Salvation* (London, 1981); R. P. C. Hanson, *The Search for the Christian Doctrine of God* (Edinburgh, 1993); R. Lyman, 'A Topography of Heresy: Mapping the Rhetorical Creation of Arianism', in M. R. Barnes and D. H. Williams (eds.), *Arianism after Arius; Essays in the Development of the Fourth Century Trinitarian Conflicts* (Edinburgh, 1993); R. P. Vaggione, *Eunomius of Cyzicus and the Nicene Revolution* (Oxford, 2000); Maurice Wiles, *Archetypal Heresy: Arianism through the Centuries* (Oxford, 1996); R. D. Williams, *Arius: Heresy and Tradition* (London, ²2001).

S. PARVIS

ARISTOTELIANISM

Aristotelianism is a philosophical tradition which finds its principal source and inspiration in the works of the ancient Greek philosopher Aristotle (384–322 BC). This article will first examine briefly some of Aristotle's key ideas before assessing the history of Aristotelianism and the influence of Aristotle's work within Christian theology.

Key ideas

Ethics

Aristotle was a pupil of Plato, and the extent to which Aristotle developed or departed from his master's teachings is much contested (see L. Gerson, *Aristotle and Other Platonists*). Aristotle followed Plato closely in his understanding of the good life and the importance of the virtues (see *Nichomachean Ethics*, I.x–xiii; II). For Aristotle, a virtue (*aretē*) is an excellence in the fulfilment of a certain function or task (*ergon*). These functions or tasks will be particular to certain creatures such as human beings, and in the virtuous performance of such tasks we will find our 'happiness' or 'fulfilment' (*eudaimonia*). Such happiness is not merely 'cheerfulness', but rather a state of spiritual and physical well-being or fulfilment which can be more or less intense. Virtue and happiness are not states but activities: in being happy, one displays excellence in the performance of a certain activity such as generosity (a moral virtue) or learning (an intellectual virtue). The virtues are to be practised and honed over a whole lifetime in pursuit of the 'happiness' which is humanity's goal and fulfilment. Aristotle's ethics, like the whole of his philosophy, is therefore profoundly teleological.

Metaphysics and physics

Aristotle's *metaphysics includes three key distinctions. The first is between potency and act (see *Metaphysics* IX). This refers to the distinction between the qualities or states that something has *potentially*, and the qualities or states which something has *actually*. For example, a bowl of cold water is *potentially* hot, and by the application of heat it might become *actually* hot.

Secondly, Aristotle distinguishes between *substance (the essence or particularity of something; not, as the English term might suggest, simply its material qualities) and accident (the variable characteristics which a substance might possess 'accidentally', such as height in a human being) (see *Metaphysics* VII). This allows Aristotle to distinguish between substantial change and accidental change. For example, if a person were to dye their hair a different colour, they would still remain a person; this would be an accidental change, or a change to one of the person's variable qualities known as 'accidents'. A substantial change involves an alteration in what something is, for example, the turning of a tree into a desk.

Finally, Aristotle supports so-called 'hylomorphism', which can be found in the teachings of Plato. This is the view that substance can be analysed in terms of 'form' and 'matter' (see *Physics* II). Matter is the underlying material element of any substance and, of itself, is purely potential. All matter is qualified as a certain kind of thing (e.g. a bird or a desk) by possessing a 'form' (say the form of a bird or a desk). The 'form' is what makes something a particular kind of thing (e.g. a man rather than a tree). For Plato, the Forms exist more truly in a realm independent of the physical, visible reality we inhabit. For Aristotle, 'form' is immanent within particular things.

Regarding the concept of 'cause' in metaphysics and physics, Aristotle makes the important distinction between material, formal, efficient and final causes (see *Metaphysics* I.3). The most important of these is the final cause, namely the goal of an effect, or the reason why something happens. For example, we might ask what causes someone to go shopping for food. Aristotle would say that the most important causal explanation for someone shopping for food is the desire for food and the need to satiate hunger. This is the 'goal', or final cause of, and the reason for, the shopping trip.

Sciences and logic

Aristotle wrote a number of treatises on logic and the relationship between the increasingly independent subject areas included within the broad pursuit of philosophy (see esp. *Prior Analytics* and *Posterior Analytics*). This was an attempt to delineate more clearly the relative certainty of different subject matters such as physics and metaphysics, their appropriate methodologies, the way in which less certain areas of knowledge require the support of more certain areas of knowledge, and the rules of logic, including syllogism.

Reception and influence

The early church was deeply influenced by ancient Greek philosophy. The notion that this constitutes an 'infection' of a 'pure' biblical theology cannot be maintained; there never was a time when Christian theologians were not influenced positively and negatively by the philosophy of ancient Greece. The teachings of Platonism were much more influential than Aristotelianism in the early church. It was thought that Plato, in speaking more readily of the transcendent nature of the Good and the Forms, was more conducive to Christian theology than the supposedly more materialistic teachings of the Aristotelians.

Despite the deployment of Aristotle's thought by prominent theologians such as *Boethius, Aristotelianism's influence was not considerable until the recovery of Aristotle's writings, beginning in the ninth century with his teaching on logic. Certain of Aristotle's writings in natural philosophy were well known in the Islamic East (particularly in the work of Avicenna [980–1037] and *Averroes) and later transmitted to the Latin West. It was not until the twelfth century that Aristotelianism began to have significant impact on Christian theology. The first known Latin commentary on a work by Aristotle since Boethius, on the *Posterior Analytics*, was written in the 1220s by Robert Grosseteste (c. 1170–1253). Aristotelian philosophy reached the height of its influence in the thirteenth-century work of *Albertus Magnus and *Thomas Aquinas. Aquinas wrote many commentaries on Aristotle's works and deployed his metaphysical categories extensively in his writings on the existence of God, grace and sacramental theology. However, Aquinas often deploys these categories in quite un-Aristotelian ways (e.g. in his use of substance and accident in the discussion of transubstantiation), so the extent to which Aquinas can be termed 'an Aristotelian' is much contested. It is clear that in the thirteenth century Aristotelianism is introduced into Christian theology in the context of Neoplatonism's continued prevalence.

In the late thirteenth century certain Aristotelian teachings became suspect and were condemned as heretical by the Bishop of Paris, Stephen Tempier. Of particular concern was Aristotle's view that the universe is of endless time. While Aquinas thought this a rationally defensible claim, it nevertheless appeared to contradict the Christian teaching that God created the universe *ex nihilo*.

Aristotelian teachings were particularly conducive to Christian theology in three areas. First, the categories of act, form, substance and final cause could be applied to the doctrine of *God. In being distinct from creation, God was to be understood as pure act (having no potentiality), pure form (having no matter), a substance with no accidents, and the final cause of motion by being the object of creation's desire (see *Metaphysics* XII). Secondly, the Aristotelian understanding of virtue aided the exposition of what would constitute the good Christian life within the *polis* of the church. To Aristotle's ethical teachings were added the theological virtues of faith, hope and love and the Christian understanding of the final goal of human life (*eudaimonia*), namely the beatific vision (see *Vision of God). This aspect of Aristotelianism has recently been very influential in Christian ethics, particularly in the work of Alasdair *MacIntyre, Stanley *Hauerwas and John *Milbank. Finally, Aristotelian teaching on the relation of the different spheres of human knowledge (the so-called 'subalternation of the sciences') influenced Boethius and Aquinas in their attempts to articulate the distinctive nature of Christian theology or 'holy teaching' (*sacra doctrina*) in relation to other disciplines, particularly metaphysics.

The extensive use of Aristotle's texts in the schools and universities of Europe alongside the proliferation of commentaries on his works ensured that Aristotelianism was the predominant philosophy of the Renaissance. Of particular importance were Aristotle's logic and natural philosophy. However, the direct influence of Aristotelianism on Christian theology waned during the Reformation, indicating the extent to which philosophical learning was increasingly divorced from theology. Aristotelian natural philosophy was to remain dominant until the late sixteenth and seventeenth centuries when the advent of modern science and philosophy, particularly Newtonian mechanics and Cartesian philosophy, recast the intellectual landscape of Europe.

The commendation of Thomistic Aristotelianism in Pope Leo XIII's 1879 encyclical *Aeterni Patris* ensured that the influence of Aristotelianism as expounded by Aquinas would be considerable in late nineteenth- and early twentieth-century *Roman Catholic theology. More recently, the Aristotelian influence on the doctrine of God, particularly the notion of the 'unmoved mover' from *Metaphysics* XII, has been widely and very controversially criticized by those of the *process and *open schools of theology. These schools argue that Aristotelianism renders God 'static' and 'apathetic' in contrast to the personal God of the Bible. It has been suggested that this is, in fact, a misunderstanding of the Aristotelian view of divine causation. To refer to God as the 'unmoved mover' is to suggest that God is beyond movement and rest, and most fully 'dynamic'.

While the exact nature of Aristotle's influence on key theologians such as Thomas Aquinas remains contested, the importance of neo-Aristotelian virtue ethics in contemporary Christian theology cannot be denied.

See also: PLATONISM; PLATONISM, CHRISTIAN.

Bibliography

Works: Aristotle's works are available in many editions and translations. The following are the best recent single-edition translations of those works mentioned in this article: *Metaphysics*, tr. Hugh Lawson-Tancred (London, 1998); *Nicomachean Ethics*, tr. R. Crisp (Cambridge, 2000); *Physics*, tr. R. Waterfield (Oxford and New York, 2008); *Posterior Analytics*, tr. J. Barnes (Oxford, ²1994); *Prior Analytics*, tr. R. Smith (Indianapolis, 1989).

Studies: H.-G. Gadamer, *The Idea of the Good in Platonic-Aristotelian Philosophy*, tr. P. C. Smith (Yale, 1988); L. Gerson, *Aristotle and Other Platonists* (Ithaca, new edn 2006); S. Hauerwas and C. Pinches, *Christians among the Virtues: Theological Conversations with Ancient and Modern Ethics* (Notre Dame, 1997), esp. part I; M. Jordan, *Ordering Wisdom: Hierarchy of Philosophical Discourses in Aquinas* (Notre Dame, 1987); *idem*, *Rewritten Theology: Aquinas after His Readers* (Oxford and Malden, 2006); D. Knowles, *The Evolution of Medieval Thought* (London and New York, ²1988), esp. parts 3 and 4; J. Lear, *Aristotle: The Desire to Understand* (Cambridge, 1988); D. A. D. Liscia, *Method and Order in Renaissance Philosophy of Nature: The Aristotle Commentary Tradition* (Aldershot, 1998); A. MacIntyre, *After Virtue: A Study in Moral Theory* (London, ³2007); J. Milbank, *Theology and Social Theory: Beyond Secular Reason* (Oxford, ²2006); S. Oliver, *Philosophy, God and Motion* (London and New York, 2005), chs. 2 and 4; C. Pinnock, *Most Moved Mover: A Theology of God's Openness* (Grand Rapids, 2001).

S. A. OLIVER

ARMINIANISM

Jacobus Arminius (1560–1609) was a Dutch theologian educated at Leiden, Basel and Geneva, at which latter place he studied under *Beza. Upon returning to the Netherlands, he served as pastor in Amsterdam before becoming professor at Leiden in 1603. He questioned some basic assumptions of *Reformed theology, arousing a bitter and vituperative controversy.

Central to Arminius' theology was his radical view of *predestination. He attacked the speculative supralapsarianism of Beza on the grounds of its lack of Christocentricity, Christ being not the foundation of election but only the subordinate cause of an already foreordained salvation, resulting in a split between the decree of election and the decree concerning salvation through the incarnate Christ. This Christocentric concern led Arminius to invert the order of election and *grace. For Reformed orthodoxy, the historical manifestation of God's grace was dependent on election. For Arminius, election was subsequent to grace. God decrees to save all who repent, believe and persevere. Election is conditional on man's response, dependent on God's foreknowledge of his faith and *perseverance. The possibility of a true believer totally or finally falling from grace and perishing is not denied. Consequently, there could be no *assurance of ultimate salvation. Moreover, God gives sufficient grace so that man may believe on Christ if he will. His *will is free. He can believe or he can resist God's grace. Redemptive grace is universal not particular, sufficient not irresistible; man's will is free not bound, and cooperates with God's grace rather than being vivified by it. Effectively, Arminius was saying that God does not choose anyone, but instead foresees that some will choose him. This was a position with *Pelagian and Greek patristic roots.

Arminius' views were developed by his followers in the five theses of the Remonstrant Articles (1610): (1) Predestination is conditional on a person's response, being grounded in God's foreknowledge; (2) Christ died for each and every person but only believers are saved; (3) a person is unable to believe and needs the grace of God; but (4) this grace is resistible; (5) whether all the regenerate will persevere requires further investigation. The resultant controversy assumed convulsive national importance, culminating in the Synod of *Dort (1618–19) which condemned the Remonstrant Articles (see *Dort, Canons of) and removed and exiled the Remonstrant ministers. To the Contra-Remonstrants it appeared that the followers of Arminius had adopted a *Semi-Pelagian view of grace, had destroyed the doctrine of assurance by questioning perseverance and, through their inversion of predestination, were introducing a conditional gospel which threatened the *atonement and *justification.

Some of the fears of the Contra-Remonstrants appear soon to have been fulfilled. Simon Episcopius (1583–1643), Remonstrant leader at Dort, a prominent figure behind the Remonstrant Articles and professor at Leiden, made further developments in his own theology. Reiterating a conditional doctrine of predestination, he held that only the Father had deity of himself, the Son and the Holy Spirit being subordinate not simply in terms of generation and spiration but also in essence (see *Trinity). His stress was on Christ as exemplar, with doctrine subordinated to ethics.

The commitment to universal atonement (see *Atonement, extent of) led followers of Arminius to oppose the penal *substitutionary view of the atonement held by Reformed orthodoxy whereby Christ actually paid the penalty of all the sins of all his people and thus made effective atonement. For Arminianism, since Christ was held to have suffered for everyone, he could not have paid the penalty for their sins, since all are not saved. His death simply permits the Father to forgive all who repent and believe. It makes salvation possible, but does not intrinsically atone for anyone in particular. In fact, the atoning death of Christ was not essential for salvation by virtue of God's own nature as both loving and righteous, but was rather the means God chose to save us for prudential administrative reasons. Hugo *Grotius, an Arminian, was the first clearly to expound the governmental theory of the atonement.

Despite initial suppression in the Netherlands, Arminianism spread pervasively throughout the world, eventually permeating all Protestant churches. In particular, its growth was facilitated by the impact of John *Wesley. Wesleyan Arminianism allowed that depravity was total, affecting every facet of man's being, thus highlighting the need for grace. However, synergism (see *Will) was retained, for the work of Christ was related to all men, delivering all from the guilt of Adam's first sin and granting sufficient grace for repentance and faith, providing people 'improve' or appropriate it. Hence, the stress falls on human appropriation of grace. Additionally, the possibility of a true believer falling from grace was expressly accepted with the consequence that while one could have assurance of present salvation, there could be no present assurance of ultimate salvation. The leading Wesleyan theologian, Richard Watson (1781–1833), in his *Theological Institutes* (1823), did not even include election in his table of contents, regarding it as a temporal act subsequent to the administration of the means of salvation.

In recent years, Arminianism has become intermingled with *Baptist and *dispensationalist ideas, particularly in its contact with American *fundamentalism. However, strictly speaking, it should be disentangled from such extraneous accretions so as to focus on its own intrinsic tenets: election based on foreknowledge, partial depravity, universal non-efficacious atonement, universal resistible grace, a voluntaristic view of faith, a Semi-Pelagian co-operation of a person with God's grace and the possibility of a true believer falling from grace with concomitant undermining of assurance.

Bibliography

Works: J. Arminius, *Works*, 3 vols. (London, 1825, 1828, 1875).

Studies: C. Bangs, *Arminius* (Grand Rapids, ²1985); A. H. W. Harrison, *Arminianism* (London, 1937); P. K. Jewett, *Election and Predestination* (Grand Rapids, 1985); R. Olson, *Arminian Theology: Myths and Realities* (Downers Grove, 2006); J. Owen, *Works*, vol. 10 (repr. London, 1967); R. E. Picirill, *Grace, Faith, Free Will* (Nashville, 2002); C. H. Pinnock (ed.), *Grace Unlimited* (Minneapolis, 1975); P. Schaff, *The Creeds of Christendom* (New York, 1919 edn); C. W. Williams, *John Wesley's Theology Today* (London, 1969).

R. W. A. LETHAM

ART, see AESTHETICS

ASBURY, FRANCIS (1745–1816)

Francis Asbury, though English, was the principal architect of the Methodist Episcopal Church in the USA. He was born in Handsworth, Staffordshire, and as a teenage apprentice was drawn to evangelical preaching and then to Wesleyan *Methodism. He became a class leader in the Methodist society at West Bromwich Heath in 1762 and a local preacher the following year. In 1767 Asbury was appointed an itinerant preacher by the Wesleyan Conference, and after four years' travelling in English circuits he volunteered to go to America. From 1771 until his death in 1816, Asbury played a crucial role in shaping American Methodism. He navigated the tense years of the War of Independence, and secured the formal establishment of the Methodist Episcopal Church as a separate body from the British Wesleyan Connexion at the 'Christmas Conference' of 1784. Ordained deacon, elder and superintendent on the authority of John *Wesley, Asbury acquiesced in the adoption of the title 'bishop' (to Wesley's dismay), but set an example of frugality, discipline and ceaseless itinerancy which saw American Methodism grow by 1816 to 214,000 members.

Bibliography

F. Baker, *From Wesley to Asbury: Studies in Early American Methodism* (Durham, NC, 1976); D. Salter, *America's Bishop: The Life of Francis Asbury* (Nappanee, 2003); J. A. Vickers, *Francis Asbury* (Peterborough, 1993); J. Wigger, *American Saint: Francis Asbury and the Methodists* (New York, 2009).

M. WELLINGS

ASCENSION [AND HEAVENLY SESSION OF CHRIST]

The ascension helps Christians address an obvious but central question: how should we understand *Jesus' physical absence? His physical absence might suggest his indifference to, desertion of, or impotence towards, this present world, or even that his incarnation is now over. All this would leave Jesus less central to Christians' lives now.

Traditional theology has seen the ascension as the transition from Jesus' state of humiliation to his exaltation (Dan. 7:13 arguably depicts this). It is the precursor to his session (being seated) at the right hand of God the Father. Omitting the ascension therefore risks overemphasizing his state of humiliation, while understating the benefits of his exaltation. Yet equally, the ascension does not simply reverse the humiliation, for the Son's *incarnation, which is central to his humiliation (Phil. 2:7), continues in the ascension: it is the God-Man Jesus who ascends, and his incarnation continues.

Biblical material

Both Nicene and Apostles' Creeds contain the ascension, suggesting its importance. Although extensive biblical material is relatively scant, the *creeds' emphasis is warranted. Acts 1:9–11 recounts the event, where a cloud, readily associated with God's glory, hides the risen Jesus from his disciples (cf. Luke 24:51). Ascension motifs are not exclusively Lucan, but occur throughout the NT, notably in John (e.g. 14:2), Ephesians (1:20–22; 4:8–10) and Hebrews.

Discussion of the ascension's significance can usefully begin with the ascension as the fulfilment of three psalms. Further fulfilment themes can be drawn, for example, from Dan. 7.

Psalm 110

In Eph. 1:19–21, Christ's resurrection and ascension are associated with power and fulfilment. God the Father is powerful enough to establish his Son as raised, ascended and seated with him, so fulfilling the enthronement promises of Ps. 110. This matters since Ps. 110 is so pervasive in NT understandings of Jesus (especially in Heb.). If Ps. 110, as interpreted by the NT, includes the ascension, then adequate understandings of Jesus must include it too. Jesus' ascension relates to God's plan for the cosmos to be united under Jesus' headship (Eph. 1:10), and demonstrates his ability to execute his promises and his faithfulness to them.

Ps. 110 speaks of one who is both king and priest, and Hebrews develops this extensively, applying Ps. 110's priestly language to Jesus who, having ascended into the heavens (Heb. 4:14), intercedes now for his people (Heb. 7:25–26).

Psalm 68

In Eph. 4:8–10, Paul envisages fulfilment of the promises of Ps. 68:18 that Yahweh, or his anointed, will ascend in victory. This victory element clarifies the enthronement of Eph. 1:20–21: enthronement occurs despite opposition (cf. Ps. 110 and Ps. 2) and relates not to mere attempts at power, but to victory won. Finally, Eph. 4:8–10 asserts that 'the ascender' is identical with 'the descender': the one who ascends in victory is he who visited humanity in humility. This identification of ascender with descender allays fears that the ascension is merely victorious power: it is the victorious power of the humble, servant Son. Theologies of exaltation and humiliation are joined.

Psalm 8

Arguably Heb. 2:5–9 sees Ps. 8 fulfilled in Jesus as ascended: he is the human in whom God's creation plan for a sovereign humanity is fulfilled. This indicates the importance of Jesus' continuing incarnation. Without him, there would be no 'last Adam' now to be the head of the new, re-created race, and the cosmos would continue to lack its perfected human head.

Consequences

This ascension theology has profound and glorious consequences. First, God's faithfulness to his promises is confirmed, but, vitally, since what Pss 2 and 110 promise to the Son is so vast (cosmic kingship), if God can keep this promise, we are assured he will keep others. In particular, Jesus' ascension is linked to a promise of his return (Acts 1:11). Paradoxically, the ascension, properly understood, underscores the certainty of Jesus' return, not his absence.

Secondly, the ascension speaks of victory won: the decisive battle is past (the nations conspire 'in vain', Ps. 2:1). Jesus' 'absence' is not weakness or desertion, tempting us perhaps to see Christian life in the present as something to do on our own, whose outcome even depends fundamentally on us. Instead, the ascension as victory focuses the Christian on the Jesus who reigns now. This challenges how much we trust, for clearly Jesus' rule is still contested, and gives theodicy questions a Christological dimension.

As victory, the ascension relativizes human power and legitimacy. It underlines Jesus' rule as universal, over all people for all time, not simply of Jews in the first century. Resistance to Jesus thus appears both illegitimate (Jesus' cosmic kingship is God's eternal plan) and ultimately futile (Jesus is already decisive victor). The ascension has current political applications, necessarily subverting human claims to autonomous power, whether totalitarian oligarchy or tyranny of the majority, and including claims to power within the church (see *State).

This subversive aspect is heightened when we remember that believers are currently united by faith with the ascended, reigning Jesus. To the world, believers may seem simply oppressed, but they are also united to the ascended Christ and sit with him (Eph. 2:6). Christian experiences of oppression remain real and agonizing, but this renders them less absolute and final.

Thirdly, the Hebrews material implies the ascended Jesus' priestly work is necessary and sufficient. This should allow us to approach God with confidence (Heb. 4:16) and suggests that constructing further priesthoods offering saving sacrifices or saving intercession fail to grasp the ascended Jesus' priestly work; they imply his work is unnecessary or insufficient.

Fourthly, the ascension relates to Jesus' gifts to the current church. The *Holy Spirit is sent by the Father at Jesus' behest after he has ascended. Jesus comments (John 16:7) that it is to our advantage that he departs, so that the Spirit may come. This indicates how precious he considers the gift of the Spirit, and that his ascension is the necessary precursor to Pentecost. The victorious Jesus also sends *gifts on his church (Eph. 4:7, 11), to build her common life under his headship. An ascension-less church therefore risks being a church that has not properly understood or accepted Jesus' gifts for her life now.

See also: ESCHATOLOGY; KINGDOM OF GOD.

Bibliography

D. Farrow, *Ascension and Ecclesia* (Edinburgh, 1999).

M. OVEY

ASCETICISM AND MONASTICISM

Asceticism and monasticism are almost synonymous terms, since the origins of the ascetical life are the origins of monasticism. Asceticism (from Gk *askesis* = practice, training or exercise) describes a system of spiritual practices designed to encourage interior vigilance so as to combat vices and develop virtues by means of self-discipline and self-knowledge in the context of seeking God. Its chief preoccupation is the desire to master the lower nature and gain freedom from the disordered passions through renunciation of the world and the flesh as part of the great struggle against the devil. The religious practice of renouncing worldly pursuits in order to fully devote one's life to spiritual work also describes monasticism (from Gk *monachos* = solitary, alone) and is found in many religions.

Asceticism was practised in biblical times, and events like the temptations of Jesus in the wilderness and the lifestyle of John the Baptist in the desert were later regarded as helpful models when monasticism became the leading representation of asceticism.

As an example of early asceticism, *Eusebius of Caesarea (d. 339) refers to the first successors to the apostles as following the Lord's counsel to distribute their possessions to the poor and become travelling preachers of the gospel. These preachers were often celibates who by the mid-second century constituted a clearly distinguishable group in the church, alongside those who were to marry. By the third century, ecclesiastical writers such as *Clement of Alexandria and *Origen were providing spiritual guidance for celibates and virgins, with voluntary poverty, self-denial and obedience to the local bishop seen as the normal Christian life.

The practice of seeking seclusion from the world in order to better practise ascetic ideals was not unknown in the third century, but it was not until the conversion of *Constantine that it became general. By the beginning of the fourth century a new expression of the ascetical life was introduced to the church in two forms: eremitical and cenobitic monasticism.

Christian monasticism first emerged as a distinct movement in the early fourth century, but it was not so much an innovation as a fresh expression of the ascetic spirit present in Christianity from the start (K. Ware, *The Oxford History of Christianity*, Oxford 1990, p. 139).

The rise of monasticism at this time is attributed to the huge changes in the church brought about by the Emperor Constantine's conversion. These included the acceptance of Christianity as the main Roman religion and the subsequent laxity following the realignment of the church along more material and political lines. The end of persecution also meant that *martyrdom by blood was no longer an option to prove one's piety, and instead the long-term 'martyrdom' of the ascetic became common.

Monastic development

The history of monasticism begins with Antony of Egypt (251–356) as he was the first monk about whom anything was written. He was the pioneer of anchorite monasticism, the solitary life of the hermit. After years of solitary existence in lower Egypt, he formed a colony of hermits and undertook to organize the monks who had sought him out for spiritual guidance and had become his disciples.

Monasticism soon adopted a more communal form, and the two great founders of this form of monastic life are Pachomius of Egypt (286–346) and Basil the Great of Caesarea (330–79). The 'common life' form of monasticism became widespread primarily in Egypt and Asia Minor. Pachomius's communities were found around Tabbennisi in Thebaid, near the Nile and in areas of Egypt less remote than that of Antony. A gifted organizer, his idea was an ascetic *koinonia* based on the primitive Jerusalem community where monasteries were self-sufficient colonies developed along military lines. Chastity and poverty were presupposed, and to these Pachomius added obedience as a necessary condition for life in community. Organization required obedience, and so a rule of life was introduced.

Asceticism and monasticism

In Asia Minor, Basil also strongly encouraged the cenobitic form of monasticism as being more suitable for most people than the eremitic style. His model of a monastic community as a brotherhood of love and service counteracted his fear that the eremitic life could lead to a neglect of the gospel call to charity, philanthropy and issues of social justice. He also insisted on monastic obedience as a check on those given to excessive display of extreme ascetical practices that were bringing the monastic movement into disrepute. His more informal counsels became the ascetic rule, or *Ascetica*, the rule still used today by the Eastern Orthodox Church of which he was the patriarch.

While Pachomius and Basil set the pattern for monasticism, the most important figure in its development was *Benedict of Nursia, who created his famous rule at his monastery in Monte Cassino, Italy (529). Largely influenced by the contemporary but anonymous *Rule of the Master* as well as the writings of Basil and Pachomius, Benedict softened the severity of the primitive ascetic practices of earlier monasticism and made it a more practical life-choice. The Benedictine asceticism of silence, obedience, solitude, humility, manual labour and liturgical prayer were designed to unite people with Christ and with one another. His desire to make monasteries 'a family, a home for those seeking God' proved more suitable to the peoples and conditions of the West.

Less than half a century after Benedict's death, Augustine (of Canterbury) and his fellow monks in 597 brought the Benedictine Rule to England. However, they found a system of monasticism already established bearing the characteristics of the main features of the Egyptian model: namely, Irish Celtic monasticism.

Characteristic of the rigorous asceticism of this system was an emphasis on missionary work – a voluntary exile of wandering for the love of God (*peregrinati*). For example, Columbanus (540–615) was a native of Ireland, but his voluntary exile took him to Gaul, Burgundy, and finally to northern Italy. He founded the monasteries of Luxeuil in Gaul, St Gall in present-day Switzerland, then Bobbio in northern Italy. Monks like Columbanus took with them their rule and their culture, establishing monasteries under the sole direction of the abbot. Columbanus wrote a more austere rule which existed side by side with Benedict's at Luxeuil and Bobbio, but by the mid-seventh century it had ceased to exist as a separate rule.

Spread to the West

Those who shaped the monastic movement and its eventual spread to the West are many, but include *Athanasius whose *Life of Antony* was a classic in his lifetime, and Evagrius Ponticus (d. 399) who taught ascetic life in Nitria, numbering among his pupils Palladius and Rufinus. It also includes such luminaries as Ambrose in Milan (d. 397), who as bishop planted monasteries, and the scholar *Jerome in Rome, who championed the ascetical life and translated the rule of Pachomius into Latin. *Augustine of Hippo in North Africa founded a monastery at Hippo; when he became bishop in 396 he turned the episcopal house into a monastic community, thus propagating the monastic life. Martin of Tours, a pioneer in Gaul, founded a monastery at Liguge (*c.* 361), and in 371 at Marmoutier, near Tours, where he became bishop. John Cassian (d. 435), who founded a monastery at Marseilles, was an expert on Egyptian asceticism and (drawing from Evagrius) wrote his *Institutes* and *Conferences* (*c.* 415–30) which influenced the Benedictine Rule. Along with the recorded counsel known as the 'sayings of the desert fathers' on the ascetical life, the works of Cassian were regarded as classics for centuries.

Over the next three centuries the Benedictine monasteries became centres of learning and culture in Europe, and their missionary work was the principal reason why Christianity spread throughout Europe. Until the eleventh century nearly all monks in the West were Benedictines, but the institutionalization of the monastic tradition had by that time led to a serious relaxation of the primitive ideals of poverty, chastity and obedience. The growing pressure of nation states and monarchies also threatened the wealth and power of the orders. The system broke down in the eleventh and twelfth centuries as religion became far less a preserve of the religious elite.

The eleventh to the thirteenth centuries saw a number of reforms being initiated, with the result that about this time new monastic orders sprang up, most of which originated in France or Italy. These included the Cistercians who began in Citeaux (Latin = *Cistercium*), France, in 1098 and set about 'interpreting the rule in the spirit of the desert fathers'. They expanded under *Bernard of Clairvaux, who organized sixty-five monastic houses in France alone. The *Franciscans began in 1209, setting an example in simplicity and poverty at a time of great clerical wealth. The *Dominicans were founded in 1216 as a teaching and preaching order following the Augustinian Rule.

After the Black Death (1346–49) the depopulation of Western Europe was too great to support monasticism on a large scale, and the orders began to decrease. By the time of the Reformation many monasteries were in decline, and their lands and assets were seized with little resistance. At the same time, many of the leading Reformers, notably Martin Luther, were monks who had left the cloister. They abandoned the traditional forms of monastic piety, but sought to recover the underlying spiritual ideals in a way which was not overtly ascetic.

New expressions of the monastic heart

In the next centuries, religious orders for both men and women (combining aspects of the contemplative orders and the active orders) had spread across the world. By the mid-twentieth century, in a deviation from the traditional orders, many different expressions of the monastic 'common life' appeared. In 1938 George McLeod founded the Iona Community in Scotland. In 1946 Roger Schutz, known as Brother Roger, founded the Taizé Community in France as an independent religious order. In 1947 Mother Basilea Schlink founded the Lutheran Evangelical Sisterhood of Mary, in Darmstadt, Germany. The popularity of the writings of the Trappist monk Thomas *Merton brought monasticism to the wider church and the wider world. Monastic spirituality lived outside the cloister as a community of the heart. This was continued in the United States by the Cistercian monks Thomas Keating and Basil Pennington and Benedictine monk John Main (d. 1982). Along with others, they initiated a monastic renewal touching the contemporary secular world. As a result of this new interest in monasticism, the late twentieth century spawned a movement often referred to as 'a new monasticism'. Citing Dietrich *Bonhoeffer's Life Together (1938), a written account of his experimental Christian community in Finkenwalde at that time and his earlier statement that 'the renewal of the church will come from a new type of monasticism', the movement saw asceticism in terms of the daily spiritual disciplines needed to fulfil the 'one thing necessary' of seeking God in the midst of life.

It seems no coincidence that these monastic expressions started during a time of enormous social upheaval as the church is experiencing exile within society and there is a growing dissatisfaction with the pervading popular culture. This is the context in which new monasticism is flourishing, as Christians seek an alternative way of being together in the world, much like the first founders of monasticism.

See also: MONASTIC THEOLOGY.

Bibliography

D. J. Chitty, *The Desert a City* (Oxford, 1966); M. de Dreuille, *Seeking the Absolute Love* (Leominster and New York, 1999); D. Knowles, *Christian Monasticism* (London, 1969); C. H. Lawrence, *Medieval Monasticism* (London and New York, 1984).

J. T. MILLER

ASIAN CHRISTIAN THEOLOGY

Asian Christians share a common concern to relate their Christian faith to real life in various Asian contexts. Reflecting on the nature and content of theology, Asian theologians have come to believe that every form of theological production is culturally conditioned. As a result, on the one hand there has been a critical evaluation of traditional theology developed in the West and imported to Asia, and, on the other, an enthusiastic pursuit of contextual theology that speaks to the actual questions people in Asia are asking today in the midst of changing social and political situations. Asian theology has started the growing process, and is already bearing fruits of different kinds. This article attempts to point out some observable trends and salient features of Asian theology, at the risk of overgeneralizing a complex development.

From c. 1970 there has been a shift of emphasis in Asian theology from 'indigenization' to '*contextualization'. The former tends to be 'past-orientated' and remains a static concept, with its stress on the relation of the gospel to traditional cultures; the latter is 'future-orientated' and dynamic, concerned also with the gospel in relation to social change. On the whole, most evangelicals are slow in responding to this change, and have not really gone beyond the 'indigenization' stage.

Theology serves to articulate one's understanding of the eternal truth in terms of one's given locale and context. The Bible, being the foundation and the source, provides the content of any Christian theology. With the Christian gospel as the God-given answer to human problems, it is the task of indigenous theology to discover what the real questions are, in order that Asian theology may assume a systematic form dictated by the salient emphases of Asian culture. The issue involves *gospel and *culture, and centres on the presentation of the gospel in different contexts, such as *Hindu, *Buddhist, *Islamic and totalitarian contexts. In theology, this means that particular contexts help to decide what particular area of faith should receive special emphasis. Raimon Pannikar utilized the Hindu concept of the *avatar* for his doctrine of the cosmic Christ; Aloysius in Sri Lanka tried to relate the gospel to Buddhism; and Lee Jung-Young has tried to use the Daoist concept of *yin* and *yang* in trinitarian theology. Discussions on the relationship between *evangelism and social responsibility (see *Missiology and *Society, theology of) have prompted evangelicals to face seriously some of the important issues in Asia (see *Lausanne Covenant). These include communism (see *Marxism and Christianity), *poverty, overpopulation, hunger, suffering, war (see *Pacifism and peace), bribery and *secularism.

Bong Rin Ro categorizes Asian theologies into four models: *syncretism, accommodation, situational theology and biblically orientated theology. His analysis reflects a common evangelical caution against contemporary Asian theology: fear of syncretism and accommodation whereby the gospel is diluted and biblical truth compromised. The key issue in the whole argument of contextual theology, as he sees it, is 'whether the biblical and historical doctrines of the Christian Church can be preserved without compromise in the process of contextualization'. The strength of evangelical theology lies in its insistence on the *uniqueness of the Christian gospel, the *revelatory nature of biblical truth and the necessity of *salvation. Its weakness may be described as a self-imposed limitation which does not adequately appreciate the richness of Asian religions and cultures, or urgently recognize the gravity of the demonizing effects of social and political evils.

Theological reflection in ecumenical circles often takes a different point of departure. *Ecumenical theologians have reacted against the merely conceptual, abstract and confessional nature of traditional theology. To them theology is more than an articulation of beliefs or a formulation of Christian doctrines (see *Confessions and *Creeds). Its task is rather to reflect on the contemporary situation in the light of the Christian faith. Therefore, the totality of life is the raw material of a living and confessing theology.

This approach to Asian theology, in terms of methodology and content, is very much determined by the context. Asian distinctives are used as a frame of reference in the theological task. These include plurality and diversity; colonial experience in the past; present nation-building, modernization and the resurgence of traditional religions. Asian theology is committed to address such issues as social injustice, poverty, violation of human rights, oppression and exploitation of the poor.

High on the Asian theological agenda is the theme of *suffering. In *Japan, Kazoh Kitamori (1916–98) brings out the centrality of suffering in the gospel and the reality of human suffering. The divine and the human are thus joined together in suffering, through which one comes to realize the love of God. Choan-Seng Song (b. 1929) further develops this theme by emphasizing that God commits himself totally to the suffering of this world. His theology of the *cross depicts the crucified God (see *Moltmann) not so much as the God who vicariously suffers and dies for the world (see *Atonement) as the God who suffers and dies with the world. Vicariousness is in fact replaced by identification.

Concern for humanity and *freedom is another important theme. From South *Korea we have *Minjung* theology, using a political concept (*minjung*) denoting people who are ruled and dominated (different from the Marxist proletariat which is defined socio-economically), and applying Christian themes of messianic *kingdom and *resurrection to interpret *history and give meaning to its vision. History is the process in which the *minjung* realize their own destiny to be free subjects through sufferings and struggles against oppressive powers. It may not be inaccurate to label this as a Korean version of *liberation theology. In *India, *dalit* theology spoke to the disadvantages experienced by the *dalit* people, the outcasts and untouchables under the Hindu caste system.

What about the long history of Asian peoples and the significance of their cultures? In what ways can we perceive the work of God among them? C. S. Song suggests that the frontiers of Asian theology must move from the history of Israel and the history of Christianity in the West to the history of Asia, in order to gain insights into God's ways with the nations, and to discover what place history beyond the Jewish-Christian traditions plays in God's saving purposes in the world. Probing in such a direction may present a challenge to some and a problem to others.

The creative efforts and insights of ecumenical theologians offer contributions to Asian theology that cannot be ignored. Their strength lies in their relevance to contexts, openness to new ideas and boldness to search into the dark. Yet these may also turn out to be disastrous if basic biblical foundations are forsaken in favour of other assumptions.

See also: CHINESE THEOLOGY; CONFUCIANISM AND CHRISTIANITY.

Bibliography

D. Aikman, *Jesus in Beijing* (Washington DC, 2003); S. Chan, *Grassroots Asian Theology: Thinking the Faith from the Ground Up* (Downers Grove, 2014); J. Elwood (ed.), *Asian Christian Theology* (Philadelphia, 1980), esp. essays by S. Coe, S. Athyal and E. P. Nacpil; J. C. England (ed.), *Living Theology in Asia* (London, 1981); K. Gnanakan (ed.), *Salvation: Some Asian Perspectives* (Bangalore, 1992); Hwa Yung, *Mangoes or Bananas? The Quest for an Authentic Asian Christian Theology* (Oxford, 1997); Kazoh Kitamori, *Theology of the Pain of God* (London, 1958); A. P. Nirmal (ed.), *A Reader in Dalit Theology* (Madras, 1991); V. Ramachandra, *The Recovery of Mission: Beyond the Pluralist Paradigm* (Grand Rapids, 1996); idem, *Faiths in Conflict: Christian Integrity in a Multi-cultural World* (Downers Grove, 1999); Bong Rin Ro, 'Contextualization: Asian Theology', in Bong Rin Ro and R. Eshenaur (eds.), *The Bible and Theology in Asian Contexts* (Taichung, Taiwan, 1984), pp. 68–75; Choan-Seng Song, *Third-Eye Theology: Theology in Formation in Asian Settings* (Maryknoll, 1979); idem, 'New Frontiers of Theology in Asia', in D. T. Niles and T. K. Thomas (eds.), *Varieties of Witness* (Singapore, 1980); Kim Yong-Bok (ed.), *Minjung Theology* (Singapore, 1981).

W. W. CHOW

ASSURANCE

Assurance of *salvation can be defined as someone's personal conviction that they have been eternally saved by God's *grace in Christ. Historically, such assurance has been a particular issue for Protestant and evangelical Christians. Other traditions have tended to view claims to absolute certainty of salvation as presumption: it is at the final judgment when the verdict will be given. Until then we wait, hope, and seek to live faithfully. But this has not satisfied *Protestants, who have grappled with two linked questions regarding assurance. First, can someone really be sure, in this life, that they are saved and that this salvation cannot be lost? Secondly, if such security is possible (or indeed normative for a Christian believer), then how is this assurance to be known?

These questions came to the fore at the time of the European Reformation. The Magisterial Reformers (see *Reformation theology) reacted against the doctrine of *penance and the close linkage of assurance with ecclesial authority as taught by the medieval Roman Catholic Church. Against this, Martin *Luther stated: 'I have been baptized and I have the Word, and so I have no doubt about my salvation as long as I cling to the Word' (*Works*, vol. 54, p. 57), and John *Calvin asserted that assurance and 'security' were to be found by looking to Christ and especially his cross (*Institutes*, 2.16.6, 2.16.19). Assurance of salvation was possible, indeed it was part of normal Christian experience. The guarantees of such assurance were found in the *atonement and the gracious promises of God to his people, appropriated by *faith.

Later *Reformed theologians, for example many sixteenth- and seventeenth-century English *Puritans, continued to focus on the objective work of Christ as grounds for assurance, but also stressed a need for believers to reflect on their own growth in practical holiness. The doctrine of 'temporary faith', developed by William *Perkins, was important here. A profession of faith might be made by someone who was not, in fact, truly regenerate. The sign that a 'professor' had really exercised saving faith was significant progress in holy living. Without such progress any assurance a 'believer' possessed would likely be proved false. In practice this led to significant doubts concerning assurance and a stress on rigorous 'self-examination'. Those who had professed faith were to search their experience for signs that they were truly part of the elect. In this tradition assurance was often achieved only after a long struggle and was, according to the Puritan Thomas Brooks, 'a pearl that most want, (but) a crown that few wear' (*Heaven on Earth*, p. 15).

In eighteenth-century evangelicalism there was a shift of emphasis again. According to David Bebbington, evangelicals such as Jonathan *Edwards believed that assurance was 'normally given at *conversion' and was 'the result of simple acceptance' of God's gift of salvation (*Evangelicalism in Modern Britain*, pp. 42–50). Assurance was of the essence of faith and normative for believers, although it was still expected that there would be significant changes in the way Christians lived subsequent to conversion. Nevertheless, this more confident view of assurance could have a significant impact on the life of a believer. The Baptist theologian Andrew *Fuller had been reared in a religious atmosphere dominated by High Calvinists who practised a heightened form of self-examination with a strong tendency towards introspective soul-searching and doubt. Fuller's conversion, in the years following 1780, to a more evangelical, moderate Calvinism led him away from the despondency which had characterized his earlier spiritual life towards what, by his own testimony, was a deeper joy and trust in God.

John *Wesley certainly believed that assurance was of the essence of faith, stressing a 'felt' assurance, the classic description of which was Wesley's own account of his conversion and his heart being 'strangely warmed'. Wesleyan Methodists differed from Calvinistic evangelicals, however, in believing salvation could still be lost. A Christian could 'fall away' by rejecting Christ or failing to live as a believer. Thus Wesley refused to affirm the Calvinistic teaching regarding 'the final perseverance of the saints'. But Reformed evangelicals who were committed to final *perseverance have also spoken of a 'felt' assurance in terms reminiscent of Wesley. Sometimes this has been described as a 'baptism' or 'filling' of the Spirit subsequent to conversion. One of the sermons printed in Martyn *Lloyd-Jones's *Joy Unspeakable: The Baptism of the Holy Spirit* is entitled 'Blessed Assurance' (Eastbourne, new edn, 1995, pp. 33–48). However, it has been conceived, assurance has always been an important feature of evangelical spirituality.

Significant work has been done on the doctrine of assurance by twentieth-century theologians such as *Berkouwer, *Barth and *Moltmann, as questions of eternal security have continued to exercise the minds of Protestant thinkers. The fundamental point at issue is whether assurance is a confidence in Christ alone or the result of an additional work of the Spirit or a period of self-reflection. Barth speaks of the vain search for a 'guarantee of the guarantee' (*CD* 1/1, p. 465). But others have sought to insist that all true, regenerate believers will show some signs of growth in holiness, and that some evidence of the work of the Spirit is an important part of a biblical doctrine of assurance. What is certain is that the way questions of assurance are answered has deep implications for the way the Christian life is conceived and lived.

Bibliography

K. Barth, *CD*; D. W. Bebbington, *Evangelicalism in Modern Britain: A History from the 1730s to the 1980s* (London, 1989); M. C. Bell, *Calvin and Scottish Theology: The Doctrine of Assurance* (Edinburgh, 1985); G. C. Berkouwer, *Faith and Perseverance* (ET, Grand Rapids, 1958); T. Brooks, *Heaven on Earth* (London, 1961 [1654]); J. Calvin, *Institutes of the Christian Religion* (ET, London, 1961); M. Luther, *Works* and *Table Talk* (ET, Philadelphia, 1967 [1532]); J. Moltmann, *Theology of Hope* (ET, London, 1967).

P. J. MORDEN

ATHANSIAN CREED, see ATHANASIUS; CREEDS

ATHANASIUS (300–73)

One of the greatest of all Christian theologians, Athanasius of Alexandria is particularly revered by the Orthodox churches, but also has a central place in the thought as well as the affections of many Protestant and Catholic theologians past and present. His tenacity and rhetorical brilliance were key to the eventual acceptance of the *Creed of Nicaea as normative for subsequent generations, and his theology of the *incarnation has been inspirational to those attempting to move beyond the classical Western forensic approach to soteriology. His implication in the violence of the times (from which he himself also suffered considerably) nonetheless remains something of a blot on his character.

Athanasius was an Egyptian of humble origins, possibly a native Coptic speaker, but his abilities and Christian devotion attracted the notice of Bishop Alexander of Alexandria, who seems to have been responsible for his education. As a deacon he accompanied Alexander to *Nicaea, and on Alexander's death in 328 was consecrated bishop, at slightly under the legal age of twenty-nine. He was bishop for nearly forty-six years, seventeen of them spent in exile (he was exiled five times in all). Athanasius' many works include major contributions to some of theology's most important topics – the *Trinity, the incarnation, soteriology (see *Salvation), the *Holy Spirit – and he also evidences great pastoral concern in his annual *Festal Letters*, and a prolonged interest in monasticism (see *Asceticism and monasticism) in his *Life of Antony*.

Athanasius, as deacon and secretary to Alexander, may have been the author of an early encyclical letter condemning Arius, but his earliest lengthy work is usually held to be the double treatise *Against the Greeks* and *On the Incarnation*. Since it contains no explicit reference to the *Arian controversy, the theological dispute which dominated most of his life and works, the work is sometimes dated as early as 318, though others have suggested 325 (on Athanasius' return from Nicaea), 335–7 (during his first exile), or even later.

Athanasius assails the pagan religious system in fairly conventional terms, largely on the basis of Rom. 1:18–32 (one of his favourite texts). His own account of salvation history is a mixture of two traditions. The first is a noetic, *Origenist picture. Here human beings turn their minds away from intelligible reality and from contemplation, becoming fixated instead in their own desires. This demands a revelation which will turn them back towards the true God. Athanasius' treatment of the subject, however, is vivid and original, for he has a strong sense of the seriousness of the problem: human beings are recalcitrant and ignorant and not inclined to take any of the necessary steps to fix their minds on God or to learn about God from creation. For Athanasius, the Son is like an infinitely patient teacher, ready to try anything, no matter how undignified, to help his unpromising pupils to understand the true nature of God. So he becomes incarnate to show what God is like by the clearest, simplest and most inescapable means, the inappropriateness of the action for a divine being merely underlining the boundlessness of God's love.

The second strand of Athanasius' incarnational thought is an *Irenaeus-influenced doctrine of the importance of the flesh in making human beings what they are. According to this strand, human flesh is the weak point in creation, being inherently unstable, and now subject once again because of the *fall to the corruption and decay from which God had earlier preserved it. Only the original Creator could restore it (it is very important for Athanasius that the Son as well as the Father is Creator), doing so by himself assuming flesh. The very presence of the Word transforms human flesh simply by being joined to it, burning out its corruption and decay like sparks in a stubble field. The Word, life itself, undergoes anguish and tastes death in the flesh to break the hold of suffering and death over it, fulfilling and bringing to an end the death sentence given for Adam's disobedience, freeing humanity from slavery to the devil, and making human beings adopted children of God through their new kinship with the one who is Son of God by nature.

Probably while in Rome during his second exile, during the years 339–41, Athanasius wrote his three *Orations against the Arians* (the so-called Fourth Oration is now thought to be by another hand). These are the fullest expression of his mature trinitarian thought. They represent an extensive engagement with the Scripture exegesis of Arius and his early supporters, Eusebius of Nicomedia and Asterius the Sophist. These had argued on the basis of Phil. 2:9 ('Therefore God exalted him to the highest place'), the Septuagint text of Prov. 8:22 ('The LORD brought me forth as the first of his works') and various Johannine texts that the Word was in principle mutable, having been promoted by God; that the Word was not eternal, being created rather than uncreated; and that the Word received power from God rather than having it of himself. Athanasius, devoting essentially one oration to each of these texts, together with others used by his opponents in the same way, insisted that the Word, being true Son of God by nature, image of the Father and proper to the Father's essence, must be eternal (John 1:1), equal to God (John 5:18), creator (Col. 1:16) rather than created, immutable (Mal. 3.6), and the true wisdom and power of God (1 Cor. 1:24). Scripture texts that imply otherwise are speaking about the created human flesh assumed by the Word, not about the Word per se.

The Arian controversy forced Athanasius to think through the inner relations of Father and Word or Son, as well as their relation to the world. *God exists eternally as Father, Son and Holy Spirit, quite independently of the created order, the persons of the Trinity being one in both substance (*homoousios*) and in action. Any *dualism excluding God from acting in his true being in his own world, such as was implicit in Arianism, was radically rejected. In the *Orations against the Arians* Athanasius developed further his sense of the wonderful harmony and order or created rationality within the world, a rationality not to be confused with, yet connected to and indicative of, God's rationality or Word. God is known, however, not through creation alone but primarily through *Scripture, and Athanasius evidences a profound grasp of Scripture and *hermeneutics.

Considerable differences lie between Athanasius' earlier and later thought in his understanding of the human being who is God. His soteriology was completely rethought and deepened. Prominent, as before, is the necessity, for the sake of our salvation, of the incarnation of the Word of God, and the inseparability of incarnation and atonement is reinforced. Reconciliation occurs in the first place within Christ himself, between God and the human being he assumed, this being the ground for human salvation, knowledge and receiving of the Spirit, for humankind is incorporated into Christ. The Word of God and the human being in Christ must be thought of according to their respective natures, never divorced yet not mixed either, with the centre of the Word-human always being the Word. The very awareness of the difference in being between God and human beings rests ultimately on the incarnation. In recent study of Athanasius, the question has been raised whether Athanasius was an early *Apollinarian. While many eminent theologians argue that he was, convincing reasons can be adduced to the contrary.

Concerning human knowledge of God, in the *Orations against the Arians* Athanasius moves again more in a trinitarian perspective, the incarnation again being central. All knowledge of God as Father and Creator occurs only in and through the Son. Human knowledge of God is always creaturely but not therefore false, for God has *accommodated himself to our way of knowing. Words used of God must be understood in the light of his being and nature, but certain words used of him, such as 'father' and 'son', apply properly only within the Trinity and only by participation to humankind.

In his four *Letters to Serapion Concerning the Holy Spirit*, written during his third exile in the late 350s, Athanasius, faced now with a denial of the Godhead of the Spirit, developed further his trinitarian thought, integrating the Spirit much more fully into his theology. Whereas his previous references to the Spirit tended to the more formal (apart from the third *Oration against the Arians*, where his mature understanding of the person and work of the Spirit is clearly emerging), in his *Letters* a rich understanding of God as Father, Son and Holy Spirit is evident, not only in intra-trinitarian relations, but also in relation to the world.

The key to Athanasius' theology is the Nicene word *homoousios* – the Son is 'one in substance' with the Father, which means that it is truly God who becomes incarnate. The term, though not occurring in Scripture, was for Athanasius a vital declaration safeguarding what Scripture affirms against the mis-readings of his opponents (as he argues in *On the Decrees of Nicaea*). The eternal and true Word, truly God in substance, really did become incarnate in order to save us, both joining our flesh to his divine nature forever and bringing to light the whole work and being of the triune God.

Bibliography

Works: A. Robertson (ed.), *Athanasius: Select Works and Letters*, tr. J. H. Newman (Massachusetts, 1994); R. W. Thompson (ed. & tr.), *Contra Gentes and De Incarnatione* (Oxford, 1971).

Studies: K. Anatolios, *Athanasius: The Coherence of His Thought* (London, 1998); T. D. Barnes, *Athanasius and Constantius: Theology and Politics in the Constantinian Empire* (Cambridge, 1993); J. D. Ernest, *The Bible in Athanasius of Alexandria* (Leiden, 2004); R. P. C. Hanson, *The Search for the Christian Doctrine of God* (Edinburgh, 1988); C. Kannengiesser, *Arius and Athanasius: Two Alexandrian Theologians* (Brookfield, 1991); E. P. Meijering, *Orthodoxy and Platonism in Athanasius: Synthesis or Antithesis?* (Leiden, 1968).

S. Parvis

ATHEISM

At its simplest, atheism is the belief that no God exists. This statement, however, needs to be qualified in two ways. First, it is complicated by the fact that there are various concepts of *God. For example, *pantheism is, strictly speaking, the belief that God is identical with nature, a position that has sometimes, though not always, been regarded as a species of atheism. Atheism certainly denies both the existence of any transcendent divine reality apart from the world and that the world is 'in God' (a position that can be described as 'panentheism' on some interpretations of that phrase). Secondly, the term 'atheism' is often used to describe a specific phenomenon in Western culture, namely, the rejection of all theisms (Judaism, Christianity and Islam) or beliefs in any 'gods'. Thus, although classical *Buddhism holds no belief in the existence of God and its philosophy entails the virtual denial of God's existence, it originated in a non-Western cultural environment, and to call it 'atheistic', while not inaccurate, risks subsuming it under an alien framework.

In Western thought, a materialist philosophy which rejected belief in the existence of any gods was present in the Greco-Roman world before the advent of Christianity. The long domination of Christianity in Europe marginalized anything that we might call 'atheism', but forms of *materialism began to make their appearance in the post-Reformation world and to flower on a culturally significant if still relatively small scale in eighteenth-century France, sometimes under the influence of English thought. Materialism took the view that humanity should not be explained in terms of an immaterial soul shaped by a non-embodied Creator.

In the nineteenth century, atheism made a big impact on Europe. Ludwig Feuerbach (1804–72) is sometimes regarded as the father of modern atheism; he argued that the notion of God was a projection of human self-consciousness. Various proposals were then made both to explain the human, material and social world atheistically and to offer some account of the origin and existence of religious belief. Marx (1818–83), *Nietzsche and Freud (1856–1939) were three of the most influential proponents of these views. Atheism spread widely in the twentieth century. It is currently popular in the English-speaking world under the rubric 'The New Atheism', associated with a number of thinkers, including Richard Dawkins, Daniel Dennett, Christopher Hitchens and Sam Harris.

It is sometimes denied that true atheism exists, on the ground that Paul teaches a universal natural knowledge of God, albeit distorted and suppressed (Rom. 1:19–21). But it is doubtful whether Paul means to affirm categorically that no time, space, culture or person can ever be properly atheistic; he does not appear to set theoretical limits to the degeneration of cultures. Christian converts from atheism sometimes affirm the profound and thoroughgoing nature of their former intellectual disbelief. However, this is not to deny that much of what passes for atheism is a conscious or subconscious suppression of the awareness of God.

Atheism is a wide-ranging and complex phenomenon which defies easy description and simplistic engagement. We can apply to atheism at the range of social and educational levels some words by Paul Holmer: 'Just what religious unbelief is among the educated today is . . . difficult to say. Exactly what the breakdown of concepts has to do with it is a very complicated matter' (*The Grammar of Faith*, New York, 1978, p. 125). Concepts of God and the self are at issue in the conflict between atheistic and Christian (or more broadly religious) worldviews, and arguments over the existence of God, evil and suffering, life after death and the nature of human freedom are staple fare in the classic debates. The nature and credibility of Scripture is obviously another crucial issue. Yet what Nietzsche wrote in the nineteenth century helpfully puts these disagreements in context: 'What decides against Christianity now is our taste, not our reasons' (*The Gay Science*, section 132).

If we accept the force of this remark, this does not entail denying the importance of reasons and the discussion of reasons; probably nothing is more pressing on this score than the problem of *evil and suffering, even if we believe that Christianity offers no 'rational' resolution of the problem. But Nietzsche's words alert us to the presence of a significant dimension in the conflict of worldviews, to a phenomenon that is sometimes elusive and intellectually rather intractable, but exceedingly important to recognize and address. Jesus Christ must be apprehended as the one who integrates our human lives in all their dimensions. This should enable people to see that

Christian faith is, first, meaningful; then, salutary; then, true.

If Western atheism or the atheism of the English-speaking world is riveted to one particular worldview (and it may not be), perhaps we should single out a naturalistic evolutionary worldview. Human origins, rather than cosmic origins, are in question here. It is important that Christians try to get clear on the relationship of Christian faith to evolution and rigorously present the grounds for their beliefs about human origins, nature and destiny. There is a variety of types of belief in evolution, and the phrase 'evolutionary worldview' can mean more than one thing, but it is widely believed popularly that evolution entails naturalism, which is disbelief in any supernatural agency. In fact, naturalism is not entailed in evolution, but evolutionary naturalism is a bulwark of much atheism. The supposedly anti-rationalist culture of postmodernity has apparently done little to diminish the urgency of the questions that arise in the public square in this connection.

The phrase 'practical atheism' is sometimes used, as opposed to 'theoretical atheism'. It signifies the fact that belief or disbelief is suspended on the intellectual plane, but that lives are lived as though there were no God. Practical atheism is more widespread than theoretical atheism, and the issues surrounding it can be different, though no less urgent, requiring attention to matters of will and motivation as much as to mind in the narrower intellectual sense. Here, the question of taste kicks in again. The presence of practical atheism shows how the atheistic claim that God is a projection of the human will and desire to believe can be turned on its head. That is, it shows how denial of God might be a projection of the human will and desire to disbelieve and how *agnosticism (which often undergirds practical atheism) may be a strategy of evasion. It is certainly not claimed here that all atheism or agnosticism is to be explained in this way. But the psychological causes of practical atheism are just as important for us to investigate as are the intellectual causes of theoretical atheism, just as we must admit that religious belief also often has psychological causes that must be uncovered. *Pascal's thought is important here, for he emphasized that, in practice, we all decide to live as though there were God or no God, even if we say that the issue is theoretically open, and he pressed opponents of Christianity to explain and justify their practice, if they maintain that the existence of God is a genuinely open question. It is crucial that we keep in mind, in any consideration of, and discussion with, atheism, that the issue at stake is existentially deep and that the Christian idea of God is the idea of a living and acting subject, not an object of dispassionate contemplation.

See also: MARXISM AND CHRISTIANITY; SCIENCE AND THEOLOGY.

Bibliography

M. Buckley, *At the Origins of Modern Atheism* (New Haven, 1990); H. Küng, *Does God Exist?* (New York and London, 1980); A. MacIntyre and P. Ricœur, *The Religious Significance of Modern Atheism* (New York, 1969); M. Martin (ed.), *The Cambridge Companion to Atheism* (Cambridge, 2007); A. McGrath, *The Twilight of Atheism* (New York and London, 2004); J. J. C. Smart and J. J. Haldane, *Atheism and Theism* (Oxford, 2003); J. Thrower, *A Short History of Western Atheism* (London, 1971); M. Westphal, *Suspicion and Faith: The Religious Uses of Modern Atheism* (New York, 1998).

S. N. WILLIAMS

ATONEMENT

The biblical basis

The traditional symbol of Christian faith (like the crescent in Islam) is the *cross*. The use of the symbol of the *cross has been central to Christianity, especially in the Western church, with the crucifix used as the focus of devotion from the eleventh century onwards, and with 'crucicentrism' being an acknowledged hallmark of evangelical Protestantism. The reason is obvious enough: the apostolic message contained in the NT sees the death of Jesus Christ on the cross as the source whence the benefits of salvation (divine forgiveness, fellowship with God and eternal life) flow for believers.

'At-one-ment' is the main word used in English-speaking Christendom for this cross-centred understanding of *salvation (whereas in languages of the Latin family, one finds '*redemption' as the first-rank term). Together with the verb 'atone', it corresponds fairly closely to the key OT root *kpr* which combines the meaning of 'reconciliation', the restoration of positive relationships between estranged parties (e.g. Gen. 32:21), and 'expiation', the removal of sin and its stain (cf. the link between *Versöhnung* and *Sühnung* in German).

In the NT there is a partial correspondence with the noun *katallagē*, 'reconciliation' and its cognates (taken from the vocabulary of inter-personal and political relationships), which are used in a small number of Pauline passages (Rom. 5:10–11; 2 Cor. 5:18–20; Eph. 2:16; Col. 1:20–22) and are implicit in others, for example, those that speak of peace being made between God and humankind (Rom 5:1; Col 1:20). There is also a partial correspondence with the noun *hilasmos* and its cognates (1 John 2:2; 4:10; but also found in Rom. 3:25; Heb. 2:17), whose primary focus is the idea of placating divine wrath ('propitiation'), but whose meaning also involves the idea of 'expiation' since, in the biblical view of God, *sin is the object that arouses his holy anger and this subsides if sin is done away with. However, biblical passages that are relevant for the doctrine of the atonement are not restricted to the ones where the foregoing terms occur; they also include passages which refer to forgiveness, acceptance, renewal, purification (sacrifice), fellowship, life-giving union, liberation, etc.

The Fathers and schoolmen

The ancient (orthodox) church bowed before the authority of Scripture, but lacked the tools and interest to explain with systematic clarity the *how* of Christ's atonement. Almost all the *Fathers were pastors and preachers, with little or no knowledge of Hebrew; they mixed several schemes for understanding the saving efficacy of Christ's work, with more or less literal import, while their main focus was on defending the truth of the incarnation against attack from various heresies.

One can disentangle three main types of thinking about atonement in the Fathers. First, there was an 'Isaiah 53' emphasis on the Righteous One bearing the sins of sinners, undergoing in their stead the punishment of *death they had deserved, so that legal justice is satisfied. The *Epistle to Diognetus* (IX.2) wonders at the 'sweet exchange' and, although many of the Fathers lack precision, statements by *Eusebius (*Demonstratio evangelica*, X.1), John *Chrysostom (*In I ad Timotheum, hom.* VII.3) and *Athanasius (*De Incarnatione Verbi*, 6, 9–10) are unequivocal and forceful. However, even with them, this first approach was not central and determinative for the rest of their theology.

A second type of thinking was also popular (though it does not deserve the tendentious epithet 'classic' that Aulén introduced for it). This focused on the supreme battle that was fought on the cross between God (in Christ) and the evil powers, and the freedom that was won for humankind through Christ's victory in this battle. Beyond the bare proclamation of Christ's liberating victory over Satan, many Fathers imagined that a ransom had been paid to the *devil. The wisdom of God trapped Satan, in that while the death of Christ was the price he received in exchange for humankind, he was not able to hold on to it. On the third day Christ rose triumphant (see *Resurrection), and Satan was left with neither his original prisoners nor the ransom. *Gregory of Nyssa develops this idea further. Christ's humanity was the bait, which the devil thought he could swallow, but his deity was the hook, and the Evil One was caught (*Oratio catechetica*, 22–24, 26).

The third type is often called 'mystical' or 'physical', because it is interested in what happens to the divine and human natures. The at-one-ment is the effect of the union in the person of Jesus Christ of the divine and human natures. The infusion of divine energies into our weak and corrupt 'flesh' transforms it, divinizes it – God became man that we might become gods. Although his theology focuses on universal 'recapitulation' rather than simply human divinization, *Irenaeus introduced this type of thinking into Christian theology (*Adversus haereses*, III.9.1; III.18.7, etc.). It is central with Athanasius (e.g. *Contra arianos*, III.33) and it became dominant among theologians, especially in the *Eastern church. Whereas the first two approaches presuppose the incarnation but do not see it as in itself the atoning event, the third approach makes it so, with the cross and resurrection expressing what has already taken place through the union of the two natures.

Fearing that the divine-human distinction might be blurred, Western theology exercised a little more restraint on divinization and kept closer to juridical categories. 'Merit' and 'satisfaction' played an important role in this regard, but with a weak sense of substitution: the emphasis fell on *adding* human merits and works of satisfaction to those of Christ.

*Anselm of Canterbury made the first great step forward in producing a more satisfactory approach. As he tried to understand what he believed, he put forward a limpid scheme that related incarnation to redemption and achieved a coherent theory of atonement. His starting-point was human helplessness: he dismisses earlier theories (including the idea of a ransom paid to the devil) with the refrain: 'You have not yet considered how heavy a weight sin is.' Sin is *lèse majesté*. Crime is measured by the dignity of the one offended. God's honour demands a compensation of infinite value, which humans are utterly unable to provide. Yet, God does not wish to send all humans to hell (he wishes to restore the perfect number of heavenly citizens); he is able to provide the satisfaction that humans cannot provide. Man ought to, God can. God became man to pay the price for our salvation (*Cur Deus homo*, II.6), in the form of the gift of perfect obedience offered to God by Christ on our behalf, the merit for which is credited to us since Christ does not need it for himself. Anselm's concern is not retributive justice: his logic contrasts the two alternatives: either satisfaction or penalty (ibid., I.15).

Soon after Anselm, Pierre *Abélard introduced the so-called 'subjective' theory, in which the main function of the cross is to touch our hearts through the demonstration of divine love (*Expositio in Epistulam ad Romanos*, II.3). A fuller synthesis came with *Thomas Aquinas (*Summa theologica*, IIIa, q.48, a.1–4), whose understanding of atonement includes the idea of the payment of the penalty owed to divine justice, but focuses on the sacrifice of loving devotion jointly offered to God by Christ and his church.

The Reformers and their successors

The major Reformers (see *Reformation theology) followed a path parallel to Anselm's, but they substituted justice and *law for his concept of feudal honour. For them sin is the breaking of divine law, and the essence of the atonement is that Christ paid the penalty for our law-breaking. He stood in the place of sinners, and since he bore their punishment on the cross, it no longer falls on them; hence the message of *justification by faith alone, without works. *Luther preached Christ's victory over Satan, but saw it as grounded on the satisfaction of justice (the penalty *is* the satisfaction); in his paradoxical manner, in strongest terms, he stressed the 'joyful exchange' by which Christ becomes our sin and we become his righteousness (e.g. his *Commentary on Galatians*, supremely on 3:13). Calvin's treatment (see *Reformed theology) is noteworthy for clarity, balance and exegetical groundwork. It sets the atonement in the wider context of Christ's threefold office, with his death on Calvary as the antitype of all OT atoning sacrifices and the main work of the priestly office (followed by his heavenly intercession), but also the paradoxical way in which he establishes his kingdom, and a prophetic testimony to God's holy love and human sinfulness (*Institutes*, II.15–17).

Already in the sixteenth century, the *Socinians (followers of Fausto Sozzini) bitterly attacked the idea of vicarious punishment: sin is not something that can be transferred from one person to another. If God forgives, he does not exact the penalty; it is abhorrent to think of the Father's beloved under the curse. The 'orthodox', such as John *Owen and Francis Turretin, fought back, and *Arminians, such as Hugo Grotius, softened the classical Protestant doctrine, but two centuries later Socinian arguments prevailed among *liberal theologians, who then fell back on Abelard's 'subjective' theory.

Contemporary *liberalism, especially among feminists, has cried out against the penal view, using the term 'divine child abuse' to describe it. Meanwhile, evangelicals such as Leon Morris, J. I. *Packer and John Stott have continued to defend the penal approach of the Reformers.

Recent attempts at reinterpretation

With the waning of older forms of liberalism, theologians have attempted new constructions. At times Karl *Barth sounds close to Protestant orthodoxy, writing about the Judge judged in our stead undergoing the punishment we had deserved; yet, on closer inspection, there are important differences. Barth repudiates the idea of satisfaction and expressly distances himself from the Anselmian line (*CD*, IV.1, p. 253). Rather than a transfer of guilt which is then paid for, he affirms a dialectical event in which the old humanity is annihilated in Christ and a new being of righteousness, including all human beings, the only *real* man, is established in him instead.

The views of the French anthropologist René Girard have influenced theologians, even though fellow anthropologists have been reticent about them. He sees the origin of *sacrifice, religion, and, indeed, of all human institutions, in the crisis of mimetic violence, in the murder of an innocent person subsequently declared to be guilty and divinized. Only in the Bible is this lie uncovered (partially in the OT and fully in the NT) with the consequent rejection of the sacrificial idea. Girard's views, together with the ascendency of pacifism among intellectuals, have resulted in an emphasis on the theme of a *non-violent* atonement; one looks to Jesus, first of all, as a model of non-violent devotion.

Many writers, among whom Jürgen *Moltmann stands out as widely influential (although his views have shown a degree of variation through the diverse periods of his career), have interpreted the atonement in view of *theodicy*. The following traits are common: (1) the 'scandal' is no longer so much sin towards God as it is human suffering, especially when it has political origins; God is no longer the judge on the bench but the accused in the dock! (2) God's powerlessness relieves him from sharing in the guilt for evil. This is preached as 'good news' and as the true 'theology of the cross', and is further buttressed by the reference to the divine 'self-emptying' (*kenōsis*, Phil. 2:7) (see *Kenoticism); (3) Christ's suffering on the cross is construed as God's, and it is the divine sympathy or solidarity which is the heart of atonement. It comforts us, it remedies our estrangement from God and it teaches us like attitudes. In his most Hegelian book, *The Crucified God*, Moltmann attempts to resolve the problem of the distinction between God and Christ by making the cross the foundation for the Trinity, with the *man* Jesus and human suffering being introduced into the life of the Godhead. The fact that suffering is taken up into God is what is seen as overcoming evil.

In the maze of theories about the atonement and arguments for or against 'vicarious punishment' (with or without additions from other perspectives), decisions depend first of all on the authority ascribed to Scripture and, to a lesser degree, on hermeneutical choices concerning biblical metaphors and their cognitive import. The next issue is the validity of retributive justice, which many people today now question. The final issue, which is raised by approaches to the atonement that are influenced by Hegelian dialectics, is the importance of upholding the framework of orthodox (Chalcedonian) *Christology, which cannot be rejected without serious consequences.

The central, *crucial* truth of Christian preaching being at stake, the most rigorous and consistent use of one's faith-criteria is called for – indeed!

See also: JESUS; JUDGMENT OF GOD.

Bibliography

K. Barth, *CD*; R. T. Beckwith and M. J. Selman, *Sacrifice in the Bible* (Grand Rapids and Carlisle, 1995); H. Blocher, 'The Sacrifice of Jesus Christ: The Current Theological Situation', *European Journal of Theology* 8, 1999, pp. 23–36; *idem*, 'Biblical Metaphors and the Doctrine of Atonement', *JETS* 47, 2004, pp. 629–645; H. Boersma, *Violence, Hospitality, and the Cross: Reappropriating the Atonement Tradition* (Grand Rapids, 2004); J. Denney, *The Death of Christ* (London, 1951); S. Gathercole, *Where Is Boasting? Early Jewish Soteriology and Paul's Response in Romans 1–5* (Grand Rapids and Cambridge, 2002); J. Goldingay (ed.), *Atonement Today* (London, 1995); C. E. Hill and F. A. James (eds.), *The Glory of Atonement* (Downers Grove, 2004); I. H. Marshall, *Aspects of the Atonement* (Milton Keynes, 2007); A. T. B. McGowan, 'The Atonement as Penal Substitution', in McGowan (ed.), *Always Reforming: Explorations in Systematic Theology* (Leicester, 2006); J. Moltmann, *The Cross in the New Testament* (Grand Rapids, 1965); *idem*, *The Crucified God* (ET, London, 1974); L. Morris, *The Apostolic Preaching of the Cross* (London, [3]1965); J. I. Packer, 'What Did the Cross Achieve? The Logic of Penal Substitution', *TynB* 25, 1974, pp. 3–45; J. G. Stackhouse, Jr, *What Does It Mean to Be Saved?* (Grand Rapids, 2002); J. R. W. Stott, *The Cross of Christ* (Leicester and Downers Grove, 1986).

H. A. G. BLOCHER

ATONEMENT, EXTENT OF

For whom did Christ die? In the history of the church there have been two basic answers to that question. Most Christians have taught that Christ's death is of saving significance for every individual, whilst others have contended that its benefits extend only to the elect. The former are spoken of as holding to a universal understanding of the *atonement, whilst the latter teach that it is limited, definite or particular in extent.

While a small minority have believed that all humans will be saved because of the work of

Christ (*universalism), most Christians have believed that though the atonement makes *salvation possible for all, its saving effect is realized only when some further factor is present, i.e. *faith, or faith and godly works. This has been the view of the Eastern churches, and very much the majority position in those of the West.

Those who have believed in the limited intention of the atonement have flourished only amongst those who hold that human salvation ultimately depends upon divine *predestination, a topic which came to the fore in Christian theology in the West through the work of *Augustine. However, it was a minority amongst those who held to the general Augustinian position who also thought it to imply that the work of Christ atoned only for the sins of the elect. Amongst these were Prosper of Aquitaine, Thomas *Bradwardine and John Staupitz. The general late-medieval consensus was summed up by Peter *Lombard in his *Sentences*, to the effect that while the death of Christ was sufficient to cover the sins of the human race, it was efficacious only for the elect.

This definition was accepted by *Calvin in his *Commentary on 1 John* as being formally true, but not applicable to the writer's intention in the passage on which he was commenting (1 John 2:2). In Calvin's other writings there are passages which suggest he held to the view that the saving benefits of atonement were intended only for the elect, whilst others seem to imply a more universal view of its extent. This fluid position seems to have been general in the Reformed churches until the outbreak of the *Arminian controversy, when those of that persuasion, in their *Remonstrance* of 1610, the second article, expressed the view that Christ died for all people, though only believers benefited. If this were accepted, it would imply that divine predestination was not the sole, primary cause of salvation, but that human faith led to its actualization. The mainline Reformed churches and theologians resisted this, and in the second article of the Canons of *Dort (1619) affirmed that Christ died for his people, thus the benefits of the atonement extended only to the elect. This for the following century and a half was the mainline position of the Reformed churches.

Gradually, however, under the growth of the practice of the general offer of the gospel which marked the evangelical revival, it came under critical scrutiny on the grounds that this understanding undermined the integrity of the practice of offering Christ to all people, and also that the doctrine had serious negative effects on developing appropriate Christian *assurance in believers, leading to a withdrawal into inwardness and moralism in the hope of gaining certainty of one's election.

Both sides in the controversy could appeal to certain texts in the Bible. Defenders of a universal atonement would appeal to such passages as John 3:16, Rom. 5:18 and 1 John 2:2, whilst those in favour of the limited understanding would quote Matt. 1:21, 20:28 and John 17:9. Taking into account the nuances of the language and the idiom of the writer, it is doubtful whether any of these support decisively the contention of either side (cf. John 6:44 with 12:32). So in the last resort it seems that it is theological consistency and the evaluation of the practical consequences of a particular stance in the church which are decisive.

See also: Hyper-Calvinism; Reformed Theology.

Bibliography

M. C. Bell, *Calvin and Scottish Theology: The Doctrine of Assurance* (Edinburgh 1985); W. R. Godfrey, 'Reformed Thought on the Extent of the Atonement to 1618', *WTJ* 37, 1974–5, pp. 133–171; P. Helm, 'The Logic of Limited Atonement', *SBET* 3, 1985, pp. 47–54; J. B. Torrance, 'The Incarnation and "Limited Atonement"', *EQ* 55, 1983, pp. 83–94.

S. Russell

AUGSBURG CONFESSION

The Augsburg Confession is a *Lutheran symbol, written by Philipp *Melanchthon in 1530. Emperor Charles V had demanded that a statement of faith be presented at the planned Diet of Augsburg by those German princes who had sided with Luther, and so Melanchthon wrote the Confession between April and June 1530; it was signed by seven rulers on 23 August. It is included in the *Book of Concord* (1580), which is accepted as the doctrinal standard of many Lutheran churches. The Confession, however, has wider acceptance as a standard, and a place of prominence amongst the other distinctively Lutheran texts in the *Book of Concord* (which also includes the three ecumenical creeds), and so it can be regarded as the definitive Lutheran symbol.

It is composed of two parts, one positive, stating doctrines, or 'chief articles of faith', and one apologetic, rejecting various perceived 'abuses' common within the Roman Church. The positive doctrine of the Confession is carefully arranged to begin by locating the Lutheran churches within classical (Catholic) Christianity, noting agreement with the *Nicene Creed, condemning by name various classical and contemporary heretics (*Arians, *Pelagians, *Donatists, *Anabaptists, etc.), and generally offering a careful and unobjectionable statement of received ecumenical doctrine. Even on the points which would become the crucial issues in *Reformation polemics, the Confession is notably restrained (e.g. Article IV on *justification). This might be because, this early in the Reformation, disputes still centred on practices, and had not yet become doctrinal. Certainly, the seven issues treated in the more *polemical second part (which include priestly celibacy, auricular confession and monastic vows) would tend to support such an interpretation.

The Confession visibly takes its stand on Scripture, repeatedly citing texts in support of positions, and including quotations where a position might be regarded as controversial. Church Fathers are also quoted from time to time (e.g. Ambrose in Art. VI, defending the claim that salvation is by faith alone).

The Confession in fact exists in two distinct versions: the *invariata* (Melanchthon's original text of 1530) and the *variata* (a revised version published by Melanchthon in 1540). (In fact, Melanchthon had been continually tinkering with the text between these dates, but the 1540 edition differs on matters of substance, not merely on phrasing, being more accommodating to *Calvinistic views on the presence of Christ in the Eucharist, for instance.) The *Book of Concord* preserves the *invariata*, the edited edition being condemned remarkably strongly by some later Lutheran theologians.

See also: CREEDS; CONFESSIONS OF FAITH.

Bibliography

Latin text with English translation may conveniently be found in P. Schaff, *Creeds of Christendom*, 3 vols. (rev. edn, Grand Rapids, 1994).

Studies: J. A. Burgess (ed.), *The Role of the Augsburg Confession* (Philadelphia, 1980); B. W. Teigen, *I Believe: A Study of the Augsburg Confession and the Apology of the Augsburg Confession* (Mancato, 1980).

S. R. HOLMES

AUGUSTINE (354–430)

An African from present-day Algeria, Augustine was the greatest of the Latin theologians of the early church, and one of the greatest Christian thinkers of all time. His influence dominated medieval Christianity in the West (where he became one of the four Doctors of the Church), and provided the most powerful non-biblical stimulus to the Reformation. For both Catholics and Protestants he remains a major theological resource.

Life

He was born in Tagaste in Roman North Africa (modern Souk Ahras in Algeria) to Patricius and his wife, the devout Christian Monica, who enrolled Augustine as a catechumen from infancy. (Patricius himself became a Christian only later in life.) His *Confessions* (a kind of spiritual and intellectual biography full of profound reflections on the call of God in childhood, adolescence and adult life) are the main source for tracing his early development. During his education, locally and at Carthage, his connection with Christianity became tenuous, for which he partly blames his parents' decision to give him the good pagan education necessary at the time for social success. He excelled in literature and rhetoric (he was particularly touched by the Dido and Aeneas story as told in Virgil's *Aeneid*), though he never mastered Greek. During this period he formed a long-term relationship with a woman who was not his social equal (and therefore whom he was not expected, even by his mother, to marry), with whom he had a child, the much-loved Adeodatus (372–c. 389).

His reading of Cicero's lost *Hortensius* (373) kindled in him a consuming love of divine wisdom (philosophy), on the grounds that its goal was to seek the truth (in contrast to rhetoric, which countenanced lies as long as they were beautifully told). The Scriptures struck him as puerile at this period, and he turned instead to *Manichaeism, remaining on the fringes of the movement as his career as a teacher of rhetoric progressed, and he moved from Africa to Rome (383) and then Milan (384).

But his growing disenchantment with Manichaeism's intellectual pretensions coincided with a rediscovery of the merits of Christianity, helped by his mother's prayers and the preaching of Ambrose, the bishop of Milan, who introduced Augustine to allegorical readings of the OT, and whose eloquent wisdom deeply impressed him. He was at this period persuaded (probably by his mother) to send his concubine away so that he could marry a girl of good family, but the girl was below the normal marriageable age of twelve (he was now thirty), and he took another concubine in the meantime.

The Neoplatonic writings of Plotinus and Porphyry convinced him that the *materialist Manichaean view of God was wrong. The impact of the *ascetic movement from the East spoke to his growing distaste for his own career as a teacher of rhetoric (teaching the forensic lawyers of the future how to speak well so they could argue that innocent men and women should be executed), as well as for his future marriage and present disordered domestic arrangements. Augustine was converted in 386 to Christianity, celibacy and, initially, monasticism, forming a contemplative community for sacred conversation and writing with his mother, son and various friends. He was baptized in Easter 387, alongside his son Adeodatus, and returned to Tagaste to form an ascetic community there, though his mother died in the Roman port of Ostia on the way.

His writings from this period, partly directed against Manichaeism, show how profoundly Neoplatonism (see *Platonism) had influenced him. Several are dialogues in the Platonic mould. He confidently expected that Platonic philosophy would unlock the treasures of the faith of the Catholic Church (cf. *True Religion*, 389–91). To vindicate the roles of faith and authority in religion against Manichaean objections, he argued that faith must precede understanding (cf. Isa. 7:9, LXX), but that faith has its own grounds – which he found in the moral and numerical achievements of the worldwide church (cf. *The Usefulness of Believing*, 391–92). Against Manichaean *determinism, he insisted that culpable sin proceeds only from the abuse of free will (cf. *Free Will*, 391–95). Against Manichaean *dualism he stressed the goodness of creation and adapted the Neoplatonic approach to evil by viewing it as the absence of good, lacking substantial reality. His Christian Platonism entertained a high estimate of human moral and spiritual potential.

In 391 Augustine was press-ganged into the church's ministry at Hippo (modern Annaba), and was soon bishop of its Catholic congregation (396), turning the bishop's house into an ascetic seminary-cum-chapter. The needs of the church increasingly determined his theological output. He gave himself more solidly to the study of Scripture, especially Paul, under the stimulus of Tyconius (*fl. c.* 370–90), a nonconformist Donatist from whom Augustine learned at several significant points. Exposure to pastoral realities also steadily eroded his earlier more humanist optimism, encouraging a deeper awareness of human frailty and perversity. This shift in perspective is put to good use in the searching analysis of his own sinfulness and the generosity of God's grace of the brilliant *Confessions* (397–401), which takes the story of the prodigal son as its overarching narrative. Augustine's emotional, intellectual and spiritual honesty in this work made it one of the classics of Christian literature of all time. Another fruit of this shift was *To Simplician, on Various Questions* (396), in which Rom. 9:10–21 convinced him of the basic interrelations between election, grace, faith and free will that he would later defend against the *Pelagians. Not until that subsequent controversy did he conclude that Rom. 7:7–25 must refer to the Christian, not a person under law prior to grace, as he argues in *To Simplician*.

At Hippo, Augustine continued to refute Manichaean errors. In defending the OT against their criticisms, he presented the most substantial Christian case to date for the just war (in *Against Faustus*, 397–98). But the counter-church of Donatism, far stronger in North Africa than the Catholic communion, now became his main preoccupation, evoking important contributions to Western doctrines of *church and *sacraments (especially *Against the Letter of Parmenian*, 400; *Baptism, Against the Donatists*, 400–01; *Against the Letters of Petilian*, 401–05; *The Unity of the Catholic Church*, 405). Augustine's teachings built on Tyconius and Optatus of Milevis (*fl. c.* 365–85), Catholic Africa's sole prior critic of Donatism of any theological substance.

Donatism

To *Donatism's exclusive claims Augustine opposed both the universality (or *catholicity) of the church as foretold in Scripture and its mixed character, embracing both tares and wheat until the judgment. The quest for a pure community was doomed to failure (for only God knows who are his) and contrary to Scripture. The church's holiness is not that of its members, but of Christ its head, to be realized only eschatologically. Augustine so emphasized the bond between Christ and his body that he could even speak of them as 'one Christ loving himself', even 'one person' compacted by love or the Spirit (which Augustine closely identified – see below).

Since *schism is supremely an offence against love, Augustine argues, schismatics are bereft of the Spirit of love. Although they profess the catholic faith and administer the catholic sacraments, these remain profitless to them until they enter the catholic fold which is the sole sphere of the Spirit. Reinforcing the fourth century's abandonment of the original African position (see *Cyprian), Augustine argued that schismatic or heretical sacraments are valid (but not regular), for their validity hinges not on the worthiness of the human minister, but on Christ, who is the true minister of the sacraments. So Augustine could accept Donatists into the church without requiring their rebaptism or re-ordination.

Augustine also provided a theological justification for the coercion of heretics and schismatics (*Epistle* 93 [408]; *Epistle* 185 [417]). Threats and sanctions were essentially corrective (and so could never include the death penalty), which was the special service to religion of Christians holding secular office. Augustine originally assented to this policy for pragmatic reasons, but defended it by a rather adventurous use of Scripture (including texts like Luke 14:23), and in terms of how God dealt with recalcitrant humanity – by the harsh discipline of his 'benevolent severity'. It was in this context that Augustine uttered his widely quoted dictum, 'Love, and do what you will', as a defence of paternal chastisement.

Pelagianism

Augustine's most influential legacy to Protestantism per se was his anti-Pelagian corpus (411–30). From the first of his many writings (*The Merits and Remission of Sins and Infant Baptism*, 411–12), he wove the Pelagians' diverse emphases into a single '*heresy'. The controversy unfolded in three stages: against Celestius and Pelagius (411–18; *The Spirit and the Letter, Nature and Grace, The Perfection of Human Righteousness, The Grace of Christ and Original Sin, Epistle* 194); against Julian (419–30; *Marriage and Concupiscence, Against Two Letters of the Pelagians, Against Julian, Unfinished Work against Julian*); and against the misnamed semi-Pelagian monks of Africa and Gaul (427–30; *Grace and Free Will, Correction and Grace, Epistle* 217, *The Predestination of the Saints, The Gift of Perseverance*).

The long conflict witnessed Augustine's construction of an evermore impregnable and forbidding theological fortress. Its building blocks included the following: an exalted view of the perfections of Adam and Eve, and hence of the disastrous consequences of the fall; the insistence that, because all sinned 'in Adam' (on which Augustine appealed to Ambrosiaster's biological reading of Rom. 5:12), all are bound by the penalties for that *sin – spiritual death, guilt and the diseased disordering of human nature; 'concupiscence', from which no sexual acts of fallen humanity are free (even within Christian marriage), as the locus of transmission of original sin from parents to children; the impossibility of even 'the beginning of faith' without the gift of prevenient *grace by whose power 'the will is prepared' to turn to God; the restriction of this grace to the baptized, so that infants dying unbaptized are condemned to hell, if perhaps to its milder reaches, and to the 'fixed number' of the elect, who receive it by God's sovereign free mercy alone, with the rest of humankind left to their just deserts (Augustine rarely speaks of a divine *predestination to condemnation parallel to predestination to salvation); the denial that God 'will have all persons to be saved', and the disjunction of election and baptism, for not all the baptized belong to the elect; the infallibility of the eternal redemption of the elect, in whom God's grace works irresistibly (but not coercively) and who receive the 'gift of perseverance'; and the conclusive appeal to the inscrutability of God's judgments when mere human beings dared to question them.

The church in both East and West repudiated basic Pelagian beliefs, but did not canonize the full scope of Augustine's refutation, either then or at the Second Council of Orange (529). Within Augustine's own thinking, undoubted development is identifiable at important points, especially on the nature and transmission of original sin when compared with the voluntarist approach to sin of *Free Will* (391–95). Questions have often been raised (e.g. by Harnack) whether the institutional doctrine of the church and baptism in the anti-Donatist writings can survive the heavy anti-Pelagian stress on the *certus numerus* of the elect. Dogmatically, one might question the disjunction between the loving God who elects some and the just God who condemns the rest. But at its least controversial (e.g. in *The Spirit and the Letter*), Augustine's theology provides an impressive exposition of the Pauline gospel.

The Trinity

The Trinity (399–419) is one of Augustine's most influential works: it controlled the terms of Western *trinitarian thought until very recently. He had been concerned about what he would have called '*Arian' views (modern scholars would call them 'homoian' views) from the time of his baptism, for homoianism (the view that the Son is 'like' the Father [*homoios*], rather than consubstantial with the Father [*homoousios*]) remained a strong tradition in Milan from the time of Ambrose's predecessor as bishop there, Auxentius, one of the stars of the movement. Such debates were given a new urgency after the occupation of the Western half of the Roman Empire by Germanic and other invaders, themselves largely homoian, began in 405.

Augustine pays his respects to the great Greek-speaking trinitarian theologians, but himself articulates a theology which is much more emphatic in its insistence on the unity of God and the equality of the Three than, say, the Council of *Constantinople of 381. He starts not with the Father as the fount of Godhead, but with God himself, whom he speaks of as 'essence' rather than 'substance' (the more traditional Latin term since the days of *Tertullian), to avoid implications derived from Aristotelian categories.

Augustine's theology breathes new life into the familiar notion that the difference between the persons of the Trinity is best described as a difference of relations, grounding his trinitarian thought in the love of the Father for the Son and the Son for the Father. That love (*caritas*) is the *Spirit, which is also the Trinity's gift to us, uniting God's people: Augustine thus links Trinity and church. The Spirit is unambiguously the Spirit of both Father and Son, so that Augustine is a clear witness to the *filioque* (see *Creeds).

The later chapters turn to analogies of the human mind to make further sense of the way in which God is Three in One. Since human beings are made in the image of God, they must in some way bear the stamp of the Trinity within. (Augustine plumps firmly for the mind as image of God, ignoring the tradition of *Irenaeus that it is rather the flesh that would be taken on by Christ which is made in the image of the God who would wear it.) He suggested the threeness of memory, understanding and will, or mind, mind as known and mind as loved, as appropriate analogies. Closer still was the model of the mind remembering, knowing and loving God. Contemplating the image of the Trinity in human beings leads them to strive to conform ever further to the divine image. Theology, worship and holiness have here a fruitful meeting point.

The *City of God*

The *City of God* also occupied Augustine over many years (413–26). It provides a wide-ranging crystallization of his thinking on *history and society. Its catalyst was the three-day sack of Rome by a Gothic army in 410, and the consequent pagan charge that Christianity had destroyed the Roman Empire by undermining its traditional mores. Augustine responds by deconstructing the whole of Roman history and religion, and replacing the mystique of the city of Rome with the spiritual reality of the two cities of the afterlife, the city of God and the city of Babylon, the fruits of the two loves on earth, of God or of self, that make all human beings citizens of either the one or the other.

Roman history is replaced by salvation history, based on the common Christian conception of the seven day-ages of the world. The church era is the sixth day, prior to the eternal Sabbath, the millennium of Rev. 20. Decisively abandoning the chiliasm (*millennarianism) of earlier Christianity (which he had once held himself), Augustine views the whole period between incarnation and *parousia* as homogeneous. He rejects the *Eusebian theology of the Christian Roman Empire as a new stage in God's purposes: the *City of God* consistently plays down the significance of secular history, even of Rome under Christian rulers. The pilgrimage of the city of God on earth is ultimately independent of *state or society. Augustine's notion of the role of government is minimalist; it exists to curb the excesses of sin, although Christian rulers have, as Christians, duties to promote the church. He is far from implying any kind of theocratic church power.

Like a good Christian Platonist and biblical theologian, Augustine projects solid reality beyond this world, to heaven and the future. In doing so, he gave Christians of the post-Roman world a way of making sense of what had happened, and the tools with which to face the chaotic times ahead.

Bibliography

Works: J. E. Rotelle (ed.), *The Works of Saint Augustine: A Translation for the 21st Century* (New York, 1990 – in progress).

Studies: G. Bonner, *St Augustine of Hippo: Life and Controversies* (London, rev. edn, 1986); P. Brown, *Augustine of Hippo: A Biography* (London, 1967); H. Chadwick, *Augustine: A Very Short Introduction* (Oxford, 1986); A. D. Fitzgerald (ed.), *Augustine through the Ages: An Encyclopedia* (Grand Rapids, 1999); E. Hill, *The Mystery of the Trinity* (London, 1985); R. A. Markus, *Saeculum: History and Society in the Theology of St Augustine* (Cambridge, 1970); *Revue des études augustiniennes*; J. M. Rist, *Augustine: Ancient Thought Baptized* (Cambridge, 1994); E. TeSelle, *Augustine the Theologian* (New York, 1970); F. Van der Meer, *Augustine the Bishop*, tr. B. Battershaw and G. R. Lamb (London, 1961).

S. Parvis

AUGUSTINIANISM

The influence of Augustine has been so pervasive in Western Christianity that this survey can only be selective, concentrating chiefly on his (anti-Pelagian) 'doctrines of *grace', to which Augustinianism as a theological system most commonly refers.

Critical reactions against Augustine's writings began in his lifetime with the *Pelagians and *Semi-Pelagians. The outcome of these controversies was the canonizing of the heart of Augustine's teaching in the fifth and sixth centuries. In 531 Pope Boniface II confirmed the decrees of the Second Council of Orange.

Legacy

Already Augustine enjoyed high esteem. Caesarius of Arles (d. 542) often seems little more than an adapter of Augustine, and other late Fathers, like Gregory the Great and Isidore of Seville (c. 560–636), treated him with deferential appreciation. Many digests and florilegia of his writings were produced, for example by Prosper of Aquitaine (d. 463), Eugippius, an abbot near Naples (d. 535), Bede (d. 735) and Florus of Lyons (d. c. 860). In the Carolingian renaissance, of which one inspiration was Augustine's charter for Christian education and culture, *On Christian Doctrine*, the homiliaries of Paul Deacon (d. c. 800) and others, and the biblical commentaries and theological compilations of Alcuin (d. 804), Walafrid Strabo (d. 849), Rabanus Maurus (d. 856) and many more made heavy use of Augustine.

In the ninth century, Gottschalk was a controversial exponent of Augustinianism, in particular of double *predestination and supralapsarianism. Among his opponents was the Neoplatonist Eriugena, who owed much to another side of Augustine, while among his supporters was Ratramnus, whose more spiritual view of the *Eucharist was directed against the more 'realist' teaching of Paschasius Radbertus. Both were able to appeal to Augustine – a regular feature of later eucharistic disputes.

Both *Anselm, the pioneer of the new scholastic approach to theology, and *Bernard of Claivaux, one of its keenest critics, were indebted to Augustine. Augustine's correlation of *faith and reason appeared a ready-made justification for scholasticism, while Bernard's spirituality and his teaching on grace and free will used him to quite different effect. Although *scholasticism substituted *Aristotle for Plato as the philosophical handmaid of theology, Augustine remained a dominant authority, not least in Peter *Lombard and *Thomas Aquinas, but the schoolmen increasingly inclined towards explanations of the relation between human free will and merit and divine grace that were in effect Semi-Pelagian.

The Franciscans in particular accorded a prominent place to Augustine in their theological study. *Bonaventura, for example, was more of a *Platonist than an Aristotelian, with a theory of illumination not unlike Augustine's. *Duns Scotus also picked up Augustinian motifs in his emphasis on God's freedom and on will and love.

Augustine's legacy was also acknowledged by the monastic movements (see *Asceticism and monasticism) named after the Rule of Augustine. (The Rule became influential only in the eleventh century. The authenticity of its different versions is still disputed.) The Augustinian (Austin) Canons ('canons regular') were organized during the eleventh-century Gregorian reform, not in a single order but in separate 'congregations'. Among these were the Victorines at Paris who constituted a leading school of Augustinian thought and spirituality. The Windesheim congregation in the fourteenth and fifteenth centuries included the chief monastic representatives of the renewal movement known as the *Devotio Moderna*, whose ranks embraced Geert de Groote (1340–84), the founder of the Brethren of the Common Life, and Thomas à Kempis (see *Spirituality). Erasmus, much influenced by those stirrings which fed into the Reformation at several points, was also an Augustinian Canon for a time.

The Augustinian Hermits or Friars were formed as an order in the thirteenth century. They were originally hermitic but soon became mendicant. Gregory of Rimini, a general of the order, was a thoroughly Augustinian theologian. Scholars debate the strength and significance of a renewed Augustinianism among the Augustinians in the pre-Reformation centuries. Later some of the Friars' congregations became Reformed (i.e. strict 'Observants' of the Rule), including the German one which Luther joined at Erfurt in 1505. Its vicar-general was John Staupitz (1460/69–1529), Luther's predecessor as professor of the Bible at Wittenberg. He was an uncompromising exponent of Augustine's doctrine of election, with which he correlated a unilateral covenant whereby God appointed Christ to be the mediator of *justification for the elect. He stressed the praise of God, fostered by humanity's total dependence upon divine election and justification and by his assurance of the personal presence of the risen Christ. Staupitz's influence on Luther was significant at a critical time, pointing him to God's love in the cross, and interpreting his temptations as signs of God's election. *Karlstadt, Luther's colleague and radical critic, dedicated his commentary on Augustine's *The Spirit and the Letter* to Staupitz, although it was Luther who drove him to study Augustine afresh.

The Protestant Reformers

All the Magisterial Reformers sat at Augustine's feet. They benefited from the Renaissance rediscovery of Christian antiquity. Several new editions of Augustine were printed, notably by Erasmus. The Reformation protest was directed against the prevalence in late medieval theology, for all its professed allegiance to Augustine, of one equivalent or other of Semi-Pelagianism. The *nominalists, such as *William of Ockham and Gabriel *Biel, taught that doing what was within one's natural power (*facere quod in se est*) merited the first infusion of grace from God (*meritum de congruo*). The Englishman Thomas *Bradwardine strongly opposed Ockham's Semi-Pelagianism with a somewhat extreme Augustinianism.

The Reformers highlighted different notes in Augustine. *Calvin more thoroughly systematized his predestinarianism, while *Luther was drawn to his grim portrayal of fallen humanity, probably going beyond Augustine's account of the bondage of the will. On some elements, such as free will and original sin, other Reformers too favoured divergent formulations, but the kernel of Augustinianism was everywhere the heart of the Protestant gospel (see *Reformation theology).

Roman Catholicism

But Rome could not concede the Protestants' claims to be the true interpreters of Augustine. The two centuries after the Reformation were marked by controversies within Catholicism about the import of Augustine's teachings. In undiluted form they repeatedly raised the spectre of crypto-Protestantism infiltrating the fold. Michel Baius (de Bay, 1513–89) was a Louvain theologian who claimed to have read the anti-Pelagian works seventy times! In 1567 a papal bull condemned many propositions from his writings. He undoubtedly espoused a sharper version of Augustinianism than counterreform Catholicism could tolerate. This became evident in the new Jesuit Order's official adoption of Molinist opinions which were in substance Semi-Pelagian. Dominicans who accused the Jesuits of Pelagianism were themselves accused of Calvinism. A papal ruling in 1607 allowed both main currents of teaching. Renewed controversy broke out a century later over Henri Noris (1631–1704), an Augustinian hermit and author of a learned history of Pelagianism and defence of Augustinianism against Molinism. The outcome was another authorization of different systems of thought within the church. In practice, the Jesuits' Semi-Pelagian Molinism widely prevailed (see *Jesuit theology).

1640 saw the publication of a posthumous work called *Augustinus* by Cornelius Jansen (1585–1638), a Dutchman who taught at Louvain. It sparked off a far more intense conflict, especially in France, where the Cistercian convent of Port-Royal, with two houses in and near Paris, became the headquarters of *Jansenism, under the lead of St Cyran (Jean Duvergier de Hauranne, 1581–1643, the abbot of St Cyran), Antoine Arnauld (1612–94) and his sister Jacqueline Angélique (1591–1661), the abbess of Port-Royal. Support came from Dominicans, *Pascal and others sympathetic to a movement standing also for renewal of piety and devotion. The Jansenists' main target was Jesuit theology, especially Molinism. In 1653 Pope Innocent X condemned five propositions, allegedly extracted from Jansen's book, which affirmed that God's commands cannot be fulfilled without grace; grace is irresistible; fallen man is free from coercion, not from necessity; the Semi-Pelagians' error was denial of the irresistibility of grace; it is Semi-Pelagian to say that Christ died for all mankind. Jansenists contested this presentation of Jansen's teaching, and dispute persisted. In 1713 a more comprehensive papal condemnation was given of a work by the French Oratorian, Pasquier Quesnel (1634–1719). Port-Royal was closed in 1709, but Dutch Jansenists formed an independent bishopric which has survived as part of the Old Catholic Church. This long controversy stimulated extensive study of Augustine and the Pelagian episodes. One fruit was the edition of his works, still the best complete one, by the Maurist Benedictines (1679–1700). Jansenist sympathies had been observed among the Maurists.

Since the eighteenth century, Augustinian theology has been a less controversial subject for Catholics. Study of his works has continued to grow, with several periodicals and research centres, especially the Institut des Etudes Augustiniennes in Paris. In constructive theology, other aspects of his thought have increasingly kindled keener interest than the anti-Pelagian corpus.

Protestantism

Within Protestantism, the legacy of (anti-Pelagian) Augustinianism has been largely subsumed within the Lutheran and *Reformed traditions. Platonic dualism has been held to be a major structural fault in Augustine's teaching by theologians in the Barthian tradition, which also blames him for the Western preoccupation with anthropology rather than Christology. Reinhold *Niebuhr's 'Christian realism' was explicitly indebted to Augustine, and his *Nature and Destiny of Man* has been seen as a modern-day *City of God*.

In much of modern theology across different traditions, Augustine's creativity attracts continuing attention, from his teaching on the just war and his spiritual theology to his ideas on language and culture more generally. His emphasis on the relation between sexual disorder and human sinfulness is viewed as a still damaging legacy, while his role in the development of Western notions of the individual inner self is variously assessed.

See also: AUGUSTINE.

Bibliography

P. Cary, *Augustine's Invention of the Inner Self: The Legacy of a Christian Platonist* (Oxford, 2000); H.-U. Delius, *Augustin als Quelle Luthers* (Berlin, 1984); A. Hamel, *Der Junge Luther und Augustin* (Gütersloh, 1934–35); L. Kolakowski, *God Owes Us Nothing: A Brief Remark on Pascal's Religion and on the Spirit of Jansenism* (Chicago and London, 1995); H. de Lubac, *Augustinianism and Modern Theology* (London, 1969); H. Marrou, *St. Augustine and His Influence Through the Ages* (London, 1957); H. A. Oberman, 'The Augustine Renaissance in the Later Middle Ages', in H. A. Oberman (ed.), *Masters of the Reformation* (Cambridge, 1981); H. A. Oberman and F. A. James (eds.), *Via Augustini: Augustine in the Later Middle Ages, Renaissance, and Reformation: Essays in Honor of Damasus Trapp* (Leiden and New York, 1991); J. M. J. L. van Ravenswaay, *Augustinus Totus Noster: das Augustinverständnis bei Johannes Calvin* (Göttingen, 1990); A. Sedgwick, *Jansenism in Seventeenth-Century France* (Charlottesville, 1977); L. Smits, *S. Augustin dans l'oeuvre de Jean Calvin* (Assen, 1957–8); D. C. Steinmetz, *Misericordia Dei: The Theology of Johannes von Staupitz in Its Late Medieval Setting* (Leiden, 1968); D. Trapp, 'Augustinian Theology of the Fourteenth Century', *Augustiniana* 6, 1956, pp. 146–274.

D. F. WRIGHT

AULÉN, GUSTAF (1879–1977)

Professor of systematic theology in Lund and Bishop of Strängnäs in the Swedish Lutheran Church, Aulén was (with *Nygren and *Wingren) one of the foremost Scandinavian theologians of the modern era. A student of Nathan

Söderblom (1866–1931) at Uppsala, his contributions to *ecumenism and to the revival of Lutheran theology and church life in Sweden were many and various.

Much of his theological writing is characterized by a high appreciation of *Luther's dramatic presentation of the realities of sin, grace and redemption, and by a correspondingly low view of *scholasticism, whether medieval or Lutheran.

He is chiefly known for his short work on the *atonement, *Christus Victor*, which attempts to reinstate the so-called 'classic' view of the atonement. This interpretation, traced by Aulén in the NT, and also in *Irenaeus and Luther, envisages the cross as God's mighty act of triumph over powers of evil hostile to his will, and distinguishes itself from Latin ideas of *satisfaction and from 'subjective' or 'exemplarist' accounts. His work draws not only on some of the central preoccupations of *Reformation theologies of the cross and of grace, but also on the techniques of 'motif-research' of which Anders Nygren is the chief exponent.

Aulén was also the author of a systematic theology, *The Faith of the Christian Church*, and of books on ecclesiology and sacramental theology. Towards the end of his life he published *Jesus in Contemporary Historical Research*, arguing forcefully against historical scepticism applied to the Gospels. He was also a noted musician and composer.

Bibliography

Main works in ET: *Christus Victor* (London, 1931); *The Drama and the Symbols* (London, 1970); *Eucharist and Sacrifice* (Edinburgh, 1958); *The Faith of the Christian Church* (London, 1954); *Jesus in Contemporary Historical Research* (London, 1976); *Reformation and Catholicity* (Edinburgh, 1961).

J. B. WEBSTER

AUSCHWITZ, see HOLOCAUST

AUTHORITY

Christian theology makes the simple claim that *God, the author of all created reality, is the source of true authority in creation. The creative Word or Wisdom of God has given his creation forms of authority reflecting divine right and justice, as for example the authority of just law is attributed by the apostle Paul to God (Rom. 13) for the order and protection of society. Authority in this sense is mediated in the created order in many ways (e.g. J. Calvin, *Institutes*, I. iii. 1–3; II. ii.17), including human reason and sensitivity to beauty in the cosmos: great works of art are said to have an authority, which some theologians attribute to the 'mind of the Maker', as Dorothy Sayers entitled one of her books. Moral authority, likewise, is acknowledged in people and systems of government which reflect integrity, truth and justice, all ultimately having their source in God. All forms of human authority are, however, corruptible, as is evident, for example, in the biblical narratives of kingship; and even church authorities can fall into the direst of sin. Sociology of authority points to charismatic authority, and to institutional authority, a description not incompatible with theological analysis; in fact, *Weber took his inspiration from charismatic prophetic authority becoming 'routinized' into institutional authority in the early church.

Christian theology understands divine authority as self-defined by *Jesus Christ, his life, death and resurrection. Therefore the criticism of *theism, that it presents an authoritarian deity of pure power evoking a terrified submission, cannot be true of the God who was in Christ reconciling the world to himself by the *cross. Divine authority cannot be separated from divine love, which seeks to evoke covenant or communion by responsive love; this is truly 'the omnipotence of love' (J. Oman). The reconciling death of Jesus unites *love with justice in revealing and upholding divine authority and holiness in human history. Here God speaks his final authoritative word to humankind – indeed to the cosmos – the saving act of the divine Word renewing creation and all authorities. The authority of God is revealed as Christlike rather than domineering. The authority of God is also an eschatological reality, breaking into sinful and idolatrous history, conquering the false gods of brutal authoritarian power, propaganda and deception by the *kingdom of God, revealed in Jesus and still to be wholly fulfilled, the church being the beloved, if fallible, covenant partner of Christ in history.

The *Spirit of God brings home the divine authority in human hearts, working through human will and consent, a theme expounded by *Calvin in terms of 'the internal testimony of the Spirit'. Divine authority is therefore no dry objective reality facing us only with challenge and summons, but a life-giving movement in which we participate: 'God sent the Spirit of his Son into our hearts, the Spirit who calls out, "*Abba*, Father!"' (Gal. 4:6). Worship of God the Father is the ultimate expression of our acknowledgment of divine authority, a matter of joy and love, of being caught up into the life of God. There is no need therefore to overbalance in the direction of lifeless objectivity nor of disordered subjectivity in seeking to know divine authority.

The risen Christ is Lord of the church, the canonical Scriptures informing the church and the world of this Lord, his historical and theological significance; these *Scriptures themselves being guided and inspired by the Spirit in such a way as to reflect the divine patience with human historical character and circumstance, charting the history of the covenant as like a river rather than an artificial canal blasted through rock with mathematical and mechanical force (J. Oman). The authority of God works with human creaturely resources rather than by pure external power. The Scriptures are authoritative over the church as well as in a sense being products of the people of God, inspired for particular purposes, acknowledged by the community as such and recorded faithfully. The Scriptures give the church direct access to the preaching and teaching of the apostles and prophets, whose voices therefore can and do speak now in the church, mediating the authority of Christ with clarity and power, teaching the 'apostolic' message to the church today. Karl *Barth spoke of the 'threefold form of the Word' – Christ as the 'revealed Word', the proclamation of the church as the 'preached Word' and the Scriptures the 'written Word' – arguing that these three coalesce in the Spirit again and again in the church. Few would disagree with this, but might wish to add that the truth of the written word stands as true and authoritative in a way that avoids the charge of 'occasionalism' or a Kantian epistemological dualism of faith and unfaith, that is to say, the text seems to become true in the moment of faithful reading. For Barth, that is the moment of inspiration when the Spirit brings the words to life as revelation.

Debates about the categories most apt to describe the inspired and authoritative Scriptures ('inerrant', 'infallible', 'reliable', for example) have served to underline the key importance of the Bible in the church, and theology as the basic authority in terms of the 'order of knowing', always pointing beyond itself to God, the role of Scripture. Scripture mediates the authority of God to the church and the world, a fundamentally 'personal' authority, wholly reliable and inexhaustibly rich, as witnessed by its challenge and interest from generation to generation; the Scriptures are never summarized so as to become redundant. The wide and deep range of literature, inspired and forged by the Spirit in human crises and triumphs, speaks of God's nature and purposes for the human race. This authoritative teaching is public *truth, not just for a special elite of initiates, and so all are called to attend to the message, bringing all their questions with them.

Church tradition, seeking to clarify and serve scriptural teaching about God's self-revelation, remains subject to the authority of Scripture and is not an extended mode of the canon bearing equal status. Likewise, the authority claimed by some theologians for contemporary cultural experience must be carefully discerned in terms of the witness of Scripture, especially in terms of ethical questions. The authority of individual desires or drives, for example in debates over sexual *ethics, must be related to the gospel summons of true humanity being defined in Christ. The church will never be free from debates concerning the interaction of contemporary questions and scriptural principles.

Politically, too, claims to absolute authority by the *state represent a form of false authority equating to idolatry and in need of the clarity of the criterion of the scriptural witness to Christ as Lord. The authority of God relates to creation as well as church. It is therefore to be seen as applicable to issues of culture and politics; indeed it was the realization of God's authority over political authority that led reformers such as Wilberforce in Britain to campaign for the abolition of the slave trade.

The church will never be free of contested questions arising from clashes of Christian authority with problems of *culture, and must be constantly aware of the danger of being blinkered by traditions to the radical claims of Christ mediated through Scripture and stimulated by the Spirit. In this regard the challenge of *postmodernism to authority in the form of text with a given meaning always requiring 'deconstruction', or established institutional authority needing to be regarded with suspicion as disguised power play, is interesting to Christianity. On the one hand, postmodern deconstruction brings down Enlightenment 'idols' such as rationality and morality (Nietzsche) or 'sexuality' (Foucault), but on the other hand, it has no place for the authority of God nor a final purpose to the endless 'text' of human existence. Christian theologians influenced by postmodernism have rejected 'onto theology', that is, a doctrine of a dominating deity over against the world and not participating in it, representing power rather than Christlike authority.

The authority of God mediated in Christ and the Spirit is a personal kind of authority rather than a mode of rigid rules and regulations, the issue over which Jesus clashed with the Pharisees. This is not to say that divine authority is unclear or relativist, but rather that its manner accommodates graciously to human conditions and characteristics, speaking to us through Jesus and drawing us into the life of God by the Spirit. This authority is ultimately purposive: to bring us to the glory of the kingdom and fulfil the goal of the cosmos in all respects.

Bibliography

H. Arendt, 'What Is Authority?' in P. Baehr (ed.), *The Portable Hannah Arendt* (London, 2003); P. T. Forsyth, *The Principle of Authority* (London, 1952); C. Gunton, *Enlightenment and Alienation* (Basingstoke, 1985); O. O'Donovan, *Resurrection and Moral Order*, pt. 2 (Leicester and Grand Rapids, 1994); H. E. W. Turner, *The Pattern of Christian Truth* (London, 1954); J. B. Webster, *Word and Church* (Edinburgh, 2001).

T. BRADSHAW

AUTONOMY

Autonomy refers generally to the capacity to set one's own laws and administer one's own affairs, and to one's right to do so. The term originated in ancient Greece to describe the political and legal status of city-states, but came in the *Enlightenment to be predicated of human persons. It thus extended its sphere of reference from political and legal domains to the realms of philosophy, theology and ethics, where it had previously been subsumed under the concept of freedom. For Immanuel *Kant, autonomy referred to the property of the human will to be a moral law for itself independently of any external sources. Relying for authoritative principles on other sources, whether material inclinations or desires, human institutions or conventions, or the will of God, would by contrast constitute heteronomy.

Importantly for Kant, human autonomy was neither arbitrary nor idiosyncratic, but was rather bound to the universal law of reason. In certain later Enlightenment traditions, however, autonomy was construed in a more radical way such that its goal was posited as an absolute self-determination in which every external point of reference is relativized or eliminated. These latter construals of autonomy in particular represented a view of human freedom which stood in some tension with traditional Christian views of human freedom in which a relationship with God was a central feature. In the course of responding to such Enlightenment conceptions of autonomy, Christian theology has offered a number of different approaches.

In the nineteenth century, theologians sympathetic to the Enlightenment – such as *Schleiermacher, *Hegel, and *Ritschl – sought in their different ways to correlate the idea of human autonomy, at least in its milder, Kantian formulation, with the idea of Christian *freedom in the context of theonomy, the condition of being ruled or governed by God. In the twentieth century, this theological task continued in diverse ways, as the importance of the concept of autonomy and the complexity of its relation to Christian freedom were increasingly recognized. The Roman Catholic Church at the Second Vatican Council affirmed human autonomy for the first time, with the proviso that all created things depended on God, and no created thing could be used by humanity without any reference to God as Creator. For Karl *Barth, meanwhile, there was no contradiction between autonomy and theonomy, because it was precisely the theonomy of God which willed the autonomy of the individual. Thus, human autonomy is simultaneously graciously affirmed and divinely circumscribed. For Paul *Tillich, autonomy was the obedience of the individual to the law of reason, but this autonomy was in perpetual conflict with heteronomy. Reconciliation of the two was to be found in theonomy, for God was the law for both the structure and the ground of reason. As autonomy continues to be a significant, if contested, concept in contemporary political thought and ethical theory, so the theological task of appropriately conceptualizing human autonomy – in relation both to God and neighbour and to the concept of Christian freedom – continues to be a pressing task.

Bibliography

K. Barth, *CD*, vol. II/2 (Edinburgh, 1957); I. Kant, *Groundwork of the Metaphysics of Morals* (Cambridge, 1998); P. Tillich, *Systematic Theology*, vol. 1 (Welwyn, 1953); Vatican Council, 'Gaudium et Spes', in *Vatican Council II: Constitutions, Decrees, Declarations* (New York, 1996).

P. T. NIMMO

AVERROISM

Averroism is a branch of the *Aristotelian philosophical tradition inspired by the Arab philosopher Averroes (Lat. for Ibn-Rushd, 1126–98), the most influential commentator on the writings of Aristotle. Although Averroes was the greatest Islamic philosopher, his influence was felt primarily in the Latin West (he came from Cordoba in Spain), at the University of Paris in the thirteenth and early fourteenth centuries and at the Universities of Bologna and Padua from the thirteenth to the middle of the seventeenth centuries. More recently, this movement has been called 'radical or heterodox Aristotelianism'. This name is appropriate because the primary aim of its masters was to teach the philosophy of Aristotle. Their goal was not to follow Averroes, but simply to present Aristotle's thought. Most famous among these masters at the University of Paris are Siger of Brabant (*c.* 1235–*c.* 1282) and Boetius of Dacia (*fl.* mid-thirteenth century). Among Italian Averroists, the best known is Caesar Cremoninus (*c.* 1550–1631), who is supposed to have been the friend of Galileo who refused to look through a telescope because this might compel him to abandon Aristotelian astronomy.

There are three areas in which Aristotle's thought presented a direct challenge to Christian teaching. Aristotle asserted that the world is eternal and this is opposed to the doctrine of *creation. He also seems to have held that there is one immaterial soul for all men, and this calls into question the teaching of personal *immortality and the possibility of reward or punishment after death. Finally, he supposed that man can achieve perfection following reason alone, and this opposes the Christian teaching that faith is necessary for salvation (see *Faith and reason). Because of these problems, the assimilation of Aristotle into the Christian West was difficult. Some wished to reject Aristotle entirely; others like *Thomas Aquinas used Aristotle, but only after criticizing and modifying his thought. The Averroists tended to adopt Aristotle without reservation and so appeared to be maintaining teachings contrary to the faith. Averroism was opposed by Aquinas and others, and the Christian Averroists were condemned by the church in the 1270s.

For a long time the double-truth theory was attributed to Averroists. According to this theory, a thesis could be true in philosophy and its contradictory thesis could be true for faith (see *Duns Scotus). For example, according to philosophy the world has existed eternally, but according to faith the world has had a beginning. In fact, neither Siger nor anyone else claims that such contradictory truths are compatible; rather, in cases where philosophy and faith are in conflict, truth is always held to be on the side of faith. However, even while these masters say that truth is on the side of faith, they give the impression that they remain attached to the conclusions of philosophy. This gives the impression that they hold two contradictory propositions to be true, and indeed their opponents tried to attribute the double-truth thesis to them to show the untenability of their position.

In the Averroists' concern for reason, there was not an interest in freedom of thought, as one might suppose, but rather an excessive regard for the philosophical tradition. Siger of Brabant states that to treat matters philosophically is to be concerned with determining the thought of the philosophers rather than discovering the truth. This same attachment to the philosophers, especially Aristotle, seems also to have dominated Cremoninus. Averroism was the most conservative and sterile form of Aristotelianism.

Bibliography

E. Gilson, *History of Christian Philosophy in the Middle Ages* (London, 1955); L. Sonneborn, *Averroes (Ibn Rushd): Muslim Scholar, Philosopher, and Physician of the Twelfth Century* (New York, 2006); F. van Steenberghen, *Thomas Aquinas and Radical Aristotelianism* (Washington, DC, 1980).

A. VOS

BAILLIE, DONALD MACPHERSON (1887–1954)

Donald Baillie was born at Gairloch, Ross-shire, where his father was a minister of the Free Church of Scotland; he was the younger brother of John *Baillie. He graduated in philosophy at Edinburgh, before studying for the ministry of the United Free Church of Scotland at New College, Edinburgh, under Hugh Ross *Mackintosh. Thereafter, he studied at Marburg under Wilhelm *Herrmann and at Heidelberg under Ernst *Troeltsch. He was ordained to the ministry in 1918 and served at Inverbervie, Cupar and Kilmacolm, before becoming Professor of Systematic Theology at St Andrews in 1934. In common with a majority of the United Free Church, he entered into the Church of Scotland in the Union of 1929.

His earliest significant work, *Faith in God and Its Christian Consummation* (1927), seeks to provide an apologetic ground for the reality of faith. Here we see Baillie developing his position within the theological parameters set by Albrecht *Ritschl, as interpreted by Herrmann; the influence of Ritschl, and German theology in general, was particularly marked in the late nineteenth and early twentieth centuries in Scotland. Nevertheless, *Faith in God* may be said to typify the end of an era within Scottish theology, and in Baillie's most significant work, *God Was in Christ* (1948), we see him engaged with 'the central problem of *Christology . . . What do we mean by saying that God was incarnate in Jesus?' (pp. 106ff.). Baillie seeks to present an essentially *Chalcedonian understanding of the incarnation and to do so through 'the paradox of Grace'. The concept of '*paradox' is already evident in *Faith in God*, but assumes a central place in *God Was in Christ*, where Baillie identifies it as 'characteristic of Christianity' as evidenced in Paul (1 Cor. 15:10) and elsewhere (p. 114). Thus, beginning with 'the paradox of Grace', Baillie seeks to develop an analogy which will more fully disclose 'the paradox of the Incarnation'. He contends that if the life of Christ can be 'regarded as in some sense the prototype of the Christian life, may we not find a feeble analogue of the incarnate life in the experience of those who are His "many brethren", and particularly in the central paradox of their experience: "Not I, but the grace of God"?' He further asks, 'If this confession is true . . . is it not the same *type* of paradox, taken at the absolute degree . . . of which we say that it was the life of a man and yet also, in a deeper and prior sense, the very life of God incarnate?' (p. 129).

The posthumously published *The Theology of the Sacraments* (1957) seeks to rediscover the significance of the *sacraments, particularly from the perspective of the Reformed tradition. This concern reflects Baillie's wider ecumenical outlook; he was actively involved in the *Faith and Order conferences in Edinburgh (1937) and in Lund (1952), as well as being joint editor of the volume *Intercommunion* (1952).

Bibliography

Works: *Faith in God and Its Christian Consummation* (Edinburgh, 1927); *God Was in Christ: An Essay on Incarnation and Atonement* (London, ²1956 [1948]); *To Whom Shall We Go?* (Edinburgh, 1955); *The Theology of the Sacraments* (London, 1957); *Out of Nazareth* (Edinburgh, 1958). Ed. with J. Marsh, *Intercommunion* (London, 1952).

Studies: J. Baillie, 'Some Comments on Professor Hick's Article on "The Christology of D. M. Baillie"', *Scottish Journal of Theology* 11, 1958, pp. 265–270; D. A. S. Fergusson (ed.), *Christ, Church and Society: Essays on John Baillie and Donald Baillie* (Edinburgh, 1993); D. A. S. Fergusson (ed.), *John and Donald Baillie: Selected Writings* (Edinburgh, 1997); J. Hick, 'The Christology of D. M. Baillie', *Scottish Journal of Theology* 11, 1958, pp. 1–12; G. Newlands, *John and Donald Baillie: Transatlantic Theology* (Oxford, 2002); D. W. D. Shaw (ed.), *In Divers Manners* (St Andrews, 1990).

J. L. McPake

BAILLIE, JOHN (1886–1960)

Baillie was a Scottish churchman and theologian brother of Donald *Baillie. His life mirrored Presbyterian reunion in Scotland – son of a Free Church manse, student in the United Free Church's New College, Edinburgh, Moderator of the Church of Scotland's General Assembly (1943), as well as wider ecumenism – steward at the 1910 Edinburgh Conference, president of the WCC, signatory of the *Bishops Report* commending Anglican episcopacy to the Church of Scotland (1957). He was the distinguished helmsman of the Church's Commission for the Interpretation of God's Will in the Present Crisis, 1940–45 (*God's Will for*

Church and Nation, 1946; cf. his *What Is Christian Civilization?*, 1945).

Baillie taught philosophy in Edinburgh, and then theology in the USA and Canada (1919–34), before becoming professor of divinity at Edinburgh (1934–56), and latterly also dean of the faculty and principal of New College (1950–56). Perhaps at his best as an apologist (cf. *Invitation to Pilgrimage*, 1942), he has been called 'a mediating theologian' (W. L. Power, *USQR* 24, 1968, pp. 47–68). A decided *liberalism followed the undermining of his father's Calvinism. It earned *Bonhoeffer's critical judgment in New York, and is reflected in writings like *The Roots of Religion in the Human Soul* (1926). About 1930 he shifted towards a 'liberal *neo-orthodoxy' (cf. *And the Life Everlasting*, 1933; *Our Knowledge of God*, 1939), but subsequently a greater confidence in reason reasserted itself, as he predicted a strong reaction against Barthianism. *The Belief in Progress* (1950) was followed by *The Idea of Revelation in Recent Thought* (1956), an influential survey of anti-propositional positions, and his posthumous (undelivered) *Gifford Lectures, *The Sense of the Presence of God* (1962). His best-known work was the frequently translated *A Diary of Private Prayer* (1936). Baillie combined a contemplative devotion with a humane Christian liberalism, which discriminated between competing theological tendencies.

Bibliography

Works: Collected essays in *Christian Devotion* (London, 1962), with a memoir by I. M. Forrester; and *A Reasoned Faith* (1963). Unpublished papers in New College Library, Edinburgh. Appreciations by D. S. Klinefelter, *SJT* 22 (1969), pp. 419–436; John A. Mackay, ibid. 9 (1956), pp. 225–235.

Studies: D. A. S. Fergusson, *John and Donald Baillie: Selected Writings* (Edinburgh, 1996); P. B. O'Leary, *Revelation and Faith in Our Knowledge of God According to the Theology of John Baillie* (Rome, 1968); T. F. Torrance, *Religion in Life* 30 (1961), pp. 329–333.

D. F. WRIGHT

BALTHASAR, HANS URS VON (1905–88)

Hans von Balthasar was a leading Swiss Roman Catholic theologian and spiritual writer. After studies in philosophy and literature, he became a member of the Society of Jesus before founding a secular institute (the *Johannesgemeinschaft*) and engaging in wide-ranging literary and publishing activities. He published voluminously, producing works of Christian theology and philosophy and interpretative studies in the history of culture and spirituality, as well as editing and translating the work of others.

His magnum opus, destined to become one of the classic pieces of twentieth-century theological writing, is a multi-volume work in three parts, synthesizing theology, philosophy and literature in a massive study of the beautiful, the good and the true. The first part, *Herrlichkeit* (appearing in English as *The Glory of the Lord*), examines revelation from the vantage point of theological *aesthetics. In the seven volumes of the first part of his trilogy, von Balthasar urges his readers to look at Christian theology under the sign of beauty, which is made manifest in the 'luminous form' (*Gestalt*) of Jesus Christ, the Word of God become flesh, making his view of the Christian faith irreducibly *incarnational. Divine beauty, which is glory, is profoundly different from natural or worldly beauty, because it embraces the cross and the disfigurement of Christ as its manifestations.

Von Balthasar is careful to distinguish a 'theological aesthetics' from an 'aesthetic theology' which disassociates beauty from the other transcendentals – truth and goodness – thereby rendering aesthetics a secular discipline. Through what he calls the 'circuminsession' of the transcendentals, von Balthasar was able to treat aesthetics as integral to reasoning and ethics: beauty is also truth and goodness, and all three are Being, 'the first of the Transcendentals'. Furthermore, the principle of *analogy postulates a peculiar relationality between divine and worldly beauty which allows von Balthasar to commandeer the science of aesthetics as a conceptual framework for his theology.

If *Herrlichkeit* treats Christian theology primarily under the rubric of 'contemplation', *Theodramatik* deals with divine and human action. For von Balthasar, the goal of theology is not the contemplation of God in blissful *stasis* in which the created world is left behind. Contemplation should result in obedient response to God's revelation, that is, it should lead to lives lived for the sake of goodness, truth and love. Contemplation flows into action, and the five volumes of *Theodramatik* seek to describe Christian existence in light of the dramatic *revelation of God. Although von Balthasar begins with the metaphor of the theatre and devotes much time to playwrights and dramatists in volume 1, he makes very little reference to actual plays in subsequent volumes. The literary dramatic form with which he began *Theodramatik* merely offers a new perspective to the divine revelation. Von Balthasar's main concern is to present a profound meditation on the love of God in Christ and the church's response as the basis of the relationship between God and man.

In the third part of the trilogy, *Theologik*, von Balthasar deals with the intelligible structure of *salvation. Here von Balthasar completes the conceptual building blocks he has put in place in *Herrlichkeit* and *Theodramatik* by reflecting on the nature of *truth. According to von Balthasar, an infinite truth has taken on finite form in the incarnation, and this event has enabled human beings to participate in the mystery of the trinitarian life, where truth sets them free. Theological logic is therefore *christologic*, the revelation of the incarnate Logos which invites human beings into the fullest possible participation of being, which is everlasting life. This truth is appropriated only by the Spirit, whose work is co-extensive with that of the Son: the Spirit interprets the Son as Son of the Father.

The virtually unrestricted range of von Balthasar's knowledge and interests testifies to the catholicity of his thought, which was directed by a vision of the universality of God's self-manifestation in Christ: here his debt to some of the Fathers (see *Patristic theology) is evident. The breadth of his vision is intrinsically related, however, to a firm adherence to the particularity of Christ who is the form of God, the divine *glory concentrated and focused in an unsurpassable way.

Von Balthasar's work was much influenced by that of *Barth, upon whom he wrote with great perceptiveness and to whom he was particularly indebted for his vigorous Christocentrism (especially in constructing the doctrine of God on a Christological base) and for an understanding of the theological task as directed by the givenness of revelation. Von Balthasar's use of the category of 'beauty' to describe the nature of God in his self-manifestation to creation is a means of recovering a sense of self-evidence, authority and necessity of revelation in a way closely similar to Barth's own understanding of God's self-manifestation as irreducible and needing no authentication beyond itself.

The gracious character of God's relation to man is a central preoccupation in von Balthasar's theology, and some of his emphases here owe much to the work of E. Przywara, whose account of analogy laid greater stress on the distinction between God and the world than the 'Transcendental Thomism' later made famous by Karl *Rahner.

But perhaps, most of all, von Balthasar's work was deeply impressed by his close relationship to the mystic Adrienne von Speyr (1902–67). From her experiences he developed a remarkable theology of the Holy Saturday, in which Christ's descent into hell becomes a leading motif in Christology, soteriology and *trinitarian theology. As the ultimate act of self-emptying by the Son of God, Holy Saturday furnishes a theology of reconciliation as Christ's solidarity with the damned. It also provides the basis for a theology of the trinitarian relations centred, like other contemporary trinitarian theories, on Calvary.

Von Balthasar is increasingly recognized as a thinker who made a potent restatement of the persistent themes of classical Christian theology, notably in the area of incarnational and trinitarian doctrine. His interweaving of theological and cultural references, however, along with the integrative and speculative tone of much of his writing, may not commend him to strands of contemporary theology more concerned with the critical grounding and appraisal of Christian truth-claims and less confident about the objectivity of revelation.

Bibliography

Works: *Elucidations* (London, 1965); *Love Alone, The Way of Revelation* (London, 1968); *Prayer* (London, 1971); *Engagement with God* (London, 1975); *The Glory of the Lord: A Theological Aesthetics*, 7 vols. (Edinburgh and New York, 1983–90); *Theo-drama*, 5 vols. (New York, 1988–98); *Theo-logic*, 3 vols. (New York, 2001–05).

Studies: R. Chia, *Revelation and Theology: The Knowledge of God in Balthasar and Barth* (Bern, 1999); M. Kehl and W. Löser (eds.), *A Von Balthasar Reader* (Edinburgh, 1983); A. Nichols, *The Word Has Been Abroad: A*

BANGS, NATHAN (1778–1862)

A participant in the second great awakening in Canada and the United States, Bangs was the first major American Methodist theologian. Born in Connecticut and largely self-educated, he worked as a teacher and a surveyor before moving to Canada in 1799. There, through the ministry of Methodist itinerants, he underwent a spiritual struggle that culminated in his profession of conversion in 1800 and entire sanctification in 1801. By 1802 he was preaching to large crowds, and spent the next seven years fanning the flames of the awakening in Upper Canada.

Moving to New York, Bangs became enormously influential in the Methodist Episcopal Church. A prolific author, he edited three periodicals, led the publishing house, and was chief architect of the Methodist Missionary Society.

He defended *Arminianism in *The Errors of Hopkinsianism* (1815) and *Predestination Examined* (1817), arguing that while Methodists share with Calvinists a belief in total depravity, they teach that prevenient grace enables sinners to respond freely to God.

A proponent of entire *sanctification, Bangs supported Phoebe *Palmer's ministry and frequently attended her Tuesday Meetings. However, in 1857 he criticized her belief that receiving entire sanctification required no further evidence than its promise in Scripture, and defended the necessity of both a witness and fruit of the Spirit as taught by John *Wesley and John Fletcher.

See also: METHODISM.

Bibliography

T. A. Langford, *Practical Divinity: Theology in the Wesleyan Tradition* (Nashville, 1998); idem, *Practical Divinity: Readings in Wesleyan Theology* (Nashville, 1999); G. A. Rawlyk, *The Canada Fire* (Kingston and Montreal, 1994); A. Stevens, *Life and Times of Nathan Bangs, D.D.* (New York, 1863); A. H. Tuttle, *Nathan Bangs* (New York, 1909).

H. H. KNIGHT III

BAPTISM

Baptism in the patristic period

In the primitive church, baptism was an integral part of the kerygma (e.g. Acts 2:38) and an essential part of the process of becoming a Christian (*conversion-initiation), so much so that the NT knows no unbaptized believers (1 Cor. 12:13). While baptism was clearly symbolic, it was also an effective *symbol (Gal. 3:26–27; Col. 2:12; see A. R. Cross, *Recovering the Evangelical Sacrament*, pp. 51–83, who shows that all the benefits attributed to faith are also attributed to baptism; and also D. F. Wright, *What Has Infant Baptism Done?* who uses the term 'baptismal realism', p. 93).

While the NT theology of baptism as the occasion of the reception of the Spirit and forgiveness of sins (Acts 2:38), union with Christ in his death and resurrection (Rom. 6:2–11), incorporation into the church (1 Cor. 12:13) and salvation (1 Pet. 3:21) is repeated in the early Christian writings (e.g. *Barn.* 11; Hermas, *Vis.* 3.3.1; *Mand.* 4.3.3; *Sim.* 9.13.3–6; Theophilus, *Autol.* 2.16; Irenaeus, *Dem.* 3 and 42; Clement of Alexandria, *Paed.* 1.6.25–32), there were, nevertheless, developments. Where scholars differ is on the legitimacy of these.

In the apostolic church, instruction followed baptism on acceptance of the gospel (Acts 2:41; 8:35–39; 16:30–33; cf. Matt. 28:19), but this pattern changed by the turn of the second century (cf. *Did.* 7, and Justin's *1 Apol.* 61, where, e.g. moral teaching, prayer and fasting precede baptism). The reason for the abandonment of immediate baptism most plausibly occurred when Christianity moved from a predominantly Jewish milieu, where converts were familiar with monotheism and the ethical instruction of the OT, to a Gentile one in which converts needed purifying and releasing from the defilements of paganism.

From the turn of the second century, then, we find a developing catechumenate, which varied regionally and could last up to three years, with baptism taking place at Easter. By the fourth and fifth centuries, catechetical classes involved regular attendance at daily meetings during Lent, during which the *creed was expounded (see *Catechisms). The baptismal rite included invocation of the Spirit, various exorcisms, the disrobing of the candidate, renunciation of Satan, anointing with oil, a threefold baptismal interrogation and either a single (e.g. Gregory the Great, *Ep.* 43) or threefold (as in the Eastern churches) immersion in the name of the Trinity. This was followed by further anointings, reclothing and the laying on of hands, at which point the candidate would share in the Eucharist and enter into a period of post-baptismal teaching known as mystagogy. The various components of the service varied from region to region – West and East Syria, Egypt, North Africa, Italy, Gaul – and extensive examples of catechetical instruction, mystagogical catecheses and sermons survive (in e.g. Cyril of Jerusalem, John Chrysostom, Theodore of Mopsuestia, Ambrose of Milan and Augustine).

While the NT church practised immersion (however, I. H. Marshall, in *Dimensions of Baptism*, pp. 8–24, argues also for sprinkling and pouring), alternative modes developed in time. The *Didache* 7 allowed for the threefold pouring of water on the head when sufficient water was lacking, while Cyprian of Carthage permitted its adoption for those bedridden (*Ep.* 75).

In the NT period, 'baptism upon personal profession of faith is the most clearly attested pattern in the New Testament documents' (*Baptism, Eucharist and Ministry*, p. 4), and many continue to maintain that paedobaptism is present either in the accounts of household baptisms or implicitly in the correspondence of the two covenants (see e.g. G. W. Bromiley, *Children of Promise*, Grand Rapids, 1979, and G. Strawbridge [ed.], *The Case for Covenantal Infant Baptism*, Phillipsburg, 2003). However, paedobaptism is not explicit until *c.* 200 when Tertullian acknowledges it, though disapprovingly, as, for him, people are made, not born Christians (*On Baptism* 18). Paedobaptism here appears to be relatively new, for it is absent from the *Apostolic Fathers, though this silence is variously interpreted. In less than a generation, though, Origen claimed it to be apostolic (*Comm. Rom.* 5.9).

The most cogent argument for paedobaptism's origins is that it grew out of child believer's baptism, and many paedobaptist scholars argue for the legitimacy of the development of infant baptism after the NT era solely and adequately on the grounds of the practice of the church (e.g. N. P. Williams, *The Ideas of the Fall and of Original Sin*, London, 1929, pp. 550–554). According to *Tertullian, children were in 'an age of innocency' (*On Baptism* 18; cf. also Hermas, *Sim.* 9.29.1–3; *Barn.* 6), but the intimate association of baptism with original sin and guilt developed by *Cyprian (*Ep.* 64) was developed by *Augustine (e.g. *Sermon* 174) and became the almost universal practice till the Reformation.

In the third century, Cyprian rejected baptism administered by anyone outside the church, while Stephen I regarded the use of water and the trinitarian name as valid irrespective of the standing of the administrator. In the fourth century, the *Donatist controversy raised the issue again when they claimed that those who had compromised their faith during persecution, or were guilty of moral laxity, negated the efficacy of baptism. This position was countered by Augustine (*Ep.* 98), thereby establishing that baptism is effective *ex opere operato*.

Due to the frequency of persecution some were *martyred before receiving baptism, giving rise to the doctrine of the baptism of blood (e.g. Cyprian, *Ep.* 73.22).

Baptism in the medieval period

With the establishment of Christendom, paedobaptism soon became first the norm, then the only form of baptism. The once-lengthy catechumenate was reduced to the first part of the baptismal rite. In the missionary expansion following Constantine's conversion, adult baptism continued as mission baptism, though within Christian Europe itself paedobaptism alone was practised. Anyone who reinstated believer's baptism was condemned by the Justinian Code and treated as a heretic (e.g. the Paulicians). Mass conversions were marked by mass baptisms and necessary for salvation, unless there was the baptism of desire in those who died before they could be baptized. In the rite, the promise once made by the candidates was now made by godparents, and the faith necessary was that of the church. Paedobaptism cleansed from original sin, whilst *penance cleansed from actual sin.

The term '*sacrament' first arose as the Latin translation of the NT 'mystery', and was widely used in the Fathers. However, it was not until the medieval period that its definition became more precise, definitively by Peter *Lombard (*Four Books of the Sentences* 4.1.4: 'it is a sign of the grace of God and a form of invisible grace, so that it bears its image and exists as its cause'), who also established it among the seven sacraments of the Catholic Church (see *Roman Catholic theology). This medieval theology was defended against the sixteenth-century Reformations by the Council of Trent, which reasserted that infant baptism is effective *ex opere operato* and condemned its rejection.

Baptism in the sixteenth-century Reformations

The Reformers rejected the Catholic Church's seven sacraments in favour of the two of dominical origin, though their theologies of baptism differed as they related it to their new understandings of grace, faith, salvation and the church (see *Reformation theology).

For Martin *Luther, there is no sacrament without faith, but he justified the continuation of infant baptism – which, though lacking NT support, was validated by the ancient practice of the church – by positing infant faith. He also believed that baptism conveys God's promise of salvation.

For a while Huldrych Zwingli looked as though he would reject paedobaptism, but once some of his disciples became *Anabaptists (lit. re-baptizers), he backtracked, developing his argument for paedobaptism on the basis of the correspondence of the two covenants and their respective initiatory rites (circumcision and baptism), and that the faith of the parents and church sufficed for the efficacy of infant baptism. In this he was followed by the likes of Heinrich Bullinger and John Calvin, the latter of whom developed the link between baptism and the doctrine of predestination (see *Reformed theology). However, while Zwingli drove a wedge between spirit and matter, Calvin maintained the sacramental connection between the sign and the thing signified.

While the Church of England steered its *via media* between Catholicism and the continental Reformers, understanding paedobaptism as regenerative and bringing the elect into salvation, the *Puritans moved in a more Reformed direction, seeing baptism as the seal of the covenant and a badge identifying the baptized with the church.

The *radical Reformers, however, parted company with the Magisterial Reformers. The Anabaptists rejected paedobaptism for a restored believer's baptism, rejecting the argument from the covenants and circumcision, maintaining baptism followed repentance and faith, i.e. conversion (e.g. the *Schleitheim Confession, art. 1). While those like Melchior Hoffmann were prepared to accept the temporary suspension of baptism, some radicals, such as David Joris and Sebastian Franck, were spiritualists and dispensed altogether with outward rites. As to the mode, many adopted pouring, though others practised immersion.

Though many radicals suffered imprisonment, exile or martyrdom from both Catholics and Protestants, under such leaders as Menno Simons, Anabaptist communities survived, finding havens in Holland and Eastern Europe, where baptism symbolized personal conversion and discipleship, and entrance into a separatist fellowship of believers.

Baptism to the present day

There were few developments in baptismal theology or practice between the sixteenth and eighteenth centuries, but one of the most significant was the emergence of the *Baptist movement in the early seventeenth century. Its significance lies in its contemporary numbers worldwide and the fact that they represent the tip of a baptistic iceberg – a tradition that includes Disciples/Churches of Christ, many Pentecostals, charismatics, Restorationists and other independent evangelical churches.

In 1609 a group of English Separatist exiles baptized one another by affusion, and through their covenanting to 'walk together' the first Baptist church was founded, returning to London in 1612. The practice of immersion does not appear to have been adopted till around the 1630s.

Another important development is represented by the Society of Friends, whose rejection of the outward sacraments continues the separation of spirit and matter encountered at various stages in church history. *Quaker views probably influenced The *Salvation Army, who rejected the traditional rites as obstacles to true holiness, seeking instead the true baptism of the Spirit. However, they replaced them with quasi-sacraments, the dedication of children, the swearing-in of soldiers and the presenting of the flag. The separation of Spirit- from water-baptism also emerges with the rise of the *Pentecostal movement in the early twentieth century and later charismatic and Restorationist movements.

The modern systematic study of baptism was sparked by the work of Emil *Brunner, who coined the phrase 'the divine–human encounter' (*The Divine–Human Encounter*, ET, London, 1944), and Karl *Barth (*The Teaching of the Church Regarding Baptism*, London, 1948), though he later abandoned any notion of baptismal sacramentalism. While both dismantled the theological basis for paedobaptism, they nevertheless retained it. This revived interest tied in with the earlier work of the Faith and Order conferences which later produced *Baptism, Eucharist and Ministry* in 1982. BEM marked the change from earlier comparative studies to seeking theological convergence, proposing that different traditions accept infant and believer's baptism as equivalent alternatives (common baptism or dual practice), and asserting that anything resembling re-baptism should be avoided.

Ecumenical discussions have continued to provide productive contexts for the study of baptism. Among many dialogues at national and international levels are those between the Anglican Communion and the Baptist World Alliance, and the BWA and the Roman Catholic Church, with the former suggesting recognition of different stories of initiation. Such discussions have built on the work on baptism within various traditions, perhaps the best known of which is the *Rite of Christian Initiation of Adults* which arose out of Vatican II, which has inspired and informed the examination of baptism within the wider context of initiation.

Finally, baptism has not held a prominent place in *evangelical thought, either in its paedobaptist or credobaptist expressions. Many evangelicals hold a merely symbolic view of baptism (but see S. K. Fowler, *More Than a Symbol*, Milton Keynes, 2002), and this was fuelled by antipathy towards the reassertion of the *ex opere operato* doctrine propounded by the Oxford Movement (see *Anglo-Catholic theology) in the mid-nineteenth century. Under the influence of Enlightenment individualism and Gnosticism, evangelicals have often maintained a spirit-matter dualism and, despite Calvin's influence on so much evangelical theology, evangelicals have adopted a more Zwinglian than Calvinist baptismal theology. However, through increasing ecumenical involvement, renewed biblical studies, rediscovery of the doctrine of the Spirit and growing openness to and awareness of the traditions of the church, an increasing number of evangelicals have argued for a renewed biblical and sacramental theology of baptism (both infant and believers' baptists), recognizing the realism of the NT language of baptism and arguing for the renewal not just of baptismal theology but also baptismal practice.

Bibliography

R. Armour, *Anabaptist Baptism* (Scottdale, 1966); J. E. Colwell, *Promise and Presence* (Milton Keynes, 2005); P. Cramer, *Baptism and Change in the Early Middle Ages c. 200–c. 1150* (Cambridge, 1993); A. R. Cross, *Recovering the Evangelical Sacrament* (Eugene, 2013); Faith and Order, *Baptism, Eucharist and Ministry* (Geneva, 1982); J. D. C. Fisher, *Christian Initiation: Baptism in the Medieval West* (London, 1965); idem, *Christian Initiation: The Reformation Period* (London, 1970); P. J. Jagger, *Christian Initiation 1552–1969* (London, 1970); M. E. Johnson, *The Rites of Christian Initiation* (Collegeville, 1999); K. McDonnell and G. T. Montague, *Christian Initiation and Baptism in the Holy Spirit* (Collegeville, ^{2}1994); Murphy Center for Liturgical Research, *Made, Not Born* (Notre Dame, 1976); J. Pelikan, *The Christian Tradition: A History of the Development of Doctrine*, 5 vols. (Chicago and London, 1971–89); S. E. Porter and A. R. Cross (eds.), *Baptism, the New Testament and the Church* (Sheffield, 1999); idem, *Dimensions of Baptism* (Sheffield, 2002); J. W. Riggs, *Baptism in the Reformed Tradition* (Louisville, 2002); B. D. Spinks, *Early and Medieval Rituals and Theologies of Baptism* (Aldershot, 2006); idem, *Reformation and Modern Rituals and Theologies of Baptism* (Aldershot, 2006); E. C. Whitaker and M. E. Johnson, *Documents of the Baptismal Liturgy* (London, ^{3}2003); D. F. Wright, *Infant Baptism in Historical Perspective* (Milton Keynes, 2007); D. F. Wright, *What Has Infant Baptism Done to Baptism?* (Milton Keynes, 2005); L. J. Vander Zee, *Christ, Baptism and the Lord's Supper* (Downers Grove, 2004); E. Yarnold, *The Awe-Inspiring Rites of Initiation* (Edinburgh, ^{2}1994).

A. R. Cross

BAPTISM IN THE SPIRIT

Three assertions generated this phrase: John the Baptist's, that whereas he baptized with water, his successor would baptize in (*en*) the *Holy Spirit (Mark 1:8; cf. Matt. 3:11; Luke 3:16; John 1:33); Jesus', that his disciples would soon be baptized in the Holy Spirit (Acts 1:5;

cf. 11:16); and Paul's, that Christians have been baptized in one Spirit into one body (1 Cor. 12:13). The idea of Spirit-baptism became theologically and devotionally important when it was taken to signify a post-conversion blessing of life-transforming significance. This occurred occasionally in *Wesleyanism, widely in nineteenth-century evangelical *pietism, and universally in twentieth-century *Pentecostalism with its worldwide charismatic offshoots.

Biblical

In these three assertions, Spirit-baptism appears not as a technical term with normative force, but as a theological image denoting the spiritual reality that water-*baptism signifies: namely, unitive, regenerative, purificatory and purgative initiation into the death and risen life of the now glorified Lord Jesus Christ, the divine Saviour (see Rom. 6:1–11; Col. 2:11–14; 1 Pet. 3:21–22; *Salvation). Baptism as such is a symbolic washing, and the conceptual parallel is that both baptisms carry the thought of dirt being washed off the begrimed, thus fitting them for *fellowship with God, water-baptism signifying the inner cleansing that Spirit-baptism actually imparts. At and after Pentecost this Spirit-baptism was constantly accompanied by tongues and prophecy celebrating Christ (Acts 2:4; 10:44–47), and absence of this accompaniment among groups was thought anomalous (Acts 8:12–17; 19:1–6), though whether every single Christian received these charismata is not made clear. Though water-baptism and the gift of the Spirit were held to belong together as aspects of initiation into Christ (Acts 2:38; 10:47), they did not always go together in time (8:12–17).

Historical

In ancient and medieval theology, baptism in the Spirit was not a subject of focused discussion. Prevailing *sacramental realism assimilated Spirit-baptism into water-baptism and proclaimed baptismal regeneration. Later, Protestant pietism developed in various ways the idea that the apostolic experience of Acts 2 is a paradigmatic model and a personal necessity for all Christians, thus:

(1) John Fletcher (1729–85), Wesley's designated successor, and some later Reformed teachers also, spoke of repeatable baptisms in the Spirit, meaning intensifyings of *assurance and enhanced enablings for holy living and powerful witness.

(2) Charles *Finney, D. L. Moody (1837–99), R. A. Torrey (1856–1928), Andrew *Murray, A. B. Simpson (1844–1919) and others, echoing this, adjusted it in different ways to the *Wesleyan idea of a single 'second-blessing' experience that raises one's life to a permanently new level (see *Holiness movements).

(3) Pentecostals and *charismatics generally see Spirit-baptism in this essentially Wesleyan way, but broaden the concept, relating it to full reception, recognition and/or release of the Spirit within one, in assurance, emotional exuberance, *glossolalia*, uninhibited liberty in speaking for Christ, and the blossoming of all kinds of gifts of *ministry, including in some cases (so it is claimed) prophetic and healing gifts. Tongues are often made the touchstone of Spirit-baptism (see *Gifts of the Spirit).

Theological

Guidelines for theologizing baptism in the Holy Spirit would seem to include the following:

(1) Since, biblically, the concept is initiatory, it is not proper to view Spirit-baptism as essentially a post-conversion blessing, however much particular post-conversion experiences may match initiatory experiences recorded in Acts.

(2) Since the reason why the apostles had a two-stage Christian experience was that they became believers before the Spirit's full new-covenant ministry, which Jesus promised (John 14:16–17; 15:26; 16:7–15), actually began; and since they themselves expected others to enjoy that ministry from conversion on (Acts 2:38; 5:32; cf. 9:17–18), it is not proper to make the two-stage experience a universal norm.

(3) Since the characteristic core of all so-called Spirit-baptism experiences is the intensifying of assurance as the Spirit witnesses to God's saving love in our reconciliation and adoption, and to our security in that love, it is best to theologize these experiences in just those terms, as Paul does in Rom. 5:5; 8:15–17, 31–39 (cf. John 14:16–23).

(4) Since believers receive the Holy Spirit to indwell them simultaneously with, indeed as part of, their life-giving *union with Christ through *faith, it is not proper to construe any post-conversion experiences of and in the Spirit as receiving him, on the supposition he had not been within us before; and Luke's narrative reference to the Spirit falling on and being given to and received by the Samaritans should be understood simply of charismatic manifestations (Acts 8:14–17).

(5) Since deep experience of intensified assurance (the 'seal' or 'witness' of the Spirit, as the Puritans called it) is rare and desirable, it will be proper to ask God constantly to lead us into it, by whatever name we call it and in whatever theological frame we set it. All Christians always need to enter more deeply, through the communion and commitment that penitent faith in Christ brings, into the experienced reality of Christ's resurrection life, which is what the image of Spirit-baptism is ultimately about.

Bibliography

C. O. Brand (ed.), *Perspectives on Spirit Baptism: Five Views* (Nashville, 2004); F. D. Bruner, *A Theology of the Holy Spirit* (Grand Rapids, 1970); J. D. G. Dunn, *Baptism in the Holy Spirit* (London, 1970); K. McDonnell and G. T. Montague, *Christian Initiation and Baptism in the Holy Spirit: Evidence from the First Eight Centuries* (Collegeville, 1991); J. I. Packer, *Keep in Step with the Spirit* (Grand Rapids and Leicester UK, ²2005); T. Smail, *Reflected Glory* (London, 1976); K. D. Yun, *Baptism in the Holy Spirit: An Ecumenical Theology of Spirit Baptism* (Lanham, 2003).

J. I. PACKER

BAPTIST THEOLOGY

Baptists share certain characteristics of belief and practice generally, despite variation across various Baptist bodies. First, Baptists have held that the church must be regenerated anew each generation, so insisting upon personal confession of Christ as Lord (see *conversion) and believers' *baptism upon this confession. Discipleship, understood as following Jesus, and concomitant growth in holiness have been likewise important convictions. They have in the third place shown a concern to ground faith and practice in scriptural teaching and patterns, a conviction that has led to elements of their diversity in the absence of a normative interpretive tradition. Finally, Baptists have valued freedom, as demonstrated by their congregational polity and historic commitment to religious freedom in the civil realm. One would be justified in saying freedom has been the core of Baptist theological identity.

As important as these broad commonalities are on a basic level, Baptists are at least as diverse as they are united. 'From their beginnings . . . Baptists have demonstrated beliefs and practices so diverse as to make it difficult to compile a consistent list of distinctives applicable to all segments of the movement at all times' (B. J. Leonard, *Baptist Ways*, Valley Forge, 2003, p. 1). Adequate grasp of Baptist theology must take account of this diversity. Baptists can point to no single founding figure or event emerging and growing strong in various milieus. This is but one of several factors that have produced great diversity among Baptists throughout the world. A comprehensive and universally acknowledged theological tradition is impossible. Thus, while various Baptist bodies have produced confessions and catechisms, there is no normative Baptist theology from which the challenges of particular settings may be addressed.

Because Baptists have no touchstone by which doctrine may be stated and judged even in dissent, history emerges as a crucial factor in their theological identity, both historically and currently. There are two principal consequences. First, Baptists have shown greater pliability of identity as they define themselves either within or against their social, political, intellectual and religious contexts. These contexts include most notably Calvinism, Arminianism, various millenarianisms, revivalism, Pietism, Tractarianism, liberalism, modernism and fundamentalism; but also Jeffersonian republicanism, Jacksonian anti-elitism, laissez-faire capitalism, Communism and consumerism. Second, arguments about Baptists' theological identity tend to be arguments about their *history. Mercer University historian Walter Shurden has observed, '[T]heological identity for [Baptists] is inevitably related to historical origins and subsequent history' ('The Baptist Identity and the Baptist Manifesto', *PRS* 25, 1998, p. 321). Ironically, while claims for Baptist theological identity purport to be the outworking of Baptist history, quite often one finds interpretations of Baptist history guided by uncritical theological presuppositions.

One may see both of these consequences in Baptist understanding of *freedom throughout their history. Baptists appeared in the English-speaking world first in the seventeenth century, emerging from *Puritanism. Their beliefs and practices evinced a passion for freedom, above all the freedom of God. Sharing the Reformed impulse against idolatry, they believed that God was to be free from all forms of human encroachment upon divine prerogative. On this basis, they rejected the union of church and state. In such union, the state arrogated to itself that which is God's due alone: to bring persons into the community of the redeemed. Likewise, on this basis they rejected infant baptism by both established and dissenting churches, which they saw as similar usurpation of divine right. Indeed, they refused all claims of *ex opere operato* sacramentalism and claims that any church and its rites are necessary for salvation. Yet they also affirmed that God is free to bring persons to salvation through the word and Holy Spirit, embodied in and mediated through the life of the community of faith. From this affirmation, they affirmed the ecumenical creeds, sacraments of baptism and the Lord's Supper, and the church where the word was truly preached and sacraments duly administered were all necessary to salvation. Human and divine freedom are incommensurate, and so human beings cannot cast aside that which God has ordained.

Particularly in the United States, following the Revolution and informed by the liberal democracy of the new republic, Baptists underwent a shift in thinking. Freedom was still crucial, but throughout the nineteenth century and beyond, human freedom was emphasized. They still rejected the church-state union and infant baptism, but on the basis of their infringement on free human conscience. More significantly, they rejected sacraments as such and creeds on the same basis, something earlier Baptists had explicitly warned against. Sharing in the American impulse against tradition's authority and resulting loss of historical awareness, Baptists came soon to project the pre-eminence of human freedom onto their forebears, claiming that Baptists had always held this view. The decisive expression of this came in 1908 when E. Y. Mullins declared that the historical significance of Baptists was their consistent championing of the competency of the soul in religion. This perspective has informed much Baptist theology through the twentieth century. It is unable, however, to offer a consistent interpretation of the earliest Baptists who affirmed certain ecclesial practices that more recent Baptists have rejected in the name of being Baptist. Yet because tradition is dismissed, heritage is more often invoked than interrogated.

The past two decades have seen the emergence of considerable vitality in Baptist theology. The past is being more carefully interrogated by a growing number of scholars, with the result of less parochial, more ecumenically engaged and aware, Baptist theologies. Signal among these efforts has been the three-volume theology of James Wm. McClendon, Jr, written from a more inclusive 'baptist' orientation. Also significant has been work by historians David Bebbington and Bill J. Leonard and theologians Stephen R. Holmes and Curtis W. Freeman; monographs in the Studies in Baptist History and Thought (SBHT) series by Paul S. Fiddes and Steven R. Harmon; the collected volumes *Baptist Sacramentalism* and *Recycling the Past or Researching History?* in SBHT; and Chris Ellis's *Gathering*, the first Baptist liturgical theology. Emerging as significant in recent years have been non-Anglo-American Baptists Puerto-Rican Orlando Costas, Latvian Valdis Teraudkalns, Estonian Tarmo Toom and Nigerian Osadolor Imasogie.

See also: CHURCH; CHURCH GOVERNMENT.

Bibliography

D. W. Bebbington, *Baptists Through the Centuries* (Waco, 2004); A. R. Cross and P. E. Thompson (eds.), *Baptist Sacramentalism*, SBHT 5 (Carlisle and Waynesboro, 2003); C. J. Ellis, *Gathering: A Theology and Spirituality of Worship in the Free Church Tradition* (London, 2004); P. S. Fiddes, *Tracks and Traces: Baptist Identity in Church and Theology*, SBHT 13 (Carlisle and Waynesboro, 2003); C. W. Freeman, *Contesting Catholicity: Theology for Other Baptists* (Waco, 2014); S. R. Harmon, *Towards Baptist Catholicity: Essays on Tradition and the Baptist Vision*, SBHT 27 (Carlisle and Waynesboro, 2006); B. A. Harvey, *Can These Bones Live? A Catholic Baptist Engagement with Ecclesiology, Hermeneutics, and Social Theory* (Grand Rapids, 2008); S. R. Holmes, *Baptist Theology* (London, 2012); W. L. Lumpkin and B. J. Leonard, *Baptist Confessions of Faith*, 2nd revd edn (Valley Forge, 1959, 2011); J. W. McClendon, Jr, *Systematic Theology*, 3 vols. (Waco, 2012).

P. E. THOMPSON

BARCLAY, ROBERT, see QUAKER THEOLOGY

BARCLAY, WILLIAM (1907–78)

A Scottish biblical scholar, Barclay was born in Wick, and educated at Glasgow and Marburg.

He ministered on industrial Clydeside before his appointment in 1947 as lecturer in New Testament (professor from 1964) at Glasgow University. He combined classical scholarship with an ability to communicate with all classes, whether in shipyard, lecture room, print, or through television. His *Daily Study Bible* (NT) series sold some 1.5 million copies, was translated into numerous languages including Burmese and Estonian, and brought him a further ministry through correspondence worldwide. Theologically, he called himself a '*liberal evangelical'. He claimed to be the only member of his divinity faculty who believed Matthew, Luke and John wrote the Gospels attributed to them. Nonetheless, he was a *universalist, reticent about the inspiration of *Scripture, critical of the doctrine of substitutionary *atonement, and given to views about the *virgin birth and *miracles which conservatives would find either heretical or imprecise. He once described *Bultmann as the most evangelical preacher he had ever heard, because all his writings aimed at confronting the individual with Christ. In the context of marked decline in Church of Scotland membership, he deplored the virtual disappearance of *church discipline and suggested a two-tier category of membership: those 'deeply attracted to Jesus Christ', and those prepared to make total commitment.

Bibliography

Selected works: *Testament of Faith* (London, 1975), also published as *A Spiritual Autobiography* (Grand Rapids, 1975).
Studies: R. D. Kernohan (ed.), *William Barclay: The Plain Uncommon Man* (London, 1980); J. Martin, *William Barclay* (Edinburgh, 1984); C. L. Rawlins, *William Barclay: The Authorized Biography* (London, 1998).

J. D. Douglas

BARMEN DECLARATION

The Barmen Declaration (1934) comprised six articles issued by German Protestant representatives in opposition to the Nazi-supported 'German-Christian' movement. When it became increasingly clear that the latter was adding extreme nationalism and anti-Semitism to a theologically liberal stance, Martin Niemöller (1892–1984) and other pastors, including Dietrich *Bonhoeffer, organized the first synod of the *Confessing Church at Barmen in the Ruhr. German-Christians had gained ascendancy in some regional churches and probably intimidated others, but to Barmen came representatives from Lutheran, Reformed and United churches. The declaration did not purport to be a comprehensive statement, but against contemporary deviations it stressed the headship and finality of Christ, and the pre-eminence of Scripture for belief and as the guide to practical action for Christians. There was pointed repudiation of the German-Christian subordination of Christ's church to the state. Written mainly by Karl *Barth, the Barmen Declaration was very much a document born out of political developments of the age, and pointed out the fatal fallacy of any compromise with National Socialism under Hitler.

Bibliography

Text in J. H. Leith, *Creeds of the Churches* (Richmond, ²1973) and, with discussion, in W. Niesel, *Reformed Symbolics* (Edinburgh and London, 1962).

J. D. Douglas

BARTH, KARL (1886–1968)

Karl Barth was the most significant theologian of the twentieth century. His multi-volume *Church Dogmatics* (CD) constitutes the weightiest contribution to Protestant theology since *Schleiermacher.

Life

Born into a Swiss theological family, Barth studied in Berne, Berlin, Tübingen and Marburg under some of the leading teachers of the day, notably *Harnack and *Herrmann, and after a brief period working for the journal *Die christliche Welt* (*The Christian World*) and as an assistant pastor in Geneva, he became a village pastor at Safenwil in the Aargau (1911–21). Over the course of his ministry there Barth became increasingly dismayed with the resources of his *liberal theological education, and his gradual rediscovery of Scripture as revelation eventually led to his explosive commentary on Romans. From 1921 to 1930 he taught in Göttingen and Münster, played a leading role in the co-called '*dialectical theology' movement, and published very widely, including an abortive prolegomena volume *Christian Dogmatics*. After moving to Bonn, Barth began the *CD*, and became increasingly involved in opposition to Hitler, giving substantial theological weight to the *Confessing Church, notably at the *Barmen Synod in 1934. This led to his dismissal, and appointment to a chair in his native Basel, where he remained for the rest of his career and retirement, and where the several volumes of the (finally unfinished) *CD* were written.

Decisive for an understanding of his earlier thought is his eventual rejection of the liberal heritage of his theological mentors. Along with his fellow-pastor, Eduard Thurneysen (1888–1974), Barth became increasingly dissatisfied with the historico-critical method as a way of handling Scripture. Combined with a reading of *Kierkegaard, *Nietzsche, *Dostoevsky and Franz Overbeck (1837–1905), Barth's rejection of liberal constructions of the Christian faith led to a renewed emphasis on the eschatological, supernatural element of Christianity. His refusal of any synthesis between the church and culture was given a further decisive twist under the influence of Christoph Blumhardt's (1842–1919) radical Christian socialism, and of thinkers such as Hermann Kütter (1863–1931) and Leonhard Ragaz (1868–1945). The fruits of these profound mutations in theological outlook are to be found in Barth's sermons and occasional writings during the First World War, but above all in *The Epistle to the Romans*.

Commentary on Romans

First published in 1919 and then completely rewritten for a second edition in 1922, the commentary is not so much an exegesis as a sustained and intense reflection on what Barth would later call 'the Godness of God'. Into the book Barth poured all his discontent with the synthesis of God and man which he found in the liberal religious ideal, and emphasized the radical disjunction between God and man in which God became man's interrogator, the one who initiates a crisis in the continuity of human history. Both the content and the style of the book are at times *apocalyptic, and it attracted heavy criticism from the academic establishment. Nevertheless, Barth, now a professor, continued his assault on the heartlands of liberalism. He followed his work on Romans with expositions of 1 Corinthians 15 (1924) and of Philippians (1927), and in a famous published debate with Harnack in 1923 criticized the historico-critical method (which for Harnack was the expression of disciplined inquiry into objective truth) for its failure to treat Scripture as a revelation which disturbs. An early collection of essays, *The Word of God and the Word of Man*, develops Barth's hostility to human *religion, and similarly his published lectures from the 1920s demonstrate how radical was his confrontation with what he understood as the theology of subjectivity, as in his Göttingen lectures on Schleiermacher (1923–4) and in the slightly later Münster lectures on ethics (1928–9).

Dogmatics

Towards the end of the 1920s Barth began serious work on dogmatics, and his *Christian Dogmatics in Outline* was published in 1927. Barth later came to see this volume as a halfway house between the writings of the earlier 1920s and the *CD*. Whilst more constructive than the earlier ground-clearing writings, it retained vestiges of liberal Protestant theological method, which Barth finally corrected only through intensive study of *Anselm. It was through his reading of Anselm, partly in debate with the philosopher Heinrich Scholz (1884–1956), that Barth left behind the 'dialectical theology' of his earlier period, and was able to expand a more solid basis for dogmatics than had been afforded either by the theologians of the religious consciousness or by his own eschatological and frequently aggressive rejection of their work. Barth's work on Anselm's theological procedure (which bore fruit as *Fides Quaerens Intellectum* [*Faith Seeking Understanding*] in 1931) enabled him to clarify the relationship between faith and rational inquiry (see *Faith and reason) in a more sophisticated way than the earlier debate with Harnack, and so furnished the methodological underpinnings for the *CD*. In particular, Barth came to envisage theology as an inquiry moulded by the object into which it inquires; the theologian's task is not to establish the object of inquiry (by, for example, naturally available 'proof' of God) but to be guided by the inherent rationality of the object itself. Theology presupposes an objective order of being, apprehended in the church's Credo, which alone provides the basis for rational discourse about God. Associated with this work on *theological method is Barth's polemical rejection of *natural theology in debate with an earlier fellow traveller, Emil *Brunner, and a series of expositions of creeds and Reformation confessions.

In Bonn and then in Basel, in the midst of a host of controversial political and theological concerns, Barth began work on the *CD*. Originally delivered as lectures and then revised for publication, the *CD* is, for all its inner consistency, the record of a process of growth and change over thirty years: Barth is not simply mapping out a system. Perhaps the most remarkable feature of the work is Barth's ceaseless capacity for astonishment: at one level, the *CD* is the record of Barth's captivation by the sheer weight, beauty and variety of Christian truth.

The heart of the enterprise, both methodologically and substantively, is *Christology. For Barth, Christology is not simply one doctrine alongside others, but the centre from which all other Christian doctrines radiate. Because of this, Barth's theological procedure takes a distinctive form: Christian doctrine is constructed by inference from the person of Jesus Christ, who is the locus of all truth about God and man. This leads not only to Barth's resolute *realism and his hostility to all abstract metaphysical or anthropological foundations for theology, but also to his distinctive handling of *analogy. In effect, Barth reverses the usual direction of analogy: instead of moving by analogy from the known realities of creation towards knowledge of the divine, Barth moves from God in Christ as the fundamental given towards affirmations concerning creation and humanity. It is the profundity of Barth's exploration of this theocentricity which makes the *CD* one of the most important pieces of Protestant theology.

The *CD* as it stands comprises four volumes, on the doctrine of the word of God, the doctrine of God, the doctrine of creation, and an unfinished volume on the doctrine of reconciliation. A fifth volume on the doctrine of redemption was projected but never begun before Barth's death. Each volume is subdivided into part-volumes, expounding and meditating on a series of theses, and includes a great wealth of detailed historical and exegetical discussion, as well as treatment of the ethical consequences of the main dogmatic discussion. Volume one weaves together the doctrines of *revelation and the Trinity, proposing that theology takes its rise from the self-positing of the divine subject. Revelation, as God's gracious self-repetition, creates the experience of faith in the church, and constitutes man as a recipient of God's word, which is God's self-disclosure. The theological task is that of the self-scrutiny of the church against its objective referent, from which theology receives its status as a science.

From the outset, Barth's consistent theological realism is evident: his starting point, quite different either from his liberal heritage or from his contemporary *existentialist peers, is the given actuality of the self-revealing God. This surfaces in volume two in the discussion of the *knowledge of God, the capacity for which resides not in man's readiness for God, but in God's readiness to share his own knowledge of himself with man: God's self-knowledge is graciously reduplicated in the receiver of revelation. Accordingly, Barth expounds a severely negative evaluation of natural theology and of what he understood to be traditional doctrines of analogy. The discussion of the being of God in volume two is one of the most important treatments of the theme since *Calvin. God's being is described as his being-in-act, that is to say, God is himself or becomes himself in the loving act of creating fellowship with man in Jesus Christ. In effect, Barth radically recasts the doctrine of God by making the person of Christ central for theology proper. God's absoluteness is therefore nothing other than his freedom for loving action. And similarly, the doctrine of election is a statement about God's choice to be himself in Jesus Christ, and so to choose humankind as his covenant partner, who is given the task of obedience to the divine command.

The reality of man as God's partner is treated at length in volume three. Barth refuses to handle the doctrine of *creation as a truth that is naturally available. Instead, he links creation to covenant: man's creatureliness derives from his adoption into the covenant of God with humankind made actual in Jesus Christ, who is both electing God and elected man. Thus history and human being as such are what they are because of God's own assumption of historical, creaturely existence in the incarnation. Barth expounds the theme in particularly significant discussions of human temporality and human sin, again rigorously deploying the method of analogy from Christology, which comes to assume an increasingly large role in the argument.

When Barth turns to Christology in volume four, his style and thinking become increasingly concrete. At the time when Barth was working on volume four, he published an important essay on 'The Humanity of God', in which he corrected some of his earlier 'dialectical' thinking, and focused with even greater concentration on the man *Jesus as the beginning and end of the ways of God with man. In this late stage of the growth of the *CD*, his writing becomes increasingly narrative in its handling of the Christological theme of abasement and exaltation. The ethical section of volume four, which was never finished (parts were published as a last fragment, *CD* IV.4, and parts as the posthumous *The Christian Life*), contains an increasingly realistic account of human ethical agency. This is expounded in Barth's handling of water-baptism, whose sacramental status Barth denies in order to affirm its proper character as a human act of obedient response. Volume four is the maturest expression of Barth's convictions about Jesus Christ the God-man, who furnishes a character-description of God and the origin of human participation in the covenant of God and creation. These writings also contain many suggestions for revision of aspects of his earlier theology, notably in their increasingly interactive account of the relationship of God and the natural order.

After retirement, Barth worked a little more on the *CD*, took a lively interest in the work of Vatican II, and published some smaller pieces, including his final lectures at Basel, *Evangelical Theology*. A full appraisal of his work would need to take note of his published sermons in Basel prison, *Deliverance to the Captives and Call for God*, his collections of essays such as *Against the Stream* and *Theology and Church*, and his reflections on past theologians and philosophers in *Protestant Theology in the Nineteenth Century*.

Interpretations

Barth's work substantially affected the course of Protestant theology in Europe and beyond; although Barth resisted pressure to become the centre of a school, his work has been interpreted and extended by many, notably H. Gollwitzer (1908–93), O. Weber (1902–66) and E. *Jüngel in Germany, and T. F. *Torrance in Britain. Critical appraisal of Barth often focuses on his account of the relation of God to his creation, asking whether his method and his fundamental theological convictions lead him into offering only an ambiguous affirmation of the value and reality of the natural order. In terms of his account of the knowledge of God, *Pannenberg, for example, argues that Barth's confidence in the self-evidence of the object of theology leads him into a *fideism which refuses to offer any sort of bridges between the knowledge of revelation and knowledge of the human world. Something of the same set of issues emerge in discussions of Barth's doctrine of man. Some critics suggest that by grounding the reality of man so completely in the humanity of God in Christ, Barth fails to give real weight to the natural order. Hence in his account of human freedom, sin and rejection of God, some find a lack of a real sense of man over against God. Or again, in the ethical sections of *CD*, particularly before volume four, he is interpreted as having so grounded man's agency in Christ that the impetus for human obedience is removed, and sanctification is not recognizable as a human process. Catholic theologians in particular sense an 'actualism' or 'occasionalism' in Barth's *anthropology, in that he does not appear to lay sufficient emphasis on the continuity of man as the recipient of divine grace. The effect of Barth's concentration on Christology upon his doctrine of the Trinity forms another area of discussion. By envisaging the Spirit as essentially the 'applicatory' or 'subjective' dimension of the work of Christ, Barth seems to lack a fully personalist account of the Spirit as a distinct divine agent. This is bound up with more general questions about the apparent 'modalism' (see *Monarchianism), in that his preference for the term 'mode of being' rather than 'person' suggests a high evaluation of the divine unity at the expense of a proper sense of plurality within God.

Many critiques of Barth are flawed by treating his theology too systematically, without sensing the checks and balances within the corpus of his work. Barth's great strength perhaps above all was his ability to keep starting again. The several changes of course within his work were far from fickle; much more were they part of his restless reappraisal of his own thinking, and they bear witness to his ruthlessly interrogative and constantly fresh engagement with the matter of theology. Barth never settled down, and his readings of Scripture as well as of classical theologians from the past – Calvin and Schleiermacher above all – were constantly submitted to reappraisal and critique. Barth's work is not simply a persuasive restatement of the main lines of the Christian faith; it also constitutes one of the major critical responses to the *Enlightenment, with a significant place in the intellectual history of Europe.

Bibliography

Works: *Collected Works: Gesamtausgabe* (Zurich, 1971–). *Academic Writings*: for a useful chronological bibliography see E. Busch, Karl Barth (London, 1976). *Chief Works*: *The Christian Life* (Edinburgh, 1981); *CD*, I:1–IV:4; *Credo* (London, 1936); *Dogmatics in Outline* (London, 1949); *The Epistle to the Romans* (Oxford, 1935); *Ethics* (Edinburgh, 1981); *Evangelical Theology* (London, 1963); *Fides Quaerens Intellectum* (London, 1960); *The Göttingen Dogmatics*, 2 vols. (Grand Rapids, 1990–93); *The Humanity of God* (London, 1961); *The Knowledge of God and the Service of God* (London, 1938); *Prolegomena zur christlichen Dogmatik* (Munich, 1928); *Protestant Theology in the Nineteenth Century* (London, 1972); *The Resurrection of the Dead* (London, 1933); *Theology and Church* (London, 1962); *The Theology of Schleiermacher* (Edinburgh, 1982); *The Word of God and the Word of Man* (London, 1928).

Studies: See bibliography in M. Kwiran, *An Index of Literature on Barth, Bonhoeffer and Bultmann* (*Sonderheft to Theologische Zeitschrift*, 1977). See especially: H. U. von Balthasar, *The Theology of Karl Barth* (New York, 1971); G. C. Berkouwer, *The Triumph of Grace in the Theology of Karl Barth* (London and Grand Rapids, 1956); G. W. Bromiley, *An Introduction to the Theology of Karl Barth* (Edinburgh, 1980); C. Brown, *Karl Barth and the Christian Message* (London, 1967); Sung Wook Chung, *Karl Barth and Evangelical Theology* (Milton Keynes/Grand Rapids, 2006); C. Gunton, *Becoming and Being* (Oxford, 1978); idem, *The Barth Lectures* (London, 2007); T. Hart, *Regarding Karl Barth* (Carlisle, 1999); E. Jüngel, *Barth-Studien* (Gütersloh, 1982); idem, *The Doctrine of the Trinity* (Edinburgh, 1976); idem, *Karl Barth: A Theological Legacy* (Edinburgh, 1987); H. Küng, *Justification* (London, 1964); B. L. McCormack, *Karl Barth's Critically Realistic Dialectic Theology* (Oxford, 1997); idem, *Orthodox and Modern: Studies in the Theology of Karl Barth* (Grand Rapids, 2008); K. Runia, *Karl Barth's Doctrine of Holy Scripture* (Grand Rapids, 1962); S. W. Sykes (ed.), *Karl Barth* (Oxford, 1979); J. Thompson, *Christ in Perspective* (Edinburgh, 1978); T. F. Torrance, *Karl Barth* (London, 1962); J. Webster, *Barth* (London/New York, 2000); J. Webster (ed.), *The Cambridge Companion to Karl Barth* (Cambridge, 2000); R. E. Willis, *The Ethics of Karl Barth* (Leiden, 1971).

J. B. WEBSTER

BASIL OF CAESAREA (c. 329–379)

Basil of Caesarea, also called Basil the Great, was the leading figure of the group of three Cappadocian Fathers who championed Nicene orthodoxy against the *Arians in the later fourth century. *Gregory of Nazianzus, the second of the group, formed a close friendship with Basil while they were students in Athens. The third member of the group, Basil's younger brother, *Gregory of Nyssa, was educated at home. On returning to Cappadocia, Basil devoted himself to an *ascetic and devotional life and became a pioneer of coenobitic monasticism. He and Gregory of Nazianzus compiled an influential selection from the writings of *Origen, the Philocalia. Basil's intellectual and administrative gifts led to his election as metropolitan bishop of Caesarea, the Cappadocian capital, in 372. After the death of *Athanasius the following year, he was the chief pillar of orthodoxy in the East, defending the deity of the Son and Spirit against Arians and Pneumatomachi. He thus became the chief architect of the Cappadocian doctrine of the *Trinity, which became definitive for East and West. He was also a noted liturgist.

Basil's two most important works are *Against Eunomius*, a reply to extreme Arianism, and *On the Holy Spirit*. Eunomius argued that since only creatures were begotten, the Son, being begotten, could not be God. Basil denies that 'unbegottenness' is an adequate definition of the essence of God, and defends the doctrine (inherited from Origen and Athanasius) of the eternal generation of the Son (see *Christology). The generation of creatures is physical and temporal. The generation of the Son is ineffable and eternal.

Basil's second main treatise, *On the Holy Spirit*, written to defend the glorifying of the Spirit in his doxology, must be set against the emergence of the so-called Macedonians and Pneumatomachi, who denied the deity of the *Spirit. Basil clearly accepts the deity of the Spirit in his letters, but stops short in this treatise of declaring in so many words that the Spirit is God and consubstantial (*homoousion*) with the Father. This was politic, not giving his enemies an opportunity to dethrone him, and diplomatic. Without offending those hesitant to make an explicit confession of the Spirit's deity, he argued that the Spirit cannot be a creature (the only alternative to being creator) and is to be worshipped.

Here Basil makes his distinctive contribution to trinitarian doctrine. Athanasius and the older Nicenes had defended the deity of the Son by insisting that he was consubstantial (*homoousios*) with, of the same essence or *substance (*ousia*) as, the Father. Basil made a distinction between *ousia* and *hypostasis* (which, confusingly, may also be literally translated as 'substance'), hitherto used interchangeably. He spoke of one *ousia* of God, but three *hypostaseis*, the *hypostasis* of the Father, the *hypostasis* of the Son, and the *hypostasis* of the Holy Spirit. This became the definitive doctrine of the Trinity in the East. Cappadocian doctrine greatly influenced the West through *Ambrose, although the West began from the oneness of God and spoke of three 'persons'.

Bibliography

Selected Works in ET in *NPNF*, 2nd series, vol. 8, and in FC series.

Studies: L. Ayers, *Nicaea and Its Legacy* (Oxford, 2004), pp. 187–221; P. J. Fedwick, *The Church and the Charisma of Leadership in Basil of Caesarea* (Toronto, 1979); idem (ed.), *Basil of Caesarea: Christian, Humanist, Ascetic*, 2 vols. (Toronto, 1981); J. N. D. Kelly, *Early Christian Doctrines* (London, ⁵1977); G. L. Prestige, *God in Patristic Thought* (London, 1952); idem, *St Basil the Great and Apollinaris of Laodicea* (London, 1956); P. Rousseau, *Basil of Caesarea* (Berkeley, 1994); I. P. Sheldon-Williams in *CHLGEMP*, pp. 432–438; E. Venables in *DCB* 1, pp. 282–297.

T. A. NOBLE

BAUR, F. C., see TÜBINGEN SCHOOL

BAVINCK, HERMAN (1854–1921)

In 1882 Herman Bavinck was appointed professor of dogmatic theology in the Reformed Seminary at Kampen, Netherlands. In 1902 he took the same chair in the Free University, Amsterdam, as the successor to Dr Abraham *Kuyper who had become prime minister. Bavinck was an outstanding theologian, deeply rooted in the Reformed tradition. Although he had a thorough knowledge and deep appreciation of post-Calvinian theology, he preferred to go back to *Calvin himself. At the same time he wanted to develop *Reformed theology in constant interaction with the theological and philosophical thinking of his own day. His major work is his four-volume *Reformed Dogmatics* (*Gereformeerde Dogmatiek*, ⁴1928–30). Characteristic of his method is his firm foundation in biblical theology, his thorough grasp of historical theology and his synthetic approach. He always tried to incorporate all elements of truth which he found in other theological systems. Within Reformed theology itself, he tried to bring various strands of thought together in a new synthesis (e.g. infra- and supralapsarianism – see *Predestination; creationism and traducianism – see *Soul, Origin of). In the Netherlands his *Reformed Dogmatics* is still regarded as a standard work.

Bibliography

Works in ET: *The Philosophy of Revelation* (Grand Rapids, 1953); *The Doctrine of God*, vol. 2 of *Gereformeerde Dogmatiek* (Grand Rapids, 1955); *Our Reasonable Faith*, a popularized version of *Gereformeerde Dogmatiek* (Grand Rapids, 1956).

Studies: E. P. Heideman, *The Relation of Revelation and Reason in E. Brunner and H. Bavinck* (Assert, 1959); C. Jaarsma, *The Educational Philosophy of H. Bavinck* (Grand Rapids, 1935); B. Kruithof, *The Relation of Christianity and Culture in the Teaching of Herman Bavinck* (Edinburgh, 1955); *Scottish Bulletin of Evangelical Theology* 29:1 (Bavinck Issue, Spring 2011).

K. RUNIA

BAVINCK, JOHAN HERMAN (1859–1964)

A nephew of Herman *Bavinck, Johan Bavinck studied theology in Amsterdam and Erlangen. His doctoral dissertation (1919) dealt with the medieval mystic Henry Suso (c. 1295–1366). He served as a minister in the Dutch East Indies and then in Holland at Heemstede, where he studied and wrote on psychology. On his return to the East Indies to Java, his knowledge of religious psychology and mysticism enabled him to communicate the gospel effectively to

Javanese mystics. In 1934 he published a book on the confrontation between the gospel and Eastern *mysticism.

He spent over fifteen years as a missionary, including a few years teaching theology in Jokja, and in 1939 became the first professor of *missiology in the Kampen seminary of the Reformed Churches of the Netherlands, and also professor extraordinary of missiology at the Free University of Amsterdam. From 1955 he combined the latter position with the chair of homiletics, liturgy and pastoralia at the Free University.

Although very well-versed in mysticism, psychology and non-Christian religions, and hence sensitive to the demands of the missionary approach, Bavinck was an ardent opponent of *syncretism and compromise of the gospel. Salvation in Jesus Christ was quite different from the salvation offered by the (mystical) religions, he explained in a book on religious awareness and the Christian faith in 1949. His major work, translated as *An Introduction to the Science of Missions* (Philadelphia, 1960), emphasized both the missionary's call to share the life and culture of the community around him and the vast gap between the Christian faith and non-Christian religions. Superficial similarities when investigated become profound differences. One of his last books, on religions and worldviews in 1961, stressed the uniqueness of the gospel over against attempts to harmonize the world's religions into a common front.

See also: CHRISTIANITY AND OTHER RELIGIONS.

Bibliography

Works in ET: *The Impact of Christianity on the Non-Christian World* (Grand Rapids, 1948); *The Riddle of Life* (Grand Rapids, 1958); *Faith and its Difficulties* (Grand Rapids, 1959); *The Church between Temple and Mosque* (Grand Rapids, 1966).

Studies: J. du Preez, 'Johan Herman Bavinck on the Relation between Divine Revelation and the Religions', *Missionalia* 13, 1985, pp. 111–120; J. Verkuyl, *Contemporary Missiology* (Grand Rapids, 1978); P. J. Visser, *Heart for the Gospel, Heart for the World: The Life and Thought of a Reformed Pioneer Missiologist, Johan Herman Bavinck (1895–1964)* (Eugene, 2003).

J. A. E. VERMAAT

BAXTER, RICHARD (1615–91)

Baxter was a leading *Puritan clergyman. In 1641–42 and 1647–61 (he was a parliamentary army chaplain, 1642–47) he exercised at Kidderminster, Worcestershire, the most fruitful Puritan pastorate anywhere recorded, converting almost the whole town. Under Cromwell's church settlement (establishing Independency) he formed the interdenominational Worcestershire Association of pastors, pledged to practise congregational evangelism by catechizing families and to maintain parochial *church discipline, with member ministers as the informal consistory court. At the Restoration, Baxter was offered the bishopric of Hereford, but declined it. At the 1661 Savoy Conference he pleaded fruitlessly for the non-prelatical, synodical form of episcopacy devised by his deceased friend Archbishop Ussher (1581–1656), and for a Puritan revision of the Prayer Book. After the 1662 ejections he lived in the London area, an acknowledged leader among the ejected, and wrote constantly, becoming the most voluminous of all British theologians.

His output included three folios. *A Christian Directory* (1673) summarizes in a million words all Puritan 'practical', 'experimental', '*casuistical' divinity (i.e. ethical and devotional teaching); *Catholick Theology* (1675), 'Plain, Pure, Peaceable: for the Pacification of the Dogmatical Word-Warriors', as the title proclaimed, embraces Calvinist, Arminian, Lutheran and Roman Catholic (Dominican and Jesuit) views about *grace in a tour de force of ecumenical accommodation; and *Methodus Theologiae Christianae* (1681) is a Ramist-style analysis of Christian truth in Latin, trichotomizing instead of dichotomizing as *Ramus and other Puritans did. Three more landmark books were *The Saints' Everlasting Rest* (1650), an 800-page classic that established Baxter as Puritanism's supreme devotional author; the passionate *Reformed Pastor* (1656; 'Reformed' means not just 'Calvinistic' but 'revived'), a volume which the Broad Church bishop Hensley Henson described in 1925 as 'the best manual of the clergyman's duty in the language'; and the electrifying *Call to the Unconverted* (1658), a pioneer evangelistic pocketbook that sold by tens of thousands. Also, Baxter's elaborate chronicle of his life and times, *Reliquiae Baxterianae* (1696), is a primary and trusted source for seventeenth-century church history.

Miscalled a Presbyterian, Baxter was a reluctant nonconformist who favoured monarchy, national churches, liturgy and episcopacy, and could accept the unsympathetically revised 1662 Prayer Book. But the 1662 Act of Uniformity required renunciation on oath of Puritan ideals of reformation as a condition of incumbency in the restored Church of England, and Baxter balked at that.

Baxter's gospel presents Christ's death as an act of universal *redemption, penal and vicarious though not strictly substitutionary, in virtue of which God has made a new law offering amnesty to penitent breakers of the old law. As obedience to the new law, repentance and faith are one's personal saving righteousness, which effectual calling induces and preserving grace sustains. Called 'Neonomianism', this scheme is substantially *Amyraldian, with *Arminian 'new law' teaching added. Its obvious legalistic tendency, unrecognized by Baxter, was much criticized in his own day. Baxter also argued the reasonableness of Christianity on the basis of its coherence with *natural theology, a method that boomeranged by producing *unitarianism among his English Presbyterian followers after his death.

Bibliography

Works: *Practical Works*, ed. W. Orme, 23 vols. (London, 1830).

Studies: C. F. Allison, *The Rise of Moralism* (London, 1966); W. M. Lamont, *Richard Baxter and the Millennium* (London, 1979); Hugh Martin, *Puritanism and Richard Baxter* (London, 1946); G. F. Nuttall, *Richard Baxter* (London, 1965); F. J. Powicke, *A Life of the Reverend Richard Baxter* (London, 1924); idem, *The Reverend Richard Baxter under the Cross* (London, 1927).

J. I. Packer

BECK, JOHANN TOBIAS (1804–78)

A German biblical theologian, Beck was a professor in Basel (1836–43) and Tübingen (1843–78). Often a lonely campaigner against rationalism and historical criticism, he was influenced by the *pietism of Württemberg, although he was occasionally at variance with individual pietists. While identified with 'biblicism', he cannot be squeezed into any particular mould. Among his pupils were C. A. Auberlen (1824–64) and Martin *Kähler.

A 'Society for the Promotion of Christian-theological Knowledge and Christian Life' took Beck to Basel to create a balance to the criticism of Wilhelm De Wette (1780–1849).

Beck demanded a 'pneumatic exegesis of Scripture'. Without faith it is impossible to arrive at 'an understanding with the spirit of Christianity'. The Bible is a unified system of teaching, 'the faithful image (*Abbild*) of the revelation of which it is the transmitted presentation'. We should be determined by neither the confessions of the church nor dogmatic presuppositions, but by Scripture alone.

The 'divine plan for the world' is expressed in the kingdom of God. The latter is already present but not yet visible. Only God can bring it to pass. Beck believed in the *millennial reign of Christ. Prophecy is a fundamental pillar of the Bible.

Beck presses for 'moral separation' from the world, 'personal appropriation' of the truth, and 'moral purification'. Here *sanctification lives on as the central concern of pietism.

Bibliography

Major work: *Die Christliche Lehr-Wissenschaft nach den Biblischen Urkunden* ('Christian Science of Education according to the Biblical Sources', Stuttgart, 1841); in ET only: *Outlines of Biblical Psychology* (Edinburgh, 1877); *Outlines of Christian Doctrine* (Madras, 1879); *Pastoral Theology of the New Testament* (Edinburgh, 1885).

Studies: K. Barth, *Protestant Theology in the Nineteenth Century* (London, 1972), ch. 25; German life in B. Riggenbach, *Johann Tobias Beck* (Basel, 1888); H. M. Wolf in *TRE* 5, pp. 393–394.

G. Maier

BEING

Being, or *ontology (what there *is*), is a very difficult term to pin down, and different thinkers have meant quite different things by it. Rather than give a survey of different ways in which this term has been used in the philosophical literature, fascinating though that is, what follows is restricted to consideration of several important ways in which this notion has been discussed by theologians, or by those with a theological context in mind. Of particular interest here is what is meant by the use of the term 'being' with respect to God, and with respect to creatures.

In contemporary philosophical theology, *God is often spoken of as a being. This idea has its roots in classical theology, particularly the work of St *Anselm of Canterbury, from whom many contemporary 'perfect-being theologians' take their cue. According to modern Anselmians, God is an entity in the class 'divine', which necessarily has just one instance. He fulfils all the requirements for belonging to such a class (having all great-making properties that are compossible), and is, therefore, God. Much here depends on intuitions about what counts as a great-making property, which is both the strength and Achilles' heel of this way of conceiving the divine being. But, that aside, some think it rather odd to place God in a class of entities called 'divine'. Surely God is *sui generis* and belongs to no *class* of entity whatsoever. Certain medieval theologians thought like this, and came up with a concept of God according to which he is a being like no other: he is, in fact, pure act (*actus purus*). This view of God, which owes much to *Pseudo-Dionysius and *Thomas Aquinas, states that God is without any passivity, or unrealized possibility, because he is without parts. He is a simple, single, timeless act, which has numerous temporal effects in the world. Not only is this classical conception of the divine nature difficult to get one's mind around, it also has the consequence that there is no distinction to be made between God's essence (his 'being') and existence, as there is in all other created entities. If this is true, then God is not at all like the sort of created beings we are used to encountering, if he is a being at all (in anything more than an analogous sense of the word 'being').

Nicholas Wolterstorff has very helpfully distinguished the medieval ontology (doctrine of being) from more modern conceptions. He says medieval ontology was a 'constituent' ontology, according to which objects are composed of various parts (God excepted), which constitute a concrete particular, or given object. A fundamental object in this ontology is a *suppositum*. Yet in the incarnation, we have one entity – the second person of the *Trinity – that assumes a human nature that is not a *suppositum* independent of the Word. Unlike other human beings who are also human persons (you and I included), the relevant '*suppositum*' in the case of the incarnation is the Son of God. He is a divine person with a human nature. So this medieval ontology, with its careful metaphysical distinctions about 'being' had at least one important theological application. But many contemporary metaphysicians speak instead of what Wolterstorff calls a 'relational' ontology whereby entities exemplify properties in relation to other things (e.g. 'being discussed by Crisp', where the referent is Wolterstorff). This also has theological application, but application of a different sort. To return to the example of the *incarnation, in becoming incarnate, God the Son takes upon himself the property of human nature, just as all other humans have the property of human nature. In this respect, *Christ has a relation to all other human beings in virtue of sharing with them the property of human nature.

Modern theologians have thought of the being of God in different ways. *Process theologians, influenced by the work of the Cambridge mathematician-turned-metaphysician, Alfred North Whitehead, think of all reality as composed of events, and construe the divine nature in very untraditional ways as a limited being with the world as his body (*panentheism). But this view is no longer as popular as it once was. Others, like Paul *Tillich, have claimed that God is so exalted that he is beyond being, as such. The idea motivating much of Tillich's concern seems to be that to number God amongst other (created) beings, as one amongst many – even one exalted being amongst many – is to diminish God in some fashion. He is above and beyond our petty conceptualizations of him. But not only that, it turns out on Tillich's theology that God is literally not a being at all. He is supra-being, rather as, in *Kant's transcendental *idealism, the Noumenal is a realm beyond our comprehension or access. This realm exists (just as for Tillich, God 'exists', at least in some attenuated sense of that term), but is forever beyond our grasp.

The British philosophical theologian John *Hick has taken Kantian thought in another direction. He thinks of the Real – the being the *theistic faiths understand as 'God' – as the Kantian noumenal reality. The Real is not a being either, according to Hick, if we mean by that an entity like other entities in some way. For Hick's Real is beyond all conceptualization of it/her/him. We cannot predicate personal or impersonal pronouns of it/her/him because none have purchase in this exalted 'thing' that (somehow) reveals it-/her-/himself to us, or, perhaps, is gropingly conceptualized by us in our partial, incomplete religious traditions. All salvific religions on Hick's way of thinking are strictly speaking false, but approximate attempts at a phenomenological account of that which is noumenal, and therefore beyond our understanding.

Tillich's concept of God (if it is a concept of God) has not found many adherents. Hick's account of the Real has been much discussed of late, but few are willing to follow his lead. It seems that most Christian theologians want to hold on to the notion of 'being' when applied to God, even if it is an analogous notion of being, rather than one which has a univocal, or one-to-one correspondence with other, created beings. But even if that is the case, the being of God is surely very different from my being. Here we may touch upon the matter of divine necessity. Created beings are said to be contingent in some way – you or I might not have existed, and may cease to exist, if God does not conserve us in being. But the same cannot be said of God. Anselmians argue that the relevant difference here has to do with the fact that God is a necessary being, whereas creatures are not. God cannot not exist, we can not exist, and might not have existed had circumstances been different. But there are no circumstances, no states of affairs and no possible worlds in which God does not exist.

According to one much discussed argument in defence of something like this Anselmian claim, Alvin *Plantinga reasons that God possesses maximal greatness (entailing the possession of maximal excellence, that is, possession of all compossible great-making properties). He then reasons that if God possibly exists (if there is one possible world in which a divine being possessing maximal greatness exists), he necessarily exists. His argument for this conclusion relies on the S5 system of modal logic, and, in particular, the axiom 'if possibly P, then necessarily possibly P' ($\Diamond P \rightarrow \Box \Diamond P$). Perhaps unsurprisingly, not everyone has been convinced by Plantinga's reasoning, and there have been other attempts to make sense of divine necessity that do not rely upon the semantics of possible worlds (even another such attempt by Plantinga himself). But such thinking has opened up important new avenues for discussion of the necessity of God.

Finally, there are rich theological resources for speaking of the being of creatures. One issue here has to do with what human persons are composed of, and there is a considerable literature devoted to questions of whether or not humans are made up of bodies and *souls, or are some sort of purely material being – this latter being a modern development for which there is no real orthodox precedent in the tradition. Most contemporary philosophers of mind scoff at the notion of humans possessing souls, although *argument* against such substance dualism is rather thin. Amongst contemporary Christian thinkers several have been at pains to explain how it might be that humans are ensouled creatures, while an increasing number of Christian thinkers believe that, on biblical and philosophical grounds, humans are purely physical animals, or that human personhood supervenes on a certain sort of material composition (i.e. a body).

Thomas Aquinas and Karl *Barth both spend considerable time parsing out the difference between angelic and non-angelic creaturely existence, on the roles angelic beings play in the divine economy, and the relation between such exalted entities and other created beings. Strange to say, few contemporary theologians have made much of this work, although there have been one or two theologians willing to speculate about the being of ghosts. This is theologically interesting, because ghosts seem to be immaterial entities like souls (*angels are, one might think, souls of a particular kind), and yet are often reported as manifesting themselves visibly. There are, of course, many biblical references to the physical manifestations of spiritual beings (e.g. Gen. 19; 32; Josh. 5:13–15; Judg. 13; Luke 2, and so on). Are such entities capable of temporarily manifesting themselves via some sort of 'exotic matter', as has been recently suggested by philosophers Hoffman and Rosenkranz? It is difficult to say. Here we are at the outer limits of theological speculation concerning different orders of created beings, and perhaps, with the Deuteronomist, we must simply confess 'the secret things belong to the LORD our God' (Deut. 29:29).

Bibliography

K. Barth, *CD*, esp. CD III/1; Dionysius the Areopagite, 'The Complete Works', in C. Luibheid (ed.), *Classics of Western Spirituality* (New York, 1988); J. B. Green and S. L. Palmer, *In Search of The Soul: Four Views on the Mind-Body Problem* (Downers Grove, 2006); J. Hick, *An Interpretation of Religion* (London, 1989); M. Higton and S. Holmes, 'Meeting Scotus: On Scholasticism and Its

Ghosts', in *IJST* 4 (2002), pp. 67–81; J. Hoffman and G. S. Rosenkrantz, *The Divine Attributes* (Oxford, 2002); A. Plantinga, *The Nature of Necessity* (Oxford, 1974); Thomas Aquinas, *Summa Contra Gentiles, Books I & II*, tr. A. C. Pegis and J. F. Anderson (Notre Dame, 1975 [1956]); P. Tillich, *Systematic Theology*, vol. 1 (Chicago, 1965); N. Wolterstorff, 'Divine Simplicity', in J. E. Tomberlin (ed.), *Philosophical Perspectives 5: Philosophy of Religion* (Atascadero, 1991), pp. 531–552.

O. D. CRISP

BELGIC CONFESSION, see CONFESSIONS OF FAITH

BELLARMINE, ROBERT (1542–1621)

Roberto Francesco Romolo Bellarmino was born at Monte Pulciano, in Tuscany. His mother was the sister of the future pope, Marcellus II. In 1560 he joined the *Jesuits and in 1569 was sent to Louvain, to help in the struggle against a militant Protestantism. The following year he became the first Jesuit professor of theology at Louvain University. He served there for six years before returning to Rome to become professor of controversial theology at the Collegium Romanum. From 1576 to 1588 he taught English and German missionary students at Rome. He went on to become spiritual director (1588), then rector (1592), of the college, provincial of the Jesuits' Neapolitan province (1594) and theologian to Pope Clement VIII (1597). In 1599 he was appointed a cardinal. He served for a time as Archbishop of Capua (1602–5), but was recalled to Rome for a wider ministry.

Bellarmine devoted himself to the controversy with *Protestantism. He never met Protestant leaders personally, but took care to represent their positions fairly. He was prepared to acknowledge strengths as well as weaknesses in their theology. His aim was to answer Protestantism by reasoned argument, rather than abuse or naked appeal to authority. He devoted himself to the study of the Bible, the Fathers and church history, to equip himself for his task. He was a formidable opponent, and chairs of theology were founded in some Protestant universities for the purpose of refuting him. His lectures at the Collegium Romanum formed the basis of his greatest work, a three-volume *Disputations on Controversies about the Christian Faith against the Heretics of this Time* (1586–93). This was generally reckoned to be one of the best statements of Tridentine Roman Catholic theology.

Bellarmine became embroiled in some of the controversies of his time. His views of the *papacy caused him trouble. He took the papal side in a controversy with Venice over clerical immunities (1606–7). But in 1610, in refuting a work by W. Barclay of Aberdeen (1546–1608), which denied that the pope had any temporal (as opposed to spiritual) authority, Bellarmine denied that the pope has any *direct* temporal authority. Rulers receive their authority from God. The pope has only an *indirect* temporal jurisdiction. If a ruler prejudices the eternal salvation of his subjects, the pope may intervene, even to the extent of deposing the ruler and releasing his subjects from their obligation to obey him. This might appear to grant the pope considerable power, but it was not good enough for Pope Sixtus V. In 1590 he put the first volume of Bellarmine's *Controversies* (where the pope's direct temporal power is denied) on the Index of Forbidden Books.

Bellarmine was also involved in the early stages of the affair of Galileo, who was condemned for teaching that the earth rotates about the sun. The Inquisition declared in 1616 that it is the earth, not the sun, that is at the centre of the universe and that the sun moves round the earth. Bellarmine was entrusted with the task of communicating this to Galileo.

Bellarmine was also active in other ways. He was a member of the commission that produced the revised 'Sixto-Clementine' edition of the Vulgate in 1592. He wrote a Hebrew grammar and, late in life, a number of ascetic works. Soon after his death there were moves towards his canonization, but this was delayed until 1930, because of his views on papal authority.

See also: REFORMATION, CATHOLIC COUNTER-; ROMAN CATHOLIC THEOLOGY.

Bibliography

Works: Collected editions published in Cologne (1617–21), Naples (1856–62), Paris (1870–74).

Studies: R. J. Blackwell, *Galileo, Bellarmine, and the Bible* (Notre Dame, IN, 1991); J. Brodrick, *The Life and Work of Blessed Robert Francis Cardinal Bellarmine, S. J.*

1542–1621, 2 vols. (London, New York and Toronto, 1950 [1928]).

A. N. S. LANE

BENEDICT AND THE BENEDICTINE TRADITION

The pattern of monastic life set down by Benedict of Nursia (c. 480–c. 550) in the Rule for his community at Monte Cassino became in time the norm throughout Western monasticism, especially from c. 800. Monastic reforms regularly centred on a return to strict observance of the Rule, as in the widely influential Cluniac movement of the tenth to twelfth centuries. In the same era other orders, notably the Carthusians and the Cistercians, based themselves on Benedict's Rule while demanding a discipline of greater austerity. The Rule was therefore a text of extraordinary importance throughout the 'monastic centuries' of European Christianity (see *Monastic theology).

Benedict made no provision for scholarly study as such. According to *Gregory the Great, he turned his back on higher education, taking up the ascetic life 'knowingly ignorant and wisely untaught' (*scienter nescius et sapienter indoctus*). Nevertheless, he was well-read in the great Latin Fathers, and his monks spent up to four hours a day *in lectio divina*, the contemplative spiritual reading of the Scriptures and the Fathers, especially monastic writers like *Basil and John Cassian (c. 360–435). The school (to teach youngsters vowed to the monastic life), the library and the scriptorium (where manuscripts were copied) became standard features of a Benedictine community. There developed a distinctive monastic culture, with its own style of theology, which has been brilliantly analysed by an eminent modern Cistercian scholar, Jean Leclercq (1911–93), of the abbey of Clervaux in Luxemburg.

The theology of the Rule itself is unremarkable, except in its sensitive ordering of the *ascetic life in community. Benedictine theology stood in deliberate continuity with *patristic theology, and derived both its literary forms and its content very largely from the Fathers. (The Latin classics, which were taught in the monastic schools in accordance with the educational programme of the *Institutions* of Cassiodorus (c. 485–c. 580), also provided some genres.) It was therefore orientated towards tradition. Taking the *auctoritas* of the Bible and the Fathers as its basis represented, in theology, the humility so strongly inculcated by the Rule. As one writer put it, they merely gleaned after the great reapers – *Augustine, *Jerome, Gregory the Great – had done their work. They approached the Bible in a spirit of meditation, and frequently interpreted it allegorically (see *Hermeneutics).

Not surprisingly, little creative originality is evident in the luminaries of the early Middle Ages, such as Bede (c. 673–735), who was first and foremost a biblical scholar, heavily dependent on the Fathers in his commentaries and homilies. Benedictines were prominent in the Carolingian renaissance, but in theology their contribution lay chiefly in harvesting the biblical and doctrinal wisdom of the Fathers, and applying it to contemporary needs. Writers like Alcuin from York (c. 735–804), Rhabanus Maurus of Fulda (c. 776–856) and Walafrid Strabo of Reichenau (c. 808–49) were enormously prolific, while others, like *Paschasius Radbertus and *Ratramnus, both monks at Corbie, engaged in controversies on the Eucharist and predestination that hinged on the true interpretation of the Fathers.

Theology in the Benedictine tradition came to full flower in the eleventh and twelfth centuries, supremely in *Bernard of Clairvaux. Controversy with emergent scholasticism depicted its distinctiveness in sharper colours. Theology for monks was determined by the goal of monastic life – the knowledge of God – and studied in relation to monastic experience, whose heart lay in worship and prayer. It preserved a respect for mystery, and distrusted too heavy an emphasis on the technique of dialectic.

At the same time, monastic-trained theologians like *Anselm, William of St Thierry (c. 1085–c. 1148) and Ailred of Rievaulx (1109–67), 'the English Bernard', fruitfully combined an ascetic orientation with more speculative methods. Anselm's disciple, Eadmer of Canterbury (c. 1055–1124), was a pioneer expositor of *Mary's immaculate conception, and other important teachers were the reformer Peter Damian (1007–72), Peter the Venerable (c. 1092–1156), abbot of Cluny, and Rupert (c. 1070–1129), abbot of Deutz near Cologne.

In the later Middle Ages, the monasteries lost their pre-eminence as centres of Christian theological reflection. The emergence of the universities, the predominance of *scholasticism, the success of new movements such as the *Franciscans and the *Dominicans and the appeal of *humanism all eclipsed the Benedictine tradition of theology. Later the Reformation and subsequent political upheavals drastically reduced the number of communities following the Rule.

For a century before the French Revolution, the houses of the congregation of St Maur (near Cluny), especially St Germain-des-Prés at Paris, accomplished monumental feats of scholarship, including a superb edition of Augustine (with a marvellous index) which exposed them to charges of *Jansenism. Jean Mabillon (1632–1707) edited Bernard's works, and Bernard de Montfaucon (1655–1741) those of *Athanasius and *Chrysostom. Not all churchmen approved of such wholehearted dedication to learning on the part of monks.

With the resurgence of Benedictine life in the nineteenth century, the Maurists' tradition of theological scholarship has also been revived. Important abbeys are found in Belgium at Maredsous (home of the *Revue bénédictine*) and Steenbrugge (where the *Corpus Christianorum* collections of the Fathers and the medievals are edited), in Germany at Beuron and Maria Laach and in France at Solesmes. These last three have devoted themselves to the study and renewal of the liturgy, the core of Benedictine Christianity, which is called in the Rule 'the work of God' (*opus Dei*).

Bibliography

P. Barry, *St. Benedict and Christianity in England* (Leominster, 1995); C. Butler, *Benedictine Monachism* (London, ²1924); L. J. Daly, *Benedictine Monasticism* (New York, 1965); D. H. Farmer (ed.), *Benedict's Disciples* (Leominster, 1980); A. Grün, OSB, *Benedict of Nursia: His Message for Today* (Collegeville, MN, 2006); D. Knowles, *The Benedictines* (London, 1929); J. Leclercq, *The Love of Learning and the Desire for God* (New York, 1961); C. Stewart, OSB, *Prayer and Community: The Benedictine Tradition* (Maryknoll, 1998).

D. F. WRIGHT

BENGEL, JOHANN ALBRECHT (1687–1752)

Bengel was a German Lutheran, distinguished as a NT scholar. He was a pioneer of modern textual criticism, who produced an edition of the Gk NT (1734) and formulated the canon 'The more difficult reading is to be preferred.' He is chiefly remembered for his *Gnomon Novi Testamenti* (1742), a delightful, sharply focused contextual commentary. John *Wesley wrote, 'I know of no commentator on the Bible to equal Bengel', and he abridged the *Gnomon* (which here means something like 'pointer to') as the basis of his *Explanatory Notes upon the New Testament*. The *Gnomon* has been translated into English more than once (by A. R. Fausset, 5 vols., Edinburgh, 1857–58; C. T. Lewis and M. R. Vincent, 2 vols., Philadelphia, 1860–62), and it is still being reprinted.

Bengel was a Württemberg *pietist, 'who in his biblicism approximated to the attitude of orthodoxy and in his moralism to that of the Christian Enlightenment' (Barth). An heir of Johannes *Cocceius (see *Covenant) as well as an opponent of the 'neology' of the *Enlightenment, he also espoused a prophetic chiliasm (see *Millennium) in an exposition of the Apocalypse (partial ET, London, 1757) and some chronological works which fixed the start of the millennium in 1836.

Bibliography

M. Brecht in *TRE* 5, pp. 583–589 (with bibliography); J. C. F. Burk, *A Memoir of the Life and Writings of John Albert Bengel* (London, 1837); C. J. Weborg, 'Bengel, J(ohann) A(lbrecht)' in D. K. McKim, *Dictionary of Major Biblical Interpreters*, 2nd edn (Downers Grove, 2007).

D. G. DEBOYS

BERDYAEV, see RUSSIAN ORTHODOX THEOLOGY

BERENGAR (*c.* 999–1088)

Berengar was the last important opponent of transubstantiation before *Wyclif. He was rector of the schools of St Martin at Tours and archdeacon of Angers. In 1049 he addressed a letter to Lanfranc (*c.* 1005–89), then prior of Bec, and a firm upholder of the *eucharistic teaching of *Paschasius Radbertus, in which he declared himself a disciple of John Scotus *Eriugena (to whom he may also have attributed the treatise of Ratramnus) and an opponent of Paschasius. As a result of these opinions, and his persistence in them, he was condemned at a series of synods and for a time excommunicated. He was also forced to make several recantations, including the notorious 'Ego Berengarius . . .' (1059), stating that the body and blood of Christ are 'perceptibly, and not only symbolically but truly, touched and broken by the hands of the priests and ground by the teeth of the faithful'. His chief work, *De Sacra Coena* (*On the Holy Supper*), written in reply to a treatise of Lanfranc about 1068–70, was lost until 1770. The positive teaching it gives is a form of *symbolism, though Berengar devotes much of the work to vindicating his own conduct and advancing logical objections to transubstantiation.

Bibliography

Critical edition of *De Sacra Coena* in W. H. Deekenkamp (ed.), *Kerkhistorische Studien* 2 (The Hague, 1941); N. Dimock, *The 'Ego Berengarius'* (London, 1895); A. J. Macdonald, *Berengar and the Reform of Sacramental Doctrine* (London, 1930); G. Macy, *The Theologies of the Eucharist in the Early Scholastic Period* (Oxford, 1984); C. M. Radding and F. Newton, *Theology, Rhetoric and Politics in the Eucharistic Controversy, 1078–1079* (New York, 2003).

R. T. Beckwith

BERKELEY, GEORGE (1685–1753)

Berkeley was an Irish philosopher and *apologist. Born in Kilkenny and educated at Trinity College, Dublin, he was ordained in the Anglican Church in 1707, and from 1728 to 1731 was engaged in efforts to found a college in Bermuda for missionary work. From 1734 to his death he was Bishop of Cloyne.

Although his writings on the philosophy of science are also of interest, Berkeley is best known for the 'immaterialism' developed in his *Principles of Human Knowledge* and *Three Dialogues between Hylas and Philonous*. The colours, sounds and sensations ('ideas' in Berkeley's terminology) of which we are directly aware – these are real enough; so are the minds which perceive them. But there is no need to suppose any inert 'material substance' underlying ideas in some indefinable way yet unknowable except through them; indeed, such a concept is meaningless. Physical objects consist of 'ideas', and their *esse* is *percipi*, their existence consists in being perceived; a wholly unperceived object is impossible. Since, however, no-one doubts that objects exist when we ourselves do not perceive them, there must be another mind which is always aware of them all: the infinite mind of God. Furthermore, since 'ideas' do not cause one another, and there is no 'material substance' to cause them, their sources must be minds or spirits. (Scientific laws express patterns of events among things, but do not explain their existence.) We ourselves cause some 'ideas', those of memory and imagination, but most have to be ascribed to another spirit – God.

In *Alciphron*, his only purely apologetic work, Berkeley added a further argument, not dependent on immaterialism, to the traditional argument from design (see *Natural theology). The best indication of personhood is language, that is, signs used to convey meaning but having no intrinsic connection with the thing signified. And this is precisely the relationship our visual experiences have to the things they inform us about: thus, small size and faintness indicate distance, although they neither entail nor resemble it. Visual impressions are thus analogous to human language, 'the universal language of the Author of nature', whereby he instructs and guides us, and proof of his reality and personhood.

Berkeley was a philosopher and apologist, not a theologian, and somewhat doubtful of the value of theology. 'The Christian religion', he said in a sermon, 'was calculated for the Bulk of Mankind, and therefore cannot consist in subtle and nice Notions.' Its mysteries were to be accepted in humility and faith, not measured by reason. But reason could defend them against *atheist or *deist critics, show the reasonableness of religion generally, and support the idea of revelation.

Bibliography

Works: ed. by A. A. Luce and T. E. Jessup, 7 vols. (London, 1948–56); selections in *Principles of Human Knowledge* (London, 1962) and *Philosophical Works* (London, 1910).

Studies: S. H. Daniel (ed.), *Re-examining Berkeley's Philosophy* (Toronto, 2007); idem (ed.), *New Interpretations of Berkeley's Thought* (Amherst, 2008); G. Dicker, *Berkeley's Idealism: A Critical Examination* (Cambridge, 2011); A. A. Luce, *Life of George Berkeley* (London, 1949); E. A. Sillem, *George Berkeley and the Proofs for the Existence of God* (London, 1957); G. Warnock, *Berkeley* (Harmondsworth, 1953); K. P.

Winkler, *The Cambridge Companion to Berkeley* (Cambridge, 2005).

R. L. Sturch

BERKHOF, HENDRIKUS (1914–95)

Hendrikus Berkhof was Professor of Systematic Theology at the University of Leiden, and one of the most significant *Reformed dogmaticians of the twentieth century. His work combines a thorough familiarity with, and appreciation of, the traditions of classical Reformed *dogmatics with a sensitivity towards developments in contemporary theology and philosophy. His main work, *Christian Faith*, was one of the most persuasive attempts to write a *systematic theology in the later twentieth century, not least because of its lively use of biblical criticism, and because of its sympathetic but not uncritical relationship to classical orthodoxy. Berkhof also wrote on the theology of history in *Christ the Meaning of History*, which contains valuable discussions of *existentialist and *salvation-history treatments of the theme. His work on *The Doctrine of the Holy Spirit* is one of the best surveys of the territory by a recent Protestant theologian. Berkhof was also much involved in ecumenical affairs.

Bibliography

Works: in ET *Christ and the Powers* (London, 1962); *Christ the Meaning of History* (London, 1966); *Christian Faith: An Introduction to the Study of the Faith* (Grand Rapids, ²1986 [1979]); *The Doctrine of the Holy Spirit* (London, 1964); *Well-founded Hope* (London, 1969); *Introduction to the Study of Dogmatics* (Grand Rapids, 1985); *Two Hundred Years of Theology: Report of a Personal Journey* (Grand Rapids, 1989).
Studies: E. P. Meijering, *Hendrikus Berkhof: Een Theologische Biografie* (Kampen, 1997).

J. B. Webster

BERKHOF, LOUIS (1873–1957)

*Reformed theologian, influential chiefly through the use in seminaries, colleges and churches of his frequently reprinted *Systematic Theology* (1941, first published in 1932 under the title *Reformed Dogmatics*).

Born in the Netherlands, Berkhof went to the USA in 1882. He graduated from the Christian Reformed Church's Calvin College and Seminary before taking further studies at Princeton Seminary (1902–4) under B. B. *Warfield and G. *Vos. From 1906–44 he served in various capacities at Calvin Seminary, including that of president from 1931.

Berkhof was heavily dependent on the *Dutch Reformed tradition (and especially H. *Bavinck). The strength of his magnum opus lay in its presentation of that tradition in English dress and in a clear textbook format with updated discussions (e.g. of the earlier *Barth) rather than in any theological creativity.

Less well known is his earlier work which displayed considerable interest in the development of a coherent Reformed world-and-life-view (e.g. *The Church and Social Problems*, Grand Rapids, 1913; *The Christian Laborer in the Industrial Struggle*, Grand Rapids, 1916). In 1920–21 he delivered the Stone Lectures at Princeton Seminary on 'The Kingdom of God in Modern Life and Thought' (published under that title in 1951). His *Systematic Theology* has continued to enjoy widespread circulation.

Bibliography

J. D. Bratt, *Dutch Calvinism in Modern America: A History of a Conservative Subculture* (Grand Rapids, 1984); H. Zwaanstra, 'Louis Berkhof', in D. F. Wells (ed.), *Reformed Theology in America* (Grand Rapids, 1985).

S. B. Ferguson

BERKOUWER, GERRIT CORNELIS (1903–96)

A Dutch *Reformed theologian, Berkouwer served as a part-time lecturer in the Free University of Amsterdam from 1940. In 1945 he was appointed to the chair of *dogmatics, a chair which had formerly been held by A. *Kuyper, H. *Bavinck and V. Hepp (1879–1950). Undoubtedly, he felt attracted to the biblical-historical approach of Bavinck, rather than to the more speculative approach of Kuyper and the strongly scholastic method of Hepp.

Berkouwer's doctoral thesis of 1932 dealt with the relationship between *faith and *revelation in recent German theology. This relationship held his attention throughout his entire theological career. In his early years there were two main *loci* of interest, the first being the theology of Karl *Barth. In his first major work, *Karl Barth* (1936), he proved to be very critical. In his second major work (*The Triumph of Grace in the Theology of Karl Barth*, 1954; ET, Grand Rapids and London, 1956) he showed a more sympathetic understanding of Barth's intentions, although incisive criticism was by no means lacking.

Berkouwer's second focus of interest was *Roman Catholic theology. In his first major volume on Roman Catholic dogma, *Barthianisme en Katholicisme* (1940), criticism again prevailed. This was still true of the second (*Conflict with Rome*, 1948; ET, Philadelphia, 1958), although the general approach was more conciliatory. In 1961 he was invited to be an official observer at the Second *Vatican Council. Following this, he published two other volumes on Catholic theology: *The Second Vatican Council and the New Theology* (Grand Rapids, 1965) and *Nabetrachting op het Concilie* (*Reflection after the Council*, Kampen, 1968), in which he offered a penetrating analysis of both the council and recent Catholic theological thinking.

Berkouwer's main achievement, however, was his series of *Studies in Dogmatics*, in which he treated several *loci* of dogmatics (Dutch edn, 18 vols., most of which are available in ET, Grand Rapids, 1952–75).

He never wrote a formal introduction to theology (*prolegomena*), but it is quite evident that the guiding idea in all his theologizing is the correlation between faith and revelation (cf. the titles of his first *Studies in Dogmatics: Faith and Justification*, 1954; *Faith and Sanctification*, 1952; and *Faith and Perseverance*, 1958). God's revelation is never a communication of revealed truths, but it is God's coming in Jesus Christ to the sinner. This revelation can be accepted only in faith. No salvation without faith! Faith, however, is not a constitutive factor in the process of revelation, but is totally dependent upon and directed towards its object: God's salvation in Christ. This correlation makes Berkouwer's theology strongly anti-speculative and antischolastic. All theology has to be 'preachable'. Increasingly, he also turned against all causal-deterministic ways of thinking (cf. his volume on *Divine Election*, 1960). The *sola Scriptura* of the Reformers deeply appealed to him and increasingly determined his own theology. The question has been raised whether his correlation method and the return to the 'pre-scientific' *sola Scriptura – sola fide* approach of the Reformers does not lead to a limitation of the possibilities of theology and to too easy a retreat to the notion of 'mystery'.

Bibliography
Works: *A Half Century of Theology* (Grand Rapids, 1977).

Studies: A. Baker, *A Critical Evaluation of G. C. Berkouwer's Doctrine of Election* (Dallas, 1976); C. M. Cameron, *The Problem of Polarization: An Approach Based on the Writings of G. C. Berkouwer* (Lewiston, 1992); P. D. Collord, *The Problem of Authority for Dogmatics in G. C. Berkouwer* (PhD diss., University of Iowa, 1964); J. C. de Moor, *Towards a Biblically Theological Method: A Structural Analysis and a Further Elaboration of Dr. G. C. Berkouwer's Hermeneuticdogmatic Method* (Kampen, 1980); L. B. Smedes, 'G. C. Berkouwer', in P. E. Hughes (ed.), *Creative Minds in Contemporary Theology* (Grand Rapids, 1966).

K. RUNIA

BERLIN DECLARATION

The 'Berlin Declaration on Ecumenism' (BDE), entitled *Freedom and Fellowship in Christ* (1974), was a radical critique of the theological direction of the World Council of Churches (WCC). It also affirmed the theological convictions on which its criticism was based, and called for a return towards a biblically based concern for Christian unity.

It was produced by the same Theological Convention of Confessing Fellowships which issued the *Frankfurt Declaration, in cooperation with others all over the world who had responded positively to the Frankfurt Declaration. It was intended as a critical but constructive contribution to the forthcoming Fifth Assembly of the WCC which was to take place in 1975 in Nairobi under the theme 'Christ Frees and Unites'. The text was adopted at the first European Confession Congress in Berlin in May 1974, exactly forty years after the historic first Confessing Synod of the Evangelical Church in Germany which had issued the *Barmen Declaration. In 1975, prior to the Nairobi Assembly, a volume documenting the Declaration in detail (listed below) was presented to leaders of the WCC and the Lutheran World Federation as well as to the Vatican Secretariat on Christian Unity.

In twelve affirmations and refutations recent *ecumenical pronouncements on the Christological, soteriological and ecclesiological aspects of the Nairobi theme were analysed and condemned for their politicizing and *syncretizing tendencies, while the authentic biblical content of these terms was expounded. The Declaration's call for a coming together of concerned Christian groups worldwide was partly fulfilled in the formation of the *Lausanne Movement for World Evangelization later the same year.

The BDE has been used as a model for similar declarations, e.g. the Seoul Declaration on Christian Missions (1975).

Bibliography

H. Berkhof, 'Berlin versus Geneva: Our Relationship with the "Evangelicals"', *Ecumenical Review* 28 (1976), pp. 80–86; W. Künneth/ P. Beyerhaus (eds.), *Reich Gottes oder Weltgemeinschaft? Die Berliner Ökumene-Erklärung zur utopischen Vision des Weltkirchenrats* (Bad Liebenzell, 1975).

P. P. J. Beyerhaus

BERNARD OF CLAIRVAUX (1090–1153)

Bernard was born at Fontaines (near Dijon) of noble parents. At the age of twenty-one he entered the recently founded abbey of Cîteaux, at that stage the only abbey of the new and strict Cistercian order. Three years later Bernard was appointed abbot of a new monastery, at Clairvaux. Under Bernard it grew rapidly and during his lifetime became parent to some seventy new Cistercian abbeys.

Bernard went to Cîteaux to flee the world, but in time he became one of the most active and widely travelled leaders of the twelfth-century church. During the 1130s he campaigned for Pope Innocent II against the rival pope, Anacletus. Eventually he secured Innocent's victory, which gained many favours for the Cistercians. Later he opposed the teaching of Peter *Abelard, securing his condemnation at the Council of Sens in 1140 and thereafter by the pope. His authority was further enhanced when one of his own monks, Bernard Paganelli, became Pope Eugenius III in 1145. In the next two years, at Eugenius' request, Bernard preached round Europe, raising support for the Second Crusade. This was launched in 1148 but failed dismally, a severe blow for Bernard. But his reputation was great enough to survive such a setback, and his popularity has never really waned.

Bernard has been called 'the last of the Fathers'. He was the last great representative of the early medieval tradition of *monastic theology. He was a brilliant writer, earning himself the title 'mellifluous' (sweet as honey). He preached regularly and many of his sermons survive. Some are unpolished, probably much as originally preached. Others are in a highly polished literary form, designed for reading. These are mostly based on various Sundays and saints' days throughout the church year. Bernard corresponded widely and more than 500 of his letters survive, ranging from the personal and devotional to the official and political. Some are virtually treatises, on *baptism, on the office of bishop and against the errors of Abelard.

Bernard wrote a number of treatises. Three of these are on monasticism: his *Apology* for the Cistercians against the Cluniacs, *Precept and Dispensation* on the correct interpretation of the Rule of St *Benedict and a treatise *In Praise of the New Knighthood* on the new order of Templars. He also wrote a biography of Archbishop Malachy of Armagh (1094–1148), who helped to bring the Irish church into line with Roman practices.

In his early years Bernard wrote a masterly treatise on *Grace and Freewill*. In this he relates the work of *grace and of the human *will, along *Augustinian lines. He argues that our good works are at the same time entirely the work of God's grace (thus leaving no room for boasting) and entirely the work of our freewill in that it is we who perform them (thus providing a basis for *merit and reward).

Towards the end of his life Bernard wrote on *Consideration* for his former disciple, Pope Eugenius III. Bernard urges him to find time for reflection or meditation in his busy life. He sees the pope as 'the unique vicar of Christ who presides not over a single people but over all' and has fullness of power. But he is equally emphatic in his opposition to papal tyranny (see *Papacy).

Bernard is best known as a spiritual writer. His book on *Loving God* has been called 'one of the most outstanding of all medieval books on *mysticism'. His *Steps of Humility and Pride* is based on the twelve steps of humility described in the Rule of St Benedict. But his best-known spiritual work is his eighty-six *Sermons on the Song of Solomon*, allegedly commenting on Song of Solomon 1:1 – 3:1, but in reality a treatise in sermonic form on the spiritual life of the monk.

Bibliography

Works in *PL* 182–185. Critical edition: J. Leclercq, H. Rochais, *et al.* (eds.), *Sancti Bernardi Opera*, 8 vols. (Rome, 1957–77). ET of works in the *Cistercian Fathers* series (Kalamazoo, MI, 1970ff.).

Studies: A. H. Bredero, *Bernard of Clairvaux: Between Cult and History* (Edinburgh, 1996); G. R. Evans, *The Mind of St Bernard of Clairvaux* (Oxford, 1983); idem, *Bernard of Clairvaux: Selected Works* (New York, 1987); idem, *Bernard of Clairvaux* (Oxford, 2000); E. Gilson, *The Mystical Theology of Saint Bernard* (London, 1940); J. Leclercq, *Bernard of Clairvaux and the Cistercian Spirit* (Kalamazoo, 1976); E. Vacandard, *Vie de Saint Bernard*, 2 vols. (Paris, 1895).

A. N. S. LANE

BEZA, THEODORE (1519–1605)

As *Calvin's successor Beza was the acknowledged champion of Genevan orthodoxy and chief spokesman for *Reformed Protestantism. In Geneva he served as moderator of the clergy (1564–80), rector of the Academy (1559–63) and professor of theology (1559–99). In addition, through generations of students, pastors, men and women of state and merchants who knew him personally, and through correspondence, Beza's influence was felt in France, Britain, the Netherlands, Poland and Germany. It was principally through his writings, however, that Beza became established as the skilful polemicist and man of letters, indeed the authoritative guide for defining the doctrinal integrity of the Reformed faith. He wrote close to 100 treatises, mostly polemical writings on the *Eucharist, *Christology and the *church. His magnum opus, the *Novum Testamentum*, was dedicated to Queen Elizabeth in 1565.

The interpretation of Beza's thought and his role in the development of Calvinism have caused considerable controversy. His fidelity to Calvin was accepted by contemporaries, but by the middle of the seventeenth century Peter Heylyn (1600–62) in England and Amyraut (see *Amyraldism) in France found Beza responsible for hardening Calvin's theology. Such protests were largely ignored until Heinrich Heppe (1820–79) articulated this thesis in his nineteenth-century study of Beza's role in the development of the rational element in Calvinism. This challenge won few converts within nineteenth-century Calvinism, which cherished the very rational coherence of the Calvinist system that Heppe deplored. By the middle of the twentieth century the tide had turned in the historiography. By then *Barth's revolutionary theology had created a more favourable climate for a new interpretation of Calvin which celebrated the dynamic, Christological and biblical centre of his theology over against the more metaphysical and systematic structure of the Calvinism attributed to Beza.

Certainly, one finds in Beza's writings a greater openness to *Aristotelian *metaphysics and dialectic, more reliance on *patristic authority and more insistence on systematic coherence: all of which served to reshape Calvin's theology into a more tightly argued, logically unassailable body of truth. But this does not mean that he produced a rational synthesis based on a metaphysic of God's decree, or that there is a direct line from Beza to seventeenth-century Reformed scholasticism, as the German school of interpretation has insisted.

Evidence from recent studies calls for a revision of this thesis. Beza's education within French *humanism had a lasting impact on both the style and content of his theology. Using the literary models of Greek and Roman literature, humanism was drawn into the rhetorical and ethical style and concerns of the classics. Moreover, the logic and philosophy which Beza absorbed in Paris was a more broadly based Aristotelianism than the technical, impersonal and increasingly abstruse nature of medieval *scholasticism. It is this literary culture of French humanism which separates Beza from any easy identification with scholasticism and which binds him closely to the religious and biblical centre of his mentor's theology.

Bibliography

Works: Many theological treatises in *Tractationes Theologicae*, 3 vols. (1570–82); *Correspondance de Théodore de Bèze*, 20 vols. (Geneva, 1960–98).

Studies: W. Kickel, *Vernunft und Offenbarung bei Theodor Beza* (Neukirchen-Vluyn, 1967); R. Letham, 'Theodore Beza: A Reassessment', *SJT* 40, 1987, pp. 25–40; T. Maruyama, *The Ecclesiology of Theodore Beza* (Geneva, 1978); S. M. Manetsch, *Theodore Beza and the Quest* for Peace in France, 1572–1598 (Leiden, 2000); J. Raitt, *The Eucharistic Theology of Theodore Beza* (Chambersburg, PA, 1972); S. D. Wright, *Our Sovereign Refuge: The Pastoral Theology of Theodore Beza* (Milton Keynes, 2005).

I. McPhee

BIEL, GABRIEL (c. 1415–95)

The German Gabriel Biel was one of the last great *scholastic theologians. After a lengthy university career at Heidelberg (arts) and Erfurt and Cologne (theology), during which he was exposed to both the *via antiqua* ('old way') of *Thomas Aquinas and *Albertus Magnus at Cologne and the *via moderna* of *Duns Scotus and *William of Ockham at Erfurt, he became in middle life a pastor and preacher. He was cathedral preacher at Mainz, and from the 1460s onwards a leading figure in the Brethren of the Common Life, especially as the first provost of their new house at Butzbach. From 1479 he was provost at Urach in Württemberg, combining his responsibilities with the professorship of theology at the new university at Wittenberg from 1484 to c. 1490.

Biel was a true disciple of Ockham's *nominalism, but was able to be critical of all schools of thought. Though 'a faithful preserver of the impressively coherent structure of the Occamistic system' (H. A. Oberman), his teaching was more explicitly theological than Ockham's, demonstrating nominalism's potential for pastoral application (as did his friend and follower, the famous Strasbourg preacher John Geiler of Kaysersberg, 1445–1510; see the study by E. J. Dempsey Douglass, *Justification in Late Medieval Preaching*, Leiden, 1966). Biel's thought is increasingly appreciated both for its thorough grounding in earlier medieval tradition and for its influence on Catholic responses to the Reformation. He was prominent among the nominalist writers with whom *Luther's early theology critically engaged.

Bibliography

J. L. Farthing, *Thomas Aquinas and Gabriel Biel: Interpretations of St Thomas Aquinas in German Nominalism on the Eve of the Reformation* (Durham, NC, 1988); H. A. Oberman, *Forerunners of the Reformation: The Shape of Late Medieval Thought*, (London, 1967); idem, *The Harvest of Medieval Theology: Gabriel Biel and Late Medieval Nominalism* (Grand Rapids, ²1967).

D. F. Wright

BLACK CONSCIOUSNESS

Black consciousness arose to counter the blackness that whiteness created. Being black is a social construct foisted upon blacks by whites, creating confusion about their identity. It is seen in the policy of assimilation practised by the French upon their colonial subjects. Thus Léopold Sédar Senghor, later president of Senegal, suffered a crisis of identity when as a student he travelled to Paris in 1928. He had been told he was French, but in France he was treated as an African. Aimé Césaire similarly arrived in Paris from Martinique to begin his studies. In *Return to My Native Land* he had to construct an identity for himself. This was the experience of Franz Fanon, also from Martinique, when he went on to work as a psychiatrist in Algeria during the war of liberation. Identity can be withheld but it cannot be given or received as a gift: it has to be won. His therapy of violence was influential throughout Africa and America, wherever blackness sought to determine its own identity without the permission of white people.

Black consciousness defined its identity, declaring itself to be African. As whites looked back to the old country of origin, so blacks had to be able to return to Africa – at least in principle. The most famous black to have done this in practice was Edward Blyden. Originally from St Thomas, he had gone to college in the USA but soon left because of discrimination, and set sail for Liberia in 1851. He was to become a classical scholar, educator, ambassador and international statesman. He urged the black diaspora of North and South America to return to their own continent.

Marcus Garvey was the most influential figure in the development of black consciousness in two respects. First, white was still the colour of value and preference when he was born in Jamaica in 1887. But Garvey, a maroon, declared his preference for blackness. He advocated self-help and in 1914 set up UNIA (the Universal Negro Improvement Association). Blacks must be responsible for themselves, socially, politically and especially economically. Secondly, in his Pan-Africanism, he believed that Africa should be for Africans, that Africa should be able to exercise power in the world, to help and to protect blacks wherever they might live. These themes were taken up by the Black Power movement in America in the 1960s, initially inspired by Stokely Carmichael.

Edward Blyden, himself a Presbyterian minister, saw that Islam had related better than Christianity to the peoples of West Africa. Within America the Honourable Elijah Muhammad created the Nation of Islam, a non-orthodox form of Islam which called for black people to unite as a nation within a nation. This black religious consciousness declared Christianity to be the religion of slaves and enslavement. Its most famous exponent was Malcolm X, who accepted the Yacub myth about the origins of the white race and declared white people to be of the devil. His successor, Louis Farrakhan, led the Million Man March on Washington in 1995, calling on black men to pledge themselves to high moral values, respect towards women and kindness towards children. Affluent black consciousness now explores the rich variety of African-American culture, but is in danger of forgetting the poorest section of the black community, who were the special concern of Marcus Garvey.

The Black Consciousness Movement in South Africa was created by Bantu Stephen Biko. It was the genius of Steve Biko to create a movement which transformed the consciousness of ordinary black people. It was not dependent on the fate of its leaders: Mandela was imprisoned in 1964 and Biko was beaten to death in police custody in 1977, but the movement in hearts and minds could not be defeated.

See also: BLACK THEOLOGY.

Bibliography
S. Biko, *I Write What I Like* (London, 1978); F. Fanon, *The Wretched of the Earth* (London, 1961); A. J. Garvey, *The Philosophy and Opinions of Marcus Garvey* (New York, 1923).

A. KEE

BLACK THEOLOGY

Black theology arose as a response by advocates steeped in black church tradition to the pervasive presence of *racism in the United States during the climactic emergence of both the civil rights and Black Power movements (see *Black consciousness) during the 1960s. Though echoes of sociocultural, economic and political liberation sounded long before through diverse voices, the monumental work that started what has become known as the Black Theology Project is James H. Cone's *Black Theology and Black Power* (1969). Since that time the project has grown, embraced some developments and acquired determinative dialogue partners. A sign of maturing formulations is the fact that the movement has drawn critics from those identifying with this theological community and those considered sympathetic observers. In addition, black theology must face various challenges demanding response if it seeks to be a viable contributor to the black church and those seeking models of liberatory theological reflection in the global community.

Cone, black church historian Gayraud Wilmore, and philosophical theologian J. Deotis Roberts, along with other African-American theologians and philosophers, were burdened to show that the gospel of Jesus Christ was consistent with the movement toward liberation, i.e. confronting the pervasive effects of racism. Black theology was understood as:

> a theology of 'blackness'. It is the affirmation of black humanity that emancipates black people from white racism, thus providing authentic freedom for both white and black people ... The demand that Christ the Liberator imposes on all men *requires* all blacks to affirm their full dignity as persons and all whites to surrender their presumptions of superiority and abuses of power. (*Statement by the National Committee of Black Churchmen, 13 June, 1969*)

Theological formulation of this sort must draw from some traditional sources and from sources unique to the black perspective. Scripture and church tradition remain foundational, but they must be engaged with a critical eye. Critical distancing was essential because much of the oppressed community's knowledge of Christianity was channelled through exposure to a dominant white culture which often used such instruction to further the subordination of black people. The multifaceted realm of the 'black experience' was another foundational source for doing theology. This experience inculcated the history, stories, songs, poems and music arising from the black community as it struggled to make sense of an existence radically affected by widespread racial oppression in a country where ostensibly 'all men are created equal'.

Within black theology, liberatory models have been identified, focusing on the model's devotion to Scripture and church tradition, but also revealing a devotion to concrete strategies and demonstrations of behaviour resulting in freedom for themselves and for others. Thus slave insurrectionists such as Gabriel Prosser (1800), Denmark Vesey (1822), and Nat Turner (1831), whom Wilmore refers to as 'Three Generals in the Lord's Army', can be considered appropriate liberatory models because of a conviction common to all of them, namely, that God through Scripture and other experiences had called them to armed rebellion to free those enslaved. Others such as Harriet Tubman (1819–1913), who was known as 'Moses' because she was a leader on the underground railroad conducting slaves to freedom in Canada, along with Sojourner Truth (born Isabella Baumfree, 1797–1883), who travelled in various parts of the United States speaking against slavery, were models combining religious conviction with concrete acts of liberation.

Many other voices contributed to the emergence of black theology during the 1960s. The contributors shared a life oriented toward the conviction that God was ultimately against slavery, against the biblical and theological justifications offered by some advocating this institution, against the perpetual dehumanization and marginalization of people of African descent even beyond the official end of slavery. Black churchmen began to reformulate theology in such a way to encourage black people and give them a sense of dignity, propagating a view that this was what God desired for them now. An example of this early reformulation was Henry McNeal Turner (1834–1915), a bishop in the African Methodist Episcopal Church in the USA, who as early as 1894 declared that in view of the racial discrimination practised by white Christians against black people, 'God is a Negro'.

The impetus of the civil rights movement, in conjunction with the Black Power wing of the movement, provided a consummatory time for the formulation of black theology. The event, often cited as the beginnings of the modern civil rights movement, was the Montgomery (Alabama) bus boycott, beginning in 1955 precipitated by Rosa Park's refusal to give up her bus seat to a white man, whereby she was then arrested. The subsequent boycott helped galvanize the civil rights movement and catapulted Dr Martin Luther King, Jr into national attention. Related to the civil rights movement in general was the situation arousing the Black Power presence in particular. Black Power had different emphases to different people in the movement. For some it was more of a sociocultural liberatory perspective: a perspective governed by black racial dignity, self definition, self-reliance and self-expression. It was a rejection of white attempts to maintain control of black consciousness. For others Black Power had a more definitive political, economic orientation.

Black theology thus emerged as the theological expression of a number of foundational factors to black existence and what could be identified as the 'black experience'. It attempted to explicate that through the gospel of Jesus Christ, God demonstrated concern for the effects of *slavery and racism on people of African descent. He was concerned about their pain, their anger and their demands for self-determination. God was an advocate in their struggle for freedom in all spheres of existence. Cone, Wilmore and Roberts did much to set this black theological agenda.

Black theology has undergone a number of crucial developments. Among them are the reformulation of 'blackness', the emergence of a second generation of black theologians, the thought of womanist theologians and ethicists.

Cone had also addressed 'blackness' as a symbol of dehumanization, suffering and marginalization. Blackness could also symbolize hope and the inspiration to achieve liberation. This symbolic perspective facilitated much in terms of interaction and evaluation with other liberation-oriented theologies such as Latin American *liberation theology. Much comparative study had been done between black theology and *African theology. The relationship between the two in terms of similarities and dissimilarities has been debated by members in both camps. African theologians such as John Mbiti, E. W. Fashole-Luke and Harry Sawyer had little use for the theme of liberation and saw little hope for an alliance between black and African theologies. On the other hand, Cone, Desmond Tutu and Burgess Carr stressed foundational similarities in terms of the common experience of a shared contempt of blackness by many whites, the 'motherhood' of Africa, and the unity that comes through baptism and membership in the body of Christ.

The Black Theology Project has produced a second generation of theologians who facilitated further depth of study in the discipline and who are prolific writers. This group would include people like Dwight N. Hopkins, George C. L. Cummings and Will Coleman. They have contributed to developments in black theology through investigations in the nature and function of slave religion. In addition, they have aided in the consultation with other disciplines, such as sociology, economic theory and the effects of *globalization to enhance the relevance and impact of black theology.

Cone affirms that *womanist theology 'is the most creative development to emerge out of the Black theology movement during the 1980s and 1990s'. The term 'womanist' comes from Alice Walker's *In Search of Our Mother's Garden* (1983). Womanist theologians share with their black brothers a burden to confront racism in all its effects, but concurrently recognize shortcomings in black theology in light of the unique experience of African-American women. Sympathies are shared with white feminists who confront sexism, but distancing occurs, nevertheless, because white, middle-class feminists do not confront racism. Womanist theological reflection is multidimensional because it must address not only racial and gender oppression, but also classism and heterosexism. Leading formulators are Delores S. Williams, Jacquelyn Grant, Katie G. Cannon, Cheryl J. Sanders, M. Shawn Copeland and Emilie M. Townes.

Black theology has been criticized by voices sympathetic to the movement as well as those occupying a more distant evaluative position. As early as 1975 Cecil W. Cone criticized his brother, James, for his initial 'Barthian' tendencies in explicating the meaning and significance of black theology. A more recent sympathetic voice comes from Victor Anderson, who raises concerns about black theology's 'alienated consciousness'. This *alienation is multifaceted in terms of its perceived alienation from the traditions of the black church, its reliance to a problematic degree upon theological methodologies derived from white European theologians and philosophers and its attempts to negotiate a commitment to black radicalism and yet build morality upon Christian foundations. British theologian, Alistair Kee, from outside the Black Theology project, contributes the call for more critical attention to be given to the analysis of class and its effects. Cone began such deliberations in 1984 (*For My People*) by introducing Marxism as a possible tool of analysis for black theologians. Kee, however, argues that more must be done.

Black theology faces a number of challenges in the present and in the future. What is its relationship to be with the black church and the church's immediate needs in various urban communities? Will the project maintain a uniquely Christian identity? Here Jesus Christ and the meaning of the cross remain foundational points of reflection. What will be its relationship to other liberatory theologies? How will it relate to other global religions in general? To what degree are the reflections of black theologians affected by the academy and the seeking of prestigious positions in predominantly white academic institutions? These and many other questions must continually be addressed if black theology is to be faithful to its initial vision and purpose.

Bibliography

J. H. Cone, *Black Theology and Black Power* (New York, 1969); idem, *For My People: Black Theology and the Black Church* (Maryknoll, 1984); D. N. Hopkins, *Cut Loose Your Stammering Tongue: Black Theology in the Slave Narratives* (Maryknoll, 1992); idem, *Introducing Black Theology of Liberation* (Maryknoll, 1999); D. N. Hopkins *et al.*, *Black Faith and Public Talk* (Maryknoll, 1999); J. S. Mbiti, 'An African Views American Black Theology', *Worldview* 17, 1974, pp. 41–44; J. D. Roberts, *Black Theology in Dialogue* (Philadelphia, 1987); E. M. Townes, *Womanist Justice, Womanist Hope*, AAR Series 79, 1993; D. S. Williams, *Sisters in the Wilderness* (Maryknoll, 1993); G. S. Wilmore, *Black Religion and Black Radicalism* (Maryknoll, 1984); G. S. Wilmore and J. H. Cone, *Black Theology: A Documentary History 1966–1979* (New York, 1979); idem, *Black Theology: A Documentary History, Volume Two: 1980–1992* (Maryknoll, 1993); J. U. Young, *Black and African Theologies: Siblings or Distant Cousins?* (Maryknoll, 1986).

B. FIELDS

BLASPHEMY

Blasphemy (Gk *blaptein*, 'to injure', and *pheme*, 'reputation') denotes evil, slanderous or defamatory speech about God. It draws on the Hebrew verbs *nakob* and *qillel*, which mean to pronounce a curse on God (Lev. 24:10–23). In its non-trivial sense, it involves the active and conscious overthrow of the third commandment (Exod. 20:7; Deut. 5:11) and is an inversion of praise. Thomas Aquinas saw it as the opposite of the confession of faith and a mortal sin.

Blasphemy is to be distinguished from its close cousins – heresy, *idolatry, profanation, *apostasy and sacrilege – by its political dimension. Blasphemy is a form of sedition: it undermines the very basis of social and political life by calling into question the foundation of that life. In the Jewish Talmud, blasphemy is an act of treason against the King of kings. The pagan philosopher Porphyry (*c*. 300) draws out the political implications of early Christians' blasphemy against the pagan gods. As he puts it in *Against the Christians*: '[The Christians] would bring us a society without law. They would teach us to have no fear of the gods.' This political dimension was obscured for much of the medieval period in the West as ecclesial and political authorities jointly ordered society. During this period blasphemy became a sub-species of *heresy. In England, however, by the seventeenth century, the charge of heresy was seen as only an ecclesiastical offence punishable by excommunication, yet blasphemy was a common law offence against the state (as it still is to this day both in Britain and a number of other European countries). Thus, when *Nietzsche made the blasphemous declaration that 'God is dead', he intended not simply to call into question Christian belief and practice, but to challenge the very basis of Western civilization. To blaspheme is not only to reject God, but also to set oneself against the order of human life that God commands and sustains.

The trials and condemnations of Jesus (Mark 14:53–65; John 10:22–33), Stephen (Acts 6:11–14), Martin Luther, George Fox and William Penn suggest that one man's blasphemy is another's orthodoxy. The boundaries between legitimate and illegitimate dissent, deviancy and criticism shift according to changing historical situations – at different times and in different places blasphemy can mean different things. Yet blasphemy is not simply a term of abuse that gives expression to that which a society most abhors and can prosecute. There is a difference between dissent from and criticism of particular religious authorities and patterns of belief and practice, and the wilful and hostile rejection of God that blasphemy entails.

In the contemporary Western context, the theological moorings of blasphemy are lost, and it has morphed into the crime of religious hatred: the crime of intolerance against a particular sociological group rather than a crime against God and the foundations of the social and political order.

Bibliography

A. Cabantous, *Blasphemy: Impious Speech in the West from the Seventeenth to the Nineteenth Century* (ET, New York, 2002); D. Lawton, *Blasphemy* (New York, 1993); G. Nokes, *A History of the Crime of Blasphemy* (London, 1928); Thomas Aquinas, *Summa Theologica* (ET, Notre Dame, 1981).

L. Bretherton

BLOESCH, DONALD G. (1928–2010)

Donald Bloesch's grandfathers and father were pastors in the Evangelical Synod of North America that later became part of the United Church of Christ where Bloesch was a member. Bloesch was educated at Chicago Theological Seminary and the University of Chicago. He taught at the University of Dubuque Theological Seminary for thirty-five years.

Bloesch's many ecumenical encounters help explain his self-designation as a 'catholic evangelical'. Drawing on Karl *Barth, among many other theologians, Bloesch developed a historically rich confessional 'theology of Word and Spirit' as an alternative to *fundamentalism and *liberalism.

Bloesch's theological method combined the truth of the word of God and the power of the Holy Spirit for renewing the church and converting the world. His theology focused on themes crucial to evangelicalism, such as God's sovereignty, the primacy of Scripture, total depravity, Christ's deity, substitutionary atonement, salvation by grace and faith, the new birth, Christ's bodily resurrection and personal return, and heaven and hell. Yet Bloesch reworked these themes, particularly in light of what he had learned from Barth and his family heritage in *Pietism.

See also: EVANGELICAL THEOLOGY.

Bibliography
Works: *Essentials of Evangelical Theology*, 2 vols. (San Francisco, 1978–79); *Christian Foundations*, 7 vols. (Downers Grove, 1992–2004).
Studies: E. M. Colyer (ed.), *Evangelical Theology in Transition: Theologians in Dialogue with Donald Bloesch* (Downers Grove, 1999).

E. M. COLYER

BLOOD, see SACRIFICE

BODY, see ANTHROPOLOGY

BODY OF CHRIST, see CHURCH

BOEHME, JACOB (1575–1624)

Boehme was a German shoemaker and mystic of Görlitz who combined a concern for personal *religious experience, in reaction to Lutheran scholasticism (see *Orthodoxy/Scholasticism, Lutheran), with speculation about the nature of God and his relation to creation.

Most of Boehme's writings from 1612 to 1622, prompted by mystical experiences in 1600 and 1619, used language and ideas from his long study of Neoplatonism (see *Platonism), Jewish cabbalism and alchemy. Later writings, including the treatises collected in *The Way to Christ* (1624), were more clearly expressed in traditional Christian themes and images, but the thought remained complex and speculative. Boehme's writings were banned in his lifetime and subsequently often ignored, although they strongly influenced *The Spirit of Love* (1752, 1754) and other later writings of William *Law, causing a rift between Law and John *Wesley, who described Boehme's writings as 'most sublime nonsense'.

While Boehme's ideas cannot be fitted into any system, his influence can be traced in *pietism, *quietism and *idealism. The 'dazzling chaos' (Boutroux) of his thought also appealed to the imagination of artists and poets, including John Milton (1608–74), William Blake (1757–1827) and S. T. *Coleridge.

Bibliography
P. Erb (tr.), *Jacob Boehme: The Way to Christ* (London and New York, 1978); B. Nicolescu, *Science, Meaning, and Evolution: The Cosmology of Jacob Boehme*, tr. R. Baker (New York, 1991); J. J. Stoudt, *Jacob Boehme: His Life and Thought* (New York, 1968).

P. N. HILLYER

BOETHIUS (*c*. 480–524)

Despite his noble Roman birth and senatorial rank, the statesman and Christian philosopher Boethius gained real political power at the court of the Gothic ruler of Rome, Theodoric. His prominence, however, did not last. Accused of treasonable dealings with the emperor in Constantinople, he was imprisoned in Pavia, where he was eventually executed.

Boethius was a transitional figure between the classical and the medieval world. He laid the foundation of the *quadrivium* ('the four ways'), the standard introduction to serious study of philosophy (see *Philosophy and theology). More important, he was a major influence in the virtually universal acceptance by Western *Christendom of a marriage between Christian theology and the best of Greek philosophy, effectively *Aristotle and the Neoplatonists (see *Platonism). Boethius' translation of and commentary on Porphyry's *Introduction* proved particularly influential in the medieval period.

Boethius also wrote on Christian doctrines, notably the Trinity and the person of Christ. But his most influential work has been *The Consolation of Philosophy*, written in prison as a vindication of the divine *providence behind the painful demise of his own political career. The work has been criticized because of its lack of explicit reference to Scripture and its reliance on logical reasoning. Indeed, Boethius actually identifies the 'highest good' of philosophers with the Christian God. But alongside this, deliberate parallels to the wisdom literature of the OT, particularly Ecclesiastes, must be recognized.

Bibliography
Works in *PL* 64–64.
Studies: H. Chadwick, *Boethius: The Consolations of Music, Logic, Theology and Philosophy* (Oxford, 1981); M. Gibson (ed.),

Boethius: His Life, Writings and Influence (Oxford, 1981); N. H. Kaylor, Jr and P. E. Phillips (eds.), *A Companion to Boethius in the Middle Ages* (Leiden, 2012); H. Liebeschütz in *CHLGEMP*, pp. 538–555; J. Marenbon, *Boethius* (Oxford, 2003); J. Marenbon (ed.), *The Cambridge Companion to Boethius* (Cambridge, 2009).

G. A. KEITH

BOFF, LEONARDO (b. 1938)

Boff is a Brazilian liberation theologian, social activist and ecologist. Born in Concordia, Santa Catarina, he joined the order of the Franciscan Minors in 1959 and later earned a doctorate in Germany under Karl *Rahner. He taught theology at the Franciscan Theological Institute in Petropolis, Brazil and became well known through his book *Jesus Christ the Liberator*, published in Portuguese in 1971, the first systematic Christology written by a Catholic theologian from Latin America, in dialogue with European theology. With his brother Clodovis he became an important protagonist of the *liberation theology movement, both through his support of the struggles for human rights in Brazil, and through his extensive writing in an effort to systematize the main themes of classic theology from a liberation perspective, including a reinterpretation of *Franciscan spirituality. Within the Catholic Church in Brazil, which was challenged by lack of clergy and the growth of Protestantism, Boff took part in the search for renewal of pastoral work and the effort to mobilize the laity that produced the Base Ecclesial Communities.

Theological reflection about this experience was summarized in 1981 in his book *The Church: Charisma and Power*, with a strong NT component, in an effort to develop a critical ecclesiology from the liberation perspective. Translated into several languages, the book became the subject of a process by the Sacred Congregation of the Doctrine of the Faith, which could not tolerate an open challenge to traditional Roman ecclesiology. Boff was sanctioned by the Vatican with censorship and restrictions to his teaching and priestly activity, though the sanction was lifted in 1986. His theology evolved as he became an activist in the issues of *ecology and *poverty, and he could not tolerate new restrictions imposed by the Vatican. In 1993 he abandoned the priesthood, got married and was appointed as a professor at the Rio de Janeiro State University. He currently lives in Jardim Araras, Brazil and is a Professor Emeritus of Ethics, Philosophy of Religion and Ecology.

Bibliography

Works: *Jesus Christ Liberator: A Critical Christology for Our Time* (Maryknoll, 1978); *Liberating Grace* (Maryknoll, 1979); *Church, Charism and Power: Liberation Theology and the Institutional Church* (New York, 1985); *Ecclesiogenesis: The Base Comunities Reinvent the Church* (Maryknoll, 1986); *Cry of the Earth, Cry of the Poor* (Maryknoll, 1997).

With Clodovis Boff: *Salvation and Liberation: In Search for a Balance between Faith and Politics* (Maryknoll, 1984); *Liberation Theology: From Confrontation to Dialogue* (San Francisco, 1986); *Introducing Liberation Theology* (Maryknoll and London, 1987).

Studies: D. W. Ferm, *Profiles in Liberation: 36 Portraits of Third World Theologians* (Mystic, 1988); A. T. Hennelly (ed.), *Liberation Theology: A Documentary History* (Maryknoll, 1990).

S. ESCOBAR

BONAVENTURA (1221–74)

Bonaventura was a *scholastic theologian, born in Tuscany, who became the greatest *Franciscan mystic after St Francis himself. Earning the MA degree at Paris, he joined the order (1243) and studied under some of its most renowned scholars, including Alexander of Hales (*c.* 1170–1245). In 1248 he began lecturing on the Scriptures and theology, but he was not formally received into the masters' guild at Paris until 1257 because of a dispute between the friars and the secular teachers. However, by that time he was no longer actively teaching, because he had been elected minister-general of the Franciscans (1257) and had resigned his position so that he could spend time on his administrative duties. Despite many other responsibilities he continued to encourage Franciscan involvement in academic life. Although often absent on business for the order and the church, whenever possible he preached at the university on matters of philosophical and theological importance to the faculty and students. Declining the position of Archbishop of York (1265), he was persuaded to become Bishop of

Albano (1273) and was also made a cardinal. He attended the Council of Lyons (1274) and contributed to an agreement to reunite the Western and Eastern churches.

Bonaventura was a mystic scholastic, as distinct from other Franciscans who were scientific scholastics and the *Dominicans such as *Thomas Aquinas who were rational scholastics. His leadership of the Franciscans temporarily saved the order from division by achieving a compromise between the two opposing factions. His most original thought, expressed in books including *The Seven Journeys of Eternity* and *The Journey of the Mind to God*, centres on mysticism, and this caused him to be remembered as 'the Seraphic Doctor'. The works are profoundly influenced by *Augustine, whom he regarded as a balance to the emphasis on *Aristotle and the Arabic commentaries which were so popular in his time.

The knowledge of God, according to Bonaventura, comes not through formulating propositions but by experience with him in the soul (see *Religious experience). Rational *knowledge of God is actually impossible because he is different from humans in a qualitative sense. Information about the divine is hazy, equivocal and analogous. An understanding of God comes through a long and arduous struggle of the spirit, rather than by means of a series of logical progressions. Preparation for an encounter with God requires separation from material concern. Then a person must look for God through shadows or reflections of the divine in things of the world. After one perceives God's presence in the world, one can see God through one's own being. For example, the human will demonstrates his goodness and the intellect shows his truth. This leads to an appreciation of the grace and transcendence of God, but another leap of faith is required to accept the mystery of the Trinity. At this stage in the mystical quest, Bonaventura warns, a period of testing, monotony and spiritual fatigue often sets in; but then, like the light of dawn, comes the gift of the Spirit consisting of an experience of the ineffable joy of the divine presence.

Bonaventura influenced and foreshadowed the great period of mysticism during the fourteenth and fifteenth centuries, which produced such individuals as Meister Eckhart, John Tauler and Thomas à Kempis (see *Imitation of Christ). The *Augustinianism and individual devotion that he emphasized helped to prepare the way for the Protestant Reformation.

Bibliography

E. Bettoni, *Saint Bonaventure* (Notre Dame, 1964); J. G. Bougerol, *Introduction to the Works of Bonaventure* (New York, 1964); L. Costello, *Saint Bonaventure* (New York, London, etc., 1911); E. Gilson, *The Philosophy of St Bonaventure* (New York, 1965); G. F. LaNave, 'Bonaventure', in P. L. Gavrilyuk and S. Oakley (eds.), *The Spiritual Senses: Perceiving God in Western Christianity* (Cambridge, 2011), pp. 159–173; J. F. Quinn, *The Historical Constitution of St. Bonaventure's Philosophy* (Toronto, 1973).

R. G. CLOUSE

BONHOEFFER, DIETRICH (1906–45)

Theologian and leader of the Confessing Church in Germany until his *martyrdom by the Nazis, Bonhoeffer remains one of the most provocative voices in contemporary Christianity, despite the fragmentary and occasional character of much of his writing.

Bonhoeffer was born into a leading German family and educated in Berlin, Tübingen and Rome, and his earliest theological work, *Sanctorum Communio*, attempted to bridge the theology of *revelation and philosophical sociology by describing the way in which the transcendent is encountered in corporate life. This early work contains many seeds of his more famous later writings, as does another early study on the place of ontology in systematic theology, *Act and Being*.

A spell in New York at Union Theological Seminary led Bonhoeffer into a strong reaction against *liberal theology and confirmed his nascent attraction to *Barth, at that time beginning work on the *Church Dogmatics*. On his return to Germany, Bonhoeffer taught in Berlin. His published lectures *Creation and Fall* (a highly charged interpretation of Gen. 1–3) and *Christology* are much under Barth's influence.

At the same time, Bonhoeffer became increasingly involved in the young ecumenical movement and in opposition to Hitler, and in the mid-1930s he emerged as a leader of the *Confessing Church which refused any alliance between Christianity and Nazism. Until its enforced closure, he ran a seminary for the Confessing Church at Finkenwalde.

From this period of his work come some of his well-known writings on spirituality, notably *Life Together* and *The Cost of Discipleship*. Until his arrest in 1943, he was at work on his posthumously published *Ethics*. His prison writings, collected as *Letters and Papers from Prison*, became one of the most influential theological documents of the century, notably for their attempts to phrase questions about the relationship between Christianity and the apparatus of human religion.

Proponents of the so-called 'theology of secularity' sought an antecedent in Bonhoeffer, but generally missed the nuances of his work. Behind the *Letters and Papers* is not so much a confidence about human powers as Bonhoeffer's eventual departure from Barth's account of the relation of revelation to human history. It is this, rather than denials of the possibility of all objective language about God, which should provide the starting point for appraisal of Bonhoeffer's fragmentary assertions about 'religionless Christianity' or man's 'coming of age'. In effect, Bonhoeffer seeks to correct Barth by reintroducing an emphasis on the relative autonomy of the natural order as the sphere of God's presence and action. In this way, Bonhoeffer moves towards a theological account of human responsibility, a theme which was to occupy Barth himself in his later years. Bonhoeffer's own biography, from which his theology is inseparable, shows a parallel growth into consciousness of responsibility for history. He lived through a critical phase of European political and intellectual history, and condenses many of its tragedies in his own life.

Bibliography

Works: *Life Together* (London, 1954); *Gesammelte Schriften*, 6 vols. (Munich, 1958–74); *The Cost of Discipleship* (London, 1959); *Creation and Fall* (London, 1959); *Act and Being* (London, 1962); *Sanctorum Communio* (London, 1963); *No Rusty Swords* (London, 1965); *The Way to Freedom* (London, 1966); *Letters and Papers from Prison* (London, ²1971); *True Patriotism* (London, 1973); *Christology* (London, 1978); *Ethics* (London, 1978). *Studies*: E. Bethge, *Dietrich Bonhoeffer* (London, 1970); A. Dumas, *Dietrich Bonhoeffer, Theologian of Reality* (London, 1971); J. D. Godsey, *The Theology of Dietrich Bonhoeffer* (London, 1960); K. L. Johnson and T. Larsen (eds.), *Bonhoeffer, Christ and Culture* (Downers Grove/Nottingham, 2013); E. Metaxas, *Bonhoeffer: Pastor, Martyr, Prophet, Spy* (London, 2011); H. Ott, *Reality and Faith* (London, 1971); J. A. Phillips, *The Form of Christ in the World* (London, 1967); R. Gregor Smith (ed.), *World Come of Age* (London, 1967).

J. B. WEBSTER

BOOK OF CONCORD, see CONFESSIONS OF FAITH

BOSSUET, JACQUES-BÉNIGNE (1627–1704)

Educated by Jesuits (Dijon) and mentored by Nicolas Cornet (Paris), Bossuet served as Archdeacon of Metz (1652), Bishop of Condom (1669) and Bishop of Meaux (1681). He was a gifted speaker, gaining a considerable reputation from his sermons and orations. Many of these in fact were delivered to the French court, with which Bossuet built important connections: in 1670 serving as tutor to the dauphin, and becoming Louis XIV's spiritual counsellor in 1675. Bossuet supported the 'Gallican thesis' – claiming that the French king's authority was derived directly from God, and not subordinated to the Pope's.

Bossuet entered into debates with contemporaries such as Hobbes, *Leibniz, Simon, Malebranche and Fénelon. Against Malebranche, who reduced divine governance to a 'general will', Bossuet insisted on God's *particular* *providence (to which, among other things, kings owed their absolute sovereignty). In the clamorous *quietism debate of the late 1690s Bossuet criticized Archbishop Fénelon's ideal of 'disinterested' love of God. Apart from deeming it alarmingly elitist, Bossuet saw in it a threat to the very foundations of Christianity – the knowledge and enjoyment of God's *goodness*. Finally, Bossuet felt much challenged by the Protestants, whom he encountered especially during his days in Metz. While attacking the Protestants in his writings, he nevertheless made attempts towards reconciliation between them and the Catholic Church.

Bibliography

Works: *Discourse on Universal History*, ed. O. Ranum (Chicago, 1976); *Politics Drawn from the Very Words of Holy Scripture*, ed. P. Riley (Cambridge, 1990).

Studies: H. L. S. Lear, *Bossuet and His Contemporaries* (London, 1880); E. K. Sanders, *Jacques-Bénigne Bossuet* (London, 1921); W. J. S. Simpson, *A Study of Bossuet* (London, 1937).

G. DE GRAAFF

BOSTON, THOMAS (1676–1732)

Boston was a Church of Scotland minister (see *Presbyterianism) and an accomplished theologian. Born in Berwickshire, Scotland, he graduated MA from Edinburgh University and studied theology there for one term, later completing his course under presbyterial supervision. He was minister, successively, at Simprin and Ettrick in the Scottish borders.

Boston published several books during his lifetime, the most famous being *Human Nature in Its Fourfold State*, which later ranked alongside *Pilgrim's Progress* in its popularity among Scottish Christians. Boston's treatises on the covenant of works and the covenant of grace rival even Herman Witsius (1636–1708) and Johannes *Cocceius (1603–69) in their cogent presentation of *covenant theology.

Boston was also an accomplished Hebraist, and his *Tractatus Stigmologicus Hebraicus* on the divine inspiration of the Hebrew accents (published posthumously in Lat. in 1738) earned him high praise from Hebrew scholars all over the world, albeit that later scholarship has demonstrated its main thesis to be untenable.

Boston's name is best known through his involvement in the Marrow Controversy. In the early eighteenth century there was a legalistic strain in Scottish theology. This came to the surface in a dispute between the Presbytery of Auchterarder and a student whom they refused to license because of his understanding of the doctrine of *repentance. The Presbytery had asked the student to subscribe to the following proposition: 'I believe that it is not sound and orthodox to teach that we forsake sin in order to our coming to Christ.' The student refused and the General Assembly of 1717 supported him, censuring the Presbytery. Boston agreed with the intention of the so-called 'Auchterarder Creed', although he had some reservations about the precision of its formulation.

In the context of this dispute, Boston began to recommend Edward Fisher's *The Marrow of Modern Divinity* (1645). It was a compilation of Reformed writing including passages from *Luther, *Calvin and English *Puritan divines, set in the form of a debate. Boston asserted that it had helped him to understand and preach the doctrines of *grace. James Hog of Carnock republished the book in 1718.

At this stage the two schools of thought within the church became apparent. Principal James Hadow (*c.* 1670–1747) of St Mary's College, St Andrews, opposed the book, which was ultimately banned by the General Assembly. Boston and eleven others (the 'Marrow Men') made unsuccessful representations to have this ban lifted. Both sides claimed to represent the position of the church's subordinate standard, the *Westminster Confession of Faith.

In retrospect, we can say that Hadow and those who supported him were guilty of a legalistic adaptation of covenant theology. They made repentance a condition of salvation and restricted the gospel offer in the belief that a universal offer required as its basis a universal redemption. Boston and the others represented covenant theology as a theology of grace. As for Hadow's view that the Marrow and the Marrow Men were opposed to the Westminster Confession, it is significant that the 1645 edition of the Marrow appeared with a preface by Joseph Caryl (1602–73), who had been specifically appointed by the Westminster Assembly to 'revise and approve theological works for the press' (D. Beaton, *Records of the Scottish Church History Society* I).

Boston later re-issued the Marrow with his own notes (in *Works*, vol. 7). This is the edition which is most significant for a proper understanding of the debate.

Bibliography

Works: *Memoirs*, ed. G. H. Morrison (Edinburgh, 1899); *Works*, ed. S. McMillan, 12 vols. (Edinburgh, 1853).

Studies: D. Beaton, 'The "Marrow of Modern Divinity" and the Marrow Controversy', *Records of the Scottish Church History Society* I, 1926, pp. 112–134; J. P. Mackenzie, 'The Reformed Doctrine of the Will of God in the Theology and Pastoral Practice of Thomas Boston', PhD thesis (Aberdeen, 2011); A. T. B. McGowan, *The Federal Theology of Thomas Boston* (Carlisle, 1997); P. Ryken, *Thomas Boston as Preacher of the Fourfold State* (Carlisle, 1995).

A. T. B. MCGOWAN

BRADWARDINE, THOMAS
(*c.* 1290–1349)

Sometimes called 'Doctor profundus', Bradwardine was a member of Merton College, Oxford, and a student of mathematics and theology. He was chosen Archbishop of Canterbury a few weeks before he died of the Black Death.

Bradwardine's chief work, *De Causa Dei Contra Pelagium*, is a massive and profound metaphysical polemic against both the characteristic doctrines of *Pelagianism and the Pelagian temper. The work was edited in 1618 by Sir Henry Savile, with the help of William Twisse (1575–1646), who later became the prolocutor of the Westminster Assembly. In that work the *Augustinian (and biblical) themes of the bondage of the *will, *predestination and the need for prevenient *grace are developed with an unrivalled subtlety and precision, from a dominantly theocentric standpoint: that of a God who in timeless eternity unchangeably wills and controls all that comes to pass, without being the author of sin. The extent to which this represents a hardening of Augustine's position is a matter of continuing debate.

Bradwardine is regarded (with, for example, *Wyclif) as an important influence preparing the way for the *Reformation in England, and thus as an important element of continuity between the medieval church and the *Lutheran Reformation and its effects.

Bibliography
Works: *De Causa Dei Contra Pelagium*, ed. H. Savile (repr. Frankfurt, 1964 [1618]).
Studies: E. W. Dolnikowski, *Thomas Bradwardine: A View of Time and a Vision of Eternity in Fourteenth-Century Thought* (Leiden, 1995); G. Leff, *Bradwardine and the Pelagians* (Cambridge, 1957); H. A. Oberman, *Archbishop Thomas Bradwardine* (Utrecht, 1965).

P. HELM

BRIGGS, CHARLES AUGUSTUS
(1841–1913)

Born in New York City, the son of Alanson Briggs and Sarah Mead Berrian, Briggs attended the University of Virginia. Converted during the 1858 revival, he decided to prepare for pastoral ministry. The Civil War temporarily diverted his plans, and he served in the Union Army before entering Union Theological Seminary in 1861.

Ordained a Presbyterian in 1866, he pursued doctoral studies at the University of Berlin. Returning in 1869, he pastored in Roselle, New Jersey before accepting a teaching position at Union in 1874. Introducing the higher critical method in biblical studies to a US audience, Briggs became a lightning rod between conservatives and liberals in the waning years of the nineteenth century. His problems with *Presbyterianism were exacerbated when he published *Whither? A Theological Question for the Times* (1889) in which he advocated changes in the *Westminster Confession. The controversy led to charges of heresy. In a show of solidarity, the faculty of Union voted to disaffiliate with the Presbyterian Church. Briggs was ordained in the Episcopal Church and continued teaching at Union until 1904.

See also: LIBERAL THEOLOGY.

Bibliography
R. L. Christensen, *The Ecumenical Orthodoxy of Charles Augustus Briggs: 1841–1913* (Lewiston, 1995); M. S. Massa, *Charles Augustus Briggs and the Crisis of Historical Criticism* (Minneapolis, 1990).

D. W. FAUPEL

BROWN, WILLIAM ADAMS
(1863–1943)

Brown was a *Presbyterian minister and theologian, born in New York and educated first at Yale, then Union Theological Seminary, with which his family had strong associations. Following further study in Germany under *Harnack, he taught at Union from 1898 to 1936, beginning his career as the controversy surrounding C. *Briggs and biblical authority was reaching its height, and being appointed Professor of Systematic Theology in 1897. He was accused of *heresy at his own denominational Assembly in 1913 following a speech on 'The Old Theology and the New', delivered at Harvard two years earlier. Union Seminary Principal Francis Brown rallied support and averted formal charges.

Early in his career, Brown became engaged in home mission work with poorer and immigrant communities. Later he was active in opposition to commercialized vice and political corruption in the city, and was a key activist in Union Settlement Involved at East Harlem, a seminary initiative that provided education, health and social support services. Further ecumenical work included war-time chaplaincy coordination, and interest in ministerial training. Following retirement in 1930, he became Research Professor of Applied Christianity until 1936. Brown published fifteen books, including *Christian Theology in Outline*; his reminiscences are in *A Teacher and His Times*.

See also: LIBERAL THEOLOGY.

Bibliography

Works: *A Teacher and His Times: A Story of Two Worlds* (New York, 1940).

Studies: G. Dorrien, *The Making of American Liberal Theology: Idealism, Realism and Modernity* (Louisville, 2003); R. Handy, *A History of Union Theological Seminary in New York* (New York, 1987).

J. GORDON

BRUNNER, EMIL (1889–1966)

A Swiss Reformed theologian, Brunner was initially a pastor before becoming a professor of systematic and practical theology in Zurich from 1924 to 1955. He travelled widely, having a lifelong interest in ecumenism and mission, and spent the concluding two years of his teaching career in Japan.

In reacting against *Schleiermacher's theology, and that of the *liberal Protestant school, Brunner has been identified with *Barth and others as part of the *neo-orthodox movement, whose theology, couched in dialectical terms, was influenced by *Kierkegaard and *Buber.

Brunner considered that the *revelation on which Christianity was based consisted of a person-to-person encounter. Thus God's revelation, occurring uniquely in the life, death and resurrection of Jesus, is completed only when the individual acknowledges that Jesus is Lord. *Scripture itself is not revelation, for it is not verbally inspired and infallible, but it may be the bridge used by the Spirit to bring a person to faith. Brunner admitted that there was historical uncertainty about the gospel events, but affirmed that the divine and human natures were united in Jesus Christ. Thus he embodies and accomplishes mediation between God and man; hence Brunner's *Christology is entitled *The Mediator* (London, 1934).

It was Brunner's conviction that belief in Christ necessitated universal revelation of God in creation, history and human conscience. This brought him into sharp conflict in 1934 with Barth, who completely rejected any notion of general revelation. (See Brunner's 'Nature and Grace' to which Barth replied with 'No!' Both are printed in *Natural Theology*, with an introduction by John *Baillie, London, 1946.) However, Brunner was not suggesting that general revelation offered the first reliable step into knowledge of God which special revelation completed. Rather, fallen man retains something of the *image of God which enables him to perceive distorted truth about God. Special revelation brings this truth into focus, confirming what is right, and reforming what is wrong.

Brunner's major exposition of doctrine is to be found in his three-volume *Dogmatics* (London: vol. 1, 1949; vol. 2, 1952; vol. 3, 1962).

Brunner inherited from his family an interest in social issues, which was kept alive by the questions arising from two world wars and the advance of Communism. Although man's revolt against God has led to despair and guilt, nevertheless the unbeliever is still related to and responsible to God. This theme, developed in *Man in Revolt* (London, 1939), lies behind his *ethics found in *The Divine Imperative* (London, 1937). God gives man the opportunity to obey his command to love both God and man. Love for humanity is appropriately expressed as one recognizes the different orders of society: family; the community, understood economically, legally (the state) or culturally; and the church. Both books opposed the totalitarianism found in Hitler's National Socialism and in the Communist bloc on the grounds that they promoted the godless dehumanization of society and were to be identified with Antichrist. Consequently, both were banned in Hitler's Germany.

Brunner made a positive contribution to post-war reconstruction through his book *Justice and the Social Order* (London, 1945), which discussed both the principles and the practice of justice at different levels of society. That this dogmatic theologian also concerned himself with practical issues sprang from his conviction that dogmatics and ethics are inextricably linked both in the NT and in proclamation and in Christian experience.

Bibliography

J. E. Humphrey, *Emil Brunner* (Peabody, 1991); C. W. Kegley (ed.), *The Theology of Emil Brunner* (New York, 1962).

C. A. BAXTER

BUBER, MARTIN (1878–1965)

Grandson of the famous Midrash scholar Solomon Buber, philosopher, theologian, Zionist and lover of the pietistic, messianic Hasidim, Buber's influence on *Judaism and Christianity is enormous.

Jews will think of Buber in three areas:

Hasidism. This movement of ultra-orthodox and mystical Judaism was founded in the eighteenth century and had its base in Eastern Europe. Buber's youthful contact with Hasidic communities led, in his adult years, to his editing the *Tales of the Hasidim* and other works telling the legends and beliefs of the Hasidim. His love for Hasidic communities brought him to see the importance of community witness whereby the life of Israel should permeate the Gentile world. He noted the formative Jewish influence on Christianity, Islam and Marxism. He saw Israel as the 'gateway of the nations', fusing the spirit of the East and West in fruitful reciprocity.

Zionism. Buber became a Zionist at university and later edited the paper *Die Welt* (*The World*). During both World Wars he laboured tirelessly for Jews under German occupation. Having supported Jewish colonies in Palestine all his life, he migrated to Israel in 1938, where he was Professor of Social Philosophy in Jerusalem. As a *Zionist, he advocated 'peace and brotherhood with the Arab people'.

The Bible. Buber dedicated himself to the translation of the Hebrew Scriptures into German for German-speaking Jews. Ironically, his translation is now mainly used by Gentile Christians, the community for which it was intended having been largely exterminated. His biblical studies led also to a significant work on *The Kingship of God* as well as the books *Moses* and *The Prophetic Faith*.

Christians will know Buber best for his book *I and Thou* and for his work on dialogue. Both spring from the influence of *existentialism in the 1920s. Supported by Hasidic teaching that there is good in all things, Buber stressed the need for 'education', which unfolds what is in man, rather than 'propaganda'. He taught the need for an I-Thou relationship of love and appreciative understanding, not the proselytizing I-It confrontation which uses the other approach. But in his *Writings on the Dialogue Principle*, he also maintains that 'dialogue does not mean a mutual relativization of convictions, but the acceptance of the other as a person'.

The influence of Buber's I-Thou thought spread through Emil *Brunner to such 'Christian presence' thinkers as Max Warren (1904–77) and John V. Taylor (1914–2001). He also played a formative part in the unfolding of Christian thought on dialogue and proselytization. But in this context it should be noted that Buber steadily upheld the calling of Israel to bring salvation to the nations.

Bibliography

Works: *Tales of the Hasidim* (New York, 1947); *On Judaism* (New York, 1967); *I and Thou* (New York, 1970).

Studies: M. L. Diamond, *Martin Buber, Jewish Existentialist* (New York, 1968); M. Friedman, *Martin Buber: The Life of Dialogue* (Chicago, 1955); idem, *Martin Buber's Life and Work*, 3 vols. (New York, 1981–8); D. J. Moore, *Martin Buber: Prophet of Religious Secularism* (New York, 1996); M. Zank (ed.), *New Perspectives on Martin Buber* (Tübingen, 2006).

M. F. GOLDSMITH

BUCER (BUTZER), MARTIN (1491–1551)

A native of Sélestat in Alsace, Bucer (or Butzer) became a Dominican (1506), but Alsatian *humanism prepared him first for *Erasmus and then *Luther, who captivated him at the Heidelberg disputation in 1518. He left the cloister, was married in 1522 and excommunicated, and took refuge in Strasbourg (1523), where he soon became the leader of reform.

Bucer was prominently involved in the Protestant Supper-strife (see *Eucharist). After supporting the approach of *Zwingli and *Oecolampadius, he formulated a mediating (South German) position from *c*. 1528, insisting that Luther and Zwingli were fighting merely about words. Strasbourg did not at first subscribe to the *Augsburg Confession (1530), submitting instead, in the interests of Protestant concord, the Tetrapolitan Confession. Eventually Bucer and *Melanchthon reached agreement on the Eucharist in the Wittenberg Concord (1536). While unhappy with some Lutheran formulae, Bucer stressed that even unworthy believers (but not rank unbelievers) partake by faith of the true (real) presence of Christ's body and blood, presented and conveyed (*exhibere*) by and with the elements in a 'sacramental union'. Not all applauded Bucer's almost scholastic facility in formulating agreed statements. This applied also to his efforts with Melanchthon to negotiate doctrinal accord with Catholics in Germany (*c.* 1540). Provisional agreement on justification was reached at Regensburg in 1541. In pursuit of consensus, Bucer made much of the pure unity of the early church.

The strength of Bucer's theology lay in his ecclesiology. He was more deeply committed than Luther to the ordered life of a community renewed according to the biblical pattern and marked by mutual love and service in the Spirit. The civil authorities had, in his view, an important role in religious reform. His insistence on church *discipline reflected in part his responsiveness to some of the demands of Strasbourg's numerous Radical Reformers (see *Reformation, Radical). On this and other issues (e.g. the four orders of ministry, the ordering of worship, congregational singing, education), *Calvin learned much at Strasbourg (1538–41), and Bucer's vision of a reformed *church and a Christian society found fuller realization in Geneva and elsewhere than proved possible in Strasbourg.

So strong was Bucer's emphasis on spiritual renewal that he could acknowledge a twofold *justification. True faith, which he defined as a sure persuasion, was always 'active through love' (Gal. 5:6). He was more disposed than Luther and Calvin to speak of free will in the unregenerate.

Bucer's last years (1548–51) were spent in exile, chiefly as regius professor in Cambridge. There he influenced the *Book of Common Prayer* (1552), and *English Reformers such as John Bradford (*c.* 1510–55), Matthew Parker (1504–75) and John Whitgift (*c.* 1530–1604). He produced for Edward VI a remarkable blueprint for a Christian England, *The Kingdom of Christ*, and, as one of the Reformation's ablest expositors, contributed to the shaping of the English exegetical tradition.

See also: REFORMATION THEOLOGY.

Bibliography

Works: Collected edition in progress: German (Gutersloh, 1960–); Latin (Paris, 1954–5; Leiden, 1982–); *Correspondence* (Leiden, 1979–). In ET, selections in: D. F. Wright, *Common Places of Martin Bucer* (Appleford, 1972); W. Pauck (ed.), *Melanchthon and Bucer*, LCC 19 (London, 1970).

Studies: H. Eells, *Martin Bucer* (New Haven, 1931); W. P. Stephens, *The Holy Spirit in the Theology of Martin Bucer* (London, 1970); D. F. Wright, *Martin Bucer: Reforming Church and Community* (Cambridge, 1994).

D. F. WRIGHT

BUDDHISM AND CHRISTIANITY

'The Buddha' is not a name but a Sanskrit word meaning 'enlightened one', or 'one who is awake to everything that is going on around him'. This title is used for Siddhattha (personal name) Gotama (clan name) after his alleged enlightenment at the age of thirty-five. Each world and period of time has a Buddha, a being who discovers the *Dharma* (true nature of all things) by himself and reaches out to help humankind toward liberation from *suffering. The way of liberation taught by Siddhattha, the Buddha of our time, will one day become overgrown as humankind abandons appropriate living. A new Buddha will then emerge and rediscover the *Dharma*. This next Buddha is referred to as Metteyya, and Siddhattha (sometimes referred to as the historical Buddha) predicted he would come 5,000 years after his passing away.

Siddhattha Gotama was born around 480 BC in Lumbini, in present-day Nepal. His father, Shuddhodhana, often referred to in Mahayama Buddhism as Shakyamunit, was a leading nobleman of the Shakya tribe. His mother, Maya, died seven days after his birth, and his mother's sister later married Shuddhodhana and brought up Siddhattha.

An astrologer called Asita went to visit his father five days after the child's birth. Observing physical marks of a future Buddha on Siddhattha, he said that the child would become either a great monarch or an enlightened being. He added that if Siddhattha saw what life was really like for ordinary people, then he would forsake palace life and seek spiritual enlightenment. The father kept his son within the palace, surrounded him with luxury and pleasure and hoped that he would become a great warrior. Siddhattha did, however, have exposure to the outside world and saw the sufferings of ordinary people. This led him at the age of twenty-nine to leave his wife (Yashodhara) and young son (Rahula) in order to become a mendicant. His quest was to strive after truth, in particular the cause and cure of suffering, through the traditional mendicant's disciplines of thinking, exchanging ideas, meditation, asceticism and the practice of yoga.

After five years Siddhattha went through an intense and extended experience when he allegedly became enlightened and able to recall his previous existences and the reincarnations of world systems. He gained insight into what is known as the Four Noble Truths:

- Suffering (*dukkha*), a reality for all sentient beings, is unhappiness, a lack of satisfaction due to the changing nature of existence.
- The cause of suffering is our craving and thirst (*tanha*).
- Suffering can be reduced and eradicated by stopping our craving and striving.
- The way leading to the cessation of suffering, or enlightenment, *nirvana*, is following the Middle Way, also known as the Eight-Fold Path.

The initial response of the Buddha (as he should now be referred to) was not to teach the *Dharma*, since it would be difficult for people to understand and accept it. Yet out of compassion he began to teach. His first sermon, *The Discourse of Setting the Wheel [of the Dharma] in Motion*, was in the Deer Park, near Benares, to the five ascetics he had trained with prior to his enlightenment. The Buddha and the five ascetics, who one by one became enlightened, travelled around as monks (*bhikkhus*) teaching the *Dharma* and the extinguishing of suffering, and modelling good behaviour. They were offered food, basic medicines and robes by lay supporters, who viewed this as part of their spiritual practice. The community of monks were referred to as the *sangha*, and in time developed rules for monastic behaviour (*vinaya*). Five years after the monastic order was established, an order of nuns (*bhikkhsunis*) began. The Buddha passed away (*parinirvana*) at the age of eighty without appointing a successor, since he expected the monks to be instructed by the *Dharma* and to adhere to monastic discipline.

What does a Buddhist believe?

An essential feature of Buddhism is taking refuge in the 'Triple Gem': that is, respect/devotion for the Buddha, appreciation for the *Dharma*, the ultimate truth of everything, and respect for the *sangha*, the community of practising Buddhists (sometimes the monks alone).

A Buddhist will keep the Five Precepts. Viewed positively, these are important rules for character development. Indeed, each precept begins with 'I undertake the rule of training to abstain from (I) harming living beings; (II) "taking what is not given"; (III) misconduct concerning sense pleasures [generally understood to mean no illicit sex]; (IV) false speech and (V) unmindful states due to alcoholic drink or drugs' (P. Harvey, *An Introduction to Buddhism*, p. 199). Buddhists may well attend temples on holy days; these occur on the new, full and the two quarter phases of the moon. On these occasions, and at retreats, the Five Precepts are often increased to Eight Precepts.

The Eight-Fold Path is central to the Buddhist belief system. When the Middle Way is followed at the higher level, then it will ultimately lead to *nirvana*, the cessation of suffering. The path is first followed at the ordinary or mundane level. This generates merit and leads to good rebirths; this is sometimes described as karmic Buddhism. The Buddhist may then experience the true nature of things, entering the *Dharma* stream, and follow the Path at the supramundane level. The Path is then referred to as the Noble Eight-Fold Path. There are eight interconnected aspects to the Path regardless of whether it is followed at the ordinary or the higher level. They are as follows: (1) right view or understanding of the nature of reality; (2) right intention to follow the teachings of the Buddha for one's own eventual liberation but also for the benefit of others; (3) right speech – to be truthful, accurate and gentle with one's words; (4) right action – keeping the rules of training, e.g. the Five Precepts; (5) right livelihood – an occupation which brings suffering is an unskilful way of making a living; (6) right effort – working hard to purify the mind as this determines who we become; (7) right mindfulness – being aware of how we cause ourselves and others to suffer, and working with mindfulness as this leads to a safer and more efficient working environment; (8) right concentration – achieved through meditation which expands the mind, enabling it to move beyond its conditioning, bringing insight into reality.

Karma is a key Buddhist doctrine; it is moral cause and effect – action and reaction. It is viewed by Buddhists as a natural law like the law of gravity. Actions have to be intentional if they are to generate karmic fruit. Bad karmic fruit, for example, is not generated if one accidentally hurts someone else. *Karma* should not be thought of as a reward or punishment by a deity, as there is no god in Buddhism; it is simply the working out of a principle, or law.

A moment passes away and does not leave anything but an impression which is picked up by the next moment. Within this 'impression' is a trace of all that has gone before in terms of karmic action. This trace may be seen as determining our next moment. The rebirth process (transfer from one life to the next) is similar to the transfer of an impression from moment to moment. Karmic seed (intentional action whether skilful or unskilful) is passed on and becomes karmic fruit in the future. *Karma*, then, determines the location/state of our rebirth. Thus, we continue to be reborn until the fires of greed, hatred and delusion are extinguished and we become enlightened, entering the state of *nirvana*. A person who reaches this stage will not be reborn.

Two major schools of Buddhism may be distinguished. Theravada Buddhism emphasizes the solitary life of religious discipline, but Mahayana Buddhism, founded by the philosopher Nagarjuna, puts more emphasis on the life of compassion and reveres the *bodhisattva*, the sage who delays *nirvana* until all are saved from suffering and rebirth.

Four basic dissonances between Buddhism and Christianity

First, in Buddhism, salvation (defined as liberation from suffering) is achieved through attending to the Eight-Fold Path. While some confidence and faith are placed in one's teachers, the ability to liberate one's self lies within. When Christians attempt to show Buddhists that *salvation is all of God, it can create the impression that spiritual discipline and good deeds are unnecessary.

Secondly, Christians define *sin as lack of conformity to God's moral will. In Buddhism, there is no god or law giver. The Buddha showed people an overgrown path, which, if followed, will lead to liberation. Buddhists view 'sin' as unskilful action based on a misunderstanding of reality (ignorance). This unenlightened behaviour causes suffering.

Thirdly, many Buddhists believe that this world of suffering is the effect of a bad cause. If a god created it, he may have had great power but was not a compassionate and wise being. Ignorance could only be responsible for this world of suffering from which we must all escape. Christians attest that a loving and powerful God devolves genuine moral choice to humankind. Suffering is a corollary of selfish choices.

Fourthly, knowledge of ultimate reality for a Buddhist is gained from living a morally upright life and listening to Buddhist teachers. Primarily, however, meditation, the developing and purifying of the mind which leads to knowing truth, is the key to advancement. For the Christian, what we need to know is revealed by God in our prayerful engagement with the Christian Scriptures.

See also: CHRISTIANITY AND OTHER RELIGIONS.

Bibliography

D. Cush, *Buddhism* (London, 1993), a highly accessible introduction; J. R. Davis, *The Path to Enlightenment: Introducing Buddhism* (London, Sydney and Auckland, 1977), contains some Christian perspectives on and responses to Buddhism; P. Harvey, *An Introduction to Buddhism* (Cambridge and New York, 1990); C. Prebish and D. Keown, *Introducing Buddhism* (New York and Abingdon, 2006).

R. MACKENZIE

BULGAKOV, SERGEI (1871–1944)

Sergei Bulgakov was born in 1871, the son of a Russian priest. As a young man, he lost his faith and graduated from Moscow University with a doctorate in economics, having become a convinced Marxist. After the failure of the 1905 revolution, he, along with other members of the intelligentsia, gradually found his way back to the Russian Orthodox Church, and was a lay member of the 1917–18 synod, or *Sobor*, that restored the patriarchate and sought to reform the church, but was cut short by the Communist Revolution of 1918. In that year he accepted ordination as a priest. In 1922, as one of the intellectuals deemed of no use to the new Communist state, he was expelled from Russia, and after a short time in Prague, arrived in Paris in 1925. He became Professor of Dogmatic Theology, and then Dean, of the newly founded Institut St-Serge, where he remained until his death in 1944.

Bulgakov's earliest writings were on economics, though gradually economics became for him an understanding of the way the human shared in God's care for his creation, and so exercised both a divine role in relation to the created order and also as human became a kind of priest of nature. This interest in what one might call the 'interface' between God and his creation Bulgakov came to pursue through the notion of the divine wisdom or *sophia*, a notion based on the wisdom literature in the Bible (Proverbs and the Wisdom of Solomon), developed by the Church Fathers (see *Patristic theology; *Wisdom in early Christology), celebrated in Christian liturgy, especially in relation to the virgin Mother of God, and given modern form in the works of Vladimir Solov'ev, an enormous influence on the Russian Christian intelligentsia. This 'sophiology', as he called it, was controversial, especially among conservative elements reacting against the Russian revolution, and he was condemned in the early 1930s, though exonerated by the Russian jurisdiction to which he belonged.

In Paris, he became one of the most articulate voices of the Russian diaspora and sought to communicate the insights of *Russian Orthodoxy to the Western Christian world that had welcomed him. He was deeply committed to Christian ecumenism. In exile, he wrote voluminously, including two great theological trilogies: a smaller one between 1927 and 1929, and a larger one, *On Godmanhood*, begun in 1933 and still incomplete at his death.

Bibliography

Works: The small trilogy: *The Burning Bush* (1927), *The Friend of the Bridegroom* (1927; ET, Grand Rapids, 2003), *Jacob's Ladder* (1929); The great trilogy: *The Lamb of God* (1933, ET, 2008), *The Comforter* (1936; ET, Grand Rapids, 2004), *The Bride of the Lamb* (1945; ET, Grand Rapids, 2002).

Studies: A. Nichols, *Wisdom from Above: A Primer in the Theology of Father Sergei Bulgakov* (Leominster, 2005); R. Williams, *Sergii Bulgakov: Towards a Russian Political Theology* (Edinburgh, 1999).

A. LOUTH

BULLINGER, JOHANN HEINRICH (1504–75)

Born at Bremgarten, Switzerland, the son of the parish priest, Bullinger was educated at Emmerich, then Cologne, where he studied the Fathers, felt the impact of *Erasmus, *Luther and *Melanchthon, and commenced a direct investigation of the NT. Back in Switzerland in 1522, he lived in Bremgarten, lectured at Kappel, and took courses at Zurich, where he supported *Zwingli and was elected a delegate to the Berne Disputation. Ordained in 1528, he ministered at Bremgarten, marrying a former nun in 1529.

The defeat at Kappel (1531) forced him into refuge at Zurich, and here, rejecting offers from Berne and Basel, he succeeded Zwingli as virtual leader of church life in both city and canton. He remained in this post until his death, exercising a quietly effective pastoral ministry, strengthening fellowship with other churches, and entertaining refugees, especially Anglican exiles under Mary, such as John *Jewel (1522–71).

In addition to his regular duties, Bullinger carried through an extensive literary programme; he himself collected his chief writings into ten volumes. Prominent among his works are commentaries, polemical treatises against the *Anabaptists and Lutherans, doctrinal writings on the *Eucharist and Scripture, sermons on the Christian sacrifice and the Lord's Supper, a diary, and a history of the Reformation. Of special interest to *Anglicans are the *Decades*, five books of ten sermons each on the heads of Christian doctrine which, by Archbishop Whitgift's order in 1586, became prescribed reading for the English clergy in an effort to meet Puritan protests against scholarly inadequacy.

More important, perhaps, than the academic labours were Bullinger's confessional contributions, which began in 1536 when, with *Bucer and Leo Jud (1482–1542), he drew up the First Helvetic Confession (see *Confessions of Faith) in a futile attempt to reach agreement with the Lutherans. Irenically disposed, Bullinger achieved greater ecumenical success in 1549, for in that year, after discussions with Calvin, the *Consensus Tigurinus* (Zurich Consensus), consisting of twenty-six articles on the sacraments, united Zurich and other German-speaking Swiss churches with Geneva and Neuchâtel. Bullinger's crowning confessional achievement came in 1566 when, at the request of the elector Palatine, he issued a statement of beliefs which, commonly known as the Second Helvetic Confession, found wide acceptance in Switzerland, France, Scotland, Hungary, Poland and the Netherlands as well as Germany.

Noteworthy among Bullinger's emphases in both his writings and his confessions are his commitment to the *creeds, his regard for the Fathers, and his conviction that the Reformation was restoration, not innovation. In the tradition of Zwingli, creeds and Fathers remain subordinate to the word of God in its threefold form as incarnate, spoken and written. The Spirit's role in the interpretation as well as the inspiration of Scripture receives attention, although not at the expense of scholarly, if prayerful, exegesis. Bullinger maintained Zwingli's position on the baptismal *covenant, but added positive insights to the more negative eucharistic teaching. His presentation of election had an interesting Christological focus. He shared common *Reformation views on such matters as *justification, *atonement, church and papacy. His position on *adiaphora and on church-state relations brought him into sympathy with early Elizabethan Anglican church leaders against their Puritan critics.

Bibliography

Works: F. Büsser *et al.* (eds.), *Works* (Zurich, 1972–c. 92); ET selections in G. W. Bromiley (ed.), *Zwingli and Bullinger* (London, 1953); T. Harding (ed.), *The Decades of Henry Bullinger*, 5 vols. (Cambridge, 1849–52);

Studies: J. W. Baker, *Heinrich Bullinger and the Covenant* (Athens, 1981); E. Campi and P. Opitz (eds.), *Heinrich Bullinger: Life, Thought, Influence* (Zurich, 2007); B. Gordon and E. Campi (eds.), *Architect of Reformation: An Introduction to Heinrich Bullinger, 1504–1575* (Grand Rapids, 2004); D. J. Keep, *Henry Bullinger and the Elizabethan Church*, unpub. diss. (University of Sheffield, 1970); C. P. Venema, *Heinrich Bullinger and the Doctrine of Predestination* (Grand Rapids, 2002).

G. W. BROMILEY

BULTMANN, RUDOLF (1884–1976)

NT scholar and theologian, influential most especially through his work on the existentialist interpretation of the Christian faith. After studying at Tübingen, Berlin and Marburg, Bultmann taught at Breslau, and from 1921 to 1951 was professor of NT at Marburg. His theology is expounded in his *Theology of the New Testament*, in a variety of studies of NT and theological issues, in his various collections of essays, and in his large-scale commentary *The Gospel of John*.

Bultmann's basic proposals about existentialist interpretation were conceived early in his theological development, although the terminology of '*kerygma' and '*myth' did not emerge until late in the 1930s. For Bultmann, the interpretation of the NT involves 'demythologizing', i.e. a proper interpretation of the mythological language in which its kerygma or message about human existence is couched. 'Myth' is a flexible term in Bultmann's usage, but most commonly denotes 'objectifying' language. Such language projects reality 'out there', speaking of it as an object essentially unrelated to human self-understanding and existence. To 'demythologize' the biblical writings is not to eliminate their mythology while retaining some non-mythological material: such selectivity Bultmann criticized in the attempts of some nineteenth-century liberal theologians to disentangle Jesus' moral teaching from his eschatology, for example. Demythologizing is rather a process of interpreting mythology consistently, in terms of the understanding of human existence which it articulates. Thus, for example, to demythologize creation myths is not to repudiate them as untrue, but to interpret them as objectified expressions of man's understanding of himself as *contingent.

To some extent, demythologizing is an *apologetic exercise, seeking to distinguish between the Christian faith and an obsolete supernatural worldview in which it finds expression and which is no longer available to us. But philosophical and theological factors are more determinative upon Bultmann's programme than such considerations. Bultmann drew heavily on the work of his Marburg colleague Martin *Heidegger, whose book *Being and Time* (1927) is one of the fundamental texts of German *existentialism. Heidegger's analysis of human existence in that book was especially influential over the question of man as a subject within *history, whose selfhood is not the expression of a pre-given nature but rather created in historical acts of decision and choice. This sense of man as 'history' rather than 'nature', which surfaces in Bultmann's treatment of theological *anthropology in his *Theology of the New Testament*, was bound up with the further influence of the Marburg Neo-Kantian philosophy of Hermann Cohen (1842–1918) and Paul Natorp (1854–1924), with its radical dualism of 'fact' and 'value'. These philosophical influences are, however, absorbed within what is essentially a theological project. Behind the programme of demythologizing lies a tradition within nineteenth-century Lutheranism according to which knowledge of objective facts constitutes human 'works', that is, the attempt to secure the self against encounter with God by a codified account of the divine being and acts. In effect, demythologizing is for Bultmann the *epistemological equivalent of *justification by faith: both meritorious works and objectified knowledge of God are attempts to guarantee the self over against God. Here Bultmann owes a great deal to the turn-of-the-century Lutheran theologian Wilhelm *Herrmann, who laid emphasis on faith as encounter with God in the present rather than as mere assent to objective realities doctrinally described. From this perspective, it should be added, Bultmann's early attraction to the *dialectical theology of the early *Barth and Friedrich *Gogarten is readily comprehensible, in so far as he, like Barth in *The Epistle to the Romans* (1919), is rejecting any ground for human security against interruption by God.

This account of demythologizing or 'de-objectification' helps account for Bultmann's radical scepticism about the historicity of the NT records. Along with other early form-critics such as Martin Dibelius (1883–1947), Bultmann concluded in *The History of the Synoptic Tradition* (1921) that the Gospels contain almost no authentic historical information about Jesus, but rather material shaped and frequently created by the early Christian communities. Bultmann's theology can support such scepticism, however, precisely because objective historical facts simply constitute 'knowledge after the flesh'. Real knowledge of Christ is encounter with him in the word of the kerygma as one who summons man now to meaningful existence. Bultmann thus excises the 'Jesus of history' (see *Historical Jesus, quest for) from *Christology; historical interest in the personality and deeds of Jesus both cannot and should not be satisfied, since it merely furnishes the occasion for human evasion of the claim of God by adhering to objective realities. Like Martin *Kähler, whose book *The So-Called Historical Jesus and the Historic, Biblical Christ* deeply influenced him, Bultmann envisages the concern of Christology to be the 'Christ of faith', Christ encountered in believing existence (or, as earlier Protestants would state it, in his *benefits*), rather than in abstract historical observation.

While Bultmann's influence on the course of twentieth-century theology and biblical interpretation was immense, subsequent critical scholarship has qualified much of his historical scepticism. Many pupils of Bultmann associated with the so-called 'New Quest of the Historical Jesus' (such as E. *Käsemann, E. Fuchs, 1903–83, and G. *Ebeling) have found a stronger historical anchor for the kerygma in the history of Jesus than Bultmann allowed; others have radically criticized his reading of the influence of *Gnosticism and *Hellenism on primitive Christianity.

In systematic theology and philosophy, Bultmann acutely rephrased some fundamental questions concerning the relation of faith to history and the nature of divine presence and action in a way which remains fundamentally determinative for some contemporary theological reflection. Bultmann consistently attempted to construct a theology in which the question of God and the question of human existence would be inseparable. But because of his theological roots in Lutheranism and the influence of both *dualist and existentialist philosophy, he found acute difficulty in talking of God's transcendence and his action in history, since he always suspected such talk to be objectifying. Bultmann's theology is thought by many to lack any ontological reference in its interpretation of the Christian faith, and thus to be radically subjective, translating statements about God into statements about man. However, while this may be true of some followers of Bultmann such as F. Buri (1907–95), Bultmann himself always strove to retain the necessity of talking of God, if only paradoxically: 'The fact that God cannot be seen or apprehended apart from faith does not mean that he does not exist apart from faith' (*Jesus Christ and Mythology*, p. 72).

Along with his close contemporary, Karl Barth, Bultmann decisively reshaped the landscape of Protestant theology in Germany and beyond, and his work continues to set the terms of reference for some theological traditions.

Bibliography

Works: *Essays* (London, 1955); *Existence and Faith* (London, 1964); *Faith and Understanding* (London, 1969); *The Gospel of John* (Oxford, 1971); *History and Eschatology* (Edinburgh, 1957); *The History of the Synoptic Tradition* (London, 1963); *Jesus and the Word* (London, ²1958); *Jesus Christ and Mythology* (London, 1960); *Primitive Christianity* (London, 1960); *Theology of the New Testament*, 2 vols. (London, 1952, 1955).

Studies: H. W. Bartsch (ed.), *Kerygma and Myth*, 2 vols. (London, 1962, 1964); G. Ebeling, *Theology and Proclamation* (London, 1966); D. Fergusson, *Bultmann* (London, 1992); R. A. Johnson, *The Origins of Demythologizing* (Leiden, 1974); C. W. Kegley (ed.), *The Theology of Rudolf Bultmann* (London, 1966); J. Macquarrie, *An Existentialist Theology* (London, 1955); idem, *The Scope of Demythologizing* (London, 1960); S. M. Ogden, *Christ without Myth* (London, 1962); H. P. Owen, *Revelation and Existence* (Cardiff, 1957); R. C. Roberts, *Rudolf Bultmann's Theology* (London, 1977); J. M. Robinson, *A New Quest of the Historical Jesus* (London, 1963); W. Schmithals, *An Introduction to the Theology of Rudolf Bultmann* (London, 1968); A. C. Thiselton, *The Two Horizons* (Exeter, 1980).

J. B. WEBSTER

BUNYAN, JOHN (1628–88)

A Baptist pastor and author, Bunyan's fame has been chiefly the result of one of his more than sixty books: his masterpiece *The Pilgrim's Progress* (1678/1684), which had appeared in around 1,300 editions by the late 1930s and has been translated into more than 200 languages.

Bunyan's early years were spent in the village of Elstow, Bedfordshire. After leaving school in the late 1630s with the rudiments of reading and writing, he learned his father's trade of a brazier. At sixteen he joined the New Model Army, in which he served until being discharged in 1647. To what extent Bunyan actually saw action in the English Civil War is disputed. No significant battles were fought near Newport Pagnell, where he was stationed, but the realism of the battle scenes in his later allegory *The Holy War* (1682) has led some scholars to think that he did see fighting.

Bunyan returned home to Elstow, where his reading of *Puritan literature encouraged him to become religious. During the early 1650s, however, he came to the conviction that religiosity is of no salvific value if Christ is absent from the heart. After a lengthy period of profound spiritual torment, recorded in his spiritual autobiography *Grace Abounding to the Chief of Sinners* (1666), he arrived at a place of spiritual rest in late 1657 or early 1658.

By that time he had been baptized and joined what is probably best described as an open-membership Calvinistic *Baptist church in Bedford, pastored by an ex-Royalist officer named John Gifford (d. 1655). He was soon being asked to speak in front of small groups, to share his testimony and to expand the Scriptures. While preaching in Bedfordshire, he encountered various Quaker missioners, including George Fox (1624–91). These encounters, in turn, led to his earliest attempts as an author, a series of rebuttals of *Quaker theology.

After the restoration of the monarchy in 1660, Puritan preachers like Bunyan found themselves in trouble with a state that was determined to destroy the political power of the Puritans. On 12 November 1660, Bunyan was arrested as he was about to preach in Lower Samsell, a hamlet near Harlington, Bedfordshire. Tried and convicted under the Elizabethan Conventicle Act of 1593, Bunyan spent the next twelve years in prison. But his imprisonment proved to be the catalyst for developing his gifts as an author. Here he wrote his powerful apology for his nonconformity, *I Will Pray with the Spirit* (1662), as well as a rebuttal of *antinomianism, *Christian Behaviour* (1663), and his classic *Grace Abounding to the Chief of Sinners*, which went through six editions in his lifetime.

Before his release from prison in the spring of 1672, Bunyan had been called as pastor of the Bedford congregation. Almost immediately he plunged into controversy with the publication of *A Confession of My Faith* (1672), largely a response to closed-communion Baptist critics of his ecclesial practice of allowing Christians who had not been baptized as believers to participate fully in the life of his congregation. This controversy was continued by Bunyan in two further books in 1673–4 and is surely the reason Bunyan was not an influential figure among the Calvinistic Baptists of that era.

Generally speaking, Bunyan embraced the Calvinistic *covenant theology (see *Reformed theology) typical of the Puritan movement. In one key particular, though, the relationship between *faith and *justification, he came to reverse the traditional Puritan perspective and argued that faith is a sign of justification and not its cause (see his *Discourse upon the Pharisee and the Publican*, 1685). Bunyan's indebtedness to the Reformation, particularly Martin *Luther, is seen in his emphasis that acceptance with God is utterly dependent on God's free grace. Bunyan has sometimes been accused of fostering an unbliblical individualism, for example, in the first part of *The Pilgrim's Progress*. Although none of his writings elaborates a formal doctrine of the church, his writings frequently reveal his rich sense of the vital importance of communal experience for the Christian's growth (see *The Pilgrim's Progress, Part II*).

Bunyan's ability to preach out of his spiritual experience made him an extremely popular preacher – his preaching was known to the king, Charles II (r. 1660–85), for example. On a preaching trip to London in August of 1688 Bunyan was soaked to the skin in a heavy rainstorm and subsequently developed a fever from which he died on 31 August, 1688. He was buried in the famous nonconformist cemetery in London, Bunhill Fields.

Bibliography

Works: *The Works of John Bunyan*, 3 vols., ed. George Offor (Glasgow, 1853–4); *The Miscellaneous Works of John Bunyan*, 13 vols., eds. R. Sharrock et al. (Oxford, 1976–94); *Grace Abounding to the Chief of Sinners*, ed. W. R. Owens (Harmondsworth, 1987); *The Pilgrim's Progress*, ed. W. R. Owens (Oxford and New York, 2003).

Studies: J. Brown, *John Bunyan (1628–1688): His Life, Times, and Work*, rev. F. M. Harrison (London, 1928); R. L. Greaves, *John Bunyan* (Abingdon, 1969); idem, *Glimpses of Glory: John Bunyan and English Dissent* (2001); C. Hill, *A Turbulent, Seditious and Factious People: John Bunyan and His Church* (Oxford, 1988); N. H. Keeble (ed.), *John Bunyan: Conventicle and Parnassus: Tercentenary Essays* (Oxford, 1988); G. Wakefield, *Bunyan the Christian* (London, 1992).

M. A. G. HAYKIN

BUSHNELL, HORACE (1802–76)

Horace Bushnell, graduate of Yale College and Divinity School, was a *New England theologian and the pastor of North Congregational Church in Hartford, Connecticut (1833–59). Though converted in a revival, his most influential work, *Christian Nurture* (1861), ran counter to America's predominant evangelical ethos. Bushnell argued that children raised in the nurture of a Christian church and family should be taught from an early age to regard themselves as God's children and as part of the church, and should never be taught differently. The thesis provoked controversy from Protestants, who regarded Christian *conversion as the only reliable path to salvation. Bushnell advanced a version of the moral influence theory in his trilogy on the *atonement: *God in Christ* (1849), *The Vicarious Sacrifice* (1866), and *Forgiveness and Law* (1874). He also explored the relationship between faith and *doubt in *Nature and the Supernatural* (1858). He accepted Jesus' divinity, but held that the Trinity reflected a human way of apprehending God, not God's essential nature. An attempt to try him for heresy on this point was thwarted. Bushnell was a transitional theologian in the mid-nineteenth-century shift toward a more liberal American Protestantism. His collected works first appeared in eleven volumes published from 1876 to 1881.

Bibliography

R. B. Mullin, *The Puritan as Yankee: A Life of Horace Bushnell* (Grand Rapids, 2002); D. L. Smith, *Symbolism and Growth: The Religious Thought of Horace Bushnell* (Chico, 1981); H. S. Smith (ed.), *Horace Bushnell* (New York, 1965).

S. INGERSOL

BUTLER, JOSEPH (1692–1752)

Bishop Butler, 'the philosopher of Anglicanism', was outstanding in his century as a religious *apologist and moral philosopher. His *Analogy of Religion* constituted the most successful published refutation of *deism. In it, Butler argued that, granted that God is the author of nature, the veracity of Christian revealed religion attains a significant probability. This is because features are contained in it which are analogous to those found in natural religion, as we see when we properly interpret *miracle, prophecy and messianic mediation. Rational probability provides an adequate ground for practical assent to Christianity.

Butler's moral philosophy (see *Moral theology), contained mainly in his sermons, analyses the empirical actualities of human nature and psychology. It contains elements of intuitionism (where something is presented in moral experience as self-evidently right or true), utilitarianism (where moral obligation is directed or related to what produces happiness) and naturalism (where, in this case, behaviour in accordance with one's nature is morally advocated). Theologically, Butler ascribed importance to the role of *conscience in the moral sphere.

While the contemporary climate of discussion in the relevant areas is largely uncongenial to Butler's approach, *Hume's respect for him and the huge acclaim of the following century signal something of his stature as a religious thinker.

Bibliography

J. H. Bernard (ed.), *The Works of Bishop Butler*, 2 vols. (London, 1900); C. Cunliffe (ed.), *Joseph Butler's Moral and Religious Thought: Tercentenary Essays* (Oxford, 1992); A. Duncan-Jones, *Butler's Moral Philosophy* (Harmondsworth, 1952); A. Jeffner, *Butler and Hume on Religion: A Comparative Analysis* (Stockholm, 1966); D. M. Mackinnon, *A Study in Ethical Theory* (London, 1957), ch. 5; E. C. Mossner, *Bishop Butler and the Age of Reason* (New York, 1936); T. Penelhum, *Butler* (London, 1985).

S. N. WILLIAMS

CALLING

The term translated 'calling' in the NT is used in more than one sense there, and in the history of Christian theology has come to have a great variety of usage. A basic distinction may be drawn between the outward call of the *gospel, through preaching or some other means (e.g. Matt. 22:14), and an inner, personal call, when that message is willingly answered by an individual person (1 Cor. 1:26). That God calls through preaching is hardly a matter of controversy, but the reception of that call, a personal 'calling', has been variously understood. These understandings are largely determined by a set of considerations having to do with the doctrine of *grace.

In *Augustinianism (endorsed by a major tradition of the church and significantly by the Magisterial Reformers [see *Reformation theology], with the possible exception of Melanchthon), the inner call is understood to be the result of divine mercy and the energizing work of the *Holy Spirit in illumination and regeneration. It accomplishes God's saving purpose for that person. In this sense the call is 'effectual'. In the account that Augustine provides of his conversion in the *Confessions*, he puts up enormous resistance to this inner call; nevertheless, God's grace proves invincible. The connection between such an effectual call and bondage to *sin, and then to election, *predestination, the gift of faith and *perseverance in grace can easily be seen. It is part of a monergistic understanding of the teaching of the NT, especially of Rom. 8 and 9, Eph. 1 and John 6.

However, where it is held that the human will has the power freely to cooperate or not with the outward 'call', then the 'inner call' correspondingly weakens in force. It is not unconditionally effectual, but its efficacy is conditioned by a person's freely willed compliance. The response may be aided by divinely provided helps of various kinds, but its independent, unilateral activity is indispensable. Such an understanding is characteristic of *Pelagian, *Semi-Pelagian and *Arminian theologies. A distinction between an outward and an inward call is still preserved, yet the inwardness of the latter is understood in terms of preparing and alluring the person, not energizing her; persuading the living, rather than bringing life to the dead. At the extreme, the call is indistinguishable from the idea that through God's goodness everyone has the same opportunity and innate power to respond. In less extreme versions, God is said to give the grace of faith to those who make good use of some prior grace, and who therefore in some sense 'merit' it. A fundamental principle here is that 'ought implies can'. If a person ought to heed God's call, then he must have the innate power to do so. Such views of calling are synergistic, ineffectual without human cooperation, a case of the divine power in synthesis with human power.

Less centrally, the NT also refers to 'calling' as synonymous with a job or profession or 'place in life' (1 Cor. 7:17–24) (see *Work). In the history of the Christian church such *vocations have been variously estimated. A deepening contrast between the secular and the sacred, and especially the valuing of celibacy, led by the time of the later Middle Ages to the assumption that the priestly vocation and the monastic life were different in kind from any lay activity. The Reformers, with *Luther in the lead, reversed that trend. It was recognized that a worldly calling is legitimate in itself for, though principally concerned with 'things below', and not with the 'things above' of the kingdom of God, it could nevertheless be undertaken with godly consecration and to the good of human society. In *Calvin such callings – in literature, philosophy, law, science and commerce, for example – are the expression of God's gifts of 'general grace', and arise from his conviction that God's gifts are not only to be used but also to be enjoyed. It is argued (e.g. by *Weber and Tawney) that such convictions, undergirded by honesty in business and frugality, lie at the heart of the rise of *capitalism.

In *pietism and *fundamentalism, a much sharper, ethical separation is made between the Christian life and the pursuit of an earthly calling, indicating almost a reversion to medieval categories, in which only what is 'spiritual' is worthwhile.

Bibliography

P. Helm, *The Callings* (Edinburgh, 1987); H. R. Niebuhr, *Christ and Culture* (New York, 1951); R. H. Tawney, *Religion and the Rise of Capitalism* (Harmondsworth, 1938 [1926]); M. Weber, *The Protestant Ethic and the Spirit of Capitalism* (London, 1976 [1904]).

P. Helm

CALVIN, JOHN (1509–64)

Calvin was born at Noyon in Picardy, France. He spent much of his youth at school in Paris, being trained for the priesthood. His study of medieval scholastic theology was followed by a period of training for the legal profession, which brought him into touch with the Christian humanism current in France at the time, through teachers such as Lefèvre d'Étaples (1455–1529) and Guillaume Budé (1468–1540). He was greatly attracted by such learning and wrote, as his first work, a commentary on Seneca's *De Clementia*. He underwent, however, a 'sudden conversion', the date of which is uncertain. The effect of this was to detach his mind from his former studies, as he became more committed to the study of Scripture and the *Reformation teaching. In 1536 he published in Basel the first edition of his *Institutes of the Christian Religion*. Thereafter, a short and unsuccessful ministry in Geneva was followed by an enriching experience of teaching and pastoral work in Strassburg from 1538 to 1541. Calvin then allowed himself to be recalled to Geneva. There he patiently worked and struggled for many years, seeking to put into practice his beliefs about the gospel, church and society.

When he began his theological work, the Reformation was entering an important second phase in its development. The word of God, under *Luther and others, had powerfully broken through the old forms which had for centuries restricted the *Spirit and obscured the truth. The movement had inspired innumerable sermons, writings, conferences and controversies, and had brought about important changes in social and political life. People had been introduced to new experiences, ideals and hopes. The removal of old restraints, however, had given rise to wild speculations which threatened the dissolution of moral standards and social order.

In the midst of the confusion, Calvin took the lead in defining the new forms of Christian life and *work, of church and community life, which under the newly discovered teaching of the Bible, and the power of the Spirit, were relevant to conditions in Europe in his day. Moreover, he was able to help his contemporaries to attain a clarity of vision and an orderliness in theological thought and expression, which gave them a firmer grasp of the *gospel in its fullness. At the same time, by the power of his preaching, the convincing clarity and simplicity of his teaching, and his practical ability and moral integrity which gave him finally an undisputed leadership in his community, he was conspicuously successful in achieving his aims in his own city-parish. His work in Geneva added greatly to the widespread fame which his writings had already brought him. His whole life-work, therefore, is an important and challenging illustration of how our *theology, if it is healthy, should be related to our life-situation.

Calvin's theology is a theology of the word of God. He held that the *revelation given to us through Scripture is the only reliable source of our *knowledge of God. Though *nature also

Calvin, John

reveals God, and all men and women have a natural instinct for *religion, yet our human perversity prevents us from being able to profit from what nature presents to us. We must therefore turn to the witness to revelation given by God to his prophets and servants in the OT, and to the apostolic witness to Christ in the NT. The Scriptures themselves were inspired, and indeed 'dictated' by God. Their statements, stories and truths must be regarded as having infallible *authority.

Calvin believed that there is a basic unity in the teaching of Scripture, and that the theologian must seek to clarify and give expression to this unity in the orderly setting out of its doctrines. As a theologian, he sought to do justice to the whole content of the written word of God.

He also recognized, however, that *Scripture was given to us by God not simply to present us today with truths and doctrines, but also to introduce us to the living revelation to which the written word bears witness. At the heart of this revelation which the apostles and prophets wrote about, there was for them a personal encounter with the Word of God himself, the second person of the *Trinity. Even though they may have been the recipients of truths and doctrines, the biblical witnesses also knew themselves as men before God himself in personal love and majesty. Calvin believed that the theologian, in his approach to Scripture, must seek to find himself, and must regard himself, in this position too. He must therefore seek through the Scripture to be brought into communion and confrontation with the Lord himself, and in giving shape to his theology must take account of all the original events in and through which God revealed himself to his people. Calvin at times uses the language of *mysticism to describe how faith enables us through the word and Spirit to grasp in vision much more than can be comprehended immediately by the understanding. In his approach to Scripture and his theological task, therefore, the prayerful quest for a fuller understanding of what he had already to some extent grasped, and for a closer communion with the living God, also played an important part.

Calvin did not therefore attempt to create a *systematic theology by subjecting the truths of Scripture to any controlling principles of human thought or logic. He tried rather to allow his thinking to be controlled by the whole word which God had spoken in Christ. The order in which he was able to cast his thought was an order which he found in the revelation which impressed itself upon his mind.

Calvin wrote commentaries on nearly all the books of the Bible. These had a vast circulation and are still of great use. He applied the methods of humanistic scholarship to the Bible to find out the exact meaning of the words of a text, and the circumstances of the history involved (see *Hermeneutics). His belief in the authority and integrity of the word meant that while he read the text critically in the sense of discerningly, he never read it critically in the sense of rejecting its teaching. Though he allowed for a text to have various senses, he was sparing in his use of the allegorical method of interpretation. He believed that Christ was present to the people of God in the OT, though the *revelation then given took different forms from that in the NT. He gave a lead in recognizing the use of typology as a clue to understanding the unity of the two testaments. His belief in this unity enabled him to interpret one text by the whole of Scripture. In his exegesis and theological work he always put himself into debt to other scholars. He was especially influenced by *Augustine, and he was a careful student of the Greek as well as of the Latin Fathers. He gave final expression to his theology in the last edition of the *Institutes* in 1559 (French, 1560). The work is in four parts, following to some extent the order suggested by the Apostles' Creed: Book I, God the Creator; Book II, God the Redeemer; Book III, The Way We Receive the Grace of Christ; Book IV, The Church.

On the doctrine of *God, Calvin avoids discussion of the hidden essence of God (what God is) and confines himself to the biblical teaching on the nature of God (of what kind he is). God himself proclaimed his 'eternity and self-existence' when he uttered his name, 'I am that I am'. Calvin's stress was always on the moral attributes or 'powers' of God. He finds such qualities adequately listed in two specific texts: Exod. 34:6–7 and Jer. 9:24, which dwell especially on his mercy and justice. In his practice, too, in church and civil administration, Calvin tried always to show that God was both 'a just God and a saviour', without one aspect of his goodness cancelling out the other. In discussing the doctrine of God, he does not mention the '*sovereignty of God', which was not always (as some think) a dominating principle in his theology. For him, *glory was a special attribute of God, revealed everywhere in the world, shining out in all his redemptive works, but most fully displayed in the humiliation and *love revealed in the cross. Calvin brings the *Trinity into the centre of his discussion on the nature of God, since revelation admits us into the heart of the mystery of the divine Being himself. Often in his theology Calvin reminds us that God has revealed himself fully in Christ, and that we must turn to no other source than the gospel for our *knowledge of him.

When he discusses how God acts in *providence, we find ourselves often being spoken to pastorally (a characteristic of much of Calvin's theology). He assures us that God is always at work sustaining and guiding the whole of his *creation, and directing the whole course of human history with gracious fatherly concern. The *church and the Christian, however, are under especial care in the hands of God, as Christ was in the hands of God. We are never in the hands of 'fate' or 'chance'. Calvin's discussion of providence presents us with difficulty, however, when he suggests that by a decree of God from the remotest eternity, the plans and wills of people are so governed as to move exactly on the course which he has destined. When he discusses *predestination, he traces the rejection of the non-elect back to this decree of God, which he describes in the Lat. word *horribile*, 'fearful, awesome'. It is at this point that many today would raise questions, and ask whether Calvin was himself being faithful to the central thrust of his own teaching on God, and whether he was doing justice to the *freedom with which in the Bible God seems to act and react within developing situations. We have to remember that Calvin several times revised his *Institutes* as he wrote his commentaries, and did not regard his theology as having attained ultimate finality.

In his discussion of the person and work of Christ, Calvin repeated concisely and accurately the teaching of the Church Fathers and councils (see *Christology). He emphasized the mystery concealed in the person of the *mediator, affirming that 'the Son of God descended from heaven in such a way that, without leaving heaven, he willed to be born in the virgin's womb, to go about the earth, to hang upon the cross; yet continuously filled the world even as he had done from the beginning'. Yet he so emphasized at times the limitations and frailty of *Jesus' humanity that he was suspected by some of not believing in his divinity. He realized that we have to try to understand the person of Jesus in terms of the functions he fulfilled rather than in terms of the essence he concealed. He was the first theologian systematically to interpret Christ's work in terms of the threefold office of prophet, priest and king. He stressed the penal element in Christ's sufferings on the *cross, yet he also emphasized the value placed by God on his lifelong obedience, both active and passive, and his sympathetic self-identification with us in our humanity. The *incarnation created a 'holy brotherhood' between him and ourselves so that he might 'swallow up death and replace it with life, conquer sin and replace it with righteousness'.

Discussing how the *fall has affected humanity (see *Anthropology), originally made in the *image of God, Calvin will allow us to use the phrase 'total depravity' only in the sense that no aspect of man's original being or activity has been left unaffected by his *sin. In all our dealings with others, we ourselves must still regard each person as being still in that image, no matter how low he seems to have sunk. There are two spheres in which human life is set by God – the spiritual and the temporal. With regard to spiritual or heavenly matters, humankind has been wholly deprived of all true knowledge and ability. With regard to temporal or earthly activities, the natural man still retains admirable qualities and abilities by which to conduct his manifold human affairs. Calvin admired, for example, the divine light which shone on the ancient heathen lawgivers in forming their legal codes, and he recognized that man has been endowed by God even in his fallen estate with brilliant gifts to adorn his existence, to allow him comfort, a measure of enjoyment and artistic self-expression in his earthly life. Calvin reminded his readers that in creation God has provided for our use not only the things that are necessary to sustain our life, but also many precious and beautiful things which are designed to give us pleasure and enjoyment. In Geneva one of his final achievements was to found an academy where the 'liberal arts and sciences' were taught by teachers trained in humanistic studies. Calvin was, however, concerned that the development and use of such arts and *sciences should be in accordance with the law of God, and that they should be especially used in the service of the word of

God and in the furtherance of a stable Christian community.

Calvin sought to continue and complete the work begun by Luther and other Reformers. He frequently re-echoed his predecessors' criticisms of *Rome for denying the common man any place of personal security before a gracious God. Nine chapters of the *Institutes* were devoted to the doctrine of *justification by *grace alone, and the Christian liberty this involved. Yet Calvin felt called upon by the situation prevailing around him to insist more firmly than had been already done on the importance of *sanctification or repentance, and to define more clearly for his own day the new pattern of Christian living which alone could form a fitting and worthy response to God's grace and call in Christ. Therefore, in the final edition (1559) of his *Institutes*, he preceded his nine chapters on justification with nine on sanctification or repentance. He thus stressed the fact that there can be no forgiveness without repentance, since both graces flow from our *union with Christ and neither can be prior to the other. He insisted that nothing which Christ suffered or did for us in his redeeming work is of any use if we are not united to him by faith, in order to receive personally from him the grace which he seeks to give us. He taught that this 'mystical union' between us and Christ is a work of the Holy Spirit.

The Christian must not only be united to Christ, but must live in conformity to Christ in his *death and *resurrection. He listens to the imperative command of God: 'Be holy for I am holy', and to the call of the Lord to deny self, take up the cross and follow. Calvin attacks the root of human sin in self-love, and shows that self-denial can alone be the basis of outgoing love to all people. He urges the triumphal acceptance of every form of *suffering to conform us to the image of Christ. Each of us gives obedient expression to our Christian faith as we pursue our earthly *vocation. We are meant to enjoy and use the earthly benefits which God often showers upon us as we pursue our path in life, yet even in such enjoyment we must remain detached, aspiring always towards the life to come, of which even now we enjoy some foretaste.

Calvin's desire to help the individual to live the *Christian life with full assurance led him to give due place to the doctrine of predestination in his discussion. He believed that no Christian could be finally victorious and confident unless he had some sense of his election to salvation. He believed that while Scripture taught this doctrine, it also pointed out that those who refused to believe must be predestined to damnation (see *Judgment). Attacks on his writing on this matter forced him to defend himself in several treatises on the subject. We must not imagine, however, that this was the central doctrine in his theology. It is significant that next to his chapters on predestination in the *Institutes* Calvin places his magnificent chapter on *prayer, in which we are urged to exercise our free *will in intercession before God and in seeking answers to the prayers we make.

A large section of the *Institutes* deals with the *church and its *ministry. Calvin was concerned that the form of ministry within the church, especially by the pastor, should reflect Christ's own ministry of utter humility, concern for each individual and faithfulness to the truth exercised in the power of the Spirit. He was concerned with instruction, *discipline and poor-relief. Therefore, along with the pastor in the ministry, he believed God had placed teachers or 'doctors' (experts in Scripture and theology), elders and deacons. He found such offices indicated in Scripture, but he did not insist that every detail of the church's ordered life required explicit scriptural warrant. He admired the *development of doctrine and *liturgy during the first six centuries of the church's life and had no hesitation in reproducing features of this development. He believed that the 'bishop' of the NT and the early church corresponded to the pastor of a congregation in a truly reformed church. All ceremonies in the church must be simple and clearly intelligible and justifiable in the light of Scripture. He believed that the second commandment forbade not only the use of images in worship, but also the invention of ceremonies merely to stimulate religious emotion. He encouraged congregational singing, but felt that musical instruments gave too uncertain a sound to be the accompaniment of rational *worship.

Calvin followed Augustine in regarding a *sacrament as a visible sign of an invisible grace. Only *baptism and the Lord's Supper (see *Eucharist) were sacraments with dominical authority. He denounced the doctrine of transubstantiation and the idea that a sacrament was efficacious by virtue of its merely being performed as a ritual. He also rejected the view that the bread and wine were given by Christ as mere symbols representing his body and blood, meant simply to stimulate our memory, devotion and faith. The sacraments give what they represent, he insisted. We are not asked by the Lord merely to look, but to eat and drink. This is a sign that between him and us there is a life-giving union (in relation to which Calvin even uses the word 'substantial'). This union is given and created when the word is preached and responded to by faith; it is also increased and strengthened when the sacrament is received by faith. Calvin rejected current *Lutheran explanations of this mystery of the efficacy of the sacrament. He often stated that the body of Christ, on which we feed, remains in heaven, and our souls are raised there by the wonderful power of the Spirit to feed upon him. Calvin insisted that a sacrament was inefficacious apart from the faith of the recipient. He justified the *baptism of infants by his view of the unity of the old and new covenants, and by urging that the efficacy of a sacrament need not be tied to the moment of its administration.

The relationship between church and *state was an acute issue in Calvin's lifetime. His struggle in Geneva involved him in a determined stand against attempts by the civil authority to interfere in matters relating to church discipline, which he felt should be entirely under the control of a specifically ecclesiastical court. He had a high view of the state, and stressed the duty of citizens to obey the law and to give honour to their rulers. He also stressed the duty of rulers to care, like shepherds, for each of their subjects. He advised obedience even to tyrants, and the acceptance of unjust suffering rather than the resort to revolutionary plotting. Yet he believed that a tyrant could be overthrown by the deliberate action of a justly constituted lower authority within a state, or by an 'avenger' from elsewhere raised up and elected by God.

See also: REFORMED THEOLOGY.

Bibliography

Works: *Institutes of the Christian Religion*, tr. F. L. Battles, ed. J. T. McNeill, 2 vols. (London, 1961); *Commentaries on the NT*, tr. and ed. by D. W. Torrance and T. F. Torrance, 12 vols. (Edinburgh, 1959–72); H. Beveridge and J. Bonnet (eds.), *Selected Works of John Calvin: Tracts and Letters* (Grand Rapids, 1983 reprint).

Studies: F. L. Battles, *Analysis of the Institutes of the Christian Religion of John Calvin* (Grand Rapids, 1980); B. Gordon, *Calvin* (New Haven, 2009); A. N. S. Lane, *A Reader's Guide to Calvin's Institutes* (Grand Rapids, 2009); D. K. McKim (ed.), *The Cambridge Companion to John Calvin* (Cambridge, 2004); R. A. Muller, *Calvin and the Reformed Tradition: On the Work of Christ and the Order of Salvation* (Grand Rapids, 2012); M. A. Mullett, *John Calvin* (London, 2011); T. H. L. Parker, *Calvin's New Testament Commentaries* (Edinburgh, 1993); C. Partee, *The Theology of John Calvin* (Louisville, 2008); H. J. Selderhuis (ed.), *The Calvin Handbook* (Cambridge, 2009); F. Wendel, *Calvin: The Origins and Development of His Religious Thought* (London, 1963).

R. S. WALLACE

CALVINISM, see REFORMED THEOLOGY

CALVINISTIC METHODISM

Calvinistic Methodism was the product of the eighteenth-century evangelical awakening in England and Wales. Its chief representatives were George *Whitefield and Daniel Rowland (1713–90). Its theology found expression in their sermons, in the prose and poetical works of William Williams of Pant-y-celyn (1717–91), and in the *Confession of Faith which appeared in 1823 from the Welsh Calvinistic Methodists.

It can be described as theology for the heart, giving expression to a mainline Calvinism within an experimental and practical framework. It drew heavily and heartily on earlier *Puritanism, and yet shared unashamedly the individual pietism of contemporary (*Arminian) *Methodism. As such, it confessed a biblical authority for matters of faith and conduct, and a trinitarian, *Protestant and *evangelical faith.

The distinctives of Calvinistic Methodism lie in the prominence given to the *Holy Spirit's influences in man's salvation, and in the experimental ethos of its soul culture. Light and life, holiness and love, submission to the divine will and the realization of human dignity, were to be held in biblical balance. They were also to be enjoyed and nurtured in the disciplined context of warm but heart-searching fellowship or 'society' meetings.

In England, Calvinistic Methodism waned after the passing of Whitefield, but in Wales it remained vigorous for another century. It did so for two main reasons: able leadership from men like Thomas Charles ('of Bala', 1755–1814) and John Elias ('of Anglesey', 1774–1841), and repeated, powerful revivals. The Calvinistic passion for order later spilled over into church polity as well, determining for Welsh Calvinistic Methodism a place among the *Presbyterian family. *Liberalism and *ecumenism in the twentieth century contributed to the decline of Calvinistic Methodist theology.

Bibliography
E. Evans, *Daniel Rowland and the Great Evangelical Awakening in Wales* (Edinburgh, 1985); idem, *Howel Harris* (Cardiff, 1974); idem, 'The Confession of Faith of the Welsh Calvinistic Methodists', *Journal of the Hist. Soc. of the Presb. Church of Wales* 59, 1974, pp. 2–11; G. T. Hughes, *Williams Pantycelyn* (Cardiff, 1983); D. M. Lloyd-Jones, 'William Williams and Welsh Calvinistic Methodism', *The Manifold Grace of God* (The Puritan and Reformed Studies Conference) (London, 1968); W. Williams, *Welsh Calvinistic Methodism* (Bridgend, 1998 [1884]).

E. EVANS

CAMBRIDGE PLATONISTS

At the beginning of the seventeenth century, much Protestant theology was closely interwoven with *Aristotelian philosophy. *Puritan commitment to a reasoned faith and a liveable theology, English interest in the Fathers and dissatisfaction with the aridity of theological systems led a group of scholars in Cambridge to restate theology in a *Platonic mode which emphasized the *deification of the believer.

While cherishing many previous insights, the Cambridge Platonists sought the fundamentals of authentic Christianity outside the *Augustinian tradition. Their reading of Plato, Plotinus and Fathers such as *Origen gave them new perspectives and optimism about the role of reason. 'Our reason is not confounded by our Religion, but awakened, excited, employed, directed and improved' (Benjamin Whichcote, 1609–83). Whichcote, Henry More (1614–87), Ralph Cudworth (1617–88) and John Smith (1618–52) were the leaders of this movement. They rejected the dominant *Reformed theology of the Church of England. At times they were accused of *Socinianism because of their critique of Protestant orthodoxy, their commitment to *toleration, their plea for essentials and their insistence on the inseparable connection between truth and holiness. They were not, however, interested in theological reductionism, but sought to ground faith securely in a more adequate *metaphysic, which safeguarded the heart of Christianity from the fanaticism of enthusiasts and the misunderstanding of materialist philosophers such as Thomas Hobbes (1588–1679). Their optimism about an alliance between revelation and reason was not uncritical. More was initially an admirer of *Descartes, but he saw Descartes less and less as an ally and had rejected him by 1671.

In books such as Cudworth's *The True Intellectual System of the Universe* (1678) they sought to uphold a spiritual account of reality against *determinism and *materialism. The complexity of their thought limited their influence to this field, but their theology of *creation provided the context for their account of Christ as the one who enlivened the divine seed within us and moulded us into the divine likeness. Their striking aphorisms were more easily remembered than their subtle and detailed arguments about the spiritual and rational.

While they gave an impressive account of the reality of the soul, they did not always do justice to human sinfulness and the insights of Protestant soteriology. They provided an important alternative to Puritan denigration of natural reason and virtue. The letters between Whichcote and Anthony Tuckney (1599–1670) brought out sharply the extent of the differences between Platonist and Puritan. The group's academic and religious stature provided important ingredients for the restatement of English theology after 1660, helping to create a more generous and tolerant spirit. Unfortunately, some of their admirers lacked the depth of their mentors. The resulting *latitudinarianism could sometimes pass readily into *deism. Nevertheless, they shared the creative power of partnership between revelation and reason. Their emphasis on God's love and rationality provided a vital alternative to the doctrine of God in the *Westminster Confession. They made lasting contributions to ethical reflection, as well as exploring contemporary philosophical and scientific issues with an authority and insight that is all too rare among theologians.

Their style of writing often makes them difficult for modern readers, but they represent one of the high points of the English theological tradition.

Bibliography

G. R. Cragg, *The Cambridge Platonists* (Oxford, 1968); C. A. Patrides, *The Cambridge Platonists* (London, 1969); J. D. Roberts, *From Puritanism to Platonism in Seventeenth Century England* (The Hague, 1968).

I. BREWARD

CAMPBELL, ALEXANDER (1788–1866)

Alexander Campbell led a movement to restore primitive Christianity. Born in County Antrim, Ireland, he studied at the University of Glasgow, but grew disenchanted with Calvinist doctrine and Presbyterian sectarianism. He emigrated to Pennsylvania in 1809, joining the Christian Association of Washington, a free church founded by his father, Thomas. In 1812 the Campbells were rebaptized by immersion and forged Baptist ties, but by 1830, wary of Baptist confessions, Alexander headed an anti-creedal movement whose adherents simply called themselves 'Disciples'. He held that Christian unity through the disappearance of *sects and creeds would precede Christ's postmillennial advent (see *Millennium) and that believers' *baptism by immersion was essential for salvation. He edited the monthly *Christian Baptist* and later *The Millennial Harbinger*. His systematic theology, *The Christian System*, appeared in 1839. A bold, logical thinker, he engaged in notable debates, including one in Cincinnati, Ohio, in 1829 with Robert Owen, utopian free-thinker, over Christian evidences. In 1832 the 'Disciples' united with a similar group of 'Christians' led by Barton W. Stone of Kentucky. Despite its anti-sect stance, the 'Stone-Campbell movement' eventually gave rise to three distinct denominations: Disciples of Christ, Churches of Christ, and the independent Christian Church.

Bibliography

'Alexander Campbell', *Dictionary of American Biography*, vol. 3 (New York, 1929), pp. 446–448; L. Garrett, 'Alexander Campbell', in D. A. Foster *et al.* (eds.), *The Encyclopedia of the Stone-Campbell Movement* (Grand Rapids, 2004), pp. 112–134; D. E. Harrell, *Quest for a Christian America* (Nashville, 1966); R. T. Hughes, *Reviving the Ancient Faith* (Grand Rapids, 1996); S. C. Pearson, 'Alexander Campbell', in M. G. Toulouse and J. O. Duke (eds.), *Makers of Christian Theology in America* (Nashville, 1977), pp. 222–227; R. Richardson, *Memoirs of Alexander Campbell*, 2 vols. (Philadelphia, 1868).

S. INGERSOL

CAMPBELL, JOHN MCLEOD (1800–72)

The theology of John McLeod Campbell provokes contrasting reactions. Central to the debate is his soteriology, outlined in *The Nature of the Atonement*, which must be interpreted within the wider context of his life and theology.

John McLeod Campbell was born in May 1800, the eldest son of Rev. Donald Campbell, minister of the united parish of Kilninver and Kilmelford. He went to Glasgow to begin studies at the university in November 1811, entering the Divinity Hall in 1817. Licensed to preach the gospel in 1820, he spent several years awaiting the call to his first church. In May 1825 he was presented to the parish of Row (Rhu) by the Duke of Argyll and was ordained minister of the parish later that year.

Campbell's contacts with his parishioners made him aware of a problem, which he described as *'the want of living religion'*. He concluded that this lack of assurance was the legacy of federal Calvinism (see *Reformed theology), which was the prevailing theological orthodoxy. Having been taught that Christ died only for the elect, church members had no *assurance that they belonged to God's elect. Looking into their own lives for 'evidences of election', people found that their fluctuating feelings offered no firm basis for Christian assurance.

Campbell became convinced that the only foundation for genuine assurance was in believing that Christ died for the sins of all. Preaching this message led to accusations of *heresy, and his case was referred to the disciplinary courts of the Church of Scotland. Debate centred on three main themes: the extent of atonement, universal pardon and the doctrine that assurance is of the essence of faith.

149

Campbell believed that his teaching about the universal extent of the atonement and universal pardon did not lead to *universalism. However, his contemporaries, who assessed everything in the light of the *Westminster Confession, concluded that his teaching tended towards universalism. The ecclesiastical courts decided that his doctrines contradicted the teaching of the Westminster Confession of Faith, the Church of Scotland's principal 'Subordinate Standard of Faith'. In May 1831 the Kirk's General Assembly voted to depose Campbell from its ministry.

Campbell became pastor of an independent congregation in Glasgow. In 1856 he published an influential book, *The Nature of Atonement*, which explored what the atonement was intended to accomplish. For Campbell, the traditional emphasis upon what he termed the 'retrospective' aspect of atonement (what Christ had saved people *from*) had to be seen alongside an equal concern for the 'prospective' aspect of God's redemptive work (what Christ saves people *for*).

He described his approach as 'moral and spiritual', in contrast to prevailing penal approaches to the *cross. Not surprisingly, some conclude that he advocated a moral influence model of atonement. George Carey asserts that 'Campbell evacuates the atonement of any "objective" content', so that we encounter only 'a variation of the "moral influence" theory' (*The Gate of Glory*, London, 1986, p. 125).

The most controversial aspect of Campbell's theology was the idea of Christ offering a perfect confession of sin. In 1856, writing in the *National Review*, James Martineau asked, 'Is vicarious contrition at all more conceivable than vicarious retribution?' However, the controversial terms 'vicarious confession' or 'vicarious repentance' are not actually used by Campbell. Leanne Van Dyk suggests that these terms 'can be usefully employed in a description of Campbell's own atonement theology in a representative sense rather than a substitutionary sense. Provided one understands that the vicarious aspect of Christ's confession is that Christ confessed **on our behalf so that we too can confess**, the term is legitimate' (*The Desire of Divine Love*, p. 113). Campbell's idea has sometimes been described as 'vicarious penitence'. This does not appear to be a term which he used, but is rather the terminology used later by R. W. Moberly (*Atonement and Personality*, London, 1901).

James B. Torrance suggested that the OT symbolism associated with the work of the high priest on the Day of Atonement provides the background for Campbell's thinking. When the high priest entered God's presence, 'all Israel entered *in his person* . . . Conversely, when he vicariously confessed their sins, and interceded for them before God, God accepted them as his forgiven people *in the person of their high priest.*' ('The Vicarious Humanity of Christ', in T. F. Torrance (ed.), *The Incarnation*, Edinburgh, 1981, p. 139.)

In his earlier sermons Campbell had claimed that Christ had identified himself fully with fallen human nature, arguing that 'the flesh of Christ differed not in one particle from mine; but Christ did present his flesh, which was even my flesh, without spot to God through the eternal Spirit' (J. McLeod Campbell, *Notes of Sermons*, Paisley, 1831, p. 7).

Seen against this background, it is possible to interpret Campbell's language in terms of Christ confessing to the Father that human nature is so riddled with sin, that the only way to deal with such fallen flesh is to put it to death and recreate it. If Christ assumed sinful human nature, then whilst he is not personally guilty of sin, he would be able to confess that human flesh needs more than just the verdict of 'not guilty'. Such fallen flesh needs to be redeemed and recreated, and this is accomplished in Christ's representative death and resurrection.

If the idea of 'vicarious repentance' is deemed inadequate, it seems logical to conclude that Campbell's version of exemplarism is theologically deficient. However, his proposal about Christ's confession on the cross is only one part of a more complex soteriology outlined in *The Nature of the Atonement*. Taken in isolation, the notion of Christ's 'perfect confession' clearly does not provide an adequate way of understanding Christian atonement. When it is read alongside the other elements at the heart of his high priestly, incarnational understanding of the nature of atonement, a more objective assessment becomes possible.

Trevor Hart suggests that in spite of differences in emphasis, there are significant areas of theological convergence between *Anselm and Campbell. He argues that both theologians have a strong sense that atonement is the objective accomplishment of God. For, 'the atonement is something that God does, and not something that we do. It is the product of his prevenient love for sinful man, and not something which man brings to placate an angry and otherwise unforgiving deity' (T. A. Hart, *EQ* 62, p. 322).

Earlier assessments have not paid sufficient attention to sermon transcripts from Campbell's ministry, which supply vital insights into his theology. His sermons proclaim that the Son of God assumed fallen human nature, presenting it spotless to God in the power of the Holy Spirit. Such a *Christology, which he may have derived from his friend Edward *Irving, sheds fresh light on *The Nature of Atonement*. For if Christ assumed sinful fallen nature, then it may be more plausible to talk about Christ making a perfect confession of sins. Acknowledgment of Campbell's Christology does not remove all the difficulties associated with his soteriology, but enables a more accurate view of it to emerge.

See also: ATONEMENT; SALVATION.

Bibliography

Works: *Christ the Bread of Life: An Attempt to Give a Profitable Direction to the Present Occupation of Thought with Romanism* (London, ²1869); *The Nature of the Atonement* (Grand Rapids and Carberry, 1996).

Studies: J. C. Goodloe, *John McLeod Campbell: The Extent and Nature of the Atonement, Studies in Reformed Theology and History* (Princeton, 1997); T. A. Hart, 'Anselm of Canterbury and John McLeod Campbell: Where Opposites Meet?', *EQ* 62, 1990, pp. 311–333; P. K. Stevenson, *God in Our Nature: The Incarnational Theology of John McLeod Campbell* (Carlisle, 2004); T. F. Torrance, *Scottish Theology from John Knox to John McLeod Campbell* (Edinburgh, 1996); G. M. Tuttle, *John McLeod Campbell on Christian Atonement: So Rich a Soil* (Edinburgh, 1986); L. Van Dyk, *The Desire of Divine Love: John McLeod Campbell's Doctrine of the Atonement* (New York, 1995).

P. K. STEVENSON

CANON, see SCRIPTURE

CANON LAW

The Greek word *kanōn* means a rule, and canon law comprises the disciplinary regulations of the church. These began to be formulated in the early centuries by local and ecumenical *councils, and are distinct from the decisions which the ancient councils made on matters of belief. However, they are likewise expressions of a NT concern for order and moral discipline in the church. The common law of the Eastern church still consists essentially of the canons of the early councils (in which they include the so-called *Apostolic Canons*, appended to the fourth-century *Apostolic Constitutions*, and the numerous canons of the 692 Quinisext Council, not recognized in the West).

Influential individual bishops also issued decrees which became embodied in canon law, and this was especially the case with the decrees of *popes, which continued to be added through the Middle Ages. The ninth-century *False Decretals* were also drawn upon. The twelfth-century *Decretum* of Gratian of Bologna gained its fame as being a much-needed systematic and annotated arrangement of Western canon law, and was taken bodily into the official corpus (*Iuris Cononici*) of Roman canon law. The *Corpus* was codified in 1917, has several times been modified, and was fully revised in 1983. A separate code for Eastern-rite Catholic churches was promulgated in 1990.

Whether Roman canon law was binding in England during the Middle Ages has been disputed, perhaps wrongly, but since the Reformation the only parts considered by the courts to retain their force are those which have long been incorporated in the statute or common law of the realm and do not conflict with post-Reformation statute or custom. The Reformers proposed a new code of canon law entitled the Reformation of the Ecclesiastical Laws but, owing to the death of Edward VI, it was never enacted, though it was published by John Foxe in 1571. However, in 1603–04 a brief new code of canons was drawn up and approved by Convocation and received the royal assent. They became binding on the clergy of the Church of England (but not the laity, not having been submitted to Parliament). They were clearly Reformed in character, though with an anti-Puritan tendency, and remained in force until a fresh and less stringent code replaced them in 1969. This has since been revised by the General Synod on several occasions.

See also: CHURCH GOVERNMENT.

Bibliography

J. A. Brundage, *Medieval Canon Law* (Harlow, 1995); *The Canons of the Church of England* (London, 1969); *New Code of Canon Law* (London, 1983); Earl of Halsbury, *Ecclesiastical Law*, ed. R. P. Moore (London, ⁴1957); E. W. Kemp, *An Introduction to Canon Law in the Church of England* (London, 1957); R. C. Mortimer, *Western Canon Law* (London, 1953).

R. T. BECKWITH

CANONIZATION, see SAINT

CAPITALISM

An economic system is a structure for organizing the production and distribution of provisions. In the modern era there have been only two basic economic systems: capitalism and command economies. The key feature of capitalism is the private ownership of the means of production combined with reliance on a free-market system to order production and distribution. Command economies, such as communism in the former Soviet Union, take public ownership of the means of production and centralize decision-making about how to produce and distribute goods.

Capitalism has been astonishingly successful in the production of goods: even its sternest critics, Karl Marx and Friedrich Engels, stated that it had assembled more colossal forces of production than all previous generations together (*The Communist Manifesto*). Following the collapse of the Soviet Union and the increasing development of private enterprise and a market economy in China, modern economic discussion is focused on the relative merits of different capitalist systems, rather than alternatives to them.

While aspects of capitalist economy have antecedents in the ancient world, the development of it as a system originates in England between the sixteenth and eighteenth centuries, as the producers of cloth and then other industries invested their profits in expanded and more efficient production. The peerless theorist of capitalism is Adam Smith, whose 1776 work *The Wealth of Nations* began the modern discipline of economics. Smith argued that the key difference between wealthy nations and others was how they ordered production. He observed how developments in the division of labour – workers becoming more specialist in a particular task – could lead to huge advances in the efficiency of production, and if the surplus generated in this way could then be traded in freely operating markets, the wealth generated could be raised by several orders of magnitude. He also argued that the needs of society for goods could be best satisfied by allowing each individual to pursue their own advantage, as the 'invisible hand' of the free market would ensure that there was an economic incentive to produce the goods people wanted in an efficient way. While Smith's analysis continues to be foundational, there have been very significant developments in capitalism since the eighteenth century, not least the expansion of the public provision of social services in many Western nations in the mid-twentieth century and, towards the end of the century, the acceleration towards a globalized economy and the rapid expansion of international financial markets, the value of which now far exceeds trade in goods and services.

At the beginning of the twentieth century Max *Weber argued that one of the major causal factors in the development of capitalism was the Protestant Reformation. Martin *Luther's doctrine of *vocation gave Christians confidence that they could serve God through secular employment, and John *Calvin's doctrine of *predestination left them anxious about whether they were part of the elect who would be saved. The combination, Weber argued, was a powerful contribution to the diligent production and reinvestment of wealth required for a capitalist economy to be successful, though the significance of Weber's thesis has since been a matter of dispute.

While there can be little doubt over the success of capitalism in enabling production, there have been many critics who have been concerned about the nature and consequences of capitalist production of goods together with defects in the way it distributes the fruits of production. A century after *The Wealth of Nations* Karl Marx argued in *Das Kapital* (vol. 1, 1867) that capitalism was fundamentally unjust in exploiting the labour of workers to enrich the capitalist owners of the means of production, and that markets were unfair in allowing the economically powerful to take advantage of the poor. He objected to the way capitalism functioned to *alienate, or separate and distance, workers from the products of their labour, which then became fetishized as commodities with a value independent of the process of their production. Marx also argued that capitalism was fundamentally unstable: when investment opportunities become apparent it creates an economic boom, but this is followed by recession when the boom comes to an end. He noted that the impact of successful companies buying out the assets of less successful ones concentrates financial power into bigger and bigger firms.

While Marx believed that this cycle would end finally with the collapse of capitalism and the birth of a socialist economy, others have argued that the worst effects of the features of the capitalist system Marx diagnosed can be avoided through appropriate government regulation. John Maynard Keynes's work in the mid-twentieth century was influential in arguing for a significant government role to compensate for the inherent instabilities of capitalist systems. Keynesian economics has since been challenged by economists such as Milton Friedman who have argued for *laissez-faire* policies of state non-intervention in economic affairs.

Theological critiques of capitalist economic systems date back to the nineteenth century in the work of F. D. Maurice and Charles Kingsley, and in the papal encyclical *Rerum novarum* published by Pope Leo XIII in 1891, which expressed concern for the exploitation of workers. In the twentieth century it is notable that major figures of diverse theological opinions expressed moral concern about the workings of capitalism: Karl *Barth, Paul *Tillich and Reinhold *Niebuhr all displayed a preference for *Christian Socialism. Towards the end of the century the critique of capitalism was a significant aspect of South American *liberation theology. Many liberation theologians have found Marxist economic analysis a useful tool in their attempt to understand and respond to the oppression of the poor and they have come to doubt whether a capitalist economy can adequately serve the interests of the poor, though their association with Marxist thought has led to critique from ecclesial authorities.

Timothy Gorringe and Ulrich Duchrow are prominent recent theological critics of capitalism. Other theologians have come to the theological defence of capitalism in reaction to what they see as theological naïveté. Michael Novak, for example, claims that socialist critics of capitalism forget the significance of the economic problem of production in their concern about the issues of distribution, and suggests that capitalism, democracy and Christianity are ideally suited to define the economic, political and religious spheres of modern democracy. Between these two extremes, thinkers such as Ronald Preston have sought a middle way that takes a clear-sighted view of the defects of capitalism while appreciating both its merits and the lack of viable alternatives.

See also: MARXISM AND CHRISTIANITY; POVERTY AND WEALTH; WORK.

Bibliography

M. Friedman, *Capitalism and Freedom* (Chicago, 1962); T. Gorringe, *Theological Ethics and Economic Order* (London and Maryknoll, 1994); J. M. Keynes, *The General Theory of Employment, Interest and Money* (London, 1936); K. Marx, *Capital* (ET, London, 1970); K. Marx and F. Engels, *The Communist Manifesto*, ed. D. McLennan (Oxford, 1992); J. Miranda, *Marx and the Bible: A Critique of the Philosophy of Oppression* (London, 1982); M. Novak, *The Spirit of Democratic Capitalism* (New York, 1982); R. H. Preston, *Religion and the Ambiguities of Capitalism* (London, 1991); A. Smith, *The Wealth of Nations*, eds. R. H. Campbell *et al.* (Oxford, 1976); M. Weber, *The Protestant Ethic and the Spirit of Capitalism* (ET, London, 1992).

D. L. CLOUGH

CAPPADOCIAN FATHERS, see BASIL OF CAESAREA; GREGORY OF NAZIANZUS; GREGORY OF NYSSA

CARNELL, EDWARD JOHN (1919–67)

An American evangelical apologist, theologian and president of Fuller Theological Seminary (1954–9), Carnell was a major figure in the mid-twentieth-century development of an intelligent and articulate exposition of *evangelicalism in the USA. He was the author of books on *Kierkegaard (*The Burden of Søren Kierkegaard*, Grand Rapids, 1965) and Reinhold *Niebuhr (*The Theology of Reinhold Niebuhr*, Grand Rapids, 1951), and of three influential *apologies. In the first of these, *An Introduction to Christian Apologetics* (Grand Rapids, 1948),

Carnell proposes 'systematic consistency' (that is, 'obedience to the law of non-contradiction' and conformity with 'the totality of our experiences') as the test of truth. He attempts to show that the Christian worldview passes this test, while other religions and worldviews cannot.

A Philosophy of the Christian Religion (Grand Rapids, 1952) adds to the author's earlier work an apologetic based on values (axiologies). Carnell surveys 'a set of typical value options' for which an individual might live and die. In each case he gives reason why 'one must move on from the lower to the higher'. The 'lower immediacies' of material goods and pleasures, the 'higher immediacies' of the pursuit of knowledge, and the 'threshold options' of devotion to man and to sub-Christian gods, are all unable to provide ultimate satisfaction, which can be found only through faith in the person of Christ.

The argument of *Christian Commitment* (New York, 1957) is moral rather than axiological or rational. Carnell proposes 'a third way of knowing', in addition to knowledge by acquaintance and knowledge by inference. 'Knowledge by moral self-acceptance', or knowledge of truth as rectitude, is intimately involved in knowing persons, including oneself and God. But one cannot have this kind of knowledge without being 'morally transformed by the realities that already hold one'. Carnell's third apology is both an argument from 'the judicial sentiment' to God who is its source, and a call to humble ourselves in order to know the person of God.

Bibliography

K. D. Boa and R. M. Bowman, *Faith Has Its Reasons* (Colorado Springs, 2001); M. Erickson, *The New Evangelical Theology* (Westwood, 1968); R. Nelson, *The Making and Unmaking of an Evangelical Mind* (Cambridge, 1987); B. Ramm, *Types of Apologetic Systems* (Wheaton, 1953); J. A. Sims, *Edward John Carnell: Defender of the Faith* (Washington DC, 1979).

D. W. CLOWNEY

CAROLINE DIVINES

During the first half of the seventeenth century there were three main parties in the English church: the *Puritans, critical of the Elizabethan settlement and its spirituality as but half a reformation; the school of Richard *Hooker, appealing to the God-given principle of human reason as a guide to the Christian in 'things indifferent', and questioning the Puritan appeal to an exclusively biblical regulative authority; and what came eventually to be known as the 'High Church Party', led successively by Richard Bancroft (1544–1610) and William Laud (1573–1645), Archbishops of Canterbury. Among this group emerged a number of able moral and controversial theologians, most of whom held high office in the church during the reigns of Charles I and Charles II. They were known collectively as the Caroline Divines, and included such churchmen as Jeremy Taylor (1613–67), Herbert Thorndike (1598–1672), Gilbert Sheldon (1598–1677) and Henry Hammond (1605–60).

Although they gave a high place in their theology to the authority of the Bible, their main theological inspiration was the writings of the Fathers of the early church: probably no other group in English church history has been so skilled in *patristics. As a consequence, their spirituality reveals an openness to mystery and the more subliminal and less verbal aspects of relationship to God which was at odds with the Puritan preoccupation with the word. One practical effect of this was the 'beauty of holiness' programme conducted by Laud in the 1630s, restoring colour, music and beauty to the worship of the church. In this, as in other things, their instinct was to emphasize those features of the Church of England which reflected its continuity with the pre-Reformation church. They were, however, keen supporters of the Elizabethan settlement as a *via media* between the extremes of papacy and sectarianism, and had no hesitation in rejecting papal claims to supremacy. At the same time, however, they accepted (as others did not) that the Church of Rome was a genuine Christian church.

Their attitude towards other Protestant churches was more ambivalent. Increasingly they tended to question their right to be regarded as authentic churches unless they were episcopally ordered (see *Ministry). Indeed, they regarded the bishop as the *sine qua non* of the true church, and saw it as the peculiar glory of the Church of England that it had both bishops and a history of reformation. But in order to protect this insistence on episcopacy against the attacks of Puritans, they forged an alliance with the monarch, thus attaching episcopacy as a theory to the doctrine of the divine right of kings which they did much to promote.

During the Interregnum the majority of the Caroline Divines went into exile with the king, and it was in this context that their apologia for the Church of England was finally formulated in dialogue with Catholic and Protestant critics, both of whom regarded the *via media* as an experiment that had failed. Not surprisingly, the sufferings of this time led to an intransigence towards the Puritan party once the Restoration had occurred. The few who remained in England seem to have adopted more irenic attitudes: Richard *Baxter deeply regretted the death of Henry Hammond, formerly canon of Christ Church, Oxford, in 1660, because of his known willingness to seek grounds for the comprehension of dissenters within the church.

Theologically, the Caroline Divines were usually regarded as *Arminian, but this reflects more their antipathy to Puritanism than their views on salvation. They shared with the Puritans, however, the seventeenth-century preoccupation with the study of cases of conscience (see *Casuistry); Robert Sanderson (1587–1663), Bishop of Lincoln, was probably the leading English *moral theologian of the century. They were deeply committed to the *Book of Common Prayer*, and their corporate and private piety was focused on the Holy Communion. Their influence declined during the closing decades of the century, but was revived with the rise of the Oxford Movement in the nineteenth century (see *Anglo-Catholic theology), which held them to be the authentic tradition of *Anglicanism after the Reformation.

Bibliography

R. S. Bosher, *The Making of the Restoration Settlement* (London, 1951); I. M. Green, *The Re-Establishment of the Church of England, 1660–1663* (Oxford, 1979); B. Guyer (ed.), *The Beauty of Holiness: The Caroline Divines and Their Writings* (Norwich, 2012); H. R. McAdoo, *The Structure of Caroline Moral Theology* (London and New York, 1949); J. Sears McGee, *The Godly Man in Stuart England* (New Haven, 1976); P. E. Moore and F. L. Cross, *Anglicanism* (London, 1935); J. W. Packer, *The Transformation of Anglicanism, 1643–1660* (Manchester, 1969); N. Sykes, *From Sheldon to Secker* (Cambridge, 1959); H. R. Trevor-Roper, *Laud* (London, 1962).

D. D. SCEATS

CASUISTRY

The application of moral principles and the determination of right and wrong in particular cases (Lat. *casus*) in light of the peculiar circumstances and situation. The need for casuistry arises because it is not possible to frame or express general moral rules relevant to every situation and case without exception. Casuistry seeks to make the general rule more specific, and apply it directly to the actual moral situation. This may be seen positively as making the law more specific and removing obscurity and doubt as to its application. In *Puritanism it accompanied a scrupulousness over 'cases of *conscience'. Unfortunately, however, casuistry in Christian history has been seen negatively as providing excuses and permitting exceptions where there ought to be none, particularly among *Jesuits in the seventeenth century. The term often suggests a debater able to justify even what is wrong by a process of reasoning based on exceptions. Casuistry thus bears some resemblance to 'situation' *ethics. Theologically, casuistry takes seriously the fallen nature of the world and of humankind and recognizes the complexity of moral decisions. Therefore, to cope with the ambiguity and finitude of human existence, people require moral guidance given in a detailed way.

Bibliography

J. C. Ford and G. Kelly, *Contemporary Moral Theology*, 2 vols. (Westminster, 1958–63); K. E. Kirk, *Conscience and Its Problems: An Introduction to Casuistry* (London, 1927); P. Lehmann, *Ethics in a Christian Context* (London, 1963).

E. D. COOK

CATECHISMS

From its earliest days, the church was concerned to instruct its converts and nurture its members. Before being baptized and admitted to communion, new Christians were generally enrolled in beginners' classes for a programme of instruction known as *catechesis*. Manuals for their instruction were written by a number of leading theologians, most notably Cyril of Jerusalem (fourth century) and *John of Damascus (675–749). By the latter date, however, widespread conversion had apparently made this kind of activity unnecessary in the eyes of many. In any case, the decline of learning in Western Europe following the collapse of the Roman Empire made it practically impossible. The only reminder of it to survive was 'the departure of the catechumens', a ritual exercise between the ministry of the word and the sacrament during public worship which lost all real meaning as there were no catechumens to depart!

The need for theological instruction remained acute, of course, and in the twelfth century, Peter *Lombard, the Archbishop of Paris (d. 1160), devised a question-and-answer method of teaching which became standard in the medieval schools and survived up to and beyond the Reformation. What Lombard intended for theological students was simplified and extended to parish clergy by men like John Peckham, Archbishop of Canterbury (1279–92), who shortly after taking office issued a famous canon, *Ignorantia sacerdotum* ('the ignorance of priests') in which he ordered all ordination candidates to demonstrate their competence in expounding the Apostles' *Creed and other subjects, like the seven deadly sins and the seven sacraments as originally expounded by Lombard. By the early fourteenth century it was usual for them to have to show adequate knowledge of the creed, the Ten Commandments and the Lord's Prayer, which represented the pillars of Christian doctrine, discipline and devotion.

The extension of this form of training to lay people was slow and greatly hindered by the difficulty of producing texts in sufficient numbers and the prevailing illiteracy. With the invention of printing and the gradual revival of primary education in the late fifteenth century, it became feasible to produce such documents in large quantities, and the need to spread the teachings of the Reformation made it imperative to do so. The Lutherans seized the initiative, and by 1529 *Luther himself had produced a Long Catechism (mainly for students and priests) and a Short Catechism (mainly for children and lay people). Luther put the Ten Commandments first and followed them with the Apostles' Creed, which reflected his own understanding of the *gospel. The *law came first, in order to reveal the nature of *sin. *Faith then appeared as the cure for sin, and the Lord's Prayer, followed by the *sacraments, illustrated the Christian life of *grace. Luther also subdivided the Creed into its *trinitarian parts and linked them to the divine works of *creation, *redemption and *sanctification.

A more traditional approach was followed by John *Calvin in his Genevan catechism of 1541, where the primacy of faith over law was restored. This catechism is noteworthy for the way in which it deals at some length with such topics as the descent of Christ into hell, and for its *Reformed emphasis on the Lord's Supper (see *Eucharist). Calvin also stressed the importance of the union of the believer with Christ (see *Union with Christ), which can be found right through the catechism. The most famous Reformed catechism is that of *Heidelberg (1563), composed by Zacharias *Ursinus (1534–83) and Caspar *Olevianus (1536–87). It is structured in three parts, to correspond with each of the persons of the Trinity, and places considerable emphasis on the doctrine of Christian *assurance. Overall it is an attempt to mediate between Lutheran and Reformed sacramental teaching and has remained in use among Dutch and French Protestants in particular.

The first English catechism appeared in 1549 and was the work of Alexander Nowell, dean of St Paul's (d. 1602). Its theology generally followed Calvin's, but the emphasis on union with Christ was toned down to some extent. Nowell's work was clearly designed to prepare candidates for *confirmation, though it did not contain any reference to the sacraments. That was not added until 1604 and is generally thought to have been the work of John Overall, Nowell's successor as dean of St Paul's. In 1662 the catechism was separated from the order of confirmation in the *Book of Common Prayer* and given an independent place, which may have unintentionally contributed to the relative neglect which it suffered in later years.

The Puritans were great believers in catechisms, and even in the sixteenth century, William *Perkins (1558–1602) composed one which he regarded as supplementary to that which was found in the *Book of Common Prayer*. The main difficulty with the official form was that it presupposed belief on the part of the student, whereas Perkins aimed his work at the need to convert his pupils as much as to instruct them. The famous products of the Puritan tradition were undoubtedly the Larger and Shorter Catechisms of the Westminster Assembly, which first appeared in 1648 after having been ratified for use by parliament. The Larger Catechism has never been widely used, but the Shorter one became and long remained a mainstay of *Presbyterian instruction.

The Westminster divines kept the traditional order, but replaced the Apostles' Creed with their own confession of faith (see *Westminster Confession), which they regarded as more complete and satisfactory, even though it was too long to be committed to memory. The brilliance of the Shorter Catechism lay in its brevity and depth of theological insight, which made it ideal for use in homes, schools and churches. The aim was to produce a well-instructed congregation which would be able to use the knowledge thus gained as a basis for appreciating sermons and Christian literature. It was an attempt to create a perceptive response to the teaching of the Bible, which it endeavoured to structure in a way that corresponded to the development of the Christian life – a motivation strikingly reminiscent of John Peckham's canon, even if the authors of the Catechism were scarcely aware of it.

How successful catechisms were in inculcating the Reformed faith is a matter of some debate. There were certainly a great many of them composed and distributed, and the method was soon copied by the Roman Catholic Church. As early as 1555 the Jesuit Peter Canisius (1521–97) had produced one for the laity, and this was soon followed (1563) by one for priests authorized by the Council of Trent. Non-Christian groups also produced catechisms, of which the most famous was the *Socinian Racovian Catechism of 1605. That in itself is testimony to their effectiveness, at least for a time, and as long as rote learning was the accepted norm, it seems that catechisms found a logical place in the pattern of religious instruction adopted by most Christian churches. As that declined, however, and as other books became more widely available, catechisms receded into the background, and by the twentieth century were no longer being widely used. They have survived to some extent as witnesses of the Reformation and may even be recognized as subordinate standards of faith, but intimate knowledge of them is now quite rare.

From time to time there have been attempts either to revive the traditional catechisms or to compose new ones, but it cannot be said that a widespread movement to this effect has so far developed in the Protestant world. The Roman Catholic Church, on the other hand, presents an interesting contrast to this neglect. After many years of consultation following the Second Vatican Council, an official *Catechism of the Catholic Church* was eventually published (1992), which has now been translated into most of the world's major languages. Drafted in French (though technically it is the Latin version which is 'official'), this *Catechism* is a major statement of current *Roman Catholic theology and is more like a university textbook than anything else. It is certainly far beyond anything that could be used for the instruction of children. Its extensive notes provide a ready guide to the sources of Catholic doctrine and to the way in which they have been officially interpreted since Vatican II, so much so that it is now common to quote the *Catechism* as the most accessible authoritative source of Catholic teaching. It is organized along traditional lines, but each section is a vastly expanded version of anything found in earlier catechisms. Thus, part one is a lengthy exposition of Christian theology using the Apostles' Creed as its basis, part two examines the sacraments, part three covers the moral dimension of the Christian faith (including the Ten Commandments) and part four deals with the Christian's devotional life, which culminates in an exposition of the Lord's Prayer.

The *Catechism* was a major publishing event at the time and has been widely used in the Roman Catholic Church, occasionally leading to calls from some Protestants that similar ones should be produced, but to date very little has materialized, and it remains to be seen how influential the Catholic *Catechism* will turn out to be in the longer term. The Eastern Orthodox churches have not produced any official catechisms, though there have been occasional suggestions that they should try to do so. Several Orthodox writers have published introductions to their faith which have a catechetical character to them. On the whole, though, it must be said that in most churches the catechetical tradition is moribund at the present time. An interesting exception to this general tendency is the Evangelical Lutheran Church of Finland, which has recently published a new catechism with considerable success, but whether (or to what extent) that will be imitated elsewhere remains to be seen.

Bibliography

H. Bonar, *Catechisms of the Scottish Reformation* (London, 1866); *Catechism of the Catholic Church* (London, 1995); D. Janz, *Three Reformation Catechisms: Catholic, Anabaptist, Lutheran* (New York, 1982);

E. Norman, *An Anglican Catechism* (London, 2003); G. Strauss, *Luther's House of Learning* (Baltimore, 1978); G. I. Williamson, *The Westminster Shorter Catechism* (Philadelphia, 2003).

G. L. BRAY

CATHOLICITY

Catholicity is an aspect of the *church, applied to her in the historic *creeds ('I believe one holy, *catholic*, apostolic Church . . .'). It is fundamentally an ecclesiological category, often viewed as one of the church's essential 'marks'. In popular usage, it can refer simply to formal styles of theology and worship that draw on practices and interests associated (either now or in the past) with: the Roman Catholic Church; the undivided church of the early Christian centuries; the pre-Reformation Western church; or finally, the broader ecumenical community of contemporary churches. In this broader way, 'catholic' can be a term of liturgical, historical, or ecumenical reference.

The term itself comes from the (non-Scriptural) Greek phrase denoting wholeness or comprehensiveness. Ignatius of Antioch (*Letter to the Smyrneans*, 8.2) early applied it to the whole church of Christ as represented in the bishop, and it soon came to designate the true Christian church as distinguished from the idiosyncratic bodies of *heretics and *schismatics. Confession of 'the catholic church' entered the common creeds of East and West by the mid-fourth century.

A key to its meaning is given in the early description of certain NT letters as 'Catholic Epistles' (e.g. of James, Peter, John and Jude, by Eusebius and Jerome), addressed not to particular local congregations but to the breadth of the church. 'Catholic' here pointed to the word of God spoken to 'all'. It implied a *common* reception of God's call as it goes out to the world. This notion of commonality of life, teaching and subjection to God's extending word (cf. Acts 2:42–47; Eph. 4:4–6) stands at the root of catholicity and of the early belief that the bishop is its natural living embodiment. The development that saw communion with the Bishop of Rome in particular (cf. *Irenaeus) as a mark of catholicity derives from this.

There are problems in the use of the term when the church divides over time, and when various groups out of communion with one another and without mutually recognized ministries of oversight confess the creed simultaneously. What could commonality mean in this case? One possibility is that the term refers to a visible church that alone is catholic in a 'full sense', and to others only partially if at all. Roman Catholics, for instance, have articulated a vision of ordered inclusivity over time, through which separated churches in 'imperfect communion' with Rome through baptism may be moving through history towards gradual fullness, along with the human race as a whole, as they are finally embraced by the Roman Church (see *Roman Catholic theology). That there are levels of catholicity among churches, however, is difficult to demonstrate quantitatively, and 'fullness' here is reduced to a providential hope.

Another possibility is to identify catholicity with an invisible reality, generally of a personal nature, that is tied to the desire and faith that binds an individual or group to Christ, and only through Christ to others. Protestants like Barth and even Roman Catholics like de Lubac, from very different perspectives, have adopted this view, which is based on a rejection of 'extrinsic' measures of divine action – material, institutional and visibly evaluated – that might somehow rest within human control apart from God's gracious initiative. If catholicity is here reflected in ecclesial structures (as clearly it is for someone like de Lubac), these represent a history of changing ecclesial relations that manifest Christ. There is, in this perspective, little historical verifiability to claims of catholicity in this world, and the word itself risks becoming a confusedly broad synonym for the indwelling presence of the Holy Spirit in its trinitarian life.

More recently, following the Second Vatican Council, catholicity has been reconnected to its divine missionary roots. As the accountable receipt in time and space of God's word, catholicity refers to the church's own *conversion* within history to God's love for the whole world (1 Tim. 2:4). To be catholic, in this renewed understanding of the term, is to subject oneself to the mandated movement of the church through the Holy Spirit to embrace all people in the formal life of 'all things in common' as willed and embodied by the Father through his self-offering of love in his Son. Hence, there is a *moral* basis to catholicity, located in the embodied charity of heart and will, that extends to the world's corners. The church, as a whole or as divided churches, is thereby judged according to her catholicity – that is, her enacted communion – and not the reverse. This, finally, coheres with part of the definition given by Cyril of Jerusalem in his eighteenth catechetical lecture, that, in addition to its extent and comprehensive doctrine, the church 'is called Catholic . . . because it brings into subjection to godliness the whole race of mankind, governors and governed, learned and unlearned; and because it universally treats and heals the whole class of sins . . . and possesses in itself every form of virtue which is named, both in deeds and words, and in every kind of spiritual gifts' (18.23, tr. E. H. Gifford).

Bibliography

K. Barth, *CD*, Vol. 4: *The Doctrine of Reconciliation* (ET, Edinburgh, 1969); *Catechism of the Catholic Church* (New York, 2003); H. de Lubac, *The Christian Faith: An Essay on the Structure of the Apostles' Creed* (ET, San Francisco, 1986); J. Pearson, *An Exposition of the Creed* (1659), rev. and ed. T. Chevallier and R. Sinker (Cambridge, 1899); R. Williams, 'Catholicity', in A. Hastings (ed.), *The Oxford Companion to Christian Thought* (Oxford, 2000); J. Zizioulas, *Being as Communion: Studies in Personhood and the Church* (ET, Crestwood, ²1997).

E. RADNER

CELIBACY, see SEXUALITY

CELTIC CHRISTIANITY

Christianity appeared in the ancient Roman province of Britannia in the second century, mainly among the Romano-British population, but also apparently spreading to the Celtic tribes to the north and west. A delegation of British bishops participated in the Council of Arles in 314, and later in the century, Ninian, the first missionary to the southern Picts beyond the empire in Caledonia, established his *candida casa* (white house) at Whithorn in Galloway. Roman rule finally ceased in Britain in 410, and in 429, Germanus, the bishop of Auxerre near Paris, sent a mission to the British church to counter the influence of the doctrines of *Pelagius, a Celtic monk who had travelled throughout the Roman Empire. After the collapse of Roman rule, the immigration into southern and eastern Britain of the pagan tribes of Angles, Saxons and Jutes from Germany led to the isolation of the Celtic churches of the north and west. But in the fifth century, the Romano-British missionary, Patrick, completed the evangelization of Ireland, and in the sixth century, David emerged as the leading bishop and saint in Wales. In 563, Columba crossed from Ireland to establish a monastery on the island of Iona off the west coast of the Scottish kingdom of Dalriada, which had been settled by Gaels from Ireland.

Iona became the centre from which the Picts of north-eastern Scotland were evangelized. From there too Aidan went to the Angles of the kingdom of Northumbria in 635 at the invitation of its king, Oswald, establishing a monastery on Lindisfarne. By this time, Pope Gregory the Great had sent Augustine to England, leading first to the conversion of King Ethelbert of Kent and the establishing of a church in Canterbury in 597. From there, the mission from the Roman church spread to the other southern Saxon kingdoms, and in fact in Northumbria, Oswald's predecessor had already been influenced by them. The long years of the isolation of the Celtic church were coming to an end, and the Synod of Whitby in 664 established the practices of the Roman church in Northumbria.

For about 200 years, therefore, the church in the Celtic lands of Wales, Ireland and Scotland developed practices which distinguished it from the rest of Western Christianity, centred in Rome. In Ireland particularly it became more dominated by its monasteries than elsewhere, and the abbot could be more powerful than the bishop. The monasteries were centres of learning, conserving Christian culture and civilization when most of Continental Europe had succumbed to the barbarian invasions. The *Book of Kells*, dating from the late eighth century, is one outstanding example of an illuminated manuscript of the four Gospels in Latin, thought to have been produced by Columban monks, possibly in Iona. Celtic art, with conventions such as the circular representation of eternity, is also to be seen in the large stone Celtic crosses which still survive. The monasteries were also bases for missionary work; missionaries not only evangelized in the Celtic countries, but established the great monasteries of the Alpine region, re-establishing the Christian church there.

159

Celtic spirituality has attracted much interest in the last few decades, but too often a contemporary agenda has been read into a romanticized version of the life and thought of the Celtic saints. Their spirituality was certainly marked by a strong sense of God's presence in *creation and also by a strong focus on the *Trinity. Both of these features are represented in the hymn known as 'St Patrick's Breastplate': 'I bind unto myself today the strong name of the Trinity.' Patrick certainly gave priority to the role of the bishop as a teacher, and his *Confessio* includes an exposition of the faith which is clearly related closely to the Nicene *Creed. There was also a strong *asceticism and a fierce penitential discipline in Celtic Christianity. A movement to return to earlier austerity developed in the Irish church in the late eighth century: their Gaelic title, 'Servants of God', came into English as the 'Culdees'. The Synod of Whitby, which marked the increasing integration of the Celtic churches into the wider Western church, did not have to address any outstanding theological differences, but only practical issues such as the date of Easter, the shape of the monks' tonsure and the procedure for the consecration of bishops.

Bibliography

I. Bradley, *Celtic Christianity: Making Myths and Chasing Dreams* (Edinburgh, 1999); T. Cahill, *How the Irish Saved Civilization* (New York, 1995); B. Lehane, *Early Celtic Christianity* (London, 2005); D. Meek, *The Quest for Celtic Christianity* (Edinburgh, 2000); T. O'Loughlin, *Celtic Theology: Humanity, World and God in Early Irish Writings* (London, 2000).

T. A. Noble

CHALCEDON, COUNCIL OF

On 8 October 451 the Council of Chalcedon opened with over 500 bishops in attendance, the pope being represented by his legates. The issue confronting the Council was how to conceive and express the truth that *Jesus is the Son of God incarnate. The majority of bishops did not want to promulgate a new creed, but rather simply to ratify again the *Nicene-*Constantinopolitan *Creed, Cyril's *Second Letter to Nestorius* (see *Cyril of Alexandria), and Pope Leo's *Tome to Flavian*. However, the emperor realized the need for a new definition, one to which all could agree. This new definition included the following important points.

First, the Fathers three times used the phrase 'one and the same' and five times used the phrase 'the same'. Who is the 'one and the same' and 'the same'? It is the eternally only-begotten Son/Word. There are not two 'sons' (*contra* *Nestorius). There is only one subject or person – the Son/Word.

Second, the one and the same – the Son/Word – is perfect in Godhead and perfect in manhood. The same is consubstantial with the Father (*contra* *Arius), and the same is consubstantial with us with a human soul and body (*contra* *Apollinarius). Because Jesus is the one and the same Son existing as God and man, *Mary can truly be called Mother of God, for the Son of God was born of her as a man (*contra* Nestorius). Moreover, because the Son of God actually existed as a man, he is 'made known in two natures' (*contra* Eutyches).

Third, the act of *incarnation – the 'becoming' – establishes a union whereby the natures are not confused or changed, nor are they divided or separated. The reason the natures are not confused or changed is because the incarnational union – the 'becoming' – is not the compositional union of natures which would give rise to a new third kind of being. Yet, the natures are not divided or separated, because they are united to the one person or subject of the Son/Word.

Fourth, because the Council established a proper understanding of the incarnation, it equally confirmed the proper use of the communication of idioms, that is, because it is one and the same Son who exists as God and as man then both divine and human attributes (idioms) can be predicated of one and the same Son. The Son can truly be said to be born, thirst, hunger, suffer, die and rise, because the Son actually lived an authentic human life as a man.

The Council of Chalcedon did not bring about complete unity and peace. Some Antiochenes believed that it relied too heavily on the theology of Cyril and so tended to *Monophysitism. (The Coptic Church in Egypt is still Monophysite.) Some Alexandrians believed that the stress on the two natures after the union was a profession of Nestorianism. (There are still Nestorians in Iraq today.) Nonetheless, the Council of Chalcedon is a Christological landmark, and its creed continues to be the doctrinal basis for most Christian denominations.

See also: CHRISTOLOGY; COUNCILS.

Bibliography

M. Forlin Patrucco and M. Simonetti, 'Chalcedon', in *EEC Church*; P. T. Camelot, in *NCE* 3, pp. 363–366; J. McGuckin, *Saint Cyril of Alexandria and the Christological Controversy* (Crest Wood, 2004); R. V. Sellers, *The Council of Chalcedon* (London, 1953); T. G. Weinandy, *Does God Change?: The Word's Becoming in the Incarnation* (Petersham, 1985).

T. G. WEINANDY

CHALMERS, THOMAS (1780–1847)

A professor of divinity at Edinburgh from 1828 until his death, Chalmers was famous as a preacher, parish minister and leader of the *evangelical party in the Church of Scotland, and of the Free Church of Scotland after the Disruption of 1843. Although his reputation rests here, and his disdain for theological systems was well known if not well remembered, his influence on generations of Scottish students of theology was profound. He retained many of the finer values of the moderate tradition which he had embraced prior to his conversion in 1811, and came to represent the evangelical tradition which finds its major concerns in the proclamation and application of the gospel, rather than in overprecise formulation of its content. The *atonement was central to the mission of the church in personal and social transformation, but he told his students not to preach *predestination; that was God's business, not theirs. The liberalization of *Presbyterian adherence to the harsher aspects of the *Westminster Confession of Faith which took place some thirty years after his death reflects many of the theological values of his preaching and lectures. His sermon, 'The fullness and freeness of the gospel offer', summarizes in title and content his basic understanding of the Christian message. His *Theological Institutes* are volumes 7 and 8 of his *Posthumous Works* (1847–9), and other relevant writings can be found in his *Works* (1836–42).

Bibliography

S. J. Brown, *Thomas Chalmers and the Godly Commonwealth* (Oxford, 1982); A. C. Cheyne (ed.), *The Practical and the Pious: Essays on Thomas Chalmers (1780–1847)* (Edinburgh, 1985); W. Hanna, *The Life and Writings of the Rev. Thomas Chalmers,* 4 vols. (Edinburgh, 1849–52); S. Piggin and J. Roxborogh, *The St Andrews Seven* (Edinburgh, 1985); J. Roxborogh, *Thomas Chalmers: Enthusiast for Mission* (Edinburgh, 1999).

W. J. ROXBOROGH

CHARISMATIC MOVEMENT/THEOLOGY

The Charismatic Movement, which many of its adherents prefer to describe as the Charismatic Renewal, exercised great influence in the thinking, worship and expectations of all the historic Christian denominations in both First and Majority World contexts during the second half of the twentieth century.

To insist on calling it a renewal rather than a movement is not without significance, because it has for the most part sought to be not a movement alongside or even outside the churches, but a renewal or rediscovery within the life of the church of the charismatic dimension of the work of the *Holy Spirit. The characteristic emphasis has been on the recovery of the charismatic gifts listed in such NT passages as 1 Cor. 12, and often with a particular insistence on the exercise of the gift of tongues as the validating sign of the so-called *baptism in the Holy Spirit.

The renewal from one point of view was a spillover of the *Pentecostalism of the first half of the twentieth century, but it was integrative rather than sectarian in its intention. It found an often controversial place in all the mainline Protestant denominations, and from the sixties onwards in the Roman Catholic Church, whose authorities both welcomed and at the same time supervised it to make sure that its spontaneity was contained within the sacramental and liturgical practices of the church.

It has been said, with considerable insight, that the charismatic renewal which was penetrating the churches in this powerful way in the second half of the twentieth century was a movement looking for a theology. One might argue with equal plausibility that, at least in its early stages, theological reflection was one of the lowest of its priorities. Charismatics were much more concerned to experience the Holy Spirit and his gifts than they were to think about them. In fact, the whole movement could be seen as a mighty swing of the religious pendulum from the cerebral to the experiential, from a faith for the mind to a faith for the heart. If you had a direct contact with God, what need had you for theological theories and defined doctrine, especially if the theories were seen as liberal subversions of the given gospel and the doctrines seemed to require intellectual assent more than a personal engagement with a living God?

However, as the movement matured, it soon became obvious that the way it presented itself implied a theological framework which was therefore open to assessment and revision. Its teaching about a baptism in the Holy Spirit that was distinct from and subsequent to new birth and *conversion and that evidenced itself in the exercise of spiritual gifts (see *Gifts of the Spirit), notably the gift of tongues, made it clear that it had often unreflectingly inherited a Pentecostal theology that was distinct from, and in considerable tension with, the doctrinal traditions in which the mainline charismatics had come to Christian faith and understanding. Such teaching exposed them to theological criticism from people in their own tradition who read the biblical evidence differently and interpreted the gospel in less Pentecostal ways. Furthermore, they themselves remained faithful to the traditions in which they had been nurtured in faith and so had to face questions about how the new experience of the Spirit could be integrated with the understanding of the gospel that they had inherited and still wanted to affirm.

The charismatic renewal has, after the initial excitement in which many rediscovered the power of the Spirit and his gifts, given rise to a theological debate in which its proponents have both corrected and been corrected by the more established theologies of their churches.

In terms of biblical theology, writers like James Dunn have argued convincingly that in the NT being baptized in the Holy Spirit is integral to Christian conversion rather than a second blessing subsequent to it. Tongues as the invariable evidence of Spirit baptism has very little support in Scripture, and many charismatics accept that conclusion. On the other hand, the typical Protestant teaching that the charismata of 1 Cor. 12 were withdrawn when the canon of Scripture was established has also been shown to lack credible biblical authentication and has been practically refuted by the credible, if still contested, claims of charismatics to exercise these very gifts today.

Theologians both inside and outside the charismatic constituency have attempted to integrate charismatic experience with inherited theology in terms of sacramental theology (L. J. Suenens), Lutheran teaching on justification (F. D. Bruner), Barthian Christocentrism (T. A. Smail), Puritan teaching about assurance (J. I. Packer) and liberation theology of peace and justice (M. Welker).

More widely there has been concern to relate the resurrection spirituality of the charismatics, with its dangers of a superficial triumphalism, to a continued insistence of the centrality of the cross to all authentic Christian experience. The whole discussion has been given theological depth by the more recent trinitarian emphasis that the chief work of the Spirit is not the distribution of dramatic gifts, but the relating of people to the Father and the Son, with a view to their enlistment in the triune God's mission of reconciliation to his whole creation.

Bibliography

A. Anderson, *An Introduction to Pentecostalism* (Cambridge, 2004); S. M. Burgess and E. van der Maas (eds.), *New International Dictionary of Pentecostal and Charismatic Movements* (Grand Rapids, rev. edn, 2002); J. D. G. Dunn, *Baptism in the Holy Spirit* (London, 1970); P. Hocken, *Streams of Renewal: The Origins and Development of the Charismatic Movement* (Carlisle, rev. edn, 1997); S. Hunt, M. Hamilton and T. Walter (eds.), *Charismatic Christianity: Sociological Perspectives* (Basingstoke, 1999); T. A. Smail (ed.). *Charismatic Renewal: The Search for a Theology* (London, 1993).

T. A. SMAIL

CHEMNITZ, MARTIN (1522–86)

Martin Chemnitz was a *Lutheran theological conciliator. After university study at Frankfurt an der Oder and Wittenberg (1543–7), service with Albrecht Duke of Prussia at Königsberg (1547–53) and a brief time teaching at Wittenberg, he was called to Braunschweig (Brunswick) in 1554, joining his long-time friend Joachim Mörlin in church ministry, teaching and wider reform, and contributing to several territorial statements of church doctrine.

Chemnitz was the leading drafter of the *Formula of Concord (1577, published in the *Book of Concord*, 1580), intended to reconcile the disputing parties of 'True-Lutherans' (Gnesio-Lutherans), represented by Mörlin and Flacius Illyricus, co-ordinator of the Protestant church history known as the *Magdeburg Centuries*, and the 'Philippists', adherents of *Melanchthon widely suspected as revisionists. Chemnitz sought to do justice to both *Luther and Melanchthon, on whose *Common Places* he had long lectured. His own *Common Places*, published posthumously, were a commentary on Melanchthon's. In substance, Chemnitz sided with the Gnesio-Lutherans, following Melanchthon chiefly only in method and style, despite their early friendship.

A considerable scholar, Chemnitz wrote a massive *Examination of the Council of Trent*, and a work rich in patristic learning on *The Two Natures in Christ*. Other works, especially on the Lord's Supper (see *Eucharist), helped to stabilize mainstream Lutheran doctrine amid challenge and dispute (e.g. on *justification by faith against *Osiander). His modification of the traditional notion of the omnipresence of Christ's human nature (which Melanchthon rejected) was known as multivolipresence: a presence in as many places as Christ wished. Chemnitz's importance for Lutheran orthodoxy is reflected in the common dictum: 'If the second Martin had not come, the first Martin [Luther] would not have survived.'

Bibliography

Works: *Examination of the Council of Trent*, tr. F. Kramer (St Louis, 1971–86); *The Two Natures in Christ*, tr. J. A. O. Preus (St Louis, 1971); *Common Places*, tr. J. A. O. Preus, 2 vols. (St Louis, 1989).

Studies: E. F. A. Klug, *From Luther to Chemnitz: On Scripture and the Word* (Grand Rapids, 1971); J. A. O. Preus, *The Second Martin: The Life and Theology of Martin Chemnitz* (St Louis, 1994); B. W. Teigen, *The Lord's Supper in the Theology of Martin Chemnitz* (Brewster, 1986).

D. F. WRIGHT

CHICAGO SCHOOL OF THEOLOGY

The leading proponent of theological modernism and the radical wing of the *liberal movement in American Protestantism, the Chicago School of Theology is associated largely with the Divinity School of the University of Chicago during the half century from 1890 to 1940. Reaching its summit while Shailer Mathews (1863–1941) was dean (1908–33), other prominent members of the Chicago School included George Burman Foster (1858–1918), Shirley Jackson Case (1872–1947), Gerald Birney Smith (1868–1929), Edward Scribner Ames (1870–1958) and Henry Nelson Wieman (1884–1975). Incorporating a wide variety of perspectives, the Chicago modernists championed an *empirical and pragmatic approach to religion which stressed its functional values and betrayed an indebtedness to the philosophies of William James (1842–1910), John Dewey (1859–1952), George Herbert Mead (1863–1931) and Charles Peirce (1839–1914).

Chicago modernism celebrated the 'spirit of the age' in both its scientific and democratic dimensions. Theologically, this entailed a rejection of special *revelation as the basis for theological authority in favour of an appeal to experience as the criterion of truth in religion. However, their emphasis on experience was not in the *Schleiermacheran tradition of using personal *religious experience, but the more radical approach of securing scientific legitimacy for religion by appealing to experience in the public domain – that is, that which is accessible to and verifiable by all enquirers. A socio-historical method for studying religious phenomena as human behaviour, and not divine, was urged, since all theological traditions were thought to evolve with time. Thus an openness to radical questioning of theological forms, a willingness to experiment with new conceptions of God, and an affirmation of human ideals and values – with an accompanying drift toward *humanism – all characterized the school.

Culturally, the Chicago modernists were also virtually apostles for a 'religion of democracy'. Exuding optimism about altruistic human nature and an evolutionary ascent that boded well for man's future, they combined and confounded Christianity and democracy. This liberal belief in an immanent and democratic deity was sorely tested by the new spirit of pessimism and cynicism emerging from the First World War and the economic depression which followed it.

Bibliography

C. H. Arnold, *Near the Edge of Battle: A Short History of the Divinity School and the Chicago School of Theology 1866–1966* (Chicago, 1966);

W. J. Hynes, *Shirley Jackson Case and the Chicago School: The Socio-Historical Method* (Chico, 1981).

S. R. POINTER

CHICAGO STATEMENT

The Chicago Statement on Biblical Inerrancy came from the first 'summit' conference (1978) of the International Council on Biblical Inerrancy. ICBI was a coalition of conservative scholars who over ten years sponsored conferences and books to vindicate the full truth and trustworthiness of the Bible as a basic and necessary Christian certainty, so countering liberal Protestant opinion and also revisionist advocacy of 'limited inerrancy' and 'non-inerrantist evangelicalism' in their own ranks. (The latter factor prompted ICBI's formation.) Against all forms of the thesis that biblical authority and integrity of faith were compatible with disbelieving at least some assertions and assumptions in both Testaments, ICBI urged that methodological and epistemological coherence in theology depends on treating all canonical *Scripture as trustworthy instruction from God, a view learned from the explicit attitude of the NT writers and the historical Jesus himself to their Scriptures, that is, our OT. ICBI thus revitalized the polemic maintained in scholarly form by such as B. B. *Warfield at the turn of the twentieth century, and by *fundamentalism throughout that century, and with growing academic strength by evangelicals (see *Evangelical theology) for some decades before ICBI was born.

The Statement is defensive, not adventurous, pursuing no new paths but clarifying a consensus. Its three parts are: a summary of ICBI's view, nineteen 'articles of affirmation and denial' elaborating it, and an extended exposition of it. The Bible's divine origin and full humanness; its consistent Christ-centredness; its total reliability as a guide, both informationally and imperatively; the ministry of the Holy Spirit as its inspirer, authenticator and interpreter; and its final authority for the church and every Christian, are the points emphasized.

ICBI's second consensus document, the Chicago Statement on Biblical Hermeneutics (1982), complements the first by exploring principles of interpretation in twenty-five further affirmations and denials. The two together have become a reference point for many American evangelicals and evangelical institutions.

See also: INFALLIBILITY AND INERRANCY OF THE BIBLE; LIBERAL THEOLOGY; SCRIPTURE, DOCTRINE OF.

Bibliography

N. L. Geisler (ed.), *Inerrancy* (Grand Rapids, 1979) – contains the text of the statement; J. Hannah (ed.), *Inerrancy and the Church* (Chicago, 1984); G. R. Lewis and B. Demarest (eds.), *Challenges to Inerrancy: A Theological Response* (Chicago, 1984).

J. I. PACKER

CHINESE THEOLOGY

Since Robert Morrison (1782–1834) baptized the first Chinese converts almost 200 years ago, Chinese theology has gone through several phases of development. The first phase was dominated by concerns for indigenization. Morrison's colleague, William Milne, blazed the trail with just a handful of Chinese converts. His *Zhang Yuan Liang You Xianglun* (*Dialogues Between Two Friends, Zhang and Yuan*) remains one of the most inspiring indigenous attempts. The Confucian vision of humanity is affirmed, but regarded as less than comprehensive, and can only be realized in Jesus Christ, the manifestation of God's love in the overcoming of sin. *Jing Shi Liangyan* (*The Word for Awakening the Age*), written by Liang Fa (1789–1855), represents the first genuine Chinese indigenous attempt. Integrating Confucian ethics with the *kingdom ethics of righteousness and equality, the book inspired Hong Xiuquan, the leader of the Taiping Rebellion (1851–65).

This signalled the coming of the second phase, which was marked by socio-political turmoil, with the Qing Dynasty crumbling, and the imperial expansion of the West encroaching. A deep sense of crisis sent China into a feverish quest for cultural transformation and national salvation. Modernization, scientism, iconoclastic rejection of Confucianism and religions, carried the day. Christianity was seen not only as irrelevant, but also as an accomplice for Western imperialism.

Leading Chinese Christian thinkers like Zhao Zichen and Wu Leichuan formed the Apologetic Group in 1920 in Beijing, aiming to regenerate Chinese society through the Christian faith. To do so, Zhao believed, Christianity had to be radically reinterpreted in the light of the modern scientific worldview. The essence of the gospel had to be uncovered from the rubble of unscientific dogmas and outdated traditions. Denominationalism had to be abandoned. The centre of the Christian faith was the person of *Jesus, a man who became the Son of God through radical consciousness of being one with God, thus becoming the embodiment of God's personality, at the heart of which is *love. God's love was manifested in the self-giving sacrifice of Jesus, which reveals what authentic personhood should be. The regeneration of Chinese society hinged on the widespread acceptance of Jesus as the model of an authentic person. Wu saw Jesus as a revolutionary, attempting to bring in a radically new socio-political order, where private property would be abolished, and all goods equally shared, with equal rights for everybody.

In the same vein, Wu Yaozong regarded Jesus' gospel as a *social gospel, pointing to a social order based on communal labour and communal ownership. The communist ideal was evident as a shaping force in theology even before 1949. But Wang Mingdao attacked the idea of building an ideal society on earth, since all social evils come from corrupt human nature. The key to social transformation is personal repentance and regeneration through faith in Jesus Christ.

After 1949, the church faced a different sort of challenge. Under communist rule, the church was under pressure to provide a positive interpretation of the communist revolution, which claimed to be liberation accomplished, dwarfing all forms of social gospel or *liberation theology, making pietistic theology totally irrelevant. How was the church to assess the revolution theologically? What were the implications?

From the 1950s onward, theology in China entered into its third phase. Shen Yifan rejected the duality between revelation and history, creation and redemption, the sacred and the profane. He proposed an incarnational-sacramental theology. The glory of God and his redemptive act can find expression in profane history such as the communist revolution. Ding Guangxun saw history as progression in God's continual creation. The 'Cosmic Christ' was the omega point where creation comes to its fullness, with love permeating all things, reconciling all contradictions. Even among atheists or unbelievers, we can see the love of Christ at work. The doctrine of 'justification by faith' was deemed exclusivist and should be replaced by 'justification by love'.

Outside mainland China, socio-cultural context remains a vital concern. C. S. Song sees indigenous cultural identity, religious pluralism, political oppression and suffering as the main issues. His 'transpositional theology' weaves biblical stories into stories of Asian people. Transposition is incarnation in action. When the crucified Jesus is transposed from Jerusalem to Asia, Jesus means the crucified people in Asia. Highly critical of Western imperialism, he nevertheless was mute about oppression in China, in particular the immense suffering during the Cultural Revolution. He even suggested that the new China undergoing cultural revolution was a secularized version of salvation history.

Since the 1980s, theologians in Hong Kong have emerged as a significant force in public discourse, as Christians were actively involved in shaping the future of Hong Kong. Jonathan Chao, Carver Yu and a few others drafted the *Christian Declaration of Faith in the Face of Socio-political Uncertainty in Hong Kong* in 1984, acknowledging God as the Lord of history, affirming Christian solidarity with the people of Hong Kong, and calling the people to become the subject of history, both for Hong Kong and China.

Chao subsequently developed a kingdom theology, with Christian transformation of Chinese culture as part of the kingdom mission. Yu believes that current contextual theologies merely touch the surface of the present cultural context. The breakdown of personhood, the uprooting of spiritual values by market-driven functional rationality, is the heart of the matter. *Covenant is the answer to the postmodern culture of narcissism shaped by market *capitalism.

Phee Seng Kang actively promotes theology as public discourse. To him, the real challenge for Chinese theology lies in communicating the Christian faith and its rationality in the public forum and the academy, rejecting privatization and marginalization, refusing to allow public values shaped only by the secular market place. Theology should prophetically expose the poverty of scientific naturalism and secular *humanism, setting a new paradigm for inter-disciplinary, cross-cultural and multi-perspectival quest for truth.

See also: SCIENCE AND THEOLOGY.

Bibliography

D. H. Bays, *Christianity in China: From the Eighteenth Century to the Present* (Stanford, 1996); T. C. Chao, 'The Basis of Social Reconstruction', *Chinese Recorder* 53, 1922, pp. 312–318; A. Hunter and K. K. Chan, *Protestantism in Contemporary China* (Cambridge, 1993); Kang Phee Seng, 'From Believing to Professing: Maintaining Distinctiveness in a Pluralistic Culture in Asia', *Quest: An Interdisciplinary Journal for Asian Christian Scholars* 1, 2002, pp. 35–47; idem, 'Religious Discourse in the Public Forum', in S. Chan (ed.), *Truth to Proclaim* (Singapore, 2002); Lam Wing-hung, *Chinese Theology in Construction* (Pasadena, 1983); Lutheran World Federation/Pro Mundi Vita, *Christianity and the New China* (South Pasadena, 1976); Yi-fan Shen, 'Theological Reflections in the Chinese Church', *Chinese Theological Review*, Vol. 4, 1988, pp. 22–31; C. S. Song, *The Compassionate God* (New York, 1982); idem, *Jesus, The Crucified People* (New York, 1990); B. Whyte, *Unfinished Encounter: China and Christianity* (London, 1988); C. Yu, *Being and Relation: A Theological Critique of Western Individualism and Dualism* (Edinburgh, 1987).

C. T. YU

CHRIST, JESUS, see CHRISTOLOGY; JESUS

CHRISTENDOM

The word 'Christendom' in English has had a peculiar history that partially distinguishes it from related words in other languages: the German *Christentum*, for example. But that peculiar history serves to highlight a problem that is important – and ambiguous – theologically. The word is first found in Old English at the end of the ninth century. The suffix, '-dom', was originally a noun that meant 'jurisdiction', and -dom words were coined to describe a certain state in either a concrete or an abstract sense. Thus, one could speak of a 'kingdom' as a concrete thing, a state, a polity, or of 'wisdom' as the abstract condition of being wise. 'Christendom' had both those senses (and *Christentum* [*-tum* is cognate with '-dom'] retains something of both). It was used in Old English to mean the Christian faith, Christianity as a system. But it was also used to mean the whole body of Christians and the society (or one of the polities) in which they lived.

In the post-Reformation world the abstract senses tended to be hived off onto other words (such as 'Christianity'), while 'Christendom' came almost exclusively to mean the place, the social and political sphere in which 'Christianity' was found and, ideally, embodied. And over the last fifty years or so the word has inevitably lost some of its currency: both theologians and politicians are increasingly unlikely to use it without either explanation or apologia.

The idea of a society embodying Christian values only really became thinkable at all in the aftermath of the conversion of *Constantine in the early fourth century, and it was probably only around the year 350 that Christians achieved numerical parity with non-Christians in the Roman Empire. But the late Empire never really became coextensive with Christianity as a system of belief, for two reasons. On the one hand, in both the Eastern and Western halves of the Roman and post-Roman world there were for centuries large clusters of 'pagans' living under Christian overlordship. And on the other, there was always an awareness of large numbers of Christians living beyond Christian political dominion – in the Persian Empire, for example.

Four things radically altered this situation: the rise of Islam and the consequent fragmentation of the Mediterranean world; the evolution of a new and distinctively, or at least self-consciously, Christian civilization in the high Middle Ages (partly in response to Islam); the collapse of the short-lived Crusader states in the East; and, finally, the expansion of Ottoman power into the heartland of Europe. There gradually emerged an increasing sense of living in a sphere – social, political and intellectual as well as religious – that was uniquely shaped and defined by Christian belief – in other words, a *Christiandom* formed by *Christianity*. So 'Christendom' in this sense (the sense in which the word passed into the modern world) was in part a product of cultural isolation and in part a product of conflict – a painful awareness of standing over against a non-Christian 'other'. In that sense the existence of Islam as at once a social and political structure and a faith to be affirmed helped shape the counter-notion of 'Christendom'.

But the vision of a Christianized society and the idea that the levers of secular power should be used to bring that about entered Christian discourse much earlier, indeed as soon as the political possibility began to exist. Constantine, for example – the first Christian emperor – issued a long series of laws which he at least regarded as promoting Christian values and Christian moral teaching. For example, in 316, he prohibited the branding of criminals on the face because the face expressed the image of God (but they could be branded anywhere else). Other laws drastically restricted legal grounds for divorce, and in theory at least put an end to the cruelty of gladiatorial shows (though the latter was never really enforced). Other measures under Constantine and his successors used the means of the state to further the interests of the church. Clergy received substantial tax privileges, for example, and various civil penalties were imposed on an ever-expanding catalogue of heretics – though the latter were at best only spasmodically enforced. That vision survived the political break-up of the Empire. In both Byzantine East and Latin West (after the coronation of Charlemagne by Pope Leo III on Christmas Day 800) there remained an ideal of a universal empire supporting and supported by a universal church. Their particular interests and their means of operation might be different, but in theory at least the harmonious union of church and state was the unquestioned precondition and ideal of Christian civilization. And that vision was not undermined, in either East or West, by the frequent reality of bitter conflict between the two orders. Indeed, it was precisely that vision of harmonious union that made such conflict inevitable when either the sacred or the secular power seemed to the other to be getting out of step.

Even the fragmentation of 'Christendom' at the Reformation did not destroy the notion of a uniform society of church and state. It undid the universal power of the papacy over the church in Western Europe, but in different ways theologians such as *Luther, *Calvin and *Hooker continued to believe in and work for a united form of Christian social order with complementary roles for church and state.

Profound changes were wrought in the early modern period by massive intellectual shifts, such as the *Enlightenment and the development of a pluralistic social order. There were, nonetheless, thinkers in the twentieth century who believed it right to try to recover a Christian form of society. The Christendom movement, which had some influence in England in the 1920s and 1930s, supported and enabled by men such as V. A. Demant (1893–1983) and Maurice B. Reckitt (1888–1980), was an example of such thought. T. S. Eliot, in his book *The Idea of a Christian Society* (1939), is a further example of commitment to a Christian social order. And in America thinkers in the *Social Gospel tradition, such as Walter *Rauschenbusch and – in a more nuanced and ultimately more radical form – Reinhold *Niebuhr were passionate in their affirmation of the need for the Christian message to take its place in the public arena.

What, in the end, are we to make of the ideal of 'Christendom'? It can be – and often is – argued that it is an idea past its sell-by date. On the one hand, internally as it were, there is the fact that Western society has entered a so-called post-Christian phase. It is not just a failure of Christian nerve here that leads to a rethink. Rather, it is the fact that Christian values – at least explicitly Christian values – may no longer command the measure of public consensus that can in and of itself be appealed to in order to justify their deployment in the framing of social policy. And on the other hand, there is an increasing awareness of the ever-growing importance theologically and ecclesially of various forms of Christianity in the non-Western world. Indeed, at the beginning of the twenty-first century the most vigorous centres of Christian growth are in Africa and Asia. Where and what, then, is 'Christendom'?

So those two facts together subvert any lingering sense that 'Christendom' is something that can be located on a map. But the dream of trying to realize – in some measure at least – Christian values in the here and now of social and political life will not, and should not, go away. A model for trying to understand what the concept of Christendom might mean for the twenty-first century is perhaps provided by a theologian who was himself living on the cusp between two ages. *Augustine began his *City of God* (it was to occupy him on and off for nearly fifteen years) in the aftermath of the sack of Rome by Alaric's Goths in 410. The invaders were themselves Christian – though, like most of the Germanic tribes, they had been converted to a form of *Arianism – but those three days of destruction brought the self-confidence of a society that had increasingly come to define itself as Christian crashing to the ground.

Augustine's response was a profound rethinking of the real though hidden ways in which God's purposes are worked out in history. This meant, first, an unwavering conviction that all of human history is somehow in God's hands. Second, the whole of human history is structured by a tension between two 'cities', the city of God and the city opposed to it, distinguished and defined by two 'loves' – two patterns of response to and relationship with God. Third, the city of God, though partially manifested and partially realized in time and space, can never be identified with any concrete, earthly polity. The purposes and policies of even the greatest of human rulers have been at least partially compromised by pride and self-aggrandizement. And therefore, finally, the city of God is and must remain an eschatological reality. It is something towards which we – as individuals, as a Christian people, as the whole of humankind – are ineluctably moving, but which will only become a reality at the end of all things, when all the redeemed stand in the presence of God, united in their love for him and for each other (see *Eschatology; *Kingdom of God).

The peculiar way in which the usage of the word has developed in English can perhaps help us retrace something of Augustine's journey. Christendom as a polity is distinct from Christianity as a system of belief. It cannot neatly be located on a map – as many in late medieval, or even the nineteenth, centuries were often tempted to do. But the public sphere does lie open to Christian influence and is one of the arenas in which Christian life is to be lived out. Christendom remains a task, a goal and a dream.

See also: SOCIETY, THEOLOGY OF; STATE.

Bibliography

C. Gore et al., *The Return of Christendom* (London, 1922); R. A. Markus, *Saeculum: History and Society in the Theology of St Augustine* (Cambridge, ²1989); R. Niebuhr, *The Nature and Destiny of Man*, 2 vols. (Hitchen, 1941–3); O. O'Donovan and J. L. O'Donovan (eds.), *From Irenaeus to Grotius: A Sourcebook in Christian Political Thought 100–1625* (Grand Rapids, 1999); W. Rauschenbusch, *Christianity and the Social Crisis* (London, 1907); M. B. Reckitt (ed.), *Prospect for Christendom* (London, 1945).

P. PARVIS

CHRISTIAN LIFE

While sanctification, spirituality and the Christian life each concern Christian transformation, the Christian life particularly concerns the character human life takes under the determination of God's grace. It has to do with how Christians are claimed by the *gospel, the spiritual postures and practices that rightly relate to God's *salvation.

As a subset of *sanctification, a theology of the Christian life will derive from soteriology. Different accounts, then, will diverge according to their respective accent upon salvation, that is, their different understandings of the nature of God's *grace and how such is received. And because the diversity is due to variations on a common root, making it impossible to categorize them in any straightforward way, the following will classify different versions according to emphasis. But these designations are primarily pedagogical and need not be mutually exclusive.

Ethical

Conceptions of the Christian life which locate obedience at its heart attempt to account for the moral claim God's salvation places upon its recipients and are influenced by the role discipleship played in Christ's ministry. One of the earliest of these was the dilemma of the 'two ways' in which Christians faced a constant choice between 'the way of light' and the 'way of darkness'. The former typically consisted of obedience to the Bible's moral imperatives (see *The Epistle of Barnabas*, chs. 19–20).

Desiderius *Erasmus proffered his *philosophia Christi* (philosophy of Christ), a less mystical, more humanist version of Thomas à Kempis' *Imitatio Christi* (*imitation of Christ). This urged learning the mind of Christ through obedience to the ethics of the Sermon on the Mount.

Dietrich *Bonhoeffer, while in accord with what is here labelled the 'relational' view, emphasized obedience and discipleship for Christian living and thus deserves mention. Bonhoeffer loathed 'cheap grace', 'grace without discipleship, grace without the cross, grace without the living, incarnate Jesus Christ' (*Discipleship*, Minneapolis, 2001, p. 44). He thus intertwined faith and obedience, arguing for the equal truth of the two statements: 'only the believers obey, and only the obedient believe' (ibid., p. 63). His explanation shows his sensitivity to and care in trying to avoid transgressing the Protestant doctrine of *justification: 'Because we are justified by faith, faith and obedience have to be distinguished. But their division must never destroy their unity, which lies in the reality that faith exists only in obedience, is never without obedience. Faith is only faith in deeds of obedience' (ibid., p. 64). Here again, the Sermon on the Mount was central.

The potential pitfalls concern the role assigned to good works. There are the pastoral perils of legalism which can both give the impression that the success of one's Christianity depends upon oneself and make for grudging obedience. There are also the theological errors of *Pelagianism and *Semi-Pelagianism. These underestimate both the extent of human depravity (see *Sin) and the priority of God's grace. While Bonhoeffer avoids these, Roman Catholic moralism was subject to the ire of Martin *Luther who was certain of violation on both counts. By making discipleship part of the believer's relationship with God, Catholics changed salvation into law. Law turned obedience into slavish duty and therefore made it superficial, whereas the gospel, in freeing Christians from law through justification, enables genuine obedience rendered out of love, not fear (see his *On Christian Liberty*). Luther specifically targeted Erasmus' *Diatribe on the Freedom of the Will* which said there were two causes of salvation: grace and human will. Luther's *The Bondage of the Will* replied that the human will is enslaved to sin, unable to cooperate with God's grace. Moreover, since God's salvation is a gift, human cooperation is inappropriate.

Mystical

Medieval *mysticism, prompted by the beatitude, 'the pure in heart will *see* God', saw salvation as mystical/spiritual communion with God. Accordingly, the Christian life is cultivating intense experiences of God by contemplating the incomprehensible divine essence. *Augustine outlined three stages of spiritual ascent: purgation, illumination and union (the beatific *vision). Most mystical works delineate degrees of knowledge through which the mystic must progress. Experiencing the transforming love of God is a frequent theme, as the writings of *Bernard of Clairvaux and Richard of St Victor show. Recently, mystical practices have seen Protestant attention on the 'spiritual disciplines' which urge fasting, *lectio divina* (meditative Bible reading) and divine hours (see Richard Foster, *The Celebration of Discipline*, New York, 1988).

Karl *Barth's rejection of Christianity as a 'religion' is an example of a critique. Since the doctrine of justification means that a believer's relationship with God is perfectly established in the finished work of Christ, Barth argued that the Christian life cannot concern sinful humans anxiously attempting to deepen or develop through religious activities what is already fully present (see *CD* I/2, 17).

Relational

The Reformers followed the Renaissance return to simple biblical morality, though they set it within the context of God's prior justification of the Christian. Their approach is 'relational', because it emphasizes above all the relationship forged by God in Christ and understands any act of moral obedience as the *fruit* of this relationship, not something constitutive of it.

Luther distinguished between two types of *righteousness: righteousness *coram Deo* (before God) and righteousness *coram homine* (before humanity). *Coram Deo*, good works of discipleship, have no place, for only Christ's righteousness is adequate. *Coram homine*, however, they are necessary and pleasing to God, though without faith they are insincere and therefore presuppose a relationship with Christ. Discipleship is thus *communio cum Christo* (communion with Christ) not *imitatio Christi*; it is Christ's character shining through the believer united to him in justification.

John Calvin and the *Reformed tradition developed Luther's notion of union with Christ, argued that obedience stemmed from gratitude for God's grace, and spoke of law more positively as instructive and motivating for Christian obedience. The Reformed tradition also emphasized the close relationship between word and Spirit, holding that the justifying word is never without the sanctifying Spirit. While John *Wesley had a more progressive and optimistic understanding of sanctification, he still believed it was a gift of God's love, not something earned. The Christian life was being perfected by God's love and sharing that love with the world through evangelism and charity (see bibliography).

Despite its best intentions to preserve both grace and obedience, this view of the Reformers is charged with *antinomianism by Roman Catholics and some Protestants. It is alleged that if good works have no material role in salvation, then obedience is optional. God's grace appears to make his commands ring hollow, and grace should never become an excuse for inaction.

Ecclesial

Because Christ is head of the church, Christians can grow in Christ only as members of his corporate body. Thus, Bonhoeffer claimed the Christian life is 'life together'. In his classic book bearing that title he described how, because of the *incarnation, Christian existence is physical, and therefore being present with other believers is a comfort. He also discussed how believers hear Scripture together, receive sacraments together, confess sins to each other and have both ministries to fulfil and gifts to exercise in the church.

Another ecclesial view is found in the so-called 'cultural-linguistic' or postliberal school of theology. Following the insights of recent sociology which show how humans develop through social conventions, proponents argue that the practices of the church – sacraments, fellowship, corporate prayer and public Scripture reading – give meaning to the Christian life. The church is not just one space in which the Christian life can be practised, but the primary locus for spiritual formation. From an ethicist's perspective, Stanley *Hauerwas has similarly stressed that the church forms Christian character (see bibliography).

Kevin Vanhoozer, without diminishing the church's role in spiritual formation, has sought to restore the authority of the word in this schema. He argues that what gives meaning and power to these 'ecclesial practices' are the prior 'canonical practices', activities commanded by and instituted in the Bible. For Vanhoozer, the Christian life is first hermeneutical, a matter of interpreting and fittingly performing one's role within God's drama of redemption as relayed in Scripture (see his *The Drama of Doctrine: A Canonical-Linguistic Approach to Christian Theology*, Louisville, 2005).

Sacramental

In *Roman Catholicism and *Eastern Orthodoxy, salvation includes being ontologically transformed. While differing in the specifics, both consider the *sacraments integral to this process. They thus become the focus of the Christian life. Christians begin with regeneration in baptism which gives them power over sin. They mature in confirmation (Catholic only), are continually renewed in penance and nourished by the Eucharist. Disagreements about the nature and function of the sacraments become important for the success of this version.

Political

Christ announced the *kingdom of God – a message with political overtones – and the NT speaks variously of Christians in political terms (e.g. believers are 'citizens of heaven'). Accordingly, some promote a political account of the Christian life. Here, God's grace is socially liberating, and his salvation is more about the optimization of human society through Christian ethics than personal betterment or individual rescue from sin and eternal damnation.

These sentiments lie behind the *Social Gospel movement in America in which the Christian life consisted of being politically and publicly active, assisting the transformation of society through advocating for the disenfranchised, serving the poor and combatting inequality. Similarly, *liberation and *Black theologies stress Christian *praxis*, the work of Christians in revealing and opposing oppressive societal forces. John Howard *Yoder proffered yet another political view of the Christian life where being a Christian is being political. He believed the integrity of the Christian political vision should never be dulled by complicity with the state. Instead, Christians must have a prophetic voice in culture and practise a radical ethics of nonviolence. As with the sacramental view, most objections concern the interpretation of the political dimensions of the gospel. At the very least, critics contend the social benefits of the gospel should not come at the expense of classical theories of salvation.

Bibliography

K. Barth, *Church Dogmatics* IV/4 (ET, Edinburgh, 1969); S. Ferguson, *The Christian Life: A Doctrinal Introduction* (Edinburgh, 1981); S. Hauerwas, *A Community of Character: Toward a Constructive Christian Social Ethic* (Notre Dame, 1981); D. H. Knight, *The Eschatological Economy: Time and the Hospitality of God* (Grand Rapids, 2006); J. Webster, 'Discipleship and Obedience', *Scottish Bulletin of Evangelical Theology* 24.1 (Spring 2006), pp. 4–18; J. Wesley, *A Plain Account of Christian Perfection* (Peabody,

2007); D. Willard, *The Divine Conspiracy: Rediscovering Our Hidden Life in God* (New York, 1998); J. H. Yoder, *Discipleship as Political Responsibility* (Scottdale, 2003); P. F. M. Zahl, *Grace in Practice: A Theology of Everyday Life* (Grand Rapids, 2007).

J. R. A. MERRICK

CHRISTIAN SCIENCE, see SECTS

CHRISTIAN SOCIALISM

The Christian Socialist movement is usually thought to have begun in the nineteenth century. The interest of Christian thinkers and practitioners in the ideals of common ownership and of a universal society of human brotherhood is much older. It has often been said that the experiment in Acts 2:44–45 of holding all things in common is the first Christian socialist experiment. The commitment to such themes can be found in the early Fathers and in the development of the *monastic movement. Nevertheless, the name 'Christian Socialist' came to be used in relation to British nineteenth-century developments, many of which had their roots in the Church of England (see *Anglicanism).

Robert Owen's (1771–1858) social experiments at New Lanark, Scotland, marked the first nineteenth-century attempt at a form of socialist organization. There were some clergy who took an interest in it. A few clergy were also to be found sympathizing with the working-class political reform movement, Chartism, in the 1840s. However, the beginnings of an organized movement of Christian leaders sympathetic to socialism came with the joining of J. M. F. Ludlow (1821–1911) with F. D. Maurice (1805–72). It was Ludlow's experience of socialism in Paris that provoked him to see the need for socialism to come under the influence of Christian thought. It was they, together with Charles Kingsley (1819–75) and Thomas Hughes (1822–96) for a time, who began to respond to the failure of the Chartist movement by experimenting in thought and action and who called their work 'Christian Socialism'.

F. D. Maurice stressed the universal character of the *kingdom of Christ. The Christian gospel reveals the true state of man. The starting point for Christian thought and the perspective from which we should view human life in the world is the kingship of Christ and the fact that God has both created and redeemed humankind in Christ. Maurice's theology is inclusive and *universalist. It was this fact of faith which Maurice brought to bear in his political interests in an age of social unrest as Britain moved into its industrial age and class-structured social order. Following the failure of the Chartist movement in 1848, Maurice and his friends sought to experiment in co-operative workshops, in the development of the Working Men's College and in journalism and tracts such as 'Politics for the People' and 'Tracts on Christian Socialism'.

The development of Christian Socialism took on a number of forms in the nineteenth century. In the 1870s a group of *Anglo-Catholics began to organize themselves and in 1877 formed the Guild of St Matthew. Stewart Headlam (1847–1924) was the founder priest of the guild. It was more radical and activist in kind than Maurice's group had been at an earlier stage. The Guild attacked social injustice wherever it found it and made many public statements as to what needed to be done. It pressed for action by Parliament on housing, education and working conditions. It produced the magazine *The Church Reformer*. Many dedicated Anglo-Catholic priests who worked hard in the slums of east and south London saw their commitment to the working classes as the proper expression of an incarnational understanding of Christian faith. Their commitment to action and radical reform was for them a direct consequence of a truly *incarnational theology.

The Christian Social Union, founded in 1889, was much more respectable ('wishywashy' was Headlam's judgment of it!). It was less concerned with direct action than with establishing social principles from Christian faith. It was more given to organizing study groups and encouraging writing. B. F. *Westcott, Bishop of Durham in the last years of the nineteenth century, was one of the most distinguished presidents of the Christian Social Union. His socialism, like that of Maurice, took its form from his conviction of our union and unity in Jesus Christ. 'Men are "one man" in Christ, sons of God and brethren' (quoted in A. R. Vidler, *F. D. Maurice and Company*, London, 1966, p. 26). Westcott took a leading role in the settlement of the 1893 Durham miners' strike.

It was in the twentieth century that the Christian Socialist movement began to have an increasing influence on public life in Britain, and on theology and church life. People such as R. H. Tawney, J. H. Oldham and William *Temple began to organize conferences and gatherings to address the growing challenge of the market economy. R. H. Tawney helped draft Labour Party manifesto material and wrote a seminal work, *Religion and the Rise of Capitalism* in 1948. George Lansbury, Labour leader following Ramsay MacDonald, was an active Christian and a pacifist. In the post-war Labour Government of 1945, Sir Stafford Cripps, who became Chancellor of the Exchequer, was a deeply committed Anglican in the Catholic tradition.

In the wider world facing huge levels of *poverty, oppression and inequality, the developing world gave birth to the movement of *liberation theology which, in different ways, sought to respond to the *Marxist agenda and the demand for revolutionary change. This movement was especially powerful in the 1970s in South America and was driven by the work of theologians such as Gustavo *Gutiérrez and Jon *Sobrino. Their commitment to a theology and praxis arising from the communities of the poor and excluded held a vision of a revolutionary future fed by gospel imperatives.

In more recent times when the language of both Marxism and socialism has become increasingly difficult, the Christian Socialist Movement has changed its name to 'Christians on the Left'. The increasing inequalities of our age bring the historic agenda of the socialist movement to the fore in our own time. It will be interesting to see how thoughtful Christians respond to these challenges and whether they will link to this history of radical thought.

Bibliography

T. Christensen, *Origin and History of Christian Socialism, 1848–54* (Aarhus, 1962); D. Hay, *A Christian Critique of Capitalism* (Bramcote, Nottingham, 1975); K. Leech, *The Social God* (London, 1981); F. D. Maurice, *The Kingdom of Christ* (1838; several edns); E. R. Norman, *The Victorian Christian Socialists* (Cambridge, 1987); R. H. Tawney, *Religion and the Rise of Capitalism* (Penguin, 1948); idem, *Equality* (Open University, 1964).

For general background history: C. Bryant, *Possible Dreams: A Personal History of British Christian Socialists* (London, 1996); idem, *Stafford Cripps* (London, 1997); G. Gutiérrez, *The Liberation of Theology* (Maryknoll, 1976); E. Hobsbawm, 4 vol. history, from *Age of Revolution* (1962) to *Age of Extremes* (1994)

(London); J. Sobrino, *The True Church and the Poor* (London, 1985); E. P. Thompson, *The Making of the English Working Class* (London, 1968).

J. GLADWIN

CHRISTIANITY AND OTHER RELIGIONS

Although Christianity has always existed in a world of religious diversity, the reality of our post-Christendom, post-colonial, post-holocaust, post-9/11 and 7/7, multi-ethnic and multicultural context has meant that more than ever Christians are acutely aware of systematic, pastoral and *missiological issues posed by other religions. The missiologist Gerald Anderson has stated that 'No issue in missiology is more important, more difficult, more controversial, or more divisive for the days ahead than the theology of religions . . . This is the theological issue for mission in . . . the twenty-first century' ('Theology of Religions and Missiology: A Time of Testing', in A. F. Glassner, C. E. Van Engen, D. S. Gilliland and P. E. Pierson (eds.), *The Good News of the Kingdom: Mission Theology for the Third Millennium*, Maryknoll, 1993, p. 201).

As a discipline, the 'theology of religions' has had a meteoric rise to fame and quickly become its own distinct category in theological studies. The 'theology of religions' must be distinguished from the allegedly 'neutral' discipline of academic 'religious studies', for although being sibling rivals striving to occupy the same space, the 'theology of religions' locates itself in the tradition of *fides quaerens intellectum* ('faith seeking understanding'): 'The theology of religion asks what religion is and seeks, in the light of Christian faith, to interpret the universal religious experience of humankind; it further studies the relationship between revelation and faith, faith and religion, and faith and salvation' (J. Dupuis, *Toward a Christian Theology of Religious Pluralism*, Orbis, 1997, p. 7). Although the focus of the 'theology of religions' has often concentrated on the issue of salvation, a truly comprehensive Christian theology of religions includes not only questions pertaining to salvation, but questions pertaining to truth in other religions, and questions pertaining to the phenomena of human religiosity.

In 1983, Alan Race, an Anglican priest and theologian, developed a threefold typology that has largely set the terms of debate over the last twenty years within the 'theology of religions' (*Christians and Religious Pluralism*, London, 1983). Netland (*Dissonant Voices*, p. 9f.) neatly summarizes these positions:

> *Exclusivism* maintains that the central claims of Christianity are true, and that where the claims of Christianity conflict with those of other religions the latter are to be rejected as false. Christian exclusivists also characteristically hold that Jesus Christ is the unique incarnation of God, the only Lord and Saviour. Salvation is not to be found in the structures of other religious traditions . . . *Inclusivism* . . . holds that [although] God has revealed himself definitively in Jesus Christ and that Jesus is somehow central to God's provision of salvation for humankind, they are willing to allow that God's salvation is available through non-Christian religions . . . *Pluralism* parts company with both exclusivism and inclusivism by rejecting the premise that God has revealed himself in any unique or definitive sense in Jesus Christ. On the contrary, God is said to be actively revealing himself in all religious traditions . . . Christian faith is merely one of many equally legitimate human responses to the same divine reality.

Historical context

Historically, the dominant theme regarding Christian approaches to other religions has been exclusivistic. While philosophical and socio-cultural factors have played their part, the foundational authoritative basis for historical affirmations of exclusivism has been the strongly exclusivistic tenor of the Bible (both OT and NT) which Christians have understood to be a true and unified revelation of God's works and words *in history*. The constant theme throughout the history of Israel and in the founding of the Christian church is both the incomparability (none *like* him) and transcendent uniqueness (no *other* God) of YHWH, and Jesus Christ who is God incarnate (cf. C. J. H. Wright, *The Mission of God*, Nottingham, 2006, p. 82).

As a consequence of the nature and activity of God comes a secondary affirmation of the incomparability and uniqueness of both Israel and the church. There is no other covenant community like them, and there is no other community with a history like theirs, because the incomparable and unique God has covenanted with them alone and intervened salvifically on their behalf alone (see *Covenant; Salvation). However, with this theme of particularity also come complementary themes of universality, inclusion, diversity and tolerance (e.g. attitudes towards the alien and stranger; attitudes towards ethnic diversity, including the eschatological hope of Christians being drawn from all nations and languages; God's universal care and sustenance of creation; the universal scope of the gospel and the universal mandate to take the gospel to the nations, etc.). Such exclusivity should never lead to vain glory or malice, for both Israel and the church are chosen by the sheer grace of God to display his glory, and have a unique responsibility and calling to be a light for the nations in both word and deed.

Although the exclusivist mood of the biblical testimony continued into the early church, the writings of some of the early Fathers, such as Justin, Irenaeus, Origen and Clement of Alexandria, indicate a willingness to speculate on the relationship between Christianity and other philosophies in matters of truth and salvation. However, it is *Cyprian in *The Unity of the Catholic Church* who is responsible for the slogan most often associated with exclusivism, '*extra ecclesiam nulla salus*' ('outside the church there is no salvation'), remembering his focus was that of schismatics and heretics rather than other religions per se. With Augustine, this axiom was strengthened. *Augustine's teaching on original guilt, predestination, God's sovereignty and efficacious grace gave a far more substantial theological and philosophical basis and reinforced Christian particularity. Within Roman Catholic teaching, exclusivistic interpretations of *extra ecclesium nulla salus* (albeit with some modifications) continued until the Second Vatican Council, when many acknowledge that in terms of the threefold typology, Roman Catholic teaching shifted from the exclusivist paradigm into the inclusivist paradigm (see F. A. Sullivan, *Salvation Outside the Church? Tracing the History of the Catholic Response*, London, 1992).

The Protestant Reformers largely continued the exclusivist heritage, not so much under the banner of *extra ecclesiam nulla salus*, but rather under their five *solas* of the *Reformation: *sola Scriptura, solus Christus, sola fide, sola gratia, soli Deo Gloria*. Calvin affirmed a universal natural revelation of God in all humanity, a *sensus divinitatis* or *semen religionis*, but claimed that because of the sinfulness of man, such knowledge was always twisted and distorted away from God (*Institutes*, 1.3.1–2) (see *Reformed theology).

For those coming under its sway, the *Enlightenment, with its own ultimate commitment to autonomous human reason, signalled a paradigm shift in the theology of religions: the death knell for exclusivism, but the breeding ground for what would become inclusivism, pluralism and the scientific study of religion (religious studies). Changes in fundamental doctrinal loci would mean changes in the Christian attitude towards the religious other. However, not all were influenced by Enlightenment presuppositions, and the early modern missionary movement continued to be propelled by an exclusivist engine fuelled on the uniqueness of Christ and the uniqueness of the Christian message. This culminated in intense debate at the first three world missionary conferences of Edinburgh (1910), Jerusalem (1928) and Tambaram (1938), where a wide range of missiological issues were discussed, underlying which was the relationship of Christianity to the world religions. One exclusivist scholar inextricably linked to and towering over these conferences, in particular Tambaram, was the Dutch missiologist Hendrik *Kraemer, whose multi-disciplinary approach combined theological, missiological, linguistic and phenomenological insights. Kraemer's main works, *The Christian Message in a Non-Christian World* (1938), *Religion and the Christian Faith* (1956), and *World Cultures and World Religions* (1960), remain some of the most detailed, nuanced and sophisticated statements within the exclusivist paradigm, and have influenced (though not without criticism) subsequent generations of exclusivist missiologists from the 'Reformed' tradition, most importantly J. H. *Bavinck, Johannes Verkuyl and Lesslie *Newbigin.

Within the contemporary scene, different versions of exclusivism, inclusivism and pluralism can be found at both popular and academic levels, together with the emerging voices of post-liberalism (with its social and political emphasis) and comparative theology (which, in fact, argues against an all-encompassing a priori theology of religions, focusing more on a posteriori engagement between living religious traditions).

Rethinking the terms of the debate

As the 'theology of religions' continues to mature as a discipline, an important debate concerns the 'terms' on which the debate has been conducted. Increasingly, many scholars are dissatisfied with the threefold typology. First, as a classificatory system, the tradition-specific nature of all theology means that the theology of religions is a parasitic discipline dependent on other a priori theological commitments. Whilst recognizing the pedagogical usefulness of all typologies and taxonomies, there is no real 'generic' exclusivism, inclusivism or pluralism, and if such generalizations are made, they must be recognized as a rather blunt analytical tool. At the very least, exclusivism, inclusivism and pluralism must be seen as points along a spectrum, rather than hermetically sealed positions. For example, 'exclusivism' is a broad enough category to posit a number of different configurations and interpretations concerning issues pertaining to salvation and truth and human religiosity. Exclusivism certainly does not *necessarily* entail a parsimony regarding salvation.

Second, a number of scholars have argued that there is an inbuilt prescriptive bias in the way the threefold typology has been construed, a bias *against* exclusivism often portrayed in overly emotive and 'sensationalistic' terms, and *for* pluralism (and to a lesser extent inclusivism) portrayed not only as more enlightened and tolerant than the other positions but more significantly religiously and epistemologically 'neutral'. D'Costa has argued that 'pluralism' is itself a 'myth' and in reality a covert form of hardline exclusivism: ' "pluralism" represents a tradition-specific approach that bears all the features of exclusivism – except that it is liberal modernity's exclusivism' (*The Meeting of Religions and the Trinity*, p. 22). Far from enabling tolerance and diversity, pluralism does the opposite, for it 'privileges liberal modernity as a mastercode within which all the religions are positioned and neutered' (*Religions and the Trinity*, p. 91). His conclusion is that 'pluralism' becomes something other than Christian, a worshipping of the god of modernity rather than the triune God.

The debate within evangelicalism

Despite there being scholarly disagreement amongst evangelicals regarding a plethora of issues regarding soteriological, truth and missiological questions, *evangelicalism is still largely a confessionally exclusivistic movement, stressing the authority of the Bible, the uniqueness of Christ and the necessity of faith in Christ. Three important international symposia have articulated exclusivist themes in their official statements: the *Frankfurt Declaration (1970), the *Lausanne Covenant (1974) and the Manilla Manifesto (1992), and several evangelical theologians and missiologists have articulated nuanced and constructive exclusivist positions: e.g. Harold Netland, Don Carson, Chris Wright, Vinoth Ramachandra, Gerald McDermott and Terrance Tiessen. More controversially, there are also a handful of evangelical theologians like Clark *Pinnock and John Sanders who can be located more comfortably within inclusivism than exclusivism. Generally speaking, and compared to other traditions, evangelicals have a lot more thinking to do in this area of theology.

Any evangelical 'theology of religions' must recognize at one and the same time both continuity and discontinuity between the quest for God in other faiths and the fullness and finality of the knowledge of God 'in the face of Jesus Christ'. Non-Christian religion, alike in its most debated and most elevated manifestations, always bears the dual impress of God's gracious *revelation of himself to all humankind in creation and humankind's universal exchange of the truth of God for a lie. So long as these twin biblical perspectives are maintained, there may be scope for legitimate differences in the way Christian theology balances and correlates them in its evaluation of other religions. The two perspectives are tellingly presented in Paul's address at Athens. Despite the universality of God's providential care and presence (Acts 17:24–28), the Athenians' religiosity suppressed the knowledge of the true God. Their abundant images and idols attested their ignorance of him (17:16, 22–23, 29–30), and even their awareness of that ignorance (17:23). Paul's message came to hearers whose refusal to know the living God had left its mark upon their religion. Because idols are distortions and perversions of truth and so 'related' to truth, like Kraemer one might cautiously say that Christianity is the 'contradictory or subversive fulfilment' of the human religious quest (Kraemer, 'Continuity or Discontinuity', in W. Paton (ed.), *The Authority of Faith*, London, 1939, p. 5).

See also: BUDDHISM AND CHRISTIANITY; CONFUCIANISM AND CHRISTIANITY; HINDUISM AND CHRISTIANITY; ISLAM AND CHRISTIANITY; JUDAISM AND CHRISTIANITY; RELIGION; RELIGIONS, THEOLOGY OF; SHINTOISM AND CHRISTIANITY; TAOISM AND CHRISTIANITY; ZOROASTRIANISM AND CHRISTIANITY.

Bibliography

J. H. Bavinck, *The Church Between Temple and Mosque* (Grand Rapids, 1966); J. Calvin, *Institutes of the Christian Religion*, tr. F. L. Battles (London and Philadelphia, 1961); D. A. Carson, *The Gagging of God: Christianity Confronts Pluralism* (Leicester and Grand Rapids, 1996); G. D'Costa, *The Meeting of Religions and the Trinity* (New York, 2000); V. Kärkäinen, *An Introduction to the Theology of Religions: Biblical, Historical and Contemporary Perspectives* (Downers Grove, 2003); H. Kraemer, *The Christian Message in a Non-Christian World* (New York, 1938); G. McDermott, *God's Rivals* (Downers Grove, 2007); H. Netland, *Dissonant Voices* (Grand Rapids and Leicester, 1991); idem, *Encountering World Religions: The Challenge to Christian Faith and Mission* (Leicester and Grand Rapids, 2001); T. Perry, *Radical Difference: A Defence of Hendrik Kraemer's Theology of Religions* (Ontario, 2001); A. Plantinga, 'Pluralism: A Defense of Religious Exclusivism', in T. D. Senor (ed.), *The Rationality of Belief and the Plurality of Faith* (London and New York, 1995); D. Strange, *The Possibility of Salvation Among the Unevangelised* (Carlisle, 2002); T. L. Tiessen, *Who Can Be Saved? Reassessing Salvation in Christ and World Religions* (Leicester and Downers Grove, 2004).

D. S. STRANGE

CHRISTOLOGY

An account of the identity of *Jesus of Nazareth, especially of his humanity and divinity or of his relation to *God. It tends now to be distinguished from the closely related topic of soteriology (see *Salvation), which treats Jesus' saving work.

NT Christology

Jesus was a first-century Jewish man who attracted a considerable following as he travelled Palestine healing, exorcizing and proclaiming a message of repentance as preparation for God's coming *judgment. Christology began as, during his ministry, this man presented himself, and was understood by others, in terms adapted very largely from the Judaism of his day (particularly Jewish apocalypticism). After his execution as a trouble-maker, his followers proclaimed that his tomb had been found empty, that he was risen from the dead, and that he had appeared to many of them. Christology developed as they made sense of Jesus as the crucified and risen one, drawing on a wide variety of Jewish and Hellenistic sources (and it is important to recognize that Judaism and Hellenism were already interacting in complex ways in this context). Who was this man? they asked. What part did he play in God's plans? They sought adequate terms to express their sense that God had spoken to them, laid hold of them, and saved them through the life, death and resurrection of Jesus Christ (see *Cross: Resurrection of Christ).

Older discussions of early Christology tended to focus on the titles which Jesus used of himself or which were used by others: Rabbi, Prophet, King, Christ, Son of Man, Son of God, Saviour, Lamb of God, Logos, etc. More recent discussions have tended to explore more complex ways in which existing Jewish and Hellenistic ideas and narratives were drawn into the process by which Jesus made sense of himself and was made sense of by others. Such ideas were transformed as they were given a new context in early Christian community life, evangelistic endeavours, and above all devotion. After all, 'a noteworthy devotion to Jesus emerges phenomenally early in circles of his followers' and it 'was exhibited in an unparalleled intensity and diversity of expression, for which we have no true analogy in the religious environment of the time' (L. W. Hurtado, *Lord Jesus Christ*, p. 2). Yet Jesus appears to have been the recipient of devotion by Christians who nevertheless regarded themselves still as monotheists, worshipping the one God now as the Father of Jesus Christ, and Jesus as that Father's Son and viceroy, and as the exemplar and enabler of human life acceptable to God.

The NT writings are the primary evidence for early Christological developments. In Paul's letters, for instance, we see Jesus identified as the supremely obedient Son, the embodiment of divine wisdom, the Lord of Christian life; in John's Gospel he is God's Word made flesh, sent to show God's character and enact God's saving purposes; in the book of Revelation, he is the conquering, slaughtered Lamb of God who receives the worship of the saints.

Patristic Christology

The second and third centuries saw many different attempts to make sense of the relationship of Jesus to the one he called 'Father' (see *Fatherhood of God). There were those who interpreted Jesus either as an angel who had come down to earth and been clothed with human flesh, or as a human being who had at some point been appointed to angelic power and status or adopted as God's Son and representative – a view sometimes called *adoptionism. The result of both views was a Jesus who was not quite divine and not quite human, and theologians like Ignatius of Antioch and *Tertullian demurred, stressing (against *Docetism) Jesus' full humanity and the reality of his suffering, and insisting (against *adoptionism) that he had been fully divine from the very moment of his conception, so that divinity was not a matter of his achievement and God's response, but simply of God's gracious gift.

*Gnostic Christologies, while having much in common with some angel Christologies, tended to claim that the God revealed in Jesus Christ was not the Creator God of the OT, convinced as they were that Christ saved people from the disastrous mess that was the created world. They were opposed by such theologians as *Irenaeus of Lyons, who presented Christ's incarnation as the summation of a salvation history of cosmic scope, bringing God's work in creation and in the covenant with Israel to its proper completion. According to Irenaeus and others, Christ's advent initiates the salvation *of* the world, rather than being a catalyst for salvation *from* the world.

At the start of the fourth century, a controversy erupted around an Alexandrian presbyter named *Arius, who stated more clearly than others before him the idea that the divine Son who had become incarnate in Jesus was a creature, albeit the first and greatest of all creatures. The Father's relation to the Son was therefore the result of a specific action on the Father's part, rather than being eternally characteristic of him. Arius's created and originate Son is of a fundamentally different order of reality from the creating and unoriginate Father. Arius was condemned at the Council of *Nicaea in 325, which asserted (without clarifying exactly what the term meant) that the Son was *homoousios* ('of one substance') with the Father. Arius's views later became a foil for the theology of *Athanasius of Alexandria, who argued that to know God as the Father of the Son is to know him truly, for he is eternally and essentially a Father-who-has-a-Son. For Athanasius, there is no foreign God hidden behind the familiar face that God turns to the world in Jesus Christ.

There were debates in the fourth and fifth centuries amongst those working with the Johannine idea that Jesus is the incarnation of God's Word or *Logos. The divine Logos is the expression of God's wisdom and the template for creation, and came to be seen as a distinct *hypostasis (often translated '*person', but meaning here 'distinguishable reality'), eternally united with the Father in the Godhead. Some theologians, who tend to be identified with the city of *Alexandria, insisted that this divine Logos was in the incarnation united to human flesh in such a way as to produce a single resultant reality (and fifth-century Alexandrians could insist that Christ had one *physis* or 'nature' in order to speak about the unity of this reality). This emphasis cohered with a stress in their theologies on the union of *all* humanity with God which God has made possible through Christ. The difficulty lay in defining 'flesh', a word that could refer to the fullness of human life, but that was sometimes taken simply to refer to Jesus' physical body, as with the version of this thinking promoted by *Apollinarius, who argued that in place of a human soul Christ had the divine Logos. Other theologians, who tend to be identified with *Antioch, insisted against this tendency that the incarnate Lord consisted of the divine Logos united not just to 'flesh' but to a distinct, complete human individual. The strong version of this thinking, attributed (probably unfairly) to *Nestorius, suggested that Christ consisted of two distinct realities (two *hypostases*), one divine and one human.

Rejecting the extremes associated with Apollinarius and Nestorius, and drawing on vocabulary developed in the 'Tome' of Pope *Leo I, the Council of *Chalcedon in 451 offered a formula intended to unite Alexandria and Antioch. It claimed that Christ was one *person* in two *natures*: the former reflecting the Alexandrian insistence, associated with men like *Cyril of Alexandria (a theologian whose thinking was particularly formative for Chalcedon), the latter reflecting the Antiochene insistence, associated with theologians like Theodore of Mopsuestia. That is, one should never so speak of the humanity and of the divinity of Christ as to suggest that he consists of two distinct realities, artificially joined together; Christ is one distinct reality (one *hypostasis* or 'person') 'without division, without separation'. Equally, one should never so speak of the unity of this reality that one fails to distinguish between the unqualifiedly complete human life (or 'nature') and the unqualifiedly complete divine life (or 'nature') that this one reality bears ('the distinction of natures being in no way annulled by the union'). Chalcedon did not offer a coherent metaphysical theory of how this unity-in-distinction was possible, but rather laid down a set of parameters and provided a language that allows the emphases of both sides to be articulated. This attempted settlement was rejected by a significant number of more '*monophysite' ('one-nature') Alexandrian theologians, who believed that its insistence on attributing two distinguishable natures to Christ underplayed his unity, and who insisted that Christ could only be one person if he had a single, divine-human nature. For much of the church, however, the Chalcedonian formula became the chief foundation of classical Christology.

An attempt to spell out a fuller conceptual articulation of the Chalcedonian settlement was hammered out in Byzantine Christological controversy in the period after Chalcedon (451–787). One way of approaching that explanation is to recognize that a constant problem for theologians before this period had been the presence in the Gospels of witness on the one hand to Jesus' miracles, and on the other to moments in which he displayed weakness and ignorance. The former made it seem to many as if Jesus' human flesh had been 'divinized' by the indwelling presence of the Logos (for how otherwise would he have been able to walk on water, and how else could people have been cured simply by touching him?). The latter seemed to show aspects of Christ's humanity that were antithetical to his divine nature, for if Jesus' humanity was empowered or enhanced, receiving the properties of the divine nature with which it was united, how could there be room for human weaknesses? Athanasius and others were reduced to saying that Jesus had only pretended to be ignorant or weak as a way of teaching his disciples. Later Byzantine theology insisted that the unqualifiedly complete human life of Christ, bearing all the limitations that are essential to human being, and consisting of an entirely human body, mind, soul and will, was brought into being (that is, given distinct 'hypostatic' reality) as the human life belonging to the person (the 'hypostasis') of the divine Word. That human life has no distinct reality of its own, outside of this union (it is 'anhypostatic'); it is given its distinct reality (its 'hypostatic' existence) only in and by this union ('enhypostasis'). The Word remains fully divine in the process (with fully divine nature and will), but assumes in addition this new, creaturely way of being itself. Any communication of attributes (*communicatio idiomatum*) from the divine nature to the human nature (any partial 'divinizing' of the flesh) is an important but secondary matter, providing God-given signs of the deeper, 'enhypostatic' unity that truly constitutes Christ's divinity.

Modern Christology

Theologians in the medieval and Reformation periods made many significant contributions to Christology proper – whether it was *Anselm of Canterbury's examination of the soteriological grounds for the *incarnation in *Cur Deus Homo*, or the debate between the Magisterial Reformers (see *Reformation theology) on the ubiquity of Christ's risen humanity. More dramatic developments in discussions of the doctrine emerged, however, in the modern West. Traditional Christological doctrine came under fire during the European *Enlightenment thanks to (1) the rise of historical criticism of the NT and of the development of doctrine, (2) an increasing tendency to reject the possibility of miracle and the growth of a *deistic theology that posited a Creator God who did not interfere with the well-ordered running of the world, and (3) the development of *pietistic forms of Christianity that regarded Christological discussion as useless speculation, divorced from the life of faith. In more recent years a fourth line of fire has been established: scepticism about the claim that one individual Jewish male human being can be God's ultimate word to a world of multiple races, religions, cultures and genders.

Many modern theologians and historians argued that incarnational doctrine arose as a late development only marginally connected to the real life of Jesus and the proper concerns of his followers. In particular, it was often claimed (e.g. by David Friedrich *Strauss) that incarnational doctrine took its rise from a misunderstanding of the *mythic nature of early Christian testimony, with the formulators of doctrine taking too literally the pictorial and metaphorical ways in which early believers had conveyed the deep impact that Jesus of Nazareth had had upon them.

Even amongst those who retain a commitment to incarnational theology, the tendency has been for Jesus' full humanity to be accepted readily and unequivocally, and for most of the conceptual labour to be expended on justifying the claim that this fully human being could nevertheless also have been divine. In the nineteenth and twentieth centuries, various '*kenotic' theories were suggested (e.g. those of Gottfried Thomasius [1802–75] or A. M. Fairbairn [1838–1912]), seeing the 'self-emptying' of the divine Son as a process in which he divested himself of, or suppressed, divine attributes so as to be capable of union with a finite human life. In the twentieth century, there were enquiries that owed much to analytical philosophy, and which argued about the coherence and appropriateness of a number of models for the relationship of humanity and divinity in Christ, such as Thomas V. Morris's 'two minds' model, which tries to understand how Christ could have had a fully divine and a fully human mind, interrelated as fully as the nature of the two minds allows.

On the more doctrinal or systematic theological side there has also been a great deal of debate. For instance, there is a theological tradition, particularly associated with the nineteenth-century German theologian Friedrich *Schleiermacher and followers of his such as Wilhelm *Herrmann, but also seen in many other theologians, which holds that there is a potential for awareness of, and even union with, God built in to human nature, discoverable with the right philosophical and psychological analysis. In this tradition the idea that divine revelation takes place in history tends to be interpreted as meaning that the religious consciousness common to all human beings has been activated or energized, and given a distinct shape and direction, by particular historical circumstances. Such revelation is a fulfilment of inherent human possibilities at the very same time that it is a gracious gift from God. In this tradition, the incarnation consists in Jesus' (God-given) perfect realization of this universal human religious potential, and this realization is seen as the supreme catalyst for all other human beings who are realizing the same religious potential in themselves.

There is a counter-tradition, particularly associated with the Swiss Reformed theologian Karl *Barth, which regards the potentiality that is actualized in the incarnation not as a potentiality in human nature, but as a possibility open to God. Barth held that the doctrines of incarnation and Trinity speak primarily of an openness in God towards the sharing of God's life with human beings. What that sharing actually looks like in human lives is not the actualization of some potential buried deep in human inwardness, but human lives caught up into Christ-like patterns of life and thought – patterns that from a human perspective must look entirely contingent, but which from a divine perspective are the human form of the life of God. This tradition tends to go along with a deep suspicion of all attempts to analyse a deep religious structure universal in human consciousness, or of any focus on human inwardness as the site of union with God. The incarnation, in this perspective, consists in the fact that God gives the whole life of Jesus to the world as a divine word spoken in a creaturely medium. Jesus' life, by the specific and particular shape that God gives to it, both communicates and makes possible godly life within history.

In more recent debates, the full humanity of Jesus has come to the fore in new ways, with stress laid by *feminist theologians and others on the recognition that Jesus was fully bodily, that he gained his identity in relationship with others, that he was nurtured in a particular (Jewish) culture – and that the salvation that he brings cannot therefore be thought of as a release *from* bodiliness, socialization and culture, but must be seen as the redemption *of* those things. (A similar idea has been promoted by some theologians with environmentalist concerns who have stressed that, if Jesus is the Word of *God the Creator*, then he is a Word calling all humanity *to* full life in the world, rather than to escape *from* it.)

This stress has, however, gone with a renewed questioning of incarnational claims as theologians ask how one who is so temporally, bodily and culturally specific can be of universal significance. In particular, some feminist theologians have asked whether the claim that a male human being was God inevitably gives maleness a theological privilege. Other theologians have sought for ways to argue afresh that Jesus is God's Word addressed to all humanity, male and female, regardless of race or culture, by arguing that this Word does not call all human beings to become *identical* to Jesus, but rather to become fulfilled in *relation* to him as the unique gendered, bodily, culture-bound people that they are.

This debate is bound up with the claim that Jesus is not simply 'fully human' in the sense that he is unrestrictedly bodily, finite and creaturely, but that he reveals the fullness of human life to which all people are called. This theme has been taken up by some theologians who, whilst seeking to avoid the pitfalls just mentioned, wish to stress that to be fully human is to be fully caught up, as Jesus was, in God's mission of love for the freedom, healing and flourishing of the whole world, and that therefore full humanity is not simply a static nature possessed by Christ, but a dynamic form of life marked by active, relational, even political engagement.

See also: Trinity.

Bibliography

C. Allen, *The Human Christ* (London and New York, 1998); K. Barth, *CD*, esp. vols I/2 and IV; D. F. Ford and M. A. Higton, *Jesus* (Oxford, 2002); J. Behr, *The Way to Nicaea* (Crestwood, 2001); A. Grillmeier, *Christ in Christian Tradition*, vol. 1 (Atlanta and London, ²1975); L. W. Hurtado, *Lord Jesus Christ* (Grand Rapids, 2003); T. V. Morris, *The Logic of God Incarnate* (Oxford and Ithaca, 1986); F. D. E. Schleiermacher, *The Christian Faith* (Edinburgh, 1928); C. Tuckett, *Christology and the New Testament* (Edinburgh, 2001); R. Williams, *Arius* (London, 2001).

M. Higton

CHRYSOSTOM, JOHN (c. 345–407)

John Chrysostom, theologian and bishop, was born to a wealthy family in Antioch. He trained in rhetoric, but gave up practising law in 368 when he was baptized, and joined the followers of Diodore (a future bishop of Tarsus). He then retreated to the desert, where he lived for four years under a Syrian monk, and then alone in a cave for two years where he committed much of Scripture to memory. Bad health forced him to return to the city, where he spent twelve years as presbyter of the Church of Antioch. He was consecrated Bishop of Constantinople in 398, but his exhortations against the abuse of power and wealth earned him powerful enemies, such as the Empress Eudoxia and Theophilus, the patriarch of Alexandria. In 404 he was exiled to Armenia, and he eventually died in a forced march to Pontus, 407. Though his eloquence as a preacher was well known even after his death, it appears that it was not until the sixth century that he was described as Chrysostom, which means 'Golden Mouth'.

Chrysostom's work presents an excellent example of the *Antioch school of exegesis, which involved an extremely close reading of biblical texts. His works tend to fall into three categories: sermon, diatribe and *apologetic treatise. Most of his sermons begin with an exposition of Scripture, and then continue into exhortation against a vice or towards a virtue. He preached to the wealthy, but also made a point of venturing out among outlying villages, as well as slums within the city.

Chrysostom's work is marked by his personal desire to achieve a holy and ascetic life, with the recognition of the difficulties encountered by most of his flock attempting to live a Christian life in a wealthy and decadent society. Chrysostom wrote apologia for *asceticism, such as *Against the Opponents of the Monastic Life*. His acknowledgment of the gap between the ideal and the reality of most citizens' lives in Antioch and Constantinople is recognized in *On Compunction*. He also wrote a few, now controversial, treatises against Judaizing Christians, which demonstrate the still-prominent connection between Jewish and Christian groups at this time; Chrysostom, however, strongly denounced those who refused to choose between Judaism and Christianity.

His enemies, however, objected less to his discourses on monasticism or Judaism, than to his opposition to the abuse of wealth (see *Poverty and wealth) and power that was common among the aristocracy of Constantinople. He railed against high taxation, and a desire to indulge in opulence rather than show charity and help to one's neighbour. For Chrysostom faith ought to inspire deeds of kindness and generosity; he felt that the rich were stewards of wealth, saying, 'the rich man who keeps all his wealth for himself is committing a form of robbery'. He placed emphasis upon on a Pauline doctrine of self-giving love, rather than self-aggrandizement. It is this defence of the helpless that earned him the love of so many, as well as the enmity of some of those in power.

Bibliography

Works: *The Early Church Fathers: Nicene and Post-Nicene Fathers*, vols. IX-XIV, <http://www.ccel.org/fathers2/>; *John Chrysostom: The Golden Voice of Protest*, ed. R. Van de Weyer (Evesham, 1996); *PG*, vol. 47–64.

Studies: J. N. D. Kelly, *Golden Mouth: The Story of John Chrysostom – Ascetic, Preacher, Bishop* (London, 1993); W. Mayer and P. Allen, *John Chrysostom* (London, 2000); Palladius, *Dialogue on the Life of St John Chrysostom* (ET, New York, 1985); M. A. Schatkin, *John Chrysostom as Apologist* (Thessaloniki, 1987); R. L. Wilkin, *John Chrysostom and the Jews: Rhetoric and Reality in the Late 4th Century* (London, 1983).

For a more extensive bibliography, see <http://www.cecs.acu.edu.au/chrysostombibliography.html>.

J. P. MITCHELL

CHURCH

'Ecclesiology' is the term for the area of theology considering the doctrine of the church, a topic that has been much disputed throughout Christian history. Universally agreed is that the church is the church of Jesus Christ and those who participate in the *salvation of *Jesus constitute the church.

The church is the entire company of believers, and yet more than just the collection of individuals since they share together in Christ through the *Holy Spirit. Disciples therefore belong to one another in an organic way, and share together in suffering and joy as 'the body of Christ'. The church therefore is human, yet divinely created and inspired, caught up in the life of *God the Holy *Trinity in its worship; Paul tells the Galatians that 'God sent the Spirit of his Son into our hearts, the Spirit who calls out, *Abba*, Father!' (Gal. 4:6).

The bond between Saviour and saved, Christ and his church, is the *grace of Christ, specifically the self-giving of Jesus on the cross and his rising to overcome sin and death, a new life given to his disciples, the church. The very earliest practices of *baptism and Communion (see *Eucharist), focused on the grace of Christ crucified and risen, emphasize this divine origin of the church: the redeemed, Spirit-filled humanity, worshipping the Father in and through the Son, living out the way of his *kingdom.

The debate as to whether the church is 'visible' or 'invisible' relates not to some mysterious hiddenness of the church in history, as if it were 'docetic' as to its human reality, but rather to the church from God's angle, since God alone knows the depths of the heart and of authentic faith. The church is filled with the invisible Spirit of God, but is to serve in the blood, sweat, toil and tears of this world.

Church as communion/*koinonia*

Recent ecclesiology has highlighted this trinitarian understanding of the church in a way attracting consensus from the major traditions. The *Eastern Orthodox have always stressed this basis of their ecclesiology, the church taken up into the divine life, especially in its eucharistic worship. From that tradition, John *Zizioulas's seminal book *Being as Communion* commended the idea of mutuality and love, found in the Trinity, as at the heart of the new life of the church. Many Western theologians have been influenced in this Eastern direction, attracted in part by its rejection of individualistic notions of human life in favour of more corporate and participatory categories to define humanity. The Reformed theologian Jürgen *Moltmann's *Church in the Power of the Spirit* takes the Eastern trinitarian line, stressing the communal interrelationship of the divine persons as the pattern for the church, but the structure of the church emerges very differently from that of Zizioulas, who commends bishops as key to the being of the church, over against Moltmann's pluralism.

The concept of communion, *koinonia*, has been taken up in *ecumenical theological agreements fruitfully, and tends to give a full place to the local congregations as they share together in being the one church. The Roman Catholic Church's Second Vatican Council formally declared a move away from its rigid clericalism towards viewing the church as 'the whole people of God', catching this note of common communion in Christ for all believers (see *Roman Catholic theology), although the pontificate of Pope John Paul II has been widely seen as reversing this movement back to a centralist model. The Anglican-Roman Catholic International Commission (ARCIC)'s *Final Report* (1982) used the idea of *koinonia*, derived from the NT, as the spiritual bond of the believers with Christ and with one another in the local congregation of faith, needing the local minister to safeguard and build up this *fellowship or 'communion' after the teaching and lifestyle of the apostles. The individual churches or congregations share together in a way going beyond mere voluntary association, since communion with Christ holds them all together in a common body in the Spirit.

ARCIC develops this pattern in terms of ministers representing local churches and developing wider forms of leadership: bishops, which in turn produce archbishops, and ultimately – and very controversially – a world leader for the church. The *Reformed tradition, deriving from the teaching of Calvin, could agree with much of this, certainly the importance of the ordained minister, but not the final deduction about regional and global ministerial leadership. The Eastern Orthodox understand their bishops as the local ministers of local churches, their dioceses, and strongly reject the notion of any jurisdiction from a papal figure. Protestant churches tend to focus on the local congregation as the primary unit of the church worldwide. Nevertheless, it is possible to discern much common agreement about the very being of the church as communion with the Father, through the Son, in the Spirit, historically lived out locally and yet as a single entity, however differently the ministerial structures are worked out. Baptism and Holy Communion speak of sharing in Christ's great sacrifice in responsive self-giving and thanksgiving, at a local level but also more widely.

The Baptist theologian Miroslav Volf in his *After Our Likeness, the Church as the Image of the Trinity* set out a 'free church' or 'separatist' view of trinitarian communion as the basis of the church, stressing the local congregation as primary over against church with a wider historical being. He engaged with Zizioulas, and also with Joseph *Ratzinger, who became Pope Benedict XVI, for whom *koinonia* is understood centrally as being in communion with Rome first and foremost, rather than the diversity of the local churches as primary. This is a major difference between Rome and both the Eastern Orthodox and *Protestant churches, including the *Anglicans, none of which can agree that communion with and obedience to the global jurisdiction and occasional infallibility of the papacy is a condition of being a church. To start with *koinonia* as a key ecclesial concept is to make the church itself, rather than the structures of its ministry, the primary fact, although Orthodox and some Anglican ecclesiology urge that episcopal structure is essential. Most non-episcopally ordered churches regard any regional or national levels of leadership to be best organized by way of groups of ministers, meeting to 'oversee' (the meaning of the Greek term *episcope*) churches in synods or presbyteries. The Brethren are unusual in rejecting any formal ordained ministry whatsoever.

One, holy, catholic and apostolic

From this understanding of church as *koinonia* the notions entailed in the well-known phrase found in the Nicene *Creed of 381, 'one, holy, catholic and apostolic', open up easily and ecumenically. The unity of the church is in Christ, not a mere uniformity, but unity in diversity, a fellowship of self-giving love, bonded by the Holy Spirit. The unity is of very different disciples, and also between local churches. The church is holy in that disciples and churches are set apart for, and redeemed by, Christ, seeking to do his will through his grace, and in constant need of repentance, as church history shows. The *catholicity of the church means its global scope (*kath holos*) across the whole world. Like a geological stratum, local churches worldwide will show distinctively Christian ways of life and worship that are the same in essence, coloured by local cultural differences. Whether the church is 'catholic' also in embracing the *communion of saints now in heaven is an interesting issue: theologically, the present church must be linked to those fellow disciples now in the eschatological fellowship, but there is no biblical encouragement at all for believers in space and time now to seek to commune with or pray for those who have gone before. This opens up the notion of *purgatory and the great debate about indulgences that triggered *Luther's protest and the *Reformation.

This debate is an important instance of the 'apostolicity' of the church, focused on loyalty to the teaching and practice of the *apostles, accessible now through the NT alone. The principles found in the NT seem, for example, difficult to square with an idea of purgatory, let alone indulgences. Church practices and teachings diverging plainly from the NT are not 'apostolic'. The question then is raised of interpretation of the text. Roman Catholicism claims to possess a 'magisterium' which flows by a historical succession from the apostle Peter, enabling it to read the apostolic texts aright. Again, this idea is not found in the NT or the early church, and so is neither apostolic nor catholic. Indeed, the church is most 'Petrine' when acknowledging its fallibility, as did Peter on his threefold betrayal of Jesus.

The place of the canon of *Scripture is crucial to the church's apostolicity and authority, in particular to emphasize that the church did not 'create' the texts, but rather acknowledged their authority and submitted to them as normative. The church's place is to sit under this authority of the prophets and apostles, found in Scripture and made alive now by the Spirit. Interpretation of difficult texts, which are in fact surprisingly few and peripheral, is a matter of the Spirit working gradually in and through patient and generous Christian attentiveness. There can be legitimate disagreement on matters such as infant or believers' baptism, but the core message of the church, redemption of our sins and newness of life through Christ and the Spirit, is totally clear and uncontested as the way, the truth and the life of the church.

Church praxis

Avery Dulles's book *Models of the Church* discusses several ways of understanding the church and its functions, one very important being the church 'as servant'. This reflects the life and ministry of Jesus, indeed his acceptance of death itself for us as a great moral act of redemptive love. *Love for human beings, for the sick and destitute, has been a crucial outworking of the church's *koinonia* with Christ in the world and itself an evangelistic sign. This has been evident in individual disciples' 'good works', for example Wilberforce's lifelong campaign against slavery, Elizabeth Fry's prison reform, Josephine Butler's stand for women against state-sponsored prostitution, Shaftesbury's campaigns for improved factory conditions, and the provision of hospitals and schools. Christianity is at the root of most of Western welfare institutions.

*Liberation theologians, including such thinkers as Gustavo Gutiérrez, Leonard Boff and Miguel Bonino, working out of a context of grinding poverty in Latin America, urge church '*praxis' to claim the 'structures' of society and so gain a political and economic footing. They have rejected an exclusive emphasis on the 'otherworldliness' of church concerns and emphasize the needs of real people in *poverty and powerlessness. For them the kingdom of God embraces the quest for justice and plenty for all, which includes political activism. This ecclesiological emphasis has brought with it interesting ways of interpreting *eschatology, such as 'the powers and principalities' including institutions oppressing people, which for example could be unfair trading patterns, or Western economic 'idols' needing to be deconstructed by the kingdom of God.

Liberation theology offers an important model of church, albeit one which deploys some *Marxist concepts while claiming to avoid Marx's secular assumptions. The 'contextual' and local aspects of church are important to this ecclesiology, often at loggerheads with the Vatican and its centralist control systems. Local 'base communities' have been important expressions of church, with Bible reading and practice a key part of churchly *koinonia*, the key question being not 'what did I learn?' but 'what did I do after reading that text?', praxis trumping theory, and the incarnational shape of Christian faith emphasized. A criticism of this emphasis can be that it neglects personal salvation in the interests of corporate and social good, but this is not necessarily so. *Evangelical ecclesiology can engage fruitfully with liberation theology. The *Pentecostal movement is an interesting alternative to liberation ecclesiology in Latin America, as David Martin has detailed in his *Tongues of Fire* (Oxford, 1990): 'The church has opted for the poor, but the poor have their own options'; the highly emotional style of Pentecostalist worship has attracted many among the poor. Praxis for the Pentecostals is primarily collective worship in the Spirit.

Church and state

As is evident from the book of Revelation, the church has been engaging with the *state from the very start of its life, at times suffering persecution at its hands, at times overly integrated into the state and its projects, as in the Middle Ages when popes could dictate to kings and bishops chosen by secular rulers. The *Barmen Declaration of 1934 constitutes a fundamental evangelical protest against the church allowing itself to be coordinated into the state's structures, as was Nazi policy. This crystalline statement of ecclesiology, written largely by Karl *Barth, classically declares: 'We reject the false doctrine that the church could have permission to hand over the form of its message and of its order to whatever it itself might wish or to the vicissitudes of the prevailing ideological and political convictions of the day.' This in effect was a rejection of 'cultural Christianity' by one of the twentieth century's deepest theologians, engaged in a desperate struggle with a totalitarian regime bent on conforming the church to evil, but popular, purposes.

The principle of Barmen, however, remains pertinent in less dramatic and fraught contexts, a declaration that the church is God's church, the church of Jesus Christ, not an organization to be run by the state or other groupings, however worthy. Barmen sounds a standing challenge to any established church wherein the government of the day has any say in choosing church leaders, thereby also recruiting the church as its political agency for cultural propaganda. The movement calling itself *Radical Orthodoxy stresses the radical difference of the church community and politics of peace from that of the state with its underlying deployment of violence, the church being the embodied presence of God in time and space. The work of Stanley *Hauerwas similarly stresses that the church is totally different in its way of life as a community; it is to change the world rather than unwittingly adopt secular and nationalistic ways. The church as the one place of honest reconciliation (see *Atonement) has also been a fruitful topic, revealing church as a way of being reconciled and reconciling. How the church should relate to the world and the state remains an ongoing and changing problem, one not to be ignored if William Temple's dictum is true, that 'the church exists for the benefit of its non-members'.

Church as mission

Allowing the church's message to be shaped by alien forces is a real danger in the global era which preaches the equivalence of all religions and rejects the notion of Christian preaching to other faiths as provocative and divisive. The church cannot become an agency for muting its own gospel message and adjusting it into a multi-faith compromise, at the expense of the word of the *cross, which always was provocative: 'foolishness to Gentiles' (1 Cor. 1:23) and upsetting to the purveyors of idols, obvious and subtly respectable in consumer culture.

The church is summoned openly to live out its fellowship, *koinonia*, with the Father, through Christ, in the Spirit, and to declare this message and enact it in the world. In the early twenty-first century the suffocating pressures against this clear mission of the church are immense, pressures to mute the distinctive message of Christ as the hinge of history, the start of a renewed humanity. While clearly God can and does work in the world outside the church, and in that sense the kingdom is wider than the church, this does not mean that the church is just one means of divine action and revelation among others. The church is not a general religious institution, but the very particular 'body of Christ', redeemed by the sacrifice of Christ into peace with God the Father in the power of the Spirit, and at the heart of God's redeemed creation.

See also: CHURCH GOVERNMENT.

Bibliography

K. Barth, *CD*, 4.2; J. Calvin, *Institutes of the Christian Religion* (1559); A. C. Cochrane, *The Church's Confession under Hitler* (Eugene, 1962); A. Dulles, *Models of the Church* (New York, 1987); P. S. Fiddes, *Tracks and Traces: Baptist Identity in Church and Theology* (Carlisle, 2003); P. T. Forsyth, *The Church and Sacraments* (London, 1917); G. Gutiérrez, *A Theology of Liberation* (London, 1988 [1971]); S. Hauerwas and W. H. Willimon, *Resident Aliens* (Nashville, 1989); R. Hütter, *Suffering Divine Things* (Grand Rapids, 2000); R. W. Jenson, *Systematic Theology* (Oxford/New York, 1999); J. Milbank, *Theology and Social Theory* (Oxford, 1993); J. Moltmann, *The Church in the Power of the Spirit* (London, 1977); O. M. T. O'Donovan, *The Desire of the Nations* (Cambridge, 1996); A. M. Ramsey, *The Gospel and the Catholic Church* (London, 1990 [1936]); E. Schillebeeckx, *Church: The Human Story of God* (London, 1990); J. L. Segundo, *Theology and the Church* (London, 1985); M. Volf, *After Our Likeness: The Church as the Image of the Trinity* (Grand Rapids, 1998); J. Webster, *Word and Church* (Edinburgh/New York, 2001); J. Zizioulas, *Being as Communion* (New York, 1988).

T. BRADSHAW

CHURCH DISCIPLINE

Although contemporary Christians are often wary of the term (which has been used primarily in the Reformed and Anabaptist traditions), church discipline has historically been seen as an integral aspect of the church's ministry of teaching and pastoral care, designed to promote individual *sanctification as well as to maintain the holiness of the church. In a broad sense, all members share in discipline as they exhort one another to holy living; but most Christian traditions have seen this responsibility as given concrete form in the prerogatives of the ministry to watch over, guide, admonish and (where necessary) formally exclude erring members. Discipline has usually been seen as applying to both doctrinal and moral aspects of Christian life.

A church's understanding of church discipline is influenced by its thinking on such matters as whether the church is to be pure or mixed, how it is governed, and the role played by the *ministry and the *sacraments in mediating salvation. These dictate who is seen as responsible for the practice of discipline – the priesthood, the whole body of the faithful, or civil rulers. In general, those who are seen as responsible for the church's government are the ones charged with primary responsibility for maintaining its discipline.

This article will focus on theological concepts which shaped differing approaches to church discipline, as space precludes discussion of how these worked out in practice.

Early and medieval

In seeking to apply NT teaching, early development of the church's penitential system drew on synagogue precedents for maintaining community standards and cohesion. The ultimate sanction, exclusion, was regarded as constituting (or representing) the individual's exclusion from the body of those who would be saved. Persecution during the third and early fourth centuries resulted in *schism as church leaders disagreed over what to do with those who had lapsed: was the church an army of saints or a hospital for sinners? What degree of restoration was possible? Did certain sins, notably *apostasy, put individuals beyond all possibility of restoration? Was the church's holiness to be understood in terms of its head, Christ (so Augustine), or its members (so the *Donatists)? Such challenges accelerated the development of an elaborate system designed to restore the individual who had sinned and to limit the spread of infection; it also encouraged individuals to delay baptism in order to lessen the likelihood of falling foul of strictures against post-baptismal sin. As the church came to be understood increasingly in institutional and hierarchical terms, its discipline received expression as part of *canon law, which laid down appropriate *penances for various categories of sinner and formal procedures for exclusion and readmission, as well as attempting to formalize the expectations laid on individuals. Some sins required public discipline, but the rise of auricular confession led to most being dealt with confidentially through priestly counsel and absolution. With the rise of the *monastic orders came a comprehensive approach to Christian discipline which dealt with inward as well as outward aspects of Christian living.

Orthodoxy sees itself as inheriting the patristic tradition of pastoral care. However, it has not, for the most part, shared the Western liking for juridical modes of thought and action, and although it has disciplinary canons and procedures of excommunication, and encourages auricular confession, it has been wary of speaking in terms of 'church discipline'. Nevertheless, since the church is the locus for the healing of the individual through transformation into the likeness of Christ (*deification), discipline in the broader sense is integral to the church's functioning.

In medieval Roman Catholicism, the 'power of the keys' became an important instrument for strengthening the *papacy's political standing. Whole nations were on occasion put under an interdict forbidding the regular celebration of the sacraments, because their rulers clashed with the papacy.

Reformation and post-Reformation

Chronologically, the *Anabaptists were the first of the sixteenth-century traditions to develop a coherent approach to church discipline, following the pattern laid down in Matt. 18:15–20. Members were responsible to watch over one another, but congregational leaders bore ultimate responsibility for maintaining the church's purity as a community of believers called out of the world. At *Schleitheim in 1527, one of the issues on which agreement was reached was the 'ban', which thereafter became a distinctive (and controversial) feature of discipline in the believers' church tradition. Anabaptism has been seen as an attempt to apply monastic standards of discipline to the whole body of believers.

The *Lutheran tradition has tended to oppose *law and gospel, and hence it was reluctant to introduce anything savouring of legalism, works-righteousness or the medieval penitential system. The gospel was seen as the divinely appointed means for achieving personal change. Furthermore, since civil rulers took on governing responsibility as 'emergency bishops', the church's freedom to function independently was in practice limited.

*Reformed Protestantism, however, had a more positive estimate not only of the place of the *law in the life of believers and churches, but also of the formalization of this in terms of codes of conduct and mechanisms for dealing with erring members. Civil powers were expected to uphold the church's decisions and in certain serious cases to implement them, but the church was seen (in theory, though not always in practice) as free to discipline its members as it saw fit. Influenced by contact with Anabaptism, *Bucer argued that, along with the preaching of the word and the right administration of the sacraments, the practice of discipline represented a mark of the true church, though he was careful to expound it as part of a comprehensive programme of Christian education. Catholicism saw a renewed emphasis on discipline in broader and narrower senses, especially as a result of the Council of *Trent. *Anglicanism, too, continued the medieval practice of public formal discipline.

In England and North America, *Puritanism worked out Reformed thought concerning discipline, attempting to make visible the clear distinction between the elect and the world. English Dissent and Scottish Presbyterianism continued this Reformed disciplinary tradition. However, the consistency with which discipline was practised varied between congregations, and the eighteenth century saw a decline in the frequency of formal disciplinary cases, reflecting that in other traditions. Wider cultural trends were at work here, including a more positive estimate of human nature. More recent factors accelerating this decline have included changing understandings of the nature of justice, reflected in changing approaches to *punishment, and a decline in confidence regarding the church's divine institution and authority.

Churches today, as throughout history, adopt varying standpoints on a range of matters involved in church discipline: how strictly it should be applied, what offences should be dealt with through formal procedures, the authority accorded to canon law or its equivalents, and the extent to which human discipline reflects the divine mind. As in the patristic era, internal tension results from disagreement. Overall, however, more emphasis is laid than before on the broader context of pastoral care and mutual ministry, and less on formal disciplinary procedures: when the latter are exercised, as in a few high-profile *heresy trials, they attract a disproportionate amount of attention.

See also: CHURCH; CHURCH GOVERNMENT.

Bibliography

P. Benedict, *Christ's Churches Purely Reformed* (New Haven and London, 2002); G. C. Berkouwer, *The Church*, Studies in Dogmatics (Grand Rapids, 1976); D. Bridge, *Spare the Rod and Spoil the Church* (Bromley, 1985); G. R. Evans (ed.), *A History of Pastoral Care* (London and New York, 2000); S. L. Greenslade, *Shepherding the Flock* (London, 1967); M. Jeschke, *Discipling the Brother* (Scottdale, 1972).

T. GRASS

CHURCH FATHERS, see PATRISTIC THEOLOGY

CHURCH GOVERNMENT

Modern critical scholarship has made it more difficult than in the past to appeal to the Bible or the early church for a blueprint of church government. It is generally agreed that the NT does not reveal a single definitive pattern of polity, that nomenclature for various offices varies within the NT, and that there was a process of development in the communities. The liberal-Protestant antithesis, associated with F. C. Baur and A. von *Harnack, between the charismatic Corinthian community and the proto-catholic structures of the Pastoral Epistles, was exaggerated, but had a point.

This relaxation of ecclesiastical claims grounded in Scripture weakens the case for differences of polity becoming causes of serious division between the churches. It also generates a search for the deeper ecclesiological principles that inform the structure of the church in the NT. Both of these factors are at work in *ecumenical theology. The Anglican-Roman Catholic International Commission (ARCIC) renounced a direct appeal to the Petrine texts of the NT in support of the universal primacy of the Bishop of Rome, and looked instead to a providentially guided process of development in history. *Baptism, Eucharist and Ministry* (1982) discerned three dimensions of ministry – personal, collegial and communal – at work in the NT, and urged that they be reflected at every level of the churches' life.

The main structures of ecclesiastical polity are episcopal, papal, presbyterian, independent (congregational) and conciliar. They are not necessarily mutually exclusive.

Episcopal

By the mid-second century, a threefold ministry of bishop, presbyter and deacon was firmly and widely, but not universally, established, as appears in the writings of Ignatius of Antioch (*c*. 115) and Polycarp (mid-first to mid-second century). *Irenaeus and *Tertullian give no inkling that they were aware of a time when there were no bishops. Advocates of episcopacy point to the roles of James, who had a presiding role at the Council of Jerusalem, and to Timothy and Titus, who had a more than presbyteral authority, as apostolic delegates. Bishops are seen as successors of the *apostles, not in the latter's unique role as witnesses to the resurrection, but as carrying on their ministry of teaching, oversight of the *sacraments, and exercising discipline in the community, especially with regard to other ministers. However, while the apostles were mainly itinerant, bishops are localized.

The late nineteen-century scholars J. B. Lightfoot and E. Hatch held that the episcopate emerged out of the presbyterate, as Jerome had stated with regard to the church in Alexandria. But Charles *Gore attacked this view, maintaining that bishops were the lineal descendants of the apostles. The Roman Catholic Church holds that the episcopal college, with the pope at its head, is the continuation of the apostolic college, in which Peter presided. While the 1550–1662 Anglican Ordinal maintained that the orders of bishops, priests and deacons had existed since the times of the apostles, the modern Church of England ordinals (*Alternative Service Book* and *Common Worship*) simply state that the church maintains the historic threefold pattern of ordained ministry.

Related to the question of origins is the question of necessity. One medieval view was that a bishop is a priest with wider jurisdiction. There was no higher calling or authority than to celebrate the *Eucharist and perform the miracle of transubstantiation. On that basis, the episcopate could not be the crown of orders. The English Reformers (see *Reformers, English) generally saw episcopacy as an inherited, expedient form of church government, one that had the support of 'the magistrate' (the civil ruler). Only after the early *Presbyterians had claimed divine right for their favoured system did some Anglicans begin to match that claim with regard to episcopacy. Richard *Hooker, however, did not go that far; while holding that bishops were 'apostolical' and God-given, he recognized that divine positive laws could be changed by the consent of the church if circumstances altered, and he went as far as to envisage that, if the episcopate were to be abolished, it could be reconstituted (presumably from the presbyterate). The High Church divines of the seventeenth and eighteenth century Church of England did not regard episcopacy as absolutely of the being (*esse*) of the church, because they refused to unchurch the non-episcopal Reformed churches on mainland Europe and recognized their superintendents (Gk *episkopos*) as *de facto* bishops. The Non-Jurors, who saw themselves as the continuing Church of England, and then the more extreme Tractarians (see *Anglo-Catholic theology), began to make episcopacy necessary to the existence of the church. Gore believed that the abolition of episcopacy by certain churches at the Reformation was a breach of the divine order.

However, this stance has not shaped the Church of England's ecumenical policy; that church has entered into agreements of mutual ecclesial recognition with several churches that do not have bishops (or bishops in the historic succession). However, the traditional *Anglican concern to affirm episcopacy without absolutizing it is reflected in the fact that these agreements do not bring about the interchangeability of ministries; for that episcopal ordination in intended visible historical continuity from the apostles is required. Among episcopalians, some hold that only bishops have the inherent authority to ordain and that episcopal ordination is not simply a matter of good order, but is the only true ordination, while others hold that while bishops and presbyters share the same power of order, it is fitting that bishops should ordain as an expression of their oversight. In episcopally ordered churches, presbyters lay on hands with the bishop at the ordination of presbyters: some interpret this as a gesture of solidarity, an acceptance into the college of presbyters; others believe that the presbyters are actually sharing with the bishop in the ordination.

Episcopacy belongs in the context of the threefold ministry. A bishop is first a deacon and then a priest and retains these orders on being made bishop. All episcopally ordered churches, except the Roman Catholic Church, involve other clergy and the laity in synodical structures of church government. The Church of England is conciliar as well as episcopal – though not quite 'episcopally led and synodically governed', because there are lay leaders, and bishops have a special role in government. There is an ecumenical consensus that the visible unity (or communion) which the churches seek will involve episcopacy.

Papal

The monarchical, centralized character of Roman Catholicism was the product of gradual development spread over more than a millennium. The exact connection between the apostle Peter and the church in the city of Rome is obscure. Clement of Rome uses 'bishop' and 'presbyter' interchangeably at the end of the first century. The first Western writer to assert that Peter was superior to the other apostles and alone received the keys to the kingdom of heaven, which he then shared with the other apostles, was Optatus (*c.* 370). *Leo I (mid-fifth century) made explicit what had long been implicit; the identification of the Bishop of Rome with Peter, not only in his office, but in his actions: he could speak and decide with the authority of Peter. Nicholas I (mid-ninth century) claimed that Rome was mistress, mother and head of all the churches and that its bishop was Peter's vicar. The investiture contest around 1100 over the respective rights of pope and emperor, bishop and king, intensified papal claims. The concentration of power in the *papacy was enhanced by Gregory VII (Hildebrand) from 1073; he claimed, 'Blessed Peter answers by me' and styled himself 'vicar of Peter' rather than the familiar 'vicar of Christ'. The seeds of the later dogma of universal jurisdiction are found in the notion, supported by forged documents, of a transfer of Roman imperial authority to the pope. The doctrine of 'fullness of power' (*plenitudo potestatis*), which included temporal (political) power, as well as spiritual authority, goes back to Leo I and was articulated by *Bernard of Clairvaux. It was enunciated by Innocent III at the beginning of the thirteenth century: the pope was between God and man, higher than man but lower than God; he judged all, but could be judged by none. This succoured the notion of papal world monarchy, promoted just when the papacy was at its most vulnerable. Boniface VIII's reign (1294–1303) saw the high watermark in papal claims (*Unam Sanctam*, 1302), but his claims were punctured in the contest with Philip IV of France.

The struggle with conciliarism (see below) eventually strengthened the papacy, as did the Reformation conflict, when the Council of *Trent brought greater doctrinal and administrative coherence to the Roman Catholic Church. The accepted doctrines of universal jurisdiction and infallible teaching authority were given dogmatic status at the First Vatican Council (1870–71), though the latter decree can be seen as an attempt to contain the excesses of Ultramontane aspirations for unlimited papal authority. There was an attempt at the Second Vatican Council (1962–65) to counterbalance a centuries-long process of centralization with the notion of episcopal collegiality (see *Vatican Councils). The Council magnified the office of bishop to counteract the dominance of the papacy; the episcopate represented the fullness of holy orders, and bishops received their authority directly from Christ. However, the practical application of collegiality has not been encouraged by the still highly centralized Roman Catholic Church.

In theological dialogue, some of the Roman Catholic Church's ecumenical partners have recognized that there could be a place for a universal pastor who would serve the unity of the Church, but they have not shown themselves willing to accept the papacy without major reform. In the encyclical *Ut Unum Sint* (1995) Pope John Paul II, in an unprecedented way, offered his primacy for ecumenical interrogation and sought the help of other traditions in elucidating what it might mean in an ecumenical climate.

Presbyterianism

The basic features of Presbyterian church government were laid down by John *Calvin, who followed Martin *Bucer in discerning a fourfold ordained ministry in the NT: pastors, teachers, elders and deacons (*Institutes*, IV, iii–iv). Calvin was not opposed in principle to bishops in the way that he was to the papacy. The exclusive claim for Presbyterianism came with Calvin's successor in Geneva, Theodore *Beza. The system was elaborated in seventeenth-century Scotland and England and became entrenched in polemics with Anglicans. Presbyterians take their cue from the fact that, in the NT, the words *presbuteros* and *episkopos* are often used interchangeably. This remained the situation reflected in the *Didache*. The first bishops were the pastors of parish-sized communities and presided in the council of presbyters. Classic exponents of Presbyterianism, such as G. Gillespie, held that church government should be modelled on that of the synagogue, where elders were drawn from among the people.

The parity of ministers is an axiom of Presbyterian polity (though in practice ministers of word and sacrament have more prestige than ruling elders), and all have equal authority. There should be a plurality of them in every congregation. The councils or courts of the church are composed solely of presbyters. Elders are regarded as ordained, but as of the people (*laos*). However, they are called to rule and to govern; their decisions are binding.

Some Reformed churches have given up the claim that Presbyterian government is by divine right, and this makes them open to insights from other traditions, especially episcopal. The Church of Scotland now has a twofold ordained ministry of presbyters and deacons (as does the Methodist Church in Great Britain), though it is not a pure form of Presbyterianism, as it involves lay people in the governance of the church and sees the whole church as a single 'connexion', governed by the Conference, which exercises corporate *episkope*. Both churches have recently shown themselves to be resistant to taking episcopacy into their systems.

Independency

The independent or congregational form of polity goes back to the English separatists of the late sixteenth century, but has been refined by such writers as John *Owen and R. W. Dale. In England most *Congregationalists merged with the Presbyterians to form the United Reformed Church in 1972, so compromising their traditional polity. *Baptist and *Pentecostal churches are the dominant form of independency in England, though the Baptist principle of 'association' moderates the autonomy of the local congregation. Independents believe that 'church' in the NT refers either to the church universal or to particular local churches that were autonomous. They believe that this local congregation is essentially independent of external control and should not become part of a larger unit, though they have a place for forms of co-operation and consultation. Most independent churches have also been congregationalist; in other words, they have been governed by the meeting of all the members, gathered in the church meeting. They see themselves as guided by Christ, the only head of the church and as directly responsible to him. However, many independent churches are led by a group of elders, who are elected by the meeting, but, once elected, have intrinsic authority.

Conciliarism

Conciliarism exists only in conjunction with other models of church government. It gives a high place to the church gathering in council through its representatives. It holds that authority should be constitutionally defined and that the assent of the governed is required for legitimate authority. Conciliarism looks back for legitimation to the first council of the church, in Acts 15, and to the early *councils, from Nicaea (325) onwards. It is generally recognized that councils that took place after the schism between East and West in 1054 cannot have the same authority as those of a virtually united church. There has not been an 'ecumenical' council in the East since then.

During the split in the papacy in 1378, first into two, later into three, contenders traumatized Western Christendom and generated the conciliar theories derived from canon law and ecclesiology. They appealed to the whole body to redress the failings of the centre. The early fifteenth-century councils (principally Constance, 1414–18) united the papacy, but failed to reform the church 'in head and members'. The Reformation continued the conciliar aim of reform by other means. The sixteenth-century Reformers inherited the conciliar doctrine and some (e.g. *Luther and *Cranmer) appealed to a free general council to vindicate their stance. Conciliarism is still under a cloud in the Roman Catholic Church, because it is seen as a threat to the papacy (which does not have any constitutional constraints). But conciliar principles have shaped not only parliamentary forms of government, but all the major traditions of the Christian church.

See also: CHURCH; COLLEGIALITY AND CONCILIARITY.

Bibliography

P. Avis, *Beyond the Reformation? Authority, Primacy and Unity in the Conciliar Tradition* (London, 2006); idem (ed.), *The Christian Church: An Introduction to the Major Traditions* (London, 2002); E. Duffy, *Saints and Sinners: A History of the Popes* (New Haven and London, 1997); J. S. Gray and J. C. Tucker, *Presbyterian Polity for Church Officers* (Louisville, 1999); W. Henn, 'Historical-Theological Synthesis of the Relation between Primacy and Episcopacy during the Second Millennium', in *Il Primato del Successore di Pietro* (Vatican City, 1998); H. Küng, *Structures of the Church* (New York, 1964; London, 1965); O. O'Donovan and J. L. O'Donovan, *From Irenaeus to Grotius: A Sourcebook in Christian Political Thought* (Grand Rapids, 2004); F. Oakley, *The Conciliarist Tradition: Constitutionalism in the Catholic Church* (Oxford, 2003); C. Podmore, *Aspects of Anglican Identity* (London, 2005); B. Tierney, *Religion, Law and the Growth of Constitutional Thought* (Cambridge, 1982); W. Ullmann, *The Growth of Papal Government in the Middle Ages* (London, ²1962).

P. D. L. AVIS

CIVIL RELIGION

The debate about 'civil religion' became a major academic issue in the late 1960s with the seminal article by sociologist Robert Bellah (b. 1927), entitled 'Civil Religion in America' (*Daedalus* 96, 1967, pp. 1–21; repr. in W. G. McLaughlin and R. N. Bellah [eds.], *Religion in America*, Boston, 1968). Bellah's essay develops the argument of Jean-Jacques *Rousseau (1712–78), who in *The Social Contract* (1762) discussed the role of civil religion in society. Rousseau argued that, by introducing a distinction between church and *state based on the trans-national loyalty demanded by the God of the Bible, Christians actually undermine civil society. Bellah does not discuss Rousseau's obvious sympathy for pagan Rome, but concentrates instead on his outline of the essence of a civil religion. In Rousseau's views, belief in the existence of God, the life to come, the reward of virtue and the punishment of vice, and the rejection of religious intolerance, are all important for the smooth running of a state. All other religious beliefs may be held privately by individuals, but they must not be allowed to affect social duties or fundamental loyalty.

Bellah argues that the founding fathers of the United States shared a common outlook with Rousseau. He goes on to argue for the existence of an 'American civil religion' which is consciously or unconsciously appealed to by American leaders, especially presidents. To prove his point, Bellah analysed various presidential speeches, from Washington's first inaugural in 1789 to Kennedy's in 1960. Behind these speeches Bellah found a strong affirmation of the purpose and destiny of America and a call for patriotic values based upon biblical imagery and archetypes.

Bellah's article sparked a lively and stimulating debate among theologians, philosophers, sociologists and historians. Eventually, five types of religious activity were identified as civil religion. (1) Folk religion and American values, which seem to arise out of the actual lives of Americans. (2) A transcendent universal religion of the nation or religion of the republic. This view was propounded by Sidney Mead (*CH* 36, 1967, pp. 262–283) and assumes an essentially American prophetic faith. (3) A religious nationalism which glorifies American leaders and policies. Martin Marty (in R. E. Richey and D. G. Jones [eds.], *American Civil Religion*, pp. 139–157) argued that this type of religious response could be seen in the speeches of Richard Nixon, which identified American policies with Nixon's own policies. (4) A generalized democratic faith which sees America as the pinnacle of democratic institutions and their highest expression in a providential history. (5) A Protestant civic piety which identifies American with *Protestant moralism, individualism, activism, pragmatism and work ethic.

Against all of these views, various theologians have made major criticisms of an implicit idolatry. Herbert W. Richardson argued in his powerful essay 'Civil Religion in Theological Perspective' (in Richey and Jones, *American Civil Religion*, pp. 161–184) that the term civil religion 'unites two terms: the civil order and the religious order', and that this was an essentially unbiblical and anti-Christian position. He acknowledges that civil religion has had great influence in America, but says it deserves strong condemnation from Christians.

In Richardson's view, American civil religion is a growing force which is a corruption of the original ideals of American *Puritans and a potential threat to the future freedom of religion.

In addition to discussing civil religion in America, various authors have applied the theory to their own situation. Probably the most extensive discussion of civil religion outside America has taken place in South Africa. Here sociologists and theologians debated the use of biblical imagery by Afrikaner nationalists in relation to apartheid (see *Race). T. Dunbar Moodie's *The Rise of Afrikanerdom* is an excellent example of the application of this perspective to South African history. Apart from helping Christians to understand how a state can manipulate religious symbols, Moodie also helped to discredit the popular but false notion that apartheid was a natural historical development due to the influence of Calvinism.

Although there are many problems in identifying what exactly is meant by civil religion and how it operates in a society, the idea is a creative one which sensitizes Christians to the misuse of religious symbolism by secular groups. In the work of Bellah and Moodie, the existence of a civil religion is found at the heart of political and social life in modern states. But this need not always be the case. In British history, groups like the British Israelites represent an attempt to create a civil religion which would have legitimated British imperialism. Similarly, many observers find in the Unification Church or Moonies (see *New religions; *Sects) elements of civil religion which glorify South Korea and America (Thomas Robbins, 'The Last Civil Religion: Reverend Moon and the Unification Church', *Sociological Analysis* 37, 1976, pp. 111–125).

Among modern evangelicals the works of Francis *Schaeffer come close to propounding an evangelical civil religion, as can be seen from books such as *How Should We Then Live?* (1976). In Schaeffer's case his intention is clearly to promote a biblical appreciation of history. But in practice, among theologically unsophisticated people, this theological history often translates into something completely different and quite unbiblical. It is the ease with which biblical ideas can become sources for an idolatrous glorification of the state which is, from a Christian perspective, the true danger of civil religion.

Bibliography

T. D. Moodie, *The Rise of Afrikanerdom: Power, Apartheid and the Afrikaner Civil Religion* (Berkeley, CA, 1975); G. Müller-Fahrenholtz, *America's Battle for God: A European Christian Looks at Civil Religion* (Grand Rapids, 2007); G. Parsons (ed.), *Perspectives on Civil Religion* (Aldershot, 2002); R. E. Richey and D. G. Jones (eds.), *American Civil Religion* (New York, 1974).

I. Hexham

CLARKE, WILLIAM NEWTON (1841–1912)

Baptist minister and theologian, Clarke is generally considered the first systematic theologian of theological liberalism in the US. Born in Cazenovia, New York, son of a Baptist pastor, Clarke studied for the ministry at Madison (now Colgate) University and Theological Seminary in Hamilton, New York. He pastored Baptist churches in the US and Canada for twenty years. Between 1883 and 1887 he taught NT at the Baptist Theological School in Toronto, Canada. After a brief return to the pastorate in Hamilton, New York (1887–90), Clarke became professor of theology at Colgate Theological Seminary where he taught until 1908.

Clarke published his best-known work, *An Outline of Christian Theology* (1898), after failing to find a textbook for his courses that systematically addressed both the intellectual ferment of his time and classical theological ideas and emphases. Drawing from evolutionary thinking, critical-historical approaches to the Bible, comparative religions, and especially the theology of Friedrich *Schleiermacher, Clarke articulated a theology that was anchored primarily in religious experience, which emphasized that the character of God is revealed pre-eminently in Jesus, and which asserted that God is active everywhere throughout the creation, including in non-Christian religions. Clarke's aims were essentially conservative, to frame Christian ideas in contemporary thought forms and language. Within the wide range of 'liberal' theologies, Clarke was an 'evangelical liberal' (*see* *Liberal evangelicalism).

See also: Liberal Theology.

Bibliography

Works: *An Outline of Christian Theology* (New York, 1898); *What Shall We Think of Christianity?* (New York, 1899); *The Use of Scripture in Theology* (New York, 1905); *The Christian Doctrine of God* (New York, 1909).
Studies: E. A. Clarke (ed.), *William Newton Clarke: A Biography* (New York, 1916); C. L. Howe, Jr, *The Theology of William Newton Clarke* (New York, 1980).

H. E. Raser

CLEMENT OF ALEXANDRIA (*c.* 150–*c.* 215)

Clement was a Christian philosopher, probably born in Athens, who succeeded his teacher Pantaenus as head of a Christian (catechetical?) school in Alexandria some time after 180. He left Alexandria around 202.

Apart from fragments preserved by various authors, his extant works consist of the *Protrepticus* (*Exhortation to the Greeks*), a polished work of Christian apologetics; the *Paedagogus* (*The Tutor*), a detailed guide for Christian life and conduct; the *Stromateis* (*Miscellanies*), a rich assortment of notes and outlines on a wide variety of topics; and *Quis Dives Salvetur?*, an extended sermon on the rich young ruler in Mark 10:17–31.

In many respects his thinking stands in the line of the Greek *apologists, but he represents a contrast to contemporary (Western) writers in his positive evaluation of Greek philosophy, his speculative bent and his deliberate lack of system. Alexandria having been the home of *Philonic allegory (see *Hermeneutics) and various brands of *Gnosticism, it is necessary to note Clement's use of allegory (not yet systematized as it is by *Origen) and his description of the perfect Christian as a 'true Gnostic'.

Though he vigorously opposes Gnosticism, Clement apparently retains *docetic elements in his *Christology, by denying emotions and certain corporeal functions in the man Jesus. He frequently uses the trinitarian formula, emphasizing the distinction between Father, Son (*Logos) and Holy Spirit and affirming the eternity of the Son's existence, without however coming to any clear definition of the nature of the *Trinity.

Before the incarnation, knowledge of God was given to the Jews through the law and to the Greeks through philosophy, which was inspired by the Logos, i.e. by Christ. The Logos became incarnate to impart knowledge and to serve as our model. Clement uses the language of *atonement and conquest of *evil with respect to Christ, but his main emphasis is on Christ as teacher. Though faith, understood as assent to the teaching of Christ, is sufficient for salvation, the true Gnostic moves beyond faith to knowledge, a full understanding of Christ's teaching, coupled with an exemplary mode of living (which corresponds closely to *Platonic and *Stoic ideals). This knowledge leads to perfect love and to a *mystic relationship with God, fully consummated only after death, when the believer becomes (like) God.

Salvation is obtained in relation to the church, and through baptism one is made a member of the church. In his arguments against the heretics, Clement emphasizes the antiquity and unity of the catholic church, the tradition handed down orally in the church from the apostles and the importance of interpreting the Scriptures (which for Clement included rather more than our present canon) in accordance with the 'rule of the church'.

Clement strongly affirms the freedom of the *will and the need for man to co-operate with God by accepting salvation. He apparently conceives of the possibility of repentance even after death.

Bibliography

Works in ET: in *ANCL* and *ANF*; selections in G. W. Butterworth (ed.), *Clement of Alexandria*, LCL (London, 1919); H. Chadwick and J. E. L. Oulton (eds.), *Alexandrian Christianity*, LCC (London, 1954).

Studies: H. Chadwick, *Early Christian Thought and the Classical Tradition* (Oxford, 1966); H. F. Hägg, *Clement of Alexandria and the Beginnings of Christian Apophaticism* (Oxford, 2006); S. R. C. Lilla, *Clement of Alexandria: A Study of Christian Platonism and Gnosticism* (Oxford, 1971); E. F. Osborn, *The Philosophy of Clement of Alexandria* (Cambridge, 1975).

T. G. DONNER

COBB, JOHN B. Jr (b. 1925)

Cobb is an American theologian known for his significant contributions to *process theology, the theology of *ecology, and dialogue between *Christianity and other religions. Born to Methodist missionaries serving in Kobe, Japan, in 1940 Cobb was sent to live with his grandmother in Georgia to attend high school. After graduating, he attended junior college and the University of Michigan, and was thereafter admitted to an interdepartmental masters programme at the University of Chicago where he concentrated on modern criticisms of Christianity. When that experience left his faith in tatters, Cobb transferred to the Divinity School, and there he discovered resources in Whitehead's cosmology for constructing a Christian vision that took modernity seriously while transcending its reductionistic worldview. In 1949, he earned an MDiv, and three years later completed a PhD. He joined the faculty of the School of Theology at Claremont in 1958, where he co-founded the Centre for Process Studies with David Griffin, and the academic journal, *Process Studies*, with Lewis Ford. In the late 1960s, Cobb became aware of the ecological crisis, and worked to integrate a theology of ecology with process theology. He has also worked to link interfaith dialogue with process thought by suggesting that Whitehead's vision of metaphysical ultimacy as a plurality (creativity–God–world) grounds such diverse religious notions of ultimate reality as the Christian doctrine of God and the Buddhist concept of emptiness.

Bibliography

Selected works: *A Christian Natural Theology* (1965); *Is It Too Late? A Theology of Ecology* (1972); *Christ in a Pluralistic Age* (1975); *Beyond Dialogue: Toward a Mutual Transformation of Christianity and Buddhism* (1982).

Studies: G. Dorrien, *The Making of American Liberal Theology: Crisis, Irony, and Postmodernity 1950–2005* (Louisville, 2006); D. R. Griffin and T. J. J. Altizer (eds.), *John Cobb's Theology in Process* (Philadelphia, 1977); D. R. Griffin and J. C. Hough (eds.), *Theology and the University: Essays in Honor of John B. Cobb* (Albany, 1991).

J. R. WILSON

COCCEIUS, JOHANNES (1603–69)

Johannes Cocceius was a prominent seventeenth-century Bible scholar, who worked in the tradition of advanced humanist scholarship (see *Humanism, Renaissance) and *Reformed theology. German by birth, he taught at Bremen, Franeker and Leiden. He was a prolific author, and his writings include commentaries on all the biblical books, a Hebrew and Aramaic lexicon, works on philology and ethics, and volumes on theology, especially his famous *Summa doctrinae de foedere et testamento Dei* (1648).

In this work he developed a *covenant theology which described all of human history by introducing the structure of consecutive covenants or *foedera*. By using the biblical concept of *foedus* (covenant), he sought to do justice also in systematic theology to the historical nature of the biblical narrative. He defined this covenant as 'nothing other than a divine declaration of the way of perceiving the love of God and of obtaining union and communion or friendship with God' (*Summa doctrinae*, ch. I § 5). He distinguished two fundamental forms of God's covenant in salvation history: the covenant of works before the *fall and the covenant of *grace after the fall. The former was violated by the disobedience of Adam and Eve; the second was promulgated immediately after the fall. The covenant of grace Cocceius chiefly divided in two periods: *ante et post Christum natum* (before and after Christ's birth). But the establishment of the covenant of grace, he argued, did not entail an abrupt end of the original, failed covenant in paradise. Therefore, he described the whole biblical history after the fall as a series of events by which the covenant of works was abrogated step by step, until the salvation promised in the covenant of grace is revealed in full glory and liberty. By means of this abrogation theme he infused his view on the covenant with a powerful dynamic, and with an eschatological perspective.

This *eschatological orientation also emerged in his interpretation of biblical prophecy. On the basis of a supposed analogy of the prophecies of especially Daniel and Revelation, he subsequently interpreted the Bible as a prolonged prophecy of the Christian church until the end of time, divided into seven periods. Elements of this 'prophetic theology' were elaborated in the works of a later generation of Cocceians.

Cocceius's followers, however, were not servile imitators of his covenant system and prophetic theology. While some of them incorporated elements of Cartesian philosophy in the Cocceian covenant system (Fr. Burman), others developed a more pietistic model that influenced Reformed Puritan circles in the Netherlands (via H. Witsius and also Scottish covenant theology) and Lutheran pietistic theologians such as Ph. J. Spener and J. A. *Bengel.

Although the term *Heilsgeschichte* was coined in the nineteenth century, Cocceius can be viewed as the founding father of this concept in the Reformed tradition. Finally, his federal theology was of considerable importance in the theological and political history of Europe and the United States and forms the framework for much Reformed theology in the past three centuries.

Bibliography

W. J. van Asselt, *The Federal Theology of Johannes Cocceius (1603–1669)* (Leiden, Boston and Cologne, 2001); H. Faulenbach, *Weg und Ziel der Erkenntnis Christi: Eine Untersuchung zur Theologie des Johannes Coccejus* (Neukirchen-Vluyn, 1973); C. S. McCoy, *The Covenant Theology of Johannes Cocceius*, PhD diss. (Yale University, 1956); G. Schrenk, *Gottesreich und Bund im älteren Protestantismus vornehmlich bei Johannes Coccejus* (Darmstadt, 1967 [1923]).

W. J. van Asselt

COLERIDGE, SAMUEL TAYLOR (1772–1834)

Coleridge was one of the most important pioneering figures to appear on the English theological scene during the nineteenth century. Most probably the originator of the term '*existentialist', he also scored a 'first' as a psychedelic theologian. The impact of his work permeated the entire religious spectrum in England. Among those influenced by him were such important figures as J. S. Mill (1806–73), Thomas Carlyle (1795–1881), J. C. Hare (1795–1855), J. H. *Newman, Thomas Arnold (1795–1842), James Martineau (1805–1900), Rowland Williams (1817–70), F. D. Maurice (1805–72; see *Christian Socialism) and F. J. A. Hort (1828–92).

In 1795 Coleridge married Sara Fricker but soon felt they were incompatible. Eventually, they agreed to separate. While suffering the torment of domestic tension he became addicted to opium. At about the same time he was making the acquaintance of the Wordsworths and emerging from his fascination with the *determinism which had captivated him at Cambridge University.

Opium introduced Coleridge to a vast uncharted spiritual domain. The appeal of the experience of the new dimension of existence was heightened by the sensation of freedom from the limitations of time and space. At such times reason was able to enjoy the unhindered realization of its potential in perceiving spiritual truth. The implications of these discoveries were, he considered, revolutionary. 'Need we wonder,' he enquired, 'at Plato's opinions concerning the body, at least, need that man wonder whom a pernicious drug shall make capable of conceiving and bringing forth Thoughts, hidden in him before . . . is it not, that the dire poison for a delusive time has made the body . . . a fitter instrument for the all powerful soul?'

The nature of his *religious experience led him to insist, 'All revelation is *ab intra* [from within]'. The intellectually arid, law-court theology of the eighteenth-century apologist was a disservice to the cause of true religion. 'Evidences of Christianity,' he expostulates, 'I am weary of the word. Make a man feel his want of it . . . and you may safely trust it to its own Evidences.'

To safeguard religion from the assaults of the sceptic, Coleridge adopts *Kant's distinction between reason and the understanding, but adapts these concepts to suit his own purposes. In particular, he insists that reason is able to 'behold' truth, and 'is the Source and substance of truths above sense'. The understanding has no jurisdiction over suprasensible knowledge. It cannot comprehend the essence of true religion. Its faltering attempts to articulate the truths of reality are, inevitably, incomplete and erroneous. History, theology, the natural and human sciences fall within the province of the understanding.

He held that, as a historical document expressing 'ideas' or truths in human terms, the Bible contains much ineffectual and erroneous material. Those who adhere to the doctrine of the inspiration (by which he meant dictation) of *Scripture are branded as 'orthodox liars for God'. We discern the truth contained in Scripture by virtue of the fact that 'whatever finds me, bears witness for itself that it has proceeded from a Holy Spirit'.

In differing ways, Coleridge appealed to and influenced theologians of every standpoint. Many of the questions he raised remain as burning issues today.

Bibliography

Works: ed. W. G. Shedd, 7 vols. (New York, 1953), especially: *Aids to Reflection* (1825); *On the Constitution of Church and State* (1820); *Confessions of an Inquiring Spirit* (1840).

Studies: J. R. Barth, *Coleridge and Christian Doctrine* (Cambridge, MA, 1969); T. McFarland, *Coleridge and the Pantheist Tradition* (Oxford, 1969); B. Willey, *Samuel Taylor Coleridge* (London, 1972).

J. H. ELIAS

COLLEGIALITY AND CONCILIARITY

These two concepts are concerned chiefly with the *government or *ministry of the church. *Vatican II's *Constitution on the Church* (*Lumen Gentium*) spoke of the college of the apostles and of the college of bishops as successor to it (II:22–23). This was an attempt to redress the imbalance of Vatican I's exclusive concentration on the primacy of the bishop of Rome. The use of the concept of collegiality has not resolved the Roman problem of the relation between the *papacy and the rest of the bishops in governing the church, but it has encouraged regional episcopal conferences (virtually synods) and fostered more generally a co-operative, collegial spirit and style in church life.

The Faith and Order report, *Baptism, Eucharist and Ministry* (Geneva, 1982), set up the ideal of a collegial, as well as a personal (i.e. individual) and a communal, dimension of ministry at every geographical level. This pattern finds clear expression in *Presbyterianism, at the congregational level in the body of elders (including any ordained presbyters) and at broader levels in presbytery, synod and assembly.

In the Roman and Orthodox traditions, *councils comprise only bishops, so that collegiality and conciliarity inevitably overlap. But in so far as the latter is applicable to other churches, decision-making in synods, assemblies or conferences normally involves laity as well as ordained ministers, perhaps of different orders. 'Conciliar fellowship' as a way of describing the goal of church unity has been prominent in World Council of Churches circles, especially since the Nairobi Assembly (1975). This speaks of a unity between churches that is publicly manifested when their representatives assemble for a council whose decisions will be authoritative for all the participating churches. Such conciliarity allows for the continuation of some diversity among the churches. 'Conciliar' is also used to denote a quality of life within each local church – one that integrates and coordinates rather than excludes the gifts of individual members.

Conciliarity is thus a more comprehensive ideal than collegiality, although their more generalized applications are closer to each other. They both bear comparison with the concepts of *sobornost and *koinonia.

Bibliography
Faith and Order: Louvain 1971 (Geneva, 1971); L. Vischer, 'After the Debate on Collegiality', Ecumenical Review 37 (1985), pp. 306–319.

D. F. WRIGHT

COMMON GRACE, see GRACE

COMMON-SENSE PHILOSOPHY

This is the name given to a number of anti-sceptical philosophical positions adopted in reply to David *Hume, which stressed the philosophical importance of common-sense beliefs (e.g. about the existence of the self, the external world, the past and other minds), and also to common sense as a method of settling philosophical disputes. More weakly, the appeal to common sense may be regarded as a dialectical move, placing the onus of proving scepticism on the sceptic. Common-sense philosophy received its most able expression and defence from the theological 'moderate' Thomas Reid (1710–96), but the basic tenets of the 'Scottish common-sense philosophy' were taken over by numerous evangelical theologians (particularly those influenced by *Princeton College and Seminary, probably through the influence of the Scot John *Witherspoon), as providing both the epistemological and ontological basis of their natural theology and their philosophical ethics. Common-sense philosophy withered under its own internal difficulties, particularly the vagueness of the criterion of common sense, but more especially under the impact of continental *idealism. It enjoyed a revival in the twentieth century through the appeal to common sense by G. E. Moore (1873–1958) and to ordinary language by philosophers such as J. L. Austin (1911–60), and through the epistemology of R. M. Chisholm (1916–99).

Bibliography
R. M. Chisholm, Theory of Knowledge (Eaglewood Cliffs, ²1977); T. Cuneo and R. van Woudenberg (eds.), The Cambridge Companion to Thomas Reid (Cambridge, 2004); H. A. Harris, Fundamentalism and Evangelicals (Oxford, 1998); J. McCosh, The Scottish Philosophy (London, 1875); G. E. Moore, Philosophical Papers (London, 1959); essays by N. Wolterstorff and P. Helm, in H. Hart et al. (eds.), Rationality in the Calvinian Tradition (Lanham, 1983); N. Wolterstorff, Thomas Reid and the Story of Epistemology (Cambridge, 2006).

P. HELM

COMMUNICATO IDIOMATUM, see CHRISTOLOGY

COMMUNION OF SAINTS

A theological term meaning 'fellowship of believers' which is found in the classical *creeds. It was originally inserted in order to express the belief that the living and the dead were united in the body of a single church, but it soon came to have a number of additional meanings which grew out of the ways in which the words '*saint' and 'communion' were defined.

In medieval theology, the word 'saint' was usually restricted to a relatively small category of Christians, including those whose names appeared in the Bible, who were *martyrs for their faith, or who had lived a life of exceptional piety and devotion. The most important single criterion, however, was doctrinal orthodoxy, and so the '*fellowship of the saints' came to mean the confession of Christ which the church formulated in creeds and other statements of a similar nature. The inclusion of both the living and the dead ensured that this confession had not changed over time, even if it had been periodically reformulated to deal with particular heresies. In later medieval theology, the term came to be understood as 'sharing in holy things', interpreting the Latin communio sanctorum as communio in sanctis. That view has been popular in Roman Catholic circles, where it is often associated with the church's requirement that a person must be in communion with the see of Rome in order to partake of the sacraments, but although this remains the official view, most Catholic scholars today recognize that it is at best an extension of the credal sense and not the term's original meaning.

The *Protestant Reformers rejected the medieval understanding of sainthood; following the NT, they used the term to refer to all Christians. The fellowship of the saints thus came to mean the common life of any given congregation of believers, as well as the acceptance of the traditional teachings of the leading theologians and martyrs of the past. Doctrinal orthodoxy remained fundamental, but the scope of the term was broadened to embrace different spiritual gifts and ministries which were meant to be shared within the body of Christ. In the context of a divided Christendom, the communion of saints also came to be understood as the belief that all truly spiritual Christians were united with each other, regardless of their particular political situation or denominational affiliation. Because of this, it can be said that the doctrine of the communion of saints is one of the main theological pillars of the modern *ecumenical movement. A practical problem which it has encountered has been the need to distinguish between an essentially invisible church of 'true believers' on the one hand, and the largely nominal membership of institutional ecclesiastical bodies on the other. Many Protestants have tried to resolve this difficulty by seceding from 'mixed' denominations and creating what they see as 'pure' congregations of the saints. This tendency helps to account for the fissiparous nature of so much Protestantism, particularly as the 'pure church' remains an elusive ideal. Today most Protestants recognize their spiritual kinship with others who share their core beliefs, thus re-emphasizing the centrality of doctrinal orthodoxy in the definition of the communion of saints, and minimizing the significance of visible ecclesiastical divisions. Many Roman Catholics also think along these lines nowadays, as do some members of the Eastern Orthodox churches, though both Catholics and Orthodox give greater importance to the visible church as a means of defining what the boundaries of the communion of the saints are than Protestants usually do.

Theologically speaking, the doctrine of the communion of saints is interpreted in relation both to time and to space. In relation to time, it is taken to mean the fellowship of Christians in every age, past, present and future. Roman Catholics believe that it has a direct bearing on the church triumphant in heaven, and use the doctrine as a justification for praying to the dead, especially to the officially canonized 'saints'. Most Protestants vigorously reject that interpretation on the ground that prayer should be offered only to God, both because Jesus Christ, not the saints, is the one mediator between God and man (1 Tim. 2:5) and because the church triumphant has entered into eternal rest.

In relation to space, the doctrine means that all true Christians are united in fellowship with each other, regardless of nationality, language, social status or culture. The emergence of a truly worldwide Christianity has given this dimension of the doctrine a new significance, as theologians, church leaders and many ordinary believers from developing countries make an ever greater impact on the traditional 'Christian' world of the West. It seems almost certain that this phenomenon will become even more important in the future than it already is and that the implications for the communion of saints in the body of Christ will be worked out most fully in the mutual acceptance and even integration of different cultures and forms of worship in an increasingly globalized church.

See also: CHURCH.

Bibliography

E. Clowney, *The Church* (Leicester, 1995); Lutheran Church of Germany, *Communio Sanctorum: The Church as the Communion of Saints*, tr. D. R. Smith (Collegeville, 2005); B. L. Marthaler, 'Interpreting the Communion of Saints', *Liturgy* 5, 1985, pp. 89–93; M. Perham, *Communion of Saints: An Examination of the Place of the Christian Dead in the Belief, Worship and Calendars of the Church* (London, 1980); D. H. Steele, 'With All God's People: Towards a Protestant Reclaiming of the Communion of Saints', *Theology Today* 51, 1995, pp. 539–547; K. Ware, 'One Body in Christ: Death and the Communion of Saints', *Sobornost* 3, 1981, pp. 179–191.

G. L. BRAY

CONCILIARITY, see COLLEGIALITY AND CONCILIARITY

CONCUPISCENCE, see AUGUSTINE; SIN

CONFESSING CHURCH

The Confessing Church (*die Bekennende Kirche*) comprised that section of the German evangelical church which resisted the nazification of Protestantism during the Third Reich, 1933–45. The extreme nationalism that brought Hitler to power at the end of January 1933 was accompanied by religious movements such as the 'German Christians' (*Deutsche Christen*) that sought to transform the Protestant faith into a religion of Germanic racial purity and subservience to the state. This would have included the banning of all 'non-Aryan' (i.e. of Jewish descent) pastors from office and the imposition of a dictatorial 'Führer-principle' into church government.

There resulted the 'Church Struggle' (*Kirchenkampf*) from the spring of 1933 onwards. At church-political level the opposition was led by Pastor Martin Niemöller, who formed the 'Pastors' Emergency League' that soon had 6,000 members, while the theological resistance was mainly nerved by Karl *Barth, who was then teaching at Bonn. At the end of May 1934 a Free Synod met at Barmen and unanimously adopted the Theological Declaration of *Barmen. Inspired largely by Barth and his christocentric emphasis upon revelation, this rejected the beliefs and methods of the 'German Christians' as inimical to the biblical faith and Reformation doctrine, and declared Jesus Christ as the one Word of God to be obeyed in contradistinction to all other claims to divine truth, power and authority. Thereafter, those pastors, congregations and regional (*Land*) churches that adhered to Barmen denoted themselves as the Confessing Church. A second synod at Berlin-Dahlem in October 1934 set up alternative church structures. The Confessing Church was never a majority in German Protestantism, and did not as such politically oppose the Nazi state. But adherence to it was costly, and until the end of the Reich its very existence represented almost the only public form of denial of Hitler's claims to total allegiance.

See also: BONHOEFFER, DIETRICH.

Bibliography

E. Bethge, *Dietrich Bonhoeffer: A Biography* (Minneapolis, rev. edn, 1999); K. Scholder, *The Churches and the Third Reich*, 2 vols. (London, 1987 and 1988).

K. CLEMENTS

CONFESSIONS OF FAITH

Confession has from the outset been constitutive of Christianity. The Jesus movement was distinguished from the rest of Judaism by its declared conviction that Jesus was Messiah. In various contexts in the developing life of the church, distinctive Christian beliefs were summarized in formulas of greater or lesser fixity in structure and wording (cf. 1 Tim. 3:16; O. Cullmann, *The Earliest Christian Confessions*, London, 1949). The *martyrs in particular made their confession before the world as they faced death (cf. 1 Tim. 6:12–13); the martyr-designate was a 'confessor'.

To serve the needs of the church there developed in the second century the 'rule of faith' and later the *creeds. These may all be described as confessions of faith. So too may other statements such as the Chalcedonian Definition (see *Christology), technically not a creed, which begins, 'We all with one voice confess our Lord Jesus Christ.'

Normally, however, the phrase designates the formal presentations of belief produced mainly by Protestants in the church divisions of the Reformation, including writings not calling themselves 'confessions', such as the decrees and creed of the Council of *Trent, the Heidelberg Catechism, the Thirty-Nine Articles and the Canons of Dort. Many of these confessions have remained authoritative doctrinal standards in their ecclesiastical traditions (hence 'confession' is also occasionally used with reference to such communions).

The survey given below restricts itself to the Reformation and post-Reformation confessions, and is still necessarily selective. But confessions continued to be formulated, such as the *Methodist Articles of Religion (Wesley's revision of the Thirty-Nine Articles, adopted by American Methodists in 1784) and the Lambeth Quadrilateral (1888, stipulating the *Anglican essentials for church unity). Significant twentieth-century examples are the *Barmen Declaration (1934), the expanded but still very brief confessional basis of the *World Council of Churches approved at New Delhi in 1961, the *Lausanne Covenant (1974), and the Confession of 1967 of the United Presbyterian

Church in the USA. This last was included in the church's *Book of Confessions* (1967), along with the Apostles' and Nicene Creeds, the Scots and Second Helvetic Confessions, the Heidelberg Catechism, the Westminster Confession and Shorter Catechism, and the Barmen Declaration (cf. E. A. Dowey, Jr, *A Commentary on the Confession of 1967* and an *Introduction to the Book of Confessions*, Philadelphia, 1968). The ecumenical movement has produced many doctrinal formulations, including the widely based *Baptism, Eucharist and Ministry* of 1982.

The contemporary pluralistic confusion in theology has not been conducive to the writing of new confessions. The *Book of Confessions* represents one solution to the churches' difficulties with their sixteenth- or seventeenth-century confessional documents, which often speak disparagingly of the pope or inappropriately of the relation between church and civil power, as well as possibly being excessively doctrinally rigid in places. Another solution is relaxation of the terms in which office-bearers are required to subscribe to them. (The Church of Scotland requires acknowledgment of only the fundamental doctrines [unspecified] in the Westminster Confession, with liberty of opinion on issues not part of the [undefined] substance of the faith.) Or, again, churches have relegated confessions to the status of 'historic' statements of their faith.

In this debate, confessions are often compared to their disadvantage with the creeds, but the contrast is frequently overdrawn. Most confessions were certainly productions of dividing or divided churches, but so too was the Chalcedonian Definition. Both confessions and creeds were formed to exclude erroneous beliefs; both were historically conditioned by the heresies they refuted. The creeds' limitations (e.g. none mentions the Lord's Supper; they together contribute little on the *atonement) and obscurities (cf. '*descended into hell' in the Apostles' Creed, to say nothing of the technical terms of Nicaea and Chalcedon) are far more obvious than those of the confessions, which are normally more balanced and thorough. If confessions are more controversial, creeds are more minimal and have in practice lost more completely than confessions their originally basic function as touchstones of orthodoxy. This is, however, not true of the Apostles' or Nicene Creeds.

Conservative Christians may in response be found defending confessions undiscriminatingly, forgetting that for Protestants they (like creeds) can only be secondary to Scripture, and are subject to the judgment and revision of Scripture, as many of them explicitly state. Among some major traditions, e.g. the Baptist, churchmen have often refused subscription to any creed or confession; but claims to be 'Bible-only' Christians or churches ignore the quasi-confessional force of other forms, such as church constitutions, patterns of worship and practice, hymnaries and traditional schemas of biblical interpretation. In so far as most churches have found they cannot do without confessions in some form, the best defence of the Reformation confessions lies in their wider use in the teaching activities of the congregation.

Survey of confessions

Virtually all the confessions discussed below are given in English translation in J. Pelikan and V. Hotchkiss, *Creeds and Confessions in the Christian Tradition*, 4 vols. (New Haven, 2003). Many are also found in P. Schaff, *The Creeds of Christendom*, 3 vols. (New York, 1877ff., best edn 1919); J. H. Leith, *Creeds of the Churches* (Richmond, VA, ³1982); A. C. Cochrane, *Reformed Confessions of the Sixteenth Century* (London, 1966).

**Schleitheim Confession* (1527), seven articles drafted by Michael Sattler (*c.* 1490–1527) and adopted by the Swiss Brethren, 'the free church of the Zwinglian Reformation'. They give a clear statement of the distinctive views of mainstream *Anabaptists.

**Augsburg Confession* (1530), the first major Protestant confession, a moderate account of Lutheran teachings compiled by *Melanchthon and presented to the imperial Diet (Parliament) of Augsburg. It retains an unrivalled status throughout *Lutheranism. In 1531 Melanchthon wrote an *Apology* for it in response to a Catholic *Confutation*. His subsequent revision of the Confession, softening in particular its assertion of Christ's real presence in the Supper, brought bitter controversy. It was the original, unaltered (*Invariata*), that was reaffirmed as the basic document of Lutheranism in the *Book of Concord* (see below). It starts with the Trinity, condemns ancient heretics and Anabaptists and says nothing on predestination (T. G. Tappert, *The Book of Concord*, Philadelphia, 1959).

Tetrapolitan Confession (1530), submitted to the same Diet by 'four cities' of South Germany led by Strasbourg (hence largely *Bucer's work). It was unable to follow the Lutherans' Augsburg Confession on the Lord's Supper, on which, *inter alia*, it sought to mediate between Lutherans and *Zwinglians (see *Eucharist).

First Helvetic (Swiss) Confession (1536), the first common confession of the Swiss Reformed cities, drawn up by *Bullinger and others, with help from Bucer and Capito (1478–1541), still hoping to reconcile the Swiss and the Lutherans. It begins with Scripture, gives prominence to church ministry, and covers temporal government (whose supreme task is to promote true religion) and marriage. It is also known as the Second Confession of Basel, where it was agreed. The First Confession of Basel (1534) was typical of earlier Swiss statements in having only local authority.

Genevan Confession (1536), produced by *Calvin and *Farel as part of the constitution of the city's newly reformed church. It was unique among the Reformation confessions in demanding subscription by all Geneva's citizens and residents – an impossibility, as events proved. Its twenty-one brief articles begin with Scripture as God's word, and include excommunication and the 'Christian vocation' of magistrates, but not predestination.

Second Helvetic (Swiss) Confession (1566), a revision of Bullinger's personal confession, approved at Zurich by the Swiss Reformed cities now including Geneva (but not Basel). Although a short book, it has been widely translated and as influential as perhaps the most mature of the Reformed confessions. It is marked throughout by a concern for continuity with the catholic orthodoxy of the early church, and by a practical, pastoral outlook. Article 1, on Scripture, declares that 'the preaching of the Word of God is the Word of God'. The involvement of Geneva built on the Zurich Consensus (*Consensus Tigurinus*, 1549) on the Lord's Supper, between Calvin and Farel for Geneva and Bullinger for the more Zwinglian Swiss churches. The approach of the latter probably predominates in the Consensus.

Gallican (French) Confession (1559), adopted at the first national synod of the Reformed churches at Paris. It was a recasting into forty articles of a draft sent from Geneva, with some significant deviations from the latter. Article 2 declares that God reveals himself first in creation and 'secondly, and more clearly' in his word, which the Genevan draft placed alone as Article 1. It acknowledges the three creeds, without Calvin's reservations. The synod at La Rochelle in 1571 reaffirmed it after minor revisions.

Scots Confession (1560), the first confession of the reformed Church of Scotland (superseded by the *Westminster Confession in 1647), drawn up by John *Knox, assisted by five other Johns – Douglas, Row, Spottiswoode, Willock and Winram. It rings with a spontaneous and even disorderly vigour, reflecting the critical haste of its production. It draws on a wide range of Reformed sources, spanning Knox's experiences on the continent and in England. God and creation come first, but election appears between incarnation and the cross. 'Out of this Kirk there is neither life nor eternal felicity' – but 'this Kirk is invisible, known only to God'. The notes of the true church include discipline as well as the word and sacraments. Condemned is the notion that the sacraments are merely 'naked and bare signs'. This lively, combative confession has enjoyed considerable modern appreciation (G. D. Henderson and J. Bulloch [eds.], *The Scots Confession* [modern English version], Edinburgh, 1960; K. Barth, *The Knowledge of God and the Service of God*, London, 1938).

Belgic Confession (1561), drawn up by Guido de Brès (1522–67) as an apologia for the persecuted Reformed of the Low Countries, finally becoming, at Dort in 1619 (see *Dort, Synod of), one of the doctrinal standards of the Dutch Reformed Church (with the *Heidelberg Catechism and the Canons of *Dort). It closely follows the Gallican Confession, e.g. in its apologetic dissociation from 'Anabaptists', although its statement on natural revelation is more careful.

Thirty-Nine Articles (1563), the basic confession of the Reformed Church of England (and hence of most other Anglican churches). Under Elizabeth I they were distilled from Cranmer's Forty-Two Articles of 1553, with a final change in 1571. Intended as an instrument of national religious unity, a *via media* between Rome and Anabaptism (not between Rome and Geneva), they reflect diverse continental influences – more Lutheran on predestination and in allowing beliefs and practices not contrary to Scripture, more Reformed on the sacraments. Their interpretation has been keenly disputed (cf. *Newman's *Tract 90*) (W. H. Griffith Thomas, *The Principles of Theology*, London, ^{5}1956; O. O'Donovan, *On the Thirty-Nine Articles*, Exeter, 1986).

Formula of Concord (1577), a long document which resolved Lutheran controversies between the 'Philippists', who followed the accommodating Melanchthon, and the 'Gnesio-Lutherans', the 'authentic' disciples of Luther himself. Compiled largely by James Andreae (1528–90), who also wrote an *Epitome*, and Martin *Chemnitz, its carefully balanced exposition had the effect of excluding rapprochement with the Calvinists, which the Melanchthonians hoped for. It was included in the Lutherans' *Book of Concord* (1580) together with: the three creeds; the Augsburg Confession and its *Apology*; Luther's *Smalcald Articles* and Melanchthon's *Treatise on the Power and Primacy of the Pope* (both 1537); and Luther's *Large* and *Small Catechisms*. This collection comprises all the generally accepted doctrinal standards of Lutheranism and is accepted by most Lutheran clergy at ordination (T. G. Tappert, *The Book of Concord*; E. Schlink, *The Theology of the Lutheran Confessions*, Philadelphia, 1961).

An irenic response to the Formula of Concord was the *Harmony of the Confessions of Faith of the Orthodox and Reformed Churches* published at Geneva in 1581. Produced by Jean Salvart (d. 1585), *Beza and others, this harmony of fifteen Protestant confessions, including Augsburg, argued that Protestant unity was not to be despaired of, but it had little appeal beyond the Reformed constituency (Peter Hall, *The Harmony of Protestant Confessions of Faith*, London, 1842).

Westminster Confession (1646), a highly systematic exposition of Calvinist orthodoxy (see *Reformed theology), of remarkable comprehensiveness, balance and precision, which was adopted by the Church of Scotland in 1647 and subsequently became the confession of most Presbyterian churches, and, with appropriate changes, of Congregationalists (and Particular Baptists) in Britain and America. It was the work of the Westminster Assembly's largely *Puritan divines, commissioned to produce a confession to unite Scotland and England. It purveys a developed, so-called 'scholastic' Calvinism, reflecting the influence of Puritan *covenant theology and of the Irish Articles of 1615 (which were briefly adopted by the [Episcopal] Church of Ireland, despite saying nothing about the necessity of episcopal ordination and the three orders of ministry, being chiefly written by James Ussher, 1581–1656). Its more controversial features include double predestination (alongside free *will and contingent 'second causes'), the covenant of works with *Adam, a Puritan doctrine of *assurance and a sabbatarian view of Sunday. Even its critics recognize its solidity and majesty (S. W. Carruthers [ed.], *The Westminster Confession of Faith ... with Notes*, Manchester, 1937; B. B. Warfield, *The Westminster Assembly and Its Work*, New York, 1931; A. I. C. Heron (ed.), *The Westminster Confession in the Church Today*, Edinburgh, 1982).

Cambridge Platform (1648) and *Savoy Declaration* (1658) were the fundamental formularies of, respectively, American and English *Congregationalism. In doctrine they essentially reproduced the Westminster Confession, with the changes needed to provide for a church polity of independent congregations (Schaff; Leith; W. Walker, *The Creeds and Platforms of Congregationalism*, New York, 1893).

Second London Baptist Confession (1677), known also as the Philadelphia Confession, similarly adapted Westminster Calvinism to *Baptist polity and baptism. It was the most widely accepted of Calvinist Baptist confessions (W. L. Lumpkin, *Baptist Confessions of Faith*, Valley Forge, rev. edn 1969). The New Hampshire Confession (1833) was a milder statement of Baptist Calvinist faith.

Confession of Dositheus (1672), the most important *Orthodox confession of modern times, defining Orthodox theology against Protestantism, but showing evidence of indebtedness to Roman Catholic thought; Orthodox are thus wary of placing too much weight on it as a statement of their faith. Dositheus (1641–1707) was patriarch of Jerusalem and presided over the synod there which canonized this confession. Its specific 'Calvinist' target was Cyril Lucaris (1572–1638), the patriarch of Constantinople who was strongly attracted to Protestantism. His own *Confession of Faith* (Geneva, 1629; G. A. Hadjiantoniou, *Protestant Patriarch*, Richmond, 1961) is a thoroughly Calvinist interpretation of Orthodox doctrine.

Bibliography

W. A. Curtis, *A History of the Creeds and Confessions of Faith* (Edinburgh, 1911); J. Pelikan, *Creeds and Confessions in the Christian Tradition*, vol. 4, *Credo* (New Haven and London, 2003); C. Plantinga, Jr, *A Place to Stand: A*

Reformed Study of Creeds and Confessions (Grand Rapids, 1979); E. Routley, *Creeds and Confessions* (London, 1962).

D. F. WRIGHT

CONFIRMATION

The rite called 'confirmation' has become a 'rite in search of a theology'. It developed in the Western church from the separation of a secondary part of the third-century baptismal rite from the actual (water) *baptism, and in the fifth century gained the Latin title '*confirmario*'. Whereas it appears to rest upon the apostolic precedent of a post-baptismal laying on of hands (Acts 8:14–17; 19:1–7), in fact no direct continuity of usage can be traced to these occurrences, and, even if they do provide some precedent, it is doubtful whether they should be viewed as normative for Christian initiation in the way that water baptism is.

The Gospels give no warrant for such a rite; the Acts of the Apostles has many instances of the use of water baptism without a subsequent laying on of hands (so that these instances in fact appear as exceptions); the two instances themselves have very little in common with each other (and in particular the Acts 8 passage has the laying on of hands far apart in time from water-baptism, whereas the Acts 19 passage has it in immediate sequence); and the Pauline corpus (whether understood narrowly or broadly) has no mention of this rite, though much about water baptism. The only further possible biblical evidence is the obscure reference in Heb. 6:2 (where *baptismōn* does not necessarily refer to baptisms at all, and is not always translated as baptisms in the English versions). In general, there is silence, and there is no theology of initiation (whether outward and sacramental, or inward and regenerative) which would correspond to such a ceremony. There is reference to water baptism in some of the earliest post-apostolic authors, notably Ignatius of Antioch, the *Didache*, the *Shepherd of Hermas* (see *Apostolic Fathers) and Justin Martyr (see *Apologists). However, they too are silent about a post-baptismal laying on of hands or *anointing. The most primitive traceable practice, whether in the West or in the East, seems to have been simply water baptism, for adults and probably for infants, and this led straight into participation in Communion (see *Eucharist).

A post-baptismal laying on of hands in initiation is first to be discovered in the West in the late second century in *Tertullian and soon after in *Hippolytus. The East did not follow this until the second half of the fourth century, and then used anointing (the 'seal'). It still continues this practice to the present day (giving both water baptism and the 'seal' even to infants in one single rite of initiation which leads them into Communion). In the West the complex rite of water baptism (with or without anointing), laying on of hands, giving of the kiss of peace, and participation in Communion, held sway till around the sixth century, but afterwards broke into separate parts in most places. *Augustine's doctrine of original *sin, and the necessity of baptism immediately subsequent upon birth where any chance of death existed, led to clinical baptism of infants from the early Middle Ages. Confirmation (as it was called from the fifth century onwards) could not then take place at the same time (as it usually still required a bishop to give it), and the age of confirmation floated upwards in an unplanned way to suit the actual circumstances in which a bishop might be present to confirm. The title '*confirmatio*' was used from the fifth century onwards of the detached episcopal laying on of hands. Thus the rite came, in process of time, to be interpreted not as initiatory, but (as its use declared it to be) 'confirmatory'. *Thomas Aquinas has it so far detached from baptismal initiation that he allows that ordination can proceed without the candidate having being confirmed!

Thus the Reformers inherited a pattern in which confirmation was given by anointing, and was viewed as a sacrament of strengthening or growth, for candidates at any age from infancy (though that was rare by the sixteenth century) to adulthood, though a mean age may have been between three and nine. The Reformers agreed that water baptism was the sole sacramental initiation, and did not wish to add confirmation to the rite of baptism, which in general they still administered to infants. Instead, they took the medieval pattern to its logical conclusion, raised the age of confirmation to between thirteen and sixteen, required massive *catechizing to precede it, and used it as a rite for adult admission to Communion. In this they were assisted by some bogus early church history promulgated by *Calvin, and believed on his authority. In fact, the new usage was unprecedented. What happened was that the outward sign reverted to the laying on of hands, which replaced 'the Bishop of Rome's buttering'. The Church of England *Book of Common Prayer* adopted exactly this discipline of Calvin's, and it has run to the present day. On the other hand, Article XXV of 1563 (see *Thirty-Nine Articles) added to the Edwardian Article a paragraph which said that confirmation is not to be counted as a sacrament of the gospel, as it arises from the corrupt following of the apostles, and has no visible sign or ceremony ordained of God. The *Book of Common Prayer* corresponded to this in that the prayer at the laying on of hands had no sacramental content or character ('Defend, O Lord, this thy servant with thy heavenly grace . . .'); and, when a section on the *sacraments was added to the Anglican Catechism in 1604, even though it occurred within the confirmation service and was preparing candidates for confirmation, it asserted that there are but two sacraments of the gospel, and made no reference to confirmation whatsoever.

The twentieth century saw differing attempts to produce a satisfying theology, and to bring pastoral and liturgical practice into accord with it. Non-episcopal churches have followed Calvin's pattern. Anglicans have first flirted with the notion that water-plus-the laying-on-of-hands equals full initiation, and have attempted to 're-integrate' the 'disintegrated' parts of the primitive (i.e. Hippolytan) rite; but more latterly they have been ready to see water baptism as full sacramental initiation, and have started to move towards child and even infant Communion on the basis of it. Roman Catholics have greatly widened the use of presbyteral confirmation (which has a long history in that church), and have sought in some places to associate it with first Communion. But thinness of the theological foundations in both Scripture, history and systematic theology still generally leaves it a rite in search of a theology.

Bibliography

R. J. Bastian, *The Effects of Confirmation in Recent Catholic Thought* (Rome, 1962); J. Behrens, *Confirmation, Sacrament of Grace: The Theology, Practice and Law of the Roman Catholic Church and the Church of England* (Leominster, 1995); C. Buchanan, *Anglican Confirmation* (Nottingham, 1986); G. Dix, *The Theology of Confirmation in Relation to Baptism* (London, 1946); J. D. G. Dunn, *Baptism in the Holy Spirit* (London, 1970); J. D. C. Fisher, *Confirmation Then and Now* (London, 1978); G. W. H. Lampe, *The Seal of the Spirit* (London, 1951); B. Neunhauser, *Baptism and Confirmation* (Freiburg, 1964); E. C. Whitaker, *Sacramental Initiation Complete in Baptism* (Nottingham, 1975).

C. O. BUCHANAN

CONFUCIANISM AND CHRISTIANITY

Confucianism has been the most significant philosophical system for centuries among the Chinese, Japanese and Korean peoples in providing ethical principles and contributing to the stability of society. While Mao Tse-tung (Mao Zedong) and other communist leaders in mainland China tried to exterminate Confucianism from Chinese society for hindering the cause of the communist revolution, Confucianism was strongly rejuvenated in Asia by the governments of the Republic of China (Taiwan) and Singapore in line with the resurgence of traditional values.

Confucianism is considered by the Chinese as a philosophy rather than a religion; but 'philosophy' is not here used in the normal sense of the word in the West. Confucianism is more than a philosophy, as it combines philosophy with life itself.

There are similarities between Confucianism and Christianity in their *ethical teaching and their concern for peace in family, society and nation. However, the methods of achieving peace and tranquillity in society are radically different in the two.

(1) Confucius (551–479 BC) taught the golden rule and the moral perfection of the individual through harmony in five basic human relationships: between ruler and subject, husband and wife, parents and children, brother and sister, and brother/sister and friends. The ideal man in Confucianism is called Jün Tze (gentleman). He is not necessarily an aristocrat, but one who cultivates the moral characteristics of *Jen* (benevolence, love of others), *Shiao* (filial piety) and *Li* (sense of propriety), and who keeps the five virtues of courtesy, magnanimity, good faith, diligence, and kindness. The ideal man knows how to cultivate himself, how to rule his family, and how to govern his nation properly. The chief objective of Confucianism is to establish peace and order in society through a strong moral basis with the help of rituals and music.

In Christianity, Jesus' Sermon on the Mount (Matt. 5–7) in the NT and the Ten Commandments (Exod. 20) in the OT similarly emphasize a moral and peaceful society. This may provide a starting place for communication between Confucianism and Christianity.

(2) In Confucianism, a man's chief concern should be the duties of the present life rather than what will happen after death. There is, therefore, an emphasis on the 'now' of this present world. When Confucius was asked how a man should serve the spirits of the dead, he replied, 'As you are not yet able to serve the living, how will you be able to serve the spirits of the dead?' (*Analect* XI.11). When he was asked about death, he said, 'As you know nothing yet about life, how can you know anything about death?' (ibid.). Death and life must be accepted with resignation as the result of natural law, and they are determined by the 'will of heaven' (*Ming*) rather than either fate or divine *predestination.

By contrast with biblical teaching on *sin, Confucianism considers wrongdoing as improper, inexpedient and antisocial, without any reference to man's direct responsibility to a higher being or God. Most important is human reformation. Scripture, on the other hand, presents a doctrine of *salvation, *repentance, and forgiveness of sins from God (see *Guilt and forgiveness).

The Bible, in addition, gives due weight to both present and eternal existence, and stresses that people's earthly lives possess significance for them and God precisely in the light of their future existence (see *Eschatology; *Judgment of God).

There is also a radical difference between Confucianism and Christianity in the areas of *epistemology and methods of achieving human goals. The former starts with man and nature (humanism), the latter with the self-revelation of God (in a supernatural, theocentric and Christocentric outlook in life). Confucius was an agnostic and taught the basic goodness of human nature which man can cultivate for the betterment of humankind. For Confucius, man can achieve the peaceful society by his own ingenuity.

On the other hand, the Christian Bible teaches that individuals can do nothing apart from God and his *grace, and are totally dependent upon him for moral and spiritual life (John 15:5). The question of whether people need God for their moral and spiritual life distinguishes Christianity from Confucianism. Those in the West who deny supernatural elements in Christianity are attracted to Confucianism, while others in the Orient who see finitude and failure in humanism are open to Christianity.

Bibliography

Ching Feng, quarterly magazine produced by Tao Fong Shan Ecumenical Centre, New Territories, Hong Kong; Julia Ching, *Confucianism and Christianity* (Tokyo, 1977); Paul E. Kauffman, *Confucius, Mao and Christ* (Hong Kong, 1978); Bong Rin Ro (ed.), *Christian Alternatives to Ancestor Practices* (Talchung, Taiwan, 1985); Xinzhong Yao, *Confucianism and Christianity* (Brighton, 1996); J. D. Young, *Confucianism and Christianity: The First Encounter* (Hong Kong, 1983).

BONG RIN RO

CONGAR, YVES (1904–95)

Yves Congar was one of the leading Catholic theologians of the twentieth century. He regarded his vocation as being 'at once and by the same vein, priestly and religious, *Dominican and *Thomist, ecumenical and ecclesiological'. He contributed to the recovery of the biblical images of the church which emphasize its mystical nature. Congar's vision for ecclesial renewal led to a profound transformation of the Catholic Church, its relationship with the other churches and the world. The Second *Vatican Council (1962–5) became the catalyst for this change, and its documents gave authoritative expression to his most important ideas on the church. As he explains, 'I was filled to overflowing. All the things to which I gave special attention issued in the Council: ecclesiology, ecumenism, reform of the Church, the lay state, mission, ministries, *collegiality, return to the sources and Tradition.' Congar viewed his immense work at the Council as a part, albeit the most important part, of a vocation dedicated to the service of truth. Honoured as a pioneer of church unity and a champion of the laity, it is true to say that, for many in the Catholic Church, his role as reformer is ambiguous and his theology remains obfuscated to the present day.

Bibliography

V. Dunne, *Prophecy in the Church: The Vision of Yves Congar*, European University Studies

23 (Frankfurt, 2000); G. Flynn, *Yves Congar's Vision of the Church in a World of Unbelief* (Aldershot, 2004); *idem* (ed.), *Yves Congar: Theologian of the Church* (Louvain, 2005); E. T. Groppe, *Yves Congar's Theology of the Holy Spirit* (New York, 2004); A. Nichols, *Yves Congar* (London and Wilton, 1989).

G. FLYNN

CONGREGATIONALISM

The origins of Congregationalism may be traced back to England in the reign of Queen Elizabeth I (1558–1603). Her objective for the church was an enforced uniformity, but there were those who wanted to see the national church reorganized on *presbyterian (see also *Church government) rather than episcopal lines. Others, however, repudiated the whole concept of a state church and favoured the 'gathered church' principle. These became known as 'Separatists' (later 'Independents') and were the forerunners of the Congregationalists. They contended that the *church should consist only of those who had personally responded to the call of Christ, and who had covenanted with him and with one another to live together as his disciples.

A leading figure among the early Independents was Robert Browne (1553–1633), a Cambridge graduate who has been called the father of English separatism. In 1582 he published in Holland his famous *Treatise of Reformation without Tarrying for Anie* in which he set forth congregational principles. He asserted that 'the Church planted or gathered is a company or number of Christians or believers, which, by a willing covenant made with their God, are under the government of God and Christ and keep his laws in one holy communion'. Such churches, he claimed, are subject to neither bishops nor magistrates. Ordination is not vested in elders, but is at the hands of the whole church.

In various areas, companies of men and women put Browne's teaching into practice. Rather than submit to ecclesiastical regimentation, many sought religious freedom in Holland. Some of these later crossed the Atlantic where churches of the congregational pattern became one of the formative influences in the New World. It was from John Robinson's (*c.* 1575–1625) church at Leiden that the 'Pilgrim Fathers' set off in 1620 in the *Mayflower*. Congregationalism became the recognized church order in Connecticut and Massachusetts and continued to be so until the first quarter of the ninteenth century. Meanwhile, in England the pattern of church life taught by Robert Browne spread with the formation of Congregational and *Baptist churches throughout the country, particularly in the later seventeenth century. Following the Act of Uniformity (1662), over 2,000 clergy opted for nonconformity rather than conform to the *Book of Common Prayer* and an episcopal order. The faith and beliefs of the Congregationalists were expressed in the Savoy Declaration of 1658, just as the Westminster Confession a few years earlier had expressed the Presbyterian viewpoint.

During the following century there was less obvious growth in nonconformity, but two great Independents of this period call for mention – the hymn writers Isaac Watts (1674–1748) and Philip Doddridge (1702–51). A number of Independent and Presbyterian churches at this time became virtually *unitarian in doctrine, and dissenters lost much of their earlier zeal.

The Evangelical Revival, however, brought new life to the churches as a whole. In 1831 the Congregational Union was formed with the primary objective of 'promoting evangelical religion in connection with the Congregational denomination'. Insistence upon the independence of the local Christian community was never regarded as precluding a loose fellowship of independent local churches for purposes of mutual consultation and edification.

One of the great names in Congregationalism during the second half of the nineteenth century was that of R. W. Dale (1829–95). He was one of a long line of distinguished ministers at Carrs Lane Congregational Church in Birmingham. Dale combined moral fervour, intellectual power and intense religious conviction. He was the embodiment of nonconformity's interest in social and educational reforms. He maintained that Christian convictions either issued in political action or evaporated in pietistic sentimentality. He became a national figure and sat on the Royal Commission for Education, and was the ally and friend of leaders of the Liberal Party. It was said that in the city of Birmingham no major municipal decision would be taken before Dale's views had been canvassed. Dale found time to write a History of Congregationalism and was also instrumental in the founding of Mansfield College, Oxford (1886), the first principal of which, A. M. Fairbairn

(1838–1912), was a significant mediator of German critical scholarship in Great Britain.

During the latter part of the nineteenth century the influence of biblical criticism was increasingly felt in Britain; Congregationalists and Presbyterians were, in many cases, ready to imbibe the teachings of '*liberal' theologians. 'Congregationalists drank more deeply of [them] than did any of the others. Congregationalism, freed by its new federation from the bondage of parochialism, and freed traditionally by its intellectual ethos from any risk of becoming mentally stagnant, offered enthusiastic hospitality to the new critical teachings on the Bible which came from Germany. There has always been a keen and energetic "modernist" movement in Congregationalism' (E. Routley, *The Story of Congregationalism*).

In Britain, Congregationalism took a decisive step in 1966 when local Congregational churches were invited to covenant together to form the Congregational Church. This step was later followed by the union of the Congregational Church with the Presbyterian Church of England, leading to the formation of the United Reformed Church. With this new development, Congregationalism, as traditionally understood, largely disappeared from the scene in England, but not in Ireland, Scotland and Wales, although it remains the basis of church order in Baptist churches as well as in a growing number of independent evangelical churches.

A group of Congregationalists, determined to save historic independency, formed themselves into the Congregational Federation. Their quarrel with the scheme of union was not so much on theological grounds, but on the issue of the freedom of the local church to govern its own affairs under the direction of the Holy Spirit. The Federation believes strongly in the value of unity in diversity and deplores any tendency towards regimentation. A number of strongly evangelical Congregational churches did not enter the scheme of union, on the grounds that it was one further example of ecumenical compromise. They were critical of the scheme on the grounds of its theological ambiguity, as well as its abandonment of the principle of independency. They are linked together in an Evangelical Fellowship of Congregational Churches.

Worldwide, Congregationalism has been closely involved with the *ecumenical movement. This fact no doubt explains to some extent the underlying reasons for the various mergers which have taken place in different parts of the world between Congregational, Presbyterian and – in some cases – Methodist churches. The general trend in Congregationalism worldwide has been away from independency.

The Congregational system of church government has often been wrongly described as democratic. Ideally, the church is seen as being under the rule of Christ, and the church meeting seeks to discern his will. It is hardly surprising that many Congregational churches have been relatively small in membership – a large congregation finds it harder to work out the principle of 'Christocracy' through the medium of the church meeting. In a Congregational church the members are empowered to elect their own church officers and to choose their own minister. Membership of the church is on profession of personal faith in Christ, and new members are normally welcomed by being given the right hand of fellowship at a Communion service.

Bibliography

R. W. Dale, *Manual of Congregational Principles* (London, 1884); D. Jenkins, *Congregationalism: A Restatement* (London, 1954); A. Peel, *A Brief History of English Congregationalism* (London, 1931); E. Routley, *The Story of Congregationalism* (London, 1961); A. P. F. Sell, *Saints: Visible, Orderly and Catholic: The Congregational Idea of the Church* (Allison Park, 1986); W. Walker, *The Creeds and Platforms of Congregationalism* (New York, 1893); B. R. White, *The English Separatist Tradition from the Marian Martyrs to the Pilgrim Fathers* (Oxford, 1971).

G. W. KIRBY

CONGRUISM, see MERIT

CONSCIENCE

Although the language of conscience (Lat. *conscientia*; Gk *syneidesis*) was partially inherited from Roman Stoicism, the *patristic usage of the terms attempted to reflect scriptural concepts. For example, Ambrose of Milan wrote of conscience as a reflective self-opening whereby men are encountered and probed by God in grace and in judgment. Since the Fathers, Christian accounts of conscience have mainly been shaped by two distinctions.

Prospective and retrospective conscience

The first distinguishes between whether conscience is prospective (looking towards future action; 'directive') or retrospective (judging past action).

Prospective: The medieval period developed the most thorough systematization of a prospective account of conscience whereby it became an integral aspect of practical reason. *Thomas Aquinas first revised *Jerome's influential concept of *synteresis* (a linguistic corruption of *syneidesis*) to interpret it as an error-free, innate, human habit which contains the basic principles of natural law, and then defined conscience (*conscientia*) as an act (not a faculty) in which these principles are discursively applied to specific situations. As M. G. Baylor says, 'Conscience, for [Aquinas], was pre-eminently a part of the operations of the practical intellect as it reasoned to a decision about what should be done in concrete situations that confront the individual' (*Action and Person*, p. 42). Since, for Aquinas, the conscience can err, subsequent prospective accounts have tended towards a pastoral concern for correcting the conscience so that it gets the application right. This is often, though not necessarily, to the exclusion of conscience's retrospective function and, indeed, any essential reference to God.

Retrospective: Accounts which argue for an exclusively retrospective function have traditionally responded to this tendency by repositioning conscience within an explicitly soteriological framework. The Fathers characteristically failed to connect conscience to the *cross, while the scholastic treatments were aiming at an account of created human anthropology. But *Luther, the leading proponent of a return to a retrospective conscience, explained conscience as basic to a person's encounter with God in *judgment. On the one hand, conscience is how a person experiences the coincidence of his own painful awareness of sin and the terrifying condemnation of God. This experience is available to believer and unbeliever alike. On the other hand, by faith in God's grace, conscience is how a believer experiences the justificatory declaration of God's righteousness. On this account, which many believe reflects New Testament usage (cf. C. A. Pierce, *Conscience in the New Testament*), a Christian conscience, following *justification by faith, is characterized by assurance of peace with God. A logical corollary is that conscience becomes secondary to faith not only in soteriology, but also in *moral theology. For conscience under the influence of faith does not operate primarily as a judge of particular acts, but rather focuses on God's judgment on the whole person: *simul iustus et peccator*. Thus retrospective accounts have argued that conscience is a power of the soul rather than a habit of natural moral knowledge which instructs action. *Synteresis* slips out of sight to be replaced by *faith as the spring of ethical life.

Theological and psychological accounts

The second distinction pertains to conscience as theological and eschatological on the one hand, and psychological and sociological on the other. Historically, this distinction can be traced through the Renaissance, Freud, *Nietzsche and *Barth among others. Conceptually, this distinction focuses on whether conscience can be separated from the gracious presence of God. In the aftermath of the Reformation, some Renaissance thinkers' description of conscience as a form of 'God's providential government', separable from God's gracious activity, led to its development into an unforgiving demand for personal self-authenticity (O. O'Donovan, *The Ways of Judgment*, p. 307). This approach is congruent with, though not necessarily responsible for, modern accounts of the liberty of conscience which have found favour with contemporary Roman Catholic scholars. However, the decisive conceptual break was made by Freud and Nietzsche, who sought to explain conscience as a pathology which simply reflected back parental or societal norms rather than as something essentially theological. This psychological account, supported by modern sociological trends and the now largely discredited behaviourist school, has been accused of committing the genetic fallacy of mistaking mechanistic origin for total explanation. There remains too the question of whether accounts of conscience should start from the agent or from the moral field within which the agent operates, the latter lending itself more to theological interpretations.

A more radical analysis emerges from Christian *eschatology and, specifically, pneumatology. Karl Barth argued that conscience is present only in Christians and is judicial not executive. He proposed that conscience is the voice of God and the voice of the eschatological 'I' prayerfully united in the *Holy Spirit as a judgment from the future upon the present self.

However, these eschatological judgments are largely incommunicable to others because of fallen, human epistemology and so cannot be saved up as a store of moral knowledge. This eschatological reassertion of the traditional Reformation emphasis on soteriology, although involving the loss of a natural conscience, has refocused discussion of conscience today in Protestant theology. The early twentieth-century Roman Catholic emphasis on autonomy, critiqued by Barth, has been overtaken by sophisticated accounts such as that presented in the papal encyclical, *Veritatis Splendor*.

Bibliography

K. Barth, *Ethics* (ET, Edinburgh, 1981); M. G. Baylor, *Action and Person: Conscience in Late Scholasticism and the Young Luther* (Leiden, 1977); John Paul II, *Veritatis Splendor* (ET, London, 1993); O. O'Donovan, *The Ways of Judgment* (Grand Rapids, 2005); C. A. Pierce, *Conscience in the New Testament* (London, 1955); Thomas Aquinas, *Summa Theologiae* 1a2ae q.18–19; Vatican II, *Dignitatis Humanae* in A. Flannery (ed.), *Vatican Council II: The Conciliar and Post Conciliar Documents* (Dublin and Clonskeagh, 1975); J. Webster, 'Conscience', in J. Y. Lacoste (ed.), *Encyclopaedia of Christian Theology* (London and New York, 2005).

J. W. S. Hordern

CONSERVATIVE THEOLOGY

The correlative terms 'liberal' and 'conservative' were coined in the early nineteenth century to express opposing political traditions and later transferred into Christian theology. The tradition of 'liberal' theology from F. D. E. *Schleiermacher to Paul *Tillich attempted to commend Christian faith to the sceptics of 'modern' *Enlightenment thought, but conservative theologians took the view that in the attempt, the liberal tradition was conceding too much to '*modernity'. Rather than visualizing two completely separate and opposed traditions, however, it is better to recognize a spectrum of theological views from liberal to conservative. Different kinds of conservative theology also need to be recognized, depending on which particular Christian tradition is being 'conserved'.

The nineteenth-century Roman Catholic Church was opposed to both political and theological liberalism, and their conservatism was formulated in the First *Vatican Council (1869–70) which promulgated the doctrine of papal infallibility. This strong conservatism led to the condemnation of Catholic 'modernism' early in the twentieth century, and was dominant in Rome until the Second Vatican Council (1962–5). In the Church of England, the Tractarian movement of the 1830s initiated a conservative *Anglo-Catholic tradition which tried to deny that the Church of England was Protestant and attempted to revive the liturgy and practices of the medieval period. In Protestant Germany, 'conservative' theology, represented by figures such as Adolf *Schlatter, was overshadowed by the major figures of Liberalism in the Ritschlian school (see *Ritschl, Albrecht). But after the First World War there was a more conservative reaction led by Karl *Barth and Emil *Brunner, which saw itself as reviving the emphases of the Reformation and embraced 'conservative' doctrines such as *Chalcedonian *Christology, the *Trinity and substitutionary *atonement.

In the English-speaking world meantime, the growing strength of *evangelical Christianity in the nineteenth century had to meet questions raised by Darwinian science, and the introduction of the historical-critical approach to the Bible. A strongly conservative Calvinist theology (see *Reformed theology), emphasizing the authority of Scripture, was maintained particularly in America by the 'Old *Princeton' school (whose heirs were later to dismiss Barth and Brunner as 'modernists'), and their belief in biblical inerrancy (see *Infallibility and inerrancy of the Bible) was one of the ingredients in the emergence of popular '*fundamentalism'. Many fundamentalists also embraced premillennialism (see *Millennium) or *dispensationalism and regarded Darwinian evolution as contrary to belief in creation.

The end of the twentieth century saw the decline of liberal theology, the rise of 'post-liberalism' in North America, and a widespread revival of 'conservative' doctrines of Christology and the Trinity across the church at large. A revived evangelicalism, fed by an increasingly vibrant tradition of conservative biblical scholarship, distanced itself from fundamentalism, but remained doctrinally conservative and grew in influence in Protestant Europe and North America as more liberal churches declined. Churches originally founded by conservative evangelical missionaries in Africa, Asia and

South America grew even more. In North America (but not elsewhere) conservative theology is often linked with political and social 'conservatism'.

See also: LIBERAL THEOLOGY.

Bibliography

D. W. Bebbington, *Evangelicalism in Modern Britain: A History from the 1730s to the 1980s* (London, 1989); A. I. C. Heron, *A Century of Protestant Theology* (London, 1980); G. M. Marsden, *Understanding Fundamentalism and Evangelicalism* (Grand Rapids, 1991); P. Toon, *Protestants and Catholics* (Ann Arbor, 1984).

T. A. NOBLE

CONSTANTINE (c. 272–337)

Constantine the Great reigned as Roman Emperor between 306 and 337. It is hard to overstate his impact on the history of the Christian church and on the development of Christian thought. He was the first Roman emperor to declare himself a Christian when, at the Milvian Bridge in Rome in 312, he saw a vision calling him to conquer in Christ and replaced the pagan insignia of his army with the cross. His Edict of Milan in 313 announced religious toleration for Christians and brought an end to a severe period of persecution of the church. He convened synods and *councils to resolve doctrinal disputes and encourage unity among Christians, notably in Arles (314) and *Nicaea (325). Under his reign, the church was given the opportunity to engage with the politics of the Roman Empire for the first time and had quickly to come to terms with its new imperial role.

While there is no doubt about the significance of Constantine for the church, there has been controversy about the genuineness of his faith and how to evaluate his impact. The first Christians beneficiaries of the change in the church's fortunes were enthusiastic about the virtues of their emperor. In his *Oration in Praise of Constantine* (335), Eusebius of Caesarea (*c*. 260–*c*. 340) called Constantine the paradigm of true religion, ordained by God to show the proof of the conquest of Christ through the rise of the Roman Empire. Christians of later times and different political contexts sometimes saw things differently, however: an Anabaptist tract published around 1530 is representative in dating the 'fall of the church' to its involvement with temporal power and the sword following Constantine's conversion (W. R. Estep, *The Anabaptist Story*, Grand Rapids and Cambridge, ³1996). John *Wesley thought that the golden age of the church had been corrupted by riches, honours and power given to its ministers under Constantine and wrote that with Constantine 'not the golden but the iron age of the church commenced' (T. Jackson [ed.], *The Works of John Wesley*, Grand Rapids, 1978, vol. 6, pp. 261–262).

More recently, Stanley *Hauerwas has repeated the Anabaptist critique that the church was wrong to use the power of this world for the sake of the kingdom, but Oliver O'Donovan has argued in response that contemporary Christians saw Constantine's conversion as a sign that the powers had become subject to the rule of Christ in accordance with biblical prophecy. Jacob Burckhardt suggested in 1853 that Constantine took up Christianity driven merely by ambition and lust for power, but most have doubted the validity of this judgment.

See also: CHRISTENDOM; STATE.

Bibliography

T. D. Barnes, *Constantine and Eusebius* (Cambridge, 1981); N. H. Baynes, *Constantine the Great and the Christian Church* (London, ²1972); J. Burckhardt, *The Age of Constantine the Great* (ET, London, 1949); H. A. Drake, *In Praise of Constantine: A Historical Study and New Translation of Eusebius' Tricennial Orations* (Berkeley, 1976); *idem*, 'Constantine and Consensus', *Church History* 64, 1995, pp. 1–15; S. Hauerwas, *After Christendom* (Nashville, 1991); A. Kee, *Constantine Versus Christ: The Triumph of Ideology* (London, 1982); O. O'Donovan, *The Desire of the Nations: Rediscovering the Roots of Political Theology* (Cambridge, 1996).

D. L. CLOUGH

CONSTANTINOPLE, COUNCIL OF

The First Council of Constantinople met in 381 and, although it only included 150 bishops from the Eastern Roman Empire, is regarded as the second ecumenical council, the first being the Council of *Nicaea of 325. It was called by the newly appointed emperor, Theodosius, and ended the *Arian controversy (at least within the empire). It rejected the various alternatives and re-affirmed the doctrine of the Nicene Creed of 325 that the Son was *homoousios* with the Father. This word, meaning 'of the same being' (sometimes translated 'consubstantial') had been rejected not only by Arians, but by many who are misleadingly called 'Semi-Arians'. The council acknowledged the deity of the Son and by 381 they had been convinced that the affirmation of this term was the only way to rule out Arianism.

The documents of the council have not survived, but it is regarded as certain that the Nicene-Constantinopolitan Creed, documented seventy years later at the Council of *Chalcedon (451), must have been approved in 381. It is different in detail from the original Nicene *Creed of 325, but is recited today as 'the Nicene Creed'. In the third article the council gave a much fuller doctrine of the *Holy Spirit, thus excluding from the church the 'Macedonians', who accepted the deity of the Son, but not of the Spirit.

The council was not however entirely harmonious. After the death of its first chairman, Meletius of Antioch, *Gregory of Nazianzus, now recognized as archbishop of Constantinople, took the chair. But he was evidently unhappy that the deity of the Spirit was only strongly implied by saying that the Spirit 'proceeds from the Father' and was to be 'worshipped and glorified'. This followed the preference of his late friend Basil, whose brother, Gregory of Nyssa, was a member of the council. Gregory of Nazianzus would have preferred an explicit statement that the Spirit was God, *homoousios* with the Father and the Son. He had also been displeased that the strict Nicene Paulinus had not been recognized as bishop of Antioch in place of his late rival, Meletius. When a party of Egyptian bishops arrived, led by Timothy, the new archbishop of Alexandria, and objected to Gregory's recognition as archbishop of Constantinople (since he had already been *de jure* bishop of Sasima and *de facto* bishop of Nazianzus), Gregory resigned in disgust. The council elected a layman, Nectarius, as archbishop and third chairman of the council.

See also: Councils; Trinity.

Bibliography
G. L. Bray, *Creeds, Councils and Christ* (Leicester, 1984); R. P. C. Hanson, *The Search for the Christian Doctrine of God* (Edinburgh, 1988); J. N. D. Kelly, *Early Christian Creeds* (London, 1972); idem, *Early Christian Doctrines* (London, 1978); A. M. Ritter, *Das Konzil von Konstantinopel und sein Symbol* (Göttingen, 1965).

T. A. Noble

CONSUMERISM

Consumerism is a possibility where a significant proportion of a human population has surplus wealth after providing for their basic needs. Once needs are met, further spending must be on goods that are chosen because they are desired rather than needed, and manufacturers of unnecessary goods seek to stimulate these desires and encourage this spending. Consumerism characterizes a society where the consumption of luxury goods has become a significant aspect of personal and social identity and members of society are predominantly understood as consumers of goods and services. Scholars differ on when consumerism originated, but there is strong evidence of a significant increase in consumer goods in late seventeenth- and eighteenth-century England. One of the features of a consumerist society is that the motif of consumption tends to expand well beyond products on sale: citizens become consumers of education, politics and even interpersonal relationships. Interaction with others in these spheres is then reduced to whether consumers are getting 'value' for the 'price' they are paying. Another is that the satisfaction promised after consumption turns out to be illusory because the desires promoted must be insatiable in order to sustain the markets that depend upon them.

Different theories have been offered to explain how choices are made in such a consumerist context. Thorstein Veblen sought to understand economic activity through neo-Darwinian natural selection and saw consumption as a competitive behaviour, aimed at impressing others and gaining social status. Here, the motivation to buy an expensive car is to be seen as someone wealthy enough to be able to afford it. This fails to account for consumption that is not apparent to others, however, as well as being inattentive to complexities such as disagreements about how status should be assigned to goods. Peter Sedgwick argues that theologians have depended too heavily on Veblen to understand consumerism, and draws on the work of Jürgen Habermas to argue that consumerism is a quest for personal identity in a *postmodern context where the institutions that used to provide identity no longer command allegiance. He argues that instead of condemning consumer culture, Christians should attempt to pose a creative alternative to consumerism. Others such as Timothy Gorringe and Sallie McFague call for resistance to consumerism rather than engagement with it, so that consumption of goods is related to human need instead of manufactured desire.

See also: POVERTY AND WEALTH.

Bibliography
C. Bartholomew and T. Moritz (eds.), *Christ and Consumerism* (Carlisle, 2000); Z. Bauman, *Work, Consumerism and the New Poor* (Milton Keynes, 1998); T. Gorringe, *Fair Shares: Ethics and the Global Economy* (New York, 1999); J. Habermas, *Legitimation Crisis* (Boston, 1975); S. McFague, *Life Abundant: Rethinking Theology and Economy for a Planet in Peril* (Minneapolis, 2001); N. McKendrick, J. Brewer and J. H. Plumb (eds.), *The Birth of a Consumer Society* (Bloomington, 1982); W. Schweiker and C. Mathewes (eds.), *Having: Property and Possession in Religious and Social Life* (Grand Rapids and Cambridge, 2004); P. Sedgwick, *The Market Economy and Christian Ethics* (Cambridge, 1999); D. Slater, *Consumer Culture and Modernity* (Cambridge, 2007); R. Tawney, *The Acquisitive Society* (New York, 1920); T. Veblen, *The Theory of the Leisure Class: An Economic Study of Institutions* (London, 1925).

D. L. CLOUGH

CONTARINI, GASPARO (1483–1542)
Born into a Venetian aristocratic family, Contarini was influenced in his youth by the civic *humanism widespread in Italy, and even as a lay person combined a passion to reform the pastoral and educational work of the church with a personal study of Scripture and particularly the Pauline letters. His understanding of *justification by faith, which he shared with a fascinating circle of friends, lay and clerical, men and women, led him to be critical of meritorious good works. As a Venetian diplomat, he became aware of the strength of reforming movements in Germany, and urged the reform of the *papacy, especially its civil service, or Curia. Pope Paul III appointed him a cardinal in 1535, and he headed a reforming group which sought to regain unity of the church by dialogue with moderate Lutherans. In 1541 the emperor, Charles V, briefly favoured such attempts at reconciliation at Regensburg, and Contarini as papal representative encouraged an agreement with the Lutherans on justification; discussion broke down, however, on the sacraments and church authority. Contarini died in 1542, and the Council of *Trent effectively ended such mediatory attempts.

Bibliography
E. G. Gleason, *Gasparo Contarini: Venice, Rome and Reform* (Berkeley and Los Angeles, 1993); P. C. Matheson, *Cardinal Contarini at Regensburg* (Oxford, 1972).

P. C. MATHESON

CONTEMPORARY THEOLOGICAL TRENDS
Contemporary theology is characterized by such greatly divergent methods and proposals that any neat map of the territory is exceedingly difficult to draw. Partly this is because some dominating models of an earlier generation have substantially been replaced (*Bultmann) while others have receded (*Tillich), but still others have been revived (*Barth); partly this is because much modern theology is pluralist, spanning different confessional and sometimes religious traditions; and partly this is because theology's conversation partners are no longer simply history, ethics and philosophy, but also, for example, social theories and the natural sciences.

Questions of *method remain at the forefront, with heightened interest in issues of pluralism. Despite some revisionist versions of *liberalism (D. Tracy), approaches labelled '*post-liberal' often hold the momentum. Traditional areas of prolegomena, such as the relation of *faith and reason or the scope of *natural theology, remain under discussion, along with efforts to appropriate *hermeneutical thinkers such as H. G. Gadamer and

P. *Ricœur, and topics such as the role of the *imagination or non-literal language. However, 'non-' or 'post-foundationalist' approaches desire to dominate, building on S. *Hauerwas's emphasis on the specific virtues of Christian communities, H. Frei's recovery of biblical narrative, and G. Lindbeck's 'cultural-linguistic' definition of doctrine as the second-order regulative grammar for first-order religious speech such as prayer. The nature of '*narrative theology' remains unclear and the scope of postliberalism broad, but the Anglo-American world now sees renewed interest in Barth and in serious dogmatic theology without apologetic nervousness. Recent interest in the Roman Catholic Hans Urs von *Balthasar has turned some attention to theological *aesthetics (as also in the Eastern Orthodox theologian D. B. Hart), with drama as a motif for connecting interest in narrative more clearly to the real world and to redemptive history (K. Vanhoozer). Hermeneutical attention has galvanized a movement known as 'theological interpretation of Scripture' with contributions from biblical scholars in critical dialogue with B. Childs's 'canonical' approach (F. Watson, S. Fowl), as well as from theologians interested in pre-critical exegesis (D. Yeago).

Besides increasing the prominence of ecclesiology (see *Church), such trends regarding method have accompanied sophisticated recoveries of classic theological figures. Historians are demonstrating that the Church Fathers (see *Patristic theology) were not simply in thrall to 'substance metaphysics' or Greek philosophy in general, as the older history of *dogma or *doctrinal criticism suggested. Rather, classical theists used the language of Hellenism to resist its adoption at points that threatened the biblical *gospel, as in the case of *Arianism. Explorations of *Augustine and Eastern Fathers recognize many more points in common than previously thought (L. Ayres, M. R. Barnes), and recoveries of *Thomas Aquinas demonstrate him to be a scriptural, not just philosophical, theologian (M. Levering, J-P. Torrell). A contemporary movement that has expressed considerable devotion to medieval Catholic theologians (and *Platonism) is the '*radical orthodoxy' pioneered by J. Milbank. However, the overall shape of its narrative – after certain glories of Christendom, a downward spiral from *nominalism to the absolutism of the modern secular state – has been questioned, along with some subplots.

Radical orthodoxy has highlighted the *secularism of social theory along with other academic and cultural practices. Thus theology and social science have increased interaction, but with more variety and tension. 'Political' or 'liberation' theologians have called into question characteristic assumptions about the primacy of theory and highlighted political identification with the poor and oppressed as a prime datum for theology. While it originated in the Majority World, notably Latin America (G. Gutiérrez), the theology of *liberation now permeates Western agendas also, through, for example, *black (J. Cone) or *feminist (R. R. Ruether, M. M. Fulkerson) theologies which seek to counter the ideological effects of much traditional reflection. Theologians outside these categories now turn more attention to issues of justice and *globalization, and hence (slowly) to non-Western theologies themselves. At the same time, the vitality of liberationist movements per se may have weakened, partly due to the responses of ecclesiastical and academic structures. Sophisticated engagement with political questions has also come from more traditional quarters (O. O'Donovan; J. H. Yoder).

Recovery of 'Christian self-description' (in H. Frei's terms) brings the reminder that theology should concern *God, not just socio-political concerns or *religious experience or talk about God. Influenced by Barth and K. *Rahner, along with more recently a host of others, *trinitarian theology is a contemporary focus. Here some Asian theologians and L. Boff have made oft-cited contributions. The Orthodox theologian J. *Zizioulas has led many to appropriate the Cappadocian Fathers in a way that defines personhood as constituted by relationship. Strong analogies are then drawn between the divine being as a communion of three co-equal persons through *perichoresis*, and human personhood as fundamentally social, oriented democratically to egalitarian relations. Such 'social' forms of trinitarianism have become popular in *postmodern contexts, even among fairly traditional theologians (C. Gunton) who criticize Western luminaries such as Augustine, Thomas, and Barth for over-emphasizing divine unity. Likewise, postmodern contexts have elicited further focus on the suffering of God in Jesus Christ, as emphasis on *Luther's 'theology of the *cross' has been recovered notably since J. *Moltmann. Forms of '*open' or 'freewill' or 'relational' theism, making use of this theme, have stirred controversy among evangelicals in particular, with the claim that divine foreknowledge must be limited by the decision to engage human creatures in meaningful relationship. More broadly, while *process theology per se may have waned somewhat, forms of *panentheism abound.

Among reasons for thus conceiving God's being as embracing the world's becoming, perhaps on the analogy of the world as God's body, are not only attention to evil but also philosophy of science (P. Clayton). Yet defences of traditional approaches to the freedom of the Trinity (P. Molnar) and attributes such as divine immutability or impassibility (T. Weinandy) have been forthcoming as well, in addition to defences of the classical heritage against the *Hellenization thesis. Nevertheless, in the wake of terrorism, tsunamis and hurricanes, theologians must query how God relates to *suffering. Moreover, the possibilities and need for a post-supersessionist Christian theology must be on the agenda in the wake of the *Holocaust (R. K. Soulen, B. Marshall), along with the shape of inter-religious dialogue (G. d'Costa), especially among monotheistic 'peoples of the book' (the Society of Scriptural Reasoning) (see *Christianity and other religions).

Apart from the internal concerns and ongoing conversations of specific ecclesiastical communions, soteriology (see *Salvation) joins theology proper as a crucial area of doctrinal controversy. The *Lutheran-Roman Catholic *Joint Declaration on the Doctrine of Justification* issued from substantial biblical, historical and dogmatic groundwork, and resulted in ongoing disputation. Meanwhile, Evangelicals and Catholics Together also produced 'The Gift of Salvation' which brought fresh attention to the doctrine of *justification by faith. Subsequently, the nature of *atonement has been a matter of both heat and light. Historical objections to the dominance of penal *substitution theories, favouring a *Christus Victor* model, have been joined to biblical and moral objections concerning the nature of metaphor, the appearance of divine child abuse, and so forth. Postmodern interests, such as the scapegoat theory of the French thinker R. Girard, have also come to the fore, with penal substitution theorists seeking new construals in response. Apart from postmodern theorizing about the self, practical concerns such as bioethics, *sexuality and *gender have tended to dominate theological *anthropology, while popular aberrations have driven most theologians away from the *eschatological field since Moltmann and W. *Pannenberg. Constructive contributions to *Christology, despite the ferment in biblical studies regarding the *historical Jesus, have been modest, although non-Western theologies highlight the need for, and possibilities of, attention to Christ's humanity (D. Stinton). Also modest until very recently have been efforts toward a full-scale dogmatics, with exceptions such as Pannenberg and D. Bloesch. But now the feminist and traditionally trinitarian projects of S. Coakley and K. Sonderegger are harbingers of several fresh efforts.

Controversies of various kinds have left institutional *ecumenism in a somewhat stagnant condition. Nevertheless, there are contemporary examples of 'ecumenism of the trenches': besides Evangelicals and Catholics Together, there is 'In One Body through the Cross' (the Princeton Proposal for Christian Unity). Such a movement coalesces around 'Nicene Christianity' or the 'evangelical catholic' theology associated with C. Braaten and R. Jenson. Ecclesiology is also shaped by attention to the church's missional character. *Mission is not just one thing the church *does*, but what the church *is* throughout – sent by the triune God, participating in the dynamic of the Son and Spirit being sent. Thus the church's mission must be holistic, for it participates in the very *missio Dei* (D. Bosch), and always cross-cultural, for it embodies the gospel in every local culture (L. *Newbigin). Embodiment entails attention to sacramental theology and practice, perhaps even to the church having a sacramental character.

On the whole, while there is much faddishness, the best recent theology is increasingly sophisticated methodologically and seriously engaged with the classical texts of the Christian tradition – so much so that many now speak of 'retrieval' as a theological mode. While remaining an exercise in critical reflection, much contemporary theology now pays attention to scriptural, ecclesiastical and creedal authorities. Accordingly, as evidenced in recent years by theologians having significant ecclesiastical roles (R. *Williams as Archbishop of Canterbury; Joseph Cardinal *Ratzinger as Pope Benedict XVI), theology is more preoccupied with constructive responsibilities.

See also: ASIAN CHRISTIAN THEOLOGY; EVANGELICAL THEOLOGY; ROMAN CATHOLIC THEOLOGY; EASTERN ORTHODOX THEOLOGY.

Bibliography

W. D. Buschart and K. D. Eilers, *Theology as Retrieval: Receiving the Past, Renewing the Church* (Downers Grove, 2015); D. Ford with R. Muers (eds.), *The Modern Theologians* (Oxford, ³2004); P. Hodgson and R. King (eds.), *Christian Theology* (Minneapolis, 1994); H. Schwarz, *Theology in a Global Context* (Grand Rapids and Cambridge, 2005); C. Seitz (ed.), *Nicene Christianity* (Grand Rapids, 2001); K. Vanhoozer (ed.), *The Cambridge Companion to Postmodern Theology* (Cambridge, 2003); J. Webster and G. Schner (eds.), *Theology after Liberalism* (Oxford, 2000); D. Yeago, 'The New Testament and the Nicene Dogma', *Pro Ecclesia* 3, 1994, pp. 152–164. Among new journals, *Modern Theology*, the *International Journal of Systematic Theology* and *Pro Ecclesia* represent some trends described here.

D. J. TREIER AND J. B. WEBSTER

CONTEXTUAL THEOLOGIES

Background

'Contextual theologies' connote the range of theologies which have arisen as a result of a growing sensitivity toward the role of context and experience in the doing of theology. Although a number of terms have been used to refer to such theologies, including 'indigenous theologies', 'local theologies', 'ethnotheologies', and reference to the process of 'inculturation', 'contextual theologies' arguably is the most utilized.

The term 'contextualization' first originated in the 1972 *Ministry and Context* report by the WCC and responds to concerns raised by contemporary theologians and global ecumenical movements that theology must be rooted in the historical, material realities of particular communities. Key factors influencing this shift towards context include first, the turn toward the human subject or the '*anthropological turn'. This highlighted that knowledge could not be separated from the knowing subject and thus called for a shift away from classical theological deductive approaches (where knowledge was perceived as filtering 'from above'; i.e. from 'received' sources) to more inductive approaches ('from below') which recognized the human subject as the starting point of theological investigation.

Second, the expansion of the Western missionary movement in the nineteenth century gave rise to questions surrounding the role of culture in mission and consequently to the term 'indigenization', a term which tended to reflect a colonial view of mission as the transportation of a fixed, unchanging gospel into the fixed and static setting of non-Christian communities. However, as the movement developed, there became a growing sense of dissatisfaction amongst many Christian communities, particularly in parts of Africa and Asia, with the theology inherited from the colonizing West, thus leading to a subsequent growth in Majority World theologies (see *African Christian theology; *Asian Christian theology). Third was the arrival of *liberation theology at the Latin American Episcopal Conference (CELAM) in Medellín in 1968. Although not the first example of contextual theology, this increased the church's awareness of the importance of context, through its insistence that theology be rooted in the material and historical circumstances of the poor in Latin America.

Radical contextual theologies

More radical approaches to contextualization tend to articulate present experience and therefore 'context' as the starting point of theological method. Theology, it is maintained, is always done from particular locations. Rosemary Radford *Ruether, a prominent American feminist theologian, thus argues that all theology is grounded in experience. What have been seen as the universal and objective sources of theology – Scripture and tradition – are nothing more than codified collective human experience, and more importantly, *male* experience (R. R. Ruether, *Sexism and God-Talk*, p. 12). Hence, rather than seeing theology as the 'deposit of faith', received through *Scripture and tradition, contextual theologies such as *black theologies, *womanist theologies, *feminist theologies, Filipino theologies, Asian theologies, African theologies, and so on, tend to look with suspicion on such a perspective, noting how it often serves to reinforce white, Western, affluent, male experience as both normative and universal. In this sense, radical contextual theologies seek to expose the particularized nature of all theology by giving voice to those who have previously been excluded from theological conversation.

Here, Scripture and tradition are not considered to perform the function of redeeming culture and context from a 'sinful' condition. Instead, context is seen as a source of divine revelation and a lens through which Scripture and tradition should be read and a criterion against which they should be judged. Hence, Jacquelyn Grant, a contemporary womanist theologian, asserts that '[T]o do Womanist Theology, ... we must read and hear the Bible and engage it within the content of our own experience. This is the only way that it can make sense to people who are oppressed' (in *Feminism and Theology*, p. 303). It is only by placing the text in conversation with present experience that it can assist in particularized struggles towards a better world.

Conservative contextual theologies

Many evangelicals have been concerned to uphold the primacy of *Scripture and to avoid *syncretism (the collapse of theology into culture). Integral to this has been a desire to maintain belief in an 'authentic' trans-cultural Christian message. David Wells thus argues that the task of theology is to de-contextualize Scripture by discovering what God has said and then re-contextualizing this so that it coheres with the cognitive assumptions and social patterns of our age (*The Use of the Bible in Theology*, pp. 175–176).

Others, however, have noted problems with this. Harvie Conn, for instance, maintains that it is problematic to insist that the 'husk' of culture can be stripped away to reveal the 'kernel' of the Christian faith, preferring to talk about a gospel 'centre' as opposed to a gospel 'core'. For him, the redemptive activity of God through Jesus Christ constitutes the 'centre' of the gospel, since this remains the same despite the particular context of the culture within which it is communicated. The role of the Bible, however, is to instruct and transform contemporary culture. Although there is continuity between biblical writers and people today (since both share in the same redemption history), the former must always address the latter because their testimony is 'God-breathed and inerrant', whereas ours is always 'tentative and in need of correction' (*Eternal Word and Changing Worlds*, p. 227).

Other evangelicals, however, afford culture a more formative place within theological method. Stanley Grenz insists that neither the gospel nor culture constitute pre-existing, fixed realities since both inform one another. Culture can help us interpret the Bible because the same Spirit speaks through both. Indeed, Grenz argues that since the Spirit's speaking always meets its hearers within specific historical-cultural settings, the Spirit cannot speak through the Bible except without speaking through culture. The Spirit communicates what is the 'word of God' for particular communities, hence there can be no foundational reading of the Bible. This arguably provides a more nuanced contribution to evangelical debate on the grounds that it avoids talk about the 'essence' of Christianity and recognizes that there can be no theology without context.

See also: CONTEXTUALIZATION; CULTURAL THEORY AND THEOLOGY; CULTURE.

Bibliography

S. B. Bevans, *Models of Contextual Theology* (Maryknoll, rev. edn 2002); H. M. Conn, *Eternal Word and Changing Worlds: Theology, Anthropology and Mission in Trialogue* (Phillipsburg, 1984); D. L. Gelpi, *The Turn to Experience in Contemporary Theology* (New York, 1994); J. Grant, 'The Challenge of the Darker Sister', in J. M. Soskice and D. Lipton (eds.), *Feminism and Theology* (Oxford, 2003), pp. 302–311; S. J. Grenz, 'Articulating the Christian Belief-Mosaic: Theological Method after the Demise of Foundationalism', in J. G. Stackhouse (ed.), *Evangelical Futures: A Conversation on Theological Method* (Grand Rapids and Leicester, 2001), pp. 107–136; S. J. Grenz and J. R. Franke, *Beyond Foundationalism: Shaping Theology in a Postmodern Context* (Louisville and London, 2001); R. R. Ruether, *Sexism and God-Talk: Towards a Feminist Theology* (London, 1983); R. J. Schreiter, *Constructing Local Theologies* (Maryknoll, 1994); M. Stackhouse, *Apologia: Contextualization, Globalization, and Mission in Theological Education* (Grand Rapids, 1988); C. F. Starkloff, 'The Problem of Syncretism in the Search for Inculturation', *Mission* n.s. 1.1, 1984, pp. 75–94; D. F. Wells, 'The Nature and Function of Theology', in R. K. Johnston (ed.), *The Use of the Bible in Theology: Evangelical Options* (Atlanta, 1985), pp. 175–199.

H. J. BACON

CONTEXTUALIZATION

Contextualization is a dynamic process of the church's reflection, in obedience to Christ and his mission in the world, on the interaction of the text as the word of God and the context as a specific human situation. It is essentially a *missiological concept. The interpreter or one engaged in this process may be part of the context or, as a cross-cultural communicator, represent a second context in a three-way process.

Contextualization is not a passing fad or a debatable option. It is essential to our understanding of God's self-revelation. The *incarnation is the ultimate *paradigm of the translation of text into context. Jesus Christ, the Word of God incarnate as a Jew, identified with a particular culture at a limited moment in history though transcending it. In his life and teaching he is the supreme *model of contextualization. His every command was *de facto* a command to contextualization, whether to love one's neighbour or to disciple the nations. The implication of this process is seen in the apostolic witness and the life of the NT church. The difference in theological emphasis and preaching method between Paul's address to the synagogue in Pisidian Antioch (Acts 13:16–41) and his address to the Areopagus in Athens (Acts 17:22–31) is but one notable illustration of the sociological and theological inevitability of contextualization. In the history of dogma the affirmations of the truths of God's revelation in Scripture have always involved a selection of themes and contextualized language in response to the particular theological and ethical issues confronting the church in that moment of history. The *creeds, *confessions and statements of faith reflect this process.

With the rapid expansion of the Western missionary movement in the nineteenth century, missionary strategists Henry Venn (1725–97), Rufus Anderson (1796–1880) and others developed the concept of indigenization, whereby the unchanging gospel was transplanted into the static and generally 'primitive' cultures of non-Christian peoples. This movement was primarily concerned with indigenizing the forms of worship, social customs, church architecture and methods of evangelism. It led in the twentieth century to a new appreciation of the importance of cultural anthropology for the preparation of missionaries and for the study of missions. The failure to indigenize resulted in the perpetuation of colonialism and the growth of a ghetto mentality among Christian communities. But the adequacy of the indigenization principle was seriously questioned. After the Second World War, the rise of nationalism, the decline of Western colonialism, and the spread of political revolution leading to military dictatorship or socialist and Marxist governments engulfed an increasing number of nations. The explosion of human knowledge, science and technology, and the spirit of materialism and secular humanism which permeated all modern societies resulted in a crisis of faith and a search beyond indigenous identity for truth and relevance.

The need to move from indigenization to contextualization was also accelerated by issues raised by modern theologians and the global ministry of conciliar *ecumenical movements. These issues include: the situational *hermeneutics of R. *Bultmann; the call to the church in the midst of rapid social change to be action-orientated, made for example at the World Conference on Church and Society at Geneva (1966); the questioning of the distinction between *salvation-history and world history at the WCC Assembly at Uppsala (1968); the acceptance of the principle of humanization and *universalism in salvation at the WCC Commission on World Mission and Evangelism at Bangkok (1972); and the search for the unity of mankind at the WCC Assembly at Nairobi (1975). The focusing on issues of social reconciliation, humanization and liberation led to a shift of priority from interpreting the text to reflection on suffering and oppression in particular contexts. Contextualization has become a way of doing politicized theology (see *Political theology).

The origin of the term 'contextualization' is credited to Shoki Coe and Aharoan Sapsezian, directors of the Theological Education Fund of the WCC in their 1972 report, *Ministry and Context*. They suggested that the term 'contextualization' implies all that is involved in the term 'indigenization', but goes beyond it to take account of 'the process of secularity, technology and the struggle for human justice which characterised the historical moment of nations in the third world'.

Radical interpretations

Modern scholars, and *liberation theologians in particular, have made extensive use of the concept of contextualization as part of a wider

Contextualization

theological debate. They begin by rejecting the traditional view of divine revelation as inscripturated in the Bible, since the word of God cannot be equated with any particular form, whether Scripture or theological systems. They deny that the Bible contains propositional truths and argue that since all Scripture is culturally and historically conditioned, its message is relative and situational. Further, they hold that there is no truth outside of the action of concrete historical events of human struggle. There can be no epistemological split between thought and action, truth and practice. Thus all authentic theology must be participatory theology. Theological knowledge comes only from participation in action and reflection on *praxis. As a result radical theologians hold that the hermeneutical process does not begin with the exegesis of Scripture, but with a prophetic 'reading of the times', discerning God's act of humanization and liberation in the general historical process and in particular situations. Gustavo *Gutiérrez argued that theology is reflection on praxis in the light of faith. It is a dialectical movement between action and reflection. The hermeneutics of Scripture give place to the hermeneutics of history. Evangelical Latin American theologians René Padilla, Emilio Antonio Núñez and others, while recognizing the validity of the deep concerns raised by liberation theologians, argued that this way of doing theology leads to a truncated gospel, a secularized political theology and ultimately to the demise of the institutionalized church and of the centrality of evangelism.

Conservative interpretations

Evangelical scholars, missionaries, church and lay leaders have taken seriously the validity of the shift from indigenization to the enlarged agenda of contextualization. A beginning was made at the *Lausanne Congress on World Evangelization (1974) and followed up at the Gospel and Culture consultation in Bermuda (1978). Nevertheless, for many evangelicals the task of contextualization is restricted to the faithful and relevant communication of the unchanging message into the language and cultural thought forms of those to whom it is communicated. This concern takes seriously the issues of the cultural conditioning of the biblical message, the communicator's self-understanding and the receiving community's response to the message. In this way, contextualization is understood in terms of 'dynamic equivalence', whereby the biblical message is seen to bring forth in the receiver a response equivalent to that which the biblical text produced in those to whom it was first addressed.

However, the task of contextualization calls for a more profound understanding of translating the gospel in its relationship to the contemporary historical situation. The time-honoured grammatico-historical method of biblical exegesis continues to be accepted as fundamental to authentic contextualization, giving clarity and understanding as to what the biblical writers said and meant in their own context. However, contextualization takes place only when the faithful exegesis of the text enters into a dialogical encounter with the issues of the human situation. This encounter will be both theological and ethical, in which belief and action are interdependent. It takes place in dependence on the Holy Spirit who is the hermeneutic key to relating text and context.

The interpreter's critical reflection on his or her own cultural pre-understanding is an essential part of this three-way process. While drawing on the insight of Bultmann's hermeneutical circle, scholars such as Orlando Costas find an alternative symbol in a dialogical spiral that points to an eschatological goal. This dynamic process of critical reflection and interpretation takes place as the interpreter identifies by faith with the text of the Scripture and at the same time distances himself from it in study and reflection. At the same time the interpreter identifies with and distances himself also from the context. Authentic contextualization takes place when these horizons meet. In the dialogue between text and context, the questions raised by the context are brought to the text for answers, while the text in turn raises new questions that confront the context. For example, the context may focus on specific issues of violence, while the text raises issues concerning sin and demonic power. Since the text is given and authoritative, and the context relative and changing, the dialogical movement will always be from text to context. In this way, the process of reflection differs sharply from that of the more radical views. However, while recognizing that there can be no absolute and final system of theology, the interpreter works in the confidence that the Spirit of God gives increasing clarity and assurance on the nature of the gospel and its relevance to every human situation.

Evangelicals recognize that valid contextualization takes place only where there is unreserved commitment to the path of discipleship. First and foremost, this calls for loyalty and commitment to Jesus Christ as Saviour and Lord of all of life, personal and social, and to his gospel. Evangelicals share with liberation theologians their commitment to the historic Jesus in his humility and suffering and his prophetic rebuke of hypocrisy and injustice. But they are equally committed to the Christ of faith – incarnate Son of God, crucified, risen from the dead and coming again at the end of time to consummate his kingdom. This commitment to Jesus Christ is within the trinitarian framework of God the Father and God the Holy Spirit.

Furthermore, true contextualization demands commitment to the *church as the people of God. The church with its openness to God in worship and fellowship is also called to obedience in humble service, especially to the poor, and to proclaim to all people that salvation is in Jesus Christ alone. Contextualization takes place primarily within the sphere of the church and only secondly within the world. Reflection and interpretation are the work of the church. The priesthood of all believers and the work of the Holy Spirit in illuminating Scripture emphasize that the church is the sphere in which contextualization takes place. It is not the prerogative of a professional theological élite alone, but is open to all God's people. The church as the body of Christ with the Spirit-given diversity of gifts of ministry ensures that this dynamic process of contextualizing theology and practice takes place.

True contextualization warns against the dangers of *syncretism in theological beliefs, religious practices and ethical lifestyles, but it is not driven to inertia or to maintenance of the status quo by fear of this danger. A willingness to take risks and commitment to clear missiological goals enables the communicator to overcome this fear. The Holy Spirit as the divine Communicator is the pioneer and enabler in the fulfilment of this task.

In this dialogical relationship between the biblical text and the human context all forms of idolatrous beliefs and practices, whether religious or secular, are judged and stand condemned. The church is committed to their destruction. Though all of culture is tainted with sin, it still reflects the truths and beauty of God's general revelation. Therefore that which is compatible with the law of God must be purified, transformed and put under the lordship of Christ.

Contextualization culminates in the good news breaking into every situation, with the newness of redemption from sin, guilt and demonic power, liberation from human despair and social injustice, and the actualization of faith, hope and love. Thus contextualization is a central task of the church in its mission in the world.

See also: CONTEXTUAL THEOLOGIES; CULTURE.

Bibliography

R. Bauckham, *The Bible and Mission: Christian Witness in a Postmodern World* (Grand Rapids, 2003); J. Miguez Bonino, *Doing Theology in a Revolutionary Situation* (Philadelphia, 1975); O. E. Costas, *The Church and Its Mission* (Wheaton, 1974); J. D. Douglas (ed.), *Let the Earth Hear His Voice* (Minneapolis, 1975); B. C. E. Fleming, *Contextualization of Theology* (Pasadena, 1980); D. Flemming, *Contextualization in the New Testament* (Downers Grove, 2005); D. S. Gilliland, *The Word among Us: Contextualizing Theology for Today* (Dallas, 1989); D. J. Hesselgrave, *Theology and Mission* (Grand Rapids, 1978); J. A. Kirk, *Theology and the Third World Church* (Exeter, 1983); C. H. Kraft, *Christianity in Culture* (Maryknoll, 1979); L. J. Lutzbetak, *The Church and Cultures* (Pasadena, 1976); I. H. Marshall (ed.), *New Testament Interpretation: Essays on Principles and Methods* (Exeter, 1977); B. J. Nicholls, *Contextualization: A Theology of Gospel and Culture* (Exeter, 1979); Bong Rin Ro and R. Eshenaur, *The Bible and Theology in Asian Context* (Taichung, 1984); V. K. Samuel and C. Sugden (eds.), *Sharing Jesus in the Two-Thirds World* (Bangalore, 1983); J. R. W. Stott and R. T. Coote, *Gospel and Culture* (Pasadena, 1979); J. Sobrino, *Christology at the Crossroads: A Latin American Approach* (Maryknoll, 1978); TEF staff, *Ministry in Context* (London, 1972); A. C. Thiselton, *The Two Horizons* (Exeter, 1980).

B. J. NICHOLLS

CONTINGENCY

All propositions are logically either contingent or necessary. They are logically contingent if their denial is consistent. States of affairs are causally either contingent or necessary. They are causally contingent if their existence depends on the existence of something else, causally necessary if not.

God's existence may be thought of as being causally necessary (he is uncaused) and even logically necessary (his non-existence is inconceivable), and these positions may be thought to have a scriptural basis (Ps. 90:2). Conversely, the universe may be thought of as causally and logically contingent, the expression of the free (i.e. unconstrained) goodness of God (Gen. 1). The contingency of the universe may seem to require an explanation, and this thought has been the basis of numerous 'cosmological' arguments for God's existence, most of them of dubious validity (see *Natural theology). *Anselm's ontological argument, if cogent, would be a demonstration of God's logical necessity. Philosophers since *Hume and *Kant have claimed that all logically necessary truths are uninformative, and hence that 'God exists' is, at best, a contingent truth.

Thinkers of an *existentialist cast of mind have given prominence to the mystery of human contingency as an element in what is in their view the meaninglessness of human life. By contrast, the Bible gives the recognition of such contingency as one reason for awe, reverence, humility and thanksgiving (Pss 90:12; 100).

Bibliography

D. R. Burrhill (ed.), *The Cosmological Arguments* (Garden City, 1967); A. Plantinga, *The Nature of Necessity* (Oxford, 1974); T. F. Torrance, *Divine and Contingent Order* (Oxford, 1981).

P. HELM

CONVERSION

The term conversion in Christian usage refers to the transformation of one's life brought about through the hearing of the *gospel and through the recognition of the call of God (see *Calling) upon one's life. Commonly referred to as 'new birth' or *regeneration, conversion involves the reorientation of a person's life to the truth of God made known in *Jesus Christ. It is a change of heart and mind and results also in a change of conduct as the convert is transformed according to the likeness of Jesus Christ.

There has been some dispute in the Christian tradition about how the work of God in conversion is related to the action of the individual. While most theologians have recognized the need for a freely chosen response to the gospel, most are also agreed that conversion must first be understood as the action of the *Holy Spirit in bringing people to see, understand and share in the *salvation wrought through the life, death and resurrection of Jesus. The response of *faith is thus a response made possible by God's *grace. The Protestant Reformers (see *Reformation theology) typically claimed that baptism marked the decisive point of conversion and that the practice of infant baptism expressed clearly the utter dependence of conversion upon divine grace. Others have contended, however, that the grace of God is active only in response to the individual's repentance and confession of faith.

A further point of disagreement concerns whether conversion is best understood as a discrete episode in which the individual accepts the gospel and responds in faith, or as a lifelong process of transformation. In the latter case, conversion is closely related to *sanctification, the process whereby believers are gradually conformed to the likeness of Christ. Reports of the conversions of Paul, *Augustine and John *Wesley, to name three well-known instances, trace conversion to a particular moment and experience, but many Christians claim that their faith in Christ has grown over a long period, with no identifiable point of conversion. Within the *evangelical tradition, conversion has usually been understood to refer to a particular point in one's life. A particularly insistent expression of this understanding occurred in Puritan New England where, for a time, church membership was restricted to those who could recount a conversion experience.

Whether conversion is understood as a singular event or as a process, it involves in both cases the transformation of one's life, a dying to the old self, and a rising to new life in Christ. So important is this transformation that, for John Wesley, a lack of evidence of a holy life was taken as a sure sign that a person had not been converted at all. Concomitantly, a holy life could be taken by believers as an assurance of their conversion and faith.

In evangelical thought, conversion is closely associated with *repentance. The reorientation of one's life to the truth made known in Jesus

Christ involves, simultaneously, a turning from the life of the 'old Adam' and a turning toward new life in Christ. With that turning comes sorrow and confession that the person now born anew had for so long persisted in the life of sinfulness and disobedience. A point of debate has been whether Christ himself may be understood to offer that repentance on our behalf so that the decisive event of our conversion back to God takes place, not at some point in our own personal journey but in the life, death and *resurrection of Jesus, through which the world is reconciled to God. It is argued by some, in the *Reformed tradition especially, that Christ does for us what we cannot do for ourselves. That is, Christ offers a true repentance on our behalf, bears the consequences of our sinfulness, and thus turns us back to right relationship with God. Those awakened to this conversion are called to respond with *worship and praise for the wonders of God's grace. Such worship is to be expressed through every facet of the believer's life.

It is important to stress that while the new life of the believer has ethical ramifications, it is fundamentally concerned with a new relationship. Believers are made new because they are reconciled with God and made members of the body of Christ. It has been a weakness of the evangelical tradition to construe conversion in excessively individualistic terms. While conversion is necessarily personal, it is not the institution of a private relationship with God. An essential dimension of conversion is the believer's incorporation into the community of faith in Jesus Christ (see *Church). The call to discipleship is a call to participation in the community of believers who are together established as the body of Christ and who together are charged with proclaiming the gospel in the world. The converted life is one oriented both to God and to neighbours in faithful and loving service.

Bibliography

J. Baillie, *Baptism and Conversion* (London, 1964); G. Gutiérrez, 'Conversion for Evangelisation', in G. Gutiérrez, *The Power of the Poor in History* (ET, Maryknoll and London, 1983); W. James, *The Varieties of Religious Experience*, ed. M. E. Marty (Harmondsworth, 1983 [1902]); H. T. Kerr and J. M. Mulder (eds.), *Famous Conversions* (Grand Rapids, 1983); T. Smail, 'One Cross – Baptism into Communion', in T. Smail, *Once and for All: A Confession of the Cross* (London, 1998).

M. A. RAE

COPTIC CHRISTIANITY

The Coptic Church is essentially the church centring on the ancient patriarchate of *Alexandria, the Egyptian Church (Arabic *qibt*, Ethiopic *qibs*, 'Egypt'). We may identify four groupings: the *monophysite Orthodox Copts; the Melkites ('Emperor's men'), adherents of the Chalcedonian position; the Eastern Catholic Copts, dating from 1741; and the *Ethiopian Orthodox Church, Coptic only in its historic links with Alexandria. The term Coptic Church is used properly only of the first of these four groups.

The Coptic Church should not be subsumed under the heading of the *Eastern Orthodox churches as it belongs to the *Oriental Orthodox family of churches (formerly often known as monophysite). The distinction arose in the *Christological debates of the fifth century, which were brought to a focus at the Council of *Chalcedon in 451. The conclusions of that Council are not accepted by the Oriental Orthodox. Their view is that there is only one (divine-human) nature in Christ. The Copts reject the extreme position of Eutyches (c. 378–454), but subscribe to the formula attributed to *Cyril of Alexandria, 'one *physis* (which can be understood as 'nature' or 'person') of the incarnate Word'. Monophysitism is, in fact, peripheral to the theology of the Copts, and their initial acceptance of the monophysite view might be attributed in part to national pride, injured by the deposing and banishment of their patriarch, Dioscorus (d. 454), at Chalcedon, as well as to traditional Egyptian religion which conditioned Egyptian thinking to divine-human unity, and to the influence of philosophy. The Oriental Orthodox Church recognizes the formulations of the *Councils of Nicaea, Constantinople and Ephesus. In recent decades, dialogue between Eastern and Oriental Orthodox has led to the acknowledgment that both traditions share the same faith, and closer relationships are being sought.

Three ranks of clergy are recognized: the diaconate, the priesthood and the episcopate, although in theory the laity are seen to act with the clergy in giving effect to liturgy and sacrament. The Coptic patriarch is a monk, reflecting the historic importance of *monasticism, which may be said to have originated in Egypt with Antony (c. 251–356) and Pachomius (c. 287–346). Monasticism has seen a measure of renewal in recent decades.

Although no particular stress is laid on the number, seven *sacraments are recognized. Infant baptism is followed by *anointing with consecrated oil (chrism) and *confirmation. Communion is taken by the clergy in both kinds, but the laity more commonly take it in one kind only. The three orders of priesthood are referred to above. Penance follows confession. Marriage is in theory indissoluble, although this view is modified by reference to a sacramental eternity for the relationship. Anointing of the sick is the seventh sacrament.

The Coptic liturgy is very rich, employing the Coptic language or Arabic. Lectionaries are widely used, as are *synaxaria*, lives of the saints, related to the church calendar. Fasting is widely practised. There is a strong evangelical element in the Coptic Church, and nineteenth-century Western influence stimulated it to develop a flourishing Sunday School movement, which is led by well-trained teachers. It is estimated that 10% of the population of Egypt belong to the church, but it has experienced opposition in recent decades from Islamic extremists.

Bibliography

A. S. Atiya, *A History of Eastern Christianity* (London, 1968); idem (ed.), *The Coptic Encyclopedia*, 7 vols. (New York, 1991); C. Chaillot, *The Coptic Orthodox Church* (Paris, 2005), with further bibliography; W. H. C. Frend, *The Rise of the Monophysite Movement* (Cambridge, 1972; this includes a magnificent bibliography); P. Gregorius, W. H. Lazareth and N. A. Nissiotis (eds.), *Does Chalcedon Divide or Unite?* (Geneva, 1981); O. F. A. Meinardus, *Christian Egypt, Faith and Life* (Cairo, ²1977); idem, *Two Thousand Years of Coptic Christianity* (Cairo, 2002); J. H. Watson, *Among the Copts: Beliefs and Practices* (Brighton, 2000).

F. P. COTTERELL

CORPORATE PERSONALITY

In Scripture and in human experience, self-awareness, moral and legal responsibility, blessing and trouble, reward and punishment are corporate as well as individual realities. Thus Israel and other nations can speak as 'I' as well as 'we' (Num. 20 – 21); the fate of a family can be bound up together (Josh. 7); one generation can bear the consequences of earlier generations' sins (Matt. 23:35); a church can be addressed as a person invited to open its 'heart' to Christ (Rev. 3:20).

For a period in the mid-twentieth century, under the influence of the work of H. Wheeler Robinson (1872–1945), the OT version of this common phenomenon was given a rather mystical connotation by being described in terms of 'corporate personality' connected with a primitive way of experiencing reality that was different from our modern way. The theory was used to explain passages in the Psalms which alternate between 'I' and 'we', and the servant passages in Isa. 40 – 55 with their changing identification of the servant. But it is now discredited, and such passages are better approached in other ways. There is no need for the hypothesis that OT or NT people's corporate or individual self-awareness was radically different from our own.

Bibliography

P. Joyce, 'The Individual and the Community' in J. Rogerson (ed.), *Beginning Old Testament Study* (London, 1983); J. R. Porter, 'The Legal Aspects of the Concept of "Corporate Personality" in the Old Testament', *VT* 15 (1965), pp. 361–380; H. W. Robinson, *Corporate Personality in Ancient Israel* (Philadelphia, ²1980); J. Rogerson, 'The Hebrew Conception of Corporate Personality: A Re-examination', *JTS* 21 (1970), pp. 1–16; Sang-Won (Aaron) Son, *Corporate Elements in Pauline Anthropology* (Fort Worth, 2001).

J. GOLDINGAY

COTTON, JOHN (1584–1652)

Cotton studied at Cambridge, UK, encountering the preaching of *Perkins and *Sibbes. Converted under Sibbes' preaching, he was in turn instrumental in the conversion of John Preston. Ordained in the Church of England, Cotton agitated for a fully Reformed church and promulgated Calvinist doctrine (see *Reformed theology). In 1615 he encouraged those with an assurance of salvation to covenant together 'to follow after the Lord in the purity of his worship', thus distinguishing the elect from the generality of those in a state church.

In 1633 Cotton emigrated to New England, where he served as pastor in Boston, and was first engaged in controversy with Roger Williams over liberty of conscience and the nature of the gathered church, then in defence of a group accused of antinomianism, including Anne Hutchinson and John Wheelwright. He later disassociated from them. Cotton was a strong defender of *Congregationalism, seeking a middle road between Presbyterianism and separatism. He became a pivotal and influential leader of English *Puritanism, his Calvinism giving shape and scope to his soteriology and ecclesiology. His distinctive views on grace, the role of affections and assurance in post-regeneration experience, are largely consistent with other Cambridge Puritans such as Sibbes and Preston.

Bibliography

Works: *A Treatise of the Covenant of Grace* (1659); *The Way of the Church of Christ in New England* (1645).

Studies: E. Emerson, *John Cotton* (Boston, 1990); E. B. Holifield, *Theology in America: Christian Thought from the Age of the Puritans to the Civil War* (New Haven, 2003); M. Schuldiner, *Gifts and Works: The Post-Conversion Paradigm and Spiritual Controversy in Seventeenth-Century Massachusetts* (Macon, 1991); L. Ziff, *The Career of John Cotton: Puritanism and the American Experience* (Princeton, 1962).

J. Gordon

COUNCILS

A church council is a gathering of all those members of the church who are responsible for guarding the deposit of the apostolic faith.

1. In Christian theology

Councils are summoned to settle disputes of interpretation, or to pass judgment on matters not found in *Scripture, and their decisions are regarded as binding if they are 'received' by the *church as being in accordance with Scripture and its traditional interpretation. A general or ecumenical or universal council is one for which universal 'reception' by the church is claimed.

This theory has a number of weaknesses, and is in fact understood in different ways. To begin with, there is disagreement as to who has the right to summon a council. According to Byzantine tradition, which is followed by the Church of England (Article VIII), only the secular authority has this power. The Roman Catholic Church, on the other hand, believes that it is the prerogative of the *papacy. Other churches do not define this right, but in practice it is conferred on representative synods or officials, who are elected by more or less democratic means.

It is not agreed who has the right to participate and vote in a council. The Eastern churches restrict both participation and voting to bishops. Rome allows wider participation, but also restricts voting to bishops, whereas *Protestants invariably believe that representatives of the whole church should take part and vote.

The *authority of councils is also a subject of debate. The Eastern church believes that councils are infallible because they are inspired by the Holy Spirit, who speaks not only in the unanimous voice of the bishops but also in the answering echo of the church, which must receive and find the proper application for the decisions taken. The practical difficulties with this are that dissenting bishops have had to be silenced or excommunicated in order to achieve unanimity, and that there have been notable instances of conciliar decisions which have subsequently been rejected by the church, largely on non-theological grounds.

The Roman position is that the pope is the ultimate arbiter and executor of conciliar decisions. No council is valid unless he has given it his approval. The difficulty with this is that the great councils of the early church were held without Roman approval or participation, at least in some cases, though Rome has always accepted them as authoritative. This position also creates a tension between papal monarchy and episcopal oligarchy, which is a standard feature of the life of the Roman Church and which remains unresolved.

Following the schism of 1378 which led to two rival popes, the theory of papal monarchy which had grown up in the Middle Ages was called into question by many churchmen. They wanted to see the church governed by councils which would meet in principle every five years. The membership of these councils would be chosen on a national basis, and their authority would be at least equal to that of the papacy, which would still retain its ancient primacy. The

Conciliar movement, as this trend came to be called, reached its highest point at the Council of Constance (1414–18), where it was agreed to set up the appropriate conciliar machinery. A council of the new type actually met at Basel in 1431, but by that time the papacy had regained much of its former prestige, and slowly it strangled the Conciliar movement. First it disrupted proceedings at Basel, and then it transferred the council to Ferrara, where it could be more easily manipulated. By the time it ended, the papacy had regained complete control, and the Conciliar movement was effectively dead. However, memories of it survived, and were to be influential at the time of the Reformation, when various theologians were to propose its revival as an answer to the Protestant breakaway.

Protestants attach no infallible authority to councils, and recognize their decisions only in so far as they can be shown to be in accordance with Scripture. Indeed, for most Protestants, councils of the type described above no longer play any role in church life. There is no agreed machinery for calling an interdenominational council, or for making its decisions binding on participants. The word has now come to be used mainly to describe interchurch organizations such as the *World Council of Churches, whose constitution explicitly eschews any interference in the internal life and doctrine of member churches.

See also: COLLEGIALITY AND CONCILIARITY.

Bibliography

B. Lambert, *Ecumenism: Theology and History* (London, 1967); P. Sherrard, *Church, Papacy and Schism* (London, 1978); G. Tavard, *Holy Writ or Holy Church: The Crisis of the Protestant Reformation* (New York, 1959); B. Tierney, *Foundations of the Conciliar Theory* (Cambridge, 1955).

G. L. BRAY

2. Survey of councils

What has been called the first council of the leaders of the church was held at Jerusalem in AD 48 or 49, in order to settle the dispute about the reception of Gentile converts into the covenant community (Acts 15). After that time, a number of local synods were held, at Antioch, Carthage and Alexandria, as well as Serdica (Sofia), Lyon and other places, to settle doctrinal disputes and heal schisms of different kinds. Some of their decisions have been preserved in church tradition and become authoritative in the wider Christian world. The most famous series of local synods were those held at Toledo between 400 and 694. Tradition records eighteen in all, and their canons are an invaluable source for the history and theology of the Spanish church during those centuries.

There is little doubt, however, that the most important church councils have been those which have received the title ecumenical, or universal. The Roman Catholic Church recognizes twenty-one of these, though other churches accept far fewer. Unlike the Roman Church, they have never given this title to an assembly consisting exclusively of members of their own church or communion.

The ecumenical councils may be conveniently grouped by historical period, with those which were held in ancient times having the greatest claim to universal recognition. The First Council of *Nicaea (325) and the First Council of *Constantinople (381) established the divinity of Christ and of the Holy Spirit. They have been traditionally linked together by the so-called Nicene, or Niceno-Constantinopolitan, Creed (see *Creeds), which is supposed to have been composed in 381 on the basis of the creed promulgated in 325. Modern scholars doubt this tradition, but there is no doubt that the creed, the councils and their theology have been accepted by virtually all the major branches of the Christian church.

The third ecumenical council was held at Ephesus in 431. It was concerned with the *Christological issues raised by *Nestorius, who was eventually condemned, in circumstances which did the church little credit. The council was followed twenty years later by the fourth, held at Chalcedon in 451, which condemned the Christology of Eutyches (c. 378–454), a monk who had championed and misrepresented the Alexandrian tradition. The council's famous Definition, perhaps the most significant Christological statement in the history of the church, decreed that Jesus Christ was one divine person in two natures, one human and one divine. This eventually drove the Egyptian and Syrian Churches into schism, because they supported a doctrine of *monophysitism, according to which Christ had only one nature.

The fifth council was the Second Council of Constantinople (553), which tried to heal the breach with the monophysites. It decreed that the human nature of Christ was not independent, but received its identity by being united with the divine person of the Son of God. This attempted compromise failed, however, and the breach became permanent after the sixth council, the Third Council of Constantinople (680), which declared that Christ had two wills, a human and a divine, which the monophysites and some of their orthodox supporters had denied.

In 691–92 a synod was held in the palace of Trullum, in Constantinople, which endeavoured to complete the work of the fifth and sixth councils. For this reason it is known as the Quinisext (Fifth-Sixth) Council in Trullo. It established the *canon law of the Eastern church, but it was rejected by Rome, whose traditions were somewhat different, especially in liturgical practice. As a result, this council is not included in the list of ecumenical councils.

List of ecumenical councils

Ancient councils

1.	Nicaea	325
2.	Constantinople I	381
3.	Ephesus	431
4.	Chalcedon	451
5.	Constantinople II	553
6.	Constantinople III	680
5–6.	*In Trullo*++	692
7.	Nicaea II	787
8.	Constantinople IV+	870
	Constantinople IV++	880

Medieval councils

9.	Lateran I+	1123
10.	Lateran II+	1139
11.	Lateran III+	1179
12.	Lateran IV+	1215
13.	Lyons I+	1245
14.	Lyons II+	1274
15.	Vienne+	1311–12
16.	Constance+	1414–18
17.	Basel/Ferrara/Florence/Rome+	1438–45
18.	Lateran V+	1512–17

Modern councils

19.	Trent+	1545–63
20.	Vatican I+	1869–70
21.	Vatican II+	1962–65

++ Not recognized by the Western church(es)
++ Not recognized by the Eastern churches

The seventh ecumenical council was the Second Council of Nicaea (787), which was called to settle the *iconoclastic controversy. It authorized the veneration of icons on the grounds that it was possible to portray the divine person of Christ after the incarnation, and that honour paid to the image passed to the one represented. This decision was rejected at the Council of Frankfurt (794) and it has never affected the practice of the Western church, although it was later accepted by Rome. The Protestant Reformers all rejected it, but in the Eastern church it has come to occupy an important place as the last of the officially recognized ecumenical councils.

The eighth council, recognized as such only by the West, is the subject of dispute even today. Roman canonists have traditionally claimed that it was the council held at Constantinople in 870. This council condemned and deposed the Patriarch of Constantinople, Photius (*c.* 820–*c.* 895) who had broken with Rome over the double procession of the Holy Spirit (the *filioque* clause in the Nicene Creed) and the evangelization of Bulgaria. However, Photius was rehabilitated at another council of Constantinople, held in 880, and Rome apparently approved of this decision at the time. Modern scholars believe that the canonists of the eleventh century preferred to make the earlier council ecumenical, because by that time the two churches were in *schism and it suited the Roman canonists' case to argue that the Eastern church had been condemned in the person of Photius. In the modern ecumenical climate, research by Roman Catholic scholars has altered our understanding of events, and it is at least possible that both Rome and the Eastern churches may one day be able to declare the council of 880 to have been the eighth ecumenical council.

The next series of councils are the ten which were convened by the Western church during the Middle Ages. None of these is recognized today by the East, and their status among Protestants is undetermined. The first four were held at the Lateran Palace, the pope's official residence in Rome, and are of importance largely because they mark successive stages in the rise of papal power in the medieval church. At the first of these, in 1123, the church condemned lay investiture, which meant the practice of rulers in effect appointing the higher clergy in their realms. It also enjoined the monastic practice of celibacy on all clergy. The second council inveighed against false popes (1139), and the third against the *Albigensian heretics, who were fomenting rebellion in the south of France (1179). The Fourth Lateran Council (1215) asserted the unique primacy of the Roman see over all Christendom, and it is usually held to represent the high point of papal power in the Middle Ages. It also officially defined the dogma of transubstantiation (see *Eucharist).

Later medieval councils pursued similar themes, but the circumstances and locations in which they were summoned indicate a waning of papal power. The First Council of Lyons (1245) attacked the Holy Roman Emperor, Frederick II (1194–1250), but he paid little attention, and the pope was obliged to turn to France for support. The Second Council of Lyons (1274) attempted to heal the breach with the Eastern church. The Byzantine Emperor Michael VIII (1259–82) agreed to accept papal authority of a limited kind in return for aid against the Turks and the Normans (in Sicily), but help was not forthcoming, his own subjects repudiated him, and the union lapsed after his death. The Council of Vienne (1311–12) was called in order to dissolve the Crusading Order of the Knights Templar, on the ground that they were indulging in magical practices.

The Council of Constance (1414–18) was called to heal the papal schism which had broken out in 1378 and had resulted in the existence of three rival popes. The council resolved the schism, and also condemned Jan *Hus to be burned at the stake for *heresy. It decided to weaken the papacy by decreeing that the church would thenceforth be governed by synods meeting at five-yearly intervals. The scheme was not put into effect until 1429, when a council met at Basel, without the support or participation of Pope Eugenius IV (his predecessor had called it, and then died). The popes were determined to crush the Conciliar movement, and the opportunity to do so came in 1438, when the Byzantine Emperor John VIII (1425–48) offered church union to the West in exchange for support against the Turks. The pope called a council of his own (nominally a continuation of that at Basel), which met at Ferrara, only to be moved to Florence after a few months, because of an outbreak of plague. Eventually it was moved to Rome, where it was finally wound up in 1445. The Council of Florence, as it is most generally known, promulgated union with the different Eastern churches, including the Nestorians and monophysites, but these unions were forced, were dependent on aid against the Turks (which materialized, but did not succeed) and were concerned chiefly to back papal claims against the Council of Basel, which gradually petered out as its members withdrew their support and turned back to Rome. In the East, church union was not even proclaimed openly until 1452, and it was immediately repudiated when Constantinople fell to the Turks the following year. Nevertheless, the Council's decrees remain the basis of most of the Eastern Rite Catholic Churches (formerly known as 'Uniates'), who are Eastern in ritual but owe allegiance to Rome.

The last medieval council was the Fifth Lateran Council (1512–17), which tried to introduce some modest reforms into the church, but was overtaken by events in Germany which led to the Reformation.

Since the *Reformation, the Roman Catholic Church has held three councils, to which it has given the name ecumenical, even though no other church recognizes them. The first and most important of these was the Council of *Trent, which met in three distinct stages between 1545 and 1563. After initial attempts to include at least some Protestants, the council's attitude hardened and became extremely hostile to them. Trent spent its time defining and regulating Roman doctrines and practices which the Reformers had attacked, and it did so in a way which polarized the church and drove Rome into a Counter-Reformation which characterized it until the twentieth century (see *Reformation, Catholic Counter-). It produced a very influential *catechism, and the Tridentine Mass, authorized as the official Roman canon from 1570 until 1970, which enshrined the doctrines of transubstantiation and eucharistic sacrifice in a way which came to be regarded as typically Catholic. The abandonment of this Mass after 1970 even caused some conservative Catholics to accuse the church of having sold out to Protestantism.

The First *Vatican Council (1869–70) completed the work of Trent by defining the infallibility of the pope when making official (*ex cathedra*) statements in matters of faith and morals. The Second Vatican Council (1962–65) has been widely interpreted as a reaction against the Counter-Reformation spirit of Trent and the First Vatican Council, although it did not repudiate any of their decisions. The

Second Vatican Council adopted some of the Reformers' principles, such as the use of the vernacular in worship, and many radical Catholics have since appealed to it as justification for their ideas. It is undoubtedly true that the Roman Church is more open to outside influences than it was before the Second Vatican Council, though the long-term effects of this are still unclear. Rome is now committed to ecumenical dialogue in a way in which it was not previously, and it must be wondered whether the pope will ever again summon an ecumenical council without the active participation of other churches. On the other hand, it is far from certain whether the Eastern Orthodox or the Protestant churches would be prepared to attend a council under papal chairmanship, something which never happened in the undivided church of the early centuries.

Bibliography

The Seven Ecumenical Councils (texts), in *NPNF* series 2, vol. 14; G. Albertigo, *A Brief History of Vatican II* (Maryknoll, 2006); A. P. Flannery (ed.), *Vatican Council II: The Conciliar and Postconciliar Documents* (Dublin, rev. edn, 1992); C. J. Hefele, *A History of the Christian Councils*, 5 vols. (Edinburgh, 1883–96); P. Hughes, *The Church in Crisis: A History of the Twenty Great Councils* (London, 1961); H. Jedin, *Ecumenical Councils of the Catholic Church* (Freiburg, 1960); H. J. Margull (ed.), *The Councils of the Church: History and Analysis* (Philadelphia, 1966); R. V. Sellers, *The Council of Chalcedon* (London, 1961).

G. L. BRAY

COUNTER-REFORMATION, see REFORMATION, CATHOLIC COUNTER-; ROMAN CATHOLIC THEOLOGY

COVENANT THEOLOGY

Patristic and medieval church

No systematic use of covenant emerged during the ancient church, but *Irenaeus based his millennialism on the land promises of the OT covenant, and *Chrysostom spoke of the sacraments as covenants. *Augustine defined a covenant as an agreement between two parties, emphasized the unity of the OT and NT and proposed a pre-fall covenant between God and Adam.

The medieval period saw the development of three covenantal ideas: (1) Papal absolutists developed a baptismal covenant of the Christian with the pope. Disobedience to the pope was a breach of covenant entitling the pope to resist even a king. Covenant-breaking was grounds for resisting authority. (2) Sacramental theologians explained the saving properties of the mass's re-sacrifice of Christ as a covenant of God. (3) Gabriel *Biel devised a covenant of *merit, whereby God justified a man for doing his best: 'to the ones who do their best, God does not deny grace.' This doctrine of justification by works in God's covenant of merit was held by Luther until with his rediscovery of justification by faith in 1517, he became an opponent of medieval covenant theology.

Early Reformed theology

Luther's law/gospel distinction resulted from a repudiation of Biel's covenant thought, and subsequently, the concept of covenant was developed neither in Luther nor in the Lutheran tradition. In *Reformed theology, however, from Zwingli and Calvin onwards, covenant became a key theme.

*Zwingli emphasized the covenant with Abraham for the relationship of the Christian with God, becoming his main argument for infant *baptism. In 1534, *Bullinger wrote the first treatise on the covenant, *Of the One and Eternal Testament or Covenant of God*. Bullinger argued that the Scriptures must be interpreted by the Abrahamic covenant in which God graciously offers himself to man, and demands that man 'walk before him and be blameless'.

*Calvin developed the covenant in his *Institutes* (1559) in several areas: the unity of the OT and NT, the mutuality and conditionality of the covenant, the benefits of *salvation, the *Christian life (law, prayer, repentance, assurance), *predestination (predestination explains how the covenant works), the reformation of the church (Rome had broken the covenant, and should be resisted), the sacraments. Where Calvin wrote of the one covenant of God, later scholastic 'federal' Calvinism (from *foedus*, Lat. for 'covenant') developed schemes of two or more covenants.

Students of Calvin developed a pre-*fall covenant of works and a pre-temporal covenant of redemption. In 1562, Zacharias *Ursinus spoke of a pre-fall covenant of law between God and *Adam that demanded perfect obedience with the promise of life, and threatened disobedience with the penalty of death. In 1585, Caspar *Olevianus presented a pre-temporal covenant between the Father and the Son for the salvation of man. This coupled with the covenant of grace resulted in the federal theology of theologians such as Johannes *Cocceius. The covenants of works and grace received confessional status in the *Westminster Confession and catechisms.

By the post-Reformation era, one can distinguish: (1) the covenant idea of the Bible, (2) covenant theology – the unity of the covenant of grace throughout salvation history, and (3) federalism, the distinction between a pre-fall covenant of works and the redemptive post-fall covenant of grace. This federal scheme sometimes included the eternal pre-temporal covenant of redemption or *pactum salutis* between the Father and the Son.

Later developments in Reformed covenant theology

Cocceius is important for covenant theology because he developed a theology of the history of the covenant, reflecting God's gracious abrogation of the covenant of works by bringing eternal life. As an acknowledged infralapsarian, he did not develop his covenant views to blunt predestination as has been claimed.

Other Reformed theological controversies revolving around the covenant include: (1) political resistance to tyranny as in Samuel *Rutherford's *Lex Rex* (1644); (2) *Arminius's view that God's covenant with his creation was the basis for his right to judge them for disobedience; (3) the denial of a pre-fall covenant of works by certain schools of Reformed theology; (4) the denial by the school of Saumur, led by Moses *Amyraut, that the Mosaic covenant was to be included in the covenant of grace; (5) the covenant as a central point in the *New England Puritans' discussions concerning legalism and antinomianism; as well as (6) the New England Congregationalists' famous 'halfway covenant' that allowed non-communing adults who had been baptized as infants to bring their infants to be baptized.

Baptist theology

The Baptist movement emerged from English nonconformity. While agreeing with the Anabaptists on believers' baptism, some *Baptists in the Calvinist tradition had affinity with aspects of covenantal thought. Theologians such as John *Gill and Andrew *Fuller were influenced by the hermeneutics and theological covenants of federalism.

Baptist covenant theologians such as Nehemiah Coxe, however, distinguished circumcision from believers' baptism by a bi-covenantalism in the Abrahamic covenant. By developing two covenants in Abraham's relationship with God, Baptists could affirm continuity between the Abrahamic covenant and the NT teaching on salvation, but discontinuity between baptism and Abrahamic circumcision.

John Gill developed a strong contrast between the conditionality of the Old Covenant with Israel and the unconditionality of the New Covenant with the Christian. He also lessened the tension between the *sovereignty of God and the responsibility of man that is often an emphasis of Calvinistic covenantal teachings of salvation. Gill also postulated a trinitarian covenant of redemption that recognized the role of the Holy Spirit in the pre-temporal covenant.

Modern theology

Covenant theology remains important in modern Reformed theological discussion, particularly in terms of the covenant of works, the prelapsarian covenant of creation made by God with Adam. Federal theology, however, has come in for sharp criticism in respect of *the* covenant of works and its allegedly contractual colouring (cf. J. B. Torrance in *SJT* 23, 1970, pp. 51–76, and 34, 1981, pp. 225–243). Karl *Barth developed his doctrine of covenant in relation to *creation, characterizing the creation as the outer basis of the covenant and the covenant as the inner basis of creation (*CD*, III.1, 41). This gave expression to what has been called his 'refined supralapsarianism' in seeing the goal of creation in God's people, the church.

Some have alleged that Calvin's theology is incompatible with the way in which federal Calvinism developed. Barth summarizes, 'In Calvin there can be no question of the Law destroying the character of the covenant as a covenant of grace, nor can we find any combination of the covenant concept with a primitive *lex naturae*. This idea came in as a result of the influence which Melanchthon came to exercise on Reformed theology . . .' (*CD*, IV.1, 58).

Within traditional federal Calvinism, adherents of covenant theology such as John *Murray and Meredith Kline debated the primacy of God's grace or the primacy of God's law in the 'Adamic Administration' or the 'Covenant of Works'. Questions discussed include: Was the original covenant based on divine law and human merit, or was it fully gracious for unfallen humanity? Did Christ's death satisfy completely for man's salvation (the imputation of Christ's passive obedience) or did his perfect obedience to God's law satisfy the covenant of works for all the elect in Christ (the imputation of Christ's active obedience)?

Bibliography

T. K. Ascol, 'The Doctrine of Grace: A Critical Analysis of Federalism in the Theologies of John Gill and Andrew Fuller', PhD dissertation (Southwestern Baptist Theological Seminary, 1989); J. W. Baker, *Heinrich Bullinger and the Covenant: The Other Reformed Tradition* (Athens, OH, 1980); L. D. Bierma, *German Calvinism in the Confessional Age: The Covenant Theology of Casper Olevianus* (Grand Rapids, 1996); Jeong Koo Jeon, *Covenant Theology: John Murray's and Meredith G. Kline's Response to the Historical Development of Federal Theology in Reformed Thought* (Lanham, 1999); N. Coxe and J. Owen, *Covenant Theology from Adam to Christ*, eds. R. D. Miller, J. M. Renihan and F. Orozco (Palmdale, 2005); P. A. Lillback, *The Binding of God: Calvin's Role in the Development of Covenant Theology* (Grand Rapids, 2001); C. S. McCoy and J. W. Baker, *Fountainhead of Federalism: Heinrich Bullinger and the Covenantal Tradition* (Louisville, 1991); J. Murray, 'Covenant Theology', in *EC*, vol. III; S. Preus, *From Shadow to Promise* (Cambridge, MA, 1969); S. Strehle, *Calvinism, Federalism, and Scholasticism: A Study of the Reformed Doctrine of Covenant* (Bern, 1988); G. Vos, 'The Doctrine of the Covenant in Reformed Theology', in R. B. Gaffin, Jr (ed.), *Redemptive History and Biblical Interpretation* (Philipsburg, 1980), pp. 234–267; D. A. Weir, *The Origins of the Federal Theology in Sixteenth-Century Reformation Thought* (Oxford, 1990).

P. A. LILLBACK

COVENANTERS

Scottish *Presbyterians who from 1638 resisted attempts by Stuart monarchs to impose and maintain an episcopal system of *church government. Previously uneasy about the modified episcopacy established under James VI (d. 1625), the country became increasingly alarmed when Charles I not only made friendly overtures to Rome, but imposed upon the Scottish church a Book of Canons (1636) and a liturgy (1637) without the endorsement of General Assembly or parliament. These documents demanded explicit acknowledgment of the royal supremacy, transferred full power to the bishops, and threatened excommunication on those who rejected episcopacy (see *Caroline Divines).

When the king ignored their protests, Scots leaders prepared a legal bond of association known as the National Covenant (1638). After repeating a 1581 Confession condemning Roman Catholic errors, including 'tyrannous laws made . . . against our Christian liberty', the Covenant detailed those Acts of Parliament which had established the *Reformed faith and church government, and subscribers bound themselves to defend the Presbyterian religion and 'the King's majesty . . . in the preservation of the foresaid true religion'.

Charles prevaricated, Archbishop Laud (1573–1645) was unmoved; so a General Assembly met in Glasgow to reject Erastian tendencies (see *State) and royalist pretensions by proclaiming Christ as the only head of the church. The Scottish bishops were deposed, offending ecclesiastical legislation was condemned, and the notorious Court of High Commission abolished. The king, who was embroiled also in conflict with the English Parliament, lost the battle of Newburn against the Covenanting forces, and was forced to yield to Scottish demands. The Glasgow Assembly was given legal validity, and the Kirk with dubious wisdom asked the Privy Council to require all Scots to sign the Covenant. Thus the Covenanters took upon themselves the power they had denied to the crown, but more blame attaches to a king who had obtusely converted a protest against episcopacy into a rebellion against himself.

Basic to the Covenanting position was the firm opposition of the Reformed Church of Scotland to two principles: the authority of the civil power in spiritual matters, and the prelatic superiority of one minister over others. Among the early Covenanters who guided the Kirk in its return to Presbyterianism were Alexander Henderson (1583–1646), George Gillespie (1613–49) and Samuel *Rutherford, all of whom had a prominent part in the Westminster Assembly. Henderson, meanwhile, was the chief drafter of the Solemn League and Covenant, a religious alliance between the Scots and the English parliamentary party, though one essentially forced on the latter by political expediency.

Soon after the Restoration of 1660, Charles II had two leading Covenanters executed: the Marquis of Argyle and James Guthrie, minister of Stirling. Episcopacy was reimposed upon the land and church government vested in the Crown. Covenanter-ministers were ejected from their parishes, the process helped by a dissolute court, a Scottish Council of profligate nobles, and military leaders who carried out a policy of savage repression. Latterly known as 'the killing times', the persecution of Covenanters continued until James VII fled in 1688 and the Revolution Settlement vindicated the rebels and re-established Presbyterianism.

Cameronian or Reformed Presbyterian churches maintain a Covenanting succession, on both sides of the Atlantic.

Bibliography

J. D. Douglas, *Light in the North: The Story of the Scottish Covenanters* (Exeter, 1964); J. K. Hewison, *The Covenanters*, 2 vols. (Glasgow, ²1913); A. Smellie, *Men of the Covenant* (repr. London, 1975 [1908]); E. Whitley, *The Two Kingdoms* (Edinburgh, 1977).

J. D. DOUGLAS

CRANMER, THOMAS (1489–1556)

Thomas Cranmer came to his mature doctrinal views only gradually. Typical of the Catholic *humanism of John Fisher's Cambridge, he was trained at Jesus College in *scholasticism, the Fathers and the Bible (BA, 1511; MA, 1515; BD 1521; DD 1526). During the 1520s he followed *Erasmus, emphasizing Scripture over scholastic reasoning, rejecting Luther's bondage of the will, and preferring *conciliarism to papal authority. Hence, he was able to work for Henry VIII's 'divorce'. Nevertheless, during the 1530s Cranmer accepted *justification by faith as the true Augustinian exegesis of Paul. His conversion to evangelical teaching most likely dates from his 1532 residency in Germany, while serving as the king's ambassador to Charles V, when he married a relative of the Nuremburg Reformer Andreas Osiander.

Unexpectedly, Cranmer was called back by Henry VIII to become Archbishop of Canterbury in 1533. After the split from Rome the following year, Cranmer worked with limited success to convince the king to introduce the Reformation into England. Only with the 1547 accession of Henry's young son Edward VI did Cranmer have the opportunity to reshape the teachings of the English church according to his own now clearly *Protestant principles.

First, he oversaw the publication of the *Book of Homilies* (1547). This collection of required sermons for parish clergy taught the supremacy and sufficiency of Scripture as well as justification by faith. Secondly, he compiled a new national *liturgy. The 1549 *Book of Common Prayer* used English exclusively, institutionalized the systematic reading of Scripture, removed all references to personal merit and emphasized a eucharistic sacrifice of praise and thanksgiving only. The next year Cranmer published a similarly revised Ordinal. His 1552 combination Prayer Book and Ordinal contained even more Protestant changes. The traditional order of the prayers in the Canon of the Mass was broken up so that the thanksgiving of the people was now their response to the grace received with the elements, not its grounds. In addition, the prayers themselves were altered to clarify that Christ's eucharistic presence was spiritual in nature, a holy communion in the heart of the believer through personal faith. Finally, Cranmer drew up an official statement of essential theological beliefs called the *Articles of Religion* (1553). Crucial for the future development of the Anglican Communion, the Forty-Two Articles (see *Thirty-Nine Articles) distinguished saving truth, which served as the basis of church unity and had to be clearly established by Scripture, from ecclesiastical traditions and ceremonies, which every nation was free to adapt to their own culture, so long as the result was not contrary to Scripture.

Although Cranmer was burned as an archheretic under Mary, his three formularies were adopted with only minor modifications by the Elizabethan church. Consequently, Cranmer's doctrinal and liturgical legacy served as the foundation for the emergence of *Anglicanism.

Bibliography

P. N. Brooks, *Thomas Cranmer's Doctrine of the Eucharist* (London, ²1992); D. MacCulloch, *Thomas Cranmer: A Life* (London, 1996); idem, *Tudor Church Militant: Edward VI and the Protestant Reformation* (London: 1999); A. Null, 'Official Tudor Homilies', in P. McCullough, H. Adlington and E. Rhatigan (eds.), Oxford Handbook of the Early Modern Sermon (Oxford, 2011), pp. 348–365; *idem*, *Thomas Cranmer's Doctrine of Repentance: Renewing the Power of Love* (Oxford, 2000).

J. A. NULL

CREATION

The Christian doctrine of creation has been the object of immense controversy during the modern era, especially since the rise of evolutionary theory in the nineteenth century and developments in cosmology during the twentieth. Such controversies have significantly truncated the range of theological reflection on this doctrine. They have also deflected popular Christian engagement with this topic to an unduly narrow focus on the questions of cosmological and biological origins. In fact, in its classical expressions the Christian doctrine of creation addressed questions of origins only within the wider context of interest in the nature, purpose and status of creation, the structures appropriate to creaturely existence, the relationships between the various creatures, and the nature of *sin and *evil.

Nevertheless, it is reflection on the nature, status and purpose of creation – as these are framed through the NT's nexus of *Christology and creation – which lies at the heart of the Christian doctrine of creation. The biblical foundations and theological development of these themes will be the focus of what follows.

The New Testament

There can be few more all-encompassing claims for Jesus Christ than those contained in the prologue to the Gospel of John. Here, *Jesus, the one who 'made his dwelling among us' (1:14) is none other than the Word who was 'in the beginning' (1:1) and through whom 'all things were made' (1:3). Nor is this text alone. Col. 1:15–17 and Heb. 1:2 similarly identify Christ as the mediator of creation. Also noteworthy are those texts which identify Christ as the goal of creation (e.g. Eph. 1:9–10; 4:10; Phil. 2:9–11; Rev. 22:13). Notwithstanding assorted points of exegetical controversy, these texts point to a significant consensus across different strands of the NT literature around the Christological interpretation of creation. It is not just that Christ is being portrayed as a figure of cosmic significance – which he is – but that he is portrayed as *the* ground and purpose of creation. As such, these texts point to a strong affirmation of both the goodness of creation (how could it not be good if it was created by Christ?) and the fact that Christ's redemptive work is the redemption *of*, not a redemption *from*, creation. As statements, therefore, of the unity of creation and *redemption these texts specify Christologically one of the strands of OT teaching about creation.

The Old Testament

OT references to creation cannot be isolated from claims about monotheism, divine sovereignty and the order of creation, and these as articulated in polemical encounters with rival worldviews, theologies and cosmologies. Where, for instance, other ancient beliefs involved postulating creation as the outcome of battles between warring divinities, Gen. 1:1 – 2:4 affirms creation both as the good work of the sovereign will of the one *God and also as a reality distinct from God. And, where other cosmologies saw creation permanently threatened by various chaotic forces, OT writers envisaged the act of creation as God's ordering of (Pss 89:9–10; 104:7), or at least imposing limits on (Job 38:8–11), chaos. What remains unresolved in the OT is the tension between creation as an ordering (of already existent realities) and creation as the absolute beginning (of all that is not God). This tension will later yield, in both Christianity and Judaism, to a doctrine of *creatio ex nihilo*.

Also significant in the OT is the place which human beings have in God's creation. Alone among the creatures, they are the *image of God and are given dominion over the rest of creation (Gen. 1:26–28). On the basis of both etymological considerations and its canonical context, this designation cannot be taken either to licence any human exploitation of creation (e.g. Gen. 2:15–17; Deut. 20:19; 22:6) or to imply any divine indifference to the non-human creation (e.g. Gen. 8:21–22). After all, it was the very community which ascribed this specific status to humanity which also had a well-developed understanding of the role of the whole creation in the praise of God (e.g. Ps. 148).

Theological developments

As it moved into the world of classical Greek thought and as it struggled with *Gnosticism,

Christianity encountered yet further rival views of the origin, nature and purpose of creation, such as the eternal existence of creation, an understanding of creation as the fashioning of pre-existent matter by an inferior divinity, and, concomitantly, redemption being a form of release or escape from the reality of creation. Reflecting the multi-layered context of the biblical references to creation, the Christian response to these issues was neither isolated from other areas of belief nor univocal. Nevertheless, the NT's consensus on the Christological unity of creation and redemption certainly forced the rejection of any understanding of creation as inferior, chaotic or evil. Nor can the impact of nascent patristic Christological debates (ultimately addressed directly in the Arian controversy) upon these reflections be underestimated. The clarification for Christological purposes of the distinction between *creating* and *begetting* both reflected and informed the developing Christian understanding of creation as a contingent event which brought into being a reality distinct from God. Herein lies the foundation of the Christian commitment to the idea of *creatio ex nihilo*. It does not rest on the disputable exegesis of particular verses (i.e. Gen. 1:1–2), but on the considered combination of various theological convictions.

Awareness of these various background convictions is essential for the full articulation of the doctrine of creation. In fact, what has often been lost in the reception and defence of this doctrine is precisely its Christological – and ultimately trinitarian – context. Placed in that context, the doctrine of creation depends for its coherence on maintaining various tensions which are proper to the doctrine. An insistence on the sovereignty of the divine creative will cannot be at the expense of an awareness that this same will is as loving, gracious and purposeful as it is sovereign. Equally, and for similar reasons, an emphasis on *creatio ex nihilo* can overlook God's continuing and eschatologically open relationship with creation. An unbalanced emphasis on the unity of creation and redemption can too easily surrender the distinction between the two. At the same time, an emphasis on the distinction of creation from God must not render creation alien to God, nor blind the believer to God's order in creation. Observing how these tensions play out in various theologians is always instructive. *Thomas Aquinas, for instance, affirmed the doctrine of *creatio ex nihilo*, but sought to describe the relationship between God and the creation through an appeal to a continuous hierarchy of causes (see *ST* 1a, 44–46), thus potentially threatening the *distinction* between God and creation. Karl *Barth defined creation as the external basis of the *covenant and the covenant as the internal basis of creation (see *CD* III/1, pp. 94–329). His appeal to covenant reflects the Christological *telos* of creation, but in deeming creation 'external' to the covenant, he potentially rendered problematic God's continuing *relationship* to creation. The debates surrounding these equally sophisticated proposals reflect the tensions inherent in doing justice to all the dimensions of the distinctively Christian understanding of creation.

Contemporary issues

Modern controversies related to the doctrine of creation often reflect the dissolution of one or more of the various tensions just discussed.

Creation and science

That the development of evolutionary theory and discoveries in cosmology turned the relationship between science and Christianity (see *Science and theology) into one of conflict was due to many factors, of which the interpretation of Genesis was only superficially the most important. More telling was the fact that the prevailing theology in the relevant contexts (i.e. *deism) had dissolved the tension between contingent origin and Christological purpose entirely in favour of the former. Consequently, the ordered openness of nature described by evolution, cosmology and quantum physics was wrongly perceived to be *necessarily* at odds with Christian teaching. More theologically balanced doctrines of creation in T. F. *Torrance and Alister McGrath allow for constructive dialogue between science and theology. Specifically, a Christological understanding of creation's origin and purpose allows McGrath to propose that the rationality discerned by the natural sciences is the same rationality as 'embedded in creation and embodied in Christ' (*Scientific Theology* I, p. 188). The discernment of order in creation can therefore be interpreted Christologically and need not merely become, as it risks becoming in Intelligent Design, the basis of an explanatory appeal to a 'god of the gaps'.

Creation, revelation and natural theology

A closely related issue is whether creation reveals God. Does the unity between creation and redemption extend to revelation? A negative answer to that question led Karl Barth to his vigorous attack upon '*natural theology'. Barth believed that natural theology rested on a *necessary* connection between God and human beings (thus dissolving the tension between creation's distinction from God and God's covenantal relationship with creation). Barth's fear was that any such necessary connection implied a source of *revelation independent of that given uniquely and redemptively in Christ. The intensity of Barth's polemic against natural theology has often obscured from his readers the positive statements he did make about the *contingent* role of creation in revelation. In fact, consistent with his particular understanding of creation and covenant, he was quite able to endorse faith's recognition of a divinely given order in creation (see *CD* IV/3, pp. 135–165). Such a move justifies a 'theology of nature' which allows observations (scientific or otherwise) of nature's order to be given an appropriate (albeit non-foundationalist) place in theological discourse.

Creation and the environmental crisis

The human exploitation of the earth which lies behind this crisis is often explained as the direct consequence of the Judeo-Christian teaching about the dominion granted by God to human beings (see *Ecology). As noted above, the texts themselves resist such interpretation. In fact, more problematic for many contemporary critics is the ideological function of the doctrine of creation more generally. The distinction between God and creation is said to justify the objectification of creation. Furthermore, the sovereignty ascribed to God is said to be illegitimately transferred to human beings. Thus, so the critics argue, is the exploitation of nature ideologically justified. The counter-proposal is an account of creation which deliberately surrenders the distinction between God and creation in a form of *pantheism (which tends also to dissolve several of the other tensions noted above). The actual intellectual and ethical advances of such proposals, the coherence of their criticisms of the orthodox doctrine, and their accounts of the latter's reception are all issues likely to be vigorously debated for the foreseeable future.

See also: CREATION AND EVOLUTION; CREATION-CENTRED SPIRITUALITY; NATURE, THEOLOGY OF.

Bibliography

K. Barth, *CD*; D. Fergusson, *Cosmos and Creator: An Introduction to the Theology of Creation* (London, 1998); C. Gunton, *The Triune Creator: A Historical and Systematic Study* (Grand Rapids, 1998); G. May, *Creatio Ex Nihilo: The Doctrine of 'Creation out of Nothing' in Early Christian Thought* (ET, Edinburgh, 1994); G. McCulloch, *The Deconstruction of Dualism in Theology: With Special Reference to Ecofeminist Theology and New Age Spirituality* (Carlisle, 2002); S. McFague, *The Body of God: An Ecological Theology* (Minneapolis and London, 1993); A. McGrath, *A Scientific Theology, vol 1: Nature* (Edinburgh, 2001); J. Moltmann, *God in Creation: An Ecological Doctrine of Creation* (ET, London 1985); Thomas Aquinas, *Summa Theologiae* (ET, London, 1911); T. Torrance, *Divine and Contingent Order* (Edinburgh, ²1998).

G. J. THOMPSON

CREATION AND EVOLUTION

To gain clarity in this area, hotly debated by some Christians, it is necessary to differentiate between the doctrine of *creation, which is not a scientific theory but a doctrine of the Christian faith confessed in the historic creeds, and the theory of evolution, which is a scientific theory and indeed a cornerstone of natural science today. The doctrine of *creatio ex nihilo*, that the world (that is, the universe, everything other than God) was created by God out of nothing, was formulated in the second century by the early Christian bishops, *Irenaeus of Lyons and Theophilus of Antioch, on the basis of Scripture and has been held by all major theologians and branches of the church ever since. The theory of evolution, that all animal species evolved from a common ancestry, was proposed before Darwin, but was established as the dominant paradigm of the science of biology and related sciences such as geology, following the publication of his book, *The Origin of the Species*, in 1859. It remains today the dominant and accepted view of the scientific community. Charles Darwin himself (1809–82) came from a Unitarian family, and his theory (along with the problem of evil) brought him to a crisis of faith. But it was his disciple, Thomas Henry Huxley (1825–95), who took up Darwin's theory as a weapon to fight for the place of science in the universities in opposition to classics and theology, and as an argument for what he called '*agnosticism', a position which today is largely synonymous with secular *humanism. Richard Dawkins presents a contemporary version of Huxley's position.

Despite the notorious debate at Oxford between Huxley and Bishop Samuel Wilberforce, many leading church leaders of the day (including such evangelicals as B. B. *Warfield of Princeton, Henry Drummond of Edinburgh, and James *Orr of Glasgow) accepted some form of evolution and did not see it as contrary to the doctrine of creation *ex nihilo*. After all, before evolution could begin there had to be matter, and science had not given any explanation for the origin of the material universe itself. The theory was disturbing, however, for many ordinary Christians, because they did not distinguish the doctrine of creation from their literal interpretation of the first chapters of Genesis. Ironically, the *fundamentalist movement which developed mainly in America in the 1920s was in fact agreeing with Huxley against many theologians that belief in creation was a scientific theory held by Christians in opposition to Darwinism, and 'creationists' today continue to take that view.

The case for 'creationism' was revived in the 1960s by the publication of *The Genesis Flood* by John C. Whitcomb and Henry Morris. Today a significant percentage of American Christians accept their 'Young Earth' view that the earth was created 10,000 years ago in seven days and that much of the fossil record is due to the flood. Battles have continued in the courts as to whether these views can be accepted as reputable science. 'Old Earth' creationists, however, interpret the 'days' in Gen. 1 as long periods of time (as did Augustine), and often accept micro- as distinct from macro-evolution. Over against creationism as scientific theory, the case for 'theistic evolution' as compatible with the doctrine of creation has been maintained by evangelical leaders in the United Kingdom, including John Stott, Oliver Barclay and the geneticist, R. J. Berry.

In the 1990s, new opposition to Darwinism appeared in the advocacy of 'intelligent design' by an American law professor, Phillip Johnson, supported by William Dembski (a mathematician and philosopher) and the biochemist, Michael Behe. Rather than proceeding from Scripture, these writers attacked the presumptions of 'naturalism' in science and pin-pointed problems in the theory of evolution, particularly the problem of the 'irreducible complexity' at the biochemical level. These thinkers seem to advocate a revived teleological argument for God as Creator, rather than a fundamentalist form of creationism. They have defended 'intelligent design' against the accusation that it simply revives the 'god of the gaps', using God to explain aspects of science that we do not yet understand.

While the idea of the evolution of the species (and indeed the evolution of the cosmos over 13.7 million years since the Big Bang) may be logically compatible with a belief in the creation of the universe *ex nihilo*, advocates of 'theistic evolution' face greater problems in reconciling evolution with the Christian doctrine of humanity created 'in the *image of God' and with the traditional understanding of the doctrine of the *fall.

See also: ADAM; ANTHROPOLOGY; SCIENCE AND THEOLOGY.

Bibliography

D. Alexander, *Creation and Evolution: Do We Have to Choose?* (Oxford and Grand Rapids, 2008); R. J. Berry and T. A. Noble, *Darwin, Creation and the Fall* (Nottingham, 2009); M. C. Cunningham, *God and Evolution: A Reader* (London and New York, 2007); G. Finlay, S. Lloyd, S. Pattemore and D. Swift, *Debating Darwin* (Milton Keynes, 2009); K. W. Giberson, *Saving Darwin* (New York, 2008); D. N. Livingstone, *Darwin's Forgotten Defenders* (Grand Rapids and Edinburgh, 1987); E. Lucas, *Can We Believe Genesis Today?* (Leicester, 2001); S. Meyer, *Signature in the Cell* (New York, 2009); P. Nelson, R. C. Newman and H. J. Van Till, *Three Views on Creation and Evolution* (Grand Rapids, 1999).

T. A. NOBLE

CREATION-CENTRED SPIRITUALITY

A term originally associated with the work of theologians like Matthew Fox and Thomas Berry, and their dissatisfaction with an over-emphasis in Western theology on the moral categories of fall and redemption, with an accompanying devaluing of *creation and *incarnation. Fox argues that this has engendered an unbiblical dualism between humanity and divinity that alienated people from the natural world, and by differentiating the physical and spiritual aspects of human nature has created much of the ecological, social and personal dysfunction that characterizes contemporary life. A worldview that takes seriously the creation-incarnation axis of biblical teaching would start with 'original blessing' rather than 'original sin', and in doing so can offer reconciliation to a broken world, by recognizing the divine wholeness that already exists ('*panentheism' – God is not exclusively transcendent, but is also immanent in all things), and which invites an affirmation of diversity in people and the natural world. Virtually anything can therefore be regarded as a pathway into God, including the ancient traditions of many peoples as well as contemporary science. In the hands of Matthew Fox, this leads to an inclusive vision of the entire cosmos transformed through a common passion for justice for the natural world as well as for people and systems. It has also been criticized for incorporating a form of *syncretism, and a tendency to downplay the reality of *evil, though Fox denies this.

The notion that God can be found in the natural world as well as through direct revelation is deeply rooted in the Bible, and is also found in the teachings of the Greek Fathers, along with the theories and practices of medieval mystics such as *Hildegard of Bingen, *Thomas Aquinas, Meister Eckhart and Nicholas of Cusa, among others. It is undoubtedly the case that Christians have often used the notion of original sin (not a biblical term) as a form of control, and that the role of the natural world in the divine economy has largely been ignored. The same can be said of mystical experience, which has frequently been marginalized in favour of rational reflection. The rise of Pentecostal theology has to some extent reinstated experience as an authentic vehicle for the Spirit, while Rom. 8:19–23 indicates that concern for the environment (see *Ecology) is intrinsic to a biblical doctrine of salvation. Other questions raised by creation-centred spirituality include the nature of human beings as made in God's image (Gen. 1:27) (see *Image of God), and the role of *imagination and creativity in worship as well as theology.

Bibliography

T. Berry, *The Dream of the Earth* (San Francisco, 2006); L. Boff, *Cry of the Earth, Cry of the Poor* (Maryknoll, 1997); J. Drane, 'Matthew Fox', in T. A. Hart (ed.), *The Dictionary of Historical Theology* (Grand Rapids, 2000); M. Fox, *Creation Spirituality* (San Francisco, 1991); idem, *Original Blessing* (New York, ²2000); idem, *A New Reformation: Creation Spirituality and the Transformation of Christianity* (Rochester, 2006).

J. DRANE

CREEDS

A creed (from the Lat. *credo*, 'I believe') is an authoritative statement of the main articles of the Christian faith to which believers are expected to assent. Broadly speaking, biblical religion has always been credal. Biblical and post-biblical Judaism confessed Yahweh's absolute unity and uniqueness by the Shema': 'Hear, O Israel: the LORD our God, the LORD is one' (Deut. 6:4). The genesis of the church's symbols (as creeds have been called from early times) resides in protocredal statements of faith and worship embedded in the NT (see *Confessions of Faith). With the confession, 'Jesus is Lord' (Rom. 10:9; 1 Cor. 12:3), early Christians acknowledged that the Nazarene was to be spoken of in the same terms as Yahweh of the OT. The text interpolated at Acts 8:37, 'I believe that Jesus Christ is the Son of God', represents a primitive Christian baptismal affirmation. Other NT credal formulas affirm Christ's incarnation, saving death and glorious resurrection (Rom. 1:3–4; 1 Cor. 15:3–4; 1 John 4:2). The great Christological passage, Phil. 2:6–11, may have been sung at early Christian baptismal services. 1 Cor. 8:6 affirms the unity of God and the co-ordination of the Father with Jesus Christ. Finally, in the NT a *trinitarian confessional pattern emerged (Matt. 28:19; 2 Cor. 13:14), which became the paradigm for later credal formularies.

The *Apostolic Fathers reflect what J. N. D. Kelly calls 'quasi-credal scraps', and the *apologists a growing corpus of teaching that distils the essence of the Christian faith. What scholars refer to as the Old Roman creed (c. 140, Harnack) was an expanded trinitarian baptismal formula: 'I believe in God the Father

Almighty and in Christ Jesus his Son, our Lord, and in the Holy Spirit, the holy Church, and the resurrection of the flesh.' In the writings of *Irenaeus, *Clement of Alexandria, *Tertullian and *Hippolytus is found the 'rule of faith', or 'the tradition', which was an informal corpus of teaching provided to catechumens. The so-called Apostles' Creed, while not apostolic in authorship, is nevertheless apostolic in content. Its present form (eighth century) represents a lengthy development from simpler trinitarian baptismal formulas, particularly the Old Roman creed. The Apostles' Creed indirectly refuted various heresies (e.g. *Ebionites, *Marcion, *Gnostics, *docetists) and was widely used in the West for instruction and worship. 'The Creed of creeds' (P. Schaff, *The Creeds of Christendom*) contains the fundamental articles of the Christian faith necessary to salvation.

The Creed of Nicaea (325), which was probably based on earlier creeds from Jerusalem and Antioch, was drafted to refute the *Arian claim that the Son was the highest creation of God and thus essentially different from the Father (see *Christology). The Nicene Creed as we know it today represents in effect an enlargement of the teaching of the Creed of 325, probably approved by the Council of *Constantinople (381). It affirms the unity of God, insists that Christ was 'begotten from the Father before all time', and declares that Christ is 'of the same essence [*homoousios*] as the Father'. Thus the Son is God in every respect. The Creed also upheld the divinity of the *Holy Spirit and his procession from the Father. In the West the phrase 'who proceeds from the Father' was later altered to read, 'from the Father and the Son'. This so-called *filioque* clause, which affirms the double procession of the Spirit, followed the teaching of *Hilary, *Ambrose, *Jerome and *Augustine and appears in the Athanasian Creed, but was rejected by the Eastern Church (see *Eastern Orthodox theology). It became the major doctrinal issue in the schism between East and West that came to a head in 1054.

The Athanasian Creed, or *Quicunque vult* (from the opening words of the Latin text), was written by an unknown author in the *Augustinian tradition in Southern Gaul about the mid-fifth century. It contains a clear and concise statement of the Trinity and the *incarnation of Christ, both of which must be believed for salvation. Concerning the Trinity, the Creed affirms that 'the Father is God, the Son is God, and the Holy Spirit is God; and yet there are not three Gods but one God'. The articles on Christ uphold his eternal generation from the substance of the Father, his complete deity and complete humanity, his death for sins, resurrection, ascension, second coming and final judgment. The East never recognized the Athanasian Creed.

The Chalcedonian Definition was prepared by over 500 Greek bishops at the Council of *Chalcedon in 451. In response to erroneous interpretations of the person of Christ advanced by *Apollinarius, *Nestorius and Eutyches (see *Monophysitism), the Definition states that Jesus Christ is perfectly God and perfectly man, that he is consubstantial with God as to his divinity, and with mankind as to his humanity. Moreover, humanity and deity are joined in the God-man 'without confusion, without change, without division, without separation'. Chalcedon represents the definitive statement, albeit in Greek ontological language, of how Jesus Christ was God and man at the same time.

Creeds have served a variety of functions in the church. Initially elemental creeds were used in a *baptismal context. By responding to questions or reciting certain formulas which later became fixed, the baptismal candidate made confession of faith in Christ. Moreover, creeds were used for *catechetical purposes, i.e. for instructing new Christians in the essentials of the faith. The creeds (especially the 'rule of faith') were also employed for confessional purposes, that is, to refute and expose the heretical teachings of the docetists, Gnostics, *Monarchians, Arians and others. And finally, the creeds served a *liturgical purpose as they were recited at various places in the worship services of the churches.

As for the authority of the creeds, the Eastern Orthodox churches ascribe authority to the decrees of the seven ecumenical *councils, from the First Council of Nicaea (325) to the second at Nicaea (787). The Eastern churches have not accepted the Western doctrinal creeds and reject the *filioque* addition to the Nicene Creed. Rome, on the other hand, claims infallibility for all the pronouncements of the magisterium. Traditionally, the Apostles', Nicene and Athanasian creeds were known as 'the three symbols'. According to Rome, the ancient credal formulas contain truths revealed by God and thus authoritative for all time. The

Protestant Reformers accepted the Apostles' Creed and the decrees of the first four councils by virtue of their agreement with Scripture, the only rule of faith and practice. *Luther said of the Apostles' Creed: 'Christian truth could not possibly be put into a shorter and clearer statement' (*LW* 37, p. 360). *Calvin said of the formulas of the ecumenical councils: 'I venerate them from my heart, and would have all of them held in due honour' (*Institutes* IV.ix.1). The main branches of *Protestantism value the four creeds discussed above as faithfully embodying the teachings of Scripture. Beginning with A. von *Harnack, critical scholarship has attacked the classical creeds for their reliance upon an alleged alien Greek philosophical system and an outmoded cosmology. Thus Protestants such as *Tillich, *Bultmann and J. A. T. *Robinson claim that the ancient creeds possess little cash value in the modern world. Even Roman Catholics such as H. *Küng and the Dutch compilers of the New Catechism (1966) claim that the creeds are human statements formulated in cultural contexts foreign to our own and are thus beset with serious limitations and even errors.

Orthodox Protestantism views each of the above-mentioned creeds as a *norma normata*, i.e. as a rule that is ruled by the final authority of the word of God. In general terms, the creeds expound 'what has always been believed, everywhere, and by everyone' (Vincentian Canon; see *Catholicity). But ultimately, even the best human formularies must be ruled by the infallible word of God. In sum, by virtue of their general agreement with Scripture, the orthodox creeds provide a valuable summary of universal Christian beliefs, refute teachings alien to the word of God, and are serviceable in Christian instruction and worship.

See also: CONFESSIONS OF FAITH; COUNCILS.

Bibliography

G. Bray, *Creeds, Councils and Christ* (Leicester, 1984); P. T. Fuhrmann, *Introduction to the Great Creeds of the Church* (Philadelphia, 1960); J. N. D. Kelly, *The Athanasian Creed* (London, 1964); idem, *Early Christian Creeds* (London, ³1972); J. H. Leith, *Creeds of the Churches* (Richmond, ³1982); P. Schaff, *The Creeds of Christendom*, 3 vols. (New York, 1877ff., best edn, 1919).

B. DEMAREST

CREMER, HERMANN (1834–1903)

Hermann Cremer was a Lutheran biblical scholar and theologian with a very wide influence on conservative *Protestant thought in Germany in the latter part of the nineteenth century. Born into a family deeply influenced by the *pietist movement, he moved away from that spirituality towards a more biblicist orientation, especially in his mature years as a professor at Greifswald from 1870. A determined and forceful personality, and a thinker of exceptional cogency, Cremer became a stout opponent of what he regarded as the destructive legacy of the *Enlightenment, rejecting the alliance with human *culture which he found among many contemporary Protestants.

Besides his work on the language of the NT (which bore fruit in his *Biblico-Theological Lexicon of New Testament Greek*, ET, Edinburgh, 1878, widely used in both Germany and Britain at the end of the nineteenth century), he is remembered particularly for his work on the doctrine of *justification, where he urged a strong doctrine of human *sin and a forensic account of the work of Christ. Cremer was a leading figure in church politics, and deeply influential on pupils and colleagues (notably the biblical and doctrinal theologian Adolf *Schlatter), as much by his character as by his theology. Towards the end of his life he became a noted opponent of *Harnack, then at the height of his influence in German intellectual life.

Bibliography

H. Beintker in *TRE* 8, pp. 230–236 (with German bibliography); G. Friedrich in *TDNT* X, pp. 640–650 (on his *Lexicon*); W. Koepp in *RGG* 1, cols. 1881–2.

J. B. WEBSTER

CROSS, THEOLOGY OF THE

The term *theologia crucis* was first used by Martin *Luther to describe his Reformation theology in its early period. It refers not simply to the doctrine of the cross, in which the cross is seen as the focal point of Christ's work of salvation (see *Atonement), but to an understanding of the whole of theology as theology of the cross, in that the cross is seen as the focal point of God's revelation of himself and therefore as the foundation and centre of all truly Christian theology. In the theology of the cross, the cross becomes a methodological key to the whole of theology. In Luther's epigram: *Crux probat omnia* ('the cross is the criterion of all things', *Weimarer Ausgabe* 5, p. 179). Hence Luther could claim that 'the cross alone is our theology' (p. 176), a claim which recalls Paul's words (1 Cor. 2:2) in a passage which was of fundamental significance for Luther's concept of a theology of the cross (1 Cor. 1 – 2).

In the Heidelberg Theses (1518) Luther contrasted his *theologia crucis* with the theology of glory (*theologia gloriae*), a term which sums up his objections to late medieval *scholastic theology. The two terms represent two approaches to the *knowledge of God: the theologian of glory perceives the glory of God – his power, wisdom and goodness, manifest in the works of creation; while the theologian of the cross perceives God hidden in the suffering and humiliation of the cross. Luther does not deny that there is a natural knowledge of God to be had from the created world (see *Natural theology), but in the soteriological context in which he insists that our knowledge of God must belong, it is useless. Indeed, it can be worse than useless, because the sinner distorts it to create an idol who supports his own attempts at self-justification by moral and intellectual achievement. But in God's revelation of himself in the cross, God shatters human preconceptions of divinity and human illusions about how God may be known. In the cross God is not revealed in the power and glory which natural reason can recognize as divine, but in the very opposite of divinity, in human disgrace, poverty, suffering and death, in what seem to us weakness and foolishness. Paradoxically, therefore, Luther says that God is hidden in this revelation (see *Hidden and revealed God), because he is not here immediately recognizable as God, but can be perceived only by faith. To recognize God in the crucified Christ is to realize that God is not truly knowable by those who pride themselves on their progress towards divine wisdom and goodness, but can only be known at the point where human wisdom is silenced and human ethical achievements are worthless.

Finally, it is important for Luther's concept of the theology of the cross that the humiliation and suffering of Christ, in which God hides his revelation, correspond to the humiliation and suffering of the sinner, for whom God conceals his real work (*opus proprium*) of salvation behind his strange work (*opus alienum*) of humiliation, which furthers it. Only the humbled sinner, struck down by the experience Luther calls *Anfechtung* ('spiritual conflict') can know the God who for his justification underwent the humiliation and condemnation of the cross. Hence Luther, in a famous sentence, insisted on the experiential basis of the theology of the cross, against any purely speculative theology: 'Living, or rather dying and being damned make a theologian, not understanding, reading or speculating' (*Weimarer Ausgabe* 5, p. 163).

The central and critical role of the cross in Christian theology has rarely been perceived as clearly as it was by Luther, but in modern times theologians as diverse as K. *Barth, K. *Rahner, J. *Moltmann and E. *Jüngel have attempted to do justice to it, and in some respects have pressed it further than Luther. In particular, they and others have sought to revise our (and the theological tradition's) preconceptions of God in the light of the cross. Barth, for example, insists that it is in the humiliation of the cross that Christ's divinity is most fully revealed. In the humanity, lowliness and suffering of the cross, the true God truly expresses his divine nature, which is his freedom to love humanity in this way, by contrast with all the false gods who cannot do so. A strong tradition of English theology in the twentieth century, as well as other theologians such as the Japanese Lutheran Kazoh Kitamori (1916–98), have argued that the cross is not taken seriously until a doctrine of God's suffering love replaces the traditional notion of divine *impassibility.

Two of the most notable recent attempts to develop a theology of the cross are Moltmann's (in *The Crucified God*) and Jüngel's (in *God as the Mystery of the World*). Moltmann, whose treatment owes much to Luther, aims to recover 'the profane horror and godlessness of the cross' from behind its religious interpretations. Jesus' godforsaken death is to be understood as the loving solidarity of the incarnate Son of God with godless and godforsaken men and women. Here, as in Luther, God is revealed in his opposite – in abandonment by God – because he is love which identifies with what is alien. But the implications of this revelation of God in the cross Moltmann wishes to pursue as far as 'a revolution in the concept of God', rejecting all notions of God not derived from the cross. The death of Jesus, as death, not of God, but in God, as an event between God and God, in which God abandons God to death, makes it necessary to conceive of God in terms of a *trinitarian history. The cross is the event of God's love in which the Son suffers abandonment by the Father, the Father suffers the death of the Son, and the Holy Spirit is the powerful love which spans the gulf between Father and Son and so reaches godforsaken humanity. Thus Moltmann finds a consistent *theologia crucis* to require both a trinitarian doctrine of God and a doctrine of divine passibility, and further claims that such a *theologia crucis* thereby opens a way through the impasse of both metaphysical *theism and *atheism in the face of the problem of *suffering. Rather similarly, Jüngel makes the cross the starting point for a trinitarian understanding of God which transcends the modern dispute between metaphysical theism and atheism.

Bibliography
E. Jüngel, *God as the Mystery of the World* (Edinburgh, 1983); A. E. McGrath, *Luther's Theology of the Cross* (Oxford, 1985); J. Moltmann, *The Crucified God* (London, 1974); W. von Loewenich, *Luther's Theology of the Cross* (Belfast, 1976).

R. J. Bauckham

CULLMANN, see SALVATION-HISTORY

CULTS, see NEW RELIGIONS; SECTS

CULTURAL THEORY AND THEOLOGY

The concept of *culture began to develop at the end of the nineteenth century and into the twentieth. It is more accurate to think of this in terms of a multiplicity of concepts as scholars have defined and understood cultures through different analytical lenses. The following are especially noteworthy.

Functionalist approaches are common in definitions of culture. Functionalism understands culture as that which is comprised of various elements that are structurally integrated to form a whole that then provides a functional order working for the best of the individual and society.

Structuralist approaches are exemplified in the work of Claude Lévi-Strauss, the father of modern *anthropology. *Structuralism draws heavily upon an application of linguistic theory. It understands culture as a system of signs, and is concerned with uncovering the structures that generate the patterns that make up a society.

Another worth considering is the *worldview approach*. This includes a certain set of cognitive presuppositions about the construction of reality. The worldview approach involves various assumptions: that worldview is the primary foundation of culture; that culture is related to certain basic philosophical categories; that cultural order is primarily cognitive; that human beings have a strong drive for *rational order and consistency; and that humans act rationally, given their cognitive assumptions. The worldview approach to culture is a common one among *evangelicals.

Considering the different approaches to studying culture, the following are common elements in defining it: culture is acquired through a process of learning, but it should not be understood as being purely cognitive; it is shared by members of a society; it is comprised of *symbols and meanings; and it involves structure and patterns.

*Theology relates to culture in that it involves a message that must be understood in differing cultural contexts, both the original cultural contexts of the biblical texts (Ancient Near Eastern and first-century Palestine) as well as the contemporary cultural contexts. Theology is also related to culture as it is communicated cross-culturally. Understood in this sense, it is better to think of cultural theories and theologies as different cultural ways of understanding, meaning-making and concerns, necessitating the development, expression and communication of diverse theologies for various cultural contexts.

H. Richard *Niebuhr's *Christ and Culture* has been influential among Christians in charting a relationship between theology and culture. His volume articulated five ways of viewing the relationship, to include 'Christ against Culture', 'Christ of Culture', 'Christ above Culture', 'Christ and Culture in Paradox' and 'Christ the Transformer of Culture'. Although influential, Niebuhr's approach has been the subject of significant critique.

Missionaries and *missiologists have often been at the forefront of developing and communicating theologies tailored for specific cultures. In the history of Christian missions the goal has often been to develop theologies within a particular culture and which best connect with its members. This type of theologizing has been labelled variously, including '*contextualization', 'inculturation', 'localization' and 'indigenization'. More recently the term 'incarnational' has been used, as theologians and missiologists base their theological method within culture on the *incarnation of Christ, communicating transcendent theological ideas within a specific cultural context.

Contextual theology or local theology can be defined as 'the dynamic interaction among gospel, church, and culture' (Schreiter, *Constructing Local Theologies*, p. 22). This process begins 'with the opening of a culture, that long and careful listening to a culture to discover its principal values, needs, interests, directions, and symbols' (ibid., p. 28). Pastors, theologians and missiologists then shape theologies to best communicate within a culture.

Finally, changing global dynamics impact the development of theologies in relation to culture. This includes the process of *globalization, the changing face of Christianity with the shift of vitality and growth from the global North to the South and East, as well as the interactions of Christians with adherents of non-Christian religions (see *Christianity and other religions).

Bibliography

C. Geertz, *The Interpretation of Cultures* (New York, 1973); P. Jenkins, *The Next Christendom: The Coming of Global Christianity* (Oxford, 2011); C. Klassen, *Religion and Popular Culture: A Cultural Studies Approach* (Ontario, 2014); C. Kraft, *Christianity in Culture: A Study in Dynamic Biblical Theologizing in Cross-Cultural Perspective* (Maryknoll, 1979); G. Lynch, *Understanding Theology and Popular Culture* (Malden, 2005); H. R. Niebuhr, *Christ and Culture* (New York, 2001 [1951]); C. Ott and H. Netland, *Globalizing Theology: Belief and Practice in an Era of World Christianity* (Grand Rapids, 2006); L. Sanneh, *Whose Religion Is Christianity? The Gospel beyond the West* (Grand Rapids, 2003); R. Schreiter, *Constructing Local Theologies* (Maryknoll, 2002); K. Tanner, *Theories of Culture: A New Agenda for Theology* (Minneapolis, 1997).

J. W. MOREHEAD

CULTURE

'Culture' derives from the Latin *colere*, 'to cultivate', originally associated with agriculture and animal husbandry. It concerns the activity as well as the products of world-building, whereby the natural world is refashioned into one more fit for human habitation. More precisely, culture refers to the world of human making – a symbolic and concrete social order – regarded as an essentially meaning-making enterprise: 'man is . . . suspended in webs of significance he himself has spun' (C. Geertz, *The Interpretation of Cultures*, p. 5).

Culture in the Bible

In Christian theology, culture seldom received extensive attention as such before the nineteenth century. Several factors may account for this. First, no precise equivalent OT or NT term exists: *kosmos*, 'world', is its closest approximation, but with only neutral (John 21:25; 1 Cor. 14:10) or negative (Gal. 6:14; 1 John 2:15–17) connotations. Thus culture often goes untreated by biblical theology (summarizing scriptural teaching principally according to its idiomatic categories). Nonetheless, the creational accounts portray the cultivation of community and the earth's latent potential as components of humanity's calling to image and serve God (Gen 1:26 – 2:4; 2:15–24), a motif called 'the cultural mandate'. Culture's positive, ante-penultimate value in God's redeeming purposes is seen in the doctrines of (1) the *incarnation of Christ (redemptively embracing humanity and the world as a dwelling-place for God, John 1:1–14); (2) ecclesiology (Pentecost beginning to undo humankind's fragmentation occasioned by defiance of the cultural mandate at Babel, Gen. 11:1–8; Acts 2, and the translational mode of mission and Christian formation, Acts 15:1–35) (see *Church); and (3) *eschatology (the nations' cultural gifts purged of all evil and preserved in some fashion in the ultimate order of life with God in the renewed heavens and earth, Rev. 21:1 – 22:5).

Secondly, while theology is always shaped by specific socio-historical circumstances, a long-held, mistaken view of objective understanding as eliminating cultural conditioning led to widespread underestimation of culture's influence and value. Contemporary trends related to *globalization, the increasingly influential *postmodern outlook in many quarters, and the location of the church's most rapid growth centres in the global South now require a direct engagement with culture.

The culture concept

Culture, according to anthropology's nineteenth-century founder, is 'that complex whole which includes knowledge, belief, art, morals, custom, and any other capabilities and habits acquired by man as a member of society' (E. B. Tylor, *Primitive Culture*, p. 1). Two evangelical benchmark statements assume this classical definition. The Willowbank Report (1978) defines culture as 'an integrated system of beliefs (about God, or reality, or ultimate meaning), of values (about what is true, good, beautiful, and normative), of customs (how to behave, relate to others, talk, pray, dress, work, play, trade, farm, eat, etc.), and of institutions which express these beliefs, values and customs (governments, law, courts, temples or churches, family, schools, hospitals, factories, shops, unions, clubs, etc.), which bind a society together and give it a sense of identity, dignity, security, and continuity'. The *Lausanne Covenant (1974) maintains the biblical tension of affirmation and critique: 'because man is God's creature, some of his culture is rich in beauty and goodness. Because he is fallen, all of it is tainted with sin and some of it is demonic.'

This approach casts culture as a largely unitary, coherent entity: ideas, practices and structures that a population universally maintains. Social scientific study of late modern societies, manifesting diversities of various kinds, challenges this view. Such accounts stress contradictions within traditions, societal divisions and the power and economic interest-driven character of human interaction. Meanwhile, globalizing structures introduce and accelerate interchange among all locales within their networks.

This multiplicity within and between societies indicates that cultures associated with ethnic groups and national polities are not static, singular systems, but rather, relatively fluid, hybrid sets. *Niebuhr's fivefold typology of the Christ-culture relationship (opposition, agreement, synthesis, dualism, conversion) is problematic not only because it construes cultures as monolithic, but also because historical communities continually reassess, debate and adapt inherited traditions, borrowing from elsewhere to address emergent needs. More complex, dynamic, and nuanced analyses are needed.

Theological analysis of culture

For theological analysis of cultural phenomena, two definitions from cultural theory provide helpful direction: culture refers to 'a particular way of life, whether of a people, a period or a group'; and it can be examined as 'a signifying system through which a social order is communicated, reproduced, experienced and explored' (R. Williams, *Keywords*, p. 90). Cultural products and practices resemble texts and can be exegeted similarly. A theological interpretation investigates the explicit and implicit claims, values, and functions a particular item exemplifies (e.g. according to its producers, distributors, users) in the context of members' self-understood 'way of life' and as related to the wider society. A multiperspectival 'thick description' (Williams, *The Sociology of Culture*, p. 13) of a work's many aspects must include the theological dimension – identifying and interacting with its ultimate concern, its religious import – to be complete.

Gospel, church and cultures

Theology's task does not end with analyses of current phenomena. While the gospel seeks to make its home in every cultural system and finds resonances there, a culture's redemption also requires the correction and reconfiguration of specific sociocultural values and practices in accordance with the *gospel (the 'indigenizing' and 'pilgrim principles', A. F. Walls, *The Missionary Movement in Christian History*, p. 9).

Thus, theological reflection continually returns to Scripture as its creative catalyst and norm (the decisive criterion for weighing claims from church tradition, reason and experience). A deepening, detailed grasp of biblical teaching (both parts and whole) is paramount for paradigmatic ethical reasoning as well as for theological understanding. The Scriptures, of course, brim with diverse examples, each implementing a measure of redemption within its concrete social and redemptive-historical situation. One helpful proposal suggests that comparative biblical-theological analysis can lend additional clarity regarding what can and cannot be ascribed to the 'redemptive movement' toward an 'ultimate' (eschatological) social ethic that the Scriptures display (which contemporary interpreters are to extend in their own contexts). A more systematic use of cultural analysis and intracanonical criteria (tracing texts' connections to patterns of coherence, discontinuity and development related to the unfolding biblical storyline) may further distinguish the consistent and the more contingent within the body of scriptural teaching concerning a given practice (see *Hermeneutics).

Theological-ethical discernment about one's own sociocultural world grows in proportion to awareness of its differences from the characteristic patterns of canonical teaching. Since every culture is contingent, human theological judgments and the statements, acts and products they generate (themselves enculturated) are, at best, partial, provisional grasps of the realities to which the Scriptures attest. All human activity thus requires critical examination and further refinement. The ultimate realization and regathering 'in Christ' of the new humanity, and the truth and goodness of its multicultural inheritance, are prefigured and presently tasted only as Christians intentionally press beyond instinctual ethnocentrism to engage in cross-cultural, multiethnic fellowship, offering their varied gifts and openheartedly receiving from one another whatever proves 'right, whatever is pure, whatever is lovely, whatever is admirable' (Phil. 4:4), sifted in the light of the cross of Jesus Christ, the risen, reigning Lord.

See also: CULTURAL THEORY AND THEOLOGY; SOCIETY, THEOLOGY OF.

Bibliography

P. Berger and T. Luckmann, *The Social Construction of Reality* (New York, 1967); C. Geertz, *The Interpretation of Cultures* (New York, 1973); P. Jenkins, *The Next Christendom* (New York, 2002); Lausanne Theology and Education Group, 'The Willowbank Report' (Wheaton, 1978); A. MacIntyre, *After Virtue* (Notre Dame, 1984); R. J. Mouw, *When the Kings Come Marching In* (Grand Rapids, 1983); R. J. Mouw and S. Griffioen, *Pluralisms and Horizons* (Grand Rapids, 1993); H. R. Niebuhr, *Christ and Culture* (New York, 1956); L. Sanneh, *Translating the Message* (Maryknoll, 1989); E. Y. Sung, 'Culture and Hermeneutics', in K. Vanhoozer (ed.), *Dictionary for Theological Interpretation of the Bible* (Grand Rapids, 2006); P. Tillich and R. C. Kimball, *Theology of Culture* (New York, 1959); E. B. Tylor, *Primitive Culture* (New York, 1877); K. J. Vanhoozer, 'Everyday Theology', in K. Vanhoozer (ed.), *Everyday Theology* (Grand Rapids, 2006); A. F. Walls, *The Missionary Movement in Christian History* (Maryknoll, 1996); W. J. Webb, *Slaves, Women and Homosexuals: The Hermeneutics of Cultural Analysis* (Downers Grove, 2001); R. Williams, *Keywords* (New York, 1985); idem, *The Sociology of Culture* (New York, 1982); N. J. Wolterstorff, 'Suffering, Power, and Privileged Cognitive Access', in D. Hoekema and B. Fong (ed.), *Christianity and Culture in the Crossfire* (Grand Rapids, 1997); C. J. H. Wright, *Old Testament Ethics for the People of God* (Downers Grove, 2004); J. H. Yoder, 'How H. Richard Niebuhr Reasoned', in G. Stassen, D. M. Yeager and J. H. Yoder (eds.), *Authentic Transformation* (Nashville, 1996).

E. Y. SUNG

CYPRIAN (c. 200–58)

Latin Church Father, and Bishop of Carthage from about 249 until his death, Cyprian was a pagan who was converted to Christianity in middle age and quickly rose to the office of bishop. He was well educated and a gifted speaker, able to unite and inspire a church which was undergoing severe persecution. Cyprian himself fled to safety in 250, but this left him ill-prepared to deal with the rigorist element in the church, which demanded that no concessions be made to backsliders. Cyprian disagreed, and began to preoccupy himself with the underlying issues of church order which had surfaced during the controversy.

His writings are less voluminous than those of *Augustine and less varied than those of *Tertullian, but they are an important source for our knowledge of the period and its problems. Cyprian's lasting importance for theology lies in his 'high' view of the *church, which he developed to counter the *schismatic tendencies which were latent in North Africa. He held an advanced theory of apostolic succession, and was insistent in demanding that his rights as a bishop be respected, ceding his authority to no-one, not even to the bishop of Rome (see *Church government; *Ministry). He was also determined to insist that outside the church there is no salvation (*extra ecclesiam nulla salus*), and he presided over the Council of Carthage (256), which expressly decreed that schismatic and heretical *baptisms were invalid (see *Rebaptism). This decision was repudiated by Rome, and is not held today, but it was typical of the rigorous outlook of the North African Church. Cyprian is an important witness to infant baptism, whose necessity he linked to original sin, and to the application of priestly and sacrifical terms to the ministry and sacraments of the church.

Cyprian might have been forced, ironically, into schism with Rome had it not been for a renewed outbreak of persecution, which claimed his life, and perhaps that of the bishop of Rome as well. After his death, Cyprian became the patron saint of the North African church, and the authority to whom later rigorists and schismatics, notably the *Donatists, would appeal.

Bibliography

Works: A. Brent (ed. and tr.), *St Cyprian of Carthage: Selected Treatises* (New York, 2007); idem, *St Cyprian of Carthage: Selected Letters* (New York, 2007); P. Campbell (ed.), *The Complete Works of Saint Cyprian* (Sydney, 2013).
Studies: A. Brent, *Cyprian and Roman Carthage* (Cambridge, 2010); P. Hinchliff, *Cyprian of Carthage* (London, 1974); G. S. M. Walker, *The Churchmanship of St Cyprian* (London, 1968).

G. L. Bray

CYRIL OF ALEXANDRIA (375–444)

Born and raised in Alexandria, Cyril succeeded his uncle Theophilus (fl. 385–412) as bishop of the city in 412. His early career (412–28) was dedicated to the exposition of the Scriptures and the refutation of heretics and unbelievers. The second period of his episcopate (428–33), more intense and fruitful than any other, was marked by his opposition to *Nestorius. Cyril's stand, strengthened by his alliance with the Church of Rome, led to the summoning of the Council of *Ephesus (431) which ended with Nestorius' condemnation. The last period of Cyril's life (433–44), was reasonably peaceful, though he had to explain his teaching to critics from both the *Alexandrian and the *Antiochene sides.

Cyril was a prolific writer who wrote in Attic Greek and had an extensive knowledge of the classics, the Scriptures and the Fathers, especially *Athanasius and the Cappadocians. His many commentaries demonstrate his biblical orientation. He employed the typological and historical methods of interpretation which are most clearly set out in his writings, *On Worship in Spirit and in Truth* and the *Glaphyra on the Pentateuch*. Cyril's anti-heretical dogmatic works are numerous, the most substantial being: *Thesaurus on the Holy and Consubstantial Trinity*, *Dialogues on the Holy and Consubstantial Trinity*, and *Five Books of Negation against Nestorius' Blasphemies*. In the last-named he argues for a true and personal (*kath'hypostasin*) union of the divine Logos/Son with the flesh born from Mary, against Nestorius' Christology based on a conjunction between the divine Logos and the man born from Mary. Cyril also argues for two births of one and the same (divine) Son, one (divine) in eternity and one (human) in time, whereas Nestorius' argument implies two sons, one divine and one human, who are conjoined in Christ.

Cyril also wrote many homilies, and about seventy of his letters are extant. Some of these played a central role in the conflict with Nestorius (see T. H. Bindley, rev. by F. W. Green, *The Oecumenical Documents of the Faith*, London, 1950, and L. R. Wickham, *Cyril of Alexandria: Select Letters*, Oxford, 1983).

Cyril is one of the most distinguished theologians of the early church, recognized by his contemporaries and his successors in the East (Chalcedonian Orthodox and anti-Chalcedonian *monophysites) and in the West (Roman Catholics and Protestants). He is the first Father to establish firmly the *patristic argument, which appeals to the earlier Fathers of the church for the right understanding of the apostolic preaching and the gospel of Christ.

Following Athanasius and the Cappadocians, Cyril accepted the Nicene *homoousios*, the three *hypostaseis* of the Father, the Son and Holy Spirit and the unity of the divine *ousia* (see *Substance) seen in the three *hypostaseis* and expressed in their common will and activity. He is not as original in the content of his triadology as in the presentation of it, and he is not so much interested in the 'essential *Trinity' as in the 'economic', because of his soteriological interest which he inherited from Athanasius. As far as the essential Trinity is concerned, Cyril emphasizes both the coinherence of the three *hypostaseis* or persons and the primacy of the Father from whom the Son is born and the Spirit proceeds. But Cyril does speak of the procession of the Spirit from both the Father and the Son, not, however, with reference to the hypostasis of the Spirit, but with reference to the common essence of the Spirit with the Father and the Son.

*Christology is the key to Cyril's theology and the topic to which his contribution became decisive for the early church and subsequent generations. His terminology initially presented certain problems, because it was flexible and equivocal, but his thought was clear and helped to clarify and eventually settle problems relating to linguistic formulations. He followed Athanasius' principle that theological disputations were not about terms, but about the meaning embedded in them. This is why Cyril could use the term *physis* (nature) as equivalent to both *hypostasis* or person and *ousia*, and so speak of 'one nature of God the Word incarnate' and 'one person of God the Word in (from) two natures'. Thus it is unfair to argue that he changed his mind in Christology from a *monophysite to a dyophysite standpoint. Cyril has been unfairly accused of *Apollinarianism both by his Nestorian opponents and by modern patristic scholars who wish to stress the humanity (or, specifically, the psychology) of Christ almost independently of the Logos/Son of God. Equally unfair is the modernist charge that Cyril's Christology is only a Christology 'from above'. The doctrine of the two births of Christ does not imply the either/or of the schema 'from below' and 'from above', but brings the two together in the mystery of Immanuel, his *kenosis, his economy, his hypostatic union of two natures, his communication of idioms (properties) and, above all, in his virgin mother who is true *theotokos* (see *Mary).

Cyril understands *salvation in terms of both participation in and imitation of the human nature in relation to the divine nature, objectively in Christ and subjectively appropriated by human beings through the Holy Spirit who acts in and through the sacraments (for his eucharistic doctrine, see Ezra Gebremedhin, *Life-Giving Blessing*, Uppsala, 1977). The objective aspect of salvation in Christ is particularly stressed in his doctrine of justification of grace, developed in a masterly way in his evangelical interpretation of the law in *On Worship in Spirit and in Truth*.

Cyril's theological legacy has been influential in all Christian contexts in the East and in the West. A contemporary positive reassessment of this legacy would prove especially beneficial for the current ecumenical dialogue, since it affirms the basic dogmatic perceptions of classical Christianity.

Bibliography

Works listed in *CPG* III, nos. 5200–5438, and, with secondary literature, in J. Quasten, *Patrology*, vol. 3 (Utrecht, 1960), pp. 116–142.

Selected studies: A. M. Bermejo, *The Indwelling of the Holy Spirit According to St Cyril of Alexandria* (Oña, Spain, 1963); essays on Cyril's Christology by J. N. Karmiris, J. S. Romanides, V. C. Samuel, in *Does Chalcedon Divide or Unite?* (Geneva, 1981); C. Dratsellas, *Questions of the Soteriological Teaching of the Greek Fathers with Special Reference to St Cyril of Alexandria* (dissertation, Edinburgh, 1967), in *Theologia* 38 (1967), pp. 579–608, 39 (1968), pp. 192–230, 394–424, 621–643; A. Grillmeier, *Christ in Christian Tradition*, vol. 1 (London, ²1975); F. J. Houdek, *Contemplation in the Life and Works of St Cyril of Alexandria* (unpub. dissertation, University of California, Los Angeles, 1979); A. Kerrigan, *Cyril of Alexandria, Interpreter of the Old Testament* (Rome, 1952); J. McGuckin, *Cyril of Alexandria and the Christological Controversy* (New York, 2004); S. A. McKinion, *Words, Imagery, and the Mystery of Christ* (Leiden, 2000); T. F. Torrance, *Theology in Reconciliation* (London, 1975); T. G. Weinandy and D. E. Keating, *St Cyril of Alexandria* (London, 2003).

G. D. Dragas

DABNEY, ROBERT LEWIS (1820–98)

A leading Southern Presbyterian theologian, educator, author and social critic, who taught for many years at Union Theological Seminary, Richmond, Virginia. Dabney firmly adhered to the conservative Calvinist 'Old School' tradition of American *Presbyterianism. His popular textbook, *Lectures in Systematic and Polemic Theology* (²1878; repr. Edinburgh, 1985), owes much to the writings of *Calvin, the British *Puritans and especially the *Westminster Confession of Faith. His approach to the philosophical and theological currents of his day is influenced by Scottish *common-sense realism.

Dabney's exposition of such topics as the decrees of God (see *Predestination), *sovereignty and responsibility, the imputation of *sin and *eschatology is marked by the same non-speculative sobriety of statement found in the Westminster Standards. He gave much attention to *anthropology, particularly human psychology and the proper organization of social institutions. He endeavoured throughout to base his theology on the clear meaning of relevant texts of Scripture.

See also: PRINCETON THEOLOGY.

Bibliography

Works: *Discussions*, 4 vols. (1890–97), repr. as *Discussions: Evangelical and Theological*, 2 vols. (London, 1967); *Discussions: Philosophical* and *Discussions: Secular* (Harrisonburg, 1980 and 1979); *The Practical Philosophy* (repr. Harrisonburg, 1984 [1897]).

Studies: T. C. Johnson, *The Life and Letters of Robert Lewis Dabney* (repr. Edinburgh, 1977 [1903]); D. F. Kelly, 'Robert Lewis Dabney', in D. F. Wells (ed.), *Reformed Theology in America* (Grand Rapids, 1985); S. M. Lucas, *Robert Lewis Dabney: A Southern Presbyterian Life* (Phillipsburg, 2005); M. H. Smith, *Studies in Southern Presbyterian Theology* (Jackson, 1962).

D. F. KELLY

DALE, R. W., see CONGREGATIONALISM

DARBY, JOHN NELSON (1800–82)

The Anglo-Irish Darby was a founding father of the Brethren movement, a formative influence on modern forms of *dispensationalism, and an influential exponent of premillennialism (see *Millennium). While serving as curate in the Church of Ireland at Calary, Co. Wicklow, he became disillusioned with the establishment and started to associate with those of separatist tendency in the late 1820s. He developed distinctive views, particularly on the 'ruin of the church' as a structured body. He taught the duty of believers to gather for unstructured worship associated with 'breaking bread', to preach the gospel to unbelievers, and to lead lives of sacrificial devotion to Christ in expectation of his second coming (which would be preceded by the 'secret rapture' of believers).

In 1845 Darby broke with B. W. Newton (1807–99) of Plymouth and in 1848–9 with George Müller (1805–98) and Henry Craik (1805–66) of Bristol, leading to permanent division between those Brethren who followed him ('Exclusives') and those who did not ('Open'). Despite their turgid style, his voluminous writings on controversial, expository, doctrinal, apologetic and devotional themes have attracted both readers and popularizers (notably C. H. Mackintosh, 1820–96). His Bible translations in German, French and English reflect serious scholarship. Darby travelled extensively in Western Europe and, later, in North America, the West Indies and New Zealand. Though his ecclesiology has had little influence beyond the Exclusive Brethren, his *eschatology has attracted much support, particularly in North America.

Bibliography

Works: *Collected Writings of J. N. D.*, 34 vols., ed. W. Kelly (London, 1867–1900; repr. Winschoten, Holland, 1971); *Letters of J. N. D[arby]*, 3 vols. (Kingston-on-Thames, n.d.).

Studies: J. D. Burnham, *A Story of Conflict* (Carlisle, 2004); T. Grass, *Gathering to His Name: The Story of Open Brethren in Britain and Ireland* (Bletchley, 2006); H. H. Rowdon, *The Origins of the Brethren 1825–1850* (London, 1967); M. S. Weremchuk, *John Nelson Darby* (Neptune, 1992); P. Wilkinson, *For Zion's Sake: Christian Zionism and the Role of John Nelson Darby* (Carlisle, 2007).

H. H. ROWDON

DARWINISM, see CREATION; CREATION AND EVOLUTION

DEATH

In biblical usage the word has four main senses. Physical death generally denotes the irreversible cessation of bodily functions (2 Sam. 14:14; Rom. 6:23; Heb. 9:27), but occasionally the gradual weakening of physical powers (2 Cor. 4:12, 16). Spiritual death describes man's natural alienation from God, his lack of responsiveness to God, or his hostility to God, because of sin (Gen. 2:17; Matt. 8:22; John 5:24–25; 8:21, 24; Rom. 6:23; Eph. 2:1; Jas 5:20; Jude 12; Rev. 3:1). The 'second death' refers to the permanent separation from God that is the destiny of the unrighteous (Matt. 10:28; Rev. 2:11; 20:6, 14–15; 21:8). Death to sin involves the suspension of all relations with sin that results from being alive to God through dying and rising with Christ (Rom. 6:4, 6, 11).

By divine decree, physical and spiritual death is the consequence and penalty of sin (Ezek. 18:4, 20; Rom. 5:12; 6:23; 7:13; Eph. 2:1, 5) and is the common lot of mankind because all have sinned (Josh. 23:14; 1 Kgs 2:2; Eccl. 9:5; Rom. 5:12; Heb. 9:27). Man and woman were not created unable to die but were created able not to die, although after the fall death became a universal biological necessity. God takes no pleasure in death (even of the wicked, Ezek. 18:23), yet premature death may be the result of divine displeasure (Ps. 55:23; 1 Cor. 11:29–30).

So pervasive and devastating is the influence of death that the NT can depict death as a realm where the devil reigns (Heb. 2:14; Rev. 1:18; 20:13), as a warrior bent on destruction (Acts 2:24; 1 Cor. 15:26; Rev. 6:8; 20:14), or as a domineering ruler (Rom. 5:14, 17). But by his death and resurrection, Christ robbed death of its power (Rom. 6:9; 14:9; Col. 1:18; 2 Tim. 1:10) and emancipated its captives (Rom. 8:2, 38–39; 1 Cor. 3:21–22; Heb. 2:14–15; Rev. 1:18), and through his second advent it will be finally destroyed (1 Cor. 15:23–26, 54–55; Rev. 20:14; 21:4).

Christians view physical death as a destructive force, because through it the bodily tent is permanently dismantled (2 Cor. 5:1) or stripped off (2 Pet. 1:14) and all links with the securities of earthly existence are severed (2 Sam. 12:23); there is a loss of physical corporeality and corporateness. Yet, positively, death may be seen as God's reclaiming of the breath of life (Ps. 104:29; Eccl. 12:7), as resting from one's labours (Rev. 14:13), as the surrender of the spirit into divine hands (Luke 23:46; Acts 7:59), or as the believer's departure from this life (Luke 2:29; 2 Tim. 4:6; 2 Pet. 1:15) to the immediate presence of the Lord (2 Cor. 5:8; Phil. 1:23; contrast with this Pss 6:5; 88:5), where the believer enjoys an enriched form of the intimate fellowship with Christ enjoyed on earth. Through resurrection the believer becomes immortal (Luke 20:35–36; John 11:25–26; 1 Cor. 15:52–54). That is, he or she becomes immune from any type of decay or death through a direct sharing in the life of God who alone is inherently immortal (1 Tim. 6:16). The Christian's attitude to physical death is therefore ambivalent; it should be neither welcomed nor feared.

The imminent advent of death or uncertainty about the time of death ought to prompt *repentance and preparation to meet God (2 Kgs 20:1; Luke 12:16–20), for death terminates all opportunity to repent (Heb. 9:27).

The Roman Catholic and Eastern Orthodox churches teach that after death those who have died in fellowship with the church but who lack Christian perfection enter an intermediate period of suffering in *purgatory that 'purges' them of venial sins and fits them for an eternal life of heavenly bliss with God (2 Macc. 12:39–45). *Luther, on the other hand, taught that at death all remaining traces of original depravity are eradicated from the believer's soul; death marks the final purgation of the soul.

See also: IMMORTALITY; INTERMEDIATE STATE; RESURRECTION, GENERAL.

Bibliography

L. R. Bailey, Sr (ed.), *Biblical Perspectives on Death* (Philadelphia, 1979); L. O. Mills (ed.), *Perspectives on Death* (Nashville, 1969); L. Morris, *The Wages of Sin: An Examination of the New Testament Teaching on Death* (London, 1954); J. Pelikan, *The Shape of Death: Life, Death, and Immortality in the Early Fathers* (London, 1962); K. Rahner, *On the Theology of Death* (London, 1972).

M. J. HARRIS

DEATH-OF-GOD THEOLOGY

A short-lived but widely publicized theological trend of the 1960s which took Friedrich *Nietzsche's slogan 'God is dead' as its *leitmotiv*. It was associated with the writings of Thomas Altizer (b. 1927) and William Hamilton (1924–2012). Altizer argued that God had become fully human in Christ, thereby losing his divine attributes in what can perhaps best be described as an extreme form of *kenoticism. Hamilton said that modern people are no longer able to believe in God, and so the church ought to dispense with him as well. Paul van Buren (1924–98) followed linguistic philosophers in arguing that the concept of God was 'cognitively meaningless' because God's existence is not scientifically verifiable, and therefore belief in him has no solid grounding.

In many ways, the death-of-God movement was an amalgam of currents present in modern neo-Orthodox theologians. Like Karl *Barth in his early commentary on Romans, it held to a radical separation between the divine and the secular spheres, but did not follow Barth's later modifications of this radical position. It also reflected something of his tendency to focus all theological and religious issues on Jesus Christ, but it understood him as a mere human being, whereas Barth always insisted that *Jesus was the incarnate Son of God. From Paul *Tillich it borrowed its prejudice against all forms of personalist and mythological language about *God. From Rudolf *Bultmann it borrowed the idea that objective ontological and dogmatic language about God is meaningless, so that theological language is reduced to language about human self-understanding in the light of Jesus. It was also influenced to some extent by John *Robinson, whose best-selling *Honest to God* (1963) was largely a popularization of Tillich, and by a particular interpretation of Dietrich *Bonhoeffer, who claimed that the modern world was one in which man had come of age and had to live without God.

The authors of the death-of-God debate are still alive and writing a generation later, but the extent of their influence is difficult to measure. Discontent with the traditional picture of God has become a feature of many left-wing tendencies in Christian theology, but few of these have tried to dispense with him altogether. Concentration on the humanity of Jesus at the expense of his divinity is also widespread in some circles, but most of these tend to assume that Jesus reflects God, not that he has replaced him. Radical *feminists and so-called '*open theists' have both tried to reinvent the Christian doctrine of God to suit their particular emphases, but again, this does not amount to abolishing him altogether. It would seem that theological radicalism has pulled back from this particular extreme, and that those who have been persuaded by it have become straightforward atheists. In retrospect, the death-of-God theology will probably be regarded as a transition from belief to unbelief which affected a certain number of leading intellectuals in the latter part of the twentieth century who continued to regard themselves as 'Christians' in a cultural sense, but who in reality had evacuated the Christian faith of any real meaning.

Bibliography

T. J. J. Altizer, *The Gospel of Christian Atheism* (Philadelphia, 1966); T. J. J. Altizer and W. Hamilton, *Radical Theology and the Death of God* (New York, 1966); J. Ice and J. Carey (eds.), *The Death of God Debate* (Philadelphia, 1967); J. Montgomery, *The 'Is God Dead?' Controversy* (Grand Rapids, 1966); J. Montgomery and T. J. J. Altizer, *The Altizer-Montgomery Dialogue* (Chicago, 1967); C. Van Til, *Is God Dead?* (Philadelphia, 1966).

G. L. BRAY

DECONSTRUCTION

The notion and practice of deconstruction comes to philosophy from French philosopher Jacques *Derrida, though it has multiple origins and its applications range far beyond Derrida's interest. First suggested in his 1967 book *Of Grammatology*, Derrida envisioned a method of philosophical inquiry that refuses to conform to the metaphysical or logical parameters that have defined philosophy historically. Deconstruction is offered not as a new philosophical system, or even a new methodology, but as a rigorous manner of reading and interpretation. Since its introduction and implementation by Derrida, deconstruction has become a tool utilized in literature, art, theology and a wide range of other disciplines.

Philosophy habitually protects its sacred and vulnerable concepts, ideas that hold together epistemology, politics, ethics and religion. At times, centuries of sedimentation piles atop an original and perhaps questionable concept. Investigating such ideas requires a disregard for the venerated traditions of philosophy. For deconstruction there can be no safe, unquestioned foundation for constructive thought; originary concepts must be discovered and then interrogated. In questioning the 'logos' of Western philosophy, for instance, Derrida knows he may be pulling out the lynchpin for the very structures of truth. He envisions the practice of deconstruction to be simultaneously faithful and violent.

Deconstruction originally evolves out of a method suggested by Martin *Heidegger, Derrida's teacher. Heidegger understood that words and concepts carry unseen baggage, accumulations from culture, accident, tradition, history and the pressures of philosophical systems. Words and concepts do not part easily with these accretions, and the act of investigating and peeling back layers will often threaten the survival of the concept itself. Deconstruction follows, in part, the boldness of Friedrich *Nietzsche, who routinely challenged the sacred nature of philosophy's most guarded ideas.

For Derrida, deconstruction takes the form of intensely careful readings. In the careful examination of a text, deconstructive readers look for small contradictions and unseen dependencies. Contradictions or coincidences, however slight, serve as fissures for pulling apart the seams of an argument. Deconstruction seeks to identify the missing leaps and assumptions that other readings unknowingly presume. There is a leap between every sign and its signifier, between every word and its reception. This slippage in meaning, which Derrida names *différance*, masquerades as a trivial loss, but may at times unravel the whole system. Attention to the unseen assumptions in an idea may also lead to more faithful understanding.

Bibliography

J. Caputo, *Deconstruction in a Nutshell: A Conversation with Jacques Derrida* (New York, 1997); J. Derrida, *Speech and Phenomena and Other Essays on Husserl's Theory of Signs* (Evanston, 1967); idem, *Of Grammatology* (Baltimore and London, 1967); C. Norris, *Deconstruction: Theory and Practice* (New York, 2003).

E. SEVERSON

DECREES, see PREDESTINATION

DEIFICATION

Deification, in Gk *theosis,* is perhaps best expressed in the affirmation made by no small number of Church Fathers, namely that 'God became man so that man might become God'. Predominantly present in the *Eastern Orthodox tradition, deification is at once understood as both a divine gift and the supreme goal of human existence. Biblical support is maintained for this doctrine through appeal to such passages as Ps. 82:6, John 10:34–35 and 2 Pet. 1:4. The expression used by the apostle Peter has become a sort of 'motto' of Orthodox theology's view of deification: to be deified means to become 'partakers of the divine nature'. In the view of the vast majority of Eastern theologians, whether past or present, any interpretation of these passages and these expressions other than an organic, realistic one would represent a negation of Scripture itself.

The concept of *theosis* is a complex one, being closely linked to a number of key theological terms, and being expressed in terms of a variety of models. We thus find references to deification as adoption, union, participation, fellowship, salvation, and so on. The models of deification to which appeal is most frequently made are the metaphorical, ethical and realist or *ontological models. The last is the one against which Western theologians (both Catholic and Protestant) most frequently raise objections, pointing out that it offers far more than can actually be attained in reality. In essence, this model affirms that human deification is not merely the attempt to grow in semblance to God, that is, to reproduce divine attributes in one's own life by imitation, but presupposes something far beyond this, namely the transformation of human nature along the lines of the Christological model of the *incarnation. Just as Christ assumed a human nature and deified it, in the same way it is possible for a human being to assume the divine nature so as to be deified in a very real sense. Of course, even if the entire deifying process is 'real', this does not mean that any sort of identification with the divine nature takes place. At the end, one still finds that what is in view is an imitation of the divine nature, received by grace. The concepts and language associated with deification appear far too daring to Christian theologians unfamiliar with the mysticism and *asceticism practised in the East. On the other hand, to an Eastern theologian these ideas sound familiar, and also stimulating, for nothing could be greater than to experience deification.

The Eastern theologian's familiarity with the idea of deification stems from the mode in which theology itself is understood in the East. Theology itself is *mystical – that is to say, it has a contemplative aspect, to which the concept and practice of *theosis* belong. The believer can attain the level of a real, true knowledge of God. In a way that resembles Neo-Platonic (see *Platonism) or Evagrian mysticism, knowledge is understood to have many stages, the last of which is unity with the divinity. Of course, one can never achieve a perfect union, inasmuch as the *knowledge of God is inexhaustible. Nevertheless, God chose to make himself known to humankind, or in other words, to make himself accessible to us. This encourages the mystic to dare to proceed further still, seeking to attain to the more advanced stages of deification.

Essentially, the possibility of human *union with God, or deification in terms of the ontological model, implies the replacement of human activity with the divine for a greater or shorter length of time. Human nature transcends itself, or more precisely, is raised above its natural limits by the deification process. This move beyond the limits of human nature is expressed by *Gregory of Nyssa in terms of *epektasis* or progress, by Maximus the Confessor in terms of the soul's 'ever-moving rest', and by Gregory *Palamas in terms of the experience of divine light. Although opening itself to suspicions of *pantheism, this approach cannot be accused of identifying Creator and creation in a complete unity. Human participation in the deification process is only by *grace, and not by nature.

See also: CHRISTIAN LIFE; IMAGE OF GOD.

Bibliography

P. M. Collins, *Partaking in Divine Nature: Deification and Communion* (London, 2010); V. Lossky, *The Mystical Theology of the Eastern Church* (Crestwood, 1997); N. Russell, *The Doctrine of Deification in the Greek Patristic Tradition* (Oxford, 2005); A. N. Williams, *The Ground of Union: Deification in Aquinas and Palamas* (Oxford, 1999).

E. BARTOS

DEISM

Deism is the name given to a movement which started late in the seventeenth century and persisted long into the next, with its programme for replacing traditional by rational religion. It is popularly regarded as belief in a remote creator, uninvolved in the world whose mechanism he devised; but this does not readily serve as a defining or even essential characteristic of the movement. Deism is hard to define, and deists are sometimes hard to identify. Broadly, deism stands for the abolition of *dogma founded on alleged *revelation and promulgated by an authoritarian priesthood such that the principle of rational scrutiny is quashed and its results disavowed. Constructively, deists often sought to promote a natural religion, universally bestowed on humanity by an impartial and benevolent God, its content in conformity with the unchanging moral law. Assault on the principle of revelation in *history (if it proclaims more than what reason can, or does, know independently) and on the claim that it occurred (if founded on belief in *miracles, *prophecies or inerrant *Scripture) was meant to vindicate reason over against superstition. Deists, remarked the English poet John Dryden, are 'rationalists with a heart-hunger for religion'. Prominent representatives included: in England, John Toland (1670–1722), Anthony Collins (1676–1729) and Matthew Tindal (1655–1733); in Germany, Hermann Reimarus (1694–1768); in France, *Voltaire; and in America, Thomas Paine (1737–1809).

Deism has seldom been regarded as of high intellectual calibre; its representatives were commonly outmatched at the level of pure debate. Arguably, however, they drew forth from their opposition a defence that would ultimately prove unable to sustain orthodox claims, in the form of concessions (for example) to reason and natural religion. At the least, deism demonstrates what forces were at work in the eighteenth century to undermine classical Christianity. Its perception of God exhibits the revulsion felt at what was perceived to be the primitive deity of the OT and the arbitrary deity of historically particular revelation; its understanding of man indicates the confidence of the day in the sufficiency of rational morality for life and salvation. Its view of *nature illustrates how the stable harmonies in which *Newton had apparently enfolded the world could call forth a non-Christocentric worship of God; its assessment of the clergy shows how the structure of socio-ecclesiastical power revolted a free-thinking fraternity, sick of aggressive dogmatism masquerading as the prime Christian virtue. In the midst of this, the biblical scheme of fall and redemption was dismissed, and its literary presentation regarded as crude, corrupt and variously flawed. Scripture was discredited as the sole, sufficient or necessary foundation of religion.

Deism has long been regarded as a spent force and a non-combatant in twentieth- and twenty-first-century theological battles. Yet it could earmark a set of ideas, such as those involved in the divine perfection or the morality of rational discrimination in religion, which had great potential for overthrowing the traditional scheme. Meeting the thrust if not the actual particulars of the deists' arguments may still promote fruitful reflection on the nature of Christianity.

Bibliography

G. R. Cragg, *Reason and Authority in the Eighteenth Century* (Cambridge 1964);

J. Redwood, *Reason, Ridicule and Religion: The Age of Enlightenment in England, 1660–1750* (London, 1976); L. Stephen, *English Thought in the Eighteenth Century*, vol. 1 (London, 1962); R. E. Sullivan, *John Toland and the Deist Controversy: A Study in Adaptations* (Cambridge, 1982).

S. N. WILLIAMS

DEITY OF CHRIST, see CHRISTOLOGY

DEMYTHOLOGIZATION

Rudolf *Bultmann announced his programme of demythologization in a lecture in 1941, 'New Testament and Mythology', and developed it in *Jesus Christ and Mythology* (1958). He declared: 'We cannot use electric lights and radios and, in the event of illness, avail ourselves of modern medical and clinical means and at the same time believe in the spirit and wonder world of the New Testament.' Although he had reacted against the 'classic' *liberal theology of the *Ritschlian school, like all the theologians of the broader liberal tradition, Bultmann was engaging in an apologetic presentation of the gospel to the era of *modernity. He assumed that modern science ruled out talk of miracles, of another world of spirits, angels and demons, and of a three-storied universe of heaven above, the earth, and hell beneath us. All such language in the Bible was no longer to be taken literally, and we had to recognize frankly that it was *myth.

The programme of demythologization which he proposed was the key feature linking the two sides of his thought. First, it was part of his sceptical view of the historicity of the NT. Not only were miracles such as the virgin birth and resurrection of Jesus ruled out by modern science, but the Gospels had been composed from oral traditions, and these stories took certain typical forms. 'Form criticism' could therefore trace how these had been shaped in the telling, and the Gospels therefore told us much about the theology of the early Christians, but little or nothing dependable about Jesus. But secondly, this fitted neatly with Bultmann's reinterpretation of 'faith' according to the *existentialist philosophy of Martin *Heidegger. Faith had nothing to do with believing that certain events had objectively happened. Faith was the decision to live authentically, and it was the *kerygma, the proclamation of Jesus as the Christ, which enabled us to come to this existential self-understanding. It was sufficient to know that he lived and was crucified.

Demythologization struck a chord in the mid-twentieth century when Western culture was self-consciously 'modern'. John A. T. *Robinson drew on Bultmann's ideas in his popular presentation of the Christian faith in *Honest to God* (1963). In *The Myth of God Incarnate* (1977), edited by John *Hick, a group of scholars used the concept of myth to develop a sophisticated denial of the *incarnation. And although some of Bultmann's former doctoral students rejected his extreme historical scepticism about the NT in their 'New Quest' for the *historical Jesus, they did not differ from him in rejecting *miracles and reinterpreting 'myth'. John Dominic Crossan and the scholars of the Jesus Seminar share the same perspective.

Various criticisms have been made of demythologization. First, Bultmann had a view of science which was already outdated when he was writing. Even the existentialist theologian John *Macquarrie commented, 'He is still obsessed with the pseudo-scientific view of a closed universe that was popular half a century ago', assigning anything which did not fit into that to 'myth' (*An Existentialist Theology*, London, 1955, p. 168). He shared the *deistic view of high modernity that science prescriptively ruled out any divine 'intervention' in the world. Secondly, and partly arising out of that, he shared the *positivistic historiography which was formulated by Ernst *Troeltsch. History dealt with outward facts which could be objectively determined. Thirdly, it is not always clear exactly what is meant by the word 'myth'. In ancient Greece the word *mythos* came to mean a tale or story, usually about the gods, which came to be regarded as legendary rather than factual, and was often the basis for religious ritual. But 'myth' can mean any story which explains the origins of anything or expresses a universal truth in story form. It can simply refer to the literary genre or it can be used to imply that it is an imaginary tale which has no basis in historical fact. It is not always clear which of these is in view. Fourthly, although demythologization claimed to keep the kernel of the gospel and throw away the cultural husk, many scholars have judged that it is not true to the gospel as presented in the NT. Oscar Cullmann criticized Bultmann for separating *faith and history, whereas for the NT writers in continuity with the Old, faith was inseparable from God's action in *history (*Salvation in History*, London, 1967, pp. 138ff., 148ff.). It was a serious misinterpretation to say that their focus was on the existential decision of faith rather than on their claims for the incarnation, death and resurrection of Jesus. Fifthly, existentialist philosophy itself now appears a highly individualistic philosophy of a passing era. Bultmann's interpretation of 'justification by faith' in Heidegger's terms may have seemed relevant and 'modern' at the time, but new 'postmodern' interests in the corporate, in community and indeed in history and language, have blunted its apologetic appeal.

Bibliography

H.-W. Bartsch (ed.), *Kerygma and Myth* (London, 1972); J. D. G. Dunn, 'Demythologizing – the Problem of Myth in the New Testament', in I. H. Marshall (ed.), *New Testament Interpretation* (Exeter, 1977); D. Fergusson, *Bultmann* (London, 1992).

T. A. NOBLE

DEMYTHOLOGIZING, see MYTH

DENNEY, JAMES (1856–1917)

James Denney was born in Paisley, educated at Glasgow University and Free Church College, and became minister of East Free Church, Broughty Ferry (1886–97), before being appointed first to the chair of systematic theology (1897), then NT language, literature and theology (1900), and finally principal of the United Free Church College, Glasgow.

Denney's voluminous literary output and correspondence reveals a man of great spiritual stature, of whom H. R. *Mackintosh said, 'I have never known his equal for making the New Testament intelligible as the record and deposit of an overwhelming experience of redemption.'

Passionate scholarship wedded to a burning conviction about the power of the gospel were hallmarks of a theological position centred on the *atonement. W. Robertson Nicoll (1851–1923) maintains that his wife 'led him into a more pronounced evangelical creed', inducing him to read *Spurgeon, whom he came to admire greatly, and who was instrumental in constraining him to proclaim the atoning death of Christ as the heart of the gospel. The cross became for him the centre of all Christian theology and the heart of all true preaching. He was influenced in some measure, however, by the critical theological spirit of his age: his attitude to matters such as the inspiration and authority of *Scripture (cf. his *Studies in Theology*), and *confessional subscription, which he proposed should be abandoned in favour of a simple confession of faith in God through Jesus Christ (cf. *Jesus and the Gospel*), became matters of debate, as did his trinitarian position and his eschatology.

Bibliography

J. M. Gordon, *James Denney* (Milton Keynes, 2006); J. R. Taylor, *God Loves Like That!: The Theology of James Denney* (London, 1962), contains complete bibliography.

J. PHILIP

DEPRAVITY, see SIN

DERRIDA, JACQUES (1930–2004)

Jacques Derrida was born into a Sephardic Jewish family in Algeria. He studied and subsequently taught philosophy in Paris, and latterly in America. He was influenced by many figures associated with Continental philosophy, notably Husserl, *Heidegger and *Levinas, but his own influence is most associated with that phenomenon of post-structuralism termed '*deconstruction'. Where structuralism had argued for or assumed stable structures of linguistic meaning, Derrida challenges the notion that there is any stable, fixed meaning.

The father of *structuralism, Ferdinand de Saussure, was interested in how signs signified, and he sought to show that the meaning of a word or phrase is generated by a verbal sign's associations with and differentiations from other verbal signs. But Derrida argues that in this chain of signs, signification is generated not only differentially but is also deferred: one sign in turn signifies another – the signifier becomes the signified – in a potentially temporally infinite series. Derrida calls this '*différance*' and suggests thereby both the 'difference' between signs and the 'deferring' of any finally signified 'thing' at which the chain of signs ends. In the jargon of deconstruction, there is neither 'transcendental signifier' nor 'transcendental signified' external to and upholding the meaning of any chain of signs. Whereas it had once been thought that the possibility of stable meaning was underwritten by reason, truth, God, being or a 'metaphysics of presence', this is now ruled out.

Although it is largely ignored by analytic philosophers, Derrida's work has some similarities to the later *Wittgenstein, and he wrote on speech-act theory in *Limited Inc*. *Death-of-God theologians were the first to introduce it to Anglophone theology in the 1980s, but since then it has had a widespread influence on *hermeneutics and *systematic theology, especially among those who pursue theologies of correlation.

Bibliography

Works: *Of Grammatology* (Baltimore and London, 1976); *Limited Inc* (Illinois, 1988).
Studies: H. Coward and T. Foshay (eds.), *Derrida and Negative Theology* (Albany, 1992).

A. J. Moore

DESCARTES, RENÉ (1596–1650)

Descartes, a Frenchman who worked largely in Holland, is often termed the father of modern philosophy. In a bid to reconstruct the foundations of human knowledge, he inaugurated a method of intellectual enquiry whose procedure and results have commanded the attention of generations of successors.

In the Reformation era, the problem of validating claims to knowledge was acutely raised: differing religious convictions, scientific enquiry and the recovery of classical scepticism were all contributory factors. Descartes set about methodically *doubting all and any received certainties in order to discover the criterion and content of indubitable truth. This led him, by arguments that can be both described and assessed in different ways, to formulate the principle: *cogito, ergo sum* – 'I think, therefore I am.' The very act of doubting one's own existence constitutes a demonstration of that existence, for only an existing self can think or doubt. Once Descartes attained this, he established successively the existence of God and of the external world (cf. *Natural theology). The former is proved in more ways than one: the idea of a perfect being, implied in the knowledge of one's own imperfection, cannot come from a source other than such a being. Again: as the idea of a triangle contains the equality of its three angles to two right angles, so the idea of a perfect being contains the real existence of God. Further, if (as we can conclude) God is benevolent and not deceitful, we must infer that the world we perceive really exists, for God's goodness guarantees the correspondence here between what appears and what is the case. Scepticism has been vanquished.

Theologically, important consequences followed from another set of convictions, those pertaining to the relation of mind and body. Descartes was a *dualist, holding that a human being is composed of these two substantially distinct entities (mind, or soul, and body) characterized respectively by thought and extension. Moreover, it is the immaterial soul, not the corporeal body, that constitutes the person. This conviction, quite apart from Descartes' attempts to expound and defend it, has come in for heavy criticism especially in the philosophy of the twentieth century (see *Anthropology). But some Christian philosophers (e.g. H. D. Lewis, 1910–92) hold that a form of 'Cartesian dualism' is indispensable to Christian belief, including belief in life after death. In theology and ethics, in different ways, this issue is a vital one.

Descartes was more than a philosopher; he was a mathematician of distinction, using algebraic notation to describe spatial relations in his 'analytic geometry', and was also a keen scientist. His continental successors, preeminently *Spinoza and *Leibniz, have been labelled, along with Descartes, 'rationalists', to draw attention to the role of the mind apart from the senses in possessing and acquiring knowledge.

See also: Rationalism.

Bibliography

D. Clarke, *Descartes: A Biography* (Cambridge, 2006); J. Cottingham (ed.), *The Cambridge Companion to Descartes* (Cambridge, 1992); J. Cottingham, R. Stoothoff and D. Murdoch, *The Philosophical Writings of Descartes* (Cambridge, 1985); E. M. Curley, *Descartes against the Skeptics* (Oxford, 1978); A. Kenny, *Descartes: A Study of His Philosophy* (New York, 1968); B. Williams, *Descartes: The Project of Pure Enquiry* (Harmondsworth, 1978).

S. N. Williams

DESCENT INTO HELL

The term derives from the clause in the Apostles' *Creed (also included in the Athanasian Creed): Christ 'descended into hell' (*descendit ad inferna*). 'Hell' here refers not to the hell of eternal punishment (Gehenna), but to the realm of the dead, the underworld (OT Sheol, NT Hades). Hence modern translations of the Creed read 'he descended to the dead'.

That Christ in his human soul departed at death to the place of the dead, until his resurrection, is stated in the NT (Acts 2:31; Rom. 10:7; Eph. 4:9) and amounts to saying that he really died. According to one interpretation of 1 Pet. 3:19; 4:6, he preached the gospel to those who had died before his coming, in order to make salvation available to them. But it should be noted that this interpretation, first attested in *Clement of Alexandria, was rejected by *Augustine and many medieval exegetes, and was not until modern times a major exegetical basis for the doctrine of the descent. Although it is an interpretation which is still vigorously defended by some (e.g. E. *Schillebeeckx, *Christ: The Christian Experience in the Modern World*, London, 1980, pp. 229–234), many modern exegetes take 3:19 to refer to Christ's ascension, during which he proclaimed his victory to the rebellious angels imprisoned in the lower heavens, while 4:6 refers to Christians who died after the gospel was preached to them (see W. J. Dalton, *Christ's Proclamation to the Spirits*, Rome, 1965).

That Christ's descent effected the transference of OT believers from Hades to heaven has been thought to be implied by Matt. 27:52; Heb. 12:23. This notion is certainly found in the earliest post-apostolic writings (Ignatius, *Ascension of Isaiah*) along with Christ's preaching of the gospel to the dead (Hermas, *Gospel of Peter*, *Justin Martyr, *Irenaeus). This was the normal understanding of the descent in the patristic period. Although the *Alexandrian Fathers included the pagan dead among those whom Christ delivered from Hades, the prevailing view, which became the orthodox medieval view, was that only believers of the pre-Christian period were recipients and beneficiaries of Christ's preaching in Hades.

Alongside the theme of the preaching to the dead, another motif which was associated with the descent from a very early period (*Odes of Solomon, Ascension of Isaiah*, *Hippolytus) was Christ's victory over the infernal powers in order to liberate the souls they kept imprisoned in Hades. The earliest credal reference to the descent (in the 'Dated Creed' of Sirmium, 359) clearly alludes to this theme, and it would have been in the minds of those who recited the words, 'he descended into hell', when this clause appeared in some Western creeds from the fifth century and eventually in our Apostles' Creed. Christ's triumph over the devil and death in his descent was vividly narrated in the *Gospel of Nicodemus*, which became very popular in the medieval West, and it was graphically portrayed in medieval art. Although this theme of 'the harrowing of hell' strictly referred only to the salvation of pre-Christian believers, it represented symbolically Christ's liberation of all believers from death and the powers of evil. It dramatized the *Christus victor* theme in *atonement theology for the ordinary medieval Christian.

*Luther continued to make pedagogic use of the idea of the harrowing of hell, and it became Lutheran doctrine in the Formula of Concord. But *Calvin (*Institutes* II.xvi.10) interpreted the clause in the Creed as a reference to Christ's vicarious endurance of the torments of hell on the cross, and this became a common Reformed view.

In the nineteenth century, the descent into hell and an appropriate interpretation of 1 Pet. 3:19 became part of the relatively novel idea of opportunities of salvation after death for all who had no opportunity in this life, and even of a hope for *universal salvation based on 'extended probation' after death (the classic treatment is E. H. Plumptre, *The Spirits in Prison*, London, 1885). Among contemporary theologians who take the descent to symbolize the possibility of salvation through Christ for those who have not heard the gospel in this life are Schillebeeckx (*loc. cit.*) and W. *Pannenberg (*The Apostles' Creed*, London, 1972, pp. 90–95).

Bibliography

F. Loofs, *ERE* IV, pp. 654–663; J. A. MacCulloch, *The Harrowing of Hell* (Edinburgh, 1930).

R. J. Bauckham

DETERMINISM

Most discussions of determinism are bedevilled by confusion between several different uses of the term.

1. In *science* it stands strictly for the hypothesis that the form of every physical event is determined uniquely by the conjunction of events preceding it. Science attempts to discover the pattern of interdependence and express it in 'laws'. Note that this hypothesis does not necessarily imply that all events are *predictable-by-us*, nor even that they are *predictable-for-us* (see below). It is also consistent with (but distinct from) the biblical theistic doctrine that every physical event depends on God for its coming into being (Col. 1:16–17; Heb. 1:3).

In physics, Heisenberg's 'Uncertainty Principle' (1927) asserts that *observable* data can never suffice for exact predictions of physical events; but (despite common assertions to the contrary) it does not logically deny strict determinism.

2. *Theological* determinism is the doctrine that the form of all events is determined according to 'the determinate counsel and foreknowledge of God' (Acts 2:23, KJV). This neither depends on nor implies scientific determinism: it could apply even in a world that was scientifically indeterminate.

3. In *philosophy* determinism often stands for the doctrine that the future of human beings is inevitable-for-them, so that freedom of choice is illusory. This doctrine is often thought to follow from scientific determinism, and Heisenberg's principle has been invoked as a defence against it; but 'compatibilists' (including the writer) consider both these moves to be mistaken. A future event E may be physically determinate without being inevitable-for-an-agent-A, if its form *depends* (among other things) upon *what A thinks or decides about it*.

Suppose, for example, that the physical states of A's brain reflect what A thinks and believes, so that no change can take place in what A believes without a corresponding change in his brain-state (as assumed in mechanistic brain science). It follows that no completely detailed specification of the immediate future of A's brain can claim to be equally accurate regardless of what A thinks of it, for (*ex hypothesi*) it must *change* according to what A thinks of it! In other words, no completely determinate specification of A's future exists, even unknown to A, which A would be correct to believe, and mistaken to disbelieve, if only he knew it. What does exist is a range of options, any one of which will be realized, if, and only if, A opts for it, and none of which is inevitable-for-A. This is a rational basis for holding A responsible for the outcome, whether or not it was predictable-for-others. There is here a principle of relativity: what others might be correct to believe about A's future is not what A would be correct to believe.

Notice that the question here is not what A would do if offered a prediction. The question is whether A's future is inevitable-for-A, in the sense of having one, and only one, determinate specification (unknown to A) with an unconditional *logical claim* to A's assent. The argument shows that no such specification can exist.

This disproof of 'philosophical determinism' requires us neither to assume nor to deny determinism in either its scientific or theological senses.

Bibliography

G. Dworkin (ed.), *Determinism, Freewill, and Moral Responsibility* (London, 1970); D. M. MacKay, *Human Science and Human Dignity* (London, 1979), pp. 50–55; G. Watson (ed.), *Freewill* (London, 1982).

D. M. MACKAY

DEVELOPMENT OF DOCTRINE

We possess, on the one hand, the Bible as a collection of books written over many centuries, and, on the other, a continually increasing number of doctrinal statements produced by individuals and groups over the centuries (see *Confessions and *Creeds). Development of doctrine may refer to the relation of the Bible's later teaching to its earlier teaching (e.g. that of the doctrine of the *resurrection of the body to the concept of a shadowy existence in Sheol). However, the expression is more often used with reference to (1) the relation of the doctrine/theology produced within the church of post-apostolic times to that contained within the books of the Bible (e.g. the dogma of the *Trinity as found in the Athanasian Creed to the doctrinal statements about Father, Son and *Holy Spirit in the books of the NT); and (2) the relation of a *dogma or precise doctrinal statement which appeared late in the history of the church, to earlier expressions of the same basic teaching (e.g. the doctrine of *justification as taught by *Luther to that taught by *Augustine of Hippo).

Given that there is a difference – which may be in emphasis, arrangement of words, *contextualization, language, aim or purpose –

between the teaching that appears in the Bible and the church's doctrinal statements allegedly based on the original scriptural information, the question arises: How best can this difference be explained? What kind of *models help us to understand the (often subtle) changes? There is the further question: What are the primary factors in a given situation which lead to the formulation of a doctrine for the first time, or to the more precise formulation of a doctrine already confessed within the church; and what models give helpful insight into these processes?

Before the middle of the nineteenth century, the word 'development' was not used to refer to these processes within history and human thought. *Roman Catholic apologists emphasized the immutability of doctrine, that one doctrine had been preserved unchanged from the apostolic teaching recorded in the Bible in the teaching of the (Roman, Western) church throughout the centuries: verbal changes were not of the essence of the matter; the concept had always been the same. In response, *Protestants emphasized the corruption of doctrine – especially after the *patristic period through the medieval era – and saw their own doctrinal emphases and insights as recovery of the pristine, original teaching of the apostles and the early Fathers.

However, it was J. H. *Newman in his important work, *An Essay on the Development of Doctrine* (1845), who insisted on the very fact of development as a new model replacing the models of immutability and corruption. He knew that there was a real difference between biblical data and statements from the church, as well as between earlier and later pronouncements from the church. He suggested models based on the way in which an idea enters the mind, grows and develops before it is expressed as a clear concept. However, Newman still needed the existence of the *papacy to guarantee that the development of doctrine within the mind of the church was the one approved by God. Thus, since Newman's work, it has become customary to talk about the problem of the development of doctrine. Though some Protestants still think that their doctrinal statements are direct modern-day equivalents of biblical data, most scholars are very much aware that an account has to be offered of the formulation of new doctrines and dogmas, as well as of the relationship between these as they exist within the continuing church. It is probably true to say that during the twentieth century, while Roman Catholics were much more absorbed with the problem of development, Protestants were more absorbed with the problem of *hermeneutics – how to interpret the Bible today. Of course these are related, and both exercises are necessary.

Bibliography
O. Chadwick, *From Bossuet to Newman* (Cambridge, ²1987); R. P. C. Hanson, *The Continuity of Christian Doctrine* (New York, 1981); N. Lash, *Newman on Development* (London, 1975); P. Toon, *The Development of Doctrine in the Church* (Grand Rapids, 1978).

P. TOON

DEVILS AND DEMONS

Although the biblical writers encourage no speculation concerning the nature of evil powers, there is no doubt that they take them with intense seriousness, elaborating upon them with a variety of terms and images. Beginning with the reference in Gen. 1:1–2 to a chaos which is 'formless and void', the biblical story offers a picture of an ordered creation continually threatened by powerful and effective adversaries, supremely Satan or the devil, and the demons. The nature, origin and defeat of these adversarial spiritual powers, 'demonology', has been a theme within Christian theology, with the majority opinion finding their origin in some transcendent angelical fall or catastrophe. *Origen was the first to systematize this idea, equating Lucifer (Isa. 14:12–15) with Satan, who with other created angelic powers revolted and fell from heaven because of pride. *Augustine followed Origen, although not his opinion that the devil could finally be reconciled to God. *Thomas Aquinas held that the devil, who is the cause of all sin, was once probably the very highest *angel who, through pride, fell immediately after creation, seducing those who followed him to become his subjects. *Calvin likewise identified the devil as an angel whose malice came as a result of his revolt and fall.

More modern theologians have found such notions hard to digest. *Schleiermacher, often seen as the father of modern theology, questioned the conception of a fall among good angels. Instead, Jesus and his disciples drew their demonology from the common life of the period rather than from Scripture, so that the conception of Satan is not a permanent element in Christian doctrine. In contemporary theological enquiry, *Bultmann still sums up the prevailing view: 'It is impossible to use electric light and the wireless and to avail ourselves of modern medical and surgical discoveries, and at the same time believe in the New Testament world of daemons and spirits' (*Kerygma and Myth*, p. 5). Many modern theologians and others are therefore content to divorce the ministry of Jesus from its biblical context in a mission to 'destroy the devil's work' (1 John 3:8). The worldview of metaphysical *materialism has little room for supernatural powers of any kind, yet must itself be considered an unproven and unprovable philosophical assumption. It is by no means self-evident that a scientific methodology precludes that on which science is unable to adjudicate.

Conversely, NT scholars of varying convictions or lack of them have become increasingly persuaded that Jesus was an exorcist, whatever the precise nature of the forces he encountered. The demonic cannot therefore be excised from the NT without loss. The experience of global Christianity suggests that engagement with the demons continues to be a vital and significant aspect of Christian *mission, involving the manifestation of phenomena remarkably parallel to those recorded in the Gospels. Neither are such phenomena unknown in the West. Furthermore, theological enquiry post-Second World War has shown a renewal of interest in the NT language of 'principalities and powers' prompted by the need to make sense of the 'demonic' experiences of a Nazi state, the *Holocaust and Hiroshima. In a world where the 'Lordless Powers' (Barth) are rampant, perhaps this language still speaks of fallen and destructive supra-human realities from which humans need liberation and which in themselves need either to be overcome or redeemed. Opinions on the powers range from identifying them as fallen angels, or as social institutions and agencies, or as some pre-modern composite of the two. Far from being outmoded, however, the language is useful in locating realities which otherwise we would not have the power to name: the 'spirituality' (good or bad) of the frameworks within which we live our lives.

The NT world of demons and spirits needs not to be jettisoned but rather re-understood. A more conservative way of appropriating the language insists that it refers to a truly existent world of spiritual, ontological realities which, although unseen, impinge upon our present world. The devil is real, powerful and personal, although in principle defeated at the *cross. The powers and principalities are fallen angels which hold sway in the social and political realm and cause havoc. They may be counteracted through prayer. Demons are subordinate spirits which can tempt, possess and disturb people, yet whose activity can be nullified in the name of Christ, the Victor. Difficulties with this view include finding an adequate biblical basis for the concept of an angelic fall (surprisingly meagre). In addition, what it means to call the devil 'personal' gives pause for thought. If personhood involves being made in the image of the triune God, then to apply this to the devil is problematic: not even angels are described as being made in the image of God. If the devil is personal, and certainly the Bible ascribes agency to the devil, it is personality of a radically different kind from that of human beings.

A more experimental theological perspective, albeit rooted in discussion long present in the church's theology, denies ontology to the powers of evil, seeing them rather as the power of the negative, that destructive emptiness created by the displacement of the living God from the affairs of humankind. Evil is privation of the good. This is not to deny its power or its dynamic, since a vacuum, although nothing, can have devastating effects; and *death, which is the absence of life, is a power closely associated with evil itself which exercises great power through fear (Heb. 2:14–15). In this construct Satan is not an invisible, spiritual individual of the most intense form of evil, but the spirituality of a fallen society, a power generated out of the world and the flesh, the malicious and destructive spiritual dynamic produced by the cocktail of human sin and chaos. A difficulty with this perspective, besides its apparent complexity, might be that it lacks the focus of the ontological approach and so reduces the energy and clarity with which it is opposed by the people of God.

See also: EVIL.

Bibliography

K. Barth, *CD* III/3, pp. 289–531 and *CD* IV/4, pp. 213–233; G. A. Boyd, *Satan and the Problem of Evil* (Downers Grove, 2001); R. Bultmann,

'The New Testament and Mythology', in H. W. Bartsch (ed.), *Kerygma and Myth*, vol. 1 (London, 1953); E. M. B. Green, *I Believe in Satan's Downfall* (London, 1981); A. N. S. Lane (ed.), *The Unseen World: Christian Reflections on Angels, Demons and the Heavenly Realm* (Carlisle, 1996); E. Langton, *Essentials of Demonology* (London, 1949); S. H. T. Page, *Powers of Evil: A Biblical Study of Satan and Demons* (Leicester, 1995); J. B. Russell, *Satan: The Early Christian Tradition* (Ithaca, 1981); G. H. Twelftree, 'Spiritual Powers' in T. D. Alexander and B. S. Rosner (eds.), *New Dictionary of Biblical Theology* (Leicester and Downers Grove, 2000); W. Wink, *Engaging the Powers: Discernment and Resistance in a World of Domination* (Minneapolis, 1992); N. G. Wright, *A Theology of the Dark Side* (Carlisle, 2003).

N. G. WRIGHT

DEWEY, JOHN (1859–1952)

Dewey was a leading American pragmatist philosopher and liberal social reformer whose work remains influential in the fields of philosophy, psychology and pedagogy. Educated at the University of Vermont and Johns Hopkins University, Dewey's intellect was formed by the cross-currents of *Hegelianism, New England transcendentalism, reformist Congregationalism and the emerging sciences of evolutionary biology and psychology. After holding faculty posts in Michigan, Minnesota and Chicago, he moved to Columbia University, where he taught until his retirement in 1930.

Fundamental to Dewey's project is the suggestion that we abandon philosophical preoccupation with *epistemology – i.e. with the question of how we know the real world – in favour of understanding human knowing as a social practice by means of which we adjust to our environment and project possible futures for ourselves. On this account, ideas are always tools in the service of some plan of action, and the true test of any knowledge is its success or failure in bettering human life over time.

Dewey's chief contributions to religious thought were made in his 1929 *Gifford Lectures, *The Quest for Certainty*, and developed further in *A Common Faith* (1934). These works advance a thoroughly naturalistic interpretation of the 'religious quality of experience'. His aim was to emancipate this quality from any necessary connection with the dogmas and institutional forms of organized religion. Dewey held that *religious experience had no discrete object, act or internal state; neither did it have a supernatural origin. Rather, any experience can acquire religious force. An experience functions religiously when it incites an imaginative and harmonious alignment of our entire being with the social and natural world as a whole. Dewey's interest in religious experience lay in the potential of its stirring visions of ideal possibilities to direct our present willing and doing towards humanistic ends.

Dewey's work continues to inspire contemporary applications of pragmatic philosophy to the study of religion and Christian theology.

See also: PHILOSOPHY OF RELIGION.

Bibliography

H. L. Friess, 'Dewey's Philosophy of Religion', in J. A. Boydston (ed.), *Guide to the Works of John Dewey* (Carbondale and Edwardsville, 1970), pp. 200–217; L. Hickman and T. M. Alexander (eds.), *The Essential Dewey*, 2 vols. (Bloomington, 1998); B. Kuklick, *Churchmen and Philosophers: From Jonathan Edwards to John Dewey* (New Haven, 1985); S. Rockefeller, *John Dewey: Religious Faith and Democratic Humanism* (New York, 1991); J. P. Soneson, *Pragmatism and Pluralism: John Dewey's Significance for Theology* (Cambridge, MA, 1993).

P. ZIEGLER

DIALECTICAL THEOLOGY

Also called 'crisis' theology after the Greek for 'judgment', dialectical theology arose in the crisis of the First World War (1914–18), an event which shook the foundations of European cultural confidence and broke up former optimistic attitudes. Karl *Barth is the theologian most deeply linked, as its primary inspiration, to this movement in German theology, notably through his famous 1922 commentary *The Epistle to the Romans*. This was not only a commentary on the text of St Paul's NT letter, but a radically new theological manifesto or summons to reject liberal Protestantism, for a long time dominant in German academic theology (see *Liberalism, German). Such was its impact that the Roman Catholic theologian of the time, Karl Adam, called it 'a bombshell

Dialectical theology

in the playground of the theologians', indicating also its spiritual seriousness. Barth strongly felt that the prevailing *liberal Protestant theology was revealed as bankrupt in its attitude to the catastrophe of the First World War, since many well-known theological professors had supported the Kaiser's disastrous nationalistic and militaristic policies in the name of Christianity. For Barth, such *Kriegstheologie*, or theology of war, called for condemnation not blessing, an instance of the pressing need to recover divine judgment over against the chaos and sin of human pride at work in history. A parallel to Barth at this time was P. T. *Forsyth and his *The Justification of God* (1917), likewise arguing that the cross of Christ in history is the great eschatological act of *judgment on sin.

Barth's *Romans* set out to sound the alarm against 'cultural Christianity' by emphasizing again the transcendence, unknowability and sheer holiness of *God, and the danger of 'domesticating' God into morality, aesthetical sense, or any other human cultural or psychological activity. God for Barth is 'wholly other', of 'infinite qualitative' distinction from the created order, which is also deeply fallen. Indeed, we cannot speak of God with our merely human capacities since God's being eludes human concept and speech, and theology must therefore be 'dialectical' in constantly negating what it affirms. The unknowable God is known in the revelation of Christ, but the 'early Barth' stressed the negative.

He rejected conservative biblicism as seeking to objectify truth about God. Liberalism is even more roundly criticized for identifying God with human ethics. Roman Catholicism is rejected for identifying the divine with the institution of the church. Barth does wish to return to the Bible, but in its capacity to point us to God, as someone might point to a moving bird in flight. Liberal theologians in Germany felt Barth was rejecting reason and scholarship in favour of supernaturalism, whereas Barth responded that if God is transcendent, then only a dialectical approach is truly theological. We tread on holy ground. Barth had a sharp exchange of correspondence with Adolph *Harnack, his former teacher, illustrating well their complete difference in theological approach. For Barth, following *Anselm, theology has to be 'faith seeking understanding'. Following *Kierkegaard, he stressed personal faith in Christ, the one who transcends the merely human and historical and brings judgment strange to the complacent European culture of the day. Luther's message of judgment and grace meeting at the cross influenced both Kierkegaard and Barth.

Dialectical theology sought to recover a Christian *eschatology, by which was meant the inbreaking of God into history in divine strangeness and awe, over against human self-confidence and arrogance. Franz Overbeck was a key influence on Barth for this aspect of his early theology. The theme of the *kingdom of God coming with Christ into human history, bringing a new way of life into the selfishness of society, a way of life compatible with the socialist message, was gained by Barth from the Blumhardts.

Besides Barth, other theologians writing under the banner of dialectical theology included Rudolph *Bultmann, Friedrich *Gogarten and Emil *Brunner. Barth broke with Bultmann and Gogarten since they based their dialectical theology on human existence in dialectic with God, whereas Barth's dialectic was rooted in the event of *revelation and its judgment on human existence and experience. This eschatological emphasis on the inbreaking of the divine in judgment and grace on human culture and its various forms of idolatry was one of radical discontinuity, even dualism, over against the liberal tendency towards historicism and finding God in human experience.

The movement in fact contained different emphases and interests within itself, and the four theologians disagreed over various issues. Barth criticized Brunner for suggesting that the human being had a capacity for God, a 'point of contact', whereas Barth believed that God alone could supply that by grace. Barth was confirmed in his dialectical approach by the onset of Nazism in the 1930s, when many Christians sought to integrate Nazism into the church. Barth wrote, with two others, the *Barmen Declaration of 1934, radically pointing to Christ as 'the one Word of God'. Human *culture was corruptible and not a source for truth about God. Bultmann's path took a radically subjective turn, perhaps showing that dialectical theology itself was subject to dialectical polarization. For Bultmann, we can know by faith only that God exists and that the message of the gospel is that Jesus himself had authentic faith. It is open to us to accept this faith as we hear the gospel preached and take up an 'authentic' way of life.

Epistemologically, Bultmann is with Barth in rejecting any 'natural theology' or pathway from reason to faith: they both insist on a radical disjuncture. But in terms of ontology, Barth developed his dialectical theology in a much more objective and traditional direction, with Jesus revealed to faith as the trinitarian Son incarnate. For Bultmann, this is a return to metaphysics and *myth. Barth's dialectical theology insisted on the Kierkegaardian point at which the divine became human, a total mystery, a contradiction even, the holy God conquering human sin. The sheer otherness of God is most sharply focused at the *cross where God reveals and conceals himself, dialectically. This dialectic again owes much to Luther's 'God of the cross', and seeks to transcend the 'yes' and 'no' of affirmative and negative theologies (see *Apophatic theology) so as to preserve the Absolute of faith from fixed formulations devised by human thought. Barth's dialectical theology seeks to point to God as veiled and unveiled, neither pole of the dialectic being available to inspection without the simultaneous impact of the other. The dialectic deployed by Barth owes far more to Kierkegaard than *Hegel, whose dialectic of thesis, antithesis and synthesis was said to be the engine of historical development. Barth's dialectic aims at precisely the reverse in that it radically blocks any human grasp of the Absolute. Barth's dialectical theology likewise blocks any 'secret identification of God with man' in terms of the church, which Barth warns must not be regarded as deified in any sense, contrary to Roman Catholic ecclesiology. The church herself is not holy but, dialectically, awaits the touch of the Spirit.

Other cultural influences shaping dialectical theology in addition to Kierkegaard's writings and polemics against cultural Christianity include the novels of *Dostoevsky exploring the reality of sin and evil. The pessimistic side of human nature and history was pitted against liberal optimism, an optimism killed off on the barbed wire of the Somme. Artistically, this inter-war era was one of discontinuity and radical questioning. T. S. Eliot's poem, 'The Waste Land', portrayed a pessimistic, bleak European culture, adrift from its moorings. Expressionism in art, with its fractured and broken imagery, disturbing the conventional and establishment views, notably Picasso's *Guernica* on the Spanish Civil War, echo dialectical theology. Indeed, Barth's *Romans* is full of the imagery of lightning splintering trees, of mountain rivers gushing headlong downwards, of the crater left by the meteorite, that is, of the aftershock of grace encountering sin in judgment, but without an ongoing restored relationship. Barth later acknowledged that his dialectical phase, 'the rolling thunder of Romans', was a necessary overemphasis against the ruling liberal Protestantism of the day. He developed his dialectics in Christological fashion in his *Church Dogmatics*, following the logic of the incarnation that God has acted to assume full humanity in Christ.

Dialectical theology was overwhelmingly a German theological movement, and an attack on liberal theology which proved extremely successful. It also, however, swept away the conservative evangelical tradition of such theologians in Germany as Adolph *Schlatter, a scholarly biblical theologian. *Roman Catholic theologians too acknowledged Barth as their greatest critic and dialogue partner. The movement never really found a favour in England, but Scotland proved far more receptive. Today Barth and his dialectical way of doing theology has returned to fashion with the advent of *postmodernism and its rejection of 'foundationalism' or the building up of a rational basis for theology. Just as modernism is accused of rationalistic objectivism, so Barth's dialectics rejected the notion of God as an object accessible to human capacities and 'domestication' by reason, feeling, morality or spirituality. Our speech about God depends on the grace of God. Divine revelation, like the burning bush drawing Moses towards it, is to be approached in fear and trembling, pointing beyond itself. Scripture functions as this pointing finger. Barth remained a dialectical theologian in an important sense (according to Bruce MacCormack), but his early phase was radically so, almost dualistic in terms of both *ontology and *epistemology.

There has been a considerable renewal of interest in Barth in English-speaking theological circles, as liberal theology has lost touch with grassroots Christianity and fundamentalism is regarded as verging on bibliolatry. Dialectical theology declines any claim of human enlightenment or rationality to define God. It also refuses to allow a deification of any text or institution, albeit Scripture or church. They may 'become' witnesses to God as the Spirit acts. Dialectical theology tried to find a way of affirming God's reality and sovereign holiness as disclosed in the narratives of 'the strange new world of the Bible', while preserving divine freedom from capture by human language and concept. It has now gained the attention of postmodern thinkers, and is likely to remain relevant in any Christian critique of Western culture now struggling to find meaning.

Bibliography

C. Asprey, *Eschatological Presence in Karl Barth's Göttingen Theology* (Oxford, 2010); H. U. von Balthasar, *The Theology of Karl Barth* (Chicago, 1971); K. Barth, *The Epistle to the Romans* (ET, London, 1933 [1922]); N. MacDonald, *The Strange New World within the Bible* (Milton Keynes, 2001); B. McCormack, *Karl Barth's Critically Realistic Dialectical Theology* (Oxford, 1995); J. D. Smart, *The Divided Mind of Modern Theology* (Philadelphia, 1967); T. F. Torrance, *Karl Barth: An Introduction to his Early Theology 1910–1931* (London, 1962).

T. BRADSHAW

DIDYMUS, see ALEXANDRIAN SCHOOL

DILTHEY, WILHELM (1833–1911)

Wilhelm Dilthey was professor of philosophy at Basel from 1866, Kiel from 1868, Breslau from 1871 and Berlin from 1882 until his death. At the beginning of his university career he studied theology with the intention of entering the ministry, but, realizing that he could not accept the traditional doctrines of the Christian faith, soon abandoned this course. Henceforth his labours were devoted to philosophical, psychological and sociological studies, in which he developed a *relativistic approach and methodology to the *Geisteswissenschaften* (cultural or human sciences) in contrast to the *Naturwissenschaften* (natural sciences). In Dilthey's methodology there is no place for the *supernatural; knowledge of life comes from understanding the mental processes and worldviews (*Weltanschauungen*) of human beings, and seeing these as part of the ongoing flow of universal history.

In theological circles, Dilthey is best known for his biography of *Schleiermacher (1870), but his greatest importance lies in his development of a philosophy of *history in which – over against the biblical understanding of history – God has no place. This scheme of history in turn provided a basis for the *phenomenology of Edmund Husserl (1859–1938), the historicism of R. G. Collingwood (1889–1943), and the *existentialism of Martin Heidegger (1889–1976), which was to influence *Bultmann. Although Dilthey lies outside the main stream of theological scholarship, his approach to the philosophy of history was to influence the whole course of twentieth-century historical methodology, not only in the philosophical field, but also in the theological.

Bibliography

I. N. Bulhof, *Wilhelm Dilthey* (The Hague, 1980); H. A. Hodges, *The Philosophy of Wilhelm Dilthey* (London, 1952); R. A. Makreel, *Dilthey: Philosopher of the Human Studies* (Princeton, 1993); J. de Mul, *The Tragedy of Finitude: Dilthey's Hermeneutics of Life* (New Haven, 2004); H. P. Rickmann, *Wilhelm Dilthey* (London, 1979).

H. HARRIS

DIODORE OF TARSUS, see ANTIOCHENE SCHOOL

DIONYSIUS OF ALEXANDRIA, see ALEXANDRIAN SCHOOL

DIONYSIUS THE AREOPAGITE, see PSEUDO-DIONYSIUS THE AREOPAGITE

DISPENSATIONAL THEOLOGY

Dispensationalism rests on the view that God's dealings with men have proceeded through 'well-defined time-periods' (L. S. Chafer) – 'dispensations' – in each of which God reveals a particular purpose to be accomplished in that period, to which men respond in faith or unbelief. Dispensationalists deny that they teach more than one way of salvation, admitting only that the content of faith varies according to the revelation given in each dispensation. Scriptural support is derived from passages which distinguish between, for example, past ages (e.g. Eph. 3:5; Col. 1:26), the present age (e.g. Rom. 12:2; Gal. 1:4) and the age to come

(Eph. 2:7; Heb. 6:5), and especially the use of *aiōnas* in Heb. 1:2 and 11:3.

Dispensationalists differ in identification of the dispensations, but it is fairly general to distinguish those of innocency (Adam before the fall), conscience (Adam to Noah), promise (Abraham to Moses), Mosaic law (Moses to Christ), grace (Pentecost to the rapture) and the *millennium. The sharp distinction drawn between Israel and the church (except during the dispensation of grace) is crucial. The systematization of modern dispensational theology owes much to J. N. *Darby and the Scofield Reference Bible (1909, by the American Congregationalist, Cyrus I. Scofield, 1843–1921).

The basic *hermeneutical principle is literal interpretation, which does not rule out symbols, figures of speech and typology, but does insist that, throughout, 'the reality of the literal meaning of the terms involved' is determinative (C. C. Ryrie, *Dispensationalism Today*, p. 87). Consequently, the promises of an earthly kingdom given to Israel as a nation must be fulfilled literally in a future, millennial kingdom (on the analogy of the literal fulfilment of the messianic promises relating to Jesus). Dispensationalists accept that believing Jews – as individuals – find their place in the church during the dispensation of grace, but the promises made to the natural seed of Abraham await the premillennial return of Christ with his church for their fulfilment. Then will be initiated the dispensation during which the material blessings promised to Israel will be bestowed and will be characteristic, though not to the exclusion of the spiritual dimension.

Some details are in dispute among dispensationalists. These include the number and designations of the dispensations and the point at which the dispensation of grace began. The most extreme view is that of E. W. Bullinger (1837–1913) who commenced the church age with the ministry of Paul after Acts 28:28, held that Paul's prison epistles are the only Scriptures addressed primarily to the church, and denied that water baptism and the Lord's Supper are for this age. There is less disagreement over the *terminus ad quem* of the dispensation of grace, though some believe the rapture of the church (which marks its termination) will not take place until the end (a few say the middle) of the great tribulation.

See also: ESCHATOLOGY.

Bibliography

L. S. Chafer, *Systematic Theology*, 8 vols. (Dallas, 1947); R. G. Clouse (ed.), *The Millennium: Four Views* (Downers Grove, 1977); A. H. Ehlert, 'A Bibliography of Dispensationalism', *BS*, *passim* (1944–6); S. Grenz, *The Millennial Maze* (Downers Grove, 1992); V. Poythress, *Understanding Dispensationalists*, 2nd edn (Phillipsburg, 1993); C. C. Ryrie, *Dispensationalism Today* (Chicago, 1965); E. Sauer, *From Eternity to Eternity* (Exeter, 1954); J. F. Walvoord, *The Millennial Kingdom* (Findlay, 1959).

H. H. ROWDON

DIVORCE, see SEXUALITY

DOCETISM

Among the cluster of movements that arose in response to the life, teachings, death and resurrection of Jesus emerged a tendency that came to be called Docetism, which responded with a 'no' to questions like – 'Was Jesus a real human being?', 'Did Jesus really suffer?' and 'Did Jesus actually die on the cross?' The proponents of this tendency, which was strongly affirmed among various *Gnostic groups, based their response on a particular way of understanding scriptural texts like 1 Cor. 15:45, which speaks of the last Adam being 'a life-giving Spirit', and 1 Cor. 15:47, which speaks of the 'man from heaven'. For those who held docetic opinions, Christ only seemed to be human and only appeared to have a human body.

The word 'docetism' derives from a Greek work which has the meanings of 'seeming' and 'appearing'. This was used to think about the humanity of Christ as being a disguise which concealed his true spiritual nature. There were several early teachers of faith for whom this tendency was incompatible with a Christological understanding of Jesus, who suffered in the flesh and who experienced the reality and finality of death. Prominent among these were Ignatius and *Irenaeus. Ignatius, writing at the beginning of the second century, argues that it is not possible to accept an ethereal disembodied view of Christ, since it is Christ's actual suffering in the body that establishes the model for people to follow. He also denies the docetic tendency to spiritualize the resurrection and argues that Jesus remained in the flesh even after the resurrection, shown by the accounts of his eating and drinking with the disciples even while he was spiritually united with the Father. Only this reality could play a role in the transformation of human beings.

Irenaeus, writing toward the end of the second century, argues vehemently against Docetic teachings. In his major piece of writing against heresies, he hotly opposed the view of teachers like Simon the Samaritan, Saturninus, *Marcion and Basilides, that Jesus only appeared to be human. He contradicts Basilides' teaching that Simon of Cyrene, who had been compelled to carry Jesus' cross, had been transformed to look like the crucified Jesus, while the real Jesus stood by laughing.

Evidence for Docetic inclinations can be found in a variety of 'Gnostic' texts, including apocalyptic writings attributed to various disciples. Alternate views of what happened during the crucifixion is present in 'acts' and 'gospels' attributed to different disciples. A church leader like Serapion of Antioch, who was bishop during the turn of the second century, is recorded by the church historian Eusebius to have exposed the docetic nature of writings like the so-called 'Gospel of Peter'.

Christological thinking that tends to minimize the humanity of Jesus is always in danger of falling into Doceticism, and this is an ongoing challenge to those who continue to respond to the question as to who Jesus is.

See also: CHRISTOLOGY; JESUS.

Bibliography

J. K. Elliott, *The Apocryphal Jesus: Legends of the Early Church* (Oxford and New York, 1996); A. J. Hultgren and S. A. Haggmark (eds.), *The Earliest Christian Heretics: Readings from Their Opponents* (Minneapolis, 1996); J. Stevenson, rev. W. H. C. Frend, *A New Eusebius: Documents Illustrating the History of the Church to* AD *337* (London, new edn, 1987).

J. J. SEBASTIAN

DOCTRINAL CRITICISM

Doctrinal criticism is the appraisal of the truth and adequacy of doctrinal statements. The term owes its currency in British theology to a programmatic essay by G. F. Woods (1907–66), setting out the task of the doctrinal critic as that of subjecting doctrinal statements to the same kind of critical scrutiny brought to bear upon the biblical writings by biblical *criticism. As well as analysing the capacity of human symbols to articulate the transcendent, the critic assesses doctrines in the light of the historical setting in which they were formulated and in the light of contemporary understandings of reality. Woods's suggestions were extensively developed and applied in the work of Maurice Wiles (1923–2005), notably in the area of *Christology. While doctrinal criticism contributed much to the renewed interest in *systematic theology of recent years, it inherited a changed perspective on the authority and self-evidence of *revelation which stems from the *Enlightenment, according to which no *contingent statement or system may be accorded a position of privileged immunity from critical examination.

See also: CONTEMPORARY THEOLOGICAL TRENDS.

Bibliography

B. L. Hebblethwaite, *The Problems of Theology* (Cambridge, 1980); *idem*, *Th* 70, 1967, pp. 402–405; M. F. Wiles, *Working Papers in Doctrine* (London, 1976); *idem* (ed.), *Explorations in Theology*, vol. 4 (London, 1979); G. F. Woods, 'Doctrinal Criticism', in F. G. Healey (ed.), *Prospect for Theology* (London, 1966).

J. B. WEBSTER

DOCTRINE

Doctrine is generally understood to be communally agreed and communally authoritative teaching. More specifically, Christian interest in doctrine stems from the fact that the Christian faith has a constitutive cognitive content summarized in the claim, 'Jesus is Lord.' Although this claim is confessed, expanded and articulated principally in narrative form within the canonical Scriptures, doctrine serves to point to the unity, identify the emphases, expound the implications and specify the plot of the scriptural narratives. Classically, the result is a body of teaching focused on such topics as *God, *Christ, the *Holy Spirit, the *Trinity, *creation, humanity, *salvation, the *church and *redemption. Whilst such teaching is often presented as a systematically ordered body of doctrines in *creeds, *catechisms and *confessions, it is also embedded in liturgies, hymns and church polity.

Christian doctrine often emerges with particular clarity and energy when the church is required to specify its essential beliefs vis à vis the claims of alternative and/or hostile communities. The Nicene Creed, for instance, specifies the unity and basic plot of the Christian faith within a narrative framework of creation, *incarnation and redemption, whilst simultaneously identifying the triune character of God in contrast to prevailing forms of both monotheism and polytheism.

The identity-marking function of doctrine can, however, also be used as the basis of separation between Christians. Paradigmatic of this was the continental Reformation and the subsequent disintegration of *Protestantism into a multiplicity of denominations. Such disintegration was often justified by the appeal to particular doctrines (e.g. *justification, election – see *Predestination; inspiration – see *Scripture, doctrine of) abstracted from a broader doctrinal framework.

Awareness of this church-dividing function of doctrine made the whole doctrinal tradition ripe for criticism. Adolf von *Harnack argued that the doctrinal articulation of the Christian faith belonged to the *Hellenization of Christianity in which the Hebraic focus on narrative was replaced and obscured by an alien Greek tendency to objectify and systematize. More generally, modern (especially liberal Protestant) theologians sought to avoid the embarrassment of doctrinal division by explaining doctrine as diverse and distorted linguistic 'expressions' of some common pre-cognitive, pure experience of God.

Nevertheless, recent discussions display a lively retrieval of the doctrinal tradition. The Hellenization thesis is regarded as dependent on an exaggerated antithesis, and the appeal to pre-cognitive experience is deemed both conceptually flawed and itself alien to the Christian faith. Seminal in these discussions has been George *Lindbeck's *The Nature of Doctrine* (1984). Rejecting expressivism, Lindbeck argues that doctrine is to faith as grammar is to language. Just as grammar regulates language in ways that enable effective communication, so doctrine regulates the practice of faith in ways that enable authentic experience of and response to God. Alongside widespread endorsement of his rejection of expressivism, Lindbeck's critics have worried that stressing doctrine's regulatory role undermines confidence in its capacity to state the truth of the gospel. At the same time, nervousness about naïve propositionalism has seen claims for doctrine's truthfulness draw on wider discussions of critically realist correspondence theories of *truth. Such theories propose that truth-claiming statements are not merely projections of the human mind onto reality, but are themselves determined by and correspond to reality, even if imperfectly and therefore in ways subject to modification. Additionally, attention to the role of doctrine has led to explorations of the mutual interplay of thought and practice. Discussions about the truthfulness of doctrine also focus on its relationship to Scripture from which it derives. Appeals to such metaphors as 'performance' and 'drama' are leading these latter discussions into fruitful areas of enquiry.

Bibliography

E. T. Charry, *By the Renewing of Your Minds: The Pastoral Function of Christian Doctrine* (New York and Oxford, 1997); C. E. Gunton, 'A Rose by Any Other Name: From "Christian Doctrine" to "Systematic Theology"', *IJST* 1, 1999, pp. 4–23; R. Hütter, *Suffering Divine Things: Theology as Church Practice* (ET, Grand Rapids, 1997); N. Lash, 'Performing the Scriptures', in N. Lash, *Theology on the Way to Emmaus* (London, 1986); G. A. Lindbeck, *The Nature of Doctrine: Religion and Theology in a Postliberal Age* (Philadelphia, 1984); A. E. McGrath, *The Genesis of Doctrine: A Study in the Foundation of Doctrinal Criticism* (Oxford, 1990); N. Murphy, *Beyond Liberalism and Fundamentalism: How Modern and Postmodern Philosophy Set the Theological Agenda* (Valley Forge, 1996); S. W. Sykes, *The Identity of Christianity: Theologians and the Essence of Christianity from Schleiermacher to Barth* (London, 1984); K. J. Vanhoozer, *The Drama of Doctrine: A Canonical Linguistic Approach to Christian Theology* (Louisville, 2005).

G. J. Thompson

DODD, CHARLES HAROLD (1884–1973)

Charles Dodd was probably the leading twentieth-century British NT scholar. He showed that Jesus taught that the *kingdom of God was already present during his ministry. Dodd tried to understand his teaching, especially the parables, on the assumption that he did not expect any future apocalyptic events; later he modified this position. Dodd's recognition of 'realized' *eschatology was a necessary reaction to the 'futurist' eschatology of A. *Schweitzer and others. Dodd also gave a profound analysis of the use of Jewish ideas in a *Hellenistic framework in John's Gospel, and analysed its historical contents to show that it contained valuable historical traditions independent of the other written gospels. Dodd emphasized the combination of historical facts plus interpretation in *revelation. He was thus at the opposite end of the theological spectrum from R. *Bultmann, and he showed that it was possible and legitimate to write about the historical *Jesus. Dodd also showed how a basic pattern of preaching (*kerygma) lay at the root of *NT theology, and how this theology was developed from a study of various 'fields' of OT Scriptures. Despite some 'liberal' elements in his interpretation of Scripture, he made a positive and lasting contribution to NT scholarship.

Bibliography

F. F. Bruce, 'C. H. Dodd', in P. E. Hughes (ed.), *Creative Minds in Contemporary Theology* (Grand Rapids, 1966), pp. 239–269; F. W. Dillistone, *C. H. Dodd, Interpreter of the New Testament* (Grand Rapids, 1977).

I. H. MARSHALL

DOGMA

This Gk word was used in the pre-Christian world of public ordinances, judicial decisions or statements of principle in philosophy or science. In the LXX, it is used of government decrees in Esth. 3:9; Dan. 2:13; 6:8. In the NT, the judgments of the law are so referred to in Eph. 2:15 and Col. 2:14 and the decisions of the Council of Jerusalem in Acts 16:4.

In the Christian church 'dogma' became teaching which was considered authoritative. Throughout the first three centuries, the Lat. and Gk writers were inclined to call everything related to faith 'dogma'. *Chrysostom used the word specifically for those truths revealed by Christ and above reason. *Thomas Aquinas and the *scholastics did not often use the term and preferred to speak of the articles of faith.

From the Reformation onwards, the word came to designate those articles of faith which the church officially formulated as the truth which had been revealed. It reflected therefore a common recognition by the Reformed and Roman churches that dogmatic formulation is an activity of the church, often arising out of theological controversy or the need to clarify the faith to be embraced.

The Reformed milieu

In the debate over the nature of authority, the *Reformed understanding of dogma reflected its anchorage of authority in Scripture rather than in the church. The response of the church to doctrinal controversy was seen to be *materially* based upon Scripture. *Formally*, dogma bears the marks of the intellectual and cultural ethos in which it is formulated. It is not infallible, but nevertheless provides grounds for unity and stability within the church catholic.

*Pietism challenged the *formal* dimension of dogma in perceiving it as perpetuating an arid and intellectual scholasticism, far removed from the experience of God in the life of the believer. The *Enlightenment increasingly undermined the classic *material* substance of dogma, by challenging the church's identification of the word of God with Scripture. A new understanding of dogma and how it develops emerged. This is found in the writings of *Schleiermacher, *Ritschl and specifically in *Harnack's *History of Dogma*. Here the focus is upon the religious and ethical experience of the Christian community in which divine revelation is authenticated. Dogma is the articulation by and for that community of their perception of the revelation of God.

The return to orthodoxy spearheaded by Emil *Brunner and Karl *Barth in post-war Germany sought to purge the Reformed faith of seventeenth-century scholasticism while preserving the ground of dogma in the revelation of God in Jesus Christ. Dogma was seen as the articulation of the church's understanding of this revelation as the Holy Spirit bears witness to Christ in the Scriptures. Unlike their immediate *liberal predecessors or *existential successors, the neo-orthodox school did not view dogma as an attempt to understand and express human experience of God, but as the necessary and scientific response to 'the light of the knowledge of the glory of God in the face of Jesus Christ'. The *modus operandi* for dogmatic formulation has its roots in the nature of God and his revelation and not in the nature of man and his religious awareness. What is then the role of Scripture? It remains, in this framework, the source of the material content of dogma, but only in so far as its equation with the Word is indirect, for the Word of God is the revelation itself, i.e. Jesus Christ.

Dogma is essentially a corollary of orthodoxy. The increasing pluralism within Reformed confessional churches and their inability to function with objective criteria of *authority have produced a growing ambivalence to the articulation of dogma. Only in pragmatic areas of morality do the Reformed churches appear to speak with authority.

The Catholic stance

The *Roman Catholic Church has sought to affirm its understanding of dogma under the same pressures as that of the Reformed community. The traditional view in the Catholic Church is that dogma is truth revealed by God in Scripture and/or tradition and formulated by and for the church against error. Such truth is irrevocable, unchangeable and infallible. Dogma, therefore, does not add to what has been revealed but merely defines and declares it.

Although not denying this view of dogma, since the nineteenth century many Catholic theologians have queried the static and scholastic manner in which the church is perceived to have stated dogma. *Newman argued for a dynamic process of dogmatic *development in the church. Truth was implanted like seeds in the mind of the church and organically developed, so that latent truth became under the focus of controversy a full-grown dogma explicitly approved by the church.

A further stage in Catholic reflection is the awareness that there is a continual process of uncovering the meaning of what is expressed in dogma. Apart from truth transcending human thought and requiring analogical language to communicate, it was increasingly recognized that church pronouncements are the product of their age and reflect the cultural, philosophical and linguistic norms of the period. Most Catholic theologians would want to argue that the reality expressed will remain unchanged and unchanging, and that dogmas have an objective content whose meaning is valid for all ages. Nevertheless, *the form* of expression can be subject to revision.

Three further convictions have affected the contemporary Catholic stance. First, revelation is not the divine communication of abstract truths which dogma would put into propositions. Second, all truth is organically interrelated and finds its central focus in Jesus Christ. Third, revealed truth is self-authenticating in that it demands an existential response. Karl *Rahner argues that dogma is deduced from revelation, which is a 'saving event' wherein 'the incarnate Word' communicates the reality of God himself. Dogmas are not therefore merely statements about God, but are 'exhibitive' words with a 'sacramental' nature; i.e. 'what [a dogma] states actually occurs and is posited by its existence'. Dogma, therefore, when rightly affirmed and personally assimilated, is 'life'. This view he would wish to incorporate within the traditional twofold distinction between the formal (expressed by the church explicitly and definitively as a revealed truth) and the material (belonging to Christian revelation as it is found in the word of God addressed to us in Scripture and/or tradition).

*Neo-orthodoxy in the Reformed and Roman Catholic churches continues to grapple with how to draw from revelation truths which are organically interdependent, whose logic stretches traditional models to breaking point, and yet when articulated in dogmatic form may receive the allegiance of the faithful.

*Ecumenism and social and economic realities are in practical terms the two most powerful influences upon the major Christian traditions in their revaluation of dogma. Today ecumenical dialogue has heightened the awareness of the influence of Western/Greco-Roman thought forms upon dogmatic formulations which, in the eyes of cultures more akin to the world of the OT and NT, are a distortion of the revelation with unsettling moral and spiritual ramifications. The socioeconomic conditions to which the gospel is to speak expose the bourgeois nature of the churches' historic dogmatic statements and their failure to emphasize those aspects of the revelation which hold together *creation and *redemption in cosmic deliverance.

See also: CONTEXTUALIZATION; LIBERATION THEOLOGY; POLITICAL THEOLOGY; SYSTEMATIC THEOLOGY.

Bibliography

K. Barth, *CD* 1:1; E. Brunner, *Dogmatics 1: The Christian Doctrine of God* (London, 1949); A. Harnack, *History of Dogma*, vol. 1 (London, 1894); A. Lecerf, *An Introduction to Reformed Dogmatics* (London, 1949); J. Orr, *The Progress of Dogma* (London, ³1908); W. Pannenberg, *Basic Questions in Theology*, vol. 1 (London, 1970), pp. 182–210 ('What Is a Dogmatic Statement?'); O. Weber, *Foundations of Dogmatics*, vol. 1 (Grand Rapids, 1981).

T. W. J. MORROW

DOMINIC AND THE DOMINICANS

The Dominicans, officially known as the Order of Friars Preachers (O.P.) and more popularly called the Black Friars, are one of the four great mendicant orders of the Roman Catholic Church. The founder of the order, Dominico (Dominic) de Guzman (1170–1221), was a Spaniard whose early career began in Castile. Educated at the University of Palencia, which was later moved to Salamanca, he became a member of the religious community attached to the cathedral at Osma. Because of his impressive ability he was sent to southern France to help convert the *Albigensian heretics. Dominic came to believe that the only way to reach them was with evangelical preaching accompanied by a lifestyle of apostolic poverty. To accomplish this task he set out on preaching missions in market-places and roadsides, living in poverty so extreme that he wore no shoes or sandals and begged for his food. At first his policy met with little success, and his mission was forced to end when Pope Innocent III (1198–1216) began to use force against the heretics in 1208.

Inspired by this vision of a group of preachers who would win *heretics and heathen by preaching the word and living a simple life, Dominic attracted a group of followers (1214). He prepared them for their task by careful instruction and by sharing his dream of a learned preaching order of mendicant friars. Despite the rather impressive nature of the group, they were denied recognition by the Fourth *Lateran Council (1215), but later Pope Honorius III (1216) sanctioned their mission, and in 1220 their rule, adopted from the *Augustinians with added requirements of preaching and apostolic living, was confirmed. Dominic spent the remainder of his life travelling in Italy, France and Spain organizing his order. He was canonized in 1234. A man of intelligence, courage and zeal, he was also an extremely effective administrator.

From its inception the order has accepted from its founder its synthesis of an active ministry with a spiritual life. The members live in community, observe diet and fast rules, and conduct liturgical rites, but, according to their constitution, time is to be given for study and preaching. Dominicans are governed by a relatively democratic order. However, a balance is maintained between the elected representative bodies, or chapters, and strong but elected superiors. In contrast to other orders of its time, the Dominicans were not a collection of autonomous houses, but were an army of preachers organized in provinces under a master general and prepared to go wherever they were needed. This organization has served as a model for many monastic movements, organized after the Dominicans took form.

From the beginning they insisted that no-one should preach without three years of theological training. Within forty years of the founding of the order their scholars were teaching at Oxford, Paris, Bologna and Cologne. Dominican intellectual activity led to the founding of several universities, where they emphasized the teaching of languages, including Greek, Hebrew and Arabic, in addition to the more standard curriculum of scriptural studies and theology. Some of the great masters of medieval thought, led by *Thomas Aquinas and *Albertus Magnus, were Dominicans who sought to harmonize *faith and reason in a series of massive volumes (see *Scholasticism). They lived at a time when Muslim scholars had made the works of *Aristotle available for the first time to medieval Europeans. These books, which presented a complete explanation of reality without any reference to the Christian God, challenged the academic minds of the thirteenth century. After a period of conflict and uncertainty, the thought of Thomas, bringing the Aristotelian and Christian systems together, was accepted as the basis for *Roman Catholic theology.

The academic pursuits of the Dominicans did not divert them from their mission to combat heresy and seek conversions. They continued to work among the Albigensians and extended their efforts to include the Jews and Moors in Spain. Their evangelistic efforts led them to preach to the non-Christian peoples in Eastern Europe and in Asia. When the Inquisition was established, Dominicans were assigned to help carry it out because of their dedication to the church and orthodoxy. They entered the new world as the first and most energetic missionaries under the Spanish and Portuguese explorers.

The Dominican order has experienced periods of achievement and of decline. During the fourteenth and fifteenth centuries, discipline relaxed as Europe suffered from plague, warfare and division in the church. However, the sixteenth century witnessed a period of Thomistic renewal under leaders such as Francisco de Vitoria (c. 1485–1546) and Thomas de Vio Cajetan (1469–1534; see *Luther). During this period, Dominican studies were revised to meet the challenge of *humanism and *Protestantism. At the Council of *Trent (1545–63), attended by many Dominicans, *Thomistic theology was made the basis for the dogmatic decisions. With some modern revisions, it still remains basic to much of Roman Catholic thought. Despite this recognition, there were forces at work that undermined the order. The rise of new groups such as the *Jesuits and the loss of much of Eastern Europe to Western control began to push the Dominicans into the background. The eighteenth-century Enlightenment also dampened enthusiasm, weakened discipline and made recruiting difficult.

The order continues into modern times, standing firmly for orthodoxy and opposing novelty in theology. Paradoxically, many Dominicans have been active in the reform movement that resulted from the Second *Vatican Council, including theological reform (e.g. E. *Schillebeeckx). They have also led in the worker-priest movement, spoken decisively for the Majority World and made extensive use of the fields of radio, television, films and the stage in their preaching ministry.

Bibliography

W. R. Bonniwell, *A History of the Dominican Liturgy* (New York, 1944); W. A. Hinnebusch, *The History of the Dominican Order* (Staten Island, NY, 1966); B. Jarrett, *Life of St Dominic (1170–1221)* (London, 1924); idem, *The English Dominicans* (London, rev. edn, 1937); P. F. Mandonnet, *St Dominic and His Work* (St Louis, MO, 1944); idem, in *DTC* 6, 1920, cols. 863–924; S. Tugwell (ed.), *Early Dominicians: Selected Writings* (New York, 1982); M. H. Vicaire, *Saint Dominic and His Times* (London, 1964); R. Woods, *Mysticism and Prophecy: The Dominican Tradition* (London, 1998).

R. G. Clouse

DONATISM

Donatism was a *schism which broke out in North Africa c. 313 and persisted until after the Muslim conquest in 698. Donatism is so called because its leading spirit was a man named Donatus, whom the schismatics elected as Bishop of Carthage in 313, shortly after the outbreak of controversy.

The origins of the schism were bound up with personal rivalries at Carthage, and later took on social and political implications in that the Donatists drew much of their support from the less-Romanized Berber tribespeople of the country. Yet the main and enduring cause was religious and theological. The Donatists were rigorous in their support of the spiritual rewards of *martyrdom, and it was the lax policy of the church at Carthage towards *traditores* (those who had 'handed over' their copies of the Scriptures to be burned during the Great Persecution of 303), which caused the bad feeling and led to schism. The election as bishop in 312 of Caecilian, who seemed unenthusiastic about the martyrs, and his consecration by a suspected *traditor*, caused a scandal among the rigorists and led to separation. Donatists regarded themselves as the true *church, and claimed *Cyprian's authority in *rebaptizing Catholics.

In the fourth century, Donatism possessed gifted teachers in Parmenian (against whom *Augustine later wrote) and Tyconius (fl. c. 370–90), a layman who was a somewhat nonconformist Donatist and exercised a major influence on Augustine (who incorporated the essence of his *Book of Rules*, the first Latin Christian treatise on *hermeneutics, into his *Christian Instruction*) and on Western interpretations of the Apocalypse of John. Tyconius taught that the church was truly universal, a 'bipartite' mixture of the 'cities' of God and of the devil. His Paulinism also influenced Augustine.

It is sometimes said that the Donatists were against the links which the emperor, Constantine, was beginning to forge between church and *state at the moment the schism erupted, but the fact that they were prepared to appeal to the emperor for support argues against this conclusion. Donatist opposition to the Roman authorities stemmed from the attempts of the latter to persecute them. These attempts started in 317 and continued intermittently thereafter. A conference held at Carthage in 411 tried to reintegrate the Donatists into the Catholic Church, with some success. Augustine wrote against them, and justified their forcible coercion, and by the time he died, Donatism was a declining force. Its remnants may have partly merged with the Catholic Church during the Vandal occupation of North Africa (439–533) and the final phase of Roman rule (533–698).

Bibliography

W. H. C. Frend, *The Donatist Church* (Oxford, 1952); M. A. Tilley, *The Bible in Christian North Africa: The Donatist World* (Philadelphia, 1997); idem (tr.), *Donatist Martyr Stories* (Liverpool, 1996).

G. L. BRAY

DOOYEWEERD, HERMAN
(1894–1977)

A Dutch Christian jurist and philosopher, at the time of his death Dooyeweerd was professor emeritus at the Free University of Amsterdam and editor-in-chief of *Philosophia Reformata*, the scholarly journal of the Association for Calvinistic Philosophy. He was the founder, together with his colleague D. H. Th. Vollenhoven (1892–1978) and others, of the Christian philosophy now called the 'Philosophy of the Cosmonomic Idea'.

Dooyeweerd was born into a family that had a strong attachment to the movement in the Netherlands which was headed by the Dutch theologian, journalist and statesman Abraham *Kuyper.

Dooyeweerd approached philosophy by way of investigating his own field of jurisprudence, penetrating to its foundations, which, he said, could be understood only in terms of a radically Christian world-and-life view. The great turning point of his thought came when he discovered that all thinking, and indeed all of life, has a religious root. He began to examine the foundations of jurisprudence and statecraft as adjunct director of the Abraham Kuyper Foundation in the Hague (1922–26). After assuming his professorship at the Free University in 1926, he worked out his principles more broadly and in greater detail and published in 1935–6 his magnum opus, the three-volumed *Philosophy of the Law-Idea* (or *Cosmonomic Idea*). The appearance of this seminal work marked the beginning of a new philosophy, which sought to base itself on the teachings of the Scriptures and to participate in the reformation of all of life in the name of Jesus Christ.

In all science and philosophy, Dooyeweerd argued, thought is guided by a threefold idea: that of the coherence (how things hang together), the deeper unity (where and how things come to a single focus), and the origin of all things (how, in this focusing, they manifest their dependence on the Creator-God, who has expressed and continues to express his will in his law, i.e. in the created order that holds for the entire cosmos). Dooyeweerd attempted throughout to demonstrate that thought, by its very nature, is dependent on underlying presuppositions, and ultimately on basic religious motives. He argued, furthermore, that science and philosophy can perform their respective tasks successfully only on a sound Christian foundation. Thus he entered, along with other reformational thinkers, into a critique of systems of thought that attempt to build on non-Christian foundations or seek to combine Christian and non-Christian (apostate) motifs.

Because of the intrinsic relation of thought and religion, Dooyeweerd's critique is fundamentally a critique of theoretical thought itself, a theme that assumed greater prominence as his career progressed. Dooyeweerd's philosophy has also made many positive contributions to other disciplines; for instance, in its examination of the foundations of jurisprudence, in its development of a theory of individuality structures as a foundation (e.g. of a Christian sociology), and in settling forth a new theory of the intertwining (*enkapsis*) of such individuality structures in man's body, as a foundation for a Christian *anthropology.

Closely associated with Dooyeweerd's name are those of the other original representatives, broadly speaking, of this philosophy, who, following the lead of Abraham Kuyper, have attempted to reform scholarship in the name of Christ: D. H. Th. Vollenhoven (history of philosophy); H. G. Stoker (b. 1899; psychology); and C. *Van Til (apologetics).

See also: PHILOSOPHY AND THEOLOGY.

Bibliography

Works: *The Collected Works of Herman Dooyeweerd*, eds. D. F. M. Strauss *et al.* (Lewiston, 1996–).

Studies: V. Brümmer, *Transcendental Criticism and Christian Philosophy* (Franeker, 1961); J. Chaplin, *Herman Dooyeweerd:*

Christian Philosopher of State and Civil Society (Notre Dame, IN, 2011); Yong-Joon Choi, *Dialogue and Antithesis: A Philosophical Study on the Significance of Herman Dooyeweerd's Transcendental Critique* (Cheltenham, 2006); C. T. McIntire (ed.), *The Legacy of Herman Dooyeweerd: Reflections on Critical Philosophy in the Christian Tradition* (Lanham and Toronto, 1986).

R. D. KNUDSEN

DORT, CANONS OF

The *Synod of Dort (Dordrecht, 1618–19) was an ecclesial gathering whose main concern was to address theological controversies that surrounded the ideas of James *Arminius (Dutch name Jakob Hermandszoon). In 1610, after Arminius' death, his followers wrote five key articles of remonstrance (from which they get their name, Remonstrants) that outline their disagreement with key Calvinistic doctrines.

Since the Canons of Dort are a direct response to the Remonstrants' five articles, they are sometimes known as the 'Five Articles against the Remonstrants'. In actuality, however, there are really only four headings or points in the Canons, since Dort combines the third and fourth Remonstrance headings, treating them together. Each section contains articles of affirmation, as well as articles of rejection.

The five major heads were as follows. The First Head is on divine *predestination. It affirms not only the justice and love of God, but also that his sovereign election is based on his own good pleasure and not founded on 'foreseen faith'. In this section the language of 'passed by' is employed for the non-elect, ensuring God is not understood as the 'author of sin', since he merely leaves them to their own rebellion. The Second Head is on the death of Christ, and it emphasizes the infinite worth and value of the *atonement, which is given with 'saving efficacy . . . to all the elect'. Christ died on the cross for his people, and not merely for a potential number that may be saved. The Third and Fourth Heads, which are combined, focus on the extent to which humanity, after the fall of Adam, is wholly affected by *sin in mind, heart, will and affections. Thus, sinful humanity is neither 'able nor willing to return to God' in light of their depravity, and it thus takes God's Spirit to bring life where there is only death and rebellion. The Spirit does not merely make regeneration possible, but rather actual, bringing faith and true conversion. In this light the gospel should be preached 'to all nations, and to all persons . . . without distinction'. Finally, the Fifth Head explores the *perseverance of the saints, which really emphasizes God's faithfulness and preserving grace, rather than the saints' consistency.

While there was unity about these doctrines, and agreement that they should be preached 'in due time and place', there was clear concern to avoid potential abuse – they must be handled with 'the spirit of discretion and piety'. Rightly handled, these doctrines 'enliven' and 'comfort' God's people and should not be used to 'investigate the secret ways of God'.

See also: REFORMED THEOLOGY.

Bibliography
'The Canons of the Synod of Dort' in J. Pelikan and V. R. Hotchkiss (eds.), *Creeds and Confessions of Faith in the Christian Tradition* (New Haven, 2003); 'Canones Synodi Dordrechtanae' in P. Schaff (ed.), *The Creeds of Christendom: The Evangelical Protestant Creeds* (Grand Rapids, 1996); P. Y. De Jong (ed.), *Crisis in the Reformed Churches: Essays in Commemoration of the Great Synod of Dort, 1618–1619* (Grand Rapids, 1968); D. Nobbs, *Theocracy and Toleration: A Study of the Disputes in Dutch Calvinism from 1600 to 1650* (Cambridge, 1938); W. van 't Spijker, *et al.*, *De Synode Van Dordrecht in 1618 En 1619* (Houten, 1987).

K. M. KAPIC

DORT, SYNOD OF

This was a gathering of representatives of the international *Reformed community intended to end disagreements over the doctrine of *predestination which had persisted through the late sixteenth century. The synod was held in 1618–19 in Dort or Dordrecht by invitation of the government of the Netherlands, after civil war in which the party which favoured the more predestinarian position gained power. There were sixty-two representatives of the Dutch provinces and twenty-four foreign delegates.

Very considerable dissension had arisen in the Netherlands at the beginning of the century concerning the understanding of divine *sovereignty. This centred for a period in the teaching of *Arminius, but continued unabated after his death. In 1610 a document known as the Remonstrance was issued by those who were restless with the Reformed doctrine of predestination as it had developed under *Calvin and *Beza. It affirmed: (1) God's election is of all those who, according to his foresight, will have *faith in Christ and *persevere to the end; (2) the intent of the redemptive work of Christ was the salvation of all human beings but forgiveness is actually given only to those who believe; (3) fallen humanity is incapable of any good and specifically of saving faith, except by the intervention of the *Holy Spirit; (4) while *grace is necessary for all good, it is not irresistible; (5) the question of perseverance must be more carefully studied from *Scripture before any firm conclusion can be reached.

A number of conferences, notably at The Hague (1611) and at Delft (1613), did not resolve the questions. Resolution was therefore sought in a large gathering in which not only the Dutch churches but the international Reformed community would be represented. The issues were considered in the order of the Remonstrance, with the understanding that the third and fourth points were considered jointly. In the deliberations the Remonstrants did not have a part; they were viewed as accused of *heresy and subject to trial, rather than as members of the synodical party. The conclusions of the synod were set out in what are known as the *Canons of Dort, consisting of four chapters with a number of articles and a rejection of errors. The chapters relate respectively to sovereign predestination, definite *atonement, radical depravity (see *Sin) and effectual grace, and the perseverance of God with the saints. It is from this document that the articulation of five-point Calvinism has arisen.

In spite of certain differences among the delegates, particularly concerning the second point, there was a general approval of the Canons. They were worded at times in such a way as to accommodate certain differences of emphasis. In particular, the rejection of errors has often been thought to embody a very harsh repudiation of Arminianism. The Canons, complete with rejection of errors, were approved as a formulation of the faith of the Reformed Church of the Netherlands, and ministers were required to subscribe to them. This requirement was not maintained seriously in later times, but it still functions in the Netherlands and in churches of Dutch extraction in South Africa and the United States. In 1620 at the National Synod of Alais, French Reformed pastors were similarly enjoined to subscribe to the Canons.

Those who oppose the conclusions of Dort are almost unanimously in thinking that the synod was unduly harsh with the Arminian leaders and their views and that the Canons embody a scholastic form of doctrine which is foreign to the Scriptures. Those who approve of them ordinarily judge that the Reformed consensus on these difficult topics was expressed in a proper and balanced manner, and that a grievous deviation was thus warded off for at least a century in Reformed thinking. The subsequent history of the Arminians in the Netherlands, and the direction of Arminian bodies since that time, tend to confirm this opinion in the minds of traditional Calvinists, although some feel that if Arminian leaders had been treated more amicably at Dort and later, they might not have so quickly moved into positions which were in stark opposition to Reformed orthodoxy.

Bibliography

A. Hoekema, 'A New English Translation of the Canons of Dort', *CTJ* 3, pp. 133–161; P. Schaff, *Creeds of Christendom* (New York, 1919). A modern translation is found in the *Acta* of the 1985 Synod of the Christian Reformed Church.

Studies: P. Y. De Jong (ed.), *Crisis in the Reformed Churches* (Grand Rapids, 1968); W. R. Godfrey, *Tensions within International Calvinism: The Debate on the Atonement at the Synod of Dort, 1618–1619*, PhD diss. (Stanford, 1974); W. R. Godfrey and J. L. Boyd III (eds.), *Through Christ's Word* (Phillipsburg, 1985); J. I. Packer, 'Arminianisms', *The Manifold Grace of God* (Puritan and Reformed Studies Conference Papers, London, 1968); T. Scott, *The Articles of the Synod of Dort* (Utica, 1831).

R. NICOLE

DOSTOEVSKY, FYODOR MIKHAILOVICH (1821–81)

Brought up in a pious Russian Orthodox home, as a young man Dostoevsky went through a period of serious doubt. Exile in Siberia (1849–59) helped him to reaffirm his commitment to Christian principles, as embodied in the traditions and spirituality of the Russian church, and to develop a sense of the 'messianic destiny' of the Russian people. As a novelist,

Dostoevsky gave expression in different ways to concepts such as the tremendous power of evil, the dangers of Roman Catholicism and socialism (which Dostoevsky tended to equate with each other), of individualism, indeed of any philosophy which did not give God his rightful place and recognize the salvific value of *suffering.

Dostoevsky was not, however, a systematic thinker. He did not write works of philosophy and theology, still less novels about abstract ideas. As a brilliant, creative writer, he has left us a series of unforgettable characters motivated by many different kinds of ideas and passions, some of which were those of the author himself. Undoubtedly, the most powerful exposition of ideas occurs in the 'Legend of the Grand Inquisitor' (*The Brothers Karamazov*, Book 5, ch. 5), of which Dostoevsky makes Ivan Karamazov the author. Dostoevsky aimed to portray the bankruptcy and pernicious influence of the philosophy of Ivan Karamazov/the Grand Inquisitor which led to man's putting himself in the place of God. This, Dostoevsky felt, was the heresy both of Roman Catholicism, whose 'Grand Inquisitor' condemns Christ for rejecting the three temptations in the wilderness, and also of socialism.

Bibliography

J. Frank, *Dostoevsky*, 5 vols. (Princeton, 1976–2003); A. B. Gibson, *The Religion of Dostoevsky* (London, 1973).

M. DOWLING

DOUBT

While there are many categories that explain the concept of doubt, one of the recognizable forms was expressed by René *Descartes. For Descartes, to move forward in knowledge and understanding was to move from doubt to certainty, so his first principle of knowledge was to begin in doubt. By employing this method, he believed that he avoided prejudice and misleading judgments. Descartes explained, 'The first of these was to accept nothing as true which I did not clearly recognise to be so; that is to say, carefully to avoid precipitation and prejudice in judgments, and to accept in them nothing more than what was presented to my mind so clearly and distinctly that could have no occasion to doubt it' (*Discourse on Method*, p. 82). For Descartes, doubt was the first step in producing clarity for truth statements. Yet elsewhere Descartes wrote of such an experience of doubting, 'It feels as if I have fallen unexpectedly into a deep whirlpool which tumbles me around so that I can neither stand on the bottom or swim up to the top' (*Meditations on First Philosophy*, 'Second Meditation', p. 16). Into this philosophical account of doubt Descartes appeared to think of knowledge, understanding and perception as grounded in propositional statements. Doubt thus prepared the way for statements on *truth and falsity, but he could also include distrust as part of doubt. Thus one could believe in the existence of God but doubt whether God could be trusted.

Søren *Kierkegaard established a different model for creating knowledge, understanding and perception in relation to doubt. Kierkegaard used the OT character, Abraham, as a type of dialogue partner in attaining knowledge. In *Fear and Trembling*, Abraham began in obedience, moved to uncertainty (the command to sacrifice Isaac), and then to understanding and trust. Doubt, or uncertainty, was not the starting point for knowledge, yet doubt was not disconnected from human experience. With Kierkegaard, doubt was part of the move to clearer understanding, yet clarity through obedience overcomes doubt. In this sense, as developed by Kierkegaard, it is possible to interpret one of the healing miracles of Jesus. Just before Jesus healed a young boy and enquired whether the father believed, the father responded, 'I do believe; help me overcome my unbelief!' (Mark 9:24).

While both Kierkegaard and Descartes accepted that it is possible to believe in the existence of God yet doubt that 'God was reconciling the world to himself in Christ' (2 Cor. 5:19), they would differ on the method of overcoming such doubt. Kierkegaard was not confident in the rationalist approach of Descartes and, instead, placed greater confidence in the priority of obedience. If Kierkegaard expressed a closer alignment to the theological task, in one sense we can understand that the theological task is never a completed project. Serious deconstructive doubt can only be reconstructed in obedience to the objective reality of a God who established communication through *revelation. With this in mind, doubt can be overcome along Kierkegaardian lines in the priority of obedience, or the continuous thinking in fresh ways through obedience.

Doubt, then, is not simply a 'No' to propositions as is the tendency with Descartes' *rationalistic philosophical system. Doubt can be more fluid and dynamic, but it still raises important questions within the Christian faith. Doubt, for Karl *Barth, can pertain to the experience of remaining uncommitted: it is uncertainty without resolution. According to Barth, such doubt or uncertainty can be resolved in obedience to God's word (*Evangelical Theology*, p. 125). This approach is closer to Kierkegaard than Descartes, and in this sense, doubt can be resolved in the healing or transformation of the mind through God's grace. Unresolved doubt is more familiar to the non-theological world, and for a Christian to live in such a world creates disorder. Barth used the metaphor of disability, stating that such a person is 'a theologian lame and limping on one foot' (*Evangelical Theology*, p. 129).

Barth's articulation of doubt provides a hermeneutic for Jas 1:6–8. To doubt, according to the epistle, is to be tossed by the wind in the sea without a rudder. In other words, using secular philosophical approaches leaves a person unstable in a double-minded situation. Such a condition leaves a person outside the full understanding of God's grace.

No-one can escape doubt in its various forms, but there is no ultimate despair, since doubt does not have the final word. As Barth prayerfully insisted, '... again he may obtain a glimpse when he begs God, "Thy Kingdom come!" Even within this boundary, without being able simply to do away with doubt, he can still offer resistance ...' (*Evangelical Theology*, p. 112).

Bibliography

K. Barth, *Evangelical Theology: An Introduction*, tr. G. Foley (Grand Rapids, 1963); R. Descartes, 'Discourse on the Method of Rightly Conducting the Reason and Seeking for Truth in the Sciences', in *Key Philosophical Writings* (ET, Hertfordshire, 1997); idem, *Meditations on First Philosophy* (ET, Cambridge, 1996 [1641]); S. Kierkegaard, *Fear and Trembling*, tr. W. Lowrie (Princeton, 1954).

D. L. RAINEY

DOXOLOGY

Doxology is the profound note of worship from believing Christian communities at the heart of all offering of true praise and worship to *God. The exaltation of the living God, revealed to people in the Lord Jesus Christ and affirmed in the lives of believers through the indwelling of the *Holy Spirit is central to the Christian experience. It has a primary association with the offering to the triune God of formal worship within communities of Christians, but in more recent times has also become associated with an approach to theological reflection which is worked out in a context of worship.

The classic doxological text from liturgy might be seen in the words of the hymn:

Praise God, from whom all blessing flow;
Praise Him, all creatures here below;
Praise Him above, you heavenly host;
Praise Father, Son and Holy Ghost.
(Thomas Ken, 1637–1711)

In such a text the key themes of doxology are exposed. The context is worship, the expression of praise is orthodox trinitarian, the scope of the praise is from the whole *oikoumenē* (created and inhabited earth), together with the company of heaven, and the central affirmation is that the triune God is the true source of blessing and hope. For many theologians, it is an axiom that true primary theology begins in the context of the community of faith. Furthermore, the gathering community of faith is formed in the life of worship and immersion in the *Scriptures. From such a beginning, discipleship, diaconal life, theological engagement and missionary enterprise flow. The exploration of theology or doctrine becomes a barren and fatal exercise when divorced from the offering of praise and worship, a mere intellectual discipline lost in the world of academia. Theology rooted in doxology takes seriously the NT imperative to be 'transformed by the renewing of your mind', so that you 'will be able to test and approve what God's will is' (Rom. 12:1–2), and by the activity of the Holy Spirit enabling believers to make the affirmation of praise, 'My Lord and my God!' (John 20:28).

Doxology, then, is not simply a note, a subtheme or point for analytical reflection within the general theological enterprise. It is an undergirding in both worship and theological construction from beginning to end of the whole response that believers in the normative experience of the community in Christ, and by derivation, as individuals, make to the gracious offering of salvific love by the triune God.

Doxological affirmations are 'expressions of praise to the God who enters into relationship with us' (W. Pannenberg, *Basic Questions in Theology*, vol. 1, pp. 236–238). It is both an Alpha and an Omega of the worship and of the theologizing of the believing community arising out of community reflection in the Scriptures. Such community engagement and reflection takes place where there is a Christological hermeneutical key asserting that 'at the name of Jesus, every knee should bow' (Phil. 2:10), and where the Scriptures themselves are understood to be the divinely inspired: OT and NT Scriptures having supreme authority as the written word of God and being fully trustworthy for faith and conduct.

Doxology is at the heart of the life of communities of faith, not only in worship – especially in the celebration of the *Eucharist where the resounding note is doxological as believers engage in the *anamnesis* ('remembrance') of the passion and resurrection of Christ and enjoy an *arrabōn* (foretaste) of the banquet of the kingdom of God – but in the orthopraxy of the community lived out day by day. This is actualized in the way such believing communities fulfil their missional lives in the midst of the world. Doxology does not cease in worship, but is affirmed in the ministries of the communities and is a mark of authentic discipleship. Thus, there is a natural flow from the praise of the community gathered in worship, breaking open the word of God and breaking open the bread, into the offering of prayers – thanksgiving, intercession and supplication – by the individual believer, and on into the orthopraxy of the life of the believers as communities and individuals engaged in the realities of the world, affirming in all that they do the essential goodness of creation and the loving goodness of the Creator, who is drawing the faithful towards his kingdom where eternity will ring with the doxology of praise.

See also: LITURGY; WORSHIP.

Bibliography

T. Bradshaw, *Praying as Believing: The Lord's Prayer and the Christian Doctrine of God* (Macon, 1998); S. J. Grenz, *Theology for the Community of God* (Carlisle, 1994); D. W. Hardy and D. F. Ford, *Jubilate: Theology in Praise* (London, 1984); J. W. McClendon, Jr, *Systematic Theology*, 3 vols. (Nashville, 1986–2000); A. E. McGrath, *Christian Theology: An Introduction* (Oxford, 1994); W. Pannenberg, *Basic Questions in Theology*, 3 vols. (London, 1973); G. Wainwright, *Doxology* (London, 1980).

K. JONES

DUALISM

The term 'dualism' refers generally to the existence within any particular domain of two fundamental (i.e. irreducible) kinds of substances or principles. Dualism must be distinguished, then, from *monism, according to which there is only one fundamental kind, and (less commonly) with pluralism, according to which there are multiple such kinds. It thus faces two key tasks. First, it must defend its assertion that there are two and only two kinds in any particular domain. And second, it must offer some account of the relationship that obtains between them. This latter task is typically complicated by the fact that dualism tends to emphasize the differences between the two in order to ward off any attempt to conflate them.

In Christian theology it is possible to discern at least four different domains in which it seems necessary to affirm or deny some form of dualism.

God and creation. Christian theology has often manoeuvred between two poles in its understanding of the relationship between *God and *creation: that of affirming God's radical transcendence (i.e. God is completely separate from and wholly other than creation) and that of maintaining God's immanence (i.e. God is intimately involved in and possibly even inseparable from the world). The former offers a dualistic account, positing God and creation as distinct kinds. The latter tends toward a monistic understanding, at times even going so far as to affirm a *pantheistic identification of God and creation. Traditionally, most theologians have endeavoured to affirm that God is distinct from creation as its Creator, while remaining intimately involved in all of its myriad aspects.

The mind and the body. Similarly, the human body can be understood dualistically, comprising a mental and physical substance, or monistically, either as a single material substance or, rather less commonly, as a mental or spiritual substance.

On a dualistic account, the human person is understood to comprise two distinct substances.

For some, this involves identifying the human person with a 'higher' substance (the mind) trapped in a 'lower' substance (the body), from which it longs to be freed (*Platonic dualism). Others distinguish the two substances primarily in terms of their radically differing properties (Cartesian dualism, see *Descartes). Both approaches have come under significant criticism for their ostensible denigration of the physical and their apparent inability to explain how such discrete substances could interact.

More recently, the advances of modern science, with its awareness of the extent to which a person's physical body affects his or her mental life, and developments in biblical studies, with a growing consensus that the Bible presents the human person as a whole person, have contributed to a move away from these earlier forms of dualism. In response, many have retained the dualistic framework, along with some of its concomitant problems, while arguing for a greater appreciation of the intimate interrelation between the two substances and the importance of identifying the person with their union, rather than with one substance alone ('holistic' dualism). Others have rejected the dualistic framework entirely. Opting for a monistic approach, these thinkers contend that we should view the human person as an entirely physical being, albeit one with mental aspects ('non-reductive', 'emergent' or 'dual aspect' physicalism). This approach has been criticized in turn by those who argue that the biblical texts affirm a duality within the whole human person, and by others for being unable to maintain the causal significance of the mind in an exclusively physical being (i.e. how ideas or thoughts can affect a physical thing).

Moral and physical evil. Some systems of thought have attempted to account for moral and physical evil by positing two principles, one good and the other evil, locked together in conflict (e.g. Zoroastrianism). Although some have seen a similar form of cosmic dualism in the 'war' between God and Satan (see *Devils and demons), Christian theology has consistently rejected the idea that God and Satan are equal powers. Instead, Christian theologians typically explain the existence of *evil as the result of the free (and in the Augustinian tradition God-ordained) moral actions of God's creatures.

Reason and revelation. According to many theologians and philosophers, we must distinguish between truths that are humanly ascertainable through reason or sense experience, and those that may be known only through divine *revelation. In its weaker form, this epistemological dualism maintains that the truths of revelation are fully rational, even if they transcend the ability of human reason to fully comprehend their rationality. A stronger form stipulates that revealed truths are so discontinuous with human reason as to be ultimately irrational. Rejecting this dualistic emphasis, others have argued for a form of epistemological monism that views revealed truths as a mere restatement of that which is otherwise discernible by reason.

Bibliography

W. S. Brown, N. C. Murphy and H. N. Malony (eds.), *Whatever Happened to the Soul? Scientific and Theological Portraits of Human Nature* (Minneapolis, 1998); J. W. Cooper, *Body, Soul, and Life Everlasting* (Grand Rapids, 2000); K. Corcoran (ed.), *Soul, Body, and Survival: Essays on the Metaphysics of Human Persons* (Ithaca and London, 2001); J. Foster, *The Immaterial Self: A Defense of the Cartesian Dualist Conception of the Mind* (London, 1991); J. L. Green and S. L. Palmer (eds.), *In Search of the Soul: Four Views on the Mind-Body Problem* (Downers Grove, 2005); J. P. Moreland and S. B. Rae, *Body and Soul: Human Nature and the Crisis in Ethics* (Downers Grove, 2000); R. Swinburne, *The Evolution of the Soul* (Oxford, 1986).

M. CORTEZ

DUNS SCOTUS, JOHN (1255/6–1308)

Born in Scotland, at Maxton-on-Tweed or Duns, Duns Scotus was accepted for the *Franciscan order at the age of fifteen. In 1291 he was ordained priest, having studied theology, probably at Oxford and at Paris, where he also studied between 1294 and 1297. By 1302 he was teaching at Paris, having already taught at Oxford and Cambridge. But the following year he was forced to leave Paris and return to Oxford. In 1304 he returned to Paris, to resume his teaching. But again his stay was brief; in 1307 he was transferred to Cologne, where he taught at the Franciscan House of Studies until his premature death.

Because Duns died young, he never wrote a *Summa Theologica*. He wrote two commentaries on Peter *Lombard's *Sentences*, of which the

Opus Oxoniense (*Oxford Work*), a synthesis of his various sets of lectures on the *Sentences*, is his most important work, outlining his thought as a whole. Unfortunately, he did not live to revise it fully, and this task was continued by his disciples. The modern critical edition seeks to restore it to the form in which Duns himself left it. Duns's second most important work, and probably his last, is his *Quaestiones Quodlibetales* (*Various Questions*). This is clearer and more methodical than his earlier works and so provides a valuable supplement to the *Opus Oxoniense*. Duns's writings are not easy to read, due partly to his style and partly to the fact that he died before he could present his thought in a definitive form. Their difficulty earned him the title 'Subtle Doctor'. The sixteenth-century humanists and Reformers were less polite and coined the word 'dunce' from his name.

As a Franciscan, Duns followed in the *Augustinian tradition of *Bonaventura. He attacked the rival *Aristotelian tradition, especially the teaching of *Thomas Aquinas. But Duns was not an uncritical supporter of the Franciscan tradition. He revised it in the light of Aristotelian philosophy, rejecting Bonaventura's theory of divine illumination, for instance.

Thomas believed in the primacy of reason and knowledge over the *will. The will follows what reason presents to it as the highest good. God's will can therefore be explained by the use of reason. Duns, by contrast, stressed the primacy of the will. Reason shows the will what is possible, but the will is free to choose whichever option it wants to. The freedom of the will means that it does not simply follow whatever reason dictates.

Two major implications follow from this. Duns stressed the freedom of God. Things are the way that they are, not because reason requires it, but because God freely chose it. But God's will is not arbitrary or beyond all constraint. He cannot contradict himself, for instance. One aspect of God's freedom lies in his *predestination. First, he predestines Peter (representing the elect) to eternal glory. Secondly, he decides to give Peter the means to this end – grace. Thirdly, he permits both Peter and Judas (representing the reprobate) to sin. Finally, Peter is saved by God's grace, while Judas is justly rejected because he perseveres in sin.

Duns's stress on the freedom of God means that the role of reason and philosophy is necessarily limited. While earlier apologists, such as *Anselm, had sought to demonstrate rationally that the incarnation and the cross had to happen, Duns held that they happened because God chose that they should. This emphasized God's freedom, but also limited the possibility of showing such doctrines to be reasonable. In his stress on God's freedom, Duns went so far as to suggest that the Son would have become incarnate even had man not sinned, thus making the incarnation a free choice on God's part, not a necessity imposed upon him by man's sin. Duns believed that reason and philosophy could prove God's existence and some of his attributes. But much that Thomas believed to be demonstrable by reason (God's goodness, justice, mercy, predestination) Duns held to be known only by revelation. Such doctrines are accepted by faith alone, not proved by reason. But Duns agreed with Thomas that the truths of theology are never contrary to reason.

Duns is famous as the first major advocate of the doctrine of *Mary's immaculate conception. The predominant view at this time was that Mary had been freed from sin after her conception, but before her birth. Duns was the one who began to turn the tide, and he did this in a way that was remarkable for one with so little confidence in the power of reason to tell us about God. He argued that it is more perfect to preserve someone from original sin than to liberate them from it. Jesus Christ, as the perfect Redeemer, must have redeemed someone in the most perfect way possible – and who more fittingly than his mother? By presenting Mary's immaculate conception as the most perfect form of redemption, Duns defused the major objection to the doctrine: that it would mean that Mary did not need redemption. He himself claimed no more for the immaculate conception than its probability. But he argued that if there are a number of options, all of which are consistent with the teaching of Scripture and the church, one is to be chosen which ascribes the most glory to Mary. This principle, in addition to his argument for the immaculate conception, is of great value to those who wish to further the growth of Mariology, and Duns has been duly rewarded with the title 'Marian Doctor'.

See also: FAITH AND REASON.

Bibliography

Works: *Critical edition*: C. Balic (ed.), *Opera Omnia* (Vatican City, 1950ff.).

Studies: E. Bettoni, *Duns Scotus: The Basic Principles of his Philosophy* (Washington, DC, 1961); W. A. Frank and A. B. Wolter, *Duns Scotus, Metaphysician* (West Lafayette, 1995); J. K. Ryan and B. M. Bonansea (eds.), *John Duns Scotus 1265–1965* (Washington, DC, 1965); T. Williams, *The Cambridge Companion to Duns Scotus* (Cambridge, 2002).

A. N. S. Lane

DURKHEIM, EMILE (1858–1917)

A French sociologist in the *positivist tradition, generally regarded, with Max *Weber, as a founder of modern sociological theory. His most significant work on religion was *The Elementary Forms of the Religious Life* (1912). He argued that one of the basic characteristics of religion is the classification of all things into two categories, the sacred and the profane. 'Beliefs, myths, dogmas and legends are . . . representations which express the nature of sacred things' (*The Elementary Forms*, p. 37). These representations are also collective, since they arise from human experience in society. The primal type of a 'collective representation' is the totem which is 'at once the symbol of the god and of the society' which means that 'the god and the society are only one' (p. 206). The symbols are created as a result of collective emotion, which means that Durkheim, who was influenced in this by W. Robertson Smith (1846–94), emphasized the primacy of ritual over *myth in the formation of religious traditions. Durkheim's views had some direct, if ephemeral, influence on biblical studies through the work of scholars such as A. Lods (1867–1948) and C. A. H. Guignebert (1867–1939), but he is more significant as the fountainhead of the sociological way of viewing religion in terms of its function, which has become a part of contemporary thought and with which contemporary theology has to come to terms.

See also: Sociology of Religion.

Bibliography

Works: *The Elementary Forms of the Religious Life*, tr. J. W. Swain (London, 1915).
Studies: S. Lukes, *Emile Durkheim* (Harmondsworth, 1973); idem, *Emile Durkheim: His Life and Work* (Stanford, 1985); J. Macquarrie, *Twentieth-Century Religious Thought* (London, ⁵2001); W. S. F. Pickering, *Durkheim's Sociology of Religion: Themes and Theories* (Cambridge, 2009); K. Thompson, *Emile Durkheim* (London, ²2002).

D. A. Hughes

DUTCH REFORMED THEOLOGY (SOUTH AFRICA)

As the epithet 'Dutch' implies, Dutch Reformed theology had its origins in the Reformation in the Netherlands. The early Dutch settlers, who came to the refreshment post established at the most southern point of Africa to supply ships on their trade route to the East, transplanted the Dutch Reformed Church from Dutch soil to African soil. For almost two centuries this theology developed in close contact with and along similar lines to Reformed theology in Holland. The three earliest Christian ecumenical confessions (i.e. the Apostles', the Nicene and the Athanasian *creeds) together with three Protestant *confessions of faith (*viz.* the Belgic Confession, the Heidelberg Catechism and the Canons of *Dort) formed its confessional basis. It is still mandatory for at least twelve sermons on the *Heidelberg Catechism to be preached annually in all congregations of the Dutch Reformed Church, and a summary of the catechism is still used in preparing catechumens for church membership.

When Britain finally took over the Dutch colony at the Cape in 1806, Presbyterian ministers from Scotland were imported to serve the Dutch Reformed Church with the intention of influencing the white inhabitants. This, in turn, introduced a strong evangelical-Puritan type of Scottish *Presbyterian theology, directed more at Scripture and its direct implications for the personal life of the individual, into the more confession-orientated Dutch Reformed theology, which tended to centre upon the teaching of the church and its way of existence. Under Andrew *Murray, in particular, this influence increased and spread, eventually turning Dutch Reformed theology into a strong *evangelical, *Puritan and conservative type of *Reformed theology.

After the Anglo-Boer War early in the twentieth century, the Dutch Reformed Church in the northern provinces (the Orange Free State and the Transvaal) identified strongly with the downtrodden Boers (Afrikaner people). Consequently Dutch Reformed theology became more people-orientated, which may be interpreted as a form of indigenization. Dutch Reformed theology gradually became deeply embedded in the newly awakened and growing nationalism of the white Afrikaans-speaking (Afrikaner) section of the South African population and subsequently developed in isolation from the rest of the country.

In the early 1930s the Dutch Reformed Church in South Africa experienced a severe theological crisis when a professor at the theological seminary for the training of ministers was accused of *heresy concerning the divine/human nature of Christ. As a result of this controversy, most of the theological students started to go to the Free University of Amsterdam instead of the University of Utrecht, where the majority had previously studied. The Free University of Amsterdam was considered to be more orthodox in its theological teaching. It was started by Abraham *Kuyper, who represented a strong confessional type of Reformed theology. The university stressed the confessional aspect of Reformed theology rather than the existing evangelical/Puritan types.

One aspect of confessional Reformed theology in particular, which developed strongly in the late 1930s, was the emphasis on the pluriformity in creation as stressed by Abraham Kuyper. This emphasis in Dutch Reformed theology eventually supplied the main motivation and justification for apartheid – the separation of *races in South Africa. Kuyper had strongly emphasized the variety in the created order. He insisted that because God loved this variety it must be preserved. This element in his theological thinking had a profound influence on some professors of theology in Holland, and it also found fertile ground in which to grow in South Africa. Variety was seen also to apply to people, and was given biblical sanction, it was believed, in the division of people at Babel and by Paul's words in Acts 17:26. The essence of pluriformity was that God created humankind as pluriform as the rest of creation. Therefore each race has a God-given responsibility to maintain its identity.

Another aspect of Dutch Reformed theology which should be mentioned is that it developed in Africa but in total isolation from Africa. The separation between Westerners and Africans (whites and blacks) caused this theology to remain almost purely Western with very little African influence. Dutch Reformed theology thus lost relevance for the African context in which it developed. A multiracial education in Reformed theology may eventually turn Dutch Reformed theology into African Reformed theology, which will certainly contribute significantly towards the Christianization of the African context (see *Contextualization).

Bibliography

L. Cawood, *The Churches and Race Relations in South Africa* (Johannesburg, 1964); J. W. De Gruchy, *The Church Struggle in South Africa* (Cape Town, 1979); W. A. Landman, *A Plea for Understanding: A Reply to the Reformed Church in America* (Cape Town, 1968); *Reply of the Dutch Reformed Church to the Report of the General Synod of Haarlem, 1973–1975, in Connection with the 'Programme to Combat Racism'* (Cape Town and Pretoria, 1976); J. M. Sales, *The Planting of the Churches in South Africa* (Grand Rapids, 1971); J. H. P. Serfontein, *Apartheid, Change and the N. G. Kerk* (Johannesburg, 1982).

N. J. SMITH

DYOTHELITISM, see CHRISTOLOGY

EASTER

The earliest and greatest annual festival of the Christian calendar, called *pascha* in Greek (which also means Passover). On the basis of the evidence quoted by *Eusebius (*EH* 4.24.1–8), its existence can certainly be traced back to the time of Anicetus and Polycarp (*c.* 155) and probably to the time of the birth of Polycrates (*c.* 125). The reference in *Epistle of the Apostles* 15 may also date from *c.* 125. It is likely that the festival arose at Antioch *c.* 110, out of the weekly commemoration of Christ's resurrection on Sunday, the intention being to give special prominence to that Sunday which fell nearest to the actual season of the resurrection: the Sunday next after the Jewish Passover on 14 Nisan.

In the second century, the small Roman province of Asia observed Easter on 14 Nisan itself, whereas virtually the whole of the Christian world outside observed it on the Sunday following, and this has given rise to an alternative explanation of the origin of Easter. It has been supposed, notably by B. Lohse, that the practice of the province of Asia was the original Christian practice, and was a continuation of the observance of the Passover itself by Jewish Christians in NT times. However, it is very hard to understand why Jewish-Christian practice should have been preserved in Asia (a largely Gentile area, evangelized by the author of Col. 2:16–17 and Gal. 4:9–11) but not in Palestine or Syria (where there were more Jews than anywhere else, and where Jewish Christianity had its centre). So it is better to see the practice of Asia as presupposing the existence of Easter Sunday, and as an attempt to achieve greater precision than the rest of the Christian world, by transferring Easter from the Sunday after the Passover to the Passover itself. There is no evidence, incidentally, for the hypothesis that the church of Asia was celebrating Christ's death and the rest of the church his resurrection. The ancient Easter day celebrated both events (the separate Good Friday first appears in the fourth century).

The practice of Asia gave rise to an internal controversy between Melito and Claudius Apollinaris (c. 150–60) and to the worldwide Quartodeciman ('about the fourteenth') controversy (c. 190) in which the non-Asian view prevailed. Up to this point, all Christians dated Easter by following the decision made each year by the Jews about the Passover, which was still being fixed by observation; so they kept Easter either on the Sunday following the Jewish festival or (in Asia) on the actual Jewish festival day. However, since this dependence aroused Jewish mockery, in the third century Christians began to fix Easter independently, by astronomical calculation. The problem they faced was to reconcile the Jewish lunar year with the standard solar year of the Roman Empire. For this purpose the Roman church used a doubled eight-year cycle, and later an eighty-four-year cycle, while the Alexandrian church used the Metonic cycle of nineteen years, which was the most accurate of the three, and ultimately prevailed everywhere. In the meantime, however, the second great Easter controversy arose, between those who had begun to fix Easter astronomically, and those who continued to be guided by Jewish practice, and to hold it on the Sunday after the Passover. This controversy (often confused with the Quartodeciman, causing Quartodecimanism to be thought more lasting and widespread than it was) was resolved in principle by the Council of Nicaea in 325, the decision being in favour of the new method. The dissidents this time were not the church of Asia, but the churches of Syria, Cilicia and Mesopotamia.

The subsequent Easter controversies arose from the different methods of calculating Easter. The seventh-century controversy over the Celtic Easter was due to the Celtic churches having retained the eighty-four-year cycle after Rome had abandoned it. The controversy extending from the sixteenth century to our own day over the Julian and Gregorian calendars is due to the slight but accumulating inaccuracy in the Roman solar year, as established by Julius Caesar. By 1582 this had become significant enough for Pope Gregory XIII to have it corrected, but churches out of communion with Rome were naturally slow in adopting his reform. It was not adopted in England until 1752, when new Easter tables were introduced into the *Book of Common Prayer*; many of the Eastern churches have still not adopted it. Since Easter is a movable festival, related to the moon, it coincides in the Julian and Gregorian calendars about once every three years; but the fixed festivals, such as Christmas, now fall thirteen days later in the Julian calendar than in the Gregorian. The modern secular concept of a fixed Easter, which would mean abandoning the Jewish lunar year altogether, has met with some degree of favour in the Western churches, but none in the Eastern, where the only interest is in an agreed Easter.

Already in the second century the Easter celebrations were being continued over the following seven weeks, and a preparatory period of one or more days of fasting (the ultimate source of the later Lent) was also being added. The uniquely early origin of Easter, the scale of its celebrations, and the heat with which its date was debated, all bear witness to the unrivalled importance of Christ's death (see *Atonement) and *resurrection (the actual fulfilment of the ancient *pascha*) in primitive Christian thinking.

Bibliography

R. T. Beckwith, 'The Origin of the Festivals Easter and Whitsun', *SL* 13, 1979, pp. 1–20; P. F. Bradshaw and L. A. Hoffman (eds.), *Passover and Easter: Origins and History to Modern Times* (Notre Dame, 1999); J. G. Davies, *Holy Week* (London, 1963); A. A. McArthur, *The Evolution of the Christian Year* (London, 1953); T. Talley, 'Liturgical Times in the Ancient Church: The State of Research', *SL* 14, 1982, pp. 34–51; *idem*, *The Origins of the Liturgical Year* (New York, 1986).

R. T. BECKWITH

EASTERN ORTHODOX THEOLOGY

'Eastern Orthodox' refers to the churches in communion with the patriarchate of Constantinople (Istanbul). These include the national churches of Greece, Cyprus, Bulgaria, Romania, Serbia, Russia and Georgia, as well as the ancient patriarchates of Antioch, Jerusalem and Damascus. There are smaller Orthodox churches in a number of other countries, notably the USA, Britain and France, though these are composed mainly of immigrants and expatriates from Orthodox countries.

History

The historical development of Eastern Orthodox theology can be conveniently divided into five main stages. The first of these is the *pre-Chalcedonian period* (to 451). During this time the foundation of later Orthodoxy was laid in the writings of the Greek Fathers, of whom the most notable are *Athanasius, John *Chrysostom, *Cyril of Alexandria and the 'Three Hierarchs', known in the West as the Cappadocian Fathers. These are *Basil the Great, of Caesarea, *Gregory the Theologian, of Nazianzus, and Basil's brother, *Gregory of Nyssa. These men, most of whom were virtually contemporaries, expounded the theology of the first ecumenical council, held at *Nicaea in 325, and ensured that their interpretation would carry the day at the second (*Constantinople, 381) and third (*Ephesus, 431). The main influence came from the *Alexandrian School of theology, which strongly emphasized the unity of the divine Christ, both before and after his *incarnation. There was also a great development of *trinitarian theology, largely thanks to Basil of Caesarea. The period ends with the fourth ecumenical council, held at *Chalcedon in 451. There the doctrine of Christ as one divine person in two natures, one human and one divine, was upheld (see *Christology), in spite of the objections of the Alexandrians (who favoured a doctrine of one nature in Christ), and the *Nestorians (who regarded the person as the result, not the cause, of the incarnation). After Chalcedon these groups split off to become the Nestorian Church, now a very small body of 50,000 members, and the *Monophysite Church, known in Egypt as *Coptic and in *Syria as Jacobite (after its sixth-century leader, Jacob Baradaeus). These churches still flourish, both in their countries of origin and in areas where they have spread, notably Ethiopia (Coptic) and South India (Jacobite).

The next phase was the *early Byzantine period* (451–843). This was dominated by Christological controversy, first against the Monophysites, and then against the *iconoclasts. The fifth ecumenical council (Constantinople, 553) tried to reconcile the churches of Egypt and Syria, but without success, and the attempt was formally abandoned at the sixth council (Constantinople, 680). The seventh and, in Orthodox eyes, last ecumenical council (Nicaea, 787) condemned the iconoclasts. The leading theologians of this period were Leontius of Byzantium (see *Hypostasis) and his namesake Leontius of Jerusalem (both sixth century), Maximus the Confessor and *John of Damascus. They gave Orthodox Christology a shape which reflects a deep and sophisticated appropriation of the dogmatic pronouncements of the Council of Chalcedon. The period is also notable for the development of Orthodox spirituality, especially the veneration of icons, the great liturgies, and the canonical regulations which govern the church's life. These were codified at the so-called Quinisext Council, or Synod *in Trullo*, held at Constantinople in 691–92. The canons regulated such practices as clerical marriage, and the use of leavened bread in the Eucharist, which were rejected by the Western church. Many of the visible differences between Orthodoxy and Roman Catholicism can be traced to the canons of this council.

The third stage may be called the *late Byzantine period* (843–1452). During this time, Orthodoxy engaged in increasingly bitter polemic against Western theology and, as a counterweight to it, developed tendencies which were latent in the Eastern tradition. The main cause of dispute was the *filioque* clause, added to the Nicene Creed in the sixth century in Spain, and adopted officially at Rome *c*. 1014. The addition raised the question of papal authority in matters of doctrine, as well as the theological issue of the double procession of the *Holy Spirit. Photius, Patriarch of Constantinople from 858–67 and again from 880–86, led the opposition to the *filioque* clause, and his views are still repeated by Orthodox theologians today. On a more positive note, the period also witnessed a remarkable spiritual revival, which bore fruit first in the conversion of the Slavs (850–1000) and then in the practice of devotional meditation. The great names whose counsels are still followed by Orthodox monks today are *Symeon the New Theologian and Gregory *Palamas. The latter championed a monastic movement known as *Hesychasm, which practised a system of spiritual exercises not unlike yoga. This was bitterly resisted by Westernizing influences at Constantinople, but was declared to be orthodox in 1351. The Westernizers, who had been gaining in strength since the abortive union of the churches at the Council of Lyons in 1274, were now put on the defensive. A second union was promulgated at the Council of Florence in 1439, but it was never popular and was abandoned after Constantinople fell to the Turks in 1453.

Ironically, it was during the period of Turkish domination (1453–1821) that Western influence reached its peak in the Orthodox world. After the Reformation, all parties courted the Eastern churches, who were able to send many of their students to be educated in the West. This did not win Orthodoxy either to Rome or to the Protestant cause, but it made Orthodox theologians much more Western in their theological method and interests. In the seventeenth century, the patriarch successively of Alexandria and Constantinople, Cyril Lucaris (1572–1638), composed a Calvinistic *confession of faith, which was published at Geneva in 1629. This provoked a Catholicizing reaction, which can be seen in the *Confessions* of Peter Mogila (1596–1646) and Dositheus of Jerusalem (1641–1707). Both these confessions are now regarded as more faithful to Orthodoxy than that of Lucaris, but many modern Orthodox reject them because they reflect a theological method which is foreign to the Eastern tradition.

The *modern period* (1821 to the present) has been characterized chiefly by a recovery of the monastic traditions of Byzantine Orthodoxy and by the struggle of the church against persecution from both communism and Islam. During the nineteenth century, the established theological tradition of both Greece and Russia was almost completely subservient to German liberal Protestantism, and this trend has continued to some extent up to the present time. There developed an Orthodox dogmatic theology modelled on the West, as can be seen in the works of Chrestos Androutsos (1869–1937), J. Karmiris (1904–92) and P. N. Trembelas (1886–1977; *Dogmatique de l'église orthodoxe catholique*, 3 vols., Chevetogne, 1966–68). An almost heretical *mysticism characterizes the leading *Russian theologians of the period, notably Alexis Khomiakov (1804–60) and Sergei *Bulgakov. These trends have produced a reaction, however, which is now very powerful. Beginning in the eighteenth century, with the edition of patristic texts known as the *Philokalia*, monastic ideas began to revive in the Orthodox world. These bore fruit in the twentieth-century revival of neo-Byzantinism, associated with the work of the Russians, Vladimir *Lossky and John *Meyendorff and with the Romanian theologian Dumitru *Staniloae. Orthodoxy is torn between liberal and conservative tendencies, with the latter appearing to be gaining the upper hand.

Characteristics

Orthodox theology differs from both Roman and Protestant teaching in a number of important respects. In general terms, it relies more on the philosophical base of Neoplatonism (see *Platonism), which the West in the main abandoned in the thirteenth century. It has a strongly mystical flavour, and fights shy of dogmatic definition as much as it can. Its authority is derived from 'tradition', which includes both the Scriptures, decisions of the *councils, especially the *Nicene Creed, and the Greek Fathers. The Latin Fathers before the eleventh century are honoured as part of this tradition as well, but in practice they are ignored. Also important are the testimony of the *liturgies, which have not changed for over a thousand years, and the veneration of icons, which is much more 'theological' in tone than any comparable devotion in the West.

The Orthodox doctrine of the *Trinity is superficially the same as the Western one, with the exception of the *filioque* clause, but in conception it is very different. The Orthodox put the primary stress on the persons of the Godhead, and tend to regard the Father as the hypostatization of the divine essence. He is the unique fountainhead of Deity (*pēgē tēs theotētos*), which explains why the Orthodox cannot accept that the Holy Spirit derives his being from the Son as well as from the Father. They also place great emphasis on the energies of God, a concept which is strange to Western minds. The Holy Spirit, for example, is said to proceed from the Father but to rest on the Son, whose energy he becomes. The concept is analogous to the Catholic notion of grace, though the Orthodox insist that they do not see the divine energy as a substance which can be infused into the believer.

This naturally affects their doctrine of *sanctification, and their sacramental theology. Orthodox believe in baptismal regeneration, and administer chrismation (confirmation) and Holy Communion to the newly baptized, including infants. They believe that the Holy Spirit descends on the elements of bread and wine by liturgical invocation (*epiclēsis*; see *Eucharist), but resist Roman Catholic ideas of transubstantiation. The believer is called to a life of *deification, which means transfiguration into the image and likeness of God. The supreme manifestation of this can be found in the ecstasy of the contemplative life, which occupies a much more important place in Orthodox spirituality than it does in Roman Catholicism.

By Western standards, Orthodoxy has a weak doctrine of *sin and *atonement. Sin is regarded as the effect of death and finitude, not as its cause. Salvation therefore tends to be seen primarily in terms of freedom from death, not as a release from guilt. In modern times this soteriology has made a great impact on Western theologians who for various reasons have recoiled from the Reformed doctrine of the atonement, and its influence can be seen in recent liturgical revisions.

Since 1961, Orthodox churches have participated in the World Council of Churches, which has forced them to take an interest in other kinds of theology. They have established very friendly relations with the non-Chalcedonian churches of the East, and have made some moves in the direction of Rome and the Protestant churches as well. On the whole, however, they remain by far the most closed of the major branches of Christendom. At the WCC their influence has mostly been exercised in favour of a more theological approach, and against political involvement. Today creative Orthodox thinking is more vital than at any time since the fourteenth century, and it offers itself as a conservative challenge to Western Christendom. There are a number of signs that its influence may be growing, and it is certain to become a major force in ecumenical circles in the future.

See also: ORIENTAL ORTHODOX THEOLOGY.

Bibliography

D. B. Clendenin, *Eastern Orthodox Christianity: A Western Perspective* (Grand Rapids, 1994); idem (ed.), *Eastern Orthodox Theology: A Contemporary Reader* (Grand Rapids, 2003); M. B. Cunningham and E. Theokritoff, *The Cambridge Companion to Orthodox Christian Theology* (Cambridge, 2008); V. Lossky, *The Mystical Theology of the Eastern Church* (Cambridge, 1957); G. A. Maloney, *A History of Orthodox Theology since 1453* (Belmont, 1976); J. Meyendorff, *Byzantine Theology* (London, 1974); T. Ware, *The Orthodox Church* (London, 1993).

G. L. BRAY

EBELING, GERHARD (1912–2001)

Ebeling studied theology at Marburg under *Bultmann, at Zurich with *Brunner and at Berlin. After a time as a colleague of *Bonhoeffer in the theological seminary at Finkenwald (1936–7), he took charge of a provisional congregation of the *Confessing Church in Berlin. In 1946 he became Professor of Church History in Tübingen, moving to Systematic Theology in 1954. Two years later he transferred to Zurich to the chair of Systematic Theology, History of Theology and Symbolics. Here he founded the Institute of Hermeneutics (1962), finally retiring, as Professor of Fundamental Theology and Hermeneutics, in 1979.

Ebeling's theological thought shows him to be indebted equally to *Luther and *Schleiermacher. He was one of the editors of the Weimar edition of Luther's works (*Weimarer Ausgabe*) and of a complete edition of Schleiermacher. His unusually wide-ranging (historical, exegetical, dogmatic) monographs all concentrate on the attempt to interpret the relationship between God, man and the world as a continuum of living reality, to be experienced, understood and articulated by faith. His *Dogmatik des christlichen Glaubens* (*Dogmatics of the Christian Faith*, 3 vols., Tübingen, 1979) offered the Bultmann school's first substantial, systematic conspectus. In it Ebeling not only inculcates the basic and essential theological differentiations (e.g. between God and the world, visible and eternal life, political and evangelical use of biblical teaching), but also, with noteworthy impressiveness, makes us conscious that the proof of all Christian theology is prayer.

Bibliography
Many *works* in ET, including: *God and Word* (Philadelphia, 1967); *Introduction to a Theological Theory of Language* (London, 1973); *Luther: An Introduction to His Thought* (London, 1970); *Word and Faith* (London, 1963); *The Word of God and Tradition* (London, 1968).
Studies: S. P. Schilling, *Contemporary Continental Theologians* (London, 1966), ch. 6.

R. E. Frische

EBIONISM

The Ebionites were a Jewish-Christian *sect, first mentioned by Irenaeus, drawing its name from Hebrew (*'ebyônîm*; 'the poor') but later dropping the title when it became a term of abuse (poverty of spirit and faith). Tertullian and Hippolytus erroneously believed the title referred to the sect's founder, Ebion. Early commentators on Ebionism (e.g. Origen and Eusebius) generally rely on hearsay and documents rather than first-hand evidence. However, Epiphanius and the Pseudo-Clementines provide important information on their doctrine, as does the *Gospel of the Ebionites*, which is heavily dependent on Matthew, the only Gospel they used. Their Christology was essentially *adoptionist. Jesus was a man who became the Messiah through obedience to the Jewish law (thus others might similarly become christs). They denied his pre-existence and the virgin birth; the Christ was believed to be an angelic being that entered Jesus at his baptism. Although they stressed the need of Jewish law, the Ebionites removed what they saw as interpolations, rejecting the sacrificial cult, monarchy, the validity of biblical prophetic books and anthropomorphic language used for God, and adopting vegetarianism, holy poverty and ritual ablutions. Sceptical of visions, Paul and his epistles were rejected on the grounds that he had not been an eyewitness of the earthly Jesus.

Bibliography
J. K. Elliott (ed.), 'The Gospel of the Ebionites', in *The Apocryphal New Testament* (Oxford and New York, 1993), pp. 14–16; A. F. J. Klijn and G. J. Reinink, *Patristic Evidence of Jewish-Christian Sects* (Supplements to *Novum Testamentum* 36; Leiden, 1973), pp. 19–43; H.-J. Schoeps, *Jewish Christianity: Factional Disputes in the Early Church* (ET, Philadelphia, 1969).

A. D. Rich

ECCLESIOLOGY, see CHURCH

ECKHART, see MYSTICAL THEOLOGY

ECOLOGY

Ecology (the study of *ecos* or place) was formally recognized as a separate discipline within biology by Ernst Haeckel in 1866; he defined it as 'the comprehensive science of the relationship of the organism to the environment'. Theologically, ecology, together with the related subject of environmentalism (which is wider in scope, involving the interaction of physical and geological factors as well as biological ones), can be regarded as the scientific study of *creation (Ps. 111:2).

The starting point for a theology of ecology is that the world belongs to *God (Ps. 24:1) and that God continues in active relation to the world as Creator (Isa. 42:5; John 1:1–3; Rev. 4:11), Redeemer (Eph. 1:10; Col. 1:20) and Sustainer (Ps. 104:27; Col. 1:17; Heb. 1:3). He rejoices in it, independently of any human witness (Job 38 – 39; Ps. 104:4–23), and he has committed its care to us (Gen. 1:28; 2:15). This responsibility is pictured in the relationship of Israel to the Promised Land: if Israel obeys YHWH, the created order within the land will be abundantly fruitful, but if Israel disobeys, the land itself will turn against them and ultimately drive them into exile. The treatment of the land is intimately linked with God's *covenant with his people (Deut. 27 – 30; Isa. 40 – 55).

Our privilege and task of creation care is commonly referred to as 'stewardship'. This term is disliked by some on the grounds that it implies an absent landlord, a feudal-style male hierarchy, an impossible task, or an arrogant assumption; such critics prefer a word such as 'trustee', 'co-worker', 'partner', 'priest', 'manager' or 'factor'.

Human actions have certainly damaged the world (over-fishing and over-grazing, deforestation, greenhouse gas emissions, release of toxic chemicals, etc.). Contrary to common assumptions (and former scientific conclusions), there is no intrinsic 'balance' or 'equilibrium' in the natural world. The illusion that there is derives from over-extrapolating the analogy between macrocosm ('nature') and microcosm ('individual bodies') or the recovery which often follows local disturbance.

Our ecological failures are traditionally linked to effects of the *fall described in Gen. 3, but this assumption needs examination: nature was certainly 'red in tooth and claw' before the advent of humankind (e.g. many species disappeared, predatory animals abounded, dinosaurs had arthritis), and there is no evidence from archaeology of any change in ecology when humans appeared on earth. The curses in Gen. 3 focus on the *relationships* of Adam and Eve with other creatures and with the land, rather than on the properties of the land itself. It should be noted, too, that Adam and Eve continued to exist physically after their expulsion from Eden – indeed all their children were born outside Eden, although Adam had been warned that he would die 'the day' that he ate the forbidden fruit (Gen. 2:17). The death introduced into the world by Adam's disobedience can best be understood as a break in relationship with God, a break healed by Christ's redeeming work (Eph. 2:1, 5, etc.). These considerations make it very difficult to maintain the traditional Western orthodoxy of a 'cosmic fall'. Apart from the overtly messianic passage in Isa. 11:6–10 (and 65:17–25), there is nothing in the OT to imply that the natural world itself is fallen or distorted in any way. God's declaration that creation is good in his eyes has not changed.

Ecological disorder is often attributed to Christian doctrine, following a much reprinted article on 'the historical roots of our ecologic crisis' by an American historian, Lynn White. In it, White placed the blame on 'an Occidental, voluntarist realization of the Christian dogma of man's transcendence of, and rightful mastery, over nature . . . [Our attitude is that] we are superior to nature, contemptuous of it, willing to use it for our slightest whim' (White, in *Science* 155, p. 1206). Whilst there is some historical truth in this judgment, it is based on a non-biblical understanding of human dominion as well as ignoring the widespread and influential *Benedictine tradition of stewardship.

Christian attitudes as parodied by White have certainly been prominent in those parts of the world influenced by the Western church and science, but they need to be qualified by two other important traditions – of the Orthodox Church and the 'Celtic' Church. Both of these are explicitly Christocentric whilst both are open to the dangers of *panentheism. For the Orthodox, our calling is to be 'priests of creation', continuing God's blessing in creation, preserving its beauty and nurturing its faithfulness, while the modern practice of 'Celtic Christianity' tends to spill over into *animism. Moreover, neither tradition fully incorporates the wildness and 'otherness' of the non-human world.

An important passage for a mature understanding of the environment is Rom 8:19–22, climaxing Paul's argument in Rom. 5 – 8 that the renewal of God's covenant results in the renewal of God's creation. Moule interprets Rom. 8:19–22 as meaning that 'man is responsible before God for nature. As long as man refuses to play the part assigned him by God, so long the entire world of nature is frustrated and dislocated. It is only when man is truly fitting into his proper position as a son in relation to God his father that the dislocation of nature will be reduced' (*Man and Nature in the New Testament*, p. 12). When Christ's *redeeming work and the empowering of the Spirit come together, we are enabled to recover the stewarding role we lost through the fall. Paul's message is one of hope for creation, just as the liberation of God's people from exile is linked by Isaiah with the rejoicing of all creation (Isa. 55:12–13). Kidner comes to the same conclusion in his Tyndale Commentary on Genesis: 'Leaderless the choir of creation can only grind in discord' (p. 73). Blocher argues similarly: 'If man obeys God, he would be the means of blessing the earth; but in his insatiable greed . . . and in his short-sighted selfishness, he pollutes and destroys it. He turns the garden into a desert (cf. Rev. 11:18). That is the main thrust of the curse of Genesis 3' (*In the Beginning*, p. 184).

Our understanding of the natural world should be *theocentric* – based on caring for a world created and sustained by God: neither *anthropocentric* (that the world is here chiefly for our use and enjoyment) nor *bio-* (or *eco-*) *centric* (that we are no more than a trivial component of an interdependent biosphere, as represented by the 'deep ecology' of Arne Naess or by James Lovelock's 'Gaia'). We share a common interest in and responsibility for the sustainability of the creation with all humankind and have no excuse for not making common cause with them; we differ from non-believers in being able to give a reason for the world's existence and hope for its future. The centuries-old concept that God is the author of both a Book of Words (the Bible) and a Book of Works (creation) is a powerful image. The books are written in very different languages, but only if we study them both will we have a full understanding of their author and our proper response (Ps. 19).

Christian awareness of the importance and implications of ecology has been rising rapidly in recent years, stimulated by secular concerns but spurred by rediscovering theological truths. Influenced by Jürgen *Moltmann, the World Council of Churches in 1983 changed its long-standing 'Peace with Justice' programme into 'Justice, Peace and Integrity of Creation'. The General Synod of the Church of England produced major reports on the subject in 1969, 1986 and 2005; successive Lambeth Conferences have drawn attention to Christian responsibilities in the area; many denominations have issued their own environmental policies. In 2015 Pope Francis asserted that 'a true ecological approach must integrate questions of justice in debates on the environment, so as to hear both the cty of the earth and the cry of the poor' (*Laudato Si'*, para 49), and many Catholic Bishops' Conferences have issued statements calling for Christian action (e.g. Christiansen and Grazer, 1996). Bartholomew of Constantinople (the 'Green Patriarch') has been particularly active in calling for environmental action; in 1995, he castigated crime against the natural world as sin. In 2006, the US National Association of Evangelicals issued an 'Evangelical Climate Initiative'. Many development agencies have pointed out that environmental care and *poverty relief are tightly linked; there are important issues of environmental justice. Perhaps most importantly, the environment is increasingly seen as a fundamental doctrinal issue rather than nothing more than an enthusiasm for a minority.

See also: NATURE, THEOLOGY OF

Bibliography

R. Bauckham, *Bible and Ecology* (London, 2010); R. J. Berry (ed.), *Environmental Stewardship* (London and New York, 2006); *idem* (ed.), *When Enough Is Enough* (Leicester, 2007); J. J. Bimson, 'Reconsidering a Cosmic Fall', *Science & Christian Belief*, 18, 2006, pp. 63–81; H. Blocher, *In the Beginning* (Leicester, 1984); S. Bouma-Prediger, *For the Beauty of the Earth* (Grand Rapids, 2001); W. Brueggemann, *The Land* (Philadelphia, 1977); D. Christiansen and W. Grazer (eds.), *'And God Saw That It Was Good'* (Washington DC, 1996); D. G. Horrell, C. Hunt, C. Southgate and F. Stavrakopoulou (eds.), *Ecological Hermeneutics* (London and New York, 2010); D. J. Moo, 'Nature in the New Creation', *Journal of the Evangelical Theological Society* 49, 2006, pp. 449–488; C. F. D. Moule, *Man and Nature in the New Testament* (London, 1964); M. S. Northcott, *The Environment and Christian Ethics* (Cambridge, 1996); Pope Francis, *Laudato Si'* (London, 2015); L. White, 'The Historical Roots of Our Ecological Crisis', *Science* 155, 1967, pp. 1203–1207; R. S. White, *Who Is to Blame?* (Oxford and Grand Rapids, 2014); N. T. Wright, *New Heavens, New Earth* (Cambridge, 1999); *idem*, 'Creation and Covenant', in *Paul: Fresh Perspectives* (London, 2005).

R. J. BERRY

ECONOMY

The canonical tradition of the Orthodox Church employs the term 'economy' in a variety of meanings. Following the usage common from the classical period, economy means 'to administer'. I Constantinople Canon 2 uses economy in this sense when it directs the bishop of Alexandria 'to administer the affairs in Egypt alone'. Byzantine penitential discipline used economy similarly, but in the administration, or application, of a 'remedy . . . for the illness of sin', as enshrined in Trullo Canon 102. In this context, economy can be according to a strict observance or a lenient approach.

A subtle difference in meaning occurs whereby the latter meaning of economy has a sense akin to *dispensatio* in the West. In other words, the canons admit the possibility of canonical leniency, due to the 'necessity of the times' (Trullo Canon 37), in the administration of church life. As such, economy offers Orthodox canonists an accommodation to pastoral exigencies instead of the strict application of the text of the canons (*akriveia*). This meaning has developed further, most notably since the eighteenth century. It became understood less in the context of application, and more as principle of canonical leniency by itself, as a group of theologians, typically, though not exclusively, from the Greek-speaking world, put forward various explanations of how and when churchman can use economy. Others, usually from the Russian Orthodox Church, have argued that this view of economy presents merely an opinion and does not accurately reflect the tradition of the church.

See also: EASTERN ORTHODOX THEOLOGY.

Bibliography

J. Erickson, 'The Problem of Sacramental "Economy"', in J. Erickson, *The Challenge of Our Past* (Crestwood, 1991); A. de Halleux, '"Oikonomia" in the First Canon of Saint Basil', *The Patristic and Byzantine Review* 6, 1987, pp. 53–64; F. J. Thomson, 'Economy: An Examination of the Various Theories of Economy in the Orthodox Church', *Journal of Theological Studies*, n.s. 26, 1965, pp. 367–420.

A. RENTEL

ECUMENICAL MOVEMENT

Ecumenism is the attempt to foster unity between distinct groups of Christians. It typically entails the reconciliation or mutual recognition of doctrines, organizational structures and acts of witness and service. The more specific phraseology of the 'ecumenical movement' is associated with particular manifestations of ecumenism that have developed since the early twentieth century, but ecumenism as such has much deeper historical roots.

The term 'ecumenical' is derived from the Greek *oikumene*, meaning the whole inhabited earth. It is used in the NT both in this general sense (Luke 2:1; Acts 11:28), and more specifically in relation to the global mission of God (Matt. 24:14; Heb. 2:5). As the early church realized its part in this mission, so its identity as a universal body came to be designated as ecumenical. Hence the seven 'ecumenical *councils' that took place between the fourth and the eighth centuries, at which Western and Eastern churches were represented, and at which key creeds, declarations and policies were agreed. This 'undivided Church' subsequently fragmented in the Great Schism of 1054, in the splitting of Protestants from Roman Catholics at the *Reformation, and in subsequent intra-Protestant divergences such as those between *Lutherans, *Presbyterians, Independents and *Anabaptists. Henry VIII's breach with Rome in the 1530s was not so clearly a Protestant move, but the establishment of the Church of England (see *Anglicanism) with Henry as 'Supreme Head' constituted another significant fracture point. In time even finer distinctions would develop within specific Protestant traditions, so that by the late eighteenth century a host of Reformed, Baptist, Methodist and other sub-varieties would exist on both sides of the Atlantic, often with their respective churches and chapels in the same town.

The expansion of empire from this time fostered in many British Christians a more international perspective, and with it, a heart for world mission (see *Missiology). Often this was married to an enthusiasm generated by the various evangelical revivals that had taken place since the 1730s. While many of the mission agencies and movements that were formed in response to these developments had a singular denominational identity, some favoured a more interdenominational approach. The London Missionary Society was founded in 1795 by a group of Congregationalists, Anglicans, Presbyterians and Wesleyans and urged its missionaries to forswear ecclesial partisanship in their preaching. Similarly, the China Inland Mission was founded by Hudson Taylor in 1865 as an avowedly interdenominational body.

Reflecting these and other such endeavours, a diverse network of Protestants from Britain, America and the European continent joined together in 1846 to form the World's Evangelical Alliance. With its annual conferences, weeks of prayer and lobbying for religious liberties, the Alliance has justifiably been seen as a forerunner of the modern ecumenical movement. However, the birth of that movement proper is generally recognized as having taken place somewhat later, at the World Missionary Conference held in Edinburgh in June 1910. This conference was convened to review the mission work of 160-odd societies and churches, but its 1,200 delegates were also challenged to seek greater interdenominational cooperation. Similar challenges had been issued at earlier gatherings of Protestant missions, but Edinburgh also included Anglo-Catholics and gave a more prominent role to leaders of indigenous churches formed as a result of missionary activity. Not least thanks to its American chairman John R. Mott (1865–1955) and its

British chief organizer Joseph Oldham (1874–1969), Edinburgh 1910 also bore a significant legacy. A Continuation Committee was formed which helped to generate three key ecumenical organizations. The first of these was the International Missionary Council (IMC). This was formed in New York in 1921 and went on to sponsor significant conferences in Jerusalem (1928), Madras (1938) and Whitby (1947). Having secured the rights of German missions after the war, the IMC focused on developing appropriate frameworks for mission among Jews and Muslims, as well as fostering greater coordination between mission agencies in Africa, Asia and Latin America.

The second major organization flowing from Edinburgh 1910 was the Life and Work Movement. Pioneered by the Swedish Archbishop Nathan Söderblom (1866–1931), this operated as a network of churches committed to shared Christian service and action, most notably in the area of reconciliation and peacemaking (see *Pacifism/peace). Inaugurated at Stockholm in 1925, it convened for a second conference at Oxford in 1937. The report of this latter conference, *Church, Community and State*, represents a landmark in modern Christian *social teaching.

Edinburgh 1910 largely avoided those matters of doctrine and polity which had been the 'presenting issues' of past church division, and the early days of the Life and Work Movement had in fact been associated with the slogan 'Doctrine divides, service unites'. However, a third organization arose which would tackle these difficult areas head-on.

The *Faith and Order movement was constituted at Lausanne in 1927 under the guidance of the American Episcopalian bishop Charles H. Brent (1862–1929). Some 400 attendees from ninety churches identified core areas of theological agreement and disagreement, and a further conference was held at Edinburgh in 1937. This latter gathering was chaired by William *Temple, then Archbishop of York, later to become Archbishop of Canterbury. This Edinburgh conference also echoed calls for a closer-knit global ecumenical structure, proposing that the Life and Work and Faith and Order movements should come together in a '*World Council of Churches' (WCC). An inaugural assembly was planned for this new body in 1941, but the Second World War intervened.

Eventually, in August 1948, the first assembly of the WCC was held in Amsterdam with 351 delegates from 147 churches present. However, the Roman Catholic Church did not join the Council, and despite increased engagement in more recent years, is still not a full member. In 1928, Pope Pius XI had attacked the fledgling ecumenical movement in his encyclical *Mortalium animos*, but by 1949, Pius XII's decree *Ecclesia sancta* struck a far more conciliatory note: although the largely Protestant membership of the WCC was 'dissident from the Catholic church', their common witness to the gospel was, it declared, 'an inspiring grace of the Holy Spirit'.

At Amsterdam the WCC had defined itself as 'a fellowship of churches which accept our Lord Jesus Christ as God and Saviour'. This minimal basis of faith remained for the second WCC assembly at Evanston, Illinois in 1954, but at the third in New Delhi in 1961 it was adapted and expanded: the WCC was now to be 'a fellowship of churches which confess the Lord Jesus Christ as God and Saviour according to the Scriptures, and therefore seek to fulfil together their common calling to the glory of the one God, Father, Son and Holy Spirit'. The trinitarian addition pleased the Eastern Orthodox churches who had joined the Council in 1948, and whose presence was now bolstered by the Russian Orthodox. In 1920 the Holy Synod of the Church of Constantinople had issued an encyclical, *Unto the Churches Everywhere*, which envisaged an antidote to the devastation of the First World War in a global Christian fellowship in analogy with the League of Nations. Now the Orthodox began to play a fuller part in making this a reality.

The 1961 New Delhi assembly also saw Roman Catholic interaction with the WCC progress when the Vatican allowed delegates to attend the Council as observers. The following year Pope John XXIII convened the epochal Second *Vatican Council. Not only were observers allowed to attend Vatican II from non-Roman denominations; the Council's *Decree on Ecumenism* (1964) defined these denominations as 'separated brethren' rather than dissident outsiders. In the wake of this, Roman Catholic representatives became full participants in the Faith and Order strand of the WCC.

Another major development at New Delhi was the incorporation of the International Missionary Council into the WCC. Ostensibly, this recognition of missiological priorities should have encouraged evangelicals and

Pentecostals, but in fact many in these traditions had been suspicious of the WCC from its foundation, and remained so after 1961. For some this was due to minimalism of its statement of faith, which was only partly mitigated by the additions made at New Delhi. By this time, too, theological *liberalism had become dominant in the seminaries and councils of many of the historic Protestant denominations that comprised the majority of the WCC's membership. Typically, evangelicals and Pentecostals saw liberalism as a false gospel, and viewed 'liberal' and 'ecumenical' as virtually synonymous. This scepticism intensified as the WCC appeared to recast traditional models of mission in terms of left-wing political and social activism. By the fourth WCC Assembly at Uppsala in 1968, it did indeed seem that the Council was allowing its agenda to be shaped along socialist and even Marxist lines, similar to those that would define the '*liberation theologies' developed in Latin America and elsewhere during the next decade or so.

This leftist socio-political orientation effectively eclipsed the Faith and Order work of the WCC for some time after Uppsala, but priorities changed significantly with the adoption of the 'convergence document' *Baptist, Eucharist and Ministry* at Lima in 1982. This text articulated a striking degree of consensus between major Christian traditions in the three areas stated, and offered a realistic account of how outstanding differences might be addressed. It went on to become the most influential report of the modern ecumenical movement, attracting constructive responses from around 200 churches and Christian organizations, several of them evangelical and Pentecostal. *BEM* in turn spurred a number of bilateral or multilateral conversations and unions. Precedents for these had existed from the formative days of the WCC, when the Church of South India had brought episcopal and non-episcopal traditions together in a new ecclesial structure (1947), and in later developments such as Pope Paul VI's and Patriarch Athenagoras' nullifying of the anathemas of the Great Schism (1965), the formation of the Anglican-Roman Catholic International Commission (1970), the inception of the United Reformed Church in Great Britain (1972), and the Leuenberg Concord between Lutheran and Reformed Churches in Continental Europe (1973). Following *BEM*, however, the level of such activity has risen considerably, and has included full communion agreements between Anglican and Lutheran churches in northern Europe (Porvoo, 1992) and between Lutheran, Reformed, Episcopalian and Moravian communities in the USA (1997–99). At Augsburg in 1999, the Vatican and the Lutheran World Federation signed a *Joint Declaration on the Doctrine of Justification* which recognized ongoing doctrinal differences in this area but which classed them as non-church-dividing, and which rescinded the mutual condemnations levelled in relation to them at the Reformation. Dialogues and agreements between other traditions and denominations continue apace.

*Evangelical and *Pentecostal engagement in ecumenism has also increased on national and international fronts in more recent times. The World's Evangelical Alliance was reconstituted in 1951 as the World Evangelical Fellowship (WEF), partly in response to the founding of the WCC, but for the reasons cited above its initial stance towards the WCC-style ecumenism was limited to 'benevolent neutrality'. In 1974 the *Lausanne Covenant offered an alternative to the perceived politicization of the WCC in the form of a fresh evangelical vision of mission based on both personal conversion and social transformation. Later, the WEF restyled itself as the 'World Evangelical Alliance', took on a fuller observational role at WCC assemblies, and participated in an extensive dialogue with the Pontifical Council for Christian Unity (1993–2002).

While fundamentalists and certain more conservative evangelical bodies continue to make disavowal of the ecumenical movement an article of faith, the decline of liberal modernist influence and the growth of evangelical and Pentecostal churches since the 1980s has been a factor in prompting the WCC to shift from a relatively 'centripetal' model of visible institutional unity to a relatively 'centrifugal' or devolved model more in keeping with mainstream evangelical and Pentecostal approaches to cooperation. One major expression of this was the founding in 1998 of the Global Christian Forum, an informal network in which WCC members could interact with leaders of non-WCC affiliated bodies on matters of mutual concern. Another was the establishment in 2000 of a Joint Consultative Group on Pentecostalism, which proceeded on a more open-textured, relational basis than had pertained in earlier Faith and Order dialogues. One notable outcome of this process occurred in August 2010, when the WCC General Secretary, Olav Fykse Tveit, offered a formal greeting to the 22nd World Pentecostal Conference in Stockholm – an unprecedented move which confirmed that, 100 years on from Edinburgh 1910, ecumenism was once again undergoing significant change.

Bibliography

C. E. Braaten and R. W. Jenson (eds.), *In One Body through the Cross: The Princeton Proposal for Christian Unity: A Call to the Churches from an Ecumenical Study Group*, Center for Catholic and Evangelical Theology (Grand Rapids and Cambridge, 2003); H. van Beek, *Revisioning Christian Unity: The Global Christian Forum* (Eugene, 2009); J. Briggs, M. Oduyeye and G. Tsetsis (eds.), *A History of the Ecumenical Movement, vol. 3, 1968–2000* (London, 2004); H. E. Fey, *A History of the Ecumenical Movement, vol. 2, 1948–68: The Ecumenical Advance* (Eugene, 2009); T. E. Fitzgerald, *The Ecumenical Movement: An Introductory History* (Westport, 2004); M. Kinnamon and B. E. Cope, *The Ecumenical Movement: An Anthology of Key Texts and Voices* (Geneva and Grand Rapids, 1997); R. Rouse and S. C. Neill, *A History of the Ecumenical Movement, vol. 1: 1517–1948* (Geneva, ³1993).

D. H. K. Hilborn

ECUMENICAL THEOLOGY

Ecumenical theology can be construed to mean many things. For example, it could refer to the expression of the apostolic faith as articulated by the first four (ecumenical) *councils, that is, the councils of the undivided church as they articulated orthodox doctrine when challenged by various heresies, a process which led to the definition of the trinitarian faith of the *church (see *Creeds). At the opposite extreme in the story of the church, ecumenical theology can describe attempts to identify the theology of the contemporary church in all its diverse forms, embracing all the riches of the experiences of Christians from every continent. But these must be riches tested by the apostolic faith as set forth in Scripture, for ecumenical theology must not stand for a form of confessional pluralism in which diverse and often contradictory understandings are placed side by side as of equal legitimacy. Equally, ecumenical theology cannot be allowed to stand for a lowest-common-denominator theology – that which all Christians can agree upon shorn of all contentious elements. But ecumenical theology remains still very different from denominational theologies, or even *evangelical theology, with its focus around a range of agreed doctrinal priorities. By contrast, ecumenical theology has to be concerned about handling differences within an overall Christian commitment.

The basis of the *World Council of Churches itself points to certain fundamental agreements for ecumenical fellowship. As amended in 1961, it states that the WCC 'is a fellowship of churches which confess the Lord Jesus Christ as God and Saviour according to the scriptures, and therefore seek to fulfil together their common calling to the glory of the one God, Father, Son and Holy Spirit'. Accordingly, it insists on a theology which is biblical, trinitarian, church-focused and missionary, with its vocation focusing on Jesus Christ as God and Saviour, that is to say, it centres on the *incarnation and *atonement. For many evangelicals, it lacks defining detail, but on the other hand it makes an essential statement about the Christian churches in worldwide fellowship without imposing a *credal statement on any church at the behest of an external council. That said, the Council has in recent years, partly out of concern for the consciences of its Orthodox members, but also in recognition of the concerns of evangelicals, introduced mechanisms to ensure that member churches take the basis seriously. Since clearly there are diversities of outlook within the church of Jesus Christ, its theology cannot be narrowly equated with an exclusively evangelical perspective, thus necessitating that theological discussion will accordingly range beyond the limits of evangelical thinking.

Whilst ecumenical theology seeks to be faithful to the inherited apostolic faith, it also seeks to relate this to the contemporary scene in both word and action (see *Culture). Thus, its concern for a wide-ranging diakonial ministry represents its understanding of Christ's concern for a needy world. Seriousness about the coming of God's *kingdom is seen in its concern to promote peace and justice and to be effective stewards rather than ruthless exploiters of God's good creation. Thus, traditional concerns for social justice and peace are now supplemented by the promotion of a green agenda (see *Ecology) in the context of the biblical doctrine of *creation, whilst increasingly difficult *ethical issues in biotechnology claim attention. In all such programmes the theological sources and resources are critical, providing the essential defences preventing such concerns declining into feverish activism fuelled by mere political ideology. More concerned these days with mission than missions (see *Missiology), the *Missio Dei* is now seen as God working through all his people in every nation. Interfaith dialogue appears on the ecumenical agenda with new urgency, but there is no one agreed theology of dialogue. As over against the view that the WCC is only concerned with a political agenda, it is theologically concerned to explore the nature of spirituality. Discussions about the church as an inclusive community are essential for some churches, but contentious for others.

Because ecumenical theology is a theology which champions the oneness of Christ's church, it will necessarily want to place all divisions and differences within the context of that unity which is Christ's gift to the church, distinguishing between a legitimate diversity of understandings, and that sectarian temper which unchurches all other than itself. A theology of unity certainly does not mean uniformity; rather, it celebrates legitimate diversity – ethnic, cultural, historical – within an essential unity, within a recognition of Christ's presence in different Christian groups. In this respect, it is important that it is the church as a body which patiently undertakes the theological task, never surrendering it to articulate individuals who, heedless of the corporate voice, by their action privatize theology.

The sole criterion for working out ecumenical theology must then be, as one Orthodox theologian (Nicholas Lossky) explains, 'God, himself, Jesus Christ, image of the Father, bearer of the Spirit who reveals Christ, and cries "Abba, Father" in the hearts of all the baptized.' Thus 'Ecumenical theology implies total humility and intellectual honesty; it implies being prepared to be guided into all truth by the Spirit of truth', a stance which involves 'a permanent crucifixion for the intellect'.

Bibliography

P. Avis, *Reshaping Ecumenical Theology: The Church Made Whole?* (London, 2010); J. Briggs, M. A. Oduyoye and G. Tsetsis, *A History of the Ecumenical Movement, 1968–2000* (Geneva, 2004); G. R. Evans, *Method in Ecumenical Theology: The Lessons So Far* (Cambridge, 2009); W. Kasper, *Harvesting the Fruits: Aspects of Christian Faith in Ecumenical Dialogue* (New York, 2009).

J. BRIGGS

EDWARDS, JONATHAN (1703–58)

An American theologian and philosopher, Edwards was reared in a Christian home and culture, studying at Yale University. The first period of his ministry (in the Congregational Church, Northampton, MA, 1727–33) was a time of relative obscurity, followed by great popularity and success (1734–47), which ended with rejection (1750) and virtual burial in a little Indian outpost (Stockbridge, 1751–57) where he did his greatest work (*Freedom of the Will*; *Original Sin*; *End of Creation*; *True Virtue*). He was called to the presidency of the then nascent Princeton College shortly before his death.

According to Edwards' thought, 'nothing is more certain, than that there must be an unmade and unlimited being' (*The Insufficiency of Reason as a Substitute for Revelation*). *On Being* maintained that eternal being alone can be thought, and *Freedom of the Will* that 'we first prove *a posteriori* . . . there must be an eternal cause . . . and prove many of his perfections *a priori*'. In spite of this, apart from biblical revelation, man is 'naturally blind in the things of religion' (*Sermon* on Ps. 94:8f.). This is partly because of the complexity of metaphysical questions and mainly because of the noetic influence of sin. The Bible evidences its own inspiration by its shining 'bright with the amiable simplicity of truth' (*Observations on Scripture*), as well as in the external certification by its authors' God-enabled powers (*The Miracles of Jesus Not Counterfeited*).

By natural reason and Scripture God reveals his purpose in creating the world for his glory and therein the blessedness of his people (*End of Creation*) which consists in their disinterested benevolence toward his being-in-general (*Religious Affections*; *True Virtue*). Adam was first created upright, but fell into temptation (not calling on the efficient grace available to him) and brought the race which was 'constituted' one with him into ruin (*Original Sin*). Through the covenanted work of the God-man (*On Satisfaction*), God redeems the elect (*Efficacious Grace*), leaving the non-elect to their inexcusable unbelief and judgment (*The Justice of God in the Damnation of Sinners*).

This work of Christ is brought to the elect usually through the preaching in which the Spirit arouses previously 'sottish' people (*Sinners in the Hands of an Angry God*) to 'seek' (*Pressing into the Kingdom*; *Ruth's Resolution*). Of the many called, few are the chosen (see *Predestination). Only those who give a credible profession of faith and life are rightly admitted to and remain in the membership of the church and are entitled to her *sacraments (*Qualifications for Communion*), others being barred or excommunicated (*The Nature and End of Excommunication*).

A general awakening (see *Revival, theology of) that was occurring in the American colonies made Edwards believe the 'latter day' *millennium was dawning (*Thoughts on Revival*), which would be followed by the general judgment, conflagration, eternal hell and heaven (*The Portion of the Wicked*; *The Portion of the Righteous*). The awakening under Edwards, in addition to its immediate effects, had considerable power in preparing established churches for disestablishment after the American Revolution and, according to some scholars, in bringing about the Revolution itself. B. B. *Warfield thought that Edwards' defence of Calvinism (see *Reformed theology) had delayed the *Arminian conquest of New England for a hundred years.

Edwards is still regarded today as perhaps America's profoundest theological and philosophical mind.

See also: New England Theology.

Bibliography

Works: many editions, e.g. 2 vols. (Edinburgh, 1974–75); *The Works of Jonathan Edwards*, 26 vols., ed. Paul Ramsey (New Haven, 1989–2009).

Studies: C. Cherry, *The Theology of Jonathan Edwards: A Reappraisal* (New York, 1966); D. J. Elwood, *The Philosophical Theology of Jonathan Edwards* (New York, 1961); S. R. Holmes, *God of Grace and God of Glory* (Edinburgh, 2000); G. Marsden, *Jonathan Edwards: A Life* (New Haven, 2003); I. H. Murray, *Jonathan Edwards: A New Biography* (Edinburgh, 1987); O. E. Winslow, *Jonathan Edwards, 1703–1758: A Biography* (New York, 1940).

J. H. Gerstner

ELECTION, see PREDESTINATION

ELLUL, JACQUES (1912–1994)

Historian, social scientist and lay theologian, Ellul was born in Bordeaux, France, and worked as a professor at the Institute of Political Studies in the university there. In his youth he was converted to the Christian faith, and he was an active lay-preacher in the French Reformed Church.

His prolific writings fall into five categories:

(1) *History*. He wrote an extensive history of institutions.

(2) *Sociology*. In *The Technological Society*, his most important study, he examines the influence of 'modern technique' on all spheres of society, as well as on the human mind. Technique is considered an independent factor which functions in accordance with its own rules and which is developing into the 'technical system'.

(3) *Social criticism*. He proved himself to be a debunker of many a modern commonplace. For instance, he questioned whether modern man has ever come of age and whether modern society has really become secular. In his view, modern man is subject to the requirements of technique and believes his future and well-being are dependent on it, as if it were 'God himself'.

(4) *Biblical studies*. Some remarkable commentaries deserve attention (Jonah, 2 Kings, Apocalypse). His (biblical) study on *The Meaning of the City* is fundamental to an understanding of his theological thinking. The city stands for civilization and is the outcome of the efforts of men to build a world without the living God, which includes systems of religion, of morals, of defence, of insurance, etc. Man is now doomed to live in this city, which is judged by God. However, the Christian knows that God has promised a transformation of the works of men. The end of history is marked not just by the terror of Babylon, but also by the coming of the New Jerusalem.

(5) *Ethics*. These are based on 'the meaning of the city'. In his ethical works he attempts to escape the dangers of idealism, of moralism or of planning a sound society which can only lead to a well-ordered system which controls everything and everybody. What is left is the individual person, who is encouraged to be realistic about the situation he is in, determined by technical and political necessities, who is

also encouraged to accept his responsibilities and to continue to hope for the impossible: true dialogue, righteousness, peace, freedom, love.

In this theological thinking, the influence of Karl *Barth is noticeable. Characteristic of his work is the dialectical tension between biblical revelation and modern technical consciousness. Also characteristic is his insistence on the importance of personal freedom and of the dialogue between God and the human person, which is continually obstructed by human systems.

Bibliography

Works: *The Technological Society* (New York, 1964); *The Meaning of the City* (Grand Rapids, 1970); *The Politics of God and the Politics of Man* (Grand Rapids, 1972); *The Ethics of Freedom* (Grand Rapids, 1976).
Studies: C. G. Christians and J. M. van Hook, *Jacques Ellul: Interpretive Essays* (Champaigne, 1981); J. M. Hanks, assisted by R. Asal, *Jacques Ellul: A Comprehensive Bibliography* (Greenwich and London, 1984); B. Kristensen, 'Jacques Ellul', CG 29:4 (1976), pp. 106–110.

B. KRISTENSEN

EMERSON, RALPH WALDO (1803–82)

Ralph Waldo Emerson was an American writer who championed the creative self and exhorted others to believe they could retain the essence of Christian experience without the substance of Christian belief or practice. Born into a long line of New England clergymen, Emerson served a brief tenure as a *Unitarian minister before resigning his position and breaking with the church forever. He then launched a writing and speaking career that would bring him oracular status in his own day and an enduring reputation as one of the foremost figures in American literature.

In a series of works, including *Nature*, 'The American Scholar', 'The Divinity School Address', and *Essays: First Series*, Emerson sharply dismissed key particulars of Christian doctrine, including belief in the divinity of Jesus, the authority of the Scriptures, and the efficacy of the sacraments. According to him, instead of preaching 'a faith like Christ's in the infinitude of man', the church 'has dwelt, it dwells, with noxious exaggeration about the *person* of Jesus'; it preaches 'not the doctrine of the soul, but an exaggeration of the personal, the positive, the ritual'. Emerson instead encouraged his audience to 'dare to love God without mediator or veil' by seeking access to the deity without the aid of Scripture or the Son of God.

In espousing the innocence of human nature, in substituting intuition for revelation, and in proclaiming a glorious future for an essentially secular humanity, Emerson gave powerful voice to *romantic notions that were to become a central facet of the American experience.

Bibilography

L. Buell, *Emerson* (Cambridge, MA, 2003); B. Packer, *The Transcendentalists* (Athens, Georgia, 2007); R. D. Richardson, *Emerson: The Mind on Fire* (Berkeley, 1995).

R. LUNDIN

EMPIRICISM

Empiricism is the view that the source of all knowledge is sense-experience. It is based on the common perception that our senses provide us with knowledge. Its roots stem from the ancient Greeks, but it flourished as a reaction to *rationalism and its belief that reason was the basis of certain knowledge. In contrast, John *Locke, Bishop *Berkeley and David *Hume argued that all knowledge was based on the senses. This response was part of that critique of scepticism which operates by finding a source of absolutely certain knowledge. Hume divided what we know into matters of fact and relations of ideas. The realm of the relation of ideas is that of logic and mathematics. The truths of mathematics and logic are true by definition, necessary (i.e. they could not be false) and are known a priori. These truths are not part of the real world. In contrast, matters of fact stem from ordinary sense-experience. They are contingently true – they could be otherwise. They are known only by direct experience and a posteriori. They give genuine knowledge of the way the world is, and may be used to check what is said and claimed on the basis of experience. Common sense claims that we have ideas and concepts as well as sense-experience. Hume argued that these ideas or concepts either are relations of ideas, or can be analysed into having sensations or reflecting on them. For Hume, impressions were the actual content of the mind in the moment of perception. Ideas were less vivid copies of impressions, which could be amalgamated into complex ideas by the imagination. In the end, however, empiricism claims that there is nothing in the mind which was not previously in the sense.

Modern empiricism

Empiricism provides an answer to the sceptic and a unified source of all knowledge. This has developed in two ways. The search for certainty has led to the analysis of experience into irreducible, infallible units of experience called sense-data. These are the raw basics of our experience (e.g. a reddish blur) about which we cannot be mistaken. This approach highlights the problems of the reality of the external world and of the self. *Logical positivism has turned empiricism into a search for meaning based on ostensive definition, which sees knowledge as like learning a language, in which we give a name and point out an object so that no other understanding is possible. Verifiability has been the other basis for meaning, in which a statement is meaningful if, and only if, it can be verified by sense-experience. This was modified and even became a 'Principle of Falsifiability', which based knowledge on the failure to disprove. Empiricism is still based on *verification by sense-experience, using the methods of the empirical and inductive sciences as a solution to scepticism. It has created doubt about the truth and validity of religious statements and doctrines, based on a narrow view of experience being reducible to sense-experience alone.

Bibliography

A. J. Ayer, *The Problem of Knowledge* (Harmondsworth, 1971); D. Hume, *An Inquiry Concerning Human Understanding*, ed. L. A. Solby-Bigge (Oxford, ³1975); R. G. Meyers, *Understanding Empiricism* (Chesham, 2006); H. Morick (ed.), *Challenges to Empiricism* (Belmont, 1972).

E. D. COOK

ENHYPOSTASIA, see HYPOSTASIS

ENLIGHTENMENT, THE

Between the close of the seventeenth and the eighteenth centuries, the intellectual history of Europe and America underwent such signal development that the whole age has been named after it. This is the era of Enlightenment. The Enlightenment varied from nation to nation; it took moderate or radical forms; one may speak of a 'High' or a 'Low' Enlightenment; and it also developed, rather than existing unchanged. These and other considerations suggest that to identify a single 'Enlightenment' is, perhaps insuperably, difficult. Nor can its nature be properly grasped if treated as a purely intellectual or literary phenomenon. For example, demographic studies, such as those revealing the facts about decline in infant mortality in some nations where there was Enlightenment, show the vital social context of themes such as '*progress'. Whatever the contours or conclusions of future studies, however, to understand and to evaluate 'modernity' we need to go back to the Enlightenment.

In their religious thought, prominent Enlightenment thinkers were markedly hostile to traditional Christianity. The *Reformation and its aftermath witnessed the dissipation, not demise, of *dogma, as alternative interpretations of Christianity claimed its authentic inheritance and condemned each other as well as unbelief. Bloodshed and persecution accompanied this, so that Enlightenment thinkers attacked the consequences as well as content of traditional dogma. Negatively, they rejected the principle of the rule of dogma, and with it a range of ideas both formal (such as *revelation, where it provided exclusive, necessary knowledge) and material (such as the accepted doctrine of *original sin). Positively, they sought the rule of reason, and with it the adumbration of new formal ideas (such as the nature of morality) and material ones (such as the relation of God to physical nature). *Kant defined Enlightenment as the spirit's determination to exercise its intellectual faculties in unfettered integrity – 'Dare to know.' He who did so had some claim to be called an 'enlightened' thinker.

But if the term 'reason' is used to pick out a typical Enlightenment attitude, it requires cautious treatment. Comprehensive metaphysical constructions, based on rational deductions, could be criticized in the name of practical philosophy. Cold analytic reason, conceived as the instrument of universal understanding, could be censured in the name of passionate sensibility. If the Enlightenment is the age of reason, reason must be understood either as the alternative to dogma or in terms of broad intellectual autonomy. Nor did Enlightenment thinkers abandon religion or revelation. Atheistic materialism could develop in France certainly, but it had its anti-Christian critics (such as *Voltaire). Revelation might be deprived of sole religious authority, of the right to impart anything not knowable by reason, or of the ability even to provide significant incentive for the religious life; yet it could be domesticated (as in German neology) rather than eliminated.

It is hard to account for the forces behind Enlightenment thought without offering, in this case, a theological interpretation. The rise of modern science was a major factor: *Newton, sometimes almost deified in the eighteenth century, had impelled the search for scientific explanation that would lead to interpreting the physical world in terms of physical law. The growth of historical criticism was significant: while the Enlightenment is often regarded as deficient in real historical understanding, it could distinguish between its own and the biblical world. Yet Newton found no quarrel with Christianity at points where his later admirers did, and antiquity as such was not alien to the Enlightenment thinkers, as the prestige of the ancient Roman world revealed. Unless one suspects that the logic of scientific method – whether in physics or in history – is hostile to faith, one may look for a broader context, in which scientific explanation could develop into the rival, rather than the complement, of religious explanation; and in which historical criticism could develop into the opponent, rather than exponent, of Christian doctrine. This is neither to commend Newtonian science, nor to accept the operative principles of early historical criticism – but neither is it to hold them intrinsically responsible for what followed.

This broader context is surely supplied by the explicit or implicit sense of human autonomy. Indeed, in any comprehensive account, this must be related to political and economic change and policy. But, in the present perspective, 'autonomy' has both a relative and an absolute meaning. It was *relative* to the Christian claims about man. It was *absolute* in its willingness in principle to dispense with external, even divine, authority if that was where its logic led. Christianity opposes autonomy on grounds of creation, fall and redemption. The Enlightenment could relegate the Creator to a remote caretaker or irrelevant possibility, deny the incapacity of human nature to attain heaven by its own created resources and affirm that the moral life, conducted in good faith, if not complete knowledge, fulfils the basic purpose of existence. If God is finally disposed of, as he dramatically was in the nineteenth century, it is because he is not needed; if he is not needed, it is not because he is simply intellectually disposed of, but because the heart is satisfied – or satisfied to look – elsewhere. In such matters, the will, as well as the intellect, is at work.

This brief summary cannot avoid, any more than can other generalizations, misrepresenting the Enlightenment in some of its aspects. It is also no more disinterestedly neutral than any other fundamental interpretation. But, in a truistic or profounder sense, *autonomy is compatible with the phenomenon of Enlightenment thought in its flow or formulations. *Hume, Edward Gibbon (1737–94), Voltaire, Jean Jacques *Rousseau, Christian Wolff (1679–1754), *Lessing, Giovanni Battista Vico (1668–1744), Thomas Jefferson (1743–1826) – these represent a cultural and intellectual range in the Enlightenment. There may be others more significant, for the question of who is significant, and why, will continue to be debated, as will the significance of the Enlightenment itself, if it is to be retained as a viable concept. To reject or accept the 'Enlightenment' overall seems futile. If calamitous consequences flow from the adoption of some of its axioms, note that there were calamitous aspects to the preceding history of Christianity. Karl Popper (1902–94) remarked that the urge to improve the lot of our fellows is both 'admirable and dangerous' and was rooted in the 'longing of uncounted, unknown men to free themselves and their minds from the tutelage of authority and prejudice'. By considering what is here claimed or assumed about the motives of the 'Enlightened', we grasp and estimate the nature and significance of the enterprise.

See also: FRANKFURT SCHOOL; MODERNITY.

Bibliography

A. Broadie (ed.), *The Scottish Enlightenment: An Anthology* (Edinburgh, 2001); E. Cassirer, *The Philosophy of the Enlightenment* (Princeton, 1951); P. Gay, *The Enlightenment: An Interpretation*, 2 vols. (London, 1970); N. Hampson, *The Enlightenment* (Harmondsworth, 1968); M. Jacob, *The Radical Enlightenment: Pantheists, Freemasons and*

EPHESUS, COUNCIL OF

The third Ecumenical Council was called by Emperor Theodosius II in 431 to resolve the *Nestorian controversy, which was arguably as important as the *Arian crisis for clarifying *Christological doctrine. In 429 Nestorius had disputed the traditional title *Theotokos* (God-mother) for Mary since, strictly speaking, this would suggest that she was some form of 'goddess'. He also rejected *Anthropotokos* (man-mother) proposed by Constantinopolitan monks (doubtless to draw out his theology), which suggested Christ was merely a man. He sought to reconcile the problem by proposing *Christotokos* (Christ-mother). These titles point to the heart of the dispute: the nature of Christ as both God and man united in one integrated person, as in the Nicene Creed or, as Nestorius was claimed to imply, two sons or natures joined in one human being. *Cyril of Alexandria entered the debate defending Nicene orthodoxy, only to be accused of *Apollinarism. At the council, Nestorius and his doctrines were condemned and Cyril's doctrine held to be in agreement with *Nicaea. Eight canons were passed at the council, seven dealing with the doctrinal question and confirming the Nicene Creed as the basis of faith, and one with the autonomy of the church of Cyprus. The manner in which the council was conducted did the church little credit.

See also: Councils; Creeds.

Bibliography

The Seven Ecumenical Councils, in NPNF ser. 2, vol. 14; J. McGuckin, *Saint Cyril of Alexandria and the Christological Controversy: Its History, Theology, and Texts* (New York, 2004); N. P. Tanner, *The Councils of the Church: A Short History* (ET, New York, 2001); idem (ed.), *Decrees of the Ecumenical Councils*, 2 vols. (ET, London and Washington, 1990).

A. D. Rich

EPICLESIS, see EUCHARIST

EPISCOPACY, see MINISTRY

EPISCOPIUS, see ARMINIANISM

EPISTEMOLOGY

The term comes from the Gk word for knowledge or science (*epistēmē*). Epistemology is the study of the nature and basis of experience, belief and knowledge. It asks what we know and how we know it. It is concerned to differentiate knowledge from feeling sure or believing. It asks how we justify claims to know, whether we can be wrong about what we know, if we can know only if it makes sense that we can also not know, and whether we know that we know something. There are many areas of difficulty in knowledge: e.g. knowing the self, the past, the future, universal facts, scientific laws and the facts of philosophy, aesthetics, morality, religion, logic and mathematics. Various modern philosophers have introduced distinctions to help analyse the nature of knowing. Bertrand Russell (1872–1970) distinguishes knowledge by acquaintance, which is direct and immediate, from knowledge by description, which is indirect. Gilbert Ryle (1900–76) distinguishes knowing how to do things, from knowing that such and such is the case.

Rationalism and empiricism

*Descartes sought absolute certainty in knowledge. He stressed that reason alone provided the route to absolute certainty. This *rationalist emphasis was countered by the *empiricism of *Locke, *Berkeley and *Hume, who argued that certainty was to be found through the senses alone. These key strands in philosophy share in a common debate over the origin of knowledge, are aware of the problems of universals and abstract ideas, use rational and scientific approaches, and engage in a search for certainty. Both are responses to the sceptical challenge to knowledge. The sceptic queries the reliability of knowledge, and argues that it is always possible to doubt. Rationalism and empiricism are attempts to cure doubt. *Kant offered a bridge between the senses and reason with his stress on the synthetic a priori categories of understanding which make knowledge possible. Knowledge of these categories was not derived from experience, yet was a condition of the comprehensibility of experience. His synthetic a priori claims have been much disputed. More recent philosophers have argued variously. G. E. Moore (1873–1958) and *Wittgenstein have set aside the issues of doubt and analysed knowledge in terms of meaning through linguistic usage. Ordinary language and common sense have little problem with philosophical doubt and offer a simple solution to it. *Polanyi has stressed the personal nature of knowing and its tacit dimension in which we know more than we can say. The *logical positivists have taken empiricism along the road of *verification and falsification as means for testing knowledge and truth claims, often using sense data as the ultimate source of certainty. A. J. Ayer (1910–89) offers an analysis of knowledge in terms of its being justified true belief. The key issues in epistemology seem to concern: the role of justification and its nature; ways of setting aside, or coping with, *doubt, and whether the sceptic's position makes any sense; the nature of what is known (whether it be in terms of ideas or what is real); an adequate theory of *truth (whether in terms of coherence or correspondence with reality); and the relationship between objectivity and subjectivity, in terms of whether we can know something totally objectively and to what extent subjectivity intrudes or is seen to be problematic.

Epistemology in theology

Traditionally, the distinction between belief and knowledge has taken the form of *faith and reason in theology. Biblical writers do not seem hesitant about making claims that God is known and that Christianity is not simply a question of faith, but also one of knowledge. *Anselm argues that faith seeks understanding, while others similarly assert that we believe in order that we may understand. Theologians express the various sources of knowledge in religion in terms of *revelation and experience. Revelation is usually divided into special and general. Special revelation includes the incarnation, the resurrection and the miracles, where God reveals himself in a 'special' way to particular people. General revelation is open to all and is usually seen in terms of *natural theology. This looks to the nature of the world and the nature of humanity as revealing something of the nature of God. He may be known by deducing his nature from the world or humanity. *Religious experience seems to offer a direct knowledge of God as seen in the call of the prophets and the many direct experiences of God and Christ as recounted in Scripture. Distinctive religious experiences, or simply interpreting the world or events in one's life or in the world's life as God's activity, have allowed personal claims to know God directly.

These knowledge claims have been criticized by philosophers, especially logical positivists, because of the absence of the kind of proof required by theories of verification and falsification. Theologians have responded in various ways. Some argue that religious experience is self-authenticating. Others argue that the positivist view of experience is too narrowly defined in terms of sense-experience. Religious experience has been interpreted as a disclosure model or situation parallel to scientific discoveries (see *Ramsey, Ian). John *Hick offers eschatological verification as the ground of knowing God. Others have argued that reason does not offer absolute knowledge in any realm and that belief is the best that any area of study and life can offer. Thus, Christian presuppositions are no worse or better off than any other set of presuppositions.

If we follow the biblical balance between faith and knowledge, it is crucial to deal with questions of truth and justification whenever claims of knowledge and belief are made. Both sets of claims require evidence and support, and the theologian must not shrink from seeking the best evidence and offering the strongest justification for knowledge and belief claims. Nevertheless, we must recognize the limits of reason and when there are unreasonable and inappropriate demands for proof and justification. This may be demonstrated by showing that nothing would count as satisfying these demands. Christians need to reflect on what would count against knowledge and belief in God. Biblical Christianity does not claim immunity from criticism, nor assume automatic acceptance by its hearers; it offers good reasons for the hope that is within us.

Bibliography

A. J. Ayer, *The Problem of Knowledge* (Harmondsworth, 1956); S. T. Davis, *Faith*,

Skepticism and Evidence: An Essay in Religious Epistemology (Cranbury, 1978); J. Greco and E. Sosa, *Blackwell Guide to Epistemology* (Oxford, 1999); D. W. Hamlyn, *Theory of Knowledge* (London, 1971); C. Hay, *The Theory of Knowledge: A Coursebook* (Cambridge, 2008); J. Hick, *Faith and Knowledge* (London, 1966); T. Penethum, *Problems of Religious Knowledge* (London, 1971); D. L. Wolfe, *Epistemology* (Leicester, 1982).

E. D. COOK

ERASMUS, DESIDERIUS
(*c.* 1469–1536)

The most renowned scholar of his time, Erasmus of Rotterdam was a complex and cosmopolitan Christian *humanist. Although courted by universities, popes, kings and an emperor, this frail intellectual carefully protected his independence. His consuming passion for piety and unity was best served, he felt, through the power of his pen.

Overcoming the stigma of an illegitimate birth, Erasmus was raised in a clerical world of monastic schools and rules. Although ordained in 1492, the young priest sought a release from his *Augustinian order to pursue university studies in Paris. He was steeped in classical literature and became a consummate Latinist.

A visit to England in 1499 proved to be a turning point when he was both captivated and challenged by an Oxford lecturer, John Colet (*c.* 1466–1519), the future dean of St Paul's Cathedral, who fired his imagination with the ideals of Christian humanism and specifically the importance of a return to the normal sense of the biblical text. Such a goal, the two agreed, would best be realized through a working knowledge of the original languages of the Bible.

The next years were given to travel and research, especially the study of Greek grammar. Inspired by the chance discovery of an obscure manuscript by Lorenzo Valla (1407–57) which criticized the accuracy of the Latin Vulgate, Erasmus gave himself to the production of a new Latin NT based on a critical Greek NT. In 1516 this *New Instrument*, as he titled the first edition, was published. Its influence was immense. With one book, Erasmus put the Greek NT within reach of preachers and scholars.

As his fame grew, Erasmus began to direct his influence against various abuses in the Roman Catholic Church. The satirical *In Praise of Folly* blasted away at the foibles of contemporary monasticism. He stood squarely against the misuse of indulgences (see *Purgatory), and when Luther delineated his Ninety-Five Theses, Erasmus gave his support. As *Luther became more strident, however, the irenic Erasmus began to distance himself from the controversial Reformer. Correspondence between the two churchmen became increasingly bitter. Goaded by Rome to strike out at the Lutheran heresy, Erasmus wrote a treatise *On the Freedom of the Will* in 1524, which took Luther to task on the thorny issue of *predestination and human freedom. The differences between the two men, however, were by no means solely theological. Erasmus sincerely wanted reform, but not at the expense of unity. The humanist defended Luther's freedom to criticize abuses, but he could never condone an ecclesiastical rebellion against authority.

The Reformers faulted Erasmus for vacillation and timidity, and various popes put his works on the Index of Forbidden Books, but his influence was enormous. Protestants and Catholics alike quoted and cited him freely on matters of biblical and theological interpretation. Calvin's *Institutes* are more indebted to him than appears on the surface. His *Paraphrases on the New Testament*, which were translated into many languages, had a sustained popular influence. His editing of the collected writings of major early Church Fathers was probably his most important contribution next to the 1516 NT.

Erasmian studies burgeoned in the twentieth century. Several biographical works were published, as well as major new editions of his works and letters.

Bibliography

Works: *The Collected Works of Erasmus*, eds. J. K. McConica *et al.* (Toronto, 1974–); *Luther and Erasmus: Free Will and Salvation*, LCC 17, eds. E. G. Rupp *et al.* (London, 1969); *Opera Omnia*, eds. C. Reedijk *et al.* (Amsterdam, 1969–).

Studies: C. Augustijn, *Erasmus: His Life, Works, and Influence* (Toronto, 1991); R. H. Bainton, *Erasmus of Christendom* (New York, 1969); A. G. Dickens and W. R. D. Jones, *Erasmus the Reformer* (London, 1994); J. McConica, *Erasmus* (Oxford, 1991); E. Rummel, *Erasmus* (New York, 2004).

N. P. FELDMETH

ERASTIANISM, see STATE

ERIUGENA, JOHN SCOTUS (c. 810–c. 877)

Eriugena was a philosophical theologian of Christian Neoplatonism (see *Platonism). Reared in Ireland (as both 'Scotus' and 'Eriugena' tautologically indicate), John became the most original thinker of the Carolingian renaissance, spending over thirty years from c. 840 as the leading light of Charles the Bald's palace academy near Laon in Gaul. Late in life he may have taught in England.

John's knowledge of Greek (rare in the West at the time and probably acquired in Ireland) equipped him to Latinize the thought of Greek Christian Neoplatonism. As well as works by *Gregory of Nyssa and Maximus the Confessor, he translated and commented on the influential corpus of *Pseudo-Dionysius. He was also indebted to *Boethius' interpretation of *Aristotelian logic; his dialectical style has earned him the title 'the first *scholastic'.

His most important work, *Periphyseon* or *The Division of Nature* (c. 862), was condemned in the thirteenth century. Its apparent fusion of biblical teaching and Neoplatonism (for he viewed both reason and *revelation as manifestations of divine wisdom, and virtually equated philosophy and religion) verged on *pantheism. All creation proceeds outward from God as source, by 'division' or 'progress', and by a circular motion of 'resolution' or 'regress' returns to him as goal. John's thought bears the typical marks of Neoplatonism: a preference for *apophatic or negative theology, a poetic, almost mystical ardour and intensity, a hierarchical scale of being, the *deification of all creatures, and the 'restoration of all things' proposed by *Origen. Nature and grace could scarcely be separated in John's system.

He opposed *Gottschalk on predestination. Appealing to *Augustine's early anti-Manichaean works, he advanced what seemed a *Pelagian appreciation of humankind's moral abilities, and denied that Augustine taught double predestination. No credible version of predestination or election survived in John's thought, any more than did eternal punishment or hell.

In the *eucharistic controversy associated with *Paschasius Radbertus and *Ratramnus, Eriugena taught a refined symbolist interpretation of the sacrament. Christ is offered and eaten 'not dentally but mentally' (*mente non dente*). In his vision of reality, all visible and corporeal things signified something incorporeal and intelligible.

Recent Irish scholarship has rediscovered John as the greatest Irish philosopher (except perhaps for *Berkeley). He has been too often depicted as a lonely outpost of Greek thought in the medieval West. Yet he worked among a colourful community of scholars, and must not be detached from the tradition that derives from Augustine. He posed in an acute form the perennial question of the relation between *faith and reason.

Bibliography

Most *works* in PL 122; for list see I. P. Sheldon-Williams in *JEH* 10 (1960), pp. 198–224; *Periphyseon*, ed. and tr. Sheldon-Williams (Dublin, 1968ff.).

Studies: H. Bett, *Johannes Scotus Erigena* (Cambridge, 1925); CHLGEMP, pp. 518–533 (Sheldon-Williams), 576–586 (H. Liebeschütz); D. Carabine, *John Scottus Eriugena* (Oxford, 2000); D. Moran, *The Philosophy of John Scottus Eriugena: A Study of Idealism in the Middle Ages* (Cambridge, 1989); J. J. O'Meara, *Eriugena* (Oxford, 1988); J. Pelikan, *The Growth of Medieval Theology (600–1300), The Christian Tradition*, vol. 3 (Chicago and London, 1978), pp. 95–105.

D. F. WRIGHT

EROS, see LOVE

ERSKINE, THOMAS (OF LINLATHEN) (1788–1870)

Thomas Erskine was an outstanding Scottish lay theologian, who combined the roles of leisurely laird and theological author and correspondent. Denominationally uncommitted, Erskine travelled theologically from an initial Calvinism (see *Reformed theology), through Irvingism, to a final though far from easygoing *universalism. His first book, *Remarks on the Internal Evidence for the Truth of Revealed Religion* (1820), argued that Christianity's truth was demonstrated by its correspondence with man's moral needs. It was well received by the orthodox world. His *Unconditional Freeness of the Gospel* (1828), however, provoked bitter criticism for its advocacy of universal atonement. In 1828 Erskine met John McLeod *Campbell, and enthusiastically supported him during his trial and deposition from the Church of Scotland. They became lifelong friends. Campbell's mature Christology is seminally present in Erskine's *Brazen Serpent* (1831). Erskine also encountered Edward *Irving at this period, and adopted his views on premillennialism (see *Millennium), Christ's humanity and the *gifts of the Spirit. *The Doctrine of Election* (1837) concluded Erskine's breach with Calvinism.

Erskine's thought shows increasing preoccupation with *conscience as the criterion of truth. He regarded God as a universal Father who is educating all men into a filial relationship with himself, and in later years saw the ultimate salvation of all as the essential gospel. Always a deeply pious and charming man, Erskine's writings and personal influence contributed notably to the liberalizing of nineteenth-century British theology.

Bibliography

Other works: *An Essay on Faith* (1822); *The Gifts of the Spirit* (1830); *The Spiritual Order* (1871).

Studies: J. S. Candlish, in *British and Foreign Evangelical Review* 22 (1873), pp. 105–128; W. Hanna, *Letters of Thomas Erskine*, 2 vols. (Edinburgh, 1877); T. Hart, *The Teaching Father: An Introduction to the Theology of Thomas Erskine of Linlathen* (Edinburgh, 1993); H. F. Henderson, *Erskine of Linlathen* (Edinburgh, 1899); D. Horrocks, *Laws of the Spiritual Order: Innovation and Reconstruction in the Soteriology of Thomas Erskine of Linlathen* (Milton Keynes, 2004); N. R. Needham, *Thomas Erskine of Linlathen: His Life and Theology 1788–1837*, unpubl. PhD thesis (Edinburgh, 1987); idem, *Thomas Erskine of Linlathen: His Life and Theology* (Edinburgh, 1990); T. F. Torrance, *Scottish Theology from John Knox to John McLeod Campbell* (Edinburgh, 1996); D. F. Winslow, *Thomas Erskine: Advocate for the Character of God* (New York, 1993).

N. R. NEEDHAM

ESCHATOLOGY

Eschatology is the doctrine of the end (*eschaton*) or the Last Things (*eschata*). Christian eschatology has its roots in the eschatology of Second Temple Judaism in which there was generally an expectation of the end of 'the present evil age' when Israel was oppressed, and the dawn of the 'age to come' when God would intervene to establish his rule. This was expressed in highly figurative *apocalyptic literature. In the NT, this perspective of Judaism was subtly altered so that, while in one sense the age to come had *already* come with the coming of Jesus, his resurrection and the giving of the Holy Spirit, in another sense it had *not yet* come. While Jesus was raised from the dead, his followers died and were *not yet* raised and evil was still rampant. Christians therefore still prayed: 'Your kingdom come'.

Patristic eschatology

As the Christian church became increasingly separated from its Jewish roots, its eschatology was affected by its cultural context. A strong *dualism in Greco-Roman culture separated the physical from the spiritual in both metaphysics and anthropology. The spiritual was eternal and of ultimate value; the physical (including the human body) was either inferior (as in *Platonism) or considered evil (as in various *Gnostic sects). In this cultural context, the early teachers of the church, such as *Justin Martyr, *Irenaeus or *Tertullian, still defended the clear NT teaching of the resurrection of the body and even the belief in a literal millennium when Christ was to return in his resurrection body to rule on earth.

But the strong influence of Platonism led to the increasing 'spiritualization' of Christian doctrine. *Origen was strongly committed to the Christian faith, but he taught that Christ's coming would not be physically in one place, that there would be no literal *millennium or reign on earth, and that the body would keep the same form, but be materially a 'spiritual body'. Most notably, he speculated that hell referred to spiritual anguish, a punishment that would be reformative so that eventually all (even the devil) would be saved. His Platonism even led to the speculation that since 'spirit' is eternal, all human souls have existed from, and would exist to, all eternity

While there was strong reaction against Origen, by the end of the patristic period Christian eschatology emerged from Greco-Roman culture in a somewhat different form. The expectation of Christ's return or parousia remained, and the last *judgment was expected, but the resurrection body would be 'spiritual' rather than material, and the idea of a literal millennium had largely disappeared. *Gregory of Nyssa, one of the leading Fathers of the Eastern church, shared Origen's universalism, but *Augustine in the West and John *Chrysostom in the East maintained that the punishment of the wicked would be eternal. Augustine broadened eschatology into a whole philosophy of history in his work, *The City of God*. Two cities, the city of God and civilization in opposition to God, battled through the ages, but eventually the city of God would prevail. But the doctrine of the resurrection of the body and the new creation, while still present in his thought, is overshadowed by his more Platonist vision of an eternal heaven in which the saints will gaze enraptured at the beatific vision. Only then will the pure in heart see the triune God.

The medieval and Reformation period

In the medieval period, descriptions of heaven and hell as the final destiny for human souls were heightened. In the *Four Books of Sentences*, which became the standard textbook for theology in the monastic schools and the new universities, Peter *Lombard defined the 'four Last Things' as *death, judgment, heaven and hell. Eschatology thus defined came as the final *locus* (theme) of theology in all standard treatments. Dante's vivid description of his journey through hell, purgatory and paradise in his *Divine Comedy* gripped the medieval imagination. Millenarianism made its appearances on the fringes of medieval Christianity, for example, in the thirteenth-century *Joachamites, whose teaching took the three ages of Joachim of Fiore as a starting point.

At the Reformation, Luther rejected the medieval doctrine of *purgatory which had become the basis for the abuse of indulgences, and the Magisterial Reformers, although they agreed that the pope was the *Antichrist, generally rejected millennialism as fanaticism. Calvin wrote commentaries on almost every book of the Bible, but not the book of Revelation. Among some of the *Anabaptists, however, there was a renewed interest. The various groups varied widely, but at one extreme, Thomas Münzer, a renegade follower of Luther, applied the apocalyptic visions of Daniel and Revelation literally to the politics of his own day, and during the Peasants' War led an army of peasants to their deaths at Frankenhausen, promising that Christ would intervene.

Evangelical millennialism

Millennialism flourished again among various sects during the English Civil War (1638–49) and the succeeding dictatorship of Oliver Cromwell, notably among the Fifth Monarchy Men. But earlier in the century, two Puritan writers, Thomas Brightman and Joseph Mede, both Cambridge scholars, initiated (respectively) postmillennialism and premillennialism. Postmillennialism was the view that Christ would return after (Lat. *post*) the millennium. That implied that the gospel would spread and the world become increasingly peaceful before the second advent. Premillennialism was the view that Christ would return before (Lat. *pre*) the millennium. That implied that conditions on earth would become progressively worse until Christ defeated evil at the second advent. In the eighteenth century, the leaders of the Evangelical Revival, such as Jonathan *Edwards, leant towards postmillennialism, although John *Wesley appears to have held the more complex view of the great pietist scholar of Halle, Johann Albrecht Bengel (1687–1752), that there would be two millennia, one before and one after the second advent.

The evangelical movement for 'foreign *missions' led by William Carey, Thomas Chalmers, John Venn and many others was accordingly predominantly postmillennialist. The spread of the gospel would usher in the universal reign of Christ. This vision continued to inspire the American revivalist, Charles Finney, and the Scottish missionary, David Livingstone in the mid-nineteenth century. The missionary societies therefore engaged in medical and educational work to improve society, Livingstone advocating an alliance of Christianity, commerce and civilization to counter the Arab slave trade in East Africa.

But from the 1820s a more pessimistic premillennialism began to stir. Edward *Irving's teaching led to the Albury Park conferences, and despite Irving's rejection by evangelicals, leaders such as Horatius Bonar, Lord Shaftesbury and Henry Grattan Guinness advocated the premillennial view. John Nelson *Darby developed out of this the more elaborate scheme of *dispensationalism, adopted by some but rejected by others in the new movement of Christian Brethren. The OT prophecies applied to Israel, not to the church, and at the end of the present dispensation, Christian believers would be caught up to meet the Lord in the air in the 'rapture' before the great tribulation, which in turn would end with the second advent which would initiate the millennium. Darby was more successful in propagating his views in the USA. Dispensationalism became widely known through the annual Niagara Bible Conferences from 1883 to 1900 and was taught in the notes of the widely influential Scofield Bible (1909).

Postmillennialism continued to influence the wider evangelical movement, although the watchword of the Student Volunteer Movement (founded 1886), 'The evangelization of the world in this generation', was interpreted both ways. But premillennialism (though not necessarily dispensationalism) was stronger among the more conservative evangelicals in Britain in the early twentieth century. The leading Baptist preacher, F. B. Meyer, founded the Advent Testimony and Preparation Movement in 1917, while the fall of Jerusalem to General Allenby and the Balfour Declaration promising Jews a home in Palestine were hailed as events of epochal significance (see *Judaism and Christianity). Full-blown dispensationalism flourished in America, strengthened by the founding of Dallas Theological Seminary by Lewis Sperry Chafer. From the 1970s it was promoted in popular literature by Hal Lindsey in *The Late Great Planet Earth* and the 'Left Behind' series of novels by Tim LaHaye and Jerry Jenkins. While American evangelicalism continues to include all views, British evangelicalism and evangelical scholars in both countries and around the world generally reject the idea of a literal millennium as a misreading of Rev. 20:3 and adopt the amillennial views of Augustine and the Reformers.

Modern and contemporary theology

In academic theology, eschatology began to play a more significant role even in *liberal thought with the teaching of Albrecht *Ritschl. Hegel's thought had made theologians more conscious of the significance of time and history, but Ritschl rejected both the metaphysical approach of *Hegel and *Schleiermacher's focus on religious experience to turn to a more historical approach. This began with Jesus' proclamation of the *kingdom of God, understood as a historical movement of moral and social progress initiated by Jesus and continued by the church. This perspective contributed (along with evangelical postmillennialism) to the general nineteenth-century belief in progress. At the same time, Karl *Marx, a baptized but apostate Jew, rejected this progressive view for the belief that the revolution of the proletariat would eventually lead to the classless society, a secularized form of eschatology. The '*social gospel' of Walter *Rauschenbusch at the beginning of the twentieth century was more in line with the liberal theology of Ritschlian thought.

By that time, however, Ritschl's view of the kingdom of God had been rejected by his son-in-law, Johannes Weiss, who argued that Jesus was not a figure comparable to a modern social reformer, but rather a wild Jewish apocalyptic visionary proclaiming the end of the world. This was taken up by Albert *Schweitzer in his rejection of the '*quest for the historical Jesus' which had projected modern progressive views on to Jesus. Jesus had preached the ethic of love, but (according to Schweitzer) had sacrificed his life in the false belief that God would intervene to save him from the cross and usher in the new age of the kingdom. The kingdom of God was not the consequence of liberal social policies, but (in the misunderstanding of Jesus) could only come with the dramatic crisis of divine intervention.

Schweitzer's view was challenged by C. H. *Dodd, who argued that Jesus proclaimed that the kingdom of God, expected by many Jews of his day, had *already* come in his ministry. This idea of 'realized eschatology' was corrected, however, by several NT scholars, including W. G. Kümmel, Oscar Cullmann and George Eldon Ladd. They characterized the eschatology of Jesus and of the NT as paradoxical. In one sense the kingdom God had *already* come with the presence of Jesus, but in another sense it had *not yet* come. This has become the standard and widely accepted interpretation of NT eschatology: this paradox is thought to recapture the structure of thought soon lost as the church lost contact with its Jewish roots and was shaped by the culture of the Greco-Roman world. That being so, the implication for *systematic theology is that eschatology is not merely the doctrine of the Last Things, to be treated as the final topic, as it has been since Peter Lombard. Rather, it shapes the whole of Christian theology: it is the key in which the whole music is set.

This conclusion was somewhat influential in the theology of Karl *Barth, although the early Barth at least still tended to think in terms of the Eternal invading time directly 'from above'. It was in the theology of Wolfhart *Pannenberg and Jürgen *Moltmann that it began to be taken as the starting point for theology. They were linked together in what was called the 'Theology of Hope' in the 1960s, but actually there are significant differences between them.

Pannenberg rejected Barth's view of *revelation as the word of God, substituting the idea that revelation came as history. The whole, total *history of the world would reveal God only at the end, but the end had come proleptically in Jesus. We could establish his resurrection by the historical-critical method and so enter rationally into faith in Jesus as the revelation of God. Moltmann's first significant publication was entitled *The Theology of Hope* (1964), and his theology has since developed from this starting point of eschatology. Hope arises from faith in the crucified Jesus in whom God shared in our suffering, and it is this eschatological perspective which motivates Christians to crusade for social justice in the present. Without following either Pannenberg or Moltmann, evangelical Christianity has recovered a sense of the wholeness of the mission of the church in both evangelism and social action from this recovery of the eschatological perspective. But in articulating eschatology itself, N. T. Wright sums up the new perception that the Christian *hope is not the long-held and rather Platonist one of a disembodied existence as disembodied souls or spirits in an eternal heaven, but that, while at death believers go to be with the Lord, the real hope is for 'life after life after death'. It is hope not just for individual souls, but hope for *resurrection 'transphysical' life in the new creation.

In *The Progress of Dogma* (1906) James *Orr thought that the edifice of Christian theology was virtually complete except for some additions to eschatology. But instead, eschatology now shapes the whole building. While popular speculative millenarianism survives, the serious study of NT eschatology is providing new insights into the whole of Christian theology and into the *mission of the worldwide church today.

Bibliography

G. C. Berkouwer, *The Return of Christ* (Grand Rapids, 1972); E. Brunner, *Eternal Hope* (London, 1954); R. Bultmann, *History and Eschatology* (Edinburgh, 1957); O. Cullmann, *Christ and Time* (London, 1951); idem, *Salvation in History* (London, 1967); C. H. Dodd, *The Parables of the Kingdom* (London, 1936); M. J. Harris, *Raised Immortal* (London, 1983); A. A. Hoekema, *The Bible and the Future* (Grand Rapids, 1979); S. Holmes and R. Rook (eds.), *What Are We Waiting For? Christian Hope and Contemporary Culture* (Milton Keynes, 2008); H. Küng, *Eternal Life?* (London, 1984); G. E. Ladd, *The Presence of the Future* (Grand Rapids, 1982); S. H. Travis, *Christian Hope and the Future of Man* (Leicester, 1980); N. T. Wright, *Surprised by Hope* (London, 2007).

T. A. NOBLE

ESSENCE OF CHRISTIANITY

Although association with *Feuerbach's *The Essence of Christianity* (1841) and *Harnack's *What Is Christianity?* (1900) has suggested that the subject is of interest only to historians of nineteenth-century thought, or one whose pursuit inevitably leads to abstract generalizations or reduction of living religion to sociological or ethical principles, these are not necessary conclusions. In fact, the issue is a central one of permanent and even increasing contemporary significance in at least five areas.

Definitions of the essential features of Christianity, which include *religious experience, *worship and *ethics, as well as doctrine, are: (1) offered in varying degrees by all *creeds, *confessions of faith and *catechisms, both ancient and modern; (2) the basis of *ecumenical discussions promoting reunion of the churches; (3) necessary for undertaking intra-religious dialogue; (4) entailed in every attempt at the *contextualization or cross-cultural communication of the gospel, which is a particularly sensitive issue for the Roman Catholic Church in different parts of the world (cf. *Concilium* 135, 1980; 171, 1984); and (5) the implicit or explicit basis of every work of *systematic theology or *apologetics.

Looking at the breadth and implications of the subject in this way makes it clear that there is a distinction to be made between understandings of the essence of Christianity that seek to reduce it to one or more key ideas, and those that attempt to do full justice to its complex elements. In this respect there are important differences between the approaches taken by Feuerbach and Harnack and those adopted by contemporaries such as *Schleiermacher or *Newman.

The constant tendency of a search for an 'essence' to de-historicize Christianity has to be resisted both by careful consideration of its components – religious experience, worship, ethics and doctrine – and by due regard for the unity and diversity of their manifestation from earliest times.

The question of 'essence' thus turns out to be closely related to the question of the *development of doctrine. It may therefore be useful to consider the arguments of Newman's celebrated *Essay on the Development of Doctrine* (1845, ³1878). Whether or not his understanding of the church's role in interpreting the mystery of *revelation is felt to be completely satisfactory, two of Newman's conclusions are worth noting. The first is that Christian truth may be organized around one idea, in his case the *incarnation, providing it does not exclude another aspect of revelation. The second is that ultimately revelation is a mystery that cannot be systematized or exhausted in words, a timely reminder that knowledge of God comes through the response of the whole person.

Bibliography

J. D. G. Dunn, *Unity and Diversity in the New Testament* (London, 1977); G. E. Gunton, *Yesterday and Today; A Study of Continuities in Christology* (London, 1983); N. Lash, *Theology on Dover Beach* (London, 1979); H.-G. Link (ed.), *Apostolic Faith Today*, Faith and Order Paper 124 (Geneva, 1985); R. J. Schreiter, *Constructing Local Theologies* (London, 1985); S. Sykes, *The Identity of Christianity* (London, 1984).

P. N. Hillyer

ETERNAL LIFE, see ESCHATOLOGY

ETERNITY, see TIME AND ETERNITY

ETHICS

The field of 'ethics' has been defined as 'disciplined reflection on that dimension of human life denoted "moral"' (A. Verhey, *Dictionary for Theological Interpretation of the Bible*, Grand Rapids and London, 2005). 'Christian ethics', then, is disciplined *Christian* reflection on the moral dimension of human life. In the light of the comprehensive claims of God over human existence as Creator and Lawgiver, and the equally comprehensive scope of his redeeming and sanctifying intentions, 'the moral dimension of human life' should be construed as embracing every conceivable facet of human activity. There are no aspects of human activity in which we are not constantly and inescapably confronted by questions of right conduct (moral action) or questions of virtue (moral character). Indeed, on such a broad definition, the moral dimension would also include every facet of the human relationship to the non-human creation, so that ecological and technological questions are also part of the subject matter of 'ethics'.

Modern challenges to classical Christian ethics

This all-embracing understanding of the scope of ethics was, in the classical Christian era, associated with a particular view of the ground of ethics. Ethics was construed as grounded in 'natural' order. Nature was understood as 'creation', that is, as ordered by and revelatory of inherent, divinely established moral purposes (*tela*) accessible in principle to unprejudiced human reason. Nature as *creation, then, was governed by moral laws, and communicated moral truths. Such truths were seen as confirmed, clarified and expanded in Scripture, the highest authority in matters of ethics. This was the central conception underlying various versions of 'natural law theory' which dominated Christian ethical thinking from patristic times until the late Middle Ages, attaining its most systematic formulation in the work of *Thomas Aquinas. The Reformers later insisted that whatever moral knowledge 'nature' might communicate was only imperfectly discernible by the fallen human mind and could only be rightly apprehended through the correcting and judging lens of Scripture. Yet whatever disagreements there were over how, and how reliably, humans might gain access to natural moral truths, the core assumption of natural law theory – that created nature discloses moral truths – prevailed in European thought until the modern period.

Such a view came to be fundamentally challenged by influential modern thinkers. The challenge gathered momentum under the influence of seventeenth-century *empiricism, which began to reconceive 'nature' in mechanistic terms, dispensing with the Thomistic-Aristotelian moral teleology that had long underpinned the notion. This was a radically novel conception, representing a fundamental departure from the classical Christian view. Initially, this led to a new conception of 'natural laws' as observable or deducible causal regularities in the physical world. While this was a fruit of the seventeenth-century 'scientific revolution', inspired in part by the new *Reformation theology of creation, this view of physical nature was gradually extended into more and more areas of human nature as well. The eventual outcome of applying the new scientific method to human nature was a reductionist view of natural morality profoundly at odds with the prior integrated understanding of nature (including human nature) as saturated with moral purpose and revelatory of divine intentions. The challenge to the classical Christian view reached a new peak in David *Hume, who argued that it is impossible to derive an evaluative proposition from a descriptive one – an 'ought' from an 'is'. Such an attempted derivation later came to be termed 'the naturalistic fallacy', because, so it was argued, 'nature' itself was incapable of embodying or conveying moral obligations.

The course of ethical theory since Hume may be construed as a continuing struggle to make sense of the relationship between the 'is' and the 'ought' which Hume had attempted to sever, and the efforts of *Kant and *Hegel were of particular importance in this regard. Kant sought to found a universally valid ethic of obligation (often termed a deontological ethic) on autonomous practical reason alone, rejecting the idea that 'nature', or the empirical world generally, could yield any moral duty. Hegel, Kant's most searching critic, attempted to reconnect morality with human experience, but he did so not by invoking the earlier biblical notion of nature as creation, but rather by seeking to ground morality in history, thus generating a powerful historicist conception of ethics.

The nineteenth century witnessed a wide variety of responses to the impact of rationalist and historicist ethics. Neo-Kantianism sought to revive the flagging Kantian legacy, giving rise to a reformulation of the Humean bifurcation between 'is' and 'ought' as one between 'fact' and 'value'. Mediated by *Weber and *Durkheim, among others, this distinction came to exercise a massively powerful hold over the emerging social sciences of the late nineteenth and early twentieth centuries. It lay behind the eventual dominance of *positivist methodologies whose influence is still evident wherever contemporary social scientists assert that the conclusions of their research are 'value-free', untainted by moral evaluation or personal commitment. Other scientifically oriented theories of ethics emerged alongside positivism, including utilitarianism and social Darwinism. These schools made renewed attempts to derive an 'ought' from an 'is', though they now conceived that which 'is' in positivist fashion, as explicable in terms of the methods of the natural sciences. *Marxism (not addressed here) generated quite another variant of 'scientific' ethics. In the first half of the twentieth century, other schools, such as *existentialism (which placed the 'authenticity' of the moral agent at the centre of ethics) and emotivism (which claimed that evaluative propositions were nothing but expressions of emotion carrying no empirical or cognitive content), added further to the mix.

These modernist ethical theories collectively posed major questions to the public credibility of traditional Christian ethics. An even more fundamental challenge had already been launched in the late nineteenth century by *Nietzsche. By pushing the logic of historicism to an extreme conclusion, he claimed not only that it was impossible to know reliably whether moral claims were universally valid, but also that the very pretension to make claims of universal validity was itself an inherently oppressive move, necessarily doing violence to those who were to be subjected to such supposedly universal principles. This sweeping Nietzschean critique was the driving force behind much late twentieth-century deconstructionism, whose stock-in-trade was the relentless attempt to expose widely endorsed and supposedly universal ethical principles such as liberty, justice, toleration, democracy and rights as mere instruments of political domination and exclusion.

Christian responses

Christian ethicists have attempted in various ways to come to terms with and respond to the successive waves of ethical theorizing thrown up by secular modernity and postmodernity. Some Christian theologians and philosophers have responded in what has been thought to be accommodationist fashion, incorporating one or other school of modern ethical theory into a supposedly Christian framework. Yet while charges of accommodation continue to be levelled today, it is noteworthy that increasing numbers of Christian ethicists display a concern to stand in continuity with biblical and traditional modes of thought. For some, this concern has come to expression primarily in their attempt to reassert the radical distinctiveness of Christian ethics over against, and in judgment upon, modern secularist conceptions (e.g. the radically Christocentric ethics of *Barth, *Yoder, *Hauerwas). Others, in more reconstructive mode, have devoted their energies essentially to reviving and restating the core insights of the classical Christian ethical tradition (e.g. the variegated contributions of *Bonhoeffer, *Ramsey, *Thielicke, Finnis, *O'Donovan, the later *MacIntyre).

Still others have construed their contributions principally as a critical engagement with prevailing schools of secular ethics in order to reformulate core biblical and theological concerns within the terms of prevailing discourse, while also attempting to address its deficiencies. Many have done so principally in dialogue with one or more *modern* intellectual currents (e.g. Fletcher, *Niebuhr, *Gutiérrez, *Moltmann, *Taylor). These encounters have been evaluated very differently. Some have evoked renewed charges of accommodation (e.g. against Fletcher's now largely discredited 'situation ethics'). Others have earned admiration in some quarters for the powerful critiques and constructive proposals issuing from such encounters (e.g. Taylor's critical exposure of the sources of the modern 'self').

More recently, however, a growing number of Christian ethicists have claimed to find *postmodern* currents more conducive to constructive dialogue. Commentators have certainly differed sharply over whether the Nietzschean school might, after all, turn out to provide resources for the cause of a reconstituted postmodern, post-secular Christian ethics. But some 'Christian postmodernists', often drawing also on phenomenology, have discerned particular significance in the 'ethical turn' in postmodern philosophy, its renewed appreciation of the ethical claims of personhood, and its repudiation of all forms of violence (see e.g. the contrasting appropriations of Derrideans such as Caputo, and the '*Radical Orthodoxy' of Milbank).

It may seem remarkable that there should have been a notable revival of the classical Christian theory of natural law in such seemingly inauspicious circumstances, although defenders of natural law see this as a predictable rediscovery of a common, enduring human nature out of the cacophony of contemporary ethics. Such a revival has been witnessed not only in orthodox Roman Catholic circles (e.g. Finnis, George), but also in some sections of evangelical Protestantism (e.g. Budziszewski). One of the many challenges such a movement faces is, in the first instance, to persuade other Christians that some version of 'ethical naturalism' (the view that created nature discloses moral truths) is at all credible in a 'post-metaphysical' and 'postmodern' intellectual climate.

By contrast, the contemporary school known as narrative ethics (see *Narrative theology) is critical of what it sees as the longstanding tendency within Christian ethics to formulate objective general principles of morality in a deductive fashion (whether from Scripture or from practical reasoning). They claim that much modern Christian ethics has unwittingly absorbed a Kantian preference for abstract rational principles and neglected the historical character of Scripture itself. In rejecting modernist ethics, narrativists identify themselves as 'postliberal' and, to some degree, 'postmodern'. They propose instead that Christian ethics is the practice of a faithful ecclesial community, and that Christians come to discern ethical principles only by committed engagement in such a community and by embodying its distinctive gospel virtues (i.e. by 'living its story'). Most narrativists acknowledge, however, that an ecclesial community can only be 'faithful' insofar as it acknowledges the authority of *Scripture (and tradition). Yet, seeking to honour a core insight of historicism, they insist that that the process of ethical discernment does not involve the rational apprehension of abstract and unchanging universal principles (whether located in Scripture or nature) by the individual mind. Rather, it involves the participatory exploration of the contemporary shape of discipleship within a believing and worshipping community. The future capacity of Christian ethics both to remain faithful to its own authoritative sources and to speak authentically and relevantly to contemporary culture may, in part, depend on whether these two creative strands of ethical reflection can adequately inform and complement each other.

Christian ethics facing the twenty-first century

As Christian ethics enters an already turbulent twenty-first century, it confronts a series of momentous challenges, many inherited from the twentieth, but bringing with them newly perplexing dilemmas and, more often than not, global dimensions.

Violence, war and peace

The experience of two devastating world wars in which tens of millions lost their lives in conflicts fought between supposedly 'Christian' nations could not but impose a posture of chastened humility upon Christian ethicists in the post-war period. A revived classical 'just war' theory, intended to restrain nationalist and imperialist militarism, then found itself confronting the awesome dilemmas of an escalating Cold War arms race. This race now threatens to gather renewed pace as a revived and aggressive Russian nationalism confronts an America conscious of itself as but declining sole superpower in a dangerous world with weak international institutions, nervous to protect its own political and economic interests, and possessed of military bases all over the globe. The outbreak of terrible regional wars and civil conflicts since 1989, and, of course, the scourge of terrorism since 9/11, have forced yet further rethinking of the ethics of war, peace-building and reconciliation in a persistently and perplexingly violent age. In these circumstances, Christian ethics must think far beyond the traditional 'pacifism vs. just war' debate to envisage the shape of a stable global order in which international power is effectively and collaboratively put to the service of justice and *peace.

Political authority, democracy and human rights

The traumatic experiences of political authoritarianism and totalitarianism in mid-twentieth-century Europe were deeply formative on Christian political ethicists. Many proposed that 'ethics after Auschwitz' must strive for a radically deepened sensitivity to the reality of enormous human evil. Later, *liberationist ethicists, first in Latin America and then in other regions of the Majority World, argued that the 'idealist' ethics of the Christian West had to be brought down to the level of the concrete struggles against oppression in those contexts. Liberationist ethics, informed initially (and problematically) by Marxist social analysis and later by post-colonial theorizing, in time spawned novel regional expressions, especially in African and Asian countries suffering under authoritarian regimes. Yet the widespread failures of many post-independence Majority World states – their endemic corruption, their institutional dysfunctionality, their persistent violations of *human rights – have chastened earlier liberationist optimism and pressed the question of whether there are not vital cultural and perhaps even religious preconditions necessary for the realization of a stable and just constitutional democracy. Given the potentially huge influence of a rapidly expanding Christian presence in many Majority World states, Christian political ethics is called to forge a credible notion of constitutional representative government, which firmly resists authoritarianism in any form, but is more than a mere transposition of Western models.

Globalization and ecology

The multi-faceted phenomenon of late-twentieth-century *globalization has evoked a revival of Christian economic ethics – from some quarters in defence of the supposed blessings of global *capitalism, from others, against its widely perceived deformations. The seemingly uncontainable power of markets apparently dominated by transnational corporations and international finance (albeit shaken by the 2008 banking crisis), and the growth of abject yet avoidable *poverty in the Majority World – as well as in pockets of the Western world – have demanded new responses to the question of how to fashion global economic relations in accordance with an authentically Christian conception of economic justice. The near-universal scientific consensus on global warming, and mounting evidence of other kinds of irreversible environmental degradation, have produced a flourishing body of original Christian environmental thought (see *Ecology), yet one which has yet to bring about the far-reaching lifestyle changes that would be required if such catastrophic outcomes are to be averted.

Science, technology and the human person

These military, economic and environmental challenges are leading instances of persistent ethical dilemmas thrown up, at least partly, by the exponential advance of science and technology since the last century. Developments in vanguard disciplines such as biology, medicine, information technology (IT) and nanotechnology have continued to thrust novel and highly complex ethical dilemmas upon the attention of Christian ethicists. The possibilities opened up by stem-cell research and reproductive technologies, for example, are demanding ever more profound reflection on the relation between personhood and embodiment. And mounting evidence that the unprecedented advances in IT may actually be reshaping human relationships, often in damaging ways – for example, by corroding the internal life of families – deserves greater attention from Christian ethics than it has received (see *Science and theology).

Family, gender and sexuality
As if the foregoing external pressures were not enough for *families to cope with, the precipitous internal decay of this most vital social institution seems to continue unabated. On the one hand, Christian ethicists (at least in the West) were, by and large, favourably disposed towards the emancipation of women in the second half of the last century. This discovery of the concrete social implications of the biblical principle of gender equality was widely (though by no means uniformly) seen as a major advance in Christian ethics. Yet the troubling questions inevitably posed thereby to the expectations of marital and family relationships (e.g. the nature of parental authority, the meaning of 'femininity' and 'masculinity'), and the implications of changed family structures for wider society (e.g. the sharp decline in the pool of available volunteers and carers as women entered paid employment), threw down far-reaching challenges which Christian ethicists have been slow to take up. The task here is to think beyond a mere reiteration of narrowly modernist views of 'equality' and postmodernist deconstructions of '*gender', in order to reprise a profoundly biblical understanding of 'family' and 'marriage' for a rapidly changing social landscape. Such an understanding, coupled with a similarly biblical conception of 'friendship', should also be the deeper starting point for an adequate ethical view of homosexual orientation, and indeed of *sexuality in general.

Pluralism

The simultaneous advance of secularization and the growth of cultural and religious pluralism in many historically 'Christian' cultures, and the continued existence of pluralism in other *cultures, continue to pose the dilemma of how Christian ethics might speak with both confidence and sensitivity in such seemingly inhospitable contexts. On the one hand, some Christians in 'post-*Christendom' contexts still need to come to terms with their loss of inherited privilege and begin to reckon with, and make the best of, their new status as one minority among many. On the other, others in such contexts need to eschew post-Christendom breast-beating and learn to speak unapologetically with a Christian voice in the public sphere, resisting the newly assertive secularist campaign to privatize religious faith. In other contexts, the dilemmas of Christian public witness in religiously plural societies vary very widely depending on the size and strength of the Christian minority and the attitudes towards it of rival religious groups, which can range from benign indifference to outright hostility. In this as in all ethical challenges facing the twenty-first-century church, serious, respectful and biblically inspired national and global dialogues within the community of faith will be an essential precondition of effective Christian ethical witness beyond it.

Bibliography

D. Atkinson and D. Field (eds.), *New Dictionary of Christian Ethics and Pastoral Theology* (Leicester, 1995); M. Banner, *Christian Ethics and Contemporary Moral Problems* (Cambridge, 1999); N. Biggar, *Behaving in Public: How to Do Christian Ethics* (Grand Rapids, 2011); J. P. Burnside, *God, Justice and Society: Aspects of Law and Legality in the Bible* (New York, 2011); A. J. B. Cameron, *Joined-Up Life: A Christian Account of How Ethics Works* (Nottingham, 2011); R. Gill (ed.), *The Cambridge Companion to Christian Ethics*, 2nd edn (Cambridge, 2002); S. Hauerwas and S. Wells (eds.), *The Blackwell Companion to Christian Ethics* (Malden, Oxford and Carlton, 2004); G. Meilaender and W. Werpehowski (eds.), *The Oxford Handbook of Theological Ethics* (Oxford, 2005); O. O'Donovan, *Resurrection and Moral Order: An Outline for Evangelical Ethics* (Leicester and Grand Rapids, ^{2}1994); G. H. Stassen and D. P. Gushee, *Kingdom Ethics: Following Jesus in Contemporary Context* (Downers Grove, 2003).

J. P. CHAPLIN

ETHIOPIAN ORTHODOX THEOLOGY

The principal classical texts currently recognized, in addition to the Scriptures (the canon of which is considerably larger than that of most other churches, including such works as the *Shepherd of Hermas*), as sources for the theology of the Ethiopian Orthodox Church are the Ethiopic Liturgy (pre-anaphora with fourteen anaphoras) and the work *Haymanotä abäw* ('The Faith of the Fathers', a collection of excerpts on the *Trinity and *Christology).

The Ethiopian Orthodox Church is heir to a rich theological tradition which cannot be described briefly. A full account would need to note what is more central to the tradition, and what is more peripheral; it would describe the historical doctrinal disputes with other churches, and within the Ethiopian Orthodox Church itself, which led to the production of theological literature; it would review the actual shifts which have taken place in the mainline Ethiopian Orthodox Church tradition; and it would portray the close integration of belief and practice in the daily life of the faithful, who now number at least 40 million. This tradition has given rise to certain distinctive practices, including the observance of the Sabbath as well as Sunday as holy days, and the imposition of dietary restrictions which resemble those of Judaism.

The *creeds accepted by the Ethiopian Orthodox Church are those contained in the Ethiopic Liturgy, namely the 'Creed of the Apostles' (not the Western 'Apostles' Creed'), and the Niceno-Constantinopolitan creed (without the *filioque* clause).

A framework which is commonly used for expositions of Ethiopian Orthodox theology is that of the 'five pillars of mystery', namely the doctrines of the Trinity, the incarnation, baptism, the Eucharist and the resurrection of the dead. Not infrequently, texts of the 'five pillars' are preceded by accounts of creation, and Ethiopian preaching of the gospel often follows this pattern: 'Adam was created, then fell, and Christ came to set him free.'

Modern Ethiopian theological state-ments also commonly contain an account of the 'seven sacraments' – baptism, post-baptismal anointing, Eucharist, repentance, orders, marriage, unction – but such systematization is less evident in the classical texts, and may have arisen in response to Roman Catholic teaching.

Further study of specific Ethiopian theological positions must take account of the actual language in which these are expressed. A bald statement such as that the Ethiopian Orthodox Church 'teaches transubstantiation' or 'honours icons' is misleading, as such ideas are differently conceived in Ethiopia, or at least have sets of associations different from those of Western theology.

The principal issue dividing the Ethiopian Orthodox Church from most other churches has been Christological, namely that it does not accept the *Chalcedonian Definition, and specifically rejects the phrase 'in two natures'. The Ethiopian position has been termed '*monophysite' or 'non-Chalcedonian', but the preferred description is 'unified' (*Tweahedo*), a word which forms part of the church's official title.

See also: EASTERN ORTHODOX THEOLOGY; ORIENTAL ORTHODOX THEOLOGY.

Bibliography

J. Bank, *An Annotated and Classified Bibliography of English Literature Pertaining to the Ethiopian Orthodox Church* (Metuden, 1984); C. Chaillot, *The Ethiopian Orthodox Twahedo Church Tradition* (Paris, 2002); D. Crummey, *Priests and Politicians* (Oxford, 1972); M. Daoud (tr.), *The Liturgy of the Ethiopian Church* (Addis Ababa, 1954); S. H. Sellassie (ed.), *The Church of Ethiopia: A Panorama of History and Spiritual Life* (Addis Ababa, 1970); E. Ullendorff, *The Ethiopians: An Introduction to Country and People* (London, ³1973).

R. W. COWLEY

EUCHARIST

Eucharist, or 'thanksgiving', is the most popular name given to the central sacramental rite of Christians. But the rite has other names which emphasize different aspects of the service, such as the Lord's Supper, Holy Communion, the Mass, the Breaking of Bread, the Holy Mysteries, the Qorbana, and so forth. The earliest record we have of this rite is Paul's injunction to follow the example and command of the Lord at the Last Supper with his disciples, to take bread and wine and eat and drink together as a memorial, or *anamnesis* of the Lord's death and rising again (1 Cor. 11:23–26)

Eucharist

(see *Salvation). This was following the example of Jesus, who on the night of his arrest shared a ritual meal with his disciples.

Eucharist and Passover

According to the Synoptic Gospels, the Last Supper was a Passover meal; John's Gospel suggests that it was a short time before the Passover. Passover imagery is evident in the way the Eucharist has developed, and thus provided a singular interpretation of the sufferings and death of *Jesus as the Lamb of God. Paul declares that every time believers break the bread and take the cup, they proclaim publicly the death of the Lord, until he comes (1 Cor. 11:26). John's Gospel suggests that the meal was before the Passover, and the meal led into the foot washing, followed by the farewell discourses. But for John's Gospel too the Last Supper is full of Passover imagery.

Passover was, and is, a family festival celebrated annually in every pious Jewish home. For the disciples gathered as Jesus' family in the upper room it must have been in paradoxical fashion a festive occasion and a ritual so familiar to the disciples that they must have found security in the midst of stress as they heard the familiar words and took part in the well-remembered actions of Passover, so rich with associations, and speaking so powerfully of the things of God.

Jesus must have startled and disconcerted his disciples by giving the Passover a new meaning and a quite unexpected and puzzling significance. When he performed the traditional ritual of taking unleavened bread – food for a journey – he said, 'This is my body which is for (or broken for) you.' And when he took the cup he said, 'This is my blood of the new covenant which is poured out for many.' In doing and saying these things, Jesus was linking together in the strongest and most dramatic of ways what happens at the Supper and what was to happen on the *cross the next day. The two events interpreted one another, and remain indissolubly linked in the Supper. The foot washing in John's Gospel is not only an example to the disciples of how they should behave; it also evokes the OT image of the Suffering Servant who gives himself for his people.

The meals that Jesus shared with his disciples after the resurrection also enrich our understanding of the presence of the Lord in the Supper. On the Emmaus Road the Lord opens the Scriptures to the puzzled disciples, and he is 'made known to them when he broke the bread' (Luke 24:35). And he reveals himself to the confused disciples who have returned in doubt and uncertainty to their fishing when he invites them to share with him in a fish breakfast beside the lake (John 21:1–14).

The fellowship of the table

Jesus' willingness to welcome all sorts of people to his table caused scandal at the time. 'How can a holy man feast with all sorts of people, including notorious sinners?' they asked (Luke 15:2). And in the early church where the breaking of bread was the regular weekly worship, from the beginning there was a strict discipline, excluding from the table evildoers, including, perhaps, many whom Jesus would have welcomed (1 Cor. 11:27–34). But causing scandal within the *fellowship was a grievous offence, and one Christian going hungry while others guzzled at the Lord's table was a serious offence which caused scandal both within the congregation and outside.

The hospitality at the Lord's table did not continue in the early church, and before long disciplinary procedures – later called 'the fencing of the table' – were instituted in most denominations. And it was not only notorious sinners who were excluded and denied hospitality, but believers of other traditions and denominations who were not allowed to share in communion. This refusal of hospitality continues today, and what is often declared to be a festival of reconciliation or a 'converting ordinance' is often an occasion of painful exclusion. And this denial of hospitality continues even when there is a notable convergence in understanding the theology of the Eucharist.

The early church

There is evidence to suggest that in the early church the Eucharist was a major element in the weekly *agape*, or love-feast, when the congregation gathered for a meal, for a celebration of the Eucharist and to hear the word expounded. Fairly early on, the agape meal and the Eucharist became separated, and from the second century we have a few rather incomplete orders of worship which indicate how Christian congregations celebrated the Eucharist. In some situations Jewish Christians found it very hard to share in the Lord's Supper with Gentile Christians. Some said it did not matter if there were separate celebrations for Jews and Gentiles. But Paul thought otherwise. For him the universality of the gospel and the work of Christ in tearing down barriers among people must be displayed in celebrations of the Lord's Supper at which there was no discrimination, no recognition or sanctioning of the age-old suspicion and hostility between Jew and Gentile. Paul withstood Peter to his face because he had equivocated on this vital issue (Gal. 2:11–16). And very similar issues have been wrestled with in the churches in modern time, in apartheid South Africa or in caste-dominated India, for example.

About AD 110, the Proconsul in Asia Minor reported to the Emperor Trajan on the strange practice of the Christians, who met together for a meal each week. The early second-century *Didache* gives an account of the weekly meal with breaking of the bread and taking of the cup with thanks, and after the meal a magnificent prayer of thanksgiving. Justin Martyr, who was converted to Christianity about 150, gives two accounts of the Lord's Supper in his *First Apology*. In the first, a baptism is followed by a Eucharist, including prayers of intercession and the 'kiss of peace'. In the second service, there is reading of 'the records of the apostles or writings of the prophets', followed by a homily. Hippolytus's *The Apostolic Tradition* was probably written in the early third century, and it contains the earliest text of a eucharistic prayer. It comes from a time before Eastern and Western liturgical traditions began to diverge significantly, and it has been amazingly influential in a wide range of modern liturgical revisions.

During the Middle Ages the *liturgies of the Eastern and the Western churches diverged significantly. For the Eastern churches the heart of the liturgy was the *epiclesis,* or invocation of the Holy Spirit to bless the bread and the wine and be present with the people of God. In a typical Orthodox Church the priest celebrates the Eucharist behind a screen, or *iconostasis,* with pictures of the saints. The priest's voice can be heard, but the actions cannot be seen by the people. In the Western church the priest stood at the altar with his back to the people, and the rite was held to transform *ex opere operato* the elements of bread and wine into the body and the blood of the Lord. The Lord was present in the elements, and continued to be present in the church through the reserved *sacrament. The faithful participated primarily through their presence, and while they were expected to be present at Mass frequently, they received the sacrament – in one 'kind' only – on infrequent occasions. There was an increasing tendency to concentrate attention on the elements of bread and wine rather than the rite as a whole, and to narrow down the understanding of Christ's presence in the bread and wine. This went with an underplaying of Christ's role as the host and master of the feast; his presence according to his promise whenever two or three are gathered in his name; his presence in the word; his presence in his body, the church; and his presence in the needy neighbour.

The Reformation

The Reformation came as a corrective to what was denounced as 'the idolatry of the Mass'. Like most correctives, it perhaps went too far, so that many Protestants tended to see the Lord's Supper as no more than a commemoration, to deny the real presence, and to refuse to see any sacrificial or eschatological connotations whatsoever. Sometimes Protestant church leaders found strong resistance from their people to many desirable changes, such as frequent Communion. *Luther taught a theology of 'consubstantiation', a theory that the presence of Christ was 'in, with, and under' the bread and the wine, as against the Roman Catholic assumption that in the sacrament the bread and the wine become the very body and blood of Christ. *Zwingli taught that the Lord's Supper was no more than a memorial meal. The Calvinists taught that in the Lord's Supper believers are lifted up to share something of the life of the *kingdom, and in particular the heavenly banquet (see *Reformed theology).

Eucharistic convergence

The twentieth century was a time of remarkable ecumenical convergence in eucharistic theology and practice, in almost all branches of the Christian church. It started with scholarly theological and historical work, which found its way into the renewal of eucharistic practice in one denomination after another. Eastern Orthodoxy contributed scholarly work from theologians such as John *Zizioulas and Alexander Schmemann, but there was little change or experiment in liturgy, and a fairly complacent belief that the Orthodox liturgy needed no improvement or revision. The Second *Vatican Council of the Roman Catholic Church authorized and encouraged the development of a fresh vernacular Mass which was popular all around the globe, but was denounced by conservatives as 'a Protestant liturgy'. Altars were moved from the east wall of churches so that the faithful could gather around, and the priest faced the congregation, who were encouraged to participate in all sorts of ways which had been unthinkable a generation before. Fresh and exhilarating liturgies of the Eucharist were produced, most notably perhaps the *Book of Common Worship* of the recently united Church of South India. The World Council of Churches Faith and Order Commission produced in 1982 a remarkable 'convergence document', *Baptism, Eucharist and Ministry*, which demonstrated a remarkable agreement between the major churches on the understanding and celebration of the Eucharist. It is not unfair to suggest that this generation is experiencing a major renewal in eucharistic faith and practice in most of the major Christian denominations.

See also: WORSHIP.

Bibliography

P. F. Bradshaw (ed.), *The New SCM Dictionary of Liturgy and Worship* (London, 2002); D. Forrester, H. I. H. McDonald and G. Tellini, *Encounter with God* (London, ²1996); R. C. D. Jasper (ed.), *The Eucharist Today: Studies on Series 3* (London, 1974); J. Jeremias, *The Eucharistic Words of Jesus* (London, 1966); A. Schmemann, *The Eucharist* (New York, 1988); B. D. Spinks and I. R. Torrance (eds.), *To Glorify God: Essays on Modern Reformed Liturgy* (Grand Rapids, 1999); M. Thurian, *The Eucharistic Memorial* (London, 1960); idem, *The Mystery of the Eucharist: An Ecumenical Approach* (London, 1981); G. Wainwright, *Eucharist and Eschatology* (London, 1971).

D. B. FORRESTER

EUNOMIANS, see ARIANSIM

EUSEBIUS OF CAESAREA
(*c*. 265–*c*. 339)

Eusebius is chiefly famous for his *Ecclesiastical History* (definitive edition *c*. 325), but theologically for pronouncements upon the *Trinity at the time of the *Arian controversy. He adopted the strains in *Origen's teaching which most leant towards a subordinationism, being imbued, like Origen, with a sense of God's unique self-existence as the author of all things. While insisting that the Son or *Logos existed before all the ages and all times, he nevertheless denied that the Son was coeternal with God, and he associated his generation with the Father's will. The focus of unity between Father and Son rested with a shared glory. Not surprisingly, Eusebius was embarrassed by the *homoousios* formula of Nicaea, probably because it recalled the spectre of Paul of Samosata (see *Adoptionism). The Holy Spirit fared even worse at his hands, being described as a 'third' rank and power and, as Origen said, 'one of the things which have come into existence through the Son'.

Eusebius was radical, but not as radical as Arius himself, though possibly drawn by the fear of Sabellianism (see *Monarchianism) into the circle of Arian influence. Those who were not Arians (but could not be counted among the more moderate opponents of *Athanasius) readily identified with his views.

The other strand of Origenism in Eusebius was his approach to *Christology. He continued the tradition of emphasizing the pre-incarnation *mediatorial function of the Word, but pressed the centrality of the Word in *incarnation even further, so that the human soul was eclipsed altogether. Thus, in some measure he anticipated the developments which led up to *Apollinarianism.

Perhaps Eusebius' greatest influence derived from his role as the apologist of the 'Constantinian revolution'. His theology of the Christian empire and the Christian emperor, correlating them with the kingdom of God and the Logos, laid down the main lines of Byzantine thought for centuries to come, but had less impact on the West.

Bibliography

H. W. Attridge and G. Hata (eds.), *Eusebius, Christianity, and Judaism* (Detroit, 1992); H. A. Drake, *In Praise of Constantine: A Historical Study and New Translation of Eusebius' Tricennial Orations* (Berkeley, 1976); R. M. Grant, *Eusebius as Church Historian* (Oxford, 1980); J. N. D. Kelly, *Early Christian Creeds* (London, ³1972); idem, *Early Christian Doctrines* (London, ⁵1977); C. Luibhéid, *Eusebius of Caesarea and the Arian Crisis* (Dublin,

1981); D. S. Wallace-Hadrill, *Eusebius of Caesarea* (London, 1960).

R. KEARSLEY

EUTYCHES, see MONOPHYSITISM

EVANGELICAL THEOLOGY

Contemporary evangelical theology has deep roots. Some consider that it was primarily shaped in reaction to theological liberalism, and while it is true that this conflict has lent a certain complexion to evangelical theology, its substance is drawn from the heritage of orthodox Christian theological formation. As one of its most prominent advocates, John Stott, insisted, evangelical faith is 'neither an eddy nor a backwater but mainstream Christianity'. In concert with the creeds and councils of the early church, evangelical theology affirms that: the Bible is the truthful revelation of God, and through it the life-giving voice of God speaks; God is a *Trinity of Father, Son and Holy Spirit; God is the almighty Creator and we are his dependent creation; God has entered history *redemptively in the *incarnation of Jesus Christ; Jesus *Christ is fully divine and fully human; the power and judgment of sin is a reality for all humanity; God graciously takes the initiative by *saving us in Jesus Christ and by the Holy Spirit; Jesus Christ is building his church, and the consummation of history will be expressed in his second advent, in the general resurrection, and in final judgment to heaven or hell (see *Eschatology).

Evangelical theology also has strong links with the early medieval church. It draws heavily upon the satisfaction view of the *atonement enunciated by *Anselm of Canterbury and shares the concomitant stress upon the passion of Jesus Christ expressed by no-one more fully than *Bernard of Clairvaux.

Evangelical theology becomes more distinctive, however, in relation to the Protestant Reformation. In 1531 Thomas More referred to the *English Reformers as 'Evaungelicalles', and in Continental Europe the term still widely functions as a synonym for 'Protestant'. Although it would later acquire an even more particular meaning in Britain and America, evangelical theology reflects signature *Reformation emphases on the plenary divine inspiration and supreme authority of *Scripture, on interpreting it as naturally as possible, and on disseminating it in the vernacular. Likewise, it emphasizes a scriptural approach to worship and witness in which *preaching is central. Evangelical theology also draws from the Reformation its commitment to *justification by *grace through *faith, in which acceptance with God is received by trusting his loving self-disclosure and not by any human accomplishment. Against the same background it emphasizes that the *church is composed of all believers who have thus been incorporated by the Holy Spirit, and who have direct personal access to the Father.

The Reformation expressed itself in various institutional structures, and in these many of the diversities of evangelical theology arose. The Reformers and their successors differed on the *sacraments, *liturgy, *predestination, the *millennium, *church government, Christian assurance and the relation of church and *state. Hence evangelicals may be variously *Lutheran, Calvinist (see *Reformed theology), Zwinglian, *Anglican, *Anabaptist, *Baptist or *Arminian in their more detailed convictions, just as their preferred polity may be episcopal, presbyterian, congregational or connexional. Further variations on these diverse approaches were later developed in different forms of *Methodism, Brethrenism and *Pentecostalism. However, these specific ecclesiastical distinctions would be held by most evangelicals today as secondary to the shared convictions listed above. Indeed, the readiness of evangelicals to transcend such distinctions for the sake of common witness and service – to operate 'pan-evangelically' – is one of the defining characteristics of evangelical theology.

A definitive expression of this interconfessional ethos came with the series of evangelical awakenings and revivals which began in the 1730s. Jonathan *Edwards, John and Charles *Wesley, George *Whitefield, Howell Harris, William McCulloch and others led these movements from a variety of denominational and doctrinal backgrounds, but all reaffirmed the theology of the great and received tradition while laying special emphasis on the theology of the *Christian life. The imperative of *conversion was continually to the fore, as was the consciousness of God's love and the *sanctification which accompanied it. No doubt there were differences on the instantaneousness of conversion and the possibility of perfection, but these were usually overridden

Evangelical theology

by a shared impulse to renew the church, evangelize the world and improve social conditions. On these foundations were built the *mission societies of the following century, and the great movements of British evangelical social reform associated with William Wilberforce (anti-slavery), Lord Shaftesbury (factory acts), Hannah More (education) and William Booth and the *Salvation Army (evangelization and care of the poor). Between the 1780s and the 1820s a 'Second Great Awakening' in the United States spurred evangelicals there to a similarly deep concern not only for personal holiness but also for social and national well-being, as exemplified in the *revivalist theology and methods of Charles G. *Finney.

By the mid-nineteenth century evangelicalism was showing hopeful signs of marrying these practical preoccupations with *holiness, evangelism and civic service to serious scholarly endeavour. 1846 saw the formation of the World's Evangelical Alliance, an early expression of modern *ecumenism which attracted several leading academic theologians from Britain, Europe and the United States. From 1875 the Keswick Convention (see *Higher-life theology) coupled influential guidance on 'practical holiness' with teaching from prominent British and overseas expositors. However, evangelical theology was profoundly challenged in the later 1800s by the rise of theological *liberalism. In this climate, evangelicals tended either to seek accommodation with liberals (see *Liberal evangelicalism) or retrench into *pietistic or oppositional ghettos. Key legacies of this retrenchment were the decline in evangelical social concern characterized by David Moberg as the 'Great Reversal', and the development of *fundamentalism in the early twentieth century. Fundamentalism, in particular, tended to combine ecclesiological separatism with forms of *millenarian theology that mediated a typically pessimistic and *quietistic view of political and cultural engagement.

These trends meant that at the start of the twentieth century evangelical theology lacked both internal dynamism and external impact. However, a foretaste of more holistic approaches to come arose in the *Dutch neo-Calvinist school that developed around the scholar and statesman Abraham *Kuyper and the dogmatician Herman *Bavinck. This group affirmed the orthodox tradition while offering a rich theology of the Christian life in all its ramifications – one which engaged keenly with issues and worldviews arising in contemporary *society. Otherwise, much evangelical theological energy in the 1920s and 30s was expended either on intramural debates about the limits of evangelical soundness or on responding to the then-dominant liberal agenda. By the onset of the Second World War, sharper distinctions were being drawn between fundamentalists who advocated clear separation from the any liberal influence, and evangelicals who were prepared to remain within 'mixed' denominations and seminaries, or at least to interact ecumenically and theologically with non-evangelicals. In America many in this latter group came together to form the National Association of Evangelicals (1942), and the cooperative ethos of NAE was evident in the founding of the Evangelical Theological Society in 1949. ETS, in fact, both reflected and facilitated a significant revitalization of American evangelical theology in the post-war period. This revitalization was part of a wider 'neo-evangelical' movement that even more explicitly rejected fundamentalism while seeking to reposition its scholarship in the theological mainstream. As well as espousing a more open ecclesiology, neo-evangelicals characteristically endorsed theologies of *social responsibility which reclaimed the public vision of the previous century. A landmark in this process was Carl F. H. *Henry's book *The Uneasy Conscience of Modern Fundamentalism* (1947), which presented an avowedly biblical case for social involvement distinct from the liberal '*social gospel'. Later, more radical evangelical social theologies would follow from the Mennonites John Howard *Yoder and Ron Sider, while a new generation of Dutch neo-Calvinists, including Herman Dooyeweerd, Gerrit Berkouwer and Hans Rookmaaker, modelled a fresh engagement with contemporary thought and *culture – an engagement continued more recently still in the work of Stanley *Grenz, Kevin Vanhoozer, Nancy Murphy and others.

The 1940s also saw various key institutions founded on both sides of the Atlantic which would contribute significantly to the development of evangelical theology in the next few decades – most notably London Bible College (1943) (now London School of Theology), Tyndale House, Cambridge (1944) and Fuller Seminary in California (1947). Along with Henry, neo-evangelical theology found eloquent advocates in Bernard *Ramm and Donald *Bloesch. Like Ramm and Bloesch, several neo-evangelicals were influenced by Karl *Barth, including the US-based British historical theologian Geoffrey Bromiley, who edited the English translation of Barth's *Church Dogmatics* along with the Edinburgh theologian, T. F. *Torrance. However, another Briton teaching in North America, J. I. *Packer, won support for a relatively more conservative line which was nonetheless distinguished from fundamentalism. Tensions between these two 'left' and 'right' wings of American evangelicalism have continued, not least with respect to the precise terms in which the authority of Scripture is understood. Nonetheless, most American evangelical theologians maintain a commitment to the inerrancy of Scripture (see *Infallibility and inerrancy of the Bible), and this remains a requirement of ETS membership. In 2003 the distinguished ETS members Clark *Pinnock and John Sanders faced censure for advocating a 'free will theism' (see *Open theism) which questioned traditional attributes of God such as omniscience and impassibility, yet both were allowed to retain their membership. Building on the pioneering work of the English evangelical Sir Norman Anderson, Sanders has also been at the forefront of burgeoning evangelical theological reflection on other faiths. While divergence exists here, as in debates about justification in Paul, penal *substitutionary atonement and the nature of hell, evangelical theology is arguably more fertile now than at any time in the past 150 years.

In Britain, fundamentalism and the discourse of inerrancy have always been less prominent than in the USA, and this may explain why the earliest shoots of post-war evangelical theological renewal in Britain were seen in the field of biblical studies, notably through the contributions of F. F. Bruce, Donald Guthrie and I. H. Marshall. Later, James Dunn, N. T. *Wright and Richard Bauckham gained world-class reputations for their work on the historical background to the NT, while Anthony Thiselton and John Goldingay did much to introduce evangelicals to the principles and methods of *hermeneutics. In other fields not directly related to biblical scholarship, evangelical theologians have nonetheless brought sophisticated biblical sensibilities to bear: e.g. Oliver *O'Donovan in *ethics, Robert Jenson in *systematics and Alister McGrath in *historical theology and *apologetics.

Although considerable debate surrounds the extent to which Pentecostalism can be classed as an evangelical movement, in practice the majority of *Pentecostal theologians are aligned with evangelical networks. While earlier expressions of Pentecostal faith often tended towards anti-intellectualism, increased links with historic denominations and mainline evangelical bodies, and ongoing relationships with the resultant charismatic movement, have spawned a vibrant community of Pentecostal scholars, journals and societies. From pioneers like Donald Gee and J. Rodman Williams to younger Pentecostal academics like Vinson Synon and Amos Yong, it is a community set to make an increasingly important contribution to theology in the twenty-first century. The charismatic movement itself, as it has shared the emphasis of Pentecostal theology on the Spirit, and particularly the *gifts of the Spirit, has grown rapidly within the older denominations, and has influenced many evangelical theologians from those communities.

The rise of Pentecostalism and Pentecostal scholarship serve as a salutary reminder that evangelical theology can no longer be defined on Western terms alone. Indeed, the greatest church growth today is in non-white Majority World contexts, much of it Pentecostal and *charismatic. Whereas resources for theological scholarship in these contexts were once scarce, macroeconomic shifts and increased funding from first-world Christian bodies have ensured that a new generation of theologians is emerging from beyond the traditional evangelical axis of Britain, Europe and North America. The pivotal *Lausanne Congress (1974) consolidated neo-evangelical commitment to social action alongside evangelism, but through Sam Escobar, René Padilla and Vinay Samuel it also confirmed the rise of authentic 'global south' perspectives in evangelical theology. Latterly, evangelicals in non-Western contexts have been key shapers of indigenous theological approaches – e.g. the Dalit theology of Tamil Christians in India (see *Indian Christian theology).

Finally, it should be emphasized that evangelical theology is a spiritual theology. The Bible is not only central to the theological enterprise, but it is meditated upon and prayed over in Christian community. Thus the goal of evangelical theological work is not so much to know theology as to know and to glorify God.

Bibliography

D. W. Bebbington, *Evangelicalism in Modern Britain: A History from the 1730s to the 1980s*

(Baker, 1992); A. Besançon Spencer and W. D. Spencer, *The Global God: Mulicultural Evangelical Views of God* (Grand Rapids, 1998); D. G. Bloesch, *The Future of Evangelical Christianity: A Call for Unity Amid Diversity* (New York, 1983); G. A. Boyd and P. R. Eddy (eds.), *Across the Spectrum: Understanding Issues in Evangelical Theology* (Grand Rapids, 2002); D. W. Dayton and R. K. Johnson (eds.), *The Variety of American Evangelicalism* (Downers Grove, 1991); S. J. Grenz, *Renewing the Center: Evangelical Theology in a Post-Theological Era* (Grand Rapids, 2000); C. F. H. Henry (ed.), *The Uneasy Conscience of Modern Fundamentalism* (Grand Rapids, 1947); idem, *Christian Faith and Modern Theology* (New York, 1964); T. Greggs, *New Perspectives for Evangelical Theology: Engaging with God, Scripture and the World* (Abingdon and New York, 2009); T. Larsen and D. J. Treier (eds.), *The Cambridge Companion to Evangelical Theology* (Cambridge, 2007); G. M. Marsden, *Understanding Fundamentalism and Evangelicalism* (Grand Rapids, 1980); G. McDermott (ed.), *The Oxford Handbook of Evangelical Theology* (Oxford, 2010); J. I. Packer, *God Has Spoken: Revelation and the Bible* (London, 1979); B. L. Ramm, *The Evangelical Heritage: A Study in Historical Theology* (Waco, 1973); J. R. W. Stott, *Evangelical Truth: A Plea for Unity* (Leicester, 1999); C. Trueman, T. J. Gray and C. L. Blomberg (eds.), *Solid Ground: 25 Years of Evangelical Theology* (Leicester, 2000); N. T. Wright, *Scripture and the Authority of God* (London, 2005); A. Yong, *The Spirit Poured out on All Flesh: Pentecostalism and the Possibility of Global Theology* (Grand Rapids, 2005).

D. H. K. Hilborn

EVANGELICALISM, POSTCONSERVATIVE

'Postconservative' was first used as a term by Clark H. *Pinnock (1990) and more recently by Kevin J. Vanhoozer (2005) to denote *evangelicals who critically and constructively engage with *postmodern thought and culture, thereby distinguishing themselves from evangelical theologians more at home in *modernity. Gary Dorrien (1998) used the term to describe a diverse collection of evangelicals who see the demise of modernity as theologically advantageous; Roger E. Olson subsequently defined postconservatism more precisely and popularized its usage in a number of books and articles. Not everyone so labelled is happy with the term – Nancey C. Murphy, for example, prefers 'postmodern evangelical'. But 'postconservative' has become the most common term among both adherents and critics.

A harbinger of constructive engagement with postmodern thought and culture was Dave Tomlinson's *The Post-Evangelical* (1995), which sought 'to take as given many of the assumptions of evangelical faith, while at the same time moving beyond its perceived limitations' (p. 7). Tomlinson criticized the dogmatic certainty, rationalism and individualism of the evangelicalism with which he was familiar, and called for a less systematic and more communal form, with a critical *realist *epistemology, an understanding of Scripture as mediating the word of God, and a *spirituality that welcomes imagination, doubt and growth. The book sparked a major debate in Britain, but even many critics believed Tomlinson had identified crucial issues for the future of evangelicalism.

Postconservative evangelical theologians address similar concerns, but do so with greater theological precision and faithfulness to historic *orthodoxy. Central to their theology is their rejection of the *Enlightenment claim that the truth of knowledge requires it to be rationally established on the foundation of facts or experience that cannot in themselves be doubted. There is, they believe, no universal, neutral knowledge. Instead, they embrace a form of postfoundationalism which holds that all knowledge is necessarily perspectival, shaped by narratives within a community and tradition. While engaging a wide range of postmodern thinkers, postconservatives do not accept the relativism of neopragmatists and *deconstructionists. Most are attracted to those postmodern philosophers and linguists for whom it is not truth itself that is relative but our knowledge of it, such as Alasdair McIntyre, Michael *Polanyi, W. V. O. Quine, J. L. Austin and the later Ludwig *Wittgenstein.

As a result, postconservatives reject the scriptural propositionalism and rational *apologetics that dominated evangelical theology in the twentieth century. For them Scripture is not essentially a book whose truth is to be rationally demonstrated and propositions theologically systematized, but the central means to encounter Jesus Christ, and be personally, communally and missionally shaped by that encounter.

*Revelation is thus more transformational in purpose than informational.

The truth of Scripture is conveyed in the form of narratives and imagery such as metaphors that are used by the Holy Spirit to shape faithful imagination and transform hearts and lives. Through indwelling the biblical narrative, persons are enabled both to know and live the truth. Indeed, for N. T. *Wright and especially Vanhoozer, Scripture is essentially dramatic and used by the Holy Spirit to enable the church to participate in the drama of the gospel.

Thus, like *postliberals such as George *Lindbeck, postconservatives are concerned with the ecclesial embodiment of biblical narrative. But unlike postliberals, they locate *truth not only in the intertextual coherence and faithful embodiment of Scripture, but in its fundamental historicity and divine inspiration. Scripture shapes communities truthfully because it corresponds to divine revelation in history.

Because God is known in and through *history, there is no ahistorical *revelation. While the *gospel is *contextualized within every culture, it also exerts transformative influence on culture. As the gospel is lived out over time in a multiplicity of *cultures, the church as a whole grows in its understanding of the fullness of the gospel and its meaning for life.

Postconservatives emphasize relationality and community over the autonomous individualism characteristic of modernity. This relationality is central to their understanding of church, salvation and humanity, and most especially the triune God. While their doctrines of God vary, all critique the classical *theist preoccupation with divine attributes and instead seek to emphasize the personal and relational nature of God, and especially the love of God as revealed in *Jesus Christ.

Theologians often classed as 'postconservative' include Clark H. Pinnock, Stanley J. *Grenz and Kevin J. Vanhoozer. Others include Nancey C. Murphy, Roger E. Olson, John R. Franke, Henry H. Knight III, John Sanders, F. LeRon Shults, Rodney Clapp, N. T. Wright and Lesslie *Newbigin.

Bibliography

Post-evangelicalism: G. Cray, et al., *The Post-Evangelical Debate* (London, 1997); D. Tomlinson, *The Post-Evangelical* (London, 1995).

Postconservative evangelicalism: G. Dorrien, *The Remaking of Evangelical Theology* (Louisville, 1998); M. J. Erickson, *The Evangelical Left: Encountering Postconservative Evangelical Theology* (Grand Rapids, 1997); idem (ed.), *Reclaiming the Center: Confronting Evangelical Accommodation in Postmodern Times* (Wheaton, 2004); J. R. Franke, *The Character of Theology: A Postconservative Evangelical Approach* (Grand Rapids, 2005); S. J. Grenz and J. R. Franke, *Beyond Foundationalism: Shaping Theology in a Postmodern Context* (Louisville, 2001); S. J. Grenz, *Revisioning Evangelical Theology* (Downers Grove, 1993); idem, *Renewing the Center* (Grand Rapids, ²2006); H. H. Knight III, *A Future for Truth: Evangelical Theology in a Postmodern World* (Nashville, 1997); R. Middleton and B. J. Walsh, *Truth Is Stranger Than It Used to Be* (Downers Grove, 1995); N. C. Murphy, *Beyond Liberalism & Fundamentalism: How Modern and Postmodern Philosophy Set the Theological Agenda* (Valley Forge, 1996); Lesslie Newbigin, *The Gospel in a Pluralist Society* (Geneva and Grand Rapids, 1989); R. E. Olson, *Reformed and Always Reforming: The Postconservative Approach to Evangelical Theology* (Grand Rapids, 2007); C. H. Pinnock, *Tracking the Maze* (San Francisco and London, 1990); K. J. Vanhoozer, *First Theology: God, Scripture and Hermeneutics* (Downers Grove, 2002); idem, *The Drama of Doctrine: A Canonical Linguistic Approach to Christian Theology* (Louisville, 2007); N. T. Wright, *Scripture and the Authority of God* (London and San Francisco, 2013).

H. H. KNIGHT III

EVANGELISM, THEOLOGY OF

Evangelism takes its shape and form from the *evangel*, the good news, or *gospel. In the NT, the gospel is variously described as the 'good news of Jesus' (Mark 1:1; Acts 8:35; 10:36; 11:20) or 'the good news of the kingdom' (Matt. 4:23; 9:35; 24:14; Luke 4:43; 8:1; 16:16; Acts 8:12). There is therefore a crucial link at the heart of evangelism between the person, work and identity of Christ and the announcement and in-breaking of the *kingdom of God. Kingdom language of course picks up a rich vein of OT history and imagery, running through the Israelite monarchy to God's rule over the creation itself. The OT can be read as

Evangelism, theology of

the story of God's search for someone to whom he can entrust rule over his *creation. This is the primary calling of humanity – to rule over creation in God's name (Gen. 1:28), yet the subsequent entry of sin and evil into the world through human disobedience (see *Fall) renders that prospect fraught with danger. The monarchy, reaching its high point in King David, a 'man after God's own heart' (1 Sam. 13:14) can be seen in the same light. Even David flatters to deceive and yet is promised a king from his offspring (2 Sam. 7) to rule forever. The coming of Jesus, the Son of David (Matt. 1:1; 20:30; 21:9, etc.), proclaiming and demonstrating the kingdom of God, is the culmination of this theme, with the rest of the NT indicating the start of the time when the kingdom is to be preached and lived in the present age, in anticipation of the *eschatological fullness of the reign of God in due time (Acts 1:6–8).

The content of the evangel can therefore be identified as the gospel of the kingdom, which is at the same time the gospel of *Jesus Christ. It is the announcement that *God has again set up his kingdom in the world, that he is its rightful ruler; that God's reign is the ultimate reality towards which all history tends; and that this reign has now broken into human history in a new way in the person of Jesus. To put it another way, as the early Christians would say, 'Jesus is Lord' (Rom. 10:9; 1 Cor. 12:3). Evangelism therefore has a clear Christological focus – it takes its reference from the nature of Christ as God's Son, the second *Adam, who is now seen as Lord of all through the *resurrection (Rom. 1:4) and who could truly be entrusted with power over creation. A high and robust *Christology will lead to confident evangelism; a tentative and diffident Christology will lead away from it. The message of the kingdom of God come in Jesus is gospel because if Jesus is Lord, then he has the final say over human destiny and the whole created order. The future of creation is not in the hands of blind chance or faceless biological processes, but in the trustworthy hands of God's King, the 'friend of sinners'.

This message is also controversial. If Jesus is Lord, then no political despot or system has the last word – neither do disease, hunger or *poverty. The proclamation of the kingdom of God and the lordship of Christ is a direct challenge to *idolatry of various kinds. It has a clearly political edge to it, as the claim of Christ to be Lord means a challenge to ways of human relating that devalue 'those for whom Christ died' (Rom. 14:15; 1 Cor. 8:11), or destroy the creation itself.

In the light of this discussion, evangelism can be described as the proclamation of the rightful and gentle rule of Jesus Christ, and the gracious invitation to bring a person or community's life under that rule, to learn its disciplines, its privileges and culture. It involves the announcement of God's willingness to overlook *sin through the sacrifice of Christ, and to send the *Spirit to indwell and fill the one who believes in Christ and who seeks to live his or her life under God's rule. It also establishes an inextricable link between the proclamation of the gospel of the rule of God in Christ and its demonstration. Jesus' words of invitation pointed out the significance of what was happening in his works of healing, the overcoming of evil and his mastery over creation (Matt. 12:28; Luke 11:20). In these works it was possible to see the reality of the kingdom, not in all its fullness (not everyone in Palestine was healed or raised from the dead), but in part. In the same way, the verbal proclamation of the reign of God today needs to be able to point to evidence of its reality in the present, in lives turned around, bodies and communities healed, creation transformed.

This leads to the central place of the *church in a theology of evangelism. The church is the community called out of the world to live out and proclaim the lordship of Christ over creation. Therefore the church is shaped by its evangelistic task. Rather than beginning with the church as a fixed institution that has a number of roles in the world, one of which happens to be evangelism, the church is to be ordered around its central identity and task: to embody and proclaim the rule of God. This gives a criterion for the order of the church. Whatever aids or contributes to this is to be embraced. Whatever deflects from it is to be questioned. It also helps to relate the ministry of evangelism to other ministries in the church. The role of theology is to test and protect the message: to 'make sure that what gets transmitted by the church's words and deeds is the Good News of what God has done in Christ, rather than some other message' (K. Vanhoozer, p. 73). *Worship, pastoral care and community action are not in competition with evangelism, but in harmony with it, as these are the ways in which the church lives out and demonstrates God's loving rule over and care for the creation in which the church is placed.

Bibliography

W. J. Abraham, *The Logic of Evangelism* (London, 1989); D. J. Bosch, *Transforming Mission: Paradigm Shifts in Theology of Mission* (Maryknoll, 1991); W. Brueggemann, *Biblical Perspectives on Evangelism: Living in a Three-Storied Universe* (Nashville, 1993); M. Green, *Evangelism in the Early Church* (Crowborough, 1984); L. Newbigin, *The Open Secret: An Introduction to the Theology of Mission* (London, 1995); G. Tomlin, *The Provocative Church* (London, 2002); R. E. Webber, *Ancient-Future Evangelism: Making Your Church a Faith-Forming Community* (Grand Rapids, 2003); K. J. Vanhoozer, *The Drama of Doctrine* (Louisville, 2005).

G. TOMLIN

EVIDENTIALISM

Evidentialism is a theory about epistemic justification, or whether believing a given proposition (or set of propositions) is justified. While every proposition is either true or false, there are three different attitudes one could take regarding the truth of that proposition. One may believe the proposition, or deny the proposition. To believe a proposition is to hold that the proposition is true; to deny a proposition is to hold that it is false. But there is a third possibility, and that is to withhold judgment, and neither believe nor deny the proposition. It will be convenient to think of these three different attitudes as 'belief policies'. Epistemic justification is concerned with the degree to which any of these three belief policies is reasonable *from the epistemic point of view*.

'The epistemic point of view' is language used by epistemologists to refer to the natural human interest in acquiring true belief in a responsible way. Epistemic justification, then, is *truth-oriented. The epistemic justification of a person's belief policy depends on the degree to which the basis for that policy makes it likely that the proposition is true. In other words, justification is 'truth-conducive' or 'truth-indicative', though it need not be a guarantee of truth.

As one of many theories of epistemic justification, evidentialism stresses the importance of evidence in determining the degree to which a particular belief policy is justified. Epistemic justification, according to this view, depends entirely on the character of a person's evidence. This account excludes the relevance of such factors as: how the belief happens to be caused, whether there are non-evidential motives a person may have for believing a proposition, and whether a person's belief-forming mechanisms happen to be functioning normally or properly.

There are varieties of evidentialism. They are best distinguished in terms of how each variety answers three central questions. First, what counts as evidence? Second, what is meant by 'a person's evidence'? (Presumably, it means 'evidence possessed by a person'. So the question becomes: What is it for a person to 'have evidence'?) Third, what is it about the evidence that justifies a person's belief policy regarding a particular proposition? This is a question about the relation between evidence and the likelihood that a proposition is true.

Some evidentialists deny that intellectual duties and cognitive virtues have a bearing on the justification of a person's belief policy. But if a theory can be developed showing how the possession of evidence is tied to the fulfilment of intellectual duties or having cognitive virtues, then there is the possibility that an evidentialist account can include these factors.

Critics of evidentialism often complain that evidence cannot be required for epistemic justification, since many beliefs are justified without argument or explicit reasons. But this is mistaken. Evidence should not be confused with argument, and some versions of evidentialism allow that a person may possess evidence in support of his or her belief, without consciously regarding it as evidence per se. Many evidentialists are *foundationalists, who hold that there are justified beliefs whose justification depends on direct acquaintance with evidence, rather than on the basis of an inference from other beliefs. This kind of evidence is made available through direct experiential acquaintance a person has with the object his or her belief is about. In an act of perception, for example, one has 'the evidence of one's senses'. But the evidentialist holds that for something to count as evidence in support of a person's belief, it must be epistemically apt – making it likely, from the person's point of view, that his or her belief is intellectually responsible.

In Christian *apologetics (see P. Hicks, 'Evidentialism', in *New Dictionary of Christian Apologetics*, IVP, 2006), strong or 'classical' evidentialism has been widely rejected by *Reformed epistemologists. While good evidence may be adduced for Christian beliefs, in the end only the work of the Holy Spirit can bring fallen minds to faith.

See also: EPISTEMOLOGY.

Bibliography

J. E. Adler, *Belief's Own Ethics* (Cambridge, MA, 2002); L. BonJour, *The Structure of Empirical Knowledge* (Cambridge, MA, 1985); R. Chisholm, *The Foundations of Knowing* (Minneapolis, 1982); *idem*, *Theory of Knowledge* (Englewood Cliffs, ²1977, ³1989, 2nd edn is best); *idem*, 'Firth and the Ethics of Belief', *Philosophy and Phenomenological Research* 50, 1991, pp. 119–128; R. Feldman, *Epistemology* (Upper Saddle River, 2003); R. Feldman and E. Conee, *Evidentialism* (Oxford and New York, 2004); S. Haack, *Evidence and Inquiry* (Oxford, 1993); P. Moser, *Knowledge and Evidence* (Cambridge, 1989).

R. D. GEIVETT

EVIL

'Evil' refers primarily to our intentional actions that cause undeserved harm or suffering serious enough to be addressed. Although generally we use 'evil' in contrast with 'good', 'evil' particularly can connote the horrendous or unthinkable – the demonic. Thus, for example, although we term murder evil, we use 'evil' emphatically when speaking about especially brutal murders, the systematic rape of women in war, or genocides. Traditionally, evils performed by humans are referred to as *moral evils*: evils for which human agents can be held morally accountable. In a theological context, moral evils, while committed against our neighbour, are also sins against God.

Evil refers not only to human actions but also to human dispositions to act in ways that cause harm or fail to meet certain standards. Thus, dispositions to lie, cheat, steal or covet are evils (vices) that may indicate a person's character. Classical ethics was more concerned with these dispositions than the actions themselves, since our actions flow from our character.

'Evil' can also refer to pain, suffering and dysfunction, and derivatively to things like diseases and natural disasters that cause these. This kind of evil, for which humans are not morally responsible, is termed *natural* or *physical evil*. However, not all (e.g. Barth) see the shadowsides of creation – pain, suffering, dysfunction, death – as evil, since as part of creation they participate in creation's goodness.

Origin and nature of evil

If *God is the ultimate source of everything, does evil come from God? Some, such as *Gnostics and Manichees (see *Dualism), viewed good and evil dualistically as independent powers eternally in combat. However, the Christian theological tradition is more greatly influenced by Plotinus and Neo-*Platonism. Just as matter is what remains when the emanation of the One ends, so evil is what remains when the Good runs out. Evil, having no independent existence, is a privation, yet none the less real for that. Like matter, evil is qualityless, mere potency; yet in having a nature it exists outside of and other than Being. Although evil cannot produce because production is good, it has effects. Evil as turning from the Good characterizes the individual soul whose descent into matter weakens it for subsequent enslavement, which is sin.

This view influenced *Augustine, for whom evil has its origin neither in God (for all God makes is good; *Confessions*, VII, 5, 12) nor in randomness, but is caused wilfully by created beings. Consonant with Neo-Platonism, evil is not a substance but a privation of the good, a deficiency or imperfection in the will, originating in the mind, that occurs when we intentionally turn from the Good. Though a privation, evil is real; darkness is the privation of light but nonetheless is real. Evil is found not primarily in the act itself, but in the intention. In his later works, Augustine insists that evil persists in us, making it impossible for sinners to comprehend divine truths. God's grace given in illumination of the mind is necessary to assist the sin-damaged will. Seven centuries later *Abelard echoes Augustine when he writes that sin, defined negatively, is non-being; it rests not in the act, but in *consenting* to not do what we truly believe God desires that we ought to do (*Ethics* III).

The view of evil as privation is more fully developed in the theology of *Barth, who identifies evil with nothingness (*das Nichtige*). Influenced by *Heidegger and Sartre, Barth sees nothingness as an alien power, a real enemy, that has its existence in the 'No' or rejection of God. For Barth nothingness has its own being in being not-willed by God. *Das Nichtige* is uncreated, but arises when God separates his creation from chaos. A menacing power, *das Nichtige* is a continuing threat that, apart from God's sustaining providence, would pull creation into non-being. *Das Nichtige* reveals itself as evil, not merely by posing the threat of non-being, but in opposing and resisting God and his grace. Sin occurs when the created gives itself up to that which opposes God.

Many (e.g. Boyd) attribute the source of evil to a being (Satan) who, as an external, aggressive, powerful adversary of God, seeks to pervert those who would do good, and to destroy the good that is done. Though as created by God Satan is good, God's gift of freedom allowed Satan to depart from the good of divine obedience and become an instigator of evil. Along with the demons over which he rules, Satan, the 'prince' (*archon*) of this age, has seized creation and with his demonic powers wars with God to maintain his authority. Natural evils, including sickness and suffering, can be caused by the demonic and are contrary to God's design. Although on the *cross Christ defeated the satanic forces, Satan remains, if not in control of the earth, powerfully active for evil until his promised final defeat.

Evil and the human predicament

The world religions affirm that a world with evil contravenes the ideal state. Buddhists view life as being evil (*dukha*: unsatisfactory, characterized by suffering found in birth, old age, sickness and death), rooted in ignorance, cravings and hatreds. Evils arise in dependent origination from prior conditions, as we cling to the permanence of things and of self when in reality nothing is permanent. The goal of life is to eliminate suffering by identifying its causes in us and by taking appropriate action to eliminate them in accord with the Eight-Fold Path of moral action and right meditation.

For Christians, evil was not part of the original state, but entered through wilful disobedience of God's commands. Christians understand evil not so much as suffering but as *sin (though sin results in suffering). Its origin lies not in creation, which the Creator viewed as good, but in the wills of conscious agents who, in morally culpable ways, did and continue both to do wrong and to develop non-virtuous dispositions. Paul interprets the sin of the first human as creating a predisposition in his descendants to do evil (original sin), a predisposition that weakens our ability to resist sinning. As a result of our sin, evil also affects the institutions that were intended for good: sexuality and child-bearing, work and agriculture, and family relationships. Thus, Christianity responds to the question, why we do evil by affirming that, contrary to a common view of humans, we have a disposition to do evil (classically, we have a sinful nature) and need divine *grace not to sin.

Why do humans do horrendous evils?

Burned into the twenty-first-century conscience is the question of how humans can be the intentional and responsible source of so much cruelty to other persons or to creation. The genocides of the twentieth century (see *Holocaust), continuing into this century, make vivid human diabolicalness. While some argue that horrendous evils require a group mentality or a pathological disposition, others suggest it can arise from ordinary people. The psychologist Waller suggests a model that invokes diverse factors such as an ancestral shadow, cultural belief systems and moral disengagement from the victims, a culture of cruelty, and an attitude of dehumanization toward or blaming the victim, to explain (not justify) how ordinary people can do extraordinary evil.

Addressing evil

All religions affirm that evil can be overcome. The paths to overcoming evil differ among the various religions. Whereas South Asian religions emphasize liberation from the evil of the human predicament by ethical action and meditation, for Christians Christ's *atonement addresses evil in humans and in the world. Different theories of atonement invoke diverse metaphors or paradigms – ransom, conquest, penal substitution, satisfaction, healing – that indicate the power of God to resolve the human sinful condition. Salvation requires a recognition of and repentance of our own evils and an acceptance of the incarnational suffering of Christ on our behalf.

Evil and the existence of God

The theodicist tradition

One major issue facing Christian theism concerns how evil can be compatible with the existence and nature of God. The critical philosophical/theological challenge comes in two forms, deductive and inductive. The *deductive* argument from evil or suffering claims incompatibility among the following propositions: God exists; God has the properties of omnipotence (God can do that which is logically self-consistent), omniscience (God knows anything that can be known, including the future) and omnibenevolence (God is virtuous and only does good actions); evil exists, and a good being eliminates evil as far as it can. The critic contends that these propositions entail that God would eliminate all pain and suffering in the world, which contradicts the contention that evil or suffering exists. Although some have sought to defuse the problem by qualifying God's properties (e.g. God is limited in power, knowledge or goodness), such solutions suffice only if the limitations were so significant that they would in turn jeopardize any significant conception of God. Others have constructed a (free will) *defence* to show that the atheologian cannot generate such a contradiction.

According to the *inductive* argument from evil, it is improbable that God exists, given the quantity and quality of evil and suffering in the world. The presence of seemingly divinely preventable, horrendous evils, such as the Asian tsunami or the Jewish, Cambodian or Rwandan genocides, renders God's existence unlikely.

Attempts to provide morally sufficient reasons for the existence of evil are termed *theodicies* (defences of God's justice). Theodicies for *moral evils* generally invoke the greater good of human freedom. God bestows on agents the freedom necessary for agents to be able to do good acts or be virtuous at all. Given the freedom to choose between good and evil, humans are morally responsible for moral evils. God permits our doing evil, but does not contribute to or desire the evil actions we perform.

Theodicies for the *natural evils* are more diverse. Both the OT and NT suggest that some (though not all) pain and suffering result from punishment for sin. Those in the so-called *Irenaean tradition suggest that God permits pain and suffering to build our characters: much as resistance builds muscles, evil is soul-building. The fact that death can occur without opportunity for life-changes or that the suffering proves to be too much for the person suggests that this explanation is at best partial. A third suggestion is that natural evils result from natural laws affecting psychophysical beings. Though God at times intervenes in nature, constant divine intervention in nature to prevent all evils would conflict with the human freedom needed for rational decision-making and moral action. God is the Creator of our creaturely nature and therefore of our finitude (our subjection to natural laws). Since laws are a necessary feature of any creation, and since the creation results in good, God is justified in creating finite beings subject to the vicissitudes of nature. The worry with this theodicy is that it tends toward *deism in limiting God's significant action in nature. Although each theodicy may provide a partial sufficient reason for evil, none is totally sufficient by itself.

Some Christians argue that since every event serves a divine purpose, evil events likewise serve a divine purpose. Such a strong view of divine *providence (often termed meticulous providence) reintroduces the problem of evil, for one would have to assert that God intends the evil we suffer in some way or other. It is more likely that many evils are the gratuitous by-products of freely chosen actions or natural laws, permitted by God in line with the above theodicies but not willed or intended by God. The traditional ethical principle of double effect (i.e. evil by-products are justified when they satisfy the following criteria: the act must be good or morally neutral, the overall outcome must be good, the intention must be good and the evil effect must not be a means to the good end) might be invoked to justify God's allowance of evil in such cases.

The anti-Theodicist tradition

Following the lead of *Kant, who contended that theodicies are impossible because, given the disparity between God and the world, we cannot know how God causally relates to the world or how the world connects to God's moral wisdom, some contemporary theologians reject the attempt to construct theodicies or defences. Theodicies reflect the *Enlightenment project, stemming from its rationalist presuppositions, of providing evidence for or justifying one's beliefs about God. They treat God as an object about which our human language and grammar can speak, while they treat evil in abstraction, apart from the historical and social horrors and personal tragic suffering.

To the contrary, since no 'order' or 'ratio' exists between the infinite God and the finitude of ourselves and our language, we cannot know the mystery that is God, let alone treat him as theodicists do merely as a possessor of divine perfections, apart from fullness of the Christian doctrines such as the Trinity, incarnation, redemption and life after death. The problem of evil is not a rational issue of how to justify God's existence to the unbeliever, but a historical issue addressing how God in Christ responds to human sin and suffering, and how through conversion and holiness we respond to evil. Evil engenders epistemological crises between the personal narratives of victims and their suffering and the narratives of the Christian community, forcing us to evaluate our historical and cultural position to enable us to respond to those suffering.

Ultimately, the existential or practical questions we must face concern our apathy toward evils and how we respond to our own and others' evils and the resultant suffering. Jesus' model was to condemn demonic evil in no uncertain terms and to extend compassion and assistance to those who suffered evil. The theology of the cross, of a saving God who as incarnate shares in suffering and in the atonement addresses human sin, becomes central to addressing evil. We cannot resolve evil, sin and suffering by ourselves through merely identifying with the victims; divine grace, as Augustine saw, remains necessary to transform us.

See also: DEVILS AND DEMONS; FALL; SUFFERING.

Bibliography

M. M. Adams, *Horrendous Evils and the Goodness of God* (Ithaca, 1999); *idem*, 'Theological Contributions to Theodicy', *Faith and Philosophy* 13, 1996, pp. 469–608; H. Arendt, *Eichmann in Jerusalem: A Report on the Banality of Evil* (New York, 1965); G. Boyd, *Satan and the Problem of Evil* (Downers Grove, 2001); G. R. Evans, *Augustine on Evil* (Cambridge, 1982); G. Graham, *Evil and Christian Ethics* (Cambridge, 2001); M. Peterson, *God and Evil* (Westview, 1998); A. Plantinga, *God, Freedom, and Evil* (Grand Rapids, 1974); K. Surin, *Theology and the Problem of Evil* (Blackwell, 1986); J. Waller, *Becoming Evil* (New York, 2002).

B. R. REICHENBACH

EXCOMMUNICATION, see CHURCH DISCIPLINE

EXISTENTIALISM

Existentialism is a reaction against *romanticism and *rationalism. It concentrates on human existence and the human situation. Existentialists range from theists like *Kierkegaard and *Dostoevsky to atheists like Sartre, Camus, *Heidegger and *Nietzsche. In literature, drama and poetry, the themes of anxiety (*angst*), dread and death, absurdity and meaninglessness and the individual and choice are presented, often obliquely. Particularly through Heidegger, existential theology has emphasized the existential moment in *hermeneutics and preaching in which each of us is challenged to respond to the direct call of God to live authentically. *Tillich stresses that God is not so much a being but the 'ground of being', and Weil and *Marcel have adopted a more participative and incarnational approach grounded in human experience. *Buber argues for dialogue and communication with the individual 'I' relating to the eternal 'Thou'. In recent philosophical work, there has been a shift towards *phenomenology, *postmodernism and *deconstructionism, often taking existential themes, approaches and interpretations to their logical extremes.

Theological engagement

Much of modern theology, particularly in the early twentieth century, shaped the theological writings both positively and negatively, focusing on the themes of subjectivity, authenticity, truth, faith and ultimately even the '*death of God'. Barth, Brunner and Bultmann all stressed the need for faith to be a personal, inner reality. Following Kierkegaard's notion of a 'leap of faith', the stress was on making truth one's own and the importance of the individual in terms of belief and action and biblical interpretation. Faith was to be abstract and remote but seen by works and ways of living. Authentic faith was a continual choosing to live with the whole of one's being. Sin and inauthenticity were part of the human failure to be what we were created to be.

Existentialism offers a frightening account of fear, suffering, separation and death in human existence. It can see life and the world as having no meaning, humanity as devoid of purpose, and no meaning in any one thing or in everything together. Life is absurd. For the theist this emphasized the need for a step of faith and the centrality not just of personal

Existentialism

relationships, but of an 'I-Thou' relationship with God. For the atheist, humanity was alone and that meant not only was there no God, but we had to create our own meaning, reality and morality. The individual alone and isolated must take responsibility for that creation. Life is eternally making choices to live authentically, even if 'Hell is other people' (J. P. Sartre) and there is no comfort or help from outside humanity. There is no God to relieve our predicament.

Existentialism recognizes the danger of trying to escape from the reality of the here and now by retreating into the past, the present or the future, rather than living each moment in light of the past and open to the future. Jesus is often depicted as the genuine authentic human being – the man for others – but there can be little or no sense of his divinity and salvation through his death and sacrifice.

This life is usually the extent and limit of human existence, and our choices are significant because they affect every aspect of how we live and impact the world and others. Confronted by the absurdity and meaningless of everything, we can only seek to create our own sense and meaning though our choices.

Theological critique

Most existentialists allow no room for the Creator and Sustainer *God. They do not see the world, human existence or history as having purpose or meaning. Existentialism is reductionistic and focuses narrowly on the negative aspects of human existence without the Christian notions of hope and salvation. *Barth reacted against this kind of subjectivity by emphasizing the sheer objectivity of God in Christ and the importance not only of his revelation but also of the very capacity to receive that revelation. Grace not only gives human beings genuine choices, but also the capacity to choose well and in line with God's revealed will. Humanity is created by God to live in community. It was not good for man to be alone (Gen. 2:18). In creation and final redemption, humanity is social. The role of society, culture and family are crucial in gaining a sense of identity, and this communal aspect is mirrored and developed in the church.

The *gospel directly challenges the hopelessness of humanity. The *grace of Christ in the incarnation, cross and resurrection and the gift of the Holy Spirit make it possible for human beings to be transformed and to live authentically in the church.

Existentialists use exceptional examples to make their case, but life is regular and patterned by God's good providence. The human sciences are possible only because of such regularity.

The very statement of existentialism needs to be challenged. It is self-contradictory to state that 'everything is meaningless' and claim that statement is actually meaningful. We have been given the ability to make sense of a world which makes sense because of the Creator. There also needs to be a proper balance between the subjective process of making our own what we learn from the objective realities of God, the world and other people. Likewise, human will cannot be separated from the whole of what it means to be human, made in the image of God with physical, psychological, volitional and spiritual natures.

Morality is not simply a human construct, but stems from the revealed will of God in the nature of the world and humanity, in the various covenants which express the law and will of God, and most of all in the person, teaching and work of Jesus, who embodies the divine will and the perfect human response and obedience to that will. Morality is not only about the will, which Paul shows can fail (Rom. 7:15–20), but about the whole person in relationship to God in Christ by the grace and power of the Holy Spirit.

While Kierkegaard, Dostoevsky and Buber stress genuine faith in God, many question whether the strong subjective stress of a 'leap of faith' needs to be balanced by a clearer understanding of the objectivity of the triune God and of the good reasons to embrace and exercise *faith. God is neither dead nor absent. He reveals himself and his will in Christ, who not only restores and reconciles us with God, but shows that it is possible for a human being to live out and up to God's moral standards.

Philosophically and theologically, Christians will recognize that modern theology has many roots in and connections with existentialism. The account of human existence gives a dramatic picture of life apart from God and the awful predicament of isolation and separation from God. But Christians will want to question and debate the nature of the meaning, purpose and content of human being and beings, truth, meaning, faith, subjectivity and choice. There are competing views of human nature and the complexity of each holistic individual in the context of and in relationship with the human community and the world itself. What is at issue is the reality of God and his work in creating and sustaining the world, providence, revealing his law, his prophetic word and his moral standards, linked to a full account of the divine-human nature of Christ expressed through his incarnation, crucifixion, resurrection and return in glory. All of this is only known and responded to in faith and living obedience through the power and influence of the Holy Spirit.

Bibliography

J. Macquarrie, *An Existentialist Theology* (London, 1955); *idem*, *Existentialism* (London, 1972); D. E. Roberts, *Existentialism and Religious Belief* (New York, 1957).

E. D. COOK

EX OPERE OPERATO, see SACRAMENT

EXORCISM

Exorcism, often also known as 'deliverance', has long been a ministry exercised by the church. Its roots are in the gospel traditions about Jesus, who is portrayed as particularly successful in expelling demons from people (Mark 1:23–26). Exorcism in the name of Jesus continued into the apostolic missions recorded in Acts (16:18; 19:11–15) and was common in the post-apostolic church, becoming formalized in catechetical rituals as converts passed from paganism into Christian faith. Exorcism was seen as the driving out of demonic activity from the fallen creation in the name of Christ. Anointing came to symbolize both purgation from *evil in preparation for baptism in water and the bestowal of the Spirit. Since the third century exorcism has been practised as part of *baptism; in the East this is of a threefold nature. In time it was accompanied with the laying on of hands and the sign of the cross, as well as Bible readings, prayers, adjurations and execrations. By 252 in the West, exorcists formed one of the four minor orders of clergy. A rite of pre-baptismal exorcism was contained in the Anglican first *Book of Common Prayer*, but was dropped in 1552. Until 1969 exorcism was part of the rite of infant baptism in the Roman Catholic Church and is still retained in adult baptism. The various strands of the church possess therefore a considerable body of literature, well-winnowed by tradition and experience, which touches upon ministries of deliverance. Found here is the distinction between *minor* and *major* exorcisms. The former is performed by calling down blessing upon the afflicted, and the latter by the intentional expulsion of an unwanted spirit deemed to be in possession of an individual. In some traditions major exorcisms are only permitted after episcopal approval.

Since the study of human pathologies has hugely increased, questions inevitably arise about how exorcism is to be understood today. In pastoral contexts there are still those who present symptoms remarkably similar to those recorded in the Gospels; but are these to be interpreted psychiatrically? Are they, following traditional interpretations, attributable to fallen spirits? Might they even be the spirits of the dead or, more complexly, 'hypostases of nothingness' (Karl Barth)? Even if some biblical depictions of 'evil spirits' might now be identified as psychiatric disorders, notably Saul's 'evil spirit from God' (1 Sam. 18:10), the same conclusion is not so easily drawn about the Gospel accounts. Given the complexity of human nature, the various ways of interpreting the human condition available to us need not exclude the need for deliverance ministry. Martin Israel's language of 'removing evil influences' appears helpful at this point in naming the presence of powers that go beyond reductionist explanations, while at the same time maintaining a proper agnosticism concerning the precise nature of those disturbing and destructive entities which apparently have power to afflict people and places. Whatever is not understood about the form taken by evil powers, Christians can certainly know that 'Jesus is Victor!'. In Christ's name there is authority to deliver.

Guidelines drawn up by the House of Bishops for the Church of England in 1975 insisted that the ministry of exorcism must be (1) in collaboration with the resources of medicine, (2) in the context of prayer and sacrament, (3) with the minimum of publicity, (4) by experienced persons authorized by the diocesan bishop and (5) followed up by continuing pastoral care. All who are called to this ministry, wherever they are located in the church, should work with responsible practice of this kind.

See also: DEVILS AND DEMONS.

Bibliography

K. Barth, *CD* III, 3, §51,3 (Edinburgh, 1960); Church of England, *A Time to Heal* (London, 2004); M. Israel, *Exorcism: The Removal of Evil Influences* (London, 1997); K. McDonnell and G. T. Montague, *Christian Initiation and Baptism in the Holy Spirit: Evidence from the First Eight Centuries* (Collegeville, 1991); M. Perry (ed.), *Deliverance: Psychic Disturbance and Occult Involvement* (London, 1987); N. G. Wright, *A Theology of the Dark Side* (Carlisle, 2003).

N. G. WRIGHT

EXPIATION, see ATONEMENT; SACRIFICE

FAIRBAIRN, A. M., see CONGREGATIONALISM

FAITH

In English, the word 'faith' refers to an attitude of belief, trust or reliance in the word or character of another, whereas the word 'faithfulness' refers to a virtue or quality of character seen in ongoing dependable action. Both meanings are found in the Hebrew '*aman* word group and in the biblical story. Abraham had *faith in* God (Gen. 15:6), but is more commonly said to be *faithful to* God. Later Jewish writings emphasize the latter (e.g. 1 Macc. 2:52). Both meanings, *trust in* another and *faithfulness to* the other, make sense within the context of personal relationships.

In the NT, James picks up this double meaning (Jas 2:21–23), dismissing so-called faith (*pistis*) in God which does not issue in faithful action. Paul's complementary emphasis, aware of the *un*faithfulness of OT Israel, is on the primacy of faith (*pistis*) as trust in another, specifically in the word and character of God revealed in *Jesus Christ. This is his understanding of Hab. 2:4, 'The righteous will live by faith', in Rom. 1:17 (see also Gal. 3:11). He establishes from Gen. 15:6 that Abraham's faith in the God who justifies the ungodly is the model for ours (Rom. 4:3–5). Recent scholarship has explored the idea that the Pauline phrase, *pistis Iesou Christou*, often understood in the past as our faith *in* Christ, can be understood to mean the faith *of* Christ, that is, the faith which Christ himself had *in* God and his faithfulness *to* God. In the Johannine writings, faith is that trust in Christ which is also 'knowledge', not knowledge of the abstract, but the knowledge of personal acquaintance.

The Fathers tended to think of faith as belief and to use other words (obedience, love) to refer to the Christian's faithful character. But thinking in a cultural context which valued the abstract idea as real, faith was understood more as 'faith that' (i.e. belief in a truth or doctrine) rather than 'faith in' a person. It was accepting and believing true statements, particularly the 'rule of faith' (*regula fidei*), a summary of Christian doctrine which came to be encapsulated in the creeds. In the medieval scholastics, this was formulated in a distinction between *assensus*, the acceptance of the truths or doctrines of Scripture as interpreted by the authority of the church, and *fiducia*, personal trust in God. The accent was often more on 'the faith', meaning the Christian faith, the doctrine to be believed (*fides quae creditur*), than on the faith which believes (*fides qua creditur*).

The Reformation can be seen as a revival of emphasis on faith as belief (*fides qua creditur*). This was to be understood not merely as *assensus*, acceptance of doctrine, but as *fiducia*, personal trust. Luther's interpretation of '*justification by faith' in Paul saw faith as 'the wedding ring' which unites the believer to Christ. We are not saved by our *faithfulness*, a view which Luther saw in some late medieval teaching and rejected as *Pelagian (salvation by works), but by our *faith* in Christ. But neither was this faith a good work, something we did by which we were justified: it was the gift of God. *Salvation was therefore not only by faith alone (*sola fide*) but, as Augustine had taught, by *grace alone (*sola gratia*). 'Justification by faith' became the doctrine of all the *Reformers and the subsequent Protestant churches, and *Luther regarded it as 'the article [of doctrine] by which the Church stands or falls' (*articulus stantis vel cadentis ecclesia*).

At the Council of *Trent, the Catholic theologians of the Counter-Reformation were afraid that the Protestant doctrine encouraged *antinomianism, that is, a disregard for the moral law and the need for personal holiness. For them, faith was to be understood not just as *faith* in God but as *faithfulness* to God. The same anxiety that some Lutheran and Calvinist doctrine could lead to antinomianism was echoed in some *Anabaptist thinking. Later, the leaders of German *pietism and of the evangelical revival in Britain and her American colonies reacted against the tendency of Protestant orthodoxy to lapse back into thinking of faith as *assensus*, the acceptance of orthodox doctrine. Accordingly, they emphasized a living, personal faith (*fiducia*) in Christ. But along with the pietists, *Wesley, while fully adopting the doctrine of justification by faith from Luther and Calvin, also emphasized that it was 'faith expressing itself through love' (Gal. 5:6). Faith led to *sanctification (faithful living) as well as justification.

The philosophers of the *Enlightenment tended to polarize faith and knowledge. The search for certain knowledge by the exercise of human *reason tended to marginalize and eventually to dismiss the claims of the Christian faith based on the authority of Scripture and the tradition of the church. In reaction to the focus on orthodoxy in the Lutheran church and the attempt of Hegel to present Christian doctrine as merely illustrative of his metaphysical system, Søren *Kierkegaard spoke of 'the leap of faith'. Like the Pietists, he argued that Christian faith was not a system of doctrine, but a personal commitment. For him it was the subjective decision of the will to embrace the paradoxes of the faith (particularly the incarnation of the Eternal in time) as truth.

In the twentieth century, secular *existentialist philosophy drew upon Kierkegaard, and influenced theologians such as *Bultmann and *Tillich who interpreted faith as a 'leap' or decision to live 'authentically', that is, open to God's future rather than clinging to the dead past. In reaction to that existentialist view of faith, theologians such as *Pannenberg and many evangelicals emphasized that Christian faith was not an irrational 'leap', but a fully rational belief in the gospel which in turn was based in history. Karl *Rahner proposed that many who did not explicitly believe the gospel of Christ had 'implicit faith' (see *Anonymous Christianity).

To be true to the NT, a Christian understanding of faith must begin with *Christ. If in him the God of Israel was ultimately *faithful* to his promises of salvation, and if he as our representative demonstrated perfect human *faith in* God and *faithfulness to* God, then salvation has been completed for all who are 'in him' by *faith*. It is not that our faith is a good work which saves us, but that he saves us through our *faith* in him and is transforming us already into his *faithful* people.

Bibliography
D. M. Baillie, *Faith in God and Its Christian Consummation* (Edinburgh, 1927); G. C. Berkouwer, *Faith and Justification* (Grand Rapids, 1954); R. B. Hays, *The Faith of Jesus Christ* (Grand Rapids, 2002).

T. A. NOBLE

FAITH AND HISTORY

Christian faith is grounded in events reported in the Bible (see *Scripture) and centred on the life, death and resurrection of *Jesus Christ. The reliability of these reports became a matter of doubt and public debate in the post-Reformation era and has been widely disputed since the time of the Enlightenment. But if it is held that faith can no longer be grounded in the conviction that certain events occurred, what is its basis? How is it related to history? The issues surrounding these questions constitute what is known as 'the problem of faith and history'. Among the various approaches to it are the following:

(1) Biblical accounts of events are fundamentally or entirely reliable, but historical investigation cannot demonstrate their truth or probability. Faith is grounded in the actuality, but not the rational verifiability, of their occurrence.

(2) Biblical accounts of events are fundamentally or entirely reliable and historical-critical reason can give a significant measure of support to such belief. Faith may not be dependent on the results of historical investigation, but it gains strength and support from it.

(3) Faith is somewhat dependent on the results of historical investigation, but these results are provisional and faith contains a significant element of risk. This is in the nature of faith; faith is not certainty.

(4) Faith is indeed possessed of certainty, but it is not a certainty that particular events have taken place. Faith is not based on history and is independent of it. It is based on self-validating experience or encounter with God.

(5) Traditional ways of posing and answering the question of faith and history are misconceived. Scripture communicates and commends a mode of existence rendered through the medium of narrative, but narrative is a vehicle

for absorbing our lives into its story independently of any correspondence between its account and external events.

(6) Faith is independent of both historical events and the narrative world of the Bible. It is a way of being in the world which may take its inspiration and values from the portrayal of Jesus in the NT, but it is self-supporting and self-sustaining as far as history or Scripture are in question.

These options are rather crudely described, can be modified or alternatively formulated and do not exhaust the possible ways of relating faith and history. However, they illustrate something of the range of positions adopted since the issue began to be debated in modern times. In approaching the question of faith and history, we might keep in mind at least five things.

First, Scripture contains a variety of literary genres, and we should try to identify and distinguish them as we consider what kind of 'history' is contained in the Bible. Our judgments will sometimes be provisional, since our customary ways of describing genres (e.g. prose, poetry, chronicle, narrative, legend) may impose inappropriate categories on the biblical materials.

Secondly, those who believe that faith is grounded in historical events must make distinctions, including some already mentioned. One is the distinction between the actuality and the demonstrability (or demonstrable probability) of an occurrence. Another is between events of greater and of lesser significance for religious faith.

Thirdly, even if we maintain that there are no such things as uninterpreted events, there is a distinction between an event and its interpretation. The fact that Jesus died may be essential for faith, but it is the interpretation of that death as an *atonement which provides the content of faith. Even an extraordinary occurrence like a resurrection only has saving significance if it is interpreted in a particular way.

Fourthly, an intellectual persuasion that an event has occurred – however we attain it – is not the same as saving faith. Saving faith is trust in and acceptance of Jesus Christ. Events may ground or may even, in some sense, be objects of faith, but mere belief (*fides historica*) is not saving (*fides salvifica*).

Fifthly, the hinge on which the testimony of the Christian Scriptures turns is the *resurrection of Jesus from the dead, with its twofold witness to an empty tomb and appearances of the risen Christ. However we conceive the metaphysics of the resurrection or the nature of the assurance of faith, the testimony itself is fundamental. Differences on whether historical investigation can or cannot, should or should not, be used to support this witness, should not obscure its centrality.

Diverse methods of approaching the Bible, especially since the last quarter of the twentieth century, have made 'the question of faith and history' appear rather antiquated to many biblical scholars and theologians. However, as long as the testimony of Scripture is considered seriously on its own terms, it is a question that should not go away.

See also: FAITH; HISTORY; INFALLIBILITY AND INERRANCY OF THE BIBLE.

Bibliography

C. Braaten, *History and Hermeneutics* (London, 1968); S. Evans, *The Historical Christ and the Jesus of Faith: Incarnational Narrative as History* (Oxford, 1996); H. W. Frei, *The Eclipse of Biblical Narrative: A Study in Eighteenth and Nineteenth Century Hermeneutics* (New Haven and London, 1974); M. R. Licona, *The Resurrection of Jesus: A New Historiographical Approach* (Nottingham, 2010); W. Pannenberg, *Basic Questions in Theology*, vols. 1 & 2 (London, 1970, 1971); L. Perdue, *The Collapse of History* (Minneapolis, 1994); N. T. Wright, *The New Testament and the People of God* (London, 1992).

S. N. WILLIAMS

FAITH AND ORDER

Together with the Life and Work movement and the International Missionary Council, Faith and Order was one of several strands of *ecumenical activity founded after the Edinburgh Missionary Conference of 1910, enabling the churches to explore their common mission. Persuaded by Bishop Charles Brent, the effective father of the movement, the American Episcopal Church campaigned to obtain the support of other churches in the setting up of a commission to prepare for the convoking of a first Faith and Order Conference, which met in Lausanne in 1927, bringing together churches of the Reformation, the Orthodox and the Anglican Communion. At this and subsequent conferences the wide degree of agreement between the churches was identified, as well as those areas where serious disagreements remained, affirming a unity which is both gift and goal. In 1937, at the second Faith and Order world conference in Edinburgh, Faith and Order agreed to unite with the Life and Work movement to seek to form a council of churches, which came into being after wartime delays in 1948.

The Faith and Order movement has a semi-autonomous existence within the *World Council of Churches. Its staff are employed by the WCC, which also funds its activities, but it has its own separate membership which since 1968 has included the Roman Catholic Church, together with an increased representation from the Orthodox Churches and from the non-Western world. It operates through a standing commission (thirty members), and a full commission (120 members), which meets approximately every four years, with world conferences being held more intermittently. It embodies the world's most representative theological forum. The third world conference was held at Lund in 1952, the fourth at Montreal in 1963 and the fifth at Santiago de Compostella in 1993.

Its aim, according to its bylaws, is 'to proclaim the oneness of the church of Jesus Christ and to call the churches to the goal of visible unity in one faith and one Eucharistic fellowship, expressed in worship and in common life in Christ, in order that the world may believe'.

Some of its more recent work has been a programme entitled, 'Towards the Common Expression of the Apostolic Faith Today', the production of its consensus document on *Baptism, Eucharist and Ministry* (1982) and the associated Lima Eucharistic text, which have been extensively studied by the churches who have widely responded to them, for clearly not all is acceptable to all, since profound differences cannot simply be bridged by ambiguous words. More recently the commission has been exploring the theme of 'The Unity of the Church as Koinonia' to see how this can help a divided church come together.

Bibliography

G. Gassmann (ed.), *A Documentary History of the Faith and Order Movement 1963–1993* (Geneva, 1993); L. Vischer (ed.), *A Documentary History of the Faith and Order Movement, 1927–63* (St Louis, 1963).

J. BRIGGS

FAITH AND REASON

Because conceptions of both faith and reason have varied so widely in the Christian church, there is no one answer to the question of the relationship between the two. However, a few broad patterns may be distinguished.

If by 'reason' is meant the faculty of reasoning – drawing deductive and inductive conclusions from data – there is a broad measure of agreement within the Christian church that faith (whether understood as 'the faith' or as the act of faith) is compatible with reason; indeed, it requires reason both in order to understand what is believed, and to articulate what is believed in an orderly, coherent and systematic way. Christians have recognized such logical influences on the very surface of the Bible (e.g. Matt. 12:26; Luke 6:39) and in the outworking of the mysteries of the faith in *creeds and confessional formulae (e.g. the Nicene Creed). This attitude of reason to (the) faith has found classic expression in the words of the *Westminster Confession, that 'the whole counsel of God, concerning all things necessary for his own glory, man's salvation, faith and life, is either expressly set down in Scripture, or by good and necessary consequence may be deduced from Scripture' (I.vi). Even *Luther, who was capable of making very uncomplimentary remarks about philosophers such as Aristotle, did not shrink from writing a first-rate work of systematic theology, *De Servo Arbitrio* (*On the Bondage of the Will*; 1525).

In both the medieval period and in the *Enlightenment (as well as less dominantly in other periods), 'reason' came to mean not only the faculty of reasoning from data but also the ability to certify certain data as 'reasonable'. This has operated, destructively, in rationalist attacks upon the Christian gospel from outside the church. But also, from within the church, it has operated in three discernibly different ways.

(1) In the classical medieval position, and in all forms of *natural or rational theology since then, reason is said to provide a stock of initial propositions or data 'evident to the senses' or acceptable to all rational people, from which certain theological conclusions can be deduced which act as the *praeambula fidei*. Not that all Christians are capable of making the requisite inferences; but they can all be assured that such inferences are possible. Weaker senses of 'reasonable' also operated in anti-*deist writers

such as Joseph *Butler and William *Paley, and those influenced by them. The religious and theological danger of this approach, quite apart from the success or otherwise of the 'proofs' of God's existence, lies in its abstract rationalism.

(2) It was a characteristic position of the eighteenth-century Enlightenment that, in *Kant's words, religion should be confined 'within the limits of reason alone'. What this meant, in practice, was the excision of all supernatural references from Scripture, or the adopting of a *hermeneutic which effectively 'naturalized' them by regarding Scripture as a retelling of the truths of reason in figurative and emblematic form for popular consumption, and (in the case of Kant and his immediate followers) the distilling of the pure essence of religion in terms of individual ethics (Kant), sentiment and pious affection (*Schleiermacher) or social engagement (through the implementation of the ethics of Jesus; *Ritschl). It is of the utmost importance to recognize that such appeals to 'reason' and 'logic' are not neutral and objective, as they may appear to be, but incorporate substantive ontological, *epistemological and sometimes moral positions.

(3) 'Reason' has been appealed to in order to set up a barrier against the incursion of what has been regarded as mystical or enthusiastic excess. Thus John *Locke, writing against the background of what he regarded as the sectarian chaos of seventeenth-century England, could write: 'If anything shall be thought *revelation* which is contrary to the plain principles of reason and the evident knowledge the mind has of its own clear and distinct ideas, their reason must be hearkened to, as to a matter within its province' (*Essay* IV.xviii.8). Locke himself is somewhat equivocal in the way in which he employs this criterion, employing it not only in order to assert that no credible revelation can be unintelligible gibberish, but also to assert a more substantive control of what may count as revelation.

There has been a fairly definite correlation, and perhaps a logical connection, between views of the place of reason in articulating, reconstructing or delimiting the faith, and views of *faith. In the medieval church, and in much present-day Roman Catholic theology, faith is primarily, if not exclusively, assent to the basic doctrines of 'the faith'. The credibility of these doctrines is attested by the church's authority which is in turn based upon an appreciation of the rational arguments for God's existence, divine revelation, and the church as the infallible teaching authority. Faith is thus assent (sometimes explicit, often implicit) to those propositions certified by the church.

At the other extreme, faith is seen by many, particularly those influenced by *existentialism from Søren *Kierkegaard onwards (some would find antecedents in Luther and *Pascal, probably mistakenly), as a leap in the dark. It is an act of trust in God which goes beyond the evidence, and in some cases goes against the evidence. (This distrust of reason has sometimes been called 'fideism'.) It is clear that it would be difficult to hold such a view along with an acceptance of natural theology. But it would be a mistake to suppose that because faith requires no reasons, no reasons can be given for this view of faith.

In classical Protestantism, faith is trust in Christ for salvation, the Christ to whom the Scriptures exclusively bear witness. Though some have ventured to attempt to authenticate the Scriptures as the divine revelation by reason, appealing to certain of its unique features to do so, in general in Protestantism the Scriptures have been regarded as self-authenticating. God, by his Spirit, bears testimony to his people to the divine and saving character of his word not by investing that word with a set of private, Gnostic meanings, but by bearing testimony in the mind and conscience of the regenerate, in a dynamic, ongoing fashion, to the divine authority of Scripture. Faith in Christ is thus of a piece with faith in the trustworthiness of the Scriptures, which reveal and testify to Christ. It is not the 'reason' alone to which the Scriptures appeal, but the whole person in the context of the fellowship of the church.

See also: EPISTEMOLOGY; PHILOSOPHICAL THEOLOGY; PHILOSOPHY AND THEOLOGY; PHILOSOPHY OF RELIGION.

Bibliography

G. H. Clark, *Religion, Reason and Revelation* (Nutley, 1961); K. J. Clark (ed.), *Philosophers Who Believe* (Downers Grove, 1993); P. Glynn, *God – The Evidence: The Reconciliation of Faith and Reason in a Postsecular World* (Rocklin, CA, 1997); P. Helm, *The Varieties of Belief* (London, 1973); J. Hick, *Faith and Knowledge* (London, 1967); T. Keller, *The Reason for God: Belief in an Age of Skepticism*

(New York, 2008); C. Michalson, *The Rationality of Faith* (London, 1964); K. Ward, *God and the Philosophers* (Minneapolis, 2009).

P. HELM

FALL

Since patristic times, the Eden story (Gen. 2 – 3) has been given a decisive significance by Christian theologians, under the title 'The Fall' (introduced by Origen and Hippolytus Romanus, used by Gregory of Nyssa and Gregory Nazianzen). The rise of biblical criticism, the development of evolutionary theories, post-Enlightenment rationalism (and irrationalism) in idealistic and historicist forms, have led to a new questioning of the doctrine of the fall ('originating original sin'), with its presupposition of original *righteousness and its consequence of 'originated original sin'. Was there ever an historical Adam and, if there was, how can the sin of one individual affect the whole of humanity? Was there ever a state of perfect integrity? Did the fall make nature 'red in tooth and claw'? Modernity has seen a swarm of interpretations that take the Genesis narrative as a *mythical* account of the condition of all humankind through all time (including readings that imply a fall *upwards*, *Hegel, some *feminists).

Though the evidence is rather diffuse and lacks formal elaboration, the data of the OT warrant the traditional understanding of the fall as a particular event which destroyed a prior condition of harmony and fellowship with God, and had lasting catastrophic effects for all the descendants of the first couple. Were it not for the prestige of the rival scenario drawn from the theories of natural sciences, few interpreters would have adopted the 'mythical' reading of Eden.

The formal features of the biblical narrative contrast with those of myth; 'most probably', as James Orr wisely summarized, to be identified 'as old tradition clothed in oriental allegorical dress' (*The Christian View of God and the World*, Kerr Lectures 1890–91, Grand Rapids, repr. 1960, p. 185). It is the first link in a chain of historical sequence, in tune with the biblical valuation of *history, with *Adam as the first ancestor. The etiological intention is obvious, concerning death, birth-pangs, strained relationships of the sexes, and effects beyond human nature (the ground) which are difficult to measure (cf. Rom. 8:20–21, but also Ps. 104:20–22 and Job 38 – 41 for phenomena ascribed to God's *creative* wisdom) (see *Ecology). The sinfulness of human nature (flesh), even from birth, is everywhere acknowledged, and there are some hints that the fountainhead might be found in the first father, even a few possible references to the Gen. 3 disobedience (e.g. Hos. 6:7: NIV is literal, 'Like Adam, they have broken the covenant'; Ezek. 28:12–19, Adam being the figure behind the King of Tyre; Eccl. 7:28–29).

Intertestamental Judaism echoed that teaching (Ecclus. 24:25; Wisdom 2:23–24; 2 Baruch 48:42–43; IV Ezra 7:118f.), though, especially in apocalyptic literature, the fall of angels (Gen. 6:1–4; cf. Jude 6) loomed larger as the source of evils in the world. Adam originated the evil 'impulse' (*yetser*, Gen. 6:5) in all human hearts (IV Ezra 3:21–22; 7:48), which coexists with the good impulse in rabbinic texts (Qumran leans on a more deterministic side).

The NT doctrine of sin denounces more strongly the corruption of human nature and the universal bondage it involves. Matt. 19:8 suggests an original defection from a previous state of purity. The Johannine corpus insists on the devil's role 'in the beginning' (John 8:44; 1 John 3:8; Rev. 12:9; 20:2). Paul's interest is more anthropological; he mentions Eve's role (2 Cor. 11:3; 1 Tim. 2:14), and focuses on Adam's: it is part of the First-Adam/New-(Last)-Adam scheme he develops to unfold the meaning of Christ's work on our behalf. Universal death is traced back to this origin: all die 'in Adam' (1 Cor. 15:21–22); more explicitly, Adam's disobedience is said to have introduced sin into the world, and consequently death (the wages of sin) for all humans (Rom. 5:12–21), and even more precisely to have secured the condemnation of all, who were 'constituted sinners' (vv. 18–19). Since the parallel Adam/Christ is asymmetrical, their two roles being both alike and unlike (vv. 12, 14–16, 18–19), interpretations vary on the way Adam's brings about such a state of affairs.

*Irenaeus may be called the first theologian of the fall (he rather spoke of 'apostasy'), with an influence both Eastern and Western (he had been trained in Asia Minor and was the bishop of Lyons). He does maintain its historical character, and that Adam lost the prospect of immortality for his descendants; he more vaguely alludes to moral corruption, though Satan's tyranny he emphasizes implies the bonds of condemnation (*Against Heresies*, III.23.1). He tends, however, to minimize the guilt of Adam and Eve, whom he considers to have been children (also sexually, III.22.4) and easily duped by the Serpent/devil (IV.38.1–2): this view is subservient to his main interpretation of salvation as growth, progressive conformation to God, owing to the 'recapitulation' effected by Christ. Despite human bondage, Irenaeus affirms that free *will was not annihilated; this is the common emphasis among the Fathers, who fought pagan, astral fatalism. Among the Greek Fathers, the fall has entailed the reign of death and demonic influence, and the spread of evil desires; of sin itself and guilt, there is little talk (though *Athanasius speaks of sin 'passing', and Didymus the Blind of its 'transmission', *diadochè*). *John Damascene, while stressing free will, could teach that man, having broken the divine command 'passed on to his generation the impulse towards matter and far from God, and wrath come from the one authentic enemy of his salvation' (*Orthodox Faith*, Book II.30). *Eastern Orthodox theology heightens its differences from the Augustinian tradition; it affirms that the fall (historical) entailed mortality but no guilt nor total depravity; the advantages of the pre-fall state are lowered, the fall somewhat de-dramatized, and salvation is seen primarily as deification (*theôsis*) rather than restoration.

In the West, a sterner view of sin prevailed, with the phrase 'original vice' coined as soon as *Tertullian, but free will was also emphasized. When *Pelagius, however, pushed further the logic of free will and all but denied any effects of Adam's fall (for him, men and women were born in the state of Adam prior to his fall, were free from his guilt and the pollution of his sin, only exposed to the bad influence of his example), *Augustine took up the cudgels against him and for the first strong doctrine of original sin. His carefully constructed account of the connection between Adam's sin and guilt and those of all humanity gave the fall a dramatically efficient role. He highlighted the privileges of original righteousness and the magnitude of the fall from it. He saw pride as the root of Adam's transgression, and as the cause of that disorder of desire, concupiscence (lust), which was to him a central form of sin. Since all were germinally present in Adam (after the logic of Heb. 7:9–10), all actually participated in Adam's sin (the so-called 'realist' interpretation; Augustine understood the last clause in Rom. 5:12: 'in whom (Adam) all have sinned'). Therefore all are born both corrupt and guilty. The union of Adam and his descendants makes it possible to maintain both the radical necessity of sin (bondage), in everybody born, and its responsibility, since Adam had full free will when he violated the divine prohibition. The transmission of Adamic sinfulness Augustine attached to the conditions of human reproduction: the disorder of concupiscence even affects the lawful conjugal act, and thus every child is conceived and born in sin (Ps. 51:5, cf. Heb. 7).

Augustine's interpretation was largely confirmed at the Council of Orange (529) and remained official dogma. His understanding of concupiscence was influential in the development of monastic *asceticism and the value set on *Mary's virginity (considered to be perpetual). Scholasticism brought only refinements to the doctrine. *Anselm explained original righteousness in terms of *rectitude* and highlighted the negative dimension of loss in the fall: humans were deprived as much as they became depraved. Successors, in line with their Nature-Grace ground-motive, considered original righteousness as a *super-added* gift, above nature (supernatural or, rather, praeternatural): it was entirely lost, but nature itself was only weakened. This was *Thomas Aquinas' view; he was also able to clarify the hereditary transmission of Adamic sinfulness: it does not happen through concupiscence in the sexual conjunction, but because procreation is the transmission of *nature*, and human nature is fallen. Following *Duns Scotus' emphasis on will, the later medieval *nominalistic trend (especially among Franciscans) moved away from Augustine and his pessimistic/realistic outlook.

The Magisterial Reformers were Augustinians and (with the notable exception of *Zwingli) reaffirmed the dogma. Martin *Luther stressed the corruption and utter inability of fallen nature; it lies helplessly under the wrath of the God of law; the will no longer deserves to be called 'free', but, according to the title of Luther's reply to Erasmus, it is a 'slave-will' (*servum arbitrium*) which only pure grace can rescue. Adam's sin, which initiated that condition, was first and foremost *unbelief*.

John *Calvin followed Luther (and also owed more to Aquinas than meets the eye). His definition of original sin is worth quoting: 'a hereditary depravity and corruption of our nature, diffused into all parts of the soul, which first makes us liable to God's wrath, then also brings forth in us those works which Scripture calls "works of the flesh"' (*Institutes*, II.i.8). His intention is clearly to bind together guilt (incurring God's wrath) and depravity; he insists on Adam's sin being our own, since we *are* sinful, rather than merely 'alien'. To establish the connection, he relies on metaphors (sin flowing down) and the thought of God's ordinance: original sin is the outcome of a judgment, imputing Adam's sin to all, just as Christ's righteousness is imputed to all believers. *Beza and later *Reformed orthodoxy elaborated the doctrine of this ordinance: Adam's role depended on his appointment as 'federal Head and representative' ('federal': of the creational 'Covenant of works'); since he acted as the lawful representative of all, his disobedience can be imputed to all. Some theologians, such as Charles *Hodge, can interpret depravity as the first *punishment*, inflicted on the ground of imputed guilt. Calvin and his tradition gave prominence to a thought that is already found among the Fathers, that of the *probationary* character of Eden and the prohibition; it was a test of obedience and, had not Adam and Eve failed, they would have been raised afterwards to a higher form of life. *Berkouwer and a few others have observed that there is not the slightest hint in Scripture that it was so; the thought has to be read into the text. The Reformers departed from medieval tradition by rejecting the difference that was made between the 'image' and the 'likeness' of God; not without some ambiguity, they affirmed that the fall had defaced the image-likeness, only restored in Christ; this has consequences for the use of reason, which is first among 'image' faculties (see *Image of God).

Liberal and modernist theology, generally, has discarded the Augustinian dogma. Karl *Barth, though retrieving part of its language, offers a radical reinterpretation. He rejects any thought of 'inherited sin' (*Erbsünde*, the usual term for the dogma in German), though he does speak of 'original sin' (*Ursünde*). He remains ambiguous on the historical reference of the 'saga' (*Sage*) of Gen. 2–3, which he differentiates both from myth and from history in the ordinary sense, but he is clear that there never was a pre-fall state of innocence (nor any other covenant than the covenant of grace). One should not talk of transmission: rather 'Adam' is the title or label (*Überschrift*) placed over the whole of human history. Death (future non-existence) as such is no consequence of a fall but part of the goodness of creation. The most original feature is the Christological foundation of original sin: Jesus Christ is truly the *first* Adam, and also as regards sin. The priority of Christ (required by Barth's dogmatic Christological principle) is not only noetic (we know our sin in the light of Christ) but ontic, in the order of being. He could write:

> He is the man whom God in His eternal counsel, giving Him the command, treated as its transgressor, thus rejecting Him in His righteous wrath, and actually threatening Him with that final dereliction. That this was true *of Adam*, and is true of us, is the case *only because* in God's counsel, and in the event of Golgotha, it became true *first of all* of Jesus Christ (*CD* II.2, p. 739; emphasis added).

This reversal is bound with Barth's interpretation of evil as uncreated, yet real, 'nothingness' and his claim that sin is 'ontological impossibility'; it has no clear precedent and conflicts sharply with Calvin's emphasis on the Creation-Fall-Redemption sequence.

In the field of dogmatics, after Barth, one may mention the work of Wolfhart *Pannenberg, whose strength resides in his perspicacious treatment of the history of the dogma; he discerns Augustine's intention, but he believes he can do without a true historical fall, through a combination of free will and a metaphysical near-inevitability of sin in the relationship of Finite and Infinite. The main contribution has come from a philosopher, Paul *Ricœur, whose *Symbolism of Evil* (1960) broke new ground and finely perceived the intention of Genesis. Ricœur highlights the unique character of the Adam story (he says 'myth'), the only one that separates radically between the origin of being (all good) and the origin of evil (later); he sees the import of that historical beginning for evil: the goodness of the monotheistic Creator, the source of being, is safeguarded, indignation is preserved ('Evil becomes scandalous at the same time as it becomes historical'), the sinner's guilt is established, repentance is possible and called for; he notes that it is consonant with the prophetic call to conversion. Nevertheless, he thinks that scientific results rule out a simple, naive acceptance of historicity; he tries to exploit the meaning 'as if' the fall were really historical and promotes a 'symbolic' interpretation; his sentiment that the 'tragic myth' (evil part of the fabric of being), ultimately, cannot be overcome shows that he slides back into ontological accounts of evil.

The example of Ricœur's work suggests that the key issue today concerning the fall in Eden is that of historicity (see *Faith and history). The alternatives are an interpretation of sin (cardinal evil) as the misuse of freedom against the perfectly good God, perversion and corruption of his gifts, and an ontological interpretation which sees in it a component of being (which may be called, relatively, non-being). The latter view blunts the edge of any imputation of guilt and any call to repentance. The former view finds its counterpart in the glorious news of a similarly *historical* *redemption.

See also: DEATH; EVIL; SIN.

Bibliography

K. Barth, *CD*, IV.1; G. C. Berkouwer, *Sin* (ET, Grand Rapids, 1971); H. A. G. Blocher, *Original Sin: Illuminating the Riddle* (Leicester, 1997); J. Calvin, *Institutes*, II.i-ix; M. Luther, *The Bondage of the Will* (ET, Cambridge, 1957 [1525]); J. Murray, *The Impartation of Adam's Sin* (Grand Rapids, 1959); W. Pannenberg, *Systematic Theology* II (ET, Grand Rapids and Edinburgh, 1994); P. Ricœur, *The Symbolism of Evil* (ET, Boston, 1967); P. Ricœur, *The Conflict of Interpretations* (ET, Evanston, 1974); H. Rondet, *Original Sin: The Patristic and Theological Background* (Shannon, 1972); N. P. Williams, *The Ideas of the Fall and Original Sin* (London, 1929).

H. A. G. BLOCHER

FAMILY

Our understanding of what a family is has changed throughout history and is continuing to evolve. Traditionally, the family was both a means of having and caring for children and ensuring inheritance and the family's name. Marxists and feminists have offered critiques of traditional understandings of the family on economic, hierarchical and patriarchal grounds. There have been attempts to replace the family unit with wider communities where childcare was shared or given to specific specialists. With increasing levels of divorce and remarriage, single-parent families, homosexual partnerships and new biological reproductive technologies, many feel that the family is under threat. Such social, political and legal changes should make the church ask: what do we mean by 'family', and how can we prepare people for family life and support families through the pressures and demands of modern life?

Definitions

While there is great diversity in the social and cultural forms and expressions of family life, there are some central features which seem universal. It provides individual and social identity. It provides for the biological, social and emotional needs of its members. It is a formalized, social structure to ensure the procreation, nurture and education of children. Inevitably, society and the law create demands, pressures and expectations, and they constrain what family members may do to and with each other and how and when society may intervene and regulate family life and relationships. At root, family provides for the well-being and flourishing not only of children but all its members.

In biblical and historical times, 'family' included the whole household who lived and worked in the same location and shared, in some sense, worked on and benefited from the land which belonged to the family. Family is a setting where roles, duties, responsibilities and rights are balanced and where and how we learn how to navigate our social and practical worlds. Historically, our notion of family has been in flux. Today our families are smaller, more mobile, with more choice and higher life expectancy. In our societies we are surrounded by greater ethnic and cultural variety of models of family. Caring for elderly parents and relatives is creating a new set of demands, balancing the continuing concerns of nurture and education of children and the well-being of each family member. No family is an isolated unit, but works with schools, neighbours, communities and society to ensure that all its members are protected and flourish.

Theological and biblical perspectives

The Trinity expresses God's fundamental nature as three persons in one unity, a family community. Many see in the *Trinity a model for family relationships, with each person being unique, yet living and being in close spiritual and communal contact. The family is the basic unity of human life in creation. Men and women made in the *image of God are set in creation as a family. It was not good for man to be alone, and humanity is to be fruitful and multiply (Gen. 1:28). Marriage and family are the context for *sexual intimacy.

While polygamy, concubinage and levirate procreation were not unknown in biblical times, the Christian pattern has been monogamy. The leaving, cleaving and becoming one flesh blend sexual expression and family life. Childlessness, widowhood and parental death are serious matters and require God's special care and our human responsibility for those in need (e.g. Sarah, Rachel, Hannah; Lam. 1:5; 5:3; 1 Tim. 5:1–16). God is not just the Creator of humanity but the Father of all humanity (Eph. 3:14–15). We are all in his family, made in the image of our heavenly Father (Gen. 1:26).

The *fall reveals how family relationships can and do break down (Gen. 3 and 4). Sin undermines family relationships, between husband and wife, parents and children, brothers and sisters and brothers. There is enmity between Adam and Eve, Cain kills Abel, Noah is disgraced by his son, Abraham presents Sarah as his sister, Jacob and Esau and Joseph and his brothers are dysfunctional, and Absalom rebels against his father David. The OT balances pictures of, and advice on, how family relationships ought to be conducted with a brutally honest account of the disasters between husbands and wives, parents and children, brothers and sisters.

In biblical times, family was not so much our modern nuclear notion, but included folk bound by kinship and extended tribal relationships. It was more like a clan. The family is central in God's covenant purposes (Gen. 12:3; 17:11–14).

It is clear that in the giving of the Law and Commandments, honouring father and mother is mandated (Exod. 20:12). In both the Pentateuch and Wisdom literature parents are given specific instructions and advice about how to educate (especially spiritually) and bring up their children (Deut. 6:4–7; 5:13–15; 29:9–11; Exod. 12:24–27; Prov. 31). This is paralleled in Eph. 6:4 with the command to bring up children in the training and instruction of the Lord.

Jesus was not only incarnate in human flesh, but incarnated in a particular society, culture and family. Matthew is careful to delineate Jesus' descent from the house of David and lists his full genealogy. Jesus grew up in a family with other children and worked for his father. His first miracle was performed at the behest of his mother (John 2:1–11). Some suggest that Jesus' warning that to follow him might mean hating father, mother and the rest of the family undermines the importance of the family (Luke 14:26; 9:59–62; 12:52–53; Matt. 10:34–39), but this is rather a question of priority of claims and responsibilities and what is vital. If a choice has to be made, then following Christ is more important than family obligations.

In the Gospel accounts, Jesus is at pains to teach how important honouring parents is (Matt. 15:4–8) and chides the Pharisees for using the practice of Corban to break the command of parent honour and escape their financial obligations (Mark 7:9–13). His teaching is full of the importance of parents and of children (Matt. 19:14; Mark 10:14; Luke 18:16) and of how good parents behave towards their children, drawing a parallel with God as their loving heavenly *Father. Even on the cross, Jesus shows family concern and indicates that John will take care of his mother, Mary (John 19:26–27).

Scripture stresses the importance of the people of God in his purposes for the world. Followers of Christ are adopted into the family of God, the *church (Eph. 1:5; Gal. 4:5; Rom. 8:15–23). God is pictured as showing both a mother and Father's *love (Isa. 66:13; John 14:23; 16:27; 1 John 3:1). Jesus himself is the Son of God (Matt. 4:6; 27:43; Mark 3:11; Luke 1:35; John 1:34; 3:18), Son of Man (Matt. 9:6; 24:30; Mark 2:10; 13:26; Luke 19:10; John 3:14; Acts 7:56), our brother (Matt. 12:48–50; Luke 8:21), and members of his household are under his authority (Heb. 3:6). Jesus and his Father are closely bound (Matt. 11:25–27; John 5:19–30). His great high priestly prayer in John 17 reveals the integrated nature of their being. At Jesus' baptism, God recognizes that this is his 'beloved Son' in whom he is well pleased (Luke 3:22). Jesus constantly prays to his Father and even in the garden of Gethsemane and on the cross addresses his prayers to the Father, asking for the cup to pass and the Father to receive his spirit (Matt. 26:39–42; Mark 14:35–36; Luke 23:46). Jesus encourages his disciples to pray to God as their 'Father' (Matt. 6:9; Luke 11:2) and to expect that the Father will respond positively as a good father (Matt. 6:11; Luke 11:13). Jesus commends the faith of children as an example of genuine faith and warns against the abuse of children (Matt. 18:1–10).

The followers of Jesus experience the love of their Father (see *Love of God) and are called the children of God (1 John 3:1). Family relationships, experiencing and showing love, are the marks of being in Christ and born of God (1 John 4:7; 5:18). Time and again Christians are called brothers and relate to each other with brotherly love (2 Thess. 2:13–15; 1 John 3). Family and household relationships in the NT are reciprocal, with mutual duties and responsibilities under submission to Christ (Col. 3:18 – 4:1; 1 Pet. 2:18 – 3:7; Eph. 5:20 – 6:9). In Acts, households hear the gospel preached and respond together (Acts 10:24). Theologians have debated the extent to which the children of believers are included as members in the people of God, and see christening, naming, infant baptism and dedication as ways of expressing the status of children and families within the church. This often revolves around the nature of *baptism and confirmation and focuses on when children are admitted to Communion. Christ is pictured as a bridegroom, with the church as his bride (Rev. 19:7; 21:2), and the unity of the church and Christ is paralleled in the husband-wife relationship (Eph. 5:25–33). There is clearly a model here of husband-wife, church and Christ interconnectedness.

Theological ethics

Doctrine leads to practice. Theological truth is meant to be lived. Catholic theology emphasizes that the family manifests Christ's living presence to the world in a community of love and faithfulness. The family is a context of fulfilling mutual roles and responsibilities, helping each member mature and grow from the dependency of a new-born baby to interdependence and independence (Eph. 5; Col. 3; 1 Pet. 2 – 3). When the church emphasizes the family today, it can isolate the single, divorced and widowed, but it needs to teach what it means to found and be a family, and to be a family member, through marriage preparation and family support.

The phenomena of the house church and the home schooling movements raise key theological and ethical questions about how to balance the danger of adopting cultural norms and how to retain and recover biblical ideals. The idealization of children, concern with child abuse and the growing problem of caring for the elderly pose fresh challenges for the church. This is not just about helping individual families. Christians must consider how best to encourage social and political practices and laws, tax systems, housing and educational policies which enable and support families rather than do them harm.

Bibliography

S. C. Barton (ed.), *The Family in Theological Perspective* (Edinburgh, 1996); R. Clapp, *Families at the Crossroads* (Leicester, 1994); John Paul II, *Familiaris Consortio: The Christian Family in the Modern World* (Vatican, 1981); H. Pyper (ed.), *The Christian Family: A Concept in Crisis* (Norwich, 1993); J. H. Rubio *Family Ethics* (Georgetown, 2010).

E. D. COOK

FAREL, WILLIAM (GUILLAUME) (1489–1565)

William Farel was born in Gap, France. He matriculated at the University of Paris (1509) and came under the influence of Jacques Lefèvre, who directed Farel to the Scriptures, especially Paul's doctrine of *justification by faith. After persistent struggle, Farel experienced an evangelical breakthrough in 1516. In 1520 he followed Lefèvre to Meaux to preach reform in the French church. His banishment from France in 1522 caused him to itinerate among the Swiss cantons while engaged in debate against Roman theology.

During this period he composed his *Sommaire* (1525), a pocket-sized manual presenting a theology for the laity based heavily on Scripture. Along with forensic justification, Farel stressed a doctrine of the Christian life with a strong emphasis on obedience to the law through good works and ardent devotion. Expositions of the Lord's Prayer and the Apostles' Creed (neither extant), and a liturgy, completed a trilogy of writings explaining the 'new' theology.

Farel's fame lies in securing a hearing for Protestantism in Geneva, from 1532 to 1535. His forceful charge to young *Calvin to remain in Geneva is memorable. Later, from 1541 to 1565, he devoted himself to preaching in Neuchâtel, where he faced intense opposition. Those struggles among 'the lost sheep' portray a tireless evangelist with compassion for the common people.

Bibliography

H. Heyer, *Guillaume Farel: An Introduction to His Theology* (Lewiston, 1990); R. Hower, *William Farel, Theologian of the Common*

Man, and the Genesis of Protestant Prayer (unpubl. ThD thesis, Philadelphia, 1983); D. H. McVicar, *William Farel, Reformer of the Swiss Romand: His Life, His Writings, and His Theology* (unpubl. ThD thesis, New York, 1954); S. E. Ozment, *The Reformation in the Cities* (New Haven, 1975).

R. G. HOWER

FARMER, HERBERT HENRY (1892–1981)

Farmer was born in Highbury, London and studied at Cambridge University and Westminster College, Cambridge, which was, at that time, the theological college of the Presbyterian Church of England. In 1931 he joined the staff of Hartford Theological Seminary, Connecticut, as Riley Professor of Christian Doctrine and Ethics. In 1935 he returned to England to succeed John Oman and, in 1949, succeeded C. H. Dodd as Norris-Hulse Professor of Divinity at Cambridge, a post he held until his retirement in 1960. In 1951 he delivered the *Gifford Lectures at the University of Glasgow, the first series of which was published as *Revelation and Religion* (1954). The second series, with which he was not entirely happy, was published posthumously as *Reconciliation and Religion* (1998).

Farmer was the most significant mid-twentieth-century British thinker to develop a theology shaped by Wilhelm *Herrmann, Albrecht *Ritschl, Freidrich *Schleiermacher and, particularly, John Oman. However, because of Karl *Barth's popularity during this period, his work always appeared a little out of step with contemporary theological trends.

Farmer's most important work and the best introduction to his thought, *The World and God* (1935), interprets all religious experience in terms of divine-human personal encounter. For Farmer, this encounter has two primary elements, 'absolute demand' and 'final succour'. Humans become aware of God as unconditional 'will' calling for obedience at any cost and also as ultimate succour, in that God is also absolute love seeking our highest good, forgiving us, and supporting us when we fail.

Farmer is one of the most important theologians in the personalist tradition, for which humans are persons living in a moral universe, the source and ground of which is a personal *God, the ultimate reality, who is rational intelligence, purposive will and experienced as absolute goodness. As wholly good, God brings into existence good personal life (i.e. 'the world of persons'), a life that is only fully realized in fellowship with God. 'The conviction that God is personal, and deals personally with men and women, lies at the heart of Christian experience and thought.' As personal beings, we are constituted by the nature of the relationships we form with other persons, particularly the relationship we form with the 'Eternal Personal' (to be distinguished from the notion of a 'person'). The self, other selves and God constitute 'an ultimate and continuous order of personal relationships'. That is to say, persons are always in relation to the Eternal Personal *in and through* their relationships with one another, and, *in and through* their relationship with God they are related to each other: 'The self does not stand in two relations, one to God and one to his neighbour, but in one relation with, as it were, two poles; he is related to his neighbour in God and to God in his neighbour; it is a single and personal continuum or order.'

Perhaps Farmer's most significant popular influences on Anglo-American Christianity were his sermons and his homiletics, which were rooted in his theological personalism. He was widely recognized as one of the most important and engaging preachers of his generation, and his *The Servant of the Word* (1941) is still considered to be one of the most insightful studies in preaching.

Bibliography

Works: *The World and God: A Study of Prayer, Providence and Miracle in Christian Experience* (London, ²1935); *The Servant of the Word* (London, 1941); *Towards Belief in God* (London, 1943); *Revelation and Religion: Studies in the Theological Interpretation of Religious Types* (London, 1954; Lewiston, 1999); *The Word of Reconciliation* (London, 1966); *Reconciliation and Religion: Some Aspects of the Uniqueness of Christianity as a Reconciling Faith*, ed. C. H. Partridge (Lewiston, 1998).

Studies: P. Donovan, 'Phenomenology as Apologetics', *SJT* 27, 1974, pp. 402–407; F. G. Healey (ed.), *Prospect for Theology: Essays in Honour of H. H. Farmer* (Welwyn, 1966); T. A. Langford, 'The Theological Methodology of John Oman and H. H. Farmer', *Religious Studies* 1, 1966, pp. 229–240; C. H. Partridge, *H. H. Farmer's Theological Interpretation* of *Religion: Towards a Personalist Theology of Religions* (Lewiston, 1998); idem, 'Henry Herbert Farmer', in S. Brown (ed.), *Dictionary of Twentieth-Century British Philosophers* (Bristol, 2005), pp. 274–276.

C. Partridge

FARRER, AUSTIN MARSDEN (1904–68)

A graduate in 'Greats' (classics and philosophy) and theology, chaplain of St Edmund Hall, 1931–5, and of Trinity College, 1935–60, and warden of Keble 1960–68, Farrer was a brilliant Christian thinker of quintessential Oxford type.

His prolific writings on philosophy, theology, and NT exegesis show an independent, lucid, agile, argumentative and articulate mind, fastidiously whimsical, witty in the matter of a metaphysical poet, *Newmanesque in sensitivity, incantatory in expression, and committed to a rational credal orthodoxy. He embodied a devotionally robust Anglican catholicism comparable to that of his peers, Kenneth Kirk (1886–1954), E. L. Mascall (1905–93) and C. S. *Lewis. He is difficult to read, for his informality of style, alternately musing and leaping, gives an appearance of waywardness to his tightest arguments.

His philosophical theology (*Finite and Infinite*, 1943; *The Freedom of the Will*, 1957; *Love Almighty and Ills Unlimited*, 1961; *Faith and Speculation*, 1964) has roots in both the substance-philosophy of medieval *scholasticism and the modern *metaphysics of action and clarification, based on linguistic usage (see *Religious language). His exegesis of Matthew, Mark and Revelation is heavily (some would say, fantastically) typological. In *The Glass of Vision*, 1948, he argued for *images rather than sentences as bearers of God's revealed truth.

Bibliography

C. C. Conti (ed.), *Reflective Faith: Essays in Philosophical Theology* (London, 1972); P. Curtis, *A Hawk among Sparrows: A Biography of Austin Farrer* (London, 1985); J. C. Eaton, *The Logic of Theism: Analysis of ⁾e Thought of Austin Farrer* (Lanham, 1983); ⁾. Eaton and A. Loades (ed.), *For God and ity: New Essays in Honor of Austin Farrer* ⁾urgh, 1983); D. Hein and E. H. Henderson (eds.), *Captured by the Crucified: The Practical Theology of Austin Farrer* (London, 2004).

J. I. Packer

FATHERHOOD OF GOD

Christian use of the name 'Father' in reference to God derives from Jesus' own use of the equivalent Aramaic term, *Abba*. Though not entirely without precedent in biblical Judaism (e.g. Isa. 63:16), the significance accorded its use by Jesus for the NT writers is signalled both by explicit remembrance of the Aramaic original even in clearly alien contexts (e.g. Rom. 8:15), and by the distinctive ways in which the name in Greek translation continues to be used. God is not only 'Father', and 'the Father' in the NT, but also, more tellingly, 'the Father of our Lord Jesus Christ', and 'our Father'.

The distinctive Christian doctrine of God the Father is closely bound up with this basic Christological reference. Hellenism could refer to Zeus as 'father', and Plato spoke of the divine 'father' and 'maker' of the universe in *Timaeus* 28c, in a text which greatly influenced Christian thought. The generic idea of the 'fatherhood of God', taken to be indicative of the divine creative power and providential care, owes much to these sources. The Christological reference implicit in NT usage, by contrast, has more specific implications: that there is a logical connection between the 'Son's' relation to God and ours; and that use of the name 'Father' must bear directly upon the substance of the Christian doctrine of God.

It was the burden of the trinitarian question elaborated in patristic theology to clarify the implications of biblical, liturgical and theological reference to God as 'Father' and 'Son'. The idea of the 'eternal generation' of the Son developed by *Origen in third-century *Alexandrian Christianity implied the eternity also of divine fatherhood, and rendered reference to the creative and providential activity of God in this context purely secondary and analogical. In the context of the *Arian crisis of the fourth century, this reasoning was further extended: central to *Athanasius' defence of the Nicene faith (see *Creeds), especially in his *Orationes contra Arianos*, was the claim that the Father-Son relation is in fact integral to the meaning of the word 'God'. Since God is eternally the Father of the Son, and since no creature can belong by nature to this relation, the Son can only be 'of one substance with the Father' (P. Widdicombe, *The Fatherhood of God from Origen to Athanasius*, pp. 159–222). In a complementary though distinctively Western argument, *Augustine later maintained that the name 'Father' is meaningful only to the extent that the name 'Son' is correlative with it, since the names of the persons strictly denote those eternal relations subsisting in God that have been opened to view in creation and redemption (e.g. Augustine, *De Trinitate*, VII). Modern Christianity, influenced by Enlightenment antipathy to the trinitarian question, has tended to conceive of God's 'fatherhood' mainly in terms of God's care for the world, but the concept in the older Christian tradition is fundamentally determined by these more strictly 'theological' concerns.

What the trinitarian dynamic also helps us to grasp is the basis upon which we call God 'Father'. This possibility rests not upon a generic divine attribute of fatherhood such as that of the *Timaeus*, or upon the naïve assertion that humans are all alike 'God's children', but rather, upon being drawn by the action of the Holy Spirit specifically into union with Jesus Christ, God's Son and our Lord, by virtue of union with whom we also are 'adopted' to become children ('sons') of God (see *Salvation). Thus in adoption we come to participate in the mutual love of the Father and the Son, not only being pardoned in justification, and being conformed to the image of Christ in discipleship, but also being made to share – though undoubtedly at a creaturely distance – the relations proper to the divine trinitarian life.

See also: CHRISTOLOGY; GOD; TRINITY.

Bibliography

J. Barr, 'Abba Isn't "Daddy"', *JTS* n.s. 39, 1988, pp. 28–47; J. Jeremias, *The Prayers of Jesus* (ET, London, 1967); A. F. Kimel, Jr (ed.), *Speaking the Christian God* (Grand Rapids and Leominster, 1992); K. Rahner, 'Theos in the New Testament', in K. Rahner, *Theological Investigations*, vol. 1 (ET, London, 1961); T. Smail, *The Forgotten Father* (London, 1980); P. Widdicombe, *The Fatherhood of God from Origen to Athanasius* (Oxford, 1994).

G. D. BADCOCK

FATHERS, see PATRISTIC THEOLOGY

FEDERAL THEOLOGY, see COVENANT

FELLOWSHIP

Seeking the restoration of communion with the divinity is a mark of our inclination toward the religious, an incurable feeling present in every human being. Contrary to secular pragmatism and scepticism, the Christian religion claims that the fellowship of human beings with the divinity is possible. The revelational and historic Christian sources assert the fundamental teaching that to have fellowship with the divinity (i.e. with an infinite and personal God) is the goal of human existence. The context that God the Creator decided for human beings to inhabit is the context of the *covenant, defined by the acceptance of a reciprocal relationship between God and humankind, with privileges and responsibilities (Gen. 3:8). We were not created to live in isolation, but in fellowship with other personal beings.

The concept of fellowship or communion (*koinonia*) is promoted by Christians mainly because of its participative and communitarian dimension. More precisely, in the Christian religion fellowship is defined in relationships. Therefore, the worship and fear of God, living in holiness and spreading unconditional love among people, trace the matrix in which one can rediscover real fulfilling fellowship, the objective testimony against present individualism and neopaganism.

Before everything else, the fellowship of believers is influenced and empowered by the model of the fellowship among the persons of the Holy *Trinity. The call of believers is to fellowship 'with the Father and with his Son, Jesus Christ' (1 John 1:3; 1 Cor. 1:9), and to 'the fellowship/communion of the Holy Spirit' (2 Cor. 13:14). The invitation refers to the experience of personal knowledge by *faith, and not to a mystical absorption or an ontological identification. That caused the Church Fathers to use a special term for this unique nature of relationship: *perichoresis*. Strictly speaking, the perichoretic relationship is the intimate relationship and reciprocal habitation of the persons in the Godhead: the Father, the Son and the Holy Spirit. The specific dynamics of life in the Trinity suggests the prototype of the fellowship expected within the Christian community.

This life is possible because human beings were created after God's *image, which at the beginning included also the dimension of uncorrupted fellowship. The *fall of humankind distorted the divine image in themselves and the intimate relationship of creature and Creator. The constant longing of humankind for this communion is real, but the initiative for its accomplishment can come only from the divine. Therefore, any kind of fellowship enjoyed by human beings is a divine gift. At the centre of the Christian revelation stands the truth that by sharing/communication of God himself in the divine *Logos, in the person of Jesus Christ, he came to re-establish the initial state of fellowship. Therefore, anyone who enters into a real fellowship with the Son of God by faith can have fellowship with God the Father (John 1:1, 14, 18).

The trinitarian pattern of fellowship is made manifest in the ecclesial pattern. All those who answer to the divine call and enter into fellowship with the Son are integrated into the *church, 'the fellowship of the saints' (*communio sanctorum*). The restoration of personal fellowship with God brings the restoration of fellowship among believers through the work of the word and the Spirit. This new type of Christian communion manifested itself from the beginning of church history through a new form of *worship, prayer, Eucharist, teaching, edifying and sharing of goods (Acts 4:32–35; 1 Cor. 10:16–17). In the church, as the body of Christ, the principle of incorporation in the same body eliminates independence (1 Cor. 12), relationships come before activities, sharing comes before accumulating (Acts 2:46), and the harmony of fellowship is perfected in partnerships and common ministries (2 Cor. 8:3; Phlm. 6). Thus fellowship does not reduce itself to some common social activity, in which one interacts with the opinions, ideas or habits of others, but it embodies the perichoretic life of the Trinity in consecration, *ministry and sacrifice. The fellowship extends itself in public testimony, in *mission and social ministry, in generosity and collection, all proving to be a real investment in the context of covenant. Following the model of Jesus in his relationship with his disciples (cf. John 13:29), the fellowship of the church implies communitarian relationships through participation in the process of giving and receiving. Christians stay together because they share not only the spiritual, but also the material; not only the joys, but also the sorrows (1 Cor. 15:27; Phil. 1:7; 3:10; 4:15; 1 Pet. 4:13). Finally, the ethical model gathers and actualizes the relational and the ecclesiastic models.

The condition of being partakers of the divine nature (2 Pet. 1:4) is to walk in the light (1 John 1:7). Fellowship and purity go together. You may enjoy authentic fellowship only if you live in the light, that is, in truth. To have authentic fellowship with God means to be open toward him, to refuse to live in darkness and decide to live in the light (cf. 1 Tim. 5:22).

See also: CHRISTIAN LIFE; DEIFICATION.

Bibliography

S. J. Grenz, *Theology for the Community of God* (Nashville, 1994); J. M. Lieu, *The Theology of the Johannine Epistles* (Cambridge, 1997); A. J. Torrance, *Persons in Communion: An Essay on Trinitarian Description and Human Participation* (Edinburgh, 1996); J. D. Zizioulas, *Being as Communion: Studies in Personhood and the Church* (London, 1985).

E. BARTOS

FEMINIST THEOLOGY

One of the first things to be noted in relation to 'feminist theology' is that we should, rather, talk of 'feminist theologies'. Although such theologies may have much in common (origins, concerns, methodologies), it is crucial to recognize distinct foundations, approaches and outcomes which may differentiate them. Feminist theology is an approach, or set of concerns, raising fundamental questions for Christian theology. Indeed, it might be said that it is the range of questions which is the common ground, but whether and where answers are found – and the nature of the answers – depends on the stance and approach being taken. It is a mistake to prejudge or dismiss feminist theology because of an assumption that it is one particular set or type of answers.

History and development

Within a circular hermeneutical model (ch. 1 of *Sexism and God-Talk*, London, 1983) Rosemary Ruether presents feminist theology as arising from a crisis faced by Christianity – a crisis comparable to that which led to the Reformation and which she understands as a disjunction between past tradition(s) and present experience's needs and questions. Tradition here is a broad term encompassing the 'codifications' which make up a religion: texts, beliefs, practices, doctrines, symbols, rituals, law codes, moral codes and so on; the 'shape' which a religion takes as it seeks to understand, explain and apply the initial revelatory experience(s) on which it is founded.

Each generation, Ruether argues, will inevitably approach and utilize religious traditions from the perspective of its own historically and culturally located experience. Of course, the nature and relative authority both of tradition and of our experience may be understood very differently, and we will return to this point below. However, it seems axiomatic that questions about *gender and *sexuality – like other issues, notably about race – arise out of the response of particular individuals and groups: 'but what about me?'

Feminist theology can thus also be seen as a significant case study of the ways in which Christianity might respond to the challenges of expressing Christian faith in a manner which is relevant and meaningful in specifically contemporary and culturally varied contexts (see *Contextualization).

This process has been very much related to global changes in the last two centuries. Paradigm shifts in relation to reform and equal rights movements may be related to earlier questioning and protest, but have been dramatically new in scale and in the pace of resultant change. It is also hard to overestimate the impact on theology of the participation of women in education and 'public life' in general. Christian faith was a key motivation for many of the nineteenth-century reformers, and it seems both inevitable and right that Christianity should continue to engage with and respond to these paradigm shifts and the contemporary issues which have emerged from them.

Women have, of course, always been centrally part of Christianity, and so, unsurprisingly, there have always been questions about gender. It is important to note that the questions raised by feminist theologies are not always or necessarily new questions. What has been new is the way in which gender has arguably become (for some) a way of approaching theology per se, rather than simply a concern of theology; a major determinant of the agenda, rather than simply a possible agenda item. This development can be seen as part of what has been described as a movement from 'first-wave' to 'second-wave' feminism.

The first wave of feminism emerged within the nineteenth-century political context of – and very much associated with – other movements such as those for the abolition of slavery and welfare reform. Its immediate impetus was concern over specific inequalities or exclusions (notably suffrage and education), and early feminist theology was similarly concerned with specific exclusions of women in the church, with campaigns for the ordination of women raising an increasingly far-ranging set of questions about *Scripture and tradition.

It is worth noting, however, that the work of Elizabeth Cady Stanton in the 1890s, with her assertion of the androcentric bias of the Bible, pre-empted some of the more 'second-wave' and radical concerns of the 1960s. Like feminism in general and like *liberation theologies to which it is related, feminist theology in this period turned its attention increasingly to fundamental and structural issues which were seen to underlie specific inequalities. Feminism began to discuss issues about female/male nature, *power, gender roles and stereotyping, and the concepts of sexism and patriarchy became central to much feminist analysis. The question had now been raised explicitly as to whether the specific gender inequalities identified within Christianity were also due to patriarchal assumptions and beliefs which might have shaped not only the practice of Christianity, but also the transmission and interpretation of Christian belief in texts and teaching. Such questions have led to re-examination of history and texts and to discussion about *hermeneutics, the nature of traditions and in fact the very way we understand God.

An early example of this development, regularly cited as both influential and indicative, was Valerie Saiving's article, 'The Human Situation: A Feminine View'. Her suggestion that Christian understanding of *sin has been shaped by particularly male perspectives and experience illustrates the impact within theology of the kinds of gender issues being raised in other discipline areas, and she draws specifically on the work of Margaret Mead. Some significant theologians of and after this period – such as Mary Daly and Daphne Hampson – would eventually conclude that Christianity was so essentially patriarchal as to be incompatible with feminism. Others – such as Kari Borrensen, Catharina Halkes and Rosemary Ruether – are convinced that the central truths of Christianity are not only compatible with feminist concern for equality and unity, but may provide a basis, resources and empowerment for such concern:

Feminist theology

a 'place to stand' (Ruether, *Sexism and God-Talk*, p. 18).

Tasks

Feminist theology shares not only some of its origins and history with feminism, but also important aspects of its past and present preoccupations. The tasks with which feminist theologies engage range from specific, 'first-wave' concerns with particular roles and texts to 'second-wave' discussions such as those about traditional associations of women with nature and motherhood, or God-Talk.

Having identified feminist theology as arising from the crisis of disjunction between tradition and current experience and/or needs, Ruether sees it as inevitable and right that such crisis propels us to re-examine not only our experience and needs, but also tradition – the 'codifications' of religion.

There is a 'relativizing' element in feminist theology in recognition of the ways in which Christianity as a faith may be shaped by historical and cultural aspects. It questions how far the teachings, doctrines and practices of the church might have been distorted through and by the processes of codification, subject as they might be to a range of historical, cultural, political, personal and other influences. Whether or not this question is extended from church teaching and practice to include Scripture itself is a defining decision to be taken by any Christian thinker, and feminist theologians take a range of different views on this.

A useful example here is that of the ordination of women, since it uncovers questions from first and second waves of engagement. Initially, Christian thinkers sought to explore how women might be included in the existing ecclesiastical set-up, and whether leadership was necessarily male. They returned to their received traditions and sought biblical models of female leadership, sometimes re-examining the role of women among Jesus' first disciples and the earliest Christian church (such as the work of Elisabeth Fiorenza, *In Memory of Her*, London, ²1996, and many other works), as well as the specific contested texts. They asked, 'Are there inclusive and egalitarian elements of the teaching and practice of Christ which have been lost or sidelined in the ways Christianity has developed and been practised?' From such engagements, Christian feminists argued for a pattern of inclusion and mutual submission as a true reflection of the intention, teaching and practice of Jesus Christ. Has the 'original revelatory experience' been obscured or even jettisoned in following centuries as later patriarchal contexts and their assumptions about gender roles became entrenched in the codifications of Christian tradition?

Second-wave questions took this interrogation further, asking what kind of ecclesial models would best reflect the 'original revelatory experience'. The ways in which these questions are answered have implications beyond ecclesiology (see *Church government). Approaches to church leadership reveal and reflect assumptions about the nature of the divine, the nature of priesthood, of authority, of what it fundamentally means to be male or female. Christian feminists found that received traditions, despite often claiming to be based only on Scripture, may in fact mask presuppositions about femininity and masculinity and ideas of propriety for which there is no clear Christian mandate.

This re-examination reflects a desire, according to Ruether, to 'go back' to the beginning, to set the original revelation against (some of) the possibly patriarchal ways in which Christianity has developed – and also to see how the original revelation might relate and speak to current experience and needs. There are varying views, of course, about the viability and possibility of such a 'return'.

Traditions or 'codification' are also re-examined with an interest in the ways in which it has reached us – not only the contents, but the process of transmission is under scrutiny. Is there important evidence about the role of women in early Christianity which is lost or obscured through the ways in which the texts have been written, assembled, translated and interpreted? Translation of key terms like *diakonos* and passages like those about Junia (Rom. 16:7) were identified early on as a crucial area for analysis. Furthermore, the omission of women from Paul's list of witnesses to the resurrection (1 Cor. 15), when set against the Gospel accounts to which women are central, raised new questions about the way in which the story has been told, and the kinds of factors which might have shaped its telling.

So feminist theologians talk frequently of the 'hermeneutics of suspicion'. It is necessary not only to re-examine the story, but also to be aware of who is telling the story and what differences that might make, a point that is relevant to all who interpret the Bible.

Importantly here, Christian feminism has sought to return to a theology where the person and teaching of *Jesus is central. Christian feminism has often been portrayed as the woeful ousting of Christocentric faith for something enshrining a secular ideology. As we have suggested, this would ignore and misrepresent the work of a great many Christian feminists who strive to unearth an original experience of Christianity where the practice and intention of Jesus Christ is central.

Feminist theology today

A century of concerted engagement with the findings and challenges of feminism has resulted in a spectrum of theological positions. In common with its secular equivalent, Christian feminism has both radical and liberal interpretations: those who desire a brand new order of human relationality, and those who seek equality within the existing schema. We can identify extreme positions and a number of mid-points. Most importantly, positions along the spectrum are determined by the weight given to experience and to tradition in shaping the resultant theology. Unfortunately, some critiques of feminist theology have focused on the two extremes, whereas most work done in relation to theology and gender in fact falls into the middle ground.

At one end of the spectrum, the radical frontier of Christian feminism, contemporary experience has the prerogative in deciding which elements of the Christian tradition are relevant and which should be rejected. Here some feminists have concluded that Christian tradition is ultimately inconsistent with the women's liberation movement. Viewed from this position, Christian feminism is an oxymoron. Having been examined and found wanting, some radical feminists suggest that Christianity should be rejected in favour of post-Christian spiritualities. This edge has been termed 'revolutionary', in that it finds the Christian tradition irredeemably patriarchal and oppressive and needing to be cast off in a radical way. This position is evident in the writings of Mary Daly (most famously in *Beyond God the Father*, London, ²1986) and Daphne Hampson (*Theology and Feminism*; also *After Christianity*, London, ²2002).

At the other extreme, some Christian engagements with feminism have conversely privileged received traditions entirely over contemporary experience, rejecting the possibility that contemporary experience may question or shape Christian tradition at all. Feminism may be judged as aberrant and an alien intrusion of secular ideology into Christianity. Acute conservative positions view the Bible as instigating prescribed gender roles and an intractable worldview that must not be challenged. The gospel message is viewed as inseparable from the received traditions circumscribing it. Questioning tradition implies undermining the gospel itself. Given this, an attempt is made to allow received tradition to define contemporary experience fundamentally. At this end of the spectrum, engagement with feminism leads to the retrenchment of a supposed biblical worldview that is seen as under attack. W. Oddie's book *What Will Happen to God?* (San Francisco, ²1993) is a good introduction to views at this end of the spectrum.

For both the radical and the acutely conservative, there is a tendency towards an either/or mentality in the interaction between received tradition and contemporary experience. The majority of Christian responses to feminism fall somewhere between these positions and involve a process of mediation between experience and tradition. Here, within what have been termed 'reformist' responses, there is the recognition that the Christian *gospel holds an indispensable role in human liberation, possessing a means to combat oppression and injustice in all its forms. While upholding the unique libratory potential of the gospel, reformist Christian feminists accept that this gospel has been filtered through human experience and invariably marked by the sinful effects of centuries of patriarchy. As such, this received tradition requires interrogation and reformulation. The interface between Christianity and feminism gives rise to a process of deconstruction where the gospel's emancipatory power is to be uncovered and reclaimed like a 'golden thread'; a process that leads not to destruction, but to expression of a renewed Christian tradition. (The term 'golden thread' is Hampson's, *Theology and Feminism*, pp. 25ff.) Such reformist positions are held (in quite different ways) by many notable theologians, including Rosemary Radford Ruether, Sallie McFague and Elaine Storkey.

Emerging themes

Christian feminism is at the forefront of engaging with twenty-first-century issues, foremost of which are environmental concerns, an appreciation of the relevance of ethnicity and race to theory, and the challenges of postmodernity. We believe that that there is a methodological capacity within Christian feminism that makes it an efficient respondent to changing concerns. Lessons learned in the deconstruction of the codifications of traditions and in hermeneutics of suspicion in the twentieth century make it well placed to engage with twenty-first-century interests.

First, contemporary Christian feminists form part of the vanguard relating theology to *ecology, giving rise to a movement termed 'Christian eco-feminism'. Rosemary Ruether, Sallie McFague and Celia Deane-Drummond are notable in exploring this interface. They identify ways in which roots of ecological destruction are linked to those of social oppression. The solution to both the oppression of women and the earth is to be found in a holistic, anti-hierarchical paradigm available through a renewed Christianity. Christian feminists contend that spiritual conflict and sin, structural as well as individual, lie at the heart of ecological exploitation. They identify the root causes of oppression and offer spiritual as well as practical solutions, a concern shared by some other ecologists who identify a link between environmental concern, gender and spirituality. From this engagement, Christian eco-feminists draw both ethical implications concerning the way we live in our environment and a theological model of an organic relationship between God and the world.

A second twenty-first-century concern has been the recognition of the global context for faith. Within feminism, there is a growing appreciation of the way in which women's experiences are shaped by *race or ethnicity and that many women have suffered a double oppression. *Black and Asian women theologians respond negatively not only to exclusion from patriarchal and Eurocentric forms of religion, but also in identifying a further exclusion from Western feminist theologies. They recognize the need for black women to find their own voice, insisting on the importance of particularity in resistance to universalizing and essentialist tendencies they identify within Western feminism, which should not claim to speak for them. Accordingly, they have taken it upon themselves to reapprehend Scripture and tradition in light of their own experiences. Some of these approaches have been termed 'womanist', and Mercy Oduyoye and Chung Hyun Kyung are foremost examples. *Womanist writers have been especially interested in using literature, exploring the role and power of narrative in theology and faith, and celebrating culture as an expression of their religious, black, female identity.

Perhaps this willingness to listen to the voices beyond the master narrative has also equipped Christian feminism, thirdly, with a means to engage with the challenge of *postmodernism. Today multiculturalism and diversity provide the framework for political, cultural and social theories. All have been required to consider voices from the margins and resist imposing a false hegemony. This global context for faith, coupled with post-structuralist theories of language (see *Deconstructionism) and the dissipation of meaning, have shaped a twenty-first-century paradigm that has become termed 'postmodernity'. In relating to this context, some Christian feminists have found an ally in postmodern theory as they dismantle the rigidity of universalism and the hierarchies imposed by dualistic thinking. This is evident in the writing of Maggie Kin, Susan M. St Ville and Susan M. Simonaitis. Such theorists extend critique of patriarchy and *modernism to encompass feminism itself, suggesting that all universal categories are oppressive. They use a post-structural philosophy of language and discourse theory to argue for a plurality of perspectives. Others are more suspicious of the tenets of postmodernism, especially the notion that meaning is purely constructed in language. Elaine Storkey (*Created or Constructed?*) provides an introductory overview of feminist theology's engagement with post-feminist and post-structuralist approaches. In engaging with postmodernism, Christian feminists have joined the debate as to the place of psychoanalysis within theories of subjectivity, the nature of epistemology, the relationship between gender and sex, and the decentring of heterosexuality.

In all these areas of discussion we see the full spectrum of possibilities in relating experience and tradition. We also see the breadth which might be encompassed in the term 'feminist theology' and the scope of its concerns and possibilities. Christian feminist theologians are committed to the task of interpreting Christianity for a contemporary audience, and the questions they raise as they weigh contemporary experience and received tradition are precisely those which confront all those seeking to present an authentic Christian faith for the twenty-first century.

Bibliography

D. Carmody, *Christian Feminist Theology* (Oxford, 1995); E. S. Fiorenza, *In Memory of Her* (London, ²1996); D. Hampson, *Theology and Feminism* (Oxford, 1990); U. King, *Feminist Theology from the Third World: A Reader* (Oxford, 1994); M. van Leeuwen (ed.), *After Eden* (Paternoster, 1996); A. Loades (ed.), *Feminist Theology: A Reader* (London, 1996); S. McFague, *Models of God* (London, 1987); R. Muers, 'Feminism, Gender, and Theology', in D. F. Ford (ed.), *The Modern Theologians* (Oxford, Malden, MA and Victoria, ³2005); R. R. Ruether, *Women and Redemption* (London, 1998); V. Saiving, 'The Human Situation: A Feminine View', *The Journal of Religion* 49, 1960, pp. 100–112; E. Storkey, *Created or Constructed?* (Paternoster, 2000).

S. E. ALSFORD AND S. MANN

FEUERBACH, LUDWIG ANDREAS (1804–72)

Feuerbach was the best-known nineteenth-century proponent of the view that *religion arises as a projection of human aspirations. After study with *Hegel in Berlin (and several years as a convinced Hegelian), Feuerbach underwent a philosophical conversion. The result appeared first in *The Essence of Christianity* (1841) and then in a series of works which explicated both his anti-Hegelianism and his distinctive convictions about religion. Feuerbach's arguments rested upon a post-Kantian conception of reality. That is, since we cannot know the world in itself, our minds contribute to our conception of what actually exists. Feuerbach also drew on *Schleiermacher's assertion that religion consists in an inner conviction, or sense, of absolute dependence. Feuerbach, however, differed from *Kant and Schleiermacher, who were *theists. He insisted that if these thinkers are correct, they demonstrate that all our supposed knowledge of God is merely an enlargement of ideas about ourselves and human experience. 'God,' Feuerbach wrote in 1841, 'is himself the realized wish of the heart, the wish exalted to the certainty of its fulfilment . . . the secret of theology is nothing else than anthropology – the knowledge of God nothing else than a knowledge of man!' (*Essence of Christianity*, pp. 121, 207). Thus, when humans talk about their God or religion, they do nothing more than abstract and externalize their own experience. Feuerbach claimed the support of *Luther, since Luther had emphasized the way in which God expressed his divinity in human qualities through the incarnation. Feuerbach also went further to make a general statement about the basis of reality. Against Hegel, who postulated ideas or intelligence as the foundation, Feuerbach contended that 'Nature, Matter, cannot be explained as a result of intelligence; on the contrary, it is the basis of intelligence . . . Consciousness develops itself only out of nature' (*Essence of Christianity*, p. 87). Feuerbach felt that the *atheism which resulted from his views was not a message of despair, but a testimony to the nobility of humanity. If humans could project such an ennobling and altruistic faith as Christianity, this spoke very well indeed for the quality of humanity itself.

Feuerbach's ideas had a significant influence on Karl *Marx and Friedrich Engels, who drew from him the belief that the material realm is the basis for all ideology. For Marx, Feuerbach established true materialism and true science by demonstrating that human social experience establishes our conception of humankind. Yet Marx also criticized Feuerbach for not breaking cleanly enough with Hegel. The key for Marx was not idealized humanity, but people in their concrete social and economic relationships. Feuerbach's influence can also be seen in Sigmund Freud's treatment of religion as an 'illusion', and in Martin *Buber's concentration upon inter-human relationships as the source of knowledge and ethics.

The mark of Feuerbach was especially great on twentieth-century theology. Radical thinkers such as John A. T. *Robinson concede that 'in a real sense Feuerbach was right in wanting to translate "theology" into "anthropology"' (*Honest to God*, London, 1963, p. 50). Other theologians have contended against Feuerbach. Chief among these was Karl *Barth, whose insistence upon God's transcendence is, among other things, an effort to repudiate Feuerbach. When Barth denies the value of *natural theology, and when he contends that Christianity is not a religion, he is responding to Feuerbach's description of faith as mere human projection. The seriousness of Barth's response to Feuerbach suggests that while the latter's human-centred atheism is important for understanding nineteenth-century German philosophical history, it is even more important as a continuing challenge to those who believe in divine *revelation, the *supernatural and the otherness of God.

Bibliography

Works: *The Essence of Christianity*, tr. G. Eliot (New York, 1957); *The Essence of Faith According to Luther* (ET, New York, 1967).

Studies: K. Barth, *Protestant Thought from Rousseau to Ritschl* (ET, New York, 1959); M. Buber, 'What Is Man?' in *Between Man and Man*, tr. R. G. Smith (Boston, 1955); V. A. Harvey, *et al.*, *Feuerbach and the Interpretation of Religion* (Cambridge, 1997); K. Marx, 'Theses on Feuerbach' (1845), in *Marx and Engels on Religion* (ET, New York, 1964); E. Schmidt, 'Ludwig Feuerbachs Lehre von der Religion', *Neue Zeitschrift für systematische Theologie und Religionsphilosophie* 8 (1966), pp. 1–35.

M. A. NOLL

FICHTE, JOHANN GOTTLIEB (1762–1814)

Fichte was one of the founders of *German idealism. In his main philosophical works he attempted to provide a rigorous philosophical foundation for Immanuel *Kant's (1724–1804) critical philosophy. His philosophy of religion was in many ways similar to Kant's, especially in identifying the substance of religion with morality and in deriving religious belief from the demands of the moral life. Accordingly, he argued that any supposed historical revelation of God must be judged by whether the content of the alleged revelation agrees with the content of the moral law. Revelation, therefore, adds nothing to morality; its purpose is to motivate us to perform our moral duties. This emphasis on morality is due to the driving force of Fichte's philosophy, the need to vindicate the claims of human freedom over against philosophical theories of naturalism and determinism, especially that of Benedict *Spinoza (1632–77). Fichte achieved public notoriety in 1798–99 when charges of atheism arose in the wake of some his published works. Although Fichte was not an atheist, he did hold that God cannot be regarded as personal or self-conscious. Instead, he presented God as the creative ground of the universe's moral order. We are not able to form a clear conception of this ground, although Fichte referred to it as reason, will, life and being.

Bibliography

Works: *Attempt at a Critique of All Revelation*, tr. G. Green (Cambridge, 1978); *The Vocation of Man*, tr. P. Preuss (Indianapolis, 1987); 'The Basis of Our Belief in a Divine Governance of the World', tr. D. Breazeale, in *Introductions to the Wissenschaftslehre and Other Writings (1797–1800)* (Indianapolis, 1994); D. Breazeale (ed.), *The Popular Works of Johann Gottlieb Fichte*, tr. W. Smith (London, facsimile edn, 1999).

Studies: D. Breazeale and T. Rockmore (eds.), *Fichte: Historical Context/Contemporary Controversies* (Atlantic Highlands, 1993); *idem* (eds.), *New Perspectives on Fichte* (Atlantic Highlands, 1996).

S. M. POWELL

FIDEISM

Fideism is the view that an appropriate basis of belief, including religious belief, is not the intellect, but the will, or perhaps the emotions or preferences. Thus *Pascal claims that it is reasonable, in the absence of compelling evidence, to wager on God's existence, since more is lost if God exists and one fails to believe in him than if he does not exist and one believes. William *James argued that one may believe (in the absence of sufficient evidence) if the choice is live (one that arises out of present beliefs and desires), forced (that is, one cannot avoid making a choice), and momentous. As can be seen from these cases, fideism is not necessarily irrational, since there may be 'second-order' reasons for being fideistic. However, fideism depends on the controversial claim that belief may depend on the *will. The problem is: If I have good reason for believing that today is Thursday, how can I 'will to believe' that it is Friday? However, this objection does not rule out that one may set oneself to believe some proposition over a longer period, by choosing to concentrate on certain factors (e.g. that such a proposition is comfortable), and by neglecting others (e.g. the evidence against it).

Bibliography

W. Clifford, 'The Ethics of Belief', in *Lectures and Essays* II (London, 1879); P. Helm, *Belief*

Policies (Cambridge, 1994); W. James, 'The Will to Believe', *The Will to Believe and Other Essays* (New York, 1917); S. Kierkegaard, *Concluding Unscientific Postscript to 'Philosophical Fragments'*, ed. and tr. H. V. Hong and E. H. Hong (Princeton, 1991); B. Pascal, *The Pensées*, tr. J. M. Cohen (London, 1961).

P. Helm

FILARET (PHILARET) DROZDOV (1782–1867)

A *Russian Orthodox theologian and churchman, Filaret was a monk who, after teaching biblical studies, theology and philosophy at St Petersburg, became archbishop (1821) and metropolitan (1826) of Moscow. Through his lectures and sermons, and his Christian *Catechism of the Orthodox Catholic Eastern Greco-Russian Church (1823), he exercised a wide influence on nineteenth-century Russian theology. Having assimilated Protestant elements in his youth (especially from the works of Feofan Prokopovich, 1681–1736), he exemplified an intense biblicism (which led to attempts to purge his Catechism of its 'Lutheranism'). He keenly supported Bible Society work, dissented from declarations that Western Christians were heretics, and reflected the abandonment of the *scholastic style in theology in favour of the *patristic. He was enormously influential in affairs of church and state, despite the restrictive rule of Nicholas I (1825–55), which he survived long enough to become the honoured author of the 1861 manifesto emancipating Russia's peasants from serfdom. He was canonized by the Russian Orthodox Church in 1994.

Bibliography

ET of *Catechism* in P. Schaff, *The Creeds of Christendom*, vol. 2 (New York, 1877), pp. 445–542; G. Florovsky, *Ways of Russian Theology, Part One* (*Collected Works*, vol. 5: Belmont, 1979).

D. F. Wright

FILIOQUE, see CREEDS; EASTERN ORTHODOX THEOLOGY; HOLY SPIRIT; TRINITY

FINNEY, CHARLES GRANDISON (1792–1875)

For Finney, the 'father of modern revivalism', the doing of theology was always an eminently practical matter. Whether serving as itinerant evangelist, pastor, professor of theology or college president, his fundamental goal remained the same: to secure the *conversion of sinners and to set them to work in preparing the way for the coming *millennial kingdom.

Finney was trained as a lawyer, but after his dramatic conversion in 1821 sought ordination in the Presbyterian Church and began his labours as a missionary to the settlers of upstate New York. Using such 'new measures' as the anxious seat, protracted meetings and allowing women to pray in public, a series of *revivals soon began to sweep across that region with such frequency that it came to be known as the 'Burned-over District'. Although Finney was involved in promoting revivals throughout his lifetime, even travelling to England for that purpose (1849–50, 1859–60), the period 1824–32 remained the high-water mark of his revival career.

When illness began to curtail his travels, he became pastor of the Chatham Street Chapel in New York. He subsequently held pastorates at the Broadway Tabernacle of New York (1836–7) and the First Congregational Church of Oberlin, Ohio (1837–72). In 1835 he became professor of theology at the newly formed Oberlin Collegiate Institute in Ohio (now Oberlin College). He later served as president of Oberlin College (1851–66).

Theologically, Finney is best described as a New School Calvinist (see *New Haven theology). His preaching and teaching, always pointed and dramatic, stressed the moral government of God, human ability to repent and create new hearts, the perfectibility of human nature and society, and the need for Christians to apply their faith to daily living. For Finney, this included the investment of one's time and energy in establishing the millennial kingdom of God on earth by winning converts and involving oneself in social reform (including anti-slavery, temperance and the like).

Throughout his lifetime, Finney produced a variety of books, sermon collections and articles. Among the more important were his *Lectures on Revivals of Religion* (1835; repr., ed. W. G. McLoughlin, Cambridge, MA, 1960), a kind of manual on how to lead revivals; his

Lectures on Systematic Theology (Oberlin, 1846), reflecting his special brand of '*Arminianized Calvinism', and his *Memoirs* (1876), recounting his involvement in the great revivals of the earlier nineteenth century.

Bibliography

C. E. Hambrick-Stowe, *Charles G. Finney and the Spirit of American Evangelicalism* (Grand Rapids, 1996); K. J. Hardman, *Charles Grandison Finney (1792–1875)* (Syracuse, 1987); W. G. McLoughlin, Jr, *Modern Revivalism: Charles Grandison Finney to Billy Graham* (New York, 1959); G. M. Rosell, 'Charles G. Finney: His Place in the Stream of Evangelicalism', in L. I. Sweet (ed.), *The Evangelical Tradition in America* (Macon, 1984).

G. M. ROSELL

FIORENZA, ELISABETH SCHÜSSLER (b. 1938)

Elisabeth Fiorenza is a leading feminist theologian renowned for her pioneering work in biblical interpretation. Born in Romania, fleeing to West Germany during the Second World War, Fiorenza remained committed to *Roman Catholic theology, becoming the first woman to take the licentiate in practical theology at the University of Würzburg (1962). She is the Krister Stendahl Professor of Divinity at Harvard Divinity School, having lectured previously at the University of Notre Dame and the Episcopal Divinity School in Cambridge, Massachusetts. She is co-founder and editor of the *Journal of Feminist Studies in Religion*, co-editor of *Concilium*, and the first woman to be elected as president of the Society of Biblical Literature (1987). She has published widely and is best known for her ground-breaking book *In Memory of Her: A Feminist Theological Reconstruction of Christian Origins* (1983, translated into twelve languages).

In Memory of Her argues for a feminist biblical *hermeneutic that questions the authority and use of the biblical text. Informed by the feminist critique of androcentrism and *Foucault's account of the extent to which historical narratives reflect underlying power struggles, Fiorenza questions the traditional interpretation of Christian origins. Hence, by rereading the text 'in a different key', Fiorenza reconstructs Christian *history in order to de-naturalize female subordination. On the grounds that traditional interpretations of the texts reflect androcentrism and since there is a lack of proof concerning the non-participation of females in history, she supposes that it is 'possible' that females contributed to the shaping of the early church. Thus, by employing a fluid notion of the canon and by conceiving of the Jesus movement as a 'discipleship of equals', Fiorenza is able to reconcile feminism and Christianity. In *Bread Not Stone* she examines the Bible as a dual resource for female empowerment and continued victimization, while *But She Said* contains the radical assertion that biblical texts which fail to liberate oppressed groups are untrue or misinterpreted. From the 1990s Fiorenza has been leading the way with her use of the terms 'kyriarchy' (master-rule) rather than patriarchy to acknowledge a multiplicity of oppressions and oppressors, 'G*d' to highlight the inadequacy of androcentric god-language, 'wo/men' to avoid implying that all women have the same experience, and the biblical *ekklēsia* (assembly) rather than church (belonging to lord/master) to emphasize equality.

Fiorenza's critics accuse her of finding more egalitarianism in the early church than is warranted, but this criticism misses the point, since her aim is to highlight the political, cultural and ethnic biases that are at work in the transmission of history and serve to legitimate patriarchal structures in the Christian religion: thus, Fiorenza insists that all accounts of Christian origins, whether feminist or traditional, are constructions rather than historical facts. Consequently, her corpus is a formidable challenge to readings of the biblical text that marginalize women's place in church and theology; she calls them to account both in terms of the gendered history on which they are founded and in respect of the political values they continue to advocate.

See also: FEMINIST THEOLOGY; GENDER.

Bibliography

Works: *In Memory of Her: A Feminist Theological Reconstruction of Christian Origins* (London and New York, 1983); *Bread Not Stone: The Challenge of Feminist Biblical Interpretation* (Boston, 1984); *But She Said: Feminist Practices of Biblical Interpretation* (Boston, 1992); *Discipleship of Equals: A Critical Feminist Ekklēsia-logy of Liberation* (London, 1993); *Jesus: Miriam's Child,*

Sophia's Prophet – Issues in Feminist Christology (London, 1994); *Jesus and the Politics of Interpretation* (New York and London, 2000).

E. McIntosh

FLACIUS, see LUTHERANISM

FLOROVSKY, GEORGES (1893–1979)

Georges Florovsky was born in 1893, the son of a Russian priest. He graduated in arts from Odessa University in 1916, and later lectured there. He left Russia in 1920, first for Sofia and then for Prague, where he lectured in law 1922–6. In 1926 he became Professor of Patristics at the Institut St-Serge in Paris, being ordained priest in 1932. After the Second World War, he moved to the United States, and became the Dean of St Vladimir's Orthodox Theological Seminary 1948–55, then taught at Harvard 1956–64, and at Princeton from 1964.

His patristic scholarship is mostly found in his Paris lectures, published in the 1930s. His greatest scholarly work was his *Ways of Russian Theology* (1937), which gave a doleful account of Russian theology, subject to a 'Babylonian captivity' of the West, reaching its apogee in the religious thought of his contemporary émigrés. Russian theology needed to embrace a patristic 'Christian Hellenism': a 'Neo-patristic synthesis', as he came to call it, that is, a theology recovering the insights of the Greek Church Fathers from the Apostolic Fathers to St Gregory Palamas. Although he had reservations about some aspects of the inchoate *ecumenical movement, he came to be deeply involved in it and was one of the architects of the theological statement endorsed at the first meeting of the *World Council of Churches at Amsterdam in 1948. During his time in the States he became an immensely revered Orthodox voice on the theological scene.

See also: Russian Orthodox Theology.

Bibliography

Works: *Collected Works*, ed. R. S. Haugh, 14 vols. (Vaduz, 1987–9).

Studies: A. Blane (ed.), *Georges Florovsky: Russian Intellectual, Orthodox Churchman* (Crestwood, 1993); P. L. Gavrilyuk, *Georges Florovsky and the Russian Religious Renaissance* (Oxford, 2013).

A. Louth

FORGIVENESS, see GUILT AND FORGIVENESS

FORMULA OF CONCORD

The Formula of Concord is a confessional document devised in 1577 to resolve several doctrinal disputes among Lutherans that arose shortly after the death of Martin Luther. To a large extent, these disputes were prompted by different reactions to the resurgence of Catholicism (see *Reformation, Catholic Counter-) and the spread of Calvinism (see *Reformed theology) in Germany during that era. One party of theologians, known as the Gnesio-Lutherans, argued that the Philippists, another group widely influenced by the teachings of Luther's co-worker Philipp *Melanchthon, were endangering the purity of the Lutheran movement by their openness to ideas more closely associated with those other competing theological traditions. The most important disagreements concerned the role of the will and the significance of good works in the process of salvation, as well as the nature of Christ's presence in the Lord's Supper.

In defence of the stress on salvation by grace expressed in 1530 in the *Augsburg Confession, the Formula of Concord noted more explicitly that the human *will, after the fall, is unable to do anything to render itself fit to receive grace. The Formula condemned some Philippists who suggested that the will was able to cooperate, though weakly, with grace, and some Gnesio-Lutherans, on the opposite extreme, who declared that human nature was so substantially infused with original sin that it no longer bore a trace of the image of God.

Martin *Chemnitz and Jakob Andreae, the mediating theologians who composed the Formula of Concord, condemned radical statements made by some Philippists and Gnesio-Lutherans who, in the heat of debate, had argued that good works were either necessary for, or harmful to, salvation. Concerned to avoid both works-righteousness and moral irresponsibility, they stated more simply that good works will surely follow true faith.

On the issue of the Lord's Supper (see *Eucharist), the Formula of Concord sought to differentiate more clearly between the theology of the Swiss Reformers and the Lutherans. In contrast to Calvin and some Philippist Lutherans, it specified that both true believers and unbelievers receive the true body and blood of Christ by mouth along with the sacramental bread and wine.

The Formula of Concord never received as wide an official endorsement among Lutheran churches as the Augsburg Confession, but in 1580 it was included in the Book of Concord, the collection of confessional writings that continues to be the most authoritative standard of theology for the majority of Lutherans down to the present.

See also: CONFESSIONS OF FAITH; LUTHERANISM AND LUTHERAN THEOLOGY.

Bibliography

The Book of Concord: The Confessions of the Evangelical Lutheran Church, eds. R. Kolb and T. Wengert (Minneapolis, 2000).
Studies: F. Bente, *Historical Introductions to the Book of Concord* (St Louis, 1965 [1921]); E. Klug and O. Stahlke, *Getting into the Formula of Concord* (St Louis, 1977).

E. LUND

FORSYTH, PETER TAYLOR (1848–1921)

Forsyth was born and educated in Aberdeen in Scotland. On advice from his friend William Robertson Smith, he studied theology under *Ritschl at Göttingen, then at New College, London, after which he spent the rest of his life as a pastor and theologian. Both words are required to explain the power and passion of Forsyth's theological oeuvre. He was Congregational pastor for twenty-five years in Shipley (1876), Manchester (1885), Leicester (1888) and Cambridge (1894), followed by twenty years as Principal of Hackney College in London. In 1899 and 1907 he visited the United States, in 1905 was Chairman of the Congregational Union, and in 1910 was appointed Dean of the London Faculty of Theology.

During his early pastoral years his theological position moved from liberal theologian heavily indebted to German thought, and impatient with traditional formulations of doctrine, to that of 'classical Christianity' with an enduring focus on the *cross as the 'magnetic north' on the Christian compass. The consequences of Forsyth's theological and personal 'conversion' was an abandonment of earlier humanistic ideas, while retaining the tools of liberal higher criticism used now with discriminating purpose (see *Liberal theology). In 1896 the potent mix of critical scholarship, personal tragedy on the death of his wife, and evangelical experience were distilled into an address entitled 'The Holy Father', in which Forsyth announced the main emphases of his future theological manifesto.

From 1897 when *The Holy Father and the Living Christ* was published, until 1918 when his last book *This Life and the Next* was issued, Forsyth produced a steady flow of constructive, pastoral, occasional and at times polemical theological publications. The range of interest and subjects indicates the non-systematic but contextually engaged style of Forsyth's theology. He wrote important, original constructive treatments of the *atonement and *Christology; presented fresh construals of ecclesiology and the sacraments combined with bold statements on issues of church relations and polity; produced bracing and robust reflections on prayer and spirituality which while eschewing mystical speculation do not lack a sense of the profound, transformative power of encounter with God in Christ; and his lectures on preaching and art indicate the breadth and depth of Forsyth's awareness of the pastoral realities and *cultural constraints that must inform and challenge contemporary articulation and proclamation of the gospel. There is no discernible overarching programme in Forsyth's theological writing and development other than the pervasive, recurring attention he pays to the cross as the work of Christ.

Forsyth's secure grasp and trenchant expression of both evangelical essentials and critical scholarship made him a key opponent of R. J. Campbell's so-called New Theology, and a recognized theological leader within and beyond English *Congregationalism. Gratefully confessing that he had been turned 'from a love of God to an object of *grace', his emphases in some respects anticipated Barth. The objectivity and primacy of grace, the 'Christological concentration' on Jesus Christ crucified and risen as the centre of theology and revelation, and biblical exegesis as the primary basis and essential content of dogmatics, are emphases shared by the two theologians without traceable dependence.

Like his contemporary, James *Denney, Forsyth presented the atonement as a reality beyond the conceptual control of one theory. Reconciliation, judgment, substitution, victory, regeneration, sacrifice and satisfaction provide a complex nexus of ideas that are woven together into a continuing exposition of the cross. However, in seeking an understanding of atonement adequate to its significance for Christian faith, the holy love of God became both the dogmatic background and kerygmatic foreground of Forsyth's exposition (see especially *The Cruciality of the Cross* and *The Work of Christ*). Rejecting any sentimental or 'soft' view of divine love and Fatherhood, and dismissive of reductionist views of sin to psychological or social forces, he insisted on the ontological reality and radical moral and eternal consequences of sin. 'Do not say God is love. Why atone? ... The New Testament says God has atoned! What love! ... you can go behind love to holiness, but behind holiness you cannot go.' The purpose of God in the cross was to redeem, to create a new moral order through 'the Son's sinless obedience and the Father's, holy satisfaction' (L. McCurdy, *Attributes and Atonement*).

The cruciality of the cross derives, for Forsyth, from the centrality of Christ as God's self-revelation of holy love, the overcoming of sin by 'a holy God, self-atoned in Christ [as] the centre of the world'. In his Christology (particularly *The Person and Place of Jesus Christ*), Forsyth explored a form of *kenosis which sought to do justice to divine immutability and the reality of God incarnate in Christ, primarily by asserting the crucial connection between incarnation and atonement, and by balancing divine kenosis with the notion of divine *plerosis*, 'making dogmatic room for Christ's growth in grace, personality and achievement until he was filled with the fullness of God'(McCurdy, *Attributes and Atonement*).

'Love is only divine as it is holy; and spirituality is Christian only as it meets the conditions of holy love in the way the cross did, as the crisis of holy judgement and holy grace.' In *Christian Perfection* and *The Soul of Prayer* Forsyth expounded Christian *spirituality as a matter of will directed to obedience, as inner moral urgency generated by grace finds expression in an outward and active engagement with the world. Rather than contemplative cultivation of spiritual experience, Forysth urged the energizing exertion of will, wrestling with God, because 'resisting His will may be doing His will', and 'our soul is fulfilled if our petition is not'. Unanswered prayer is never a reason for thinking ill of God: 'He says no in the spirit of yes.' Through prayer moral personality is renewed in the regular encounter of the soul with the God who is Holy Love. The cross gives prayer its guarantees and its moral power. Thus the Christian life is 'repentant praise', because 'we confess much more than sin – a Saviour to our own worst depths and to the wide ends of the earth'.

In his thinking and writing, Forsyth ranged widely across cultural and theological fields. Almost a third of his library included German theologians, amongst them Ritschl, *Kähler, Zahn and *Schlatter. He expressed conscious indebtedness to the great Congregational Puritans, *Owen and *Goodwin, whose writings 'not only tingle, they soar', and live on in the spiritual life. From English theologians such as Maurice, Forsyth derived important insights on the nature of faith, and from Dale a permanent conviction of the centrality of Jesus in constructive theology of the atonement, and the cross as the primary focus of Christian theology. An early reader of the astringent *Kierkegaard, appreciative of *Pascal's epigrammatic fire, suspicious of mysticism 'used as the sufficient basis of religious certainty for a whole church', he nevertheless insisted, 'Bernard is my favourite saint and his Canticles a great delight.' The poets were read with receptive admiration (Dora Greenwell, a favourite), with critical appreciation (Browning) or outright disagreement (Whittier). The mind of Forsyth was both free-ranging and theologically assimilative, but to the powerfully centred end of expounding the person and work of Christ in terms that, while never adequate, would at least seek 'to stretch to the measure of eternal things without breaking under us somewhere'.

The theology of Forsyth continues to inspire postgraduate research and theological reflection in such contemporary writers as Fiddes, *Gunton, *Bloesch.

Bibliography

Works: *The Work of Christ* (London, 1938); *The Person and Place of Jesus Christ*

(London, 1946); *The Church and the Sacraments* (London, 1947); *The Cruciality of the Cross* (London, 1948); *Positive Preaching and the Modern Mind* (London, 1949); *The Soul of Prayer* (London, 1949); *The Holy Father and the Living Christ* (London, 1957); *Christ on Parnassus* (London, 1959); *The Church, The Gospel and Society* (London, 1962).

Studies: W. L. Bradley, *P. T. Forsyth. The Man and His Work* (London, 1952); J. M. Gordon, 'Peter Taylor Forsyth and Alexander Whyte', in J. M. Gordon, *Evangelical Spirituality. From the Wesleys to John Stott* (London, 1991); T. Hart (ed.), *Justice the True and Only Mercy: Essays on the Life and Theology of P. T. Forsyth* (Edinburgh, 1995); M. Husbands, 'Forsyth, P. T.', in *BDE*; L. McCurdy, *Attributes and Atonement. The Holy Love of God in the Theology of P. T. Forsyth* (Carlisle, 1999). With comprehensive bibliography; L. McCurdy, 'Forsyth, P. T.', in *DHT*.

J. Gordon

FOUCAULT, MICHEL (1926–84)

Michel Foucault, a philosopher and historian, is best known for exploring the ubiquity of power relationships in *modernity. In his surveys of the asylum, healthcare, prisons and sexuality, he argues that what masquerades as truth or rationality is in fact procedures of power. In *Madness and Civilization* (1961), he undertakes a historical enquiry into how madness has been managed across the centuries. He argues that though the modern age appears as more enlightened – in that it no longer simply incarcerated the insane, but sought to treat them – the reality was that we merely substituted one form of imprisonment for another. In *The Order of Things* (1966), his analysis of knowledge charts a series of 'epistemes' or guiding frameworks, in which our categorization and thinking take place. His conclusion is that knowledge is 'culture-bound instead of universal, epoch-relative instead of cumulative . . . no more than our persistent self-delusion'. Foucault is frequently accused of inconsistency for this apparent 'universal' critique of universal knowledge. However, he is best understood as providing a critique 'from within'. His later works emphasized the development of the self, drawing on Greek and early Christian literature to address issues such as confession and conscience, especially in relation to sexuality.

Bibliography

P. Rainbow (ed.), *The Foucault Reader* (London, 1984; J. K. A. Smith, *Who's Afraid of Postmodernism?* (Grand Rapids, 2006).

J. Thacker

FOUNDATIONALISM

Foundationalism is a term from the theory of knowledge concerning how beliefs become rationally acceptable (or justified), which has developed wider application to other disciplines, including theology.

Narrowly conceived, foundationalism is a dominant family of views in Western thought which affirm that knowledge-beliefs are of two sorts: basic beliefs, which do not receive rational support from other beliefs, and non-basic beliefs, which are inferred from other beliefs. The architectural metaphor of a 'foundation' comes from the fact that inferred beliefs are based or grounded on basic beliefs. The critical aspect of any foundationalist theory concerns its criteria for basic beliefs as those beliefs which do not require inference from other beliefs to ground knowledge. The dual attraction of foundationalism is its ability to halt scepticism by providing a stopping point in the justification process and its common sense acknowledgment that some non-inferential beliefs are rationally appropriate. Following René *Descartes, modern foundationalists believed that basic beliefs must possess an infallible guarantee of truth. The majority of Western philosophers now reject this view, opting instead for a modified foundationalism, because modern foundationalism is overly restrictive to the point of failing its own test for knowledge. Modest foundationalists believe that basic beliefs are fallible, providing a basis for knowledge that is *defeasible*, or able to be defeated or revised in light of further evidence.

In theology, foundationalism is a broader, somewhat contestable term referring to Western Christian theological discourse whose goal is to construct an infallible body of theological knowledge. In modern Christianity, conservative theological foundationalists look to Scripture as the foundational source of inerrant, infallible propositions (as declarative sentences), whereas their liberal counterparts appeal to some form of human rational experience.

For each, the goal of theology is to articulate theological propositions that can be known for certain. Discussions of theology and foundationalism frequently conflate foundationalist justification with modern foundationalism and thereby ignore the implications of modest foundationalism for theology.

There are two basic lines of objection to foundationalism. One questions the foundationalist account of knowledge, while the other, *postmodern, line challenges the need to, and even the moral permissibility of, prescribing knowledge foundations at all. Modest foundationalism has launched an effective response to the former. The latter objection, however, challenges the entire foundationalist project on philosophical and moral grounds, and it is unclear whether the foundationalist response is adequate or even appropriate, particularly alongside increasing acknowledgment of non-Western and postcolonial thought.

See also: Conservative Theology; Liberal Theology; Infallibility and Inerrancy of the Bible.

Bibliography

J. Beilby, 'The Implications of Postmodernism for Theology: On Meta-Narrative, Foundationalism and Realism', *The Princeton Theological Review* XII, 2006, pp. 11–16; L. Bonjour, 'The Dialectic of Foundationalism and Coherentism', in J. Greco and E. Sosa (eds.), *The Blackwell Guide to Epistemology* (Oxford and Malden, 1999); J. R. Franke, 'Christian Faith and Postmodern Theory: Theology and the Nonfoundationalist Turn', in M. B. Penner (ed.), *Christianity and the Postmodern Turn: Six Views* (Grand Rapids, 2005); J. R. Franke and S. J. Grenz, *Beyond Foundationalism: A Postconservative Theological Approach* (Grand Rapids, 2000); P. Klein, 'Foundationalism and the Infinite Regress of Reasons', *Philosophy and Phenomenological Research* LVIII, 1998, pp. 919–926; J. P. Moreland and G. DeWeese, 'The Premature Report of Foundationalism's Demise', in M. J. Erickson, P. K. Helseth and J. Taylor (eds.), *Renewing the Center: Confronting Evangelical Accommodation in Postmodern Times* (Wheaton, 2004); A. Plantinga, 'Reason and Belief in God', in A. Plantinga and N. Wolterstorff (eds.), *Faith and Rationality* (Notre Dame, 1983); M. Westphal, 'Hermeneutics as Epistemology', in J. Greco and E. Sosa (eds.), *The Blackwell Guide to Epistemology* (Oxford and Malden, 1999).

M. B. Penner

FOX, GEORGE, see QUAKER THEOLOGY

FRANCIS AND THE FRANCISCAN TRADITION

The founder of the Order of Friars Minor (the Franciscans), Francis of Assisi (1182–1226), is one of the most admired figures of Christendom. Reared in an atmosphere of luxury, parties and polite society, during his youth he dreamed of a career of military glory, and composed love poetry in the style of the Provençal troubadors. Francis's father (Pietro Bernardoni) believed that his son should become a knight or a merchant, but in his early twenties Francis experienced a religious *conversion which was expressed in a number of dramatic ways. One of them involved the distribution of some family goods for religious purposes. By 1209 he began to live in 'apostolic' *poverty and wandered the countryside clothed in a ragged cloak and a robe belt from a scarecrow – hence the distinctive dress of the Franciscans. He attracted followers to the lifestyle of poverty, love and brotherhood that he taught and exemplified. They begged from the rich and ministered to the sick and the poor while they preached the gospel to the outcasts of medieval society.

In 1210 Pope Innocent III allowed Francis to organize a religious order, the Little Brothers, based upon poverty and service to others. A second order was founded in 1212 when an influential woman named Clare was commissioned by Francis to perform many of the same activities as the brothers. Thus was formed the order for women called the Poor Clares. In addition to his activities among Christians, Francis was concerned with missionary activity and went to Syria (1212), Morocco (1213–14), and Egypt (1219) to evangelize the Muslims. Illness and other misfortunes prevented much success in these endeavours.

Because of the rapid growth of the Order and the need for organization beyond the few simple rules formulated by Francis, a new set of regulations was approved by Pope Honorius III in 1223. A cardinal was named protector of the group, but this displeased Francis, who became less involved in the order. He spent the remainder of his life in solitude, prayer and writing. It was during this period that he produced the 'Canticle to the Sun', his *Admonitions* and his *Testament*. In 1224 he allegedly received the stigmata, a series of wounds on his body similar to those inflicted on Jesus as he was crucified. He was canonized (see *Saint) by Gregory IX in 1228.

Of all the achievements of Francis, the one which may be of greatest interest today is the respect he showed for God's *creation. His enthusiastic, sacred outlook on the world led him to view everything as a living comrade. Many sources report his sermons to the birds, which included the charming line: 'My brother birds, much ought you to praise your Creator and to love him . . .'

Despite his personal example, it was probably inevitable that the Order founded on the principles of simplicity, poverty and service could not adhere to them once it became a successful movement. The Franciscans developed into one of the leading thirteenth-century orders of friars that sought to meet the spiritual needs caused by rapid urban growth and the spread of heresy. Unlike earlier groups of monks, the friars lived among the people, ministering the gospel as well as providing social services to the needy. The problem was that such large-scale enterprises needed financing and organization. All such businesslike activities were discouraged by Francis, who left a will asking that the vow of poverty should not be changed among his followers. Only four years after his death, Pope Gregory IX declared that the will was not binding, thus permitting the Order to hold property. A conflict arose between the Spirituals or Fraticelli, who insisted on keeping the founder's request, and those who accepted the new approach. The main body of the Franciscans, the Conventuals, agreed with the changes. During the latter half of the thirteenth century, tension between the two groups eased under the leadership of *Bonaventura, who maintained a balanced approach between structure and spirit. As an outstanding intellect, he represented the increasing role of scholarship within the Order, which began working in the new urban universities.

As the Franciscans increased their material wealth, Europe entered a difficult time during the fourteenth and fifteenth centuries, experiencing plague, warfare and papal division. The Order declined during these years, but a reform movement, the Observants, developed in its ranks. They wished to re-establish a strict rule and were granted ecclesiastical recognition in 1415. The new group was opposed by the more moderate Franciscans represented by the Conventuals. In 1517 Leo X officially separated the Order into two independent branches: the Friars Minor of the Regular Observants and the Friars Minor Conventuals. Further discord among the Observants led them to divide into several factions, including the Capuchins, the Discalced (Shoeless) and the Recollects. Increasing division caused Leo XIII (1897) to unite all the Observants except the Capuchins.

Despite the admonition of Francis that the Christian faith 'consists not in working miracles . . . nor in learning and knowledge of all things; nor in eloquence to convert the world', his followers have been heavily involved in theological scholarship, preaching and missions and even in politics. During the medieval period all branches of *scholasticism were influenced by Franciscan contributions. Because the order is so diverse, it included those, such as *Duns Scotus and *William of Ockham, who undermined the theological system of *Thomas Aquinas through *Aristotelian logic; while others followed Bonaventura and emphasized the role of meditation and prayer in Christian thought; and a third group supported the outlook of Robert Grosseteste (*c.* 1175–1253) and Roger Bacon (*c.* 1214–92) and insisted on the centrality of observation in arriving at truth. However, all groups of Franciscans were agreed in opposing the synthesis of *faith and reason elaborated by Thomas Aquinas.

The Franciscans have also been active in preaching the gospel. Their missionary journeys took them to China as early as 1294, and they accompanied the Portuguese and Spaniards on their pioneering journeys to India and America. Currently, Franciscans are found working in every mission field of the world.

Many popular devotional practices of the Roman Catholic Church have been encouraged by Franciscan influence. Among the better-known of these are devotion to the Christmas Crib, the Sacred Heart, the Precious Blood, and the Stations of the Cross.

Today the Franciscans are divided into three major branches: the Observants, the Conventuals and the Capuchins. The largest of these is the Observants. They revised their constitution after *Vatican II and have defined the Order's goal as that of a movement which continually reinterprets the gospel in the light of current problems. Many of these friars look on their role as that of the conscience of the church. Such an attitude has led individuals including Leonardo *Boff, a Brazilian theological professor, to apply *Marxist ideas to the problem of the poor. The support that his *liberation theology has received has caused conflict between the Order and the Vatican. Other Franciscan groups have remained more conservative and continue to apply the teachings of their leading medieval scholars such as Bonaventura to contemporary issues.

The Franciscans have contributed in an important way both to Catholicism and to Christendom in general. Their work in evangelizing the new towns of the Middle Ages, developing Christian scholarship and serving in a variety of missionary and social ministries, has helped to make faith in Christ a living reality.

Bibliography

L. Boff, *Church: Charism and Power* (New York, 1985); idem, *St Francis: A Model for Human Liberation* (London, 1985); I. Brady (ed. and tr.), *The Marrow of the Gospel: A Study of the Rule of St Francis of Assisi* (Chicago, 1958); L. Cunningham (ed.), *Brother Francis: An Anthology of Writings by and about S. Francis of Assisi* (New York, 1972); O. Englebert, *Saint Francis of Assisi* (Chicago, 1966); E. H. Gilson, *History of Christian Philosophy in the Middle Ages* (New York, 1955); M. A. Habig, *St Francis of Assisi: Writings and Early Biographies* (Chicago, 1973); H. Holzapfel, *The History of the Franciscan Order* (Teutopolis, 1948); J. R. H. Moorman, *A History of the Franciscan Order: From Its Origins to the Year 1517* (New York, 1988); K. Osborne, *The History of Franciscan Theology* (New York, 1994); N. Şenocak, *The Poor and the Perfect: The Rise of Learning in the Franciscan Order, 1209–1310* (New York, 2012); A. Thompson, OP, *Francis of Assisi: A New Biography* (New York, 2012).

R. G. CLOUSE

FRANKFURT DECLARATION

The Frankfurt Declaration on the Fundamental Crisis of Christian Mission (1970) reaffirmed the basic elements of biblical mission over against their distortions in contemporary *missiological thinking, particularly in the *ecumenical movement since the integration of the former International Missionary Council with the *World Council of Churches in New Delhi in 1961. The Declaration was promulgated by a gathering of German theologians who had joined the struggle of the confession movement 'No Other Gospel' to counteract the effects of radical biblical criticism on the life of the church. The Declaration was occasioned by the unhappiness of many evangelical mission leaders and theologians about Section II, 'Renewal in Mission', of the Fourth Assembly of the WCC in Uppsala, 1968, and might be considered as a German equivalent to the *Wheaton Declaration (1966). Both stand in the tradition of modern confessional statements, of which the *Barmen Declaration of the *Confessing Church in Germany in 1934 is the most outstanding example.

In fact, the form of the Frankfurt Declaration is modelled on the Barmen Declaration. Its seven affirmations, each one introduced by a biblical key text, restate the classical understanding of mission and condemn opposing modern theological concepts. The 'Seven Indispensable Basic Elements of Mission' are intended to safeguard: (1) the sole authority of the Bible over against situational *hermeneutics; (2) the primacy of *doxology over against humanization as the goal of mission; (3) biblical Christology over against an anonymous Christ-presence in human history; (4) the significance of personal faith in salvation over against *universalism; (5) the spiritual nature of the church over against a merely functional understanding of it; (6) the uniqueness of the *gospel over against other religions; (7) the reality of Christ's second coming for the eschatological orientation of mission over against an ideology of *progress or *revolution.

The original purpose of the Declaration was not a call for separation from the WCC's Commission of World Mission and Evangelism, but a call to it to return to its former biblical tradition, seen most clearly in the pronouncements of the World Missionary Conferences of Whitby (1947) and Willingen (1952). This call went largely unheeded. Rather, the actual effect of the Frankfurt Declaration was to stir up an intense debate not only in Germany, but all over the world. In Germany it contributed to the split between the conciliar organization of mission societies and the 'working fellowship of evangelical missions' which became final after the Bangkok World Missionary Conference of 1973. The basic concerns of the Declaration influenced the *Lausanne Covenant in 1974.

Bibliography
CT XIV:19 (19 June, 1970), pp. 3–6; P. Beyerhaus, *Missions: Which Way?* (Grand Rapids, 1971); idem, *Shaken Foundations* (Grand Rapids, 1972).

P. P. J. Beyerhaus

FRANKFURT SCHOOL

Founded in 1923 as the Institute for Social Research, the School's influence may be dated from Max Horkheimer's directorship in 1930. Its members left Germany under the Third Reich, settling in New York, but returned to Germany after the Second World War as the only surviving institution from the Weimar Republic.

In the earlier generation of scholars, key figures are Max Horkheimer (1895–1973), Theodor Adorno (1903–69) and Herbert Marcuse (1898–1979). The leader of the younger generation is Jürgen Habermas (b. 1929). An eschatological character in the School's thought reflects the influence of *Hegel and *Marx, but the Jewish background of many of the members is a distinct and conscious influence. The major theme in their work is critique of the *Enlightenment, both its philosophy and its impact on 'mass-culture'. Closely linked with this is their analysis of Nazism.

The School has consistently attacked the *positivism central to the Enlightenment theory of knowledge, and with it the view that *nature should be made subject to human control, and that this subjection/domination should become the chief purpose of knowledge; that 'whatever does not conform to the rule of computation and utility is suspect' (Adorno and Horkheimer, *Dialectic of Enlightenment*, 1944, repr. London, 1979, p. 6). A world dominated by technology is the material realization of the Enlightenment goal.

Positivism and technology are linked by a popular view of physical science as both the model form of knowledge and the bringer of material benefit to the world. In this way they legitimate one another. The result is that 'the fully enlightened world radiates disaster triumphant' (ibid., p. 3); for man, 'existent social practice, which forms the individual's life down to its least details, is inhuman, and this inhumanity affects everything that goes on in society' (Horkheimer, 'Traditional and Critical Theory', 1937, in P. Connerton, ed., *Critical Sociology*, Harmondsworth, 1976, p. 220).

The Frankfurt School's *anthropology has, therefore, a dialectical character; in this inhuman world, 'critical thought has a concept of man as in conflict with himself' until inhumanity is overcome. There are parallels here and elsewhere with the thought of Jacques *Ellul.

A right view of reality is imperative; central to it is a refusal of the *Kantian distinction between subject and object. 'Social reality' is not 'extrinsic' to the individual. The critical thinker rejects analyses of the world which cut him off from 'the experience of the blindly dominating totality and the driving desire that it should ultimately become something else' (Adorno, et al., *The Positivist Dispute in German Sociology*, London, 1976, p. 14). 'Totality' here has more than rhetorical significance: 'totality is what is most real' (p. 12), but it is also illusory (it hides the fact that a really human world would be different).

Public debate, even in a democracy, is seen as deformed. Habermas's primary concern is to criticize forms of rationality which lead to such distorted discourse (drawing on insights from psychoanalysis as well as from classical philosophy), and to construct a theory of 'communicative action' in which a genuinely consensual generalized ethics can develop. Theory-building in this sense is a salvific activity; 'theory is the *telos*, not the vehicle' (ibid., p. 113).

Bibliography
T. Bottomore, *The Frankfurt School and Its Critics* (London, 2002); P. Connerton, *The Tragedy of Enlightenment* (Cambridge, 1980); J. Habermas, *Knowledge and Human Interests* (London, 1978); D. Held, *Introduction to Critical Theory* (London, 1980); M. Jay, *The Dialectical Imagination* (London, 1973); H. Marcuse, *From Luther to Popper* (London, 1972); T. Wheatland, *The Frankfurt School in Exile* (Minneapolis, 2009).

H. W. Smart

FREEDOM, CHRISTIAN

The Christian understanding of freedom is rooted in the OT, where the exodus is the paradigmatic event of God's liberation of his people from slavery. Importantly, this was not just liberation *from* oppression, but also liberation *for* the service of God. God's rule, unlike Pharaoh's, made Israel a society free from structures of privilege and exploitation.

In the NT, freedom acquires further dimensions: from the inner compulsion of sin, from the entail of guilt, from subjection to death (see *Guilt and forgiveness). The image of the exodus is used to portray Christ's work as the liberator of his people from all that disables and threatens human life. But as, in the OT, freedom means equally freedom for the service of God and Christ. Freedom is not licence to sin, but a new enablement to serve voluntarily, to make God's will one's own, to do good from the heart rather than under constraint. In Paul's theology, where freedom is especially a prominent theme, this is the work of the Spirit, for 'where the Spirit of the Lord is, there is freedom' (2 Cor. 3:17).

Freedom in the Spirit is associated with being sons and daughters of God, since ideally, unlike slaves, children obey parents with the glad and free obedience of love. But the image of Christians as slaves is also, paradoxically, used, and was powerfully enacted by Jesus himself when he washed his disciples' feet, performing the servant's role as an example to his disciples to do the same for each other. The image of slavery is re-functioned to make the humblest form of service a matter of voluntary love. The NT, instead of replacing a model of society in which there are masters and slaves with one in which everyone is his or her own master, replaces it with a model in which everyone is the willing servant of all. Thus Christian freedom does not lead to competitive individualism, but to loving community.

In the theological tradition, discussion of Christian freedom has focused on the issue of *grace and free *will, attempting to do justice both, on the one hand, to the sense in which humans are enslaved to sin and cannot free themselves, and, on other hand, to the fact that freedom and coercion are contradictory. While this discussion has divided Christians, it has also highlighted the important truths that the human plight is one of profound internal subjection to *sin, and that the kind of freedom worth having is not mere freedom of choice, but the freedom to choose good.

In the modern period, freedom has become a dominant value of Western culture, and Christian theology has had to engage with the new ideas of freedom that have emerged from the Renaissance and the *Enlightenment. One strand in this modern thinking has been the conception of freedom as absolute self-determination, such that the destiny of humanity is to appropriate the absolute freedom of God and to transcend all limits. This led to the catastrophic project of domination over the rest of creation (see *Ecology). Secondly, freedom has been conceived as autonomy. For *Kant, obedience to God's commands was inconsistent with human autonomy, and morality could rest only on recognition of universal moral truths. For *Nietzsche, even this contradicts autonomy, which must be the freedom to create one's own values, a notion that has become widespread in *postmodernity. What is valued has come to be freedom of choice as such (the freedom of consumerism), rather than the freedom to choose well. Finally, modern freedom is highly individualistic. The truly free person is the sovereign individual, free of all dependence, relating to the world only by mastery. Many of the dilemmas of contemporary Western society are rooted in a misconception of freedom as the opposite of all dependence, belonging and society.

In this context, Christian theology must reconceive freedom as not only contradicted by oppressive relationships, but also enabled by the kind of belonging and relationships we find in fellowship with God and in Christian community. We must point out that mere freedom from quickly becomes a new enslavement, while the freedom worth having is the freedom to choose well and to serve God and others in voluntary love.

Bibliography

R. Bauckham, *God and the Crisis of Freedom* (Louisville, 2002); C. E. Gunton (ed.), *God and Freedom* (Edinburgh, 1995); A. J. McKelway, *The Freedom of God and Human Liberation* (London, 1990); J. Moltmann, *The Trinity and the Kingdom of God* (London, 1981); D. Nicholls, *Deity and Domination* (New York, 1989).

R. J. BAUCKHAM

FREEDOM OF WILL, see WILL

FREE WILL, see WILL

FREI, HANS (1922–88)

Hans Frei was an American theologian best known for his work on biblical *hermeneutics and for his contributions to *postliberal theology.

His early work examined modern attempts to interpret those biblical narratives characterized by literary realism, particularly various portions of the Gospels. Some modern interpreters have taken these texts simply as evidence for 'the facts', others as expressions of a certain flavour of religious consciousness. Frei suggested instead that they should be seen as providing a narrative identification of their central character, Jesus Christ, and that their meaning simply is this story that they tell. This is a meaning that can be grasped before any questions of factuality or of significance for the reader are raised, and Frei argued that the story can therefore dictate when and how those questions are posed. With regard to factuality, he argued that it is in the resurrection narratives that the question of historical reference is pushed most urgently by the stories themselves. With regard to significance for the reader, he argued that typological interpretation (which sees realities in the present as 'types' of biblical realities) is the best way to explore the significance of realistic narrative texts like these for personal, ecclesial and political life.

Frei later conceded that his claims could not be justified simply by appeal to the literary qualities of the Gospel texts. Only a deep consensus in Christian reading practices (the *sensus literalis*), which has involved taking the Gospels primarily as realistic depictions of Jesus, can provide the soil in which his kind of reading will flourish. Frei also developed a typology distinguishing theologians who present theology as the internal discourse of a particular community, describing its idiosyncratic ways of thought and practice, from those who present it as the re-interpretation of Christian claims according to some universal philosophical scheme. He argued that his hermeneutical claims would flourish best amongst theologians who let their philosophical claims about realism, reference and meaning be governed by the particular shape of the Gospel narratives as they are read in distinctive ways within the Christian church.

See also: NARRATIVE THEOLOGY.

Bibliography

Works: *The Eclipse of Biblical Narrative* (New Haven, 1974); *The Identity of Jesus Christ* (Philadelphia, 1975); *Types of Christian Theology*, ed. G. Hunsinger and W. C. Placher (New Haven, 1992); *Theology and Narrative*, ed. G. Hunsinger and W. C. Placher (New York, 1993).

Studies: G. Green (ed.), *Scriptural Authority and Narrative Interpretation* (Philadelphia, 1987); M. A. Higton, *Christ, Providence and History* (London, 2004); J. Springs, *Toward a Generous Orthodoxy* (New York, 2010).

M. HIGTON

FULLER, ANDREW (1754–1815)

Andrew Fuller was an English Particular (Calvinistic) *Baptist whose reputation as a theologian largely rests on his *Gospel Worthy of All Acceptation* (1785). This challenged the High Calvinism (see *Hyper-Calvinism) associated with John *Gill by contending that it was the 'duty' of all who heard the gospel to believe, whether they were part of the elect or not. Consequently, preachers could, and should, 'offer' the gospel to their hearers by directly inviting all to respond. Fuller based his argument closely on Scripture, but also made use of a distinction between 'natural' and 'moral' ability derived from Jonathan *Edwards' *Freedom of the Will* (1754). People's inability to come to Christ apart from the Holy Spirit's work was wholly 'moral', and therefore all who refused to respond were culpable. The *Gospel Worthy* constitutes the classic statement of 'Edwardsean' evangelical *Calvinism in a British context. Its stress on human responsibility provided Particular Baptists with a rationale for applied evangelistic preaching. Fuller put his principles into practice through his work as a pastor and, especially, as the energetic secretary of the Baptist Missionary Society, which he helped found in 1792.

Fuller also wrote a large number of other theological and apologetic works, the most significant of which is probably *The Gospel Its Own Witness* (1800), which sought to combat *deism and was widely respected.

Bibliography

Works: A. G. Fuller (ed.), *Works*, rev. edn, J. Belcher, 3 vols. (Harrisonburg, ³1988 [1845]).

Studies: C. Chun, *The Legacy of Jonathan Edwards in the Theology of Andrew Fuller* (Leiden, 2009); P. J. Morden, *The Life and Thought of Andrew Fuller (1754–1815)* (Milton Keynes, 2015).

P. J. MORDEN

FUNDAMENTAL THEOLOGY

Fundamental theology is one of the most problematic and creative areas of Christian theology. An established discipline in *Roman Catholic theology, fundamental theology is also recognized as a useful demarcation of a vital area of *Protestant theology. Attempts have been made to explore the possibilities of an *ecumenical fundamental theology that is politically aware and socially self-critical.

Traditionally, fundamental theology examined the presuppositions of the Christian faith – the existence of *God, the reality of *revelation and man's capacity to receive it (the sensitive area of the relation of revelation and reason; see *Faith and reason) – in a systematic way as a prolegomenon to the study of *dogma. But the fundamentals were already given, rather than proposed as hypotheses to be established. At its best, this approach could be seen as 'faith seeking understanding' (see *Anselm); at its crudest, it could appear to be an attempt to prove revelation, a purely formal way of handling the most basic questions of theology.

The current conception of fundamental theology stems from *Rahner's reassessment of the discipline and the encouragement this derived from the Second Vatican Council's *Constitution on the Church in the Modern World* (see *Vatican Councils). This approach is the beneficiary of the old discipline of *apologetics. It is motivated by a concern to commend the faith to the world and to establish its credentials in the light of modern thought, but it seeks to do this by a critical presentation of the whole self-expression of the Christian faith, rather than by an artificial abstraction from the contents of Christian doctrine (see *Systematic theology). Rahner set out to reconstruct fundamental theology in union with dogmatic theology so as to impart to the whole enterprise of Christian theology an open and apologetic character that responds to the questions raised by man's subjectivity in the modern world.

Fundamental theology is in a vulnerable position, as it mediates between Christian doctrine and other relevant disciplines. But it is a theological, not a pre-theological, discipline, since it is conducted from the standpoint of faith. Here it is distinct from both *philosophy of religion (see also *Philosophical theology; *Philosophy and theology), which does not require *faith, and apologetics proper, which, though obviously conducted from the standpoint of faith, does not presuppose faith in its audience.

A new departure in Roman Catholic fundamental theology has been initiated by J. B. *Metz, who, though in sympathy with Rahner's approach, regards it as naively theoretical – neither acutely aware of its ideological determinants, nor committed to the struggle against oppression at the level of *praxis (see also *Political theology). Metz proposes a practical fundamental theology structured by the three practical *hermeneutical categories of narrative, memory and solidarity, in relation to which the standard themes and problems of fundamental theology – the actuality, character and credibility of revelation, and the subjects, conditions and consequences of its reception – would be interpreted.

In Protestant theology, the discipline of fundamental theology owes its momentum to G. *Ebeling, for whom it is concerned with the question of the *truth of theology through a process of *verification and self-criticism in an integrated dialogue not only with other theological disciplines, but with all relevant sources of information and insight. This is of course conspicuously and intentionally lacking from *Barth's *CD*, but was strongly attempted in *Tillich's *Systematic Theology*.

Some degree of coherence can be imposed on this varied scene if fundamental theology is understood as analogous to the philosophy of science or of history, in other words, as a theological *epistemology or as the discipline of theological method comprising the sources, scope, aims and rationality of theology in dialogue with the whole range of theological studies. Such a fundamental theology would have a public aspect and serve an apologetic function as the meeting point of Christian doctrine and other relevant disciplines.

Bibliography

P. Avis, *The Methods of Modern Theology* (Basingstoke, 1986); A. Dulles, *The Craft of Theology: From Symbol to System* (New York, 1992); G. Ebeling, *The Study of Theology* (London, 1979); H. Fries, 'Fundamental

Theology', *SM* II, pp. 368–372; *idem, Fundamental Theology* (Washington, 1996); H. H. Knight, *A Future for Truth: Evangelical Theology in a Postmodern World* (Nashville, 1997); R. Latourelle, 'A New Image of Fundamental Theology', in R. Latourelle and G. O'Collins (eds.), *Problems and Perspectives of Fundamental Theology* (Ramsey, 1982); G. A. Lindbeck, *The Nature of Doctrine: Religion and Theology in a Postliberal Age* (Philadelphia, 1984); A. E. McGrath, *The Genesis of Doctrine: A Study in the Foundations of Doctrinal Criticism* (Oxford, 1990); J. B. Metz, *Faith in History and Society: Towards a Practical Fundamental Theology* (London, 1980); J. B. Metz and P. Avis, *SJT* 35, 1982, pp. 529–540; K. Rahner, *Foundations of Christian Faith: An Introduction to the Idea of Christianity* (London, 1978).

P. D. L. AVIS

FUNDAMENTALISM

Fundamentalism developed its distinctive characteristics primarily in North America, and has had its widest influence in the USA where revivalist *evangelicalism has been the dominant religious heritage. Although it has many missionary exports and also many parallels in anti-modernist Protestant movements in other countries, we can best understand its distinguishing features by looking at the prototypical and widely influential American developments.

The word 'fundamentalism' originated in the USA in 1920 as the designation that editor Curtis Lee Laws (1868–1946) used for his anti-modernist party in the Northern Baptist Convention. The term was soon used to describe a broad coalition of evangelical Protestants who fought militantly against *modernist (i.e. liberal) theology and against some features of *secularization of modern culture. This remains the most accurate way to use the word. Essential to being a fundamentalist is that one be (1) an evangelical *Protestant; (2) an anti-modernist, meaning that one subscribes to the fundamentals of traditional supernaturalistic biblical Christianity; and (3) militant in this anti-modernism or in opposition to certain aspects of secularization. A fundamentalist, then, is a militantly anti-modernist evangelical.

This picture is complicated by a number of other broader and narrower usages. Sometimes the word is used generically to designate any religious anti-modernist group, hence 'Islamic fundamentalists'. Martin Marty and R. Scott Appleby promoted this use in their multivolume *Fundamentalism Project* (Chicago, 1991–5). Opponents of Protestant fundamentalism may use the term loosely to describe almost any of the features, especially the more extravagant or anti-intellectual ones, of evangelical *revivalism, such as those especially common in the American South. Such usage invites confusion of fundamentalism with revivalism generally and with several closely related movements with revivalist roots. For instance, the *holiness movement, which arose in the middle decades of the nineteenth century, was distinguished especially by emphasis on experiences of outpourings of the Holy Spirit leading to lives of sinless *perfection. *Pentecostalism, arising in the early twentieth century, was marked by stress on receiving spectacular spiritual powers. Fundamentalist anti-modernist militancy was sometimes also adopted by these groups, so that they often became 'fundamentalistic'. These movements tended to remain distinct and ecclesiastically separate, although some Pentecostals and members of the holiness movement did affiliate with fundamentalist institutions and initiatives. Nonetheless, these three movements were ultimately related by common origins to the broader and still more diverse heritage of nineteenth-century American revivalism, and many of their traits commonly called 'fundamentalist' are more accurately called 'revivalist'.

In America, 'fundamentalism', when used carefully, has come to refer to the more narrow phenomenon of the main groups of militantly anti-modernist white evangelicals. (American black evangelicals are often revivalist in style, fundamental in doctrine, and anti-modern in ethics, but they do not typically call themselves 'fundamentalists'.)

The characteristics of the distinctively 'fundamentalist' movement can be seen best from its history. As Ernest R. Sandeen has shown in his important study, *The Roots of Fundamentalism: British and American Millenarianism, 1800–1930* (Chicago, 1970), one major source of fundamentalism was the premillennial prophecy movement originating from the work of J. N. *Darby and others. Although in England this movement produced primarily the Plymouth Brethren who left the traditional churches, in the United States its main expression in the late nineteenth century was within major northern denominations, such as the Presbyterian and the Baptist. *Dispensationalism was the distinctive feature of this movement and became almost canonized in the notes of C. I. Scofield's famous *Reference Bible* (New York, 1909). Many American dispensationalists also adopted the moderate holiness teachings fostered by England's Keswick Convention.

Dispensationalism, which predicted the ruin of the church in this epoch, encouraged militancy against the rise of aggressive theological modernism in the early twentieth century. In the USA, especially, where modernism was strong, dispensationalists found many allies who wished to defend the fundamentals of the faith against modernism. Among the northern Presbyterians, conservatism was strong, bolstered by the intellectual leadership at Princeton Theological Seminary (see *Princeton Theology). Conservative Presbyterians first developed the strategy of defending lists of fundamental doctrines. Dispensationalists also organized the publication, from 1909 to 1915, of *The Fundamentals*, defending traditional doctrines. Many fundamentalist groups had lists of 'fundamental' doctrines, though no one list was ever standard. The most common points were the inerrancy of *Scripture (see *Infallibility and inerrancy of the Bible), the deity of Christ, his *virgin birth, the substitutionary *atonement, Christ's *resurrection, and his second coming (see *Eschatology).

During the 1920s fundamentalists fought hard against modernist gains in the major northern Presbyterian and Baptist denominations. Smaller fundamentalist controversies occurred in other denominations, and parallel splits between conservatives and liberals took place in a number of churches in the United States and Canada. Meanwhile, fundamentalists took on a cultural as well as an ecclesiastical dimension as they attacked aspects of moral erosion after the First World War. The campaign led by William Jennings Bryan (1860–1925) to keep evolution from being taught in American public schools was the chief expression of such concern. The spread of evolutionary teaching was seen as undermining the authority of the Bible in American life and as fostering moral relativism. Marxism, Romanism, alcohol, tobacco, dancing, card-playing and theatre attendance were other major targets for fundamentalist attacks. Amid these conflicts, fundamentalism grew as a coalition of anti-modernist Protestants from many traditions, throughout the USA, north and south, other English-speaking countries and their missionary outposts. At the centre of the coalition were American dispensationalists, whose fundamentalism was least tempered by other traditions.

By the 1930s fundamentalism was beginning to take a distinctive ecclesiastical expression. Increasingly, the most militant fundamentalists felt that they should separate from groups which contained modernists, and from independent congregations or denominations. Most such fundamentalists became Baptist and were dispensationalist. Separatism was becoming a test of true faith.

What had been the broader militant anti-modernist coalition of the 1920s thus began to split by the 1940s. One major group in America softened its militancy and tried to retain contact with mainline denominations. Led by spokespersons such as Harold John Ockenga (1905–85), Carl F. H. Henry (1913–2003) and Edward J. Carnell (1919–67), they at first called themselves 'neo-evangelicals', and by the later 1950s simply 'evangelicals'. Their association with Billy Graham (b. 1918) signalled the growth of this inclusivist wing of 'evangelical' ex-fundamentalists. Meanwhile, militant separatists, such as John R. Rice (1895–1980), Bob Jones (1883–1968) and Carl McIntire (1906–2002), claimed they were the only true fundamentalists. After 1960, 'fundamentalism' in America could be used to distinguish this separatist sub-group from the broader 'evangelicalism', which included ex-fundamentalists and Bible-believing Christians from many traditions.

Separatist fundamentalism continued to grow, although it probably never constituted more than 10% of America's estimated 40 to 50 million 'evangelicals' in the 1970s and 1980s. By the 1980s, especially with the rise of Baptist fundamentalist Jerry Falwell's (1933–2007) Moral Majority, the political concerns of fundamentalists to preserve traditionalist Christian mores in American public life had become prominent again, as they had been in the 1920s. Fundamentalist politics now included strong support for the state of Israel, important to dispensational prophetic interpretation. While holding to a dispensationalist premillennialism that believed in the inevitable decline of human history, Falwell was hopeful that political moral reform on issues such as abortion and homosexual marriage might temper this downward spiral. This later tendency became one of the more visible marks of fundamentalist and evangelical involvement with politics throughout the 1990s and into the 2000s. During the 2004 presidential election in which influential fundamentalists like Falwell, James Dobson and Bob Jones III publicly supported the Republican incumbent George W. Bush, both homosexuality and abortion were among the more important 'moral issues' on the conservative platform.

Bibliography

D. O. Beale, *In Pursuit of Purity: American Fundamentalism since 1850* (Greenville, 1986); J. A. Carpenter, *Revive Us Again: The Reawakening of American Fundamentalism* (New York, 1997); G. M. Marsden, *Fundamentalism and American Culture* (New York, ²2006).

G. M. MARSDEN AND J. D. HANKINS, JR

GALLICANISM, see PAPACY

GENDER

The concept of gender refers to the understanding of human identity in terms of the perceptions of masculinity and femininity. Gender is a complex issue, for it influences our stance towards God, ourselves and others, as well as being itself informed by the convictions we hold as organic beings. The awareness of the importance of this aspect of ourselves has been reflected in the growing field of gender studies, including their relationship to religion.

Gender identity and gender relations represent a significant aspect of societal fabric and its interpretation, and therefore vary accordingly. In contemporary studies, especially under the influence of feminist scholarship, it has become increasingly common to distinguish between the notion of sex and that of gender. The first denotes biological differences between women and men, whereas the second refers to the interpretation of those differences in their social contexts. Thus, gender is commonly understood as socially constructed and reflecting the variables of cultural norms of a given tradition. Other researchers, among whom both traditionalists and feminists can be found, point to what they see as inescapable biological and physiological differences between the sexes and therefore subscribe to essentialism of some sort (e.g. C. Gilligan, *In a Different Voice*).

Much of gender studies has been woman-centred, in reaction to the dominance of hermeneutics carried out from the male point of view. The emerging 'men's studies' represent a response to the current crisis in male self-understanding in the Western world, caused by radical social changes which have greatly affected the patterns of gender roles. Gender studies also address the perceived Platonic divide between spirit/mind and body and the complications and clashes of the two, typically resulting in explorations in transcending the limitations of the body so that the body corresponds to how the person feels 'inside', rather than the other way around.

Theological reflections on gender are a fertile field, ranging from radical gender polarization to focus on the enrichment of the concepts of both femaleness and maleness in the light of the dynamic changes taking place in contemporary societies. It is often related to discussion on *God in regard to gender terms, especially by pointing to the features of God which are characteristic of both genders as well as to the disassociation of God from sexual characteristics in the Judeo-Christian tradition.

For Christians, gender is a component of the story of God and human beings. It starts with the creation of humanity as male and female and the union of the two; continues through the story of the Jewish nation characterized by differing expectations regarding men's and women's roles, although with some notable exceptions, such as Deborah or Esther; through the way Jesus engaged with men and women and his redefinition of family with its radical reorientation of the purpose of human life no longer bound to procreation; through the affirmation of the epistles that in Christ there is no longer male and female, whether in marriage or singleness; to the vision of the Day of the Lord when the renewed community of God's creation will celebrate life in its fullness (though views would differ in regard to whether gender would still play any role).

One of the continuing debates in Christian communities concerns the makeup of the relationships between, and the social roles of, men and women, often with reference to the so-called household rules or codes (e.g. Col. 3:18 – 4:1; 1 Tim. 2:8–15; 1 Pet. 2:18 – 3:7). These are interpreted either in a very literal sense as fundamental for overcoming the current crisis of the institution of the *family in the Western world, or as functioning in the framework of the cultural norms of the ancient world which was oppressive towards the marginalized, and therefore to be discarded today as not true to the liberating spirit of Christ. This is reflected in the debate between the complementarians (those arguing that because women and men are biologically different, this will be reflected in their social roles) and egalitarians (who are concerned with the equal treatment of men and women in terms of worth, giftedness and calling). Another way to look at the issue, however, is to see household codes as reflecting creative reconstruction of personal and social forms of life in a given culture in the light of the good news of the in-breaking *kingdom of God. In that case, a Christian community is engaged in the challenging yet indispensable invitation to live out the eschatological reality of the new household of God (cf. J. H. Yoder, *The Politics of Jesus*, Grand Rapids, 2003, pp. 162–192; J. G. Stackhouse, Jr, *Finally Feminist*).

As some theologians would argue, even when assuming the same roles, males and females often tend to operate in differing ways. Whether gender differences are seen as mutually exclusive or interchanging, and how the liberty of beings created in the *image and likeness of God interplays with biological factors, will shape the way gender is appropriated inside and outside the church. As both the witness of Scripture and the experience of those living in the Majority World indicate, a comprehensive approach to individual gender identity requires the framework of communal identity in which humans can see themselves and others as embodied beings, and the social meaning of human embodiment can be measured by faithfulness to the vision of the fullness of Christ.

See also: FEMINIST THEOLOGY.

Bibliography

S. C. Barton, 'The Epistles and Christian Ethics,' in R. Gill (ed.), *The Cambridge Companion to Christian Ethics* (Cambridge, 2001); L. S. Cahill, 'Gender and Christian Ethics', in R. Gill (ed.), *The Cambridge Companion*; C. Gilligan, *In a Different Voice: Psychological Theory and Women's Development* (Cambridge, 1993); C. Penner (ed.), *Women and Men: Gender in the Church* (Waterloo and Scottdale, 1998); J. G. Stackhouse, Jr, *Finally Feminist: A Pragmatic Christian Understanding of Gender* (Grand Rapids, 2005).

L. TOTH (ANDRONOVIENE)

GENERAL REVELATION, see REVELATION

GENERATION, ETERNAL, see TRINITY

GERMAN IDEALISM

The term 'German idealism' refers to developments immediately after Kant, principally including J. G. *Fichte, G. W. F. *Hegel and F. W. J. Schelling (1775–1854). Their shared goal, executed with significant differences, was to chart a path between the philosophical tendencies of *Spinoza and *Kant. They were highly influential on *Barth, *Bonhoeffer, *Balthasar and *Rahner.

The German idealists inherited the powerful notions of a single determining 'substance' from Spinoza and free 'subjectivity' from Kant. The task they set themselves was to relate the two notions in a systematic and comprehensive theory.

The central themes of the German idealists are the thinking subject, nature and culture, and the ways these are related to each other. Are humans part of nature, and thus links in a great chain of causality, as Spinoza had claimed? Are the products of culture related to nature, and if so, how? If humans are free, and yet part of nature, what does this imply about nature?

Fichte claimed, in the various versions of his *Science of Knowledge*, that the human subject is radically free and in some sense 'posits' or 'places' the world for itself, restrained in some way from unrestricted freedom by its own internal checks. This action he called a 'deed-act' (*Tathandlung*). The ground of knowledge is thus the free act of the subject. Schelling, in his earlier work, claimed that human action is fully part of nature which is itself free. The ground of knowledge is the 'absolute' identity which exists prior to its differentiation into different 'things'. There is no direct access to the absolute, which is prior to ontology and language; it is the products of art such as painting and music that perform a conscious relation to the unconscious absolute, through the insights of the genius. Hegel, in his famous works, claimed that the one substance is also 'subject' in Kant's sense. Nature and culture are all the products of this self-developing 'spirit' (*Geist*), which achieves higher levels of self-consciousness and conceptual clarity, from nature, through religion and art, to the pinnacle of philosophy. The absolute is a result of a process of dialectic which is reached at the end of the process. Schelling, in his later works, claimed that Hegel's account was 'merely logical' and failed to grasp that the ground of reality is an origin that cannot be grasped by thought.

The first issue of relevance to theology is the description of the human subject developed by the German idealists, and the difference between Fichte and Hegel. At stake are the freedom and constraints that characterize human action. In orthodox Christian theology human action is *free and graced. Its fruits are characterized by estrangement from God owing to sin, and reconciliation to God owing to Christ's life, death and resurrection. The activity of the soul cannot be separated from its receptivity to God's *grace, which is mediated in many different ways. Fichte claimed, following Kant, that the subject is radically free, and extended this insight to the claim that the subject 'posits' (*setzt*) the world. The model for this radical freedom in the earlier tradition is God's creation of the world. Fichte appears to attribute this divine creativity to humanity. Its product is an account of human action that is almost unconstrained. Hegel claimed, following Spinoza and Kant, that while the subject is free, its agency is a matter of recognition between subjects who inhabit a community. Radical freedom produces actions that have no significance. It is freedom as it participates in the life of the spirit that produces meaningful, significant action. Again, the arguments supporting these claims are complex. Their significance for theology lies in their implications for debates about the ways in which human freedom and divine grace are related.

The second issue of relevance to theology is the relation of thinking to its ground, and the difference between Hegel and Schelling. At stake is the scope of thinking. In orthodox Christian theology God appears in creation in a way suited to human perception: as a man who speaks human languages (see *Accommodation). Knowledge of God is obtained though knowing creatures, and any language used to describe God will be a language whose most familiar use is the description of creatures. God is the Creator of creatures. God is also the Giver of life to creatures. There is more of God than can appear in ways suited to human perception or, by extension, conception. To say that God as Creator and as life cannot be conceived is the historically relevant claim behind Hegel's claim that the 'absolute' is the product of a developing self-consciousness of spirit which can be conceived, and Schelling's counter-claim that the 'absolute' is the origin of the world and language and reasoning which cannot itself be conceived. The arguments supporting these claims are complex. Their significance for theology lies in their implications for debates about the degree to which God, and thus the grounds of faith, can be adequately conceptualized in *philosophy.

Bibliography

K. Ameriks (ed.), *The Cambridge Companion to German Idealism* (Cambridge, 2000); A. Bowie, *Schelling and Modern European Philosophy* (London, 1993); D. Henrich, *Between Kant and Hegel* (London, 2003); T. Pinkard, *German Philosophy 1760–1860* (Cambridge, 2002); G. Zöller, *Fichte's Transcendental Philosophy* (Cambridge, 1998).

N. ADAMS

GIFFORD LECTURES

The Gifford Lectures refer to the lectureships endowed at the ancient Scottish universities (Aberdeen, Edinburgh, Glasgow, St Andrews) by the will of Adam Gifford (1820–87), who as a judge of the Court of Session took the honorary legal title of Lord Gifford. A follower of *Spinoza, Gifford wished to promote 'the study of *natural theology, in the widest sense of that term, in other words, the knowledge of God', to be pursued as 'a strictly natural science, the greatest of all possible sciences . . . that of Infinite Being, without reference to or reliance upon any supposed special exceptional or so-called miraculous revelation. I wish it studied just as astronomy or chemistry is.'

Starting in 1888, the lectures have featured the most distinguished religious thinkers within and beyond the English-speaking world, and have been issued in numerous significant publications. Lecturers have included: John *Baillie, *Barth (who justified his series as an exposition of 'a totally different theology' without whose challenge natural theology loses its vitality),

*Brunner, *Bultmann, Christopher Dawson, John Dewey, A. S. Eddington (*The Nature of the Physical World*), Austin *Farrer, J. G. Frazer, E. *Gilson, J. S. Haldane, W. C. Heisenberg, W. R. Inge, W. Jaeger, William James (*The Varieties of Religious Experience*), John MacMurray, G. Marcel, E. L. Mascall, *Moltmann, F. Max Müller, Reinhold *Niebuhr, Michael Polanyi, A. E. Taylor (*The Faith of a Moralist*), William *Temple, Paul *Tillich, Arnold Toynbee, C. C. J. Webb and A. N. Whitehead (*Process and Reality*).

In recent decades, lecturers have included R. J. Berry, Noam Chomsky, Antony Flew, Stanley *Hauerwas, John *Hick, Alasdair *MacIntyre, Donald M. *Mackay, Raimundo Pannikar, Jaroslav *Pelikan, Roger Penrose, Alvin *Plantinga, John *Polkinghorne, Paul *Ricœur, Carl Sagan, Stephen Toulmin, David *Tracy and Nicholas Wolterstorff.

Such a selection illustrates how generously the founder's terms have been interpreted.

Bibliography

S. L. Jaki, *Lord Gifford and His Lectures: A Centenary Retrospect* (Edinburgh, 1986); B. E. Jones (ed.), *Earnest Enquirers after Truth: A Gifford Anthology* (London, 1970); L. Witham, *The Measure of God: Our Century-Long Struggle to Reconcile Science and Religion* (San Francisco, 2005).

D. F. WRIGHT

GIFT, THEOLOGY OF

Discussion of the theology of 'gift' became prevalent in North America and Continental Europe during the first decade of the twenty-first century and was particularly promoted by the writings of John Milbank and Kathryn Tanner. Its origins, however, lie in the writings of the French anthropologist, Marcel Mauss, who published his study, *The Gift*, as long ago as 1924. Mauss claimed that primitive society, long before the rise of individualistic and competitive capitalism, operated with a system of 'gift-exchange' which promoted social cohesion. The free giving of goods and services elicited similar responses. Jacques *Derrida argued, however, that a 'pure gift' must be given without any expectation of return or exchange, and this became a code for the divine *revelation which cannot ever be fully expressed or reduced to a linguistic formula, but only by endlessly deferred meaning. Jean-Luc *Marion reinterpreted the notion of 'pure gift' as 'saturated phenomenon' – that is to say that the intuitive knowledge of the divine cannot be conceptualized.

John *Milbank drew on this train of thought from French anthropology and philosophy in his essay, 'Can a Gift be Given?' (1995). He rejected Derrida's idea of 'pure gift' as an impossible dream and reinterpreted the concept of 'gift' in fully doctrinal, trinitarian terms. Reverting to Mauss's original notion of 'gift-exchange', he wanted to recast *systematic theology under the 'transcendental category' of 'gift' in order to provide a basis for a *Christian socialism, and began this project with his book, *Being Reconciled* (2003). The divine self-gift elicits a human response leading to 'participation'.

Kathryn Tanner in turn criticized Milbank and sees the concept of 'gift-exchange' from Mauss as sharing the same individualistic competitiveness and contractualism as *capitalism. In line with her reading of Calvin, she advocates instead a form of 'pure gift', a divine 'unilateralism' in which the persons of the *Trinity give themselves unconditionally and without any competition. When this is received, it issues in a 'reflected' human generosity to those in need. Despite the key difference, however, both Milbank and Tanner are attempting to draw on *patristic trinitarian theology and the notion of 'participation' in the Trinity to combat the structures of global capitalism.

The more traditional theological language for 'gift' is 'grace'. *Charisma*, the Greek word for 'gift', is derived from *charis*, translated 'grace'. Etymologically, *charis* comes into Latin as *caritas*, translated into English as 'charity' or 'giving love'. The English word 'grace' is derived from the parallel Latin term, *gratia*. The debate about 'gift' can therefore be seen as a continuation of the long-standing debate about *grace, and indeed Milbank criticized *Reformation theology, and particularly Calvin (see *Reformed theology), for its concept of 'unilateral' grace, unconditionally given and only 'passively' received. Following the more catholic *Augustinian tradition, Milbank noted that 'gift' is a name given to the Holy Spirit in Augustine's *De Trinitate*. He interprets *Augustine's trinitarian ethic of love in terms of gift-giving. Human beings are brought by the Spirit into the trinitarian 'gift-exchange'. Rather than passively receiving God's self-giving, we are to be engaged in 'active reception', that is to say, in actively giving the love one receives from God to one's neighbour. Indeed, without that, one cannot receive God's love. The divine gift is therefore 'coincident with relation', and 'reciprocity' is inseparable from receiving the gift. In contrast to Marion's notion of a 'saturated phenomenon' in which the divine self-giving is overwhelming and cannot be comprehended or resisted, Milbank sees an ecstatic reception in which we actively participate in the trinitarian exchange in the community of the church.

J. Todd Billings has argued that Milbank has not fully understood Calvin, and particularly his 'double grace' (*duplex gratia*) of *justification and *sanctification as two aspects of *union with Christ. Believers are passive in receiving the pardon and *adoption which is ours in justification. We do nothing to merit this reception of grace. But as we receive grace through the gift of faith, we will necessarily be active in holiness, for, since 'Christ cannot be torn into parts', justification and sanctification cannot be divorced.

Despite any failure to understand Reformation theology, however, and despite their differences, Milbank and Tanner are challenging traditional evangelical theology to think of grace not merely in individualistic terms, but also in terms of how Christian theology addresses economic and social questions.

Bibliography

J. T. Billings, 'John Milbank's Theology of the Gift and Calvin's Theology of Grace: A Critical Comparison', *Modern Theology* 21:1, 2005, pp. 87–105; S. Coakley, 'Why Gift? Gift, Gender and Trinitarian Debates in Milbank and Tanner', *SJT* 61: 2, 2008, pp. 224–235; M. Mauss, *The Gift: The Form and Reason for Exchange in Archaic Societies* (London, 1990); J. Milbank, 'Can a Gift Be Given?', *Modern Theology* 11, 1995, pp. 119–161; idem, *Being Reconciled: Ontology and Pardon* (London, 2003); K. Tanner, *Jesus, Humanity and the Trinity* (Minneapolis, 2001); idem, *Economy of Grace* (Minneapolis, 2005).

T. A. NOBLE

GIFTS OF THE SPIRIT

The beginning of the twentieth century saw the rise of a new form of the *Pentecostal movement, emphasizing the gifts of the Spirit and resulting in new denominations. In the 1960s the emphasis on the gifts spread to existing churches (including the Roman Catholic Church) through the *charismatic movement. Both movements emphasized the recovery of the gifts of the Spirit in the church's ministry, but often tended to focus on the more miraculous gifts such as tongues (*glossolalia*), prophecy and healing. In classic Pentecostalism the gifts were regarded as the evidence of the *baptism of the Spirit coming subsequent to the new birth, but that was not always held in the charismatic movement. Other Christians take the 'cessationist' view (held by the Reformers) that the more miraculous gifts associated with revelation ceased once the NT books were written.

All Christians, however, agree on the diversity of roles and spiritual gifts in the *ministry of the church. These are found in the Pauline writings, especially 1 Cor. 12; 14; Rom. 12:3–8 and Eph. 4:7–13. Clearly, Paul links the use of spiritual gifts to the work of Christ as well as the Holy Spirit.

For Paul, the concern in establishing the use of spiritual gifts is the unity of the *church. With the prior emphasis on one Lord, one faith, one baptism, the exercise of spiritual gifts should not disrupt the unity in the *fellowship established by God. Although Paul may imply a type of hierarchy in the practice of the gifts, there is no elitism, and so each person finds an appropriate ministry in light of the variety of gifts given to the church. With the emphasis on unity, there is importance given to the spiritual depth exhibited in the church through the gifts. While some of the gifts appear as 'offices' of leadership in the church (see *Church government), other gifts appear to be designed for the supportive structure of the fellowship. This includes not only mission to the world, but the provision for inner cohesion.

Theologically, it is important that our understanding of the gifts of the Spirit should be an integral part of pneumatology, the doctrine of the *Spirit, and so viewed in trinitarian perspective. The use of gifts of the Spirit should be closely related to the fruit of the Spirit in Gal. 5. Only as Christians evidence the fruit, spiritual depth and maturity, can the spiritual gifts further the unity and healthy growth of the church.

Bibliography

G. Fee, *God's Empowering Presence: The Holy Spirit in the Letters of Paul* (Carlisle, 1994);

S. Ferguson, *The Holy Spirit* (Leicester, 1996); R. Martin, *The Spirit and the Congregation: Studies in I Corinthians 12–15* (Grand Rapids, 1984); S. Schatzmann, *A Pauline Theology of Charismata* (Carlisle, 1987); T. Smail, *The Giving Gift: The Holy Spirit in Person* (London, 1994); M. Turner, *The Holy Spirit and Spiritual Gifts: Then and Now* (Carlisle, 1994).

D. L. RAINEY

GILL, JOHN (1697–1771)

John Gill was an English Particular *Baptist theologian and pastor whose prodigious written output earned him the nickname 'Dr Voluminous'. Probably his best-known work was *The Cause of God and Truth*, published in four parts (1735–8), which defended Calvinistic soteriology (see *Reformed theology). But he also produced a multi-volume *Exposition of the Holy Scriptures* (1746–66), together with numerous other works, many of which were polemical in intent.

Gill was associated with the theology known as 'High Calvinism' (see *Hyper-Calvinism) which exalted the divine decrees in a way that downplayed the importance of human responsibility. In practice, this led to an insular ecclesiology and a refusal to offer the gospel to all, as only the elect could properly respond. Some recent scholarship has sought to rebut the charge that Gill was a High Calvinist. But he disliked the 'open offer', and his influence almost certainly discouraged applied evangelistic preaching. In the years following his death his continuing influence was anathema to many evangelical Baptists, with the nineteenth-century preacher Robert Hall memorably describing Gill's writings as a 'continent of mud'. A balanced assessment of Gill will, however, seek to avoid reading him against the background of later missiological debates and acknowledge that his writings probably helped Particular Baptists to resist the rationalist thinking which was making inroads into church life elsewhere.

Bibliography

J. Gill, *Exposition of the Old and New Testaments*, 9 vols. (Paris, Arkansas, 1989 [1746–66]); M. A. G. Haykin (ed.), *The Life and Thought of John Gill (1697–1771): A Tercentennial Appreciation* (Leiden, 1997); J. Rippon, *A Brief Memoir of the Life and Writings of the Late Rev. John Gill, DD* (London, 1838).

P. J. MORDEN

GILSON, ÉTIENNE (1884–1978)

Étienne Gilson taught medieval philosophy in France, chiefly at the Sorbonne (1921–32) and the Collège de France (1932–51), and then at the Pontifical Institute of Medieval Studies in Toronto, which he had directed since its inception in 1929. Resident again in France from 1959, he wrote prolifically until his death, producing over a hundred books and articles after his seventy-fifth birthday.

Gilson was early influenced by H. Bergson (1859–1941), the French philosopher and champion of 'intuition' and creative evolution. From studies of *Descartes he moved to the medieval era, with monographs on *Bonaventura (1924), *Augustine (1928; ET, *The Christian Philosophy of St Augustine*, London, 1961), and *Bernard of Clairvaux (London, 1934). His *Gifford Lectures of 1930–31 were translated as *The Spirit of Medieval Philosophy* (1936).

Gilson always presented himself as a *Christian philosopher*, refusing to modernize *Thomism as though its essence could be independent of theology. Among the different *scholastic syntheses of medieval Christian philosophy, the Thomist was for him, as for his ally Jacques *Maritain, the best creative basis for interpreting modern culture. He defended teleology for both philosophy and biology, and called himself a dogmatist, while insisting that unchanging *dogma requires ever-fresh expression.

A man of public life, honoured by the French resistance and at one time a senator in the government, he enjoyed universal recognition as perhaps the most distinguished historian of medieval philosophy.

Bibliography

M. McGrath, *Etienne Gilson. A Bibliography* (Toronto, 1982); F. A. Murphy, *Art and Intellect in the Philosophy of Étienne Gilson* (Columbia, 2004); A. C. Pegis, *A Gilson Reader* (New York, 1957); P. A. Redpath (ed.), *A Thomistic Tapestry: Essays in Memory of Étienne Gilson* (Amsterdam, 2002); L. K. Shook, *Etienne Gilson* (Toronto, 1984).

D. F. WRIGHT

GLOBALIZATION

Globalization may be defined as the big idea that the world has changed to become much more interconnected than it was in previous eras. Precisely when this happened is disputed, especially by sociologists, and exactly what it looks like is also debatable. Zygmunt Bauman labels the term itself as a 'fad' word that everyone uses and few understand, which further frustrates the situation on account of the term's ubiquity in everyday and academic writing. The concept, 'globalization', is difficult to understand due to the sheer scope of what it seeks to account for, embracing the entire social, economic, geographical, technological and political situation of our present world.

The word is often used as a given to describe where the world currently finds itself, or a current scenario that has taken over all things: 'now that globalization has shaped the world ...'; or 'since globalization has happened ...'; or, 'in a world shaped by globalization ...' The idea, however, is best understood as a *process*. Jan Aart Scholte describes this process as including five features: (1) cross-border international exchange relations; (2) economic liberalization that challenges artificial state restrictions on borderless markets; (3) the universalization of local cultures into a wider synthesis; (4) the overall Westernizing or modernizing of the wider world; and (5) increased transplanetary connectedness. According to political theorist David Held, globalization refers to the deeper, wider, faster forms of interconnectedness of all of social life, including the cultural, criminal, financial, and even spiritual.

Colonialism: assertion from above

The powerful forces of globalization find precedence in the earlier processes of imperialism and colonialism. Imperialism refers to the practice of establishing the power and presence of a nation-state (or civilization), as ancient empires would exercise their rule on foreign territories through military and political control. Often foregoing actual settlement, imperial rule established itself though indirect forms of domination (especially economic) over other groups. Colonialism, on the other hand, set out to settle its people on the newly conquered territories, establishing colonies which would then exploit the places of settlement in ways that benefitted the home country both economically and strategically. In the ancient world, the Greeks, Romans, Moors, Ottomans and many others set up colonies in this way.

By the sixteenth century, however, colonialism took on a new shape as technological advancements in navigation and nautical engineering allowed explorers to connect with a wider range of the world. Faster ships could sail more speedily to distant ports, enabling closer connections between home countries and colonies. Thus a deeper form of ongoing exploitation was established through planned permanent settlement. This is how European countries exerted their political control over other parts of the 'newly discovered' world, including the Americas, Australia, New Zealand, Africa and other places. This process continued from major power groups, including forms of colonialism by the USA (over places like the Philippines and Puerto Rico), establishing colonies on other territories until just after the Second World War, and especially in the 1960s when different national liberation movements emerged to establish societal and political forms of independence from the colonial occupiers.

It was during this same period during the mid-twentieth century that Lesslie *Newbigin, British missionary to India, noted that the old style of colonialist Christian missionary engagement had met its demise. The older colonial model of *missions accompanied the earlier colonization, since occupying a territory or region meant not only establishing a civic centre, but additional, spiritual motivating factors also aimed to establish a spiritual centre of life for the foreign people groups (e.g. the Spanish pueblos and early Franciscan missions in colonial California). As such, a new model of indigenous missionary engagement emerged in the mid-twentieth century, paying greater attention to the integrity of local indigenous *cultures. Newbigin is a classic example in this regard, submitting himself to the authority of the local leaders in the church where he served in South India, which in turn appointed him as bishop of the newly established Church of South India in 1947.

Globalization: assertion from below

In contrast to the top-down approaches of imperialism or colonialism, globalization indicates a form of cultural exchange that is not imposed in such hegemonic ways. Instead, cultural exchange most naturally takes place in our current world through various dynamic formal and informal networks of exchange, without the essential value projections of an earlier era. It arises more naturally, through the process of advanced forms of migration, education and exchange, valuing more regional and localist approaches to life and culture.

Bilateral in its manner of exchange, and capturing strongly ambitious impulses, it is difficult to tell whether globalization may be a new form of colonialization, whether Euro-centric, American or something else. Whatever globalization may be, however, it seems to include an opportunity for increasing the common experience of humanity as a whole. It runs multi-directional, through social classes and transnational identities. While exhibiting abuses, where major transnational companies have exploited foreign workers, or terrorist networks develop new angles, so also it has provided new possibilities of more just treatment of oppressed people groups, more responsible approaches to resources and the environment, and better approaches to life on this earth.

There have been many responses to globalization, from capitalism's various forms of innovation and exploitation, to a postcolonial consciousness among contemporary European and American scholars. Globalization is perhaps most seen in major urban centres, from cultural producers like Los Angeles or Mumbai, to economic centres like Shanghai, Tokyo, London and New York. Yet amid the dynamic life these places have cultivated, the latter half of the twentieth century often gave way to suburban 'white flight' from many centres only now to be met with the reverse trend of gentrification, uprooting urban communities by forcing higher costs of living and other powerful expressions of cultural elitism and oppression.

Christianity and globalization

Latin American *liberation theologians provided sharp resistance to globalization, declaring the system as evil and unbiblical. Yet this approach often failed to acknowledge various developmental goods offered to the global South. Christianity in its various expressions – localized, regional and transnational – is both a product and agent of globalization. As such, it affirms the local as well as the universal and transcendent, including the significance of particular settings as meaningful places to do theology *from*. Roland Robertson suggested that this new emphasis on localization itself is a feature of globalization. Thus globalization may indeed provide a platform not only for sharing the gospel more locally in today's increasingly interconnected world, but also allow for a deeper understanding of and participatory sharing in the particularities of other localized expressions of Christianity, especially where it faces extraordinary difficulties throughout the world. This is especially important as Christians seek to love one another and the neighbours to whom we are increasingly connected over time and through the globalization process.

See also: CONTEXTUALIZATION.

Bibliography

L. Bretherton, *Resurrecting Democracy* (Cambridge, 2015); D. S. Browning, *Globalization and Grace*, vol. 2 (London, 2001); Y. H. Ferguson and R. W. Mansbach, *Globalization* (Abingdon, 2012); S. Kim, *Theology in the Public Square* (London, 2011); L. Newbigin, *The Gospel in a Pluralist Society* (Grand Rapids, 1989); F. Sanders and J. S. Sexton, *Theology and California* (Farnham, 2014); M. L. Stackhouse, *Globalization and Grace*, vol. 1 (London, 2000); idem., *Globalization and Grace*, vol. 3 (London, 2001); idem., *Globalization and Grace*, vol. 4 (London, 2008).

J. S. SEXTON

GLORY OF GOD

A multifaceted term used in the Bible to describe the honour, splendour, majesty and power of *God. The Hebrew word *kabod* originally meant 'weight' or by extension 'importance', and its Greek equivalent *doxa* meant 'opinion' or by extension 'reputation'. The theological concept contains both these ideas in equal measure. It can be applied to creatures as well as to God, since everything has its own value or importance which ought to be recognized. The key here, however, is that each person or thing should be honoured with the glory appropriate to it. When God's glory is compromised by being attributed to a creature, the result is *idolatry, something which from the beginning has always been recognized as one of the worst sins. On the other hand, believers are entitled to share in God's glory to some extent, because their salvation is entirely his work and enhances his reputation when it becomes known. Those whose lives are transformed by the indwelling presence of his Holy Spirit become people of light (an image frequently used to describe God's glory) and bring honour to him as they manifest the signs of holiness and moral goodness in their lives.

The centrality of God's glory for Christian *worship and living has always been recognized, but until the twentieth century it was not developed as a separate subject in its own right. The glory of God was an aspect of the doctrine of *creation, and in particular of the creation of the human race, the supreme manifestation of the divine glory. The created order demonstrated by its regularity, and also by its inaccessibility to mere human minds, the supreme honour which had to be paid to the Creator. Men and women, created in the *image and likeness of God, manifested that glory on earth, but as a result of the fall, it was corrupted and virtually effaced. One of the main motives for God's intervention to save us from our sins, put forward by almost every major theologian from Irenaeus to Calvin and beyond, was precisely for the restoration of this tarnished glory.

In modern times a different emphasis has emerged. One factor which has contributed to this has been the renewal of interest in *liturgy and the appreciation that worship is essentially an act of giving glory to God. The belief of many liturgists that prayer shapes theology, often expressed in the Latin phrase *lex orandi, lex credendi*, has been very influential in this respect, and has led to the appearance of systematic theologies grounded in the concept of worship or *doxology. The chief objection to this approach is that worship is the expression of theology, not the other way round, and that it is quite possible to compose liturgies or write hymns which do not do justice to the glory of God as they should – the theologically problematic or simply pedestrian quality of many modern productions in this field being regarded as ample evidence of this.

At a somewhat different level, there has also been a growing understanding of the importance of beauty as a theological concept, and the idea that the whole creation reflects the glory of God (cf. Ps. 19) has led some thinkers to apply this principle to a Christian understanding of the universe in which the creation and salvation of the human race is the crowning achievement which brings glory to God the Creator and Redeemer. This idea can be found, for example, in the work of the eighteenth-century American theologian Jonathan *Edwards, but it has been most extensively developed in the work of the twentieth-century Roman Catholic theologian Hans Urs von *Balthasar, who reacted against the apparent denigration of creation which he and others perceived in the work of Karl *Barth. Balthasar wrote a seven-volume work called *The Glory of the Lord* in which he developed the importance of *aesthetics for our understanding of God, and in the process reinterpreted the concept of God's glory by concentrating on the beauty of the divine perfection as its principal manifestation.

If this approach is to be adopted, the paradoxical quality of the revelation of God's glory needs to be taken into account. Christian theology is primarily a *theologia crucis*, stressing that the glory of God is revealed most fully and profoundly in the suffering and death of Jesus Christ, who became sin for us and died in order to take that sin away. In doing this, 'he had no beauty or majesty to attract us to him' (Isa. 53:2). A *theologia gloriae* which ignored or downplayed this point would fail to do justice to biblical teaching and is unlikely to strike deep roots in the Christian tradition.

Bibliography

H. U. von Balthasar, *The Glory of the Lord*, 7 vols. (Edinburgh, 1982–91); G. Wainwright, *Doxology: The Praise of God in Worship, Doctrine and Life: A Systematic Theology* (London, 1980).

G. L. BRAY

GNOSTICISM

The modern terms 'gnosis' and 'gnosticism' derive from the Greek words *gnōsis* ('knowledge') and *gnōstikos* ('pertaining to knowledge'). Such knowledge originally referred to what could be perceived through reason and later to mystical knowledge. However, the use of the term in late antiquity as a title for a specific group of people and their heretical beliefs as opposed to describing various forms of such belief has been called into question. Modern use of the term 'gnosticism' appears to date from the seventeenth century, derived from the word *gnōsis* in the full Greek title of Irenaeus' *Against Heresies*. Some recent scholars have called for the term to be redefined or abandoned on the grounds that it is either an unhelpful means of describing a wide range of phenomena or suggests a single identifiable sect or religion, a position that is debated. Similarly, the current tendency to understand gnosticism as originating in pre-Christian Jewish Sethianism has been questioned, seeing it instead as a *heresy arising from within Christianity.

Patristic sources

Following the discovery of the Nag Hammadi gnostic texts in 1945, it became apparent that while the writers used a range of self-designations (including Christians, race of Seth and immoveable race), they did not use *gnōstikos* (or a Coptic equivalent) for this pupose. Before this discovery the primary source of information on gnostics came from early heresiologists and polemicists such as *Justin Martyr, *Irenaeus, *Origen, *Tertullian, Hippolytus and Epiphanius. Although their works preserved extracts of gnostic writings, their principal aim was one of self-definition, establishing a Christian identity distinct from heresy, Judaism and Greco-Roman society and thought. Of particular significance and influence has been Irenaeus' *Against Heresies* (which may be dependent in part upon Justin Martyr) in which he identifies a range of figures and groups holding gnostic beliefs which he describes and then argues against their theological positions. Hippolytus, drawing on Irenaeus, similarly identified and countered gnostic sects in his *Refutation of all Heresies*, and Epiphanius' *Panarion* ('Medicine Chest'), if somewhat unreliably, identifies a number of gnostic sects, seeking to explain how they related to others.

Gnostic leaders

Justin, Irenaeus and Hippolytus all claim that Simon Magus (Acts 8) was the founder of gnostic heresy (and, for Irenaeus, many other sects as well), but this is now doubted not least because of the confusing and conflicting descriptions of the beliefs associated with him. According to Irenaeus, Simon's successor was another Samaritan, Menander, who also worked in Antioch and claimed that anyone baptized into him would not die. The second-century Saturninus of Antioch and Basilides of Alexandria were both understood to be dependent upon Simon and Menander. Irenaeus explains that the former held that an unknown father created angels (one of whom was the 'God of the Jews') who then created human beings and that he had a *docetic view of Christ. The account of Basilides' teaching is differently reported: by Irenaeus, who attributes to him a dualistic system, and by Hippolytus a *monistic system. Cerinthus, from Asia Minor and teaching in the early second century, also held that the world was created by lesser beings than the supreme unknown God and maintained a docetic *Christology, but he is also associated with the *Ebionites. There is some dispute as to whether *Marcion of Sinope should be regarded as gnostic. His Christology was docetic, and he distinguished between the Creator God of the Jews and the God revealed by Christ, rejecting the OT and establishing the first canon of the NT, consisting of Luke's Gospel and ten Pauline letters from which he excised anything that he regarded as a Jewish interpolation or corruption of the original text. However, he does not exhibit traits that scholars commonly associate with gnosticism: his emphasis on faith rather than *gnōsis*; his rejection of allegorical interpretations of Jewish scripture; the lack of a myth associating the God of Jesus with creation; and the absence of any teaching on humans having within them a divine spark destined to return to its original spiritual realm.

Before the discovery of the Nag Hammadi texts, the most famous gnostic teacher was Valentinus, an Alexandrian Christian who gained a wide following in Rome when he moved there (*c*. 140). Irenaeus records that Valentinus adapted gnostic thought to his own system, but describes his teaching based primarily on the development of his thought taught by his disciple Ptolemy. From the realm (*plērōma*) of the good, unknown God there emanates an elaborate series of aeons or eternities, and it is from the lowest and fallen of these, *Sophia* (wisdom), that there came into being the demiurge or God of the OT who created the visible world; there is thus a dualistic separation of the spiritual and material worlds. The aeon Christ was understood to have descended into Jesus at his baptism in order to teach people about their heavenly origin and enable them to return to the heavenly realm. Valentinus thus divided humanity into three categories: pneumatics (i.e. Valentinians) to whom this *gnōsis* is given; psychics who are Christians living by faith but can only reach the middle realm of the demiurge; and hylics, the rest of humanity destined for destruction.

Gnosticism

In the Nag Hammadi *Gospel of Truth*, often attributed to Valentinus or to the Valentinian school, Christ is said to reveal the truth of the Father and restore unity with him through his teaching and resurrection.

Gnostic sources

Before the twentieth century three Coptic gnostic codices were discovered. The fifth-century *Codex Brucianus* contained two works, one untitled and the other the *Books of Jeu*. The latter, probably dating originally from the late third century, contain revelations of Christ to his disciples; the various names of the 'true God' and Father of Christ, Jeu (a variant of YHWH), are illustrated with ideographs. The *Books of Jeu* are referred to in the fourth-century *Pistis Sophia* (*Codex Askewianus*) which contains further revelations of Christ to his disciples. The fifth-century *Codex Berolinensis* (published in 1955) contains four works: the *Gospel of Mary*, which consists of a dialogue between Jesus and his disciples, including a special revelation to his favourite, Mary Magdalene; an *Apocryphon* ('secret book') *of John*; the tractate *Sophia of Jesus Christ* containing mythological material; and an *Act of Peter*. The first two codices were held to represent a later form of gnosticism that offered little of importance concerning the origins of gnosticism and Christianity, and so they received little serious attention.

The Mandaean community of modern Iran and Iraq has been held out as the last surviving gnostic sect. The study of Mandaean materials has suggested to some a pre-Christian oriental origin for gnosticism. *History of religions scholars used this material to reconstruct an artificial gnostic redeemer myth which, while it is found in no single ancient literary source, has had a considerable influence on how gnosticism has been understood. *Manichaeism had a much less positive view of the demiurge and the world. It arose in Iran in the third century and has been seen not only as influenced by gnostic ideas, but also as a later development of gnosticism that for the history of religions school could shed light on its origins.

The Nag Hammadi library, containing a large body of mainly gnostic material, has had a significant impact on gnostic studies in recent years. Although matters of authorship, origin and date are still debated, it has been seen as a collection of material arising from a community that saw itself as Christian with a unifying myth and rite of initiation. The correlation between this heterogeneous collection of texts and heresiological accounts of gnostic thought is limited and the diverse perspectives and literary genres contained within them has led to much debate on such matters as classification, origins and definitions. It has also been suggested that it was originally part of a Christian monastic library, though whether for heresiological or edificatory purposes is uncertain. The variety in the material has also suggested that the distinction between orthodoxy and heresy in early Christian Egypt was not clearly defined. The fifty-two writings in the library frequently reflect biblical literary genres, and several of the works appear more than once. Particularly significant among these is the *Apocryphon of John*, of which there are three copies (a fourth copy is extant in another manuscript further suggesting its importance); some of the Church Fathers, especially Irenaeus, appear to have been familiar with some version of it. Mythological in nature, the *Apocryphon of John* describes secret mysteries revealed to the apostle by Christ after the resurrection on such matters as the nature of divinity and levels of it, humanity (including its fall and salvation), the heavenly realm, visible creation (including how it came into being and the subdivine powers that control it), the origin of evil and how to escape this evil world and return to the heavenly realm. The library also includes the well-known *Gospel of Thomas*, which does not seem to have been gnostic originally, but appears to have been influenced by gnostic ideas as the text was edited. It contains numerous supposedly secret sayings of Jesus (many with NT parallels) which develop a theme of self-recognition in order to discover what is hidden; by gaining knowledge of one's divine origin, salvation is achieved through leaving behind all that binds one to the corruptible world.

Common features

Although there is no systematic gnostic theology and a wide variety of gnostic ideas are found in both Christian polemical and gnostic writings, beliefs common to different gnostic systems can be identified, some of which have already been noted. Anticosmic ('world rejecting') *dualism is frequently seen as a distinctive characteristic of gnosticism; the world is regarded as evil, as sometimes is its Creator, the demiurge often seen as the God of the OT, who is separate from the good, supreme and unknown God. However, this needs to be treated with caution, as the Nag Hammadi texts do not support such a generalized and consistent view. Sparks of divine light are said to be trapped in the bodies of the elect élite (pneumatics), or sometimes all people, who are unaware of their divine origin. A redeemer (often a docetic Christ) is therefore sent to give them secret *gnōsis* of their true nature and enable them to escape the evil world and return to the world of light. The archons (rulers of this world) attempt to prevent the soul's ascent through the aeons to be reunited with God, but the use of secret formulae provided by Jesus facilitates the journey. However, the redeemer myth is not so consistently expressed as this might suggest. It has long been held that the gnostic negative view of the world coupled with the need of *gnōsis* rather than faith or works for salvation perhaps goes some way to explaining the ascetic and licentious behaviour associated with gnosticism; both responses can be seen as rejection or means of overcoming the evil world. Gnostic texts do advocate or at least imply forms of ascetic self-denial and renunciation aimed at achieving something of the perfection and serenity that would be fully enjoyed when the soul had returned to the *plērōma*. The libertine model of gnostic ethics has been challenged, not least because of the lack of evidence for this in the Nag Hammadi texts. It has been suggested that the only direct, if debatably gnostic, evidence of sexual licence is found in the extensive quotations by Clement of Alexandria from Epiphanes' *Concerning Righteousness*. Epiphanes, not unlike his father Carpocrates, if Irenaeus' depiction of him is accurate, regarded monogamy as an unnatural limitation imposed by human law on God's plan for sexual freedom. However, there is far more evidence for *asceticism than for libertinism. Rites such as baptism, which included chrismation with scented ointment, and the Eucharist tended to be spiritualized as symbols of *gnōsis*.

Conclusion

There is no clear consensus on how gnosticism should be defined, and the diverse nature of the evidence for gnostic beliefs from Christian polemicists and gnostic texts suggests a variety of thought rather than a single system. Although gnostic texts provide evidence of the context in which Christianity developed, the extent to which, for example, the extracanonical gospels contribute to our understanding of Jesus hinges largely on their date. However, the contemporary fascination with such texts and the appeal of gnosticism to, for example, New Age groups demonstrates the importance of contemporary engagement with them.

Bibliography

C. A. Evans, *Fabricating Jesus: How Modern Scholars Distort the Gospels* (Nottingham, 2007); H. Jonas, *The Gnostic Religion* (London, ²1992); K. L. King, *What Is Gnosticism?* (Cambridge, MA and London, 2003); B. Layton, *The Rediscovery of Gnosticism*, 2 vols. (Leiden, 1980–81); A. H. B. Logan, *The Gnostics: Identifying an Early Christian Cult* (London and New York, 2006); C. Markschies, *Gnosis: An Introduction* (ET, London and New York, 2003); B. A. Pearson, *Gnosticism and Christianity in Roman and Coptic Egypt* (London and New York, 2004); J. M. Robinson, *The Nag Hammadi Library in English* (San Francisco, 1988); K. Rudolph, *Gnosis: The Nature and History of an Ancient Religion* (ET, Edinburgh, 1983); M. A. Williams, *Rethinking 'Gnosticism': An Argument for Dismantling a Dubious Category* (Princeton and Chichester, 1996); E. M. Yamauchi, *Pre-Christian Gnosticism: A Survey of the Proposed Evidences* (Grand Rapids, ²1983).

A. D. RICH

GOD

The church confesses, worships and serves God, as he has revealed himself in Scripture.

The identity of God

In Christian *monotheism, following biblical *revelation, God is understood in two ways: through the doctrine of the *Trinity; and through an account of the divine perfections.

Monotheism

History demonstrates a variety of views of the divine. Christian accounts are *theistic, rather than *deistic or *pantheistic, and monotheistic rather than *polytheistic. Deism, first formulated in the seventeenth century, sees the cosmos as a closed system with its maker outside it, and so denies God's direct providential control of events and his miraculous creative interventions into the ongoing life of the world.

God

Pantheism, which pre-dates Christianity in Oriental religions (see *Buddhism and Christianity; *Hinduism and Christianity), recognizes no creator-creature distinction, but sees everything, good and evil included, as a direct form or expression of God. As *Coleridge put it, for a pantheist, God minus the universe leaves nothing; for a theist, God minus the universe leaves God, entire and complete.

Polytheism is more directly denounced in Scripture, as the constant form of Ancient Near Eastern and Greco-Roman religion. It posits many divine beings, limited by each other, none omnipotent. Worship must therefore be spread and allegiance divided amongst them all. (Early Christians were routinely accused of 'atheism' for their refusal to worship any and every god with which they were presented.) Monotheistic belief stresses the uniqueness of God, his independence from the world, and his involvement with the world.

Trinitarianism

Belief in God's tri-unity is distinctive, and basic, to Christian theism. While developed trinitarian theology only appears in the fourth century AD, the later theology is a faithful response to God's self-presentation in the biblical revelation. Divine works, such as creation (e.g. Col. 1:15–18) and redemption (e.g. 2 Thess. 2:13–14) are presented as the work of Father and Son, or (more rarely) Father, Son and Spirit. More tellingly, monotheistic affirmations of faith from the OT are expanded to include the Son in the NT (1 Cor. 8:6), and worship is offered to Father, Son and Spirit indifferently and together. Blessing is often given in triadic form (2 Cor. 13:14; Rev. 1:4–5). The early theologians, supremely the Cappadocian Fathers and *Augustine of Hippo, found language in which to speak of God which was adequate to this biblical data. God is one – or, perhaps better, unique (the *patristic theologians would have hesitated to 'count' God); this unique God exists eternally in three persons: Father, Son and *Holy Spirit.

The Cappadocian discussion stressed the unity of divine action (*Basil, *On the Holy Spirit*; *Gregory of Nyssa, *Ad Ablabius*; see also *Gregory of Nazianzus). God's saving act, for instance, is decreed by the Father, carried forth by the Son, and perfected by the Spirit. It remains, however, one act of one God. In this, they were simply working carefully through the necessary logic of the NT witness. Augustine switched the focus to God's eternal life. God is triune, not just in his actions in the world, but in himself from all eternity.

The divine names in the Bible

Divine names begin in the Scriptures. Although 'God' functions in Christian *worship as a proper noun, in the OT God is named in many ways, expressing the various aspects of his perfect life:

1. *El, Eloah, Elohim* (in English translations of the Bible, typically 'God'); *El Elyon* ('God most high'). These names suggest a transcendent being, superhumanly powerful, and with inexhaustible life in himself, on whom everything that is not himself depends for its being and life.
2. *Adonai* ('Lord'). One who rules over all else.
3. *Yahweh* ('the LORD'), *Yahweh Sabaoth* ('LORD of hosts' or 'LORD Almighty'). Yahweh is God's personal name for himself, by which his people were to invoke him as the Lord who had taken them into covenant with himself in order to do them good. When God first revealed this name to Moses (Exod. 3), he explained it as meaning 'I am what I am', or perhaps more accurately, 'I will be what I will be'. It is thus a declaration of independent, self-determining existence.

The NT identifies the God who is Father of Jesus Christ as the God of the OT, the only God there is, and it sees Christian *salvation as the fulfilment of God's promises. There is thus no space for '*Marcionism', or any other system that sets the God of the OT against the God of Jesus. God is named in the NT as 'Father' (see *Fatherhood of God). 'Lord' (*kurios*; translating *Adonai*) becomes the regular term for characterizing, confessing and invoking the risen and enthroned Christ (Acts 2:36; 10:36; Rom. 10:9–13; 1 Cor. 8:6; 2 Cor. 12:8–10; Rev. 22:20, etc.). Christians are to be baptized into the 'name' (singular) of 'the Father, the Son and the Holy Spirit' (Matt. 28:19). This is God's 'Christian name', as Barth happily put it.

The language of belief

Human language is all that we have for worshipping, confessing and discussing God. It is adequate, but it has to be systematically adapted for the purpose. God co-opts or commandeers our language to enable it to refer adequately to him. Scripture, in presenting God in *anthropomorphic terms, quietly witnesses to this adaptation or co-option. God's life, thoughts, attitudes and actions are presented as basically comparable to our own, although they contrast with ours in being free both from the limitations of our creaturely finiteness and from the moral flaws that are part and parcel of our fallenness. The words are thus used in Scripture in a sense analogous to, though never quite identical with, the sense they would carry if used of humans.

In the early development of theology, Basil and Gregory of Nyssa stressed in their debates with Eunomius that our language concerning God is a product of *epinoia*, or human construction. The words which we use to speak of God thus refer genuinely, but only imperfectly. The classic development of this theme comes in the work of St *Thomas Aquinas, who developed a nuanced account of *analogy based on the similarity of being that exists between God and the creatures because of God's own gracious gift of his life to other beings. St Thomas's account was almost immediately criticized by John *Duns Scotus, who believed that any analogy must, logically, be based on an underlying univocity, and so suggested that existence itself is true in exactly the same way for God and the creatures. God is; we are; these two statements are not distinguishable. However, an account of analogy similar to that of St Thomas was accepted on all sides of the *Reformation debate.

In the Eastern church, St Gregory *Palamas introduced the notion of the 'divine energies', which effectively removed the perfections as descriptions of God's life at all. What we know are the energies, which serve to mediate God's presence to the world; God's life in itself remains completely unknown to us. The Western church opposed Palamas on this point, claiming that such a doctrine made speech about God too unavailable to us.

More recently, Karl *Barth has criticized what he understood Aquinas to be saying, and argued for a reversal in the direction of the analogy. We do not understand justice (say) in human terms, and then find it echoed in God; true justice is divine justice, and any human analogue is a pale and distorted shadow. Whether Barth was right to accuse Aquinas of arguing the former must be questioned; his positive point, however, is significant. God is the primary reality; creaturely existence is secondary, derivative and dependent. 'This is love: not that we loved God, but that he loved us, and sent his Son as an atoning sacrifice for our sins' (1 John 4:10).

The perfections of God

The 'perfections of God' are ways in which God is properly named, or described. Any word or concept that adequately completes the sentence 'God is . . .' is a perfection of God. Classically, the perfections of God are divided into two classes: 'uncommunicated' perfections, which are realities true only of God, and 'communicated' perfections, which are realities granted in some analogical measure to other creatures.

The uncommunicated perfections

1. God is self-existent (*a se*), self-sufficient and self-sustaining ('divine aseity'): God exists necessarily, with no need of help or support from the created order (cf. Acts 17:23–25). Divine aseity is God's quality of having life in and from himself. It denies any account of God which suggests he needs the world to be who he is.

2. God is simple (i.e. totally integrated), perfect and immutable: God is wholly and entirely involved in everything that he is and does. His nature, intentions and ways of acting do not change, either for the better (because the perfect cannot become better) or for the worse. His immutability is not the changelessness of an eternally frozen pose, but the moral consistency that holds him to his own principles of action and leads him to deal differently with those who change their own behaviour towards him (cf. Ps. 18:24–27). In the medieval *scholastic tradition, God was understood to be *actus purus*: pure activity. His changelessness must be understood under this rubric, as the constancy of a perfectly dynamic and active life.

3. God is infinite, bodiless (a spirit), omnipresent, omniscient and eternal. These words affirm that God is not bound by any of the limitations of space or time that apply to his creatures. He is always present everywhere, though imperceptibly, and is at every moment aware of all that ever was, is or shall be, and all that could have been.

4. God is purposeful, omnipotent and sovereign. God has a plan for the universe which guides its *history. In executing this plan, he governs and controls all created realities. Without violating the nature of things,

and without at any stage infringing on human free agency (see *Freedom, Christian; *Will), God acts in, with and through his creatures so as to do everything that he intends exactly as he intends it. By this overruling action, despite human disobedience and demonic obstruction, he achieves his intended goals.

5. God is both transcendent over, and immanent in, his world. These nineteenth-century words express the thought that on the one hand God is distinct from his world and does not need it; while on the other hand he permeates the world in sustaining creative power (see *Creation), shaping and steering it in a way that keeps it on its planned course.
6. God is impassible. This means, not that God is impassive and unfeeling (a frequent misunderstanding), but that no created beings can change God's intentions or life without his previously intending it. God enters human suffering and grief, as Scripture testifies abundantly, and the *cross proves beyond all doubt, but he does so by his own deliberate decision. He is never simply acted upon by his creatures. Recent theology has often criticized the idea of divine *impassibility (see, classically, *Moltmann, *The Crucified God*), arguing that it is an improper accretion from Greek philosophy, foreign to the gospel story, and that belief in God in a suffering world is rendered difficult or impossible by the doctrine. Against this, we should note that divine impassibility is not a claim that God is unable to sympathize with our sufferings, but a claim that no creature can harm, damage or impede God. Only if God is *sovereign and omnipotent in this way can we hope that he will be able to overcome the troubles and evil of the world and bring, finally, the eschatological *kingdom where 'there will be no more death or mourning or crying or pain' (Rev. 21:4).
7. God is incomprehensible. After listing all these perfections of God, it is important to stress again that God's life cannot be encompassed by human language. Our words point, haltingly and imperfectly, towards the single, simple perfection that God is. However, we do not understand or define God's nature. We witness to the nature of his perfection, far beyond our understanding, with worship and awe.

The communicated perfections

In God's dealings with humanity we see many divine perfections displayed that have analogues in human life. God's justice is comparable to human concepts of *justice, even if it is infinitely beyond any human reality. God is Jesus-like, for *Jesus is God in the flesh. The key affirmations we can make concerning God's character would seem to be these:

1. God is holy *love (see also *Love of God): the essence of all love is giving prompted by goodwill, with joy in the recipients' benefit. The statement, 'God is love' (1 John 4:8), is explained in context as meaning that God gave his Son as a propitiatory *sacrifice for human sin to bring believers to new life (see *Atonement). Love that gives freely, without regard for the worth of the recipient, is at the heart of the NT account of God's life – not just in his relationships with the world, but in his own inner life, according to John 5:20 and 14:31. Giving in order to make the recipient great must be understood as the moral shape of the triune God's own life.

God is also 'the Holy One'. Holiness, in the Bible, suggests separateness from the world, purity and hatred of moral evil (see *Sanctification). Accounts of love that ignore such realities are simply deficient, biblically. Rather, God's love is holy love, and God's holiness is loving holiness. The cross is classically understood as the place where God demonstrates both his holiness and his love to the utmost degree.
2. God is moral perfection. God is not just awesome but also adorable. His moral perfections, such as his truthfulness, faithfulness, *grace, mercy, loving-kindness, patience, constancy, wisdom, justice, goodness and generosity, are supremely beautiful and inspire adoration, devotion and praise. Theology has not begun, and God has not been known at all, unless the study of God's nature and character results in heartfelt worship.

See also: CHRISTOLOGY.

Bibliography

K. Barth, *CD*, I.1, II.1, 2; H. Bavinck, *The Doctrine of God* (Grand Rapids, 1952); D. G.

Bloesch, *God the Almighty* (Downers Grove, 2005); G. Bray, *The Doctrine of God* (Leicester, 1993); A. Coppedge, *Portraits of God* (Downers Grove, 2001); J. M. Frame, *The Doctrine of God: A Theology of Lordship* (Phillipsburg, 2002); C. Kaiser, *The Doctrine of God: An Historical Survey* (London, 1982); V.-M. Kärkkäinen, *The Doctrine of God: A Global Introduction* (Grand Rapids, 2004); R. H. Nash, *The Concept of God* (Grand Rapids, 1983).

S. R. HOLMES

GOGARTEN, FRIEDRICH (1887–1967)

Gogarten was a German Lutheran pastor turned systematic theologian who taught in Jena (1925–31) and later became Professor in Breslau (1931–5) and Göttingen (1935–55). Gogarten partnered with Karl *Barth, Eduard Thurneysen (1888–1977) and George Merz (1892–1959) to found the journal *Zwischen den Zeiten (Between the Times)* and the dialectical theology movement along with Emil *Brunner and Rudolf *Bultmann. A staunch opponent of Weimar Germany, but never a National Socialist, Gogarten was briefly associated with the German Christians in 1933, directly criticizing Barth and the *Confessing Church, but retracting his position only months later when German Christian anti-Semitism became explicit.

Gogarten's early theology attempted to avoid the 'timeless truths' of both idealism and orthodoxy and eventually located one of the foundations for theology in an *existentialist anthropology by reversing Martin *Buber's formula to Thou-I in order to de-emphasize the priority of the self, an overall *anthropological turn earning Barth's public disavowal. The later Gogarten relied on Bultmann's programme of *demythologization to endorse Christianity as the world's pre-eminent secularizing force that ended public mythology by relating Christianity to faith and worldly affairs to reason. Both periods are united by Gogarten's interests in anthropology, law and gospel, history and ethics.

Bibliography

Works: *Ich Glaube an den dreienigen Gott* (Jena, 1926); *Demythologizing and History* (ET, London, 1955); *Der Mensch Zwischen Gott und Welt* (Stuttgart, 1967); *Christ the Crisis* (ET, London, 1970).

Studies: L. Shiner, *The Secularization of History: An Introduction to the Theology of Friedrich Gogarten* (Nashville, 1966).

D. A. GILLAND

GOODWIN, THOMAS (1600–80)

Academically gifted and religiously sensitive, Goodwin left Norfolk for Cambridge University when he was still just twelve years old. Graduating at sixteen, he excelled in his academic development, yet he was initially more interested in popularity than spiritual reality. This changed in 1620 when, hearing a funeral sermon, he was deeply disturbed about his sin and spent seven years looking for peace. When Goodwin had a very definite experience of 'new birth', he was a transformed man: as the living God 'created the world and the matter of all things by a word, so he created and put a new life and spirit into my soul, and so great an alteration was strange to me'. This experience helps to explain the experimental warmth throughout the ministry of Goodwin.

Goodwin became a *Congregationalist in 1634, and in 1643, along with his friends Nye, Burroughs, Bridge and Simpson, he was appointed to the Westminster Assembly, leading the Congregationalist party and later working to produce the Savoy Declaration of 1658. At the Restoration Goodwin felt that he could no longer maintain his work in Oxford, and in 1660 he left the university and settled in London, later establishing City Temple in Holborn. The members of his Oxford congregation followed him to London where he remained throughout the plague and the Great Fire. He spent his life studying how Jesus is the total answer to the sin and corruption of *Adam, and on his deathbed Goodwin confessed, full of assurance, that he had 'the whole righteousness of Christ'.

Bibliography

The Works of Thomas Goodwin, 12 vols., facsimile of 1861–66 version of Nichol's *Standard Divines* (Grand Rapids, 2006).

P. R. BLACKHAM

GOOD WORKS, see SANCTIFICATION

GORE, CHARLES (1853–1932)

Gore was an Anglo-Catholic leader and scholar, and Bishop of Worcester (1902–5), Birmingham (1905–11) and Oxford (1911–19). Scion of an aristocratic family, Gore was educated at Harrow where his early 'Catholic' spirituality was nurtured by, among others, B. F. *Westcott. An outstanding undergraduate at Balliol, Oxford, he was elected fellow of Trinity College in 1875. As vice-principal of the newly founded theological college at Cuddesdon (1880–83), and as first Principal Librarian of the new *Anglo-Catholic study centre in Oxford, Pusey House (1884–93), Gore exerted a personal and spiritual influence comparable to that of J. H. *Newman. These early years were also Gore's most significant theologically, as he controversially sought to imbue traditional Tractarianism with the modern spirit of a critical scripturalism in his quest for an effective popular dogmatic. His *The Ministry of the Christian Church* (1888, new edn 1919) is, however, a spirited conservative defence of High Church views of the historical origins of episcopacy. His liberal catholicism came to fruition in his contribution to, and editorship of, the controversial volume of Oxford essays by like-minded scholars, *Lux Mundi: A Series of Studies in the Religion of the Incarnation* (1889). Traditional Tractarians were further discomfited by Gore's Bampton Lectures, *The Incarnation of the Son of God* (1891), which not only contained a Greek patristic reaffirmation of the dogmatic centrality of the incarnation, but also claimed that Christ's full earthly humanity involved a voluntary self-emptying (*kenosis) of his divine knowledge and a resultant human ignorance.

No narrow-minded academic aristocrat, Gore was passionately concerned for social justice and for a credible grass-roots manifestation of Christian thought and life: hence, his lifelong involvement with the Oxford Mission to Calcutta and the *Christian Socialist Union, and his civic involvement and support of the Workers Educational Association when Bishop of Birmingham. Gore wedded an Anglo-Catholic apologetic to this concern for Christian social action. His *Dissertations* (1895), *The Body of Christ* (1905), *Christ and Society* (1928), and exposition of the *Sermon on the Mount* (1896) reveal a Catholic sacramental dogmatic accompanying his call for Christian service in church and world.

Despite successful episcopal labours, Gore became increasingly isolated, vigorously and unpopularly denouncing a progressive Anglo-Catholicism which commended liturgical supplementation (e.g. reservation of the Eucharist) and credal laxity. He devoted his last years in London to teaching and writing, notably in defence of the Christian faith (cf. his dogmatic trilogy *Belief in God*, 1922, *Belief in Christ*, 1922, *The Holy Spirit and the Church*, 1924) and of his Anglo-Catholic position (e.g. his critique, *The Anglo-Catholic Movement Today*, 1925).

Bibliography

J. Carpenter, *Gore, A Study in Liberal Catholic Thought* (London, 1960); W. R. Inge, in *Edinburgh Review* 207 (1908), pp. 79–104; G. L. Prestige, *The Life of Charles Gore: A Great Englishman* (London, 1935); A. R. Vidler, 'Charles Gore and Liberal Catholicism' in *Essays in Liberality* (London, 1957); A. T. P. Williams in *DNB* (1931–1940), pp. 349–353.

C. D. HANCOCK

GOSPEL

The gospel describes the core proclamation of the Christian faith, centred on *Jesus Christ and the divine plan of *redemption fulfilled in his life, death, resurrection and renewal of creation. The Old English word *godspel* translated the Greek term *euangelion*, meaning 'glad tidings' or 'good news'. Lutheran dogmatics tends formally to distinguish the 'law' of the old covenant from the 'gospel' of the new, but lexically at least *euangelion* and its variants appear in both the LXX and the NT. In Isa. 40:9 and 52:7–10 the returning exiles become heralds of joy to Jerusalem, Judah and the nations. In Isa. 61:1–2, an anointed redeemer preaches good news to the poor and liberty to captives. Jesus significantly applies this Messianic text to himself when launching his own mission (Luke 4:18–21). Indeed, while the key accounts of Jesus' ministry were not formally named 'Gospels' until the second century, it is significant that Mark identifies his narrative from the outset as 'the gospel about Jesus Christ, the Son of God' (Mark 1:1).

Matthew and Mark in particular associate the gospel with the 'kingdom' or 'reign' of God, as demonstrated most vividly in Jesus' miracles and parables (Matt. 4:23; 9:35; Mark 1:14–15;

4:26). Whereas certain more pietistic traditions have presented 'gospel ministry' largely in terms of individual *conversion, growing theological appreciation of this link between gospel and *kingdom over the past century or so has led most Christian bodies to articulate a broader understanding which relates the gospel to social justice, communal well-being and *ecological stewardship, as well as to personal *salvation. Echoing the Hebrew concept of *shalom*, this definition underlies the *Barmen Declaration, drafted by the German Confessing Church in opposition to Nazism. It is also reflected in the evangelical *Lausanne Covenant, with its emphasis on the 'whole church' taking the 'whole gospel' to the 'whole world'.

Euangelion and its cognates appear even more often in Paul's letters than in the Synoptics. Here the message proclaimed by Jesus is seen more explicitly to have been embodied by him in the fact that he died for sinners, was buried and was raised from the tomb (1 Cor. 15:3–5). Thus, Jesus not only declares the good news; he *is* the good news (Rom. 1:1–4, 9; 1 Cor. 9:12b; 2 Cor. 4:4). Just as he is divine, eternal and unparalleled, so is the gospel; and just as this gospel must be proclaimed, so also it must be faithfully heard, received and applied for *salvation (1 Cor. 9:16–23). Thus for individuals, societies and the world as a whole, the gospel is nothing less than a matter of life and death.

'*Evangelical theology' is the term given to that historical tradition of theology and church life which, since the Reformation, has centred on the *euangelion*. Although at various times in the past evangelical understanding of the gospel has tended towards more personalized forms of conversion, in other periods and situations evangelical commitment to the authority of *Scripture has prompted a broader understanding of the gospel as concerned not only with individual salvation, but with corporate, societal and cosmic dimensions of the 'good news'. This has become especially apparent in recent mainstream expressions of evangelicalism. For these as for other authentic accounts of the gospel, while contexts may change and while understanding may grow, what has not altered, and cannot alter, is that the gospel is personified and centred in the Lord Jesus Christ.

Bibliography

C. E. Braaten, *That All May Believe: Theology of the Gospel and the Mission of Church* (Grand Rapids, 2008); M. J. Erikson, *Christian Theology* (Grand Rapids, ²1998), pp. 1069–1076; G. Friedrich, '*Euangelizomai, euangelion, proeuangelizomai, euangelistēs*', in *TDNT* 1 vol. edn, abridged G. Bromiley (Grand Rapids, 1985), pp. 267–273; I. H. Marshall, *New Testament Theology: Many Witnesses: One Gospel* (Leicester, 2004); J. R. W. Stott (ed.), *Making Christ Known: Historic Mission Documents from the Lausanne Movement, 1974–1989* (Carlisle, 1996); R. H. Strachan, 'The Gospel in the New Testament', in G. A. Buttrick (ed.), *The Interpreter's Bible*, VII (New York, 1951), pp. 3–31.

D. H. K. HILBORN

GOTTSCHALK (*c.* 803–69)

Gottschalk was a *Benedictine theologian, poet and monk who caused an argument over *predestination that agitated the church in France and Germany during the Carolingian era. His father, Berno, a Saxon noble, placed him in the monastery at Fulda, but when he came of age he asked to be released from his vows. This request was granted by the Synod of Mainz (829), but Louis I the Pious, on an appeal from the abbot of Gottschalk's monastery, Rabanus Maurus, reversed the decision. Gottschalk was then moved to the monastery at Orbais, where he began an intensive study of the work of *Augustine. Becoming a priest, he visited Rome and later served as a missionary in the Balkans. His constant emphasis upon double predestination led to his condemnation at the synods of Mainz (848) and Quiercy (849 and 853). He was dismissed from the priesthood, beaten until he almost died and imprisoned for life at the monastery of Hautvillers.

His view of predestination included the belief that God foreordains those he wishes to heaven or to hell, that one can have absolute certainty of salvation or damnation, that God does not will that all shall be saved, that Christ died only for the elect, and that no-one can exercise free *will for the doing of good works but only for performing evil acts. Several theologians wrote in support of his views, including *Ratramnus, Prudentius of Troyes (d. 861) and Remigius of Lyons (d. 875). When three opponents of Gottschalk's teaching, including Hincmar of Reims (*c.* 806–82), sent letters to Remigius to justify the harsh treatment he had received, Remigius responded in the name of the Church of Lyons with a *Reply to the Three Letters*, which criticized the treatment given to the monk, clarified the issues and partially supported Gottschalk's position.

The lively debate over predestination demonstrates that the issues raised in the earlier *Pelagian controversy had not been settled. They were to surface again at the time of the *Protestant Reformation and in more recent times as a result of the *Wesleyan movement. These discussions, accompanied by a certain amount of rancour, continue to divide evangelicalism in modern times. There was little new ground broken in the ninth-century phase of the argument and neither party prevailed, nor was any compromise reached. Some of Gottschalk's fellow monks tried to free him by appealing to the pope, but this attempt failed. He remained in prison unreconciled to his ecclesiastical superiors. The resentment he felt because of the severe treatment he had received probably led to the mental illness he experienced before his death. A man of great literary talent, he left several thoughtful poems that rank with the finest literature produced by the Carolingian Renaissance.

Bibliography

G. W. Bromiley, *Historical Theology* (Grand Rapids, 1978); J. Jolivet, *Godescale d'Orbais et la Trinité* (Paris, 1958); J. Pelikan, *The Growth of Medieval Theology (600–1300): The Christian Tradition*, vol. 3 (Chicago, 1978); K. Vielhaber, *Gottschalk der Sachse* (Bonn, 1956).

R. G. Clouse

GRACE

In its primary meaning, grace is undeserved favour, usually that extended from a superior to an inferior. The Hebrew term for this is *hen* and the Greek is *charis*, a word closely related to *charisma*, which means a gift of (divine) grace. As traditionally understood, the grace of God is first of all the free act by which he reaches out to sinful human beings and rescues them from condemnation, even though they have done nothing to deserve this favour. It is manifested within the context of the *covenant that God made with Israel, the nation which he chose of his own free will to represent him on earth, and in the NT to 'all people, especially of those who believe' (1 Tim. 4:10) and who, as the church, are the new people drawn from every nation and chosen for salvation in Christ, again without any action on their part which might have earned it. But the word is also used to refer to God's transforming power in those who have become his children.

It follows from this that every aspect of human *salvation is an act of divine grace, from the original *calling (election), through *redemption, *justification, *conversion, *sanctification and finally glorification by incorporation into the risen and ascended body of Christ in heaven. Its all-embracing character within the context of salvation has given rise to a number of theological developments, some of which have come to characterize particular types of Christianity. Indeed, it is not too much to say that it is the different understandings of grace, as much as anything else, which have created the main divisions within the Christian church as we know them today.

The doctrine of grace was little developed in the early church until the time of *Augustine, who was forced to respond to the challenge presented by the teaching of *Pelagius. Pelagius believed that human beings were capable of contributing to their salvation by their own efforts, though the grace of God was still required in order to bring those efforts to fruition. Augustine condemned this teaching on the ground that every aspect of our salvation is a work of God's grace to which we can add nothing. According to him, baptism is *prevenient grace*, given by God at the very beginning of the Christian life in order to take away the guilt of original sin. This is then complemented by *co-operating grace*, which God gives to souls regenerated by baptism, so that they might grow to be more like God. Then there is *sufficient grace*, which was given to Jesus of Nazareth so that in his human flesh he could live without sin in the world, and finally *efficient grace*, which sanctifies us and makes us fit to dwell in the kingdom of heaven.

In medieval *scholastic theology these different types of grace were codified and linked to different ministries of the church, which came to be seen as the great dispenser of God's grace in the world. The ways in which it was communicated to believers were known as the *means of grace*, which were listed and analysed by a series of medieval theologians. The church itself was a means of grace, but so too were things like prayer, the reading and exposition of Scripture, and above all the seven *sacraments. A person in good standing with the church had access to the means of grace which its ministry made available, but the church had the power to cut people off from them if it so chose (excommunication). In theory, excommunication was reserved for the most serious sins, but as time went on, it was routinely used for even minor matters of church discipline such as failure to pay tithes, and its original force was compromised accordingly.

Medieval theologians also developed the notion that grace builds on nature and perfects it. This idea gained ground after the reintroduction of pagan philosophy, in particular the science of *Aristotle, into Western Europe in the twelfth and thirteenth centuries. *Thomas Aquinas and others concluded that human reason could advance only so far on its own, and that in order to receive the fullness of truth it had to be supplemented by divine revelation, which was an act of grace. In this way, they came to believe that the Bible accepted and addressed an essentially Aristotelian view of the universe, which it then rounded out with knowledge which could only be communicated by God. It was this conviction, as much as anything else, which provoked the intellectual crisis of the sixteenth century, when it was realized that Aristotle was fundamentally mistaken in many of his supposedly scientific assertions. The nature-grace dualism which scholastic theology had erected on the understanding that Aristotle and the Bible were both infallible in their respective spheres was strongly challenged and either overthrown (in Protestant countries) or reasserted by force (in Catholic countries). The tension is most clearly visible in the medieval doctrine of transubstantiation, which rested on the belief that grace transforms nature and perfects it by turning simple bread and wine into the body and blood of Christ (see *Eucharist). Scientific discoveries made this distinction untenable, and transubstantiation was accordingly rejected by Protestants, whereas the unfortunate Galileo was condemned and imprisoned for having reached the same conclusion in a Catholic environment.

*Protestantism redefined the means of grace, putting preaching at the top of the list and firmly subordinating the sacraments (now reduced in number to two) firmly to it. The work of God in the life of a believer was effected chiefly through the reception of the preached word of God, and the sermon rapidly became the central act of Protestant worship. The effects of preaching were carefully analysed into conviction of sin, righteousness and judgment, followed by conversion, sanctification and *assurance of salvation – all of them works of saving grace.

Protestantism also asked whether God's grace was aimed primarily at the forgiveness of sins or of sinners, and by opting for the latter fundamentally changed the nature of medieval theology and religious practice. By asserting that God sent his Son into the world to die for people and not for things, the Reformers raised a host of new questions which had to be answered. Did Christ die for everyone, or only for those whom he had chosen by grace before the foundation of the world? Was it possible to resist the grace of God once it got to work in a person's life? Debates over these and related questions divided the Reformed churches (see *Reformed theology) into those who answered that Christ died only for the elect, and that grace was irresistible ('strict Calvinists'), and those who believed that Christ's atoning death was universal, and individual human beings were enabled by grace to respond in faith ('mild Calvinists' or 'Arminians'). Some so-called *Arminians defended 'free will' and so were regarded by critics as proposing a revamped form of Pelagianism and therefore as deeply heretical. But Arminians true to Arminius (such as John *Wesley) insisted that the very freedom to believe was the gift of prevenient grace, but that grace was not irresistible. It is probably true to say that most Protestants today, not to speak of other Christians, hold beliefs which are closer to the Arminian position than to the Calvinist one.

Within Calvinist circles there has been a debate about the extent of God's grace, touched off mainly by questions about the status of those who do not belong to the company of the elect (see *Predestination). Nineteenth-century theologians like Charles *Hodge and Abraham *Kuyper came to believe that God had made a covenant with Adam, which was renewed in Noah and which applies to the entire human race. This is a covenant of temporal preservation, but not of eternal salvation. Under it, unbelievers are permitted to share in the work of having dominion over the creation, and within that context there is no difference between them and believers. In such fields as art, music, literature and the natural sciences, Christians are free to work alongside others to develop the creation mandate common to them both. This is why this covenant has come to be known as the covenant of *common grace*.

Distinct from this, though not entirely separate, is another covenant, made originally with Abraham and sealed in Jesus Christ. This is the covenant of eternal salvation which is granted only to the elect. In this world it is manifested primarily in the different thought patterns which govern the lives of believers and set them apart from others, but the real effects of this will only become fully apparent in the next life, when those who are called to believe in Christ will go to reign with him in his heavenly glory. This is the covenant of *special grace*. It is clearly the duty of the church to bear witness to this grace, but Protestant theologians, unlike their *Roman Catholic counterparts, do not see the church as the exclusive vehicle of it. The Christian family, Christian schools and even Christian political parties may also have a role to play in ministering God's special grace, which is not confined to a clerical élite, but to a *priesthood which extends to all believers. There is thus no real distinction between the 'sacred' and the 'secular', because everything is sacred in God's eyes. Nor can it be said that there is a radical distinction between nature and grace, since everything belongs to the realm of grace, whether people are conscious of this or not.

In practice, many Christians find it very difficult to absorb the notion of common grace, and most of the time the term refers only to God's initiative in salvation. At the same time, Protestants are much more likely than Roman Catholics to reject clericalism and to believe that the grace of God is given to all believers. The ordained clergy may be trained to fulfil certain functions within the church, but they have not received a particular grace which sets them above the laity in any objective sense.

The *Eastern Orthodox tradition has developed a very different understanding of grace from anything found in the West. It has steadfastly refused to analyse it or separate it into different theological compartments, and despite some similarities with Roman Catholicism, it has consistently attacked the Roman doctrine (and by implication the Protestant ones as well) for holding to a doctrine of 'created grace' which can be quantified and dispensed in varying proportions. To the Orthodox mind, grace is fundamentally a charismatic experience of God which can take many forms, of which the highest is the beatific vision of the Lord granted to those who have been transfigured by the divine light, or 'deified' as Orthodox theologians somewhat misleadingly tend to phrase it. In this understanding, although grace can be given to anyone, it is most clearly present in the lives of those who have forsaken the cares of the world for a life of mystical contemplation in preparation for the perfect union with Christ in heaven.

Varied though its manifestations are, the basic connection between grace and salvation remains at the core of Christian teaching even today, and at the popular level it is as visible and influential as ever. The popularity of a hymn like 'Amazing Grace', even outside church circles, is a clear reminder of this. More elaborate schemes remain the province of minorities, but for ordinary Christians grace is a term associated most readily with the saving work of Christ, which remains at the heart of all Christian worship and proclamation.

Bibliography

J. P. Burns, *The Development of Augustine's Doctrine of Operative Grace* (Paris, 1980); W. D. Buschart, *Exploring Protestant Traditions* (Downers Grove, 2006); D. Engelsma, *Common Grace Revisited* (Grandville, 2003); J. M. Ensor, *The Great Work of the Gospel: How We Experience God's Grace* (Wheaton, 2006); A. T. Evans, *The Grace of God* (Chicago, 2004); D. Fairbairn, *Grace and Christology in the Early Church* (Oxford, 2003); M. S. Horton, *God of Promise: Introducing Covenant Theology* (Grand Rapids, 2006); R. K. Johnston et al., *Grace upon Grace: Essays in Honor of Thomas A. Langford* (Nashville, 1999); R. T. Kendall, *Grace* (Lake Mary, 2006); G. I. Mantzarides, *The Deification of Man* (Crestwood, 1984); J. Oman, *Grace and Personality* (Cambridge, 1931); C. Ryder Smith, *The Bible Doctrine of Grace* (London, 1956); T. F. Torrance, *The Doctrine of Grace in the Apostolic Fathers* (Edinburgh, 1948); C. Van Til, *Common Grace* (Philadelphia, 1947); G. A. Wilterdink, *Tyrant or Father? A Study of Calvin's Doctrine of God* (Bristol, 1985).

G. L. Bray

GRATIAN, see CANON LAW

GREGORY OF NAZIANZUS (*c.* 329–90)

Gregory, also known as Gregory the Theologian, was one of the three great Cappadocian Fathers (with *Basil and *Gregory of Nyssa). He formed a close friendship with Basil, later the leading figure of the group, while they were students in Athens. After his return to Cappadocia, Gregory reluctantly submitted to be ordained a presbyter to help his aged father, the Bishop of Nazianzus. A sermon preached subsequently (*Oration* II) is a seminal work of pastoral theology. Later Gregory was consecrated bishop against his will to help Basil, by then the metropolitan Bishop of Caesarea, in an ecclesiastical power struggle. After Basil's death, he was called to lead the tiny remnant of orthodox Christians in Constantinople, capital of the Eastern Roman Empire. Gregory's outstanding oratory and the accession of the Emperor Theodosius I led to the triumph of orthodoxy over *Arianism. After becoming Bishop of Constantinople and briefly presiding at the Council of *Constantinople (381), Gregory resigned and retired thankfully to Cappadocia.

Gregory's theology is to be found in his sermons, letters and poems. The five *Theological Orations*, preached in Constantinople in 380, contain his classic exposition of the doctrine of the *Trinity. After emphasizing the purification necessary for the theologian and the incomprehensibility of *God, he expounds the doctrine of the Trinity in terms of relationships within the Godhead. The Father is the begetter and emitter, the Son is the begotten and the Holy Spirit is the emission. The begetting of the Son and the procession of the Spirit are beyond time, so that all three are coeternal. While the Father may be greater than the Son in the sense that he is the cause, he is not greater by nature, for the two are of the same nature. The names, Father and Son, make known to us an intimate relation within the Godhead.

On this basis, Gregory strongly defends the deity of the *Holy Spirit. The Spirit must be either a creature or God, and only the latter alternative can give coherence to Christian doctrine. The Spirit, however, is neither begotten nor unbegotten, but the one who proceeds (*to ekporeuton*). The distinction of the three is thus preserved in the one nature. Gregory unequivocally proclaims what Basil had expressed so guardedly, that the Spirit is God and consubstantial with the Father.

Gregory's main contribution to the development of *Christology was in his opposition to *Apollinarius. He argued that the whole of human nature which fell in Adam must be united to the Son, body, soul and mind, 'for the unassumed is the unhealed'.

Bibliography

Works: ET of selected works by C. G. Browne and J. E. Swallow in *NPNF*, second series, vol. 7 (1894; repr. Grand Rapids, 1974); cf. also E. R. Hardy and C. C. Richardson, *Christology of the Later Fathers* (LCC 3, London, 1954).

Studies: C. A. Beeley, *Gregory of Nazianzus on the Trinity and the Knowledge of God* (Oxford, 2008); B. Daley, *Gregory of Nazianzus* (London and New York, 2006); J. L. González, *A History of Christian Thought*, vol. 1 (Nashville, 1970); J. N. D. Kelly, *Early Christian Doctrines* (London, ^{5}1977); J. A. McGuckin, *St Gregory of Nazianzus: An Intellectual Biography* (New York, 2001); F. W. Norris, *Faith Gives Fullness to Reasoning: The Five Theological Orations of Gregory Nazianzen* (Leiden, 1991); R. R. Ruether, *Gregory of Nazianzus: Rhetor and Philosopher* (Oxford, 1969); I. P. Sheldon-Williams in *CHLGEMP*, pp. 438–447; J. H. Srawley in *ERE* III, pp. 212–217; H. H. Watkins in *DCB* II, pp. 741–761; D. F. Winslow, *The Dynamics of Salvation: A Study in Gregory of Nazianzus* (Cambridge, MA, 1979).

T. A. NOBLE

GREGORY OF NYSSA (*c.* 335–95)

Gregory was the youngest of the three Cappadocian Fathers (together with his elder brother *Basil of Caesarea, and their friend *Gregory of Nazianzus). In the late ninth century, he helped to bring about the victory of Nicene orthodoxy over *Arianism and give definitive shape to the doctrine of the *Trinity. Gregory lacked the university education of the other two, but became like them a teacher of rhetoric and surpassed them as a speculative thinker. He was created Bishop of Nyssa in 372 by Basil to assist him in an ecclesiastical power struggle. After Basil's death, Gregory was one of the leading figures at the Council of *Constantinople in 381.

Gregory's contribution to the Cappadocian doctrine of the Trinity is most succinctly expressed in his short treatise, *That We Should Not Think of Saying There Are Three Gods*.

The Cappadocians had balanced the emphasis of *Athanasius and the older Nicenes on the unity and common *ousia* (*substance) of the Trinity with an emphasis on the distinctiveness of the three *hypostaseis* (persons). But this could lead to the danger of *tritheism, especially if the analogy of three men sharing the same substance of humanity is used. But Gregory argues that we ought not to speak of three gods sharing the same substance of deity (or Godhead), because it is actually inaccurate and misleading to speak of three men when the 'man' (i.e. the human nature) in them is one and the same. Furthermore, the analogy falls short, in that three men may pursue activities separately, whereas in God, each act towards the created world is common to all three, having its origin in the Father, proceeding through the Son and being perfected by the Spirit. Gregory's dogmatic works also include an important treatise *Against Eunomius* and a treatise against *Apollinarius.

A fuller account of Christian doctrine is given in *The Catechetical Oration*, written to help the instruction of converts. Here the influence of Neoplatonism (see *Platonism) and of *Origen is evident in his interpretation of the Christian doctrines of *creation, humanity (particularly *sexuality) and *evil.

Gregory is more faithful to the orthodox tradition than Origen, yet he clearly teaches *universalism, a redemption and restoration of the whole creation (including the devil). Those not purified in this life will be purified by fire after death. Gregory's originality is seen particularly in his doctrine of the *atonement and of the *Eucharist. He explains the atonement in terms of the paying of the ransom (the life of Christ) to Satan (see *Redemption), who took it 'like a greedy fish' swallowing 'bait', not realizing that the Godhead was concealed within the flesh 'like a fishhook'. This grotesque imagery, together with any idea of a ransom being paid to the devil, has generally been rejected by the church. The merits of Gregory's theory lay in its objective and cosmic view of the atonement and in the way in which he linked it to the divine attributes of goodness, power, justice and wisdom. His doctrine of the Eucharist arises from his understanding of the physical aspect of salvation in the *resurrection of the body. He taught that *salvation was communicated to the body through the Eucharist. The bread and wine became the elements of the body of Christ through the words of consecration, so that as we receive them our bodies share in divine immortality.

Gregory is also noted for his influential *mystical writings in which he traces three stages in the ascent of the soul from *apatheia*, freedom from passion, through *gnōsis*, mystical knowledge in which the senses are left behind, to *theōria*, the highest stage of contemplation in which (since a created soul cannot see God) one passes into the limitless ascent into the divine darkness.

Bibliography

Works: ET of selected works by W. Moore and H. A. Wilson in *NPNF*, second series, vol. 5 (1890; repr. Grand Rapids, 1976); cf. also E. R. Hardy and C. C. Richardson, *Christology of the Later Fathers* (LCC 3, London, 1954).

Studies: L. Ayres, *Nicaea and Its Legacy* (Oxford, 2004), pp. 344–363; S. Coakley et al., *Re-thinking Gregory of Nyssa* (Oxford, 2003); J. L. González, *A History of Christian Thought*, vol. 1 (Nashville, 1970); J. N. D. Kelly, *Early Christian Doctrines* (London, ^{5}1977); M. Ludlow, *Gregory of Nyssa: Ancient and Post(modern)* (Oxford, 2007); A. Meredith, *Gregory of Nyssa* (New York, 1999); I. P. Sheldon-Williams in *CHLGEMP*, pp. 447–456; J. H. Srawley in *ERE* III, pp. 212–217; L. Turcescu, *Gregory of Nyssa and the Concept of Divine Persons* (Oxford, 2005); E. Venables in *DCB* II, pp. 761–768.

T. A. NOBLE

GREGORY OF RIMINI (c. 1300–58)

Gregory was born at Rimini in Italy. Having become an Augustinian friar, he proceeded to study and then to lecture in theology. From 1341 to 1351 he taught at Paris. In 1351 he returned to the Augustinian house at Rimini, becoming in 1356 and 1357 vicar general and prior general of the order. His most important surviving work is a commentary on the first two books of Peter *Lombard's *Sentences*.

Gregory's theology has been described as an *Augustinian response to the questions of the fourteenth century. He accepted, with his contemporaries, the separation of *faith and reason, revealed truth and natural knowledge. He emphasized the limits of reason and the inscrutability of God's ways. He based theology on God's *revelation, allowing little scope for a *natural theology. He was a philosophical *nominalist. Thus far, Gregory was in accord with the dominant and radically untraditional Ockhamist school (see *William of Ockham). But Gregory's theology, more traditional than theirs, was a return to the teaching of Augustine. Together with his contemporary *Bradwardine, he opposed the current *Semi-Pelagianism. He stressed the sovereignty of God and our total dependence upon grace for salvation. Fallen humanity can do no good without God's grace. Election is God's sovereign and unmerited choice of us. Gregory followed Augustine in teaching that those who die unbaptized in infancy are condemned to hell, for which he earned the title *tortor infantium*. But a fairer assessment of his theology as a whole is found in the more traditional title, *doctor authenticus*.

Bibliography

G. Leff, *Gregory of Rimini* (Manchester, 1961).

A. N. S. LANE

GREGORY THE GREAT (*c*. 540–603)

Gregory renounced a secular career as prefect of Rome in order to become a monk following the *Benedictine rule (see *Asceticism and monasticism). Out of the proceeds of his own estates he founded monasteries in Sicily and Italy. Even as pope, an office he held from 590, he retained a monk's garb and lived with his clergy under a strict rule. His most influential work was his *Pastoral Rule*, which had a decidedly monastic tone.

Gregory's *papacy fell during chaos and internal strife for Italy. In a power vacuum Gregory took various initiatives, appointing governors to Italian cities and providing materials for the war against the Lombards. Thus he effectively extended the temporal power of the papacy.

Though Gregory asserted the sovereign authority of the apostolic see, whenever he suspected heresy or uncanonical procedure, he preferred not to interfere with the authority of other bishops. He abhorred the title 'ecumenical patriarch' adopted by the Patriarch of Constantinople as uncanonical and arrogant. In reaction he adopted for himself the humble title of 'the servant of all the servants of God'.

Gregory combined a learned *Augustinianism with various traits of popular piety. He published *Dialogues* full of accounts of bizarre prodigies and visions of Italian saints, which he credulously accepted. He gave the doctrine of *purgatory an important extension when he made it a dogma that souls in purgatory would be released by the sacrifice of the Mass. Again, though not himself approving the worship of *images, he allowed them a place in the worship of the illiterate.

Gregory also played an active role in the expansion of the church. His initiative behind the mission of Augustine of Canterbury to England is well known, but he also took steps to strengthen the church in Spain, Gaul and North Italy.

Bibliography

J. Cavadini (ed.), *Gregory the Great: A Symposium* (Notre Dame, 1995); F. H. Dudden, *Gregory the Great*, 2 vols. (London, 1905); G. R. Evans, *The Thought of Gregory the Great* (Cambridge, 1986); R. A. Markus, *Gregory the Great and His World* (Cambridge, 1997).

G. A. KEITH

GRENZ, STANLEY J. (1950–2005)

Born 7 January 1950, Grenz was ordained to *Baptist ministry (1976) and completed his doctorate under Wolfhart *Pannenberg at the University of Munich (1978). After a short stint as a pastor, he taught at Sioux Falls Seminary for nine years and then, excluding a brief Distinguished Professorship at Baylor University (2002–03), taught theology at Carey Theological College in Vancouver, Canada for his remaining career.

Arguably the leading North American evangelical theologian at the turn of the century, and certainly the most significant Canadian Protestant theologian, during his lifetime Grenz authored, co-authored or edited twenty-eight books, and over 100 articles, essays and reviews.

Central to Grenz's methodology was the role of *Scripture (theology's *norma normans*), tradition (theology's *norma normata*) (see *Scripture and tradition) and *culture as the context from which theology draws its questions, borrows language, but ultimately speaks with the *gospel message of *salvation through Christ. Although third by order of priority in the theological endeavour, because culture was not seen as a 'source' for theology at all, Grenz received significant critique within evangelicalism, even as he prodded evangelicals to move toward more constructive theology for the church's *mission. Remaining conservative on the gay issue, having written much on *sexuality, he was still criticized for his engagement with *postmodern culture.

His methodology led him to emphasize three dominant motifs in theology: *Trinity, community, *eschatology. In different ways, each of these can be traced back to Pannenberg, after whom Grenz was working to develop a distinctly trinitarian theology for evangelicalism. His theological project began to emerge in the multi-volume Matrix of Christian Theology series, which unfortunately was cut short with his untimely death on 12 March, 2005.

Bibliography

Selected works: *Revisioning Evangelical Theology* (Downers Grove, 1993); *The Social God and the Relational Self* (Louisville, 2001); *The Named God and the Question of Being* (Louisville, 2005)
Studies: B. S. Harris, *The Theological Method of Stanley J. Grenz* (Lewiston, 2011); J. S. Sexton, *The Trinitarian Theology of Stanley J. Grenz* (London, 2013); D. Tidball, B. Harris and J. S. Sexton, *Revisioning, Renewing, Rediscovering the Triune Center* (Eugene, 2014).

J. S. SEXTON

GROTIUS, HUGO (1583–1645)

Huig de Groot was a Dutch jurist, publicist, statesman and theologian. Precocious in study and attainment, Grotius imbibed rational humanism from both his family and his studies at Leiden University which he entered in 1595. After being granted the degree of LL.D by the University of Orleans, he practised as a lawyer in Holland, and held important public offices.

In 1610 the followers of *Arminius published a Remonstrance stating the five points on which they departed from strict Calvinism (see *Reformed theology). The debate was, however, complicated by its being embroiled in questions as to the relative powers of the Dutch Provinces and central authority. Grotius, of the Arminian persuasion, strove for peace and urged moderation in *Ordinum Pietas* (1613). He also drafted the Resolution for Peace (1614) by which the States-General forbade preaching on controverted doctrines, and commended toleration. Politically the dispute was dealt with by a coup, Maurits of Nassau, Prince of Orange and leader of the Calvinists, seizing major cities in 1618. Jan van Oldenbarnevelt, the leader of the Arminians and supporter of provincial autonomy, was executed for treason, and Grotius was imprisoned for life. The Synod of *Dort (1619) asserted the five points of Calvinism against the Remonstrance of the Arminians.

In 1621 Grotius escaped and settled in Paris. He returned briefly to Holland in 1631, retiring thereafter to Germany. From 1635 to 1645 he was Swedish ambassador to Paris. He died at Rostock as a result of shipwreck off Danzig.

Grotius had a literary reputation, his early drama *Adamus Exul* (1601) influencing Milton's *Paradise Lost*. In law his *Mare Liberum* (1609) first expounded the freedom of the high seas, and his works in civil law are still used. His *De Iure Praedae* (1604, but published 1868) foreshadowed *De Iure Belli ac Pacis* (1625), a seminal work of modern international law, in the course of which Grotius indicated that the principles of *natural law might be based as much on reason and social order as on revelation, and be valid even if there were no God – a hint which others took much further.

In theology Grotius moved to a creedless position, moderation and *toleration being paramount. His *De Veritate Religionis Christianae* (1627) stated the common core of Christianity irrespective of denomination and theology, and recommended trust in God and the following of Christ's teaching. It was translated for missionary purposes into Arabic, Persian, Chinese and other languages. Other works, such as the *Via ad Pacem Ecclesiasticam* and the *Votum pro Pace Ecclesiastica* (both 1642) were attempts to promote reunion and peace. However, these were rejected by many as sacrificing too much of the Protestant and Reformed cause. His *Annotationes in Vetus et Novum Testamentum* (1642) rely on philology, science and history to explicate the texts commented on in a way unusual at a time when received doctrines of inspiration would have excluded such methods.

His *Defensio fidei catholicae de satisfactione Christi adversus Faustum Socinum Senensem* (1617, ²1636), an attack on *Socinianism of doubtful effect, contains what has become known as the governmental or rectoral theory of the atonement, which derives from, but is tangential to, penal theories of the atonement (see *Substitution, penal). Coloured by then developing notions of the role of the sovereign, the theory anticipates some modern views. God's pardon of sinners is within his absolute unfettered discretion, the death of Christ being accepted by him as ruler or governor, not as creditor or offended party. As ruler, God's interest is in the good government of the world. The death of Christ illustrates the punishment which sin may attract, and therefore serves good government by acting as a deterrent. It also forms a contrast with the mercy shown through God's forgiveness of sinners, thus bringing home to humankind the depths of that mercy.

Bibliography

ET of *De Iure Belli ac Pacis* by F. W. Kelsey (London and Washington DC, 1923–8; repr. New York, 1964); E. Dumbauld, *The Life and Legal Writings of Hugo Grotius* (Norman, 1969); W. S. M. Knight, *The Life and Works of Hugo Grotius* (London, 1925; repr. New York and London, 1962); R. W. Lee, 'Hugo Grotius', *Proceedings of the British Academy* 16 (1930), pp. 3–61; J. ter Meulen, *Concise Bibliography of Hugo Grotius* (Leiden, 1925); idem and P. J. J. Dietmanse, *Bibliographie des écrits imprimés de Hugo Grotius* (The Hague, 1950); C. A. Stumpf, *The Grotian Theology of International Law: Hugo Grotius and the Moral Foundations of International Relations* (Berlin, 2006); H.-J. van Dam, J. M. Henk and N. and E. Rabbie (eds.), *Hugo Grotius – Theologian* (New York, 1994).

F. LYALL

GUILT AND FORGIVENESS

Biblical data

God proclaims two characteristics of himself to Moses: he is 'forgiving iniquity and transgression and sin' but also 'by no means clearing the guilty' (Exod. 34:7, NRSV). Without acting against the guilty, God seems unjust. Without acting in forgiveness, God seems merciless. How can he be both? Further, if *God is perfect, as traditional theology asserts (see e.g. in the West, Anselm, *Thomas Aquinas, *Turretin; and in the East, *John of Damascus), then he must be both perfectly forgiving and perfectly just, rather than one attribute predominating at the other's expense.

This is no minor tension since guilt and forgiveness bulk so large in *salvation history: judgment is exercised justly on guilty 'Gentile' Sodom and Gomorrah (Gen. 19), on guilty Israel and Judah in the exile (Dan. 9:14) and God's final just *judgment awaits (Rev. 19:1–2 underlines God's judgments as just). Yet salvation history also speaks in the covenant with Abraham of blessing for all nations (Gen. 12:3), a blessing fulfilled in the forgiveness of sins (Acts 3:19, 25–26). Dealing with sin is a major focus of OT sacrifice (e.g. Lev. 16:16 on the Day of Atonement), but this is anticipatory shadow rather than reality. The final or real sacrifice is that of Jesus, the final high priest, who offers a perfect *sacrifice for sin (Heb. 10:1–19; see *Atonement).

The new covenant stresses interiority (dealing with the heart) and forgiveness of sin (Heb. 8:12; 10:17). This centrality of forgiveness is present in Paul's citation of Ps. 32:1–2 in Rom. 4:7: 'Blessed are those whose iniquities are forgiven, and whose sins are covered' (NRSV). Forgiveness acquires here a strong 'law' association since forgiveness is of 'iniquities' and stands in parallel with covering sin. This dealing with sin and iniquity is unearned (Rom. 4:4–6), while 'guilt' is established as liability for sins committed (Rom. 3:9–19; cf. Jas 2:10), and is the precondition for condemnation. Both guilt and forgiveness relate to *sin, something constituted by the law of God. Hence guilt is predominantly associated with sin as offence against God, even though the immediate expression may be actions or omissions at the expense of another human. Thus David says he has offended only against God (Ps. 51:4), yet he has also wronged Uriah by murder and Bathsheba by sexual predation. Since sin is offence against God, it is God's prerogative both to judge it and to forgive. In the NT fulfilment, *Jesus is both judge (John 5:27–29) and able to forgive sin (Mark 2:10). Dealing with guilt and providing forgiveness ultimately centres on Christ.

Law, guilt and forgiveness

Since the guilty are forgiven of some breach of law, guilt is objective in that it is a liability under a law that lies outside oneself. Lack of a subjective sense of guilt does not guarantee innocence, nor does its presence conclusively indicate guilt. 'Legal breach' here does not simply refer to the Law of Moses. First, Paul indicates in Rom. 1:18–22 that humanity has obligations to God (to *worship him as God and to be thankful to him) that arise simply from the relationship of creator and creature. The relationship carries duties outside the Sinaitic law. Further, this underlines that legal breach does not preclude personal relationship: it is precisely wrongdoing within the relationship that grounds God's judging actions in Rom. 1:18–32. Similarly, God imposed the exile for breaches of a personal covenantal relationship. Secondly, since aspects of the OT law are fulfilled in Christ, it is important when explaining legal guilt today to show how those outside the Sinaitic covenant are lawbreakers. This is often done in terms of the creator-creature relationship, Jesus' summary of the law in terms of love, and the detailed commands retained in the NT epistles.

Who deals with guilt?

With these considerations in mind, the place of God becomes central. He establishes the *law and relationships within which sin occurs and is the arbiter of guilt. He is also the one who forgives. This theocentric emphasis is strongly developed by *Athanasius in his account of divine mercy and forgiveness. He reasons (*De Incarnatione* 6, 7) that since God has established a law (Gen. 2:17) and is utterly truthful, he cannot simply extend mercy for *Adam's sin by *fiat*. That would involve him 'unsaying' his own laws. God must be true to himself. The law imposing death for disobedience must be kept, and ultimately this means that only God can restore creation since he alone can bring new life. Further *Anselm in *Cur Deus Homo* reasons that we cannot ourselves make satisfaction to God by paying him back with meritorious acts (see *Penance) since we owe God every good act anyway. We must consider, he repeats, the seriousness of sin. As such, we cannot provide satisfaction to God ourselves to deal with guilt, but God himself must do so for us as a human being.

This theocentricity is intensified by Luther's perception that sin lurks, not just in our worst, but in our best actions (*Heidelberg Disputation*, 1518, thesis 3), since we do apparently holy things to serve ourselves and our pride rather than God. In fact, reasons Luther, 'The person who believes that he can obtain grace by doing what is in him adds sin to sin so that he becomes doubly guilty' (*Heidelberg*, thesis 16). Hence *Reformation thought in both *Lutheran and *Reformed versions insisted that God's grace was alone in forgiving sins, with no meritorious human contribution possible.

Guilt freely forgiven

For both Lutheran and Reformed alike God's *grace in *freely* forgiving sins was critical (notably Martin *Chemnitz, esp. *Loci Theologici*, locus XIII). The idea 'freely' here (taken from Rom. 3:24) has a double aspect. From God's side, forgiveness is free because no law outside him binds him to forgive (that would deny his *sovereignty). Nor is he providing a reward or wage to the deserving: rather he is disposing of his blessing as he wills and in accord with his own character. He forgives freely because he is that kind of God. From our side, God's forgiveness is free, since we do, and can do, nothing to earn it, for the reasons Anselm and Luther give.

The Anglican Homily 'A Sermon of the Salvation of Mankind' (*Homilies*, book 1, 3) is broadly representative of such Reformation syntheses. Both God's mercy and justice are fulfilled: '. . . with his endless mercy he joined his most upright and equal justice'. This is possible because Christ perfectly keeps God's law for his people: 'He for them fulfilled the law in his life. So that now in him and by him every true Christian man may be called a fulfiller of the law . . .'

This work of Christ is appropriated by *faith alone, but a common note for both Lutheran and Reformed theologians of the Reformation was that this goes beyond just 'general assent' to a belief that God in Christ is merciful to oneself as an individual (e.g. Melanchthon, *Apology for the Augsburg Confession* on article 12; Calvin, *Institutes*, III.2.7).

Criticisms of free forgiveness for guilt

An important criticism of the Reformers was that they opened the door to licence. However, both Lutherans (e.g. Melanchthon in the *Apology*) and *Calvin (*Institutes*, III.3–6) stress the importance of the fruits of repentance. A key point of difference was that the *Roman Catholic Council of *Trent envisaged a meritorious place for human works in *justification (see Sixth Session 1547, canons 24, 32) and that justification was not through faith alone (canon 12). In fact, the bulk of the Reformers did stress the need for law and obedience (see *Christian life; *Sanctification). In their reaction to the *antinomianism of Johannes Agricola and others, Luther and others envisaged that 'law' must be taught to humble proud hearts to seek mercy in Christ alone and not in themselves (see *Melanchthon and Chemnitz on the *law-gospel relation).

This emphasis on teaching the law is pertinent in a Western cultural milieu which can stress entitlement (see e.g. J. M. Twenge, *Generation Me*, New York, 2006) and a therapeutic approach (see e.g. O. J. Madsen, *The Therapeutic Turn*, London, 2014) to human predicaments. The accountability implicit in objective guilt challenges entitlement thinking as well as assumptions that *all* one needs is appropriate cure/treatment. That said, guilt is not the only dimension to human problems – being guilty does not preclude being a genuine victim in need of healing and liberation.

Finally, some theologies reduce the tension between guilt and forgiveness by elevating *love as God's primary attribute (a recent example is the *Open Theism movement: see e.g. Richard Rice in *The Openness of God*). The traditionalist answer is that it is not wrong to see God's love as primary, but we must see God's justice as equally primary and how he has fulfilled both (see *Righteousness).

Implications of free forgiveness

This understanding of guilt and forgiveness suggests three things for the *church's life. First, a church is a community of forgiven sinners, none of whom may look down on their neighbours. Secondly, the church will explain guilt, not to obscure grace, but precisely so that forgiveness may be seen fully. Thirdly, the church will be a community of mutually forgiving sinners: while forgiveness is God's in the first instance, he has also instructed us to forgive each other in a secondary way, precisely because he has first forgiven us (Col. 3:13).

Bibliography

J. Calvin, *Institutes*, III.3; J. Edwards, 'Sinners in the Hands of an Angry God', sermon 8 July 1741, <http://www.ccel.org/ccel/edwards/sermons.sinners.html>; P. Melanchthon, *Apology for the Augsburg Confession*, on article 12; idem, 'Sermon of the Salvation of Mankind', Homily 3 in Book I of *The Homilies*; J. Owen, 'An Exposition upon Psalm 8 CXXX', in *The Works of John Owen*, vol. VI: *Temptation and Sin*, ed. W. H. Gould (Edinburgh, 1967), pp. 323–326; J. Wesley, Sermons 5 and 6, 'Justification by Faith' and 'The Righteousness of Faith', in *The Works of John Wesley*, vol. 1 (Nashville, 1984), pp. 181–216; C. Williams, *He Came Down from Heaven and the Forgiveness of Sins* (Berkeley, 2005).

M. OVEY

GUNTON, COLIN EWART (1941–2003)

Colin Ewart Gunton was the leading English *systematic theologian of his generation, perhaps of the twentieth century. Taught by Robert Jenson, he pioneered a theological style that was seriously interested in dogmatic questions, and basically conservative and *Reformed in orientation. His early work explored the doctrine of God (his doctoral thesis, comparing Karl *Barth and Charles Hartshorne, published as *Becoming and Being*), Christology (*Yesterday and Today*, a profound defence of classical Christology), and the doctrine of reconciliation (*The Actuality of Atonement*, an exploration of theological method and how it affected what was said about the atonement). It was meeting John *Zizioulas on the British Council of Church's Study Commission on the Trinity that enabled Gunton to develop his mature voice. In *The Promise of Trinitarian Theology*, he developed a nuanced social *trinitarianism, stressing the personhood of the three hypostases, and the relationships between them, but without collapsing it so bluntly into an account of society, as some recent trinitarian theology has done. This was increasingly allied to a stress on the gospel history as the primary locus of God's revelation – the primary triune relations were to be understood and interpreted through the narratives of the Jewish man *Jesus of Nazareth, and his relationship with the God he called Father. This led to a sustained interest in the nature of particularity (hinted at already in his work on Christology), and questions of the mediation between God and creation.

Building from these basic insights, he produced incisive social commentary (particularly in his Bampton Lectures, *The One, the Three and the Many*) and profound constructive theology. Books on revelation (*A Brief Theology of Revelation*, his Warfield lectures), creation (*The Triune Creator*) and the divine attributes (*Act and Being*) all showed how a focus on the Trinity might reshape these doctrines. At the same time a regular flow of essays, a one-volume summary of Christian doctrine, *The Christian Faith*, and a projected three-volume *Dogmatics* hinted at how the approach might develop in other areas also.

Gunton maintained a lifelong interest in English theology, particularly in its nonconformist forms (he himself was a convinced Congregationalist, and a minister of the United Reformed Church; two books of his sermons have been published). Amongst his essays, attempts to re-ignite theological interest in such figures as Samuel Taylor *Coleridge, Edward *Irving or John *Owen testify to this. He also encouraged research students to work and publish on these, and similar, figures. His interest in English theology was not confined to its history; he served the churches and the academic theological community cheerfully and tirelessly in a variety of ways.

Bibliography

B. G. Green, *Colin Gunton and the Failure of Augustine* (Eugene, 2011); L. Harvey (ed.), *The Theology of Colin Gunton* (London, 2010).

S. R. HOLMES

GUTIÉRREZ, GUSTAVO (b. 1928)

Gutiérrez is a Peruvian Roman Catholic priest known for his creative and formative role in the development of Latin American *liberation theology. Born in Lima, he abandoned medical school and studied for the priesthood in Chile. He took graduate studies in psychology in Louvain followed by theology at the University of Lyon, both influential schools on Latin American progressive *Catholicism. Ordained as a secular priest in 1959, Gutiérrez was an advisor to the Union of Catholic Students and taught at the Catholic University of Lima. Starting from a pastoral concern for the decline of Catholicism in Latin America, he proposed a new social practice for the church, one that was being pioneered by missionaries from Europe and North America, based on taking sides with the poor in the acute social conflicts of the 1960s. Such activism was made possible by the Second *Vatican Council, and its application to Latin America through the Bishops' Conference (CELAM) of Medellín in 1968. The documents from this gathering call the church to take 'a preferential option for the poor' in language and categories formulated by Gutiérrez. His thinking was eventually condensed in the book *A Theology of Liberation* (1971), published in English in 1973; it started with a social analysis of Latin America and suggested radical pastoral changes based on a new reading of Scripture and tradition 'from the perspective of the poor'. After 1979 under Pope John Paul II, Gutiérrez' theology was the subject of an inquiry to which he responded in his book *Truth Shall Make You Free* (1986). Gutiérrez decided to remain within Roman Catholic orthodoxy, and accordingly *A Theology of Liberation* was revised for its fifteenth anniversary edition, eliminating *Marxist vocabulary about class struggle. During those fifteen years Gutiérrez had become known around the world and received honorary doctorates from universities such as Nimega (1981). In his later book *We Drink from Our Own Wells* (1983) he outlined a spirituality of liberation, followed by biblical studies on Job (1986) and the *God of Life* (1989). In 1993 his massive work *Las Casas: In Search of the Poor of Jesus Christ* was published in English. It is an exhausitve study of the development of a theology of conquest and forced Christianization in the sixteenteen-century conquest of Latin America, and the defence of the Indians that was articulated by the Dominican Bartolomé de las Casas. In 1998 Gutiérrez entered the Dominican Order. Through the years he has kept his parish work in Rímac, a shanty town of Lima.

See also: POVERTY AND WEALTH.

Bibliography

Works: G. Gutiérrez, *A Theology of Liberation*, rev. edn (Maryknoll and London, ²1988 [1973]); *The Power of the Poor in History* (Maryknoll, 1983); *We Drink from Our Own Wells: The Spiritual Journey of a People* (Maryknoll, 1984); *On Job: God-Talk and the Suffering of the Innocent* (Maryknoll, 1987); *The Truth Shall Make You Free* (Maryknoll, 1990); *The God of Life* (Maryknoll, 1991); *Las Casas: In Search of the Poor of Jesus Christ* (Maryknoll, 1993); *Sharing the Word Through the Liturgical Year* (Maryknoll, 1997).

Studies: R. M. Brown, *Gustavo Gutiérrez: Makers of Contemporary Theology* (Atlanta, 1980); C. Cadorette, *From the Heart of the People: The Theology of Gustavo Gutiérrez* (Oak Park, 1988); M. H. Ellis and O. Maduro (eds.), *The Future of Liberation Theology: Essays in Honor of Gustavo Gutiérrez* (Maryknoll, 1989); E. J. Muskus, *The Origins and Early Development of Liberation Theology in Latin America: With Particular Reference to Gustavo Gutiérrez* (Carlisle and Waynesboro, 2002).

S. ESCOBAR

HALLESBY, OLE (1879–1961)

Ole Hallesby was a Norwegian evangelical theologian who originally lost his evangelical convictions through the influence of *liberalism at the University of Oslo, but was converted shortly before graduation (1903). He was called to be a preacher of the 'Inner Mission' within the (Lutheran) Church of Norway, and his preaching resulted in widespread spiritual revival.

In 1909 he received his PhD from Erlangen and became a professor of systematic theology at the Free Faculty of Theology in Oslo, recently founded (1907) in reaction against the liberalism dominant in the state university.

From 1919 Hallesby took a clear stand in preaching, teaching and writing for the biblical faith against liberal ideas that denied the truth of the Apostles' Creed. He advised *evangelicals not to cooperate with liberal theologians and pastors. Though he strongly emphasized the need for *conversion and vital Christian experience, Hallesby remained a firm Lutheran, laying strong emphasis upon the teaching of the confessions of the Lutheran Church in Norway. In this respect he is typical of many of the leaders of the 'free' organizations within that church. He initiated the establishment of a variety of institutions sponsored by such voluntary societies.

During the Second World War, Hallesby was a member of the Christian Council that resisted Nazi control of the church. For this reason he was imprisoned, together with other Christian leaders in Norway.

The author of textbooks on dogmatics and ethics, Hallesby is best known outside Norway for his works on *Prayer* (ET, London, 1948) and *Why I Am a Christian* (ET, London, 1950).

N. YRI

HARNACK, ADOLF (1851–1930)

Harnack (created von Harnack in 1914), a German church historian, was the son of the Lutheran theologian Theodosius Harnack. After studying at the universities of Dorpat (where his father held a chair) and Leipzig, he taught at the universities of Leipzig (1874–9), Giessen (1879–86), Marburg (1886–9) and Berlin (1889–1921). From 1905 to 1921 he was director of the Prussian State Library; in 1910 he became president of the Kaiser Wilhelm Gesellschaft for the promotion of learning and science. With Emil Schürer he founded the Theologische Literaturzeitung in 1876, and in 1882 he became founding editor, with Oscar von Gebhardt, of the series *Texte und Untersuchungen zur Geschichte der altchristlichen Literatur*. His literary output continued without intermission from his collaboration with von Gebhardt and Theodor von Zahn in an edition of the *Apostolic Fathers (1876–78) to his final study of 1 Clement (1929).

In theology he was generally a *Ritschlian. With the publication of his popular series of lectures *What Is Christianity?* (1900; ET, 1901), he came to be viewed as the spokesman of *liberal Protestantism. He perceived the *essence of Christianity to lie in the fatherhood of God, the infinite worth of the individual soul, the higher righteousness and the commandment of love. This work, by stimulating Alfred Loisy to write *L'Évangile et l'Église* (1908), indirectly precipitated the modernist crisis in the Roman Church (see *Modernism, Catholic). Another modernist, George Tyrrell, observed that 'the Christ that Harnack sees, looking back through nineteen centuries of Catholic darkness, is only the reflection of a Liberal Protestant face, seen at the bottom of a dark well' (*Christianity at the Crossroads*, London, 1909, p. 44).

Jesus' simple message, Harnack believed, had been distorted and corrupted by Catholicism, resulting from the alien intrusion of Greek *metaphysics. This belief was elaborated in his study of the Apostles' Creed (*Das apostolische Glaubensbekenntnis*, 1892) and in his multi-volume *History of Dogma* (1886–90, ⁶1922; ET, 1894–99).

His work in early church history is of abiding value. One of his greatest works was his study of *Marcion (1921, ²1924), a *heretic with whose outlook (especially on the OT) he felt considerable sympathy. Also worthy of honourable mention are his *Geschichte der altchristlichen Literatur bis Eusebius*, 3 vols. (1893–1904), *The Mission and Expansion of Christianity* (1902, ⁴1924; ET, 1904–5); *The Constitution and Law of the Church* (1910; ET, 1910) and *Die Briefsammlung des Apostels Paulus* (1926).

In his monographs on NT criticism he reached increasingly conservative conclusions. In his *Sayings of Jesus* (1907; ET, 1908) he reconstructed the text of Q (the source presumably underlying the non-Marcan material common to Matthew and Luke) and argued that it was 'a document of the highest antiquity', reflecting in places 'the memory of an apostolic listener' and presenting a reliable portrait of Jesus. *Luke the Physician* (1906; ET, 1907) argued that Luke and Acts were composed by one man, an associate of Paul, and in particular that this man was the author of the 'we' narratives of Acts. Further evidence on this last point was adduced in *The Acts of the Apostles* (1908; ET, 1909), which also investigated the sources underlying the earlier chapters. In *The Date of the Acts and of the Synoptic Gospels* (1911; ET, 1911) he dated Luke-Acts (and *a fortiori* Mark) not later than AD 64 and Matthew shortly after AD 70.

Bibliography

W. H. C. Frend, *JEH* 52, 2001, pp. 83–102; K. Nowak *et al.* (eds.), *Adolf von Harnack: Christentum, Wissenschaft und Gesellschaft* (Göttingen, 2003); W. Pauck, *Harnack and Troeltsch: Two Historical Theologians* (New York, 1968); M. Rumscheidt (ed.), *Adolf von Harnack: Liberal Theology at Its Height* (London, 1989); A. von Zahn-Harnack, *Adolf von Harnack* (Berlin, ²1951).

F. F. BRUCE

HARTSHORNE, CHARLES, see PROCESS THEOLOGY

HAUERWAS, STANLEY (b. 1940)

Stanley Hauerwas, the Gilbert T. Rowe Professor of Theological Ethics at Duke University Divinity School, was born in Pleasant Grove, Texas. The son of a bricklayer, he was educated at Southwestern University, Georgetown, Texas, and then Yale Divinity School, where he earned a PhD. More recently he received an honorary DD from Edinburgh University. Before moving to the Methodist University of Duke in 1984, he taught for fourteen years at a Catholic institution: the University of Notre Dame. He is a prolific writer and outspoken speaker, making him one of North America's best-known and perhaps most controversial theologians.

His publications are extensive and wide-ranging. Hauerwas has produced over two dozen books, many made up of essays. Among contemporary theologians he is a leading exponent of the short essay as a form of theological expression. Many of his essays, such as *From System to Story: An Alternative Pattern for Rationality in Ethics* (1977), co-written with David Burrell, are widely cited. Here and elsewhere Hauerwas was critical of 'quandary ethics', in which scholars analyse difficult individual cases in order to derive ethical principles or foundations. In its place he has highlighted an approach to *ethics rooted in the formation of virtuous character. This is a recurring theme for Hauerwas. The primary issue is not what the moral subject should do, but rather what kind of person we should become. Through his writing and teaching Hauerwas has encouraged Christians from widely diverging traditions to think further about the importance of nurturing virtues for the Christian life. He was influenced not only by *Aristotle and *Thomas Aquinas in this move, but also by twentieth-century theologians such as John Howard *Yoder and philosophers such as Iris Murdoch and Alasdair McIntyre.

Two of his best-known books are *A Community of Character* (1981) and, a text commonly described as his most 'unified' book, *The Peaceable Kingdom* (1983). Within these and other publications he developed further the themes of virtue, character, narrative and non-violence. Hauerwas is a passionate pacifist who has challenged earlier twentieth-century theologians such as Reinhold *Niebuhr and Paul Ramsey, especially their defence of just war (see *Pacifism/peace). Throughout the 1980s and beyond, his thinking has continued to evolve, with more nuanced accounts of the place of narrative and a greater emphasis upon the importance of the church for Christian discipleship. Hauerwas has consistently emphasized the centrality of the story of *Jesus' life, death and resurrection for Christian ethics. An academic, linked with the United Methodist Church and more recently the Anglican Church, who regularly speaks beyond academia at local churches, he has made significant contributions to debates related to medical, legal and political ethics, as well as the importance of welcoming the stranger, the outsider or the disabled. In his sixties he highlighted the importance of *worship for Christian ethics and continued to challenge aspects of American patriotism, nationalism and liberalism, as well as produce notable publications, including an original Barthian reading of *natural theology in *With the Grain of the Universe* (2001), a theological commentary on the *Gospel of Matthew* (2006) and a critical reflection upon *The State of the University* (2007).

Bibliography

Selected Works: *Vision and Virtue: Essays in Christian Ethical Reflection* (Notre Dame, 1974); *Character and the Christian Life: A Study in Theological Ethics* (San Antonio, 1975); *A Community of Character: Toward a Constructive Christian Social Ethic* (Notre Dame, 1981); *The Peaceable Kingdom: A Primer in Christian Ethics* (Notre Dame, 1983); *Against the Nations: War and Survival in a Liberal Society* (Minneapolis, 1985); *Suffering Presence: Theological Reflections on Medicine, the Mentally Handicapped, and the Church* (Edinburgh, 1986); *Resident Aliens: Life in the Christian Colony* (with William Willimon) (Nashville, 1989); *Naming the Silence: God, Medicine and the Problem of Suffering* (Grand Rapids, 1990); *After Christendom: How the Church Is to Behave If Freedom, Justice, and a Christian Nation Are Bad Ideas* (Nashville, 1991); *Unleashing the Scripture: Freeing the Bible from Captivity to America* (Nashville, 1993); *Dispatches from the Front: Theological Engagements with the Secular* (Durham, NC, 1994); *Wilderness Wanderings: Probing Twentieth-Century Theology and Philosophy* (Boulder, 1997); *Sanctify Them in Truth: Holiness Exemplified* (Nashville, 1998); *A Better Hope: Resources for a Church Confronting Capitalism, Democracy and Postmodernity* (Grand Rapids, 2000); *With the Grain of the Universe: The Church's Witness and Natural Theology* (Grand Rapids, 2001); *The Blackwell Companion to Christian Ethics* (with Samuel Wells) (Oxford, 2004); *Performing the Faith: Bonhoeffer and the Practice of Non-Violence* (2004); *Matthew*, Brazos Theological Commentary on the Bible (Grand Rapids, 2006); *The State of the University: Academic Knowledges and the Knowledge of God* (Oxford, 2007). *Studies*: J. Berkman and M. Cartwright (eds.), *The Hauerwas Reader* (Durham, NC, 2001); this includes an annotated bibliography and wide selection of readings. J. Stout, *Democracy and Tradition* (Princeton, 2004); S. Wells, *Transforming Fate into Destiny: The Theological Ethics of Stanley Hauerwas* (Carlisle, 1998).

J. P. MITCHELL

HEALING

Health

A theological understanding of healing must be based on a theological understanding of health and illness. The standard secular definition of health is that of the World Health Organization, stated thus: 'A state of complete physical, mental and social well-being and not merely the absence of disease and infirmity'. Some theologians have criticized this definition, arguing among other things that complete well-being is impossible in earthly life. Consensus as to what it actually means is difficult to achieve given that there is controversy over whether mental illness overlaps with spiritual as well as social dis-ease. Definitions of mental health and illness vary in practice geographically and historically, and debates over them have a major impact on the reading of biblical stories of healing and exorcism by OT prophets and by Jesus and his disciples. Some Christians have tried to promote Jesus Christ as the model of mental health. Problems arise in the implicit correlation or even the conflation made between modern psychological models of mental health and the sinlessness of Jesus as the Incarnate Son.

The healing *miracles of Jesus demonstrate his intent and ability to restore the sick to adequate physical and mental health. The purpose of those miracles is to witness to the glory and authority of God bringing in the new creation through Christ. Health in Scripture and the Christian tradition is a gift from God intended to witness to his *glory. It is not simply a right, though many Christians accept that access to healthcare is a right in modern societies with welfare systems. However, pressure on welfare state systems due to the ageing populations of Western countries are provoking governments to act on lifestyle-induced patterns of ill health such as alcohol abuse and eating problems. Christian theological reflection and practice in relation to health and illness is therefore still important in the secular West, as more people increasingly struggle to be healthy. The goal of lifelong complete physical, mental and social well-being is strictly impossible given that even the healthiest people must die in the end. The rise of the hospice movement from within the Christian community witnesses to the continued need to promote mental health and spiritual well-being even for the terminally ill who will never recover physically.

Illness

Illness is the result of the intrusion of *evil into creation, thereby thwarting God's purpose of physical, mental and spiritual well-being for all his creatures. It is also present in human life due to the condition of original *sin. This does not entail that all sickness is the result of individual sinful intentions and acts, i.e. the individual sufferer is not necessarily to blame for their illness, nor is there a sense in which medical care should be administered only to those who supposedly 'deserve' it. Christian theology has generally counselled that sick persons should fight their illness and not give into it. This is due to the traditional Christian view of *death, the ultimate outcome of illness, as the enemy of humanity, and of suicide as a form of murder and a rejection of God's gift of life.

Healing

The definition of healing is closely related to the definition of humanity restored in Christ. This means that Christians can accept that healing may not necessarily be complete until the believer is *resurrected for eternal life with God. This eschatological perspective on healing is strongly emphasized in Paul's Corinthian correspondence. It is a perspective that has been emphasized by Christians working with disabled people.

A problem arises if Christians teach that healing from a particular condition can be accomplished only through faith in Christ. Both the biblical witness and the scientific evidence for most illnesses disprove such a claim. Rather it shows that Christian faith in particular, and religious faith in general, is correlated with a slightly higher probability of being healthy. This is famously true of healing from addictions such as alcoholism as a result of participation in Alcoholics Anonymous. Participants in AA are told to enlist the support of their chosen 'higher power', who may or may not be the Christian God. Empirical studies tend to show that healing is more likely in such cases if a person's adoption of faith is intrinsic rather than extrinsic, i.e. if their main goal is submission to the divine will regardless of the consequences.

A Christian understanding of healing is particularly important as regards mental illness, given the often troubled relationship between Christianity and the mental health professions. The question of whether a person's condition is to be diagnosed as resulting from mental illness or as a result of a combination of sinful self-chosen acts and being damaged by being sinned against by others is always pertinent for Christians. For example, the concept of personality disorders entered psychiatry only in the last few decades, having previously been labelled more moralistically as character disorders.

Healing ministries in the global church

A theological account of healing requires a trinitarian framework. In the Western church Augustine of Hippo was influential in developing a theological understanding of healing as a gift from God that is available to believers throughout history. Some charismatic and Pentecostal theologians argue that Jesus Christ is the ultimate source of all healing through his *redemption of all creation and his self-sacrifice on the cross. Typically, those who accept that gifts of healing are still operative in the church derive those gifts from the view that the Holy Spirit mediates those gifts given by Christ to his disciples (see *Gifts of the Spirit). As the church is the community of believers born again of Christ's eternal Spirit in every historical age, many *charismatic, *Pentecostal and other evangelicals argue that the gifts of healing are available to believers in every age.

The ministry of healing and the attestation of healing miracles is central in conversion to evangelicalism, especially its Pentecostal and charismatic strands, globally today. Evangelical controversies have arisen in the last few decades over the so-called 'Gospel of Health and Wealth', the belief that God grants health and prosperity to those who have a strong enough faith in him (see *Poverty and wealth). Churches espousing these beliefs have multiplied in the global South, but have also grown in the United States.

The prevalence and depth of theologies and ministries of healing in the global churches has social dimensions. Healing ministry is a more mainstream part of evangelicalism in the United States than in Western Europe, and this is partly attributable to a fit between certain theologies of healing and a therapeutic, optimistic, goal-oriented social worldview together with the lack of a welfare state system with its concomitant promise of free healthcare for all citizens. Likewise, healing may be more mainstream in certain non-Western, especially African churches, due to theologies of healing filling a void owing to lack of state healthcare, as well as to the attractiveness of diverse Christian theological anthropologies for some people in comparison to their previous indigenous religions. Globally the church today supports medical and spiritual healing, thus continuing in the spirit of the early church which founded the first hospitals in the fourth century as a communal and institutional means of healing illness, and as an antidote to the magical attitudes to healing prevalent in the classical world.

Bibliography

K. E. Alexander (ed.), *Pentecostal Healing: Models in Theology and Practice* (Blandford Forum, 2006); D. X. Burt, 'Health, Sickness', in A. D. Fitzgerald, *Augustine Through the Ages: An Encyclopaedia* (Grand Rapids, 1999), pp. 416–419; S. E. Lammers and A. Verhey (eds.), *On Moral Medicine: Theological Perspectives in Medical Ethics* (Grand Rapids, 1987); E. Lucas, *Christian Healing: What Can We Believe?* (London, 1997); F. MacNutt, *Healing* (London, 1989); M. Maddocks, *The Christian Healing Ministry* (London, 1995); D. McConnell, *The Promise of Health and Wealth: A Historical and Biblical Analysis of the Modern Faith Movement* (London, 1990); M. A. Yarhouse, R. E. Butman and B. W. McRay (eds.), *Modern Psychopathologies: A Comprehensive Christian Approach* (Downers Grove, 2005).

C. A. E. Moseley

HEAVEN, see ESCHATOLOGY

HEGEL, GEORG WILHELM FRIEDRICH (1770–1831)

Hegel is one of the three major figures in *German idealism, together with *Fichte and Schelling. Hegel's significance for philosophy is assured by two significant contributions. The first is his use of *Aristotelian themes (sociality, community) to repair the rationalist (especially *Kantian) emphasis on autonomy and freedom. The second is his emphasis on the historicity of concepts to develop the Kantian insight that human knowledge is tied to judgment, and that judgment relies on concepts. By describing the human agent as social as well as free, and by insisting that human judgment relies on concepts that are historically determined, Hegel's work produced one of the most important descriptions of human judgment.

Hegel is the most influential philosopher to develop an account of what it means to be 'modern'. He notices that people take certain things to be authoritative; he asks how they come to take them as authoritative. To be *modern, for Hegel, is to refuse to take something to be authoritative at another's insistence, and to embrace that something positively and freely. The modern community is self-determined and self-reflective. Modern philosophy, in the modern university, is likewise a matter of self-determination and self-reflection, and that includes paying attention to real contradictions in the world rather than allowing them to be solved, or merely appear to be solved, by appeals to external authorities. His method of 'dialectic' is his way of describing the significance of 'negation' for thinking and for social life.

Hegel's significance for theology rests on his significance for philosophy. Hegel insists that knowledge is 'mediated', which means (following Kant) that we do not know things by direct intuition (*Descartes, *Leibniz), but must judge what our senses give us by means of things (concepts, ideas, ways of thinking) that do not accompany the objects we seek to know. This is indebted to Christian theology. Knowledge of God is mediated by Jesus Christ: no-one has seen God by direct intuition. Revelation is mediated by the Holy Spirit: no one can faithfully interpret Scripture unaided by God. Hegel's tendency to extend the notion of mediation to all knowledge carried risks, and his philosophy was criticized from the start for seeming to claim that concepts are like the incarnation, or that the community is like the Holy Spirit. Christians worship Jesus Christ and the Holy Spirit. Are concepts divine? Can the community claim divine sovereignty?

Hegel's emphasis on 'thinking' has stimulated theologians in various ways. Hegel often claims that it is the significance of objects and events, rather than their brute existence or occurrence, that is the concern of the thinking person. It is their manner of being 'thought' that matters. This draws attention to the contexts in which things appear, and the presuppositions of those who relate to them. It can also give the impression that Hegel's idealism is a matter only of 'thinking' and not of 'reality'. For Hegel what is real is determined by its significance for someone, rather than its brute existence of occurrence. Yet Hegel also says that 'religion' is a matter of sensual practices and metaphorical language: bread and wine, incense, music, Scripture; 'philosophy' by contrast is a matter of thinking: concepts, logic, reflection. This leads Hegel to claim that liturgy is a lower activity whose concerns are not only clarified in philosophy, but surpassed by it. Hegel was criticized for this claim by Schelling, who argued that the ground of thinking is an origin that cannot be thought. He can also be criticized for seeming to think that concepts are not metaphorical.

Hegel's claims about God go significantly beyond emphasizing the mediation of objects through concepts, or stressing the significance rather than the mere existence of objects. Hegel tends to think teleologically in three of his most theologically significant texts. He speaks of 'absolute knowing' at the end of the *Phenomenology of Spirit* (1807), of 'the absolute idea' at the end of the *Science of Logic* (1816) and of 'the completed religion' at the end of his lectures on the philosophy of religion. His tendency is to arrive at completion or absoluteness at the end of the process of human inquiry.

This can be viewed as theologically dangerous and even heterodox. Premodern theology tended to think of the mystery of creation and the mystery of the eschaton as being illuminated, in a partial but abundantly generous way, by the person of Jesus Christ and the gift of the Holy Spirit. By contrast, and drawing on both *rationalist (Leibniz, Kant) and so-called *mystical (Böhme, Oetinger) traditions, Hegel tended to think of inarticulate realities at the beginning, which become developed and conceptualized realities at the end. God becomes progressively known; the Spirit becomes progressively more self-conscious. Hegel tends to try to reason in a 'presuppositionless' fashion in a way that intends to be suitable for 'modern' thinkers, but also rules out Scripture. Hegel appears to believe that philosophy can finally not only arrive at a concept of God, but do so without attention to Scripture.

The most famous claim that serves the project of achieving the absolute idea (a claim that is less theologically significant than that project as a whole) is that history is the developing self-consciousness of the 'absolute' or 'spirit' (*Geist*). The word 'absolute' here signifies that which is the ground of reality. It is what unifies difference and makes difference possible. It is the process which contains negation. It is substance (in Spinoza's sense) that is subject (in Kant's sense). The word 'spirit' signifies that the absolute is both nature and culture, fully self-conscious.

Debates about how to interpret Hegel, which have intensified in recent years, partly concern how best to understand his claims about the 'absolute idea' in the *Science of Logic* and the 'eternal idea' of God in the lectures on the philosophy of religion, and the relation between the two. On one reading Hegel seems to claim that God can be conceptualized. On another Hegel is interested only in conceptualizing God's significance for us. There is disagreement among scholars on these issues, but the task is largely agreed: the most fruitful theological investigation is one that offers the fullest account of the relation between the *Phenomenology*, the *Logic* and the lectures.

See also: PHILOSOPHY AND THEOLOGY.

Bibliography

F. Beiser, *Hegel* (London, 2005); P. Hodgson, *Hegel and Christian Theology* (Oxford, 2005); S. Houlgate, *Introduction to Hegel* (Oxford, 2005); T. Pinkard, *Hegel: A Biography* (Cambridge, 2000).

N. ADAMS

HEIDEGGER, MARTIN (1889–1976)

A key twentieth-century philosopher, Heidegger famously reopened the 'question of *being'. He contended that while philosophers have always investigated entities of different kinds, they have largely neglected the underlying question of what it means for an entity 'to be'. Heidegger sought to retrieve the 'meaning of being' and expose how faulty *ontological assumptions embedded in the history of Western philosophy have damaged human understanding. To avoid perpetuating those mistaken assumptions, he discarded traditional metaphysical language, choosing to craft his own custom vocabulary.

In his formidable masterwork, *Being and Time* (1927), Heidegger analyses the nature of human being in the hope of uncovering what it more generally means for something to be. Dispensing with traditional scientific and theological anthropologies, he repurposes the phenomenological method of his mentor, Edmund Husserl, in order to access the distinctive type of being humans possess. Heidegger's analysis finds that humans are not self-contained subjects standing apart from the world – as modern philosophy since Descartes had taught – but are characterized by 'existence': fundamentally, humans have their 'being in the world' and are composed of a set of relations to things, others, their potentialities and possibilities. He uses the colloquial German word *Dasein* (the 'presence' or 'there-ness' of a thing) in place of other anthropological labels, such as 'rational animal' or 'person', because it uniquely conveys the idea that humans 'exist'. Although the work remained unfinished, Heidegger's analysis of *Dasein* includes innovative discussions of anxiety, authenticity and finitude – core existentialist themes. Moreover, the work suggests that the meaning of being is *time*, since temporality is shown to be basically and inseparably constitutive of *Dasein*'s various structural items.

Perhaps on account of Heidegger's failure to complete *Being and Time*, the 1930s witnessed a major change in his approach to the question of being, which he himself labelled 'the turn'. Dropping *Dasein* as his starting point, Heidegger now attempted to think being from the standpoint of being itself, a move that led him to philosophize in an often quasi-mystical way about the truth of being's 'essential unfolding'. Emblematic of this phase is his view that the early Greeks originally experienced being through the 'self-showing' of entities, and that in forgetting this insight, Western philosophy has precipitated the present age of technology in which entities have been catastrophically reduced to mere things for manipulation. Crucially for Heidegger, poetry and art may retrieve the West from the nihilism of technological thinking, insofar as they reconnect humans with the basic experience of being. His proposal in *Contributions to Philosophy* is that, far from rejecting technology, humans should inhabit the technological world in a manner that 'shelters' the truth and openness of being.

Heidegger's active involvement in Nazism is a subject of ongoing controversy. Nevertheless, his work paved the way for significant advances in French philosophy (Derrida), hermeneutics (Gadamer) and political theory (Arendt). Heidegger's relationship to Christian theology is also of considerable importance, not least because, having initially trained for the priesthood, much of his pre-turn conceptuality is the product of serious engagement with St Paul, Augustine and Kierkegaard.

The early theological reception of Heidegger's work focused on the *Dasein* analytic, which Bultmann and Tillich used as a resource in the development of their existential theologies. More recently, studies by Marion and Caputo have traced the implications of Heidegger's post-turn thought for theology, particularly with regard to his critique of Western philosophy. They ask, if theology must no longer rely on traditional metaphysical understandings of being, then what language is appropriate for conceiving God's nature and activity? After the 'end of metaphysics' what does it mean for God 'to be'?

Bibliography

H. Dreyfus, *Being-in-the-World: A Commentary on Heidegger's Being and Time, Division 1* (Cambridge, MA, 1991); J.-L. Marion, *God without Being* (Chicago, 1991); R. Safranski, *Martin Heidegger: Between Good and Evil* (Cambridge, MA, 1998); J. Wolfe, *Heidegger and Theology* (Bloomsbury, 2014).

A. McFarlane

HEIDELBERG CATECHISM

The Heidelberg Catechism had its genesis in the volatile confessional climate of the late Reformation. Between 1546 and 1559, the Palatinate emerged as one of the most powerful Protestant territories in Germany. During the first years of the reign of Elector Frederick III (r. 1559–76), theological controversy between conservative (*Gnesio*) *Lutherans, followers of Philipp *Melanchthon, as well as Calvinists and Zwinglians, exploded within the university faculty at Heidelberg and disrupted the Palatinate churches. Frederick responded by sponsoring a theological disputation and dismissing contentious faculty members, actions that tipped the balance toward the Reformed camp. Further, the elector commissioned a team of professors, ministers and church superintendents to prepare a new catechism for his realm, with the aim of providing Christian instruction for children and achieving confessional harmony among his subjects. This doctrinal statement, known as the Heidelberg Catechism, was published in German and Latin editions in early 1563.

Scholars continue to debate the authorship of the Heidelberg Catechism. Whereas the traditional view ascribed principal authorship to Reformed theologian Zacharias *Ursinus and minister Caspar *Olevianus, most interpreters now believe that the catechism was the cooperative effort of a team of scholars overseen by Frederick himself, with Ursinus providing primary theological leadership. Like other Protestant catechisms of the period, the Heidelberg Catechism employs a question/answer format in treating the Apostles' Creed, the Lord's Prayer, the Ten Commandments and the sacraments. Beginning with the question 'What is your only comfort in life and in death?', the Catechism proceeds in 129 questions/answers to address three primary dimensions of the Christian gospel: human guilt, God's grace in Jesus Christ and the Christian's response of grateful service. That the Catechism seeks consensus within a moderate Reformed and Melanchthonian theological perspective is particularly evident in its treatment of sacramental theology and its inclusion of law under the rubric of the Christian life. Likewise, it avoids detailed discussion of more 'angular' Reformed doctrines such as election, reprobation and covenant. Although not entirely free of religious polemic – for example, *Anabaptism is proscribed, the Catholic Mass is deemed 'accursed idolatry' (phrase inserted in the second edition), and the Lutheran doctrine of ubiquity is rejected – the Heidelberg Catechism on the whole evinces an irenic tone and warm, devotional character. Zurich Reformer Heinrich *Bullinger praised it as 'the best catechism ever published' (quoted in F. H. Klooster, *The Heidelberg Catechism*, p. 196).

In the century after its initial publication, the Heidelberg Catechism went through no less than sixty-five editions and was translated into Dutch, English, French, Czech, Greek, Hungarian and Romansch. Today, it serves as a widely accepted confessional standard in German, Dutch and Hungarian Reformed churches.

See also: CATECHISMS; REFORMED THEOLOGY.

Bibliography

L. D. Bierma, *An Introduction to the Heidelberg Catechism: Sources, History, and Theology* (Grand Rapids, 2005); I. J. Hesselink, 'The Dramatic Story of the Heidelberg Catechism', in W. F. Graham (ed.), *Later Calvinism: International Perspectives* (Kirksville, 1994); F. H. Klooster, *The Heidelberg Catechism: Origin and History* (Grand Rapids, 1982); B. Thompson (ed.), *Essays on the Heidelberg Catechism* (Philadelphia, 1963); D. Visser (ed.), *Controversy and Conciliation: The Reformation of the Palatinate 1559–1583* (Allison Park, 1986).

S. M. MANETSCH

HEIM, KARL (1874–1958)

A German Protestant systematic theologian, Heim taught at Tübingen. His theological development was strongly influenced by *pietism, especially by its evangelistic emphases. His major theological legacy is a six-volume work of apologetics, *Der evangelische Glaube und das Denken der Gegenwart* (*The Protestant Faith and Contemporary Thought*) (Tübingen, 1931–52), translated into English in a variety of volumes.

Heim attempted to mediate between Protestant theology and modern worldviews, notably those he found presupposed in natural science, and tried to develop a critical role for Christian theology in the contemporary world. His work was for a time influential on teachers and pastors in Germany, and he remains one of the few German theologians to address himself seriously to natural science.

Bibliography

Works: *God Transcendent* (ET, London, 1935); *Spirit and Truth* (ET, London, 1935); *Christian Faith and Natural Science* (ET, London, 1953); *The Transformation of the Scientific World-View* (ET, London, 1953); *Jesus the Lord* (ET, Edinburgh, 1959); *Jesus the World's Perfecter* (ET, Edinburgh, 1959).

Studies: I. Holmstrand, *Karl Heim on Philosophy, Science and the Transcendence of God* (Stockholm, 1980); C. Michalson, 'Karl Heim' in D. G. Peerman and M. E. Marty (eds.), *A Handbook of Christian Theologians* (Nashville, [2]1984).

J. B. WEBSTER

HELL, see ESCHATOLOGY

HELLENIZATION OF CHRISTIANITY

By this is meant the penetration into Christianity of beliefs and practices which originated in the pre-Christian or non-Christian culture of ancient Greece. Generally speaking, this is now regarded as a positive development by most Roman Catholic and Orthodox theologians, whereas most Protestants tend to think of it as a corruption of the faith.

The facts of Hellenization, beyond the superficial level, are almost impossible to document with any degree of certainty. The NT was written in Greek, but this followed the established practice and style of Hellenized Judaism and was not a Christian innovation. There is much debate as to whether the apostolic interpretation of the OT was seriously affected by Greek ideas or not. At one time it was widely believed that John 1:1–14 reflected a Middle Platonic *logos doctrine, possibly mediated through *Philo of Alexandria, but this has been strongly challenged by modern scholarship, which tends to emphasize John's Hebraic roots.

Matters are more complex when we turn to the post-apostolic period. Christianity spread in the Hellenized Roman Empire more than it did elsewhere, and this certainly left its mark. *Justin Martyr thought that Socrates and Plato were Christians before Christ, and the belief that *Platonism was a kind of Gentile OT, preparing the Greeks for the coming of Christ, later became widespread. There were a number of syncretistic sects, now known collectively as '*Gnostic', which tried to merge pagan and Christian ideas in different ways. Perhaps the most significant development along these lines was the widespread adoption of the allegorical method of interpretation (used earlier by Jewish writers such as Philo), to overcome difficulties which Greek minds felt in the literal text of Scripture. By using this method, *Origen and others were able to harmonize Christianity with late Middle (and later Neo-) Platonism, much to the detriment of the former.

How far Hellenizing tendencies were responsible for the development of Christian doctrine is a matter of considerable controversy. Conservatives generally argue that the *creeds and other doctrinal statements were a reaction against the influence of Hellenism, which after the fourth century became a term of abuse, even among the Greeks (who subsequently called themselves *Rōmaioi* rather than *Hellēnes*). Liberals, however, argue that *dogma is itself a philosophical concept. According to them, a non-Hellenized Christianity would have been much more pluralistic in its theology, and would probably not have insisted that Jesus Christ was God incarnate. Some of them even regard Islam as a Semitic reaction against Hellenized Christianity, though that is certainly an oversimplification of what was a very complex development.

Bibliography

J. Daniélou, *Gospel Message and Hellenistic Culture* (London and Philadelphia, 1973); E. Hatch, *The Influence of Greek Ideas on Christianity* (New York, 1888); M. Hengel, *Judaism and Hellenism*, 2 vols. (London, 1974); R. H. Nash, *Christianity and the Hellenistic World* (Grand Rapids, n.d.).

G. L. BRAY

HELVETIC CONFESSIONS, see CONFESSIONS OF FAITH

HENOTHEISM, see MONOTHEISM

HENRY, CARL F. H. (1913–2003)

The Protestant theologian Carl Henry was widely recognized as an intellectual spokesman for evangelical Christianity. Converted in 1933 as a New York journalist, he studied at Wheaton College (MA), Northern Baptist Theological Seminary (BD, ThD) and Boston University (PhD). He taught theology at Northern Baptist (1940–47) and at Fuller Theological Seminary (1947–56), prior to becoming founding editor (1956–68) of the influential *Christianity Today* magazine. Always an understanding encourager and adviser of younger Christian writers, Henry from 1968 devoted himself to research and writing. He was chairman of the World Congress on Evangelism (Berlin, 1966), and also presided over the Evangelical Theological Society (1967–70) and the American Theological Society (1980–81).

Among his numerous books are *The Uneasy Conscience of Modern Fundamentalism* (1948), which spurred conservative Protestants in America out of cultural isolation into social engagement; and *Christian Personal Ethics* (1957), now a standard textbook. His magnum opus is *God, Revelation and Authority* (Waco, 1976–82), the six volumes of which are also available in Korean and Mandarin. Henry was a founder of the Institute for Advanced Christian Studies which produces literature directed at secular university students. As lecturer-at-large for World Vision International from 1974, he gained a global ministry of teaching, lecturing and preaching.

Bibliography

Works: *Confessions of a Theologian* (Waco, 1986).
Studies: G. Fackre, 'Carl F. H. Henry', in D. G. Peerman and M. E. Marty (eds.), *A Handbook of Christian Theologians* (Nashville, ²1984); Bob E. Patterson, *Carl F. H. Henry* (Waco, 1984); C. Wright Doyle, *Carl Henry: Theologian for All Seasons* (Eugene, OR, 2010).

J. D. Douglas

HERBERT OF CHERBURY
(*c*. 1583–1648)

Edward, first Baron of Cherbury, brother of the poet, George, made his reputation as a philosopher, historian, diplomat and adventurer. He has been styled 'the father of *deism' but his system differs significantly from much later deist thought, and the extent of his influence upon it is debatable.

In his foundational work, *De Veritate* (*On the Truth*), he sought to refute the sceptical denial of the possibility of knowledge, by adumbrating an original method of discovering the truth. His theory of universal 'Common Notions' provided the grounds for cognitive certainty and produced a scheme of rational religion when extended into that sphere. The five 'Common Religious Notions' are: (1) there is a supreme God; (2) he ought to be worshipped; (3) virtue and piety constitute the main elements of such worship; (4) sin must be expiated by repentance; (5) there are future rewards and *punishments. Herbert passionately advocated a form both of religious tolerance and of religious liberation for the laity. To the extent that he assimilated religious to general *epistemology and maintained that the practice of natural religion can lead to eternal blessedness, Herbert heralded an approach to religion that became broadly characteristic of much seventeenth- and eighteenth-century British and European thought.

Bibliography

Works: M. H. Carré (tr. and ed.), *De Veritate* (Bristol, 1937).
Studies: R. D. Bedford, *The Defence of Truth: Herbert of Cherbury and the Seventeenth Century* (Manchester, 1979); R. H. Popkin, *The History of Scepticism from Erasmus to Spinoza* (Berkeley, 1979).

S. N. Williams

HERESY

Heresy is teaching or belief which claims to be Christian and yet is contrary to orthodox doctrine. One of the meanings of the Greek word *hairesis* is a sect or school of philosophy, and the word is used in that sense in the Acts of the Apostles (5:17; 15:5; 24:5; 26:5; 28:22). Paul refers to *haireseis* in 1 Cor. 11:19 (translated as 'factions' in the NRSV) and in Gal. 5:20 ('party-spirit'). The adjective *hairetikos* ('factious') occurs in Titus 3:10, and 2 Pet. 2:1 refers to false prophets who will bring in 'destructive heresies' (*haireseis*). 'Heresy' therefore came to mean false teaching arising within the church and causing division. Among the Apostolic Fathers (see *Patristic theology), bishop Ignatius of Antioch refers to heresy as poison or a deadly drug (*Trall*. 6:1–2) and to heretics as 'ravening dogs' from whose bite one must flee (*Eph*. 7:1).

But to define heresy, or heterodoxy, wrong or other (*heterē*) opinion or belief (*doxa*), requires a prior definition of what constitutes orthodoxy, straight or right (*orthē*) belief. For Christians, that is determined by apostolic teaching, embodied in the books of the NT, and yet more must be said, for the unavoidable question arises of how the NT is to be interpreted.

Towards the end of the first century, the word 'heresies' appeared in the title of the first major treatise of Christian theology, the *Adversus Haereses* of *Irenaeus, bishop of Lugdunum (Lyons) in Gaul (France). This includes a catalogue of numerous sects grouped under the name of '*Gnosticism', who generally worked with a *dualism between the realm of the divine or the spiritual, comprising numerous levels or *aeons* of divine beings, and the realm of matter which was essentially evil. This gave rise to

*Docetism, the heresy that Christ only appeared (*dokei*) to be human. At this early period, the boundaries of the church were fairly fluid, for although the Gospels and the epistles were read widely throughout the churches, the NT canon had not yet been definitively determined and no council of the whole church had yet given guidance on interpreting the NT or defining the limits of Christian orthodoxy, and it was easy for this popular Gnostic religiosity to infiltrate. (This led to the modern theory of Bauer, answered by H. E. W. Turner, that what was later accounted 'orthodoxy' was merely one variation post-dating the 'heresies'.) One rich Christian, *Marcion, also seeing the world as evil, attributed its creation to the vengeful god he saw in the OT and differentiated the loving God and Father of our Lord Jesus Christ as a different deity. At the same time, there were Jews (the *Ebionites or 'Poor') who claimed to be followers of Jesus, and yet insisted that he was a man chosen by God, rejecting any confession of his deity.

The solution proposed by Irenaeus to these heresies already wracking the church in the late second century was that orthodox Christian doctrine could be recognized within the living tradition of the church, specifically the bishops appointed by the apostles together with their successors. But it could also be summarized in the 'rule of faith' (*regula fidei*), not found in any specific agreed formula, but always bearing the same triadic shape. It was belief 'in one God, the Father Almighty, Maker of heaven and earth . . . and in one Lord Jesus Christ, the Son of God, who became incarnate for our salvation, and in the Holy Spirit, who proclaimed through the prophets . . .' (*Adversus Haereses*, I, 10, 1). This summary of the faith arose from Matt. 28:19, was used as a confession made at baptism and variously expanded in different churches. Yet there remained the question of how this triadic faith was to be interpreted, and in the third century, the heresy of Sabellius, that the one God was Father, Son and Spirit in three successive modes (modalism), had to be rejected (see *Christology).

But it was in the fourth century that serious heresy prompted the development in which the baptismal confession became the basis for a more official creed. The creed approved at the Council of *Nicaea in 325 was formulated specifically to exclude the heresy of *Arianism, the belief which was already present within the church before Arius, that the Word (*Logos) or Son of God was not to be identified with God himself, but was the first of the creatures through whom God created the world. Instead of the One God of Sabellius who was not really or eternally Three, the 'Arians' in effect posited a kind of hierarchical tritheism. The controversy raged for another sixty-five years before the Nicene *Creed was approved in revised form by the Council of *Constantinople (381), insisting on the full deity of Christ. The phrasing was rather different, but the key formula of the Creed of Nicaea was retained – that the Son was 'of one Being with the Father' (*homoousion tō Patri*). Contemporary scholarship argues, however, that to classify many of the fourth-century views as 'Arian' or 'Semi-Arian' is misleading, and that Arius was a minor figure whose name was attached by Athanasius to a variety of views within the church.

With the Nicene-Constantinopolitan Creed, there was now a standard of orthodoxy approved by an ecumenical council and accepted by the church. But heresies about the doctrine of the person of Christ still flourished. *Apollinarianism (that Christ had no human mind) had been condemned at Constantinople (381), but at the later Council of *Chalcedon, *Nestorianism (that there were in effect two persons in Christ, the Son of God and the Son of David) and Eutychianism (that the humanity of Christ was deified in such a way that there was no longer a distinct human nature) were both condemned. The 'Symbol' of the Council of Chalcedon added a clarification of the second article of the Creed to insist that we should speak of Christ as one person (the Son of God) in 'two natures', deity and humanity, distinct but not separate. The trinitarian and Christological heresies therefore are those which deny the doctrine of the *Trinity formulated in the creed and the doctrine of the person of Christ as further clarified in the Chalcedonian Symbol. However, it should also be noted that the Coptic, Syrian and Armenian churches, while they reject the *Monophysitism of Eutyches, are 'Miaphysites': they insist on speaking of the 'one nature' (*mia physis*) of Christ, and although this was regarded as heretical by the Greek and Latin churches, it is now often understood as a difference in the use of language, since they clearly asserted (and still affirm) both his true deity and his true humanity.

But even while the Christological heresies were causing dispute in the early fifth century, several other heresies particularly affected the Latin-speaking church of the West. *Manichaeism was like Gnosticism both in holding to a metaphysical dualism between two ultimate principles (or 'gods') of good and evil, and also in that it arose outside rather than from within the church. *Donatism arose from within as a movement in north Africa to preserve the purity of the church and was rejected by *Augustine's doctrine that the church was only holy by *grace. *Pelagianism, the more outright heresy that salvation could be attained by human merit, was also rejected by Augustine on the grounds that salvation was by *grace. It was condemned by the second Synod of Orange (529).

Subsequent disputes, such as that between Greek East and Latin West over the *filioque* clause in the creed, led to mutual anathemas, but these would now be regarded as disputes within the church. The *Reformation led to further disputes which are now generally accepted as divisions within the church, but some of the ancient Christological and trinitarian heresies arose again, notably in the teaching of Servetus (who rejected the doctrine of the Trinity) and *Socinus. Socinianism arose out of a strong biblicism which rejected the credal, trinitarian interpretation of Scripture and went beyond Arianism (rejecting the full deity of Christ) to what became known as *Unitarianism (rejecting even his pre-existence as a subordinate deity). Unitarianism flourished particularly in the eighteenth century as *deism became popular.

*Schleiermacher presented an analysis of heresy. Since the heart of the Christian faith is the experience of Jesus as the Redeemer, the four 'natural heresies' are Pelagianism, which denied the need for redemption; Manichaeism, which regarded creation as beyond redemption; Ebionism, which denied that Jesus was any different from us and so could not provide redemption; and Docetism, which said that Jesus only appeared to be human and so could not provide the kind of redemption we need. But this does not take trinitarian heresies into account, and it was the 'liberal' tradition following Schleiermacher which reproduced in *Harnack and many others a revival of several of the ancient heresies.

While 'heresy hunting' often displays an unchristian spirit, and while the history of the church is replete with the persecution of heretics in ways we now deplore, the Christian church cannot dispense with the category of 'heresy' if the Christian faith is not to lack definition and mean anything and everything. It is important to distinguish, however, between doctrinal disagreements between authentic Christians, and heretical doctrines which deny the faith.

See also: SCHISM.

Bibliography

W. Bauer, *Orthodoxy and Heresy in Earlier Christianity* (Philadelphia, 1971 and London, 1972); R. Olson, *The Mosaic of Christian Belief: Twenty Centuries of Unity and Diversity* (Leicester, 2002); G. L. Prestige, *Fathers and Heretics* (London, 1977); B. Quash and M. Ward, *Heresies and How to Avoid Them: Why It Matters What Christians Believe* (London, 2007); K. Rahner, *On Heresy* (New York, 1964); H. E. W. Turner, *The Pattern of Christian Truth: A Study in the Relations between Orthodoxy and Heresy in the Early Church* (London, 1954).

T. A. NOBLE

HERMENEUTICS

Hermeneutics (a term derived from the Gk verb *hermēneuō*, to interpret) is the study of interpretation. General hermeneutics can take as its subject matter the interpretation and understanding of any act of communication, whether written or oral, verbal or non-verbal, and as such tends to include fundamental questions about the nature of language, meaning, communication and understanding, and the possibility of 'correct' interpretation. Biblical hermeneutics focuses specifically on the interpretation, understanding and appropriation of biblical texts. It can be understood (1) as a specific application of a general hermeneutics, albeit as one which might push general hermeneutics to its limit in some way; or (2) as having a character all of its own thanks to the unique nature of the biblical texts, and specifically their relationship to God and God's ways with the world; or (3) as being the unique foundation of a revised and theologically informed general hermeneutics, which sees *all* communication as somehow caught up in the communication of God to the world displayed most clearly in the Bible.

Pre-modern biblical hermeneutics

Beginnings

For biblical hermeneutics to exist, there must first be scriptural texts that exist in some relatively stable form and are regarded as capable of shaping life in the present, and then there must be some kind of explicit reflection upon the nature and limits of the processes by which the text's life-shaping potential is realized by readers. The Hebrew Bible contains significant amounts of textual interpretation (scribal glosses, the inclusion and arrangement of pre-existing material, direct quotation and commentary, the Chronicler's reworking of the traditions found in Kings, and so on), but there is no clear sense of a fixed canon of text to be interpreted, nor any explicit reflection on the processes of interpretation involved. Similarly, the expansively paraphrasing Aramaic translations of Hebrew Scripture known as Targums are certainly interpretation of classic texts for present situations, but they too don't assume the fixity of the classic texts, and don't tend to include reflection upon their own production. Some examples from Qumran and early Rabbinic midrashic interpretation do seem to assume that there are relatively fixed texts to be interpreted, and that because the texts cannot simply be reshaped so as to apply to contemporary needs and situations, some process of fairly sophisticated interpretation is needed if the texts' life-shaping potential is to be unlocked. It is, however, only with early rabbinic codifications of the rules by which valid midrashic interpretation could proceed (such as Rabbi Hillel's seven 'rules' – *middoth* – of interpretation) that we see explicit reflection on these processes, and so only then that biblical hermeneutics proper begins to appear.

There is a great deal of scriptural interpretation in the NT, most of which does seem to assume the relative fixity and contemporary authority of the texts used, but there is rather less that explicitly reflects on the nature and limits of the interpretive process. Two examples, however, capture well the most important characteristics of early biblical hermeneutics. On the one hand, we have the claim in 2 Tim. 3:16 that 'all Scripture is God-breathed and is useful for teaching, rebuking, correcting and training in righteousness'. The pervasive assumption of early Christian scriptural readers is that the texts are intended by God to lead readers deeper into knowledge of God and into service to God's mission in the world; interpretation is the process by which scriptural texts that may not initially seem to serve this divine intention are worked on until their divine educative potential is unlocked.

A second example of explicit biblical hermeneutics can be found in the writings of Paul the apostle, as he justifies Christian claims to true understanding of Hebrew Scripture, and distinguishes Christian readings of those texts from others. In 2 Cor. 3 – 4, he draws on the narrative of the veiling of Moses not just to make claims about the stages of God's salvific plan, but in order to justify his hermeneutics, explaining how the advent of Christ allows a different and truer construal of the meaning of Hebrew Scriptures than is available without Christ. As Paul explained this point further, he deployed (as one part of a more complex array of diverse and interlocking metaphors) language about 'letter' and 'spirit', contrasting a reading of Scripture informed and enlightened by Christ's advent (one that in his view can lead us deeper into the glory of God) with one that is constructed without attention to Christ. In so doing, Paul provided terminology that was later to be widely used to distinguish between literal or plain sense readings of a text and the spiritual readings that fully unearth that text's educative potential. That contrast (with which one may compare the contrast between *peshat* and *darash* in rabbinic interpretation) was to become a basic distinction in Christian biblical hermeneutics for centuries to come.

Patristic and medieval exegesis

The distinction between 'literal' and 'spiritual' readings in the patristic period became a distinction between 'grammatical' readings governed by the ordinary procedures for making sense of texts in Greco-Roman culture, and 'figural' readings which went beyond this and employed the techniques of allegorical or typological exegesis to explore the full Christ-centred tutelary potential of the texts. It was assumed that the Scriptures formed a single text with a unified central meaning (the depiction of, and induction into, God's ways with the world culminating in Christ), and that Christ was a recap or concluding summary of the whole.

The theory and practice of allegorical interpretation goes back to pre-Christian times. Many *Stoic philosophers respected Homer as a classic text, but were embarrassed by the crudities and absurdities of stories about the gods and goddesses of ancient polytheistic Greek religion. Some interpreters in the Stoic and *Platonic tradition reduced this tension by interpreting the stories of these gods and goddesses as disguised accounts of human qualities or elements of nature. Plato spoke of a 'meaning below' (*hyponoia*) the surface of the text, and many first-century writers describe this as *allegoria*. From Greek thought, this method of reading a text found its way into Jewish circles. *Philo wrote as a Jew seeking to commend Jewish faith to educated Greeks and Romans, and used allegorical interpretation as a device for rereading passages in the early chapters of Genesis that he found embarrassingly anthropomorphic, or passages in Leviticus that described the minutiae of animal sacrifice. Thus the method was established in Jewish and Greek circles before its growth within the Christian church.

Allegorical interpretation has had an ambivalent status in Christian tradition. *Origen argued that Paul himself provided precedent for allegorical interpretation in his identification of the wilderness rock with Christ in 1 Cor. 10:1–4. There has always been controversy about whether this passage and Gal. 4:22–26 constitute genuine examples of allegorical interpretation. Much depends on definition and questions about Paul's purpose. Many draw a firm distinction between allegory, which depends on a correspondence between *texts*, and typology, which depends on a correspondence between the *events* to which those texts point. Some argue that Paul uses typology but not allegory; others have argued that the distinction is not clear-cut in the NT and patristic periods, and that much allegorical exegesis has at least elements of the typological and vice versa.

Clement of Rome (*c*. 96) provides a very early example of Christian allegorical interpretation. Commenting on Josh. 2:18, he observes that the Israelite spies gave Rahab a sign 'that she should hang out a scarlet thread from her house, foreshadowing that all who achieve and hope in God shall have a deliverance through the blood of the Lord' (1 Clement 12:7). Clement of Alexandria, a century later, argued that the interpreter should expect to find hidden meanings in the biblical writings, because the mystery of the gospel transcended the meaning of any particular passage. Origen, one of the most influential of early Christian exegetes, spoke of the body of the text which taught readers truly about God's economy, but did so in ways that were sometimes difficult and obscure and so could drive them to a deeper level of spiritual reading which laboured to see the whole text as a unified educative structure leading to contemplation of God. There were some, notably theologians associated with Antioch in the late fourth century (see *Antiochene School), who in large part rejected the allegorical method, but for the most part it was the common inheritance of patristic exegesis.

In the medieval period, the practice of spiritual exegesis developed until interpreters could talk regularly of a fourfold sense of Scripture. The plain or literal sense of a passage was expanded by allegorical reading that asked what light the text threw on the divine economy (or, more narrowly speaking, on matters of Christian doctrine), by tropological or moral reading that drew out the text's significance for practical conduct, and by anagogical reading that considered the text's relation to the culmination of God's purposes in eternity.

Reformation hermeneutics

For the Reformers no less than for patristic and medieval readers, Christ is the sum and substance of the Scriptures: the Bible is, in Luther's metaphor, the manger in which the infant Jesus is to be found. For the Reformers, Scripture was God's sermon, addressing sinful humanity with words of law and of grace – words that are made effective within the hearer by the work of the Spirit (see *Reformation theology). The Scriptures are sufficient for this purpose, and with the aid of the *Spirit these words can be clearly and unambiguously heard. These divine words have certainly been spoken in Scripture by means of human words, and the Reformation saw various aspects of literal or grammatical reading flourish as the Reformers drew on the textual and philological techniques of Renaissance *humanism to assist them in reading the texts afresh in the languages of their human authors. Spiritual exegesis was not, however, rejected, and figural or typological reading remained for most of the Reformers an important part of the reading process.

Modern biblical hermeneutics

The end of the pre-modern consensus

There was a rough consensus in pre-modern biblical hermeneutics that literal and spiritual senses combined could lead the reader into an understanding of and participation in the one divine economy centred on Christ; in that sense, the Scriptures presented a 'world' within which the reader could find him- or herself. As early modernity progressed, a reversal began to take place. With the rise to prominence of non-theological disciplines thought capable of giving comprehensive accounts of the world (the natural sciences, philosophy, history), the question for biblical interpreters became: How do the Scriptures and what they speak of fit into this world? Historical criticism, in particular, developed in the seventeenth century and became the dominant force in biblical interpretation in academic circles (and often more widely) from the eighteenth. The prime question to ask of texts was how they stood up as evidence by the canons of historical criticism, and whether the events they depicted really happened. Whether the answers given were conservative or radical, the religious application of Scripture frequently became a matter of tracing the implications of the facts to which the texts pointed, rather than finding the Scriptures as such to be a unified and multi-layered school for Christian life. The exploration of spiritual senses began to be seen as a distraction from or even corruption of this new form of literal-historical reading.

Romantic hermeneutics

*Romantic hermeneutics provided, in the hands of theologians like Friedrich *Schleiermacher, one way of rescuing the religious significance of scriptural texts after the demise of pre-modern spiritual exegesis. Romantic interpreters focused on the texts not as evidence for historical facts, but as the creative expressions of religious individuals or communities – expressions from which the quality of the authors' religious consciousness could be reconstructed and shared by a sympathetic reader. Schleiermacher stressed the spiralling nature of such hermeneutical investigation: the interpreter has to undertake a creative leap into a provisional understanding of the experience that the text expresses, but this depends on an understanding of that text's component words and phrases. Yet the meaning of those words and phrases in turn depends upon their context within the text as a whole, for the consciousness encoded in the text is an organic whole rather than an aggregate of individual thoughts and impressions. This understanding of the 'hermeneutic circle' was later taken up by the philosopher Wilhelm *Dilthey, who drew on it to develop an influential account of the distinctiveness of the human sciences, grounded as they are in the interpretation of expressions of human experience.

It is as an heir to this Romantic tradition that much twentieth-century biblical hermeneutics (as, for instance, the existentialist hermeneutics of Rudolf *Bultmann, or the New Hermeneutic of Ernst Fuchs and others) turned to examining the ways in which biblical texts could disturb and reshape patterns of perception and thought in the reader that lie deeper than those that can be verbalized in clear propositions or theories – repainting the 'horizon' against which all a person's individual experiences and thoughts are perceived. In the second half of the twentieth century, these conversations were much influenced by the philosophical hermeneutics of Hans-Georg Gadamer, who described interpretation as a matter of the 'fusion of horizons', whereby the interaction between the worldview encoded in a text and the worldview embodied in the reader leads that reader to a transformed understanding.

The hermeneutics of suspicion

The hermeneutics of suspicion is another child of the attempt to see where the Scriptures fit into the world described by non-theological disciplines. A hermeneutics of suspicion argues that the claims and descriptions offered by biblical texts cannot necessarily be taken at their face value, but are determined by and cloak forces at work beneath the surface. With the right analytical tools, the texts may be seen both to promote and to disguise the power of their authors or of the groups for which they speak – whether that is the power of one particular faction in the struggles of early Christianity, or the power of the ruling or wealthy classes, or the power of patriarchy. Similarly, attempts to interpret these texts may be shown up as determined not by a disinterested commitment to the texts themselves, but by a variety of unspoken interests that subtly or more blatantly shape what the interpreter thinks he or she sees in the text. In neither case is it necessary to accuse the author or interpreter of conscious deception: the ideology that determines the text or interpretation may well be invisible to those whose interests it serves and to those whom it disempowers.

*Feminist hermeneutics can take both of these forms, looking either at the shaping of biblical texts or of their reception history by patriarchal ideology. *Liberation hermeneutics tends to focus more on the latter, pointing to the ways in which the revolutionary sociopolitical message of the Scriptures has been neutered by powerful and privileged interpreters simply incapable, from their vantage point, of seeing what was before their noses. Deconstructionist hermeneutics can be seen as a radical form of the hermeneutics of suspicion, chasing the play of interlocking and evolving ideologies that have shaped not just the text and the history of its interpretation, but the very idea of a unified text to be interpreted, or of unified readers capable of disinterested interpretation.

Hermeneutics and dogmatic theology

In a rather different vein, a renewed attempt to think through biblical hermeneutics in the light of credal convictions about the divine economy, drawing only unsystematically on non-theological philosophical hermeneutics, was pursued by such twentieth-century theologians as Karl *Barth and Hans Urs von *Balthasar, and their followers. Barth, for instance, claimed that Scripture is to be understood within a thoroughly trinitarian and incarnational frame. The Word of God to the world is in the first place Jesus of Nazareth. That incarnate Word is then present in a second form, in the form of witness, in Scripture, and in a third form as the church's proclamation of Christ on the basis of the scriptural witness. It is only when we read the diverse texts of the Bible as a unified canon witnessing to Christ, for the sake of proclamation, that we read them as Scripture (and this incidentally means that theological exegesis can treat the results of historical criticism only as initial steps in exegesis, clarifying the nature of some of the raw materials, but incapable on its own of coming to terms with the real subject matter of the Bible). To say that Scripture is a witness to Jesus Christ is not, for Barth, to say that we should think of it primarily as a source of correct information about him; it is, rather, a witness to Jesus Christ as the Word of the Father, and we hear that Word only to the extent that we find ourselves grasped by him, our sins judged by him, and the love of God proclaimed to us in him. And, for Barth, the hearing of that divine Word is in no sense a human achievement, the outcome of appropriate hermeneutical techniques correctly applied; it is the work of the Spirit on us and in us, converting us to the Word. Other theologians have stressed even more than Barth the extent to which the Spirit who allows us to hear the Word is the Spirit who animates and unifies the body of Christ, so that a true 'spiritual' interpretation cannot be the product of an individual reader, however inspired, but must emerge out of the conversation between readers who are the diverse members of the body of Christ.

Postliberal hermeneutics

In the later decades of the twentieth century, a number of *postliberal theologians have turned away from the attempt to construct a philosophical hermeneutics of general applicability, or from the attempt to develop a purely dogmatic biblical hermeneutics, and have instead turned to tracing the specific ways in which the Bible has been and is used by real Christian communities. A postliberal theologian might trace the settlements within a particular community by which its specific ideas and practices shape the way in which it approaches Scripture, with Scripture in turn, when approached in that way, supporting the ideas and practices of the community. There is an unavoidable circularity here, but postliberals tend to be non-*foundationalists – that is, they assume that such circularity is ultimately unavoidable: in the end, no reading practice can be justified simply on a priori grounds. Differing approaches to Scripture sustained by different communities of interpretation can nevertheless be compared to a certain extent according to how coherent and comprehensive they are, and by the extent to which they allow Scripture to shape and inform the community's life in a wide range of contexts. The focus on community use does not mean straightforwardly accepting that the community can make of Scripture what it likes. Postliberals such as Hans *Frei have pointed to the fact that central amongst the reading practices of mainstream Christian groups have been ones which genuinely allow the Scriptures to stand over against the community as a source of judgment and critique.

See also: HISTORICAL THEOLOGY; SCRIPTURE; SCRIPTURE, DOCTRINE OF.

Bibliography

K. Barth, *CD*, esp. I.I; H. W. Frei, *The Eclipse of Biblical Narrative* (New Haven, 1974); A. J. Hauser and D. F. Watson, *A History of Biblical Interpretation*, vol. 1 (Grand Rapids, 2003); J. Holcomb, *Christian Theologies of Scripture* (New York, 2006); H. de Lubac, *Medieval Exegesis*, 2 vols. (Grand Rapids and London, 1998–2000); C. Rowland and M. Corner (eds.), *Liberating Exegesis* (London, 1990); F. D. E. Schleiermacher, *Hermeneutics* (Oxford, 1978); A. C. Thiselton, *Hermeneutics: An Introduction* (Grand Rapids, 2009); idem, *New Horizons in Hermeneutics: The Theory and Practice of Transforming Biblical Reading* (Grand Rapids, 1992; idem, *The Hermeneutics of Doctrine* (Grand Rapids, 2007); P. Trible, *Texts of Terror* (London, 2003); F. Watson, *Paul and the Hermeneutics of Faith* (London, 2005); F. Young, *Biblical Exegesis and the Formation of Christian Culture* (Cambridge, 1997).

M. Higton

HERRMANN, WILHELM (1846–1922)

Herrmann grew up under *pietist influences, but during his theological studies embraced the up-and-coming theology of Albrecht *Ritschl and became his foremost disciple. After a period as a lecturer at Halle, he was appointed professor of theology at Marburg in 1879, where he remained to the end of his life. His most famous work is *The Communion of the Christian with God* (1886; ET, 1971), which deals with the doctrine of God and the Christian's relationship with him.

'God' for Herrmann is not the traditional three-in-one of orthodox Christianity, but rather 'the personal vitality and power of goodness'. Jesus is not the Son of God in the sense traditionally understood by the church, but rather a man in whose exemplary character the power of God, i.e. the power of the highest good, was revealed. For Herrmann there are no supernatural miracles. Jesus demonstrated that the highest good is a life of love. It is the beauty of Jesus' life that reveals God.

In contrast to the scepticism of the 'Did Jesus live?' movement, Herrmann maintained that the evangelists' portrayal of Jesus is completely independent of historical reality; even if Jesus had never existed, the portrait of him would still remain permanently valid for its purpose. He therefore discounted the results of the higher-critical investigation of the Bible as in no way requiring amendment of the picture of Jesus contained in the Gospels. In Herrmann's opinion, the portrait would stand for all time as a model of how we should live, even if it were completely devoid of historicity. Christianity did not need a historical apologetic.

Bibliography

R. T. Voekel, *The Shape of the Theological Task* (Philadelphia, 1968).

H. Harris

HESYCHASM

Hesychasm (i.e. quietism, from Gk *hesychia* = quietness), though generally regarded as a theological movement in fourteenth-century Byzantium stemming from a particular type of Christian spirituality, finds its beginnings in the early development of anchoritic *asceticism. In the beginning it was a matter of practice, but from the fourth century onwards, with the rise of great figures like *Basil the Great, Evagrius Ponticus (346–99), *Macarius, *Pseudo-Dionysius the Areopagite, *Maximus the Confessor, John Climacus (*c.* 570–649) and *Symeon the New Theologian (see *Eastern Orthodox theology), ascetic hesychasm was given a theoretical or theological basis. The fourth-century hesychast was one who attempted to be totally freed from visible realities, through mastery over passions and acquisition of virtues, illumination of the mind by contemplation and prayer of the mind (or heart), so that he might arrive at quietness in God or *vision of God.

From the sixth century onwards 'monologic' prayer, consisting in the rhythmic repetition of one sentence, phrase or word, usually the name of the Lord Jesus Christ, became the means of attaining divine *hesychia*. In the seventh century St Catherine's Monastery at Sinai became the centre of a type of hesychasm epitomized in *The Ladder* of John Climacus (tr. C. Luibhèid, London, 1982). In the second half of the tenth century Symeon the New Theologian gave hesychasm a new impulse by linking it with a purely Christocentric vision of the 'divine light' (cf. *Symeon the New Theologian: The Discourses*, tr. C. J. de Catanzaro, London, 1980; G. A. Maloney, *The Mystic of Fire and*

Light: St Symeon the New Theologian, Denville, 1975). Growing out of this, a psychological technique of prayer was developed. The central element was the ceaseless repetition in solitude of 'Lord Jesus Christ, have mercy on me a sinner', to which the posture of the body and the manner of breathing could be added as secondary elements. The end of it all was the vision of the 'uncreated light' of God.

In the fourteenth century both the vision of the 'divine light' and especially the method used for its attainment became the subjects of bitter controversy. Opposition to hesychasm was led by Barlaam of Calabria (c. 1290–1350) and George Akindynos (c. 1300–49). The 'uncreated' light of the hesychasts was held to imply ditheism. *Gregory of Palamas was the greatest apologist of hesychasm, putting forward the distinction between God's essence (*ousia*) and energies, linking the latter with the uncreated divine light and arguing that God, who is invisible, unapproachable and incommunicable in his essence, becomes visible, approachable and communicable in his energies.

After intense conflict, a decisive synod of 1351 endorsed Gregory's distinction, and also the principles: (1) that the energies are uncreated, (2) that God is not composite, (3) that the word 'divine' can be attributed not only to the essence, but also to the energies of God, and (4) that men do not participate in the essence, but in the energies and grace of God. Henceforth, Barlaam and Akindynos would be regarded as heretics, and Palamas as the mouthpiece of orthodoxy. Yet disputes over hesychasm continued, especially as a result of Latin influence from the West. Hesychasm lives on in the Orthodox East, especially on Mount Athos; it exercises a measure of influence in the West, partly through the compilation of eighteenth-century hesychist writings known as the *Philokalia*.

Bibliography

Works: Gregory Palamas, *The Triads*, tr. N. Gendle (London, 1983); *The Philokalia*, 5 vols., tr. G. E. H. Palmer, P. Sherrard and K. Ware (London, 1979–95).

Studies: L. Clucas, *The Hesychast Controversy in Byzantium in the Fourteenth Century*, unpubl. diss., 2 vols. (Los Angeles, 1975); C. D. L. Johnson, *The Globalization of Hesychasm and the Jesus Prayer* (London, 2010); J. Meyendorff, *Byzantine Hesychasm* (London, 1974); *idem*, *St Gregory Palamas and Orthodox Spirituality* (New York, 1974); *idem*, *A Study of Gregory Palamas* (London, 1962); G. C. Papademetriou, *Introduction to St Gregory Palamas* (Brookline, MA, 2004).

G. D. DRAGAS

HICK, JOHN HARWOOD (1922–2012)

Hick was a philosopher of religion and a radical theologian. He was educated in Edinburgh, Oxford and Cambridge, and was formerly a minister of the United Reformed Church in Britain. He held numerous academic positions, including latterly emeritus professor at Birmingham University and the Claremont Graduate University, California. He was a Fellow of the Institute for Advanced Research in Arts and Social Sciences, University of Birmingham, and a Vice-President of the British Society for the Philosophy of Religion and of the World Congress of Faiths.

Hick's earlier works were concerned with central traditional issues in the *philosophy of religion (cf. *Philosophy of Religion*, Englewood Cliffs, NJ, ³1983; *Faith and Knowledge: A Modern Introduction to the Problem of Religious Knowledge*, New York, 1957; and essays on the existence of God, etc.). His most significant book in this field is *Evil and the God of Love* (London, ³1985), which prefers a so-called *Irenaean to an *Augustinian approach to the problem of *evil, and also appeals to an eschatological resolution that will be unveiled only at the end.

Hick's attention then turned to questions about the *uniqueness of Jesus as the incarnate Son of God in the context of the other world religions (cf. *God and the Universe of Faiths*, London, 1973). He argues for the reduction of the 'high' Christology of the Nicene Creed and the Chalcedonian definition of the faith (cf. Hick, ed., *The Myth of God Incarnate*, London, 1977). It can be established that there has been a historical development in Hick's *Christology from an earlier orthodoxy to the later rejection of it. This is due to his assumptions that: no special revelation of God is possible; unconditional *universal salvation is certain (cf. *Death and Eternal Life*, London, ²1985); and all world religions are equal in their theological aspirations and claims. Hick argued that the traditional arguments for the uniqueness of Jesus Christ are invalid, regressive and even harmful to the harmonious co-existence of people of different faiths which is the need of the hour. He therefore pleads for a return from a Christocentric to a theocentric theology, with all the great religious systems alike providing access to the 'ultimate reality' of God.

Hick delivered the 1986–87 *Gifford Lectures, and in 1991 was awarded the Grawemeyer Award for Religion.

See also: CHRISTIANITY AND OTHER RELIGIONS.

Bibliography

C.-R. Brakenheim, *How Philosophy Shapes Theories of Religion* . . . (Lund, 1975) – with special reference to Hick; G. D'Costa, *John Hick's Theology of Religions: A Critical Evaluation* (New York and London, 1987); N. Jason, *A Critical Examination of the Christology of John Hick, with Special Reference to the Continuing Significance of the 'Definitio Fidei' of the Council of Chalcedon, AD 451* (unpubl. dissertation, University of Sheffield, 1978); T. R. Mathis, *Against John Hick: An Examination of His Philosophy and Religion* (Lanham, 1985); C. Sinkinson, *The Universe of Faiths: A Critical Study of John Hick's Religious Pluralism* (Carlisle, 2001).

N. JASON

HIDDEN AND REVEALED GOD

A concept particularly associated with the theology of Martin *Luther and Karl *Barth.

Meaning of terms

To speak of God as revealing himself is to imply that God is a hidden God: the *Deus revelatus* still remains a *Deus velatus*. Moses, Jacob, Job, the psalmists and prophets are all aware of the 'hiddenness' of God, even in his act of revealing himself. *Clement, *Origen, Chrysostom (*c.* 344/54–407), *Augustine, doctors, mystics, schoolmen were all conscious of the unknowability of God, and Luther intensely so. Modern, secularized humanity may have lost its earlier awareness of the mystery of God, that divine holiness which transcends all human experiences, aesthetic, intellectual and moral. Nevertheless, the mystery of God remains, as well as the question: 'How do I know him?'

In the Bible *revelation is disclosure of truth about God by the agency of God, as distinct from man's discovery of truth as he investigates his secular experience. In the NT it is expressed as God's disclosure in his Messiah in judgment and salvation, an event already effected in the advent of Jesus, though still to come on the last day.

The OT left unresolved the problem of how the God of Israel can be 'squared with' the history of Israel. The NT sharpened this poignantly in the disclosure of the work of God who, in showing his righteousness and mercy, yet suffered on the cross. The revelation of God cannot simply be read off from history or human experience. The crucial question still remains: How can the hidden God be revealed to me? How shall I find a gracious God?

The hidden God revealed in Christ

No theologian has tackled the problem of God as hidden and revealed more penetratingly than Luther. Luther argued that knowledge of God was twofold: (1) General, that there is a God, that he created heaven and earth, that he is righteous, and that he punishes the wicked. This knowledge was open to all humankind. (2) Particular or 'proper', that God loves us and seeks our salvation. This was revealed only in Christ.

Luther did not share the scholastic view of *Thomas Aquinas, or even of *Duns Scotus and *William of Ockham, that the general knowledge of God was attained by inference, and that reason was the foundation on which the proper knowledge of God revealed in Christ could be erected. He argued biblically that noone can see God and live. We cannot say what God is like in himself, but only what he does for us. In any dealings with man, God has to wear a 'mask' (*larva*), and these 'masks' describe the way God meets man in his concrete existence (i.e. through the ordinances he established, and through the human beings he had created doing God's work in their appointed roles).

This had an exact parallel in the incarnation. Just as we do not infer God's existence, nature and attributes from his masks or veils, but recognize that God comes to meet us in them, so is it none other than God who comes to us and meets us in Christ. God gives no gifts less than himself. This was the supreme revelation wherein the hidden God is revealed: 'He who has seen me has seen the Father' (John 14:9); 'No man comes to the Father but by me' (John 14:6). We see by, and in, faith alone. Similarly, the faculty of reason, though of divine origin, cannot of itself find God or the road to salvation.

In a striking passage in the Heidelberg Disputation (1518), referring to God's 'face' and God's 'back' (Exod. 33:23), Luther argued against the 'theology of glory' of the schoolmen in favour of the 'theology of the *cross'. God's 'back' means his humanity, his weakness, his foolishness (1 Cor. 1:21, 25; cf. Isa. 45:15), i.e. the *incarnation. God is always revealed 'under a contrary form'; weakness is strength, foolishness is wisdom, death is life. In this simple truth of the gospel lies the divine secret, the disclosure supreme. We must stoop to learn about God from God as revealed in Christ, and not from our own understanding.

Deliverance by faith

The problems of election and *predestination, of *suffering and the *wrath of God remain, but they are delivered by faith out of our minds into the hands of God where they belong: they now appear as solutions, not problems. Luther never speculated on these problems, for he never faltered in faith: it is faith alone and only faith which fortifies and safeguards a soul from doubt, speculation, despair. In those memorable words, *Wer glaubt, der hat* (if you believe, you already possess), he argued that sufficient truth for man had been revealed in Christ, and only the believing heart which had grasped (or rather had been grasped by) the theology of the cross could see this. Even then, God is more deeply hidden in Christ crucified than he is in creation or in history. Power in weakness, glory in suffering, life in death, all show how hidden he is. This paradox of the cross and of God working in 'contrary form', reveal him as hidden, and leave him open to faith only. Election and predestination Luther experienced as God's love, without whose prior move he would have known nothing and been lost. Even in the wrath of God is hidden God's love, for wrath is but the annihilating reaction of the love of God to man's sin and disobedience: it disguises God's care and concern to redeem man. Similarly, in weakness, fear and suffering, all we need to know is that grace is sufficient, and strength is made perfect in weakness.

When Barth (as Luther before him) argued that we can know God only in Christ, he meant that it is only in a faith-experience of Christ that a person becomes open to revelation: the problems of wrath, predestination, suffering, the painful hiddenness of God, are all transmuted into an experience of the love, the care and the mercy of God. All experiences of life, evil and good, now become the raw material of the good life in which the believer experiences God's loving care in all things. In this experience of Christ, the hidden God becomes the revealed God.

Bibliography

J. Atkinson, *Luther's Early Theological Works*, LCC 16 (London, 1962); J. Dillenberger, *God Hidden and Revealed* (Philadelphia, 1953); B. A. Gerrish, 'To the Unknown God: Luther and Calvin on the Hiddenness of God', *JR* 53, 1973, pp. 263–292; A. E. McGrath, *Luther's Theology of the Cross* (Oxford, 1985).

J. ATKINSON

HIGHER-LIFE THEOLOGY

A pattern of Christian holiness teaching (see *Holiness Movement) popularized by the American Presbyterian minister, William Edward Boardman (1810–86), in his *Higher Christian Life* (1859). Boardman's book, which sold over 100,000 copies on both sides of the Atlantic, asserted that the experience of *sanctification is a distinct work of grace, clearly separable from *justification, if not in theory, then certainly in practice. He insisted that it is not to he confused with Wesleyan *perfectionism (Boardman's bête noire), and that it has been enjoyed throughout the centuries by outstanding Christians such as *Luther, *Baxter, Jonathan *Edwards and (surprisingly, in view of his aversion to *Wesley's teaching) some early *Methodist people such as Hester Ann Rogers (1756–94) and William Carvosso (1750–1835). The book's immediate popularity released Boardman for an itinerant convention ministry during which he met, and was later joined by, Robert Pearsall Smith (1827–98) and Hannah Whitall Smith (1832–1911), a couple who were to give his teaching wider popularity throughout Britain.

Emphasizing sanctification as a crisis experienced by faith, Boardman accepted neither the Wesleyan nor *Reformed doctrine of holiness, believing that Wesley claimed too much whilst the *Puritans and Reformers did not expect enough. Robert Pearsall Smith endeavoured further to meet the demand for popular holiness literature by writing *Holiness Through Faith* (1870). His wife, Hannah, added to the partnership some further concepts from her *Quaker background (particularly stillness and guidance), and this unusual fusion of Wesleyanism and Quakerism, expounded in her book, *The Christian's Secret of a Happy Life* (1875), was to become one of the most remarkable features of late nineteenth-century holiness teaching, combining the idea of a dramatic crisis with the 'rest of faith' ('Let go and let God').

The Boardman and Pearsall Smith message came to be presented in England at holiness conventions held at Broadlands (1874), Oxford (1874), Brighton (1875) and Keswick (1875). In its infancy the movement was in danger of concentrating on subjective experiences rather than objective teaching; some of its earlier addresses were more in the nature of extemporaneous talks and testimonies than carefully prepared expositions of Scripture. Over successive decades the teaching of the annual interdenominational Keswick Convention, held each July, gradually changed. Throughout its history the Convention Council has refrained from formulating a closely defined theology of sanctification, leaving its speakers free to expound and apply the various facets of scriptural teaching concerning personal and practical holiness. While recognizing that for some Christians the appropriation of their unique resources in Christ may find its focus in a particular moment of crisis, the Convention has given greater prominence to central biblical themes such as promised deliverance from known sin, continual cleansing by and identification with Christ, the practical implications of his lordship and the perpetual filling of the *Holy Spirit (see *Baptism in the Spirit), equipping Christians for service in the world. A strong missionary and evangelistic concern has been present from its earliest days and is integral to the Convention's main message.

Bibliography

S. Barabas, *So Great Salvation: The History and Message of the Keswick Convention* (London, 1952); D. Bebbington, *Holiness in Nineteenth-Century England: The 1998 Didsbury Lecture* (Carlisle, 2000); *The Keswick Week* (London, 1892–); J. C. Pollock, *The Keswick Story* (London, 1964); C. Price and I. Randall, *Transforming Keswick* (Carlisle, 2000); W. B. Sloan, *These Sixty Years: The Story of the Keswick Convention* (London, 1935); B. B. Warfield, *Perfectionism*, 2 vols. (New York, 1931).

R. BROWN

HILARY OF POITIERS (c. 315–67)

Hilary was born of a pagan, noble family. Like *Augustine after him, he found pagan philosophy a useful preliminary to the Christian gospel. Shortly after his conversion he was made Bishop of Poitiers. Subsequent resistance to *Arianizing trends within the Gallic church led to a term of banishment in Asia Minor.

During his exile Hilary gained firsthand experience of Eastern theology, and was particularly influenced by the *Origenism of men like Basil of Ancyra (*fl.* 340–60). His work *On the Synods* dates from this period. It was an attempt to reconcile fellow Westerners to the different theological approach of the anti-Arians in the East.

His exile was also the occasion for his *On the Trinity*, the outstanding Latin theological treatise of the Arian controversy. Hilary added little to the orthodox view on the relationship of the Father and the Son or on the role of the Holy Spirit; but he did make an original contribution in *Christology, for he saw the most effective counter to Arian insistence on the human weakness of Christ in the postulation of three distinct stages in Christ's existence.

In the first stage, Christ was pre-existent as the Son of God, united with his Father in a mutual indwelling. At the incarnation (the second stage) he was born as a man without in any way ceasing to be God. Nevertheless, since Christ appeared in the form of a servant for man's benefit, effectively a breach was created within the Godhead. The human nature which Christ assumed was separated by an infinite distance from God the Father, though it was indissolubly linked to the divinity of God the Son. It was the latter's task to raise the human nature to the level of the divine – a task accomplished at his resurrection and ascension. In the third stage, Christ was restored to that glory which he shared with his Father before the incarnation. Believers, therefore, might hope that they too would share in the glory to which Christ had elevated human nature.

The key to Hilary's soteriology is the *deification of humanity, which God had purposed from the beginning. Its achievement had merely been complicated, not first inspired, by sin. Hilary has a clear concept of the two natures in the incarnate Christ, as well as of the unity of his person. His treatment, however, of the events of Christ's life falls into *docetism. He argued that Christ possessed a unique sort of body – a heavenly body, because its owner, who had come down from heaven and was on earth, was still in heaven. This body might fulfil all the functions of a human body and go through suffering, but it did so only by special condescension, and even then it did not really feel pain. According to its own nature, the body was free of human needs, and evinced the sort of power shown in the miracles and in the transfiguration. In effect, he had reached the polar opposite position from the Arians on the incarnate Christ. For him the miraculous displays of power were the rule, not the exception, for Christ's human body.

Bibliography
Select works in ET in *NPNF*.
Studies: C. Beckwith, *Hilary of Poitiers on the Trinity: From* De Fide *to* De Trinitate (New York and Oxford, 2009); P. Galtier, *Saint Hilaire de Poitiers* (Paris, 1960); C. B. Kaiser, 'The Development of Johannine Motifs in Hilary's Doctrine of the Trinity', *Scottish Journal of Theology* 29, 1976, pp. 237–247; E. P. Meijering, *Hilary of Poitiers on the Trinity* (Leiden, 1982); G. M. Newlands, *Hilary of Poitiers: A Study in Theological Method* (Berne, 1978); Lionel R. Wickham (ed.), *Hilary of Poitiers* (Liverpool, 1997).

G. A. KEITH

HILDEGARD OF BINGEN
(1098–1179)

Hildegard was first a novice at Disibodenberg, in the Rhineland area of Germany, then convent mistress in 1136. From 1141 her occasional visions became expressed in words, which coincided with moving to Rupertsburg near Bingen. She spoke of being fairly constantly 'in the shadow of the living light' in spite of her pain. The living light itself which brought joy and release in visions was less common. The authority she believed herself to have was that of a 'Marian' mystical knowledge, for which self-annihilation made room.

Known as 'the Rhineland Sibyl', her express desire was to clarify the tradition of orthodox theology with some 'pictures'. Yet the world and humanity are both the puzzle and the solution to each other; and she awaited the answer of the Holy Spirit to clarify her visions, which became texts for 'exegesis'. The imagery of the visions are replete with OT influences as well as the Rule of *Benedict and a number of Church Fathers. *Bernard of Clairvaux was her staunch defender, getting Pope Eugene III to read her works when she was suspected of heresy.

A true representative of the high Middle Ages, her imagery was pastoral rather than domestic, as in the case of later medieval spiritual writing. She thought of God as an artist who in salvation history came to improve on his work in the human soul. As artists in his image, we are called to co-operate in this task. Her innovations in musical composition she viewed as part of this operation. Yet, for Hildegard, Jesus Christ shows us the fullness of the revelation of the divine artist.

See also: SPIRITUALITY.

Bibliography
J. L. Baird (ed.), *The Personal Correspondence of Hildegard of Bingen: Selected Letters with an Introduction and Commentary* (Oxford, 2006); F. Bowie and O. Davies (eds.), *Hildegard of Bingen: An Anthology* (London, 1990); Hildegard of Bingen, *Scivias* (New York, 1990).

M. W. ELLIOTT

HINDUSIM AND CHRISTIANITY
Frederic Spiegelberg has commented that, 'As we study the religions of the modern world we immediately become aware of one outstanding phenomenon – that the Occident and the Orient are apt to conceive the basic concepts of which the human race is capable in diametrically opposed ways' (*Living Religions of the World*, London, 1957, p. viii).

Superficial acquaintance may convey a different opinion, but it remains an indisputable fact that Hinduism and its derivatives, *Buddhism, Jainism and Sikhism, stand in diametrical divergence from Christianity on every major doctrine of faith and practice. A brief survey of Hindu teachings basic to the understanding of human destiny and salvation will amply demonstrate the truth of this statement.

Scripture

Hindu theology places a high premium on the Vedas as the revealed scriptures, rooted in the divine omniscience and 'received' by sages in deep transcendental meditation. The Vedas are referred to with reverence, and at first sight appear to have the same claim to authority as the Bible does in Christianity. Yet in spite of the insistence on the divine origin of the Vedas, another doctrine completely alters the nature of scriptural authority. This is well stated later in the Gita, probably the most popular scripture in present-day Hinduism: 'As is a pool of water in a place flooded with water, so are all the Vedas to a person who has attained Enlightenment' (2:46), i.e. once the seeker has attained *Moksha* or 'the Enlightened Consciousness' or 'Nirvana' or 'God-realization' (all of which signify *salvation in Hinduism), even the revealed scriptures no longer have a claim on him. In effect, this doctrine elevates the subjective experience of God-realization beyond the claim of the objective word of scripture. As a consequence, probably not even a handful of Hindus have ever read the entire Vedas. Aspirants prefer to bypass the close study of scripture in pursuit of experience in meditative practice (see *Religious experience). In this hazardous retreat into the subjective world of private experience, each individual is supreme and above authority.

God

There is no conception of God in Hinduism similar to the Christian doctrine of a sovereign *God who created the universe and governs it in the exercise of his omnipotent power (see *Sovereignty; *Creation; *Providence). In Hinduism, God is utterly beyond form and definition; he is the totally Other, unknowable and unknown. A distant omniscience in the heavenlies, he is also immanent in the universe, so that everything in nature is shot through with the divine. It is for this reason that the worship and propitiation of the forces of nature, or even of great men, comes so easily to Hindus.

Incarnation

Hindus have a doctrine of incarnation. The unknowable Divine becomes incarnate in flesh and blood during times of world crisis, and dwells among men in order to restore righteousness. But by contrast with the finality of Christ's *incarnation, in Hinduism incarnation is a process and is recurrent whenever the world is threatened by upheaval. The concept of a God of *love, especially the sacrificial love that is inherent in the Christian gospel, is foreign to the Hindu understanding of the Divine.

Humanity and its destiny

In Hinduism, the human person is a perfectible being. It is freely admitted that he is imperfect and prone to evil, but the cause of this is nothing inherent in his nature but ignorance (*Avidya*). This ignorance is his absence of understanding of his true divine nature. He is essentially a spiritual being with the divine spark as his core. If this were truly realized and made manifest, his radiant spiritual nature would shine forth. The highway that leads to this state is spiritual practice, especially silence, meditation, intense self-abnegation and the chastening of one's gross carnal nature. Thus man is the architect of his own salvation and needs no *mediator, still less a saviour or redeemer. Hinduism is par excellence a blueprint for auto-salvation. The individual achieves his own deliverance from the knot of human bondage into the liberty of God-realized people of spirit.

Karma and reincarnation

These twin doctrines are characteristic of all oriental mysticism, especially in the Indo-Aryan world. The law of Karma is simply the law of causality applied rigorously in the moral and conceptual realm as well as the physical. 'As a man thinketh, so is he' is an example of this law as it works in the realm of thought and moral intent. The law of rebirth or reincarnation (see *Metempsychosis) is the safety valve in Hinduism. If a seeker fails to realize his destiny of God-consciousness in this life, he can always lay the foundations of a second chance to labour for his salvation in another incarnation. Probation does not exhaust itself in one life; there is always a second opportunity for those who cannot face the rigours of the discipline prescribed for the spiritual athlete who sets himself single-mindedly to break through the coils of his earthly bondage. Divine grace is operative only at the fringes of the process, almost at the end of the human effort.

Hindu-Christian dialogue

It is an essential Hindu doctrine that all religions are pathways to God and that no religion can justifiably make any claim to exclusiveness (see

*Christianity and other religions; *Uniqueness of Christ). Any religion that insists on being the only true one is unwarrantedly restrictive and narrow, in the light of the all-embracing amplitude of the divine will. Here Christ and Hinduism emerge in clear conflict (cf. John 14:6).

However attractive Hinduism may appear, especially with its techniques of meditation and spiritual practice, from a Christian point of view its 'Achilles' heel' is its failure to address itself meaningfully to the cold, hard, inescapable fact of *sin. Christians see sin, by which they mean that alienation of humanity from God which leads to alienation from our fellows and, above all, from ourselves, as the great harasser of humankind. For Christians this is dealt with by the divinely appointed method, namely, reconciliation by repentance and self-surrender through faith in the Lord Jesus and his redemption (see *Atonement); anyone who gives himself to meditation and spiritual discipline, however sincerely, is playing a dangerously losing game.

These profound differences between Hindu and Christian beliefs have not deterred writers and teachers from both traditions attempting to identify and build on points of contact between the two. Reforming Hindus such as Sri Aurobindo (1872–1950) have drawn on the Bible and Christian teaching to correct what they have seen as the weaknesses of Hinduism. Christians such as Raimundo Panikkar (1918–2010) have urged the use of Hindu concepts to commend Christianity to Hindus. Panikkar's book, *The Unknown Christ of Hinduism* (London, ²1980), finds common ground in the humanity shared by Hindu and Christian and brought to true focus in the incarnation – for Hindus have not found it impossible to regard Jesus as an incarnation of deity. But other Indian Christian theologians (e.g. S. Kulandran, *Grace: A Comparative Study of the Doctrine in Christianity and Hinduism*, London, 1964) continue to view the two faiths as incompatible, and the approach of Panikkar as verging on *syncretism.

Bibliography

J. Brockington, *Hinduism and Christianity* (London, 1992); J. M. Brown and R. E. Frykenberg (eds.), *Christians, Cultural Interactions, and India's Religious Traditions* (Grand Rapids, 2002); H. Coward (ed.), *Hindu-Christian Dialogue: Perspectives and Encounters* (Delhi, 1993); J. Kalapati, *Dr Radhakrishnan and Christianity: An Introduction to Hindu-Christian Apologetics* (Delhi, 2002); S. Nirved-Ananda, *Hinduism at a Glance* (Calcutta, 1957); S. Radhakrishnan, *The Hindu View of Life* (London, 1960); B. Robinson, *Christians Meeting Hindus: An Analysis and Theological Critique of Hindu-Christian Encounter in India* (Oxford, 2004); D. S. Sarma, *Hinduism Through the Ages* (Bombay, 1967); H. E. W. Slade, *Schools of Oriental Meditation* (London, 1973); H. Smith, *The Religions of Man* (New York, 1957); R. Tagore, *The Religion of Man* (London, 1966); T. C. Tennent, *Christianity at the Religious Roundtable: Evangelicalism in Conversation with Hinduism, Buddhism and Islam* (Grand Rapids, 2002).

P. M. KRISHNA

HIPPOLYTUS (c. 170–c. 236)

Hippolytus came to Rome from the Eastern Mediterranean, perhaps Egypt, and was the last major ecclesiastical writer in Greek at Rome. A presbyter and then counter-bishop in the church at Rome, he was exiled (c. 235) under Emperor Maximin to Sardinia, where he died.

The facts of his life are obscure, and the authorship of some works attributed to him is disputed. His major work, *Refutation of All Heresies* (*Philosophumena*), attempts to trace the origin of *Gnostic systems and other erroneous teachings to Greek philosophies. He was indebted to *Irenaeus for much of his information on heresies (as he was for much of his theology), but he had access to other sources. His *Commentary on Daniel* is the earliest surviving orthodox commentary; it placed the return of Christ at 500 years after his birth and so sought to quiet anxiety about the end. Similar eschatological concerns are found in *On Christ and Antichrist*. The *Apostolic Tradition* is important for liturgical practices and theology, especially with reference to baptism, Eucharist, ordination and the love feast. Recovery of its text is difficult because it survives mainly in later (expanded) versions. *Against Noetus* opposes the modalism (see *Monarchianism) of Noetus of Smyrna, active at the end of the second century.

Hippolytus led his followers into *schism shortly after Callistus was elected Bishop of Rome in 217. The two men were personal rivals: Hippolytus was educated and came from cultured circles; Callistus was a former slave whose practical abilities had made him a leading deacon. The two men clashed on church *discipline: which sinners could be reconciled to the *church and on what terms, and what would be the church's attitude in fellowship on social and moral questions. Callistus favoured taking a forgiving and moderate approach, willing to reconcile those guilty of sexual sins and to recognize marriages not sanctioned by Roman law. Since the church is a saving society, it should be inclusive in membership. Hippolytus favoured keeping serious sinners under discipline until their deathbed, leaving forgiveness in the hands of God. He wanted a church of the pure. The two men also represented rival *Christologies. Callistus emphasized the oneness of God, trying to walk a middle way between the modalism of Sabellius and what he called the ditheism of Hippolytus. The latter developed his doctrine of Christ from the *Logos Christology of the *apologists and from Irenaeus. The Logos, immanent in God, is eternal, but came forth to have a separate existence in connection with creation and separate personality in the incarnation, when he became fully Son of God.

Hippolytus and Pontianus, Callistus' second successor, were exiled at the same time. They apparently became reconciled, for the two parties reunited and commemorated both men as martyrs. A statue of Hippolytus has been found containing a list of his writings and tables which he prepared for determining the date of *Easter.

Bibliography

A. Brent, *Hippolytus and the Roman Church in the Third Century: Communities in Tension before the Emergence of a Monarch-Bishop* (Leiden, 1995); J. A. Cerrato, *Hippolytus between East and West: The Commentaries and the Provenance of the Corpus* (Oxford, 2002); G. Dix, *The Treatise on the Apostolic Tradition of St Hippolytus of Rome* (London, ²1968); J. H. I. von Döllinger, *Hippolytus and Callistus* (Edinburgh, 1876); D. G. Dunbar, 'The Delay of the Parousia in Hippolytus', *VC* 37, 1983, pp. 313–327; J. M. Hanssens, *La Liturgie d'Hippolyte, Orientalia Christiana Analecta* 155 (Rome, ²1965); J. B. Lightfoot, *The Apostolic Fathers*, part 1, vol. 2 (London, 1890); P. Nautin, *Hippolyte et Josipe: Contribution à l'histoire de la littérature chrétienne du troisième siècle* (Paris, 1947); D. L. Powell, 'The Schism of Hippolytus', *SP* 12, 1975, pp. 449–456; J. E. Stam, 'Charismatic Theology in the "Apostolic Tradition" of Hippolytus', in G. F. Hawthorne (ed.), *Current Issues in Biblical and Patristic Interpretation* (Grand Rapids, 1975); C. Wordsworth, *St Hippolytus and the Church of Rome* (London, ²1880).

E. FERGUSON

HISTORICAL JESUS, QUEST FOR

This phrase achieved currency as the title of the English translation of Albert *Schweitzer's famous survey of attempts to rewrite the life of Jesus (originally published in German under the title *Von Reimarus zu Wrede* – 'From Reimarus to Wrede'). In this work, Schweitzer summarized the main 'lives of Jesus' that were written between the end of the eighteenth century and the beginning of the twentieth. Such works reflected the impact of *Enlightenment *rationalism on NT research: scepticism towards the miraculous, combined with reflection upon the discrepancies between the Gospel accounts (the 'Synoptic Problem'), resulted in a generally low estimation of the value of the canonical Gospels as historical accounts. The 'lives of Jesus' sought to reconstruct the reality behind the texts of the Gospels, assuming that the 'real' Jesus was an ordinary person around whose memory legends had developed and a 'supernatural nimbus' had grown. In fact, Schweitzer saw the scholars behind these lives as projecting their own values onto the figure of *Jesus, memorably likened by George Tyrrell to staring down a deep well and seeing their own faces reflected. A disturbing aspect of this, now a matter of sensitivity in biblical studies, was the extent to which the scholarly reconstructions were based on a belief that the Judaism of Jesus' day was ossified and lifeless and that Jesus came to liberate those who would follow him from its darkness.

The last figure discussed by Schweitzer was William Wrede (1859–1906), who argued that the Gospels were never intended to be historical works, but were theologically motivated and coloured throughout. This made it doubtful whether much reliable information about Jesus could be extracted from them. Such a position was reinforced by such scholars as Rudolph *Bultmann, who used form-criticism to identify secondary additions to the tradition and concluded that the actual historical Jesus is virtually inaccessible to the historian: all that we possess of historical worth is a handful of his sayings. Bultmann himself was, in any case, much more concerned with the development of the *kerygma, the Christian faith that was projected on to Jesus through the construction of *myths. For him, the secondary additions to the Jesus tradition were just as valid as objects of study as the historical Jesus. To appreciate the significance of this, it is important to locate Bultmann within the context of the German theological movements of the early twentieth century, particularly with regard to their concept of *religion. Subsequently, however, many have simplistically taken his project of '*demythologization' as foundational to any historically defensible study of the life of Jesus.

Ernst *Käsemann, one of Bultmann's former students, believed that his teacher had been too extreme in his assessment of the historical worth of the Gospels. Using the 'criterion of dissimilarity', whereby sayings that fit neither within ancient Judaism or early Christianity are deemed plausibly to be the authentic teaching of Jesus, Käsemann sought to retrieve genuine sayings of Jesus. This sparked what James M. Robinson (b. 1924) came to label 'A New Quest of the Historical Jesus' (in more recent times, this has come to be referred to as the 'Second Quest', for reasons explained below). In fact, Robinson's label is slightly misleading; outside of the circle of scholars affected by Bultmann's thought, there had always been scholars who believed, on sound historical grounds, that the Gospels contained reliable information – and rightly so, despite the sweeping indictment of their method by Robinson. Within Germany we should mention Joachim Jeremias (1900–79) and at least spare a thought for K. Bornhäuser (1868–1947), Bultmann's contemporary at Marburg. Outside Germany there was the great British trio of C. H. *Dodd, T. W. Manson (1893–1958) and Vincent Taylor (1887–1968), among others. Despite such misgivings, the label 'New/Second Quest' has endured, probably in part due to the fact that in the early 1980s, N. T. *Wright coined the phrase 'The Third Quest for the Historical Jesus' to denote the new stage of Jesus research that he saw reflected in the work of Ben Meyer, among others. It has now become more or less standard to use this label to denote the current corpus of historical Jesus research.

Again, however, the label may be misleading: it is difficult to see much unity in this corpus of the kind that might allow us to see it as a movement. It is extensive and diverse, reflecting a broad range of opinion on the methods that ought to be used in handling our sources and of the picture of Jesus that can be reconstructed from them. Some contributions, such as those made by the Jesus Seminar collective (which famously voted on the authenticity of Jesus' sayings using coloured balls) are scarcely different from those made by the Second Quest scholars, being largely sceptical of the authenticity of the contents of the Gospels and for the most part focusing on Jesus' sayings, rather than narratives about his actions. Others, however, such as N. T. Wright, have been strikingly conservative, arguing that the Gospels are, in fact, largely reliable accounts and that our picture of Jesus must be reconstructed from his actions as much as from his teachings. Even the common view that the Third Quest has restored to pre-eminence the Jewishness of Jesus needs to be qualified as being too simple an assessment: scholars such as John Dominic Crossan (b. 1934) and Burton Mack have emphasized Hellenistic influence within Galilee and presented Jesus as being rather like the Greco-Roman Cynic philosophers.

Nevertheless, there are some characteristics of the Third Quest that set it apart from its predecessors. Most obviously, the social location of Jesus is a prominent concern; in this respect, the Third Quest reflects the burgeoning interest in the social sciences within biblical studies in recent years. It also, however, reflects the fact that a much more complex methodology is employed in research into the historical Jesus. It is no longer the case that discrete criteria are applied to the Gospel sources in order to distinguish the authentic from the secondary: now the criterion of dissimilarity is balanced by the criterion of plausibility (whether a saying or story of Jesus can be regarded as plausible in the context of first-century Galilee) and others. Another distinctive feature of the Third Quest is the willingness of many of its contributors to question the hegemony of Enlightenment rationalism, often building upon the philosophical explorations of *postmodernity. While many scholars continue to regard the supernatural as either myth or misunderstanding, others are unwilling to dismiss it so easily. As a consequence, the Third Quest has seen at least some constructive theological contribution from biblical scholars, notably N. T. Wright, who has written on

Christological themes and on concepts of justification. Most recently, Pope Benedict XVI (see *Ratzinger, Joseph) has engaged with the Third Quest, dialoguing with its findings as he presents his own more theological understanding of Jesus of Nazareth.

Bibliography

B. Chilton and C. A. Evans, *Studying the Historical Jesus: Evaluations of the State of Current Research* (Leiden and New York, 1994); I. H. Marshall, *I Believe in the Historical Jesus* (London, 1977); J. Ratzinger, *Jesus of Nazareth* (Milan, 2007); B. Witherington III, *The Jesus Quest: The Third Search for the Jew of Nazareth* (Downers Grove, ²1997); N. T. Wright, *The New Testament and the People of God* (London, 1992); idem, *Jesus and the Victory of God* (London, 1996); idem, *The Resurrection of the Son of God* (London: 2003).

G. Macaskill

HISTORICAL THEOLOGY

Since Christian *theology always stands in a tradition in which theologians refer to those who went before them, it has always had a historical dimension. Even the earliest bishops and teachers refer to the apostolic writings of the NT. But it was only with the development of the historical-critical method in the nineteenth century that historical theology developed as a distinct discipline. Before then writers in many fields tended to think of the past as very similar to their present and so often tended to read their own ideas and categories back into previous generations. The new historical consciousness, an awareness that the past was often subtly different from the present, stimulated to some degree by the Romantic movement, led to the development of 'scientific history' in which primary documents from the past were examined critically to establish 'what really happened'. This new ideal of 'scientific objectivity' to establish 'objective facts' separate from interpretation also affected the study of the history of Christian theology.

One key figure, John Henry *Newman, undertook the study of *Patristics, continuing an Anglican tradition of appealing to the Fathers to argue (against Rome) that the Anglican tradition was true to the ancient Catholic Church. But his seminal idea in the *Essay on the Development of Christian Doctrine* (London, 1845), published in the year that he became a Roman Catholic, was to bear fruit in eventual acceptance by Protestants and Roman Catholics that change in doctrine was not necessarily a departure from the faith, but was, at least in the central tradition of Christian theology, a drawing out of previously unseen implications. This challenged the claim of the Roman Catholic Church to be always the same (*semper eadem*), and opened the way to the later *ressourcement* movement ('back to the sources') which prepared the way for the Second *Vatican Council.

But whereas Newman put historical theology at the service of Christian orthodoxy, Adolf von *Harnack, who was to emerge as a spokesman of *Ritschlian *liberalism, believed that objective historical study demonstrated that Christian orthodoxy had departed from the teachings of Jesus. The doctrines of incarnation, Trinity and the atonement were a distortion of his simple message by Greek metaphysics. Harnack's multi-volume *Dogmengeschichte* (1886–90; ET, *History of Dogma*, 1894–99) set new standards of scholarly thoroughness, but despite that, his 'scientific' method did not guarantee the vaunted 'objectivity'. James Orr's *History of Dogma* (1901) deliberately countered Harnack's interpretation, arguing (like Newman) that the historical development was the drawing out of the implications of the Christian message, and his book marked the acceptance of Newman's thesis by evangelicals. Numerous studies since then have generally borne out the Newman-Orr thesis.

The striving for objectivity has had considerable success. One outstanding instance of this is the way in which Roman Catholic scholarship which in the past treated Luther with vituperation has come to a more balanced and positive assessment of his place in the *development of doctrine. Numerous outstanding and definitive works have appeared, including specialist studies of the Fathers such as J. N. D. Kelly's *Early Christian Doctrines* (London, ⁵1977) or R. P. C. Hanson's *The Search for the Christian Doctrine of God* (Edinburgh, 1988) and comprehensive surveys such as Jaroslav Pelikan, *The Emergence of the Catholic Tradition* (5 vols., Chicago, 1971–89), or Justo González, *A History of Christian Thought* (3 vols., Nashville, 1970–75). However, historical research no longer pretends that it can attain absolute objectivity by completely separating 'objective facts' from interpretation.

The question also remains whether historical theology is only a species of *history employing the historical-critical method, or whether it should not also still play its more ancient role within the methodology of Christian theology. The concession that absolute objectivity is a myth raises the question of what presuppositions are acceptable. Theologians may also ask whether the insistence that theologians of the past should be seen only within the context of their own time and *culture does not preclude consideration of the truth of their claims about the God who is not a creature of time or culture. Theologians might well claim that when the historical-critical method rules, the result is actually theological *history*, a branch of the history of ideas, and that true historical *theology* must rather follow a theological methodology. Theologians such as, for example, John *Zizioulas (*Being as Communion*, London, 1985) or T. F. *Torrance (*The Trinitarian Faith*, Edinburgh, 1988), while still paying attention to historical fact and to primary documents, are less interested in the distinctive cultural setting of past theologians, and more interested in engaging them as conversation partners and guides in the task of Christian theology today. This would argue that to reduce historical theology to theological history is to *relativize theological claims. In contrast, however, it could be argued that such an approach raises questions about the methodology of theology itself and how far it is shaped, and should be shaped, by cultural, *contextual circumstances.

See also: DOGMA.

Bibliography

J. Pelikan, *Historical Theology* (New York and London, 1971).

T. A. NOBLE

HISTORY

History, in the sense of the historical process, is recognized by Christians as the sphere of earthly existence where God has dealings with humanity. Although the whole chain of world events, past, present and future, was rarely, if ever, described as 'history' before the late eighteenth century, discussion of its significance has formed part of theology down the ages. In the Bible there are ample materials for constructing an understanding of history, even if (as has been much debated) it contains little elaboration of a theology of history as such. In the OT God is presented as an agent in the historical process. Supremely in the exodus from Egypt, but also in many other events, God displays his power (e.g. Ps. 136). By contrast with the nature deities of surrounding nations, *God *reveals himself primarily in history. In the NT God takes a decisive part in human affairs through Christ, his purposes begin to unfold through the church and it is promised that history will come to an end with Christ's return for *judgment. So the chief biblical convictions about history are that (1) God has been shaping the overall course of the historical process from the beginning in *creation; (2) he intervenes in particular events, usually in judgment or mercy; and (3) he will bring his plans to a triumphant conclusion in the last things. By contrast with the cyclical view of history, widespread in ancient and oriental civilization, that events regularly recur on the seasonal pattern of nature, Christians have therefore held a linear view of history as a process moving towards a climax predetermined by God. His control they have described as *providence; the future climax is the ground for their *hope.

Different Christian estimates of the future have frequently been based on beliefs about the millennium. In particular, if the bliss of the *millennium was to be expected before the end of history, hope could be intensified into an ebullient optimism. By the fourth century, such millenarianism was fading before an 'imperial theology' holding that the Roman Empire was earning God's favour by adopting the Christian faith. Voiced most eloquently by *Eusebius, the first great historian of the church, the imperial theology, together with millenarianism, was sharply challenged by *Augustine. In *The City of God* he propounded a magisterial theology of history according to which the welfare of the community of believers in every age does not depend on temporal power and the millennium is identified with the present history of the church. Augustine's periodization of time into seven epochs was to haunt the medieval Christian imagination. It was not until the rise of *Joachimism in the thirteenth century that Augustine's framework was significantly modified. The teaching of Joachim that history is approaching a new age of the Spirit freed from ecclesiastical forms was to inspire a range of groups including many associated with the *Radical Reformation. Nevertheless, Augustine remained the main influence over the classical Reformers at the same time as cyclical motifs drawn from ancient literature were re-injected into Christian thought by the Renaissance. The last *Augustinian theology of history, the *Discourse on Universal History* (1681) by Bishop J. B. Bossuet (1627–1704), was to be ridiculed for its parochialism by *Voltaire. The *Enlightenment generated its own view of history, a *secularization of the Christian understanding, in the idea of *progress. Philosophies of history, however, were most in vogue in the *Romantic era, when the scheme of *Hegel was but the most elaborate. From the same soil sprang the German tradition of historicism, according to which each society produces its own distinctive values in the course of its history. The tradition could incline, as it did in the hands of F. C. Baur of the *Tübingen School, to discount the possibility of *miracle in history. It eventually led, in the thought of *Troeltsch, to the belief that, without God, all values are relative.

With Troeltsch we enter the lively twentieth-century debates on the relation of faith to history. Perhaps the chief stimulus was the *existentialist claim of *Bultmann that history is irrelevant to faith, a claim to which the new phase of the *quest for the historical Jesus was a response. Another source has been interest in Hegel, the chief influence over both the contention of *Pannenberg that all history is revelatory and the critique of traditional Catholicism in Gustavo *Gutiérrez and some other exponents of *liberation theology. Biblical studies, specially in Gerhard von Rad (1901–71) and Oscar Cullmann, have drawn attention to the centrality of '*salvation-history'. And *Moltmann has argued that *eschatology is the key to understanding history as well as theology. Meanwhile, others have tried to state a Christian understanding of history for our time. Nicolas Berdyaev from an Eastern Orthodox standpoint (see *Russian Orthodox theology), Herman *Dooyeweerd from a Dutch Reformed standpoint and Eric Voegelin (1901–85) from a Lutheran standpoint have wrestled with the issue. Most influential, however, have been Reinhold *Niebuhr, with his rejection of the idea of progress, and Sir Herbert Butterfield (1900–79), a Methodist historian whose *Christianity and History* (1949) discerns God at work in the past. Looming behind these studies is the central question for any Christian philosophy of history, the problem of *suffering, which is perhaps treated most tellingly by P. T. *Forsyth in his wartime work, *The Justification of God* (1916).

Bibliography

D. W. Bebbington, *Patterns in History* (Leicester, 1979); D. P. Fuller, *Easter Faith and History* (London, 1968); V. A. Harvey, *The Historian and the Believer* (London, 1967); C. T. McIntire (ed.), *God, History and Historians: Modern Christian Views of History* (New York, 1977); K. Popper, *The Poverty of Historicism* (London and New York, 1993).

D. W. BEBBINGTON

HISTORY-OF-RELIGIONS SCHOOL

History-of-Religions School is the English translation of the German phrase, *Religionsgeschichtliche Schule*. It designates a group of scholars who in the late nineteenth and early twentieth century attempted to understand the religious developments of the OT, the NT and the early church by relating them to the context of other religious movements. Inspired by *positivist principles, these scholars used historical and philological approaches to explain the origin of biblical religion.

The Old Testament

Hermann Gunkel's *Schöpfung und Chaos in Urzeit und Endzeit* (*Creation and Chaos at the Beginning and End of Time*, Göttingen, 1895) derived much of the OT's themes of creation and chaos from Babylonian mythology. As opposed to Julius Wellhausen (1844–1918), Gunkel (1862–1932) placed this derivation not in the exilic period but in the second millennium BC. Hugo Gressmann (1877–1927) in *Der Ursprung der israelitischjüdischen Eschatologie* (*The Origin of Israelite-Jewish Eschatology*, Göttingen, 1905) attempted to demonstrate the antiquity of the mythological themes found in the prophets. Rudolf Kittel's (1853–1929) *Geschichte des Volkes Israel* (*History of the People of Israel*, rev. edn, Gotha, 1912) maintained that Moses had taught not a monotheism but an 'ethical monolatry'.

The New Testament

Wilhelm Heitmüller (1869–1926) argued in 1903 that Paul's understanding of the *Eucharist was not derived from the original teachings of Jesus but from the Hellenistic world. Wilhelm Bousset (1865–1920) examined the early church as a Hellenistic-Jewish phenomenon. His greatest work, *Kyrios Christos* (1913; ET 1970), set forth the thesis that it was the Gentile Christians in the context of their worship who first addressed Christ as Kyrios ('Lord') in place of the title 'the Son of Man', which derived from Jewish eschatology. Some of the Christians who had been members of the mystery cults thus reinterpreted Christ as their new 'mystery god'.

In his work, *Hauptprobleme der Gnosis* (*The Main Problems of Gnosticism*, 1907), Bousset explained *Gnostic teachings as the result of a transformation of older oriental Hellenistic philosophy. He held it self-evident that Gnosticism existed prior to Christianity.

Richard Reitzenstein (1861–1931) was a philologist who studied the role of mysticism in Hellenism. His *Poimandres* (1904; repr. Darmstadt, 1966) suggested that the Hermetic tractate Poimandres was the source of Johannine thought. He also used late Mandaean (see *Gnosticism) texts to reconstruct the background of Christian baptism in *Die Vorgeschichte der christlichen Taufe* (*The Pre-history of Christian Baptism*, 1924; repr. Darmstadt, 1967).

In his most famous book, *Die hellenistischen Mysterienreligionen* (*Hellenistic Mystery-Religions*, Stuttgart, 1910; ET 1978), Reitzenstein argued that Paul was profoundly influenced by Hellenistic religious traditions such as the mystery religions and Gnosticism. In fact, he went so far as to call Paul the greatest of all the Gnostics.

In his work, *Das iranische Erlösungsmysterium* (*Iranian Mystery Religion*, 1921), Reitzenstein used recently discovered documents from Turkestan to recover the alleged Iranian roots of a pre-Christian Gnosticism – without realizing at the time that these were Manichaean texts. Later he maintained that Manichaeism must have preserved some very ancient Iranian Gnostic traditions.

Appraisal

The views of such scholars as Reitzenstein and Bousset had a great impact upon Rudolf *Bultmann, one of the leading NT scholars of the twentieth century. Despite the enormous impact of the writings of Bousset and Reitzenstein in Europe, their writings were not translated into English in their lifetimes.

The use by the history-of-religions scholars of late and unrelated sources to explain Paul's religion or to reconstruct a hypothetical pre-Christian Gnosticism has been severely criticized. In Earle Ellis's trenchant phrase, 'There is a tendency to convert parallels into influences and influences into sources' (*Paul and His Recent Interpreters*, Grand Rapids, 1961, p. 29).

Bibliography

W. Bousset, *Kyrios Christos* (ET, Nashville, 1970); H. F. Hahn, *The Old Testament in Modern Research* (rev. edn, Philadelphia, 1966), ch. III, 'The Religio-Historical School and the Old Testament'; R. Reitzenstein, *Hellenistic Mystery-Religions* (ET, Pittsburgh, 1978); E. M. Yamauchi, *Pre-Christian Gnosticism* (Grand Rapids, ²1983).

E. M. YAMAUCHI

HODGE, CHARLES (1797–1878)

Charles Hodge was the best-known proponent of the conservative Calvinistic theology that came from the Presbyterian seminary in *Princeton, New Jersey, from its founding in 1812 to its reorganization in 1929. Hodge arrived from his native Philadelphia in 1812 to study at Princeton College, where he was converted during a period of revival. He then entered the seminary and soon became a devoted student and close friend of Archibald Alexander (1772–1851), the professor of theology. Hodge became professor of oriental and biblical literature at Princeton in 1822; in 1840 he was transferred to the chair of exegetical and didactic theology, a position which was augmented by the professorship of polemic theology at Alexander's death in 1851.

Well before then, however, Hodge had proven his mettle as a forceful voice for conservative *Reformed theology against a wide variety of alternatives. Especially in the pages of the *Princeton Review*, which he edited for nearly fifty years, Hodge was a lion in controversy. His adversaries ranged across the theological spectrum – from *Schleiermacher and other Romantic theologians of inward subjectivity, through representatives of the Oxford Movement (see *Anglo-Catholic theology) and nineteenth-century conservative Roman Catholicism, to Americans such as Charles G. *Finney, Horace *Bushnell, John W. Nevin

(1803–86) and Philip Schaff (1819–93) of *Mercersburg, and Nathaniel W. Taylor (1786–1858) and Edwards Amasa Park (1808–1900) from *New England. Hodge's point of view was consistent. He contended for sixteenth- and seventeenth-century understandings of Calvinism. He proclaimed the dangers of unchecked religious experience, whether in the form of sophisticated European *Romanticism or frontier American revivalism. He championed scientific method, understood in terms of Francis Bacon's *empiricism, as the proper way to organize the *infallible teachings of Scripture. But what most troubled him were positions which undercut high Calvinistic convictions about divine sovereignty in salvation or which valued too highly the moral capacities of unregenerate human nature. Hodge could sometimes appear overly rationalistic in these polemics, and he occasionally misread his opponents to their disadvantage; but by and large, he conducted his polemics on a very high plane. After Hodge's death, the Lutheran theologian C. P. Krauth said that 'next to having Hodge on one's side is the pleasure of having him as an antagonist' (A. A. Hodge, Life of Charles Hodge, p. 616).

Although Hodge exerted his greatest efforts in the defence of Calvinism, his interests ranged very widely. He was the author of major commentaries on Romans, Ephesians and 1 and 2 Corinthians. He wrote frequently on Presbyterian ecclesiastical affairs. He penned numerous expositions of Christian teaching for laymen, of which *The Way of Life* (1841) was perhaps the most notable in its limpid prose and affective power. He wrote a not inconsiderable objection to Darwin's apparent assault on the idea of design (*What Is Darwinism?*, 1874). He often commented cogently on public affairs, taking generally conservative positions on social issues. His lifetime's classroom instruction was summed up when he published his *Systematic Theology* in 1872, a work which like many of his other writings remains in print and in use to this day.

It has been noted that Hodge's *Systematic Theology* and some of his polemical essays play down the role of the Holy Spirit and the noncognitive dimensions of the faith. In other writings, however, like his commentaries and works for the laity, these aspects of Christian experience receive much fuller consideration. Hodge probably did not integrate the various aspects of his thought as carefully as one could wish. But his work remains the most effective nineteenth-century American presentation of Calvinism. It is wide-ranging in its concerns, spiritually sensitive in its insights, and thought-provoking in its defence of Reformed distinctives.

Bibliography

Works: *Essays and Reviews: Selections from the Princeton Review* (New York, 1857); *Systematic Theology*, 3 vols. (New York, 1872–3).

Studies: W. S. Barker, 'The Social Views of Charles Hodge (1797–1878): A Study in 19th-century Calvinism and Conservatism', *Presbyterion. Covenant Seminary Review* 1, 1975, pp. 1–22; P. Gutjahr, *Charles Hodge: Guardian of American Orthodoxy* (Oxford, 2011); P. A. Hicks, *The Philosophy of Charles Hodge* (Lewiston, NY, 1997); A. A. Hodge, *The Life of Charles Hodge* (New York, 1880); J. O. Nelson, 'Charles Hodge (1797–1878): Nestor of Orthodoxy', in Willard Thorp (ed.), *The Lives of Eighteen from Princeton* (Princeton, 1946); J. W. Stewart and J. H. Moorhead (eds.), *Charles Hodge Revisited: A Critical Appraisal of His Life and Work* (Grand Rapids, 2002).

M. A. NOLL

HODGSON, L., see ANGLO-CATHOLIC THEOLOGY

HOLINESS, see GOD; HOLINESS MOVEMENT; SANCTIFICATION

HOLINESS MOVEMENTS

Holiness movements in modern Protestantism generally trace back to John *Wesley's teaching that Christians could have an undivided desire to serve God and a 'perfect love' for God that excluded sin. For Wesley, this doctrine of 'Christian perfection' was the 'grand *depositum*' given to 'the people called Methodists'. *Sanctification was the developing work of God from *regeneration to 'entire sanctification' and beyond. But he rejected the term 'sinless perfection' as he recognized continued human weakness and the need for confession of faults and failings (see *Perfection, perfectionism).

In the nineteenth century Wesley's doctrine was refashioned, particularly in America. Phoebe *Palmer, the wife of a New York doctor, led the 'Tuesday meetings for the promotion of holiness' in her home, and went with her husband on preaching tours in Britain and America. She advocated what she called a 'shorter way' to holiness by total consecration, 'laying all on the altar', signified by kneeling at the communion rail. Two prominent Congregationalists, Charles G. *Finney (the most prominent revivalist of the 'second awakening') and Asa *Mahan, both of Oberlin College, Ohio, advocated the view that the day of Pentecost was the 'entire sanctification' of the apostles. This gave them a biblical proof text for the 'second blessing', a 'crisis' in the Christian life. They therefore equated Wesley's 'entire sanctification' with the *Pentecostal 'baptism of the Holy Ghost' (see *Baptism in the Spirit).

By the 1870s the holiness movement had become very influential across American *Methodism. It included two breakaway denominations, the Wesleyan Methodist Church of 1843 and the Free Methodist Church of 1860. The National Camp Meeting Association for the Promotion of Holiness was established at Vineland, New Jersey, in 1867. Of the many smaller churches begun independently, the Pilgrim Holiness Church (1897, uniting with the Wesleyan Methodists in 1968 to form the Wesleyan Church) and the Church of the Nazarene (1908) became the largest. But the holiness tradition also remained within mainstream Methodism, leading to the foundation of Asbury Theological Seminary in 1923.

The holiness movement which began in Methodism was also influential across other American denominations. Congregationalists such as T. C. Upham and R. A. Torrey (D. L. Moody's successor), Presbyterians such as W. E. Boardman (author of *The Higher Christian Life*, 1959), Baptists such as A. B. Earle, as well as Quakers, Mennonites and Episcopalians, all belonged to the '*higher life' movement. Many of them followed Finney's emphasis on the power for service brought by the 'baptism of the Holy Ghost' rather than the Wesleyan emphasis on sanctification and purity of heart.

In Britain (and then around the world), the *Salvation Army emerged as the largest denomination in the Wesleyan holiness tradition. William and Catherine Booth were deeply influenced by Phoebe Palmer (not least in her strong advocacy of women preachers). In British Methodism, those committed to Wesley's doctrine launched the Methodist Southport Convention in 1885, and Cliff College in 1903. Other independent leaders of holiness missions were Richard Reader Harris, QC, who founded the Pentecostal League of Prayer, Francis Crossley of Star Hall, Manchester, Paget Wilkes of the Japan Evangelistic Band, and Oswald Chambers, author of the popular devotional book, *My Utmost for His Highest*.

A further variant of holiness spirituality began with a conference in 1874, when about one hundred people met at Broadlands, in Hampshire, the home of William and Georgina Cowper-Temple. The main speakers, Robert Pearsall Smith and his wife, Hannah Whitall Smith (author of *The Christian's Secret of a Happy Life*, 1875), were Quaker manufacturers from New Jersey who testified to receiving 'the blessing' of victory over sin at a Methodist camp meeting.

Much larger meetings in 1874 and 1875 led to the establishment in 1875 of the annual interdenominational Keswick Convention. Evan Hopkins, one of the early Anglican Keswick leaders, outlined three views of sanctification within *evangelicalism: the Calvinist tradition that holiness was achieved by earnest effort (strongly advocated in this period by Bishop J. C. Ryle), the Wesleyan tradition of the 'clean heart', and the Keswick position of the perpetual 'counteraction' of the sinful nature through 'full surrender'. Keswick teaching gradually found widespread acceptance among British evangelicals in the first half of the twentieth century. The emphasis on consecration, as in the hymns of Francis Ridley Havergal, strongly influenced the Student Volunteer Movement in which hundreds offered themselves for missionary service.

Leading Keswick speakers, who helped to spread the Convention's message of holiness, included Bishop Handley Moule of Durham (previously a Cambridge professor), Andrew *Murray of South Africa, and the Baptist minister Graham Scroggie (awarded a DD by Edinburgh). The Keswick approach has often been regarded as inward-looking, but the speaker who united inner-directed piety and outward-directed social concern was F. B. Meyer, a Baptist minister who became Keswick's leading international speaker. He stressed the power of the Spirit for holiness. In 1955, Keswick's devotional and practical teaching was strongly challenged from the *Reformed perspective in an article by James I. *Packer.

The traditional Keswick emphasis was maintained by speakers such as George Duncan, minister of St George's Tron, Glasgow, but gradually Keswick embraced a more general evangelical spirituality. Both the Wesleyan and Keswick traditions rejected the focus on the *gifts of the Spirit which characterized the new Pentecostal movement after 1900.

In recent years there has been some revival of interest in Wesleyan holiness and in the Keswick tradition, in part because of extensive historical work being done on both evangelicalism and *spirituality. In 2000, in *Transforming Keswick*, Charles Price described Keswick teaching as Bible-based, Christ-centred, Holy Spirit-enabled, practical, and mission orientated. The Wesleyan holiness denominations continue to grow around the world and through the scholarly rediscovery of John Wesley are recovering his more nuanced understanding of sanctification.

Bibliography

S. Barabas, *So Great Salvation: The History and Message of the Keswick Convention* (London, 1952); D. W. Bebbington, *Holiness in Nineteenth-Century England* (Carlisle, 2000); D. Bundy, *The Global Impact of the Wesleyan Traditions and Their Related Movements* (Portland, 2002); M. E. Dieter, *The Holiness Revival of the Nineteenth Century* (Metuchen, 1980); C. E. Jones, *Perfectionist Persuasion* (Lanham, 1974); W. C. Kostlevy, *Historical Dictionary of the Holiness Movement* (Portland, 2001); C. Price and I. M. Randall, *Transforming Keswick* (Carlisle, 2000); I. M. Randall, *Evangelical Experiences* (Carlisle, 1999).

I. M. RANDALL

HOLL, KARL (1866–1926)

Karl Holl was a distinguished German church historian, who was professor of church history at Tübingen (1901–6) and Berlin (1906–26). His *Habilitationsschrift* was on Greek monasticism (1896), followed by works on *John of Damascus (1897), and Amphilochius of Iconium (c. 340–95) in 1904. He later assumed the editorship of the 'Berlin Corpus' of the Greek Fathers (*Griechische Christliche Schriftsteller*), and in this series published his renowned three-volume edition of Epiphanius (c. 315–403) (1915–33). During these years of intensive research on the Greek Fathers he also worked on *Luther, as well as *Calvin and the Enthusiasts (see *Reformation, Radical). These years culminated in his epoch-making *Gesammelte Aufsätze* (*Collected Essays*, vol. 1, 1921, ⁷1948; vols. 2–3, 1928, ²1932). It was his immense knowledge of patristics which, reinforced with his unique grasp of Luther, gave both originality and independence to his judgments as well as an interest in *systematic theology. He was no party man, for his interests were wide, covering Russian as well as English church history; this breadth of outlook gave him a balanced and informed mind. He reacted against certain emphases of Lutheran orthodoxy, notably the forensic view of *justification (as formulated by *Melanchthon rather than Luther). More than any other single person it was he who was responsible for the Luther renaissance of the 1920s.

His contribution lies first in that he made the sole basis of his thought the exact historical and philological study of sources. Secondly, he related Luther to the whole spiritual and historical development of the West, thereby making Luther of intense contemporary significance. Thirdly, he showed Luther's to be a theocentric religion based on man's relation to God, a theology of *conscience.

Bibliography

W. Bodenstein, *Die Theologie Karl Holls* (Berlin, 1968); A. Jülicher and E. Wolf, *RGG* III, cols. 431–433; W. Pauck, introd. to ET of Holl's *The Cultural Significance of the Reformation* (New York, 1959); J. M. Stayer, *Martin Luther, German Saviour: German Evangelical Theological Factions and the Interpretation of Luther, 1917–1933* (Montreal, 2000); J. Wallmann, *TRE* XV, pp. 514–518.

J. ATKINSON

HOLOCAUST

The genocide of around 6 million Jews in Europe through systematic/industrialized murder by the Nazis in the years 1941–45 is commonly known as 'Holocaust'. Some interpretations would include the beginning of the Second World War in 1939, or the onset of state persecution of Jews with the Nazi rise to power in Germany in 1933 in their definition of Holocaust. Derived from the Greek word in the LXX for a wholly burned offering (e.g. Lev.

6:23), and originally used figuratively of wholesale sacrifice, the term has been used since the late 1950s for this specific series of events. Some definitions also include 5 million non-Jews who were murdered by the Nazis between 1933 and 1945 across Nazi-occupied Europe. While the history of the term 'holocaust' suggests that prior to this time it had been commonly used to describe catastrophes of both human and natural origin, the sacrificial connotations of the term as well as its undifferentiated use for different groups of victims of the Nazis have been criticized. In order to clarify the distinctive aim (total annihilation) of the organized racist persecution of Jews by Nazi Germany, many prefer the Hebrew term *Shoah*, meaning complete destruction. Equally biblical in origin (e.g. Job 30:14; Ps. 35:8; Isa. 6:11) the term does not refer to sacrificial contexts. In modern Hebrew, *shoah* is also used to refer to other disasters caused by humans or nature. In some religious Jewish circles, the Yiddish/Hebrew term *Hurban* is preferred, as it stresses the continuity of the Nazi genocide with other events in Jewish history such as the destruction of the First and Second Temples, the Crusades, etc.

Christians have responded to the Holocaust with increased theological reflection on the relationship of Christians to Jews, the church to the synagogue. This includes reflection on Christian responsibility for anti-Semitism and Christian complicity in Nazi policies and their application, as well as a rethinking of Christian aims to convert Jews to Christianity. Johann Baptist *Metz and Jürgen *Moltmann are two theologians whose theologies are motivated in part by reflection on the Holocaust and the consequences of this genocide for the future of Christianity and Christian-Jewish relations. Metz's political theology asks students of theology to beware of theologies that purport to be the same before and after the Holocaust. Moltmann's recasting of the major themes of systematic theology is influenced by his reading of Holocaust literature (notably Elie *Wiesel's *Night*) and works by Jewish religious scholars such as Abraham Joshua Heschel. The works of Franklin Littell and Roy Eckardt as well as Paul van Buren focus explicitly on the Holocaust, arguing that because of Christian culpability for the development of racist anti-Semitism, reflection on this genocide should form the centre of Christian theology after 1945. There is general agreement among these theologians that the Holocaust marks such a break in human history that history can no longer be understood as an evolution from lower to higher forms of civilization.

Jews have responded to the Holocaust with systematic reflection as well as practical social restructuring and rebuilding. Theologically, both Jews and Christians raise the question, 'Where was God?' in the Holocaust. While Jewish theologians struggle with the question of whether God abandoned God's people, the covenant and the implications of the Holocaust for *theodicy, questions regarding the responsibility of humanity ('Where was "man"?') are often foregrounded. Jewish theological reflections on the Holocaust are rarely 'systematic' in the sense this term carries in Christian theology. Rather, they address a concrete historical situation and aim to derive insights from history as well as contemporary Jewish practice in order to establish possible interpretations of the Holocaust which would be helpful for Jewish life in the present. It is characteristic that the majority of Jewish theologians who make the Holocaust a central focus of their work are at home in Reform and Liberal Jewish movements, while for the most prolific Orthodox scholars of the twentieth century the Holocaust, though certainly central to their experience and interpretation of Jewish life, does not become a sustained theological trope. In addition, interpretations of the Holocaust in other areas, such as art, literary criticism, sociology and history, can equally be seen as ways in which Jews struggle with the legacy of the Holocaust. An increased movement towards memorialization is recognizable in Israel and many Western countries which, though sometimes motivated by Jewish concerns, has also captured the interests of wider society.

Most church statements relating to the Holocaust and Christian-Jewish relations are formulated in Western countries who share concerns associated with the Holocaust. Arguably, this is due to the fact that churches in Europe were historically affected by the Holocaust and its aftermath, and churches in North America share historical ties with European churches, often feeling the need to reflect on their own church politics during the Holocaust. With the exception of North America, churches outside of Europe have, in the majority, not come forward with declarations on the Holocaust and Christian-Jewish relations.

It should be noted that Christian theology that explicitly focuses on the Holocaust is the province of few, mostly liberal Christian scholars. A few evangelical theologians have recently also begun to engage in this field, often with an interest in the interpretation of the State of Israel for contemporary Christian views of Jews. Some Christian theologians reflecting on the Holocaust construct a dependence of Christianity on Jews, suggesting more or less strongly that after the Holocaust Christian worship and the future existence of the church depend on the continued existence of the Jewish people as Jews. These theologies also posit a close salvation-historical connection between Jews and Christians, arguing that without the continuity of God's covenant with Jews, the Christian connection with the God of Israel is severed.

As far as the wider Christian community is concerned, these positions do not enter the mainstream, hence are not part of theological controversies. Conservative Christians do not focus theological reflection on the Holocaust, and in the majority object to the theological and doctrinal demands of Christian Holocaust theologians, perceiving these as distortions of Christian doctrine.

See also: JUDAISM AND CHRISTIANITY.

Bibliography

Z. Braitermann, *(God) After Auschwitz: Tradition and Change in Post-Holocaust Jewish Thought* (Princeton, 1998); P. M. van Buren, *A Theology of the Jewish-Christian Reality, Parts I-III* (San Francisco, 1981–8); J. S. Conway, 'The Changes in Recent Decades in the Churches' Doctrine and Practice Toward Judaism and the Jewish People', in Y. Gutman and A. Saf (eds.), *Major Changes Within the Jewish People in the Wake of the Holocaust: Proceedings of the Ninth Yad Vashem International Historical Conference, Jerusalem, June 1993* (Jerusalem, 1996), pp. 589–612; D. Engel, *The Holocaust: A History of the Third Reich and the Jews* (Harlow, 2000); R. P. Ericksen and S. Heschel (eds.), *Betrayal: German Churches and the Holocaust* (Minneapolis, 1999); E. S. Fiorenza and D. Tracy (eds.), *The Holocaust as Interruption*, Concilium 175 (Edinburgh, 1984); S. R. Haynes, *Prospects for Post-Holocaust Theology* (Atlanta, 1991); S. L. Jacobs (ed.), *Contemporary Christian Responses to the Holocaust*, Studies in the Shoah V (Lanham, 1993); *idem, Contemporary Jewish Responses to the Holocaust*, Studies in the Shoah V (Lanham, 1993); S. T. Katz, *Post-Holocaust Dialogues: Critical Studies in Modern Jewish Thought* (New York and London, 1983); J.-B. Metz and J. Moltmann, *Faith in the Future: Essays on Theology, Solidarity, and Modernity* (Maryknoll, 1995); Secretariat for Ecumenical and Interreligious Affairs, and National Conference of Catholic Bishops (eds.), *Catholics Remember the Holocaust* (Washington DC, 1998).

K. H. HOLTSCHNEIDER

HOLY SPIRIT

A formulated doctrine of the Holy Spirit was a relatively late arrival on the Christian theological scene and has never been developed in as full and detailed a way as many other dogmatic themes. In the early centuries attention was concentrated on controversies about the *Trinity and the person of Christ rather than on the Spirit. As *Gregory of Nazianzus puts it in the fourth century, 'It was not right while the deity of the Father was not yet acknowledged plainly to proclaim the Son, nor when that of the Son was not yet received to burden us further . . . with the Holy Spirit' (Gregory of Nazianzus, *Fifth Theological Oration on the Holy Spirit*, para. XXXVI).

That quotation not only describes the order in which the doctrinal questions were historically addressed; it hints that to speak theologically of the Spirit has special difficulties that make it a 'burden'. More than that, it reflects the NT perspective summed up in the words of Jesus about the Spirit: 'He will not speak on his own' (John 16:13). There is a reticence about the Holy Spirit in that he constantly points us away from himself as he initiates us into knowledge of and relationship with the Father and the Son.

The Spirit and the *creed

Pneumatology, the technical term for the doctrine of the Holy Spirit, has three main concerns: (1) the relationship of the Spirit to the Father and the Son within the trinitarian life of *God; (2) the work of the Spirit in imparting knowledge of God and new life in Christ to the Christian community and individual believers within it; and (3) the relation of the Spirit to God's purposes of creation and re-creation in the world. This article will deal almost exclusively with the first two of these headings because they have been the central concerns of the mainline theological tradition; the third has remained marginal until our own day.

Concentration on the theology of the Holy Spirit emerged in the fourth century with *Athanasius' *Letters to Serapion*. This was followed by *Basil of Caesarea's important treatise, *On the Holy Spirit* (c. 350), which proved highly influential for all that was to follow. The first detailed dogmatic statement about the Spirit, along the lines laid down by Basil, is in the third article of the *Nicene Creed as it was revised at *Constantinople in 381, where the Spirit is confessed as 'the Lord, the giver of life, who with the Father and the Son is to be worshipped and glorified'.

Here the divinity of the Spirit is clearly affirmed, he has the same title of divine lordship as the Father and the Son and along with them is a proper object of worship. That implies that the Spirit is not an impersonal divine energy, nor simply a way of describing how the Father and the Son relate to us and act upon us, but is himself a source of personal action who, in his own special way, expresses in his relationships and actions the same sovereign love as the Father and the Son.

According to the basic NT witness, the distinctive work of the Spirit is to enable us to confess God as *Abba*, Father (Rom. 8:15) and Jesus as *Kyrios*, Lord (1 Cor. 12:3). According to John 16:14, it is the Spirit who brings to the Son the glory of being known and loved by the company of believers. All this requires that he should be recognized as one who shares the divine nature, but who interacts personally with the Father and the Son in the work of salvation. Later both Eastern and Western tradition followed Athanasius and Gregory Nazianzen in affirming the Spirit as well as the Son to be *homoousios* (of the same being) with the Father, so making the affirmation of his essential divinity secure.

In the creed of 381 the emphasis of the third article is on the Spirit's trinitarian relationships: his relationship to us both in creation and redemption is affirmed in the most general terms as the 'giver of life' and the one who has 'spoken through the prophets'. This is quite inadequate to the rich NT material on the work of the Spirit and cries out for fuller development.

A further inadequacy in *patristic teaching about the Spirit comes to light in the *Christology promulgated at *Chalcedon in 451, in which Christ is declared to be both fully God and fully man without reference to the Spirit as the agent of his incarnation, who comes upon him in his baptism and who, as he himself confesses at Nazareth (Luke 4) inspires and energizes his ministry. The neglected role of the Spirit in the constitution of the person and work of Christ has become a subject of keen theological debate in our own day.

Son and Spirit in East and West

In the following centuries the *Orthodox East and the *Catholic West increasingly diverged in the way that they developed their trinitarian theology, not least in the way that they understood the relationship between the Spirit and the Son. This came to a head in the so-called *filioque* dispute, in which the East insisted that the Spirit like the Son had his eternal origin only in the Father, while the West, under the influence of St *Augustine, insisted that the Spirit proceeded 'from the Father *and the Son*' (Lat. *filioque*). At first sight this looks like an ancient dispute without contemporary relevance, but on closer examination, we can see that it involves issues that are central to a proper understanding of the Christian gospel.

The Catholic West alleged that the position of the Orthodox East did not take adequate account of the dependence of the work of the Spirit upon the work of the Son and at least opened the door to a possibility of relating to the Spirit without at the same time relating to the Son. This could lead to a unfocused spirituality to which the person and work of Christ was not central or even to a pluralistic understanding of other religions as works of the Spirit even when they rejected Christian claims about Christ.

The East retorted that such fears were unfounded, because the confession that both Son and Spirit were *homoousios* with the Father, and so with each other, meant that any possibility of relating to the one without relating to the other was totally excluded.

Eastern theologians in turn alleged against the West that its *filioque* teaching subordinated the Spirit to the Son and was in danger of understanding the Spirit simply as the way in which the ascended Christ acted in and among his people. This could lead to a binitarian

(= two person) rather than a properly trinitarian (= three person) doctrine of God.

The East claimed that the scriptural data pointed not to a one-way dependence of the Spirit upon the Son, but to a mutual interdependence in which the incarnate Son was totally reliant upon the Spirit whom he received from the Father, while the Spirit was sent into the world through and as a result of the ministry and atoning work of the Son. As the first systematic theologian, *Irenaeus of Lyons, put it in the second century, the Son and the Spirit were the two hands of God who were sent from the Father and worked in total co-ordination to inaugurate, execute and complete his creative and saving purposes in the world.

The East-West dialogue on the relation of Son and Spirit, broken off by the schism between them, has been resumed in our own day with positive prospects and the suggestion that the legitimate claims made by both sides might be reconciled and satisfied if the disputed creedal phrase were amended to read 'who proceeds from the Father *through* the Son'. The point that is relevant to both evangelical and charismatic Christians in our own day is to insist that there can be no dealing with the Spirit that does not involve a dealing with the Son and no dealing with the Son that does not involve a dealing with the Spirit.

In the Catholic West the *filioque* clause was incorporated into the creeds and either accepted or defended by all the major shapers of the theological tradition from Augustine, through Anselm and Aquinas, Luther and Calvin to Karl Barth in our own day.

The Spirit in the Catholic West

The way that tradition developed gave substance to the Orthodox claim that it involved a downgrading of the Spirit and his work. In Augustine's trinitarianism the Father and Son were seen as the Lover and the Beloved, and the Spirit as the love that bound them together. Love, however, is a relationship between persons rather than itself a third person, so that such a model lends itself to the depersonalization of the Spirit.

It is not therefore surprising to find that when the West began, as it increasingly did, to reflect on God's interaction with us in the giving and receiving of salvation, it spoke not of an interpersonal transaction between the Spirit and the believer, but rather of an impersonal infusion of grace through the sacraments mediated or even controlled by the ordained priesthood. In such a context there was not much interest in the person and work of the Spirit.

The Reformation approach

The Reformation marked a new approach to pneumatology, notably in the theology of John *Calvin. Calvin saw the appropriation of the salvation which had been achieved once for all in Christ as the personal action of the Holy Spirit. What Christ did *for* us remained ineffective until the Spirit brought us to faith and joined us to Christ. This established the closest connection between the Holy Spirit and our justification and sanctification in Christ (see *Salvation).

For the *Reformation tradition with its emphasis on the authority of *Scripture (see doctrine of), the inspiration of the authors of Scripture by the Spirit was of central importance and has led to an ongoing debate about exactly how that inspiration is to be understood. Calvin taught that the Spirit was at work not only in the biblical writers but also in their readers. It was the 'internal witness of the Spirit' that persuaded us that the Bible was the written word of God and enabled us to believe its message. This teaching has been expanded as an integral part of Karl Barth's doctrine of *revelation where the Spirit not only opens the Scriptures to us, but through their witness enables us to believe in Jesus Christ as the Word of God incarnate for our salvation through whom we know the Father.

The neglected theme of the Christological dimension of the Spirit's part in the constitution of Christ's person was explored by the Puritan John *Owen in the seventeenth century, a subject developed by Edward *Irving in the nineteenth century. Irving's distinctive contribution has been more valued in our day than in his own but remains controversial.

*Pietism and the eighteenth-century evangelical revival led by Wesley and Whitefield brought a new emphasis on 'the new birth'. In *evangelical theology in general the Spirit was characteristically presented as the agent of our regeneration and sanctification and led to a keen debate between Calvinists and Arminians about how the divine initiative of the Spirit and the human response of faith were related to each other.

The rise of Pentecostalism

In the nineteenth century the *Holiness movement radically interpreted, or (some would say) distorted, John Wesley's teaching on sanctification with a new focus on Pentecost as evidence of a 'second blessing' beyond regeneration described as 'the *baptism in the Holy Spirit', which could be experienced by those who fulfilled the requisite conditions for its reception.

This gave rise to a variety of second-blessing theologies, some of which looked to the Spirit to confer complete cleansing from sin or *perfection, but others to a filling with the Spirit that empowered people for mission and service and bestowed on them some of the charismatic *gifts described in 1 Cor. 12. This latter teaching was the distinguishing mark of the *Pentecostal movement and, from the time of the revivals of the early twentieth century, the initial evidence of this Spirit-baptism was characteristically held to be the exercise of the gift of tongues.

In the mid-twentieth century this experience of renewal in the Spirit began to be sought and found in nearly all the mainline Christian denominations, Catholic and Protestant, and gave rise to much debate about the soundness of the theological presuppositions on which it was based, with various attempts to reinterpret what was happening in terms of more traditional Reformed, Catholic or Anglican doctrinal approaches.

Whatever their practical and theological excesses and shortcomings, the Pentecostal and *Charismatic Movements have been transforming both for individuals and churches and have helped us to reappropriate the NT emphasis on the Spirit not just as the giver of new birth and personal holiness, but the powerful driving force that motivates and equips Christians for participation in God's *mission in the world. Pentecostal Christianity has been a major force in the massive spread of the gospel in the third world.

The Spirit and the trinitarian revival

This new openness to the Spirit has been replicated in mainline theology. In the pneumatology that predominated in nineteenth-century Protestant liberalism the distinction between the immanent human spirit that is our possession and the transcendent Spirit who is God's gift in Christ became at best unclear, with the danger that more attention was paid to religious experience than to biblical revelation.

That trend was challenged and to a large extent reversed by the revival of trinitarian theology starting with Karl *Barth and Karl *Rahner. The Spirit was again seen as the gift of the Father conferred through his Son to regenerate and sanctify his people and to resource them for their witness to the world. This emphasis on the Spirit as the inspirer and enabler of missionary outreach to the world, echoing as it does the first chapters of Acts, has been characteristic of contemporary pneumatology and has found eloquent and insightful expression in the work of the Anglican, John V. Taylor.

Barth himself remained true to the Western theological tradition by defending the *filioque* and maintaining a one-way dependence of the Spirit on the Son. The post-Barth theologians have not all followed him in this. Jürgen *Moltmann has argued for a distinctiveness of the divine persons that has opened him to a charge of incipient tritheism. Wolfhart *Pannenberg has proposed a trinitarian doctrine of *creation in which the order and reliability of the creation is seen as having its basis in the Son who is also the Logos, while the dynamic movement of the creation from its divine origin to its divine fulfilment is the work of the Spirit who is the Lord and Giver of Life.

In terms of ecclesiology (the doctrine of the *church), the Orthodox theologian, John *Zizioulas, has suggested that the life of the people of God is *in*stituted by the Son but *con*stituted by the Spirit. What Christ has done once for all in his own humanity at the beginning is reproduced and reflected by the Spirit so that the life of the people of God is constituted by what he does among them. This is reflected in the sacrament which was instituted by Jesus, but has its power and efficacy through the Spirit who makes Jesus savingly present to those who in faith eat his bread and drink from his cup.

So also in contemporary understanding of *worship, in line with Rom. 8:26–27, emphasis is laid on prayer and praise as themselves the gift and work of the Spirit, rather than the product of human attempts to reach God.

All in all, this is a time of great pneumatological debate and creativity in which the person and work of the Spirit are being explored within the trinitarian context where they belong and in the context of experience and worship that testify to their reality. If different times in Christian history have concentrated on the different theological themes that their situation called upon them to clarify, our own day may be credibly described as the era when the theology of the Holy Spirit is at last coming into its own.

Bibliography

J. Calvin, *Institutes of the Christian Religion* (Philadelphia, 1960); Y. Congar, *I Believe in the Holy Spirit* (London and New York, 1980); G. Fee, *God's Empowering Presence* (London, 1994); A. I. C. Heron, *The Holy Spirit* (London, 1983); J. Moltmann, *The Spirit of Life* (London, 1992); J. I. Packer, *Keep in Step with the Spirit* (Old Tappan and Leicester, 1984); T. A. Smail, *The Giving Gift* (London and Eugene, 1994); J. V. Taylor, *The Go-Between God* (London, 1972); M. Vischer (ed.), *Spirit of God, Spirit of Christ* (London, 1981); J. M. Welker, *God the Spirit* (London, 1994); J. Zizioulas, *Being as Communion* (London, 1985).

T. A. SMAIL

HOMOOUSIOS, see ARIANISM; ATHANASIUS; CREEDS; TRINITY

HOMOSEXUALITY, see SEXUALITY

HOOKER, RICHARD (c. 1553–1600)

Hooker was an *Anglican theologian and apologist. Apart from a famous controversy with the *Puritan Walter Travers (c. 1548–1635) at the Temple Church in 1586, Hooker's life was uneventful (Fellow of Corpus Christi College, Oxford, 1577–84, master of the Temple, 1585–91, and rural incumbencies), but his later years were devoted to the writing of his masterpiece, *Of the Laws of Ecclesiastical Polity*, of which Books I–IV were published in 1593 and Book V in 1597. The remaining books, which Hooker apparently failed to put into final form, were published after his death (VI and VIII, 1648, VII, 1662). The authenticity of these last three books, once discredited because their views on monarchy and episcopacy were not those of the later seventeenth-century Church of England, has been vindicated by modern scholarship. Hooker's aim in the *Polity* was to defend the Elizabethan Church of England against Puritan criticisms of its polity, ceremonies and liturgy.

Like most Anglican theologians of his day, Hooker was at first preoccupied with apologetic against Rome, and only after his controversy with Travers did he make the defence of the Elizabethan ecclesiastical establishment against the Puritans his major concern. Although his Puritan critics, including Travers, regarded him as dangerously sympathetic to the Church of Rome, and traditional interpretation of Hooker has praised his ecumenical outlook, in fact his attitude to Roman Catholicism was only a little more generous than that of most of his Protestant contemporaries. His allegiance to the royal supremacy (the monarch's role as governor of the Church of England) and the doctrine of separate national churches, and his firm conviction that *justification by faith alone is essential to true Christianity, made him view the Roman Catholic doctrines of the *papacy and justification as extremely serious errors. However, without surrendering a fundamentally *Protestant position, Hooker's very independent theological development produced, in the *Polity*, a theology less influenced by continental Reformed theology and more influenced by the Fathers and, especially, the medieval scholastics, than that of any of his Anglican contemporaries.

Hooker's approach to anti-Puritan apologetic in the *Polity* differed from that of other Elizabethan apologists, who debated detailed differences over polity and *liturgy on the basis of a common Calvinist theological position (see *Reformed theology). Hooker's method was to produce a broad theological structure on which to base his defence of the details of the ecclesiastical establishment. By broadening the whole discussion and setting the immediate issues of the controversy in the context of a comprehensive theological structure of his own creation, Hooker produced a work of controversy which was also an enduring contribution to the English theological tradition. His theology is not at all representative of the 'Anglican' theology of his day, but later became a major influence on the emergence of a distinctively Anglican theological tradition.

In opposition to what he saw as the Puritans' unbalanced reliance on Scripture alone as a sufficient guide in all religious and ecclesiastical matters, Hooker went back to the scholastic (especially *Thomist) synthesis of reason and *revelation, with its appropriation of both the *Aristotelian and *Platonic philosophical traditions (see *Faith and reason). On this basis, Hooker created a vision of the universe ordered by reason expressed in *law. All reality is or should be governed by a harmonious structure of rational law, which extends from the eternal law of God's own being, through the natural laws of creation and human reason, and the positive divine law revealed in Scripture, to the human positive laws of church and state. As all being, in its various levels, derives from God, so all law, in its various levels, derives from the rational law of God's being. Thus both Scripture and human reason, expressed in antiquity, tradition and political authority based in implicit consent, belong within a universal and hierarchical rational order. The stress is on harmony rather than conflict, so that reason in the form of tradition and authority may be expected to complement and interpret revelation.

From this structure the profound conservatism of Hooker's thought follows, making his work a massively uncritical defence of the status quo in church and *state. An organic, hierarchical, law-governed concept of the universe supports an organic, hierarchical, law-governed concept of human society. The rational nature of hierarchy, law and tradition provides the rational basis for the necessity of obedience to the established order. The harmony of revelation and reason supports the integral harmony of church and state, as co-extensive aspects of the one Christian society.

In his defence of the Anglican liturgy against the Puritans, Hooker extols the value of beauty and order in external ceremonies and signs, plays down the necessity for preaching, and gives a central role to the sacraments. Within a general context of the harmony of nature and grace (see *Natural theology), Hooker's theology is incarnational and sacramental. The *sacraments effect our participation in Christ who is humanity's participation in God.

Hooker had little influence in his lifetime, but during the seventeenth century, with the growth of an Anglican theology which distanced itself from Calvinism, he attained his position as the Anglican apologist par excellence. Especially this was the case after the Restoration (1660), when, with the aid of Izaac Walton's tendentious and unreliable biography, the Restoration bishops promoted Hooker's theology as the quintessence of Anglicanism, while at the same time creating an image of Hooker more in line with the principles of the Restoration Church of England than the historical Hooker was.

To the influence of Hooker, traditional Anglican theology owes much of its reasonable moderation, its sense of the harmony of *Scripture and tradition, faith and reason, grace and nature, church and state, its boast of representing the golden mean between Roman and Protestant extremes, and its social and political conservatism.

Bibliography

Works: *Of the Laws of Ecclesiastical Polity*, 4 vols. (Folger Library edn, Cambridge, MA, 1977–82); *The Works of Mr Richard Hooker*, ed. J. Keble, 7th edn rev. by R. W. Church and F. Paget, 3 vols. (Oxford, 1888).

Studies: R. K. Faulkner, *Richard Hooker and the Politics of a Christian England* (Berkeley, 1981); W. Speed Hill (ed.), *Studies in Richard Hooker* (Cleveland, 1972); P. E. Hughes, *Faith and Works: Cranmer and Hooker on Justification* (Wilton, 1982); O. Loyer, *L'Anglicanisme de Richard Hooker*, 2 vols. (Lille, 1979); A. S. McGrade (ed.), *Richard Hooker and the Construction of Christian Community* (Arizona, 1997); P. Munz, *The Place of Hooker in the History of Thought* (London, 1952/1971).

R. J. BAUCKHAM

HOPE

In Christian theology the understanding of hope initially rests in God's promises communicated to humanity. In other words, hope is grounded in the God who established a relationship with all of creation, but is specifically revealed in God's creation of humanity. Eventually, the final *revelation on which hope rests is interpreted through Christ. In this the final revelation is expressed in Christ's victory over sin, death and hell through his *resurrection.

In the mid 1960s Jürgen *Moltmann articulated the meaning of Christian hope in his book, *The Theology of Hope*. Moltmann set the agenda for insisting that the centre for theological thought was in the eschatological hope in Christ. The concept of hope and the related idea of *eschatology became the hermeneutic for theology and a basis for rethinking Christian *social ethics. Wolfhart *Pannenberg continued this theme with the publication *Revelation as History*. For Pannenberg, God is ahead of us, making all things new. The future is now to be brought into the present through Christ the God-man. Crucial to both Moltmann and Pannenberg was Karl *Barth's Christology, which countered the previous influence of

Friedrich *Schleiermacher's liberalism. Although both Moltmann and Pannenberg have received a wide variety of critical assessments, they set the agenda for a rigorous *Christological focus on Christian hope.

For both Moltmann and Pannenberg, their work continued on a biblical focus regarding the affirmation of the historical *Jesus as an eschatological prophet. Through Jesus' words and deeds we gain an insight into the future hope in the present. Jesus proclaimed, 'The *kingdom of God has come near' (Mark 1:15), meaning that the future has now become present, and, in his eventual death and historical resurrection, there now was confidence in Christ as the hope for the future for both humanity and all of creation. The resurrection of Christ was the culmination of his entire ministry from birth to death. At every stage of Jesus' life he defeated the powers of evil and won a decisive victory. Hope now centred in the person of Christ and in his work. Importantly, the affirmation was clear that in Christ came the universal hope for all (Col. 1:20).

With Christ bringing the future into the present, Christian theology was now to run counter to the world of *evil powers. This meant that patience, a fruit of the Spirit, does not translate into inactivity. Since God's mission is reconciliation (see *Atonement), the church is given the ministry of reconciliation to the world (2 Cor. 5:18–19), as difficult as this may be. Here, with active patience, the future expectation does not lose sight of God's presence with us (Matt. 1:23). Trials and tribulations are to be expected, but they do not lead to despair (Rom. 5:1–5), for it is the ministry of the church, in light of Christian hope, that protests against the prevailing evil powers. This leads to the conclusion that no political system deserves ultimate allegiance, so a theological protest is always necessary since the hope for the future is made secure in God's mission to the world.

Christian hope is to be understood in light of the *trinitarian activity. The Father who sent the Son to take human flesh (John 1:14) and live with humanity, also sent the eschatological Spirit who brings Christ's victory over sin, death and hell into the Christian experience. Holiness, then, is not only a specific human spiritual reality, but with the Spirit there is holiness and renewal in the Christian community, and within the Christian community the emphasis on renewal and reconciliation is displayed at the Lord's Table in sacramental action. This leads to a renewed emphasis on the interpretation of God's *creation as a 'new heavens and a new earth' (Isa. 65:17–25). Such a mission is accomplished through Christ, empowered by the *Holy Spirit. With our hope in Christ we have been sealed with the Holy Spirit (Eph. 1:12–13) as the foretaste of how the present is to be recreated. God's promised hope is 'Yes' in Christ (2 Cor. 1:20–22) and is made present in the power of the Holy Spirit.

Near the end of Moltmann's early work on Christian hope he made it abundantly clear that hope creates *mission, and so it is the church's mission to establish hope throughout the world. Moltmann stated, 'One of the first senses in which this happens is in the missionary proclamation of the gospel, that no corner of this world should remain without God's promise of new creation through the power of the resurrection' (*Theology of Hope*, p. 328). Primarily, hope does not begin in human effort. Hope begins in the resurrected Christ with whom the church is empowered by the Holy Spirit. It is this eschatological community, in mission, that brings hope into every corner of the world.

Bibliography

R. Bauckham and T. Hart, *Hope Against Hope: Christian Eschatology in Contemporary Context* (London, 1999); K. E. Brower and M. W. Elliot (eds.), *'Let the Reader Understand': Eschatology in Bible and Theology* (Leicester, 1997); J. Moltmann, *Theology of Hope* (ET, London, 1967); W. Pannenberg (ed.), *Revelation as History* (ET, London and New York, 1969).

D. L. RAINEY

HOPE, THEOLOGY OF

'Theology of Hope' refers principally to two theologians, Wolfhart *Pannenberg and Jürgen *Moltmann. 'Hope' designates their emphasis on the future as the place of divine action. Pannenberg and Moltmann are best understood as responding to two impulses in twentieth-century theology: Karl's *Barth's focus on divine revelation and the recovery of *eschatology. They accepted Barth's focus, but criticized him for presenting revelation as the Word that existentially encounters us. In response, borrowing an idea from G. W. F. *Hegel, they held that history in its totality is the revelation of God. Eschatology thus became for them a critical theme, for the totality of *history, which is God's revelation, is in our future. Yet this eschatological future is not simply in the future; in the resurrection of Jesus Christ it has entered into the midst of our history. Hope is thus grounded in a revelatory future that has, in a preliminary way, already taken place. In later developments, Pannenberg and Moltmann placed increasing emphasis on the doctrine of the Trinity, emphasizing the social analogy in contrast to Barth's Augustinian approach. They also articulated powerful ways of understanding the doctrine of creation. Additionally, Moltmann expressly connected the principle of hope to *liberation theology and to Martin Luther's theology of the cross.

Bibliography

J. Moltmann, *The Crucified God: The Cross of Christ as the Foundation and Criticism of Christian Theology*, tr. R. A. Wilson and J. Bowden (New York, 1974); J. Moltmann, *Theology of Hope: On the Ground and Implications of a Christian Eschatology*, tr. J. W. Leitch (Minneapolis, 1993); W. Pannenberg, *Systematic Theology*, tr. G. W. Bromiley, 3 vols. (Grand Rapids, 1991–1998); idem (ed.), *Revelation as History*, tr. D. Granskou (New York, 1968).

S. M. POWELL

HUBMAIER, BALTHASAR (1481–1528)

Born in Friedberg in Bavaria, Hubmaier studied in Ingolstadt, and was appointed to Regensburg as the chaplain at a significant Marian shrine. He made an impact on the city through his preaching, a skill that was to remain important throughout his ministry. His commitment to the 'ordinary people' was also evident, there taking the form of anti-Semitic preaching, since he identified the Jewish community with financial exploitation, as well as being significantly shaped by the pervasive anti-Semitism of the period.

He moved from Regensburg to Waldshut, and in 1522–3, he began to move towards reform, reading the writings of Luther, going to Zurich to meet Zwingli, and marrying – a well-recognized sign of a preacher who wished to identify with Reform.

The community of Waldshut was deeply affected by the Peasants' Uprising of 1524–25. In 1525, Reublin, an *Anabaptist evangelist, arrived and preached believers' baptism. Hubmaier and sixty others were baptized, and what was effectively a civic-sponsored Anabaptist church was inaugurated.

Later in 1525 Hubmaier returned to Zurich. Arrested there, he was required to recant. Although in his first recantation appearance, he actually preached on believers' baptism, following torture, he did recant, and was released. He fled to Nikolsburg in Moravia, and there succeeded in converting the politically powerful in the city. Most citizens followed, and again, Hubmaier inaugurated a civic-based Anabaptist church.

In 1527 he was re-arrested and taken to Vienna, where again he was required to recant. He did not, and was burned in 1528, three months before his wife was executed, by drowning.

Hubmaier was not a typical Anabaptist. His conviction that civic society and the church could be identified set him apart. He also rejected the position of pacifism which marked most sixteenth-century Anabaptists. As one of the few who had a university education, his theological thinking was more highly developed than most others. As well as preaching, he also wrote effectively and his writings remained influential. The most distinctive parts of his theology, apart from his understanding of church and state, was his tripartite *anthropology, and also his conviction that the justification given by Christ was imparted, imputed and an ontological change, when most thinkers at the time adopted only one of those positions.

His most important contribution to our understanding of Anabaptism was the preparation of an Anabaptist communion liturgy, which demonstrates much of his theology, and in particular the 'horizontal' aspect of the table, with the 'Pledge of Love' which forms a part of the service. This expression of mutual commitment among believers was characteristic of the Anabaptist sense of practical discipleship (see *Fellowship). The other major contribution for which he is noted is his motto: *Die Warheit ist untodtlich* ('Truth is immortal or unkillable').

Bibliography

T. Bergsten and W. R. Estep, *Balthasar Hubmaier: Theologian and Martyr* (Valley Forge, 1978); W. R. Estep, *Balthasar Hubmaier* (Nashville, 1978); H. W. Pipkin and J. H. Yoder,

Balthasar Hubmaier: Theologian of Anabaptism (Scottdale, 1989).

R. GOULDBOURNE

HÜGEL, FRIEDRICH VON (1852–1925)

Baron Friedrich von Hügel was one of the leading Roman Catholic intellectuals of his day and widely influential in cultured religious circles in England, where he settled after 1867. A man of the broadest intellectual interests, embracing philosophy, theology, history, spirituality and science, and of wide religious sympathies with diverse traditions, von Hügel was acquainted with leading thinkers of his day, notably the Roman Catholics George Tyrrell (1861–1909) and Maurice Blondel (1861–1949), and the Protestant historian and theologian Ernst *Troeltsch. He was an early supporter of critical views concerning the OT and became associated with Roman Catholic *modernism in the early part of the present century, although his own work was not condemned like that of others more central to that movement. His chief literary legacy, apart from a voluminous correspondence with scholars and those seeking spiritual counsel, is his book *The Mystical Element in Religion* (2 vols., London, ²1923), which, through a study of Catherine of Genoa (1447–1510), argues that the religious life needs to hold together emotional, institutional and intellectual elements. His thought is developed in a number of directions in his once widely known *Essays and Addresses*.

Bibliography

Works: *The Mystical Element in Religion* (London, 1908); *Eternal Life* (Edinburgh, 1912); *Essays and Addresses* (First Series: London, 1921; Second Series: London, 1926); *The Reality of God* (London, 1931).

Studies: L. F. Barmann, *Baron Friedrich von Hügel and the Modernist Crisis* (Cambridge, 1972); M. de la Bedoyère, *The Life of Baron von Hügel* (London, 1951); J. J. Kelly, *Baron Friedrich von Hügel's Philosophy of Religion* (Louvain, 1983); E. M. Leonard, *Creative Tension: The Spiritual Legacy of Friedrich von Hügel* (Scranton, PA, 1997); J. A. McGrath, *Baron Friedrich von Hügel and the Debate on Historical Christianity (1902–1905)* (San Francisco, 1993).

J. B. WEBSTER

HUMANISM (MODERN)

In the twentieth century, the term 'Humanism' (now a proper name) was adopted by an alliance of groups formerly known as secularists, rationalists, scientific naturalists, ethicists, universalists, free thinkers, atheists or agnostics. The first Humanist Manifesto, published in 1933 in the United States, was followed in 1941 by the formation of the American Humanist Association. H. J. Blackham, the leader of the Ethical Union in the UK, initiated international contacts which led to the formation of the International Humanist and Ethical Union following an inaugural congress in Amsterdam in 1952. The British Humanist Association was first formed in 1963 at a meeting at the Houses of Parliament chaired by Sir Julian Huxley. With the exception of Huxley, British Humanism has tended towards a more aggressive secularism, while American Humanism includes those (e.g. in the Universalist-Unitarian Church) who retain a certain religious or mystical feeling for life or the transcendent.

Although the membership of the Humanist organizations remains very small, the Humanist outlook or 'life-stance' is widespread in Europe and English-speaking cultures around the world. It has largely overtaken Christianity as the dominant assumption in the universities and the media and (except in America) in every part of society. Although it only emerged in the twentieth century, H. J. Blackham saw it as the culmination of a long European tradition with roots in Protagoras, Epicurus, Thucydides and Pericles, Lucretius and Renaissance *Humanism. *Voltaire, *Rousseau and particularly *Hume were formative, together with Thomas Paine and the Declaration of the Rights of Man during the French Revolution. In the mid-nineteenth century there was a more obvious movement of thought towards *atheism in the writings of John Stuart Mill, Auguste Comte, Ludwig Feuerbach and George Eliot, but it was Darwin's theory of evolution which led to a significant pressure group led by T. H. Huxley, the grandfather of Sir Julian.

Huxley propagated the 'conflict thesis' that science and 'religion' had always been in opposition (see *Science and theology) and campaigned for science to be given an equal place in education, which was then dominated by the Latin and Greek classics and the church. The propaganda that science was essentially 'agnostic' (Huxley's new word), rational and forward-looking, while 'religion' was authoritarian, dogmatic, superstitious and backward-looking was highly influential, largely thanks to the genius of writers such as Herbert Spencer, George Bernard Shaw and H. G. Wells. The intellectual attraction of the new Humanism has been powerfully articulated by leading philosophers such as Bertrand Russell, William James, John Dewey, A. J. Ayer and Antony Flew, along with leading scientists, such as Sir Herman Bondi, Sir Fred Hoyle, Francis Crick and Richard Dawkins, together with literary figures and journalists in Europe and the English-speaking countries.

Humanism may be summed up in four basic convictions (Humanists would refuse to think of them as 'dogmas'), which may be conveniently labelled *rationalism, naturalism, anthropocentrism and liberalism. Their rationalism begins from the belief that each individual human being must think for himself or herself and refuse to accept the authority of tradition. It is rationalism in the *empiricist tradition of *Locke and Hume, restricting knowledge to what may be known through the five senses. This leads to 'naturalism', meaning here 'secularism', the rejection of any supernatural, spiritual or transcendent realities (such as a god or gods or immortal souls) which cannot be empirically proved by the senses. That negative conviction (not fully shared by some American 'religious' Humanists) may also be expressed more positively as 'scientific naturalism', a commitment to modern science, and it leads on to the positive conviction of 'anthropocentrism', expressed in the chosen designation, 'Humanism'. 'Man is the measure of all things' (Protagoras). Perhaps this should rather be seen as the most fundamental conviction of all, since it is basic to the epistemological conviction that there is no authority higher than human reason. For Humanists, the highest value attaches to the human, to humanity, to being 'humane' and so also to the 'humanities'. The arts therefore are in effect the devotional exercises of what *some* (but not all) Humanists accept is in fact a kind of religion. The fourth conviction, democratic liberalism, emerges out of the others. In this, Humanists are not unique, but it can be seen how their passion for civil liberties, tolerance and human rights arises out of a history of being shunned and marginalized by a dominant Christianity.

Organized secular Humanism emerged at the height of the celebration of '*modernity', and with the development of a conscious 'postmodernity' which rejects the universal claims of rationalism and 'scientism', it remains to be seen whether secular Humanism can adapt. It also faces continuing claims that the only true humanism is Christianity.

See also: FAITH AND REASON.

Bibliography

J. Bequette, *Christian Humanism: Creation, Redemption and Reintegration* (Lanham and Oxford, 2004); H. J. Blackham, *Humanism* (London, 1968); A. Bullock, *The Humanist Tradition in the West* (Oxford and New York, 1985); O. Chadwick, *The Secularization of the European Mind in the Nineteenth Century* (Cambridge, 1975); D. W. Ehrenfeld, *The Arrogance of Humanism* (Oxford, 1981); R. W. Franklin and J. M. Shaw, *The Case for Christian Humanism* (Grand Rapids, 1991); J. Herrick, *Humanism* (Amherst, 2005); P. Kurtz, *Living Without Religion* (Amherst, 1994); idem, *Humanist Manifesto 2000: A Call for a New Planetary Humanism* (Amherst, 2000); J. I. Packer and T. Howard, *Christianity: The True Humanism* (Waco, 1985); D. Shepherd and K. Arisian, *Humanism and Postmodernism* (New York, 1994).

T. A. NOBLE

HUMANISM (RENAISSANCE)

The renaissance of interest in the art and literature of ancient Greece and Rome in the fifteenth century gave birth to what nineteenth-century historians called 'humanism'. The word was derived from *umanista*, a slang term used in the fifteenth century for a teacher of *studia humanitatis* (grammar, rhetoric, history, literature and philosophy) from Latin and Greek texts. The Renaissance was a new focus of interest in all things human, seen as a 'modern' rebirth of ancient culture in reaction to the *scholastic theology of the despised 'Middle Ages'. Francesco Petrarch (*c.* 1304–74) and Lorenzo Valla (*c.* 1406–57) initiated the new literary criticism, while Marsilio Vicino (1433–99) and Giovanni Pico del Mirandola (*c.* 1463–94) tried to hold this together with Christian faith. Some humanists, such as Machiavelli and later Montaigne, presented a fairly secular approach in their writings, but Renaissance humanism did remain largely

Christian, and humanist scholars in northern Europe brought the new learning to the study of the Scriptures.

*Erasmus, the 'prince of humanists', emphasized that Christian theology should work from its original sources in Scripture, thus requiring both knowledge of the biblical languages and textual criticism to establish accurate texts. John Colet (c. 1466–1519) undertook a grammatical-historical interpretation of the biblical texts, Jacques Lefèvre d'Etaples (c. 1455–1536) produced a French translation of the NT, and Johannes Reuchlin (1455–1522) wrote *Rudiments of Hebrew*, thus initiating Christian Hebraic studies. Robert Estienne (1503–59) and John Froben (c. 1460–1527) became publishers, utilizing the new technique of printing. Some of the leading Reformers, including *Calvin, *Cranmer, *Melanchthon and *Zwingli, benefited from a humanist education.

Bibliography

J. Hale, *A Concise Encyclopaedia of the Italian Renaissance* (Oxford, 1981); C. G. Nauert, *Humanism and the Culture of Renaissance Europe (New Approaches to European History)* (Cambridge, 2006).

T. A. NOBLE

HUMAN RIGHTS, see RIGHTS, HUMAN

HUME, DAVID (1711–76)

Such is Hume's influence on philosophy in the English-speaking world of the twentieth century that he has been described as the founder of modern *philosophy of religion. He himself, in his general philosophy, can be regarded as a radical descendant of *Locke, using and developing the latter's emphasis on the role of sense-experience (see *Empiricism) in knowledge to achieve *epistemological scepticism. Whatever the merits of such a characterization, Hume announced distinctive and independent theses which are still lively – for example, on the mistaken ascription of moral judgments to reason rather than feeling, and on the error of supposing that observation or inference establishes causal connections as matters of empirical fact.

Two aspects of Hume's religious thought have commanded special attention. First, in the celebrated Book X of the *Enquiry Concerning Human Understanding* (1748) he challenged the reasonableness of belief in *miracles. The probability of their having occurred is less than the probability of false report; therefore one cannot claim a rational basis for belief in them. Hume's definition of miracle, its relation to the laws of nature and his asseverations concerning scientific impossibility tempt one to conclude that he disallowed miracles even in principle. But, especially in the context of the entire *Enquiry*, this verdict has no safe warrant. Investigating the regulative grounds of assent to particular claims suffices to show that miracles cannot constitute the foundation of a credible religion.

Second, in the posthumously published *Dialogues Concerning Natural Religion* (1779), Hume challenged the validity of an argument from the world considered as an order to the existence of the one God of traditional Christianity. Not only does the argument fail, but it cannot remotely succeed in demonstrating God's moral attributes as traditionally described. Hume's classic discussion deals with a number of perennially significant issues in *philosophical theology, such as the problem of *evil and the coherence of *theism. However, in the context of the eighteenth century, demolishing the argument from 'design' in itself constituted a major threat to the grounds of theistic belief.

Some have maintained that Hume, in freeing Christianity from false dependence on ill-conceived ideas of 'rationality', has rendered a service to faith. But certainly there is little direct comfort for the religious believer to be found in his work. He may not have been an atheist, but his whole enterprise jeopardized traditional ways of speaking of or believing in God without providing a positive alternative obviously compatible with Christianity. His tribe, embodying both his spirit and his argumentation, lives on.

Bibliography

Works: *Dialogues Concerning Natural Religion*, ed. N. K. Smith (Edinburgh, 1947).
Studies: R. M. Burns, *The Great Debate about Miracles: From Joseph Glanvill to David Hume* (London, 1981); A. Flew, *Hume's Philosophy of Belief* (London, 1961); J. C. A. Gaskin, *Hume's Philosophy of Religion* (London, 1978); E. C. Mossner, *The Life of David Hume* (Oxford, 1980); P. Russell, *The Riddle of Hume's Treatise: Skepticism, Naturalism and Irreligion* (Oxford, 2008);

N. K. Smith, *The Philosophy of David Hume* (London, 1941).

S. N. WILLIAMS

HUS, JOHN (1372/3–1415)

Czech Reformer and martyr, Hus was a powerful preacher as well as a scholar and theologian. He held it as a basic truth that Scripture possesses unique authority as the 'law of God'. At the same time he considered the tradition of the church, especially the teaching of the early Fathers up to *Augustine, to be a source of doctrine, but with the proviso that it too was subject to the superior authority of the Bible. The same proviso applied to the declarations of church leaders at all times. Even laymen were entitled to challenge such declarations if they were inconsistent with Scripture. For this reason he firmly believed that the Bible should be made available in translation to the public.

This was the basis of his sharp criticism of the abuses of power and wealth by the church in his own day. It was these views, especially as expressed in his impressive book, *De Ecclesia* (*The Church*, 1413) that led to his condemnation and death at the hands of the Council of Constance in 1415. The *church in the real sense of the word is the whole company of the elect. This is the mystical body of Christ, whose only head is Jesus Christ. The pope cannot be head of the church in this sense. As an earthly institution, however, the Roman Church is a mixed company, since the 'foreknown' – the non-elect – belong to it. Office in the church does not of itself place anyone among the elect. This Augustinian understanding of the nature of the church implied that even the pope himself as well as the cardinals might belong to the 'foreknown' rather than the elect. Indeed, the stark contrast between the extravagant lives of these men and the poverty of Christ raised deep suspicions about their spiritual status.

The true church is wider than the communion of the Roman Church, and includes all those in the world who confess with Peter that Christ is the Son of the living God. This faith is the rock upon which the true church is founded. Hus understood faith in the Catholic sense as 'faith formed by love accompanied by the virtue of perseverance'.

If the pope emulates Christ's virtuous life, he is Christ's vicar. But his authority is spiritual, not civil. It is unfitting that any priest should exercise coercive power, and so Hus drew the conclusion that there is no justification for using violence to uproot heresy.

Hus accepted that there were seven sacraments, but called for a firmer emphasis on their spiritual character. Thus, with regard to *penance, he insisted that God alone can forgive sin and that the priest has authority only to declare God's forgiveness in absolution. He adhered to the doctrine of transubstantiation in the *Eucharist, but insisted that Christ's body is not present in a material way in the elements; it is a sacramental presence.

It is incorrect to think of Hus's teaching as a mere echo of *Wyclif's. He revered his predecessor but was a discriminating user of his books. Hus was a moderate Catholic Reformer, but is admired by Protestants because in his attitude to biblical authority, his passion for reform and insistence upon Christ's lordship over the church, he paved the way for the spiritual enlightenment that culminated in the Protestant Reformation.

Bibliography

Works: *De Ecclesia*, tr. S. H. Thompson (Boulder, 1956); *The Letters of John Hus*, tr. M. Spinka (Manchester, 1972).

Studies: H. Kaminsky, *A History of the Hussite Revolution* (Berkeley and Los Angeles, 1967); M. Spinka, *John Hus* (Princcton, 1968); J. K. Zeman, *The Hussite Movement and the Reformation in Bohemia, Moravia and Slovakia (1350–1650): A Bibliographical Study Guide* (Ann Arbor, 1977).

R. T. JONES

HYPER-CALVINISM

Hyper-Calvinism is a conservative form of traditional *Reformed theology that holds to the five points of Calvinism as formulated by the Synod of *Dort. In contrast with mainstream Calvinism, however, it denies the free offer of the gospel. Many Hyper-Calvinists also reject the historic Reformed doctrines of common *grace and duty faith (i.e. that it is the duty of all who hear the gospel to savingly believe in Christ). They contend that free offers, common grace and duty faith are *Arminian concepts and are incompatible with the Five Points. Their justification for their position is that God sincerely desires the salvation of only the elect, not all men. All Hyper-Calvinists have been supralapsarian, but not all supralapsarians have been Hyper-Calvinist (see *Predestination).

The movement is mainly associated with the Strict and Particular Baptists in England and the Protestant Reformed Church in America. It began in England around the year 1700. The first significant work was *God's Operations of Grace, But No Offers of Grace* (1707) by Joseph Hussey. The leading theologian has been John *Gill, whose *Body of Divinity*, *The Cause of God and Truth* and other works continue to be reprinted. Other leaders include John Brine, William Huntington, William Gadsby, Joseph Charles Philpot, B. A. Ramsbottom and George Ella. The English movement was much curtailed by Andrew *Fuller's *The Gospel Worthy of All Acceptation* (1785) and the ministry of C. H. *Spurgeon. Herman Hoeksema (1886–1965) has been the leading American exponent, as in his *Reformed Dogmatics* (Grandville, ²2004). Homer Hoeksema, David Engelsma and Herman Hanko have continued his tradition, which has been opposed by Cornelius *Van Til, John *Murray and others. The movement has always been a very small minority in the Reformed community.

Bibliography

C. D. Daniel, *Hyper-Calvinism and John Gill* (unpublished PhD thesis, University of Edinburgh, 1983); A. De Jong, *The Well-Meant Gospel Offer* (Franeker, 1953); D. Engelsma, *Hyper-Calvinism and the Call of the Gospel* (Grandville, ²1994); M. A. G. Haykin (ed.), *The Life and Thought of John Gill (1697–1771)* (Leiden, 1997); I. H. Murray, *Spurgeon v. Hyper-Calvinism* (Edinburgh, 1995); J. Murray, *The Free Offer of the Gospel* (Edinburgh, 2001); R. W. Oliver, *History of the English Calvinistic Baptists, 1771–1892* (Edinburgh, 2001); P. Toon, *The Emergence of Hyper-Calvinism in English Nonconformity, 1689–1765* (London, 1967).

C. D. Daniel

HYPOSTASIS

Hypostasis is a Greek noun (plural *hypostaseis*) which became the standard designation in Eastern theology of a 'person' of the divine Trinity. Its nearest Latin equivalent was *persona*.

Hypostasis had a wide range of non-technical meanings (cf. its NT occurrences in 2 Cor. 9:4; 11:17; Heb. 1:3; 3:14; 11:1), but in philosophy and theology it denoted 'being, substantial reality', with reference either to the stuff or substance of which a thing consisted (cf. Heb. 1:3) or to its particularity. Against *Monarchianism, *Origen insisted that Father, Son and Spirit were eternally distinct *hypostaseis*. Until the later fourth century (e.g. in the Creed of Nicaea of 325), hypostasis was used almost interchangeably with *ousia* (see *Substance), but *Basil and his fellow-Cappadocians vindicated its appropriateness to designate the three objective presentations of God, while restricting *ousia* to the single Godhead. This differentiation broadly corresponded to Latin theology's one *substantia* and three *personae* – which bred confusion, since *substantia* was the etymological equivalent of *hypostasis*, not of *ousia*.

The difference between *hypostasis* and *ousia* is subtle, for both speak of single entities or beings. *Ousia* has more reference to internal essence or nature (God in respect of his Godness), while hypostasis more to the objective, concrete individuality of the three 'persons' (to which a closer Lat. counterpart would be *subsistentia*).

In *Christology, the Council of *Chalcedon (451) distinguished between the one *hypostasis* of Christ's incarnate being and the two *physeis*, 'natures' (divine and human), which were united in what *Alexandrian theologians called 'the hypostatic union'. (They had earlier used *physis* almost in the sense of *hypostasis*, for the single being of Christ.) After Chalcedon, debate continued on the integrity of Christ's human nature – whether it lacked a personal centre or focus and was strictly 'non-personal' (*anhypostatos*), as theologians in the mould of *Cyril of Alexandria taught. (Some *Antiochene divines liked to ascribe a *hypostasis* to the human nature.) The one *hypostasis* affirmed by Chalcedon was normally interpreted as that of the divine Word.

A resolution of the difficulty was provided by Leontius of Byzantium (d. c. 543), whose life remains obscure, although he was probably a Palestinian monk who spent several years at Constantinople. He wrote against both *Nestorians and *Monophysites, using *Aristotelian categories in a new way in the service of Christological definition. According to the traditional interpretation, his basically Cyrilline teaching declared that Christ's humanity, although *anhypostatos*, was *enhypostatos*, 'inpersonal, intrahypostatic', i.e. had its personal subsistence in the person of the Logos, while still preserving, as Chalcedon affirmed, its own characteristic properties. God incarnate thus encompassed within himself the perfection of human nature. This notion of *enhypostasia* (a form not found until much later; *enhypostatos* had earlier been used by Neoplatonists) was developed by *Maximus the Confessor and *John of Damascus.

A recent reinterpretation by D. B. Evans (*Leontius of Byzantium: An Origenist Christology*, Washington, 1970) claims that for Leontius both divine and human natures were enhypostatized, in the *hypostasis* of Jesus Christ which was not that of the Logos. This view (which makes him an Origenist in Christology, indebted to Evagrius Ponticus [346–99], a pioneer writer on monastic spirituality) has found some acceptance (e.g. J. Meyendorff, *Christ in Eastern Christian Thought*, New York, ²1975) but much resistance (e.g. J. J. Lynch in *TS* 36, 1975, pp. 455–471, and B. Daley in *JTS* n.s. 27, 1976, pp. 333–369).

Bibliography

J. N. D. Kelly, *Early Christian Doctrines* (London, ⁵1977); G. L. Prestige, *God in Patristic Thought* (London, 1959); H. M. Relton, *A Study in Christology* (London, 1917); M. Richard, *Opera Minora*, vol. II (Turnhout and Louvain, 1977), chs. on *hypostasis* and on Leontius.

D. F. WRIGHT

ICONOCLASTIC CONTROVERSIES

A series of debates about the place of *images (Gk *eikones*, icons) in worship which took place in Byzantium between 726 and 843. The first controversy began when the emperor, Leo III (717–41), issued a decree ordering the destruction of pictures in churches (726). His motives may have been partly religious, though they were certainly very mixed, and there is no evidence that the Islamic prohibition of image-worship had any effect on his thinking. Leo's policy was continued by his son Constantine V (741–75), and by Leo IV (775–80), but after Leo's death it was gradually reversed by his widow Irene, acting in the name of her son, Constantine VI (780–97). At the Seventh Ecumenical *Council, held at Nicaea in 787, iconoclasm (i.e. the destruction of icons) was condemned and outlawed.

The Council's decisions were strongly supported by the papacy, which had never approved of iconoclasm, but they were rejected by the Frankish Church at the Council of Frankfurt in 794. In 815, during the reign of Leo V (813–20), there was a renewed outbreak of what was now a heresy, which was not finally overcome until 842. The restoration of the images was formally proclaimed at the so-called Triumph of Orthodoxy, on 11 March 843, the first Sunday in Lent. Since that time, this Sunday has been specially commemorated in the Eastern Church.

Iconoclasm had great social and political implications, but it was fundamentally a theological controversy. The iconoclasts appealed to the second commandment, and to passages like John 4:24, as evidence to support their belief in a purely spiritual worship of God. Their opponents, the so-called iconodules (Gk *douleia*, service), accused the iconoclasts of denying the reality of the *incarnation. The great exponent of this view was *John of Damascus, who made the classical distinction between worship paid to God (*latreia*), honour paid to the saints (*douleia*), and veneration given to created objects (*proskynēsis*).

John argued that man was the *image of God, that Christ was the image of the invisible God and that the Christian's destiny was to be re-formed in the image of God's Son. Those who had met Jesus in the flesh had seen God, whether they had recognized that fact or not. To say otherwise was to fall into the heresy of *Arius, who had denied the divinity of Christ.

In the second period of iconoclasm, John's mantle was taken up by a monk of Constantinople, Theodore the Studite (759–826). Theodore argued that an icon was a true representation of the *hypostasis* (i.e. person) of its subject, but that it had a different nature (*ousia*; see *Substance). An icon of Christ was thus able to bring the believer into direct contact with his person, but it was not an idol.

Theodore also championed the compulsory veneration of icons, claiming that they were a necessary part of Christian worship. This became the teaching of the Eastern Church after 842, but it has never really caught on in the West, even in those churches which use images in worship, although icons have become popular as objects for contemplation. It should be noted, however, that the Eastern Church does not tolerate statuary in worship, on the grounds that it is idolatrous. This is because the third dimension, which in an icon is believed to be the transcendent divine reality, is contained by statuary within the finite realm.

Bibliography

L. Brubaker, *Inventing Byzantine Iconoclasm* (Bristol, 2012); A. Bryer and J. Herrin (eds.), *Iconoclasm* (Oxford, 1977); A. Giakalis, *Images of the Divine: The Theology of Icons at the Seventh Ecumenical Council* (Leiden, 1994); John of Damascus, *On the Divine Image* (Crestwood, 1980); L. Ouspensky, *The Theology of the Icon* (London, 1977).

G. L. Bray

IDEALISM

As a metaphysical doctrine, idealism is the view that all that really exists are minds and their ideas. Though it is possible to have secular versions of idealism (e.g. phenomenalism), its most notable exponent, George *Berkeley, advanced a theistic version, a chief reason for which was to combat the allegedly atheistic consequences of John *Locke's doctrine of material substance, the view that the objects of the external world were substances possessing sets of primary and secondary qualities. If it is allowed that a thought is a mental image, it is possible to give a plausible idealist version of Christian theology, as Berkeley shows and Jonathan *Edwards and others appear to have held, but this can scarcely be regarded as the most natural view. For though God's decree or thought that x shall exist or happen is a necessary and sufficient condition of x existing or happening, it does not follow that x is itself only an idea in God's mind.

In the philosophies of *Kant and *Hegel, idealism is a consequence of Kant's 'Copernican revolution' – his view that the knowing mind contributes to the character of what is known. According to Hegel, reality develops historically in dialectical fashion towards the absolute idea, and the distinction between the knowing subject and a known object is a convenient and conventional one rather than one which corresponds to reality as it is.

The influence of transcendental or absolute idealism upon Christian theology is chiefly through versions of post-Kantian idealism. Denying, with Kant, any possibility of knowing God through either reason or revelation, idealism came to understand the Christian faith in immanent and largely ethical terms. The Christian gospel is not the proclamation of redemption from sin by the self-offering of the God-man, but a way of life consisting in observing the ethical teachings of Jesus of Nazareth in an effort to bring about the kingdom of God on earth. This outlook is characteristic of the theology of e.g. Albrecht *Ritschl.

Idealism became influential in England and the English-speaking world through the writings of S. T. *Coleridge and F. D. Maurice (see *Christian Socialism) in England and the Cairds (Edward, 1835–1908, and his brother John, 1820–98) in Scotland, and is one important source of theological *liberalism in Protestantism.

Kant gave prominence to the so-called moral proof of God's existence, but for him morality is severed from divine command, and stress is laid on human autonomy in devising and endorsing the moral law. Put in terms of Christian theology, in Kant's philosophy the creature assumes some of the roles of the creator, giving the world its character, and legislating the moral law.

In a less technical sense 'idealism' concerns the holding and propagating of ideals, as opposed to ideas. While holding out perfect conformity to the will of God, or to the *imitation of Christ, as ideals, much Christian theology has cautioned against the thought that such ideals are attained or attainable in this life, regarding this as *perfectionism, which fails to take the effect of indwelling sin, even in the regenerate, with sufficient seriousness.

See also: German Idealism.

Bibliography

A. C. Ewing, *Idealism: A Critical Survey* (London, 1969); P. H. Neujahr, *Kant's Idealism* (Macon, 1995); B. M. G. Reardon, *From Coleridge to Gore* (London, 1971); W. H. Walsh, *Hegelian Ethics* (London, 1969).

P. Helm

IDEOLOGY

According to Marx and Engels, the ideology of a particular historical era is the sum of the ideas of the dominant social class. This links to class struggle resulting from the division of labour. The mode of material production sets conditions to how history unfolds. Historical existence is 'life', which in turn determines 'consciousness'. Ideology conceals the contradictions within modes of production (e.g. unjust wages for socially valuable manual work), so that the oppressed will not have their consciousness opened to the need to transform reality. The criticism of ideology can free the consciousness of the oppressed classes from the dominant ideology, so that their new consciousness can come out of revolutionary practice. Marx did not say under what conditions such criticism was possible. The Leninist and Communist response was that within the proletarian class, the Party was conscious of its own history and created a competing ideology by its political and educational work. Lenin believed that historical conflicts passed through new ideologies. *Liberation theologian Gustavo *Guttiérez contrasts ideology to utopia, which is 'a condemnation of the existing order' and a commitment to a new social consciousness and new types of relationships based on hope in Christ given by God. In speaking to political, social and economic issues, Christian theology has to be careful not to become captive to any ideology.

See also: MARXISM AND CHRISTIANITY.

Bibliography
G. Gutiérrez, *Essential Writings*, ed. J. B. Nicholoff (New York, 1996); K. Mannheim, *Ideology and Utopia: An Introduction to the Sociology of Knowledge* (London, 1966); K. Marx and F. Engels, *The German Ideology* (London, 1998 [1846]); V. Westhelle, 'Ideology', in *DEM*.

C. A. E. MOSELEY

IDOLATRY

The word 'idolatry' literally means 'the worship of images', deriving from two Greek terms: *eidōlon*, image; and *latreia*, worship or service. In its broader sense, idolatry means giving worship to anyone or anything other than God, but it is often associated with the false worship of an idol or the divine as represented by an image.

Idolatry in historical theology
Early Christians confronted the issue of idolatry in both the iconoclasm of Judaism and their Hellenistic cultural context. As far as is known, Christian art did not develop until after the NT era. The earliest artworks by Christians were wall paintings in the Roman catacombs from about the third century, but the crucifixion was not a regular symbol until centuries later.

On the whole, theologians of the early church and patristic era attacked idolatry. *Justin Martyr rejected all worship of idols on the basis that they were lifeless images created by immoral artisans that could not capture God's nature. *Tertullian considered idolatry the gravest of sins because it encompassed all others, and *Augustine critiqued idolatry in *City of God*. In an oft-quoted argument, Pope *Gregory the Great prohibited the adoration of images yet maintained that illiterate people could learn from them, so he did not forbid their making.

In the eighth and ninth centuries, idolatry became a central matter of dispute in the *iconoclast controversies over the use of *images in Byzantine worship. Around 725, Emperor Leo III prohibited icons because they could not represent Christ's divinity and prevented the conversion of Jews and Muslims. The use of icons was defended by *John of Damascus and Theodore of Studios, and they were reinstated by Empress Irene. The Second Council of Nicaea affirmed the iconodule position in 787, allowing icons on the basis of Christ's incarnation and the notion that in venerating an image, one venerates the person represented. After Leo V reintroduced the proscription against icons, they were finally restored under Theodora in 843 and affirmed by the Fourth General Council of Constantinople in 869. Ever since, icons have held an important place in *Eastern Orthodox worship.

Medieval theology drew a distinction between *latria*, worship due only to God, and *dulia*, veneration of the Virgin *Mary and the saints. *Thomas Aquinas regarded idolatry as unduly giving 'divine honour to a creature' (*Summa Theologica*, 2.2, 92.2, London, 1922, p. 172). The Protestant *Reformers of the sixteenth century, however, believed that the theology and worship of the church had been corrupted, and many of them called into question the place of images within worship, though they were far from uniform in their opinions.

In contrast to *Karlstadt's radical iconoclasm in Wittenberg, *Luther was more moderate. He allowed for images as long as they were not worshipped, stating that they were 'neither evil nor good, we may have them or not, as we please' (H. Lehmann [ed.], *Luther's Works*, vol. 51, Philadelphia, 1959, p. 86). Meanwhile, *Zwingli and *Calvin, in Zurich and Geneva respectively, held more strict positions, asserting that images were forbidden by Scripture and inevitably lead to idolatrous worship (see *Reformed theology). In addition, Calvin challenged the church to teach the uneducated better, rejected the distinction between *latria* and *dulia*, and restricted artistic representation to things 'which the eyes are capable of seeing' (John T. McNeill [ed.], *Institutes of the Christian Religion*, 1.xi.12, London, 1960, p. 112). In its articulation of the Catholic Counter-*Reformation, the Council of Trent reaffirmed the veneration of images.

Idolatry in systematic theology

Theological reflection upon the Christian understanding of and opposition to idolatry considers scriptural prohibitions from the OT, notably the first and second commandments (Exod. 20:3–6; Deut. 5:7–10) and narratives or prophetic warnings about the temptation to worship idols (Exod. 32; Judg. 8:22–27; Ps. 115:4–8; Isa. 44:6–20; Jer. 51:17–18), as well as NT admonitions concerning actual and metaphorical idolatry (Acts 17:16–31; 19:23–41; Rom. 1:22–23; 1 Cor. 8:4; 10:14; Gal. 5:19–21; Eph. 5:5; Col. 3:5; 1 Thess. 1:9; 1 John 5:21; Rev. 21:8). At the same time, the NT affirmations of God's self-revelation in the incarnate person of Jesus Christ (John 1:14; Phil. 2:5–11) and the declaration that Christ is the *image of God (2 Cor. 4:4; Col. 1:15–20; Heb. 1:3) have been interpreted to counter opposition to the use of images within *worship and to demonstrate true worship.

Idolatry is related to several theological doctrines: God's freedom and unrepresentable nature; *creation, in particular the juxtaposition of divine creation *ex nihilo* with human creativity; *Christology, regarding the implications of the *incarnation of Christ for the material world; pneumatology, concerning the inspiring presence of the *Holy Spirit; *ecclesiology, especially the legitimacy and function of images within worship; and *ethics, particularly questions related to artistic activity.

Bibliography

S. C. Barton (ed.), *Idolatry: False Worship in the Bible, Early Judaism and Christianity* (London and New York, 2007); G. K. Beale, *We Become What We Worship: A Biblical Theology of Worship* (Downers Grove, 2008); W. Brueggemann, *Israel's Praise: Doxology against Idolatry and Ideology* (Philadelphia, 1988); W. A. Dyrness, *Reformed Theology and Visual Culture: The Protestant Imagination from Calvin to Edwards* (Cambridge, 2004); C. M. N. Eire, *War against the Idols: The Reformation of Worship from Erasmus to Calvin* (Cambridge, 1986); P. C. Finney, *The Invisible God: The Earliest Christians on Art* (New York and Oxford, 1997); T. Hart, 'Protestantism and the Arts', in A. McGrath and D. Marks (eds.), *The Blackwell Companion to Protestantism* (Oxford, 2004); G. E. Thiessen (ed.), *Theological Aesthetics: A Reader* (Cambridge and Grand Rapids, 2004); R. Viladesau, *Theological Aesthetics: God in Imagination, Beauty, and Art* (New York and Oxford, 1999).

D. W. McNutt

IGNATIUS OF LOYOLA (1491–1556)

Ignatius, a Spaniard, was the founder of the Society of Jesus (*Jesuits). Following his conversion from a military career to a determination to be a soldier of Christ, Ignatius went into retreat at Manresa (1522–23), and his meditations and mystical experiences at that time formed the basis for his *Spiritual Exercises*, which were complete by 1535 and became the major instrument in forming Jesuit *spirituality thereafter. It is in the *Exercises* that Ignatius' spiritual theology comes to clearest expression.

The *Exercises* provide instructions for a month of intensive, supervised retreat, with the object especially of discovering and committing oneself to God's particular will for one's life, or of renewing such a commitment. Following the fundamental meditations on the Kingdom of Christ and the Two Standards, in which the exercitant receives the call of Christ the King to enlist in his service in the battle against Satan, the *Exercises* focus on contemplation of the gospel history of Jesus, through which the exercitant encounters the living Christ and commits himself to discipleship following Christ's way of service to God and victory through the cross. Ignatius' spirituality is primarily one of service through love, in which, out of his realization of Christ's love for him, the Christian always asks, 'What *more* can I do for Christ?'

See also: Reformation, Catholic Counter-.

Bibliography

P. Caraman, *Ignatius Loyola: A Biography of the Founder of the Jesuits* (San Francisco, 1990); W. Meissner, *Ignatius of Loyola: The Psychology of a Saint* (New Haven, 1992); N. W. O'Malley, *The First Jesuits* (Cambridge, MA, 1993); H. Rahner, *Ignatius the Theologian* (London, 1968).

R. J. BAUCKHAM

IMAGE OF GOD

According to Gen. 1:26–27, men and women are both created 'in the image and likeness of God', a feature which distinguishes them from other creatures. In 1 Cor. 11:7–9 the apostle Paul elaborates on this by saying that the male is in 'the image and glory of God', but the female is 'the glory of the male'. This statement does not diminish the position of women or make them inferior to men, but explains that the image of God in them must be understood in relation to the image in men, for 'the head of the female is the male' (1 Cor. 11:3).

The Hebrew words *ṣelem* and *děmût*, translated into Greek respectively as *eikon* and *homoousios*, seem to have referred initially to statues put up to represent a king or governor. If this was the meaning intended in Genesis, the terms would imply that human beings have been appointed as God's representatives on earth, which would tie in with the statement that they have been given dominion over the creatures. This theme has always had a place in Christian theology, though the rediscovery of the original context in modern times has made it more prominent in recent theological thinking. Attempts have sometimes been made to differentiate the meaning of the two words, but nowadays it is generally accepted that in theological terms they are synonymous and refer to a single reality.

It must be said, however, that this was not the case in the early church, which regarded the image and the likeness as two quite different things. The general opinion was that the likeness of God had been lost at the *fall but that the image had been retained. By making this distinction, the Fathers were able to do justice to the divine qualities still present in the human race without diminishing the catastrophic effects of the fall. It was only in the sixteenth century, as the study of Hebrew revived, that theologians came to realize that the two terms were virtually identical. This meant that a new explanation of the effect of the fall had to be devised. Some theologians claimed that the image/likeness had been lost by Adam and Eve, but the majority held to an intermediate position, saying that the image was still present in fallen man though severely wounded, corrupted or ruined. In effect, this allowed them to reappropriate the patristic inheritance, and their interpretation still enjoys a wide currency today.

In recent times it has been pointed out that the term 'image of God' occurs infrequently in the Bible, a fact which has led some theologians to question its overall importance. However, as has often been pointed out, the phrase occurs at significant moments and its substance underlies virtually everything in Scripture, even when it is not mentioned specifically. Today most theologians regard it as fundamental for a Christian *anthropology, and the image of God remains a prominent theme in modern theological discussion. It has a particular relevance to questions relating to evolutionary theories, because of the implication that the human race is somehow fundamentally different from the animals. It is also important in the study of psychology because it asserts that we have a special relationship with the divine which seems to go beyond the purely physical aspect of human nature. The result is that the precise meaning of the term is a matter of debate among specialists in those disciplines as well as among theologians.

Given the doctrine's history, it is odd to note that nowhere in the Bible is there any suggestion that the 'image and likeness of God' suffered in any way from the fall of Adam. On the contrary, the prohibition against killing human beings in Gen. 9:5–6 is justified by appealing to our creation in God's image, and the same principle is invoked in Jas 3:8–9, where Christians are told not to curse other people because they have been created in the likeness of God. The image therefore appears to retain its power and authority even in fallen human beings. If this is so, there is no objective difference between the humanity of believers and that of unbelievers, both of whom continue to share the creation mandate.

The early Christians were impressed by the fact that the image of God appeared to be what distinguishes human beings from other creatures, and they were therefore inclined to identify it with the rational soul, which they regarded as something uniquely human and even intrinsically divine. This equation led *Augustine to suggest that the image of God was an image of the Trinity, and he proceeded to find a tripartite element in the human mind. This he described as 'being, knowing and willing' and as 'memory, intelligence and act(ion)', but either way, the inner processes of the mind were held to reflect the character and constitution of the triune God. Interestingly, Augustine's reflections on this are still taken seriously today and he is sometimes hailed as the virtual founder of modern psychology.

Interesting as such theories are, there is no scriptural evidence for them and there are serious objections to them. For example, the equation of the image with the rational soul might lead some people to think that less intelligent or mentally handicapped people have ceased to be fully human (and might therefore be suitable candidates for euthanasia). It might also suggest that intellectuals are closer to God than others, and that Christians are more intelligent than non-believers. For all these reasons, theologians since the sixteenth century have preferred to locate the image of God elsewhere. Rather than focus on a particular part of human nature, they have generally preferred to see the whole man as created in the image of God, including even the body, which must also reflect the divine presence. The means by which the image is made known is the moral and spiritual awareness which human beings possess and which is not directly related to intelligence. As moral awareness was corrupted by the fall but not removed, it chimed in with *Calvin's understanding of the image very well. This view is still found today, particularly (though not exclusively) in theologically conservative circles.

The spiritual dimension is more complex because it raises the question of whether the faith-relationship which Christians have with God can be regarded as a (partial?) restoration of the image which was lost or corrupted by sin. Though some have held this view, there is no biblical warrant for it and it creates a divide between Christians and others, including Jews, which is unwarranted by the evidence. However, the spiritual nature of human beings is expressed in the fact that all people, believers and unbelievers alike, have an inbuilt relationship with God. This relationship went wrong at the fall but it was not destroyed, and now every human being must take responsibility for it. In other words, creation in the image and likeness of God gives meaning to *sin and *guilt, which would not exist if we did not have to answer to God for our thoughts and behaviour. The image of God may thus be understood as the human capacity for relationship(s), which reflects the divine character but is not present elsewhere in creation. In this sense it comes close to the concept of 'person', and in recent years theologians have been exploring the extent to which the two terms can be regarded as synonymous.

The personal and relational nature of the divine image has naturally led to a new focus on the social or *covenantal dimension which the term is believed to express. According to this, human beings have been created for community, so the image of God cannot be regarded as primarily an individual possession. It is given to individuals, of course, but only in order to establish them in relationships for which they must take responsibility. Our primary relationship is with God in Jesus Christ, who on this view becomes the archetypal image of God (as in the theology of Karl *Barth), but the image has implications for all human relationships, which are established and maintained in and by Christ, the true image of the divine. Furthermore, our behaviour towards other people must reflect the fact that they too are created in the image of God, so that if we mistreat them we show disrespect to him.

This communitarian emphasis ties in very well with the concept of dominion (see *Creation) over the earth, which is given to the entire human race and not to a particular individual. It underscores the belief that all human beings are equal to each other and therefore entitled to a fair share of the world's goods. It has the added advantage of being close to the original meaning of the word in Hebrew and can therefore be represented as a return to the biblical standpoint. Practically speaking, however, this approach has difficulty in coming to terms with the effects of the fall, which has distorted the pattern of human and divine relationships in ways which will not be put right until the end of time, when the entire creation will be renewed and restored.

Today, the concept of the image of God continues to have an important bearing on theological anthropology, particularly where ethical questions of life and death are concerned. Is a foetus, for example, created in the image of God? Does this belief make euthanasia murder, and perhaps even blasphemy? Would a cloned human being be made in God's image, and if not, what difference would that make? These questions and others like them have ensured that the question of the image of God is now at the interface of religious belief and modern science (see *Faith and science) and promises that there will be considerable discussion of what it really means in the foreseeable future.

See also: RIGHTS, HUMAN.

Bibliography

D. R. Alexander, *Cloning Humans: Distorting the Image of God?* (Cambridge, 2001); K. E. Børresen, *Image of God: Gender Models in Judaeo-Christian Tradition* (Minneapolis, 1995); G. L. Bray, 'The Significance of God's Image in Man', *TynB* 42, pp. 195–225; J. A. Clanton, *In Whose Image? God and Gender* (London, 1990); D. Keyes, *Beyond Identity: Finding Yourself in the Image and Character of God* (Carlisle, 1998); V. Lossky, *In the Image and Likeness of God* (New York, 1985); R. Ruston, *Human Rights and the Image of God* (London, 2004).

G. L. BRAY

IMAGES

Christian traditions differ substantially in their attitudes and practices with regard to the use of images and more generally the arts (see *Aesthetics) in Christian worship and life. Well-established pre-modern Christian traditions (Eastern Orthodox, Roman Catholic, to a certain extent Anglican and to a lesser degree Oriental churches) have used arts in Christian worship. They make use of a wide range of artistic expressions such as icons and frescoes; sculptures, woodcarving and monumental art (including architecture, mosaics, stained-glass work, floor-patterns, cross features); banners and symbolic colours, textiles and gestures; lights and smells; hymnody, a cappella singing and instrumental music; liturgical reading and dramatic expressions. Reformed, evangelical, holiness and radical Christian movements are much more constrained in drawing on artistic forms in worship.

In the context of cultures saturated by symbolic images of deities, the use of any representations of humans, animals or plants, whether carved or painted, had been prohibited by the Torah (Exod. 20:4–5). In other parts of the Hebrew Scriptures, however, images are mentioned and used by Hebrew heroes of faith (Moses in Num. 21:9; the Ark of the Covenant with the cherubim in Exod. 25:18–22; artistic decoration of Solomon's temple in 1 Kgs 6:18–35, etc.). In the intertestamental period, for pious Palestinian Jews, worshipping or venerating any material creation was idolatry – serving the creature rather then the creator. But, as the lively mosaic decorations of Jewish synagogues testify, the code was much less stricter in the diaspora.

While growing out of the Jewish spiritual matrix and synagogue patterns of worship, Christianity adapted its message to the diverse contexts of the expanding missionary outreach to the Gentiles. The early churches transferred their base from a Jewish minority, with a stricter code regarding images in worship and daily living, to a largely Gentile majority and its cultural patterns. Apart from the influence of Hellenistic culture on the development of early Christian worship, the use of images in worship can be seen also as a deliberate departure from Jewish ways. Images constituted a visible theological expression of a new and broader perspective on God and humanity and a moving away from all things Jewish. 'To the orthodox [in the later iconoclastic controversies], an iconoclast was simply one with a Jewish mind . . .' (J. Pelikan, *The Christian Tradition*, p. 201).

While there is no direct mention of imagery in the NT or in early Christian writing, there is sufficient evidence of its use in Christian worship practices from the paintings in catacombs, church mosaics and sarcophagi, some of which date from the late second century. The earliest Christian visual art had a symbolic and didactic rather than aesthetic function. After the period of persecutions of Christians in the Roman Empire was over, sacred images came to play an ever-increasing part in the church's spiritual practices. In the west of Europe the appropriation of images also embraced the use of statues. From the time of *Constantine 'the Great', Christian artistic expressions were looked upon as an evidence for Christianity being victorious. The artistic paraphernalia of the cathedrals served as an encyclopaedic display of theology, history, hagiography, morality, natural history, learning, crafts and trades.

The disproportionate use of images both in worship, in monasteries and in the private lives of Christian communities in the Byzantine Empire, as well as the pressure from the widespread popular movements hostile to the use of images (such as the *Monophysites, Paulicians and Bogomilians, and also Islam, which diminished the human side of the incarnation), led to the notorious *iconoclastic controversy that lasted for more than a century (726–843). The opponents of icons saw them as unscriptural and as a chief obstacle to missionary witness among the Jews and Moslems, and unleashed systematic persecutions against image-users, particularly against the monks who were the most zealous defenders of icons. In the West the opposition to the use of artistic expressions in the churches was almost non-existent.

The proponents of the use of sacred images claimed a fuller hold on the theological significance of the *incarnation: God had become visible by taking human nature. The high Christology of Col. 1.15–20 speaks of Christ as the image (icon) of the invisible God, having in himself the full nature of God and yet in truly human form. From this perspective, it was argued, there should not be any obstacle to the use of images of humans and of living nature, nor to the artistic creativity of humanity in the service of the true worship of God. The champions of the veneration of icons (monastic communities, *John of Damascus, Theodore of Studious and later *Thomas Aquinas) used the Christological argument of incarnation to carry on their theological apologia. The patristic backing for this position was found in the works of the Cappadocian Fathers, particularly of *Basil 'the Great' (of Caesarea), who thought that the honour paid to the image passed on to its prototype. So the use of icons is not worship of an image but an honour to and adoration of the archetype.

Due to the abuses which had grown up around the worshipping of icons and human objects (relics) in the Latin Church, the Protestant *Reformers, particularly the Swiss wing of the Reformation, fiercely opposed the use of images. They were followed in this by English Puritans and the descendants of the *Radical Reformation. The gradual turn from mystery to reason, alongside the Protestant and later the evangelical theological concern for the primacy of the biblical text (*sola Scriptura*), coupled with the widespread use of printing technologies in the early modern period, firmly established the pre-eminence of a word-centred means of worship in Protestant and evangelical communities – at the expense of non-verbal and artistic forms. There are, however, signs that this is changing. Current discussions about the relationship of creativity and imagination to spirituality are part of a larger debate about the relationship of theology to the arts and spiritual expressions of cultures.

See also: WORSHIP.

Bibliography

J. Begbie (ed.), *Behold the Glory: Incarnation through the Arts* (Grand Rapids, 2001); L. W. Hurtado, *At the Origins of Christian Worship: The Context and Character of Earliest Christian Devotion* (Carlislie, 1999); R. P. Martin, *Worship in the Early Church* (London, 1964); J. W. McClendon, Jr, *Witness: Systematic Theology*, vol. 3 (Nashville, 2000); L. Ouspensky and V. Lossky, *The Meaning of Icons* (Crestwood, 1999); J. Pelikan, *The Christian Tradition: A History of the Development of Doctrine*, vol. 2 (Chicago, 1974).

P. R. PARUSHEV

IMAGINATION IN THEOLOGY

Imagination has long been an orphan in Western philosophy and theology. *Plato disqualified all image-making activity as intrinsically deceptive: imaging pictures what is not really there, yielding neither knowledge nor truth. The King James Version of the Bible (1611) does not help matters by speaking of the imagination of the human heart as evil (Gen. 6:5; 8:21) and of those who fail to honour God as becoming 'vain in their imaginings' (Rom. 1:21).

The rehabilitation of imagination

In his *Critique of Judgment* (1790) *Kant distinguished the ability to picture images of things no longer there (the 'reproductive' imagination) from the ability to create order and unity – a sense of wholeness – out of diverse and unrelated experiences and ideas (the 'productive' imagination). The imagination here appears, like reason, as a cognitive faculty. Where reason explains the working of the world by means of scientific laws, however, the special remit of the imagination is to think in terms of relating parts to wholes. Science and logic think in the necessary terms of causality and inference, but the imagination thinks in terms of teleology, in terms of meaningful wholes.

*Schleiermacher linked the imagination to *aesthetic and religious feelings, in particular, to the taste for the infinite and the sense of dependence on the absolute. Theology is imaginative in the bad sense when it projects an image of some human ideal onto the heavens and calls it 'God'. Here aesthetic invention is *idolatrous and, as such, susceptible to *Feuerbach's critique that theology is really only *anthropology.

The imagination's stock has risen considerably in the eyes of philosophers thanks to its association with creative language. Indeed, the imagination comes into its own only when we consider its verbal rather than pictorial application. P. *Ricœur argues that metaphors have a cognitive rather than a merely cosmetic function because they are paradigm instances of semantic innovation: metaphors redescribe reality, enabling us to explore unfamiliar territory in terms of the more familiar (e.g. light as wave or particle). Metaphors with staying power become scientific models, pictures that orient our thinking (e.g. the universe as mechanism; God as Father). Jesus' parables, to take another example, describe the kingdom of God in terms of ordinary life. Yet Jesus' imaginative lessons subverted the worldview of his hearers, redescribing reality not to gain scientific knowledge of its surface features, but to awaken hearts to its eschatological depths.

Narratives are another species of creative language that do more than convey information. Narratives 'configure' a series of events into a meaningful whole; they explain by 'emplotting' (Ricœur). M. Nussbaum has made a compelling case for appreciating the unique contribution that literature can make in ethics, arguing that literary form is not separable from content, but an integral part of the search for and statement of truth.

To generalize: Where reason analyses and breaks things (and texts) up into their constituent parts, imagination synthesizes, making connections between things that otherwise appear unrelated.

Imagination and the Bible

D. Kelsey's *Proving Doctrine: The Uses of Scripture in Recent Theology* shows that it is not enough to affirm biblical authority; one must decide how to use the Bible (see *Scripture) in formulating and justifying doctrine. Kelsey argues that every theologian makes an 'imaginative construal', deciding to read the Bible as evincing a certain kind of wholeness (e.g. history, universal truth, myth, story, etc.).

Yet the difference between true religion and idolatry depends on grasping patterns in Scripture that are God-given rather than man-made. A Christian conception of the imagination will distinguish vain imaginings (mere human projections) from the virtuous imaginings in the Bible (divine *accommodations) that render the truth of the gospel in a variety of literary forms and canonical colours.

It takes imagination rightly to grasp the way in which God presents himself in and through the medium of the biblical texts. What faith hears in Scripture is neither a philosophy nor a system of morality but a gospel: good news from God about what God has done. The various books of the Bible comprise a vast theodrama, a divine comedy in which the triune God has the leading part and in which the plot advances via God's words and God's acts.

Theological interpretation and the theodramatic imagination

Beyond analytic exegesis, reading Scripture theologically further requires imagination, the faculty which makes sense of things, locating particular bits and pieces within larger patterns. Moreover, to the extent that theology serves a way of life, one needs the imagination if one is to locate everyday reality within a biblical pattern, that is, if one is really going to indwell the world of the biblical text. To live in such a way that the biblical world is one's primary interpretative framework is an imaginative, practical, and spiritual enterprise.

Ultimately, the theodramatic imagination discerns not only the pattern of meaningfulness in the Scriptures themselves (say, the typological connections between the old and new covenant persons and events) but the way in which the church's current situation fits into that same meaningful pattern. The church requires theodramatic imagination in order to see how it fits into the strange new (*viz.* eschatological) world of the Bible. Theology must not be content merely with stating truth, but must take every imagination captive to Scripture so that we can see, taste and judge the world as it is: made new in Christ.

Yes, there are vain imaginings. But this no more disqualifies the imagination from serving theology than the existence of logical fallacies disqualifies reason. A false picture of the imagination – as the power of conjuring up the unreal

– has held us captive. We do more justice to the image of God in humanity and to the nature of Scripture itself when we view the imagination as the power of synoptic vision: the ability to synthesize heterogeneous elements into a meaningful pattern; the ability to see as whole what those without imagination see only as a meaningless jumble. Only those with an imagination nurtured from Scripture will discern theo-dramatic fittingness and so see God, the world and ourselves – as well as truth, goodness and beauty – as they really are, in light of their relation to the one in whom all things hold together: Jesus Christ.

See also: HERMENEUTICS; THEOLOGICAL METHOD.

Bibliography

G. Green, *Imagining God: Theology and the Religious Imagination* (San Francisco, 1989); R. L. Hart, *Unfinished Man and the Imagination* (Freiburg, 1968); J. Hartt, *Theological Method and Imagination* (New York, 1977); J. McIntyre, *Faith, Theology and Imagination* (Edinburgh, 1987); M. Nussbaum, *Love's Knowledge: Essays on Philosophy and Literature* (Oxford, 1990); P. Ricœur, *Figuring the Sacred: Religion, Narrative, and Imagination* (Minneapolis, 1995); K. Vanhoozer, *The Drama of Doctrine* (Louisville, 2005); idem, *Pictures at a Theological Exhibition: Scenes of the Church's Worship, Witness, and Wisdom* (Downers Grove, 2016); M. Warnock, *Imagination* (London, 1975).

K. J. VANHOOZER

IMITATION OF CHRIST

The expression of this ideal of Christian discipleship has varied widely, and its meaning, possibility and validity have often been questioned. Yet whenever discipleship has been taken seriously, the ideal has re-emerged, prompting re-examination of its biblical foundation.

The imitation of Christ is implied throughout the Gospels and more explicitly taught in the epistles (cf. 1 Cor. 11:1; Phil. 2:5; Heb. 12:1–3; 1 Pet. 2:21; 1 John 2:6; 4:7–11). In Christian thought after the NT the theme can be traced from the *Apostolic Fathers onwards. Sometimes, as with *Francis of Assisi, it appears in literal form; more usually it features in devotion to the humanity of Christ in mystical theology. It continued in Catholicism after *Teresa of Avila as a theme of seventeenth-century French spirituality and inspired several later reformers and idealists, including Charles de Foucauld (1858–1916) and his heirs, the Little Brothers and Little Sisters of Jesus.

The work of this title, normally ascribed to Thomas à Kempis (i.e. from Kempen; *c.* 1380–1471), has had enormous appeal. Thomas was reared in the reforming piety of the Brethren of the Common Life, and spent his life in an Augustinian house near Zwolle. The title applies in fact only to the first chapter. The book as a whole is a guide to spiritual communion with God.

In Protestantism *Luther's difficulties with the doctrine have obscured *Calvin's acceptance of it. Luther did not find in the distinctions made in medieval spirituality between active and passive imitations of Christ a proper reflection of biblical teaching on *grace and *union with Christ. Declaring, 'It is not imitation that makes sons, but son-ship that makes imitators', Luther preferred to speak of conformity to Christ. He also emphasized individual Christian vocation against ideals of any fixed pattern of imitation, such as the *monastic life or the literal approach adopted by many radical Reformers (see *Reformation, Radical).

Despite Luther's influence, the ideal surfaced again whenever people like William Law or *Kierkegaard recalled believers to serious discipleship. Interpretation of the imitation of Christ in twentieth-century Protestant theology may be described as the combining of a partial assimilation of Kierkegaard and a reaction against *Schleiermacher and his successors for appearing to stress Christ the example at the expense of Christ the redeemer. This produced either significant yet unfinished movements towards a fresh understanding (*Bonhoeffer); qualified approval (*Barth); or rejection (*Bultmann).

Much recent NT exegesis has tended to play down imitation of Christ, resolutely interpreting 'imitation' as 'following' and 'obedience' alone (cf. W. Michaelis, 'mimeomai', TDNT IV, pp. 659–674). It may, however, be asked how much such interpretation has been affected by agnosticism about the historical Jesus or presuppositions about the *existential nature of faith. In Bultmann's case these clearly involve an emphasis on the words rather than the actions of Jesus and a tendency to see Jesus' connection with the believer solely in terms of isolated individual responses to commands. This not only eliminates practice of the virtues in imitation of Christ, it also leaves almost no content to the idea of Christian character, a position unknown in traditional *moral theology. Removal of imitation of Christ from *ethics or its confinement to mystical theology or individual *spirituality is also challenged by *liberation theology. This maintains that the imitation and following of Jesus should take its place in systematic theology as a source of knowledge in *Christology, for 'It is the real following of Jesus that enables one to understand the reality of Jesus' (J. Sobrino).

Bibliography

R. A. Burridge, *Imitating Jesus* (Grand Rapids, 2007); E. Cothenet, *Imitating Christ* (St Meinrad, IN, 1974); J. M. Gustafson, *Christ and the Moral Life* (New York, 1968); E. Malatesta (ed.), *Imitating Christ* (Wheathampstead, 1974); C. A. Snyder, *Following in the Footsteps of Christ: The Anabaptist Tradition* (London, 2004); E. J. Tinsley, *The Imitation of God in Christ* (London, 1960).

P. N. HILLYER

IMMANENCE, see GOD

IMMORTALITY

The term 'immortality', in its straightforward sense, means not being subject to *death. Because it has been the destiny of all human beings so far to have lived that their lives come to an end, it might seem uncontentious to say that human beings are not immortal. By all outward appearances human beings die and their bodies decay. 'Ashes to ashes, dust to dust' is the phrase commonly used in affirmation of this reality. Despite appearances, however, many cultures and religious traditions have claimed that human beings are, after all, immortal. There are three main variants to this belief, namely, reincarnation, immortality of the soul, and the Christian belief in resurrection.

Reincarnation is the belief that the soul of a dead person re-enters the world in the body of some other living organism in order to be punished for former sins or to continue the journey toward perfection. Of the three main variants of belief in immortality, reincarnation has been the least influential in Western culture.

While some ancient cultures apparently believed in an afterlife consisting of the shadowy existence of a replica of the body, it has been more common in Western thought to assert the immortality of a disembodied soul. Classical Greek philosophy, with the notable exception of *Stoicism, advocated such a view. *Plato, for example, offered several arguments in favour of the claim that human beings possess a soul that, in virtue of its incorporeality, is not subject to death. In the *Phaedo*, Plato has Socrates assert that 'the soul is immortal and imperishable, and our souls will truly exist in another world'. According to this view, our essential individual identity is not subject to death, but persists beyond the body's demise. *Aristotle, while rejecting Plato's arguments, attributed the quality of immortality to our 'active intellect', but it remains unclear precisely what this involves.

In the Renaissance and Enlightenment periods the newly discovered arguments of Arabic scholars against the immortality of the soul prompted a resurgence of interest among Western thinkers. *Descartes considered the denial of an immortal soul to be a grave error that would lead the individual from the paths of virtue. Like his Greek philosophical forebears, Descartes rested his belief in immortality on the independence of the soul from the body and upon its immateriality. David *Hume, by contrast, considered belief in immortality to be no more than wishful thinking, and offered a number of arguments in favour of the finality of death. The doctrine of immortality was defended by Immanuel *Kant, however, who claimed that immortality is a necessary postulate of practical reason. Without such a doctrine our sense of moral obligation would lack a coherent intellectual basis.

On account of Christianity's extensive interaction with the Greek philosophical tradition, the *dualistic thinking seen in Plato and Descartes has sometimes passed over into Christian thought. A dualistic conception of the human condition is evident in the Westminster Confession, for example, which in chapter XXXII reads, 'The bodies of men, after death, return to dust, and see corruption: but their souls, which neither die not sleep, having an immortal subsistence, immediately return to God . . .'

A dualistic anthropology of this kind is theologically dubious. A stronger case can be made, both biblically and theologically, for a holistic conception of the person as a psychosomatic unity. Nor can Christian theology endorse the view that immortality is an intrinsic property of the soul or that survival of death is the natural outcome of human existence. God alone is immortal by nature, whereas God's creatures are finite and subject to death. Originating with *Athanasius (*De Incarnatione* 3–4), there has been some debate about whether human mortality is a consequence of the *fall or whether human beings even in their pre-lapsarian state were destined to die. Whatever one's view on that question, mortality is evidently a characteristic of our post-lapsarian human condition.

Christian faith holds that death is overcome through the *resurrection of Jesus Christ. The term 'immortality' has in this context been used to indicate that the death that we surely die is not the last word for those who live in Christ. The power of God to give life where there was none yet remains, and this, rather than the inherent immortality of the soul, is what is affirmed through Christian faith in the resurrection of the dead. Thus, the immortality that it may be possible to affirm theologically is not a natural property of human life, but is dependent on one's life in God. The 'life everlasting', affirmed in Scripture and in the Apostle's Creed, is a hope fulfilled only through the power of God to give new life to those who die in the Lord. It is further contended within Christian faith that death is the outcome of sin. Death can be overcome, therefore, only to the extent that *sin is overcome. Just because the soul is affected by sin, so it has no immunity from death. The total human being, mind, body and soul, is plunged into the bondage of death and has no hope for life beyond death except through the grace and mercy of God.

Whether the eternal life brought about through resurrection, and beginning with baptism, should be seen as a species of immortality has been a moot point in Christian tradition. With careful qualification one might speak of immortality as the *outcome* of resurrection, so that those who were once subject to death are no longer so, but the common use of the term immortality to designate a natural capacity to survive death encourages a more explicit distinction between immortality and resurrection. That is the view taken by Oscar Cullman, in a 1958 monograph on the subject, and more recently by Murray Harris and Jürgen *Moltmann. Refuting the underlying dualism in the doctrine of the immortal soul, it is argued that what Christian faith promises is not the avoidance of death by some incorruptible part of us, but the resurrection of those who are wholly given up to death. Cullmann contends that immortality and resurrection are mutually exclusive. If the soul is immortal, there is no need for a resurrection, for the essential self does not die. Harris, while agreeing with Cullmann's basic point, is nevertheless willing to say that those who die in the Lord are raised to immortality. The Christian hope for life beyond death is grounded, not in anthropology, but in theology, not in assertions about the immortal nature of the soul, but in the love and mercy of the God who raised Jesus from the dead.

Bibliography

O. Cullmann, *Immortality of the Soul or Resurrection of the Dead?* (London, 1958); M. Harris, *Raised Immortal: Resurrection and Immortality in the New Testament* (Grand Rapids, 1985); J. Moltmann, 'The Immortality of the Soul or the Resurrection of the Body?' in *The Coming of God: Christian Eschatology* (ET, London, 1996).

M. A. RAE

IMPASSIBILITY, see GOD

IMPASSIBILITY OF GOD AND HUMAN SUFFERING

Impassibility is that divine attribute whereby *God is said not to experience inner emotional changes of state, whether enacted freely from within or affected by his relationship to and interaction with human beings and the created order. More specifically, impassibility denies that God can experience suffering and pain, and thus does not have feelings that are analogous to human feelings. Divine impassibility follows upon his immutability, in that, since God is changeless and unchangeable, his inner emotional state cannot change from joy to sorrow or from delight to suffering. Within contemporary theology and philosophy this divine attribute is frequently denied, the argument being that if God is impassible, he is then utterly devoid of love, mercy and compassion.

Biblical foundation

The Bible does not address the philosophical question of whether or not God is impassible. Nonetheless, within the OT, God reveals through his immanent actions within time and history that he is personal and loving. He is the one God who is Saviour, Creator and Sanctifier. These very same immanent divine acts also reveal that God transcends all else that exists, that is, he does not exist in the same manner as created reality. He is completely 'other', and so cannot be numbered among all else that exists. Thus, God is present and active within the created order of time and history as the one who, as the 'Wholly Other', transcends it, in that he exists distinct from and outside of the created order of time and history. Such revelation is the biblical basis for God's impassibility.

Because God exists in a manner unlike the manner in which creatures exist, God reveals himself, unlike creatures, to be wholly perfect. While creatures undergo change, and human beings, in particular, undergo emotional changes of state, God, because he is perfect, does not change and so does not undergo emotional changes of state either, that is, he is impassible. Therefore, he is unchangeably perfect in his passionate love.

Within this OT context, God, nonetheless, is seen as displaying a variety of emotions, such as groaning, suffering, anger and grieving. The traditional defence for God's impassibility, in the light of such passages, was to argue that the OT is using anthropomorphic language (see *Accommodation), and so cannot be taken literally. Therefore, God does not literally 'groan', 'suffer' or 'grieve'. While the OT is undoubtedly using anthropomorphic language, yet it is nonetheless attempting to say something that is actually true about God. The very superlative, extravagant, and even excessive, expression of the love, the compassion, the forgiveness and, indeed, the anger, accentuates that the one who displays all of this intense passion is someone who transcends what is beyond the merely customary and human. The Lord is 'God and not mortal'.

The Christian tradition

While the Fathers of the church inherit the term impassibility from Greek philosophy, they nonetheless interpret it, for the most part, from within a biblical understanding of God's transcendence. Because God differs from created reality, in that he is eternal and incorruptible, *Justin Martyr professes that Christians dedicate themselves to the 'impassible God' (*Apologia*, 1:13). Similarly, *Irenaeus argues that because God as Creator is unchangeably perfect, he is impassible (*Adversus Haereses*, 2:12, 1; 2:17, 3; 8). *Tertullian states that because God is eternal, and thus outside of time, he does not change or suffer (*Adversus Marcionem*, 1:3; 8). Yet, precisely because God is perfectly and unchangeably good, Tertullian holds that creatures experience this goodness in differing manners – anger toward sinners and mercy toward the repentant (*Adversus Marcionem*, 2:13). *Origen holds that one cannot interpret literally those passages which speak of God being subject to any humanlike emotion, for 'God must be believed to be entirely without passion and destitute of all these emotions' (*De Principiis*, 2:4, 4). Nonetheless, because the Father is moved by our sinful plight, Origen can also state that 'the Father is not impassible' (*In Ezechielem Homiliae*, 6:6). Origen is not contradicting himself. God is impassible in the sense that he does not undergo emotional changes of state, but he is not impassible in the sense that he is devoid of passionate love. It is precisely because of his unchanging and abiding all-consuming love that he comes to our aid. In attributing impassibility to God, then, the Fathers of the church are primarily denying of him anything that would place him within the changeable created order, which might suggest he could undergo emotional changes of state. Moreover, in their denial, they wish to enhance the absolute perfection of God's unchanging passionate love.

*Thomas Aquinas discusses God's impassibility within the context of perfect love. Because God's love is fully actualized, unlike the love of human beings, all facets of his love are similarly fully actualized. This love embraces goodness, kindness, mercy, compassion, justice, admonition, anger, correction, etc. God need not undergo passible changes in order lovingly to reprimand the sinner or be lovingly merciful to the repentant. Thus, God is merciful and compassionate, not in the sense that he 'feels' pain or suffering, but in the sense that his perfect love embraces those who suffer. His mercy is primarily expressed by acting to alleviate the cause of the suffering, something that even compassionate human beings are often unable to do. For Aquinas, God's omnipotence is ultimately expressed in his mercy, the alleviation of sin and death, and in the outpouring of grace and the bestowal of eternal life. The theologians of the later Middle Ages as well as the great theologians of the Reformation, such as Luther and Calvin, continued to uphold this common Christian biblical and theological tradition concerning God's impassibility.

Contemporary issues

From the later part of the nineteenth century to the present the majority of Christian theologians have come to deny the universal and continuous Christian tradition that God is impassible by specifically asserting that God must suffer. There are three reasons for this radical shift.

(1) The experience of immense *suffering within the world, especially as exemplified in the *Holocaust and similar horrendous events, ardently yearns for the consolation of knowing that God suffers in solidarity with those who unjustly suffer. An impassible God, it is asserted, is aloof to human suffering and thus indifferent.

(2) The Bible bears witness to a passible and so suffering God. As seen above, within the OT God is said to suffer with, on behalf of and because of his people. Moreover, through the incarnation, the Son of God must not only suffer as man but also as God. Equally in the crucifixion the Son not only suffers the loss of his Father, but the Father equally suffers the loss of his Son.

(3) Contemporary philosophy, as specifically exemplified in process philosophy, has fostered the notion that God's immanence within the world and its history demands that he changes and develops in relation to the world and its history (see *Philosophy and theology). Thus he experiences time and changeable emotional states such as suffering.

In response to this denial of God's impassibility, a number of points can be made. As seen above, to say that God is impassible is not a positive statement affirming that God is static, inert and lifeless, and so aloof and indifferent. Rather, it is a denial of those 'human' characteristics, such as change and corruptibility, or sinful passions, such as unjust anger and lust, that would make him less than fully loving. God is impassible precisely because he need not undergo passible changes of state that would make him more loving. God is pure and perfect love fully and dynamically actualized.

Because God possesses all his attributes fully actualized, he cannot suffer the loss of any these perfect goods and so he cannot experience the suffering due to their loss. If God did suffer, not only would his love not be perfect, but his love would also not be entirely altruistic and beneficent in the face of human suffering. He would now act so as relieve his own suffering.

While God is immanent within the world, he is immanent as the one who is wholly other than the world. Thus, while God is in the midst of evil, the evil of the created order does not reverberate back into his divine being and so cause him to suffer. If God did suffer, it would mean that he was a member of the created order, not the Creator, thus, as a suffering member of that order, would himself need to be freed from evil. He would no longer be the omnipotent God of mercy who could act so as to surmount the causes of suffering such as sin, death and damnation. Divine impassibility protects the biblical notion of God.

Similarly, a number of points can be made with regard to the suffering of Jesus. The church's doctrinal understanding of the *incarnation demands that, since the divine Son of God actually existed as man, all human attributes could truly be predicated of him. The Son of God as man hungered, cried, suffered and died; however, within his divine nature he remained impassible. In wanting to assert that the Son of God, within his incarnate state, suffers as God, contemporary theologians rob the incarnation of its authentic salvific value. What is important is that the Son of God experiences authentic human suffering in an authentic human manner and not that he experiences human suffering in a mitigated divine manner. It is the Son of God as man who offers his human life to the Father as a sacrifice for sin that is salvific. On the cross the Son of God as man may humanly experience being forsaken by the Father, but he equally trusts that he is not so forsaken and that the Father will come to his aid.

While Jesus, as the Son of God incarnate, is now gloriously risen from the dead, yet as head of his body, he continues to suffer in union with his body – the church. This is central to Paul's conversion experience. 'Saul, Saul, why do you persecute me? . . . I am Jesus, whom you are persecuting' (Acts 9:4–5; see 1 Cor. 12:26). This brings true consolation to human beings in the midst of their suffering, not that God suffers in his divine nature, but that Christ, who has conquered all evil, continues to suffer in union with his body so as to assure his people that they too will triumph with him. 'For as we share in Christ's sufferings, so through Christ we share abundantly in comfort too' (2 Cor. 1:5; see Rom. 8:17; Phil. 3:10; 1 Pet. 4:12; 5:1).

Bibliography

R. Bauckham, '"Only the Suffering God Can Help": Divine Passibility in Modern Theology', *Them* 9, 1984, pp. 6–13; N. M. de S. Cameron (ed.), *The Power and Weakness of God* (Edinburgh, 1990); M. Dodds, *The Unchanging God of Love* (Fribourg, 1985); idem, 'Thomas Aquinas, Human Suffering, and the Unchanging God of Love', *Theological Studies* 52, 1991, pp. 330–344; P. Fiddes, *The Creative Suffering of God* (Oxford, 1990); T. E. Fretheim, *The Suffering of God: An Old Testament Perspective* (Philadelphia, 1984); R. Goetz, 'The Suffering God: The Rise of a New Orthodoxy', *New Christian Century* 103, 1986, pp. 385–389; G. Hanratty, 'Divine Immutability and Impassibility Revisited', in F. O'Rourke (ed.), *At the Heart of the Real* (Dublin, 1992); W. Hill, 'Two Gods of Love: Aquinas and Whitehead', *Listening* 14, 1979, pp. 249–265; John Paul II, *Salvifici Doloris* (1984); J. Lambrecht and R. F. Collins (eds.), *God and Human Suffering* (Louvain, 1990); J. Moltmann, *The Crucified God* (London, 1974); J. K. Mozley, *The Impassibility of God: A Survey of Christian Thought* (Cambridge, 1926); Thomas Aquinas, *Summa Theologica*, I.20; II–II:30 (New York, 1947); idem, *Summa Contra Gentiles*, I.89–91 (Garden City, 1955); T. G. Weinandy, *Does God Suffer?* (Edinburgh, 2000); H. R. Wheeler, *Suffering, Human and Divine* (New York, 1939).

T. G. WEINANDY

INCARNATION

Within *Christology (the doctrine of the person of Christ), the word 'incarnation' may be taken to refer particularly to the humanity of the Son of God. The word literally means 'enfleshment' and the idea that the Word or Son of God 'became flesh' appears most clearly in the NT in the Johannine literature (John 1:14; 1 John 4:2). While this focuses on the act or event of becoming flesh, the term is also used to refer to the resulting humanity of the divine Son or to his being as a human.

Since the Council of *Chalcedon (451), orthodoxy has always used the terminology it made official (see *Creeds), confessing the one 'Person' of Christ 'recognized in two natures' (divine and human) 'without confusion, without change, without division, without separation' (see *Hypostasis; *Substance). But more recently, while the term 'Person' is favoured in the current revival of *trinitarian thought, alternatives have been suggested to the term 'nature'. Recognizing that the Council intended to give certain parameters to be observed, ruling out unacceptable heresies rather than providing a positive and tight definition, it has been suggested, for example, that 'two natures' might be translated into 'two different terms of reference' (O'Collins). Some scholars have proposed that the NT suggests a lighter terminology, such as 'the divine identity of Jesus' (Bauckham) or divine presence 'in' or 'to' him (N. T. Wright).

Chalcedon was an attempt to accommodate the insistence of the *Antiochene theologians on the full humanity of Jesus within the insistence of the *Alexandrians that the one Person must not be divided. But full humanity requires that 'flesh' be understood (in opposition to *Apollinarianism) to include all aspects of humanity (particularly the intellectual and volitional dimensions) and not merely the physical, and modern Christology has been most concerned to emphasize, with the Antiochenes, Christ's full and true humanity.

Such an emphasis raises the question of whether, if Christ underwent the full range of human experiences, he was different from us in any way. Heb. 4:15 makes it clear that he 'has been tempted in every way – yet was without sin', while Paul speaks of his coming 'in the likeness of sinful man' (Rom. 8:3) or in 'human likeness' (Phil. 2:7). This has been taken to mean *not* that Christ was only 'like' a human being, but that he *was* a human being, only unlike us in the sense that sin was absent. Since *sin is held to be a defect in humanity and not something one has to have to be fully human, this is believed not to compromise his full humanity. Christ therefore was not different in that he was endowed with some superior 'religious' consciousness, but since divine and human, eternal and temporal existed together in him by virtue of the hypostatic union, he was different only in that he was God as a man.

Medieval theology wrestled with the idea of two different natures or realities co-existing in the same individual. How could two *perfecta* exist in the same place? Was there something about his humanity which added something to the pre-existent Son, and in that sense to God? Did the incarnation involve any risk to God? Was there even a possibility of the incarnate Son sinning against the Father? Cyril's doctrine of *anhypostasia*, which was affirmed at Chalcedon, asserted that the One Person (*hypostasis*) of the Word united to himself, not (*an*) to a distinct human person (*hypostasis*), but that human nature which was common to all. Later Leontius of Byzantium suggested the *enhypostasia*: that even though there was no second 'person' in Christ, the common human nature had its being in (*en*) the Person (*hypostasis*) of the Son of God.

The West resisted any idea that the humanity of Christ was 'nothing'. It was even demeaning to a perfect humanity to think that, even if there were something like two consciousnesses, they could be compared to two 'tracks' running (in Thomas Morris's model), one of which is not conscious of the information stored in the other, in which divine 'electrodes' were standing by ready to kick in should the one fail. Rather, as a man, Jesus grew to be supremely perfect, without sin, even if by nature sin was possible.

That of course is also a question. O'Collins thinks that it would demean the perfection of Christ's humanity if it were possible for him to veer from the path, and so he suggests that sin was only psychologically but not ontologically possible. Yet if God could suffer *as a man*, could he not also have sinned *as a man*? A perfect humanity needs to be tempted with a risk of falling if its overcoming is to be true. John 1:5 ('and the darkness has not overcome it') suggests that sin, suffering and even death were encountered by the God who was in Christ (2 Cor. 5:19), but that they did not enter into his being. *Duns Scotus' way was to insist that the humanity assumed by God was dependent on, but not overwhelmed by, the divine presence, as suggested by Col. 1:19 ('fullness indwelling').

One attempt to deal with the question of 'oneness and twoness' in Christ is *Thomas Aquinas's way of affirming the mystery by using the language of predication. 'It is truly the Son of God who *truly* is man and so suffers *truly* as man, but remained unaffected as God' (T. Weinandy, *Does God Suffer?*, p. 175). The union is such that, in the incarnation, God *is* man and suffers as man, not *in* a man; just as he did not turn into a man but acted as a man, not in a man, so immediate is the union. Similarly, *Barth, drawing on a long and honourable Christian *Platonist tradition, wrote how it was *humanitas* (humanity) not a *homo* (man) which is assumed. Yet with *William of Ockham he pointed out that Christ was a particular *homo*, not a universal *humanitas* who was dependent on God (as Duns Scotus agreed). An alternative would be to say that he is universal not as humanity, but because the Word or *Logos himself who identifies with that human being is the universal principle of everything, so that this particular man had universal significance.

Why did the incarnation happen? Would it have happened if there had been no sin in order that the one perfect creature should be shown to the world, or was it simply in order to remove sin? Did God already forgive humanity before sending his Son? Indeed, could God so love the world without having already forgiven it? Of course, the question is really about what happens to humanity, not to God, in God's reconciling of the world to himself. The notion that human beings are to grow up into Christ does not mean that as children they are innocent in nature only, needing a more perfect model to follow. The revelation of the divine Christ shines through the contradiction of sin and the need for *atonement.

Yet how did the incarnation happen? Given the principle of *infinitum capax infiniti* (the infinite is capable of the finite), but not vice versa, John 1:11 suggests enough of a compatibility between the Word and the human Jesus (according to Pannenberg), a full-blown self-emptying (*kenosis* as in Phil. 2:5–11), so that the pre-existent Word becomes limited and the humanity becomes 'Son' in being Father-centred. One should then speak of the 'obedience' of sonship as the overlap, coterminous with the obedience of faith (Rom. 16:26). Jesus did not lack personhood, but could be defined as being the Son to the Father in his living a life completely to God and in this way as fully obedient as Adam before the fall.

For the *Reformed tradition, there can be no loss of God's sovereignty in the incarnation. According to the doctrine sometimes known as the *extra Calvinisticum*, the Logos, while incarnate in Jesus of Nazareth, is also *extra carnem*, not contained in the flesh, but still upholding the universe. Thus Jesus is the Word and vice versa, because his humanity is elevated in the divinity rather than his divinity becoming lessened through *kenosis (see e.g. Karl Barth, CD IV.2.183). To this those who defend *kenosis* would argue that Jesus always had divine power, but that doing justice to a true humanity, let alone several biblical passages, demands that he was not always conscious of that power. Even if we think that Christ's *kenosis* reached down to the depths of hell, this was only a *vision* of the second death (see Rev. 20:14; 1 Pet. 3:22; 4:6; also Eph. 4:8–10). On the *descent to hell, *Bonaventura was not too far from *Calvin: 'In what concerns the pain of suffering, *passio*, Christ suffered more intensely in his sensibility. In what concerns the pain of co-suffering, *compassio*, he suffered more intensely in his spiritual nature. But the pain of his co-suffering was greater than the pain of suffering' (*In III SentLibros d.16, a.2*). Christ was still divine even in the depths of his *kenosis*. What is essential to God is having the property of being omnipotent-unless-freely-and-temporarily-choosing-to-be-otherwise (S. Davis, 'Is Kenosis Orthodox?', in C. S. Evans [ed.], *Exploring Kenotic Theology* [Oxford, 2006]).

The post-Enlightenment problem was whether there could be such a thing as a metaphysical 'nature', whether divine or human. From Schleiermacher to some recent theologians, *Jesus was special because he was inspired to think, feel and act as a human dependent on God to the utmost degree. It is Jesus who needs to relate to the Father, not the Word who presumably is in touch with God the Father, and there cannot really be a relationship between two 'natures'. The Spirit draws Jesus to a realization of himself as the Word – into who he really is. The Spirit of God is present to Jesus in a complete, fully effective way, in a most intense manner. The uniqueness of Jesus is understood in terms of his vocation, mission, and appointment by God to be 'the firstborn of many'. Thus, Jesus was only the symbol of God and no metaphysical exchange took place. His uniqueness lay only in that to which he pointed, and Christ tells us only a little about who God is. Or, he is only the supreme instance of the paradox of grace given to all the saints (so John *Hick). With Karl *Rahner (*Theological Investigations* I), it all seems a bit much like a fusion of Spirit and spirit, especially when tied to his statement that the Word assumed all of human history, not just a 'static' humanity.

But as G. O'Collins has rightly said, a priori we do not know enough about God in order to rule that such a thing as incarnation is impossible. God coming to live as a human being in limitation and concreteness will always be a stumbling block.

Bibliography

K. Barth, *CD* IV.2; S. Davis, D. Kendall and G. O'Collins (eds.), *The Incarnation* (Oxford, 2002); C. S. Evans, *The Historical Christ and the Jesus of Faith: The Incarnational Narrative as History* (Oxford, 1996); J. Hick, *The Metaphor of God Incarnate* (London, 1993); T. Morris, *The Logic of God Incarnate* (Ithaca, 1986); G. O'Collins, *Christology* (Oxford, 1995); T. Weinandy, *In the Likeness of Sinful Flesh: An Essay on the Humanity of Christ* (Edinburgh, 1993); idem, *Does God Suffer?* (Notre Dame, 2000); N. T. Wright, *Jesus and the Victory of God* (London, 1996).

M. W. ELLIOTT

INDIAN CHRISTIAN THEOLOGY

There are three major strands in Indian Christian theology.

The dominant strand for many centuries was the reflection of converts from the upper castes of *Hinduism, principally Brahmins. There are no clear landmarks. The early churches in India, which claim to date their existence from the apostle Thomas, were in the Orthodox tradition. They broadly followed the theology of the *Eastern Orthodox churches and made some points in the debates with Rome. But being set in Indian soil made little or no difference to them. They were upper caste in membership and the church was treated as one of the higher castes. This tradition still continues.

In the seventeenth century the Jesuit Robert De Nobili (1577–1656) attempted in theory and practice to relate the Christian faith to the practice of the Indian caste system. He did not so much reflect theologically on Christianity and the caste system as attempt to come to terms with socio-religious realities.

Christian involvement in India from Western countries between 1600 and 1900 at first developed a largely negative attitude to Indian religions. The concern of Christian theology was to point out the errors and supposed irrationality of Hindu religions.

At the same time Orientalists from the West helped spark a renewal in Hinduism. Hindu leaders sought to encourage the best in their own religion, and some, such as Vivekananda (1862–1902), responded to the impact of Christian mission in India by taking Christ seriously as the revealer of God.

Christian leaders, who were all personal converts from the Brahmin upper castes, responded to this movement of renewal and reform in Hinduism. This marked the birth of Indian Christian theology. These upper-caste converts were also shaped by the liberal tradition in Western Christianity, which had responded to the *Enlightenment challenge that a supernatural God could not exist, by locating God solely in the individual's inner experience. It identified Christianity with personal religious experience. Indian Christian theologians then searched for parallels in Hindu *religious experience in seeking the most adequate terms to express Christian faith. Proponents of this method were Ram Mohan Roy (1772–1833), Brahmabandhab Upadhyaya (1861–1907) and P. Chenchiah (1886–1959).

A second major stream related Christian faith to the process of nation-building, in order to identify the role Christians should play in pre-independent and post-independent India. India became independent in 1947. Some leading Indian Christian theologians addressed the social and economic realities that confronted the new state. P. D. Devanandan (1901–62), M. M. Thomas (1916–96), K. M. George and J. R. Chandran took the lead. They urged Christian commitment to nation-building and to the ecumenical movement as a pledge and sign of Christian commitment to the unity of humankind. Christians could hardly argue for a united India if their own ranks were rent with division.

Evangelical Christians were slow to respond to these issues. But in the 1970s the formation of the Evangelical Fellowship of India's Committee on Relief and its involvement in both relief and development projects stimulated increasing theological work on the biblical basis of social involvement. Documents like the Madras Declaration on Evangelical Social Action reflect this.

A third stream is now emerging, in Indian Christian reflection from the context of the poor and the outcast. In previous centuries no theology has been done by converts from the lower castes of Hinduism and from poor people. This is especially striking since over ninety per cent of India's Christians come from this background. The Roman Catholic theologian Sebastian Kappen, though not from this background, has sought to identify with them.

A number of key issues have occupied Indian Christian theologians in the period since 1947. One major issue was how far Christianity was continuous with the experience and even the revelation of other religions. H. *Kraemer insisted that Christianity was totally discontinuous, but M. M. Thomas responded by speaking of a Christ-centred *syncretism. He pointed out that in every society Christianity took over and endorsed some aspects of the life and experience of society in order to communicate its meaning. By its very nature Christianity was syncretistic. The issue was whether this syncretism was centred on Christ. According to Thomas, an important way of harnessing all religions for the task of nation-building was the specific focus of humanization. He saw the Christian faith as providing a definite force for humanization and as a dynamic in dialogue with the vertical foci of other faiths pushing them in the direction of new horizontal relationships in concern for humanity.

J. N. Farquhar (1861–1929) had posited Christianity as the crown of Hinduism. Post-independence reflection did not accept this judgment. The most dominant thought came through Raimundo Panikkar (1918–2010) and M. M. Thomas who spoke of the hidden Jesus in Hinduism which found expression in Hindu compassion and justice. S. M. Samartha focused on *religious experience as a way of relating to other religions. He regarded dialogue as a method not of evangelism, but of relating in an open-ended pilgrimage where experience of different religions influences pilgrims in their search for truth and true religious experience.

A second major issue was how to witness to the *uniqueness of Christ in an atmosphere of religious universalism and philosophical pluralism. Hinduism finds everything in Christ prefigured in its own religious experience. So how could unique claims be made of Christ? Furthermore, Hinduism, while open to receive insights from all religions, is fundamentally centred on personal experience. It is therefore impossible to make objective judgments, since everyone's religious experience is equally valid. In this context how could someone claim that the experience of salvation through Christ is uniquely valid without appearing arrogant and thus undermining their very claim by their pride?

A third issue is whether it is proper to use Hindu categories to describe Christian faith. In Hindu mythology many gods appeared on earth as men, as avatars. Could the incarnation of Jesus be described in these terms? Could Hindu religious language be used for Christian realities without compromising Christian truth?

A fourth issue concerns the socio-economic context of India. How does the gospel contribute to building a united nation out of many fragmented groups? This issue was addressed at the time of independence when the Christians declined an offer by the government to have a certain number of parliamentary seats reserved for Christians elected by Christian constituencies. Their reason was that the Christian goal was not to be one sect among many, but to contribute in every group to the unity of the whole.

In the socio-economic sphere the church is also grappling with how to be a prophetic voice on behalf of the poor. Sixty per cent of India's population live below the poverty line. Should the church work with structures of the establishment, whether government agencies or business interests, to secure its own institutions which were founded to serve the poor but increasingly serve the rich? Or should the church work with action groups in the grass roots of society? Should the church encourage people to discover their identity as the creatures of God with equal rights to the earth's resources by the process of welfare provision or through political protest?

Important thinking has been done in this area by Roman Catholic theologians of the Jesuit Order. The Indian Social Institute, John Desrochers (*Jesus the Liberator*, Bangalore, 1976), Sebastian Kappen (*Jesus and Freedom*, Maryknoll, 1978), Desmond D'Alreo and Stanley Lourduswamy have contributed important perspectives which share much in common with *liberation theology from Latin America.

A fifth issue concerns the relationship between the church's role in the socio-economic spheres and its concern to challenge people to accept Christ. What is the true biblical relationship between social responsibility and evangelism? This issue specially focuses on whether the church should require people to renounce caste on becoming Christian or allow caste-churches to emerge.

A sixth issue is how to express Christian worship and communication in appropriate cultural forms (see *Contextualization). Can Hindu patterns of architecture, dance, worship and prayer express Christian devotion and worship, or does the fact that Hindu spirituality excludes the poorest people make it totally inappropriate? Would an outcaste person feel at home in Hinduized Christian worship? While Western forms of church practice may appear foreign in the Indian context, for many the only alternative to Hindu practices which completely excluded them has been a total break. Such people are now discovering that the Western practices themselves compromise biblical priorities in some aspects and are looking for new models. Important work is being done in this area by the Roman Catholic D. S. Amalorpavadass of the National Biblical Catechetical and Liturgical Centre in Bangalore, and by the Christian Arts and Communication Services in Madras.

In summary, the responses of Indian Christians to the Hindu religious reality have been described in a number of ways: (1) the cosmic Christ includes all the various pluralities of religious experience; (2) Christianity takes shape within a pluralistic environment and so becomes a Christ-centred syncretism; (3) Christ is the unknown force for justice within Hinduism; (4) Christ is the goal of the religious quest of Hinduism; (5) Hinduism is related to Christianity as its OT Scriptures; (6) Christianity is totally discontinuous with Hinduism; (7) the Hindu context produces a particular form of Christian, an Indian Christian; (8) Hinduism must be addressed with the question of the poor and marginalized as the question about religion which Jesus validated.

See also: CHRISTIANITY AND OTHER RELIGIONS.

Bibliography

R. Boyd, *Indian Christian Theology* (Madras, 1969); V. Samuel and C. Sugden, *The Gospel among Our Hindu Neighbours* (Bangalore, 1983); G. Shiri, *Christian Social Witness* (Madras, 1983); M. M. Thomas, *The Acknowledged Christ of the Indian Renaissance* (Madras, 1969); *idem*, *Man and the Universe of Faiths* (Madras, 1975); *Tr* 2:2 (1985) – issue on Caste and the Church.

C. M. N. SUGDEN AND V. K. SAMUEL

INDULGENCES, see MERIT

INFALLIBILITY AND INERRANCY OF THE BIBLE

A distinctive mark of *evangelical Christianity is belief in 'the divine inspiration and infallibility of Holy Scripture as originally given and its supreme authority in all matters of faith and conduct' (UCCF doctrinal basis). Some evangelicals use the term 'inerrancy': 'The Bible alone and the Bible in its entirety, is the Word of God written, and therefore inerrant in the autographs' (The Evangelical Theological Society). In practice, those who use the term 'infallibility' assert the truth of the doctrinal teaching of the Bible, whereas those who speak of 'inerrancy' include also historical and other factual information, although the boundaries between the positions are inevitably fuzzy.

Such terms express an understanding of the Bible long taken for granted in the church and held by many contemporary Christians. The two statements quoted were formulated to indicate how evangelical doctrine differs (1) from *Roman Catholic teaching that asserts the infallibility of church and pope alongside and sometimes even above the authority of Scripture; and also (2) from *liberal Protestant teaching that the Bible is one, fallible source of Christian truth alongside human reason and secular sources of knowledge.

Belief in the inspiration and infallibility or inerrancy of *Scripture may have two sorts of basis.

First, it can be regarded as an implication of accepting the divine authority of Christ and of the authors of Scripture as God's agents mediating his revelation to humanity. Many biblical books were written by people who claimed to be, or who were believed to be, directly inspired by God; in particular, the books of the OT were treated as authoritative revelation by Jesus and his immediate followers. Having come to faith in Christ, we should accept his view of Scripture. The statement that 'all Scripture is God-breathed' (2 Tim. 3:16; cf. 2 Pet. 1:21) epitomizes this belief; its author was not saying anything unusual or controversial. Other biblical statements indicate a belief that the *Holy Spirit influenced what was written. Many texts purport to express what God was saying ('the word of the Lord') through revelations to prophets or other divinely accredited messengers. In addition to these examples of direct inspiration, God could and did work through human biblical authors in such matters as the recording of history (often using other sources) so that their ordinary human compositions were inspired and authorized by him. N. Wolterstorff has helpfully developed the concept of God giving his imprimatur to human compositions which expressed what he wants to say, although he recognizes that there must be something about such works that makes them apt for this purpose. Scripture, then, is fully trustworthy, since God is the omniscient God of truth and cannot lie; the doctrinal statements are true, the commands are binding, and the historical statements refer to events as they really happened.

Second, such belief may be supported by the claim that, wherever the Bible can be tested for factual accuracy, it passes the test; if so, it is probable (but beyond proof) that it is also true and reliable in matters of faith and ethical teaching (as well as in factual matters more generally). Clearly, to base belief exclusively on such testing of the Bible would be a dubious procedure, since it makes acceptance of the truth of the Bible dependent upon the shifting sands of historical and scientific investigations. If the Bible can be shown to be reliable where it can be tested, this would at most confirm faith, but it cannot be the basis of faith.

However, there are innumerable points where the trustworthiness of the Bible has been questioned. To this there are two types of response. One is to produce explanations of how statements in the Bible may be accurate despite appearances to the contrary (e.g. by offering ways of harmonizing different accounts of the same event or by producing historical evidence that corroborates a biblical account). Some such explanations are more ingenious than persuasive. The other approach is to insist that, although there is at present no solution, nevertheless one may be discovered in the future, and that in any case we should 'honor God by trusting His assurance that His Word is true, despite these appearances' (N. L. Geisler, *Inerrancy*, p. 501). Once this is said, however, it is clear that a belief in inerrancy is just that, a 'belief', and therefore not something that can be demonstrated in such a way as to carry conviction for people who are not believers.

The function of a belief in infallibility or inerrancy, therefore, is in-house. It is a confession of faith that what may be deduced about the nature of Scripture from its own testimony is that it is a reliable record of 'divine disclosure', thanks to its being 'God-breathed', and hence it functions as the supreme authority for Christian faith and practice.

Within evangelicalism there is a range of understanding of this character of Scripture. On the one hand, there is the position most powerfully articulated by *Warfield and expounded in 'The *Chicago Statement on Biblical Inerrancy' (accessible in Geisler, *Inerrancy*, pp. 493–502). Inspiration is the concursive activity of the Holy Spirit, that caused the various human authors to write what God wished them to say while writing freely in normal human ways; in no sense did the Spirit dictate what to say to them, although the results of inspiration are the same as if dictation had actually taken place.

But 'inerrancy' is a slippery term and needs some exposition. Scripture was written at particular times and places in the past and uses the appropriate modes of expression; for example, it may use approximations rather than precise measurements. Scripture may contain fictitious material intended as such and readily identifiable (e.g. the parables). Statements can be misunderstood if not read in their contexts. The parts must be interpreted in the light of Scripture as a whole. There is certainly development in understanding over the long period of composition (e.g. the recognition of the Son and the Holy Spirit as persons within the divine identity), even if there is no change in essential teaching. Although the old and new covenants stand in continuity with one another, some teaching has been abrogated; the sacrificial legislation in the OT is no longer binding now that Christ has offered the perfect, final sacrifice for sin. In this kind of way phenomena that might be thought to argue against inerrancy can be accommodated within the definition.

Over against 'inerrancy' stands the view of other scholars who hold equally firmly to the inspiration and authority of Scripture as 'infallible', but allow for the possibility that Scripture might not be wholly free from error, or who argue that the categories of errancy and inerrancy are inappropriate. Such scholars argue that (for example) the actual text of Scripture has not been preserved without errors in the copying of the manuscripts which makes it difficult, if not sometimes impossible, to reconstruct the original text, but they insist that the extent of such uncertainty is not sufficient to place the message of Scripture in any real doubt. But if readers have to live with this undeniable uncertainty in the transmitted text, some would question whether it is necessary to believe that absolute accuracy is necessary, or has actually been provided, in the teaching of the original text.

Within this infallibilist position there is a greater willingness to recognize that the genres and forms of the biblical texts may permit the inclusion of matter that is not literally historical (e.g. the early stories in Genesis) (see *Myth), and that the accepted practices of ancient authors might include greater freedom in interpretation and presentation than would be considered appropriate by contemporary historians. The composition of many books was an extended, complex process in which various individuals and communities were concerned, rather than being akin to the writing of a document by a single author (e.g. the book of Isaiah contains later additions to the work of the eighth-century prophet). It is arguable that a strict doctrine of inerrancy is threatened by death by a thousand qualifications.

Assessing these two views depends to some extent on the relative weights attached to a doctrinal, a priori approach that argues from what is perceived to be the teaching of Scripture on its own character and to an empirical approach that examines the actual phenomena in Scripture (e.g. the variations in the wording of sayings of Jesus in the Gospels).

The importance of the doctrine is undeniable. In the late nineteenth century it was developed particularly over against the growth of the kind of biblical criticism which hypothesized about the sources and dating of the biblical books (especially the OT) on various grounds, including the detection of alleged contradictions. The historicity of the recorded events that were held to be the locus or the proof of divine activity in history was assailed; if the Israelites never escaped from Egypt in the way described in Exodus, then this non-existent event could not have been a divine event. More importantly, if the details in the accounts of the resurrection appearances of Jesus appear to contradict one another, then the fact of the resurrection as God raising Jesus from the dead is also called into question. The fact that 'higher' criticism was largely carried on by opponents of orthodox, evangelical Christianity or of Christianity itself created a powerful reaction of fairly total rejection on the part of evangelicals. At the present time, controversy centres more on the validity of scriptural teaching on such matters as the sinfulness of homosexual practice or the status of adherents of other religions at the last judgment.

At the very least, all evangelicals would affirm that the inspiration of Scripture implies that it is fully adequate for the purposes for which God caused it to be written. As a collection of writings expressing what God considers it needful for us to know, it is fundamentally true, but this leaves open questions regarding the nature of its truth. Evangelicals need to be at the forefront in the task of biblical *hermeneutics, the science of understanding how to go about the interpretation of an authoritative text. Although, then, there is something of a spectrum of beliefs among evangelicals regarding just in what sense the Bible is trustworthy and infallible (or inerrant), there is a united acceptance that Scripture is the inspired word of God and its character is such as to make it the final authority in faith and conduct.

See also: REVELATION; SCRIPTURE, DOCTRINE OF.

Bibliography

G. C. Berkouwer, *Holy Scripture* (Grand Rapids, 1975); N. L. Geisler (ed.), *Inerrancy* (Grand Rapids, 1979); J. Goldingay, *Models for Scripture* (Grand Rapids and Carlisle, 1994); I. H. Marshall, *Biblical Inspiration* (London, 1982); J. Orr, *Revelation and Inspiration* (London, 1910); J. I. Packer, *Fundamentalism and the Word of God* (London, 1958); idem, 'Hermeneutics and Biblical Authority', *Them* 1, 1975, pp. 3–12, <http://www.biblicalstudiesorg.uk/article_herm_packer.html>; C. H. Pinnock, *The Scripture Principle* (Grand Rapids, ²2006); B. B. Warfield, *The Inspiration and Authority of the Bible* (London, 1951); N. Wolterstorff, *Divine Discourse* (Cambridge, 1995).

I. H. MARSHALL

INFALLIBILITY, PAPAL, see PAPACY

INFANT BAPTISM, see BAPTISM

INFRALAPSARIANIAM, see PREDESTINATION

INSPIRATION, see SCRIPTURE

INTERCESSION OF CHRIST, see OFFICES OF CHRIST

INTERMEDIATE STATE

Given the Christian hope of the general *resurrection at the end of the age, the question necessarily arises of the 'state' of the dead in the intermediate time between their death and resurrection. If the future general resurrection is linked to the redemption of the cosmos (Rom. 8:18–23) in such a way that the resurrection body has its habitat within the new creation (Rev. 21:1–4), then some kind of personal continuity has to be posited between the moment of the individual's death and the future resurrection. Paul certainly teaches such a personal continuity in 2 Cor. 5 where he refers to the body as an 'earthly tent' and the expected resurrection body as a 'heavenly dwelling', and expresses the desire not to be 'naked', but to be 'further clothed'. Through the mixed metaphor of 'clothing' and 'dwelling', this passage certainly implies a personal continuity of the 'I', but does not name that as a 'spirit' or 'soul'. Christian tradition from the earliest days has used such language, however, and, influenced perhaps by Hellenistic and particularly Platonist anthropology, has generally understood that the human *soul will exist between death and resurrection in a bodiless state.

Further reflection on this has arisen in the light of the OT understanding of the state of the dead. Until the hope of the resurrection arose late in the OT period, the general belief was that the dead went forever to *Sheol* (Gk, *Hades*), a place of shadowy half-life, otherwise referred to as 'the grave' or 'the Pit'. It was not, however, originally thought of as a place of punishment. That concept emerged in Second Temple Judaism with the term *Gehenna*, a word coined from the valley of Hinnom outside Jerusalem where the rubbish of the city was burned, and a term used by Jesus (Matt. 5:22, etc.). References to Christ's preaching 'to the spirits in prison' (1 Pet. 3:18–22; 4:6) led to the belief that those of OT times, particularly the faithful, had been released from *Sheol* through Christ's *descent into hell between his death and resurrection. This later developed into the medieval notion of the 'harrowing of hell', resulting from the victory of Christ over the devil.

The question remained, however, as to what 'state' the OT saints presently enjoy along with those who have since believed in Christ, and the question was complicated by the rise of belief in *purgatory. This latter belief arose in the early centuries of the church as the answer to the question of how God dealt with post-baptismal sin. The belief that there was no forgiveness after the initial repentance, faith and conversion gave way to a belief that baptized Christians could be forgiven for later sin if they performed works of *penance, and this in turn led to the belief that Christians who did not complete such penance and who had not progressed sufficiently in *sanctification would be purged in 'purgatory' before final admittance to heaven.

The doctrines of penance and purgatory were rejected by the *Reformers, but the question still remained as to the 'state' of both believers and unbelievers in the intermediate period between death and resurrection. Luther and some Anabaptist groups tended towards belief in 'soul sleep'. The classic passage for that belief is in 1 Thess. 4:13–18, where Paul writes that those who are 'asleep' in Christ will not be left behind at the coming of the Lord. By contrast, John Calvin interpreted 'sleep' as simply a metaphor for death and was totally opposed to the notion of soul sleep, writing his first published work, *Psychopannychia*, to refute it. The souls of the elect enter immediately on death into the *kingdom of God. Christ 'receives them into paradise' (*Institutes*, III.25.6) and there they rest consciously, but do not sleep, until they enter into their full glory after the Last *Judgment. The reprobate 'are chained up like malefactors until the time when they are dragged to the punishment that is appointed for them'. Perhaps the classic passage which has been used to reject 'soul sleep' is the parable of the rich man and Lazarus (Luke 16:19–31), in which 'a great gulf' has been fixed between the blessed and the damned, but both are conscious. Scholars today, however, may question whether that conclusion may be drawn from what is evidently a story told to make a different point.

Where popular religion has lost the Christian doctrine of the resurrection and imagines instead a disembodied life forever in 'heaven', the question of the intermediate state does not arise. But as N. T. Wright has emphasized, Christians believe in 'life after life after death' and therefore some concept of the intermediate state seems to be required. A certain mystery remains and the focus of Christian *hope is not there but in the resurrection. Yet Christian theology has generally asserted that while the nature of the intermediate state may not be entirely clear, nor needs to be, those who are 'absent from the body' are 'present with the Lord' (2 Cor. 5:8), resting from their labours (Heb. 4:10; Rev. 14:13) until the Lord's coming. Protestant theology rejects, however, the idea of any direct communication with the dead in Christ, either in the form of prayers to the saints or the popular notion that those who are 'with the Lord' are able to observe our present life.

Bibliography

M. J. Harris, *Raised Immortal* (London, 1983); B. Hebblethwaite, *The Christian Hope* (London, 1984); S. Travis, *Christ Will Come Again* (London, 1997); N. T. Wright, *Surprised by Hope* (London, 2007).

T. A. NOBLE

INTERPRETATION, see HERMENEUTICS

INVOCATION, see EUCHARIST; SAINT

IRENAEUS (*c.* 130–*c.* 200)

A vigorous anti-heretical writer devoted to the biblical faith, Irenaeus, whose lifetime connected the sub-apostolic church to the old Catholic church, was a pivotal figure in the development of Christian theology. Coming from Asia Minor, where he heard Polycarp of Smyrna teach, and becoming a presbyter and then bishop at Lyons, he united Asian and Western theological traditions. Maintaining contacts with Rome, he attempted to mediate in the paschal (see *Easter) and *Montanist controversies in order to preserve the unity of the church, which was so important to his theology.

Irenaeus' *Demonstration of the Apostolic Preaching* elaborates catechetical instruction according to biblical history as the saving plan of God. Following a literal history of the mighty acts of God – beginning with creation and continuing through the events of Genesis, the Mosaic covenant, the taking of the Promised Land, the sending of the prophets, the coming of Christ, the sending of the apostles, and the general resurrection – the work treats the spiritual sense of Scripture in which OT prophecies are presented as testimonies to Christ's pre-existence, his divine and human nature, his virgin birth, miracles, passion, resurrection and calling a new people through the apostles.

The chief fame of Irenaeus rests on his *Against Heresies*. The first two books expound various *Gnostic systems and offer rational arguments against them. Books 3–5 undertake the refutation of Gnostic teachings from the apostolic writings and words of the Lord. Although primarily a theologian, Irenaeus was knowledgeable about philosophy and employed rhetorical devices in structuring his treatise.

One can interpret Irenaeus as a 'biblical theologian' for his emphasis on Scripture, creation, redemption and resurrection; or one can interpret him as a theologian of the developing Catholic tradition for his arguments from tradition, apostolic succession (see *Ministry), the importance of Rome, and *Mary as the new Eve. Since *Scripture and tradition had the same content for Irenaeus (i.e. the gospel), biblical theology is the substance of his thought. The 'Catholic' elements appear primarily as polemical arguments against the Gnostics and *Marcion. Likewise, the doctrines he emphasizes are those challenged by heretics.

Irenaeus argued for the unity of Scripture as the historical revelation of 'one and the same God' who had initiated different covenants with human beings. Thus the OT is in harmony with the NT, although the law of Moses is now superseded by the gospel of Christ. The historical pattern of *revelation was the prophets, Christ and the apostles; but the essential content throughout was Christ. Whereas the Gnostics interpreted the Bible according to their mythical views of reality, Irenaeus defended the interpretation of the Bible according to the 'canon (rule) of truth'. This consisted of summaries of the apostolic preaching as representing the proper content of Scripture. He argued that the correct understanding of apostolic teaching was preserved in the churches which went back to apostolic times and had personal acquaintance with the apostles (cf. E. Molland in *JEH* 1, 1950, pp. 12–28). Contrary to Gnostic claims to a secret tradition handed down from the apostles, Irenaeus insisted that the apostles would have appointed as bishops and presbyters those to whom they would have revealed any secrets. The succession in doctrine and life was transmitted from one holder of the teaching chair in each church to the next (not from ordainer to ordained). The consistency of the teaching in the churches of Irenaeus' day with the apostles' teaching was assured by its public character. Its correctness was further guaranteed by its agreement in each locality.

Irenaeus contributed to the explanation of the *Trinity the image of God's Word and Wisdom (Christ and the Holy Spirit) as the 'two hands of God'. The image expressed God's direct action in creation and revelation. The one God created all things out of nothing. God's providence exists alongside human free will. Adam was created as a child and so was easily deceived into sin.

The fully divine Son of God became Son of Man for human salvation. The incarnation through the virgin birth involved his assuming real flesh and retracing the steps of humanity in order to bring humanity to perfection in himself (recapitulation). His contact with every circumstance of human experience sanctified all ages and conditions of life. Christ's perfect obedience reversed the effects of the first Adam's disobedience, the blood of his death bringing forgiveness of sins and his resurrection a triumph over death, and so the devil was defeated.

Baptism brings regeneration and the gift of the Holy Spirit. The addition of the Holy Spirit to the human person, consisting of body and soul, restores the likeness of God lost in the first transgression. Salvation is progressively realized, a process to be completed only in the end-time. As the Spirit becomes accustomed to dwell in the flesh, so the person grows in the fullness of salvation, leading to communion with God and participation in immortality. The availability of grace to all, and the human freedom to respond to grace were important to his argument against Gnosticism.

The human creature in its wholeness, including the flesh, is saved. Thus Irenaeus' eschatology includes an earthly kingdom of the Lord at his second coming, a renewed material world and a literal resurrection of the flesh. The *millennial kingdom is the last stage of preparation for the ultimate perfection of the *vision of God.

The *eucharistic elements of bread and wine, by receiving the invocation of God, come to consist of two realities, one earthly and one heavenly. The human bodies nourished by the body and blood of the Christ become capable of the resurrection and eternal life.

The *church contains the deposit of truth, and in the church the Holy Spirit is found. The presbyters, including bishops, when they succeed to their teaching chairs, receive the apostolic teaching (the deposit of truth) to transmit to others. The church at Rome, as founded by Peter and Paul, was especially important to Irenaeus as preserving the apostolic tradition (see *Papacy). In a passage which has been given many interpretations (*Against Heresies* III.3.2) Irenaeus seems to say that all must agree with the church at Rome. Rome was a model of sound doctrine, and the agreement must be primarily with that sound doctrine preserved at Rome and secondarily with the church there as exemplary of the apostolic teaching (cf. J. F. McCue in *TS* 25, 1964, pp. 161–196).

Bibliography

Works: *Against Heresies*, Books 1–5, tr. A. Roberts and W. H. Rambaut, *The Ante-Nicene Fathers*, vol. 1 (Grand Rapids, 1987); *St Irenaeus: Proof of the Apostolic Preaching*, tr. J. P. Smith, *Ancient Christian Writers*, vol. 16 (New York, 1952).

Studies: R. Berthouzoz, *Liberté et grâce suivant la théologie d'Irénée de Lyon* (Paris, 1980); D. Farkasfalvy, 'Theology of Scripture in Irenaeus', *RBén*; 78 (1968), pp. 319–333; P. Foster and S. Parvis (eds.), *Irenaeus: Life, Scripture, Legacy* (Minneapolis, 2011); R. M. Grant, 'Irenaeus and Hellenistic Culture', *HTR* 42 (1949), pp. 41–51; idem, *Irenaeus of Lyons (The Early Church Fathers)* (London and New York, 1997); J. Lawson, *The Biblical Theology of Saint Irenaeus* (London, 1948); J. T. Nielsen, *Adam and Christ in the Theology of Irenaeus of Lyons* (Assen, 1968); W. R. Schoedel, 'Theological Method in Irenaeus', *JTS* 35 (1984), pp. 31–49; G. Vallee, 'Theological and Non-Theological Motives in Irenaeus's Refutation of the Gnostics', in E. P. Sanders (ed.), *Jewish and Christian Self-Definition*, vol. 1 (Philadelphia, 1980), pp. 174–185; G. Wingren, *Man and the Incarnation: A Study in the Biblical Theology of Irenaeus* (Philadelphia, 1959).

E. FERGUSON

IRVING, EDWARD (1792–1834)

Born and brought up in the small town of Annan in southern Scotland, Irving never lost a sense of the importance of close-knit communities founded on shared values. He studied at Edinburgh University, and was licensed to preach in 1815 by the Presbytery of Kirkcaldy, where he was a schoolmaster. Only in 1819, however, did he secure a ministerial post, as assistant to Thomas *Chalmers. The delay did much to fuel his disillusionment with contemporary Christianity and convince him to attempt something better. From 1822 he ministered to what became the National Scotch Church in London, but increasing criticism of his theology and practice led to his eviction by the trustees in 1832 and his deposition as a minister for heresy by the Church of Scotland in 1833. Thereafter he played a vital but subordinate role in what would become the Catholic Apostolic Church, although already ill with the consumption which killed him.

Irving has been seen as making contributions in three areas of theology: Christology, *eschatology and pneumatology (see *Holy Spirit). In each, his views proved controversial and continue to stimulate debate. But others also deserve attention.

In *Christology, Irving's passionate argument that Christ assumed fallen human nature, being upheld sinless (see *Sinlessness of Christ) by the indwelling Holy Spirit, has attracted attention from Catholic and Orthodox as well as Protestant and Pentecostal theologians. His motivation was pastoral, to give believers a Christ who could identify with them as their high priest, but it has been argued that the result was a somewhat confused account, alleged by some to verge on *Nestorianism. Set against contemporary evangelical failure to do justice to the humanity of Christ, it may be seen as a timely corrective, however.

It is arguable that Irving's pessimistic assessment of the contemporary church and of the prospects for Christendom was given considerable force by his friendship with *Coleridge. At any rate, he did much to popularize premillennial (see *Millennium) thought in evangelicalism, though this also served to accelerate the movement's fragmentation. He was the leading light in the Albury conferences on prophecy (1826–30).

Well before his 'charismatic' years, Irving as a *Romantic was developing a fuller theology of the Holy Spirit. Influenced by his assistant A. J. Scott (1805–66), Irving came to believe that miracles should still be occurring, and that the charismata had not been finally withdrawn from the church (see *Charismatic theology/ movement). Perhaps the most fateful aspect of this was his exposition of the Gospel miracles as performed by Jesus as man in the power of the Spirit, which encouraged some to expect such things to occur in the ministry of contemporary churches. The 'manifestations' in Scotland and London from 1830 were a direct result.

Other areas of Irving's thought also call for comment. In 1824 he preached a lengthy sermon on behalf of the London Missionary Society, the first part of which appeared in 1825 as *For Missionaries after the Apostolical School*. He argued that the contemporary emphasis on doing *mission though voluntary parachurch bodies lost sight of the fact that God's appointed mission agency remained the church, and that its emissaries should go forth like the Twelve and the Seventy, without visible human means of support. His thinking was reflected by early protagonists of the 'faith mission' movement, some of whom had read this work.

A somewhat neglected aspect of his thought is that of theology as 'public truth', and the duty of Britain as a nation in covenant with God to make due acknowledgment of its dependence on God and to frame its laws and its practice in areas such as economics and education in line with the word of God (see *State). This led him to some forthright social critique, especially earlier in his ministry. Especially after the Emancipation Act (1829), giving civil rights to Catholics, he argued that the covenanted nation had become an apostate nation, ripe for divine judgment.

Irving's theology should be taken as a whole. This relates to his sense of calling as a pastor, responsible to ensure the provision of a balanced diet for his flock. In assessing his thought, three points should be made regarding how he did theology. First, Irving came to fame as a preacher, perhaps more for the style than the content of his sermons. He regarded preaching as the lynchpin of his ministry. His early claim to pioneer new styles of communication, the 'argument' and the 'oration' (*For the Oracles of God*, 1823), was not maintained, but he did consider that his preaching ranged far more widely in divine truth than that of his contemporaries, especially the evangelicals. Many of his doctrinal works began life as lengthy series of sermons, a fact which should be borne in mind when reading them. Secondly, he was a pastorally driven theologian. For all his early love of theoretical speculation, Irving's concerns were essentially practical. At Annan in 1833, he asserted that his Christology (for which he was on trial) was motivated by concern for the sanctification of his flock. Thirdly, we may call Irving a practitioner. He early came to be recognized as a man of integrity who sought to live out his faith in every aspect of his life. As one memorial tribute asked, 'If it is the written Word of God, shall it not be the acted Word too?'

Twentieth- and twenty-first-century debate on Irving has sometimes taken one or another aspect of his thought and studied it in isolation. Furthermore, his early death means that we are left with multiple suggestions about 'what might have been', his thought being capable of application in widely differing directions. More recently, attention has been given to the Romantic strain in his thought, e.g. in his emphasis on supernatural divine action. Although born on the same day as the poet Shelley, he took Romantic ideas in a very different direction, an indication of the likely fruitfulness of further study of early nineteenth-century Romantic thought about religion and *spirituality. He remains a controversial figure.

Bibliography

Works: *Preliminary Discourse to the Work of Ben Ezra* (London, 1827); *Collected Writings*, 5 vols. (London, 1864–6); *Prophetical Works*, 2 vols. (London, 1867/70).

Studies: P. Elliott, *Edward Irving: Romantic Theology in Crisis* (Bletchley, 2014); T. Grass, *The Lord's Watchman: A Life of Edward Irving* (Bletchley, 2011); G. Macfarlane, *Christ and the Spirit: The Doctrine of the Incarnation According to Edward Irving* (Carlisle, 1996).

T. GRASS

ISLAM AND CHRISTIANITY

Islam has had continuous and wide-ranging contact with Christianity throughout its history. Arabia, the cradle of Islam, was surrounded by Christian countries and civilizations. To the north and west were Syria (see *Syrian Christianity), Egypt (see *Coptic Christianity) and Palestine (all part of the Byzantine Empire), while to the south and east were Ethiopia and her colonies (such as the Yemen). Biographical accounts record that Muhammad (*c.* 570–632), the founder of Islam, had early contact with both groups. Furthermore, there were Arab Christian individuals and settled communities in Arabia itself with which the earliest Muslims interacted.

The Qur'anic view of Christians and Christianity is ambiguous. On the one hand, it recognizes particular qualities such as humility (5:85) and a degree of commonality (2:136; 29:46). But the Qur'an also includes a fundamental polemic directed against certain basic Christian beliefs, such as the divine sonship of Jesus Christ (see *Christology) and the doctrine of the *Trinity. This sets the stage for more pointed pronouncements in the *Hadith*, where Muhammad is reported to have said, '[H]e who amongst the community of Jews or Christians hears about me, but does not affirm his belief in that with which I have been sent and dies in this state [of disbelief], he shall be but one of the denizens of Hell-Fire' (*Sahih Muslim*, Bk 1, Ch. 71, No. 284). Such a critique informed early contacts between Muslims and Christians, with Christian apologists from this period, such as *John of Damascus and later Timothy of Baghdad (eighth to ninth centuries), attempting to respond to this early Islamic polemic.

The enlargement of the territorial domains of Islam to the north and west of Arabia came primarily at the expense of Christianity, especially Byzantine Christianity. The years between the death of Muhammad (632) and the First Crusade (1096) witnessed rapid and extraordinary military expansion by Muslims throughout the Middle East, North Africa and the Iberian peninsula, resulting in a series of Muslim empires. Christians, Jews and others became subject peoples, or *dhimmis*. They were divided into *millats* (or communities) which corresponded to the different Christian sects (Melkite, Jacobite or *Nestorian).

The Christian experience under Islamic Empire was mixed. Some more enlightened Caliphs promoted individual Christians to positions of prominence within the Islamic bureaucracy. In this way, Christians made a significant contribution towards the development of classical Islamic civilization, transmitting classical Hellenistic learning (particularly science, medicine and philosophy) to the Muslim Arabs. This learning was then brought to Western Europe through Muslim Spain.

However, some oppressive Caliphs destroyed churches, humiliated and killed Christians. Overall Christian *dhimmis* were second-class citizens within the Islamic realms, due in large part to attitudes engendered by negative references to non-Muslims within the Islamic sacred texts, and to prescribed roles within Islamic law.

The Crusades represented a Christian military response to over 450 years of retreat and territorial loss in the face of Islamic expansion. Many of the images of Christianity in the Muslim mind today date from this period, with Muslim memories of the bloody Crusader conquest of Jerusalem in 1099 preserved in popular culture and media. Even during the Crusades, however, there were Western Christians such as Raymond *Lull and *Francis of Assisi who advocated a peaceful approach to Islam.

The European colonial period and the advent of the Western missionary movement brought increased Christian-Muslim contact. From the seventeenth to the twentieth centuries European powers built empires to rival the great Muslim empires of earlier times. European colonial expansion opened the way for the establishment of new churches in Muslim lands for the first time since the rise of Islam. Simultaneously, Ottoman Turkish colonial expansion into Eastern Europe was accompanied by Islamic missionary activities, leading to conversion of some southern European communities, such as Albanians, to Islam.

Doctrine

In doctrinal matters there are certain areas of convergence between Islam and Christianity: belief in a Creator God; prophets; final judgment. However, there are also key areas of significant doctrinal difference, including the following:

(1) *The Islamic rejection of the doctrine of original sin.* Muslims generally believe that human beings are born innocent but weak. Although human beings are regarded as able to *sin, there is no general belief in the human disposition to sin.

(2) *The doctrines of the Trinity and the deity of Christ.* The differences in these areas are encapsulated by the late Pope John-Paul II, who wrote that the God of Islam 'is ultimately a God outside of the world, a God who is only Majesty, never Emmanuel, God-with-us ... There is no room for the Cross and the Resurrection. Jesus is mentioned, but only as a prophet ... not only the theology but also the anthropology of Islam is very distant from Christianity' (*Crossing the Threshold of Hope*, London, 1993, p. 93).

(3) *The rejection of the Christian doctrine of the *atonement* and a radically different view on the means of attaining a right relationship with God. Orthodox Muslims usually hold that the Qur'an denies the death of Christ (3:55; 4:157), teaching that he was raised bodily to heaven at the time of his arrest. Muslims therefore consider a right relationship with God derives from obedience to his will as revealed in the Qur'an and subsequent prophetic tradition and law.

(4) *The integrity of the Christian Scriptures.* Muslims often claim that the Jews and the Christians have altered their Scriptures and that this accounts for the disagreement between the Bible and the Qur'an, but some commentators hold only that Jews and Christians have falsified the true interpretation of the text. The question of the reliability of the Scriptures is thus raised at an early point in Christian-Muslim encounter.

(5) *The nature and authenticity of Muhammad's religious experience.* This is also a controversial area, with Muslims calling Christians to accept the prophetic status of Muhammad and the authority of the Qur'an, and Christians responding that given an anti-Christian polemic within the Islamic sacred texts and the Islamic rejection of the doctrine of atonement, acceptance of Muhammad and the Qur'an would be tantamount to abandoning the Christian faith.

Modern-day relationship

Muslim-Christian relationships today vary according to location. In some countries Muslims and Christians live happily side by side, interacting positively and fully. However, discrimination against Christian minorities living in Islamic majority countries increased in the late twentieth century, due to the legacy of *dhimmi* teachings within Islamic legal codes, given a new lease of life by the resurgence of political Islam.

Many Muslim-majority governments have increased the influence of Islamic *shari'ah* law on state legal systems, even creating specific departments promoting Islamic values and teachings. At the same time, non-Muslims are commonly forbidden by law to engage in mission among Muslims, with such policies justified by reference to Islamic sacred texts and law which emphasize the exclusivist claims of Islam. This has sometimes had an impact on Christian worship, with Christian minorities having difficulty gaining authorization for church construction and repair in some Muslim countries.

Such developments have led to a significant outflow of Christians from the Muslim world, especially from the Middle East, seeking greater opportunities and freedoms in Western countries. This exodus has accelerated as a result of increased tension between Islam and the West in the wake of the 9/11 attacks of 2001 and the subsequent wars in Afghanistan and Iraq.

While Christians have been leaving Muslim countries at an increasing rate, Muslim minorities have grown rapidly in Western countries during the last quarter of the twentieth century, benefiting from the religious freedom of those countries. In 1975, the Muslim community in Britain numbered just 400,000; in 2006 this figure had grown to over 2 million. Similar growth can be seen in other Western countries such as France, Germany, Denmark, Holland, Australia, Canada and the United States. With Muslim community growth has come rapid and widespread construction of mosques and Islamic community centres. There is thus a situation of asymmetry between the experiences of Christian minorities in Muslim-majority countries and Muslim minorities in Western, majority-Christian countries.

Muslims believe that they have a serious obligation to conduct *da'wah* (invitation) to Islam, and do so with great energy in Western countries. It is important for Christians to affirm that they too have an obligation to share the good news of Jesus Christ, his person, work and teaching, with everyone, including Muslims. In the work of commending the gospel to Muslims, Christian apologists to Islam need to call upon a wide spectrum of theological scholarship. They need to take account of critical research on the Bible as Muslim interlocutors are quite likely to be aware of it; they also need to familiarize themselves with emerging critical research on the sacred literature of Islam. Christians engaging with Muslims also need to express the doctrines of the Trinity, the incarnation and the atonement in ways which are both faithful to Scripture and Christian tradition as well as comprehensible to a Muslim. Furthermore, Christians need to be aware of contemporary social issues and the distinctive Christian response to them, as well as the whole range of responses which may be found in the Muslim world.

See also: ARAB CHRISTIAN THOUGHT.

Bibliography

K. Cragg, *Muhammad and the Christian: A Question of Response* (London, 1984); M. Durie, *Revelation? Do We Worship the Same God? Jesus, Holy Spirit, God in Christianity and Islam* (Mt Gravatt, 2006); S. Masood, *The Bible and the Qur'an* (Carlisle, 2001); C. Moucarry, *The Search for Forgiveness: Pardon and Punishment in Islam and Christianity* (Leicester, 2004); B. Musk, *Kissing Cousins? Christians and Muslims Face to Face* (London, 2005); M. J. Nazir-Ali, *Conviction and Conflict: Islam, Christianity and World Order* (New York, 2006); P. G. Riddell, *Christians and Muslims: Pressures and Potential in a post-9/11 World* (Leicester, 2004); P. G. Riddell and P. Cotterell, *Islam in Conflict* (Leicester, 2003); P. Sookhdeo, *Islam: The Challenge to the Church* (Pewsey, 2006); R. Spencer (ed.), *The Myth of Islamic Tolerance: How Islamic Law Treats Non-Muslims* (New York, 2005); B. Ye'or, *Islam and Dhimmitude: Where Civilisations Collide* (Lancaster, 2002).

P. G. RIDDELL AND M. J. NAZIR-ALI

JAMES, WILLIAM (1842–1910)

William James was a prominent American philosopher and psychologist who made a substantial contribution to the study of *religion. In *The Varieties of Religious Experience* (1902) he developed an empirical and scientific approach to religion. This meant, first, that there is no essence of religion, for religious phenomena are irreducibly diverse. However, this approach also meant distinguishing the central aspect of religion from the peripheral aspects. For James, the central aspect is what he called 'personal religion', which is the feelings and acts of individuals as they experience themselves in relation to what they understand to be divine. The peripheral aspect consists of the institutional and doctrinal sides of religion, which, in James's conception, are rooted in personal religion and, as its residual effects, are definitely secondary to it. They emerge when the experiences of deeply religious individuals (such as the founders of religious traditions) are translated into forms that are more accessible to people with less profound experiences. As a result, religious institutions and doctrines are valid only in so far as they are expressions and interpretations of personal religion.

Besides his contribution to the empirical study of religion, James wrote substantially on the topic of belief (especially in *The Will to Believe*, 1897). James sought to defend the propriety of religious belief in the face of *rationalists who insisted that belief should always be withheld whenever the available evidence is not fully compelling. In response, James argued that in religion we are faced with options that are forced and momentous. They are forced because there is no possibility of not choosing (since withholding belief is equivalent to unbelief). They are momentous because they bear on the things that are most significant to human existence. Additionally, James noted, our beliefs do not rest upon evidence and logic alone. He asserted that our 'passional nature' plays an important and valid role in belief-formation. Consequently, we are epistemologically justified in believing in God once the demands of our passional nature are taken into account.

James's own theology was in keeping with his pragmatic theology. Although he believed in the existence of a divine being, he held that such belief is important and valid because it best accords with the rest of our beliefs and best helps us make sense of the totality of our experience. In other words, we accept belief in God as true because it promotes the good life of ethical activity, hope and intellectual coherence.

Bibliography

Works: *The Meaning of Truth* (1975); *Pragmatism* (1975); *The Will to Believe and Other Essays in Popular Philosophy* (1979); *The Varieties of Religious Experience* (1985); all in *The Works of William James*, 18 vols., ed. F. Burkhardt (Cambridge).

S. M. POWELL

JANSENISM

Jansenism was a movement of theological and disciplinary renewal within *Roman Catholicism during the seventeenth and eighteenth centuries, mainly in France, but also in the Low Countries and northern Italy. It takes its name from Cornelius Jansen (1585–1638), a Flemish theologian whose work on Augustine's theology of *grace, the *Augustinus* (1640), was posthumously condemned by the Vatican (1653) because of its seemingly severe reading of human incapacity before God. Several French theologians favourable to Jansenius' emphases (e.g. Duvergier de Hauranne ['Saint-Cyran'], Antoine Arnauld, Pierre Nicole and Blaise *Pascal) became the actual leaders of the movement. Controversies first focused on monastic and spiritual discipline (tied especially to the convent of Port-Royal), and soon flowered into a full-blown effort to renew the ecclesial life of France. The Jansenists' grace-centred theology gave rise to a unique commitment to Scripture as divine narrative moulding the church's history, and encouraged pioneering work in biblical catechesis, historical research, missionary theory, liturgical renewal and finally ecclesiological reflection. These efforts in turn influenced eighteenth-century struggles for social reform and religious freedom.

Jansenism is often divided into three main periods. First, the initial work of Saint-Cyran and Arnauld, which revolved around the idea of a morally decadent church and the nature of God's healing of the human heart. An ongoing aspect of this period was open conflict with *Jesuits over issues of moral rigour, penitential demand, and missionary practice, with Jansenists generally defending non-accommodationist positions with respect to Christian teaching and local culture. (These controversies, and later political ones, contributed to the eventual expulsion of the Jesuits from France in the mid-eighteenth century.) The second period was one of energetic and imaginative resistance following the condemnation, in the Bull *Unigenitus* (1713), of Pasquier Quesnel's works of scriptural commentary, which maintained a strict reading of grace over works, and was viewed by the Vatican as crypto-Protestant in orientation. French clergy were asked to subscribe to the papal condemnation, a demand that most Jansenists rejected. This period, known as Appellancy after those Jansenists who 'appealed' to a General Council to resolve their dispute with Rome, was highlighted by the work of scriptural theologians like J.-J. Duguet and J.-B. le Sesne de Ménilles d'Etemare, and included widely publicized episodes of charismatic holiness, gifts and symbolic convulsions, punctuated by the experience of persecution.

Finally, Jansenist conflicts with authority converged with the widening political reform movement of both church and state that culminated in the Synod of Pistoia (1786), and gave rise to the vagaries of the Constitutional Church of the French Revolution. During this time, many Jansenists became aligned with forces seeking greater national control over their churches vis-à-vis the Vatican (cf. the 'Gallicans' in France). Already in 1724, a formal schism between the diocese of Utrecht (Holland) and Rome had taken place when, after several years of estrangement between the two parties, a Jansenist bishop was consecrated without Vatican approval. (This schism has continued and, with later groups joining it after the First Vatican Council, has taken the form of the Old Catholic Church.) Some Jansenists were also active in pressing for those civil liberties that would protect individual conscience. The career of Henri Grégoire (1750–1831), Jansenist priest, revolutionary leader, advocate of civil liberties for Jews and Africans, bishop in the Revolutionary Constitutional Church, courageous opponent of Jacobin anti-Catholicism, and finally irreconciled but popularly embraced exile from the restored Roman church in France, captures the final evolution and integration of Jansenism into the new conflicts of modern political life. As a self-defined movement, however, Jansenism disappeared in the destruction of the Revolution, many of its elements merging into general attitudes of nineteenth-century French Catholicism, or taken over by liberal politics, or waiting for vindication in aspects of Second Vatican Council reforms.

As a theology, Jansenism's radical *Augustinian reading of original *sin and grace was distinguished from Protestant attitudes by its foundational commitment to the embodied life of the Church Catholic. Its strong and mystical *predestinarianism, according to which only a few are saved even though unknown to all but God, meant that the church's forms and structures, granted by God, assumed an obligatory weight within history. In contrast to the Utrecht and Revolutionary schisms, most Jansenists refused to break with Rome, and deliberately submitted to the sanctions and persecutions of the institutional church, adopting a profound spirituality of the cross, of patience and of self-giving. Precisely their sense of historical uncertainty and mystery meant that Jansenists clung to the particularities of the Christian faith, especially in its scriptural, liturgical, moral and missionary witness. This outlook founded Jansenism's paradoxical merging of a theology of total grace with unparalleled efforts at lay formation within the church.

Bibliography

L. Cognet, *Le Jansénisme* (Paris, 1968); W. Doyle, *Jansenism: Catholic Resistance to Authority from the Reformation to the French Revolution* (London, 2000); C.-L. Maire, *De la Cause de Dieu à la Cause de la Nation: Le Jansénisme au XVIIIe Siècle* (Paris, 1998); E. Radner, *Spirit and Nature* (New York, 2002); C. A. Saint-Beuve, *Port-Royal* (Paris, ^{4}1953 [1840–59]); A. Sedgwick, *Jansenism in Seventeenth-Century France: Voices from the Wilderness* (Charlottesville, 1977); A. G. Sepinwall, *The Abbé Grégoire and the French Revolution: The Making of Modern Universalism* (Berkeley, 2005); D. Van Kley, *The Religious Origins of the French Revolution* (New Haven, 1999).

E. RADNER

JAPANESE THEOLOGY

The 'Christian century in Japan', beginning with the arrival of Francisco Xavier, a Jesuit missionary, was tragically closed in 1549 with prohibition of the Christian faith and total isolation from Western culture, without having produced any academic theology despite the temporary success of the Catholic mission. Since the country was reopened in the late nineteenth century, however, we have seen a wide spectrum of theological reflections, ranging from syncretistic liberalism to a more biblical conservatism.

Many of the early Christian leaders in the late nineteenth and early twentieth centuries, having a 'Samurai' (warrior) background, reveal a more or less Confucian ethos. Most conspicuous were Kanzo Uchimura, the founder of the unique '*Mu-kyokai* (non-Church) movement', advocating an uninstitutionalized church; Danjo Ebina, who accepted liberal theology imported from the West; and Masahisa Uemura, who defended orthodoxy against Ebina.

This last evangelical line was taken up by Tokutaro Takakura, who argued that Catholicism and modernism are an amalgam of paganism and the Bible. It appears that Takakura paved the way for the later emergence of dialectic theologians like Yoshitaka Kumano, Kuwata Hidenobu and Yoshio Yoshimura. Liberalism, on the other hand, was pursued by those who tried to produce a 'Japanese Christianity' influenced by Shinto. Another stream was a socialistic movement whose advocates claimed social love to be the highest form of redemptive love.

In the mid-twentieth century, a Catholic theologian, Soichi Iwashita, laid a foundation for medieval studies, and his student, Yoshihiko Yoshimitsu, proposed Neo-*Thomism as one answer to decaying modernism.

One of the most notable theologians after the end of the Second World War was Kazoh Kitamori, who proposed his 'Pain of God theology' (see *Impassibility of God and human suffering), which came to be highly valued because of its originality. He criticized Barth's infinite qualitative distinction between God and man and yet refused liberal ideas of God's love which excludes his pain. Another creative attempt was the so-called 'Water Buffalo Theology' of Kosuke Koyama, who translated the Christian faith into terms understandable to Thai farmers. A more recent effort to achieve a much-needed theological reformulation was made by Nozomu Miyahira, who explained the Trinity in terms of the Japanese traditional idea of *sankan ichiwa* which means 'three betweenesses, one concord'.

The most urgent theological agenda in Japan today is the confirmation of God's sovereignty over the Japanese nation and the emperor, and the establishment of a Christian theology of religion in the face of predominant traditional religions and religious pluralism.

See also: ASIAN CHRISTIAN THEOLOGY.

Bibliography

Y. Furuya and H. Ohki, *Nihon no Shingaku (Japanese Theology)* (Jordan-sha, 1989); Y. Furuya *et al.*, *Nihon no Shingakushi (A History of Japanese Theology)* (Jordan-sha, 1992); C. Germany, *Protestant Theologies in Modern Japan* (International Institute for the Study of Religions, 1965); S. Ono, *Nihon Purotesutanto Kyokaishi (A History of Japanese Protestant Churches)* (Seikeijusanjo, 1986).

K. UCHIDA

JASPERS, KARL, see EXISTENTIALISM

JENSON, ROBERT W. (b. 1930)

Robert Jenson has been described as 'America's theologian'. Influenced by Jonathan *Edwards, the American Norwegian is among the foremost theologians of his day. A 'theologian of culture', Jenson's theology covers a wide array of disciplines, issues and art-forms.

First trained at Luther College, Jenson taught in Oxford, Gettysburg, Minnesota and Princeton, publishing over twenty-five monographs and hundreds of essays and articles. Describing himself as a 'theologian of the *one* church', he co-founded *Pro-Ecclesia*, a journal dedicated to Catholic and Evangelical theology.

Having completed his doctoral research on Karl *Barth, under Peter Brunner, the systematic style and scope of Jenson's work reflect the grand tradition of G. W. F. *Hegel. Refusing to blindly accept the language of Western philosophy, particularly when influenced by Greek religion, Jenson's metaphysics are rooted in the biblical narrative and gospel story.

'Who is God?' Regularly returning to this question, Jenson's answer proves persistent. God is whoever raised Jesus from the dead. This discovery leads to a triple identification. As Father, Son and Holy Spirit, the triune God assumes the revelatory lead role in the biblical drama. The coalescence of biblical exposition and *trinitarian doctrine comprise Jenson's contribution to twentieth-century theology's trinitarian revival.

Jenson's trinitarian commitments and systematic approach are evident in his treatment of time and the church. Dismissing the notion of 'timelessness' as the erroneous import of Greek philosophy, Jenson posits a biblical alternative. Not timeless but eternal, God's triune life comprises a unique and unending temporality. Thus, in creation, God makes time for us. Certain critics allege that this leads to *pantheism, or *panentheism.

Unperturbed, Jenson's ecclesiology proves similarly immanent. In his radical ecumenist rendition of Luther's *totus Christus*, Jenson proclaims the church as the presence of the resurrected Christ in time and space. This claim alone underlines the courage, drama, relevance and importance of Robert Jenson's work.

Bibliography

Works: *Story and Promise: A Brief Theology of the Gospel about Jesus* (Philadelphia, 1973); *Essays in Theology of Culture* (Grand Rapids, 1995); *Systematic Theology: The Triune God*, vol. 1 (New York, 1997); *Systematic Theology: The Works of God*, vol. 2 (New York, 1999).

Studies: C. E. Gunton, *Trinity, Time, and Church: A Response to the Theology of Robert W. Jenson* (Grand Rapids, 2000).

R. ROOK

JEROME (c. 347–420)

Jerome was baptized as a young man into the church at Rome. He retained a lifelong attachment to the Roman church, though he spent his last years in the East.

Early on, Jerome attempted to lead a solitary, monastic life in the desert, but found the isolation uncongenial. He remained, however, a keen exponent of the ideals of virginity and a modified *asceticism. Through this and his reputation as a biblical scholar Jerome won the admiration of a group of pious aristocratic Roman women to whom he acted as teacher and counsellor.

Jerome's greatest achievement lay in biblical translation. A vigorous advocate of reference to the original languages, he completely revamped current Latin translations. The fruit of this work was the Vulgate. Jerome's attempts, however, to restrict the OT canon to what was written in Hebrew (see *Scripture) met with no response until the *Reformation.

Alongside this, Jerome embarked on a series of commentaries, particularly on OT prophets. These contain invaluable comments on philological and topographical matters, but rarely give much theological insight. Nor did Jerome contribute significantly to contemporary theological debates, to which he invariably brought an acrimonious taste. His anti-Origenism seems to have been determined more by personal circumstances than by considered theological reflection, since in his early days he had greatly admired *Origen's vast scholarship. A similar verdict applies to Jerome's anti-*Pelagianism, for Jerome does not reveal much understanding of the theological issues at stake.

Bibliography

J. N. D. Kelly, *Jerome: His Life, Writings, and Controversies* (Peabody, 1998); S. Rebenich, *Jerome* (London and New York, 2002).

G. A. KEITH

JESUIT THEOLOGY

Among the 'Rules for Thinking with the Church', which *Ignatius Loyola, the founder of the Jesuits, added to his Spiritual Exercises after encountering Protestantism at Paris, is the injunction 'to praise both positive and *scholastic theology'. 'The positive doctors' such as *Augustine, *Jerome and *Gregory the Great promote the love and service of God, and 'the scholastic doctors' such as *Thomas Aquinas, *Bonaventura and Peter *Lombard 'define and explain for our times the things necessary for eternal salvation, and refute and expose all errors and fallacies'. Ignatius' *Constitutions* (finalized 1550–51) name *Aristotle as the Jesuits' authority in philosophy, and Thomas in scholastic doctrine. Their adoption of Thomas (see *Thomism and Neo-Thomism), confirmed by the order's *Ratio Studiorum* (*Scheme of Study*) in 1598, helped to make him Catholicism's dominant theologian, displacing Peter Lombard. On certain topics Thomas's opinions were declared to be not binding. In particular, the minority (Scotist) belief in *Mary's immaculate conception was espoused by the Jesuits, who subsequently proved ardent Mariologists. The early generals of the order, especially Claudius Aquaviva (1543–1615), were concerned to ensure 'solidity and uniformity of doctrine' in its varied teaching activities.

Although Ignatius had declared that 'the scholastic doctors, being of more recent date, ... have a clearer understanding of the Holy Scripture and of the teachings of the positive and holy doctors', the Jesuits' polemical engagement with *Protestantism and later Jansenism demanded increasing attention to the branches of 'positive' theology, especially the Bible, the Fathers and church history. The Dutchman Peter Canisius (1521–97) produced a widely used Catechism (*Summa Doctrinae Christianae*, 1554) and worked tirelessly against Protestantism in Germany and beyond, but the prolific and learned *Bellarmine was the Jesuits' supreme anti-Protestant controversialist. They had powerful centres of study at Louvain, Paris (Collège de Clermont), Cologne, Ingolstadt, Würzburg, Vienna, Prague, Alcala, Valladolid, Cracow and elsewhere, and their ranks included a remarkable number of weighty theologians and scholars, such as Francisco de Toledo (1532–96, scholastic), Jakob Gretser (1562–1625, historical-patristic controversialist), Peter de Fonseca (1528–99, 'the Portuguese Aristotle'), and Leonhard Lessius (1554–1623, dogmatic and moral theologian).

Ignatius' 'Rules' had warned against detracting from free *will and good works by speaking too much of *predestination and *faith. From 1613, by a decree of Aquaviva, the Jesuits' official teaching on grace became what was known as 'Molinism', from the Spaniard Luis de Molina (1535–1600). His *Concordia . . .* (*Harmony of Free Will with the Gifts of Grace*, 1588) taught that the efficacy of grace lay not 'intrinsically' in the gift itself, but in the divinely foreknown co-operation with it of human free will. Efficacious grace, distinguished from sufficient grace, was defined as the grace to which a person consents. Francisco de Suárez (1548–1617), perhaps the greatest of Jesuit theologians, spoke of this as 'congruism'. God bestows *gratia congrua* (i.e. grace 'congruent' with its profitable use by the recipients), which is foreknown by God's special knowledge (*scientia media*). This obviously anti-Protestant position provoked a sharp dispute with the *Dominicans, who were more faithful Thomists in following Augustine on the primacy of (irresistible) grace. A special congregation at Rome (*De Auxiliis*, 1597–1607) ended with toleration of both viewpoints, but subsequently the Jesuit one has more generally prevailed in the Roman church.

In the mid-seventeenth century the Jansenists accused the Jesuits of *Pelagianism and *Semi-Pelagianism. Jesuits were to the fore in the campaigns against *Jansenism. The French patristic experts, Denis Petau (Petavius, 1583–1652) and Jean Garnier (1612–81), contested Jansenist interpretations of Augustine and the Pelagian movements. About a century earlier the teaching of Michel Baius of Louvain (1513–89) represented in effect an anticipation of Jansenism, and was condemned by Jesuits like Bellarmine and Lessius.

Jansenists also criticized the Jesuits' zeal for *papal supremacy, which went back to Ignatius himself. Two of his original associates, Diego Lainez (1512–65) and Alonzo Salmeron (1515–85), contributed effectively to the Council of *Trent as (anti-conciliarist) 'theologians of the pope'. Canisius was also active at Trent. Lainez insisted that bishops possessed their power of jurisdiction immediately from the pope, not from Christ. Later Jesuits were forceful in preparing for the definition of papal infallibility at the First *Vatican Council (1870). They were essentially ultramontane and anti-Gallican theologians. Early Jesuits also accorded to the pope an 'extraordinary and indirect' power in the temporal realm. This belief was an element in the justification of lawful rebellion and tyrannicide advanced by Juan de Mariana (1536–1623), Bellarmine, Suárez and other Jesuits (along lines similar to contemporary Calvinists). Such political theology brought damaging accusations of sedition upon Jesuits in England and France in particular.

Jesuits also developed *ascetic theology and spirituality, based on Ignatius' *Spiritual Exercises*. In India and the Far East, Jesuit missionary pioneers like Matteo Ricci (1552–1610) and Robert de Nobili (1577–1656) were adventurous in the theology as well as the practice of mission (see *Missiology). Jesuit moral theology has given too great a place to casuistry, and has earned the order a degree of notoriety. Its stress on 'responsibility' meant that one could not culpably sin without knowledge of what one was doing, and hence 'good faith' was always a valid excuse. Its 'probabilism', developed by Suárez and others and condemned by the Jansenists as 'laxism', in effect removed a moral obligation as soon as any serious doubt arose on informed and conscientious reflection. It was based on the principle that, in any doubtful case, it was lawful to follow a merely probable course of action contrary to the established norm, even if a more probable opinion favoured the norm itself. The system was subject to extended controversy in Catholic moral theology.

The golden age of the Society of Jesus was its first century, when it was a major factor in the reinvigoration of post-Reformation Catholicism (see *Reformation, Catholic Counter-). Although a prey to controversies, and suppressed by Rome from 1773 to 1814, it remained a bastion of scholastic orthodoxy and fidelity to the papacy. As recently as 1916 the general of the order promulgated an instruction *On Increasing Devotion to the Teaching of St Thomas* in the Society. Although a few years earlier George Tyrrell (1861–1909) had been expelled from the order for his Catholic *modernism, it was not until Teilhard de *Chardin and the Second Vatican Council that the traditional image of Jesuit theology markedly changed. Jesuits remain at the centre of Catholic theological endeavour, with their own universities (e.g. the Gregorian at Rome) and numerous periodical publications, but their ranks have included some of Catholicism's most controversial, as well as most important, modern theologians – *Lonergan, *Rahner, the Dutchman Piet Schoonenberg (1911–99), the Latin American *liberation theologian Juan Luis Segundo (1925–96), Josef Jungmann (1889–1975), theologian of liturgy Henri de Lubac (1896–1991) and Jean Daniélou (1905–1974). With few exceptions (e.g. Jean Galot), Jesuit theologians can no longer be characterized straightforwardly as defenders of traditional orthodoxy.

Bibliography

X. le Bachelet *et al.*, in *DTC* 8 (1924–25), cols. 1012–1108; G. E. Ganss (ed. and tr.), *Ignatius of Loyola: Spiritual Exercises and Selected Works* (New York, 1991); J. de Guibert, *The Jesuits: Their Spiritual Doctrine and Practice* (Chicago, 1964); D. Mitchell, *The Jesuits: A History* (London, 1980); J. W. O'Malley, *The First Jesuits* (Cambridge, 1993).

D. F. WRIGHT

JESUS

Jesus is the personal name of the man Jesus of Nazareth, known to Christians as Jesus the Messiah (Christ). For Christian faith he is not only a real historical figure of the past, but also, by virtue of his *resurrection and exaltation to divine lordship (see *Ascension and heavenly session of Christ), the living person in whom Christians believe. For classical Christian theology, Jesus is the incarnate Son of God, that is, the divine Son or *Logos, the second person of the *Trinity, incarnate as a human being (see *Christology, *Incarnation). As Jesus, the divine Son lived a fully human life and now retains in heaven his full humanity, glorified as ours will be in the new creation.

The name Jesus, itself a common Jewish name (Yeshua) in first-century Palestine, directs our attention to the human, historical and particular identity of the Jewish man of Nazareth, who lived and died and rose from the dead as the Gospels relate. This article will therefore focus on this human particularity of Jesus, which can easily be obscured when theological discussion focuses on the incarnation as God become 'man' or human in a general sense, rather than as God become *this* particular man, Jesus.

Jesus in classical Christology

Following a long process of reflection and controversy, the Fathers at the Council of

*Chalcedon defined the orthodox understanding of the person of Jesus Christ in a definition that became normative for mainstream Christian theology thereafter. It spoke of the personal unity of 'one and the same Son and only-begotten God the Word, Lord Jesus Christ', in whom are united two natures, divine and human, each complete, neither confused nor divided but united, such that the one person is both 'truly God' and 'truly human'. The completeness of the humanity is specified as 'consisting of a rational soul and body', ruling out the view that Jesus was a divine mind in a human body. Jesus is said to have participated in the same common human nature as all of us ('of one substance with us as regards his humanity'), like us in all respects except sin. Of his particular human story, the definition refers only to his birth from *Mary.

The Council's insistence on the full integrity of both natures is an essential warning against the all-too-common tendency to think of the divinity and the humanity of Jesus as, so to speak, competitive, as though the more human he was the less divine he could be, and vice versa. It is also of great soteriological importance. The Fathers often used the slogan, 'He became what we are in order that we might become what he is', or 'He became human so that we might become divine.' They meant that the divine Son assumed humanity so that we humans could come to share the life of God. For this purpose it was essential that he assumed complete humanity, became all that it means to be human. Had he assumed, for example, only a human body, only human bodies would have been redeemed, not human minds.

The particular philosophical cast of the Fathers' thinking inclined them to think of Jesus' humanity in terms of general human nature, and to neglect the fact that to be a human being one must not only share human nature in general, but also be a particular human with a unique history. Of course, nothing they say denies that, and it is important that, like any abstract statement of Christology, their definition was not meant to stand alone, but to serve as a framework within which to read the Gospels and to tell the story of Jesus. The *Tome of Leo*, one of the Christological treatises that the Council authorized as orthodox, does root its understanding of the two natures in the particularities of the Gospel story.

The 'Jesus of history' and the 'Christ of faith'

For Christian faith and theology down to modern times, Jesus Christ was without question the Jesus of the Gospels. The one and only real Jesus was both a historical person, whose story was told reliably in the Gospels, and the exalted Lord, who was the object of faith and worship. But the development of critical historical study of the Gospels in nineteenth-century Europe set this in question, and the result was the Quest for the *Historical Jesus, which aimed to reconstruct the life and personality of Jesus on the basis of a solely historical enquiry.

Much of the impetus for the quest in nineteenth-century Germany came from the desire of *liberal Protestant scholars to discover a Jesus different from the dogmatic Christ of the church's faith, a non-supernatural Jesus who would be a more credible figure on which to base their understanding of Christianity. This historical Jesus was primarily a teacher of ethics who taught, in Adolf von *Harnack's phrase, 'the fatherhood of God and the brotherhood of man'. Albert *Schweizer's definitive survey of the quest up to 1906 exposed its tendency to produce a Jesus who expressed the ideals of the scholars who reconstructed him, and Schweizer himself proposed instead an apocalyptic Jesus utterly strange to late nineteenth-century culture. The quest has continued in other forms down to the present day. Many scholars, especially in the British tradition, have taken a relatively high view of the value of the Gospels as historical sources and portrayed a historical Jesus not seriously at odds with the Jesus of the Gospels, while others, including recently those associated with the Jesus Seminar in the USA, have been much more sceptical of the historicity of the Gospel traditions.

A fundamental problem in the quest has been the assumption that, in order to get to the 'real' Jesus, we have to strip away the interpretations, deriving from early Christian faith, that permeate the Gospels. The whole enterprise was criticized especially by Martin *Kähler and Rudolf *Bultmann. While Bultmann denied we could know anything about Jesus relevant to faith, Kähler argued that the 'Christ of faith' of the early Christians was in fact rooted in the history of Jesus, so that the attempt to prise history and faith apart was misleading. Some recent scholars, such as Dunn and Bauckham, have argued that the faith of the first disciples is our way of access to the historical Jesus, not a barrier to be jumped. In this way historical study of the Gospels can illuminate the human, historical particularity of Jesus that is essential to Christian faith and theology. One particular gain from historical study of Jesus since 1970 has been to highlight his Jewishness and his rootedness in Jewish tradition, so obvious in the Gospels but much neglected in Christian history, including earlier phases of the quest.

Jesus in the Christology of the NT

In the nineteenth-century liberal Protestant view, the purely human 'historical Jesus' was obscured by his transformation into a divine figure, an object of faith and worship, for which Paul was held largely responsible. This view is still widely held, especially outside NT scholarship. More recently, however, it has become clear that Jesus was an object of faith and worship as far back as we can trace early Christian tradition, and such worship cannot be ascribed to a lapse from Jewish monotheism as Christianity moved into a pagan environment (see *Judaism and Christianity).

A more plausible view is that the earliest Christians took the quite deliberate step of including Jesus in the identity of the one God of Jewish *monotheism. In early Jewish theology, dependent on the Hebrew Bible, the uniqueness of the God of Israel was often defined by saying that he is the only Creator of all things and the only sovereign Ruler over all things. The first Christians believed that the risen Christ had been exalted to sit with God on the divine throne from which God rules creation (Ps. 110:1, used to make this point, is the OT text most quoted in the NT). That amounted to claiming that he belongs to the unique identity of the God of Israel. Associating the pre-existent Christ with God in the uniquely divine work of creation was a step that evidently soon followed (1 Cor. 8:6), making even clearer the inclusion of Jesus in the divine identity.

This understanding of Jesus' divinity did not eclipse his particular human identity, which for early Christians was axiomatic. Rather, Jesus' particular identity was seen to belong to the identity of God, without any loss to the former. The Jesus who was exalted to God's throne was precisely the Jesus whose story the Gospels tell.

The particular human identity of Jesus

A key task of Christology is to maintain the particularity of Jesus along with his universal significance. There is a perennial temptation to make the latter intelligible by reducing the former. Jesus then becomes a generalized notion of ideal humanity or of divine presence in human life, and the specific features of Jesus of Nazareth fall away. Especially since the *Enlightenment many thinkers have supposed that only what is universally discernible can be of universal significance. Gotthold *Lessing famously stated that contingent facts of history cannot be the basis for 'necessary truths of reason'. Christian faith, however, finds the universal significance of Jesus *in*, not despite, his historical particularity as the figure the Gospels portray. Since human identity is not static but formed by the dynamics of a particular life and particular relationships, we should think of it as a narrative and relational identity. Just such an identity is narrated in the Gospels. Who Jesus is, as the particular first-century Jewish man he was, happens in the story of his life, death and resurrection, and in the relationships he had, especially with God his Father. The Gospels, therefore, give us the historical particularity of Jesus narrated in such a way as to show his universal significance.

So in what way can we find the universal significance of Jesus in his historical particularity? We should think first of the early Christian proclamation of Jesus as Messiah, which was the earliest expression of his universal significance. In his messianic identity Jesus is the one man to whom God has given a unique vocation to reveal God and to bring *salvation, the *kingdom of God, to Israel and to all the nations. In this sense his identity includes a unique task, undertaken for the sake of all people, which takes place in the events of his life as the Gospels narrate them. This messianic identity also includes a unique relationship with God. Jesus knows God as his Father in a very special way that entails his own *sonship to God as something unique. From the perspective of his exaltation we can see that this relationship was *divine* sonship: it was his own Son that the Father sent to complete his purpose for all humanity. The one who in the Gospels acts and speaks for God and reveals God is himself God.

Relationships are the way in which a particular human can transcend his or her particularity without losing it. Jesus was not only uniquely related to the one God, but also uniquely related to his fellow-humans. Jesus has often been seen, as in Paul's parallel between *Adam and Christ (Rom. 5:12–21), as the representative of all humanity before God. But this representative role may seem to imply only generic humanity unless we can relate it to the particular history of Jesus in the Gospels. One way of doing so is the notion of Jesus' *loving identification* with other men and women.

This can be understood not simply as an abstract identification of himself with humanity in general, but as something that occurred in Jesus' actual relationships with other people, as he empathized with them, took part in their lives, lived his own life for their sake, and in the end suffered for identifying with their cause. This identification with others was limited in the sense that it was with the actual men and women Jesus encountered in his earthly life, but not in the sense that Jesus called a halt to it and excluded anyone from his love. So it was in principle unlimited and potentially universalizable. This potential universality became actual by means of his resurrection and his post-resurrection presence in the *Holy Spirit. Hence Paul, whom Jesus never knew, can say that 'the Son of God loved *me* and gave himself for *me*' (Gal. 2:20).

These two forms of unique relationship – Jesus' unique identification with his Father's will and his potentially unlimited, loving identification with other men and women – together make him the one who embodies *God's* loving identification with *all* men and women. This way of understanding the matter recognizes Jesus as a man who is unique in his universal significance without abolishing his particularity. Rather, his universality is found in the actual ways he communicated God's loving presence to actual men and women. It is found in his dealings with Martha and Peter, with the paralytic and the Gerasene demoniac, with the high priest's slave and the penitent thief, and no generality can replace the stories of these concrete relationships in Jesus' particular human story. This particular story is not just an illustration of God's *love for all humanity, but is actually the way in which God brings his love for all humanity into actual human lives.

This way of finding Jesus' universality in his loving identification with others frees us from a certain sort of problem about the universal relevance of Jesus that frequently recurs in Christology. A good illustration is the argument of Christian feminists who find Jesus' maleness a problem. How can Jesus as a man be the human figure of supreme religious relevance to women? But Jesus' maleness is one aspect of his particularity. There are comparable problems in the fact that Jesus was a Jew and not a Gentile, an unmarried man who had no experience of sexual love or of parenthood, a person with no physical or mental disabilities, a young man who died before experiencing old age. How can Jesus be the figure of supreme religious significance for Gentiles, married people, parents, disabled people, elderly people? If Jesus' universal significance has to mean that he lived, in his own human significance, all the diversity of human experience, then he could not be a particular human person, only a kind of cipher, a symbolic Everyperson with whom everyone can identify because he is specifically no-one. But if Jesus is universally relevant through his loving identification with others, then his particularity is no problem. Jesus practised the kind of love that transcends all barriers between people and all the varieties of human experience and really identifies with the experience of others. The evidence of Christian history is that people of both sexes, all ages, all races and cultures and conditions, have experienced Jesus' loving identification with them. They have found it in the particularity of the man who lived the story presented in the Gospels.

The particularity of God in Jesus

The biblical *God reveals himself by making himself identifiable in the world. He comes out of his infinite mystery and gives himself a particular identity in the world, as the God who has done such-and-such or the God of so-and-so or the God who dwells somewhere-or-other. He is known as the universal God in relation to all worldly reality: the God who created all things and is sovereign over all things. But God also makes himself more specifically identifiable through relationship to particular worldly realities – events which are particular acts of God, places where God appears or dwells, people to whom God relates in specific ways. In an important sense God particularizes himself and gives himself a particular identity by which he may be known. By relating to the patriarchs and entering into covenant with them, God becomes the God of Abraham, Isaac and Jacob. By bringing Israel out of Egypt, giving Israel the Torah, by giving Israel the land, and by being accessible to Israel in the temple, God becomes the God of his people Israel. This particular identity enables him to be known, not in abstraction, but in encounter and relationship.

From this OT perspective, the incarnation of God as Jesus the Jew from Nazareth is in significant continuity with the way God revealed himself to Israel. Just as God's identity as the God of Israel is a narrative identity that takes place in the story of Israel, so the incarnation means that God is known in the particular story of Jesus, which the NT presents as the continuation and climax of the OT story. But in the latter case God particularizes himself in an even more radical way, not just as closely related to Jesus, but *as* the particular man Jesus. God's definitive *revelation, his identity for us, is now Jesus. Jesus, in his human, historical particularity, is the identity God has given himself in the world, by which he can be known. Finally, we should note that this form of revelation is at the same time salvific. In the history of Jesus God gives himself for human salvation. His love reaches us and reconciles us, overcoming sin, through Jesus' ministry of identifying love, his death for the sake of all, and his resurrection on behalf all. Only in this particular story is Jesus the visible image of the invisible God.

Bibliography

R. J. Bauckham, 'Jesus the Revelation of God', in Paul Avis (ed.), *Divine Revelation* (London and Grand Rapids, 1997), pp. 174–200; idem, *Jesus and the God of Israel* (Milton Keynes, 2008); M. Bockmuehl (ed.), *The Cambridge Companion to Jesus* (Cambridge, 2001); J. D. G. Dunn, *Jesus Remembered* (London 2003); C. S. Evans, *The Historical Christ and the Jesus of Faith* (Oxford, 1996); D. F. Ford and M. Higton (eds.), *Jesus* (Oxford, 2002); H. W. Frei, *The Identity of Jesus Christ* (Philadelphia, 1975); L. W. Hurtado, *Lord Jesus Christ* (Grand Rapids, 2003); G. O'Collins, *Jesus: A Portrait* (London, 2008); J. Pelikan, *Jesus through the Centuries* (New Haven, 1985); G. Theissen and A. Merz, *The Historical Jesus* (London, 1998); N. T. Wright, *Jesus and the Victory of God* (London, 1996).

R. J. BAUCKHAM

JEWEL, JOHN (1522–71)

Born in Devonshire, John Jewel was educated at Oxford, where he became Reader of Humanities and Rhetoric. He was ordained a priest in 1551. When Mary Tudor (r. 1553–58) as queen attempted to restore Catholicism in England, Jewel lost his Readership and fled to the Continent.

Jewel returned to England in March 1559 after the accession of Elizabeth I and was appointed bishop of Salisbury on 27 July 1559. As the first major apologist for the reformed Church of England (see *Anglicanism), Jewel wrote the *Apology of the Church of England* (1562, 1564) and his far more voluminous *Defense of the Apology* (1567, 1570). The central argument running through both these works is that the reformed Church of England was established upon the Scriptures, the first four ecumenical councils, the early Fathers, and the example of the primitive church. In enacting the Elizabethan Settlement, England returned to the ancient and apostolic church. This for Jewel provided the framework in which he defended the right of a national church to regulate matters of doctrine and worship by means of its own regional and national synods apart from general councils and the duty of the godly prince to initiate national ecclesiastical reform. Jewel died while on episcopal visit on 23 September 1571.

Bibliography

Works: *An Apology of the Church of England*, ed. J. E. Booty (New York, 2002); *Works of John Jewel, Bishop of Salisbury*, ed. J. Ayre (Cambridge, 1850).

Studies: J. E. Booty, *John Jewel as Apologist of the Church of England* (London, 1963); G. W. Jenkins, *John Jewel and the English National Church: The Dilemmas of an Erastian Reformer* (Burlington, 2006); W. M. Southgate, *John Jewel and the Problem of Doctrinal Authority* (Cambridge, 1962).

A. A. GAZAL

JEWISH-CHRISTIAN RELATIONS

Judaism and Christianity 'encounter' one another textually. There is also a tradition of organized, institutional relations. More common are interactions between Jews and Christians as historical actors, which shape individuals' perceptions of each other's (and their own) faiths. Some Christians actively seek dialogue with Jews, hoping to explore Christianity's 'roots' or to address the history of Christian anti-Judaism. Conversely, Jews may engage Christians because they are conscious of living in a predominantly Christian culture, and hope to prevent future conflicts. Recently, some Jews have made theological space for Christianity, welcoming the fact that through it, millions of people relate to Israel's God.

Ancient agendas influence contemporary Jewish-Christian relations. Arguably, Judaism is Christianity's point of departure, both theologically and historically speaking. The early Jesus movement decided that observance of the commandments was not required of Gentiles. Church Fathers extended and consolidated this position, regarding faith in Jesus Christ as alone capable of reconciling people to God. For centuries, Christianity was ambivalent, dismissing Judaism as redundant but affording Jews some protection, since they were the Scripture's first guardians. In contrast, once Christianity had become fundamentally Gentile, Judaism found it to be of little doctrinal interest.

It is only really since the *Holocaust that many churches have re-evaluated their approach to Judaism: Nazism depended on *race theory for its notion of the biologically inferior Jew, but centuries of anti-Judaism had meant that few Christians included Jews within their sphere of care and concern. Much post-war dialogue focuses on commonalities between Judaism and Christianity, emphasizing Jesus' Jewishness and arguing that his death admitted Gentiles into the God-Israel *covenant or created a new parallel covenant for them, but did not signal the end of God's relationship with Jews. Joint mission is explored as a replacement for Christian mission to Jews. Such ideas inform statements like *Nostra aetate* (1965) and subsequent Catholic documents, and the Jewish text, *Dabru emet* (2000). Of course, some Christian groups hold to supersessionism and *conversionary mission. Orthodox Jews regard Judaism as the unique embodiment of a divinely revealed teaching. However, belief that Judaism and Christianity are essentially different does not preclude positive relations (even as it creates problems for theological discourse), which may then explore social, political matters.

As previously, future relations will be influenced by historical contingencies as much as theology. The post-Holocaust reconstruction of relations is still in its infancy, and questions such as the place of Messianic Jews/Hebrew Christians (Jews who believe that their Jewishness is completed in their accepting of *Jesus as Messiah, and that there should be now, as in the earliest period, a distinctive Jewish Christianity) remain largely untouched. Many churches are becoming increasingly less Eurocentric, and in future this may influence their interest in Jewish-Christian relations. Judaism is affected by high rates of intermarriage and disputes over conversion procedures. If dialogue is to stay relevant to the experience of actual Jews and Christians, it must recognize the contemporary contestedness of Jewish identity.

The story of Jewish-Christian relations does not make for easy reading. But in recent decades, dialogue has chipped away at the heritage of mistrust and opposition, opening up avenues of genuine reconciliation.

See also: JUDAISM AND CHRISTIANITY; ZION.

Bibliography

T. Frymer-Kensky, P. Ochs, D. Novak, D. F. Sandmel and M. A. Signer (eds.), *Christianity in Jewish Terms* (Boulder, 2000); E. Kessler and N. Wenborn (eds.), *A Dictionary of Jewish-Christian Relations* (Cambridge, 2005); E. Kessler and M. J. Wright (eds.), *Themes in Jewish-Christian Relations* (Cambridge, 2005); M. Saperstein, *Moments of Crisis in Jewish-Christian Relations* (London and Philadelphia, 1989); M. Shermis and A. E. Zannoni (eds.), *Introduction to Jewish-Christian Relations* (New York and Mahwah, 1991).

M. J. WRIGHT

JOACHIMISM

Joachim of Fiore (c. 1135–1202) developed an elaborate and very influential theological interpretation of *history and the future, which he expressed both in exegetical writings and in symbolic pictures (*figurae*). He understood the development of history in terms of the activity of the Trinity (in history) so that history reflects the trinitarian relationships. As the Spirit proceeds from the Father and the Son, so an age (status) of the Spirit will develop out of the OT age of the Father and the NT age of the Son. Among many other ways of thinking of this third age of the Spirit, Joachim identified it with the *millennium of Revelation. Unlike some of his radical followers, he did not hold that the NT gospel of Christ would be superseded in the age of the Spirit, but that the full spiritual meaning of both testaments would be realized in this period of peace and contemplation before the end of history. Joachim's thought constituted a revolution in medieval *eschatology: for the first time in medieval Christianity he made it possible to envisage progress of a theologically significant kind within the future history of this world. If the subtlety of his theology was lost on many of his followers, the potent expectation of a third age of the Spirit inspired many people in the late medieval period (especially the Spiritual Franciscans), in the sixteenth century (both Catholics and Protestants), and even down to modern times.

Bibliography

E. R. Daniel, *Abbot Joachim of Fiore and Joachimism: Selected Articles* (Farnham, 2011); B. McGinn, *The Calabrian Abbot: Joachim of Fiore in the History of Western Thought* (New York, 1985); M. Reeves, *Joachim of Fiore and the Prophetic Future* (London, 1976); idem, *The Influence of Prophecy in the Later Middle Ages* (London, rev. edn, 1993); D. C. West (ed.), *Joachim of Fiore in Christian Thought* (New York, 1975); A. Williams (ed.), *Prophecy and Millenarianism* (London, 1980).

R. J. BAUCKHAM

JOHN OF DAMASCUS (c. 652–c. 750)

Born and raised in Damascus in an eminent Christian family called Mansur, John at first assumed high civil office, but later (after the eruption of Emperor Leo Isaurian's *iconoclastic policy) joined his adopted brother Cosmas as a monk at the monastery of St Saba near Jerusalem. He was ordained to the priesthood and devoted the rest of his life to writing books and composing church hymns for which he has become most famous. Some of these hymns are used in English today, e.g. 'Come, Ye Faithful, Raise the Strain' and 'The Day of Resurrection! Earth, Tell It out Abroad'. John defended the use of icons and as a result was personally condemned by the iconoclastic Synod of 754. He died at a very advanced age, most probably some time before the Seventh Ecumenical Synod (Nicaea II, 787), which reinstated him in the church and acknowledged his contribution. Later generations called him Chrysorroas, 'gold-pouring', because of his erudition and his inspiring hymns.

It was at St Saba, where one can still see his cell, that John wrote most of his works, using material from earlier authors but arranging it in a superbly methodical and original way. They were translated into various languages and utilized by many authors (e.g. Peter *Abelard and *Thomas Aquinas in the West and practically all systematic theologians in the East). The Greek *Life* divides them into four categories, the 'melodic hymns', the 'panegyric orations', the 'sacred Bible and divinely inspired tablet' (i.e. his most important systematic/dogmatic work, *The Fountain of Knowledge*) and the 'treatises on the icons'. Modern patrologists divide them into exegetical, dogmatic, antiheretical, polemical, ethical, homiletical, hagiographical and poetical.

As a theologian, John of Damascus was a traditionalist who wanted to follow the Scriptures and the accredited Fathers, because he saw both as inspired by the Holy Spirit. He was interested in particular theological questions and issues, but he was supremely a *systematician who wanted to supply a comprehensive summa of theological knowledge. Thus he covered almost all theological topics both broadly and in detail. He made use of philosophy in an eclectic manner, making a clear distinction between true (psychical) and false (demonic) philosophical knowledge and holding that philosophy was related to theology as a servant was related to a queen. He held that God is transcendent in his being and immanent in his grace, i.e. his creative and redeeming acts through which are revealed respectively the divine attributes (eternity, immutability, majesty, etc.) and the divine persons (the three *hypostaseis* of the Father, the Son and the Holy Spirit). Following the doctrine of the Greek Fathers and especially of the Cappadocians (see *Basil of Caesarea, *Gregory of Nazianzus, *Gregory of Nyssa), he always began with the *Trinity and moved to the unity of the Godhead which he expounded in terms of communion (*koinōnia*), while always retaining the priority of the Father who begets the Son and projects (*ekporeuein*) the *Holy Spirit. The world, consisting of spiritual and material creatures without any *dualism (anti-*Manichaean), is contingent and destined to last in order to reveal God's plans, especially through the activities of *angels and men. Yet a free *fall (he decisively opposed Muslim *predestination) from goodness into evil led to the frustration of this destiny and caused slavery and death. Some angels have been turned into demons, and human beings have fallen into *sin, which is not only a loss of God's grace, of life and understanding, but also subjection to corruption and death through procreation. The solution to these problems is given in Christ the Saviour. For John of Damascus, Christ is in his person not a deified man but an 'inhominated' God, consisting of two natures, the divine and the human, resembling every human being in consisting of two parts, one immaterial and another material, but differing from them in not forming 'another out of the two' but remaining 'one in the two'. In this John followed both Chalcedonian orthodoxy and post-Chalcedonian clarifications, especially Leontius of Byzantium's doctrine of *enhypostasia* (see *Hypostasis) and *Maximus the Confessor's and the Sixth Ecumenical Synod's 'two natural energies and wills' which remain distinct though harmonized, whereby he exposed both errors, the *Nestorian and the *Monophysite (see *Christology). Christ's saving work comprises his teaching, his life and his sacrifice on the cross with its outcome in his resurrection, ascension and final parousia, which become gifts offered to, and ends to be freely attained to by, believers through the reception of the sacraments and the response of personal faith and works respectively.

For John of Damascus, Christian works were summed up in the Christian *ascetic ideal of the renunciation of 'the world'. Closely connected with this emphasis on Christian works was the doctrine of the final judgment which is to follow after the general bodily resurrection of all human beings (forcefully asserted in his work *Against the Manichaeans*), as well as the memorial services and prayers for the dead which were of particular benefit for the living. John regarded the Virgin *Mary and the *saints as living epistles of the saving truth of Christ ('friends of Christ' and 'children of God'), with whom they were to be honoured and exalted but not worshipped. This point became clearer in his defences of the use of icons, whereby he affirmed, not only that 'the veneration of honour given to the icon goes to the prototype', but also that there was a crucial distinction between veneration of honour given to the icons (*proskynēsis*, *timē*) and true worship (*latreia*) offered only to the Trinity. But as with his doctrine of Mary and the saints, so also with his doctrine of icons, John had Christ as his focus and aimed at expounding the appropriation of Christ's gift of salvation by human beings. This was probably why, like most of the Eastern Fathers, he did not develop any explicit doctrine of the church.

Bibliography

Works in ET: *NPNF*, vol. ix; M. H. Allies, *St John Damascene on Holy Images Followed by Three Sermons on the Assumption* (London and Philadelphia, 1898); D. Anderson, *St John of Damascus, On the Divine Images* (New York, 1980); F. C. Chase, *St John of Damascus' Writings* in *FC* 37.

Studies in English: D. Ainslee, *John of Damascus* (London, ³1903); B. Altaner, *Patrology* (Freiburg, 1960), pp. 635–640; P. M. Baur, *The Theology of St John Damascene's 'De Fide Orthodoxa'* (Washington DC, 1951); F. Cayré, *Manual of Patrology and History of Theology* (Paris, Tournai, Rome, 1940), pp. 326–339; A. Fortescue, 'John of Damascus', in *The Greek Fathers* (London, 1908), pp. 202–248; J. H. Lupton, *John of Damascus* (London, 1882); V. A. Michell, The Mariology of St John Damascene (Kirkwood, 1930); D. J. Sahas, *John of Damascus on Islam* (Leiden, 1972).

G. D. DRAGAS

JOHN OF THE CROSS, see MYSTICAL THEOLOGY

JOY

Joy is an essential ingredient of all true Christianity as it was a conspicuous feature of Hebrew religion at its best. The basis of Christian joy lies in the main theological doctrines of the faith. This necessitates viewing the subject through clear theological lenses, which will include *creation, the *Trinity, *Jesus, *salvation, humanity and *sin, the *church and *eschatology.

Joy forms the bookends that stand at either end of biblical revelation. It begins with God's delight in his good creation and ends with the beatific vision of redeemed humanity seeing the face of God. Between them spreads a tangled history of joy shattered through human sinfulness and joy restored at great cost through the redeeming work of Christ.

Throughout history Christians have approached the subject of joy via many different routes; these might be narrowed down to three broad categories: contemplative, Reformed or evangelical, and charismatic. Each strand of

Christian spirituality has its own distinctive contribution to make to our theological understanding of joy.

Contemplative

*Augustine provides an early expression of Christian joy in contemplating God: 'My God, I give thanks to you, my source of sweet delight, and my glory and my confidence' (*Confessions*, 1.XX 31). This strand is also reflected in the writings of medieval mystics (see *Mysticism), such as *Hildegard of Bingen and *Teresa of Avila, who derived joy from contemplating the character of God and his works in creation. The contemplative tradition can also be observed in the growing influence of Orthodox *spirituality. Its celebration of the whole of life can be seen as an echo of the joy that exists within the Trinity: a joy that explodes into life in creation, redemption and the climax of history.

Reformed/Evangelical

The Reformed view is echoed in the comment that: 'Joy is not an isolated or occasional consequence of faith, but is an integral part of the whole relation to God' (Hendry). The Westminster Shorter Catechism is unequivocal: 'Man's chief end is to glorify God, and to enjoy him forever.' Barth describes the glory of God as beauty. This is the beauty of one who is the source and giver of joy. 'The beautiful in God is what makes us rejoice in him' (Moltmann). One of the major expressions of the Reformed view of joy is the massive meditation on 1 Pet. 1:8 in Jonathan Edwards' *The Religious Affections*. Published in the eighteenth century, this work continues to have an impact through the contemporary writing of authors like John Piper, with his ideas of desiring God and 'Christian hedonism'. Edwards has also been used as a resource in the charismatic movement.

Charismatic/Pentecostal

Although Pentecostal type groups have emerged throughout twenty centuries of church history, the twentieth century was particularly marked by the joyful vitality and growth of first the Pentecostal and then the *charismatic movements. The charismatic/Pentecostal movements have had in the past century a truly global impact; their emphasis on joy in the Holy Spirit has been reflected in a fresh explosion of new church structures, new songs and a renewed zeal for communicating the gospel. Joy finds expression in a new attitude to life as a whole and in revitalized *worship.

David F. Ford is one contemporary writer who has managed to successfully combine the contemplative, Reformed and charismatic strands of joy. He has done so by utilizing their complementary contributions in a way that restructures our understanding of what it means to have joy in God. Joy refocuses and reshapes our lives so that we can rediscover our centre in God. In this way we regain our intended shape as image-bearers of the blessed Trinity.

Bibliography

Augustine of Hippo, *Confessions* tr. H. Chadwick (Oxford, 1991); J. Edwards, *Religious Affections*, vol. 2 in *Works of Jonathan Edwards* (Yale, 1977); D. F. Ford, *The Shape of Living* (London, 1997); idem, *Self and Salvation* (Cambridge, 1999); J. Piper, *Desiring God: Confessions of a Christian Hedonist* (Leicester and Downers Grove, ²2004).

J. D. WOODS

JUDAISM AND CHRISTIANITY

To speak of Judaism and Christianity might be taken to suggest that there are two comparable entities founded on similar principles. Only from the late eighteenth century did Jews conceptualize observances and communal organization along the lines of what may be called '*religion'. The task in hand was to make themselves acceptable to a society which, notably in France and the German principalities, privileged the Christian traditions adhered to by the majority of the population. Thus the Jewish community became a religious organization alongside Christian churches, its organizational structure partly copied from the churches, but retaining distinctly Jewish characteristics.

Before emancipation (1792 onwards), Jewish communities in Europe were founded on the basis of contractual arrangements with the relevant local or provincial authorities and/or on *canon law. Christians regarded the members of these Jewish communities as 'foreigners', and even Jews accepted that they were admitted for a particular purpose and could be expelled. Indeed, some have cast this period of Jewish history in Europe as a long list of expulsions and persecutions at the hand of Christian communities and authorities. This perspective may be extended into the modern era. Even with emancipation, persecutions did not come to an end, but rather, with the development of modern racist anti-Semitism, took a different turn, the consequences of which can be observed in the *Holocaust.

Jews in Europe understood their own communities as much as an ethnic entity as a community of faith. Faith in a set of doctrinal propositions did not determine membership in the Jewish community. Jews were born into the Jewish community and, unless converting to another faith, did not, and often could not, leave the Jewish community. While individuals propagating positions deemed contrary to the unity of the community could be cast out as heretics, these bans were localized judgments of limited duration. Hence, Jewishness can be conceived as an ethnicity (see *Race), and has also been cast in terms of belonging to a people or, in its modern sense, a nation.

Christian conceptualizations of Jews are as old as the beginnings of the church. The primary problem of the largely Jewish early church was not its attitude to Jewish religious backgrounds, but rather the question of Gentiles becoming believers in the God of Israel and in the Jewish Messiah. Must Gentiles become Jews in order to become followers of Jesus, with all that this entails in terms of the observance of Jewish law? In Gal. and Rom., Paul evaluates the ways in which Christians of Jewish origin and the increasing number of Gentile Christians can successfully live together. Acts 15:1–29 suggests the danger of a split between a community comprised mainly of Jewish Christians and communities outside of the land of Israel whose members are mainly Gentile. Paul also develops a theological foundation for the relationship between Jews and Gentiles in Rom. 9–11 which, in recent theology, has given biblical foundations to *covenant theology.

Recent scholarship on the 'parting of the ways' of church and synagogue suggests that this was a long process extending into the fifth century. During the first five centuries both the Christian and Jewish communities developed the principles on which their respective observances and organizational structures for the following thousand years were founded, and which in significant respects survive today, even after the separation between Constantinople and Rome, the transformations of *Reformation, *Enlightenment and *secularization, and in spite of the development of distinctly modern Jewish movements. Polemics between communities abound in the early centuries of the church and, with Christianity's rise to dominance during Constantine's reign, became integral to parts of Christian theology. NT texts can be read as embodying polemics against certain Jewish practices and communities, but their history of interpretation contains strong anti-Semitic currents, in particular where references to 'the Jews' are applied to Jews at all times. *Augustine's interpretation of Jews as 'witness people' whose existence demonstrates the glory of Christ and the salvific power of Christianity became central to church teaching. While this interpretation ensured the possibility for Jewish communities to live as tolerated minorities in Christian society, it also contributed to the restrictions placed on Jewish communities. Christian persecution of Jews, tolerated by the church, found theological justification in the accusation of Jews as 'Christ killers', leading to the accusation of deicide. On the one hand, Jewish communities often enjoyed the protection of Gentile authorities. On the other, Christian persecution, whether by the masses such as during the Crusades or of monarchs such as Ferdinand and Isabella of Spain, led to the massacre of whole communities (e.g. in the Rhineland during the Crusades from 1096 onwards) and the murder or expulsion of Jews who did not submit to forced conversions from much of Western Europe (e.g. expulsion from Spain in 1492). The 'Pale of Settlement', encompassing much of Poland, Belorussia, the Ukraine and parts of Western Russia, became home to the largest population of Jews in northern Europe. There Jews found a geographical and social space of relative autonomy and freedom that allowed some economic prosperity (while many continued to live in poverty) and scholarly excellence, though interrupted by pogroms (notably in 1648 by Cossacks under Bogdan Chmielnicki). A sharpening of nationalism and anti-Semitism at the end of the nineteenth century, the Russian Revolution of 1917, and the Holocaust brought this period of Jewish life in Europe to an end.

After the Holocaust, some churches reflected on the close connection between Christian teachings about Jews and the medieval and modern racist anti-Semitism. Some churches, in particular in Europe and North America, have revised their interpretation of continued

Jewish communal and religious life alongside Christian communities. Jews are no longer perceived as representing a rival option of salvation which dispenses with the need for Christ and which thus may be seen as challenging the efficacy of the Christian message. Rather, this kind of Christian theology has begun to speak of Jewish religious life in an affirmative way. Drawing heavily on Rom. 9 – 11, theories of a single and double covenant theology developed, both of which suggest that Jews have no need of being drawn into a relationship with God through Christ, since the covenant of Sinai on which the Jewish relationship with God is founded is still valid. *Vatican II's *Nostra Aetate* 4 affirm the continuing validity of the Jewish relationship with God and, along with statements of individual local Protestant denominations, reject Christian mission to convert Jews to Christianity. At the same time, Christians as individuals as well as representatives of churches have begun to develop a Christian-Jewish dialogue which aims to foster better understanding between Jews and Christians and to aid the Christian re-evaluation of its interpretations of Jews.

Such change to Christian theological thought and practice is located on the margins of the churches and embraced by few. The majority of the Christian community remains untouched by these developments. This may be due to theological objections to such enterprises or a perceived irrelevance of Christian-Jewish relations to their particular context. In particular, conservative Christian circles in both Catholic, Protestant and Orthodox churches object to changes to traditional Christian teaching about Jews, as this would challenge *salvation-historical doctrine.

See also: JEWISH-CHRISTIAN RELATIONS; RABBINIC THEOLOGY.

Bibliography

C. E. Braaten and R. W. Jensen (eds.), *Jews and Christians: People of God* (Grand Rapids, 2003); P. M. van Buren, *A Theology of the Jewish-Christian Reality, Part I–III* (San Francisco, 1981–8); N. Cohen (ed.), *Essential Papers on Jewish-Christian Relations in the United States* (New York, 1990); D. Cohn-Sherbok (ed.), *The Future of Jewish-Christian Dialogue* (Lewiston, 2000); A. T. Davies (ed.), *Antisemitism and the Foundations of Christianity* (New York, 1979); E. J. Fisher (ed.), *Visions of the Other: Jewish and Christian Theologians Assess the Dialogue*, Studies in Judaism and Christianity (New York, 1994); S. R. Haynes, *Jews and the Christian Imagination: Reluctant Witnesses* (Basingstoke and London, 1995); G. I. Langmuir, *History, Religion and Antisemitism* (Berkeley, 1990); M. Perry and F. M. Schweitzer (eds.), *Jewish-Christian Encounters over the Centuries: Symbiosis, Prejudice, Holocaust, Dialogue*, American University Studies Series IX: History, vol. 136 (New York, 1994); M. Saperstein, *Moments of Crisis in Jewish-Christian Relations* (London and Philadelphia, 1989); M. Shermis and A. Zannoni (eds.), *Introduction to Jewish-Christian Relations* (1991); G. Wigoder, *Jewish-Christian Relations since the Second World War* (Manchester and New York, 1988).

K. H. HOLTSCHNEIDER

JUDGMENT OF GOD

God's judgment reflects the character of God himself in relation to creation and all human history. This judgment has been initiated and revealed in Jesus Christ, bringing God's *kingdom into history, a kingdom to be finally and totally implemented at the last judgment or second coming of Christ. The NT sees human history existing between these two moments of judgment, with an era of divine forbearance until the final judgment, related theologically as 'realized' and 'thoroughgoing' *eschatology. The relation between these points is *Jesus Christ, 'the judge judged in our place' at Calvary and raised victorious over sin and death (K. Barth, *CD*, 4.1), in whose light all will be judged at the end of their lives. Barth argues that Jesus Christ destroyed sin by his great sacrifice at Calvary, passing judgment on it victoriously, and the last judgment is where the absolute destruction of *sin takes place, the completion of this judgment. The dead are raised to judgment, for eternal life or death, the moment transcending therefore our space and time continuum. The human race will be judged by its attitude to Christ and his revelation of God's holy love, shown by the episode of the repentant thief on the cross (Luke 23:42).

Judgment of holy love

The judgment on sin revealed and enacted at Calvary shows the truth of *Calvin's view that this bearing of human judgment by God the Son flows from holy *love (*Institutes*, II.XVII. 2). Divine judgment is the divine attitude to sin; a wider category than just moral wrong according to human standards, God's judgment attends to the heart and to the full circumstances of a person. A person is judged according to their deeds and to what the whole person has become as a result. Divine forbearance in judging is a permeating theme in the Bible. God's verdict is given at the end of a life, and this verdict is in a sense also the verdict of the person being judged: 'This is the verdict [judgment]: Light has come into the world, but men loved darkness instead of light' (John 3:19).

Rudolph *Bultmann's 'demythologizing' existential interpretation of eschatological judgment stresses exclusively an inward aspect of self-judgment in the light of Jesus in the here and now, but he makes the mistake of rejecting an objective final divine judgment. We can harden our hearts, or open our hearts to God, and according to the parables of Jesus strict religiosity can lead to a deadening and anthropocentric moralism, whereas a genuine sense of our own unholiness is mandatory for the disciple who trusts solely on God's mercy, exemplified in the parable of the Pharisee and the tax collector (Luke 18:9–14). Divine judgment is therefore 'relational' in Christian theology, not a matter of detached rejection or acceptance: rather the relationship is already one of judgment or *grace, of our rejection of or trust in God, a theme linked to Abrahamic faith and hence the unevangelized (Rom. 4:3). The gospel teaches that Christ crucified and risen is the true anchor for such trust. The disciple shares in the identity and human status of the second *Adam or remaker of humanity, dead to sin and alive in a new resurrection life (Rom. 8:1). Barth points out that the presupposition of divine judgment is divine love: 'His love lives and rules before and over and even in His judgment. Thus even as the ineluctable judgment of wrath, which is the form it necessarily takes, is the instrument of His love' (*CD*, II.2, 735).

The justice of divine judgment

God cannot be true to his own being simply to 'excuse' wrongs. Our actions matter and cannot be overlooked in a moral universe. Liberal theology has contested the need for divine judgment to be enacted since God is love, anticipated by Heinrich Heine's dying words in 1856: 'Of course God will forgive me, that's his business.' The response to this by theologians such as *Forsyth and *Barth has been that God is holy and cannot implicitly connive at wrong by overlooking it; to do so is not love in any deep sense. Sociologist Peter Berger makes one of his 'signals of transcendence' 'the argument from damnation', that is, the human sense of the need for 'a retribution that is more than human' in the case of monstrous evil, such as Nazi mass murder (*A Rumor of Angels*, New York, 1970, p. 87). This kind of example of evil evacuates the indulgent liberal view of divine judgment, having no theological depth in terms of divine holiness or human sin. The truth of divine judgment on human wrong is necessary in a moral universe, upholding the goodness of God, respecting the dignity of humanity. Doctrines of heaven and hell arise from this.

Christ enacts and bears divine judgment as the suffering servant, absorbing human sin and dealing with the human predicament in every dimension, including that of justice and responsibility. Objectively and subjectively, Jesus' painful and unjust death expresses divine judgment on human sin, unmasking it and triumphing over evil in history (see *Atonement).

Judgment in and on history

Judgment emerges as both a *point* of final verdict in the comings of Christ, and also a *process* at work in the world, whereby God allows humanity to suffer the spiralling consequences of sin (Rom. 1) and become aware of the need for *salvation. Into this maelstrom of human sin came Jesus Christ to reveal and enact decisive divine judgment, and after Calvary the Spirit convicts the world of 'guilt in regard to sin and righteousness and judgment' (John 16:7). The last judgment is still to happen, and yet has been anticipated in Christ, 'who will judge the living and the dead' with true authority. We are bidden not to judge others, but leave judgment to God (Job; Luke 13:4).

A major twentieth-century emphasis has been to put God into the dock of judgment on the grounds of mass suffering of two world wars and the *Holocaust, stressing God's fellow-suffering rather than undergoing of judgment for sin (see *Impassibility of God). The NT weaves these two themes together: innocent suffering is taken into God's mercy by Jesus, who identifies himself as the suffering servant of Isa. 53 (Mark 14:24); God passes judgment on sin through his bearing of injustice and suffering in Christ.

This has been interpreted as the process of 'the creative suffering of God' (P. S. Fiddes), the notion that God waits for his wayward creation to return to him, a painful process grieving the heart of the divine revealed at Calvary, shocking us into transforming self-judgment. The sovereign act of judgment upon history becomes a process immanent with it, drawn by divine persuasion. J. A. T. Robinson's *In the End, God* argued that nothing finally will be able to resist God's love, and so all will be saved, a kind of *universalism akin to the Eastern Orthodox doctrine of *apokatastasis*, the idea that all will be cleansed through the fire of divine judgment. The last judgment will totally eradicate all evil (including the *devil) that has not responded to Christ's love and challenge to repent. Christ's *resurrection, including yet transcending time, is linked theologically with this moment of destroying all evil and delivering the kingdom to the Father (1 Cor. 15:24).

Bibliography

K. Barth *CD*, II/2, 39; 4.1, 59; J. Calvin, *Institutes*, Book II (ET, London and Philadelphia, 1960 [1559]); P. S. Fiddes, *Past Event and Present Salvation* (London, 1989); P. T. Forsyth, *The Justification of God* (London, 1917); C. S. Lewis, *The Great Divorce* (London, 1946); J. Moltmann, *The Crucified God* (ET, Minneapolis, 1974); W. Pannenberg, *Jesus, God and Man* (Philadelphia, 1970); J. A. T. Robinson, *In the End, God* (Cambridge, 1968).

T. Bradshaw

JULIAN OF NORWICH (*c.* 1342–*c.* 1416)

We know little about Julian's life: she tells us she was 'a devout woman', living as a recluse at Norwich. She was born in *c.*1342, fell seriously ill at the age of thirty, and believed herself to have been granted a series of revelations, or 'shewings'. She spent the rest of her life reflecting on what they meant, eventually writing first a short and later a longer version of what in the text is called 'A Revelation of Love', but which later came to be called *Showings* or *Revelations of Divine Love*. Both versions begin with the suffering of Christ on the cross: Julian sees the passion of Christ as the key, not just to understanding her own *suffering, but to making sense of the world as a whole. For her, the God we see revealed in Christ is our mother by virtue of God's loving, nurturing and suffering love for us. By that love alone we are set free from the power of both sin and evil. Her theology is profoundly Pauline and Christ-centred, rooted in a lifelong contemplation of the NT and its relevance to the sufferings of her own day: she was born when the Black Death was at its height, hence her relevance to a post-Holocaust age.

See also: Mystical Theology; Spirituality.

Bibliography

Works: *Showings*, tr. E. Colledge and J. Walsh (New York and London, 1978).

Studies: D. N. Baker, *Julian of Norwich's Showings: From Vision to Book* (Princeton, 1994); G. Jantzen, *Julian of Norwich* (London, ²2000); G. Mursell, *English Spirituality*, vol. 1 (London, 2001).

G. Mursell

JÜNGEL, EBERHARD (b. 1934)

Jüngel is emeritus professor of systematic theology at the University of Tübingen, and a leading contemporary Protestant theologian. He has published widely on the NT, historical and dogmatic theology, and philosophy of religion. His work is deeply influenced by Ernst Fuchs' (1903–83) theories of language and by *Barth's rigorous Christocentrism. Three main areas of theological concern can be identified. (1) Jüngel expounds an incarnational and trinitarian understanding of God, rooted in God's humble self-identification with the crucified Christ. Much of his work is preoccupied with the theological and ontological implications of Calvary. (2) He uses the motif of justification to develop an *anthropology emphasizing man as receptive and relational rather than self-realizing. (3) He has tried to rephrase *natural theology as a theology of the natural, that is, as an exploration of the universal implications of God's particular self-revelation. All three themes contribute to a theology whose intention is to give an account of the proper distinction between the human God and his human creation. Jüngel has also published perceptive studies of Barth, essays on analogy, metaphor and ontology, and a book on death.

Bibliography

Works: *Death* (ET, Edinburgh, 1975); *The Doctrine of the Trinity* (ET, Edinburgh, 1976); *God as the Mystery of the World* (ET, Edinburgh, 1983).

Studies: P. DeHart, *Beyond the Necessary God: Trinitarian Faith and Philosophy in the Thought of Eberhard Jüngel* (Atlanta, 2000); D. Nelson, 'The Indicative of Grace, the Imperative of Freedom: An Invitation to the Theology of Eberhard Jüngel', *Dialog* 44:2 (2005), pp. 164–180; J. B. Webster, *Eberhard Jüngel: An Introduction to His Theology* (Cambridge, 1986); idem, *The Possibilities of Theology: Studies in the Theology of Eberhard Jüngel* (London, 2006).

J. B. WEBSTER

JUSTICE, see RIGHTEOUSNESS

JUSTIFICATION

The doctrine of justification pertains to the reconciliation (see *Atonement) that has been effected between God and humanity through the person and work of Jesus Christ. This reconciliation is for those in the church a present reality and for those outside a possibility. As such it is a central doctrine. Luther stated that '. . . where this article is upheld so is the church, and where this article is overthrown so is the church' (WA 40/3. 352.3). Eighteenth-century Protestantism echoed this sentiment, stating that justification was the 'article upon which the church stands and falls' (*articulus stantis et cadentis ecclesiae*). Likewise, in the twentieth century, ecumenical dialogues saw agreement on this doctrine as a possible foundation for greater unity.

Historical development

Early church

The doctrine of justification was not a topic of extensive theological debate in the early church. The concept was primarily discussed within exegetical contexts. Of particular interest is the way in which some of the Greek Fathers developed a doctrine of free choice (*autexousia*). For them humanity was free to choose good or evil over against the Stoic concept of fatalism (cf. *Justin Martyr, *II Apology*, ch. 7). This concept was further advanced by Pelagius, a British monk, during the late fourth century, whose theology led to a larger-scale discussion about the forgiveness of sins and whether it came about by grace or by natural moral effort.

Augustine

It seems that Pelagius believed that human beings were created good and that God, through the law, had given humanity all that it needed to live a holy life. Thus *Pelagianism became known as advocating the idea that one could take the initial steps toward *salvation apart from a special gift of grace, thus emphasizing the free will of humanity in salvation. In opposition to this theology, *Augustine developed his theology of *grace. It is important to note, that Augustine, the fountainhead of Western theology, was concerned with articulating a sound theology of grace rather than a theology of justification (see D. Wright, 'Justification in Augustine', in McCormack [ed.], *Justification in Perspective*, pp. 55–72). It is his theology of grace that laid the foundation for later discussions on justification.

Augustine's theology of grace has three important emphases that provided the foundation for later discussions about justification. (1) It is associated with his doctrine of election based on God's eternal decree of *predestination. For Augustine grace was God's complete freedom to act without any external necessity. God's freedom established his sovereignty. Predestination, therefore, was 'God's arrangement of his future works in his prescience, which cannot be deceived and changed' (PL 45:1019). In this way predestination was a necessary precursor for the gift of grace. (2) In Augustine's thought, *faith was seen as a gift of God's grace. This gift of justifying faith was defined by Augustine as faith which is operative through love (Gal. 5:6). *Love plays a pivotal role in his thought. He once stated: 'Love begun is righteousness begun; love developed, righteousness developed; great love, perfect righteousness; love out of a pure heart and a good conscience and faith feigned' (PL 40:286). (3) Lastly, via propagation from Adam all humanity was born with original *sin, which resulted in a corrupt freedom. This corruption could only be healed by grace. Only then could a person choose to love God and only then because God first loved them.

In addition, Augustine's theology of grace was developed within a sacramental framework.

Thus he spoke of the *sacraments as the main channels of grace, that is, the sacraments of the church mediated grace to believers. 'There is no other valid means of making Christians and remitting sins, except by causing men to become believers by the institution of Christ and the church, and through the sacraments' (*CSEL* 60:149).

It was within this wider context of grace that Augustine occasionally spoke of justification (Lat. *iustificatio, iustificare*). Thus, he primarily understood it to mean 'to make righteous', so that in his treatise *The Spirit and the Letter* he stated: 'What else does "having been justified" mean than "having been made just", that is, by the one who justifies the ungodly, so that from being ungodly one becomes righteous?' (*PL* 44:228). This transformative view of justification was predominant in his thought; however, as the Reformers would highlight, Augustine's thought was broad enough that he did not exclude a declarative view of the forgiveness of sins from justification.

Middle Ages

Following Augustine the Middle Ages developed an elaborate sacramental theology within which the doctrine of justification found its home. As Alister McGrath states: 'The characteristic medieval understanding of the nature of justification may be summarized thus: justification refers not merely to the beginning of the Christian life, but also to its continuation and ultimate perfection, in which Christians are made righteous in the sight of God and of humanity through a fundamental change in their nature, and not merely in their status' (*Iustitia Dei*, p. 59). Within this setting justification was most clearly seen as a transformative progression in grace. A person began their progression in justification first as a child who was baptized, then their grace was strengthened through confirmation and the participation of the Lord's Supper. If this person then sinned, their progression in grace was halted and they would have to be reintroduced to grace through the sacrament of penance. This cycle of being in a state of grace or sin dominated one's religious life.

Thus it was during this time that an intricate theology developed around *penance and the question: 'What must I do to be saved?' After someone commited a sin, what then was required for the restoration to grace? The medieval school of the *via moderna* constructed a covenantal theology, which held that God had ordained that all that was necessary for a person to be saved was 'to do only what they are capable of' (*facere quod in se*). Accomplishing 'what one was capable of' was seen as an initial move toward receiving grace, and this initial move was then accepted by God as worthy of the forgiveness of sins.

This initial step was spoken of as a *merit of congruity, or a half-merit (i.e. merits that were not worthy of grace in and of themselves but are merits only because God's covenant ordained to accept them as such). After one was infused or imparted grace one progressed in merits of condignity (i.e. merits stemming from grace that are accepted as having merit to save). This intricate system of merit was advanced via the papal bull *Unigenitus* (1343), which established the idea of a treasury of merit from which merit could be borrowed through the church by means of indulgences. From this point on an elaborate system of merits was established so that the Christian life was seen as a progression of accumulating more and more merit, until in *purgatory one accomplished perfect satisfaction for one's sins. This process was theologically understood as justification.

Reformation

*Luther devised his theology of justification in response to this theology of merit. In the system of merit, he emphasized the declarative aspect of the forgiveness of sins based on Augustine's theology of grace. The forgiveness of sins was not earned but given. For Luther justification came about by faith alone (*sola fide*) and not by works. With the aid of Philipp *Melanchthon, Luther developed a forensic understanding of justification that held negatively that a person's sin was no longer held against them (i.e. it was not imputed to them as sin), and positively that Christ's merits (an alien *righteousness) were imputed to them (i.e. Christ's saving work was credited to the believer). On this account, the Lutheran doctrine of justification has been often explained by the phrase *simul iustus et peccator* – a Christian is at one and the same time a sinner and righteous. 'What then? Are we sinners? No, rather we are justified, but by grace.' Righteousness is not situated in those qualitative forms, but in the mercy of God. In fact, if you take mercy away from the godly, they are sinners, and really have sin, but it is not imputed to them because they believe and live under the reign of mercy, and because sin is condemned and continually put to death in them' (*LW* 32, p. 208). This dialectical teaching overthrew the penitential cycle of the medieval church based on a cycle of being in a state of sin and then a state of grace. Thus the majority of Reformers held that a Christian was in both states at once – there is no fluctuation between being sinful and righteous; justification was an event of God's grace rather than a process (see *Reformation theology). It should be noted that in Luther studies, the twentieth-century Finnish school has brought to light the more transformative elements in Luther's thought, sometimes in terms of *theosis*.

Though not characteristic of the early days of the Reformation, the Reformers gradually spoke of the transformation that develops from justification as *sanctification. Thus what the medieval church held together in the doctrine of justification (i.e. forgiveness of sins and moral transformation or progression), the Reformers began to distinguish. As Anthony Lane explains, justification and sanctification are like the two legs of a pair of trousers: they are distinguishable but cannot be separated (A. N. S. Lane, *Justification by Faith*, p. 18).

During the sixteenth century the *Roman Catholic Church responded to this Reformation doctrine of justification and its forensic leanings at the Council of *Trent. At the sixth session (1547) of this council they rejected the Reformation teaching of *sola fide* and insisted on the imparted nature of grace rather than an imputed understanding of justifying grace. Hence, the Catholic Church focused on the transformative element of justification, seeing it more as a process than an event. This dichotomy between event and process, declaration and transformation, Protestant and Catholic, has characterized much of the modern understanding of justification to the present day.

Current issues

Ecumenical movement

In Hans *Küng's work *Justification: The Doctrine of Karl Barth and a Catholic Reflection*, he argued that the Roman Catholic and Protestant positions over justification were actually compatible. This work acted as a catalyst for larger cross-confessional dialogues over the topic of justification. The largest and most successful of these dialogues has been between the *Lutheran Church and the Catholic Church. On 31 October 1999 the Lutheran World Federation and the Roman Catholic Church signed the *Joint Declaration on the Doctrine of Justification*. In this document both sides affirmed that the condemnations of the sixteenth century no longer applied and stated, 'Together we confess: By grace alone, in faith in Christ's saving work and not because of any merit on our part, we are accepted by God and receive the Holy Spirit, who renews our hearts while equipping and calling us to good works' (*Joint Declaration*, para. 15). This agreement has led to a greater healing of the division between Protestants and Catholics.

New perspective

Concurrent with the ecumenical dialogues, NT scholars were rigorously investigating first-century Judaism, and these investigations began to change certain scholars' views about Paul's thought in regard to the law (esp. E. P. Sanders, James Dunn, N. T. Wright) (see *Law and gospel). Rather than seeing the works of the law as moral works, this new school tends to understand that when Paul refers to the works of the law he is referring to the laws that defined a Jew over against a Gentile. The way in which one understands Paul's understanding of the works of the law is pivotal for understanding what Paul means by justification. The verdict is still out on this new perspective; however, it has reinvigorated Pauline studies as well as theologians' views on justification.

With the various ecumenical dialogues and new investigations into Paul's theology the new debate over the doctrine of justification is providing opportunities for reconciliation between brothers and sisters of different denominations. We need no longer speak of either or, but both and, as Karl Barth eloquently stated: 'There is no room for any fears that in the justification of man we are dealing only with a verbal action, with a kind of bracketed "as if", as though what is pronounced were not the whole truth about man. Certainly we have to do with a declaring righteous, but it is a declaration about man which is fulfilled and therefore effective in this event, which corresponds to actuality because it creates and therefore reveals the actuality. It is a declaring righteous which without any reserve can be called a making righteous' (*CD* IV.1, p. 95).

See also: GUILT AND FORGIVENESS.

Bibliography

H. G. Anderson, T. A. Murphy and J. A. Burgess (eds.), *Justification by Faith: Lutherans and Catholics in Dialogue VII* (Minneapolis, 1985); D. E. Aune (ed.), *Rereading Paul Together: Protestant and Catholic Perspectives on Justification* (Grand Rapids, 2006); K. Barth, *Church Dogmatics*, tr. by G. W. Bromiley and T. F. Torrance, IV/1 (Edinburgh, 1956); J. D. G. Dunn, *Jesus, Paul and the Law: Studies in Mark and Galatians* (London, 1990); M. Husbands and D. J. Treier (eds.), *Justification: What's at Stake in the Current Debates* (Downers Grove, 2004); R. Jenson, 'Justification as a Triune Event', in *Modern Theology* 11 (1995), pp. 421–427; *Joint Declaration on the Doctrine of Justification* (Grand Rapids, 2000); E. Jüngel, *Justification: The Heart of the Christian Faith*, tr. by J. Webster (Edinburgh, 2001); H. Küng, *Justification: The Doctrine of Karl Barth and a Catholic Reflection*, 2nd edn (London, 1964); A. N. S. Lane, *Justification by Faith in Catholic-Protestant Dialogue: An Evangelical Assessment* (London, 2002); M. Luther, *Kritische Gesamtausgabe* (Weimar, 1883–); idem, *Luther's Works*, J. Pelikan and H. T. Lehmann (eds.) (St Louis, 1955–76); T. Mannermaa, *Christ Present in Faith: Luther's View of Justification* (Philadelphia, 2005); B. L. McCormack (ed.), *Justification in Perspective: Historical Developments and Contemporary Challenges* (Grand Rapids, 2006); A. E. McGrath, *Iustitia Dei: A History of the Christian Doctrine of Justification*, 3rd edn (Cambridge, 2005); A. B. Ritschl, *A Critical History of the Christian Doctrine of Justification and Reconciliation* (Edinburgh, 1871); W. G. Rusch (ed.), *Justification and the Future of the Ecumenical Movement: The Joint Declaration on the Doctrine of Justification* (Collegeville, 2003); E. P. Sanders, *Paul and Palestinian Judaism: A Comparison of Patterns of Religion* (Philadelphia, 1977); N. T. Wright, *Justification: God's Plan and God's Vision* (Downers Grove, 2009); idem, *What St. Paul Really Said* (Oxford, 1997).

B. LUGIOYO

JUSTIN MARTYR (c. 100–162/7)

Justin is perhaps the most significant Greek-speaking *apologist of the second century. Autobiographical statements and material from Eusebius' *History* suggest he was born at Flavia Neapolis (near Shechem) into a pagan family c. 100. Justin recounts how, after investigating different pagan philosophies, an old man instructed him in true philosophy, Christianity. Justin probably taught in Rome on two occasions, and was martyred 162–7 under Marcus Aurelius, possibly because of the enmity of his Cynic opponent, Crescens.

Many works are attributed to him, but only the *First* and *Second Apologies* and the *Dialogue with Trypho* can be assigned with confidence. The *Apologies* and the *Dialogue* have different targets, the former dealing with the position of Christians within a pagan society and the latter the relationship between Christian and Jewish beliefs.

The *First Apology* is in form an appeal for justice from the emperor Antoninus Pius, and the *Second* an address to the Romans. In the *Apologies*, Justin employs arguments which became typical of Christian *apologetic. He argues that Christians should not be persecuted for the 'name alone', but only for specific crimes. He contrasts Christian moral life with pagan immorality, and trenchantly criticizes the immorality of Greco-Roman mythology, arguing that pagan religion is demonic deceit.

In the *Dialogue* two key strategies emerge: the OT law was not a path to salvation, and OT prophecy refers to Christ. Justin characteristically construes OT theophanies as appearances of the Son, an interpretation that persisted until *Augustine, and has followers today.

Justin is associated with a positive evaluation of pagan philosophy and his idea of the *logos spermatikos*, at work in all human beings. In fact Justin weighs this work, and its results in pagan philosophy, against the revelation of the divine Word in Jesus, which alone he sees as complete. Hence his stance that Christianity is the true philosophy.

Bibliography

Works: *The Apologies of Justin Martyr*, ed. A. W. F. Blunt (Eugene, 2006); *Dialogue with Trypho*, eds. M. Slusser and T. Halton (Washington DC, rev. edn, 2003).

Studies: R. M. Grant, *Greek Apologists of the Second Century* (London, 1988).

M. OVEY

KÄHLER, MARTIN (1835–1912)

Kähler was a German Protestant theologian who studied law at the University of Königsberg and theology at the universities of Heidelberg, Tübingen and Halle. Following a brief time at Bonn (1864–67), he served as professor of systematic theology and NT exegesis at Halle (from 1879). His magnum opus was a three-volume work on Christian doctrine (*Die Wissenschaft der christlichen Lehre*, 1883–87), but the work for which he is remembered today is a small booklet entitled *The So-called Historical Jesus and the Historic Biblical Christ* (tr. with intro., C. E. Braaten, Philadelphia, 1964; *Der sogenannte historische Jesus und der geschichtliche, biblische Christus*, 1896), in which he rejected the terms of reference of the liberal 'quest of the *historical Jesus' with its implied separation of faith from history, of the *Jesus who lived from the church's kerygma concerning him. The attempt to get behind the data of the Gospels to the 'real Jesus', he argued, is futile. He raised critical, dogmatic and apologetic objections to the work of the liberal 'questers'. Their critical basis was flawed by their assumption that the Gospels give us the material necessary to construct a coherent, developmental life of Jesus; they were never intended to give us this. Theologically, they mistakenly presupposed that Jesus was a mere man like themselves. And, apologetically, they made the faith of the ordinary Christian believer the captive of the latest results of scholarly opinion, rather than allowing him direct access to the object of his faith, the historic Jesus portrayed in the Gospels and proclaimed by the apostles. The united confession of the early church that 'Jesus is Lord' was no mere theological construction, but was firmly rooted in history.

Bibliography

C. E. Braaten, 'Martin Kähler on the Historic, Biblical Christ', in Braaten and R. A. Harrisville (eds.), *The Historical Jesus and the Kerygmatic Christ* (Nashville, 1964), pp. 79–105; Braaten and Harrisville (eds.), *Kerygma and History* (Nashville, 1962); A. E. McGrath, *The Making of Modern German Christology, 1750–1990* (Grand Rapids, 1994); D. K. McKim, *Dictionary of Major Biblical Interpreters* (Downers Grove, 2007).

W. W. GASQUE

KANT, IMMANUEL (1724–1804)

For many years professor of logic and metaphysics at the University of Königsberg, East Prussia, Kant is now seen as a seminal figure of the *Enlightenment period. His immense influence on the whole range of human enquiry, including theology, stems out of his distinctive understanding of the nature of human knowledge and belief.

The background to Kant's thinking here was the development of two philosophical traditions: British *empiricism and Continental *rationalism. The former, in its understanding of the nature of human belief, placed a primary emphasis on experience. The latter stressed the importance of innate principles and ideas within the human mind. Kant at once unites, and stands at the climax of, both traditions. Thus he affirms the importance of sense-organ experience in human knowledge. But Kant also argues that the human mind is not a wholly passive receptor of these sense experiences. On the contrary, the mind is constantly active in organizing and classifying the raw materials of experience. In this way the human mind imposes on experience its own distinctive categories and concepts. (These 'Forms of Intuition' or 'Pure Ideas' are what Kant terms the synthetic a priori dimension of human understanding.) Here, however, an obvious question arises: If we are constantly imposing our own ideas and categories on the world of experience, is this not a source of distortion and prejudice? We may constantly wear red-tinted spectacles. If so, then everything without exception will appear to be red. But this does not mean that the whole of reality is actually red.

It is, in effect, Kant's response to this problem which constitutes his most important contribution to philosophy. Kant maintains that we cannot know things in themselves: all knowledge is from a certain perspective and through a particular mode of understanding. But he also argues that, whilst the human mind does impose its own forms of understanding on the world, nevertheless, the world must be of a certain character in order to receive these forms of understanding.

An example here is his teaching about causality. The Scottish philosopher, David *Hume, had argued that sense-experience could, by itself, never furnish us with the idea of causal connection, but only that of constant conjunction. (For example, we never have a genuine sense-experience of the actual causal relationship between the hot stove and the boiling water. All we ever experience is the constant conjunction or co-existence of these two events.) So where does the idea of causality come from? Hume's answer had been that the mind is psychologically (a-rationally) predisposed to make the step from constant conjunction to causal connection. But, he provocatively urges, the fact that human beings happen to have these particular psychological tendencies does not mean that the material world is actually of a certain character. This is the basis of Hume's scepticism.

Kant's philosophy of knowledge is best understood by reference to the way in which it departs from Hume's at this crucial point. For Kant's fundamental position is this: our actual experience of nature (and in particular the orderliness, regularity and consistency which characterizes this experience) must entail a world to which causal laws are applicable. Only a certain sort of a world would be able to *receive* our causal pre-understandings. An order of reality characterized by natural anarchy and unqualified random chance could never *conform to* our fundamental categories of cause and effect. There is philosophical disagreement as to just how much Kant has established here. Nevertheless, the departure from Hume is clear. For Kant, the idea of causation is established as an authentic part of rational human judgment because it is a belief – alongside other fundamental beliefs about the material world – which expresses the *conditions of the possibility of experience*.

But if for Kant this philosophical approach establishes the possibility of a distinctive *knowledge* of the material world, it also confirms our inability to *know* anything beyond it: to know of God, the soul or life beyond death. This is the case since, for Kant, there is no theological proposition whose truth is necessary in order to explain the character of the experiences which we actually have. (In saying this, Kant had already dispelled, to his own satisfaction, the traditional proofs of God's existence. See *Natural theology.) For Kant, the essential problem with religious knowledge is not a shortage of raw data (as a detective might despair of a lack of clues). Rather, it is that the infinite God must forever elude our pre-understandings. He is beyond our limited conceptual apparatus, and thus we cannot in any substantial sense know him. The categories through which we apprehend the world of sense-experience are simply inappropriate for the infinite, the non-conditioned, the eternal metaphysical. And thus in religion, demonstrative reason must give way to *practical faith*.

The implications for theology here were obviously immense. If God is, in the strictest sense, unknowable, then the proper object and study for theology is not God, but man's religious states and sentiments and their individual and communal expressions. Theology becomes anthropocentric. (Witness, for example, the direct impact of Kant's thinking on *Schleiermacher's theology.) Similiarly, within such anthropocentricism, the Scriptures will be seen as a descriptive record of human religious experience, but as having no authority beyond this.

What then is practical faith? And is it wholly divorced from reason? While, for Kant, human beliefs about God, transcendence, human freewill, the soul and immortality are not within the scope of demonstrative reason, they are *practical presuppositions* of the moral life. Kant does not (contrary to what is sometimes stated) argue here that God is the only possible source of moral judgments – of an objective morality. Rather he argues that to be committed to the moral life is to make the practical presupposition of a beneficent being of sufficient power to unite full virtue and happiness (that is, to bring about the *summum bonum*), and also of a future state in which the soul will enjoy this union.

The idea (anticipated by Hume) that our minds are constantly imposing their own pre-understandings on to the successive items of experience is today part of common intellectual currency. Thus, for example, it is an idea which is central within the present debates about biblical interpretation (cf. *Hermeneutics). It is also, to cite just two further examples, a key concept in the sociology of knowledge and in much of our thinking about personal relationships. Furthermore, it is a conception which, not least through the writings of the later *Wittgenstein, continues to play a significant part in formal philosophy. All of this testifies to the considerable historical importance of Kant's contribution to human thought. As a figure of the Enlightenment, his self-sufficient reliance on human understanding and reason separates him sharply from the most fundamental principles of Protestantism. But it would be unwise to underestimate his influence on the modern mind.

Bibliography

Works: *A Critique of Pure Reason*, tr. N. Kemp Smith (London, 1929); *The Critique of Practical Reason*, tr. T. K. Abbott (London, ⁶1909).

Studies: C. D. Broad, *Kant: An Introduction* (Cambridge, 1978); S. Köorner, *Kant* (Harmondsworth, 1955); D. J. O'Connor (ed.), *A Critical History of Western Philosophy* (New York, 1964); R. Scruton, *Kant: A Very Short Introduction* (Oxford, 2001); T. K. Seung, *Kant: A Guide for the Perplexed* (London, 2007).

M. D. Geldard

KARLSTADT, ANDREAS BODENSTEIN VON (1486–1541)

Andreas von Karlstadt was a leading German Reformer whose very popular writings championed lay discipleship. Trained in arts, law and theology, the Wittenberg professor was won over to Luther's understanding of grace by 1517, but moved in a more radical direction. He respected OT revelation and German mysticism, with its emphasis on resigning oneself wholly to God, and on the work of the Spirit in the 'abyss' of the soul. At the famous Leipzig Disputation of 1519 he stood side by side with *Luther and during the former's enforced absence after the Diet of Worms effectively took over the leadership of the reforming movement in Wittenberg. Impatient of compromise, he abolished the Mass and urged the removal of statues and paintings from the churches. He also came to reject infant baptism and the real presence in the Lord's Supper (see *Eucharist). When the Peasants' War broke out in 1524, Karlstadt was caught between the fronts, deploring its violence, but identifying himself with the poor. In later life he taught and preached in Zurich and Basel. His passion for inward faith foreshadowed many of the concerns of *Pietism.

See also: Reformation Theology.

Bibliography

E. J. Furcha (ed.), *The Essential Carlstadt* (Scottdale, 1995); R. J. Sider, *Andrew Bodenstein von Karlstadt: The Development of His Thought* (Leiden, 1974).

P. C. Matheson

KÄSEMANN, ERNST (1906–98)

A student of *Bultmann, Käsemann was professor of NT successively in Mainz, Göttingen and Tübingen, and was also identified with the German *Confessing Church during the Third Reich. His main achievements have been significant and necessary modifications in the dominant Bultmannian hypothesis.

(1) He initiated the so-called 'new quest for the *historical Jesus', pointing out that to have the 'Christ of faith' without historical anchorage led to potential *docetism. He still insisted, however, on the importance of demythologizing (see *Myth) the Gospels as the necessary corollary of *justification by *faith alone. (Faith must not be based on history, according to the Bultmannian school, lest it turn into a 'work': see 4. below.)

(2) He argued that *apocalyptic, not *Gnosticism, was the 'mother of early Christianity', i.e. that Christianity, including *Paul's theology, was essentially Jewish in origin.

(3) He argued that 'the righteousness of God' was not, as in Bultmann (and, so he claimed, in Luther), a status or attribute given by God to people, but God's own 'salvation-creating power'.

(4) He understood Paul's theology as revolving around the 'justification of the ungodly' as opposed to an immanent process of developing *salvation-history (which he saw, embryonically, in Luke).

He was active in World Council of Churches circles, speaking on ecclesiology and the political implications of the gospel (see his *Jesus Means Freedom*). In 1977 he left the Lutheran church to become a Methodist following a dispute over student protest in Tübingen, but later returned. Alongside shorter works on Hebrews and John, his magnum opus is the commentary on Romans (1973: ET, London and Grand Rapids, 1980), for which he prepared with three volumes of essays on NT theology, particularly that of Paul. A collection of essays in his honour was published in 1976 under the title *Rechtfertigung* ('Justification'), edited by J. Friedrich *et al.* (Tübingen).

Bibliography

R. Harrisville and W. Sundberg, *The Bible in Modern Culture: Theology and Historical Critical Method from Spinoza to Käsemann* (Grand Rapids, 2002), pp. 238–261; R. P. Maran, 'Ernst Käsemann', in D. K. McKim (ed.), *Historical Handbook of Major Biblical Interpreters* (Downers Grove, 1998), pp. 500–505; R. Morgan, *The Nature of New Testament Theology* (London, 1973), pp. 52–65; D. V. Way, *The Lordship of Christ: Ernst Käsemann's Interpretation of Paul's Theology* (Oxford, 1991); N. T. Wright, *Pauline Perspectives* (London, 2013; idem, *Paul and His Recent Interpreters* (London, 2015), pp. 46–57, 145–150.

N. T. Wright

KEBLE, JOHN (1792–1866)

John Keble, son of an Anglican gentleman-parson living in Gloucestershire, was educated at Oxford, where he became a fellow of Oriel College (1811–23). While in Oxford, Keble became a beloved figure, and was renowned for his good nature and wisdom even more than for his undoubted academic brilliance. Unusually, he regarded his tutorial role as a 'species of pastoral care' and before long was ordained and left Oriel, first to help his father and then in 1836 to take up what he felt was his true calling, the curacy of a small parish in Hursley, Hampshire, which he held until he died.

When a volume of Keble's devotional verses for Sundays and Holy Days entitled *The Christian Year* was published in 1827, it became extremely popular, and some of the poems are still used as hymns today. From 1831 until 1841, Keble was Professor of Poetry at Oxford; this led to his preaching the Assize Sermon in 1833, published under the title *National Apostasy*. His concept of the catholic and apostolic church in this sermon seemed startlingly new to most contemporary Anglicans, but to Keble himself, bred in the tradition of the *Caroline Divines, it was something dear and familiar. The sermon quickly became famous, and is widely considered to have initiated the revival in the Anglican Church known as the Oxford Movement (see *Anglo-Catholic theology). For the rest of his life, John Keble endeavoured to reaffirm what he regarded as the supreme importance of the sacraments and liturgy within *Anglicanism.

Bibliography

Works: Many editions of *The Christian Year* (1827); *Lyra Innocentium* (1846); *Sermons Academical* (1848); *Life of Bishop Wilson* (1863); *Sermons Occasional and Parochial* (1867).

Studies: G. Battiscombe, *John Keble: A Study in Limitations* (London, 1963); K. Blair (ed.), *John Keble in Context* (London, 2004); J. T. Coleridge, *A Memoir of the Rev. John Keble*, M.A., 2 vols. (Oxford, 1869); W. Lock, *John Keble* (London, 1895); G. Rowell, *The Vision Glorious* (Oxford, 1983); C. M. Yonge, *Musings over the 'Christian Year' and 'Lyra Innocentium', Together with a Few Gleanings of Recollections of the Rev. John Keble, Gathered by Several Friends* (Oxford, 1871).

M. M. Szurko

KENOTICISM

Kenoticism, from the Gk *kenōsis*, meaning (self-) 'emptying' (used in Phil. 2:6–7), refers to a number of related *Christological theories concerning the status of the divine in the incarnate Christ. While the term is found in a number of patristic writers and formed a key point of controversy between the Lutheran theological faculties of Tübingen and Giessen in the seventeenth century, kenoticism is usually associated with a group of German theologians in the mid-nineteenth century: G. Thomassius (1802–75), F. H. R. von Frank (1827–94) and W. F. Gess (1819–91) and a group of British theologians in the late nineteenth and early twentieth centuries: Charles *Gore, H. R. *Mackintosh, Frank Weston (1871–1924), P. T. *Forsyth and O. C. Quick (1885–1944).

The German kenoticists took the idea of self-emptying beyond its usual bounds of voluntary self-restraint of the divine nature by the God-man (the position of the Giessen faculty). Instead, they believed that the divine *Logos limited itself in the act of *incarnation. The actual theories varied. Thomassius separated the metaphysical attributes, omnipotence, omnipresence and omniscience, from the moral attributes, love and holiness. The Logos gave up the former while retaining the latter. Other German kenoticists (Frank and Gess), however, took more radical positions, which stripped Jesus of any of the attributes of divinity and called into question the use of the term 'incarnation'.

The British kenoticists had a more positive orientation. Although often accused of developing kenoticism simply as a means of accommodating the results of biblical criticism by admitting the possibility of human ignorance in Jesus, it would be more true to say that

487

British kenoticists, under the impact of a more historical reading of the Gospels, came to the conclusion that traditional Christologies did not do justice to Jesus' human life. Thus, it was the Gospel records of the human and limited consciousness of Jesus that the British kenoticists asserted over the strongly *docetic dogmatic tradition. Among the individual kenoticists the actual manner in which the divine self-emptying was believed to have occurred varied, but in general the emphasis was on the gracious character of the divine condescension and not on the precise metaphysical explanation of the act.

The current status of kenoticism is difficult to assess. On the one hand, although kenoticism is not a popular way of expressing the nature of the incarnation among conservative Christians, it should be noted that many of the major themes of the British kenoticists have been incorporated into modern evangelical Christologies. The reality of Jesus' temptations, his single (as opposed to double) consciousness, and the depth of pathos of the cry of dereliction from the cross are universally affirmed today. In the nineteenth century these were often considered part of the kenoticists' heretical innovations. On the other hand, modern evangelicalism is justifiably sceptical of any metaphysical speculation concerning the process of incarnation and sees the use of kenotic language as almost always inviting such speculation.

Bibliography

P. Dawe, *The Form of a Servant: A Historical Analysis of the Kenotic Motif* (Philadelphia, 1963); C. S. Evans (ed.), *Exploring Kenotic Christology: The Self-Emptying of God* (Oxford, 2006; Vancouver, 2010); P. T. Forsyth, *The Person and Place of Christ* (London, 1909); O. C. Quick, *Doctrines of the Creed* (London, 1938).

B. E. Foster

KERYGMA, KERYGMATIC THEOLOGY

The Greek word *kērygma* is usually translated proclamation, preaching or announcement and, outside of the NT, it was used generally of a public notice proclaimed by a herald whereby that which was announced became effective by the act of announcing it.

The usage of the word within the NT makes no distinction between the act of proclamation and the content of that proclamation, though C. H. *Dodd and others have tried to trace a single core of content in the *gospel proclamation of the primitive church as recorded in the sermons and letters of the NT. Though one may presume a unanimity among the writers of the NT concerning the essential elements of the gospel message, there is little evidence of any fixed or definitive '*creed' to which the proclamation of the primitive church invariably conformed. In this sense, the content of the kerygma as recorded in the NT must be discerned from each specific context of proclamation.

However, the word 'kerygma' has acquired a more specific philosophical and technical significance in modern theology through its usage by Rudolf *Bultmann. Bultmann suggested that the writing of the NT documents occurred within the context of the proclamation of the primitive church, and therefore the documents themselves were kerygmatic in character. He then argued that it is both inappropriate and futile to probe behind this kerygma of the primitive church as recorded in the NT documents in order to discern the underlying historical data. The attempt to legitimize the kerygma in historical terms was considered by Bultmann to be symptomatic of a lack of *faith; the quest to discover the '*historical Jesus' behind the 'Christ of faith' had to be dismissed as invalid. Bultmann then considered that, since the kerygma of the NT is expressed in the terms of a primitive worldview, this kerygma had to be demythologized (see *Myth) and reinterpreted in the terms of an *existentialist philosophy. This stretching of the term 'kerygma' and the resultant wedge that was driven between the 'Jesus of history' and the 'Christ of faith' was both unhelpful and misleading. It is hard to avoid the conclusion that through this process of demythologization and an existentialist reinterpretation of the kerygma Bultmann had arrived at a 'different gospel' (Gal. 1:6).

Bultmann's hermeneutic developed from the seed-bed of *dialectical theology which is sometimes itself referred to as kerygmatic theology and which was characteristic of the early writings of Karl *Barth. In reaction to the *liberalism of nineteenth-century German theology, Barth proclaimed the radical discontinuity between God and man. The authentic subject of theology is not man and his religion, but God and his word: the word that demands obedience; the word that authenticates itself; the word that does not therefore require historical legitimization. Though Barth in his *Church Dogmatics* continues to reject any authentication of God's word by means of historical criticism, he avoids the dualism implicit in Bultmann's distinction between the 'Jesus of history' and the 'Christ of faith' and also rejects Bultmann's process of demythologization: the *resurrection of Jesus Christ is a real event of space and time, albeit an event which will not yield to the scrutiny of positivistic historical science.

Bibliography

H. W. Bartsch (ed.), *Kerygma and Myth*, 2 vols. (London, 1953, 1962); R. Bultmann, *Theology of the New Testament*, 2 vols. (London, 1952, 1955); C. H. Dodd, *The Apostolic Preaching and Its Developments* (London, 1936); M. D. Gibson, 'Does Jesus Have a Say in the Kerygma? A Critical Remembrance of Bultmann', *SJT* 58, 2005, pp. 83–103; V. A. Harvey, *The Historian and the Believer* (London, 1967); J. I. H. McDonald, *Kerygma and Didache: The Articulation and Structure of the Earliest Christian Message* (Cambridge, 1980).

J. E. Colwell

KESWICK, see HIGHER-LIFE THEOLOGY

KIERKEGAARD, SØREN AABYE (1813–55)

In philosophical terms Kierkegaard can be seen as the father-figure of *existentialism. He consciously opposed *Hegel's philosophy, stressing by contrast the role of individual decision and active engagement with truth within the confines of concrete, finite existence. Truth must be true 'for me'. In religious terms, he saw the purpose of his writings as that of showing what it meant to be a Christian. This was very different from being a 'name-Christian' in the Danish state church of his day. In theological terms he rejected an over-intellectualist notion of *faith and reflected extensively on the role of ethical decision and a stage of faith which might be said to transcend it.

Kierkegaard was born and educated in Copenhagen. Three sets of events or relationships have special importance for an understanding of his writings.

(1) He grew up under the shadow of a dominating father who was himself plagued by a sense of guilt. Mikaël, the father, believed that his own act in childhood of cursing God could never be forgiven. He exacted high standards of academic success from Søren, who tried his best to please his father in this dismal atmosphere of duty, anxiety and guilt. But Søren was deeply shocked when he discovered that his father was not the morally upright man he had assumed him to be. His authority figure collapsed and now he sought to discover what it meant to live as and for himself. For a period he experienced moral decline, but self-discovery led on further to an experience of repentance and faith.

(2) Kierkegaard resumed his studies, and had begun pastoral ministry in the Lutheran Church when he fell deeply in love with Regine Olsen. But as soon as they became engaged, he was filled with a sense of utter unworthiness. He felt compelled to withdraw both from the engagement and from the life of a Lutheran pastor. He interpreted his 'sacrifice' of Regine in terms of the divine call to Abraham to sacrifice Isaac. For Abraham to slay the son of promise was on one level paradoxical and a suspension of the ethical. Nevertheless, God's call took precedence over the seemingly rational and ethical. For him, the broken engagement was the way of authentic discipleship in all its loneliness and contradiction of convention.

(3) Kierkegaard now lived a withdrawn life. He began to write prodigiously, producing more than twenty books in the twelve remaining years before his premature death. A third event, however, contributed even further to his distress. He attacked the low standards of a satirical paper *The Corsair*, and the paper responded by making Kierkegaard effectively the object of public ridicule. Its devastating caricature made him the laughingstock of Denmark. He interpreted this as the price for authentic Christian obedience, and set this in contrast to the easygoing pseudo-faith of 'name-Christians' in the Danish church.

Individualism

Kierkegaard's life seemed to turn on a radical contrast between authentic individual first-hand faith and the inauthentic acceptance of second-hand values. Kierkegaard saw this contrast in religious terms. He writes: 'The most ruinous evasion of all is to be hidden in the crowd in an attempt to evade God's supervision . . . in an attempt to get away from hearing God's voice as an individual' (*Purity of Heart Is to Will One Thing*, London, ²1961, p. 163). Each one, he continues, 'shall render account to God as an individual'. In modern secular existentialism this principle has become a largely negative one, as it is traced through *Nietzsche to Camus and Sartre. Authentic existence is seen in terms of throwing off the conventions of Western bourgeois society and its predetermined expected roles. But Kierkegaard's criticisms were directed towards a second-hand claim to Christian faith: 'Christianity has been abolished by expansion – by these millions of name-Christians . . .' (*Attack upon 'Christendom'*, London, 1944, p. 237). The notion of a 'Christian' state, for example, is 'shrewdly calculated to make God so confused in his head by all these millions that He cannot discover that He has been hoaxed, that there is not one single Christian' (ibid., p. 127). In the venture of faith the individual stands alone before God. Kierkegaard chose for his own epitaph only the words: 'That Individual'. He paid a price for his individualism. In his isolation from the church, his faith was always shot through with agonizing doubt, though he saw this as a mark of its authenticity.

Participation and subjectivity

It is impossible simply to acquire *truth passively from others, because the appropriation of truth involves active engagement with truth on the part of the individual human subject. It is crucial to Kierkegaard's position that 'everyone who has a result merely as such does not possess it; for he has not the way' (*The Concept of Irony*, London, 1966, p. 340). Actively to become engaged in decision, struggle and response is what Kierkegaard calls 'the task of becoming subjective'. Subjectivity, in his use of the term, does not mean the arbitrary elevation of personal opinion over the claims of objective evidence. He defines subjectivity as 'being sharpened into an "I" rather than being dulled into a third person' (*Journals*, London and Princeton, 1938, p. 533). 'The objective accent falls on WHAT is said; the subjective accent on HOW it is said . . . Thus subjectivity becomes the truth' (*Concluding Unscientific Postscript*, Princeton, 1941, p. 181).

Finitude and indirect communication

Kierkegaard ironically called Hegel's philosophy 'the System'. He attacked Hegel for claiming, in effect, that reality can be viewed 'eternally, divinely, theocentrically', when in fact the philosopher is 'only a poor existing human being not competent to contemplate the eternal either eternally or divinely or theocentrically' (ibid., p. 190). Kierkegaard would not have followed secular existentialists in effectively reducing truth to a matter of 'viewpoints'. But he insisted that the communication of truth proceeds indirectly or dialectically. Truth is not to be presented on a plate, as if it can be reduced to the dimensions of a single package. In his earlier writings Kierkegaard wrote under pseudonyms, leaving the reader to judge between competing perspectives in such a way that truth was perceived through struggle, engagement and decision. Truth cannot be 'surveyed' from a comfortable armchair, situated somewhere beyond or above the confines of human finitude. 'Truth becomes untruth in this or that person's mouth' (ibid., p. 181).

Bibliography

Works: *Kierkegaard's Writings*, H. V. and E. H. Hong (tr. and eds.), 26 vols. (Princeton, 1978–2000).

Studies: L. C. Barrett, *Kierkegaard* (Nashville, 2010); N. J. Cappelørn, H. Deuser, *et al.* (eds.), *Kierkegaard Studies Yearbook 1996–* (Berlin and New York, 1996–); C. Carlisle, *Kierkegaard: A Guide for the Perplexed* (London, 2006); C. S. Evans, *Kierkegaard on Faith and the Self: Collected Essays* (Waco, 2006); M. J. Ferreira, *Love's Grateful Striving: A Commentary on Kierkegaard's Works of Love* (Oxford, 2001); J. Garff, *Søren Kierkegaard: A Biography*, tr. Bruce Kirmmse (Princeton, 2005); A. Hannay, *Kierkegaard: A Biography* (new edn), (Cambridge, 2003); A. Hannay and G. Marino (eds.), *The Cambridge Companion to Kierkegaard* (Cambridge, 1998); H. V. Hong and E. Hong, *The Essential Kierkegaard* (Princeton, 2000); B. Kirmmse, *Encounters with Kierkegaard* (Princeton, 1996); G. Pattison, *The Philosophy of Kierkegaard* (Montreal, 2005); R. L. Perkins (ed.), *International Kierkegaard Commentary* (Macon, 1978–).

A. C. THISELTON

KINGDOM OF GOD

An expression found mainly in the Synoptic Gospels, where it is presented as central to the teaching of *Jesus. It (or one of its variants) occasionally occurs in other parts of the NT but not in the OT, although the underlying theme is fundamental to the entire biblical narrative. God is presented throughout Scripture as a King because he is the Creator of the universe to whom everyone and everything owes allegiance. In its early years, Israel was God's earthly kingdom in the sense that the Israelites did not have a recognized human ruler, though this eventually gave way to a kingdom along contemporary Near Eastern lines. After an unhappy start, this kingdom was blessed by God in the person of David, who was assured that his descendants would reign 'for ever' over the Lord's people. This promise plays a significant role in the NT, where Jesus' descent from David is recorded as a fundamental element of his mission and ministry.

That God remained the ultimate ruler of Israel, and indeed of the entire world, is frequently recalled in the OT, particularly in post-exilic eschatological prophecy. At a time when the Jews were subject to a series of foreign rulers and had little hope of regaining their freedom, the divine message was clear: the Lord was on his heavenly throne and would one day reveal himself as the ruler in *Zion. At that time all nations and kings on earth would be drawn to him and submit to his rule.

Jesus proclaimed the coming of the kingdom in and through him. Some people evidently thought that he would rebel against the Romans and re-establish the Davidic monarchy in its original form, but although Jesus claimed the Davidic inheritance, he did not interpret it in that way. In his teaching, the kingdom of God involved the forgiveness of sins and the restoration of the broken relationship between man and God (see *Atonement). This he accomplished in his death and resurrection, and his *ascension into heaven was the claiming of his kingdom in this sense. Seated at the right hand of God the Father, the glorified Christ is now the ruler of the universe, and by the sending of his Holy Spirit he is now making his rule felt in the hearts and minds of those who believe in him.

However, it must also be said that his vision of the kingdom was largely *eschatological, conforming in this respect to the picture already familiar from the OT. Jesus performed healing miracles as signs of the coming kingdom, and the picture we have of it is that when it arrives in its fullness all sickness, disability, poverty and ignorance will be swept away. Whether, and to what extent, the kingdom of God has already arrived on earth is the great theological question which forms the substance of contemporary debate.

The first Christian to develop a detailed theology of the kingdom was *Augustine (354–430). Motivated by criticisms that the fall of Rome was due to the abandonment of the ancient gods and the acceptance of Christianity as the state religion, Augustine wrote a massive history of the world in which he claimed that there was an age-old struggle between two kingdoms (or 'cities' as he called them) – the city of God and the city of this world. The latter took the form of empires and states which flourish for a time but which are inevitably overcome and disappear. The former, however, remains constant and will grow stronger until the end of time, when it will be revealed in its fullness. The city of God is present in the *church but is not identical with it, since the church too is a mixed body which contains both believers and unbelievers. This subtle analysis was simplified in later centuries, and for practical purposes, the church came to be regarded as in essence the kingdom of God on earth. As such, it not only claimed a special status in secular society, but regarded itself as superior to it. Secular rulers were expected to submit to the church as the voice of God, church officials and property were exempted from secular jurisdiction, and many aspects of life, which were regarded as primarily 'spiritual' (e.g. matrimony), were removed from the secular courts and treated as religious questions (see *Christendom).

It was only with great difficulty that secular rulers were able to assert their rights against such a church, but the sixteenth-century Reformation gave them their opportunity as many broke with Rome and established national churches of which they were the temporal rulers. This committed them to furthering the cause of the kingdom of God in their own earthly jurisdictions, and great efforts were made to ensure that the law of the state conformed to the teachings of the Bible. The observance of Sunday as an official day of rest was a prime example of this, and in Protestant countries at least, it became a prominent symbol of the dominant religious culture. It also led to the establishment of free schools, of workhouses for the poor and even of hospitals. How far the drive to establish a 'godly commonwealth' (as this kind of Christian state was often termed) ought to go was one of the main issues of debate in seventeenth-century England, where a persistent and dedicated minority, known today as *Puritans, did everything it could to establish the kingdom of God on earth. Unfortunately, the Puritans disagreed among themselves about the precise form their godly society should take and this weakened their cause. They were further hindered by the fact that sin could not be eradicated, especially when only a minority of the population was truly chosen by God. Efforts to restrict the government to the so-called 'saints' were doomed to fail, and in the end the Puritan experiment became a dictatorial tyranny under Cromwell, suppressing everything which did not agree with its own vision.

Nevertheless, the long-term effect of Puritanism was to establish that a secular *state whose laws were fashioned in accordance with Scripture was effectively a kingdom of God, to which not only ordinary Christians but even the kings themselves owed allegiance. A king who betrayed his trust by claiming to be above the law could be deposed, something which actually happened in 1688 (in England) and again in 1776 (in America). Those who rebelled were often convinced that they were re-establishing the kingdom of God in its purest form, and the virtual identification of this type of state with God's rule remained a commonplace of political and theological discourse until the twentieth century. Yet the close alliance between church and state continued in European monarchies. Membership in the Church of England was regarded as essential in principle to full participation in national life well into the nineteenth century, while in the newly established German Empire, the *Ritschlian school tended to identify the kingdom of God with economic and social progress and particularly (by implication) with advanced German culture.

Change came in continental Europe when the confessional states established after the Reformation came crashing down in the First World War and its aftermath. After 1918 theologians like Karl *Barth and Emil *Brunner began to speak of the 'post-Constantinian era', which forced them to reassess not only church-state relations but the whole meaning of the 'kingdom of God' as this was found in the NT. The events of 1939–45 only confirmed them in this view, and from an attitude of general conformity to the traditional link between 'throne and altar' many theologians turned to radical opposition to the established order. In some cases this led them to espouse revolutionary doctrines and to support 'freedom struggles' in different parts of the world as the true manifestation of God's kingdom on earth (see *Liberation theology).

The naivety of this was gradually exposed as revolutionary regimes became tyrannies and various liberation movements were shown to be far less noble in practice than in theory, but the view that the 'kingdom of God' is somehow opposed to earthly states has remained and continues to provide the chief motivation for much modern thinking on this subject. The English-speaking world, always more conservative than continental Europe, and relatively unscathed by the troubles of the twentieth century, has been slower to embrace this new model. There is still a powerful element, especially in the United States, which adheres to the earlier view that the secular state is the kingdom of God as long as it is ruled by godly people. This explains why the religious views of the president and other top officials are so important in a country where church and state are formally separate.

The collapse of the traditional order in Europe coincided with, and to some extent provoked, a revival of interest in the biblical concept of the kingdom of God. It came to be recognized once more that not only was this a fundamental part of Jesus' teaching, but that the coming of the kingdom was essentially an eschatological event, which is heralded in the present and will be fulfilled at some point in the future. Today almost everyone accepts these basic points, but there are divergent ways in which they are interpreted. Some evangelicals continue to emphasize the 'spiritual' interpretation of the kingdom, associating it primarily with personal conversion to Christ and world evangelization (see *Evangelical theology). These people are often criticized for neglecting the social dimension of Christian witness, but although they certainly tend to hold conservative political views, the charge is unfair. Christians of this kind have often been in the forefront of social mission, both in the developing world and in the inner cities, and have not been afraid to strike out on their own when their consciences have dictated it.

Others see the 'kingdom of God' in essentially social and political terms (see *Social gospel) and spend a good deal of time and effort in campaigning for various causes, ranging all the way from supporting political prisoners and refugees on the one hand to supporting environmental conservation on the other. In their eyes, the kingdom of God comes when peace and justice prevail on earth. The main difference of opinion among them is between those who are pacifist in their outlook and those who are activist. Pacifists like the late John Howard *Yoder remain vocal, but in recent years it is the activists who have gained the upper hand, going so far as to advocate the invasion of 'rogue states' and the imposition of 'regime change' on countries which have failed to respect the international order based on their principles. The main criticism of such efforts is that they tend to submerge specifically Christian values and affirmations in a desire to co-operate with people of many different beliefs. The intentions may be good, but in the end a Christian vision of the world and its future cannot be sustained by people who are not themselves Christians, and the attempt to do so runs the risk of being rejected by the latter as another form of 'imperialism'. Whatever else may be said of it, the kingdom of God will not come without an explicit recognition of his *sovereignty, a fact which people of this tendency are liable to forget.

There has been a good deal of theological writing on the subject of the kingdom of God, but how influential it has been in shaping people's approaches is uncertain. Biblical scholarship which seldom ventures beyond the pages of the NT has had little impact on modern discussion. Those like Oliver O'Donovan, who adopt the 'spiritual' perspective, are more likely to be guided by their own consciences than by a specific theological programme, and their writings on the subject tend to be theoretical proposals for political action which make little impact on those who would be expected to implement them. Others may claim to have been influenced by the writings of men like Abraham *Kuyper and Reinhold *Niebuhr, but how far this is really true may be doubted. Perhaps the main difficulty is that it is always hard to turn theory into practice, and the latter may not look much like the former once it is implemented. Nevertheless, it can be said with some confidence that the expectation of the coming of the kingdom of God is alive and well in modern theology, despite the many differences of approach, and that Christians today feel obliged to justify their thoughts and actions in the light of this concept to a degree which is perhaps unprecedented in Christian history.

Bibliography

M. Erdmann, *Building the Kingdom of God on Earth* (London, 1999); L. Green, *Urban Ministry and the Kingdom of God* (London, 2003); R. A. Horsley, *Jesus and Empire: The Kingdom of God and the New World Order* (Minneapolis, 2003); M. L. Humphries, *Christian Origins and the Language of the Kingdom of God* (Carbondale, 1999); P. Johnson and C. Sugden, *Markets, Fair Trade and the Kingdom of God* (Oxford, 2001); O. O'Donovan, *The Desire of the Nations: Rediscovering the Roots of Political Theology* (Cambridge, 1996); A. Robertson, *Manifesto for a Revolution: The Kingdom of God on Earth* (Manchester, 2000); M. W. G. Stibbe, *The Kingdom of God and Human Society* (Edinburgh, 1993); J. H. Yoder, *The Politics of Jesus* (Grand Rapids, 1972).

G. L. BRAY

KIRK, KENNETH E., see ANGLO-CATHOLIC THEOLOGY

KNOWLEDGE OF GOD

To arrive at an adequate definition of the term 'knowledge of God', we must consider what it means to know generally, and what it means to know an object which is qualitatively distinct from every other. These considerations are related because the idea of God entails the notion that the world of knowable objects, including knowing human subjects, is constitutively related to God as its Creator. Christians may infer from this that knowing, an essentially relational enterprise, reflects the triune character of God. If biblical passages suggesting that God's knowledge is eternal are read in light of trinitarian doctrine, God's eternal life may be depicted as a *perichoresis* of *knowing* and *being known* (Matt. 11:27; 1 Cor. 2:11). The work of creation manifests the *noetic* character of the triune life (Prov. 8:30; John 1:3) in which creatures live, move, know and are known (Acts 17:28; 2 Pet. 1:3–4; cf. F. LeRon Shults, *Reforming the Doctrine of God*, Grand Rapids, 2005, pp. 205–234).

All knowing occurs in relations between knowers and objects of knowledge, wherein knowers are informed by their objects.

Whether knowing happens thus depends on whether the relation between a knowing subject and the object to be known is appropriate to the character of the object. For example, a frog may arguably be known truly by a subject who relates to it via dissection, while a person will never be truly known in such a relationship. In that objects of knowledge exercise authority over knowing subjects, Colin Gunton noted that all *truth, true knowing, is a species of *revelation. Gunton did not mean that knowers passively receive data, but rather that an active knower is acted upon; knowing requires a subject's thinking to become object-shaped. Perhaps, therefore, knowing is most adequately thought of as a dialogical enterprise involving moments of discovery and disclosure.

This understanding of knowledge generally bridges the conceptual separation between 'natural theology', which is sometimes taken to suggest that knowledge of God is a product of human activity, and gracious or 'revealed theology', which can be taken to mean that human knowledge of God occurs without human participation. The terms 'nature' and '*natural theology', and their juxtaposition with '*grace' and 'revealed theology' have the unfortunate tendency of suggesting that a modicum of theological knowledge is either a datum of human nature conceived apart from its relation to God's creative activity, or a product of autonomous human endeavour, such as extracting evidence of God's existence from nature and/or history.

Materially, however, this is not the case, for as Wolfhart *Pannenberg suggests, even so-called natural knowledge of God is due to the activity of God's *Spirit. All knowing involves activity on behalf of the knowing subject and the object known. When the object of knowledge is God, the knowing subject, the subject's capacity for knowing, and the content of the subject's knowledge are constitutively dependent upon God's revealing activity in creation and redemption. This holds true whether the knowledge of God is 'natural' or 'revealed'. Both forms of theology involve divine and human activity, and the distinction between divine and human agency in either form of theology is the *qualitative* difference between finite knowing and the infinite knowledge of God on which it is dependent. Pannenberg writes in this regard:

The founding of theology on divine revelation is not a determination that is foreign to its nature, as the later distinction between natural and revealed theology might seem to imply. Instead, the knowledge of God that is made possible by God, and therefore by revelation, is one of the basic conditions of the concept of theology as such. Otherwise the possibility of the knowledge of God is inconceivable. It would contradict the very idea of God (*Systematic Theology*, p. 2).

According to this view, natural and revealed theology differ in the relative significance they attribute to the creative and redemptive moments of God's revelation. Natural theology focuses on general revelation in *creation, while revealed theology prioritizes special or specific revelation in the history of *redemption. The terms general and specific revelation have been used to express two biblical understandings of God's revealing activity. Natural theology and gracious or revealed theology attempt to describe the noetic implications of these biblical understandings. General revelation expresses the biblical view that God's activity in creation is available to all persons (Ps. 19:1; Rom. 1:19–20). Special or specific revelation, on the other hand, refers to the biblical teaching that God is known only by *Jesus Christ and those to whom Jesus Christ discloses God (Matt. 11:25–27; John 1:18).

Natural theology, which holds that all humans know God 'naturally', is one way of conceiving the noetic implications of Scripture's view that God is disclosed in and through God's creative activity. According to this theory, knowledge of God grounded in general revelation is true knowledge, but is insufficient for *salvation, and needs to be completed by knowledge grounded in God's specific revelation in Jesus Christ. This conception of the *relation* between knowledge grounded in creation and that disclosed in the history of redemption has proven unsatisfactory to a number of influential thinkers who have proposed alternative views of the relationship. H. Richard *Niebuhr's typology concerning the relation between Christ and culture gives a sense of the range of available options for construing the relation between natural knowledge (nature) and revealed knowledge (grace). There are five types: (1) grace against nature; (2) the grace of nature; (3) grace above nature; (4) grace and nature in paradox; and (5) grace as the transformer of nature.

Niebuhr argued that the first two types are extremes to be avoided. Natural theology resembles the third type, which emphasizes continuity between creation and redemption, while recognizing that grace also transcends nature. The fourth type places great stress on the discontinuity between grace and nature in its present sinful state, and tends to portray creation and redemption as separate divine activities. The final type, which Niebuhr favoured, mediates between the third and fourth.

If type three focuses on the distinction between the infinite and the finite and asks how much knowledge of the infinite God finite objects are capable of mediating, types four and five are more concerned with the noetic effects of *sin. According to the fourth type, sin destroys the ability to know God from creation, while the fifth holds that knowledge of God from creation remains but is distorted and in need of transformation. No ideal type is likely to capture the complexities of any actual proposal, but theological positions fall nearer or farther from one or another of the types. Natural theology, and its most nuanced representative, *Thomas Aquinas, falls somewhere nearer type three than either the fourth or fifth type. Emil *Brunner sought to approximate the fifth type in his *Nature and Grace*, but in *No!*, Karl *Barth depicted it as an expression of the third type, and defended a position that is nearest to the fourth type. That has recently been defended by Stanley Hauerwas's *Gifford Lectures.

Protestant *Reformers, such as Martin Luther and John Calvin, seemed to operate between the idea that grace and nature exist in a paradoxical relation and the notion that grace transforms or converts distorted nature. *Luther leaned toward the fourth type, while *Calvin gravitated toward the fifth. Both men affirmed a twofold knowledge of God, but described the two ways of knowing and the relation between them differently. Luther spoke of general and specific knowledge, but depicted general knowledge (the knowledge that God exists, is the world's Creator, is righteous and will judge the wicked) as a worthless way of knowing because it does not include any understanding of God's intention for our lives. He reserved the designation 'true and proper knowledge of God' for knowledge of 'what God proposes concerning us, what he wants to give and do, so that he might deliver us from sin and death' (*Commentary on Galatians*, in Alister E. McGrath (ed.), *The Christian Theology Reader*, Malden, ³2007, pp. 98–100).

Calvin, on the other hand, distinguished between knowledge of God as the Creator and knowledge of God as the Redeemer, but did not regard knowledge of God the Creator as synonymous with so-called natural or general knowledge. Calvin began with knowledge of God as Creator not only because it is disclosed in creation, but also because Scripture teaches us that God is our Creator before it describes God as our Redeemer in Christ. Thus for Calvin, the first way of knowing God is disclosed by general and specific revelation. However, despite the clarity of revelation, humans cannot know God the Creator truly because sin clouds our ability to read either revelatory source rightly; that is, unless and until we receive knowledge of God as the Redeemer in Christ. Calvin writes in this respect that 'since we have fallen from life into death, the whole knowledge of God the Creator that we have discussed would be useless unless faith also followed, setting forth for us God our Father in Christ' (*Institutes*, 2.6.1). Knowing God as the Redeemer in Christ through the Holy Spirit *transforms* our noetic relation to creation and Scripture, and therefore to God as our Creator.

Perhaps this is also what Luther had in mind when he wrote, 'God does not want to be known except through Christ', but his negative assessment of the objective value (rather than merely its efficacy given the reality of sin) of general knowledge, and his notion that God's will for us is disclosed exclusively in Christ, suggests a paradoxical more than a transformational view of the relation between nature and grace. Ultimately, however, this difference between Luther and Calvin is less significant than their common conviction, which was also shared by Aquinas, Brunner and Barth, that receiving the gracious disclosure of God in Jesus Christ is essential to the discovery of a right (noetic) relationship to God.

See also: EPISTEMOLOGY; GOD.

Bibliography

E. A. Dowey, Jr, *The Knowledge of God in Calvin's Theology* (Grand Rapids, 1994); C. Gunton, *A Brief Theology of Revelation* (Edinburgh, 1995); S. Hauerwas, *With the Grain of the Universe: The Church's Witness and Natural Theology* (Grand Rapids, 2001);

W. Pannenberg, *Systematic Theology*, vol. 1 (Grand Rapids, 1991); R. Sokolowski, *The God of Faith and Reason: Foundations of Christian Theology* (Washington DC, 1995); P. R. Sponheim, *God – The Question and the Quest: Toward a Conversation Concerning Christian Faith* (Philadelphia, 1985); Thomas Aquinas, *Summa Theologiae: A Concise Translation*, ed. T. McDermott (Allen, 1989).

J. R. WILSON

KNOX, JOHN (*c.* 1514–72)

The principal theologian and architect of the Reformed Kirk of Scotland, Knox was born at Haddington and educated at St Andrews University, possibly under John Major (1467–1550), an advocate of *scholasticism and conciliarism. Following his ordination in 1536, Knox held minor posts as a notary and a tutor. Shortly after his conversion to *Protestantism he came under the influence of George Wishart (*c.* 1513–46), from whom he learned an amalgam of *Lutheran and *Reformed ideas, including the views of Martin *Bucer on the Lord's Supper (see *Eucharist). Knox's conception of his calling as a prophet also dates from this period. While supporting a group of Protestant rebels in the castle at St Andrews, he was captured by the French and enslaved on a French ship. During his imprisonment he prepared a summary of the compendium of Lutheran thought by Henry Balnaves (d. 1579). Thus by 1549, when he was released and returned to England, Knox's theology was characterized by its eclectic fusion of the principles of Lutheran and Reformed thought, particularly with respect to the doctrines of *justification and the Lord's Supper.

In England Knox's preaching at Berwick, near the Scottish border, attracted so many Scots that the government became nervous. He accepted an invitation to preach to Edward VI's court, but declined an offer to become Bishop of Rochester. During the revision of the first *Book of Common Prayer*, he was instrumental in the inclusion of the 'Black Rubric', which stipulated that kneeling during Communion did not imply transubstantiation. When the Catholic Mary Tudor became queen in 1553, Knox struggled with his conscience over the duty of martyrdom before deciding he should flee the country. His years of exile were spent at Frankfurt, where he lost a battle to continue reforming the second *Book of Common Prayer*, and Geneva, where he was influenced by John *Calvin. At Geneva he wrote a series of tracts on political disobedience to idolatrous rulers, particularly the well-known *First Blast of the Trumpet Against the Monstrous Regiment of Women*, which generally denied the right of females to rule, excepting only those rare individuals such as the Hebrews' Deborah who had a divine calling. In these political tracts he developed the revolutionary view that common people had the right to overthrow a tyrannical and idolatrous sovereign (see *Revolution, theology of). During his exile he also wrote a lengthy and tendentious defence of the Calvinist doctrine of *predestination against the work of an unknown Anabaptist.

Knox's exile was interrupted in 1555–6 by a return to Catholic Scotland, where he was fortunate to escape a charge of heresy. A group of Protestant lords invited him to return in 1559, and his preaching and leadership in the ensuing year was a major factor in the success of the Scottish Reformation. With a select group of colleagues, he helped draft the *Scots Confession of Faith (1560), a classic of Reformed Protestantism, and the *Book of Discipline*, with its pattern for church government and an ambitious blueprint for educational reform. After Mary Stuart returned to Scotland in 1561, Knox confronted her in three emotionally charged interviews in which he uncompromisingly condemned idolatry. His years in Scotland were characterized by major theological controversies with Catholics, the first with Ninian Winzet (*c.* 1518–92) over ordination and the second with Quintin Kennedy (1520–64) over the Mass. Knox's greatest achievement in these years was the writing of his *History of the Reformation of Religion within the Realm of Scotland* (ed. W. C. Dickinson, 2 vols., Edinburgh, 1949). The status of Protestantism in Scotland was assured when Mary Stuart abdicated in 1567 and Knox preached the coronation sermon for her infant son, James VI.

See also: REFORMERS, SCOTTISH.

Bibliography

Works: *Works*, 6 vols., ed. D. Laing (Edinburgh, 1846–52); *John Knox: Political Writings*, ed. M. Breslaw (Cranbury, 1986).

Studies: R. L. Greaves, *Theology and Revolution in the Scottish Reformation: Studies in the Thought of John Knox* (Grand Rapids, 1980); R. G. Kyle, *The Mind of John Knox*

(Lawrence, 1984); R. K. Marshall, *John Knox* (Edinburgh, 2000); R. A. Mason (ed.), *John Knox and the British Reformation* (Aldershot, 1998); W. S. Reid, *Trumpeter of God* (New York, 1974); J. Ridley, *John Knox* (Oxford, 1968).

R. L. Greaves

KOINONIA

This English transliteration of the NT Greek term often translated '*fellowship*' is in common use in *ecumenical theology, particularly in discussions involving Roman Catholics and Anglicans. It is presented as the key concept underlying the Agreed Statements of the Anglican-Roman Catholic International Commission on the Eucharist, ministry and ordination, and authority in the church (*The Final Report*, London, 1982). In ecumenical circles, a definitive statement was produced by the World Council of Churches at its 1991 Canberra assembly: *The Unity of the Church as Koinonia: Gift and Calling*. The meaning of *koinonia* is near to 'communion', a relation between individual Christians or Christian communities resulting from their common participation in one and the same reality. 'Κοινονια with one another is entailed by our *koinonia* with God in Christ.' It has thus become the controlling model for understanding the nature of the church, which is not the case in the NT. Its currency, often with a somewhat fluid meaning, attests the prevalence of the notion of the church as 'mystery' over more institutional or social approaches to the church. A somewhat comparable concept in Eastern Orthodoxy is *sobornost*.

Bibliography

T. F. Best and G. Gassmann (eds.), *On the Way to Fuller Koinonia* (Geneva, 1994); B. C. Butler, *The Church and Unity* (London, 1979); A. Dulles, *Models of the Church* (Garden City, expanded edn, 2002); L. F. Fuchs, *Koinonia and the Quest for an Ecumenical Ecclesiology* (Grand Rapids, 2008); C. Hill, 'Seeking the One, Holy, Catholic and Apostolic Church: Do Bishops Exhibit or Obscure It?', in P. Avis (ed.), *Paths to Unity: Explorations in Ecumenical Method* (London, 2004); J.-M. R. Tillard, in *Dictionary of the Ecumenical Movement* (Geneva, ²2002).

D. F. Wright

KOREAN THEOLOGY

Korean Christianity has two main branches: the more liberal branch that focuses on social activism and writes theology reflecting Korea's social context of suffering, and the more conservative evangelical branch that writes theology from a biblical viewpoint but is sympathetic to the spiritual and social needs of Koreans.

The most distinctive contribution to theology is *minjung* theology. *Minjung* means theology of the masses. It is political, a people's theology of *liberation, and is about people who are dominated by oppressive political power. It reflects the cultural milieu of Koreans as they have prevailed over oppression and suffering. It involves 'han' (righteous anger), something felt by an oppressed people.

There are numerous theologies suggesting various themes for Korean theology, such as the Yin-Yang way of thinking in theology, God as a fellow-sufferer, 'trace of the Trinity' theology based on the Korean myth of origin (the Tangun myth), some process theology based on the thinking of Alfred North Whitehead and Korean Confucian-Christian theology, with an emphasis on filial piety, the Confucian concept of social relations as the basis of its hierarchical understanding of social structure.

See also: Asian Christian Theology.

Bibliography

Commission on Theological Concerns of the Christian Conference of Asia (ed.), *Minjung Theology: People as the Subjects of History* (Maryknoll and London, 1981); D. J. Elwood (ed.), *Asian Christian Theology* (Philadelphia, 1980); J. C. England (ed.), *Living Theology in Asia* (Maryknoll, 1981); Bong Rin Ro and R. Eshenaur (eds.), *The Bible and Theology in Asian Contexts: An Evangelical Perspective on Asian Theology* (Seoul, 1984).

R. Stults

KRAEMER, HENDRIK (1888–1965)

Kraemer was a Dutch layman who deeply influenced international missionary thinking in the period 1930–60. After the early death of his father and mother he was sent to a diaconal orphanage. There he began to study the Bible and, at the age of fifteen, went through a deep spiritual experience which led him to the

Christian faith and into the Christian church. He first received training as a missionary, but then went on to study Indonesian languages, and in 1922 was sent to Indonesia in the service of the Dutch Bible Society. Here he obtained a wide and deep knowledge of Javanese mysticism and Indonesian Islam. He greatly assisted the Indonesian churches in their struggle for independence.

In 1928 he attended the International Missionary Conference at Jerusalem and participated in the discussion about the relationship between the Christian faith and other world religions. At the invitation of the International Missionary Council, he wrote as a study guide for the Third World Missionary Conference held at Tambaram, India, in 1938, *The Christian Message in a Non-Christian World* (London, 1938). In a way this was a reply to the report *Re-thinking Missions of the Laymen's Foreign Mission Inquiry* (1932), which asserted that the aim of missions is 'to seek with people of other lands a true knowledge and love of God, expressing in life and word what we have learned through Jesus Christ'. In his own book Kraemer strongly emphasized the radical discontinuity between 'biblical realism' and non-Christian *religious experience. Acknowledging that our Christian *religion also stands under the judgment of God, he maintained that the Christian *revelation is incomparable and absolutely *sui generis*, because it is 'the record of God's self-disclosing and re-creating revelation in Jesus Christ . . . giving the divine answer to this demonic and guilty disharmony of man and the world'. He did not deny the reality of 'general revelation', but for him this revelation did not lead to true religion, but was itself an object of faith, because it could be discovered only in the light of the 'special revelation' in Christ. Co-operation with non-Christian religions and a combined search for further truth, therefore, would mean a betrayal of the word of God.

In 1937 Kraemer was appointed professor of the science of religion at Leiden. During the Second World War he was imprisoned as a hostage by the Germans. After the war he was very active in the reorganization of the Netherlands Reformed Church. Largely due to his influence the new church order mentioned missions as an essential element of the life and work of the church. From 1948 to 1958 he served as the first director of the Ecumenical Institute at Bossey, near Geneva.

Kraemer was one of the most influential missionary and ecumenical thinkers of the twentieth century. Other important books of his published in English are: *Religion and the Christian Faith* (London, 1956); *The Communication of the Christian Faith* (Philadelphia, 1956); *A Theology of the Laity* (London and Philadelphia, 1956); *World Cultures and World Religions: The Coming Dialogue* (London, 1958).

See also: CHRISTIANITY AND OTHER RELIGIONS; MISSIOLOGY.

Bibliography
C. F. Hallencreutz, *Kraemer towards Tambaram: A Study in Hendrik Kraemer's Missionary Approach* (Uppsala, 1966); idem, *New Approaches to Men of Other Faiths*, WCC Research Pamphlet no. 18 (Geneva, 1970); A. Th. van Leeuwen, *Hendrik Kraemer, Dienaar der Wereldkerk* (Amsterdam, 1959); T. S. Perry, *Radical Difference: A Defence of Hendrik Kraemer's Theology of Religions* (Waterloo, 2001).

K. RUNIA

KÜNG, HANS (b. 1928)

A Swiss Roman Catholic theologian, who has taught at Tübingen since 1960. Küng's theological work has been dominated by three main concerns: *apologetics, *ecumenism and reform in the Roman Catholic Church. He sees his most important task as a theologian to be that of using all the resources of modern theology to present the Christian gospel as a credible and relevant message for the modern world. Especially in his *On Being a Christian*, which he called 'a kind of small "Summa" of the Christian faith', but which for all its theological weight was aimed at and achieved a very wide readership, Küng expounded a Christianity centred on the historical Jesus as its distinguishing feature, and a Christian faith compatible with modern critical rationality and the aspirations and achievements of modern *humanism. Jesus is presented as the true man who makes it possible for modern men and women to live in a genuinely human way. Further works on the existence of God and life after death have continued Küng's apologetic work.

His ecumenical concerns go back to his first book, in which he attempted the tour de force of reconciling the Protestant and Roman Catholic doctrines of *justification by comparing the teachings of the Council of *Trent (see *Roman Catholic theology) and Karl *Barth on this classic point of denominational division. His ecclesiological studies also demonstrate a strong ecumenical concern, and in general it could be said that Küng's theological approach results in an ecumenical, rather than specifically Roman Catholic, theology. It belongs to the 'evangelical Catholicity' or 'Catholic evangelicity' which is obligated to the whole church but brings everything to the 'evangelical' test of the gospel, which is Jesus himself as the criterion of Christian faith.

Since the point in the Second *Vatican Council when it seemed to Küng that the progressive direction initiated by Pope John XXIII was being frustrated by the reactionary authoritarianism in the church, he has seen himself in the role of 'his Holiness's loyal opposition'. His reforming critique of the church is based on the twin principles of the normative priority of the historical Jesus and the NT gospel over all subsequent developments of the tradition, and the need to be open to the critical rationality and liberal attitudes of the modern world. These principles characterize much recent progressive Roman Catholic theology, but Küng's radical, often polemical and provocative application of them makes him virtually a Protestant in conservative eyes.

Criticism of his theology focused on his *Christology, since in *On Being a Christian* he interpreted the ontological Christology of incarnational dogma in purely functional terms, and on his explicit denial of the dogma of ecclesiastical (not only papal) infallibility. In the latter case, his deliberate rejection of the teaching of the First and Second Vatican Councils and his demand for frank recognition that the church has unequivocally erred in doctrinal statements in the past, constitute a radical break with the principles and method of traditional Roman Catholic theology. Protracted investigations of his work by the Congregation for the Doctrine of Faith led in 1979 to the Vatican's withdrawal of his canonical mission, i.e. his authorization to teach as a Catholic theologian. In recent years, Küng's work has focused on the relationship between Christianity and other world faiths (see *Christianity and other religions). He also played a major role in drafting a 'global ethic', which could be subscribed to by members of all faiths.

Bibliography

Works: *Justification* (London, 1965); *The Church* (London, 1967); *Infallible?* (London, 1971); *On Being a Christian* (London, 1977); *Does God Exist?* (London, 1980); *Eternal Life?* (London, 1984); *Christianity and the World Religions* (London, 1987); *Judaism* (London, 1992); *Christianity and Chinese Religions* (London, 1993); *A Global Ethic for Global Politics and Economics* (London, 1997); *Disputed Truth: Memoirs*, 2 vols. (London, 2008–9).

Studies: K.-J. Kuschel and H. Häring (eds.), *Hans Küng: New Horizons for Faith and Thought* (London, 1993); C. M. LaCugna, *The Theological Methodology of Hans Küng* (Chico, 1982).

R. J. BAUCKHAM

KUYPER, ABRAHAM (1837–1920)

The son of a Dutch Reformed Church minister, Kuyper was born in Maasluis, the Netherlands. At the University of Leiden he distinguished himself as a brilliant student and strong advocate of liberalism. During his first pastorate, in the small fishing village of Beesd, Kuyper experienced an evangelical conversion after reading the English novel *The Heir of Redclyffe* by Charlotte Yonge. Influenced by the simple, Calvinist piety of his parishioners, he renewed his study of theology to become the leader of the Dutch neo-Calvinist movement.

Kuyper wrote hundreds of books and articles, the majority of which have never been translated into English, on topics as diverse as art, politics, literature, philosophy and social issues. In all of these he sought to develop a consistent Christian world-and-life-view. He founded two newspapers, the weekly religious magazine *De Heraut* ('The Herald') and the daily newspaper *De Standaard* ('The Standard').

In 1874 he entered the Dutch parliament as a representative for the newly founded AntiRevolutionary party which, following the lead of Groen van Prinsterer (1801–76), was opposed to the principles expressed by the French Revolution and political liberalism. He became prime minister in 1900, but lost office in 1905 largely because of his controversial handling of the bitter railway strike of 1902. From 1908 to shortly before his death in 1920 he was a member of the Dutch Second

Chamber of Parliament and continued to edit *De Standaard*.

Kuyper was active in the 'Christian school struggle' and fought for state aid for private Christian schools. He founded the Free University of Amsterdam in 1880 and led a successful secession from the State Church to found the independent Gereformeerde Kerk (Reformed Church) in 1886.

Theologically, Kuyper developed *Calvin's teachings about common *grace to provide a basis for Christian social action. He also placed great emphasis on the importance of the *kingdom of God, an idea he seems to have picked up from F. D. Maurice (1805–72; see *Christian Socialism). His greatest contribution is in his development of the notion of 'sphere-sovereignty' which is similar to Michael Novak's and Peter Berger's (b. 1929) idea of 'mediating structures' as a basis for the development of religious, social and political pluralism. Many contemporary Christian movements can be traced to Kuyper's work. Probably the best-known evangelical to be influenced by Kuyper is Francis *Schaeffer whose work helped popularize some of Kuyper's ideas with, amongst others, the so-called 'Moral Majority' in America. However, left-wing Christian activists have also been influenced by Kuyper, and in North America there is a growing interest in his work.

See also: DUTCH REFORMED THEOLOGY.

Bibliography

Works: *Lectures on Calvinism* (Grand Rapids, 1898); *Principles of Sacred Theology* (Grand Rapids, 1898); *The Work of the Holy Spirit* (Grand Rapids, 1900).

Studies: P. S. Heslam, *Creating a Christian Worldview: Abraham Kuyper's Lectures on Calvinism* (Grand Rapids and Cambridge, 1998); T. Kuipers (ed.), *Abraham Kuyper: An Annotated Bibliography, 1857–2010* (Leiden, 2011); F. Vandenberg, *Abraham Kuyper* (Grand Rapids, 1960).

I. HEXHAM

LACUGNA, CATHERINE MOWRY (1952–97)

LaCugna was a feminist *Catholic systematic theologian. While on the faculty of Notre Dame she produced a significant contribution to the ongoing renewal of trinitarian thinking, *God For Us: The Trinity and the Christian Life* (1991). The main thrust of her claim could be paraphrased as follows: at the heart of the doctrine of the *Trinity is the mystery of God's *love that has come to us 'in the face of Christ and the activity of the Spirit'. This mystery of God reaching out to the creature means that God's life does not belong to God alone; God exists 'for us', and thus, God's life is our life. The mystery of triune love is the mystery of salvation where our lives are now lived together as God lives. As the Spirit of God reaches out and gathers us up into the body of Christ and incorporates us into the *koinonia* of the triune God, we are made to 'live from and for God, from and for others'. The triune God is 'God for Us' and this makes the doctrine of the Trinity the church's most 'practical doctrine with radical consequences for Christian life'. Critics (e.g. Colin *Gunton) have asked whether LaCugna's virtual rejection of any doctrine of the immanent Trinity does not deny God's grace and fall into a kind of *pantheism.

Bibliography

Works: *God for Us: The Trinity and Christian Life* (San Francisco, 1993).

Studies: C. E. Gunton, *Father, Son, and Holy Spirit* (London, 2003); R. E. Olson and C. A. Hall, *The Trinity* (Grand Rapids, 2002).

K. S. MCCORMICK

LAITY

The term 'laity' has travelled a long way from its simple biblical meaning of people, crowd, or people of God. The original term is indiscriminate and inclusive. All who come to Christ are the *laos* of God. People of every tribe and nation gather to Christ.

The radical nature of Christianity in not having a priesthood as some kind of intermediary between God and humankind is breathtaking among religions. The Jewish priesthood was limited, and stood beside God's revelation through the law and the prophets. *Jesus more fully rejected a priesthood, showing the directness of each person's relationship with God. He was the only way to peace with God, and priests were out of business. Christ's ironic but complete identification of the temple with his own body showed the end of the priestly class and the new birth of the *laos* of God.

Gradually, however, the priesthood reasserted itself from among a range of offices like teacher, elder, prophet, evangelist and pastor, servant roles in the Christian community. The threefold structure of bishop, presbyter and deacon emerged soon after the NT books were written. The presiding role of the bishop or presbyter at the Lord's Supper developed into a sacerdotal act. Within this conception, linked to imperial and feudal structures, the people of God became passive recipients of this and other *sacraments. The laity became non-priests, though this was mitigated by a series of Catholic orders emphasizing different kinds of Christian service and obedience.

The medieval development of a distinct order of 'clergy' was blown open in the Reformation by the rediscovery of direct *salvation by God's *grace though human *faith. The sacramental monopoly of the priesthood, including indulgences and priestly mediated salvation, was challenged. Luther and Calvin emphasized the *vocation of all Christians. Lutherans, Anglicans and others retained ministers or pastors as overseers of churches and modified the sacramental nature of the Eucharist, while retaining a distinction between the clergy or priesthood and the laity.

However, various *Anabaptist groups broke much more radically with this priestly/lay polarity and recognized the status of Christians as invited friends of Jesus (the *Quakers), as people living under the rule of Christ (*Mennonites) or just as people of faith. Within this tradition there was a growing sense of the multiform ministries that occur among the people of God, involving not just institutional church activities like teaching and pastoring, but broader callings to service like building, farming, family, science, education and peacemaking. The renewed sense of Christian community – sharing faith, love and values – marked this development.

A similar move took place within the *Reformed tradition. As well as callings to minister and preach, the wider callings of the laity to marriage, *family, *work, business, the magistrate, politics and education were recognized. Here all of life is lived before God and in discipleship to Christ, and the difference in callings between clergy and laity are obliterated by acting in conformity to the will and purposes of God, reclaiming the creation for obedience to God. These Reformed traditions firmly closed the church doors outside Sunday, so that prayer and worship would take place in the home and all work and employment would be done as service to God.

The *Pentecostal movements of the twentieth century were laicized. Though they still sometimes had ministers or pastors, the direct work of the Holy Spirit in the lives of Christians was in no way mediated by ministers, and those who carried the gospel needed no pattern of ordination. In *Charismatic movements, patterns of leadership are shaped by spiritual fruit and maturity rather than through ordination.

Churches who retain priests and ministers have responded in three ways. First, they acknowledged a range of lay ministries which could be incorporated into the activities of the institutional church. Second, they deconstructed the role of the priesthood into different sacramental, pastoral, preaching, organizational and other tasks. Third, they increasingly professionalized these roles. Nevertheless, the priestly/lay distinction is often challenged in the modern West and lay initiatives are shaping the church worldwide.

See also: CHURCH GOVERNMENT; MINISTRY; PRIESTHOOD OF ALL BELIEVERS.

Bibliography

Church of England General Synod, *All Are Called: Towards a Theology of the Laity* (London, 1986); D. Clark, *Breaking the Mould of Christendom: Kingdom Community, Diaconal Church and the Liberation of the Laity* (Peterborough, 2005); Y. Congar, *Priest and Lay-man* (London, 1967); C. Cross, *Church and People, 1450–1660; The Triumph of the Laity in the English Church* (London, 1976); R. Etchells and G. Carey, *Set My People Free: A Lay Challenge to the Churches* (London, 1995).

A. STORKEY

LAMBETH QUADRILATERAL, see ANGLICANISM

LATERAN COUNCILS

The Lateran Palace in Rome had been a convenient place for ecclesiastical gatherings from the fourth century (when it became the official residence of the bishop of Rome). Five *councils held there from the twelfth to the sixteenth century are regarded as ecumenical councils by the *Roman Catholic Church. The First Lateran Council (1123) was concerned with relationships between the church and the Holy Roman Emperor; the Second (1139) with healing a schism that had arisen with the election of an antipope. These two councils also formalized the ban on clerical marriage within the Roman Church. The Third Lateran Council (1179) addressed similar concerns again: another antipope had been elected, and was supported by the emperor. It also condemned various heretical groups, including the Cathars (see *Albigenses).

The Fourth Lateran Council (1215) was called to address the relative failure of the Crusades. It followed the Third Council in placing restrictions on Jews and Muslims within Europe (requiring, for instance, the wearing of distinctive clothes to mark them out as non-Christian). Canon 21 required auricular confession at least annually from all Catholics; this, however, was a regulation of a customary position, not something new. It is the most interesting of the Lateran Councils theologically: the first Canon defined transubstantiation as dogma (see *Eucharist), and offered the definitive statement of the Western position on the procession of the Holy Spirit; the second Canon condemned *Joachim of Fiore's trinitarian theology, suggesting that Joachim taught that the unity of the three Persons of the *Trinity was merely collective and not substantial.

The Fifth Lateran Council (1512–17) was preceded by extensive dispute on the relative powers of councils and *popes, with some on the conciliarist side hoping that a new council could adequately address the perceived abuses in the church. In the event, its decrees were rather limited, and any proposals for reform were rapidly overtaken by events: mere months after it closed, Martin *Luther proposed his Ninety-Five Theses, and the question of the reform of the church took on a new, and highly political, character.

Bibliography

H. J. D. Denzinger, *Enchiridion Symbolorum* (Würzburg, 1854), contains extracts from the decrees of all five councils; full texts are only available in older editions which (particularly in the case of the Fourth Lateran Council) are often based on inadequate manuscript traditions.

S. R. HOLMES

LATITUDINARIANISM

This term describes the attitudes and opinions of those in the English church of the late seventeenth and eighteenth centuries who sought a pattern of religious belief and experience free from what were perceived as the opposing extremes of *Puritan fanaticism and High Church extremism. As the name suggests, it was characterized by breadth and variety, but its most salient features were the appeal to reason as authoritative in religious questions, the pursuit of *toleration and irenicism in theological and ecclesiastical debate, and a deep-seated horror of 'enthusiasm'. The movement marks the emergence of that tendency to liberal and pluralistic opinions which is so characteristic of the broad middle ground within the Church of England (cf. *Anglicanism).

The origins of Latitudinarianism can be traced back to Richard *Hooker's appeal to the light of reason as a supplementary authority to the Bible, which was taken up in the early seventeenth century by divines such as William Chillingworth (1602–44). The original Latitudinarians were a group including Chillingworth who were associated with Lord Falkland at Great Tew in Oxfordshire during the 1630s. The term was also applied to the *Cambridge Platonists of the Interregnum because of their breadth of sympathy and rejection of the personal animosities which characterized Puritan controversial theology. However, the term is most commonly used today of a wide group of leading churchmen of the late seventeenth century, many of whom were disciples of the Cambridge Platonists, but who neglected their *mysticism and emphasis on *religious experience in favour of their appeal to reason as 'the candle of the Lord' in the soul. And even in this respect the Latitudinarians were less than completely faithful to their mentors, for where the Platonists saw reason as a divine light permeating the whole personality, they tended to identify it with common sense. As a result, by comparison, they appear worthy, but pedestrian and pragmatic.

The background to the emergence of Latitudinarianism was the low level of personal morality characteristic of Restoration court circles, and the rise of natural science in the intellectual world. In this context its adherents appealed to reason as a defence against what they saw as the unbridled 'enthusiasm' of the dissenting sects. As the counterpart of the new natural science they emphasized *natural theology and the ability of the rational mind to grasp the fundamentals of religion without recourse to *revelation, and this led to a tendency to formulate the faith in minimal terms. For them the basic religious motivation was the hope of immortality, and on this foundation they erected a utilitarian appeal to moral behaviour, commending religion for its advantages, as in John Tillotson's (1630–94) sermon *The Wisdom of Being Religious* (London, 1664). They were opponents of all kinds of superstition and of the dogmatism which had characterized the Calvinist theology of the preceding age. Theological complexity was regarded with suspicion as a plot by divines to keep simple people from perceiving the truth, and they cultivated a preaching and writing style of dispassionate simplicity. Their preaching lacked the drama of the Puritan pulpit, but appealed to an age that had grown weary of religious controversy. Pastoral care was a high priority, though its substance was of a piece with their whole approach. They knew something of the inwardness of religion, though they rejected the public expression of emotion. Like the Platonists before them, they passed on to succeeding generations less than all that they were, and their evacuation of feeling from religion was an important contribution to that emotional starvation which made the Evangelical Awakening of the mid-eighteenth century so cathartic an experience for so many.

Bibliography

G. R. Cragg, *From Puritanism to the Age of Reason* (Cambridge, 1950); idem, *Reason and Authority in the Eighteenth Century* (Cambridge, 1964); N. Sykes, *From Sheldon to Secker* (Cambridge, 1959); B. Willey, *The Eighteenth Century Background* (Harmondsworth, 1972).

D. D. Sceats

LAUSANNE COVENANT

In July 1974 an International Congress on World Evangelization, convened under the leadership of the evangelist Dr Billy Graham (b. 1918), was held at Lausanne, Switzerland. At the end, the vast majority of the 2,700 participants put their name to a document called the Lausanne Covenant.

The Covenant is a statement of intent concerning the unfinished task of *evangelization. It consists of fifteen paragraphs affirming God's purpose to create a special people for himself, Jesus Christ as the world's only Saviour, the nature and urgency of evangelism, Christian social responsibility, evangelism across cultures, *human rights (particularly religious freedom), the Holy Spirit in evangelism and the hope of Christ's return. Its evangelical thrust is underlined in a paragraph on the authority and power of the Bible.

The document was originally drawn up from statements in the main speakers' papers and revised in the light of the participants' contributions, especially those from a Majority World perspective. The title 'covenant', rather than 'declaration', is meant to emphasize commitment to the task of world evangelization.

The Covenant's significance lies in the breadth of its vision of the church's missionary task, its courage in handling controversial issues, its ability to combine different evangelical traditions and its subsequent extensive reception by the evangelical constituency worldwide as a fresh theological charter, expressing basic convictions about the church's multiple task in a changing world.

The conference gave rise to a continuing movement, the Lausanne Committee for World Evangelization, which convened a second major congress at Manila in 1989. The resulting 'Manila Manifesto' reaffirmed the groundbreaking commitment made at Lausanne to social responsibility as an integral part of the evangelistic task. Many other smaller-scale consultations have taken place, focusing on such topics as outreach to particular ethnic groups and faith communities, cultural contextualization of the gospel, and the quest for social justice.

Bibliography

J. D. Douglas (ed.), *Let the Earth Hear His Voice* (Minneapolis, 1975); K. Lundström, *Gospel and Culture in the World Council of Churches and the Lausanne Movement* (Uppsala, 2006); A. Nichols (ed.), *The Whole Gospel for the Whole World: The Story of Lausanne II Congress on World Evangelism, Manila 1989* (Charlotte, 1989); C. R. Padilla (ed.), *The New Face of Evangelicalism* (London, 1976); J. R. W. Stott, *The Lausanne Covenant: An Exposition and Commentary* (Minneapolis, 1975); idem (ed.), *Making Christ Known:*

Historic Mission Documents from the Lausanne Movement, 1974–1989 (Carlisle, 1997).

J. A. KIRK

LAW

Law, understood theologically, is the expression of the commands of God to his people, which demonstrate the will of God concerning all major aspects of life. It is therefore a moral concept as opposed to a merely social one. The moral law of God is summarized in the Decalogue.

All major evangelical theologians historically have accepted that no human being has ever perfectly fulfilled the precepts of the divine law, due to having their hearts corrupted by the condition of original *sin and therefore turned away from the worship and love of God. Jesus Christ alone, as the incarnate Son of God, perfectly fulfilled the law.

Legalism and antinomianism

*Jesus Christ came 'not to abolish the Law or the Prophets . . . but to fulfil them' (Matt. 5:17). The law pointed to his *incarnation and saving work, and was perfectly fulfilled by his obedience to the Father in all aspects of his life, death (see *Atonement) and *resurrection. Thus Christ is the New *Adam who perfectly fulfils the will of God. Two types of attitude threaten any Christian approach to law, namely legalism and *antinomianism.

The history of Christianity demonstrates that there is a recurrent danger for some people to consider that Christ came to abolish the divine law codified in the Decalogue, thus making a libertarian attitude central to Christian moral reasoning and living. This is known as antinomianism. The tendency is often criticized for substituting inspiration by the Spirit for obedience to the law. While such criticism has some basis, it is also necessary to recall that the role of the Spirit as the Spirit of Christ is to work in the hearts of believers to bring them closer to the will of God. Antinomianism needs to be judged from a theological framework that is properly rooted in acceptance of all three persons of the Trinity, without omitting to understand the role of the *Holy Spirit in the discernment of the will of God and the conduct of the Christian life. Otherwise the resulting criticism risks being merely a legalistic one.

Legalism is typically defined as people's tendency to attempt to fulfil the requirements of divine law (and even perhaps believe that they are capable of fully doing so) in order to be acceptable in the sight of God. Some theologians argue that Paul does not attack legalism in his letters to the Galatians and the Romans, rather that he challenges nomism. This can be characterized as the sense that the people who have been saved by God through his *grace must follow the law of Moses. This implies that the Jewish Christians portrayed in Acts as wishing to retain Jewish circumcision for males are nomistic. In turn some early Christians, some of them Jewish converts, accused Paul of 'antinomianism', saying that his gospel invited people to abandon moral restraints perceived to be unnecessary to the Christian life. In response, therefore, Paul said that people had been freed to live under the lordship of Christ and in the power of the Spirit (see *Sanctification). To clarify then, legalism is definable as the tendency for humans to attempt to make themselves just in the eyes of God through doing the works of the law, i.e. doing so without reliance on the Spirit that is given by Christ to believers. This tendency is known especially within the Protestant tradition since Martin Luther as 'works-righteousness'. It is evident that the controversies over legalism and nomism are still relevant for *Jewish converts to Christianity both in Israel and globally today. Arguably, they may also be relevant to converts from *Islam to Christianity, given the centrality of law to traditional Islam, and the affinities between Islamic law and ancient Jewish law.

The Christian concept of natural law

The early Church *Fathers used Paul's claim that the Gentiles had 'the law written on their hearts' (Rom. 2:15) as validating their case for Christian adoption of classical Greek and Roman notions of natural law. Gentiles are described by Paul as having some knowledge of the attributes of God through creation (this is taken by most historic theologians to be '*natural theology'). The law of God written on the hearts of Gentiles has been understood by most Christian theologians as corresponding to classical notions of natural law. However, they did not honour God and their hearts were 'darkened', the consequence being unwillingness to obey the law of God.

The major Christian formulation of natural law theory was made in the thirteenth century by the Italian theologian *Thomas Aquinas. For Thomas, natural law is the first way in which humans as rational creatures participate in eternal law, which is divine *wisdom. When God created humans, he ordained for them an end which is harmonious with their nature. The law of human conduct is deemed natural because it is implanted in human nature by God, and because it is accessible to humans through the natural medium of reason (as opposed to the supernatural medium of *revelation). Thus the precepts of natural law according to Thomas are both universally binding and universally knowable. The *Reformers also worked with a Christianized concept of natural law, though *Calvin in particular emphasized that the rational faculty is corrupted by original sin and requires redemption through the work of the Holy Spirit. It is necessary to distinguish between pre-modern appeals to natural law insofar as it was seen within the doctrines of *creation and *Christology, and modern appeals that rely on scientific and evidence-based approaches. The latter involve an inductive approach that looks for common themes across faiths and cultures in order to formulate a theory of natural law acceptable in multi-faith and secular societies (see *Christianity and other religions). They tend to appeal to a doctrine of God as Creator but not as Redeemer.

Uses of the law in the Magisterial Reformers

The Magisterial Reformers John Calvin and Philipp *Melanchthon taught that the law has three uses: theological, civil and didactic. According to Calvin, they were articulated in the Decalogue and mediated by Christ. The three uses of the law according to Calvin are as follows. First, the pedagogical use of the law is that it demonstrates divine righteousness by reflecting the sinful nature of humanity to humans, making us aware of our condition and that we are condemned for this. The second use of the law is the civil use of the law, to restrain evil in society. The Mosaic law was given partly for this reason. The Pauline injunction that the state be 'a terror to bad conduct' (Rom. 13:3–4) exemplifies this use of law as statute law. For Martin *Luther, the number of true Christian believers in the European states of his time (the sixteenth century) was small, therefore the state could and should not assume that the population which it governed would always obey the divine and natural law embedded in its statutory laws. The third use of the law according to John Calvin relates to believers, and is its principal use as the moral law. From it believers learn each day what God's will is for their lives and how they may please him. The law is thus the instrument which the Holy Spirit uses in the sanctifying of the people of God. For the contemporary Anglican theologian Oliver *O'Donovan, it is best to use the term 'law' only to refer to the law of Moses given to Israel, and 'positive community law'. This can facilitate recognition that the 'third use of the law' refers to Christian moral teaching.

Theological matters arising in engagement with state and society

From the early church on, Christians have differed on matters such as whether the *state should enact laws based on Christian moral reasoning, ultimately based on Christian theology and anthropology. In Calvinist terms, this is a disagreement about the second use of the law. In AD 313 the Edict of Milan was passed under Constantine I, granting freedom of religion to all religions within the Roman Empire, including Christianity. By the end of the century the practice of non-Christian religions was illegal. During that time the Roman state passed a number of laws which were based upon a Christian understanding of law and anthropology, including rendering abortion illegal. Some of these laws built upon existing Roman laws which were perceived as coextensive with Christian theological ethics. Jurisprudence and legal reasoning were practised within a Christian framework in Western countries down until the late eighteenth/early nineteenth century. Christian attitudes to the establishment of the church, i.e. its closeness to the state authorities in terms of its rights and responsibilities, are related to diverse Christian attitudes to law as well as government. The matter is ultimately theological and not merely political in the classical sense. Establishment is an arrangement that stems from a theological and social worldview where monarchy was the main accepted form of government, where seeing Christ as King posed little problem, and where democracy was either non-existent or seen as morally inferior. Such a worldview can accept without too much difficulty the idea of divine law as the basis of jurisprudence and statute law. The wars of religion, fought between different Christian states in Western Europe in the seventeenth century, provoked many theological minds to attempt to base Christian natural law theory on a rational basis as much as on a theological one. The foremost exponent of this was the Dutch *Arminian thinker Hugo *Grotius.

The relationship between law and morality is central to a theological understanding of law.

The traditional Christian approach has been to work within the classical tradition of natural law theory. The historicist view of law is that law is the expression of the common consciousness of a nation forged by its history. This is a view often held by conservative political thinkers. *Positivist theories of law base law in 'the rules issued or sanctioned by the State without intrinsic moral connotations'. Human rights theories of law are interpreted by some scholars as a secularization of older Christian natural law and natural right theory. Other Christians, however, see human rights law as anti-Christian and atheistic, in that it does not protect human life from beginning to end given that it tends to favour the 'pro-choice' stance on abortion and euthanasia. Human rights law is also criticized by some Christians as tending to privilege the rights of the individual over the right of the community, thus endangering the common good and the welfare of future generations.

The current international growth of *Islam, including the increasing public presence of Muslims in Western post-Christian countries, poses challenges and opportunities for revisiting Christian theological understandings of law. Key issues include the status and treatment of women, the limits of state law in handling personal morality, especially sexual behaviour, freedom to proselytize, freedom to convert and leave a religion, and freedom to practise and also criticize religious beliefs.

Bibliography

M. Cromartie (ed.), *A Preserving Grace: Protestants, Catholics, and Natural Law* (Washington DC, 1997); J. Ellul, *The Theological Foundations of Law* (ET, New York, 1960); J. M. Kelly, *A Short History of Western Legal Theory* (Oxford, 1992); E. F. Kevan, *The Grace of the Law: A Study in Puritan Theology* (London, 1964); F. Klug, *Values for a Godless Age: The Story of the United Kingdom's New Bill of Rights* (London, 2000); Byung-Ho Moon, *Christ the Mediator of the Law: Calvin's Christological Understanding of the Law as the Rule of Living and Life-Giving* (Milton Keynes, 2006); O. O'Donovan, *Resurrection and Moral Order: An Outline for Evangelical Ethics* (Leicester, 1994); S. J. Pope, 'Natural law and Christian Ethics', in R. Gill (ed.), *The Cambridge Companion to Christian Ethics* (Cambridge, 2001), pp. 77–95; J. Witte, *Law and Protestantism: The Legal Teaching of the Lutheran Reformation* (Cambridge, 2002).

C. A. E. MOSELEY

LAW AND GOSPEL

The *law is God's holy will for human life, and the *gospel is the good news of the reconciliation of the world to God in Jesus Christ (see *Atonement). Christian theology traditionally treats both as forms of the eternal word of God. The relationship between law and gospel constitutes a major point of emphasis in biblical exegesis, doctrine, preaching, ethics and the Christian life, and is handled diversely in Christian history and doctrine.

In the sixteenth century, Martin *Luther recognized several errors in medieval theology that made law and gospel virtually identical and turned the gospel into 'the new law'. In this format *justification became contingent upon both faith and works, thereby hindering the assurance of faith and causing corruptions in the functioning of the church. In response, Luther emphasized an ongoing relationship of contrast, or dialectic, between law and gospel based on justification by *faith alone, making possible the assurance of *salvation and demanding the reformation of certain church practices.

Following the thrust of Luther's thought, the Reformation generally recognized the law as God's will for creaturely life that Adam voluntarily obeyed (see *Reformation theology). As a result of Adam's sin (see *Fall), humanity became corrupt in its very nature and was unable to fulfil the law, which now came in between humanity and God as a witness to God's wrath and *judgment of *sin. The law subsequently given to Moses was an expression of God's will for his chosen people, Israel, serving as their tutor until the fulfilment of the covenant promise given to Abraham. Although Israel served other gods and abused the law, God kept the covenant promise in Jesus Christ, who served as the mediator between God and humanity by perfectly fulfilling the law and bearing humanity's punishment for sin as an atoning sacrifice. Accordingly, the Reformers stressed justification by faith in Christ alone, apart from works, and the imputation of Christ's *righteousness to the believer.

While the Reformers stressed the fulfilment of the law by Jesus Christ, they maintained an understanding of the law as God's word and eternal will in perceiving three uses for the law. First, the law has a civil or political use in which it is understood to provide for societal order and restrain sin. Second, the law has a theological use, which reveals sin and functions as a tutor leading to Christ through *repentance. Third, the law serves as a guide to the Christian life. Following *Calvin, the Reformed maintain a reverse ordering of the first and second uses given above and place greater weight on the third use than the Lutherans, although it is now recognized that Luther articulated a role for the law in the Christian life.

*Lutheran theology stresses the dialectical nature of the law and gospel relationship, often using it as an organizing principle governing theology. Thus, the law and gospel dialectic is often used as a rubric for mediating between the natural and revealed knowledge of God, reason and faith (see *Faith and reason), or philosophy and theology. It is foundational for the doctrine of the two kingdoms and an essential element in Lutheran homiletics. Several forms of philosophical existentialism have employed aspects of the Lutheran law and gospel dialectic.

*Reformed theology typically places law and gospel within a covenantal scheme, either as a distinction of administration within the *covenant of grace, or in the relationship between a covenant of works given to Adam and covenant of grace established by Christ. While the use of law and gospel is often implicit in Reformed thought, it is nonetheless a foundational distinction.

The nature of the law and gospel relationship is a continual subject of debate and was considered by Luther to be the essence of theology. A particularly important aspect of this task has been the determination of the nature and purpose of the law. The relationship between the revealed or Mosaic law to natural law and the law written on the heart, as well as the nature and unity of the ceremonial, civil and moral elements of the Mosaic law have all been determinate elements for comprehensive treatments of law and gospel in Christian theology.

Karl *Barth argued for the order 'gospel and law' based on their mutual unity as God's word, emphasizing that the gospel determines the law-gospel relationship because the law is only properly known as God's word in its fulfilment by Jesus Christ. Although Barth also maintained a usage for the traditional order and expressed an infinite difference between law and gospel, his view has been criticized for being overly harmonizing. Barth's position on gospel and law has profound ramifications for his theology, especially in his doctrine of God, anthropology, sin and his placement of ethics within dogmatics.

The two most notable errors deriving from an improper balance between law and gospel are legalism and *antinomianism. Legalism or moralism can occur through improper or excessive stress on the place and role of the law in justification and sanctification. It can undermine justification by faith, Christian *assurance, and lead to excessively individualistic and introspective piety.

Antinomianism in its classical form emerged when an associate of Luther and Philipp *Melanchthon, John Agricola (c. 1494–1566), insisted that the preaching of repentance belonged to the gospel because the law could not justify. Rather, the law had been fulfilled by Christ, was not to be preached prior to the gospel and was not a guide to the Christian life. Agricola's teaching explicitly rejected the law as a form of the word of God, and therefore the entire dialectic of law and gospel, although he maintained a political use for the Decalogue. Both legalism and antinomianism have appeared and been combated at various times in the history of the church and are continuing but unavoidable dangers for theology.

*Dispensationalism treats law and gospel as strictly antithetical, placing them in the distinct dispensations of Israel and the church. Most modern dispensationalism teaches that while justification is by grace in every dispensation, the Mosaic law served a binding regulatory function for Israel's sanctification that is not binding on the church. Consequently, the law is not a guide for the Christian life; rather, the 'law of Christ' is written on the heart of the believer. However, as a biblical revelation of God's holy nature, the law points out sin and the need for grace, but is itself antithetical to grace.

*Liberal theologies often avoid both the traditional dialectical and covenantal notions by implicitly treating law and gospel as progressive stages or contrasts in humanity's religious perception. Higher forms of religion emphasize God's affirming love and offer emancipation from primitive legalism. Such notions are frequently related to abandonment or relativizing of the OT, rejection of the law as God's word and the approach to theology from the standpoint of religion in general, instead of *revelation.

Study and examination of the distinction and unity of law and gospel is an essential task for the church in its exegesis, theology, ethics and preaching. While the task of defining the relationship between law and gospel should rely heavily on the contributions of systematic and historical theology, it is foremost a task of biblical exegesis and should at its base represent an interpretation of the entirety of Scripture.

Bibliography

K. Barth, 'Gospel and Law', in *God, Grace and Gospel* (Edinburgh, 1959); I. U. Dalferth, *Theology and Philosophy* (Oxford and New York, 1988); C. H. Dodd, *Gospel and Law* (Cambridge, 1951); G. Ebeling, *Word and Faith* (London, 1963); G. Forde, *The Law-Gospel Debate: An Interpretation of its Historical Development* (Minneapolis, 1969); S. Gundry (ed.), *Five Views on Law and Gospel* (Grand Rapids, 1996); E. Jüngel, 'Gospel and Law', in *Karl Barth: A Theological Legacy* (ET, Philadelphia, 1986); B. Lohse, *Martin Luther's Theology* (ET, Edinburgh, 1999); O. Weber, *Foundations of Dogmatics*, vol. 2 (ET, Grand Rapids, 1983); T. Wengert, *Law and Gospel: Philip Melanchthon's Debate with John Agricola of Eisleben over Poenitentia* (Grand Rapids, 1997).

D. A. GILLAND

LAW, WILLIAM (1686–1761)

William Law was an Anglican devotional writer and mystic. Born in Northamptonshire and educated at Cambridge, his promising academic and ecclesiastical career was cut short in 1716 by his Jacobite and nonjuring sympathies. His early writings attacked the Latitudinarian theology of Benjamin Hoadly and the *deism of Matthew Tindal, but he gradually turned from polemics to *mysticism. His best-known work, *A Serious Call to a Devout and Holy Life* (1728), urging total devotion to God, was greatly admired by John *Wesley. From the mid-1730s, however, Law came under the influence of Jacob *Boehme, and his earlier High Church orthodoxy and rigorous asceticism were overlaid, if not replaced, by a strand of theosophy emphasizing the mystical way as the path to union with God. This led to a breach with Wesley in 1738.

Law's later works, *The Spirit of Prayer* (1749 and 1750) and *The Spirit of Love* (1752 and 1754), provoked Wesley's *A Letter to the Revd Mr Law* (1756), accusing him of denying God's omnipotence and justice, and misunderstanding justification and the new birth. In 1740 Law returned to his birthplace of King's Cliffe, living a life of charity, celibacy, prayer, study and writing in a household community of three: himself, Hester Gibbon (sister of his former pupil Edward and aunt of the historian) and the widowed Mrs Elizabeth Hutcheson.

Bibliography

J. H. Overton, *William Law, Nonjuror and Mystic* (London, 1881); I. Rivers in *Oxford Dictionary of National Biography* (Oxford, 2004); A. K. Walker, *William Law: His Life and Thought* (London, 1973).

M. WELLINGS

LAYING ON OF HANDS

In Christian practice the laying on of hands has several resonances, theologically rooting back to *Jesus' empathy, healing and empowerment with the Spirit; Jesus refocuses the Hebrew traditions he inherited. Touching signifies care, compassion and love. As *Wittgenstein would say, such sympathetic action is a form of life, not to be explained in terms of anything else, just a given practice common to humanity. It is an instinctive human and pastoral gesture, and it has wide scriptural warrant as a gesture of blessing, healing, caring, commissioning for Christlike service in his church, and empowering for membership of this body. Theologically, the role of the *Spirit is never absent from this Christian gesture. We might use the distinction between synchronic and diachronic: the Spirit and Jesus emphasized respectively.

It is clearly a sign of blessing in the OT (Gen. 48:17) and of commissioning for a role or task, which is where it finds its great emphasis in the NT. Jesus blesses (Matt. 19:13) and heals (Mark 6:5) using the laying on of hands with prayer. In Acts we find the laying on of hands used with prayer for commissioning for apostolic preaching (Acts 13:2–3), along with a deep sense of the Holy Spirit's agency at work, or indeed of receiving the Spirit (Acts 8:18) or 'spiritual gifts' (2 Tim. 1:6).

Churches practising the rite of *confirmation as part of commitment as disciples invariably use the laying on of hands, and call on the Holy Spirit's empowerment and gifts. The theological signification of laying on of hands for Christianity therefore brings together divine blessing and commissioning in the power of the Spirit. *Tertullian and *Cyprian witness to a distinctive and influential model for the structure of Christian initiation, in which water *baptism is followed by anointing and by hand-laying and then receiving the Eucharist, the components being considered as a whole. Tertullian is emphatic that it is at the laying on of the hand that the Spirit is given, although he like other early writers talks of the rite, water baptism and confirmation, as a whole.

Ordination to pastoral *ministry has come almost universally to involve this practice of laying on of hands, some denominations also valuing the sense of continuity down the generations of church ministry. Ordination has been linked to the gesture since 200. As historians and theologians such as *Schillebeeckx argue, the ordained ministry had a pastoral emphasis for the first millennium of church history, only then acquiring the notion of a special power, *potestas*, given by the laying on of bishops' hands in asserted succession back to Peter and Jesus. The gesture of laying on of hands clearly signifies corporate pastoral service rather than bestowing a separate power to an individual over the community. At ordination the whole community is acting in Christ to commission for Christlike service.

This Christian practice is best interpreted always Christologically: whether in healing, caring, commissioning, praying for or blessing, this is the act of Christ helping and supporting his flock, exercising his ministry through others and graciously bestowing the Spirit in the particularities and exigencies of life. Ultimately, the laying on of hands is an act representative of the whole Christ-indwelt community.

Bibliography

J. K. Coyle, 'The Laying on of Hands as Conferral of the Spirit', in E. A. Livingstone (ed.), *Studia Patristica* 18 (Louvain 1989); G. W. H. Lampe, *The Seal of the Spirit* (London, 1952); J. V. Taylor, *The Go-Between God* (London, 1972); C. H. Turner, Χείρτόνία in *JTS* 24, 1922–3, pp. 496–504.

T. BRADSHAW

LEGALISM, see LAW AND GOSPEL

LEIBNIZ, GOTTFRIED VON (1646–1716)

German mathematician and philosopher. According to Leibniz, the full definition of anything involves describing all things from its unique standpoint; each thing is an independent 'monad' 'mirroring' the rest. The highest monad, and creator of all others, is God.

Leibniz produced classical versions of the arguments for the existence of God (adding one of his own from the 'pre-established harmony' needed to ensure that the monads mirror one another accurately; see *Natural theology), and a famous rebuttal of antitheistic arguments from *evil, holding that this is the best of all possible worlds, at least in being the best possible sequence of events moving towards perfection, even if it is not perfect yet; evil elements in it are essential ingredients in the whole. He was the first to use the word '*theodicy'.

Leibniz was also the promoter of unsuccessful schemes for reunion between Catholic and Protestant churches, and between Calvinists and Lutherans. Later he drifted towards a more purely 'natural' religion, and declined the assistance of any minister at his deathbed.

Bibliography

Works: Only some are available in English. L. Strickland (ed.), *The Shorter Leibniz Texts* (London, 2006); R. S. Woolhouse and R. Francks (eds.), *Leibniz: Philosophical Texts* (Oxford, 1998).

Studies: S. Brown, *Leibniz* (Brighton, 1984); N. Jolley (ed.), *The Cambridge Companion to Leibniz* (Cambridge, 1994); B. C. Look (ed.), *The Continuum Companion to Leibniz* (London, 2011); B. Mates, *The Philosophy of Leibniz* (New York and Oxford, 1986); G. M. Ross, *Leibniz* (Oxford, 1984).

R. L. STURCH

LEIDEN SYNOPSIS

The *Synopsis purioris theologiae* (1625) is a theology textbook explaining and defending mainstream *Reformed orthodoxy as it stood after the Synod of *Dort (1618), in the form of fifty-two theological disputations. It is known as the Leiden Synopsis after the four professors of theology at Leiden who co-authored it: J. Polyander, A. Waleus, A. Thysius and A. Rivetus. These academic disputations were presented at Leiden by students of the authors, under their close supervision and authority, and with their editorial control and additions (thus such disputations were considered ultimately the work of the supervisor).

The work follows a traditional 'commonplaces' arrangement, moving from discussion of the nature of theology, Scripture and the triune God, to creation, humanity, Christ, salvation, the church and the last things. There are in addition disputations throughout, more or less flowing from this topical arrangement, which address issues hotly contested among the various confessional blocs. The Synopsis was quite popular, going through five editions in the seventeenth century.

Bibliography

Polyander et al., *Synopsis purioris theologiae, disputationibus quinquaginta duabus comprehensa*, ed. H. Bavinck (Leiden, [6]1881); *Synopsis of overzicht van de zuiverste theologie* (Dutch tr., Enschede, 1964).

Studies: G. P. van Itterzon, *Het gereformeerd leerboek der 17de eeuw* ('s-Gravenhage, 1931).

B. E. ELLIS

LEO THE GREAT

Leo, who held the office of pope from 440 to 461, magnified the *papacy in various ways. Not only did he see himself as the successor to Peter, but he believed that Peter actually spoke through all he preached or wrote. Hence he expected all his statements as pope to be accepted without question. On the political front he obtained from the Emperor Valentinian III (425–55) effective jurisdiction over the Western Empire. If any bishop resisted papal authority, the pope could now resort to secular authority. Leo also added the decretals of his predecessors to Western *canon law, of which he became the effective guardian.

Leo enhanced his political standing by his achievements in negotiation with Rome's enemies, the Huns and the Vandals. Again, he boosted the city of Rome's own Christian tradition by claiming Peter and Paul as its patrons in succession to Romulus and Remus.

Leo made a significant contribution to the Eastern *Christological controversies of his time. Shortly before the 'Robber Council' of Ephesus in 449 Leo came out decisively against Eutyches (see *Monophysitism) and wrote a *Tome* to Bishop Flavian of Constantinople (d. 449) to confirm him in his stance against Eutyches. Leo hoped that the promulgation of his own doctrine would render a general council unnecessary, but it was not to be. At Ephesus Leo's *Tome* was not even read, and the supporters of Eutyches held the day. Leo immediately pressed for the decisions of this council to be overthrown. Circumstances following the death of Theodosius II (in 450) favoured this. A new general *council was held at *Chalcedon in 451, where the *Tome* was acclaimed among other documents as an orthodox statement.

The *Tome* was designed to refute Eutyches, whom Leo understood to be denying that it was real human flesh which Christ derived from *Mary. Leo, by contrast, held that Christ had to assume true human nature if he was to restore to humanity by his divine power that which it had once lost through sin. It was equally vital that Christ should have lost nothing of his divinity. In the one person of Jesus Christ each of the two natures retained its own natural properties unimpaired, and yet they always acted in concert with one another. Not surprisingly, this aspect of the *Tome* raised misgivings at Chalcedon among Illyrian and Palestinian bishops, who thought Leo was guilty of the *Nestorian error of dividing the natures and seeing in Christ two persons. This undoubted ambiguity in the *Tome* may be explained by its immediate purpose – to answer Eutyches. Elsewhere Leo disowned Nestorianism, which he interpreted as a form of *adoptionism. Thus Leo would stress the indivisible connection which was achieved when the two natures came together in Jesus Christ. But the fact remains that Leo did not explain the unity of Christ's person as well as he did the manifestation of the two natures in the life of the incarnate Christ.

Bibliography

T. G. Jalland, *The Life and Times of St Leo the Great* (London, 1941); J. N. D. Kelly, *Early Christian Doctrines* (London, [5]1977).

G. A. KEITH

LEONTIUS OF BYZANTIUM, see HYPOSTASIS

LESSING, GOTTHOLD EPHRAIM (1729–81)

A pioneer in modern German drama, Lessing was one of the most elusive and seminal religious thinkers of his age. Even in its essentials, his thought has been interpreted in widely varied and incompatible ways. Lessing apparently sought to adopt a theological stance that avoided the deadlocked rationalism and orthodoxy of his day, but he can be regarded either as crypto-rationalist or as providing an alternative non-rationalist position to that held by the orthodox. There are at least two reasons for these, and other, discrepant verdicts. First, Lessing was a subtle author whose real views, it has been maintained, defy easy access. Secondly, he did not obviously correlate his main ideas coherently and gave no comprehensive, systematic account of them. One may therefore put it in terms which he himself applied to religion: it is the spirit of Lessing's enterprise, not the letter of his writing, that guides us best in the interpretation of his thought.

Such thought gains its unity, in part, from its preoccupation with a set of questions, namely, those that cluster around the issue of religious truth and how it is apprehended. In particular, Lessing propounded several theses on the general relation of *religion and *history, of which the following are among the most significant. (1) The Bible, including its historical record, is open to critical investigation. Lessing momentously published the *Wolfenbüttel Fragments* of H. S. Reimarus' (1694–1768) work between 1774 and 1778 and vindicated at least the critical principle adopted by the latter in his attack on the orthodox approach to the Bible. (2) True religion antedates its literary expression and furnishes us with a spiritual criterion for assessing the force of the 'letter'. Hence it is not the historical account that actually authorizes our religious beliefs. (3) Historical testimony is technically 'uncertain' in the sense that, at its most reliable, it cannot warrant our absolute conviction. Its credibility therefore does not establish its religious authority. (4) Historical truths are, logically, of a different order from 'necessary truths of reason'. The former are contingent (an event, for example, might not have happened); the latter are necessary (their contradictories cannot be supposed). (5) History is process, and the communication or apprehension of religious truth can vary with its change. Revelation can be conceived as the education of the human race so that eventually it may be possible to comprehend the truths of morality and religion without recourse to earlier, partial ways of apprehension.

Certainly, such theses may be described differently, related in different ways and supplemented with others of note. Furthermore, their abstract statement fails to capture the fluid, suggestive, thrusting style of their author. Lessing appears to have deemed orthodoxy totally unrealistic in its religious foundations and rationalism quite ineffective by its failure to break new ground. It is hard to chart with precision the direct or indirect influence of Lessing's thought, but the various ways in which he organized the issue of *faith and history continue to command attention. When Lessing wrote that the endeavour to find truth is preferable to its possession in itself, it may reveal much of the man and his thought: in the spirit of this, one is perhaps more intellectually indebted to him for his attempts than his accomplishments.

Bibliography

H. E. Allison, *Lessing and the Enlightenment* (Ann Arbor, 1966); K. Barth, *Protestant Theology in the Nineteenth Century* (London, 1972); H. Chadwick (ed.), *Lessing's Theological Writings* (London, 1956); B. Fischer and T. C. Fox (eds.), *A Companion to the Works of Gotthold Ephraim Lessing* (Woodbridge, 2005); L. P. Wessell, *G. E. Lessing's Theology: A Reinterpretation* (The Hague, 1977).

S. N. WILLIAMS

LEVINAS, EMMANUEL (1906–95)

Levinas was a twentieth-century philosopher, born in Lithuania and naturalized a French citizen in 1930. He studied with Martin *Heidegger and Edmund Husserl in Strasbourg, where he also began a lifelong friendship with the philosopher Maurice Blanchot. He was drafted into French military service in 1939, but his army unit was routed and he was taken prisoner. Levinas spent most of the Second World War in a Nazi labour camp. After the war Levinas learned that his parents and brothers had been murdered by Nazi soldiers, though his wife and daughter survived in hiding. His philosophical work, which had begun to move away from Heidegger before the war, did so dramatically afterwards. In 1947 Levinas published his first book, *Existence and Existents*, much of which was handwritten during his time in the Nazi stalag. He spoke and wrote very little about his wartime experiences, though they exerted significant influence on his philosophy.

His first major work, *Totality and Infinity*, appeared in 1961 and presents a serious challenge to the history of philosophy. Levinas claims that philosophy has failed to realize that the relation with the other person exceeds the totality of *being. The encounter with the face of the other is a transcendent event, an encounter with the holy. For this reason *ethics should have the first and last word in philosophy. Levinas challenges philosophies of totality, from Parmenides to *Hegel, which he claims remain philosophies of the self. The other person summons from beyond any philosophical construction, before the construction of any system of ethics. For Levinas, responsibility precedes reason, metaphysics, philosophy and cognition.

Levinas gives preference to the face of *suffering, echoing biblical concern for the widow, the orphan and the stranger. He utilizes *religious language to express philosophical concepts and also wrote explicitly religious reflections on the Jewish Talmud. These essays often served to incubate ideas that later appear in his explicitly philosophical writings. Key ideas about holiness, goodness, time and radical responsibility first appear in readings of the Talmud.

Levinas's second major book, *Otherwise than Being or Beyond Essence*, appeared in 1974. Here Levinas presses obligation to even higher registers. Responsibility to the other is expressed as primordial summons, a calling to holiness and sacrifice that is older than time itself. His final works explore the dynamics of time and language in light of this infinite and original debt to the other person and to God.

Bibliography

Works: *Time and the Other* (Pittsburgh, 1947); *Existence and Existents* (Pittsburgh, 1947); *Totality and Infinity* (Pittsburgh, 1961); *Otherwise than Being or Beyond Essence* (Pittsburgh, 1974).

Studies: A. Peperzak, *Beyond: The Philosophy of Emmanuel Levinas* (Evanston, 1997); D. Perpich, *The Ethics of Emmanuel Levinas* (Stanford, 2008).

E. SEVERSON

LEWIS, CLIVE STAPLES (1898–1963)

Born in Belfast, Lewis took a triple First at Oxford, and after a short time teaching philosophy became Fellow of Magdalen College and University Lecturer in English. He had abandoned Christian belief in adolescence, but was converted to *theism in 1929 and to Christianity two years later. For an account of his life up to conversion, see his *Surprised by Joy* (London, 1955). He was for many years the centre of a group of friends, the 'Inklings', which included the writer and lay theologian Charles *Williams and J. R. R. Tolkien (1892–1973), author of *The Lord of the Rings*. From 1954 he was Professor of Medieval and Renaissance English at Cambridge.

Lewis was a prolific writer, whose specifically Christian writings fall mainly into three classes. His fiction includes a series of three 'science fantasy' novels (*Out of the Silent Planet*, *Perelandra* – later retitled *Voyage to Venus* – and *That Hideous Strength*), a retelling of the myth of Psyche (*Till We Have Faces*) and his seven 'Narnia' books for children. In them Christian themes are introduced unmistakably and yet naturally; Lewis hoped that by setting them in new contexts he could help readers see them as they were, not spoilt by 'stained-glass and Sunday school associations'.

Avowedly *apologetic works include the broadcast talks collected in *Mere Christianity*, the studies *The Problem of Pain* and *Miracles*, and the allegorical *Pilgrim's Regress*. Here Lewis sought, without limiting himself to any one philosophical or theological position, to defend the common ground of traditional Christian orthodoxy, blending logical argument with insight into the workings of the human mind (especially the *conscience) and leading on to the transformed worldview that follows conversion.

Of his writings on the Christian life, the best known is *The Screwtape Letters* (from a senior devil to a novice tempter, advising on traps for the patient's soul). *Letters to Malcolm*, closer to theology proper than most of his work, deals with problems raised by *prayer. *The Four Loves* analyses in turn affection, friendship, eros and charity and the part they play in natural and Christian lives. *Reflections on the Psalms* is not a commentary but an exploration of Christian use of the psalter.

Lewis was probably the best-known apologist of his day, and his popularity continues. His works are characterized by his command of lucid and enjoyable English, enough philosophy to make his arguments coherent and persuasive without becoming technical, and his ability to lead his reader from the everyday, even the humorous, to hints of glory. His appeal was chiefly to the imagination and the intelligence, but though he seldom went very deep (except perhaps in *A Grief Observed*, written after his wife died), the fact that there were depths beyond was always made clear.

Bibliography

H. Carpenter, *The Inklings* (London, 1978); D. C. Downing, *The Most Reluctant Convert: C. S. Lewis's Journey to Faith* (Downers Grove, 2002); B. L. Edwards (ed.), *C. S. Lewis: Life, Works, and Legacy*, 4 vols. (Nestport, 2007); J. Gibb (ed.), *Light on C. S. Lewis* (London, 1965) (essays by friends and pupils); R. L. Green and W. Hooper, *C. S. Lewis* (London, 1974); A. Jacobs, *The Narnian: The Life and Imagination of C. S. Lewis* (San Francisco, 2005); W. H. Lewis (brother) (ed.), *Letters of C. S. Lewis* (London, 1966); M. Mühling, *A Theological Journey into Narnia: An Analysis of the Message Beneath the Text* (Göttingen, 2005); V. Reppert, *C. S. Lewis's Dangerous Idea: In Defense of the Argument from Reason* (Downers Grove, 2003); S. Schwartz, *C. S. Lewis on the Final Frontier: Science and the Supernatural in the Space Trilogy* (Oxford, 2009); C. Walsh, *The Literary Legacy of C. S. Lewis* (San Diego, CA, 1979); G. Watson (ed.), *Critical Essays on C. S. Lewis* (Menston, 1992); E. J. Wielenberg, *God and the Reach of Reason* (Cambridge, 2007).

R. L. STURCH

LIBERAL EVANGELICALISM

The term 'liberal evangelicalism' came to prominence at the beginning of the twentieth century, when it defined a 'progressive' or 'modernizing' network of evangelical clergy within the Church of England. It was subsequently applied to evangelicals from a range of denominations.

In the later 1800s Anglican evangelicals found themselves challenged on two key fronts. On the one hand, *liberals were commending higher criticism, embracing Darwinian evolution and rejecting *substitutionary *atonement – trends which many evangelicals saw as heretical. On the other, *Anglo-Catholics were promoting forms of worship which traditional evangelicals rejected as 'ritualistic'. However, not all evangelicals reacted with such hostility. Some emerged who thought it possible and indeed desirable to review historic evangelical interpretations in the light of modern scientific and cultural insights, and who were open to more liturgical forms of devotion. One such was A. J. Tait, who in 1906 gathered like-minded clergy into a 'Group Brotherhood' which included F. S. Guy Warman, later Bishop of Manchester. The Group soon attracted high-profile churchmen like T. Guy Rogers, E. W. Barnes and Cyril Bardsley. While 'clinging to the fundamental spiritual truths of Evangelicalism', the Group's manifesto declared that 'old doctrines had to be set forth in modern language'.

Following the 1914–18 war the Group Brotherhood was reconstituted as the Anglican Evangelical Group Movement, and enjoyed significant growth. Several AEGM figures contributed essays to the landmark volumes: *Liberal Evangelicalism* (1923), and *The Inner Life: Essays in Liberal Evangelicalism* (1925). By this time, the Movement had acquired its most dominant advocate: Vernon F. Storr was a Canon of Westminster Abbey and personified the AEGM's resolve to engage constructively with the wider church. However, Storr provoked controversy when suggesting that the Bible's spiritual value had been enhanced by critical scholarship, and that it was not wholly free from errors. He agreed with Rogers that modern evangelicals had become 'dissatisfied with some of the older and cruder penal substitutionary theories of the Atonement', and emphasized moral influence theories instead. Meanwhile Barnes championed theistic evolution, in opposition to the many traditional evangelicals who maintained a creationist view (see *Creation and evolution). Liturgically, Rogers, F. T. Woods and others embraced the 'catholic' eastward position at Communion, while a number of AEGM members replaced their 'Protestant' cassock and preaching scarf with an alb and stole. Retreats and non-Protestant traditions of prayer were also encouraged.

Unsurprisingly, these moves led to division. In 1922 conservatives within the Church

Missionary Society broke away to form the Bible Churchmen's Missionary Society. In 1928 the AEGM launched an annual conference at Cromer, as an alternative to the more traditional Keswick Convention (see *Higher-life theology). These Anglican tensions were reflected in other contexts. The interdenominational Student Christian Movement came under liberal evangelical influence, and in 1928 the Inter-Varsity Fellowship was formed by those convinced that it had compromised the gospel. The contours of evangelicalism developed somewhat differently in the USA, but the growing divergence of fundamentalism from 'neo-evangelicalism' there bore echoes of what was happening in England.

Storr's death in 1940, and the move of Barnes, Charles *Raven and others into full-blown liberalism led to the decline of the AEGM: the last Cromer convention took place in 1948. 'Liberal evangelical' is not a designation many would own now, and continuities between it and more progressive forms of evangelicalism today are not direct. Both the centrist neo-evangelicalism of Billy Graham, Carl *Henry or John Stott and more 'open', 'radical' or 'left-wing' forms of evangelicalism might accept biblical criticism, assimilate evolution, engage positively with contemporary culture and cooperate with Catholics. Yet unlike many liberal evangelicals of the 1920s and 1930s these constituencies would characteristically still affirm the primacy of Scripture and substitutionary (if not necessarily penal) accounts of the atonement. This may change, but as things stand, the legacy of liberal evangelicalism is seen as much in thoroughgoing liberal and 'post-evangelical' approaches as it is in groupings that would still identify themselves as evangelical.

Bibliography

O. R. Barclay, *Whatever Happened to the Jesus Lane Lot?* (Leicester, 1977); D. W. Bebbington, *Evangelicalism in Modern Britain: A History from the 1730s to the 1980s* (London, 1989), ch. 6; I. M. Randall, *Evangelical Experiences: A Study in the Spirituality of English Evangelicalism, 1918–1939* (Carlisle, 1999), ch. 3; G. T. Rogers et al., *Liberal Evangelicalism: An Interpretation* (London, 1923); idem, *The Inner Life: Essays in Liberal Evangelicalism* (London, 1925); M. Wellings, *Evangelicals Embattled: Responses of Evangelicals in the Church of England to Ritualism, Darwinism and Theological Liberalism, 1890–1930* (Carlisle, 2003).

D. H. K. Hilborn

LIBERAL THEOLOGY

The adjective 'liberal' comes from the Latin word for 'free' and so was applied in ancient times to the 'liberal arts', those educational pursuits of 'free men' who were not slaves. But in the early nineteenth century, it came to apply to those who favoured democratic government in the tradition of the French revolutionaries, or at least favoured representative parliamentary government on the Anglo-Saxon model. It acquired the meaning of 'forward-looking' (in contrast to 'conservatives' who wanted to conserve the best of the past) and strongly emphasized the liberty of the individual over against the community and the state.

It was first applied in theology to the heirs of F. D. E. *Schleiermacher, who were thought to be 'liberal' in the sense that they were forward-looking and willing to re-articulate the Christian faith in a way which appealed to the modern age. Schleiermacher, called 'the father of liberal theology', did this by thinking of Christian faith as one example or development (albeit the most 'advanced') of '*religion', that subjective 'feeling' or 'consciousness' of the divine and the eternal found in all humanity. In contrast, *Hegel and his heirs saw the Christian faith as a pictorial version of his *idealist metaphysics in which God (*Geist*, meaning 'mind' or 'spirit') realized itself in the history of the world. Towards the end of the nineteenth century, this classic German *liberalism was represented by the *Ritschlian school which followed Schleiermacher in rejecting *metaphysics, but prioritized the ethical. In Adolf von *Harnack, their focus on the 'kingdom of God', understood as a historical movement for social reform, led to a denial of the orthodox doctrines of the atonement, the incarnation and the Trinity. In the United States, Walter *Rauschenbusch's '*social gospel' optimistically saw social progress dealing with sin and evil and ushering in the *kingdom of God through following the moral teaching of Jesus. Other-worldly notions were dismissed.

The First World War brought the demise of this classic liberalism. The 'dialectical' theology of Barth, Brunner, Bultmann and *Gogarten strongly reacted against it in favour of a 'theology of the word'. But in fact many of the characteristic notes of classic nineteenth-century liberalism survived. *Barth and *Brunner returned to the doctrines of incarnation, Trinity and atonement and the doctrines of the Reformation, but they remained suspect to some conservatives because they did not adopt the full intellectual system of *scholastic post-Reformation Protestant 'orthodoxy'. They were dismissed by some as 'neo-orthodox', along with Reinhold *Niebuhr. Niebuhr's strong emphasis on sin and evil in his *Nature and Destiny of Man* (1941) led him to reject the optimism of classic liberalism, but his theological method was more akin to it than was Barth's focus on biblical revelation.

In the 1950s and 1960s the survival of the approach of liberal theology was even more evident in the thought of Rudolf *Bultmann. Although he had rejected classic liberalism, the historicism seen in Harnack, *Troeltsch and Rauschenbusch issued in his extreme historical scepticism about the Gospels and his classifying any talk of miracles, angels or demons, or indeed of God's action in the world as '*myth'. When the NT was '*demythologized', however, its core message remained, and this proved to be virtually identical to the *existentialist philosophy of Bultmann's colleague, Martin *Heidegger. To be 'justified by faith' (Bultmann was a Lutheran) was to live deciding authentically to embrace the future and reject the dead old historical past.

Paul *Tillich similarly adopted an existentialist stance, but whereas Bultmann was an NT scholar, Tillich was a philosophical theologian and articulated a method of 'correlation'. Human philosophy and culture posed the great questions of human life, and Christian theology supplied the answers. God was to be thought of not as a person 'up there', but as the ground of our *being, and all religion was a matter of 'ultimate concern'. Popular versions of the theologies of Bultmann and Tillich appeared in John A. T. *Robinson's *Honest to God* (1963). John *Hick moved from the more conservative position of his youth to a gradually more 'liberal' one, eventually letting go of the doctrine of the incarnation as an editor of *The Myth of God Incarnate* (1977), and adopting a fully pluralist and universalist position (*God Has Many Names*, 1980).

Although this tradition is mainly Protestant, Roman Catholic theologians such as Hans *Küng are frequently identified as 'liberal'. And while the term is more strictly applied to the largely German nineteenth-century schools, some features characterize the whole tradition from Schleiermacher to Tillich and Hick.

First, the broader liberal tradition had an *apologetic motive. Its aim (as the title of Schleiermacher's major work put it) was to commend 'religion' to its 'cultured despisers'. It arose therefore in response to the attack on Christian faith by the *Enlightenment and tried to adapt Christian theology to meet the challenge of '*modernity'. It might therefore be better termed 'modernist'.

Secondly, it was characterized throughout by the method of correlation which was most clearly articulated by Tillich. It was therefore essentially *anthropocentric rather than theocentric, and often appeared to be concerned more with human well-being and 'self-understanding' than with the glory of God. While it had commendable social concern, it often tended to come down to a 'private' or individualistic religion which fitted the individualism characteristic of the era of modernity. While an early optimism was abandoned, a tendency to emphasize human need rather than human sin and the fall persisted.

Thirdly, in line with this strong human and even *humanist concern, it was characterized by a strong *historicism. In line with modern philosophy and what was seen as scientific method, the Christian faith had to be explained historically along with all 'religion' in terms of a closed continuum of cause and effect. The transcendence of God was sacrificed to an accent on immanence which sometimes verged on *pantheism or at least panentheism.

Fourthly, this led to radical revision of Christian theology, rejecting not only the rigid scholasticism of Protestant *orthodoxy, but the Reformation doctrine of substitutionary *atonement, and even the patristic and creedal doctrines of incarnation and the Trinity. Miracles, including the central *miracle of the resurrection, were regarded as contrary to 'modern science'. Attempts were made by some to develop a non-incarnational Christology, but at best these often fell short of affirming the full deity of Christ, and frequently developed into *universalism and pluralism.

Fifthly, the Christian *Scriptures were merely human products, inspired only in the same sense that all great literature was said to be 'inspired', a resource for faith, but to be corrected in the light of human reason and experience.

Liberal theology today is often said to be in decline as 'modernity' gives way to '*postmodernity'. The so-called 'postliberalism' of George *Lindbeck and Stanley Hauerwas classifies it as an 'experiential-expressive' model in opposition to the 'cognitive-propositionalist' model of 'conservative' theology, and advocates instead a post-liberal 'cultural-linguistic' model. It remains to be seen, however, whether this is a genuine departure from liberalism, or whether this simply replaces an individualistic human focus with a community-based one. The question is whether any theology can escape liberalism if it makes no cognitive claims to speak of the true and living God.

Bibliography

G. Dorrien, *The Making of American Liberal Theology: Imagining Progressive Religion, 1805–1900* (Louisville, 2001); D. F. Ford (ed.), *The Modern Theologians: An Introduction to Christian Theology in the Twentieth Century* (New York and Oxford, ³2005); S. J. Grenz and R. E. Olson, *20th-Century Theology* (Downers Grove, 1992); A. I. C. Heron, *A Century of Protestant Theology* (London, 1980); N. Murphy, *Beyond Liberalism and Fundamentalism: How Modern and Postmodern Philosophy Set the Theological Agenda* (Valley Forge, 1996).

T. A. NOBLE

LIBERALISM, GERMAN

The roots of nineteenth-century German liberalism are mainly to be found in the eighteenth-century *Enlightenment, the French Revolution, and the *romanticism and *idealism of the turn of the century. The philosophical and political ideas generated during this period permeated both secular and ecclesiastical thinking, producing a growing reaction against traditional institutions and beliefs.

Within the circle of theological liberalism one must distinguish between liberalism of doctrine and liberalism in biblical scholarship. The former was an undermining or denial of the traditional doctrines of the Christian faith, while the latter challenged the authenticity, historicity and divine inspiration of the Bible. These two forms of liberalism were generally connected in varying degree, yet one might hold one without necessarily holding the other.

In the realm of Christian doctrine, German liberalism may be traced back to *Kant and *Lessing, but above all to *Schleiermacher, who drastically reinterpreted the fundamental doctrines of Christianity from an anthropocentric viewpoint. For Schleiermacher, theology must begin from human 'religion' which resulted from a universal 'God-consciousness' or 'feeling of dependence'. For Christians it was the absolute God-consciousness of Jesus, impressed upon the Christian community, which constituted his redemptive work. Classical *Christology and the doctrine of the *Trinity were all but dismissed as speculation irrelevant to true piety.

The first serious challenge to the authenticity of the NT writings was *Strauss's *Life of Jesus* in 1835. With this book Strauss proclaimed that the *supernatural elements of the gospel history were unhistorical '*myth'. In this same year appeared Peter von Bohlen's (1796–1840) commentary on Genesis and Wilhelm Vatke's (1806–82) *Biblischen Theologie*, both of which demonstrated that Strauss's non-supernatural approach could also be applied to the OT. These works evoked a flood of literature dealing with the Bible and its reliability. In the forefront came the *Tübingen School, which from a non-supernatural theological and historical perspective examined the history of the early church and determined the dating and authorship of each book according to its own particular 'tendency'. The Gospels were all pronounced to be productions of the second century, and apart from Romans, 1 and 2 Corinthians, Galatians and Revelation, no book was authentic.

In the realm of the OT came the documentary theory in which the Pentateuch was divided up into at least four different sources or documents, all thought to have originated at different times several centuries after Moses. This hypothesis was fully developed by Karl Heinrich Graf (1815–69), Abraham Kuenen (1828–91) and Julius Wellhausen (1844–1918), who brought it to its dominant position at the end of the nineteenth century.

Implicitly underlying the whole critical investigation of the Bible was the idealistic philosophy which developed from the Enlightenment in the second half of the eighteenth century and culminated in the writings of J. G. Herder (1744–1803), *Hegel, J. G. *Fichte, F. W. J. von Schelling (1775–1854) and J. W. von Goethe (1749–1832). God was conceived as an Absolute Spirit manifested in many different forms and ways, but chiefly as immanent in nature and revealed in history and humanity. This *revelation was thought of as a general revelation throughout history in all peoples and cultures, and not as special and miraculous revelation to one particular nation, i.e. Israel. Thus the Jewish religion was regarded simply as one natural religion among others, its myths and folklore parallel to that of other primitive cultures, with its development from simple beginnings to a complex priestly cultus following a pattern which could be traced more or less clearly in the history and culture of every nation. And just as the Tübingen School had fitted the NT books into Baur's historical perspective, so the OT scholars fitted the literature of Israel into this evolutionary scheme of religion, determining the date and provenance of every part and section according to how its 'tendency' best fitted into the predetermined historical and religious framework.

Following Strauss's *Life of Jesus* came a host of other works of the same genre, each advocating the author's own interpretation of Jesus' life – G. H. A. von Ewald's (1803–75) rationalistic portrayal (1855), K. T. Keim's (1825–78) tedious three-volume account (1867–72), Strauss's *New Life of Jesus* (1864), and J. E. Renan's (1823–92) sentimental embellishment (1863) – to name only the most widely read. By the 1880s these and a host of lesser works were being eagerly translated into English. In Great Britain it was primarily this scholarship which was regarded as liberal. Only in the 1880s and 1890s did liberalism come to possess the narrower sense originating with *Ritschlian theology.

In the 1880s the Ritschlian school became the dominant influence in the realm of dogmatics, and it was the liberalism of this school which largely determined non-orthodox theology until the First World War. For Ritschl the *kingdom of God was an ethical and moral kingdom which would develop and grow to maturity, with Jesus as the great example for humanity to follow. Sin was not the radical evil of the will, but rather ignorance which could be corrected by moral upbringing and education. For Ritschl's pupil W. *Herrmann, the portrait of Jesus contained in the Gospels provided man with the example to which he himself should aspire. For A. *Harnack, Jesus himself did not even belong in the gospel: 'Not the Son, but the Father only, belongs in the gospel, as Jesus proclaimed it.' For others Jesus was merely a great moral teacher who taught a purely ethical kingdom of goodness, kindness, tolerance and love for one's neighbour. His death was regarded not as an atonement for sin – that was a relic of primitive Judaism – but as a wonderful example of moral fortitude and resolution. Above all, liberalism desired an undogmatic form of Christianity, free from the constricting trammels of the traditional doctrines and creeds, while still retaining an outward vestige which might pass for orthodoxy.

Such was the essence of German liberalism at the turn of the nineteenth century. There were other movements which denied the authenticity of the Scriptures, such as the *history-of-religions school, but these were not necessarily identified with the doctrinal liberalism of the Ritschlians. For the orthodox, however, who regarded all non-orthodox literature as liberal, unbelieving or atheistic, fine distinctions between these various viewpoints were not of great significance.

Two main causes led to the decline of theological liberalism in Germany. The first was the onslaught of the rationalists during the decade preceding the First World War. Led by Albert Kalthoff (1850–1906) and Arthur Drews (1865–1935), who argued that Jesus had never lived, the rationalists regarded the liberal view of Jesus as a compromise between the supernatural Jesus of orthodoxy and their own rationalistic explanations. Either one or the other, but not half and half! Thus ensued a long and acrimonious controversy in which many flaws in the liberal viewpoint were exposed.

The second cause was the First World War itself, which shattered the liberal idea of a civilization growing upwards in goodness and perfection. It became evident that the world was not getting better. The evil which was laid bare struck a mortal blow against the old liberal idea that evil was only ignorance which might be corrected by education. After the war came Karl *Barth, who radically opposed the pre-war liberal theology, and proclaimed that the God of the Bible must not be confused with human ideas about God. Yet while it is true that doctrinal liberalism received a severe check, liberalism in biblical scholarship continued unabated in the demythologization (see *Myth) programmes of the *Bultmannians. Doctrinal liberalism also took new forms in major thinkers such as *Tillich, who continued the apologetic intention of the German liberal tradition to commend 'religion' to its 'cultured despisers' and helped to make it dominant for a time in America. By the end of the twentieth century, however, the liberal tradition, aiming to correlate theology with 'modern' thought, appeared to many to be outmoded by the rise of '*postmodernism'.

Bibliography

A. I. C. Heron, *A Century of Protestant Theology* (Guildford and London, 1980); H. R. Mackintosh, *Types of Modern Theology: Schleiermacher to Barth* (London, 1937); B. M. G. Reardon, *Liberal Protestantism* (London, 1968); C. Welch, *Protestant Thought in the Nineteenth Century, vol. 1: 1799–1870* (New Haven, and London, 1972).

H. HARRIS

LIBERATION THEOLOGY

The name 'Liberation theology' was first coined by Catholic theologians from Latin America in the 1970s. Their initial vision of theology as a way of reflecting on the Christian faith 'from the perspective of the poor' was adopted by a variety of theological movements such as *Black, Hispanic and Amerindian theologies in the United States, anti-apartheid theologies in Africa, and *feminist theologies elsewhere. In its origins, the concept of 'liberation' had political and cultural connotations reflecting the revolutionary attempts radically to change the social structures in Latin America following the Cuban revolution (1959). As some Catholic clergy, bishops and lay people adopted that revolutionary stance, when they reflected about their faith they found biblical and historical motifs that related to it. According to Gutiérrez, 'The theology of liberation offers us not so much a new theme for reflection as a *new way* to do theology. Theology as critical reflection on historical *praxis*' (*A Theology of Liberation*, 1988, p. 12). Theology becomes a second act after Christians make a political choice and act accordingly. From that perspective every theology is also to be understood as a product of historical circumstances.

Historical context

Latin American nations became independent from Iberian colonialism between 1810 and 1824. The Roman Catholic Church, which had been imposed through military conquest, was a key component of the colonial structure and *scholastic theology provided an ideological explanation for the role of Christians in society. The modern creed of the independence leaders taken from the French and American revolutions was condemned by the church, which remained as a conservative force. Scholastic theology became irrelevant to the cultural life of these societies and unable to stand the onslaught of *positivism in the nineteenth century and *Marxism in the twentieth. In the early nineteenth century *Protestantism arrived in Latin America and saw itself as a transformative force in society, its theology being more akin to the ideas of liberalization, democracy and progress. However, Latin American theologies of liberation have been predominantly a Roman Catholic phenomenon that emerged as an outcome of transformative processes within that church.

The first conference of bishops (CELAM I, 1955) in Rio de Janeiro opened doors for Catholic missionaries from Europe and North America to help the church that felt threatened by the growth of communism and Protestantism. The new wave of missionaries after the Second World War became concerned with the social conditions and the decline of the church, and though at first influenced by the anti-communist stance of the Cold War, their encounter with the appalling conditions of the poor brought a change of mission practice in a twofold direction. Europeans applied social analysis to understand church and society, and North Americans became activists in a variety of grassroots actions for the poor. Their approach coincided with the change of political outlook and alignment of Catholic lay leaders, especially those related to the Catholic Action movement of workers and students, such as Brazilian Paulo Freire (1921–97). Active involvement in these processes was part of the formative experience of theologians such as Juan Luis Segundo (1925–96) from Uruguay and Gustavo *Gutiérrez from Peru. Their ideas became influential at the time of the second Conference of Bishops in Medellín, Colombia (CELAM II, 1968), which was an effort to apply *Vatican II to Latin America. Key concepts and vocabulary of these theologians were adopted by the hierarchy in the final documents they issued, and the church called her new position a 'preferential option for the poor'.

According to Gutiérrez, liberation theology came as reflection on that new practice, but it was to be done 'in light of God's Word'. The French Bible-centred pastoral renewal was influential in many of the missionary priests from Europe, and the use of biblical scholarship and biblical categories also became a new source of theological reflection within Catholic circles, as a result of Vatican II. Influential theologians such as Marie-Dominique Chenu (1895–1990), Yves *Congar, Johannes Baptist *Metz and Karl *Rahner had pioneered an approach sanctioned later by *Conciliar decrees. This placed the Bible as the chief source of theology, and as the centre of the curriculum for the training of priests. In the use of biblical material and motifs, theologians of liberation that represented this new moment in Catholicism were Severino Croatto (1930–2004), Leonardo *Boff, and Porfirio Miranda (1924–2001).

There was also interaction between Catholic liberation theologians and some Latin American Protestants related to the *ecumenical movement, such as Emilio Castro (b. 1927) from Uruguay, José *Míguez Bonino from Argentina and Rubem Alves (1933–2014) from Brazil, all of whom adopted liberation perspectives. In 1978 Alan Neely surveyed Protestant antecedents of liberation theologies, one of them being the study carried out by the WCC about churches in situations of rapid social change, which reached its peak in a conference about 'Christians in the Technical and Social Revolutions of Our Time' (Geneva 1966). The theological contributions of Harvey Cox (b. 1929), Paul Lehmann (1906–94) and Jürgen *Moltmann were influential in this process. It was understood that unjust structures and oppression in society had a dehumanizing effect contrary to God's design, and that God's action in history was aimed at humanization, 'to make and to keep human life human'. Consequently, Christians were called to take part in the historical process of the twentieth century, in which revolution represented the cutting edge of humanization. This agenda was to be implemented by the movement Church and Society in Latin America (ISAL), which first publicized the writings of Rubem Alves, Paulo Freire and Richard Shaull (1919–2002). Alves' book *A Theology of Human Hope* (1969) represents a Latin American interpretation of Barth, Bultmann, Cox, Lehmann and Moltmann that preceded by two years the original Spanish edition of the classical book of Gustavo Gutiérrez, *A Theology of Liberation* (1971, ET 1973).

Theological method

Both Míguez Bonino (1975) and Gutiérrez (1988) in their classic overviews emphasize the fact that for liberation theology the starting point is the committed action of the Christian people. In this theological itinerary, Christians first perceive God moving in *history to bring liberation for the poor (see *Poverty and wealth), and consequently throw their lot with him in obedience; secondly, they go to Scripture or to Christian tradition in order to read, understand and expound the Christian faith. Only from the ground of commitment does one have access to the reality of biblical truth, because, as Míguez Bonino says, 'There is no truth outside or beyond the concrete historical events in which men are involved as agents. There is, therefore, no knowledge except in action itself, in the process of transforming the world through participation in history' (*Doing Theology in a Revolutionary Situation*, 1975, p. 88). Croatto argues that this corresponds to a pattern found in the Bible itself, in which the biblical message wells up from the salvific happening. This determines a method in which 'I do not first carry out an exegesis of the biblical passage and subsequently relate it to the facts of our world or our oppressed continent. Rather, the facts must be and are prior to my interpretation of the biblical Word' (*Exodus: A Hermeneutics of Freedom*, 1981, p. 11).

For these theologians, in Latin America *praxis* meant involvement in the cause of social and political liberation as defined by a Marxist analysis of history and of social reality. In 1975 Míguez Bonino stated that 'the thought of these men is characterized by a strict scientific-ideological analysis, avowedly Marxist. This is clearly seen in their way of relating *praxis* and theory and in their insistence on the rationality, conflict and radical nature of the political realm. It can also be seen in the recognition of class struggle' (*Doing Theology*, p. 71). Therefore Marxism offered a tool for social analysis and a view of history permeated by a messianic and eschatological bent involving what Míguez Bonino called 'a certain discernment of the future' (ibid., p. 35). Class struggle was the key to understanding current social reality, and the coming of an end to that struggle was to be achieved in the classless society that revolution would bring. Gutiérrez, Míguez Bonino and Hugo Assman (1933–2008) were explicitly critical of *capitalism, and rejected political options that could be described as 'developmentalism', 'reformism' or a third way between Marxist socialism and capitalism. Gutiérrez stated, 'The goal is not only better living conditions, a radical change of structures, a social revolution; it is much more: the continuous creation, never ending, of a new way to be human, a permanent cultural revolution' (*Theology of Liberation*, 1988, p. 21).

The use of Marxism in liberation theology has been criticized by Catholics such as James V. Schall and Michael Novak, and by evangelicals such as Emilio Núñez and others. This was also the main thrust of official criticism from the Vatican in the Instructions of the Sacred Congregation for the Doctrine of the Faith (1984, 1986), issued by Cardinal Joseph *Ratzinger. In response to it some liberation theologians clarified and refined their position. In his responses to criticism from the Vatican, Gustavo Gutiérrez was explicit about the limits he had set to his own use of Marxism. He argued that some Marxist elements were part of the social sciences used for analysis, and he pointed to the fact that CELAM in their assemblies of Medellín and Puebla did the same: 'Social analysis has been a resource in order to know a situation and not for the study of matters considered more strictly theological' (Gutiérrez, 1984, p. 83).

The collapse of the socialist world symbolized by the fall of the Berlin wall in 1989 affected the validity of the Marxist theoretical construct that had guided the liberation theology method. However, the rise of neo-liberalism and a new world order shaped by it did not bring an end to poverty and injustice in the world. Even in Latin America the context from which liberation theologies had risen continues to be a challenge to the Christian conscience. The most recent work of Gutiérrez in his massive book, *Las Casas: In Search of the Poor of Jesus Christ* (1993), studies the development of the theology of *mission that backed the Spanish conquest of America and contrasts it with the theology of the Dominican Bartolomé de las Casas that proposed a different missionary approach. It is an effort to prove that liberation theology is in line with a form of theology that has been present in Christian history, and that it is not an outcome of Marxism. Theologians such as José Comblin and Leonardo Boff have continued to work along similar lines.

Liberation theologies outside Latin America emphasized the common situation of oppression in their origins, but in some cases dismissed the use of Marxism. Thus Black American theologian J. Deotis Roberts (b. 1927) says that 'It is rather easy for black theologians to enter into dialogue with Latin American liberation theologians because both are tuned in on an oppressed human situation' (*A Black Political Theology*, 1974, pp. 205–206). But he also contrasts the Catholic milieu, the reaction against totalitarian governments and the influence of Marxism in Latin America, with the context of Black theology which is mainly Protestant, comes from a pluralistic society, and faces the specific question of *race. Moreover, 'Black theologians are not bound by church dogmas; neither do they seek church approval for their reflection' (ibid., p. 207). Roberts also emphasizes the intense and lively spirituality of the Black church within which Black theology was born and the North American experience of reconciliation to which it was related.

Theologies from other cultures have taken cues from liberation theologies but have also criticized it. Aloysius Pieris, a Jesuit from Sri Lanka, stresses the validity of the great religions and rejects the Marxist criticism of religion. For him, 'This Afro-Asian critique of Marxist occidentalism is also an implicit judgment on the militant stream of Latin American theology, which maintains a methodological continuity with Western Marxism and a cultural continuity with European theology' (in V. Fabella and S. Torres, *Irruption of the Third World*, 1983, p. 119). On the other hand, in his book *Mañana* (1990), historian Justo L. González (b. 1937) articulated a Christian theology from a Hispanic perspective in the United States. Using perceptions from liberation theologies, he stresses the *contextual nature of every theology and the need to make room for perspectives that come from minorities that are not always given a voice in the dialogue within the churches and the academic world. From an intentional evangelical stance, Orlando Costas (1942–87) offered a similar reflection in *Liberating News* (1989).

Some key themes

What comes closer to a systematic exposition of liberation theology is the book *Mysterium Liberationis* (1993), edited by Ignacio Ellacuría and Jon Sobrino. Its method and hermeneutical approach are better perceived in some of the themes that have been privileged by these

Liberation theology

theologians: poverty and Christian *praxis*, Christology and history. Christian *praxis*, which is the starting point of doing theology, is to be understood with help from the social sciences. The so-called 'option for the poor' taken by some Catholics in Latin America is seen as a pastoral and political alignment, because biblical categories cannot be applied to our contemporary situation without the mediation of the social sciences. 'The poor' is not a vague term, but it points out to the existence of social classes and social struggles. For Gutiérrez, 'Poor and oppressed people are members of a social class which is overtly or covertly exploited by another social class. The proletariat is simply the most belligerent and clear-cut segment of this exploited social class' (in R. Gibellini [ed.], *Frontiers of Theology in Latin America*, 1979, p. 8). The poverty of the poor demands a new *praxis*, which rather than engaging in acts of generosity to alleviate their plight, must be 'a compelling obligation to fashion an entirely different social order' (ibid., p. 8).

The *hermeneutics of liberation theologies may be better perceived in their Christological and ecclesiological proposals. The *Christology of Jon Sobrino, from Spain and El Salvador, intentionally starts from the biblical text rather than from the dogmatic statements of the church, and seeks to focus on the historical Jesus in order to provide a basis for Christian action: 'The course that Jesus took is to be investigated scientifically, not just to aid in the quest for truth but also in the fight for truth that will make people free' (*Christology at the Crossroads: A Latin American Approach*, 1978, p. 35). Reading the texts of the Gospels, with due attention to their social and political context, Sobrino emphasizes the political dimension of the death of Jesus as the historical outcome of the kind of life he lived, and his suffering for the cause of justice which becomes the central challenge for discipleship today. Accepting the validity of this approach, which provides a fresh understanding of the biblical text, René Padilla (b. 1932) has criticized it for overemphasizing the political significance of Jesus' death and not paying enough attention to its soteriological significance, which is also an important part of the text (in V. Samuel and C. Sugden, *Sharing Jesus in the Two Thirds World*, p. 28).

An *ecclesiology carrying the logic of liberation theologies was explored especially by the Brazilian, Leonardo Boff, who has tried to articulate the experience of the basic Christian communities, the grassroots small groups in which poor people started to revive their Catholic faith, relating it to their daily experience in Latin America. For Boff 'A true "ecclesiogenesis" is in progress throughout the world, a Church being born from the faith of the poor' (*Church: Charisma and Power*, 1985, p. 9). The concept of the church as the people of God that was emphasized in Vatican II, has been an incentive for new pastoral practices, but according to Boff, 'true ecclesiology is not the result of textbook analysis or theoretical hypothesis; it comes about as a result of ecclesial practices within the institution' (ibid., p. 1). Boff has been very critical of hierarchical authoritarianism and clericalism that he sees practised in the Catholic Church, and proposes 'new ministries and a new style of religious life incarnated in the life of the people' (ibid., p. 10). He argues that the key elements in his proposals that come from *praxis* are characteristics of the model of church life that we also find in the NT, and on the basis of the biblical data he questions some dogmatic assumptions.

The new way of understanding history derived its critical dynamism from the Marxist concept. Application of class analysis and emphasis on the social role played by the institutional churches brought a new reading of their history that had a shocking effect, especially when used for a critical understanding of missionary action within the frame of European imperial expansion after the sixteenth century. From that perspective both Catholic and Protestant missionary work has been criticized, provoking what Míguez Bonino calls a crisis of conscience 'when Christians discover that their churches have become the ideological allies of foreign and national forces that keep the countries in dependence and the people in slavery and need'(*Doing Theology*, p. 17). Historians who have adopted the liberation perspective, such as Enrique Dussel (b. 1934) from Argentina and Eduardo Hoornaert (b. 1930) from Brazil, have modified the Marxist view, turning it more into a new outlook 'from the perspective of the poor' (Dussel, 1981; Hoornaert, 1988).

What Gutiérrez calls the 'irruption of the poor' would be part of the general movement of history towards *liberation* in which he distinguishes three levels: 'liberation from social situations of oppression and marginalization', 'a personal transformation by which we live with profound inner freedom in the face of every kind of servitude', and 'liberation from sin, which attacks the deepest root of all servitude' (*Theology of Liberation*, p. xxxviii). In other theologians, awareness about the irruption of the poor in history has become part of the agenda of a theology of the Christian mission that must interpret the significance of the growth and flourishing of the Christian faith in the southern hemisphere parallel to the decline of Christendom in Europe. It brings to the debate the *eschatological question which for Gutiérrez has been expressed in his insistence upon the concept that there is no sacred history within a world history, but only *one history* 'one human destiny, irreversibly assumed by Christ the Lord of history' (ibid., p. 86).

The publication of a revised edition of the classic work of Gustavo Gutiérrez, fifteen years after the first, was an occasion to see the wide repercussions of this theology around the world, and the form in which it has been incorporated in a variety of church and missionary situations. Within Protestantism there were efforts to demonstrate that in spite of its Catholic origins liberation theologies incorporate some of the main tenets of the Protestant Reformation, but there are also critical approaches, coming especially from evangelicals, that point to important and insurmountable differences.

See also: ROMAN CATHOLIC THEOLOGY; REVOLUTION, THEOLOGY OF.

Bibliography

R. Alves, *A Theology of Human Hope* (St. Meinrad, 1969); L. Boff, *Church: Charisma and Power: Liberation Theology and the Institutional Church* (New York, 1985); J. M. Bonino, *Doing Theology in a Revolutionary Situation* (London and Philadelphia, 1975); J. Comblin, *Called for Freedom: The Changing Context of Liberation Theology* (Maryknoll, 1998); O. E. Costas, *Liberating News: A Theology of Contextual Evangelization* (Grand Rapids, 1989); J. S. Croatto, *Exodus: A Hermeneutics of Freedom* (Maryknoll, 1981); E. Dussel (ed.), *The Church in Latin America 1492–1992* (London, 1992); I. Ellacuria and J. Sobrino (eds.), *Mysterium Liberationis* (Maryknoll, 1993); M. H. Ellis and O. Maduro (eds.), *The Future of Liberation Theology: Essays in Honor of Gustavo Gutiérrez* (Maryknoll, 1989); S. Escobar, *Changing Tides* (Maryknoll, 2002); *idem*, *Liberation Themes in Reformational Perspective* (Sioux College, 1989); V. Fabella M. M. and S. Torres (eds.), *Irruption of the Third World* (Maryknoll, 1983); R. Gibellini (ed.), *Frontiers of Theology in Latin America* (Maryknoll, 1979); J. L. González and O. González, *Christianity in Latin America: A History* (Cambridge, 2008); G. Gutiérrez, *We Drink from Our Own Wells: The Spiritual Journey of a People* (Maryknoll, 1984); *idem*, *A Theology of Liberation*, rev. edn (Maryknoll, ²1988); *idem*, *The Truth Shall Make You Free* (Maryknoll, 1990); E. Hoornaert, *The Memory of the Christian People* (Maryknoll, 1988); A. P. Neely, *Protestant Antecedents of the Latin American Theology of Liberation*, Thesis, American University, Washington (Ann Arbor, 1977); M. Novak, *Will It Liberate? Questions about Liberation Theology* (New York, 1986); E. A. Núñez C., *Liberation Theology* (Chicago, 1985); J. D. Roberts, *A Black Political Theology* (Philadelphia, 1974); Sacred Congregation for the Doctrine of the Faith, *Instruction on Certain Aspects of the 'Theology of Liberation'* (Boston, 1984); *idem*, *Instruction on Christian Freedom and Liberation* (Boston, 1986); V. Samuel and C. Sugden (eds.), *Sharing Jesus in the Two Thirds World* (Grand Rapids, 1983); J. V. Schall SJ, *Liberation Theology in Latin America* (San Francisco, 1982); D. S. Schipani (ed.), *Freedom and Discipleship: Liberation Theology in Anabaptist Perspective* (Maryknoll, 1989); P. E. Sigmund, *Liberation Theology at the Crossroads* (New York, 1990); C. Smith, *The Emergence of Liberation Theology: Radical Religion and Social Movement Theory* (Chicago, 1991); J. Sobrino, *Christology at the Crossroads: A Latin American Approach* (Maryknoll, 1978); R. S. Sugirtharajah (ed.), *Voices from the Margin: Interpreting the Bible in the Third World* (Maryknoll, 1991).

S. ESCOBAR

LIMBUS

In Roman Catholic theology this word (Lat. *limbus*, 'order, hem, edge') denotes the region on the border of hell thought to be inhabited by those who do not experience the pangs of hell or the joys of heaven (or *purgatory). On this view *limbus* (cf. Eng. 'limbo') is the abode of two categories of the dead. (1) Those who on earth never gained the use of reason and were not baptized, whether infants (*limbus infantium*, 'the limbo of infants') or the mentally incompetent. Although they were innocent of personal *guilt, their original sin had not been removed by *baptism. According to Pope Innocent III (1160–1216), the punishment of original sin is deprivation of the beatific vision of God. Some writers maintain that such infants are in some way conscious of their permanent exclusion from eternal beatitude; others believe that they are unaware of this loss or are in a state of natural happiness such as Adam enjoyed before the *fall. (2) OT saints prior to their liberation by Christ on his '*descent into hell' and their ascent into heaven (see *Eschatology) (*limbus patrum*, 'the limbo of the fathers', sometimes referred to as *sinus Abrahae*, 'Abraham's bosom', based on Luke 16:22). In 2007, Pope Benedict XVI (see *Ratzinger, Josef) authorized the publication of a report by a commission which allowed that there were grounds for hope that unbaptized infants would be saved and that 'the theory of limbo' was a 'possible theological hypothesis' rather than a formal 'dogmatic definition' of the *Roman Catholic Church.

Bibliography

P. Gumpel, 'Limbo', *SM* III, p. 319; International Theological Commission, *The Hope of Salvation for Infants Who Die without Being Baptised* (Rome, 2007).

M. J. Harris

LINDBECK, GEORGE (b. 1923)

George Lindbeck is an American Lutheran theologian, who until 1993 taught at Yale University. After attending the Second *Vatican Council as an observer, he became a prominent commentator on Roman Catholicism and a prolific contributor to *ecumenical debates. Although he is most often mentioned in connection with the rise of *postliberal theology, his work in that regard was largely a by-product of his ecumenical work.

In *The Nature of Doctrine* (1984), Lindbeck asked what account of doctrine would make sense of ecumenical debates in which long-separated partners reached doctrinal agreements, and yet claimed to remain faithful adherents of traditions that had previously found each others' views unacceptable. He rejected both the 'cognitive-propositional' view that sees doctrinal statements as straightforward factual claims, and the 'experiential-expressive' view that sees them as the expressions of one's religious consciousness. He suggested instead that religions or denominations should be seen as analogous to communities with distinctive languages, and doctrinal statements as analogous to grammatical rules for these languages – a view he dubbed the 'cultural-linguistic' approach.

Controversially, Lindbeck claimed that doctrinal statements need not be understood as themselves making direct truth claims. Rather, it is the lives that are governed by doctrinal rules that should be thought of as truth-claiming. So the Nicene *Creed's claim that the Father and the Son are of one substance is not itself a direct claim about the being of God. Rather, it states a rule for Christian life, insisting that all Christian practices that refer to the Father must treat him as the Father of Jesus Christ. Nevertheless, Lindbeck claims that lives governed by this and other doctrinal rules do indeed witness truly to God.

According to this view, the conceptual vocabulary used in a doctrinal statement is not necessarily crucial. The Nicene Creed, for example, does not mandate the adoption of substance metaphysics. Doctrinal statements that employ very different conceptualities and appear to be at variance can be found in ecumenical debate to encode identical or similar rules.

Much of Lindbeck's later work argued that Christian reading of Scripture should be guided by a new doctrinal rule: it should avoid all *supersessionism in which the church is read as the fulfilment of which the people of Israel was the shadow. Rather, the church and Israel should be seen as two forms of the people of God, and Jesus Christ as the true fulfilment to which they both point. The church is, for Lindbeck, a transformative movement witnessing to this fulfilment in Christ within a people of God now made up of Jew and Gentile; it has not taken Israel's place as the recipient of God's promises.

Bibliography

Works: *The Nature of Doctrine* (Philadelphia, 1984); 'The Story-Shaped Church', in G. Green (ed.), *Scriptural Authority and Narrative Interpretation* (Philadelphia, 1987); *The Church in a Postliberal Age*, ed. J. J. Buckley (Grand Rapids and Cambridge, 2002).

Studies: M. A. Higton, 'Reconstructing the Nature of Doctrine', *Modern Theology* 30 (2014), pp. 1–31; B. D. Marshall (ed.), *Theology and Dialogue* (Notre Dame, 1990); P. Ochs, 'George Lindbeck and the Church as Israel', in *Another Reformation* (Grand Rapids, 2011), pp. 36–62; T. R. Phillips and D. L. Okholm (eds.), *The Nature of Confession* (Downers Grove, 1996).

M. HIGTON

LITURGICAL THEOLOGY

Although the concept has always probably existed in liturgical churches (those which use settled forms of corporate *worship, including settled forms of the spoken texts), liturgical theology has attracted wider interest only during the last half-century, owing to the growing interest in liturgy itself. It is an attempt to provide a theological interpretation of traditional forms of liturgy, not merely a devotional or historical interpretation, and to understand what theological significance has been attached by Christians to the liturgy they have offered. More specialized than the theology of worship in general (which includes non-liturgical worship), it also follows a different method. It begins not from the Bible, tracing the development (good and bad) of biblical principles in and from historical practice, but from historical practice, examining how, and how far, this can be understood in terms of biblical principles. In addition, it explores the relationships between liturgical worship and dogmatic theology.

The primitivist view that Christian worship should as far as possible reproduce NT practice unchanged allows no validity to the historical development of worship, and therefore none to liturgical theology. The *Lutheran, *Anglican and (to some extent) Calvinist (see *Reformed theology) approach is different, however, taking history seriously and making allowance for changed conditions, but seeking fully to implement biblical principles in the context of those changed conditions. On this view, the development (for example) of daily services, services for marriage and burial, particular texts for these services and others, and a calendar of annual festivals, is not invalidated merely by showing that they did not exist in biblical times, but only by showing that they do not accord with biblical principles.

Jewish synagogue practice of the first century, in which Jesus and his disciples shared, appears to have included many features which neither go back to the OT nor are mentioned in the NT. It is this pattern of worship which was refashioned but not abolished by the impact of the *gospel, and evolved into historic Christian practice. Its origins, therefore, are good, and, just as it is the true task of liturgical revision to reform it by the teaching of the Bible, so it is the task of liturgical theology to interpret it by the teaching of the Bible, in order that it may be understood and used in the most edifying way.

See also: DOXOLOGY; LITURGY.

Bibliography

J. J. von Allmen, *Worship: Its Theology and Practice* (ET, London, 1965); S. Chan, *Liturgical Theology* (Downers Grove, 2006); D. Fagerberg, *Theologia Prima: What Is Liturgical Theology?* (Mundelein, 2004); A. Kavanagh, *On Liturgical Theology* (New York, 1984); A. Schmemann, *Introduction to Liturgical Theology* (ET, London, 1966); G. Wainwright, *Doxology: A Systematic Theology* (London, 1980).

R. T. BECKWITH

LITURGY

Inheritors of the Reformation have lived with a commonly held distinction between 'liturgical' worship and 'free' worship. Typically, this distinction marked the difference between those churches that relied upon centrally agreed liturgical texts (e.g. Roman Catholicism, Anglicanism and Orthodoxy) and churches that were free to generate their own local orders of worship (e.g. Congregational and Baptist). This distinction continues to shape contemporary discussions, for example in the way that charismatic worship is often portrayed as 'free' in comparison with the 'liturgical' worship of the historic denominations. However, maintaining a sharp distinction between these two terms has become increasingly difficult. One of the fruits of the ecumenical conversations fostered by the twentieth-century liturgical movement has been the recognition that free worship has liturgical habits, such as various forms of repetition and the often unacknowledged deep patterns within public worship. Similarly, liturgical worship is more than a recitation of a 'text' and may contain a considerable amount of flexibility (such as the directions to those who lead intercessory prayer to use set or 'other suitable words').

The word 'liturgy' is derived from the Greek *leitourgia* which referred to the work of the citizens' assembly in the ancient Greek city states, particularly Athens, where it connoted the representative task of citizen-legislators. It was a term that described 'good works' done for the benefit of the wider community. *Leitourgia* was used in the LXX to describe the service of OT priests and Levites, and it also came to be used of Christian acts of worship, especially the *Eucharist. Eastern Orthodox churches have retained this tradition and use the term 'the Liturgy' to refer specifically to the Eucharist. However, the term is used more generally to refer to the action of public worship as 'the work of the people'. This frames the practice of public worship, which will include varying degrees of set forms of words and actions, as primarily an activity of the *church in service to God and also for the world. As such, 'at the heart of liturgy is an understanding of public worship that goes beyond the personal encounter with God (without denying it) to the corporate drama of being the people of God' (M. Earey, *Liturgical Worship*, p. 18). The importance of liturgical patterns for the church can be summarized under three headings:

Liturgy and the Bible

There is a very close relationship between the Bible and the worshipping assembly; the NT letters, for example, were written in order to be read aloud in the receiving churches. Liturgy helps the church engage with the Bible at a number of levels. The public reading of the Bible has been traditionally organized by the use of a lectionary (designated Bible passages ['lections'] ordered according to each Sunday or weekday). This allows exposure to the breadth of the biblical message. A sermon focuses the congregational response to the Bible reading. The Bible also informs the language of prayer used by the church, the most obvious example being the ancient tradition of incorporating psalms in public worship, which may be used for congregational song or in responses (such as 'O Lord open our lips'; R: 'And our mouth shall proclaim your praise', Ps. 51:15).

Liturgy and tradition

Liturgy is a vital carrier of tradition, the practices and associated beliefs that centre the church upon God's loving action in Christ. *Baptism and Eucharist (also known as Holy Communion, Mass, the Breaking of Bread or the Lord's Supper) are the two most prominent practices of the tradition. The term 'ordinance', preferred by some Christians, roots the regular practice of the welcoming of new Christians and celebration of the gift of Christ at the table in faithful obedience to the command of Christ (Matt. 28:19 and 1 Cor. 11:23–25); the alternative term '*sacrament' locates these practices in the gift of God, who creates and sustains the church in and through Christ by the Spirit.

Liturgy and doctrine

The public assembly is the place where the content of the Christian vision of God is embodied and affirmed. The Orthodox tradition has affirmed that all true theology is 'doxology'; the term 'orthodoxy' means giving right glory to God. One obvious example of this is the inclusion of creedal formulae in liturgy. The Apostles' *Creed was used originally by baptismal candidates as an affirmation of faith, and the *Nicene Creed was introduced into worship after the fourth century as a way of countering the continuing threat of Arianism. In worshipping traditions that have not used creeds, such as the Nonconformists, the doctrinal content of the faith is very often celebrated in congregational song. When John Wesley wrote his 'Preface' to the first Methodist hymn book in 1779, he declared that the book 'is large enough to contain all the important truths of our most holy religion'.

See also: DOXOLOGY; LITURGICAL THEOLOGY; WORSHIP.

Bibliography

S. Burns, *SCM Study Guide to Liturgy* (London, 2006); M. Earey, *Liturgical Worship: A Fresh Look, How It Works, Why It Matters* (London, 2002); C. Ellis, *Gathering: A Theology and Spirituality of Worship in Free Church Worship* (London, 2004); J. R. K. Fenwick and B. D. Spinks, *Worship in Transition: The Liturgical Movement in the Twentieth Century* (Edinburgh, 1995); M. C. Ross, *Evangelical Versus Liturgical? Defying a Dichotomy* (Grand Rapids, 2014); F. C. Senn, *Introduction to Christian Liturgy* (Philadelphia, 2012); J. H. S. Steven, *Worship in the Spirit: Charismatic Worship in the Church of England* (Paternoster, 2002).

J. H. S. STEVEN

LLOYD-JONES, DAVID MARTYN (1899–1981)

Although born in Wales, Lloyd-Jones completed his education at Marylebone Grammar School and St Bartholomew's Hospital, London. A distinguished career as a physician lay before him when, after severe inner struggle, he committed himself to the Christian ministry in 1926. Following a notable pastorate at Aberavon (1927–38), he was called as colleague and then successor to G. Campbell Morgan (1863–1945) at Westminster Chapel, London. He played an early leadership role in the Inter-Varsity Fellowship (now UCCF) and was also involved in the founding of such new evangelical agencies as the Evangelical Library, the London Bible College and the International Fellowship of Evangelical Students.

While he gave much time to helping students, ministers and missionaries, the pulpit was Lloyd-Jones's most important work. By authoritative exposition and application of the Scriptures he sought to restore the true nature of *preaching, rejecting the prevalent opinion that scientific knowledge had outmoded commitment to the inerrancy of Scripture (see *Infallibility). He saw faith in the word of God and dependence upon the Holy Spirit as the foremost needs in contemporary Christianity, and regarded human unbelief as moral rather than intellectual (see his *Truth Unchanged, Unchanging*, London, 1951). He reintroduced consecutive expository preaching, with subsequent publications on *The Sermon on the Mount* (London, 1959–60), *Ephesians* (Edinburgh, 1974–82), *II Peter* (Edinburgh, 1983) and *Romans* (London and Edinburgh, 1970–). But the majority of his preaching was evangelistic as he itinerated constantly for over fifty years (including Europe and the United States in summer vacations). Thoroughly committed to *Calvinistic Methodism, Lloyd-Jones's ministry did not harmonize with the prevailing religious ethos in Wales or England, and while constantly helping many evangelical agencies, his convictions on the importance of *Reformed theology kept him from any full identification. He was, however, closely involved with a resurgence of interest in Reformed theology commenced through the IVF, the Puritan Conferences and the Banner of Truth Trust (subsequently to be his principal publisher).

In his later years, faced with a general decline of Christianity in England, Lloyd-Jones called for the priority of evangelical unity above denominational loyalties. He did not propose a new denomination, but urged the importance of the true unity of churches (which he hoped to see expressed in the British Evangelical Council) and warned that evangelical neutrality to the *ecumenical movement was contributing to the spread of low views on saving faith.

Resigning from Westminster Chapel in 1968, he remained active in preaching and in the preparation of sermons for publication until shortly before his death. By his preaching and books he profoundly influenced the whole English-speaking world, as one who stood in the tradition of the Reformers and *Puritans, *Whitefield, *Edwards and *Spurgeon. Emil *Brunner once described him as 'the greatest preacher in Christendom today'.

Bibliography

With the works above, *Preaching and Preachers* (London, 1971) gives invaluable insight into his views of the ministry. **Biography**: C. Catherwood (ed.), *Chosen by God* (Crowborough, 1986); I. H. Murray, *D. Martyn Lloyd-Jones: The First Forty Years, 1899–1939* (Edinburgh, 1982); idem, *D. Martyn Lloyd-Jones: The Fight of Faith, 1939–1981* (Edinburgh, 1990).

Studies: A. Atherstone and D. Ceri Jones (eds.), *Engaging with Martyn Lloyd-Jones* (Nottingham, 2011); J. Brencher, *Martyn Lloyd-Jones (1899–1981) and Twentieth-Century Evangelism* (Carlisle, 2002); M. A. Eaton, *Baptism with the Spirit: The Teaching of Martyn Lloyd-Jones* (Leicester, 1989); J. Peters, *Martyn Lloyd-Jones: Preacher* (Exeter, 1986).

I. H. MURRAY

LOCKE, JOHN (1632–1704)

John Locke combined a career in academic work at Oxford where, technically a physician, he collaborated with natural scientists (Boyle and Newton) and became physician-secretary to Lord Shaftesbury in London from 1667 and secretary of the Board of Trade which included some time researching persecuted Protestantism in France. He was forced into exile in Holland for his anti-catholicizing activities and spent formative years there, writing *An Essay Concerning Human Understanding*, until his vindication and return with William and Mary in 1688. The last decade of his life was marked by essays on toleration and serving once more on the Board of Trade.

For Locke the contrast with the strong Calvinism (see *Reformed theology) of many of his contemporaries regarding toleration and inwardness was a conscious one, and showed the impact of *Grotius (from whom the emphasis on faith as freely chosen) and *Descartes. More so than for the latter, 'the self' was central, but reason still allowed that objective, 'necessary' truths would come to mind. Reason was not just for science, but also for belief. No-one could really be certain of one's salvation, since one could be deceived. Coercion was antipathetic to belief, whether from divine or human pressure. Belief in the Messiah could not be enforced, since belief is a matter of will and not for anyone else's sake. However, atheism was dangerous for losing the transcendent and should be silenced. Locke was also influenced by Chillingworth and then by his contemporary and friend Archbishop Tillotson (d. 1694). The source of all truth is ultimately experience – Locke was an empiricist as against those (rationalists) who thought that truth began in the mind – and that includes much of what we find in the Bible.

Locke's *Reasonableness of Christianity as Delivered in the Scriptures* was published anonymously in 1695. He stood against Bible proof-texting, and preferred the simple sense of Scripture with a lighter amount of dogmatic complexity. Putting the life and teachings of Jesus (less so his miracles) as the centre of authority for Christian teaching, he relegated the NT epistles to a lower place. The test for being a Christian was simply to be able to say that Jesus was the Messiah of the one true God who would as resurrected return to judge/rule the world. That may be all one has to believe, but there is a lot more to be *done* by the Christian. From the premise that all have capacity for abstraction which distinguishes us from beasts, his *Essay Concerning Human Understanding* concluded: 'They have light enough to lead them to the knowledge of their Maker.' Yet in *Reasonableness* he notes that we wrongly take for granted the Christian *revelation and its great impact on civilization and mistake its contribution for some sort of innate knowledge. He thought of 'revelation' as Jesus' clarifying of the moral law without giving absolute moral certainty to us but also popularizing theology for the benefit of us all, not just labourers. For morality is too hard for unaided reason. Yet there is a capacity for moving towards knowledge of the moral and the divine, towards revelation's fullness.

Belief in the natural equality of humankind meant that he argued that the state should enforce a less radical charity (e.g. finding work for the poor). Jesus and Paul were the main influences on Locke here. Equality as its foundation comes before utility. Locke built on scriptural proofs as well as on natural law. He stressed that both Adam and Eve in the beginning shared dominion; God predicted but did not cause Eve's distress in her loss of immortality, which was not punishment.

Bibliography

J. Dunn, *Locke: A Very Short Introduction* (Oxford, 2003); P. Helm, 'A Forensic Dilemma: John Locke and Jonathan Edwards on Personal Identity' in P. Helm and O. D. Crisp (eds.), *Jonathan Edwards: Philosophical Theologian* (Aldershot, 2003); V. Nuovo (ed.), *John Locke and Christianity: Contemporary Responses to the Reasonableness of Christianity* (South Bend, 1997); idem (ed.), *John Locke: Writings on Religion* (Oxford, 2002); P. L. Quinn, 'Disputing the Augustinian Legacy: John Locke and Jonathan Edwards on Romans 5: 12–19', in G. B. Matthews (ed.), *The Augustinian Tradition* (Berkeley, 1999); A. Sell, *John Locke and the Eighteenth Century Divines* (Cardiff, 1997); J. Waldron, *God, Locke and Equality: Christian Foundations of John Locke's Political Thought* (Cambridge, 2002); N. Wolterstorff, *John Locke and the Ethics of Belief* (Cambridge, 1996); idem, 'Locke's Philosophy of Religion', in *The Cambridge Companion to Locke* (Cambridge, 1994).

M. W. ELLIOTT

LOGIC IN THEOLOGY

Logic is the study of the conditions of valid inference and the methods of proof. In its broadest sense it concerns the structures and principles of reasoning and sound argument. Logic is relevant to every area of life where argument is used. Its methods distinguish between correct and incorrect reasoning, good and bad arguments. Logicians are interested in the form of the argument rather than the content, so there is no requirement that a logically valid argument be based on true premises. If the premises are false, the argument may still be valid. In examining the relation between the premises of an argument and its conclusion, there are two main forms of inference. Deduction implies a necessary relation, so that acceptance of the premises means accepting the conclusion. Induction implies only a probability in the relation between premises and conclusion. Deductive logic rests on the principle of non-contradiction and is concerned with validity rather than truth. Inductive logic is more concerned with the standards of reasoning used in empirical and scientific reasoning, where what is reasonable or probable is not based on avoiding contradiction.

If logic is concerned with form, then it is neutral and simply a tool to enable proper argument to take place. Varieties of logical systems and notations seem, however, to suggest some assumptions about the nature of reality and need to be examined on that basis.

Theologians use arguments in the discussion and presentation of the Christian faith. Accordingly, it is crucial that they understand and use logical means properly, to avoid contradictions and to present the truth of what is claimed by valid argumentation. Medieval theologians used various deductive and inductive arguments of the ontological and cosmological variety to prove the existence of God (see *Natural theology). They argued deductively that, from an acceptance of the concept of God as 'that than which nothing greater can be conceived', God must necessarily exist, for to exist is more perfect than not to exist. This led to a philosophical debate over the nature of existence, necessity, perfections, concepts and their relation to reality. Cosmological arguments argued inductively from features of our experience of the world, such as motion, causation, being, values or purpose to a source of these things, which was called God. The critique of these arguments centred on the relationship between each premise in the argument and its claimed relationship to the conclusion. It was argued that these arguments made an illicit leap from experience of this world to a transcendent realm.

Modern theology has revitalized the proofs of God's existence, but uses logical argument more to defend theology from philosophical attacks. These attacks stress the contradictions in theology, whether in the nature of God or in our talk about God, Christ, the Spirit and other doctrines. The task of the Christian theologian is to clarify the nature of the premises, the validity of the conclusions and the truth of the claims made by Christians using both deductive and inductive reasoning.

See also: Faith and Reason.

Bibliography
G. J. Dorrien, *Kantian Reason and Hegelian Spirit: The Idealistic Logic of Modern Theology* (Oxford, 2012); E. J. Lemmon, *Beginning Logic* (London, 1965); S. E. Toulmin, *The Uses of Argument* (Cambridge, 1958); J. C. Puddefoot, *Logic and Affirmation: Perspectives in Mathematics and Theology* (Edinburgh, 1987); N. Wolterstorff, *Reason within the Bounds of Religion* (Grand Rapids, 1984).

E. D. Cook

LOGICAL POSITIVISM

There are two main sources of logical positivism. The first is David *Hume and *empiricist philosophy with its emphasis on sense experience leading to certainty about matters of fact, which it contrasted to relations of ideas which told nothing about the real world. The second is Auguste Comte (1798–1857), who coined the word '*positivism' to cover six features of things: being real, useful, certain, precise, organic and relative. His desire was to apply a scientific attitude not only to science but also to human affairs. These came together in the Vienna Circle of the 1920s and 1930s, whose main members were M. Schlick (1882–1936), R. Carnap (1891–1970), O. Neurath (1882–1945), F. Waismann (1896–1959), with *Wittgenstein and K. Popper (1902–94) on the fringe, and C. G. Hempel (1905–97) and A. J. Ayer (1910–89) as allies. The general aim was to develop and systematize empiricism using tools and concepts derived from logic and mathematics, especially from the early works of Wittgenstein and Bertrand Russell (1872–1970).

The approach was highly critical of theology and *metaphysics as meaningless. Their statements were either nonsense or interpreted like those of ethics and aesthetics as expressing feelings, attitudes or matters of taste. The Vienna Circle focused on the nature of meaning and developed the '*verification principle'. This stated that a statement or proposition was meaningful only if it were verifiable by sense experience. Thus for a statement to have a truth value, it must be known what would count for or against it in terms of sense experience; if it could not be tested by sense experience, it was dismissed as meaningless. The positivist, following the empiricist, divided knowledge into either (1) relations of ideas which were tautologies, like the truths of mathematics and logic, and were true by definition but uninformative, or (2) matters of fact which were known only by sense experience. Theology and metaphysics were neither and their statements were therefore meaningless.

The positivists ran into problems over the status of the principle of verifiability and whether the aim was verification in principle or practice, in a strong or weak sense. Popper turned to falsifiability as a better test for scientific laws, while Carnap and Ayer tended to stress testability or confirmability. Much of their debate was over attempts to preserve the notion of verification, but this tended to lose ground in view of the struggle over the exclusion of scientific laws and historical propositions. Logical positivism stressed the underlying unity of science and the strong belief that reality could be fully expressed by translation into statements about physical objects or sense experience, and that this would ultimately have the form of logic or mathematics. The role of philosophy was not to establish philosophical doctrines, but to elucidate meaning or call attention to the lack of meaning. With the failure of the strict notion of verification, there tended to be a drift towards less dogmatic forms of linguistic and conceptual analysis (see *Religious language). Nevertheless, the themes of meaning, verification, anti-metaphysics and unified science have continued to exercise a powerful influence on modern philosophy, and provided a major challenge to religion and theology through the work of Ayer and A. Flew (1923–2010).

Bibliography

A. J. Ayer, *Language, Truth and Logic* (London, ²1946); idem (ed.), *Logical Positivism* (London, 1959); R. B. Braithwaite, *An Empiricist's View of the Nature of Religious Belief* (Cambridge, 1955). **Critiques**: H. D. Lewis (ed.), *Clarity Is Not Enough: Essays in Criticism of Linguistic Philosophy* (London, 1963); E. L. Mascall, *Words and Images* (London, 1957); I. T. Ramsey (ed.), *Christian Ethics and Contemporary Philosophy* (London, 1966); A. Richardson and T. Uebel (eds.), *The Cambridge Companion to Logical Positivism* (New York, 2007); S. Sarkar, *The Legacy of the Vienna Circle: Modern Reappraisals* (New York, 1996).

E. D. COOK

LOGOS

The Greek term *logos* can mean word, discourse or reason. In John 1:1–18, Jesus Christ is the incarnation of the pre-existent divine Logos (Word). Logos is the intermediary through whom God created the world and reveals himself to humanity. The way John used the word *logos* has interesting parallels in Greek philosophy, but it also has its own distinctives.

The *Stoics (c. 300 BC onward) understood logos as the active principle, the dynamic reason or plan, the 'divine' fire, which organizes and gives forms to passive unformed matter. Likewise, the soul of man, understood as an emanation from the 'divine' logos (*logos spermatikos*), pervades the body, giving it form, organization and character. The presence of logos in humans enables them to comprehend reality. The logos in its entirety permeates the universe and could be described as God (*pantheism) or the soul of the universe (*panentheism). But logos for the Stoics was not a personal being and could be thought of as a material substance – a fiery vapour pervading matter and organizing it.

*Philo borrowed ideas about logos from the Stoics, but believed in the personal God of Israel. He fused these ideas with *Wisdom theology (Prov. 8) and the idea of God creating the world by his word in the OT, and suggested that logos is God's agent in *creation and its government. The 'divine' logos is the thoughts in God's mind which are projected into formless matter, making it a real and rational universe. The logos is also the means by which the human mind comprehends God. Philo's understanding of logos is closer to John's prologue than the Stoics by virtue of his belief in the personal God. But to him logos was not a personal being.

It was in this milieu of Hellenistic Judaism and Greek Stoicism that the author of John chose to use the word *logos* to convey some important aspects of the divine Son of God to his audience – his role as the agent in creation and his giving light to humanity, which have echoes both in the Stoics and Philo. But the author radically transformed the former meanings by acknowledging the Logos' personal being, his eternity and his full divinity. Furthermore, he declared that the Logos has become a true member of humanity (flesh), and his presence on earth, characterized by grace and truth, reveals the glory of the Father.

In the post-NT writings, the *logos* concept was used to articulate the relationship between the Son and his Father, in particular their oneness in eternity and in time (see *Christology; *Trinity). The apologist Justin understood (1) logos as the Father's immanent thought or rationality before creation (cf. *logos endiathetos* in Stoicism), and (2) logos as the expression of the Father's thought in creation (cf. *logos prophorikos* in Stoicism and the parallels in Philo). Justin used the analogy of the unity of the speaker, his thought and his word to illustrate the Father's unity with the Son/Logos in eternity and in time. He also affirmed that the Logos is numerically distinct from the Father who communes with him. However, the notion of the Logos as the Father's immanent thought and expressed speech does not sit easily with this notion of numerical distinction and personal communion. One's awareness of one's thought and speech cannot be construed as communing with another. The speaker-thought-speech model, borrowed from Stoicism, though illuminating some aspects of the divine relationship between the Father and the Son, admittedly has its own limitation and therefore cannot be taken too far (see a similar difficulty in Karl Barth, *CD*, I.1, pp. 295–314; critiqued in D. So, *Jesus' Revelation of His Father*, pp. 60–64). The question of the unity and distinction between the Father and the Son (and the Spirit), i.e. the mystery of the Trinity, remained to be saluted and enquired into through the first few centuries and beyond.

Justin also spoke of *logos spermatikos* (seminal *logos*), which before the coming of Christ was present in human beings and enabled them to perceive some fragmentary aspects of truth. It has been seen that some aspects of logos in Stoicism and Philo bear fragmentary resemblance to the divine personal Logos in John's prologue. Could this resemblance be genuinely accounted for by Justin's suggestion? This question in its generalized form (cf. Justin) has *missiological implications. Related to this is another missiological question. The creative use of Logos by the author of John for his own purpose witnesses to his wisdom and his understanding of the audience's culture and linguistic concepts which bore some contact points for easing the entry of the gospel. Could this kind of creative use of some elements in the linguistic concepts of the local/target cultures be useful in contemporary missiological endeavours?

Bibliography

K. Barth, *CD* I.1; P. Cotterell, *Mission and Meaninglessness* (London, 1990); A. Debrunner *et al.*, in *TDNT* IV, pp. 71–136; G. Fries *et al.*, in *NIDNTT* III, pp. 1081–1117; J. N. D. Kelly, *Early Christian Doctrines* (London, ⁵1977); G. E. Ladd, *A Theology of the New Testament* (Grand Rapids, 1974); G. L. Prestige, *God in Patristic Thought* (London, 1952); D. W. K. So, *Jesus' Revelation of His Father: A Narrative-Conceptual Study of the Trinity with Special Reference to Karl Barth* (Milton Keynes, 2006).

D. W. K. So

LOISY, A. F., see MODERNISM, CATHOLIC

LOMBARD, PETER (*c.* 1100–59)

Peter Lombard was born in the Novara region of Lombardy. He studied at Bologna, Reims and Paris universities. From *c.* 1140 he taught at Paris. In 1158 he became bishop of Paris, where he died the following year.

Twenty of Peter's sermons survive, together with commentaries on the Psalms and on Paul's letters, the latter written between 1139 and 1142. But he is remembered primarily for his *Four Books of Sentences* (*Sententiarum Libri Quatuor*). They cover the Trinity, providence and evil (Book I), creation, sin and grace (Book II), incarnation, redemption, virtues and commandments (Book III), sacraments and the four last things (Book IV). In this work Peter discusses various theological questions and resolves them by reference to the Bible, the Fathers (especially *Augustine) and other later authorities. He quotes extracts (*sententiae*, 'sentences', meaning maxims or opinions) and uses reason, dialectic and *logic to arbitrate between them. In this he was following the methods of the *canon lawyers (such as Gratian) which had been applied to theology by Peter *Abelard. But while Abelard had run foul of authority, Lombard was to meet with general approval. *Bernard of Clairvaux, who had hounded Abelard, commended Lombard. While Lombard used Abelard's *methods*, he combined them with a respect for authority uncharacteristic of Abelard. His aim was not to introduce new ideas, but simply to decide the truth on the basis of the established authorities.

In one area Peter did break new ground – in the theology of the *sacraments. He was probably the first to give what is now the standard Roman Catholic list of seven sacraments. The concept of seven sacraments met with rapid approval, seven being the perfect number. But not all agreed with Peter as to which seven rites should be included in the number. In due course Peter's list prevailed and it was defined as orthodoxy by the Council of Florence in 1439. Peter's limitation of the number of sacraments to seven was based on the distinction between a sacrament proper, supposed to have been instituted by Jesus Christ himself, and other less important rites, called sacramentals. Peter also argued that a sacrament is not simply a 'visible sign of an invisible grace' (Augustine), but also the effective *cause* of that grace. Here again, Peter's view prevailed.

Peter's theology did not meet with immediate acceptance. At first the orthodoxy of his teaching on the doctrines of the Trinity and the person of Christ was questioned, by *Joachim of Fiore (*c.* 1135–1202) among others. But at the Fourth Lateran Council in 1215 Lombard was fully vindicated and this encouraged the use of his *Sentences*. They became the standard theological textbook until the time of the Reformation and beyond. For centuries, writing a commentary on Lombard's *Sentences* was a standard part of the preparation for a doctorate in theology. Not inappropriately, Peter came to be known as the 'Master of the Sentences'.

Bibliography

Works in *PL* 191–192; *Libri IV Sententiarum*, 2 vols. (Quaracchi, ²1916). Selections in ET in E. R. Fairweather, *A Scholastic Miscellany: Anselm to Ockham* (LCC 10; London, 1956), and R. McKeon, *Selections From Medieval Philosophers*, 2 vols. (New York, 1929–30).

Studies: M. L. Colish, *Peter Lombard* (New York, 1994); P. Delhaye, *Pierre Lombard: sa vie, ses oeuvres, sa morale* (Montreal and Paris, 1961); J. de Ghellinck, 'Pierre Lombard' in *DTC* 12, cols. 1941–2019; E. F. Rogers, *Peter Lombard and the Sacramental System* (New York, 1917);

P. W. Rosemann, *Peter Lombard* (Oxford, 2004); *idem*, *The Story of a Great Medieval Book: Peter Lombard's 'Sentences'* (Peterborough, Ontario, 2007).

A. N. S. LANE

LONERGAN, BERNARD (1904–84)

After teaching in his native Canada (1940–53), Lonergan, a *Jesuit theologian, was professor of theology at the Gregorian University in Rome until his retirement in 1965, after which he lived in North America. His life work was the study of intellectual enquiry in general and theological *method in particular. In his early works on specific Christian doctrines he was beginning to develop his method, and his work on *Thomas Aquinas also prepared the way for his own study of method. In *Insight* (1957; London, ³1983) he studied the structure of human understanding in all fields of knowledge, and then, especially in *Method in Theology* (London, 1972), he applied his thinking to theological method.

Lonergan pursues a 'transcendental method' of reflecting on the activity of knowing, an enquiry into enquiry. This reveals a basic cognitional structure common to all human knowing in all areas of knowledge. There are three operations (experience, understanding and judgment) involved in all knowledge, and a fourth (decision) in which we decide to act on what we know. The activity of knowing can thus be summed up in Lonergan's four 'transcendental precepts': be attentive, be intelligent, be reasonable, be responsible. Through the transcendental method of reflecting on this dynamic structure of all knowing, there takes place a heightening of consciousness and a move to interiority, 'a personal appropriation of one's own rational self-consciousness', which Lonergan calls intellectual conversion.

In a very complex discussion, *Insight* moves from cognitive analysis through *epistemology to *metaphysics and a kind of *natural theology. The three steps involved in knowing take one beyond naive realism and *idealism to the kind of critical realism which is implied in the combination of the three steps. Knowledge is objective knowledge of reality, and reality is intelligible. Humanity's unrestricted desire to know intelligible reality points towards God.

In his work on theological method, Lonergan takes up his scheme of mental operations, but also divides the theological task into eight 'functional specialties'. These are not the usual subject specializations of theology (OT studies, patristics, etc.), but 'distinct and separate stages in a single process from the data to ultimate results'. There is a sequence of specialties in two phases. Those of the first phase (research, interpretation, history, dialectic) are concerned with understanding religion in the past: assimilating and assessing the tradition. Those of the second phase (foundations, doctrines, systematics, communications) are concerned with contemporary appropriation, interpretation and communication. All four levels of mental operation (experience, understanding, judgment, decision) operate in each specialty, but in each they operate to achieve the end proper to one level. Thus (in the first phase) research corresponds to experience, interpretation to understanding, history to judgment, and dialectic to decision.

Of special interest is the transition from the first phase to the second, through dialectic and foundations. Dialectic sorts out and clarifies the fundamental conflicts which arise in and from the religious tradition, and which can be decided or overcome only on the basis of a fundamental intellectual, moral or religious outlook. Such an outlook results from conversion (intellectual, moral or religious) and is expressed in the fifth specialty, foundations. Thus whereas the specialties of the first phase do not presuppose conversion, those of the second do. A personal appropriation of the tradition is required for its contemporary mediation.

In delineating this series of interdependent stages in a single process of theological work, Lonergan aims to unify the whole area of theological endeavour and to provide 'a framework for collaborative creativity'. His method as such is not *confessional, but *ecumenical, in that it provides a methodological framework for the study and assessment of all religious traditions, but in a properly theological, not merely *phenomenological, way. Lonergan has found enthusiastic disciples, but the results of his method remain to be seen.

Bibliography

Works: *Collection* (London, 1968); *A Second Collection* (London, 1974); *The Collected Works of Bernard Lonergan*, 25 vols. projected (Toronto, 1990–).

Studies: P. Corcoran (ed.), *Looking at Lonergan's Method* (London, 1975); F. E. Crowe, *Lonergan* (Collegeville, 1992); *idem, Developing the Lonergan Legacy* (Toronto, 2003); P. Lambert and P. McShane, *Bernard Lonergan: His Life and Leading Ideas* (Vancouver, 2010); H. A. Meynell, *An Introduction to the Philosophy of Bernard Lonergan* (London, 1976); M. C. O'Callaghan, *Unity in Theology: Lonergan's Framework for Theology in Its New Context* (Lanham, 1983); D. Tracy, *The Achievement of Bernard Lonergan* (Freiburg, 1970).

R. J. BAUCKHAM

LORD, see CHRISTOLOGY; GOD; JESUS

LORD'S DAY, see SABBATH

LORD'S SUPPER, see EUCHARIST

LOSSKY, VLADIMIR (1903–58)

Vladimir Lossky was born in 1903, the son of the Russian philosopher, Nicolas Lossky. He studied at the University of St Petersburg, and then, after the expulsion of the intellectuals in 1922, in Prague and at the Sorbonne. He spent the rest of his life in France, after the Second World War attached to the Centre National de la Recherche Scientifique, working on a thesis on the medieval theologian and mystic, Meister Eckhart, which found expression in his largest work, published posthumously in 1960. Among the émigrés in Paris, he was unusual in remaining loyal to the Moscow Patriarchate, despite the compromises forced on it by the Communist regime, and was involved in its condemnation of *Bulgakov's sophiology. He was a founder member of the Confrérie de Saint Photius, and after the war the Institut Saint-Denis, both of which sought to make the insights of Orthodox theology accessible in the West. His most important contribution to Orthodox theology was his book, *The Mystical Theology of the Eastern Church*, published in 1943; there are also various articles and short books, including a work that he co-authored with Leonid Ouspensky, *The Meaning of Icons* (1952), but his contribution to theology was cut short by his early death in 1958. Despite this, he is one of the greatest Orthodox theologians of the twentieth century. His work explores what *Florovsky called the 'Neo-patristic synthesis', and his principal contribution was, perhaps, his understanding of the centrality of *apophatic theology, understood not simply as knowing God through denial (*apophasis*) of the attributes asserted of him, but rather as the 'repentance of the human person before the face of the living God'. Understood like this, theology became 'mystical theology', in which the contrasts between theology and spirituality, thought and life, individual experience and corporate worship, are transcended.

See also: EASTERN ORTHODOX THEOLOGY; RUSSIAN ORTHODOX THEOLOGY.

Bibliography

Works: *The Mystical Theology of the Eastern Church* (ET, London, 1957); *In the Image and Likeness of God* (ET, Crestwood, 1957); *The Vision of God* (ET, London, 1963); *Orthodox Theology: An Introduction* (ET, Crestwood, 1989); *Seven Days on the Roads of France: June 1940* (Yonkers, 2012).

Studies: O. Clément, *Orient-Occident Deus Passeurs: Vladimir Lossky, Paul Evdokimov* (Geneva, 1985); R. Williams, 'Lossky, the *Via Negativa* and the Foundations of Theology', in R. Williams, *Wrestling with Angels: Conversations in Modern Theology*, ed. M. Higton (London, 2007).

A. LOUTH

LOVE

The triune love

The statement from 1 John 4:16, that *God is love, is the natural beginning of any theology of love. The standard Western articulation of this idea comes primarily from *Augustine, who understood love to be God's nature. Augustine borrowed from Neo-Platonism the idea of God as being itself, and as such the divine love is thought to pervade all things. All creation participates in the being of God, and thus all human love is love 'in God'.

Although Augustine understood God as Father, Son and Spirit, his philosophical influences led him to still conceive of God as a single subject. Only in the twentieth century has a more robust conception of the *Trinity been recovered in Western theology, beginning with the thought of Karl *Barth. For Barth, 'God is' means 'God loves', and the very being of God as the mutuality of Father, Son and Spirit is already love. There is no outside other that can contribute to the love of the divine life. Hence God's love for the creature is absolutely free.

Wolfhart *Pannenberg goes even further in articulating the intra-trinitarian relations which identify God as love. For him, the Father loves the Son and the Son responds to this love by being obedient to the Father, that is, by *faith. This dynamic is mediated by the *Holy Spirit, who has often been conceived in the tradition since Augustine as the bond of love between Father and Son (e.g. Peter *Lombard). Furthermore, like Augustine, Pannenberg conceives of God closely with being, particularly as the all-determining reality. Since this reality, the Trinity, *is* love, Pannenberg concludes that God's love pervades all cosmic processes. This he understands as the work of the Spirit.

Perhaps the chief insight to be gained from these and other recent theologians is that love is not a static substance, but a category of power and activity. It is inherently eventful, hence the giving and being given to among the persons of the Trinity can be understood as an articulation of the biblical assertion that God is love.

Key to this activity of love is the aspect of faithfulness. The Son's love for the Father is expressed in his faith in and obedience to the Father (cf. John 10:17). We can also say that the Father's love for the Son is expressed in faithfulness to the Son, quintessentially in his resurrection of the Son. This dimension of mutual faithfulness is also significant for all other relations of love.

The triune love for us

It has been maintained throughout the Christian tradition that God's love for creatures precedes all human love, including both love for God and love for others. This is professed already in the biblical statement of 1 John 4:19 that 'we love because he first loved us'. Meditating on John, Augustine asserts that our reconciliation to God in *salvation does not initiate God's love for us. Rather, we were reconciled to him who already loved us. Moreover, God's love is the origin and condition of all creaturely life. This is only a logical conclusion from our earlier discovery that God's love for the creature comes from the freedom of the triune life. Creation is already an act of divine love.

The *Reformers concentrated on the undeserved *grace of God to people. Love cannot be earned, and there is no human ability or power to secure the love and grace of God. It is pure gift. Here they followed Paul's emphasis on divine love as redemption from sin. For Luther and Calvin, this grace is mediated chiefly by church and sacrament.

According to Moffatt, that *Jesus is called the Father's 'Beloved' in the Bible means that he is meant to represent the Father's love to creation. Williams suggests that the mutual love of Father and Son is the pattern of communion between God and humanity. God's love for us *is* the Father's love for the Son, as is seen in Jesus' love for others. For Barth, God's love to creation comes chiefly in the gift of *Christ to us by the power of the Spirit.

Here as well we can understand the love of God for creatures as faithfulness. In the Hebrew Scriptures this is understood chiefly through the *covenant. That this is initiated by God is simply an expression of the fact that he loved us first, and his keeping of the covenant in spite of consistent disobedience on the part of Israel shows his love as faithfulness. This commitment to creation is manifested climactically *in Christ*, whose love for sinners simply *is* the love of the Father for the world. As demonstrated in the idea of Jesus as the 'first fruits', the resurrection of the Son is not only an act of faithfulness between the Father and the Son, but also between the Father and all of creation.

Our place in the triune love

Love for God

The biblical command to love God (e.g. Deut. 6:5 and Mark 12:29–30) is obviously the basis for any theology of love for God. Most of the Western tradition adopted Augustine's understanding of *eros* in articulations of love for God. This was drawn from Plato and conceived of love for God as a striving after the supreme good. In NT times, however (a few centuries after Plato), *eros* had been associated more with lust in the surrounding Greco-Roman world, which is one reason why NT authors avoid its use. For them *agape* was the preferred term, and referred to the free gift of God in the sending of the Son.

In modern theology there has been a turn toward conceiving of love for God chiefly as faith. For Barth, love for God is to keep his commandments (cf. 1 John 5:3), but this is in the context of choosing God to be our Lord, of grasping our future, which is God himself. Pannenberg also prefers faith to love when it comes to our relation to God, but articulates this in a more trinitarian way. For him and others, we love God by letting him be God to us in the same way that Jesus let the Father be God to him. This is made possible by the power of the Spirit, through whom we share with Jesus his sonship to the Father. In this sense we are his brothers and sisters (Heb. 2:11). This, we might say, is a fuller articulation of what the NT means by *agape* with regard to our love for God, since our love is a faithful response to the gracious sending of the Son.

Love for neighbour

Many theologians insist that the primary way in which we share in the Father's love of the Son is to love our neighbours. This is against the tendency in some circles to separate the two main commandments which Jesus gives: to love God, and your neighbour as yourself. 1 John is rather simple: to love God is to lay down your life for others. This is really by the power of the Spirit, by whom we abide in God. Hence the first among aspects of the fruit of the Spirit is love (Gal. 5:22).

The unity of love for God and love for others is expressed in the distinction between faith and love. Pannenberg suggests that faith is how we relate to God, and love is how we relate to others. They are two sides of the same coin, if you will. Here we are given a new opportunity for *eros*, for in its classical sense this denotes a deep desire for a perceived good. All human loves, however much they can be perverted, are expressions of desire, for true love of another cannot be coerced. The agapic *eros* which characterizes Christian love simply affirms the desirability of the neighbour, both by us and in the eyes of God.

Yet even here the aspect of faithfulness is paramount. Not only is (agapic) love for neighbours an act of faith in God, but (erotic) love requires the kind of desire which stands with the neighbour through the unpredictability of time. Such is the love of God for us, that he is faithful in spite of disobedience and change. Sharing in the Father's love for the world, then, means continuing to love in spite of the neighbour's response to that love. It is a faithful love which awakens love from the neighbour in turn where there was not before.

See also: LOVE OF GOD.

Bibliography

K. Barth, *CD* I.2; J. Burnaby, *Amor Dei* (Norwich, 1990 [1938]); J. Moffatt, *Love in the New Testament* (New York, 1930); G. Newlands, *Theology of the Love of God* (London, 1980); W. Pannenberg, *Systematic Theology*, vol. 3 (ET, Grand Rapids, 1998); F. L. Shults, *Reforming the Doctrine of God* (Grand Rapids, 2005); D. D. Williams, *The Spirit and the Forms of Love* (Washington, 1981).

A. R. MILLS

LOVE OF GOD

The love of God is less a discrete locus of theology than a theme that pervades all aspects of the doctrine of God: essential attributes, interpersonal relations of the Trinity, and God's relation to the world. Its familiarity breeds not contempt but confusion when attempts to explain it begin in human experience rather than the history of *redemption. Western culture's tendency to sentimentalize love has encouraged contemporary theologians to associate it with suffering rather than sovereignty, where it properly belongs, but only when we let the acts of Father, Son and Spirit define both love and divine *sovereignty.

Biblical theology

First things first: the 'love of God' in Scripture usually refers to God's love for humanity rather than human love for God. A human being *has* love but God *is* love (1 John 4:8). Humans can 'love' non-personal things like music and mashed potatoes, but God loves persons.

God shows his love to Abraham by establishing an everlasting *covenant that includes a gift of land and a promise of everlasting loyalty. God bases his election of Israel to be his treasured possession not on something Israel was or had done but on his own loving initiative (Deut. 7:6–9). 'I have loved Jacob, but Esau I have hated' (Mal. 1:2–3). God's love is always prevenient: 'We love because he first loved us' (1 John 4:19).

God reveals himself to Moses as 'compassionate and gracious, slow to anger, abounding in steadfast love and faithfulness' (Exod. 34:6). This puts the lie to the common misconception that the God of the OT is wrathful whereas the God of the NT is loving. God's steadfast love (*hesed*) stands at the core of his covenant and is on conspicuous display throughout Israel's history, especially when the people go astray like a faithless wife (see Hos. 1 – 3). God initiates a new and better covenant with the whole world. God 'demonstrates his own love for us in this: while we were still sinners, Christ died for us' (Rom 5:8; cf. John 3:16). God gives himself not only in the person of his Son but also in the person of the Holy Spirit (Acts 2:38; 11:17; Rom. 5:5) who unites disciples to Christ and adopts them into God's family (Rom. 8:15–17; Eph. 1:4–5).

'God is love' (1 John 4:8): this claim summarizes the nature and character of the one who brings Israel out of Egypt and pours himself out on the cross to bring sinners out of the bondage of sin and death.

Historical and systematic theology

The *history of theology showcases the love of God in striking fashion primarily because it appears in so many doctrinal guises.

Attribute and action

Standard systematic theologies locate the love of God among the moral attributes (e.g. goodness). God's love is his unselfish interest in the well-being of others. *Thomas Aquinas defines love in terms of benevolence (*bene volere* = 'good willing'). Yet a generic 'willing of the good' falls short of God's special affection for and delight in his chosen people.

Karl *Barth argues from the incarnation that God is free because his existence is self-determined, and love because he determines himself to be for another. The event of Jesus Christ demonstrates that God is 'the one who loves in freedom'. Accordingly, Barth views all the divine perfections as qualifications either of God's freedom or his love.

God is also light (1 John 1:5). Love and justice are often seen to be at odds (love unites; holiness separates) but in fact converge in God's loving justice accomplished on the cross. The event of Jesus Christ reveals God's being as love: 'a still greater selflessness within a very great self-relatedness' (E. Jüngel, *God as the Mystery of the World*, p. 317).

Relation and union

The love of God begins in God's own immanent life: the mutual relations of Father, Son and Spirit (see *Trinity). Love in this perspective appears less an attribute of a subject than a relation between persons. Augustine, for example, focuses on the relation between the Father and Son depicted in the Fourth Gospel (John 3:35; 5:20; 14:30–31) as indicating a relation of eternal mutual love. The Spirit is the overflowing of the Father and Son's love and the love between them.

Richard of St Victor (see *Victorines) further develops this inner-trinitarian shape of divine love. Love is perfect only when shared with another. The God-world relationship is not an example of perfect love because the world is not equal to God. Perfect love requires of the divine lover a divine beloved. Love between two only, however, is selfish. Richard therefore concludes: 'the perfection of charity requires a Trinity of persons' (i.e. lover, beloved and co-lover).

Jürgen *Moltmann is representative of contemporary process, feminist, openness and panentheist theologians generally who, going further than the tradition, argue that God's love for the world means that God 'opens' up a space for the world in the trinitarian history. Love is a mutual relation of give and take between God and the world and, as the *incarnation and *cross of Jesus attest, God's love for the world involves God's suffering. Where the theistic tradition emphasizes love as action, *panentheists link love with passion (i.e. God's willingness to be affected – to suffer – by what is not God).

Communication and communion

God's love for his covenant partner involves not simply giving good gifts but the gift of *salvation, that is, the gift of triune fellowship: communion. The love of God is the Father giving the gift of himself to his adopted children through the Son in the Spirit. 'In his general goodness God bestows various gifts upon the creature; in His love He gives Himself and holds nothing back' (G. Vos, in *Redemptive History*, p. 440).

God's self-communication is something that God *does* and *is*. God's loving actions in history correspond to the love God is in himself. The basis of God's love *ad extra* is the Father's love for the Son and the Son's love for the Father to which the Spirit bears witness and in which the Spirit participates by communicating it abroad.

Is God's love a substantial attribute (e.g. benevolence) or a personal relation? The truth may lie somewhere in between if we view the love of God as *God's active disposition to communicate the Father's communion with the Son to others in the Spirit.*

See also: GOD; LOVE.

Bibliography

V. Brümmer, *The Model of Love: A Study in Philosophical Theology* (Cambridge, 1993); D. A. Carson, *The Difficult Doctrine of the Love of God* (Wheaton and Leicester, 2000); E. Jüngel, *God as the Mystery of the World* (Grand Rapids, 1983); J. McIntyre, *On the Love of God* (London, 1962); J. Moltmann, *The Trinity and the Kingdom: The Doctrine of God* (New York, 1981); J. C. Peckham, *The Love of God: A Canonical Model* (Downers Grove, 2015); K. J. Vanhoozer, *Nothing Greater, Nothing Better: Theological Essays on the Love of God* (Grand Rapids, 2001); G. Vos, 'The Scriptural Doctrine of the Love of God', in *Redemptive History and Biblical Interpretation: The Shorter Writings of Geerhardus Vos* (Phillipsburg, 1980).

K. J. VANHOOZER

LULL, RAYMOND (*c.* 1232–1316)

Lull's father participated in the armada which delivered Majorca from the Muslim Moors. The young Raymond grew up with influential contacts, allowing considerable travel and contact with Moors. A series of visions of Christ turned him from a dissolute life to an assurance of sins forgiven and a total dedication to mission among Muslims. His aim was threefold: (1) to write books on *apologetics, particularly for Muslims; (2) to inspire popes, prelates and princes to found colleges for the study of Christian sciences and Arabic; (3) to give his life as a martyr among Muslims.

Lull broke the medieval tradition by writing not only in Latin, but also in his native Catalan and in Arabic. He was prolific, producing some 290 books of which about 240 still survive. He loved religious allegories with apologetic aims. *The Book of the Gentiles* and the *Three Wise Men* and *Blanquerna* typify this. But he also wrote the semi-autobiographical *The Book of Contemplation* in seven volumes in Arabic and some more directly apologetic works – e.g. *The Great Art* for which he was examined at Paris University in 1287 and awarded the title Master. In *The Great Art* he seeks to supply incontrovertible answers to questions of theology (particularly the doctrines of the *Trinity and the *incarnation), metaphysics and natural science. Thus *Aristotelian philosophy and *scholastic theology are fused – as also in *Thomas Aquinas, Al Ghazzali (the formative Muslim theologian, 1059–1111) and the Jewish Maimonides (1135–1204).

Lull travelled widely and frequently to share his vision of training colleges with popes, prelates and princes. Frequently, however, his visits coincided with events which prevented these leaders giving attention to his aims. He persuaded King James of Majorca to establish such a college in Miramar with thirteen friars, but to Lull's grief it lasted only sixteen years. Then in 1285 Pope Honorius IV was persuaded to set up a school of Arabic and other languages in Paris. Lull himself not only spent nine years after his conversion in concentrated study of Arabic and Latin, but also then lectured in the University of Montpellier and worked in Paris, where he combated the heresies of the *Averroists. Lull's struggle with Islam-related Averroism was motivated by the hope that the heretics might then preach the pure Christian truth to Muslims. Lull's concern for pure doctrine always had a missionary purpose.

Lull engaged in three major missionary journeys to North Africa in 1291, 1307 and 1313. His pattern was to challenge leading Muslims to debate, with the pretext that he would become a Muslim if persuaded. He also did evangelistic preaching in marketplaces and streets. Like the apostle Paul, he experienced shipwreck, preaching to visitors in prison and mob violence. (Only on his third journey at the ripe age of eighty did he see people converted, both leading Moors in Tunis and simpler folk in villages.) Finally, he was stoned in the streets of Bugia and died virtually a martyr.

See also: ISLAM AND CHRISTIANITY.

Bibliography

A. Bonner, *The Art and Logic of Raymond Llull: A User's Guide* (Leiden, 2007); E. A. Peers, *The Fool of Love: The Life of Ramon Lull* (London, ²1948); F. A. Yates, *Lull and Bruno* (London, 1982); S. M. Zwemer, *Raymond Lull: First Missionary to the Moslems* (New York and London, 1902).

M. F. GOLDSMITH

LUTHER, MARTIN (1483–1546)

Martin Luther was not the author, but became the accidental instigator of the *Protestant Reformation through his famous protest about the abuse of indulgences in 1517. He remains one of the Christian church's most influential theologians, who gave his name (unwillingly, it must be said) to a whole denomination and initiated a new way of Christian living, praying and believing across Europe.

Born in 1483, in Eisleben, Germany, Luther matriculated at the University of Erfurt in 1501. A dramatic experience in a thunderstorm in 1505 led to his entry into a monastery of the Augustinian Order in the same city to begin life as a friar. This event did not indicate a termination of his study, merely a refocusing around the study of theology. He was ordained priest in 1507, and transferred formally to the new university of Wittenberg in 1511 to become Professor in Biblical Studies, a post he held until he died.

During his time in Erfurt and the early years in Wittenberg, Luther began to question the theology and church practice he had been taught from his youth. The nature and timing of this is both complex and disputed. Sometime over the period between 1514 and 1520, Luther's own theological understanding, particularly of the doctrine of *salvation, was transformed. This led to a decisive break from the theology and piety of his contemporaries, and eventually from the papal church itself.

In the autumn of 1517, Luther became concerned about the abuse of indulgences, certificates issued by the church that remitted punishments imposed as part of the medieval penitential system (see *Roman Catholic theology). Indulgences had recently begun to be applied not only to the church's earthly requirements, but to punishments to be endured in *purgatory as well. They could also be applied to deceased relations who were believed to be suffering the torments of purgatory. An indulgence backed by Archbishop Albrecht of Mainz, and preached near Wittenberg by the renowned indulgence-seller Johann Tetzel drew Luther's fire. His basic complaint was that these certificates offered a form of cheap grace, and 'false assurance', encouraging people to trust in letters of indulgence rather than God's mercy. They encouraged Christians to avoid the true and painful contrition which alone rendered the sinner receptive to God's grace.

Luther's protest took the form of ninety-five theses, posted as a challenge to academic debate. These were rapidly printed and distributed, and came to be interpreted as an attack both on clear conciliar teaching and papal authority. This was clearly not Luther's intention when the controversy began. Over this period from late 1517 to 1520, in dispute with papal theologians such as Cajetan, Prierias and Eck, the implications of Luther's developing theology were slowly drawn out. The similarities between his ideas and those of the executed Bohemian heretic Jan *Hus were established, as was the clear water between his own teaching and that of recent *councils (especially the Council of Constance in 1415) and papal decretals. The result was excommunication in January 1521, followed by an appearance before Emperor Charles V at the Diet at Worms later the same year, after which Luther was placed under the imperial ban, an edict which was never fully implemented in Luther's lifetime.

For the rest of his life, Luther found himself embroiled in further disputes, this time with other reformers within the evangelical movement itself. These debates were to divide the Reformation movement profoundly. Some centred on political theology, over the tactics of the 'Peasants Revolt' of 1525, and his subsequent development of his idea of the 'two kingdoms' in response to the peasants' use of violence to achieve their aims, and the confusion between political and ecclesiastical power in the late medieval church.

A particularly significant debate focused on the theology of the *sacraments. Luther originally clashed with Andreas von *Karlstadt over the interpretation of the Mass or Lord's Supper (see *Eucharist), but later faced stronger opposition from Swiss theologians, particularly Huldrych *Zwingli from Zürich, over the same issue. While Luther had long abandoned the medieval doctrine of transubstantiation as an unnecessary piece of speculative Aristotelian theory, he consistently held to the idea of the Real Presence, the notion that 'in the Supper we eat and take to ourselves Christ's body truly and physically'. Zwingli, however, denied the real bodily presence of Christ in the elements of bread and wine, insisting that the Lord's Supper was primarily a communal meal whereby Christians pledge their allegiance both to Christ and one another. A series of lengthy treatises and counter-treatises culminated in the 'Marburg Colloquy' which brought together the main figures in the evangelical movement at the time, including Luther, his close Wittenberg colleague Philipp *Melanchthon, Zwingli, *Bucer, *Oecolampadius and *Osiander. The debate was inconclusive. While agreement was acknowledged on a remarkably wide range of theological issues, over the contentious issue of sacramental presence, the parties agreed, reasonably amicably, to differ. Even so, it became clear in time that both still felt the fundamental issue had not been resolved. Luther thought Zwingli's refusal to recognize the embodied way in which God presents himself to us in sacraments was an implicit denial of the incarnation, and so jeopardized the reality of the gift of Christ to sinners. Zwingli thought Luther's insistence on the real bodily presence of Christ in the sacrament encouraged a false trust in the elements themselves rather than in Christ, and compromised God's spiritual freedom to act as he chooses, independent of physical forms.

For the remainder of his life, Luther was based in Wittenberg. He spent many hours and words working on the reformation of the church in Saxony, his home region, and in a project which was always among the closest to his own concerns, the translation of the Bible from the original languages into a colloquial and accessible German. He died in 1546.

Justification

A central feature of Luther's theology was a renewed understanding of the '*righteousness of God' (*iustitia Dei*). Luther referred to his discovery of this in a late recollection, the famous 'autobiographical fragment' of 1545. As he pondered the scriptural use and meaning of the phrase, particularly its occurrence in Rom. 1:17, Luther turned from a view, common within systematic works of theology at the time, of this as 'active righteousness', or God's own righteousness by which he actively condemns sinners. Instead, he began to understand it as 'passive righteousness', a righteousness which God works in sinners, and which is received by *faith. Hence God's *iustitia* became for Luther not demand but gift (see *Justification). Acceptance of sinners by God as truly righteous came at the start of, and as the essential precondition for, the grateful living of Christian life, rather than a goal to be achieved at the end of it. Christians were not partly righteous and partly sinful, with the Christian life as the slow process, to be completed in purgatory, whereby such sin as remained could be removed, until final acceptance by God was achieved. Instead, Christians were, in Luther's well-known phrase, 'at the same time righteous and sinful': fully righteous by virtue of the righteousness of Christ received by faith, despite and yet simultaneous with the real presence of sin.

Faith is hearing the promise of God that he justifies the ungodly (Rom. 5:6), and simply believing it. Faith therefore includes both a positive and negative aspect. Positively, it lays hold of and clings tightly to the word of promise which offers forgiveness and *grace; negatively, it refuses to try to earn any kind of personal merit before God on the basis of which a claim might be made for his favour. Faith resolves to take God at his word and therefore eschews the attempt to impress God with works: it is by definition the opposite of 'works' – passive receptiveness of grace, not active co-operation with it.

All previous versions of scholastic medieval soteriology (see *Salvation) suggested to varying degrees that the granting of salvation required the actual and gradual transformation of the penitent from within, with the help of God's grace, so that they became meritoriously righteous within themselves, and it was on the basis of this internal righteousness, once complete, that justification was bestowed. Luther, however, insisted that the righteousness which justifies a Christian is not his or her own internal righteousness, but is instead, an external or strange righteousness (*iustitia externa* or *aliena*), the 'righteousness of another, namely Christ'. The practice of good works flows from justification, but does not in any way contribute to it. Salvation did not depend on the performance of meritorious works, even those performed with the assistance of grace. Justification was granted solely on the basis of the merits of Christ, imputed to the believer through faith alone.

This view of justification led Luther to a furious falling-out with the great Dutch humanist, *Erasmus. Erasmus advocated a simple freedom for the human will to choose to turn towards God or not, and stated his belief that further precision on such questions was impossible due to the lack of clarity of Scripture on these points. For Luther, this position was untenable on two main counts. First, it re-opened the door to uncertainty in the doctrine of justification. If any part of the justification was dependent on human action or choice, it re-introduced subjectivity and hence uncertainty, which robbed the sinner of the joyful certainty of God's grace and promise.

Second, it undermined the clarity of Scripture. Only if the promise of Scripture was clear and unequivocal could it be trusted and hence bring security and peace. For Luther, Erasmus's casual assertion of Scripture's opaqueness on such questions removed the Christian's hope and freedom.

Scripture

This emphasis on *Scripture marks one of the other distinguishing points of Luther's theology. His focus on 'Scripture alone' as the final authority for Christian life and thought emerged from two distinct but related aspects of his early development. During the course of his controversy with papal theologians before his excommunication, Luther appears to have been surprised by their failure to tackle him on the grounds he wanted to argue – the teaching of the Bible. Instead, all he encountered was the repeated charge that his ideas were opposed to both papal and conciliar teaching, and therefore to be condemned. While he began the indulgence controversy with a somewhat naïve expectation that Scripture, pope, councils and canon law would be seen to be in agreement, these controversies soon drove a firm wedge between Luther's reading of Scripture and these other authorities. The failure of his opponents to answer him with Scripture compelled him towards asserting the authority of Scripture over against these other authorities, rather than complementary with them.

The other force which shaped his emerging doctrine of Scripture was experiential. Luther's experience of Christian life from early times, and subsequently in the monastery, was marked by what he later called *Anfechtung*, the experience of doubt and despair, especially focused on the question of whether God looked on him with favour or condemnation. His theological discoveries did not banish these experiences; they simply gave him means of dealing with them. Such experiences were particularly acute during the controversy with the papacy, and produced a consequent need for reassurance which could be trusted. *In extremis*, Luther found that a human word such as papal teaching, the pronouncement of a council or the word of eminent theological authorities could not give him the solid ground he needed. Only a word from God in Scripture presented itself as an unyielding foundation on which he could stand firm while the storms of conflict or conscience raged around him. As a result, his famous stand before the emperor to whom he was summoned at the Diet of Worms in 1521 took the form of an appeal to Scripture: he was '. . . bound by the Scriptures I have quoted and my conscience is captive to the Word of God'.

The question of the interpretation of Scripture is of course another matter. The debate with Zwingli over the Eucharist showed the inability of evangelicals who held in common the final authority of Scripture always to agree on what it meant, or the central principles by which it should be interpreted. However, this does not gainsay the vital role played by Luther in establishing the central role of Scripture within Protestant theology, and the principle of the role of theology as exegesis – that theology is essentially a response to the prior word of God revealed in Christ and in the Scriptures, a human word in response to God's word.

Christology

Luther's theology is also characterized by a focus on *Christ, as God's gift. For Luther, the Christian holds onto the gift of Christ as the eternal pledge of God's favour and grace, over against any voice of accusation or experience of abandonment that might suggest God is unmerciful. God's act in Christ of becoming human for us pledges him to us once and for all, and is the foundation of Christian faith and peace: 'If you see . . . that God is so kindly disposed towards you that he even gives his own Son for you, then your heart must grow sweet and disposed towards God.' Luther's Christology also held that Christ's divine and human natures were not separate entities co-existing within the same body, but a unified substance – a divine-human nature. This preserved for Luther the notion that Jesus' human life and nature expressed perfectly the nature and heart of God. The *incarnation, as God's gift of Christ to us, to be received by faith, is a true expression of the heart of God as turned towards humanity in love and favour. It reveals the innermost identity and will of God, not as the demanding judge, but as the generous giver. This is how we know what God is like.

In addition, this Christology profoundly affected his understanding of the way God communicates himself to humankind. Justification consists in the promise and gift of the righteousness of Christ to sinners, received only by faith. Because Luther could not conceive of any separation between Christ's divine and human nature, this gift could not be thought of as just a spiritual thing, but it had to take embodied form, just as in the incarnation. Hence, Luther thought of God's approach and availability in very physical forms. It is this Christological perspective that lies at the root of Luther's insistence on the real presence of Christ in the elements of bread and wine in the Mass. God's word of promise, which comes in the form of both preaching and sacrament, does not just refer to the gift of Christ; it actually conveys what it promises. It is no mere legal fiction, but effects a real union between the believer and Christ at the most intimate level, in which the believer's sin is exchanged with Christ's righteousness. If, as Luther insists, Christ is one human/divine nature, then it cannot be that Christ is offered to us spiritually, while his physical presence or flesh is elsewhere. Both belong together, and Christ and his benefits are offered to us bodily in the sacrament, to be received in faith.

Luther is one of the most creative and influential figures in Christian history. His writing, voluminous and seldom dull, extends over a very broad range of Christian theology and practice, and remains accessible and stimulating even 500 years later.

See also: LUTHERANISM AND LUTHERAN THEOLOGY; REFORMATION THEOLOGY.

Bibliography

M. Brecht, *Martin Luther: His Road to Reformation, 1483–1521* (Philadelphia, 1985); *idem*, *Martin Luther: Shaping and Defining the Reformation, 1521–1532* (Minneapolis, 1990); *idem, Martin Luther: The Preservation of the Church, 1532–1546* (Minneapolis, 1999); G. Ebeling, *Luther: An Introduction to His Thought* (London, 1972); B. Lohse, *Martin Luther's Theology: Its Historical and Systematic Development* (Minneapolis, 1999); H. A. Oberman, *Luther: Man Between God and the Devil* (New Haven, 1989).

G. TOMLIN

LUTHERANISM AND LUTHERAN THEOLOGY

The Lutheran Reformation was pre-eminently a theological movement. Although it had a profound effect upon the political, social and academic life of Western Europe, it did not start out, primarily, as an effort to change political and social structures. Unlike earlier medieval reform movements in the Western church, which generally aimed at moral renewal or institutional change, Martin Luther's reform efforts in sixteenth-century Germany were rooted in a concern for doctrinal reform. Arising from his own struggle with sin and his breakthrough to a new understanding of God's *grace, Luther sought to lead others, and the church as a whole, to a fuller realization that *salvation is a divine gift received by sinners through an act of trust in the righteousness of Christ. All of Luther's significant contributions in liturgy, catechetics and hymnody, even his deep concern for social and ecclesiastical reform, came about as a result of his pursuit of this great soteriological goal.

There are three sources for an understanding of the nature and structure of traditional Lutheranism. First, the Lutheran confessions collected in the *Book of Concord*; second, the writings of Luther; and third, the writings of other Lutheran church leaders, most notably from the first three generations of the Lutheran movement. Since Luther was a prolific but unsystematic writer, the whole corpus of his printed works could not easily function as a concise standard for Lutheran theology. The *Book of Concord*, assembled some sixty years after the start of the Lutheran Reformation, served this purpose. It collected Luther's two *catechisms and joined them to several doctrinal summaries from key moments in the development of the Lutheran church. To the three ecumenical creeds shared by Eastern and Western Christians, it added the *Augsburg Confession written by Luther's close associate Philipp *Melanchthon in 1530, the Smalcald Articles prepared by Luther himself in 1537 and the *Formula of Concord written in 1577 to settle doctrinal disputes that had arisen among Lutherans after Luther's death.

The Lutheran confessions do not vary on any significant point from the theology of Luther himself. However, this does not mean that all of the early Lutheran church leaders thought alike. Philipp Melanchthon inspired a party of theologians known as the Philippists who clashed over several issues with another group, the Gnesio-Lutherans (so-called 'authentic' Lutherans), led by Matthias Flacius (1520–75) among others. The Formula of Concord was an effort to restore consensus to the Lutheran movement. Written principally by Martin *Chemnitz and Jacob Andreae (1528–90), it clarified Lutheran teachings about a number of important articles of faith, such as original *sin and the bondage of the human *will, the role of good works in the Christian life, law and gospel, the nature of Christ's presence in the Lord's Supper (see *Eucharist) and *predestination. Lutheran theology in the seventeenth century, the so-called Age of Orthodoxy, was devoted to the task of defending the doctrinal heritage articulated in the *Book of Concord*. Chemnitz was the most important transitional figure between the late Reformation and the Age of Orthodoxy. He wrote an extensive defence of Lutheran theology in response to criticisms of it expressed in the decrees of the Council of *Trent. Theologians in this era wrote increasingly massive doctrinal textbooks using biblical exegesis and philosophical argumentation to clarify how Lutheran theology differed from the tenets of other traditions such as Roman Catholicism and Calvinism. Most notable among these university-based dogmaticians was Johann Gerhard (1582–1637).

On the fundamental articles of the Trinity, the person of Christ, the centrality of Christ's saving work and the work of the Holy Spirit through word and sacrament, Lutheran theology consciously follows the great Eastern and Western creeds and Fathers of the early church. Luther and later Lutheran theologians deliberately constructed their confessions and dogmatic disquisitions according to a trinitarian scheme and pattern of thought. The distinct contribution of Lutheran theology in the history of Christian theology is in two areas: the authority of God's word in the church, and soteriology.

The theology of the word

The sacred Scriptures are the word of God brought to humanity through prophets and apostles, and as such carry with them the authority and truthfulness of God himself. Against the authority of the papacy, church councils, reason and personal experience, Lutheran theology teaches that Scripture alone (*sola Scriptura*) is the source of all theology and the rule and norm for judging all teachers and teachings in the church. The unity of Scripture consists in its witness to Christ, promised in the OT and made manifest in the NT (see *Scripture, doctrine of).

The books of Scripture and words proclaimed on the basis of Scripture have a soteriological purpose, and to this end are inherently powerful to raise consciousness of sin and to reveal the remedy made available by the saving work of Christ. The word of God comes in the form of *law, which judges and condemns sinners, and *gospel, which comforts the distressed and promises forgiveness. The word must be preached in both forms in order to be effective for salvation (see *Law and gospel).

The word of gospel (proclaimed through the spoken word and the 'visible word' of baptism and Eucharist) actually creates and sustains the church, which is the community of all believers everywhere. Or, more precisely, the Holy Spirit works always and only through these means of grace to call, build, comfort and save the church. The doctrine of the real presence of Christ's body and blood in the Communion bolsters this function of the sacrament as means of grace, for by his body and blood Christ procured forgiveness of sins for all. Furthermore, the gospel and all its articles, that is, the doctrine drawn from Scripture, is the Spirit's means to reform the church and to unite it against all schism. For church unity and external fellowship, unity in biblical doctrine is necessary.

The theology of the cross

Although Luther and subsequent Lutheran theologians have used various motifs to describe the saving work of Christ, the tradition has always affirmed that the Son of God has done what other humans were unable to do for themselves. As reconciler, propitiator, and victor over sin and death, Jesus Christ alone provides the way for sinners to find favour with God. In *justification (God's effective forensic act of forgiveness and acquittal for Christ's sake), God reckons to the sinner the very righteousness which Christ acquired by his perfect obedience and atoning death on the cross.

The article of justification through faith, so central in Lutheran theology, builds upon Luther's theology of the *cross. Through *faith alone (*sola fide*), the sinner receives and appropriates to himself all the benefits Christ has acquired for the world – Christ's righteousness, God's forgiveness, peace and *reconciliation with God and eternal life. Thus, the reality of the sinner's justification through faith offers abundant comfort and certain *assurance to troubled Christians. As the theology of the word affords the Christian certainty of his doctrine and confession, the theology of the cross affords the Christian certainty of God's grace and of his own personal salvation.

The faith through which a sinner is justified is wrought by the Holy Spirit through word and sacrament. It is not a human accomplishment. In fact, sinners contribute nothing to their salvation by acts of their own wills or by their best efforts or works. Salvation and all things pertaining to it are by God's grace alone (*sola gratia*). Good works are not the cause of salvation, but are manifested in the life of a Christian as fruits of faith. Emphasizing what the apostle Paul said, Lutherans see all signs of new life in the reconciled sinner as faith becoming active in love. In gratitude for what Christ has done for them, faithful believers devote themselves to the welfare of others.

From the eighteenth century onwards, there have been movements within the Lutheran churches that have sometimes shifted the language and emphasis of theology. The *Pietist reform movement increased interest in personal religious experience and added more stress on the process of regeneration or *sanctification. Rationalists during the Enlightenment elevated the role of reason and diminished the significance of some articles of faith. Influences from philosophy and historical-critical studies created various schools of thought during the nineteenth and early twentieth centuries However, the original principles of Lutheran confessional theology have been repeatedly recalled to a central place throughout the centuries. Since the middle of the twentieth century, many Lutheran theologians have been increasingly committed to ecumenical dialogue and have thereby come to a greater appreciation of commonalities shared with some other Protestant traditions and Roman Catholicism. This is even true with regard to previously divisive issues such as the doctrine of justification and the nature of the sacraments.

See also: LUTHER, MARTIN; REFORMATION THEOLOGY.

Bibliography

W. Elert, *The Structure of Lutheranism* (St Louis, 1962); E. Gritsch and R. Jenson, *Lutheranism: The Theological Movement and Its Confessional Writings* (Philadelphia, 1976); B. Hanson, *Grace that Frees: The Lutheran Tradition* (Maryknoll, 2004); B. Lohse,

Luther's Theology: Its Historical and Systematic Development (Minneapolis, 1999); The Lutheran World Federation and the Roman Catholic Church, *Joint Declaration on the Doctrine of Justification* (Grand Rapids, 2000); A. McGrath, *Luther's Theology of the Cross* (Oxford, 1990).

E. LUND

MACARIUS (PSEUDO-)

This Greek *ascetic teacher was active in Asia Minor or Syria-Mesopotamia between *c.* 380 and 430. Many of his homilies and letters have been ascribed to Macarius of Egypt (*c.* 300–*c.* 390) (wrongly) or Symeon of Mesopotamia (perhaps his true name), and so he is sometimes referred to as Macarius-Symeon. The scope and significance of his corpus, clarified only in recent years, remain the subject of keen research.

Macarius had links with the Messalians, ascetic extremists who stressed prayer to the virtual exclusion of outward religion and were inclined to denigrate matter (like *Manichaeans). The movement was condemned in the Eastern church in the late fourth and early fifth centuries. But Macarius was also related to the more central tradition of ascetic and *mystical theology stimulated by *Origen and notably exemplified in *Gregory of Nyssa, one of whose works was dependent on Macarius' *Great Letter* on the monastic life (or perhaps vice-versa; scholars disagree). The *Fifty Spiritual Homilies* have been much admired in the West, not least by John *Wesley, who translated several of them. Macarius inculcated an interiorized quest for Christian perfection, freedom from all earthly passions, and mystical enlightenment.

Bibliography

Works: CPG, nos. 2410–2427; *Pseudo-Macaire, oeuvres spirituelles*, ed. V. Desprez, vol. 1 (SC 275–, 1980–); *Fifty Spiritual Homilies*, tr. A. J. Mason (London, 1921); *Pseudo-Macarius: The Fifty Spiritual Homilies and the Great Letter*, tr. G. A. Maloney, (New York, 1992).

Studies: W. Jaeger, *Two Rediscovered Works of Ancient Christian Literature: Gregory of Nyssa and Macarius* (Leiden, 1954); V. Desprez, in *DSp* 10, cols. 20–43.

D. F. WRIGHT

MACDONALD, GEORGE (1824–1905)

George MacDonald was born in Huntly in rural Aberdeenshire, Scotland, the son of a bleacher. He was to write nearly thirty novels, several books of sermons, a number of abiding fantasies for adults and children, short stories and poetry. His childhood is captured in his semi-autobiographical *Ranald Bannerman's Boyhood* (1871). Like C. S. *Lewis and J. R. R. Tolkien (1892–1973), MacDonald was a scholar as well as a story-teller. He entered Aberdeen University in 1840, and had a scientific training. Much later he was for a time professor of literature at Bedford College, London. After a short spell in the Congregational ministry, he found freer rein in the precarious life of a writer and lecturer. His broad theology allowed him to approve of both C. H. *Spurgeon and F. D. Maurice (see *Christian Socialism). It is, however, for his theology of the *imagination, and its outworkings in his writings, that he is memorable. His psychological grasp of the unconscious laws upon which the human making of meaning is based predates Freud and Jung. His sense that all imaginative meaning originates with the Christian Creator became the foundation of C. S. Lewis's thinking and imagining. Two seminal essays, 'The Imagination: Its Functions and Its Culture' (1867) and 'The Fantastic Imagination' (before 1882), remarkably foreshadow Tolkien's famous essay 'On Fairy Stories' (1947), the gist of which persuaded C. S. Lewis of the truth of Christianity on a windy night in 1931. Writes MacDonald, 'One difference between God's work and man's is, that, while God's work cannot mean more than he meant, man's must mean more than he meant.'

Bibliography

R. N. Hein, *The Harmony Within: The Spiritual Vision of George MacDonald* (Grand Rapids, 1982); C. S. Lewis (ed.), *George MacDonald: An Anthology* (London, 1946); G. MacDonald, *George MacDonald and His Wife* (London, 1924); K. Triggs, *The Stars and the Stillness: A Portrait of George MacDonald* (Cambridge, 1986); R. L. Wolff, *The Golden Key: A Study of the Fiction of George MacDonald* (New Haven, 1961).

C. P. DURIEZ

MACHEN, JOHN GRESHAM (1881–1937)

John Machen was a NT scholar, apologist and popular theologian, the last major advocate of the *Princeton theology, who by training and disposition was cut out for a life of scholarship, but who as a result of a tumultuous ecclesiastical conflict became a creator of new institutions to carry on conservative Presbyterian Calvinism in America.

Machen came from a well-to-do family in Baltimore, MD, and studied at Johns Hopkins University, Princeton Seminary (under B. B. *Warfield), Princeton University and in Germany. From 1906 to 1929 he taught NT at Princeton Theological Seminary. When his appointment to a chair of theology was denied at the same time as the governing structure of the seminary was changed in favour of 'inclusive' *Presbyterianism, Machen left Princeton to found Westminster Theological Seminary in Philadelphia. Shortly thereafter, in an effort to certify the orthodoxy of missionaries, he helped establish a missions board independent of the Presbyterian General Assembly. This move led to Machen and several other conservative leaders being ousted from the large Northern Presbyterian Church. As a result, the Orthodox Presbyterian Church was formed to maintain a 'true Presbyterian' witness in the United States. Machen, who never married, was a careful scholar, a tireless organizer, and most of all a personal inspiration to many others, especially young ministers, who were troubled about the theological drift of American Presbyterianism.

Machen's best-known scholarly efforts were books defending traditional understandings of NT topics. His *Origin of Paul's Religion* (London, 1921) provided a careful rebuttal of the fashionable belief that Paul had propounded a gospel heavily indebted to Gk philosophy and strikingly at odds with the simple teachings of Jesus. His study *The Virgin Birth* (London, ²1932) carefully sifted through biblical, historical and philosophical scholarship to conclude that no valid reasons existed for questioning the church's belief in the supernatural conception of Jesus (see *Virgin birth). In these and similar works Machen displayed the type of thorough orthodox scholarship that had marked Old Princeton since its founding in 1812, but which had become a rare commodity in the heated days of the *fundamentalist-*modernist controversy.

Machen's popular works presented logical and intelligent arguments for traditional Christian faith. Among these, his *Christianity and Liberalism* (Grand Rapids, 1923) has rightly received the most attention. Here Machen examined theological *liberalism with respect to beliefs about God and humanity, the Bible, Christ, salvation and the church. His conclusion was that 'the chief modern rival of Christianity is "liberalism." An examination of the teachings of liberalism in comparison with those of Christianity will show that at every point the two movements are in direct opposition' (*Christianity and Liberalism*, p. 53). The argumentation in this volume is careful, yet compelling. The critic Walter Lippman, who was no friend to any variety of Christianity, called it a 'cool and stringent defense of orthodox Protestantism' (*Preface to Morals*, New York, 1929, p. 32).

With Machen's premature death on 1 January 1937, American conservative Presbyterians lost more than just an important leader. He had been at once a model of scholarship and a rallying point for consistently Reformed churchmen. Friendly critics have suggested that his thought was perhaps too closely tied to intellectual conventions of the nineteenth century and that he was overprone to independence. But critics and supporters alike have acknowledged the integrity of his work and the influence of his life.

Bibliography

D. G. Hart, *Defending the Faith: J. Gresham Machen and the Crisis of Conservative Protestantism in Modern America* (Grand Rapids, 1995); G. M. Marsden, 'J. Gresham Machen, History, and Truth', *WTJ* 42 (1979), pp. 157–175; W. S. Reid, 'J. Gresham Machen', in D. F. Wells (ed.), *Reformed Theology in America* (Grand Rapids, 1985); C. A. Russell, 'J. Gresham Machen: Scholarly Fundamentalist', in *Voices of American Fundamentalism* (Philadelphia, 1976); N. B. Stonehouse, *J. Gresham Machen: A Biographical Memoir* (Grand Rapids, 1954).

M. A. NOLL

MACINTYRE, ALASDAIR CHAMBERS (b. 1929)

Alasdair MacIntyre was born on 12 January 1929, in Glasgow, Scotland. He has served on philosophy faculties at numerous universities, first in the UK, at Oxford University, and then in the United States, where he is permanent senior research fellow at Notre Dame University. MacIntyre has published numerous books and articles, starting with *Marxism: An Interpretation* (London, 1953). A religious interest has been evident from the very beginning, leading to the collection which he edited together with Anthony Flew, *New Essays in Philosophical Theology* (London, 1955). However, it was after his conversion to Catholic Christianity that he published his most influential books. It would not be an exaggeration to say that his contributions to the fields of *ethics, political philosophy and the history of philosophy have significantly altered our understanding of *rationality in general, but also theological rationality in particular.

His 1981 classic, *After Virtue*, was a watershed in both ethics and theology. Exhibiting a fresh philosophical methodology, which combined philosophical argument with historical narration, MacIntyre stressed the inseparability of reason and tradition. He described the contemporary moral morass as resulting from the fact that liberal reason had divorced moral concepts from the traditions and practices which are their rightful context. Moral, philosophical, theological, political arguments cannot be settled by appeal to tradition-neutral criteria, but only by setting them against the background of some tradition. He defines a living tradition as 'an historically extended, socially embedded argument, and an argument precisely in part about the goods which constitute that tradition' (*After Virtue*, p. 207). This led MacIntyre to speak about tradition-constituted and tradition-constitutive rationality.

At the time, MacIntyre was not the only philosopher emphasizing the so-called social construction of knowledge. But what distinguished MacIntyre from others, beyond his insistence that tradition is not a barrier to knowledge, was his optimism with regard to inter-traditional rationality. His *Whose Justice? Which Rationality?* (1988) insisted that, while reason is always embedded in traditions, both perspectivism and *relativism must be rejected. It is possible, he forcefully argued, to see transitions from one tradition to another as improvements in understanding. MacIntyre rejects *foundationalism and the correspondence theory of truth while insisting on arguments about the relative superiority of one tradition over another. His *Gifford Lectures, published as *Three Rival Versions of Moral Enquiry* (1990), are such a non-foundationalist and historicist argument for the superiority of the tradition of Augustinian *Thomism in ethics, as opposed to modern liberal encyclopaedia and postmodern deconstructionist genealogy.

MacIntyre has been very influential in the development of *narrative (or *postliberal) theology, as well as in the development of so-called virtue ethics.

Bibliography

Works: 'Epistemological Crises, Dramatic Narrative, and the Philosophy of Science', *The Monist* 60, 1977, pp. 453–472; *After Virtue* (Notre Dame, ²1984); *Whose Justice? Which Rationality* (Notre Dame, 1988); *Three Rival Versions of Moral Enquiry* (Notre Dame, 1990); *The Tasks of Philosophy: Selected Essays*, vol. 1 (Cambridge, 2006); *Ethics and Politics: Selected Essays*, vol. 2 (Cambridge, 2006).

Studies: M. Fuller, *Making Sense of MacIntyre* (Aldershot, 1998); C. S. Lutz, *Tradition in the Ethics of Alasdair MacIntyre: Relativism, Thomism, and Philosophy* (Lanham, 2004); M. C. Murphy (ed.), *Alasdair MacIntyre* (Cambridge, 2003).

A. Vidu

MACKAY, DONALD M. (1922–1987)

Donald MacKay was an internationally known British neuroscientist who was Granada Research Professor of Communication and Neuroscience at the University of Keele (1960–82), where he led an interdisciplinary research team on the organization of the brain. All his work, both in this area, and in his more philosophical reflections on the human person, and on science and faith, were motivated by a strong Christian faith. He was reared in the strong *Reformed faith of the Free Church of Scotland.

Theologically, MacKay's work is important for two bold metaphysical theses which he developed with great thoroughness and tenacity. MacKay insisted that *science and religion stand in a logically complementary relationship. Science expresses the physically measurable and testable aspects of created reality. The findings of science are not exhaustive – MacKay was a fervent antireductionist – but are complemented by other levels of significant description, among which is that of the Christian religion. Thus the description of an event as 'confession of sin' is not a rival to the description of the same event in terms of physical changes in the brain, but complements it. Both science and Christian theology make claims which are objectively true or false, and the Christian faith has nothing to fear from scientific enquiry. Both science and faith progress, in different ways, in a humble, listening and enquiring attitude to the data.

The roots of MacKay's approach to science and religion lay in his view about the relation between the brain and the mind, and in his *Augustinian emphasis upon the divine timeless upholding of all things. God is not active in the 'gaps' of our present understanding, nor does he interfere with the working of otherwise immutable physical laws.

MacKay also gave prolonged and intense effort to defending the view that free choices are logically indeterminate (see *Determinism; *Will). For the chooser there is no future specification of any of his free actions which it would be correct for him now to believe, even though such specifications can, in principle, exist for another human observer, and do exist in the mind of God.

These views were expounded in numerous articles and reviews and in several books, including: *Christianity in a Mechanistic Universe* (London, 1965); *Science, Chance and Providence* (Oxford, 1978); *The Clockwork Image* (London, 1974); *Brains, Machines, and Persons* (London, 1980). His *Gifford Lectures, given in 1986, were published as *Behind the Eye* (Oxford, 1991).

Bibliography

J. W. Haas, Jr, 'Donald MacCrimmon MacKay (1922–1987)', *Perspectives on Science and Christian Faith*, 44 (1922), pp. 55–61.

P. Helm

MACKINNON, DONALD M. (1913–94)

MacKinnon held chairs in moral philosophy at Aberdeen and in philosophy of religion at Cambridge until 1978. His work represents a powerful and consistent rejection of *idealism in philosophy and theology in favour of a realism given its distinctive shape by the doctrines of the person of Christ and the *atonement. His main concerns lay in the overlapping areas of theology, metaphysics and moral philosophy. MacKinnon was especially concerned to explore the ontological and *metaphysical implications of Christian beliefs about the person and work of Christ, and it is here that his restless and interrogative analysis is at its best. His ethical work is much preoccupied with offering a realist account of the nature and significance of human action and moral freedom, especially as this determines the character of human political action. He has also written perceptively on the history of philosophy (notably on *Kant and *Butler), on *Marxist-Leninism, and on sacramental and dogmatic theology. Much of his best work is highly complex and allusive, approaching issues tangentially through particular historical incidents or texts. Partly because of this, and partly because his preferred form is the suggestive essay rather than the systematic treatise, his work has not received the attention which it deserves.

Bibliography

Works: *Christian Faith and Communist Faith*, ed. MacKinnon (London, 1953); *A Study in Ethical Theory* (London, 1957); Gifford Lectures 1965–66; *Borderlands of Theology and Other Essays*, eds. G. W. Roberts and D. E. Smucker (London, 1968); *Making Moral Decisions*, ed. MacKinnon (London, 1969); *The Problem of Metaphysics* (London, 1974); *Explorations in Theology*, vol. 5, ed. MacKinnon (London, 1979).

Studies: D. Hardy, 'Theology through Philosophically Mediated Life: Donald M. MacKinnon and Nicholas Lash', in D. Ford (ed.), *The Modern Theologians* (Oxford, 1997), pp. 272–278; B. Hebblethwaite and S. Sutherland (eds.), *The Philosophical Frontiers of Christian Theology: Essays Presented to D. M. MacKinnon* (Cambridge, 1982); P. G. Wignall, 'D. M. MacKinnon: An Introduction to His Early Theological Writings', *New Studies in Theology* 1, 1980, pp. 75–94.

J. B. Webster

MACKINTOSH, HUGH ROSS (1870–1936)

Mackintosh was a Scottish theologian born in Paisley and educated at Edinburgh and in Germany. He ministered in Tayport and Aberdeen before appointment in 1904 to the chair of systematic theology in New College, Edinburgh, which post he held until his death. His early experience on the continent gave him a continuing interest in nineteenth-century German Protestant writers whose work he sought to publicize in Scotland, particularly by his participation in translating *Schleiermacher and *Ritschl. As with a later Scottish scholar, William *Barclay, he would accept the classification of '*liberal evangelical'. The two were alike in recommending their students to have a number of non-religious interests. Mackintosh rejected the view that saw propitiatory or punitive features in the *atonement. His works, which have proved more durable than those of other early twentieth-century scholars, include *The Doctrine of the Person of Jesus Christ* (Edinburgh, 1912), *The Christian Experience of Forgiveness* (London, 1927) and *Types of Modern Theology* (London, 1937), which latter presents developments from Schleiermacher to *Barth.

Bibliography

J. W. Leitch, *A Theology of Transition: H. R. Mackintosh as an Approach to Barth* (London, 1952), with bibliography; T. F. Torrance, 'H. R. Mackintosh: Theologian of the Cross', SBET 5:2 (1988); idem (ed.), *H. R. Mackintosh: The Person of Jesus Christ* (Edinburgh, 2000).

J. D. Douglas

MACQUARRIE, JOHN (1919–2007)

Macquarrie taught in Glasgow, New York and latterly in Oxford. Born into a Scottish Presbyterian family, he became one of the best-known Anglican theologians of the late twentieth century, having published very widely in the areas of Christian doctrine and philosophy of religion. Much of his writing shows the influence of a variety of thinkers in the *existentialist tradition. His earlier books *An Existentialist Theology* (London, 1955) and *The Scope of Demythologizing* (London, 1960) are particularly concerned with the resources to be found in *Bultmann's theology, though they do not counsel uncritical acceptance. His much-used textbook *Principles of Christian Theology* (London, 1966, ²1977) draws heavily on *Tillich's thought, among others, in its reinterpretations of central Christian doctrines. He is also well known for his history of *Twentieth Century Religious Thought* (London, 1963), and for a variety of other books on such topics as *ethics, *spirituality, theological language and Christian eschatology. Macquarrie's later work is to be found in two large treatises on the Christian doctrines of God and man, *In Search of Deity* (London, 1984) and *In Search of Humanity* (London, 1982). Best read as essays in *natural theology, these volumes are particularly good examples of the range of theological and philosophical reference, both historical and contemporary, which his work commands.

See also: Myth.

Bibliography

Additional works: *Studies in Christian Existentialism* (London, 1966); *God-Talk* (London, 1967); *God and Secularity* (London, 1968); *Paths in Spirituality* (London, 1972); *Existentialism* (Harmondsworth, 1973); *Christian Hope* (London, 1978).

Studies: T. Bradshaw, 'John Macquarrie', in A. E. McGrath (ed.), *SPCK Handbook of Anglican Theologians* (London, 1998); O. Cummings, *John Macquarrie: A Master of Theology* (New York, 2002); E. T. Long, *Existence, Being, and God: An Introduction to the Philosophical Theology of John Macquarrie* (St Paul, MN, 1985).

J. B. Webster

MAHAN, ASA (1799–1889)

Asa Mahan was a pastor, theologian and educator, influential in many reform causes popular among English-speaking evangelical Protestants during the nineteenth century. He grew up as a *Presbyterian in the highly *revivalistic 'burned over district' of western New York. He graduated from Hamilton College (1824) and from Andover Theological Seminary (1827). Following seminary, he was an agent for the American Tract Society, then minister of Presbyterian churches in New York State (1829–31) and Cincinnati, Ohio (1831–5).

In 1835 Mahan became president of Oberlin College in Oberlin, Ohio. Together with Charles *Finney (the first professor of theology there) and a cohort of other 'progressive' New School Presbyterians and others, Mahan helped to make Oberlin a centre of 'reformism', and a model for many evangelical Protestant colleges of the time. Oberlin enrolled women, the poor, and African Americans. It propagated abolitionism (see *slavery), the doctrine of Christian *perfection, various health reform causes, and advocated that Christians live as simply as possible and give away all surplus to the poor. In 1850 Mahan left Oberlin for other work in Christian education. From 1859 to 1871 he was president of Adrian College, Michigan, a school founded by the abolitionist Wesleyan Methodist Church.

While at Oberlin and following, Mahan became increasingly active in the *Holiness Movement. His first major book was *The Scripture Doctrine of Christian Perfection Stated and Defended* (1839). A later work, *The Baptism of the Holy Ghost* (1870), became a standard exposition of holiness/*Higher Christian Life teaching. From 1872 until his death in 1889 Mahan lived in England, where he preached occasionally, edited several periodicals and published his autobiography (1882).

Bibliography

Works: *The Scripture Doctrine of Christian Perfection; with Other Kindred Subjects, Illustrated and Confirmed in a Series of Discourses Designed to Throw Light on the Way of Holiness* (Boston, 1839); *The Baptism of the Holy Ghost* (New York, 1870); *Autobiography, Intellectual, Moral, and Spiritual* (London, 1882).

Studies: E. H. Madden and J. A. Hamilton, *Freedom and Grace: The Life of Asa Mahan* (Metuchen, 1982).

H. E. RASER

MAN, see ANTHROPOLOGY; FEMINIST THEOLOGY

MANICHAEISM

Once regarded as a Christianized form of *Zoroastrianism, Manichaeism is now generally accepted as one of the last and most complete manifestations of *Gnosticism. It was founded by the Syro-Persian Mani (216–76) who was brought up in a Jewish-Christian sect in south Babylonia and subsequently rebelled against it. The Manichaean *gnōsis* embodies a complex cosmic drama which centres on a primordial battle between the originating principles of Light and Darkness. An initial invasion of Light by Darkness led to a counter-attack by Light which was designed to fail, tricking the powers of Darkness into swallowing particles of Light. The universe was then created to redeem and purify this captive light and to punish and imprison the archons of Darkness. Through their concupiscence some of this defiled Light escaped from the archons' bodies and became plant life. They also brought forth humankind through a series of horrific acts involving abortion, incest and cannibalism; this resulted in the imprisonment of Light-particles, the soul, in a body which is utterly evil and corrupt. The soul could, however, be awakened by *gnōsis* and be made aware of its divine origins.

Jesus in Manichaeism is one of a series of Gnostic saviours, and his historical manifestation was purely *docetic. The individual details of the Manichaean cosmic drama are derived mainly from Jewish and Christian apocrypha and from the cosmogonic teaching of the Edessan philosopher Bardaisan (154–222). Mani was also heavily influenced by *Marcion, from whom he acquired a strong 'Pauline' *antinomianism and claimed the title of 'Apostle of Jesus Christ'.

The Manichaean sect was extremely hierarchical, and was divided into elect and hearers; the former were priests who had to observe sexual abstinence and strict food taboos including vegetarianism so that they could enable the liberation of the Light particles trapped in the plants. The hearers, the lay followers, had to attend to the needs of the elect, and were not bound by the same rigid rules. Easily organized into small units, the religion was able to spread swiftly and to survive persecution.

A combination of missionary zeal and persecution by Sassanian authorities resulted in the religion being diffused in the Roman Empire and the lands east of the River Oxus. It was particularly well established in Roman Africa where it passed itself off as a more perfect form of Christianity, including the young *Augustine among those who were captivated by its 'higher criticism' of the Jewish and Christian Scriptures. The *dualism of Manichaeism was later seen by church authorities in the Middle Ages as having been inherited by heretical movements such as the Paulicians, the Bogomils, the Paterenes and the Cathars (see *Albigenses). In the East, the religion gradually expanded along the Silk Road and eventually reached China where it was outlawed. After the ninth century, however, the religion became strongly established in Central Asia. Later the sect went underground in China and survived as a secret religion in the south until the sixteenth century.

The Manichaean canon consists of a corpus of seven works by Mani, none of which has survived in a complete form. Besides a large body of polemical writings on the sect by the Church Fathers, our knowledge has been greatly increased by the discovery of genuine Manichaean writings from Turfan, Dunhuang (both in China), Medinet Medi (Egypt) and Theveste (North Africa). In the 1970s and 80s a small papyrus codex from Egypt, belonging to the papyrus collection of the University of Cologne, containing a hagiographical version of the life of the founder (the Cologne Mani Codex), was successfully restored and edited. It shows beyond doubt that the sect had its origins in the fringe of Judeo-Christianity and not in Iranian religions.

Bibliography

Sources: A. Adam (ed.), *Texte Zum Manichäismus* (Berlin, ²1969); A. Böhlig and J. P. Asmussen (eds.), *Die Gnosis*, vol. 3: *Der Manichäismus* (Zurich and Munich, 1980); R. Cameron and A. J. Dewey (eds.), *The Cologne Mani Codex* (Missoula, 1979).

Studies: N. J. Baker-Brian, *Manichaeism: An Ancient Faith Rediscovered* (London, 2011); J. K. Coyle, *Manichaeism and Its Legacy* (Leiden, 2009); H. J. Klimkeit, *Manichaean Art and Calligraphy* (Leiden, 1982); S. N. C. Lieu, *Manichaeism in the Later Roman Empire and Medieval China: A Historical Survey* (Tübingen, ²1992); idem, *Manichaeism in Mesopotamia and the Roman East* (Leiden, 1994); H.-Ch. Puech, *Sur le Manichéisme et autres essais* (Paris, 1979).

S. N. Lieu

MARCEL, GABRIEL (1889–1973)

Gabriel Honoré Marcel was a French philosopher and playwright who played a pivotal role in the development of *existentialism. His work shows a consistent concern for the modern pressures of technology and materialism, forces that threatened to annihilate the individual. Marcel is most famous for his existential philosophy, which he preferred to call 'Philosophy of Existence' to distance his work from that of his friend Jean-Paul Sartre. Marcel also penned dozens of plays, often using the scripts to depict characters caught in the interpersonal problems that he identified in his strictly philosophical writings. Raised an atheist, Marcel converted to Catholicism in 1929 and his work is sometimes considered Christian existentialism.

In his best-known, two-volume work *The Mystery of Being* (1951), Marcel demonstrates his consistent commitment to concrete philosophy and ordinary language. The human world is broken, Marcel claims, because people have lost sight of their relation to *being. Without any sense of ontology, humans are oriented only by function, and defined by superficial realities instead of what is truly exigent. Unlike the problems of science, *ontology opens not toward solutions and technology, but toward mystery and the relation with the other person.

Bibliography

Works: *The Mystery of Being, Volume 1: Reflection and Mystery* (London, 1951); *The Mystery of Being, Volume 2: Faith and Reality* (London, 1951); *Man Against Mass Society* (Chicago, 1962).

Studies: J. G. Hernandez, *Gabriel Marcel's Ethics of Hope: Evil, God and Virtue* (New York, 2011); T. Michaud, 'Gabriel Marcel and the Postmodern World', *Journal of French Philosophy* VII, 1–2, 1995, pp. 5–29.

E. Severson

MARCELLUS OF ANCYRA (d. *c.* 374)

Marcellus was bishop of Ancyra in Galatia. He first became prominent as a supporter of *Athanasius and the Nicene term *homoousios* (the Son being 'of one substance' with the Father). From this perspective he attacked the teaching of *Arius' supporters, Asterius (d. *c.* 341), Eusebius of Nicomedia (d. *c.* 342) and *Eusebius of Caesarea, but in so doing exaggerated the oneness of the Father and the Son before and after the incarnation. Eusebius of Caesarea responded with his *Contra Marcellum* and *De Ecclesiastica Theologia*, charging Marcellus with Sabellianism (see *Monarchianism). Marcellus was accordingly condemned by a synod of Constantinople (336). In exile in Rome he gained the support of Pope Julius I, and with the arrival of Athanasius (339) he was cleared of 'the falsehood of Sabellius, the malice of Paul of Samosata, and the blasphemies of Montanus' (Rome, 341; Sardica, 343). He was, however, again removed from his see by the Emperor Constantius (347) and died in exile, his teaching being repudiated by Basil and condemned by the Council of Constantinople (381).

Marcellus's ideas *On the Subjection of the Son* are preserved by Eusebius and in his own letter to Julius. According to Basil, he taught that only to the incarnate *Logos is the title 'Son' properly applied. By the return or contraction of the Son to the pre-incarnate state, his temporary separate existence came to an end. 'He returned again to him whence he came forth and had no existence before his coming forth, nor *hypostasis after his return' (Basil, *Letter* 69). It was to counter Marcellus' teaching that the phrase 'whose kingdom shall have no end' was included in the Nicene Creed.

See also: CHRISTOLOGY; CREEDS; TRINITY.

Bibliography

L. Ayres, *Nicaea and Its Legacy: An Approach to Fourth-Century Trinitarian Theology* (Oxford, 2004); R. P. C. Hanson, *The Search for the Christian Doctrine of God* (Edinburgh, 1988); J. N. D. Kelly, *Early Christian Doctrines* (London, 1977); J. T. Lienhard, *Contra Marcellum: Marcellus of Ancyra and Fourth-Century Theology* (Washington DC, 1999); A. H. B. Logan, 'Dark Star: The Rehabilitation of Marcellus of Ancyra', *The Expository Times* 118, 2007, p. 384; S. Parvis, *Marcellus of Ancyra and the Lost Years of the Arian Controversy 325–345* (Oxford, 2006).

H. D. McDonald

MARCION (c. 80–c. 160)

Marcion was reared in Sinope of Pontus (modern Turkey), where his father was reported to have been a bishop and himself a wealthy ship-builder. He was active as a teacher in Asia Minor, perhaps as early as the opening decades of the second century, before going to Rome. The rejection of his teaching by the leaders of the main Christian centres led him to set up a rival church which in a few years was nearly as widespread as the great church.

Marcion is best known for his work on the text and canon of the Bible (see *Scripture). He rejected the OT as a Christian book and collected the earliest known Christian canon, composed of an abbreviated version of Luke's Gospel and ten edited Pauline epistles (lacking the Pastorals). He presented his theological views in the *Antitheses*, in which he set out contradictions between the OT and the NT. His works do not survive, so his positions must be reconstructed from the refutations made by his opponents, the fullest of which is *Tertullian's five books *Against Marcion*.

Marcion was convinced that *Paul was the only true apostle and that the original twelve, by 'Judaizing', became false apostles. Galatians was placed first in his collection of Paul's letters. The opening words of the *Antitheses*, 'O wealth of riches! rapture, power, amazement! seeing that there can be nothing to say about it, or to imagine about it, or to compare to it!' express his wonder before the Pauline gospel of grace. From Paul, Marcion deduced an exaggerated contrast between *law and gospel. In agreement with his contemporary Aquila of Pontus, he practised a literal interpretation of Scripture, rejecting all allegory (see *Hermeneutics). Marcion went far beyond Paul in concluding that there are two Gods: the God of the OT, the Creator, who is a God of law and justice and who predicted the Jewish Messiah; and the previously unknown God of the NT, the Father of Jesus Christ, who is a God of mercy and salvation.

Jesus Christ revealed the Father in the fifteenth year of the Emperor Tiberius, for Marcion omitted the birth narratives from the gospel. Jesus' death purchased human salvation, and Jesus raised his own soul from the grave. Marcion advocated *asceticism: the avoidance of sex frustrates the Creator God. Marcion administered baptism only to the unmarried or abstinent before the end of life. Water was substituted for wine in the Lord's Supper. To the charge of antinomianism in the absence of law, he responded with 'God forbid'.

The Church Fathers objected to Marcion's separation of salvation from *creation and of the church from its OT heritage. Marcion's challenge accelerated the church's recognition of a NT canon and sharpened its emphasis on certain doctrines in the rule of faith (see *Creeds). Marcion shared in common with *Gnosticism such things as the idea of the unknown God, a negative view of the created world and a depreciation of the OT; but he differed in his lack of speculative, mythological interest, rejection of allegory, emphasis on faith rather than 'knowledge', and concern to establish a church.

Bibliography

B. Aland, 'Marcion: Versuch einer neuen Interpretation', *ZTK* 70, 1973, pp. 420–427; A. Amann, in *DTC* 9, cols. 2009–2032; D. Balás, in *Texts and Testaments: Critical Essays on the Bible and Early Church Fathers*, ed. W. Eugene March (San Antonio, 1980); G. Bardy, in *DBS* 5, cols. 862–877; E. C. Blackman, *Marcion and His Influence* (London, 1948); E. Evans, *Tertullian: Adversus Marcionem*, 2 vols. (Oxford, 1972); A. Harnack, *Marcion: Das Evangelium vom fremden Gott* (Leipzig, 1960 [²1924]); R. J. Hoffmann, *Marcion: On the Restitution of Christianity* (Chico, 1984); J. Knox, *Marcion and the New Testament: An Essay on the Early History of the Canon* (Chicago, 1942); G. Ory, *Marcion* (Paris, 1980); R. S. Wilson, *Marcion: A Study of a Second-Century Heretic* (New York, 1980 [1933]).

E. Ferguson

MARION, JEAN-LUC (b. 1946)

Jean-Luc Marion, Professor of Philosophy at the University of Paris and of the Philosophy of Religion and Theology at the Divinity School of the University of Chicago, is a leading phenomenologist, an authority on *Descartes and one of the most prominent figures in the 'theological turn' of recent Continental philosophy. Marion was a student of Deleuze, *Derrida, Daniélou, de Lubac and von *Balthasar. *Kierkegaard, Husserl, *Heidegger and *Levinas have deeply influenced him as well. In his most overtly theological work he has contrasted 'love' and 'being'. 'God is love' signifies that God is free in relation to 'being' and ruptures it from the outside in the gift of the incarnate Christ, a gift that cannot be comprehended. Through a liturgical, iconic witness to Christ, God's hallowing gaze disrupts intellectual fixation. The gift of God thus works a *kenosis* of the centred self, a *metanoia* that abandons idolatry.

Bibliography

Works: *God Without Being* (ET, Chicago, 1991); *The Idol and Distance* (ET, New York, 2001); *Prolegomena to Charity* (ET, New York, 2002); *The Crossing of the Visible* (ET, Stanford, 2004).

Studies: K. Hart (ed.), *Counter-Experiences: Reading Jean-Luc Marion* (Notre Dame, 2007); R. Horner, *Jean-Luc Marion: A Theological Introduction* (Aldershot and Burlington, 2005).

C. S. Keen

MARITAIN, JACQUES (1882–1973)

Jacques Maritain was a French philosopher and a key figure in the Roman Catholic revival of the first half of the twentieth century. He converted to Roman Catholicism in 1906. His main contribution lies in reinterpreting the insights of *Thomas Aquinas as foundations for modern metaphysics, politics and ethics. His work impacted on theology in at least five major ways. First, he restated the role of Christian philosophy as a passionate search for truth. He provided a metaphysical base, through his concept of 'intuition of being', for *existentialist theology. Of major importance are his writings on political philosophy. A friend of Popes John XXIII and Paul VI, his vision of a democratic state founded on Christian values influenced them and the conciliar church (see *Collegiality and conciliarity). He also gave a firm natural law basis for the post-war discussion on human *rights. Finally, he was a lifelong opponent of anti-Semitism, and his writings underlie, but go further than, the Second Vatican Council's *Nostra Aetate*. Maritain exercised an important influence on, especially, French theology in the mid-twentieth century, but also on figures such as *Lonergan or *Rahner and their transcendental *Thomism. He remains significant also for his work on the church's political role, and on *aesthetics.

Bibliography

The Collected Works of Jacques Maritain, ed. R. McInerny, vols. 1, 7, 11, 20 (Notre Dame, 1995–).

T. A. Noble

MARRIAGE, see SEXUALITY

MARROW CONTROVERSY, see BOSTON, THOMAS

MARTYRDOM

The word 'martyr' derives from the Greek *martus*, meaning 'witness', while the verb *martureo* is commonly translated 'to bear witness'. Both words regularly recur in the NT, especially in John, Acts and Revelation. Stephen is described by Paul as your 'witness', whose blood was shed (Acts 22:20), while Rev. 2:13 refers to a 'witness', Antipas, who was killed for his faith. Towards the end of the second century the word 'martyr' was increasingly connected with this idea of a 'blood witness', someone who gave up their life for their faith, though it was probably not until the middle of the fourth century that the term was used exclusively in this way. The oldest surviving account of a Christian martyrdom outside the NT, the *Martyrdom of Polycarp* (*c*. 155), uses 'martyr' in this sense (see *Apostolic Fathers).

An extensive literature about martyrdom emerged from early Christian communities. First, the *passiones* or *martyria*, which describe the final days and actual death of the martyr(s) (*The Passion of Perpetua and Felicitas*); second, the *acta* or *gesta*, which provide accounts of the trials of the martyrs (the *Acts of Justin* or the *Acts of Carpus*); third, exhortations, which reflect upon martyrdom and are largely intended to encourage Christians facing persecution (Tertullian, *To the Martyrs*; Origen, *Exhortation to the Martyrs*; Pseudo-Cyprian, *Glory of Martyrdom*); fourth, eulogies or panegyrics on the anniversaries of martyrdoms, which celebrate the virtues of martyrs in order to edify their listeners (sermons by Basil, Gregory of Nyssa and John Chrysostom). Some descriptions embellish the events, transforming the martyrs into early Christian saints with supernatural powers over the beasts, the fires or their gladiatorial executioners.

'The blood of the martyrs' (cf. Tertullian, *The Apology*, 50) planted a seed in some imaginations. *Justin Martyr claims to have been drawn to Christianity by seeing martyrs die (*Second Apology*, 12). Martyrs were perceived as following in the footsteps of Christ, inspired by the Holy Spirit and assured of immediate access to heaven. Some early Christians, like Ignatius of Antioch, yearned for martyrdom, while others urged caution to those who sought it (*Martyrdom of Polycarp*, 4). The theological significance bestowed upon martyrdom contributed to the development of the cult of martyrs, which became widespread in the third century. Their 'remains' ('relics') were venerated, their stories retold, and their memories commemorated through liturgies, pilgrimages, books and buildings. Such practices have a long history. Stories of martyrdom were put to various uses in John Foxe's *Book of Martyrs* (1559) and the *Martyr's Mirror* (1660). Both ancient and modern stories about martyrdom are repeated, amplified, contested and elaborated upon through different media. The statues of ten twentieth-century martyrs at Westminster Abbey, London, illustrate the ongoing significance of martyrdom.

See also: SUFFERING.

Bibliography

G. W. Bowersock, *Martyrdom and Rome* (Cambridge, 1995); T. van Braght, *Martyr's Mirror* (aka *The Bloody Theater*, 1660); E. Castelli, *Martyrdom and Memory: Early Christian Culture Making* (New York, 2004); J. Foxe, *Foxe's Book of Martyrs* (also known as *Acts and Monuments of Happening in the Church* (Latin, 1554; English ^{4}1583); W. H. C. Frend, *Martyrdom and Persecution in the Early Church* (Oxford, 1965); L. Grig, *Making Martyrs in Late Antiquity* (London, 2004); J. Leemans (ed.), *More than a Memory: The Discourse of Martyrdom and the Construction of Christian Identity in the History of Christianity* (Leuven, 2005); P. Middleton, *Radical Martyrdom and Cosmic Conflict in Early Christianity* (London, 2006); H. Musurillo, *The Acts of Christian Martyrs* (Oxford, 1972); A. Trites, *The New Testament Concept of Witness* (Cambridge, 2004); B. Wicker (ed.), *Witnesses to Faith? Martyrdom in Christianity and Islam* (Aldershot, 2006).

J. P. MITCHELL

MARXISM AND CHRISTIANITY

Marxism refers to a socio-political project put forward in a series of treatises by Karl Marx (1818–83) and Friedrich Engels (1820–95) or to any of several systems of thought or approaches to social criticism derived from their works. The term is used narrowly to designate a cluster of socio-political structures generated by dominant Communist parties in different parts of the world in the twentieth century.

Marxism is an intellectual tradition, or a family of interrelated traditions, offering a secular 'interpretation of human existence' (A. MacIntyre, *Marxism and Christianity*, p. 2).

But there is more to Marxism than philosophical rationality. Marx's view that philosophers have interpreted the world but that the point is to change it, indicates the visionary and inspirational nature of Marxism while disclosing key themes of context and power in Marxist thought. Throughout the twentieth century practically all radical movements of emancipation drew upon Marxism for socio-political critique and aspiration. Marxism, as the official state-sponsored ideology of socialist regimes, evoked a kind of religious commitment. Marxist movements have an intellectual tradition, an ideology and a revolutionary vision. They intersect with Christian traditions on all three levels.

Marx did not produce a systematic exposition of his thought. The philosophical ideas of Marx and Engels evolved, and were challenged, revised, enriched and broadened by a variety of intellectuals and political activists. The philosophical aspect of Marxist discourse is often called dialectical *materialism. It is dialectical because it incorporates *Hegel's idea of inherent change, and materialistic because it follows *Feuerbach's rejection of German metaphysical *idealism and argues for economic, social and physical embodiment.

For several decades, after the Bolshevik and other revolutions, broad agreement concerning Marxist doctrine was developed and politically enforced. This resulted in 'orthodox' Marxism (or 'scientific' Marxism-Leninism). It placed heavy emphasis on historic determinism and the inevitability of the replacement of *capitalism by a socialist and eventually a communist economy. Socialism takes the equality of all individuals as its ideal. It favours control over the means of production and redirecting that for the welfare of the socialist state. The means of production can be controlled by the elite (Lenin's centralist socialism) or democratically. Marx envisioned that socialism would naturally transform itself into communism. Work for the common good becomes its own reward. This leads to the abolition of private property and brings full harmony between people's talents and needs: from each according to ability, to each according to needs. Orthodox Marxism is a totalizing and even totalitarian ideology. Western forms (humanist or critical Marxism) differ (sometimes substantially) from 'orthodox' versions, and emphasize the cultural relativity of Marx's project or the philosophical, ethical, socio-critical or aesthetic dimensions of his thought.

Marxism and Christianity

The Marxist vision has fascinating religious qualities. Its attractive power is sustained partly by an excessive confidence in the supremacy of the human reason and partly by an appeal to the goodness and equality of each individual: freedom, equality and brotherhood for all. What appears on the surface to be a logical, rational philosophy of life turns out to be based on faith-like commitments. Belief in the eventual arrival of communism requires almost as great a faith-commitment as belief in God. In many ways Marxism embodies a secularized Christian eschatology, both in form and content.

As with other foundationalist religions, 'orthodox' Marxism is founded on the uncontested truth of the narratives of the founders, such as Marx, Engels and Lenin. Others interpreted the texts and true doctrines were derived. They were systematized and enforced. Rival groups were condemned and suppressed. New party members were inducted into the privileged group through special rituals. Shrines, icons and statues of the founders of the struggle for Communist dominance were regularly visited and venerated. Psalmodies were created to praise the achievements of the Party and the glorious future. Processions of the faithful with banners of the leaders past and present (members of the Politburo) were organized annually.

The relationship of Marxism and Christianity can be viewed in terms of affinities and antagonism. Hoping for and working toward a 'bright future', with a just society that removes the problems of suffering and injustice, is appealing and evokes major Judeo-Christian concerns. Marxism owes to Judeo-Christianity the understanding of human imperfection and alienation and a search for means to overcome them, as well as a fascination with the meaning of life. Following the Hegelian lead, Marxism also takes over the understanding of a linear, progressive and teleologically determined direction in *history, a history which has meaning and purpose (union with God for Christians; eschatological justice for Communists). Marxist collectivism also draws from the way of life of radical Christian communities – shared property ownership, sacrifice for others, fellowship and mutual care.

From Marx on there is a history of interaction between Christians and Marxists. Some Christians have tried to emulate Marxist social criticism. Theologians from *Rauschenbusch (a Baptist) and the *social gospellers, through Reinhold *Niebuhr and Protestant proponents of *Christian Socialism, to Catholic *liberation theologians, have found Marxian themes of alienation, exploitation, inequality and political activism compatible with Christian social concerns. For them, as long as social divisions (elitism, wealth, class, gender, ethnicity and race) domination and asymmetric distribution of power continue, Marxism is an essential and challenging dialogue partner. Fundamentalist and conservative Christians, by contrast, have associated Marxism primarily with oppressive regimes led by Communist parties. They have regarded 'orthodox' Marxism as a satanic pseudo-religion and a threat to Christian faith. In the mid-twentieth century, anti-communism became a defining characteristic of some conservative evangelicals, particularly in the United States.

In spite of many common concerns and the qualified applicability of Marxian critical tools within Christian social thought, there is an essential narrative incompatibility of the two belief systems: that of Prometheus as the benefactor of humanity (a god against gods in early Marx) and of Immanuel, God with us, the wounded Saviour of the world, in Christianity. Marxism's explicit *atheism has a clear anthropological focus. It sets emancipated humanity at the centre and subsumes people's dignity and fate under the collective well-being. Marxist morality serves only this end. Such views are antagonistic to Christian ideas of a transcendent moral order. From a Christian perspective, Marx's accounts of the human condition and liberation are reductive and deficient. They underestimate the importance of the human spirit in relation to God and the potential of the radical politics of Jesus to transform the social order (see *Kingdom of God).

Theological implications

Currently Marxism is largely out of fashion; however, saying farewell to Marxism is premature. Marxisms share a hermeneutic of suspicion towards powerful social structures – a commitment to identifying, explaining and confronting gross inequality, social domination and abuse, particularly economic. To undermine the Marxist critique of religion, a rational apologetic defence is insufficient. The 'truth of belief in God must be proven, tested, [and] verified in practice' (H. Küng, *Does God Exist?* p. 260).

Christianity must not retreat into unalloyed individualism, deriding the creation, serving earthly powers or sanctioning injustice. Rather, there should be 'practical proof that Christian faith has social-ethical potential and social-critical relevance, that Christianity requires a readiness for change and active commitment, that the expectation of the kingdom of God does not exclude but includes the emancipation of the weary and heavy burdened' (Küng, p. 260).

Bibliography

J. C. Bennett, *Christianity and Communism* (New York, 1949); M. Hoelzl and G. Ward (eds.), *Religion and Political Thought* (London, 2006); A. Ignatov, *Psychologie des Kommunismus* (München, 1985); L. Kołakowski, *Main Currents of Marxism*, 3 vols. (Oxford, 1976–78); H. Küng, *Does God Exist? An Answer for Today* (New York, 1995); A. MacIntyre, *Marxism and Christianity* (London, ³1995); S. Malpas and P. Wake (eds.), *The Routledge Companion to Critical Theory* (London, 2006); P. Scott and W. T. Cavanaugh (eds.), *The Blackwell Companion to Political Theology* (Oxford, 2004); D. R. Stiver, *Theology after Ricœur: New Directions in Hermeneutical Theology* (Louisville, 2001).

P. R. PARUSHEV

MARY

The Roman Catholic doctrine of Mary is a classic example of the gradual *development of doctrine. From the nineteenth century the development has accelerated, stimulated by alleged appearances of Mary at Lourdes, Fatima and elsewhere. Some Catholics were hoping that the Second *Vatican Council (1962–5) would further the process by proclaiming Mary 'CoRedemptrix' (Co-Redeemer with Christ), but others felt that the greater need was to curb the excesses of popular piety. The first group wanted a separate document on Mary, but by a tiny majority the Council voted instead to devote to her a chapter of the *Dogmatic Constitution on the Church*. The decision to view Mary as a *member* of the church was itself a significant moderating step. But the document reaffirms all of the traditional Marian doctrines, albeit with certain qualifications. The aim was 'carefully and equally [to] avoid the falsity of exaggeration on the one

Mary

hand, and the excess of narrow-mindedness on the other' (67). (Here and hereafter numbers in brackets refer to the sections of ch. 8 of the *Constitution*.)

The Eastern Orthodox view of Mary is similar, with two main qualifications. The Orthodox are hesitant about the doctrine of Mary's immaculate conception and incline towards rejecting it. They also object in principle to the Roman Catholic elevation of these beliefs and practices to the status of dogmas.

Theotokos (53, 61, 66)

In Luke 1:43 Mary is called 'the mother of my Lord'. In the early Alexandrian tradition this was made more explicit by the term *theotokos* ('one who gave birth to God', traditionally translated 'mother of God'). The initial concern was *Christological, not Mariological, to affirm the deity of Christ and the reality of the incarnation. At the Council of Antioch in 325 the term was used to state the deity of Christ, in opposition to *Arius. In the next century *Nestorius attacked the term (preferring *Christotokos*). As a consequence, *theotokos* was affirmed by the Council of Ephesus in 431 as a safeguard against *adoptionism. Thus far the concern was Christological, although Nestorius did, in a sermon, warn his hearers to 'beware lest you make the Virgin a goddess'. This warning was timely in that the cult of Mary burgeoned during the Middle Ages. She came to be seen as Queen of Heaven, a title that enjoys no favour in Scripture (Jer. 7:18; 44:17–19, 25). She was increasingly venerated with a worship (*hyperdoulia*, Gk *hyperdouleia*) above that offered to other saints (*doulia*, Gk *douleia*) but below that offered to God (*latreia*).

Mediatrix (60–62)

In the Middle Ages the practice grew of praying to *saints. Mary became especially popular. There was a tendency to see Jesus Christ as stern and unapproachable, and so the faithful were directed to Mary as a sympathetic figure who could *mediate between the believer and Christ. This view of Mary as mediatrix was forcefully stated in 1891 by Pope Leo XIII in an encyclical: 'Nothing is bestowed on us except through Mary, as God himself wills. Therefore as no one can draw near to the supreme Father except through the Son, so also one can scarcely draw near to the Son except through his mother.' The Second Vatican Council reaffirms Mary's role as mediatrix, but states that it should be so understood as 'neither [to] take away from nor [to] add anything to the dignity and efficacy of Christ the one mediator' (62; cf. 60, where 1 Tim. 2:5–6 is quoted).

Immaculate conception (59)

By the beginning of the Middle Ages it had come to be believed that Mary had lived without *sin. But when had she been delivered from sin? *Anselm held that she was born with original sin (*Cur Deus Homo?* 2:16). *Bernard of Clairvaux held that she was *conceived* with original sin but purified before birth (*Ep.* 174). This view was also held by *Thomas Aquinas and the *Dominican school. It was *Duns Scotus who popularized the idea that Mary was conceived without original sin. This new idea did not meet with universal acceptance, and Pope Sixtus IV in 1485 and the Council of *Trent (see *Roman Catholic theology) in 1546 both left the matter undecided. But eventually Duns Scotus' view prevailed, and in 1854 Pope Pius IX proclaimed it a dogma in his bull *Ineffabilis Deus*: 'We declare, pronounce and define that the most blessed Virgin Mary, at the first instant of her conception was preserved immaculate from all stain of original sin, by the singular grace and privilege of the omnipotent God, in virtue of the merits of Jesus Christ, the saviour of mankind, and that this doctrine was revealed by God and therefore must be believed firmly and constantly by all the faithful.'

This doctrine was proclaimed on the basis of the unanimity of the *contemporary* church. There was no scriptural basis for it. It was asserted that this doctrine had always been held in the church as a revealed doctrine. But this is not so much an appeal to tradition (which does not support the doctrine) as the triumph of dogma over tradition. The definition of the immaculate conception is rightly seen as a 'trial run' for the doctrine of papal infallibility, to be defined sixteen years later at the First Vatican Council.

Assumption (59)

In the fourth century there arose the legend that Mary had been assumed into heaven, like Enoch and Elijah in the OT. During the early Middle Ages it came to be generally believed. From the seventh century there was pressure for its definition as a dogma, and this finally took place in 1950. Pope Pius XII defined it in his apostolic constitution, *Munificentissimus Deus*: 'Since [Jesus Christ] was able to do [Mary] so great an honour as to keep her safe from the corruption of the tomb, we must believe that he actually did so . . . The majestic mother of God . . . finally achieved, as the supreme crown of her privileges, that she should be preserved immune from the corruption of the tomb and, like her Son before her, having conquered death should be carried up, in body and soul, to the celestial glory of heaven, there to reign as Queen at the right hand of her Son, the immortal king of the ages.'

Again, the basis for the definition is said to be its theological suitability and the consensus of the *contemporary* Roman Catholic Church. It should be noted that the doctrine concerns more than an (alleged) episode in Mary's personal history. It is the basis for belief in her as Queen of Heaven and as mediatrix.

Co-Redemptrix

Some had hoped that Mary would be proclaimed 'Co-Redemptrix' at the Second Vatican Council, but this did not happen. But while the *term* was avoided, the *concept* is clearly stated. Mary plays a (subsidiary) role in Christ's work of redemption. The incarnation could not occur without Mary's permission or 'fiat' (Luke 1:38). Mary 'gave life to the world' (53); 'Death through Eve, life through Mary' (56). She suffered grievously with Christ at the cross and 'lovingly consented to the immolation of this Victim which she herself had brought forth' (58). She 'was united with [Christ] in suffering as he died on the cross' and co-operated 'in the Saviour's work of restoring supernatural life to souls' (61).

Mother of the church (53f., 61f.)

At the Second Vatican Council Mary is seen both as 'a preeminent and altogether singular member of the church' and as the mother of all Christians (53). While the Constitution does not actually refer to her as 'mother of the church', Pope Paul VI used the title in promulgating the document in 1964.

Protestants as a whole reject these doctrines. While the *virgin birth is scriptural and while *theotokos* can be seen as an affirmation of the biblical doctrine of the incarnation, the other Marian doctrines are seen as a classic example of the *bad* development of doctrine, of the way in which unscriptural if not pagan devotional practices can become dogmas. They can be seen as a striking proof of the need to test all doctrine by *Scripture and of the dangers of making ecclesiastical tradition infallible.

See also: SCRIPTURE AND TRADITION.

Bibliography

D. Attwater, *A Dictionary of Mary* (London, New York and Toronto, 1956); H. Graef, *Mary: A History of Doctrine and Devotion*, 2 vols. (London and New York, 1963 and 1965); G. Miegge, *The Virgin Mary* (London, 1955); P. F. Palmer, *Mary in the Documents of the Church* (London, 1953); M. Warner, *Alone of All Her Sex: The Myth and Cult of the Virgin Mary* (London, 1976); D. F. Wright (ed.), *Chosen by God: Mary in Evangelical Perspective* (London, 1989).

A. N. S. LANE

MASCALL, ERIC, see ANGLO-CATHOLIC THEOLOGY; THOMISM AND NEO-THOMISM

MATERIALISM

Materialism is the doctrine that whatever exists is either physical matter, or depends upon physical matter. Thus stated, the doctrine is vague enough to have had numerous expressions, from the materialism of Democritus (*c*. 460–*c*. 370 BC) and Epicureanism, in which everything is reducible to the movements of atoms, to the mechanical materialism of Thomas Hobbes (1588–1679) and the physicalism both of *logical positivism and the dialectical materialism of Karl *Marx. Besides being a philosophical position with definite ontological explanations (the denial of the existence of minds or spirits), materialism may also be regarded as a research programme and research methodology with no such implications.

Materialism is opposed both by forms of mind-body *dualism (e.g. that of *Descartes) and by a more general anti-reductionism, which warns that although the universe has a materialistic aspect, it is invalid to conclude that it is 'nothing but' matter. At first glance the biblical stress on humanity as part of the creation may seem hospitable to a wholly material *creation, but the biblical doctrine of personal continuity after bodily death (2 Cor. 5:1–10) appears to rule this out (see *Immortality; *Intermediate state).

'Materialism' may also refer to an ethical outlook which regards the only worthwhile pursuit to be that of wealth and sensual gratification, but there is no logical connection between the philosophical doctrine of materialism and this ethical stance.

Bibliography

P. K. Mowser and J. D. Trout (eds.), *Contemporary Materialism: A Reader* (London, 1995); J. R. Smythies (ed.), *Brain and Mind* (London, 1965); R. C. Vitzthum, *Materialism: An Affirmative History and Definition* (Amherst, NY, 1995).

P. HELM

MATHER, COTTON (1663–1728)

Grandson of John Cotton and son of Increase *Mather, Cotton Mather represented two leading *Puritan families in America. Serving with his father in the ministry at Old North Church in Boston, Cotton Mather's theology and life is well represented in his writing, since he produced hundreds of books and pamphlets.

Several examples of his diverse writings are representative of the challenge of categorizing this man. In *Memorable Providences Relating to Witchcraft and Possessions* (1689), Mather described his pastoral work with a young woman who recovered slowly from apparent demonic possession. Later, despite some private reservations about the legal proceedings surrounding the Salem witchcraft cases, he also wrote *The Wonders of the Invisible World* (1692), which at times defends the judges of the trials. Mather is often viewed in an entirely negative light because of this association.

However, Mather is not easily stereotyped, as his incredible scientific abilities demonstrate (e.g. his early use and advocacy of smallpox inoculations, plant hybridization, and astronomical views). Elected into the fellowship of the Royal Society in 1713, Puritans like Mather believed their positive utilization of science was the natural outgrowth of their theology.

Mather's other works include his massive *Magnalia Christi Americana* (1702, which told of God's providential leading many from Europe to establish Christian New England) and the well-known *Bonifacius: Essays to Do Good* (1710; though mocked early on by the young Benjamin Franklin, it was later praised by him). His *Manuductio ad Ministerium* (1726) was an often-used text for seminarians preparing for ministry. Reading his *Diary* (repr., 1957) shows the warm-hearted side of a man who found the German Lutheran *Pietism of August Herman Francke appealing.

Bibliography

D. Levin, *Cotton Mather: The Young Life of the Lord's Remembrancer* (Cambridge, 1978); R. Lovelace, *The American Pietism of Cotton Mather* (Grand Rapids, 1979); R. Middlekauf, *The Mathers: Three Generations of Puritan Intellectuals, 1596–1728* (New York, 1971); K. Silverman, *The Life and Times of Cotton Mather* (New York, 1984); B. Wendell, *Cotton Mather: The Puritan Priest* (repr. New York, 1963); M. P. Winship, *Seers of God: Puritan Providentialism in the Restoration and Early Enlightenment* (Baltimore, 1996).

K. M. KAPIC

MATHER, INCREASE (1639–1723)

Known as one of the leading American *Puritans, Increase Mather was a graduate of Harvard (1656) and completed his MA at Trinity College in Dublin (1658). Eventually he returned to Boston where he served in ministry for nearly sixty years at Old North Church (1664–1723). During this time he also functioned as president of Harvard College (1685–1701).

Publishing over 130 books and pamphlets, Mather's writings covered numerous topics, including theology, science, politics and history. As a leading churchman, he was also deeply involved in political affairs. For example, at one point he travelled to England and stayed for four years, representing concerns regarding the Massachusetts charter.

As his life progressed his rhetoric against what he saw as the spiritual decline among the people of New England grew. Although originally opposing any relaxing of the requirements for baptism, eventually he ended up defending the Half-Way Covenant (see *New England theology). Nevertheless, he always encouraged the people to look to previous generations for examples of faithfulness.

During the Salem trials of 1692 he ended up warning against the manner in which people were being found guilty. In *Cases of Conscience Concerning Evil Spirits*, 1693, he cautions against accepting 'spectral evidence'. Using his influence, especially among leaders like Governor Phips, he helped finally end the growing chaos and executions.

He and his wife Maria Cotton (daughter of the eminent John Cotton) had ten children; among them was their firstborn, Cotton *Mather.

Bibliography

M. Hall, *Increase Mather: The Last American Puritan* (Middletown, 1988); M. I. Lowance, Jr, *Increase Mather* (New York, 1974); C. Mather, *Parentator: Memoirs of . . . Increase Mather* (London, 1725); I. Mather, *The Autobiography of Increase Mather*, ed. M. G. Hall (repr. Worcester, 1962); R. Middlekauf, *The Mathers: Three Generations of Puritan Intellectuals, 1596–1728* (New York, 1971); K. B. Murdock, *Increase Mather: The Foremost American Puritan* (Cambridge, 1925).

K. M. Kapic

MAURICE, F. D., see CHRISTIAN SOCIALISM

MEDIATION

Literally, mediation is the function or condition of coming between two parties for the purpose of encounter, transaction or reconciliation. In Christian thought it pertains both (legitimately) to Christ's supreme interposition between God and man, and (illegitimately) to the active ministry of other heavenly or earthly intermediaries.

The principle of mediation is common to any of the world's religions, as various religious mediators (e.g. priests, medicinemen, rainmakers, sorcerers) interpose with supernatural or natural powers between a transcendent order (and often an offended deity) and a terrestrial realm (and offending earthly party). The OT describes a multiplicity of 'mediations' and mediators, e.g. the patriarchs, Moses, judges, prophets, kings, and Levitical priests. Fundamentally, a twofold pattern of mediation exists: the prophetic (manward), in which an appointed agent reveals, proclaims and interprets God's will to people; and the priestly (Godward), in which God is approached, reconciled and besought on man's behalf by an appointed representative. This pattern of mediation is consummated in Christ. He is both the consummation of antecedent mediation and the redefinition of mediation.

The Christian faith centres on the person and work of Christ as mediator. The NT presents Christ's unique mediatorship directly and indirectly. He is directly declared to be 'the one mediator (*mesitēs*) between God and men' (1 Tim. 2:5), and the mediator of a new and better covenant. He is indirectly portrayed, in his person and work, as the unique intermediary, the principle of cosmic unity, who in himself not only fulfils a prophetic ministry of revelation, proclamation and interpretation of God's will, but also a 'priestly' ministry of approach, reconciliation of sinful man to God by sacrifice, perpetual intercession and heavenly blessing. The NT portrays Christ's mediation as both an active function (as the agent of salvation) and a static condition (uniting in himself God and man, heaven and earth). Both strands have at times come to the fore in subsequent Christian reflection.

Patristic and *scholastic thought emphasized Christ's static mediation as the God-man as the basis or prerequisite of his active mediation of *salvation though his death, resurrection and exaltation, and Eastern Orthodox thought has usually followed this line, placing greater stress on the *incarnation in this connection than the West has usually done. *Thomas Aquinas, somewhat artificially, located Christ's mediation in his taking of perfect manhood, which distinguished him both from God and sinful humanity. The Protestant Reformers reaffirmed Christ's active salvific mediatory work, and *Reformed theology expounded Christ's person and work as mediator in terms of his threefold 'office' as prophet, priest and king (see *Offices of Christ). In addition, against medieval Roman Catholic sacerdotalism, the Reformers affirmed the *uniqueness, finality and permanence of Christ's mediation. Most later Protestant tradition has repudiated both an official human priestly caste, with the power to forgive sin (in absolution) and to offer *sacrifice (in the *Eucharist), and additional heavenly intermediaries (e.g. *Mary and the *saints), stressing rather the perfection of Christ's atoning sacrifice and continual intercession, and the priestly prerogative of access for all believers in Christ (see *Ministry; *Priesthood of believers). At the Second *Vatican Council, Roman Catholicism explicitly reaffirmed Christ as 'the one Mediator', although its adherence to a human derivative priesthood, co-operative with Christ, the great High Priest, an outlook largely shared by Orthodox and High Anglicans, continues to present a stumbling-block to many Protestants, especially in non-English-speaking areas.

Bibliography

L. Berkhof, *Systematic Theology* (London, 1969); E. Brunner, *The Mediator* (London, 1934); J. Calvin, *Institutes* II.xii-xv; A. Oepke in *TDNT* IV, pp. 598–624; T. F. Torrance, *The Mediation of Christ* (Colorado Springs, new edn, 1992).

C. D. HANCOCK

MELANCHTHON, PHILIPP (1497–1560)

Born in Bretten, Germany, a grand-nephew of the humanist Johannes Reuchlin (1455–1522), Melanchthon was a child prodigy and became a Protestant Reformer. His scholarly output started when he was only seventeen and was admired by *Erasmus as early as 1515. At this stage he was a humanist. In 1518 he came to Wittenberg to be professor of Greek. He quickly absorbed *Reformation theology, and this, together with his brilliance both as a scholar and as a teacher, ensured that he was much admired by *Luther. In 1521 he produced the first edition of his *Loci Communes* (*Commonplaces*) which developed throughout his life as a Lutheran dogmatic textbook.

Melanchthon was more a scholar than a man of action and displayed weaknesses when faced with situations of conflict. When he was confronted by the demands of *Karlstadt and the Zwickau prophets (see *Reformation, Radical) for a very radical and rapid reform of Wittenberg in 1521–22, he proved incapable of providing the strong leadership that was necessary. Despite this, supported by Luther, he exercised an important influence on the Colloquy of Marburg (1529) and drew up the *Augsburg Confession (1530) and the accompanying Apology (1531). The Augsburg documents were highly significant for the Reformation, and Melanchthon's temperament and skills were well suited to their irenic objectives. These skills were again demonstrated at the Colloquy of Regensburg (1541) when Melanchthon and *Bucer and Catholic representatives including John Eck (1486–1543) and Gasparo *Contarini reached agreement on *justification without being able to persuade their respective sides of its appropriateness. Typically, Melanchthon signed the Schmalkaldic Articles (1537) with the proviso that if the pope would allow the gospel he would concede him superiority over the bishops.

Throughout Luther's life Melanchthon declined to involve himself as fully in theology as Luther desired. He never, for example, took his doctorate in theology. He was, however, an independent thinker. On the *Eucharist he leaned towards *Calvin, on *predestination and free will more towards Erasmus and on *justification towards a more forensic view than that of Luther. When Luther died (1546), Melanchthon was his natural successor. He could not quite cope with the task. He compromised with the Catholics after the Protestant defeat in 1548 by accepting the Leipzig Interim which in effect allowed Protestant theology but required Roman Catholic ritual. This degree of compromise undermined his authority and, for the remainder of his life, he was involved in a series of conflicts within Lutheranism; with Andreas *Osiander over justification, with Nicholas von Amsdorf (1483–1565) over predestination and with a variety of Lutherans over the Lord's Supper. He died praying for deliverance from the 'fury of the theologians'. He was very widely learned and retained his humanistic interests. He was a most significant educational reformer, making an important contribution to university and school education in Germany.

Assessments of Melanchthon vary. He can be interpreted as a figure somewhat alien to the true direction of the Reformation. However, in an age which recoils, as Melanchthon did, from some of Luther's most vehement polemic, Melanchthon stands as a rational, moderate, ecumenical figure, more able than Luther to find rapprochement and to look for a middle way.

Bibliography

Works: ET of *Loci Communes* (1521) in W. Pauck, *Melanchthon and Bucer*, LCC 19 (London, 1969); *Melanchthon on Christian Doctrine: Loci Communes 1555*, tr. C. L. Manschreck (Oxford, 1965).

Studies: E. W. Gritsch, *A History of Lutheranism* (Minneapolis, 2002); N. Kuropka, *Melanchthon* (Tübingen, 2010); C. L. Manschreck, *Melanchthon, the Quiet Reformer* (New York, 1968); R. Stupperich, *Melanchthon* (ET, London, 1966); T. J. Wengert, *Philip*

Melanchthon, Speaker of the Reformation: Wittenberg's Other Reformer (Farnham, 2010).

C. P. WILLIAMS

MENNONITE THEOLOGY

The roots of Mennonite theology are to be found in sixteenth-century Dutch, German and Swiss *Anabaptism. Menno Simons, Pilgram Marpeck (c. 1495–1556), Conrad Grebel (c. 1498–1526) and others provided the theological inspiration for the movement which later took the name Mennonite from its major Dutch leader, Menno Simons (1496–1561). Historically, the Mennonite tradition has assumed the substance, if not always the authority, of the early Christian *creeds. Confessionally – in statements of faith, doctrinal writings, *catechisms, sermons, hymns, devotional literature and worship – it has stressed scriptural themes often omitted in the historic creeds and *confessions, especially Christ's way of suffering love, the life of Christian discipleship and obedience (see *Christian life), and the nature of the believers' *church as separated from the world. Moreover, it has also affirmed the triune understanding of God, the substitutionary atoning death and exemplary nature of Christ's life, sin as a voluntary act of disobedience, human accountability for faithfulness in the Christian life, the return of Christ and the primacy of Scripture for all theological reflection.

The doctrine of the church is the most central theme in Mennonite theology. Its hallmarks are *regeneration, holy living, believers' baptism, the Lord's Supper, footwashing, church *discipline, nonconformity, integrity, non-resistance (see *Pacifism), religious liberty and the separation of church and *state.

In the course of its migrations, in both Europe and the Americas, the Mennonite movement came under the influence of *pietism. The effects were frequently beneficial and revitalizing, especially in regard to mission and to the personal dimensions of salvation. The experience-oriented pietism, however, also tended to erode Mennonite theological distinctives pertaining to Christian discipleship and ethics.

Mennonites sympathized with the *fundamentalist struggle against modernism, but did not formally join those ranks, even though certain sectors were strongly influenced by it. In general, Mennonite theology has been conservative and *evangelical. *Liberal theology has not had a great impact on Mennonite thought in North America and most other continents, although common *ethical interests are more evident in recent times. During the nineteenth and twentieth centuries, however, most of the Dutch and many of the North German Mennonites turned towards liberalism. Their assimilation into mainstream European culture also meant the abandonment of many traditional doctrinal positions. Some theological renewal has taken place since the Second World War. Today, Mennonite theology in northern Europe is more ecumenical in its interests.

The development of the Mennonite theological tradition can be characterized by the struggle for greater confessional unity (seventeenth and eighteenth centuries), the quest for religious and cultural stability (eighteenth to early twentieth centuries) and, more recently, a search for theological identity (twentieth century). Since the Second World War, Mennonite theology and ethics have explored their sixteenth-century roots in the *Radical Reformation. This 'recovery of the Anabaptist vision' has sought to recapture the biblical-ethical emphasis in discipleship, ecclesiology and non-resistance, the challenge of social responsibility and the nature of Mennonite theological identity as it relates to Mennonite ethnocentrism, cultural pluralism, contemporary evangelicalism and historic Anabaptism.

Representing the free-church tradition, Mennonite faith and life have contributed to an understanding of the church as a covenant community of faithful believers. Its greatest internal challenge today is the quest for theological identity and the integration of its ecclesiology with the changing relationship of the church to society.

See also: YODER, JOHN HOWARD.

Bibliography

H. S. Bender et al. (eds.), *The Mennonite Encyclopedia*, vols. I–IV (Scottdale, 1955–1959); L. Driedger and D. B. Kraybill, *Mennonite Peacemaking: From Quietism to Activism* (Scottdale, 1994); C. J. Dyck (ed.), *An Introduction to Mennonite History* (Scottdale, 1967); H. J. Loewen, *One Lord, One Faith, One Hope and One God: Mennonite Confessions of Faith in North America – An Introduction* (Newton, 1985); J. D. Weaver, *Keeping Salvation Ethical: Mennonite and Amish Atonement*

Theology in the Late Nineteenth Century (Scottdale, 1997).

H. J. LOEWEN

MERCERSBURG THEOLOGY

A movement named after the small town in central Pennsylvania where in the nineteenth century the theological school of the German Reformed Church was located. From 1844, under the direction of John W. Nevin (1803–86), formerly an Old School Presbyterian theologian (see *Princeton theology), and Philip Schaff (1819–93), a young historian from Germany, the school attempted to provide a classical Calvinist alternative to what it perceived to be the decline of American New England and Princeton Calvinism (see *Edwards, Jonathan; *New England theology; *New Haven theology; *Reformed theology) into 'Puritan' revivalist subjectivism. Emphasis was placed on the ecumenical *Christological theology of the ancient church (see *Creeds), the significance of the institutional *church with its *sacraments, *ministry and catechetical method, and the organic development of that church throughout history.

Its theological thrust may be regarded as the American counterpart of English *Anglo-Catholicism and German high-church *Lutheranism in the same period, reflecting the philosophical shift from the subjectivism of *Kant and *Schleiermacher to historical and corporate expressions of reality in *Hegel and *Ritschl, which in Germany must be seen against the background of evangelical *pietism.

In much evangelical piety, the reality of personal salvation had made denominational, *confessional and particularly sacramental concerns substantially irrelevant. Heaven will be populated with representatives from all confessions, it was said. The important issue was not *baptism or church membership, but whether one had made a personal commitment to Christ. While awakenings divided denominations, their adherents regarded them as unifying true believers. Nevertheless, within the American context, the multiplicity of denominations seemed to conflict with the unity experienced in the awakenings (see *Revival).

Resolutions to this tension were varied. Princeton theologians ordinarily considered Calvinism as the most consistent expression of awakening theology. *Methodists and others expressed themselves similarly. Others thought it necessary to repudiate all existing denominations and 'restore' the primitive church, now possible in a time of 'latter-day' blessing (as in the Church of Christ, the Adventists and the Latter Day Saints; see *Sects).

Mercersburg's response was to see the Reformed church as the embodiment of the Protestant and ecumenical church. This was seen not as sectarian, but rather as an expression of a developing church with its roots in history. This led to the repudiation of the innovative conversion experience in favour of catechetical instruction (Nevin's *Anxious Bench*), and to an emphasis on the real presence of Christ in the Lord's Supper (see *Eucharist) in the place of revivalist subjectivism. (American Calvinism's view of the Supper had to some extent weakened into naive *Zwinglianism, and Nevin's understanding of the Reformed sacramental heritage was more accurate than that of Charles *Hodge.) Renewed interest in Reformed liturgy and the nature of the ministerial office was also characteristic. Following the lead of German research into Calvinism, Mercersburg concluded that a *Melanchthonian lack of interest in the divine decrees and rejection of reprobation (see *Predestination) was more typical of Calvinism than the New England and Princeton direction. Perhaps that was encouraged by the way it considered *Puritanism to have misused election.

While Mercersburg produced helpful insights and correctives in a confusing period in American church history, it did not provide lasting direction. Its ecumenical stance was seen to be too sympathetic towards Roman Catholicism, and it failed to give substantial leadership in the emerging arena of biblical authority (see *Fundamentalism; *Scripture). Nevertheless, questions about the value of confessions and sacraments in a pluriform American evangelical community are still present, and Mercersburg's answers may still be studied with profit.

Bibliography

L. J. DeBie, *Speculative Theology and Common-Sense Religion: Mercersburg and the Conservative Roots of American Religion* (Eugene, 2008); D. G. Hart, *John Williamson Nevin: High-Church Calvinist* (Philadelphia, 2005); W. B. Littlejohn, *The Mercersburg Theology and the Quest for Reformed Catholicity* (Eugene, 2009); G. A. Mast, *The Eucharistic Service of the Catholic Apostolic Church and*

Its Influence on Reformed Liturgical Renewals of the Nineteenth Century (Metuchen, 1998); J. H. Nichols, *Romanticism in American Theology* (Chicago, 1961); idem (ed.), *The Mercersburg Theology* (New York, 1966).

D. C. DAVIS

MERIT

Merit is that quality of a good action which entitles the agent who performs it to a reward. In the history of Christian theology, how to conceive of human merit has led to particular controversy in connection with the questions of *justification and *salvation.

In the time of *Augustine, controversy arose with regard to the teaching of *Pelagius. Pelagius had an optimistic view of human freedom, believing that God had given the Christian the gifts of the capacity to choose freely how to act and of the guidance of the Scriptures. With these gracious gifts and without further assistance, the Christian could perform good actions and merit divine grace. For Augustine, however, this view meant that grace would no longer be grace. By contrast, Augustine believed that an individual was justified and saved not by the merit of works but by the free *grace of God.

The later, medieval view of merit is perhaps best represented by a figure such as *Thomas Aquinas. Aquinas accepted Augustine's starting point that the Christian could not merit justifying grace, and noted that any human merit before God could only exist on the presupposition that God had ordained it. Moreover, he believed that if Christians did what they ought, by the grace of God but also through their own free will, then they merited reward. He distinguished two types of merit: condign merit, which was a matter of strict justice between God and those in a state of grace, by which God was (freely) bound to reward a good work; and congruent merit, which reflected God's generous character as he rewarded the acts of those who did not satisfy the strict conditions for merit. For Aquinas, insofar as a good work proceeded from the grace of the *Holy Spirit, it would merit eternal life condignly, while insofar as a good work proceeded from an act of the free will, it would merit eternal life congruently. Meanwhile, Aquinas also believed that the saints of the church had performed meritorious good works beyond what was required of them, and that their resultant merits, together with those of Jesus Christ, were part of the property of the church and could be dispensed accordingly.

At the time of the Reformation, Martin *Luther and John *Calvin wrote vehemently against this conception of merit. The Reformers agreed that grace and salvation were made possible through the merit which Jesus Christ had graciously obtained through his obedient life and death (see *Reformation theology): that sinless life and death of Jesus Christ, as *Anselm had already observed, was so excellent and so glorious as to make not only ample but infinite satisfaction for the sins of the world. The Reformers also agreed that a Christian could not perform good works without the grace of God. However, the Reformers insisted that a Christian could not in any way merit either grace – for herself or for others – or eternal life by her works. The grace of justification came to the Christian only by faith in Jesus Christ, and the resultant righteousness was alien and extrinsic and thus not meritorious. This latter point served theologically to divide the *Roman Catholic Church – which stated its views at the Council of *Trent – from the Reformation churches on this issue. For the former, the justification of the individual involved an intrinsic change in the individual by an infusion of divine grace, such that the resultant good works were done not only through the grace of God but also through the co-operation of the free will of the agent, and thus to that agent's merit. For the latter, however, justifying grace did not effect any internal righteousness in the Christian, and thus good works brought forth by grace were to be ascribed to God alone and not to that person's merit.

The issue lay dormant for many years, but re-emerged in the late twentieth century in ecumenical discussion between Roman Catholics and *Lutherans. The discussion concluded that many antitheses might be overcome if the term 'merit' were considered in the light of its biblical meaning of 'wage' or 'reward'. However, the resultant Joint Declaration did not attempt this, nor did it resolve the issue of the meritorious value (or otherwise) of good works.

Bibliography

Anselm, 'Cur Deus Homo?' in *Basic Writings* (Indianapolis, 2007); Augustine, 'On the Grace of Christ and on Original Sin', in *Basic Writings of Saint Augustine*, vol. 1 (New York,

1948); M. Luther, *Lectures on Galatians – 1535* (St Louis, 1963); J. Calvin, *Institutes of the Christian Religion*, vol. 3 (Louisville, 2001); *The Canons and Decrees of the Council of Trent*, Session 6 [1547] (Rockford, 1982); Lutheran World Federation and the Catholic Church, 'Joint Declaration on the Doctrine of Justification' (Grand Rapids, 2000); M. Root, 'Aquinas, Merit, and Reformation Theology after the *Joint Declaration on the Doctrine of Justification*', MT 20, 2004, pp. 5–22; Thomas Aquinas, *Summa Theologiae*, vol. 30 (Cambridge, 2006).

P. T. Nimmo

MERTON, THOMAS (1915–68)

Merton, an American Trappist-Cistercian monk, helped to shape post-Second Vatican Council Catholic, ecumenical and interfaith *spirituality. His acclaimed autobiography, *The Seven Storey Mountain* (New York and London, 1948), recounts his early life. He was born in France to artist parents, schooled in Europe, orphaned at fifteen, landed on Long Island at eighteen to live with relatives, completed studies at Columbia University, converted to Catholicism and, in 1941, entered Gethsemani Abbey, Kentucky, taking the monastic name Louis. Poet, essayist, teacher of novices, letter-writer, literary and social critic, his life and diverse writings attest to the relevance of monasticism to a world undergoing significant turmoil and change. Rooted in the True Self (the Christ within) and the ascetical discipline of his monastic community, he branched outward to embrace increasingly diverse others, modelling contemplation as both withdrawal from and engagement with others. His move in 1965 to a hermitage on the monastery grounds increased his ability to receive leaders of the American civil rights, peace and ecumenical movements. A 1968 trip to Asia to dialogue with Buddhist monks established him as a bridge-builder among world religions. His accidental death there (Thailand) has not diminished his continuing influence as a Christian who reflected God's mercy in making room for 'the other'.

See also: Asceticism and Monasticism.

Bibliography

Works: *New Seeds of Contemplation* (New York, 1961); *Conjectures of a Guilty Bystander* (Garden City, 1966); N. Burton, J. Laughlin and P. Hart (eds.), *The Asian Journal of Thomas Merton* (New York, 1973); L. S. Cunningham (ed.), *Thomas Merton: Spiritual Master: The Essential Writings* (New York, 1992); P. Hart and J. Montaldo (eds.), *The Intimate Merton: His Life from His Journals* (New York, 1999).

Studies: J. J. Harford, *Merton and Friends: A Joint Biography of Thomas Merton, Robert Lax, and Edward Rice* (New York and London, 2006); G. Kilcourse, *Ace of Freedoms: Thomas Merton's Christ* (Notre Dame, 1993); W. H. Shannon, *Thomas Merton: An Introduction* (Cincinnati, 2005).

D. S. Hardy

METAPHYSICS

Metaphysics may be defined as the attempt to work out the most basic structure of reality, not by observation and experiment, as in science, but by systematic and critical thought, seeking to analyse, test and connect such concepts as 'cause', 'quality', 'matter', 'mind' and 'event'. Metaphysicians may simply try to describe the form taken by our normal thought about the world when set out systematically; or, more often, to revise and improve on this, and, it may be, to demonstrate a reality behind the appearances. In the former class might be found such thinkers as *Aristotle, *Locke and perhaps *Thomas Aquinas, in addition to some twentieth-century thinkers such as Sir Peter Strawson (1919–2006); in the latter class, *Plato, *Spinoza, *Leibniz, *Berkeley and *Hume. Most metaphysicians have of course included elements of both these approaches; and some might hold, with R. G. Collingwood (1889–1943), that as the presuppositions of our thought vary over the years, even the first kind of metaphysics needs constant revision.

Metaphysicians have at times made spectacular claims: to show, for instance, that time is an illusion; that the whole of existence forms a single unity, all else being at best only partially real; that mind and matter are both constructed out of a more basic 'neutral stuff'; or, more relevantly to the Christian, that reason can prove or disprove the existence of God or of the human soul. The frequent conflict between these claims, and the failure of metaphysicians to convince one another, have cast some suspicion on the whole enterprise. Indeed, a number of philosophers have thought that metaphysics may be in principle impossible, except perhaps in our first sense, the description rather than the revision of our normal thought. Thus *Kant argued that the 'categories' which made science (and experience generally) possible, such as unity, limitation, substance and cause, are not part of reality in itself, but only conditions of our experiencing of it. They cannot therefore be used to go beyond that which we experience, to argue, for example, that the world is or is not limited in extent or duration, or that it was or was not created and caused by a god. More recently, the *logical positivism of the 1920s and 1930s argued that metaphysical claims had no real meaning at all. Since they did not provide any way for us to test whether they were true or false, how could they be said to assert anything? To the Christian believer, this was a more disturbing criticism than Kant's; for he had left it possible (and indeed himself believed) that the reality of God might be known by faith, though not proved by reason, whereas it was now argued that all metaphysical propositions, including those which Christians would wish to make, were totally meaningless and asserted nothing at all that could even be believed in faith.

Accordingly, some philosophers have seen metaphysics not as a system of factual assertions, but as a way of seeing and interpreting the world; while others have retained some metaphysical arguments as analyses of our concepts, while abandoning hope of any all-inclusive system. A number, however, remained obstinate. They could reply that as they were seeking the necessary structure of any world, it was absurd to demand that particular features of the world prove or disprove the reality of this structure; and that if it was legitimate to analyse concepts like time or cause, it was also legitimate to see whether, for instance, there were contradictions in the idea of time, or whether belief in causes should entail belief in a first cause, God.

Some metaphysical systems, such as those of *Hegel or Spinoza, were explicitly offered as substitutes for (and improvements on) traditional religious beliefs. Others, such as those of Thomas Aquinas, *Descartes or Leibniz, while avowedly Christian, claimed that human reasoning was able to prove such religious truths as the reality and goodness of God, and so seemed, to some, to depreciate *revelation (see *Natural theology). Accordingly, some theologians have wished to repudiate metaphysics altogether. And clearly there is no need for Christians to construct a metaphysical system, or accept an existing one. But many Christian concepts and beliefs involve metaphysical assertions, even when they are not argued for by metaphysical methods: the ideas of *creation, *miracle, spirit, revelation, *grace and, above all, of *God, all carry implications about the structure of reality, and may well need metaphysics, not for their discovery, but for explanation and defence. It seems a mistake therefore for the theologian to reject metaphysics completely. The truth of Christianity surely implies that some metaphysical systems (e.g. *atheist or *materialist ones) are false, and this suggests that some system – perhaps known only to God – is true; unless, indeed, with a few extreme radicals, we abandon the idea of supernatural truths and reduce Christianity to a way of life (while repudiating much of the beliefs and teaching of the Christ who founded that way). Whether in fact reason (with or without the aid of God's revelation given to us) is adequate to work out the fundamental nature of reality can only be found out in practice.

See also: FAITH AND REASON; PHILOSOPHY OF RELIGION.

Bibliography

A. J. Ayer, *The Central Questions of Philosophy* (London, 1973); B. Blanshard, *Reason and Analysis* (London, 1962); C. D. Broad, 'Critical and Speculative Philosophy', in J. H. Muirhead (ed.), *Contemporary British Philosophy* (London, 1924); R. G. Collingwood, *An Essay on Metaphysics* (London, 1940); R. M. Gale, *The Blackwell Guide to Metaphysics* (Oxford, 2002); E. E. Harris, *The Restitution of Metaphysics* (New York, 2000); I. Kant, *Prolegomena to any Future Metaphysics* (ET, Manchester, 1957); J. Kim and E. Sosa (eds.), *A Companion to Metaphysics* (Malden, MA, 2000); idem (eds.), *Metaphysics: An Anthology* (Oxford, 1999); R. Le Poidevin et al. (eds.), *The Routledge Companion to Metaphysics* (New York, 2009); M. J. Loux, *Metaphysics: A Contemporary Introduction*, 3rd edn (London, 2006); E. J. Lowe, *A Survey of Metaphysics* (Oxford, 2002); J. McTaggart, 'Introduction to the Study of Philosophy', in his *Philosophical Studies* (London, 1934); D. F. Pears (ed.), *The Nature of Metaphysics* (London, 1957); W. H. Walsh, *Metaphysics* (London 1963).

R. L. STURCH

METEMPSYCHOSIS

Metempsychosis is (the belief in) the 'transmigration of souls', i.e. that human or animal souls pass through more than one bodily existence in this world. In some forms the reincarnation of human souls is restricted to human bodies, but in others may extend to animals (and hence its advocates are often also vegetarians). The purpose of metempsychosis is often presented as progressive purification or evolutionary development, which is not infrequently related to the view that the soul's entry into bodily life is in some sense a punitive confinement, e.g. following a pre-existent or pre-cosmic fall.

Reincarnation is widely believed in Eastern religions such as *Buddhism and *Hinduism, and was taught by influential Gk traditions, especially Pythagoreanism, *Platonism and Neoplatonism. From such sources it was adopted by many *Gnostics (and hence by *Manichaeans and their later counterparts, the Cathari or *Albigenses). It was consequently much discussed by the early Church Fathers, normally with unqualified hostility, although they sometimes observed, for apologetic reasons, that it bore a partial similarity to the Christian belief in the resurrection of the body (cf. *Tertullian, *Resurrection of the Flesh* and *The Soul*), as too did the *Stoic doctrine of a cyclical succession of worlds.

Whether *Clement of Alexandria and *Origen espoused metempsychosis remains a matter of debate. Origen undoubtedly accepted the eternal pre-existence of souls (see *Soul, origin of), but may well have envisaged only a single bodily 'incarnation' (at least in this world). He certainly resisted any fatalist kind of reincarnation. If he did entertain it, he would have exploited it, like the soul's pre-existence, apologetically, to help explain some of life's apparent injustices and inequalities.

In later centuries, metempsychosis has found occasional advocates, e.g. among the Neoplatonists of the Italian Renaissance, in *Lessing, among spiritualists and theosophists, such as Emanuel Swedenborg (1688–1772; see *Sects) and Annie Besant (1847–1933), as well as among a few Christian thinkers of a liberal cast of mind.

The theory not only lacks biblical support but is also incompatible with central doctrines, such as the *resurrection of the body. It is also dependent on the notion, now largely abandoned by Christian theology, of the soul as a substance or essence different from the body (see *Anthropology).

Bibliography
Q. Howe, Jr, *Reincarnation for the Christian* (Philadelphia, 1974); G. MacGregor, *Reincarnation as a Christian Hope* (London, 1982).
Critique: M. Albrecht, *Reincarnation: A Christian Appraisal* (Downers Grove, 1982); R. A. Morey, *Reincarnation and Christianity* (Minneapolis, 1980).

D. F. WRIGHT

METHODISM

Methodism began as a renewal movement of religious societies within the Church of England, under the leadership of John *Wesley and his brother *Charles, during the evangelical revival of eighteenth-century Britain. Although the movement was united by a 'catholic spirit', early Methodism suffered various internal disputes over theology and practice; the most significant division was between followers of Wesley's *Arminianism and the *Calvinism of George *Whitefield.

Methodism in America had its origins in Wesley's own visit to Georgia, but grew through the ministry of early Methodist migrants and later missionaries sent by Wesley to direct the work. After the Revolutionary War, Wesley commissioned Thomas Coke and Francis *Asbury to preside over the emergence of Methodism as a separate church in America. Shortly after Wesley's death, and against his intention, British Methodism also formally separated from the established church.

Subsequent divisions in British and American Methodism led to a variety of Methodist denominations, independent Methodist churches and other movements in the pan-Wesleyan family, such as the *Salvation Army, Free Methodists and Nazarenes. Prolific missionary activity through the nineteenth and twentieth centuries resulted in the spread of these Wesleyan traditions throughout the world. Those with roots in British Methodism are now largely independent communions, while those originating from American mission activity have retained their episcopal connection to United Methodism in America.

Wesleyan genes

The following are some Methodist family traits, having their origins in Wesley's theology and the practices of early Methodism. The founding constitutions of most Methodist denominations contain reference to Wesley's published *Sermons* and *Notes upon the New Testament* as standards of doctrine and theology.

Scriptural holiness

Wesley believed that the Methodist movement had been providentially raised up to spread 'scriptural holiness': that is, a way of discipleship summed up by love for God and neighbour, with Christian *perfection or 'perfect love' as its spiritual goal. Wesley's theological influences include patristic sources from East and West, Anglican divines, Catholic mystics and *Moravian pietists. Holiness is a way of love which encompasses heart and life, subsists in constant communion with God through the means of grace, and is founded upon the evangelical gifts of personal faith, new birth and the assurance of sins forgiven. It is both a 'relational', imputed righteousness that God has accomplished *for us* in Christ, bringing freedom from the guilt of sin (*justification); and a 'real', imparted righteousness that God accomplishes *in us* by the Spirit, bringing freedom from the power of sin (*sanctification). Methodist theology affirms the Reformation emphasis on justification by faith, but makes it the ground of sanctifying grace which denies the intractability of sin even in this life. For Wesley, sanctification is a *gradual process* of transformation, punctuated by the experience of perfect *love as an *instantaneous gift*. The doctrine of Christian perfection has invited a variety of interpretations and a good deal of controversy: including the sense in which it implies freedom from sin; whether it is a once-and-for-all state; and if it can be spoken of by those who have attained it.

Practical discipleship

Holy living is pursued by the means of *grace – both works of piety and works of mercy – by which justifying and sanctifying grace are communicated, and the responses of repentance and obedient faith are embodied. They constitute the whole of life as an arena for working out one's salvation: a life which combines personal spirituality, disciplined fellowship, evangelistic witness and loving service. Methodist theology affirms the central *Reformation commitment to salvation by 'grace alone', but strives to maintain the scriptural connections between law and gospel, faith and works. For Wesley, divine grace always works preveniently, to enable human responsibility in the way of salvation, thus avoiding the errors of both *Pelagianism and *antinomianism. (See especially John Fletcher's *Checks to Antinomianism*, 1771–5.)

Disciplined fellowship

Methodist theology extends the Reformation understanding of the law – as that which brings conviction of sin and drives us to the grace of Christ – to include the way Christ sends us back to the law in grace-filled obedience (see *Law and gospel). The practice of disciplined *fellowship embodies the covenant realities of divine grace and human responsibility in the activities of mutual confession, intercessory prayer and exhortation to grow in grace. 'Solitary Christianity' is denied by the doctrine of 'social holiness'. In other words, personal salvation subsists in Christian fellowship, and holy living is for the sake of witness and service in the world. The Calvinist doctrine of *perseverance is rejected, since both advancement and backsliding, even to the point of apostasy, are possible in the way of salvation.

Evangelistic mission

An 'evangelical Arminian' doctrine of *salvation has been the centre, if not the circumference, of Methodist theology, and is usefully summarized by the so-called 'Four Alls' of Methodism. First, that *all must be saved* affirms the doctrine of original sin, particularly against deistic accounts of natural virtue. Second, that *all can be saved* challenges the Calvinist doctrine of *predestination as unconditional election, by affirming that prevenient grace is free for all and in all, and that the benefits of the *atonement are universal in scope. Third, that *all can know they are saved* affirms the witness of the Spirit as normal Christian experience, against accusations of religious 'enthusiasm'. Fourth, that *all can be saved to the uttermost* challenges the intractability of sin, by affirming that holiness and perfect love can be accomplished in this life. Methodists have also stressed holiness as a 'present salvation', which cannot ultimately be separated from God's eschatological purpose to renew creation as a whole. The doctrine of God and the nature of the church are understood in terms of this evangelistic-missional priority: that God is the one who saves, and that the salvation of souls is the end of all ecclesiastical order (see *Evangelism, theology of).

Historic expressions

The history of Methodist theology and practice can be interpreted as more or less diverse expressions of this Wesleyan genome.

Christian perfection

Wesley claimed that the doctrine of Christian perfection was the 'grand depositum' of Methodism, and regular attempts have been made at restating its significance in British Methodism. From the work of William Burt Pope (1822–1903) onwards, scholars have reaffirmed Wesley's view that perfection is not absolute, but a dynamic state of spiritual maturity, utterly contingent on the grace of Christ, that can be gained and lost. R. N. Flew's *The Idea of Perfection in Christian Theology* (London, 1934) locates Wesley's teaching in the historical development of the doctrine, and highlights the moment-by-moment nature of perfect love in the context of human relationships. W. E. Sangster's *The Path to Perfection* (London, 1943) relates the doctrine to trends in psychology, while emphasizing the saintly calling of ordinary Christians. Eric Baker's *The Faith of a Methodist* (London, 1958) argues that the gift of Methodism to the church catholic is a theology in which the doctrine of perfection is systematically central. For the development of this doctrine in America, see John L. Peters' *Christian Perfection and American Methodism* (New York, 1956).

Revivalist spirituality

The early Methodist movement was born in the midst of *revival, and revivalism continued as a common feature through the nineteenth century. As a means of both renewal and conversion, revival meetings have had a place both inside and outside the church: from camp meetings to itinerant evangelism, campaigns and crusades. A renewal of Christian values in society was also expected to come through the work and witness of holy lives. In Britain, William Arthur's *Tongue of Fire* (London, 1856) was most influential. American Methodism has been significantly shaped by the camp meeting tradition, the Holiness Movement, and the formulation of revival meetings found in Charles *Finney's *Lectures on Revival* (1835).

Holiness Movement

The *Holiness Movement interpreted Christian perfection through the lens of Pentecost, anticipating a 'second blessing' in which the presence and power of sin is finally overcome by Spirit baptism (see *Baptism in the Spirit). The experience of 'entire sanctification' or 'full salvation', as an instantaneous work of grace, becomes the foundation for a divinely empowered life of witness and service. The origins of the movement in America can be traced back to Phoebe *Palmer, especially her *Way of Holiness* (1843), as well as the work of H. Orton Wiley (1877–1961) and Mildred Bangs Wynkoop (1905–97). Samuel Chadwick's *Way to Pentecost* (London, 1932) and *The Call of Christian Perfection* (London, 1936) made Cliff College a centre for the Holiness Movement in Britain.

Social responsibility

The pattern set by early Methodists in founding medical dispensaries, alms houses, schools, orphanages and other charities has continued through various movements of social responsibility, such as temperance, the development of Sunday schools, the abolition of *slavery, and agencies dedicated to relieving problems of poverty. At its best, the Methodist commitment to works of mercy has harnessed both social responsibility and evangelical zeal. Hugh Price Hughes (1847–1902) related Christian faith to its social context in a fusion of the Holiness Movement, radical discipleship and the 'non-conformist conscience'. John Scott Lidgett (1854–1953) continued the tradition of 'social evangelism' as a means for the 'perfecting' of society. In the late nineteenth and early twentieth centuries, Methodism in America was influenced by women's suffrage, notably through Frances Willard (1839–98), and the *Social Gospel movement, conferring a strong impulse to the pursuit of human *rights and social justice (see *Righteousness).

Methodist ecclesiology

Methodism has inherited the tension bequeathed by a *renewal movement* turned *institutional church*: such as, catholic spirit vs denominational distinctives; charismatic organization vs authorized structures; discipline vs inclusivity. This has been expressed in familiar debates about the conditions of membership, the nature of ministry and the administration of sacraments. In British Methodism, J. H. Rigg

(1849–1902) articulated the nature of Methodist connexionalism as an ecclesiastical and spiritual principle; while the catholic spirit in R. N. Flew's *Jesus and His Church* (London, 1938) rooted ecclesiology in the community of disciples called and sent by Jesus, as a spiritual reality prior to any particular church order. Geoffrey Wainwright's *Methodists in Dialog* (Nashville, 1995) presents Methodism as a broad tradition marked by the importance of both disciple-making fellowship and ecumenical relations for the sake of unity and mission (see *Church government).

Academic scholarship

Methodist theology after Wesley was initially shaped by the biblical commentaries of Adam Clarke (1760–1832), the systematic work of Richard Watson's *Theological Institutes* (1823–24) and William Burt Pope's *Compendium* (1875–76). While remaining faithful to Wesleyan emphases, they were less concerned to use Wesley himself as a source of authority.

British Methodism, however, has consistently made its most significant contribution in the field of biblical studies, reflecting Wesley's own commitment to scriptural exposition in the service of preaching. Scholars of note include W. F. Moulton (1835–98), J. H. Moulton (1863–1917), A. S. Peake (1865–1929), Vincent Taylor (1887–1968) and more recently, James Dunn, Morna Hooker and I. Howard Marshall.

This biblical scholarship fuelled much theological reflection on the meaning of atonement. The themes of identification with Christ, the mediatorial role of his sacrifice, and moral persuasion to a cruciform life were developed in W. F. Lofthouse's *Ethics and Atonement* (London, 1906) and Russell Maltby's, *Christ and His Cross* (London, 1935). The general impulse to go beyond theories of penal *substitution, clearly seen in John Scott Lidgett's, *The Spiritual Principle of the Atonement* (London, 1897), was an attempt to keep the *atonement central to both evangelical conversion and the pursuit of social holiness.

In America, early Methodist theology was given direction by the systematics of Nathan Bangs (1778–1862), Thomas O. Summers (1812–82) and John Miley (1813–95). Later theological movements steered Methodism into the broad philosophical currents of *liberal Protestantism: such as Boston personalism, led by Henry Clay Sheldon (1845–1928) and Borden Parker Bowne (1847–1910); and *process theology, by John Cobb and Schubert Ogden.

Methodist theology has also been enriched by a number of scholars around the world, writing in a self-consciously Wesleyan mode. Significant voices include Theophil Sporri (Switzerland), Vilem Schneeberger (Czechoslovakia) and Manfred Marquardt (Germany); Harald Lindstrom, Thorvald Kallstad and Ole Borgen (Scandanavia); José Bonino (Argentina), Elsa Tamez (Costa Rica), Daniel T. Niles (Sri Lanka) and Emerito Nacpil (Philippines).

Contemporary variations

Since the mid-twentieth century, there has been a renewal of interest in the theology of John Wesley himself, the distinctive genes of the Wesleyan traditions and their significance for contemporary Methodism. Beginning with Harald Lindström's *Wesley and Sanctification* (Stockholm, 1943) and William Canon's *The Theology of John Wesley* (Nashville, 1946), the field of Wesley Studies has continued to emerge through contributions such as Randy Maddox's *Responsible Grace* (Nashville, 1994) and Kenneth Collins' *The Theology of John Wesley* (Nashville, 2007). The current *Wesley Works* project (1959–), pioneered by Frank Baker, Albert Outler and Robert Cushman, is providing essential critical editions and commentaries on primary texts for this scholarship. There is also a gathering interest in the work of Charles Wesley, and especially the theological contributions of his hymnody: for example, S. T. Kimbrough, *Charles Wesley: Poet and Theologian* (Nashville, 1993); and Newport and Campbell (eds.), *Charles Wesley: Life, Literature and Legacy* (London, 2007).

In Britain, Philip Watson, Gordon Rupp, Peter Stephens, Rupert Davies and Geoffrey Wainwright are Methodist scholars of historical and ecumenical theology who have placed an emphasis on specifically Wesleyan thinking. United Methodist theology has been deeply influenced by the '*Wesleyan Quadrilateral' of Scripture, tradition, reason and experience, though its exact formulation as a theological method, and the extent to which it is actually Wesleyan, remains a matter of scholarly debate. While promoting considerable theological diversity, it has nevertheless provided a method for sustained theological engagement with John Wesley and the Methodist tradition.

Official theological reflection in British Methodism has tended to be fixed by prevailing trends in theology and pressing social issues, rather than a prior commitment to Wesleyan doctrine as such. On this basis, what counts as Methodist theology tends to be just what the Methodist people have agreed at any given time in their history. In the missional context of 'emerging church' conversations and 'fresh expressions' of church, however, it would appear that the Wesleyan genes and their distinctive historic expressions are gaining a renewed attention.

Bibliography

K. Collins, *The Theology of John Wesley: Holy Love and the Shape of Grace* (Nashville, 2007); K. Cracknell and S. White, *An Introduction to World Methodism* (Cambridge, 2005); R. Heitzenrater, *Wesley and the People Called Methodists* (Nashville, 1994); S. Jones, *United Methodist Doctrine* (Nashville, 2002); T. Langford, *Practical Divinity: Theology in the Wesleyan Traditions*, vols. 1–2 (Nashville, 1999); R. Maddox, *Responsible Grace: John Wesley's Practical Theology* (Nashville, 1994); P. Meadows, *The DNA of Wesleyan Discipleship* (Cambridge, 2013); H. Rack, *Reasonable Enthusiast: John Wesley and the Rise of Methodism* (Peterborough, 2002); G. Rupp (ed.), *A History of the Methodist Church in Great Britain*, vols. 1–4 (Peterborough, 1965–88); K. Wilson, *Methodist Theology* (London, 2011).

P. MEADOWS

METZ, JOHANNES BAPTIST (b. 1928)

Johannes Metz is a professor at the University of Mainz, and a leading Roman Catholic representative of *political theology. A student of Karl *Rahner, some of whose earlier works he has reissued, his theology is particularly concerned with the political dimensions of Christian faith and theological reflection. Strongly opposed to any reduction of religion to a merely private option in secular society, he understands Christian faith, and its expressions in corporate life and theological activity, as a force of critical and liberating potential. In particular, he envisages theology as not simply a discipline internal to Christianity, but as a constructive critique of social reality, and in this way he sees theology as a dialogue with the world over the future shape of society. The relationship of theology to politics is not one of consequence or application; politics is intrinsic to the theological exercise. Moreover, theology has a critical role in the church, in so far as it enables the identification of ideological elements within the hierarchical forms of church life, and so contributes to the emergence of a 'post-bourgeois church'. Much of this theology rests on the basis of a powerful doctrine of *creation and on an understanding of *salvation as concerned primarily with man in his bodily, corporate and political existence.

Bibliography

Works: *Theology of the World* (ET, London, 1969); *Faith in History and Society* (ET, London, 1980); *A Passion for God: The Mystical-Political Dimension of Christianity* (ET, New York, 1998).

Studies: J. K. Downey (ed.), *Love's Strategy: The Political Theology of Johann Baptist Metz* (Harrisburg, 1999); R. D. Johns, *Man in the World: The Political Theology of Johannes Baptist Metz* (Chico, 1976).

J. B. WEBSTER

MEYENDORFF, JOHN (1926–92)

John Meyendorff was born in Paris, the son of Russian émigré parents. Educated in Paris, he graduated from the Institut St-Serge in 1949 and submitted his *Doctorat ès lettres* at the Sorbonne in 1958. In the same year he was ordained to the priesthood. In the following year, the fruits of his doctorate were published: a major work on St Gregory *Palamas, inaugurating serious study of Palamas and the *hesychast controversy, and his edition of Palamas' major work in defence of the hesychasts, the *Triads*. In 1959, too, Meyendorff left Europe for America, becoming Professor of Patristics at St Vladimir's Orthodox Theological Seminary, and also maintaining links with Dumbarton Oaks, the centre for Byzantine Studies in Washington DC, and with Fordham University, where he held an adjunct chair. In 1983, on the death of Alexander Schmemann, he became Dean, resigning in 1992 and dying shortly afterwards.

As a scholar, Meyendorff was primarily a church historian with deep knowledge of both Byzantium and Russia, but he wrote widely on theological matters. Perhaps his greatest work was *Byzantium and the Rise of Russia* (1981), which traced the influence of hesychast monastic culture in the formation of Muscovite Russia. His work on hesychasm made Palamas accessible as never before, with the result that the Orthodox 'Neo-patristic synthesis' increasingly came to involve an endorsement of the theological terms of Palamas' defence of the hesychasts, especially the distinction drawn between God's unknowable essence and his knowable energies and an emphasis on the authenticity of a deifying experience of God attained through prayer. In the States, he became involved in both inter-Orthodox affairs (notably the establishment in 1970 of an autocephalous – self-governing – Orthodox Church of America, uniting most Orthodox of Slav descent under an American hierarchy) and in ecumenical matters. With his early death, the articulate and learned Orthodox voice America had known since *Florovsky and *Schmemann fell temporarily silent. In his final years, glasnost and perestroika enabled him to visit his ancestral Russia, where the wisdom and insight of his words found eager listeners.

See also: EASTERN ORTHODOX THEOLOGY; RUSSIAN ORTHODOX THEOLOGY.

Bibliography

Most of Meyendorff's works in English and English translation are published by St Vladimir's Seminary Press, Crestwood. See especially: *The Orthodox Church* (London, 1960); *Byzantine Theology: Historical Trends and Doctrinal Themes* (London, 1974), both now published by SVSP.

A. LOUTH

MÍGUEZ BONINO, JOSÉ (1924–2012)

Known as the dean of Protestant theologians in the Spanish-speaking world, Bonino was also the only Latin American Protestant observer during the Second *Vatican Council. Born in Rosario, Argentina in 1924, he studied theology in Buenos Aires, and did graduate work at Emory University and Union Theological Seminary in New York. A Methodist pastor from 1947, he served in several local parishes in Argentina. From 1954 to 1985 he taught at the Higher Institute for Theological Studies (ISEDET) in Buenos Aires, of which he was also a Dean. Active in the *ecumenical movement, he became one of the presidents of the World Council of Churches and a spokesperson for ecumenical Protestantism from Latin America. He also participated with evangelicals in the Latin American Theological Fraternity. His book, *Doing Theology in a Revolutionary Situation*, is probably the most comprehensive introduction to *liberation theology from a sympathetic but not uncritical position. The same irenic approach is characteristic of his book *Christians and Marxists: The Mutual Challenge to Revolution*. His theological reflection has a Christological and ethical bent and is characterized by clarity and consistency, an acute analytical ability and familiarity with the Protestant theological traditions, especially in his later books such as *Towards a Christian Political Ethics* and *Faces of Latin American Protestantism*.

Bibliography

Works: *Doing Theology in a Revolutionary Situation* (Philadelphia and London, 1975); *Christians and Marxists: The Mutual Challenge to Revolution* (London, 1976); 'For Life and Against Death: A Theology That Takes Sides', *Christian Century*, 1980, pp. 1154–1158; *Towards a Christian Political Ethics* (Philadelphia, 1983); *Faces of Latin American Protestantism* (Grand Rapids, 1997).

S. ESCOBAR

MILBANK, JOHN (b. 1952)

John Milbank is an Anglican theologian and Professor of Religion, Politics and Ethics at the University of Nottingham. After studying history at Oxford and then theology at Cambridge University with Rowan *Williams, former Archbishop of Canterbury, Milbank went on to teach at the Universities of Lancaster, Cambridge and Virginia. Along with other theologians with Cambridge connections (Catherine Pickstock and Graham Ward) Milbank edited a volume of essays in 1999 called *Radical Orthodoxy: A New Theology*. Since that time, Milbank's scholarship has become closely associated with a 'theological sensibility' known as *Radical Orthodoxy.

Milbank's first major work to elicit widespread attention was *Theology and Social Theory: Beyond Secular Reason* (1990). In this work, Milbank gives a genealogy of 'secular reason', arguing that the attempt in modern social theories to have scientific 'objectivity' actually veils implicit anti-theological *ontologies in these theories. Wide-ranging in scope, Milbank interrogates the key thinkers in the development of modern sociology, economics and political theory to find an underlying common strand: they assume an 'ontology of violence', in which the necessity of conflict is a basic assumption about the way the world is. As an alternative to this, Milbank reconstructs an Augustinian 'ontology of peace', in which the most basic ontological status of the universe is grounded in the harmony of differences and participation in the beauty of the triune God. *Theology and Social Theory* seeks to liberate theology from captivity to modern norms, which claim to be based on social scientific 'facts'. Theology itself should critique the implicit ontologies in these social theories.

Milbank's current work focuses on the articulation of a *trinitarian ontology. In *Being Reconciled* (2003), Milbank begins a series of books on this ontology using the concept of 'gift' as 'a kind of transcendental category in relation to all the *topoi* of theology, in a similar fashion to "word"'. The focus on 'gift' in particular reflects Milbank's trinitarian focus upon how the work of the Spirit brings human beings into relationships of mutual interest and exchange, as opposed to a vision of love which sees the true gift as a 'free gift' with no return. Milbank thinks that Anders *Nygren has falsified the notion of Christian agape by excluding concerns for mutuality – and that a similar glorification of sacrifice for its own sake is also displayed in the thought of *Kant and *Derrida.

Milbank has also written monographs which fit within the Radical Orthodoxy sensibility more generally, including works on Vico (his dissertation), Thomas Aquinas, Henri de Lubac, Christology and theological *aesthetics.

Bibliography

Works: *Theology and Social Theory: Beyond Secular Reason* (Oxford, 1990); *Being Reconciled: Ontology and Pardon* (Oxford, 2003).

J. T. BILLINGS

MILLENNIUM

The term refers to the period of 1,000 years mentioned in Rev. 20:2–7 as the time of the reign of Christ and the saints over the earth. Although the term 'millenarianism' has come to be used much more loosely, in this article we are concerned with millennial belief in the strict sense, referring to interpretations of the millennium of Rev. 20. Three main views of the millennium are usually distinguished (premillennialism, postmillennialism and amillennialism), but these views as they have emerged in the history of Christianity can be best understood as five traditions of interpretation:

1. Premillennialism (or chiliasm) in the early church

Many of the early Fathers, including Papias (*c*. 60–*c*. 130), Justin (*c*. 100–*c*. 165), *Irenaeus, *Tertullian, Victorinus of Pettau (d. *c*. 304) and Lactantius (*c*. 240–*c*. 320), were premillennialists, i.e. they expected the personal coming of Christ in glory to inaugurate a millennial reign on earth before the last *judgment (see *Eschatology). This belief was not only an interpretation of Rev. 20, but also a continuation of Jewish *apocalyptic expectation of an interim messianic kingdom. The framework of Rev. 20 was filled with content derived from Jewish apocalyptic and especially from OT prophecies, with the result that the millennium was understood primarily as a restoration of paradise. Amid the abundant fruitfulness of the renewed earth and peace between the animals, the resurrected saints would enjoy 1,000 years of paradisal life on earth before being translated to eternal life in heaven. The 1,000 years were explained either as the originally intended span of human life on earth or as the world's sabbath rest at the end of a 7,000-years' 'week' of history. It was the materialistic nature of this millennialism which made it objectionable to others of the Fathers, including *Augustine, whose highly influential rejection of it led to the virtual disappearance of premillennialism until the seventeenth century.

2. Augustinian amillennialism

The interpretation of Rev. 20 which held the field for most of the medieval period and remained influential down to the present was pioneered by the fourth-century *Donatist Tyconius, whose ideas were taken up by Augustine. According to this view, the millennial reign of Christ is the age of the church, from the resurrection of Christ until his parousia. Augustine took the figure 1,000 itself to be symbolic, not the actual length of time. This interpretation of Rev. 20 is often called amillennialist, because it rejects belief in a future millennium. For the earthly kingdom expected by the chiliasts, it substituted a twin emphasis on the present rule of Christ and other-worldly eschatological hope.

The Protestant Reformers adopted a modified form of this view. They took the millennium to be an actual period of 1,000 years in the past (variously dated), during which the gospel flourished. Satan's release at the end of this period (Rev. 20:7) marked the rise of the medieval *papacy. For the future, the Reformers expected the imminent coming of Christ, leading at once to the last judgment and the dissolution of this world.

3. Joachimism and Protestant postmillennialism

The ideas of the twelfth-century abbot *Joachim inspired a new form of eschatological expectation which in the later Middle Ages and the sixteenth century was the major alternative to the Augustinian view. Before the end of history there would be an age of the Spirit, a period of spiritual prosperity and peace for the church on earth, which was identified with the millennium of Rev. 20, though not primarily derived from that text. This expectation can be called post-millennialist, since it held that the millennium would be inaugurated by a spiritual intervention of Christ in the power of his Spirit, not by his bodily advent, which would follow the millennium.

Joachimism appealed to some early Protestants, who saw in the success of the Reformation gospel the dawning of a new age of prosperity for the church. Joachimist influence, Protestant optimism about the trends of history, and exegesis of Revelation combined to produce Protestant postmillennialism, whose first influential exponent was Thomas Brightman (1562–1607) and which first flourished in the seventeenth century. In this view, the millennium would come about through the Spirit-empowered preaching of the gospel, resulting in the conversion of the world and the worldwide spiritual reign of Christ through the gospel.

The eighteenth century was the great age of postmillennialism, which played a key role in the development of missionary thinking. The revivals were seen as the first ripples of the movement of conversion which would engulf the world, and a view which gave human activity a significant role in God's purpose of establishing his kingdom was a major stimulus to missionary activity. But in the nineteenth century, postmillennial expectation increasingly approximated to the secular doctrine of *progress and merged into *liberal theology's identification of the *kingdom of God with moral and social improvement. The modern decline of postmillennialism coincides with the loss of Christian credibility that doctrines of progress have suffered.

4. Protestant premillennialism

Protestant premillennialism originated in the early seventeenth century, especially under the influence of Joseph Mede (1586–1638). It differs from postmillennialism in expecting the personal advent of Christ and the bodily resurrection of the saints to precede the millennium, and therefore tends to stress the discontinuity between the present and the millennial age more than postmillennialism does. It enjoyed a major revival in England in the 1820s, from which its modern forms derive. Whereas postmillennialism thrived on observing hopeful signs of the approaching millennium, premillennialism gained popularity in circles whose view of the current situation was deeply pessimistic. Not the influence of the church, but only the personal intervention of Christ could establish his kingdom on earth.

Premillennialists have taken many views on the character of the millennial reign, but nineteenth-century premillennialism tended towards a literal interpretation of prophecy, including OT prophecies applied to the millennium. This tendency reached extreme form in the *dispensationalist theology pioneered by J. N. *Darby, in which a 'secret rapture' of the church, preceding the coming of Christ, is to bring the age of the church to an end, while the millennium functions as the time of fulfilment for the OT prophecies to Israel.

5. Symbolic amillennialism

Many proponents of views 2, 3 and 4 above have taken the figure 1,000 in Rev. 20 to be a symbolic number, but have still interpreted the millennium as a period of time. A view found occasionally in the modern period takes the millennium to be a symbol, not of a period at all, but of the complete achievement of Christ's kingdom and his total victory over evil at the parousia.

The various views are, of course, based in part on the debated details of exegesis, but in a broader sense they represent differing attitudes to the relationship between the kingdom of Christ and the history of this world. In all its forms, millennial belief represents, in opposition to a completely other-worldly eschatology, the conviction that it is part of God's purpose to realize his kingdom in this world.

Bibliography
O. Blöcher, G. G. Blum, R. Konrad, R. Bauckham, 'Chiliasmus,' *TRE* VII, pp. 723–745; R. G. Clouse (ed.), *The Meaning of the Millennium: Four Views* (Downers Grove, 1977); J. Daniélou, *The Theology of Jewish Christianity* (London, 1964); S. Grenz, *The Millennial Maze* (Downers Grove, 1992); P. Toon (ed.), *Puritans, the Millennium and the Future of Israel* (London, 1970).

R. J. BAUCKHAM

MINISTRY

Ministry is a term that refers to the work of the *church – its service in the world, proclamation of the gospel and administration of the sacraments. It can refer to the activities of the whole people of God; or equally to individuals with specific vocations (e.g. teacher, pastor, priest, evangelist, bishop, prophet, etc.). Ministry describes both the general work and service of the church, as well as the type of vocation that is particular to an individual, which may involve ordination, licensing or some kind of recognition.

Contexts and shaping
To a large extent, the range of ministry and ministers that one can encounter across the denominational spectrum will be characteristic expressions of ecclesiological outlooks. For example, Lesslie *Newbigin contrasts associational (or congregationalist) models of the church with those that are parochial. Avery Dulles has developed five models of the church: institution, mystical communion, herald, servant and sacrament. James Hopewell suggests four models: mechanistic, organic, contextual and symbolic. Each of these models presented by the authors are suggestive of a different kind of ministry – in terms of character, style, substance, ethos and foci – that is offered by the church. Thus, a sacramental understanding of the church (Dulles) requires an emphasis on priesthood; whereas an understanding of the church as herald might lead to an emphasis on the ministry of preaching.

Ministry is never shaped in isolation from its context. Whether it is the ministry of the church or the individual minister, the environment in which a church finds itself located will have some kind of impact upon the shaping of ministerial identity. The political contexts of South and Central America play a significant part in the shaping of *liberation theology, and of the ministry offered through base communities in some of the world's poorest slums. It is less likely that a theologian in a developed country enjoying relative stability and prosperity could have generated this kind of theology and ecclesiology.

Context matters. As Richard *Niebuhr demonstrated, the social sources of denominationalism (e.g. economic, race, class, gender, caste, etc.) will have some bearing on the shape of ministry, and upon ministerial identity. Whilst theological priorities will still be more significant than other factors, here is no escaping, for example, the alignment of class identity and early Methodism in England.

In terms of contemporary contextual factors that shape ministry, current British church-going habits correlate with the two main religious economies that can be observed in Europe. The first is a market model, which assumes voluntary membership will become the norm. The second model is utility-based, where membership is ascribed rather than chosen. In the first model, individuals opt in to become members. In the second model, all in some sense are deemed to belong, unless they opt out. The two models are in partial tension, and arguably depend upon each other.

One may further characterize these differences as intensive and extensive forms of ecclesial polity. Ministries that centre on intensity tend to build strong congregational identity (cf. Newbigin's notion of 'associational' churches), which can be based on a charismatic leader, a particular programme or some kind of significant emphasis (e.g. doctrinal, worship, liturgical, pastoral, political, etc.). In contrast, extensive forms of ecclesial polity tend to be more open and accommodating, and focus on being the church for the whole community, which leads to a breadth of expression. In turn, this may compromise both definition and numerical growth, although this is not necessarily the case.

As a general rule, North American churches, irrespective of their denominational tradition,

Ministry

will have a primary proclivity for market and intensive models of the church, as religion is fundamentally a matter of choice. Many European countries, in contrast, are still shaped by utility-extensive expectations by virtue of the Christian faith being 'by law established' (e.g. Presbyterian in Scotland, Lutheran in Sweden, Anglican in England, etc.). But Europe, like many parts of the world, is now increasingly influenced by market-models of faith.

How, then, can one account for the particularity and praxis of ministry being so variable, even within a relatively confined area such as one suburb or small town? A fertile notion that might help explain this comes from the vocabulary of sommeliers. *Terroir* is a Gallic word for which there is no English equivalent. The term refers to the combination of factors that make one wine slightly different from another, even when they are geographically proximate. Sunshine and temperature; north- or south-facing, and the amount of rainfall; the height of the land (and the drainage), the type and acidity of the soil; the types and subtypes of grape, and their progeny; local know-how and human skill; the amount of time permitted for a wine to mature, and the types of barrels chosen: all combine to make wines taste different.

This accounts for why one type of Burgundy tastes quite different from another, even though they might be from the same village. And this analogy is suggestive for theology in relation to the composition of local ecclesial identity and the expression of ministry. So on one level, church is church, just as wine is wine. Yet to the refined palate, the differences are detectable and telling. The ecclesial history and ethos of one church might be composed through all manner of factors: denominational identity, buildings, local history, various forms of organization, social factors such as wealth, ethnicity and education, and more obviously ecclesial and theological accents. In an adjacent church, even of the same denominational hue, and in a similar context, the flavour of ecclesial praxis and ministry may turn out to be markedly different.

Sources

Theological rationales for ministry will have several traceable roots. These may include emphases drawn from biblical, patristic, Reformation and contemporary Christian sources. But they might also include more current cultural perspectives. Some forms of modern ministry make no apology for being enculturated expressions of faith, even to the point of becoming somewhat heterodox. (See e.g. the emergence of ministers who are exemplars of the power of positive thinking in the health, wealth and *prosperity movements.)

The scriptural sources for ministry are rooted in the person and example of *Jesus, what is known about the organization of the early church, and what the NT teaches more generally about collective discipleship, which is effectively ministerial *praxis. The ministry of Jesus is focused on teaching, proclaiming the *kingdom of God, *healing (which includes deliverance) and *prayer. Generally, the ministry of Jesus can be characterized as reaching out to the lost or marginalized. For the most part, this is a costly ministry of service and inclusiveness, where Jesus takes radical steps to either cut through or challenge the social or religious constructions of reality of his day, that in delineating are also discriminating. For example, there are over forty healing miracles recorded in the Gospels, and yet the names of the individuals healed seem to be unknown to the evangelists, suggesting that the persons receiving this ministry from Jesus had little social or religious status.

Jesus' ministry of dedicated service is of course an expression of his *incarnation. Paul's deep and profound Christological hymn (Phil. 2:6–11) talks about Jesus 'taking the form of a slave', which echoes the early established gospel tradition identifying Jesus not as one who came to be served, but to serve (Matt. 20:28; Mark 10:45; Luke 22:27; John 13:4–17). This ministry – arguably the core paradigm for all forms of Christian ministry, whether individual or collective – is ultimately expressed in the *cross. Several NT writers understand the crucifixion as priestly, sacrificial and ultimately reconciling (see Heb. 10:5–14; Rom. 5:2; Eph. 2:13–18; 1 John 2:1–2; etc.).

The ministry of the early church focused on prayer, further workings of miracles, signs and wonders amongst the poor (Acts 5:12–16) and diaconal acts of service (Acts 6:1–7). Stephen, the first Christian martyr, was one of these deacons, and the form of his commission involved him being identified for a specific ministry (i.e. selected, with the role and tasks described) and the apostles *laying their hands upon him in order to set him aside for this ministry, in the company of six others.

As the early church began to mature, and to some extent develop the initial foundations that are fundamental for organizations and institutions, the reflections on the nature of ministry and the identity of the church began to converge. Thus, Paul describes the church as 'the body of Christ', and in so doing offers a vivid analogy of mutuality, intra-dependence, differentiation and diversity (Rom. 12:4–8; 1 Cor. 12; Eph. 4). The analogy allows a variety of different spiritual *gifts (and their holders) to be identified, yet without individual ministries becoming competitive. Thus, some are prophets, others teachers, and still others evangelists or apostles: 'but all are one in Jesus Christ'.

The New Testament also began to develop a sense of 'officers' of the church, although this is more nascent than concrete. The Twelve (following the election of Matthias, after the death of Judas) are identified as apostles. Deacons were appointed almost from the outset. Paul's letters, on the other hand, merely refer to 'fellow workers' who may lead and guide the church. However, there is mention of 'overseers' (i.e. *episkopoi*) in Philippi – the forerunner of bishops. Yet the NT does not leave a clear pattern that links tasks to roles. Thus, no one office is singled out for the task associated with the presiding over and administration of the Lord's Supper (1 Cor. 11:17–33). The book of Acts mentions the appointment of elders and presbyters (e.g. 14:23; 15:2; 20:17, 28; 21:18). Again, it is not clear what these titles indicate, and it may even be the case that the roles were rather fluid in the early church, and varied from city to city and state to state. Deacons emerge as a category within the pastoral epistles, and as with the other named offices, would have included women (e.g. Rom 16:1, 3, 6).

So whilst there is plenty of biblical warrant for patterns of ministry, and also for the identification of the roles and tasks that might pertain to ministers, the NT does not per se, offer a complete and concrete blueprint for ministry. The early church had not yet organized itself around agreed creeds, a canon of Scripture, or authorized ministers. But the early church was not disorganized either. Living between the fluid and concrete, it was, rather, unorganized. It was developing an emerging, nascent shape for its ministry, and roles and task for ministers that would soon be ordered, albeit variable (by degrees) according to the context and environment in which the new faith was expressing itself.

Development

The development of orders follows a relatively standard trajectory that is familiar to sociologists of religion. Namely, after a period of original and charismatic leadership, the phase of development that enables maintenance, development and further growth is more dependent on routinization and bureaucratization. Thus, *Methodism is the 'system' that develops and concretizes after the death of the *Wesley brothers.

It was no different in the early church, where the passing of the apostles, and then those that had known them first-hand, soon led to the establishment of bishops, presbyters and deacons. As the Christian faith expanded, and became increasingly diverse in its cultural expressions, it became more and more important to preserve its catholicity. Gradually, a shape for Christian ministry began to emerge that was recognizable putatively across different cultural contexts. This was driven both by numerical and geographical increase, leading to bishops being persons who presided over several eucharistic communities, whilst presbyters became more identified with single local congregations, presiding on behalf of the bishop.

In the early third century, writers such as *Tertullian and Hippolytus were beginning to describe the roles of bishops and presbyters with the use of sacerdotal terminology, thereby conflating the ministry of the priest with the priestly ministry of Christ. This trajectory continued to develop throughout the medieval period, with minor orders being added to the church, such as reader, acolyte, exorcist, pardoner, deacon and sub-deacon. The growth of monastic life also contributed to a flourishing, rich and variegated economy of recognized ministries within the church. These evolved and acquired denser identities, allowing for further delineation (e.g. celibacy for priests from the eleventh century onwards, but not for deacons; different kinds of liturgical apparel to symbolize offices and their functions; which offices are responsible for which sacraments, etc.). The maturing of ministry, in other words, cannot be separated from the development of ecclesiology.

The Reformation period witnessed a reappraisal of ministry. Whilst the *Reformation was in fact several movements rather than just one, and a complex alloy of nationalist, theological and revisionist sentiments, all of which were supported by the emergence of mass-produced and vernacular publications, the impact of the Reformers on the shape and identity of ministry was arguably the most substantial in Christian history. In general, the Reformers rejected the idea that the identity and existence of the church was dependent upon a sacerdotal understanding of priesthood.

The consequences of this manifested themselves differently, according to the nature of the reformation and the context in which it was emerging. In many (early) Reformed churches, the distinction between clergy and laity was still perpetuated – but with the clergy now focusing their identity on a highly professional pastoral and teaching office. (Hence John Milton's dictum that the 'new Presbyter is but old priest writ large'.) In the Church of England, the office of the presbyter still had sacramental responsibility, but the pastoral and teaching foci had moved to being just as important (see *Anglicanism). This is expressed in classic writings and exemplary figures such as George Herbert, Richard *Hooker and John Donne. In more radical groups such as the *Quakers, however, the gift of *preaching was now no longer attached to an office or to ordination, and to all intents and purposes, the boundary between clergy and laity had been dissolved. Some Reformed churches emerged where ministry was simply the activity of the whole people of God, and not the particular and distinct responsibility of one person set aside for certain and unique tasks (see *Priesthood of all believers).

As the Reformation developed, differences between emerging Protestant denominations began to take place. Some of these are related to distinctive theological outlooks, whilst others arise from subtle cultural conditions. Thus, some congregations had the right to choose and dismiss their ministers, whereas in other denominations, appointment and dismissal could be done only by a bishop (or the equivalent person or body). The Church of England continued to observe a threefold distinction of ordained ministries: bishop, priest and deacon. The Anglican understanding of ministry is, therefore, still medieval in its functionality and roots, but largely stripped of its sacerdotal theology.

In the nineteenth century, however, the *Anglo-Catholic movement sought to restore pre-Reformation understandings of ministry to Anglican ministerial identity. The movement expressed itself in spirituality, hymnody, architecture and liturgical renewal. The impact of this is now widespread, albeit extremely dissipated. The underlying theology that was supposed to support this neo-gothic renaissance did not have the intensive influence that *Keble, *Newman and others had hoped. The legacy of Anglo-Catholicism today is expressed mainly in style rather than substance.

Meanwhile, and in some Reformed churches, deacons and elders are lay appointments, and the minister is a trained professional who chiefly exercises a ministry as the primary teacher and pastor. In the twentieth century, the emergence of house churches and charismatic renewal has witnessed a resurgence in new forms of recognized lay ministry, many of which depend on the authorization and validation of the local congregation, or perhaps a wider network of affiliated churches. This has led to some house church leaders being recognized (or self-designated) as *apostles, and functioning very much like primitive bishops from the early church.

More recently, church historians and sociologists now agree that the most decisive period for impacting upon ministry and ministerial identity in Britain, after the Reformation, is the Victorian era. The onset of industrialization – something begun in the eighteenth century, but which primarily came to dominate the landscape of British society in the nineteenth century – resulted in significant changes for churches. Several factors need noting.

First, the mass migration of people from rural to urban contexts led to a range of consequences. Many new churches were built in cities, although statistics tend to show that these were not necessarily well-attended. But the social upheaval created a fertile environment for *revivals. Second, training for clergy began in earnest, in order to equip ministers for the new challenges presented by an industrialized society. Theological colleges were born, which shifted the identity of clergy life from being a gentlemanly pursuit to being a profession. Third, the funding of churches began to move from being a widely held social responsibility to being that of the congregation. Fourth, clergy roles gradually became less public as the state and local government took on more responsibility. Consequently, clergy became more intensely focused on their congregations, and on the styles of theology that differentiated them. The response to gradual marginalization is invariably intensification, and some patterns of ministry now anticipated clergy becoming 'technologists of the sanctuary' – specialists in discrete areas of ritual and performance. Fifth, whilst the emerging clerical profession of the nineteenth and early twentieth centuries gave birth to better educated clergy, it was ironically for a more disconnected church. Thus, the current accent on training, formation and education in theological colleges – which includes practical work and reflective practice – is rightly regarded as an essential component in preventing clerical identity and development from becoming too rarefied.

Current developments

In more recent times, all denominations and congregations have begun to renew their understanding of ministry in the light of the problems and possibilities presented by contemporary *culture. An increased emphasis on the ministry of the laity is now common to many denominations. Yet whilst there is ample scriptural warrant for the recovery of this tradition, it also has to be acknowledged that the increased emphasis on lay ministry may also be prompted by a shortage of resources to train clergy, and, in some cases, far fewer vocations to ordained ministry. Britain and Ireland have witnessed a sharp fall in the number of priestly vocations for the Roman Catholic Church, and a steady fall in the number of nonconformist ministers.

Some commentators have observed that this correlates with a general decline in the social status of the clerical profession. However, the decline is not uniform, since the Church of England continues to ordain and licence significant numbers of men and women to a variety of ministries. And as new forms of church emerge (i.e. cell, 'fresh expressions' and other alternatives), new types of ministers are now beginning to be trained (e.g. pioneer minister). That said, no modern pattern of ministry can claim to replicate a pure and untainted version of what is presented in the NT. To claim complete scriptural warrant for a pattern of contemporary ministry is both hermeneutically doubtful and ecclesiologically hazardous.

Several significant changes in ministry for churches have taken place in Western culture in the post-war era. The rise of consumerism is altering the cadence and contours of church membership. As global culture increasingly moves from one of religious assumption to consumption, in which believing and belonging are matters of conscious choice rather than a set of inherited suppositions, churches and ministers find themselves competing with other leisure activities. This is a direct consequence of concepts such as obligation and duty being eclipsed by cultures of choice.

More positively, *charismatic renewal has brought a flexibility and exuberance to ministry that has led to experimentation in patterns of organization, *worship and types of ministry. The increased presence and recognition of ordained women has also transformed the ecclesial landscape. Although this development is still confined to mainline Protestant churches (i.e. not Roman Catholics and Orthodox, but including Anglicanism), it is a development that many denominations have embraced.

Another significant development is the growing ecumenical convergence on the functions and identity of ministry. This leads denominations still to value their differences, yet also entering into formal associations that recognize the ministry practised by others. So whilst differences of organization, and the theological rationales behind them, continue to inhibit unity, there is a growing recognition that all ministries belong to Christ, who is the head of the body.

See also: CHURCH GOVERNMENT.

Bibliography

R. S. Anderson (ed.), *Theological Foundations for Ministry* (Edinburgh, 1979); Anglican-Roman Catholic International Commission, ARCIC: *The Final Report* (London, 1982); *Baptism, Eucharist and Ministry*, Faith and Order Paper No. 111 (Geneva, 1982); J. M. Barnett, *The Diaconate: A Full and Equal Order* (New York, 1981); C. K. Barrett, *Church, Ministry and Sacraments in the New Testament* (Exeter, 1985); A. Coxon and R. Towler, *The Fate of the Anglican Clergy: A Sociological Study* (London, 1979); G. Guiver (ed.), *Priests in a People's Church* (London, 2001); M. Harris, *Organizing God's Work: Challenges for Churches and Synagogues* (London, 1998); A. T. and R. P. C. Hanson, *The Identity of the Church: A Guide to Recognizing the Contemporary Church* (London, 1987); R. P. C. Hanson, *Christian Priesthood Examined* (Guildford, 1979); U. Holmes, *The Future Shape of Ministry* (New York, 1971); H. Küng, *Why Priests?* (London, 1972); P. C. Moore (ed.), *Bishops – But What Kind? Reflections on*

Episcopacy (London, 1982); D. M. Paton and C. H. Long (eds.), *The Compulsion of the Spirit: A Roland Allen Reader* (Grant Rapids, 1983); M. Percy, *Clergy: The Origin of Species* (London, 2006); A. Russell, *The Clerical Profession* (London 1980); E. Schillebeeckx, *The Church with a Human Face: A New and Expanded Theology of Ministry* (London 1985); E. Schweizer, *Church Order in the New Testament* (London, 1961); M. Thurian, *Priesthood and Ministry: Ecumenical Research* (London, 1983).

M. Percy

MIRACLE

The word 'miracle' (from the Latin *miraculum*, a wonder) is traditionally used to describe a special *supernatural intervention in the 'natural' course of events in the world. As such, it covers any supernatural activity of God, including divine *revelation and answers to *prayer, as well as healings, exorcisms, nature miracles, and the two great 'wonders' of the life of Jesus, the *incarnation and *resurrection.

In keeping with the biblical worldview and the majority culture of its day, the church in the early centuries readily accepted the reality of miracles, but initiated continuing debates on two issues: their relationship with natural events (did they contradict or complement them?), and the extent to which they should be expected to continue in the post-biblical age.

Miracles and natural events

The medieval church largely followed Augustine, who rejected any radical discontinuity between miracles and natural events, arguing that since God is *Creator both are equally his work. This view fitted well the medieval synthesis between Platonism and Christianity which viewed God as immanent and rational in all his ways. The rediscovery of *Aristotle, however, and the infiltration of his teaching into Christian thinking, especially through Thomas Aquinas, began to open up a gulf between the natural and the supernatural. This slowly widened, encouraged by the success of early Western *science, giving the natural order more and more autonomy until it became the 'clockwork machine' of the eighteenth century, a fixed order of cause and effect into which, it seemed, even God could not break. This set the stage for the great Enlightenment debate over the possibility of miracles which is still with us today.

It is important to note, however, that this debate arises from the presuppositions of the European *Enlightenment, and its significance for the concept of miracle in the rest of the world is strictly limited. When, from the eighteenth century on, missionaries took Christianity to Asia, Africa and South America, they found cultures which had no difficulty at all in accepting the biblical concept of miracle and incorporating it readily into their understanding of the natural world. Despite the universality of technology, this continues to be largely the case; even, say, in China, despite decades of indoctrination in secular materialism, Christians have no difficulty fitting the reality of miracles into their worldview, causing them to look on the continuation of the Enlightenment debate as largely irrelevant. Foisting this debate upon the rest of the world, particularly in a post-Enlightenment age, is an unfortunate example of Western intellectual and theological imperialism.

The classic Enlightenment objections to miracles were summed up by David *Hume in his *Enquiry Concerning Human Understanding* (1748), section 10. By defining a miracle as 'a violation of the laws of *nature' and asserting that 'firm and unalterable experience has established these laws', he was able to claim 'entire' proof against miracles. Faced with so many instances of 'natural law', he said, it will always be the case that the evidence against a miracle claim will be greater than the evidence for it. Additionally, Hume argued that those who claimed to be witnesses to miracles were frequently ill-educated or living in obscure parts of the world or prone to exaggeration. So any sensible person must necessarily always reject a reported miracle. As for the Protestant claim that miracles established the validity of the Christian revelation, Hume pointed out that different religions claim miracles, so they cannot be used to validate Christian truth claims.

None of these arguments has the cogency in our post-Enlightenment age that they had in Hume's day. No contemporary scientist holds Hume's concept of 'the laws of nature'. Radical changes in our understanding of physics and developments in the philosophy of science mean that most scientists have a much more 'open texture' understanding of the way the natural world operates than the eighteenth century 'clockwork universe' view. We have learnt to be less dismissive of the experiences of 'ignorant and barbarous nations' and are much more ready to accept counter instances to observed regularities than Hume would allow. And the debate on the relationship between the natural and the supernatural, between science and religion, has opened new ways of accommodating one to the other. In particular, a number of creative suggestions have been made by Christian thinkers to help us picture how the 'divine action' of the personal God of Christianity can be reconciled with the observed consistency of the world around us. Rather than trying to find ways in which God is enabled to break in to an autonomous natural process, we are more inclined to view the process itself as the action of *God, who incorporates the specific 'miraculous' events into the whole. At the other end of the scale, unpredictability and openness at the sub-nuclear level open up the possibility of totally unexpected events without subverting the observed principles of physics.

The continuance of miracles

Although *exorcisms, *healings and the like were accepted as part of both Christian and non-Christian cultures in the early Christian centuries, some, such as *Irenaeus, suggested that the pattern of miracles seen in the Gospels and Acts was not to be expected as the norm, and that miracles were gradually dying out. Miracles continued, however; *Augustine, for instance, gives us a list of contemporary (fifth-century) miracles for which he could personally vouch, including spectacular instantaneous healings. As the centuries went by, miracles continued to occur, but they tended to be linked with special sanctity and with martyrs and their relics, a concept which has continued to be significant in the Orthodox and Catholic traditions. But in the eyes of the Protestant Reformers this led to abuses, and, in a classic case of overreaction, much of European Protestantism developed a theology that the purpose of miracles was to confirm the validity of revelation, and so, once the Bible was complete, all miracles ceased. With delightful inconsistency, however, most Protestants (apart from Deists and some liberals) remained committed to the concept that God still acts today in the world and answers prayer, even prayer for healing.

This strange compromise was challenged by missionary contact with non-European cultures in the nineteenth century, by the rise of *Pentecostalism at the beginning of the twentieth century, and by the development during the twentieth century of a richer understanding of the purpose of miracles, particularly as an expression of the inbreaking of the kingdom of God. Pentecostals not only rejected the doctrine of the cessation of miracles as having no biblical foundation; they also produced abundant evidence that miracles were still happening, particularly, again, among those whose culture did not present a barrier to their acceptance. The influence of Pentecostalism and of the subsequent charismatic renewal has been felt by all denominations and has produced a widespread, though not yet universal, acceptance of the concept of contemporary miracles. At the same time, a recovery of a holistic concept of *salvation, in which God is seen to be concerned for the physical as well as the spiritual, has made it harder to limit the sphere of his action in the world.

Bibliography

C. Brown, *Miracles and the Critical Mind* (Grand Rapids and Exeter, 1984); N. L. Geisler, *Miracles and the Modern Mind* (Grand Rapids, 1992); R. D. Geivett and G. R. Habermas (eds.), *In Defence of Miracles* (Downers Grove and Leicester, 1997); K. J. Hacking, *Signs and Wonders, Then and Now* (Leicester, 2006); C. S. Lewis, *Miracles* (London, 1947); J. C. Polkinghorne, *Science and Providence* (London, 1989); R. Swinburne, *The Concept of Miracle* (London and New York, 1970).

P. A. HICKS

MISSIOLOGY

Missiology is a discipline within theology which studies the Christian faith and community as they cross frontiers in mission. Its particular interest is in the nature of their encounter with the non-Christian world. The frontier may be geographical or cultural, and includes other worldviews, ideologies, religious beliefs and practices. NT examples of these frontiers might be pagan rituals in the case of food offered to idols (1 Cor. 8), syncretistic beliefs in Colossae or the political authority of the Roman Empire (Rom. 13:1–7; 1 Pet. 2:13–17).

Missiology focuses on what happens at the border, where Christian people engage with

Missiology

non-Christian beliefs and practices. It surveys the activities of the church *ad extra*. So, missiology examines the expansion (or retraction) of the Christian faith as carried throughout the world by a self-consciously distinct community, beginning in Jerusalem around AD 30 and spreading throughout the inhabited world.

In recent years there has been a considerable debate about its relationship to theological studies. Traditionally, it has been viewed as one discipline among others in the theological curriculum. Often it has been studied as a field in practical theology only after a groundwork in biblical and systematic studies has been undertaken. Sometimes it has been offered only as an optional subject. However, as the church's calling to mission has become increasingly prominent throughout the worldwide Christian community, a growing number of people believe that missiology is an integrating factor for all the disciplines. Given the constant missionary concern of the God revealed in Jesus Christ and in the Spirit's testimony within the church, some speak of the inescapably missionary nature of all theology.

Whatever the precise way of understanding the theological task, missiology relates closely to all the classic theological subjects. Thus, biblical study investigates the basis and rationale for the expansion of the Christian community in the *missio Dei*, highlighted in the calling of Abraham to be a blessing for all peoples (Gen. 12:1–3), the election of Israel to be a light to the nations (Isa. 49.6), Jesus' commission to his disciples to be his witnesses to the ends of the earth and the end of time (Matt. 28:18–20; Acts 1:8), the work of the Spirit (John 15:26; 16:7–11), the universal offer of salvation (1 Tim. 2:3–4), the new community of the reign of God (Matt. 11:11) and the promise of new heavens and a new earth (2 Pet. 3:13, Rev. 21). Historical study surveys the expansion of the *church at various periods, assesses its impact on different societies and cultures and investigates what factors have encouraged or discouraged its growth (e.g. the rise of *Christendom, the coming of *Islam, the challenge of the *Enlightenment, Western colonialism). *Systematic theology studies the self-understanding of Christian faith in the context of approval, opposition, indifference or rapid change (such as the encounter with other faiths, modern *science, cultural and ethical pluralism and *globalization) and how it adjusts its message to communicate better with the changing assumptions behind a society's prevailing values. Ethical studies are incorporated into missiology to evaluate the legitimacy of ends and means in mission and orientate the church in its responsibility to declare God's will for the whole of life (see *Ethics; *Social ethics). Pastoral theology has to deal with problematic questions that occur on the frontiers of *culture, such as the practice of baptism in hostile environments, polygamy, the veneration of ancestors, the caste system and same-gender relations. It may also consider the use of cultural symbols and artforms in the church's worship and other activities (see *Contextualization; *Cultural theory and theology).

Due to the wide scope of missiology, it has an important role to play in the integration of other areas of theology. Every aspect of theology has an inescapably missiological dimension, for, by its nature, theology exists as a critical companion of the church's mission. Missiology has a descriptive and analytical task: explaining how and why the Christian faith has expanded across frontiers. It also has a critical dimension in assessing good and bad mission practice, according to criteria which themselves have to be kept under review. Finally, it has a constructive role to play in contributing to a discussion on more adequate mission thinking and practice. In other words, it has both descriptive and normative tasks to fulfil.

In popular imagination, mission is often conceived only in terms of Christians crossing national frontiers to spread the gospel. This view reflects a past age when Christians tended to divide the world neatly into Christian and non-Christian. Today, however, 'the missionary frontier runs around the world. It is the line which separates belief from unbelief.' Mission takes place from and to all continents and within each nation. It is both global and local.

Some Christians want to restrict mission to *evangelism, understood as proclaiming the good news about Jesus Christ and inviting people to believe in him for salvation. Others, on the contrary, believe that every aspect of mission (e.g. serving the needs of the poor) is evangelism. A third group accept that mission is more than evangelism and not all mission is evangelism, yet suppose that evangelism is the primary calling of the church. However, there also exists a new impulse to discover an integral mission, which overcomes all false dichotomies.

Mission conveys the biblical idea of 'being sent', classically expressed in Jesus' saying: 'As the Father has sent me, I am sending you' (John 20:21). The parallel between God sending Jesus and Jesus sending his disciples describes both the method and the content of mission. The church is sent by Jesus, its head, in the power of the Spirit into every part of the world to be an agent and embodiment of God's new order of righteousness (see *Kingdom of God). It does not include everything the church does nor everything God does in the world. Nevertheless, 'the church is by its very nature missionary' (*Ad Gentes*). 'A church exists by mission as a fire exists by burning' (Emil Brunner).

There are a number of diverse, but intimately related, models or paradigms of mission. Each is vitally important. By stressing one more than the others, different groups of Christians have tended to see them as alternatives. Ideally, there is no choice. The Christian community's vocation is to ensure that each is fully implemented in its overall life.

(1) The care of the environment. This means encouraging a wise and sustainable use of the natural order created by God, by engaging in the numerous aspects of conservation and the elimination of pollution (see *Creation, *Nature, theology of). The church will point to the Creator's gift of life, which implies there are sufficient resources for all to have enough, as long as a small minority renounces the ambition of an expanding consumerist lifestyle and learns to enjoy material goods in a restrained way. Only then will future generations inherit an earth restored to health, that is able to support fully everyone's basic needs.

(2) Service among human beings without distinction and whatever their needs. This means a particular concern for vulnerable people, such as those economically excluded from society, the disabled, old people, the bereaved, children at risk and families in tension, refugees, the victims of drought and famine, bonded-labourers and those who suffer as the result of their misuse of alcohol, drugs and gambling (see *Poverty and wealth). It has a particular responsibility to work in the rehabilitation of criminals. The church will fulfil its mission by helping to set up projects that will strengthen the ability of all to decide their own future, such as development schemes, micro-industries, literacy campaigns, health care, education and housing programmes. It will provide shelter for the victims of violence and offer rehabilitation programmes for those suffering from destructive lifestyles.

(3) Witness to 'the truth as it is in Jesus' (Eph. 4:21). This includes a number of tasks, like *apologetics, personal evangelism and church planting. Bearing witness means both the verbal communication of the apostolic gospel and the visual demonstration of its power to bring new life and hope to human relationships and communities.

(4) The promotion of God's justice and healing in society (see *Righteousness; *Society, theology of). To this end, Christians will challenge the damaging effects (including modern slavery) of present global economic forces (see *Globalization), the corrosive effects of affluence (especially political corruption), the destructive fruits of poverty and any policy which serves the powerful rather than the powerless. In places of conflict and violence they are to be peace-makers (see *Pacifism/peace). In particular, the church will be active in promoting and defending the integrity of *family life against easy divorce, abortion, casual or abnormal sexual relationships, pornography, the exploitation of women and children (see *Sexuality), and experimentation on early human life. Finally, it will protest against the immoral arms trade between rich and poor nations.

(5) The practice of being a reconciled and liberated community. It is sent to demonstrate the reality of God's unmerited *grace by loving the enemy, practising forgiveness (see *Guilt and forgiveness), sharing goods and resources, eliminating prejudice and supicion, and exercising *power as servanthood, not as domination and control.

Missiology engages in serious historical and theological reflection on all these aspects of the church's mission. In addition it has focused in recent years on a number of specific issues. Is it right for Christians to be involved in violence to overthrow non-elected, repressive regimes (see *Revolution, theology of)? What is the right approach in sharing Christ with people of other faiths – dialogue, proclamation or simply presence among them? (See *Christianity and other religions.) Is it even legitimate to evangelize them at all? Should communities of ethnically and culturally homogeneous groups be encouraged for the sake of church growth? Is there a task for mission towards the whole of a culture or subculture? What does the gospel as *public* truth mean (Newbigin)? What role, if any, should mission agencies, which exist independently of any church, play in evangelism, relief or development? How may human and financial resources be shared in genuine Christian partnership between different parts of the worldwide church in a way which commends the gospel? Each of these questions has many practical entailments. They are not fully resolved. They will constitute part of the missiological agenda for many years to come.

Bibliography

R. A. Ahonen, *Mission in the New Millenium: Theological Grounds for World Mission* (Helsinki, 2006); S. B. Bevans and R. P. Schroeder, *Constants in Context: A Theology of Mission for Today* (New York, 2004); D. Bosch, *Transforming Mission: Paradigm Shifts in Theology of Mission* (Maryknoll, 1991); S. Escobar, *The New Global Mission: The Gospel from Everywhere to Everyone* (Downers Grove, 2003); D. L. Guder, *The Continuing Conversion of the Church* (Grand Rapids, 2000); J. A. Kirk, *What Is Mission? Theological Explorations* (London, 1999); L. Newbigin, *The Gospel in a Pluralist Society* (London, 1989); H. Peskett and V. Ramachandra, *The Message of Mission* (Leicester, 2003); V. Ramachandra, *The Recovery of Mission: Beyond the Pluralist Paradigm* (Carlisle, 1996); L. Sanneh, *Whose Religion Is Christianity? The Gospel beyond the West* (Grand Rapids, 2003); D. Smith, *Mission after Christendom* (London, 2003); T. Sundermeier, *The Theology of Missions* (New York, 1997); N. Thomas, *Classic Texts in Mission and World Christianity* (Maryknoll, 1995); A. Walls, *The Missionary Movement in Christian History: Studies in the Transmission of Faith* (New York, 1996); T. Yates, *Mission in the Twentieth Century* (Cambridge, 1996).

J. A. KIRK

MOBERLY, ROBERT CAMPBELL (1845–1903)

Robert Moberly was a creative *Anglo-Catholic theologian. The son of Bishop G. H. Moberly of Salisbury, he was educated at Winchester and New College, Oxford. Moberly was successively principal of St Stephen's House, Oxford (1876), the Diocesan Theological College, Salisbury (1878), incumbent at Great Bedwyn, Cheshire (1880–92), and Oxford's regius professor of pastoral theology from 1892 until his death. He was self-consciously a writer and is remembered primarily for his theological works. A *liberal Anglo-Catholic, Moberly contributed an essay 'The Incarnation as the Basis of Dogma' to the controversial Oxford publication *Lux Mundi* (1889). His influential *Ministerial Priesthood* (London, 1897) reflects a High Anglican justification of Anglican orders and centres on Christ's priesthood as determinative of the basis and nature of a 'ministerial priesthood' in the church (see *Ministry). *Atonement and Personality* (London, 1901) is a more significantly liberal reinterpretation of the *atonement, based on *Hegelian views of personality and the redemptive power of Christ's exemplary life and *satisfaction for sin. His other noteworthy works are *Sorrow, Sin and Beauty* (London, 1889), *Christ Our Life* (sermons, London, 1902), *Undenominationalism as a Principle of Primary Education* (London, 1902) and *Problems and Principles* (collected papers, London, 1904).

Bibliography

Appreciations by: A. Clark, *DNB*, Second Supplement 1901–11, vol. 2, pp. 624–626; W. H. Moberly, *JTS* 6 (1905), pp. 1–19; W. Sanday, *JTS* 4 (1903), pp. 481–499.

Studies: R. S. Franks, *A History of the Doctrine of the Work of Christ*, vol. 2 (London, 1918); M. Hutchison, 'Classics Revisited: Ministerial Priesthood, R. C. Moberly', *Anvil* 2, 1985, pp. 247–253; T. A. Langford, *In Search of Foundations: English Theology 1900–1920* (Nashville and New York, 1969).

C. D. HANCOCK

MODELS

'Model' became a technical term in theology in the second half of the twentieth century, having been borrowed from the scientific world. In science a model is a kind of 'visual aid' – a set of ideas, or a natural process, or some other series of known phenomena, which can be used as a guideline for investigating relatively unknown areas. A simple example of this is the old picture of the nervous system as similar to a network of ropes, levers and pulleys. This example also serves to show that as scientific knowledge advances, certain models have to be discarded as inadequate, and replaced by others – for example, the picturing of the nervous system as a series of electrical impulses.

Theology has in fact always needed to use models, for the reality being described transcends the world from which language is taken and used to describe that transcendent reality. A classic example of a model in theology is the use of 'word' in the OT and John 1, and from the history of doctrine we could take the *Logos concept of the *apologists, *Augustine's trinitarian analogies, or the body-soul picture of the union of natures in Christ. One of the major issues in *Christology today is whether language about 'two natures' is itself a model that needs to be discarded, or at least revised. There is the danger, however, that the introduction of new models can lead, not to a greater understanding of the mystery of Christ, but to the elimination of that mystery, as Christ is reduced to the status of a mere man.

The concept of a theological 'model' has also been linked to questions about *religious language, particularly the role of metaphors. Sallie McFague proposed 'Metaphorical Theology' as a correction to abstract conceptual *systematic theology, relating theology more closely to the 'first-order' language of experience. A 'model' was an extended and relatively permanent metaphor which became definitive and was used systematically to organize thought and so draw practical and ethical implications. McFague saw the parables of Jesus as such extended metaphors, although (in line with feminist thought) she also argued that new models for God (such as mother, lover and friend) were needed to counter the patriarchal and hierarchical models in the Christian tradition which had become idolatrous. Without subscribing to the view that new models could critique biblical models, other theologians have explored the use of such definitive metaphors or models in Christian doctrine. John McIntyre and Colin *Gunton examined the use of models in the doctrine of the *atonement. Gunton particularly emphasized that although doctrine had to use models, these were not to be regarded as fictions, but were necessary ways of referring to the reality of God's saving action.

See also: ANALOGY; PARADIGM; RAMSEY, IAN THOMAS.

Bibliography

I. G. Barbour, *Myths, Models and Paradigms* (London, 1974); C. Gunton, *The Actuality of Atonement* (Edinburgh, 1998); S. McFague, *Metaphorical Theology: Models for God in Religious Language* (Philadelphia, 1982); *idem*, *Models of God: Theology for an Ecological, Nuclear Age* (Philadelphia, 1987); J. McIntyre, *The Shape of Christology* (London, 1966); *idem*, *The Shape of Soteriology* (Edinburgh, 1995); I. T. Ramsey, *Models and Mystery* (London, 1964).

M. DOWLING

MODERNISM (CATHOLIC)

Roman Catholic modernism is the term applied to a loose-knit movement at the end of the nineteenth and beginning of the twentieth centuries in which scholars, working in a number of different fields, tried to bridge the gap between Christianity as traditionally understood by the Roman Catholic Church and the world of modern thought and knowledge. Since the Counter-Reformation Rome had increasingly presented Christian truth as a logically watertight, *scholastic system. Against this static, unhistorical understanding, and against the authoritarianism by which it was imposed, a diverse group of scholars protested. They claimed that crucial questions about the historical origins of the Bible, the *development of doctrine, the self-understanding of the church and the relation of religion to *science were going unheard. The 'modernists', as they were called by Rome, and as some of them came to call themselves, insisted that these questions had to be faced. Pope Leo XIII (1878–1903) appeared to give some encouragement to the attempt.

Alfred Loisy (1857–1940) was a brilliant biblical scholar who dedicated himself to the application of modern, critical methods. In 1890 he became Professor of Holy Scripture at the Institut Catholique in Paris. Loisy taught, as 'permanent acquisitions of knowledge', that the Pentateuch in its present form cannot be the work of Moses, that the first chapters of Genesis do not contain an exact and reliable account of the beginnings of humankind, that the historical books of the Bible, including those of the NT, were composed 'in a looser manner than modern historical writing', and that there is a real development of doctrine within Scripture. Through the ineptitude of his rector, he lost his job in 1893 and became chaplain of a girls' school for five years. When Adolf *Harnack published his classic liberal Protestant account of Christian origins, *What*

Is Christianity? (1900), Loisy already had to hand all the material for a comprehensive refutation, which was critical of Harnack's individualistic understanding of the gospel and his rejection of *apocalyptic, but in some respects was even more radical than Harnack on questions of gospel criticism. In *L'Evangile et l'église* (Paris, 1902), Loisy stressed the continuity between the ministry of Jesus and the life of the church: 'Jesus foretold the *Kingdom and it was the church that came.' The sharp distinction he made between history and faith, and the concession he allowed at the historical level, were unacceptable to Rome. Loisy made his meaning even clearer in a second book, and five of his works, including *L'Evangile et l'église*, were placed on the Index in 1903. Understandably, Loisy could not accept the condemnation as a comment on his historical work, but, largely because of political relations between France and Rome, he was not excommunicated until 1908.

A second important name is that of the British *Jesuit, George Tyrrell (1861–1909). He was not a scholar in the same sense as Loisy, but was the most gifted writer of the movement. In a series of brilliantly readable books and articles on devotion, ethics and apologetics, written between 1897 and 1909, he pleaded for a new synthesis between Christianity and 'science' and particularly *history. He became an ever more outspoken critic of the rationalist and authoritarian mentality of Rome. From 1900, he was in serious conflict with his Jesuit superiors. In 1906 he was dismissed from the Jesuits, and when, in 1907, he published in *The Times* a searing critique of the anti-modernist encyclical *Pascendi*, he was excommunicated. Tyrrell, like Loisy, rejected the notion that the *dogmas of the church had been revealed in propositional form. He stressed '*revelation as experience' and dogma as the human attempt to speak about that experience. The function of dogma is not primarily to inform the mind, but to promote the life of charity. The key to religious life is not theology, but prayer and love, and the test of religious truth is pragmatic, the truth of dogma being measured by its power to promote sanctity.

An important influence upon both Loisy and Tyrrell was the philosopher Maurice Blondel (1861–1949). In *L'Action* (Paris, 1893), he presented a *phenomenology of man as an integrated being, active in the world. It was Blondel, with Lucien Laberthonnière (1860–1932), who showed how the *supernatural could be regarded not as an alien element imposing itself from without upon the natural, but as the transcendental presupposition of all human action. The supernatural is not 'extrinsic' to the natural life of man, but discerned within the natural by 'the method of immanence'.

If there was a coherent Catholic 'modernist movement' in France, Italy and England, the common factor among the scholars involved was friendship with Baron Friedrich von *Hügel, himself a biblical scholar and critical historian of *mysticism. Von Hügel sought them out, corresponded with them, and brought them into touch with each other. Like Blondel, he eluded condemnation.

From the accession, in 1903, of Pius X, a man of simple and intolerant devotion, scholars such as these were regarded as a deadly threat to the Catholic faith. In 1907, the encyclical *Pascendi* warned against 'the doctrine of the modernists', and presented the picture of a composite 'modernist' who, as philosopher, founded his religious philosophy on agnosticism; as believer, rejected the notion of propositional revelation; as theologian, believed that dogmas represent divine reality only in 'symbolical' fashion; as historian, was a rationalist who excluded the miraculous; as critic, believed that Scripture is a human summary of religious experiences; and as apologist, tried to promote *religious experience, not the acceptance of religious truth. 'Modernism' (which was never a system) was branded as 'the synthesis of all heresies', and from 1910 an anti-modernist oath was imposed on Roman Catholic clergy. Not until after the Second *Vatican Council (1962–65) did Roman Catholic scholarship recover confidence in critical study of the Bible and of Christian origins.

Bibliography

A. F. Loisy, *L'Evangile et l'église* (Paris, 1902), ET, *The Gospel and the Church* (London, 1903); idem, *Mémoires pour servir l'histoire religieuse de notre temps*, 3 vols. (Paris, 1930–31); M. O'Connell, *Critics on Trial: An Introduction to the Catholic Modernist Crisis* (Washington DC, 1994); E. Poulat, *Histoire, dogme et critique dans la crise moderniste* (Paris, ²1979); G. Tyrrell, *Christianity at the Crossroads* (London, 1909); A. R. Vidler, *The Modernist Movement in the Roman Church* (Cambridge, 1934).

N. Sagovsky

MODERNISM (ENGLISH)

English modernism was a school of late nineteenth- and early twentieth-century theology loosely united by the belief that the proper response to modern thought is to make radical alterations in Christian doctrine. This is an assumption on which much religious thinking has proceeded since the *Enlightenment, but in modernism the assumption became an explicit principle.

The name was first given to a school of Roman Catholic theologians, represented in France by A. F. Loisy (1857–1940) and in Britain by Baron F. von *Hügel and by G. Tyrrell (1861–1909), which was condemned by Rome in 1907. It adopted a far-reaching biblical criticism and a sceptical attitude towards Christian origins and traditional *dogma, emphasizing ethical conduct and, sometimes, *mystical devotion (see *Modernism, Catholic).

In the different context of English Protestantism, modernism displayed many of the same features. There was the same rationalistic demolition of biblical authority and traditional doctrine, the same emphasis on *ethics (the moral example and moral teaching of Jesus being particularly emphasized), and in some writers, notably Dean W. R. Inge (1860–1954), the same concern for mystical devotion. The affirmation of human goodness and of historical *progress in rational and moral thought, and the denial of any real distinction between the natural and the *supernatural or between *Christianity and other religions, were frequent themes. The divinity of Jesus was often explained as different only in degree from the divinity of every person made in the image of God.

Though theology of this kind had many representatives in the free churches, it attracted most notice in the Church of England, where its proponents were linked together by the Modern Churchmen's Union (founded 1898; now the Modern Churchpeople's Union), and where one of them, E. W. Barnes (1874–1953), became in 1924 Bishop of Birmingham. In this position he gained notoriety by his attacks on what he regarded as Anglo-Catholic superstition and especially by the publication of his sceptical book *The Rise of Christianity* (London, 1947), after which the archbishops of both Canterbury and York publicly called on him to resign. Modernism was by this date rapidly declining. Its ideas of human goodness and progress had been discredited by the experience of Nazism, culminating in the events of the Second World War, and its Anglican representatives had always had conscientious problems with the supernaturalism of the *Book of Common Prayer* and especially with the obligation to use the *creeds. The radicalism that arose in the 1960s, when the war was sufficiently far past and the Prayer Book revision had started, brought back many of the ideas of the modernists, but not their strong ethical emphasis (cf. *Robinson, John Arthur Thomas).

In many ways the most distinguished of the English modernists was Hastings Rashdall (1858–1924), teacher of philosophy at Oxford and afterwards dean of Carlisle. Apart from his standard history of the European universities, he wrote a great variety of theological works, notably *The Theory of Good and Evil* (Oxford, 1970), propounding a modified utilitarian ethics, *Philosophy and Religion* (London, 1909), defending *idealism as a basis for religious philosophy, and *The Idea of Atonement in Christian Theology* (London, 1919), upholding the *Abelardian or exemplarist theory of the *atonement, and rejecting the idea of *substitutionary *sacrifice as abhorrent to modern conceptions of justice. Rashdall was also strongly opposed to mysticism, thus demonstrating the variety of opinion possible among modernists.

Bibliography

P. Badham, *The Contemporary Challenge of Modernist Theology* (Cardiff, 1998); H. P. V. Nunn, *What Is Modernism?* (London, 1932); M. Rayner, 'The Theology of Hastings Rashdall' (PhD theses, University of Gloucestershire, 2005); A. M. G. Stephenson, *The Rise and Decline of English Modernism* (London, 1984).

R. T. BECKWITH

MODERNITY

In cultural discourse, 'modernity' refers to the culture that developed in Europe and North America, coming to full flower by the early twentieth century. The use of science to investigate nature, and the development of industrialization, coupled with democratic politics and market-based economies, have led to an astonishingly rapid rise in material wealth. It is this process of high-speed development that marks contemporary Western culture out as unique in world history.

The roots of modernity are complex and controversial. Some writers will trace it as far back as the Reformation, seeing a rejection of tradition and an invitation to individual intellectual enquiry there, which eventually leads to the *Enlightenment and modernity. Certainly the development of the method of natural science in the seventeenth century is an important ingredient in the mix, as are the new political and economic ideas of the eighteenth century, and the industrial revolution of the nineteenth century. However these relative influences are evaluated, by 1910 (say) a culture has come into being that is able to develop technologically and economically with increasing rapidity.

Modern culture borrowed a rhetoric of *rationality and progress from the Enlightenment, understanding itself in wholly positive terms, and assuming that further technological advance, and so an increase of modernity, would supply the solution to any problem still remaining in society. This mythology was already criticized in the first half of the nineteenth century, by both artists (Shelley's *Frankenstein*) and social activists (the Luddites). The history of the twentieth century has generated increasing disenchantment and criticism: technology has led to the most terrible wars ever seen, to the possibility of industrial genocide in the *holocaust/shoa, and to the threat of nuclear destruction. At the same time, rising understanding of the environment (see *Ecology) has led to an appreciation of the real costs of industrial growth, and post-colonial theorists have questioned the extent to which Western development was based simply on imperialism and the oppression of non-Western peoples. Further, the experience of *alienation and loss of meaning even in the midst of unparalleled wealth has led to disenchantment within modern culture. These streams of criticism have coalesced into the rise of *postmodernity, although in economic and social terms, Western culture remains resolutely modern.

Christianity has not flourished in modernity, although the rise of evangelicalism might be the one great exception. In the nineteenth century there was a general assumption that Christianity and modernity belonged together; with the critique of modernity, there has been an increasing realization that modern culture, too, needs to be challenged and transformed by the gospel. This was crystallized for many in the works of Lesslie *Newbigin.

Bibliography

L. Cahoone (ed.), *From Modernism to Postmodernism: An Anthology* (Oxford, 2003); C. E. Gunton, *The One, the Three and the Many: God, Creation and the Culture of Modernity* (Cambridge, 1993).

S. R. HOLMES

MÖHLER, JOHANN ADAM (1796–1838)

Johann Möhler was a German Catholic theologian and church historian, who taught at Tübingen and Munich. He gained an early acquaintance with the work of leading contemporary Protestant theologians, notably J. A. W. Neander (1789–1850) and *Schleiermacher, and much of his work is implicitly concerned to mediate between Catholicism and Protestantism, most especially in his *Symbolik* (Mainz, 1832; ET, *Symbolism, or Exposition of the Doctrinal Differences* . . . , 2 vols., London, 1843), where established confessional divergences are deliberately de-emphasized. His other chief works are *Die Einheit der Kirche* (*The Unity of the Church*) (Tübingen, 1825), *Athanasius der Grosse* (*Athanasius the Great*) (Mainz, 1827) and *Neue Untersuchungen* (*New Enquiries*) (Vienna, 1834). His earlier work drew charges of unorthodoxy, notably in its assertion of the priority of spiritual church unity over institutional unity guaranteed by communion with the ecclesiastical hierarchy. Later writings shift towards a more positive evaluation of visible, institutional forms of organization, possibly under the influence of *Hegel's theory of religion. Many Catholic *modernist theologians drew inspiration from Möhler's work, which remains one of the decisive influences on post-*Enlightenment Catholic thinking.

Bibliography

J. Fitzer, *Möhler and Baur in Controversy* (Tallahassee, 1974); R. H. Nienaltowski, *J. A. Möhler's Theory of Doctrinal Development* (Washington DC, 1959).

J. B. WEBSTER

MOLTMANN, JÜRGEN (b. 1926)

Moltmann is a Protestant theologian, Professor of Systematic Theology at Tübingen (1967–94), and probably the most influential German theologian in the period since 1960.

His major works comprise two series. There is the trilogy of early works: *Theology of Hope* (London, 1967), *The Crucified God* (London, 1973) and *The Church in the Power of the Spirit* (London, 1977). These approach theology from three complementary perspectives: *eschatology, the *cross, and pneumatology (see *Holy Spirit) (including ecclesiology). The second series, comprising six 'contributions' to theology, make up a dogmatics: *The Trinity and the Kingdom of God* (London, 1981), *God in Creation* (London, 1985), *The Way of Jesus Christ* (London, 1990), *The Spirit of Life* (London, 1992), *The Coming of God* (London, 1996) and *Experiences in Theology* (London, 2000).

Thematically Moltmann's theology is notable, first, for rehabilitating futurist eschatology as not only credible but essential to contemporary Christian faith; secondly, for addressing the theodicy problem 'after Auschwitz' from the perspective of the *suffering of God in the cross of Christ; thirdly, for developing a thoroughly trinitarian understanding of God; fourthly, for conceiving the relationship of God and the world as reciprocal and as internal to God's own trinitarian relationships; fifthly, for breaking out of the modern paradigm of reality as human history and giving theological weight to the reciprocal relationship of humanity and the rest of nature.

In his earliest work Moltmann established his theology's *Christological centre*, in the particularity of Jesus' history, and its *eschatological orientation*, in hope for the whole of God's creation. The two events of Jesus' cross and resurrection are understood dialectically, representing the contradiction between what reality is now, in its subjection to *sin, suffering and *death, and what God promises to make it in new creation. Because Jesus in his death was identified with the world in its godlessness, godforsakenness and transitoriness, his *resurrection is God's promise for a new future for all reality. It is this all-embracing eschatological perspective that grounds Moltmann's consistently holistic view of both theology and the church's mission. Christian hope is not for the spiritual rather than the material, or for the individual rather than the social, or for the personal rather than the political, or for humans rather than the rest of creation. It is an eschatology that aims to promote involvement in the world, promoting change in anticipation of the coming kingdom and openness to the future that only God can give his creation. Moltmann's *political theology stemmed originally from this eschatological approach.

On the other side of the dialectic, the cross is God's loving solidarity in love with the godless and the godforsaken. By recognizing God's presence, as the incarnate Son of God, in the abandonment of the cross, Moltmann brings the dialectic of cross and resurrection within God's own experience. God's love is such that it embraces and suffers what is most opposed to God in order to overcome the contradiction. Moreover, this suffering is internal to God's own trinitarian relationships. On the cross Jesus suffers dying in abandonment by his Father, while the Father suffers in grief the death of his Son. As such, the cross is the act of divine solidarity with the godforsaken world, in which the Son willingly surrenders himself in love for the world and the Father willingly surrenders his Son in love for the world. At the point of their most painful separation, Father and Son are united in their love for the world, and from this event of suffering love comes the power of the Spirit to overcome all that separates the world from God.

In *The Crucified God* Moltmann's theology became strongly *trinitarian. He developed an understanding of the *trinitarian history of God* with the world, in which the mutual involvement of God and the world is increasingly stressed. God experiences a history with the world in which he both affects and is affected by the world, and which is also the history of his own trinitarian relationships as a community of divine Persons who include the world within their love. This trinitarian doctrine dominates Moltmann's later work, in which the mutual relationships of the three Persons as a perichoretic, social Trinity are the context for understanding the reciprocal relationships of God and the world. The dialectic of cross and resurrection, now developed in a fully trinitarian way, becomes the decisive moment within this broader trinitarian history, which retains the eschatological direction of *Theology of Hope* and the crucified God's suffering solidarity with the world, but also goes further in taking the whole of *creation and *history within the divine experience. Essential to this trinitarian narrative of God and reality is the third divine Person, the Holy Spirit. As Moltmann's thought becomes increasingly *pneumatological*, he recognizes the Spirit as the immanent presence of God in creation and also the Spirit's equal role as one divine Subject in the reciprocal relationships of the Trinity.

With Moltmann's understanding of the Trinity as constituted in the loving and changing relationships of three divine Subjects goes a general principle of *relationality and reciprocity*. This governs the way Moltmann thinks about the relationship of the *church to other movements and forces in world history; about the relationship of persons in society and in the church; about the relationship of humanity and other creatures; and about the relationship between God and creation. In all these areas Moltmann thinks of relationships of mutuality rather than of dominance or even hierarchy. Whereas 'monotheism' (by which Moltmann means *unitarianism) has in his view constantly legitimated human domination, both of other humans and of nature, social trinitarianism understands God as in himself a fellowship of *love, and so finds relationships of free friendship between humans as most adequately reflecting God and constituting his 'kingdom'. In the political sphere, this principle of mutuality grounds democracy; in the ecclesiological sphere, it coheres with Moltmann's vision of the church as an open society of friends; while in the *ecological sphere, it highlights the interdependence of humanity and the rest of nature.

Moltmann also applies to such relationships the traditional trinitarian term perichoretic. It is in their *perichoresis* or mutual indwelling in love that the three divine Persons are both three and one. Similarly, God's relationship to his creation is one of mutual indwelling (sometimes called *panentheism). Because God is transcendent beyond the world, it dwells in him, but because, as the Spirit, he is also immanent within the world, he dwells in it. With this dominant notion of the Spirit in creation, Moltmann is able also to take the non-human creation into his general concept of the trinitarian history of God. The whole of creation from the beginning is oriented towards the future goal of its glorification through divine indwelling. The Spirit in creation co-suffers with creation in its bondage to decay, keeping it open to God and to its future with God. Humanity's eschatological goal does not lift us out of the material creation, but confirms our solidarity and relatedness with it.

Moltmann's theological project is now complete, and in *Experiences in Theology* he reflects on its general character. Throughout the nine major and many minor works Moltmann has combined a creative faithfulness to the central themes of biblical and historical theology with a critical and *praxis-oriented openness to the contemporary world as well as a conviction that theology's task is not only practical but also *doxological.

Bibliography

R. Bauckham, *Moltmann: Messianic Theology in the Making* (London, 1987); *idem*, *The Theology of Jürgen Moltmann* (Edinburgh, 1995); *idem* (ed.), *God Will Be All in All: The Eschatology of Jürgen Moltmann* (Edinburgh, 1999); G. Müller-Fahrenholz, *The Kingdom and the Power: The Theology of Jürgen Moltmann* (London, 2000); J. L. Wakefield, *Jürgen Moltmann: A Research Bibliography* (Lanham and Oxford, 2002).

R. J. BAUCKHAM

MONARCHIANISM

In the third century, under the general name 'monarchianism', the heresies of *ebionism and *docetism of the second century reappeared. Its basic doctrine that God is one, the sole principle of all existence, was itself an accepted truth of the ethical monotheism of the OT of which Christianity was heir. The term *monarchia* applied to God had an honourable history. It was used by Plato and Aristotle, and with a more religious connotation by *Philo. *Tertullian, who first gave the name 'monarchianism' to its specific heresy, declares, after examination of its Greek and Latin usage, that *monarchia* has no other meaning than 'single and individual rule' (*Against Praxeas* 3).

The heresies of monarchianism developed naturally as a consequence of their initial interest. Where the theological concern was the stronger, it was found necessary to stress the *oneness* of God against pagan polytheism. The tendency here was to exalt the unity of God at the expense of Christ's divinity. The result was the elaboration of a new form of ebionism, or as now designated 'dynamic monarchianism'. Christ is here conceived as the subject of a special influence or *dynamis* (Gk 'power') of the one *monarchia* which came to reside in the man Jesus. For introducing this 'God-denying heresy' that 'Christ was a mere (indwelt) man', Theodotus of Byzantium was expelled from the church in Rome *c.* 190. Its most formidable exponent was, however, Paul of *Samosata, bishop of Antioch (260–72). For him only a matter of degree marked the difference between Jesus and other men. Jesus entered progressively into such an ethical relationship with God that he became the more penetrated with the divine *ousia* (see *Substance) until 'out of man he became God'. Paul was condemned by a synod of Antioch in 268. He used the word *homoousios* to deny that the Son and the Father were distinct beings.

Modalist monarchianism, otherwise designated patripassianism and Sabellianism, started from a firm conviction of Christ's divinity free from all compromising emanationisms and subordinationisms. However, it called in question the integrity of Christ's body and thus verged towards docetism. It sought to unite the deity of the Son and the oneness of God by declaring the designations Father and Son to be modes, or expressions of manifestation, of the one divine being. The view was first elaborated by Noetus of Smyrna (*c.* 200–25), who 'introduced a heresy from the tenets of Heraclitus' (according to *Hippolytus), and was developed by the anti-*Montanist Praxeas, who brought in the Holy Spirit as the third mode of representation of the one God and thus 'did a twofold service to the devil at Rome: he drove away prophecy and brought in heresy; he put to flight the Paraclete, and crucified the Father' (Tertullian, *Against Praxeas* 1).

The name of Sabellius (in Rome *c.* 198–220) is now identified with modalist monarchianism. In the interest of strict monotheism, Sabellius declared that, although the names Father, Son and Holy Spirit were biblical, they were attached to the one being. Thus God as a single monad is manifest in three distinct and successive operations of self-revealing. The unity of God is thus secured at the expense of the divine tri-unity of persons within the Godhead. The Son and the Holy Spirit are but temporary modes of self-expression of the one Father of all. It was the Father who became incarnate as the Son and was crucified (patripassianism, lit. 'Father-suffering'). *Origen's strong assertion of the *Logos as at once eternal with, yet subordinate to, the Father gave the decisive blow to monarchianism.

See also: ADOPTIONISM; MONOTHEISM; TRINITY.

Bibliography

J. F. Bethune-Baker, *An Introduction to the Early History of Christian Doctrine* (London, 1903); J. L. Gonzalez, *A History of Christian Thought*, vol. 1 (Nashville, 1970); J. N. D. Kelly, *Early Christian Doctrines* (London, ⁵1977); G. L. Prestige, *God in Patristic Thought* (London, 1956).

H. D. MCDONALD

MONASTIC THEOLOGY

If theology is the contemplation of God, then monastic theology is devoted to the inner life, practices and spiritual disciplines that nurture that contemplation. Put simply, the term 'monastic theology' refers not just to the local setting of the theologians but to the approach that they adopted. They worked in an atmosphere of commitment and devotion, within the framework of a way of life that has its focus not on externals but on seeking God (from Gk *monachos*: alone, solitary). Their goal was not the pursuit of knowledge for its own sake, but edification and worship. Their approach was one of meditation and adoration. The theologian was not a detached academic observer studying his material from outside, but a committed, involved participant.

Monastics have been among the most productive spiritual and theological writers down the centuries, and at some periods, notably those up to the Middle Ages, the story of monastic *spirituality is almost indistinguishable from that of theology in general. In later centuries, there arose another form of theology – *scholastic theology. Theology came to be studied outside of the cloister – in the university and other 'secular' (non-monastic) settings. The goal was objective intellectual knowledge. The approach was one of questioning, logic, speculation and disputation as theology became a detached objective science. This approach did not eliminate the older monastic approach, but it was to displace it from the front line of theology. *Bernard of Clairvaux (d. 1153) is called 'the last of the Fathers', although he does not end the list of those who have continued to contribute to monastic spirituality.

The age of monastic theology

Many great names dominate the age of monastic theology: *Clement of Alexandria

(d. 199) and later *Origen (d. 253) developed the ideas on which monastic life and theology was founded. They interpreted the exodus from Egypt, the Sabbath rest and the life of John the Baptist in the desert as symbolizing the need of withdrawal from the desires of the world in order to fully seek and serve God.

In the Writings of Clement of Alexandria and especially of Origen all the essential elements of an ascetical theology may already be found. (H. Chadwick, *The Early Church*, p. 177)

The Life of Antony was written by *Athanasius, bishop of Alexandria, famous for the part he played in defending orthodoxy at the Council of Nicaea. The biography of Antony of Egypt defined and propagated the monastic life to both East and West, not least in precipitating the conversion of *Augustine of Hippo.

John Cassian (d. 435), a monk in Bethlehem and Egypt, produced a comprehensive monastic theology dependent largely on the teaching of Evagrius Ponticus (d. 399) and their common inspiration, Origen. Having mastered both Greek and Latin he was in a unique position to facilitate monasticism in the West, where he established monasteries in Gaul.

Cassian's writings strongly influenced Benedict of Nursia (480–547), who recommends in his 'rule' that all monks read his *Institutes* and *Conferences* (see *Benedict and the Benedictine tradition). *Gregory the Great used Cassian's teaching on compunction and prayer and built on his teaching about the active and contemplative paradox of monastic theology. Cassian is the only Latin author to be found in the 'Sayings of the Desert Fathers' *(Apophthegmata)* and the Greek *Philokalia*.

Both Cassian and Augustine remind us that the essence of monastic life lies with the aspiration and intention with which it is lived rather than in its structures or disciplines. They are nothing without a renunciation of the heart towards love. The monastic life has no meaning if it does not turn the soul towards God. The quest for purity of heart and the seeking of God alone in both the contemplative and practical aspects of life, all of which finds its fulfilment in heaven, is a theme taken up by all writers on monastic theology and popularized in the twentieth century by the Trappist monk and writer, Thomas *Merton.

Monastic theology was lived, preached and written in the monastery and was above all a theology rooted in experience. Theologians are those who can write or talk about God with the authority of their own experience of God. The writings of Augustine were prized especially for their spiritual teaching, and the *mystical teaching of Gregory and Bernard are among the greatest achievements of monastic theology.

Fundamental themes of monastic theology include the concept of spiritual warfare, which the monk is called to wage against evil spirits that threaten him on all sides (see *Devil and demons). This conflict takes place in the heart, and the struggle against evil thoughts, the need for vigilance, guarding the heart, and discernment of spirits is a daily battle. Honesty and confession to a spiritual father is useful because even when beaten the discovery of our weakness through self-knowledge helps our humility. It also strengthens our virtue and brings the reward of being able to help others similarly afflicted.

Monastic theology was based primarily on Scripture which, together with the Fathers, was read daily in the *lectio divina* ('divine reading'). Although Scripture was central, the aim was not a literal, scientific exegesis. Nevertheless, monastic exegesis was disciplined, with a strong emphasis on Scripture being interpreted by Scripture in handling the sacred text. Also of great importance was the allegorical interpretation of the Bible, with special emphasis on the Song of Solomon and the life of Moses, together with the Genesis account of the earlier patriarchs. This was because the monastic tradition regarded the individual soul as the bride of Christ, and interpreted OT love poetry in this sense. The patriarchal period was attractive, because of its emphasis on desert life, which corresponded to the origins of monasticism.

In summary, monastic theology is that which is characteristic of the reflections and disciplines of those leading an ascetic life either in contemplative seclusion or following a common life in a monastery.

The scholastic endeavour is to a greater degree occasioned by the need for action in the Church: controversy, pastoral administration or again the solution of new questions. Monastic thought is less affected by the concerns of the moment: rather it is governed only by the enduring necessities of the search for God. (J. Leclercq, *The Love of Learning and the Desire for God*, pp. 279–280)

See also: ASCETICISM AND MONASTICISM.

Bibliography
H. Chadwick, *The Early Church* (New York, 1968); P. King, *Western Monasticism* (Michigan, 1999); J. Leclercq, *The Love of Learning and the Desire for God* (New York and London, ²1974); C. Stewart, *Cassian the Monk* (New York, 1998).

J. T. MILLER

MONISM

As a philosophical theory, monism is the view that all reality is ultimately one, not twofold (as in *dualism) and not many. The one, however, may be understood either quantitatively or qualitatively. In the first sense everything is numerically one, and any plurality that appears is either illusory (e.g. Parmenides and the Greek Eleatic school, sixth–fifth centuries BC) or else a transitory mode of operation of the underlying one (e.g. *Spinoza). In the second sense everything is of one kind, which may be either physical (as in naturalism and *materialism), or immaterial and spiritual (as in *idealism), or else neutral with regard to the matter-spirit distinction. Quantitative monism applied to religion erases the God-creation distinction that is basic to *theistic belief, thereby leading to forms of *pantheism or *panentheism as in Neoplatonic and *Hegelian theology. Qualitative monism applied to religion takes theism to be a kind of metaphysical idealism (e.g. *Berkeley) or else a panpsychism (e.g. *process theology).

The difficulty with monism is that when everything is treated as one, the over-generalization involved elides important distinctions, and so tends to a reductionist position. Mind or spirit is reduced to a by-product of physical processes, individuality is diminished, any ultimate distinction between good and evil is eroded, and the transcendence of God (either numerically or qualitatively) is lost. In some Eastern religions, and in F. H. Bradley (1846–1924), God is therefore one manifestation of the all-inclusive Absolute Being, rather than himself the one eternal reality.

Bibliography
J. Schaffer, 'Monism: The Priority of the Whole', *Philosophical Review* 119:1 (2010); T. Sider, 'Against Monism', *Analysis* 67:1 (2007), pp. 1–7.

A. F. HOLMES

MONOPHYSITISM

The seeds of monophysitism, that the person of the incarnate Christ was of one nature only (*monos*, 'single'; *physis*, 'nature'), are present in *Cyril of Alexandria's polemic against *Nestorius. Cyril's *That Christ Is One* affirms that 'there is one nature (*mia physis*) of God the Word incarnate, but worshipped with his flesh as one worship'. While, according to *Harnack, Cyril's theory is pure but unintentional monophysitism, he cannot be said to state the view precisely. That was done by Eutyches, the aged anti-Nestorian monk of Constantinople (c. 378–454). Eutyches supported Cyril against Nestorius at the Synod of Ephesus, 431, but was himself accused by Eusebius of Dorylaeum in 448 of confounding the two natures and was deposed by Flavian, bishop of Constantinople (d. 449). By court support Eutyches had Flavian's decision reversed at the Latrocinium (Robber Synod) of Ephesus, 449. Both put their case to *Leo of Rome for judgment. Leo's decision went against Eutyches, and his doctrine was consequently repudiated at *Chalcedon (see *Christology) and Eutyches again deposed and exiled.

Eutyches' view was simply a reaction from Nestorianism in favour of *Apollinarianism. Faced with the question whether he confessed two natures in the incarnate Christ, Eutyches declared 'our Lord to have become out of two natures before the union. But I confess one nature after the union.' He conceived of Christ as a mingling of two natures, which constituted him a *tertium quid*. In the union the divine had the major share, the humanity being merged with deity as a drop of honey mingled with the ocean.

Leo's *Tome* in which he repudiated Eutyches' monophysitism became one of the bases of the dogma of Chalcedon. Chalcedon declared for the two natures after the union, but gave no explanation of how they unite in the one Christ. The Chalcedonian Definition was not, however, well received everywhere in the East. The Cyrilline formula, 'one nature of the Word made flesh', had popular allegiance and was sometimes defended with outbursts of violence.

After Chalcedon monophysitism diverged into two main streams. The more moderate, the Severans, following Severus the monophysite Patriarch of Antioch (*c.* 460–538), adhered closely to Cyril, considering the two natures to be a mere ideal abstraction. They strongly asserted the humanness of the resultant nature which they declared capable of corruption in itself like ours. Monophysites of this type were sometimes called *phthartolatrai*, worshippers of the corruptible, by their opponents. The other group, the Julianists, after Julian, bishop of Halicarnassus (deposed *c.* 518), adopted the stance of Eutyches. For them Christ's human body was so modified by union with the divine as to be rendered incorruptible. Christ suffered by an act of his own will, and not because he possessed a corruptible human nature. They were consequently referred to as the *aphthartodokētai*, teachers of the incorruptible, or as the *phantasiastai*, declarers of Christ's body as merely phantasmal.

Another group, who flourished *c.* 519 in Constantinople and taught that one of the Trinity suffered in the flesh, were called *theopaschitai* by their opponents for teaching that 'God suffered'.

The usurper Basiliscus' (d. 477) Encyclion of 476, pressing on all Eastern sees the 'one nature' doctrine, and the Emperor Zeno's *Henoticon* of 482, declaring the *Nicene *Creed as alone binding, served merely to intensify opposition to and support for Chalcedon. In the sixth century Leontius of Byzantium (see *Hypostasis), by interpreting Chalcedon in a Cyrilline sense, succeeded in bringing most of the East and West finally to concur in affirming the Chalcedonian dogma.

Monophysitism remains the official interpretation of Christology in the *Oriental Orthodox churches. However, recent decades have seen an increasing awareness of Christological convergence between these churches and the Chalcedonians, both (Eastern) Orthodox and Roman Catholic.

Bibliography

C. Chaillot and A. Belopopsky (eds.), *Towards Unity: The Theological Dialogue Between the Orthodox Church and the Oriental Orthodox Churches* (Geneva, 1998); R. C. Chesnut, *Three Monophysite Christologies* (Oxford, 1976); W. H. C. Frend, *The Rise of the Monophysite Movement* (London, 1972); A. A. Race, *Monophysitism, Past and Present* (London, 1920); W. A. Wigram, *The Separation of the Monophysites* (London, 1923); F. Young, *From Nicaea to Chalcedon* (London, 1983).

H. D. McDonald

MONOTHEISM

Monotheism is the term used to describe the concept of believing in and worshipping one God, as opposed to *polytheism, which is the belief in and worshipping of many gods, or *henotheism*, which presupposes the existence of several gods but accepts only one God as the supreme authority. The term is most commonly associated with the faiths of Judaism, Christianity and Islam because of what many scholars perceive as their common heritage in Abraham who is regarded as the common ancestor of all three faiths.

These world faiths describe themselves as monotheistic in different ways. Judaism, the oldest of the three, calls for a monotheism that recognizes that God is unique in relation to creation and not part of it. Judaism requires a rigorous adherence to the first commandment of the Decalogue: 'You shall have no other gods before me' (Exod. 20:3). The sole lordship of God is summarized in the central Jewish confession, the *Shema*: 'Hear, O Israel, the LORD our God, the LORD is one' (Deut. 6:4). Implicit in Jewish monotheism is the hope that one day all people of the world will recognize the God of Israel as the one and only God: 'The LORD will be king over the whole earth. On that day there will be one LORD, and his name the only name' (Zech. 14:9).

Christian monotheism is better described as trinitarianism. For Christians, the one and only God of Israel is decisively revealed in the self-giving love of the crucified and risen Jesus, in the love of the Father who sent him, and in the life-giving Spirit who pours God's love into the hearts of believers. The doctrine of the *Trinity thus affirms that God is one with the eternal *Logos of God incarnate in the crucified Jesus, and one with his life-giving Spirit. The one God freely *loves in God's own being in all eternity and freely shares that love with humanity, drawing humanity into communion with God and each other. The chief end of human existence is therefore to take part in the triune love of God extended to humanity by Jesus Christ in the power of the Holy Spirit (see *Love of God).

Islam, the youngest of the three monotheistic faiths, understands itself as radical and uncompromising monotheism. Allah is uniquely one. For Muslims this precludes any notion of multiple deities or of creatures sharing in the being of the one God. Islam rejects the doctrine of the Trinity. The confession of three persons in God is tantamount, from an Islamic perspective, to *tritheism. Islam also rejects the doctrine of the deity of Jesus. This follows logically from the Islamic understanding of the oneness of God. God has no partner. God is not divided and no creature is equal to God or can be associated with God. Thus Islam rejects the Christian teaching that Jesus Christ the Son of God was crucified for the salvation of the human race.

Despite obvious and deep theological differences amongst these monotheistic faiths there is growing consensus, following the terrorism most traumatically revealed in New York and Washington on 11 September 2001, for members of these faith communities to share, in principle at least, the responsibility to struggle for human justice and peace, both individually and corporately before God. There is also growing consensus for a theological commitment from each faith to achieve greater understanding of each other's tradition as well as clarification of what each faith has in common with the others and where they diverge in their understandings of God and of God's revelation to humanity. It is felt that these are responsibilities which Christians, Jews and Muslims share because of their connection to Abraham and God's promise to him.

Other philosophies and belief systems believe in one god, but cannot be regarded strictly speaking as forms of mono*theism* since they virtually exclude that god from the universe (*deism), or identify that god with the universe (*pantheism).

See also: GOD; ISLAM AND CHRISTIANITY; JUDAISM AND CHRISTIANITY.

Bibliography

D. F. Ford, 'An Interfaith Wisdom: Scriptural Reasoning between Jews, Christians and Muslims', *Modern Theology* n.s. 22.3, 2006, pp. 345–366; A. J. Heschel, 'One God', in J. Neusner (ed.), *Understanding Jewish Theology: Classical Issues and Modern Perspectives* (New York, 1973), p. 17; B. Klappert, 'Abraham eint und unterscheidet: Begründungen und Perspektiven eines nötigen "Trialogs" zwischen Juden, Christen und Muslimen', in Rudolf Weth (ed.), *Bekenntnis zu dem einen Gott? Christen und Muslime zwischen Mission und Dialog* (Neukirchen-Vluyn, 2000), pp. 98–122; H. Küng, *Judaism: The Religious Situation of Our Time* (London, 1992); idem, *Islam: Past, Present and Future* (Oxford, 2007); D. Migliore, *Faith Seeking Understanding: An Introduction to Christian Theology* (Grand Rapids, ²2004); idem, *The Power of God and the Gods of Power* (Louisville, 2008); J. Moltmann, 'Human Rights, the Rights of Humanity and the Rights of Nature', in H. Küng and J. Moltmann (eds.), *The Ethics of World Religions and Human Rights* (London and Philadelphia, 1990), pp. 120–135; M. Wyschogrod, 'Der eine Gott Abrahams und die Einheit des Gottes der jüdischen Philosophie', in C. Thoma and M. Wyschogrod (eds.), *Das Reden vom einen Gott bei Juden und Christen* (Bern, 1984), pp. 29–48.

G. A. CHESTNUTT

MONOTHELITISM, see CHRISTOLOGY

MONTANISM

Montanism was a prophetic movement originating *c.* 170 in Phrygia, where a Christian named Montanus began to utter *prophecies in a state of convulsive frenzy. He and his supporters claimed that his ecstatic condition was a sign that he was totally possessed by the Holy Spirit, who was inaugurating a new dispensation of divine *revelation. They demanded unhesitating recognition for the new prophecy.

Others demurred at this because the ecstatic mode of prophecy was contrary, they said, to recognized church tradition. Some, believing Montanus to be demon-possessed, even tried to have him *exorcized, but they were frustrated by his supporters. Several local church councils did condemn the Montanist prophecies, but were powerless to prevent the Montanist movement running its course and creating a split within the churches. The Montanists looked exclusively to Montanus and two women, Prisca and Maximilla, as their prophets, and saw to the widespread circulation of their oracles. They did not suggest that every believer should claim the prophetic gift. Indeed, when the last of these prophets, Maximilla, died c. 189, she left a prophecy that there were to be no further prophets before the end of the age. Thereafter in Phrygia the movement turned into a cult in memory of the three prophets and their writings. Elsewhere the movement gained some acceptance in a diluted form. It was taken as one piece of evidence that God had new revelation to give to his people. In this form the 'new prophecy', as it was termed, gained its most outstanding convert in the African writer, *Tertullian.

Tertullian was attracted to the movement by its strict discipline. For example, the prophecies proscribed remarriage after being widowed as unlawful, and added both to the length and frequency of those fasts which had become statutory within the church. Tertullian believed that this development was directly in line with the teaching in John 16:12–13 that the Holy Spirit had further truth to bestow. The church by Tertullian's time had reached such maturity that it could tolerate standards previously beyond its capacity. But opponents of Montanism contended that these developments were innovations contrary to Scripture.

The influence of Montanism on the church lasted about a generation. At first it provoked an inconclusive debate on the validity of ecstatic prophecy, but attention later turned to the more important issue of whether the church was to expect further revelation after the apostolic era. Montanism failed in the end to convince the church that it was a valid addition to recognized *Scripture. For one thing, the movement lost the phenomenon of prophecy in its directly inspired form, while its position on second marriage was considered contrary to Scripture. The mainstream church was left with a heightened appreciation of the apostolic teaching, and prophecy in all forms virtually disappeared from the church.

Bibliography

R. D. Butler, *The New Prophecy and 'New Visions': Evidence of Montanism in the Passion of Perpetua and Felicitas* (Washington DC, 2006); R. E. Heine, *The Montanist Oracles and Testimonia* (Macon, 1989); W. Tabbernee, *Montanist Inscriptions and Testimonia: Epigraphic Sources Illustrating the History of Montanism* (Macon, 1996); idem, *Fake Prophecy and Polluted Sacraments: Ecclesiastical and Imperial Reactions to Montanism* (Leiden, 2007); idem, *Prophets and Gravestones: An Imaginative History of Montanists and Other Early Christians* (Peabody, 2009); C. Trevett, *Montanism: Gender, Authority and the New Prophecy* (Cambridge, 1996).

G. A. KEITH

MOONIES, see NEW RELIGIONS; SECTS

MORAL REARMAMENT

Moral Rearmament (MRA) originated through Frank Buchman (1878–1961), an American Lutheran. After an experience of conversion while at Keswick (see *Higher-life theology) for the convention in 1908, he gradually became concerned about reforming the world. He founded the Oxford Group in 1929, and this became MRA in 1938. The movement spread beyond the Christian faith, and welcomed any who sought to change society through practising the four absolutes, namely absolute purity, absolute unselfishness, absolute honesty and absolute love. Every legitimate means was used to spread the message and enrol supporters. Groups and houseparties were used from the beginning, and the general public were reached through plays and films, the Westminster Theatre in London being a centre for plays.

Buchman himself received many honours from world leaders, and after his death his place was taken by Peter Howard (1908–65), who himself wrote some of the MRA plays. At Howard's death control of the movement passed to directors in USA, but there are strong local centres at Caux in Switzerland, in Japan and other countries.

The absolutes accord with Christian ideals, but MRA members remain in their own religion, generally, but not always, Christianity. Some evangelicals who, like Buchman, already have a clear experience of salvation in Christ and his death, have held that in MRA they are united in a corporate expression of Christian standards. Others believe that there is no need for a separate organization to promote Christian values; and the promotion of values, without basic Christian doctrines, is not the NT gospel.

Bibliography

K. D. Belden, *Reflections on MRA* (London, 1983); G. Ekman, *Experience into God* (ET, London, 1972); P. Howard, *The World Rebuilt* (Poole, 1951); D. Johnston and C. Sampson (eds.), *Religion, the Missing Dimension of Statecraft* (Oxford, 1994); C. Pignet and M. Sentis, *World at the Turning* (ET, London, 1982).

J. S. WRIGHT

MORAL THEOLOGY

Although theology, especially in the West, has always been concerned with questions of Christian morality, the recognition of moral theology as an independent discipline dates from the late sixteenth century. The expression *theologia moralis* is found a century earlier in connection with the medieval confessionals, which elaborate the purpose of the penitentials of the early Middle Ages: to give guidance to the priest on suitable *penances for various sins. With the moral theology of the Counter-Reformation (see *Reformation, Catholic Counter-) the concern is more profound and the theological roots more extensive. It aims to guide the perplexed *conscience of the individual believer confronted with complex practical deliberations. It draws on the theology of law and psychology of moral judgment developed by *Thomas Aquinas, on the *canon law, and on the common theological understanding of man's orientation to God as the *summum bonum* which derived from *Augustine. It attended closely to the detailed examination and analysis of moral cases – hence the modern word '*casuistry'. In the seventeenth century, as theological concern shifted from the doctrinal questions of the Reformation, English Protestantism was attracted by this orientation to deliberative questions, and major contributions to moral theology were made in English by *Puritans (e.g. William *Perkins) as well as by Laudians (e.g. Jeremy *Taylor).

The validity of the traditional moral theology was always controversial. Typical of the seventeenth century in which it flowered, it was individualist in its conception of the agent, lay-orientated in its concern for life in the world, yet looked to impose order upon subjective moral perceptions more by the authoritative guidance of the institutions than from Scripture. Modern critics (e.g. *Barth) objected to its authoritarianism, contemporaries (e.g. *Pascal) to its accommodation of lax standards. Both criticisms have some justice. So do objections to its formalist analysis of moral problems, its focus on the pathological and exceptional phenomena of the moral life, and its scholastic traditionalism. Nevertheless, it contributed considerably to an understanding of the nature of moral discernment, and so pointed towards a Christian moral thinking that was neither legalistic nor subjective. The tradition fell into disrepute in Protestant circles in the eighteenth century, while in Roman Catholicism it reached its height with the work of Alphonsus Liguori (1696–1787), and achieved new vigour in the nineteenth (Antonio Rosmini, 1797–1855), only to lose favour in the twentieth.

From the early eighteenth century, Protestant thinkers turned increasingly to philosophical sources for moral guidance, and from the late eighteenth century were under the influence of *Kant. The resulting tradition of 'Christian *ethics' has been marked by a persistent anxiety about how the Kantian doctrine of ethical autonomy can be at home in a theological context. Never as successful as moral theology in the detailed analysis of recurrent moral situations, it has often appeared to be at a loss in the face of new social challenges, driven back upon a pragmatic consequentialism in matters of ethical substance. By contrast, the moral-theological tradition produced strong and sometimes controversial directions on such questions as the conduct of war (see *Pacifism/peace), medical practice and the place of labour in industry.

There have been frequent calls, notable among them that of the Second Vatican Council, for a reformation of moral theology/Christian ethics (the distinction has no more than historical usefulness) into a more wide-ranging intellectual enterprise with greater responsiveness to Scripture. The following pointers serve to guide this worthy ambition:

(1) Moral theology is distinct from 'spiritual theology' (the study of *prayer and *worship; cf. *Liturgical theology; *Spirituality) and from 'pastoral theology' (the study of the tasks of Christian *ministry), being concerned with questions that are more worldly than the one and more lay-orientated than the other. Yet there will always be interaction between these three fields.

(2) The primary task of moral theology is to clarify *Christian moral concepts*, showing how the distinctive Christian ways of posing moral questions (in terms of the command of God [see *Law], *love for the neighbour, the *freedom of faith, the *sanctification of the believer, the forms of created orders, etc.) arise from the

Scriptures, and comparing them with other ways in which moral questions may be put.

(3) Moral theology has to develop in detail certain aspects of *the Christian doctrine of human nature*, especially of *society and government, of *sexuality, and of life and *death. This continues the work of *systematic theology in these areas, and draws upon the relevant biblical commands and injunctions in reaching a systematic view.

(4) Moral theology must address the *deliberative questions* faced by individuals or societies in a way that applies what has been learned. These questions will often present themselves in three forms: (a) asking about the conduct of the individual believer who has to make a decision for himself (the agent perspective); (b) asking about how a believer or the church may advise others who have particular decisions to make (the counselling perspective); (c) asking about the form of an appropriate social rule that might govern practice (the legislative perspective). When these three forms of deliberative questioning are not kept distinct, confusion results.

(5) There is no value in the division of moral theology into 'personal' and '*social ethics' – which fosters the mistaken conception that the personal and the social constitute separate *fields* of moral enquiry, whereas every serious deliberative matter has both personal and social *aspects* to it, as outlined by the threefold distinction in (4) above.

Bibliography

R. M. Adams, *Finite and Infinite Goods* (New York, 2002); H. U. von Balthasar, 'Nine Theses in Christian Ethics', in *Principles of Christian Morality* (San Francisco, 1975); M. Banner, *Christian Ethics: A Brief History* (Chichester 2009); Barth, CD III.4; R. Cessario, *Introduction to Moral Theology* (Washington DC, 2001); G. Grisez, *The Way of the Lord Jesus*, 3 vols. (Chicago, 1993); J. Gustafson, *Protestant and Roman Catholic Ethics* (London, 1979); S. Hauerwas, *The Peaceable Kingdom: A Primer in Christian Ethics* (London, 1984); R. B. Hays, *The Moral Vision of the New Testament* (San Francisco, 1996); S. D. Long, *John Wesley's Moral Theology* (Nashville, 2005); B. Mitchell, *Morality: Religious and Secular* (Oxford, 1980); O. O'Donovan, *Resurrection and Moral Order* (Leicester, 1986); *idem*, *Self, World, and Time* (Grand Rapids, 2014); J. Pieper, *Faith, Hope, Love* (San Francisco, 1997); S. Pinckaers, *The Sources of Christian Ethics* (Washington DC, 1995); P. Ramsey, *Deeds and Rules in Christian Ethics* (New York, 1967); T. Rendtorff, *Ethics*, 2 vols. (Philadephia, 1986); H. Thielicke, *Theological Ethics*, 3 vols. (Grand Rapids, 1966–81).

O. M. T. O'DONOVAN

MORAVIAN THEOLOGY

The worldwide Moravian Church (*Unitas Fratrum*), also known as the Moravian Unity, is organized and governed by the terms of *Church Order of the Unitas Fratrum (Moravian Church)*, at the core of which is the Ground of the Unity.

The Ground of the Unity begins with an explicit Christocentric statement:

> The Lord Jesus Christ calls His Church into being so that it may serve Him here on earth until He comes. The Unitas Fratrum is, therefore, aware of its being called in faith to serve humanity by proclaiming the Gospel of Jesus Christ. It recognizes this call to be the source of its being and the inspiration of its services. As is the source, so is the aim and end of its being based upon the will of its Lord. (*Church Order*, 2002, p. 13)

After statements on the belief of the church and personal belief, the Ground of the Unity addresses God's word and doctrine from a broad ecumenical perspective:

> The Unitas Fratrum takes part in the continual search for sound doctrine. In interpreting Scripture and in the communication of doctrine in the Church, we look to two millennia of ecumenical Christian tradition in the wisdom of our Moravian forebears in the faith to guide us as we pray for fuller understanding and ever clearer proclamation of the Gospel of Jesus Christ. But just as the Holy Scripture does not contain any doctrinal system, so the Unitas Fratrum also has not developed any of its own. It knows that the mystery of Jesus Christ, which is attested to in the Bible, cannot be comprehended completely by any human mind or expressed completely in any human statement. (*Church Order*, p. 14)

It is therefore not possible to define or describe a Moravian theology per se. However, the Moravian Church through the centuries has recognized the importance of the great *creeds and *confessions of the Christian church in aiding the formulation of a scriptural confession, and in marking the boundaries of heresy. Furthermore, the orthodoxy and catholicity of belief in the Moravian Church can be seen in the recognition and acceptance of the Apostles', Athanasian and Nicene Creeds; and the *Protestant Reformed tradition in the list of confessions: Confession of the Unity of the Bohemian Brethren of 1535; Twenty-One Articles of the unaltered *Augsburg Confession; Shorter *Catechism of Martin Luther; Synod of Berne of 1532; *Thirty-Nine Articles of the Church of England; Theological Declaration of *Barmen of 1934; and the *Heidelberg Catechism.

Particular emphases within the broader spectrum of ecumenical theology can be seen in the concluding statements of the Ground of the Unity. There is the goal of unity itself:

> We confess our shared guilt, which is manifest in the severed and divided state of Christendom. By means of such divisions we ourselves hinder the message and power of the gospel . . . Since we together with all Christendom are pilgrims on the way to meet our coming Lord, we welcome every step that brings us nearer the goal of unity in Him. (*Church Order*, p. 15)

There is a distinct Moravian ecclesiology (see *Church, doctrine of), which emphasizes strong sociological and missiological imperatives with regard to the church as a fellowship, emphasizing the equality of humankind regardless of ethnic origin, sex or social standing; the church as a community of service, following Christ's example of coming not to be served but to serve; serving our neighbour, recognizing the needs of and reaching out to all God's children; and serving the world, challenging humankind with the message of God's love.

Bibliography

Church Order of the Unitas Fratrum (Moravian Church) 2002 (Bethlehem, 2002). *Church Order* is revised and republished every seven years following the meeting of Unity Synod.

D. J. NEWMAN

MORMONS, see SECTS

MÜNTZER, THOMAS (c. 1490–1525)

Thomas Müntzer used to be regarded by Lutheran historians as a blood-stained fanatic and by Marxists as a heroic revolutionary, but he is now widely recognized as a significant radical theologian and liturgist. As a young priest he was influenced both by *humanism and by *Luther, but like *Karlstadt, German mysticism also marks his thought and language. He spent some time in Prague, and *Hussite ideas appear to have added an apocalyptic dimension to his ministry. A conscientious pastor and preacher, his translations of the Lord's Supper and other services in the little Saxon town of Allstedt proved highly popular with local artisans and peasants. His emphasis on the immediate inspiration of the Spirit led to a critique both of academic theology, whether Lutheran or Roman Catholic, and of obedience to those secular authorities he regarded as 'pagan'. Gradually coming to recognize the right to armed resistance, he wrote movingly about social justice and became a prominent leader in the Peasants' War in Thüringen. After the battle of Frankenhausen in 1525 he was arrested, tortured and executed. His hymns, liturgies and scriptural interpretations kept his name alive after his death.

See also: REFORMATION, RADICAL.

Bibliography

P. C. Matheson (ed.), *The Collected Works of Thomas Müntzer* (Edinburgh, 1989); T. Scott, *Thomas Müntzer: Theology and Revolution in the German Reformation* (Basingstoke, 1989).

P. C. MATHESON

MURRAY, ANDREW (1828–1917)

Andrew Murray was a South African religious leader, evangelist, educator, author of over 250 books and numerous articles on theology, missionary strategy, pastoral concerns and personal devotion. The son of a Scottish Dutch Reformed Church (DRC) minister, he was born in Graaf-Reinet, South Africa, and educated at Aberdeen and Utrecht. He was ordained in 1849 and returned to South Africa to become the first regular DRC minister north of the Orange River. After nine years on the frontier he returned to the Cape Colony where he engaged in a series of theological and legal disputes with liberal clergymen. In 1860 a *revival movement began in his Worcester pastorate which quickly swept through South Africa. Murray became known as a 'revivalist' preacher, and in 1879 began a series of highly successful evangelistic tours throughout South Africa, Europe and America. He is best remembered for his books on personal piety, such as *With Christ in the School of Prayer* (London, 1885), *The New Life* (London, 1891) and *Absolute Surrender* (London, 1895), as well as for his study of Hebrews, *The Holiest of All* (London, ²1895).

Although not a Pentecostal in the modern sense, Murray was deeply influenced by *Methodist *holiness tradition, and through his books, *The Spirit of Christ* (London, 1888), *The Second Blessing* (Cape Town, 1891), *The Full Blessing of Pentecost* (London, 1907), and *Divine Healing* (London, 1900), he helped shape modern *Pentecostalism. Bengt Sundkler has argued, in *Zulu Zion* and *Some Swazi Zionists* (London, 1976), that Murray's teachings and emphasis on Christian experience contributed to the rise of *African independent churches. His works clearly influenced the rise of inter-denominational movements such as Inter-Varsity (Christian) Fellowship in the USA and UK, and the theology of the Chinese Christian leader Watchman Nee (1903–72). Nee's work, in turn, encouraged the growth of trans-denominational 'Bible' churches in North America which are similar in many ways to 'independent church' movements in Africa and the Majority World.

Although he preached a *pietist message, Murray was involved in South African social life and strongly opposed the growing Afrikaner nationalist movement as well as British imperialism. He was a gifted and unusual man whose influence is still felt in evangelical Christianity.

See also: DUTCH REFORMED THEOLOGY.

Bibliography

L. F. Choy, *Andrew Murray: Apostle of Abiding Love* (Fort Washington, 1978); W. M. Douglas, *Andrew Murray and His Message* (London, 1926); J. Du Plessis, *The Life of Andrew Murray of South Africa* (London, 1919).

I. HEXHAM

MURRAY, JOHN (1898–1975)

John Murray was born in Scotland, but studied at Princeton Theological Seminary. After fulfilling a promise to teach there for one year (1929–30), Murray joined the faculty of the newly formed Westminster Seminary, Philadelphia, which J. G. *Machen and others had founded (following the appointment to the Princeton Board of two signatories of the Auburn Affirmation, 1924, which was essentially a plea for the toleration of theological diversity within the Presbyterian Church).

An eloquent and thoughtful advocate of the classical orthodoxy of the *Westminster Standards, Murray married that theology to strong personal piety and a deep appreciation of the significance of biblical theology for *dogmatic thought (an element in his work traceable to the influence of the teaching of G. *Vos; see *Collected Writings*, vol. 2.). Murray's teaching and writing were consequently often marked by the close exegetical and theological argument characteristic of his *Commentary on Romans* (Grand Rapids, vol. 1, 1960; vol. 2, 1965).

Of special interest in his thought are: (1) his understanding of biblical *covenants as oath-bound promises, which led to his reticence to adopt the classical dual covenant thought of *Reformed theology (*Covenant of Grace*, London, 1954; *Collected Writings*, vol. 2, pp. 49–50); (2) his rooting of the Christian *ethic in the ordinances of creation (*Principles of Conduct*, Grand Rapids, 1957); (3) his exposition of immediate imputation (*The Imputation of Adam's Sin*, Grand Rapids, 1959; see *Adam; *Sin); and (4) his reworking of the doctrine of *sanctification to reflect more fully its definitive as well as progressive character (*Collected Writings*, vol. 2, pp. 277–317).

A deeply committed churchman, Murray served as Moderator of the General Assembly of the Orthodox Presbyterian Church, USA, in 1961.

Bibliography

Collected Writings, 4 vols. (Edinburgh, 1976–83), including I. H. Murray, *The Life of John Murray*, vol. 3; *Bibliography*, vol. 4.

S. B. FERGUSON

MUSCULUS, WOLFGANG (1497–1563)

Musculus (Müslin) was a second-generation German *Reformed theologian who joined the Reformation in 1527, leaving the Benedictine order to assist Martin *Bucer at Strasbourg. Musculus became pastor at Augsburg in 1531. While there, he participated in the Wittenberg accords (1536) and Worms discussions (1540), though he eventually left in response to the anti-Protestant Augsburg Interim (1548).

Musculus declined an invitation from the Archbishop of Canterbury to join Bucer in England after the Interim, instead heading for the Swiss territories. From 1549 he served as professor of theology at Bern, where he remained an important Reformed leader until his death. Although self-taught, Musculus was broadly learned and quite prolific. He wrote many occasional and polemical works, several biblical commentaries, and translated and edited multiple volumes of the writings of various Church Fathers.

Bibliography

Works: *Common Places of Christian Religion* (ET, London, 1563); P. Romane-Musculus, 'Catalogue des Oeuvres imprimées du théologien Wolfgang Musculus', *Revue d'histoire et de philosophie religieuses* 43.3, 1963, pp. 260–278.

Studies: R. Bodenmann, *Wolfgang Musculus (1497–1563): Destin d'un autodidacte lorrain au siècle des réformes* (Genève, 2000); R. Dellsperger et al. (eds.), Wolfgang Musculus, *1497–1563, und die oberdeutsche Reformation* (Berlin, 1997); C. S. Farmer, *The Gospel of John in the Sixteenth Century: Johannine Exegesis of Wolfgang Musculus* (New York, 1997).

B. E. ELLIS

MYSTICAL THEOLOGY

Like mysticism, mystical theology has been defined in so many ways that it is necessary to distinguish its various connotations.

(1) It can mean, as it did in the Middle Ages, simply personal experience of God and reflection upon it (see *Religious experience). In this sense every medieval theologian was a mystic because he wrote about what he himself experienced. Thus Karl *Rahner can affirm that 'the devout Christian of the future will either be a "mystic", one who has "experienced" something, or he will be nothing at all' (*Theological Investigations*, vol. 7, London, 1971, p. 15). Theology and mysticism are equally inseparable in *Eastern Orthodox theology: 'If the mystical experience is a personal working out of the content of the common faith, theology is an expression, for the profit of all, of that which can be experienced by everyone' (V. Lossky, *The Mystical Theology of the Eastern Church*, London, 1957, p. 9).

Writers who understand mystical theology in this way as a loving awareness or knowledge of *God see nothing unusual in describing *Jesus and *Paul as mystics, and their teaching about *prayer, *union with God and Christ, or life in the Holy Spirit, as mysticism. They will also point out how deeply steeped in Scripture are mystics like Teresa of Avila and John of the Cross (see below).

(2) A more restricted usage of the term confines it to the higher stages of mystical prayer which, like other *gifts of the Spirit, are given as God wills to some and not to others. In this sense mystical theology is distinguished from *ascetical theology, which describes the stages of prayer from the beginnings to the prayer of 'loving attention' or 'simple regard' that goes beyond words. Many writers on prayer consider that this latter type of contemplation is open to every Christian.

(3) Protestant writers, though well aware of the relationship between theology and experience of God, have usually been reluctant to speak of mystical theology. The term 'mystical' has suggested confusion with the Greco-Roman mystery religions, identification with the Neoplatonism of the *Mystical Theology* of *Dionysius, and the errors of *Gnosticism and *quietism. It has also been maintained that mystical theology overlooks the prominent prophetic or ethical element in Scripture (cf. A. *Nygren, *Agape and Eros*, 3 vols., London, 1932–39; G. *Ebeling, *Word and Faith*, London, 1963). Some mystics may have laid themselves open to such charges, sometimes through their attempts to describe the indescribable, but it is impossible to categorize all mystical theology in this way. Each example must be examined in context and assessed on its own merits.

A survey of Western mystical theology down to the thirteenth century would include the Fathers from *Augustine to *Bernard of Clairvaux, *Francis of Assisi and his disciple and biographer *Bonaventura, not forgetting the mystical side of *Thomas Aquinas. Bernard's devotion to the humanity of Christ, maintained in the writings of Aelred of Rievaulx (1110–67), had lasting influence in European mysticism.

The other major influence was the *apophatic theology of Dionysius, translated from Greek into Latin by *Eriugena in the ninth century and into a modified English version in the late fourteenth century by the anonymous author of *The Cloud of Unknowing*. *The Cloud* (which also introduced English readers to the third contemporary influence in European mysticism, the school of St Victor; see *Victorines) appeared c. 1370, between the works of Richard Rolle of Hampole (c. 1295–1349) and the other flowers of English mysticism: *The Scale of Perfection* of Walter Hilton (d. 1396), the *Showings or Revelations of Divine Love* to the anchoress Julian of Norwich (c. 1342–1416) and *The Book of Margery Kempe* (c. 1373–1433).

Mysticism also flourished during this period in movements of spiritual renewal in Germany and Flanders inspired by Meister Eckhart (c. 1260–1327), John Tauler (c. 1300–61) and Henry Suso (c. 1295–1366). The three were involved with the Rhineland Friends of God (which produced the *Theologia Germanica*, an anonymous plain man's guide to mysticism which Luther later printed) and indirectly contributed to the Brethren of the Common Life in Flanders by their influence on Jan van Ruysbroeck (1293–1381). Ruysbroeck's disciple Gerard Groot (1340–84) founded the Brethren, thus promoting a spirituality which achieved lasting expression during the following century in the writings of Thomas à Kempis (1380–1471) (see *Imitation of Christ).

If some of the writings mentioned above suggest that a mystic is concerned only with the inner life of the soul, such an impression would be corrected by a study of the lives of Italian and Spanish mystics such as Catherine of Siena (1347–80), Catherine of Genoa (1447–1510), *Ignatius of Loyola, or Teresa of Avila (1515–82), the Carmelite reformer who produced, like her disciple the poet John of the Cross (1542–91), analyses of the stages of the mystical life which have never been surpassed.

More recent wrestlings with the relation between prayer and action are found in the writings of *Bonhoeffer and liberation theology. It is a substantial theme in Thomas *Merton (cf. *Contemplation in a World of Action*, London, 1971), whose work is also important as a pioneering contribution to the increasingly pressing question of the relationship between mystical theology and religious experience in Christianity and other religions.

Bibliography

Individual volumes in the *Classics of Western Spirituality* series (London and New York, 1978–); A. Bancroft, *The Luminous Vision* (London, 1982); L. Bouyer (ed.), *A History of Christian Spirituality*, 3 vols. (London, 1963–69); P. Grant, *A Dazzling Darkness* (London, 1985); G. Gutiérrez, *We Drink from Our Own Wells* (London, 1984); W. Johnston, *The Wounded Stag* (London, 1985); A. Louth, *The Origins of the Christian Mystical Tradition* (Oxford, 1981); M. A. McIntosh, *Mystical Theology: The Integrity of Spirituality and Theology* (Oxford, 1998); S. Tugwell, *Ways of Imperfection* (London, 1984); G. S. Wakefield (ed.), *A Dictionary of Christian Spirituality* (London, 1984); R. Williams, *The Wound of Knowledge* (London, 1979). Earlier literature, including the classic studies by Otto, Underhill and von Hügel, may be traced through the bibliography in R. Woods (ed.), *Understanding Mysticism* (London, 1981).

P. N. HILLYER

MYTH

Myth is a confusing and slippery term in theology; it is used in so many ill-defined ways by individual theologians that it would be no bad thing if its use were prohibited. In popular parlance the word is used to refer to stories that are fictional, and hence it has come to have a pejorative sense. Traditionally, it refers to invented stories about the gods in which they behave like human beings with superhuman powers. Closely associated with this sense of the word is its usage to refer specifically to the stories which may accompany and allegedly form the basis for religious rituals. Thus the Greek myth of Demeter and her daughter Persephone (who married Pluto and spent six months of each year in the underworld with her husband and six months with her mother on earth) was recited in the rites of the mystery religion celebrated at Eleusis near Athens, and was regarded as the justification for performing them. A number of modern writers would argue that such myths reflect in some ways fundamental aspects or modes of human thinking.

As the term is used technically in theological discussion it seems to have four nuances, any or all of which may be present at any one time.

(1) A myth may be a story which attempts to explain the origins of things without the use of modern historical and scientific investigation. Myth can thus be represented as pre-scientific thinking, and this may lead to a negative evaluation of it. (2) A myth may depict some aspect of human experience in the form of a story about the past. The story of an original 'social contract' which expresses the structure of society by a fictitious example of 'how it began' would be a myth of this kind. (3) A myth may be a story which is presented in terms of some symbolism and thus has a poetic or emotional appeal and is capable of reinterpretation in the light of fresh experiences. Some of the deepest feelings of people about the human predicament may find expression in mythical form. (4) The term is often used to refer to any kind of story which involves the gods or other supernatural actors.

The story of the *fall of man in Gen. 3 can be seen to function in these ways. (1) It is meant to explain how sin and disobedience came into the world. (2) It is expressive of the present fallen state of humankind, summed up in the statement: 'Each of us has become our own Adam' (2 Baruch 54:19). It describes our plight in the form of a story. (3) The language contains symbolism that is capable of further development and that may evoke fresh ideas and deeper understanding. (4) The story includes among its actors God and a serpent who miraculously speaks.

To say that this story performs the functions of a myth enables us to recognize a number of facts. First, to say that a story is a myth is not to pronounce on its historical truth or falsity; it is to say something about how it functions (just as a parable may be historical or fictional). A myth may or may not employ historical materials. For example, F. F. Bruce has commented on the way in which Exod. 1 – 15 functions as the *mythos* of the annual Passover ritual in Israel: 'But – and herein lies the whole differentia of Israel's faith as contrasted with the surrounding religions of Old Testament days – the *mythos* in this instance is . . . the recital of something that really happened in history, interpreted as the mighty, self-revealing act of Israel's God' (in C. Brown, *History, Criticism and Faith*, p. 80).

Second, the important question about a myth is whether it is valid, or invalid in the point that it makes: a myth which tells us that man is fallen is clearly valid, whereas a myth asserting that man is not really sinful would be invalid.

Third, myth is a well-recognized literary genre, and there is no reason in principle why the Bible should not contain mythical material. The question regarding the historical truth of a myth must be separated from the question of its validity; a myth may well be valid even though the story is fictitious, just as in the case of parables. A verdict on the literal truth or historicity of Gen. 3, for example, will depend on general considerations regarding the nature of the story and how it came to be composed, and also on how we evaluate the NT references to *Adam as a historical person.

The question of the presence of myth in the Bible raises various problems. Some of the NT writers themselves reject the use of what they call 'myths' (1 Tim. 4:7; 2 Pet. 1:16), and thereby indicate that the substance of Christian belief is not akin to pagan myths. So far as the OT is concerned, the writers on the whole did not take over pagan mythology, although, as we have seen, the use of material functioning as myth should not be excluded. One can find some parallels in pagan mythology to biblical concepts and stories in the NT, but again the influence, if any, is marginal.

Difficulties arise when material which appears to be historical is labelled as myth in the sense of being unhistorical. A powerful body of opinion extending from D. F. *Strauss to R. *Bultmann and then to the 'myth of God incarnate' school has argued in one way or another that some central affirmations of Christian faith – the *incarnation, sacrificial death (see *Atonement), *resurrection and second coming of Jesus (see *Eschatology) – are mythical in this sense. Some scholars simply reject such myths and argue that they must be dropped from Christian theology; others hold that these myths 'really' express an understanding of humanity which must be released from its mythological expression (i.e. demythologized) and then re-expressed in other terms which will be intelligible to modern men and women who cannot believe in the supernatural.

This proposal is open to basic objections. Fundamentally, it assumes that the modern scientific, materialistic frame of reference is to be the criterion by which the truth of biblical teaching is to be assessed, and it does not sufficiently recognize that such a godless understanding stands judged by biblical teaching. Further, as a result of the slipperiness of the term, it may lump together as 'mythical' a whole set of varied concepts and fail to differentiate between them. For example, the 'three-decker' view of the world held by many ancient people is not essential to the expression of biblical truth and need not be shared by modern people. But to reject this as being 'mythical' or 'pre-scientific' is quite different from rejecting the truth of the incarnation. The danger is to argue that stories involving God are 'mythical' like the three-decker universe, and to fail to recognize that, if myth is defined in terms of 'stories involving God', it is not possible to dispense with myth. To say that the myths are 'really' expressions about the nature and existence of humanity is to fail to recognize that the biblical writers were making the point that any expressions about the existence of humanity must inevitably also be statements about the nature and existence of God. This is not to deny that we may need to find ways of translating the biblical expressions to make them intelligible to modern people; but the whole point of translation is that it faithfully renders in our language what was originally said in another. It would be better to recognize that much of what is often called mythical language is really *analogical or *symbolical language in which we talk about the God who lies beyond the grasp of ordinary literal expressions in terms of analogy with human persons.

Bibliography

H.-W. Bartsch (ed.), *Kerygma and Myth* (London, 1972); C. Brown (ed.), *History, Criticism and Faith* (Leicester, 1976); D. Cairns, *A Gospel Without Myth?* (London, 1960); J. D. G. Dunn, 'Demythologizing – the problem of Myth in the NT', in I. H. Marshall (ed.), *New Testament Interpretation* (Exeter, 1977); R. Johnson, *The Origins of Demythologizing* (Leiden, 1974); G. Stählin in *TDNT* IV, pp. 762–795.

I. H. MARSHALL

NARRATIVE THEOLOGY

There are several different kinds of narrative theology. There are, for instance, 'story theologies', popular since the 1960s, and indebted to earlier theologies of '*myth'. They focus upon narrative as a means by which people evoke and express their deepest ways of seeing the world. Jesus' parables are often presented as key exemplars of such stories (e.g. by Robert Funk): they are stories that lure their audience in by familiarity of setting and cast, but which then explode narrative bombshells, provoking moments of revelation in which the hearers' ways of seeing the world are transformed. Parables are taken to work on their hearers at a preconceptual level, reshaping patterns of perception and thought that lie deeper than can be verbalized in clear propositions.

Then there are *postliberal theologies of 'realistic narrative', developed since the 1970s. Theologians like Hans *Frei focus on narrative portions of the Gospels that appear to tell the story of characters and incidents in the real, historical world. These theologies focus not on the response evoked in the reader, but on the ways in which the narratives employ literary techniques and patterns to depict a public world of character and circumstance that has a certain objectivity over against the reader. The meaning of the narrative text is not the 'way of seeing' that is evoked by it, but simply the story that is told.

The meaning of the Gospels is the portrayal of a character who can be identified most properly simply by telling his story. The question of historical factuality can be temporarily bracketed whilst this narrative identification is being explored and understood, but the question of the relationship between the depicted *Jesus and the Jesus of history (see *Historical Jesus, quest for) remains urgent and must be posed when it is clear where the weight of the realistic narrative identification falls (e.g. on the crucifixion–resurrection sequence). All other attempts to define the identity of Jesus, whether by reconstructing the likely facts referred to by the texts, or by amassing doctrinal statements, or by identifying the 'mode of being in the world' that these texts convey, are held to be thoroughly subordinate to his identification by narrative means. The *significance* of these narratives can be found by asking how the reader might take the world depicted to be his or her own world, or by exploring how the characters and incidents of the story can become 'types' of the reader's own world.

Then there are theologies that focus on the relationship between narrative and reasoning. To ask what appropriately follows from a set of propositions differs from asking what appropriately follows from an incomplete narrative. So, for instance, in Christian ethics theologians committed to narrative reasoning can eschew sets of principles that supposedly dictate what is and is not right and instead concentrate on exploring the drama of Jesus and the church, and to asking what ways of living 'follow' this drama appropriately. Theologians like Stanley *Hauerwas who value narrative reasoning tend to share with theologians of realistic narrative a focus on the history-like narratives of Jesus and the church, but also share with story theologians an interest in narrative as a pervasive human way of making sense.

Bibliography

H. W. Frei, *The Eclipse of Biblical Narrative* (New Haven, 1974); *idem*, 'On Interpreting the Christian Story', in *Reading Faithfully* (Eugene, 2005); R. W. Funk, *Language, Hermeneutic, and Word of God* (New York, 1966); S. Hauerwas, *A Community of Character* (Notre Dame and London, 1981); S. Hauerwas and L. G. Jones (eds.), *Why Narrative?* (Grand Rapids, 1989); G. W. Stroup, *The Promise of Narrative Theology* (Virginia and London, 1981 and 1984).

M. HIGTON

NATURAL LAW, see LAW

NATURAL THEOLOGY

Natural theology is the attempt to attain an understanding of God's existence, nature and relationship with the universe by means of rational reflection, without appealing to special *revelation such as the self-revelation of God in Christ, in Scripture or in church tradition. Sometimes (as in *deism) this is thought to arise from unaided human reason (see *Rationalism), and sometimes from God's general revelation in *nature.

The early high point of popularity for natural theology was medieval *scholasticism. Anselm and Thomas Aquinas are the most important representatives of this theological approach, although their epistemologies differ significantly. *Anselm, in *Proslogion*, structures his argument as an a priori demonstration of the logic of God's existence. His argument (which Kant later designated the *ontological argument) begins from the definition of God as 'that than which no greater can be conceived'. Anselm claims that, in addition to attributes of perfection such as omnipresence, omnipotence, omniscience and others, we must include the characteristic of existence, because that which exists in reality surpasses that which exists only in the mind. Thus, the definition of God as 'that than which no greater can be conceived' logically entails the actual existence of God.

The intent of Anselm's argument has been hotly debated recently. On the one hand, many have noted that it is presented in the form of a prayer and is introduced under Anselm's affirmation, 'I do not seek to understand so that I may believe, but I believe so that I may understand.' This leads some commentators to argue that the ontological argument should not be taken as a philosophical proof for God's existence, but as an argument that requires prior faith. On the other hand, others have noted that Anselm seems to expect that the Fool (Anselm's conversational foil in the first part of *Proslogion)*, who 'says in his heart, "There is no God"' (Ps. 14:1; 53:1), should be convinced of the logical necessity of God's existence apart from any pre-existing faith.

Anselm's ontological argument remained popular for many centuries among those committed to an a priori epistemology. A notable example can be found in *Descartes' modified versions of the ontological argument in his *Meditations on First Philosophy*. While Anselm's intent may be ambiguous, it is clear that Descartes expects the ontological argument to stand as a philosophical demonstration of God's existence. However, this argument suffered a significant blow from Kant, who argued that existence is not a predicate. Existence, properly understood, refers to the instantiation of a being that has proper predicates, such as omnipotence, and is therefore not an attribute itself. Despite Kant's criticism, the ontological argument still has proponents today.

Natural theology's other major proponent in the medieval period was *Thomas Aquinas. In contrast to Anselm's a priori *epistemology, Aquinas relied on an a posteriori approach. This method works from our experience of the world's existence and orderly operations and derives from this the conclusion that God must exist. Aquinas' arguments, commonly referred to as the 'five ways', are generally thought to be reducible to two arguments. The first four arguments (although there is some debate about the extent to which the fourth conforms to the pattern of the first three) are usually categorized as the cosmological argument. This argument, in its simplest form, says that the world and everything within it is contingent. Thus, the world is an effect that requires a cause. However, an infinite regress of causes is logically impossible. Without some first cause, which does not itself require a cause, no subsequent effects could possibly exist. Since these effects do in fact exist, an Uncaused Cause (which, Aquinas says, 'all people call God') necessarily exists as well.

The fifth of the 'five ways' is referred to as the teleological argument, or the argument from design. In sum, the teleological argument observes that order and logical structure is evident, not just in the activities of beings that possess intelligence, but also in the activities of entities that do not themselves have intellect. Aquinas' conclusion is that we can only account for orderly processes in unintelligent things by the imposition of order by an external intelligent reality. In other words, because design is a manifestation of an intelligent agent, the design evident in the universe points to a divine designer.

The emergence of *nominalist philosophy in the later medieval period diminished interest in natural theology. Unlike earlier forms of medieval scholasticism, nominalism rejected Aquinas' concept of the analogy of *being, which argues that while God's mode of existence differs from that of anything in the created order, language from our experience within the latter could be properly applied to God provided that we understood it analogically. The nominalist tradition, which tended to interpret Aquinas' analogy of being as an analogy of proportion, claimed instead that God was decisively Other than creation, and thus sharply distinguished between the realms of philosophy and theology. While the former is an adequate tool for discerning and analyzing the created order, only theology provides access to the divine. This has the effect of eliminating the entire category of general revelation, which functions as the foundation of natural theology.

The theology of the magisterial *Reformation viewed creation as deeply implicated in the fall, and was therefore more negative toward the prospects of natural theology. *Luther, educated in the nominalist tradition, rejects any possibility that philosophy can discover theological truths apart from special revelation. *Calvin's position was somewhat more nuanced. He argued that God was revealed through nature and God's providential governance of it. As a result each individual has a sense of the divine (*sensus divinitatis*), which is the origin of human religious sensibilities. However, the corrosive effects of *sin are so extensive that our rational capacities offer no certainty of God or God's nature. Clarity of God is available only by means of Scripture.

The English Reformation, whose break with the Roman Catholic Church was not as radical as that of the magisterial Reformation, was more optimistic about the prospects of natural theology. In combination with Lockean empiricism, the *Anglican tradition yielded two closely related but distinct approaches to natural theology that dominated the British world of the eighteenth and early nineteenth centuries. The first type is most evident in works of Anglican authors such as William *Paley and Joseph *Butler. Paley, in his *Natural Theology*, offers what is probably the most famous restatement of Aquinas' teleological argument for God's existence – the watchmaker analogy. This analogy draws a link between the intricately interconnected and orderly structures of a watch and those found within the natural realm to argue for the existence of a divine designer. Butler's natural theology in his *Analogy of Religion* attempts to demonstrate God's existence through a cumulative argument, although he focuses heavily on the moral structure of the universe to make his case.

The second type of natural theology in Great Britain during this time was *deism. Deists argued that God's nature and will, to the extent that they can be known, are revealed within the structures of *creation. Typically, they asserted that the natural order reveals the existence of God, and the moral structure of our minds could detect, in its interaction with the external world, the ethical nature of this Creator. While deists quite frequently appealed to the same arguments for God's existence or to delineate our moral obligations as Anglican natural theologians, they differed in two significant ways. First, the orthodox Anglicans did not limit themselves exclusively simply to natural theology, but also accepted the validity of special revelation as a necessary supplement to what could be known by means of general revelation. In contrast, deism generally argued that what could be known about God should be limited solely to what could be gleaned from rational understanding of the natural realm. Thus, Scripture, church tradition or any other form of special revelation should be accepted only so far as it conformed to the dictates of natural reason. All else should be discarded as unwarranted superstition. Second, since God reveals himself only through the natural realm, no event that is inexplicable in terms of natural processes is possible. Thus, miracles, resurrection, theophany, and similar events that violate the general laws of nature must be dismissed as delusion or untruths.

Natural theology encountered two severe sources of criticism in the eighteenth and nineteen centuries. The first was philosophical in nature, and grew primarily out of the thought of Hume and Kant. Both challenge cosmological and teleological arguments for God's existence by calling into question the concept of causality. *Hume's argument is that within a sequence of events, perception cannot distinguish between a sequence of events that we take to be causally linked and events that are merely a series. Thus, sense experience provides no foundation for claiming a causal connection between two events, no matter how frequently they might occur in sequence. He concludes that all we can say with certainty is that our mind habitually joins together certain sequences because (1) two objects in a sequence become contiguous to each other and (2) we are able to predict with accuracy, because of a resemblance to other observed sequences, what event will follow upon this contiguity. However, perception provides no means of knowing whether that which the mind draws into causal connection corresponds with any causal reality that exists beyond our mind.

*Kant comes at it somewhat differently by arguing that cause and effect simply do not apply to the divine realm. Causation is a category within the mind by which pure reason organizes the data of perception. However, since God is not an entity accessible by perception, causal arguments are not possible. Kant argues that we gain access to the metaphysical realm by means of practical reason only.

While the arguments of Hume and Kant cast significant doubt on natural theology, perhaps a more serious blow came from the natural sciences. Darwinian evolution (see *Creation and evolution) agrees that the universe manifests order, but argues that this order should not be confused with design. Cases of apparent design can be explained instead by the purely natural evolutionary processes of adaptation to a constantly shifting environment.

While natural theology was at a low ebb outside *Roman Catholic circles in the nineteenth and early twentieth centuries, forms of this approach survived in the philosophical and theological systems that stressed God's immanence. *Hegel's idealism (see *German idealism) rejects the dichotomy between nature and the divine. Instead, God (Spirit) is embedded in the processes of history. As historical processes evolve toward conformity with the Absolute Spirit, our consciousness is able to discern the divine as it properly understands the nature and movement of history and its social institutions. Thus, knowledge of the natural realm is, at the same time, knowledge of God. From *idealism, it is a short jump to get to the natural theology at the foundation of *process philosophy and theology. God, in God's absolute primordial nature, lures the universe toward loving responses. However, the universe is also identical to God in God's consequent nature, and this gives a responsive impulse to all things toward love. Thus, it is possible to discern the nature and will of God to the extent that the universe responds to the divine lure.

A major impetus for contemporary discussions of natural theology has been the *Gifford Lectures. This lectureship was established by Adam Lord Gifford in 1888 to 'promote and diffuse the study of Nature Theology in the widest sense of the term – in other words, the knowledge of God'. Lecturers have included some of the most significant thinkers across a broad array of disciplines.

The most visible debate on natural theology in the twentieth century took place between Karl Barth and Emil Brunner. In this interchange, *Barth rejected all natural theology on the grounds that God reveals himself in his word. It was therefore pointless to look elsewhere for revelation. This view was questioned by *Brunner, who believed that Barth had overstated his case. Brunner pleaded for a Protestant natural theology which he wanted to base on such ideas as the image of God, general revelation, preserving grace, divine ordinances, point of contact, and the contention that grace does not abolish nature, but perfects it. Barth's later theology offers a highly qualified place for natural theology. He speaks of creation as a 'token of revelation'. By means of the incarnation, all creation, if properly seen through Christ, can be a witness to the word of God.

Presently, two currents of theological reflection have added new elements to the discussion of natural theology. First, the emergence of *postmodernism has raised new questions about the possibility of a neutral and universal rationality. Such unbiased rationality is generally thought to be the starting point for natural theology. Thus, those sceptical that we are able to conceive of reason apart from cultural and temporal conditioning will take a similarly sceptical view of natural theology's prospects. Secondly, a minor revival of interest in natural theology is evident in the work of many natural scientists and philosophers and theologians who are engaged with the sciences. While one cannot speak of developments in this area as monolithic, a sizeable number within this group argue that natural laws raise questions that can only receive satisfactory answers by appeal to a divine agent. In other words, science generates issues that science itself lacks the tools to address, and this calls for a philosophy or theology of *science that includes divine causation and guidance. While this appears to reflect Aquinas' theological approach, advocates within this movement tend to be more modest in their claims about what the natural realm reveals about God.

Bibliography

J. Barr, *Biblical Faith and Natural Theology* (Oxford, 1993); E. Brunner and K. Barth, *Natural Theology* (London, 1946); J. Cobb, *A Christian Natural Theology* (Philadelphia, 1965); S. Hauerwas, *With the Grain of the Universe* (Grand Rapids, 2001); N. Kretzmann, *The Metaphysics of Creation* (Oxford and New York, 2001); A. McGrath, *The Science of God* (Grand Rapids, 2004); J. Polkinghorne, *Science and Theology* (London and Minneapolis, 1998); R. Swinburne, *The Coherence of Theism* (Oxford and New York, 1993).

S. WILKENS

NATURE, THEOLOGY OF

The term 'nature' translates the Gk *physis*. If it is taken to connote underived self-existence, it is in opposition to the biblical concept of *creation, according to which nothing comes to be of itself, but only by God's word (cf. John 1:3). Understood, however, in the sense of 'that which exists prior', i.e. prior to some supervening activity, it is used extensively in Christian theology, with two main references: that which is prior to human cultural activity, i.e. the natural world; and that which is prior to God's saving grace, i.e. human nature.

Nature prior to human culture

In some classical Gk thought *physis* and *nomos* ('law' or 'convention') are in opposition: *physis* in this connection refers to the human nature common to all, a given constant admitting only of simple acceptance; *nomos* designates the sphere of moral, social and political practice, which may differ between cultures. Another strand of Gk thought, however, intimates that of itself nature is shaped by *law. Biblical teaching resembles this latter, differing from it in ascribing the law in nature to divine promulgation. Thus Paul's dictum that 'Gentiles who have not the law (*nomos*) do by nature (*physis*) what the law requires' (Rom. 2:14, RSV) assumes an embodiment of God's law in human nature: the application of the same principle to the non-human world may be inferred from certain passages in the OT (e.g. Ps. 19).

The divine declaration that creation is 'very good' (Gen. 1:31) establishes the natural world as the proper context for human fulfilment. Humankind's *vocation is to be found in respect for nature and the *stewardship of its order, not in escape from it to a 'higher' freedom. The denial of the goodness of the material universe, contrary to the biblical view, was a feature of certain second-century *Gnostic sects and of the *Manichaean heresy (third–fifth centuries): they typify the recurrent tendency in the West to assert a radical opposition between inert nature and imposed human ordering. In the modern period the *idealist polarization of nature and spirit and the rejection of the medieval sacralization of nature have frequently led to the denial that the natural order is either knowable or valuable. At the same time the understanding of human vocation has shifted from stewardship of a God-given order to technological manipulation of a recalcitrant environment. Similarly, values have come to be grounded in the purposes imposed on an indifferent universe by the historical creativity of the human spirit (cf. *Teilhard de Chardin's doctrine of universal 'hominization'). This relocation of the ground of morality has been rationalized in terms of the supreme value of freedom and the alleged impossibility of deriving 'values' from 'facts'. The discussion of *ecological problems and of the character of stewardship demands serious reconsideration of the biblical teaching concerning an inherent order of value in creation. The natural world bears an intrinsic dignity and ordering anterior to its usefulness for human purposes: it may not be treated simply as raw material to be exploited at the convenience of a technologically minded civilization.

The incorporation of law within nature also suggests a role for natural law within Christian *ethics, though the concept is admittedly fraught with difficulties. There are common threads within the many Christian and non-Christian conceptions of natural law: (1) moral and legal precepts are 'objective' (i.e. true independently of the will or affections of human agents); (2) they are founded on nature; and (3) they are known to all through reason (however these terms are construed). Thus human morality, despite its apparent diversity, is fundamentally homogeneous; to be human is to share in certain basic conceptions, however much they may be denied through self-interest, passion or corrupt sophistication. Natural law therefore stands against accounts that identify moral reasoning with the mere articulation or expression of preferences (subjectivism and emotivism), the prediction of consequences (utilitarianism), the unguided response to necessarily particular situations (situationism), or the reflection on untranscended communal tradition (communitarianism).

In the classic Christian exposition of natural law (that of *Thomas Aquinas, in *Summa Theologica* II:1:90–105), only a part of moral knowledge is derived from unassisted human reason, namely the basic principles: these comprise the law of non-contradiction and the principle that the good is to be pursued and the bad avoided; also primary precepts concerning murder, lying, stealing, duty to parents, etc. The greater part of the substance of moral teaching is provided by divine law (revealed in *Scripture) and conventional human law. But natural law also has a function here: it explains how we can recognize moral truths as necessary implications of the basic principles once we have received instruction in them from revelation or *culture. Thus the doctrine of natural law is not meant to explain how we come by all our moral insights or even (since it is admitted that culture plays a role) how we come by those that are widely accepted. Moreover, it can be given an interpretation compatible with the claim that all knowledge is ultimately dependent on grace.

Nature prior to divine action

In *Protestant theology 'nature' refers most commonly to the unfitness of humankind for God's presence prior to God's intervening act of *grace. Thus 'we were by nature children of wrath' (Eph. 2:3, RSV). In this context the term points to the fallen condition of human nature originally created good but now corrupted. Failure to set the *fall within the context of creation has sometimes left theology misleadingly polarized. Catholicism on the one hand has avoided an unacceptable severance of God the Redeemer from God the Creator through its division of human nature into a 'natural' part (which is substantially unaltered by the fall) and a 'supernatural' part (which is bestowed by grace), but has been tempted to a *Pelagian optimism about human capacity for good. Protestantism on the other hand has recognized that every part of human nature has been corrupted by *sin, but in its proper emphasis on the absolute human dependence on grace has leant towards a Manichaean denial of creation.

However, the limits of human nature prior to grace, even regardless of the fall, must also be stressed. Against naturalism Christian theology teaches that human beings are not self-sufficient, but require the gracious self-disclosure of God in order to achieve the goal of their existence. Debate about revelation and the possibility of *natural theology must be set within this perspective. Through his work of salvation God gave himself to humankind in a new way, not already implicit in creaturely human existence. The knowledge of God is given as a 'mystery hidden for ages . . . but now . . . manifest' (Col. 1:26, RSV): in the person of Christ is imparted the fullness of grace and the promise of glory. Human nature is called to fulfilment in the supernatural, which transcends but does not abolish or destroy it. The same may be said about created nature as a whole: it is God's plan to 'unite all things in [Christ], things in heaven and things on earth' (Eph. 1:10, RSV).

Bibliography

K. Barth, *CD*, III.1–2; J. Finnis, *Natural Law and Natural Rights* (Oxford, 1980); C. S. Lewis, *The Abolition of Man* (Oxford, 1943); A. E. McGrath, *A Scientific Theology: Vol. 1. Nature* (Edinburgh, 2001); J. Moltmann, *God in Creation* (London, 1985); D. J. O'Connor, *Aquinas and Natural Law* (London, 1967);

O. O'Donovan, *Resurrection and Moral Order* (Leicester, 1986); J. Polkinghorne, *The Way the World Is: The Christian Perspective of a Scientist* (London, 1992); idem, *One World* (London, 1986); idem, *Science and Creation* (London, 2006); T. F. Torrance, *Divine and Contingent Order* (Edinburgh, 1998).

O. M. T. O'DONOVAN AND R. J. SONG

NEO-ORTHODOXY

This title is applied to a twentieth-century development in theology, which is 'orthodox' inasmuch as it emphasizes key themes of Reformed theology, but 'neo-', i.e. 'new', inasmuch as it has taken serious account of contemporary cultural and theological developments. It originated with continental theologians: *Barth, *Brunner, *Bultmann and Friedrich *Gogarten, but others have become associated with it such as *Aulén, *Nygren, *Tillich, C. H. *Dodd, *Richardson, J. *Baillie, D. M. *Baillie, Reinhold *Niebuhr and H. Richard *Niebuhr. It was in no sense an organized movement, and precise definitions or boundaries are impossible.

Neo-orthodoxy emerged in reaction against the *liberal Protestantism which had dominated the end of the nineteenth century and the beginning of the twentieth. In particular, it rejected the notion that historical investigation could provide absolute certainty as to the events recorded in *Scripture, upon which scholars had hoped to build secure theology. Further, it renounced the attempt to make man's experience of God a starting place for theology (cf. *Religious experience). The crisis in human *culture epitomized by the First World War precipitated a recognition of the bankruptcy of a theology which had been naively optimistic.

In searching for a new way to do theology, the work of *Kierkegaard, the rediscovery of *Luther, and the novels of the Russian author Fyodor *Dostoevsky became influential. Driven back to the Bible, and spurred on by the need to be able to engage with contemporary social issues, a new method of theology was developed which nevertheless could not ignore the discoveries which had been made by the application of the historical-critical method to Scripture (see *Hermeneutics).

Neo-orthodoxy affirmed the absolute transcendent 'otherness' of God whom man cannot know except God reveal himself. This he has done primarily through Jesus Christ, but also in the events of *salvation-history to which Scripture bears witness. Neo-orthodoxy accepted the results of historical inquiry showing Scripture to be a human, fallible and errant document, because its certainty was thought to lie in the fact that God has chosen to make himself known through it. It is theologically reliable as a means whereby God in Christ may be encountered.

This foundation seemed a more secure basis for theology than questionable historical events or religious experience capable of alternative secular explanations.

On the basis of an encounter with the word of God, incarnate, written and preached, the neo-orthodox theologians affirmed the sinful predicament of humanity redeemed through the *grace of God in Christ alone. Receptive *faith was the only way to enter a saving relationship with God; indeed, only those who believe can know God, or know how to please him. They thus espoused the key *Reformation principles of *sola gratia* and *sola Scriptura*.

While some common theological features characterized those dubbed neo-orthodox, sharp disagreements arose as to how to work these out in a systematic theological way. For example, Tillich and Bultmann were prepared to be influenced by contemporary philosophy more than Barth thought permissible; and Brunner's espousal of general *revelation (cf. *Natural theology) caused a sharp dispute.

Classic critiques of this position suggest: (1) Neo-orthodoxy can offer no justification for basing itself on God's revelation known only by faith (lest faith become sight), since this renders its foundation impervious to *verification or falsification. (2) The emphasis on the transcendent 'otherness' of God led to extreme scepticism about whether talk about God was possible, and indeed whether such a God any longer existed (see *Death-of-God theology). (3) *Pannenberg and others challenged its view of secular history as essentially uncertain, susceptible of differing interpretations and separable from God's activity in the world, for they regarded revelation as history. (4) Neo-orthodoxy can have no reply to those who claim to have encountered God through other religions and would therefore adopt an alternative basis to their theology.

Bibliography

G. C. Berkouwer, *A Half Century of Theology* (Grand Rapids, 1977); J. Livingston, *Modern*

Christian Thought (London, 1971); H. R. Mackintosh, *Types of Modern Theology* (London, 1937); W. Nicholls, *Pelican Guide to Modern Theology, vol. 1: Systematic and Philosophical Theology* (Harmondsworth, 1969); S. Sykes, *The Identity of Christianity* (London, 1984).

C. A. BAXTER

NEO-PLATONISM, see PLATONISM

NESTORIUS (*fl.* 428–*c.* 451)

Nestorius, Patriarch of Constantinople, as an extreme exponent of the *Antiochene *Christology has his name attached to the heresy of the two persons, a divine and a human, existing in juxtaposition in the incarnate Christ. A pupil probably of Theodore of Mopsuestia (*c.* 350–428), Nestorius was a monk and presbyter at Antioch before his elevation to the see of Constantinople by Theodosius II. His Christology, for which he was eventually condemned, was elaborated in relation to the question of the legitimacy of the term *theotokos* ('bearer of God', commonly translated 'mother of God') in reference to the Virgin *Mary. His chaplain at Constantinople, Anastasius, objected to its increasing usage, especially by monks. Nestorious gave him his support and himself declared the designation unscriptural and going 'best with those who deny Christ's true humanity'. Instead Nestorius preferred *anthropotokos* ('bearer of man') or *Christotokos* ('bearer of Christ'). In his structure of Christ's person, Nestorius made a clear-cut distinction between the human and the divine natures (which he seems to have equated with 'persons') in Christ, denying any real organic union between the man Jesus and the indwelling divine *Logos.

The extant fragments of his sermons and his 'Twelve Counter-Anathemas' reiterate, 'Not one nature but two are we constrained to concede to Christ' (*Fragments* 216). The theme is constant: Christ 'is not divided', 'the Son of God is double in his natures'. Throughout, the *theotokos* issue is discussed and the conclusion restated, 'The Virgin bore indeed the Son of God, but since the Son of God is twofold in his nature, she bore the manhood, which is Son because of the Son who is joined thereto' (*Sermons* x).

*Cyril of Alexandria's vehement opposition and his 'Twelve Anathemas against Nestorius' brought about the patriarch's condemnation by the Council of *Ephesus (431). He died in exile somewhere in the East.

Nestorius maintained his orthodoxy, declaring that the Scriptures show Christ to have been truly divine and as such not involved in human suffering and change. The same Scriptures present Christ as having lived a truly human life of growth, temptations and suffering. The only way to understand the relation of these two distinct elements, that of full Godhead and of full manhood, is to acknowledge their separate presence in a 'common *prosōpon*' of union. 'Christ is indivisible in that he is Christ, but he is twofold, in that he is both God and man, he is one in his Sonship, but he is twofold in that which takes and in that which is taken. In the *prosōpon* of the Son he is an individual, but as in the case of two eyes he is separate in the natures of manhood and Godhead' (*Fragments* 297).

Although Nestorius was condemned for heresy by the excessive zeal and vindictiveness of Cyril, the question of his actual unorthodoxy has persisted. The discovery of Nestorius' *The Bazaar of Heracleides* in a Syriac translation in 1910 reopened the issue. Opposing verdicts have been returned. J. F. Bethune-Baker declares that Nestorius was no Nestorian; while F. Nau upholds his condemnation. The *Bazaar* is consistent in its rejection of the designation 'Mother of God', while strongly asserting the full manhood of Christ as necessary for salvation. Cyril's objections are countered one by one and his *monophysitic statements rebutted. Nestorius denies that he admits only a moral union of the two natures, by declaring it to be 'syntactic' and 'voluntary'.

Nestorius' defence of his orthodoxy was accepted by several Eastern bishops who continued to acknowledge his primacy after the Council of Ephesus and united to form a separate Nestorian Church. The Nestorian Christians, characterized by a vigorous missionary zeal, carried the gospel to India and Arabia. In the thirteenth and fourteenth centuries their adherents suffered greatly in the Mogul invasions. Groups of 'Assyrian Christians' survive who consider themselves Nestorians and prohibit the designation 'Mother of God'.

Bibliography

G. R. Driver and L. Hodgson (tr.), *Bazaar* (Oxford, 1925); A. Grillmeier, *Christ in Christian Tradition*, vol. 1: *From the Apostolic Age to Chalcedon* AD 451 (London, ²1975); R. V. Sellers, *Two Ancient Christologies* (London, 1940).

H. D. McDonald

NEW AGE

The term 'New Age' has been used since the mid-1980s to denote the so-called 'alternative' spiritualities that came to prominence in the cultural revolution of the 1960s, and which are now so widely adopted that they may be regarded as the mainstream religious viewpoint in many places. Some identify it with the 'Age of Aquarius', thereby locating this movement within the Western mystical tradition that arose after the French Revolution and whose historical roots can be traced, through Rosicrucians, Freemasons, Cathars (see *Albigenses) and *Gnostics, back to the metaphysical traditions of ancient Babylon and Egypt. On this account, the New Age is primarily an occultic phenomenon, linked to astrological theories which understand history in terms of a series of different dispensations, each one more spiritually sophisticated than its predecessor.

To regard the New Age as exclusively – or even mainly – an occult phenomenon is, however, to miss its major significance on the spiritual landscape of contemporary *culture. It is better understood as part of what is often referred to as *postmodernity, at the heart of which is a dissatisfaction with the Western worldview inherited from the *Enlightenment, and with roots in the abstract analytical philosophy of ancient Greece. By the late twentieth century there was a growing disillusionment with the self-confidence of Western *rationality and its vision of inevitable progress that would improve the human condition. This was fuelled by a new awareness that, far from getting better, the quality of life was actually getting worse, something that was highlighted by the sheer violence and brutality of the twentieth century, exemplified by the enormous loss of life of the First World War, followed by the industrialized genocide of the Nazis (see *Holocaust), the threat of nuclear destruction, and ultimately the realization that the planet itself is under threat, with all that would imply for human safety and survival (see *Ecology). By the beginning of the twenty-first century, it was generally assumed that the vision that inspired our forebears would no longer serve to take us forward into the future, and that far from providing solutions, much of what the West regarded as 'progress' was actually part of the problem.

Faced with this reality, many people retreat into hopelessness and nihilism. Others see it as a spiritual problem, located in a *dualistic worldview that distinguished spirit from matter, body from soul, people from nature, men from women, and Westerners from the rest of the world, and therefore a more holistic outlook will be required to redress the balance. For individuals who think this way, and seek a renewed spiritual vision, the New Age is often where they turn. This is especially true of those whom social scientists call 'the creative class', who are the trendsetters of this generation, which helps to explain the widespread knowledge of these nostrums even among those who reject them.

Some of the perspectives embraced by this emerging *spirituality are indeed new, for example, the way in which 'new science' is perceived as being the antithesis of the old mechanistic – and therefore destructive – science of the past. Other strands, however, are decidedly old, if not ancient. Beginning with an awareness of the deficiencies of *modernity, those who are searching for new ways of being intuitively conclude that anything that is not traditionally Western is bound to offer insight into meaningful ways of being. Consequently, a wide variety of therapies, spiritualities, worldviews, rituals and lifestyles are embraced, with no obvious intrinsic connection apart from the fact that they are not conventional.

In this context, Christianity is often regarded as a major source of the discredited outlook that has created a dysfunctional world, with the matching assumption that it is unlikely to contribute to the creation of a new future. The history of *Christendom provides plenty of evidence to support that opinion. It is significant, however, that in searching for ways of reconnecting with the wisdom of the past, many New Age people look further back, and find the spirituality of medieval mystics or Celtic saints – not to mention the biblical prophets, and indeed Jesus – inspirational in relation to the challenges facing us today. Similar trends can be found within the church, as *missiologists reflect on the heritage of *Constantinianism and seek to reimagine the gospel for a new cultural context. A biblical text that is being adopted as a model for creative theological appreciation of the New Age is the account of St Paul's visit to Athens, a city that was arguably the ancient equivalent of today's New Age spiritual emporium (Acts 17:16–34). The underlying assumption of that story is what today would be called the *missio Dei*, which enabled the apostle to recognize God at work even in unlikely places, and therefore to be able to acknowledge the spirituality of the culture (in this case, the 'unknown god') while also sharing the story of Jesus.

Bibliography

J. Drane, *Do Christians Know How to Be Spiritual: The Rise of New Spirituality and the Mission of the Church* (London, 2005); D. Kemp, *New Age: A Guide* (Edinburgh, 2003); G. Lynch, *New Spirituality* (London, 2007); S. Sutcliffe and M. Bowman, *Beyond New Age: Exploring Alternative Spirituality* (Edinburgh, 2000).

J. DRANE

NEW ENGLAND THEOLOGY

This is a general name for the theological tradition which stretched from Jonathan *Edwards to Edwards Amasa Park (1808–1900). Although the New England theologians all called themselves Calvinists (see *Reformed theology), they did not share entirely similar beliefs. Rather, it was a common approach to theology combining practical morality with philosophical speculation and a common fascination for issues like the freedom of the human will which set the tradition apart.

Jonathan Edwards' efforts to describe and defend the revival in colonial America known as the Great Awakening defined the distinctive concerns of the New England theology. To an unusual degree, Edwards brought together penetrating insight into *religious experience, sophistication in the use of current philosophy, and firm commitment to Calvinistic convictions. His books such as *The Freedom of the Will* (1754) and *Original Sin* (1758) defended divine *sovereignty in *salvation over against contemporary views arguing for autonomous moral action. His works of practical divinity such as *A Treatise on the Religious Affections* (1746) and *The Nature of True Virtue* (1765) provided tests to judge the reality of spiritual experiences. The major emphases of Edwards' theology were the greatness of God, total dependence upon God for salvation, and the intrinsic value of the holy life. By promoting these concerns through careful attention to both practical Christianity and recondite philosophical argumentation, he marked out the path for his followers.

Two of Edwards' students, Joseph Bellamy (1719–90) and Samuel Hopkins (1721–1803), provided a transition to the major New England theologians of the nineteenth century. Bellamy defended at length Edwards' belief that church membership should be reserved for those who made credible profession of saving faith. Hopkins developed Edwards' *ethics into an entire system of what he called 'disinterested benevolence'. But as they adopted their teacher's ideas, they also began subtly to change them. Bellamy gave more emphasis to a governmental view of the *atonement whereby God's sense of right and wrong, rather than his wrath, was the key to understanding the work of Christ. Hopkins came to regard *sin as a quality not so much of human character as of human action.

The New Englanders who came after Bellamy and Hopkins made still further alterations in the Edwardsean legacy, but like them they shared Edwards' twin commitment to *revival and theological precision. Jonathan Edwards, Jr (1745–1801) more firmly set aside the view of God as jealous sovereign. Timothy Dwight (1752–1817), a grandson of Edwards, placed greater stress on the reasonableness of Christian faith and on the natural powers of the human will. Dwight's most influential student, Nathaniel William Taylor (1786–1858), became the most prominent exponent of New England views during the mid-nineteenth century. From his position in the chair of theology at the Yale Divinity School, Taylor reversed the elder Edwards on the will by contending for a natural power of free choice. The last major theologian of this school, E. A. Park, held forth over a long career from Andover Theological Seminary near Boston. He attempted to draw back closer to Edwards, but still held views on natural human capacity and the character of sin which were more characteristic of his century's moral optimism than of Edwards' moral realism.

All of the New England theologians were 'close' reasoners. This strength could sometimes lead to dry preaching, but it could also result in a fruitful conjunction of practical piety and learned theology. In the 1930s when theologians like Joseph Haroutunian (1904–68) and H. Richard *Niebuhr rediscovered this tradition, they concentrated their attention on Edwards rather than his successors. To them, Edwards had seen more clearly the dangers to Christianity of optimistic opinions about human nature. Historians since Haroutunian and Niebuhr have not so much altered their judgments as pointed out the care and intelligence with which Edwards' successors also went about their work.

See also: NEW HAVEN THEOLOGY; WILL.

Bibliography

A. C. Cecil, *The Theological Development of Edwards Amasa Park: Last of the Consistent Calvinists* (Tallahassee, 1983); J. A. Conforti, *Samuel Hopkins and the New Divinity Movement* (Grand Rapids, 1981); F. H. Foster, *A Genetic History of the New England Theology* (Chicago, 1907); J. Haroutunian, *Piety Versus Moralism: The Passing of the New England Theology* (New York, 1932); B. Kuklick, *Churchmen and Philosophers: From Jonathan Edwards to John Dewey* (New Haven, 1985); H. R. Niebuhr, *The Kingdom of God in America* (New York, 1937); D. A. Sweeney and A. C. Guelzo (eds.), *The New England Theology: From Jonathan Edwards to Edwards Amasa Park* (Grand Rapids, 2006); B. B. Warfield, 'Edwards and the New England Theology', in *The Works of Benjamin B. Warfield*, vol. IX: Studies in Theology (New York, 1932).

M. A. NOLL

NEW HAVEN THEOLOGY

New Haven theology was the last important stage of the *New England theology which had begun with the work of Jonathan *Edwards. Its name derived from the Divinity School at Yale College in New Haven, Connecticut. The first professor of theology at that seminary, Nathaniel William Taylor (1786–1858), was also its most influential proponent.

Taylor's background included several divergent aspects of New England's theological history. He grew up in an 'Old Calvinist' community which questioned the rigorous views promoted by Jonathan Edwards. He then attended Yale College, where a grandson of Edwards, Timothy Dwight (1752–1817), was president. Dwight was not only a winsome individual and a solid theologian in his own right; he was also an ardent promoter of revival in the manner of his grandfather. In his later work, Taylor would reflect this early training. He was wary of traditional Calvinistic (or *Augustinian) solutions to problems such as the nature of sinfulness, the innate capacity of the human will, and the character of divine justice, but he was also fervently committed to *revival and societal reform.

Timothy Dwight's theological work helped prepare the way for Taylor. Dwight's concern for revival led him to emphasize the natural human ability to respond to the gospel more heavily than Edwards had. And his efforts to defend the faith reasonably gave it more of a rationalistic tone than had been the case with his famous grandfather.

Taylor, first as pastor of an influential Congregational church in New Haven and then as Yale's professor of theology, engaged in lengthy polemics against both the emerging *Unitarian party and Calvinists who were more conservative than himself. Although Taylor still regarded himself as a successor of Edwards, he went even further than Dwight in modifying Edwards' views, especially in regard to human nature. In his day Taylor was best known for his argument that people always had a 'power to the contrary' when faced with the choice for God. He also contended that human sinfulness arose from sinful acts, not from sinful nature inherited from *Adam. Everyone did sin, Taylor held, but this was not a result of God's predestinating action or the imputation of Adam's guilt.

One of the things that explains Taylor's theological convictions is the fact that he was much impressed with the Scottish philosophy of *common sense. Unlike the Presbyterian Calvinists of *Princeton Seminary in New Jersey, who used the Scottish philosophy mostly as a guide to theological method, Taylor made the Scottish conception of an internal 'moral sense' a critical feature of his *ethics. For Taylor, the intuitive deliverances of this 'moral sense' – for example, that the will had a self-determining power – constituted conclusive theological demonstration.

The New Haven theology became a powerful engine for revival and reform when it was taken up by activists such as Taylor's friend, Lyman

Beecher (1775–1863). Beecher and like-minded revivalists used its principles in evangelizing the western United States and in promoting the moral reform of the country. The New Haven theology traced its origins to a colonial Calvinist, Jonathan Edwards, but it exerted its greatest influence in an America which had largely set aside the earlier Calvinistic convictions of its Puritan ancestors.

See also: REFORMED THEOLOGY.

Bibliography

O. D. Crisp and D. A. Sweeney (eds.), *After Jonathan Edwards: The Courses of the New England Theology* (Oxford, 2012); F. H. Foster, *A Genetic History of the New England Theology* (Chicago, 1907); B. Kuklick, *Churchmen and Philosophers: From Jonathan Edwards to John Dewey* (New Haven, 1985); S. E. Mead, *Nathaniel William Taylor: A Connecticut Liberal* (Chicago, 1942); D. A. Sweeney and A. C. Guelzo (eds.), *The New England Theology: From Jonathan Edwards to Edwards Amasa Park* (Grand Rapids, 2006); N. W. Taylor, *The Moral Government of God* (New York, 1859).

M. A. NOLL

NEW RELIGIONS

The history of religions is the history of new developments, reforms, revivals, novel emphases, and the passing away of older forms of *religion. Hence, new religions have always been part of the flow of religious history, just as the identification of *heresy and the persecution of perceived heretics have accompanied them. It is, of course, always worth bearing in mind that the major world religions were, at one time, 'new', 'alternative' minority religions that experienced persecution until they achieved a position of social and cultural dominance. Hence, it is important to understand that the terms used to identify minority religions tell us just as much, if not more, about those using them as they do about the groups they seek to describe. The term 'cult' (Lat. *cultus*, worship), for example, is nowadays typically used pejoratively to identify a religion as 'other' and, therefore, possibly dangerous or profane in some sense. That is to say, the term 'cult' immediately indicates how a minority religion is perceived by mainstream society.

Regarding terminology, 'new religions' carries essentially the same meaning as a range of other terms, including 'new religious movements', 'fringe religions', 'alternative religions' and 'minority religions'. However, while terminology is often a matter of personal preference, for the reasons outlined above, most scholars interested in objective analysis avoid the popular term 'cult'.

What religions should be considered *new*? This is a complex issue about which there is a lack of consensus. Generally speaking, a religion is considered *new* if it has *emerged* or has *risen to prominence* or *has migrated to a new social context* during the previous century: UFO religions are new because they *emerged* following the first wave of UFO sightings in America in 1947; in the West, a non-Western group, such as the Hare Krishna movement, while belonging to the ancient Hindu bhakti tradition, can be considered new in that it *migrated* to the West with A. C. Bhaktivedanta Prahbupada in the 1970s; organizations such as the Jehovah's Witnesses, the Mormons and Christian Science, all of which were founded in the nineteenth century, can be considered new in that they all *rose to prominence* within the last hundred years. Finally, all 'new religions' are minority traditions, which, to some extent, stand over against mainstream religion and society. In this sense, they can be usefully distiguished from, for example, denominations.

As an area of analysis rooted in sociological methodology, scholars have been keen to construct typologies in order to provide some way of ordering and analysing the growing variety of new religions. No typology, however, is entirely satisfactory. Much early analysis built on the work of the Protestant theologian Ernst *Troeltsch and the sociologist Max *Weber, who distinguished between churches and sects. Churches enjoy social and cultural dominance and allow varying levels of commitment. Sects are smaller authoritarian groups, which typically reject the prevailing culture, challenge civil authorities, and exert significant demands on their members. Sects are also voluntarist, in that membership requires an explicit decision to accept the teachings of the organization. Later sociologists developed an understanding of 'cult', before it acquired its current unhelpful baggage. Rodney Stark and William Sims Bainbridge, for example, disguished between 'audience cults', 'client cults' and 'cult movements', each of which offers 'compensators' or rewards (spiritual and/or material) for the commitment of members. Audience cults lack formal organization and disseminate their ideas through literature and other social media. There is no requirement to join as such, simply an encouragement to follow the published guidance. Client cults offer a service to people for a fee, such as astrological and tarot readings, spiritual therapies, and so on. Cult movements are minority religions which, while similar to sects, are not schismatic (i.e. have not broken away from a larger, parent tradition), but are rather novel religious developments that have emerged within particular social contexts as a result of 'mutation or migration'.

Other scholars, such Gordon Melton and Robert Moore, have sought to distinguish new religions according to a typology of 'families', each of which represents 'a common thought world, life-style and heritage'. The *Latter-Day Saint family* are 'held together by a shared belief in the revelations of Joseph Smith', the founder of Mormonism. The *communal family* is made up of alternative religions that emphasize communal living. The *metaphysical family* draws on ideas developed within the nineteenth-century New Thought movement in America. Essentially, this family denies the reality of evil and emphasizes the power of the mind over matter and personal health. Individuals, it is believed, can determine their own health, wealth and happiness by positive thinking. The *psychic-spiritualist family*, the largest of the families, focuses on psychic phenomena, the paranormal and the occult. Drawing on spiritualism, revelations are, it is believed, communicated through mediums or channels. The *ancient wisdom family* consists of groups (many of which overlap somewhat with the previous family) that believe individuals to have the ability to access powerful, occult knowledge from an ancient and mythic past. Such groups will often emphasize important truths that have been passed down within secret traditions. The *magical family* overlaps somewhat with the previous two families, in that, again, there is an emphasis on ancient wisdom and the paranormal. However, groups within this family seek to harnass natural and *supernatural forces and contact spiritual entities by means of ritual magic. Typical of this family would be the Order of the Golden Dawn, Ordo Templi Orientis, and some Satanist organizations. Melton also includes in this family pagan traditions such as Druidry and Wicca. The *Eastern family* draws inspiration from 'Eastern religions'. Often these groups have a single teacher or guru who will tutor them in certain techniques, disciplines and philosophies. The *Middle Eastern family* consists of those religions, sects and spiritualities that have their roots in faiths, such as Islam, which have their origins in the Middle East. While an approach such as this has its merits, it is problematic in that it fails to account for the enormous variety of new religions, some of which are related to a number of families and some of which cannot easily be identified with any of the families. Furthermore, it seems a little odd to allocate a separate category to the Latter-Day Saint groups.

Another popular way to classify new religions was developed by the sociologist Roy Wallis. He argued that new religions could be classified according to their relationship to society, as 'world-affirming', 'world-renouncing' or 'world-accommodating'. *World-affirming* new religions accept many of the values, goals and aspirations of society, but believe that they can offer a more effective route to attaining such goals and provide a better model of such values. They teach that problems can be solved by adjusting the individual's relationship with the world. The world itself is not flawed. Movements such as Transcendental Meditation and Scientology are typically world-affirming. *World-renouncing* new religions view the world as corrupt and detrimental to spiritual growth. As such, members are required to separate themselves from the influence of the world, including, sometimes, their non-believing families. Such groups typically require total commitment and absolute obedience. Moreover, theologically, because there is often an enormous *dualistic emphasis on the 'sinfulness' of the present age, such groups are often *millenarian, emphasizing an imminent apocalypse. In extreme cases, the renunciation of the world can lead to acts of violence, including mass suicide. This is what happened on 18 November 1978, when 918 members of Jim Jones' (1931–1978) Peoples Temple committed suicide in Jonestown, Guyana, and also on 26 March 1997 when thirty-nine members of the UFO religion Heaven's Gate evacuated their 'earthly containers' (i.e. bodies) to meet the occupants of a spacecraft trailing the Hale-Bopp comet. Finally, located between these two types of new religion are the *world-accommodating* movements which, while not entirely rejecting the world, do claim that humanity has, so to speak, 'backslidden'. Humans are not living as they were intended to live. Hence, there is a need to recommit oneself to the spiritual life and to increase one's devotion. However, while Wallis identifies such movements as Neo-*Pentecostalism and charismatic Christianity as being 'world-accommodating', strictly speaking, such a view applies to most major religious traditions. Hence, while helpful, this last category of Wallis's highlights a problem with the typology, namely that it is rather too broad.

Scholars have also sought to analyse the role of charismatic leadership in new religions, in that most groups are organized around an individual claiming to be 'set apart' in some sense, often as a result of certain exceptional spiritual qualities, such as supernatural gifts or unique access to new knowledge. The influence such individuals seem to have over their followers, particularly when this has led to acts of violence, has resuted in accusations of 'brainwashing'.

The largely unsubstantiated theory of brainwashing in new religions is the result of bemusement about why people would commit themselves to apparently irrational beliefs and engage in extreme behaviours in the service of eccentric leaders. Also, in the 1960s and 1970s, new religions seemed to be targeting young people and turning them against their families and the faiths in which they had been raised. Hence, encouraged by anticult activists, the families and friends of new religious adherents rejected the idea that they had freely converted and became convinced that they had been brainwashed. This was the only theory that made sense of what appeared to be their irrational behaviour. However, following significant research, little evidence has been found to support the brainwashing hypothesis and very few scholars nowadays, outside the anticult movement, would want to defend it. For example, the sociologist Eileen Barker, in her important research over a six-year period into why people joined the Unification Church ('the Moonies'), an organization subjected to numerous brainwashing allegations, found that, not only was there no evidence for it, but the organization's retention rate was extremely low.

See also: CHRISTIANITY AND OTHER RELIGIONS; NEW AGE; SPIRITUALITY.

Bibliography

E. Arweck, *Researching New Religious Movements* (London, 2006); G. Chryssides and B. Zeller (eds.), *The Bloomsbury Companion to New Religious Movements* (London, 2014); P. B. Clarke (ed.), *Encyclopedia of New Religious Movements* (Abingdon, 2006); L. Dawson, *Comprehending Cults: The Sociology of New Religious Movements* (New York, 2005); J. R. Lewis (ed.), *The Oxford Handbook of New Religious Movements* (New York, 2004); *idem*, *Violence and New Religious Movements* (New York, 2011); J. R. Lewis and J. A. Petersen (eds.), *Controversial New Religions* (New York, ²2014); C. Partridge (ed.), *Encyclopedia of New Religions: New Religious Movements, Sects and Alternative Spiritualities* (Oxford, 2004); *idem*, *UFO Religions* (London, 2003); R. Stark and W. S. Bainbridge, 'Of Churches, Sects and Cults: Preliminary Concepts for a Theory of Religious Movements', *Journal for the Scientific Study of Religion* 18 (1979), pp. 117–133; R. Wallis, *The Elementary Forms of the New Religious Life* (London, 1984).

C. PARTRIDGE

NEWBIGIN, JAMES EDWARD LESSLIE (1909–98)

Newbigin, probably the most influential British *mission theologian of the twentieth century, was born in Newcastle-on-Tyne, the son of a ship owner. He came to Christian faith at Cambridge (where he read geography and economics) in the context of the Student Christian Movement (SCM), and after graduation became an SCM Secretary in Scotland, marrying another SCM Secretary, Helen Henderson, a missionary candidate. Convinced of his own missionary vocation, he entered Westminster College, Cambridge, following a course of private study from which he emerged, as he wrote later, 'much more of an evangelical than a liberal'. Missionary service in India under the Church of Scotland began in 1936. Formative experiences included interaction with Hindu scholars in the sacred city of Kanchipuram, sharing study of Hindu and Christian scriptures, responsibility for the Christian education of village Christians (his book *Sin and Salvation* was first written in Tamil) and involvement in the negotiations leading to the formation of the

Church of South India. At the inauguration of that church in 1947 he became a bishop with responsibility for Madurai and Ramnad. The status of the church was controversial in some Anglican circles; Newbigin's theological advocacy brought him to prominence in the International Missionary Council (IMC), and he had much responsibility for the IMC's Willingen Conference of 1947. In 1959 he was seconded by the Church of South India to be General Secretary of the IMC, with a brief to integrate it with the still young *World Council of Churches (WCC). This accomplished (he believed it would encourage mission as integral to the life of the churches), Newbigin became the first director of the WCC's Division of World Mission and Evangelism, also editing the *International Review of Missions*. His secondment over, he returned to India in 1965, being elected Bishop of Madras, though still active in ecumenical affairs. He retired to Britain in 1974. He had always been a prolific writer; this period (despite the demands of teaching at the Selly Oak Colleges and pastoring a run-down city congregation) produced some of his finest work, analysing the post-Christian West, developing a critique of the effect of the *Enlightenment on Western thinking, and directing a movement concerned with 'the Gospel and our *Culture'.

Newbigin, an atheist in youth and theologically liberal as a young Christian, was largely self-directed in theological formation. He read Barth seriously only late in life. His theology was developed in his own awakening to faith, and in dialogue with Hindu *monism and Western *secularism, and shaped by the life of the Indian church. He developed an essentially trinitarian three-dimensional theology of mission, *proclamation* based on the Father's authority, *presence* rooted in the Son's work and *prevenience* arising from the Spirit's preparatory activity. His soteriology, influenced by James *Denney, centred on the *cross as demonstrating both God's love and God's judgment, divinity 'receiving the wages of sin'. The cross also reveals the principalities and powers behind the working of the universe represented in, but not wholly identical with, political figures and institutions. The proclamation of the *gospel has thus not only individual but societal relevance: it is *public* truth. Newbigin's epistemology, always expressed in terms of personal relations, expanded in his last period through the influence of Michael *Polanyi, stressing that knowledge of God, like scientific knowledge, is external to the knower. The church is chosen (the election [see *Predestination] of Israel, and of the church, with corresponding privilege and responsibilities, is another recurrent Newbigin theme) to proclaim and demonstrate that reality.

Bibliography

Selected works: *The Household of God: Lectures on the Nature of the Church* (London, 1953); *A Faith for This One World?* (London, 1961); *The Finality of Christ* (London, 1969); *Foolishness to the Greeks: The Gospel and Western Culture* (London, 1986); *The Gospel in a Pluralist Society* (London, 1989); *An Unfinished Agenda: An Updated Autobiography* (Edinburgh, ²1993); *The Open Secret: Sketches for a Mission Theology* (London, ²1995). P. Weston (ed.), *Lesslie Newbigin, Missionary Theologian: A Reader* (London, 2006) provides a useful selection of writings.

Biography: M. T. B. Laing, *From Crisis to Creation: Lesslie Newbigin and the Reinvention of Mission* (Eugene, 2012); G. Wainwright, *Lesslie Newbigin: A Theological Life* (Oxford, 2000).

A. F. WALLS

NEWMAN, JOHN HENRY (1801–90)

Newman was an Anglican and Roman Catholic theologian and philosopher. Undergoing at fifteen a gradual intellectual conversion which he later described as an experience of falling 'under the influence of a definite creed', Newman wrestled continually with the doctrine of the *church and questions about its *authority and apostolic role as the guardian and teacher of Christian truth, finding much inspiration in the patristic studies he began in his first book, *The Arians of the Fourth Century* (London, 1833).

Newman's *Parochial Sermons* at St Mary's, Oxford, had considerable spiritual impact on hearers and readers, and his contributions to *Tracts for the Times* (London, 1834–41) played a significant role in the formation of the *Anglo-Catholic theology of the Oxford Movement. He supported for a while the theory that the Church of England was the true heir of the early church and a *via media* between the errors of Rome and Protestantism, but gradually changed his mind. Shocked by public and ecclesiastical condemnation of his attempt in

Tract 90 (1841) to reconcile the *Thirty-Nine Articles with official Roman Catholic teaching, Newman retired to nearby Littlemore. Here he lived a semi-monastic life and worked on his *Essay on the Development of Christian Doctrine* (London, 1845), which appeared soon after Newman was received into the Catholic Church in 1845.

The high feelings aroused in both Anglicans and Catholics by Newman's conversion were cooled by the honesty of his spiritual autobiography, *Apologia Pro Vita Sua* (London, 1864), but his independent habits of mind found little recognition in a Catholic Church moving towards the first *Vatican Council and the definition of *papal infallibility (1870). Newman was convinced about papal supremacy and the pope's place as the divinely appointed and visible centre of unity in the church. But he did not equate authority with authoritarianism and absolutism, or confine the church's teaching office to papal pronouncements. However, Newman's suggestions 'On Consulting the Faithful in Matters of Doctrine' (1859) earned him the reputation at Rome of being the most dangerous man in England. His argument for a creative interrelationship between the church's prophetical (teaching), priestly (worshipping) and kingly (ruling) functions – which was outlined in the preface to the third (London, 1877) edition of *Lectures on the Prophetical Office of the Church* (London, 1837), now retitled *The Via Media of the Anglican Church*, vol. 1 – was almost a century too early.

Although Newman was made a cardinal in 1879 and officially cleared of *modernism in 1908 (he was beatified in 2010), his theology was generally neglected or misunderstood until Vatican II (1962–65) focused the whole Roman Catholic Church's attention on many parallel issues. It then became clear that Newman had touched on many questions of enduring importance, even if his own answers had proved to be fragmentary, illustrative rather than explanatory, inspirational rather than definitive. Newman's relevance to recent theology can be seen in two of his works in particular: the *Essay on the Development of Christian Doctrine* (London, 1845, ⁸1891) and *An Essay in Aid of a Grammar of Assent* (London, 1870).

The first of these, although primarily the intellectual cause and justification of Newman's conversion to Catholicism, had the much wider function of pioneering the idea of *development in doctrine, fifteen years before Darwin's *Origin of Species* popularized the concept of evolution. It also, in its final (1878) form, made a significant contribution to the question of defining the *essence of Christianity, a question now often discussed in terms of *contextualization.

The second essay, which contains Newman's analysis of the movement from implicit to explicit belief, may be criticized for assuming that faith is chiefly a matter of believing theological propositions, and for describing 'assent' in terms of an act of will towards a truth that we grasp, rather than a truth that grasps us. Elsewhere, however, in his *Lectures on Justification* (London, 1838), in his sermons and in hymns such as 'Lead, Kindly Light', Newman does emphasize divine grace. But the *Grammar of Assent*'s focus on what Newman called an 'illative sense' or instinctive capacity to make sense of a mass of diverse evidence, determining 'the limit of converging probabilities, and the reasons sufficient for a proof' was an important step towards present recognition of the significance of intuition. *Lonergan has acknowledged his debt to Newman and sought to explain more fully what Newman described. *Wittgenstein's *On Certainty* (Oxford, 1984) and H.-G. Gadamer's *Truth and Method* (ET, London, ²1979) have made major contributions in this area. Many other studies on the place of *imagination in faith and the relationship between faith and *doubt have found inspiration in Newman's *Grammar of Assent*.

Bibliography

Works: Many editions of *Apologia Pro Vita Sua*, *Essay on the Development of Christian Doctrine*, *Idea of a University* (1852), and poem *The Dream of Gerontius* (1865); *On Consulting the Faithful in Matters of Doctrine*, ed. J. Coulson (London, 1961).

Studies: O. Chadwick, *Newman* (Oxford, 1983) and J. M. Cameron, 'John Henry Newman and the Tractarian Movement', in N. Smart *et al.* (eds.), *Nineteenth Century Religious Thought in the West*, vol. II (Cambridge, 1985), pp. 69–109; S. Gilley, *Newman and His Age* (London, 2002); I. Ker, *John Henry Newman: A Biography* (Oxford, 2009); I. Ker and T. Merrigan (eds.), *The Cambridge Companion to John Henry Newman* (Cambridge, 2009); N. Lash, *Newman on Development: The Search for an Explanation in History* (London, 1980); B. Martin, *John Henry Newman* (London, 2000); *idem*,

John Henry Newman: His Life and Work (London, 2001); P. Misner, *Papacy and Development* (Leiden, 1976); T. J. Norris, *Newman and his Theological Method* (Leiden, 1977); F. M. Turner, *John Henry Newman: The Challenge to Evangelical Religion* (New Haven, 2002).

P. N. HILLYER

NEWTON, ISAAC (1642–1727)

Professor of mathematics at Cambridge (from 1699) and president of the Royal Society (1703–27), Newton was the most eminent physicist of his day. His most far-reaching achievement was to formulate the universal law of gravitation to explain the motion of the planets and the behaviour of everything in the solar system. The publication of his theory in *Principia Mathematica* (1687) heralded great advances in science. The universe was seen no longer as an irrational chaos or the place of God's constant and unpredictable intervention. It functioned according to laws that could be calculated and, in principle at least, all its secrets could be discovered by patient and logical inquiry.

Although Newton himself, a deeply religious man like many of his scientific contemporaries, believed he was discovering laws established by the Creator and that it was necessary for God to intervene from time to time to correct irregularities in the solar system that would otherwise occur due to loss of energy, this view did not prevail long. As the eighteenth century progressed, it was increasingly felt that any apparent irregularities would be accounted for in due course by refinements of scientific theory. The 'God of the gaps' would disappear, along with any concept of *miracle or *providence.

While Newton's scientific views were revolutionary, his religious beliefs were unremarkable for the period. He maintained the convention of not linking *science and religion in public debate, and kept his researches into biblical and world chronology, prophecy and alchemy to himself, along with his doubts about the doctrine of the *Trinity. Newton's private papers suggest that he did not see himself as a *Unitarian, as he criticized *Arius as well as *Athanasius for being among the many before and since who had corrupted the plain meaning of Scripture with *metaphysics. Newton does not seem to have been aware that his difficulty in taking the *incarnation seriously was entirely consistent with his understanding of space and time. For if, as Newton held, absolute space and time are attributes of God, God becomes the 'container' of the universe and his incarnation in it becomes unthinkable.

By the beginning of the nineteenth century experiments with magnetism and electricity were calling in question the universal application of Newtonian principles and paving the way for relativity theory and quantum mechanics. It has been argued that the scientific revolution associated with Albert Einstein (1879–1955) has produced a new climate of thought favourable to the Christian understanding of creation as contingent and open, 'finite and unbounded' (*Torrance).

Bibliography

S. L. Jaki, *Science and Creation* (Edinburgh, 1974); F. E. Manuel, *A Portrait of Isaac Newton* (Oxford, 1968); idem, *The Religion of Isaac Newton* (Oxford, 1974); J. Moltmann, *God in Creation* (London, 1985); T. F. Torrance, *Divine and Contingent Order* (Oxford, 1981); idem, *Space, Time and Incarnation* (London, 1969); R. S. Westfall, *Science and Religion in Seventeenth-Century England* (New Haven, 1958); idem, *Isaac Newton* (Cambridge, 2007).

P. N. HILLYER

NICAEA, COUNCIL OF

This council was a meeting of several hundred bishops (traditionally 318), convened by the Emperor *Constantine, which took place in 325. Given the number, the council is often described as the First Ecumenical Council. In fact, the bishops were mainly from the eastern provinces of the Roman Empire (a handful of Western representatives were there, including Hosius, bishop of Cordova), and the principal occasion was the teaching of the presbyter *Arius, although the Council also stated canons on points of ecclesiastical polity.

When teaching in Alexandria, Arius had adopted the idea that the Son was a second, lesser being than God and was created (as in the motto 'once the Son was not'). Arius was disciplined by Alexander, bishop of Alexandria, but fled, finding support from *Eusebius, bishop of Caesarea and Eusebius, bishop of Nicomedia. Constantine therefore had considerable political incentives to have the matter resolved.

The consensus of the council was surprisingly large, given the intense debate preceding it. There were, apparently, only two dissentients from the most important formulation of the council, a creed. This creed is designed to rebut Arianism, asserting the Son is 'begotten not made' (contradicting Arian claims that the Son was a creature), and that he is true God. It anathematizes the ideas that the Son is created or of a different substance from the Father, and asserts that the Son is 'of one/the same substance' as the Father (*homoousios*), possibly because of the interventions of Hosius. This term has ambiguities, conceivably meaning 'of numerically one substance' or 'of the same kind of substance'. Perhaps this contributed to the breadth of consensus, yet *homoousios* was not initially central to later debates over Arianism which followed the council. However, the principal defender of the Nicene settlement, *Athanasius, Alexander's successor at Alexandria, came to focus on *homoousios* as vital, and explained it in terms of 'of numerically one substance', a point taken up by his followers, the Cappadocian Fathers.

The Creed of Nicaea is of first importance. It was crucial in refuting Arianism, but was also the inspiration for the creed of 381 formulated at the Council of *Constantinople (our present 'Nicene' Creed), dealing with the deity of the Spirit, as well as the Christological definition of the Council of *Chalcedon 451, and remains of enormous ecumenical significance in the common trinitarian theology of Protestant, Roman Catholic and Orthodox churches.

See also: CHRISTOLOGY; COUNCILS; CREEDS; TRINITY.

Bibliography

G. Bray, *Creeds, Councils and Christ: How the Early Church Developed Doctrine* (Fearn, 1997); L. D. Davis, *The First Seven Ecumenical Councils (325–787): Their History and Theology* (Wilmington, 1987).

M. OVEY

NICENE CREED, see CREEDS

NICHOLAS OF LYRA (*c.* 1265–1349)

Lyra was the most influential biblical exegete of the late Middle Ages. Born in Normandy, he entered the *Franciscan order before studying theology at the University of Paris and then teaching there. An able Hebraist, he was familiar with Jewish commentaries on the OT. He was appointed provincial of his order in France and later in Burgundy. He became involved in a controversy about the beatific *vision, in reaction against the view of Pope John XXII that the souls of those who die in grace do not enjoy this until after the last judgment. Lyra had a profound concern for the conversion of Jews, as is reflected in both his preaching and writing.

He was the author of numerous works, some of which still remain unpublished. His major achievement lay in his contribution to *hermeneutics as represented by his commentary on the whole Bible in two parts, the first (written 1322–31) expounding the literal sense and the second (1339) the mystical or moral. These *Postillae* established themselves as recognized text books widely cited by other biblical scholars. When published (1471–2) they had the distinction of being the first printed commentary on Scripture and soon ran through several editions. Lyra also produced a tractate comparing the Vulgate OT with the Hebrew text, and two treatises contesting Jewish interpretations of Christ.

Lyra's *Postillae* were so highly regarded as to be adopted as a supplement to the standard *Glossa Ordinaria* and indeed to be set alongside it in some editions. These two commentaries are looked upon as the crown of medieval exegesis. In the prologue to his first volume Lyra declared that the primary function of Scripture is to reveal divine truth; he described it as the sole source of theology. He conceded that Scripture may bear more than one meaning, but insisted nevertheless that the literal sense is basic and that other senses depend upon it. He therefore proposed to avoid the confusing variety of interpretations which had so hampered the *scholastic approach, and to use the historical-grammatical meaning as the overall criterion.

With this principle to guide him, Lyra realized how important it was to recover the authentic biblical text which had been obscured by the carelessness of copyists and the ineptitude of some emendations. He stressed the need to get behind the Vulgate to the Hebrew original as a corrective. Lyra's indebtedness to Rashi (Rabbi Solomon ben Isaac, 1040–1105) has been the subject of much discussion. He was not the first Christian expositor to pay attention to Rashi, but he did so more thoroughly, if cautiously, than others. Latterly his independence grew more apparent.

He displayed a similar attitude to church tradition, claiming that the opinions of the Fathers were not to be accepted as definitive in themselves, but were subject to the final jurisdiction of Scripture. In this, as in his insistence on the primacy of the literal sense, Lyra anticipated *Luther and the other Reformers. Luther, in turn, often referred to him, ranking him among the most useful commentators because his aim was to discover the exact meaning intended by the biblical writers themselves.

Bibliography

P. D. W. Krey and L. Smith (eds.), *Nicholas of Lyra: The Senses of Scripture* (Leiden, 2000); H. Labrosse, 'Biographie de Nicolas de Lyre', *Etudes Franciscaines* 17, 1907, pp. 489–505, 593–608; A. Skevington Wood, 'Nicolas of Lyra', *EQ* 33, 1961, pp. 196–206.

A. S. WOOD

NIEBUHR, H. RICHARD (1894–1962)

Richard Niebuhr, who taught at Yale from 1931 to his death, and was Reinhold *Niebuhr's brother, represented the left wing of American *neo-orthodoxy. He aimed at a holistic and critical Christian worldview.

Niebuhr's most important theological work was *The Meaning of Revelation* (1941), which advocates 'perspectival *relativism' and counsels Christians to adopt a 'confessional' stance. He maintains that any perception of truth is historically and culturally conditioned, but he repudiates *agnosticism. He holds that in revelatory experiences we truly perceive the Absolute, but our perception itself is not absolute. Thus we need not disparage other revelations and faiths in order to affirm our own. *Revelation is primarily personal, not propositional. Meaning, not information, is revealed, and different meanings have been revealed to others. The task for Christians is to view all of life according to the 'pattern' of Jesus Christ.

Niebuhr pursued this task in his famous *Christ and Culture* (1951). He delineates five possible models for relating the two: (1) 'Christ against Culture' rejects the world as evil. Believers must retreat to the elect community, shunning politics, art, the military, and worldly entertainments. Revelation is preferred to 'the whole Reason'. Christ has given the law of the kingdom in the Sermon on the Mount, and his disciples must live as sojourners in a foreign land. (2) 'The Christ of Culture' makes Christ the figurehead of one's *culture, embodying the culture's values yet providing a basis for culture's critique. Revelation is accommodated to reason, the line between God and world is blurred, and Christ's salvation is mere 'moral influence'. (3) 'Christ above Culture' describes a schema like *Thomas Aquinas', wherein cultural institutions are grounded in 'natural law' (see *Law), which is yet limited in scope. Christ's supernatural law is revealed to enable us to reach salvation. Nature is supplemented and fulfilled by grace, both coming from Christ. (4) 'Christ and Culture in Paradox' proposes the world as radically corrupt yet not abandoned by God, who has set up social structures to stem the tide of chaos. We live in this world of necessary evils as sinners justified by grace, resulting in a predominantly private, personal Christian morality. (5) 'Christ the Transformer of Culture' sees the world as fallen, but capable of sanctification, both socially and personally.

In his third major theological work, *Radical Monotheism and Western Culture* (based on lectures given in 1957), Niebuhr calls for an integrative approach to culture, politics, science, religion, etc. We ought to reject '*polytheism' (the fragmented pursuit of many distinct value centres) and 'henotheism' (partisan championing of one finite value centre, e.g. one country, sect or political party, against others) in favour of '*monotheism' (a trusting and loyal adherence to Being-itself, the source and integration point of all penultimate value centres).

Niebuhr's other works all evidence both his integrative vision and his gift for creating helpful typologies.

Bibliography

L. A. Hoedemaker, *The Theology of H. Richard Niebuhr* (Philadelphia, 1970); J. Irish, *The Religious Thought of H. Richard Niebuhr* (Atlanta, 1986); D. F. Ottali, *Meaning and Method in H. Richard Niebuhr's Theology* (Lanham, 1983); P. Ramsey (ed.), *Faith and Ethics: The Theology of H. Richard Niebuhr* (New York, 1957).

R. M. PRICE

NIEBUHR, REINHOLD (1892–1971)

The development of Christian thought in the face of the social and political challenges of the middle years of the twentieth century in Western history was dominated by Reinhold Niebuhr. Senior politicians on both sides of the Atlantic and across the political parties have spoken of their debt to his thinking.

After graduating in 1914 from Yale, Niebuhr took a pastorate in the Presbyterian Church in Detroit. His experience of ministry among Ford workers and in the face of the developing corporate power of the motor industry profoundly transformed his thinking. He abandoned the social ideas of liberal Protestantism which had been dominant in the early years of the century. Its utopianism seemed inadequate in the face of the hard realities of collective power in the contemporary world. After the publication of his first book *Does Civilization Need Religion?* (New York, 1927) he left Detroit to become Professor of Applied Christianity at Union Theological Seminary, New York. He remained there until his retirement. 1932 saw the publication of one of his most influential books, *Moral Man and Immoral Society* (New York). In it he demolished liberal Protestant responses to the social structures of the age, and set about constructing a theology of justice as the true response of biblical faith to the realities of power. In coming to terms with the structural issues of social order and political life, Niebuhr showed a sympathy for aspects of *Marxist analysis. He sometimes described himself as a Christian Marxist. However, the roots of his growing theological work could be found in the developing *neo-orthodoxy represented by *Barth and *Bonhoeffer in Europe. In many ways he stood in the tradition of *Calvin and *Augustine, demanding a full, structured statement of the transcendence and *righteousness of Christ to meet the forces of power which threatened such disastrous consequences for human experience in the middle years of the twentieth century. *The Nature and Destiny of Man* (1941 and 1943, 2 vols.) (his *Gifford Lectures of 1939) is the fullest theological statement he made. It was regarded as a masterpiece of contemporary exposition of fundamental Christian themes.

Niebuhr has been criticized, in his stress on the corporate manifestations of power, for being too pessimistic about human nature and for overstressing the fallenness of humanity. It was for these reasons, so the criticism runs, that he could not see a way to relate the radically Christian understanding of *agapē* (see *Love) directly to social issues. This is why he interposed the notion of justice as the only way Christian faith could relate to the collective issues of the time.

After the Second World War he became increasingly concerned with the effects of the Cold War. His book *Children of Light and Children of Darkness* (London, 1945) attempts to provide a fuller and more substantial justification of democracy than could be provided in liberal thought: 'Man's capacity for justice makes democracy possible; but man's inclination to injustice makes democracy necessary' (p. xiii). He foresaw the weakness of the optimism of liberal notions of democracy and the dangers of the optimism of Marxist ideas of social order. Throughout, he kept a vision of world community and the need, in the face of the Cold War, to find practical realistic understandings and policies to move the world towards it (see *Political theology).

Bibliography

H. Beckley, *Passion for Justice: Retrieving the Legacies of Walter Rauschenbusch, John A. Ryan, and Reinhold Niebuhr* (Louisville, 1992); C. C. Brown, *Niebuhr and His Age: Reinhold Niebuhr's Prophetic Role in the Twentieth Century* (London, 1992); K. Carnahan, *Reinhold Niebuhr and Paul Ramsey: Idealist and Pragmatic Christians on Politics, Philosophy, Religion, and War* (Idaho Falls, 2010); J. P. Diggins, *Why Niebuhr Now?* (Chicago, 2011); G. Fackre, *The Promise of Reinhold Niebuhr*, 3rd edn (Grand Rapids, 2011); R. Harries and S. Platten (eds.), *Reinhold Niebuhr and Contemporary Politics* (Oxford, 2010); D. F. Rice (ed.), *Reinhold Niebuhr Revisited: Engagements with an American Original* (Grand Rapids, 2009); D. F. Rice, *Reinhold Niebuhr and His Circle of Influence* (Cambridge, 2013); H. A. Warren, *Theologians of a New World Order: Reinhold Niebuhr and the Christian Realists, 1920–1948* (Oxford, 1998).

J. W. GLADWIN

NIETZSCHE, FRIEDRICH (1844–1900)

Probably no critic of Christianity had more influence on twentieth-century thought than

Friedrich Nietzsche. Born into a Lutheran parsonage, he began to move towards *atheism during his teenage years. Appointed young to a chair in Classical Philology in Basle, he was pensioned off in his mid-thirties on account of ill health, and the decade until his mental collapse in 1889 was spent in a somewhat nomadic existence in various parts of Western Europe. Nietzsche never recovered his faculties, but during the last years of his life he became a celebrity.

Nietzsche believed that reason (see *Rationalism), whether applied in biblical, philosophical or scientific investigation, had undermined Christianity. In this respect, he was the heir of eighteenth-century thought. However, he maintained that European unbelievers had not absorbed the consequences of 'the *death of God' and that the moral legacy of Christianity had to be extirpated root and branch. If God is dead, moral values have no objective grounding in a metaphysical worldorder and so humans must be creators of value. This takes hardness and strength. Christianity has produced a sickly type of human being – a weak, vengeful, stupid herd-creature, submissive to a God of its own invention. It has pronounced as evil the natural instincts of human life, including self-affirming aggression. Nietzsche is unsparing: 'I call Christianity the *one* great curse, the *one* great intrinsic depravity, the *one* great instinct for revenge for which no expedient is sufficiently poisonous, secret, subterranean, *petty* – I call it the *one* immortal blemish of mankind' (*The Antichrist*).

No single writing of his conveys all Nietzsche's thought, but he regarded *Thus Spoke Zarathustra* as his most important work. Although it is open to various interpretations, it certainly explores the hope that a new kind of human being will emerge from post-Christian civilization, even if the vast majority of people remains contemptibly feeble. The implications of the notions surrounding this idea have been widely debated. Nietzsche has often been held responsible for Nazi ideology, but this has long been disputed. Whatever we conclude, Nietzsche certainly did not believe that the strong should be subject to moral restraint by a standard external to the egoistic impulses of their own nature.

In recent years, much attention has been given to Nietzsche's influence on *postmodernism, and his views on language, truth and perspective have undoubtedly been significant in this respect. Yet while his criticisms of Christianity are connected to these views, he concentrates his attack on the substantive content of Christian teaching on *sin and *redemption. This, above all, is what makes Christianity loathsome. In his way, Nietzsche was here echoing criticisms that went back as far as the earliest Christian centuries. It is sometimes argued that Nietzsche opposed not authentic Christianity but a distorted interpretation of it, but Karl *Barth was far nearer the mark when he said that Nietzsche 'resolutely and passionately and necessarily rejected, not a caricature of the Christian conception of humanity, but in the form of caricature the conception itself' (*CD* III/2, p. 231).

At present, there is no sign of abatement in the interest in Nietzsche and he has fulfilled at least elements of a prophecy which he made in *Ecce Homo*: 'I know my fate. One day there will be associated with my name the recollection of something frightful ... of a decision evoked *against* everything that until then had been believed in, demanded, sanctified.' Opinions differ on the intellectual force of Nietzsche's work, but it is impossible to deny his influence and hard to deny the rhetorical power of much of his writing. His anti-Christianity was not just one component in Nietzsche's thought; it lay at its heart. Nietzsche arguably brings clearly and dramatically into the open the point of collision between Christianity and a central strand in European atheism, even if his beliefs about nature, morality and power are unacceptable to many who share his dislike of Christian religion. How much he is our contemporary emerges in words written in 1882: 'What decides against Christianity now is our taste, not our reasons' (*The Gay Science*).

Bibliography

R. J. Hollingdale, *Nietzsche: The Man and His Philosophy* (Cambridge, 1999); B. Magnus and K. Higgins, *The Cambridge Companion to Nietzsche* (Cambridge, 1996); R. Safranski, *Nietzsche: A Philosophical Biography* (London and New York, 2002); J. P. Stern, *Nietzsche* (London, 1985).

S. N. WILLIAMS

NOMINALISM

Nominalism is the view that only particular instances exist, and that our general terms or names are convenient ways of grouping these particulars, and nothing more. Our use of the language of properties is therefore a mere shorthand way of referring to groups of particulars, the groups formed as a matter of convenience. There is no property 'greenness', but only particular green things. Nominalism is contrasted with *realism, the view that properties exist independently of the mind. Realism has more than one version, however: for example, that a general property exists only if there are instances of it; or that a general property may exist even if there are no instances. If there are universals, existing independently of the mind, and of particular instances, how are they accessed? In some direct fashion, or through the familiar mental process of abstracting general features from particular instances? The view that universals exist independently of the mind is usually associated with Plato and *Platonism, the other view with Aristotle and *Aristotelianism. Conceptualism, the view that properties exist but depend on the mind for their existence, is a mid-way view.

Discussion of 'universals' had its heyday in Christian theology in the Middle Ages, controversies initiated by Roscelin (c. 1050–1125) and *Abelard. *Ockham's nominalism concerned not so much an issue in logic as in *epistemology, the nature of our knowledge of matters of empirical fact, including our knowledge of *revelation. This is important because of Ockham's commitment to the idea of divine absolute power, as well as to a theological agnosticism that seems to be implied by this view. The controversy regarding universals may seem to be arcane, but even arcane issues may signal important issues in theological *metaphysics.

So in fact (as in Ockham's case) a nominalistic attitude can be applied to particular things discernible in human experience as well. Such an attitude would claim that the division of the world into individual things grouped in kinds or classes takes place not in accordance with their essences or natures (since they may not have essences, or such things may be inaccessible), but our language about particular things is developed simply as a matter of convenience. An extreme form of nominalism is conventionalism as regards language and even as regards truth, the view that what we assert and deny is simply a matter of tacit human agreement, and assertions do not correspond (or fail to correspond) to a distinct reality.

Where nominalism is taken to be an expression of voluntarism the nominalist-realist debate engages with issues in Christian theology. Such a voluntarist-nominalist attitude may have different motivations. One sort may be epistemological, the view that reality, and especially divine reality (in whole or in part), may be undisclosed or undisclosable to us (for various reasons, such as human finitude or sin). So even divine revelation may be taken to be not a disclosure of objective or independent truth which it is possible to come to know, but the language of revelation is taken to possess a practical function, such as providing ways of coping with human need, made available by God.

So, on such a view, theological doctrines may simply be a matter of what the Christian community agrees upon as means of furthering these practical teachings found objectively disclosed in divine revelation. For the realist, by contrast, such doctrines express the natures of things, the nature of God, or of man, for example. So essentialism coheres with realism, whereas nominalism fits best with non-essentialism, though the language of essentialism may be retained in a half-way house position such as the idea of a 'nominal essence' employed by John *Locke. For expressivist, non-cognitive views of religious language, the nominalism-realism issue as regards our understanding of God is a non-issue.

Historically, nominalism and a nominalistic attitude have therefore usually been attractive to theological thinkers who are sceptical about the capacity of the human mind to receive a divine revelation, or whose view of the Christian religion is predominately ethical and not metaphysical, and who are prepared to understand ethical ideas in non-realist terms. Christian thinking about God influenced by the theological agnosticism of Immanuel *Kant is invariably nominalistic, as is that influenced by the anti-essentialism of Ludwig *Wittgenstein. Realism at the human level may be coupled with nominalism at the divine level if human ignorance of the divine nature is stressed.

Bibliography

N. Kretzmann, A. Kenny and J. Pinborg (eds.), *The Cambridge History of Later Medieval Philosophy* (Cambridge, 1982).

P. HELM

NON-REALISM

In some ways, non-realism can be viewed as a radical version of earlier outlooks such as the *Death-of-God theology. Influential exponents of various forms of non-realism have included two English Anglican priests, Don Cupitt and Anthony Freeman, and the New Zealand Presbyterian Lloyd Geering, and it is disseminated through the *Sea of Faith network; a parallel movement of thought is Reconstructionist Judaism. Non-realism asserts the impossibility of speaking meaningfully about an objectively existing God or about any supernatural realm or dimension. 'God' is simply a construct giving expression to ultimate human values, an attempt to make sense out of profound dimensions of human experience. (Advocates may draw on *logical positivist denials of meaning to unverifiable statements, such as those about a transcendent God, or on *postmodernist assertions regarding the relationship between language and reality.) Nevertheless, spirituality and worship remain important for such 'Christian humanists' as ways of binding together a community of people and stimulating them to respond to contemporary ethical concerns.

Bibliography
C. Crowder (ed.), *God and Reality: Essays on Christian Non-Realism* (London, 1997); D. Cupitt, *The Long-Legged Fly* (London, 1987); idem, *Taking Leave of God* (new edn, London, 2001); A. Freeman, *God in Us* (London, 1993); L. Geering, *Christianity Without God* (Wellington, 2002); D. Hart, *Faith in Doubt: Non-Realism and Christian Belief* (London, 1993).

T. GRASS

NOVATIAN (*fl*. 249–51)

Novatian was a highly educated priest, theologian and writer, who led the Roman clergy during the vacancy between popes Fabian and Cornelius in 250–51. During this time he corresponded with *Cyprian of Carthage. After the Decian persecution when many believers lapsed from the faith, Novatian opposed any readmission of these people into the church. Because his severe denial of reconciliation was opposed to Catholic practice, Novatian was excommunicated by a Roman synod. He set up a schismatic church, which lasted to the eighth century.

According to *Jerome, Novatian wrote several works, including *On the Passover*, *On the Sabbath*, *On Circumcision*, *On the Priesthood*, *On Prayer*, *On Standing Fast*, *On Jewish Foods*, and many others (some of which are extant), 'especially a great volume on the Trinity'.

In his *On the Trinity*, Novatian's theology advances beyond *Tertullian's earlier thought in maintaining the eternal sonship of Christ (cf. *Christology). Novatian gives a clear explanation of biblical *anthropomorphisms in terms of God's *accommodation to human language. He uses the doctrine of trinitarian circumincession, and anticipates what later theology came to call the 'hypostatic union' of the two natures of Christ in one person, and the 'communication of idioms' between the natures.

Bibliography
Works: ed. G. F. Diercks (*CCL* 4, 1972), tr. R. J. DeSimone (*FC* 67, 1974); *De Trinitate*, ed. W. Y. Fausset (Cambridge, 1909), tr. H. Moore (London, 1919).

D. F. KELLY

NUMINOUS, see OTTO, RUDOLPH

NYGREN, ANDERS (1890–1977)

Anders Nygren served the Swedish Lutheran Church as bishop and professor of theology in Lund. Along with that of Gustav *Aulén, his work represents a Scandinavian parallel to German *dialectical theology in the 1920s and 1930s, especially in its critical attitude towards the then dominant *liberal theology. Nygren, however, was more interested than either *Barth or *Bultmann in the analysis of Christianity as a human religious system, and became one of the few significant Lutheran *philosophers of religion. His method of analysis is usually labelled 'motif-research', in that it attempts to uncover basic distinguishing motifs of Christianity by historical analysis and contrast with other religious systems. His best-known work along these lines is the now classic *Agape and Eros*, which presents a historical account and theological analysis of the contrast between the motif of *agapē* (Gk, unmotivated self-giving love) and that of *erōs* (Gk, love which desires to attain a higher good). The presentation of these motifs offers Nygren the opportunity to discuss basic theological issues in such areas as revelation, atonement and ethics. The book's historical analysis has been the subject of much debate, as has its sharp distinction between *agapē* and *erōs*. Critics suggest that Nygren lacks interest in *love as a human phenomenon, and that his theology shows a general deficiency in the area of the doctrine of creation. Behind the motif analysis there certainly lies a strong theology of grace as a divine accomplishment requiring no human ethical response. Such emphasis on the priority of divine action is also expressed in a brief work on the doctrine of the atonement, *Essence of Christianity*, and is pervasive throughout the *Commentary on Romans*. Nygren's philosophy of religion can be studied in more detail in his *Meaning and Method*.

Bibliography

Works: *Agape and Eros*, 2 vols. (ET, London, 1932–39); *Commentary on Romans* (ET, London, 1952); *Essence of Christianity* (ET, London, 1960); *Meaning and Method* (ET, London, 1972).

Studies: T. Hall, *Anders Nygren* (Waco, 1978); C. W. Kegley (ed.), *The Philosophy and Theology of Anders Nygren* (Carbondale, 1970); G. Wingren, *Theology in Conflict* (ET, Edinburgh, 1958).

J. B. Webster

O'DONOVAN, OLIVER (b. 1945)

Oliver O'Donovan was born and schooled in London, reading classics and theology, and completing doctoral research on Augustine, at Oxford, where he was ordained into the Church of England ministry. Having taught in Toronto, in 1982 O'Donovan returned to Oxford as Regius Professor of Moral and Pastoral Theology and Canon of Christ Church Cathedral, before taking up the Chair of Christian Ethics and Practical Theology at the University of Edinburgh in 2006.

His landmark study *Resurrection and Moral Order* argues against a false polarity between creation and kingdom in Christian *ethics. It explores the objective reality of moral order, known in Christ and secured by his resurrection, wherein the pluriform good of creation is given back to us, as the Holy Spirit subjectively authorizes free action.

O'Donovan's work is based on sustained biblical exegesis in the light of his strong conviction of the *authority of Scripture for theology. This, in turn, directs his attention to history as *salvation-history, ordered towards the eschatological fulfilment of creation and human sociality, fuelled in particular by a recurrent engagement with the book of Revelation and his interpretation of Augustine.

From a sustained and careful reading of the tradition of Christian political thought emerges the two-part project of *The Desire of the Nations* and *The Ways of Judgment* which elaborates a contemporary Christian political conceptuality. The fullness of the Christ-event in advent, passion, restoration and exaltation, recapitulated in the life of the church, is the key to understanding God's rule, and the secular task of government as judgment in the wake of the gospel. One notable achievement of this project is the sustained emphasis on mission as the proper motor of *political theology. Moral and political theology, for O'Donovan, are apologetic disciplines for Christian public engagement.

With a strong vocational commitment to preaching, O'Donovan's churchmanship is further evidenced in contributions to Anglican, evangelical and ecumenical discussions.

Bibliography

Works: *Resurrection and Moral Order* (Leicester and Grand Rapids, [2]1994 [1986]); *The Desire of the Nations* (Cambridge and New York, 1995); *The Ways of Judgment* (Grand Rapids and Cambridge, 2005).

A. J. Draycott

OBEDIENCE OF CHRIST

This is a biblical concept of particular importance in *Reformed theology and piety.

Filial obedience

The NT clearly depicts Jesus' whole life as one of perfect, sinless and conscious obedience to God as his Father (e.g. 1 John 2:2; 3:5; 1 Pet. 2:22), whose will for his life was learned through prayerful meditation on OT Scripture (Matt. 3:15; Luke 22:37; John 8:29, 46). Such obedience was based on trust and love of the Father, and it involved a real experience of temptation by Satan, acting both directly and through others, to try to make him doubt the Father's goodness and deviate from his plan for his life (Matt. 4:1–11; 16:22–23; 26:53–54). Such temptation was overcome by the spiritual weapons of prayer, the word of God and fasting, in a genuinely human life of faith. John emphasizes that Christ's ministry and teaching were all based on obedience to what his Father showed him and gave him to do and say. A military background enabled a Roman centurion to perceive that such submission to God was the source of Jesus' authority over evil and disease (Matt. 8:8–10; John 5:19–20; 7:16).

While Christ's obedience also included submitting himself to other God-given human authorities, even when imperfectly exercised (Mark 14:61–62; Luke 2:51; John 19:11; 1 Pet. 2:23), his obedience to God involved a resolute adherence to the Father's specific will in every situation, sometimes rejecting another morally allowable course in order to see that perfect will done in his life and death.

Representative obedience

As man and as Messiah, Jesus learned the meaning and cost of obedience in experience through what he suffered (Mark 8:31; Heb. 5:7–9), and became obedient even to death on a cross (Phil. 2:5–8). This was a conscious and voluntary act of obedience right up to the point of death itself (John 10:17–18; 19:30). Since Satan and evil had no place in his righteous life, death could not in fact hold on to him (John 14:30; 16:10–11; Acts 2:24; Rom. 1:4). Paul contrasts the obedience of Jesus with the disobedience of *Adam, seeing the two as representative figures acting on behalf of the old and the new humanity. Christ's obedience right to the cross won *justification and eternal life for the many people on whose behalf he lived and died (Rom. 5:18–19; cf. also 1 Cor. 15:20–22, 45–49).

Christ's obedience as understood by the Christian church

Jesus' obedience and sinless life have been drawn upon in at least four ways by the church down the years: (1) As the example of perfect obedience by a Son of the Father, his life gives inspiration to all God's children to live obedient lives (1 Pet. 2:18ff.); (2) The one who was tempted and did not yield can help us when we are tempted (Heb. 2:18; 4:14–16); (3) Only his righteous life could be laid down on behalf of sinners as an effective atoning sacrifice (2 Cor. 5:21; Heb. 7:26–27; 1 Pet. 3:18; 1 John 2:2); (4) The *Holy Spirit of Christ dwells within Christians to reproduce Christ's life and image in them (Rom. 8:9–30). Calvin rightly states that we are saved by 'the whole course of his obedience' (*Institutes* II.xvi.5). In keeping with this, Reformed theologians have often distinguished between Christ's active obedience (his life of filial obedience to the Father) and his passive obedience (his suffering of the Father's judgment against covenant-breakers). These terms were not intended to denote that Christ was at any point inactive ('passive') in his obedience. Passive is used here in the Latinate sense (*patior*: suffer, submit). Nonetheless, the fullness of his obedience is now commonly clarified in terms of his preceptive and penal obedience.

Bibliography

G. C. Berkouwer, *The Person of Christ* (Grand Rapids, 1954); L. W. Grensted, *The Person of Christ* (London, 1934); D. Guthrie, *New Testament Theology* (Leicester, 1981); J. Murray, *Collected Writings*, vol. 2 (Edinburgh, 1977), pp. 151–157; B. B. Warfield, *The Person and Work of Christ* (Philadelphia, 1950).

J. P. BAKER

OCHINO, BERNARDINO (c. 1487–1564)

An Italian Reformer, popular evangelist and author, Ochino was born in Siena, joined the *Franciscans at the age of eighteen and studied medicine at Perugia. Transferring to the newly founded Capuchins in 1534, he was elected Vicar-General of the Order in 1538 and 1541.

His preaching was directly inspired by the Gospels and won rapturous response throughout Italy, particularly delighting Charles V at Naples in 1536. Many turned to Christ. But his 'Lutheran' doctrine began to arouse suspicion, and in July 1542 he was summoned to appear before the recently reconstituted Inquisition in Rome. Instead he quit Italy for Geneva, his flight causing a national sensation.

In 1547 Thomas *Cranmer invited him to England, and he spent six years in London; here he wrote his most ingenious work, *Tragoedie* (1549), which influenced Milton. He pastored exiled Italian communities in Germany and Switzerland, but his questing and questioning mind made him an uncomfortable bedfellow. No orthodoxy satisfied him, and he was suspected of anti-trinitarianism. A stream of published sermons and speculative dialogues – such as *Labyrinthi* (1561) – culminated in *Dialogi XXX* (1563), which included the scandalous *Dialogus de Polygamia*.

Banished from *Bullinger's Zurich, denied asylum in Nuremberg, he sought refuge in Poland, was again banished and died an outcast from Christendom in Moravia.

Bibliography

R. H. Bainton, *Bernardino Ochino, esule e riformatore senese del cinque cento, 1487–1563* (Florence, 1940); C. Benrath, *Bernardino Ochino of Siena* (London, 1876); P. M. J. McNair (ed.), *Patterns of Perfection: Seven Sermons Preached in Patria by Bernadino Ochino, 1487–1564* (Cambridge, 1999); M. Taplin, *The Italian Reformers and the Zurich Church, c. 1540–1620* (Aldershot, 2003).

P. M. J. McNair

ODEN, THOMAS CLARK (b. 1931)

Thomas Oden, a United Methodist minister and theologian, was born on 21 October, 1931, in Altus, Oklahoma. He retired from Drew University in 2004, where he remains as Emeritus Professor. His early theological career was characterized by liberalism, with a strong emphasis on humanistic psychology. Around 1965 Oden returned to an evangelical orthodoxy, in whose revitalizing he has been actively involved ever since. He is best known for encouraging a return to an ecumenical 'paleo-orthodoxy', by which he means an understanding of the essential nature of Christianity rooted in the teachings and exegesis of the Church Fathers from the first five centuries (see *Patristic theology). Oden argues that this corpus constitutes a consensual tradition leading to the maxim that 'in the worldwide community of believers every care should be taken to hold fast to what has been believed everywhere, always, and by all'. According to Oden, the recovery of the patristic tradition is not 'a simplistic, sentimental return to premodern methods', but 'a rigorous, painstaking rebuilding from the crash of modernity using treasures old and new for moral formation and spiritual reconstruction'. As part of this project, Oden authored numerous theological books, including a massive three-volume systematic theology. He is also the general editor of the *Ancient Christian Commentary on Scripture*.

Bibliography

Works: *The Care of Souls in the Classic Tradition* (Philadelphia, 1984); *The Rebirth of Orthodoxy: Signs of Life in Christianity* (New York, 2003); *Systematic Theology*, 3 vols. (Peabody, 2006).

Studies: A. G. Padgett, 'Methodist Theology Today: A Review Essay of Thomas C. Oden, Systematic Theology', *Evangelical Quarterly* 64, 1992, pp. 245–250; K. Tanner and C. A. Hall (eds.), *Ancient and Postmodern Christianity: Paleo-orthodoxy in the 21st Century: Essays in Honor of Thomas C. Oden* (Downers Grove, 2002); R. C. Wood, 'Rediscovering the Radical Christian Consensus: The Theology of Thomas Oden', *Perspectives in Religious Studies* 17, 1990, pp. 253–260.

A. Vidu

OECOLAMPADIUS, JOHN (1482–1531)

Born in Weinsberg in Württemberg, Germany, Oecolampadius attended Heidelberg University and was soon in touch with a *humanist circle which included Jacob Wimpfeling (1450–1528), Johannes Reuchlin (1455–1522), *Melanchthon and *Bucer. After a period as a tutor to the children of Landgrave Philip I of the Palatinate, he became a preacher at Weinsberg (1510). Further study at Tübingen University led to a mastery of Greek, Latin and Hebrew and thence to work with *Erasmus on his NT (1515). In 1518 he was awarded his doctorate at Basel. He rapidly became a considerable patristic scholar, particularly interested in the Greek Fathers. In 1518 he was appointed penitentiary in the Münster at Basel. His studies continued and for a short time in 1521 he entered a Brigittines Monastery at Altomünster. He was, however, moving in a Reformed direction and soon left. In 1522 he returned to Basel and published the first of his translations of Chrysostom.

Already under the considerable influence of *Zwingli, he soon became the leading figure of the Reformed cause in Basel. In 1525 he was made professor of theology and, in typical Swiss fashion, furthered the Reformation cause by formal disputations. In Basel he was successful; in Catholic Baden (1526), faced by John Eck (1486–1543), much less so, but later in Berne (1528), and with the help of Bucer, Zwingli and Wolfgang Capito (1478–1541), he was part of the process which won Berne to the Reformation cause.

In the following year, under his influence, Basel committed itself to the Reformation. He made proposals for setting up a body composed of pastors, town councillors and church elders which sought to avoid the dependence for church *discipline upon the council, which characterized Zurich. These were a foretaste of later developments by Bucer and *Calvin.

Oecolampadius' theology developed towards a view of Christ's spiritual presence in the Eucharist. Though he followed Zwingli at this point, he had an independent mind and cited patristic sources to support his convictions. He was involved in the Colloquy of Marburg (1529) (see *Luther; *Eucharist). Like Zwingli, he found himself troubled by the *Anabaptists and in 1529 disputed with them. They were driven from Basel.

He died shortly after the Battle of Kappel (1531). A scholarly, retiring man, he was a significant *Reformation figure in Switzerland. He had continued to work in close collaboration with Erasmus in translating Chrysostom. His role in keeping Erasmian and patristic learning within the early Reformation circle is important.

Bibliography

D. Poythress, *Reformer of Basel: The Life, Thought and Influence of Johannes Oecolampadius* (Grand Rapids, 2011); G. Rupp, *Patterns of Reformation* (London, 1969).

C. P. WILLIAMS

OFFICES OF CHRIST

Historical discussion

The Gospels record *Jesus acknowledging that he was the *Christ, the anointed one (Heb. *messiah*), long expected by Israel. The name 'Christ' became an official title for him after his resurrection. Behind this lay the *anointing with oil of priests and kings in the OT, and the declaration that the Messiah was to be anointed to office (Isa. 61:1–3). While the church reflected on Christ as a royal priest from its earliest days, it was *Calvin who recognized that sometimes the prophets too were anointed. In his *Institutes* he considers Christ as mediator between God and man in terms of his being prophet, priest, and king. This pattern became commonplace in *Reformed theology, *The Westminster Larger Catechism* (36–45) of 1648 adopting the threefold office to unfold the work of Christ. It has been repeated in standard systematic theologies up to the present. It is not so evident in other traditions. The *Catechism of the Catholic Church* (pp. 1544–1545) refers only cursorily and in passing to Christ as priest. For its part, Orthodoxy is more interested in the incarnation and deification than the work of Christ, let alone Christ's offices (see R. Letham, *Through Western Eyes: Eastern Orthodoxy; A Reformed Perspective*, Tain, 2007, pp. 243–268).

Biblical background

The offices of Christ are based on the pattern of Israel in the OT, in line with the Jewish roots of the NT. The Christ was the anointed one, long expected as the one who would come to deliver his people. Jesus was anointed by the Holy Spirit at the Jordan at his installation in office (Matt. 3:13–17). This approach to the work of Christ follows the pattern of the three great functions or offices in Israel. Priests in Israel, who were to administer the *sacrificial system and to represent the people before Yahweh, were taken from the tribe of Levi, the high priest from the sons of Aaron. Kings, after Saul, were descendants of David, from the tribe of Judah. There was a clear separation of the two – occupants of one office could not function in the other. Prophets, however, were called directly by Yahweh as his mouthpieces. The striking point about Jesus Christ is his fulfilling and occupying all three offices.

Criticisms

The idea of the threefold office has come in for much criticism. Wolfhart Pannenberg argued in *Jesus – God and Man* that only the prophetic office could possibly be said to characterize Jesus' earthly ministry. Indeed, there is no explicit or clear-cut evidence that Jesus claimed any of these offices for himself. He could not be a priest in Israel, since priests were taken exclusively from the tribe of Levi and Jesus belonged to Judah. Jesus himself warned against the popular demand to make him king, since his *kingdom was of a different kind, not of this world (John 18:36–37). Moreover, he set himself apart from the OT prophets, for he was the Son of the living God (Matt. 16:13–16). Besides, there is an inherent difficulty in considering Christ as a prophet. Prophets spoke the word of God, whereas Jesus is identified as *the* Word of God (John 1:1–18). They authenticated their message with 'thus says the Lord'. Jesus spoke on his own authority, declaring 'I say unto you'. Therefore he is greater than a prophet.

On the other hand, it is impossible for us to understand Jesus' identity and work outside the struggles Yahweh had with Israel down the years. Israel was heir to a long process in which God had revealed himself and his saving purposes. Torrance has argued in *The Mediation of Christ* that this is itself revelatory; the national structures of Israel are reflective of God's self-revelation. Attempts to set this Jewish background aside and construct some other alternative from outside the context of Israel raise the inevitable question of anti-Semitism.

Jesus may not have claimed these offices explicitly, but the overall context points to his fulfilling everything they represented. Just as the prophets did, Jesus spoke the word of God; in his case, the biblical authors claim he was equal to, and identical with, God. His own word was the standard of authority. Behind this was the eschatological expectation of a prophet like Moses, whose word was to be heeded (Deut. 18:15–19). In Hebrews, his *death and intercession is seen in priestly terms throughout. The epistles portray the risen Christ as King over the church and the world as the Lord (Col. 1:15–20; Heb. 1:1).

The criticisms of the threefold office of Christ have largely stemmed from the twentieth century predilection for a Christology from below, in which the humanity of Christ is in the foreground. The weaknesses of this approach were exposed by Colin Gunton (in *Yesterday and Today: A Study of Continuities in Christology*, London, 1997); the result was a Christ who was not quite God and not quite man, who could hardly be held to have identified with us. In recent decades, growing interest in patristics, both theological and exegetical, has led to a re-appropriation of the classic *Christology of Athanasius and Cyril. In answer to the question of *who* Jesus Christ is, these Fathers identified him as the eternal Son who has assumed human nature into permanent union. Such a retrieval undermines the force of much of the above criticisms.

The mutual interconnection of the three offices in Christ

The work of Christ is not portioned into a series of isolated actions. His ministry, life, death, resurrection, ascension and heavenly session is one integral work 'for us and our salvation'. His activity in all three offices is interconnected and mutually interpreting.

Prophetic office

As the supreme prophet, Jesus declares the truth of God, and reveals God, since he is one with the Father (John 14:1–11). He declares, represents and realizes the justice of God in his priestly work of atonement, while in his resurrection he makes known his kingly rule. Karl Barth focused much of his theology on Christ the living Word of *revelation.

Priestly office

As our great high priest, Christ represents his people in making *atonement, offering intercession (his presence as a man at the right hand of the Father), and in benediction (his final act in his ascension betokening his continued ministry in and to the church). This raises the question of the extent of the human race he represents and incorporates. The fate of the unevangelized has loomed large in recent discussion. Karl Rahner suggested a class of 'anonymous Christians', the evangelical Clark Pinnock has proposed that God's mercy is wider than hitherto believed, while the traditional view that – apart from such instances as the case of elect infants dying in infancy – conscious faith in Christ is necessary for *salvation continues to find advocacy. Additionally, the penal *substitutionary doctrine of the atonement has come under attack at various times. Hugo *Grotius adopted what Oliver Crisp calls penal non-substitution, in his exposition of God's upholding his moral government of the universe, while Tom Smail wishes to maintain substitution but without the penal element. That Christ underwent punishment for our sins is considered barbaric. However, its advocates maintain that it demonstrates the trinitarian love of God; the Son willingly and freely offering himself in place of his people. It is the trinitarian context, and the threefold office, that provides the context to understand the atonement.

Kingly office

At his *resurrection, Christ was exalted to the right hand of the Father, to rule all things until his enemies are all subjugated (Matt. 28:18–20; 1 Cor. 15:20–28). He reigns in effective priestly intercession and sent the Holy Spirit to reveal the truth to his apostles (John 16:12–15). However, focus on Christ's kingship has seen a range of triumphalist ideas develop. The prosperity gospel, and some in the theonomic movement, have focused on the material benefits of Christ's present reign, with suffering, poverty, human atrocities and injustice largely unaddressed (see *Poverty and wealth). It is more generally recognized that Christ's reign is inaugurated but fully consummated only eschatologically.

Bibliography

K. Barth, *CD* I.2, 83–87; II.1, 152ff., 397ff.; II.2, 408ff., 443ff.; III.2, 61f.; IV.1, 137ff., 275.; IV.2, 155ff., 291ff., 518f.; H. Bavinck, *Reformed Dogmatics*, vol. 3 (ET, Grand Rapids, 2006); J. Calvin, *Institutes of the Christian Religion* 2:12–17 (ET, London and Philadelphia, 1960); R. Letham, *The Work of Christ* (Leicester and Downers Grove, 1993); W. Pannenberg, *Jesus – God and Man* (ET, Philadelphia, 1968); T. F. Torrance, *The Mediation of Christ* (Grand Rapids, 1983).

R. W. A. LETHAM

OLDHAM, JOSEPH HOULDSWORTH (1874–1969)

Oldham was a Scottish layperson who was led to Christ by D. L. Moody at Oxford and served as secretary of the British Student Volunteer Missionary union and the Inter-Varsity Christian Union. After three years with the YMCA in India and further studies at Edinburgh he worked as Mission Study Secretary for the Free Church of Scotland. He was recruited by John R. Mott as secretary of the 1910 Edinburgh International Missionary Conference, subsequently becoming secretary of its Continuation Committee and founding editor of the *International Review of Missions* (1912). After the First World War Oldham designed and became secretary of the International Missionary Council and for the next twenty years was the single most influential figure on the international *ecumenical stage, his major interests including Africa, missions and education, *race relations and (in the 1930s) the growing totalitarian menace in Europe. In the 1920s he played a key role in opposing forced labour in Kenya and in establishing in British colonial policy the principle of the 'paramountcy' of the interests of Africans in East and Central Africa, and in persuading the government to devote more study and resources to African needs as a whole, especially education.

Oldham was study organizer of the Oxford Conference on Church, Community and State (1937), and the constitution of the *World Council of Churches laid down in 1938 was largely his design. At the same time he was critical of the tendency of large-scale institutions to become self-serving bureaucracies, and much of his energy from 1938 was devoted to small-scale groups bringing together 'the best minds' to work on social issues in light of Christian faith. Particularly important here were 'The Moot' (1938–47), which included figures as diverse as T. S. Eliot, Karl Mannheim and John *Baillie, and the Christian Frontier Council founded by Oldham in 1942 in order to bridge the growing gulf between the churches and secular people wrestling ethically with social issues. A prolific writer, his most substantial work was the pioneering *Christianity and the Race Problem* (1924). No less significantly, his little *Devotional Diary* (1925) enjoyed huge popularity for nearly thirty years, while his weekly bulletin *The Christian News-Letter* was widely influential in stimulating popular discussion of vital topics throughout the Second World War and for several years afterwards.

Bibliography

K. Clements, *Faith on the Frontier: A Life of J. H. Oldham* (Edinburgh and Geneva, 1999).

K. CLEMENTS

OLEVIANUS, CASPAR (1536–87)

Caspar Olevianus (Olevian) was a Reformed theologian in Heidelberg and Herborn. Raised in the Roman Church, he converted to the Reformed faith in university. After briefly practising law, he studied theology in Geneva with John *Calvin and Theodore *Beza and in Zürich with Heinrich *Bullinger. Returning to Trier, he attempted to begin a Calvinist congregation but was jailed by the archbishop. He was rescued and given a position in Heidelberg by Frederick III, the Elector Palatinate. From 1561 until 1576 he served first in the university, then as pastor of Holy Spirit Church and as a teacher in the seminary. Upon Frederick's death in 1576, he and the Reformed theologians were expelled. In Herborn he founded and led, until his death in 1587, an influential Reformed seminary.

Olevianus is best known for his collaboration with Zacharias *Ursinus in the formation of the *Heidelberg Catechism (1563), but he also wrote an important early account of Reformed federal (*covenant) theology, *De substantia foederis gratuiti inter Deum et electos* (1585). He wrote three popular summaries of the faith and several biblical commentaries, the most significant of which, on Romans, was published in 1579.

See also: REFORMED THEOLOGY.

Bibliography

Works: *A Firm Foundation. An Aid to Interpreting the Heidelberg Catechism*, tr. L. D. Bierma in R. A. Muller (ed.), *Texts and Studies in Reformation and Post-Reformation Thought* (Grand Rapids, 1995); *Exposition of the Symbole of the Apostles*, tr. J. Fielde (London, 1581); *Der Gnadenbund Gottes 1590: Faksimile-Edition Mit Einem Kommentar*, eds. F. Gunther, J. F. G. Goeters, W. Holtmann and K. Müller (Köln, 1994); *Monatshefte für Evangelische Kirchengeschichte des Rheinlands* 38–39 (1988–89).

Studies: L. D. Bierma, *German Calvinism in the Confessional Age* (Grand Rapids, 1997); R. S. Clark, *Caspar Olevian and the Substance of the Covenant: The Double Benefit of Christ*, in D. F. Wright (ed.), *Rutherford Studies in Historical Theology* (Edinburgh, 2005).

R. S. CLARK

OMAN, JOHN WOOD (1860–1939)

John Oman was born in Orkney and educated at Edinburgh and Heidelberg. He was Presbyterian minister at Alnwick, Northumberland, from 1889 to 1907 before becoming professor at, and principal of, Westminster College, Cambridge. Deeply concerned about the crisis for Christianity brought about by the *Enlightenment, he developed an interest in *Schleiermacher and in the inner authority of truth which verifies and helps elucidate all other experiences. But this inner illumination is not just absoluteness of value; it attaches itself to that objective reality we call the *supernatural. Oman's 'sacredly discerned' seems not unlike R. *Otto's 'idea of the holy', though Oman criticized the latter, probably unfairly. Oman believed strongly in man's progress to ultimate freedom and exalted the individual religious *conscience at the expense of all external *authority, including the *creeds and the *church. In his thinking the *kingdom of God has a similar primacy: his doctrine of the church and ministry is thus rather impoverished. In all, he wrote thirteen books, notably *The Natural and the Supernatural* (1931), but the Germanic cast of his thought does not make for easy reading. Oman's pupil, H. H. Farmer (1892–1981), went on to stress the personality of the supernatural, feeling that his teacher had not done justice to this aspect of deity.

Bibliography

G. Alexander and H. H. Farmer, in J. Oman, *Honest Religion* (Cambridge, 1941), pp. xv–xxxii (memoirs); F. G. Healey, *Religion and Reality: The Theology of John Oman* (Edinburgh, 1965); Y. Woodfin, *John Wood Oman (1860–1939): A Critical Study of His Contribution to Theology* (unpublished dissertation, New College, Edinburgh, 1962).

I. SELLERS

ONTOLOGY

Although the term ontology (literally, the study of being) was first used in scholarly writing in the early seventeenth century, ontological considerations begin in Greek thought. They underlie *Plato's (fourth century BC) description of reality in the *Republic*, where he differentiates the realm of appearances from the intelligible world of mathematical objects and Forms. *Aristotle (fourth century BC) in his *Metaphysics* and later *Thomas Aquinas in the thirteenth century systematically studied being by investigating substances in terms of their essences. In the twentieth century, Martin *Heidegger noted that 'being' must be understood through the being of the enquirer, *Dasein* or human beings, whose being-in-the-world he explores. In a later work, Heidegger continues to explore being by asking what he takes to be the most fundamental question, 'Why is there something rather than nothing?'

In studying what it is to exist, the general features that are characteristic of all beings, and being's most fundamental categories and the relationships that hold between them, ontology raises fundamental questions about reality: What is being? What is it to be or exist? What are the primary categories of being? What laws govern these categories? What kind of being, for example, do universals or numbers have? What gives an existent both its identity and its uniqueness? Ontology thus addresses the objective side of our experience, in contrast to but in conjunction with *epistemology, which addresses how the subject knows that reality.

Bibliography

Aristotle, *Metaphysics*, in R. McKeon (ed.), *The Basic Works of Aristotle* (New York, 2001); M. Heidegger, *An Introduction to Metaphysics* (Garden City, 1961); idem, *Being and Time* (Albany, 1996); Thomas Aquinas, *On Being and Essence* (Notre Dame, 1965).

B. R. REICHENBACH

OPEN THEISM/OPENNESS THEOLOGY

These terms have been given to a type of theology which has emerged in evangelical circles to question some of the fundamental assumptions of classical Christian *theism. Openness theology asserts that the traditional doctrine of *God is 'closed', mainly because of its belief that God is by nature both immutable and impassible (see *Impassibility of God). Open theists claim that these statements derive from Hellenistic philosophy and not from the Bible, which is supposed to reveal a God who is deeply affected by human activity and whose nature can change to respond to this if he wishes it to do so. They quote passages which refer to God 'repenting' of previous threats or promises because of subsequent human action, as evidence for this, often taking quite literally expressions which theologians have traditionally interpreted in a more metaphorical sense (see *Accommodation). They are particularly opposed to traditional conceptions of divine 'foreknowledge', and argument over the true meaning of this has characterized much of the recent debate in North American circles. The principal motivation of open theists is pastoral, and springs from a perceived need to preach a God who can relate to suffering human beings in a meaningful way. Open theists assume that a God who cannot change or experience suffering cannot understand the realities of human life and therefore cannot relate to us. They claim that the biblical picture of a 'suffering God', revealed most fully on the *cross of Jesus Christ, contradicts this essentially philosophical view and offers us a God who can be known and understood as one who genuinely cares about our experiences of life.

Open theism clearly owes much to the theology of Jürgen *Moltmann who has promoted the idea of a suffering God in order to account for the horrors of Auschwitz and the like. There is also some indebtedness to the *process theology of Charles Hartshorne (1897–2000), according to which God grows and develops along with his creation. At the same time, open theism is distinguished from those approaches by its typically *evangelical insistence on a high doctrine of *Scripture. Open theists contend that their view is the right interpretation of the Bible, which was obscured by a false philosophical direction taken by classical theology which the Reformers and their successors were unwilling or unable to overcome. However much of their approach may have been influenced by recent social and political trends, they insist that they are doing no more than recover what God originally revealed of himself to his people. In this sense, open theists claim to be deeply conservative and orthodox, a stance which sets them apart from men like Moltmann and Hartshorne.

Openness theology has made some impact within evangelical circles but has largely been ignored outside them, and it is unclear whether it will have much of a future. Its critics, who are almost all evangelicals, believe that 'openness' is merely a code word for 'liberalism', a term which evangelicals generally want to avoid because of its associations with a theology which ignores or compromises the supreme authority of Scripture. They argue that although open theists have a high regard for the authority of Scripture, in practice they undermine this by an inadequate hermeneutic.

The main objection to open theism is that it is superficial. Its critics do not deny that God is involved in human affairs and they insist that believers have a genuine relationship with him which is rooted and grounded in his love for us. As they see it, the problem with the open theist approach is that it fails to distinguish adequately between the persons of the Trinity on the one hand, and the nature of God on the other. In his nature, God can neither change nor suffer because he is both perfect and sovereign. For him to change would mean either that he was not perfect to begin with or else that he has now abandoned his earlier perfection, neither of which options is possible within the parameters of biblical theology. For him to suffer would mean that he is vulnerable to the power of an inferior being, which amounts to a denial of his sovereignty over all creation.

Critics of open theism insist that the love of God is not part of his nature but a quality of his persons, and it is in terms of personal relationship that human beings come to know him. In his personal aspect, God is fully capable of entering into fellowship with human beings, even to the point where one of his persons, the Son, took on a human nature in order to be able to suffer and die for us in the ultimate act of identification with our suffering and need. At the same time, the cross is not the end of the story, which continues until the final victory over sin and death is obtained through the resurrection, ascension and glorification of Christ. This can happen because in another way God remains untouched by human failure and is therefore able to save us from its consequences. In his nature, God is quite different from human beings, and it is this difference which makes it possible for him to be our Saviour. Our *salvation depends on the fact that God cannot change, because his immutability is the assurance that what he has done is guaranteed to remain the same for ever. By overemphasizing relationality at the expense of the divine nature, open theists have failed to appreciate that what they are trying to affirm has always formed an essential part of classical theology. Although much of the traditional Christian theological vocabulary may have been borrowed from ancient philosophy, its substance is more purely biblical than open theists are prepared to allow. For all these reasons, most evangelicals have rejected open theism or openness theology, which remains a minority voice even in the circles where it has attracted a certain amount of attention.

Bibliography

G. L. Bray, *The Personal God: Is the Classical Understanding of God Tenable?* (Carlisle, 1998); J. B. Cobb, Jr and C. H. Pinnock, *Searching for an Adequate God: A Dialogue Between Process and Free Will Theists* (Grand Rapids, 2000); C. H. Pinnock (ed.), *The Openness of God: A Biblical Challenge to the Traditional Understanding of God* (Downers Grove, 1994); J. Piper, J. Taylor and P. K. Helseth (ed.), *Beyond the Bounds: Open Theism and the Undermining of Biblical Christianity* (Wheaton, 2003); D. Strange, *The Possibility of Salvation among the Unevangelised: An Analysis of Inclusivism in Recent Evangelical Theology* (Carlisle, 2002); B. A. Ware, *God's Lesser Glory: A Critique of Open Theism* (Leicester, 2001).

G. L. BRAY

ORANGE, COUNCIL OF, see SEMI-PELAGIANISM

ORDINATION, see MINISTRY

ORDO SALUTIS

Ordo salutis (Lat. 'order of salvation') is the systematic ordering of the various elements in personal *salvation. It answers the question: how are, for example, *regeneration, *faith, *repentance, *justification, *sanctification and glorification related to each other?

The term is common in *Reformed theology, but first appeared in the *Lutheran dogmaticians Franz Buddeus (*Institutiones Theologiae Dogmaticae*, 1724) and Jakobus Karpov (*Theologia Revelata Dogmatica*, 1739). The concept, however, has an older pedigree, stretching back into pre-Reformation theology's attempt to relate the various experiential and sacramental steps to salvation (see *Penance). In this context Luther's personal struggle may be viewed as a search for a truly evangelical *ordo salutis*.

The *ordo salutis* seeks to establish, on the basis of Scripture, a pattern common to all believers, although experienced with different degrees of consciousness by each individual. The order involved is logical, not chronological (even if certain temporal implications seem to be implied).

Controversies over apparently isolated issues of soteriology are frequently related to contrasting expositions of the *ordo salutis*. This is well illustrated by the desire of some theologians (e.g. A. *Kuyper) to safeguard the justification of the ungodly by placing justification prior to regeneration in the *ordo*, and teaching a justification from eternity. Others, meanwhile, seek to safeguard man's responsibility by giving faith priority over regeneration, while yet others give regeneration (God's sovereign work) priority over *conversion (man's response) in order to safeguard divine *sovereignty.

Important (though often neglected) in such discussions is the recognition of the fluidity of theological language. Not all theologians have used their terminology in the same way. For example, Calvin uses 'regeneration' to denote the whole process of renewal, repentance, mortification and vivification (new life), in contrast to later evangelical theology's use of the term in an inaugural sense (new birth).

In recent years the concept has come under widespread criticism because: (1) It is heavily dependent on a passage (Rom. 8:28–30; cf. W. *Perkins' [see *Puritan theology] 'Golden Chain') which does not reflect on the order, but rather on the fullness of salvation (e.g. O. Weber, *Berkouwer).

(2) It distorts the basic NT (Pauline) emphasis on *historia salutis*, substituting for it a less than biblical emphasis on personal experience (H. N. Ridderbos). It transforms the NT's *via salutis* (Christ, John 14:6) into a 'psychologizing' (*Barth) or 'spiritualizing' (*Weber) of salvation. This subjective focus means that man's basic orientation as *incurvatus in se* ('turned in on himself', Luther) is unresolved.

(3) It reduces to one level (*ordo*) elements belonging to disparate dimensions of salvation (the divine activity and human responsibility). This 'lowest common denominator' approach minimizes the riches of God's *grace and virtually nullifies the NT emphasis on the *eschatological (already/not yet) character of Christian experience.

Some of these criticisms are salutary, but: (1) We cannot avoid thinking about salvation in a coherent (order-ly!) fashion. H. Berkhof is correct to say of Barth that 'he too needs a kind of logical order' (*The Christian Faith*, p. 479). (2) Following *Calvin, we should stress that the disparate elements in soteriology all have their centre in Christ. All evangelical blessings are ours only in him (Eph. 1:1–14). *Union with Christ must therefore be the dominant motif in any formulation of the application of redemption and the dominant feature of any 'order' of salvation.

Bibliography

K. Barth, *CD* IV.2; G. C. Berkouwer, *Faith and Justification* (Grand Rapids, 1954); J. Calvin, *Institutes*, III; R. B. Gaffin, *The Centrality of the Resurrection* (Grand Rapids, 1978); M. Garcia, *Life in Christ: Union with Christ and Twofold Grace in Calvin's Theology* (Paternoster, 2008); A. A. Hodge, 'The *Ordo Salutis*; or Relation in the Order of Nature of Holy Character and Divine Favor', *PTR* 54, 1878, pp. 305–321; J. Murray, *Redemption – Accomplished and Applied* (Grand Rapids, 1955); O. Weber, *Foundations of Dogmatics*, vol. 2 (Grand Rapids, 1983).

S. B. Ferguson

ORIENTAL ORTHODOX THEOLOGY

The Oriental Orthodox churches are those Eastern jurisdictions which accepted the decrees of the first three *ecumenical councils but not those of the fourth, the Council of *Chalcedon (451). They comprise the Armenian Apostolic Church; the *Coptic Orthodox; the *Ethiopian Orthodox; the *Syrian or Syriac Orthodox (sometimes called Jacobite after its most important theologian, the missionary bishop Jacob Baradaeus, c. 490–578); the now-divided Syrian Orthodox of India (some of whom continue to owe allegiance to the Syrian patriarch); and (since 1994) the Eritrean Orthodox. The Nestorians or Church of the East represent a different Christological tradition, belonging to neither Eastern nor Oriental Orthodoxy, rooted in the approach of *Nestorius, a fifth-century patriarch of Constantinople.

Traditionally, the distinctive aspect of Oriental Orthodox theology, in comparison with that of (*Eastern) Orthodox churches which upheld the Chalcedonian Definition, has been their *Christology. This has been called *monophysite. However, the Oriental churches dislike this term because of its perceived pejorative connotations, and recent investigation has shown that part of the disagreement in the fifth century was (as so often during Christological debate) caused by linguistic ambiguity: the term *physis*, which appears in *Cyril of Alexandria's slogan 'the one *physis* of the incarnate Word' could be taken as meaning 'nature' or 'person'. Furthermore, it has been increasingly acknowledged that politics and resentment at perceived Greek and Roman domination of church life and thought were major factors in the fifth-century division; these churches were developing in different cultural worlds from that of the Greeks. Accordingly, dialogue assisted by the *World Council of Churches between Orthodox and Oriental Orthodox (unofficial since 1964, official since 1985) has led to agreement that both traditions are essentially orthodox in their confession of Christ, affirming both Christ's deity and his full humanity, along with the four negative adverbs used at Chalcedon affirming that the union of divinity and humanity was without confusion, change, division or separation. Indeed, it has gone so far as to describe the differences as matters of terminology rather than substance, although the two traditions continue to differ over whether the later ecumenical councils may properly be seen merely as elaborating the Nicene faith. As a result, full eucharistic communion has been restored between the two traditions in the area under the patriarchs of Antioch, although in most other areas this process is less advanced.

Testimony to the essential unity of Orthodox and Oriental Orthodox in Christology comes from the fact that both traditions venerate icons as part of worship, and do so on similar grounds. This is all the more significant since it was only at Nicaea II (787, long after attempts to heal the division had failed) that the practice received formal affirmation.

Certain other theological and ecclesiological distinctives appear in one or more Oriental Orthodox jurisdictions, but as far as the tradition as a whole is concerned, apparent differences from Eastern Orthodox theology are probably primarily cultural, the result of many centuries of separate development.

Bibliography

A. S. Atiya, *A History of Eastern Christianity* (London, 1968); J. Binns, *An Introduction to the Christian Orthodox Churches* (Cambridge, 2002); C. Chaillot, *The Syrian Orthodox Church of Antioch and All the East* (Geneva, 1998); C. Chaillot and A. Belopopsky (eds.), *Towards Unity: The Theological Dialogue between the Orthodox Church and the Oriental Orthodox Churches* (Geneva, 1998); P. Gregorios, W. H. Lazareth and N. A. Nissiotis (eds.), *Does Chalcedon Divide or Unite?* (Geneva, 1981); D. P. Teague (ed.), *Turning Over a New Leaf: Protestant Missions and the Orthodox Churches of the Middle East* (London and Lynnwood, ²1992).

T. GRASS

ORIGEN (c. 185–c. 254)

As learned exegete, creative philosopher, master of the spiritual life, and active churchman, Origen was one of the great figures of the ancient church. He was born in *Alexandria of Christian parents. After the martyrdom of his father in the Severan persecution (202), Origen supported the family by teaching. When he was asked to instruct catechumens preparing for baptism, he gave up secular teaching and adopted an *ascetic life. Devoting himself to the study of Scripture, he was often called to other places to participate in theological discussions. On a trip to Palestine (c. 215) he was invited to preach by the bishops of Caesarea and Jerusalem. His bishop Demetrius, perhaps spurred by jealousy of Origen's influence, took exception to this. On a later visit to Palestine (c. 230) he was ordained a presbyter so that there would be no objection to his preaching. Demetrius was furious, and Origen chose to move his teaching activities to Caesarea. His pupil, Gregory Thaumaturgus (c. 213–c. 270), in his *Panegyric on Origen*, described his educational methods: he provided an encyclopedic education, encouraged the reading of all the non-atheistic philosophers, employed the Socratic method and taught more by example than by instruction. Imprisoned and tortured during the Decian persecution, Origen died not long after at Tyre.

Origen's great work of scholarship was the *Hexapla*, a study edition of the OT, presenting in parallel columns the Hebrew text, a Greek transliteration and the translations of Aquila, Symmachus, the Seventy (Septuagint) and Theodotion. His exegetical work found expression in *scholia* (brief notes) on difficult passages, numerous homilies preached regularly in Caesarea and directed to ordinary believers, and full-scale scholarly commentaries on major books (significant portions of John and Matthew survive). The climax of Christian *apologetic literature in Greek was reached in his *Against Celsus*; in replying to this pagan critic's *True Word*, Origen, in addition to the usual themes of Christian apologetics, made extensive use of the argument from the moral excellence of Jesus and the beneficent influence of Christian teaching. The treatises *On Prayer* and *Exhortation to Martyrdom* show the saintly spirituality and fervent faith of a man often remembered only as a scholar and theologian. Origen's major work of theology was *On First Principles*, treating in four books God and heavenly beings, the material world and human beings, free will and its consequences, and the interpretation of Scripture. Opposition to his teachings on the pre-existence of souls (see *Soul, origin of) and *universal salvation, climaxing in their condemnation at the Fifth Ecumenical Council in Constantinople (553), adversely affected the circulation of his works, many of which survive only in Latin translations of sometimes doubtful accuracy.

Origen was educated in the milieu of emerging Neoplatonism (see *Platonism), and his theological construction works with its philosophical concepts. His basic presuppositions are the unity and benevolence of God and the freedom of his creatures. Origen contributed significantly to the doctrine of the *Trinity with his teaching on the eternal generation of the Son by the Father. This assured that the Son was eternally of the same nature as the Father but derived from him. The *Holy Spirit, whose exact relation to the Father and Son is not clear, is in the third rank as the chief of spiritual beings. The universe includes a variety of functions united as in a body, so there are various ranks of angels and demons, their nature determined by their free choice. Some spiritual beings by choosing evil became demons; others whose transgression was not so serious fell into bodily existence, becoming the souls of human beings. Origen seems to make a more significant division between beings which are pure spirits (bodiless) and those having bodies, than between uncreated and created beings. Jesus Christ was a union of the *Logos, a soul that had not fallen into sin, and a human body.

In his doctrine of *redemption Origen drew on traditional Christian themes, such as the victory of Christ over the wicked spiritual powers, but at other times he described it as an educational process. The process continues in successive worlds, in which punishment is disciplinary and corrective (see *Metempsychosis). The love of God eventually triumphs in the salvation of all beings, who finally choose freely to love God. The church is important as the school of Christ. As with the human nature of Christ, the material aspect of the sacraments is not neglected, but the emphasis is on the spiritual aspect and what benefits the soul of the recipient. The true leaders of the church are concerned with the care of souls.

Origen's most enduring influence on the practice of the church was his biblical interpretation (see *Hermeneutics). Scripture is inspired by the Holy Spirit, which means that every text has a spiritual meaning whether it has a literal meaning or not. The same Spirit must be in the interpreter for him to discern this meaning, and divine power must be added to the words to make them effective. Not every part of Scripture appears to have a lofty spiritual sense, because God has accommodated it to human language and not every person is at the same stage of spiritual growth. Problems in the text are to make the reader look beyond the literal to a non-literal sense. Since the human being is body, spirit and soul (see *Anthropology), so Scripture has three senses: the actual story, the meaning for the church and Christian doctrine and the moral lesson. This is Origen's normal order, and in his homilies in church he went directly from the historical sense to the application to the souls of his hearers. The non-literal meanings were justified on the basis that since Scripture is spiritual, it must have a meaning worthy of God and be inerrant in spite of apparent difficulties. Controls on the non-literal interpretation were provided by the history of salvation and the articles of faith, but the understanding of the nature of man and God allowed philosophical ideas to influence the interpretation. The allegorical (spiritual) interpretation was elevated to prominence by Origen's followers, who thereby lost the control exercised by the moral purpose.

Bibliography

H. Crouzel, *Origen* (Edinburgh, 1989); J. Daniélou, *Origen* (London, 1955); B. Drewery, *Origen and the Doctrine of Grace* (London, 1960); W. Fairweather, *Origen and Greek Patristic Theology* (Edinburgh, 1901); R. P. C. Hanson, *Allegory and Event* (London, 1959); idem, *Origen's Doctrine of Tradition* (London, 1954); R. E. Heine, *Origen: Scholarship in the Service of the Church* (Oxford, 2010); J. W. Trigg, *Origen: The Bible and Philosophy in the Third-Century Church* (Atlanta, 1983); idem, *Origen: The Early Church Fathers* (London, 1998).

E. FERGUSON

ORIGINAL RIGHTEOUSNESS, see FALL

ORIGINAL SIN, see SIN

ORR, JAMES (1844–1913)

Scottish theologian, apologist and polemicist, Orr was educated for the most part at Glasgow University, where he distinguished himself in philosophy and theology. After seventeen years of pastoral ministry, he delivered a lecture series which was published as *The Christian View of God and the World* (1893). This work, which proved to be his magnum opus, was widely acclaimed and launched him on a prolific academic career. He was the leading United *Presbyterian theologian at the time of the United Free Church of Scotland union of 1900, and he came to exercise a significant influence in North America.

Orr's adult life corresponded to a particularly dynamic period in Protestant theology, and within this milieu he sought to defend evangelical orthodoxy in the face of various challenges. He was one of the earliest and principal British critics of Albrecht *Ritschl's thought. In *The Ritschlian Theology and the Evangelical Faith* (1897) and elsewhere, Orr insisted that Ritschlianism was opposed to genuine Christianity, and was intellectually untenable because of its limitation of the role of reason in Christian thought and experience. He also opposed Julius Wellhausen's documentary hypothesis on the Pentateuch. In *The Problem of the Old Testament* (1905), Orr argued for the 'essential Mosaicity' of the Pentateuch, and for the traditional construction of OT history. Further, Orr treated Charles Darwin's theory of man's origin as a serious threat to the Christian doctrines of man and sin. Initially he appeared comfortable with theistic evolution (see *Creation), but later, in *God's Image in Man* (1905), he stressed the necessity of supernatural interruptions of the evolutionary process to account for man as an embodied soul, and still later, in *Sin as a Problem of Today* (1910), he argued that the idea of moral evolution undermined the seriousness of sin and man's accountability for it.

There are some distinctive elements in Orr's apologetical thought. In *The Progress of Dogma* (1901), for example, Orr tried to counter Adolf *Harnack's negative verdict on the history of dogma by arguing that it has unfolded according to a recognizable inner logic. By regarding this logical movement as a manifestation of God's hand in history, Orr sought to vindicate the orthodox doctrines that the movement produced. With respect to *Scripture, Orr affirmed its plenary inspiration and remarkable accuracy, but regarded inerrancy as apologetically 'suicidal' (see *Revelation and Inspiration*, 1910). Finally, in such works as *The Virgin Birth of Christ* (1907), Orr defended theologically as well as biblically the *virginal conception of the Mediator.

The significance of Orr's theological contribution lies in neither its brilliance nor its originality, but in the breadth of his grasp of orthodox theology, the exhaustiveness of the reading upon which his conclusions were based and the vigour with which he defended and diffused his views. His voice seemed omnipresent in his day, and his last great work as editor of *The International Standard Bible Encyclopaedia* (1915) constituted a substantial and enduring means of extending conservative orthodoxy's line of defence. He was also a contributor to the twelve-volume series *The Fundamentals* (1910–15).

Three themes pervade Orr's work. The first is an appreciative insistence that *evangelical orthodoxy offers a unified and coherent worldview, a satisfying *Weltanschauung*. The second follows from the first: since Christian doctrine is an interconnected unity, no part can be negated or even altered without serious consequences for the whole. This determined Orr's apologetic agenda, and he ranged with remarkable competence across many disciplines in his efforts to buttress orthodoxy. The third decisive theme is the conviction that virtually all modern deviations from evangelical orthodoxy are prompted by anti-supernatural presuppositions.

Bibliography

J. Rogers and D. McKim, *The Authority and Interpretation of the Bible* (San Francisco, 1979); G. G. Scorgie, *A Call for Continuity: The Theological Contribution of James Orr* (Vancouver, 2004); P. Toon, *The Development of Doctrine in the Church* (Grand Rapids, 1979).

G. G. SCORGIE

ORTHODOXY/SCHOLASTICISM, LUTHERAN

The era of Lutheran orthodoxy refers to the century and a half of Lutheran theological development, elaboration and polemic, roughly situated between the confessional codification that took place with the Book of Concord (1580) and the various factors which contributed to an alternative paradigm for theology characterized by the concerns and approaches of the *Enlightenment, regnant in church and academy by the middle of the eighteenth century.

Lutheran orthodoxy arose in the context of the establishment within Lutheran territories of a common confessional position. Building upon the insights of the first and second generation Reformers, these later theologians sought to establish and defend such a confessional orthodoxy in church and academy. This process occurred, not only amid somewhat parallel developments within the *Reformed and *Roman Catholic confessional blocs, but also amid fundamental changes in philosophy, the sciences and biblical criticism which swept Western Christendom in the post-Reformation era.

Approach

A historiographical paradigm upheld by A. Tholuck and many others since the early nineteenth century has often evaluated Lutheran orthodoxy quite negatively, picturing it as coldly philosophical and scholastic (in a rationalistic, metaphysical sense) in contrast to the warm biblicism of their *Reformation-era forebears. This paradigm has serious shortcomings, not the least of which is the counterevidence of Lutheran orthodoxy's thoroughly exegetical approach to Scripture and the practice of theology, as well as the remarkable wealth of its devotional literature and hymnody.

Robert D. Preus began a much more sympathetic contemporary reassessment, although his historical-theological work found precedent in that of H. Schmid, and the more recent work of W. Elert, among others. Preus also appealed to the dialogue with orthodoxy among dogmaticians such as F. Pieper. Preus's approach represents a notable historiographical and historical-theological advance, however, in that he sought to explore 'how these Lutherans of a former day arrived at their theological position, the basis for their assertions, the way they thought and reasoned' (Preus, *Theology of Post-Reformation Lutheranism*, 1.16). In doing so, Preus has shown a deep continuity in theological approach and conclusions between Luther, Melanchthon and their contemporaries, and their Lutheran heirs, while not ignoring development and change in formulation, presentation and setting. Although mainly discussing Reformed orthodoxy, R. Muller has advanced and improved upon Preus's discussion in several ways, most notably regarding the nature of Protestant orthodoxy's 'scholasticism' and its role in academic theology.

Character

Preus highlighted several central characteristics of Lutheran orthodoxy: (1) a doctrinal position that grew out of and mutually informed exegesis; (2) 'catholicity and confessionalism', or commitment to the truth of Scripture as summarized in the Book of Concord, and as recognized – at least implicitly – by the universal church; (3) an abiding doctrinal unity, stemming from both confessional moorings and a strong loyalty to early Lutheran writings; and (4) a vigorous polemical stance, in line with their firm confessional position and closely reflecting the controversial tone of the day.

Periodization and representatives

Preus further suggested dividing Lutheran orthodoxy into three periods:

1. *The golden age of orthodoxy*, from the *Formula of Concord (1577) to the second decade of the seventeenth century; a time of exegetical and doctrinal fruitfulness in which the structure of a comprehensively 'Lutheran' systematic and polemical theology was put in place, largely on the model of *Melanchthon's Loci communes. The work of L. Hutter is notable in this respect.

2. *High orthodoxy*, extending to mid-century; characterized by increasing awareness of issues of prolegomena, further stress on technical formulation and distinctions, and a more standardized polemical stance, together with an emphasis on the practical outflow of theology for the Christian life. J. Gerhard is considered its chief representative, who was also influential in introducing an extensive use of philosophical language and categories in the context of academic Lutheran theology.

3. *The silver age of orthodoxy*, reaching somewhat indefinitely into the first half of the eighteenth century; continued development took place simultaneously with various theological and philosophical movements which were increasingly undermining Lutheran orthodoxy's position in church and academy. A. Calov is often considered the pinnacle of the development of Lutheran orthodoxy in this

period, although the vastness, thoroughness and clarity of J. A. Quenstedt's work arguably carried it to its furthest extent. Throughout this era, the Lutheran 'seats of orthodoxy' remained the universities at Wittenberg, Tübingen, Strasbourg, Leipzig and Jena; Rostock and Königsberg were also influential.

See also: LUTHERANISM AND LUTHERAN THEOLOGY.

Bibliography

Select Works: A. Calov, *Biblia Illustrata* (Frankfurt am Main, 1672–76); idem, *Systema locorum theologicorum* (Wittenberg, 1655–77); M. Chemnitz, *Examen Concilii Tridentini* (Frankfurt am Main, 1566–73); idem, *Loci theologici* (ET, St. Louis, 1989); J. Gerhard, *Loci theologici* (Jena, 1610–21); J. Hutter, *Compend of Lutheran Theology* (ET, Philadelphia, 1868); J. Quenstedt, *Theologia didacticopolemica sive Systema Theologiae* (Leipzig, 1702).

Studies: W. Elert, *The Structure of Lutheranism* (ET, St Louis, 1962); R. Muller, *Post-Reformation Reformed Dogmatics* (Grand Rapids, ²2003); F. Pieper, *Christian Dogmatics* (ET, St Louis, 1951); R. D. Preus, *The Theology of Post-Reformation Lutheranism* (St Louis, 1970); H. Schmid, *The Doctrinal Theology of the Evangelical Lutheran Church* (ET, repr. Minneapolis, 1961).

B. E. ELLIS

ORTHODOXY/SCHOLASTICISM, REFORMED

Reformed Orthodoxy was a theological movement which began in the immediate aftermath of the *Reformation and came to an end by 1800, although the Orthodox remained influential on later theologians, including *Schleiermacher and *Barth. Much was written in the twentieth century on the differences between the Reformers and the Reformed Orthodox (particularly in the 'Calvin against the Calvinists' debates), suggesting a range of changes, some material, some methodological, which made later *Reformed theology different, and inferior, from the vision of the Reformers. The theology of the Reformation thus stood out in stark contrast from medieval scholasticism preceding and Reformed scholasticism following. Some recent scholarship has instead emphasized broad theological continuity from the medieval schools through the Reformers to the Reformed Orthodox.

Following the Reformation, the new Reformed churches were faced with the need both to define their own beliefs and to defend themselves against Roman Catholic (and Lutheran) polemic. The early period of Orthodoxy (c.1560–1620) is therefore marked, on the one hand, by a preoccupation with the production, evaluation and explication of *confessional material, and on the other by a controversial interest. The natural method chosen to expound the new doctrinal systems was the scholastic method; Roman Catholic *polemics (particularly Bellarmine's influential *Disputationes de controversiis christianae ...* of 1586) drew extensively on scholastic arguments and distinctions. It is no surprise, therefore, that the conscious adoption of the scholastic method was felt to be a natural development for Reformed theology.

The Synod of *Dort might be taken as a turning point: Reformed dogmatics had now achieved a degree of stability, and the churches were no longer under immediate threat. With Dort, the pressing questions became internal. Theologians began to produce works intended to offer a comprehensive summary and examination of Reformed doctrine, directed as much to the resolution of internal disputes as defence against external attacks. The polemical element thus becomes broader; indeed, in the 'elenctic' method, which shaped the whole system of Francis *Turretin, doctrine was taught and developed exclusively by considering disputed questions. Turretin is an extreme example, but Peter van *Mastricht (for example) included an 'elenctic part' under each locus, alongside the exegetical, dogmatic and practical parts.

Much of the seventeenth century, therefore, was marked by a relative stability in Reformed *dogmatics. The questions, although sharp, were defined, and the great systems advanced the arguments by assuming what had come before and proposing refinements, rather than by offering completely new constructions (the negotiations of the superlapsarian-infralapsarian debate [see *Fall] by Turretin or van Mastricht provides a pair of fine examples). The rise of federal theology (see *Covenant theology), associated with Johannes *Cocceius, was a new development within the tradition, and one which occasioned some debate and discussion, but it was not perceived as a fundamental rupture in the system. This period may be characterized as 'high orthodoxy', and offers perhaps the purest examples of the spirit and method of Reformed Orthodoxy.

This stability was most marked in those locations which had achieved a Reformed settlement: Geneva, parts of what is now Germany, the Netherlands. England produced notable contributors to Reformed Orthodoxy, notably William *Ames, William *Perkins and John *Owen, but the continued polemical context of English theology shaped the careers of these writers. Owen's work, for instance, is often polemical and occasional, and he never produced the sort of extended system of theology which a settled stability allows.

With the rise of the *Enlightenment and the beginnings of biblical criticism, old assumptions about theological method could no longer be simply assumed. More-or-less traditional theology in the Reformed Orthodox tradition continued to be produced during the eighteenth century (Endemann's *Institutiones* of 1777–8, and *Compendium* of 1782 might be taken as the last truly significant and recognizably Orthodox works), but it lacked the calm assurance, or the intellectual vigour, of the great high Orthodox systems of the previous century. Schleiermacher's *Christian Faith* cites the Orthodox repeatedly, but, in terms of method, Schleiermacher finds the need to reconstruct theology from the ground up, on wholly new foundations, in order to render it credible in a changed age. The period of Orthodoxy was over.

The Orthodox method was carefully logical and assumed the truth of *revelation, which was found in Scripture. Philology was interesting insofar as it served exegesis, but history, and particularly historical criticism, was largely ignored. The great Orthodox systems are masterpieces of logical acuity, built on a simple assumption that any and every text of Scripture may be assumed to be the direct self-revelation of God. This fundamentally exegetical basis should be the subject of further research; older attempts to demonstrate that the methodology of the Orthodox was, despite their own claims, in fact the logical working out of a central dogma across all other areas of theology have been shown to be false, but a careful analysis of the ways in which *Scripture was in fact used as the source of theology would be extremely valuable.

Bibliography

Primary texts available in English translation include: W. Ames, *The Marrow of Theology*, tr. J. D. Eusden (Grand Rapids, 1997); F. Turretin, *Institutes of Elenctic Theology*, 3 vols., tr. G. M. Giger (Philipsburg, 1992–97); J. Wollebius, *Compendium Theologiae Christianae*, in J. W. Beardslee (ed.), *Reformed Dogmatics* (Oxford, 1965), pp. 26–262.

Studies: W. J. van Asselt and E. Dekker (eds.), *Reformation and Scholasticism* (Grand Rapids, 2000); R. A. Muller, *Post-Reformation Reformed Dogmatics*, 4 vols. (Grand Rapids, 2003); C. R. Trueman and R. S. Clark, *Protestant Scholasticism: Essays in Reassessment* (Carlisle, 1999).

S. R. HOLMES

ORTHOPRAXIS, see PRAXIS AND ORTHOPRAXIS

OSIANDER, ANDREAS (1498–1552)

Osiander was born at Guzenhausen near Nuremberg, studied Hebrew at the University of Ingolstadt and became an able Hebraist. He was ordained in 1520, joined the *Augustinians and taught Hebrew in Nuremberg. He revised the Latin Vulgate in the light of the Hebrew (1522). He attached himself to the Reformation cause and became an ardent advocate of *Lutheran doctrinal and liturgical principles in Nuremberg.

He had a difficult personality and irritated others remarkably easily. Nonetheless, his ability ensured that he was present as a Lutheran representative at the Colloquy of Marburg (1529). He was aggressive by temperament and had little sympathy with the irenic compromises of *Melanchthon at Augsburg (1530). It was not thought appropriate that he should take part in the delicate negotiations at the Colloquy of Regensburg (1541).

In 1542 he went to the Palatinate to further the Lutheran Reformation. After the Leipzig Interim (1548), with which he did not agree, he went to Königsberg (1549) and joined the theological faculty. It was from there that he became involved in a controversy with Melanchthon over *justification. He argued that Melanchthon overstated imputation. He maintained correctly that Luther spoke not only of external imputation but also of a real union with Christ. However, he exaggerated the point so that he taught that genuine *righteousness was achieved, and thus lost the Lutheran tension (*simul* *peccator, simul justus*, 'always a sinner, always justified'). His emphasis was on the indwelling of the divine Christ, at the expense of the justifying consequences of the human death of Christ. The human nature of Christ and his work consequently receded in importance.

Characteristically, Osiander conducted the controversy with much invective and won considerable opprobrium. *Calvin attacked both his view of justification and his understanding of the image of God in man. His writings 'prove him to have been perversely ingenious in futile inventions' (*Institutes* I. xv. 3). On the Lord's Supper (see *Eucharist) he was a strong Lutheran. He was also very interested in science and wrote the anonymous preface to Copernicus's *De Revolutionibus Orbium Caelestium* (*Revolutions of the Celestial Spheres*, 1543). It has been argued that by speaking of Copernicus's theory as a 'hypothesis', Osiander was undermining his work. He was in reality seeking to find a way round the opposition and was using a well-accepted philosophical word.

Bibliography

J. Dillenberger, *Protestant Thought and Natural Science: A Historical Interpretation* (London, 1961); D. C. Steinmetz, *Reformers in the Wings* (Philadelphia, 1971).

C. P. WILLIAMS

OTTO, RUDOLF (1869–1937)

Rudolf Otto, German Lutheran theologian, was professor of theology at Breslau (1914–17) and at Marburg (1917–29). A man of profound religious experience, he found his intellectual roots in *Luther, *Kant and *Schleiermacher.

His overriding concern was to defend the integrity of *religious experience as opposed to other types of human experience. He began by defending it from the threat posed by materialistic science, but then went on to explore its essential nature. To this end he visited India in 1911 and took up serious study of Sanskrit.

The main fruit of this inquiry was *Das Heilige* (1917; ET, *The Idea of the Holy*, Oxford, 1923), one of the classic studies of *religion in the twentieth century. The subtitle is *An inquiry into the non-rational factor in the idea of the divine and its relation to the rational*. Otto was concerned to reject the rationalistic emphasis of comparative religion or the history of religion, and to stress the non-rational and irreducible element in religion. For him there was at the heart of religion an experience which could not be reduced to any other category. This he described as the experience of the holy.

In Kantian terms he argued for the addition of the holy to the categories of the understanding and the categorical imperative. However, he was not perfectly at ease with the term 'holy', since it had become too identified with the moral category; so he coined the term *numinous* (Lat. *numen*; spirit, divinity) to replace it. Since, for Otto, this experience of the numinous is essentially supra-rational, all *religious language is an attempt to express the inexpressible. He also recognizes that any terms he might use to describe this experience can but point towards or evoke it. Thus his famous formula describing the numinous as *mysterium tremendum et fascinans* is to be taken as a series of ideograms and not a rational definition. But in attempting to evoke the numinous experience, Otto is not completely subjective. For example, he considered *Schleiermacher's definition of religion too subjective since it does not point clearly enough to the presence of the numinous object as the ground of the numinous experience. Thus the experience of the *mysterium* is described in terms of creature-feeling, the feeling of dependence upon that which stands over and above man as 'wholly other'. This *mysterium* is, on the one hand, absolutely unapproachable or awe-inspiring (i.e. *tremendum*), overpowering and replete with energy or life, while on the other hand, there is something in it that entrances and attracts (i.e. the aspect of *fascinans*), which is expressed conceptually in terms of love, mercy, pity and comfort.

While emphasizing that this numinous experience is the foundation of all religion, Otto also emphasizes the necessity of constructing a rational superstructure upon it, if it is to be of any benefit to humankind. To be a blessing, mere feeling must be transmitted into belief; and belief is only possible in rational terms. Thus the comparison of religions is possible, and Otto goes on to argue for the superiority of Christianity because of its superior conceptualization of the numinous.

Bibliography

Works: *The Idea of the Holy* (Oxford, 1923); *The Philosophy of Religion* (London, 1931); *Religious Essays: A Supplement to 'The Idea of* *the Holy'* (Oxford, 1931); *Mysticism East and West* (London, 1932).

Studies: P. C. Almond, *Mystical Experience and Religious Doctrine* (Berlin, 1982); D. A. Crosby, *Interpretive Theories of Religion* (Berlin, 1981); R. F. Davidson, *Rudolf Otto's Interpretation of Religion* (Princeton, 1947); T. A. Gooch, *The Numinous and Modernity: An Interpretation of Rudolf Otto's Philosophy of Religion* (Berlin and New York, 2000); R. R. Marett, *The Threshold of Religion* (London 1909); M. Raphael, *Rudolf Otto and the Concept of Holiness* (Oxford, 1997); N. Smart, *Philosophers and Religious Truth* (London 1964). See also 'The Piper at the Gates of Dawn', in K. Grahame, *The Wind in the Willows* (London, 1908).

D. A. HUGHES

OUSIA, see SUBSTANCE

OWEN, JOHN (1616–83)

Called by some 'the Calvin of England' and by others 'the greatest of the Puritan scholastics', Owen is widely considered *the* theological giant among the *Puritans. Born in a home of Puritan persuasion, young John was educated at Queen's College, Oxford University, receiving first a BA and then an MA. During his life Owen would minister in several churches, serve as a chaplain to Oliver Cromwell, become dean of Christ Church, Oxford, and finally receive the high honour of becoming the vice-chancellor of Oxford University (1652–57). As one committed to the 'Congregational way', Owen always valued the local church, and he spent the final decades of his life ministering primarily through his preaching and writings.

A prolific author, Owen's many books have consistently remained in print for more than 350 years. Writing significant doctrinal expositions on almost every key area of the Christian faith, Owen consistently displays both theological depth and pastoral wisdom, even though his complex sentences and detailed outlining apparatus are taxing to the reader. Owen's massive corpus (containing twenty-four volumes in the standard nineteenth-century edition) continues to stimulate readers, as his work is being rediscovered not only by historians, but also by contemporary theologians (e.g. Carl Trueman).

Several ideas in his corpus deserve mention. First, a *trinitarian sensitivity guides much of his thinking on all manner of subjects. His work *Of Communion with God the Father, Son, and Holy Ghost* (1657), for example, attempts to describe how saints commune with each divine person distinctly, while not compromising the reality that believers worship one God. This book displays pastoral sensitivity and theological creativity. For Owen, a biblical trinitarian theology always found its centre in Jesus Christ, who was the perfect image of God and to whom the Spirit always pointed. Two other treatises (*The Person of Christ* [1679] and *The Glory of Christ* [1684, 1691]) make this *Christological focus clear, tying together classic orthodoxy with fresh exegesis and practical application.

Owen's exploration of the person and work of the *Holy Spirit was arguably the most exhaustive treatment of the subject yet published at that point in history. Broken up into five works published from 1674 to 1693 (see vols. 3–4 of his *Works*), Owen's reflections follow Puritan tendencies to focus on the Spirit's application of Christ's work to the lives of believers. Here Owen holds together an unflinching commitment to the sovereignty of God while at the same time attempting not to diminish a high view of human responsibility. The Spirit is key in navigating through these difficulties. Throughout this work Owen also provides stimulating proposals for understanding the Spirit's work in the life of the incarnate Lord. Interestingly, Owen's work on the Spirit is in many ways an attempt to chart a path between what he viewed as the extreme rationalists (i.e. Socinians) on the one hand and the 'enthusiasts' (e.g. Quakers) on the other. One view seemed to deny the personal Spirit, while the other seemed to separate the Spirit from Christ.

Despite stereotypes, Owen, like many of his fellow Protestant scholastics, engaged in a great deal of exegetical work, and often he was wary of philosophical speculations. His massive multi-volume exposition of the *Epistle to the Hebrews* displays his knowledge of historical and linguistic backgrounds.

Owen's high view of Scripture (see *Scripture, doctrine of) is apparent throughout his work. At times his comments seem to present a flat dictation view of inspiration; while at other times he readily recognizes the biblical authors' distinctive styles, personalities, etc. What is consistent is Owen's emphasis on the work of the Spirit *both* in the original writings of the sacred texts and in the continuing reception of those texts by believers throughout the ages (see his *Vindiciae Evangelicae* [1655], *Pro Sacris Scripturis Exercitationes adversus Fanaticos* [1658], *The Reason of Faith* [1677]).

Bibliography

Works: *The Works of John Owen*, ed. W. H. Goold, 24 vols. (repr., London, 1965 [1850–55]); *Biblical Theology* (ET, Morgan, 1994).

Studies: K. M. Kapic, *Communion with God: The Divine and the Human in the Theology of John Owen* (Grand Rapids, 2007); S. Rehnman, *Divine Discourse: The Theological Methodology of John Owen* (Grand Rapids, 2002); P. Toon, *God's Statesman: The Life and Work of John Owen: Pastor, Educator, Theologian* (Exeter, 1971); C. Trueman, *The Claims of Truth: John Owen's Trinitarian Theology* (Carlisle, 1998); idem, *John Owen* (Aldershot, 2007).

K. M. KAPIC

OXFORD MOVEMENT, see ANGLO-CATHOLIC THEOLOGY

PACIFISM/PEACE

Christian pacifists believe that their discipleship means renouncing the use of violence. While the term 'pacifism' dates back only to 1902, the Christian rejection of violence originates in Jesus' instruction to his followers to 'turn the other cheek' when struck by their enemies (Matt. 5:39). Early Christian writings make a strong link between Christian faith and living in peace: *Justin Martyr saw Isaiah's prophecy of swords being beaten into ploughshares (Isa. 2:4) fulfilled in his time: 'we who formerly used to murder one another do not only now refrain from making war upon our enemies, but also . . . willingly die confessing Christ' (*First Apology*, 39); *Clement of Alexandria wrote that 'it is not in war, but in peace, that we are trained' (*The Instructor*, I, 12); *Tertullian asked, 'How will a Christian man war, nay, how will he serve even in peace, without a sword, which the Lord has taken away?' (*On Idolatry*, 19); *Origen explains that Christians 'no longer take up "sword against nation", nor do we "learn war any more", having become children of peace, for the sake of Jesus, who is our leader' (*Against Celsus*, V, 33); and third-century church orders stipulate excommunication for soldiers. Recent scholarship has shown, however, that this clearly stated position was not universally observed.

The position of the church changed radically following the Emperor *Constantine's Edict of Milan in 313. Church orders from 314 stipulate that Christians would be excommunicated for leaving the army. Later in the fourth century both *Ambrose of Milan and *Augustine of Hippo agreed that warfare was appropriate in certain circumstances, and by 416 Theodosius II could issue an edict specifying that only Christians could serve in the army. From the fourth century onwards, Christian renunciation of violence was restricted to monks and clerics, until a diverse range of Christian movements in the medieval and Reformation periods took it up as a return to the original witness of the church, including the Cathars (see *Albigenses), *Waldenses, Lollards, *Hussites, and later the *Mennonites, Hutterites, *Quakers and the Brethren. In the twentieth century, there was widespread protest by labour unions against war before the First World War. The mass killing of troops during that war led to disillusion about warfare as a means of resolving conflicts, and peace movements grew, inspired by the example of Mahatma Gandhi effectively resisting British Imperial rule in India with non-violent action. This belief in the effectiveness of non-violence faltered with the Second World War, though non-violent action continued afterwards, especially in opposition to nuclear weapons.

Christian pacifism is a diverse phenomenon: while rejecting the use of violence by Christians, Tertullian and Origen agree with St Paul that the political authorities rightly bear the sword (Rom. 13) and assure the Romans that the church prays for the success of Roman armies. Their pacifism is therefore *communal* – relevant only for the Christian community – rather than *universal* in application. Another difference between pacifists is whether their renunciation of violence is *principled* and valid in every circumstance, or *strategic* – chosen for its effectiveness in a particular situation (e.g. Emil *Brunner said he was pacifist because modern weaponry meant warfare could no longer achieve its purpose). Some pacifist groups have withdrawn into *separatist* communities and renounced responsibility for the wider world;

others have been *integrationist* in seeing their vocation in the midst of responsibility for a diverse society. Finally, some pacifists are *absolute* in rejecting every use of violence (e.g. Leo *Tolstoy, who thought policing and prisons were incompatible with Christianity), whereas *classical* pacifists are prepared to accept the use of violence in policing contexts and peace-keeping operations.

Christians have always seen Christ as the fulfilment of Isaiah's prophecy of the coming of the Prince of Peace (Isa. 9:6), and have recognized that the Hebrew concept of *shalom* includes justice (see *Righteousness) as well as peace. Those who have judged war permissible have done so only on the basis that it is the only way to establish this just and peaceful order among sinful human beings. The development of the just war tradition following Ambrose and Augustine is an attempt to specify the conditions under which wars could be fought appropriately with the aim of doing justice and establishing peace. Christian pacifists and those in the just war tradition agree that violence should be avoided and what makes for the building of peace pursued; they differ in the judgment about whether violence is appropriate as a last resort when all other means of establishing justice and peace have been exhausted.

Bibliography

Clement of Alexandria, *The Instructor* in *The Ante-Nicene Fathers: Translations of the Writings of the Fathers down to A.D. 325*, vol. 2, eds. A. Cleveland Coxe *et al.* (Edinburgh, 1997); D. Clough and B. Stiltner, *Faith and Force: A Christian Debate about War* (Washington DC, 2007); J. Helgeland *et al.*, *Christians and the Military: The Early Experience* (London, 1987); Justin Martyr, *First Apology*, in ANF, vol. 1; Origen, *Against Celsus* in ANF, vol. 4; R. Niebuhr, *Christianity and Power Politics* (Hamden, 1969); P. Ramsey, *The Just War: Force and Political Responsbility* (Savage, 1983); Tertullian, *On Idolatry*, in ANF, vol. 3; J. H. Yoder, *Nevertheless: A Meditation on the Varieties and Shortcomings of Religious Pacifism* (Scottdale, 1971).

D. L. CLOUGH

PACKER, JAMES INNELL (b. 1926)

J. I. Packer (born in Gloucester, England) is an esteemed theologian in the (*Anglican) Calvinistic tradition (see *Reformed theology). He currently serves as the Board of Governors' Professor of Theology at Regent College in Vancouver, British Columbia.

The son of a clerk for the Great Western Railway, Packer won a scholarship to Oxford University where he studied at Corpus Christi College, gaining his BA in 1948, later gaining his MA (1952) and PhD (1955). In 1949 he entered Wycliffe Hall, Oxford to study for his doctoral thesis on the life and theology of the Puritan theologian, Richard *Baxter of Kidderminster. His work was published in 2003 under the title *The Redemption and Restoration of Man in the Thought of Richard Baxter*.

J. I. Packer was ordained as a deacon in the Church of England in 1952 and as a priest in 1953. He became an Assistant Curate of Harborne Heath in Birmingham 1952–4, lecturer at Tyndale Hall, Bristol 1955–61, librarian of Latimer House, Oxford 1961–2, and Principal 1962–9. In 1970 he became Principal of Tyndale Hall, Bristol and from 1971 until 1979 he was Associate Principal of Trinity College, Bristol, formed by the amalgamation of Tyndale Hall with Clifton College and Dalton House-St. Michael's. In 1979 Packer moved to Regent College, Vancouver as the Sangwoo Youtong Chee Professor of Theology, a position he held until his retirement.

A prolific writer and co-signer of the *Chicago Statement on Biblical Inerrancy*, Packer was named as 'One of the 25 most Influential Evangelicals in America' by *Time* magazine (Feb. 2005). He is best known as the author of *Knowing God* (1973), and *Fundamentalism and the Word of God* (1958), the former having sold over a million copies. He has been a frequent contributor and an executive editor of *Christianity Today*.

Packer has devoted much of his life to Anglican and *Puritan studies, especially the latter's relevance to contemporary Christian spirituality. Controversially, Dr Packer has been an advocate of dialogue with Roman Catholics (see *Evangelicals and Catholics Together: Toward a Common Mission*, 1994, eds. C. Colson and R. J. Neuhaus).

Packer served as a general editor of the Bible translation *English Standard Version*, an evangelical revision of the *Revised Standard Version*.

Bibliography

Selected works: *Fundamentalism and the Word of God* (Eerdmans, 1958); *Knowing God*

(London, 1973); *Concise Theology* (Wheaton, 2001); *The Collected Shorter Writings of J. I. Packer*, 4 vols. (Carlisle, 2002).

Studies: Alister McGrath, *J. I. Packer: A Biography* (Grand Rapids, 1997).

D. W. H. Thomas

PAEDOBAPTISM, see BAPTISM

PALAMAS, GREGORY (*c.* 1296–1359)

Gregory Palamas was born into a noble family, probably in Constantinople, in about 1296. Drawn to the monastic life from his youth, in about 1318 he went to Mount Athos, where he encountered the *hesychast tradition of solitary use of the Jesus prayer. The Turkish advance forced him to flee to Thessaloniki, where he was ordained priest in 1326. He returned to Athos in 1331. In the later 1330s, he became involved in controversy with a Calabrian monk, Barlaam. Initially the controversy concerned the doctrine of the procession of the *Holy Spirit. Attacking the Latin doctrine of the *filioque* clause, Barlaam invoked God's unknowability; for Palamas knowledge about God could be demonstrated, and he refuted the *filioque* in two 'apodeictic treatises' on the procession of the Holy Spirit. Controversy then turned to claims made by hesychast monks that in their prayer they could experience ('see') the uncreated light of the Godhead. Barlaam rejected such a claim as illusory, since God is unknowable in himself. Palamas countered by maintaining that the hesychasts indeed experienced the uncreated light of the Godhead, reconciling this with the unknowability of God by making a distinction between God's essence, which is indeed unknowable, and his activities ('energies', an over-literal translation of *energeiai*) through which he makes himself known; God, known in his activities, is God himself, not some created symbol. Central to the argument was the meaning of the transfiguration of the Lord, Palamas arguing that the light, radiating from Christ and perceived by the apostles, was the uncreated light of the Godhead, experienced now by the hesychast monks. The fourteenth century was a period in which *Augustine and some of the scholastic theologians, such as *Thomas Aquinas, became known in the Byzantine world, and this new factor played a not-yet-clearly understood role in the controversy. The controversy was also caught up in the divisions of Byzantine society which resulted in civil war in the 1340s. A series of synods, held on Mount Athos and in Constantinople, upheld Palamas' teaching, though Barlaam was not lacking in support. In 1347, Palamas was consecrated Archbishop of Thessaloniki, though political conditions prevented him going there until 1350. In 1354, on his way to Constantinople, he was captured by the Turks and spent a year in captivity, during which he encountered and held discussion with Muslim theologians. He died in 1359 and was declared a saint in 1368.

See also: Eastern Orthodox Theology.

Bibliography

Works: *Suggrammata*, ed. P. Chrestou (incomplete, 5 vols., Thessaloniki, 1962–92); *Triads in Defence of the Holy Hesychasts*, abridged, ed. J. Meyendorff (Louvain, ²1973); *The Triads*, Classics of Western Spirituality (Mahwah, 1983); *150 Chapters* (ET, Toronto, 1988).

Studies: J. Meyendorff, *A Study of Gregory Palamas* (abridged, London, 1964 [1959]).

A. Louth

PALEY, WILLIAM (1743–1805)

Paley is chiefly remembered for his use of the analogy of the watch and the watchmaker as a defence of the existence of God. He studied at Christ's College, Cambridge, of which he eventually became a Fellow, leaving in 1775 to take up an ecclesiastical career in the diocese of Carlisle. In an age when the universities were at something of a low ebb, Paley was a gifted and conscientious teacher whose lectures were popular.

Paley's theology was in the tradition of *latitudinarianism, and he wrote a number of apologetic works against the prevailing scepticism of the eighteenth century which had its roots in *deism. He was not an original thinker, but had the great virtue of being a clear one, and his writings are more in the nature of textbooks than original treatises. His major theological works were *A View of the Evidences of Christianity* (1794), *Natural Theology, or Evidence of the Existence and Attributes of the Deity Collected from the Appearances of Nature* (1802) and *Principles of Moral and Political Philosophy* (1785). This last is one of the clearest statements of the utilitarian morality propounded by the latitudinarian divines of the eighteenth century, anticipating many of the arguments of Jeremy Bentham (1748–1832), though Paley appeals, as Bentham does not, to the supernatural sanction as an inducement to moral behaviour. His definition of virtue was 'doing good to mankind, in obedience to the will of God, and for the sake of everlasting happiness'.

Despite his rejection of scepticism, however, Paley's own theological views appear to have been tinged with *Unitarianism. Early in his career as a university lecturer he took the view that subscription to the *Thirty-Nine Articles of the Church of England could only be construed as an action of 'peaceableness', since they included, on his estimate, 'some 240 distinct propositions, many of them inconsistent with each other'. On these grounds he continued to adhere nominally to the creeds, although on a conservative interpretation of them his views were at odds with the Christian understanding of the incarnation. He was, however, entirely sincere in his belief that the doctrines he did accept were logically demonstrable.

The watchmaker analogy, which appears in his *Natural Theology*, is a classic statement of the argument from design (the teleological argument) for the existence of God (see *Natural theology). Paley introduces it by comparing his likely reaction in crossing an empty heath to discovering, on the one hand, a stone, and, on the other, a watch. One might reasonably account for the stone in terms of its having always been there, but no-one would account for the watch in that way. Watches evidence purpose and design. In short they are mute testimonials to the existence of a watchmaker, and this is the conclusion any sensible person would infer from the discovery of one. The conclusion is not invalidated by the discoverer never having seen a watch made, nor by the watch not being accurate, nor by parts of it having an unknown function; neither could its existence be satisfactorily explained by appeals to impersonal laws or chance. What it demonstrates is the fact of design. Paley concludes, 'Every indication of contrivance, every manifestation of design, which existed in the watch, exists in the works of nature . . .', and the conclusion is therefore irresistible that nature too has its maker.

It is one of the ironies of history, and an example of the gap that frequently occurs between the discussions of theologians and philosophers, that twenty-three years before the publication of Paley's *Natural Theology*, David *Hume had already published the classic critique of the argument from design in his *Dialogues Concerning Natural Religion*.

Bibliography

Works: *Natural Theology*, with introduction and notes by M. D. Eddy and D. M. Knight (Oxford, 2006).

Studies: M. L. Clarke, *Paley: Evidence for the Man* (Toronto, 1974); D. L. LeMahieu, *The Mind of William Paley* (Lincoln, NE, 1976).

D. D. SCEATS

PALMER, PHOEBE WORRALL (1807–74)

An American Methodist revivalist, theologian and author, Phoebe Palmer was born in New York City and grew up active in the Methodist Episcopal Church. In 1827 she married Dr Walter C. Palmer; they had six children, three of whom survived to adulthood. After a profound religious experience in 1837 she became a leader of a movement to keep John *Wesley's doctrine of Christian *perfection at the centre of Methodist teaching and life during a time when *Methodism in the US was expanding rapidly both numerically and geographically and undergoing significant changes in leadership. In time Palmer became the principal spokesperson for this '*holiness movement', which also spread beyond Methodism to influence other Protestant denominations in North America and the British Isles.

Palmer published nearly twenty books, many in multiple editions, beginning with *The Way of Holiness* (1843). She led a well-known weekly religious gathering, the Tuesday Meeting for the Promotion of Holiness, for over thirty years. She travelled thousands of miles, speaking and teaching in churches, camp meetings, colleges and seminaries and public auditoriums, becoming one of the most widely recognized revivalists in the world. In addition, she edited an influential journal, *The Guide to Holiness*, for ten years (1864–74). Palmer also supported a wide variety of compassionate and humanitarian ministries throughout her life, and was an advocate for the ministry of women in the churches.

Bibliography

Works: *The Way of Holiness; with Notes by the Way* (New York, 1843); *The Promise of the Father; or, a Neglected Specialty of the Last Days* (New York, 1859).

Studies: T. C. Oden, *Phoebe Palmer: Selected Writings* (New York, 1988); H. E. Raser, *Phoebe Palmer, Her Life and Thought* (New York, 1987); R. Wheatley, *The Life and Letters of Mrs. Phoebe Palmer* (New York, 1876); C. E. White, *The Beauty of Holiness: Phoebe Palmer as Theologian, Revivalist, Feminist and Humanitarian* (Grand Rapids, 1986).

H. E. RASER

PANENTHEISM

Panentheism is the view that the universe is God, though God is more than the universe. It should be clearly distinguished from *pantheism, in which God and the universe are strictly identical. For the panentheist God has an identity of his own, that is, he is something which the universe is not. On the other hand, the universe is part of the reality of God. It is God.

The actual term was first used by contemporary *process theology, but it could be used of several earlier theories. Plotinus (c. 205–70; see *Platonism), who influenced early medieval theology, held that the world emanates from God. It is an overflow of his creative being. God creates out of himself, not out of nothing.

Some *idealists, for example George *Berkeley, held that the world has reality only as a thought of God's mind. The very reality of the universe consists in its being the contents of God's ideas, and is, therefore, God himself. Though very different from Plotinus' view, here too God has his own reality, but the universe is real only as God.

Alfred North Whitehead and Charles Hartshorne each developed slightly differing versions of panentheism which have become the philosophical basis of process theology. For Whitehead this view is demanded by his general view of causality, coupled with the insistence that God cannot be an exception to the basic principles of reality, but must rather be their chief example. Whitehead thought of reality as composed of multiple series of events, not objects. Since only actual entities can be causes, and since each preceding event is past and not actual, events must determine themselves. And yet something must create the possibility of each event. This, Whitehead argued, must be God. Causal relations, including that of knowing, are real connections. They are events, hence God who creates and knows each event cannot be separate from them. They are just his experience, and he is just the subjectivity that feels all events.

Charles Hartshorne supplies a more detailed view of God. In his earlier writings especially, he begins by arguing for a new concept of perfection. If God is related by inclusion to all events, then be cannot be perfect in the classical sense of being unaffected by the limitations of the universe. Rather, God is perfectly relative. He is all he can be because he feels and retains all there is. And, by constantly including novel events, God is in perpetual change in new and more complex states. God grows in a creative advance as he experiences the universe he includes.

Hartshorne and his theological followers often compare God's relation to the universe to a person's relation to his body. I depend on my body as the source of my experience, but I also transcend it. Just so, while God depends on his body, the universe, he also transcends it as a mind that knows all of the possibilities for future events. In addition to the panentheism of process thought, panentheism can be seen in the theology of Teilhard de Chardin, Paul Tillich, Jürgen Moltmann and Wolfhart Pannenberg (cf. Cooper).

Bibliography

D. Brown, R. James and G. Reeves (eds.), *Process Philosophy and Christian Thought* (Indianapolis, 1971); J. W. Cooper, *Panentheism: The Other God of the Philosophers – From Plato to the Present* (Nottingham, 2007); L. Ford, *The Lure of God* (Philadelphia, 1978); C. Hartshorne, *Omnipotence and Other Theological Mistakes* (New York, 1984); A. N. Whitehead, *Religion in the Making* (London, 1926).

W. D. BECK

PANNENBERG, WOLFHART (1928–2014)

A German Lutheran theologian, Pannenberg studied theology under Karl *Barth in 1950–1 in Basle, leading on to doctoral work in

Heidelberg where he gained a keen interest in *Hegel, and worked with a group of younger theologians in the development of a new approach to the theology of revelation, in terms of both biblical interpretation and *systematic theology. This work resulted in the seminal symposium *Offenbarung als Geschichte*, edited by Pannenberg (1961; ET *Revelation as History*, 1968). In 1961 he moved from his first teaching post at the Lutheran Seminary in Wuppertal to Mainz as Professor of Systematic Theology. Pannenberg engaged in dialogue at Chicago University 1963, and Harvard and Claremont 1966–7, notably with *process theologians. In 1968 he became professor at Munich in the Protestant Faculty of Theology, where he taught until his retirement, writing prolifically. He proved an important dialogue partner for discussions between *science and religion. He was also a significant figure in ecumenical life.

Pannenberg's essays in *Revelation as History* broke sharply from the predominant German-speaking theologies of *Bultmann and Barth and the 'theologies of the word', based on *revelation alone and rejecting '*natural theology' as a possible source of the knowledge of God. Pannenberg argued that the approach he criticized was *dualistic, sundering faith and reason, and led theology and church into a ghetto, cut off from the questions of the secular world. Pannenberg criticized Bultmann's theology for its individualistic focus and radical disjunction between critical reason and existential faith. He criticized Barth's *epistemology as offering a form of *fideism, divorced from critical questions and the insights of reason and culture. Pannenberg did not, however, reject Barth's understanding of revelation as divine self-disclosure, but sought to widen this out and root it in historical research and interpretation. Pannenberg regards theology that does not take account of secular insights as failing to do justice to God as 'die *Alles bestimmende Wirchlichkeit*', 'the all-determining reality' of the whole world and its truth.

This programme he presented in what may prove to be his most lasting theological legacy, his *Christology, *Grundzüge der Christologie* (1964; ET *Jesus – God and Man*, 1968). This tour de force took up his idea of 'indirect self-revelation', that is to say, divine self-disclosure through the events of *history as interpreted aright. From a formal position of openness and free enquiry into facts and meanings of events of history, Pannenberg concluded that the figure of *Jesus, his life and fate, did indeed rise from death. Pannenberg's arguments involve historical points; he is particularly impressed by the 'appearance traditions' and does not think that these are explained by psychological factors. He also makes use of what he takes to be differences in the NT texts as evidence against collusion and falsification by the authors and editors. He argues that philosophically the new and unique event is not to be ruled out on a law of naturalistic historicism, and that the resurrection is therefore a possibility. Having argued that historically the best explanation for the data about Jesus is that a resurrection did take place, he then went on to say that this event has to be interpreted in the thought context of its day, which he took to be that of apocalyptic expectation. Jewish expectation was that the end time, the time of final revelation of the meaning of all things and of God, was to be a time of resurrection of the dead (see *Eschatology). Pannenberg argued that Jesus' resurrection anticipated this expectation, and so constituted the end-time event of revelation in advance or 'proleptically'. From here he argued that this event therefore entails Jesus' 'revelational unity of essence' with God. Moreover, since in his life Jesus had shown himself totally dependent on God as his Father, this part of his identity carries forward to entail a trinitarian bond: God reveals himself indirectly, through the process of historical events and their meaning, as Father, Son and Spirit. Pannenberg stresses Jesus' humble 'self-differentiation' from God in his life, and this is taken into the divine identity of unity and differentiation.

Especially in this early Christology Pannenberg teaches that history really affects *God, and yet God sends history from the future to its present. The result has been called a 'theology of the future perfect': history is open and free, yet its final meaning always was going to have been given by Christ. The structure of this theology is one of epistemological anticipation and ontological 'retroaction': Jesus' *resurrection constitutes his identity as the Son of God, and this is read backwards into his life. Pannenberg has executed an argument for the Trinity from reason alone, but reason guided by the Spirit at work in all the historical process, and here the reader perceives the influence of Hegel, although with the distinctive future orientation given by Pannenberg's use of apocalyptic. In an important set of essays, not translated into English, *Grundfragen systematischer Theologie band* 2 (1980), Pannenberg made clear that his doctrine of history and God of the future were deeply *trinitarian. The Father conveys events from the freedom of the future, the Son represents the past event, and the Spirit creatively synthesizes the process as it moves forward, while originating in the open future. Jesus' filial relationship with the Father during his life is taken up into his identity at the decisive and constitutive event of the resurrection. Pannenberg's mature theology endorses a doctrine of the immanent Trinity, understood through divine eschatological self-revelation.

This pattern shapes his doctrine of humanity which is essentially open and orientated to the future. Who we really are lies in our final future or judgment: an example might be that of Mozart, who died a pauper, but whose true identity is now revealed with the verdict of the future. In the case of Jesus, the resurrection event revealed him to be the divine Son or *Logos, a concept Pannenberg has rehabilitated in his later work after rejecting it as useful for Christology earlier. Sin is the phenomenon of human refusal of the divine goal and turning in on itself. We are open to God and open to the world in our existence, and our freedom is a crucial factor in being human, a factor that no atheistic philosophy seems able to ground, notably Marxism. Pannenberg's theology is at the same time an ongoing dialogue and apologetic with other worldviews. This flows from 'revelation as history': they are two sides of one coin, theology and reason are partners in interpreting the world, and God is the best concept for making sense of the totality of reality. *Faith and reason share the same structure, as they trust in the coherence and unity of the world and our thought, a coherence needed if there is to be any thinking at all. Pannenberg produced an acclaimed book on theology in dialogue with secular learning, *Wissenschaftstheorie und Theologie* (1973; ET, *Theology and the Philosophy of Science*, 1976), and a work of massive erudition, *Anthropologie in theologische Perspektive* (1983; ET 1985).

Pannenberg insists that his conclusions are 'provisional' in that he is formally open to new evidence appearing that might undermine his argument, in which case he would have to revise his position, that of being led to faith in the God of Jesus through a thoroughly rational process of argumentation. He distinguishes between logical and psychological certainty: logically believers must formally be open to the possibility of new negative evidence against Christianity, but psychologically the believer can be certain of faith.

In his final theological work, the three-volume *Systematische Theologie* (1988–93; ET 1991), Pannenberg sets out his theology in its widest scope, showing that he is first and foremost a theologian, but one of great learning keen to take all criticism seriously and to harvest the fruits of secular thought, while challenging *atheism to consider the God hypothesis as the best account of truth and reality. His ideas have proved particularly interesting to those at the interface of science and faith, notably his idea of the Spirit as 'field force'. He is defended from postmodern charges of *rationalism by those who point to his stress on openness and provisionality. His theology creatively meshes Hegelian thought with biblical apocalyptic and the Christian dogmatic tradition in a genuinely new synthesis.

Bibliography

Works: *The Apostles' Creed* (ET, London, 1972); *Basic Questions in Theology*, vols. 1–3 (ET, London, 1970–73); *Ethics* (ET, London, 1981); *Christianity in a Secularised World* (ET, London, 1989); *Metaphysics and the Idea of God* (ET, Edinburgh, 1990).

Studies: C. E. Braaten and P. Clayton (eds.), *The Theology of Wolfhart Pannenberg* (Minneapolis, 1988); T. Bradshaw, 'The Trinitarian Theology of Wolfhart Pannenberg: The Divine Future Perfect', in P. Duce and D. Strange (eds.), *Getting Your Bearings: Engaging with Contemporary Theologians* (Leicester, 2003); A. D. Galloway, *Wolfhart Pannenberg* (London, 1973); S. J. Grenz, *Reason for Hope: The Systematic Theology of Wolfhart Pannenberg* (Oxford, 1990); C. Rausch Albright and J. Haugen (eds.), *Beginning with the End: God, Science and Wolfhart Pannenberg* (Chicago, 1997); F. L. Shults, *The Postfoundational Task of Theology: Wolfhart Pannenberg and the New Theological Rationality* (Grand Rapids, 1999); E. F. Tupper, *The Theology of Wolfhart Pannenberg* (London, 1974).

T. Bradshaw

PANTHEISM

The word 'pantheism' derives from Gk *pan* (all) and *theos* (God). Literally, it means 'all is God'.

Specifically, pantheism's metaphysic, its view of reality, affirms two things: the unity of all reality and the divineness of that unity. Pantheism parallels naturalism on the first point in that both assert only one reality. But in contrast to naturalism, it calls reality divine. Pantheism is like *theism on the second point, for both recognize that the world depends on God. But unlike theism, it does not hold the world's existence to be separate from God's.

Pantheism often teaches that logical opposites coalesce in the divine being. Conceptual pairs like good/evil, personal/ impersonal, and even A/non-A cannot be separated in God. These function only at the level of logical thought. At the highest levels of reality, conceptual distinctions break down because they treat as divided what is actually undivided. Since language depends on logic, pantheists usually assert *God to be ineffable or indescribable.

*Epistemologically, in their ways of knowing, pantheists fit into two general categories. Religious pantheists are often *mystical. Mysticism teaches a communion with God which bypasses discursive thought. Through *ascetic or meditative practices, mystics claim to experience God directly, intuitively and/or ineffably. Philosophical pantheists often use rationalism, the method of reason unadulterated by sense-data, for knowledge of God. Representatives of this latter group include Benedict *Spinoza and Georg W. F. *Hegel.

Religious pantheisms appear in each of the world's five major religions. Most prominently, major religions which sprang from India, *Hinduism and Mahayana ('Greater Vehicle') *Buddhism, presuppose the pantheism of the ancient Hindu scriptures, the Upanishads. Modern proponents include the Hindu Sarvepalli Radhakrishnan (1888–1975), and the Zen Buddhist D. T. Suzuki (1870–1966). But pantheists have also been found among the theistic religions, Judaism, Christianity and Islam. In Christianity, mystics like John Scotus *Eriugena, Meister Eckhart (c. 1260–1327) and Jacob *Boehme at least border on pantheism because of the influence of the Neoplatonic mystic, Plotinus (c. 205–70; see *Platonism).

Theists, however, have generally resisted pantheistic expressions. They often hold that pantheism destroys God's personality and goodness for it affirms that God is beyond such conceptual opposites as personality/ impersonality and good/evil. They also criticize pantheism for implying that life in this world, including ethics, has little importance. Biblical Christianity in particular finds pantheism unacceptable, for it blurs the distinction between the *Creator and his creatures.

Philosophers who argue against pantheism raise several questions. What empirical evidence could ever count for pantheism's claim of unity? Further, what reasons could be given to call this unity divine?

Bibliography

Texts: Jacob Boehme, *Works*, ed. C. J. Barber (London, 1909); G. W. F. Hegel, *Lectures on the Philosophy of Religion*, tr. E. B. Speirs and J. B. Sanderson, 3 vols. (London, 1962); Meister Eckhart, *Meister Eckhart: The Essential Sermons, Commentaries, Treatises, and Defense*, tr. E. Colledge and B. McGinn (New York, 1981); S. Radhakrishnan, *Indian Philosophy*, 2 vols. (London, 1929); B. Spinoza, *The Chief Works*, tr. R. H. M. Elwes, 2 vols. (New York, 1951).

Studies: N. Geisler, *Christian Apologetics* (Grand Rapids, 1976); C. Hodge, *Systematic Theology* (1872–3, repr. Grand Rapids, 1981); H. P. Owen, *Concepts of Deity* (New York, 1971); C. E. Plumptre, *General Sketch of the History of Pantheism* (Cambridge, 2011); D. T. Suzuki, *Essays in Zen Buddhism*, 3 vols. (New York, 1949).

D. K. CLARK

PAPACY

In Roman Catholicism the papacy describes the office and court (or Curia) of the Bishop of Rome, who occupies a primary role among bishops and as such exercises 'full, supreme and universal power over the whole church' (*Lumen Gentium*, 22). Although the terms *pappas* and *papa* (Gk and Lat. 'father') were applied to various church leadership roles from the third century, more specific designations evolved in relation to the patriarch of Alexandria in the east and to the Bishop of Rome in the west. However, whereas patriarchal authority in the east developed along more plural lines, Rome's assertion of a monarchical universal primacy reflected its historic place at the centre of empire and its relatively wider territorial reach. It also rested on certain key theological claims.

Rome was associated with the martyrdom of Peter and Paul, who respectively represented the Jewish and Gentile missions of the church. On this basis *Irenaeus and *Tertullian hinted at a primary role for Rome – a primacy which Stephen (254–257), Siricius (384–398) and Innocent (401–447) institutionalized in various ways before Leo I (440–461) appropriated the pagan title *pontifex maximus* ('great bridge-builder'), intervened decisively in the Council of *Chalcedon (453), and declared that 'fullness of power' resided with the pontiff. Gelasius I (492–496) asserted this power further by declaring himself 'Vicar of Christ'. The title 'pope' itself had by now become largely reserved to Rome – an exclusivity which would be formalized in 1073.

As the concept of Roman primacy developed in the early medieval period, it was expounded increasingly in relation to Peter rather than Paul. Matt. 16:18–19 ('You are Peter, and on this rock I will build my church') had been cited in favour of this bias from at least the second century, but Stephen and Leo inferred from it a unique Petrine *succession* through a continuous lineage of popes. As it has developed, this notion has become perhaps the most contentious aspect of Roman Catholic dogma with respect to the papacy.

The general importance of Peter in the NT is clear. He was the first disciple to be called by Jesus (Matt. 4:18–19), comes first in the list of apostles (Matt. 10:2), is first to confess Jesus as Messiah (Matt. 16:16), is first among the Twelve to see the risen Christ (1 Cor. 15:5), and preaches as the church is formed on the Day of Pentecost (Acts 2:14). He is also identified as the author of two canonical epistles. However, Roman Catholic ecclesiology moves more debatably beyond these basic points to infer a strong continuity from the apostles on whom the church is founded (Eph. 2:20), to the bishops who emerged as metropolitan and regional overseers in the second and third centuries of the church's life. Within this logic, the chief apostle, Peter, is taken to be the first bishop in both a chronological and a primatial sense. Moreover, because the church is eternal, it is held that Peter must have initiated a line of successors who would embody the continuity of that church. Further support for this is claimed from Jesus' charges to Peter in Luke 22:32 ('Strengthen your brothers') and John 21:15–17 ('Feed my sheep').

This model of Petrine succession was elaborated as the papacy gained power and influence during the Middle Ages. Following the sack of Rome, Gregory I ('the Great', 590–604) restored the Western church's confidence by evangelizing the Lombards and sponsoring mission across northern Europe. However, the Lombard threat persisted and in 756 Pope Stephen II sought an alliance against them with the Frankish king Pepin III. In return for papal patronage, Pepin confirmed the Curia's right to large tracts of land in central Italy, which became known as the Papal States and which remained in the church's hands until 1870, when the pontificate's civic jurisdiction was restricted to Vatican City.

In 800 Pope Leo III anointed Pepin's successor Charlemagne as Holy Roman Emperor, yet as the papacy assimilated the trappings of imperial power, tensions mounted between lay and ecclesiastical rule. Indeed, overweening politicization was one of several charges laid against it by the Eastern Church at the Great Schism of 1054. Gregory VII (1073–85) went so far as to assert Petrine papal supremacy over secular as well as sacred rulers, and Boniface VIII (1294–1303) carried two swords to symbolize both spiritual and temporal power. Boniface's bull *Unam Sanctam* (1302) insisted that there was no salvation outside the church, but more specifically defined this church as the Church of Rome and justified its claim with an extensive apologetic for Petrine primacy. The *Council of Florence (1438–45) subsequently asserted the superiority of the pope over all councils. This was exploited by Leo X (1513–21), whose granting of indulgences (see *Penance) to fund the renovation of St Peter's basilica spurred the protest of Martin Luther and so helped to provoke the *Reformation.

In the seventeenth and eighteenth centuries it was not only Protestants who questioned papal power. Catholic groups including the Gallicans and *Jansenists in France and the Febronians in Germany variously argued for their national churches' independence from Rome, and for the submission of pontifical to conciliar authority. In reaction, the movement which came to be known as Ultramontanism sought to centralize yet more power within the papacy, and saw many of its aims fulfilled at the First *Vatican Council of 1870 – not least in that Council's declaration of papal infallibility.

According to Vatican I, the Pontiff's Petrine lineage means that he is 'teacher of all Christians'. When he invokes this teaching authority *ex cathedra* to explain 'a doctrine of faith or morals to be held by the Universal Church', he 'operates with that infallibility with which the divine Redeemer wishes that His church be instructed'. Considerable debate followed on what might retrospectively be considered *ex cathedra*. As it was, only Pope Pius IX's pronouncement of the immaculate conception of *Mary (1854) was clearly defined as such. In the decades after Vatican I various papal challenges to theological and cultural modernism were published, but were not deemed infallible. Then, in 1950, infallibility was accorded to Pope Pius XII's affirmation of the bodily assumption of Mary.

Critiques of papal infallibility typically derive from broader biblical and historical critiques of Petrine succession. They point out that the discourse of ecclesial leadership in the NT sees pastors, teachers, deacons, presbyters and overseers deployed in various configurations (see *Church government), and that it is thus far more complex than a straight line from apostles to bishops, or from Peter to the papacy, would suggest. They underline that Peter's authority is shared with the other apostles (Matt. 18:18), and that in his own terms he is 'an apostle' rather than the chief apostle (1 Pet. 1:1). It is often added that Peter is very obviously flawed – earning Jesus' rebuke (Matt. 16:23), denying him after his arrest (Matt. 26:69–75), and reneging on support for Paul's Gentile mission (Gal. 2:11). While papal infallibility does not rest on the thoroughgoing sinlessness of Peter, it is nonetheless argued that the criteria for infallible pronouncements are unclear. It is because of this, perhaps, that infallibility has been so rarely applied, and then only to two marginal, and biblically questionable, Marian dogmas.

The Second Vatican Council of 1962–65 took place in an ecclesiastical and cultural context very different from that which marked Vatican I. The rise of the *ecumenical movement and the related interaction of Catholic, Protestant and Orthodox scholarship were influential, and while Petrine succession and papal infallibility were reaffirmed, Vatican II placed far more emphasis on the whole 'college' of bishops, in which the Bishop of Rome is 'first among equals'. While this college could not function without the Supreme Pontiff at its head, it was nonetheless seen to express 'the variety and universality of the people of God' (*Lumen Gentium*, 22).

Since Vatican II the Roman Catholic Church has engaged in various dialogues with other churches on supremacy. The Anglican-Roman Catholic International Commission agreed on the special place of Rome in the early church, and affirmed in principle the desirability of universal primacy. Yet it has failed to reach consensus on existing papal arrangements, and on infallibility in particular. Similar conclusions have been reached in bilateral conversations between Rome and Lutheran and Orthodox churches. Unsurprisingly, non-episcopal denominations have found it harder to identify common ground in this matter, with certain more conservative Protestants viewing the very concept of universal primacy as intrinsically antithetical to the gospel.

While theological debate about the papacy will continue, its global profile has been developed in more recent decades, not least by John Paul II (1978–2005) and Benedict XVI (2005–13), whose extensive international travelling and harnessing of modern communications have ensured that it remains one of the most significant offices held by any individual on earth.

See also: ROMAN CATHOLIC THEOLOGY.

Bibliography

C. E. Braaten and R. W. Jenson (eds.), *Church Unity and the Papal Office* (Grand Rapids, 2001); R. E. Brown, K. P. Donfried and J. Reumann (eds.), *Peter in the New Testament* (London, 1974); E. Duffy, *Saints and Sinners: A History of the Popes* (New Haven and London, ³2006); A. Flannery (ed.), *Vatican Council II: Constitutions, Decrees, Declarations* (Northport, 1996); K. Schatz, *Primacy from Its Origins to the Present* (Collegeville, 1996); J. M. R. Tilliard, *The Bishop of Rome* (London, 1983).

D. H. K. HILBORN

PARADIGM

A paradigm is literally an example, especially a normative example, in the light of which the whole class is to be understood. The word may be used theologically in the following ways.

In philosophy, 'paradigm case' arguments are sometimes used against sceptical positions. So, if it is denied that free will exists, the argument would be that 'freedom' is to be understood in terms not of some abstract definition, but of paradigm cases such as lovers deciding to marry. Such cases certainly exist; so therefore does freedom. Critics reply that this would have 'proved' the reality of witchcraft. Moreover, concepts so defined are of limited use: is 'freedom' thus understood the 'freedom' relevant to moral responsibility?

Martin Dibelius (1883–1947) used the term for gospel passages used by early Christian preachers as examples of 'that which Jesus was and brought into being'. Paradigms end in thoughts useful for preaching purposes, usually a saying of Jesus. Dibelius thought paradigms historically valuable, though sometimes modified by preachers or evangelists.

In recent decades theologians and ecumenists have drawn on the approach of the philosopher of science, Thomas Kuhn (1922–96). Controversially, he argues that the development of science is characterized by the alternation of periods in which 'normal science' solves the problems which arise in connection with the overarching framework of understanding provided by a paradigm, with periods of revolutionary changes in understanding which are precipitated when the amount of anomalies and unsolved 'puzzles' becomes too great for a paradigm to bear and it is replaced by a new one.

Bibliography

G. Carey, *I Believe in Man* (London, 1977); M. Dibelius, *From Tradition to Gospel* (ET, London, 1934); E. Gellner, *Words and Things* (London, 1959); H. King and D. Tracy (eds.), *Paradigm Change in Theology* (Edinburgh and New York, 1989); T. S. Kuhn, *The Structure of Scientific Revolutions* (Chicago and London, ²1970); K. Raiser, *Ecumenism in Transition* (Geneva, 1991); P. Schilpp (ed.), *The Philosophy of G. E. Moore* (New York, ²1952).

R. L. STURCH

PARADOX IN THEOLOGY

A paradox (from Gk *para* and *doxa*, 'against opinion') is *an apparent contradiction or logical absurdity*. Paradoxes may be divided into three broad categories:

(1) *Rhetorical* paradoxes. Here the contradiction appears only at the surface verbal level. When the statements are understood with the appropriate qualifications, they are seen to be logically consistent, but restating them in a non-paradoxical form sacrifices the rhetorical impact. Biblical examples include 'the last will be first, and the first last' (Matt. 20:16) and 'when I am weak, then I am strong' (2 Cor. 12:10).

(2) *Philosophical* paradoxes. Some of our commonsense intuitions about basic notions, such as being, change, truth, rationality and free choice, can be shown to entail apparent contradictions. The identification and resolution of such paradoxes has been a central theme in the history of philosophy. Famous examples include Zeno's paradoxes (seeking to show that our assumptions about the reality of motion entail contradictions) and the Liar Paradox ('This statement is false' appears to be false if true, and true if false). Proposed resolutions typically require us to repudiate one of the intuitions or assumptions involved.

(3) *Theological* paradoxes. It has been traditionally held that theology involves propositional truth claims about *God: his attributes, his relationship to the world, his actions within the world, and so forth. Theologians occasionally make claims which seem to them (or to others) to entail contradictions, either within the claims themselves or with respect to other firmly held beliefs. The problem is acute when the claims in question are taken to be essential tenets of orthodoxy or strongly supported by inspired Scriptures.

Examples of theological paradoxes within mainstream Christianity include: the *Trinity (the three persons of the Godhead are distinct, and each is fully God, yet there is only one God); the *incarnation (the transcendent, immutable God became a man in space and time); the *hypostatic union (Christ is one person with both a divine nature and a human nature, and thus is omniscient and limited in knowledge, omnipresent and limited in location, impeccable yet susceptible to temptation, etc.); and the claim that God has infallible foreknowledge of human *free choices. Some traditions within Christianity face their own distinctive paradoxes (e.g. the Reformed teaching that God foreordains all things, yet we are morally responsible for our actions; see *Predestination).

Such paradoxes present a challenge to the rationality of Christian beliefs. Various approaches to theological paradoxes have been proposed, including: (1) The paradoxes involve real contradictions, but God is not bound by 'human logic'. (2) The paradoxes involve real contradictions, and therefore some traditional doctrines need to be revised or (more radically) abandoned. (3) Through creative philosophical reflection the relevant doctrines can be explicated in logically consistent ways without compromising orthodoxy, thus showing that the apparent contradictions are *merely* apparent. (4) The paradoxes do not ultimately involve real contradictions, but they resist resolution on account of divine incomprehensibility and the limitations of the human mind. The same approach need not be followed in every case, but which approach is favoured will depend largely on one's broader theological and philosophical commitments.

Bibliography

J. N. Anderson, *Paradox in Christian Theology* (Eugene, 2007); R. W. Hepburn, *Christianity and Paradox* (London, 1958); R. M. Sainsbury, *Paradoxes* (Cambridge, ³2009).

J. N. ANDERSON

PAROUSIA, see ESCHATOLOGY

PASCAL, BLAISE (1623–62)

Pascal, whose early genius emerged in mathematics, experimental physics and practical inventions, was converted to *Jansenism at Rouen in 1646. He participated in the social, intellectual and cultural life of Paris until his 'night of fire' (1654), an experience of intense assurance, joy and peace through Christ, leading to the total consecration of his life to God. Visiting the Jansenist community at Port-Royal, he was invited to rally public support for their leader, Antoine Arnauld, accused of heresy by the Sorbonne. In fourteen months he wrote a series of anonymous pamphlets, ten addressed to a provincial priest and eight to the Jesuits. With biting satire *The Provincial Letters* exposed the intellectual dishonesty of Arnauld's opponents and the moral hypocrisy of the Jesuits, who were the leading faction.

His chief legacy is an *apologia of the Christian religion, aimed at the educated unbeliever of his day. Ill health restricted it to sketches, some developed, others telegraphic, which the Jansenists published posthumously as the *Pensées*. Pascal eschews the traditional proofs for the existence of God, based on pure reason or deduced from the cosmos. Human reason is faulty, affected by instincts, illnesses and delusions, subject to pride, incapable of establishing first principles (*contra* *Descartes), let alone of bringing us to a knowledge of God and of our eternal destiny; at best it establishes only an abstract God and is powerless to move the heart (in the biblical sense, Ps. 119:36) – the highest order of human awareness, which is persuaded by grace alone. Instead, Pascal the *empiricist starts with the data, notably the inexplicable phenomenon of humankind: unquestionably corrupt, subject to inconstancy, boredom, anxiety and selfishness, doing anything in the waking hours to divert the mind from human wretchedness, yet showing the vestiges of inherent greatness in the mind's realization of this condition. Humankind is also finite, suspended between the twin infinities revealed by telescope and microscope, and aware of an inner emptiness which the finite world fails to satisfy. No philosophy makes sense of this. No moral system makes us better or happier. One hypothesis alone, creation in the divine image followed by the fall, explains our predicament and, through a redeemer and mediator with God, offers to restore our rightful state. Pascal proceeds to challenge his reader to commitment to Christ and to eternal life, particularly in his famous 'wager' passage, and then presents evidence for the truth of Christianity by showing its perpetuity from the first man until the end of time and Christ's excellence as mediator in perfectly combining human greatness with human degradation on the cross; further, the whole OT finds fulfilment in him, whose redemption relieves despair, humbles pride and empowers us to do good while not rendering us totally sinless.

The *Pensées* remain striking by their almost unique approach to apologetics, their deep, compassionate understanding of humankind without God and the persuasive prose of some of the developed sections. Their readership has multiplied in our affluent, anxious generation; many modern writers who reject Pascal's solution show the influence of his analysis of the human condition.

Bibliography

Works: A. Krailsheimer (ed.), *Pensées* (Harmondsworth, 1966); *idem* (ed.), *The Provincial Letters* (Harmondsworth, 1967).

Studies: D. Adamson, *Blaise Pascal: Mathematician, Physicist, and Thinker about God* (New York, 1995); J. H. Broome, *Pascal* (London, 1965); D. Groothuis, *On Pascal* (Belmont, CA, 2002); J. Jordan, *Pascal's Wager: Pragmatic Arguments and Belief in God* (Oxford, 2006); A. Krailsheimer, *Pascal* (Oxford,

1980); J. Mesnard, *Pascal: His Life and Works* (London, 1952).

D. G. Preston

PASCHAL CONTROVERSIES, see EASTER

PASCHASIUS RADBERTUS
(*c*. 785–*c*. 860)

The theologian Paschasius Radbertus was the first explicit proponent of transubstantiation. Monk, and for a time abbot, of the Benedictine monastery at Corbie in modern France, he issued in 831 the first separate treatise on the doctrine of the Holy Communion, *De Corpore et Sanguine Domini* (*On the Body and Blood of the Lord*). It brought to a head the tendencies of the immediately preceding centuries, by interpreting the emphatic language of many of the Fathers about the presence of Christ in the sacrament, or in the elements, in a strictly literal sense, as meaning that the true body and blood of Christ which suffered on the cross are present, through being made out of the substance of the bread and wine – though without altering the appearance or taste of the latter (see *Eucharist). The doctrine of transubstantiation was defined by the Fourth *Lateran Council (1215), and Paschasius is a saint of the Roman calendar. He seems to have expected opposition, and the revised edition of his book (844) was given by King Charles the Bald to *Ratramnus, and perhaps to John Scotus *Eriugena, for them to answer. Paschasius wrote various other works, including a long commentary on Matthew.

Bibliography

Works: in *PL* 120; extracts, with translations, in C. Herbert, *The Lord's Supper: Uninspired Teaching* (London, 1879); discussion in N. Dimock, *The Doctrine of the Lord's Supper* (London, 1910).

R. T. Beckwith

PATRISTIC THEOLOGY

The contribution of the early teachers of faith, a heterogeneous group ranging from those who wrote (or writings) ranging from the time that the NT was coming into being to seven or eight centuries after that, fall into a category traditionally called the teachings of the 'Fathers' (Lat. *patres*) or patristics. It has now been recognized that this understanding is too narrow and that we have to acknowledge the role and contribution of women writers and theologians of this period also. The writings range from liturgical material and directions for the ordering of worship, to apologetic and polemical writings, from teachings on the sacraments to speculations on the Trinity, from responses to questions on Christian life and practice, to analysis of 'heretical' teachings, from considerations about the link between the humanity and divinity of Christ, to questions regarding the relationship between the church and the state. These writings, which span the range of theological, ethical, poetic, linguistic, ritualistic, historical and polemical, and philosophical genres are mainly available in Latin, Greek and Syriac sources, although other local languages were also used. Some writers, because of a long tradition of transmission of manuscripts, are well-represented, and a wide range of their writings are available; others are known to us only through allusion or references in other writings, and their own contributions are lost.

Some of the writings and writers who are important in considering patristic theology are Clement of Rome, the *Didache*, Ignatius of Antioch, accounts of martyrdom like the description of the deaths of Perpetua and Felicitas, *Clement of Alexandria, *Tertullian, *Origen, *Cyprian of Carthage, *Athanasius, *Cyril of Alexandria, *creedal formulations like the Nicene-Constantinopolitan Creed, the church historian *Eusebius, *Ambrose, *Augustine, *Basil of Caesarea, *Gregory of Nazianaus, *Gregory of Nyssa, John *Chrysostom, *Jerome, Aphrahat, Ephrem and John Cassian. This is by no means a comprehensive list and there are many others who have contributed to patristic theology, a contribution that is not limited to formal writings alone, but can also be found in tombstone inscriptions, worship patterns, church architecture, laws and legal codes, and editions of the Scriptures. Some of those represented have been considered 'orthodox' in their views and teachings, and others have been derided as exhibiting 'heretical' tendencies. Some who became prominent in one region were looked upon with suspicion by those from another region, and some who were considered to be championing 'orthodoxy' at one period were held to have been schismatics or *heretics by those holding other ideological or theological positions. Debate, dialogue, confrontation, uncertainty, deliberate misunderstanding and attempts at consensus marked patristic theology through and through.

The variety and range of writers and writings exhibited by those who contributed to patristic theology are an indication that 'consensus' regarding faith and order was always elusive. Even when attempts were made through more or less representative *councils or 'synods' to arrive at consensus, not all were pleased at the outcome, and tensions because of strongly held views continued to be a mark of this period. In addition, historical vicissitudes also played a major role in the process of how doctrines, teachings and practices came into being.

In spite of these caveats, the teachings and examples of the early teachers of faith continue to be of importance in extremely significant ways to Christian theology and the life and witness of the church today. In that sense we reach back to patristic theology in order to move forward in our ecumenical quest today. Although there are ebbs and flows in how certain writers have been appropriated or ignored, nevertheless these writings offer us a rich treasure trove of material to which we can return time and again with profit, to be illumined and admonished. Even though the church is now a global phenomenon, the writings of the early teachers of faith are a repository to which those coming from various regions and locations, and also from varied traditions, can return to, even when there may not be a direct genealogical or geographical link to particular 'Fathers'.

Some of the perennial questions which continue to enliven the life of the church are questions with which patristic theology struggled. Although these struggles may not be of direct relevance to those of us in the twenty-first century, one can benefit from a study of how in another time and place and under very different situations real people struggled and dealt with similar issues and themes. In that sense the dead continue to speak to us, feeding into the living stream of tradition, which is watered from many sources. Such questions include those regarding the nature of *theology and theologizing, the attributes of *God, the meaning of the affirmation that God was in *Christ, the role and function of the *Holy Spirit, intra-*trinitarian dynamics, God-*creation-world inter-relationships, the destiny of human beings, the understanding of life, death and eternal life, hope in the second coming of Christ, the ends of God and the end of the world (see *Eschatology).

There are several other areas that would benefit from such a conversation with long-dead seekers of salvation, healing and wholeness, to say nothing of nasty church politicians, scheming bureaucrats, those condemned as heretics by one group of people and venerated as saints by another, faithful and misunderstood disciples, seekers of varied ways of responding to the living out of the Christian faith in complex intercultural situations. Some of these areas are the study of our *liturgical traditions, the attitude to women in our churches, the understanding of the *history that has shaped us, the search for new symbols and images for faith articulation, an analysis of Christology in its encounter with cultures, the methodology of biblical interpretation (see *Hermeneutics), the search for a genuine and meaningful *spirituality, the understanding of *poverty and prosperity, the changing patterns of *family life, and the quest for *ecumenical inter-relationships across doctrinal divisions.

The writings of the early teachers of faith which form patristic theology have been influential directly and indirectly in all forms of theologizing up to the present, and in this sense continue to offer us the ongoing possibility of bringing out of *our* treasure what is new and what is old (Matt. 13:52).

Bibliography

P. M. Blowers *et al.* (eds.), *In Dominico Eloquio – In Lordly Eloquence: Essays on Patristic Exegesis in Honor of Robert Louis Wilken* (Grand Rapids, 2002); P. Brown, *The Body and Society: Men, Women, and Sexual Renunciation in Early Christianity* (New York, 1988); B. E. Daley, *The Hope of the Early Church: A Handbook of Patristic Eschatology* (Peabody, 2003); W. H. C. Frend, *The Rise of Christianity* (Minneapolis, 1986); C. A. Hall, *Reading Scripture with the Church Fathers* (Downers Grove, 1998); idem, *Learning Theology with the Church Fathers* (Downers Grove, 2002); A. J. Malherbe, F. W. Norris and J. W. Thompson (eds.), *The Early Church in Its Context: Essays in Honor of Everett Ferguson* (Leiden, 1998); J. J. Sebastian, *Enlivening the Past: An Asian Theologian's Engagement with the Early Teachers of Faith* (Piscataway, 2009); C. A. Volz, *Pastoral Life and Practice in the Early Church*

J. J. Sebastian

PELAGIANISM

Pelagianism was a current of teaching in the *ascetic movement in the West in the fifth century, of which Pelagius is commonly regarded as the fountain head. Its theological outlook was characterized by: an insistence on the adequacy of created human nature, essentially unimpaired by Adam's *fall, to fulfil the will of God; the denial of original *sin as either *guilt or corruption transmitted from *Adam to all humankind; the highest moral and spiritual expectations of the baptized Christian who must be capable of a life of perfect holiness, because God commands him thereto; and an understanding of the gifts of grace that excludes, or at best drastically minimizes, that enabling power without whose inner working we can do nothing acceptable to God.

In reality, the Pelagian movement was neither uniform nor united by Pelagius's sole inspiration. Nevertheless, the traditional terminology remains useful. The label 'Pelagian' is often loosely invoked to damn any doctrine felt to threaten the primacy of *grace, faith and spiritual regeneration over human ability, good works and moral endeavour.

Pelagius was a British layman who gained acceptance in Rome *c.* 400 as a teacher of Christian asceticism. He wrote letters of ascetic counsel, some treatises (including a credally orthodox *Faith in the Trinity*) and a commentary on the Pauline epistles. These works drew on several Christian sources, including *Origen, Ambrosiaster and *Augustine. Strongly persuaded of the goodness of the created order, he opposed whatever denigrated it, such as *Manichaeism and even *Jerome's more extravagant asceticism. One gift of grace was God's inviolable endowment of the human creature with self-determination. Although the fall set in train a habit of sinning, to the detriment of subsequent generations, the created abilities (*posse*) of the *will, though overlaid with inveterate custom or obscured by forgetfulness or ignorance, remained as God made them, and needed only our act of will (*velle*) to make the accomplishing of God's will a reality (*esse*). To this end was added the grace of revelation and illumination, by both *law and *gospel. In conversion and baptism (assumed to be that of the responsible believer), the grace of the forgiveness of past sins was assured (unlike Paul, Pelagius wrote explicitly of *justification 'by faith *alone*'). Thereafter, however, the Christian was deemed capable of realizing the potential of his created powers. Above all, there was no room for the dismal defeatism or fatalism in the face of sin that Pelagius claimed to find in Augustine's *Confessions*. The church must be a community zealous for Christian perfection.

The Gothic advance on Rome in 410 dispersed Pelagius and his supporters, southwards to Sicily and Roman Africa, and eastwards to Palestine in particular. His associate Celestius was the first 'Pelagian' to incur the censure of the church, at Carthage in 411. Similar in background to Pelagius, he was nevertheless a more combative and possibly less guileful spirit. He clumsily offended received Catholic beliefs in Africa by asserting that Adam was mortal before his fall, which injured no-one but himself, and that infants were baptized not for the remission of sin (for there was no original sin), but to obtain sanctification or the kingdom of heaven. These opinions of Celestius were apparently disowned by Pelagius in Palestine in 415, when he was acquitted by two synods of Eastern bishops. Celestius had himself appealed to one Rufinus 'the Syrian' in defence of his denial of the transmission of sin. This shadowy figure (not to be confused with Rufinus of Aquileia) illustrates both the diversity of 'Pelagian' views (for, unlike Celestius, he taught that Adam would not have died had he remained sinless) and the ultimate Eastern roots, or at least affinities, of Pelagian ideas (although his role is exaggerated by the writer who depicts him as the inspirer of Pelagius himself). Rufinus rejected the traducianist theory of the origin of the *soul, which suited belief in the transmission of original sin, and was a sharp critic of Origen. The disputes about Origen's speculative doctrines, not least the pre-existence of souls, were a powerful undercurrent in the Pelagian controversy.

The condemnation of Celestius and Pelagius was spearheaded by the African episcopate instructed by Augustine. The *Council of Carthage in 418 anathematized the following teachings: the natural, rather than penal, mortality of Adam; the denial of infant baptism, and of original sin derived from Adam and requiring cleansing in baptism for the newborn; the restriction of justifying grace to the remission of past sins, excluding its help against committing future sins; the restriction of the aid that grace gives against sinning to the enlightening of the understanding, to the exclusion of the implanting of love which enables us to delight in and obey the will of God; the assertion that grace merely enables us to do more easily what we could still do without it, albeit with greater difficulty; and the denial of the plain statements of 1 John 1:8–9 and the implications of the Lord's Prayer ('forgive us our debts') in order to claim that one is in reality without sin.

African pressure was largely instrumental in eliciting a conclusive condemnation of Pelagian teachings from Pope Zosimus later in 418. Its terms are only partly recorded, but it certainly affirmed the universal transmission of sin from Adam, resulting in that captivity to sin from which all need to be set free through baptism, which has the same force for infant and adult alike. The (third ecumenical) Council of *Ephesus in 431 also condemned any who shared the opinions of Celestius.

A group of Italian bishops led by Julian of Eclanum in South Italy (c. 386–c. 455) refused to subscribe to Zosimus' verdict. Julian now became the protagonist for Pelagian beliefs, conducting an increasingly bitter controversy with Augustine until the latter's death. Fragments of his works survive largely in Augustine's replies. Extant expositions of Job and of Hosea, Joel and Amos are with considerable probability ascribed to Julian.

This phase of the controversy is important more for elaborations in Augustine's thought (which in turn provoked the anti-Augustinian reaction known misleadingly as *Semi-Pelagianism) than for significant new teachings expounded by Julian. He attributed Augustine's account of humanity's bondage to sin to his incurable Manichaeism, and generally systematized Pelagian doctrines, which made him a more formidable opponent than either Pelagius or Celestius. More central to this phase of the controversy were predestination (Julian charged Augustine's God with injustice), the sinful concupiscence persisting in the Christian after baptism, and sexual intercourse between inevitably concupiscent partners as the medium for the transmission of original sin.

Pelagianism was important for provoking new or sharper clarification of Catholic beliefs on issues untouched by earlier controversies in the East, where they were inadequately understood. Modern study has rescued Pelagius and his fellows from the ranks of the moralists and humanists, recognizing their serious religious intent and their claim to be faithful to earlier tradition in areas where much was undefined. But the Pelagian assessment of the effects of Adam's fall and understanding of grace cannot be squared with Scripture, although the church, in decisively rejecting Pelagian views, did not wholly endorse Augustine's refutations.

Bibliography

T. Bohlin, *Die Theologie des Pelagius und ihre Genesis* (Uppsala, 1957); G. Bonner, *Augustine and Modern Research on Pelagianism* (Villanova, 1972); idem, 'How Pelagian Was Pelagius?', *SP* 9, 1966, pp. 350–358; P. Brown, *Religion and Society in the Age of St Augustine* (London, 1972); R. F. Evans, *Pelagius: Inquiries and Reappraisals* (London, 1968), and *Four Letters of Pelagius* (London, 1968); J. Ferguson, *Pelagius: A Historical and Theological Study* (Cambridge, 1956); G. de Plinval, *Pélage: Ses écrits, sa vie et sa réforme* (Lausanne, 1943); B. R. Rees, *Pelagius: A Reluctant Heretic* (Woodbridge, 1988); D. F. Wright, 'Pelagius the Twice-Born', *Churchman* 86, 1972, pp. 6–15.

D. F. Wright

PELIKAN, JAROSLAV (1923–2006)

An American scholar of mixed Serbian and Slovak origin, Pelikan was Professor of History at Yale University from 1962 to 1996. A Lutheran for most of his life, he converted to *Eastern Orthodoxy in 1996, regarding this more as a natural progression than as a change in religious orientation. Pelikan specialized in the history of Christian thought, to which he contributed a large number of editions and original works. His most notable achievement was his five-volume work *The Christian Tradition* (1971–89), a magisterial, thematic study of Christian *doctrine from its beginnings to its multiple manifestations in the modern world. He also translated a number of volumes in the American edition of Martin Luther's works and more recently he supervised a project to edit and publish the *creeds and *confessions of all the major Christian denominations. In works like *Jesus through the Centuries* (1985) he demonstrated how a central theme can be treated in different ways according to the social, cultural and theological predilections of a given ecclesiastical milieu. In *Christianity and Classical Culture* (1993) he explored the way in which the Fathers of the church developed a *natural theology in order to integrate the positive insights of ancient Greek culture into their Christian vision of the world. His approach is both conservative and ecumenical, concentrating on broad trends and overall synthesis more than on detailed analysis of particular writers and subjects. In this respect he has provided the present generation with a comprehensive and coherent vision of what the Christian cultural inheritance has achieved and still has to offer today.

Bibliography

Works: *The Christian Tradition*, 5 vols. (Chicago, 1971–89); J. Pelikan and V. Hotchkiss (eds.), *Creeds and Confessions of Faith in the Christian Tradition* (New Haven, 2003).

Studies: V. Hotchkiss and P. Henry (eds.), *Orthodoxy and Western Culture: A Collection of Essays Honoring Jaroslav Pelikan on His Eightieth Birthday* (Crestwood, 2005).

G. L. BRAY

PENANCE

Early in Christian theology the Greek term *metanoia* was translated by the Latin term *poenitentia*, which has broadly been understood by the concepts penitence, penance, punishment, repentance and conversion. Penance is predominantly associated with the *Roman Catholic tradition and seen as a *sacramental process that eradicates sin after baptism, what Jerome described as a second plank after baptism able to save a person after a shipwreck (*Epistle* 130, 9).

In the early church, penance began as a form of discipline reserved for grave offences like apostasy, murder or adultery. It usually entailed a public confession, segregation from the congregation, exclusion from the *Eucharist, and adherence to a rigid course of prayer and fasting. At this stage in church history it was only allowed once in a person's lifetime. This practice, which was intended to amend the life of a baptized sinner, became theologically buttressed by *Tertullian's work *De paenitentia*, which also introduced legal concepts into Western theology (e.g. *merit and *satisfaction). With this development, early in the third century, the church began seeing penance in terms of a divine contractual obligation.

In the Eastern Church penance developed differently. Here penance provided spiritual direction and was mainly a private pastoral rite. This Eastern practice influenced the sixth-century Celtic writing of elaborate penance manuals (penitentials). Now penance was seen as the private confession to a priest, absolution and completing a light formal penance. This structure gained popularity during the early Middle Ages and influenced the move toward private penance on the continent. Through the influence of Peter *Lombard's *Sentences* (*c.* 1150), penance was seen as a sacrament, and at the Fourth *Lateran Council (1215) the rite of penance became mandatory for all Christians, requiring the confession of sins once a year.

In the Late Middle Ages the doctrine became the foundation of the *nominalist view that forgiveness could be gained through a contractual agreement that God required penitents 'to do only what they are capable of' (*facere quod in se*). Luther's doctrines of salvation by grace alone and justification by faith were partly a reaction against this nominalist view of penance. The *Reformers unanimously rejected the contractual nature of this sacrament (esp. its related ideas of satisfaction, indulgences, merit and *purgatory). Instead of a sacrament, the Reformers interpreted penance as turning one's entire life to God (cf. *Inst.* 3.3.1). More recently in both Catholic and Protestant theology, and in ecumenical dialogue, penance has been viewed broadly in terms of Jesus' summons to return to God.

Bibliography

P. Anciaux, *The Sacrament of Penance* (London, 1962); J. Bossy, 'The Social History of Confession in the Age of the Reformation', in *Transactions of the Royal Historical Society* fifth series, vol. 25 (1975), pp. 21–38; H. Connolly, *Irish Penitentials and Their Significance for the Sacrament of Penance* (Portland, 1995); Tertullian, *Treatises on Penance* (ET, New York, 1959); O. Watkins, *History of Penance* (London, 1920).

B. LUGIOYO

PENTECOST, see BAPTISM IN THE SPIRIT; HOLY SPIRIT

PENTECOSTAL THEOLOGY

Pentecostal theology has its roots in nineteenth-century *holiness groups holding John Wesley's doctrine of entire *sanctification, sometimes called the *baptism of the Spirit, and an enduement of power; the teaching of the Keswick Conventions that the 'higher Christian life' was to be experienced after a post-conversion crisis of consecration (see *Higher-life theology); the teaching of R. A. Torrey (1856–1928) that the baptism of the Spirit was a post-conversion enduement of power for witness, not sanctification; the teaching of A. B. Simpson (1843–1919) and A. J. Gordon (1836–95) that divine healing was to be received by faith; and the *dispensational premillennialism (see *Millennium) of J. N. *Darby. These streams all contributed to the 'four-square' emphases of Pentecostal preaching: Christ the Saviour, the baptizer in the Holy Spirit, the healer and the coming King.

Origins and spread

In the late-nineteenth century supernatural manifestations, including glossolalia, were reported in the United States, and in India and Korea in the first decade of the twentieth century. However, the origin of Pentecostalism has been commonly dated to 1 January 1901, when Miss Agnes Ozman, a student at Bethel Bible College, Topeka, Kansas, spoke in tongues after the principal, Charles Fox Parham, laid hands on her and prayed for her to receive the power of the Spirit. Henceforth, for Pentecostals, the supreme sign of being baptized in the Spirit would be speaking in tongues. This is considered to be the gateway to vivid experience of God, lively worship, the gifts of the Spirit (especially divine healing) and power for Christian witness and service. The beginnings of Pentecostalism were encouraged by reports of the dramatic phenomena in the Welsh revival of 1904–5.

Powerful Pentecostal phenomena occurred at a revival (1906–9) at the Azusa Street Apostolic Faith Mission, Los Angeles, led by William J. Seymour, a former student of Parham. Within a few years Pentecostalism had spread widely in the USA, especially through the considerable influence of pastors who had witnessed the revival at Azusa Street, which was visited by Christians from around the world. At least twenty-six denominations trace their Pentecostal roots to this revival.

Pentecostal teaching was introduced to Europe by Cecil Polhill (1860–1938) and the Oslo-based Thomas Ball Barratt (1862–1940), who imparted it in 1907 to the Anglican vicar of Monkwearmouth, Alexander A. Boddy (1854–1930). Boddy organized the annual Pentecostal conferences in Sunderland (1908–14), which were attended by some of the later British Pentecostal leaders. Due to the ministry of Lewi Pethrus (1884–1974), Pentecostalism gained a strong foothold in Scandinavia. Jonathan Paul (1853–1931) established Pentecostalism in Germany, where it was accused of being demonically inspired in the notorious Berlin Declaration of 1909.

Pentecostalism gave rise to considerable controversy among evangelicals in the first half of the twentieth century, especially over the baptism in the Spirit as a second experience after conversion, and the availability of the supernatural gifts of the Spirit, particularly speaking in tongues and divine *healing. Many holiness leaders rejected Pentecostalism, although some joined the growing movement after contact with those influenced by the Azusa Street Mission. Having taught that sanctification was a 'second blessing', some described the baptism of the Spirit with glossolalia as a 'third blessing'. Most Pentecostals, however, argued that sanctification was a progressive work following conversion, and so the baptism in the Spirit was a 'second blessing'.

Over the years many Pentecostal denominations have been formed throughout the world, sometimes due to schism, but more often to the growth of indigenous churches. Considerable growth occurred after the Second World War in North and South America, Scandinavia, sub-Sahara Africa and Korea. Underground Pentecostal churches were established in the former Soviet Empire, and millions have been drawn to the illegal Pentecostal house churches in communist China, despite intermittent severe persecution. The World Pentecostal Conference first met in 1947 in Zurich and has since met triennially.

The *charismatic renewal movement (initially called 'neo-Pentecostalism') began in the United States and gained national prominence in 1960, when the Episcopalian priest Dennis J. Bennett (1917–91) announced his experience of the baptism in the Spirit to his church in Van Nuys, California. The teachings of the charismatic movement influenced many in the historic denominations, due especially to the ministry of the American Assemblies of God minister David J. du Plessis (1905–87) and other well-known speakers. Around 1960 the charismatic movement spread to the historic denominations in Britain, where it was fostered by the Fountain Trust, founded by the Anglican Michael C. Harper (1931–2010), and its magazine *Renewal*. Another outcome was the establishment of a number of independent networks of charismatic new churches. Similar developments occurred in other European countries. The 'word of faith' movement pioneered by Kenneth E. Hagin (1917–2003), which promoted the teaching that it was possible for Christians always to claim health and prosperity from God (see *Prosperity theology), also spread to many parts of the world, although many Pentecostals rejected its teaching as unscriptural.

Since 1967 the charismatic movement has extended into the Roman Catholic Church, initially influential in the USA and Ireland and later in France and Italy. But apart from a series of five extended theological dialogues at the Vatican from 1972 to 2002, there has, in general, been little attempt amongst Pentecostals to foster fellowship with Roman Catholics. Charismatic Catholic theologians have usually regarded distinctive charismatic experiences as 'releases' or 'manifestations' of the Spirit that have been imparted to the believer at her baptism and confirmation, or sometimes labelled them, along with baptism in water, as baptisms in the Spirit, although many wished to avoid this term as being elitist and divisive.

A further phase of the charismatic movement, known as the 'third wave', developed in the 1980s under the influence of the teaching of C. Peter Wagner (b. 1930) and the healing missions of John Wimber (1934–98), the founder of the Vineyard fellowship of churches. This third wave taught that the baptism in the Holy Spirit occurs at conversion, that multiple fillings of the Holy Spirit are to be expected, and that the gifts of the Spirit, especially healing, are to be manifest. A derivative of the third wave was the 'Toronto experience' that originated in the Toronto Airport Vineyard Church under the leadership of John Arnott (b. 1940) in 1994, characterized by involuntary prostrations, ecstatic spiritual experiences, spontaneous laughter and shaking.

According to the statistician David B. Barrett, by 2000 the classical Pentecostal movement had grown to 65 million adherents, denominational charismatics to 175 million and the independent, indigenous charismatic movements, mainly in the developing world, to 295 million, the total representing 27% of the Christian population worldwide.

Distinctive doctrines

Pentecostal doctrines were expounded in the United States by well-known teachers such as Peter C. Nelson (1868–1942), Ernest S. Williams (1885–1981), Ralph M. Riggs (1895–1971), Myer Pearlman (1898–1943), Stanley M. Horton (1916–2014) and William W. Menzies (1931–2011) of the American Assemblies of God, and Charles W. Conn (1920–2008) of the Church of God (Cleveland, Tennessee). In Britain such teaching was promoted by key Pentecostal leaders such as Harold L. C. Horton (1880–1969), Donald Gee (1891–1966), A. Howard Carter (1891–1971) and his brother John H. Carter (1893–1981) of the Assemblies of God, and by George Jeffreys (1889–1962), William G. Hathaway (1892–1969), Percy S. Brewster (1908–80) and John Lancaster (b. 1925) of the Elim Pentecostal Church.

To support their doctrine that the baptism in the Spirit is an empowerment for mission subsequent to conversion (the 'subsequence' doctrine), Pentecostals hold that the anointing of Jesus with the Spirit after his baptism is a pattern to be followed by Christians, and occurred to the first disciples on the day of Pentecost, when they were baptized in the Holy Spirit and endued with power for the Great Commission. Pentecostals likewise argue that in the Acts of the Apostles the Samaritan converts of ch. 8 and the Ephesian disciples of ch. 19 were regenerate before they were baptized in the Spirit. Thus, in Luke's terminology, 'to receive the Spirit' is 'the same gift' as the baptism by Jesus in the Holy Spirit. The Holy Spirit is described as 'coming' or 'falling' upon believers with observable results, such as speaking in tongues and prophesying.

Pentecostals distinguish between the indwelling of the Holy Spirit as the source of saving faith and the outpouring of the Spirit that empowers for Christian witness. Supernatural gifts and miracles abounded throughout the apostolic period, and this is still Christ's will for his people. These are manifestations of Jesus' messianic lordship and his exaltation to the Father's right hand. The baptism in the Spirit is grounded in the *ascension of Jesus, just as forgiveness of sin and new life are grounded in the death and resurrection of Christ respectively. Speaking in tongues is the principal sign of being baptized in the Spirit, but many Pentecostals now recognize other *gifts of the Spirit as confirmatory signs of this experience.

Adult water *baptism is usually practised, immediately followed by prayer for the baptism in the Spirit. A purely symbolic (Zwinglian) view of the sacraments has usually predominated, although Pentecostals do emphasize a deep sense of fellowship with the risen Lord when partaking of Communion. Church government usually takes Congregational or Presbyterian forms, along with a stress on the *priesthood of all believers, although some Pentecostal denominations have approximated more in practice to the Episcopal form of church government. Prayer for the sick, accompanied by anointing with oil and the laying on of hands, has been a regular practice of Pentecostals in both evangelistic campaigns and weekly church services. Pentecostals have often adhered to the 'healing in the atonement' doctrine in which Christ is regarded as having borne our sicknesses as well as our sins. More recently, some have not accepted this view, holding to a less dogmatic doctrine of divine healing.

Recent debate on the baptism in the Holy Spirit

Only a brief outline can be given here of some of the significant contributions to this debate from amongst a vast literature. Detailed academic discussion of Pentecostal theology was initiated by the publication in 1970 of *Baptism in the Holy Spirit* by J. D. G. Dunn and *A Theology of the Holy Spirit* by F. D. Bruner. For Dunn the impartation of the Spirit to Jesus at his baptism confirmed his divine sonship and initiated the messianic age and the beginnings of the new covenant era. Hence, the reception of the Spirit within the 'conversion-initiation' complex of events in Acts 2, 8, 9, 10 and 19 imparted primarily regeneration to the first disciples, as well as their empowerment for their mission, and thus Luke's pneumatology of Christian initiation correlates with that of Paul. Bruner goes further in claiming that, for the apostles, justification and regeneration, identified as the baptism in the Spirit, occurred during baptism in water. Thus Bruner rejects the Pentecostal 'subsequence' doctrine and the claim that Spirit baptism is evidenced by the sign of glossolalia. For Bruner, the advocacy of conditions by Pentecostals for receiving the baptism in the Spirit undermines the sufficiency of the unconditional grace of the gospel for living the Christian life.

This teaching that opposed the Pentecostal 'subsequence' doctrine was answered by a number of defences of that position by Pentecostals such as H. Hunter in *Spirit-Baptism* (London, 1983) and D. Petts in *The Holy Spirit* (Nottingham, 1998) and by charismatic writers such as the Baptist H. M. Ervin in *Conversion-Initiation and the Baptism in the Holy Spirit* (Peabody, 1984) and the Presbyterian J. R. Williams in his three-volume *Renewal Theology* (Grand Rapids, 1988–92). In response to those who wished to press the texts in Acts on the impartation of the Spirit into a supposed Pauline mould, R. Stronstad argues that Luke's charismatic theology must be independently assessed in terms of his dependence upon OT texts describing anointing by the Spirit of God, the commonality of the motifs of the transfer of the Spirit, the parallels between Jesus and Elijah and Elisha, and the parallels between Luke 3:1 – 4:44, Acts 1:1 – 2:42 and subsequent experiences of impartation of the Spirit (*The Charismatic Theology of St. Luke*, Grand Rapids, 1984). Likewise, in undertaking a redactional approach to Luke-Acts, J. B. Shelton argues that Luke's distinctive pneumatology should not be forced to conform to that of Paul (*Mighty in Word and Deed*, Peabody, 1991). Careful exegesis of the key passages in Acts leads Stronstad and Shelton to maintain that, for Luke, the baptism in the Spirit reveals the God-given call to ministry and/or imparts empowerment for prophetic revelation, witness, miracles and service. Thus the baptism in the Spirit is commonly subsequent to regeneration and water baptism and should not be identified with either. But Stronstad and Shelton failed to explain adequately how Luke's pneumatology could be reconciled with that of the Pauline epistles, which appear to identify the impartation of the Spirit with regeneration.

In *Power from on High* (Sheffield, 1996) and *The Holy Spirit and Spiritual Gifts* (Carlisle, 1996), M. M. B. Turner argues that the intertestamental Jewish understanding was that the 'Spirit of prophecy' imparted not only charismatic revelation, guidance, prophecy, worship and miraculous powers, but also a salvific life-giving wisdom central to authentic faith and ethical renewal. He agrees with Dunn that, for Luke, the reception of the Spirit by the early disciples in Acts was a soteriological regenerating gift, as maintained by Paul, as well as an empowering for their mission. Likewise, the Pentecostal scholar Gordon Fee argues that, for Paul, the baptism in the Spirit is identical with regeneration and that the notion of the reception of the Spirit being subsequent to conversion is not a norm of the NT (*God's Empowering Presence*, Peabody, 1994). Fee exemplifies a departure amongst some Pentecostals from the traditional 'subsequence' doctrine.

Contrary to this, R. P. Menzies argues that the intertestamental Jewish understanding of the 'Spirit of prophecy' is commonly seen as the source of prophetic activity, but not of miracles, and only rarely as the source of life-giving wisdom (*Empowered for Witness*, Sheffield, 1994). Thus Luke retained this Jewish understanding of the Spirit in representing the impartation of the Spirit to Jesus at his baptism as the inauguration of prophetic empowerment for his messianic task, rather than the designation of Jesus' divine sonship or messianic calling. Likewise, the baptism in the Spirit of the first disciples at Pentecost empowered them for their prophetic mission, granting them special insight and inspired preaching, rather than mediating the new covenant or initiating their regeneration. According to Menzies, Luke limited the role of the Spirit to the impartation of prophetic powers, never attributed soteriological powers to him, and resisted the developing tendency in the apostolic church of regarding the Spirit as the source of miracle-working power. Menzies thus holds that Paul was the first to attribute soteriological functions to the Spirit so that his pneumatology contains both salvific and charismatic dimensions.

The Korean Pentecostal Y. Cho endorses these conclusions of Menzies, but goes further than him in showing that, for Paul, life in the Spirit for the Christian correlates with life in the kingdom of God as taught by Jesus to his disciples, whereas in Acts Luke limits the ministry of the Spirit to the empowerment of the disciples and the source of their inspired preaching, prophecies and miracles (*Spirit and Kingdom in the Writings of Luke and Paul*, Milton Keynes, 2005). Thus Menzies and Cho identify the baptism in the Spirit and such cognate phrases as 'receiving the Spirit' in Acts as a post-regeneration empowerment for the church's mission. But they do not satisfactorily say how this can be reconciled with Paul's salvific pneumatology that seems to relate such phrases to the beginnings of the Christian life.

The Finnish Pentecostal V.-M. Kärkkäinen relates Pentecostal theology to the pneumatologies of differing traditions and their theologians in his *Pneumatology* (Grand Rapids, 2002). Out of a desire to engage in ecumenical dialogue, the American Pentecostal A. Yong interprets the metaphor of baptism in the Spirit as referring to the dynamism of all the salvific work of the Spirit in regeneration, sanctification, empowerment for mission and spiritual gifts, as well as to the eschatological transformation of the believer in the new age. But this blurs the meaning of the term 'baptism in the Holy Spirit' (i.e. a metaphor for immersion in the dynamic presence of the Holy Spirit) that refers to the distinctive events of infillings of the Spirit in Acts. Jesus' anticipation that the disciples would be baptized in the Holy Spirit 'in a few days' (Acts 1:5) applies to the empowerment of the disciples that happened on the day of Pentecost, not to their whole experience of salvation.

K. Warrington, who has authored a comprehensive survey of recent debates on Pentecostal doctrines, also advocates a flexible understanding of the term 'baptism in the Spirit' as embracing the regenerating, liberating, sanctifying and empowering ministry of the Holy Spirit in the believer's life. Likewise, F. D. Macchia enlarges the concept of the baptism in the Spirit within a soteriological, charismatic and eschatological framework to identify it with a baptism in the love of God that sanctifies, renews and empowers us until, at the end of the age, Spirit baptism transforms all of creation into the final dwelling place of God. In other words, the risen and ascended Jesus baptizes believers in the Spirit in regeneration and sanctification (Paul) and in empowerment for mission subsequent to conversion (Luke). But these events prefigure the eschatological baptism of all creation in the Spirit at its transformation in the *eschaton* (cf. John the Baptist in Matt. 3:11–12).

Finally, Paul does not explain exactly what he means by Spirit baptism in his letters; perhaps because this was well known to his converts. It would seem that one either has to say that Paul's concept of Spirit baptism differs from Luke's concept of charismatic empowerment for mission in referring either to the new birth and incorporation into Christ or to the complex of events of the conversion-initiation process, or to hold that Paul's references to being baptized in the Spirit (1 Cor. 12:13), anointed with the Spirit (2 Cor. 1:21) and sealed with the Spirit (2 Cor. 1:22; Eph. 1:13) allude to a post-conversion charismatic experience as described in Acts 8 and 19.

See also: HOLY SPIRIT.

Bibliography

S. M. Burgess and E. M. van Der Maas (eds.), *The New International Dictionary of Pentecostal and Charismatic Movements* (Grand Rapids, 2002); G. P. Duffield and N. M. van Cleave, *Foundations of Pentecostal Theology* (Los Angeles, 1983); W. J. Hollenweger, *Pentecostalism: Origins and Developments Worldwide* (Peabody, 1997); S. M. Horton (ed.), *Systematic Theology* (Springfield, rev. edn, 1995); H. I. Lederle, *Treasures Old and New: Interpretations of 'Spirit-Baptism' in the Charismatic Renewal Movement* (Peabody, 1991); F. D. Macchia, *Baptized in the Spirit: A Global Pentecostal Theology* (Grand Rapids, 2006); G. B. McGee (ed.), *Initial Evidence: Historical and Biblical Perspectives on the Pentecostal Doctrine of Spirit Baptism* (Peabody, 1991); W. W. Menzies and R. P. Menzies, *Spirit and Power: Foundations of Pentecostal Experience* (Grand Rapids, 2000); V. Synan, *The Century of the Holy Spirit: 100 Years of Pentecostal and Charismatic Renewal, 1901–2001* (Nashville, 2001); K. Warrington, *Pentecostal Theology: A Theology of Encounter* (London, 2008); idem (ed.), *Pentecostal Perspectives* (Carlisle, 1998); J. R. Williams, *Renewal Theology: Systematic Theology from a Charismatic Perspective*, 3 vols. (Grand Rapids, 1988–1992); A. Yong, *The Spirit Poured Out on All Flesh: Pentecostalism and the Possibility of Global Theology* (Grand Rapids, 2005).

J. W. WARD

PERFECTION, PERFECTIONISM

Perfect (*teleios*) and perfection (*teleiōsis*) are NT terms found in the sayings of Jesus (Matt. 5:48; 19:21), the teaching of Paul (Phil. 3:12–15), the epistle to the Hebrews (6:1) and the Johannine literature (1 John 4:12, 17). Throughout Christian history attempts have been made to understand what such passages imply. In some of the early apologists, such as Aristides, Athenagoras and Justin, this was interpreted as an absolute sinlessness, and some of the writings of the so-called 'Apostolic Fathers' (e.g. the *Shepherd of Hermas*) wrestle with the question of whether sins committed after baptism could be forgiven. Some balance appeared, however, in the teaching of *Clement of Alexandria, who stated that while Christians were in one sense 'perfect' once they were baptized into Christ (*Paedagogus* I, 6), and their lives evidenced a transformation, they still had to grow to a more mature level of 'perfection' (*Stromateis*, VII, 3 and 10). Clement wisely defined this Christian maturity positively rather than negatively, that is, not as sinlessness, but as a growing knowledge and love of God which purifies the heart.

This idea of a relative perfection, a maturity which ended the instability of the divided heart, characterized the spirituality of the Eastern Fathers. Through the example of Antony, challenged as a young man by Matt. 19:21, this inward perfection or purity of heart became the goal of the monastic movement (see *Asceticism and monasticism), pursued in different ways by Pachomius, Basil, Cassian and *Benedict. Given his strong development of the doctrine of original sin, it is not surprising that *Augustine was pessimistic about the possibility of even a relative perfection in this life (see *On Man's Perfection in Righteousness*). But despite his pessimism, the 'ladder of perfection', the idea of a scale of degrees of perfection, characterized the *spirituality of the medieval period. *Bernard of Clairvaux (*On the Love of God*) identified four degrees of love: self-love, loving God for his benefits, loving God for his own sake, and loving oneself only for God's sake. The fourth degree was possibly only in the life to come, but Bernard regarded the third degree as a level of perfection possible in this life. *Thomas Aquinas similarly defined 'perfection' in terms of *love and taught that absolute perfection was possible for God alone. Even the perfection of loving God as much as we possibly can is impossible in this life. But there is a lower level where everything contrary to the love of God (such as mortal sin) is removed. There can be no love of God without this and so it is essential to salvation. It may also move a notch higher so that everything hindering the affections toward God is removed, and this is the highest perfection possible in this life (*Summa Theologica*, 2a–2ae, 84, 1).

The Reformers, reacting against the hypocrisy of much sixteenth-century monasticism, generally rejected any idea of perfection as contrary to justification by grace through faith. *Calvin's exposition of Christian *sanctification, more positive than that of *Luther, still remained extremely suspicious of it. In the seventeenth century, some *Pietists developed a more positive line, but this was defined as maturity, not sinlessness. John *Wesley (see his *A Plain Account of Christian Perfection*) similarly developed the idea of perfection as maturity, being deeply influenced by Clement of Alexandria and by homilies thought to have been written by Macarius the Egyptian. Like Bernard and Aquinas, he defined it as 'perfect love', that is, the fulfilling of the law as summarized in the great commandments. This was not attained by discipline, but was the gift of grace received in 'entire sanctification' (cf. 1 Thess. 5:23), which was an act of God, yet never apart from the believer's self-discipline and patient seeking. He refused to define this perfection as 'sinless', and ejected extreme perfectionists from his *Methodist societies, yet he did believe that loving God with a pure heart necessarily implied a cleansing from sinful self-love. Wesley's doctrine was rejected by his Calvinist allies in the eighteenth-century Awakening.

In the nineteenth century, Wesley's teaching partly inspired the '*holiness' or 'higher-life' movement, which lacked the sophistication and balance of his thought and was strongly criticized by B. B. *Warfield of Princeton. Within American Methodism, this was propagated by a doctor's wife, Mrs Phoebe *Palmer, whose 'altar theology' and emphasis on consecration constituted what she regarded as a 'shorter way' to entire sanctification. Across the denominations, the holiness movement was also influenced by the teaching of Charles *Finney, the American revivalist, that the 'baptism of the Spirit' which the disciples received as a 'second blessing' on the day of Pentecost brought them to 'perfection'. This had a strong influence on William and Catherine Booth of the *Salvation Army and on Robert and Hannah Pearsall Smith, whose teaching led to the Keswick movement. But there the influence of Finney was barely detectable. Leading speakers at the annual Keswick Convention included Anglicans such as Bishop H. C. G. Moule, Presbyterians such as Andrew Murray and Baptists such as Graham Scroggie. In the early twentieth century, the Keswick movement came to dominate evangelical Christianity in the English-speaking world and the modern missionary movement, but it is doubtful if it is rightly described as 'perfectionist'. Unlike the patristic and medieval tradition, and unlike Wesley, its focus was not so much on the positive – perfection understood as mature, wholehearted, undivided love for God and neighbour – as on the negative aspect of victory over sin through a decisive act of faith and consecration. Finney's doctrine of the 'baptism of the Spirit' was also to lead eventually to the development of *Pentecostalism, but the idea of relative perfection as 'perfect love' was largely lost in this movement too.

Bibliography

M. de Dreuille, *Seeking the Absolute Love: The Founders of Christian Monasticism* (New York, 1999); R. N. Flew, *The Idea of Perfection in Christian Theology* (Oxford, 1934); A. H. Francke, 'On Christian Perfection', in P. C. Erb (ed.), *Pietists: Selected Writings* (London, 1983), pp. 114–116; C. E. Jones, *Perfectionist Persuasion: The Holiness Movement in American Methodism, 1869–1936* (Metuchen, 1974); W. C. Kostlevy (ed.), *Historical Dictionary of the Holiness Movement* (Lanham and London, 2001); H. A. Luckman and L. Kulzer (eds.), *Purity of Heart in Early Ascetic and Monastic Literature* (Collegeville, 1999); B. B. Warfield, *Perfectionism* (Philadelphia, 1967); J. Wesley, 'A Plain Account of Christian Perfection', *Works*, vol. 13 (Nashville, 2013), pp. 132–191.

T. A. NOBLE

PERICHORESIS, see TRINITY

PERKINS, WILLIAM (1558–1602)

William Perkins has been regarded as the father of Puritanism and the greatest of all *Puritan theologians. In fact, he remained a committed member of the established *Church of England all his life, and condemned separatism in strong terms while also advocating tolerance of *Presbyterian polity within the national church. His theological influence in his day was remarkable: he was named alongside *Calvin and *Beza as one of the three writers most read by 'the godly' in England; his works were rapidly translated into Dutch, German, French, Welsh, Czech and Polish, and had an enduring influence in New England. His *Arte of Prophesying* was the standard homiletic textbook of Puritan preachers for a century or more; his *Golden Chaine* was an enduringly popular summary of the supralapsarian Calvinist scheme (see *Predestination).

Perkins begins the *Golden Chaine* with the claim, 'Theology is the science of living blessedly forever.' This quotation emphasizes the practical concern of his work, which spanned an extraordinary range of subjects (ranging from biblical exposition through doctrinal theology and ecclesiastical controversy to pastoral advice, casuistry, and even a discussion of witchcraft), but was always devoted to calling the Christian to live up to his or her profession. His theology was careful, but his expression adapted to understanding, at least by the university congregations to which he spoke. Perkins's works were generally the text of lectures or sermons given in St Andrew's Church in Cambridge, where he held a lectureship from 1585 to the end of his life.

He emphasized practical *holiness as the natural life of the true Christian, and the primary evidence of our own election. (His several works on ethical dilemmas, which began and shaped the Puritan tradition of casuistry, stemmed from this emphasis.) He was capable, however, of powerful evangelistic appeal, and of pressing the mercy of Christ to those who found themselves wanting in evidence of *sanctification. His theological method was *Ramistic, and he extended this into his advice for preachers.

Although his career was relatively short, his reputation, coupled with his strategic location in a university town, ensured that he influenced many, including such eminent successors as William *Ames and Richard *Sibbes. When the Church of England became less tolerant after his death, and the self-consciously Puritan movement was born, Perkins's writings shaped much of its thought and practice.

Bibliography

Works: there is no modern critical edition; the best of the older editions remains *Workes*, 3 vols. (Cambridge, 1608–09).
Studies: D. K. McKim, *Ramism in William Perkins' Theology* (New York, 1987); P. R. Schaefer, 'Protestant "Scholasticism" at Elizabethan Cambridge: William Perkins and a Reformed Theology of the Heart', in C. R. Trueman and R. S. Clark (eds.), *Protestant Scholasticism: Essays in Reassessment* (Carlisle, 1999).

S. R. HOLMES

PERSEVERANCE

The doctrine of the perseverance of the *saints in *Reformed theology teaches that true believers will certainly keep their faith to the end through all tests and temptations, and will finally enter into heaven. It is argued that this salvation cannot be lost because it is grounded, not in human action but in the sovereign action of God and that it follows logically from the nature of the believer's union with Christ and from his or her *justification. A great deal of NT teaching is drawn together to support such a position, not least those passages which emphasize God's free *grace towards sinners and those passages which insist that no-one can pluck the believer from God's hand nor separate the believer from the love of God in Christ Jesus.

This doctrine of perseverance can be traced back to *Augustine, but it came to full expression in the Calvinistic strand of the Protestant Reformation, being affirmed in some of the Reformed confessions and catechisms, not least in the *Westminster Confession of Faith*. *Luther was equivocal about perseverance because of the tension in his thought on grace and law, but *Calvin clarified and consolidated the Augustinian doctrine, tracing all the effective stages of Christian life to the 'pre-destination of glory'.

The doctrine was codified at the Synod of *Dordrecht in 1618–19, in response to the theology of Jacobus Arminius. After *Arminius died in 1609, his supporters issued a five-point 'Remonstrance' in 1610, arguing for a stronger place for the human will in Reformed theology. The Synod was called in order to respond to these 'Remonstrants' and did so by producing five points of its own (see *Dort, canons of). The first point concerns total depravity, not arguing that human beings are as bad as they could be, but that every human being is a *sinner, estranged from God, with a sinful nature. The second point affirms God's unconditional election of some sinners to *salvation. The third point is that Jesus Christ died on the *cross specifically for that 'elect' group of sinners and for no others. The fourth point concerns the means used by God to effect this salvation, namely, his irresistible grace in effectual calling. The fifth point is the perseverance of the saints, demonstrating that what God has started he will complete.

This doctrine of perseverance has not been unopposed, since there are a number of biblical passages which seem to envisage a possible falling away from salvation, especially in the letter to the Hebrews. Reformed theologians have tended to explain these in context as warnings against a superficial Christianity, or as purely hypothetical arguments *ad hominem*, or as urgings to seek a surer ground in holiness for Christian confidence.

Those opposed to the tenet of final perseverance, including Arminians, *Roman Catholics and the Wesleyan strand of *Methodism, often take this stance out of concern for the biblical emphasis upon the contingency of final salvation, believing that the doctrine may encourage complacency. If it has any evils, however, it has been the provoking of excessive preoccupation with *assurance* of final perseverance. In general, the result of the Calvinist conviction has not been lack of zeal, any more than non-Calvinists have, on the whole, lacked a strong Christian hope. The purpose of the teaching in the NT is to direct attention away from the always incomplete nature of Christian experience to the complete faithfulness and reliability of the God of all grace, and to strengthen the believer for the conflict with sin in the service of God. It emphasizes that the ultimate destiny of the Christian is achieved by God's grace through an enduring *faith.

See also: PREDESTINATION.

Bibliography

G. C. Berkouwer, *Faith and Perseverance* (Grand Rapids, 1958); W. Edgar, *Truth in All Its Glory* (Phillipsburg, 2004); R. L. Reymond, *A New Systematic Theology of the Christian Faith* (Nashville, 1998); *Westminster Confession of Faith*, ch. 17.

A. T. B. MCGOWAN

PERSONALISM

Personalism is a worldview, which posits the person as ultimate in *ontology (being) and axiology (value). Mostly personalism has been *theistic, but occasionally atheistic (e.g. J. M. E. McTaggart). Christian personalism argues that God as personal is ultimate in ontology and axiology, and that human persons, created as they are in the divine image, are penultimate in ontology and axiology.

Defining 'person' is philosophically very difficult and controversial. Minimally, one can say that a sufficient condition for personhood is the capacity to say 'I' as a self-conscious speech agent. In the canonical presentation, Father, Son and Holy Spirit are such speech agents (the Father in Matt. 3:17, the Son in John 17:1 and the Holy Spirit in Acts 13:2). Persons are 'thous', not 'its'. On this view, Christian personalism maintains that the one *God is personal in three self-consciously distinct but inseparable ways as the eternal *Trinity: one God in three Persons.

Christian personalism, when consciously informed by a trinitarian understanding of God, prizes relationships, since ultimate reality consists of Persons-in-relation: the eternal dance of love, which is Trinity. Christian personalism is not individualistic. Because of the high value placed on persons, Christian personalism ought to express itself in a concern and advocacy for the well-being of persons and their relations: a culture of life rather than a culture of death. Historically speaking, distinct forms of personalism have arisen in more than one place (e.g. Europe, Britain and the US). Personalism of whatever precise stamp resists any reductionist understanding of humankind, whether secular (e.g. humans are merely the highest kind of primate) or religious (e.g. *pantheism). Indeed, there is an argument that without the emergence of Christianity and its ideas of the triune God and Christ as the God-man, together with the shared view with Judaism of human beings as images of God, that personalism could not have arisen. The Roman Catholic tradition produced major modern personalists in John Paul II (Poland) and Emmanuel Mounier (France). In Britain, philosopher John Macmurray was an important personalist, and Borden Parker Bowne, Edgar Sheffield Brightman and Martin Luther King Jr were similarly important in the US.

Bibliography

R. Burrows, Jr, *Personalism: A Critical Introduction* (St Louis, 1999); J. Macmurray, *The Form of the Personal*, 2 vols. (London, 1995); P. A. Sayre, 'Personalism', in P. L. Quinn and C. Taliaferro (eds.), *A Companion to Philosophy of Religion* (Maldin and Oxford, 2000).

G. A. COLE

PHENOMENOLOGY

Philosophers have commonly distinguished between the objective world and consciousness of that objective world, and have viewed the latter, the phenomenal world, as being ontologically or epistemologically privileged. To take this view is to be an idealist. The distinction, which goes back to the Greeks, has played a central role in modern philosophy: in the work of *rationalists, such as *Descartes and in the work of empiricists, such as *Locke and *Hume. Its most celebrated exponent is Immanuel *Kant. However, although Kant's 'transcendental idealism' affirms a distinction between the 'phenomenal' and the 'noumenal' worlds, one of Kant's many famous contributions to philosophy was his 'Refutation of Idealism', his contention that knowledge claims concerning the phenomenal world necessarily presuppose knowledge of an objective world. By contrast, the twentieth-century school of thought which is called 'phenomenology' affirmed the primacy of the phenomenal world and attempted to construct a philosophy upon it.

Phenomenology is, therefore, a form of *idealism. It is a sustained attempt to describe experiences and phenomenal 'things themselves' without metaphysical speculation or commitment. In so doing, it rejects both *naturalism*, the attempt to study nature using the methods of the natural sciences, and *psychologism*, the collapsing of the normative discipline of logic into descriptive psychology, claiming to construct a distinctive science of consciousness rather than a science of material objects.

Kant's defence of a priori concepts in *The Critique of Pure Reason*, especially his contention that phenomenal description presupposes the integrity of a priori concepts, is as devastating when directed against phenomenology as when directed against Hume; and as recent work by Strawson and Stern demonstrate, the issue remains at the heart of contemporary *epistemology and *metaphysics.

Edmund Husserl (1859–1938) is viewed by many as the founder of the 'phenomenology' movement. Spells of his career spent at the universities of Halle, Göttingen and Freiberg marked significant milestones in his intellectual development.

When at Halle, he published his first major work on the philosophy of mathematics, *On the Concept of Number* (1887), which attempted to explain the synthetic unities of many-ness. These reduced to two: a physical unity, relating to the content of the mental representation; and an imposed psychical unity, based upon a unifying mental act that sets representational content into its various relationships. However, Husserl then went on to contrast with them a non-synthesized unity, the unity which is displayed by living organisms whose parts are continuous and come apart only in the process of analysis.

In *Logical Investigations* (1900) Husserl attacks 'psychologism' on the grounds that it treats logical relationships as being no different in kind from all other non-rational mental operations, mathematics thus collapsing into a branch of psychology. Timeless mathematical and logical principles would be transformed, in this account, into temporally instantiated and self-validating descriptions.

Husserl's third major work, *Ideas 1 & 2* (1913 and 1952) sees the emergence of his transcendental phenomenology, his correlation of all forms of unity in a 'principle of principles'. The unity in question was not a unity of different elements, because, logically, prior to each kind of unity there is oneness which overrides individual subjectivity to reveal a form of trans-subjectivity which is at the heart of everything.

The intelligibility and coherence of Husserl's philosophy has been widely challenged, especially in the Anglo-American analytic tradition. To be successful, his account must show how the ego secures both the unity of the known object and the unity of the knowing subject. Even if his account of this is ultimately unsuccessful – as it shows only the possibility of the noetic project rather than its success in any particular case – it constitutes the most imaginative aspect of his later work.

Later writers in the phenomenological tradition have included Martin *Heidegger, Maurice Merleau-Ponty, Jacques *Derrida and Jean-Paul Sartre. Although sharing Husserl's general approach to philosophy, these writers developed key aspects of phenomenology in original and distinctive ways. Heidegger, for example, understood 'phenomenal reduction' *ontologically and in a way that reveals 'the Being of beings'. Since the things which are under analysis – numbers, relations, colours, people – differ greatly, their being differs also. He was led, therefore, to postulate a 'pre-ontological form of being' which is independent of our understanding of any of the specific beings under analysis. Sartre, sympathetic to central phenomenological theses, developed a distinctive account of intentionality. In particular, he rejects belief in an ego which synthesizes the experiences of a given subject. The unity of consciousness is achieved, rather, through the temporal structuring of experience.

These are only a few of the ways in which later writers, though in the phenomenological tradition, differed from Husserl over important issues.

Clearly, its practitioners believed that phenomenology has implications for all of the great branches of traditional philosophy: for metaphysics, logic, epistemology and *ethics. We should also note its interaction with the study of religion.

The phenomenology of religion seeks the meaning of *religion by focusing on experiential aspects of religion, especially the consciousness of the worshipper. Writers such as Rudolf Otto and Mircea Eliade (1907–86) have tried to study systematically the universal and transcendent aspects of sacred reality, aspects of reality which evoke dread, wonder and awe. They seek to exclude analysis or rational criticism from their accounts, and so their work might be regarded as a preliminary to *philosophy of religion rather than part of that discipline itself. This phenomenological approach to religion often provides the intellectual underpinning for writers in the traditions of *liberal theology and *postmodern Christianity.

Bibliography

M. Eliade, *The Sacred and the Profane: The Nature of Religion*, tr. W. Trask (London, 1959); E. Husserl, *Logical Investigations*, tr. J. N. Findlay (London, 1973); idem, *The Essential Husserl*, ed. D. Walton (Bloomington, 1999); R. Otto, *The Idea of the Holy* (London, 1958); B. Smith and D. W. Smith (eds.), *The Cambridge Companion to Husserl* (Cambridge, 1995); R. Stern, *Transcendental Arguments and Scepticism* (Oxford, 2000); P. F. Strawson, *The Bounds of Sense* (London, 1966).

H. BUNTING

PHILO (*c.* 20 BC – *c.* AD 50)

A Hellenistic Jew from Alexandria, Philo wrote through allegorical interpretation (see *Hermeneutics) of the Pentateuch and found the teachings of Plato and the Stoics already present in Moses' words. Philo's writings can be divided into what deals directly with the biblical text, and what does not. The latter include *On The Contemplative Life* (a treatise describing the *monastic practices of Therapeutae, who claimed they experienced the *vision of God), and *Against Flaccus* and *The Legation to Gaius* (documents dealing with anti-Jewish acts of Emperor Gaius Caligula). The writings on the biblical texts consist of major divisions entitled 'The Exposition of the Law' (considering e.g. the life of Moses, Abraham, the Decalogue and rewards and punishments), 'The Allegory of the Law' (a series of expositions from Genesis), and 'Questions and Answers' (*re* Genesis and Exodus).

Philo attempted to synthesize Greek philosophy with Hebrew thought. Here he is seen as a precursor of Christianity (see *Apologists; *Hellenization of Christianity; *Platonism). Yet this observation can be misleading. Philo's influence is far more important for later *Alexandrian Christianity (e.g. *Clement and *Origen) and for allegorical exegesis and theology than for the emergence of NT Christianity. Early Christianity's *Christological understanding of the OT is only superficially like Philo's exegesis; the NT's theology, for its newness, is not the amalgamation of two different worlds of ideas, Jewish and Greek, but is fully explainable within a Jewish framework alone.

Philo's goal is the practice of *religion, culminating in the *mystic vision of (and communion with) God. His eclectic appropriation of Greek philosophy attempts to communicate the truth of Judaism to his Hellenistic contemporaries. Basic to Philo's approach is the *dualism between material and non-material. The latter, the intelligible world, is ultimately all-important to Philo, who by allegorical exegesis presses consistently beyond the material, in understanding or conduct, to Plato's transcendent realm of Ideas. Philo borrows the Stoic '*Logos' concept to mediate between the transcendent God and the material world.

How Philo is related to Palestinian (rabbinic) Judaism and the NT writings is not clear. On the former, E. R. Goodenough alleged Philo's Judaism had become a Greek mystery religion; H. A. Wolfson maintained Philo held a form of Pharisaic Judaism. S. Sandmel is right: Philo is a representative of Hellenistic Judaism. Philo's possible relation to NT writings is even more complex. His influence upon the epistle of Hebrews is affirmed by some (Spicq), arguing that the author was Philo's student, although Williamson denies direct influence. With the 'Logos' prologue and frequent contrasting of material and spiritual, the Gospel of John is also described as influenced by Philo. Scholars also found parallels to Philo in Paul's epistles. Recognizing the enormous differences between Philo and the NT, however, the best conclusion is that no NT writing reflects direct dependence on Philo, and that observed similarities reflect instead the general milieu of Hellenistic ideas that pervaded the first-century Mediterranean world.

Bibliography

C. Anderson, *Philo of Alexandria's Views of the Physical World* (Tübingen, 2011); H. Chadwick, 'Philo and the Beginnings of Christian Thought', in *CHLGEMP*, pp. 137–192; idem, 'St Paul and Philo', *BJRL* (1965–66), pp. 286–307; E. R. Goodenough, *An Introduction to Philo Judaeus* (New Haven, 1940); S. Sandmel, *Philo of Alexandria: An Introduction* (Oxford, 1979); C. Spicq, 'Le philonisme de l'Epître aux Hébreux', *RB* 56 (1949), pp. 542–572; and 57 (1950), pp. 212–242; R. Williamson, *Philo and the Epistle to the Hebrews* (Leiden, 1970); H. A. Wolfson, *Philo* (Cambridge, MA, 1947).

D. A. HAGNER

PHILOSOPHICAL THEOLOGY

Philosophy is the critical examination of the meaning, *truth and grounds of ideas, and of the methods by which ideas are arrived at. *Philosophy of religion is the critical examination of religious ideas in general. By contrast, philosophical theology pursues such an examination of the ideas of a theology associated with a particular religion.

Philosophy is not a subject which has its own autonomous subject-matter, as does astronomy, biochemistry, English literature or international law. It is an ancillary discipline which examines the ideas, truth claims and methods practised in a discipline, and seeks to elucidate and evaluate their nature. Thus there is philosophy of science, behaviour (see *Ethics), art (see *Aesthetics), knowledge (see *Epistemology), *history, education, logic and religion. In each case philosophy is not a short cut to achieving the results otherwise arduously obtained in the discipline concerned. It is rather an attempt to clarify and reflect critically on what is entailed in the truth claims and methods of the discipline. Christian philosophical theology takes the Christian faith as its starting point and examines it philosophically.

Among the questions examined by philosophical theology are the following:

Grounds for belief in the existence of God. This includes discussion of the traditional arguments for the existence of God: the ontological, the cosmological, the teleological and the moral arguments (see *Natural theology). It also examines the nature and validity of appeals to experience and revelation (cf. *Religious experience; *Scripture) as well as the claim that belief in God is a necessary presupposition for making sense of the world and our experience. It takes account of arguments for *agnosticism and disbelief in God (cf. *Atheism).

The identity of God and God's relation with the world. This includes evaluation of the competing claims of *theism, *deism, *idealism, *pantheism and *panentheism.

Religious language. Discussion of the structure, meaning and use of *religious language has been a major preoccupation in philosophical theology since the advent of *logical positivism. However, the problem of using ordinary language to describe transcendent reality was a concern of the Neoplatonists (see *Platonism) and the medieval thinkers. Logical positivism claimed that religious language is meaningless, since it is not open to verification in the way that scientific claims are verifiable. This gave rise to much discussion of *verification, falsification and ways of testing meaning and truth claims. Even scientific claims are not always strictly verifiable. Words for God are not literally true, since God is not an object in time and space. Meaningful talk about God presupposes *analogy rather than direct literal correspondence. Recent investigation into religious language has drawn attention to the richness of its variety and use, and to the complexity of symbolism.

History and religion. This includes the way God may be thought of as acting in history, the question of *miracles, and the clarification of the distinction between history and *myth.

Revelation, faith and reason. This includes discussion of *revelation as a form of knowledge, the role of *faith in cognition, assent, trust and interpretation, and the role of reason in apprehending, discerning and explaining (see *Epistemology).

Evil. How can the existence of physical and moral *evil be reconciled with belief in an almighty, loving God (cf. *Theodicy)?

Freedom. In what sense may we speak of freedom and free will, in the light of theological considerations concerning the sovereignty of God and philosophical considerations concerning human beings who are products of their physical environment and whose activities are capable of explanation in terms of physical processes?

Human identity. Are human beings more than bodies? What is meant by the mind, the self and the soul? What is the relationship between the brain and the mind and between the body and the self?

Life after death. What grounds are there for belief in life after *death, and what are its possible forms (cf. *Resurrection, general)?

Prayer. What sort of an activity is *prayer? What are the logic and implications of intercessory and other forms of prayer?

The relation of Christianity to other faiths. This includes examination of the conflicting truth claims of different religions and ways of testing them.

In recent decades, there have been particular developments in thinking about the grounds for belief in the existence of God. Basil Mitchell debated the philosophical merits of theism with the atheists R. M. Hare and Antony Flew, and was succeeded as Nolloth Professor of the Christian Religion at Oxford by Richard Swinburne. Both developed the 'cumulative case' for the existence of God. Swinburne was interested in probability theory, and wrote a series of monographs devoted to miracles, the coherence of theism, the probabilty of God's existence, the problem of evil, evolution of the soul, revelation, atonement, and the divinity of Jesus. Alvin *Plantinga and Nicholas Wolterstorff were associated with Calvin College, Michigan, where they developed a school of philosophical theology known as 'Reformed epistemology', building on the thought of Thomas Reid, the 'common sense' philosopher of the Scottish Enlightenment. Along with William Alston, they launched the journal, *Faith and Philosophy*. Wolterstorff developed a theory of knowledge, which examined the roles of *data beliefs*, *data-background beliefs*, and *control beliefs* in science and religion.

Bibliography

C. Brown, *Philosophy and the Christian Faith* (London, 1969); O. Crisp, *A Reader in Contemporary Philosophical Theology* (London, 2009); O. Crisp and M. Rea (eds.), *Analytic Theology: New Essays in the Philosophy of Theology* (Oxford, 2009); C. S. Evans, *Philosophy of Religion* (Downers Grove, 1985); A. Flew and A. MacIntyre (eds.), *New Essays in Philosophical Theology* (London, 1955); T. Flint and M. Rae, *The Oxford Handbook of Philosophical Theology* (Oxford, 2009); N. L. Geisler, *Philosophy of Religion* (Grand Rapids, 1974); J. Hick, *Faith and Knowledge* (London, ²1966); *idem*, *Philosophy of Religion* (Englewood Cliffs, ³1983); *idem* (ed.), *Classical and Contemporary Readings in the Philosophy of Religion* (Englewood Cliffs, ²1970); B. S. Mitchell, *The Justification of Religious Belief* (London, 1973); *idem* (ed.), *The Philosophy of Religion* (London, 1973); A. Plantinga, *God and Other Minds* (Ithaca, 1967/90); *idem*, *The Nature of Necessity* (Oxford, 1974); *idem*, *God, Freedom, and Evil* (Grand Rapids, 1974); *idem*, *Warranted Christian Belief* (Oxford, 2000); M. Rea (ed.), *Oxford Readings in Philosophical Theology, Vol. 1: Trinity, Incarnation and Atonement* (Oxford, 2009); *idem*, (ed.), *Oxford Readings in Philosophical Theology, Vol. 2: Providence, Scripture and Resurrection* (Oxford, 2009); N. Smart, *Philosophers and Religious Truth* (London, ²1969); R. Swinburne, *The Coherence of Theism* (Oxford, 1977); *idem*, *The Existence of God* (Oxford, 1979); *idem*, *Faith and Reason* (Oxford, 1981); K. Ward, *God and the Philosophers* (Minneapolis, 2009); N. Wolterstorff, *Reason within the Bounds of Religion* (Grand Rapids, 1976/84); *idem*, *Thomas Reid and the Story of Epistemology* (Cambridge, 2001); *idem*, *Inquiring about God: Selected Essays*, vol. I; *Practices of Belief: Selected Essays*, vol. II, ed. T. Cuneo (Cambridge, 2009); N. Wolterstorff and A. Plantinga (eds.), *Faith and Rationality: Reason and Belief in God* (Notre Dame, 1984); K. E. Yandell, *Christianity and Philosophy* (Leicester and Grand Rapids, 1984).

C. BROWN

PHILOSOPHY AND THEOLOGY

In the Christian tradition there are arguably three dominant tendencies for relating philosophy to theology: the reparative, the synthetic and the analytic. Reparative reasoning uses philosophy to interrogate *Scripture with the goal of healing the world. Synthetic reasoning brings philosophy and *theology together to illuminate each other's concerns, in the course of faith seeking understanding. Analytic reasoning tends to separate philosophy and theology in order to discover what each can achieve independently of the other. Rarely is any one of these tendencies present to the exclusion of the others. It is a matter of which tendency is dominant.

The reparative approach is dominant in *Augustine. Augustine confronted a series of problems in the church (Pelagianism, Donatism) and used philosophy as a method for interpreting Scripture in ways that addressed those problems. Augustine makes full use of the range of philosophical tools learned from *Platonic and ancient *Stoic philosophy to develop an account of the signs of Scripture that enables him to use Scripture to solve ecclesial problems. Scripture provides the patterns of reasoning and narrative that constitute the deepest resources for human action, and philosophy provides the logical tools for learning those patterns and deploying them in new and unfamiliar situations.

The synthetic approach is also present in Augustine, who claimed, 'I believe so as to understand', but is particularly intensely displayed in the thought of *Anselm of Canterbury, who coined the term 'faith seeking understanding', and of *Thomas Aquinas. Anselm's *ontological argument for the existence of God is one of the most famous examples of the synthetic approach, where prayerful naming of God is combined with intricate logical argumentation. Aquinas' project of bringing Augustinian theology into relation with *Aristotelian metaphysics is one of the most influential intellectual syntheses in the history of Western thought. Aquinas' most famous synthetic argument is his so-called 'five ways' which answer the question 'whether God exists', bringing Aristotelian styles of reasoning to bear on Exod. 3:14: 'I AM WHO I AM'. Aquinas thought of the relation between philosophy and theology as something like Jesus' transformation of water into wine at the wedding at Cana. Philosophical water accomplishes a certain amount, and can even lead the inquiring mind to infer 'that' God exists. It is consummated by theological wine that fills the mind with grace in such a way that one can know analogically 'what' is meant when one refers to God.

The analytic approach is present in Augustine insofar as he differentiates types of *credibilia*, or 'things to be believed' (e.g. history, mathematics, theology), and charts different modes of reasoning that accompany them. It is also present in Aquinas insofar as he addresses the question 'whether God can be known in this life by natural reason'. It is more vigorously pursued by John *Duns Scotus and *William of Ockham. Duns Scotus investigated very thoroughly the question of what degree of 'natural' knowledge of God can be acquired by the wayfarer who does not consult Scripture, compared with the believer's 'supernatural' knowledge of God that comes from reading Scripture. Duns Scotus developed subtle arguments attempting to demonstrate that the wayfarer can know that God is infinite. Moreover, unlike Aquinas, who, developing Henry of Ghent, claimed that speech about God is analogically related to speech about creatures, Duns Scotus argued against Henry that all analogy rests on some root univocal use of concepts. These two tendencies combine to produce an approach that develops complex patterns of reasoning about God that do not require commentary on Scripture. William of Ockham strongly separated the results of philosophical reasoning from those of theology. He claimed that 'natural' reasoning could not demonstrate the existence, unity or infinity of God. These can only be known by 'supernatural' knowledge. There is a tendency in Ockham to protect the fruits of supernatural knowledge from the scrutiny of human reasoning. In this he went significantly further than either Aquinas or Duns Scotus.

The modern period, inaugurated by *Descartes and *Spinoza, saw a thoroughgoing privileging of analytic over synthetic and reparative approaches to philosophy. Descartes' method of doubt in the *Meditations* tends to rule out appeal to Scripture, and seeks a point of certainty independent of tradition or faith. Spinoza's principal target in the *Tractatus Logico-Politicus* is any reparative approach to philosophy and Scripture, and he argues strongly that Scripture teaches only obedience to God, not knowledge. Faith is distinct and separate from philosophy. Of the two figures, Spinoza is the more consistent. The names of God Descartes eventually introduces in the *Meditations* are largely inherited from scholastic Aristotelian theology. Spinoza's own account of 'God or nature' in the *Ethics* is a significantly more austere and radical rethinking of the category of substance.

The synthetic approach by no means disappears in the modern period. *Locke wrote *The Reasonableness of Christianity* (1695) in which he attempted to show the harmony of philosophical and scriptural reasonings. *Leibniz wrote *Principles of Nature and of Grace, based on Reason* (1714), in which an attempt is made to illuminate theological topics using his own refined philosophical tools of 'necessary truths'. One can also argue that *Hegel's late 'eternal idea of God' or Schelling's late 'potencies of God' are likewise synthetic approaches to philosophy and theology.

It is arguably not until the twentieth century that one sees in Christian theology a significant embrace of reparative approaches that were eclipsed in the modern period. The theology of Karl *Barth is notable for its use of philosophical tools learned from *Kant and Hegel (and their heirs) to interpret Scripture in order to address serious political problems in the world (national socialism, certain forms of capitalism). Dietrich *Bonhoeffer's unfinished *Ethics* likewise brings philosophical tools to bear on the book of Genesis, in a striking way, in order to repair problems relating to knowledge of the good in the context of national socialism.

The contemporary university hosts a mixture of reparative, synthetic and analytic approaches. *Systematic theology tends to combine reparative and synthetic approaches. *Philosophical theology tends to combine synthetic and analytic approaches. The *philosophy of religion tends to privilege analytic approaches, although not exclusively. The decisive factor tends to be the training of a particular thinker, and the anticipated readership's standards of what counts as a respectable argument.

Bibliography

T. V. Morris (ed.), *Philosophy and the Christian Faith* (Notre Dame, 1988); *Philosophy and Theology: Marquette University Journal*, vol. 1 (1989) to present.

N. ADAMS

PHILOSOPHY OF RELIGION

The philosophy of religion is to be distinguished from both *philosophical theology and *apologetics. Unlike philosophical theology, which is concerned with ontological and logical reflection on the doctrine of God, the philosophy of religion is concerned with religion as a pervasive feature of human nature and *culture. And unlike the apologist, the aim of the philosopher of religion is to understand and evaluate religion from a philosophical standpoint rather than to defend belief in God, or a particular religion, by philosophical argument. Yet the three areas are sometimes intertwined, as in Aquinas's *Summa Contra Gentiles*, for example.

Sometimes 'religion' is used in a wide sense, to include all that any person values basically or unreservedly. So Marxism and *atheistic *materialism are sometimes dubbed 'religions' in this sense. However, the philosopher of religion is usually not concerned with religion in this broadest of senses, but in those religions which involve belief in God or gods.

Scope

It is important to note that the 'philosophy of religion' simply denotes the application of the methods, problems and conclusions of the philosophical tradition going back to classical times. It is not a separate philosophy with its own doctrines and standards of argumentation, but endeavours to apply the rich tradition of Western philosophy to issues in *religion.

Religion involves sets of human subjective states, for example, acts of worship, religious belief, moral convictions, the whole range of phenomena that comprise '*religious experience', from visions to convictions. These may give rise to claims about how things are. These are of interest to the philosopher of religion: how are things according to this individual or that religious tradition? And on what basis does he or she believe that things are like this? By what kind of appeal – to direct experience perhaps, or divine revelation or human reason and experience at the most general level? If they are like this – there's the claim that there's a God, or gods – how does this relate to other things we have reasonable beliefs or deep convictions about? How does God relate to the cosmos, or to morality, or to science?

Such enquiries involve investigations of two different kinds. There are conceptual enquiries. What does it mean to say that someone has seen a vision, or that a miracle has occurred, or that God exists and is infinitely wise? What any of these things means is partly a matter of the logical implications of claims made in particular propositions. Is saying that God exists like saying that there is a moon? Is God an object in space? If so, where is he located? If he is not in space (or time) how is his existence to be understood? Does he exist like an abstract object – goodness or beauty, say? But God acts.

Do goodness and beauty act? Is a 'miracle' the name we give to an event we cannot explain? What if there came to be a physical explanation of 'the miracle of the resurrection'? Would it cease to be a miracle?

What is religious belief? Is it like the belief that I have a left hand? Or is it more like a wager, a leap in the dark? But perhaps religious sentences are not truth-bearing, not cognitive, but emotive or expressive. 'Meaning' may be discovered in another, though related, sense, by enquiring how religion in its various elements (its symbols, utterances, practices) functions within a religion. The relation between these two senses of meaning – meaning as truth-conditions, and meaning as personal or communal significance – is itself a matter of philosophical controversy. In asking such questions, the philosopher of religion is endeavouring to understand the basic categories and commitments of religion and its associated theology.

Central to religion, and certainly to the Christian religion, are moral claims. How are these related to God? Is he subordinate to the values of a religion, simply endorsing them? Or is he superior to them? If he is superior to them, ought anything commanded by God to be obeyed? Would adultery (for example) be morally permissible if God allowed it? Could God allow it? Or is God, as an aspect of his perfection, the exemplar of moral perfection and so could not will what was at odds with that?

Besides analysing the concepts and propositions of religion in an effort to gain insight into what they mean, the philosopher of religion is also concerned about how one might reasonably be said to believe or to know that some religious claim is true or false. Here, if not before, it becomes apparent that 'the philosophy of religion' is not a distinctive kind of philosophy, but simply the main spine of philosophical interest – logic, metaphysics, epistemology, ethics – as applied to religion. Three broad answers to epistemological questions posed by religion are discernible, though these are not exclusive of each other.

Certain religious claims may be known by reason alone, by rational reflection on the concept of God (e.g. *Anselm) or by argumentation from propositions known to be true by any rational man (e.g. *Aquinas, *Locke). The main issues which arise here are over the place and legitimacy of such *natural theology, its tendency to *rationalism, and issues about the validity, soundness and strength of particular arguments.

Second, it may be claimed that God can be directly experienced, through personal encounter, vision or inspiration, or by rational reflection upon some aspect of experience. The problems concern the ambiguity or the adequacy of experience alone to provide reasonable grounds for believing that a transcendent ground of that experience exists.

A third approach is '*fideistic'. At one extreme this may be unthinking rationalism, and at the other a reliance upon the will (and not the intellect), because the issues of religion are important and yet the evidence from reason or sense experience is ambiguous, and the issues too important to be left unresolved. There may be reasons for having no reasons.

These epistemological concerns about the justification of knowledge-claims, including claims to know truths about God, have been much more dominant since the seventeenth century than they were up to the medieval period, when the reliability of reason and the senses were taken for granted, and when the authority of the church was largely unquestioned.

Such approaches have often had one common assumption, that the rationality of religious belief must be grounded in considerations which are common to all rational people. This – an assumption of the *Enlightenment – has been recently questioned by the 'Reformed' epistemologists, notably by Alvin *Plantinga. They argue that the Enlightenment requirements are not self-evidently true, and that a person is entitled (under certain conditions) to believe what is not self-evidently true to any rational person. In this connection it is interesting to note that both Anselm's ontological argument and Aquinas's 'Five Ways' were offered within the context of Christian belief, and not as providing a necessary condition of the rationality of such belief.

Immanuel *Kant initiated an important watershed in the philosophy of religion by his constructivist and anti-realist approach to metaphysical issues. Kant dismissed all natural or rational theology because in his view the very questions it raised, and the mode of argumentation, marked an illegitimate extension of human powers beyond their rational boundaries. For Kant, the existence of God could not be learned: it is a 'postulate' of the pure practical reason, not a discovery but a requirement of the rationality of morality, offering assurance that true morality will issue in true happiness. Kant's position became important and influential in post-Kantian *Protestant theology from *Ritschl to *Barth. It is also a precondition of the individualism, scepticism and communitarianism of much *postmodern philosophy.

In general, the Christian tradition has sought to occupy the middle ground between two extremes. On the one hand, in the interests of preserving the integrity of special revelation it has resisted rationalistic or a priori philosophical approaches which would reconstruct or reduce that revelation in order to conform it to some alien philosophical doctrine, and thus to eliminate the sacred mysteries of the faith. On the other hand, in the interests of being able to consider the rationality of the faith, and particularly the reasonableness of belief in God, irrationalistic attitudes have generally also been resisted. In the middle of these extremes is the broad path of 'faith seeking understanding', a programme reckoned to have been initiated by Augustine of Hippo and frequently adopted (though variously understood) since then. Anselm and Aquinas follow this tradition, as do the Magisterial Reformers, especially *Calvin, insofar as they consider the interface between theology and philosophy, and other notable thinkers such as Jonathan *Edwards.

Contemporary emphases

Much philosophy of religion in the twentieth century was dominated by the attack on *metaphysics by *logical positivists. It was alleged that theological sentences stated matters which were unverifiable or unfalsifiable empirically, and hence cognitively meaningless, which carried the consequence that religious language would not be truth-bearing. The latter decades of that century saw a rapid decline in positivism's influence, due largely to the weight of its own internal difficulties, and consequently a shift away from interest in the nature and function of *religious language. As a consequence, metaphysics has been reinstated as a legitimate philosophical enquiry, and essentialism has returned. One consequence has been the rekindling of philosophical interest in the metaphysics of theism, not only in the 'proofs' but in the entire range of theological claims of Judeo-Christianity: the nature of God, the relation between God and the creation, incarnation and the Trinity, and so forth. In fact, while the traditional stance and interests of the philosophy of religion, as mentioned above, have not gone away, they have tended to be eclipsed by a return to the 'faith seeking understanding' stance of the patristic and medieval periods.

The problem of evil

Philosophical attacks on religion have centred upon the problem of *evil. It is argued that since the existence of evil is incompatible with the existence of an essentially benevolent and all-powerful God, then such a God does not exist. Various strategies have been offered in response. For example, that there is no logical inconsistency between the existence of God and the existence of evil if men and women have libertarian freedom, since it is then up to them, and not up to God, whether there is evil, at least whether there is moral evil. (This is a 'defence' against the charge of inconsistency, rather than a full-blown *theodicy.) Others argue for a 'greater-good' defence either in terms of human 'soul-making', or in more traditionalist terms. The divine permission of a world containing moral evil is a necessary condition of the greater good of human *redemption through Christ. Such approaches are not inconsistent and so may be combined with each other to present a cumulative case. Sometimes greater-good defences are accused of adopting an ethic in which the end justifies the means.

Justification

Can the philosophy of religion be justified as a legitimate area of interest for the Christian? The Christian scholar, like it or not, must take an interest in philosophical issues because of the influence of philosophy – of Neoplatonism, or Aristotle, or Kant, to look no further – on the historical development of theology. But besides this historical enquiry, what of the activity of philosophy itself?

As noted, the current scene is marked by much less hostility to historical Christianity than a couple of generations ago. Although the philosopher's questions, 'What do you mean?' and 'How do you know?', when applied to the Christian faith, may be taken as sceptical challenges to it, they need not only be understood in this way, but rather as invitations to reflect rationally upon how the statements and other utterences of a developed religion are to be understood, and how they are to be justified. Paradoxically, it is the rich interplay between philosophy and theology throughout the Christian centuries that makes possible continued philosophical reflection on the faith. Yet the Bible, together with the main *creeds and *confessions of the church, are underdetermined both in their meaning and their truth claims when measured by current standards of philosophical rigour. The Bible is not a textbook of the natural sciences, and nor is it a textbook in metaphysics or epistemology (see *Scripture). It is best to think of the Bible as setting parameters. Within these broad but definite limits it is up to the church and the individual Christian to articulate the faith philosophically as best they can, using the resources of philosophy in an eclectic manner and not allowing the faith to be 'captured' by some prevailing philosophical fashion or unduly influenced by it.

Bibliography

B. Davies (ed.), *Philosophy of Religion: A Guide and Anthology* (Oxford, 2000); P. Helm, *Faith and Understanding* (Edinburgh, 1997); A. Plantinga, *God, Freedom and Evil* (London, 1974); idem, *Warranted Christian Belief* (New York, 2000); P. Quinn and C. Taliaferro (eds.), *A Companion to the Philosophy of Religion* (Oxford, 1997); R. Swinburne, *The Existence of God* (Oxford, 1979); C. Taliaferro, *Contemporary Philosophy of Religion* (Oxford, 1998).

P. HELM

PIETISM

Albrecht *Ritschl saw Pietism as a deviation from *Reformation Christianity, but it is more balanced to view it as a renewal movement within Germany and beyond, and with that, a missionary movement with room for women's initiatives. Though beginning in the late sixteenth century, it was carried on through the nineteenth and twentieth centuries by great leaders such as Mencken, *Beck and Blumhardt. Martin Brecht thinks the Bible is the indispensable connection between them by providing a 'meta-history' for the people of God which transcends historical contingencies. The canonical message is more than the mere kerygma of justification by faith, but includes guidance by the inspired reading and preaching of the Bible, allegiance to a community and dedication to a priesthood of believers. Yet most Pietists (the label attached to followers of Spener and Francke) would have distanced themselves from the so-called 'radical Pietism' of J. *Boehme and even the Holy Spirit experience of Zinzendorf's *Moravians (*Herrnhuter*).

One can speak of a pre-Reformation *mystical influence (e.g. Angela of Foligno, Thomas à Kempis and the *Theologia Deutsch*, which is thought to be written by Tauler) at work on Johann Arndt (1555–1622). He was a prophet of 'interior Protestantism' (A. Schweitzer). His most famous book was *True Christianity*, in which he calls the reader to follow Christ and allow his indwelling, all in a spirit of sober penitence and sanctification through prayer as conversation. Life was a process of rebirth. Faith, not learning, was the only source of all true virtues. One is to learn to know to hate the inherited abomination of original sin and his helpless misery, to ascribe all to Christ so that he may work all things by indwelling in the believer. If one cannot take up the cross with joy, one should at least take it up with humility and find interior rest as the Sabbath of God. Arndt's follower Johann Gerhard (1582–1637) believed that *spirituality and scholastic theology (see *Orthodoxy/Scholasticism, Lutheran) could be complementary. Gerhard's attempt to replace Arndt with his own textbook *Schola Pietatis* failed, yet his *Sacred Meditations* had more than 100 editions during the seventeenth century.

P. J. Spener (1635–1705) held Arndt as the one through whom the Reformation had come to fruition. Spener saw the task of dragging people out of atheism as beyond the powers of doctrine and orthodoxy, although he was indebted to English *Puritan writers and their belief in the verbal inspiration of Scripture. He encouraged believers to seek a 'new birth' with less of Arndt's sombre intensity, more on the joy of Christian life, and a call to the Christian that Christ be *in* us as well as *for* us. For Spener the Bible was certain, clear, intelligible and perfect, with an inner power, so that reading the Bible should stimulate a conversation with God, asking for guidance and receiving his answer. Central along with conversion came rediscovery of the Bible (and third, eschatological fervour, with a belief in better times for the church just ahead). He formed small (twice-weekly) meetings while remaining loyal to the Lutheran Church and encouraging regular Communion attendance and Sunday observance.

Spener had to leave Strasbourg for Frankfurt in 1665 when he came under suspicion of being a Calvinist. With him the Bible returned as the book of edification along with a new belief in the efficacy of *Scripture in the place of the Lutheran catechisms. Divine power resided in the reading of the Bible to which the medieval mystic Tauler had pointed. Bible study should not just be for learned theologians. His main work, *Pia Desideria* (1675), insisted on communities of Bible readers. For his close colleague J. J. Schütz (1640–1690) the reality of putting biblical commands into practice convinced him of Christianity's truth, and that conversion needed to go on *within* the church. By the last four years of his life, when this seemed to be failing, he and his small community, fuelled with expectation of Christ's thousand-year reign on earth (chiliasm; see *Millennium), broke off relations with the Lutheran Church.

Whereas Spener was a mystical interpreter of Luther, viewing justification as *sanctification and as practice of piety, Francke, at the Pietist centre of Halle, stressed the ethical and legalistic side of the individual's great struggle before justification, followed by a great feeling that God had done a new work, along the lines of Paul's 'change' between Rom. 7 and 8. Ministerial candidates should give testimony of their conversion. According to John 7:17, when someone does God's will, then they would know whether that teaching comes from God. The work of J. A. Bengel (1687–1752) was to produce as near as possible the NT as it left the hands of NT Christians. He disliked the text-lottery method of the Moravians. His exegesis was practical, even to the point of encouraging later south-west German Pietists to emigrate in search of the fulfilment of salvation-history of which Bengel's Bible spoke.

Around 1800 a *catechism versus Bible battle was being fought within *Lutheranism. Although one could detect Reformed influences among Swiss Pietists, the doubts about the nature of the atonement in the mid-century more reflect the internationalization of the missionary pietistic movement. This turned those who had been receivers through the Anglo-Saxon Bible societies and the Keswick *holiness movement into providers of mission. The Deutsche Christentumsgesellschaft in Basel split off from the British and Foreign Bible Society in 1824. During this period of Awakening (*Erweckungsbewegung*) a new accent on pastoral care appeared against the background of political unrest, industrial revolution and the state church's failure to give answers, and the need for the simple faith of the laypeople to step up to the challenge with a duty to use their gifts. The term 'evangelization' of an organized sort was advanced at the Gnadauer Conference of 1888.

On the academic side, Hermann Cremer's 1897 *Beiträge zur Förderung der christlichen Theologie* was an important counterweight to German *liberal theology. The significance of Adolf *Schlatter and Martin *Kähler at the beginning of the twentieth century has become increasingly appreciated. According to Martin Brecht, Kähler saw himself as one who honoured the Bible, standing in a line from *Cocceius through Menken. A split from the Pentecostal Pietists over the issue of *gifts and the possibility of *perfection was sealed as early as 1909 (Berlin Conference). For most of those 'evangelical' mission and Bible Christians who are today's descendants of Pietism, and are strong in their community churches and missions (and also with an influence on the established ones), God has come into history by the Bible in terms of its effects on the lives of believers.

Bibliography

J. Arndt, *True Christianity*, tr. and introd. P. Erb (Mahwah, 1979); H. Lehmann (ed.), *Geschichte des Pietismus*, vol. 4 (Göttingen, 2004); C. Lindberg, *The Pietist Theologians* (Oxford, 2005); P. J. Spener, *Pia Desideria*, tr. T. G. Tappert (New York, 2002).

M. W. Elliott

PINNOCK, CLARK (1937–2010)

Clark Pinnock was Professor of Theology at McMaster Divinity College in Hamilton, Ontario from 1977 to 2002. His doctoral studies were in NT with F. F. Bruce at Manchester and in his early career as a Southern Baptist theologian in the US. He defended the concept of biblical inerrancy (see *Infallibility and inerrancy of the Bible), which was modified later in *The Scripture Principle* (1984). His later works include *The Flame of Love: A Theology of the Holy Spirit* (1997). Pinnock's later career is best known, however, for his reaction against his earlier Calvinism. He came to the conclusion that the 'exclusivism' which he saw in the Augustinian-Calvinist tradition militated against the mission of the church, and, going beyond the classical *Arminian position, he became the leading advocate of '*open' or 'freewill' theism. Since he continued to believe that God's total foreknowledge and his absolute *predestination were logically tied together, he moved to a rejection of the former in order to deny the latter. This implied a reinterpretation of God's omniscience: just as God's omnipotence only meant that he could do whatever was *logically* possible, so his omniscience meant that he knew whatever was *logically* possible, and that did not include complete knowledge of the future. Open theism has been supported by biblical passages where God is said to change his mind, but it has been widely rejected as authentically *evangelical theology.

Bibliography

Works: *A Wideness in God's Mercy: The Finality of Jesus Christ in a World of Religions* (Grand Rapids, 1992); *Most Moved Mover* (Carlisle and Grand Rapids, 2001).
 Studies: B. L. Callen, *Clark H. Pinnock: Journey Toward Renewal, An Intellectual Biography* (Nappanee, 2000); D. Strange, 'Clark H. Pinnock: The Evolution of an Evangelical Maverick', *EQ* 71, 1999, pp. 327–348.

T. A. NOBLE

PLACHER, WILLIAM (1948–2008)

William Placher was a professor of *philosophy and religion at Wabash College. He is associated with the '*Yale theology' of George *Lindbeck and Hans *Frei. This theology is self-described as *postliberal theology because it attempts to move beyond the commitments of nineteenth- and twentieth-century liberal theology. It is also a form of *narrative theology because of its view that the Bible's narrative, and not experience or reason, is the foundation of theology and the source of our knowledge of God's identity. Part of Placher's agenda, accordingly, was to continue Karl *Barth's project of liberating Christian theology from any subservience to philosophy (see *Philosophy and theology). Placher, therefore, rejected theology's apologetic task, for apologetics has usually meant using philosophy to find common ground between the beliefs and values of the church and of the larger human community. For the same reason, his post-*foundationalist approach means the rejection of any attempt to secure theology's claims on the basis of a rational and universally acceptable basis. However, Placher's writings show concern about some of the implications of postliberal theology, especially its tendency to locate theological authority in the church instead of in the biblical text itself. He has also written about the need to recover the idea of truth in light of the spectre of *relativism raised by postfoundationalist theology.

Bibliography

Works: *Unapologetic Theology: A Christian Voice in a Pluralistic Conversation* (Louisville, 1989); *Narratives of a Vulnerable God: Christ, Theology, and Scripture* (Louisville, 1994); *The Domestication of Transcendence: How Modern Thinking about God Went Wrong* (1996); *The Triune God: An Essay in Postliberal Theology* (Louisville, 2007).

S. M. POWELL

PLANTINGA, ALVIN (b. 1932)

Alvin Plantinga is a prominent American philosopher, apologist and founding member of the Society of Christian Philosophers. He is John A. O'Brien Professor Emeritus at the University of Notre Dame, and inaugural holder of the Jellema chair in philosophy at his alma mater, Calvin College. Plantinga's work in epistemology, *metaphysics and the *philosophy of religion has significantly shaped contemporary philosophical discussions.

A master of the methods of analytic philosophy, and deeply engaged in its central discussions, Plantinga identifies most deeply with the tradition of *Augustine, *Calvin and Abraham *Kuyper. Like them, he believes that all human thought and action spring from broadly religious motives, and that Christian academics should act accordingly. Hence he philosophizes unabashedly as a Christian, and often directly for the Christian community. His work includes excurses into *philosophical theology (e.g. *Does God Have a Nature?* and *Warranted Christian Belief*), which integrates discussion of sin, salvation, Scripture and the work of the Holy Spirit into discussion of the knowledge of God.

Plantinga's *epistemology is developed in his 1987–8 *Gifford Lectures, since published as *Warrant: The Current Debate* and *Warrant and Proper Function*, and followed by *Warranted Christian Belief*. Knowledge, he argues, is best seen as warranted true belief, where warrant derives from the operation of properly functioning cognitive equipment designed to produce true beliefs. He goes on to claim that proper function, in biology or epistemology, makes sense only in the context of theism. From this he derives an argument to the effect that evolution, if true, makes theism rather than naturalism more likely ('Naturalism defeated').

Like Augustine and Calvin, Plantinga contends that it is natural for us to respond to divine revelation by believing in God; if not for the effects of *sin, we would do so immediately and with no need for argument. But since our sense of deity is clouded by sin, we need the testimony of the Holy Spirit working through the Scriptures to bring us to the knowledge of God. Plantinga fleshes these claims out within the context of contemporary epistemology. Partly because he believes them, he is less concerned to prove God's existence, or the truth of Christianity, than to defend Christian *theism against the charge that it is irrational or false.

However, Plantinga has produced theistic and anti-atheistic proofs, arguing that (1) belief in the existence of God is epistemologically on a par with belief in other minds, so that if the one is rationally justified, so is the other (*God and Other Minds*); (2) the ontological argument can be given a sound formulation: in brief, if a maximally perfect being *could* exist (and why think otherwise?), then such a being *does* exist (*The Nature of Necessity*); (3) God's omnipotence, omniscience and goodness are logically consistent with the existence of evil (*God, Freedom and Evil*), nor does the existence of evil render God's existence improbable ('The Probabilistic Argument from Evil'); (4) the existence of purpose in the natural world can only be explained by divine creation (*Warrant and Proper Function*).

Plantinga has also argued (*Warrant and Proper Function*) that if naturalism and evolution are both true, it is either unlikely or not rational to believe that our cognitive faculties are generally reliable. This, plus the argument from proper function to a designer, has made him popular with the advocates of Intelligent Design in the United States. Plantinga himself sees belief in evolution and Christian faith as compatible (see *Science and theology). Most of his polemics on this subject are not aimed at evolution per se, but at the naturalistic claim that the world is here by chance, with no God involved, and that this belief somehow follows from evolutionary theory. His recent reflections on science and Christian faith are enunciated in his 2005 Gifford Lectures, *Science and Religion: Conflict or Concord?*

Plantinga has been a very public apologist, frequently participating in public debates in defence of the rationality of theism. His interchange with Daniel Dennett has been published as *Science and Religion: Are They Compatible?* (Oxford, 2011). In 2012 the University of Pittsburgh's Departments of Philosophy, History and Philosophy of Science co-awarded Plantinga the Nicholas Rescher Prize for Contributions to Systematic Philosophy.

Bibliography

Works: *God and Other Minds* (Ithaca, 1967); *God, Freedom and Evil* (Grand Rapids, 1974); *The Nature of Necessity* (London, 1974); *Does God Have a Nature?* (Milwaukee, 1980); 'How to Be an Anti-Realist', *Proceedings of the American Philosophical Society* 56, 1982, pp. 47–70; *Warrant: The Current Debate* (Oxford, 1993); *Warrant and Proper Function* (Oxford, 1993); *The Analytic Theist: An Alvin Plantinga Reader* (Grand Rapids, 1998); *Warranted Christian Belief* (Oxford, 2000); *Science and Religion: Are They Compatible?* (with Daniel Dennett) (Oxford, 2011); *Where the Conflict Really Lies: Science, Religion and Naturalism* (Oxford, 2012); <http://www.calvin.edu/academic/philosophy/virtual_library/articles/plantinga_alvin/>.

Studies: J. E. Tomberlin and P. van Inwagen (eds.), *Alvin Plantinga* (Dordrecht, 1985).

D. W. CLOWNEY

PLATONISM

Platonism, the tradition of philosophy deriving from Plato of Athens (*c.* 429–347 BC), one of the most significant figures in the history of human thought, has had a major influence on Christian theology, especially through its last creative development, known as Neoplatonism.

Plato's work rests on the impressive life and death of his fellow-Athenian Socrates (469–399 BC), perhaps the first Greek thinker to devote critical philosophical attention to the bases of morality (and, for his adherence to conviction even unto death, the favourite pagan hero of early Christianity). For his last forty years, Plato taught at a grove outside Athens which gave the name 'the Academy' both to his school (which lasted until Justinian's final dissolution of pagan schools in AD 529) and to the Platonic tradition in general. He produced some twenty-five works, nearly all in dialogue form, with Socrates often a leading participant. The most significant for Christian thought come from his middle and later periods, notably the *Phaedo*, *Republic*, *Timaeus* and *Laws*.

True understanding is pursued by dialectical argument. The so-called Socratic method, best observed in *Meno* (and known from the Gk word as 'maieutic' because the philosopher acts as 'midwife'), demonstrates that we have innate knowledge (*epistēmē*) of basic realities, awareness of which is elicited by question and answer, not imparted by teaching. By such reasoning we may attain explicit knowledge of the forms (*ideai*), one of Plato's most distinctive contributions to philosophy. He emphasizes that sense experience yields only fallible opinion (*doxa*), not firm knowledge, for the observed world is in perpetual flux, and easily deceives. Behind the impermanent phenomena lie the changeless archetypal 'forms', the originals, of which all particular things are imperfect copies. Thus there exists a 'form' of the human person above and apart from all individual human beings, their perfect and eternal model, by sharing in which they are what they are. The same applies to artefacts (e.g. tables and the 'form' of the table) and to abstract realities such as beauty and wisdom. Knowledge of the 'forms' is the basis of morality and practical life.

The supreme 'form' is that of the good, which Christian thought has easily identified with God, although Plato distinguishes them. Normally, the 'forms' are independent of God, but in Timaeus they appear as his thoughts. This work had a long influence on Christian thought (later in Chalcidius' Lat. translation and commentary, *c*. AD 400), for it presents an outline cosmology. The world was fashioned by the Demiurge ('craftsman'), who is apparently God, imprinting the pattern of the 'forms' on chaotic matter. The world is both soul and body, and so in a true sense both divine and corruptible. Laws gives the earliest version of the cosmological argument for God's existence (see *Natural theology), based on the necessity for a 'perfectly good soul' as the source of all motion.

Plato believed in the *immortality of souls (*Phaedo*), which belong to the realm of the 'forms'. While subject to their imprisoning bodies, they gain knowledge of the forms by recollection (*anamnēsis*) from their previous existence. Souls are liable to reincarnation (see *Metempsychosis) until, finally released by death, they find fulfilment after judgment in a supra-mundane heaven.

The similarity of certain Platonic ideas to Judeo-Christian beliefs was highlighted by early Christian apologists. At the same time Platonic *dualism deeply tainted Christian attitudes, with its depreciation of the body and the physical world in favour of the soul and the realm of true reality accessible to reason alone.

One element in Plato's thought was developed by Arcesilaus and Carneades (third to second centuries BC) into philosophical scepticism. Knowledge was impossible; probability must serve as guidance for living. This position heavily influenced Cicero and evoked *Augustine's *Against the Academics*.

It was the Middle Platonism of the first two centuries AD (especially Albinus, Plutarch and Numenius) that most directly influenced early Christian writers such as Justin (see *Apologists) and *Clement of Alexandria. Religious concerns predominated, and Plato was mixed with elements of *Aristotelian, *Stoic, Pythagorean and even Jewish origin. Numenius described Plato as 'Moses speaking Attic Greek'. Middle Platonism heightened God's transcendence, leaving him describable only negatively (cf. *apophatic theology) and active in creation only through intermediaries (e.g. *Logos, planetary powers, world-soul). Plato's 'forms' are now unambiguously thoughts in the divine mind, and speculations about the cause of evil relate it in different ways to matter itself. Such tendencies fed into Gnosticism as well as orthodox Christianity. An eclectic Platonism pervasively coloured early Christian theology, most conspicuously in the Christian Platonists of *Alexandria, where *Philo the Jew had led the way.

The last phase of the tradition was Neoplatonism (third – sixth centuries), which developed out of Middle Platonism (especially Numenius) but took its shape from the creative genius of Plotinus (*c*. 205–270), a contemporary of *Origen at Alexandria who later taught at Rome. By *c*. 400 Neoplatonism had taken over the Athenian Academy itself, with Proclus (410–485), the most encyclopaedic Neoplatonic teacher, its leading light. The Syrian Iamblichus (*c*. 250–*c*. 325) accommodated Neoplatonism to *polytheism, magic and divination, while Porphyry (*c*. 232–303), the pupil, editor, biographer and even popularizer of Plotinus, gave it an anti-Christian twist. His *Against the Christians* was shrewd and weighty enough to demand responses from several major Christian writers.

In Plotinus' Platonism, dualism is subsumed within a higher *monism, and philosophy approaches religion and *mysticism. The source and goal of all existence is the One, which is beyond not only description but even being itself. It is accessible only by ascetic abstraction above the world of sense and even thought, culminating in rare moments of ecstatic vision in which the self is united with the One. From the One's creative overflow emanates a hierarchy of levels of being, tending towards multiplicity and inferiority and aspiring to return to the One. The first emanations are Mind and Soul, cosmic principles respectively of intelligence and animation. All being as such is good, even bare matter at the lower limit of the 'great chain of being' (hence Plotinus' polemic against *Gnosticism). *Evil is strictly nonbeing – a real possibility for those who turn away from the One.

Although it inspired ancient paganism's last major intellectual challenge to Christianity, Neoplatonism proved enormously attractive to Christian thinkers from Origen's successors onwards. The Cappadocian Fathers, *Ambrose, *Victorinus Afer, Augustine and *Pseudo-Dionysius the Areopagite were all deeply indebted to it. Through Dionysius it became perhaps the most formative factor in Christian mystical theology in both East and West (see *Eastern Orthodox theology). Through Augustine it coloured virtually the whole medieval tradition in the West. Other peaks of Christian Platonism or Neoplatonism include *Boethius, *Eriugena, the school of Chartres, Hugh of St Victor (see *Victorines) and Nicholas of Cusa (*c.* 1400–64).

Although the rediscovered *Aristotle became 'the philosopher' of *scholasticism, Platonic and Neoplatonic influence lived on. The Renaissance witnessed renewed interest, both in Italy (especially in Marsilio Ficino's [1433–99] Florentine Academy) and in England (e.g. John Colet, *c.* 1466–1519). Platonic ideas were current in some streams of the *Radical Reformation. Anglicanism has been particularly receptive, from *Hooker through the *Cambridge Platonists and the *Christian Socialists to B. F. Westcott and W. R. Inge (1860–1954; see *Modernism, English). In the twentieth century, despite widespread reactions against dualism and Greek metaphysics, the vitality of Platonism is evident in writers as diverse as A. E. Taylor (1869–1945), A. N. Whitehead (1861–1947; see *Process theology), John *Baillie, *Tillich and Iris Murdoch. *Universalism often betrays Neoplatonic influence at work.

Bibliography

A. H. Armstrong and R. A. Markus, *Christian Faith and Greek Philosophy* (London, 1960); *CHLGEMP*; E. Cassirer, *The Platonic Renaissance in England* (Edinburgh, 1953); J. Daniélou, *Gospel Message and Hellenistic Culture* (London and Philadelphia, 1973); J. Dillon, *The Middle Platonists* (London, 1977); W. R. Inge, *The Platonic Tradition in English Religious Thought* (London, 1926); J. B. Kemp, *Plato* (Nottingham, 1976); J. M. Rist, *Plotinus* (Cambridge, 1967); N. A. Robb, *Neoplatonism of the Italian Renaissance* (London, 1935); P. Shorey, *Platonism Ancient and Modern* (Berkeley, 1938); R. W. Southern, *Platonism, Scholastic Method and the School of Chartres* (Reading, 1980); A. E. Taylor, *Plato* (London, ⁶1949); *idem*, *Platonism and Its Influence* (London, n.d.); D. P. Walker, *The Ancient Theology: Studies in Christian Platonism from the Fifteenth to the Eighteenth Century* (London, 1972); R. T. Wallis, *Neo-Platonism* (London, 1972).

D. F. WRIGHT

PLATONISM, CHRISTIAN

Christian Platonism is that complex strand of theology which is influenced by the philosophy of Plato (427–347 BC) and Plato's successors. Hellenistic influence over later Jewish thought, particularly *Philo, ensured that Christianity was directly or indirectly affected by Platonic philosophy from its inception. This clear influence of Plato and *Platonism can be traced at least as far back as *Clement of Alexandria and *Origen. Alongside the Cappadocian Fathers of the East, *Augustine of Hippo is often identified as the most prominent Christian Platonist of the patristic period. His popularity amongst both Catholic and Protestant theologians during the Reformation ensured the lasting influence of Platonist thought within Christian theology. Platonism was particularly influential in the work of Christian mystics of the East (*Pseudo-Dionysius the Areopagite,

John Climacus, *c.* 570–*c.* 649) and West (John Scotus *Eriugena, *Bernard of Clairvaux). Christian theology's encounter with pagan Neoplatonism, particularly the work of Plotinus (*c.* 205–270) and Proclus (410/412–85), also ensured that Plato's influence would remain strong.

Despite the introduction of the works of Aristotle in the twelfth century, the theology of the high Middle Ages is deeply influenced by various forms of Platonism. This can be seen clearly in the work of *Thomas Aquinas. Marcilio Ficino (1433–99) did much to transmit Platonic texts and ideas in the Renaissance, while the *Cambridge Platonists of the seventeenth century called for a return to what they regarded as the Platonic roots of Christian thought. Today, Christian Platonism remains highly influential, particularly amongst those who espouse an *apophatic doctrine of God which resists the influence of *nominalism in late medieval and modern philosophy and theology. Of particular note is the theological sensibility known as *Radical orthodoxy and the work of more recent Christian mystics such as Simone Weil (1909–43).

Christian Platonism is impossible to characterize in any straightforward fashion. It is often assumed to be dualistic in character, yet this is mistaken. It is precisely in Augustine's rejection of *Manichean *dualism and his view that only the good is primordial and real, with evil being the absence or privation of the good, that we see his Platonism most clearly. It is also sometimes thought that Christian Platonism regards material nature as corrupt or corrupting. Once again, this would be too crude a reading of the Platonist tradition. Christian Platonism is perhaps most clearly characterized by the development of Plato's doctrine of the Forms. Rather than existing in an independent realm in which the visible world participates, in Christian thought the Forms are understood as ideas in the mind of God (see Thomas Aquinas, *Summa Theologiae* 1a.15). It is by participating in the divine ideas that creatures receive being and intelligibility. The importance of the soul as the hinge between the material and the immaterial, sharing characteristics of both, is also emphasized.

Bibliography

J. Cleary (ed.), *Traditions of Platonism: Essays in Honour of John Dillon* (Aldershot, 1999); J. Dillon, *The Middle Platonists: A Study of Platonism 80 BC to AD 200* (rev. edn, Ithaca, 1996); idem, *The Great Tradition: Further Studies in the Development of Platonism and Early Christianity* (Aldershot, 1997); E. J. Doering and E. O. Springted (eds.), *The Christian Platonism of Simone Weil* (Notre Dame, 2004); G. O'Daly, *Platonism Pagan and Christian: Studies in Plotinus and Augustine* (Aldershot, 2001); J. Rist, *Platonism and Its Christian Heritage* (London, 1985); A. E. Taylor, *Platonism and Its Influence* (London, 1925).

S. A. OLIVER

PLOTINUS, see PLATONISM

PNEUMATOMACHI, see ARIANISM; HOLY SPIRIT

POLANUS, AMANDUS, see REFORMED THEOLOGY

POLANYI, MICHAEL (1891–1976)

Hungarian by birth, British by adoption, Polanyi came to prominence as a scientist after the First World War. Stimulated on the one hand by the new physics of Einstein, and on the other by contacts with fascism and Marxism before his move to Britain, he devoted his later years to a wide-ranging investigation of philosophical, social and cultural questions.

His major book, *Personal Knowledge* (London, 1958), charts a path between the epistemological extremes of subjectivism and objectivism which, although bequeathed by classical philosophy, had been especially polarized since the *Enlightenment. For Polanyi faith and knowledge are not to be set in opposition, even in the physical sciences, but are properly combined in a concept of *personal knowledge*. This new *epistemology is established by reference to a wide range of examples and arguments, and helps to unify a spectrum of knowledge from science to the arts. Although he did not extend his arguments substantially into the domain of theology, he recognized the validity of this enterprise, in which theologians, most notably T. F. *Torrance, have been engaged.

After *Personal Knowledge*, besides refining his epistemological ideas in *The Tacit Dimension* (London, 1967), he began to explore corresponding questions of ontology: in what ways does the actual structure of reality affect our search for an understanding of it? His last writings, summarized in *Meaning* (Chicago, 1975), present a stratified world which human beings, with their mental activity, indwell, personally and objectively. Polanyi's analysis of the multi-levelled structure of reality may throw interesting light upon various aspects of the relationship between divine and human activity in the world.

Bibliography

For a general introduction to Polanyi's thought, see R. Gelwick, *The Way of Discovery: An Introduction to the Thought of Michael Polanyi* (Oregon, 2004). For its application to theology, see T. F. Torrance (ed.), *Belief in Science and in Christian Life* (Edinburgh, 1980); articles by R. L. Hall *et al.* in *Zygon* 17 (1982), pp. 3–87; J. V. Apczynki, *Doers of the Word: Toward a Foundational Theology Based on the Thought of Michael Polanyi* (Chico, 1982); M. Mitchell, *Michael Polanyi: The Art of Knowing* (Wilmington, 2006); D. Scott, *Everyman Revived: The Common Sense of Michael Polanyi* (Grand Rapids, 1995); W. T. Scott and M. X. Moleski, *Michael Polanyi: Scientist and Philosopher* (Oxford, 2005).

P. R. Forster

POLEMICS

A sub-discipline of confessionally oriented *dogmatic theology intended to defend the doctrinal truths of specific Christian denominations or of various branches within them, over against others. Thus polemics are essentially inter- and intra-confessional. The discipline flourished in the wake of the Protestant Reformation, as each new denomination sought to define itself as precisely as possible, but the polemical approach to theology has been present throughout Christian history. Examples of significant inter- or intra-confessional theological debates include those between Catholics and Orthodox (over the *filioque* formula; see *Creeds), Lutherans and Reformed (over the Lord's Supper; see *Eucharist), and in the Church of England between conformists and Puritans (over *church government).

Bibliography

G. R. Elton (ed.), *The New Cambridge Modern History II: The Reformation, 1520–1559* (Cambridge, [7]1976); C. Lindberg, *The European Reformations* (Oxford, [8]2002); R. A. Muller, *Post-Reformation Reformed Dogmatics, vol. 1: Prolegomena to Theology* (Grand Rapids, [2]2003); R. E. Olson, *Arminian Theology: Myths and Realities* (Downers Grove, 2006); J. Pelikan, *The Christian Tradition: A History of the Development of Doctrine, vol. 4: Reformation of Church and Dogma, 1300–1700* (Chicago, 1984); C. R. Trueman and R. S. Clark (eds.), *Protestant Scholasticism: Essays in Reassessment* (Carlisle, 1999).

C. C. Simuţ

POLITICAL THEOLOGY

Political theology in the broadest sense has meant from the beginning a theology which explains and justifies the political, social and economic orders. Thus, in the Roman Empire the cult of the divine emperor was something to which all loyal citizens were expected to subscribe, often alongside another permitted religion, *religio licita*, which did not conflict with the official cult. There was always in relation to Judaism tension between the claims of Jahweh and the formal sacrifices and so forth that were expected by the official political religion. Thus it is not without significance that Pilate insisted on putting on Jesus' cross the words 'The King of the Jews', while the Jewish leaders protested that they had no king but Caesar (Matt. 27:37; Mark 15:26; Luke 23:38; John 19:19).

Three types of political theology

In the early and patristic church three distinct types of Christian political theology emerged, each of which has its exemplars today. First of all, there was the political theology which offered a theology very much in the classical mode, suitable for the new relationship between church and empire which followed the *Constantinian settlement and the establishment of Christianity as the official faith of the Empire. Christianity took over the ancient role of civil religion, sacralizing power, legitimating the existing order of things and inculcating in the populace reverence for the authorities and obedience to orders from above. This

683

approach, which initially had as its greatest protagonist *Eusebius, continues today in those who promote a political theology that supports an establishment of Christianity as '*Christendom' and the shaping of public policy in the light of Scripture. Prominent protagonists of this position in modern times have been Abraham *Kuyper and Oliver *O'Donovan.

The second type of political theology was associated from the beginning with Tertullian and others who regarded the church as a kind of counterculture, an alternative to the Empire and the civil order. 'Nothing,' writes Tertullian, 'is more foreign to us than the state.' Christians live by their own standards, maintaining an absolutist ethic with a tendency to *pacifism. A true church should have no dealings with political power nor any involvement in the world of secular politics. Christians of this persuasion withdrew from politics in order to sustain communities of love, free from the compromises of the world of power, violence and greed. And these communities and their faith are a constant challenge to the broader society, and not only a challenge, but also the offering of an alternative to the 'way of the world', with its violence, greed and oppression. Communities of faith and love sustained faith, hope and love in the Dark Ages, according to Alasdair MacIntyre, and thus they ensured that civility remained a living option in an age of violence and disorder.

This type of political theology was sustained in monastic communities (see *Asceticism and monasticism) and in *Mennonite communities today, such as the Amish people in Pennsylvania. Its most potent advocates today are the disciples of the Mennonite, John Howard *Yoder, and the Methodist, Stanley *Hauerwas. And this voice is heard loudly and clearly in recent political theology.

The third type of political theology has its roots in the theology of St *Augustine. His great work, *De Civitate Dei*, was occasioned by the suggestion that the sack of Rome by Alaric the Goth in 410 had been caused by the abandonment of the old civil religion of Rome; the gods of Rome were angry and the virtues that had been nurtured by the traditional patriotic cult were no more in evidence. Political theologians of the school of Eusebius were incapable of responding to this onslaught, because for them the prosperity and power of Rome and the *kingdom of God had become hopelessly confused. Augustine produced not simply a tract for the times, but a theology of history and a political theology which was one of the greatest achievements of late antiquity and a classic of Christian political theology.

Augustine developed a political theology which sparked between the two poles of the earthly city and the city of God. The two cities are very different from one another, but in a real sense they are both cities of God. Augustine defines a city or a commonwealth as 'a gathering of rational beings united in fellowship by sharing a common love of the same things' (*De Civitate Dei* XIX.24). There are, of course, many loves that may bind people together in fellowship, but the highest love, which is the love of God, is the love which sustains the city of God, where alone true justice, true peace and true *fellowship are to be found. The visible church is a partial and incomplete manifestation of the city of God, and the earthly city operates in a fallen, sinful world where compromise is often the only way forward, and the task is often to provide a 'dyke against sin' rather than a complete manifestation of God's love and justice.

Augustine's political theology has been, and remains, immensely influential, but in some ways the most notable protagonists of an Augustinian approach in recent times were the American theologian, Reinhold *Niebuhr, and his many disciples such as Robin Lovin. But it was developed particularly enthusiastically by Lutherans from the Reformation period until today. This *Lutheran doctrine of the 'Two Kingdoms' allowed for dangerous and extreme accounts of the relation between the two kingdoms, as when Luther declared that a statesman is obliged, in seeming contradiction both to the law and the gospel, to resort on occasion to force, coercion and violence. And in such a case, Luther declared, 'the hand that wields this sword and slays with it is . . . no more man's hand but God's, who hangs, tortures, beheads, slays and fights. All these are His works and His judgments' (M. Luther, 'Whether Soldiers, Too, Can Be Saved', 1926, *Works*, vol. 46 [Philadelphia, 1967]). And far later, some German Lutheran theologians and church leaders in the 1930s refused to recognize that the rise of Nazism was a matter of theological concern because, they said, it belonged entirely in the secular realm.

Political theology in the twentieth century

The whole notion of political theology was for a long time deeply suspect among Christians because it was associated with theologies that were closely modelled on the old – and new – pagan political theologies, and performed the same function of legitimating the social order. This impression was reinforced in 1922 by the publication of a book called *Politische Theologie* by a German philosopher, Carl Schmitt, who taught that even in a secular age there was a necessary link between theological ideas and secular politics. Schmitt advocated a strongly nationalist form of Catholicism, and a reverence for the established order of things. Theology, he taught, is inherently conservative, and indispensable in an effective political order. Schmitt's thought had considerable influence on the emerging Nazi movement which developed as Schmitt-style political theology.

Just after the Nazi takeover in Germany, Erik Peterson published *Der Monotheismus als Politisches Problem* (1935), in which he argued that any form of monotheism provided support for totalitarianism, whereas a trinitarian theology was inherently associated with democracy.

The third 'father figure' of twentieth-century political theology was Ernst Bloch, an independent Marxist, who in 1959 published his monumental *The Principle of Hope* which suggested that a *Marxism which sustained the hope of a better future both drew heavily on the Christian tradition, and suggested that believers should strive to realize on earth a better and more just state of things. Bloch was a major influence on Jürgen *Moltmann, whose monumental *Theology of Hope* (1967) suggested that a Christian theology committed to serious debate with Marxism as well as the theological tradition could be challengingly relevant in the twentieth century and beyond.

Liberation theology

Meanwhile, in Latin America, a new kind of political theology emerged from the slums and the congregations of the poor which were called 'Base Communities'. Drawing heavily on Marxist insights and also on the experience of the poor, *liberation theologians emerged, led by Gustavo *Gutiérrez, Leonardo *Boff and others, who developed a theology which put at the centre the poor, taught that theology should present a 'preferential option for the poor', and should be deeply rooted in *praxis on behalf of the poor and listening intently to their voice. Most of the Latin American liberation theologians were Roman Catholic, which was only to be expected in Latin America, where the vast majority of Christians were Roman Catholic, although the rapid growth of Pentecostal Christianity was already under way. Liberation theologians found Marxist forms of social analysis helpful in their search for a radical political theology which actually helped the poor and stood with them in their trials. The early liberation theologians did not have the caution about Marxism that was common among the Europeans, who lived close to the communist dictatorships of eastern Europe, and were aware of the horrors of many of these regimes.

Two controversies deserve particular notice. *Míguez Bonino, a leading Protestant liberation theologian, challenged Moltmann to give concrete content to the 'identification with the oppressed' which he saw as the necessary implication of faith in the crucified God. There is, argued Bonino, no such thing as innocent detachment; even the most abstract theological reasoning has an ideological function. The way to avoid the reduction of the gospel to a political programme, Bonino suggests, is not to take refuge in critical detachment, but to illuminate what is going on with the help of the best economics and political science available. In a vigorous and incisive *Open Letter to Miguez Bonino*, Moltmann rejects the substantive charges, warns against a narrow provincialism in theology and suggests that liberation theology has problems and inadequacies of its own.

The Vatican, under a Polish pope who had experienced the tyranny of a Marxist dictatorship at first hand, and with a theologically conservative Cardinal, Josef *Ratzinger, was highly suspicious of liberation theology and issued two cautious dissuasives, in the form of Instructions, *Libertatis Nuntius* (1984) and *Libertatis Conscientia* (1986), while the pope on his visits to Latin America made clear his deep suspicion of the movement in the church that had produced liberation theology. But in some ways the two Instructions were among the most radical documents to emanate from the Vatican, embracing, for example, a preferential option for the poor. Yet in some notable cases, such as that of Leonardo Boff, individual liberation theologians were disciplined, or effectively ejected from the church. With the collapse of the European Marxist regimes in 1989, many expected liberation theology to disappear. But it survived, and in some places flourished, while the Vatican took stringent measures against some leading liberation theologians such as Jon *Sobrino.

Varieties of political theology

A range of different political theologies continue to flourish in a variety of contexts. On the right wing, 'conviction politicians', such as Margaret Thatcher or the American Neocons, declared that their policies were rooted in Christian faith, while radical political theologies continue to be active, especially in Africa, Asia and Latin America, but also among evangelicals in the United States. Political theology is far from dead.

See also: SOCIETY, THEOLOGY OF; STATE.

Bibliography

A. Fierro, *The Militant Gospel* (London, 1977); D. B. Forrester, *Theology and Politics* (Oxford, 1988); G. Gutiérrez, *A Theology of Liberation* (London, 1974); A. Kee (ed.), *Reader in Political Theology* (London, 1974); J. Míguez Bonino, *Revolutionary Theology Comes of Age* (London, 1975); C. Rowland (ed.), *The Cambridge Companion to Liberation Theology* (Cambridge, 1999); P. Scott and W. T. Cavanaugh (eds.), *The Blackwell Companion to Political Theology* (Oxford, 2004); J. Sobrino, *The True Church and the Poor* (London, 1985).

D. B. FORRESTER

POLKINGHORNE, JOHN (b. 1930)

Polkinghorne, a leading scientist in the UK, was Professor of Mathematical Physics at Cambridge University until he resigned to take up studies for ordination in the Church of England. He was ordained in 1982. Since 1984 he has published a number of important books exploring the complementary relationship between *science and Christian faith. He was elected a Fellow of the Royal Society in 1974, was awarded the Templeton Prize for Science and Religion in 2002, was founding president of the International Society for Science and Religion and the Society for Ordained Scientists, and was knighted in 1997.

Polkinghorne has been highly influential in short-circuiting the sterile antipathy between scientific *materialism and Christian revelation. He has demonstrated in particular that there is nothing at either an intellectual or scientific level that precludes faith or that makes it unlikely. On the contrary, he argues that theism makes more sense of the world and human experience than does *atheism.

He sees three areas giving rise to a presumption of *theism. The first is that our capacity for moving from an intelligence that is fit for coping practically with the everyday experiences that evolution requires of us, to one where we are able to understand the subatomic world and general relativity, takes the phenomenon of our humanity beyond the criteria required for fitness and survival. The second is the anthropic principle (in its weak and strong forms). This raises the two issues of what appears to be fine tuning of the universe to create hospitable conditions for life, and the role of the intelligent observer that the universe implicitly demands. The third is that theism makes more sense of the existence and demands of both ethics and aesthetics.

He describes his view of the world as that of critical realism. From this perspective, there is only one reality, but it is assessed, interpreted or explored from different angles by science and theology. Nature is more 'cloud-like' than 'clock-like'. Dual-aspect monism implies that 'there is only one stuff in the world' not two; but that 'I can occur in two contrasting states (mental and physical).' In his *Gifford Lectures, *Science and Christian Belief: The Faith of a Physicist*, Polkinghorne distinguishes his position from *panentheism and from *process theology, which, while allowing God to share our suffering, do not seem to believe in the God who raised Jesus from the dead. His views on time have attracted interest. He sees the eternity of the new life containing a temporal component. It comes not *ex nihilo* (out of nothing) but *ex vetere* (out of the old).

Bibliography

Works: *The Way the World Is: Christian Perspective of a Scientist* (1983; London, 1992; Louisville, 2007); *One World* (London and Princeton, 1986); *Science and Creation* (London, 1989); *Science and Providence* (London, 1989); *Reason and Reality* (London, 1991); *Science and Christian Belief: The Faith of a Physicist* (London, 1994); *Quarks, Chaos and Christianity* (London, ²2005).

G. ASHENDEN

POLYTHEISM

Polytheism is the belief in and worship of many gods. In the earlier part of the twentieth century it was believed to be a stage in the evolution of *religion from *animism to *monotheism. This view is now generally rejected, and polytheism is seen as the fruit of pre-scientific response to the natural world, since most of the gods are linked to some aspect of nature. Thus the sky, sun, moon, planets, earth, fire, water, animals and even plants have been considered divine, as well as identified with various characteristics of individual and social life. With the personification of natural phenomena as superhuman beings, polytheism is born. The world's mythologies are the accounts of the deeds of the gods which often sink to the level of the grossest immorality. Each god has a cult, the centre of which is the god's image. This can be a human being, an animal, a statue, a tree, a fire, a phallus, etc. Within polytheism one god or goddess is sometimes singled out by a particular group, and elevated to the position of supreme deity, though the existence of other gods is not denied. This is called henotheism or monolatry, and some have argued that OT patriarchal religion was this type of polytheism. Generally, however, the OT condemns the image-worship of polytheism as false attempts to represent God. The NT confirms this condemnation, and Paul even identifies the Corinthian gods with demons (Rom. 1:22f.; 1 Cor. 8:4–6; 10:19f.).

Bibliography

J. Assmann, 'Monotheism and Polytheism', in S. I. Johnston (ed.), *Religions of the Ancient World: A Guide* (Cambridge, MA, 2004); J. H. Bavinck, *The Church Between the Temple and the Mosque* (Grand Rapids, n.d.); A. Daniélou, *Hindu Polytheism* (London, 1964); M. Eliade, *Patterns in Comparative Religion* (London, 1958); P. Grimal (ed.), *Larousse World Mythology* (London, 1965); W. B. Kristensen, *The Meaning of Religion* (The Hague, 1960).

D. A. HUGHES

POSITIVISM

A philosophy and humanist 'religion' originating with Auguste Comte (1798–1857). Individuals, he held, and humankind in general, begin by being 'theological', ascribing events to supernatural powers; develop to a 'metaphysical' stage where they ascribe them to abstractions like 'force', which rename rather than explain; and finally reach the 'positive' stage where both these are abandoned, knowledge being recognized as of facts alone, or, in the sciences, regularities among facts. This progress is inevitable. It is matched by parallel progress in society; and Comte proposed a new science of sociology, to study humankind and enable society to be organized rationally and peacefully by a scientifically trained élite.

God as an explanatory hypothesis is unnecessary; religion should be based on worship of humanity as a whole. Comte devised a complete positivist 'church' with its saints, ceremonies, and so on, but this never became widely popular, nor did Comte's philosophy as such. However, his rejection of metaphysical and theological explanations, and his assertion that science was a matter of establishing neutral, objective 'facts' even in the realm of the social and human sciences, became widely influential in the philosophy of science and sociology. This contributed to the growth of 'scientific humanism' and the deep *secularism of European culture in the late nineteenth and throughout the twentieth century.

See also: LOGICAL POSITIVISM.

Bibliography

F. Copleston, *History of Philosophy*, vol. 9 (Tunbridge Wells, 1975); L. Kolakowski, *Positivist Philosophy from Hume to the Vienna Circle* (London, 1968).

R. L. STURCH

POSTLIBERALISM

Postliberalism is one of the most significant movements of Anglo-American theology and is chiefly inspired by the works of *Yale theologians Hans *Frei and George *Lindbeck. The term 'postliberalism' was introduced by Lindbeck, and the movement is called interchangeably 'postliberal' or 'intratextual' or the '[New] Yale school' of *narrative theology. In developing his ideas, Lindbeck made the most of the thought of the later Ludwig Wittgenstein and Clifford Geertz in order to propose an important new paradigm or 'research programme' which related religious experiences, traditions of interpretation and doctrinal conceptualizations for Christian thinking. With its holistic theory of knowledge and recognition of the diverse functions of *religious language, it is considered one of the earliest expressions of constructive *postmodern theological thought. Arising from his ecumenical engagement with different Christian traditions and in an attempt to combine the emphases of the well-established cognitive-propositional (characteristic of conservative theology) and 'experiential-expressive' symbolic (attributed to liberal theology) traditions, Lindbeck developed his 'cultural-linguistic' (Lindbeck, *The Nature of Doctrine*, p. 16) approach to doctrine and the function of religious language. Postliberal theologians maintain that the biblical narratives provide a categorical framework for Christian understanding of the world. According to their account, religions are communal phenomena like languages or cultures, together with their correlative forms of life. Thus, doctrines are 'regulative' (Lindbeck, *The Nature of Doctrine*, p. 18); they are 'best treated as second-order discourse – as [authoritative] rules to guide both [religious] practice and the use of first-order religious language (praise, preaching, exhortation, and the like)' (N. Murphy and J. W. McClendon, Jr, in *Modern Theology*, p. 206). The truth of theological claims is therefore 'intra-systematic' (Lindbeck, *The Nature of Doctrine*, p. 64).

Several theological camps have levelled criticisms against postliberalism, considering it a crypto-sectarian temptation that legitimizes a withdrawal of Christianity from pluralistic cultural discourse and disregards social responsibility (the criticism of revisionists and liberals), or accusing postliberalism of offering a cultural-relativistic view of religious belief and lacking commitment to *ontological truth claims (the criticism of conservative evangelicals). Some theologians sympathetic to the postliberal approach, while dismissing such criticisms as ill-founded, consider its account of how one justifies claims regarding the truth of religion as inadequate (Murphy, Vidu), or see Lindbeck's concept of 'intertextuality' as problematic (DeHart) or his regulative principles of Christological doctrinal formulations as lacking emphasis on discipleship (McClendon). The lasting legacy of postliberalism is in initiating an important conversation on the dialectical relationship of the practice of faith to theological reflections on the nature of *faith.

See also: LIBERAL THEOLOGY; CONSERVATIVE THEOLOGY.

Bibliography
P. J. DeHart, *The Trail of Witnesses: The Rise and Decline of Postliberal Theology* (Oxford, 2006); H. W. Frei, *The Eclipse of Biblical Narrative: A Study in Eighteenth and Nineteenth Century Hermeneutics* (New Haven, 1974); G. A. Lindbeck, *The Nature of Doctrine: Religion and Theology in a Postliberal Age* (Philadelphia, 1984); J. McClendon, *Doctrine: Systematic Theology*, vol. 2 (Nashville, 1994); N. Murphy, *Theology in the Age of Scientific Reasoning* (Ithaca, 1990); N. Murphy and J. W. McClendon, Jr, 'Distinguishing Modern and Postmodern Theologies,' *Modern Theology* 5, 1989, pp. 191–214; A. Vidu, *Postliberal Theological Method: A Critical Study* (Bletchley, 2005).

P. R. PARUSHEV

POSTMODERN THEOLOGY

The spirit of the postmodern age has influenced theology in two ways: as a cultural condition that intensifies capitalist consumerism ('postmodernity'), and as a philosophical rejection of the Enlightenment project of modernity ('postmodernism'). This article focuses on postmodernism: does it represent a new exodus from the bondage of modernity or a new Babylonian captivity of the church?

The postmodern *Zeitgeist*

'Postmodern' is a contrast term signifying what is 'subsequent to' or a 'reaction against' something (i.e. *modernity). The so-called '*Enlightenment project' of modernity was an attempt on the part of modern thinkers 'to develop objective science, universal morality and autonomous art' (M. Sarup, *Identity, Culture and the Postmodern World*, p. 94). In effect, it was an effort to arrive at the medieval transcendentals – truth, goodness, beauty – by pulling up our own human bootstraps (i.e. without God).

*Kant held that the enlightened person is free to use his own *reason and is not beholden to authorities and traditions. His famous 'turn to the subject' put the finishing touches on *Descartes' method of critical reasoning. The prize of such reasoning is knowledge and mastery: control of some dimension of the natural or social world. The project of modernity is a self-guided pilgrimage to the promised land of truth and liberation. Loneliness accompanies the autonomous knowing pilgrim, however, as *Voltaire well knew: 'To be modern is to be cut off from the consolations of religion or metaphysics, to be the child – happy or wretched – of science.'

Postmodern thinkers protest the Enlightenment project and its inevitable result: modern orphans who no longer belong to nurturing traditions. Postmoderns find implausible the model of the modern knowing subject and its ambition to attain universal truth (i.e. a God's-eye point of view). Postmodernism is the reminder that minds are not disembodied but embodied: knowing, seeing and thinking are culturally located. Human reason is never 'pure' but always coloured by one's social position and historical horizon. *Homo postmodernis* is *situated* being: a being-here in a particular race-gender-class.

Is postmodernism a historical epoch, a cultural context, or a mode of thought? All of the above. It is a *condition* in which one lives and moves, speaks and thinks, and has one's being; it is the shadowy 'other' of modernity, the 'return of the repressed' (Freud). To be postmodern is to have a heightened awareness of things that modernity suppressed, namely, our rootedness in a body, a culture, a tradition and a language.

Five big postmodern ideas

(1) *Language*. *Nietzsche's announcement that 'God is dead' went hand in hand with his insistence, 'There are no facts, only interpretations'. Postmodern thinkers radicalize the insight: language is irreducibly plural; it is impossible to believe that any one community's language provides a better purchase on reality than another's. Thought is language-laden; language screens us from the way things really are.

(2) *Knowledge*. *Foucault contests the modern ideal of absolute knowledge by claiming that all knowledge is relative to the interests and purposes of the institutions (e.g. the state, the academy, society) out of which such claims emerge. Knowledge for him is a political instrument, a means of exerting a certain kind of institutional or social power.

(3) *Ethics*. *Lévinas takes Foucault's analysis one step further. If knowledge is power, then claims to know are a kind of violence insofar as they attempt to 'master' that of which they speak. Modern thought is the violent attempt to 'totalize' things by appropriating them to our conceptual schemes. Whereas epistemology is the 'first philosophy' of modernity, Lévinas believes that ethics – the non-violent letting-be of things – should play that role.

(4) *The sublime*. Lyotard generalizes the above point, and in so doing brings postmodernity into focus as an aesthetic condition. Whereas modernity suppresses the 'other', postmodernity is aware of the 'sublime' nature of experience, its inability to be mastered by language or thought, words or concepts. Postmoderns distrust grand explanatory schemes, hence the oft-cited description of postmodernism as 'incredulity towards metanarratives' (*The Postmodern Condition*, p. xxiv).

(5) *Metaphysics*. For Jacques *Derrida, *metaphysics – 'the science of presence' or being – is a 'white mythology': a story told by white Anglo-American intellectuals about the ability of reason and language to map the contours of ultimate reality. *Deconstruction exposes the conditions of impossibility of this metaphysical project. 'There is nothing outside textuality' means that reason is always/already trapped inside contingent language systems whose binary hierarchical distinctions (e.g. true/false; subject/object; faith/reason) distort thought. Deconstruction exposes the arbitrary nature of conceptual schemes. Metaphysics goes the way of all metanarratives, having been exposed as the pretender it is. The emperor philosophy has no clothes. There are no philosophical facts, only poetic interpretations.

Scripture and theology

If Scripture is the 'soul' of theology, then postmodern theories of textuality that trouble the distinction between legitimate and illegitimate interpretation or proclaim the death of the author and authority represent a sickness in theology's soul. It is difficult to see how the Bible can wield significant *authority if meaning is indeterminate and if there are no universally recognized criteria for right interpretation (Vanhoozer, *Is There a Meaning in This Text?*). Postmodernism also questions the exclusive authority of historical criticism and has opened up space for other approaches, including the theological interpretation of *Scripture. Nevertheless, if the Bible is God's authoritative word, we must do more than view theological interpretation of Scripture as simply one more community interest.

For simplicity's sake, we can distinguish two broad types of postmodern theology.

'Deconstructive' theologians (e.g. D. Cupitt, C. Raschke, T. Altizer) appropriate Derrida's insights about language, textuality, knowledge, etc. and carry them through to the end, namely, a radicalized negative or 'weak' theology that limits itself to saying what God is not. The main North American representative of this postmodern type is J. Caputo, for whom the question of *atheism vs. *theism is undecidable. It is not that anything goes, but that *truth is situational, relational and pragmatic. It is ultimately a matter of doing justice to otherness rather than forcing us to conform to more-of-the-sameness.

'Reconstructive' postmodern theologies (e.g. *Radical orthodoxy; *postliberalism) accept the critiques of modern metanarratives but then go on to the more positive task of inhabiting the Christian narrative and the practices (e.g. giving and forgiving) it generates. J.-L. *Marion's work is noteworthy for its attempt to speak well of God under postmodern conditions. The 'God' of metaphysics is, for Marion, a conceptual idol. By contrast, the God who gives himself in revelation is more like an icon, a saturated phenomenon whose reality is not reduced to its appearance in consciousness. *Theos* gives itself to human *logos, but the logos cannot contain it. No amount of human reasoning could predict or explain God's self-giving on the cross of Jesus Christ. God is 'beyond being' because 'love does not have to be' (*God without Being*, p. 138). Reconstructive postmoderns thus work radicalized variations on a Kantian theme: 'I must abolish reason in order to make room for faith.'

Postmodern evangelicalism?

Evangelicals have responded to the postmodern condition in two diametrically opposed ways: critical rejection and uncritical appropriation. A number of conservative theologians and philosophers (A. McGrath; M. Erickson; D. Geivett) worry that postmodernism undermines rationality and relativizes truth, making it impossible either to commend or defend the Christian story over against competitors.

By way of contrast, postconservative, emergent and emerging theologians unapologetically embrace many characteristic postmodern themes and perspectives, including its suspicion of metanarratives, in order to contextualize the faith and 'do church' in fresh cultural ways (J. K. A. Smith). Many are content to live out the particularity of the Christian narrative without seeking to 'legitimate' it by basing it on 'foundationalist' beliefs (Grenz and Franke). They reject a strict orthodoxy that has become a tool with which to oppress others, preferring conversation to formulation of fixed truths ('always conversing') and *missional communal living to apologetic arguments. Indeed, the practices of the believing community – the form of ecclesial life – have increasingly taken the place once given to doctrinal foundations (see *Fellowship).

Conclusion

There is another, better way: critical appropriation. The church must engage postmodernity as it does every other philosophy or cultural development, with discernment, affirming 'whatever is true' (Phil. 4:8) and avoiding whatever takes us captive that is not according to Christ and his Scriptures (Col. 2:8). Postmoderns are right to protest the pride at the heart of the Enlightenment project, but the church did not need Foucault to learn about the will to power, or Marion to learn about the human tendency to manufacture *idols. Christian theology must not simply exchange philosophical masters. If modernity at its worst is guilty of pride, postmodernism at its worst succumbs to sloth: the deadly sin that cannot muster enough conviction to say, believe or do anything.

Perhaps the biggest challenge postmodernism represents to evangelical theology pertains to its Protestant heritage and future. Evangelicals are a people of the book, and biblical authority and *infallibility have long been distinguishing characteristics. The momentum in postmodernism, however, is toward according *authority to interpretive traditions (i.e. community) rather than texts (i.e. canon), thus raising the question: Will evangelicals remain on the Protestant road, defined by *sola Scriptura*, while driving under the postmodern influence?

See also: CONTEXTUALIZATION; CULTURE.

Bibliography

B. Benson, *Graven Ideologies: Nietzsche, Derrida & Marion on Modern Idolatry* (Downers Grove, 2002); J. Caputo, *What Would Jesus Deconstruct?: The Good News of Postmodernism for the Church* (Grand Rapids, 2007); D. Dockery (ed.), *The Challenge of Postmodernism: An Evangelical Assessment* (Grand Rapids, 1995); R. Greer, *Mapping Postmodernism: A Survey of Christian Options*

(Downers Grove, 2003); S. Grenz and J. Franke, *Beyond Foundationalism: Shaping Theology in a Postmodern Context* (Louisville, 2001); J.-F. Lyotard, *The Postmodern Condition* (Minneapolis, 1984); J.-L. Marion, *God without Being* (Chicago, 1991); M. Penner (ed.), *Christianity and the Postmodern Turn: Six Views* (Grand Rapids, 2005); M. Sarup, *Identity, Culture and the Postmodern World* (Edinburgh, 1996); J. K. A. Smith, *Who's Afraid of Postmodernism? Taking Derrida, Lyotard, and Foucault to Church* (Grand Rapids, 2006); G. Veith, *Postmodern Times: A Christian Guide to Contemporary Thought and Culture* (Wheaton, 1994); K. Vanhoozer, *Is There a Meaning in This Text? The Bible, the Reader, and the Morality of Literary Knowledge* (Grand Rapids, 1998); idem (ed.), *Cambridge Companion to Postmodern Theology* (Cambridge, 2003); G. Ward (ed.), *The Blackwell Companion to Postmodern Theology* (London, 2004).

K. J. VANHOOZER

POSTMODERNISM

Since the 1970s 'postmodernism' has featured prominently in philosophy, cultural studies, literary theory, the social sciences, fine art, architecture and theology. It is notoriously difficult to define, but the most influential attempt to do so was made by Jean-François Lyotard (1924–98), who depicted it as 'incredulity toward metanarratives'. As an ex-Marxist, Lyotard was aware of the potential of purportedly universal explanations or 'grand stories' to function in a 'totalizing' manner, and associated them particularly with the suspect ideologies of the 'modern' age. Colloquially, 'modern' might describe that which is up to date, so that the idea of anything being 'postmodern' seems nonsensical. Yet postmodernism is to be construed attitudinally rather than chronologically, as a critique of certain key metanarratives developed in the *Enlightenment period of the seventeenth, eighteenth and nineteenth centuries. For our purposes these metanarratives may be summarized as *rationalism, statism and scientism.

Rationalism exalts human reason as the primary source of knowledge and truth, most typically over against divine *revelation. Truth in rationalist understanding is presented as unitary and objective, while reason is related to universal precepts inferred from naturalistic processes. Hence René *Descartes interrogated the basis of all knowledge and experience and concluded that existence is verified by rational thought. Since thought takes place in the minds of individual humans, Descartes' work represented a 'turn to the subject' which became a hallmark of *modernity. Later, David *Hume would seek to recast both ethics and religion in rationalistic terms, while Immanuel *Kant would exalt the 'audacity to think for oneself' and rationalize religion as an essentially moral phenomenon.

One key outworking of Enlightenment rationalism was the rise of the modern secular *state. In the late 1700s revolutionaries in America and France sought to constitute government distinct from the church, on the basis of universal human rights rather than religious dogma. While contributing much to democracy, this approach was often exported to less apparently 'rational' cultures in colonialism, with decidedly mixed results. In the twentieth century it would reach its most distorted expressions in the statist tyrannies of Stalinism, Nazism and Maoism.

Modernity was also characterized by the scientific and technological advances of the industrial revolution. While delivering momentous gains in manufacturing, social mobility and medicine, at times this fostered what David Harvey calls 'the scientific domination of nature'. When wedded to the idea that scientific advance is its own justification apart from morality, such 'scientism' can be seen to have produced pollution, nuclear weaponry and gas chambers alongside the many benefits yielded by science as such.

In reaction to all this, postmodernism views reason and *truth in far more diffuse, provisional and relativistic terms. Driven by the failure of Communist 'reason', 'science' and imperialism, Lyotard's critique of metanarrative is closely bound up with a rejection of singular, uniform accounts of reality. In this sense the roots of postmodernism can be traced back to Friedrich *Nietzsche, who reinterpreted claims to truth as metaphors concealing self-interested bids for power. Also influential was Sigmund Freud (1856–1939), who expounded the 'irrational' and often self-deceptive drives of the unconscious, and as such construed an even more pessimistic epistemology than Nietzsche. Postmodern questioning of rationalism was also anticipated by Martin *Heidegger, who insisted that 'thinking subjects' are never detached from the contingencies of their environment, and that the language they use to make sense of life thus functions more as poetry than as a direct 'mirror' of the world.

In the work of later thinkers more directly associated with postmodernism, these themes are reinforced. Zygmunt Bauman (b. 1925) echoes Nietzsche when defining postmodernism as 'living with ambivalence' – an openness to plurality and difference which views unitary accounts of 'truth' as inevitably oppressive. Jacques *Derrida likewise accentuates difference, more specifically contrasting it with the 'metaphysics of presence' – that is, with the assumption that language can reconstruct pristine authorial intent or enshrine any fixed 'original' meaning. In the Derridean project of '*deconstruction', texts are read as volatile assemblages of writing itself, changing their nature as the spaces within them, and between them and other elements in the system of communication, are altered. For Michel *Foucault, truth, rationality and knowledge are similarly fluid – as demonstrated particularly in shifting social representations of insanity, criminality and sexual deviance. Truth and reason are no more stable in the American version of postmodernism propounded by Richard Rorty (1931–2007). Radicalizing earlier pragmatist philosophy, Rorty presents a thoroughly contingent understanding of reality in which 'truth' functions as little more than a set of rhetorical tropes that facilitate our 'loyalty to other human beings clinging together against the dark'.

These philosophical shifts from modernism to postmodernism have been reflected in various cultural forms. Whereas modernist architects like Le Corbusier and Mies van der Rohe designed housing along hard 'rationalist' lines devoid of ornamentation, postmodern structures are typically eclectic and ironically decorative in style. Whereas artists like Georges Braque and Wyndham Lewis made works influenced by logical sequences and mechanisms abstracted from contingent representation, postmodern artists like Andy Warhol, Jeff Koons and Tracey Emin celebrate contingency and ephemerality by referencing popular artefacts or deploying everyday objects in their work.

Christian theological responses to postmodernism might readily appreciate its emphasis on plurality and multiplicity: after all, the Trinity, the diversity of biblical canon or the numinous confluence of words, signs and actions in the Eucharist could hardly be exhausted by 'linear' rational explanations. In their later work Lyotard and Derrida in fact wrote suggestively about the interplay between God's presence and absence, his word and his silence, in biblical and devotional writings. Citing Derrida in particular, Kevin Hart suggests resonances between deconstruction and the 'negative' theology of mystics like *Pseudo-Dionysius the Areopagite (see *Apophatic theology). Similarly, Mark C. Taylor finds in deconstructive approaches a corollary of the divine *logos, which at once 'grounds' and 'disseminates' the 'divine milieu', and which is discerned in the space between the 'fullness of deity' in Christ and the *kenotic 'self-emptying' of Christ on the cross. For Jean-Luc *Marion, theological discourse which defines God as the fullest form of 'being' is actually idolatrous, in that it represents God as an extension of ourselves. Rather, Marion sees authentic theological discourse functioning 'iconically', mediating traces of divinity while pointing away to the God who is ultimately beyond language and being, and who is thus known by faith rather than reason. There are echoes here of Karl Barth's critique of philosophically based theology: indeed, Robert Jenson has argued on these grounds that *Barth is the quintessential *postmodern theologian.

More fundamentally, of course, it is hard to see how orthodox Christian theology could disavow metanarrative as such, since this would seem to require the denial of a divine 'author' or 'creator' distinct from the world – a Word who gives ultimate meaning to our words. The *gospel of salvation through Jesus Christ is in this sense surely the 'story which explains our stories' (John 4:29). Then again, it is a story which subverts the claims of other 'grand stories', because far from representing a malign 'bid for power', it has as its heart an act of radical, loving renunciation. Jesus 'deconstructs' the self-contradictions in domination-systems of his time, and as John Dominic Crossan and others have shown, the parables and sayings in which he does this have a playful quality that postmodern readings can illuminate. Yet it is precisely in the metanarrative of his atoning death (see *Atonement) that Jesus challenges the necessary postmodern identification of 'grand stories' with totalization and tyranny, for here the metanarrative turns on a divestment of *power in which the Lord of heaven and earth comes 'not to be served but to serve', and in which the bringer of abundant life sacrifices his own life as a 'ransom for many' (Mark 10:45).

Bibliography

The Blackwell Companion to Postmodern Theology (Oxford, 2005); L. Cahoone (ed.), *From Modernism to Postmodernism: An Anthology* (Oxford, 1996); P. Kamuf, *A Derrida Reader: Between the Blinds* (Hemel Hempstead, 1991); J. F. Lyotard, *The Postmodern Condition: A Report on Knowledge* (Manchester, 1984 [1979]); J. A. K. Smith, *Who's Afraid of Postmodernism: Taking Derrida, Lyotard and Foucault to Church* (Grand Rapids, 2006); A. C. Thiselton, *Interpreting God and the Postmodern Self* (Edinburgh, 1995); K. Vanhoozer (ed.), *The Cambridge Companion to Postmodern Theology* (Cambridge, 2003); G. Ward (ed.), *The Postmodern God: A Theological Reader* (Oxford, 1997).

D. H. K. Hilborn

POVERTY AND WEALTH

Poverty and wealth describe the situation where some people have access to and use of few of the earth's resources while others control lots of them through ownership and power. The normal forms of wealth-holding include land, raw materials, property, capital, education, technology, financial assets and direct control of workers, trade, taxes and consumption. The Bible presents a relationship between the two. Wealth, by concentrating resources into the hands of a few, undermines the access of the many. The Bible counsels against riches and for helping the poor. This principle makes sense. Even distribution of resources allows everybody to work with effect and live productive lives, while a big concentration of wealth leaves many unable to work well and encourages extravagant living among the elite. Theological responses to this issue have tended to reflect different aspects of the biblical treatment of poverty and wealth, and we therefore link each tradition to its main biblical emphasis.

The exodus shows God redeeming the children of Israel from slavery and acute poverty. They are taken into freedom and to land which God has purposed for them. In the Promised Land, territory was allotted equally among the population. The Lord commanded a revised census to be carried out (Num. 26), revealing a population of 601,730; the land was to be apportioned strictly according to the number of names (vv. 51–56). A small tribe had a small allotment of land and a large tribe a large one, so that the distribution could be equal. The radical egalitarianism of this settlement, carried out by Joshua, has been the focus of a long radical tradition since the Reformation associated with the Levellers, Diggers, Henry George, *Tolstoy and some *liberation theologians. Its emphasis is on equality in the ownership of resources and redistribution to bring it about as reflecting God's purposes.

Other decrees in the Mosaic law were designed to maintain this wide distribution of resources, preventing poverty. At a strategic level there were the Jubilee return of land and proclamation of liberty to all the inhabitants (Lev. 25). The Christian campaign in Britain with *Wesley and Wilberforce to end slavery drew from this theme, as did land distribution for migrants in the United States. Later, the rules requiring no interest and a seven-year cancellation of debt were drawn on by the Jubilee Campaign for the cancellation of debt in the Majority World, movements for forgiving personal debt and various attempts to lower interest. Credit and community banks in Europe have similarly embodied Christian attempts to centre banking on the needs of the poor rather than the revenues of the rich.

The direct provisions for the poor and needy in the Mosaic law were likewise built into the creation of what has come to be called the Welfare State in the UK. A tradition of thought and action including Shaftesbury, Chalmers, Ruskin, the early Christian Socialists, the 'Nonconformist Conscience', Lloyd George, Tawney, *Temple and others shaped a response to those in need which was a mixture of social insurance, local and national provision (see *Social ethics). This slowly moved from a patronage of the unworthy poor to a recognition that this was the right thing to do and an awareness with Lloyd George that redistributive tax was necessary. Over the last few decades this commitment has weakened with the weakening of Christianity in Britain.

Other Christians and theologians have picked up the direct commendation by Christ of the poor and poor in spirit. They have stood apart from the capitalist drive to wealth and the consumerism of the late twentieth century. In the West this has been at odds with the prevailing culture, but a mixture of people including David Sheppard, Mother Teresa, Fritz Schumacher, papal encyclicals and liberation theologians have honoured the poor, respected their mode of living and identified their needs in non-consumerist terms. *Gutiérrez and other liberation theologians identified the way in which theology has been biased towards the rich, rationalist elites of the West and ignored Christ's message of freedom for the oppressed. Now it turns out the ways of the poor are required of all of us, if we are to prevent the degradation of the planet (see *Ecology). As Christ taught, it is from the poor that we must learn blessing.

Though many theologians and thinkers have addressed aspects of Christian teaching, the evidence of the last few hundred years is that the structural, personal and economic aspects of the issue of poverty and wealth have not been held together in a coherent Christian perspective. Usually, a full Christian vision has been compromised by the secular capitalist and consumerist pressures of modern secular culture. Now we examine those trends.

Theology and economics

This biblical understanding of wealth and poverty, seeing both as a problem, has been reflected, in part, in economic and political perspectives for much of the last two millennia. Gradually, the concentration of wealth through predation, political control and economic dominance has waned. Castles, slavery, feudalism and forced labour have diminished (though they were still stronger in modern history than we usually allow). Charity, direct giving to the poor, was done and advocated by the church as a necessary immediate Christian response. Some monastic orders, especially the *Franciscans, took on vows of poverty and stood against excesses in the churches. We cannot easily estimate the impact of this long-term emphasis on European life.

The Reformation offered a deeper threat to feudal and landed control in opening up work, trade, the production of goods, investment and thrift as part of the Christian calling. Gradually, an economy not based on owned wealth and required labour emerged. At the same time this was an attack on necessary poverty. The Dutch market response of the seventeenth century was the beginning of the modern economy, and this was the time in Britain when the Levellers and Diggers attacked in Christian terms the economic control of the wealthy. Sadly, they did not win and the landed gentry re-established control, both attacking and buying off the churches. Though Protestants continued to work, improving agriculture, trade, production, science and technology, the running and understanding of the economic system moved to the kind of liberal and naturalistic view of economic life promoted by Adam Smith.

Here, especially later with Bentham, poverty was largely seen as self-imposed and was to be addressed by self-interest and tough regimes. Though the Christian influence of Shaftesbury, Chalmers and others was substantial, the dominant economic paradigm was classical. The practical reformist Christian influence produced some good results, but the intellectual opposition to classical economics came mainly from *Marx and secular socialists, though Maurice, Kingsley, Ruskin and others made important contributions. At this time, too, the self-justifications of wealth began to appear and grow. The Manchester School championed the entrepreneur and capitalist, suggesting that they were responsible for national wealth.

It was during this period that theology began to disengage from economic considerations, as though God was only interested in religion and not in the whole of life. As a result, the formation of the discipline of economics was largely without theological input, and it came to be identified as secular and supposedly value-free. Poverty and wealth were deemed outside the corpus of 'theology' for much of the twentieth century, despite the biblical content of the themes. People looked only to secular socialism to address these issues.

Some theologians moved out of this impasse, partly because of the series of papal encyclicals beginning with Leo XIII's *Rerum Novarum* (1891). Similarly important was Abraham *Kuyper's *The Problem of Poverty* (1891), which identified in Christian terms the structural links between wealth and poverty. But the theological tradition has hardly been strong.

Often the wealthy have controlled economic ideology, economic theory and business studies. Neo-liberalism lauded the value and success of the wealthy. The idea of 'wealth creation' was coined, as though the wealthy really were the engine of economic development. Though many critiques of this assertion emerged, the ideology of wealth gained weight by repetition, especially in the twenties, fifties and nineties in

America. A strong Christian perspective on wealth and poverty waned.

More recently, with global warming, the problem of quasi-slave labour in poor countries (see *Slavery), the exploitations of international trade and rampant consumerism, the problems of plutocracy are glaringly obvious. Suddenly, the deep strength of the biblical perspective is newly evident. At the beginning of the twenty-first century some kind of coherent Christian response is beginning to re-emerge from aid agencies, some theologians, Christian economists and others. At every level in Christian living, policies and economic understanding, there is vast work to do, especially in the West. When all the biblical themes, personal, structural, those involving *justice, fairness (see *Righteousness), meekness and freedom from sin, and the dangers of materialist idolatry are brought together, the resources to eliminate wealth and poverty are available to us focused in the person of Christ.

See also: CAPITALISM; MATERIALISM.

Bibliography

R. G. Clouse (ed.), *Wealth and Poverty: Four Christian Views of Economics* (Downers Grove, 1984); B. Goudzwaard and M. Vander Vennen, *Hope in Troubled Times: A New Vision for Confronting Global Crises* (Grand Rapids, 2007); G. Gutiérrez, *The Power of the Poor in History* (New York, 1983); L. J. Hoppe, *There Shall Be No Poor among You: Poverty in the Bible* (Nashville, 2004); D. Hughes, *God of the Poor: A Biblical Vision of God's Present Rule* (Carlisle, 1998); John Paul II, *Encyclical Laborem Exercens* (Vatican, 1981); A. Kuyper, *The Problem of Poverty* (Washington and Michigan, 1991); J. Ruskin, *Unto This Last* (London, 1900); D. Sheppard, *Bias to the Poor* (London, 1983); R. H. Tawney *The Acquisitive Society* (London, 1948); L. Tolstoy, *How Much Land Does a Man Need?* (London, 1993 [1886]).

A. STORKEY

POWER

Each academic discipline analyses the concept of power according to its own objectives. Here we do so in the context of Christian theology, but not ruling out engagement with other disciplines. The thinking of two political and social systems may be identified to give meaning to the concept. First, in the Greco-Roman world in which the NT was written, the use of power was based on the patron-client social system. The Greco-Roman world was a brokered empire, hierarchical in structure, with power in the hands of a few who shaped the lives of others according to this social system. Obedience was expected of all and, despite the cultural diversity, obedience was always a measure of the structured peaceful coexistence for all. Since the tentacles of this political system stretched throughout the known civilized world, to disrupt this *pax Romana* was considered a criminal activity. It was a world controlled by human political power, buttressed by an efficient military system.

Secondly, at the end of the nineteenth century a new analysis of human power emerged in the writings of Friedrich *Nietzsche, who proposed that the 'will to power' re-established self-determination as the highest endeavour for human life and the proclamation of the crucified Christ was insufficient for that. Nietzsche's model had a powerful influence on Western philosophical systems.

What helps culture identify itself are systems, institutions, structures and organizations that weave patterns by which people are expected to live. This is all necessary, but some of these systems become paradigms of *evil. What this means is that political and social systems are not necessarily understood as impersonal. So to change a system is to change it from within. Systems, organizations, institutions that refuse to change eventually become 'demonic' or diseased and lose any sense of accountability or responsibility. Neither the *pax Romana* nor the 'will to power' encompassed the required responsible or accountable controls. Power, according to these systems, was thus open to abuse. But in Christian theology everything is accountable to God, whether persons or political and social systems.

Christian theology, based on the NT, runs in a way which is counter-cultural to political systems that became paradigms of evil even while they do not recognize their own moral and ethical failures. The apostle Paul proclaimed as of first importance the good news of Christ crucified (see *Cross). This, he acknowledged, was a stumbling block and foolishness to its cultured despisers. But Paul made clear that this message, Christ crucified, was evidence of God's power and wisdom (1 Cor. 1:23–24).

First, it should be recognized that the message of Christ crucified was not contextual in the sense of arising out of, or being limited to, one specific culture. For Paul, the good news was applicable to all cultures without being watered down or corrupted (Gal. 1:6–10). The gospel was true regardless of where it was preached, and so it is possible to affirm that Christ crucified is a theological metanarrative. But it comes from God, not through human ingenuity.

The power of God is now revealed in the crucified Christ. But the crucified Christ had lived an earthly life that revealed the new meaning of power. Such titles as Messiah and King were transformed into a new definition of power through *Jesus' life, ministry, death and resurrection. Power was evident in Jesus' healings, miracles over nature, his control over demonic forces and, in each case, the message was one of restoration, overcoming systemic oppression, establishing justice and a new form of open fellowship. In these events it became evident that God's power set humanity free (Gal. 5:1). But the controversy of Jesus' ministry was not over freedom, but the manner in which it was achieved. The divine transcendence became personally visible in the powerlessness and weakness of humanity, and this could be translated as *agape* *love, a self-giving love, going out of one's self for others, which was now to be understood as God's power.

Power was thus defined by God in the actions of Jesus the King. But it was Jesus' power over the evil forces and his eventual defeat of evil at the cross and in the resurrection that clearly revealed the new meaning of power. It was God's power to raise Jesus from death that set humanity free. And now such good news was proclaimed as God's power and wisdom (Rom. 1:16; 1 Cor. 1:18).

God's power revealed in Jesus' life, ministry, death and resurrection continued in the work of the Holy Spirit. Jesus' promise to the waiting disciples was the promise of power from the *Holy Spirit (Acts 1:8). Such power took on a *missional agenda, and the earliest disciples were expected to replicate Jesus' ministry in the life of the church. Of use here is the reference in Mark's Gospel to the exercise of power. While the disciples struggled for power positions with Jesus, Jesus instead taught servanthood according to the model he had set (Mark 10:35–45). This was now the power of the Holy Spirit in the life of the disciples and in the pattern of the church's ministry.

There is a 'mindfulness' that is important in Christian thought in relation to power. This is expressed by Paul: 'Your attitude should be the same as that of Christ Jesus' (Phil. 2:5). Paul then proceeds to describe Christ's humiliation, that is, his descent into human life and death, but this is followed by Christ's exaltation, his ascent to the 'highest place'. According to this new definition of power, we are to go through all the experiences of life committed to servanthood, and only so be victorious. It is this power that is given to us in the power of the Holy Spirit.

See also: POLITICAL THEOLOGY; SOCIETY, THEOLOGY OF; STATE.

Bibliography

M. Hengel, *Christ and Power* (ET, Philadelphia, 1977); idem, *Crucifixion in the Ancient World and the Folly of the Cross* (ET, London, 1977); L. Hurtado, *One God, One Lord* (Edinburgh, 1998); N. T. Wright, *Jesus and the Victory of God* (London, 1996); W. Wink, *Powers That Be* (London and New York, 1998).

D. L. RAINEY

PRAXIS AND ORTHOPRAXIS

'Praxis' essentially means 'action'. In theology it gained currency through *liberation theology. Theology usually emphasizes orthodoxy (i.e. right belief or conceptual reflection on truth). Like *political theology, liberation theology balances this with an emphasis on action. *Gutiérrez typically complains that 'the church has for centuries devoted her attention to formulating truth and meanwhile did almost nothing to better the world'. Knowing and doing are dialectically related, and right action becomes the criterion for truth.

An epistemology that privileges *praxis* can be traced back to the preference for action over contemplation characteristic of philosophy after *Hegel, *Feuerbach and *Marx. As the Croatian theologian, Miroslav Volf, pointed out, 'a new consciousness has developed: the truth opens itself up, not to beholding but to doing and to changing . . . true thinking as opposed to false consciousness is, for Marx, thinking which reveals its power to establish the truth of this world. Revolutionary practice is the criterion of truth' (*Them* 8, p. 13). *Míguez Bonino has observed that there is a danger that theology is reduced to ethics, the vertical dimension equated with the horizontal and the concept based on Marxism. Positively, however, it can claim biblical roots. God communicates with his world in creative activity; in John's Gospel knowing truth is contingent upon doing it (John 3:21). René Padilla accepts that liberation theology is correct in criticizing the *rationalistic tendency in theology, because, from a biblical perspective, God's Logos became a historical person. However, he offers a warning against the pitfall of pragmatism, the kind of theologizing that uses the biblical text to justify a position that has been adopted on either pragmatic or ideological grounds, because 'if there is no norm for evaluating *praxis* outside of *praxis* itself, the sheer utility will provide the only grounds for its justification – the end will justify the means. Only if faith has a cognitive content outside *praxis* itself can it serve as a criterion to evaluate *praxis*' (D. S. Schipani, *Freedom and Discipleship*, p. 40).

Bibliography

L. Boff, *Jesus Christ Liberator* (London, 1980); G. Gutiérrez, *A Theology of Liberation*, rev. edn (Maryknoll and London, ²1988); J. Míguez Bonino, *Doing Theology in a Revolutionary Situation* (London and Philadelphia, 1975); C. R. Padilla, *Mission Between the Times*, revised and updated (Carlisle, 2010); D. S. Schipani (ed.), *Freedom and Discipleship: Liberation Theology in Anabaptist Perspective* (Maryknoll, 1989); M. Volf, 'Doing and Interpreting: An Examination of the Relationship Between Theory and Practice in Latin American Liberation Theology', *Them* 8/3 (1983).

S. Escobar

PRAYER, THEOLOGY OF

Prayer is often said to include adoration, thanksgiving, confession, petition and intercession. But these last two, petition for oneself and intercession for others, present a particular problem, namely: why do we ask God for certain things if God is already *sovereign and determines what will happen? Yet the Christian faith has always rejected fatalism, and Jesus himself taught that we should ask, seek and knock (Matt. 7:7). He warns us against hypocritical prayer which is merely to display our piety, against empty vain clichés, and gives us the model prayer which begins with a prayer for the hallowing of God's name and the coming of his rule on earth. Our own requests and petitions for daily bread, for forgiveness and for deliverance from evil, follow (Matt. 6:5–13). But we pray with confidence in the *fatherly love of God (Matt. 7:9–11). His teaching surely implies that petition and intercession cannot stand alone or be extracted from prayers of adoration, thanksgiving and confession.

But a Christian theology of prayer must begin not only with the teaching of *Jesus, but with his own practice of prayer as a human being. Here he follows in the line of the great intercessors of biblical history, including Abraham (Gen. 18:22–33) and Moses (Exod. 32:31–32). But at the heart of Jesus' life of prayer lies the secret of his life and ministry, namely his unique and intimate relationship with the One he called, 'Abba' (Luke 10:21). For this man, being God incarnate, has unique access to the Father. And it is that unique access that he shares with us, his disciples. It is within the context of that relationship, his gracious gift to us, that we can bring our petitions and intercessions.

Yet as we follow him in the practice of prayer, we need to take special note of the fact that at the climax and crisis of his earthly life, the prayer he offered, 'Father, let this cup pass from me', was not to be given a positive answer (as he himself immediately acknowledged). His cry of anguish and apparent despair on the cross must also be regarded as prayer (Mark 15:34). Following Jesus in his life of prayer, therefore, we have to reject the idea that God will indulgently give a positive answer to all our requests. Even more, we have to reject the false idea that we will get what we desire if we just work up enough 'faith'. The greatest faith was exemplified by Jesus, whose prayer to be spared the cross received a negative answer and who persevered nevertheless, trusting his Father by drinking the cup which he was not spared. The greatest saints are therefore surely those who persevere despite prayers that receive negative answers. Prayer is therefore to be seen as a conversation in which we have to try to discern our Father's will rather than trying to impose our own. It is not a means of having our will done in heaven, but of having God's will done on earth.

Since Jesus taught us to pray to his Father as 'our Father' (Matt. 6:9), prayer is normally directed through the Son to the Father. We pray therefore in the name of Jesus, believing that even now the one who prayed for his disciples while on earth (John 17) is the ascended Christ who presents our prayers and requests before the Father as part of his heavenly ministry (Rom. 8:34; Heb. 7:25; 1 John 2:1). That is not to say that God does not hear the prayer of those who are not in Christ, but those who have received him are given the privileges of his children (John 1:12), sharing the intimacy of the Son with the Father. Yet we also pray to Jesus as 'Lord', as did the first martyr, Stephen (Acts 7:59). In prayer we bow the knee to him as the human being on whom the Father has bestowed the divine name of 'Lord', and we thus recognize him as the one who has always been 'in very nature God' (Phil. 2:5–11).

Such intimacy with the Father and the Son is possible for Christians because of the gift of the *Holy Spirit, and here we see that Christian prayer is fully *trinitarian. It is because the Spirit of the Son has been sent into our hearts that we too are able to cry, 'Abba! Father!' (Rom. 8:15; Gal 4:6). And the Spirit enables us to pray aright by revealing to us the mind of God (1 Cor. 2:9–13). We do not know infallibly and perfectly what God's will is in every particular circumstance, but the Spirit aids our weakness, groaning more deeply that we could ever do, so that we may join in the longings of God (Rom 8:26–27). And we do know that God's will and intention is always good, so that we pray to our Father in confidence, asking for wisdom.

Since the church rejects the idea that the Holy Spirit is a creature, and therefore confesses him also to be of one being with the Father and the Son, we can also pray to the Holy Spirit and glorify him as God. All of this we do as members of the body of Christ, participating even in our private prayer in the corporate prayer of the church. That is why the church not only glorifies the Father 'through the Son by the Holy Spirit', but in the *Gloria Patri*, which dates back at least to Basil of Caesarea, prayerfully sings, 'Glory be to the Father *and* the Son *and* the Holy Spirit.'

Prayer is therefore an integral part of the *worship of the church. The traditional *liturgies from earliest times include the *kyrie*, a prayer for God's mercy (still in the original Greek), the *gloria* and the *agnus Dei*, a prayer to Christ as 'the lamb of God'. These ancient prayers remain in the Protestant liturgies of the Lutheran and Anglican traditions and were embraced by evangelicals such as Wesley and Simeon. Wesley and more recent Protestant liturgies also affirm the *epiclesis*, the prayer to the Holy Spirit at the consecration of the bread and wine. The Reformed tradition of the Swiss Reformation, together with the Anabaptist and Baptist traditions, generally reject forms of prayer, however, regarding genuine prayer as extemporary. But Wesley and Simeon also embraced extemporary prayer. Perhaps we should see then that both are helpful in the life of the church and in the practice of private prayer by each believer. Without the church's riches of forms of prayer, our prayers can become repetitive and the tradition threadbare and oversubjective. Without extemporary prayer, our prayers can become stilted, formal and unreal.

In all this, Christians therefore understand that petitions and intercessions are not a way of extracting from God what is according to our own pleasure. Rather, we only present our petitions and intercession to him as an integral part of a whole life of adoration, confession and thanksgiving. Prayer includes asking, but only within the context of the intimate relationship with the Father we have come to know in and through the Son by the Spirit.

See also: FELLOWSHIP.

Bibliography

D. G. Bloesch, *The Struggle of Prayer* (New York, 1980); E. M. Bounds, 'With Christ in the School of Prayer', in *Complete Works on Prayer* (Grand Rapids, 1990); J. Bunyan, *Prayer* (repr. London, 1965); J. Calvin, *Institutes*, III, xx; O. Hallesby, *Prayer* (London, 1961); J. Jeremias, *The Prayers of Jesus* (London, 1967); J. Murray, *The Heavenly Priestly Activity of Christ* (London, 1958); J. Owen, 'A Discourse upon the Work of the Holy Spirit in Prayer', *Works*, vol. 4 (London, 1967), pp. 235–350; W. R. Spear, *The Theology of Prayer* (Grand Rapids, 1979).

T. A. NOBLE

PREACHING, THEOLOGY OF

This is grounded in biblical conviction that *God is a speaking God who has spoken in creation (Gen. 1:3), in the incarnation of Jesus Christ (John 1:1, 14), and in the *revelation of *Scripture (2 Tim. 3:16). God has designed the universe so that words are vehicles for creative power (Isa. 55:11). Proclamation is central to the prophetic task of the OT ('this is what the Sovereign Lord says', Isa. 7:7), and to the NT where Jesus Christ is both supreme proclaimer of good news and also, by his own life, death and resurrection becomes the content (*kergyma*) of the early church's proclamation (see *Gospel). Preaching communicates God's revelation as his voice is heard through the preacher (1 Pet. 4:11). Subsequent theology has needed to wrestle with many issues.

Authority

Preaching became essential to subsequent church ministry and mission, assuming co-status as 'word and sacrament' in its liturgy. However, whenever a church has placed *authority on ecclesial tradition as well as on Scripture, preaching is more likely understood as 'the church speaking' than 'God speaking'. But a high view of scriptural authority as in the *Reformation's stress on *sola Scriptura*, re-emphasized that God himself is heard in preaching. *Calvin and *Luther both asserted that when the gospel of Jesus Christ is proclaimed, God himself is heard. This theology was vividly enshrined in the Second Helvetic Confession (1566): 'the preaching of the Word of God is the Word of God.'

Relationship between Christ, Scripture and the preacher

Karl *Barth memorably provided a formula to describe the threefold dynamic of the Word of God as: the Word *revealed* who is Jesus Christ; the Word *written* in Scripture; and the Word *proclaimed* in Scripture. Giving central place to Christ, Barth's theology binds all three 'words' together, each possessing a human and divine aspect, so that collectively they constitute God's own proclamation. Renewed engagement with the doctrine of the *Trinity in the latter part of the twentieth century (also influenced by Barth) has further heightened awareness of the preacher's spiritual dynamic. Emphasis on the 'social Trinity', with its perichoretic communion, has highlighted the interacting roles of Father, Son and Spirit in the theology of worship and the preaching event. *Moltmann further argues for an *eschatological dimension as preaching creates expectation of God's new future.

Interpretation

Ever since early church employment of 'four senses' (literal, allegorical, moral, prophetic), interpretation has raised urgent questions for the task of exegesis. More recently, Friedrich *Schleiermacher, the father of modern *hermeneutics, argued that understanding Scripture requires a pre-understanding about the authors' intent that a preacher awakens in the hearers' God-consciousness. This more subjective experiential process opened up the roles of both reader and text itself in subsequent hermeneutics. Fresh insights from *narrative theology also encourage moves towards narrative preaching, and recent emphasis in biblical studies on the literary and rhetorical shape of different genres has invited genre-sensitive reading and preaching.

Design

In the early church, suspicion of rhetoric's role as human persuasion was later countered by *Augustine, whose textbook adopted rules of classical rhetoric to preaching, forging a link between solid textual understanding and the need to design persuasive sermons. But tension continues, most recently surfacing between the so-called 'old homiletic' of propositional deductive 'outline' design, majoring on grammatical-historical analysis of authorial intention, and the 'new homiletic' of inductive narrative preaching, pioneered by Fred Craddock. In this contemporary ferment, 'exposition' needs defining in terms of submission to Scripture text rather than to a particular style of sermon design, so that message remains more important than method.

Culture

Current Western preaching faces other theological challenges. Shifts in *culture, from *modernity to so-called *postmodernity, also press for valid experiential responses to Scripture, in addition to traditional grammatical-historical research. The growing 'southern church' challenges the declining 'northern church' to recover spiritual authenticity and courage by powerful pneumatology. From a Latin American perspective Gustavo *Gutiérrez has argued for prophetic preaching that speaks into situations of powerlessness. The gospel and culture movement (pioneered by Lesslie *Newbigin) has critiqued Western preaching for its accommodation to culture and failure to build missional communities. Henry Mitchell's major contribution on African-American preaching as an expression of black culture with holistic theology also has much to teach the world church. These continue to be demanding days for the theology of preaching.

Bibliography

K. Barth, *CD*, vol. 1; F. B. Craddock, *As One Without Authority* (Nashville, 1971); G. Gutiérrez, *A Theology of Liberation* (New York, 1988); T. G. Long, *The Witness of Preaching* (Louisville, 2005); H. H. Mitchell, *Black Preaching: The Recovery of a Powerful Art* (Abingdon 1990); J. Moltmann, *Theology of Hope* (Minneapolis, 1967); M. J. Quicke, *360-Degree Preaching* (Grand Rapids, 2003); F. Schleiermacher, *The Christian Faith* (Edinburgh, 1928); J. R. W. Stott, *Between Two Worlds* (Grand Rapids, 1982).

M. J. QUICKE

PREDESTINATION

Thomas Aquinas defined predestination as 'The planned sending of a rational creature to the end which is eternal life'. There is inescapable witness to this idea in the NT (Rom. 8 and 9, Eph. 1:3–10 and John 6:37–45 being outstanding examples), while it is significant that the belief surfaces in passages in the NT which are not directly connected with this theme, as Acts 13:48.

After the NT period, the belief, though mentioned on occasion, tended to become latent rather than at the forefront of the church's thinking, probably due to the arduous battle the church was engaged in against the naturalistic determinism of the *Gnostics with which they did not wish its own message to be confused. It came, however, very much to the fore again in the career of *Augustine, who as a young convert from the determinism of Manichaeism at first wished to accord to the human *will the priority in gaining salvation, but who after closer study of the Scriptures argued from 397 onwards that the final grounds in the *salvation of a person rested solely upon the will of God. This position a decade or so later was developed at length and in depth in the controversy with *Pelagius and his followers.

According to the mature Augustinian position, empirical human beings had so fallen from the intention of God that they were incapable to turning to him, unless their wills were completely reorientated by the work of God's *grace, freely bestowed according to his determination. So the reason why some sinners are saved and others lost is to be found ultimately in God. It is according to God's sovereign purpose, his eternal decree, that some sinners are rescued whilst others are left in their sin; so in the last resort salvation depends upon the sovereign divine decision in regard to the individual. Reprobation, the shadow-side of predestination, depends equally upon the divine will, though here it is not so much a question of the positive willing of an individual to salvation as the willed leaving of a person in his or her fallenness (see *Judgment of God). It is a clear-cut doctrine which does full justice to the biblical understanding of the sovereignty of God in salvation, and it formed the basis of the predominant understanding of the matter in the medieval Western church. Its most clear statement is to be found in the writings of *Aquinas, who dealt with predestination as an aspect of providence, giving a thoroughly Augustinian account of the doctrine. A minority among some of the later Scholastics (as *Ockham) sought to base predestination on God's foreseeing the future presence, or not, of faith in an individual.

The doctrine of predestination in its traditional form was unsurprisingly affirmed by the three major Reformers, *Luther, *Zwingli and *Calvin. This was to be expected, as at a theological level the Reformation was really about the right interpretation of the general Augustinian position. Anglicanism too was fully compatible with this stance; among the Anabaptists a variety of views were held, but none seemed to be regarded as being of central importance. Lutheranism after Luther moved to emphasize only single predestination – that to eternal life, and to play down its negative aspect.

On the Protestant side, the doctrine played the most prominent role in the churches of the *Reformed persuasion. Interestingly enough, though Calvin, like Aquinas, almost treats the doctrine as an aspect of providence, he refrains from doing so, and instead expounds it as being primarily the foundation of the true life of faith. Believers should live by the assurance that as they are in Christ they are also elect, and that therefore their lives should be characterized by joyous, confident service of God and others. So for Calvin, predestination was a doctrine of comfort and assurance, which should liberate the Christian from morbid introspection or debilitating insecurity. Unfortunately, it was not understood thus by all adherents of the

Reformed faith, who turned inward and made *assurance of election the result of a lengthy process of searching and struggle on the part of the believer.

Afterwards, within the Reformed churches there arose a disagreement about the logical order of the decrees of God – was the primary decree that of predestination and reprobation, with that of the fall subsequently following for its implementation (supralapsarianism), or that of the fall primary, and the decrees of predestination subsequent to it (infralapsarianism)? *Beza and Gomarus were associated with the former view, though the majority of Calvinists always seem to have been infralapsarian.

In the early seventeenth century, a revisionary form of the Reformed faith was put forward by the Dutch theologian Jacobus *Arminius, who tended to found predestination upon the divine foreknowledge. This was strenuously resisted by the majority of Reformed theologians, but deeply influenced many Anglicans, and through them the founders of *Methodism, where it has always been the historic stance of that church. Similar controversies were also taking place in the Roman Catholic communion during the sixteenth and seventeenth centuries. Many theologians, including Cardinal *Contarini and the *Dominican order, upheld the general medieval position on the matter as represented by Aquinas. They were, however, opposed mainly by the up-and-coming missionary *Jesuit order, who held to a revisionary view put forward by Louis Molina (1535–1601) known as congruism. This taught that as God knew the future, he also knew all the conditions which then would be at work and thus could save individuals by offering them sufficient grace in circumstances that he had foreseen would result in their freely accepting that grace. Augustinianism, by contrast, teaches that salvation comes to the elect solely through efficient grace activating their free response. The debate between the Dominicans and the Jesuits on this issue was so fierce that eventually in 1594 Pope Clement VIII summoned the principal disputants to Rome, where in the congregation *De Auxiliis* they contended for eleven years until dismissed with no decision being made.

In the eighteenth century, under the influence of new revisionary modes of thought, many both within the churches and outside were contending that the final arbiter of human behaviour and belief was our inalienable free will, which even the Deity was bound to respect. To combat this and its explicit assault on any significant doctrine of predestination, Jonathan *Edwards wrote his most powerful philosophical treatise *The Freedom of the Will*, which appeared in 1754. In this he argued that the everyday usage of the notion of having a free will was in no way opposed to what was affirmed by the doctrine of predestination, also pointing out how, if God was dependent upon countless finite decisions, his overall sovereignty over the universe would be destroyed.

The great Protestant theologian of the nineteenth century, *Schleiermacher, came from a Reformed church background, and though he based his interpretation of the Christian faith on the religious consciousness rather directly upon Scripture as the word of God, he nevertheless held to a doctrine of predestination. It was not, however, balanced by the doctrine of reprobation, since those who were not in the community of faith even at death were to be regarded as being as yet passed over by God. Schleiermacher seems to have believed that eventually the whole of the old humanity would be taken up into the new. So here we meet another theological possibility, that of the predestinarian *universalist.

Discussion of the doctrine of predestination has been dominated in recent years by the daring and original contribution of Karl *Barth. He was of the opinion that the role of Jesus Christ had been unduly diminished in the classic presentations of the doctrine, being largely portrayed as the agent of an anterior divine will. To counteract this he sought to develop the long-standing supralapsarian/infralapsarian argument by insisting that we must view the two primary divine decrees, creation and election, as being integral to each other, with creation being the external basis of the covenant, whilst the covenant is the internal basis of creation. Furthermore, he argued that we must regard Jesus Christ as the complete focus of the divine predestinating activity, being at the same time the elect man, and also the one who bore the reprobation of God upon the cross. Thus in him the whole process is fulfilled. A frequent criticism of this understanding is that this logically implied universalism, a charge which Barth always rejected, though he never spelled out in detail the nature of the alternative proposed.

The doctrine of predestination, unlike in previous centuries, is hardly a matter of widespread debate and concern today in the churches.

This is largely due to their being in the grip of a pragmatism which is primarily concerned about popular impact rather than becoming clear about the foundations of Christian truth. It is hard to see how one can do justice to the fundamental biblical insight of God being sovereign Creator of all that is, without having a significant doctrine of predestination, as the only alternative would be belief in some kind of finite deity. It is inevitable that any genuine revival of the faith will mean coming to terms again with what is signified by this historic doctrine. Here the test will be how far any particular presentation does justice to the various other facets of the historic faith.

Bibliography

Augustine, *On the Predestination of the Saints*; Augustine, *On the Gift of Perseverance*; K. Barth, *CD* II.2 c. 32–35; G. C. Berkouwer, *Divine Election* (ET, Grand Rapids, 1960); J. Calvin, *Institutes*, III c. xxi–xxiv; idem, *Concerning the Eternal Predestination of God*, tr. J. K. S. Reid (London, 1960); F. Schleiermacher, *The Christian Faith*, pt. II. 119–120; Thomas Aquinas, *Summa Theologiae*, 1a Q. 23.

S. RUSSELL

PRESBYTERIANISM

Presbyterianism denotes both a form of church government by elders (presbyters) and a system of scriptural doctrine whose origins date back to the sixteenth-century *Protestant Reformation and in particular John *Calvin's reforms of church and society in Geneva. It was Calvin's *Institutes of the Christian Religion* with its distinctive emphasis upon the biblical meaning and implication of God's sovereignty that would spread from Geneva to establish and anchor the doctrine and polity of global Presbyterianism. In what follows we will examine Presbyterianism's confessional roots, doctrine, understanding of the church and governance, as well its relation to civil society and social reform.

The Presbyterian confessions

Presbyterians share with Calvin a high view of *Scripture whose ultimate authorship and authority is attributed to God. Calvin's *Institutes* and extensive biblical commentaries sought to distinguish biblical doctrine and church order from medieval traditions and practices that had distorted or departed from the faith and practice of the early church. These reforms became the seedbed of the Reformed *confessions and *catechisms of the sixteenth and seventeenth centuries, including the Confession of Faith and catechisms of the *Westminster Assembly (1634–9) that have become the confessional and catechetical backbone of global Presbyterianism. These concise and systematic restatements of biblical doctrine were drafted to distinguish, educate and unify the growing reform movement that would establish itself as Presbyterianism. Though subordinate to Scripture, Presbyterians affirm the Apostles' and Nicene *Creeds as well as selected Reformed confessions as standards for the church that clarify biblical doctrine and guide the church in its reading, understanding and application of Scripture to its governance and ministry. This confessional tradition extends into the modern era with recognition of the *Barmen Declaration, which rejected the subordination of the church and the gospel to the state and national ideology, and the Confession of 1967, which raised concern for social justice to confessional status. Nevertheless, adoption of these two latter confessions has been controversial both within and between Presbyterian denominations.

Presbyterian doctrine

It is the majesty and praise of God that emerges from the rich doctrinal tapestry of the Reformed confessions woven from the four doctrinal distinctives of Presbyterianism: the priority of the *glory of God, the pervasiveness of human depravity, *sin and guilt, the unmerited grace of *salvation and the life of gratitude that *grace enables. The priority of God's glory can be seen in Presbyterian insistence that the purpose of creation and the goal of humankind is to glorify God. Paradoxically, the emphasis on God's glory gives rise to complementary stress upon the pervasiveness of sin and human depravity. Humankind's engrained hostility towards God leaves humankind guilty and estranged from God. Yet it is the very helplessness of the human situation which reveals that *redemption and reconciliation rest solely in the grace of God in Jesus Christ, whose perfect obedience and death on the *cross atoned for human sin by satisfying God's divine justice. Moreover, it is God who seals the gift of salvation in the sending of the Holy Spirit who unites the believer to Christ by faith. Though *faith entails human will and decision, Presbyterians hold that faith is ultimately the gift of God evidenced in the election (see *Predestination), regeneration and redemption of his chosen people. Appreciation of unmerited grace is to produce the rest and assurance that ought to exemplify the life of Presbyterians and be the catalyst of a life of service lived in gratitude to God.

Ecclesiology and polity

Reform and restoration of a biblical church order begins for Presbyterians in the recognition of Christ as the head of the church and sole mediator between God and humankind. Christ rules in his church through his word and Spirit. In turn, the church is commissioned by Christ to share in his prophetic, kingly and priestly ministry as a '*priesthood of believers'. This priesthood corporately and individually bears witness to Christ in worship, governance and through service to church and society. Moreover, Presbyterians regard children of believers as members of this *covenant communion with Christ and thus share in the church's corporate ministry of worship, edification, witness and mission.

Two 'marks' identify the true church for Presbyterians: the preaching of the word and the proper administration of the *sacraments. Though all members are expected to share in the church's ministry, elders and deacons are sanctioned by Scripture to govern and maintain that ministry. Elders are made up of ministers of word and sacrament who serve as teaching and ruling elders and lay elders who share in the oversight of the church. Deacons minister to the practical needs of the church and its members, with special attention paid to the poor and those in need.

Presbyterian unity, connection and catholicity are maintained through a system of representative assemblies (courts) at the congregational, regional and national levels of the church. Congregations are overseen by the church session (consistory) made up of the ordained ministers and elected ordained lay elders. Presbyterian congregations are not independent, but united to the wider church through their representation at the Presbytery, Synod and General Assembly levels of church governance. Presbyteries are made up of ministers and elders sent from each congregation along with theological college educators and retired ministers. Numerical balance is maintained between ordained ministers and lay elders through the appointment of additional elders. At Presbytery an equal number of ministers and lay elders are elected as representative commissioners to serve in the Synod and General Assembly. Synods assist and oversee the work of the Presbyteries, while the General Assembly is the highest governing body in Presbyterianism. In all matters ruling elders are to be guided by the conscience informed by the word and Spirit of God. Presbyterians maintain that 'God alone is Lord of the conscience', and thus the decisions of elders are not to be predetermined or coerced by fellow members or their congregations. Nonetheless, recognition of the freedom of conscience and the right of private judgment neither limits the right of Sessions, Presbyteries, Synods and Assemblies to establish the polity of the church nor allow elders or members to defy the church's doctrine, rule or discipline.

Civil society and social reform

Presbyterians, like their forebears in the magisterial Reformation of Geneva and Zurich, have understood their calling to include the renewal of society through the reform of civil governance and the flowering of sciences, arts and literature. Thus, Presbyterians encourage cultivation of the life of the mind so as to better engage civil society to procure the common good. In this endeavour, historically Presbyterians have been neither naïve to the prevalence of sin in society nor cowed by its destructive force, but in wisdom have sought to reform society through reforming government institutions so as to lessen evil's influence and bind its power to destroy both individuals and society. Accordingly, the civil magistrate is recognized by Presbyterians as ordained of God to punish vice, promote virtue and safeguard the ministry of the church. Moreover, Presbyterians are not to avoid public service, but instead to seek public office so as to better reform society and establish the common good.

See also: CHURCH; CHURCH GOVERNMENT; REFORMED THEOLOGY.

Bibliography

G. D. Henderson, *Presbyterianism* (Aberdeen, 1954); J. H. Leith, *Introduction to the Reformed Tradition* (Atlanta, ²1981); *idem, Creeds of the Churches: A Reader in Christian Doctrine, from the Bible to the Present* (Louisville, ³1983); S. M. Lewis, *On Being Presbyterian: Our Beliefs, Practices, and Stories* (Philipsburg, 2006); A. E. McGrath, *Reformation Thought: An Introduction* (Oxford and Malden, ³1999); J. B. Torrance, *Worship, Community and the Triune God of Grace* (Downers Grove, 1996).

T. HARVEY

PRIESTHOOD OF ALL BELIEVERS

The doctrine of the priesthood of all believers, central to Martin Luther's teaching on the 'true' church, is a major feature of all *Protestant ecclesiologies down to the present day. It is typically derived from Peter's depiction of the *church as a 'royal priesthood', fulfilling the kingly and priestly functions of Christ insofar as the church is Christ's body. There are no texts in the NT that call leaders of any churches priests. This is significant given the existence of an all-male, hereditary priesthood in Judaism.

Priesthood of all believers in the early church

There is a wealth of historical scholarship on priesthood in general, leadership in the churches, and the doctrine of the priesthood of all believers. There was always a distinction between leaders and their flock in the early pre-Constantinian churches. Theologians disagree as to whether this was always a distinction between ordained clergy and laity, with the former having the role of administering *sacraments, or whether the distinction was merely formal. There are grounds to believe that both models existed in this period. Colin Bulley argues that *Justin Martyr and *Irenaeus were aware of the notion of the priesthood of all believers. *Tertullian develops it considerably, linking it to baptism, reception of the Holy Spirit, membership of the church as spiritual temple, and salvation. He also links believers' priesthood to prayer as believers' sacrifice. For *Clement of Alexandria, believers' priesthood is less important than his idea of the 'gnostic' Christian who is holy, knows and contemplates God and secret knowledge about him, and teaches these matters to the faithful. Later in the third century, Hippolytus, Cyprian and the *Didascalia* emphasize the priesthood of bishops and clergy. This influenced medieval notions of priesthood.

The Reformation and its consequences

The priesthood of all believers was a key doctrine that Martin *Luther used in anti-Catholic polemics, especially attacking the validity of the *papacy. For Luther, all Christians are born priests by virtue of baptism. There is debate as to whether ordained ministry was simply derived according to Luther from the priesthood of all believers, or whether it was directly instituted by God. Calvin (see *Reformed theology) based his doctrine of priesthood on Christ's *office as prophet, priest and king. For both, the priesthood of all believers is the basis for preaching, the sacraments of baptism and Communion, the keys of Christian discipline and forgiveness, ministerial ordination, and the spiritual sacrifices of believers as prayer, praise and thanksgiving. Some Protestant churches such as the *Quakers, the *Salvation Army and the Brethren do not have any form of ordination. Their ecclesiologies take the doctrine of the priesthood of all believers at its most literal and radical.

Why the doctrine matters today

In the twentieth century the international *ecumenical movement found discussion of the priesthood of all believers important due to wishes by some churches to reunite. In more modest vein, denominations have made progress in theological dialogue over the nature and function of priesthood and its relation to the notions of clergy and laity. Since the Second *Vatican Council, several liberal Roman Catholic theologians, following Hans *Küng, have argued that priesthood is a function of the whole church, refusing to term the leadership or presidency of ordained persons 'priesthood'.

In the modern period the priesthood of all believers has also been key in enabling space for discussing the validity of ordaining women, and in promoting this practice. Those Protestants who argue for women's ordination use the doctrine of the priesthood of all believers, arguing that there is no theological bar to any member of this priesthood being considered to have the necessary gifts for ordination and leadership. Opponents of women's ordination do not deny that women have spiritual gifts suitable for ministry, but sometimes point to Jesus' appointing of twelve males to be apostles, representing the male heads of the twelve tribes of Israel. This, however, moves the debate onto the nature of *apostles and leaders in Protestant churches. Some *charismatics and *Pentecostals make certain distinctions in this respect. These differences among Protestants have not, however, masked the fact that a very large number, in many cases a majority, of Protestant missionaries have been women. Their return from the non-Western to the Western world has been a factor in the rise in support for women's ordination among Anglican and other evangelicals in the last few decades. The concept of the ministry of all members of the church is an aspect of believers' priesthood that has surfaced in recent decades. Some of this is due to wanting to unburden ministers or priests at a time of declining ordination in Western countries. It coincides with the increased cultural and theological influence of evangelicalism, broadly understood, upon Protestants since the marginalization of churches from Western society in the 1960s.

Bibliography

C. J. Bulley, *The Priesthood of Some Believers: Developments from the General to the Special Priesthood in the Christian Literature of the First Three Centuries* (Carlisle, 2000); C. Eastwood, *The Priesthood of All Believers: An Examination of the Doctrine from the Reformation to the Present Day* (London, 1960); B. A. Gerrish, 'Priesthood and Ministry in the Theology of Luther', *Church History* 34(40), 1965, pp. 404–422; R. P. C. Hanson, *Christian Priesthood Examined* (London: 1979).

C. A. E. MOSELEY

PRINCETON THEOLOGY

Princeton theology was a major expression of conservative Calvinism (see *Reformed theology) in America during the nineteenth and early twentieth centuries. It owed its force to the remarkable series of theologians who taught at the Presbyterian Seminary in Princeton, New Jersey, and to the significance of that institution within the denomination and the country at large. The three most important Princeton theologians were Archibald Alexander (1772–1851), founding professor of the school, Charles *Hodge, who taught over 3,000 students in his more than fifty years as a Princeton professor, and Benjamin Breckinridge *Warfield, who upheld Old Princeton positions during a period of fading evangelical influence. These three were joined by a host of other important figures, including Hodge's son, Archibald Alexander Hodge (1823–86), two sons of Alexander, James Waddel (1804–59) and Joseph Addison (1809–60), and the NT scholar and apologist, J. Gresham *Machen.

The Princeton theologians upheld Reformed confessionalism, defended high views of biblical inspiration and authority, organized their thinking with the aid of the Scottish philosophy of *common sense, and had a surprisingly large place for the role of the *Holy Spirit in religious experience. The theologians of Old Princeton were jealous guardians of Calvinistic views on the divine pre-eminence in salvation, the unity both of the race in Adam's guilt and of the elect in the work of Christ, and the moral inability of humans apart from God's grace. They upheld these positions against continental *romanticism and *rationalism, against domestic forms of subjectivity, against the excesses of enthusiastic revivalism, against all varieties of theological *liberalism and against evangelical *perfectionism. One of the Reformed positions which the school held most doggedly was the *infallibility of the Bible. This was a central theme in the apologetics of Alexander, it was an essential foundation for Charles Hodge's *Systematic Theology* and for the polemics which he carried on in the *Princeton Review*, and it provided Warfield with the position that he defended in countless essays toward the end of the nineteenth century. The well-known monograph on 'Inspiration' in 1881 by Warfield and A. A. Hodge summed up the Princeton position: the church's historic belief in the verbal infallibility of the Bible should be maintained both because of external proofs for Scripture's divine character and because of the Bible's own testimony concerning itself.

Principles of the Scottish philosophy of common sense provided guidelines for the Princeton theologians in their organization of scriptural material and for their approach to theology. In this they reflected the teaching of two Scottish-born presidents of Princeton College, John *Witherspoon and James McCosh (1811–94), whose work influenced all of the major Princetonians directly or indirectly.

At Princeton Seminary, the Scottish philosophy was not so much a guide for convictions about the native powers of the 'moral sense', as was the case among *New England Calvinists. It provided rather a confidence in empirical science and simple inductive procedures by which to chart a theological course. The opening pages of Charles Hodge's *Systematic Theology* provide the clearest illustration of these procedural commitments. But even as the Princetonians adopted the scientific standards of the Scottish philosophy, they always retained a large place for distinctly spiritual influences. The major Princeton theologians were all powerful preachers. Although they distrusted unrestrained revivalism, they worked for renewal in the church. Charles Hodge especially, in his commentaries and some of his polemics, could write as movingly about the inward effects of the Holy Spirit as any of his contemporaries.

The Princeton theologians embodied their beliefs in powerful institutions. The seminary itself trained more ministers than any comparable institution in the United States during the nineteenth century. The *Princeton Review* and its successor journals were mighty organs, not only among northern Presbyterians but across denominational boundaries. And the school was a force to be reckoned with in the denomination, both when its positions dominated significant segments of the church and when its views became a minority position.

Critics of the Princetonians accuse them of scholastic rationalism and a mechanical biblicism. While these claims are not without a particle of truth, the larger reality is that the theologians of Old Princeton were faithful representatives of historic Calvinism, who energetically adopted their confessional position to the needs and opportunities of the American experience.

Bibliography

H. A. Harris, *Fundamentalism and Evangelicals* (Oxford, 1998); C. Hodge, 'Retrospect of the History of the Princeton Review', *Biblical Repertory and Princeton Review*, Index Volume, no. 1, 1870, pp. 1–39; A. W. Hoffecker, *Piety and the Princeton Theologians: Archibald Alexander, Charles Hodge, and Benjamin Warfield* (Phillipsburg, 1981); M. A. Noll (ed.), *The Princeton Theology 1812–1921: Scripture, Science, and Theological Method from Archibald Alexander to Benjamin Warfield* (Grand Rapids, 1983); J. C. Vander Stelt, *Philosophy and Scripture: A Study in Old Princeton and Westminster Theology* (Marlton, 1978); J. D. Woodbridge and R. Balmer, 'The Princetonians and Biblical Authority', in J. D. Woodbridge and D. A. Carson (eds.), *Scripture and Truth* (Grand Rapids, 1983); F. G. Zaspel, *The Theology of B. B. Warfield* (Wheaton, 2010).

M. A. NOLL

PRISCILLIANISM

Priscillianism, named after Priscillian, a Spanish nobleman, was an *ascetic movement which emerged within the churches of Spain and Aquitaine in the 370s. It emphasized virginity, voluntary poverty, and vegetarianism as sure means of attaining greater spiritual heights, particularly the gift of *prophecy. For the Priscillianists this meant the ability to discern special meaning both in the Scriptures and in various aprocrypha. While Priscillian, who became Bishop of Avila, accepted the current canon of Scripture, he was convinced that divine revelation was not confined to this. He also took some interest in occult literature in the belief that a successful spiritual life involved a close knowledge of the enemy and his strategy.

Priscillianism neither challenged the church authorities directly nor fostered monastic foundations, though some informal fraternities were established. Certain bishops, however, became suspicious that the activities and doctrines of the Priscillianists smacked of *Manichaeism and sorcery. Matters came to a head when these charges were brought against Priscillian and some associates before the Emperor Maximus at Trier in 385. This led to their execution – the first and almost only occasion in antiquity when a heretic suffered this fate at the hand of a civil ruler. At the time the greatest indignation was reserved for those bishops who had pressed capital charges.

After these executions there was a temporary reaction in favour of Priscillian, who in some quarters was regarded as a *martyr. A *schism was threatened within the Spanish church, but this was avoided by vigorous action from the Council of Toledo in 400. At a popular level Priscillianism continued to exercise some influence right up to the sixth century.

Bibliography

H. Chadwick, *Priscillian of Avila* (Oxford, 1976).

G. A. KEITH

PROCESS THEOLOGY

Process theology is the theological system based on the philosophy of Alfred North Whitehead (1861–1947) and Charles Hartshorne (1897–2000), developed at the University of Chicago in the 1920s and 1930s. The name itself derives from the central tenet of both of these philosophers that reality is a process of becoming, not a static universe of objects or substances. In *Process and Reality* (1929) Whitehead set out an original *metaphysical system based on the primacy of events. The notion of events combines into one the previously separated notions of space, time and matter, as indicated by Einstein's physics and theory of relativity. These events, or 'actual occasions', are the open-textured atoms of the cosmos. Each atom is a point in the process, which takes from the past and incorporates new possibilities into a new event which, in turn, contributes to the future. The highest principle in this process is that of creativity or love. It continuously brings about novelty in a 'creative advance' that maximizes good.

Beginning with several major works in the 1940s, Hartshorne developed a complete process philosophical theology, detailing especially a full concept of *God. These views were then elaborated, especially by American theologians and philosophers such as John Cobb (b. 1925), David R. Griffin (b. 1939), Schubert Ogden (b. 1928), Daniel Day Williams (1910–73) and Lewis Ford (b. 1933), the French Jesuit *Theilhard de Chardin, and among British theologians Norman Pittenger (1905–1997) and David Pailin.

Process theology is a form of *theism with a markedly immanentist doctrine of God and redefinition of his transcendence. God gives to all events their initial aim, and so is 'primordial'. Events, and their divine giver, are inwardly interrelated and mutually participatory, and by free decision they receive, 'prehend', from all other events and so choose their own development and become 'consequences' gathering up their past into their future, actualizing their possibilities. Ultimately, God is also the recipient of these actualizations, harmonizing them in accordance with his love to further 'creative advance' in the cosmos, so that his 'primordial' pole is complemented by his 'consequent' pole, affected by all cosmic events in a real way. The *suffering of God is therefore totally real for process theology, but it claims that God cannot be degraded by suffering, or indeed temptation, because of his 'primordial pole'. Some critics have asked whether this imports a *dualism into the doctrine of God, but process theologians argue it is a distinction akin to the analogy of a person's life and body. We are inseparable from our bodies, and yet transcend our physical being, while being open to suffering and new experiences from our material side.

Process God is therefore only sovereign in that he patiently, unremittingly, waits and persuades the creatively suffering God. God cannot compel change, and is open to new experiences in his 'consequent pole', but process theologians insist that God cannot fundamentally change as a result of his real and organic relation to the cosmos, and this is crucial as regards Christian basic spirituality which needs an unchangeably holy God to redeem and to be worshipped, although given the temporality of this process God, it is not immediately evident why radical change should not take hold of God. Process God works only through the freedom of the cosmos, and his judgment is a matter of a refining, sanctifying process, of luring the world towards a more loving and more joyful future, away from its self-centredness and complacency, an attitude rejected by God.

In a sense, process theology is one of continual self-incarnation of God into the material order, and Christ's *incarnation therefore exemplifies what is happening rather than proving a great disjuncture with the process. God, according to Whitehead, is not the 'exception to' the metaphysical principles undergirding reality as process, but rather the 'chief exemplification of' these principles, and Jesus discloses the heart of how things really are and should be, true openness to God. The *atonement is understood as a revelation of divine suffering and a summons to repent, along the line of the theology of *Abelard. Process Christologies, as in David Griffin, Norman Pittenger and Lewis Ford, show that Christ's life was God's in the sense that it was lived in perfect obedience to the 'lure' of God to the extent that a whole new subjectivity, a way of human living, is inaugurated, a Christology sharing much with that of *Schleiermacher. The result of the life and death of Christ is the emergence of a new kind of community, the *church. This is the meaning of *resurrection: the body of Christ is born. For Ford, this is seen as a major step in human evolution. Man is now radically different and communitarian. Add to this the view that the *Holy Spirit is to be understood as God's contribution of initial aims, and we see that process theology is unitarian, not trinitarian.

We can now see why Hartshorne rejects theism as divorcing God from the world, *pantheism as identifying God as the world, and opts for *panentheism, teaching that the cosmos is everlastingly in God, with God empathetically superintending, rather than imperiously controlling, the cosmos. The cosmos and process God were and are organically everlasting, interwined in the temporal process, not so much 'ying and yang' as co-equal but coordinated ontologically, as mind to body. As regards the doctrine of *revelation, we can see that the cosmos, the body of God, is a continual disclosure of the divine purposes and also of evil frustrating these. Christ is the key moment of disclosure of this pattern already going on in history, as God absorbs the pain of the negative (Hegel).

*Hermeneutics is seen as an attempt to retrace the revelational process to discover God's original 'lure', in a markedly Hegelian way. Thus, it has both objective and subjective components, and is possible only in the interaction of the reader.

The general features of process philosophy imply a view of man that is very close, if not identical, to that of *Heidegger, *Bultmann and other *existentialists. Ogden has been the principal figure in developing this point. A person is a series of separate events. Each point is autonomous not only in relation to all others in the series, but also to God. It is self-determinative. Thus, it is also dependent on its own existential decision. I am what I am now deciding to be.

As a result, the redemptive activity of God consists in his willingness to accept past evil, transform it into good and continue to lure each individual toward a self-authenticating acceptance of true value. A person's salvation consists in his recognition of disloyalty to communality and his willing acceptance of God's lure to be a member of the body of Christ.

The process God's ability to preserve each event as an 'eternal object' adds an *eschatological dimension to the theological system. Not only does God's continuing knowledge preserve the reality (in a subjective sense) of each occasion, but his use of the past in presenting new possibilities to the future also gives meaning to former events. Ogden and others have used this concept in Whitehead as a way of spelling out the biblical idea of eternal life and heaven. Nothing is forgotten to the love of God; all is preserved and continues to affect the future meaningfully. It should be noted, however, that this is not conscious personal continuance, and also that it is universal in application.

Ford, Cobb and others have done much to develop a general eschatology as well. It follows from their view of the church as the emergence of a higher state of human evolution (see *Creation). This understanding permits us to look forward to a time when God's aims will finally overcome the individual evil events, and bring about a true community of love and peace. Hartshorne roots this in the biblical view of love as true union.

Process theology clearly affirms much that traditional Christianity welcomes, notably the empathy of God for the world and the desire of God to work through creaturely freedom rather than iron laws and sheer power. But the question is whether in so emphasizing such factors process theology has tipped over into a system offering a depotentiated deity who is so vulnerable to the world process as to be incapable of reaching into history to save and renew. The *history of theology has seen the equivalent of process theology in nineteenth-century theology influenced by *Hegel, in which Christ becomes a symbol of the process as God reveals himself to himself. The telling criticism offered by Karl *Barth in his dialectical theology can be directed at process theology. As with all systems tending to *monism, process theology struggles to present a sufficient doctrine of radical evil, tending to regard it as part of the process, the discord contributing to the overall harmony.

Several influential theological movements of the later twentieth century have drawn on process theology, notably *feminist theology and theologians of the *ecological movement. Feminist theology applauds the process theologians' rejection of the God who is in control, as 'male', and favour the great emphasis on nurturing and organic real relations with the cosmos, on the model of the foetus in the divine womb, united but distinct, stressing the physical and affective. Ecological thinkers have produced cosmologies suggesting a panentheism, and the Gaia theory of J. Lovelock has much in common with process views. *Evangelical theology has also been deeply affected by process thought in theologians espousing *open theism, notably Clark *Pinnock. The vulnerability of God has been emphasized by some pastoral theologians along the lines of process theology as a comfort to the suffering, since God is our co-sufferer who understands, the problem being whether God can break in to heal and to save, or merely sympathizes. Critics, on the other hand, point to the theological problems entailed with a disempowered God who cannot exercise control over a universe which could spiral into chaos and total disorder; indeed such a deity would prove to be irresponsible in creating the world and risking the horror of evil triumphing. Herbert McCabe, one such critic, therefore suggests that process theology is the result of anthropocentric sentimentalism. But it cannot be denied that process theology proves a stimulating dialogue partner for many strands of Christian theology.

Bibliography

D. Brown, R. E. James and G. Reeves (eds.), *Process Philosophy and Christian Thought* (Indianapolis, 1971); J. B. Cobb and D. R. Griffin, *Process Theology: An Introductory Exposition* (Philadelphia and Belfast, 1976 and 1977); P. S. Fiddes, *The Creative Suffering of God* (Oxford 1988); L. Ford, *The Lure of God* (Philadelphia, 1978); D. R. Griffin, *A Process Christology* (Philadelphia, 1973); R. Gruenler, *The Inexhaustible God* (Grand Rapids, 1984); C. Hartshorne, *Man's Vision of God and the Logic of Theism* (Chicago, 1941); H. McCabe, *God Matters* (London 1987); D. Pailin, *God and the Processes of Reality* (1989); N. Pittenger, *Christology Reconsidered* (1970); S. Ogden, *The Reality of God and Other Essays* (London, 1966); I. Trethowan, 'Process Theology and the Christian Tradition', *Studies in Historical Theology* 5 (Still River, 1985); A. N. Whitehead, *Religion in the Making* (Cambridge, 1926); idem, *Process and Reality* (London, 1929); D. D. Williams, *The Spirit and the Forms of Love* (New York, 1968).

T. BRADSHAW

PROCESSION (OF HOLY SPIRIT), see HOLY SPIRIT; TRINITY

PROGRESS, IDEA OF

The idea characterizing nineteenth-century thinking was progress. There were many reasons for this. Britain's Industrial Revolution became the pattern for rapid economic growth and social development throughout the Western world. Scientific discovery and its application in such practical developments as techniques of mass production and advances in public health helped generate an optimistic and forward-looking mentality buttressed by the spread of Western civilization by European empires and across North America. At the same time, the influence of *Hegel's dialectical *rationalism provided the seedbed in which was sown the theory of evolution (see *Creation and evolution).

Evolutionary progress as the explanatory hypothesis of reality was therefore antecedent to the development of Darwin's theory of evolution (itself not the first scientific theory of its kind). Darwinism seemed to provide a scientific basis for the philosophical ideas which were already popular, and the use of biological evolution as the key to all historical development reached its high-water mark in the extensive writings of Herbert Spencer (1820–1903). It was typical of the mindset of the mid-nineteenth century that his scientific hypothesis should be made the basis for general philosophical constructions. Scarcely any thinker avoided being influenced by the idea of evolutionary progress, in which the development of human society and the moral development of man were seen as continuous and essentially analogous with the supposed upward progress of biological evolution.

Jesuit anthropologist *Teilhard de Chardin attempted a full-blooded marriage of Darwinism and the Christian view of humanity and redemption. Spencer's later contemporary, Henry Drummond, sought in popular evangelical terms to do something similar in his *Ascent of Man* (1894). And many more recent forms assimilating theology and science have been offered: e.g. Wolfhart *Pannenberg's view of theology as a hard science and the future's ontological priority; the work of the John Templeton Foundation, advocating that *science may provide better insights into theology.

One immediate implication of these ways of thinking was found in the understanding of *history, where evolutionary progress was used to sketch the narrative. Since the Bible largely presents an account of history, there were dramatic repercussions for how the Scriptures were read. A classic instance is William Robertson Smith's *Religion of the Semites* (1889), which attempted to find revelation in a naturalistic reading of history. It was of course not new for naturalistic explanations to be given to the biblical story. Yet such was the absorption with evolutionary progress that in the mid- and later nineteenth century the church itself began to adopt such readings of its canonical Scriptures.

The Bible does not present human history as an evolutionary progress. It tells of an original perfection from which humans have fallen (see *Fall), and the following story of failed attempts to set matters right (Babel, flood, exile), with perpetual human regress. Ultimate 'progress' comes only from God. The idea of a natural evolutionary progress, with implications for morality, is therefore antithetical to the biblical picture of humanity and religion, and so the attempt to reinterpret the biblical history has to adopt the violent methods of Procrustes, and subordinate the data to the theory. This explains in part the subsequent history of OT scholarship, which despite noticeable problems with an evolutionary paradigm is still undergirded by the inversion of the order of the law and the prophets which the theory required (since prophetic religion was held to be more simple and therefore earlier).

Later social developments – from the First World War to the rise of the radical Islamic state, with global warming and economic meltdown, to epidemics and other damaging features of the Anthropocene era – essentially show that progressive views of humanity are fraught with challenges. Indeed, the myth of endless progress is seen especially in the inability of science and technological progress to account for matters of the soul and the rest of the human experience, leaving these things often ignored. Progress is still possible, but only in ways that reckon with the possibility of the (ironic) setbacks of various forms of so-called progress. And indeed, in the face of the secularization thesis that people will progress beyond religion, the majority of people today remain religious.

Human progress has been shown to be tenuous and by no means inevitable or unending, with question marks put against the claim that humanity has advanced morally since its earliest days. Redemption, far from being a product of evolution, can only be by revolution in humanity's continually regressive moral and spiritual story. The only true idea of progress is that of the progress of God in salvation history.

Bibliography

C. Dawson, *Progress and Religion: An Historical Enquiry* (London, 1945); C. S. Lewis, 'The Funeral of a Great Myth', in *Christian Reflections* (London, 1967).

N. M. de S. Cameron

PROOFS OF GOD'S EXISTENCE, see NATURAL THEOLOGY

PROPITIATION, see ATONEMENT; SACRIFICE; WRATH

PROSPERITY THEOLOGY

With the core of its message often referred to as the 'prosperity gospel', prosperity theology is a system of thought within the wider *Pentecostal movement, asserting that God wishes everyone to be healthy and wealthy. This theology asserts that if prosperity is not present in the lives of professing Christians, then God's blessing may not be upon them.

Developed in extravagant ways in the USA during the twentieth century with various so-called faith healers (e.g. Benny Hinn, Kenneth Copeland), teachers who became well known through television and modern media, these leaders built multi-million dollar international industries and have been widely subject to accusations of exploitation.

Additionally, there is a group of prosperity teachers deemed by many in the popular evangelical world as closer to, if not part of, *evangelicalism, including Joel Osteen, T. D. Jakes and Joyce Meyer. While committed to a kind of prosperity theology, they have become more identified with the wider evangelical movement.

Prosperity teachers are often popular particularly with those from lower socio-economic situations, often in Latino, African-American, South-East and Far-East Asian communities. One small group of prosperity preachers was profiled in a two-season US reality-television show, *Preachers of L.A.* (2013–14).

Bibliography

D. W. Jones and R. S. Woodbridge, *Health, Wealth & Happiness: Has the Prosperity Gospel Overshadowed the Gospel of Christ?* (Grand

Rapids, 2010); <http://www.oxygen.com/shows/preachers-of-la>.

J. S. SEXTON

PROTESTANTISM

The term derives from the Diet of Speyer in 1529, when five German princes and fourteen cities made a formal *protestatio* against legislation to end all toleration of Lutherans in Catholic districts and demanded freedom of conscience for minorities. Protestants were marked out as stressing personal faith in Christ in Pauline fashion, and critical of Rome in so far as her practice obscured such faith. It is worth noting that groups now called Protestant existed prior to Luther and the Reformation, notably the *Waldensians, the *Hussites and Lollards. Protestantism has a longer pedigree than the *Reformation, deriving most deeply from the evangelical message of the NT, and this message has bubbled up throughout Christian history as a testimony on behalf of Christ – *protestare* in the most positive evangelical sense.

Core orientations of Protestanism

Grace and faith

The Pauline message of *salvation for believers in the crucified and risen Christ made present in the Spirit is central to original Protestantism, in fact the Protestant Reformation might be regarded as a recovery of the *Spirit in the church, overcoming clerical mediation. The Protestant Reformers stressed the divine gift of *grace, an emphasis found in Augustine, an authority much cited in this respect. But *Luther's emphasis found in Romans the doctrine of *justification by grace through *faith, the total acceptance by God of the repentant believer on the basis of the *sacrifice of Christ (see *Atonement, *Cross, *Redemption). Protestant theology and spirituality has since stressed this 'once for all' aspect of salvation, although it cannot be said that the challenge of *sanctification as a life process was neglected, notably in the writings of *Calvin. But salvation is the gift of God, even 'good works' are divinely given and empowered in 'the paradox of grace', the divine embracing the human, the glory going to God. The stress on grace as the direct gift of God, rooted solely in divine action at Calvary, is distinctively Protestant. Debates about the doctrine of *predestination, election (see *calling) and the status of human will take up deep strands of *Augustinian theology also found in less systematic form in biblical texts. Calvinistic and *Arminian emphases continue to be found within Protestantism, stressing divine and human agency respectively.

Protestantism harks back to *Scripture and its patterns of life in order to judge and reform current church practice now – *semper reformanda*. Another point worth noting is the Protestant tradition of accepting that Christians will disagree on some secondary things, *adiaphora*, but should all unite on the primary issues of the *gospel of salvation – indeed such shared basics are 'the catholic faith' for Protestants, rather as Irenaeus set out his 'rule of faith' as a summary of core beliefs in the early church. Scripture stands over church tradition for Protestantism, but the history of doctrinal tradition is a key resource in seeking to wrestle with problems of interpretation. Protestantism continues to be defined powerfully by its commitment to Scripture, and the principle *sola Scriptura* has proved a key distinguishing feature over against *Roman Catholicism. After the Enlightenment, Protestant thinkers debated the infallibility of Scripture intensively, the figure of *Schleiermacher representing a liberal view, followed by *Ritschl and *Harnack, with a conservative reply from *Pietists, *evangelicals and Tractarians (see *Anglo-Catholic theology) in England. B. B. *Warfield in America produced important scholarly defences of the inerrantist view at the end of the century (see *Infallibility and inerrancy of the Bible).

The priesthood of all believers

This emphasis on grace was gained from the NT and in effect broke the medieval synthesis of sacramental grace mediated by the priesthood, including the sacrament of *penance. The medieval hierarchical structure of salvation could not survive the radical Pauline message of Christ's reconciling grace received by personal faith. The church's ministry therefore becomes a pastoral ministry of this word, very much rooted in Scripture and lived out in practice, arguably the ministerial shape of the earliest church. Priesthood is attributed to the whole church, to all believers, as holy and set apart in Christ for the service and praise of God the Father. But the ordained ministry is very important to the church, as Calvin and many after him have taught. The minister's role has been acknowledged by most strands of Protestantism, although not by the Brethren. The ordination of women to the pastoral ministry has been accepted by many Protestant churches, but by no means all. Fierce debates about the place of homosexuals in church life may be best seen under this heading, in that salvation is by grace but Scripture seems to be clear in holding homosexual practice to be wrong, and therefore ordination of non-celibate homosexuals is not acceptable to most traditional Protestant denominations, which would seek to accept and work with homosexuals while commending abstinence for serious disciples.

While the *priesthood of all believers and a pastor-teacher ordained ministry has been the Protestant theory, history has examples of heavy-handed clericalism and even persecution, for example, the Salem witchhunts and the use of force against dissidents such as the *Anabaptists in the *Radical Reformation. Karl *Barth was scathing in his attack on the 'German Christians' who sided with Nazism in the 1930s. But the Protestant view of church history is that it is far from sinless.

The sacraments

Protestants hold to two *sacraments, taken from the NT with a strong background in the OT: *baptism and the Lord's Supper or Holy Communion (see *Eucharist). Both relate to the death of Christ as the matrix of salvation: the dying and rising with Christ in the waters of baptism; partaking of the bread and wine closely linked to Christ's Last Supper, interpreting his death to his disciples. Protestants all accept the importance of these sacraments, although they disagree about aspects of them. For example, Baptist churches do not baptize infants, and the symbolic link between the bread and wine with Christ has various interpretations, from a 'mere' sign to an 'effectual' sign conveying what it signifies. The dynamic role of the Spirit in or through the sacraments is a common Protestant emphasis, and indeed one now ecumenically agreed with Rome as seen in the Anglican Roman Catholic Agreed Statement, *The Final Report*.

Church and *state

As Scripture stands over tradition, Christ stands over his church, and Protestantism has a deep critique of any doctrine of the church that falls into a self-identification with Christ and then a dispenser of grace. The church stands in constant need of forgiveness for all her members; there is no specially holy caste distinct from ordinary believers. This tension between Christ and his church, in contrast to Roman Catholic identification of the two, is a fundamental difference. The Protestant Reformation received the protection of many German princes who prevented Luther being executed in the manner of Jan Hus earlier. This state protection was important historically, but theologically now seems dubious. Some Protestant denominations accepted state sponsorship – Lutherans and *Anglicans, for example – others very much rejected it, notably Calvinists. The Radical Reformation, leading to the Anabaptists and *Mennonites especially, taught a far deeper divide between church and state and developed a strongly *pacifist tradition, notable today through the work of John Howard *Yoder. The relationship between the church 'visible' and 'invisible' has been an important topic for Protestants: outer structures being *adiaphora* in relation to the 'inner' spiritual wholeness of Christ. This has led to charges of *dualism and other-worldliness, but Protestant history can point to an agenda of social reform and good works on a large scale. Protestantism resists sectarianism in that it recognizes fellow believers in many denominations worldwide, regarding the true church as those in communion with Christ, rather than those belonging to a particular denomination.

Many Protestant churches use the early *creeds, notably the Nicene Creed of 381, but those not favouring formal use of creeds adhere to *trinitarian doctrine upholding the deity of Christ. The English Protestant tradition includes the Anglican Church, framed by *Cranmer especially, but accused by other denominations of maintaining too many customs from Roman Catholicism and of an Erastian position of church and state. Protestantism has been associated with social action in society (see *Social ethics): nineteenth-century Britain saw Wilberforce abolish slavery and Shaftesbury introduce factory legislation; Elizabeth Fry worked in prisons; Nightingale reformed nursing; the 'Nonconformist Conscience' attacked social evils; Methodism was the tap root of the Trade Union Movement. In the twentieth century, Martin Luther King in the US famously campaigned for civil rights. One of the most significant moments in twentieth-century tensions between church and state was Karl Barth's *Barmen Declaration of 1934, summoning the German church to a total focus on Christ and against Nazi ideology. *Bonhoeffer's theology and ministry cannot be overlooked as part of this Protestant church struggle.

World Protestantism

The original Reformation was an event of immense creative power renewing faith and rediscovering Scripture. It spread through Western Europe, then to America with the *Puritans, and across the globe with missionary societies. Protestant denominations include: Lutherans, 66 million worldwide; Presbyterians, 75 million; Anglicans, 73 million; Methodists, 70 million; Baptists, 70 million; Pentecostalists, 105 million. The newer expressions of faith such as *Pentecostalism are growing faster than the older 'mainline' denominations. Protestant missionary movements flourished in the nineteenth century, but now suffer criticism for failing to distinguish sufficiently between culture and Christianity. But Protestantism has found many enculturated forms globally. The phenomenon of the 'mega churches' in South Korea are interesting new developments, associated with Pentecostalism, each church consisting of tens of thousands of members in urban contexts. Such new expressions of Christianity and new structures chime in with the advent of *postmodernity, the breakdown of older forms of identity and the formation of new bondings and modes of Christian life, especially responding to urban conditions and flexibilities of lifestyle. Denominational allegiance means less and less to Protestants, who seem happy to cross structural boundaries, especially the younger generation in an era of globalization and liquid identities.

Strands and tensions in Protestantism

Christianity has always shown change and continuity, and the Protestant Reformation refocused faith in terms of personal knowledge of Christ, and the authority of Scripture as the shaping of this Christ and the doctrine of God at work in history. The history of Protestantism shows some strands stressing personal faith at the expense of the 'propositional' doctrines based in Scripture, and vice versa. *Schleiermacher reacted against what he took to be dry formalist dogmatism by stressing personally experienced faith with the Bible as a fallible source for such experiences. *Kierkegaard focused on individual faith at the expense of all else. *Kant taught that Christianity was essentially a morality, and his influence has been very deep on intellectual Protestantism ever since in the liberal Protestant school. The early twentieth century saw a deep reaction to liberalism in the rise of 'crisis' theology by Barth, stressing the radical objectivity of God, witnessed to by Scripture, and the need for the grace of Christ and his cross. His theology spoke to many in the era of the two World Wars, although his doctrine of Scripture has been held suspect by many liberals and evangelicals, for different reasons (see *Liberal theology). *Bultmann, Barth's contemporary, developed a more individualist path, seeking to equate Christian faith with *existentialist moments of encounter and to 'demythologize' Scripture as symbolic of such moments. Subsequent theologians such as *Moltmann and *Pannenberg have criticized Barth's theological dualism in favour of deepening doctrines of divine immanence in history, reflecting the influence of *Hegel, also present in the British theologian *Macquarrie. *Jüngel develops Barth critically, and his theological work has enjoyed a renaissance in the early twenty-first century, some theologians linking it with postmodern thinkers and their emphasis on the fractured nature of human culture. It is probably true to say that the modern enterprise of biblical studies and *hermeneutics has been driven and dominated by Protestant thought.

One of the greatest challenges to Protestantism is reacting to other world faiths in an era where mission and evangelism are under secular criticism (see *Christianity and other religions). A radical relativism is now one intellectual option, pioneered by *Hick, claiming that all religions lead to God and that missionary endeavour is simply disrespectful and offensive. This view suits Western secular politics as it wrestles with the problems of multicultural societies after large-scale immigration into Europe and America of peoples with Eastern faiths. Evangelical Protestantism, however, points to the 'offence of the cross' as the essence of the Christian message and refuses to allow it to be relativized into a general religiosity. The Protestant tradition has emphasized freedom of personal faith, and tolerance, but now it is faced with the problem of being labelled 'intolerant' merely for commending its own gospel of Christ to other faiths. The classical Protestant doctrines of salvation and *revelation are at stake in such controversies. The tension of love and truth in Protestant Christianity may be posed as alternatives in this problematic situation, but the deeper issue is whether it can be loving to deny the truth of Christ to any human being. Pluralism has become a feature of Protestantism itself, embracing all manner of contemporary movements of thought, notably *feminism and *Marxism through *liberation theology, raising the question as to the limits of Protestantism.

Protestantism has historically shaped the development of Europe and its institutions, and indeed of the *cultures of other continents, including Africa, where it enjoys its most rapid growth. As its old denominational identities lose their attraction, particularly in terms of 'established' churches, it is likely that looser affiliations will develop. Deep tensions exist between evangelical and liberal Protestants over questions of sexual ethics as postmodern culture loses touch with Judeo-Christian morality in favour of ever-increasing flexibility and experiential freedom. Roman Catholic critics in particular have pointed to Luther's *sola fide* as a cause of modern individualism and fragmentation. *Tillich, a Lutheran theologian, has written of 'the Protestant Principle' along similar lines. At the level of theology Protestant and Roman Catholic scholars relate normally, and at denominational level the *ecumenical movement has brought together Protestant churches and Rome in active dialogue.

Protestant Christianity is pluriform, although bound to Scripture as its orientation to God and the world, and ultimately to the triune God focused in the saving act of sacrifice at Calvary. It is not a philosophy so much as a shared faith in the God who reaches out to humanity in *love. This view would be shared by all Protestants, with a wide range of opinion as to how Scripture functions to shape this faith in the world today. The category of 'Protestantism' indicates a very wide range of theologies, ecclesiologies and spiritualities. Troetsch's classification of 'church', 'sect' and 'mystical communion' remains useful as marking the range of Protestant modes of Christian practice and its diversity of approach. Protestantism adopts a stance over against very secular Western culture as an *eschatological voice offering Christlike acceptance and community to a lonely and deeply individualized society; and again it can seem to accept cultural developments uncritically. It is probably safe to say, however, that a focus on Christ and his work, present by the Spirit, portrayed through the Bible, is common to any Protestantism, albeit in sometimes strikingly different ways. The term Protestant itself may be in danger of gradually emptying on the one hand into the category 'evangelical', and on the other 'liberal', as the sharp emotional tone of the division between Protestant and Roman Catholic continues to soften.

See also: CHURCH; CHURCH GOVERNMENT.

Bibliography

K. Barth, *Protestant Theology in the 19th Century* (London, 1972); J. B. Cobb. *Living Options in Protestant Theology* (Philadelphia, 1962); J. Dillenberger and C. Welch, *Protestant Christianity Interpreted Through Its Development* (New York, 1954); P. Meinhold, 'Protestantism', in K. Rahner (ed.), *Sacramentum Mundi*, vol. 5 (London 1970); O. O'Donovan, *On the Thirty-Nine Articles* (Exeter, 1986); H. M. Rumscheidt, *Revelation and Theology: An Analysis of the Barth-Harnack Correspondence of 1923* (Cambridge, 1972); P. Tillich, *The Protestant Era* (Chicago, 1948); E. Troeltsch, *Protestantism and Progress* (Boston, 1958); L. Vischer and H. Meyer (eds.), *Growth in Agreement: Reports and Agreed Statements of Ecumenical Conversations on a World Level*, Ecumenical Documents II (New Jersey, 1984); M. Weber, *The Protestant Ethic and the Spirit of Capitalism* (Harmondsworth, 2002 [1903]); J. S. Whale, *The Protestant Tradition* (Cambridge, 1955); J. H. Yoder, *The Politics of Jesus* (Grand Rapids, 1994 [1972]); H. Zahrnt, *The Question of God: Protestant Theology in the Twentieth Century* (London, 1969).

T. BRADSHAW

PROVIDENCE

The idea of providence arises from the notion of God as Creator. For there must be an answer to the question, how does the 'Maker of heaven and earth' relate to what he has made? Although it is possible to consider such questions from a purely philosophical or theoretical point of view, the Christian answer is derived from the teaching of Scripture. On this view *God upholds, governs and directs the order that he has created to a final end or ends.

Within the Christian church, however, the character of this providential activity of God has been variously understood. On the one hand providence is held to be 'meticulous', reaching down to every detail of the creation, including, crucially, to human free actions. On this broadly *Augustinian outlook, largely shared by the Magisterial *Reformers, even human wills fall under the providential order, and God willingly permits evil while not himself being the author of it, just as he efficaciously renews the sinful will without externally compelling it. On a broadly *Patristic, semi-*Pelagian or *Arminian view, God 'makes room' for human free *will, foreknowing but nor foreordaining it. More radically still, for *Socinianism or modern '*openness' views, God, together with his creatures, faces an indeterminate future even though his resourcefulness is much greater than that of any creature. Each of these views, though not derived from philosophy, typically uses philosophical concepts, from *Aristotelianism or *Stoicism, for example, to articulate the view.

Providence is distinct from *creation. But accounts of this distinction also vary in their emphases. One approach stresses two different orders of causality, divine and human. God is the primary cause, creatures are (different kinds of) secondary cause, with which the primary cause mysteriously meshes and 'concurs'. For reasons to do with the Creator-creature distinction, and also with the problem of *evil, care is taken to stress the separateness of the created order from the Creator's activity, which upholds and concurs with that of his creatures but is distinct from it. Such accounts can be found in *scholasticism and those theologies influenced by it. Another approach sees the divine activity as upholding the creation from moment to moment, and even as continuously recreating it. Here creation and providence are hard to distinguish, and occasionalism, the view that God is the only real cause, and creaturely causes and effects are simply correlations of created events, becomes an option.

Whatever their differences, this spectrum of views is united in distinguishing the Christian view of providence from several others which are held to arise from sub or non-Christian sources. *Deism is the view that God's creation unfolds in time through the original impetus imparted to it by the act of creation. For the deist, divine upholding is vestigial, and miracles are either impossible or unnecessary. Fatalism is dismissed as a pagan notion. It is impersonal, and it detaches ends from their means in a way which is at odds with the Christian view. Chance (in its ontological and not merely epistemological varieties), the idea of un-caused or purely unaccountable events (which is to be distinguished from the view that events occur with no presently assignable causes), is held to be incompatible with the view of divine *sovereignty, for it appears to place elements of the creation beyond the reach of the Creator.

Besides being of theological importance, ideas of providence have important practical consequences for those who believe them. The attitude to misfortune of those who hold that all events are in some sense willed by God is very different from those who attribute some events to the human will alone, or to chance, or to impersonal fate.

Bibliography

P. Helm, *The Providence of God* (Leicester, 1993); D. M. Mackay, *Science, Chance and Providence* (Oxford, 1978); J. Sanders, *The God Who Risks* (Downers Grove, 1998).

P. HELM

PSEUDO-DIONYSIUS THE AREOPAGITE

This name is given to the unknown author, probably a Syrian, of an extremely influential group of Greek theological works in the tradition of Christian Neoplatonism (see *Platonism) in the fifth or sixth century.

The writings in question comprise four treatises and ten letters addressed to persons of the apostolic age (though hints are also made in these texts about the existence of other works which, presumably, have not survived). *The Divine Names* explains God's attributes on the basis of the divine names supplied in the Bible. *The Heavenly Hierarchy* deals with *angels and their triadic hierarchical divisions and functions (i.e. seraphim-cherubim-thrones, dominions-authorities-powers, principalities-archangels-angels, and the threefold function of purification-illumination-perfection). *The Ecclesiastical Hierarchy* deals with the church's hierarchical structures (i.e. hierarchs-priests-liturgists and therapeutes [monks]-laity-catechumens) and their liturgical/sacramental functions. *The Mystical Theology* deals with the mystical union of the human soul with God achieved by means of cataphatic and *apophatic procedures.

Clearly, the addressees of the *Epistles* and the claims of the author point to his identity with Dionysius the Areopagite of Acts 17:34. This view prevailed by 649, when the Lateran Council, summoned in Rome against Monotheletism (see *Christology), appealed to the writings as accredited theological witnesses. This view had already been accepted by such distinguished church authors as *Gregory the Great, Leontius of Byzantium (see *Hypostasis) and *Maximus the Confessor. Once it became accepted, Dionysius' writings were rapidly disseminated, exerting a profound influence, both in the East and in the West, for centuries to come.

At the close of the Middle Ages their authenticity was questioned by Lorenzo Valla (*c.* 1406–57) and especially by *Erasmus, but without procuring a universal consensus, though from now on their authorship remained in dispute. This was true both at the time of the Reformation and during the nineteenth century, until in 1895 Joseph Stiglmayr and Hugo Koch, arguing independently on internal grounds and especially from their literary dependence on Proclus (411–85) and clear reference to later liturgical forms, established that the writings belong to an author who lived in late-fifth-century Syria. Since then, many attempts have been made to identify the author, but without success. The only sure point of an emerging consensus is that he must have been either a *Monophysite or a Monophysite sympathizer.

The obvious question, how an unknown writer could exert such a tremendous influence on theologians of all contexts and ages, can be adequately answered only by reference to the profound content and exceptional quality of his thought. It represents an answer to the two great challenges to early Christianity of *Gnosticism and Neoplatonism, which is based not on the development of a dialectical antipode to either of these but on a vision of catholic wholeness which includes and transcends both. Against Gnosticism it maintains that God is unknowable (*anōnymos*), and against Neoplatonism that he is knowable (*polyōnymos*, with many names, or *apeirōnymos*, of infinite names). In other words, God is both transcendent and immanent in relation to the world, the former relating to his being and the latter to his acts and powers. This view is defended on the basis of the Scriptures as understood by spiritual masters and of a true knowledge of the natural world, and finds its anthropological presupposition in the Christian *ascetical life.

The work of Pseudo-Dionysius is in fact a theology or a philosophy of theology (this is still much debated), which comprises three stages, the cataphatic, the symbolic and the mystical. These are respectively related to the three persons of the *Trinity (theological dimension), to the soul's ascent to the Trinity (*anthropological dimension) through purification, illumination and glorification (or *deification or union with God), and also to the threefold structure of the cosmos.

The cataphatic theology, developed in *The Divine Names*, refers to man's *knowledge of God in his acts (or energies or attributes). The symbolic theology, developed in *The Heavenly Hierarchy*, *The Ecclesiastical Hierarchy* and *Epistle IX*, refers to the threefold knowledge of the world in which God's *revelation (*theophaniai*) is granted (i.e. the sensible world together with the earthly world of human beings and the heavenly world of angels) and to the soul's movement from the sensible to the ecclesiastical (purification), from the ecclesiastical to the heavenly (illumination) and from the heavenly to the divine (deification). This last stage is developed in *The Mystical Theology*.

Though none of his works represents a comprehensive system of theology, the whole teaching of Pseudo-Dionysius presents a remarkable coherence and systematic structure. The terminology is full of neologisms and superlatives. The style leaves much to be desired. The *Christology seems to fall in line with Zeno's *Henotikon* (482), and it is interesting that its central notion is that of 'a new theandric energy' (*Epistle IV*) instead of the traditional 'one' or 'two natures'. Despite the problems surrounding Pseudo-Dionysius, the study of his teaching is indispensable for historical theology in both East and West.

Bibliography

English translations: T. L. Campbell, *Dionysius the Pseudo-Areopagite: The Ecclesiastical Hierarchy* (Lanham, 1981); J. D. Jones, *Pseudo-Dionysius Areopagite: The Divine Names and Mystical Theology* (Milwaukee, 1980).

Studies: A. Louth, *The Origins of the Christian Mystical Tradition from Plato to Denis* (Oxford, 1981); E. D. Perl, *The Neoplatonic Philosophy of Dionysius the Areopagite* (New York, 2007); R. Roques, in *DSp* 3, cols.

244–286; D. Rutledge, *Cosmic Theology: The 'Ecclesiastical Hierarchy' of Pseudo-Denys: An Introduction* (London, 1964); I. P. Sheldon-Williams, 'The Pseudo-Dionysius', in *CHLGEMP*, pp. 457–472.

G. D. DRAGAS

PUNISHMENT

'Punishment' means 'retribution', 'suffering harm for harm done' (*Grotius), and identifies a practice common to every kind of society. Genesis 9:6 is best understood not a statement of the *lex talionis*, but as the basis of retributive practice itself, grounded in our common mortality which gives both crime and punishment its meaning. Theologically understood, punishment is a form of judgment, the public discernment between right and wrong required by God of human society and performed by him in the context of the covenant (cf. Jer. 10:24). Punishment is *judgment enacted on the person, property or liberty of the condemned party*. It is neither irrational, like impulsive revenge, nor inactive like reflective disapproval; it is an 'expressive act' (Feinberg), publicly authorised in the assertion of social order. The retributive idea is that something the offender has put forth returns. But what? Not necessarily equal bodily harm. 'An eye for an eye, a tooth for a tooth' is not a general principle, but simply a measure of damages for specific injuries (Exod. 21:23ff., Lev. 24:20, Deut. 19:21). Although *Kant and others believed the death penalty for murder logically implied by the retributive principle, no universal application of the *lex talionis* can be imagined. Less crudely, it is said that a certain 'advantage' gained by crime is returned by depriving the offender of goods (Finnis). Yet 'wrong is infinite' (*Hegel), and cannot simply be made good. The metaphor of debt and payment is potentially misleading, for the logic of punishment is not that of a contractual exchange. What 'returns' is a reflective response to the wrong in judgment. It is the task of punishment to represent the wrong truthfully and effectively.

As supreme judge, God is said in Scripture to punish, both in history and at the end of history. When 'the nations have sunk in the pit that they made, in the net that they hid has their own foot been caught', the Psalmist recognises that 'the Lord . . . executed judgment' (Ps. 9:15f.). The 'foundational moral intuition' (Moore) of the rightness of retribution is an insight into God's ways. But human punishment cannot be self-justifying in this way (*Grotius). When sinful humans punish one another, further justification is needed in terms of the good of human community. Judgment is intrinsically good, Christians have believed, in contrast to the utilitarian assumption that punishment is a purely instrumental means to introduce a 'motive' into the offender's calculations (Beccaria). Christian thought modified the classical tradition that identified three possible beneficiaries of punishment, the victim, the offender, and society at large, believing that any satisfaction the victim might take in it would be vengeful. The doctrine of the three goods was thus revised in Christian thought to speak of a primary good of just punishment itself and two secondary goods, the benefit to the offender and to society.

Christians of the patristic age were greatly attracted by the thought that punishment benefitted the offender, and following Plato they applied the idea also to penal sufferings after death, giving an impulse to the later doctrine of *purgatory. *Augustine spoke of a 'benign harshness' that stamped the Christian ruler's actions with paternal affection, a conception that had disturbing implications when used to justify the persecution of heretics. Paternal and political authority are not identical; attempts to replicate the reconciling power of the family within political society can often end in ideological deception, a charge frequently levelled against eighteenth-century penitentiaries devised as a remedial alternative to capital punishment. There is no technique for converting an offender, yet there is one good that is always due to him, that of judgment itself, telling the truth about his offence.

The good of society, too, is not something other than good of judgment. If we speak of a 'deterrent' value of punishment, we must understand it not as 'annexed' to a law to secure the 'general prevention' of crime 'at as cheap a rate as possible' (Bentham), but as an aspect of judgment itself, asserting the moral conditions of social existence. In the ordinary administration of justice we have no need to ask whether a given punishment serves the social good or not, for it does so simply by applying judgment consistently. In relation to any *new* experiment in justice, however, the question of whether it serves society is important, and often difficult to answer.

Judgment exercised in punishment must discriminate between innocence and guilt, but with descriptive truthfulness. It pronounces not merely on the subjective guilt of the condemned, but on the nature and seriousness of the wrong done. The scale by which a punishment can be deemed proportionate to an offence is inevitably a conventional one, a symbolic construct of some kind. Different societies will have different expectations of punishment; its severity varies (Montesquieu) in relation to the society's sensibilities, shaped by differing experiences of suffering and differing practical resources. It has meant much for Western civilisation that it has been wealthy enough, peopled enough, and technologically advanced enough to organise and maintain long-term imprisonment, supervised probation and parole etc. These depend on social conditions that have not always existed, and do not exist everywhere today.

Yet that does not imply indefinite relativity of penal practice. There are basic conditions for a just penal system: adequate differentiation between guilt and innocence and among differing degrees of guilt, a will to minimise the incidental sufferings of the innocent and to avoid contempt towards the guilty. The Deuteronomic code limits the number of stripes to be administered in a flogging to forty, 'lest your brother should be degraded in your sight' (Deut. 23:1–3), and we should see in this a categorical rejection of torture. Though their application may be relative, these constraints have been understood in Christian thought as universally important aspects of 'Natural Law'. Different considerations have inclined Christians to favour mildness in punishment to the fullest degree consistent with effectiveness: that God wills the worst sinner's conversion, and that all are involved with the criminal in the wickedness of sin. Human punishment is imperfectible, but it can reflect the evangelical message that God's last judgment will be not only a punishment but the revelation of his mercy. It is this evangelical logic that has guided Christian reflection towards minimising the use of the death-penalty, and dispensing with it when it has seemed practical to do so.

Bibliography

Augustine, *Letters* 138, 153 (*Works of Saint Augustine*, Hyde Park, NY, 2002–4); C. di Beccaria, *On Crimes and Punishments*; J. Bentham, *Introduction to the Principles of Morals and Legislation*; J. Feinberg, *Doing and Deserving* (Princeton, 1970); J. Finnis, 'The restoration of retribution', *Analysis* xxxii (1971–2); H. Grotius, *On the Right of War and Peace* II.20; G. W. F. Hegel, *Philosophy of Right* (Oxford, 1952); I. Kant, *Metaphysics of Morals* (Cambridge, 1991); M. Luther, *Temporal Authority* (*Luther's Works* vol. 45, Philadelphia, 1952); Montesquieu, *The Spirit of the Laws* (Oakland, CA, 1977); M. Moore, *Placing Blame* (Oxford, 1997); O. M. T. O'Donovan, *The Ways of Judgment* (Grand Rapids, 2005); L. Pojman & J. Reiman, *The Death Penalty: For and Against* (Lanham, MD, 1998).

O. M. T. O'DONOVAN

PURGATORY

In the early church questions were asked about the status after death of those Christians whose lives had been less than exemplary. Two different issues were involved. First, the need for purification after *death. *Origen argued that each individual soul receives purification after death, this being related to his belief in the ultimate salvation of all. The second issue was the idea of punishment. The Fathers believed that baptism washes away all sin, but what of sin committed as a Christian? *Tertullian and *Cyprian held that post-baptismal sin dishonours God. When we repent, God forgives us, but because we have dishonoured him we need to offer some compensation or satisfaction to God – by penance, works of merit, and so on. As this was later understood, the 'eternal punishment' due to *sin is waived, but there remains a 'temporal punishment' to pay. But suppose we die without having paid off this debt? The idea emerged that those who die 'insolvent' pay off what they owe by penal and expiatory suffering in purgatory.

Various biblical texts were recruited to this cause. In 2 Maccabees 12:38–45 an expiatory sacrifice is offered for those who have died in sin. If those who blaspheme against the Spirit will not be forgiven in the age to come (Matt. 12:31–32), does that mean that some sins *will* be forgiven then? Paul's statement that some will be saved as through fire (1 Cor. 3:12–15) was also interpreted of purgatory. Prayer for the dead dates back to the martyr Perpetua (*c.* 202). *Augustine famously acceded to his mother's request to be 'remembered at the altar' after her death (*Confessions* 9:12:32, 9:13:36), an important precedent. The doctrine of purgatory was developed in the Middle Ages, with considerable help from Pope *Gregory I ('the Great'). The punishment still owing at death was to be paid in purgatory, where the departed suffer the same pains as the lost in hell, with the vital difference that this is only temporary. This suffering can be mitigated by offering the propitiatory sacrifice of the mass for the departed. When the idea of indulgences arose, these were also seen as effective for the dead in purgatory.

It was, of course, the practice of indulgences that provoked *Luther's protest and his Ninety-Five Theses. The Reformers all rejected the idea of retributive punishment for believers, although recognizing a disciplinary role for punishment (see *Reformation theology). The Council of *Trent reaffirmed the full medieval system.

But what of purification? C. S. *Lewis accepted the idea of a purgatorial purification after death (*Letters to Malcolm: Chiefly on Prayer*). Recent Roman Catholic thought plays down the idea of punishment (though without losing it completely) and instead emphasizes the idea of purification (e.g. in the *Catechism of the Catholic Church* §1030–32, but cf. §1471–79 on indulgences).

Bibliography

J. Le Goff, *The Birth of Purgatory* (London and Aldershot, 1984 and 1990); H. Schwarz, *Eschatology* (Grand Rapids and Cambridge, 2000); J. L. Walls, *Purgatory: The Logic of Total Transformation* (New York and Oxford, 2012).

A. N. S. LANE

PURITAN THEOLOGY

Theology, according to William Ames, 'is to us the ultimate and the noblest of all exact teaching arts. It is a guide and master plan for our highest end, sent in a special manner from God, treating of divine things, tending towards you, and leading man to God. There is no precept of universal truth relevant to living well in domestic economy, morality, political life, lawmaking which does not rightly pertain to theology' (*Marrow of Theology*, 1623).

This comprehensive vision grew out of encounter with the God who called humankind to repentance and faith in Christ through the written and preached word, and who energized them to holiness through his Spirit. Though 'Puritan' was initially a term of abuse, historians use it for those concerned for the further reform of the Elizabethan and Stuart Church of England, because of their particular *religious experience and commitment to *Reformed theology. Their faith was shaped by their struggle with popular religious culture and Roman Catholicism.

Puritans such as Thomas Cartwright (1535–1603), Dudley Fenner (*c.* 1558–87) and Walter Travers (*c.* 1548–1643) had, by the 1580s, given Reformed theology in England a strong emphasis on purity of biblical worship and polity, as part of continued reformation. A small minority saw no hope of reformation, without separation from the Church of England, into a covenanted church of saints. Robert Browne (*c.* 1550–1633), Henry Barrow (*c.* 1550–93), John Greenwood (d. 1593) and Francis Johnson (1562–1618) provided the initial theology for this movement, but their practice and conclusions were rejected not only by the authorities, but also by most of the Puritans, who were firmly committed to a national church.

Henry Smith (*c.* 1550–91), Richard Greenham (*c.* 1535–*c.* 1594), Richard Rogers (*c.* 1550–1618) and William *Perkins worked for reformation within the Church of England and developed a theology which had increasing popular appeal among a cross-section of the nation. These preacher-theologians wrote in detail about the way God's grace could be identified in human experience, penetrating behind formal religion to an inner transformation from death in sin to life in Christ, based on full faith. Puritan diaries and autobiographies reveal how intense this struggle could be, and how personalized were the great themes of Catholic and Reformed theology.

Theologians in the Puritan tradition did not neglect the work and being of Father, Son and Spirit, or the great themes of election, calling, justification, adoption, sanctification and glorification, but their emphases on religious experience and practical piety gave their writings an accent which was unusual among Reformed theologians in other parts of Europe. John *Bunyan's *Pilgrim's Progress* (1676) is a striking example of this difference.

Though P. Helm rightly insists that differences from Calvin should not be exaggerated, shifts of emphasis in the doctrines of *predestination and *assurance reflect use of the work of *Beza and Zanchius (1516–90), as well as expansion of the use of a theology of law and *covenant. By the time the masterly

*Westminster Confession and Savoy Declaration were written, the stream of Reformed theology had cut some fresh channels, including revolutionary and apocalyptic ones. The practical emphasis of Puritan theology led to detailed attention being paid to personal and social ethics in cases of conscience, discussions of *vocation and the relationship between *family, church and commonwealth in the redeeming purpose of God.

Reform of worship and popular religious observance, hearing and obeying the word of God and sanctification of time intersected in the development of sabbatarianism, a unique function of seventeenth-century British Christianity, which was one of the most enduring legacies of applied Puritan theology. The enthusiasm with which this was taken up by many gentry and town corporations indicates how powerfully the religious seriousness of the Puritans and their theological vision of *sabbath rest integrated with more secular aspirations such as control of leisure and the discipline of the socially marginal and disorderly.

The theology of William Perkins was the first major example of a synthesis reflecting *Augustinian and *Reformed theology applied to the transformation of Elizabethan society, church and individuals. His earliest writings were on popular piety. By 1590, he expounded the Reformed tradition in *Armilla Aurea* (*The Golden Chain*) around the theme of theology as 'the art of living well', using the logic of P. *Ramus to order his themes in memorable visual charts. 'Living well' was explored in Perkins' other prolific writings on worship, ministry, family life, vocation and conscience, as well as in published sermons, anti-Roman polemic and detailed biblical commentaries. Perkins sought to give insight into the majesty of God's order and its social and personal implications.

As a preacher he was reported to be able to make his auditors' hair stand up and hearts fall down. That same intensity shines through his writing, which was translated into Dutch, German, French, Czech and Hungarian, making him the first Elizabethan theologian with an international reputation. His writing on predestination inspired *Arminius to write a refutation, which in turn precipitated one of the most important theological debates of the seventeenth century, whose reverberations are still faintly heard. Perkins' personal influence won some important disciples, who helped the further development and popularization of Puritan theology in the British Isles, New England and the Netherlands, where it helped to shape the beginnings of Reformed *pietism.

William *Ames, Perkins' most distinguished disciple, also wrote prolifically, but his forceful criticisms of the Church of England led to his exile to the Netherlands and the banning of his books in England, until the collapse of censorship under the Long Parliament. Teaching at Franeker gave him opportunity to demonstrate his theological gifts to a wide audience. His *Marrow of Theology* (1623) and *Cases of Conscience* (1630) were his best-known works, but his writings on congregational polity and covenant were also very influential. Ames died just before his intended migration to Massachusetts, but his influence there and in the Netherlands lasted into the eighteenth century. Like Perkins, he drew deeply on the Augustinian and Reformed tradition, but also read widely in the Fathers and scholastics to refute Roman Catholic criticisms of Protestant novelty. Ames' practical divinity gave a comprehensive perspective of how every part of life ought to be dedicated to the glory of God, for exact understanding of divine truth must be reflected in the appropriate meaning of every detail of daily life.

By the outbreak of civil war in Scotland, Ireland and England, many with Puritan sympathies had migrated to New England, for they saw little future for their theological tradition in the Church of England. The policy of Charles I and the Laudian bishops cut across Puritan convictions on worship, ministry and conscience. Arminian theology with its rationalizing and anti-Calvinist emphases appeared to threaten foundation doctrines. Nevertheless, Puritan theology still had some formidable expositors, such as Richard *Sibbes, Thomas *Goodwin and John *Owen. Their power as preachers, leaders and theologians gave Puritan theology both popular influence and scholarly depth, complementing the influence of popular devotional manuals like *A Plain Man's Pathway to Heaven* (1601) by Arthur Dent (d. 1607), which set out themes of Puritan theology in very accessible form. Indeed, one of the great strengths of Puritan theology was that it was popularized without being trivialized. As a result, its reading of the Scriptures penetrated every level of British society.

Sibbes, for example, was the son of a wheelwright who studied as a sizar at St John's

College, Cambridge, before becoming a Fellow, a preacher at Gray's Inn and then Master of Catherine Hall. His preaching and life gave him wide influence in the legal profession, but his educational achievements in Cambridge were also considerable. According to Izaak Walton, 'Heaven was in him, before he was in heaven.' His telling imagery and deep spiritual insight rested on solid theological foundations. He exemplified the synthesis between biblical depth and pastoral sensitivity which characterized Puritan theology at its best. His writings are practical rather than systematic, but show clearly why Puritan emphases were so thoroughly assimilated by many laity. He underlined the authority of Scripture. 'Were not faith founded on the word of an infinite God, thoroughly appeased, the soul would sink in great temptations.' Being under Christ's government was essential to profiting from God's promises. That meant the pulling down of human achievement before the temple of God could be built. Pessimistic about the natural man, theologians like Sibbes sensitively explored the relation of grace and freedom in the redeemed. Every aspect of life had to be scrutinized by constant self-examination, so that the temptations to sin were hated as sin itself. Such strenuous and precise piety could become a caricature of evangelical freedom, sinking into joyless legalism (see *Law and gospel), but, at its best, its insights into personal and corporate holiness have been unmatched. Sibbes' writings such as *A Christian's Portion* and *Christ's Exaltation Purchased by his Humiliation* reveal deep insights into creation and incarnation, not just a sharp focus on soteriology.

Goodwin was influenced by both Sibbes and John Preston (1587–1628) and seemed assured of a distinguished ecclesiastical career when he became vicar of Holy Trinity, Cambridge in 1632. He resigned in 1634 after being persuaded by John *Cotton of the rightness of independency. He was in the Netherlands briefly after continuous harassment by the English authorities, but in 1641 his sermon *A Glimpse of Syons Glory* showed that he was deeply influenced by expectations of a new divine ruler, led by the Spirit. He played an important role as an advocate of independency in the Westminster Assembly and was one of the authors of *An Apologetical Narration* (1643), which underlined the need for reformation in polity and life. He remained an orthodox Calvinist, but rejected a national church for covenanted churches freely associated by consultation. He played a prominent part in Cromwell's regime and was president of Magdalen College, Oxford. With John Owen he counter-attacked critics of the intellectual tradition of Puritan theology, warned against the dangers of the Racovian Catechism (published in England 1652) and sought to bring unity between Independents and Presbyterians in *Christ the Universal Peacemaker* (1651). Goodwin's deep personal meeting with Christ permeated all his writings, and he came close to reasoning from experience rather than Scripture in some contexts. He was more interested in biblical exposition than in systematic theology, so that his many books are occasional pieces, rather than an ordered exposition of all the great themes of Puritan theology.

It was John Owen who was, with Richard *Baxter, the great systematic thinker in the Puritan theological tradition. Educated at Oxford and thoroughly grounded in the Aristotelian tradition there, he had a long spiritual struggle for assurance that ended about 1642. His formidable intellectual gifts were given to the parliamentary cause. *A Display of Arminianism* (1643) was a vigorous exposition of classical Calvinism. Initially of Presbyterian views, he was converted to independency by J. Cotton's *Keyes of the Kingdom of Heaven* (1644) and became an influential advocate of toleration for the orthodox in *Of Toleration* (1648). His experience as an army chaplain gave him a vivid insight into the problems of a religion of inner light, but in *Christ's Kingdom and the Magistrate's Power* (1652) he sought to show the differences between civil and religious authority.

His definition of biblical authority and the unity of the Scriptures can be seen in his massive commentary on Hebrews (1668–84). A firm opponent of *Quaker teaching on the Inner Light, he also rejected attempts to give a more weighty role to reason in the formulation of theology by his critique of *Socinian and *Grotian reinterpretations of the atonement and divinity of Christ in books such as *The Death of Death in the Death of Christ* (1647). Owen's exposition of the high-priestly office of Christ and his classic work on the Holy Spirit make his contribution to British trinitarian theology of permanent importance. To the end of his life he worked for a more comprehensive national church and reconciliation of rival dissenters.

Puritan theology remained influential among some British dissenters such as C. H. *Spurgeon until the end of the nineteenth century. Many of the major Puritan theologians were republished in more accurate editions. Likewise in New England their direct influence was still strong in the eighteenth century through scholars such as Jonathan *Edwards. In the mid-twentieth century there was a revival of interest among evangelicals such as D. M. *Lloyd-Jones and J. I. *Packer. The intellectual strength and coherence of this theological tradition is increasingly recognized by historians, despite its eclipse during the heyday of liberal theology. Its success in interpreting the seventeenth-century world has made adaptation difficult in an intellectually different era. But the faithfulness of Puritan theology to the scriptural revelation, its comprehensiveness, its integration of theology with other kinds of knowledge, its pastoral and spiritual depth, its success in creating a lasting tradition of worship, preaching and lay spirituality make it a tradition of permanent importance in English-speaking Christianity and in the wider Reformed churches, despite its distrust of the arts, its over-emphasis on individualism and its tendency to devalue the sacraments into mere symbols.

Bibliography

F. J. Bremer, *The Puritan Experiment* (New York, 1976); P. Christianson, *Reformers and Babylon* (Toronto, 1978); J. T. Cliffe, *The Puritan Gentry* (London, 1984); J. Coffey and P. C. H. Lim, *The Cambridge Companion to Puritanism* (Cambridge, 2008); P. Collinson, *English Puritanism* (Historical Association pamphlet, London, 1983); P. Helm, *Calvin and the Calvinists* (Edinburgh, 1982); E. B. Holifield, *The Covenant Sealed* (New Haven, 1974); P. Miller, *The New England Mind* (New York, 1939; Boston, 1954); E. S. Morgan, *Visible Saints* (Ithaca, 1975); R. S. Paul, *Assembly of the Lord* (Edinburgh, 1984); K. L. Sprunger, *The Learned Dr William Ames* (Urbana, 1972); P. Toon, *God's Statesman* (Edinburgh, 1971); D. D. Wallace, *Puritans and Predestination* (Chapel Hill, 1982); B. R. White, *The English Separatist Tradition* (Oxford, 1971); G. Yule, *Puritans in Politics* (Appleford, 1981); D. Zaret, *The Heavenly Contract: Ideology and Organization in Pre-Revolutionary Puritanism* (Chicago, 1985).

I. Breward

QUAKER THEOLOGY

The Quakers (the Religious Society of Friends) grew out of the religious controversies of the 1650s in England. There are now 20,000 Friends worldwide, but there is no central religious authority.

Early Quaker theology contained both *Puritan and *Anabaptist elements. George Fox (1624–91) taught the apostasy of the visible church from NT times (2 Tim. 3:1–5), and claimed that Christ had now come to gather the true church. Outward belief was powerless to save, for the universal Inward Light (John 1:9–18) was the only way to Christ. The Light led Christians into unity, continually revealed scriptural truth (John 16:13), and enjoined non-violence, strict equality and a disuse of all conventional forms of address. It was active savingly also in non-Christians.

Outward sacraments were rejected as survivals of the old covenant inappropriate to the pure inward worship instituted by Christ (John 4:24). Friends considered creeds to have been created by limited and defective human intellects not under the guidance of the Light, and rejected such doctrines as imputed righteousness, total depravity, and the Trinity. The true church met for worship in silence, waiting for the Holy Spirit to inspire extempore prayers, sermons or testimonies. Ministry, unpaid and unordained, was open to all, regardless of sex.

The Apology for the True Christian Divinity by Robert Barclay (1648–90) provided structure and coherence for Quaker theology. Scripture and the Fathers were used to argue the distinctive Quaker testimonies as the central truths of NT Christianity, from which all other formal doctrines derived their cogency. So convincing was this work that no serious theological development occurred among Friends until they were forced to drop their quasi-Anabaptism and come to terms with a different intellectual climate at the beginning of the nineteenth century.

Largely due to the influence of Joseph John Gurney (1788–1847), over half the world's Quakers are now evangelicals. Scriptural inerrancy and the divinity of Christ can be harmonized with traditional Quakerism, but continuing revelation, doctrinal pacifism and atonement through the Light are harder to accommodate to evangelical principles. This branch of the Quakers calls, but does not ordain, pastors. It has adopted programmed worship, while maintaining the testimony against ordinances. *Holiness movements have had some influence. The Richmond Declaration (1887) is the standard statement of evangelical Quaker belief.

The modern non-evangelical branch combines rational, mystical and liberal tendencies deriving partly from eighteenth-century *quietist Quakerism. The doctrine of the universal Light is extended, incarnational doctrine is attenuated and the basic harmony of all religions asserted. The sense of the oneness of humanity leads this branch to be as active in peace work and social concerns as the other branch is in mission.

What divides the branches is often rival interpretations of what the original message can be understood to mean in changed circumstances. Contemporary liberal and evangelical Quakers are both being challenged by a movement to be found within both groups which takes the original message of Fox, Barclay and William Penn (1644–1718) as its datum rather than more contemporary theologies.

Bibliography

M. Abbott, M. E. Chijioke, P. Dandelion and J. W. Oliver (eds.), *Historical Dictionary of The Friends (Quakers)* (Lanham, 2003); R. Barclay, *Apology for the True Christian Divinity* (Amsterdam, 1676); L. Benson, *Catholic Quakerism* (Philadelphia, 1966); W. A. Cooper, *A Living Faith: An Historical and Comparative Study of Quaker Beliefs*, 2nd edn (Richmond, IN, 2001); J. J. Gurney, *Observations on the Religious Peculiarities of the Society of Friends* (London 1824); W. Penn, *Primitive Christianity Revived* (London, 1696); W. Pollard, F. Frith and W. Turner, *A Reasonable Faith* (London, 1885); G. Richards, *On Being Incarnate* (London, 1979).

J. A. PUNSHON

QUEER THEOLOGY

Queer theology is a distinctive theological reflection, to be understood neither as a continuation of, nor as a component in, the fields of feminist or gay and lesbian theologies. *Feminist theologies have focused on the role of gender construction in Western and Majority World theologies alike, while gay and lesbian theologies have pursued a parallel analysis concerning the role of heterosexuality. Queer theology, as a product of the late twentieth century, has gone beyond *gender criticism and specifically deconstructs heterosexual ideologies and their influence in non-heterosexual identity formation. Its points of departure are: (1) the understanding of (hetero) *sexuality as the main pervasive unquestioned ideological category in theology and religious studies and (2) a conviction that sexual identities are fluid and unstable categories. In the same way that lesbian and gay theologies criticized the essentialization of male and female identities from exclusively heterosexual perspectives, queer theology criticizes the perceived homogeneity of all heterosexual and non-heterosexual identities as deceptive. It also asserts that heterosexuality needs to come 'out of the closet', that is, to analyse its presuppositions and ideological interests. It suggests there is also a need to realize the epistemological implications of queer theory in, for instance, systematic theology, biblical interpretation and ecclesiology.

In queer theology the term 'queer' (originally a term of abuse towards non-heterosexual people) has been reclaimed in a positive way. As with *liberation theology, it has stimulated hermeneutical suspicion and has become a category mediating the critical interpretation and transformation of reality. Queer theology is more than a perspective that unveils sexual ideological formations in theology. It has its own methods and has developed reflections on new areas of theological discourse as well as in traditional areas such as Christology, Mariology and the Trinity. Queer theology is based on the theories of sexuality and gender found in the works of Michel *Foucault and Judith Butler. It uses postcolonial and *postmodern theoretical resources to 'queer' not only the identity of the assumed Christian believer, but also the sexual underpinnings of the construction of Christian dogmatics, ethics and pastoral theology.

Queer theology presents a discourse on sexuality and sexual cultures that has not been considered before in theology. It also has its own orthopraxis, especially amongst Third World queer theologians who are bringing issues of race, class and sexuality into the debate. But it remains a highly controversial project, the orthodoxy and legitimacy of which is questioned by more conservative Christian traditions.

Bibliography

M. Althaus-Reid, *The Queer God* (London, 2003); R. Goss, *Queering Christ: Beyond Jesus Acted Up* (Cleveland, 2002); E. Stuart, *Gay and Lesbian Theologies: Repetitions with Critical Difference* (London, 2003); K. Stone, *Queer Commentary and the Hebrew Bible* (Cleveland, 2001).

M. ALTHAUS-REID

QUEST FOR HISTORICAL JESUS, see HISTORICAL JESUS, QUEST FOR

QUIETISM

The term 'quietism' derives from the belief that God is only pleased to work in the heart of a person whose whole being is passive or quiet. It may be applied generally or specifically. In a general sense it denotes an attitude, found in many religions and at all periods of the history of the church, which suggests that one should 'Let go and let God' or 'Stop thinking and empty your mind of everything' and withdraw, individually or corporately, from concern with the world.

Such tendencies or teaching may have threatened orthodox belief most seriously in the Middle Ages, when they attracted the denunciation of the Flemish mystic Ruysbroeck (1293–1381); but the term quietism is usually reserved for the seventeenth-century controversy which received papal censure. The teaching of the Spanish priest Miguel de Molinos (1628–96) was condemned by Innocent XI in 1687; and the more orthodox 'semi-quietism' of the French nun Madame de Guyon (1648–1717), which was defended by Archbishop Fénelon (1651–1715), was condemned by Innocent XII in 1699.

Molinos was condemned for holding that 'one must totally abandon one's whole self in God and thereafter remain like a lifeless body', since 'natural activity is the enemy of grace and it hinders God's action and true perfection, because God wishes to act in us without us'. This may seem a very spiritual regard for grace and a rejection of works, but in fact it is the opposite. The 'natural' activities of the believer which are discarded include petitionary prayer, self-examination, worship with fellow-believers and participation in the Lord's Supper. All ordinary means of grace are rejected in favour of an infallible short cut: if the believer makes himself passive, God must raise his soul to union with himself.

Quietism also taught that such an experience of union with God was not a momentary ecstasy, nor a temporary stage on the path of prayer, but a permanent stage of 'pure love'. Furthermore, because in this 'mystical death' God was everything and the believer nothing, the believer was not only unconcerned about his own behaviour, but – on the grounds that all his acts were God's acts – he could hold that his acts were sinless by definition, even if they caused actual harm to others. Thus quietism represents an individualistic approach to salvation and an ethic similar to that found in *pantheism.

Quietism is a distortion of orthodox *mystical theology, but official condemnation of the one produced deep suspicion about the other. In Catholicism, uncertainty lasted throughout the eighteenth century and caused a virtual suspension of serious reflection on *religious experience. The effect on Protestantism was even more extended. Quietism had some influence on *pietism's understanding of the Christian life as one of sanctification and *union with Christ. But *Ritschl's rather unsympathetic *Geschichte des Pietismus* (*History of Pietism*, 3 vols., Bonn, 1880–86) did nothing to dissuade subsequent Reformed theologians from feeling that all so-called Christian mysticism was as suspect as quietism.

Bibliography

J. Aumann, *Christian Spirituality in the Catholic Tradition* (London and San Francisco, 1985); M. de Molinos, *The Spiritual Guide*, ed. and tr. R. P. Baird (New York, 2010), see esp. B. McGinn, 'Introduction: Part Two'; E. Herman, 'Quietism', *ERE* 10, pp. 533–538; D. Knowles, *What Is Mysticism?* (London, 1967); R. A. Knox, *Enthusiasm* (Oxford, 1950); E. Underhill, *Mysticism* (London, 1911).

P. N. HILLYER

RABBINIC THEOLOGY

The most important sources are the Mishnah, the Palestinian and Babylonian Talmuds, the Midrashim and the Targums. None of these, not even the Mishnah and Talmuds with their division into tractates, attempts a systematic rabbinic theology. The unity of God and his attributes of mercy and justice (these latter associated with the divine names Yahweh and Elohim respectively) are universally affirmed; most other basic tenets are subject to a diversity of interpretations which, in the Mishnah, Talmuds and Midrashim, are often presented in an unresolved dialectic. In general, the divine attributes of omnipresence, omnipotence and omniscience are acknowledged – the first represented by the concept of *šekînâ*, the radiance, presence or glory of God ('There is no place without *šekînâ*, Midrash on Exod. 2:9), and the last two balanced by a belief in human freedom ('All is foreseen, but freedom of choice is granted', Mishnah Aboth iii.16). The extent of an individual's piety or impiety determines whether the *šekînâ* is experienced as near or far.

Tôrâ ('law') is the privileged possession of Israel and what sets her apart from other nations. According to one view, it is the Jews' obedience to *tôrâ* that will decide the precise time of the Messiah's coming; others held that the time had already been appointed by God regardless of such considerations. That the Messiah would be an essentially human figure is the predominant rabbinic view, based partly on the Hebrew Scriptures and perhaps also conceived in reaction to Christians' claims about their Messiah. The principal function of the Messiah would be to relieve Israel of foreign oppression and raise her to her true status in the world (cf. Targum Isa. 53:8).

The rabbis attributed the human proneness to sin to the 'evil inclination' which infects human nature from birth, if not before. For Jews, however, there is the countervailing 'good inclination' which becomes operative at the bar mitzvah stage, a ceremony which marks the initiation of a boy at the age of thirteen into the Jewish religious community and into observance of the precepts of the Torah. As for the expiation of sins, repentance is effective in averting, or at least delaying, punishment in all manner of circumstances (Mishnah Yoma viii.8). Study of *tôrâ* and regular prayer are regarded as the particularly appropriate exercises of the faithful in an age when temple and cultus are denied even to those resident in the land of Israel. Such meritorious acts could cancel out a weight of guilt and ensure divine acceptance at the last for the one who performed them. One might also derive benefit from the meritorious deeds of someone more righteous, while, on a national scale, the merits of the fathers (patriarchs) were reckoned among the causes of prevenient grace to the people of Israel. An earthly paradise was the prospect for those, principally within Israel, who merited divine favour on the day of judgment; for those who did not, Gehenna had long since been prepared, but rabbinic humaneness is well illustrated by the tendency to limit the duration of punishment therein to a finite period, twelve months being especially favoured.

See also: JUDAISM AND CHRISTIANITY.

Bibliography

I. Epstein, *Judaism* (London, 1959); S. Schechter, *Aspects of Rabbinic Theology: Major Concepts of the Talmud* (Peabody, 1998); R. A. Stewart, *Rabbinic Theology* (Edinburgh, 1961).

R. P. GORDON

RACE

Race is a concept used to distinguish different groups of human beings. Distinctions are made according to a number of criteria, which always include physical appearance and its underlying genetic structure, but which may also include cultural, social, political and economic factors.

This method of distinguishing people is quite alien to Scripture, where the primary assertions are (1) of the unity of the human race, both in creation (Gen. 1:28; 5:1, 2; Acts 17:26) and in the scope of salvation (Gen. 12:3; Matt. 28:19; Col. 3:11; Rev. 5:9); and (2) that the main type of subdivision of humankind is that of 'ethnicity' or 'peoplehood', where the reference is mainly cultural, though religion may be a major factor. Therefore while at times the writers of both the OT and NT refer to peoples with a darker skin colour than their own (Num. 12:7; Song 1:5; Jer. 38:7; Acts 8:27; 13:1), no further significance is seen in the fact. Likewise, most modern scientists refuse to extrapolate from genetic formation to other human characteristics. On the other hand, the existence of 'peoples' is constantly acknowledged. The beginning of Israel's special calling follows from a list of surrounding nations (Gen. 10), and a major theme of both her historians and prophets is her interplay with other peoples. Her calling to be a blessing to all peoples is seen in the NT as fulfilled in Jesus, with the gospel spreading to all peoples, whose cultures are recognized (see the numerous incidental ethnic references in Acts) and affirmed

(Rev. 21:24–26), while recognizing that individuals transcend cultures (1 Cor. 9:19–23) and that ethnic identity has idolatrous potential (Phil. 3:4–9).

Biblical reflection on 'race' in the present world, therefore, eliminates the simply physical and genetic emphasis, and affirms, in a restrained way, its cultural aspect. There is, however, a further and major element in the meaning of 'race' in the modern world: namely that differences in economic well-being and political power at both the international level and within particular nations bear a definite though not absolute correlation to differences in appearance. Such injustice is sustained either by overt ideologies of racial superiority (as in apartheid), or by unacknowledged assumptions, resulting in discriminatory and oppressive behaviour. In judgment on this situation there is a mass of biblical material about God's hatred of social and international injustice, his concern for the oppressed, and his call to establish justice in the world (cf. *Liberation theology; *Political theology).

Any attempt, therefore, to justify treating people differently on the grounds of their appearance falls foul of biblical teaching. In particular, attempts in the late twentieth century to produce a theological defence of apartheid erred in the following ways. 1) They treated 'race' rather than ethnicity as the main determinant (taking Israel's relations with her neighbours as paradigmatic would logically lead to separating Afrikaans- and English-speaking, not African and European). 2) They treated racial and cultural identity as fixed, when Scripture and history show how they develop, borrow, fragment and re-form within the God-given flux of history. 3) They were blind to the ungodly brutality, oppression and economic disparity which were inseparable from the actual implementation of apartheid.

Opposition to immigration in rich Western countries can be motivated by racial prejudice, but it can also arise from genuine concerns about the social and economic effects.

See also: BLACK CONSCIOUSNESS; BLACK THEOLOGY; DUTCH REFORMED THEOLOGY.

Bibliography

J. A. Kirk, 'Race, Class, Caste and the Bible', *Them* 10:2 (1985), pp. 4–14; J. K. Carter, *Race: A Theological Account* (New York, 2008); 'The Lived Theology and Race Workgroup', <http://www.livedtheology.org/workgroup_race.html>.

J. B. ROOT

RADICAL ORTHODOXY

Radical Orthodoxy as a term arose in the mid-1990s and found its clearest expression in a 1999 book of essays called *Radical Orthodoxy: A New Theology*, edited by John *Milbank, Catherine Pickstock and Graham Ward. This book was quickly followed up with a dozen monographs in the Radical Orthodoxy Series, published by Routledge. Radical Orthodoxy does not claim to be a 'school' of thought, but a 'theological sensibility' with some of the following features: a distrust in an *Enlightenment notion of the autonomy of philosophy from theology; a critical engagement with French thinkers in *postmodern philosophy; and an attempt to retrieve features of patristic and high medieval thought for contemporary theology. While Radical Orthodoxy thinkers come from a variety of ecclesial standpoints, its three most prominent thinkers are *Anglo-Catholic (Milbank, Pickstock, Ward), and in many ways the Radical Orthodoxy sensibility is an Anglo-Catholic sensibility as well.

A key theme in Radical Orthodoxy theologies is that the history of theology itself can provide clues to the decline of doctrinal theology in *modernity. In general, Radical Orthodoxy thinkers emphasize the dependence of Augustine and the Cappadocian Fathers upon the broadly *Platonic philosophical tradition, in which creatures participate in the divine life. They also draw upon *Thomas Aquinas as seen in this Platonic light, and vigorously defend Aquinas's formulation of transubstantiation. The movement away from transubstantiation is seen as part of the decline of modernity away from its properly Platonic, participatory *ontology.

In Radical Orthodoxy's theological genealogy, the key mistake of modernity is represented by *Duns Scotus's departure from Aquinas, postulating a 'univocity of being' between God and the world rather than a 'participatory' ontology. Duns Scotus is seen to anticipate philosophies which seek to carve out a 'secular space' for inquiry, since Duns Scotus is said to deny an 'analogy of being' between God and creation. The distinctly modern trust in the autonomy of human reason from the realm of theology is seen as grounded in Duns

Scotus's denial that universals really participate in God.

While Radical Orthodoxy brings new ideas to the contemporary theological scene, its project builds upon certain streams of thought that have been developing for several decades of scholarship: renewed work on Augustine's trinitarian theology and theology of grace; a rereading of Plato in a non-dualistic mode, emphasizing the theme of participation in the One; and the theological work of Henri de Lubac and Hans Urs von *Balthasar. Much of the promise of Radical Orthodoxy lies in the rereading and retrieval of these sources. Nevertheless, the most trenchant criticisms of Radical Orthodoxy come from *historical theologians. In particular, Radical Orthodoxy's reading of Aquinas, Duns Scotus and 'modernity' is frequently contested by medieval and early modern specialists.

Bibliography

J. Milbank, C. Pickstock and G. Ward (eds.), *Radical Orthodoxy: A New Theology* (Abingdon, 1999); J. K. Smith, *Introducing Radical Orthodoxy* (Grand Rapids, 2004).

J. T. BILLINGS

RAHNER, KARL (1904–84)

Rahner was a *Jesuit who taught theology in Germany and Austria, a prolific author, and probably the most important and influential *Roman Catholic theologian of the twentieth century. Although much of his work is quite dense and thus not immediately accessible to general readers, Rahner always considered himself to be a theologian of the church. Throughout his career, his principal aim was to articulate the claims of Christianity to ordinary people of faith in an intellectually honest and practically relevant manner. He played a key role in shaping the directions and decisions of the Second *Vatican Council, and his writings continue to exert significant influence on a wide range of topics in philosophy, theology and spirituality.

At the heart of Rahner's thought is a theological *anthropology which he developed under the influence of the transcendental *Thomism of Joseph Maréchal (1878–1944) and in dialogue with the *existential philosophy of Martin *Heidegger. Rahner adopts what he calls a 'transcendental and anthropological method of theology', which, prior to considering specific theological topics, inquires into the experiential conditions that make human knowledge and activity possible. In other words, Rahner grounds his theology not in dogmatic propositions, but in basic human experience.

Rahner argues that all human beings experience transcendentality; that is, they have an original, unthematic, pre-reflective experience that renders them always and already open to the infinite mystery in and beyond the world. Such transcendental experience becomes conscious only when we reflect on the conditions for the possibility of human knowledge and agency. While this sort of reflection can take place in mundane circumstances, Rahner emphasizes that it often emerges in moments of profound hope, fear, love, longing or trust in which we recognize that there is a self-evident holy mystery which, while transcending all things absolutely, is yet constitutive of our innermost being. Religion calls this mystery 'God'. Transcendental experience thus reveals humanity's intrinsic openness to God, who is ever present to us as the eternal 'more' – the ever-receding horizon which establishes, sustains and orients our entire existence. For Rahner, God is always revealed in the dynamic, mutually conditioning relationship between unthematic, transcendental experience on the one hand, and categorical, historical reality on the other.

On this basis, Rahner aims to breathe fresh life into the traditional faith claims of the church, so that, instead of appearing as fossilized formulations in the language of neo-scholasticism, they can be seen to have existential meaning in terms of universal human experience and its specifically modern pluralistic and scientific conditioning. The message of Christianity is that the infinite mystery of God, toward which human existence is intrinsically orientated, while always remaining a mystery, is given to us eternally and absolutely in 'free and forgiving self-communication'. This grace of divine self-communication ('mediated immediacy') is present in the transcendental experience of all human beings as an offer which can be accepted or rejected, though it grounds human freedom and determines human existence even when it is rejected. Thus, for Rahner, *grace is always already present in human nature and therefore the possibility of *salvation is given by God in human experience as such. This means that grace can be accepted (and salvation realized) without knowledge of the historical Christian *revelation and without explicit faith in Christ by '*anonymous Christians'. These may be adherents of other religions, or may even be professed atheists who fail to thematize their transcendental relatedness as relation to God, but have not rejected it.

Rahner's 'transcendental *Christology' is built upon the human experience of 'transcendental hope', by which each person, in the depths of his or her being, longs and searches for ultimate fulfilment and final validity in life. This means that the need for an 'absolute bringer of salvation' is built into human existence. Rahner emphasizes that transcendental hope always takes place in the presence of its fulfilment – the event of God's definitive and irrevocable self-communication to humanity. Christianity claims that in the life, death and resurrection of Jesus, there has been an unambiguous fulfilment of God's loving pledge to humanity. In Jesus, God's offer of grace and humanity's acceptance of that offer was fully met in history, thereby opening a way for all other men and women to fulfil their destiny in acceptance of God's free and forgiving self-communication.

It would be challenging to find a topic in Christian theology that Karl Rahner has not influenced in some way. In *trinitarian thought, he is well known for his axiom, 'the economic Trinity is the immanent Trinity, and the immanent Trinity is the economic Trinity'. He is also renowned for his robust eschatology, which conceives of God as 'absolute future'. Other areas in which he has made an indelible mark include ecclesiology, the nature of *Scripture and tradition, and the relationship between Christianity and contemporary *science. He also wrote extensively on the theology of the spiritual life, where the deep roots of his own theological approach in the spiritual exercises of *Ignatius of Loyola become apparent.

Bibliography

Works: *Foundations of Christian Faith: An Introduction to the Idea of Christianity* (New York, 1978); *Spirit in the World* (New York, 1994 [1968]); *Theological Investigations*, 23 vols. (London, 1961–81).

Studies: K. Kilby, *Karl Rahner: A Brief Introduction* (Dublin, 1997; New York, 2007); D. Marmion and M. E. Hines (eds.), *The Cambridge Companion to Karl Rahner* (Cambridge, 2005); G. S. McCool (ed.), *A Rahner Reader: A Comprehensive Selection from Most of Karl Rahner* (London, 1975); L. J. O'Donovan (ed.), *A World of Grace: An Introduction to the Themes and Foundations of Karl Rahner's Theology* (New York, 1980; Washington DC, 1995); C. J. Pedley, 'An English Bibliographical Aid to Karl Rahner', *Heythrop Journal* 25, 1984, pp. 319–365; H. Vorgrimler, *Understanding Karl Rahner* (London, 1986); K. H. Weger, *Karl Rahner: An Introduction to His Theology* (London 1980).

A. HOLLINGSWORTH

RAMM, BERNARD (1916–92)

Ramm was a North American *Baptist theologian, whose primary areas of interest were *apologetics, the relation of *science to Scripture and the question of theological *authority. His early university training included study of speech and philosophy, and later, philosophy of science. From 1943 to 1992, Ramm's teaching and writing aimed to establish a secure epistemological basis for Christian truth statements. His thought moved from evidentialist and data-focused approaches, reminiscent of mid-century fundamentalism, to increasing reliance on argument and hypothesis in which the claims of Christianity could be understood as reasonable postulates.

In reaction to *fundamentalist perceptions that science and Scripture were in inevitable conflict, he argued for a more accommodating hermeneutic seeking a valid harmony between scientific and biblical truth claims. Such 'intelligent biblicism' was part of a wider programme in which Ramm urged evangelicalism to engage constructively and credibly with the modern world. Critical appropriation of Barth's view of Scripture, and adoption of a Christocentric hermeneutic embedded in a theology of Word and Spirit, shaped Ramm's later thought. His preferred approach was a creative if critical dialogue between Christianity and its cultural context in the modern world, enabling a constructive 'conversation with the reigning scientific paradigms of the day'.

Bibliography

Works: *Protestant Biblical Interpretation* (Boston, 1950); *The God Who Makes a Difference* (Grand Rapids, 1972); *After Fundamentalism* (San Francisco, 1985); 'Helps from Karl Barth', in D. McKim (ed.), *How Karl*

Barth Changed My Mind (Grand Rapids, 1986), pp. 121–125; *The Evangelical Heritage* (Grand Rapids, 2000).

Studies: G. Dorrien, *The Remaking of Evangelical Theology* (Louisville, 1998); S. Grenz, 'Ramm, Bernard', in *BDE*; K. Vanhoozer, 'The Pattern of Evangelical Theology: Hommage à Ramm', in B. Ramm, *The Evangelical Heritage* (Grand Rapids, 2000), pp. ix–xxvii.

J. GORDON

RAMSEY, IAN THOMAS (1915–72)

Ordained in 1940, Ramsey became a fellow of Christ's College, Cambridge, in 1944, professor of the philosophy of the Christian religion at Oxford in 1951, and Bishop of Durham from 1966. In his philosophy, Ramsey saw the characteristically religious situation as one combining on the one hand a discernment, in which 'the penny drops' and we become aware of something that includes the visible elements of the situation but goes beyond them; and on the other, a total commitment arising from that discernment. God can be the 'objective reference' of such a 'disclosure'. In these cases we find that any appropriate language has logical oddities; typically, it uses *models drawn from other contexts, but qualifies them so as to differentiate them from their normal use and stress the element of transcendence. Thus God is infinitely wise, eternal Father, first cause, and so on.

Bibliography

Principal writings: (cf. *Bibliography* by J. H. Pye, Durham, 1979): *Religious Language* (London, 1957); *Freedom and Immortality* (London, 1960); *On Being Sure in Religion* (London, 1963); *Models and Mystery* (London, 1964); *Religion and Science* (London, 1964); *Christian Discourse* (London, 1965); *Models for Divine Activity* (London, 1973); *Christian Empiricism* [collected papers] (London, 1974).

For critical assessment see J. H. Gill, *Ian Ramsey: To Speak Responsibly of God* (London, 1976).

R. L. STURCH

RAMUS, PETRUS (1515–72)

Pierre de la Ramée, a French *humanist, was educated at the College of Navarre, part of the University of Paris. He was appointed regius professor in 1551. He became a Protestant c. 1561 and was murdered during the St Bartholomew's Day massacre. He advocated comprehensive reform of the academic curriculum, which had been long dominated by universal dependence on *Aristotelian *logic. His stress was on method, on practical utility, on simplification. His method of dichotomous division, whereby any subject could be distributed into ever smaller components and then arranged in diagrams, enabled the whole topography of knowledge to be displayed for instant comprehension. This simplifying diagrammatic method was part of a major intellectual and cultural revolution marking the boundary between the medieval and modern worlds. The invention of printing was already dissociating knowledge from discourse and reconstructing it in spatial, visualist terms. The humanist development of *loci* (places from which knowledge in any given subject could be surveyed) had further facilitated this shift from auditive to visual categories of thought. Ramus brought this process into pedagogy.

Ramism spread rapidly, having a major impact on educational practice until c. 1650. Germany was its principal centre, 133 editions of Ramus' *Dialectic* and 52 editions of his *Rhetoric* being published there from 1573 to 1620. Ramist method was applied to biblical exposition by Johannes Piscator (1546–1625) and to systematic theology by Amandus Polanus (1561–1610; see *Reformed theology). J. H. Alsted (1588–1638) applied it to everything. Indeed, a line can be drawn from Ramus through Alsted to Diderot and modern encyclopaedism. Ramist influence was felt in Holland and also England, where Cambridge *Puritanism had its own stress on practical utility. In seventeenth century *New England it became firmly established at Harvard and Yale.

Despite his support of *Congregationalism, which brought him into conflict with Theodore *Beza, Ramus' influence on theology was indirect, his one theological work (*Commentary on the Christian Religion*, 1576) being of meagre interest. His redefinition of theology, in line with practical utility, as '*doctrina de bene vivendo*' (the doctrine of living well) and its major consequent dichotomy of faith and observance was later developed by Puritan Ramists such as William *Ames. It represented a new foundation in man's faith rather than in objective revelation, and so prepared the way for *pietism. Ramus' method also became associated with the emergent *covenant theology, its rigorous dichotomizing possibly accelerating acceptance of the double covenant idea, with a pre-fall covenant of works additional to the covenant of grace. Ramist focus on the visual could be seen as diverging from the *Reformation stress on the word. Its persistent subdivision, in imposing an arbitrary structure on theology, focused on distinctions and divisions rather than internal connections and, by its rigorous simplification, tended to obscure theology's richness and multiform complexity.

Bibliography

M. Feingold, J. S. Freedman and W. Rather (eds.), *The Influcence of Petrus Ramus* (Basle, 2001); W. S. Howell, *Logic and Rhetoric in England 1500–1700* (Princeton, 1956); R. W. Letham, 'The Foedus Operum: Some Factors Accounting for Its Development', *The Sixteenth Century Journal* 14, 1983, pp. 457–467; J. Moltmann, 'Zur Bedeutung des P. Ramus für Philosophie und Theologie in Calvinismus', ZKG 68, 1957, pp. 295–318; W. J. Ong, *Ramus, Method, and the Decay of Dialogue* (Cambridge, 1958); idem, *Ramus and Talon Inventory* (Cambridge, 1958); K. L. Sprunger, *The Learned Doctor William Ames* (Urbana, 1972).

R. W. A. LETHAM

RASHDALL, HASTINGS, see MODERNISM, ENGLISH

RATIONALISM

The term 'rationalism' is used in a number of senses. It is sometimes used in contrast to *empiricism to describe a particular philosophical tradition inaugurated by *Descartes and featuring *Spinoza and *Leibniz. Where the empirical tradition argued that all our knowledge comes through the senses, without necessarily being restricted to the senses, the rationalist tradition maintained that we possess some ideas that are innate. When the term is so used, 'Rationalist' is sometimes written with the capital letter. However, the broader use of the word is also the more familiar one, where 'rationalism' is used to designate an intellectual approach which gives pride of place to the role and powers of reason. This use of the word

'rationalism' encompasses more than one position and is easier to grasp if we take into account the history of Western thought.

The Christian message has its alleged source in divine *revelation, though it is about events in human history. Contact with Greco-Roman philosophical thought in the early centuries forced it to appraise the role of reason in religious belief, but the Church Fathers held differing views on this question, viewing it in a more or less positive light (see *Patristic theology). In the Middle Ages, translation into Latin of works by Aristotle was a particularly potent factor in highlighting the issue of reason and revelation, an issue that exercised Jews and Muslims as well as Christians. In a synthesis that eventually became extremely influential on Christian thought, *Thomas Aquinas distinguished but did not divorce faith from reason. Aquinas held that some propositions can be secured by either faith or reason (e.g. that God exists) but that others are attained by faith alone (e.g. that God is triune). Reason operates by demonstration; faith believes on authority. (We deliberately simplify here.)

Currents of thought arising from Aristotle, Islam and the Church in the context of the birth of the European University contributed intellectually to the break-up of the 'Thomistic synthesis' and to the separation of *faith and reason. The religious and social conflict arising from the Protestant Reformations of the sixteenth century gradually led a number of influential thinkers to emphasize the role of reason in regulating religious assent (testing claims) and or in determining religious belief (making claims). Although the eighteenth-century *Enlightenment was not a uniform phenomenon and included thinkers who rebelled against excessive claims for reason, Enlightenment thinkers widely judged religious truth-claims by standards of reason as part of their project for regulating the whole of human and social life by what reason could know, independently of revelation. We have arrived here at 'rationalism', as it is widely understood; 'Enlightenment rationalism' is a familiar phrase. In Western thought, modern rationalism has been very largely shaped by its relationship to Christianity.

As rationalism could appeal to both proponents and opponents of Christian (or more broadly religious) belief, so it has been rejected on non-religious as well as religious grounds. *Postmodernity is widely regarded as anti-rationalist in the sense that it does not believe in universal and rational norms ideally regulating human belief and discourse across all times, spaces and cultures. In a postmodern context and perspective, rationalism can seem both mistaken and antiquated, a judgment which may, but usually does not, derive from any particular religious conviction. However, the contemporary intellectual and cultural scene in Europe and the English-speaking world is sufficiently wide and varied for rationalism to remain prominent, whether in a conscious and intellectually defended form or as a functioning practical philosophy. For this reason, quite apart from its massively important role in challenging Western Christianity, rationalism merits no less serious consideration today than it has in the past.

In assessing rationalism, we might preliminarily indicate two limitations upon reason. First, it is difficult to identify a universal, transcultural set of norms or judgments that ought to constrain the thinking of all human beings on the basis of sheer reason. On this point traditional Christianity and postmodern thinking may be in broad agreement. Secondly, even if we persist in speaking of 'reason' as though it were some identifiable transcultural entity or ideal, in practice it may not get very far. For example, John *Locke, 'the intellectual ruler of the eighteenth century' (Sir Leslie Stephen), and often regarded as a rationalist in the broad sense, allowed reason free scope in investigation, but argued that its competence to discover religious truth was very limited, although it might test the credibility of witnesses who claimed that God had revealed something. A contemporary thinker of a very different type, Blaise *Pascal could concur: 'There is nothing so consistent with reason as this denial of reason' (*Pensées*, no. 182).

At the same time, there are at least two features of rationalism that might compel our sympathy, if not always our agreement. First, from an historical point of view, religious obscurantism, the protection and perpetration of institutional (including ecclesiastical) power, and religious strife have all conspired to make it plausible and attractive to appeal to reason as a guide to human life and a peaceful society. The historical context in which rationalism grew and began to hold sway, in Europe in particular, should elicit a measure of sympathy when we consider the religious hostilities that sprang out of, or got mixed in with, the Reformation. Secondly, historically, the appeal to 'reason' has in the past been positively connected with the appeal to 'nature', and it is an appeal that should be taken seriously. In public life, it is impossible or difficult to adjudicate moral debate in the public square by appealing to revelation or to reason, but Christians must ponder the possibility of indicating certain 'natural' constituents of the human condition and social order – for example in relation to *sexuality and the structure of the *family – which might be susceptible to description in terms of 'reason' up to a point and in some contexts. (By 'natural' here, we mean God-given elements of our humanity.)

From a Christian point of view, God's revelation and not human reason is the source of religious truth. However, the NT not only allows, but actually invites people to scrutinize its testimony (e.g. Luke 1:1–4; 1 Cor. 15:3–6), a testimony based on the three senses of hearing, sight and touch (1 John 1:1). When Jesus commended the faith of those who believed without seeing, it was not because seeing was unimportant; it was because most contemporaries and all future generations were or would be in no position to witness for themselves the phenomena in question (John 20:29). This is not to say that seeing automatically means believing, nor that the unbelieving world should be expected to acquire a dispassionate certainty, on purely rational grounds, about the things to which the apostles testified. It is just to say that Christian belief is not detached from the evidence of the senses and that there is a possibility of appealing, within limits, to the broadly rational credibility of apostolic testimony, even if we cannot assess it with rational confidence, several centuries on. But just how much weight should be attached to this possibility is a matter of dispute, even amongst those willing to make some room for it.

The term 'rationalism' is sometimes used in another way and applied to a certain methodological use of reason within theology. Theologians firmly basing their theology on Scripture and revelation, and strongly opposed to giving reason a significant role either as source or as judge of religious truth, may nevertheless make vigorous use of it in the exposition of the faith. They set forth Christian belief in a systematically ordered, logical and conceptual form, showing that reason is vitally instrumental in understanding the content of faith. This is sometimes described as a rationalist or a rationalistic approach. Here, the word is usually being used pejoratively and the question of whether or not it should be applied to vast swathes of systematic theology over centuries in the Western tradition (at least from the Middle Ages onwards) is highly contentious. On the one hand, the attempt to explain the content of Christian belief by applying logical categories can fail to recognize the limits of our reason and confuse the reality of God and his truth with our inadequate concepts. On the other hand, reason is the instrument and logic is a necessary form of thought, so if faith requires reflection and its expression requires coherence, reason is inevitably important.

Rationalism in all its forms needs to beware of the tendency of reason to master ideas by thought; objects of reflection readily become ideas at the reflective disposal of the thinker. It is easy to forget how this appears in the light of a living God. The fear of God is the beginning of wisdom, and humility is properly the cradle of reason even for the non-religious. Only when we are rightly disposed in humility, either believing that there is a divine claim on our lives or taking seriously the fallibility, frailty and bias which marks our intellectual operations, should we deploy the resources of reason in the hope or expectation that they will yield insight.

See also: PHILOSOPHY AND THEOLOGY.

Bibliography

C. Brown, *Christianity and Western Thought: From the Ancient World to the Age of Enlightenment* (Leicester, 1990); K. J. Clark, *Return to Reason* (Grand Rapids, 1990); C. S. Evans, *Faith Beyond Reason* (Edinburgh, 1998); P. Helm (ed.), *Faith and Reason* (Oxford, 1999); M. Peterson et al., *Philosophy of Religion: Selected Readings* (New York and Oxford, 2001); N. Wolterstorff, *Reason Within the Bounds of Religion* (Grand Rapids, 1984).

S. N. WILLIAMS

RATRAMNUS (d. 868)

Ratramnus, who was known to the Reformers as 'Bertram', was an opponent of the *eucharistic teaching of *Paschasius Radbertus. Other distinguished contemporaries of Paschasius have left writings at variance with his teaching, namely John Scotus *Eriugena and Rabanus Maurus (d. 856), but Ratramnus, monk of Corbie, devoted a formal treatise to the matter, at the request of King Charles the Bald. Like the treatise of Paschasius (who was abbot of Ratramnus' own Benedictine monastery), it is entitled *De Corpore et Sanguine Domini* (*On the Body and Blood of the Lord*). Corbie had for fifty years been a centre of *Augustinian teaching, and Ratramnus considered that he could appeal to the teaching of both *Augustine and *Ambrose against that of Paschasius. His positive teaching is not as clear as Eriugena's, though he emphasizes the role of *symbolism and faith; but, negatively, he firmly denies that the sacramental body of Christ is identical with the body born of Mary. Many passages from his treatise were borrowed by the Anglo-Saxon writer Aelfric (d. c. 1020), whose works were published at the Reformation by Archbishop Matthew Parker; but it had a strong direct influence as well, especially on Ridley (see *English Reformers) and in 1559 it was put on the Index. Various English translations have been published, from 1548 onwards. Ratramnus wrote also on *predestination (on the side of *Gottschalk) and on the controversy with the Eastern church. His treatise on the soul, rediscovered in the twentieth century, is to be found in D. C. Lambert (ed.), *Analecta Mediaevalia Namurcensia* 2 (1951).

Bibliography

Works in *PL* 121; J. N. Bakhuizen van den Brink (ed.), *De Corpore* (Amsterdam, ²1974) (critical edition); J. Ginther, *Westminster Handbook to Medieval Theology* (Louisville, KY, 2009); A. J. Macdonald (ed.), *The Evangelical Doctrine of Holy Communion* (Cambridge, 1933).

R. T. BECKWITH

RATZINGER, JOSEPH (BENEDICT XVI) (b. 1927)

An influential theological adviser at the Second Vatican Council, and one of the leading German *Catholic theologians in the 1970s, Joseph Ratzinger became prominent and controversial after 1981 as cardinal prefect of the Congregation for the Doctrine of the Faith. He was elected Pope Benedict XVI in 2005. Like the Catholic *ressourcement* movement, with which he shares an affinity, Benedict's theology is based in a reading of the Church Fathers, from where it derives its considerable spiritual power. Wide-ranging in theme, his extensive literary output over fifty years appeals to academic theologians and intelligent lay readers alike. Two motifs frequently recur throughout Benedict's writings, which underpin his understanding and critique of *modernity. Negatively, he argues that much modern thought arises out of a sub-Christian and *materialistic eschatology for which technocratic reason alone is capable of producing the 'new creation'. This was also the basis of his well-known disagreements with Catholic *liberation theology. Positively, he understands the church above all as a worshipping *communio*, constituted not by its own power – criticism of Benedict's 'ecclesial totalitarianism' (J. Allen, *Pope Benedict XVI*, p. 3) is generally misplaced – but primarily by Christ's self-gift and presence (esp. sacramental), as the given theological basis and living context of all its doctrine, belief and ethics.

Bibliography

Works: *Principles of Catholic Theology: Building Stones for a Fundamental Theology* (San Francisco, 1987); *Jesus of Nazareth: From the Baptism in the Jordan to the Transfiguration* (London, 2007); J. F. Thornton and S. B. Varenne (eds.), *The Essential Pope Benedict XVI: His Central Writings and Speeches* (San Francisco, 2007).

Studies: J. L. Allen, *Pope Benedict XVI: A Biography of Joseph Ratzinger* (London and New York, 2005); L. P. Hemming, *Benedict XVI: Fellow-Worker for the Truth: An Introduction to his Life and Thought* (London and New York, 2005); A. Nichols, *The Theology of Benedict XVI* (London and New York, 2005).

C. J. R. ASPREY

RAUSCHENBUSCH, WALTER (1861–1918)

Walter Rauschenbusch was a pastor, church historian and theologian of the *social gospel. Born in Rochester, New York, Rauschenbusch was educated in Germany and the US, and graduated from the University of Rochester (1884) and Rochester Theological Seminary (1886).

For eleven years Rauschenbusch was pastor of a German Baptist Church in New York City, near the notorious 'Hell's Kitchen' neighbourhood. There he learned first-hand about the devastating human impact of poverty, overcrowding, poor nutrition, disease and crime. He became active in social reform work and was increasingly dissatisfied with the traditional individualism he found in much American Christianity and the economic and political theory of the time.

During a leave from his church in 1891 Rauschenbusch studied in Germany and absorbed a number of important ideas from European thinkers, notably the concept that the *kingdom of God is the central theme in the gospel and should be the overarching theme for theology. He was also attracted to Christian socialism and its critique of laissez-faire *capitalism. In 1897 Rauschenbusch joined the faculty at Rochester Theological Seminary. It was here that he published the series of books for which he would be remembered, culminating with *A Theology for the Social Gospel* (1917). All advocated the progressive transformation of *all* human affairs by the thought and spirit of Jesus, which would lead ultimately to the consummation of the kingdom of God.

Bibliography

Works: *Christianity and the Social Crisis* (New York, 1907); *Christianizing the Social Order* (New York, 1912); *For God and the People: Prayers for the Social Awakening* (New York, 1910); *A Theology for the Social Gospel* (New York, 1917).

Studies: C. H. Evans, *The Kingdom Is Always But Coming: A Life of Walter Rauschenbusch* (Grand Rapids, 2004); P. M. Minus, *Walter Rauschenbusch, American Reformer* (New York, 1988).

H. E. RASER

RAVEN, C. E. (1885–1964)

One of the most distinguished Anglican scholars of the twentieth century, Raven's origins in the nineteenth are reflected in the diversity of his interests, which included theology, biological science and history. A clergyman who preached throughout his long life, Raven was a prodigious author. His achievements included a major biography of John Ray (1628–1705, 'the father of English natural history') and books on ornithology, botany, the ordination of women and pacifism (he was a supporter of both the latter causes). He occupied the Regius Chair of

Divinity at Cambridge and was vice-chancellor for a period.

Raven's theology was deeply influenced by his scientific interests and in particular by his enthusiastic use of the theory of organic evolution to provide an interpretative framework for religion as well as for science. So he saw an evolutionary background even to the incarnation, and sought to understand the God-man as himself within the 'evolutionary series'. Such an extended use of evolutionary theory, common in the earlier part of the twentieth century, has fallen out of fashion more recently. It is interesting that Raven's books include a volume on *Teilhard de Chardin, for like Teilhard (though with more modest proposals) he saw himself as seeking to reinterpret orthodoxy in line with what he took to be the new science.

Bibliography

Works: *Evolution and the Christian Concept of God* (London, 1936); *Natural Religion and Christian Theology*, 2 vols. (Gifford Lectures, 1951–52; Cambridge, 1953); *Science and the Christian Man* (London, 1952).

Studies: F. W. Dillistone, *Charles Raven: Naturalist, Historian, Theologian* (London, 1975); R. F. Rizzo, *Christian Vision and Pacifism: A Study of Charles Earle Raven with a Comparison to Reinhold Niebuhr* (Ann Arbor, 1974).

N. M. DE S. CAMERON

REALISM

The topic of realism is one of the most hotly debated areas of contemporary philosophy, and also in theology and religious studies. There is no single theoretical position univocally termed realism, but rather various clusters of views which, broadly speaking, stress the independence of reality from the human mind. Jarrett Leplin, reflecting on the diversity of generically realist approaches, notes that 'realism is a majority position whose advocates are so seriously divided as to appear a minority' (*Scientific Realism*, 1984). Thus, realist approaches are present in various cultural discourses, where they have different objects: the past, other minds, artistic and literary meaning, mathematical objects, aesthetic and moral values, colours, and so on.

The typical realist thesis can be divided into two. The *ontological thesis holds that these objects have an existence which is independent of the activity of the human mind. To take a simple example, mountains and chairs would exist even if there were no human mind to know them. The *epistemological thesis is that it is possible to have accurate knowledge of these objects. Some theorists would like to add a third type of realist thesis, the semantic one, which holds that it is possible to refer successfully to an independently existing reality.

The above types of realist theses are very broad and they mask a wide variety of elaborations. They do not have to be held together. An ontological realist need not be an epistemological realist, or a semantic realist. On the other hand, an epistemological realist must be an ontological realist as well.

Historically speaking, although realism can be said to have roughly characterized both the *Platonic and the *Aristotelian schools of philosophy, it first came to prominence in the Middle Ages, in the dispute with *nominalism, a philosophical school represented by Roscelin of Compiègne (c. 1050–1125), which denied that essences, or universals, have any reality at all, except as names. Realists like William of Champeaux (1070–1121), on the other hand, held that the classes to which individuals belong have an existence outside the human mind. An intermediate position, conceptualism, made famous by Peter *Abelard, held that universals were real, but they only existed as concepts located within the human mind.

While the medieval discussion revolved around the status of universals and, later, propositions, a broad consensus seemed to hold about the status of particulars, their properties, and the relations that held between them. As we approach modernity, that agreement came under severe attack from David *Hume, who attacked *Locke's *empiricism by arguing that the connections between things are not given in experience, but are imposed by the intellect. Scottish 'common-sense' realism, through its most influential advocate, Thomas Reid (1710–96), rejected Hume's scepticism and insisted that the human mind perceives external objects and their connections directly through intuitive knowledge. This is guaranteed because our mind was constituted by God to know reality directly. Moreover, God also implanted in human beings certain *common-sense beliefs, which do not require any sort of proof. Among these are the belief in the existence of the external world and of other minds, the belief in the uniformity of nature, and the belief in the existence of God.

Scottish realism had a decisive influence on the *Princeton theology of Charles *Hodge and Archibald Alexander Hodge (1823–86) by giving it a philosophical foundation for the notion of our built-in ability to perceive facts and to know reality directly. Just as the scientist gazes openly on to the book of nature, so the Bible, as God's revelation, constitutes the theologian's foundation, his 'store-house of facts'.

Another theologian standing under the influence of common-sense realism is Thomas F. *Torrance. He defended a critical realism against the background of Kant's restriction of knowledge to appearances (*phenomena*). *Kant had denied that we could know things in themselves (*noumena*), given the active participation of the mind in the epistemic process. Torrance was also responding to the so-called 'linguistic turn' which stressed the constitutive part played by language in the construction of objects of knowledge. Torrance's realism is critical in that it recognizes an interplay between what we know and how we know it. However, although we always apprehend things through a linguistic structure, this schematic framework is nevertheless derived from the inherent structure of reality and is open to constant revision in light of evidence.

Critical realism is the most common form of contemporary theological realism, both in biblical studies (N. T. *Wright and Ben F. Meyer) and in systematic theology (Alister E. McGrath, Janet M. Soskice, Donald MacKinnon, Kevin Vanhoozer). McGrath, drawing on Roy Bhaskar's concept of the stratification of reality, insists that reality cannot be reduced to any one of its specific levels, whether physical, cultural, social, and so on. Rejecting reductionist approaches to religion, McGrath encourages a 'connectivist' approach to theology, by insisting on its correlation with the various strata of reality.

On American soil, under the influence of Ludwig *Wittgenstein, Clifford Geertz and Thomas Kuhn, the influential *postliberal theology of George *Lindbeck, Hans *Frei, Ronald Thiemann and Stanley *Hauerwas (to name but a few of its protagonists) accepts the social construction of knowledge while stressing the ontological priority of God. Even while Lindbeck does claim to be a realist, it is not entirely clear that his cultural linguistic model can accommodate the important realist intuition that our epistemic frameworks stand under the judgment of an objective and structured reality. Postliberals Bruce D. Marshall and Nancey Murphy draw on recent developments in analytic philosophy to suggest that the distinction between realism and *idealism is irrelevant because it rests on an implausible notion of epistemic intermediaries (representations). However, the question of whether or not realism can be abandoned rests on whether its essential intuitions (the existence of a structured reality, the subordination of knowledge before the tribunal of reality, the ability of knowledge to put us in epistemic touch with authentic features of reality) can be preserved in post-realist epistemologies.

Bibliography

W. P. Alston, *A Realist Conception of Truth* (Ithaca, 1996); P. Byrne, *God and Realism* (Aldershot, 2003); S. Haack, 'Realism', *Synthese* 73, 1987, pp. 275–99; B. D. Marshall, *Trinity and Truth* (Cambridge, 2000); A. E. McGrath, *A Scientific Theology. Vol. 2: Reality* (Edinburgh, 2002); A. Moore, *Realism and Christian Faith: God, Grammar and Meaning* (Cambridge, 2003); S. Patterson, *Realist Christian Theology in a Postmodern Age* (Cambridge, 1999); H. Putnam, *Realism with a Human Face* (Cambridge, 1990); J. Searle, *The Construction of Social Reality* (London, 1995); T. F. Torrance, *Reality and Evangelical Theology: The Realism of Christian Revelation* (Downers Grove, 1999).

A. VIDU

REBAPTISM

Mainstream Christian theology has generally held that *baptism is unrepeatable – or more strictly, ought not to be repeated. Although often based on a misreading of Eph. 4:5 (where 'one baptism' refers to the common baptism shared by all) and an unhistorical appeal to the Nicene Creed ('one baptism for the remission of sins', which relates to the controversy over post-baptismal sin and could not have encompassed infant baptism), this teaching has its proper grounding in the once-for-all character of Christ's work of redemption and hence of the baptismal initiation into him.

Nevertheless, rebaptism (which is what its critics call it, although for clarity it is unavoidable) has not infrequently been practised and defended, chiefly for the following reasons:

(1) Denial of the validity of an earlier baptism. In the patristic era, *Donatists and other movements rejected Catholic baptism, which they regarded as administered by the fatally defiled clergy of an apostate church. The Donatists appealed to the earlier Catholic practice (cf. *Cyprian) which refused to recognize baptism given outside the Catholic fold and hence rebaptized, but by the Council of Arles (314) this position had been abandoned. Optatus of Milevis (fl. c. 370) and *Augustine provided the theological justification for this reversal.

Baptism has commonly been treated as null and void if any essential feature (notably, a flow of water and the trinitarian name) is lacking. In cases of uncertainty, some churches (e.g. Roman Catholic) have conditionally (re) baptized ('If you have not been baptized, I baptize you . . .').

Several churches at different periods have not recognized some other churches' baptism and have accordingly rebaptized 'converts'. Southern Presbyterians in the USA took this view of Roman Catholic baptism.

(2) Denial of infant baptism as true Christian baptism. The *Anabaptists (literally, 'rebaptizers') and other *Radical Reformers pioneered this position (with only insignificant medieval precedents), but since that sixteenth-century divide such rebaptism has been common, both in new churches holding to believers' baptism only and in individual cases.

In recent times, especially in the context of charismatic renewal, a second baptism has been sought by those unable to regard their infant baptism as meaningful – e.g. because of their parents' apparent lack of faith. Such requests raise acute pastoral problems, but also touch on basic issues of baptismal theology – e.g. the relation between baptism and faith (or experience).

Bibliography

R. S. Armour, *Anabaptist Baptism* (Scottdale, 1966); A. Aubry, 'Faut-il rebaptiser?', *NRT* 99 (1967), pp. 183–201; C. Buchanan, *One Baptism Once* (Nottingham, 1978); T. H. Lyle, 'Reflections on "Second Baptism"', *IJT* 21 (1972), pp. 170–182; D. F. Wright, 'One Baptism or Two? Reflections on the History of Christian Baptism', *Vox Evangelica* 18 (1988), pp. 7–23; idem, *What Has Infant Baptism Done to Baptism* (Milton Keynes, 2005).

D. F. WRIGHT

RECONCILIATION, see ATONEMENT

REDEMPTION

The term 'redemption' is often used to refer to the whole scope of *salvation or *atonement. As a theological concept, however, it speaks more specifically of the aspect of Christ's work that delivers humanity from the binding power of *sin and *evil. As such, redemption is a metaphor that draws from the world of slavery and commercial transactions to explain the significance of Christ's work in the face of the tyrannical rule of sin and evil.

Redemption through the ages

The background to the Christian use of this metaphor has been extensively researched. In the Greco-Roman world, slaves could be set free by payment of a ransom price to their owners. The OT also contains numerous examples of redemption. For the early Christians, redemption was a vivid parable of the deliverance from sin and evil that they experienced through faith in Christ, and of their subsequent obligation to live as servants of God.

Throughout the writings of the early church, redemption is consistently associated with the crucifixion of *Jesus Christ (see *Cross). His suffering and death are the ransom price for us, redeeming us from the power of sin and delivering us from the 'sharpness of death' (words from the *Te Deum*). This association has continued in much of the theology, devotional practice and art of the Western church, both Catholic and Protestant.

Redemption has also been associated more broadly with the whole of Christ's life. In the second century Irenaeus emphasized the connection between redemption and the *incarnation. The Son of God became flesh as the Second *Adam, to restore what had been lost by sin and death from the original creation. For Eastern Christians, the redemptive work of Christ often includes his descent to the dead, the 'harrowing of hell' and the *resurrection.

While all Christians agree that redemption is accomplished by Christ, the way in which we are delivered from slavery to sin has been a matter of much theological reflection. *Origen produced an elaborate account of redemption in which Satan receives the payment of Christ's life as a ransom for those who are his prisoners. Later, *Anselm taught that it was not Satan who required a payment, but God, as restitution for the obedience and praise we owe God but are not able to give him because of our sin. In subsequent developments of this strand of thought, Western theology has tended to speak of redemption as the result of Christ's *satisfaction of divine justice. An important work by Gustaf *Aulén tries to recapture what he calls the 'classic' picture of Christ's redemptive work – that of *Christus Victor*, in which Christ triumphs over the powers of sin, evil and Satan.

Some systematic issues

The overwhelmingly positive point of redemption is that Christ delivers the world from bondage to sin and evil and transfers both the Christian and, in the future, the whole of creation, into the glorious freedom of the *kingdom of God. However, as with all metaphors or parables, the image of redemption includes some aspects that we must take care to avoid. In this case, we are not encouraged to work out to whom the ransom price was paid. Origen's view gives too much power to Satan by suggesting that he was the rightful master of the world to whom a ransom must be given, and some developments of Anselm's thought could diminish the freedom of God by suggesting that he is held to ransom by his own justice.

While avoiding these misconceptions, we can affirm the importance of understanding and proclaiming redemption today. Redemption describes the cosmic significance of Christ's work, and looks both backwards to the life, death and resurrection of Jesus, and forwards to the consummation of that redemptive work in the new *creation. A theology of redemption must affirm God's love and concern for the world he has made, his immense power in overcoming evil and generating new life, and his promise to complete this work through the redemption of our bodies, the resurrection of the dead (see *Resurrection, general).

Bibliography

G. Aulén, *Christus Victor* (London, 1970); S. T. Davis, D. Kendall and G. O'Collins (eds.), *The Redemption* (Oxford, 2004); G. O'Collins, *Jesus Our Redeemer* (Oxford, 2007).

A. J. STOBART

REFORMATION THEOLOGY

The *Protestant Reformation produced a theology that was a massive reassertion of the centrality of *God, the glory of his *sovereignty, and the primacy of his *grace in the *salvation of humanity through *Jesus Christ.

Basic principles

To Martin *Luther it was a revolutionary discovery that the *righteousness of God is 'the righteousness by which we are made righteous' (*LW* 25, p. 151). Medieval thinkers, he believed, had led Christendom astray by teaching that human persistence in doing good moral and ritual actions would earn *merit in the eyes of God and enable sinners to achieve salvation. But the appalling consequences of *sin had so paralysed the *will that sinners could not take the least step towards pleasing God. Close study of the teaching of Paul, however, led Luther to the conviction that through *faith in Jesus Christ – a faith which is itself God's gift – a sinner is granted free and full pardon. He is *justified by faith, not by his own achievements but because Christ bestows upon him the merits that he (Christ) has won through his victory over *sin, *death, the *law and the *devil, the 'tyrants' which have held sinful humanity in thrall. So justification is a forensic declaration of pardon which in no way depends upon human merit.

All the Magisterial Reformers followed Luther in this matter. *Calvin indeed did insist that the hidden work of the *Holy Spirit, in bringing a sinner to exercise faith, also *regenerated him into a new life, because to believe in Christ of necessity means coming into personal *union with him. The righteousness of faith thus manifests itself in the good works that spring from that union. But this so-called 'double justification' did not jeopardize the emphasis on primary justification by faith alone. Rather was it a way of understanding the connection between justification and *sanctification. The Reformers had no wish to minimize the role of morality in Christian living, but they were adamant that it was the product of justification, not its cause.

The Reformers were also agreed upon the authority of *Scripture. For Luther, Scripture is the word of God. Its human authors wrote under the inspiration of the Holy Spirit, and that ensured its accuracy – not only in its general teaching, but also in its verbal details. This did not preclude a critical attitude to the transmitted text; knowledge of Hebrew and Greek was necessary in order to get as close as possible to the original autographs. The Bible is the possession of the whole people of God, and so translation into the various national languages is a necessity, for how could the public acquire a knowledge of the truth, asked William Tyndale, 'except ye scripture were playnly layd before their eyes in their mother tonge?' (Foreword to the Pentateuch).

God the Holy Spirit is the true expositor of the Bible, as *Zwingli explained in his book, *The Clarity and Certainty of the Word of God* (1522). The pope could claim no monopoly in expounding it. The key of interpretation, said Luther in his appeal *To the Christian Nobility of the German Nation* (1520), was given not to Peter and his successors at Rome, 'but to the whole community'. Calvin gathered into a more systematic form the insights of his predecessors. He emphasized the self-authenticating character of the Bible (*Institutes* 1.vii.2–4), as its objective witness is confirmed by the internal testimony of the Holy Spirit in the believing heart. The relation between the Holy Spirit and the Bible is therefore a very close one. To separate them from each other is to embrace either a lifeless biblicism or the vagaries of spiritual enthusiasm.

Application

The application of these two principles, *sola fide* and *sola Scriptura*, led to striking consequences. It led to a critical modification of medieval belief and practice. Church tradition could no longer be acknowledged as a standard independent of the Bible. That meant a severe curtailment of the luxurious growth of allegorical interpretation and an insistence that biblical exposition should be grounded upon the literary and historical meaning of the text. The belief in *purgatory was abandoned for lack of scriptural proof. The cults of the *saints and of the Virgin *Mary were demolished in the light of the doctrine that Christ is the sole mediator between God and man.

On the other hand, those doctrines and declarations of faith that were consonant with Scripture were retained. Thus the classical doctrines of the *Trinity and the *incarnation were retained, as well as the definitions which expressed them, such as the Apostles' Creed, the Nicene Creed and the Definition of Chalcedon. Soon the Reformers set to it to expound their own understanding of theology. Although Luther produced no systematic exposition of his theology, he made a massive contribution in a large number of publications, among which his treatises of 1520, together with his commentaries on Galatians and Romans, are crucial to an understanding of his thought. Philipp *Melanchthon attempted the first systematic exposition of *Lutheran theology in his *Loci Communes* (1521), and the Lutheran movement produced as a definitive exposition of its faith the *Augsburg Confession (1530). Zwingli had produced the most mature expression of his theology, *True and False Religion*, in 1525. But pride of place must be given to Calvin's *Institutes of the Christian Religion*. The first edition of 1536 was expanded over the years to become the impressive masterpiece of the 1559 edition. While using the pattern of the Apostles' Creed as his framework, Calvin meant his book to be a manual for Bible readers. It is unwise therefore to seek to expound his thought in terms of one dominating doctrine, such as predestination or divine sovereignty. The work is characterized by a well-balanced treatment of complementary doctrines, each contributing towards a harmonious integration of the richness of biblical teaching.

So the Protestant Reformation released a vast amount of creative theological energy which is only partially suggested by the tags, 'faith alone', 'Scripture alone', 'Christ alone', 'grace alone' and 'to God alone be glory'.

Different emphasis

Even in those theological areas where the Reformers accepted the formulations of classical Catholic orthodoxy, there were variations of emphasis. Thus, with regard to the doctrine of God, there was a new dynamism. Luther, in his exposition of the 'theology of the *cross', introduced penetrating insights as he expounded the paradox of the glorious God who reveals himself, and yet conceals himself (see *Hidden and revealed God), in the mystery of abasement and *suffering. For Calvin, similarly, God is no remote and static divinity, but one who intervenes in a dynamic and revolutionary way in human *history. For both of them divine grace is not an impersonal quality, as it so often was in medieval theology, but a personal involvement.

In *Christology again there were differences of emphasis amongst the Reformers. Luther was always concerned to accentuate the oneness of Christ's person, while Zwingli and Calvin underlined the distinction between the two natures. In the case of Calvin, his exaltation of Christ's divinity did lay him open to the charge of minimizing his human nature. On the other hand, some *Anabaptists such as the Melchiorites rejected the teaching of the Chalcedonian Definition and maintained that Jesus' body was composed of 'celestial flesh', a unique product of the Virgin's womb, substantially different from ordinary human flesh.

Yet another area where differences of emphasis emerged was in the understanding of the relationship between *law and gospel. All the Magisterial Reformers took a sombre view of the radical effects of sin and rejected the medieval doctrine that man's natural gifts were only partially affected by the fall. On the contrary, man's will had become enslaved through sin, as Luther demonstrated in his *Bondage of the Will* (1525), and his mind darkened. For Luther, the chief function of the law was to convict man of his sin. It accused but could not save. Only the gospel could save. So Luther, and his colleague Melanchthon, distinguished sharply between law and gospel. Calvin did not dismiss the accusatory aspect of the law in revealing the need for a saviour, but for him the chief function of the law was to inspire the justified sinner to aim at moral perfection. So gospel and law are to work hand in hand, for the *covenant of grace provides the setting for the law. It was this conviction that injected into Calvinism its moral activism both in the life of the individual and in society.

According to the Augsburg Confession, the church 'is the congregation of the saints, in which the gospel is rightly taught and the sacraments rightly administered'. And Calvin agrees with this definition (*Institutes* IV.i.8). Indeed, Luther and Calvin were in close agreement about the nature of the *church. The true church, known to God alone, is a company of justified sinners. But the visible church at Geneva or Wittenberg also contained hypocrites who lacked saving faith. It follows that the visible church is a mixed company, but as long as it ensures the right preaching of the gospel and the right administration of the *sacraments, it is still a true church. Calvin, unlike Luther, believed that in view of this it was necessary for the church to submit itself to constant self-examination. Its members must accept a system of pastoral *discipline to purify it, just as its ministers should be diligent to test their doctrine by the word of God. The reformation of the church is not an act but a process. The reformed church must be a reforming church, not a church which emulates Rome's boast that it is *semper eadem*, always the same.

The sacraments

It was by the stringent application of scriptural standards that the Reformers came to reject the sacramental system of the Church of Rome. The attack upon it had been launched by Luther in *The Babylonian Captivity of the Church* (1520). Christ's *sacrifice on Calvary was a complete and final oblation for the sins of the world. The doctrine that the Mass was an unbloody repetition of that sacrifice had therefore to be rejected. Nor should the offering of the Mass be considered a meritorious work. Holy Communion is Christ's gift to his people, and it is their offering to him only in the sense that it is an offering of praise and thanksgiving. Although Luther in 1520 still listed *penance as a sacrament (but only in a severely qualified sense), the Protestant consensus was that Christ had instituted only two sacraments, baptism and the Eucharist. With this radical transformation of the concept of sacrament, the Roman Church's claim to be the sole dispenser of grace was nullified, and the priesthood stripped of its quasi-magical pretensions.

Further, the Reformers sought to eradicate the Roman Catholic distinction between priest and layman. Luther put the point with characteristic vigour: 'It has been devised that the pope, bishops, priests and monks are called the spiritual estate; princes, lords, artificers and peasants are the temporal estate. This is an artful lie . . . all Christians are truly of the spiritual estate' (*To the Christian Nobility*, 1520). This is the principle of the '*priesthood of all believers'. All offices in the church are functions of the common ministry of the community of faith.

Despite the fact that the Reformers were of a common mind in their criticisms of the Roman Catholic doctrines of the sacraments, they were unable to agree about the precise nature of the biblical doctrines that should replace them. Luther and Calvin were agreed that *baptism involves washing in water in the name of the Trinity, that it is a sign of God's pledge to forgive sin, that it is to be closely connected with the death of Christ and his *resurrection, and that baptism is a commitment to lifelong *repentance. They were also agreed that it was appropriate to baptize infants on the grounds that the benefits of God's covenant with the parents applied to their offspring, and that Jesus had blessed infants and declared that 'of such is the kingdom of heaven'; also (in the case of Calvin) because the Holy Spirit may well act secretly even in the personality of an infant, as was the case with John the Baptist and Jesus (*Institutes* IV.xvi; Luther, *The Holy and Blessed Sacrament of Baptism*, LW 35; Zwingli, *On Baptism and Exposition of the Faith*).

The validity of infant baptism was challenged by the *Anabaptists. For them, baptism with water is of no avail unless it is preceded by the inner *baptism of the Spirit. Water baptism is the external sign of the commitment of faith. Since infants are incapable of exercising faith, they cannot be appropriate subjects for baptism. This was the position which drove George Blaurock and Conrad Grebel to reject infant baptism, and so to initiate the Anabaptist movement by rebaptizing those who adopted their convictions. Much was involved in their protest, because baptism on profession of faith became for them the door of entry into the church. They consequently challenged the principle, enunciated by the Magisterial Reformers, that the church was a 'mixed company'. Rather, it must be a covenanted community of sincere believers. Such a position aroused the intense opposition of the authorities; it led directly to a denial of the concept of an established church in which people, by virtue of their citizenship, were also under the pastoral jurisdiction of the church.

Similarly, there was bitter acrimony among Protestants about the Eucharist. In article 15 of the confession signed by the participants at the Colloquy of Marburg (1529) to seek a common mind on the subject, it was agreed that the Lord's Supper should be celebrated in both kinds, that the Mass was not to be deemed a good work which ensured pardon for the living and the dead, and that it is the sacrament of the very body and blood of Jesus Christ. But they failed to agree about the precise nature of Christ's presence in the sacrament. Luther held that 'in the Supper we eat and take to ourselves Christ's body truly and physically' (*That These Words of Christ, 'This is my body' &c., Still Stand Firm*, 1527). Zwingli, supported by *Oecolampadius, denied this physical presence 'in, with and under' the elements. They held that Christ's body is in heaven and could not be ubiquitous. His divine nature, however, is ubiquitous, and to be nourished by the sacrament is to partake of Christ's spirit through faith in the heart. So Zwingli did not deny Christ's presence in the sacrament, but he insisted that it was a real spiritual presence. Luther, however, was adamant. When Christ said, 'This is my body', he meant the word 'is' to be taken in a literal and not a figurative sense. The differences remained unresolved.

Calvin was dissatisfied with both positions. In Book IV of the *Institutes* he carefully expounded his own position. The sacrament has no efficacy when dissociated from the gospel. Word and sign go together. Moreover, the sacrament is made efficacious by the operations of the Holy Spirit in the heart of the participant. This is to say that in the Eucharist there is a personal, not mechanical, relationship between God and the believer. Christ is the true substance of the sacrament, and the bread and wine are signs of the invisible food which he provides, namely, his body and blood. Christ's physical body is not ubiquitous and there is no question of its being brought down from heaven to the table by the words of institution. Rather, it is true to say that, thanks to the work of the Holy Spirit, the communicants are raised to the heavenly places to share communion with their Lord. So there is a real, but spiritual and personal, presence of Christ in the Eucharist. But none of these solutions commanded general support among Protestants.

A theology of grace which emphasizes that salvation is entirely God's work is compelled to pay close attention to the biblical doctrine of divine *predestination. Salvation is entirely God's work. Faith itself is God's free gift. Is unbelief therefore also willed by God? The leading Reformers were agreed that God elected believers to eternal life and ensured their ultimate salvation on the basis of his own gracious decision, not because of any qualification in them. It was Calvin who made the most careful study of divine election. But he confessed that he could not see how it was possible to acknowledge election to life 'except as set over against reprobation' (*Institutes* III.xxiii.1). Yet he does not put them on an equal basis. God actively elects those whom he saves, but 'passes over' the reprobate. Even so, Calvin was convinced that even this 'passing over' was according to the divine plan, for the reprobate 'have been raised up by the just but inscrutable judgment of God to show forth his glory in their condemnation' (*Institutes* III.xxiv.1–4).

Those who stood on the *radical wing of the Reformation found this predestinarianism unacceptable. Thus Melchior Hofmann (*c*. 1495–1543) in *The Ordinance of God* argued that those who were in covenant with God would through *perseverance attain election. Similarly, Balthasar *Hubmaier in *On Free Will* developed the thesis that, despite the effects of sin, man is not entirely deprived of the capacity to choose: 'God gives power and capacity to all men in so far as they themselves desire it.'

The theology of the Protestant Reformation is an imposing intellectual achievement; it was to have a profound influence upon modern civilization.

See also: CONFESSIONS OF FAITH; REFORMED THEOLOGY; REFORMERS, ENGLISH.

Bibliography

Works: see under individual Reformers, and Confessions. LCC vols. XV–XXVI presents writings by all the leading Reformers. *The Documents of Modern History* series (London, 1970–83) includes volumes on Luther, Calvin, Zwingli. Note also: H. J. Hillerbrand, *The Reformation in Its Own Words* (London, 1964).

Studies: see under individual Reformers, etc. Note also: D. Bagchi and D. C. Steinmetz (eds.), *The Cambridge Companion to Reformation Theology* (Cambridge, 2004); G. W. Bromiley, *Historical Theology: An Introduction* (Edinburgh, 1978); W. Cunningham, *The Reformers and the Theology of the Reformation* (Edinburgh, 1862); R. T. Jones, *The Great Reformation* (Leicester, 1986); E. Léonard, *A History of Protestantism*, 2 vols. (London, 1965–67); C. Lindberg (ed.), *The Reformation Theologians* (Oxford, 2002); J. T. McNeill, *The History and Character of Calvinism* (New York, 1954); W. Pauck, *The Heritage of the Reformation* (Glencoe, ²1961); J. Pelikan, *Reformation of Church and Dogma (1300–1700)*, in *The Christian Tradition* 4 (Chicago and London, 1983); B. M. G. Reardon, *Religious Thought in the Reformation* (London, 1981); G. H. Williams, *The Radical Reformation* (London, 1962).

R. T. JONES

REFORMATION, CATHOLIC COUNTER-

The term Catholic or Counter-Reformation refers to the reform movement in the Catholic Church that began before the Protestant *Reformation and continued throughout the sixteenth and early seventeenth centuries. In past years Protestant historians have tended to label it the 'Counter-Reformation', suggesting that its major emphasis was to 'counter' the impact of Protestantism. Catholic historians preferred the label 'Catholic Reformation', because it emphasized the positive reforming aspects of the movement. They also argued that since Catholic reform began before the Protestant Reformation, it was not simply a reaction to it. There was a time when one could recognize the bias of the historian by the title used, but this is no longer the case. As religious bias abated, historians began to recognize that both terms have an element of truth.

Catholic reform clearly began before the Protestant Reformation. Although many of the medieval efforts at reform were thwarted by the vested interests of the church hierarchy, and the so-called Renaissance papacy was not particularly active in initiating reforms, reform movements originating from sources other than the papacy were widespread well before the beginning of the Lutheran Reformation. Cardinal Francisco Ximenes de Cisneros (1436–1517) led a major reform movement in Spain. He set about improving the calibre of the Spanish clergy and encouraged biblical study through the printing of a six-volume *Complutensian Polyglot Bible*. Unfortunately, intolerance and persecution of dissenters were also associated with the Spanish reform movement. In 1478 the Spanish Inquisition was set up as a special court to prosecute suspected *heretics, and for a period of time Cisneros served as its Inquisitor General. Another Spanish reformer was *Teresa of Avila who, with her co-worker John of the Cross, led a significant monastic reform movement. She also helped popularize a *mystical *spirituality that was to become one of the major characteristics of the Catholic Reformation.

In Italy groups called Oratories of Divine Love played a major role in church reform. These were small, urban religious societies that sought the inward renewal of their members through religious exercises and prayer as well as frequent Communion. They were also committed to putting their faith into practice through service to the poor. The original inspiration for establishment of the oratories came from the life and work of St Catherine of Genoa (1447–1510), whose life of selfless service in the care of the sick, and profound spirituality, inspired a wealthy layman to found an oratory in Genoa in 1497. Oratories were also established in a number of other important Italian cities, including Florence, Milan, Verona, Naples and Padua. The Genoa oratory eventually moved to Rome, where it included among its members many of the future leaders of the Catholic Reformation, including Jacopo Sadoleto (1477–1547), Gaetano Thiene (1480–1547), Reginald Pole (1500–58), Gian Pietro Carafa (1476–1559) and Gasparo *Contarini. The group met regularly for prayer, meditation, mutual encouragement, and discussions about reforming the institutional church. New monastic orders such as the Theatine Order, founded in 1524, also played leading roles in the Catholic reform movement.

Some of the most committed reformers were known in Italy as the *spirituali* and included members of the Roman Oratory of Divine Love, such as Gasparo Contarini, whose understanding of justification came very close to Luther's position. Pope Paul III (1534–49) made Contarini a cardinal in 1535, and he appointed him and other Catholic reformers to serve on a Papal Reform Commission that was set up to study church reform and to make recommendations. The report of the commission, issued in March 1537, was brutally honest in identifying some of the areas that needed reform. While praising Paul III for his commitment to reform, it attributed many of the evils in the church to the actions of previous *popes. It also criticized the lifestyle of the cardinals and their failure to give adequate attention to spiritual matters. In addition, the report was scathing in its commentary on the gross immorality prevalent in Rome. It was in fact so devastating in its critique of church abuses that its publication was delayed, and it was printed without authorization in 1538. Luther even published a German translation, because it so effectively detailed the abuses in the Catholic Church.

By the late 1530s the Catholic reform movement was well under way, but *Protestantism was also gaining in strength and spreading. Catholic reformers were divided on how to deal with Protestants. Contarini and other *spirituali* were committed to finding a way to reconcile them to Rome, while reformers such as Carafa believed that suppression was the only way to deal with heretics. In 1541 a colloquy was held in Regensburg, Germany where Protestants and Catholics, including Contarini, met in an effort to arrive at reconciliation. The most surprising achievement of the colloquy was that the participants reached an agreement on the doctrine of *justification. However, neither Luther nor hard-line Catholics like Carafa were pleased with the agreement, and the participants were unable to reconcile differences over the *Eucharist and papal authority. Although Contarini remained hopeful that conciliation might still be achieved, he died in 1542. Even before his death those who were committed to suppression rather than dialogue were beginning to introduce their methods. In July 1542 Pope Paul III bestowed on Carafa the power to establish an Inquisition in Italy. Thirteen years later Carafa was elected Pope Paul IV (1555–59). During his pontificate he not only promoted the Inquisition, but he also issued an *Index of Prohibited Books* that listed those books which were prohibited reading for Catholics. It initially included all vernacular translations of the Bible.

The course of the Catholic Reformation was significantly influenced by a new monastic order called the Society of Jesus that was founded by Ignatius *Loyola in 1540. Popularly known as the *Jesuits, they played a major role in the Catholic Reformation and were responsible for missionary work in the New World, Africa and the Far East. One of the most impressive Jesuit missionaries was Francis Xavier (1506–52), who, after beginning work in the Portuguese colony in India, went on to other areas of Asia, including Sri Lanka, Malaysia and Indonesia, eventually ending in Japan. He died as he was attempting to enter China. Other Jesuit missionaries, including Matteo Ricci (1552–1610), Robert de Nobilit (1577–1656) and Alexandre de Rhodes (1592–1660), continued the Jesuit missionary work in Asia, expanding their activity to China and Vietnam. The Jesuits were also responsible for establishing colleges and seminaries throughout Europe as part of their effort to confront the challenge from the Protestant Reformation, and they played a major role in the long-delayed church council which began meeting at the northern Italian city of Trent in 1545.

Although Luther and others had long sought a church *council to resolve the issues raised by the Reformation, the calling of a general council was consistently delayed by political rivalries and the reluctance of the papacy to call one. When the Council of *Trent (1545–63) was finally convened, it failed to take any positive moves towards reconciliation with Protestants. It met in three separate sessions over a period of almost twenty years, but Protestants were only represented in a limited way in the second of those sessions. Rather than reconciling differences, the Council accentuated them by issuing a series of doctrinal decrees that defined Catholic doctrine in opposition to Protestantism. The Council also enacted impressive reform legislation that held out the promise of creating a truly reformed church which would not only save Catholicism from further Protestant inroads, but could also begin the process of winning back areas that had been lost in the initial stages of the Reformation. However, for those who had hoped for reconciliation with the Protestants, the council virtually eliminated that possibility. The theological decrees condemned Protestant beliefs in such specific terms that future generations would find the canons and decrees of the Council of Trent a major stumbling block to ecumenical discussions. After Trent, it seemed the only way in which the *schism could be healed would be by Protestants surrendering their beliefs or by suppression.

A reformed papacy played a major role in the implementation of the Tridentine legislation. Pius V (1566–72) was the first of a series of popes who worked diligently to put the reforming decrees of the Council into practice. In contrast to the Renaissance papacy, Pius was noted for his austere holiness and he was careful to appoint people of similar moral commitment. He imposed such strict moral standards on Rome that he was accused of turning the city into a monastery. He completed the work of Trent by publishing a Roman catechism as well as a revised breviary and missal. Unfortunately, in his commitment to enforcing the decisions of Trent, Pius relied heavily on the Inquisition and greatly expanded its activities, at times attending its sessions in person. Equally committed reformers followed Pius V in the papal office. Gregory XIII (1572–85), although less austere and rigorous than his predecessor, worked hard to carry out the decisions of Trent and to make sure that the men appointed to the episcopacy, or who were made cardinals, were worthy of the office. He was also responsible for the revision of the calendar. Gregory proclaimed the new calendar – fittingly called the Gregorian calendar – by a papal bull in 1582. Although Catholic countries accepted it almost immediately, the divisions resulting from the Reformation were evident even in the much-needed calendar revisions. Protestant states, suspicious of a papal calendar, did not introduce it for more than a century. The popes who followed Gregory XIII, including Sixtus V (1585–90), Clement VIII (1592–1605) and Paul V (1605–21), were also committed reformers, and they took steps to implement the decisions of Trent. Thus the papacy, which had been one of the major stumbling blocks in the way of reform in the years preceding the Reformation, became its most zealous proponent. In addition, spiritual qualities and commitment to reform rather than family connections became the most important consideration in the appointment of cardinals. Thus the Catholic hierarchy was dramatically reformed. Unfortunately, the popes were equally committed to the suppression of Protestantism, and their actions are sometimes difficult to defend from a Christian perspective. For example, when Pope Gregory XIII learned of the terrible massacre of French Protestants in the St Bartholomew's Day Massacre (1572), he had thanksgiving services celebrated in Rome and issued a commemorative medallion to celebrate the massacres as a 'holy' event.

The Catholic Reformation also benefited from a significant number of reforming bishops. Charles Borromeo (1538–84), the archbishop of Milan, stands out as one of the many bishops who worked hard to reform their dioceses. He made Milan into a model archdiocese, reforming the clergy and the monastic orders, while also renovating churches and establishing schools and colleges. Nevertheless, abuses still continued in some areas of Europe. For example, in France nepotism was rampant and a significant number of bishops continued to be non-resident or pluralists. On the other hand, Ireland was blessed with conscientious and able bishops who used their powers effectively to correct abuses. However, even those bishops committed to reform did not always succeed in reforming their dioceses. One major problem was finding the resources to establish the diocesan seminaries ordered by the Tridentine decree. Although every diocese was ordered to provide a seminary where priests would receive the training necessary to carry on their ministries, only the wealthier ones could afford a seminary. Consequently, many priests still lacked an adequate education. In addition, private patrons continued to play a major role in appointing parish priests so that even reforming bishops were not always free to appoint able candidates. Nevertheless, the Catholic Reformation did succeed in improving the calibre of the parish clergy, and a new type of reformed, committed and better-educated clergy was more common throughout Europe by the middle of the seventeenth century. The Catholic Reformation also resulted in a remarkable blossoming of theology, music, spiritual literature and impressive architecture.

A central concern of the Catholic Reformation was winning back areas from Protestants, and in that sense it was also a counter-Reformation which had as one of its major objectives confronting and challenging Protestant teaching. This was achieved in a variety of ways. Whereas in the early stages of the Reformation Protestants had often defeated the poorly educated Catholic clergy in public debates, better-educated Catholic priests now challenged Protestants to public debates. Trained in the Scriptures as well as Protestant theology and methods of argumentation, the Catholic debaters were more than able to hold their own in these debates. Jesuits also used their excellent schools to attract Protestants and win them over. One of the most successful missionaries to Protestants was the Dutch Jesuit Peter Canisius (1521–97), who devoted his ministry to confronting the Protestant challenge. Travelling throughout Europe spreading the Catholic faith, he preached countless sermons and founded five Jesuit university colleges as well as a series of colleges for boys. He also prepared three *catechisms for teaching the faith – a large catechism for priests and educated adults, a mid-size one for adolescents, and a small catechism for children. Canisius was one of many dedicated priests responsible for the success of the Catholic counter-Reformation in winning back areas from Protestantism through education, debate and preaching. Other successes were achieved in far less desirable ways. In the final century of the Reformation era, France, Belgium, Austria, Bavaria, Bohemia and Poland were all restored to Catholicism largely as the result of the suppression of Protestantism by persecution, political manipulation and religious war.

Although the Catholic Reformation was directed against Protestantism and many of its manifestations were anti-Protestant, it also had much in common with the Protestant Reformation. Both Reformations sought to Christianize a European population that was often Christian in only a very superficial way, and for which popular religion was more important than official Christianity. Both movements produced the kind of educated clergy that had been to a great degree absent in the medieval church. Both movements also stressed the importance of educating the laity, and both Protestants and Roman Catholics produced catechisms and homilies for this purpose. Sadly, the two movements, which had many objectives in common, found it impossible to reconcile the areas where they differed, and the result was religious war and permanent schism in the Christian church.

See also: ROMAN CATHOLIC THEOLOGY.

Bibliography

R. Bireley, *The Refashioning of Catholicism 1450–1700* (Washington DC, 1999); A. G. Dickens, *The Counter Reformation* (New York, 1969); R. W. Heinze, 'The Catholic Reformation', in R. W. Heinze, *Reform and Conflict* (Grand Rapids, 2005), pp. 255–279; P. Po-chia Hsia, *The World of Catholic Renewal 1540–1770* (Cambridge, 2005); M. Jones, *The Counter Reformation: Religion and Society in Early Modern Europe* (Cambridge, 1995): M. Mullett, *The Catholic Reformation* (New York, 1999); J. C. Olin, *Catholic Reform from Cardinal Ximenes to the Council of Trent, 1495–1563* (New York, 1990); A. D. Wright, *The Counter-Reformation: Catholic Europe and the Non-Christian World* (New York, 1982).

R. W. HEINZE

REFORMATION, RADICAL

This term has been used to describe those who desired a more far-reaching *Reformation than that sought by the main-line or Magisterial Reformers (*Luther, *Zwingli and *Calvin). Some historians prefer the term 'left-wing' to describe the phenomenon under study. Research in the later twentieth century pointed to a measure of continuity between the radicals and late mediaeval *apocalyptic groups. *Erasmus was also a particularly important source, because he took the Bible seriously and yet reached very different conclusions from those of the Magisterial Reformers.

Origins

The origins of radicalism can be traced back to the demands for an acceleration of change in

Wittenberg in 1522 made by *Karlstadt and the Zwickau prophets. They wanted an abolition of Catholic liturgical practices; they preached that infant baptism was wrong, and the prophets claimed to have direct revelations from God. Thomas *Müntzer, who preached in revolutionary apocalyptic terms and was savagely critical of Luther for putting too much reliance on a learned ministry and for giving insufficient place to the Holy Spirit's leading of ordinary people, was very influential in encouraging the confident but hopeless resistance of the Peasants' Revolt. Finally, a group emerged in Zurich which was critical of Zwingli, and it became clear that its concerns were not only the question of how speedily the Reformers could achieve their objectives, but also what was the nature of those objectives. They sought both a total break with non-biblical traditions and a separation of like-minded people from those who 'compromised' the faith.

G. H. Williams in his definitive study has noted three very broad radical groupings, though within these further sub-groupings can be detected.

The *Anabaptists* emphasized believers' baptism, separation from the world (including the refusal to be involved in the institutions of the state) and a very literal biblicism. They are sometimes helpfully distinguished from the Reformers as those who sought a very precise 'restoration' or 'restitution' of NT Christianity (e.g. sometimes advocating communism) as opposed to a 'reformation' according to NT principles. Somewhat unfairly, the activities of a revolutionary element among the Anabaptists – who sought to set up a rule of the godly based on a rigid and authoritarian interpretation of the OT law in Münster in 1534 – became a symbol, for most contemporaries, of the dangers of radicalism. By and large they were not a threat to the state, and the followers of Menno *Simons and Jacob Hutter (d. 1536) survived through the centuries as significant groupings (see *Mennonite theology).

The *Spiritualists* put a considerable emphasis on the leading of the Spirit, sometimes at the expense of the Bible. This could lead towards a mystical understanding of the faith and a concentration on the indwelling Word. Caspar *Schwenckfeld scandalized all orthodox believers by suggesting that there should be a moratorium on the Lord's Supper as it had become so divisive.

The *Evangelical Rationalists* put reason on a par with Scripture, and often stood rather loose to doctrine, favouring a *unitarian theology. *Socinianism developed from the teaching of Laelius Socinus (1525–62) and his nephew Faustus Socinus (1539–1604).

Characteristics

It is possible to identify eight characteristics of the radicals, though the movement was so diverse that exceptions abound.

1. An emphasis on *sanctification rather than justification, rooted in the late medieval *Devotio Moderna* stress on the Christian life as one of the *imitation of Christ. Luther, they said, put too much emphasis on the Christian's continued sinfulness (*semper peccator*). Some held out, by contrast, the possibility of reaching a perfect state. Many thought that Paul's description in Romans 7 ('O wretched man that I am') did not apply to Christians.

2. A reaction against an over-intellectual faith. There was a strong conviction that the Reformers had over-intellectualized the faith in the emphasis they gave to theology and to learned ministers. What was much more important was the witness of the Spirit within.

3. A conviction that it was possible to establish a holy church. All the Reformers accepted that the visible church could not be an exact replica of the true church. The radicals had a greater confidence in the possibility of creating a church of real believers and to this end put a great emphasis on excommunication ('the ban').

4. A determination to be separate from the world. In particular, they stressed that the *state was for non-Christians and their members should have as little to do with it as possible. They consequently caused great perturbation by refusing to serve as magistrates or soldiers, and thus appeared to challenge the fabric of society which was based, in both Catholic and orthodox Protestant theory, on a close relationship between church and state. Related to this was their emphasis on following the way of Christ; war was seen as contrary to his example of love (see *Pacifism/peace).

5. The importance of believers' *baptism. Most of the radicals were strongly against infant baptism, and rebaptized those baptized as infants.

6. A liability to theological heterodoxy. The restorationist emphasis meant that the great credal formulations of the church were ignored.

The result was a tendency to unorthodox theological views particularly in relation to the *Trinity and *Christology. Many, for example, believed that Christ did not take our human flesh, but brought his own divine body to earth ('the celestial flesh of Christ').

7. A passionate commitment to *evangelism. They had a strong sense of the continuing force of the great commission which the Reformers had tended to limit to the apostolic era. This, together with their lack of interest in political boundaries and their willingness to face persecution, made them very courageous evangelists.

8. A growing conviction about *toleration. Though it is undoubtedly true that the fierce reaction they aroused within both Protestantism and Catholicism had the effect of undermining any idea of toleration, the radicals did in time have an important part to play in extending the idea that religious opinion should be left to the individual to decide without any pressure from church or state.

In background, the radicals, though often led by men of education and position, were generally simple people, often peasants and craftsmen, manifestly seeking an identity and a medium of self-expression which the Reformers' doctrine of the *priesthood of all believers had promised, but had not, it was contended, delivered. They often met in simple and informal settings. They were very prone to division. Sometimes their emphasis on the leading of the Spirit produced dangerously emotional and aberrant moral behaviour.

The existence of the radicals and their particular emphases is a good example of the not infrequent tensions in the Christian church between enthusiasm and order; between Spirit and word; between *Scripture and tradition; between seeing the *church as a communion of saints or a school of sinners; and between understanding the priesthood of all believers as giving equal *ministry to all or ministries to all but with a special ministry, involving authority, to some.

Bibliography

C. P. Clasen, *Anabaptism: A Social History, 1526–1618* (Ithaca and London, 1972); A. Friesen, *Erasmus, the Anabaptists, and the Great Commission* (Grand Rapids, 1998); H.-J. Goertz, *The Anabaptists* (London, 1996); C. A. Snyder, *Anabaptist History and Theology: An Introduction* (Kitchener, 1995); G. H. Williams, *The Radical Reformation* (Kirksville, ³1992); G. H. Williams and A. M. Mergal (eds.), *Spiritual and Anabaptist Writers* (London, 1957).

C. P. WILLIAMS

REFORMED EPISTEMOLOGY

Reformed epistemology, developed by Alvin *Plantinga, Nicholas Wolterstorff and William Alston, maintains that belief in God can be rational or justified without the support of an argument for the existence of God. This runs counter to the *Enlightenment *evidentialist view of *rationality which claims that belief in God is rational only if it can be supported by sufficient evidence.

The evidentialist view is usually rooted in a view of the structure of knowledge called 'classical foundationalism'. According to classical *foundationalism, knowledge must be built on a foundation of certitudes such as statements that are self-evident, evident to the senses, or incorrigible. Self-evident statements include truths of arithmetic and logic such as $2 + 2 = 4$ and *every statement is either true or false*. Statements that are evident to the senses include *grass is green, honey is sweet*, and *I hear a mourning dove*. Some epistemologists exclude statements that are evident to the senses from the foundations of knowledge because we make perceptual mistakes (we sometimes perceive gray mountains, for example, as purple or golden); they include incorrigibility as the criterion of foundational beliefs. Incorrigible propositions are first-person psychological states (seeming or appearance beliefs) about which I cannot be wrong such as *grass appears green to me* or *honey seems to me to be sweet*. Evidentialists claim that since the statement that God exists is neither self-evident, evident to the senses, nor incorrigible, belief in God is rational only if it can be adequately supported by foundational beliefs.

Reformed epistemologists contend that belief in God does not require the support of a theistic argument in order for it to be rational. They find inspiration in the work of John *Calvin, who claimed that God has provided all humans with a natural, instinctual sense of the divine. He writes: 'There is within the human mind, and indeed by natural instinct, an awareness of divinity ... God himself has implanted in all men a certain understanding of his divine majesty... This conviction, namely that there is some God, is naturally inborn in all, and is fixed deep within, as it were in the very marrow.' This natural, internal sense of the divine (the *sensus divinitatis*) is inscribed or written on the hearts of all people, and so belief in God is not the product of an argument. Reformed epistemologists would come to learn from the philosopher Thomas Reid whose '*common-sense' philosophy affirmed in-built cognitive faculties that are involved in a wide variety of human beliefs.

Reformed epistemologists argue that evidentialist demands for evidence cannot be met in a large number of cases with the cognitive equipment that we have. There are no sound proofs for the existence of other persons, inductive beliefs (e.g. that the sun will rise in the future), or the reality of the past (perhaps, as Bertrand Russell puzzled, we were created five minutes ago with our memories intact) that satisfy classical foundationalist requirements. So, according to classical foundationalism, belief in the past and inductive beliefs about the future are irrational.

A second criticism, first offered by Plantinga, is that classical foundationalism is self-referentially inconsistent. Classical foundationalism may be formulated as follows:

CF: A proposition p is rational if and only if p is self-evident, evident to the senses or incorrigible or if p can be inferred from a set of propositions that are self-evident, evident to the senses, or incorrigible.

Consider CF itself. CF is neither self-evident, evident to the senses, nor incorrigible; therefore, it can only be rationally maintained if it can be inferred from propositions that (ultimately) are self-evident, evident to the senses or incorrigible. Is that possible? If one considers such propositions, it's easy to see that they fail to constitute adequate evidence for CF. So, CF is not self-evident, evident to the senses or incorrigible, nor can CF be inferred from a set of propositions that are self-evident, evident to the senses or incorrigible. So, belief in CF, by its own account, is irrational!

The primary reason to believe that it might be rational for a person to accept belief in God without the support of an argument is a parity argument. We are not only naturally inclined to trust the deliverances of our cognitive faculties (beliefs in the external world, other persons, that the future will be like the past, the reality of the past, and what other people tell us – to name just a few), we are also entitled to do so. For the sake of parity, we are entitled to trust the *sensus divinitatis*.

See also: EPISTOMOLOGY; FAITH AND REASON.

Bibliography

K. J. Clark, *Return to Reason* (Grand Rapids, 1990); A. Plantinga, *Warranted Christian Belief* (New York, 2000); A. Plantinga and N. Wolterstorff (eds.), *Faith and Rationality* (Notre Dame, 1983); P. Quinn, 'In Search of the Foundations of Theism', *Faith and Philosophy* 2, 1985, pp. 469–486; L. Zagzebski (ed.), *Rational Faith* (Notre Dame, 1995).

K. J. CLARK

REFORMED THEOLOGY

The classic representative statements of Reformed theology are found in the *catechisms and *confessions of the Reformed churches: e.g. the French Confession (1559), the *Scots Confession (1560), the Belgic Confession (1561), the *Heidelberg Catechism (1563), the Second Helvetic Confession (1566), the *Thirty-Nine Articles of the Church of England (1562, 1571), the Canons of the Synod of *Dort (1619), the *Westminster Confession of Faith and Catechisms (1647) and the Formula Consensus Helveticus (1675). On a secondary level are the writings of the leading representative theologians of those churches: e.g. Ulrich *Zwingli and Heinrich *Bullinger of Zurich, Martin *Bucer of Strasburg and Cambridge, John *Calvin and Theodore *Beza of Geneva, Peter Martyr *Vermigli of Strasburg, Oxford and Zurich, together with later great synthesizers such as Amandus Polanus (1561–1610) and Francis Turretin (1623–1687).

Historical emergence

Reformed theology developed within sixteenth-century *Protestantism in distinction from *Lutheranism. Initial disagreement between Luther and Zwingli emerged on the *Eucharist, coming to an open breach at the Colloquy of Marburg (1529). Luther's so-called consubstantiation was based on his radical, innovative view of the *communicatio idiomatum* ('interchange of properties' between Christ's divine and human natures; see *Christology) as it

Reformed theology

found expression in the ubiquity of Christ's humanity. Other differences existed but were more of emphasis or else less divisive, e.g. Lutheranism tended to posit more discontinuity between *law and gospel, to allow greater autonomy to the civil magistrate and to focus more narrowly on soteriology than did the Reformed. Yet agreement was immensely more extensive. Together with Rome and Constantinople, both held to the ecumenical *dogmas on the *Trinity and *Christology. On the central affirmations of the *Reformation (justification by *faith, the denial of transubstantiation, the number of *sacraments, the authority of *Scripture) both were at one. Yet all attempts to achieve theological and ecclesiastical unity failed.

Principal characteristics

The centrality of God is a theme that pervades Reformed theology, which developed under the compelling demand of God's self-revelation in Scripture, its ultimate focus being on the Trinity, with a more immediate focus on Jesus Christ as mediator. In distinction from Lutheranism, in which Luther's personal struggles for forgiveness bequeathed a concentration on soteriology narrowly focused on justification, the Reformed attempted to bring the whole of reality under the sway of the supremacy of God. This can be seen as eminently biblical, while avoiding the perils of faddish 'emphases'. The dominance of the doctrine of God comes to expression in a number of ways:

(1) Human self-knowledge is attained only in the light of the knowledge of God. For Calvin, we are able to recognize who we are only when confronted by the supreme majesty and transcendent holiness of the living God as he makes himself known to us in his word by his Spirit. Thereby we are made cognizant of our sin and wretchedness, of the depravity that pervades our entire being. This *Augustinianism represents in reality a high view of man, since we are seen as moral beings responsible to God, known only in the light of God. Our deep-rooted alienation is floodlit by the greatness of God. Our true identity is as the *image of God.

(2) Salvation in its entirety is the work of God. Because of the pervasive impact of sin we stand under the condemnation of God, unable to change our status or condition. Hence, Reformed theology has consistently testified to the sole and sovereign activity of God in *salvation. Its origin is God's eternal purpose, his sovereign election of his people in Christ before the foundation of the world (Eph. 1:4), a choice made without regard to anything intrinsic in man. Correspondingly, although divergently nuanced, sovereign reprobation was consistently recognized. Therefore, Christ's purpose in *incarnation and *atonement was to save his people from their sins. His death was not intended to atone for every human being; for then either he would have failed, or the road would lead to *universalism, uniformly rejected as unbiblical. Nor did the cross provisionally atone for all while intrinsically accomplishing nothing, leaving atonement in suspense, contingent upon believing appropriation of Christ. Rather, Christ made effective atonement for the sins of all his people (see *Atonement, extent of). Similarly, the Holy Spirit draws us invincibly to Christ. Since we were dead in sin (Eph. 2:1) and unable because unwilling to trust Christ, faith (indeed, all Christian virtue) is entirely a gift of God. The Spirit not only brings us to Christ, but keeps us there. The whole process of *sanctification and *perseverance requires our strenuous effort in faith, but that effort itself is the Spirit's gift. Thus, Reformed theology maintained with vigour at Dort that none of the elect can finally fall away from grace so as to be lost.

Frequently, the mnemonic TULIP (Total depravity, Unconditional election, Limited atonement, Irresistible grace, Perseverance) is used to summarize the Canons of Dort and Reformed theology generally. However, this can present a truncated picture, an abridgment of the panoramic grandeur of the Reformed view of church and cosmos.

(3) The whole of personal and corporate life is to be subjected to God. Reformed theology has consistently sought to order the whole of life according to the requirements of God in Scripture. From its beginnings in Zurich, Strasburg and Geneva, strong efforts were made to model civic as well as ecclesiastical life in this way. Reformed theology has been linked with the rise of both capitalism and socialism, with the spread of education, literacy and science, besides revolution in France, the Netherlands, England, Scotland and the American colonies. Correspondingly, greater stress was laid on sanctification and the ongoing role of the *law in the Christian life than in Lutheranism. Consequently, Reformed theology has always sought to do justice to the corporate dimension

of the gospel and, while increasingly influenced by individualism as time passed, nevertheless maintained this more effectively than other branches of Protestantism. Covenant theology exerted a strong impact in this direction within Reformed theology, since, although the covenant of grace was related to individual soteriology, the notion of the covenant of works made by God with Adam before the fall was increasingly applied, from 1600, to the civic and political responsibilities of nations to God on the basis of a permanent and universally binding law of creation.

Christocentricity. In early Reformed theology, exemplified by Calvin, *Knox and Zanchius (1516–90), a consistent focus was evident on Christ as the ground of our knowledge of God, as the subject and object of election and, precisely because of the centrality of God, as the immediate focal centre of theology. Later, the impact of scholasticism, with its rigid logical deductivism, and covenant theology, with its preponderant use of the covenant concept (see below), led to the intrusion of other factors which then assumed a place of dominance. At times, attempts have been made to reassert a Christocentric trinitarianism, in extreme form by Karl *Barth. A merit of such proposals has been to call attention to tendencies to depart from Reformed theology's roots.

Pluriformity. Reformed theology is not, nor has been, monolithic. It has possessed creative vitality sufficient to encompass diversity within an overall consensus. For instance, before Dort, differences existed on the question of limited atonement. Calvin was somewhat ambiguous, if not contradictory, on the matter, and may have leaned towards universal atonement. His successor Beza opposed the common formula (sufficient for all, efficient for the elect) on the grounds that it weakened the biblical stress on limited, or definite, atonement. Dort, in fact, fashioned a compromise agreement between the powerful British delegation's universalizing tendency and the majority's particularizing concern.

The development of *covenant theology indicates diversity too. Begun with Zwingli, *Oecolampadius and Bullinger, developed by Zacharius *Ursinus and Kaspar *Olevianus, the movement came to maturity with Robert Rollock (1555–99) and was further elaborated by Johannes *Cocceius. While increasingly dominant in the seventeenth century, not all were covenant theologians in the sense of using the concept to structure their theology. Still more was this so before 1600. Differences existed on the nature of the covenant of grace: was it a unilateral and an unconditional imposition by God, or a bilateral pact with conditions to be fulfilled by man? Most early covenant theologians had one covenant, the covenant of grace. Later, the idea of the pre-fall covenant of works emerged. From 1648 a third, pre-temporal covenant was proposed. Each suggestion had its adherents. Additionally, diversity existed on questions of piety. *Puritanism in old and new England was oriented towards *praxis, sanctification and pastoralia, increasingly tending to anthropocentrism. Similar developments occurred in the Netherlands and Scotland. This represented a contrast with earlier Reformed theology and with the more scholastically oriented tradition. This pluriformity did not extend to *Arminianism, which was proscribed by Dort for undermining the gratuitous theocentricity of salvation.

Calvin and Calvinism

Classical Reformed theology is often called 'Calvinism' due to the towering impact of John Calvin. However, this is not an entirely satisfactory term. First, owing to the above pluriformity Calvin neither could nor did impose his views on others. The autonomy of the various Reformed centres saw to that. For instance, his theology is not shaped by the covenant concept in the manner of later Reformed theology, yet after his death covenant theology became increasingly influential. Second, it is doubtful whether Calvin's distinctive theology, rooted in biblical exegesis, was properly grasped by many who came later. A recrudescence of *Aristotelian scholasticism led to a greater reliance on reason and bred a markedly different theological climate, characterized by clarity of definition, rigorous deductivism, greater use of causal analysis and liberal employment of the syllogism. Calvin's more fluid biblicism went into eclipse. Consequently, many scholars posit a dichotomy between Calvin and the Calvinists. This can be overplayed, for, whatever the differences, the parties concerned saw themselves as colleagues not competitors. Despite his antipathy to Aristotle, Calvin did use Aristotelian causal analysis on occasion. However, the reintroduction of Aristotelian logic by Beza, Zanchius and Vermigli may well have encouraged the eventual ossification of Reformed theology by the late seventeenth century. The living biblical dynamic of earlier days, exemplified by a flood of biblical commentaries and trinitarian-grounded systematic treatises based on the Apostles' Creed (Calvin's *Institutes* was one), became straightjacketed in a rigid, logical, causal system. In fact, the ground was prepared for *deism, since God became simply the First Cause behind an immanent causal chain. Despite this, there was still a major contribution to the renewal of Reformed theology in eighteenth-century North America by Jonathan *Edwards.

Later developments

A revival of classic Reformed theology occurred in the nineteenth century in America, where the *Princeton theology, spearheaded by Charles *Hodge, A. A. Hodge (1823–86) and B. B. *Warfield, followed and adapted the scholastic Calvinism of Turretin. In Holland, Abraham *Kuyper and Herman *Bavinck also made a profound impact. Kuyper took his theology into public life, founding a university, a daily newspaper and a political party, eventually becoming prime minister.

In his massive reaction to liberalism, Karl *Barth's debt to the Reformed theology of the sixteenth and seventeenth centuries is obvious on almost every page of *CD*, seen in his welcome Christocentricity and his vigorous repudiation of anthropocentrism. However, it has been argued that he never entirely eradicated the *existentialism so evident in his *Romans* commentary, and represented quite a different version of Reformed theology from that of the Reformation era and subsequent centuries.

The twentieth century witnessed major application of Reformed thinking to philosophy by e.g. Herman *Dooyeweerd, and the development of a unitary theology interacting with modern physics by T. F. *Torrance. Beyond that, Reformed theology shows an ongoing capacity for self-criticism and renewal which bodes well for the future, for, as Warfield argued, the future of Christianity is inseparable from the fortunes of the Reformed faith. Its concern for consistent theocentrism, its comprehensive worldview, and its at least implicit Christocentricity all exemplify its rigorous theological exploration of the gospel, its pursuit of 'faith seeking understanding', and its movement towards the integration of creation and redemption in Christ. Indeed, whenever prayer is offered, the church is engaging in Reformed theology, acknowledging what on other occasions its theology and praxis may sometimes deny.

Bibliography

J. W. Baker, *Heinrich Bullinger and the Covenant: The Other Reformed Tradition* (Athens, 1980); J. W. Beardslee (ed.), *Reformed Dogmatics* (New York, 1965); W. R. Godfrey, *Tensions within International Calvinism: The Debate on the Atonement at the Synod of Dort, 1618–1619* (PhD diss., Stanford University, 1974); B. Hall, 'Calvin against the Calvinists', in G. E. Duffield (ed.), *John Calvin* (Abingdon, 1966); H. Heppe (ed.), *Reformed Dogmatics: Set Out and Illustrated from the Sources* (London, 1950); J. T. McNeill, *The History and Character of Calvinism* (New York, 1954); R. A. Muller, *The Unaccommodated Calvin: Studies in the Foundation of a Theological Tradition* (New York, 2003); idem, *Post-Reformation Reformed Dogmatics: The Rise and Development of Reformed Orthodoxy, ca. 1520 to ca. 1725*, 4 vols. (Grand Rapids, 1993–2003); B. B. Warfield, 'Calvinism', in *Calvin and Augustine* (Philadelphia, 1974); H. E. Weber, *Reformation, Orthodoxie und Rationalismus*, Teil 2 (Gütersloh, 1937).

R. W. A. LETHAM

REFORMERS, ENGLISH

The success enjoyed by the Protestant Reformation in England during the sixteenth century was the result of many factors, intellectual, political, theological and social, but at its heart was the work of a group of men who were personally devoted to the Protestant doctrines and fervently advocated them even at the cost of their own lives. Most prominent among their leaders were Thomas Bilney (*c.* 1495–1531), Hugh Latimer (1485–1555), Cranmer, Frith, Tyndale, Ridley, Robert Barnes (1495–1540), John Rogers (*c.* 1500–55) and John Bradford (1510–55). All of these men were burned at the stake as *heretics between the years 1531 and 1556. During the subsequent reign of Elizabeth I (1558–1603), however, the cause of *Protestantism triumphed, and, largely through the writings of John Foxe (1516–87), the testimony of the *martyrs made a profound impression on the English Christianity of the next four centuries. The writings of Tyndale, Frith, Ridley and Cranmer are of particular theological significance, and helped to shape the

Protestantism which eventually took root in England. In their turn they clearly owed a great debt to the continental *Reformation, with *Luther's early influence being moderated by the growing prestige of the *Reformed scholars of Switzerland. At the same time, the native traditions of *Wyclif and the Lollard movement had their effect as well.

The first priority for the reformation of the church was given to the accurate translation and dissemination of the Bible. William Tyndale (c. 1494–1536) devoted most of his labours to this end. His translation of the NT and parts of the OT laid the foundation for English versions to this day. In pursuing his goal so relentlessly, Tyndale exemplifed the Protestant belief that the reform of the church and the salvation of men and women depended upon dispelling spiritual ignorance through a knowledge of the sure word of God. The practical consequences of their belief in the authority and sufficiency of *Scripture can be judged by the assault on those beliefs and practices they did not find in the Bible. Using the category of 'superstition', the Reformers dismissed such elements of Catholic religion as *purgatory, the use of *images in devotion, prayers for the dead, the veneration of *saints and the belief in sacred objects and contemporary *miracles. At the same time there was a deep commitment to the Christian tradition (see also *Scripture and tradition), especially in the writings of the early Church Fathers. *Councils and Fathers (see *Patristic theology) were regarded as providing a guide to the interpretation of Scripture, although they were also thought to err on occasion and their judgments could be and were dissented from.

The doctrine of *justification by faith alone was the second great concern of the Reformers. John Frith (c. 1503–33), the brilliant younger friend and associate of Tyndale, illustrated its controlling influence, for example, in his work *A Disputation of Purgatory* (1531). It was not only the lack of scriptural support which caused Frith to dismiss purgatory; it was its inconsistency with the *Pauline view of *grace, especially that sinners are justified by faith in the merits of Jesus Christ alone, not by works. Any other view brings discredit to the cross of Christ, for it assumes that the blood of Christ is ineffective to secure forgiveness of sin (see *Guilt and forgiveness). It also underestimates the gravity of *sin and its grip on the human personality. To trust in the message of the cross is to be truly purged. The tribulation of the Christian life is also a purgatory, but it is completed at death when all are fully purified. Frith, like the other Reformers, completed his teaching on grace by espousing a doctrine of election in which God's initiative in salvation was thoroughly secured.

The doctrines of Scripture and grace thus provided the standard by which all was to be reformed. The charge levelled by their opponents that their doctrine of grace was antinomian (see *Law and gospel) led to a constant emphasis by the Protestants on the need for good works as a fruit of faith. In Tyndale, for example, this found particular expression in a use of the theme of *covenant, for which he has been somewhat unjustly suspected of legalism. Thomas *Cranmer used different language but with the same purposes in his classic *Homily of Salvation*, where he described justification by faith alone as 'the strong rock and foundation of Christian religion', and pressed home the necessity of obedience to God as the fruit of a true faith, without which a person is not saved.

The greatest controversies of the English Reformation revolved around the doctrine of the Mass (see *Eucharist). It was at this point above all that the understanding of Scripture and faith held by Cranmer, Frith and Ridley reached its most perilous expression in their own society. Holding the views of Scripture and justification which they did, they could not but differ from *Roman Catholic theology at a point regarded by Catholics of prime significance. For this they suffered the consequences at the stake.

Nicholas Ridley (c. 1500–55) argued that the whole debate on the Mass could be reduced to one key issue: whether the matter of the sacrament was 'the natural substance of bread, or the natural substance of Christ's own body'. If this question was answered in terms of Christ's body, there would follow the idea of transubstantiation, with the devotional honour due to the sacrament, the sacrificial offering of Christ by the priest on the altar, and the reception of the flesh and blood of Christ by the unworthy. Such consequences were at odds with the Christology and soteriology of the Reformers, and they asserted that the body of Christ was and remained in heaven, the bread and the wine being the sacrament or sign of the body, and that the faithful person (and he alone) fed on Christ spiritually by faith. These were the views of the mature Cranmer, and it is they which are encapsulated liturgically in the *Book of Common Prayer*, especially the 1552 revision, and in the *Thirty-Nine Articles of Religion*.

Another focus for debate was the doctrine of the *church. The struggle with Roman Catholicism over the role of the *papacy was increasingly understood in terms of the war between God and *Antichrist, with the pope supplying the latter role. This gave the Reformers a way of interpreting the history of the church and offering theological insights about the significance of current events. There remained, however, the difficult problem of the *state. Cranmer had to attempt to give royal authority a rightful place in the affairs of the church, without acceding to unlawful constraints. Tyndale strongly declared in his *Obedience of the Christian Man* the necessity of obedience to all lawful authority, but with the caveat that the Christian must obey God rather than men. At times this teaching created an alliance with the Tudors; at times its constraints proved difficult and even fatal. Ultimately, for the major Reformers, as for many others, faithfulness to Christ as the head of the church over which he rules through the Scriptures demanded an example of obedience which has resounded even to the present day.

Bibliography

R. Bauckham, *Tudor Apocalypse* (Appleford, 1978); A. G. Dickens, *The English Reformation*, 2nd edn (London, 1989); G. E. Duffield, *The Work of William Tyndale* (Appleford, 1964); C. Haigh, *English Reformations: Religion, Politics, and Society under the Tudors* (Oxford, 1993); F. Heal, *Reformation in Britain and Ireland* (Oxford, 2005); P. E. Hughes, *Theology of the English Reformers* (Grand Rapids, ²1980); D. B. Knox, *The Doctrine of Faith in the Reign of Henry VIII* (London, 1961); M. L. Loane, *Masters of the English Reformation* (London, 1954); D. MacCulloch, *Thomas Cranmer* (London, 1996); idem, *Reformation* (London, 2003); J. I. Packer and G. E. Duffield, *The Work of Thomas Cranmer* (Appleford, 1965); T. H. L. Parker (ed.), *English Reformers* (LCC 26; London, 1966); A. Townsend (ed.), *Writings of John Bradford*, 2 vols. (1848, 1853; repr. Edinburgh, 1979); N. T. Wright, *The Work of John Frith* (Appleford, 1978).

P. F. JENSEN

REFORMERS, SCOTTISH

Patrick Hamilton (d. 1527) (influenced by Luther) and George Wishart (d. 1546) (more Zwinglian), the two most prominent early preachers of the Reformation in Scotland, were both martyred in St Andrews. John *Knox, a follower of Wishart and a powerful preacher, was influential in England during the reign of the Protestant Edward VI, and became pastor of the English exiles in Geneva during the reign of the Catholic Mary I. Strongly influenced by *Calvin, he wrote there the *Book of Common Order* and encouraged the metrical version of the Psalms. He fiercely denounced the Roman Mass as idolatry and insisted that everything in worship had to be done according to Scripture. He returned to a Scotland in crisis and civil war and, as a strong advocate of resistance to 'idolatrous' rulers, led the Reformation of the Scottish church in 1560 when parliament approved the *Scots Confession and the (First) Book of Discipline*. Not only Calvin's doctrine but also his form of church structure and discipline, administered by ministers and by lay elders and deacons, were adopted in order to produce a 'Christian Commonwealth'. A fourth order of ministry, the 'doctors' in the Reformed universities, indicated an emphasis on education, also seen in the plan to have a school in every parish.

See also: PRESBYTERIANISM; REFORMED THEOLOGY.

Bibliography

W. C. Dickinson (ed.), *John Knox's History of the Reformation in Scotland* (Edinburgh, 1949); G. Donaldson, *The Faith of the Scots* (London, 1990); J. Kirk, *Patterns of Reform: Continuity and Change in the Reformation Kirk* (Edinburgh, 1989); H. R. Sefton, *John Knox* (Edinburgh, 1993); A. Ryrie, *The Origin of the Scottish Reformation* (Manchester, 2006).

T. A. NOBLE

REGENERATION

Regeneration is a theological term that indicates the moment of new birth into God's family, as well as describing what God does to bring that new birth about. In the first instance, regeneration is seen from the human perspective as an event that happens within us. In the second instance, regeneration is seen from the divine perspective as that which must be done to effect Christ's work of *redemption for individual believers. Regeneration thus marks both the point and the process of transition from life outside Christ to life within his kingdom. We can helpfully consider two questions:

When does regeneration occur?

There is considerable agreement among theologians that regeneration is a singular, instantaneous event in comparison to *sanctification, which is the ongoing growth in holiness that continues throughout the Christian life. Regeneration can thus be said to occur at the beginning of the Christian life. For those in the early church, regeneration was generally understood to accompany *conversion, and it was their experience that in turning to God in *repentance and *faith, they were met at that moment with God's regenerative activity, changing them from a state of spiritual death to spiritual life by means of a spiritual resurrection. The four elements of this change – repentance, faith, *baptism and receiving the *Holy Spirit – normally occurred together, or with only a small interval of time between them. For this reason, the early Church Fathers often identified baptism as the moment of regeneration. In baptism, the human marks of conversion – repentance and faith – were met with the regenerative action of God, symbolized by the baptism itself and received in the gift of the Spirit. By the time of *Justin Martyr in the second century, this understanding was well-established, and later theologians such as *Irenaeus and *Tertullian took it for granted that baptism was the moment of regeneration. In baptism, the individual died to the old life and was raised again to new life in the Spirit; this action could only be the divine grace of regeneration. *Augustine spoke of awaiting regeneration after his conversion and before his baptism at Easter, and so clearly assumes a connection between the two.

The rise of infant baptism did not sever this connection, though it did significantly alter the church's understanding of regeneration. In infant baptism, the inherited guilt of original *sin was annulled, and it was a later separate act of confirmation that bestowed the Spirit upon a believer. In this split between baptism and *confirmation, regeneration refers only backwards to the washing away of previous and original sin, and the intimate connection between regeneration and new life in the Spirit is in danger of being lost.

After the Reformation, some attempts were made to reconnect regeneration with the other elements of conversion by decoupling it from the practice of baptism. This led to the evangelical emphasis that regeneration occurs at the moment when someone repents and believes the good news of Jesus Christ (see *Gospel). This stress was prominent in the eighteenth-century Evangelical Awakening and the various church movements which arose out of it.

The conversion of individuals is, of course, a varied experience, and many conversions are not instantaneous. However, we may still affirm that regeneration is to be understood theologically as a single instantaneous event that occurs along with the other elements of conversion – specifically, repentance, faith and baptism.

How does regeneration occur?

While regeneration occurs alongside human repentance and faith, it is not to be seen as a human activity. Regeneration is solely the action of God upon the human life which transforms spiritual deadness into a living responsiveness in obedience and love towards him. This is, of course, an activity of the triune God (see *Trinity), as we are placed in relationship with the Father, through the Son and by the Spirit. However, regeneration is typically associated with the Holy Spirit, who is given to believers to effect their regeneration. Just as Jesus was raised from the dead by the power of the Spirit, so we are awakened from our spiritual sleep by the impartation of God's life-giving Spirit to us.

Different theological schemes will generally result in different descriptions of the event of regeneration. *Liberal Protestantism, for instance, tends to see the human condition as essentially devoid of true understanding; consequently, regeneration is seen as a moment of spiritual education or enlightenment. Alternatively, we may give an account of the human condition as one of spiritual *idolatry. In this case, regeneration is the turning of our hearts to God and the beginning of a life of communion with the Father, through the Son and by the Spirit.

In regeneration, the Spirit applies the redemptive work of Christ to our lives and brings about the initial change – rebirth – which is necessary for us to become the children of God (see *Sonship) and to be heirs of his *kingdom.

Bibliography

J. Baillie, *Baptism and Conversion* (London, 1964); K. Barth, *CD* IV.2, esp. §66.4; W. Pannenberg, *Systematic Theology*, vol. 3 (Edinburgh and Grand Rapids, 1998), esp. pp. 239–283; D. J. Pawson, *The Normal Christian Birth* (London, 1989).

A. J. STOBART

REINCARNATION, see METEMPSYCHOSIS

RELATIVISM

To say that truth is relative is to claim that it varies from one time, place or person to another, and that it depends on the changing conditions they bring: that there is no universal truth, valid for all peoples at all times and places. This claim has been repeated throughout history. Protagoras, the Greek sophist, asserted that each person is the measure of all things.

Relativism today is to be found in most areas of enquiry. Ethical relativists see moral standards as culturally relative; situational ethics rejects universally binding moral rules in favour of decisions dependent on their peculiar contexts. Religious relativists view different religious beliefs and practices as legitimate products of different historical and cultural settings. Relativism has even arisen in the natural sciences, with the realization that the growth of scientific knowledge is in measure a function of personal and sociological, rather than just experimental or mathematical, factors. Wherever subjective or sociological influences are admitted, as distinct from the objective and universal, there relativism is likely to make its appearance.

A number of historical developments have encouraged this trend. Twentieth-century studies in the sociology of knowledge uncovered influences on human learning which were previously overlooked. The extension of evolutionary concepts to the history of religion and of ethics popularized the notion that changing ideas are historically dependent. Yet running through these developments is the overall *secularization process, which turned Western culture from its theistic way of thinking to a naturalistic worldview lacking any transcendent point of reference. Theism had provided a transcendent locus for universally valid truth, in the wisdom of the eternal, self-revealing God. Without an adequate substitute for its divine locus, truth is dislocated and becomes relative to changing natural conditions.

Critics of relativism point out that even if beliefs are as diverse as the relativist claims, this does not mean that they ought to be so; many of our differences in fact yield to reason and evidence. But the diversity seems greatly overstated, for similarities plainly exist between different cultures; common human concerns arise from generic aspects of human nature and of the world in which we all live. The supposed dependency of human beliefs on cultural and historical conditions is likewise exaggerated, for critical and creative thought transcends in measure the ideas we inherit from others. Indeed, if all human beliefs vary and depend totally on local conditions, so too will belief in relativism. Total relativism cannot be unchangingly true: it is a self-refuting position. But if not all beliefs vary and not all are totally dependent, then at least some universal truths are valid for all times and places.

Relativism therefore boils down to *epistemological questions. Is there any objective locus for truth? Can human knowledge transcend its subjective and historical conditions sufficiently to apprehend universally valid truth? Does divine revelation give us access to universal truth?

Bibliography

M. Baghramian, *Relativism* (London, 2004); N. L. Gifford, *When in Rome* (New York, 1983); M. Krausz (ed.), *Relativism: A Contemporary Anthology* (New York, 2010); J. Rachels, *The Elements of Moral Philosophy* (New York, 1986), ch. 3; R. Trigg, *Reason and Commitment* (Cambridge, 1973).

See also Bibliography for *Truth.

A. F. HOLMES

RELIGION

A summary understanding of religion must take several aspects into account. This includes definitions of religion that arise from various approaches to the subject, types of religions, and the ways in which contemporary religious expression takes place in the late modern or *postmodern period.

The academic study of religion in scientific rather than theological ways in the Western world began with the study of Christianity as the dominant religious tradition (see *Religion, theology of). This gave way to include the study of other religions due to a variety of factors. This includes the Christian *mission movement of the nineteenth century that engaged other religious movements around the world and which resulted in a wealth of data for study. The *Enlightenment also contributed to a new way of study, with its emphasis on *rationality and religion related more to human than divine or supernatural activity.

As the scientific study of religion developed over time, differing approaches have been taken, and as a result 'religion' has been defined variously. One perspective of research by scholars is the cognitive approach. This method focuses on beliefs as central and explores how they lead to certain practices by religious adherents. One of the more influential practitioners of this method of studying religion was James Frazer, who studied 'primitive religion' and animism. He understood religion in an evolutionary sense of progression from the primitive to the modern, from *polytheism to *monotheism (see *Progress, idea of). For him religion was defined as 'a propitiation or conciliation of powers superior to man which are believed to direct and control the course of nature and human life' (*Golden Bough*, pp. 57–58).

Another academic way of studying religion is the functional approach. This dismisses the idea that beliefs are the appropriate starting point for understanding religion, and instead seeks to understand what religion does for individuals, groups and societies. One proponent of the functional approach was Emile *Durkheim, who is considered the father of modern sociology. He focused on the distinction between concepts of the sacred and profane in the practice of totemism. For Durkheim, religion *'is a unified system of beliefs and practices relative to sacred things, that is to say, things set apart and forbidden – beliefs and practices which unite into one single moral community called a Church, all those who adhere to them'* (*Elementary Forms of Religion*, p. 44, italics original). Max *Weber was another important scholar in the functional study of religion. He was concerned with economic considerations and its relation to society and religion.

William James signals a shift from the previous scholars in that he took a psychological and individual approach to the study of religion rather than considering it in relation to larger social systems. James was concerned with *mystical *religious experiences and the resulting feelings of union with the divine or transcendent. James defined religion as *'the feelings, acts, and experiences of individual men in their solitude, so far as they apprehend themselves to stand in relation to whatever they may consider the divine'* (*Varieties of Religious Experience*, pp. 31–32, italics original).

Mircea Eliade (1907–86) is an example of the *phenomenological study of religion. His approach involved an interest in the patterns of *symbols and the *mythical in religion as it relates to a distinction between the sacred of the extraordinary, and the profane of everyday life. Eliade's approach has also been called the '*history of religions' method.

A more recent approach to studying religion comes from anthropologist Clifford Geertz. He was not interested in methods that tried to find universal aspects running across religious traditions like those discussed above, but instead was concerned with exploring the specific elements of religions. His method involved ethnographic study called 'thick description' which explored religion as part of *culture and the shared meaning of symbols and actions they incorporate.

Yet another contemporary approach is one that explores 'lived religion'. This method moves beyond what people do in what are considered specifically religious buildings, activities and contexts to an examination of the activities of everyday life. Scholars like Gary Laderman, Meredith McGuire and Robert Orsi are examples of academics pursuing a lived religion approach.

Moving beyond various academic approaches to the study of religion and how it is defined, it is helpful to consider how scholars categorize religions by types. One major category is world religions, those religious traditions that arose during the Axial Age starting in 500 BC. As Terry Muck has noted, world religions are 'old, large, and cross-cultural' (*Handbook of Religion*, p. 44). They include *Hinduism, *Buddhism, *Judaism, Christianity and *Islam. Indigenous religions are another type. These are 'restricted to a single cultural group', and 'are the province of a single tribe or ethnic or cultural group' (ibid., p. 183). There are a number of indigenous religions found in various geographical areas, from North America,

Meso- and South America, to Europe, the Middle East, Africa, North and South Asia, China, India and Oceania. New religious movements (often called 'cults' by evangelicals) are 'new' groups that are related to world religions or other religious traditions but which involve significantly novel expressions that differentiate them from their parent religion. Examples include The Church of Jesus Christ of Latter-Day Saints (Mormons) and the Watchtower Bible and Tract Society (Jehovah's Witnesses) arising out of Christianity; the Nation of Islam arising out of Islam; Soka Gakkai arising out of Buddhism; Transcendental Meditation in connection with Hinduism; and Paganism, *Gnosticism, the New Spirituality ('*New Age'), Scientology, and Satanism with connections to the Western esoteric tradition. One other religious type of note are hyper-real or fiction-based religions. There is some overlap with new religious movements, but these are defined by Adam Possamai as 'a simulacrum of a religion, created out of, or in symbiosis with popular culture, which provides inspiration for believers/consumers' (*Handbook of Hyper-real Religions*, p. 1). Matrixism, Jediism and the Otherkin are examples of this type of religion.

Finally, it should be noted that in our late modern or postmodern context, affiliation with religions and personal religious identities are fluid rather than fixed. *Sociologist of religion Zygmunt Bauman has referred to our time as one of 'liquid modernity', and in this context people may engage in religious switching and experimentation over a lifetime, or inhabit multiple religious identities simultaneously.

See also: NEW RELIGIONS.

Bibliography

Z. Bauman, *Liquid Modernity* (Malden, 2000); E. Durkheim, *The Elementary Forms of Religious Life*, tr. K. Fields (New York, 1995 [1912]; M. Eliade, *The Sacred and the Profane: The Nature of Religion*, tr. W. Trask (New York, 1959); J. Frazer, *The Golden Bough: A Study in Magic and Religion* (New York, 1922); C. Geertz, *The Interpretation of Cultures* (New York, 1973); W. James, *The Varieties of Religious Experience: A Study in Human Nature* (New York, 1929); C. Klassen, *Religion & Popular Culture: A Cultural Studies Approach* (Oxford, 2014); G. Laderman, *Sacred Matters: Celebrity Worship, Sexual Ecstasies, the Living Dead, and Other Signs of Religious Life in the United States* (New York, 2009); M. McGuire, *Lived Religion: Faith and Practice in Everyday Life* (Oxford, 2008); T. Muck, H. Netland and G. McDermott (eds.), *Handbook of Religion* (Grand Rapids, 2014); R. Orsi, *Gods of the City: Religion and the American Urban Landscape* (Bloomington, 1999); A. Possamai (ed.), *Handbook of Hyper-real Religions* (Leiden, 2012); M. Weber, *The Protestant Ethic and the Spirit of Capitalism*, tr. T. Parsons (Mineola, 2003 [1930]).

J. W. MOREHEAD

RELIGIONS, THEOLOGY OF

Although Christianity has always existed in a world of religious diversity, the reality of our post-*Christendom, post-colonial, post-holocaust, post 9/11, 7/7, multi-ethnic and multicultural context has meant that more than ever Christians are acutely aware of systematic, pastoral and missiological issues posed by other religions. The missiologist Gerald Anderson has stated that 'No issue in missiology is more important, more difficult, more controversial, or more divisive for the days ahead than the theology of religions . . . This is the theological issue for mission in . . . the twenty-first century' ('Theology of Religions and Missiology: A Time of Testing', in C. Van Engen, D. Gilliland and P. E. Pierson (eds.), *The Good News of the Kingdom*, Maryknoll, 1993, p. 201).

As a discipline, the 'theology of religions' has had a meteoric rise to fame and quickly become its own distinct category in theological studies. The 'theology of religions' must be distinguished from the allegedly 'neutral' discipline of academic 'religious studies', for although being sibling rivals striving to occupy the same space, the 'theology of religions' locates itself in the tradition of *fides quaerens intellectum* ('faith seeking understanding'): 'The theology of religion asks what religion is and seeks, in the light of Christian faith, to interpret the universal religious experience of humankind; it further studies the relationship between revelation and faith, faith and religion, and faith and salvation' (J. Dupuis, *Toward a Christian Theology of Religious Pluralism*, Orbis, 1997, p. 7). Although the focus of the 'theology of religions' has often concentrated on the issue of salvation, a truly comprehensive Christian theology of religions includes not only questions pertaining to *salvation, but questions pertaining to *truth in other religions, and questions pertaining to the phenomena of human religiosity.

In 1983, Alan Race, an Anglican priest and theologian, developed a threefold typology that has largely set the terms of debate over the last twenty years within the 'theology of religions' (*Christians and Religious Pluralism*, London, 1983). Netland (*Dissonant Voices*, p. 9f.) neatly summarizes these positions:

> Exclusivism maintains that the central claims of Christianity are true, and that where the claims of Christianity conflict with those of other religions the latter are to be rejected as false. Christian exclusivists also characteristically hold that Jesus Christ is the unique incarnation of God, the only Lord and Saviour. Salvation is not to be found in the structures of other religious traditions . . . Inclusivism . . . holds that [although] God has revealed himself definitively in Jesus Christ and that Jesus is somehow central to God's provision of salvation for humankind, they are willing to allow that God's salvation is available through non-Christian religions . . . Pluralism parts company with both exclusivism and inclusivism by rejecting the premise that God has revealed himself in any unique or definitive sense in Jesus Christ. On the contrary, God is said to be actively revealing himself in all religious traditions . . . Christian faith is merely one of many equally legitimate human responses to the same divine reality.

Historical context

Historically the dominant theme regarding Christian approaches to other religions has been exclusivistic. While philosophical and socio-cultural factors have played their part, the foundational authoritative basis for historical affirmations of exclusivism has been the strongly exclusivistic tenor of the Bible (both OT and NT) which Christians have understood to be a true and unified revelation of God's works and words *in history*. The constant theme throughout the history of Israel and in the founding of the Christian church is both the incomparability (none *like* him) and transcendent uniqueness (no *other* God) of Yahweh and Jesus Christ who is God incarnate (cf. C. J. H Wright, *The Mission of God*, Nottingham, 2006, p. 82). As a consequence of the nature and activity of *God comes a secondary affirmation of the incomparability and uniqueness of both Israel and the *church. There is no other covenant community like them, and there is no other community with a history like theirs, because the incomparable and unique God has covenanted with them alone and intervened salvifically on their behalf alone. However, with this theme of particularity also come complementary themes of universality, inclusion, diversity and tolerance (e.g. attitudes towards the alien and stranger; attitudes towards ethnic diversity, including the eschatological hope of Christians being drawn from all nations and languages; God's universal care and sustenance of creation; the universal scope of the gospel and the universal mandate to take the gospel to the nations, etc.). Such exclusivity should never lead to vainglory or malice, for both Israel and the church are chosen by the sheer grace of God to display his glory, and have a unique responsibility and calling to be a light for the nations in both word and deed.

Although the exclusivist mood of the biblical testimony continued into the early church, the writings of some of the early Fathers, like *Justin, *Irenaeus, *Origen and *Clement of Alexandria, indicate a willingness to speculate on the relationship between Christianity and other philosophies in matters of truth and salvation. However, it is *Cyprian in *The Unity of the Catholic Church* who is responsible for the slogan most often associated with exclusivism, '*extra ecclesiam nulla salus*' ('outside the church there is no salvation'), remembering his focus was that of *schismatics and *heretics rather than other religions per se. With *Augustine, this axiom was strengthened. Augustine's teaching on original guilt, predestination, God's sovereignty and efficacious grace gave a far more substantial theological and philosophical basis and reinforced Christian particularity. Within *Roman Catholic teaching, exclusivistic interpretations of *extra ecclesium nulla salus* (albeit with some modifications) continued until the Second *Vatican Council, when many acknowledge that in terms of the threefold typology, Roman Catholic teaching shifted from the exclusivist paradigm into the inclusivist paradigm (see F. A. Sullivan, *Salvation Outside the Church? Tracing the History of the Catholic Response*, London, 1992).

The Protestant Reformers largely continued the exclusivist heritage, not so much under the banner of *extra ecclesiam nulla salus* but rather under their five 'solas' of the *Reformation: sola Scriptura, solus Christus, sola fide, sola gratia, soli Deo Gloria ('Scripture alone, Christ alone, faith alone, grace alone, glory to God alone'). Calvin affirmed a universal natural revelation of God in all humanity, a *sensus divinitatis* or *semen religionis*, but claimed that because of the sinfulness of man, such knowledge was always twisted and distorted away from God (*Institutes*, 1.3.1–2).

For those coming under its sway, the *Enlightenment, with its own ultimate commitment to autonomous human reason, signalled a paradigm shift in the theology of religions: the death knell for exclusivism but the breeding ground for what would become inclusivism, pluralism and the scientific study of *religion (religious studies). Changes in fundamental doctrinal loci would mean changes in the Christian attitude towards the religious other. However, not all were influenced by Enlightenment presuppositions, and the early modern missionary movement continued to be propelled by an exclusivist engine fuelled on the uniqueness of Christ and the uniqueness of the Christian message. This culminated in intense debate at the first three world missionary conferences of Edinburgh (1910), Jerusalem (1928) and Tambaram (1938) where a wide range of missiological issues were discussed, underlying which was the relationship of Christianity to the world religions. One exclusivist scholar inextricably linked to and towering over these conferences, in particular Tambaram, was the Dutch missiologist Hendrik *Kraemer, whose multi-disciplinary approach combined theological, missiological, linguistic and phenomenological insights. Kraemer's main works, *The Christian Message in a Non-Christian World* (1938), *Religion and the Christian Faith* (1956) and *World Cultures and World Religions* (1960), remain some of the most detailed, nuanced and sophisticated statements within the exclusivist paradigm, and have influenced (though not without criticism) subsequent generations of exclusivist missiologists from the 'Reformed' tradition, most importantly J. H. *Bavinck, Johannes Verkuyl and Lesslie *Newbigin.

Within the contemporary scene, different versions of exclusivism, inclusivism and pluralism can be found at both popular and academic levels, together with the emerging voices of *postliberalism (with its social and political emphasis) and comparative theology (which, in fact, argues against an all-encompassing a priori theology *of* religions, focusing more on a posteriori engagement between living religious traditions).

Rethinking the terms of the debate

As the 'theology of religions' continues to mature as a discipline, an important debate concerns the 'terms' on which the debate has been conducted. Increasingly, many scholars are dissatisfied with the threefold typology. First, as a classificatory system, the tradition-specific nature of all theology means that the theology of religions is a parasitic discipline dependent on other a priori theological commitments. While recognizing the pedagogical usefulness of all typologies and taxonomies, there is no real 'generic' exclusivism, inclusivism or pluralism, and if such generalizations are made, they must be recognized as a rather blunt analytical tool. At the very least, exclusivism, inclusivism and pluralism must be seen as points along a spectrum rather than hermetically sealed positions. For example, 'exclusivism' is a broad enough category to posit a number of different configurations and interpretations concerning issues pertaining to salvation and truth and human religiosity. Exclusivism certainly does not *necessarily* entail a parsimony regarding salvation.

Second, a number of scholars have argued that there is an inbuilt prescriptive bias in the way the threefold typology has been construed, a bias *against* exclusivism often portrayed in overly emotive and 'sensationalistic' terms, and *for* pluralism (and to a lesser extent inclusivism) portrayed not only as more enlightened and tolerant than the other positions, but more significantly religiously and epistemologically 'neutral'. D'Costa has argued that 'pluralism' is itself a 'myth' and in reality a covert form of hardline exclusivism: '"pluralism" represents a tradition-specific approach that bears all the features of exclusivism – except that it is liberal modernity's exclusivism' (*The Meeting of Religions and the Trinity*, London, 2000, p. 22). Far from enabling tolerance and diversity, pluralism does the opposite, for it 'privileges liberal modernity as a mastercode within which all the religions are positioned and neutered' (*Meeting of Religions*, p. 91). His conclusion is that 'pluralism' becomes something other than Christian, a worshipping of the god of modernity rather than the triune God.

The debate within evangelicalism

Despite there being scholarly disagreement amongst evangelicals concerning a plethora of issues regarding soteriological, truth and missiological questions, *evangelicalism is still largely a confessionally exclusivistic movement, stressing the authority of the Bible, the uniqueness of Christ and the necessity of faith in Christ. Three important international symposia have articulated exclusivist themes in their official statements: the Frankfurt Declaration (1970), the *Lausanne Covenant (1974) and the Manila Manifesto (1992), and several evangelical theologians and missiologists have articulated nuanced and constructive exclusivist positions, e.g. Harold Netland, Don Carson, Chris Wright, Vinoth Ramachandra, Gerald McDermott and Terrance Tiessen. More controversially, there are also a handful of evangelical theologians like Clark *Pinnock and John Sanders who can be located more comfortably within inclusivism than exclusivism. Generally speaking, and compared to other traditions, *evangelicals have a lot more thinking to do in this area of theology.

Any evangelical 'theology of religions' must recognize at one and the same time both continuity and discontinuity between the quest for god in other faiths, and the fullness and finality of the knowledge of God 'in the face of Jesus Christ'. Non-Christian religion, alike in its most debased and most elevated manifestations, always bears the dual impress of God's gracious revelation of himself to all humankind in creation and humankind's universal exchange of the truth of God for a lie. So long as these twin biblical perspectives are maintained, there may be scope for legitimate differences in the way Christian theology balances and correlates them in its evaluation of other religions. The two perspectives are tellingly presented in Paul's address at Athens. Despite the universality of God's providential care and presence (Acts 17:24–28), the Athenians' religiosity suppressed the knowledge of the true God. Their abundant images and idols attested their ignorance of him (17:16, 22–23, 29–30), and even their awareness of that ignorance (17:23). Paul's message came to hearers whose refusal to know the living God had left its mark upon their religion. Because *idols are distortions and perversions of truth and so 'related' to truth, like Kraemer one might cautiously say that Christianity is the 'contradictive or subversive fulfilment' of the human religious quest ('Continuity or Discontinuity', in W. Paton [ed.], *The Authority of Faith*, London, 1939, p. 5).

See also: CHRISTIANITY AND OTHER RELIGIONS; CONTEXTUALIZATION; MISSIOLOGY.

Bibliography

J. H. Bavinck, *The Church Between Temple and Mosque* (Grand Rapids, 1966); J. Calvin, *Institutes*; D. A. Carson, *The Gagging of God: Christianity Confronts Pluralism* (Leicester and Grand Rapids, 1996); G. D'Costa, *Theology in the Public Square* (Oxford, 2005); idem, *Christianity and World Religions: Disputed Questions in the Theology of Religions* (Oxford, 2009); G. D'Costa, P. Knitter and D. Strange, *Only One Way? Three Christian Responses on the Uniqueness of Christ in a Religiously Plural World* (London, 2011); V.-M. Kärkkäinen, *An Introduction to the Theology of Religions: Biblical, Historical and Contemporary Perspectives* (Downers Grove, 2003); H. Kraemer, *The Christian Message in a Non-Christian World* (New York, 1938); G. McDermott, *God's Rivals* (Downers Grove, 2007); H. Netland, *Dissonant Voices* (Grand Rapids and Leicester, 1991); idem, *Encountering World Religions: The Challenge to Christian Faith and Mission* (Leicester and Grand Rapids, 2001); T. Perry, *Radical Difference: A Defence of Hendrik Kraemer's Theology of Religions* (Ontario, 2001); A. Plantinga, 'Pluralism: A Defense of Religious Exclusivism', in T. D. Senor (ed.), *The Rationality of Belief and the Plurality of Faith* (London and New York, 1995); D. Strange, *The Possibility of Salvation Among the Unevangelised* (Carlisle, 2002); idem, 'For Their Rock Is Not as Our Rock': An Evangelical Theology of Religions (Nottingham, 2014); T. L. Tiessen, *Who Can Be Saved? Reassessing Salvation in Christ and World Religions* (Leicester and Downers Grove, 2004).

D. S. STRANGE

RELIGIOUS EXPERIENCE

The notion of 'experience' is famously resistant to straightforward definition. The challenges are no less formidable when attempting to define 'religious experience'. Nevertheless, expressed in admittedly very general terms,

Religious experience

experience can be understood as the accumulated impact of all that happens in and to a community or individual in that community or an individual's passive and active engagement with the world. In that case religious experience simply denotes what it is that happens to and in communities and individuals by virtue of their participation in the practices of particular religious traditions. It can refer, therefore, in a technically low-level way, to what happens in an individual's prayer life as much as it can to what happens when a Christian community gathers around the Communion table to celebrate the Eucharist or when that same community participates in prophetic protest against injustice. All of these contribute to the experience of being Christian.

More technical theological discussion of religious experience is oriented towards a set of issues which includes, among other things, the relationship between human and divine agency in such experience, whether there is a normative experience of *God, the nature and role of the *Holy Spirit, the respective weight to be given to individual and communal experience of God, and whether religious experience is a universal phenomenon. Despite the breadth of the topic, however, theological discussion of religious experience can be usefully divided into two broad strands. The first is deeply rooted in Christian thought and focuses on the comprehensiveness of the *Christian life. The second and more recent is methodological and is especially associated with modern theology.

Religious experience and the Christian life

Although not using the term 'religious experience', the biblical tradition insists on the fullness of the life of faith, pointing to the full personal encounter of the believer with God. This is indicated in descriptions of the believer's relationship with God in terms such as seeing (Ps. 34:8; John 12:45), eating (Rev. 3:20), tasting (Heb. 6:4) and intimate fellowship (John 17:21), etc. Such references should not, however, be understood in merely individual or narrowly spiritual terms: the fully personal is also both communal and ethical. Both OT and NT show a deep resistance to anything which disrupts the balance between the personal, communal and moral. For instance, the personal encounter with God is properly liturgical (see *Worship) and therefore communal (e.g. Pss 48; 122; 1 Cor. 11:20–26), but a communal/liturgical encounter with God separated from or at odds with the moral life is harshly criticized (e.g. Amos 5:21–24; Jas 1:26–27).

Such convictions have deeply shaped Christian discourse about religious experience. A prominent place is given to the concept of 'the heart' as that which, although unseen (e.g. 1 Sam. 16:7), encompasses the breadth of the human encounter with God (Pss 13:5; 51:10). In teaching which became seminal for Christian thought and faith, Jesus points to the state or inclination of the heart as the true index of *faith (e.g. Matt. 15:17–20; Mark 7:18–23; Luke 6:42–45). It is important to note, however, that this strand of Jesus' teaching was often specifically targeted against religious hypocrisy (e.g. Matt. 5:20 – 7:27; 9:13; 12:7). For Jesus, therefore, the heart is a moral category: it is the pure heart which yields righteous actions. Accordingly, appeals to the heart have often functioned as correctives to expressions of faith which involve a moral gap between what is believed and what is lived.

These issues have shaped the idea of religious experience, which Christians have often turned to as a way of challenging any merely cognitive or ritualistic expression of the faith (see *Ethics). This was evident in the various eighteenth-century movements in Britain and North America broadly designated 'The Evangelical Revival' or 'The Great Awakening', as well as later 'revivalism' including the Pentecostal movement.

Jonathan *Edwards, one of the key figures of the North American Awakening, produced one of the most theologically sophisticated accounts of the role of experience in the Christian life. In his defence of 'the doctrine of inward experience, or sensible perceiving of the immediate power and operation of the Spirit of God' (*A Treatise Concerning the Religious Affections*, p. 138), Edwards draws attention to the NT's references to the enlightening and revealing work of God (e.g. Eph. 1:17–18) by which believers personally encounter God. Edwards acknowledges the equal legitimacy of both the secret and the spectacular workings of the Spirit, but insists that both are subject to the Johannine injunction to test the spirits (1 John 4:1–6). The global *Pentecostal movement has similarly challenged any neglect of the personal dimension of the encounter with God and has also especially emphasized the need for serious theological attention to the Holy Spirit, the neglect of whom is often a contributing cause of the merely cognitive or ritualistic.

These two movements share one further feature: a tendency to describe religious experience in what are typically psychological categories, somewhat at the expense of its moral dimensions. On this basis, an emphasis on religious experience often becomes an emphasis on the inner over the external, the subjective over the objective, and the affective over the cognitive. This tendency is reinforced and systematized in works of modern theology.

Religious experience and modern theology

The methodological appeal to religious experience is, in fact, a major distinguishing mark of modern theology. The categories of '*religion' and 'experience' presented themselves as foundations which could resist – or elude – the challenges posed to Christian faith by both the natural *sciences and the *rationalism of modern philosophy. Paradigmatically, Friedrich *Schleiermacher proposed the 'feeling of absolute dependence' as just such a foundation. He contended that this particular 'feeling' was a universal human experience which could not be reduced to metaphysical or ethical categories. Schleiermacher's attempt thereby to commend the comprehensiveness of the Christian faith against its reductionist critics was laudable. In his monumental rejoinder, however, Karl *Barth objected that in grounding the possibility of theology in human experience, Schleiermacher had turned theology into *anthropology and, in fact, made Christianity more rather than less vulnerable to the various projection theories which emerged in the nineteenth and twentieth centuries. Barth proposed that theology begins not as a reflection on some or another dimension of human experience, but as an obedient response to God's self-revealing word spoken in Jesus and attested in Scripture.

Arguably, however, an equally telling criticism of the methodological appeal to religious experience is its twofold narrowing of the very experience to which it refers. First, through the cultural and intellectual processes of *secularization, 'religion' had begun to function in the modern West as a description of an apolitical, privatized and circumscribed realm. Despite, therefore, attempts to appeal to experience as a non-reductive category, qualifying it as *religious* experience necessarily narrowed the range of what it referred to. Secondly, by treating this particular experience as self-evidently universal, it was necessary to place it outside or above the particular beliefs and language of the Christian (or any other religious) community. Consequently, religious experience was located in a narrow pre-cognitive, prelinguistic realm of life. These trends are especially evident in the following classical statement from William James: 'The truth is that in the . . . religious sphere particular reasons are cogent for us only when our inarticulate feelings of reality have already been impressed in favour of the same conclusion. Then, indeed, our intuitions and our reason work together, and great world-ruling systems, like that of the Buddhist or of the Catholic philosophy, may grow up. Our impulsive belief is here always what sets up the original body of truth, and our articulately verbalized philosophy is but its showy translation into formulas' (*The Varieties of Religious Experience*, p. 73).

Here, the key features of the distinctively modern appeal to religious experience are all in place: the designation of a specifically religious 'sphere'; the priority of 'inarticulate feelings' and 'intuition'; and the designation of language and communally held beliefs as ultimately superficial. In fact, the greater the distance placed between religious experience and specific theological claims, the more tentative and imprecise become the claims for the object of the religious experience: 'the one who raised the Lord Jesus' (2 Cor. 4:14), for instance, gives way to such generalizations as 'The Sacred', 'The Divine', 'The Transcendent', 'The Ultimate Mystery', 'The Holy', etc.

Such moves press the question of just what constitutes the Christian experience of God. Nicholas Lash suggests that '[i]f . . . Christianity has an experiential "root" or "core", then it is to be found not in "fleeting" or "puzzling" transient states of private consciousness, but in the experience of Jesus in Gethsemane and on Calvary, and in the experience of his followers . . .' (*The Beginning and End of 'Religion'*, p. 110).

Christians experience God as they are incorporated by the Spirit into the eschatological drama which takes its rise from these foundational events that cannot be contained with the confines of 'religion'. In fact, Christians do not experience 'religion'. Instead, they experience God revealed in *Jesus as he is attested in the narratives of Scripture and proclaimed in the worship, witness and service of the church. The modern notion of religious experience (even if renamed with the contemporary categories of '*spirituality' or 'identity') is not, therefore, a foundation for theology, but is itself the object of critical theological reflection.

Bibliography

K. Barth, *CD* I/1, I/2; K. Berger, *Identity and Experience in the New Testament* (ET, Minneapolis, 2003); J. Edwards, *A Treatise Concerning the Religious Affections* (New Haven, 1959 [1754]); W. James, *The Varieties of Religious Experience: A Study in Human Nature* (New York, 1902); N. Lash, *Easter in Ordinary: Reflections on Human Experience and the Knowledge of God* (London, 1988); idem, *The Beginning and End of 'Religion'* (Cambridge, 1996); G. A. Lindbeck, *The Nature of Doctrine: Religion and Theology in a Postliberal Age* (Philadelphia, 1984); W. Proudfoot, *Religious Experience* (Berkeley, 1985); F. Schleiermacher, *The Christian Faith* (ET, Edinburgh, 1989); G. P. Schner, 'The Appeal to Experience', *TS* 53, 1992, pp. 40–59.

G. J. THOMPSON

RELIGIOUS LANGUAGE

For a religion of the book like Christianity, the issue of language takes on great importance. This is an issue that has two sides to it. One is that the language of religion is basically the same as non-religious language. It is not a special, sacred language unto itself. The NT, for instance, is written in the common (*koiné*) Greek of the day. Its immense variety of confession, praise, prayer, poetry, story, depiction, argumentation, and so on is not dissimilar to language used in other contexts. Second, religious language nevertheless strains ordinary language at times to its breaking point, especially when speaking of the transcendent *God. Somehow God must be spoken of without *idolatry.

Through most of Christian history, three major options emerged. One was that language about God has basically the same literal or 'univocal' meaning as when used in other contexts. This assures that words have cognitive meaning when used of God, but the danger is that it limits God. For this reason, *Thomas Aquinas rejected this option in the thirteenth century. John *Duns Scotus reaffirmed it in the next generation while rejecting Aquinas's argument for a third way, arguing that only two choices are possible: words are either univocal or equivocal. Since he accepted that cognitive revelation has occurred, then the former option is the only one possible. The view that meaning is preserved in univocal language and its corollary that symbolic or metaphorical uses of language must be translated into literal language has made bedfellows of diverse theologians in the last century such as Carl F. H. Henry, Paul *Tillich and Schubert Ogden. This view and a suspicion of figurative language have been dominant in modern philosophy, which in turn has influenced theology toward an emphasis on literal language and propositional language.

At the opposite end of the spectrum was a second option early in the church, the so-called *via negativa* or negative way, whereby all claims about God are denied, not for the sake of sceptical unbelief, but for the sake of the most intense *mystical awareness of God possible. *Dionysius the Areopagite (fifth or sixth century), who had an almost canonical status for a thousand years because he was mistakenly thought to be the Dionysius mentioned in Acts, propounded this view. The problem of course for a religion of *revelation is that this makes revelation non-cognitive. Language may be instrumentally effective in leading one to an encounter with God, but it cannot describe God. Some modern approaches such as those of Richard Braithwaite and Richard Hare have essentially followed this instrumentalist approach in making God-language helpful in living a moral way of life without necessarily affirming God. The problem is that this approach undercuts any meaningful sense of revelation as conveying a greater understanding of God.

Aquinas quotes Dionysius heavily and actually argues that one must begin with the *via negativa*. In other words, language cannot literally describe God's transcendence of the creation. Yet in an analogical sense one can apply words to God. In one place, Aquinas suggests that this is because God is the cause of all things. In saying that God is good, for example, we are saying that God is the source of goodness but is not good in the same way that creatures are good. Moreover, Aquinas thought that those words that best analogically applied to God were words that could express God's infinity, such as goodness, love, power, knowledge, and so on, as opposed to 'metaphorical' terms that were inherently finite, such as a fortress, a lion, a shepherd.

In the end, none of these approaches seemed satisfactory. Even Aquinas's explanations seemed to reduce *analogy to the univocal approach in seeing God as the cause of all things. If 'cause' is not thereby used univocally, then he is essentially making a circular argument, explaining analogy by an analogy. The twentieth century became, however, the century of the linguistic turn in general and has offered multiple resources for religious language. Developments in the philosophy of metaphor and symbol have pointed to what some see as Aquinas's main point, namely, that figurative language need not be 'translated' into univocal language to be used and understood. This in effect has rehabilitated his third way and also offered fertile resources for understanding the biblical language of poetry and parables. These need not, and cannot, be fully translated into literal language or propositions and stand on their own. As Tillich said at one point, one can say things in symbols that cannot be said in any other way. One can thus never leave the Bible behind once one has 'explained' its meaning, which has sometimes been a tendency in theology and preaching, but must return to *Scripture for insight over and over again in a *hermeneutical spiral.

This is not to eliminate the place of univocal explanation or propositions, but it makes them supplementary to such figurative language rather than replacing them. In fact, the work of the later Ludwig Wittgenstein emphasized that even univocal language is more flexible than previously thought. As he said, it has 'blurred edges', which allow for broader application (*Philosophical Investigations*, New York, 1958, p. 71). He also made the primary issue one of effective use, so a word has meaning if it has a use. The use, he additionally pointed out, is usually particular to a community, so a word might mean something literally to one group but not another. This allows for a rehabilitation of the univocal way where one might say that certain words such as holiness and love have their primary univocal meaning when applied to God. Wittgenstein's emphasis on the 'language game' or the 'form of life' (*Philosophical Investigations*, pp. 7, 19) as being essential to meaning led to warnings of the danger of 'Wittgensteinian *fideism', where no-one not 'playing' the particular religious language game can criticize it. This focus of Wittgenstein on the use of language, however, bore fruit in John Austin's work, *How to Do Things with Words* (Cambridge, 1975). Austin pointed out the descriptive fallacy, which assumes that words usually are just describing things. Rather, he indicated that people do many things with words, such as confessing, praising, praying, exhorting and commanding, which cannot be reduced to simple description. Biblical expositors such as Anthony Thiselton have shown how helpful this is for understanding multiple dimensions of biblical language. Others like Nancey Murphy, Michael Goldberg and Nicholas Wolterstorff have shown how this helps to understand the general nature of revelation.

Both of these shifts in understanding have contributed to appreciation of narrative in Scripture and fostered several forms of *narrative theology. All of these assume that narratives cannot be simply reduced to literal language, but have an integrity of their own, much like metaphor. In fact, they usually assume that literal language has its meaning only in the context of a larger socio-cultural narrative. Alasdair *MacIntyre particularly has pointed out how the modern Enlightenment emphasis on reason and univocal language is based on a narrative that did not realize it was a narrative. More recently, John *Milbank of the *Radical Orthodoxy movement has pointed out that one cannot thus out-argue one's opponents, but must in the end 'out-narrate' them (*Theology and Social Theory*, Cambridge, 1993, p. 330). Others, like James McClendon, have emphasized the centrality of biographies (my story, your story) for making sense of faith. The so-called *Yale school of postliberal theology is seen as a type of narrative theology that emphasizes not so much the cultural story (our story) but the biblical story (THE story), where we must allow the biblical world to absorb our world rather than vice versa. Paul *Ricœur and Kevin Vanhoozer have stressed that the Bible does not just contain one such genre to which everything else must be reduced, but has many kinds of language, such as narrative, law, wisdom, prophecy, and apocalyptic, each of which must be respected on its own terms.

These positive approaches to religious language have largely taken the place of the sceptical question of religious language that dominated the middle twentieth century. The *logical positivist's 'verification principle' meant that words have cognitive meaning insofar as they can be empirically verified. This was modified later by Antony Flew and others to a 'falsification principle' that stressed that a claim must be empirically falsifiable to have meaning. On these grounds, God-talk was seen not even to rise to the category of being false; it was nonsense. It was language that 'died the death by a thousand qualifications' (B. Mitchell [ed.], *The Philosophy of Religion*, p. 14). In the end, neither principle could be consistently substantiated. Some, like Ian Ramsey and Ian Crombie, however, saw that they could be valid to some extent if one allowed 'logically odd' language such as 'kingdom of God' to relate to a 'broader empiricism' or 'reference range' that could include discernment of God. Basil Mitchell pointed not to simple verification but to 'cumulative case' reasoning that involves personal and even eschatological factors (B. Mitchell, *The Justification of Religious Belief*, Oxford and New York, 1981, ch. 3). The poststructuralist deconstruction of Jacques Derrida also had influence toward a rejection of any kind of transcendent claim or metanarrative. More recently, some have found even in Derrida's thought room for a kind of negative theology. Along with other kinds of critique, it at least supports a 'hermeneutic of suspicion' that can clear the ground of ideology for a 'hermeneutic of testimony', as Ricœur suggests (*Essays on Biblical Interpretation* [Fort Worth, 1980], pp. 119–154). The effect of this wide reflection on language and specifically religious language has offered much richer and nuanced resources that are still being plumbed for understanding Scripture and theology.

Bibliography

J. D. Crossan, *In Parables: The Challenge of the Historical Jesus* (New York, 1973); M. Goldberg, *Theology and Narrative: A Critical Introduction* (Nashville, 1982); G. Lindbeck, *The Nature of Doctrine: Religion and Theology in a Postliberal Age* (Philadelphia, 1984); J. W. McClendon, Jr, *Biography as Theology: How Life Stories Can Remake Today's Theology* (Nashville, 1974); B. Mitchell (ed.), *The Philosophy of Religion* (Oxford and New York, 1971); P. Ricœur, *Interpretation Theory: Discourse and the Surplus of Meaning* (Fort Worth, 1976); D. R. Stiver, *The Philosophy of Religious Language: Sign, Symbol, and Story* (Cambridge, 1996); A. C. Thiselton, *The Two Horizons: New Testament Hermeneutics and Philosophical Description* (Grand Rapids, 1980); K. J. Vanhoozer (ed.), *The Cambridge Companion to Postmodern Theology* (Cambridge, 2003); N. Wolterstorff, *Divine Discourse: Philosophical Reflections on the Claim That God Speaks* (Cambridge, 1995).

D. R. STIVER

RENAISSANCE, see HUMANISM (RENAISSANCE)

REPENTANCE

Although the verb 'repent' (*niḥam*) is used in the OT generally to refer to the consideration of a change of plan on God's part, it can also refer to human repentance. It is usually translated in the NT by *metanoeō*, the equivalent noun being *metanoia*. The Heb. verb *šûb*, also referring to a change, 'turning around' or *conversion, is translated in the LXX as *epistrephō*. The two are closely connected. Repentance was the theme of the preaching of John the Baptist, and also accompanied Jesus' more positive proclamation of the coming of the *kingdom of God. After the descent of the Spirit on the apostles at Pentecost, repentance and *faith were required as a response to Peter's first preaching of the Christian *gospel of Christ crucified and risen. Whereas to be converted or to turn around (*epistrephō*) might seem to focus on the outward change, the word *metanoia* means literally 'a change of mind' and so may be thought to include also the inward revolution that lies at the heart of the outward behavioural change.

In the early centuries of the church, faith and repentance were prerequisites for Christian baptism, and rigorists taught that this repentance could occur only once. A Christian who committed one of the capital sins such as blasphemy, apostasy, adultery or murder was considered to be beyond redemption in the light of passages such as Heb. 6:1–6. Gradually this was softened until the practice of *penance developed, by which Christians could confess, repent and make '*satisfaction', thus being reconciled and avoiding eternal punishment. The Celtic church introduced private penitential practices, and eventually penance was defined as one of the *sacraments of the church.

The *Reformers rejected this development, not least because of the further developments of

*purgatory and indulgences out of the practice of penance. *Luther reacted particularly against a view of penance which seemed to make sufficient penitence (doing 'all that in you lies') necessary to merit forgiveness of sins. Rather, repentance came with the faith which *justifies and which was the gift of God (see *Grace). True faith, given by God, was then a mighty, active thing which brought about a change of mind and a change of life. And yet it was paradoxical: the Christian was at the same time justified and a sinner (*simul iustus et peccator*). Calvin distinguished between 'legal repentance' arising from fear of divine anger, and 'evangelical repentance' which is a consequence of faith in Christ. He defines it as 'a real conversion of our life to God proceeding from a sincere and serious fear of God and consisting in the mortification of our flesh and the old man, and the quickening of the Spirit' (*Institutes*, III.3.5).

The danger of a nominal Christian commitment and what Bonhoeffer called 'cheap grace' can only be avoided if repentance is seen to be necessary, not as a way to buy or merit grace, but as an implication of the gift of faith. While there must be a first serious step of faith and repentance, an attitude of repentance, that is to say, of confession and humility, is also regarded as necessary throughout the Christian's pilgrimage. A new appreciation today of the reality of corporate sin should also lead to practices of corporate repentance.

See also: GUILT AND FORGIVENESS.

Bibliography

J. Calvin, *Institutes*, III.3, 'Regeneration by Faith: Of Repentance'; S. Ferguson, *The Grace of Repentance* (Wheaton, 2010); Tertullian, 'On Repentance', *ANF*, vol. 3, pp. 657–666; R. S. Wallace, *Calvin's Doctrine of the Christian Life*, esp. ch. 5 (Edinburgh, 1959); J. Wesley, 'The Repentance of Believers', sermon 14, *Works*, vol. 1, pp. 335–352 (Nashville, 1984).

T. A. NOBLE

REPRESENTATION, see SUBSTITUTION AND REPRESENTATION

REPROBATION, see PREDESTINATION

RESURRECTION OF CHRIST

Situated between his *descent into hell and *ascent into heaven, Christ's resurrection is a trinitarian act of the Father raising the crucified *Jesus in the power of the Spirit to new, glorified human life after three days of burial.

From the beginning (1 Cor. 15:14) it has been a defining doctrine, vital for the integrity of the Christian faith. The early Fathers vigorously defended it against the heresies of *Docetism and *Gnosticism. It appeared in one of the earliest, most universal and apostolic confessional forms, the Rule of Faith, as well as in the Apostles' Creed. More significant is its enshrinement in the first ecumenical creed, the *Creed of Nicaea.

Crucial to the recognition and worship of the Christian God, belief in Christ's resurrection must be maintained despite modern pressures to abandon it in favour of a more ethically oriented and scientifically acceptable Christianity. As the early church protested against anti-materialist Docetism and Gnosticism, the church today must do likewise against contemporary philosophical and scientific *materialism.

The theological implications chiefly concern Christology, soteriology, sanctification, ecclesiology, eschatology and creation. Once the meaning for these *loci* has been detailed, two major attendant theological issues will be considered.

Theological implications

*Christology

As the continuation of the incarnation and his glorification, Christ's resurrection sustains and magnifies his priestly, prophetic and kingly offices. The finality of Jesus' past work should not eclipse his present ministry.

The resurrection of Christ, which dictates the mode of his ascension, confirms that the eternal Son's *incarnation was not temporary but permanent. Jesus arose from the dead not a phantom or apparition, but a genuine human being (cf. John 20:20). His bodily resurrection was quickly contested, however. Operating with Platonic anti-materialism, Docetism and Gnosticism held salvation was the immaterial soul's liberation from embodiment and thus denied any bodily component to the Saviour. This was the background for Athenagoras' *On the Resurrection of the Dead*, *Tertullian's

Resurrection of Christ

On the Resurrection of the Flesh and much of *Irenaeus' Against Heresies*, writings which defended the physicality of Christ's resurrection. Later, *Thomas Aquinas stressed the continuity between Christ's dead and resurrected body to the point where every drop of blood spilled on the cross 'rose again with his body'; this led him to qualify the blood contained in relics (see *Summa Theologica*, III, Q. 54).

There are discontinuities, however. Aquinas also argued that Jesus' resurrected body 'differed in glory'. The Gospels portray not a resuscitated Jesus, but a resurrected Jesus whose body had been glorified, made immortal and incorruptible. As Christ's glorification, the resurrection means the Son's eternal glory pervades more fully his humanity. Just how many differences exist will be partially a function of one's view of whether the Son assumed *fallen* flesh. If so, then Christ's resurrection would mean glorification *and* sanctification. Otherwise the differences would concern only the former. The important point is to maintain both continuity – Christ rose in the same body he possessed at death – and discontinuity – that body was glorified (not merely revived) as it transitioned from death to life.

Central to the logic of Christ's mediation/priestly office is the *hypostatic union. By preserving the incarnation, Christ's resurrection preserves his *mediatorial ministry, his role as sole intercessor between God and humanity. Accordingly, it is entirely appropriate to address God 'in the name of Jesus Christ'. Christians enter the presence of the Father in worship and beseech him in their prayers only through the resurrected Mediator. As the means for humanity's intimate access to God, Christ's resurrection should energize communion with the transcendent Father.

Without his resurrection, Jesus' teaching would remain scandalized by his death, particularly Israel's judgment that he was a false prophet whose death was required by OT prescriptions. So, his resurrection divinely vindicates him and his prophetic heralding of the *kingdom of God. By raising Jesus from the dead, God declared to the world that Jesus is his Son who has faithfully testified on his behalf. In this way, Christ's emergence from the tomb is the Father's reiteration in deed of the words he spoke when Jesus arose from the baptismal waters: 'This is my Son, the Beloved; listen to him' (Mark 9:7, NRSV).

Resurrected, Christ continues to tell the world about his *Father who sent him, and does so by sending his *Spirit who declares only what he hears from Christ (John 16:13). It is on this basis that the church can, even now, hear and heed Christ in Holy Scripture. The church knows and accepts the witness of the OT prophets and NT apostles because she answers to God's perfect prophet and sent one, Jesus Christ. *Scripture is living and active because its Word lives today. Christ is the living source of the biblical message; the criteria for canonicity are therefore neither arbitrary nor subjective, but Christological.

The resurrection, along with the ascension, reveals the kingship of Jesus Christ. The Son's eternal lordship is historically manifest in Jesus' resurrection, for it is the triumph of righteousness over sin and life over death (*Christus Victor*).

Jesus Christ *lives*. In him there is human life, full and true. He is thus the Lord of eternal life and new creation, imparting it to whoever is 'in Christ'. So, he is the head of the church, the new community which has received the Spirit as guarantor of an eternal inheritance.

*Soteriology

The *righteousness established in Christ's cross results in his resurrection because life is the potency of righteousness. *Justification entails resurrection. Hence, John *Calvin interpreted Rom. 4:25 to mean the 'efficacy' of justification lies in resurrection (see his Romans commentary). In his 1 Corinthians commentary he surmised that without Christ's resurrection human sin would remain imputed (cf. his *Institutes* II.xvi.13).

When humanity fell from God's intention, it fell into corruption; the depth of this plunge is seen in Christ's cross and descent into hell. However, Christ's resurrection raises humanity from its depravity, freeing it from its bondages to the devil, death and decay and restoring it to wholeness. In the general *resurrection, when Christ's resurrection becomes their own, Christians will inhabit a redeemed human nature fully alive to God.

Sanctification

Christ's resurrected body is the new humanity, and is therefore the source of *sanctification. Just as the mortification of sinful flesh depends upon Christ's crucifixion (see *Cross), so too the vivification of the 'new man' requires his resurrection. Only by the power that raised Jesus from the dead will Christians be able to live a new life, a power itself accessible only through union with the resurrected Christ.

Ecclesiology

Like the early disciples who were made witnesses by the resurrected Lord's appearances, the *church is the community specially 'set apart' and 'called out' to testify to Christ's resurrection, for through word, sacrament and Christian *fellowship the resurrected Lord appears subtly but no less profoundly. As Christ's body, the church tastes the resurrection life in advance of its final consummation in the church's glorification. Christians are those who identify with the resurrected Lord through baptism; they are 'the Easter people, and Alleluia is [their] song', as Pope John Paul II exclaimed.

Eschatology

The resurrection of Christ marks the transition to the age of God's new creation and kingdom on earth. The *eschatological life has already dawned in the resurrected Jesus; wherever he is, there the future invades the present. Christ's resurrection means eschatology must have an 'already-not yet' character: the end is already 'at hand' in the reign of the resurrected Christ, but, since the resurrected Christ is the ascended Christ, it is not yet fully realized on earth. The latter is our hope and prayer: 'Your kingdom come, your will be done on earth as it is in heaven' (Matt. 6:10).

Resurrection is God's verdict upon Christ's righteousness; God's future *judgment of the world has already been handed down in him. The resurrected Lord, therefore, is the universal criterion for God's eschatological judgment; only those found in him will receive the covenant reward of eternal life.

Creation

The continuity between Christ's dead and resurrected body indicates God's commitment to his initial *creation and humanity as the *imago Dei*. Christianity is not anti-materialist and its soteriology is not gnostic. God pronounced creation good. In Christ's resurrection he actively repeats this declaration. Yet, as the discontinuity, the glorification implicit within resurrection, means Jesus is the 'first fruits' of a redeemed world, so God's commitment to his creation in Jesus' resurrection is an act of new creation, the creation of the new heavens and new earth which we await. Christ's resurrection, then, is cosmic in scope, a reality that redemptively redirects and reconstitutes current space and time. Christianity ought to encourage an ethic of life that propels the cultivation of, and care for, God's creation in anticipation of its future renewal (see *Ecology).

Attendant theological issues

God-world relationship

As a divine act in the world, Christ's resurrection has implications for the God-world relationship. At the very least, resurrection is a strong claim about God's activity in the *world, a claim that excludes *atheism, *deism and worldviews which see God's agency as bounded by created realities. While it occurs in history, it is not a function of previous historical sequences, nor does it arise from prior natural processes. It is a divine act, and therefore in an important sense also transcends history. Consequently, it forces Christian theology to have a concept of the miraculous, a place for super-natural/-historical causation of worldly events.

Stephen Davis has thus used Christ's resurrection as an occasion to criticize both David *Hume's scepticism of miracles and scientific naturalism as well as to defend the rationality of the supernatural on a *theistic worldview (see *Risen Indeed: Making Sense of the Resurrection*, London, 1993).

Wolfhart *Pannenberg offers perhaps the most radical challenge to the naturalistic worldview. He has simply scoffed at the unscientific attempts to evade the evidentiary weight of Christ's resurrection, writing: '[T]he reconstructions [of historical critics] are more fantastic than the biblical reports themselves, and one often wonders how easily critical historians, who examine their sources with a great deal of scepticism, believe their own imaginations without checking the historical plausibility of their intuitions with comparable rigor' ('Resurrection: The Ultimate Hope', in K. Tanner and C. Hall (eds.), *Ancient and Postmodern Christianity*, Downers Grove, 2002, p. 260). He has also accused the presupposing of naturalism in modern historiography of premature biasing, using Christ's resurrection's historicity to revise historical method. Most importantly, Pannenberg has argued that Christ's resurrection sits comfortably with contemporary science's view of the universe as less a closed system of causation and more 'elastic' and 'open'.

Since an account of the reality of Christ's resurrection rests on specifically Christian theological commitments about God and the world, Christianity's defence of it will take place primarily at the worldview level. We must be careful, then, about what sort of results we hope to harvest from historical apologetics. Perhaps it is best to keep in mind that Joseph's tomb is no more historically accessible than Mary's womb. Testimonial evidence strongly supports the conclusion that Jesus came to life in both instances. But the further claims of resurrection and incarnation ascribe a very specific notion of divine agency to these events, and that requires a worldview, if not faith itself. This does not mean that Christian faith is private, only that Christianity's public discourse will assume a more prophetic tenor: Christians will call the world to faith in the God who raised Jesus Christ from the dead, expose the weaknesses of naturalism and bemoan the inevitable meaninglessness, immorality and despair of a godless world.

The relationship between faith and history

The modern period pressed the faith-history relationship in unique ways, and Christ's resurrection became a flash-point for debate. With scientific theories challenging the supernatural, the aftermath of the Wars of Religion of the sixteenth and seventeenth centuries ushering in a quest for religious tolerance which resulted in a less confessional and more ethical Christianity, and historical-criticism questioning Scripture's origin and reliability, modern theologians were forced to re-evaluate the way *faith related to *history. Do, for example, the propositions of faith stand for actual historical realities, or are they rather symbols of personal and social transformation, the claim to historicity being merely rhetorical? Two interpretations of Christ's resurrection arose: (1) psychological; and (2) historicist.

A minimalist account of the relationship between *faith and history regarding Christ's resurrection understands the historical dimension as a metaphor for faith where faith is not belief in an historical event, but the recognition of some greater truth thought to be existentially empowering. Adolf *Harnack, for example, distinguished between the 'Easter faith' and 'Easter message', deciding that the real significance of Jesus' resurrection was not the historical fact of the empty tomb, but that 'this grave was the birthplace of the indestructible *belief* that death is vanquished, that there is a life eternal'. Such a belief 'makes our earthly life worth living and tolerable' (*What Is Christianity?* New York, 1957, p. 162). Rudolf *Bultmann, believing the earliest Christians had difficulty expressing themselves, brought the *history-of-religions school's interpretation of the resurrection accounts as the disciples' translation of their appreciation for Jesus into a Hellenistic myth about a dying and rising saviour god. For Bultmann, the idea of resurrection was the way Christians conceptualized and communicated their sense for the ongoing significance of Christ's death.

For different reasons – following the trend of exchanging classic metaphysical versions of salvation for social ones – Rowan *Williams can be located within this trajectory. While personally convinced of the resurrection's historicity, he can be ambivalent toward it, focusing more on how the event constitutes a Christian identity that is received from God, not self-constructed: 'The essential point is that resurrection *is the transaction in human beings* that brings about the essence of a selfhood given not achieved [. . .] The resurrection of Jesus may be (as I for one believe) at least the empty tomb, but it is most importantly [. . .] judgement upon the attempt to construct a system of action and understanding so impregnable that it cannot live with prophetic criticism and judgement too upon our sentimental assumption that we can sustain newness of life beyond the regularities of "law" independently of relation to a "giving" reality' (*On Christian Theology*, Oxford, 2000, p. 271). Elsewhere he has given a sustained interpretation of the type of social praxis to which Christ's resurrection gives rise. For example, he suggests that by raising Christ from the dead God condemned humanity's judgment. Therefore, the church cannot be judgmental, but loving and accepting, particularly of those ostracized by society.

The historicist position sees Christ's resurrection as historical and faith in it as at least an acknowledgment of such. Reacting against what he perceived as the uncritical subjectivism of Bultmann and Karl *Barth, *Pannenberg defended the full historicity of Christ's resurrection out of a commitment to his specific configuration of the faith-history relationship, namely, 'revelation as history'. Here, biblical events have no unique character that would distinguish them from regular historical events. Faith claims must be 'rational' and therefore subject to normal historical verification.

Yet, both historicity and faith's transformative power are crucial. Faith in Christ's resurrection should not come at the expense of its historicity, and its historicity should not cost faith. Barth, who took issue with Bultmann's view but did not approach the resurrection apologetically, may represent a way forward. He agreed with Bultmann that Jesus' resurrection was comprehended by faith, not 'neutral' historical investigations. Yet Barth believed the *historical* resurrection was itself *the* determinative element for faith. Contra Bultmann, Christ's resurrection was not the product of, but *the reason for*, the earliest Christian *kerygma* (preaching). True Christian faith is communion with Christ and therefore Christ must live today. Barth thus retained the resurrection's historicity, but did not allow faith in it to be collapsed into the past. The past event was critical, not because it proves Christianity, but because of what it means for who Jesus *is*.

Ultimately, what is needed is an apocalyptic perspective on the resurrection's historicity in which the past event unveils both the fullness of the present as governed by Jesus' heavenly reign and the promised future his resurrection inaugurates. The historical significance of Christ's resurrection is not limited to the tomb, but includes his present activity as head of the church and the future he interjects. *A truly historical resurrection is thus past, present and future.* Faith, then, is not simply taking heart in the past, but submitting to Christ's present lordship and being possessed by the future of God's new creation introduced in Christ's resurrection, which may mean participating in hopeful praxis as outlined by Williams and others.

Bibliography

K. Barth, *The Resurrection of the Dead* (ET, Eugene, 2003); R. Jenson, *Systematic Theology*, vol. 1 (Oxford, 2001); W. Kunneth, *The Theology of the Resurrection* (St Louis, 1965); P. D. Molnar, *Incarnation and Resurrection: Toward a Contemporary Understanding* (Grand Rapids, 2007); G. O'Collins, *Jesus Risen: An Historical, Fundamental and Systematic Examination of Christ's Resurrection* (New York, 1987); O. O'Donovan, *Resurrection and Moral Order: An Outline for Evangelical Ethics* (Grand Rapids and Leicester, ²1994); T. F. Torrance, *Space, Time and Resurrection* (Edinburgh, 1998); J. B. Webster, 'Resurrection and Scripture', in A. Lincoln and A. Paddison (eds.), *Christology and Scripture: Interdisciplinary Perspectives* (London, 2007); R. Williams, *Resurrection: Interpreting the Easter Gospel* (London, 1982); N. T. Wright, *The Resurrection of the Son of God* (Minneapolis and London, 2003).

J. R. A. MERRICK

RESURRECTION, GENERAL

The general resurrection is the decisive future action of God upon human beings by which the redemptive work of Christ will be consummated and the eternal life of God's new *creation will begin. In the present age, the church lives in the 'sure and certain hope' of this resurrection promise (words from the Christian funeral service). Along with the *parousia* of Christ and the final judgment, general resurrection forms the content of Christian *eschatology, the doctrine of last things.

History of general resurrection

The roots of the concept of general resurrection belong firmly in the Jewish confidence that God's covenant with faithful Israel would continue, even beyond the human limit of death. Through the intertestamental period, this understanding developed to include the expectation of a bodily resurrection of all the faithful, and perhaps of the wicked too, for judgment at the 'day of the Lord'. The *resurrection of Jesus Christ in the middle of history – one man on his own – was completely unexpected, and gave rise to the intense theological reflection of the apostles and the early church. What happened to Jesus was the 'firstfruits' of what will happen to all who belong to him. The hope of general resurrection is thus close to the centre of the NT understanding of the *gospel, and was affirmed in the major creeds of the church by the phrase 'resurrection of the dead'.

The early Church Fathers were careful to emphasize that the awaited resurrection was to be a bodily renewal, and not simply the continuation of an immaterial soul after death. This emphasis directly countered the view of the *Gnostics and others influenced by Greek dualism, who believed that the soul is the only continuing element of human life, while the body perishes along with all other created matter. In response, the Church Fathers stressed the resurrection of the *flesh*, affirming both the power of God to reconstitute bodies and the necessary re-embodiment of the soul in order for it to live in full fellowship with God in eternal life. The resurrection of the flesh does not mean, however, that the resurrected body will be exactly the same as when it died. Justin Martyr and Tertullian spoke of the complete healing of the resurrection body, while Origen emphasized the transformation into a spiritual body that will take place.

During the Middle Ages, this commitment to the bodily nature of the general resurrection was upheld, and the main question concerned the period of waiting between the death of a believer and the moment of resurrection – what is known as the *intermediate state. In the twelfth century, Bernard of Clairvaux explained that the soul is in a state of incompletion until it is reunited with the body at the day of resurrection. This position reveals a belief in the continuing existence of the soul alongside the hope of bodily resurrection. The soul is in a state of sleep, or rest, until it can enjoy fellowship with God in the new creation.

The early modern period began to see a weakening of the commitment to bodily resurrection, and it was often assumed that the reconstitution of bodies after death was a scientific implausibility. This obviously affected belief in the resurrection of Jesus, with some theologians suggesting it was either a hoax or a delusion; correspondingly, the doctrine of general resurrection began to drop out of view. In popular evangelicalism, the Christian hope was often reduced to 'going to heaven when we die', which was perceived as a spiritual, rather than bodily, existence.

Recent theology, however, has begun to recover the doctrine of general resurrection. *Pannenberg, for instance, makes God's promise of future bodily resurrection programmatic for his entire theological work, and this hope also informs the project of *Moltmann. N. T. Wright has worked through the biblical material to show the central significance of this doctrine for practical Christian faith.

Some systematic issues

What happens to us after *death is often seen as an individual matter by many Christians. However, general resurrection is a reminder of the corporate hope of the Christian faith. While there may be an initial intermediate state directly after death, resurrection will happen to all simultaneously as the fulfilment of God's *redemptive work and the beginning of his new creation. General resurrection thus connects the Christian to the cosmic scope of salvation, and is a caution against a private, individualistic faith.

Ambiguity remains over whether all will be raised to face the final judgment, or only those who will inherit the *kingdom of God, for whom resurrection is their entrance into eternal life. If the risen Christ is seen as the 'firstfruits' of those who are raised, however, it seems more likely that the second view is the case.

The doctrine of general resurrection is a strong argument for the goodness of created matter and the essential unity of body and soul in the human life. That our future life in God's kingdom will involve resurrected bodies should also be a motivation to use our present ones wisely. In addition, the hope of resurrection is a cause of praise and joy for the Christian, transforming even our view of death. As the promised fulfilment of Christ's work of salvation, the general resurrection will complete the redemption of our bodies and usher us into the new creation.

See also: IMMORTALITY; JUDGMENT OF GOD.

Bibliography

K. Barth, *The Resurrection of the Dead* (London, 1933); J. E. McWilliam Dewart, *Death and Resurrection* (Wilmington, 1986); W. Pannenberg, *Systematic Theology*, vol. 3 (Edinburgh and Grand Rapids, 1998) esp. ch. 15; N. T. Wright, *Surprised by Hope* (London, 2007).

A. J. STOBART

REVELATION

As the condition of possibility for *faith, revelation is a key concept in Christian theology. In the revelation of his mystery, God does not stop being that mystery. Most theologians work with the distinction between 'general' and 'special' revelation. If general revelation is God's everyday self-communication to the world, then special revelation takes its form in events of saving *history in Israel, culminating in the NT events, and has its impact in written

*Scripture. The 'mighty acts of God' and words spoken prophetically or apostolically are each the interpretation of the other. The tradition of interpretation of Scripture is a channel for that revelation. O. Bayer, quoting Luther, counsels believers to stay within God's word as within a cradle, the context for understanding ourselves, the text which constitutes the self, although for Luther what we find in the text is first and foremost the Son of God as Jesus of Nazareth. For A. Dulles, mystery is not 'what is left over after theology has done its best', but is the source and nourishment of theology.

Yet the form of revelation is most like an address, whose aim is to bring humans to trust *God, so as to come close to him and participate in his divine life. This takes us some distance from the 'merely propositional' view of revelation, and means that information about God gets communicated in the context of an invitation to a God-human relationship. Yet to go further and call this a 'dialogue' would be a step too far. It is communication in symbolic form from God which engages the whole human being. Scripture and the word of God of course receive interpretation in doctrinal and homiletic terms, but this is secondary to the moment of revelation which was an address to a specific group of people ('prophets and apostles'), and which has then been 'forwarded' to us. In the language of *narrative theology, that forwarding of revelation refers to that process in which the personal identities of readers are reinterpreted and transformed by means of the narratives which supply a new identity in Christ. One might speak of new room in which to live, new possibilities, adding to what is already given in creation. Yet that may still be received as a surprise since we have wilfully forgotten what was given to us. Revelation is not now new, but it might be 'new to us'. Revelation has its effect and influence 'when things click into place, when a luminous perspective emerges, which both perfects the pre-given religious framework and exceeds it'. What is revealed is not so much the essential nature of who God is, as his plan and will. Only in the Bible are created things also signifiers (Alexander of Hales, tightening Augustine).

There can be a theologically *liberal interpretation of this, that since revelation is not to be identified with Scripture or *dogmas, but as an existential guide allowing the self to transcend itself, then perhaps Christianity should see itself as something fixed but not finished – as on a path of ever new tradition and translation. But if revelation is to be a framework, then it has to be an absolute rather than something provisional. Revelation is what has been established in *Scripture and tradition, and our experience of it as it 'happens' is of something which *happened once and thus for all times*. Although revelation is received according to the mode of the one receiving it, the non-reception of revelation (Rom. 1:20) does not negate this 'general revelation in creation', and even less does special revelation rely on today's reception to be itself. However, the experience of *redemption is required for revelation *to be fully received* as such, although this should not be seen as a temporal sequence. It is not impossible that people may turn to God on the basis of general revelation without reference to Christ, but in a sense the church and Christian theology are called to communicate the special revelation as well. Revelation is a wake-up call to that sleeping world which can then become a means of bridging between *creation and what is natural on the one hand and what we are to become in our action on the other. General revelation becomes transformed through our receipt of special revelation. The latter is completed, the former, renewed by the latter, ongoing.

There has been concern that to think of revelation as external to us is to suggest that it is irrelevant, lost in history or coldly propositional. Thus John Montag: 'We have seen that Thomas [Aquinas] never had cause to reify the mediation into words or propositions through which God hands things over to be believed.' So, for *Thomas, revelation takes place in the judgment and understanding, as part of the assent of *faith. Revelation does not occur on its own, as if it were a thing apart, before becoming part of human thought and experience. That which God reveals has precisely that quality which Luther sought to recover in his translation – that is, the intimate self-manifestation, the word which pours from the heart, and which animates faith. Yet for Luther, this communication comes across a gap of knowledge: it is not really 'from the heart' even if it warms the heart. For Thomas, revelation can be seen paradigmatically in the experience of the prophet: it means the removal from the mind of a veil so that the prophet can see what was always there; it is not the face of God but natural things understood in a divine light. In symbols there is something participatory, transformative, motivational and supra-discursive (Dulles, *Models*).

Yet we are not prophets or apostles and Thomas is aware of that. In Thomas's treatment (*STh 1a.Q 13ad 1*) two things are affirmed:

1. There are two elements: images (phantasms) whether naturally or divinely formed, and a divine light. Revelation comes through the images. Revelation is not something which bypasses the mind, but nor is it something created by our minds. When believers come to receive divine light, they do it *through*, not *as*, the imagination of the prophets. Ultimately revelation remains external.
2. We do not know what he is, but know certain things about him: i.e. we can call that revealed knowledge 'propositional', since it is fragmentary and 'bitty', and needs to be weaved together in our reception of it.

Montag believes that the sixteenth-century scholastic Suárez, unlike Aquinas, saw theology as founded on philosophy, and that this was why he had a view that did not accord with St Thomas. Suárez reified revelation into words, while Thomas located it in the heart. Yet it is not the case that Thomas meant to universalize the special revelatory experience of the prophets and writers of Scripture, even if he thought that it was not discontinuous with general revelation in creation. Special revelation has a special content. Moreover, from what Thomas writes, surely the truth of the matter is that there is in Scripture, through its prophetic inspiration, not only new information about God, but knowledge of his will, his purpose, even his character, which is not just seeing the earth in a certain way. Recent work on Thomas's use of Scripture seems to confirm this. 'As a corrective theological framework, Scripture broadens our theological horizon toward a more profound understanding of the revelation of God' (Valkenberg). For Suárez, wanting to stress 'objectivity' of revelation, a proposition of faith becomes the 'sufficient object of revelation'. Since the words of Scripture alone do not bear sufficient certainty, 'the revealing God confirms his revelation (the things proposed for belief) through the infused light of faith'.

The overreaction against a 'propositional' account of revelation is also critiqued by Francesca Murphy, who wisely writes: 'the defect in Christian personalism is that it thinks of experience as something *inward*, rather than *between*. For the personalist, the key is intensive encounter, which is right, unless she sinks the extension of God's actions into herself.' In other words, the encounter has to be *dramatic*. It is not so much about, e.g. superimposing the Gospel accounts of Christ to get an identikit picture, but since these point beyond themselves, the audience is encouraged to look along these 'pointings' (presumably by imagination and prayerful reflection) away from oneself to where God is speaking to his people today. Tradition is called in to help us understand how this has happened in the past and how the biblical passages have been actualized. Yet it works both ways with biblical sense breaking and remaking the tradition's concepts.

So, the Bible may well be described as a 'means of *salvation', but it is not such without cognitive content. It affects people by changing their thoughts and is not just something unconscious so as to be manipulative on the part of the Holy Spirit. Those who are moved by God are, at least at points, aware of this, such that *sanctification is not simply 'automatic', that the Bible becomes perlocutionary because it is already illocutionary. So it is not wrong to point to the Bible and say: there is revelation quite apart from faith which is needed for there to be a revelation *event* (or better, the impact of revelation). After all, the Revelation of John speaks of no-one adding to these *words*. This need not mean subscribing to a verbal inspiration theory wherein each single word has value; rather, it is the combination of words that contain and form revelation. As Barth believed, Scripture was a human word commissioned by God by his providential arranging of canon and as such is open to God's providential use. There should be something arresting and surprising – following the 'prophetic' paradigm, such that for all the reception of the Bible, one cannot tame it. For this reason the insistence of evangelical theologians of recent times, from Carl Henry to Alister McGrath and Kevin Vanhoozer, that to say revelation is *no less than propositional* is to raise an important point. If we are going to speak of biblical revelation as 'postpropositional' (Vanhoozer, p. 276), this should mean that the 'post' in 'postpropositional' does not mean 'against' but 'beyond'. There is as much revealing as commanding going on in Christian Scripture.

Kern Trembath represents a more 'Rahnerian' view. Revelation is a relationship which allows humans to become fully human; as they come to know God as love it illuminates, even reveals what matters about being human. And when they seek the good they come into relationship with God. Thus revelation is universal, as the 'foundational groundedness' for all creatures. Revelation is about our existential concerns, not about the humans as spectators. Revelation says something about how God has made us and appears to us in the natural and the mundane. This stands against a more traditional view, as represented by A. Dulles, that the text provides us with *symbols which speak to us from beyond. Following *Rahner, we do not simply encounter things against a historically specific horizon (as for G. O'Collins), but against a universal and transcendental one.

Hans Urs von *Balthasar's helpful approach to revelation is to speak of it as a perception of the divine glory. The main thesis is a phenomenological one: that there is no deeper truth to be found by the Christian than the unique *appearance* of beauty. The objectively beautiful condescended to become beautiful 'to us' and this is hardly superficial. The beauty of God's revelation is one of *glory which provokes a response of awe and surprise. For Balthasar, the evidence is dazzling. God's act includes the gifting of response in the human heart as it steps into the realm of the church. '*Ecclesiology and Mariology* form part of the basic structure of revelation.' The location of the biblical material on glory at the end of the *Herrlichkeit* series, however, is interesting: Balthasar at least seems to flirt with biblical theology as the place where the theory is worked out in all the fullness of practice. The Word is made flesh and all that he is continues to be mediated to us by words and imagery of the Gospels.

The Bible is not there to be explained or even to explain human experience, but its function is to communicate knowledge of the divine will, to transform lives and accounts of this will. In other words, as one reads the Bible giving it the benefit of the doubt concerning its authority so as to be in a freer position to make a judgment on its content. Revelation accounts for, rather than is explained by, some deep experience (such as is claimed by what Gerd Theissen calls 'the religious studies approach', as the Bible's 'implicit axioms' are internalized). The canon helps to preserve a memory of values and truths about God rather than the memory of how the text came to be as it is in its final form. That canonical approach of Brevard Childs, an attempt to read the Bible theologically, provokes responses (by e.g. John Barton) that such a canonical approach is a systematic afterthought to the work of biblical studies. But on the contrary, it is to acknowledge that there are theological roots within the Bible itself. It has been the lifework of Catholic scholars such as Lohfink and Söding to join Childs and other evangelical scholars in refusing this gulf between biblical studies and theological reading of Scripture.

*Myths have trained us with patterns to receive a content of revelation which makes sense. Reason has granted us to learn that in the world it makes sense to believe in a Creator of all. But it is the OT which has refined those myths and *natural theology so that our minds are prepared to receive the coming Christ in the right and faithful way. In this process, faith plays not just a passive but an active role and as such is able to grasp something of the life-form of the historical Jesus. Historical evidence is not the foundation of faith, but is nonetheless important, since its investigation contributes to the task of exposing the life of *Jesus as a specific divine questioning which is posed in such a way that it provokes rejection and annoyance or a resolution to gamble trustingly with this Jesus.

Bibliography

H. U. von Balthasar, *Love Alone: The Way of Revelation* (London, 1968); K. Barth, *CD* I.1; A. Dulles, *Models of Revelation* (Garden City, NY, 1983); *idem*, 'The Theology of Revelation', in *Revelation and the Quest for Unity* (Washington, 1968); C. F. H. Henry, *God, Revelation and Authority* (Waco, 1976–83); R. Latourelle, *Theology of Revelation: Including a Commentary on the Constitution 'dei verbum' of Vatican II* (Staten Island, 1966); B. McCormack, 'Revelation and Imagination', *SJT* 37 (1984), pp. 431–455; J. Montag, 'The False Legacy of Suárez', in J. Milbank, C. Pickstock and G. Ward, *Radical Orthodoxy* (London, 1998); F. A. Murphy, *The Comedy of Revelation* (Edinburgh, 2000); K. Trembath, *Divine Revelation: Our Moral Relation with God* (New York, 1991); W. G. B. M. Valkenberg, *Words of the Living God: Place and Function of Holy Scripture in the Theology of St Thomas Aquinas* (Leuven, 2000); K. Vanhoozer, *The Drama of Doctrine* (Louisville, 2005).

S. R. HOLMES

REVIVAL, THEOLOGY OF

For 250 years *pietistic *evangelicalism both sides of the Atlantic has conceived revival as a characteristic work of God visiting communities of his people to deepen his work of *grace in their lives and to extend his kingdom in this world. The Reformation, the Puritan era, the Evangelical Revival in Britain, the first and second Great Awakenings in America, the Welsh Revival of 1904–05, and the mid-twentieth-century East African Revival are among examples cited. The theological claim is that the revival pattern is normatively seen in the Acts narrative and in the spiritual conditions that the apostolic letters to churches reflect or seek to promote: God's holy presence, sovereignly manifested and vividly realized, brings conviction of the ugliness, guilt, pollution and destructiveness of *sin; exercises and gestures of *repentance (confession to God and others, restitution, public renouncing of vices) become vigorous and even violent; Christ and forgiveness through his *cross are joyfully celebrated; and there is an evangelistic overflow. The later, narrower, American usage ('revival' meaning a concentrated evangelistic campaign, and 'revivalist' meaning its leader) stems from the early ministry pattern of Charles *Finney, an innovative itinerant evangelist for over a decade following his conversion in 1821. His brilliant and still influential *Lectures on Revivals of Religion* (1835) delineated his methods and generalized from his experience.

The fountain-head theologian of revival was the latter-day Puritan Jonathan *Edwards, who after seeing revival in his own church in 1735 and in the Great Awakening of 1740 gave the world his *Narrative of Surprising Conversions* (1735), *The Distinguishing Marks of a Work of the Spirit of God* (1741), and *Thoughts on the Revival of Religion in New England in 1740* (1742). In the latter work, as in his sermons of 1739, posthumously published as *A History of the Work of Redemption*, Edwards adumbrates a cyclical view of revival as a recurring work of sovereign mercy, like successive waves breaking on the seashore, whereby God extends his *kingdom till the largely converted world of postmillennial eschatology becomes reality. God regularly initiates revival by stirring up prayer for it (see Edward's *Humble Attempt to Promote . . . Extraordinary Prayer, for the Revival of Religion, and the Advancement of Christ's Kingdom on Earth, Pursuant to Scripture Promise and Prophecies Concerning the Last Time*, 1748); Satan regularly seeks to counterfeit it and corrupt it into heretical and antinomian fanaticism; the church, however, is regularly enlarged and Christ is freshly glorified through it. Interpreting Revelation in historicist terms and believing that God's plan had already reached the outpouring of the sixth vial (bowl) (Rev. 16:2), Edwards ventured the view that the work of God's Spirit in the Great Awakening was the start of an era of worldwide revival emanating from America ('Tis not unlikely . . .'). Edward's prognostication fuelled much religious and cultural optimism in America during the nineteenth century.

The Boston pastor Charles Chauncy saw the Great Awakening as unspiritual mass hysteria, expressed in manifold intellectual, emotional and behavioural excesses. Edward's apologia was that below the acrid smoke of carnal and perverted excitement the fire of God's Spirit was demonstrably burning, advancing faith, promoting holiness and exalting Christ in a way that only God could or would do. Chauncy argued that the excesses were overthrowing godliness rather than advancing it, and that the whole movement boiled down to self-deceived 'enthusiasm' (fanatical reliance on eccentric inner impressions). Revivals, as Edwards allowed, are always disfigured by this, and have drawn similar criticisms from churchmen of an intellectualist and formalist cast of mind, both Protestant and Roman Catholic.

The *Pelagian streak in Finney's anthropology led him to reconceive Edward's morphology of revival as illustrating what he took to be the universal law that honest and urgent prayer and repenting by the church guarantees an outpouring of the *Holy Spirit in revival blessing, just as under God's kindly providence the farmer's sowing and caring for his field guarantees a crop. The arguably simplistic thought that when the church is spiritually moribund Edwardsean revival is God's immediate will if only his faithful servants will pay the price in passionate prayer and penitence has been widely influential in popular evangelical piety since Finney's day, though the finding has rarely been commensurate with the seeking. Part of the difficulty has been the one-track-minded romanticizing and stereotyping of revival in Edwardsean terms, isolating it from the theological, liturgical, ethical and structural aspects of ongoing reformation and renewal in a changing world.

It has been proposed that revival, meaning transformation fellowship with personal righteousness and strong outreach, as seen in Acts, is a permanent norm for the church and will automatically be continuous where hindrances from unbelief, misbelief, apathy and sin do not intrude. The *charismatic renewal, like original *Pentecostalism, is sometimes seen as continuous revival in this sense. Edward's theocentricity and acknowledgment of God's wise yet often inscrutable *sovereignty, which may make disciplined patience the prime calling of eager but baffled petitioners, does not however find its place in these assessments, so that disillusionment following triumphalism constantly threatens.

Today's world church seeks renewal in many forms. The renewal quest among evangelical conservatives embraces doctrinal reformation in face of liberal unorthodoxy; charismatic revitalizing in worship and giftings; liturgical enrichments of various kinds; rehabilitation of expository preaching, and of pastoral mentoring and spiritual direction; establishing lay leadership of small groups and task forces within congregations, all on the principle of every-member ministry in the body of Christ according to each person's ability; restoring adult catechesis, and regaining all-round apologetic competence and interactive presentation of God's truth to the wider secular world (John XXIII's *aggiornamento* agenda for the Second *Vatican Council). Some seek Edwardsean revival in its classic shape, with or without the above specifics. Sought in isolation, each of these goals appears partial and incomplete in relation to the fullness of the church's present-day calling and mission. To make the profoundly spiritual Edwardsean understanding of revival the frame within which to set, and into which to integrate, all the goals mentioned would seem to be a healthful and perhaps overdue project.

See also: EVANGELISM, THEOLOGY OF.

Bibliography

J. Edwards, *Works*, 2 vols. (repr. London, 1974); *idem*, *Works*, 28 vols. (New Haven, 1957–); C. G. Finney, *Lectures on Revivals of Religion*, ed. W. G. McLaughlin (Cambridge, 1960); R. F. Lovelace, *Dynamics of Spiritual Life* (Downers Grove, 1979); I. H. Murray, *Pentecost Today* (Edinburgh, 1998); J. I. Packer, 'The Glory of God and the Reviving of Religion', in J. Piper and J. Taylor (eds.), *A God-Entranced Vision of All Things* (Wheaton, 2004); *idem*, *Keep in Step with the Spirit* (Grand Rapids, ²2005).

J. I. PACKER

REVOLUTION, THEOLOGY OF

'Revolution' is used in the political sphere to describe the destruction of one social system and its replacement by another. It is more than the transference of power between rival political groups; it represents a new way of ordering society. By changing values and creating new political and economic structures and institutions, revolutionary groups believe that it is possible to eliminate the injustice and conflict of present societies.

Revolution is associated with the slogan, 'liberty, equality and fraternity', with Marx's view of the class struggle, Engels' withering away of the *state, Lenin's belief that capitalism was doomed to devour itself, and Trotsky's permanent vigilance against state bureaucracy (see *Marxism and Christianity). Revolution flows from the utopian dream that human beings can act as historical midwives bringing to birth a qualitatively new human society.

A theology of revolution may possess or combine any one of three different strands. It may be a systematic theological reflection on the basis, nature and implications of revolution. It may seek to draw out the revolutionary characteristics of Christian faith. And it may help direct the church's legitimate response to revolutionary movements.

Revolution in a distinctively modern sense dates from the American and French Revolutions in the eighteenth century. The former was a reassertion of principles dating back to the British Revolution of 1688, whereas the latter was the overthrowing of despotism and gave birth to more secular and utopian democratic hopes. But there had been political eruptions in previous centuries which had produced (or were sometimes caused by) theological thought: the English Peasants' Revolt of 1381, the Czech Taborites of the early fifteenth century, Münster in sixteenth-century Germany (see *Reformation, Radical), the revolution under John *Knox leading to the Scottish Reformation, the English Revolution of 1641 which eventually brought Cromwell and the *Puritan party to power and brought toleration for the even more socially radical and egalitarian Levellers and Diggers. Both *Calvinists and

*Jesuits in the sixteenth and seventeenth centuries argued for the justice of rebellion in certain contexts.

The church in the nineteenth century was almost uniformly hostile to the ideas that sprang from the French Revolution. There were some exceptions: theologians such as Bruno Bauer (1809–82) and David *Strauss belonged for a time (the late 1830s) to the circle of political radicals called 'the Young Hegelians'; F. D. Maurice, C. Kingsley and others formed the *Christian Socialists in 1850, and at the end of the century Rauschenbush in America and Ragaz in Switzerland were leaders in a movement called the *Social Gospel.

In the twentieth century, at least four major groups developed Christian thinking on revolutionary change. R. H. Tawney (1880–1962), the British economist, is representative of influential thinkers in the Western world who have challenged the *capitalist economic system from a Christian basis. The Czech theologian, Josef L. Hromadka (d. 1969), was a foremost exponent after the Second World War of those who challenged Christians to come to terms with a socialist state. Some theologians in Africa and Asia have given thought to the way in which decolonization and movements of national liberation impinge on Christian faith. Later in the century, Christian leaders in Latin America (see *Liberation theology) and South Africa (see *Black theology), speaking on behalf of peoples oppressed by neo-fascist and racist regimes, reflected theologically on social change.

Theologies of revolution have a number of characteristics in common. They are critical of the official church's tendency to remain non-committal when challenged to endorse sweeping political changes at times of severe social dislocation. They believe that theological reflection has to begin with the real circumstances of the poor (see *Poverty and wealth). Further, they are convinced that social analysis is a necessary part of the *hermeneutical task of making Christian obedience concrete in specific situations. Finally, they hold that theological work cannot be divorced from ideological commitment, for no intellectual discipline is neutral towards social conflict.

These theologies hold the following basic themes in common. The exodus story of God's liberation of oppressed people from Egypt is interpreted as a *paradigm of his liberating activity throughout all *history. God continues to hear the cries of those suffering from repressive government. He does not surrender to human intransigence.

Justice (see *Righteousness) is the supreme category for knowing God; it is his action on behalf of oppressed people. Only those who take 'an option for the poor' can know him truly. *Jesus, in his life and ministry, as he inaugurated the kingdom, incarnated God's justice. He seals God's intention to deliver the poor from their oppression. He died as a result of resisting the religious and political complex of power. His *resurrection displays God's triumph over all forces of death. It is the sign of hope that the economic and military idols of our time can be destroyed and a new way of justice and peace inaugurated.

Theologies of revolution represent one type of Christian response to the innate human desire to be free of external constraints to political and economic self-determination. They express the evident antagonism of the God of the Bible to the abuse of power which grinds defenceless people into the dust. They articulate God's saving work in social terms, believing that in the coming of Jesus a power has been unleashed which can break apparently invulnerable, closed, political and economic systems. They draw their inspiration from the hope that a better world can be realized within history. This, it is argued, will not happen because history is bound to unfold in a pre-determined direction, but because groups of people, motivated by the conviction that God's power is greater than the forces which cause death in today's world, struggle for change.

Two main weaknesses are apparent in this form of theological reflection. First, in the sphere of political analysis diagnosis tends to be confused with cure. A right solution to the present suffering of the poor does not spring automatically from a correct analysis of its causes. Evil is more extensively present in the world than its operation in political and economic institutions and policies.

Secondly, a new kind of society cannot emerge without people, spiritually *regenerated, walking in the new life which God offers exclusively through Jesus Christ. However, the NT emphasis on *grace, enabling people to be free of *guilt, corruption and selfishness for a life of selfless *love, is not prominent enough in theologies of revolution. Grace tends to be seen as an addition to human *power (supplementing *nature), when people are not able to eliminate power that is against change. Revolution will certainly bring change. Almost as certainly it will not bring real human transformation, unless the regenerating power of God's grace is active in human communities.

See also: POLITICAL THEOLOGY.

Bibliography
G. Gutiérrez, *The Power of the Poor in History* (London, 1983); A. Kirk, *Theology Encounters Revolution* (Leicester, 1980); J. Míguez Bonino, *Revolutionary Theology Comes of Age* (London, 1975); J. Moltmann, *The Power of the Powerless* (London, 1983); N. Wolterstorff, *Until Justice and Peace Embrace* (Grand Rapids, 1983).

J. A. KIRK

RICHARDSON, ALAN (1905–75)
Richardson was a leading Anglican theologian and ecumenist, and one of the chief exponents of the biblical theology movement in Britain. He was a distinguished contributor to systematic and *philosophical theology in the third quarter of the twentieth century. Much of his earlier work (such as *The Miracle Stories of the Gospels*, London, 1941, *The Biblical Doctrine of Work*, London, 1952, and commentaries on Genesis and John) focuses on recovering the distinctiveness and unity of the biblical message. His more technical *Introduction to the Theology of the New Testament* (London, 1958) was very widely influential, and was, along with the *Theological Wordbook of the Bible* (London, 1950) which he edited, an important monument of the biblical theology movement. Richardson's more strictly theological work made some important moves towards detaching theology from the *positivism and *empiricism of much of the philosophical climate of his day, starting with *Christian Apologetics* (London, 1947), and culminating in his major work, the Bampton Lectures on *History, Sacred and Profane* (London, 1964). The latter work developed the notion of *history as an *apologetic platform for explaining the biblical *kerygma, making use of historiographers such as *Dilthey and R. G. Collingwood (1889–1943) to expound the nature of revelation, resurrection and divine action in the world. Much recent work in both theology and philosophy has moved away from Richardson's concerns, and in particular recent developments in *hermeneutical theory and *epistemology have been such that his work has a decidedly dated air.

Bibliography
J. J. Navone, *History and Faith in the Thought of Alan Richardson* (London, 1966). Cf. R. H. Preston (ed.), *Theology and Change: Essays in Memory of Alan Richardson* (London, 1975).

J. B. WEBSTER

RICŒUR, PAUL (1913–2005)
Paul Ricœur was a French philosopher whose writings on *hermeneutics were amongst the most influential on thinking about biblical interpretation in the second half of the twentieth century.

The start and end point of his thinking concerns human identity and self-understanding, but this journey has an unavoidable hermeneutical element to it. Fault is a fundamental reality of human existence – both in the sense of human culpability but also in the sense that there is a fracture running through human being – and it can only be explained by *symbols. These symbols need to be treated with suspicion, but also need positive retrieval; explanation must lead to a holistic sense of understanding. Symbols, in turn, are expressed linguistically using metaphors, which are the primary way in which language creates new meaning, and form the basis for narrative, the primary textual way that humanity makes sense of its experience of itself within time.

The interpretation of texts is part of a wider project of the interpretation of the self in the world. And interpretation always involves a 'wager of faith' on what the meaning of a symbol or text actually is: 'beyond the desert of criticism, we must be called again.' Ricœur's advocacy of a self-aware and holistic hermeneutics which considers the text, the world 'behind' the text and the world 'in front of' the text makes his work uniquely important in the transition to a *postmodern world.

Bibliography
Works: *The Symbolism of Evil* (Boston, 1967); *The Philosophy of Paul Ricœur*, ed. C. E. Reagan and D. Stewart (Boston, 1978); *Thinking Biblically*, with A. Lacocque (Chicago, 1998).

Studies: R. Kearney, *On Paul Ricœur* (London, 2004); D. Stiver, *Theology after Ricœur* (Louisville, 2001); K. Vanhoozer, *Biblical Narrative in the Philosophy of Paul Ricœur* (Cambridge, 1990); M. Wallace, *The Second Naiveté* (Macon, 1990).

I. PAUL

RIGHTEOUSNESS

Although the righteousness of *God has often been understood in legal terms as denoting a standard of moral perfection towards which human beings must strive but which they can never fulfil, the righteousness of God revealed and exercised in *Jesus Christ places the legal conception of righteousness within the sphere of God's mercy and *grace. The righteousness of God is made known through his mercy and is thus shown to be a righteousness exercised for humanity rather than being an abstract property of God that is set over and against humanity. The realization of this central evangelical truth lay at the heart of *Augustine's discovery of the *gospel and of *Luther's discovery that *salvation depended not upon his own works but upon the unmerited grace of God.

Until the time of Luther's wrestling with Romans, he had conceived of the justice and righteousness of God as a stern righteousness that would not tolerate and would punish with eternal damnation the least hint of any human *sin that had gone unrecognized or that had not been repented of. After reading Romans, however, Luther discovered that the righteousness of God referred, not to a standard that human beings could only vainly strive for, but to God's own righteousness in justifying the sinner, and faithfully fulfilling in Christ his covenant commitment to humankind.

Without ceasing his demand upon human beings, God had revealed his own righteousness in the mercy and love that forgives sin and imparts the gift of the Spirit to enable human beings to live in fellowship with him (see *Guilt and forgiveness). For Luther, the word of the gospel was heard in all its clarity for the first time. It became true that the truth will set you free. In Luther's case he was liberated from the endless and fruitless struggle to achieve his own righteousness before God, and could simply receive the righteousness bestowed upon those who in faith give themselves into the hands of God.

To speak evangelically of the righteousness of God, therefore, we have first to speak of God's faithfulness to the *covenant established with Israel and fulfilled in Christ on behalf of all humankind. And to speak evangelically of the righteousness of humankind, we have to speak of the righteousness bestowed upon those who entrust their lives to the one who alone is righteous, who alone does what is right. In the light of this gracious bestowal of righteousness upon God's covenant people, those same people are called to a new life, the character of which is set out in the Torah and embodied in the Word made flesh.

By attending to the revelation of God as testified to in Scripture, *evangelical theology recognizes that the righteousness of God is recognized most clearly in God's pardoning of sinners, and in his *reconciling to himself a people who are not worthy. The righteousness of God is seen in God's establishment and maintenance of a covenant with those who are not God and who have no righteousness of their own. Righteousness here means 'right relationship'. It is precisely in this sense that righteousness is equated with justice. *Tsedaqah* in Hebrew, *dikaiosune* in Greek and, perhaps to a lesser extent, *iustitia* in Latin, can all be translated as both 'justice' and 'righteousness'. Justice is done when right relationship is established. It is done, for exemplary instance, when God takes the side of the poor, the widow, the alien and the orphan, pleads their cause amongst his people, and ensures their restoration to right relationship in the community. In like manner, God takes the side of all those who have no means and no basis upon which to plead their own cause. He takes the side of sinners, puts himself in their place, and restores them to the status of his covenant partner to which they had no rightful claim. It is this act of mercy and grace that constitutes the righteousness and the justice of God. By this means God justifies the sinner and overcomes all that stands in the way of his purpose to establish right relationship with and within his creation.

It is on account of this divine drama of salvation that Christ himself may be called the righteousness of God, just as he is also the way, the truth and the life. Human beings are called to trust in Christ who is in person the righteousness of God, and who exercises on humanity's behalf the true human righteousness of faithful love that both expresses and fulfils the right relationship between Creator and creatures that is creation's goal. According to the Protestant *Reformers, this righteousness of Christ is imputed to all who place their trust in him. Luther claims that all our good lies outside us, namely, in Christ, and that we participate in him only by faith and hope. Such righteousness is sometimes described as an alien righteousness, a righteousness that is not our own. And yet, for Luther, it becomes 'our' righteousness, not by right or by achievement but solely through the grace that enables our incorporation into the righteous life of Christ. The righteousness of believers, then, consists in the fact that God has acted for them in Christ and has restored them to that loving communion with himself from which their sin had alienated them. *Faith is at once both the recognition of this intervention of God on behalf of the unrighteousness, and the appropriate response of gratitude and acceptance. The imputation of righteousness is defined as a forensic act, *actus forensis*, in which sinful individuals are declared to be righteous on the basis of their faith and apart from all human merit. The *Formula of Concord views the forensic declaration of righteousness as the basis of *justification. An individual is counted as righteous because she or he is in Christ, and is incorporated, thereby, into the righteousness of Christ.

Roman Catholic theologians at the Council of *Trent, and some Protestants too, notably Andreas *Osiander who disputed the point with *Calvin, objected that the notion of imputed righteousness, *iustitia imputata*, when taken on its own, made human beings the passive recipients of righteousness rather than active participants in right relationship with God. They thus spoke of infused righteousness, *iustitia infusa*, as a gift of grace by which it becomes possible through good works to maintain oneself in right-relationship with God.

The growth in righteousness expected of those who have been justified is referred to as *sanctification. The Protestant Reformers generally made a deliberate and systematic distinction between justification (the external act by which God declares the sinner to be righteous) and sanctification or *regeneration (the internal process of renewal within the individual). Although the two are treated as inseparable, they are nevertheless to be distinguished. It is this distinction that gave rise to Luther's famous phrase that the person of faith is *simul iustus et peccator*, at once justified, made righteous, and yet a sinner. The believer's relationship with God has been put right, but the righteous status of the believer is incompletely worked out in his or her empirical existence. Whereas justification is the process by which the sinner is declared righteous *de iure*, sanctification refers to the process whereby the sinner grows in righteousness *de facto*. Righteousness thus becomes the new life and not just the new status of those who receive in faith the righteousness of Christ. The evangelical revival of the eighteenth century in Britain placed a particular emphasis on the need for Christians to strive to live righteous and holy lives. John *Wesley, for example, stressed that while justification was the free gift of grace, attained at the point of Christian conversion, the process of sanctification was a lifelong task. Wesley contended that Christians are to strive towards perfection, by which he meant that Christians are to strive to become wholly loving persons.

The imputation of righteousness cannot be understood without also hearing the summons of God to let go of our own ideas of righteousness, conceived so often in moralistic terms, and to trust in the righteousness of God by which sinners are pardoned and those who are unworthy are made sons and daughters of God. To this extent the righteousness of God is also judgment. It lays bare the falsity of self-righteousness and requires the death of the old *Adam who trusts in a righteousness of his or her own. Faith in the righteousness of Christ, therefore, is simultaneously an acceptance of God's condemnation of our self-righteousness. It is in this sense that the disputed concept of distributive righteousness, *iustitia distributiva*, with its promise of reward to the obedient and punishment to the disobedient, can be maintained. All humankind, save the one who alone is righteous, falls under this condemnation, for all have sinned. The righteousness of God discloses the reality and the nature of this sinfulness and is, as such, *judgment and condemnation. But the righteousness of God is also mercy. The one who alone is righteous takes the fate of the unrighteous upon himself and receives in their stead the distribution of justice which is due to sinful human beings. Karl Barth has put the matter clearly: the divine 'No' to human sin is enclosed within God's merciful 'Yes' to the sinner. Faith's acceptance of this merciful 'Yes' is accompanied by the sorrowful admission of the justice of God's 'No' and by the penitential recognition that the 'No' has been borne by God himself. The righteousness of believers is thus expressed through faith and *repentance, gratitude and praise.

See also: ATONEMENT; CROSS.

Bibliography

K. Barth, 'The Mercy and Righteousness of God' in *CD* II.1 pp. 368–406; E. Jüngel, *Justification: The Heart of the Christian Faith* (ET, Edinburgh, 2001); A. E. McGrath, *Iustitia Dei: A History of the Christian Doctrine of Justification* (Cambridge, ²1998); G. Yule, 'Luther's Attack on the Latin Heresy', in T. Hart and D. Thimell (eds.), *Christ in Our Place: The Humanity of God in Christ for the Reconciliation of the World* (Exeter and Allison Park, 1989).

M. A. RAE

RIGHTS, HUMAN

A right is an enforceable claim to a human good (hence the ancient motto, *Dieu et mon droit*, 'God and my right'). A 'good' in this sense is a benefit that makes for human well-being. A *human* right pertains to an individual or a group solely by virtue of their being human. It is not in principle to be forcibly overridden for any reason, including the supposed greater good of the community, though rights may be voluntarily foregone.

Among those human rights first affirmed were those to life, liberty and property. Whereas basic human rights, such as the right not to experience torture, may in many circumstances be non-controversial, other putative rights (e.g. a 'right' to choose abortion or euthanasia) may be contested – by Christians, amongst others – according to specific understandings of what it is to be human.

The notion of a 'right' (*ius*) comes from Roman law, and its development is indebted to *Stoic notions of natural law. This set limits to the positive law of the *state, which was not to infringe the acquired or the natural rights of its citizens. Similarly, the Magna Carta (1215), to which King John of England agreed, set out certain liberties (e.g. freedom from arbitrary arrest) which were not to be infringed by the monarch. *Thomas Aquinas adopts Justinian's definition of justice as 'a constant and perpetual will to render to each person their right' (*ius*).

The notions of 'natural law' and 'natural rights' were widely used to support a supposedly 'natural' social hierarchy in which the privileges of the few were upheld against those who had no such rights. The development of a notion of natural rights that could be deployed by the individual *against* the state was central to the seventeenth-century English Revolution and the later writing of John *Locke.

The American Declaration of Independence (1776) famously asserts that 'We hold these truths to be self-evident, that all men are created equal, that they are endowed by their Creator with certain unalienable rights, that among these are life, liberty and the pursuit of happiness.' This was followed by the French Declaration of the Rights of Man and of the Citizen (1789). During the nineteenth century the phrase 'human rights' became more widespread.

The Universal Declaration of Human Rights (1948) is one of the great aspirational documents of the twentieth century. It was born of the international consensus after the Second World War which looked back in horror at the state-organized persecution of the Jews by the Nazi regime in Germany and at the failure of other nations to provide protection to those who fled. The UDHR defines as a matter of right a minimum standard of provision to meet the needs of all human beings and the need for an international order which will sustain this provision (cf. article 28).

Member states of the UN have a duty to ensure these rights for their own citizens. To what extent they have a duty to ensure them for the citizens of other states is disputed. The UDHR has been followed by a number of other human rights instruments and declarations such as the International Covenant on Civil and Political Rights (1966) and the International Covenant on Economic, Social and Cultural Rights (1966). The European Convention on Human Rights (1950) was incorporated into UK law in the Human Rights Act (1998), ensuring that all future legislation would be scrutinized for its compatibility with recognized standards in human rights.

It is sometimes argued that there are three types of human rights: first-generation civil and political rights (rights to life and to political freedoms); second-generation economic, social and cultural rights (rights to the meeting of subsistence needs); third-generation solidarity rights (rights to a sustaining social order and environment). Liberals have usually emphasized the first sort of human rights; socialists the second. The list of human rights is by no means closed: 'third-generation' rights in particular are hotly debated.

Only since the Second World War have the Christian churches unambiguously supported human rights. Before then, the Roman Catholic Church in particular saw an emphasis on human rights as a secular threat to the Christian social order. However, both liberal Protestant Christians and Roman Catholics played a key role in the drafting of the UDHR and, whilst Christians may still want to distance themselves from certain interpretations of human rights, the major churches are now committed to their support. For Roman Catholics, this was made evident in Pope John XXIII's encyclical *Pacem in Terris* (1963) and at the Second *Vatican Council in the Pastoral Constitution on the Church in the Modern World (*Gaudium et Spes*, 1965).

One major shift for Christians has been to recognize freedom of worship as a fundamental human right. Acceptance of such freedom (provided, of course, it is not harmful to others) is, however, indivisible: there cannot be a right for some religious groups which does not hold for others. The right to freedom of worship thus becomes a foundation stone for an open and plural society, in which Christians support the freedom of non-Christians to practise their faith openly. The recognition that Christianity can never be commended by violence (which may overlap with pacifism, but is not to be identified with it) may be seen as a way of placing the *cross at the centre of Christian political practice (cf. 1 Cor. 2:2–5).

The term 'human rights' does not occur in the Bible. In both OT and NT there is, however, a great concern with righteousness and with justice – two ways of translating what is one word (with its cognates) in Hebrew (*ṣĕdāqâ*) and Greek (*dikaiosyne*). Right judgments on earth reflect the *righteousness/justice of God. Judges and kings are to judge according to right (Gen. 18:25; Deut. 16:18–20). God has done this in giving commandments to his covenanted people: a command like 'Do not steal' suggests a presumptive right to property amongst Israelites (one which even a king may not infringe; cf. 2 Sam 12:7–9; 1 Kgs 21:19). Nevertheless, there is no suggestion of a '*natural* right' against which divine or human judgments are to be measured. There can be no 'right' (no claim) against the Creator – something Job has to learn (cf. Job 27:6). In accord with the concern for justice, humans are to ensure that others, especially the marginalized, receive what is right for them (cf. Deut. 24:14–22; Prov. 31:8–9). Jesus recognizes the pressing nature of human needs but does not respond to this with the promise of human rights (Matt. 6:25–33). The seed of a doctrine of natural law, from which a doctrine of rights might be induced, is, however, present in Paul (Rom. 2:14–15).

Christians have been critical of human rights approaches which do not recognize the *sovereignty of God: human beings are made in the *image of God (Gen. 1:27). The human dignity affirmed by human rights is not autonomous. It is God-given. Christians have often criticized the secularism, the individualism, and the ethnocentricity with which 'human rights' are interpreted. They have wanted to stress the solidarity of human beings by virtue of creation, human rights as a gift of God's grace for the present world order, and the correlative place of human duties, especially towards the poor.

Nevertheless, the Christian churches now recognize that the vision of human flourishing embedded in documents like the UDHR provides a secure moral basis for a plural society in which Christians are called to play their full part.

Bibliography

J. Donnelly, *Universal Human Rights in Theory and Practice* (Ithaca and London, ²2003); J. Mahoney, *The Challenge of Human Rights* (Oxford, 2007); J. Nurser, *For All Peoples and All Nations* (Geneva, 2005); R. Ruston, *Human Rights and the Image of God* (London, 2004); C. Villa-Vicencio, *A Theology of Reconstruction* (Cambridge, 1992).

N. Sagovsky

RITSCHL, ALBRECHT (1822–89)

Albrecht Ritschl, a German systematic theologian, was professor at Bonn (1852–64) and Göttingen (1864–89). Through his own writings and those of his disciples, especially Herrmann and *Harnack, Ritschl was probably the most influential continental Protestant theologian between *Schleiermacher and *Barth, certainly during the period 1875–1930, the heyday of liberal Protestantism (see *Liberalism, German).

Ritschl followed *Kant in rejecting metaphysical knowledge of God and stressing the ethical elements of religion. God was to be known not in himself, but in his effects on humankind, understood in terms of Christian experience of *justification and reconciliation (see *Atonement) and progress towards the kingdom of God. In proposing this approach, most clearly expressed in vol. 3 of *The Christian Doctrine of Justification and Reconciliation* (1874; ET, Edinburgh, 1900), Ritschl rejected certain kinds of *religious experience. He judged Schleiermacher's sense of 'absolute dependence' too subjective, and ruled out all *mysticism and *pietism as individualistic, amoral and not distinctively Christian. God was to be known rather through the gospel witness to Jesus and his unique vocation to fulfil God's will for the world by inaugurating the kingdom, which Ritschl defined as the 'organization of humanity through action inspired by love'. Thus Jesus has the 'value' for us of God, and demonstrates that Christianity is like an ellipse, with justification and reconciliation as one focus and the *kingdom of God as the other.

Ritschl has been criticized for maintaining an ethical rather than a religious view of justification and reconciliation, reading *Luther very differently from someone like *Otto. His assertion that all religious doctrines are 'value judgments' that affirm or deny man's worth or value has seemed to many to drive an unacceptable wedge between fact and value, history and interpretation, objective and subjective salvation. Yet in insisting on the need for justification and reconciliation and locating them primarily in the church (rather than the heart of the believer), Ritschl moved some way beyond Schleiermacher's individualistic optimism. He may even have contributed, via Herrmann, to Barth's interest in Christology and decision to undertake a church dogmatics.

Barth himself, however, always stressed his differences with Ritschl and the Ritschlian school, seeing in his own theological teachers' support of Germany's declaration of war in August 1914 proof that their approach produced a dangerous confusion between the values of German civilization and the values of the kingdom of God. Yet the fact that Ritschlian theology produced an inadequate understanding of a this-worldly kingdom need not be allowed to obscure Ritschl's achievement in correctly identifying the kingdom of God as a central concern of the teaching of Jesus.

It can also be argued that Barth's well-known repudiation of Ritschl (cf. *Protestant Theology in the Nineteenth Century*, London, 1972) is an insufficient basis for neglecting Ritschl's influence in other areas of theology. Yet the contribution of Ritschl's concept of value judgments to *Bultmann's *existential theology has been largely overlooked, and *Pannenberg is one of the few contemporary theologians who has given Ritschl's pioneering attempt 'to build his Christology on the question about the divinity of the historical man Jesus' (*Jesus – God and Man*, Philadelphia, 1968, p. 37) the kind of attention, and reasoned disagreement, that Barth afforded to Schleiermacher.

Bibliography

D. Jodock (ed.), *Ritschl in Retrospect: History, Community, and Science* (Minneapolis, 1995); H. R. Mackintosh, *Types of Modern Theology* (London, 1937); D. L. Mueller, *An Introduction to the Theology of Albert Ritschl* (Philadelphia, 1969); B. M. G. Reardon, *Liberal Protestantism* (London, 1968); J. Richmond, *Ritschl: A Reappraisal* (London, 1978).

P. N. HILLYER

ROBINSON, JOHN ARTHUR THOMAS (1919–83)

A prolific and controversial writer, the Anglican bishop and theologian John Robinson made significant scholarly contributions in the areas of NT, *systematic theology, *apologetics, Christian *ethics, and *liturgics. He began his career as a fellow and Dean of Clare College, Cambridge (1951–59), achieved fame as the suffragan Bishop of Southwark (South London) with responsibility for Woolwich (1959–69), and ended his days as Dean of Trinity College, Cambridge (1969–83). *Honest to God* (London, 1963), which sold more than 1,000,000 copies, was an attempt to commend the Christian faith to the modern man who, he thought, was unable to receive the gospel when presented with it in traditional terms. The book infuriated most orthodox churchmen, and Robinson became England's best-known (if most radical) theologian.

His most substantial contributions were to NT studies, where many of his views were surprisingly conservative (by the standards of contemporary critical scholarship). In a series of studies on John's Gospel, culminating in the

Bampton Lectures he was preparing at the time of his death (*The Priority of John*, ed. J. A. Coakley, London, 1985), he argued for both the essential historicity and early date of the book. In *Redating the New Testament* (London, 1976) he defended the view that all four Gospels should be dated prior to the destruction of Jerusalem (AD 70) and expressed equally conservative views on other critical issues. On the other hand, *Jesus and His Coming* (London, 1957) was an influential statement of the view that Jesus did not teach or expect his future second coming (see *Eschatology), and *In the End, God* (London, 1950) propounded *universalism. His doctrine of the church was sacramentalist (see *The Body: A Study in Pauline Theology*, London, 1952), his ethics opposed love to law, while his *Christology and essential theology were modernist (see *The Human Face of God*, London, 1973).

Bibliography

Current Biography Yearbook 1984 (New York, 1985); *The Annual Obituary 1983* (Chicago and London, 1984); D. L. Edwards, *The Honest to God Debate* (Norwich, 1963); E. James, *A Life of Bishop John A. T. Robinson: Scholar, Pastor, Prophet* (Nashville, 1989); A. Kee, *The Roots of Christian Freedom: The Theology of John A. T. Robinson* (London, 1988); R. P. McBrien, *The Church in the Thought of Bishop John Robinson* (Philadelphia, 1966).

W. W. GASQUE

ROMAN CATHOLIC THEOLOGY

The term 'Roman Catholic' emerged in the sixteenth century to distinguish Christians who had remained in communion with the pope from those who had become *Protestants. The Roman church had already divided from the majority of eastern churches in the Great Schism of 1054, partly because it asserted its 'catholicity' or universality in a more monarchical way, through a 'holy father' (*papa*) who exercised primacy among other bishops and over the church worldwide, in succession to Peter's leadership of the apostles (see *Papacy).

These claims to supremacy and authenticity confirm Roman Catholic theology to be profoundly *ecclesial*, and this is underlined in the principle of papal infallibility, which holds that when the Pope speaks *ex cathedra* to explain 'a doctrine of faith or morals to be held by the Universal Church', he operates with an unerring trustworthiness willed by Christ. The Second *Vatican Council reaffirmed this principle, although it also saw Pope John XXIII famously redefine the role of his office with respect to *dogma when he said that 'the substance of the ancient doctrine of the deposit of the faith is one thing; the way in which it is presented is another'. To an extent this merely acknowledged that beyond Rome's assumed guardianship of the 'one faith', Roman Catholic theology in fact represents a synthesis of many different influences, from the early Greek and Latin Fathers (see *Patristic theology), through *Augustine, the medieval *scholasticism of *Thomas Aquinas and the renaissance *humanism of *Erasmus, to a wide diversity of more recent approaches, not least those stemming from global *charismatic renewal. However, Pope John's remark also more specifically echoed the significant work done on the '*development of doctrine' by the Victorian Anglican convert to Rome, John Henry *Newman, and the growing ecumenical theological interaction modelled by Yves *Congar, Hans Urs von *Balthasar and others.

Since the Middle Ages Rome's 'catholic' concern for the whole of humanity has been expressed in a general endorsement of *natural theology, which affirms the essential goodness of human beings despite the *fall, and distinct from their salvation by *grace. At a deeper level, modern Roman Catholic theologies differ on the extent to which grace and nature represent discrete or integrated means of knowing God. For example, since the Second World War scholars including Henri de Lubac (1896–1991) and Karl *Rahner have sought to develop a more holistic vision of 'graced nature' based on the *incarnation.

Closely linked to this alignment with natural theology is the recognition that reason, as a faculty common to all humans, may significantly mediate divine revelation. Although Rome is still popularly tarred with its censure of Galileo's cosmology in the seventeenth century, Roman Catholic thought in the past 100 years or so has been marked by extensive engagement with contemporary scientific and cultural thinking. Thus *Teilhard de Chardin sought rapprochement between Darwinian evolution and the doctrines of providence and redemption; Pierre Rousselot (1878–1915) and Joseph Maréchal (1878–1944) reconstrued Kant's philosophy in neo-Thomian terms;

Charles Péguy (1873–1914) pioneered a Catholic form of *Christian Socialism, John Courtney Murray (1904–67) argued for the compatibility of Christian doctrine and human rights, and in 1992 Pope John Paul II approved a report acknowledging the 'subjective error' of Galileo's accusers.

Another recent example of Roman Catholic theology's commitment to universality, *rationality and natural theology can be seen in its approach to non-Christian religions. In various works Karl Rahner presented the God revealed in Jesus Christ as the 'destination' of all human development – a destination which might at first be sensed implicitly rather than comprehended explicitly. From this perspective Rahner proposed those without faith in Christ who nonetheless display awareness of God may be regarded as '*anonymous Christians'. Vatican II mirrored this approach when it defined the church as a 'universal sacrament of salvation' called to treat 'whatever is of good or truth' among non-Christians as a 'preparation for the Gospel'. This definition in turn relates to those more specific *sacraments which encapsulate the doctrine, worship and ministry of Roman Catholicism.

In Augustine's definition a sacrament is a 'visible sign of invisible grace' and denotes those sensory means by which the mysteries of Christ are communicated to humans. By 1272 the Council of Lyon had delineated seven sacraments: *baptism, *confirmation, the *Eucharist, *penance, extreme unction or anointing of the sick, orders and matrimony. These sacraments are understood to function *ex opere operato* – as objectively conferring grace by their very enactment, rather than according to the condition of those ministering or receiving them.

Baptism, confirmation and the Eucharist (or Mass) are all now classed in Roman Catholic doctrine as 'sacraments of initiation'. Baptism marks incorporation into the church as well as remission from the guilt of original sin. Confirmation is associated with the distinct 'reception of the Holy Spirit' experienced by certain first-generation Christians (e.g. in Acts 8:14–17), but it did not develop as a separate rite in the Roman church until the early medieval period, when it was accompanied by anointing with oil and the laying on of hands by a bishop. It is in turn linked in Roman Catholic theology to participation in the Eucharist ('First Communion'), whereas eucharistic elements are given to newly baptized infants in the Orthodox tradition.

The Eucharist itself is construed in Roman Catholic doctrine as an 'unbloody' *sacrifice, in which the atoning death of Christ on the cross is re-presented, and in which the consecrated elements of bread and wine become his 'real presence'. Since the thirteenth century this process has been defined in terms of transubstantiation – an explanation strongly indebted to Aristotelian ontology whereby the 'substance' of the bread and wine is changed into the body and blood of Christ even though their 'accidents' or outward appearances remain unaltered. Transubstantiation was rejected by the Protestant Reformers, often on the grounds that it encouraged superstitious focus on the elements themselves rather than on the glorified Christ.

The administration of these and other sacraments is reserved in Roman Catholic doctrine to those who have been ordained, and the clerical orders of bishop, priest and deacon themselves constitute a threefold sacrament (see *Ministry). This link between Orders and sacraments is somewhat more complex in the case of marriage: here it is the couple who marry and minister to one another, even as the priest witnesses and blesses their union on behalf of the church.

Protestants reduced the number of sacraments to the two that they perceived to have been directly authorized by Christ – namely baptism and the Eucharist, although for both Luther and Calvin even these were in a sense depictions of the one true sacrament of the word of God. On this basis the authority that Rome accords to the church, the papacy and the sacraments is substantially refocused in Protestantism on the Bible. In response, at the Council of *Trent and since, Roman Catholic theology has tended to stress the interdependence of Scripture, sacred tradition (see *Scripture and tradition) and the teaching office of the church. Three prominent examples of this approach may be seen in the development of Mariology, reproductive ethics and social teaching.

In 1854 Pope Pius IX affirmed *Mary's immaculate conception as a dogma to be 'firmly and constantly believed by all the faithful'. Then, in 1950, Pius XII invoked papal infallibility to affirm her bodily assumption. Protestants have criticized these Marian dogmas as lacking scriptural warrant, yet their long development from populist devotional tenets to formal doctrines bears out the 'Scripture-Tradition-Church' matrix that defines the essential Roman theological method.

This method was also very much at work in the position taken by the Vatican on contraception in the late 1960s. Following the advent of the contraceptive pill, Pope Paul VI established a commission to report on the moral and theological implications of its use. The commission reached a majority view that the pill should be permitted under certain conditions. However, Paul VI asserted his primary teaching status to side with the more conservative minority, and in his encyclical *Humanae Vitae* (1968) rejected the pill and other forms of artificial contraception, asserting that every sexual act within marriage must have the potential for procreation.

On a broader socio-political level modern Catholic moral theology has been profoundly concerned with matters of economics, justice and *poverty. Beginning with Leo XIII's *Rerum Novarum* (1861), a succession of papal encyclicals has developed contemporary 'Catholic Social Teaching' as a mediation between capitalist emphasis on free markets and personal responsibility, socialist insistence that the state provide for weaker members of society, and the principle of 'subsidiarity', in which more localized levels of governance should retain authority unless larger structures more effectively serve the common good.

While these concerns have often been reflected in the 'centrist' policies of various Christian Democratic parties in Europe, more radical social and political thinking influenced the '*liberation theology' espoused by various Latin American Roman Catholic theologians from the late 1960s and subsequently adapted in various forms of black and feminist theologies. Gustavo *Gutiérrez, Leonardo *Boff, John *Sobrino and others married Marxist theory to hermeneutical emphasis on the exodus and the *Magnificat* to propose that a 'preferential option for the poor' lies at the heart of the gospel. As led by Cardinal Joseph *Ratzinger, later to become Pope Benedict XVI (2005–2013), the Congregation for the Doctrine of the Faith affirmed the church's obligation to the poor but disavowed liberation theology's alignment with *Marxist concepts of class struggle and revolution. This exchange highlighted the distinction between theological work granted a *nihil obstat* or *imprimatur* by the Vatican and that published by Roman Catholic scholars but not authorized by the church. The later books of the influential Swiss theologian Hans *Küng, which include a sharp critique of papal infallibility, have also fallen into the second category.

Debate about liberation and other theologies is ongoing, but it bears out a more general challenge intrinsic to the 'catholic' nature of Roman Catholic theological practice: the challenge of maintaining a core of apostolic doctrine which is deemed to be unchanging, alongside a tradition of interpretation and application which has long been mutable, diverse and contested.

See also: CHURCH; CHURCH GOVERNMENT.

Bibliography

F. S. Fiorenza and J. P. Galvin, *Systematic Theology: Roman Catholic Perspectives* (Augsburg, ²2011); A. Flannery (ed.), *Vatican Council II: Constitutions, Decrees, Declarations* (Northport and Dublin, 1996); N. Geisler and R. E. MacKenzie, *Roman Catholics and Evangelicals: Agreements and Differences* (Grand Rapids, 1995); M. Hayes and L. Gearon, *Contemporary Roman Catholic Theology: A Reader* (Leominister, 1998); H. Küng, *The Church* (London and New York, 1968); K. Rahner, *Foundations of the Christian Faith* (New York, 2008 [1978]); J. Ratzinger (Pope Benedict XVIII), *Principles of Catholic Theology: Building Stones for a Fundamental Theology* (San Francisco, 1987).

D. H. K. HILBORN

ROMANTICISM

The term 'Romantic' is commonly used by historians of literature to describe the period from about 1780 to about 1830, but in a broader sense it applies to the sensibility that arose among literary innovators in that epoch and subsequently spread to a much wider public. Romanticism is usually contrasted with the intellectual mood of the *Enlightenment that preceded it, but in Germany, where it put down deepest roots, there was substantial continuity between the two movements of thought. In England the preface to *Lyrical Ballads* (1798), a collection of poetry by William Wordsworth and S. T. Coleridge, is often seen as a Romantic manifesto against earlier neoclassical assumptions, but there was already, in such figures as William Blake and in the gothic school of literature, a flourishing movement showing many of the features of Romantic thought.

Nevertheless, Romanticism was frequently, in its early phase, a self-conscious revolt against the Enlightenment. Whereas enlightened thinkers had exalted reason, Romantics stressed the place of emotion, intuition and the will. Instead of the universal norms dictated by classical example, there was an insistence on the diversity of human experience. It was appreciated that people grow in different ways, so that the preferred metaphor for human society was no longer a machine but a tree. The Enlightenment concentration on individuals was replaced by a new emphasis on the organic solidarity of the community. Wisdom was more likely to be found among the humble poor, with their reliance on inherited custom, than within an educated 'enlightened' elite. Creativity in poetry or music would probably come from an untutored genius exercising his imagination, rather than from a slavish imitator of supposed timeless ideals. The irreligious *rationalism of the French Enlightenment was repudiated in favour of a sense of the spiritual in nature, often giving rise to a form of *pantheism.

This complex Romantic temper was associated with two other trends of thought. One was historicism, the belief that human values are moulded by historical experience. On this view there are no absolute standards to which a community should aspire, so that the notion of natural law and the idea of progress were alike rejected. Instead, each society possesses its own unique character deriving from its circumstances over time. The new appreciation of *history gave rise to the enormous popularity of the novels of Sir Walter Scott. By insisting on the distinctiveness of each land, historicism also generated the powerful current of cultural relativism that was to affect theology along with most branches of scholarship during the nineteenth century. The other trend was *idealism, a philosophical idiom that challenged the prevailing *empiricism of the Enlightenment. The central new conviction was that the mind is active in the generation of knowledge, rather than merely a passive receptor of sense experience. Immanuel *Kant taught a moderate form of idealism from the 1780s, and in the early nineteenth century G. W. F. *Hegel propounded an absolute idealism according to which the entire world is the product of mind. These two philosophers were to retain an enduring attraction for theologians touched by the Romantic spirit.

The most significant German theologian of the early Romantic era was F. D. E. *Schleiermacher, whose appeal to experience rather than dogma reflected the priorities of his age. In the English-speaking world the most influential figure among theologians was *Coleridge. Proclaiming the inadequacy of an Enlightenment 'understanding' to grasp eternal truths, he urged the merits of a Romantic 'reason' founded on intuition of the divine. Coleridge encouraged intellectual enquiry in a religious spirit, swaying many of those such as Thomas Arnold who shaped Broad Church thinking in *Anglicanism. At the same time Romantic sensibility was fundamental to the Oxford Movement that renewed High Churchmanship (see *Anglo-Catholic theology). John *Keble's collection of poetry *The Christian Year* (1827) exemplified the new taste in verse, and J. H. *Newman saw the fresh cultural mood as the precondition for his work at Oxford in the 1830s. The 'illative sense' that Newman, by now a Catholic, posited in his *Grammar of Assent* (1870) can be understood as a species of Romantic intuition. The growth within the Roman Catholic Church of Ultramontanism, an enlarged respect for the pope joined with elaborate liturgical display, also owed a great deal to Romantic attitudes.

Evangelical Christianity was far from immune to the rising Romantic tide. Edward *Irving, a minister of the Church of Scotland in London, was a youthful friend of Thomas Carlyle, the greatest of Romantic prose writers, and profoundly influenced by Coleridge. Irving transposed evangelical doctrine into a Romantic key. Christian mission, he believed, was not to use rational business methods but to go out in radical reliance on the Almighty. Irving's readiness to expect dramatic supernatural events led him to credit the appearance of speaking in tongues in his congregation. And for the same reason he rejected postmillennial hopes of the gradual spread of the gospel over the whole earth in favour of the premillennial expectation of the imminent second coming of Jesus. J. N. *Darby, another man deeply affected by the Romantic style, also adopted premillennial teaching, propounding the distinctive version known as dispensationalism (see *Millennium; *Eschatology).

The earliest stirrings of Romantic thought in America were in *Unitarianism, the seedbed of the transcendentalism of R. W. *Emerson and his circle. The *Mercersburg theology of J. W.

Nevin and Philip Schaff transferred German Romantic themes into Reformed Christianity in America. The Congregationalist Horace *Bushnell pioneered the remoulding of evangelical teaching into Romantic phraseology, initiating the avoidance of doctrinal definition that was the hallmark of liberal theological tendencies in the English-speaking world during the later nineteenth century. The German higher critical movement associated with Julius Wellhausen was discernibly founded on Romantic premises about the growth of nations. At the same time, however, conservative trends among evangelicals such as the rise of faith missions and the Keswick holiness movement bore a Romantic impress. The many-sided phenomenon of Romanticism continued to exert a conservative as well as a liberal influence on popular theology during the twentieth century (see *History of theology).

Bibliography

M. H. Abrams, *Natural Supernaturalism* (New York and London, 1971); D. W. Bebbington, *The Dominance of Evangelicalism* (Leicester and Downers Grove, 2005); J. B. Halsted (ed.), *Romanticism* (New York and London 1969); T. A. Howard, *Religion and the Rise of Historicism* (Cambridge, 2000); R. Porter and M. Teich (eds.), *Romanticism in National Context* (Cambridge, 1988); S. Prickett, *Romanticism and Religion* (Cambridge, 1976); P. H. Reill, *The German Enlightenment and the Rise of Historicism* (Berkeley and London, 1975).

D. W. BEBBINGTON

ROUSSEAU, JEAN-JACQUES (1712–78)

Rousseau was born in Geneva and became one of the principal figures of the French *Enlightenment. In 1750, he became well-known for his writing after he was awarded a first prize for his *Discourse on the Sciences and Arts*, in which he famously argued that the progress of society was the corruptor of human morality. His new-found success set him on a trajectory that led to numerous widely read and controversial works including his political treatise *The Social Contract* (1762), advocating the supremacy of the general will and '*civil religion' policies, as well as his autobiographical work *Confessions*, published posthumously.

Over the course of his life, Rousseau was engaged with issues of theology in two noteworthy situations. Disagreement arose with *Voltaire over the problem of evil, or *theodicy, in response to the Lisbon earthquake of 1755. Voltaire's *Poem on the Disaster of Lisbon* and *Candide* rejected the explanations of Alexander Pope and Gottfried *Leibniz, which Rousseau defended. Years later, Rousseau's book *Émile* (1762) received widespread condemnation for the section, 'The Profession of Faith of the Savoyard Vicar' and its advocacy of *natural theology and critique of church dogma and practices.

Bibliography

T. E. D. Braun (ed.), *The Lisbon Earthquake of 1755: Representations and Reactions* (Oxford, 2005); R. Goldberg, 'Voltaire, Rousseau, and the Lisbon Earthquake', *Eighteenth Century Life* n.s. 13.2, 1989, pp. 1–20; R. Grimsley, *Rousseau and the Religious Quest* (Oxford, 1968); idem, *Rousseau: Religious Writings* (Oxford and New York, 1970); A. F. Mettraux, 'Rousseau et Voltaire: la guerre des philosophes', *Revue des sciences philosophiques et théologiques*, n.s. 83.2, 1999, pp. 273–290; H. Rosenblatt, *Rousseau and Geneva: From the First Discourse to the Social Contract, 1749–1762* (Cambridge and New York, 1997); J. S. Spink, *Jean-Jacques Rousseau et Genève* (Paris, 1934).

J. P. MCNUTT

RULE OF FAITH, see CREEDS

RUETHER, ROSEMARY RADFORD (b. 1936)

Rosemary Ruether is an American Catholic feminist theologian. She is Carpenter Emerita Professor of Feminist Theology, Graduate Theological Union, Berkeley, California and visiting scholar in feminist theology, Claremont Graduate University and Claremont School of Theology. She taught for many years at Garrett-Evangelical Theological Seminary and was a member of the Graduate Faculty of Northwestern University in Evanston, Illinois.

Ruether's work has been extremely influential upon the whole of *feminist theology. Her contribution to the field spans decades, and her numerous writings have helped establish the foundations of Euro-American feminist theology. Ruether's feminist *liberation theology reflects a correlationist method that places the full humanity of women in critical relationship with the practices of the historic Christian tradition. She utilizes a prophetic-liberating tradition, rooted in Scripture, which understands women as one of the oppressed whom God will liberate and vindicate, thereby making the critical principle of her feminist theology the 'promotion of the full humanity of women'. Ruether is intensely critical of what she describes as the patriarchalization of Christianity and how it has led to the exclusion of women from the shaping of theology as well as to the diminishment of their full humanity.

Therefore, it follows that Ruether grounds her theology upon sources that promote the full humanity of women. Her Christology, for instance, portrays Jesus as the messianic prophet described as the paradigm of liberated humanity. Christ's identity is that which is continued in redemptive humanity and in the life of the community. It is a 'this-worldly' approach in which our responsibility is to use our time to create a just and good community, in the present and the future. Due to the oppression that women in her own Roman Catholic tradition experienced under a patriarchal system, Ruether focused her attention on the need for women-church, a gathering of the feminist community outside established patriarchal Catholicism. Nevertheless, she is careful to maintain a link with the institutional church so as to be effective in critiquing and transforming it.

Much of Ruether's work challenges a *dualistic mindset of Western Christianity that has been distorted by androcentrism. She argues that such a view makes the male normative, and concepts like heaven, spirit, mind, good and man are polarized against earth, bodies, emotions and woman. She understands feminist theology as situated in an interconnected class, *race and *gender analysis. In addition to these, issues of *ecology are also significant. Because she understands all forms of oppression to be interlinked, Ruether seeks to construct a theology that promotes equally the embodied lives of all, as well as the well-being of the earth itself. In this way, Ruether can be considered an early North American ecofeminist who recognized the connections among ecology, feminism and religion, calling for a vision of the earth that was not defined out of domination.

Bibliography

Selected works: *Sexism and God-talk: Toward a Feminist Theology* (Boston, 1983); *Woman-Church: Theology and Practice of Feminist Liturgical Communities* (San Francisco, 1985); *Christianity and the Making of the Modern Family*; and *Gaia and God: An Ecofeminist Theology of Earth Healing* (San Francisco, 1992); *Goddesses and the Divine Feminine: A Western Religious History* (Berkeley, 2005); (ed.), *Encyclopedia of Women and Religion in North America* (Bloomington, 2006).

L. PEACORE

RUSSIAN ORTHODOX THEOLOGY

Within the *Eastern Orthodox theological tradition Russian Orthodox theology has developed specific characteristics of its own.

From the beginnings to *c.* 1800

The conversion of the two most populous Slavic nations, the Poles and the Russians, began with the baptism of the Polish prince Mieszko I in 966 and was followed twenty-two years later by that of Grand Prince Vladimir of Kiev (979–1015). An apparently insignificant difference in these two conversions was to influence profoundly the development of theology in the two nations. The Poles accepted their Christianity from Latin-speaking Christians of the West, and their resulting Latin orientation integrated them into Western Europe. The Russians, however, accepted the Christian faith from Constantinople, the capital of the still vigorous 'Roman' Empire (usually called, somewhat inexactly, the Byzantine Empire), where Greek was spoken. The first Greek missionaries to the Slavs, Cyril (826–69) and Methodius (*c.* 815–85), devised the so-called Glagolithic alphabet (the forerunner of the Cyrillic alphabet used for Russian and several other Slavic languages). Cyril's translations of biblical and liturgical texts laid the foundation for Old Church Slavonic, once widely spoken and still used in the liturgy of Slavic national churches. The use of Slavonic proved a great asset in the conversion of the Slavs, but it was later to make theology and even liturgy less accessible to the Russian masses.

For about 700 years from the conversion of Vladimir to the eighteenth century, the Russian church produced no substantial original theological literature, despite the richness of its ethical and spiritual life. A number of factors contribute to this apparent stagnation. The two most prominent are (1) the wealth of the heritage of Greek *patristic theology entering Russia in Slavonic translation, and (2) the centuries-long isolation of Russia from the outside world, particularly the West, caused by the schism of 1054 between Constantinople and Rome, the more than two centuries of Mongol rule in Russia after 1237, and the capture of Constantinople by the Muslim Turks in 1453. The flood of theological and spiritual works translated from Greek into Slavonic simply submerged the Russian church and made original work seem superfluous. The isolation of Russia kept it largely unaware of theology as a science until well into the seventeenth century.

Nevertheless, one note of continuing significance for Russian theology through the centuries was sounded early, by the first non-Greek metropolitan bishop of Kiev, Ilarion (fl. 1037–54), who produced a confession of faith as well as a classical sermon, 'On Law and Grace', around 1051. It is the sermon that foreshadows the future: Ilarion sets Russia in redemptive history, giving it an *eschatological role. In addition, he takes what will come to be a typically Russian stand concerning the relationship between faith and good works – a strong theoretical emphasis on the sufficiency of *faith coupled with a very practical insistence on good works, particularly on *asceticism and charity. But for centuries Ilarion stands virtually alone as an original writer.

In the West, where it was done in Latin, theology was in constant, productive ferment from the beginning of the eleventh century, producing great thinkers such as *Anselm of Canterbury, Peter *Abelard, *Thomas Aquinas and *Duns Scotus, as well as a host of lesser figures. Russian theology, done in Slavonic, oriented towards Constantinople, and, for centuries hampered by the Mongol yoke, lacked the stimulus of contact with the West. Greek theology, which it did know, was itself highly conservative and developed largely in the area of *mysticism and the ascetic life; in the East there was no counterpart to the flourishing *scholastic theology of the West.

As Russia emerged from Mongol subjugation in the reign of the Grand Prince of Moscow, Ivan III (1462–1595), Constantinople had fallen to the Turks. Russia, with Moscow as its new power centre, self-consciously assumed the mantle of empire from Constantinople. The Russian church appropriated Greek theology in large doses, but it was not to develop this theological heritage until it began to feel the shock of the Protestant *Reformation and the pressure of Catholic expansion in the Counter-*Reformation two centuries later. Ivan married the Byzantine princess Zoé Paleologus, the niece of the last Byzantine emperor, and took up the fallen imperial mantle. This continuity was given a theological interpretation by Abbot Filofei of Pskov (fl. c. 1540). Vassily III (1479–1534), Ivan's successor, was the first Russian ruler to take the title of tsar (from the Roman and Byzantine title 'caesar') and to appropriate the Byzantine double eagle, the symbol of empire. Filofei likened the new tsar to Constantine the Great, the founder of New Rome (i.e. Constantinople), and wrote to him, 'Two Romes have fallen, a third stands, and a fourth shall not be.' This signalled the beginning of a remarkable subservience of Russian theology to tsarist ideology, partly explicable because of the fact that Russian theology derives from Constantinople rather than from Rome. Constantinople was never without a Christian emperor (apart from the brief reign of Julian the Apostate, 361–363) from its establishment to its fall in 1453. Consequently, the patriarch of Constantinople could never claim to be the head of all Christendom as the pope did, for he always stood in the shadow of the 'sacred' emperor and his quasi-divine office. The patriarchy of Moscow was established in 1589, bringing the number of Eastern patriarchs back to the traditional early-church number of five (Rome being no longer counted).

At this time, Rome firmly set the direction for Russian theology for two centuries by attempting to bring the Russian church under its influence, since Russia could no longer look to Turkish-ruled Constantinople. The project was facilitated by the fact that most of what is now western Russia then belonged to Poland, or, more properly, to Lithuania, in the commonwealth of Poland-Lithuania. Poland itself was just recovering from an affair with *Protestantism, in which the majority of the nobility briefly embraced the Reformation. Having brought most of the Protestants back into its fold, Catholicism turned east, where a few Polish and Lithuanian Catholics lived in the midst of an Orthodox majority. The flood of Catholic propaganda called forth an Orthodox reaction: Prince Konstantin Ostrozhsky (1526–1608) established a printing house to publish classical Byzantine theological works in translation, and in 1581 it brought out the Ostrog Bible, the first complete Bible in Slavonic.

King Zygmunt (Sigismund) III of Poland-Lithuania convened a church council at Brest in 1596. The resulting Union of Brest established the uniat Eastern Church (i.e. churches in communion with Rome but retaining their own language, liturgy, etc.) and, with mixed success, placed the Russians and Ukrainians in Zygmunt's realm under papal hegemony. Leading the opposition to this union was the Cretan Cyril Lucaris (1572–1638), later to become patriarch first of Alexandria, then of Constantinople. Lucaris spent five years in Poland-Lithuania in an attempt to prevent the submission of the Orthodox to Rome. Lucaris' role illustrates the interplay of Greek Orthodox and Protestant ideas in the development of Russian theology, which continued to be receptive rather than creative, in reaction rather than in action. During his years in Poland-Lithuania, Lucaris became acquainted with Protestant (chiefly *Reformed) theology and theologians. Consequently, he promoted Protestant ideas in Russia as well as in the Near East, initiating the Protestant connection that produced a two-centuries-long, three-way conflict in Russian theology. The struggle to preserve a distinctive Orthodox tradition was waged at times in alliance with Protestantism against Roman Catholic influence, at times against Protestantism under Roman Catholic influence, and at times against both. The period, which began in 1453 with the fall of Constantinople, may conveniently be seen to close with the accession of Tsar Alexander I in 1801, for under this charismatic ruler (1801–25), who was strongly influenced by German and Baltic Protestant *pietism and eschatological speculation, the Protestant influence appeared to predominate. Eventually, Alexander's patronage of Protestant and biblical piety would stimulate, largely as a reaction, the real flowering of Russian Orthodox theology in the nineteenth century.

To the generation following Ostrozhsky and Lucaris belongs the greatest name in Orthodox theology in the seventeeth century, that of Peter Mogila (1596–1646), who was born in Moldavia in 1597 and educated at the Latin school of L'vov in Polish Galacia. In 1640 he published his *Confession of Faith, containing Protestant emphases. This confession was translated and revised by another Cretan, Melitios Syrigos (d. c. 1667), somewhat undoing the Protestant influence of Lucaris. It was accepted in this form at the Synod of Jassy in 1643 as the confession of the Eastern churches. Mogila also published a Small Catechism in 1645, somewhat in response to Syrigos' revisions, as well as a liturgical handbook, the *Euchologion*, both of which again promoted Protestant tendencies. Thus the situation prevailing at the end of the seventeenth century was one in which Russian theology, without changing its officially anti-Roman and anti-Protestant stand, was permeated with Protestant influences. Patriarch Nikon (1605–81) of Moscow had revised the Orthodox liturgy in 1660, sparking the schism of the Old Believers (*raskolniki*, fallen-away ones) in reaction; it is significant that the major religious controversy of this period was based not on theological differences but on *liturgy. (The Old Believers soon developed pronounced ascetic, separatist and chiliastic tendencies, which are beyond the scope of our consideration here.)

Tsar Peter the Great (1682–1721) promoted the westernization of Russian religion in the context of his efforts to westernize all of Russian life. A small group of theologians in Moscow resisted Protestantizing tendencies, among them Stefan Iavorsky (1658–1722), who enjoyed Peter's favour until he produced his anti-Protestant polemic, *Kamen' very* (*The Rock of Faith*) in 1713 (banned in Russia). Peter turned to Feofan (Theophanes) Prokopovich of Kiev (by then in Russian hands) to counter Iavorsky's anti-Protestant polemics, which in Peter's eyes tied Russia to the past. Prokopovich was a typical Russian theologian of his day, in that he relied heavily on two orthodox Lutherans, J. A. Quenstedt (1617–88) and Johann E. Gerhard (1582–1637). In his *Introductio ad Theologiam*, Prokopovich followed the Protestants in excluding the OT apocrypha from the Bible, but in his major treatise, *On the Gratuitous Justification of Sinners through Christ Jesus*, he rejected the Protestant doctrine of the bondage of the will. Although we are 'saved by faith alone', faith is never 'lonely', but must be accompanied by good works, as Ilarion had taught 600 years earlier.

Opposed by the Moscow theologians around Iavorsky, at the tsar's request Prokopovich drafted the new church constitution, the Ecclesiastical Regulations of 1721. It abolished the patriarchate and created the 'Holy Synod' in its stead, a move that placed the Russian church thoroughly under imperial control. Peter was visited by the ecumenically minded German mathematician G. W. *Leibniz, who saw in Russia the predestined mediator between China and Europe. Leibniz unsuccessfully promoted the idea of an ecumenical council, to be summoned by Peter the Great as the successor to the first Christian emperor, Constantine the Great (just as Filofei of Pskov had said a century before!). Less spectacular but more pervasive was the influence of the German pietist theologian and educator August Hermann Francke (1663–1727), exercised through the intermediary of the German minority in Russia as well as through Swedish prisoners of war there; Russian diplomats regularly visited Francke in Halle en route to and from western Europe.

Later in the eighteenth century, Platon Levshin (1737–1812), rector of the Moscow Academy and later metropolitan (not patriarch!) of Moscow, perpetuated the Protestant tendencies of Prokopovich, like him relying heavily on the Lutheran theologian Quenstedt. Although Levshin followed the Orthodox tradition in denouncing 'popery, Calvinism, and Lutheranism' as 'devastating heresies', in fact he held Lutheran views on the sole authority of *Scripture as well as on the church as the company of believers rather than an institution. Nevertheless, Levshin's major work (*Orthodox Teaching or a Brief Christian Theology*, Moscow, 1765) marks the first attempt at a theological system in Russian (ET by R. Pinkerton, *The Present State of the Greek Church in Russia . . .*, Edinburgh, 1814, and G. Potessaro, *The Orthodox Doctrine of the Apostolic Eastern Church*, London, 1857). At this time, Russian theological education and writing were strongly coloured by Western models, Roman Catholic as well as Protestant. Such an imported theology remained a fragile transplant and could not strike deep roots in Russia. Not until the end of the period would Juvenal Medvedsky (1767–1809) compose the first truly Russian systematic theology.

As always in Russia, where theology remained more *mystical and practical than speculative, the ascetics were more influential than the Protestantizing theologians, as for example in the case of the two monks, St Tikhon of Zadonsk (1724–83) and Palsy Velichkovsky (1722–94). Tikhon relinquished an episcopate in Voronezh for the monastery of Zadonsk. He promoted a practical love ethic based on mystical reflection on the passion of Christ. Velichkovsky gave a new impetus to the *hesychast* (quietist) spirituality of the Byzantine church, which had long been popular in Russia, by publishing the *hesychast spiritual and devotional handbook *Philokalia* (*Love of the Good*) in Slavonic. The *Philokalia* emphasizes an intense personal devotion to *Jesus based on the frequent repetition of the 'prayer of the heart' or 'Jesus prayer' – the short ejaculation, 'Lord Jesus Christ, Son of God, have mercy on me!'

Although the non-dogmatic and internationalist ideas of freemasonry enjoyed a certain vogue during the reign of Catherine the Great (1762–96), Russian spirituality soon turned back to its fascination with the Russian role in the end times. The German physician Johann Heinrich Jung-Stilling (1740–1817) contributed to the nationalistic tendencies of Russian theological speculation with his conviction that the Antichrist had been at work in the French Revolution and that all true Christians were called to gather in the East, in Russia, to withstand him. Thus a note first sounded by Metropolitan Ilarion of Kiev in 1051, namely the conviction that Russia has an important role to play in initiating the last days, continued to resound for three-quarters of a millennium: Alexander I would be seen as the 'angel flying through the midst of heaven' of Rev. 8:13. Indeed, the conviction that Russia must play a central role in the last days would continue to be heard in both tsarist and communist Russia (in secularized dress) to the present day, and to echo in an altered form in the West in the speculations of those who see the Soviet Union not as God's agent but as the opposite – the apocalyptic, anti-Christian power of the end times (see *Antichrist).

Russian Orthodox theology has been consistently a conservative force, but while it preserved major elements of patristic Gk thought, it treated them as though they were Russian. From its very beginnings it had strongly nationalistic and eschatological overtones, assigning Russia a prominent role in the conversion of the world and in the culmination of salvation history. In the seventeenth and eighteenth centuries, Russian theology was deeply influenced by Protestantism, first by Lutheran scholasticism, and then by pietism. Throughout the period 1453–1801, it was never original or independent, but always borrowing, first from the Greeks, then from the Germans. Nevertheless, it was consistently eager to claim a special destiny for Moscow and the Russian people, whether in terms of the 'third Rome' (Filofei of Pskov), of the conversion of Asia (Leibniz), or in the ultimate conflicts of the end times (Jung-Stilling). Not being productive of original ideas, it has also produced very little *heresy – which may help to explain the survival of the Russian church through almost seven decades of communist oppression.

Bibliography

G. P. Fedotov, *The Russian Religious Mind*, 2 vols. (Cambridge, MA and London, 1946, 1966); G. Florovsky, *Ways of Russian Theology* (Belmont, 1979); P. Kawerau, *Die Christentum des Ostens* (Stuttgart, 1972); G. A. Maloney, *History of Orthodox Theology since 1453* (Belmont, 1976).

H. O. J. BROWN

From the nineteenth century to the present

In the nineteenth century the Russian Orthodox Church continued to be run as a department of the tsarist state. The church nevertheless continued to nurture men of great spiritual stature. One of the most beloved saints of the Russians is St Serafim of Sarov (1759–1832), an ascetic who devoted himself to the service of others. The monastery of Optina Pustyn near Tula was to become famous as a place where one could meet monks maintaining the authentic *patristic traditions of *Eastern Orthodoxy.

Tsar Alexander I (1801–25) was interested in promoting 'public enlightenment'. Archimandrite Filaret Drozdov, later Metropolitan of Moscow, reformed and extended the church's facilities for training clergy. He maintained that Russian Orthodoxy had been under too much Western influence and must return to its own roots in the apostles and the Church Fathers. He promoted the translation of the Bible into Russian. A Russian Bible Society was founded in 1812. However, the translation project fell foul of critics who suspected that Western influences were at work, and the Society was closed down in 1826.

The reformed theological schools, including the new Academies, were the cradle for the development of nineteenth-century Russian Orthodox theology within the church. Two themes were important in this theology, usually manifesting themselves as polarities: between the role of God and the role of man; and between renunciation of the world and engagement with it.

Makari Bulgakov (1816–82), a teacher of theology at St Petersburg Theological Academy and later Metropolitan of Moscow (1879–82), published five volumes of *Dogmatic Theology* (*Bogosloviye dogmaticheskoye*) (1849–53). They were systematizing rather than innovative, but for the first time theology was available in up-to-date Russian. The volumes remained central to theological teaching throughout the tsarist period.

Fedor Bukharev (1824–71) was the first Russian Orthodox theologian to call on Orthodoxy to engage with contemporary society. His book *Orthodoxy and the Modern World* (*O pravoslavii v otnoshenii k sovremennosti*, 1860) aroused considerable controversy.

Maksim Tareyev (1866–1934), a teacher of moral theology at the Moscow Academy, argued that the personal inner world of religious experience has nothing to do with the world around, which has its own laws of historical development. Meanwhile Viktor Nesmelov (1863–1920), a teacher at the Kazan Academy, made a unique effort to construct a theological system on an *anthropological basis.

Outside the church, theology, or more precisely religious philosophy, was also developing among certain sections of the intelligentsia, a stratum of individuals concerned to write and speak about the social and political situation in Russia.

Aleksei Khomyakov (1804–60) developed the theme of organic unity and community (cf. *The Church Is One*, Willits, 1974; see *Sobornost) as the distinctive genius of Orthodoxy. Khomyakov thus became one of the inspirers of the Slavophil movement, which focused attention on the originality and resources of Russian Orthodox religious culture, as opposed to the Westernizers, who as the name suggests looked to Western models of social and political development.

By the 1860s *positivist and *atheist ideas had established predominance among the intelligentsia. Yet some writers, including *Tolstoy and *Dostoyevsky, championed spiritual values, and the lay Orthodox philosopher Vladimir Solovyov (1853–1900) produced a comprehensive religio-philosophical system derived not simply from the 'official' Orthodoxy of the

Church Fathers, but from a creative reinterpretation of the faith in the light of modern realities. His system is bound together by the concept of the 'total-unity' of all reality and the concept of 'Godmanhood'. Through the *incarnation, God sanctified all creation, including matter. The whole of creation strives for reunion with God, and human beings have a key role to play in this process.

During the 1890s, the most comprehensive and rigorously scientific positivist worldview so far adopted by the Russian intelligentsia – *Marxism – began to attract an extensive following. Solovyov's own system was of a stature to challenge Marxism, and influenced a whole new generation of the intelligentsia who were growing disillusioned with Marxism's dogmatic *materialism, including Sergei *Bulgakov, Nikolai Berdyayev (1874–1948), Semyon Frank (1877–1950) and Nikolai Lossky (1870–1965). They were part of the turn-of-the-century phenomenon known as the 'new religious consciousness' or the 'Russian religious renaissance'.

Many of these religious philosophers came together in the 1909 collection of essays called *Vekhi* (*Landmarks*), which warned in a remarkably prophetic fashion about the likely totalitarian consequences of revolution in Russia.

In 1922 over a hundred intellectuals who were unsympathetic to Marxism were banished from the Soviet Union to the West. They included a large proportion of the heirs of Solovyov. The establishment of the seminary of St Serge in Paris and later that of St Vladimir in New York provided centres where these thinkers could continue their activity and train a new generation of Russian philosophers and theologians in exile.

What followed amongst these men was an attempt at a renewal of Orthodox thought in the light of the lessons of the revolution and of post-revolutionary realities. Broadly speaking, they followed two alternative avenues: re-appraising the Russian Orthodox legacy, or reviving Patristic theology (see *Church Fathers). The main spokesman for the former path was Bulgakov; leading figures following the second path were Fr Georges Florovsky (1893–1979) and Vladimir *Lossky.

Florovsky rejected the idea that Orthodox theology needed to relate to modern philosophy. In his view it was time to revive the quest for Orthodoxy's authentic roots on which Metropolitan Filaret had embarked in the early nineteenth century. He held that Russian Orthodoxy's absorption of Western *scholasticism, *deism, *pietism and *idealism from the sixteenth century had produced a pseudomorphosis of its real Byzantine heritage. A central theme in the work of Vladimir Lossky is a reappraisal of the concept of *sobornost'*, in order to distinguish between its theological meaning and its socio-political use and abuse.

Bulgakov, meanwhile, was developing his understanding of the created world as a total unity, bound together by 'Sophia' – the wisdom of God – as the principle of creation. Sophia is a third being between God and the world, and from here it is a short step to positing the existence of a fourth person of the Trinity. In the 'Sophia Controversy' among Russian émigré theologians in 1935 Bulgakov was accused of *heresy by the Moscow Patriarchate.

Some have seen the controversy between the two schools as a debate between modernists and traditionalists, or between liberals and conservatives. However, the dispute was not about whether the Orthodox Church needed renewal, or about whether the church should be engaged with the world, but about the basis for such a renewal and engagement.

By the late 1940s the neo-Patristic school had prevailed over the Russian school. The latter was cut off from its roots, while the Patristics could engage with current theology and philosophy in the West on a more cosmopolitan basis. Neo-Patristics also chimed in with counter-cultural trends in Western theology at the time, such as Karl *Barth's theology, with its stress on the transcendence of God.

It was, nevertheless, one of the Russian school, Berdyayev, who became most widely known in the West. It was a happy coincidence that he should arrive in the West at a time when *existentialism was growing in popularity: mutual enrichment followed. Berdyayev distinguishes two realms of reality: spirit, which is living and free; and nature or being, which is passive, the product of the *fall. Humanity's free creative love of God is to be the source of the salvation of humankind and the world.

What, meanwhile, was happening to Orthodox philosophy and theology in the Soviet Union? The Russian Orthodox Church was severely restricted by the state, and while it possessed theological educational establishments it could engage in no study which would relate Orthodoxy to the modern world.

According to the official Marxist-Leninist ideology, religious thought was essentially reactionary and bourgeois. There were, however, one or two individuals who maintained continuity, such as Aleksei Losev (1893–1988) and Sergei Averintsev (1937–2004), who used the vehicle of lectures on such subjects as Byzantine literature and classical philosophy to introduce their students to the thought of Solovyov, Pavel Florensky (1882–1937), Bulgakov and others.

During the last twenty years of the Soviet Union, young converts to Orthodoxy were increasingly concerned to apply their faith to Soviet reality and to employ spiritual resources to tackle problems in their lives. Now in post-communist Russia continuity is being re-established both with the pre-revolutionary tradition and with the more recent work as developed in exile. The younger generation of converts who have been engaged in theological and philosophical enquiry include Yevgeni Barabanov, Mikhail Meerson, Vladimir Zelinsky, Vladimir Bibikhin and Sergei Khoruzhi.

The conditions again exist in Russia for religion to re-enter the public arena. In a context of moral uncertainty, many are seeing Orthodoxy as a potential source of guidelines for personal and social behaviour. The often heated debate about subjects such as, for example, the role of Orthodox education in state schools, is symptomatic of the revived confrontation between those who want religion to remain 'privatized', as one option in a pluralist secular state, and those who would like to see Orthodoxy assume the role of a 'civil religion'.

The Russian Orthodox Church as an institution, however, has hardly started coming to terms with the challenges of new freedoms, or with its new role in a pluralist society, or with its own recent past. In 2000 the church, it is true, produced the first ever exposition of a social doctrine by an Orthodox church: *Foundations for a Social Concept for the Russian Orthodox Church* (*Osnovy sotsial'noi kontseptsii Russkoi Pravoslavnoi Tserkvi*). The document affirms a desire to engage with the world, but this proclaimed desire is constantly questioned in the text. The document is predominantly defensive in tone. The dominant theme is that contemporary society is degraded as the result of the rise of irreligious individualism. The text does argue for the uniqueness and dignity of the individual, but this is subordinate to the main aim, which is the protection of traditional identity through resistance to *globalization, liberalization and *secularization.

In its discussion of community, the *Social Doctrine* refers to *sobornost'*, but does not engage with the history and problematic usage of the term, although critical discussion of this kind is readily available in the writings of the Russian émigré theologians. The issue is still lively: in fundamentalist Orthodox circles in Russia today, for example, *sobornost'* tends to be used to justify collectivism, Russian national solidarity, and even the suppression of individual rights.

In the wider perspective, the *Social Concept* contains no discussion of the church's experience under totalitarianism, or of its longer history of adaptability to the requirements of the state.

Bibliography

A. Blane, *Georges Florovsky, Russian Intellectual and Orthodox Churchman* (Crestwood, 1993); F. Copleston, *Russian Religious Philosophy: Selected Aspects* (Notre Dame, 1988); J. M. Edie, J. P. Scanlan, M.-B. Zeldin and G. L. Kline (eds.), *Russian Philosophy*, vol. 3 (Chicago, 1965); C. Evtuhov, *The Cross and the Sickle: Sergei Bulgakov and the Fate of Russian Religious Philosophy* (Ithaca and London, 1997); G. Florovsky, *The Ways of Russian Theology*, 2 vols. (vols. 5 and 6 of the *Collected Works*) (Belmont, 1979 and 1987); J. D. Kornblatt and R. F. Gustavson (eds.), *Russian Religious Thought* (Madison and London, 1996); M. Raeff, *Russia Abroad: A Cultural History of the Russian Emigration, 1919–1939* (New York, 1990); E. Roberts and A. Shukman (eds.), *Christianity for the Twenty-First Century: The Prophetic Writings of Alexander Men* (New York, 1996); A. Schmemann (ed.), *Ultimate Questions: An Anthology of Modern Russian Religious Thought* (New York, Chicago and San Francisco, 1965); N. Zernov, *The Russian Religious Renaissance of the Twentieth Century* (London, 1963).

P. M. WALTERS

RUTHERFORD, SAMUEL (1600–61)

Born near Jedburgh, Scotland, Rutherford graduated at Edinburgh in 1621 and was later appointed regent of humanity there. This office he demitted in 1626 after being charged with pre-nuptial fornication. Soon afterwards, he was accepted as a divinity student and inducted in 1627 to the parish of Anwoth, Galloway.

This was done 'without giving engagement to the Bishop', though episcopacy (see *Ministry) had since 1612 been the national church policy. In Rutherford's view, episcopacy brought *Arminianism. He wrote forcibly against that danger in his *Exercitationes Apologetica pro Divina Gratia* (*Apologetical Exercitations for Divine Grace*, 1636), published in Amsterdam. This led to invitations to chairs in Dutch institutions, but also to a summons from the notorious Court of High Commission which was incensed by the author's persistent nonconformity.

He was deprived of his pastoral office, forbidden to preach, and exiled to Aberdeen – 'the first in the kingdom put to utter silence', he mourned. Aberdeen to him was full of 'Papists or of men of Gallio's naughty faith'. When in 1638 most Scots rebelled and drew up the National Covenant (see *Covenanters) against Charles I's duplicity and Laud's liturgy, Rutherford hurried down from the north to subscribe his name. In 1639 he became professor of divinity at St Andrews.

His *Lex Rex* (1644), written in reply to the 'divine right of kings' theory, caused a furore, not least at the Westminster Assembly, to which he made influential contributions. This work asserts the supremacy of the people; that the law, and no royal tyrant, is king; and that unlimited power pertains to God only. With the Restoration the author (though not the book itself) barely escaped the hands of the public hangman. Its doctrine became the constitutional inheritance of democratic countries in modern times, but not before many Covenanters had died for the only King to whom unswerving loyalty was due.

In 1649, with the principle of religious *toleration beginning to find acceptance in England, Rutherford's *Free Disputation against Pretended Liberty of Conscience* argued that such toleration was against Scripture and common sense. It allowed two religions side by side, and was outrageous ecclesiastically and sinful civilly. The magistrate as God's vicegerent sent offenders to the scaffold, not with the idea of producing spiritual results, but to strengthen the foundations of the civil order.

Rutherford did not recognize the existence of religious minorities; the contempt he expressed for Independents and others in *A Free Disputation* provoked Milton's charge that 'New Presbyter is but Old Priest writ large'. Rutherford nonetheless came to have misgivings about the assumed infallibility of the ruling Covenanting party.

While there has been a resurgence of interest in his political views in North America, he is now chiefly remembered not for his political theory but for his *Letters*. Addressed to correspondents of all classes, they still offer spiritual counsel that is both biblical and insightful, thought-provoking and imaginative; and they do so with true compassion born of experience and understanding.

Cited to answer a charge of treason, the dying Rutherford sent the Privy Council notice of non-appearance, stating that he had a prior summons from 'a Superior Judge and Judicatory'.

Bibliography

A. A. Bonar (ed.), *Letters of Samuel Rutherford* (repr., Edinburgh, 1984); J. Coffey, *Politics, Religion and the British Revolutions: The Mind of Samuel Rutherford* (Cambridge, 1997); G. D. Henderson, *Religious Life in Seventeenth-Century Scotland* (Cambridge, 1937); A. Smellie, *Men of the Covenant* (repr. Edinburgh, 1975).

J. D. DOUGLAS

SABBATH

OT

Sabbath is an important, yet contested theological theme. The likely meaning of *šabbāt* (שבת) is to 'desist' or to 'stop'. It is based on the idea of the divine rest at the climax of God's creative activity (Gen. 2:1–3). This event is adduced as the basis of the 'work break' in the fourth commandment (Exod. 20:8–11). The recasting of the command (Deut. 5:12–15) displays 'amazing interpretive freedom' (Brueggemann) in relocating its basis in the exodus liberation from slavery.

Between the accounts of creation and the giving of the law, there is only one reference to Sabbath (Exod. 14:23); there is no data available to indicate how or whether the day was observed during this period. After the giving of the law there are hints of a religious aspect to Sabbath observance (Lev. 23:3; Num. 28:9–10; Ps. 92).

The Sabbath is described as a perpetual defining 'sign' for Israel (Exod. 31:12–17); preserving this sign brought promised blessing;

infringements, threatened judgment. This dimension of Sabbath as a badge of national distinctiveness is most fully articulated in the writings of Ezra-Nehemiah, the prophets of exile (Isa. 58), and the intertestamental period.

NT

Jesus honours the Sabbath by attending synagogue worship; yet also challenges contemporary views of the Sabbath by his words and actions. These frequent and very public challenges to Sabbath custom are difficult to read accurately; they may be attempts to put the Sabbath commandment back on track by tearing away extra-biblical additions, or may challenge the very fabric of Sabbath observance in the light of the newness of the work of Christ. The key text (Mark 2:27–28), with its reference to the relationship between humans and the Sabbath, and Jesus as 'Lord of the Sabbath', appears to signal aspects of continuity and discontinuity.

Historically, Christians have viewed Sunday as important. Jesus rose on the first day of the week, Pentecost occurred on that day, and there are hints that it played a significant part in the church's calendar (Acts 20:7; 1 Cor. 16:2). The strongest reference is Rev. 1:10, where the day is designated 'The Lord's Day'. There is no command to 'keep Sunday special', or to invest it with any Sabbath-like characteristics; there are signs that the early church met on a daily basis (Acts 2:46–47). It is notable that the bridge-building advice given to Jewish and non-Jewish believers (Acts 15) does not require any form of Sabbath observance.

NT writers outside the Gospels appear to be flexible about the observance of special days (although there is doubt whether they are referring to weekly Sabbaths), seeing them as part of the shadow that has now found its substance in Christ (Rom. 14:5–6; Col 2:16–17). The most extended reflection on Sabbath locates the believer's rest in our participation in the finished work of Christ (Heb 4:9–11).

Theological positions

The evidence has been read in different ways; conclusions tend to be shaped by wider considerations of the role of Mosaic law in the life of Christians.

Strict Sabbath observance

Sabbatarian groups such as the Seventh-Day Adventists affirm that observing a weekly seventh-day Sabbath is a mark of their identity as the people of God. During the seventeenth and eighteenth centuries, a minority of English Baptists also observed the seventh day, as some Anabaptists had done.

Transference

The Sabbath is seen as a 'creation ordinance' (Murray), a vital gift for the well-being of humankind. This principle of rest predates the Mosaic law and has continuing force and value for human beings. Sunday or the Lord's Day is seen as the 'Christian Sabbath'. In its strongest form this can involve an attempt to reconstruct all of the Torah's Sabbath regulations.

Celebration

Sunday is a valuable time to pause in gratitude and celebration of the rest offered us in Christ; it is not a day that is bound by detailed prescriptions concerning the minutiae of its use. The rest achieved through Christ's redemptive work fulfils the law and relocates rest within a relationship with Christ (Matt. 11:28–30).

Bibliography

S. Bacchiocchi, *From Sabbath to Sunday* (Rome, 1977); W. Brueggemann, 'Sabbath', in *Reverberations of Faith* (Louisville and London, 2002), pp. 180–182; D. A. Carson (ed.), *From Sabbath to Lord's Day* (Grand Rapids, 1982); M. J. Dawn, *The Sense of Call: A Sabbath Way of Life for Those Who Serve God, the Church, and the World* (Grand Rapids 2006); G. F. Hasel, 'Sabbath', in *ABD*, vol. 5, pp. 850–856; J. Murray, *Collected Writings*, vol. 1 (Edinburgh, 1976), pp. 205–228.

J. D. WOODS

SABELLIANSIM, see MONARCHIANISM

SACRAMENT

The term 'sacrament' was not used in the Bible or in the earliest church, although what we would now regard as sacramental worship was at the centre of the life and worship of the church from the beginning. The term that is closest to sacrament in the NT is *mysterion*, mystery. In the synoptic Gospels we read of 'the mystery of the kingdom of God' (Mark 4:11). For Paul the mystery is God's plan of salvation, revealed in Jesus Christ. *Mysterion* was also a reality disclosing God's hidden plan (Col. 1:26). It could refer to earthly happenings related to God's great plan, and more generally to secrets that are revealed to the faithful.

The Fathers

The early Fathers of the church were cautious about referring to Christian *worship as a mystery, perhaps because they were uneasy about possible confusion with the pagan 'mystery religions' of the day. Clement of Alexandria spoke of three categories of Christian mysteries, the greater and lesser mysteries, and the supreme mystery, which is Christ himself. The Latin Fathers on the whole tended to speak of *sacramentum* rather than *mysterion*. In secular life the word *sacramentum* referred to the ritual for army recruits, involving an oath of unconditional loyalty. *Tertullian was the first to use *sacramentum* in a Christian context, specifically in reference to *baptism as the start of a new life following on a binding commitment. Cyprian understood *sacramentum* in a less military way than Tertullian. For him, *sacramentum* is a matter of symbols, figures and signs representing spiritual realities. He speaks of the *Eucharist, baptism and marriage as sacraments.

*Augustine understood a sacrament as the 'sign' of a spiritual reality, the visible form of an invisible grace. He distinguished four components, inseparable from one another: the outward and visible element; the virtue, or grace bestowed in the sacrament; the spoken formula or *verbum* which links the sign with its virtue; and the agent of the sacrament, that is, Christ himself.

After Augustine there was continuing controversy about the number and the nature of the sacraments. Peter *Lombard taught that there were seven sacraments (baptism, confirmation, Eucharist, marriage, ordination, penance and extreme unction), while the Reformers taught that there were only two – baptism and the Eucharist – on the grounds that a sacrament must be specifically instituted and commanded by the Lord. *Thomas Aquinas taught that the sacraments were effective *ex opere operato* – a way of stressing the objectivity of the sacraments, and their independence of the goodness or otherwise of the priest and the congregation. After Thomas the prevalent legal and juridical thinking resulted in the validity of the sacraments often being seen as depending on the correct performance of the rite in the prescribed form with the proper words and actions by the legally authorized minister. This legalistic understanding of the sacraments became very widespread during the later Middle Ages, sometimes almost totally obscuring a theological understanding of the rites and their significance.

The *Reformation

The Reformers' understanding of the sacraments varied widely. At one extreme were the *Zwinglians, who understood sacraments as no more than visual aids, vivid reminders of past salvific events, at the other, those who saw the sacraments as moments in which the faithful experienced the real presence of Christ with his people. In some traditions, God the Spirit was invoked in an *epiclesis* to come down and be with his people; in other, particularly Calvinist (see *Reformed theology), traditions the imagery was more in terms of the faithful being lifted up to share in a proleptic way the joys of heaven, and the heavenly banquet in particular. All the major Protestant traditions affirmed a necessary close linkage between word and sacrament. One could not, for instance, have a eucharistic service without the reading of Scripture and preaching. Only thus could the temptation to regard Christian worship as magical be avoided. Some Protestant sects – most notably the *Quakers – are often presented as non-sacramental or antisacramental. There is, however, a strong case that they regard the whole of life as sacramental, every meal as eucharistic, and so forth.

The Eastern churches

The *Eastern churches followed a very different path. For them the term mystery in their liturgies referred to the incarnation, the Eucharist, marriage, baptism and so forth as sacramental. The whole of life and all the events of our salvation should be regarded as sacramental. There should be no argument about whether there are two, or seven, or many sacraments

The liturgical movement

At the heart of the modern *liturgical revival is a recovery of the sense that sacraments are mysteries in which participants encounter the living triune God. Disciples of today, just as the disciples of long ago, in encountering Jesus come into touch with a mystery which they know to be the mystery of God's being and acts, the secret of the universe and the meaning of life. In the primary sense, then, we should speak of *Jesus Christ as being the sacrament. In Christ, the *incarnate Son, through his physical, historical and material humanity we encounter the mystery and the reality of God himself. In a secondary sense the *church, which is the body of Christ, should be regarded as a sacrament. It is the community in space and time, the visible *fellowship in which the God and Father of our Lord Jesus Christ is encountered, and as his body it represents Christ sacramentally to the world. Thus the church is to be understood as the sacrament of the unity of all humankind. It shows in sacramental form the *saving purpose of God for all humanity; it is a sign of *hope for all, the purpose of God for all humanity, a working model (to use a rather crude image) of what God wills for everyone: loving fellowship with God and with one another. And the church is a sacrament because the visible empirical reality of the fellowship points beyond itself to its Lord, to Christ.

The sacraments of the church are also sacraments, the radical Roman Catholic theologian, *Schillebeeckx argues, precisely because they are also acts of Christ himself. 'A sacrament,' he writes, 'is primarily and fundamentally a personal act of Christ himself which reaches and involves us in the form of an institutional act performed by a person in the Church who ... is empowered to do so by Christ himself' (*Christ, the Sacrament*, p. 62).

The modern liturgical movement has led to a significant coming together of the major traditions of understanding of the sacraments, most clearly perhaps in documents such as the Faith and Order Commission's convergence document, *Baptism, Eucharist and Ministry*, agreed at Lima in 1982. But it is also fair to say that these new agreements between the major churches about the nature and celebration of the sacraments have not led to many serious moves towards unity or greater intercommunion.

Bibliography

D. M. Baillie, *The Theology of the Sacraments* (Edinburgh, 1957); P. F. Bradshaw (ed.), *The New SCM Dictionary of Liturgy and Worship* (London, 2002); D. B. Forrester, J. I. McDonald and G. Tellini, *Encounter with God* (London, ²1996); P. T. Forsyth, *The Church and the Sacraments* (London, 1917); O. C. Quick, *The Christian Sacraments* (London, 1927); E. Schillebeeckx, *Christ, the Sacrament of the Encounter with God* (London, 1983); A. Schmemann, *Introduction to Liturgical Theology* (New York, 1986); *idem*, *The Eucharist: Sacrament of the Kingdom* (New York, 1988); M. Thurian, *The Mystery of the Eucharist* (London, 1983).

D. B. FORRESTER

SACRIFICE

Sacrifice is a central component of Christ's work of reconciling humans to God: Jesus Christ saw his death in terms of Jewish sacrifice, as the sacrificial lamb of Passover; God provided the Israelite institution of sacrifice; Israel made sacrifice to God through its priesthood. Sacrifice is used both literally and metaphorically in the OT and classical philosophers. The later prophets and some classical philosophers, particularly Neoplatonists, made ethical criticisms of blood sacrifice, arguing that it was unworthy of God. For example, Porphyry rejected animal sacrifice as killing animals was deemed immoral, and God could not demand an immoral act as worship. Jewish thinkers did not try to explain how sacrifice could be expiatory, i.e. how it could remove sin and *guilt from Israel. The early Christians felt compelled to develop explanations for the efficacy of Christ's sacrifice because it was considered to be unique, final and universal, i.e. once for all. This was in stark contrast to pre-Christian views of sacrifice.

Patristic and medieval views

*Patristic theologians understood sacrifice as aversion of divine punishment, propitiation and expiation. Several patristic authors focused on Christ's sacrifice as breaking the curse of God upon sinners through Christ himself becoming accursed in our place. *Athanasius articulated the view of sacrifice as propitiation of God as follows: 'The death of Christ was a sacrifice offered by God himself to satisfy the demands of his truthfulness and pay the debt to his integrity.' The underlying problem is that God, being holy, perfectly good and true, cannot have fellowship with sinful, imperfect humans. The actual problem, however, is not intrinsic to the nature of God, but due to the tainting of humans by original *sin. God can only be God if he always acts in accordance with all his attributes. Humans cannot make themselves holy, so if God and humans were ever to be reconciled, the initiative had to come from God.

Only God can effect expiation of sin. *Gregory of Nazianzus articulated the view of sacrifice as expiation when he stated that Christ cleansed the world of sin in his role as high priest and sacrificial victim. Medieval Western Christians emphasized Christ's role as sacrificial victim due to the stress on Christ's humanity in the early Latin Fathers. In his defence of the propitiation, *Thomas Aquinas makes a link with the theory that Christ's death was a 'satisfaction' on behalf of humans.

*Reformed theology

John *Calvin's theory of the atonement brings together the three roles of sacrifice in Christ's work. Calvin's theory is based upon consideration of the entire life of Christ on earth from his conception to his ascension. This is demonstrated by the fact that when he asks 'How has Christ abolished sin, banished the separation between us and God, and acquired righteousness to render God favourable and kindly towards us?', he replies that Christ 'has achieved this for us by the whole course of his obedience' (*Institutes*, II.16.5). Christ in his *obedience represents the people of God because he has taken sinful human nature upon himself. Following the authors of the NT, John Calvin states the propitiatory nature of sacrifice thus: 'Christ paid a debt to the justice of God by taking the punishment which the law of God demanded from those who breached it' (*Institutes*, II.16.3–5). Calvin's notion of sacrifice as penal *substitution rests on Christ's role as High Priest, one of his three offices.

Theological and ethical problems

Christ's death as a sacrifice needs to be seen in the context of the saving work of the *trinitarian God if it is not to be abused ethically. *Jesus Christ could only be the one, holy and perfect sacrifice in our place because he was fully divine and fully human. A merely human Jesus could not be a suitable sacrifice, not least because human sacrifice was not permitted in Israel, nor could he have been sinless. Thus recurring controversies in the churches over *Arianism can be understood as involving battles over the very possibility of salvation through propitiation. Propitiation has often been a subject of controversy in modern Western theology, this being due to its link to the notion of divine *wrath, which itself has come under suspicion. *Evangelical theologians have consistently argued that sacrifice has a necessary propitiatory element because God's wrath is personal and is an expression of his holiness. At the same time propitiation is precisely an expression of God's *love because he has restored the possibility of fellowship between a holy *God and sinful humans.

Since the *Enlightenment, sacrifice has fallen out of favour among some Western theologians as a metaphor for understanding Christ's *atonement. One reason for this includes horror at blood sacrifice of animals. In response, it must be said that seeing Christ as sacrificial victim made sense to converts to Catholic Christianity from sixteenth-century Aztec civilization, whose religion practised human and animal sacrifices. In such a cultural setting, the view that Christ's sacrifice is the end of all sacrifices carries a strong meaning. In contemporary African Christianity, the Israelite sacrificial system and Christ's fulfilment of it is intelligible in ways not possible for Western Christians. Blood sacrifice of animals is still made in Nigeria for example.

In post-war Germany, repugnance at Nazi rhetoric of sacrificial dying for one's country has made the concept of sacrifice a difficult one to use with integrity. Sacrifice needs to be carefully defined because the understanding of the Christian life depends theologically upon *Christology. Christ's sacrifice was accomplished with an atoning purpose. Humans are invited to present themselves as living sacrifices to God and to imitate Christ in the power of the *Spirit. *Feminist theology as well as contemporary psychology tend to be critical of sacrifice if it requires that the believer lives in such a way that he or she is destroyed and unable to live a good life. Christology therefore needs to be articulated with an awareness of its relationship to models of the *Christian life, and in turn their relationship to contemporary and historic models of the good life outside the church.

See also: LAW; SALVATION.

Bibliography

C. Baxter, 'The Cursed Beloved: A Reconsideration of Penal Substitution', in J. Goldingay (ed.), *Atonement Today* (London, 1995), pp. 54–72; E. Fergusson, 'Sacrifice', in E. Fergusson (ed.), *Encyclopaedia of Early Christianity* (New York and London, 1997), pp. 1015–1018; P. S. Fiddes, *Past Event and Present Salvation: The Christian Idea of*

Atonement (London, 1989); J. B. Green and M. D. Baker (eds.), *Recovering the Scandal of the Cross: Atonement in New Testament and Contemporary Contexts* (Carlisle, 2003); C. E. Gunton, *The Actuality of Atonement: A Study of Metaphor, Rationality and the Christian Tradition* (Edinburgh, 1988); S. Jeffery, M. Ovey and A. Sach, *Pierced for Our Transgressions* (Nottingham, 2007); P. Jenkins, *The New Faces of Christianity: Believing the Bible in the Global South* (Oxford, 2006); J. R. W. Stott, *The Cross of Christ* (Leicester, 1989); T. F. Torrance, *Scottish Theology: From John Knox to John McLeod Campbell* (Edinburgh, 1996); F. Young, *Sacrifice and the Death of Christ* (London, 1975).

C. A. E. MOSELEY

SAINT

In the OT, God's people are from time to time called 'saints', 'holy ones', as being set apart to the holy God. In the NT, 'saints' (*hagioi*) becomes the commonest title used of Christians in general, for the more particular reason that they have been consecrated to God by the atonement of Christ and the gift of the Holy Spirit. However, it is not surprising that the expression came in time to be applied especially to people who showed conspicuous marks of their consecration to God, or of the influence of the Holy Spirit upon them, by their character or conduct.

The inclusion of saints in the liturgical calendar began in the second century. Originally these were local observances of the death-days of *martyrs. The dedication of churches to saints began in the same way, with churches built over the tombs of martyrs. As the fame of martyrs and saints spread, observance of their festivals became more widespread, and universal calendars of saints for the Western and Eastern churches eventually resulted. Biblical saints who were not already commemorated as martyrs were inserted, and in the East this included OT saints. After the *Nestorian controversy, feasts of the Blessed Virgin *Mary, as being the *theotokos* (bearer of God), became especially numerous and popular.

In the Church of Rome, a saint qualifies for inclusion under that title in the calendar when he or she has been canonized by the pope. The requirements for canonization are heroic virtue and miracles wrought in response to the saint's intercession. Heroic virtue contributes to the 'treasury of *merits' (see *Purgatory). Miracles are believed to occur at the saint's tomb or through his or her relics or *images, or at shrines where the saint is said to have appeared, and these miracles are attributed to the saint's intercession.

Direct requests to a saint for his or her intercession or for other benefits are what is meant by 'the invocation of saints'. The practice implies that the saints can hear such requests and know how to answer them. The practice was certainly in existence by the fourth century, and was eventually introduced into the liturgy, both Eastern and Western. It was abolished by the Reformers, as equivalent to prayer, and tending to treat the saints as gods, and hence inconsistent with the sole *mediatorship of Christ.

Because of the vast numbers of saints' days, and the legends and abuses associated with them, the Reformers were inclined to remove saints from the calendar altogether, but in England and Sweden festivals of NT saints and All Saints' Day were retained.

See also: COMMUNION OF SAINTS; SANCTIFICATION.

Bibliography

W. E. Addis and T. Arnold, *A Catholic Dictionary* (London, 1960); P. Brown, *The Cult of the Saints* (Chicago, 1981); P. D. Clarke and T. Claydon (eds.), *Sainthood and Sanctity*, Studies in Church History 47 (Woodbridge, 2011); K. Donovan, 'The Sanctoral', in C. P. M. Jones *et al*. (eds.), *The Study of Liturgy* (London, 1978); M. Perham, *The Communion of Saints* (London, 1980).

R. T. BECKWITH

SALVATION

'Salvation' is given a central place in Christian faith by the very name, 'Jesus', meaning in its Hebrew form (Yeshua) 'YHWH is salvation' (see Matt. 1:21). Soteriology (from *soter*, saviour, and *soteria*, salvation) is therefore the doctrine of salvation.

In the OT, the primary story of salvation is the exodus. It was also a '*redemption' (a setting free). But the exodus was not only Israel's salvation *from* slavery; it also led *to* the covenant at Sinai. God had acted in *grace, but that led to obligations for Israel to obey God's *law. As they were faithful, Israel experienced God's salvation in *shalom* (peace and prosperity), but their unfaithfulness led to exile in Babylon. Yet God was still righteous, that is, faithful to his covenant, and therefore was the 'Saviour' who brought them back to the land (Isa. 43:11; 45:21).

The Jewish people then developed an expectation of a new era of salvation, when God would intervene to establish his just rule (or 'kingdom') over the earth and re-establish the kingdom of Israel. Out of that came the Christian hope of the NT, that the rule or *kingdom of God which has *already* come in *Jesus has *yet* to come in glory. Salvation was therefore no longer a national salvation for Israel, but salvation for the world, including the hope of *resurrection from the dead and even 'the new heavens and the new earth' (Rev. 21:1; cf. Isa. 66:22). This was now a *hope for eternal salvation in 'the age to come'.

The Greek verb 'to save' (*sōzō*) includes the connotation of 'to heal' and is used in the Gospels for the healing miracles of Jesus. But salvation cannot be restricted to physical healing, for Jesus linked it to the forgiveness of sin (Mark 2:3–12; see *Guilt and forgiveness). Salvation is not merely the restoration of health and wealth, but at its heart has to do with our reconciliation to God. In the Pauline epistles, salvation will come in the *future* at the end of the age (Rom. 13:11). But it is assured now in the *present* to those who have faith in Jesus, confessing him to be the risen Lord (Rom. 10:9). This knowledge of present salvation is effected through the power of the *gospel (Rom. 1:16), which declares God's *past* completed act of salvation in the death and *resurrection of Jesus so that we can say that by grace we '*have been saved*' (Eph. 2:5). The crucial moment of salvation then was when, on the *cross, Christ died for our sins (1 Cor. 15:1–5). In fundamental agreement with that, the Gospel of John also presents Jesus as 'the Saviour of the world' (4:42).

Several aspects arising from the biblical concept of salvation have been explored in Christian theology.

Salvation and atonement. First, soteriology centres on the doctrine of the *atonement, treated in the West since *Anselm as a distinct doctrine. The word 'at-one-ment', coined by Tyndale to translate *katallagē* (reconciliation), has since acquired the meaning of the Hebrew *kpr* or Greek *hilaskomai*, to propitiate or expiate, which provides a biblical basis for Anselm's key concept, 'satisfaction'. Christ became human to provide *satisfaction to God as our representative, for our debt of honour. But other aspects of atonement include *victory over the powers of evil (*Aulén's *Christus Victor* theme) and the way in which God's love is demonstrated by the cross (associated with *Abelard). Except for the particular *Calvinist tradition stemming from the Synod of *Dort (1619), all Christian traditions have held that the atonement was for all, but that that did not imply *universalism, the final salvation of all.

Salvation and justification. Secondly, soteriology acquired a new focus on *justification at the *Reformation. Luther's rediscovery of justification by faith involved wrestling with the puzzling question: how can God be just and yet justify the *ungodly*? As the Reformation progressed, the *Reformers generally embraced the doctrine of penal *substitution as the way to link 'subjective soteriology' (justification and *sanctification) to objective soteriology (the atonement). God in Christ not only offered satisfaction to God (as Anselm taught) by giving God the obedience we had failed to give, but he also took our place in taking the punishment we deserved. This standard Reformation doctrine has been hotly debated since the nineteenth century. But what is clear is that the moment of justification by faith has been generally considered in evangelical Protestantism to be the moment of salvation when the sinner passes from death to life.

Final salvation. With the recovery of the structure of NT (already/not yet) *eschatology in the twentieth century, there has also come a new appreciation that the expected salvation at the end of the age is to be cosmic and physical and not just spiritual. The influence of *Hellenistic thinking in the early church led to a dualism between the physical and the spiritual, so that whereas the Jewish idea of salvation was more physical, the Christian idea was 'spiritual'. It was the saving of 'souls' and to enjoy the beatific *vision of God in heaven. But while the NT certainly speaks of the dying Christian going to be 'with the Lord' (Phil. 1:23), it is clear that final salvation is to be a salvation of whole persons in the redeemed *creation. Some theologians now embrace universalism (the salvation of all), contrary to the historic doctrine of the church, or inclusivism (the salvation of some who have not believed in Christ).

Present salvation. Christian theology speaks of present salvation in the light of final (eschatological) salvation. For the individual, present salvation includes not only justification but regeneration as the beginning of *sanctification. There is not only a change in the believer's relationship to God through forgiveness, but that is necessarily accompanied by real changes in the believer's life, both in external action, and in internal motivation. Although never complete in this life, present salvation includes release from the dominance of sinful pride and self-centredness as the *saints (that is to say, all Christians, according to 1 Cor. 1:2) increase in sanctity. There is a new awareness today that such present salvation also needs to be understood more corporately within the community of the *church, the people of God.

Bibliography

Doctrine Commission of the General Synod of the Church of England, *The Mystery of Salvation* (London, 1995); W. Foerster and G. Fohrer, *TDNT* VII, pp. 965–1024; E. M. B. Green, *The Meaning of Salvation* (London, 1965); P. A. Rainbow, *The Way of Salvation* (Milton Keynes, 2005); G. Wainwright, *For Our Salvation* (Grand Rapids, 1997); D. F. Wells, *The Search for Salvation* (Leicester, 1978).

T. A. NOBLE

SALVATION ARMY

Founded in 1865 by William and Catherine Booth, the Salvation Army was formerly known as the East London Revival Society, the East London Christian Mission and the Christian Mission. In 1878, a draft copy of the organization's annual report read, 'The Christian Mission is a Volunteer Army.' By replacing the word 'volunteer' with 'salvation', Booth christened the movement, captured the spirit of an imperialistic age and encapsulated the missional activism, public engagement and commitment to the *priesthood of all believers which constitute Salvationist theology.

Called to evangelize 'the last, the lost and the least', the Army launched new congregations, innovative models of social service and imaginative methods of social activism. By 1884, the movement had more than 900 centres in Britain and Ireland and was established in thirteen countries worldwide, including America, Australia and India. 'In contemplating Victorian religion,' Owen Chadwick argues, 'we need to remember the Salvation Army as well as Oxford University.' With more than 15,000 centres in 111 countries and over one million soldiers, the Salvation Army is one of Protestantism's largest denominations and the world's largest non-governmental provider of social care.

While subject to an array of influences, William Booth's *Methodist heritage provided the Army's theological impetus. As part of the founding deeds (1878) and successive versions of the Salvation Army Act of Parliament (1931–80), the eleven Articles of Faith frame the movement's theology. Proclaiming Christ's *atonement to the whole world, the *Arminian emphasis proposes a radical view of faith whereby *salvation is offered to the 'whosoever' and is subsequently dependent 'upon continued obedient faith in Christ'.

The call to personal holiness provides the soteriological next step. 'Holiness to the Lord is to us a fundamental truth,' declared Booth, 'it stands in the front rank of our doctrines.' Influenced by North American *holiness teachers such as James Caughey, Charles *Finney and Phoebe *Palmer, William and Catherine placed women in the pulpit, pushed the chapel into the street, paired preaching with social action and pressed *Wesley's notion of 'social holiness' to the limit. By the early twentieth century, a theology of 'second blessing' had become standard Salvationist orthodoxy. Where God's saving work in conversion effects a primary blessing in the sinner's life, this secondary blessing, sometimes called the *baptism in the Spirit or the blessing of a clean heart, brings about 'sanctification', 'holiness' or 'Christian perfection'.

A Wesleyan response to the perceived dangers of *antinomianism within Reformed theology, the Arminian emphasis upon the role of free will has been said to undermine Salvationist soteriology; the danger of a lapse into salvation by works creating tension with the concurrent commitment to *justification by faith.

The movement's soteriology, combined with its inherent pragmatism, provided the foundations for subsequent missional success, doctrinal development and ecclesial organization. Prioritizing *missiology above ecclesiology, the Army considered itself part of *the* church, as opposed to being *a* church. Freed from ecclesial convention, the movement borrowed language from other institutions, most notably the armed forces. The use of military metaphors led to the adoption of distinctive uniforms, public parades, marching bands, the terms, 'soldier' and 'officer', to denote member and minister and a direct chain of command to the organization's international leader, the General. The resulting method of governance has more in common with Roman Catholicism than Protestantism or evangelicalism (see *Church government).

Coinciding with a renewed sense of *ecumenism, and addressed to the World Council of Churches, Philip Needham's *Community in Mission* (1987) outlined the distinctive vision and contribution of the Salvation Army within the worldwide church and proved to be a defining moment in the movement's growing ecclesiological self-awareness.

The Salvation Army is ecclesiologically noted for its view of the *sacraments. Although initially observed, by 1883 conflicting theologies within the ranks, growing controversy concerning infant baptism and Booth's conviction that sacramental practice was not essential to salvation, led to Communion (see *Eucharist) and *baptism being set aside for the sake of mission. While more recent statements have sought to articulate theological justifications for the position, the stance is not prohibitive and Salvationists remain at liberty to take part in the sacraments in other contexts. More importantly, the absence of these rituals does not negate the belief in Christ's real presence within the movement. In a certain sense, the Salvation Army is highly sacramental, believing that Christ is present in every act of mission and ministry.

Discussions abound as to the future identity and direction of the movement. Growth in the Majority World, the challenge of post-Christian cultures, the growth of sizeable renewal movements and tensions arising from autocratic governance amidst an increasingly diverse and democratic membership represent just some of the challenges and opportunities facing the movement. However, through all of this the Salvation Army continues to 'preach the gospel of Jesus Christ and meet human needs in his name'.

Bibliography

W. Booth, *In Darkest England and The Way Out* (London, 1890); R. J. Green, *The Life and Ministry of William Booth, Founder of the Salvation Army* (Nashville, 2005); P. Needham, *Community in Mission: A Salvationist Ecclesiology* (London, 1987); R. Sandall, A. Wiggins and F. Coutts, *The History of the Salvation Army*, 5 vols. (New York, 1947–73).

R. ROOK

SALVATION-HISTORY

In the mid-twentieth century there were two main interpretations of the relation of the biblical message to the events of *history. For R. *Bultmann, the historical basis underlying the Christian gospel or '*kerygma' was not accessible to the historian because of what he regarded as the lack of reliable evidence; in any case, to enquire after it is illegitimate for the theologian, because that would mean that *faith would be dependent on the findings of historians. Therefore, the gospel is seen as a message which announces the bare fact of the coming of the Christ, but which is essentially a challenge to the hearer to respond to the possibility of authentic existence by making himself open to the future. This 'demythologized' version may appear to conserve the bare minimum of the gospel, namely that *justification is by faith alone in Christ who is God's word of *grace to sinful man; but the appearance is deceptive. It requires us to accept a bare word which is independent of history, and, for all Bultmann's emphasis on the fact of Christ, there is no real saving event and hence no real act of grace. Over against this view, which in effect confines revelation to the word, stands the view which sees revelation as taking place in words and events.

'Salvation history' (Ger. *Heilsgeschichte*) is a term which refers to the series of historical events which are interpreted by Christian faith as the specific acts of God to save his people. The terminology is particularly associated in the past with J. C. K. von Hofmann (1810–77) and Adolf *Schlatter, but in post-Second World War theology its main protagonist was Oscar Cullmann (1902–99) who deliberately presented an alternative understanding of the Bible to that of Bultmann. Cullmann insisted that the structure of biblical thinking is historical, and that *revelation takes place through a series of events in which God is active. What actually happened matters for the believer. To be sure, Cullmann insisted that the recognition of the events as salvation-history is a matter of faith and not of historical proof, but this does not affect the point that God is now seen to be active in the world in the historical incarnation, sacrificial death, resurrection and parousia of his Son. Thus the biblical story tells of a pattern of events in which God is active, stretching from creation to the consummation, with Christ's coming as the midpoint of time, the pivot of history. Although Bultmann's followers continue to deny that salvation-history is a category used by the biblical writers (or at least by the ones whom they regard as offering the kernel of biblical teaching), there can be little doubt that this is the correct framework for the interpretation of the Bible. It has been found particularly congenial by evangelical scholars, who have seen in it a viable alternative to the Bultmannian *existentialist, demythologizing approach which dissolves history away.

The most notable evangelical attempt to write a NT theology from this standpoint is that of G. E. Ladd (1911–82). Ladd insists that revelation takes place through events, but only as they are interpreted by the word. In this way justice is done to the two modes of divine revelation in deed (supremely in Jesus Christ) and in word. Since a limitation of revelation to the word would be to deny the reality of the events of the incarnation and atonement, evangelical theology cannot do other than recognize the insights of the salvation-historical approach. With the emergence of the co-called 'new quest' and 'third quest' for the '*historical Jesus' and the fading of existentialism, it may be thought that the salvation-history perspective has been vindicated. Despite continuing historical scepticism among some scholars, the challenge to the closed causal continuum which was assumed by Bultmann and others to be 'scientific' has encouraged an understanding of 'historicity' which is open to divine action. Although moving beyond the salvation-history school, scholars such as N. T. *Wright may be seen as their heirs.

Bibliography

O. Cullmann, *Christ and Time* (London, 1951); *idem*, *Salvation as History* (London, 1967); G. E. Ladd, *A Theology of the New Testament* (Grand Rapids, 1974); D. H. Wallace, 'Oscar Cullmann', in P. E. Hughes (ed.), *Creative Minds in Contemporary Theology* (Grand Rapids, 1966).

I. H. MARSHALL

SAMOSATA, PAUL OF (*c.* 260–72)

Paul of Samosata was a bishop of Antioch who was tried for heresy on more than one occasion in the years 264–8 and condemned for what is now known as *adoptionism. Paul was appointed *procurator ducenarius* (effectively the civil governor) of the city by Queen Zenobia of Palmyra, who seized it in 260 and held it for twelve years. He was deposed when the Emperor Aurelian restored Roman rule there in 272 and no more was heard of him. Probably much of the opposition to him was politically motivated, but theological factors certainly played a role as well. Paul apparently thought of the divine *Logos as part of the unitary being of God, not as a distinct person, which dwelt in the man Jesus of Nazareth, giving him extraordinary powers but without making him God. The baptism of Jesus seems to have been the key moment in this process, which led to a fusion of wills between God and Christ which cannot now be separated. Jesus overcame the sin of Adam by his own efforts and achieved salvation by the merits of his works, making him a model for Christians who are also adopted as children of God. It seems that Paul described this union with God in terms of consubstantiality (*homoousia*), a notion which was condemned by one of the councils of Antioch. At the First Council of *Nicaea in 325 this proved to be an embarrassment, because the fathers of that council wanted to use the same word to describe the relationship of the Son to the Father in the Godhead, and opponents of the doctrine cited the condemnation of Paul as an argument against this. Paul had a small following which existed for at least a generation after his death, but it never amounted to much and faded away after 325.

See also: CHRISTOLOGY.

Bibliography

J. N. D. Kelly, *Early Christian Doctrines* (London, [5]1977); U. M. Lang, 'The Christological Controversy at the Synod of Antioch in 268/9', *Journal of Theological Studies* 51, 2000, pp. 54–80; F. W. Norris, 'Paul of Samosata, *procurator ducenarius*', *Journal of Theological Studies* 35, 1984, pp. 50–70; R. L. Sample, 'The Christology of the Council of Antioch (268 CE) Reconsidered', *Church History* 48, 1979, pp. 18–26.

G. L. BRAY

SANCTIFICATION

Sanctification defines the manner or process by which objects, places and/or people are rendered holy and acceptable to God. In the history of Christian thought, therefore, the term has periodically been used in a ritualistic as well as doctrinal and theological sense.

In the primitive church, sanctification was initially associated with holiness of the heart (1 Clement 29:1). Christians are called to be *saints (1 Clement, *Prologue*, 59:3; *Hermas, Shepherd*, *Visions* 3:1; *Didache* 10:5). Because they are holy, they aim to 'do all that belongs to sanctification' (1 Clement 30:1; cf. *Barnabas* 15:7). This includes personal discipline (1 Clement 32:2) but especially good works of caring for the poor and needy (*Hermas, Shepherd, Mandates* 8:9f.; 2:4). Christians will be highly visible in their pagan environment – theirs is a holiness in the midst of the world (*Diognetus* 5f.), therefore they must witness to God and glorify him by their daily behaviour (2 Clement 13:22; Ignatius, *Eph.* 14:2; Polycarp, *Ep.* 10:2f.; Aristides, *Apology* 15:4f.). Throughout this initial formational stage in the early church, therefore, sanctification was both a soteriological (see *Salvation) and an ethical concept, used to define the *calling and the conduct of a Christian.

Although for a considerable period of time sanctification continues within the Greek church to be a soteriological concept linked to baptism, its moral meaning slowly fades away to be replaced by the indigenous terminology of 'virtue'. At the same time, the ritual usage of sanctification begins to find fuller expression in the consecration of priests, liturgical vestments, the elements of the Eucharist, water, oil and buildings.

For *Clement of Alexandria the saint is still the Christian, in so far as his body and soul are the temple of the holy God and he continues to be sanctified in the school of the Saviour. His good works lie in the spiritual and material uplifting of his brethren. For that, he does not have to leave his situation; as a pilgrim, he 'lives in the city as if it was the desert' (*Strom.* VII. 7, 3). Two hundred years later, for Theodoret of Cyrrhus (c. 393–c. 458) the 'saints' are the small band of athletes in *asceticism who, preferably living in the desert, have distinguished themselves by brilliant feats of abstinence which are recommended for imitation. Not only has the term 'sanctification' disappeared; its application to the Christian life in terms of being and doing have also changed out of recognition.

In the Latin church, *Tertullian restores something of the moral aspect of sanctification, but limits its application by straightforwardly identifying it with sexual abstinence, 'either from birth or from rebirth', and especially with the rejection of a second marriage of the widowed. *Augustine, in particular, re-emphasizes the soteriological aspect: accusing the Pelagians of the reduction of *justification to forgiveness of sins (the believer looking after his future moral life himself). Augustine claims that God's saving grace comprises two gifts, forgiveness and the infusion of love (Rom. 5:5), which restore and equip man for his future moral life. For the Latin ear, 'justification' (making righteous) can never denote a merely declarative forgiveness of sins; it includes the effective transformation (sanctification) of the person. Thus, following Augustine, Catholic theologians normally include sanctification with the doctrine of justification, historically defining the latter as if it were the former (cf. Council of *Trent, Session VI), and traditionally emphasizing the reality and evidence of change in a Christian.

In the Middle Ages, both *Bernard of Clairvaux and *Thomas Aquinas recognize and support Paul's translation of the ritual meaning of sanctification into a moral one. Like Tertullian, Bernard equates sanctification with personal discipline and self-control. Thomas, however, recovers the richer content of the term. He expounds it as threefold: purification from sin, confirmation in the good and dedication to the service of God (*Summa Theologica* UII: 102:4; II/II: 81:8).

The ambivalence concerning sanctification arising out of the Latin concept of justification undoubtedly helped to spark the Protestant *Reformation: were human works necessary for salvation or not? To what extent was sanctification dependent solely on God's *grace, and when did sanctification occur? *Luther re-emphasizes declarative justification as the forgiveness of sins, but he links this closely with sanctification or *regeneration which in turn leads to good works. We must be made good in order to do good, not do good in order to become good (*Christian Liberty*; cf. Melanchthon's *Apology*). Originally, Luther insists that good works follow from faith automatically, as fruit from a tree, whereas *Melanchthon (and *Calvin) urge the continuing necessity of teaching or exhortation (the 'third use of the law') to prompt the believer to good works. Later in his life, Luther resolutely fought against *antinomians who failed to teach sanctification as the necessary consequence of justification. The Reformation determined civil vocation 'as the field of sanctification, good works and Christian perfection' (*Augsburg Confession, article 27) and – against popular misconceptions – postulated a progress in sanctification, although perfection would never be attained here on earth.

Calvin described the Christian life which follows justification and regeneration or *repentance in terms of mortification, meditation on the future life and the study of piety. In his *Institutes* (III. iii.14; III. xiv.9), he defines sanctification as the process by which we are 'more and more' being 'consecrated to the Lord in true purity of life' and 'our hearts formed to obedience to the law' by the indwelling of Christ through the *Holy Spirit.

Reformation theology in the seventeenth century continued to answer the former ambiguity of the doctrine of sanctification by attempting to integrate sanctification into an *ordo salutis*, or order of salvation. A series of sequential steps in the theology of grace was identified, beginning with *predestination, and proceeding via *calling, to justification, sanctification and ultimately glorification. This ordering of salvation by grace became a distinctive part of *Reformed theology and was highly influential in the development of Reformed thought, especially in England.

The section of the Edwardian *Book of Homilies* written by *Cranmer for the Church of England taught that justification must be completed in sanctification and holiness, something that was only possible for those regenerated by divine grace. *Hooker in his writings distinguishes between habitual and actual sanctification. The possession by the believer of the habits of faith, hope and love which are expected of the 'saints' is 'habitual sanctification', whereas the specific actions performed by the sanctified are examples of actual sanctification (N. Voak, *Richard Hooker and Reformed Theology*, p. 175). Hooker's view that sanctification has a qualitative effect on human behaviour, allowing them to abstain from all mortal sins, can be seen reflected in John *Wesley's initial thoughts on sanctification and what he would later term 'entire sanctification'.

Alongside *Anglican thinking, *Puritanism strongly directed Christian attention to the practice of sanctification. *Pietism reacted against the intellectualism of some Lutheran orthodoxy, fighting the 'twin pernicious errors that sanctification was neither possible nor necessary at this time' (Spener). This concern was shared by the early *Methodists as evidenced by John Fletcher of Madeley's famous 'Checks to Antinomianism' in which he insists that 'Christ is not a minister of sin but a saviour from sin.'

John Wesley's doctrine of sanctification was developed from within an *Arminian as opposed to Calvinistic framework. He stresses sanctification to the extent that 'full sanctification' is described as a 'second grace' by which believers are made perfect, not only with 'holiness begun but finished holiness' (cf. sermon 35 of his *Forty-Four Sermons*, and Charles Wesley's hymn 'God of All Power, and Truth, and Grace'). Wesley's doctrine of entire sanctification raised several key questions concerning the nature of grace and the participation of human endeavour in the process of salvation. Wesley taught that sanctification was possible before death, although he never claimed it for himself: he insisted that sanctification was more likely to occur, following justification, at the end of a long and disciplined quest.

This view was the received evangelical view up until the early 1830s, at which time a new teaching concerning sanctification by grace was introduced which appeared to promise a short cut to sanctification. Catherine Booth, who was persuaded of this teaching, wrote that sanctification is not a matter of waiting for 'a great and mighty work', but was instead an act of 'simple reception'. The underlying evangelical belief is that God gives the needed faith whenever it is needed; consequently, holiness is available to those of faith without having to wait for it.

From here, there is development to the *holiness (Keswick) movement of the nineteenth and twentieth centuries which stressed 'victorious living', not by human effort but by complete reliance on the strength of Christ living in the believer. The fact that in 1885 some 1,500 to 2,000 people attended the Keswick Convention, whereas by 1907 there were between 5,000 and 6,000, gives some indication of the growing strength of the movement. The unity and commitment of the holiness movement challenged many of the divisive beliefs about sanctification defended on doctrinal grounds by Calvinists and Arminians, and in so doing, managed to create a common Christian experience which later supported the development of the ecumenical movement.

In spite of its prominence in the nineteenth and early twentieth centuries through the rise of the *evangelical movement, many major twentieth-century theologians either ignored the doctrine of sanctification, or gave it only cursory consideration, arbitrarily stressing certain individual aspects, excluding others. For example, Karl *Barth sees sanctification strictly as a work of God only, denying the participation of man as well as the idea of progress; he complements his treatise, however, with a highly original paragraph on vocation to witness, in which he calls for the synergism of the believer with Christ. Emil *Brunner presents a balanced view, but, like Paul *Tillich, rejects the commandments as guiding principles for sanctification.

The one noticeable exception to this is in the field of Christian *ethics. 'Sanctification means driving out the world from the Church as well as separating the Church from the world' (D. Bonhoeffer, *The Cost of Discipleship*, p. 324). Theologians such as *Bonhoeffer and *Hauerwas express sanctification in terms of community rather than individual salvation. Both, however, have insisted that the language and practice of sanctification have become too 'spiritual'. Hauerwas claims that it is something that people believe that they can will or become if they just try hard enough. The use of the language of sanctification as a means of speaking of justice and equality in community and before God has led to a recovery of the eschatological dimension of the doctrine as part of its soteriological framework.

Sanctification has recently been evaluated and affirmed as a common doctrine of both the Lutheran and the Catholic Church in the Joint Declaration on the Doctrine of Justification (signed in 1999). There have similarly been cautious steps in discerning common ground concerning sanctification between Eastern and Western theologies of grace and salvation. Tentative comparisons have been drawn between the understanding of the doctrine of *theosis* and the doctrine of sanctification in ongoing dialogues between the Lutheran World Federation and the Orthodox community.

Sanctification as a work of God's grace remains a part of mainstream Christian doctrine, although it is often restated in manner more appropriate to this century. The search for sanctification is generally recognized as a necessary communal, ecclesial undertaking rather than a personal search for individual holiness. It is a gift of God to the people of God. As the complement of justification (forgiveness of sins), it is, in the first place, a work of God, more specifically of the Holy Spirit, both as a one-time act, valid for all time, and for all people, imputing and imparting holiness, and as an ongoing, progressive work. In the latter sense, it also becomes a human, community task. It takes place in our earthly lives, as a moral and spiritual cleansing and dedication of soul and body, harnessing and deploying all human faculties in the service of God, for the building up of communities of justice for the implementation of God's will in the world.

Holiness means to be at God's disposal; it is task-orientated and grace assisted. Sanctification may be sought through the communal means of grace that God provides, which includes worship, prayer and spiritual discipline, as well as the doing of good works that benefit people for time and eternity. It is the restoration of the *image of God in humanity, the gradual assimilation of the people of God into the body of Christ that they might think and act with 'the mind of Christ' (1 Cor. 2:16), and the 'demonstration of the Spirit's power' (1 Cor. 2:4). Directed by the double commandment of love of God and love of neighbour as the fullest description of human dedication, it works by the instruction and drive of the Holy Spirit through whom we fulfil the requirements of God's law (Rom. 8:4). Finally, sanctification, the eager pursuit of holiness in the midst of an unholy world, is the positive alternative to secularism, the attitude of a world turning away from God.

In the words of Bonhoeffer, 'Sanctification is the fulfilment of the divine purpose enunciated in the words, "Ye shall be holy: for I am holy," and again, "I the Lord who sanctify you am holy".' (Bonhoeffer, *The Cost of Discipleship*, p. 312).

Bibliography

K. Barth, *CD*, IV.2, IV.3; D. W. Bebbington, *Evangelicalism in Modern Britain: A History from the 1730s to the 1980s* (London, 1993); L. Berkhof, *Systematic Theology* (Grand Rapids, 1938); G. C. Berkouwer, *Faith and Sanctification* (Grand Rapids, 1952); D. G. Bloesch, *Essentials of Evangelical Theology*, vol. 2 (New York, 1982); D. Bonhoeffer, *The Cost of Discipleship* (New York, 1963); F. de L. Booth-Tucker, *The Life of Catherine Booth:*

The Mother of the Salvation Army, vol. 1 (London, ³1924); E. Brunner, *Dogmatics* (London, 1949–62); S. Hauerwas, *Sanctify Them in the Truth: Holiness Exemplified* (Edinburgh, 1998); H. G. A. Lindstrom, *Wesley and Sanctification* (London, 1961); S. Neill, *Christian Holiness* (London, 1960); J. C. Ryle, *Holiness* (repr. London, 1956 [²1877]); N. Voak, *Richard Hooker and Reformed Theology: A Study of Reason, Will, and Grace* (Oxford, 2003); D. D. Wallace, Jr, *Puritans and Predestination: Grace in English Protestant Theology, 1525–1695* (Chapel Hill, 1982); O. Weber, *Foundations of Dogmatics*, vol. 2. (Grand Rapids, 1983).

A. SHEIR-JONES

SARTRE, JEAN-PAUL, see EXISTENTIALISM

SATAN, see DEVIL AND DEMONS

SATISFACTION

The idea of satisfaction was introduced into theology by *Tertullian and *Cyprian. The post-apostolic church was clear that *baptism washes away all sin, but less clear about how to deal with (serious) sins committed after baptism. Tertullian and Cyprian came up with the idea that sin committed by baptized Christians dishonours God and that it is necessary for them to offer God some satisfaction or compensation for this dishonour. This can be done by fasting, almsgiving or some other meritorious activity. The penitential system took up this idea, with '*penances' being set as a way of offering satisfaction.

Suppose the Christian dies without having paid off this debt of satisfaction? The idea emerged of *purgatory as a place where any remaining debt is paid off. Augustine famously acceded to his mother's request to be 'remembered at the altar' after her death (*Confessions* 9:12:32, 9:13:36), an important precedent. In the early Middle Ages a full-blown doctrine of purgatory was developed. The idea also emerged that it is possible for the living to pay the debt for those who have died. In due course it was possible to buy 'indulgences', for oneself or for someone else, which offer remission for all or part of the debt that is owed. It was, of course, the practice of indulgences that provoked *Luther's protest and his Ninety-Five Theses. The *Reformers all rejected the idea of retributive punishment for believers, although recognizing a *disciplinary role for punishment.

The NT does not refer to Christ's death as a satisfaction, but the term was introduced into the doctrine of the work of Christ in the *patristic period, by Fathers such as Origen, Athanasius and Augustine. It was *Anselm, however, who made the idea of satisfaction the key to his teaching on the *cross. Human sin has dishonoured God and a suitable satisfaction needs to be offered to him to restore his lost honour. Christ, as the God-man, is able to provide this satisfaction by his unmerited death. In understanding Christ's work in terms of restoring God's honour, Anselm was simply applying to the cross the principles that underlay the penitential system. These ideas resonated with the honour-based values of feudal society.

Anselm's idea that Christ has offered satisfaction for human sin is not the same as the idea that he has borne the punishment for *sin, in our place. *Bernard of Clairvaux, who came a generation after Anselm, also occasionally speaks of Christ's death as a satisfaction, but not in the sense meant by Anselm. What is satisfied is not God's honour but his *truth and justice, by the offering of a sacrifice which placates the Father. Bernard, unlike Anselm, uses the word to refer to penal *substitution. It is in this sense that the term is used in *Reformed confessions like the Belgic Confession, article XXI, and the *Thirty-Nine Articles, article XXXI. *Calvin spoke of the cross as satisfying God's justice (e.g. *Institutes*, 2:12:3, 2:15:6, 2:16:5, 13, 19).

The Council of *Trent affirmed that Christ is the meritorious cause of our justification, having made satisfaction for us by his most holy passion on the cross. At the same time, Christians who sin need to offer God satisfaction by fasting, almsgiving, prayers and other pious exercises of a spiritual life. Through the sacrament of penance (or the desire for it) God remits the eternal punishment due to sin (hell, see *Judgment), but there remains a temporal punishment for which we need to offer satisfaction (*Decree on Justification*, chs. 7, 14). Trent also affirms that the *Mass is a sacrifice offered for the living and the dead, for their sins, penalties, satisfactions and other needs (*Canon 3 on the Most Holy Sacrifice of the Mass*).

A recent American dialogue between Lutherans and Roman Catholics in Dialogue focused on the theme of *The Hope of Eternal Life* and tackles issues such as satisfaction, purgatory, prayer for the dead, Masses for the dead and indulgences (§§1–8, 156–271).

Bibliography

L. G. Almen and R. J. Sklba, *The Hope of Eternal Life: Lutherans and Catholics in Dialogue XI* (Minneapolis: 2011).

A. N. S. LANE

SAUMUR, see AMYRALDISM

SCHAEFFER, FRANCIS AUGUST (1912–84)

Francis Schaeffer was born in the USA, studied under C. *Van Til and others at Westminster Theological Seminary, Philadelphia, was ordained to the ministry of the Bible Presbyterian Church and in 1948 moved to Switzerland. Eventually at Huémoz (Vaud) he and his wife Edith established the 'L'Abri' community which he led until his death. His special ministry was to all who had begun to realize the hopelessness of *humanistic ideals and also to Christians who were in danger of drifting with the tides of *existentialism into a *relativistic position. He restored to many Christians a fresh confidence in the truth of God. He spoke of 'true truth'. An orthodox Calvinist, Schaeffer placed special emphasis on the reliability and authority of the Bible. His apologetic approach has been described as '*cultural apologetics'. It laid more stress on common grace than did the apologetics of Van Til and the *Dooyeweerdians, and he helped the Christian to argue with the non-Christian and expose the inadequacy of his worldview, as well as affirm the objective truth of Christian doctrine and ethics. He collaborated closely with Professor Hans Rookmaaker (1922–77) in the examination of art history as a portrayal of philosophical and religious trends. His many books started to appear in 1968 and, along with his films and public seminars in the USA and Europe, gave him a worldwide influence. He did much to restore the confidence of educated evangelicals in an orthodox theology. He helped many to understand cultural trends and thereby to have both a more positive view and use of the arts and an awareness of what was seductive in humanistic culture.

Bibliography

Works: *Escape from Reason* (London, 1968); *The God Who Is There* (London, 1968); *He Is There and He Is Not Silent* (London, 1972); *True Spirituality* (London, 1972); *How Should We Then Live?* (London, 1980); *Whatever Happened to the Human Race?* with C. E. Koop (London, 1983); *Complete Works*, 5 vols. (Westchester, ²1985); L. T. Dennis (ed.), *Letters of Francis Schaeffer*, vol. 1 (Eastbourne, 1986).

Studies: C. Duriez, *Francis Schaeffer: An Authentic Life* (Nottingham, 2008); B. Hawkins, *Francis Schaeffer and the Shaping of Evangelical America* (Grand Rapids, 2008); E. Schaeffer, *L'Abri* (London, 1969).

O. R. BARCLAY

SCHILLEBEECKX, EDWARD (1914–2009)

The progressive Roman Catholic theologian Schillebeeckx was Belgian by birth and a member of the *Dominican order. Until his retirement in 1982 he was professor of dogmatics and the history of theology in the University of Nijmegen in the Netherlands. A prolific writer in all fields of dogmatic theology, his most important work has been on the sacraments, ecclesiology, Christology and hermeneutics.

His influential early work on *sacramental theology proposed a move away from mechanical and impersonal interpretations (as in the idea of transubstantiation) towards a more *existential view of the sacraments as embodiments of the personal presence of Christ and hence a means of encounter with God in Christ.

Schillebeeckx' work is controlled by his view of the *hermeneutical task of theology. This is the task of mediating between past interpretations of the Christian experience of salvation in Christ (in the Bible and tradition) and the cultural situation in which the gospel must be reinterpreted today. The substance of the faith cannot be had in a non-historical form, but only in the fluid, historical forms which it assumes in changing cultural contexts. Thus the tradition from the past cannot be the only norm for theology, but must be creatively reinterpreted in the light of an interpretation of the modern experience of the world. Into the outworking of this hermeneutic enter two further basic principles of Schillebeeckx' approach to theology. 1) He refuses to draw a sharp distinction between *nature and *grace. There is a universal history of God's salvific presence in human experience, which the Christian history of revelation only makes explicit. 2) Especially under the influence of the *Frankfurt School, Schillebeeckx insists that a theology which is to avoid functioning as a mere ideology must be closely related to liberating Christian *praxis. These two principles also help to make the political dimension of experience an important, though not the only, sphere of soteriology and praxis.

In his great work on *Christology Schillebeeckx therefore sees the task of Christology as one of relating two sources: the early Christians' interpretations of their experience of salvation through Jesus, and the experience, both Christian and non-Christian, of living in the modern world. To this end he studies in great detail the ways in which the early church interpreted Jesus within its own cultural context, in order to distil certain principles which are constant structures of Christian experience and which must still structure our own understanding of praxis of Christian faith in the very different cultural context of today. Much of the criticism of Schillebeeckx' work on Christology has focused on the significance he gives to a speculative reconstruction of the earliest Christian interpretations of Jesus, which he thinks developed out of the original interpretation of Jesus as the eschatological prophet. This interpretation is important because it preserves the significance of the message and praxis of the historical Jesus, and Schillebeeckx therefore uses it as a critique of later Christologies which neglect these features of Jesus. While he does not consider the development of an incarnational Christology in the Johannine tradition and the Fathers to be illegitimate in itself, he judges it one-sided to the extent that it left behind Jesus the eschatological prophet, with the challenge of his message and praxis.

Bibliography

Works: *Christ the Sacrament* (London, 1963); *The Understanding of Faith* (London, 1974); *Jesus: An Experiment in Christology* (London, 1979); *Christ: The Christian Experience in the Modern World* (London, 1980); *The Church with a Human Face* (London, 1985). Complete bibliography at http://schillebeeckx.nl/documenten/bibliography.pdf.

Studies: J. Bowden, *Edward Schillebeeckx* (London, 1983); M. C. Hilkert and R. J. Schreiter, *The Praxis of the Reign of God: An Introduction to the Theology of Edward Schillebeeckx* (New York, 2002); D. P. Thompson, 'Schillebeeckx on the Development of Doctrine', *Theological Studies* 62:2 (June, 2001).

R. J. BAUCKHAM

SCHISM

Schism, from the Greek *schisma*, a division in (cf. 1 Cor. 1:10), or split from, the church. In the early centuries no clear distinction obtained between schism, an offence against unity and love, and *heresy, error in doctrine. Heretics were assumed to be, in reality or tendency, outside the church (i.e. schismatics) and vice versa. Greater clarity came in response to schismatic movements (e.g. *Novatianism and *Donatism), recognized as orthodox in faith and divided only on points of discipline or order. Whereas *Cyprian regarded separation from the institutional church as spiritual death, and sacraments given in schism as worthless, later theology – especially *Augustine grappling with Donatism – accepted the reality, if not the benefit, of schismatic sacraments. Traditional Roman theology has until recently treated bodies out of communion with the papacy (e.g. the Eastern church from 1054, and the Reformation churches, including *Anglicanism) as outside the church of Christ; but most Protestant and ecumenical theology has come to view the 'one church' of the creeds as internally in schism. Reunion thus requires not the re-integration of non-church schisms into the church, but the reconciliation of fellow churches to each other.

Bibliography

G. C. Berkouwer, *The Church* (Grand Rapids, 1976); S. L. Greenslade, *Schism in the Early Church* (London, ²1964).

D. F. WRIGHT

SCHLATTER, ADOLF (1852–1938)

Born in St Gall, Switzerland, where his father was a pharmacist and lay preacher in an independent church (though mother and children attended the state Reformed church), Adolf Schlatter studied in Basel and Tübingen

(1871–75). Following brief pastoral charges in Zurich and Kasswill-Uttwill (near Lake Constance), he taught NT at Berne (1880–8), systematic theology at Griefswald (1889–93), theology in Berlin (1893–8), and NT at Tübingen (1898–1930). He was the most important figure in the faculty of theology in Tübingen during his time, and also the most influential teacher of a generation of German pastors. His biblical-historical theology and exegesis was in stark contrast to the *history -of-religions approach (see *Bultmann) and *liberal theology (see *Harnack) of others. Rooted firmly in a careful study of language and historical data, with special emphasis on the Jewish context of the NT, he sought to ground both systematic and contemporary theological concerns in the biblical text, rather than in speculative hypotheses. He resisted the call to separate faith and history, criticism and preaching, theology and life. He came to the study of the Bible quite conscious of the fact that he was a *Christian* theologian. Although he gave due weight to the differences between the OT and NT, he insisted on their underlying unity. Central to his work was the conviction that Jesus was 'the Christ of God' and the heart of the biblical revelation, and that this was the essential *hermeneutical key to the two Testaments.

Schlatter's writings were prolific; unfortunately, few are available in English. Perhaps his greatest work is his massive study of faith in the NT (1885), in which he attempted to correct the hyper-Lutheran understanding of *justification by faith. He wrote a series of popular commentaries on the entire NT, alongside more technical and extensive volumes on Matthew (1929), John (1930), Luke (1931), James (1932), the Corinthian epistles (1934), Mark (1935), Romans (1935), Timothy and Titus (1936) and 1 Peter (1937). Those on Matthew and Romans (entitled *The Righteousness of God*) are the most important. He also wrote a two-volume NT theology (1909), a history of the primitive church (1926; ET, *The Church in the NT Period*, London, 1955), as well as major works on dogmatics (1911) and ethics (1914).

Bibliography

W. W. Gasque, 'The Promise of Adolf Schlatter', *Crux* 15, June 1979, pp. 5–9; R. Morgan (ed.), *The Nature of New Testament Theology: The Contribution of William Wrede and Adolf Schlatter* (London, 1973), includes ET of *The Theology of the New Testament and Dogmatics*; W. Neuer, *Adolf Schlatter: A Biography of Germany's Premier Biblical Theologian*, tr. R. W. Yarbrough (Grand Rapids, 1995); P. Stuhlmacher, 'Adolf Schlatter's Interpretation of Scripture', *NTS* 24 (1978), pp. 433–446.

W. W. GASQUE

SCHLEIERMACHER, FRIEDRICH DANIEL ERNST (1768–1834)

Schleiermacher was a German Protestant theologian commonly thought to be the founding father of *liberal Protestantism, though he transcends that movement and is more properly ranked with the great Reformation divines.

Born into a devout family, Schleiermacher experienced a religious conversion under Moravian influences, but whilst attending a Moravian seminary found his youthful *pietist theology intellectually inadequate. He went to study philosophy at Halle, where he immersed himself in *Kant and *Plato. During his studies there, and his early work as a tutor and pastor, he began the process of reconstructing his account of the Christian faith. His mature years were spent in Halle and later Berlin, as professor, preacher and political activist. He is chiefly known to English-language theology through the third edition of his *On Religion: Speeches to Its Cultured Despisers*, and the second edition of his dogmatics, *The Christian Faith*, a formidably difficult work which, along with *Barth's *Church Dogmatics*, is the most important Protestant theological text since *Calvin's *Institutes*. His other significant writings include the methodological sketch *Brief Outline on the Study of Theology*, the posthumous *Hermeneutics* and a large body of sermons, along with translations of Plato, and a *Dialektik* and an *Ethik* which, with much of the important biographical material, remain untranslated.

Schleiermacher's theology is self-consciously church theology. He envisages theology as an intellectual exercise which has its origins in the concrete forms of the religious life. Because Christian theology is related to the corporate piety of the Christian community, it is empirical rather than speculative: the Christian faith is not primarily conceptual, and doctrines are a second-order conceptualization of its primary religious truth. In making piety central, Schleiermacher is partly seeking an alternative base for religious knowledge in response to the restrictions placed upon speculative theology by the critical philosophy of Kant and others. His account of *revelation in *The Christian Faith* is thus of a knowledge of God mediated through the corporate experience of redemption rather than of a body of doctrine propositionally revealed. Hence Schleiermacher's perspective on doctrines clearly distinguishes between their dogmatic form and the corporate realities of the religious life to which they give secondary expression, and thus they may be alternatively expressed.

The core of Schleiermacher's understanding of the phenomena of piety lies in his much-disputed notion of the 'feeling of absolute dependence'. He proposes that the primal structure of the religious life, Christian or otherwise, is the consciousness of self as determined by that which transcends the self. In talking of a 'feeling' of dependence, Schleiermacher does not mean 'emotion': much more is he talking of a fundamental structure of personal existence, prior to emotion, action or thought. Self-consciousness is consciousness of dependence, and thus consciousness of God as the 'whence' of the feeling. And so consciousness of the self as dependent is the primary locus of God's self-disclosure to his human creation.

In *The Christian Faith*, this universal understanding of piety is given a distinct *Christological shape. Whereas in the *Speeches on Religion* Schleiermacher sought primarily to commend religion as the implicit backcloth to science and art, and was only peripherally concerned with Christianity, his dogmatics explores how the Christian consciousness of God is determined at every point by the redemptive work of Christ. He understands *redemption as the impression made by Jesus' unclouded consciousness of God upon the Christian community, as their own impoverished God-consciousness is repaired through the God-consciousness of Jesus. The relationship of Christ as the archetype of God-consciousness to the history of Jesus is not clear in Schleiermacher, and has been the subject of much criticism since F. C. Baur (see *Tübingen School). Schleiermacher's manner of approaching Christology by a soteriological route means, moreover, that he discards much of the apparatus of classical Christology as an inadequate expression of the Christian self-consciousness.

Schleiermacher consistently refuses to move behind the analysis of the conditions of piety to discuss the objectivity of God in and for himself. Thus in his doctrine of God in *The Christian Faith* he passes over *trinitarian dogma, since all talk of distinctions within the Godhead is speculation divorced from piety: 'We have no formula for the being of God in itself as distinct from the being of God in the world' (172.2). Thus the doctrines of *creation and preservation are accorded prior treatment, since they relate immediately to man's consciousness of dependence, and the doctrine of the Trinity is assigned to an appendix (a move which Barth carefully reverses at the beginning of his *Church Dogmatics*).

The relation of dogma to piety is paralleled in Schleiermacher's *hermeneutics, a subject whose contemporary prominence owes much to Schleiermacher's work, notably the posthumously published material. While his earlier hermeneutical writings focus on the objectivity of language, he later understands the act of interpretation as psychological rather than grammatical, piercing through the text to the consciousness of the author to which it affords access.

Like his whole theology, Schleiermacher's hermeneutics have frequently attracted the charge of subjectivism. It is argued that by underlining the primacy of psychological interpretation, he gives priority to questions of meaningfulness rather than truth and locates the text's referent in subjective consciousness rather than objective states of affairs. Similarly, on a broader canvas, he is often thought so to emphasize the religious self-consciousness that he undervalues the objective ground of religious life and thought. Hence he is sometimes charged with initiating the process (completed by *Feuerbach) of reducing theology to *anthropology. This line of criticism was powerfully stated by Barth, who nevertheless had far deeper respect for and proximity to Schleiermacher than many who made Barth's earlier repudiation of his predecessor a fixed norm for Schleiermacher interpretation, in a way which Barth himself left behind. This critique is seriously undermined by the fact that Schleiermacher understood the 'feeling of absolute dependence' as *intentional*, i.e. referring to an external ground. The religious self-consciousness apprehends a world which transcends the self, so that through piety the 'whence' of the religious life is disclosed. This latter interpretation suggests that Schleiermacher is restating a Reformation emphasis on the coinherence of God and the life of faith, such as can be found in passages from *Luther. It remains, none the less, an open question whether Schleiermacher's theology can support any notion of God's action and presence as other than immanent. This might be borne out by his ambivalence towards *miracles and *providence. Moreover, it is debatable whether his refusal of speculative language about God's own being, in and for himself, betrays any loss of confidence in the possibility of revelation from outside the processes of human history.

After its hostile reception by many under the influence of Barth, Schleiermacher's work has attracted more positive evaluation, notably in Germany where a new critical edition has been harvesting scholarly inquiry into the development of his thought. It is certainly no longer possible to maintain the easy stereotypes by which Schleiermacher has often been dismissed. He remains the quintessential exponent of an alternative Reformation tradition from that articulated in Calvin and Barth, namely one preoccupied with human *religion as a response to God's self-disclosure. And he constitutes a type of response to *Enlightenment critiques of the possibility of theology, a response in which the reality of God is located in human historical experience.

Bibliography

Works: *Kritische Gesamtausgabe* (Berlin, 1980–); *Brief Outline on the Study of Theology* (Richmond, 1966); *The Christian Faith* (Edinburgh, 1928); *Christmas Eve* (Richmond, 1967); *Hermeneutics* (Missoula, 1977); *On Religion: Speeches to its Cultured Despisers* (London, 1894); *Selected Sermons* (London, 1890).

Studies: K. Barth, *Protestant Theology in the Nineteenth Century* (London, 1972); idem, *The Theology of Schleiermacher* (Edinburgh, 1982); R. B. Brandt, *The Philosophy of Schleiermacher* (New York, 1941); R. Crouter, *Friedrich Schleiermacher: Between Enlightenment and Romanticism* (Cambridge, 2008); B. A. Gerrish, *A Prince of the Church: Schleiermacher and the Beginnings of Modern Theology* (London, 1984); idem, in N. Smart (ed.), *Nineteenth Century Religious Thought in the West* (Cambridge, 1985), vol. 1, pp. 123–156; C. L. Kelsey, *Thinking about Christ with Schleiermacher* (Louisville, 2003); idem, *Schleiermacher's Preaching, Dogmatics, and Biblical Criticism* (Eugene, 2007); H. R. Mackintosh, *Types of Modern Theology* (London, 1937); J. Marina (ed.), *The Cambridge Companion to Schleiermacher* (Cambridge, 2006); R. R. Niebuhr, *Schleiermacher on Christ and Religion* (London, 1964); M. Redeker, *Schleiermacher* (Philadelphia, 1973); S. W. Sykes, *Friedrich Schleiermacher* (London, 1971); R. R. Williams, *Schleiermacher the Theologian* (Philadelphia, 1978).

J. B. Webster

SCHLEITHEIM CONFESSION

Anabaptism, as a movement, is generally understood as being most visible in the decade between 1525 (when the Swiss Brethren emerge as a coherent group in Zurich) and 1535. In 1527, Michael Sattler was one of those instrumental in calling together a conference of leaders in the new movement to meet in Schleitheim, in Schaffhausen. At this time, it was becoming clear that those in power who might have looked sympathetic were resistant to the radicalness of the movement. There were also those within the movement who were influenced by *Müntzer's extremism. The conference and subsequent summary document, the Schleitheim Confession, were attempts both to defend the new movement against those who saw it as heretical and dangerous, and to set some limits against extreme teachings, especially those urging violence.

Michael Sattler is generally understood to have been the main author of the document which then became a deeply significant text for the growing radical community. While it can never be said to be or to have been definitive, it was and has remained a guiding text for those identified with *Anabaptism.

The Confession, or *Brotherly Union of a Number of Children of God Concerning Seven Articles*, is not, in the conventional sense, a *confession of faith, and takes the historic *creeds for granted. The Schleitheim Confession is a description of what is distinctive about Anabaptism, and therefore focuses on the life of discipleship rather than the content of belief.

The Confession consists of seven articles:

(1) Baptism: given to believers who request it, rather than infants.

(2) The ban: exclusion from the Lord's Supper by the congregation of those whose lives do not exemplify discipleship.

(3) The breaking of bread: to be shared by those baptized as believers.

(4) Separation from the world: and the list of the institutions from which true believers were to separate themselves.

(5) The shepherds: reflecting the recognition that those who serve as leaders are both a necessity and likely not to survive long in the hostile environment.

(6) The sword: that true Christians will not wield the sword for war or justice.

(7) Oaths: a central aspect of sixteenth-century community cohesion which Anabaptists rejected as unscriptural.

The stated aim of the Confession is to provide unity among baptized believers, based on the unity of God in Trinity, and given as God's gift. The emphasis throughout is on separation from the sinful world, and the maintaining of the purity of the body of Christ.

See also: REFORMATION, RADICAL.

Bibliography

W. Klaassen, *Anabaptism in Outline; Selected Primary Sources* (Scottdale, 1981); G. H. Williams, *The Radical Reformation* (London, 1962); J. H. Yoder, *The Schleitheim Confession* (Scottdale, 1977).

R. GOULDBOURNE

SCHMEMANN, ALEXANDER (1921–83)

Alexander Schmemann was born into a Russian émigré family in Reval, Estonia, in 1921. When he was seven, his family moved to Paris, where he was educated, finally graduating from the Institut St-Serge. He continued there as a lecturer, being ordained to the priesthood in 1946. In 1951, Schmemann followed *Florovsky to America to teach at St Vladimir's Orthodox Theological Seminary. He became Dean in 1962, holding the post until his death in 1983. He came to specialize in *liturgical studies, and, in tune with contemporary developments in Roman Catholic theology, turned this subject from a drily historical discipline into a source of deeply theological reflection: 'liturgical theology'. In the 1960s, with the popularity in Protestant circles of 'secular' theology and proclamation of the 'death of God', Schmemann found in the *sacraments, and especially the divine liturgy, resources for an understanding of God disclosed in the mystery of *worship and active in the beauty of the world; as he said, 'In the light of the Eucharist we see that Christ is indeed the life and light of all that exists, and the glory that fills heaven and earth. There is nothing else to remember, nothing else to be thankful for, because in him everything finds its being, its end.' He was instrumental in the establishment of the autocephalous (self-governing) Orthodox Church of America in 1970, which united most Orthodox of Slav descent under an American hierarchy. Despite his French education and commitment to America, he retained a deep love of Russia and Russian culture, and formed a deep friendship with the exiled Solzhenitsyn.

Bibliography

All Schmemann's works are published by St Vladimir's Seminary Press, Crestwood NY, as is *The Journals of Father Alexander Schmemann 1973–1983* (2000). See especially, *For the Life of the World* (London, 1966, now published by SVSP).

A. LOUTH

SCHOLASTICISM

'Scholastic' was used first by *humanists and sixteenth-century historians of philosophy to describe the philosophers and theologians of the Middle Ages. It was a negative, derogatory term meant to indicate a tradition-bound, logic-chopping mentality, involving a slavish adherence to *Aristotle. While echoes of the old usage remain, today the term usually refers simply to the dominant form of philosophy and theology in the central and later Middle Ages. There is also a modern scholasticism, dating from about 1550 to 1830 and associated with the age of 'confessional orthodoxy', which was influential in both Protestant and Catholic universities of Western Europe (see *Orthodoxy/Scholasticism, Lutheran; *Orthodoxy/Scholasticism, Reformed). Finally, among contemporary Catholics there is a neoscholasticism which traces its roots to the Middle Ages, especially Thomas Aquinas (see *Thomism and Neo-Thomism).

When political order began to be restored in Western Europe from the ninth century onwards, education was also fostered and with it the people in the West began the task of assimilating classical culture, an intellectual tradition far richer than that of the West in that era. Consequently, much of the teaching in the *monastic and cathedral schools, and later in the universities, was built on the reading and explication of classical texts. Since the schools were founded and maintained by Christians to foster their faith, a faith rooted in the Bible as an authoritative text, a text-based method was natural to them.

The medievals were convinced that divine *revelation made available to us truth that otherwise surpassed our understanding (see *Faith and reason). Hence, Scripture, accepted as divinely inspired, was studied and commented on. It clarified spiritual things but also illumined the understanding of man and the world. With the rediscovery of all of the writings of Aristotle (see below), both a more sophisticated dialectical method and an alternative account of reality appeared on the scene. More than anything else, the problem of coming to terms with Aristotle dominated the debates in the medieval schools. Faith still remained prior, and the theologians accepted *Anselm's view that one should not seek to understand in order to believe, but believe in order to understand.

The earliest example of the kind of rational analysis of doctrine that became characteristic of scholasticism is found in *Boethius' work *On the Trinity*. Of much greater influence was *Abelard, who sought to provide explanations of the statements of faith. In his *Yes and No* he advanced theological method by making the resolution of disagreements among authorities a part of the theologian's task. Peter *Lombard's *Sentences* become the most widely used textbook in theology. It was a collection of texts from the Bible and the Fathers of the church (see *Patristic theology) on the topics of God, creatures, the *incarnation, *redemption, the *sacraments and last things (see *Eschatology). Written about 1150, this work was still being used and commentaries being written on it at the time of the *Reformation in the sixteenth century.

In the thirteenth century, study of the biblical text continued, but gradually the masters also began to treat difficult questions by themselves. So there developed the 'disputed question', a comprehensive examination of a single topic based on the Bible, the Fathers and the philosophic tradition. These questions treated such topics as truth, God's power, his will and free choice. The crowning achievement of scholasticism was the *Summa*, which was an orderly presentation of theological issues. Best known of these is *Thomas Aquinas's *Summa Theologica*, which he wrote for beginners in theology.

In it Aquinas discusses issues in an order appropriate for beginners, treating each topic more briefly than he does in his disputed questions.

Like earlier medieval thinkers in the West, Abelard and his contemporaries in the twelfth century had access only to Aristotle's logical writings, but in the thirteenth century the remainder of Aristotle's writings became available in the West. Instead of Aristotle the dialectician, Aristotle the philosopher challenged Christian thinkers. In Aristotle's *Physics, Metaphysics, Ethics*, and other works the medievals found an account of reality which was far superior to anything they had known. The difficulty was that this sophisticated account was fundamentally opposed to Christian teaching on such points as the eternity of the world, the nature of the human soul, and the end of human existence. William of Auvergne (*c.* 1180–1249), *Albertus Magnus, *Bonaventura, Roger Bacon (*c.* 1214–92) and Thomas Aquinas are the most prominent among the many masters who sought to articulate a Christian position in the context of the new Aristotle. Each of them has his own solution. In the last century historical criticism has shown that scholasticism was not a single theology or philosophy, but rather consisted of a multiplicity of positions which attempted to deal with a common problem, the challenge of Aristotle's thought.

Around 1270 the situation at Paris was complicated by the fact that certain members of the arts faculty were promoting the interpretation of Aristotle advanced by the commentator *Averroes, who held, for example, that there is only one intellectual soul for all men. Most famous of these arts masters was Siger of Brabant (*c.* 1235–*c.* 1282). He and others seem to have thought that, so far as reason goes, Aristotle had given the final word. Siger presented the thought of Aristotle without claiming that it was true but also without challenging it where it contradicts revelation. Because he did not show that Aristotle had erred, he gave the impression that natural reason inevitably contradicts revelation. This led opponents to suggest that he held a double-truth theory, the view that one thesis can be true for philosophy and its opposite true for faith. More satisfactory was the approach taken by Aquinas, who not only insisted, in principle, that all truth is one, but also criticized Aristotle and his commentators, so showing that reason does not contradict faith.

The threat of an unrestrained rationalism, as manifested in Siger and others, led to the condemnation of 1277. The bishop of Paris condemned 219 propositions. Most were those held by Averroes and his followers, but a variety of others, including some held by Aquinas, were included. More important than the content of this condemnation is the reaction which followed it. The conviction of Aquinas and others that philosophy can serve faith gave way to doubts on this score. In *Duns Scotus and *William of Ockham one sees the collaboration of faith and reason beginning to fall apart.

By 1350 scholasticism was in decline. Lectures on the Bible were no longer mandatory and study of the writings of the church fathers had also declined. Dialectical subtleties became more and more the focus. This development worsened what was already a weakness in scholasticism – its lack of historical sense. Later scholastics tended to confine themselves to extracts from the ancients and so lost the historical context and much of the meaning of the original writings. Also, there developed a tendency among these later scholastics to group themselves into schools, and then to focus on the relatively minor issues on which they differed. Ockhamists, Scotists and Thomists battled with one another, and theology became more and more remote from the life of the church. In this context it is little wonder that *Erasmus wanted to return to the simple gospel, that *Luther had no use for Aristotle, and that *Calvin repeatedly attacks the fictions of the schoolmen.

After the Reformation, nominalist, Scotist and Thomist schools continued in the Catholic universities. The most influential new thinker was Francisco de Suárez (see *Jesuit theology), whose *Metaphysical Disputations* influenced *Leibniz, Christian Wolff (1679–1754) and other philosophers. Among Protestants *Melanchthon employed a humanist Aristotelianism in his theology, while Peter *Ramus promoted an anti-metaphysical humanism. Even so, among Protestants, too, Suárez was influential. In spite of Calvin's anti-scholasticism, Francis *Turretin and other Reformed theologians adopted the scholastic method in their theology.

Contemporary scholasticism is an extensive movement in Catholic circles which started in the early nineteenth century and flowered after Leo XIII's encyclical *Aeterni Patris* (1879), in which he called for the restoration of Christian philosophy, and singled out the teachings of Thomas Aquinas for special consideration. Institutes were established and journals founded in both Europe and America. Better-known members of this movement include E. *Gilson, J. *Maritain, K. *Rahner and B. *Lonergan.

A weakness of scholasticism has been noted, but it should be added that often the schoolmen have been condemned unheard. They have sometimes been ridiculed (as by Erasmus), and more often ignored, but seldom refuted. Some opponents of scholasticism are repelled by its analytical mode of thought which by its precision places a heavy demand on the reader. But precise definitions and careful arguments are as appropriate in theology as in any other area. Historically, it is the scholastics who considered most carefully the relation of faith to reason (see *Faith and reason) and of theology to the other sciences. For these reasons the scholastics remain a source of inspiration for philosophers and theologians even today.

Bibliography

E. Gilson, *A History of Christian Philosophy in the Middle Ages* (London, ²1980); N. Kretzmann, A. Kenny and J. Pinborg (eds.), *Cambridge History of Later Medieval Philosophy* (London, 1982); P. O. Kristeller, *Renaissance Thought: The Classic, Scholastic, and Humanist Strains* (New York, 1955); J. Marenbon, *Early Medieval Philosophy (480–1150): An Introduction* (London, ²1988); idem, *Later Medieval Philosophy (1150–1350): An Introduction* (London, rev. edn 1991); G. Van Riet, *Thomistic Epistemology* (St Louis, 1963).

A. Vos

SCHWEITZER, ALBERT (1875–1965)

Born in Alsace, Schweitzer was a human dynamo possessing the combined talents, energy and accomplishments of many individuals. He earned doctorates in philosophy, theology, musicology and medicine. At the age of thirty he became a missionary doctor in French Equatorial Africa in obedience to Jesus' command to 'lose his life for my sake and the gospel's'. Through many adversities, including both World Wars, he laboured among the local people, eventually building his own hospital. He periodically returned to Europe to give lectures and organ recitals, and during the whole period he continued the writing career which he had begun in student days.

In *The Quest of the Historical Jesus* (1906; ET 1909) Schweitzer demonstrated how all the modern 'historical' reconstructions of the life of Jesus simply attributed to Jesus the liberal theology of their authors (see *Historical Jesus, quest for). Schweitzer held that Jesus believed the *apocalyptic *kingdom of God would momentarily appear, in response to the zealous piety of himself and his disciples. Thus Jesus taught an 'interim ethic', the need for absolute *righteousness if one hoped to enter the kingdom. Jesus' values of 'higher righteousness', love and faith (described in liberal terms) called for extreme application because of the extremity of the times. One must renounce possessions, turn the other cheek and endure persecutions. In the imminent tribulation Jesus and his disciples would die and rise again, Jesus as the Son of Man.

When the end tarried, Jesus concluded that he must undergo the tribulation alone, on his followers' behalf, and thus usher in the kingdom. Later, Paul reasoned that Jesus' messianic reign had indeed begun, albeit invisibly, and so had the resurrection of his predestined elect. Paul's views of *sacraments, *ethics, the *law and *justification were all a function of his *eschatology, and not influenced by the mystery religions, as many scholars held.

In *The Philosophy of Civilization* (1923) Schweitzer set forth his ethical theory of 'reverence for life', which he saw as the only way to unite world-affirmation with inner moral devotion. All creatures share the 'will to live', but only humans can recognize this common bond. We must cherish the lives of all beings equally and should try not to kill even insects and plants, though of course often we cannot avoid doing so. Schweitzer regarded 'reverence for life' as the principle implicit in the ethic of Jesus. As a child he had felt protective of all animal life, and it is possible that his study of the Hindu and Jainist doctrine of ahimsa (non-harm) strengthened him in these feelings.

Bibliography

J. Brabazon, *Albert Schweitzer: A Biography* (New York, 1975); J. L. Ice, *Schweitzer: Prophet of Radical Theology* (Philadelphia, 1971); O. Kraus, *Albert Schweitzer* (London, 1944); G. N. Marshall, *An Understanding of Albert Schweitzer* (New York, 1966); A. Schweitzer and J. Brabazon, *Albert Schweitzer: Essential Writings* (Maryknoll, 2005).

R. M. PRICE

SCHWENCKFELD, CASPAR (1489–1561)

A lay theologian and radical Reformer from Silesia, Schwenckfeld became a Lutheran in 1518 and from 1522 to 1529 was the chief adviser of Duke Frederick II in the promotion of the *Reformation. By 1524 he had embraced eucharistic views that were unacceptable to *Luther, and he went into voluntary exile. His theology as it developed put him in the ranks of the Spiritualists among the Radicals (see *Reformation, Radical).

The *Eucharist played a formative role in his thinking. The true Eucharist, he held, is not outward participation in the rite, but an inward, spiritual feeding on the heavenly bread which is the celestial flesh of Christ. Such inward feeding ensured that the communicant was transformed by full participation in the divine nature. As a result, the will, previously paralysed by sin, is liberated to exercise the love to God and man commanded by Christ. This spiritual absorption of the celestial flesh of Christ is made possible by justifying faith which incorporates the believer in the second Adam. Even those, such as Abraham, who lived before the incarnation, were equally partakers of the spiritual Christ if they exercised faith, and are to be deemed Christians. Schwenckfeld rejected Luther's forensic understanding of justifying faith, by linking faith closely with a continuous feeding upon Christ. In this way *justification is closely tied to progressive *deification. It harmonized with his sombre view of sin and his yearning to see the Reformation producing an improvement in morality.

His *Christology matches his eucharistic teaching. He held that the human nature of Christ, although received from Mary, was 'begotten, not made'. He conceived of man's human nature, like his divine nature, progressing from a state of humiliation in the earthly ministry to a glorification which is virtually deification. He insisted that Christ suffered on the cross in his divine, as well as in his human, nature. In this way, Christ's celestial flesh became available for believers by means of the Eucharist. It is difficult to discern the difference between the two natures in the state of glorification, and that is why Schwenckfeld was accused by Luther of Eutychianism (see *Monophysitism).

The contrast between 'outer' and 'inner' runs throughout Schwenckfeld's theology. The 'outer' word of God in Scripture is contrasted with the 'inner' or spiritual word in the heart. The true church is not the outward institution, but the company of people who feed spiritually upon Christ. 'Outer' baptism with water is nothing apart from the 'inner' *baptism of the Holy Spirit. Because of his conviction that the *Holy Spirit cannot be fettered by institutions and ceremonies, Schwenckfeld withdrew from communion with other churches, but without yielding his irenical belief that God's true spiritual church had members in all communions. It followed that he was a protagonist of *toleration. He argued for the separation of church and *state and yet believed that the Christian had a creative role to play in civil government.

Although he rejected infant baptism, he is not to be confused with the *Anabaptists. The differences between him and them were sharply defined in his long controversy with Pilgram Marpeck (c. 1495–1556).

Bibliography

Works: *Commentary on the Augsburg Confession*, tr. R. A. Grater (Pennsburg, 1982); *Corpus Schwenckfeldianorum*, 19 vols. (Leipzig, 1922 onwards).

Studies: P. C. Erb (ed.), *Schwenckfeld and Early Schwenckfeldianism* (Pennsburg, 1986); R. Gouldbourne, *The Flesh and the Feminine: Gender and Theology in the Writings of Caspar Schwenckfeld* (Bletchley, 2006); R. E. McLaughlin, *Caspar Schwenckfeld, Reluctant Radical: His Life to 1540* (New Haven and London, 1986); S. G. Shultz, *Caspar Schwenckfeld von Ossig (1489–1561): Spiritual Interpreter of Christianity, Apostle of the Middle Way* (Norristown, ⁴1977); G. H. Williams, *The Radical Reformation* (Kirksville, ³1992).

R. T. JONES

SCIENCE AND THEOLOGY

In this article 'science' is taken to mean the systematic study of the natural world, an activity at once intellectual, practical and social. It is thus to be distinguished from the vast corpus of empirical 'facts' accumulated by that activity and often called 'science' by the layman. The precise character of the scientific enterprise and its methodology have varied with time. 'Modern science' may be said to have originated in Western Europe at about the time of the Renaissance and Reformation. Since then its relationship with theology has been conceived in a variety of ways.

Models of the relationship between science and theology

Some have imagined a model of *total independence*, thus eliminating any of the possibilities (and problems) discussed below. Such a zero-interaction model is irreconcilable with historical evidence, which points to a continuous series of strong interactions over many centuries.

Secondly, there is a *conflict* model which was assiduously developed after Darwin by those who wished science to snatch cultural supremacy from the church in late-Victorian Britain. On the basis of undeniable episodes in which scientific evidence did undermine received traditions that were apparently based on the Bible (e.g. Galileo and Darwin), a generalized, triumphalist image for science was cultivated, owing much to the *positivist philosophy that only scientific knowledge was ultimately meaningful. Despite much evidence for the gross historical distortions introduced by such a pre-emptive generalization, its survival in popular literature even today testifies to its hold on the public mind.

A third model is that of *complementarity* which (though not by that name) may be dated back to Francis Bacon (1561–1626) in the seventeenth century. He spoke of 'two books', the book of nature and the book of Scripture, each of which had to be read and understood. Because both came from the same author they could not be in conflict. But because each had a different purpose it was idle to mix 'philosophy' (science) and divinity, and to seek scientific data in the pages of Scripture. Problems arose, however, where biblical and scientific evidence appeared to clash, and in those circumstances it was necessary to recognize the complementarity of their modes of explanation. *Calvin, drawing on the *Augustinian concept of '*accommodation', assumed that the Holy Spirit accommodated his language to that of common speech in order to teach spiritual principles. Hence biblical accounts of the days of *creation, of the structure of the cosmos, of the sun (as opposed to the earth) standing still and of a literally universal flood would be susceptible to a non-literal interpretation. In other words, the biblical and scientific accounts of natural phenomena have purposes that are complementary rather than contradictory, the Bible's concerns being spiritual and eternal. This approach has continued to our own day and may be fruitfully applied to later problems, not least the creation debate.

For all its merits the 'complementarity' model by itself fails in a number of respects, particularly by ignoring the considerable network of relationships between science and theology disclosed by recent historical scholarship. A fourth model which takes these into account may be termed *symbiosis*. This recognizes that historically, scientific and theological thinking have owed much to one another and that their growth has been mutually promoted. It conforms with a widespread acknowledgment that much human knowledge is culture-dependent, but it does not prejudice the independence of data either in the Bible or in the natural world. It merely recognizes that in the interpretation of such data, theological and scientific ideas are often intermingled in one brain, as they are indeed in one society. Hence one might expect some degree of mutual influence, and such turns out to be the case.

Influence of science on theology

The responses of theology to science have been legion. One of the earliest was *natural theology. From Robert Boyle (1627–91) to *Paley, English literature is replete with attempts to make discoveries of science the basis of a Christian apologetic; it has been argued, somewhat doubtfully, that underlying such efforts lay a quest for social stability which might be bolstered by a strong Anglican church. Its unchanging formularies were to be confirmed by the unchanging laws of science. Be that as it may, the 'argument from design' survived, albeit in a weakened form, even the onslaughts of Darwinism. With today's greater knowledge of the intricacies of the natural world, attempts have been made to revive it, though not with conspicuous success.

It was in fact the awesome regularity of the mechanical universe as emphasized by Isaac *Newton that raised urgent questions of divine intervention. Did God intervene in the running of the machine he had created, or did he not? The dilemma was crystallized in the (probably apocryphal) remark by Laplace (1749–1827) that he had 'no need of that hypothesis (God)' in his cosmology. Thus arose a powerful stimulus to the growth of *deism and its derivatives such as *unitarianism. A recognition that all natural events (not merely those explicable by known scientific laws) must be seen as God's activity was not absent in the late eighteenth century. But a God-in-the-gaps theology proved surprisingly resilient and represents another popular misunderstanding of the science/religion relationship.

A third response of theology to science has come in the area of biblical interpretation. It goes at least as far back as Galileo's famous quip of 1615 that, in Scripture, 'the intention of the Holy Ghost is to teach us how one goes to heaven, not how heaven goes' – a response engendered at least in part by his own telescopic discoveries in vindication of Copernicus. Since that time the discoveries and theories of science have not infrequently led to a revision of traditional interpretations of Scriptures. These include ancient views on the age of the earth, the structure of the universe, the extent of Noah's flood and the origins of biological species (including human beings). Few commentators disagree when this happens over cosmology, but application of an identical methodology to questions of human origins is still controversial.

It is important not to imply a unique role for science in the reinterpretation of Scripture, but it cannot be neglected. Where a theological response to science has been claimed with much less justification is in the '*demythologization*' (see *Myth) programme prescribed by *Bultmann and others. The assertion that '*miracle' is incredible in a scientific age is as unphilosophical as it is unhistorical. It ignores the fact that science is, by definition, concerned only with regularities and can therefore make no pronouncement on their breach; and it neglects to note that, at the very time when demythologization came into vogue, old-fashioned, positivistic scientific dogmatism was in decline. For this a variety of causes may be cited, notably the demise of the *deterministic world of Newtonian mechanics in the face of successive challenges by thermodynamics, relativity and quantum theory.

Finally, it may be briefly noted that the *process theology of Whitehead, Hartshorne and others sprang, at least ostensibly, from a concern to understand God's relationship to the world of nature as studied by science.

Influence of theology on science

The *origins and growth of science* may be fruitfully considered in terms of a response to biblical insights liberated at, and since, the Reformation (Hooykaas, Russell). This response may be seen in the writings of many men of science and in the morphological similarity between scientific and religious theories. Five such insights may be identified:

(1) The elimination of myth from nature: an animate, even 'divine', nature is not susceptible to scientific enquiry, nor compatible with biblical injunctions to treat nature instead as a dependent creation of God (Pss 29, 89, 104, 137, etc.) who alone is to be worshipped (Deut. 26:11; Isa. 44:24; Jer. 7:18, etc.). The replacement of an organismic by a mechanistic universe (nature's own 'demythologization') coincided with a renewed awareness of such teaching.

(2) The laws of nature: the emergence of 'laws of nature' in the seventeenth century has been shown by Zilsel (*Physical Review* 51, 1942, pp. 245–279) as a derivative of biblical doctrines, citing *inter alia* Job 28:26 and Prov. 8:29. Later writers (Whitehead, Oakley, etc.) have strengthened this thesis.

(3) The experimental method: both in English *Puritanism and continental Calvinism (see *Reformed theology) the questioning manipulation of nature was strongly encouraged as an alternative to the abstract reasoning of ancient pagan cultures. It was seen as fully compatible with biblical injunctions to 'test' all things (1 Thess. 5:21; Rom. 12:2; Ps. 34:8, etc.).

(4) Controlling the earth: Bacon and his followers saw in Scripture (Gen. 1:26; Ps. 8:6–8, etc.) a clear mandate for altering the natural world for human benefit.

(5) To the glory of God: that scientific research could add lustre to the divine name was believed even by patristic writers, but it most strongly emerged in the seventeenth century. Thus John Kepler (1571–1630), in studying those heavens which declared the glory of God (Pss 8, 19, 50), exclaimed he was 'thinking God's thoughts after him'. This of itself was a powerful motive for the scientific exploration of nature.

If science may, without exaggeration, be seen as historically dependent for its emergence on Christian theology, then, in an age when this has been largely forgotten, biblical theology has an even more important contribution to make. This is in the area of *ethical direction*. Crucial to such an impact is a renewal of the biblical concept of *stewardship, which may be seen as the only key to current dilemmas over areas of concern ranging from the pollution of the biosphere and climate change to a possible nuclear holocaust. All of these arise from technologies now made possible by science. Moreover, many aspects of modern science have been seen as eroding human dignity and worth, whether in the extrapolations of biological science to the so-called 'sociobiology', or in the naive reductionism that, in the manner of the Greek atomists, sees all phenomena in purely material terms. To an allegedly 'scientific' worldview so devoid of comfort and hope theology surely has much to say.

See also: MACKAY, DONALD M.; ECOLOGY; NATURE, THEOLOGY OF; POLANYI, MICHAEL; TORRANCE, THOMAS F.

Bibliography

I. G. Barbour, *Issues in Science and Religion* (London, 1966); R. Bube, *The Human Quest* (Waco, 1971); J. Dillenberger, *Protestant Thought and Natural Science* (London, 1961); R. Hooykaas, *Christian Faith and the Freedom of Science* (London, 1957); idem, *Religion and the Rise of Modern Science* (Edinburgh, ^{2}1973); S. J. Jaki, *The Savior of Science* (Washington, 1988); M. A. Jeeves (ed.), *The Scientific Enterprise and Christian Faith* (London, 1969); D. M. MacKay, *The Clockwork Image: A Christian Perspective on Science* (London, 1974); idem, *Human Science and Human Dignity* (London, 1979); A. McGrath, *Science and Religion: An Introduction* (Oxford, 1999); H. Montefiore (ed.), *Man and Nature* (London, 1975); A. Padgett, *Science and the Study of God: A Mutuality Model for Theology and Science* (Grand Rapids, 2003); A. R. Peacocke, *Creation and the World of Science* (Oxford, 1979); J. Polkinghorne, *Science and Theology: An Introduction* (London, 1998); idem, *Theology in the Context of Science* (London, 2008); A. Richardson, *The Bible in the Age of Science* (London, 1964); C. A. Russell, *Crosscurrents: Interactions between Science and Faith* (Leicester, 1985); T. F. Torrance, *Christian Theology and Scientific Culture* (Belfast, 1980); idem, *Theological Science* (Oxford, 1996).

C. A. RUSSELL

SCIENTOLOGY, see SECTS

SCOTS CONFESSION

The Scots Confession was one of a number of confessions and catechisms which were produced during and after the Protestant Reformation of the sixteenth century. The purpose of these confessions was to state in summary form the content of the Christian faith as understood by Protestant theologians, particularly as distinguished from medieval Catholicism. Each strand of the Reformation produced its own distinctive theology. The Scots Confession is one of the representative documents of the Calvinistic strand of the Reformation, as opposed to the Lutheran or Anabaptist strands.

It was written in 1560, the year of the Scottish Reformation, at the request of the Scottish Parliament. It was drawn up in four days by John Knox, John Winram, John Spottiswoode, John Willock, John Douglas and John Row (the six Johns). It was revised and then approved by Parliament. The majority of scholars agree that it was primarily the work of John *Knox and indeed it is sometimes referred to as 'Knox's Confession', although some would argue that the work was done more equally by the six. It consists of twenty-five short chapters, beginning (unlike later Reformed Confessions) with the doctrine of God. It remained the official confession of the Church of Scotland (see *Presbyterianism) until 1647, when it was replaced with the *Westminster Confession of Faith.

See also: CONFESSIONS OF FAITH; REFORMERS, SCOTTISH; REFORMED THEOLOGY.

Bibliography

J. H. S. Burleigh, *A Church History of Scotland* (Oxford, 1960); G. D. Henderson, *The Scots Confession of 1560* (Edinburgh, 1960); J. Knox, *The History of the Reformation of Religion in Scotland* (London, 1905); T. McCrie, *The Story of the Scottish Church* (Glasgow, 1988); J. Rogers, *Presbyterian Creeds: A Guide to the Book of Confessions* (Louisville, 1985).

A. T. B. McGowan

SCRIPTURE

Scripture (Lat. *Scriptura*, rendering Gk *graphē*, which means a writing and is used some fifty times in NT for some or all of OT) is the Judeo-Christian label for the literature that the church has historically received as God's own written witness to himself in the form of human witness to his work, will, ways and proper worship. *Graphē* bears essentially the same sense in both singular and plural: the Scriptures are all the items that make up the Bible, each viewed as part of the divine whole, and 'Scripture' means the same material viewed as one organic unit of divine instruction. 'Holy' is regularly prefixed to 'Scripture', pointing to God as both its source and its subject matter.

Beginning as a sect within Judaism, Christianity was from the start a book-religion, invoking the Hebrew Scriptures (and, since it used Greek, sometimes the Septuagint translation as well) to establish its identity, legitimacy, authority, continuity with Israel, and much of its teaching. As *Jesus had implicitly indicated that all his ministry was fulfilling all the hopes, dreams and ideals set forth in the Scriptures, so now the apostles trumpeted this claim, and it was natural that the church should soon bracket apostolic writings with the Jewish Scriptures as declaring their fulfilment of the latter by their witness to the being and doing, the character, purpose and work of the triune Creator-Saviour. (This, be it said, was from the outset the implicit, instinctive Christian conception of God, though words in which to express it were entirely lacking in the apostolic era.) Peter classed Paul's letters as Scripture, and Paul quoted the words of Jesus in Luke's Gospel as Scripture, as early as the sixties of the first century (2 Pet. 3:16; 1 Tim. 5:18).

By the end of the first century, most of our NT was collected and in use throughout the churches: the four Gospels and Acts matching the OT historical books, the apostles' pastoral letters matching the hortatory sermons of the prophets and wisdom writers, and the book of Revelation, with its symbolic anticipation of things to come, matching the visionary foreshadowings found in Daniel and some other prophets. The two collections have been regularly called the 'Old' and 'New' Testaments since the fourth century; earlier, the OT had been 'the Scriptures' and the NT 'the gospel and the apostles'.

Mainstream Christianity knows itself as a doxological response to a loving triune Creator who is now Redeemer of our race through, first, the ongoing mediation of the second divine person, the Son, who became man, died for sins, and now reigns cosmically as Jesus the Lord, and through, second, the ongoing ministry of the third divine person, the Holy Spirit, who evokes response to the Father and to Jesus, and who changes believers progressively into the moral and spiritual likeness of the incarnate Son. God the holy Three is known, and communed with, as a team, the Father as planner, promiser and provider overall, the Son and the Spirit as Saviour and Sanctifier respectively. Communion with this God calls for knowledge of his active tripersonhood, without which he is misconceived (see *Trinity); and this knowledge has been given by self-revealing communication from him, now committed to writing for permanent availability to all in an uncorrupt form. God, who equipped humankind with language for purposes of communication, now uses language to tell us the truth about himself. The end-product of *God's self-disclosure in history, and the means of its continuance in personal experience, is precisely Holy Scripture, the written word of God.

In literary terms, Scripture is a mix of prose and poetry, history and homily, letters, visions, memoirs, philosophy, love-lyrics directed both Godward and manward, law-codes, liturgical rubrics, genealogies, statistics, and more. In functional terms, it is a guide to godliness for sinful human beings, starting from wherever each person is and operating through illumination from the Holy Spirit, who helps in interpreting the biblical writings that he himself generated. In Scripture the outworking, past, present and future, of the Father's loving, Christ-centred plan of *redemption for both individuals and the cosmos is displayed; the required response (faith, repentance, hope, love, worship, service, thanksgiving, faithfulness) is analysed, verbalized, and illustrated by narratives; and Christians and churches are in effect told to live under this written word of God, where the truth of the apostolic gospel and the claims of the triune Lord are brought home. Theological discussion of Scripture should always be so oriented as to ensure that the ministry of the written word is not blocked but enhanced.

Scripture and canon

Before asking which books belong to the canon, we should ask what being canonical actually signifies. *Kanōn* (Gk) means a rule, measure or standard. Scripture is called canonical because it is God's rule for belief and behaviour. The uses of canon for a list of books that are canonical in this sense are secondary and derivative. The church has always known, more or less clearly, that it did not create a canon by discretionary fiat, but received the canon that God created for it. The OT canon (i.e. the thirty-nine books read and stored in first-century Palestinian synagogues, Jesus' Bible) came to the church from the hands, as it were, of Christ and his apostles, for whom Christianity's credentials presupposed the divine authority of Jewish Scripture, which Christian fact fulfilled. The NT canon comes in effect from the same source, for it was the *Holy Spirit whom Christ sent who enabled the apostles to speak and write the truth about Jesus, and who all along has brought about recognition of apostolic documents as canonical. The basis of that recognition was, and is, (1) apostolic authorship for authentication, (2) Christ-honouring doctrinal content, in line with the known teaching of other apostles, and (3) continuous acknowledgment and spiritually fruitful use of the books within the church from the apostolic age on – a consideration that becomes weightier and more compelling with every passing year.

The historic *Protestant claim, that the Holy Spirit authenticates the canonical books by causing them to impose themselves upon believers as a divine rule for faith and life, should be understood in corporate terms – namely, as meaning that at no time has the great body of the church rejected any book now rated canonical, and that divine authority is constantly experienced by the faithful when canonical Scripture is read and preached in the congregation.

On the extent of the canon there has not been perfect unanimity. Protestants hold to the sixty-six-book list found in Athanasius' *Festal Letter* of 367, in Jerome, and in the canons of the provincial council that met at Carthage in 397; the Council of Trent defined twelve apocryphal books into the Roman canon in 1546; the Synod of Jerusalem defined four of these (Judith, Tobit, Wisdom and Ecclesiasticus) into the Eastern Orthodox canon in 1672; Luther rejected James; and so on. But these are relatively small matters: Luther's trouble was that he misunderstood James, supposing him to contradict Paul; and the Apocrypha is not important for doctrine. More important is the fact that the principles of canonicity to which, however unconvincingly, appeal was made each time, remained constant throughout. Thus, (2) above was Luther's warrant for rejecting James, and (3) was the Roman Catholic and Orthodox warrant for canonizing apocryphal books that were no part of Christ's Bible.

Scripture and revelation

The historic Christian view, which goes back to Christ, that Scripture is verbal *revelation in writing, is unfashionable today; most contemporary theologians classify Scripture as a human record, exposition and celebration of God in history which God uses for self-revealing encounters with us in the present. This formula, though true so far (unless 'human' is taken to imply inadequacy, incoherence or incorrectness), is theologically incomplete. That Scripture is intrinsically revelation must also be affirmed (see next section). But when this affirmation is not properly related to God's saving work in history, it too becomes incomplete. Scripture depicts revelation as a complex work of *grace whereby God brings sinners into *saving knowledge of himself, and the nature of Scripture as revelation must be understood within this functional frame.

In revelation, according to the Bible, God acts at three linked levels. Level one is revelation *on the public stage of *history*, in a series of redemptive events of which God's verbal predictions and explanations at each stage formed part. This series reached a penultimate climax in the incarnation, atonement, resurrection and enthroning of the Son of God and the Pentecostal outpouring of the Spirit. Awaited now is the final climax of Christ's return for judgment and cosmic renewal, which will end history as we know it (see *Eschatology).

Within this sequence emerged level two, revelation *in the public records of Scripture*. As redemptive revelation unfolded, God caused narrational, explanatory and anticipatory writing to be done that would preserve and spread true knowledge of his ongoing work of grace.

Level three is revelation *in the personal consciousness of individuals*: that is, the gift to sin-blinded humans of a responsive understanding of the God of history and Holy Scripture. This gift is given through the enlightening ministry of the Holy Spirit, who interprets to us the contents of Scripture, in whatever form these are met. The *Reformers insisted that as only Scripture, unaugmented from philosophical or religious sources, can bring us to know God, so it is only as the Spirit opens Scripture to us and writes its teachings on our hearts that this knowledge becomes reality for us.

Undergirding Scripture's instrumental function at level three is the total trustworthiness that its divine origin guarantees. Were the 'public records' incoherent and misleading, the knowledge of God based on them would be a dangerous half-ignorance. The many who nowadays imply this to be the case by their critiquing of the historic faith call in question not only the veracity of God as Scripture's primary author, but also his wisdom and competence in communication. If documents designed to make God known to all generations are untrustworthy and so inadequate for their purpose, God has indeed failed badly. But only the various forms of *liberal theology would ever require such a conclusion.

Scripture and inspiration

The historic description of Scripture as inspired means, not that it is inspiring (although it is), but that it is 'God-breathed' (*theopneustos*, 2 Tim. 3:16), a product of the Creator-Spirit's work, always to be viewed as the preaching and teaching of God himself in and through the words of the human witnesses who were divinely moved to write it. Both Testaments cite the words of Scripture as God's own words. Paul's quoting of God's promise to Abraham and threat to Pharaoh as the utterance of *Scripture* to both (Gal. 3:8; Rom. 9:17) shows how completely he equated statements of Scripture with words of God. And by teaching and commanding in Christ's name, claiming Christ's authority because he was Christ's apostle, and insisting that both his matter and his wording were Spirit-given, Paul showed that apostolic utterances were to be treated as truth and wisdom from God in just the same way that OT declarations were to be (see 2 Thess. 3:6; 1 Cor. 14:37; 2:9–13).

Since the God who created Scripture by sanctifying his servants' authorial efforts is true and no deceiver, biblical *infallibility and inerrancy become articles of faith. Jesus, though human, did not go astray in conduct or teaching, and there is no a priori reason why the Bible, though human, should go wrong either. Those who confess a sinless Christ cannot consistently dismiss the analogous belief in an inerrant Bible. To treat the unequivocal witness of Christ and the apostles to the nature of Scripture as not settling the matter, and to go against them, is illogical, irreverent and indefensible. The phenomena of Scripture should be dealt with on the assumption that, being God-given, it is faithful to physical, moral and spiritual reality. This has been taken for granted for most of Christian history, and is taken for granted by most of the world church still.

Scripture and interpretation

As the Reformers discerned, word and Spirit go together, and it is through Spirit-led interpretation that God's communication is received. Interpreting Scripture is, however, a demanding activity. Assuming God's changelessness, Scripture's trustworthiness and the doxological goal of encounters with deity, the interpreter's task is to draw from Scripture and apply to thought and life today all those truths about God, humanity and their mutual relations that the texts yield. Since the biblical books are occasional writings addressed to people and situations of long ago, interpretive method involves unshelling those truths from the particular applications in which we find them embedded and reapplying them to ourselves. We must move from what the text meant historically to what it means as a word from God for us today. And this can be tricky (see *Hermeneutics).

To grasp what the text meant requires grammatical-historical exegesis that takes account of the text's linguistic idiom, literary genre, cultural and geographical milieu, and the life-situation of both writer and first readers, so far as this can be known. So one must ask where, when, by whom, for what reason, to what end and with what resources each book, and the part of it now being studied, was written.

Then, discerning what the text means in application today requires two things. The truths excavated by exegesis must be checked to ensure that they square with the covenantal, Christocentric, redemptive, holiness-oriented framework of canonical revelation as a whole, for only if they do so dare one believe they have been perceived aright. After that, they should be set to interrogate us for 'rebuking, correcting and training in righteousness' (2 Tim. 3:16) as they confront our inadequacies, clarify to us our calling and our hope, and animate us to the activities of obedience. Spirit-given sensitivity to our own situation must be sought from God at this stage; we cannot succeed in obeying God without it, for then we shall still be unaware of all that needs to be done.

Scripture and authority

*Authority is the basic theological issue into which discussions of biblical revelation, inspiration and interpretation finally run. At issue is the nature and extent of the motivating control that canonical Scripture should exercise over the doctrine, discipline and devotion of the church and its members. That Scripture mediates the authority of the God who gave it and the Christ to whom it testifies, that it does this by presenting the presence of this God and the realities of salvation-history in their universal significance, and that it cannot have authority further than it is true (for falsehood has no right to rule) are points of widespread contemporary agreement. That the church has no right to read into Scripture, or graft on to it, traditional ideas that cannot be read out of it, and that no individual Christian is ever entitled to back his or her judgment against it, are principles that should command full agreement, though sometimes they do not. It cannot be said too often or too strongly that submission to Scripture is one aspect of submission to Christ.

The Reformers formulated and vindicated biblical authority against ecclesiastical waywardness by three corrective assertions, covered together in the tag-phrase *sola Scriptura* (by Scripture alone):

- The *necessity* of Scripture. Only biblically taught notions of God will be true and can be trusted. Speculations lead astray.
- The *sufficiency* of Scripture. All that needs to be known for godliness and salvation is on display in the Bible. Additions lead astray.
- The *clarity* of Scripture. The canonical books exhibit their unity and build up their message from within. In that sense, Scripture interprets Scripture. Imposed interpretations lead astray.

Post-Reformation theology recognizes that the role of Scripture is to critique as well as instruct.

Scripture in the church

The Bible has always been studied, taught and preached primarily as meat and drink for feeding and forming the faithful, those already grounded in orthodox belief (the rule of faith, the *creeds, the *confessions and doctrinal bases), and who need and desire application of

God's truth to their own lives. From *Justin Martyr through *Thomas Aquinas to the Reformation and since, it has been acknowledged that doctrine can only be established from the 'literal' sense of the text (that is, the sense that the human writer directly expressed). But from *Irenaeus and *Origen through the Middle Ages devotional allegorizing, moral and mystical in thrust, was additionally practised within the bounds of orthodoxy in order to edify, and some preachers, especially outside the West, still do this, as do some Christians in their private meditations.

See also: SCRIPTURE, DOCTRINE OF; SCRIPTURE AND TRADITION.

Bibliography

J. Barr, *The Bible in the Modern World* (London, 1973); K. Barth, *CD*, I.1–2; G. C. Berkouwer, *Holy Scripture* (Grand Rapids, 1975); D. G. Bloesch, *Holy Scripture* (Downers Grove, 1994); S. Fowl (ed.), *The Theological Interpretation of Scripture* (Oxford, 1997); N. Geisler (ed.), *Inerrancy* (Grand Rapids, 1979); P. Helm and Carl R. Trueman (eds.), *The Trustworthiness of God* (Grand Rapids, 2002); C. F. H. Henry, *God, Revelation, and Authority*, vols. I–IV (Waco, 1976–9); A. Kuyper, *Principles of Sacred Theology* (Grand Rapids, 1954); B. M. Metzger, *The Canon of the New Testament* (Oxford, 1987); J. I. Packer, *God Has Spoken* (London, 2005); C. Pinnock, *Biblical Revelation* (Chicago, 1971); idem, *The Scripture Principle* (San Francisco, 1984); E. Rademacher and R. Preus (eds.), *Hermeneutics, Inerrancy, and the Bible* (Grand Rapids, 1984); A. C. Thiselton, *The Two Horizons* (Exeter, 1980); idem, *New Horizons in Hermeneutics* (London and Grand Rapids, 1992); K. J. Vanhoozer, *Is There a Meaning in This Text?* (Grand Rapids, 1998); idem, *First Theology* (Downers Grove, 2002); B. Vawter, *Biblical Inspiration* (London, 1972); B. B. Warfield, *The Inspiration and Authority of the Bible* (Philadelphia, 1948); N. Wolterstorff, *Divine Discourse* (Cambridge, 1995).

J. I. PACKER

SCRIPTURE AND TRADITION

The relationship between Scripture and tradition cannot be studied in isolation. They interact with one another only through a third party: the contemporary *church. It might help to define the two terms. '*Scripture' refers to the canonical writings of both Testaments. The early Christians inherited the Jewish (OT) Scriptures, but did not immediately acquire a parallel body of Christian Scriptures. Early moves toward it (e.g. 2 Pet. 3:14–16) came to fruition by the time of Irenaeus, by when there was a clear concept of an NT alongside the OT. The acceptance of Christian Scriptures posed the question of the relation between these writings and the Christian tradition, which included the teaching of the *apostles handed down in other ways in the church.

'Tradition' is sometimes understood narrowly to refer solely to extra-scriptural or even un-scriptural traditions. Such clearly exist, but our present concern is with tradition in the broader sense of the Christian faith as it is handed down to us from the past. Such a broad definition could logically *include* Scripture (as in Orthodox thought, in which Scripture is often seen as part of the tradition which is the expression of the work of the *Holy Spirit in the church), but since our concern is with the relation between Scripture and tradition, we shall follow normal Western usage and exclude Scripture from the definition. Every Christian group has to grapple with the relationship between these two. There is no Christian group, however informal, that has no tradition. Similarly, every Christian group, however informal, has some authority structure, some standards of what is and is not 'Christian'. It is this element, the contemporary teaching authority of the church, which must not be forgotten in considering the relation between Scripture and tradition.

The relationship between Scripture, tradition and church has been seen differently over the ages. The earliest view may be called the coincidence view; the church teaches what the apostles taught, which it receives from the apostolic Scriptures and from the apostolic tradition. Scripture, tradition and church are assumed to teach the same one apostolic message. There is no conflict between them, and the whole Christian message is found in each. It is this approach that was adopted by *Irenaeus and *Tertullian against *Gnosticism. The Gnostics appealed to their own scriptures and to their own secret traditions. Irenaeus responded with the claim that the apostles' teaching, found in their genuine writings, was handed down in an open public tradition of teaching in those churches which they had founded, where it was still taught. This threefold cord provided the most effective answer to the Gnostic claims.

In time, the coincidence view came to be overshadowed by the *supplementary view*: tradition is needed to supplement Scripture, to provide teaching not found in Scripture. The belief that apostolic tradition supplements Scripture as a guide to *practice* is found early, but it was some time before theologians came to defend *beliefs* which they acknowledged not to be in Scripture. An important step in this direction was taken by *Basil of Caesarea in his defence of the deity of the Holy Spirit, where he states that some Christian beliefs are not found in Scripture. This approach became more common in the Middle Ages, with the emergence of doctrines concerning *Mary which lacked explicit scriptural grounding. But the coincidence view was never lost sight of.

The supplementary view could be invoked to justify beliefs with no scriptural basis. But what of beliefs actually *contrary* to Scripture? As the Middle Ages drew to a close, various groups began to raise this charge against some *Roman Catholic doctrines. These charges came to a head in the Reformation. The most fundamental issue in the *Reformation was not *justification by faith, not the role of tradition, but the relationship between Scripture and the church. The Magisterial Reformers rejected the teachings of the Roman Church in the name of the scriptural gospel. In turn, they faced the charge of heresy for rejecting church doctrine. The issue was simple: Does the gospel define the church, or vice versa? The Reformers branded the Roman Catholic Church a false church for suppressing the gospel. Rome called the Reformers heretics for rejecting the teaching of holy mother church. The Reformers did not believe in 'private judgment', with every man his own theologian. But they did believe that all church teaching needs to be tested by Scripture. They had a deep respect for tradition, especially the teaching of the early Fathers. But tradition must not add to Scripture and must be tested by Scripture. The *Radical Reformers generally adopted a more negative view of tradition, although with time many developed their own traditions and some gave expression to them in authoritative *confessions of faith.

The Council of *Trent responded to the Reformers in its *Decree on Scripture and Tradition* (1546). It stated that 'the truth and discipline [of the gospel] are contained in the written books and in unwritten traditions – those unwritten traditions, that is, which were either received by the apostles from the mouth of Christ himself or were received from the apostles themselves (having been dictated by the Holy Spirit) and have come down even to us, having been transmitted as it were hand by hand'. Furthermore, Scripture and tradition are to be venerated 'with equal affection of piety and reverence'. It used to be believed that this committed Rome to the supplementary view, but more recently J. R. Geiselmann (1890–1970) and others have challenged this assumption. It is now widely accepted that Trent does not foreclose the question of the material sufficiency or otherwise of Scripture. In other words, Trent allows the view that all Catholic doctrine is found in Scripture. What is quite clear in the teaching of Trent is the role of the church, guided by the Holy Spirit. No-one shall 'presume to interpret [the Scriptures] contrary to that sense which holy mother Church, to whom it belongs to judge of their true sense and interpretation, has held and holds, or even contrary to the unanimous teaching of the Fathers'.

Many changes have taken place since the sixteenth century. Historical criticism has affected the church's approach to the Bible and has also shown how doctrine has changed over the years. Today the fact of the *development of doctrine is widely accepted by both Roman Catholic and Protestant theologians. But despite these changes, the fundamental issue, the relationship between Scripture and the church, remains much the same. At the Second *Vatican Council (1962–5), the dogmatic constitution on *Divine Revelation* expounded, in the second chapter, the relationship between Scripture, tradition and church. Due to the efforts of Geiselmann and others the question of the material (in)sufficiency of Scripture was left open. The apostolic teaching of the gospel is transmitted to us through both Scripture and tradition, which 'are to be accepted and venerated with the same sense of devotion and reverence'. Development of doctrine is acknowledged: 'there is a growth in the understanding of the realities and the words which have been handed down.' (The Council was indebted to the work of J. H. *Newman, who argued that it is the teaching of the contemporary church, guided by the Spirit, which is authoritative, and that the teaching of earlier generations should be interpreted in the light of this.) But the final authority is neither Scripture nor tradition, but the teaching office of the church: 'The task of authentically interpreting the word of God, whether written or handed on, has been entrusted exclusively to the living teaching office of the church, whose authority is exercised in the name of Jesus Christ.' Among Protestants today there is a greater willingness than before to acknowledge the importance of tradition and to ascribe to it a high role. This is seen very clearly in the report *Scripture, Tradition and Traditions of the Fourth World Conference on Faith and Order* of the WCC, which met at Montreal in 1963. But there are no signs that Protestants are willing to submit their interpretation of Scripture to 'the living teaching office of the church'.

Tradition cannot be escaped. A sermon in church, a book read at home, sharing one's faith with a friend – all of these are tradition in action. Tradition is inevitable – and also desirable. The adage that 'those who are ignorant of history are condemned to repeat it' holds true in the history of theology. Those who have arrogantly despised tradition have often ended by relearning some of the most basic lessons that the past can teach us. Karl *Barth aptly stated that the correct attitude to tradition is summarized in the fifth commandment: honour your father and mother. We must honour our theological forebears and listen with respect to the voice of the past, but we are not bound by it. With tradition, as with parents, there are times when we should say 'we must obey God rather than men'. Tradition is worthy of respect, but is subject to the word of God in the Scriptures. If a tradition represents a manifestation of the Spirit's teaching work, it will not contradict Scripture.

The Reformers coined the slogan *sola Scriptura*: Scripture alone. What does this mean? It does not mean that we should use nothing but the Bible – that there is no place for dictionaries of theology and the like. It does not mean that we should learn Christian doctrine only directly from the Bible, which would make sermons and other books redundant. It does not even mean that we should recognize no other authority than the Bible in our Christianity. Tradition and the church inevitably and properly function as authorities in some sense. But the Bible remains the decisive and final authority, the norm by which all the teaching of tradition and the church is to be tested.

Bibliography

F. F. Bruce and E. G. Rupp (eds.), *Holy Book and Holy Tradition* (Manchester, 1968); Y. M. J. Congar, *Tradition and Traditions* (London, 1966); P. C. Rodger and L. Vischer (eds.), 'Scripture, Tradition and Traditions', in *The Fourth World Conference on Faith and Order* (London, 1964); G. H. Tavard, *Holy Writ or Holy Church: The Crisis of the Protestant Reformation* (London, 1959); WCC, *A Treasure in Earthen Vessels* (Geneva, 1998).

A. N. S. LANE

SCRIPTURE, DOCTRINE OF

The task of a doctrine of Scripture is rightly to handle the distinction and the relation of the human words in the Bible to the word of God. Jesus' oft-cited formula 'It is written' (e.g. Mark 14:27; Luke 4:8) ascribes supreme authority for life and thought to just these writings (Gk *graphē* ['writing'] is rendered in Latin by *scriptura*). Applied to the Bible, then, 'faith seeking understanding' involves, among other things, articulating its clarity, unity and sufficiency.

The doctrine of Scripture sets forth the reasons why the Bible is the supreme norm for Christian theology, as well as its relation to other doctrines. This dual purpose is seen in the prominent location of the article on Scripture at or near the beginning of many Protestant confessional statements. The *Scots Confession, for example, states Scripture's authority 'to be from God', not from the church; the *Westminster Confession of Faith declares Scripture 'the Word of God written'.

Nature: revelation and inspiration

The rise of modern historical understanding and concomitant loss of a supernaturalistic worldview led many to view the Bible as the record of human experience and, at best, an expression of human religious faith. Yet to call the Bible 'Scripture' is to regard it in some way as authoritative and part and parcel of what it means to be a Christian. However, it is one thing to assign supreme authority to Scripture, and quite another to appeal to it as an authority for theology and ethics.

Historic orthodoxy acknowledges Scripture to be 'holy' (set apart for a divine purpose) as the divinely appointed medium of God's self-communication. Where theologians differ, however, is over how God in his self-revelation relates to the biblical texts.

B. B. *Warfield responded to critical views of the Bible by reasserting its divine origin. The Bible presents itself as *theopneustos* (2 Tim. 3:16), literally 'God-breathed' or 'expired', not merely inspired in the sense of spiritually uplifting. Because the human authors are borne along by God's Spirit (2 Pet. 1:21), what they say in Scripture is ultimately what God says.

Contra this 'propositional' emphasis, K. *Barth refused simply to equate the word of God with Scripture for fear of negating God's freedom and confusing God's self-revelation ('personal' in Jesus Christ) with information susceptible to human mastery. According to Barth, the Bible becomes the word of God only when God freely and actively communicates himself to human recipients by graciously commandeering the human words so that they effectively witness to their subject matter, Jesus Christ.

More recently, a number of proposals have sought to get beyond the propositionalist-personalist impasse by viewing Scripture in terms of divine speech acts or *discourse*. Saying is a form of doing, and the concept of illocution refers to what one *does* in speaking. To equate the Bible with God's word, then, is to recognize that God does more with human words than reveal information, or even himself: God also commands, warns, promises, consoles, rebukes, etc. Scripture is more than a textbook about God; it is a creaturely medium in which God personally relates to his people through a variety of communicative acts. Through literary forms such as poetry, song, parable and apocalyptic, Scripture appeals to the imagination as well as to the mind in order both to form and inform the people of God.

Authority: word and Spirit

To confess the Bible as the word of God is to locate Scripture in the broader triune economy of *revelation and *redemption. Scripture derives its *authority from its role in the mission of the divine communicative action – the movements of Word and Spirit – into the world. The ultimate authority in theology is the triune God speaking in and through the Scriptures.

B. Ramm identifies the *Protestant or 'Scripture' principle, and hence the principle of supreme authority, with the *Holy Spirit speaking in the Scriptures. To say that the words of the biblical text alone are authoritative gives rise, by contrast, to an *abbreviated* Protestant principle, a view that undermines the structure of theological authority by omitting the internal testimony of the Spirit that shaped both individuals and the church's catholic tradition. 'The temptation of biblicism is that it can speak of the inspiration of the Scriptures apart from the Lord they enshrine' (*Special Revelation and the Word of God*, p. 117).

The doctrine of Scripture should not be isolated from other affirmations about God's communicative presence and activity. Inspiration is related to *sanctification: the Spirit sets aside and shapes just these texts, their subject matter and verbal form, to serve the publication of the knowledge of God. Scripture is a creaturely means by which the triune God presents Christ, administers the covenant, and renews the world through the ministry of the word in the power of the Spirit. As such, it governs all that the church says, thinks and does by calling God's people to respond, and correspond, to what God has done as Creator and Redeemer.

Interpretation: script and performance

Scripture is not simply a source of information about God's work of creation and redemption, but an authoritative script that calls for God's people to participate in its content: what God is doing in Christ through the Spirit to renew all things. The church, living in the first scene of the last act of the drama of redemption, is to be a theatre of the gospel precisely as the community that reads, understands, and then demonstrates its understanding of God's word.

See also: INFALLIBILITY AND INERRANCY OF THE BIBLE; SCRIPTURE.

Bibliography

J. Barr, *The Bible in the Modern World* (London, 1973); J. Holcomb (ed.), *Christian Theologies of Scripture* (New York and London, 2006); D. Kelsey, *Proving Doctrine: The Uses of Scripture in Modern Theology* (Harrisburg, 1999); B. Ramm, *Special Revelation and the Word of God* (Grand Rapids, 1961); P. Satterthwaite and D. F. Wright (eds.), *A Pathway into the Holy Scripture* (Grand Rapids, 1994); K. Vanhoozer, *The Drama of Doctrine: A Canonical-Linguistic Approach to Christian Theology* (Louisville, 2005); T. Ward, *Word and Supplement: Speech Acts, Biblical Texts, and the Sufficiency of Scripture* (Oxford, 2002); B. B. Warfield, *The Inspiration and Authority of the Bible* (Philadelphia, 1948); J. Webster, *Holy Scripture: A Dogmatic Sketch* (Cambridge, 2003); N. Wolterstorff, *Divine Discourse: Philosophical Reflections on the Claim That God Speaks* (Cambridge, 1995); N. T. Wright, *Scripture and the Authority of God* (London, 2005).

K. J. Vanhoozer

SEA OF FAITH MOVEMENT

Sea of Faith (SoF) is a loosely organized movement dedicated to exploring and promoting an understanding of religious faith as a human creation. With national networks in Great Britain, Australia and New Zealand, it claims approximately 2,000 members worldwide.

The movement traces its origins to a controversial book and television series of the same name. Written and presented by Don Cupitt, an Anglican priest and philosopher of religion at Cambridge University, *The Sea of Faith* (the title is taken from Matthew Arnold's poem 'Dover Beach') traced the decline of religious certainties in the modern world and urged a revaluation of the meaning of traditional theological language. Religiously serious talk of 'God', for example, no longer is to be understood as referring to an independently existing divine being. Rather, it serves to give public voice to the spiritual and moral values that guide human life.

Cupitt's radical Christian humanism and the theological *non-realism it entailed are not universally shared within the movement he inspired. SoF has no official statement of belief; its members are united only by a common commitment to continuing exploration of the religious dimensions of human life and a deep aversion to all forms of religious authoritarianism.

Bibliography

D. Boulton, *A Reasonable Faith: Introducing the Sea of Faith Network* (Manchester, 1996); C. Crowder (ed.), *God and Reality: Essays on Christian Non-Realism* (London, 1997); D. Cupitt, *The Sea of Faith* (London, ²1994); A. Freeman, *God in Us: A Case for Christian Humanism* (London, 1993); A. Moore, *Realism and Christian Faith* (Cambridge, 2003).

D. P. Wood

SECTS

The contemporary study of sectarianism has its roots in the work of the Protestant theologian Ernst *Troeltsch and the sociologist Max *Weber, who made an important distinction between *church and sect. For Weber, traditionally, the church is not a voluntary organization, but rather a community into which one is born. Sects, on the other hand, are voluntarist and do not seek to regulate the lives of those who *do not* explicitly wish to become its members. Those who *do* wish to become members, however, must satisfy certain membership criteria in order to demonstrate their commitment to the sect. Hence, for Weber, the church-sect distinction focuses on membership – the church being inclusive, the sect exclusive.

This, however, is not a static relationship, in that successful sects tend to evolve into churches. On the one hand, the size of a sect has an impact on the internal dynamics of the movement, in that the more people that are involved, the more likely it is to progress towards a church-type institution. On the other hand, and more importantly, Weber observes the 'routinization of charisma'. A sect's charisma is usually located in a founder, an individual religious hero, the recipient of personal revelation. As the sect continues, particularly after the death of the founder, the charisma may be relocated to 'an office', such as the office of priest or the office of bishop. Successors, as they are inducted into these ministerial offices within a religious organization, inherit the charisma of the founder in much the same way as it is believed that the charisma of Jesus Christ was communicated through Peter to the *papal office and to the office of the priest (see *Ministry). Hence, churches and sects can be distinguished, not simply by the principle of membership, but also by the nature of charisma. Whereas in a sect charisma is original, attached to a leader, in a church it is routinized, attached to an office.

In *The Social Teachings of the Christian Churches*, Troeltsch employs Weber's church-sect distinction as a key tool of interpretation. In dialogue with Albrecht *Ritschl's thought, he examines the teaching of Jesus and the formation of the early church, after which he provides a detailed sociological analysis of medieval Christianity. Although much is taken from Weber, Troeltsch differed from him in several respects, the two principle differences being that he identified particular attitudes to 'the world' as a key distinguishing feature. His types can be summarized as follows: The *church type* is open to the world and, to some degree, will accept the secular order: 'The fully developed Church utilizes the *State and the ruling classes, and weaves these elements into her own life; she then becomes an integral part of the existing social order; from this standpoint, then, the Church both stabilizes and determines the social order; in so doing, however, she becomes dependent upon the upper classes, and upon their development.' The church type is most obviously represented by medieval *Catholicism, although it can also be seen in the later development of mainstream Protestant Christianity. The *sect type* of Christianity is found in relatively small voluntary groups that tend to separate themselves from church-type institutions. Moreover, sects tend to be 'connected with the lower classes, or at least with those elements in society which are opposed to the state and to society; they work upwards from below, and not downwards from above'.

While the work of Weber and Troeltsch has not gone unchallenged, the central theses have been developed in recent sociological studies of sectarianism. In particular, scholars have distinguished 'sects' from 'cults' or '*new religions'. While the latter are typically doctrinally distinct, novel developments within a particular social context, sects are schismatic movements, which, having broken away from their parent religion, are critical of its beliefs and practices, just as they are critical of the prevailing culture and civil authorities. Indeed, sects, such as the Jehovah's Witnesses, typically claim to be the defenders of true faith over against a church or a religion that has become 'lukewarm' and barely distinguishable from the surrounding society and culture. Hence, sects tend to be revivalist, enthusiastic and authoritarian organizations, which exert significant demands on their members.

Not all sects are the same. They do not, for example, all demand the same levels of commitment from their members, or the same degrees of separation from the wider society. For example, reflecting Troeltsch's analysis of sectarian attitudes to 'the world', the sociologist Bryan Wilson (1926–2004) distinguished four sub-types of Christian sect: (1) *conversionist, (2) Adventist/revolutionist, (3) introversionist/*pietist, and (4) *Gnostic.

Conversionist sects seek to alter people, and thereby to alter the world; the response is free-will optimism. The *Adventist* sects predict drastic alteration of the world, and seek to prepare for the new dispensation – a pessimistic determinism. The *Introversionists* reject the world's values and replace them with higher inner values, for the realization of which inner resources are cultivated. The *Gnostic* sects accept in large measure the world's goals but seek a new and esoteric means to achieve these ends – a wishful mysticism.

While this, of course, is not the only typology available, it has been influential and does help us to grasp the complexity and breadth of sectarian religion.

Bibliography

G. Chryssides and B. Zeller (eds.), T*he Bloomsbury Companion to New Religious Movements* (London, 2014); C. Partridge (ed.), *Encyclopedia of New Religions: New Religious Movements, Sects and Alternative Spiritualities* (Oxford, 2004); E. Troeltsch, *The Social Teaching of the Christian Churches,* tr. O. Wyon, 2 vols. (New York, 1931); M. Weber, 'The Protestant Sects and the Spirit of Capitalism', in H. H. Gerth and C. W. Mills (eds.), *From Max Weber: Essays in Sociology* (London, 1948), pp. 302–322; B. R. Wilson, *Sects and Society: A Sociological Study of Three Religious Groups in Britain* (London, 1961); idem, *The Social Dimensions of Sectarianism: Sects and New Religious Movements in Contemporary Society* (Oxford, 1990); idem (ed.), *Patterns of Sectarianism* (London, 1967).

C. Partridge

SECULAR CHRISTIANITY

*Secularization is that process in European history marking the transition from the religious worldview to the secular worldview, approximately from 1570 to 1970. At the beginning of the period religion was the fabric of society, within which everything cohered, individuals and institutions. By the end of the period meaning and value emerged from within the *saeculum*, the here and now.

The irreligious interpreted this process as the death of (God) religion. The religious agreed. Battle was joined with secularism, a militant *atheistic worldview also linked conveniently to the Cold War. There was a third possible position: secular Christianity. Rejecting secularism as an irreligious and dehumanizing ideology, some Christians welcomed secularization, a process which had enabled very positive advances in the natural, medical and social sciences, together with the spread of egalitarian values of democracy and inclusivity in society. They held that Christians should critically engage with the secular and not seek to return to the medieval world with its corruption, cruelty and injustice.

Bibliography

J. Casanova, *Public Religions in the Modern World* (Chicago, 1994); A. Kee, *The Way of Transcendence* (London, 1971); D. Martin, *A General Theory of Secularization* (Oxford, 1978); R. G. Smith, *Secular Christianity* (London, 1966).

A. KEE

SECULARIZATION

From its inception in the nineteenth century, sociology has predicted the decline of *religion in modern societies. Nowadays, while few would doubt that some form of religious diminution or 'secularization' is taking place, there has been much debate as to its nature. Indeed, there has been an increased focus on 'de-secularization', 'sacralization', 're-enchantment', and, more recently, the 'post-secular', all of which, in various ways, identify the growth of the significance of religious discourses personally, socially and culturally in post-industrial societies.

The term 'secularization' had its origin in the Peace of Westphalia (1648) designating the transfer of ecclesiastical property into princely hands. Hence, secularization came to refer to the transfer of material goods from the religious sphere to the non-religious (secular) sphere. Likewise, in sociology, secularization refers to the historical transition from a religious social context to a less or non-religious social context. As Bryan Wilson put it, secularization is 'the process whereby religious thinking, practice and institutions lose their social significance'. In other words, secularization is a complex, multi-dimensional process. Not only does it describe the decline of religious institutions, but also the decline of the importance of religion for both society and for individuals. Hence, as Karel Dobbelaere has argued, secularization needs to be analysed across three levels: the macro-level (society), the meso-level (organizations) and the micro-level (individuals).

Classic theories of secularization, which seek to explain, rather than simply to describe the process, typically argue that 'modernization' leads to the erosion of religion and 'the disenchantment of the world' (Max Weber). Central to modernization is the progress of capitalism and what Weber referred to as 'rationalization', by which he meant the focus on reason, the scientific method, and the growth of a goal-oriented culture for which efficiency is central (see *Enlightenment; *Modernity). In the modern period, traditional values and beliefs quickly succumbed to the most efficient methods of production in order to increase profit. Gradually, this had implications for religion. For example, praying for a good harvest and observing the Sabbath is less effective than spraying with fertilizers and pesticides and working seven days a week. As such, religion began to lose its place at the centre of modern social and cultural life. It was increasingly privatized, in that, while it was considered to be acceptable for those who found it personally comforting, it seemed to make little sense for progressive modern economies and societies.

Likewise, modernity encouraged the growth of individualism and the 'turn to the self'. This has contributed to secularization, in that, again, it corrodes the social bonds so central to the communities on which traditional organized religion depends. The authority of the community, the church, the clergy, the Bible and even God, are all called into question by the modern tendency to elevate the authority of individual reason and experience.

Again, modernity has witnessed the rise of the secular nation *state. That is to say, modern states have formally separated themselves from the church and taken control of large areas of social and political life. Consequently, key social functions once performed by religious organizations have been transferred to the modern state and secular agencies.

The overall effect of such developments has been a significant decline in the numbers of those who actively participate in religious communities. Many simply do not see the point of religion, and those who do, tend to pursue self-oriented, non-institutional, private forms of 'spirituality'.

Secularization

While there is a general consensus regarding secularization, there are competing theories as to the details of the process itself. Four main varieties of secularization theory can be usefully distinguished: the disappearance thesis; the differentiation thesis; the de-intensification thesis; and the co-existence thesis. The disappearance thesis, which reflects the nineteenth-century theories of Émile *Durkheim and Max *Weber, claims that religion will effectively disappear in modern societies. Similarly, Karl *Marx predicted the displacement of religion by a new 'communist society'. The differentiation thesis is more cautious, in that it argues that, while religion will retain some significance in private life, it is becoming increasingly insignificant in social life. The de-intensification thesis claims that religion will continue to have a nominal presence in society, but only in a de-intensified, weak and insubstantial form, such as a way of investing births, marriages and deaths with some form of social significance. The coexistence thesis is more positive. It argues that, while secularization takes place in particular social contexts, in other contexts religions retain their vitality, and even grow. As we will see below, some have observed that in other areas of the world, modernization has not led to secularization.

Secularization theories can also be categorized according to the particular processes of modernization identified as its principal causes. First, differentiation theories argue that the roots of secularization are to be located in the processes of 'functional' differentiation. The various functions of modern society (health, education, social services, and so on) become increasingly disengaged from religion. Secondly, theories which focus on 'rationalization' argue that secularization can be understood by attending to the processes by which a modern society becomes rationalized, bureaucratized and science-oriented in its modes of operation. Gradually, science, technology and bureaucracy dominate our understanding of the world, thereby making magic and the supernatural redundant. Thirdly, there are theories which focus on pluralization. These observe that the awareness that others hold different beliefs tends to erode an exclusive commitment to one's own beliefs and thus promotes secularization of the mind (micro-level secularization). How do I know that my own beliefs are true and not culturally relative? Perhaps *all* religious beliefs are culturally relative? Fourthly, theories which focus on individualization argue that the process by which authority is internalized is damaging to religion, since religious institutions seek to have authority over people, rather than allowing individuals to make their own choices and follow their own paths. In other words, in modern societies when the authority of the self is challenged by traditional religion, it tends to be traditional religion that suffers. Finally, following Durkheim, theories which maintain that religion flourishes at the level of the local community argue that, because the modern period has witnessed the progress of urbanization and a decline in local communities, secularization is inevitable.

So far the focus has been on religion in Western societies. However, some sociologists have argued that, just because modernization in Europe has led to secularization, does not mean that this will always and everywhere be the case. Modernization may be hostile to religion, but religions can adapt and survive depending on a number of contextual variables. For example, Peter Berger, one of the principal architects of 'the disappearance thesis', changed his mind in later life and encouraged us to consider the 'desecularization of the world'. We should not assume that the Western relationship between modernization and religion is the only one, for it is clear that modernization in other parts of the world has not led to the erosion of religion. In fact, religion beyond the West seems to be thriving. Indeed, there are now several versions of modernity and modernization gaining ground, including the notion of multiple modernities, not all of which entail secularization to the same degree.

Even in the West, strong theories of secularization that predict the disappearance of religion are being challenged by those who encourage us to look beyond traditional institutional religion. For example, while the 'turn to the self' in modern societies has contributed to the decline of traditional mainstream religion, it has also contributed to the rise of new self-oriented beliefs. In other words, what we are witnessing in the West may be less a case of the decline of religion and more a case of the relocation of religion. Some scholars have framed this in terms of a shift from 'religion' to '*spirituality'. While religious behaviours like church attendance have declined, belief in the supernatural, the paranormal, and the spiritual significance of the self remains high. Hence, the evidence suggests that, while theistic notions of a transcendent deity have suffered, there is a turn to more immanent and 'holistic' forms of spirituality. Sometimes termed 'self religion', this process has more to do with the cultivation of a unique subjective life than with conforming to divinely revealed norms. Rather than turning to traditional authorities, Western modernity has encouraged individuals to create and re-create themselves, carving out their own paths and constructing their own identities. It is not surprising, therefore, that 'religion' is giving way to new forms of 'spirituality' that offer the enhancement and cultivation of unique subjective lives. Personal growth becomes identified with spiritual growth (see *New religions).

While modern societies are typically characterized by a distrust of religion, and often hostility to it, nevertheless its presence is increasingly felt and its discourses used in 'the public sphere'. Hence, many now make use of the term 'post-secular' to describe the ways in which non-secular belief persists in secular contexts. However we understand the post-secular (and there are a variety of interpretations), it seems clear that there is a tension between the processes of secularization/disenchantment and sacralization/re-enchantment. The secular is challenged, not only by the ubiquitous presence of non-secular discourses in, for example, popular culture (typically involving paranormal phenomena), but also by the migration of communities from parts of the world where religion is still important and by the presence of religion in the media. All of this makes adherence to strong theories of secularization increasingly difficult to maintain.

In the final analysis, secularization is a powerful theory largely because it appears to make sense of what most people observe to be obviously the case, namely that societies are becoming progressively less religious. However, significant evidence of spiritual growth in Western societies has led to softer versions of secularization and, in some cases, to substantial revisions. Moreover, many now argue that, while secularization is taking place in some contexts, in other contexts we are witnessing some form of 're-enchantment'.

Bibliography

J. Beckford, 'Public Religions and the Post-secular: Critical Reflections', *Journal for the Scientific Study of Religion* 51 (2012), pp. 1–19; P. Berger (ed.), *The Desecularization of the World* (Grand Rapids, 2000); S. Bruce, *Secularization: In Defence of an Unfashionable Theory* (Oxford, 2011); K. Dobbelaere, *Secularization: An Analysis at Three Levels* (Frankfurt, 2002); P. Heelas and L. Woodhead, *The Spiritual Revolution* (Oxford, 2005); C. Partridge, *The Re-Enchantment of the West*, 2 vols. (London, 2004, 2006); K. Wiegandt and H. Joas (eds.), *Secularization and the World Religions* (Liverpool, 2009); B. Wilson, *Religion in Secular Society* (London, 1966); L. Woodhead and P. Heelas, *Religion in Modern Times* (Oxford, 2000).

C. Partridge

SEMI-PELAGIANISM

Semi-Pelagianism was a largely monastic movement of reaction against *Augustine's developed anti-*Pelagian teachings (and hence more fittingly called Semi-Augustinianism; 'Semi-Pelagian' is found no earlier than the sixteenth century). This 'revolt of the monasteries' began in Roman Africa in 427, evoking from Augustine *Grace and Free Will* and *Correction and Grace* in response to critics of his *Letter 194*. When he heard of monastic disaffection in South Gaul, where John Cassian's teaching breathed an *Origenist optimism (cf. P. Munz in *JEH* 11, 1960, pp. 1–22), Augustine wrote *The Predestination of the Saints* and *The Gift of Perseverance*. Controversy continued after his death (430), with his weightiest critic, Vincent of Lérins (see *Catholicity), whose famous *Commonitory* implicitly faults his 'non-catholic' doctrine, and Prosper of Aquitaine (*c*. 390–*c*. 463) his tireless champion. Later, Faustus of Riez (*c*. 408–*c*. 490) and Fulgentius of Ruspe (468–533) represented the two positions.

Eventually, Bishop Caesarius of Arles (*c*. 470–542) convened the Second Council of Orange in 529, which condemned Semi-Pelagian (and Pelagian) doctrines and endorsed a qualified Augustinian theology. Its decrees, compiled by Caesarius partly from Prosper's digest of Augustine, rejected *predestination to evil, affirmed that with God's *grace we can fulfil his will, and were silent on such issues as irresistible grace, the fate of unbaptized infants and the manner of transmission of original sin.

The initial point of difference concerned 'the beginning of *faith'. Augustine's critics insisted that this was an act of unaided human freedom, although grace instantly strengthened incipient faith. Augustine held that 'the will is prepared by God' by prevenient grace alone. The assault soon extended to the 'fixed quota' who were alone predestined to salvation and granted such grace, the abandonment of the rest of the 'mass of perdition' to just condemnation, the irresistibility of grace in the elect and their infallible *perseverance to the end. Objection was also taken to Augustine's denial that God 'willed all people to be saved', which even Prosper eventually abandoned.

This anti-Augustinianism arose in part out of a monastic spirituality anxious lest fatalism should encourage lethargy (monastic *accidie*) and make rebuke and exhortation, not to say prayer and evangelism, pointless. Although Augustine feared a recrudescence of Pelagianism proper, these 'semi-Augustinians' affirmed original sin and the necessity of grace for salvation, but sought a balanced antimony between grace and freedom, disliked the resort to God's hidden counsels in election and doubted whether a just predestination could avoid being based on foreknowledge.

The doctrinal issues opened up in these decades have reappeared regularly, especially in the sixteenth to eighteenth centuries (see *Jesuit theology) and in the ceaseless 'Calvinist (see *Reformed theology) vs. *Arminian' debate in modern evangelicalism.

Bibliography

Prosper's Works, tr. P. De Letter, ACW 14 (1952) and 32 (1963); E. Amann in *DTC* 14 (1941), cols. 1796–1850; P. Brown, *Augustine of Hippo* (London, 1967); N. K. Chadwick, *Poetry and Letters in Early Christian Gaul* (London, 1955); O. Chadwick, *John Cassian* (Cambridge, ²1968); G. Fritz in *DTC* 11 (1931), cols. 1087–1103; J. Pelikan, *The Christian Tradition, 1: The Emergence of the Catholic Tradition (100–600)* (Chicago, 1971); G. Weigel, *Faustus of Riez* (Philadelphia, 1938); F. H. Woods, *The Canons of the Second Council of Orange* (Oxford, 1882).

D. F. WRIGHT

SESSION OF CHRIST, see ASCENSION

SEVENTH-DAY ADVENTISM

In the late 1820s William Miller (1782–1849), a New England farmer and later Baptist preacher, became convinced by his study of the Bible that the Second Coming (Advent, see *Eschatology) would take place within the next few years. He began to proclaim this publicly, and a significant number of his hearers joined his 'Adventist' movement. Miller's expectation that the Advent would take place between spring 1843 and spring 1844 proved unfounded, but one of his followers proposed 22 October 1844 as the day of the parousia, and Miller eventually and reluctantly endorsed this. After the 'Great Disappointment' of that date, many of the faithful (including Miller) returned to their original church allegiance, but some formed new Adventist churches. The most prominent of these is the Seventh-day Adventist (SDA) Church, which came together in 1863 as an amalgamation of three continuing 'Millerite' groups: (1) a group led by Joseph Bates (1792–1872), a retired sea captain who had become convinced by his study of the Bible and by contact with Seventh-Day Baptists that Saturday (the seventh day) should be observed as the Christian *Sabbath; (2) a group led by Hiram Edson (1806–82), whose insight was that biblical prophecy did indeed point to 22 October 1844, but that Miller's understanding of its significance had been in error, and that that date marked the heavenly beginning of the last *judgment which would be executed on earth at the second coming (date unspecified); (3) a group formed around the prophetic ministry of Ellen Gould Harmon, later White, (1827–1915), whose visions served to comfort the disappointed, and later to endorse the teachings of the other two groups. These in turn accepted Ellen White's prophetic gift.

Despite its North American origins and administrative centre, the church has been missionary from a very early stage (its first official missionary, J. N. Andrews [1829–83], began work in Switzerland in 1874), and today of a world membership of more than 17 million (as of June 2011) fewer than one in ten lives in North America and the church can be found in 209 of the 232 countries and areas recognized by the UN.

Although the church in principle rejects any official creed, believing with many evangelicals that creedal statements leave the believer unable to accept any 'new light' which God may choose to reveal, in practice its faith is enshrined in the 'Fundamental Beliefs', which have varied in number over time, but currently stand at twenty-eight. (They were last revised in 2005.) These affirm many articles of faith to which most *evangelical Christians would also assent. For example, the first Belief affirms that the Bible is the inspired word of God in which he 'has committed to man the knowledge necessary for salvation'. Other central evangelical doctrines affirmed in the Fundamental Beliefs include the *Trinity (Nos. 2–5), the *fall (No. 7), the deity of *Christ, his *incarnation and his substitutionary *atonement in death and resurrection (Nos. 4 and 9). Some other of the Fundamental Beliefs, though less mainstream, are nonetheless held in common with some in the evangelical world: 'soul sleep', for example (No. 26), and the requirement that members refrain from tobacco and alcohol, though the addition here of 'the foods regarded as unclean in the Scriptures' is less usual (No. 22). However, the distinctively SDA doctrines which, as mentioned above, lie at the foundation of the church itself – the prophetic witness of Ellen White (No. 18); the perpetual nature of the seventh-day Sabbath (No. 20); and the eschatological significance of the 1844 message, with the corollary that the second coming will soon take place (No. 24) – take SDAs away from mainstream evangelical thought. These teachings lead to a self-identification of the SDA Church as God's remnant church for the last days (affirmed in No. 13), which has often led the church to take a triumphalist and isolationist stand, making co-operation with more mainstream Christian groups difficult and, as far as many on the SDA side are concerned, both undesirable and unnecessary.

One of the earliest significant critics of the SDA faith was D. M. Canright (1840–1919), originally a protégé of Ellen White and her husband James, and an SDA minister for almost twenty years. In his books, published after he left the SDA Church, he charged the SDAs with teaching works-centred salvation (the Sabbath doctrine), and Ellen White with plagiarism and false prophecy. Though the SDA Church has often attempted to refute them, these charges continue to underpin the fundamental unease felt by many evangelicals confronted by its teaching.

Bibliography and resources

Resources: The official SDA website is www.adventist.org. The official Ellen G. White website (www.whiteestate.org) includes historical and apologetic resources and links to online texts of works by and about her, including the official biography in six volumes by her grandson, Arthur L. White. Canright's works (*Seventh-day Adventism Renounced*; *The Lord's Day from Neither Catholics Nor Pagans*; and *The Life of Mrs Ellen G. White*) can be found at various anti SDA websites (e.g. www.truthorfables.com). (All online resources accessed February 2013.)

Bibliography: M. Bull and K. Lockhart, *Seeking a Sanctuary* (Bloomington, ²2006); General Conference of Seventh-Day Advent, *Seventh-Day Adventists Believe* (Nampa, ²2005); R. Numbers, *Prophetess of Health* (Grand Rapids, ²2008).

I. Graham

SEXUALITY

The subject of sexuality is undoubtedly an important one in contemporary Christian theology. Disagreements over it threaten unity among Christians, and the church's traditional teaching is also increasingly a challenge to Western society and thus significant in the church's *mission. It is important to recognize the breadth covered by the concept and acknowledge that the term is often not sharply defined. This article introduces five main areas of theological importance.

Male and female

Central to a Christian understanding of human sexuality is the Creator's differentiation of human beings, as creatures made in God's *image into male and female (Gen. 1:27; 2:18–25). This is reaffirmed by Jesus in the Gospels (Mark 10:6–9) and also shapes apostolic teaching on sexuality (1 Cor. 7; Eph. 5:21–33), although being male and female is now to be understood in the light of our unity in Christ (1 Cor. 11:8–12; Gal. 3:28).

The significance of this sexual differentiation received little detailed attention from early patristic theologians. They held various views ranging from the irrelevance of sexual difference to our humanity (Tatian), through to emphasizing the dangers and temptations sexual differentiation brings (Tertullian), limiting its significance to procreation (Clement) or even apparently seeing it as part of God's response to the fall (Gregory of Nyssa). As in many areas relating to sexuality, *Augustine's thought has proved particularly influential on later Christian tradition. He establishes the goodness of sexual difference and traces its importance through the drama of creation, God's *redemption of our fallen state and the eschatological consummation. This view became the largely unexamined Christian consensus through the medieval period and the Reformation. In recent theology a number of both Protestant (Karl *Barth) and Roman Catholic (Hans Urs von *Balthasar, Pope John Paul II) theologians have developed more systematic accounts of what it means to be male and female within their theological anthropologies. In their different ways they all highlight the importance of sexual differentiation for human *fellowship and relationship.

The issue is of contemporary significance in four main areas. First, there are ongoing debates, especially among evangelical Christians, about whether the fundamental equality of men and women is compatible with a belief in male headship and whether Scripture teaches such a hierarchical view of the relationship between the sexes (see *Ministry). Second, the extent to which, beyond biology, any differences claimed between men and women are essential and part of God's created purpose or simply social constructions of *gender identity. Third, the importance of *feminist theology. Fourth, in ethics, a theology of sexual differentiation is vital for the development of a Christian response to homosexuality and transsexuality.

Sexual desire

Scripture speaks positively of sexual desire between men and women (Gen. 2:23; Song; 1 Cor. 7:3), but also warns against lust and disordered and excessive sexual desire (2 Sam 11; Rom. 1:24), often described in terms of concupiscence within the Christian tradition. From early in church history, the latter negative emphasis has often predominated in Christian attitudes to sex. At times this has viewed all sexual pleasure in a negative light and effectively denied the goodness of being created as sexual and bodily creatures through an exaggerated *asceticism or a *dualistic understanding of humanity which has emphasized the spirit over the body and even denigrated the body and sexuality. In recent decades, the pendulum has swung back the other way with a rediscovery of a positive Christian understanding of sexual desire (e.g. Pope John Paul II's *Theology of the Body*). In some writers (e.g. James Nelson's 'body theology' and Carter Heyward's 'erotic theology') this has led to an exaltation of *eros* that departs from biblical and traditional sexual norms. In wider society, the understanding of human sexuality in terms of sexual desire is increasingly being replaced by the language of sexual orientation. This conceptualization of human sexuality in terms of a fixed, settled sexual attraction to someone of the opposite (heterosexual) or same (homosexual) sex or people of both sexes (bisexual) is only beginning to be subjected to theological analysis and critique.

Sexual identity

An important recent cultural development is the phenomenon of relating sexuality to personal identity. This has arisen as a result of a number of factors, including greater openness about sexual matters, the concept of sexual orientation and the social organization and political mobilization of groups whose sexuality has in the past led to their marginalization or persecution. Originally focused on homosexuality, the number of possible sexual identities has continued to expand and diversify further, especially among young people. These sexual identities are also now beginning to find their own distinctive theological voice in the development of gay and lesbian theologies (discussed in Elizabeth Stuart's *Gay and Lesbian Theologies*, Oxford, 2003) and *queer theology (the best guide now being Gerard Loughlin [ed.], *Queer Theology: Rethinking the Western Body*, Oxford, 2007). These new approaches increasingly extend beyond discussion of sexuality into wider, more traditional, theological subjects. It remains to be seen whether these will become as theologically influential as other contextual theologies such as *liberation theology and *black theology, but this is unlikely for at least two reasons. First, they generally work from presuppositions opposed to traditional Christian teaching on sexuality. Secondly, many Christians believe the creation of identities based on sexuality is false, even idolatrous, and a denial that our identity is given us by God in creation and in Christ: 'At the deepest ontological level, therefore, there is no such thing as "a" homosexual or "a" heterosexual; there are human beings, male and female, called to redeemed humanity in Christ, endowed with a complex variety of emotional potentialities and threatened by a complex variety of forms of alienation' (St Andrew's Day Statement, 1995).

Sexual behaviour

Scripture includes both general warnings against sexual immorality (*porneia*, e.g. Matt. 15:19; Acts 15:20; 1 Cor. 6:18) and a significant number of prohibitions relating to specific sexual behaviour. These have then been expanded within later Christian tradition. In evaluating sexual behaviour, Christian *moral theology has emphasized the procreational (Gen. 1:28) and relational (Gen. 2:18–24) goods of sexual intercourse and the divine gift of marriage between a man and a woman as the proper context for sexual union (Gen. 2:24; Exod. 20:14; Heb. 13:4). The emphasis on procreation led to the condemnation of various practices not explicitly addressed in Scripture, including masturbation, various forms of non-procreative sexual behaviour (e.g. oral and anal sex) and the use of contraception. The latter is still rejected by the official teaching of the Roman Catholic Church, but accepted by most Protestant Christians. In much contemporary Christian sexual ethics the focus of moral evaluation has shifted to the relational good of sexual behaviour and the existence of a loving relationship. Thus traditional teaching against adultery, promiscuity, paedophilia and prostitution continues to be upheld, but other non-marital sexual behaviour is more acceptable to some Christians (e.g. Adrian Thatcher, *Liberating Sex*, London, 1993).

A particular area of contention concerns homosexual behaviour. This is consistently condemned in both the OT (Lev. 18:22; 20:13) and NT (Rom. 1: 24–27; 1 Cor. 6:9–10; 1 Tim 1:9–10) and is also seen by most of the Christian tradition as unnatural sexual behaviour. A number of scholars have, however, challenged this negative stance. They have argued for a more positive response to homosexual behaviour in loving relationships. This is either because they believe the biblical prohibitions are more narrow (e.g. restricted to cultic, abusive or pederastic sexual conduct) or because of alleged new understanding of homosexuality unavailable to the biblical writers. However, the majority of biblical scholarship and almost all Christian churches are not persuaded by these claims.

The Christian church has also strongly insisted, in contrast to much contemporary popular thinking, that sexual behaviour is not essential to human flourishing. In fact, the church honours those who, like Christ himself, commit themselves to sexual abstinence, and the early and medieval church particularly exalted virginity and celibacy.

Sexual relationships

Christian moral theology has traditionally commended marriage – a lifelong, exclusive, monogamous relationship – between a man and a woman as the only holy form of sexual relationship. Augustine defended marriage (*On the Good of Marriage*) in the face of some negative Christian evaluation and excessive exaltation of celibacy. His account of the three goods of marriage (offspring, faithfulness and sacrament) shaped the Christian tradition and is still central to much contemporary sexual ethics. Marriage is significant in Christian theology both as a created institution (Gen. 2) and as a symbol of God's covenant love for his people (Hos., Eph. 5) (see *Family).

Current debates about marriage focus on its beginning and ending. The rapid rise in cohabitation has led some to question traditional teaching against all premarital sex. A strong case can, however, still be made that the meaning, significance, symbolism and consequences of sexual union all point to it being fitting only within a marital relationship. Christians have for centuries disagreed over what circumstances, other than death, can bring an end to a marriage in such a way as to make a further marriage legitimate. Those with a strong view of indissolubility reject all remarriage after divorce, some believe Scripture allows remarriage after adultery (the Matthean exception, Matt. 19:1–12) or desertion by an unbelieving spouse (the Pauline privilege, 1 Cor. 7), while others allow remarriage in other circumstances. There are also debates as to whether same-sex relationships can be treated as marriage or as equivalent to marriage.

Bibliography

C. Ash, *Marriage: Sex in the Service of God* (IVP, 2003); T. Bradshaw (ed.), *The Way Forward? Christian Voices on Homosexuality and the Church* (Hodder & Stoughton, 1997); P. E. Engle and M. L. Strauss (eds.), *Remarriage after Divorce in Today's Church: 3 Views* (Zondervan, 2006); R. Gagnon, *The Bible & Homosexual Practice* (Abingdon Press, 2001); S. Grenz, *Sexual Ethics: An Evangelical Perspective* (Westminster John Knox Press, 1999); R. B. Hays, *The Moral Vision of the New Testament* (New York, 1996), pp. 379–406;

O. O'Donovan, *A Conversation Waiting to Begin: The Churches and the Gay Controversy* (London, 2009), published in USA as *Church in Crisis: The Gay Controversy and the Anglican Communion* (Eugene, 2008); D. Peterson, *Holiness and Sexuality: Homosexuality in a Biblical Context* (Milton Keynes, 2004); P. Ramsey, *One Flesh: A Christian View of Sex Within, Outside and Before Marriage* (Grove Books, 1977); D. W. Torrance (ed.), *God, Family and Sexuality* (Edinburgh, 1997).

A. GODDARD

SHINTOISM AND CHRISTIANITY

Shintoism is a naturalistic cosmic religion, an *animistic *polytheism. It represents the original worldview and way of life of the Japanese. Its central concept is *kami*. (The Chinese character pronounced *kami* on its own is pronounced *shin* in combination.) *Kami* is usually translated as 'god' or 'gods', but also means 'above', 'superior' or 'divine'. *Kami* means anything sacred and/or extraordinary which arouses man's fear or respect (see R. *Otto). Shintoism claims that there exist 800 million *kami*, being manifested in the beneficent beauties of nature – mountains, trees, beasts and birds. Shinto shrines are dotted around the countryside. Humankind is also a part of this world, and can never be separated from it. Every being is part of the community of the entire universe and all share *kami* nature. When a person is purified (*harai*), he recovers his *kami* nature and restores his true self. In Shintoism, the heavenly and earthly realms are not sharply separated, nor the realms of life in this world and life after death. In many homes dead relatives are worshipped as *kami*, through *syncretism with ancestor worship.

The Shinto myths trace the origin of heaven and earth to the marriage of a male deity (Izanagi, he who invites) and a female deity (Iznami, she who is invited). This resulted in the birth of the sun goddess Amaterasu Oominokami. Her children came down to the human domain, and their descendant, Jimmu, is said to have been the first *tenno* (heavenly emperor) of Japan.

In the early history of Japan (fifth century AD), several clans fought to establish themselves as the political centre. Each clan possessed its clan *kami*, to whom the whole clan turned in the time of need. The leader of the clan acted as both chief priest and military commander. The *tenno* clan (whose leader has been *tenno* up to the present day) eventually united the whole country. This meant that the goddess of *tenno* was invincible. As a result, Shintoism came to play the central role in Japanese history as a patriotic imperial cult.

In the fifth and sixth centuries, Shintoism was influenced by *Confucianism and *Buddhism, which supplied respectively the ethics and the philosophy which Shintoism lacked. Shinto's simple naturalistic faith and practice became more theoretical and ritualistic. In the ninth century, a Buddhist interpreted the Shinto *kami* as local manifestations of the universal Buddha. This provided the philosophical explanation for the co-existence of these two religions (known as *Ryobu Shinto*), which lasted until the nineteenth century. Buddhist concepts of repeated rebirths (see *Metempsychosis) and of success and failure as the result of sins in earlier lives were syncretized with underlying Shinto beliefs.

Christianity came to Japan on three occasions in history as the religious element of foreign aggression. It was first introduced to Japan by the pioneer Jesuit Francis Xavier (1502–52) in 1549. At that time, Japan was nominally ruled by *tenno*, but was actually divided among feudal lords. In such a situation, Christianity spread rather rapidly and claimed several Christian feudal lords. After the Tokugawa Shogunate consolidated its political power (1603), it severely persecuted Christians because they pledged allegiance to God rather than to Shogun. It also isolated the country to prevent Christian influence.

As soon as Japan reopened after 250 years of seclusion (1854), Protestant Christian missionaries arrived and were initially successful. In 1868, the Tokugawa Shogunate was overthrown and the Meiji imperial government was established. This government introduced several Western social, educational, political and military structures, including monarchy. The leaders of the government argued that Christianity was too individualistic for the Japanese Empire and Buddhism too weak to solidify the country. They chose Shintoism to play the role which Christianity had played in European monarchies. This was the origin of state Shintoism in Japan. A rescript read daily in schools between 1889 and 1945 declared that Japan was 'the nation of the *kami*'. When nationalists and militarists thus utilized state Shintoism to enhance Japanese nationalism,

Christians were again faced with the choice between worshipping God or the emperor, as were the Christians in the early Roman Empire. The defeat of the Japanese Empire in 1945 was seen as the failure of the *kami*kaze ('divine wind') to protect the country. This caused a serious loss of face for the *kami*, and weakened Shinto for a time.

The twentieth-century interdenominational mission also began with some success, but today Japanese Christians see attempts to reinstate Shinto as the state religion as threatening. They feel that any check on Japan's economic empire might mean a return to militarism sanctioned by Shinto as a nationalist patriotic movement.

Most Christian services in Japan begin with reference to seasons or weather, which may be either desirable *contextualization in recognition of the true Creator or syncretism with Shinto! The Christian concepts of sin and cleansing are difficult to understand if one holds Buddhist preconceptions, but the Shinto ideas of defilement and ritual cleansing (perhaps explaining why the Japanese bathe far more frequently than other humans) provide a helpful way of illustrating how the Bible thinks of sin and cleansing. Outward cleansing of the body is meant to be accompanied by a cleansing of the heart.

Little theological cross-fertilization has taken place between Christianity and Shinto. The anti-Buddhist Shinto restorationist, Hirata Atsutane (1776–1843), was partly influenced by a Christian understanding of God, and some Christian elements have been incorporated into sect Shinto. An extreme 'Japanese Christianity' has only rarely been advocated. K. Kitamori's (1916–98) *Theology of the Pain of God* (1946; ET, Richmond, 1965) is a deliberate theological attempt to speak to Japanese culture.

Another writer whose theology has sought to be explicitly sensitive to Japanese tradition and experience, particularly after the atomic bombing of Hiroshima, is Kosuke Koyama, notably in *Mount Fuji and Mount Sinai: A Pilgrimage in Theology* (London, 1984).

Bibliography

Agency for Cultural Affairs, *Japanese Religion* (Tokyo and Palo Alto, 1972); H. B. Earhart, *Religion in the Japanese Experience* (Encino and Belmont, 1974); R. Hammer, *Japan's Religious Ferment: Christian Presence amid Faiths Old and New* (London, 1961); J. M. Kitagawa, *Religion in Japanese History* (New York and London, 1966); C. Michalson, *Japanese Contributions to Christian Theology* (Richmond, 1965); S. D. B. Picken, *Shinto: Japan's Spiritual Roots* (Tokyo and New York, 1980); F. Rambelli and M. Teeuwen, *Buddhas and Kami in Japan: Honji Suijaku as a Combinatory Paradigm* (London, 2002).

S. P. Kanemoto and M. C. Griffiths

SIBBES, RICHARD (*c.* 1577–1635)

Richard Sibbes [also Sibbs, Sibs] of Tostock, Suffolk, matriculated at St John's College, Cambridge in 1595, where he earned a full slate of theological degrees including a DD. Sibbes was a noted speaker, elected St John's college preacher, Sunday lecturer at Holy Trinity Church, Cambridge, and concurrently, preacher at Gray's Inn, London. He was also elected Master of St Catherine's College, Cambridge.

Sibbes combined irenic personal qualities with a certain theological boldness. In ministry he was a moderate, submitting to the ecclesial requirements of his day, yet he twice drew formal rebukes from William Laud. In his mature theology he was widely respected by virtually all English Reformed ministers despite his rejection of the newly imported and increasingly popular federal theology (see *Covenant) from Heidelberg. Sibbes dismissed the bilateral covenant of federalists and instead preached God's unilateral triune *love as a 'spreading goodness' that woos, converts and transforms souls. The Father, Sibbes held, embraces the church in love just as he does Christ. This presumed a real – not merely juridical – union of Christ and the church under the rubric of mystical marital, a position he held in alignment with *Bernard of Clairvaux, *Luther and *Calvin. Such a relational understanding of *grace dismissed the federal return to a Thomistic model of grace – as a newly created and morally enabling *habitus* – that held faith to be a human act of will offered as a human *quid pro quo* to God's infused grace that then gains salvation. Sibbes, against this, held faith to be a simple response of a formerly disaffected heart to God's disclosures of love.

In Lutheran fashion, Sibbes held that the new covenant of the gospel replaces the old covenant and called for an affective *spirituality that relies on the Spirit's immediate presence and work of illuminating the Scriptures as a guide for daily life. Thus a love for God is the central feature of spirituality, an affection engendered in the converted soul by the Spirit's immediate witness to God's prior love. Sibbes also dismissed speculative or rationalistic theologies – citing John Calvin's similar resistance – and showed no interest in composing a systematic theology.

Bibliography

Works: *Works of Richard Sibbes*, ed. A. Grosart, 7 vols. (Edinburgh, 1862–4).

Studies: M. E. Dever, *Richard Sibbes: Puritanism and Calvinism in Late Elizabethan and Early Stuart England* (Macon, 2000); R. N. Frost, ' "The Bruised Reed" by Richard Sibbes', in K. Kapic and R. Gleason (eds.), *The Devoted Life: An Invitation to the Puritan Classics* (Downers Grove, 2004).

R. N. FROST

SICKNESS, see HEALING

SIMONS, MENNO (1496–1561)

Menno Simons, a Dutch Catholic priest, demurred from eucharistic sacramentalism and infant baptism, leading him eventually into the *Anabaptist movement, which he served as pastor and theologian. Gathering together scattered and demoralized Anabaptists after the disastrous and atypical attempt to seize control of Münster, he resisted spiritualizing and apocalyptic tendencies and established peaceful and disciplined congregations from which the worldwide *Mennonite Church eventually developed.

Menno's theology was evangelical with one exception: though insisting Christ was fully human and fully divine, he taught that Jesus did not take flesh 'from' Mary but 'in' Mary. This doctrine of the 'celestial flesh', which he defended increasingly reluctantly, he had inherited from the Spiritualists via Melchior Hoffman, who founded Dutch Anabaptism.

Menno regarded *Christendom as more deeply flawed than the Magisterial Reformers acknowledged and urged a more *radical reformation. He also distrusted scholarly biblical interpretation, which he perceived as often evading the challenge of simply obeying Scripture. He sought a pure church, free from state control, comprised of true disciples, who were baptized as believers, were morally distinctive and exercised mutual admonition. He regarded as essential for church membership new birth and readiness to take up the cross.

Menno adopted a Christocentric hermeneutic (quoting 1 Cor. 3:11 in all his writings) and insisted Jesus' teaching and example were ethically normative, superseding OT practices. Consequently, Christians must not wield the sword or swear oaths, but speak the truth always and be prepared to suffer rather than fight. Menno shared the widespread – and socially disturbing – Anabaptist commitment to economic radicalism, including simple living and open-handed generosity.

Bibliography

W. E. Keeney, *Dutch Anabaptist Thought and Practice 1539–1564* (Nieuwkoop, 1968); C. A. Snyder, *Anabaptist History and Theology* (Kitchener, 1995); J. C. Wenger (ed.), *The Complete Writings of Menno Simons c. 1496–1561* (Scottdale, 1984).

S. W. MURRAY WILLIAMS

SIMPLICITY, DIVINE

'Divine simplicity' is the doctrine that *God is not composite. To be composite is in some sense to be imperfect, or less than ultimate (every composite being necessarily has a prior cause that caused its parts to cohere). Thus if God is perfect and Creator of all, God must be simple.

Divine simplicity implies that God could not be in any way other than he is without ceasing to be himself ('God's essence is his existence'). From this, it follows that God is identical with his perfections (his love, power, wisdom, etc.). Modern discussions of simplicity derive from this the claim that God's perfections are identical with each other: God's love is identical to his power, and so on. This move was resisted by many in the medieval tradition: *Thomas Aquinas insisted that there was real distinction between God's attributes, which did not amount to division (*Comm. Sent.* Lib.1); Maimonides accepted the argument, but circumvented the conclusion by denying that God has any properties to be identical with each other (*Guide for the Perplexed*). Classical accounts of divine simplicity were in fact more interested in the identity of God's being with his activity than in any account of the unity of properties.

The idea of divine simplicity was generally accepted until the Enlightenment, but is now disputed. Some deny that the idea itself is logically coherent: if God is identical to his properties, then God would appear to be merely a property, and this seems a difficult or nonsensical position. A second line of criticism accepts that God could be simple, but argues that this is incompatible with other aspects of traditional religious concepts of deity: a simple God cannot, it might be argued, be personal, or active within history, or triune, or able to become incarnate. Some have responded to this by downplaying the significance of divine simplicity, claiming it is merely an *apophatic guide to certain things that must not be claimed about God. More robust defences typically turn on a suggestion that at one point or another an illegitimate assumption has been made, one that holds true for human beings but need not hold true for God.

Bibliography

C. Hughes, *On a Complex Theory of a Simple God: An Investigation into Aquinas' Philosophical Theology* (London, 1989); B. Miller, *A Most Unlikely God: A Philosophical Enquiry into the Nature of God* (London, 1996); S. R. Holmes, 'Something Much Too Plain to Say: Towards a Defence of the Doctrine of Divine Simplicity', *NZSTh* 43, 2001, pp. 137–154.

S. R. Holmes

SIN

According to one influential Protestant catechism, sin is 'any want of conformity unto, or transgression of, the law of God' (*Westminster Shorter Catechism*, Q. 14). If this is how it is defined, then sin has a particular relation to the moral law, but there have been those in the Western theological tradition who have conceived of it as principally privative in nature (e.g. Augustine). There are differences between the way in which Eastern and Western Christians have thought about sin. In this article, the Western tradition is the primary focus of attention.

Unlike the Chalcedonian doctrine of Christ's two natures of 451, there is no single account of sin that the whole catholic church has approved. That said, there are accounts of sin that ecumenical councils of the church have deemed unorthodox. One such is the *Pelagian theory of sin. This states that the significantly free moral choices of human agents are uncaused by anything other than the agent themselves, and even then, not caused by previous choices made by the human agent. In addition, Pelagians teach that humans are without original sin and that all human sin is a result of imitation, not transmission from Adam to his progeny. So my sin is learnt from my elders and my peers. I do not inherit, or have imputed to me, some vitiated moral nature which predisposes me to sin. This theory of sin, which denies original sin, was the object of *Augustine of Hippo's ire, and was eventually anathematized at the Council of Carthage in 418.

But other theories have been put forward since then, and they are often different in important points of detail. Some such theories are properly designated 'concepts of original sin', whereas others are less specific than that, attempting merely to account for the prevalence of sin in human society. One example of the latter sort of theory is that of Immanuel *Kant, but that is a philosophical rather than a theological approach.

There are several distinct problems to be tackled in any full-orbed theological account of original sin. The first has to do with the nature of sin: what is original sin? The second concerns the transmission of sin from *Adam to his progeny, particularly how it is just for God to transmit or impute to me the sinful condition and guilt of Adam's primal sin. The latter issue has to do with the penal consequences of sin, and how Christ *atones for sin. In addition to these issues, there is the problem of the authorship of sin, but that is related more to questions of *theodicy.

Concerning the nature of sin, the Augustinian tradition took the view that, in sinning, Adam and Eve lost original *righteousness, that state of moral uprightness with which they were created (see *Fall). Additionally, many post-Reformation theologians took the view that Adam and Eve incurred a *macula*, or deformity of soul as a result of sin, which disordered their moral natures. (Some Protestants, like Huldrych *Zwingli, preferred to speak of sin as a *Präst* or disease, rather like some medieval theologians. But this has not found favour with many Protestant theologians.) This deformity of soul is often thought to be itself heinous in the sight of God independent of any actual sin a given human agent performs. If so, then even if – *per impossibile* – someone were never to commit an actual sin, but had the property of original sin, such an individual would be barred from entering heaven on account of the heinousness of their moral state in the eyes of God. Infants who die prematurely, and perhaps the insane and severely mentally handicapped, may fall into such a category. But many theologians have thought that such individuals are not moral agents and therefore not capable of being damnable or salvable, or perhaps are salvable as a class, rather than individually. Some in the Calvinist tradition (see *Reformed theology) have taught that such individuals are treated by God in just the same way as the rest of humanity, and are either elect or reprobate depending on the divine will. Still others, notably (until recently) *Roman Catholics, taught that many such agents were confined to a region on the outskirts of hell called the *limbus infantum, where they remain in something like a state of everlasting suspended animation.

In addition to the deformity of soul, which leaves all of Adam's progeny with a fallen human nature, there is original *guilt. This is often thought to comprise the *reatus poenae* (liability to punishment – on account of possessing original sin), and the *reatus culpae* (liability to guilt). The sinner, so the story goes, is guilty for Adam's sin and therefore punishable for Adam's sin, just as Adam himself was, because he acts as our representative, or because we are somehow united with Adam. Christ's atonement may deal with the penal consequences of sin, the *reatus poenae*, so that the sinner herself need not suffer in hell the *punishment due for her sin. But she remains the one guilty of possessing original sin – the *reatus culpae*. And, of course, she is also guilty of any actual sin she commits in addition to the deposit of original sin she has inherited, or had imputed to her, by God. For this reason, some theologians, like Jonathan *Edwards, speak of a double guilt: for original sin, and for one's actual sin. Christ's work may deal with the penal consequences of both, according to such Protestant thinkers.

There are real problems for a full-orbed doctrine of original sin. One problem has to do with the biblical parallel between the first Adam and the second (e.g. Rom. 5: 2–19). If Christ deals with the sin brought about by the first Adam, how are we to square this theological commitment with the findings of modern evolutionary biology? Was there a first human pair, and if so, did they 'fall' from some higher moral state to a lower one – and if they did, what could this mean? This cluster of problems has been almost universally ignored in modern theology. But this simply will not do, given the important relation between sin and *salvation.

Another issue has to do with the justice of imputing the sin of one guilty person to another. This has two aspects. First, how can God justly impute Adam's sin to me? Why am I punished for the sin of someone who lived many years before me? This seems monumentally unjust. The second aspect to this issue concerns how the penal consequences of my sin can be transferred to Christ, who is sinless and guiltless. Surely it is unjust for an innocent *substitute to be punished in my place. Yet Christ does just this (on certain views of the *atonement). There are theological responses to these problems. One of these, popular in the Reformed tradition, is to suppose God treats me 'as if' I were guilty of Adam's sin, where Adam is the representative of the whole race, rather like one might have a representative in a senate who makes decisions on behalf of the populace of a republic. The same sort of reasoning could be applied to my relation to Christ, although the relation here is a spiritual, rather than a natural, one. God treats Christ 'as if' he was the guilty party and punishes him in my stead. Again, there are precedents for this: the payment of a fine need not be demanded of the guilty party if a substitute is willing to step in. But these solutions rely on a sort of forensic, or pecuniary, 'fiction' whereby God acts *as if* I am guilty of Adam's sin, or Christ is guilty of my sin. And some theologians have found this profoundly unconvincing.

There is an alternative view. This stems from St Augustine, and is called Augustinian realism. It says that Adam and his progeny are somehow one metaphysical entity such that God may 'pass on' Adam's sin to me because he and I are parts of one greater whole, in a way analogous to my arm and my foot being parts of a larger organic whole, namely, my body. But even if sense can be made of this, how can it apply to my relation to Christ? The Saviour and the sinner are surely not parts of one metaphysical whole. At least, almost all Augustinian realists writing about the imputation of Adam's sin have baulked at applying similar reasoning to the union of the *regenerate sinner with Christ. There is a minority report in the Reformed tradition that has taken this view (the Puritan Tobias Crisp nods in this direction, as did some advocates of the *Mercersburg theology in the United States). This is difficult theological territory. But perhaps it is no more difficult than well-known contemporary philosophical problems with the composition of objects. Tibbles the cat has parts that are not ginger, like his claws. Still, he is a ginger cat. Christ and the regenerate may be parts of one whole object in the mind of God, call it 'redeemed humanity'. The fact that Christ atones for the sin of other 'parts' of this object does not necessarily mean Christ is a sinner. Analogously, Tibbles's claws being part of a ginger cat does not mean his claws are ginger. Yet they are claws of a whole object that is a ginger cat. Perhaps Christ is part of a whole object including all regenerate sinners, who are somehow mystically united together through the agency of the Holy Spirit, without confusing the different parts of this metaphysical object. This hardly constitutes a complete solution to this particular issue, but it may provide the beginnings of an interesting answer to an ancient theological conundrum.

See also: ESCHATOLOGY; JUDGMENT OF GOD.

Bibliography

Anselm of Canterbury, *On The Virgin Conception and Original Sin in Anselm of Canterbury, The Major Works*, eds. B. Davies and G. Evans (Oxford, 1997); Augustine, *Enchiridion*, tr. E. Evans (London, 1953); H. Blocher, *Original Sin: Illuminating the Riddle* (Leicester, 1997); J. Edwards, *Original Sin: The Works of Jonathan Edwards*, vol. 3, ed. C. A. Holbrook (New Haven, 1980); J. Murray, *The Imputation of Adam's Sin* (Grand Rapids, 1959); P. L. Quinn, 'Original Sin, Radical Evil, and Moral Identity', *Faith and Philosophy* 1, 1984, pp. 188–202; R. Swinburne, *Responsibility and Atonement* (Oxford, 1989); Thomas Aquinas, *On Evil [De Malo]*, tr. J. A. Oesterle and J. T. Oesterle (Notre Dame, 1995); T. Wiley, *Original Sin: Origins, Developments, Contemporary Meanings* (New York, 2002); N. P. Williams, *The Ideas of the Fall and of Original Sin* (London, 1927).

O. D. CRISP AND M. JENSON

SINLESSNESS OF CHRIST

The belief in the sinlessness of *Jesus in the history of the church grew out of reflection on a variety of biblical texts (e.g. Isa. 53:9; John 8:46; 2 Cor. 5:21; 1 Pet. 2:22; 3:18; Heb. 4:15; 7:26; 9:14; 1 John 3:5). Often its theological significance has been viewed primarily in soteriological terms (see *Salvation), in which the redemption of sinful humanity is linked with the purity of a holy and sinless Messiah. Such thinking is exemplified by the medieval theologian *Anselm, who argued that Jesus' sinlessness meant he never dishonoured God and thus he was free from the need to die. Therefore Jesus, by his voluntary death as the perfect God-man, was enabled to serve as an *atonement for others (see his *Cur Deus Homo*).

In modern theology the idea of the sinlessness of Christ has taken a number of interesting turns. Classic liberal theology, while denying that Jesus was incapable of sinning, still often placed a tremendous emphasis on the fact that Christ did not sin. *Schleiermacher, for example, declared Jesus' sinlessness as his 'absolute perfection' which distinguished him from the rest of humanity. In the followers of A. *Ritschl, a reconceived view of the sinlessness of Jesus becomes a kind of proof of his divine status.

One of the debates surrounding the sinlessness of Jesus in the past two centuries is based on the question of whether the Son of God assumed a 'fallen' (cf. 'sinful flesh') or 'unfallen' human nature. While it is sometimes debated, the evidence seems to be that the early Fathers generally affirmed that he assumed a human nature free from sin (cf. *Adam before the fall). Such an understanding appears to be the dominant position throughout the history of the church (see *Christology), but some clarification was needed.

Edward *Irving notably argued that the Son of God assumed a 'fallen' human nature, arguing that an 'unfallen' nature is unintelligible in a postlapsarian world. The concern of Irving, and those who would embrace a similar view (e.g. Barth, Torrance, etc.), grows out of a real fear of creeping *docetism in the church. The worry is clear: if the Son did not assume a 'fallen' human nature, then he must have assumed a generic nature which was not like those he came to redeem, and thus he becomes unable to act as their Saviour.

Others have responded by arguing that the Son did assume an 'unfallen' human nature, that from birth he was free from guilt and sin, and that only on the cross did he voluntarily become (i.e. assume) the sins of humanity. His temptations were real, but they did not arise from 'internal' corruption. The concern here is also clear: to say the Son assumed a 'fallen' human nature sounds to many as if Jesus was tainted with personal guilt and sin, compromising his holiness.

Sadly, often this disagreement comes more from misunderstanding than substance, since neither side appears eager to say that Jesus was either personally guilty of sin, nor was he anything less than fully human and genuinely tempted. The debate centres around what is implied by the idea of 'fallen'. Substantively, some questions require further debate, such as Jesus' relationship to original sin, how the Spirit empowers and keeps Jesus holy, how to maintain the integrity of the two natures without compromising the truth that Jesus is truly God and truly man.

Part of the confusion surrounding the sinlessness of Jesus grows out of historical developments which, although intending to heighten the doctrine, may have merely muddied the waters. Primarily through *Augustine, the discussion shifted from the extraordinary faithfulness of Jesus in resisting temptation (stressed in the temptation narratives and Hebrews), to the metaphysical conditions for Christ to be sinless from birth. Thus, the *virgin birth was given in Augustine (and many of the creeds) the significance of breaking the bond of sexually transmitted original sin. This line of reasoning is one contributing factor to understanding historic discussions about the status of Jesus' mother and the development of the doctrine of her immaculate conception (see *Mary).

More recently, discussions about the sinlessness of Jesus have focused on the Spirit's work not merely at conception, but throughout the life, death, resurrection and ascension of Jesus.

See also: FALL; SIN.

Bibliography

D. Bathrellos, 'The Sinlessness of Jesus: A Theological Exploration in the Light of Trinitarian Theology', in P. L. Metzger (ed.), *Trinitarian Soundings in Systematic Theology* (New York, 2005); O. Crisp, 'Did Christ Have a *Fallen* Human Nature?' *International Journal of Systematic Theology* 6, 2004, pp. 270–288; K. M. Kapic, 'The Son's Assumption of a Human Nature: A Call for Clarity', *International Journal of Systematic Theology* 3, 2001, pp. 154–166; D. Macleod, *The Person of Christ* (Downers Grove, 1998); G. W. P. McFarlane, *Christ and the Spirit: The Doctrine of the Incarnation According to Edward Irving* (Carlisle, 1996); T. F. Torrance, 'The Mind of Christ in Worship: The Problem of Apollinarianism in the Liturgy', in T. F. Torrance, *Theology in Reconciliation* (London, 1975); C. Ullmann, *The Sinlessness of Jesus* (Edinburgh, 1870); T. Weinandy, *In the Likeness of Sinful Flesh: An Essay on the Humanity of Christ* (Edinburgh, 1993).

K. M. KAPIC

SLAVERY

Slavery is a social institution justifying the involuntary servitude of individuals who are treated as property. Slave owners often held the power of life and death over their slaves. Historically, slavery has existed throughout the world in most periods of history. It was divided into two forms: commercial and household slavery. Commercial, or productive, slavery involved the largest number of slaves, in mines, industrial production and farming, where they were often literally worked to death.

The most surprising fact about slavery is how very little attention it has received from scholars apart from extensive discussions of the transatlantic slave trade (TST), which was actually only a small part of the overall picture. For example, almost all ancient civilizations, including Assyria, Babylon, Egypt, Greece, Rome, Persia and Sumer, were based on slavery, yet historians, particularly art historians, either overlook slavery altogether or simply mention it in passing. Even when slavery is discussed, it is usually in terms of the relatively well-treated domestic slaves, while those who were brutally treated in manufacturing are ignored.

Similarly, the role of slaves as the basis of economic production in China, India, other parts of Asia, the Middle East and most traditional societies is usually overlooked by anthropologists and historians. As Rodney Stark points out, it was not until 1990 that the Smithsonian Institute in Washington fully recognized the role of slavery among Northwest Coast native societies. Yet up to one third of Northwest Coast natives were enslaved by other native peoples to form the productive base of their economies.

The ancient Hebrews accepted and traded in slaves (Gen. 14:14; 17:23; 24:35; 26:14; Job 1:3). In theory at least, Hebrew slavery was comparatively humane, lacking the harshness found in many other cultures, to the extent that slaves were accorded some protection under the law (Exod. 12:44; 21:20–21, 26–27). To what extent these laws were enforced in actual cases is hard to determine. In the Hebrew Bible the idea of slavery was used to illustrate the relationship between God and his people Israel. The Israelites were pictured as being redeemed from Egyptian slavery by the historic deeds of Yahweh (Exod. 20:2; Deut. 5:6). As a result, the Hebrews believed that they had become the slaves of God and were dependent on him. For this reason they could neither live for themselves alone nor worship other gods (Lev. 25:42, 55; Exod. 20:2–6). A similar use of the imagery of slavery is to be found in the NT, where Christians are described as slaves of God (Rom. 1:1; 1 Pet. 2:16).

Although early Christians owned slaves and the institution is not condemned in the NT (Matt. 18:23; 1 Cor. 7:21; Phlm.), early Christian writings display a significantly changed attitude towards slaves which reveals an awareness that they are people made in the image of God (cf. Eph. 6:5–8; Col. 3:22 – 4:1; Titus 2:9–10; *The Shepherd of Hermas*). Slowly a new realization that slavery was sin grew up in Christian lands, with people like St Bathilde (d. 680), the wife of Clovis II (d. 656), working to free slaves and abolish slavery; St Ansgar (801–65), who evangelized Scandinavia, also worked hard for the abolition of slavery.

In the Byzantine Empire the monasteries and many clergy worked against slavery, with the result that laws were passed limiting the number of slaves a monastery could accept as free men. The Byzantines also enacted legislation to allow former owners to regain their slaves from monastic institutions under specific conditions. Nevertheless, by the eleventh century Byzantine slavery was in decline, although it continued to flourish in Byzantine-influenced areas like Kiev and later Russia, where it only began to decline in the seventeenth century.

All the great medieval monastic orders of Western Europe accepted slaves as free men and refused to own slaves. The Holy Roman Emperor, Conrad II (990–1039), supported by the pope, forbade traffic in slaves, thus taking a stand that is unique among world religions. During the eleventh century, St Wulfstan (1008–95), the only English bishop allowed to retain his post after the Norman Conquest, worked ceaselessly to end the slave trade centred on Bristol. Together with Anselm he urged William the Conqueror (1027–87) to support abolition, practically bringing an end to slavery in Britain. Consequently, by the twelfth or thirteenth century slavery had virtually disappeared in north-western Europe, with the result that *Thomas Aquinas, who taught that slavery was a sin, regarded it as something practised by Muslims and people living on the edge of civilization. Various popes threw their weight behind Aquinas's teachings, leading to a series of official papal pronouncements against slavery of which those of Pope Paul III (1468–1549) are a good example.

Until recently the role of papal decrees in mitigating the evils of slavery has been dismissed by most scholars as insignificant, while statements like that of Pope Paul III, who confirmed the right of clergy to own slaves as late as 1548, have been highlighted. This dismissal of Roman Catholic criticisms of slavery has been challenged by Rodney Stark on the basis of statistical evidence showing that following the Reformation slaves were far better off in Catholic than Protestant lands because papal teachings had a significant beneficial influence on the way slaves were treated while promoting the freeing of slaves on a large scale.

Aquinas's judgment that slavery flourished in border areas and the Islamic world may seem harsh today, given the claim of contemporary Muslim apologists that the Qur'an regulates slavery in Sura IV. However, this overlooks the fact that regulation is not abolition. Further, the claim that Mohammed freed some of his slaves also overlooks the fact that he kept many more. Thus both the Qur'an and Mohammed's example actually justify slavery, as all the major traditions of Islamic law readily affirm. Similarly, both Buddhist and Hindu scriptures accept slavery as part of the established order, while temple slaves were common in both religious traditions.

The neglect of slavery in most history books, be they textbooks or academic monographs, has created the perception that the issue of slavery centres on the TST, which many people interpret to mean plantation slavery in what is today the United States of America. This distorted view overlooks the fact that the TST centred on the Caribbean rather than mainland America. In fact the number of slaves imported to what became the US was relatively small. They numbered around half a million between the first shipments of slaves to Manhattan Island by the Dutch in 1626 to the banning of slave imports by the American government in 1808. By contrast, over a million slaves were imported into Barbados and Jamaica. It is equally important to recognize that during the same period French, Portuguese and Spanish ships imported large numbers of African slaves to the Americas.

Despite the grim conditions on slave ships and the enormous suffering caused by this vile trade, the impact of the TST dims in comparison to slavery as a global institution. The TST ravaged Africa between 1579 and 1807, causing between 5 and 12 million Africans to be enslaved. However, this number is small compared to estimates of the number of Africans enslaved by Muslim slavers from the eighth century to the present, which range from 10 to 200 million.

Apart from distorting the extent to which slavery existed in the past, concentration on the TST has also caused slavery to be viewed in racial terms, creating the impression that most slaves were black. Actually, throughout history the majority were enslaved regardless of race. For example, after the Battle of Lepanto (1571) over 15,000 European slaves were freed. Since most of the galleys in the Muslim fleet were sunk, the total of European slaves, who were chained to their posts, was probably ten times that number. Similarly, at least one million Europeans were enslaved in North Africa at the beginning of the nineteenth century.

During the eighteenth century various Protestant Christian writers sought to develop a theological defence of slavery. Probably the first of such works to be written in America was John Saffin's *A True and Particular Narrative . . . and A Brief and Candid Answer . . .* Both were tracts published in Boston in 1701 which sought to justify slavery as a perpetual institution created by God and ordained in Scripture. Saffin also attempted to refute the anti-slavery arguments of Judge Samuel Sewall, who attacked the institution of slavery in his *The Selling of Joseph . . .* (Boston, 1700).

Throughout the eighteenth and nineteenth centuries many other theological defences of slavery appeared. In 1772 Thomas Thompson produced *The Trade in Negro Slaves on the African Coast in Accordance with Humane Principles and with the Laws of Revealed Religions*. Later, in the 1850s Samuel A. Cartwright argued that it was impossible to 'civilize' or 'Christianize' Africans who were not slaves. In defending slavery, numerous arguments were developed, such as those linking black Africans with the curse of Ham (Gen. 9:22–27) and the notation that slaves were receiving a 'just' punishment for their corrupt natures. Josiah Priest's *Bible Defence of Slavery* (Glasgow, 1852) even argued that Lev. 18:8 indicated that Ham's sexual perversions led to slavery. Later nineteenth-century theologians in the American South, such as Robert Lewis Dabney (1820–98), did immense harm by building the defence of slavery into their theology. In these works the Confederate States were romanticized in what was essentially a pro-slavery civil religion. All these arguments eventually gave way before the force of the reasonable criticisms of slavery and the zeal of evangelical reformers.

The writings of Jean-Jacques Rousseau (1712–78) and Thomas Paine (1737–1809) led the early modern attack on slavery. Unfortunately, with the notable exception of Paine, Rousseau and other Enlightenment thinkers, such as David *Hume, also promoted vicious racial stereotypes of Africans while denouncing slavery.

It was devout Christians who pursued the cause of abolition in Britain with the utmost vigour by arguing that African slaves were equal in all respects to other people. In 1772, Grandville Sharp (1735–1813) began a campaign for the suppression of slavery. John *Wesley and the *Methodists took up the challenge, as did William Wilberforce (1759–1833) and the Anglican Clapham Sect in England. Quakers, Presbyterians and Baptists all campaigned against the slave trade. Supported by these Christian abolitionists, talks and writing by freed slaves, such as Olaudah Equiano (c. 1745–97), whose autobiography *The Interesting Narrative of the Life of Olaudah Equiano or Gustavus Vassa, the African* (1789) is a classic anti-slavery tract, made a great impact on the public mind.

Eventually the slave trade was outlawed in Britain in 1807, and in 1808 the foreign slave trade was prohibited in the United States. In 1833 slavery was abolished in the British Empire and the Royal Navy engaged in a vigorous campaign to suppress it at sea. On land David Livingston (1813–73) exposed the realities of the internal African slave trade and fought for its abolition. During much of the nineteenth century, missionary endeavour in Africa, such as the founding of Blantyre in Malawi, was part of the strategy of 'Christianity, commerce and civilization', which was intended to build up self-sufficient African communities large and powerful enough to resist raids by well-armed slave traders.

In America Christians of all persuasions, including Unitarians centred around Boston and men like the journalist William Lloyd Garrison (1805–79), joined the attack on slavery. The biggest impact, however, was made by the Congregationalist Harriet Elizabeth Beecher Stowe (1811–96), whose best-selling novel *Uncle Tom's Cabin* (1851) made an enormous impact on public thinking. Slavery was finally abolished after the Civil War in 1865.

Today traditional forms of slavery still exist in many societies, although they receive little attention and are generally considered a dead issue. Perhaps even more extensive is the growth of sex-based slavery that exploits women from former communist countries in places as far apart as Britain and Korea. Consequently, a renewed awareness of the continuation of slavery has led to the rebirth or reinvigoration of anti-slavery societies on both sides of the Atlantic, which is a sad comment on our times.

Bibliography

B. Lewis, *Race and Slavery in the Middle East* (New York, 1990); P. E. Lovejoy, 'Volume of the Atlantic Slave Trade', *Journal of African History* 23, 1982, pp. 473–501; J. J. Miller, 'The Unknown Slavery: In the Muslim World, That Is – and It's Not Over', *The National Review*, 54, 2002, pp. 41–43; G. Milton, *White Gold: The Extraordinary Story of Thomas Pellow and Islam's One Million White Slaves* (New York, 2005); A. Porter, '"Christianity and Commerce": The Rise and Fall of a Nineteenth-Century Missionary Slogan', *The Historical Journal*, 28, 1985, pp. 597–621; R. Stark, *For the Glory of God* (Princeton, 2003).

Websites: Anti-Slavery International, <http://www.antislavery.org>; Anti-Slavery Society, <http://www.anti-slaverysociety.addr.com/society.htm>; American Anti-Slavery Society, <http://www.anti-slaverysociety.addr.com/amass1.htm>.

I. HEXHAM

SOBORNOST

In Russian *sobor* means both 'church' and 'synod' or 'council'. No single English word can do justice to *sobornost*. Its use to characterize Orthodoxy's distinctive vision of the *church dates from the Russian Orthodox lay theologian Alexis S. Khomyakov (1804–60). In his view the genius of Orthodoxy lay in avoiding the polar weaknesses of Romanism (unity imposed externally from above) and of Protestantism (individualistic liberty), in a unique synthesis of freedom and unanimity, diversity and unity. This *sobornost*, or communal unity by free association in Christ, finds significant expression in the church *council, where harmony is attained by free consultation. Khomyakov also made much of the 'reception' of conciliar decisions by the church as a whole. The *sobornost* of the church is a kind of organic spiritual catholicity and conciliarity. In ecumenical discussion *sobornost* has become almost a shorthand description of Orthodoxy's distinctive approach to ecclesiology. Somewhat comparable concepts in Anglican and Roman usage are *koinonia* and (in more limited contexts) *conciliarity and collegiality.

See also: RUSSIAN ORTHODOX THEOLOGY.

Bibliography

S. Bulgakov, *The Orthodox Church* (London, 1935); A. S. Khomyakov, 'The Church Is One', in W. J. Birkbeck (ed.), *Russia and the English Church During the Last Fifty Years*, vol. 1 (London, 1969 [1895]); N. Zernov, *Three Russian Prophets* (London, 1944).

D. F. WRIGHT

SOBRINO, JON (b. 1938)

Jon Sobrino was born into a Roman Catholic family in the Basque country of Spain in 1938. At eighteen he entered the *Jesuit order and at twenty was sent to El Salvador. He attained an MA in mechanical engineering at St Louis (1965) and his doctorate in theology at Frankfurt (1975). Returning to El Salvador he became involved in *liberation theology. In 1989, when right-wing militia invaded the university and murdered six Jesuit professors, a housekeeper, and her daughter, Sobrino was in Thailand lecturing. Despite the violence,

Sobrino remained an outspoken advocate of peace and reconciliation.

Although Sobrino has published on diverse subjects such as peace, ethics, spirituality (particularly *Ignatian spirituality), ecclesiology and community, and biographies of martyred victims of the violence in Central America, his three controversial *Christological studies brought an investigation from the Vatican's Congregation for the Doctrine of the Faith. In 2007 a Notification was issued declaring that there were areas of Sobrino's Christological thought that were, 'erroneous or dangerous and may cause harm to the faithful'. Technically, this was not a form of censorship, but an indication of theological dissatisfaction by the Vatican.

Part of the controversy was about his methodology. He insisted that the 'Church of the poor' set the agenda for Christological investigation. The Vatican responded by stating that the foundation for theology is 'in the apostolic faith transmitted through the Church for all generations'. Yet early in *Jesus the Liberator*, Sobrino had written, 'Latin American Christology – and specifically as Christology – identifies its setting, in the sense of a real situation, as the poor of this world, and this situation is what must be present in and permeate any particular setting in which Christology is done' (p. 28). The Vatican was not against developing a theology for the poor (see *Poverty and wealth), but it rejected this type of *contextual theology as foundational.

Although Sobrino has never rejected the Nicene Creed (381) or the Chalcedonian Symbol (451), the Vatican also expressed reservations that in his writings the humanity of Christ tended to overwhelm his divinity. The Congregation for the Doctrine of the Faith never accused Sobrino of heresy, but insisted that Sobrino provide greater clarity about Christ's divine nature. At this time Jon Sobrino has not expressed any particular concern to alter any of his controversial statements on Christology.

Bibliography

Works: *Christology at the Crossroads* (ET, London, 1978); *Jesus the Liberator: A Historical-Theological Reading of Jesus of Nazareth* (ET, Tunbridge Wells, 1993); *Christ the Liberator: A View from the Victims* (ET, London, 2001).

Studies: L. Boff and C. Boff, *Introducing Liberation Theology* (ET, Tunbridge Wells, 1987).

D. L. RAINEY

SOCIAL ETHICS

From the days of Plato and Aristotle ethical thought has sought to contribute to human life in society. *Ethics seeks to clarify the underlying values which inform our understanding of our shared life in society and of its political practice. From the earliest days of Christian experience the church has sought to make principled sense of the social world in which it was set. Human beings are social animals. As persons called to know and love God our Creator and Redeemer, we are called to articulate what discipleship means for our place in the wider human community (see *Christian life).

Across the centuries of Christian social thinking Christian thought has produced a rich variety of traditions in this field. In the Catholic tradition (see *Roman Catholic theology), for example, with its debt to *Thomist theology, there is a strong commitment to the theme of natural law (see *Natural theology). From this tradition the church has sought to bring to the surface the inbuilt values and themes that make for healthy social living. The contemporary Catholic emphasis on 'The Common Good', which has attracted ecumenical support, is rooted in this tradition that there are given values built into the ways things are that we need to hold on to – justice, fairness, charity, to name a few.

Protestant thinking has developed parallel themes. The great social theologian of the middle of the twentieth century, Reinhold *Niebuhr, on the basis of his experience of ministry in the corporate industrial world of Detroit in the 1930s, believed that the Christian theme of agape love needed mediating through the principle of justice if it was to challenge the corporate realities of power. He went on, with great effect, to develop this theme in relation to the corrupt world of unaccountable political power facing the challenge first of Fascism and then of *Marxism.

British social ethical thinking, building on the foundations laid by Archbishop William *Temple, R. H. Tawney, J. H. *Oldham and others in the heart of the twentieth century, sought to develop the idea of 'middle axioms' as a way of mediating conversation between the Christian traditions and secular thought. R. H. Preston and latterly John Atherton have contributed to this tradition of Christian social ethical work.

Much of this came under challenge at the end of the twentieth century and into the twenty-first through the work of John *Milbank. His seminal work, *Theology and Social Theory*, sought to challenge the assumption of scientific objectivity in secular sociological thought and to recover a full Christian foundation for engagement with this field. This has led to a '*Radical Orthodoxy' as a Christian tradition holding to orthodox creedal faith and to a radical political and social agenda. This way of thinking can be seen to owe much to the *Barthian tradition of theological reasoning.

Others who believe that it is possible to move directly from biblical faith to social and political life include Alan Storkey whose *A Christian Social Perspective* remains a classic example of a tradition that is rooted partly in *Calvinist theology and in Anabaptist traditions.

On the edge of *Anabaptist life are the Mennonites and Amish communities, some of whom place strict limits on the way Christians should relate to the wider world. Distinctive in their thinking and practice are the *Quaker people who, with a strong radical understanding, engage with society believing that the light of God's Spirit is to be found across the human community. The debate will, without doubt, continue and be influenced by the way Christians sense their place in the society in which they are set and the opportunities and threats to Christian experience that they experience.

Bibliography

J. Atherton, *Christianity and the New Social Order* (London, 2011); G. Durham, *The Spirit of the Quakers* (Yale, 2010); R. J. Elford and S. Markham, *The Middle Way: Theology, Politics and Economics in the Later Thought of R. H. Preston*, Grove Booklets on Ethics (Cambridge, 2010); S. Hauerwas and C. Pinches, *Christians among the Virtues* (Chicago, 1997); C. Mathewes, *A Theology of Public Life* (Cambridge, 2007); J. Milbank, *Theology and Social Theory* (Oxford, UK and Cambridge, USA, 1990); R. Niebuhr, *Moral Man and Immoral Society* (New York, 1934); A. Storkey, *A Christian Social Perspective* (Leicester, 1979);

W. Temple, *Christianity and Social Order* (London, 1942).

J. Gladwin

SOCIAL GOSPEL

The Social Gospel was a loosely organized movement in North America from roughly 1880 to the start of the Great Depression (1929) which attempted to formulate a Christian response to the rapid social changes of the period. Its origins were both domestic and foreign. The strong link in the American revival tradition between personal holiness and social reform contributed to the movement; as did also the newer concern for scientific study of social problems that accompanied the rise of modern America after the Civil War. In addition, the example of Britons, like Thomas *Chalmers in Scotland or the *Christian Socialism of F. D. Maurice (1805–72), who attempted innovative Christian responses to the problems of industrial society, also influenced Americans desiring a Christian social reform.

Early expressions of the Social Gospel included the work of Washington Gladden (1836–1918), a Congregationalist minister in Springfield, Massachusetts, and Columbus, Ohio. While still in Massachusetts he had published *Working People and Their Employers* (1876), an appeal for fairness to workers. In his Ohio congregation were mine owners whose labourers struck twice in the mid-1880s for better wages and working conditions. Gladden's belief in the justice of their demands led to a more insistent appeal for the rights of labour and the application of the 'Golden Rule' to industrial organization. A different expression of the Social Gospel appeared in the work of Charles Sheldon (1857–1946), a clergyman from Topeka, Kansas, whose best-selling novel *In His Steps* (1897) presented a picture of what could happen in a community torn by social dissension if Christians would only ask themselves in every decision, 'What would Jesus do?'

The most important exponent of the Social Gospel was Walter *Rauschenbusch (1861–1918), a German-American Baptist who ministered for ten years in New York City's 'Hell's Kitchen' before becoming a professor of church history at Rochester Seminary in the state of New York. Rauschenbusch's first-hand experience of industrial exploitation and governmental indifference to workers made him a convinced critic of the established order. His fruitful relationships with New York City socialists like Henry George (1839–97) offered alternative models for social organization. But Rauschenbusch's main concern was to search the Scriptures for a message to the troubled circumstances of industrial society. The results of this search were published in 1907 as *Christianity and the Social Crisis*, a work that recalled the prophetic denunciations of OT prophets against social callousness as well as NT injunctions about the dangers of mammon. Rauschenbusch followed this work with other influential volumes, including *Prayers of the Social Awakening* (1910), *Christianizing the Social Order* (1912) and *A Theology for the Social Gospel* (1917). In these works Rauschenbusch combined a prophetic ideal of justice (see *Righteousness) with a commitment to building the *kingdom of God through the power of Christ.

The Social Gospel is often identified with theological *liberalism, and with some justice. Gladden, for example, was a popularizer of biblical higher criticism, and Rauschenbusch, though much more realistic about the intractably *fallen character of human nature, yet reinterpreted some traditionally supernatural elements of Christian doctrine. At the same time, however, themes of social service associated with the Social Gospel were also prominent among evangelical bodies such as the *Salvation Army or in individual evangelical leaders like A. J. Gordon (1836–1895) in Boston. Since the 1930s the Social Gospel has disappeared as a movement in its own right, but its influence remains, both in the more liberal, mainline denominations and in the renewed social concern displayed by American evangelicals since the 1960s.

See also: SOCIAL ETHICS; SOCIETY, THEOLOGY OF.

Bibliography

P. A. Carter, *Decline and Revival of the Social Gospel . . . 1920–1940* (New York, 1956); D. G. Gorell, *The Age of Social Responsibility: The Social Gospel in the Progressive Era, 1900–1920* (Marcon, 1988); R. T. Handy (ed.), *The Social Gospel in America, 1870–1920* (New York, 1966); C. H. Hopkins, *The Rise of the Social Gospel in American Protestantism 1865–1915* (New Haven, 1940); W. S. Hudson (ed.), *Walter Rauschenbusch: Selected Writings* (New York, 1984); P. T. Phillips, *A Kingdom on Earth: Anglo-American Social Christianity 1880–1940* (University Park, 1996); R. C. White, Jr, and C. H. Hopkins (eds.), *The Social Gospel: Religion and Reform in Changing America* (Philadelphia, 1976).

M. A. NOLL

SOCIETY, THEOLOGY OF

Early Christian understandings of society usually reflected the centrality of God to human relationships and institutions. They had some sense of the unity of the two great commandments: to love God and love neighbour as self. Relationships were God-given and formed; human beings indwelt them with norms of conduct and rightness given in the Scriptures. Paul, following Jesus, articulated these relationships and showed norms brought back into relationship with God.

This understanding was brought to the dominant cultures of the day. *Augustine showed that the city of God, the society of God, shown by God's revelation, transformed ordinary sinful relationships and institutions. Following the *Constantinian settlement Christianity partly settled down to dwell with Roman imperial rule. Sometimes this involved a sacred-secular dualism in which the domain of the church was set over and alongside the political and military power. Often the rule of Christ was acknowledged, but only partially and with a weak awareness of the principles of God's rule over all human society. This pattern continued through the Holy Roman Empire to medieval feudalism.

The medieval church tended to accept a hierarchical view of society in which imperial power or monarchy was sanctified before God and descending orders were seen as located in a traditional society. *Monastic orders sat outside such a view, and understandings of the mutuality of relationships, care of the poor and the equality of people before God were also part of the picture in medieval Catholicism.

The *Reformation developed a theme seen among some earlier groups, especially among *Anabaptist groups. They emphasized God's kingdom rule in the Christian community bringing interdependence, peace, reconciliation and the absence of hierarchy and human-based authority. This view looked more directly to NT relationships than had often occurred before, with an awareness of the transforming power of God though faith, love, peace and reconciliation. The long-term impact of the Reformation was to open up areas of society God-ward in a new way. *Work and industry became a calling before God. Marriage and *family life were seen in terms of covenantal love. The ruler was redefined as the servant of the people, and democratic participation based on citizenship rather than wealth or power was mooted by the Levellers and other groups. Common wealth was emphasized rather than accumulated wealth. Education opened up, both as being versed in the Scriptures and as the study of God's creation, heralding the great scientific revolution of the seventeenth century. The underlying effect was of society seen as open before God and plural in its institutions, though this effect was slower in Lutheran, Calvinist and Anglican theologies. Even great theologians like Calvin were partly locked into church and *state as their main institutional framework, following Catholic thinkers, so that they did not break out into a wider biblical theology of society, except in terms of practical precepts. *Baxter, in his *Directory*, and others teetered on the edge of a broader vision.

The *Counter-Reformation partly retreated into the institutional church as the overarching structure for a Christian society, increasingly compromised by a secular state, and in the *Enlightenment a similar *secularization of society emerged in the worldview, where natural processes, rather than God, were seen as governing state, the economy, and social forms. When sociology emerged, society was largely defined in self-referencing terms by Comte, Marx, Spencer and others. However, two developments took place which limited this secularizing dominance. The Catholic Church, after *Rerum Novarum*, began to think about society more fully, and the Reformational Movement associated with Abraham *Kuyper picked up on the underlying themes of Reformation theology and articulated them in terms of society. Kuyper identified the fact that the sovereign God has created human society and given it a plural institutional structure: of state, family, church, work, education and so on. This gave 'institutions' their original meaning, as instituted by God, and he also considered the different given purposes of these institutions as spheres of society, involving limits. He thus had a critique of totalitarianism in secular society, as it arrived. He also recognized that the *kingdom of God extended to all institutional areas of life and not just to institutional church life. The Christian response was therefore society-wide and not just narrowly churchy.

These were at odds with the secular statist and totalitarian philosophies developing in the late nineteenth and early twentieth centuries, often formed within historicist and social Darwinist perspectives. These sought to erode the integrity of church, family, education and other institutions, usually in the name of Fascist or Communist totalitarianism; apart from the Kuyperian tradition, there was no deep and strong enough theology to resist this trend. *Barth mounted a spirited theological opposition to the Nazis, though not with a full theology of society (see *Barmen Declaration). Theology had largely retreated from the arena. There was some Christian socialist thought addressing economic *poverty and exploitation, though partly in statist terms. *Temple, Tawney and the Christendom Trust opened up these themes in the 1920s to 50s. Other conservative theologies reacted to trends in *modernism in culture, family life and secularization, but few theologians were able to come to grips with the dominance of sociology in social and societal thought.

Yet, what did emerge was a slowly growing Christian theological and sociological alternative to secularism. Seminal was Jacques *Ellul. The Shaftesbury Project, the Ilkley Group and responses to the *Lausanne Covenant led to new bodies of work and new relationships between theologians and sociologists. Theologians of church, state, family, marriage, work and other areas began to identify the purposes and norms of these institutions in biblical and wider theology. These studies would examine problems in these areas and identify a Christian salvific response. Sin, expressed in culture, behaviour and the structure of relationships was identified as distorting the human relationship, not just with God, but also with one another. These studies were matched by biblical studies showing, in OT and NT, the place of relationships, institutions and whole societies in God's revelation. The prophetic concern for the state of societies and cultures before God was rediscovered as a consistent biblical emphasis by liberation theologians worldwide. John *Milbank and others opened up a theological critique of modernity in relation to social theory.

Overall, there is hope that a Christian theology of society will emerge from these studies, one that recognizes the centrality of God in all human relationships and the created structure of human life. It should also engage with the issues of relationship, *culture, change and testing that occur in these relationships, identifying the social forms of sin with which we struggle. Most of all, it should find Jesus the locus of saving persons and relationships, and in the gentle kingdom of God healing and *shalom* for much of what humankind suffers. There is hope that this will emerge, as secular sociology falters, but it is work in progress.

See also: SECULAR CHRISTIANITY.

Bibliography

R. Baxter, *The Christian Directory* (1673); J. Ellul, *The Technological Society* (London, 1965); A. Kuyper, *The Stone Lectures* (Edinburgh, 1899); Pope Leo XIII, *Rerum Novarum* (Rome, 1891); J. Milbank, *Theology and Social Theory: Beyond Secular Reason* (Oxford, 2006); A. Storkey, *A Christian Social Perspective* (Leicester, 1979); R. H. Tawney, *The Acquisitive Society* (London, 1921); E. Troeltsch, *The Social Teaching of the Christian Churches* (London, 1931).

A. STORKEY

SOCINUS AND SOCINIANISM

Two lay theologians of this name (Italian, Sozini, or Sozzini), Lelio (1525–62) and his nephew Faustus (1539–1604), had wide influence because of their persuasive reconstruction of early Christianity. The elder was one of many gifted Italian Protestant exiles. He travelled widely and discussed theology with *Calvin, *Melanchthon and *Bullinger. His learning, social status and attractive personality gave him many friends, though Calvin warned him about the spiritual dangers of his penchant for asking questions. His *Confession of Faith* (1555) used orthodox terms, but in an open-ended and enquiring manner which made some Protestants uneasy.

Faustus, largely self-educated, was a prolific writer of anonymous manuscripts. Though he did not attract the attention of the Holy Office while at the court of Isabella de Medici (1565–75), his early works show he had moved far from orthodoxy. As early as 1562 his *Explicatio* raised questions about the divinity of Christ, and in 1563 he rejected the natural *immortality of the soul. He defended the authority of the Scriptures on rational and historical grounds, rather than on the testimony of the Holy Spirit. In Basel, his *De Jesu Christo Servatore* (unpublished until 1594) dramatically reinterpreted the person and work of Christ, underlining their exemplary character.

He arrived in Poland in 1579, finding a congenial environment in the 'Minor Church'. Their simple biblical piety and quest for holiness had led to deep divisions. Socinus gave unifying leadership, which profoundly influenced younger ministers. He appears not to have been a church member since he refused believers' *baptism, but by his death he was the church's most authoritative spokesman. Those sharing his views began to be called Socinians. He was able to moderate their otherworldliness and rejection of the state, but repudiated any political resistance. Though he agreed with their anti-trinitarian theology, he guided them into a more coherent and reasoned theological position, which is well expressed in the Racovian Catechism (1605). Drawn up by Socinus' colleagues, it was very influential among Socinian churches and beyond. Emphasis on correct knowledge as the key to salvation was basic to its content. At many points, it differed from mainstream *Protestantism. Jesus did not die for *satisfaction of sin. His role was to inspire disciples to follow his example, for only those who persevered in obedience were raised from the dead.

As a system of belief and life, Socinianism appealed not only in Poland and Hungary, but to many distressed by bitter theological warfare, who sought a simpler biblical and more tolerant Christianity. The publication of Socinus' works gave his ideas wide currency. The move from a substitutionary understanding of *atonement, apologetic emphasis on Jesus' miracles and greater emphasis on the non-dogmatic interpretation of the Scriptures aroused bitter hostility. Nevertheless, the leavening influence of Socinianism continued to grow in the eighteenth century, especially with the rise of a more historical and critical approach to the Scriptures and the search for a rational rather than a revealed Christianity. By the end of the nineteenth century, Socinianism was no longer seen as one of the major threats to orthodoxy.

Bibliography

M. Martini, *Fausto Socino et la pensée socinienne* (Paris, 1967); H. J. McLachlan,

Socinianism in Seventeenth Century England (Oxford, 1951); S. Mortimer, *Reason and Religion in the English Revolution* (Cambridge, 2010); E. M. Wilbur, *History of Unitarianism*, 2 vols. (Cambridge, 1945–52); G. H. Williams, *The Polish Brethren*, 2 vols. (Chico, 1980).

I. BREWARD

SOCIOLOGY OF RELIGION

The founding fathers of sociology, Claude Saint-Simon (1760–1825) and Auguste Comte (1798–1857) were hostile to religion, believing it to belong to a past, less mature age. Yet each of the great classical sociologists who laid the foundations of modern sociology recognized the fundamental importance of *religion in shaping society. Emile Durkheim's (1858–1917) perspective was essentially collective. In *The Elementary Forms of Religious Life* (1912; ET, London, 1976) he divided the world into the sacred and the profane (the ordinary). Religious belief and ritual focused on the sacred and were collective representations of society itself. They had the function of producing social solidarity and regenerating ailing commitments.

Max *Weber, the greatest sociologist, had a more dynamic view of religion and a place for the individual social actor. He was fascinated by the theme of the increasing rationalization of his world and in *The Protestant Ethic and the Spirit of Capitalism* (1904–5; ET, London, 1965) explored the contribution Protestant, especially Puritan, religion made to rational capitalist behaviour. While shunning simplistic ideas, such as that Protestantism had caused *capitalism, he nonetheless believed that 'the Puritan stood at the cradle of modern economic man'. His investigations into other great world religions equally explained why such rational behaviour was prevented from developing among them. Weber's view may well have been formed in reaction to Karl *Marx. Marx argued that society advanced not because of ideas but on the basis of material interests. He viewed religion as an enemy of progress that by positing a false world, kept people dependent on a God or gods that did not exist. His views on religion were complex. He saw it as both a useful tool in the hands of the powerful to keep the oppressed enslaved, but also, in his famous 'opium of the people' comment, saw that religion was a way of dulling the pain of the oppressed. Only by doing away with religion would people overcome their alienation.

A further early contribution to a sociological understanding of religion was made by Ernst *Troeltsch, who in *The Social Teaching of the Christian Churches* (1912; ET, London, 1931), proposed a distinction between '*church' (an inclusive, hierarchical body which is established in a nation) and a '*sect' (a small-scale, exclusive and voluntary religious community). Subsequent discussion in relation to immigrant religions in the USA by H. Richard *Niebuhr, and the British experience by David Martin, led to the development of the concept of 'denomination'. This framework has proved extremely fertile in understanding religious organizations and especially the growth of modern sectarian religion. The concept of the sect was greatly advanced by Bryan Wilson (1926–2004) and his numerous research students. More recently, given the *postmodern context, Troeltsch's third category of *mysticism has resurfaced in the concept of the 'cult', which, as opposed to popular press definitions, in sociological terms speaks of an undogmatic and unorganized group that an individual can brush with to satisfy their religious quest at their convenience.

None of the classical sociologists was optimistic about the future of religion and this scepticism nurtured what became the reigning paradigm of the sociology of religion in the mid to late twentieth century, namely the theory of *secularization. Briefly stated, the *modern world was considered to be inhospitable to religion. A combination of factors, including the advance of science and technology, urbanization, pluralism and rationalization, were thought to undermine a religious worldview. The decline of religious practice and the marginalization of religion in society were produced as evidence. Key advocates of the theory included Bryan Wilson, Peter Berger (b. 1929) and, most recently, Steve Bruce (b. 1954). The evidence of religious vitality in the USA was always something of an embarrassment to the theory, as were the varying definitions of secularization employed by its proponents. Increasingly, the crude theory has been refined and much more attention paid to the variety of cultural histories that contribute to a nation's religious practice as well as a recognition of there being multiple modernities and trajectories that developed nations might follow. Rather than seeing the decline of religion in Europe as the typical pattern that others will follow, it is now more frequently seen as the exception that needs explaining in a world of global religious vitality.

Stephen Warner has pointed out that a new paradigm began to emerge in the late twentieth century that called into question some of the previous certainties of the discipline. Rational choice theorists used the perspective of economics to argue that religion was not irrational and that people made religious choices by calculating the cost-benefit involved as with any other purchase they made. They argued that the demand for religion was roughly constant and that variations of religious expression could not therefore be explained by a decline in demand but rather by variations of supply. Monopoly religious positions led to little participation because there was little 'marketing' of the faith, whereas the USA enjoyed a healthy religious economy because of the lack of an established religion and energetic religious competition. The theory has many deficiencies and is vigorously opposed by Bruce. But Berger has revised his earlier view and now sees pluralism not as undermining religious certainty but as contributing to its vitality.

A difference may be detected between those sociologists who write in a nuanced way with some sympathy for religion and those who write from a more detached position, leading to the question of the proper relationship between sociology and faith. In part this mirrors the long-standing debate as to whether sociology is an art or a science. The predominant stream, influenced by Weber, was to see it as an objective science which excluded any personal commitments, except in the choice of research topic. Berger was key in advocating that sociologists should 'bracket out' any personal religious commitments, lay aside questions of validity and approach religion as 'methodological atheists'. In practice such neutrality proves much harder to produce than in theory, as the writings of its advocates demonstrate. It also makes religion a phenomenon that is purely dependent on social factors, as in Berger's concept of 'plausibility structures' where he posits that the choice and maintenance of belief is heavily influenced by having a supportive group around the believer. Other sociological fields have long recognized the value of the personal commitment of its researchers, and the faith or lack of faith of sociologists of religion is now much more transparently acknowledged than previously.

With religion playing a significant role on the global political map, the discipline of sociology of religion is undergoing a creative and diverse phase. While many are looking at themes like fundamentalism or religious minorities, others are working at the impact of religion on everyday life, the role of women, and studying local congregations. While not providing the total explanation of religion, sociological insights can prove invaluable in a world and communities where religion remains a powerful and socially conditioned aspect of human experience.

Bibliography

P. Berger, *The Sacred Canopy: Elements of a Sociological Theory of Religion* (New York, 1967); idem (ed.), *The Desecularization of the West: Resurgent Religion and World Politics* (Grand Rapids, 1999); S. Bruce, *God Is Dead: Secularization in the West* (Oxford, 2002); G. Davie, *The Sociology of Religion* (Los Angeles and London, 2007); S. Warner, 'Work in Progress towards a New Paradigm for the Sociological Study of Religion in the United States', *American Journal of Sociology*, 98, 1993, pp. 1044–1093; B. Wilson, *Religion in Sociological Perspective* (Oxford, 1982); L. Young (ed.), *Rational Choice Theory and Religion: Summary and Assessment* (London, 1997).

D. J. TIDBALL

SOELLE, DOROTHEE (1929–2003)

Soelle was a radical German theologian, who was visiting professor at Union Theological Seminary in New York from 1975 to 1987. The major characteristics of her theology are her rejection of traditional *theism and her political hermeneutic. Her deep concern with the issues raised by Auschwitz (see *Holocaust) both led her to Christian faith and made the idea of God as omnipotent ruler of the world inconceivable. She shared the *Marxist criticism of traditional theism as putting people in a position of alienated dependence and encouraging the acceptance of suffering, instead of protest and political activity to abolish suffering. For Soelle, God is loving solidarity, not omnipotent superiority. She pursued this reconception of God to the extent that, in her work, God often seems to be only a symbol for human love, liberation and hope. In this she continued *Bultmann's programme of demythologizing (see *Myth), but she rejected Bultmann's *existential privatization of Christianity in favour of a political hermeneutic of the gospel. Existential concerns cannot be separated from the need for concrete application of the gospel to the oppressive realities of international politics. Soelle's passionate advocacy of a radical political theology was matched by personal involvement, especially in base communities and the peace movement of the 1980s.

Bibliography

Works: *Christ the Representative* (London, 1967); *Political Theology* (Philadelphia, 1974); *Suffering* (London, 1975); *The Inward Road and the Way Back* (London, 1979); *Thinking about God: An Introduction to Theology* (London, 1990); *Theology for Skeptics: Reflections on God* (Minneapolis, 1995); *Against the Wind: Memoir of a Radical Christian* (Minneapolis, 1999); *Dorothee Soelle: Essential Writings*, ed. D. L. Oliver (Maryknoll, 2006).

Studies: S. K. Pinnock (ed.), *The Theology of Dorothee Soelle* (Harrisburg, 2005).

R. J. BAUCKHAM

SONSHIP

The sonship of Jesus Christ

The portrait of *Jesus that emerges from Scripture quite clearly shows him to be the Son of God. Although the language of divine sonship is used sparingly in the OT (e.g. Exod. 4:22–23), it features prominently in the NT. It is frequently used of Jesus in the Synoptics, it is pervasive in the fourth Gospel, and it is common in Paul's writings and the rest of the NT. The sonship of Jesus was widely recognized by the early Christians, and it was just as widely understood to be central to his identity. But questions also abounded in the early Christian communities: does the fact that Jesus is a son also mean that he is a creature? Does sonship entail inferiority or subordination? Is Jesus the Son of God only in the *incarnation? Or does the sonship of Jesus reveal something about the nature of God?

Pre-*Nicene theology offered no consensus, and subsequent discussions served to heighten awareness of the importance of such questions. By the early fourth century, however, the Arian controversy brought these matters to the forefront of theological consciousness. The theology of *Arius and the early 'Arians' (not all of whom were members of a sharply distinguished Arian 'party') can be summarized as containing the following propositions. First, God was not always *Father; there was a time when he was simply God and not Father. Second, the Son is a creature, one who is created by God out of nothing. The third point is that there are several powers of God (subsequent to the creation of the Son), while the fourth point is that the Son is variable by nature and remains stable only by the grace of God (e.g. R. P. C. Hanson, *The Search for the Christian Doctrine of God*, pp. 20–23). Central to Arian teaching is the insistence that the Son is alien from the divine being and distinct from God – even though he can be called 'divine', he is not true God. The Son has been created for the purpose of mediation with the rest of creation, and, as a creature, his knowledge of God is imperfect. The Son is thus a created deity, a lower-order or secondary God.

Arius was happy to affirm that Jesus Christ is the Son of God; he was perfectly willing to affirm that the Son is 'begotten of the Father'. For the Arians, begetting and creating were synonymous, and to be begotten or created is to be dependent, subordinate and inferior. There is no common divine nature or substance; the Father and Son are of different essences. To be the 'Son' just *is* to be created, and of course all created beings are inferior to the One who is uncreated. The insistence of the 'Neo-Arians' of the mid-fourth century (e.g. Eunomius and Aetius) is even more pronounced: because names reveal the essence of things, and because ingenerateness is the exhaustive definition of God, then the Son who is generated must be *heteroousios* rather than *homoousios*.

To these challenges the pro-Nicenes responded with a variety of arguments. They produced exegetical arguments (from the divine works performed by the Son, from the names and titles of Christ, and from the witness to his pre-existence) to the conclusion that the Son is fully divine. They also argued that since only God is rightly worshipped, and since the worship of Jesus is universal among Christian believers and grounded in the Scriptures, then Jesus Christ must be fully and completely divine. Similarly, they argued that Jesus Christ must be fully divine because, while only God can truly be said to save us, all Christians believe that Jesus Christ is the Saviour of the world.

855

Thus they endorsed the statement that the Son is *homoousios* with the Father, and they concluded that the Son is equal to the Father in all things.

The importance of the *homoousion* for a proper understanding of the sonship of Christ was not lost upon *Athanasius and the other pro-Nicenes (perhaps most notably the Cappadocians, *Gregory of Nyssa, *Gregory of Nazianzus and *Basil of Ceasarea). They insisted that the Son is pre-existent and indeed eternal; there was no time when the Son did not exist. Furthermore, the Son is fully and truly divine, for his is not a diminished divinity. He is not subordinate to the Father in any way (other than his 'functional' or 'economic' subordination as incarnate). The Son is all that the Father is except Father, and the Son has all of the essential attributes of divinity. The Father and Son are equal in authority and power; neither the Father nor the Son have special abilities or powers not possessed by the other. Indeed, for much classical Christian theology any of the divine persons could have become incarnate. Moreover, the fact that the Son is fully divine has vast implications for our understanding of the nature of God: because God *is* Father and Son (and *Holy Spirit) the relations are inherent to the very being of God and are even essential. As the Father is Father only in relation to his Son, and as the Son is Son only in relation to his Father, so also the being of God is constituted in the loving relations of the intra-divine life.

Sons and daughters of God

The pro-Nicene theologians also understood the sonship of Jesus Christ to have implications for human identity and destiny. The only-begotten Son of God became incarnate in order that human persons could become by grace what he is by nature. Drawing from the NT language of *regeneration and adoption, these theologians insisted that salvation is entrance into God's own life of light and love. While our understanding of *salvation is to be informed by and consistent with the legal imagery of the NT, it cannot be limited to the categories of pardon and justification. Though not less than that, it is certainly more than that. While our status as creatures is never altered, we can experience spiritual adoption and regeneration. Because the Son of God became the Son of Man, we are enabled by his grace to 'receive the full rights' of children (Gal. 4:5), to cry '*Abba*, Father' (Gal. 4:6; Rom. 8:15), and indeed to 'participate in the divine nature' (2 Pet. 1:4).

See also: CHRISTOLOGY; GOD; TRINITY.

Bibliography

L. Ayres, *Nicaea and its Legacy: An Approach to Fourth-Century Trinitarianism* (Oxford, 2004); R. Cross, *The Metaphysics of the Incarnation* (Oxford, 2002); D. Fairbairn, *Grace and Christology in the Early Church* (Oxford, 2003); S. Gathercole, *The Pre-existent Son: Recovering the Christologies of Matthew, Mark, and Luke* (Grand Rapids, 2006); R. Hanson, *The Search for the Christian Doctrine of God: The Arian Controversy, 318–381 AD* (Edinburgh, 1988); T. Torrance, *The Trinitarian Faith: The Evangelical Theology of the Ancient Catholic Church* (Edinburgh, 1988); P. Widdicombe, *The Fatherhood of God from Origen to Athanasius* (Oxford, 1994).

T. McCALL

SOUL, see ANTHROPOLOGY; SOUL, ORIGIN OF

SOUL, ORIGIN OF

The way that one understands the origin of the soul depends on prior metaphysical presuppositions about what a soul is. As such, we shall consider first theories of soul origination that assume substance *dualism before briefly noting the different approach taken by a physicalist understanding of the soul.

How the soul comes to be

Pre-existentianism. As it merely makes the claim that the soul pre-existed the body, pre-existentianism is not itself a theory of the soul's origin. However, it has often been associated with an emanationist theory in which the soul emerges from God (as in some forms of *Gnosticism). The pre-existence of the soul was taught by Plato and was introduced to Christian theology by *Origen. In light of its speculative, unbiblical nature and its tendency toward a Gnostic devaluation of the body, pre-existentianism has remained a minor eccentricity in theological history.

Traducianism. Taking his cue from *Stoic thought, *Tertullian proposed that the soul is naturally propagated by human beings. This position was adopted by a number of Latin theologians and was later embraced by Martin *Luther and most subsequent Lutherans as well as a few Reformed theologians (e.g. William Shedd and Augustus Strong). Traducians argue that Adam's creation is unique (Gen. 2:7), such that human beings, like other creatures, were designed to create progeny naturally after their kind. Traducians have disagreed over how the soul is propagated, but most have argued that the process includes some form of seminal presence, a notion that they claim has biblical warrant (e.g. Heb. 7:10) and grounds a realist theory of *Adamic headship.

Creationism. The predominant theory in Eastern Christianity, and more recently in both the Catholic and Reformed traditions, the creationist position affirms that God directly creates the soul. Creationists appeal to a number of texts (e.g. Zech. 12:1), but such passages are indeterminate at best and do not clearly exclude God's creation through mediate causes. Creationists also believe their theory provides a means to ensure Christ's incarnation without fallenness, though critics charge that the theory makes God complicit in evil since he either directly creates a depraved soul, or creates a pure soul that is joined to a depraved body.

When the soul comes to be

While there has been no settled opinion on when souls come to exist, Aristotle's views (especially as mediated by *Thomas Aquinas) have been very influential. He argued that the soul proceeds through three developmental phases (vegetative, sensate and rational) with the last, constituting ensoulment proper, beginning at forty days gestation for males and eighty days for females. More recently, many theologians have identified conception as the initial point of ensoulment. The question of the soul's origin has important bioethical implications for a range of issues, including the moral licitness of abortion, abortifacient contraceptives, artificial reproductive technologies (e.g. in-vitro fertilization) and stem cell research (see *Ethics).

Rethinking the soul's origin

Many today consider the traditional substance dualist framework to have been rendered obsolete by advances in science and philosophy. Creationism in particular fits poorly with advances in evolutionary biology, neuroscience, cognitive science and psychology. For one thing, its appeal to divine action to explain conscious life looks like the widely repudiated God-of-the-gaps approach to divine action. What is more, the creationist account does not comport with the intimate relationship between genetics and the brain and personal characteristics. Still, it is not clear that traducianism fares much better, as it posits a wholly mysterious account of spiritual origination with relatively sparse explanatory payoff. If one adopts a physicalist view of the self, then the soul might be understood simply as the living being (*nephesh*), in which case the soul comes to exist when the living being comes to exist (perhaps at conception). Conversely, one might view the soul as the set of mental properties and/or events (that is, the mind) that arises out of the functioning of the brain, in which case the soul comes to exist when the brain is sufficiently developed to produce mental properties and/or events.

Bibliography

G. C. Berkouwer, *Man: The Image of God*, tr. D. W. Jellema (Grand Rapids, 1972); W. S. Brown, N. Murphy and H. N. Malony (eds.), *Whatever Happened to the Soul? Scientific and Theological Portraits of Human Nature* (Minneapolis, 1998); J. P. Moreland and S. Rae, *Body and Soul: Human Nature and the Crisis in Ethics* (Downers Grove, 2000).

R. RAUSER

SOUTHERN BAPTIST THEOLOGY

The Southern Baptist Convention (founded 1845) has distinguished itself more for practical Christian activity than profound theological writing. Nevertheless, its missionary activity has not proceeded within a theological vacuum. John L. Dagg (1794–1884), the Convention's first writing theologian, contributed theological, ecclesiological, ethical and apologetic works giving identity and direction to Southern Baptists. His *Manual of Theology* (1858) is a devotional, yet theologically cogent, exposition of evangelical Calvinism founded upon the fundamental principle of every man's duty to love God. J. P. Boyce (1827–88), founder of the first Southern Baptist theological seminary, wrote *Abstract of Systematic Theology* as a textbook. Reflecting Boyce's *Princeton education, it gives voice to the consistent Calvinism of his Southern Baptist contemporaries (see

*Reformed theology). B. H. Carroll (1843–1914), though not a systematic theologian, had great conserving effect on Southern Baptist theology through pulpit, print, classroom, personal relations (G. W. Truett, 1867–1944, and L. R. Scarborough, 1870–1945), and the founding of Southwestern Baptist Seminary (1908). E. Y. Mullins (1860–1928) retained Calvinistic views of election, the precedence of new birth to faith, justification by faith, and perseverance, but his book, *The Christian Religion in Its Doctrinal Expression*, made universal Christian experience one of the major sources of theological method, thus introducing pragmatism into twentieth-century Southern Baptist theology. W. T. Conner (1877–1952) taught systematic theology at Southwestern Seminary for thirty-nine years. His *Revelation and God* and *The Gospel of Redemption* show a clear indebtedness to Mullins and A. H. Strong. Dale Moody's (1915–92) *The Word of Truth* shows a highly eclectic relationship with modern trends in theology, a cordial receptivity to biblical criticism, and a general rejection of historic Baptist Calvinism.

Theological controversy within Southern Baptist life has focused on two issues – ecclesiology (see *Church) and *Scripture. The Landmark movement, led by J. R. Graves (1820–93), so defined Baptist origins and ecclesiology that members of non-Baptist fellowships were not embraced as Christian brethren, nor their ministers as Christian ministers. Mainstream Southern Baptists rejected the most radical features of Landmarkism.

Controversy over Scripture arose from the gradual introduction of biblical criticism into the seminaries, countered by a growing awareness of its destructive implications for the doctrines of *revelation and inspiration. The C. H. Toy controversy at Southern Seminary (1879), the evolution controversy (1923–27), the controversy over Ralph Elliott's book *The Message of Genesis* (1961–63), and the Broadman Commentary controversy (1970ff.) were actually individual eruptions produced by the tension of this one conflict. The 1980s and 1990s witnessed a vigorous debate on the issue that established a clear commitment to biblical inerrancy on the part of all the agencies and the six theological seminaries (see *Infallibility and inerrancy of the Bible). Though it involved significant personnel change, all these organizations came to affirm not only the inerrancy of Scripture but to require a conscientious subscription to the doctrinal statement of the Southern Baptist Convention, *The Baptist Faith and Message*, newly revised in 2000. The task assumed by each of these Convention entities also took a more decidedly evangelical form. This renewed affirmation of doctrinal fidelity has fuelled an energetic discussion on the Calvinistic heritage of Southern Baptists vis-à-vis the reticence of many in the denomination to embrace that earlier confessional heritage.

See also: BAPTIST THEOLOGY.

Bibliography

L. R. Bush and T. J. Nettles, *Baptists and the Bible* (Nashville, 1999); J. L. Garrett, *Baptist Theology: A Four-Century Study* (Macon, 2009); T. J. Nettles, *The Baptists*, 3 vols. (Fearn, 2005–07).

T. J. NETTLES

SOVEREIGNTY OF GOD

The assertion of God's sovereignty is essential to Christian belief. It is an amplification of the assertion that God is Ruler, King and Lord of all, what is otherwise depicted by the *trisagion* of Isa. 6 with its vision of God sitting upon a throne. It is expressed in the affirmation of the Nicene Creed, 'I believe in God, the Father almighty . . .' and is confessed by all Christian traditions. It is particularly emphasized in the *Reformed tradition stemming from John Calvin, and specifically interpreted in conservative branches of that tradition as implying God's foreordination, particularly in the doctrine of double predestination of the elect and the reprobate. Those in other traditions, and many in the Reformed tradition today, affirm God's sovereignty but reject that interpretation.

God's sovereignty in *creation is illustrated by an insistence that he creates *ex nihilo*, out of nothing. The will, the design and the execution are entirely his. It is the basis of creation's coherence and rationality, as well as of the possibility of *science. God creates not out of any metaphysical necessity or determinism but from a free act.

Traditional Christian *theism has held that God is defined as omnipotent, omniscient and omnipresent, each a variant of divine sovereignty. His power ensures that his goals are met, his designs fulfilled and, traditionally, that his *providence is essentially 'risk-free'. His power is not absolute in the sense that God can do anything (*potestas absoluta*), although that idea is present in medieval thought as well as in *Luther, *Calvin and *Zwingli. Creedal expressions of sovereignty, however, are careful to maintain that omnipotence does not mean that God can do anything, but rather that he can do all that is logically possible (e.g. he cannot deny himself). *Anselm of Canterbury (in his *Proslogion*) and *Thomas Aquinas (in his *Summa Theologica*) suggested that it is because God is omnipotent that he cannot sin. Nineteenth-century *kenoticism argued that God engaged in self-limitation or self-emptying in the *incarnation, setting aside *metaphysical* attributes (omnipotence, omniscience, omnipresence) in Christ while retaining the *moral* attributes (love, righteousness, holiness). Dietrich *Bonhoeffer spoke of Christ's incarnation as an expression of 'God's *powerlessness'. Traditional Christian theism regarding sovereignty is also recast by *process theologians who speak of God's 'dipolarity' (e.g. A. N. Whitehead, C. Hartshorne) whereby the constant unchanging polarity of God is continually adapting itself to the cosmic evolutionary process.

As to God's omnipresence, traditional theism has insisted that God is not bound by the limitations of space (or time), but that he is always present everywhere at all times, though invisibly and imperceptibly.

The belief in God's omniscience has been challenged of late by evangelical and post-evangelical *open theism (or free-will theism), in an attempt to defend a notion of human freedom. Thus, John E. Sanders can write:

> That God changes in some respects implies that God is temporal, working with us in time. God, at least since Creation, experiences duration. God is everlasting through time rather than timelessly eternal . . . We believe that God could have known every event of the future had God decided to create a fully determined universe. However, in our view, God decided to create beings with interdeterministic freedom which implies that God chose to create a universe in which the future is not entirely knowable, even for God. For many open theists, the 'future' is not a present reality – it does not exist – and God knows reality as it is (<http://www.opentheism.info/>).

Another challenge to the traditional attributes of God related to his sovereignty has been to the notion of *impassibility: that no-one can inflict suffering, pain or any sort of distress on God. In the traditional view, God may and does enter into the creature's suffering by choice and empathy, but not as a victim. Traditional orthodoxy, despite frequent claims to the contrary, has not suggested that God is a stranger to joy or does not experience emotion. But impassibility has often been equated with Aristotle's idea of the metaphysical and ethical perfection of God, *apatheia*, meaning imperturbability and dispassionateness (the Unmoved Mover).

The traditional Calvinist view of the sovereignty of God in election and preterition (in Calvinistic theology, God's sovereign decision to pass over some people in election, who are finally condemned on account of their sin: cf. e.g. Berkhof, pp. 116–117; see *Perseverance, *Predestination) has occasioned heated disagreements in the doctrine of God itself as well as soteriology. In both, the accomplishment of *redemption as well as its application in the lives of individuals, Calvinism has seen the sovereignty of God in the concept of election itself (those chosen to eternal life), insisting, in the words of W. G. T. Shedd, that the exercise of mercy is optional with God. Calvinistic theology argues that God's purposes in redemption are always achieved: the cross accomplishes and guarantees the *salvation of men and women rather than simply making salvation possible. The *ordo salutis*, it is argued, necessitates that a line be drawn from foreordination to glorification, else the notion of election is in question.

But in the *evangelical tradition from the Reformation to the present many (*Melanchthon, Arminius, Richard *Baxter, John *Wesley) have disagreed with this in some way. Many evangelicals hold that God's sovereign prevenient grace in Christ extends to all, but does not compel any, and many contemporary Western theologians take a similar line. *Barth reinterpreted election to argue that God in his sovereignty elects all in Christ, but that some may reject their salvation. Similarly, *Eastern Orthodoxy generally opposes the idea that the sovereignty of God implies the Calvinist doctrine of predestination, comparing it with Islamic fatalism.

Those issues involving the relationship of sovereignty and human responsibility become acute in several ways. First, views differ in relation to choice or 'free will', the belief that the human *will has an inherent power to choose between alternatives. In opposition to *determinism, the will is said to be free from necessary causation (libertarianism), or the will coexists with all events being determined by previous states of affairs (compatibilism). Calvinists agree that free agency is necessary to human nature, but insist that moral choices can only take place according to the condition of human nature as fallen and not in some neutral state. Human depravity necessitates moral inability. They deny absolute autonomy, insisting on prevenient grace to enable the will to respond. Classical *Arminians agree, but insist that prevenient grace is not coercive. Some later theologians (misleadingly classified as 'Arminians') disagreed with Arminius by defending a doctrine of natural free will.

Second, in relation to *evangelism, if the sovereignty of God implies his preordaining some to eternal life and others to eternal damnation (see *Judgment of God), this appears not only to deter but ultimately to cripple initiative and encourage passivity and inertia. Defenders have countered by arguing a compatibilist position: evangelism is commanded by Christ and the apostles and should be done on this ground alone, but adding that God saves through, and not apart from, *means*. Yet most theologians find the notion that God has eternally elected some to damnation blunts the appeal of the gospel and makes the sovereignty of God incompatible with his love.

Third, in relation to *ethics, responsibility in behaviour and culpability in transgression are once again viewed as compatible with overall sovereignty, nowhere seen more starkly than in Phil. 2:12: 'Work out your salvation with fear and trembling, for it is God who works in you to will and to act according to his good pleasure.'

Fourth, in relation to civic power and authority, God is sovereign in the determination of rule and government (Rom. 13:1–7).

Fifth, in relation to *evil, both in respect to its origin and continued existence, the sovereignty of God meets its most acute problem (see *Theodicy). That God does not prevent evil from existing calls into question his omnipotence or benevolence. Seeming solutions are that evil is imaginary (Christian Science), illusion (Hinduism), privation of the Good suggesting something without ontology (Augustine and medieval thought). Reformed thought in the conservative Calvinist tradition is summarized by the Westminster Confession: 'God, from all eternity, did, by the most wise and holy counsel of His own will, freely, and unchangeably ordain whatsoever comes to pass: yet so, as thereby neither is God the author of sin, nor is violence offered to the will of the creatures; nor is the liberty or contingency of second causes taken away, but rather established' (3:1). God is the 'first cause' of all things, but evil is a product of 'second causes'. In the words of John Calvin, 'First, it must be observed that the will of God is the cause of all things that happen in the world: and yet God is not the author of evil', adding, 'for the proximate cause is one thing, and the remote cause another' (J. Calvin, *Concerning the Eternal Predestination of God*, pp. 169, 181).

See also: GOD; TRINITY.

Bibliography

J. Arminius, 'Declaration of Sentiments', *Works*, vol. 3 (London, 1825), pp. 516–668; H. Bavinck, *Reformed Dogmatics, vol. 2: God and Creation*, 4 vols., ed. John Bolt (Grand Rapids, 2004); G. Bray, *The Doctrine of God* (Leicester, 1993); J. Calvin, *Concerning the Eternal Predestination of God* (London, 1982 [1552]); J. Frame, *The Doctrine of God: A Theology of Lordship* (Phillipsburg, 2002); M. Luther, *The Bondage of the Will*, tr. J. I. Packer and O. R. Johnson (London, 1973); A. McGrath, *Christian Theology: An Introduction* (Oxford, 1994); R. K. McGregor, *No Place for Sovereignty: What's Wrong with Freewill Theism?* (Downers Grove, 1996); T. C. Oden, *The Living God* (New York, 1992); R. E. Olson, *Arminian Theology: Myths and Realities* (Downers Grove, 2006); C. H. Pinnock, *Most Moved Mover: A Theology of God's Openness* (Carlisle, 2001); John Wesley, 'On Predestination', *Works*, vol. II (Nashville, 1985), pp. 413–421; *idem*, 'Free Grace', *Works*, vol. III (Nashville, 1986), pp. 542–563.

D. W. H. THOMAS

SPINOZA, BENEDICT (BARUCH) DE (1632–77)

A complex, original, Dutch thinker, prominent in public affairs, Spinoza was of Jewish origin, but was expelled from his synagogue (1656) for his unorthodox views, which were *pantheistic. There is only one reality or 'substance', which can be called equally 'God' or 'Nature'; all other things are modifications of this (similarly, mind and body are aspects of a single human unity). Since God/Nature exists necessarily, all else follows necessarily; human freedom is simply acting rationally rather than as a slave of the passions. Our greatest good is to know and love God; but God, being perfect in himself, neither loves nor hates, save in us. The common idea of *immortality is a mistake; yet in necessary knowledge we are aware of an eternal, timeless aspect of the mind.

According to Spinoza, religions such as Judaism and Christianity do not express philosophical truth; they are primarily ways of conveying moral truths to those incapable of seeing them by reason. Any religion which helps in this way should therefore be tolerated. In seeking to study the Bible dispassionately (and dating many OT books later than tradition), Spinoza has also been seen as a forerunner of biblical criticism.

Bibliography

Ethics and *De Intellectus Emendatione* (ET, London, 1910); S. Hampshire, *Spinoza* (Harmondsworth, 1951); G. Lloyd, *Spinoza and Ethics* (London, 1996); S. Nadler, *A Book Forged in Hell: Spinoza's Scandalous Treatise and the Birth of the Secular Age* (Princeton, 2011); R. Scruton, *Spinoza: A Very Short Introduction* (Oxford, 2002).

R. L. STURCH

SPIRITUALISM, see SECTS

SPIRITUALITY

Varied understandings of spirituality are offered by those writing on the subject. Some are broad enough to include most human experience, not simply what is Christian. Within the specifically Christian context, the contemporary understanding of spirituality increasingly emphasizes the holistic involvement of the person who is responding to God's revelation of himself, recognizes and affirms the community context of spirituality in worship and fellowship, and stresses that authentic spirituality is embodied in social transformation. These perspectives mean that spirituality is not taken to refer exclusively to the life of prayer or the inner spiritual exercises. Using a framework proposed by Philip Sheldrake, spirituality can be seen as concerned with the conjunction of theology, experiential communion with God and practical Christianity. Seen in this way, spirituality is increasingly a subject for study. A more academic approach to spirituality involves critical historical analysis of a broad range of 'lived experience'.

A traditional distinction has been made between *apophatic spirituality, in which any idea of using an image of God – even a mental image – is rejected, and cataphatic spirituality, which draws attention to the association between God and his creation and which is therefore open to the use of symbols and icons. Both these tendencies can co-exist within the same Christian tradition. Thus the Eastern Church has been known both for its great mystics and also for its theology and use of icons. Another distinction that has been made is between 'apostolic' or missionary approaches to spirituality on the one hand, and the more *monastic attitude on the other, which seeks to find spiritual resources in withdrawal. A more complex categorization has been proposed by Geoffrey Wainwright, who has suggested that Richard *Niebuhr's well-rehearsed typology of the relationship between Christ and culture (Christ against culture, the Christ of culture, Christ above culture, Christ and culture in paradox, and Christ the transformer of culture) could be applied to streams of spirituality.

Historically, there have been some significant differences between the approaches of the Eastern and the Western Church. However, in the patristic period and beyond, both East and West saw spirituality and theology as one, rather than as separated. The Fathers of the church emphasized and sought to integrate *prayer, study and service (see *Patristic theology). In the medieval period influential figures in the story of spirituality included *Hildegard of Bingen, *Francis of Assisi, Meister Eckhart and *Julian of Norwich, whose *Revelations of Divine Love* give her a place as the first English 'woman of letters'. The trend was towards the exaltation of the *mystical, although Francis was also an active evangelist. The sixteenth century produced those who contributed in outstanding and very different ways to an understanding of spirituality – for example, Martin *Luther, *Ignatius of Loyola, *Teresa of Avila and her assistant, John of the Cross – but from the Protestant *Reformation onwards there was a tendency in the West, on the part of both Roman Catholic and Protestant leaders, to give precedence to the theological task and to see spirituality as subsidiary, having to do only with the practice of devotion. There were notable exceptions: many of the seventeenth-century English *Puritans sought to integrate a robust doctrinal approach with a deep commitment to godly living. In the *Eastern Orthodox tradition, spirituality – particularly its corporate expression in the worship of the church – remained central.

Within Protestantism the eighteenth century saw the rise of renewal movements across Europe. In 1675 Philipp Spener, a Lutheran, wrote on the subject of 'pious desires', and the movement that took shape was nicknamed *Pietism. By contrast with the rather lifeless state of much German Protestantism at the time, Pietism soon came to be seen as embodying an important rallying call to a more vital Protestant spirituality. It reaffirmed the centrality of the Christian experience of the new birth and also wanted to renew the theology of the *priesthood of all believers, with its outworking in the recovery of lay ecclesial participation. In order to improve the level of spiritual instruction in church life, class meetings were held, in which believers would meet to teach each other, engage in singing and share Christian testimonies. Pietism was to some extent refashioned by Nicholas von Zinzendorf, a young German count who had been educated in a Pietist environment at Halle and who opened his estate in south-east Saxony in the 1720s to a group of Protestant refugees from Bohemia and Moravia. The community that was established, called Herrnhut ('under the Lord's Protection'), became the locus of a profound spiritual renewal which produced a missional spirituality and issued in remarkable ventures in world mission (see *Moravian theology).

The same period saw the emergence within Roman Catholicism of 'spiritual theology'. This was viewed as a subset of theology and was linked with the practice of spiritual direction. The Society of Jesus in particular sought to bring together 'ascetical theology', which had to do with the active seeking of perfection, and 'mystical theology', which had contemplation as its focus. Some manuals of spiritual theology were produced, although among *Jesuits the primary resource was the thinking of their founder, Ignatius of Loyola, and especially his *Spiritual Exercises*. In the development of Ignatian spirituality there has been a stress on practical Christianity lived out in daily life through entry into the gospel story, self-examination (the *examen*), the idea of the retreat as a place of guidance, an invitation to decision or 'election' – as the Holy Spirit guides the person – in the context of surrender to God, and mission in the style of the early disciples. These ideas, or variations of them, have been taken up widely in different sections of the Christian church, especially in the later twentieth century.

John *Wesley, who shaped much early evangelical thinking in the English-speaking world, recorded in his diary for 24 May 1738 the following words, which were to become among the most famous in the story of Protestant Christian experience:

In the evening I went very unwillingly to a society in Aldersgate Street [in the city of London], where one was reading Luther's Preface to the Epistle to the Romans. About a quarter before nine, while he was describing the change which God works in the heart through faith in Christ, I felt my heart strangely warmed. I felt I did trust in Christ, Christ alone, for salvation; and an assurance was given me that He had taken away *my* sins, even *mine*, and saved *me* from the law of sin and death . . . I then testified openly to all there what I now first felt in my heart.

This account, describing as it does how John Wesley came to a point of personal reliance on God's grace and Christ's work on the cross for salvation, later came to be seen as a description of a typical experience of *evangelical *conversion, although perhaps it should rather be seen as an expression of *assurance of salvation. Among the prior spiritual influences on John Wesley and on his brother *Charles, who was also an Anglican clergyman, were the seventeenth-century English Puritan movement and Catholic and Anglican High Church devotion. John Wesley was affected by his reading of the *Imitation of Christ*, by Thomas à Kempis, and the writings of the Anglican High Churchman, William Law, *On Christian Perfection* (1726) and *A Serious Call to a Devout and Holy Life* (1728). There was also the (somewhat ambiguous) influence on Wesley of the more mystical streams of spirituality, notably that expressed by German mystics such as Meister Eckhardt and Jakob Böhme, or in books like

The Life of God in the Soul of Man, by Henry Scougal of Aberdeen, a Scottish episcopalian. All these different influences contributed in some way to the shaping of John Wesley's evangelical spirituality.

In eighteenth-century North America, Jonathan *Edwards, America's greatest theologian, was a primary shaper of evangelical spirituality. In his own phrase, in one of his great works, *The Religious Affections*, 'holy affections' constituted a great part of true religion. 'The Holy Scriptures,' he asserted, 'do everywhere place religion very much in the affections; such as fear, hope, love, hatred, desire, joy, sorrow, gratitude, compassion, zeal.' Yet for Edwards, evangelical spirituality was not to be defined as fine feelings. He insisted that 'there must be light in the understanding, as well as an *affected* fervent heart . . . on the other hand, where there is a kind of light without heat, a head stored with notions and speculations, with a cold and unaffected heart, there can be nothing divine in that light, that knowledge is no true spiritual knowledge of divine things.' In the *Religious Affections*, it becomes clear that meditation on the *cross is central to 'spiritual knowledge'. 'Where,' enquired Edwards, as he spoke with heartfelt expression of Christ's sufferings on the cross, 'are the exercises of our affections proper, if not here?'

Within the English-speaking world, a number of key figures who followed on from the founding figures such as Wesley and Edwards helped to shape evangelical thinking about spirituality. In Britain these included Anglicans such as John Newton, the hymn-writer William Cowper (hymns have been crucial expressions of evangelical spirituality) and Charles *Simeon, as well as Presbyterians such as Robert Murray McCheyne and Baptists like Charles Haddon *Spurgeon. In America, Charles *Finney was among those whose influence on thinking about holiness and evangelism was profound. There has also been a significant reshaping of aspects of evangelical experience in the period since the early twentieth century, due to the massive influence on evangelical life worldwide of the *Pentecostal and *charismatic movements, with their emphasis on the power of the Holy Spirit and also the gifts of the Spirit, such as prophecy, speaking in tongues and healing. The international Pentecostal/charismatic community, to a large extent a subset of evangelicalism although also embracing Catholic charismatics, has seen phenomenal numerical growth since its beginnings about 100 years ago, and its approach to experience has presented fresh challenges.

From the 1970s and 1980s the term 'spirituality' largely replaced 'spiritual theology', and an increasing number of seminaries, including those in the evangelical tradition, began to offer courses in spirituality. It is sometimes thought that the main ingredients of evangelical spirituality have always been rather restricted – early rising, prayer and Bible study – and that little of this could be studied. However, Derek Tidball, in *Who Are the Evangelicals?* (1994), rightly questioned the close association of evangelical spirituality with the 'quiet time', as it is sometimes called, and in examining evangelical spirituality he dealt with such broader themes as grace, holiness and involvement in *society. The major topics explored by David Gillett in his study of evangelical spirituality, *Trust and Obey* (1993), are a 'twice-born' spirituality, assurance of salvation, the cross of Christ, the pursuit of holiness, the God who speaks and the God who acts. Gillett suggested that there is within evangelicalism a new openness and a welcoming of opportunities to examine varieties of Christian spirituality. Evangelicals have become more interested in areas such as contemplative prayer, *lectio divina*, spiritual direction, the place of the sacraments, an appreciation of creation, and spirituality in relation to social action – drawing, for example, from the insights of *liberation theology.

As well as the phenomenon of evangelicals exploring other Christian traditions of spirituality, they have been engaged since the 1980s in a fresh examination of their own spiritual tradition, with its varied sub-strands such as Wesleyan *holiness, *Reformed, Keswick and Pentecostal spiritualities. Most (though not all) recent studies of evangelicalism have aligned themselves with the argument advanced by Bebbington that evangelicalism is a movement comprising all those who stress conversion, the Bible, the cross and activism. All of these features can be found in other Christian traditions, but in evangelicalism they are combined in a particular way. Evangelicalism is not so much defined by its doctrines, but may be seen, rather, as a distinctive stream of Christian spirituality, since these four features are not doctrinal formulations, but have to do with 'lived experience'. At the heart of evangelical spirituality is a personal relationship with Christ.

In the current revival of interest in spirituality in the wider Christian world, a number of twentieth-century writers have been of particular significance. One has been Thomas *Merton, an American Trappist monk, who published his best-selling autobiography, *The Seven Storey Mountain*, in 1947. Another significant Catholic writer has been Henri Nouwen, a Dutch priest, who has given attention to the nature of authentic spirituality in books such as *The Return of the Prodigal*. Kallistos Ware has been one of a number of writers introducing the wider Christian community in the West to Orthodox spirituality. Perhaps the evangelical writer who has done most to highlight the richness of the varied streams of spirituality has been Richard Foster, most notably in his book *Streams of Living Water* (1999). Fresh commitment to the renewal of spirituality is currently to be found in all Christian traditions.

Bibliography

L. Bouyer (ed.), *A History of Christian Spirituality*, 3 vols. (London, 1968); K. J. Collins, *Exploring Christian Spirituality* (Grand Rapids, 2000); R. Foster, *Streams of Living Water* (London, 1999); D. Gillett, *Trust and Obey* (London, 1993); C. Jones, G. Wainwright and E. Yarnold (eds.), *The Study of Spirituality* (Oxford, 1986); G. Mursell (ed.), *The Story of Christian Spirituality* (Oxford, 2001); I. M. Randall, *What a Friend We Have in Jesus* (London, 2005); P. Sheldrake, *Spirituality and Theology* (London, 1998); idem (ed.), *The New SCM Dictionary of Christian Spirituality* (London, 1983).

I. M. RANDALL

SPURGEON, CHARLES HADDON (1834–92)

Born into an Essex Congregational home, Spurgeon experienced a dramatic conversion in his early teens and sought baptism as a believer. After a successful short ministry in rural Cambridgeshire he became Baptist minister at New Park Street Chapel, London, which later moved to the Metropolitan Tabernacle to accommodate the vast congregations which came to hear him preach. His popularity was greatly enhanced by the weekly publication (from 1855 onwards) of his sermons, the sale of which in England and the USA helped to finance the theological college he had established in 1856. The sermons give rich expression both to his firmly held Calvinistic (see *Reformed theology) convictions and evangelistic concern. In 1864 his sermon on '*Baptismal Regeneration' brought him into theological conflict with paedobaptists, including some evangelicals. Later, when *liberal theological ideas were gaining ground, he affirmed his unqualified allegiance to biblical doctrine. During his own denomination's 'Downgrade' controversy (1887–9) he expressed alarm concerning unorthodox views, and in 1887, 'with the utmost regret', withdrew from the Baptist Union. His voluminous writings (135 books), which frequently reflect his indebtedness to seventeenth-century *Puritanism, continue to be published, maintaining his immense spiritual influence throughout the evangelical world.

See also: BAPTIST THEOLOGY.

Bibliography

J. C. Carlile, *C. H. Spurgeon: An Interpretative Biography* (London, 1933); H. F. Colquitt, *The Soteriology of Charles Haddon Spurgeon . . .* (unpublished dissertation, New College, Edinburgh, 1951); I. H. Murray, *The Forgotten Spurgeon* (London, 1966); G. H. Pike, *The Life and Work of Charles Haddon Spurgeon*, 6 vols. (London, 1892–3); H. Thielicke (ed.), *Encounter with Spurgeon* (London, 1964).

R. BROWN

STANILOAE, DUMITRU (1903–93)

Dumitru Staniloae was one of the most influential and prolific Romanian Orthodox theologians. As Professor of Dogmatic Theology at the Faculty of Orthodox Theology in Sibiu and Bucharest, he wrote and translated thousands of academic books and articles, mainly from the area of patristics and dogmatic theology.

His theological career started in 1922, focusing mainly on church history, particularly the hesychast movement. In 1928 he completed his doctoral thesis on *The Life and Work of Patriarch Dositheos of Jerusalem and His Relations with the Romanian Lands*. Immediately after that, Staniloae travelled to Munich, Berlin and Paris, where he studied in the area of dialectical philosophy and theology and Byzantine mystical theology. After 1929, he taught theology at the Theological Academy in

Sibiu and at the Faculty of Orthodox Theology in Bucharest till 1973. Staniloae was imprisoned for five years (1958–64), apparently because of his part in the revival of Romanian Orthodox spirituality.

Staniloae's contribution to Romanian Orthodoxy is seen in the two major directions of his academic studies. The first direction was the recovery of patristic spirituality. For instance, in 1938 he published *The Life and Teaching of St. Gregory Palamas*, reviving the interest on *mystical theology and practice of *hesychasm. In the same period, he started to publish a compilation of spiritual patristic texts under the title *Philokalia*. The second direction was a dialogue with Western theology and *spirituality. In one of his major works, *Jesus Christ, or the Restoration of Man* (1943), the influence of dialectical and personalist philosophy can be clearly distinguished in emphasizing the ontological dimension of Christian salvation. Staniloae's magnum opus is his three-volume *Orthodox Dogmatic Theology* (1978), followed by *Orthodox Spirituality* (1981), *Spirituality and Communion in the Orthodox Liturgy* (1986) and *Studies in Orthodox Dogmatic Theology* (1991) – all published under the Communist regime.

Staniloae was a faithful apologist of Orthodoxy, a historian, *dogmatician and philosopher. His theology is considered original, creative, mystical and *personalist. There is an immense erudition packed into his texts. A single work cannot reveal the compactness of his knowledge of patristic and modern theology. Behind his theological system there is an important organizing structure. What is specific to Staniloae's Orthodox theology is: (1) the balanced approach to the apophatic-cataphatic issue, disclosing the insufficiency of cataphaticism in Western theology and the radical way of *apophaticism in Eastern theology; (2) the rationality of creation as the revelation of the *Logos; (3) the Trinity as the structure of supreme love; (4) the emphasis on the *hypostatic equilibrium between the economy of the Son and of the Spirit; (5) the unification of incarnation and deification; (6) the church as the icon of the Trinity and communion of persons; (7) the synergetic equilibrium between the free will of man and the power of uncreated energies mediated by the Spirit as sacramental power; and (8) the vision of a transfigured cosmos. The heart of this theology is found in the theology of person and communion. Staniloae's view on *deification (*theosis*) as the goal of human existence is very much informed by his communitary personalism, a motif into which the other themes are usually subsumed.

See also: EASTERN ORTHODOX THEOLOGY.

Bibliography

Selected Works: *Orthodox Dogmatic Theology*, 3 vols. (Brookline, 2005, 2011).

Studies: E. Bartos, *Deification in Eastern Orthodox Theology: An Evaluation and Critique of the Theology of Dumitru Staniloae* (Carlisle, 1999); L. Turcescu (ed.), *Dumitru Staniloae: Tradition and Modernity in Theology* (Iaşi, 2002).

E. BARTOS

STATE

Strictly the term 'state' refers to civil government and magistrature, including the executive and legislature, together with judicial, diplomatic, military and law enforcement functions – in other words, the administration of public justice. Contemporary secular political thought often tends to conceive it in broad terms, nearer to the idea of 'nation'.

The term 'state church' usually denotes a specific constitutional and legal establishment of a church in relation to the state which gives it certain privileges, e.g. political, legal, financial, religious and may also impose certain state controls upon its own inner life and government.

The contemporary state is, with relatively rare exceptions, a secular entity. Even where, as in England or Scotland, the Christian church is in some sense 'established', the state remains secular and pluralistic. Historically, until comparatively recently, a secular state was unthinkable. Every state was religious, supporting and supported by the particular religious tradition or traditions which expressed its ideals and objectives. This was particularly true for the Jews, from among whom the first disciples came, but also for every community in the ancient world.

The question of how Christians were to understand and relate to temporal power confronted the church from earliest times. It was the political demands of Rome that set Jesus' birth in Bethlehem; it was against the background of political unrest and national aspiration characteristic of an occupied territory that his ministry unfolded; and it was on the orders of the temporal power that he was executed.

The church's theological response to persecution broadly followed two lines, each drawn from the NT. Those who, like Paul, affirmed the powers of the state, sought to present the case for the toleration of Christianity without the condition of participation in the Roman cults. They argued, in effect, that Christians must always be exemplary citizens because of their perception of the divine origin of temporal power: obedience to God ensures commitment to the commonwealth. Those, on the other hand, who looked to the traditions of Jewish apocalyptic, including the book of Revelation, for their inspiration, developed a theology in which the Roman Empire was strongly rejected as the embodiment of evil and idolatry. The objective for the Christian was not rapprochement with the world, but *martyrdom – the victory by which the believer prepared the way for the ultimate overthrow of earthly states by the kingdom of Christ. The ambivalence of the NT seen in the tension between Romans 13 and Revelation 13 highlights both the positive and negative possibilities of the powers. The same tension has been evident in more recent political challenges faced by the church. The Swiss theologian Karl *Barth saw it as central to the crisis that confronted Christianity in Germany during Hitler's rise to power in the 1930s. As a member of the dissident '*Confessing Church' and a drafter of the anti-Nazi *Barmen Declaration of 1934, Barth argued that Romans 13 enjoined subordinate service rather than unqualified subjection, and that where the state has become tyrannical, it would be most faithfully served by opposition and prophetic critique. Similarly, a group of South African evangelicals set against apartheid in the 1980s declared that 'Romans 13 does not call for blind obedience to all evil systems . . .' (Concerned Evangelicals, *Evangelical Witness in South Africa: A Critique of Evangelical Theology and Practice by South African Evangelicals Themselves*, London, 1986). The contemporary abstract concept of the 'state' is unknown in the OT. There, political power is embodied in identifiable rulers who may be favourable or hostile, but who are always seen as subject to the sovereign rule of God. Thus Jeremiah's advice to the exiles in Babylon to seek the 'welfare of the city' (Jer. 29:7) has particular resonance. Israel gains strength in the midst of oppression from knowing that it has been called to live as God's chosen covenant community. Similarly, Christians in the NT gain strength from knowing that Jesus' kingdom is 'not of this world' (John 18:36). The eschatological promise enshrined in this statement makes it possible to submit to the governing authorities now (Rom. 13:1–7). However, there is a very real sense in which *everything* is God's, so that even Caesar's power is limited (John 19:11). It is also clear that where gospel ministry is curtailed by civic authorities, they may be defied (Acts 5:29). The tension between these respectively quietist and activist first-century texts is becoming increasingly poignant in twenty-first-century Britain, as Christians face growing legislative threats to historic rights and freedoms.

The religious character of states in the ancient world helps explain the eventual outcome of the conflict between Rome and the church. Once a Roman emperor became an adherent of Christianity it was inevitable, in the absence of any concept of the secular, that Christianity must become the official cultic expression of his faith to his subjects. The eventual result of the conversion of *Constantine in AD 312 was that the church changed places with the official pagan cult of Rome. In effect, the *Christendom of the Middle Ages was inaugurated. In many ways, this marked the triumph of the moderate, world-affirming theology over the martyr tradition. This 'Christendom' model pertained for the next 1,500 years.

One of Constantine's historic decisions was to build Byzantium (Constantinople) in 330, a new capital for the Eastern Empire. After the collapse of the Western Empire in 410, the Eastern Empire was known as the Byzantine Empire. From the outset Constantinople was intended as a Christian city and with state and religion in the ancient world always coterminous, its government looked to Christian principles, in contrast to pagan Rome. Constantine therefore naturally considered himself a guardian of the Christian church and accordingly intervened as a Christian emperor to settle controversies in the early church. Constantine's close friend, *Eusebius of Caesarea, developed a complete apologia for the notion of empire and church together reflecting the kingdom of heaven where the empire reflected divine universal rule in the form of strong central government which prevented political and social chaos. It was a short step for the emperor to be acting head of the church as well as head of state, responsible for the appointment and dismissal of bishops and seeking to influence the church's theology and worship. Orthodox historians object to the term 'Caesaropapism' – control of the church by secular political interests – considering the church never to have been subordinated to the state. Rather, they believe the two worked in harmony with neither exercising absolute control over the other.

The plight of Eastern Christianity following the early Islamic conquests of the Eastern and Southern parts of the Mediterranean world was far-reaching and came mainly at the expense of Christian lands. Arab armies rapidly expanded out of Arabia following the death of Muhammad, conquering Syria, Mesopotamia, Egypt, North Africa and Spain, as well as Persia, Central Asia and India. When *Islam encountered conquered peoples they were generally required to convert to Islam in exchange for peace. However, Jews and Christians were allowed to retain their own faiths as long as they surrendered and paid a tax. They were regarded as 'dhimmis' or 'protected ones', though the political reality of 'dhimmitude' reduced them to a religious minority status. When Islamic juridical power was rolled out, it instituted a collection of laws which gradually eroded any remaining rights of the dhimmis. Prior to the rise of Islam, the Orthodox Church had persecuted non-Chalcedonian churches using the arm of the Byzantine Empire to suppress heresy. Unsurprisingly, many of these communities initially welcomed the Arab invaders, ignorant of the implications of Islamic servitude. Christian minorities generally fared better during the ascendancy of the Arabs within the Muslim empire than later on when power shifted to the Ottoman Turks, who in the early sixteenth century conquered the Middle East. As the plight of minorities deteriorated, Christians suffered regular persecutions and were reduced to small groups of illiterate peoples and their churches weakened.

As either ideal or reality, the identification of church and state was to be the most pervasive feature of European society. Rome reasserted itself as the true 'spiritual heart' of empire, and amplified its claim to the 'primacy' of its own bishop as 'pontifex maximus', or 'pope'. However, this claim was severely tested when the city was captured by the Goths in AD 410. In the wake of that disaster, *Augustine of Hippo wrote his masterpiece, *The City of God*.

Although Augustine made a clear distinction between the City of Man as temporal and transitory and the City of God as spiritual and eternal, he equated the reign of Christ not simply with a perfect future kingdom, but with the ongoing life and witness of the church on earth, thus effectively justifying the Christendom compact. For all its eloquence, Augustine's apologetic could not prevent the capitulation of Rome to the Barbarians in AD 476. While this further shifted power to the East, the Roman church still asserted its superiority. In many ways the medieval church *was* the state: it had a coherent structure, a single head, an effective administration and a body of law; it had its own courts and it controlled all learning and most communications, so that even such civil power as was able to survive depended upon it. Medieval Europe was, in effect, a church-state, and relations between church and state were largely a matter of manoeuvres between laymen and ecclesiastics to exercise effective power within it.

The Protestant *Reformation brought about immense shifts in the practices and beliefs of the Western church. It marked the point at which pre-Reformation concerns with that church's corruption threatened decisively to rupture Christendom. The religious commitments of the Reformers cannot be isolated from the growing contemporary aspirations towards greater freedom and national autonomy, and for which the pertinent theological debates became something of a vehicle. In such a climate the mainstream Reformers were unable to accomplish their work without alliances with the ruling powers in their own areas. For this reason the mainstream strand of the Reformation is sometimes called 'magisterial', in recognition of its reliance upon the magistracy. For theological and pragmatic reasons, therefore, the Magisterial Reformers maintained in principle, though in modified form, the alliance of church and ruler which had characterized medieval Christendom. The mainline Protestant Reformers diverged somewhat from one another on their theology of church and state. Martin *Luther (1483–1546) developed a doctrine of 'Two Kingdoms', in which the defining concern of the church was identified as the word of God, with temporal power devolved to magistrates charged with the maintenance of the social order, and more specifically, with the protection of the church's distinct calling and mission. Within this paradigm, it did not behove the clergy to interfere in matters of government any more than it did the rulers to intervene in theological affairs. Yet *Lutheranism has frequently been charged with too compliant an attitude to social injustice because of a failure to integrate the 'two kingdoms' more coherently. John *Calvin (1509–1564) followed Luther in developing a clear distinction between the spiritual sphere in which the church operated and the civil sphere in which rulers and magistrates fulfilled their responsibilities. As with Luther, he was persuaded that the state was divinely sanctioned and that its ministers were ordained by God. One significant difference between Luther and Calvin, however, lies in the social contexts in which they worked. Luther's was a semi-feudal society in which the princes exercised personal rule over their localities and subjects. Calvin's was the city-state of Geneva, in which the emergence of an early democracy can be discerned. Church and state in this context were mutually influential, the state having the responsibility to establish true religion, and the church influencing and shaping the nature of the civil order and its practice. In the Calvinist tradition the concept of '*covenant' – the agreement between citizens and their rulers incorporating the beginnings of ideas of social contract – was to prove influential. Calvin could therefore even envisage *in extremis* the just removal of tyrants from their positions. In general, the Calvinist tradition has consistently demonstrated a high level of commitment to shaping the civil order.

Roman Catholicism has struggled to adapt to modern secular and democratic polities and the place of religion in public affairs. Some leading theologians and philosophers have turned to Thomas Aquinas for defence of orthodox Catholic teaching and as a sound means of confronting what they regard as contemporary errors and problems, especially concerning the social order. Aquinas, following Aristotle, emphasized the natural, social and political dimensions of human beings who depend on the companionship of fellow humans for human flourishing, which in turn requires wise political rule. So the purpose of government is to promote the common good, and just or unjust political governance can be measured by this standard. Jacques *Maritain in particular has been at the forefront of attempts to apply *Thomist wisdom to moral and sociopolitical philosophy, developing the idea of a Christian social philosophy that imagines a new kind of Christendom or social and political order. This is based on a social democratic and liberal view of the state, but focused on a theocentric form of humanism involving recognition of the sovereignty of God, natural law, the common good, human dignity, liberty, and human rights and responsibilities. Maritain saw church and state as cooperative institutions, with the state concentrating on temporal matters as well as the holistic human person, whilst the church focused on spiritual matters. Fruits of Maritain's thought have been seen in the UN Declaration on Human Rights as well as other national human rights declarations. The Aristotelian-Thomist concept that political society is necessary to human welfare is notable in the affirmation of society and community as the natural and beneficial location for the human person in the 1965 expression of Catholic social theology *Gaudium et Spes* – the pastoral constitution of the Second *Vatican Council. This is reinforced by emphasis on the notion of the common good. For the promotion of the common good, divinely sanctioned political authority is required supported by wide participation in the democratic processes. This approach also stresses the benefit of the church to society. All the church seeks is space and freedom – in return much will be rendered to the state in terms of moral influence.

Following the Second World War the role of the church under communism, notably in eastern Europe and China, became a focus for demands for free space within ruling systems that allowed no legal political opposition and offered few opportunities for open debate. Religion was suppressed because it competed with the Party for control of the popular mind and prevented a developed sense of collective solidarity. Believers were persecuted and religious institutions either shut down or controlled by the state. The result was to drive religion underground, and when free religious expression became once again legitimate, it became apparent that the Christian faith had not died as predicted by *Marx. At a time when traditional religion was in decline, the church attracted wider and burgeoning support from those who considered it best represented their political interests and provided a political and/or social and community alternative to the state, often facilitating discussion and awareness of social concerns such as *peace, environment, human *rights – and even providing a base from which to initiate protest movements against the state. However, some churches were accused of being too conservative or accommodating to the state, or even being vehicles of state control. The response of the state was to dismiss the church as a mere apolitical religious community on the one hand, whilst policing and if necessary suppressing any emergent radical impulses on the other. The church was often discredited by the state as fronts for Western sabotage and espionage, and church leaders were arrested and church properties monitored, whilst the general population were pressured to withdraw from the church. When it became clear that the church was not disappearing as predicted, church-state relations gradually began to improve, with concessions being won as a result of increasing dialogue. However, strict separation of church and state was maintained whilst the church was to a greater extent permitted to define its own range of religious activities, whilst always remaining vulnerable to state pressure, propaganda and veto.

Such divergences became reflected in the different models of church-state and church-nation relationships which developed. On the radical wing of the Reformation, *Anabaptists like Balthassar *Hubmaier and Menno *Simons challenged the consensus by commending an independent, 'gathered church' ecclesiology and an explicit refusal to swear oaths or serve as magistrates. We are still living with its consequences, and its legacy is now intensely debated. As Christendom has faded, such Anabaptist and dissident or nonconformist emphases are becoming more popular among evangelicals. Separation of church and state is in fact required by the American Constitution, and increasingly the norm around the world. But the legacy of Christendom is still much debated, with some commending the opportunities afforded by state support for mission, whilst others repudiate the church's collusion with power.

Bibliography

P. Avis, *Church, State and Establishment* (London, 2001); D. Fergusson, *Church, State and Civil Society* (Cambridge, 2004); O. O'Donovan, *The Desire of the Nations* (Cambridge, 1996); S. Perks, *A Defence of the Christian State* (Taunton, 1998); W. Pilgrim, *Uneasy Neighbours: Church and State in the New Testament* (Minneapolis, 1999).

D. G. Horrocks

STAUPITZ, JOHN, see AUGUSTINIANISM

STEWARDSHIP

The principle of stewardship is closely linked to the concept of *grace: everything comes from God as a gift and is to be administered faithfully on his behalf. There is thus both stewardship of the earth and stewardship of the gospel; stewardship of personal resources of time, money and talents, and stewardship of the resources of church and society. Along with questions of mission strategy and support there are issues of personal and corporate lifestyle, just wages and fair prices, *poverty and wealth, all related to explicit or implicit theologies of the *kingdom of God, *work and *nature.

The theme of stewardship as a recognition of the unity of *creation and the consequent need to care for the whole earth can be traced in Eastern Orthodoxy and in Western theology down to Calvin. Nevertheless, it can be argued that in practice a more prevalent understanding of 'dominion' (Gen. 1:28) as domination rather than stewardship has been a justification, if not a cause, of much exploitation. However, international consciousness of the relationship between *ecological and political exploitation and the need to seek a just and sustainable society has grown steadily since the pioneering Brandt Commission report *North–South: A Programme for Survival* (London, 1980). In the 1980s the pressing problems were the arms race and nuclear disarmament, and the social consequences of unemployment and technological change in industry. They remain unresolved, and are arguably more widespread than then. But, increasingly, attention inside and outside the churches has focused on the effects of climate change; on progress towards ratification of the 1997 UN Kyoto Protocol which came into force in 2005; and on the arguments put forward by those countries unwilling to participate.

Bibliography

R. J. Berry (ed.), *Environmental Stewardship* (London and New York, 2006); Church of England General Synod, *Sharing God's Planet* (London, 2005); M. Northcott, *Environment and Christian Ethics* (Cambridge, 1996); C. Sugden, *Radical Discipleship* (London, 1981); *idem* (ed.), *The Church in Response to Human Need* (Exeter, 1987); World Council of

Churches, *Solidarity with Victims of Climate Change* (Geneva, 2002).

P. N. HILLYER

STODDARD, SOLOMON (1643–1729)

Solomon Stoddard was born in Boston, Massachusetts to Anthony Stoddard, a prominent merchant, and Mary Downing, a niece of Governor John Winthrop. After graduating from Harvard in 1662, he was appointed tutor (1666) and librarian (1667) at the college before serving two years as a chaplain in Barbados. In 1669 Stoddard was called to the *Congregational Church in Northampton, Massachusetts, where he served as pastor for the next sixty years until his death in 1729. Troubled over declining membership resulting from the Half-Way Covenant (1662), he instituted open communion to all who would partake and granted full church membership based upon 'a serious profession of the true religion' even though some lacked a definite experience of saving grace. Increase *Mather's ten-year debate with Stoddard over his new innovations did little to prevent their adoption by most of the clergy in the Connecticut River valley. Also his strong evangelistic preaching and methods resulted in five distinct awakenings or 'harvests' uncommon elsewhere in New England prior to the Great Awakening (see *Revival, theology of). His remarkable success as an evangelist added to the popularity of his treatises on conversion, especially his *Guide to Christ* (1729), which was widely read by young ministers, including his grandson, Jonathan *Edwards, who succeeded him at Northampton. Though Edwards later came to reject his grandfather's views on open communion, he followed many of Stoddard's methods through the pivotal years of the Great Awakening, citing him frequently in his classic *On Religious Affections* (1746).

Bibliography

K. J. Hardman, *Seasons of Refreshing: Evangelism and Revivals in America* (Baker, 1994); D. Laurence, 'Jonathan Edwards, Solomon Stoddard, and the Preparationist Model of Conversion', *Harvard Theological Review* 72, 1979, pp. 267–283; P. Miller, 'Solomon Stoddard, 1643–1729', *Harvard Theological Review* 34, 1941, pp. 277–320; T. A. Schafer, 'Solomon Stoddard and the Theology of the Revival', in S. C. Henry (ed.), *A Miscellany of American Christianity: Essays in Honor of H. Shelton Smith* (Cambridge, 1963); J. P. Walsh, 'Solomon Stoddard's Open Communion: A Reexamination', *The New England Quarterly* 43, 1970, pp. 97–114.

R. GLEASON

STOICISM

Stoicism was founded by Zeno (335–263 BC), who taught in Athens in a *stoa* (porch), from which his school derived its name. He was succeeded by Cleanthes (331–232 BC), who breathed a more personal spirit into the Stoic conception of deity, as in his 'Hymn to Zeus'. Chrysippus (*c*. 280–207 BC) gave Stoicism its completed form and logical defence.

The Stoic worldview may be characterized as *materialistic *pantheism. Matter, however, comes in two kinds: a grosser kind, corresponding to the ordinary conception of matter, and a more refined kind, described as breath or spirit and diffused throughout reality. The latter is the ruling power and guiding force of reality and corresponds to deity, for it exercises providence, making this the 'best of all possible worlds'. The human being too is composed of these same two kinds of material reality, as is the cosmos. The present world derived from fire and will return to fire (the world conflagration), after which the same world will re-emerge to repeat the cycle (the regeneration, *palingenesia*). The ruling spirit is rational, and the Stoics contributed to logic by their efforts to represent reality rationally and to defend their system. The Stoics developed the allegorical method of interpretation as a way of attaching their physical theories to classical mythology. Their philosophy provided a defence of the traditional religion, including divination and astrology, on the basis of the interconnectedness of the universe.

The lasting influence of Stoicism came not from its pantheism and rationalism, but its moral teaching and attitude toward life. The goal of life is virtue, and virtue is to live in accord with the rational nature of reality. The emotional life was disparaged as irrational and unnatural. The only important thing in life is virtue: therefore, one is to remain unmoved by external affairs, anything that is not within one's own power, and concentrate on the attitudes and character that are within one's control. Since according to the Stoic view of providence and the cyclical nature of reality, everything is determined, a person should accept things as they are. One cannot control circumstances, but people can control the way they look at them. Everything outside of virtue is indifferent, but in the development of later Stoic ethics more and more attention was paid to what was preferred and not preferred among indifferent things.

This change in ethical concern came with the Middle Stoa of Panaetius (*c.* 185–109 BC), who adapted Stoicism for the Romans by giving more attention to political theory and allowing a greater place to emotional and aesthetic concerns. Posidonius (*c.* 135–50 BC) further broadened Stoicism to include scientific experiment, and through the theory of sympathetic relationship between all parts of the world contributed to the understanding of kinds of unity. He likened the universe to the unity of a living body. The later Stoics allowed a greater independence to the life of the soul and so weakened the earlier monism.

Roman Stoicism represented almost exclusively ethical concerns. Seneca (*c.* AD 1–65) laid bare the wickedness in human nature, and in his moral exhortations he more nearly approximated to Christian teaching than any other classical philosopher. Musonius Rufus (30–101) and Epictetus (55–*c.* 135) use language comparable to that in the NT. Stoicism ascended the imperial throne with Marcus Aurelius (131–180), an introspective and melancholy yet noble man. Thereafter we do not hear about Stoicism as a school, but it was not extinct, for its significant moral insights had become common property, one of the permanent legacies of the ancient world to Western civilization.

Many points of contact between Stoicism and the NT have been noted. For instance, Paul in Acts 17:28 quotes a Stoic commonplace from the *Phaenomena* of Aratus (*c.* 315–240 BC), a pupil of Zeno. Many terms in the NT were at home in Stoicism: spirit, *conscience, *logos, virtue, self-sufficiency, reasonable service. Even the substantive similarities, however, are set in different worldviews. Stoicism did not have a fully personal god, a creator, personal immortality, or a saviour. In ethics, where the similarities were the closest, there were fundamental differences. Stoicism told one to have the attitude to self that one has towards others; Christianity reversed the outlook. The motivation was different: in Stoicism, living in accord with the higher self; in Christianity, response to the love of God in Christ.

The pervasive influence of Stoicism in the ethical thought of the early Empire, including that of the first-century Jewish philosopher, *Philo, meant that early Christian ethical writings showed contact with Stoicism. This is evident, for example, in *Clement of Alexandria's *Instructor* (*Paedagogus*). *Ambrose's treatise *On the Duties of the Clergy* is a Christian adaptation of Cicero's *On Duties*, itself influenced by Panaetius. The Stoic view of *anthropology influenced Tatian (second century) and *Tertullian's *On the Soul*, which gives a more 'material' view of the soul than *Platonism did.

As assimilated into Christian thought, aspects of Stoicism became a part of the Christian heritage. Independent revivals of elements in Stoicism occurred in the Renaissance and early modern period. The Stoic attitude that inner character is superior to and indifferent to external affairs has continued to have appeal. Where morality has been sought apart from religion, the Stoic view that virtue is sufficient for happiness has given encouragement. The Stoic stimulation of the idea of a natural religion and its humanitarianism and cosmopolitan universalism have been absorbed into Christian thought.

Bibliography

L. Edelstein, *The Meaning of Stoicism* (Cambridge, 1966); B. Inwood, *The Cambridge Companion to the Stoics* (Cambridge, 2003); R. MacMullen, *Enemies of the Roman Order* (Cambridge, 1966); M. Pohlenz, *Die Stoa*, 2 vols. (Göttingen, 1955–59); J. M. Rist, *Stoic Philosophy* (Cambridge, 1969); F. H. Sandbach, *The Stoics* (London, ²1994); J. N. Sevenster, *Paul and Seneca* (Leiden, 1962); R. W. Sharples, *Stoics, Epicureans and Skeptics* (London, 1996); M. Spanneut, *Le Stoïcisme des pères de l'Église de Clément de Rome à Clément d'Alexandrie* (Paris, 1957); R. M. Wenley, *Stoicism and Its Influence* (New York, 1963); E. Zeller, *Stoics, Epicureans, and Sceptics* (London, 1880).

E. FERGUSON

STRAUSS, DAVID FRIEDRICH (1808–74)

David Friedrich Strauss was born at Ludwigsburg in Württemberg, south Germany, and studied at Tübingen under Ferdinand Christian Baur (see *Tübingen School). After further study in Berlin, he was appointed tutor in the theological seminary at Tübingen, where he wrote his most famous work, *The Life of Jesus*. From its appearance in 1835 we may date the open emergence of the historical-critical investigation of the Bible.

The key to understanding this work is not merely Strauss's *Hegelian ideas, but rather his underlying non-miraculous and non-supernatural presuppositions. Strauss to the end of his days explicitly denied the existence of a God who was both transcendent and personal. It followed logically from this that there could be no divine miracles, and that every miraculous story in the NT must be *ipso facto* unauthentic. Thus the Gospels were regarded by him as fictitious accounts, elaborated solely to prove that Jesus was the Messiah. If it was prophesied that the Messiah would heal the blind and raise the dead, then such miracles had to be claimed for Jesus by the evangelists in order to show that he had fulfilled these prophecies. If Enoch and Elijah were taken up to heaven, then Jesus also had to have an ascension. The Gospel stories reflected the *myth-making power of his followers' piety which was steeped in OT expectations. This mythical approach had been suggested by some of Strauss's predecessors, but Strauss was the first to apply it consistently to every part of the NT. It is quite independent of the Hegelian philosophy, and only in his concluding attempt at a positive reconstruction of Christianity was the Hegelian philosophy employed. Jesus demonstrates the realization of the Absolute in the human race.

As a consequence of his attack on historic Christianity, Strauss was dismissed from his position at the seminary. Nomination to a professorship of theology at Zurich in 1839 came to nothing, and Strauss spent the remainder of his life writing historical biographies with renewed forays into the theological field. In 1864 he produced his revised *Life of Jesus for the German People*, and in 1872 came his last work, *The Old Faith and the New*, in which he accepted a scientific materialism, rejected life after death, and espoused Darwinian evolution, the first theologian to do so.

Strauss was undoubtedly one of the most significant theological figures of the nineteenth century. His *Life of Jesus* set in motion the whole 'Quest' for the historical Jesus, and precipitated the continuing critical examination of the NT sources. Throughout the theological and ecclesiastical world, not only in Germany but also abroad, he was widely regarded as the leader of the attack against the Bible.

See also: HISTORICAL JESUS, QUEST FOR.

Bibliography
R. S. Cromwell, *David Friedrich Strauss and His Place in Modern Thought* (Fairlawn, 1974); H. Frei, 'David Friedrich Strauss', in N. Smart *et al.* (eds.), *Nineteenth Century Religious Thought in the West* (Cambridge, 1985); H. Harris, *David Friedrich Strauss and His Theology* (Edinburgh, 1982).

H. HARRIS

STRONG, AUGUSTUS HOPKINS (1836–1921)

Strong was a Baptist minister, theologian and seminary professor. Rochester, New York, was the scene of his birth, death and the majority of his ministry. Strong received his BA from Yale in 1857, graduated from Rochester Seminary in 1859, and spent 1859–60 in study in Berlin. He was minister at the First Baptist Church, Haverhill, Massachusetts, 1861–65, and at the First Baptist Church, Cleveland, Ohio, 1865–72. He served from 1872 to 1912 as president and professor of systematic theology at Rochester Seminary, and was president emeritus from 1912 to 1921. His mature thought is reflected in *Christ in Creation* and *Ethical Monism* and the 1907 edition of his *Systematic Theology*. Strong sought to maintain traditional orthodoxy within the Calvinistic framework, while adopting both evolutionary thought and biblical higher criticism. The radical immanence of Christ in creation became his key for balancing this tension. His views of creation, providence, inspiration, human sinfulness, divine justice, atonement and world missions were shaped by this principle.

See also: SOUTHERN BAPTIST THEOLOGY.

Bibliography
J. A. Aloisi, 'Augustus Hopkins Strong and Ethical Monism', PhD thesis, The Southern Baptist Seminary (2012); C. F. H. Henry, *Personal Idealism and Strong's Theology* (Wheaton, 1951); G. Wacker, *Augustus H. Strong and the Dilemma of Historical Consciousness* (Macon, 1985).

T. J. NETTLES

STRUCTURALISM

Structuralism is the name commonly applied to a movement that emerged within a circle of French linguistic philosophers following the publication of Ferdinand de Saussure's *Cours de linguistic générale* in 1916. Saussure (1857–1913) and those who follow him argue that language reflects certain universal patterns or structures, which in turn reflect universal orders within the human brain. From this it was concluded that all narrative, especially the more unconscious or 'folk' literature, will reflect in some way the settled 'deep structures' by which societal consciousness is governed.

Biblical studies

Although most French structuralists have been far more interested in primitive mythology than in biblical studies, their work has inspired a number of experiments by students of Scripture, in which the methods more than their philosophical underpinnings have been applied to biblical texts. These studies are commonly known by the name 'structural analysis', a broad umbrella term that has come to signify any approach to Scripture which looks at the material 'synchronically' (relationships are to be found within the text), rather than 'diachronically' (relationships are to be found in various historical stages of the development of the text), as in traditional biblical criticism.

An important distinction must be made between the true structuralist, whose philosophical bent has frequently led to an abandonment of *history as a category of meaning, and the various practitioners of structural analysis in biblical studies circles in the late twentieth century. Very few biblical scholars share the rejection of history which marks true structuralism, and some of the most fruitful work being done today looks for synchronic relationships, but couples the study with diachronic research as well.

A further concern of 'semiology', as structuralism is often called, is to trace the dynamics operative in the process 'text to reader', in place of traditional biblical studies' concern for the process 'author to text'. A common conviction holds that not only the structures of societal thinking which are found in the *mythologies of the past, but also the 'deep structures' of the society or group which in a later age receives the message, are important. For a full linguistic picture, then, one must look at the original mythological structures, and then the structures operative in the receiver society, comparing the two and tracing the development of the myth in that light.

Method

The object of true structuralist research is not primarily to reveal meaning in the text itself, but rather to discover how the text, as a reflection of the deeper structures which transcend time and circumstances, conveys a *symbolic and timeless structure or meaning. This has led structuralists, as opposed to the biblical 'structural analysts', frequently to prefer the category 'myth' over the study of historical narrative, and has in turn led to some rather eccentric approaches to biblical material.

Claude Levi-Strauss (1908–2009), one such structuralist, grouped together all the mythological texts of a given culture, finding in those texts 'variations of a basic myth', reducing the events of each story studied to short sentences which he calls 'mythemes'. The mythemes are then grouped together, and from them the more comprehensive 'view of reality' emerges (C. Levi-Strauss, 'The Structural Study of Myth', in *Structural Anthropology*, ET, Garden City, NY, 1963). Applying the methods of Levi-Strauss, Edmund Leach (1910–89) gives an example of how biblical studies might look from a structuralist viewpoint, in his *Genesis as Myth and Other Essays* (London, 1969), a series of essays which amply illustrate the reasons why biblical scholars have generally rejected the method in its purest form.

Turning to more traditional biblical studies, one finds a growing body of material. From an initial critique of Leach ('Some Comments on Structural Analysis and Biblical Studies', *Supplements to VT* 22 [Congress Volume, Uppsala, 1971], Leiden, 1972, pp. 129–142, and 'Structural Analysis: Is It Done with Mirrors?', *Interpretation* 28, 1974, pp. 165–181), R. C. Culley proceeded to apply the method to various groups of biblical stories, while making it clear that his philosophical and methodological approach varied significantly from that of the structuralists. (See Culley's *Studies in the Structure of Hebrew Narrative*, Philadelphia and Missoula, 1976.)

Additional biblical scholars have taken up the task, most of whom readily argue for a sharp modification of French structuralist presuppositional and methodological approaches. Some of the new work is probably little more than a shift from historical to internal structural concerns in looking at the text, but some fresh insights in how to study the Bible have emerged in the wake of the new discipline. If nothing else, the text itself, rather than some putative form of reconstructed earlier version, has again become the focus of attention, surely a needed emphasis in contemporary biblical scholarship.

This is precisely the point of Jacques Derrida's famous phrase, 'il n'y a pas de hors-texte' ('there is nothing outside of the text'). In contrast, then, to the structuralists, these mid- to late-twentieth-century largely French post-structuralist philosophers responded critically to key features of structuralism. Often linked with *postmodernism, these writers include Michel *Foucault, Gilles Deleuze, Roland Barthes, Judith Butler and Umberto Eco. While differing at important points, their approach to knowledge argued that in order to understand cultural objects (e.g. a text) it was necessary to study both the object itself and important features surrounding the text, including various formal and informal conceptual structures that gave rise to the object as well as the experiences drawn from relating to that object. In these ways, post-structuralism both destabilized and complexified knowledge in ways seeking to be more broadly engaged with cultural objects and more open to the reality of the surrounding world.

See also: HERMENEUTICS.

Bibliography

C. E. Armerding, *The Old Testament and Criticism* (Grand Rapids, 1983); J. W. Rogerson, *Myth in Old Testament Interpretation* (Berlin and New York, 1974); K. J. Vanhoozer, *Is There a Meaning in This Text?* (Grand Rapids, 1998).

C. E. ARMERDING

SUBORDINATIONISM, see TRINITY

SUBSTANCE

Substance is the word most commonly used in Christian theology to denote the objective reality of the one being of *God. Strictly speaking, it derives from the Latin equivalent (*substantia*) of the Greek word **hypostasis*, which means 'an objective reality capable of acting'. Greek theology, however, following *Origen, claimed that there were three *hypostaseis* in God, which caused confusion when *Hilary of Poiters translated this word as *substantiae* (plural) in his *De Trinitate*.

Latin usage had been determined by *Tertullian, who used *substantia* to refer to what the Greeks usually called *ousia* (essence, being). This was almost certainly because he equated *ousia* with *hypostasis*, as the single objective reality in God. Behind the confusion of terms, therefore, there lies a different approach to theology, one which seeks to discover the Trinity in the unity of God, rather than the other way round. In the creed of the Council of Nicaea (325), *homoousios*, a compound of *ousia*, was used to affirm the full divinity of the Son as 'of one substance' with the Father (see *Trinity).

The term *ousia* was widely used in pre-Christian philosophy, where its meaning was roughly equivalent to 'real thing'. However, philosophical usage was elastic, and though it certainly influenced Christian thinking, it did not possess a single, well-defined concept of *ousia*. Christians were undoubtedly convinced, primarily from the Scriptures, that the word should be used of God. This was because the God of the Bible was called by the name I AM, or He Who Is (*ho ōn*; Exod. 3:14; cf. John 8:58).

Certain branches of the Christian *mystical tradition have held that the essence of God is in some sense visible, but most theologians have maintained that it is unknowable by any creature. Its attributes were listed by *John of Damascus as 'anarchy' (i.e. without beginning), uncreatedness, unbegottenness, imperishability, immortality, eternity, infinity, limitlessness, boundlessness, omnipotence, simplicity, uncompoundness, incorporeality, immutability, impassibility, unchangeability, unalterability and invisibility.

This list was simplified and systematized by *Thomas Aquinas, whose teaching has become the foundation of classical Western *theism. The Reformers accepted this on the whole, though they dismissed speculation about God's substance and urged the church to concentrate instead on knowing him in his persons.

In modern times, the traditional language of divine substance has come under severe attack. In particular, *process theology accuses it of conveying a static view of God, even though Marius *Victorinus, and the Augustinian tradition after him, believed that God's being was motion (*esse=moveri*). Process theology follows the tradition of *natural theology in trying to understand the *ousia* of God in philosophical and scientific terms, but this cannot be done successfully. If we are to speak of the divine substance today, we must do so in the light of the Bible's teaching about God as the I AM, which is not bound to any philosophical system of interpretation.

Bibliography

J. B. Cobb, *A Christian Natural Theology* (Philadelphia, 1966); E. L. Mascall, *The Openness of Being* (London, 1971); A. Plantinga, *Does God Have a Nature?* (Milwaukee, 1980); G. C. Stead, *Divine Substance* (Oxford, 1977); R. Swinburne, *The Coherence of Theism* (Oxford, 1977).

G. L. BRAY

SUBSTITUTION AND REPRESENTATION

It is generally accepted among Christian theologians that Jesus acted as our representative in his work of *atonement. By this is meant that his life, death, resurrection and continuous intercession accrue to our benefit. His work is for us. There is also, however, in the Scriptures a dimension of substitution in the atonement of Christ and specifically with reference to his death. In Rom. 3:23–26 Christ is said to suffer in our place as a substitutionary bearer of the judgment which we deserve. This presented answers to the question of how God can be just and yet *justify the ungodly when his wrath is revealed against all ungodliness and unrighteousness of men. God the Son endures judgment as our substitute and becomes the propitiation whereby God is able to receive sinners. This emphasis is reinforced when Christ is identified as the suffering servant: 'He was wounded for our transgressions . . .' (Isa. 53:5, RSV). Two passages also speak of him as a ransom. In Mark 10:45, the Son of man gives his life a ransom for many, and in 1 Tim. 2:6 Christ is said to have given himself as a ransom for all. The ransom concept has a powerful substitutionary connotation. Similarly, the application of the OT symbolism of the scapegoat (Lev. 16:8) to Jesus is undoubtedly substitutionary (Heb. 9:7, 12, 28).

Apart from Romans, there are two primary verses on which this view is based. In 2 Cor. 5:21, Paul argues that Jesus, who is sinless, identifies with sin to such a degree that mysteriously he is said to be made sin for our sake. The concept of substitution is perceived in that he is treated not on the basis of what he is, but what we are. He became our substitute. In Gal. 3:13, Paul argues that in order for Jesus Christ to redeem us from the curse of the law, he himself must endure, in our place, the curse of sin which we deserve.

Those scholars who reject this concept of the atonement do so for at least three reasons.

(1) Vincent Taylor (1887–1968), for example, argues that Paul consistently does not use the substitutionary preposition *anti* ('instead of, in place of') but rather the representative *hyper* ('on behalf of, for the sake of') in expounding the death of Jesus. (He rejects 1 Tim. 2:6 as non-Pauline.) In response, it has been pointed out that *hyper* can have the force of *anti* in Hellenistic Gk and that, for example, in Rom. 3:25 where it is used with *hilastērion* (propitiation) it is clearly substitutionary in intent.

(2) The concept of God's personal *wrath is questioned by C. H. *Dodd, who finds it incongruous to his inherent love and pleads for the wrath of God to be seen as inevitable and inherent consequences of man's rebellious spirit. The object of atonement is therefore said to be man *and his sin*, not God and his wrath. *Hilastērion* is then translated 'expiation', which is focusing upon sin and its consequences for man, rather than 'propitiation' which has as its focus the fulfilment of the justice of God. In reply, it must be said that wrath, in biblical terms, is not uncontrolled pique, but the inevitable response of personal pure love to that which is unholy. Again, although wrath may be the need for atonement, love is the ground of atonement. God takes the initiative not only in dealing with sin (in expiation), but in removing the personal opposition to our access into his righteous presence (propitiation). Love and wrath are not therefore contradictory in God.

(3) The idea of transactional guilt, i.e. of someone else being asked to carry our responsibility in order to make reconciliation, is said to be essentially immoral. It has to be recognized that at times the notion of Christ's substitution has been presented crudely and devoid of mystery. Nevertheless, this element in the work of Christ can be seen as a corollary of grace whereby God secures for us totally and incomprehensibly what we cannot do for ourselves.

There is more to the atonement than an objective substitution by Christ in the place of sinners. This is one of a number of complementary motifs used by the biblical writers, which subjectively increases our security and excites our worship. The confidence that in Christ we cannot be condemned because he has been condemned in our stead leaves the Christian in humble and speechless wonder.

See also: CROSS; SUBSTITUTION, PENAL.

Bibliography

R. W. Dale, *The Atonement* (London, 1894); J. Denney, *The Death of Christ*, ed. R. V. G. Tasker (London, 1951); C. H. Dodd, *The Epistle of Paul to the Romans* (London, 1932); R. S. Franks, *A History of the Doctrine of the Work of Christ* (London, 1918); E. M. B. Green, *The Empty Cross of Jesus* (London, 1984); L. Morris, *The Apostolic Preaching of the Cross* (London, ³1965); idem, *The Cross in the New Testament* (London, 1965); J. K. Mozley, *The Doctrine of the Atonement* (London, 1915); J. R. W. Stott, *The Cross of Christ* (Leicester, 1986); V. Taylor, *The Atonement in New Testament Preaching* (London, 1940).

T. W. J. MORROW

SUBSTITUTION, PENAL

The central feature of the Christian doctrine of *salvation is the *atonement effected by *Jesus Christ through his death on the *cross at Calvary. In the NT, there are various metaphors or models which help to explain the meaning and significance of this atonement. Since the early Church Fathers, penal substitution has been the controlling model used by the church to explain the atonement, the other metaphors and models being used to supplement this primary model. This has been particularly true within evangelical Christianity.

Penal substitution is an explanation of the atonement which says that Jesus Christ, the Son of God, standing in the place of sinful human beings, took upon himself the wrath of God due to those sinners. The sinners for whom Jesus died are therefore pardoned and accepted by God. This pardon and acceptance is appropriated through faith in Jesus Christ.

Recently, even among evangelicals, penal substitution as an understanding of the atonement has been challenged for various reasons. First, it is argued that to speak of the Father forsaking the Son on the cross is unthinkable, given a biblical doctrine of the unity of the Trinity. Second, it is argued that since there are many models and metaphors for the atonement, no one model must be allowed to dominate. Third, it is argued that union with Christ, rather than penal substitution, should be the controlling factor in any theology of atonement. Fourth, it is argued that the notion of the Father punishing the Son constitutes a form of celestial child abuse which should have no place in Christian theology. Fifth, it is argued that the penal substitutionary view gives the impression of an angry God who only becomes a loving God after he has been appeased by the sacrifice of his Son.

Those who affirm penal substitution regard the last two of these criticisms as simply a misunderstanding of their position, but they do recognize the strength of the first three criticisms, while continuing to maintain their position. Clearly, if penal substitution is to be maintained, then first, care must be taken to expound the atonement in the light of God's trinitarian being and his overall purpose and plan; second, use must be made of every model and metaphor of atonement, albeit under the controlling model of penal substitution; and third, proper emphasis must be given to union with Christ.

See also: GUILT AND FORGIVENESS; REDEMPTION.

Bibliography

H. Boersma, *Violence, Hospitality and the Cross* (Grand Rapids, 2004); C. E. Hill and F. A. James III, *The Glory of the Atonement* (Downers Grove, 2004); S. Jeffery, M. Ovey and A. Sach, *Pierced for Our Transgressions* (Nottingham, 2007); P. Wells, *Cross Words: The Biblical Doctrine of the Atonement* (Fearn, 2006).

A. T. B. MCGOWAN

SUFFERING

The reality of human suffering has long been seen as a problem for *theism. How can the presence of *evil and suffering in the world be reconciled with belief in God? In the Greek philosophical tradition people have been wrestling with this problem at least as far back as Epicurus, who lived three centuries before

Christ (341–270 BC). In the Hebrew tradition the struggle of faith and doubt that is prompted by the existence of suffering goes back at least 300 years earlier to the books of Job, Isaiah, Lamentations and to some of the Psalms. Likewise, in other religious traditions and cultures, suffering presents itself as a challenge to belief in the divinely bestowed order and goodness of human life. Certain kinds of suffering, such as the pain caused by heat when we approach a fire too closely, are readily enough understood and present no threat to theistic belief, but cases of innocent or unjust suffering constitute a challenge to belief in a just, almighty and benevolent God. Within the category of innocent suffering we may distinguish further between the suffering inflicted by human beings upon others and the suffering that results from natural occurrences or 'acts of God', such as earthquakes, tidal waves, disease and the like. The attempt to account for the presence of both kinds of suffering while maintaining some form of belief in God is known as *theodicy.

One of the most well-known formulations of the problem is that of the Scottish philosopher David *Hume, who asks, 'Is God willing to prevent evil, but not able? then he is impotent. Is he able, but not willing? then he is malevolent. Is he both able and willing? whence then is evil?' This intellectual conundrum has exercised philosophers a great deal, but it treats the problem as essentially theoretical. Contrast this with the problem of evil and suffering posed from out of the midst of actual suffering. In this case the question is put as an agonized cry against God and requires not only philosophical consideration, but also pastoral response. This is the question of the anguished parents who sit at the bedside of their dying child, or of those whose lives have been torn apart by tragedy and the death of loved ones. In such cases the question of suffering is framed as a cry for help to a God who does not seem to answer. This is the theological and pastorally oriented question about evil and suffering which looks not for the philosophical resolution of a logical difficulty, but for a more profound theological response about the presence or absence of God in situations when darkness covers the earth.

There have been four main lines of response to the philosophical conundrum of suffering. Many of these appear, but are also contested, in the Christian tradition.

(1) The 'just deserts' theory of human suffering supposes that suffering is a consequence of *sin. According to this view, people who suffer get what they deserve, either because foolish acts lead to harmful consequences, or because God is thought to punish the guilty. In each case the appropriate response is repentance and a reformation of one's life. While there is undoubtedly a correlation in some cases between unwise or sinful human action and suffering, the just desserts theory fails to account for the vast swathes of innocent suffering inflicted on people through no fault of their own.

(2) A second view, called the harmony view, holds that suffering is not the tragedy we suppose it to be. The Greek philosopher Plotinus, for instance, argued that with a proper perspective we will see that in the grand scheme of things suffering pales into insignificance in comparison with the beauty and rationality of the universe. This is a view that is frequently judged to be unhelpful, both intellectually and pastorally.

(3) The soul-making theory of suffering proposes that suffering may be turned to God's good purpose as a means through which we become better human beings. Much like the situation of a person training for a marathon who runs on through the pain in order to achieve the high goal, suffering is perceived to be a means of 'soul-making', of perfecting the creatures God intends us to be. A sophisticated version of this view, advocated by John *Hick, holds that while God does not ordain every instance of suffering, a world that includes suffering is the best kind of world for perfecting human beings as moral and spiritual agents. While it may be true that suffering can sometimes produce good effects, the greatest difficulty confronting this view is the problem of proportionality. It fails to explain, for example, why a starving child in a war-torn country suffers so much, while others in affluence suffer so little. The soul-making theory prompted the character Ivan in Fyodor Dostoyevsky's novel, *The Brother's Karamazov*, to protest against a God who could set the world up on such terms. The innocent suffering of even one little child cannot justify some future good, Ivan contends.

(4) The free-will defence suggests that because God seeks a free and loving relation with human beings, we must be created with free *will. Evil and suffering are an unfortunate consequence of this policy, as humanity abuses

its freedom and chooses paths that lead to suffering and evil rather than to communion and love. This view has often been advocated by Christian theologians and has the dual merits of cohering with a central strand of biblical thought and taking seriously humanity's own responsibility for the causes of a great deal of human suffering. It suggests also that we must be involved in working towards the alleviation of suffering. Proponents of the free-will defence commonly acknowledge, however, that this argument does not provide an explanation of all suffering. Natural disasters commonly cause suffering that cannot be attributed to human free will.

A fundamental difficulty attending the philosophical attempts to solve the conundrum of suffering is that they tend to promote complacency in the face of suffering. If there are good reasons for suffering, then there is little incentive to take action against it. In the ministry of *Jesus, by contrast, we may discern a profound sympathy for those who suffer and a consistent effort to alleviate suffering. It is in consideration of the ministry of Jesus that we come upon the question of what God has to do with human suffering. In him we see the God who responds with compassion to human suffering. 'Compassion' means to 'suffer with'. Jesus responds to suffering by entering into the midst of it, shouldering its burden, and by becoming active against it. The manifesto of Jesus' ministry delivered in the synagogue in Nazareth (Luke 4:16–21) has the relief of suffering as a central feature of the coming kingdom of God.

The divine compassion and the divine opposition to suffering and evil lead penultimately to that event of horror and pain which lies at the heart of Christian faith. To inquire how God relates to human evil and suffering brings us through Gethsemane to Calvary and then to the foot of the *cross. It brings us to the place where Christ took upon himself the suffering of the world and places us within earshot of that agonized cry at the last, 'My God, my God, why have you forsaken me?' At Calvary, human suffering is revealed in its greatest depths. T. F. *Torrance has written that by taking these words upon his lips Jesus reveals that he enters our situation of suffering, utters our cry and asks our questions of protest, in order both to ask them in truth and to receive the answers. Jesus' cry is a cry of real dereliction and real suffering. The Christian *gospel offers the news that the Son of the Almighty God has set aside power and has come to be among us, to share in our suffering, to take our burden upon himself, and ultimately, with the resurrection, to open up the possibility of new life beyond all suffering and pain. P. T. *Forsyth, followed more recently by Jürgen *Moltmann, Kazoh Kitamori, Eberhard *Jüngel, Hans Urs von *Balthasar, Alan Lewis, and many others, contends that it is at the cross that God does his own theodicy. He answers the questions of human suffering, not with an explanation, but by meeting it with his own compassionate presence in order that it be brought to an end. The end of all suffering is therefore a key component of Christian *hope, founded upon Christ's victory over suffering and death.

This approach to the problem of suffering has occasioned a renewed discussion in recent theology of the doctrine of divine *impassibility. The patristic theologian *Cyril of Alexandria once remarked that the Son of God suffers impassibly in the flesh. The doctrine of divine impassibility is not, accordingly, a denial of the suffering of Christ, the divine Son of God, but rather involves the assertion that God is not subject to change from forces external to himself. The suffering of the impassible God is thus an exercise of God's being as love and is not his victimization at the hands of alien powers.

A final form of human suffering that has occupied Christian thinkers is the suffering of *martyrdom. Beginning with Jesus himself, it has commonly been recognized that faithfulness to God will often bring the believer into conflict with the principalities and powers of a fallen world. In its most extreme form this may result in martyrdom, but Søren *Kierkegaard, among others, has argued that suffering, if not always death, will be a mark of all Christian discipleship. To take up one's cross and follow Christ is to choose a difficult road that, when followed resolutely, will bring the suffering caused by opposition and enmity.

Bibliography

G. Gutiérrez, *On Job: God-Talk and the Suffering of the Innocent* (ET, Maryknoll, 1987); J. Hick, *Evil and the God of Love* (London, 1966); K. Kitamori, *Theology of the Pain of God* (London, 1966); A. E. Lewis, *Between Cross and Resurrection: A Theology of Holy Saturday* (Grand Rapids, 2001); J. Moltmann, *The Crucified God* (ET, London, 1974); D. Soelle, *Suffering* (ET, Philadelphia,

1975); A. Torrance, 'Does God Suffer? Incarnation and Impassibility', in T. Hart and D. Thimell (eds.), *Christ in Our Place: The Humanity of God in Christ for the Reconciliation of the World* (Exeter and Allison Park, 1989); T. G. Weinandy, *Does God Suffer?* (Edinburgh, 2000).

M. A. Rae

SUNDAY, see SABBATH

SUPEREROGATION, see MERIT

SUPERNATURAL

In the OT there is no Hebrew word equivalent to the English word 'natural', nor is there any concept of an unbreakable natural order independent of God. The world is continually dependent upon God in every respect. That which we refer to as '*nature' (e.g. the seasons changing, the rain falling), the OT perceives as the outworking of God's gracious *providence in history. In such a context any idea of the supernatural as the interruption of an unbreakable natural order of cause and effect would be totally foreign. A 'miracle' is not an event with a 'divine cause' as distinct from a 'natural cause', but is rather an event in which God's power is particularly (and sometimes unusually) evident; a 'sign' in which the grace and judgment of God's redemptive purpose are especially revealed.

The inheritance of Greek *metaphysics and the notion of God's 'otherness' led inevitably to an implicit *dualism between God and the world, the supernatural and the natural, faith and reason. In the context of Newtonian physics the world was considered as a closed system of cause and effect, a system in which a 'supernatural' event must be viewed as an unwarranted intrusion. The removal of God from a closed natural order through *deism and his identification with it through *panentheism both imply a dismissal of the supernatural, a demythologizing of Scripture and a rejection of the possibility of present-day miracle.

The use of the term 'supernatural' (other than in the colloquial sense of 'extraordinary') with its dualistic connotations is therefore neither helpful nor scriptural, but an unnecessary diversion from a biblical faith in the transcendently immanent God whose actions reveal both the covenantal faithfulness and the sovereign freedom of his grace.

Recent *Roman Catholic theology has seen the tendency to separate nature and grace, which owed much to *Thomas Aquinas, challenged by theologians such as Karl *Rahner and Henri de Lubac (1896–1991). They have developed the concept of nature as itself 'graced', the sphere of God's loving activity. This outlook helped to shape the thought of the Second *Vatican Council.

Bibliography

D. Grummett, *De Lubac: A Guide for the Perplexed* (London, 2007); C. E. Gunton, 'Transcendence, Metaphor, and the Knowability of God', *JTS* 31, 1980, pp. 501–516; H. de Lubac, *The Mystery of the Supernatural* (rev. edn, New York, 1998); J. Oman, *The Natural and the Supernatural* (Cambridge, 1950); T. F. Torrance, *Theological Science* (Oxford, 1969).

J. E. Colwell

SUPERSESSIONISM

In its narrow sense, supersessionism refers to the relationship between Israel and the church. Accordingly, the life, death and resurrection of Jesus Christ climaxes and fulfils God's covenant with Israel to make way for the new *covenant revealed in Christ and the outpouring of the Holy Spirit upon the early church. The new covenant thus renders the old covenant salvifically null and void. Some hold that the supersession of the old covenant leaves no further role for ethnic Israel in God's unfolding drama of redemption. The new covenant subsumes ethnic and national identities, uniting persons of every race and nation in the church. Other supersessionists, however, argue that Israel remains uniquely chosen of God even if that election remains frustrated apart from the recognition of Jesus Christ as the Messiah. Hence, the promise of ethnic Israel's election is superseded only to the degree that the church now participates in the salvation prepared for God's chosen people.

In its broader sense, supersessionism refers to Christianity's relationship to the history, language, knowledge and aspirations of all peoples and nations. Positively, supersession entails the extension of knowledge, history and religious yearning that is fulfilled in and through faith in Jesus Christ. Various non-Western theologians have embraced this understanding of supersession in that it presents Christianity in continuity with *culture and even serves as a catalyst for its extension and fulfilment. Supersession, however, can be viewed as countercultural, as faith in Christ deconstructs and displaces that which it regards as false and idolatrous.

Objections to biblical and theological supersessionism are raised from numerous perspectives. Various theologians and biblical scholars have argued that the church exists only in continuity with Israel. Thus, redemption ought to be understood in light of God's ongoing irrevocable election of Israel, which by grace has now been made available to Christians but not to the detriment of God's ongoing relationship with Israel. *Dispensationalists, on the other hand, believe that the church and Israel enjoy distinct covenantal dispensations, and thus the Jews will inherit the promise of the covenant in a future restoration of Israel. More radical critics of supersessionism view the doctrine as necessarily triumphalist and oppressive. They argue that failure to recognize and affirm the diversity and integrity of various ways human beings experience and respond to the divine has historically led to cultural, religious and political repression.

Bibliography:

S. Bader-Saye, *Church and Israel after Christendom: The Politics of Election* (Boulder Colorado, 1999); K. Bediako, *Theology and Identity: The Impact of Culture upon Christian Thought in the Second Century and in Modern Africa* (Oxford and Irvine, 1999); R. K. Soulen, *The God of Israel and Christian Theology* (Minneapolis, 1996); N. T. Wright, *What Saint Paul Really Said: Was Paul of Tarsus the Real Founder of Christianity?* (Oxford and Grand Rapids, 1997); D. S. Yeago, 'Messiah's People: The Culture of the Church in the Midst of the Nations', *Pro Ecclesia* 6, 1997, pp. 146–171.

T. Harvey

SUPPER-STRIFE, see EUCHARIST

SUPRALAPSARIANISM, see HYPER-CALVINISM; PREDESTINATION

SWEDENBORGISM, see SECTS

SWISS CONFESSION, see CONFESSIONS OF FAITH

SYMBOL

Symbols mediate meaning, but demand interpretation. They are grounded in the rationality and beauty of creation, but are vulnerable to idolatry and distortion within history.

Contemporary theological appropriations of the term 'symbol' take place in dialogue with a range of increasingly complex and contested philosophical uses. These dialogues reflect both perennial philosophical questions about relationships between reality and representation and more recent *postmodern inflections of 'semiotics', concerned with questions of presence and reference.

Theology must also reckon with developing disciplinary debates around the term within anthropology and psychology, as well as cultural and media studies, without forgetting its specific histories as a theological, linguistic and mathematical term.

Much of the complexity involved in defining a 'symbol' stems from application of this term to language itself, such that 'words' as well as objects or images can be symbols. For example, Aristotle's exposition in *On Interpretation* (1.16a 3–8) sets out an economy of representation in which 'spoken words are the symbols of mental experience and written words are the symbols of spoken words'.

One common problem concerns how or whether to distinguish a symbol from a sign. Responses are heavily dependent upon particular lines of argumentation, but it is now common (e.g. C. S. Peirce) to nest the term 'symbol' within the larger category 'sign' and treat it as a particular kind of sign.

Uses peculiar to Christian practice include Cyprian's third-century description of the baptismal (Apostles') creed as *symbolum apostolorum*, a sign of Christian identity and a representation of the whole Christian confession. This was later applied by analogy to other focal statements of Christian belief such as the Lord's Prayer. Within the history of Christian doctrine, the term is closely allied to debates around *sacramental theology. The Communion elements of bread and wine came to be referred to as 'the symbols' (see *Eucharist), but other key Christian symbols would also include water, blood, fire, etc.

While some Western anthropologists such as Mary Douglas and Victor Turner have stressed the 'natural' or 'organic' origins of symbols, the example of the *cross as symbol involves a more 'cultural' understanding, in which the meaning of symbols has to be construed in relation to specific narrative contexts. Following on from this, the idea of an 'unnatural' symbol may also be present to varying degrees within specific heightened narrative and poetic traditions (e.g. apocalyptic). Here we are concerned with the extent to which we should think of symbols as given (in creation), made (in history) or perceived (forged in acts of human creativity or imagination).

Theological understandings of the sacraments or ordinances of *baptism and Communion have diverged sharply in their attitude towards the language of symbol and its relation to the language of 'presence'. Those within a Catholic, Lutheran or Calvinist tradition have often critiqued 'Zwinglian' positions for advocating a 'merely symbolic' understanding, but this may in turn beg questions as to how such critics are construing both the mediation of symbol and the mode of divine presence.

Key early and medieval theological treatments of symbol/sign are found in *Augustine's *On Christian Doctrine* and *On the Trinity*, and in *Boethius, *Anselm of Canterbury, Peter *Abelard, Roger *Bacon and *William of Ockham. Within modern theology, the concept of symbol was particularly prominent in the theology of Paul *Tillich and the hermeneutics of Paul *Ricœur. Anthony Thiselton highlights the influence of psychoanalytical theory on both thinkers, with Tillich's benign, integrative view of symbol indebted to Jungian psychology and Jung's theory of archetypes, while Ricœur's more ambivalent treatment owes more to Freud. Karl *Rahner also made extensive use of the term in his Christological formulations, positing a symbolic relation between Christ's humanity and divinity.

Bibliography

C. Bell, *Ritual* (Oxford, 1998); M. Douglas, *Natural Symbols: Explorations in Cosmology* (London, 1996 [1970]); *Oxford English Dictionary*, entry on 'symbol' tracks early English language uses; K. Rahner, *Theological Investigations*, vol. 4 (Baltimore, 1967); P. Ricœur, *Interpretation Theory* (Fort Worth, 1976); J. K. A. Smith, *Speech and Theology: Language and the Logic of Incarnation* (London, 2002); A. Thiselton, *New Horizons in Hermeneutics* (London, 1992); P. Tillich, *Systematic Theology*, vol. 1 (Chicago, 1973); K. Vanhoozer, *Biblical Narrative in the Philosophy of Paul Ricœur* (Cambridge, 1990).

D. GAY

SYMEON, see MACARIUS (PSEUDO)

SYMEON THE NEW THEOLOGIAN (949–1022)

Symeon the New, or 'the Younger', is one of the most significant figures in the revival of Byzantine letters and church life that can be marked in the eleventh century. He was an aristocrat, possibly a eunuch, and was brought by his family for imperial service at Constantinople at the age of eleven. With the rise to power of the young Emperor Basil II (Bulgarocrator) in 976 his family's influence was overthrown, and the young Symeon (already a Senator by that period) moved sideways into a monastic career in which he excelled, soon becoming an independent abbot of St Mamas, a monastery in the heart of the imperial capital, from which he conducted a noisy campaign of resistance to the emperor, especially denouncing the emperor's court theologian, the Synkellos Stephen. He argued the issue that authority in the church ought to emanate only from spiritual charism. Only those who had 'seen and experienced' the grace of the Spirit of God should speak about it. His writings, chief among them the *Catecheses* and his *Practical and Theological Chapters* where he sets out his ideas on monastic life and devotion, and also his most extraordinary *Hymns of Divine Eros*, one of the most rhapsodic and ecstatic documents ever witnessed in the history of Christian literature to that date, demonstrate him to be an impassioned and lyrical writer, attempting to reclaim the great experiences and charisms of the church of times past, and lambasting those who argued that Christianity had lost those charisms in the course of growing old. He lays immense stress on the necessity of a 'spiritual father' who will mediate (and exemplify) the living charisms of Christian religion across each generation, and his work is full of references to visions of Christ in light, and sensations of the Holy

Spirit in the form of deep affections (warmth of heart and abundant tears). Posthumously, he became a highly favoured author on Mount Athos, and was something of a founding father of the (much later) *hesychast movement, which took up some of his theological ideas. In his own time, however, he seemed to have only a limited school. The emperor moved, successfully, to have him deposed from his office on the grounds of heterodoxy. He was sent into exile in 1009, across the Bosphorus at Paloukiton, where he regathered a small monastic community, and continued writing religious lyrics until his death in 1022.

See also: EASTERN ORTHODOX THEOLOGY; SPIRITUALITY.

Bibliography

B. Krivocheine, *In the Light of Christ* (New York, 1987); G. Maloney, *St. Symeon the New Theologian: Hymns of Divine Love* (New Jersey, 1999); J. A. McGuckin, 'Symeon the New Theologian and Byzantine Monasticism', in A. Bryer (ed.), *Mount Athos and Byzantine Monasticism* (Brookfield, 1996); H. J. M. Turner, *St Symeon the New Theologian and Spiritual Fatherhood* (Leiden, 1990).

J. McGuckin

SYNCRETISM

The term was first used by Plutarch, referring to the ability of Cretan warring factions to unite against a common enemy. In the seventeenth century it was applied to those such as Georg Calixtus (1586–1656), who sought unity between Protestant denominations. In the nineteenth century it was adopted by the *history-of-religions school to describe any religion that was the result of fusing two or more religions. Sikhism, which is a fusion of Hinduism and Islam, would thus be described as a syncretistic religion. Biblical scholars of this school have argued that both OT and NT religion are syncretistic in this sense – that OT religion is a fusion of Babylonian and Hebrew (Hermann Gunkel, 1862–1932) or Phoenician-Canaanite and Hebrew (Ivan Engnell, 1906–64) religion, whereas NT religion is a fusion of Hellenistic Judaism and the primitive religion of Jesus (*Bultmann). It is also used in a broader sense to describe the process of borrowing elements by one religion from another in such a way as not to change the basic character of the receiving religion. It is questionable, however, whether such a broad definition is helpful, since it makes every religion syncretistic to some extent.

Bibliography

H. Ringgren, 'The Problems of Syncretism', in S. Hartman, *Syncretism* (Stockholm, 1969).

D. A. HUGHES

SYNERGISM, see WILL

SYRIAC CHRISTIAN THEOLOGY

Roman Syria, in its wider sense, was an extensive area centred on Antioch, but embracing Mesopotamia. Much of it was bilingual, with Greek being used as well as dialects of Aramaic, of which Syriac was an eastern dialect, spoken in northern Mesopotamia around Edessa and Nisibis. It was distinguished from other dialects of Aramaic by its script, but was basically similar. For some Syriac writers, it was their sole language.

Syria bordered on Palestine (and in the wider sense included Palestine), and also contained more Jews than any other country outside Palestine. For these reasons, as well as because of the common Aramaic language, Syriac Christianity had peculiarly close links with Palestinian Christianity and with Judaism. (Some scholars have suggested the influence of the Essene Judaism of Qumran on early Syriac Christianity.) Most of the early Christian literature from Palestine and West Syria is in Greek, and though it shows clear marks of Semitic culture (cf. *Antiochene School), the marks are naturally clearer in literature written in the Semitic language of Syriac. The influence of Syriac Christianity is also evident in the early Christian literature of Armenia and Georgia.

The old Syriac translation of the Bible, the Peshitta ('plain'), probably originated in a Syriac targum on the Pentateuch, made for the kingdom of Adiabene, after its conversion to Judaism in the first century AD. Chronicles also is thought to be a Jewish translation, but the other OT books as well as the NT were translated by Christians. The canonical OT books and Ecclesiasticus were translated from Hebrew, but the rest of the Apocrypha from Greek, somewhat later than the rest. There is an older translation of the Gospels than the Peshitta (the

'Old Syriac'), but the oldest of all was the Diatessaron (harmony) of Tatian (*fl. c.* 150–72), on which Ephraim (*c.* 306–73) wrote an extant commentary.

*Gnosticism was very active in Syria, and some of the oldest Syriac Christian literature, notably the *Odes of Solomon* (perhaps translated from Greek) and the *Acts of Thomas*, has lesser or greater Gnostic tendencies. Orthodox Syriac literature survives from the fourth century onwards. Aphrahat (*fl.* 330–50), the author of twenty-two *Demonstrations* (short treatises on biblical and ecclesiastical subjects), and Ephraim both date from that century. Ephraim wrote many biblical commentaries and controversial works, but is chiefly remembered as a poet and hymnwriter. His hymns are markedly theological as well as devotional in content, and he leans strongly to *asceticism. Asceticism had been a marked feature of Syriac Christianity from early times. Celibacy was even a condition of baptism, and *Marcion's teaching had wide appeal.

After the *Nestorian and *Monophysite controversies of the fifth century, Syriac-speaking Christianity was largely out of communion with catholic Christianity, but retained many older traits. The Nestorian liturgy of *Addai and Mari* (the legendary apostles of Edessa) is an important witness to the early evolution of the eucharistic liturgy.

Bibliography

S. P. Brock, *The Harp of the Spirit* [ET of eighteen poems of Ephraim] (London, 1983); R. Murray, *Symbols of Church and Kingdom* (Cambridge, 1975); J. Neusner, *Aphrahat and Judaism* (Leiden, 1971); I. Ortiz de Urbina, *Patrologia Syriaca* (Rome, 1965); Selections of works of Ephraim and Aphrahat, tr. J. Gwynn, are in *NPNF*.

R. T. Beckwith

SYRIAN CHRISTIANITY

The Syriac Christian tradition was centred on Edessa (Urfa in modern Turkey) and, although both Greek and Syriac were used, it was Syriac (an Aramaic dialect) that became the principal language of the Syriac church. The origins of the Syriac church are unclear, but its literature and distinctive spiritual tradition emerged as the Bible began to be translated into Syriac and exercise a formative influence on Syriac writers. The early date of these translations of Scripture (and indeed of Greek patristic works), coupled with their accuracy and tendency to be literal, makes them valuable witnesses to the original texts.

Yet more influential than the translation of the whole Bible or Peshitta ('simple version') into Syriac, which was not promulgated until the beginning of the fifth century, was Tatian's Diatessaron. Probably originally written in Syriac towards the end of the second century and soon afterwards translated into Greek, the Diatessaron was a harmony of the Gospels which reflected Tatian's encratic (severely ascetical) views and was used in services until the beginning of the fifth century.

Syriac writers made extensive use of Scripture, drawing on the Diatessaron and reflecting its asceticism. The most renowned of these were Aphrahat (*fl.* 330–350) and Ephrem (*c.* 306–*c.* 373). Aphrahat's treatises on Christian doctrine serve to illustrate how Syriac spirituality was largely uninfluenced by Greek philosophical ideas and had its own theological language. Ephrem, whose works include a commentary on the Diatessaron, was a biblical exegete, controversialist, poet and hymnographer. Early Syriac poetry is found in two forms, narrative (*memra*), which often reflects the Jewish Haggadah tradition, and hymns (*madrasha*), both noted for their beauty. Other significant authors include John the Solitary, whose mid-fifth century writings on spiritual development would significantly influence later writers, Jacob of Sarug, Philoxenus of Mabbug and Stephen Bar Soudaili in the sixth century, and in the seventh Jacob of Edessa and the monastic authors Dadisho Qatraya and Isaac of Nineveh, whose influential *mystical writings stressed God's love and human response to this. The monastic writer, John Saba, in the eighth century, the Metropolitan of Amid, Jacob Bar Salibi, in the twelfth, and Gregory Abul-Faraj/Bar 'Ebroyo, who was a significant thirteenth-century writer in the brief revival of the Syriac language after it had been overtaken by Arabic, are also worthy of note.

A number of Syriac writings are of particular importance. The *Odes of Solomon*, the origin, date and original language of which are still debated, consists of forty-two poems capable of *Gnostic interpretation but nevertheless generally orthodox. The earliest known work is *The Book of the Law of the Countries* by Bardaisan (154–222), which explores the themes of fate and free will. The *Acts of Thomas* (third century) provides evidence of early baptismal and eucharistic practices. The Greek fourth-century *Pseudo-Clementine Homilies and Recognitions* are probably based on a third-century Syriac work and provide evidence of early Syrian Judaistic Christianity. The anonymous fourth-century *Liber Graduum* (*Book of Steps*) addresses the changing needs of a Christian community in a hostile world.

The *ascetic nature of early Syriac Christianity is well known, and the *Acts of Thomas* provides evidence of this. Renunciation of marriage, property, home, stability and consuming meat and wine are typical. Up to the fourth century celibacy was a prerequisite for baptism and spiritual progression towards perfection; this ideal would remain fundamental to Syriac spirituality among more determined spiritual pilgrims. The goal was the angelic life and a return to life before the fall with the Christian a stranger in the corruptible world. In the fourth century there emerged a contemplative group called the Children of the Covenant who lived out these ideals, but by the end of the century monasticism became established. Among these later, rather individualistic 'solitary ones' is Symeon Stylites (*c.* 380–459), who lived and prayed on the top of a pillar for forty years but was equally noted for his wise counsel. The biographies of thirty of these ascetics were written by Theodoret of Cyrrhus (393–466) in his *Historia Religiosa* (*History of the Monks of Syria*). Not all Syriac spirituality was extremely ascetic (as is evident from the *Liber Graduum*), but it does reflect an early and independent Christian tradition. Syriac spirituality is concerned with the movements of the soul, passions and prayer, uses symbolism, sees the natural world as a window onto God's mysteries and frequently uses feminine imagery for God.

Gnosticism, *Marcionitism, Manichaeism and other *dualistic sects all had their appeal in early Syriac Christianity, but after these it began to reflect *Antiochene thought. After the Council of *Ephesus and the fifth-century Nestorian and *Monophysite controversies the Syriac church became largely independent. However, two distinct branches within Syrian Christianity soon arose: the 'West Syrian' to the West of the Tigris, now known as the Syrian Orthodox Church of Antioch and All the East and often called Jacobite (after Jacob Baradeus) or Monophysite (although Miaphysite is preferred), and the 'East Syrian' church in Persia, known as the Assyrian Church of the East and often called 'Nestorian' (see *Nestorius).

The Assyrian church undertook extensive missionary activity in Persia, Turkestan, China and India, but its remarkable success went into decline in the later Middle Ages with the rise of Islam. Both West and East Syrian churches have survived extensive persecution throughout history and into the modern era, which has resulted in movement and dispersion. The Syrian Orthodox Patriarchate has been forced to move many times, first from Antioch to Aleppo and later to such places as Deir Al Zafaran (near Mardin, Turkey), Homs in 1933 and finally Damascus in 1959. Syrian Christianity is also scattered through the Middle East, Syria, Iraq, Lebanon, Israel, Turkey, Europe, the Americas and Australia, and the substantial Malankara Orthodox Syrian Church of India (based in Kerala) has parishes worldwide. In addition to the Orthodox Syrian churches, the Syrian Catholic Church was established in the eighteenth century and the Eastern Syrian Protestant Church (Syrian Marthomite) was founded in the nineteenth century under the influence of British and American Protestant missionaries.

Although Arabic soon became the dominant language after the Muslim conquest of Syria in the seventh century, classical Syriac continues to be used for the liturgy and Scripture of modern churches in the Syriac tradition.

See also: EASTERN ORTHODOX THEOLOGY; ORIENTAL ORTHODOX THEOLOGY.

Bibliography

A. S. Atiya, *History of Eastern Christianity* (Notre Dame, 1968); S. P. Brock, 'Early Syrian Asceticism', *Numen* 20, 1973, pp. 1–19; C. Chaillot, *The Malankara Orthodox Church: Visit to the Oriental Malankara Orthodox Syrian Church of India* (Geneva, 1996); idem, *The Syrian Orthodox Church of Antioch and All the East: A Brief Introduction to Its Life and Spirituality* (Geneva, 1998); C. Chaillot and A. Belopopsky (eds.), *Towards Unity: The Theological Dialogue between the Orthodox Church and the Oriental Orthodox Churches* (Geneva, 1998); J. H. Charlesworth (ed.), *The Odes of Solomon: The Syriac Texts* (Missoula, 1977); R. A. Kitchen and M. F. G. Parmentier, *The Book of Steps: The Syriac Liber Graduum*, CS 196 (Kalamazoo, 2004); A. F. J. Klijn, *The*

Acts of Thomas (Leiden, 1962); R. Murray, *Symbols of Church and Kingdom: A Study in Early Syriac Tradition* (London and New York, 2006); *ANF* and *NPNF* contain ET of Syriac works, including those by Aphrahat, Bardaisan, Ephrem, the Pseudo-Clementines and Tatian.

A. D. RICH

SYSTEMATIC THEOLOGY

Systematic theology is faith seeking understanding – of God, the world and ourselves – through an ordered presentation of the doctrines implicit in the biblical testimony to the history of *creation and *redemption. Both a cognitive and passionate enterprise, systematic theology exists to serve the church in coming to know and love the God of the gospel and in demonstrating its understanding through forms of obedient speech and practice, expressed via contemporary idiom and addressed to relevant cultural and intellectual issues.

Classic formulations

Theology is as old as the proclamation, explication and application of the *Scriptures as the word of *God. The fragmentation of the theological disciplines into specialized compartments (e.g. biblical, systematic, historical, philosophical, practical) was, by contrast, a later development.

*Thomas Aquinas's *Summa Theologia*, aptly called a 'cathedral of the mind' (E. Gilson), presents biblical teaching according to a topical or logical rather than canonical or chronological order and employs categories drawn largely from Aristotle's philosophy (e.g. being, substance, cause). Aquinas presents theology as the science of God which is also taught by God through his revelation in Scripture.

Protestant examples of systematic theologies range from *Calvin's *Institutes of the Christian Religion* through *Schleiermacher's *The Christian Faith* and H. *Bavinck's *Reformed Dogmatics*, to similar works by contemporary theologians such as M. Erickson, T. *Oden, W. *Pannenberg and R. *Jenson.

Contemporary challenges

The distinctive task of systematics, in contrast to the other theological disciplines, is to present a faithful and relevant articulation of the Christian faith in terms of a coherent set of interrelated doctrines. Questions concerning the central principles and structure of such systems were perhaps easier to postpone in the modern era when reason was assumed to provide thinkers with objective and universal points of view. Today systematic theology faces three common objections:

(1) *Systematic theology is abstract, not canonically concrete.* Biblical scholars sometimes worry that systematic theology is too abstract, divorced from the flow of the history of salvation. Others worry that systematicians, in their zeal for coherence, run roughshod over the particularities of the text, thus obscuring the diversity, and fullness, of the biblical testimony.

(2) *Systematic theology is *modern, hence reductionistic, and Western, hence imperialistic.* The very idea of 'system' has become suspect in the so-called 'postmodern' era in which the situatedness of the theologian is thought to trump neutrality and objectivity. Every system is constructed by persons in particular contexts who make their choice of categories and structure to be somewhat selective and contingent, and hence prone to deconstruction. Reason's universal point of view has dissolved into a host of competing rationalities; *postmoderns and some non-Western theologians alike point out that what appears to be 'systematic' is in fact only a 'local theology'.

(3) *Systematic theology is too focused on ideas rather than on the Word made flesh.* K. *Barth issues a properly theological caution against investing too much in human systems of thought derived elsewhere than from God's self-revelation. In his *Romans*, his 'system' was limited to the recognition that God is God. Later, in his *Church Dogmatics*, his system was limited to the recognition that God has chosen not to be God without his covenant partner, man. Barth's theology remains systematic because it proceeds from a concentration on the name Jesus Christ as the key to understanding God and humanity alike.

Constructive suggestions

The key question for the systematic theologian concerns the way in which one orders and coordinates what God is saying in Scripture: what are the categories that comprise one's system and where do they come from? Everything depends on how one relates the parts to the whole and on what kind of coherence one ascribes to the whole. To the extent that the *gospel of *Jesus Christ pervades the whole, systematic theology strives for the coherence neither of a philosophy nor morality but of a storied account of what the Father is doing in the Son through the Spirit to redeem and renew creation.

A softer systematics: canonical narrative

What we may term 'hard' theological systems enjoy a high degree of intelligibility vis-à-vis the intellectual framework of the day, but at a cost, namely, that the content of the Bible may be governed by a conceptual scheme – by some '-ism', like *Platonism or *existentialism – that ends up getting imposed upon the text.

For *Irenaeus, the 'whole' is more like a narrative than a system of geometry. Irenaeus's 'soft' system consisted simply in recognizing the distinction in unity of creation and redemption and the typological connections that bind the history of Israel to the history of Jesus Christ. Such systematicity requires only that one take responsibility for the overall consistency of one's beliefs.

A sapiential systematics: theo-drama

The story that unifies Scripture is perhaps best viewed as a drama of redemption, or rather, a theo-drama carried along by divine speech and action. Doctrine helps the church both to understand what God is saying/doing and to say/do that which corresponds to God's word and act. Doctrine thus directs the church to participate fittingly in the biblically scripted drama of redemption as it continues into new situations.

The kind of wholeness or coherence for which systematic theology strives is dramatic. The emphasis on drama as enacted witness also addresses a final objection to systematic theology, namely, that it is too theoretical and hence unrelated to real life. At the heart of a good systematic theology, however, is not only a design for thinking but also a design for living.

Wisdom is the connecting link between theory and practice, between systematic, moral and spiritual theology. Becoming wise in Christ means not simply apprehending doctrines on an intellectual level, but living them out. It is a matter of practising the premise, presence and promise of the triune God: 'Given what we *have* heard and seen as the gospel, what *shall* we next say and enact?' (R. Jenson, *Systematic Theology*, p. 21).

At its best, systematic theology contributes to the renewing of our minds and imaginations through discerning unifying patterns of doctrine in the manifold testimony of the Spirit to Jesus Christ. Sapiential systematics is faith seeking, and demonstrating, understanding, by bearing faithful witness in word, thought and deed to the truth of God, world and self, made known theodramatically in the written, crucified and living Word of God.

See also: DOCTRINE; IMAGINATION.

Bibliography

H. Frei, *Types of Christian Theology* (Yale, 1992); J. González, *Christian Thought Revisited: Three Types of Theology* (Orbis, 1999); T. Guarino, *Foundations of Systematic Theology* (New York and London, 2005); C. Gunton, 'A Rose by Any Other Name? From "Christian Doctrine" to "Systematic Theology"', *International Journal of Systematic Theology* 1, 1999, pp. 4–23; R. Jenson, *Systematic Theology*, 2 vols. (Oxford, 1997); A. T. B. McGowan, *Always Reforming: Explorations in Systematic Theology* (Leicester and Downers Grove, 2006); D. Migliore, *Faith Seeking Understanding* (Grand Rapids, 2004); K. J. Vanhoozer, *The Drama of Doctrine. A Canonical-Linguistic Approach to Christian Doctrine* (Westminster, 2005); idem, *Faith Speaking Understanding: Performing the Drama of Doctrine* (Louisville, 2014); J B. Webster, *The Domain of the Word: Scripture and Theological Reason* (London and New York, 2012).

K. J. VANHOOZER

SYSTEMATIC THEOLOGY, HISTORY OF

Systematic *theology seeks to organize doctrines comprehensively according to locus (term or subject). There are four major historical periods that have significantly shaped the way scholars engage in *systematic theology (although the term itself is a modern one): the *Patristic period, the Middle Ages, the Reformation and the modern period.

The Patristic period

Systematic theology began as catechesis for new Christian converts. Following the trinitarian structure of the baptismal commission (Matt. 28:19), the earliest churches expounded the meaning of the *gospel. These catechetical exercises were encapsulated in the baptismal *creeds, which were delivered to the baptizand (*traditio*) and recited back to the bishop prior to baptism (*redditio*). An example of this systematic form may be found in the catechetical lectures of Cyril of Jerusalem. A widely accepted baptismal creed was codified for general use through the ecumenical *councils of Nicaea (325) and Constantinople (381), establishing boundaries between orthodoxy and heresy.

*Origen has often been identified as the first systematic theologian. Although he did not attempt a complete systematization of doctrines, his *Peri Archon* (or, in Latin, *de Principiis, Concerning First Things*) began with a trinitarian exposition of the creed and proceeded to consider the doctrines of creation, humanity and sin, as well as angels, Scripture and eschatology. His affirmation of the unity of the Son with the Father alongside an affirmation of the Son's ontological subordination became the critical issue during the fourth and fifth centuries. After Origen, theologians such as *Athanasius and the Cappadocian Fathers debated central theological *loci*, especially the relationship of the Son and the Holy Spirit to God the Father. This resulted in the formulation of the central confession of the church's *trinitarian faith in the Nicene Creed, but produced no comprehensive systematic compendia.

Although *Gregory of Nyssa contributed a preliminary collection of theological topics in his *Catechetical Oration* (or *Address on Religious Instruction*), it was not until *John of Damascus wrote *De Fide Orthodoxa* (*Exposition of the Orthodox Faith*) that an exhaustive explanation of the Christian doctrines as defined by the councils was attempted. John brought together the teachings of Scripture and the Church Fathers in 100 chapters, organized according to important theological terms. The chapters, subsequently divided into four books, treated the doctrines of God, creation and salvation in the first three books. The final book considered the doctrines of Christ's two natures, the sacraments and eschatology.

The Middle Ages

After the barbarian invasions in the West, scholarship was preserved within the monasteries. Western theologians looked primarily to the writings of *Augustine of Hippo for their understanding of orthodoxy, but the African's works, though seemingly exhaustive, were not systematic. Although rooted in the cathedral schools established under Charlemagne, it was with the rise of the universities that systematic theology became a sustained discipline. Disputes over various controversial doctrines, for instance, the *filioque* clause, predestination and the Mass (see *Eucharist), initially dominated the landscape.

Peter *Lombard was the first Western theologian to organize Christian doctrines into a comprehensive system. Drawing upon the recent translation of John of Damascus from Greek into Latin, Lombard organized his *Sententia in IV Libris Distinctae* (*Four Books of Sentences*) by arranging the subjects of the Damascene into a tighter format. He collected authoritative citations by the Fathers and added his own arguments. In book one, Lombard considered God as Trinity, proofs for God's existence, and divine attributes. Book two assembled arguments regarding creation, angels, humanity and sin. Book three considered the doctrines of Jesus Christ and the redemption of humanity. Book four contained Lombard's treatise on the sacraments, of which he concluded there were seven, and a treatise on eschatology. Lombard's *Sentences* were required for subsequent students, and 'did more than any other text to shape the discipline of medieval *scholastic theology' (Marcia L. Colish, 'Peter Lombard', in Evans [ed.], *Medieval Theologians*, p. 182).

Lombard's coherent and comprehensive organization encouraged theologians to write extensive commentaries on the *Sentences* as a means of expositing doctrine. His structure still provides a typical, though by no means universally uniform, order for systematic theology: God, unity, Trinity; creation, angels, man, sin; Christology, redemption, virtues (or Christian life); sacraments (or ecclesiology) and eschatology. This pattern is followed, not only by medieval dogmaticians such as *Thomas Aquinas, in his *Summa Theologiae* (*Summary of Theology*) and *Summa contra Gentiles* (*Summary against the Nations*), or Gabriel *Biel, in his *Collectorium circa Quattor Libros Sententiarum* (*Collections around the Four Books of Sentences*), but also by Protestant theologians.

The Reformation

Martin *Luther's revolt against medieval theology was not concerned with the structure of systematic theology, but with its content. He expressed himself primarily in occasional writings rather than systematic works. Luther's contribution to theology has been described as an 'event of word and faith', an event which later Protestant theologians sought to codify. Gerhard *Ebeling questioned whether placing Luther's discovery into 'the framework of a traditional dogmatic outline' is possible without the event being 'taken apart and torn asunder by being cast into a sequence' (Ebeling, *Study*, p. 135). Proponents of Protestant scholasticism (see *Orthodoxy/Scholasticism) deny that systematization transformed Luther's theology.

The only systems of doctrine Luther bequeathed to posterity are found in his large and small *catechisms, in which he followed the format of the Apostles' Creed, the Ten Commandments and the Lord's Prayer. Luther's catechisms were collected into the Lutheran Church's *Book of Concord*, providing an example of how Protestant confessional literature functions as official dogma. Philipp *Melanchthon, the first systematic theologian within the Protestant traditions, revised and expanded a scholastic theology, *Loci Communes Theologici* (*Theological Commonplaces*), beginning in 1521. He also contributed a systematic theology based upon the *Augsburg Confession. Melanchthon's works, however, focused primarily on those doctrines in dispute between Roman Catholics and Reformers, and were thus not intended to be comprehensive. A catechism written for a particular tradition provided the pattern for other Reformation systematic theologies, too. For instance, Caspar *Olevianus and Zacharias *Ursinus authored extensive treatments of the *Heidelberg Catechism.

Unlike Luther, Melanchthon and the Heidelberg theologians, however, most *Reformation systematic theologians followed a scholastic model rather than a catechetical form. Ulrich *Zwingli, Martin *Bucer and Peter Martyr *Vermigli offered preliminary attempts for codifying Reformation theology, but John *Calvin's *Institutio Christianae Religionis* (*Institutes of the Christian Religion*) exercised the most influence. Working through several revisions from 1536 to 1559, Calvin intended the *Institutes* to prepare students for biblical interpretation. Calvin followed a four-book format based on the Apostles' Creed, but reflecting a Reformation emphasis, he brought an extensive discussion of Scripture and revelation to the forefront.

As the successors of the early Reformers debated with opponents, they focused less upon interpretation and reformation, and more upon preserving and expositing an established faith. With regard to content, Theodore *Beza helped make predestination foundational for some post-Reformation Protestant systems. With the rise of such *Thomist theologians as Jerome Zanchi, the style became scholastic. A comparison of Zanchi's *Opera Theologica* (*Work of Theology*) shows a structural and philosophical correspondence with Aquinas's *Summa Theologiae* (*Summary of Theology*). The structures of systematic theology in Protestant orthodoxy demonstrate a continuing dependence upon earlier and contemporary Roman Catholic theologians, both with regard to logical structure and philosophical content.

The modern period

In the modern period, there were two major challenges to systematic theology as codified in Protestant orthodoxy: *Pietism and *rationalism. Philip Jacob Spener led a pietist reaction against scholasticism out of a desire to return to the simple piety of Luther, thus presenting a heartfelt challenge to the rigid structuring of theology. The *Enlightenment, with its optimistic rationalism, presented a comprehensive intellectual challenge to Christian theology. While Pietism deplored 'dead orthodoxy', rationalism had a profound effect upon both the content and structure of systematic theology. The major question presenting itself to theologians from the eighteenth through the twentieth centuries was: 'What is the relation between the classical [orthodox] and the humanist [rationalist] traditions?' (Tillich, *Perspectives,* p. 4). David Ford and Hans Frei offer a fivefold spectrum for classifying the answers to this question, ranging from the rejection of modernity to assigning 'complete priority to some modern secular philosophy or worldview, [so that] Christianity in its own terms is only valid in so far as it fits in with that' (Ford, *Modern Theologians*, pp. 2–3).

Systematic theology continued to set forth the *loci* of Christian theology, even as tension developed between Christian identity and its modern relevance. This creative tension manifested itself early in the system of Friedrich *Schleiermacher, the father of theological *liberalism. In order to reconcile Christianity with modernity, Schleiermacher made the concept of religious feeling fundamental (see *Religious experience). While re-presenting major doctrines according to human self-consciousness, he significantly removed the Trinity from its leading place, relegating the doctrine to an appendix. Emphasizing humanity and creativity, liberalism encouraged a complex variety of theologies catering to various publics, ranging from *existentialism to *liberation theology. Evangelical orthodox theologies have maintained a presence, mostly in secondary academies, but Karl *Barth ably reintroduced the Trinity and divine grace as priorities within academic theology through his *Die Kirchliche Dogmatik* (*Church Dogmatics*). Barth's magnum opus was structured according to a fourfold paradigm of God, creation, reconciliation and redemption, following a prolegomena upon the word of God. *Ecumenical theology now dominates many discussions, even as the *Eastern Orthodox, *Roman Catholic and Protestant churches continue to field systematic proponents.

Bibliography

G. Ebeling, *The Study of Theology*, tr. Duane A. Priebe (Philadelphia, 1978); G. R. Evans (ed.), *Medieval Theologians: An Introduction to the Medieval Period* (Oxford, 2001); idem, *The First Theologians: An Introduction to Theology in the Early Church* (Oxford, 2004); D. Ford, *The Modern Theologians: Introduction to Christian Theology in the Twentieth Century* (Oxford, ²1997); J. N. D. Kelly, *Early Christian Creeds* (London, ³1972); C. Lindberg, *The Reformation Theologians: An Introduction to Theology in the Early Modern Period* (Oxford, 2002); R. A. Muller, *Post-Reformation Reformed Dogmatics: The Rise and Development Reformed Orthodoxy, ca. 1520 to ca. 1725*, vol. 1 (Grand Rapids, ²2003); P. Tillich, *Perspectives on 19th and 20th Century Protestant Theology*, ed. Carl E. Braaten (London, 1967).

M. B. YARNELL III

TAOISM AND CHRISTIANITY

In the Far East the influence of Taoism can be clearly seen in the lives of ordinary people. For example, in Taipei City, Taiwan, many Taoist temples attract thousands of worshippers and tourists. These Taoist temples are dedicated to some forty folk deities, for whom people prepare elaborate feasts and burn incense in an attempt to appease the gods and goddesses.

Some Buddhist deities are also worshipped in Taoist temples. Taoism and *Buddhism are so closely intermingled that people generally are confused about telling Taoist temples from Buddhist ones. One way of classification between the two religions is that temples with their names ending 'ssu' or 'an' are Buddhist temples, and those ending with 'kung' and 'miao' are Taoist. The influence of Taoism is also seen in a lesser degree in Korea and Japan. Since 1979 Taoism, along with Buddhism, Confucianism, Christianity and Islam, has revived in China.

Taoism was founded by Lao Tzu (604–531 BC), who lived in the period of wars and political disorders in China during the Middle Chou Dynasty (771–474 BC). He tried to find a solution to end the struggles through searching for Tao (The Way), that is, the moral and physical laws of nature. Taoism is mainly divided into two distinctive movements: philosophical Taoism and religious Taoism.

The teaching of Taoism is developed in the book *Tao Te Ching* by Lao Tzu and later writings of Chuang Tzu, his follower (399–295 BC). The basic idea of the *Tao Te Ching* is the doctrine of inaction (or *Wu Wei*, literally 'not doing') in trying to harmonize with nature. For Lao Tzu the best way to deal with pillage, tyranny and killing is to do nothing, because in human relations force defeats itself and produces reaction. He said, 'The more laws and regulations are given, the more robbers and thieves there are' (Ch. 57). Lao Tzu advocated the natural and spontaneous way over artificial regulations, organizations and ceremonies; this is why he vigorously attacked all formalities and ratifications. *Wu-Wei* does not mean that people should avoid all action in life, but they should avoid all hostile and aggressive actions against others.

Lao Tzu's ethical principle was deeply rooted in the natural law of the Heavenly Way. He wrote, 'Man follows the example of the law of the land, the land follows the example of the law of Heaven, Heaven follows the example of the Way, and the Way follows the example of the law of natural law' (Ch. 199). Lao Tzu considered that Confucius' teaching of *Jen* (virtue), *I* (righteousness), and *Li* (propriety) in '*Wu Lun*' (five human relationships) was basically human work and artificial; Lao Tzu's ethical

889

teaching went much deeper into the law of nature, known as 'the Way'.

Philosophical Taoism began to decline in the fourth century when Buddhism spread in China. Buddhists adopted Taoist terminology to express their philosophy, while Taoists borrowed religious ideas, divinities and cults from Buddhism. Thus, Buddhism and Taoism fused very well among ordinary people's thinking. This popular type of religious Taoism absorbed local nature deities, and adopted magic, fortune-telling, animism and control of spirits.

Taoism, Buddhism and Confucianism are significant religions of the Far East. While Taoism and Buddhism were more religiously oriented, Confucianism's chief significance is mainly in the area of ethics. Buddhism effectively appealed to people with its doctrine of salvation (Nirvana) from suffering, while Taoism gave the people gods of nature and national heroes to worship.

In contrast with Christianity, the Taoist concept of God is polytheistic. The people pray to many gods, including the gods of agriculture, medicine, literature, birth, city, land, goddess of the sea, and national heroes. Praying to each god will hopefully bring help and blessings to those in special need. Because of their doctrine of inaction, many Taoists are fatalists.

See also: CHRISTIANITY AND OTHER RELIGIONS.

Bibliography

H. G. Creel, *What Is Taoism?* (Chicago, 1970); A. F. Gates, *Christianity and Animism in Taiwan* (San Francisco, 1979); H. Welch, *Taoism: The Parting of the Way* (Boston, 1965).

BONG RIN RO

TAYLOR, JEREMY (1613–67)

After studying at Cambridge, Taylor became chaplain to Charles I, and Rector of Uppingham. During the English Civil War he was a chaplain in the Royalist army and after a brief imprisonment he served as chaplain to Lord Carbery at the Golden Grove in Wales. After the restoration of the monarchy in 1660 he was made Bishop of Down and Connor in Ireland, receiving additional jurisdiction over the Diocese of Dromore in 1661. He also served as Vice Chancellor of Trinity College, Dublin.

Taylor was an independent thinker whose theology was rooted in the Bible and the teaching of the Fathers, also placing great importance on the use of reason (see *Rationalism), the role of conscience and the need and possibility for repentance and holiness. In today's terms his theology might be described as a paradoxical combination of Catholic, Reformed and liberal elements. Taylor is best known for his works of *spirituality such as *Holy Living and Holy Dying*, for a slightly tortuous work of moral theology, the *Ductor Dubitantium* and for his plea for religious *toleration, *A Discourse on the Liberty of Prophesying*. He also wrote the earliest English life of Jesus, *The Great Exemplar*, and a number of works vigorously defending Anglican theology and practice against Presbyterianism and Independency on the one hand and Roman Catholicism on the other.

Bibliography

Works: T. K. Carroll (ed.), *Jeremy Taylor: Selected Works* (New York, 1990); M. Gest, *The House of Understanding: Selections from the Writings of Jeremy Taylor* (Philadelphia, 1954); R. Heber (ed.), *The Whole Works of the Right Reverend Jeremy Taylor* (London, 1928).

Studies: C. FitzSimmons Allison, *The Rise of Moralism: The Proclamation of the Gospel from Hooker to Baxter* (New York, 1966); H. R. McAdoo, *The Eucharistic Theology of Jeremy Taylor Today* (Norwich, 1988); D. Scott, *Christian Character: Jeremy Taylor and Christian Ethics Today* (Oxford, 1991).

M. DAVIE

TEILHARD DE CHARDIN, PIERRE (1881–1955)

Born in France, Teilhard de Chardin trained as a *Jesuit and as a palaeontologist. He clashed with his superiors in the Roman Catholic Church in the mid-1920s and was forbidden to continue teaching as a geologist because of his unorthodox ideas on original sin and its relation to evolution. From 1926 he lived in China, where he carried out palaeontological work, making important contributions to the study of one form of early man, *Sinanthropus* (Peking Man). On his return to France in 1946 he was forbidden to publish or teach on philosophical subjects. In 1951 he moved to New York where he worked until his death.

At the time of his death Teilhard's influence was limited. With the publication of *The

Phenomenon of Man (ET, London, 1959), his influence spread rapidly. Within a few years a spate of further books and collections of his writings appeared, including devotional works (*Le Milieu Divin*; ET, London, 1960), palaeontological writings, collections of his letters and largely speculative writings (*The Future of Man*; ET, London, 1964).

Teilhard's aim was to construct a *phenomenology of the universe, based upon scientific thinking, and providing a coherent explanation for the world. His synthesis incorporated immense evolutionary ideas, and brought together science, philosophy and theology. For him, evolution was a general condition to which all theories and systems must conform, and within which there was movement towards increasing complexity and consciousness converging ultimately towards a supreme centre, Omega.

Underlying much of Teilhard's thinking was the basic postulate that matter, like human beings, possesses a form of consciousness. All matter has a 'within' as well as a 'without'. Evolution is an ascent towards consciousness, which is supremely manifested in humanity.

Teilhard's thought consists of three main components: cosmic, human and 'Christic'. God was viewed as an integral part of the evolutionary process, since God and the evolving universe are united. Evolution therefore has a 'Christic' centre and humankind's duty is to advance this 'Christification'. The third component, the human, links the cosmic and the 'Christic', constituting the thinking layer (noosphere), which lies between the living layer (biosphere) and the ultra-human (Omega, Christ or God). Underlying Teilhard's vision was an intense optimism, an ardent desire to bring together his science and his Christianity, a strong *mystical sense, and a rejection of any form of *dualism of mind and matter. Ultimately, therefore, he viewed Christ as the organic centre of the cosmos, with Christ's body being equivalent to the cosmos itself.

Teilhard retained the basic concepts of Roman Catholic doctrine, although they were understood in terms of a world in evolution; hence his emphasis on the cosmic role of Christ rather than his redemptive role. His Christology was in the tradition of incarnational theology, with Christ as the goal and crowning point of the natural order.

Evil and sin became by-products of evolution, with sin being viewed as part of the evolutionary process and the fall as a symbol of the world's incompleteness. The incarnation of Christ took on universal evolutionary significance with limited meaning at the levels of individuals. Salvation was equated with the efforts of humankind to complete the mystical body of Christ.

See also: Creation; Science and Theology.

Bibliography

C. Cuenot, *Teilhard de Chardin* (London, 1965); R. Hooykaas, 'Teilhardism, a Pseudoscientific Delusion', *Free University Quarterly* 9, 1963, pp. 1–83; D. G. Jones, *Teilhard de Chardin: An Analysis and Assessment* (London, 1969); H. de Lubac, *The Faith of Teilhard de Chardin* (London, 1965); E. Rideau, *Teilhard de Chardin: A Guide to His Thought* (London, 1968); C. Van Til, 'Pierre Teilhard de Chardin', *WTJ* 28, 1966, pp. 109–144; J. J. Duyvené du Wit, in P. E. Hughes (ed.), *Creative Minds in Contemporary Theology* (Grand Rapids, 1966), pp. 407–450.

D. G. Jones

TEMPLE, WILLIAM (1881–1944)

Son of an Archbishop of Canterbury (Frederick Temple) and bred to succeed to the Primacy of All England, William Temple emerged as the dominating influence on the Church of England in the period between the eclipse of Bishop Charles Gore in the 1920s and his own death two decades later. He was Bishop of Manchester (1921–9), Archbishop of York (1929–42) and Archbishop of Canterbury (1942–4).

Temple's influence was felt far beyond the established church into the *ecumenical movement, which he described in his enthronement sermon at Canterbury as 'the great new fact of our era'. Unpompous, genuine and endowed with an unfailing sense of humour, perfectly uniting personality and role, Temple reached out in his ministry of preaching and teaching, through books and the spoken word, to ordinary people and was dubbed 'the people's archbishop'. His sudden premature death was felt as catastrophic for the Church of England: it changed the course of *Anglicanism.

Temple was a leading light in innumerable good causes, social, educational, political, ecumenical: president of the Workers' Educational Association (1909); member (1922) and then chairman (1925) of the Archbishops' Commission on Christian Doctrine (*Doctrine in the Church of England*, 1938); chairman of the ecumenical Conference on Christian Politics, Economics and Citizenship (COPEC, 1924); and the (Anglican) Malvern Conference (1941); chairman of the second international conference on *Faith and Order (Edinburgh, 1937); president of the provisional committee for the formation of the *World Council of Churches (1938). Temple had a finger in every good pie and could do nothing wrong.

As a theologian, Temple was formed on the Bible (John's Gospel was his favourite of all books), on the *Book of Common Prayer*, on *Plato and personal *idealism, and on *Thomas Aquinas. Charles *Gore was a formative influence, but unlike Gore, Temple seems not to have known intellectual anguish; he was not a wrestler with truth, he saw it calmly. Only towards the end of his life, as totalitarianism darkened the face of Europe, did he confess that a theology of explanation and unification must give way to a theology of transformation and judgment. He saw the point of the revolution that Karl *Barth was bringing to Protestant theology, but Temple's vision remained one of the wholeness and wholesomeness of life, irradiated by the presence of Christ as Saviour and friend. There was no dualism in Temple, and to the last he held to the validity of *natural theology for the knowledge of God and natural law for how we should live.

The Platonic-Christian synthesis is developed in *Mens Creatrix* ('Creative Mind', 1917), *Christus Veritas* ('Christ the Truth', 1924) and matures into the impressive worldview of his *Gifford Lectures, given as Archbishop of York, *Nature, Man and God* (1934). His most popular work was *Readings in St John's Gospel* (1939–40), and his most influential statement was probably the Penguin best-seller *Christianity and Social Order* (1942). This tract for the times looked beyond the horrors of war to the social and economic reconstruction of Britain. Temple sketched an anthropology and a social theology before setting out principles of human and communal well-being. Though his recipe had obvious political implications, he stopped short of explicit political agendas with his famous 'middle axioms'. Temple did not plumb the depths: he was a consolidating and synthesizing thinker, whose work remains insufficiently dialectical. But Temple gave intellectual confidence to many lesser minds and made Christian faith attractive and credible.

Bibliography

P. Avis, 'Temple, William', in A. E. McGrath (ed.), *The SPCK Handbook of Anglican Theologians* (London, 1998); A. Hastings, 'William Temple', in G. Rowell (ed.), *The English Religious Tradition and the Genius of Anglicanism* (Wantage, 1993); F. A. Iremonger, *William Temple: Archbishop of Canterbury* (London, 1948); J. Kent, *William Temple* (Cambridge, 1992); A. M. Ramsey, *From Gore to Temple* (London, 1960); S. Spencer, *William Temple: A Calling to Prophecy* (London, 2001); A. Suggate, *William Temple and Christian Social Ethics Today* (Edinburgh, 1987).

P. D. L. AVIS

TEMPTATION

The verb 'to tempt' in Western thought is almost wholly associated with allurement into sinful situations and compromise (seduction), but this is not the primary biblical usage, which is of 'making trial of' in the sense of testing. In this sense the idea may be wholly benevolent, as in testing a person's quality (strength or weakness) with a view to improving it, something God does frequently to further *sanctify his people.

Historically and systematically, temptation has been understood as enticement or allurement to *sin in the sense prayed against in the Lord's Prayer, 'Lead us not into temptation' (Matt. 6:13; Luke 11:4), or the warning to watch and pray 'that you will not fall into temptation' (Matt. 26:41; Mark 14:38; Luke 22:40, 46). In this sense, God does not 'tempt anyone' (Jas 1:13).

Sociologists reflect on primitive cultures in which the idea of temptation seems to be lacking, leading them to suggest either that it reflects the preoccupation of Western civilization with *guilt, or that it is the result of a society devoid of Christian influence. *Roman Catholic theology, following Augustine, emphasizes universal 'inclination to sin' (*concupiscence*) adding that strength to resist such inclinations is derived from prayer and participation in the sacraments of penance and the Eucharist. *Eastern Orthodoxy likewise places an emphasis upon 'mastery of passions' through prayer, fasting, voluntary obedience and regular participation in the sacraments (mysteries).

*Reformed theology, following Augustine, refers to the fourfold state of human existence: (1) primitive integrity; (2) entire depravity; (3) begun recovery; and (4) consummate happiness or misery. These in turn are states in which man is (1) able to sin, able not to sin (*posse peccare, posse non peccare*); (2) not able not to sin (*non posse non peccare*); (3) able not to sin (*posse non peccare*); and (4) unable to sin (*non posse peccare*). Temptability, therefore, exists as part of the created condition of Adam and Eve and remains as a possibility in the state of grace or regenerate condition.

Natural desires can become sources of temptation when their fulfilment is sought in unethical ways, or for impure motives, or as ends in themselves.

Differences as to the ability to resist temptation exist because of differences in understanding the extent to which the old self manifests life and influence in the regenerate. These range from a lifelong struggle requiring active human effort in resisting temptation through the means of grace, especially prayer and watchfulness, involving resistance and effortful non-compliance along patterns of mortification (*Reformation and *puritan theologians were essentially following a path defined by late medieval theologians on this point) to the possibility of (Wesleyan) *perfectionism. John Wesley believed that Christians are not wholly free from temptations. Some may not feel tempted, but this is due to non-resistance. Others will know periods of freedom but temptations will recur. Thus the 'perfection' attainable on earth differs from that in heaven.

Theologians have also debated the temptability of Christ as a category of his *sinlessness or impeccability. In a desire to retain continuity with human nature, some have insisted that Christ inherited a fallen human nature, else he could not be human (e.g. Edward *Irving, MacLeod *Campbell, H. R. MacIntosh, Karl *Barth, C. E. B. Cranfield, T. F. *Torrance), and others, wishing to maintain Christ's temptability, have been equally insistent that he could not have borne a fallen human nature (D. MacLeod).

As 'the tempter' (Matt. 4:3; 1 Thess. 3:5), theologians have also debated the role given to Satan (by God's permission or decree) to tempt by manipulation of circumstances within limits carefully established by God (cf. Job 1 – 2) (see *Devil, demons). His schemes are limited, though cunning: attempting in one way or another to cause Christians to collapse under the burden of trial through exaggeration of their difficulty, or implanting doubt as divine motives in providence, or by evisceration of the right ways of escape by persuading wrong avenues that lead instead to despair. Temptations are Satan's work, but they are always under the supervision and control of God. The exact relation between God's control and Satan's freedom is a matter of constant debate between theologians, suggesting either compatibilism or more 'risky' views in which certainty of divine victory is in varying degrees of doubt.

Bibliography

L. Berkhof, *Systematic Theology* (Grand Rapids, 1996); D. Bonhoeffer, *Temptation* (London, 1955); M. Erickson, *Introducing Christian Doctrine* (Grand Rapids, 1999); C. S. Lewis, *The Screwtape Letters* (London, 1942); J. Owen, *Of Temptation* (1658), in W. H. Goold (ed.), *The Works of John Owen*, vol. 6 (repr. London, 1965–66); D. MacLeod, *The Person of Christ* (Leicester, 1998); J. I. Packer, *Rediscovering Holiness* (Ventura, CA, 1999); *United States Catholic Catechism for Adults* (2006).

D. W. H. THOMAS

TERESA OF AVILA (1515–82)

St Teresa of Avila is among the most beloved and prominent of Christian mystics. Born in Old Castile, Spain, Teresa was raised by pious parents. Impacted by the lives of saints and the *Letters of St Jerome*, Teresa left her parents' home at age nineteen to enter the Monastery of the Incarnation of the Carmelite nuns at Avila. She went on to become a prominent *mystic, founder of the Discalced ('shoeless') Carmelites (with St John of the Cross), church reformer, spiritual writer and the first woman to be named a Doctor of the Church.

Teresa's main writings are *The Life of St Teresa of Avila* (her autobiography, 1565), *The Way of Perfection* (1566) and *The Interior Castle* (1580). They are remarkable sources of spiritual and theological reflection. Attempting to synthesize these three works does not do justice to the fact that they are based upon her own spiritual journey and experiences, involving dynamics that change over time. Therefore, in order to understand them, it is most illuminating to consider briefly the contents of each one. In the *Life*, Teresa describes her own spiritual growth and suggests the metaphor of a garden to describe progress in the life of prayer. Teresa explains that there are four ways that this garden obtains water, each one representing how a person interacts with God through prayer: first, by hand from a well (the labour of beginners); second, from a windmill and aqueducts (when one is initiated into the passive blessings of the 'prayer of the quiet'); third, by diverting a river or stream (the intensification of the prayer of the quiet); and fourth, from rain (when the soul receives divine graces and experiences union with God).

In *The Way of Perfection*, her most ascetic work, Teresa discusses the major virtues (love, detachment and humility), the practice of *prayer, and how to utilize the Lord's Prayer in the quest for union with God.

The Interior Castle, normally considered her most developed work, employs the image of a castle with seven dwelling places, each one representing a new level of intimacy with God, with the seventh place at the centre of the soul where the King of glory dwells in the greatest splendour. Those who move to this seventh stage participate in the life of the Trinity (John 14:23), which is made possible by the incarnation of Christ and the church's sacraments, especially the Eucharist.

Bibliography

Selected works: K. Kavanaugh and O. Rodriguez, *The Collected Works of St Teresa of Avila, volume 1: The Book of Her Life, Spiritual Testimonies, Soliloquies* (Washington DC, 1987); idem, *The Collected Works of St Teresa of Avila, volume 2: The Way of Perfection, Meditations on the Song of Songs, The Interior Castle*, rev. edn (Washington DC, 1980).

Selected studies: G. T. Ahlgren, *Teresa of Avila and the Politics of Sanctity* (Ithaca, 1989); E. Arenal and S. Schlau, *Untold Sisters: Hispanic Nuns in Their Own Works*, tr. A. Powell (Albuquerque, 1989); J. Bilinkoff, *Avila of Saint Teresa: Religious Reform in a Sixteenth-Century City* (Ithaca, 1989); R. Williams, *Teresa of Avila* (Harrisburg, 1991).

B. BINGAMAN

TERTULLIAN (*fl. c.* 196–*c.* 212)

Tertullian began writing in Carthage, North Africa, towards the end of the second century, his undisputed works dating from *c.* 196 to *c.* 212. Some scholars claim to detect fresh doctrinal distinctives in his later work when he was sympathetic to *Montanism. He has been characterized both as 'the last of the Greek *apologists' and as 'the first of the Latin fathers'. Both descriptions are appropriate, since he preserves in his work a compendium of mainstream Christianity, while significantly foreshadowing the Latin Church's preoccupation with *power and stressing such legal themes as confession, *penance, renunciation and *merit.

Tertullian concentrated much of his fire against 'Christian' options tolerant of *dualism, most cogently in his *Against *Marcion*. Other dualistic systems attacked were *Gnosticism and the philosophy of Hermogenes who, in Tertullian's view, raised the status of primeval matter to the level of the unique God.

Tertullian claimed throughout his writings that he defended the doctrinal *regula fidei* (rule of faith) universally held by churches in the apostolic tradition (*Against Praxeas* 2; *Prescription of Heretics* 13, 36; *Veiling of Virgins* 2). The pillars of this confession, shared by his great predecessor *Irenaeus of Lyon, affirmed one Creator of all things, the *incarnation of the divine Word and the ultimate *resurrection of the dead. When we begin, however, to unpack this simple scheme, we meet a comparable commitment to significant implied details. The *Creator, accordingly, forms the universe from nothing (*creatio ex nihilo*), since only this guarantees his uniqueness as God and protects the intrinsic worth of the creation product itself. Hence, in his opposition to *docetism, Tertullian was able to deem the 'flesh' or humanity of Christ a worthy vehicle of God's presence (*Against Marcion* 2:4, 3:10, 5:14; *Flesh of Christ* 6, 16), and boldly identified the gracious God at work in Christ with the very creator-deity whom Marcion dismissed as malevolent or weak. Tertullian went even further and included Christ himself in the functions of creation and judgment, thus effectively placing him on the divine side of the creator-creation division (*Against Marcion* 4:20, 29, 30, etc.), while still repeatedly underlining the reality of Christ's human nature (ibid., 2:27, 5:14; *Flesh of Christ* 5, 16).

The case for future general resurrection equally rested on the doctrine of creation. The power which made all things from nothing could similarly recall persons from the dissolution of death and weave a new resurrection order in nature (*Resurrection* 7, 42, 57).

The feeling for divine power pervasively present in Tertullian's thought did not mean that he had no vision of divine grace. The incarnation for him was no mere display of God's might and majesty, but an essentially saving operation (*Against Marcion* 4:37, 5:14, 17; *Flesh of Christ* 5, 14). The power which undertook our salvation reached even to the cross where Christ 'reigned from the tree' (*Against Marcion* 3:18, 19, 21). Similarly, the *Holy Spirit, by virtue of his powerful role in creation, was the re-creating Spirit of grace who was at work in *sanctification (*Against Praxeas* 12), in the *sacraments (*Baptism* 3, 4), in prayer (*Prayer* 1) and in forgiveness (*Purity* 21).

Tertullian is chiefly famous, however, for his formulations of the *Trinity, at their most mature in his work *Against Praxeas*, directed at second-century *Monarchianism. For the Monarchians there existed only one undifferentiated divine ruler, who assumed, in succession, appropriate roles in the work of redemption. Tertullian freely conceded the principle of one rule, but held this rule to be administered through the Son and the Holy Spirit as co-regents of the Father. Despite this equality of status, Tertullian nevertheless recognized a delegation of the power of the kingdom to the Son in his redemptive self-humbling. He thereby supplied a concrete distinction between Father and Son, which broke the tight monotheistic mould of Monarchianism.

In his trinitarian doctrine Tertullian made varied and complex use of the term *substantia* (*substance). Most scholars are agreed that the later trinitarian theology of *Athanasius and the ecumenical *councils should not be read into Tertullian's use of the term. The Latin term signified for him the uniquely divine spirit-substance of which the Son and Spirit partook mainly by virtue of their emergence out of the one God as agents in the work of creation. Underlying this dynamic, economic Trinity was the *Logos theology inherited from earlier apologists and which was highly subordinationist.

Balancing the *substantia* was the term *persona* (person), which primarily highlighted the Johannine conversations of the Father and Son, thus establishing real distinctions between them in the economy of redemption. One should not assume a formulation in Tertullian's mind of all that may go with the modern word 'person' (such as self-consciousness, self-determination, etc.), though the biblical setting makes some such conception natural (cf. *Hypostasis).

Tertullian's trinitarian doctrine has, rightly, been called an 'economic Trinity', since all his formulations are set within the works of creation and redemption, hardly addressing at all a Trinity within the divine nature quite apart from God's activity. This is typical of his theology generally, which bore many marks of the Latin world's practicality and functional thinking. For Tertullian, God was active rather than abstract.

In considering the death and resurrection of the Son of God, Tertullian comments that 'it is certain because it is impossible'. This apparently irrational statement highlights his famous alleged antipathy towards philosophy. Evaluation of Tertullian on this score, however, should take account of the fact that he constantly, though very selectively, plundered contemporary sources (especially *Stoicism), was severely rationalist in many of his discourses and was concerned mainly to oppose syncretistic expressions of the Christian faith rather than philosophy in general.

Although Tertullian's originality as a theologian is sometimes questioned, and although dependence on earlier apologists is freely admitted by him (*Against Valentinians* 5), his marshalling of the material and his own trenchant presentation of it produced not only an invaluable compendium of second-century thought, but many original formulations which justify his celebrated position in the history of Christian doctrine.

Bibliography

Works: Rev. Alexander Roberts and James Donaldson (eds.), *Ante-Nicene Christian Library*, vol. 7 (1867–1872), republished in *Ante-Nicene Fathers*, vol. 4 (Edinburgh, 1885).

Studies: R. H. Ayers, *Language, Logic and Reason in the Church Fathers: A Study of Tertullian, Augustine and Aquinas* (New York, 1979); T. D. Barnes, *Tertullian: A Literary and Historical Study* (1971), repr. with appendix of revisions (Oxford, 1985); G. Bray, *Holiness and the Will of God: Perspectives on the Theology of Tertullian* (London, 1979); J. Daniélou, *A History of Early Christian Doctrine before the Council of Nicaea: vol. 3, The Origins of Latin Christianity* (London, 1977); E. Evans,

THEISM

In a broad sense, theism is synonymous with belief in God, usually one God, as in *monotheism. This usage does not distinguish it from *deism and *pantheism, nor does it look beyond philosophical theory to historical religions. In a more specific sense, then, theism refers to the belief in a personal creator-God, distinct from the world (*contra* pantheism) yet constantly active in it (*contra* deism), who is therefore worthy of worship. As *Creator, the God of theism is both intelligent and powerful. As personal, he is capable of self-revelation, a moral being with just and benevolent concerns for his creatures. As alone transcendent, he is free to act sovereignly in the creation. In this immanent activity, he seeks his own good purposes for history in general and for individual persons.

In this more specific sense, three major theistic religions may be identified: *Islam, *Judaism and Christianity. Each affirms one personal creator-God, self-revealing, active in creation, and worthy of worship. Of these three, Christianity gives the fullest account of God's involvement in his creation, in terms of the incarnation and redeeming work of the eternal Son of God.

Theism as a philosophical position may be traced to *Plato in the West. It was carefully developed by medieval Moslem, Jewish and Christian thinkers, among the latter notably *Augustine, *Thomas Aquinas and *Duns Scotus. In modern times, theologians such as John *Calvin and philosophers such as *Descartes and *Kant shaped the tradition. Recent advocates include Basil Mitchell (*The Justification of Religious Belief*, Oxford, 1981), Richard Swinburne (*The Coherence of Theism*, Oxford, 1977) and Alvin *Plantinga (*God, Freedom and Evil*, Grand Rapids, 1978).

A. F. HOLMES

THEOCRACY

Originating from the Greek compound, *theokratia*, theocracy was first coined by Flavius Josephus in description of the Jewish government as 'ascribing to God the rule and power' (*Against Apion* II, 165). However, the term is also used to signify societies in which there is a union of church and state and the civil power is dominated by the ecclesiastical body (i.e. a 'hierocracy'). These two senses of the term reflect the complexity of its usage in reference to church and *state relations throughout history, and suggest how the term's general reference to the ultimate authority of God may be acknowledged irrespective of a particular government system.

Theocratic models in church history

Based upon the understanding of the term as a society dominated by the *church or its clergy, scholars have cited examples of theocracy in Byzantine Christianity, medieval Catholicism, Calvin's Geneva and Cromwell's England, to name a few.

During the early medieval period, this dynamic was made possible through the Donation of Constantine, which granted the *papacy both spiritual and temporal power over Italy. Although the document was later exposed as a forgery in 1440 by Lorenzo Valla, initially the papacy used it to claim legitimacy for the secular rule of Italy. One may consider Pope Gregory VII (*c.* 1021–85), who implemented reform based upon the belief that the 'papal monarchy' held supreme authority over matters of church and state. Consequently, the Investiture Conflict erupted between Gregory and the German Emperor Henry IV in 1076 and 1080, which was left unresolved until the Concordat of Worms in 1122. Nevertheless, this claim of papal absolute authority over the secular world was further pushed by Pope Innocent III in the following years.

Yet, theocracy does not always describe a civil society governed by clergy. For example, studies on the *Puritan migration to New England during the 1630s under the leadership of John Winthrop and John Davenport reveal the effects that theocratic ideals had upon the civil system. One of the practices instituted was the exclusion of freemen without church membership from serving in political positions or choosing magistrates. Nevertheless, insistence that the spiritual governing body would not interfere with the civil body was still maintained. As A. Zakai claims, 'In shaping their Christian commonwealth, Puritans thus aimed neither at unification nor at complete separation of Church and State' (*The Journal of Religious History* 14, p. 138). In fact, the intention was not 'to invest ministers with political power but rather . . . to appoint civil magistrates who would govern according to God's word and will' (ibid., p. 139) and uphold the church.

In a similar vein, one may perceive the dynamic between church and state relations within the Reformed context as representing a complementary model of support based upon the understanding that all authority stemmed from God. In Geneva, for example, the Reformation was regarded as both a spiritual and a political revolution wherein the well-being of the church was considered inextricably linked to the good of the state and vice versa. As J. T. McNeill clarifies in reference to Calvinism (see *Reformed theology), 'the system was a theocracy in the sense that it assumed responsibility to God on the part of secular and ecclesiastical authority alike and proposed as its end the effectual operation of the will of God in the life of the people' (*The History and Character of Calvinism*, New York, 1954, p. 185). Yet, this never meant the subordination of the civil power to the church. Indeed, one may consider *Calvin's insistence on the separate jurisdictions of the church and state within his *Institutes* (4:11). Moreover, the *Westminster Confession is additionally adamant that 'ecclesiastical persons' are not exempted from the magistrates' power (ch. XXIII. iv). That being said, the state, as much as the individual, was subject to the will of God and bound to support and protect the church.

The *Anabaptists or Radical *Reformers represent other divergent views on the relationship between church and state during the Reformation period. Thomas *Müntzer, for example, advocated the establishment of the kingdom of God on earth through punishment of the godless and protection of the elect in his *Sermon to the Princes* in 1524. Moreover, based upon the apocalyptic visions of Melchior Hoffman and the leadership of Jan van Leiden, a theocratic government wherein God's will was enacted as civil law in expectation of Christ's second coming was established at Münster in 1533. Jurisprudence was enforced there by the civil sword according to the laws of Scripture. Subsequently, the failure of this enterprise led to the rejection of such militancy under the leadership of Menno *Simons.

Thus, the complexity of the term 'theocracy' is evident by the above examples as either designating a society in which the clergy ruled the secular sphere or one in which both political and ecclesiastical authorities carried out the will of God.

Bibliography

J. Barclay, *Against Apion*, in S. Mason (ed.), *Flavius Josephus: Translation and Commentary*, vol. 10 (Leiden and Boston, 2007); H.-J. Goertz, 'Karlstadt, Müntzer and the Reformation of the Commoners, 1521–1525', in M. Baylor (ed.), *The Radical Reformation* (Cambridge and New York, 1991); K. Greyerz (ed.), *Religion and Society in Early Modern Europe, 1500–1800* (London and Boston, 1984); H. Hopfl, *The Christian Polity of John Calvin* (Cambridge, 1982); M. Pacaut, *La Théocratie: L'Église et le pouvoir au Moyen Age* (Paris, 1989); J. Roth and J. Stayer (eds.), *A Companion to Anabaptism and Spiritualism, 1521–1700* (Leiden and Boston, 2007); S. Runciman, *The Byzantine Theocracy* (Cambridge and New York, 1977); A. Zakai, 'Theocracy in New England: The Nature and Meaning of the Holy Experiment in the Wilderness', *The Journal of Religious History* n.s. 14, 1986, pp. 133–151.

J. P. McNutt

THEODICY

From Gk *Theos*, 'God', and the root *dik-*, 'just', theodicy seeks to 'justify the ways of God to man' (Milton). A theodicy is thus an attempt to reconcile the existence of an omnipotent, omniscient and loving God with the occurrence of evil and suffering in the world. Why does a supposedly loving and all-powerful *God create a world in which creatures suffer horrendous evil? The term 'theodicy' was first used by the German philosopher Gottfried Wilhelm Leibniz in his treatise on this subject published in 1710.

Theological and philosophical responses to the experience of *evil and *suffering are frequent in Judeo-Christian writings. One highly influential figure is *Augustine of Hippo who, following a tradition extending back to Plato, argued that evil is *privatio boni* – the privation, or lack, of the good. Augustine wished to emphasize that what is primary and original in creation is goodness (Gen. 1:31) and that evil is an intrusion within creation; it is the absence of goodness. Thus, for example, sickness is the absence of health, or the weapons of war indicate the absence of peace. Augustine is primarily arguing against Gnostic and Manichean traditions which were *dualist; they argued that good and evil were two opposing and co-original forces, often associating matter with evil. For Augustine, however, evil is not something 'in itself'; the good is ontologically primary, and evil is parasitic on the good because evil is merely the absence of the good. Of course, evil is *experienced* as a positive force and not merely as an 'absence'. However, Augustine is not concerned with how we experience evil, but with what evil *is* in relation to God and creation. He claims that, next to God and his good creation, evil is quite literally *nothing*. In strict terms, Augustine's approach is not a theodicy because he does not seek to *justify* the occurrence of evil. Augustine taught that only the good is justifiable because goodness is rational and intelligible. Evil, on the other hand, is intrinsically unintelligible. How could there be *reasons* for horrendous evils such as cancer in children? Famously, Augustine did not provide any reasons for the *fall, because there could be no *reason* to turn from God. Instead, Augustine writes of God's *redemptive response to evil in Christ and our role as free moral agents in bringing evil into the world.

The notion that evil is a privation of the good was highly influential until the early modern period. However, it is with the advent of modern philosophy and theology that theodicy, understood strictly as the attempt to justify God, becomes a major topic of concern. In this period, particularly under the influence of David *Hume and Immanuel *Kant, the notion of an a-theological moral standard lying outside God which can thereby be used to 'judge' God becomes influential and prominent. God becomes a moral agent. This marks the beginning of a distinction between those philosophical (or *natural theological) *arguments* which seek to justify God in the face of evil and suffering (theodicy), and those theological *responses* which refer to what God has actually done in Christ with respect to sin, evil and suffering within the economy of *salvation (soteriology).

Theodicy in its modern guise often distinguishes between 'natural evil' (those evils such as suffering caused by natural disasters which occur due to nature and not human agency) and 'moral evil' (those evils which arise because of human agency, such as war or torture). However, many philosophers and theologians reject this distinction because certain occurrences of evil and suffering seem to be neither straightforwardly 'natural' nor 'moral'. For example, the suffering due to an earthquake (natural evil) could equally be due to housing being deliberately built in high-risk areas for reasons of exploitation and profit (moral evil). It is also not clear in what sense an earthquake is evil *in itself*. Nevertheless, one of the most popular theodicies, known as the free-will defence, applies particularly to so-called moral evil. It is claimed that much of the evil and suffering in the world is not due to divine action, but to human beings who are created as free moral agents and who are therefore at liberty to perform evil as well as good acts. A world which consists of such free agents is judged to be intrinsically better than a world of automatons who necessarily (rather than freely) perform good actions. The possibility of a world of free agents who nevertheless always perform good actions is discussed in the literature (see Mackie, *The Miracle of Theism*). Alvin *Plantinga's work on free will and evil has been particularly influential (see *Will).

John *Hick's 'soul-making' theodicy has generated much discussion with regard to so-called natural evil. Hick supposedly follows *Irenaeus of Lyon in claiming that God allows evil and suffering as a means by which souls might be fashioned for eternal life. It is argued that humans are created with potential and, through the process of suffering and the making of significant free choices, mature into the likeness of God as creatures able to share the divine life. This theodicy has obvious appeal to those whose experience of evil and suffering is not only painful, but also a time of growth which changes their perspective on themselves, their neighbour and God. It is also suggested that coping with the suffering of loss teaches one to value the gifts of life in a more profound way. However, Hick's theodicy is prone to some telling criticisms. For example, in common with a large number of theodicies, evil and suffering is justified by rendering it in some way *good for us*. This does not seem to account well for the highly destructive experience of acute evil which is all too common in human lives. Hick responds to such criticisms in his *Evil and the God of Love*.

Amongst other contemporary contributions to theodicy, the English philosopher Richard Swinburne has argued that there may be reason for God to permit certain forms of suffering and evil because they allow the display of 'higher order goods'. The performance of particular forms of extreme courage or generosity, for example, are logically dependent on certain kinds of suffering. This is a variation on the argument that, in order to know or perform the good, we must also have some experience or knowledge of evil. Notice that Swinburne's position, in making certain goods logically dependent on certain evils, is the reverse of Augustine's: the good is now parasitic upon evil and not vice versa.

The traumatic suffering during the world wars of the twentieth century, and particularly the genocide perpetrated by the Nazis, provoked a number of responses with respect to evil, particularly from theologians (see *Holocaust). In contrast to much philosophical theodicy, these theologians turned to the specifics of God's revelation in *Jesus Christ. Jürgen *Moltmann has argued that God suffers in solidarity with creatures and that this experience is a crucial aspect of the divine characteristics of love and sympathy. For Moltmann, to be incapable of suffering is to be incapable of *love. Such suffering love, which is eternally present in God himself, is redemptive within human history. By contrast, Karl *Barth, in common with traditional Chalcedonian orthodoxy, maintained God's *impassibility, but emphasized God's suffering solidarity in the *incarnation and the human nature of Christ. Consistent with his rejection of natural theology, Barth resisted any philosophical notions of God's omnipotence (particularly discussions of what God might or might not do with regard to eliminating evil) in favour of an emphasis on what is actually revealed in Christ concerning the redemption of evil and suffering.

Other recent discussions of evil and suffering have sought to emphasize St Paul's teaching in Rom. 8 that we must 'consider that the sufferings of this present time are not worth comparing with the glory about to be revealed to us' (v. 18). Such responses to evil and suffering stress that, viewed *eschatologically, the experiences of this life, even the most horrific evils imaginable, are wholly overwhelmed by the richness of the heavenly life which God offers (see Adams, *Horrendous Evils and the Goodness of God* and *Christ and Horrors: The Coherence of Christology*). Meanwhile, there has been an attempt to render the discussion of evil less metaphysically and theologically abstract by examining the ways in which Jews and Christians respond in practice to the experience of evil and suffering and continue to find speech about God meaningful and rational in the face of human tragedy (see Phillips, *The Problem of Evil and the Problem of God*). Such an approach does not seek 'solutions' to the quandary of the so-called 'problem of evil' in the form of justifications of God, but rather examines why the expression of the problem of evil is itself problematic with respect to the doctrines of God and creation, and why the modern project of theodicy is open to *theological* challenge (see especially Hart, *The Doors of the Sea: Where Was God in the Tsunami?*).

Bibliography

M. M. Adams, *Horrendous Evils and the Goodness of God* (Ithaca, 1999); idem, *Christ and Horrors: The Coherence of Christology* (Cambridge, 2006); M. M. Adams and R. M. Adams (eds.), *The Problem of Evil*, Oxford Readings in Philosophy (Oxford and New York, 1990); Augustine of Hippo (tr. Henry Chadwick), *Confessions* (Oxford and New York, 1991), esp. book VII; K. Barth *CD* III/3, §50; B. Davies, *The Reality of God and the Problem of Evil* (London, 2006); S. T. Davis (ed.), *Encountering Evil: Live Options in Theodicy* (Louisville, ²2001); G. Evans, *Augustine on Evil* (Cambridge, 1982); D. B. Hart, *The Doors of the Sea: Where Was God in the Tsunami?* (Grand Rapids, 2005); J. Hick, *Evil and the God of Love* (London, rev. edn, 2007); D. Hume (ed. Stanley Tweyman), *Dialogues Concerning Natural Religion* (London and New York, 1991), parts 10 and 11; P. van Inwagen, *The Problem of Evil* (Oxford and New York, 2006); G. W. Leibniz, *Theodicy: Essays on the Goodness of God, the Freedom of Man and the Origin of Evil* (Chicago, 1985 [1710]); J. Mackie, *The Miracle of Theism: Arguments for and against the Existence of God* (Oxford and New York, 1982), ch. 9; J. Moltmann, *The Crucified God* (London, 2001); D. Z. Phillips, *The Problem of Evil and the Problem of God* (London and Minneapolis, 2004); A. Plantinga, *God, Freedom and Evil* (Grand Rapids, 1974); K. Surin, *Theology and the Problem of Evil* (Oxford and Eugene, 1986); R. Swinburne, *The Existence of God* (Oxford and New York, ²2004), ch. 11; *idem*, *Providence and the Problem of Evil* (Oxford and New York, 1998); J. Swinton, *Raging with Compassion: Pastoral Responses to the Problem of Evil* (Grand Rapids, 2007).

S. A. OLIVER

THEODORE OF MOPSUESTIA, see ANTIOCHENE SCHOOL

THEODORET OF CYRRHUS, see ANTIOCHENE SCHOOL

THEOLOGICAL EXEGESIS

Theological exegesis is the exposition of the biblical material according to theological principles considered by Christians throughout the ages to be inherent to *Scripture. It is contrasted to, but not necessarily incompatible with, historical-critical exegesis, which tends to assess biblical texts according to the norms of modern historical study. Theological exegesis can be understood as being concerned with the theological truthfulness of biblical texts, inquiring what they are saying about God the Father, Son and Holy Spirit in relation to humanity and the doctrines of *creation, *fall and *redemption. For example, theological exegesis of the Gospel texts about Jesus' resurrection would not only inquire about the likelihood of the resurrection having occurred historically, but would ask what is the theological significance of the resurrection: what does this event say about the nature, will and purpose of God for creation and humanity. Exegesis did not originate in the universities, but within the church. The growth of *patristic and medieval studies in the twentieth century among Catholic and Orthodox scholars, and the increasing interest in these fields among evangelicals, is an important part of the field of theological exegesis. The patristic era is particularly important due to its being the common heritage of all Christian denominations.

Some basic principles which emerged in the early church are necessary to grasp if the study of theological exegesis is to bear fruit. The earliest Christian writers, including the apostles and the Apostolic Fathers, assumed that the OT was a Christian book which was rightly understood as speaking prophetically about *Jesus *Christ. The testimony of the apostles to Christ was considered to be a doctrinal norm parallel to the OT. This testimony was considered to be 'tradition' in a loose non-technical sense of having been handed down by the apostles to the next generation of Christians. The use of the Bible by *heretics in the second and third centuries AD forced theologians to produce more specific principles of exegesis. *Tertullian used the 'rule of faith', which he took to be the central truths about Father, Son and Holy Spirit, as the principle by which exegesis of Scripture should be done. Given that heretics held erroneous views on Father, Son and Holy Spirit, their exegesis of Scripture was erroneous. Moreover, correct exegesis could only occur where Christian faith and discipline were upheld, i.e. in the church. Theological exegesis therefore takes place primarily in and for the church.

Theological exegesis is best seen as reading Scripture within the *communion of saints, i.e. alongside past and present generations of theologians in the service of the churches worldwide. Most great pre-modern theologians were *preachers. This means that theological exegesis involves working in theological ethics. John L. Thompson's recent work on pre-modern exegetical debates on the relationship between women and men is a good example of theological exegesis done to aid preachers. Thompson shows how pre-modern exegetes, especially the Reformers, debated with each other and asked questions that Christians continue to ask today of the texts, but also attend to the texts in a way that repays careful re-reading. At the same time, he includes modern concerns such as feminist ones in his interaction with the texts. Finally, the American scholar Philip Jenkins argues that the Bible is seen as a book that depicts social and cosmic reality to a much greater degree in the non-Western world than in the West, and this makes theological exegesis obviously based on *historical as well as eternal theological truthfulness. For example, if healing and exorcism are normal parts of life in a particular culture, theological rather than more sceptical exegesis will prevail.

Bibliography

S. E. Fowl, *The Theological Interpretation of Scripture: Classic and Contemporary Readings* (Oxford, 1997); R. M. Grant and D. Tracy, *A*

Short History of the Interpretation of the Bible (London, ²1984); C. A. Hall, *Reading Scripture with the Church Fathers* (Downers Grove, 1998); J. L. Thompson, *Reading the Bible with the Dead: What You Can Learn from the History of Exegesis That You Can't Learn from Exegesis Alone* (Grand Rapids, 2007); N. T. Wright, *Scripture and the Authority of God* (London, 2005).

C. A. E. MOSELEY

THEOLOGICAL METHOD

The term *method* is a compound of two Greek terms: *meta* (denoting a higher-order kind of reflection) and *hodos* ('way'). The early Christian movement was also called the 'Way' (Acts 9:2; 18:25–26; 24:14), and Jesus uses the same Greek term when he identifies himself as 'the way and the truth and the life' (John 14:6). Theological method is thus reflection on the way we come to a saving knowledge of *God.

The problem: how to speak of God

Three questions – 'Where do we begin?'; 'How do we proceed?'; 'What do we use to measure our progress?' – correspond to the key methodological issues: starting points, sources and norms.

By and large, theologians have appealed to sources of knowledge: Scripture, reason, tradition and experience. These four were identified as the '*Wesleyan Quadrilateral' by Albert Outler, but they are not peculiar to Wesley. As to which should be the starting point, each has had its champions, though most view the biblical story as the raw material of theology: the bricks and straw that theologians use to build doctrinal systems.

As to norms, most theologians appeal to divine *revelation (what God teaches by self-communication), though there is ongoing disagreement as to its locus. *Aquinas is representative of the Western tradition in identifying revelation with the content of Scripture. However, especially since modern times others have identified revelation with *either* truths of reason, religious experiences, *or* church tradition (see *Scripture and tradition).

General prolegomena: method-driven approaches

Method has become the predominant concern of modern thinkers. Those who view theology as an academic discipline tend to fuss about method: what matters most is having a sound procedure for getting knowledge in general. In light of the success of the scientific method in particular, some theologians believe that knowing God should be pursued as we pursue knowledge in other areas of inquiry. For these, what must be said first ('prolegomena') concerns method itself.

Scientific methods

Theologians have sought to be scientific for centuries. Aquinas considered theology a science because, like other sciences, it proceeded deductively from first principles (though in his case, the foundation was not empirical facts but the articles of faith, the revealed propositions in the Bible). Similarly, Charles *Hodge considered theology as the science of the Bible (a 'storehouse of facts'), though for him, in the context of nineteenth-century scientific method, its hallmark was the *inductive* method: the close observation of the facts of the Bible and their interrelationships – in a word, exegesis. In the late twentieth century, T. F. *Torrance compared theological method to contemporary scientific method as elucidated by Michael Polanyi and exemplified by Einstein, and this approach has been followed by Alister E. McGrath.

Hermeneutical methods

Because the Bible is the primary source for knowing God, theologians have given extensive attention to theories of textual interpretation (hermeneutics). Conservatives and liberals alike often approach the Bible 'like any other book', aiming to recover either the historical author's intended meaning or, alternately, a mode of understanding oneself and others projected by the world of the text (*Ricœur).

Special prolegomena: matter-driven approaches

Despite the advantage in employing frameworks of discourse that are intellectually respectable and in principle available to all, we must not forget that the object of theological reflection, God in self-revelation, is not like worldly objects. Those who view theology as a church-based discipline insist upon employing methods that are adequate to their unique subject matter.

Theology 'from below'

Some who begin with divine revelation nevertheless insist that we know God not as he is in himself, but only through his effects in human experience. *Schleiermacher viewed theology as the analysis of religious feelings; doctrine is religious feeling set forth in speech.

Paul *Tillich's 'method of correlation' works by discerning questions concerning the meaning of human existence implicitly posed by philosophy, the arts, even popular *culture. Cultural experience raises the questions to which the symbols in the Bible – creation, the cross – respond.

Still others begin with ecclesial experience. Theology on this view is an exercise in Christian self-description. From this perspective, Aquinas and Hodge make theology too much like geometry, beginning as they do with propositions and facts. Nancey Murphy and Stanley *Grenz call theologians to go beyond such *foundationalism: knowledge is less like a pyramid (built from the bottom up) than a web or mosaic of belief that forms a coherent whole. The 'whole' in question is a tradition that is historically extended and socially embodied in, or as, the *church. 'Non-foundationalists' view theology in terms of setting forth the coherence of Christian life and thought by offering 'thick descriptions' of the language and culture of the ecclesial community (*Lindbeck).

Theology 'from above'

Even theologians who make Scripture their primary source do not always agree on its function. Whereas theologians *traditionally* identified what is revealed in the Bible with its doctrines or propositions, Karl *Barth identified the word of God with God himself freely, actively, and personally speaking. Because Christ himself is the revelation of God, Barth reasoned that Scripture becomes a form of the word only when God freely and sovereignly acts, enabling biblical language to bear witness to the risen Christ. The goal of theology is to participate with the biblical authors in the subject matter; theological method consists largely in obedient listening (exegesis) and active response (ethics).

From *scientia* to *sapientia*: the way of wisdom

The method of theology must be adequate to its matter. Theology is faith seeking understanding, but understanding of what? Theology's subject matter – God and his relation to the world – has recently been described as 'theodramatic' inasmuch as it centres not on a philosophy or morality but gospel: on what God says and does (Gk *drao* = 'I do'). Theology sets out to understand what God was/is saying and doing in Christ. *Understanding* is the operative term, for only when we understand where we are and what is happening, can we continue walking the way.

Here we may speak of theology 'from the side' inasmuch as the focus is on God's speech and action on the plane of history, especially in the definitive word-act that is Jesus Christ ('God with us'). This *Christological first principle gives rise to two others.

Getting theodramatic understanding: the canonic principle

The canonic principle states that Scripture is the supreme authority for Christian faith, life and thought, the normative specification of the truth of Jesus Christ. Those who would understand the drama of *redemption must study its authoritative script. The task of theology has less to do with formulating grand theoretical systems than with helping disciples – the supporting actors – to understand the play and their part in it.

Such a theodramatic method affirms the new-found interest in biblical *narrative, but goes further by emphasizing the way in which contemporary readers participate in the action. In the context of drama, interpretation means performance. Doctrine helps us to understand what has already been done (by the triune God) and what remains to be done (by us).

Consequently, theological method belongs less to theoretical science than to practical wisdom. It is as much concerned with design for living as with systems of knowledge. Theology's task is ongoing, not because the gospel changes, but because the historical stage, cultural scenery, and intellectual setting of the church – the company of gospel players – is constantly changing. Doctrine serves the church by helping to form disciples with good judgment: the ability to discern what is theodramatically fitting for disciples to say and do in new contexts.

Demonstrating theodramatic understanding: the catholic principle

While Scripture is the normative specification of the substance of the faith, reason, tradition and experience enjoy ministerial authority to the extent that they help clarify and unpack the meaning of biblical testimony.

Of particular importance is tradition, the history of the church's best interpretations or 'great performances' (K. J. Vanhoozer, *The Drama of Doctrine*, p. 449). Because no single interpretative approach or community will discern all that there is to be gleaned from the Scriptures, theodramatic method also espouses a 'catholic' principle which stipulates that the ethnic and social diversity of the church is the enabling condition for an enriched and enlarged understanding. The canonic principle keeps us centred; the catholic principle keeps us bounded. Doing theology demands both canon sense and catholic sensibility.

Theological method succeeds when it sets and speeds disciples on their way, or rather the way of Jesus Christ, enabling them to speak *and do* the truth – about God and the gospel and hence about the world and ourselves – in love to the glory of God.

See also: Hermeneutics; Scripture, Doctrine of; Systematic Theology.

Bibliography

P. L. Allen, *Theological Method: A Guide for the Perplexed* (London and New York, 2012); D. Clark, *To Know and Love God: Method for Theology* (Wheaton, 2003); A. Dulles, *The Craft of Theology: From Symbol to System* (Dublin, 1992); S. Grenz, *Revisioning Evangelical Theology* (Downers Grove, 1993); T. Hart, *Faith Thinking: The Dynamics of Christian Theology* (London, 1995); D. Kelsey, *Proving Doctrine: The Uses of Scripture in Modern Theology* (Harrisburg, 1999); G. Lindbeck, *The Nature of Doctrine* (Philadelphia, 1984); A. E. McGrath, *A Scientific Theology*, 3 vols. (Edinburgh and London, 2001, 2002, 2003); N. Murphy, *Beyond Liberalism and Fundamentalism* (Valley Forge, 1996); C. Ott and H. Netland (eds.), *Globalizing Theology: Christian Belief and Practice in an Era of World Christianity* (Grand Rapids, 2006); D. Stiver, *Theology after Ricœur: New Directions in Hermeneutical Theology* (Louisville, 2001); T. F. Torrance, *Theological Science* (London, 1969 and Edinburgh, 1996); D. Treier, *Virtue and the Voice of God* (Grand Rapids, 2006); K. J. Vanhoozer, *First Theology: God, Scripture, and Hermeneutics* (Downers Grove, 2002); idem, *The Drama of Doctrine: A Canonical-Linguistic Approach to Christian Theology* (Louisville, 2005).

K. J. Vanhoozer

THEOLOGY

Theology is derived from the Gk *theologia*, compounded of two words, meaning basically an account of, or discourse about, gods or God. Among the Greeks, poets such as Homer and Hesiod were called *theologoi*. Their stories about the gods were categorized as 'mythical theology' by *Stoic writers, who spoke also of 'natural or rational theology', which was close to Aristotle's 'theological philosophy' – broadly what today would be referred to as *philosophical theology or *metaphysics.

Although *Philo called Moses a *theologos* (i.e. one who speaks of God, God's spokesman), no form of the Greek word appears in the LXX of the OT or in the NT (a few manuscripts entitle its last book 'The Revelation of John the *Theologos*'). Its Christian usage begins with the *apologists, for whom the verb sometimes means 'ascribe divinity to, call God', a meaning which it frequently has in the later disputes about the deity of Christ (see *Christology) and of the *Holy Spirit. But by AD 200 both the Greek and its Latin transliteration were being used of teaching, normally Christian teaching, about God. *Athanasius applies *theologia* to knowledge of God in his own being, as distinct from his dealings with the world, and others such as *Augustine restrict it to teaching about the Godhead. Only occasionally in the Fathers does 'theology' refer to a broader range of church doctrine. It belongs within the community of faith, and no separation is made between teaching about God and knowledge (i.e. apprehension and experience) of God. *Theologia* can even mean 'praise of God'.

It was chiefly through the *scholastic writers and the new universities of Europe that theology became a more systematic exercise, a field of study and teaching, even a discipline or a science. This usage was not entirely new – it picked up pre-Christian Greek uses and some in the Fathers also – but it foreshadowed the development of theology as an academic discipline no longer necessarily located in the Christian community. At the same time, the schoolmen increasingly distinguished between different kinds of theology, alongside a common distinction between theology and philosophy, which broadly corresponded to their distinction between *faith and reason. Although the Reformers were generally impatient of the distinctions beloved of the schoolmen, their successors in the age of confessional orthodoxy

903

or Protestant scholasticism adopted or developed an extensive categorization of different kinds of theology.

In the modern world, 'theology' is often used in a comprehensive sense, embracing all the disciplines involved in a university course or in training for church ministry (i.e. including the biblical languages, church history, homiletics, etc.). It may thus be an academic discipline alongside, for example, English literature or physics. More precisely, the word denotes teaching about God and his relation to the world from creation to the consummation, particularly as it is set forth in an ordered, coherent manner. (It is rarely used solely of the doctrine of God himself.) It is normally made more specific by one or more of a wide range of qualifiers, which may indicate the church or tradition it belongs to (e.g. *monastic, *Roman Catholic, *Reformed, *evangelical, *ecumenical), its material basis (e.g. *natural; biblical; confessional, i.e. grounded in a church *confession; symbolic, i.e. based on a church's 'symbols', which here means *creeds, etc.), its doctrinal content (e.g. *baptismal, *trinitarian), its organizing centre or dominant motif or focus (e.g. *covenant, *liberation, incarnational, *feminist, *theology of the cross – each of which denotes more than mere subject matter), its purpose as determined by its audience (e.g. *apologetic, polemical), etc.

Among the main disciplines of theological study today must be counted biblical, *historical, *systematic, *philosophical, pastoral and practical theology, and others pursued less widely, such as *dogmatic, *liturgical and *fundamental theology. Most kinds of theology have less and less a confessional or denominational character.

The acid test for all theology was well expressed by *Thomas Aquinas: 'Theology is taught by God, teaches of God, and leads to God.'

Bibliography

G. F. van Ackeren, in *NCE* 14, pp. 39–49 (a Catholic discussion, including 'positive' and 'speculative' theology); G. Ebeling, in *RGG* VI, cols. 754–769; R. Hedde, in *DTC* 10, cols. 1574–1595; F. Kattenbusch, 'Die Entstehung einer Christlichen Theologie: Zur Geschichte der Ausdrücke Θεολογια, Θεολογειν, Θεολογος', *ZTK* n.s. 11, 1930, pp. 161–205; F. Whaling, 'The Development of the Word "Theology"', *SJT* 34, 1981, pp. 289–312.

D. F. WRIGHT

THIELICKE, HELMUT (1908–85)

Born in Barmen, Thielicke graduated PhD in 1931 and ThD in 1934. He first pastored and taught in Württemberg. Having offended the Nazi regime by questioning the so-called 'orders' of *race and people, he was for a time forbidden to speak, write or travel except in a small area. Yet he had a powerful pulpit ministry during the war years and immediately after. In 1945 he took up a professorship at Tübingen and in 1954 transferred to Hamburg, where he served as rector in 1961. Famous as a preacher, he continued to address large congregations and sponsored an indirect evangelistic venture to spread Christian knowledge by discussion, pamphlets, and radio and television talks.

His main contribution, however, came through his writings, most of which have been translated into English. Even under Hitler's ban he managed to smuggle an early version of his work on death out of the country in a diplomatic bag. After the war he published selections of sermons (e.g. *The Silence of God*, *The Final Dereliction*), in which he delivered a prophetic message for an apocalyptic situation. His academic programme, apart from some early works, began with the many volumes of the *Theological Ethics*, available in three volumes in English. The three volumes of *The Evangelical Faith* developed his dogmatic thinking, and *Modern Faith and Thought* offered a commentary on recent theological history, especially in Germany. Among works designed for more general readers, *The Hidden Question of God*, *Living with Death*, and an essay in *anthropology entitled *Being Human – Becoming Human*, deserve special mention. Reminiscences (*Zu Gast auf einem schünen Stern*) provide valuable insights into his life, thought and times.

As a preacher, Thielicke addressed the deep questions of life that emerge in days of crisis. His response to them was to press through to the final issues of human nature and destiny that lie behind immediate problems. He thus reformulated the questions, so as to point to the higher divine purpose fulfilled in Christ. Proclamation of the word of Christ forms the church's primary task, in the discharge of which *preachers tread a fine line between irrelevance and false accommodation. They best achieve this by combining expository and topical material and relying on the self-evident truth of the message as it is applied by the Spirit. The issues raised in the crises of life include many *ethical problems, e.g. lying to protect victims of persecution, political assassination, and the new questions of *sex and medicine. Tackling such issues first in his scholarly work, Thielicke laid bare the theological truths which underlie their solution, namely, *creation in God's *image, the fall, the relation of indicative and imperative in the new life, the role of *natural law, the tension of *law and gospel, the question of compromise in living the Christian life in a fallen world, and the continuing need for forgiveness as we are righteous in hope (*spe*) but sinners in fact (*re*).

Discussion of ethical problems brought Thielicke to the heart of the gospel, and in *The Evangelical Faith* he explored God's answer to the plight of human alienation which comes to expression in the modern cleavage of the religious and the secular. God himself initiates restoration by accepting solidarity with us in Christ and bringing us to new life through the Spirit. Utopias hold out only false promises, and social reconstruction is impossible without individual renewal. Yet the new aeon has dawned, advance is thus possible, and by God's action, mediated by the word and Spirit, the race may again become, and be, human, notwithstanding every threat. Participating in this mediation is the church's first responsibility; on its fulfilment depends the church's life or death.

Readers may often find Thielicke wordy, repetitive and provocative, and at times obscure. Yet for those who use discernment he makes a notable contribution to preaching, ethics and *dogmatics. He raises crucial issues, displays their final significance as he pushes through them to the issue of God, and indicates their one authentic solution in the work that God has done, and does, through Christ and the Spirit.

Bibliography

Works: *Notes from a Wayfarer: The Autobiography of Helmut Thielicke*, tr. D. R. Law (New York, 1995).

Studies: G. W. Bromiley, 'Helmut Thielicke', in D. G. Peerman and M. E. Marty (eds.), *A Handbook of Christian Theologians* (Nashville, ²1984).

G. W. BROMILEY

THIRTY-NINE ARTICLES

The Thirty-Nine Articles are a statement of faith produced by the Church of England during the reign of Queen Elizabeth I (1558–1603). Together with the *Book of Common Prayer* and its accompanying Ordinal, and the model sermons known as the *Homilies*, the Articles were intended to set out a basic framework of faith and practice for the Church of England, for, as Archbishop Matthew Parker put it: '. . . the glory of God, the advancement of true religion, and the salvation of Christian souls'.

The Articles were issued in 1571 in both Latin and English. They represent a revision by Archbishop Parker and other bishops, such as John *Jewel, Bishop of Salisbury, of an earlier series of Articles, the Forty-Two Articles, which were produced by Archbishop Thomas *Cranmer in 1553.

The Articles can be divided into eight sections. Articles 1–5 are concerned with the doctrine of God, articles 6–8 with Scripture and the creeds, articles 9–18 with sin and salvation, articles 19–21 are concerned with the church and its authority, articles 22–24 with errors to be avoided in the church, articles 25–31 with the sacraments, articles 32–36 with church discipline, and articles 37–39 are concerned with Christians and civil society.

As J. I. Packer notes ('The Status of the Articles', in J. C. de Satgé *et al.*, *The Articles of the Church of England* [Oxford, 1964]), the Articles are 'consciously eclectic' in their theology: 'They set out the trinitarian faith of the ecumenical creeds (1–5) as biblical and necessary to salvation (6–8), together with *Augustine's doctrine of sin (9–10); *Lutheran teaching on justification, grace and the church (11–21, 23, 34, 37), as given in the Augsburg confession of 1530 and Wurtemburg Confession of 1552 . . . and sacramental teaching of the Swiss sort, with at one point an anti-Lutheran edge (29).' In addition to their positive teaching, the Articles also reject various aspects of the theology of the medieval Catholic Church and of the *Radical Reformation.

In the Church of England today the Thirty-Nine Articles remain one of the sources upon which the church's doctrine is grounded. Clergy, Readers and licensed lay workers in the Church of England have to declare their belief in the faith to which the Articles 'bear witness'. The Articles also remain an important part of the doctrinal inheritance of the wider Anglican Communion, although only a minority of the provinces of the Communion now make formal reference to the doctrinal authority of the Articles in their constitutions.

See also: ANGLICANISM; CONFESSIONS OF FAITH.

Bibliography

J. C. de Satgé *et al.*, *The Articles of the Church of England* (Oxford, 1964); W. H. Griffith Thomas, *The Principles of Theology* (London, ⁴1951); C. Hardwick, *A History of the Articles of Religion* (London, 1895); O. O' Donovan, *On the Thirty-Nine Articles* (Exeter, 1984); P. Toon, 'The Articles and Homilies', in S. Sykes and J. Booty (eds.), *The Study of Anglicanism* (London, 1988).

M. DAVIE

THOMAS AQUINAS (1225–74)

The greatest of the thirteenth-century scholastic theologians, known both for his theological and philosophical work, Aquinas was born the son of the Count of Aquino at Roccasecca, near Naples. As a young man he joined the *Dominicans, a new mendicant order, in spite of strong opposition from his family who wanted him to become a traditional *Benedictine monk. The Dominicans emphasized both a return to the gospel and academic learning, for their mission was to preach and hear confessions. Aquinas was immediately sent to the University of Paris to study. He spent the rest of his life teaching theology, at Paris (1256–9 and 1269–72), Rome, Naples and Viterbo.

The major problem facing the thirteenth century was that of dealing with the recently rediscovered thought of *Aristotle. Aristotle gave a much richer account of the natural world than the West had yet known; but as interpreted by Arab commentators, he also held positions opposed to Christianity, such as the eternity of the world and the existence of one agent intellect for all. Some theologians responded by rejecting Aristotle completely; others accepted him uncritically, holding that what is true in philosophy does not always agree with what is true in theology. By contrast, Aquinas welcomed what was true in Aristotle, but systematically revised what he found to be inadequate or in error. Since all truth is from God, it is one. In principle there can be no conflict between *faith and reason. Where Aquinas found conflict, he sought to show that it was because of errors in human understanding.

With regard to the eternity of the world, Aquinas argues that reason cannot prove that the world is eternal, but the fact that it has a beginning and will end is known from *revelation. On the issue of personal *immortality, Aquinas deepens Aristotle's psychology significantly, showing how man (see *Anthropology) is a single substance composed of matter and form, but his form is immaterial and so immortal. On this basis he attacked the view that there is only one soul for all people, the interpretation of Aristotle given by *Averroes and his followers. At the same time Aquinas was modifying the traditional anthropology in the Christian West, which, following *Augustine, had tended to be dualistic. Because Aquinas adapted Aristotelian methods and principles in organizing theology, he was looked upon, and even opposed, as an innovator.

Like other scholastic theologians, Aquinas began his career by writing a commentary on Peter *Lombard's *Sentences*. Because of opposition to his order at Paris his licence to teach was delayed, but was soon granted on order from the pope. Throughout his career Aquinas gave lectures on Scripture to students. Some of these have come down to us in the form of commentaries. Better known are his 'disputed questions', *On Truth*, *On the Power of God*, *On Evil*, *On Spiritual Creatures* and *On the Soul*, which are the product of university courses and formal disputations. In addition, Aquinas wrote commentaries on works of *Boethius and the Dionysian work, *On the Divine Names* (see *Pseudo-Dionysius). His greatest works as a commentator were his commentaries on the major works of Aristotle, including the logical works, *Physics*, *On the Soul*, *Metaphysics* and *Ethics*. Aquinas is best known, however, for two works produced apart from his teaching, the *Summa contra Gentiles* and *Summa Theologica*. The latter, which was intended as a summary of theology for beginners, has three parts: the first contains the doctrine of *God and how things come from God; the second treats how human creatures return to God, dealing first with moral matters in general and then giving a detailed account of the virtues and vices; the third part considers the *incarnation and *sacraments. Aquinas had completed about half of the third part when he stopped writing and died a few months later.

In the Aristotelian account of the sciences, the highest part of philosophy included theology, considering such matters as the first movers. While acknowledging this theology and using some of its results, such as the proofs of God's existence, Aquinas argues nevertheless that there is need for sacred theology in addition to the theology of the philosophers. Sacred theology is based on revelation, and it makes known truths about man's end that cannot be known through reason. In addition, it also reveals truths that reason *can* grasp, because these truths are necessary for *salvation; but through reason only a few could grasp them, and then only after much study and still mixed with many errors.

For Aquinas, sacred theology is a science unlike any other; for while all others are based on human reason, it is based on what God has revealed. A wide variety of matters are considered in sacred theology, but they are all considered from the point of view of being revealed. Because sacred theology is founded on divine knowledge which cannot err, it possesses greater certitude than any science founded on human reason. Nevertheless, because of the weakness of our ability to understand divine things, they may appear doubtful to us, even though they are certain in themselves. Because of its origin in revelation, the strongest argument in this science is to appeal to *authority – the weakest argument in the other sciences. Aquinas denies that it is possible to argue to the articles of faith, which are the principles of this science, but one can answer objections rooted in misunderstanding. It is wrong to try to use reason as a basis for believing, but it is meritorious to try to understand what one has believed (see *Faith and reason).

In discussing issues, Aquinas consistently employs the works of the Fathers and the ancient philosophers, adopting Paul's use of the poets as his model. Thus the best arguments of the philosophers show that there is a first mover, first efficient cause, etc., and Aquinas concludes in each case that this is what everyone understands to be God. Of course, God is much more than just a first mover, so from this beginning Aquinas goes on to show that God is one, good, infinite, eternal and *Trinity. Similarly with regard to the end of man, Aquinas accepts the view of the ancient philosophers that man's end is happiness, but he argues that it is to be found only in heaven, in the *vision of God of the blessed; in this life there is only imperfect happiness, which is what the philosophers grasped to a greater or lesser degree. In his discussion of *law, Aquinas argues for a natural law which is in man, a participation in the divine law and a guide for the formation of the laws made by human legislators. The Decalogue, as given to the Israelites, is held to be a divinely given formulation of the content of the natural law. For Aquinas, nature is from God and so is good, but – because of sin – divine aid is needed in order both to regain the good of nature and to return to God.

Within fifty years of his death, the Dominicans had adopted Aquinas as the doctor of their order. Centres of Thomistic scholarship have flourished in many countries from the fifteenth century on. Today he remains the most influential theologian of the medieval church.

See also: THOMISM AND NEO-THOMISM.

Bibliography

Works: *Summa contra Gentiles*, tr. A. C. Pegis et al., *On the Truth of the Catholic Faith*, 5 vols. (Garden City, NY, 1955–57); repr. as *Summa . . .* (Notre Dame, IN, 1975); *Summa Theologica*, ET in 59 vols + index (London, 1964–81).

Studies: M. D. Chenu, *Toward Understanding St Thomas* (Chicago, 1964); F. C. Copleston, *Aquinas* (Harmondsworth, 1955); B. Davies, *The Thought of Thomas Aquinas* (Oxford, 1992); E. Gilson, *Le Thomisme* (Paris, 6·1965); F. Kerr, 'Thomas Aquinas', in G. R. Evans (ed.), *The Medieval Theologians* (Oxford, 2001), pp. 201–220; M. Levering, *Christ's Fulfilment of Torah and Temple: Salvation According to Thomas Aquinas* (Notre Dame, IN, 1997); R. McInery, *St Thomas Aquinas* (Boston, 1977); T. F. O'Meara, *Thomas Aquinas: Theologian* (Notre Dame, IN, 1997); F. van Steenberghen, *Thomas Aquinas and Radical Aristotelianism* (Washington DC, 1980); A. Vos, *Aquinas, Calvin and Contemporary Protestant Thought* (Grand Rapids, 1985); J. A. Weisheipl, OP, *Friar Thomas D'Aquino* (Garden City, 1974). See also Bibliography under Thomism.

A. Vos

THOMISM AND NEO-THOMISM

Thomism is the theological tradition which springs from *Thomas Aquinas and his followers.

Aquinas's theological views

The wide-ranging writings of Aquinas covered the whole gamut of Christian thought.

Faith and reason. Like *Augustine, Aquinas based faith in God's revelation in Scripture. Support for faith was found in miracles and rational arguments. Aquinas presented 'five ways' to prove the existence of God (*Summa*, I:2:3). Since he believed sin obscures human ability to know, however, belief (not proof) is necessary for most. While belief is never *based* on reason, nonetheless believers should reason *about* and *for* their faith. Aquinas's reasons for belief that God existed were spelled out in his famous 'five ways'. He argued (1) from motion to an unmoved mover, (2) from effects to a first cause, (3) from contingent beings to a necessary being, (4) from degrees of perfection to a most perfect being, and (5) from design to a designer. In addition to truths which are in 'accord with reason', there are some (e.g. *Trinity, *Incarnation) which go 'beyond reason' and can be known only by faith.

Epistemology. Thomas held that all knowledge begins in experience. There is nothing in the mind which was not first in the senses, except the mind itself. For we are born with an a priori, innate capacity to know. All knowledge is dependent on first principles, such as (1) identity (being is being), (2) noncontradiction (being is not non-being), (3) excluded middle (either being or non-being), (4) causality (non-being cannot cause being), and (5) finality (every being acts for an end). Once these principles are properly known, they are seen to be self-evident, or reducible to the self-evident.

Metaphysics. It is the task of the wise person to know order. The order reason discerns in its own acts is *logic*. The order it produces in acts of will is *ethics*. The order produced by reason in external things is art. But the order reason contemplates but does not produce is *nature*. Nature contemplated as sensible is called *physical science*. Nature understood, in so far as it is quantifiable, is mathematics. And nature viewed in so far as it is being is *metaphysics*. The most important affirmation of Thomas's metaphysics is: 'Act in the order in which it is act is unlimited and unique, unless it is conjoined with passive potency.' Only God is pure actuality. All creatures are composed of actuality and potentiality. God has no form, but is pure actuality. Angels are completely actualized potencies (pure form). And the human being is a composition of form (soul) and matter (body) with progressive actualization.

God. God alone is pure Existence (the 'I Am'). He is Being; everything else *has* being. God's essence is to exist. He is a Necessary Being. All else is contingent. God cannot change since he has no potentiality for change. Likewise, since time involves change (from a before to an after), God is a-temporal or eternal. God is simple (indivisible) since he has no principle (potency) for division. He is also infinite (not-finite), having no potency to limit him. Besides these metaphysical attributes, God is also morally perfect (just, good) and infinitely wise.

Religious language. Our language about God is analogous (see *Analogy). It cannot be univocal, since God's knowledge is unlimited and ours is limited. Neither can it be equivocal; since creation must resemble the Creator, the effect is like its efficient cause. Nonetheless, there are great differences between an infinite God and finite humanity. Hence, the way of negation (*via negativa*; see *Apophatic theology) is necessary. We can apply to God only the perfection signified (e.g. goodness, truth), but we must negate the finite mode of signification by which these perfections are found in creatures.

Creation. God created out of nothing (*ex nihilo*). An eternal creation is logically possible, because there is no logical contradiction in a cause causing from eternity. Nonetheless, by revelation we know that the universe began. No time existed before creation. God did not create *in* time; rather, there was a creation *of* time with the world.

Humanity. Following Aristotle, Aquinas held that the human being (see *Anthropology) is a hylomorphic unity of body and soul. Despite this unity of soul-body there is no identity between them. Rather, the soul survives death and awaits reunion with the body at the resurrection. God directly creates each individual human soul in its mother's womb (see *Soul, origin of).

Ethics. There are first principles not only of thought, but also of action (called *laws). Eternal law is the plan by which God governs all creation. Natural law is the participation of rational creatures in this eternal law. Human law is the application of natural law to local communities. And divine law is the revelation of God's law through the Scriptures and the church.

There are two types of virtue: natural and supernatural. The former are the classic virtues of prudence, justice, courage and temperance. The latter are faith, hope and love.

Thomism and Neo-Thomism

Thomism is a movement which follows the thought originating with Thomas Aquinas. Upon his death, his teachings were adopted by various individuals, most notably by his *Dominican brothers. Several propositions of Aquinas were condemned by church authorities in 1277, but primarily due to Dominican efforts his system was eventually established. Aquinas was canonized in 1323.

Thomists used an *Aristotelian mode of thought and expression, in contrast to *Franciscans who were more *Platonic. This led to lively debates between the orders through the ages.

A central figure in developing Thomism was Thomas de Vio Cardinal Cajetan (1469–1534) who opposed *Luther. Cajetan held several distinctive interpretations of Aquinas. Notable is his view that analogy is best understood as the possession of an attribute by two essences, rather than properly by only one. He also thought more in terms of abstract essences than existing substances. Finally, he raised doubts concerning the provability of God's existence and man's immortality.

By the sixteenth century Thomism became the leading school of Catholic thought. The *Jesuit order (approved in 1540) aligned itself with Aquinas, and in many of its pronouncements the *Council of Trent consciously expressed itself in Thomistic phrases. In the seventeenth century John of St Thomas (1589–1644) was a major representative of Thomism. But it became ingrown in the eighteenth century and faded. Thomism experienced a revival in the nineteenth century, however, due largely to its emphasis on human dignity in the face of the Industrial Revolution. By the time of the First *Vatican Council (1869–70), Thomism was again in vogue and triumphed in 1879 when Pope Leo XIII, in *Aeterni Patris*, gave official recommendation to it, which gave impetus to a movement known as Neo-Thomism.

Neo-Thomism is a twentieth-century revival of Thomistic thought. Two main groups emerged: the Transcendental Thomists, such as Joseph Maréchal (1878–1944), Bernard *Lonergan and Karl *Rahner, adapted Thomism to *Kantian thought; others under the leadership of Reginald Garrigou-Lagrange (1877–1964), Etienne *Gilson and Jacques *Maritain sought to expound Aquinas himself. Thomism crossed denominational lines and included Anglicans such as E. L. Mascall (1905–93) and even many non-Catholics.

The distinctive teaching of Neo-Thomism is the maxim that 'existence precedes essence'. By this it is meant that one knows by intuition *that* something exists before one knows *what* it is. For this reason Maritain claimed that Thomism is the origination of *existentialism.

The Neo-Thomist tradition has been carried on by notables such as Frederick Copieston (1907–94) in Great Britain, Joseph Owens (1908–2005) in Canada, and James Collins (1917–85) and Vernon Bourke (1907–98) in the United States.

Bibliography

V. J. Bourke, *Thomistic Bibliography: 1920–40* (St Louis, 1945); T. L. Miethe and V. J. Bourke, *Thomistic Bibliography: 1940–78* (Westport and London, 1980).

R. Cessario, *A Short History of Thomism* (Washington DC, 2006); E. Gilson, *The Christian Philosophy of St Thomas Aquinas* (New York, 1956); J. Maritain, *Scholasticism and Politics* (London, ²1945); idem, *Distinguish to Unite, or the Degrees of Knowledge* (New York, 1959); G. McCool, *The Neo-Thomists* (Milwaukee, 1994). See also bibliography under Thomas Aquinas.

N. L. Geisler

THORNTON, L. S., see ANGLO-CATHOLIC THEOLOGY

THORNWELL, JAMES HENLEY (1812–62)

An eminent theologian, teacher, minister within the Presbyterian Church in the United States (PCUSA), Thornwell was one of the founders of the Presbyterian Church in the Confederate States of America (1861). As a minister he served at Lancaster, SC (1835–8) and Columbia, SC (1840–1; 1855–61). In 1847 the General Assembly elected him as moderator, the youngest man ever to be so elected. From 1841 to 1851 he was professor at South Carolina College, and its president from 1852 to 1855. He taught didactic and polemic theology at the seminary in Columbia, SC, from 1855 to 1862. Thornwell was a strong and able defender of the Westminister Standards. His polemical ability arose from a passion for truth rather than native pugnacity.

Before the PCUSA divided between North and South, the most severe conflict engaged in by Thornwell was with Charles *Hodge. The conflict culminated with an encounter in 1860, at Rochester, New York, on the issue of the administration of missions. The issue expanded into concerns over the nature of *Presbyterianism, with special reference to the importance of the regulative and constitutive principles of Scripture, the legitimacy of virtually autonomous boards for the support of benevolent activities, and whether a ruling elder is to be considered a presbyter. Thornwell contended that *church government was no less a matter of revelation than doctrine. Hodge argued that the details of the system were not given in Scripture. Thornwell contended that committees of the presbytery, rather than boards, should control church benevolences; Hodge saw nothing unscriptural in boards. Thornwell saw ruling elders as full presbyters, acting for the church in the courts, while he felt Hodge's theory distinguished too radically between clergy and *laity and created a hierarchy.

Concerning the most volatile issue of his day, *slavery, Thornwell believed that from a study of the biblical material one could not conclude that slavery per se was immoral. Moreover, it had become so highly politicized that he defended the justness of the Confederate cause and supported the separation of Southern churches to serve the new nation.

Bibliography

Works: *The Collected Writings of James Henley Thornwell*, 4 vols. (New York, 1871–72; repr. Edinburgh, 1986).
Studies: D. B. Calhoun, *A Place for Truth: The Bicentennial James Henley Thornwell Lectures* (Greenville, 1996); E. B. Holifield, *The Gentleman Theologians: American Theology in Southern Culture, 1795–1860* (Durham, 1978); B. M. Palmer, *The Life and Letters of James Henley Thornwell* (Richmond, 1875; repr. Edinburgh, 1974); T. W. Rogers, 'James Henley Thornwell', *Journal of Christian Reconstruction* 7, 1980, pp. 175–205; L. G. Whitlock, 'James Henley Thornwell', in D. F. Wells (ed.), *Reformed Theology in America* (Grand Rapids, 1985).

T. J. NETTLES

THURNEYSEN, EDUARD (1888–1974)

Thurneysen was a Swiss theologian who associated with Karl *Barth as a student at Marburg, and who renewed his friendship with Barth while he was the pastor of a small church at Leutwil, Aargau (1913–20) at the same time Barth was pastor in the nearby Swiss village of Safenwil (1911–21). During this time, the world entered the First World War, and the Kaiser's war policy was supported by Barth and Thurneysen's former teachers, highlighting the failure of German liberal theology (see *Liberalism, German) to negotiate the modern world. In the early 1920s, together with Barth, Emil *Brunner, Rudolf *Bultmann and Friedrich *Gogarten, Thurneysen was part of a generational movement against the dominant liberal theology which made humanity rather than God and God's *revelation the central theme of theology. Understood as the leading thinkers developing so-called '*dialectical theology', they discovered a new world by turning to the word of God as the real world. Between 1923 and 1933 this group published the journal *Zwischen den Zeiten* ahead of the break of Thurneysen (following Barth) with Gogarten (becoming a Nazi supporter) and Brunner (advocating *natural theology). Thurneysen advanced the eschatological idea that rather than a dualistic future world for *eschatology, it is precisely this present world where the future promise in Jesus Christ shall come to his followers.

Bibliography

H. J. Ponsteen, *Karl Barth en Eduard Thurneysen (de theologische relevantie van een levenslange vriendschap)* (Oosterbeek, 1989); K. Raschzok, *Theologische Realenzyklopädie*, 33 (2002), pp. 524–527.

J. S. SEXTON

TILLICH, PAUL (1886–1965)

Writing as a philosophical theologian, Tillich sought to mediate between Christian theology and secular thought. He viewed his task as one of apologetics, provided that we define

Tillich, Paul

*apologetics in his own way, as an 'answering theology' which is offered on the basis of a shared area of common ground. He studied and subsequently taught in several German universities, and although he emigrated to the United States when Hitler came to power in 1933, his thought remains firmly rooted in German philosophical traditions. He is indebted to the *Romantic movement (e.g. to *Schleiermacher and to F. W. J. von Schelling, 1775–1854) but also to the *phenomenology of Edmund Husserl (1859–1938) and Martin *Heidegger. He also drew heavily on the psychology of Jung, especially in his work on symbols.

Tillich's major mature work was his three-volume *Systematic Theology* (1951, 1957, 1963). Its central principle is the method of correlation: 'In using the method of correlation, systematic theology proceeds in the following way: it makes an analysis of the human situation out of which existential questions arise, and it demonstrates that the symbols used in the Christian message are the answers to these questions' (*Systematic Theology* I, p. 70). Tillich's work is then organized around five major correlations: reason and revelation; being and God; concrete human existence and Christ; life in its ambiguities and the Spirit; the meaning of history and the kingdom of God. Tillich acknowledges that these questions and answers may influence each other in their formulations. For this reason many secular philosophers have expressed suspicions about the genuineness of the 'questions', while many theologians criticize the 'answers' as representing accommodations towards the questions. But Tillich sees his own role as that of a theologian of mediation. He seeks to mediate between theology and philosophy; between religion and culture; between Lutheranism and socialism; between the traditions of Germany and those of America. He insists that no isolated system of doctrine or theology can embrace the whole truth. Fragmentation and compartmentalizing are symbols of the demonic; wholeness points to God.

This is bound up with what Tillich has termed 'the *Protestant principle'. Since no single system of thought can encompass the reality of God, theology can never be final. It must always be in process and correction. God remains above and beyond all formulations in theology, including the formulations of the Bible itself. Pastorally, Tillich sees this principle as a defence against idolatry (see *Images). It is possible to think that we have either found or rejected God, when in reality we have encountered only a reduced image of him. The God who is truly God is ultimate. In Tillich's language, he is 'ultimate concern'. Tillich attempts to argue that an attitude of ultimate concern can have only the Ultimate as its object. 'Ultimate concern' thus has a double meaning, describing both the attitude and the reality to which it is directed. By this means Tillich seeks to replace the traditional criteria of theological content by the test of an attitude of ultimate seriousness. But this double meaning of ultimate concern can seem plausible only within a particular German philosophical tradition.

Theology, Tillich insists, uses the language of *symbol. Symbols point to that which they symbolize, but they also participate in it in the kind of way that the American flag is said to participate in the dignity of the nation. In particular, Tillich stresses the power of symbols to create or to destroy, to integrate or to fragment. They open up dimensions of reality, but also resonate with the preconscious depths of the human mind. Following Jung, Tillich stresses the creative and healing power of symbols which well up from the unconscious. While cognitive statements have the effect of reducing God to 'a' being alongside other beings, Tillich believes that symbols point beyond themselves to God who is the ground of being. Symbols are born and die, as human experience changes. But although he rightly stresses their power, Tillich provides no adequate criterion to test their truth, and his theory of symbols is insufficiently grounded in a comprehensive account of language and meaning.

Bibliography

Main works include: *The Protestant Era* (Chicago, 1947); *Systematic Theology*, 3 vols. (Chicago, 1951, 1957, 1963); *The Courage to Be* (New Haven and London, 1953); *Theology of Culture* (New York, 1959).

R. C. Crossman (ed.), *Paul Tillich: A Comprehensive Bibliography and Keyword Index of Primary and Secondary Writings in English* (Metuchen, 1984).

Studies: J. L. Adams, *Paul Tillich's Philosophy of Culture, Science, and Religion* (New York, 1965); D. M. Brown, *Ultimate Concern: Tillich in Dialogue* (New York, 1965); J. P. Clayton, *The Concept of Correlation* (Berlin, 1980); K. Hamilton, *The System and the Gospel*

(London, 1963); C. W. Kegley and R. W. Bretall (eds.), *The Theology of Paul Tillich* (New York, 1952); D. H. Kelsey, *The Fabric of Tillich's Theology* (New Haven, 1967); D. W. Musser and J. L. Price, *Tillich* (Nashville, 2010); W. and M. Pauck, *Paul Tillich* (New York, 1976); R. Re Manning (ed.), *The Cambridge Companion to Paul Tillich* (Cambridge, 2009); J. Heywood Thomas, *Paul Tillich: An Appraisal* (London, 1963).

A. C. Thiselton

TIME AND ETERNITY

Popular opinion (at least in European culture) tends to think of eternity as timelessness. The world exists 'within' time, which may be represented as a line on which the world is moving from the past into the future. Since *God is not an entity in the world, then it is assumed that he exists above and beyond time 'in' a timeless eternity. But developments in the twentieth century called that popular picture in question.

First, whereas scientific thinking at least from Newton had differentiated time from space, Einstein's theory of relativity required that these two be associated as different dimensions of the same reality, the universe. Secondly, in biblical studies, scholars became more aware that the rigid distinction between time and eternity was more characteristic of Greek culture than of the thinking of the writers of the OT or even the NT. In the OT, the Hebrew word '*ōlām*, translated 'eternity', did not imply timelessness, but very long periods of time, an 'age', or even everlasting time. NT writers assumed a Jewish *eschatological framework which believed that 'this present evil age' (*aiōn*, Gal. 1:4) would come to an end (*eschaton*), and the future time of God's *kingdom would begin, 'the age to come' (Eph. 1:21). But for Christians 'the age to come' had paradoxically *already* come in Jesus, particularly with his *resurrection, in anticipation of the future coming of the kingdom.

The idea of eternity as 'timelessness' is now seen to have developed in the Greek philosophical tradition. With roots in Parmenides and *Plato, the idea of absolute timelessness emerged with Plutarch and Plotinus and was introduced into Christian thought by *Origen and *Augustine. It became seen as an implication of *creation *ex nihilo* that God must be in a timeless eternity and not be 'in' time since time was part of creation. Boethius formulated the classic definition: 'Eternity then is the whole, simultaneous and perfect possession of boundless life.' It had to be distinguished from 'sempiternity', which was his word for everlasting duration. God was held to be immutably eternal in the full sense that past, present and future were all simultaneously present to him in the 'Eternal Now'. His so-called 'foreknowledge' therefore was not looking 'forward', but simply his omniscience. *Thomas Aquinas brought this idea of the absolute timelessness, simplicity and immutability of God to its highest expression in what is now known as 'classical *theism'.

*Hegel was the genius who challenged the whole tradition back to Parmenides and argued that God's 'being' was to be understood not in terms of static timelessness, but in dynamic 'becoming'. God, or Absolute Spirit, creates an Other, the world, and then reconciles this Other to himself in Becoming. The metaphysical movement of Spirit is therefore in Being, Negation and Becoming, and this is the true meaning of what is pictured in the Christian doctrines of the incarnation and the *Trinity. The static *idealism of Plato is thus replaced with a dynamic idealism: the Platonist dualism between eternity and time is replaced with an eternity which realizes itself in everlasting time. The influence of this Hegelian metaphysic (see *German idealism) can be seen in the way in which some subsequent theologians think of God and the world, eternity and time.

Today different Christian philosophers advocate different views of the relation of God to time and eternity. Paul Helm defends classical theism, whereas Nicholas Wolterstorff argues for divine temporality. Others advocate some kind of combination of the two (William Lane Craig) or a nuanced view between the two in 'relative timelessness' (Alan Padgett). Among dogmatic theologians, Karl *Barth wanted to dispense with any idea of God's static, timeless eternity and yet to keep something of Boethius' view of the simultaneity of past, present and future to God. His distinction between created time and 'God's time' was developed by T. F. *Torrance. As Einstein rejected Aristotle's concept of time and space as 'receptacles' in which entities existed and events happened, and instead thought of time as one of the dimension of the space-time universe, so (Torrance suggests) we may think of 'eternity' as God's time. It therefore remains a mystery to us, but as time is not some reality superior to the universe 'in' which it exists, but is rather a dimension of the universe, so 'eternity', or God's time, is not something superior to God in which God exists, but is rather a dimension or function of his Being. And God cannot be portrayed as inert or static. Further, since God has become incarnate in Jesus, the co-ordination of time and 'eternity' are to be understood with reference to the God-man. Similarly Robert Jenson has criticized the foundational Western assumption that time is a progressive movement from the past into the future and argued that it must be reconceived in its relationship to the triune God who is the God of Israel.

Bibliography

J. Barr, *Biblical Words for Time* (London, 1962); K. Barth, *CD* II.1, pp. 608ff.; III.1, pp. 67ff.; III.2, pp. 437ff.; O. Cullmann, *Christ and Time* (ET, London, 1959); G. Ganssle (ed.), *Four Views: God and Time* (Downers Grove, 2001); P. Helm, *Eternal God: A Study of God Without Time* (Oxford, 1988); D. Knight, 'Jenson on Time', in C. E. Gunton (ed.), *Trinity, Time and the Church* (Grand Rapids, 2000); A. G. Padgett, *God, Eternity, and the Nature of Time* (New York, 1992); C. Tapp and E. Runggaldier (eds.), *God, Eternity and Time* (Farnham, 2011); T. F. Torrance, *Space, Time and Incarnation* (Oxford, 1969); idem, *Space, Time and Resurrection* (Edinburgh, 1976).

T. A. NOBLE

TOLERATION

Toleration is the recognition that a community can permit religious pluralism and be enriched. It is a modern idea, and only possible in societies which deny ultimate authority to state or church, cherish the liberty of the individual *conscience to reach different conclusions, and legally uphold freedom of enquiry and speech. The drawing of these boundaries is never completed. Christians with power to persecute have rarely resisted the temptation.

The beginnings of toleration are found in the sixteenth–eighteenth centuries. These are varied – the desire of Reformation Christians to worship outside Roman Catholicism, unhappiness about intolerance of national churches which led to partial separation of church and *state, pleas of individuals for an end to persecution, development of theories of natural law (see *Law) and personal rights and recognition of the tragic consequences of religious war, which destroyed the foundations of religion and society.

Sebastian Castellio (1515–63) raised important objections against the persecution of heretics such as Servetus, but his pleas fell on deaf ears. Jacobus Acontius (1492–c. 1566) sought to undermine intolerance by setting out the basic oneness and simplicity of Christian faith, deploring fierce debates about the fine points of dogma. Arguments for limited toleration were urged by persecuted Protestants and Roman Catholics alike, but only in Poland and France was this tried, ending in 1660 and 1685 respectively with the expulsion of Protestants from both countries. In Holland, remarkable toleration of variety within Protestantism emerged, and this provided a haven for religious refugees from all over Europe. Thinkers such as *Grotius and *Spinoza gave theological and philosophical justification for this. In England, the rejection of religious unity within the Church of England led to the emergence of Independents, *Baptists and *Quakers, who pleaded for liberty of conscience and religious equality. This was granted in limited form during the Commonwealth and Protectorate and was largely achieved by the early twentieth century. The American colonies of Rhode Island and Pennsylvania provided the most remarkable and lasting experiments in toleration, inspired by the convictions of Roger Williams (c. 1603–83) and William Penn (1644–1718), which ultimately made the USA a haven for religious and political refugees during the eighteenth and nineteenth centuries.

Thinkers such as *Locke, Pierre Bayle (1647–1706), *Lessing and J. S. Mill (1806–73) also provided important rational justifications of toleration, far in advance of existing law. This secular approach to toleration gained momentum during the nineteenth and twentieth centuries, when revolutions and political change steadily undermined the coercive power of national churches.

Growing *relativism has increased toleration based on secular assumptions, but contemporary repression of dissent demonstrates how fragile are the intellectual and political foundations of toleration. Developing a positive theology and commitment to toleration, which does justice to the tragedy of the *Holocaust as the supreme example of Christian intolerance, is an awesome task. Equality before the law is essential, as is legal protection for the religious freedom of ministries and individuals. Toleration, for Christians, must be grounded in creation and redemption. All bear the image of God. That is developed uniquely through Christ's new creation. The gift of inner freedom before God must be complemented by outer freedoms which enhance the potential of others before God.

Bibliography

R. H. Bainton, *The Travail of Religious Liberty* (Philadelphia, 1951); G. Barzilai, *Law and Religion* (Farnham, 2007); C. Beneke, *Beyond Toleration: The Religious Origins of American Pluralism* (Oxford, 2006); M. A. Hamilton, *God vs. the Gavel: Religion and the Rule of Law* (Cambridge, 2005); W. K. Jordan, *The Development of Religious Toleration in England*, 4 vols. (London, 1932–40); H. Kamen, *The Rise of Toleration* (London, 1967); E. Käsemann, *Jesus Means Freedom* (London, 1969); J. C. Murray, *The Problem of Religious Freedom* (London, 1969); H. Oberdiek, *Tolerance Between Forbearance and Acceptance* (Lanham, 2001); W. J. Sheils (ed.), *Persecution and Toleration* (Oxford, 1984); P. J. Wogoman, *Protestant Faith and Religious Liberty* (Nashville, 1967).

I. Breward

TOLSTOY, LEO (1828–1910)

Leo Tolstoy, the Russian novelist and social reformer, lost both his parents early in life and was brought up by aunts on the family estate near Tula. A child of the aristocracy, he knew wealth and social prestige from the beginning. He had little interest in university life and withdrew without taking a degree, but he read widely and became absorbed in the social theories of Jean-Jacques *Rousseau. To study educational systems and municipal governments he made trips to Europe in 1857 and 1860. In 1861 he liberated his serfs. The following year he married Sonya (Sofya) Andreyevna Bers, who bore him thirteen children.

The appearance of *War and Peace* (1860), one of the great novels of Western literature, brought Tolstoy wide acclaim. *Anna Karenina* (1877) is a masterly study of a strong but unhappy woman. In his fiction Tolstoy stresses the tension between moral restraint and the natural desire to live without the constraints of society. He is a master of large panoramic scenes, character study and penetrating moral insights.

Fame failed to bring inner peace to Tolstoy, however, and he cast in his lot with the peasants following a mystical experience *c.* 1880. He disowned his title, quarrelled with the Orthodox Church (which excommunicated him in 1901) and turned over his wealth to his wife and children. Setting out on a journey by rail with his daughter Alexandra, he died en route.

With genuine zeal Tolstoy fashioned his own religion, incorporating some Christian elements and urging love and charity toward all humankind. He rejected Christian supernaturalism in favour of an inner power in human nature, and took his basic principles from an adaptation of the Sermon of the Mount, emphasizing especially non-resistance (see *Pacifism) and simplicity of life. His rejection of ecclesiastical and civil authority has been described as 'Christian anarchism'.

See also: Russian Orthodox Theology.

Bibliography

Selected works: *What I Believe* (ET, London, 1885); *My Confession and the Spirit of Christ's Teaching* (ET, London, 1889); *The Kingdom of God Is Within You*, 2 vols. (ET, London, 1894).

Studies: A. H. G. Craufurd, *The Religion and Ethics of Tolstoy* (London, 1912); K. B. Feuer, *Tolstoy and the Genesis of War and Peace* (Ithaca, 1996); H. Troyat, *Tolstoy* (Garden City, 1967).

P. M. Bechtel

TORRANCE, THOMAS FORSYTH (1913–2007)

The Scottish theologian Thomas Torrance was born in Chengdu, Sichuan, China, the son of missionary parents. He gained his MA (1934) and BD (1937) at the University of Edinburgh, where his theology teachers were Hugh Ross *Mackintosh (systematic theology), Daniel Lamont (practical theology), John *Baillie (divinity) and William Manson (NT). Mackintosh's influence is particularly significant in introducing Torrance to the study of the theology of Karl Barth. Thereafter, Torrance studied under Barth at Basel, 1937–8. He was appointed Professor of Systematic Theology at Auburn Theological Seminary in 1938, but with the onset of the Second World War he returned to the UK and began further study at Oxford (1939–40). Torrance was ordained to the ministry of the Church of Scotland in March 1940, and saw service during the war years as a chaplain on the front line during the Italian campaign. He returned to Basel in 1946 and completed his doctoral thesis, *The Doctrine of Grace in the Apostolic Fathers*. He went back to parish ministry in 1947 before being appointed Professor of Church History at Edinburgh in 1950 and then to the Chair of Christian Dogmatics (1952–79). He was one of the founding editors of the *Scottish Journal of Theology* in 1948 and was co-editor (with D. W. Torrance) of Calvin's NT commentaries. He served as Moderator of the General Assembly of the Church of Scotland in 1976, and received the Templeton Foundation Prize for Progress in Religion in 1978 in addition to eight honorary doctorates.

The theology of Karl Barth

Torrance's engagement with *Barth dates, as noted above, from an early point in his career and is particularly evidenced in his books *Karl Barth: An Introduction to His Early Thought 1910–1931* (London, 1962) and *Karl Barth: Biblical and Evangelical Theologian* (Edinburgh, 1990). In the former, Torrance established a paradigm for the interpretation of Barth which remains particularly influential in the English-speaking world. Further, he was co-editor (with G. W. Bromiley) of the English translation of Barth's *Church Dogmatics*, which served to introduce Barth's theology across the English-speaking world. Torrance's interaction with, and interpretation of, Barth is fundamental to our understanding of his subsequent theological development.

Theological science

The publication of *Theological Science* (1969) signalled the beginning of an exploration of the interaction between theology and natural science which is rooted in the same concerns that animated Torrance's interpretation of Barth. That is, our concern is with 'the actual knowledge of God', disclosed by 'God in His Self-revelation', which is the 'Self-disclosure in His Being and His Act' (p. 350). Equally, Torrance is concerned to explore the nature of the discipline of theology, particularly in its interaction with the wider scientific community (see *Science and theology). Thus, he seeks to identify the place of theological science in relation to the natural sciences, particularly physics, whilst maintaining that: 'Theology is the unique science devoted to the knowledge of God, differing from other sciences by the uniqueness of its object which can be apprehended only on its own terms and from within the actual situation it has created in our existence in making itself known' (p. 281). Torrance further developed his understanding of this relation in a series of books, drawing on the parallel thinking on scientific epistemology by the Hungarian chemist, Michael Polanyi. These include: *Space, Time and Incarnation* (1969); *Space, Time and Resurrection* (1976); *Christian Theology and Scientific Culture* (1980); *The Ground and Grammar of Theology* (1980); *Reality and Evangelical Theology* (1982); *Transformation and Convergence in the Frame of Knowledge* (1984) and *Reality and Scientific Theology* (1985).

According to Torrance and Polanyi, all scientific knowledge has both an objective and subjective pole. So, for example, in *The Ground and Grammar of Theology*, Torrance's conception of theological science is developed through an ongoing dialogue with the natural sciences in an attempt to overcome a *dualist split in theological thought and to recover a unitary approach to our knowledge of God. He contends that this recovery is already evident in the natural sciences, but that theology cannot enter into dialogue with natural science because it has 'lost any common basis in the intelligibility of the created universe' (p. 16). In recovering this unitary approach, the scientist, in particular, is able to fulfil a vocation as a 'priest of creation', whose 'basic function' is 'to bring the universe to view and understanding in its inherent harmonies and regularities and thus to allow the basic design, the meaning, of the universe to become disclosed' (pp. 1–43, 110–112).

An important consequence of Torrance's approach is a transformation in the place and significance of *natural theology. Conscious of Barth's rejection of natural theology, Torrance interprets that rejection as 'a rejection of an *independent* natural theology – treated as a conceptual system on its own, antecedent to the rise and formulation of actual knowledge of God'. In response, Torrance seeks to locate natural theology within 'the material content of theology' and to regard it as 'the space-time structure embedded in a dynamic and realist theology'.

The church: one, holy, catholic and apostolic

Integral to Torrance's theological work has been his commitment to the *church, as witnessed to in his participation in the life of the Church of Scotland (see *Presbyterianism) and concern for the *Reformed theological heritage of his native land, exemplified in his early works *The Mystery of the Lord's Supper* (1958) and *The School of Faith* (1959). The Special Commission on Baptism of the Church of Scotland (1955–62), of which he was convener, shaped the law, practice and understanding of *baptism within the church for more than a generation, and is deserving of renewed study. Further, *Scottish Theology* (Edinburgh, 1996) offers a particular interpretation of the Scottish theological tradition which seeks to integrate it into an overarching and comprehensive schema.

Interwoven with this is Torrance's concern for the fullness of the life of the church and in particular with *Faith and Order considerations, and this is demonstrated in the collected papers, *Conflict and Agreement I* (1959), *Conflict and Agreement II* (1960) and in *Theology in Reconciliation* (1975), as well as by his ongoing commitment to ecumenical dialogue. Of especial note is his concern for dialogue with the Orthodox Church (see *Eastern Orthodox theology), and the tradition of the Greek Fathers, as exemplified in the edited papers, *The Incarnation: Ecumenical Studies in the Nicene-Constantinopolitan Creed A.D. 381* (1981), *Theological Dialogue between Orthodox and Reformed Churches I* (1985) and *Theological Dialogue between Orthodox and Reformed Churches II* (1993), as well as in *Trinitarian Perspectives* (1994).

The Holy Trinity

This acknowledgment of the place of the Greek Fathers is profoundly reflected in Torrance's concern for the maintenance of the Christian faith as expressed in the Nicene-Constantinopolitan *Creed (AD 381), and in his appreciation of the theological contribution of *Athanasius in securing the identity of the Son of God as consubstantial with that of the Father (see *Christology). In *The Trinitarian Faith* (1988), Torrance states that he regards the Creed as 'essentially the fruit of Eastern Catholic theology' and that: 'The basic decision taken at Nicaea made it clear that the eternal relation between the Father and the Son in the Godhead was regarded in the Church as the supreme truth upon which everything else in the Gospel depends.' Further, the identity of the Spirit as consubstantial with that of the Father and the Son is particularly developed 'from the essential structure of knowledge of God grounded in his own self-communication through the Son and in the unity of the Spirit' (pp. 2–3, 9).

Torrance's class lectures, published posthumously as *Incarnation* (2008) and *Atonement* (2009), reveal the depth of Torrance's thinking on what he always called the heart of his theology, the 'vicarious humanity' of Christ. But it was in the later part of his career after his formal retirement from teaching that Torrance emerged as a significant 'theologian of the Trinity' (Molnar). He advocated the view that a doctrine of the *Trinity which took its lead from Athanasius rather than the Cappadocians (see *Basil of Caesarea, *Gregory of Nazianzus, *Gregory of Nyssa) would avoid the difficulties which eventually led to the great division between the Eastern and Western churches on the *filioque* clause. Torrance also emphasized (in contrast to John *Zizioulas) that the Son was begotten not from the 'Person' of the Father, but from the Being (*ousias*) of the Father, as explicitly stated in the original creed of the Council of *Nicaea (325). The Being (*ousia*) of the Father could not therefore be regarded as some 'impersonal' substance, but as fully personal. Torrance was not a patrologist interested primarily in reproducing the doctrine of the Fathers, but a dogmatician who articulated an original and contemporary Reformed and evangelical reconstruction of patristic trinitarian theology.

Torrance's trinitarian theology can be seen as taking into account the contributions of Barth and *Rahner. But unlike Barth he writes of the distinct 'Persons' of the Trinity, distinguished and united by their 'onto-relations', and he is not prepared to allow 'Rahner's rule' to be interpreted in such a way as to eliminate the transcendence of the Immanent Trinity. He sees some value in the concern of those who espouse the 'social analogy', but more strongly emphasizes the unity of the Trinity. He is not driven by the desire of some to make the doctrine of the Trinity 'relevant' to social and egalitarian concerns (as with *Moltmann), but more concerned to see the deep integration of the doctrine of the Trinity with the Christian gospel and thus to articulate a trinitarian soteriology (see D. O. Eugenio, *Communion with the Triune God*). The whole trinitarian shape of his theology is deeply permeated by his Reformation perspective that *salvation is by grace.

Conclusion

Torrance's contribution to theology is at once evangelical and catholic, Reformed and orthodox, in its breadth and scope. The concern to explore the possibility of our knowledge of God in the light of his self-revelation in Christ, complemented by the concern to enter into dialogue with the physical sciences, marks his theology as one rich in promise and potential in our contemporary age. Equally, the *ecumenical implications of his theology require to be embraced in order that their depth may be fully comprehended. Torrance was undoubtedly the most prolific Scottish theologian of the twentieth century, and in the opinion of many, the most outstanding British *dogmatician.

Bibliography

Selected works: *The Doctrine of Jesus Christ: The Auburn Lectures 1938/39* (Eugene, 2001); *Calvin's Doctrine of Man* (London, 1949); *Theology in Reconstruction* (London, 1965); *The Trinitarian Faith* (Edinburgh, 1988); *The Mediation of Christ* (Edinburgh, ²1992); *Trinitarian Perspectives* (Edinburgh, 1994); *Divine Meaning* (Edinburgh, 1995); *The Christian Doctrine of God* (Edinburgh, 1996); *Scottish Theology* (Edinburgh, 1996); *Incarnation: The Person and Life of Christ* (Milton Keynes and Downers Grove, 2008); *Atonement: The Person and Work of Christ* (Milton Keynes and Downers Grove, 2009).

Studies: E. M. Colyer, *How to Read T. F. Torrance: Understanding His Trinitarian and Scientific Theology* (Downers Grove, 2001); idem (ed.), *The Promise of Trinitarian Theology: Theologians in Dialogue with T. F. Torrance* (Lanham, 2001); A. E. McGrath, *Thomas F. Torrance: An Intellectual Biography* (Edinburgh, 1999); P. D. Molnar, *Thomas F. Torrance: Theologian of the Trinity* (Williston, 2009).

Studies of particular themes: P. Cass, *Christ Condemned in the Flesh* (Saarbrücken, 2009); D. O. Eugenio, *Communion with the Triune God: The Trinitarian Soteriology of T. F. Torrance* (Eugene, 2014); Kye Won Lee, *Living in Union with Christ: The Practical Theology of T. F. Torrance* (New York, 2003); J. D. Morrison, *Knowledge of the Self-Revealing God in the Thought of Thomas Forsyth Torrance* (New York, 1997); C. Weightman, *Theology in a Polanyian Universe: The Theology of Thomas Torrance* (New York, 1994).

J. L. McPake

TRACY, DAVID (b. 1939)

David Tracy, distinguished professor of Roman Catholic studies at the University of Chicago Divinity School since 1987, received seminary training at St Joseph's in Yonkers, New York, acquired his licentiate in 1964 and a doctorate in 1969 from the Gregorian University in Rome. He was ordained a priest in the Diocese of Bridgeport, Connecticut in 1963.

Tracy's theological project – ranging from work on Bernard *Lonergan, fundamental theology, systematics, hermeneutics, church history, inter-religious dialogue and the naming of God – manifests certain characteristics. One is that Lonergan's transcendental imperatives – 'Be attentive, be intelligent, be rational, be responsible, develop and, if necessary, change' – mark Tracy's theological work. A second characteristic is the revisionist nature of his theology. In his *Blessed Rage for Order* (1975) and *The Analogical Imagination* (1981), Tracy argues for ongoing revision of traditional Christianity and traditional modernity, building on Paul *Tillich's method of correlation. Third, Tracy emphasizes the centrality of interpretation in the task of the theologian. According to Tracy, the interpretive task of the theologian includes keeping in mind the following aspects of theology: that it is 'situated', as postmoderns say; it is most fruitful when done in dialogue; it is to be public; it is pluralistic in nature; and it is ambiguous at times.

While Tracy's previous work moved along revisionist lines, his more recent research has taken him in a new direction, that of exploring *mystical and neo-*Platonic traditions of thought along with postmodern thinkers. Tracy is drawing on the notion of the 'incomprehensibility' of God in *Pseudo-Dionysius (the unknown sixth-century mystic), and on Martin *Luther's teaching on the 'hiddenness' of God (see *Hidden and revealed God). Tracy proposes that theologians should fragment and negate positive language about God (see *Apophatic theology), as well as seek to understand God through the weakness of the cross (Luther).

Bibliography

Selected works: *The Achievement of Bernard Lonergan* (New York, 1970); *The Analogical Imagination: Christian Theology and the Culture of Pluralism* (New York, 1982); *Dialogue with the Other: The Inter-Religious Dialogue* (Grand Rapids, 1990); *Plurality and Ambiguity* (Chicago, 1994); *Blessed Rage for Order: The New Pluralism* (Chicago, 1996); 'An Interview with David Tracy', by Lois Malcolm, in *The Christian Century*, February 13–20, 2002, pp. 24–30.

Selected studies: W. Jeanrond and J. L. Rike, *Radical Pluralism and Truth: David Tracy and the Hermeneutics of Religion* (New York, 1991); T. H. Sanks, 'David Tracy's Theological Project: An Overview and Some Implications', *Theological Studies* December, 1993, pp. 698–727.

B. BINGAMAN

TRADUCIANISM, see SOUL, ORIGIN OF

TRAGEDY

Although the term 'tragedy' often refers to some grave misfortune, this usage is derivative from its more fundamental sense that refers to a literary genre. The derivation arises because it is commonly thought that tragedies end in disaster, but this is actually not right – in fact, only about half of the extant Greek tragedies end badly for the protagonist.

The genre originated in Athens in the sixth century BC, with the plays part of an annual festival honouring the god Dionysius. The Greek tragic theatre continued into the Hellenistic period, but lost most of its vitality after Athens's defeat by Sparta in the Peloponnesian War. Extant Greek plays include those written by Aeschylus, Sophocles and Euripides; Roman examples include two by an unknown author and nine by Seneca. After this, we have no more extant plays (or writings on tragedy) until the Renaissance and later, with Racine being the most prominent neo-classical example. Shakespeare, of course, is a dominating figure here, and almost deserves his own category. The style continues in the works of Samuel Beckett, Arthur Miller and others.

The ancient tragic poets, more than simply entertainers, were significant contributors to political and philosophical debates, including the effects of military expeditions. Along with the sophists, they are *Plato's principal foils, and it is the tragedians on whom *Aristotle focuses in his *Poetics*. After the Renaissance, philosophers such as *Hegel, Schopenhauer, and *Nietzsche rediscovered Greek tragedy, and, abetted by conversations between philosophy and literary theory, this engagement continued in the twentieth century.

Theologians have been less enthusiastic about the value of tragedy for their craft – think of *Niebuhr's famous argument that Christianity moved humanity 'beyond tragedy'. Biblical scholars have been more receptive, with some analysis of the story of King Saul and the Gospel of Mark as tragedy. More recently, however, theologians have begun to re-engage with tragedy, especially with the rise of the field of religion and literature.

Given its engagement with social issues in rapidly changing times and with nations at war, Greek tragedy has much to offer contemporary theological *anthropology. The ancient heroes were tragic because they structured their identity according to older Homeric virtues in a world in which these roles and identifications no longer made sense. They are no longer *Homeric* heroes, but are not yet citizens of the *polis*. Repeatedly, the heroes become bewildered at the unexpected effects of their choices, and become alienated from both their society and themselves. They are beset by contradictions (able to control nature but not themselves, both guilty and innocent, able to understand social and political realities but not their own motivations) in a world in which justice, and even truth, seems to constantly shift. In this context, the tragic poets ask what it means to be a human being – a creature they can describe sometimes as noble, sometimes as a *deinos*, an incomprehensible and baffling monster. For those theologians who think we are in a postfoundationalist, *postmodern world (both contested claims), the Greek tragedies deserve serious study.

See also: CULTURE.

Bibliography

L. D. Bouchard, *Tragic Method and Tragic Theology: Evil in Contemporary Drama and Religious Thought* (University Park, PA, 1989);

J. C. Exum, *Tragedy and Biblical Narrative: Arrows of the Almighty* (Cambridge, 1992); S. L. Nicholson, *Three Faces of Saul: An Intertextual Approach to Biblical Tragedy* (Sheffield, 2002); R. Niebuhr, *Beyond Tragedy: Essays on the Christian Interpretation of History* (New York, 1937); L. A. Ruprecht, Jr, *Tragic Posture and Tragic Vision: Against the Modern Failure of Nerve* (New York, 1994); K. M. Sands, *Escape from Paradise: Evil and Tragedy in Feminist Theology* (Minneapolis, 1990); K. Taylor and G. Waller, *Christian Theology and Tragedy: Theologians, Tragic Literature and Tragic Theory* (Farnham, 2011).

J. A. KNIGHT

TRANSCENDENCE, see GOD

TRANSFIGURATION

The story of the transfiguration is recounted in all three Synoptic Gospels: Matt. 17:1–8, Mark 9:2–8 and Luke 9:28–36. John does not include it in his narrative, but there may be an echo of it in John 1:14, 'we have seen his glory, the glory as of a father's only son' (NRSV). In 2 Pet. 1:16–18, the author reveals that he and others had been with the Lord on the holy mountain, where he received honour and glory from God the Father. Luke's account does not use the word *metamorphothe*. He records only that the appearance of Jesus' face changed. The idea of transfiguration appears twice in Paul (Rom. 12:2; 2 Cor. 4:16–17), but in both instances it refers to the inward spiritual transformation of believers.

Suggestions as to the precise site of the transfiguration are conjectural at best. The timing, on the other hand, is very precise: six days after Peter's confession at Caesarea Philippi (Mark 9:2). This is probably of psychological as well as chronological significance. The transfiguration comes at the beginning of the passion narrative, and thus at a moment when Jesus stood in profound need of encouragement. As he begins the journey to Calvary, the voice from heaven assures him of his divine identity, and of the Father's love and approbation.

The event ought also to have brought encouragement to the disciples. The glimpse of his glory lent credibility to Jesus' promise that beyond the *cross lay *resurrection, and this hope ought to have sustained them in the darkness that followed. This, as *Chrysostom suggests, may have been why he brought the three disciples with him in the first place: 'to show the glory of the cross, and to console Peter and the others in their dread of the passion, and to raise up their minds.' In the event, it brought no such consolation, but this does not detract from the fact that the story of the crucifixion is framed on one side by the transfiguration as it is on the other by the empty tomb. This rhetorical arrangement is as significant for the modern reader as the original historical setting was for the disciples.

Inevitably, the historicity of the event has been questioned. Lohmeyer saw it as a purely theological construction designed to portray Jesus as the messianic fulfiller. *Bultmann saw it as a resurrection-appearance story read back into the earthly life of Jesus. In the Synoptics, however, the story of the transfiguration is no different in genre from the story of Peter's confession, which precedes it. The evangelists clearly intended to portray the one, no less than the other, as historical fact. The details bear this out. The reference to 'after six days', for example, is an extremely precise chronological marker; and Peter's suggestion that they build three tabernacles, along with Mark's reference to a 'fuller' (KJV), both supply the sort of human touches to be expected in eyewitness reports. The key details, too, are completely different from later resurrection-appearance stories, none of which portrays a transfigured Christ, and none of which alludes to heavenly visitors, a cloud or a voice from on high. On the other hand, in all the other appearance stories Jesus speaks. In this one, he utters not a word.

But, supposing it to be historical, what sort of historical incident was it? The details are hard to fit into anything purely visionary. The disciples, as well as Jesus, clearly saw and heard something. They saw his appearance change. They saw Elijah and Moses. They heard the voice from heaven, and they heard the instruction to keep the whole affair to themselves till after the resurrection. All the signs are that for both Jesus and the disciples the experience was a matter of objective sense-perception.

What was the significance of the event? First, it was a revelation of the present, underlying *glory of Jesus. This is the line taken by both *Calvin and *Barth, and it is confirmed by the presence in the narrative of the voice from heaven, which clearly endorses the divine identity of Jesus. Calvin starts with the idea of the veiling (*krupsis*) of the glory of Jesus in the *incarnation. The *kenosis* had not involved his laying aside his divine nature, but it did involve his concealing it. Here, on the mount of transfiguration, the veil is drawn aside, though Calvin (*Harmony of the Gospels of Matthew, Mark and Luke*, vol. 2, p. 198) is at pains to point out that the disciples saw only symbols of the glory, not the real glory itself: 'this was not a substantial revelation of Christ's heavenly glory, but He gave them in symbols, consonant with the capacity of their flesh, a partial taste of what they could not yet receive fully.'

Barth's approach is slightly different. He points out that though John does not report the transfiguration, he does refer to Jesus showing his glory. One clear instance of this is John 2:11, where the glory is revealed through the miracle of turning water into wine. The transfiguration, too, was a miracle, but it was a miracle with one unique feature: it was performed not by Jesus, but on Jesus. He did nothing. 'Everything suggests a theophany,' writes Barth (*CD*, III.2, p. 478). Whatever its pointers to the future, the transfiguration was a declaration that he already was what the future would declare him to be.

Yet the context demands that we also see the transfiguration as a revelation of Jesus' future glory as the Son of Man. All three Synoptics directly connect the event to Jesus' promise: 'some who are standing here will not taste death before they see the kingdom of God come with power' (Mark 9:1). The link can hardly be a coincidence. The transfiguration clearly had *eschatological connotations. It was a glimpse of the end-time.

But what sort of glimpse? Does it point to the resurrection or to the parousia? Boobyer argues strongly for the latter, but the antithesis may be unnecessary. True, in the resurrection appearances recorded in the Gospels, Jesus looks nothing like his appearance on the holy mountain, but the resurrection must be taken with the *ascension and the heavenly session, in which Jesus has already come into full possession of his glory. The Christ of Patmos and the Damascus Road is as glorious as the Christ of the transfiguration, and there is no reason to think that the body of Jesus undergoes any further glorification between his ascension and the parousia. He will come as he already is.

But for the revelation (*apokalupsis*) and appearing (*epiphaneia*) of this glory we must await the parousia. What the three saw on the holy mountain the whole world will see when the Son of Man comes in his glory. Then, too, there will be clouds, heavenly attendants and a voice from heaven.

But is even this all? In all three Synoptics, the preceding context has recorded Christ's words on the cost of discipleship, but beyond the cost lie transfiguration and glory. Hence Anselm's observation (quoted in Ramsey, *The Glory of God and the Transfiguration of Christ*, p. 119) that 'He showed them his own glory and the glory of his own.' What the three saw was a glory which would one day be their own.

See also: JESUS.

Bibliography

K. Barth, *CD*, III.2; G. H. Boobyer, *St Mark and the Transfiguration Story* (Edinburgh, 1942); J. Calvin, *A Harmony of the Gospels: Matthew, Mark and Luke* (ET, Michigan and Carlisle, 1975); Chrysostom, *Homilies on the Gospel of St. Matthew*, LVI, NPNF, vol. 10; A. M. Ramsey, *The Glory of God and the Transfiguration of Christ* (London, 1949).

D. MACLEOD

TRANSMIGRATION OF THE SOUL, see METEMPSYCHOSIS

TRANSUBSTANTIATION, see EUCHARIST

TRENT, COUNCIL OF

Protestantism was a catalyst rather than a cause of this reforming council (1545–63). From an inauspicious start with poor attendance, the Council was to go on to assert the Catholic position on four major matters: *Scripture and tradition; *justification by faith; the Mass; and the authority of the church.

John Driedo's programmatic work (*On the Church's Scriptures and Doctrines*, 1534), which stated that the church could find in Scripture and apostolic traditions teachings which were hitherto latent, was echoed in the 1546 *Decree Concerning the Canonical Scriptures*: 'that these truths and rules are contained in the written books and in the unwritten traditions, which, received by the Apostles from the mouth of Christ Himself, or from the Apostles themselves, the Holy Ghost dictating, have come down to us, transmitted as it were from hand to hand'. The traditions of the apostles and the NT Scriptures have come from the one source – the revealed gospel of Jesus Christ – and through two channels from that source should now be received as one stream. The Vulgate, including the deuterocanonical books, was reaffirmed as the authoritative translation, but the question of vernacular translations was avoided.

The emphasis of the *Decree* in 1547 was on justification as the healing and renewing of the soul. One could and should prepare for the gift of faith: eternal life would be both reward and gift. Justification by faith *alone* was denied. To be saved in Christ meant to be in the realm of his sacramental presence. So, sacrifice, not just commemoration was emphasized in the 1551 proceedings. Yet the Mass (see *Eucharist) was not a repetition of the cross, but its unbloody application. A functionalist view held that that which effects spiritual nourishment was assumed, without prejudice to the theory of transubstantiation as expounded by Lateran IV. The position is that *sacraments (and there are seven of them) confer grace on those who put no obstacles, and that they build faith, but do not require it for their efficacy. In the last session (1562–3), the Mass did not derogate from, but confirmed, the cross. The Last Supper was the fulfilment of Mal. 1:11, and the command of Christ made the apostles priests of a sacrifice.

The church was to assert its authority in local areas, not least through processions with the eucharistic host. Pius IV could make it clear that the Eucharist in both kinds was not to be permitted for the laity, and authored a *catechism to communicate the truths of Trent. Processions became celebrations of the triumph of truth over lies and error, to amaze enemies of the church with a Jesuit-influenced expectation of genuflecting, hats off, before the host.

See also: COUNCILS; ROMAN CATHOLIC THEOLOGY.

Bibliography

H. Jedin, *A History of the Council of Trent*, 2 vols. (London, 1957–61); J. O'Malley, *Trent and All That: Renaming Catholicism in the Early Modern Era* (Cambridge and London, 2000).

M. W. ELLIOTT

TRINITY

The doctrine that there is one God who exists and has manifested himself in three distinct persons is fundamental to Christianity and distinguishes it from related forms of *monotheism like Judaism and Islam. It is closely connected to *Christology, since it was the belief that Jesus Christ is God that made it necessary to develop a theology which could encompass that belief within a monotheistic framework. The term 'Trinity' is not found in the Bible, but was invented by *Tertullian as a translation of the Greek *trias*, a word which was already in use to describe the threeness of God but which did not have an explicitly theological meaning.

Whether the doctrine can be found in the Scriptures or not has long been a matter of controversy. In the early church, several attempts were made to find indications of the Trinity in the OT, and theologians frequently cited such things as the plural name of God (Elohim) and the apparent personification of both the Word and the Spirit of God as evidence for this. Of particular significance was the appearance of the three men (or angels) to Abraham at Mamre (Gen. 18), whom Abraham addresses in the singular as 'Lord'. *Philo of Alexandria (d. 50), who was not a Christian, believed that this demonstrated that the number three was somehow present in God, and it was he who first used the word *trias* to describe him. This reference was not picked up in the NT, but by the third century it had become a part of Christian apologetic and it is still frequently encountered, especially in the *Eastern Orthodox Church, where there is a long tradition of painting Abraham and the three men in an icon known as 'The Old Testament Trinity'. On a different note, Augustine believed that the *image of God (Gen. 1:26–27) in human beings is the image of the Trinity, and he used this belief to develop a highly sophisticated theory about the tripartite structure of the human mind. In spite of these venerable traditions, however, modern scholarship is virtually unanimous in rejecting these texts as a basis for the construction of a trinitarian doctrine.

The NT contains indications of trinitarian belief which may be subdivided into two distinct categories. The first of these are the direct formulaic references to the Trinity, of which there are two. The first of them occurs in Matt. 28:19, where Jesus tells his disciples to baptize all nations in the name of the Father,

Trinity

the Son and the Holy Spirit. The second is in 2 Cor. 13:14, where the apostle Paul concludes his epistle with the famous blessing which speaks of the grace of Christ, the love of God (the Father) and the fellowship of the Holy Spirit. The authenticity of the Gospel reference has been questioned by some, but there can be no doubt that a trinitarian confession of faith was associated with the rite of baptism from a very early time, and that failure to observe this pattern resulted in a defective initiation rite (Acts 8:15–17). It is hard to see why this should have been so if the command to practise a threefold baptism did not go back to Jesus himself. The Pauline blessing stresses the importance of Christology for our understanding of the Trinity and incidentally reminds us that the Father manifests the fullness of God in a special way. It is impossible to say that all undifferentiated uses of the word 'God' in the Bible refer primarily or exclusively to the Father, but it is certain that they never designate the Son or the Holy Spirit, who are always mentioned specifically. This suggests that the Father sometimes represents the fullness of God in a way that the other persons do not, and this observation has led some theologians to conclude that he is superior to the other two, something which orthodox trinitarian theology has always strenuously resisted.

More significant are the indirect references to the Trinity in the NT, of which there are more than thirty. These are texts in which all three persons are mentioned, but in a non-formulaic way. An early example is Gal. 4:6: 'God sent the Spirit of his Son into our hearts, the Spirit who calls out, "*Abba*, Father".' Another is Eph. 2:18: 'For through him [Christ] we both have access to the Father by one Spirit.' Passages like these cannot have been inserted into the original text in order to defend a later trinitarian doctrine, and they demonstrate how the Trinity functions in the spiritual life of the Christian.

This observation is especially important because it was out of Christian experience that the doctrine of the Trinity developed. The early church was obliged to confess the divinity of both Christ and the Holy Spirit, because that is the way in which believers experienced them in their lives, but at the same time they also knew that there was only one God. It was the struggle to reconcile these beliefs that led to many of the controversies which marked the life of the church in the fourth and fifth centuries. Out of them there emerged a theological vocabulary which was capable of accommodating the subtle definitions which continue to characterize trinitarian theology today.

The need to protect monotheism led many early theologians to conclude that a Trinity emerged because at some point God produced his Word and his Spirit in order to create and redeem the world. Various theories were canvassed, including one which suggested that the persons of the Trinity correspond to different epochs of divine self-revelation, the Father being the God of the OT, the Son the God of the Gospels and the Holy Spirit the God of the post-Pentecostal church. A variant of this suggested that the differences were due to the different functions which God performs in relation to his world: as Creator he is the Father, as Redeemer he is the Son, as Sanctifier he is the Holy Spirit. Theories of this kind are called 'modalist' because they claim that the differences of the persons are seen in the modes in which God acts. Modalism falls down because God's threeness is reduced to a phenomenon of time and space and because it makes it impossible for one person of the Trinity to relate to another, which clearly conflicts with the NT evidence. Modalism is sometimes regarded as the 'typical' heresy of the Western church, which supposedly stresses the unity of the one God and derives the Trinity from that.

Another approach to the doctrine which is found in the early church may be called 'subordinationist'. This is the belief that the Father is superior to the other two persons, who are defined in relation to him, whereas he stands alone. The generation of the Son was held to take place in time, at the beginning of creation (cf. Prov. 8:22). The procession of the Holy Spirit was also said to be from the Father (cf. John 15:26) and to have taken place after the generation of the Son, though it is not entirely clear when. Beliefs of this kind circulated widely in the Eastern church and eventually resulted in *Arianism, which denied the full divinity of the Son and (at least, by implication) of the Holy Spirit. It was the struggle to affirm that the Son and the Holy Spirit were fully God, and therefore equal to the Father in every respect, which eventually produced the trinitarian doctrine which became and still remains the classical, orthodox expression of the Christian faith.

A constant problem in trinitarian thought was finding the right words to express both the unity and the diversity of the Godhead. It was generally agreed that as a being, God is one and unique. This was denoted by the Greek word *ousia* and by the Latin words *substantia* and later *essentia*. By declaring that the Son was *homoousios* (consubstantial) with the Father, the first council of *Nicaea in 325 canonized this usage, which has never been seriously challenged.

Finding the right way to express the 'threeness' in God was much more difficult. *Origen used the term **hypostasis*, which he probably got from Heb. 1:3, and Tertullian used *persona*, which he took from Roman law but which went back to Greek theatre, where it meant 'mask'. The conceptual difference between these two words is that *hypostasis* refers primarily to the manifestation of a distinct identity, whereas *persona*, at least in its legal sense, stresses the activity of a subject. Unfortunately, many Greek theologians failed to appreciate this and thought that by calling the hypostases of the Godhead *personae*, Tertullian had lapsed into modalism, because to them persons were only masks which indicated the different roles which God might play in the cosmic drama. The confusion was eventually sorted out by Basil of Caesarea, who realized that *hypostasis* and *persona* meant the same thing, a conclusion which was eventually endorsed by the council of *Chalcedon in 451.

In the Middle Ages much effort was expended on defining the meaning of *persona*. *Boethius called it 'the individual subsistence of a rational nature', and later theologians defined it as 'relation', claiming that it is not possible to be a person without being in relationship with other persons. Today, this concept dominates the field, and much modern trinitarian thought is preoccupied with relationship questions, both divine and human. At the Reformation and periodically since then, attempts were made to reject this vocabulary on the grounds that it was non-biblical and too philosophical in orientation, but to date no satisfactory alternative has been found, and in recent years the traditional language has been rejuvenated as part of the general rediscovery of trinitarian doctrine as a whole.

After the council of Chalcedon in 451 the church was generally agreed in its trinitarian doctrine, even though it was divided over Christology. Controversy did not arise until some time later and became serious only in the ninth century, when Patriarch Photius of Constantinople (d. 886) wrote a detailed refutation of the Western (Latin) doctrine. The trouble was caused by the way in which the Eastern Church understood the role of the Father as the 'source of deity' in the Trinity. According to that way of thinking, the Son derived his divinity by being 'begotten of the Father', and the Holy Spirit derived his by 'proceeding from the Father'. The different modes of causation determined the distinct identity of these two persons, and the Father was defined as the one who was both unbegotten and uncaused. In contrast to this model, the Western church, following *Augustine, understood the Trinity as a community of *love. According to this way of thinking, the Father was the Lover, the Son was the Beloved and the Holy Spirit was the Love which flows between them and creates the 'bond of unity' in the Godhead. If this model is followed, it becomes evident that the Holy Spirit must not only proceed from both the Father and the Son, but that he must do so in equal measure, since otherwise their love for one another would be imperfect. In the subsequent struggle against Arianism, the Western church gradually introduced this 'double procession' of the Holy Spirit into the Nicene Creed by placing the Latin word *filioque* ('and the Son') in the third article. Photius thought that this created two sources of deity in God and so compromised the fundamental principle of monotheism.

The original dispute was papered over, but it erupted again in the thirteenth century, by which time many other factors had combined to alienate the Eastern and the Western churches. At the council of Florence in 1439 it was decided that the formula 'who proceeds from the Father *through* the Son' would satisfy the demands of both sides, but this compromise was rejected in the East. The matter has been raised again in recent ecumenical dialogues, but has proved impossible to resolve. The Eastern churches have remained adamantly opposed to any accommodation to Western thought on the matter, and the Western ones, though sympathetic to the Eastern position, have not been willing to abandon their Augustinian heritage.

The Protestant *Reformers accepted the traditional doctrine of the Trinity, though they tried to avoid any suggestion of subordinationism by stating that each of the persons of the Godhead was 'God-in-himself', and suggesting that their trinitarian relations were the result of a mutual agreement, rather than something imposed by the Father on the others. They were also concerned to develop the work of Christ and the work of the Holy Spirit as distinct theological categories, which further emphasized both the individuality of the persons and their mutual interdependence.

In the seventeenth century, a sceptical *rationalism questioned the integrity of a doctrine which said that God was three and one at the same time, and many were persuaded to abandon it in favour of *Unitarianism. Though no church formally adopted this as its confession of faith, a pragmatic unitarianism became very common, and the doctrine of the Trinity was pushed into the background. The ultimate sign of this was the fact that it was relegated to a mere appendix in Friedrich *Schleiermacher's influential dogmatic work, The Christian Faith.

It was in reaction to this that Karl *Barth reversed his theological priorities in his Church Dogmatics and put the Trinity at the forefront of his theological concerns. Barth was basically an Augustinian who conceived of the Godhead in terms of the 'revealer', the 'revealed' and the 'revelation', but he demonstrated his indebtedness to the semi-unitarian liberal tradition by rejecting the term 'person' in favour of 'mode of being'. For Barth there was only one person in God: Jesus Christ, who revealed him to the human race and in whom everything we confess about the Godhead is to be found. This Christocentric approach was much criticized, and it was often claimed that Barth was really a 'Christomonist', but he denied this.

Whatever Barth's own views were, there can be no doubt that he sparked a revival of trinitarian thought which has not yet run its course. Both in Protestant and in Roman Catholic circles there was a vast outpouring of trinitarian studies in the twentieth century, and the rediscovery of Eastern Orthodoxy, with its strongly trinitarian piety, contributed still further to this. By the dawn of the new millennium, trinitarianism had become something of a theological fad, and it now seems that it is almost impossible to write on any subject without expounding its trinitarian dimension. This is a complete reversal of the position which had obtained a century earlier, but it may have gone too far and there is a real danger that the next few years will see a reaction against the current enthusiasm. On the other hand, the recent history of this doctrine shows very clearly that classical orthodoxy has the power to rebound from criticism and reinvigorate theological discussion when that is least expected. The doctrine of the Trinity, always the chief distinguishing mark of orthodox Christianity, has once more become a living expression of faith and a creative force in contemporary theology which is sure to produce even more fruit in the years ahead.

See also: COUNCILS; CREEDS; GOD; HOLY SPIRIT; JESUS.

Bibliography

G. L. Bray, *The Doctrine of God* (Leicester, 1993); P. M. Collins, *Trinitarian Theology, West and East* (Oxford, 2001); E. J. Fortman, *The Triune God: A Historical Study of the Doctrine of the Trinity* (London, 1972); R. P. C. Hanson, *The Search for the Christian Doctrine of God* (Edinburgh, 1988); B. C. Leslie, *Trinitarian Hermeneutics: The Hermeneutical Significance of Karl Barth's Doctrine of the Trinity* (New York, 1991); R. Letham, *The Holy Trinity in Scripture, History, Theology and Worship* (Phillipsburg, 2004); T. F. Torrance, *The Trinitarian Faith: The Evangelical Theology of the Ancient Christian Church* (Edinburgh, 1988); A. W. Wainwright, *The Trinity in the Old Testament* (London, 1962).

G. L. BRAY

TRITHEISM

Tritheism is the belief that the *Trinity is not one God but three. It can arise if the persons of the Trinity are regarded as *substantial beings in their own right, sharing a common divinity only in the sense that people share a common humanity.

Tritheism has never been the official teaching of any church. It is at best an error which some Christians may have fallen into in their attempts to explain the Trinity. *Jerome accused the Greek church of holding a form of tritheism, on the ground that the Greeks referred to the persons of the Trinity as *hypostaseis*, which he took to mean 'substances'; but he was mistaken in this and had to be corrected. Christians today are sometimes accused of tritheism by Jews, and particularly by Muslims, and also by such *sects as Jehovah's Witnesses, though the accusation has always been strenuously denied and does not in fact reflect any major strand in Christian theology.

Bibliography

J. N. D. Kelly, *Jerome* (London, 1975), pp. 52–55.

G. L. BRAY

TROELTSCH, ERNST (1865–1923)

A wide-ranging German scholar who worked in the areas of history, theology, philosophy and sociology, Troeltsch taught theology in the Universities of Bonn (1892) and Heidelberg (1894) and philosophy in the University of Berlin (1915). He was the systematic theologian of the *history-of-religions school, and was chiefly influenced by Kant, *Hegel, *Schleiermacher, *Ritschl and *Dilthey. His main concern was to deal with the problem of relativism which arose through the new understanding of history. He and others were convinced of the influence of culture on the formation of religion, but that discovery threatened the normative nature of moral and religious values and the absoluteness of Christianity.

He first approached the problem in 1902 in *The Absoluteness of Christianity and the History of Religion* and last dealt with it in lectures which he would have delivered in England but for an untimely death. These were subsequently published under the overgeneralized title of *Christian Thought: Its History and Application* (1923). He both feared and was fascinated by the problem of historical relativism. He tried to resolve the problem by positing that man was irreducibly religious and that religion itself could not be reduced to non-religious factors. He argued for the superiority of the Christian religion on the grounds that it gave the greatest value to human personality through its belief in a personal God, and therefore was of a higher form than Eastern religions, which devalued the human personality. He himself became less convinced of the absoluteness of Christianity as his studies progressed, and he became increasingly uneasy about the validity of Christian missions.

He is best remembered for *The Social Teaching of the Christian Churches* (1912; ET, 1931), in which, with massive historical insight, he related the churches' ethics to their cultural situation. He developed the idea that Christianity has three basic organizational orientations, namely *church, *sect and *mysticism. His formulations, which were much influenced by the German sociologist Max *Weber, have had a profound effect on the development of the *sociology of religion.

Troeltsch was a significant churchman of a liberal Protestant persuasion and an active politician, being at one stage a government minister for education. His ideas have recently come back into favour, since in many ways they laid the foundations for theologies which believe that man has come of age. For most, however, his answers to the problems of historical relativism are unsatisfactory, not least because they sacrifice much that is essential to Christian faith.

Bibliography

R. H. Bainton, 'Ernst Troeltsch – Thirty Years After', *Theology Today* 8, 1951, pp. 70–96; J. P. Clayton (ed.), *Ernst Troeltsch and the Future of Theology* (Cambridge, 1976); B. A. Reist, *Toward a Theology of Involvement: The Thought of Ernst Troeltsch* (London, 1966).

D. J. TIDBALL

TRUTH

In the OT, *'ĕmet* signifies covenant faithfulness and reliability, a moral attribute ascribed both to God (e.g. Ps. 86:15; Jer. 42:5) and to humans (Exod. 18:21). Truth is primarily ascribed to sayings or teachings; both promises and statements are words upon which hearers may rely. Truth is not mere accuracy, eliciting intellectual assent only; it is reliability, worthy of personal commitment and trust.

Theories of truth

Western philosophy has given more attention to truth as a property of statements or propositions than to the biblical sense of truth as an attribute of personal action. According to *Aristotle, truth is a matter of saying of what is that it is, and of saying of what is not that it is not. This intuition that language reflects reality led to the traditional definition of truth as the correspondence of a statement to the state of affairs to which it refers.

While ancient and medieval philosophers were prone to think of truth as a 'metaphysical project' (R. L. Kirkham, *Theories of Truth*), an attempt to show how language measures up to the world, modern thinkers tended to view truth in terms of the human scientific, existential and aesthetic experience. For many Enlightenment thinkers, objective truth was the desired end

925

product of the scientific method (human critical thinking); *Kierkegaard, however, insisted that truth is subjectivity, by which he meant that it involves passionate commitment (*doing* the truth) and not intellectual assent only. For *Heidegger and Gadamer, the experience of the work of art became the paradigm for thinking about truth as a disclosure event that enlarges one's self-understanding.

Many contemporary thinkers tend to abandon the metaphysical project of saying how correspondence to reality satisfies the condition for truth, in favour of reducing truth to an 'epistemic project' according to which truth coheres with what we already know or are warranted in asserting. In theology, the coherence theory shows up in non-*foundationalist methods that make truth a function of what coheres with the biblical narrative. George *Lindbeck, for example, views truth as 'intrasystematic' – a matter of what can be absorbed into the narrated world of the biblical text.

Other non-foundationalists prefer a more pragmatic theory, in which what is true is a matter of serving some end (e.g. fostering love of God and neighbour) successfully. By way of contrast, a *postmodern like *Foucault, who follows Nietzsche, treats truth claims with suspicion, viewing them as masks for the will-to-power – disguised forms of political and social oppression.

The correspondence theory, then, though intuitive, is not without its rivals – and its challenges. How, for example, does language correspond to the world? The so-called 'picture theory' of meaning, in which words name objects and sentences represent facts, does not account for the diversity of what speakers and writers actually do with words. Further, the 'traditional Western concept' of truth (P. Hicks, *Evangelicals and Truth*, p. 10), with its stress on objectivity (truth is outside us), universality (truth is the same for all people) and eternity (truth lasts for ever), fails to address the postmodern emphasis on human situatedness and hence the inaccessibility of objective truth.

The gospel: trinitarian truth

Given the core kerygma ('He is risen'), however, Christians must insist that gospel truth is not only 'according to the Scriptures' but 'corresponding to reality'. The best way forward is to follow critical realists who advocate a minimalist or 'chastened' correspondence account which stipulates that true language or thought is about something real, even though we are not always able to specify the exact nature of the correspondence relation. Some things are true even though they are in principle beyond the reach of sufficient evidence or verifiability (e.g. that God is triune).

'But the Lord is the true God' (Jer. 10:10). Truth is grounded in the God who acts faithfully in accordance with his word. The fourth Gospel identifies *Jesus as the truth (John 14:6): the utterly reliable Word of God. Jesus is the 'first truth', the definitive revelation of God, humanity, and of the evangelical action. Jesus is clue and catalyst to what God is doing to renew all things. The stories of Jesus display the already/not yet reality to which all true statements must ultimately correspond.

Jesus the truth has commissioned his own witnesses. The truth of Scripture is not a function of the genius of its authors, but of its role in the economy of divine *revelation. The biblical texts are creaturely realities set apart by the Spirit for the sake of facilitating saving knowledge of God. The Spirit who inspires the biblical texts also illuminates its readers, transforming them from sinners who suppress the truth in unrighteousness (Rom. 1:21–25) to saints who are set apart as truth's witnesses (John 17:17).

The Trinity sums up what Christians want to say about truth and theology. The Father's Word, Jesus Christ, is the primary truth bearer; the Spirit seals this true Word in our hearts. As inspired testimony to Jesus Christ, the Scriptures become the ground and framework for evaluating all other truth claims. Theology ought therefore to reject the 'dependency thesis' according to which Christian beliefs depend for their truth on some other set of beliefs.

Saving truth: theodramatic correspondence

The truth made known in Jesus Christ through the Spirit of truth (1 John 5:7) goes hand in hand with God's *ḥesed* or covenant love (Exod. 34:6). Truth in the context of theology must never be merely theoretical (a correspondence relation), but practical and transformative as well (a covenantal relation). Truth is ultimately not simply something to be believed, but something to be done (the good), appreciated (the beautiful) and adored (the doxological) (see *Worship).

The truth of the gospel – that the Father is making all things new in Christ through the

Spirit – is the ultimate truth about God, the world and ourselves. Christians speak, do and suffer the truth whenever their speech and action correspond with and fit into this theodrama.

See also: EPISTEMOLOGY; PHILOSOPHY AND THEOLOGY.

Bibliography

W. Alston, *A Realist Conception of Truth* (Ithaca, 1996); D. K. Clark, *To Know and Love God: Method for Theology* (Wheaton, 2003); P. Hicks, *Evangelicals and Truth* (Leicester, 1998); R. L. Kirkham, *Theories of Truth: A Critical Introduction* (Cambridge, 1995); A. Köstenberger (ed.), *Whatever Happened to Truth?* (Wheaton, 2005); B. Marshall, *Trinity and Truth* (Cambridge, 2000); G. Sumner, *The First and the Last: The Claim of Jesus Christ and the Claims of Other Religious Traditions* (Grand Rapids, 2004); K. J. Vanhoozer, 'The Trials of Truth', in K. J. Vanhoozer, *First Theology* (Downers Grove, 2002).

K. J. VANHOOZER

TÜBINGEN SCHOOL

Tübingen is a university town in Württemberg, south Germany. The name 'Tübingen School' refers to a small group of NT scholars who, in the middle years of the nineteenth century, were associated with Ferdinand Christian Baur (1792–1860), professor of theology at the university. Prominent members of the school were Eduard Zeller (1814–1908), Baur's son-in-law, and Albert Schwegler (1819–57). More loosely attached were Albrecht *Ritschl, Adolf Hilgenfeld (1823–1907) and Gustav Volkmar (1809–93).

Although Baur is recognized as head of the school, the significance of the name 'Tübingen' begins with David *Strauss' *Life of Jesus*, for it was its appearance in 1835 which caused the name 'Tübingen' to become almost synonymous with 'unbelief'. Henceforward, the investigations into the NT by Baur and his disciples were regarded with extreme scepticism by the orthodox, since the non-miraculous theological position of Strauss was maintained by the entire school. 'With a miracle,' wrote Baur, 'all explanation and understanding ceases.' This non-miraculous viewpoint may be called the Tübingen theological perspective. From this presupposition, there began a concentrated investigation into the authorship and dating of all the books in the NT.

Within this overruling theological perspective there was a more limited *historical perspective, first developed by Baur during the 1830s. This envisaged the history of the early church as a struggle between two rival parties – the Jewish Christian party led by Peter, and the Gentile Christian led by Paul. For a century these two parties stood over against each other in bitter hostility, and only towards the end of the second century did they become reconciled in a higher irenic and mediating movement in which both were ultimately absorbed. In accordance with this historical perspective, all the NT books were now assessed in order to ascertain their 'tendency' (*Tendenz*) – whether Petrine, Pauline or mediating. Once their tendency had been established, their authorship and dating were more accurately determined by fitting the books into the historical framework which Baur had already worked out. Only five books of the NT were regarded as authentic – Romans, 1 and 2 Corinthians, Galatians and the Apocalypse of John. All other books were ascribed to unknown hands, mostly in the second century.

The high point of the school was reached in 1846 with Schwegler's two-volume work, *The Post-Apostolic Age*, which provided a comprehensive portrayal of the school's position. But from the following year the school slowly began to break up, and with Baur's death in 1860 it may be said to have reached its end. Baur's historical perspective gradually revealed itself as untenable; the historical framework into which he fitted his tendencies was based in part on a misunderstanding of the historical evidence. The *Clementine Homilies*, in which Baur perceived a caricature of the apostle Paul in the person of Simon the magician, were composed later (third or fourth century) than Baur's second-century estimate, and did not portray Paul in disguise. The investigation of the Ignatian letters (see *Apostolic Fathers) by Theodor Zahn and J. B. Lightfoot in the 1870s drove the final nail into the Tübingen coffin, in that these letters, written by Ignatius in the early second century, revealed no trace of the bitter controversy which Baur had postulated as raging between Jewish and Gentile Christians in Ignatius' day. Other evidence also disproved the late dating which Baur had assigned to the NT books.

In its influence on NT scholarship the Tübingen School was undoubtedly the most important movement in nineteenth-century theology, in that non-miraculous presuppositions constituted the basis of its methodology. Prior to 1835, biblical scholarship had examined historical and theological questions under the implicit presupposition of the authenticity and general veracity of the biblical records. With Strauss that theological perspective was completely overturned, in that no miracle was henceforth to be admitted. Christianity in its origin and development was to be regarded as completely *un*supernatural. With Baur this same position was maintained – a non-supernatural theological and historical perspective determined all biblical interpretation.

Bibliography

H. Harris, *The Tübingen School* (Oxford, repr. 1990 [1975]); P. C. Hodgson, *The Formation of Historical Theology* (New York, 1966); A. E. McGrath, *The Making of Modern German Christology* (Oxford, 1986); R. Morgan, 'Ferdinand Christian Baur', in N. Smart *et al.* (eds.), *Nineteenth-Century Religious Thought in the West* (Cambridge, 1985).

H. HARRIS

TURRETIN, FRANCIS (1623–87)

François Turrettini was one of the most important Reformed systematic theologians of post-Reformation *Protestant orthodoxy. His influence on subsequent *Reformed theology has been considerable, although he is little known in contemporary theological circles.

Turretin was born to a wealthy mercantile family that originated in Lucca, Italy, but had fled the Inquisition and settled in Switzerland. Francis was educated in Geneva and visited intellectual centres in the Netherlands and France. He returned to Geneva to become pastor of the Italian congregation in 1648 and was appointed Professor of Theology at the Academy in 1653, having turned down the chair in philosophy in 1650. He retained both positions until his death.

Turretin wrote a number of controversial works, and was involved in the composition of the *Formula Consensus Helvetica* of 1675, along with John Henry Heidegger. Aside from this, his most enduring theological achievement is his *Institutes of Elenctic Theology*. This was the product of his encyclopaedic knowledge of the history of Christian doctrine, as well as deep engagement with the theological and philosophical currents of his own age, making this work one of the most important dogmatic systems of the period. It is a didactic and at times polemical work, being an instance of the 'school method' practised by medieval and post-Reformation divines. This means each *locus* is cast in a question-answer format, covering each topic in a comprehensive, logical manner. Turretin's work has suffered at the hands of some nineteenth- and twentieth-century theologians, for whom post-Reformation Reformed theology was an arid '*scholasticism', in contrast to *Reformation thought. More recent scholarship has overturned this mistaken account of the development of Reformed theology. One of the most important distinctions made in this literature is between the scholastic (i.e. elenctic) method dogmaticians like Turretin appropriated from medieval thinkers, and the content of that theology, which is arguably a legitimate development from the Reformation theology of Calvin.

Turretin's *Institutes* was recognized as a major achievement in Europe. But it was in the USA that it had its most enduring impact. His *Institutes* was adopted as a textbook by *Princeton Theological Seminary where Charles *Hodge commissioned an English translation, carried out by the Princeton classicist, George Musgrave Giger. This work forms the basis of the current English translation of Turretin's opus.

Bibliography

Works: *Institutes of Elenctic Theology*, 3 vols., tr. G. M. Giger, ed. J. T. Dennison, Jr (Phillipsburg, 1992–1997); *The Atonement of Christ*, tr. J. R. Wilson (Grand Rapids, 1978 [1859]).

Studies: W. J. van Asselt, *Introduction to Reformed Scholasticism* (Grand Rapids, 2011); W. J. van Asselt, J. M. Bac and R. T. de Velde (eds.), *Reformed Thought on Freedom: The Concept of Free Choice in Early Modern Reformed Theology* (Grand Rapids, 2010); O. D. Crisp, 'Francis Turretin on the Necessity of the Incarnation', in Crisp, *Retrieving Doctrine: Essays in Reformed Theology* (Downers Grove, 2011), pp. 69–91; J. T. Dennison, Jr, 'The Twilight of Scholasticism: Francis Turretin at the Dawn of the Enlightenment', in C. R. Trueman and R. S. Clark (eds.), *Protestant Scholasticism: Essays in Reassessment* (Carlisle, 1999), pp. 244–255; P. Helm, '"Structural Indifference" and Compatibilism in Reformed Orthodoxy', *Journal of*

Reformed Theology 5.2, 2011, pp. 184–205; R. A. Muller, 'Scholasticism Protestant and Catholic: Francis Turretin on the Object and Principles of Theology', *Church History* 55, 1986, pp. 193–205; S. Rehnman, 'Alleged Rationalism: Francis Turretin on Reason', *CTJ* 37, 2002, pp. 255–269; idem, 'Theistic Metaphysics and Biblical Exegesis: Francis Turretin on the Concept of God', *Religious Studies* 38, 2002, pp. 167–186; P. Wallace, 'The Doctrine of the Covenant in the Elentic Theology of Francis Turretin', *Mid-America Journal of Theology* 13, 2002, pp. 143–179.

O. D. Crisp

TYCONIUS, see DONATISM

TYNDALE, WILLIAM, see REFORMERS, ENGLISH

TYPOLOGY, see HERMENEUTICS

ULTRAMONTANSIM, see PAPACY

UNDERHILL, EVELYN (1875–1941)

Evelyn Underhill was in private life Mrs Hubert Stuart Moore. She was an English *Anglo-Catholic expositor of mysticism (see *Mystical theology) and Christian *spirituality. In her copious writings, as in her own Christian pilgrimage, she wrestled with the problem of relating personal spiritual experience (which, she believed, underlies every living religion) to the formal theology of the church. Her classic analytical survey *Mysticism* (London, ^{12}1930 [1911]) presented Christian doctrines as symbolic maps or diagrams of subjective encounters, both individual and corporate, with 'ultimate reality'; but under the influence of the Roman Catholic theologian Baron Friedrich von *Hügel she came to see these doctrines as expressing objective truth about God's historical and ongoing interaction with his creation, and as thereby holding together the experiential, biblical, liturgical and sacramental channels of divine *revelation to which they provide an interpretative key. This position was perhaps most clearly articulated in *Man and the Supernatural* (London, 1927) and *The School of Charity: Meditations on the Christian Creed* (London, 1934), but was also reflected in many other writings of her later years, which culminated in the magisterial study *Worship* (London, 1936). Her thesis that mystical experience and orthodox Christian theology are mutually complementary, together with her tireless ministry as a retreat conductor, spiritual counsellor, religious journalist, public speaker and broadcaster, contributed significantly to the revival of widespread British interest in the interior life of faith during the first half of the twentieth century.

Bibliography
C. J. R. Armstrong, *Evelyn Underhill* (Oxford, 1975); L. Barkway, 'Evelyn Underhill in Her Writings', in L. Menzies (ed.), *Collected Papers of Evelyn Underhill* (London, 1946), repr. in E. Underhill, *The Mount of Purification* (London, 1960); A. Callahan, *Evelyn Underhill: Spirituality for Daily Living* (Lanham, 1997); M. Cropper, *Evelyn Underhill* (London, 1958); D. Greene, *Evelyn Underhill: Artist of the Infinite Life* (Notre Dame, 1998); C. Williams (ed.), *The Letters of Evelyn Underhill* (London, 1943).

S. J. Smalley

UNIFICATION CHURCH, see SECTS

UNION WITH CHRIST

An ongoing task facing Christian reflection is to conceive how the life, death and resurrection of *Jesus can be of benefit to those who believe. How are his spiritual achievements, his dramatic history and his unique status able to transform the lives and standing before God of those who are temporally, geographically and culturally far removed from him? The church's various attempts to respond to these questions are brought together under the doctrine of 'union with Christ'.

Incarnational union

A widespread view among the Fathers of the early church that continues to be upheld in the *Eastern Orthodox tradition is that the *incarnation, the act of the eternal Son of God whereby he took human nature to himself, is not merely the foundation of our salvation, but is a constituent element of it. The incarnation is viewed as salvific in and of itself. The idea is that in *Christ God became one with us in order to make us one with him; he stooped to take our nature, in order that we might be restored and so become partakers of his divine nature. The nature which he assumed to himself he healed from its tendency towards sin and decay. This understanding of the divine Word's union with human nature as that which, at least in part, effects our *salvation is dependent on the notion that 'human nature' has some form of corporate reality apart from its particularization in individual humans. It is held that when the Son of God became incarnate, human nature was itself transformed, and all humans as participants in that nature potentially share in the renewal of their being. Some, however, find it difficult to conceive how the incarnate Christ can be both a particular human being and also the realization of human nature in general. Others have a concern that this theory interprets Jesus' birth, rather than his life, death and resurrection, as central to his saving ministry and so appears to run counter to the emphasis of the NT authors on the salvific centrality of the Easter events. An incarnational union is sometimes spoken of as a 'physical' theory of the *atonement in that it gives priority to matters of substance and being rather than those of obedience and faith in its understanding of human salvation.

United by faith

The Protestant emphasis on *faith as that which unites us to Christ owes much to the German Reformer Martin *Luther. Luther argued that humans have no ability of themselves to do anything of value to achieve salvation. In fact they no longer have the freedom to do anything at all that is truly good. Consequently, their salvation must come completely from Christ and not from any human endeavour. The individual's recognition of their inability and of Christ's sufficiency is the impetus for the exercise of faith. On the one hand, the human soul is full of *sin, death and damnation. On the other, Jesus Christ is full of *grace, life and salvation. Faith is that which unites the soul with Christ as a bride is united with her bridegroom. Luther argued: 'Let faith come between the soul and Christ and sins, death and damnation will be Christ's, while grace, life and salvation will be the soul's; for if Christ is a bridegroom, he must take upon himself the things which are his bride's and bestow upon her the things that are his' (*Selections from His Writings*, p. 60). This theory of a 'double imputation' was formative in the development of the Lutheran, and so Protestant, view of *justification. The difficulty with it, for some, is that it suggests that human faith is the bond that binds the believer to Christ, and so, contrary to Luther's original intention, the believer's union with Christ is held to depend on an unreliable human faculty.

Covenantal union

The *Reformed tradition sought to explain the church's union with Christ from the perspective of *covenant, that is, the divine institution of mutual obligations between God and humankind. The covenant provides the framework for the exercise of human faith, *love and obedience within the secure divine commitment to forgive, transform and safeguard his people. Consequently, a covenantal union understands Christians to be united with God through Christ in a relationship grounded on the divine promises that have their foundation in Christ's mediatory work. Within the general covenant character of God's dealings with humankind, one aspect of Paul's teaching, sometimes called federal union, has been especially noted and developed within later Reformed tradition. The way in which men and women are dealt with by God 'in Christ' is seen to parallel his dealings with humankind 'in *Adam'. God deals with 'the many' through a representative person, or 'federal head', in the one case imputing Adam's sin to his descendants, in the other, Christ's *obedience and *atonement to his followers, with all that flows from that. Being united to Christ is understood then as participation in this covenantal union with him as our 'federal head'. The covenant has its ultimate foundation in the eternal decision of God to be gracious rather than in the temporal response of the believer to the gospel. This means that the concept of grace or election (see *Predestination) has priority over the human act of faith, which is itself viewed as a gift of grace. Some are concerned that this suggests an arbitrariness in God's dealings with humankind.

Sacramental union

The *Catholic tradition, in particular, has laid stress on the *sacraments as the means of initiating and continuing union with Christ. Christian incorporation into Christ, by which one becomes a member of his body, is through *baptism as the outward sacramental rite of initiation coupled with repentance and faith in Jesus Christ as the inner means of appropriation. Baptism in Christ's name unites the baptized with Jesus Christ, especially with his death, burial and resurrection. Similarly, the *Eucharist or Holy Communion, as the covenant rite or sacrament of continuance in Christ and his body, enables Christians to nurture, deepen and strengthen their relationship or union with Christ and with one another, as they truly partake of Jesus through the elements of wine and bread. Communion focuses on Christ's death as the self-sacrificing event of divine reconciliation and the source of a Christian's new life in him. Sacramental union is closely related structurally to a union of faith. Historically, however, the nature of the relation between the agency of the sacraments and that of saving faith in uniting us to Christ has been vigorously contested, and the interpretation of both baptism and Holy Communion has been the cause of much hostility and division among the various branches of the church.

Experiential union

The Son of God became human, shared in our condition and lived a life that is the paradigm or primary example for all Christians. However, nearly all the traditions have emphasized that it is the privilege of believers not merely to follow him but to actually participate in Jesus' life, death and *resurrection. Union with Christ is understood to mean that we share through baptism in his death so that the dominance of sin should no longer be determinative of our own individual experience. It also means that the believer participates in Christ's resurrection, not simply at the end of the age, but during this present life through the empowerment of the *Spirit. Christians share Jesus' status, relationship and privileges as sons and daughters of God and are called to suffer with him, to pass through physical death to ultimate physical resurrection and so reign with him in glory. His eternal inheritance as man is also theirs. En route to that goal all Christians are called into progressive conformity to his *image, continually renewing and transforming their characters into God's likeness by the power of his Holy Spirit and by the application of God's revealed will to every aspect of their lives. In short, it is through union with Christ that Christians are *sanctified or made to be holy (see *Christian life).

Spiritual or mystical union

The final perspective on union with Christ, stressed particularly by the *mystical, *pietist and *charismatic traditions, is that the Christian is united to Christ in his or her conscious experience. This is sometimes called 'mystical union', and is rooted in the mystery of the encounter of the spirit of man and the Spirit of God or of Christ, often using the analogy of a bride and her groom. It originates in a new birth brought about within a person by the Holy Spirit, and centres on the hidden life of *prayer, meditation, contemplation and *worship. The object of these spiritual disciplines is to deepen one's knowledge of the Lord and one's love-relationship with him. It requires the submission of the whole of one's life to him in trust and obedience, knowing that such a submission of love in response to love is the route to our greatest possible fulfilment. It is believed that those fully renewed in God's image will enjoy unfettered and unclouded fellowship with him, freed from every delusion of independence which would block the free flow of pure love, truth, trust, cooperative obedience and delight between themselves, their Creator and the other creatures. Some are concerned that such an emphasis on personal devotion can be idealistic and inward-looking and tends to undermine the calling for Christians in humility and brokenness to serve God in the world.

Informed by the perspectives of these various traditions we could say that our union with Christ has its foundations in the loving purpose of a covenanting God; is established by the saving ministry of his incarnate Son; is entered into through the outward (sacramental) response of an inner trusting faith in the promises of the gospel; sanctifies us by transforming us into the likeness of Jesus as the Spirit baptizes us into his life and privileges; and introduces us to an intimate loving relationship with Christ, and through him to the Father, which we shall experience through time and eternity.

Bibliography

J. Dillenberger (ed.), *Martin Luther: Selections from His Writings* (New York, 1961); Gregory of Nazianzen, *Epistle to Cledonius the Priest against Apollinarius* (The Nicene and Post-Nicene Fathers, second series, vol. 7); M. Horton, *God of Promise: Introducing*

Covenant Theology (Grand Rapids, 2006); A. Murray, *Abide in Christ* (New Kensington, 2002); J. Murray, *Redemption Accomplished and Applied* (London, 1961); J. I. Packer, *Knowing God* (London, 1975); A. J. Spence, *The Promise of Peace: A Unified Theory of Atonement* (London, 2006).

A. J. SPENCE

UNIQUENESS OF CHRIST

The contemporary questions about the uniqueness of Jesus Christ are: 'In what is he claimed to be unique?' and 'Is that claim valid?' In one sense, everything and everyone is unique. So how has the church advanced the claim that *Jesus is unique?

The NT narrative acknowledges that Jesus was not alone in being thought to be a miracle worker or a messiah. Other miracle workers and messiahs had appeared. He was not alone in being thought to be divine – there were many gods and lords in the Romano-Greek world. However, the NT also makes clear that Jesus made the outright claim in public that he was unique (John 14:6), and others made the claim about him based on what he said and did (Acts 4:12; 17:31). Though there were many gods and lords, Jesus was the Lord of lords and King of kings (1 Cor. 8:5–6; Rev. 17:14).

The claims made for the uniqueness of Jesus centred mainly on his death and resurrection.

He was not just any crucified malefactor. He claimed to be in person the anointed bringer of God's hoped-for *kingdom, the renewal of humankind and all creation according to the promises of the OT (Matt. 1:22–23; 2:5–6). His healing miracles were witness to this (Luke 7:22; cf. Isa. 35:1–6).

His death on a *cross appeared to wipe out all these claims. How could Jesus be messiah if he himself died under God's curse? How could he have brought God's kingdom of eternal life if he ended up dead? The *resurrection was the vindication of his claim to have brought the kingdom of God active in power into this world. If Jesus had overcome death, then the kingdom was here in power.

The NT gives evidence of this present power of the kingdom of God through the work of the *Holy Spirit in the community formed by faith in Jesus as the Christ. This power was particularly evident in bringing people together in this community across the accepted boundaries of hostility in society: race, class and gender (Gal. 3:28; Eph. 2:15–16). This community experienced and pointed to the unity of all things in Jesus who created them (Col. 1:20).

This posed a further question. Since death is for *sin, and Jesus did not die for his own sin, since death could not hold him, for whose sins had he died? The answer from the Scriptures was for the sins of the whole world.

Jesus' *atoning death for sinful humanity is unique in world religions in that sinful humanity is held to be saved not by any works of righteousness in response to his example, but by faith in his death and resurrection.

Jesus' role was therefore clear: his death and resurrection had achieved *salvation from sin and the presence of the kingdom. The completion of salvation would be when Jesus returned with the glory of God to establish the kingdom openly and fully, recognized by all (1 Thess. 4:16–17; Phil. 2:10–11) (see *Eschatology).

But the early church faced a problem as it expanded beyond Palestine. In the Greek culture, God could not be said to suffer. Since Jesus suffered, he must in some way be less than God. This problem was addressed from the point of view of salvation. The straightforward claim was made that only God could save humankind, no-one else. So to save us, Jesus had to be God. But to save us, and not others than us, Jesus also had to be like us, a human being. The Christian creeds upheld the biblical witness to Jesus' uniqueness by defending both his true deity and his true humanity. This claim to full divinity and full humanity in one person is a claim unique to Christianity (see *Christology).

How then is the claim that Jesus is unique validated? This claim has always been contested. The NT is full of controversy about Jesus. It calls for controversy, proclamation, contending for and defence of the faith. Religion is always a contested area. The church's claims that Jesus is unique have always been against the background of those who would deny that Jesus was King of kings and Lord of lords.

Therefore Jesus' own actions as a miracle worker, or teachings as a prophet, or statements of his relationship with his Father, do not of themselves establish his uniqueness. People have questioned the possibility of miracle, of one person being God and man, and of God restricting his universality to one particular *revelation. In the religious climate of the twenty-first century, people make many claims for religious leaders who have carried out miracles, given spiritual teaching and have a special relationship with God. The claim for Jesus' uniqueness is then held to be a claim about the unique position he is given in the lives of his followers, not about his unique position for all humanity.

But the full nature of the biblical and Christian claim for Jesus is unparalleled for any other person. How then is the claim validated in twenty-first-century religious culture that Jesus alone brings salvation and is alone in being able to be God to save us and to save humanity? The truth of this claim is to be established by whether it coheres with what is known to be true on other grounds. Does it fit with the evidence and does it fit with experience?

The evidence centres on Jesus' sinless life and character, the factual reality of his death and the evidence for his bodily resurrection. That evidence is consistent with the claim that God was in Jesus reconciling the world to himself, that Jesus was God bearing the world's rebellion against him and that Jesus rose from the dead victorious over the forces of evil and death. If the dead body of Jesus is discovered, then those claims fall to the ground as flying in the face of the evidence. The evidence is consistent with, but does not prove, the claims.

Do the claims fit with experience? For many, the claims of Jesus fit with their own personal experience of life – whether it is one of sin, oppression, need for identity, purpose and fulfilment, forgiveness from God or others, addictions, healing or hopelessness. It is here that many hundreds of millions have found Jesus to be the one who enabled them to experience their potential as the image of God.

But these claims are not only verifiable in personal experience.

Historically, Christian faith has grown on the margins of society. In the NT, Jesus' ministry was in Galilee. After the fall of the Roman Empire, Christian faith continued on the edges of Europe in its northern islands. In the twentieth and twenty-first centuries, the number of Christians in Africa grew from 10 million to over 360 million. The centre of gravity of Christians is among the poor. This experience fits with the claim of the Bible that God delivers, protects and brings good news to the poor, and that the same God is suspicious of the actions and agendas of the rich and powerful.

The claim for the uniqueness of Jesus is that he is the unique revelation of the action of the God of the Bible, who is the God who delivered Hebrew slaves from Egypt and brought good news to the poor in Jesus (see *Gospel). Entirely consistent with this action is the action of those who in the name of Jesus fought for the freedom of slaves in the nineteenth century. He is the unique revelation of the God who reconciles all things to himself. Entirely consistent with this is the experience that in the Roman Empire the Christian faith was the only one open to people of all races and position.

This way of presenting the claims of Jesus is especially relevant today in a world which is particularly aware of the plight of the *poor and the division between the rich and the poor, which in Christian terms is an expression of human sin. Who can save people from this sin and its effects? To whom are poor people turning to find their salvation? And who is turning the hearts and the minds of the non-poor to consider the poor? By saying that his message and activity was good news to the poor, Jesus was tying his claims to verifiable evaluation. That verification depended on the obedience and actions of his followers.

Bibliography
Michael Nazir-Ali, *The Unique and Universal Christ* (Paternoster 2008).

C. M. N. SUGDEN

UNITARIANISM

Though Unitarians reject *creeds and have a wide spectrum of beliefs, they stress the oneness of God and deny the divinity of Jesus Christ and the Holy Spirit. They are committed to freedom, reason and tolerance as the context essential to a religion that is truly personal and social. Organized ecclesiastically only since the Reformation, they have some precursors such as the *Monarchians and *Arians.

Renewed attention to the literal meaning of the Scriptures led scholars such as Juan de *Valdés, Bernardino *Ochino and Michael Servetus (1511–53) to claim that *trinitarian theology had little biblical foundation. Servetus believed that purging Christianity of such corruptions would complete the restitution of primitive Christianity and hasten the conversion of Jews and Muslims. His views were widely rejected, but his execution in Geneva did nothing to prevent other radicals raising similar issues in Hungary and Poland, where anti-trinitarian ideas were widely held.

Unitarianism

In Holland and England, the influence of *Socinianism and reaction against Calvinist orthodoxy led to important questions being raised about the relation of Scripture and dogma by such distinguished thinkers as Grotius and John Milton (1608–74). Unitarian ideas were taught by John Biddle (1616–62), but he was severely dealt with by the authorities and died in prison. His concern for purifying doctrine of unbiblical additions went with deep concern for holiness of life. This seriousness was an abiding note of the Unitarian way.

Convictions about the credibility of the doctrine of the Trinity were weakened as many dissenters rejected subscription to creeds and *confessions as unscriptural. In the Church of England, many moved to a loosely 'Arian' position, because, like Samuel Clarke (1675–1729), they could find no scriptural justification for the doctrine of the Trinity. While denial of the Trinity was an offence until 1813, many simply ceased to preach and teach what they did not believe, rather than risk the penalties of public denial. Many Presbyterian congregations in England and Ireland moved steadily away from Westminster orthodoxy (see *Westminster Confession) into a less dogmatic, more simply biblical Christianity. Richard Price (1723–91) and Joseph Priestley (1733–1804) rejected foundation doctrines such as the divinity of Christ and the inspiration of Scripture. That opened up entrance to new philosophical, scientific and religious ideas, where the authority of reason and experience was given increasing weight.

A different tributary of Unitarianism came from Theophilus Lindsey (1723–1808), who resigned from the Church of England because of his anxieties about worship being corrupted by pagan philosophical additions. He drew up a new liturgy for his followers, and came to believe that the narratives of Jesus' birth were legendary and that Jesus was fully and solely human. For these early Unitarians, worship was to be addressed only to the Father. They reverenced Jesus and underlined his religious authority, but argued that correct understanding of the Scriptures led to a necessary distinction between the Father and Jesus in worship.

As they became more aware of German biblical criticism, their use of Scripture as authoritative changed. They had to search for a new basis for religious authority. Thomas Belsham (1750–1825) organized the first general Unitarian Society in 1791 and specifically excluded Arians. From this time onwards the term 'Unitarian' developed a more particular ecclesiastical meaning in Britain, and more slowly, in the USA, as well as indicating a wide range of theological positions. In England there were two major strands of thinking. One stressed human religion rather than God's reality and was politically radical. The other had mystical tendencies and emphasized the intrinsically divine character of Christianity. James Martineau (1805–1900) was especially important in this area; he did much to deepen the theology and spirituality of Unitarian congregations. Reason's place was one of the distinctive features of Unitarianism by the end of the nineteenth century. Unitarians found it hard to balance generous fellowship and definite teaching. They were deeply involved in parliamentary and civic reform, social welfare, education and intellectual life, but in the twentieth century their religious influence steadily waned with the decline of the free churches. Sustaining a distinctive religious community without boundaries has proved an almost impossible task.

Similar trends occurred in the USA, where many *Congregational churches moved into a non-dogmatic Arian position, rejecting Calvinistic emphases on original sin, atonement and predestination in favour of convictions about the perfectibility of humankind. The liberalizers won control of Harvard early in the nineteenth century, and, with leaders like William Ellery Channing (1780–1842), who sought to free Christianity from past corruptions so it could perfect human nature, the movement gathered momentum. More radical leaders such as Theodore Parker (1810–60), who shocked conservative Unitarians by his insistence that Christianity did not depend on the historical existence of Jesus, but on the truth of his teaching, had a powerful influence.

Unitarian views seemed to many educated Americans the growing edge of Protestantism. Convictions about the unipersonality of God were only a part of the movement's appeal. Openness to new knowledge and commitment to social reform helped to Christianize post-revolutionary and scientific optimism in the USA, as well as providing a sympathetic approach to other religions. Their emphasis on Jesus' humanity, and their rejection of traditional soteriology and worship, led to Unitarianism becoming a liberal religion of self-improvement and benevolence, free from credal and ecclesiastical boundaries.

Its influence declined in the twentieth century, as the theistic and biblical heritage has become less formative, and it became shaped more and more by the American social context. In an increasingly illiberal and pessimistic world, the varied Unitarian message seems increasingly limited culturally. The lack of denominational identity in the Unitarian Universalist Association, formed in 1961, may make survival difficult, for Unitarians have never displayed a strong missionary spirit. Nevertheless, they have played a significant role in the *liberalization of Protestant orthodoxies by their approach to revelation, their emphasis on reason and experience, their passion for freedom of theological enquiry and their distrust of human creeds and organization as an adequate context for the best insights of Jesus.

Bibliography

C. G. Bolam et al., *The English Presbyterians from Elizabethan Puritanism to Modern Unitarianism* (London, 1968); H. McLachlan, *The Unitarian Movement* (London, 1934); E. M. Wilbur, *A History of Unitarianism*, 2 vols. (Cambridge, 1946–52); C. Wright, *The Liberal Christians* (Boston, 1970).

I. Breward

UNIVERSALISM

The word 'universalism' has been used in two senses in Christian theology. Of these, the first is generally accepted, and the second usually rejected, in orthodox thinking.

In reference to biblical thought, 'universalism' frequently denotes the view, common to OT and NT that the purposes of God are not limited to any one nation or race, but extend worldwide. Based on *monotheism, this idea comes to expression in the worldwide scope of the promises to Abraham (Gen. 12:3, etc.), in the welcome afforded to those coming into the people of God from other nations (Rahab, Ruth, etc.), and above all in the frequent prophetic vision of the nations of the world coming within the scope of that salvation planned by God for his people. This last takes two forms in particular: the Gentiles will come and worship Israel's God on Mount Zion (Isa. 2:1–5, etc.); salvation will extend beyond the borders of Israel, out into the pagan world (Mal. 1:11, 14, etc.). In the NT this belief in the worldwide scope of salvation comes to expression in the mission to the Gentiles, which Paul bases explicitly on monotheism itself (Rom. 3:27–30; 10:12–13), understood in the light of Christ and the Spirit. The emphasis here is that people from every nation, race, tribe, language (and indeed every moral background) are welcome in the kingdom of God; there is 'neither Jew nor Greek, slave nor free, male or female, for you are all one in Christ Jesus' (Gal. 3:28). The one God has one family. This doctrine has come under attack since the Second World War from those who maintain that God has two *covenants, one for Jews and one (the Christian one) for everybody else (see *Judaism and Christianity), but this position has no basis in Scripture.

The second use of the word denotes the belief that all human beings, without exception, will eventually attain salvation. This belief has taken various forms:

(1) In the patristic period it was maintained by *Origen and others, with varying degrees of certainty, that God would eventually restore the entire created order, including Satan himself, to a perfect state (hence the Gk *apokatastasis*, 'restoration', is often used to designate this belief). Though this can claim some apparent biblical foundation (e.g. Col. 1:18–20), it was seen to be more Platonic than biblical, and was condemned at the Council of Constantinople in 553.

(2) The powerful influence of *Augustine ensured that this form of universalism did not regain popularity until the *Reformation, when it was embraced by some of the extreme Radical Reformers (see *Reformation, Radical), being condemned again in ch. 17 of the *Augsburg Confession.

(3) Contemporary universalism stems largely from *Schleiermacher (with some predecessors in the seventeenth century). He argued that the sovereign love of God is bound to save all eventually, and that heaven would be spoilt if its inhabitants were forced to witness the eternal sufferings of the damned. Nineteenth-century English theology debated this topic with some acrimony. Many theologians broke away from the traditional doctrine of hell without forming one consistent alternative, some opting for 'conditional immortality', which avoids Schleiermacher's second argument, others for the idea of a second chance after death, which allows for his first. The notion of continued spiritual growth and development, which has influenced much

contemporary universalism, has a good deal in common with the evolutionism of the *Romantic movement. Some universalist groups founded new churches in the nineteenth century, some of whose members later (1961) joined with *Unitarian groups.

(4) In the twentieth century universalism spread further, partly due to a relaxing of biblical authority. Although, strictly speaking, neither *Barth nor *Brunner taught universalism proper, both held it to be a possibility for which one might hold out hope. *Tillich regarded hell as a symbol which had lost its character of 'eternal damnation'. J. *Hick argued that only universalism makes sense of worldwide *suffering and prevents Christianity from becoming triumphalistic in its attitude to other faiths. In some modern Roman Catholic theology the adherents of such faiths are regarded as '*anonymous Christians' (*Rahner), either despite the fact that they are in error or because their religions are really disguised versions of the truth. In modern universalism, appeal is often made to the apparent teaching of such passages as Rom. 11:32, held to be in tension with passages predicting *judgment, and recourse is often had to the idea of the limitless ages of future time, after death, during which the love of God will eventually draw all people freely to accept the proffered salvation. In writers such as Hick the doctrine is allied to a considerable relativizing of traditional Christian claims about, e.g. the divinity of Christ. In writers such as J. *Moltmann, universalism is held together with a doctrine of the Trinity and the deity and humanity of Christ. In recent debate an attempt has been made to argue for universalism within an evangelical theology, giving full weight to the authority of Scripture.

Arguments which can be marshalled against this second kind of universalism are as follows:

(1) The biblical evidence for the certainty of future judgment and condemnation of at least some is extremely strong, strong enough to function as a warning even for professing Christians (1 Cor. 3:12–15; 10:12), and the texts commonly held to teach universalism can be shown to admit of other, more probable, explanations. There is no biblical warrant for the idea of a 'second chance' after death.

(2) The second sort of universalism undercuts the first (which is clearly scriptural), in that it makes Christianity one way, one family, among many. This is to compromise *Christology, the doctrine of the *Holy Spirit, and monotheism itself (by providing at best a radically different alternative to biblical monotheism, seeing all the gods worshipped in the world, including the God of Abraham, Isaac and Jacob, the Father of Jesus, as different manifestations of the one god who lies behind all, a view which has some echoes at least of the sin of the golden calf [Exod. 32:4]).

(3) The responsibility of human beings to choose to obey their Creator God is seriously undercut by universalism. (This is more than simply to say that universalism cuts the nerve of *evangelism and moral exhortation, though that can also be true.) A doctrine of hell can thus be part of an affirmation of God's intention to let his human creatures exercise their human responsibility. Orthodox Christianity need not lapse into the *dualism, rightly rejected in universalism, of seeing hell as a kind of concentration camp in the middle of heaven. To choose that which is not God is to choose that which distorts, fragments and ultimately destroys genuine humanity itself.

(4) Universalism, particularly the modern variety, tends to reduce the seriousness of *sin. In a world which continues to witness moral evil of frightening proportions and dimensions, a failure to condemn absolutely would be evidence of basic moral blindness.

(5) Although a biblical theology does not forbid the notion that some may worship the true God, and genuinely serve him, without ever hearing the message of the gospel (so, according to some, Rom. 2:14–16), it does not encourage the idea that there will be a large company of such people.

See also: CHRISTIANITY AND OTHER RELIGIONS; ESCHATOLOGY.

Bibliography

R. Bauckham, N. T. Wright *et al.*, in *Them* 4:2, 1979, pp. 48–69; N. M. de S. Cameron (ed.), *Universalism and the Doctrine of Hell* (Carlisle and Grand Rapids, 1992); J. Hick, *Evil and the God of Love* (London, ²1977); *idem*, *God and the Universe of Faiths* (London, ²1977); *idem*, *Death and Eternal Life* (London, 1976); C. S. Lewis, *The Problem of Pain* (London, 1940); R. Parry and C. Partridge, *Universal Salvation? The Current Debate* (Carlisle, 2003); J. A. T. Robinson, *In The End, God* (London, ²1968); G. Rowell, *Hell and the Victorians* (Oxford, 1974); D. P. Walker, *The Decline of Hell*

(London, 1964); N. T. Wright, *Surprised by Hope* (London, 2007), ch. 11.

N. T. WRIGHT

URSINUS, ZACHARIAS (1534–83)

Zacharias Ursinus was a Silesian Reformed theologian. Born into a Lutheran home, he studied with *Melanchthon in Wittenberg (1550–7) before taking a teaching post in his home town of Breslau (1558–60). During a year of study with Peter Martyr *Vermigli in Zurich (1560–1), he gradually moved into the *Reformed theological orbit. In 1561 he accepted an invitation to become rector of the Sapience College (seminary) in Heidelberg and later served also as Professor of Dogmatics at the University of Heidelberg (1562–8). Forced to flee in 1577 when the city reverted to Lutheranism, he spent the remainder of his life teaching at the Casimirianum, a Calvinist university in nearby Neustadt.

Ursinus is best known as the primary author of the *Heidelberg Catechism (1563), a consensus confession that sought to unify the diverse theological parties in the German Palatinate. He was also an important early Reformed covenant theologian, the first ever to use *covenant as the organizing theme in a system of theology and to speak of a pre-fall 'covenant of creation' (*Summa Theologiae*, 1562). Finally, he contributed in a significant way to the rise of Reformed orthodoxy, synthesizing the theology of second-generation Reformers like *Calvin and *Bullinger with the established methods of *scholasticism.

Bibliography

L. D. Bierma et al., *An Introduction to the Heidelberg Catechism: Sources, History, and Theology* (Grand Rapids, 2005); D. Visser, *Zacharias Ursinus: The Reluctant Reformer – His Life and Times* (New York, 1983).

L. D. BIERMA

VALDÉS, JUAN DE (c. 1498–1541)

Valdés was a Spanish Catholic author of evangelical writings. He was born at Cuenca, studied at Alcalá de Henares, corresponded with *Erasmus and became one of Spain's leading Erasmians. Falling foul of the Spanish Inquisition with *Diálogo de Doctrina Cristiana* (1529), he was declared a *heretic, but escaped the consequences by leaving Spain for Rome. Here he found favour with Pope Clement VII and was ordained. On the election in 1534 of Pope Paul III (whom he detested) he settled in Naples, where he remained in communion with the Roman Catholic Church until his death. The unique and deepening spirituality of his later years followed some profound experience when 'Christ was revealed' to him; it is first sensed in *Alfabeto Cristiano* (1536) and fully felt in his commentaries on Scripture (Matt., Rom., 1 Cor., etc.). He lived like an otherworldly recluse, yet exerted incalculable influence on a select circle of society ladies, *humanists and distinguished clerics: Pietro Carnesecchi (1508–67), Celio Secundo Curione (1503–69), Marc Antonio Flaminio (d. 1550). *Ochino, *Vermigli and countless others came under the fascination of his teaching. The linchpin of his doctrine was *justification by faith (with a pre-Quaker emphasis on inner light), and he drew on Protestant sources, especially Calvin's *Institutes*. His major work is his *The Hundred and Ten Considerations* (c. 1540; ET, Oxford, 1638), of which the Spanish original has not survived.

See also: REFORMATION, CATHOLIC COUNTER-.

Bibliography

D. A. Crews, *Twilight of the Renaissance: The Life of Juan de Valdés* (Toronto, 2008); J. C. Nieto, *Juan de Valdés and the Origins of the Spanish and Italian Reformation* (Geneva, 1970).

P. M. J. MCNAIR

VAN MASTRICHT, PETER (1630–1706)

Peter van Mastricht, a major figure in post-Reformation *Reformed orthodoxy, was born in Cologne, in Germany, in 1630 and was educated at the Universities of Duisburg and Utrecht before serving pastorates in Cleves and Gluckstadt. He was then called first as Professor of Oriental Languages at Frankfurt in 1662, then as Professor of Theology at Duisburg from 1669 until he succeeded Gisbert Voetius as Professor of Theology at Utrecht in 1677 where he served until his death. His most famous work was his *Theoretico-Practica Theologia* (1682–7), which served as a representative example of what historian Richard A. Muller refers to as 'high orthodoxy'. This work was later translated into Dutch and was influential on such seminal Reformed theologians as Jonathan *Edwards. Muller argues that it was well received during the *Dutch Nadere Reformation.

Mastricht maintained a very high view of *Scripture, arguing that the Holy Spirit infallibly directed the human writers of Scripture to produce a Bible that is without error. The personal weaknesses of biblical authors such as Moses, who complained to God that he was not a good speaker, pointed to the powerful role that the Holy Spirit exercised in the composing of the biblical text. Mastricht also includes his discussion of faith within the rubric of the doctrine of Scripture. Salvific faith, he said, is the act of *faith that is required for salvation. Faith includes knowledge, assent and the faithful apprehension of divine truth. Faith for Mastricht was no mere intellectual assent to a set of doctrinal propositions, but included the practical application of the will.

The section from the *Theoretico-Practica Theologia* on the topic of *regeneration was translated into English in 1770 and has been republished in 2002 under the title *A Treatise on Regeneration*. Mastricht dealt with the necessity of regeneration, its irresistible nature, the fact that it flows from God and not from our free will, and its practical application for the spiritual life of the believer. For Mastricht, regeneration comes logically prior to faith and is given to the believer by the Holy Spirit. Once the believer is regenerated, they develop religious affections by which they desire to be obedient to God and detest whatever is contrary to God's will. It is this emphasis on religious affections that the famed American Reformed theologian Jonathan Edwards developed. On the cover of the English translation, Edwards is quoted as saying, 'This book [*Theoretico-Practica Theologia*] is much better than any other book in the world, excepting the Bible, in my opinion.'

Bibliography

Works: *A Treatise on Regeneraton*, ed. B. Withrow (Orlando, 2002).

Studies: A. Goudriaan, *Reformed Orthodoxy and Philosophy, 1625–1750: Gisbertus Voetius, Petrus van Mastricht, and Anthonius Driessen* (Leiden, 2006); R. A. Muller, *Post-Reformation Reformed Dogmatics: The Rise and Development of Reformed Orthodoxy, ca. 1520–1725*, 4 vols. (Grand Rapids, 2003).

M. I. KLAUBER

VAN TIL, CORNELIUS (1895–1987)

A Reformed theologian and presuppositional apologist, Van Til was born at Grootegast in the Netherlands to a pious Calvinist family, who migrated to the United States in 1905 and became active in the Christian Reformed Church (which was Dutch in origin).

He studied at the Christian Reformed Calvin College and Seminary in Grand Rapids, and continued his education at Princeton Seminary and University. There he studied under Geerhardus *Vos, Casper W. Hodge (1870–1937), Robert Dick Wilson (1856–1930), Oswald T. Allis (1880–1973) and J. Gresham *Machen. At the university, he studied under the personalist idealist philosopher, A. A. Bowman (1883–1936). Also influential in his Princeton training was the biblical and dogmatic theologian B. B. *Warfield.

In 1925, Van Til married Rena Klooster (d. 1978). In 1927, he was ordained and called by the Spring Lake Church of Classis Muskegon in Michigan, his first and only pastorate. Van Til taught *apologetics at *Princeton Seminary in 1928, but, along with Wilson, Allis and Machen, he resigned from the Seminary in 1929 owing to its reorganization under a theologically more liberal board of directors. That same year, Van Til became one of the original professors of the newly organized Westminster Theological Seminary in Philadelphia, which carried on the conservative *Reformed tradition of Old Princeton. He remained at Westminster as professor of apologetics until his retirement in 1975. He joined the Orthodox Presbyterian Church soon after its inception in 1936.

From the 1940s until the late 1970s, Van Til was a most prolific writer. His major contribution was in the area of apologetics, with particular reference to the foundational questions of introductory theological *methodology and structure. Van Til's distinctive approach is 'presuppositionalism', which may be defined as insistence on an ultimate category of thought or a conceptual framework which one must assume in order to make a sensible interpretation of reality:

The issue between believers and non-believers in Christian theism cannot be settled by a direct appeal to 'facts' or 'laws' whose nature and significance is already agreed upon by both parties to the debate. The question is rather as to what is the final reference-point required to make the 'facts' and the 'laws' intelligible. The question is as to what the 'facts' and 'laws' really are. Are they what the non-Christian methodology assumes they are? Are they what the Christian theistic methodology presupposes they are? (*Defense of the Faith*, Philadelphia, ³1967)

Not only to 'prove' biblical Christianity, but to make sense of any fact in the world, Van Til holds that one must presuppose the reality of the 'self-contained' triune God and the self-attesting revelation of the Scriptures. From this basis, the redeemed person then reasons '*analogically', attempting 'to think God's thoughts after him'. This means humans may know reality truly (for God, in whose image they are created, knows it truly), but not exhaustively (for God is infinite and they are finite).

The presuppositionalist endeavours to convince the unregenerate first by demonstrating that, on unregenerate presuppositions of chance occurrence in an impersonal universe, one cannot account for any sort of order and rationality. Next, he tries to show that life and reality make sense only on the basis of Christian presuppositions.

Van Til vigorously criticized the traditional apologetic approach of both Catholics and Protestants as failing to challenge the non-Christian view of knowledge, as allowing sinners to be judges of ultimate reality, and of arguing merely for the probability of Christianity. He considered himself in the line of *Kuyper and *Bavinck in his presuppositionalism, and opposed the 'evidentialism' of *Thomas Aquinas, Joseph *Butler and Warfield.

Both Van Til's apologetic stance and his stringent critique of Karl *Barth (as a 'new modernist') have created continuing controversy. G. C. *Berkouwer, James Daane (1914–83), J. W. Montgomery (b. 1931), John Gerstner and others in the evangelical and Reformed traditions have written at length against Van Til's position as lacking in exegesis of Scripture, and as tending to irrationalism, *fideism and 'reasoning in a circle'. Other students of Van Til have sought to develop his insights and apply them to theology and ethics.

Bibliography

G. Bahnsen, *Van Til's Apologetic: Readings and Analysis* (Philipsburg, 1998); J. Frame, *Cornelius Van Til: An Analysis of His Thought* (Philipsburg, 1998); J. R. Muether, *Cornelius Van Til: Reformed Apologist and Churchman* (Philipsburg, 2008); D. Vickers, *Cornelius Van Til and the Theologian's Theological Stance* (Wilmington, 1976); W. White, *Van Til, Defender of the Faith* (Nashville, 1979).

D. F. KELLY

VATICAN COUNCILS

The First Vatican Council occurred under the *papacy of Pius IX (1846–78) in 1868, and was completed by 1870. The purposes of the council were to define the constituent parts of the Catholic faith and to establish the doctrine of papal infallibility – the notion that because the pope is Christ's representative on earth, his decrees are without error. The *Dogmatic Constitution on the Catholic Faith* and the *First Dogmatic Constitution on the Church of Christ* were the two main documents of the council, addressing Catholic doctrinal theology and papal infallibility, respectively.

Sensing the need to define more clearly the social role of the Catholic Church, particularly during the turbulent decades of the mid-twentieth century, the Second Vatican Council was convened in 1962 under Pope John XXIII (1958–63). It concluded in 1965 under a different pope, Paul VI (1963–78).

The Second Vatican Council has significantly more documents – sixteen – than that of the first council. Though many of the theological ideas remain unchanged from the first council to the second, the tone of Vatican II is notably geared toward a more progressive social ethic than that of Vatican I. Thus, the documents of Vatican II still promote natural moral law theology, the notion that humans possess a universal rational faculty that is 'naturally' inherent to them, and that through the exercise of their reason, they are capable of making morally sound judgments. Vatican II also still allows for the doctrine of papal infallibility, though this idea receives considerably less attention than it did in Vatican I.

In terms of the social ethics of Vatican II, the two most important documents are *Lumen Gentium* and *Gaudium et Spes*. *Lumen Gentium* is only one of two dogmatic constitutions in the entirety of Vatican II (*Dei Verbum* is the other), and its primary concern is to define the Catholic Church for today. It stresses the church's mysterious nature, particularly in regard to its unique relationship with Jesus Christ on the one hand, and in its role as an historical instrument of Christ on the other. *Gaudium et Spes* focuses its attention on the particular social ethics of the church defined in *Lumen Gentium*, giving special attention to the anthropocentric and existential concerns of humanity that were indicative of so much of the social philosophy from that same time period. Of the two councils, Vatican II continues to have the greater influence in Catholic moral theology today.

See also: COUNCILS; ROMAN CATHOLIC THEOLOGY.

Bibliography

W. M. Abbott (ed.), *The Documents of Vatican II: All Sixteen Official Texts Promulgated by the Ecumenical Council 1963–1965* (London, 1966); R. F. Bulman and F. J. Parrella (eds.), *From Trent to Vatican II: Historical and Theological Investigations* (Oxford, 2006); E. C. Butler, *The Vatican Council, 1869–1870: Based on Bishop Ullathorne's Letters* (London, 1962); R. Charles, *The Social Teaching of Vatican II: Its Origin and Development – Catholic Social Ethics, an Historical and Comparative Study* (Leominster, 1982); J. Mahoney, *The Making of Moral Theology: A Study of the Roman Catholic Tradition* (Oxford, 1987).

J. K. BURK

VERIFICATION AND FALSIFICATION

Verification is simply the procedure carried out to determine whether a statement is true or false. The usual tests of a statement's truth are coherence, correspondence with reality, and pragmatism. The coherence view stresses that a statement is true because it fits in or coheres with all other statements. The correspondence theory argues that true statements are those which accurately correspond to or picture reality as it is. The pragmatic theory stresses that what is true is what works in practical terms. In modern philosophy, the *logical positivist school based on the Vienna Circle produced a programme for verification and falsification.

Logical positivism and empiricism

The positivists, following the *empiricist approach to knowledge, stressed that for any sentence to be meaningful it must express a statement or proposition which is either analytic (true by definition, by necessity, or a priori) or empirically verifiable. The empirically verifiable statements were thus a posteriori, concerned with contingent facts known only by sense-experience. This division was used by the positivists to dismiss theology and metaphysics as meaningless using the 'verification principle'.

Verification principle (principle of verifiability)

This declared that a statement is meaningful if, and only if, it can be verified by sense-experience. Statements in *logic and mathematics were meaningful on an analytic basis for they were true by definition, though they gave no information about the real world. Statements of science or empirical fact were meaningful, for they could be tested by sense-experience. Statements of ethics and aesthetics were not literally meaningful, but rather expressed feelings, attitudes, taste and one's emotional response. This approach developed in positivism and empiricism the 'emotive' theory of ethics, which suggested that all ethical judgments were expressions of feeling and attempts to arouse similar feelings in others. Statements of metaphysics (e.g. about reality or creation) or theology were literally meaningless. They were either expressions of personal taste or nonsensical. They could not be true and were not objective according to the verification principle. Philosophy was no longer to make claims beyond the clearly observable, but only to clarify meaningfulness in the here-and-now realm of scientific fact.

This position seemed to give victory to the empiricist and to dismiss religion's and theology's claims to truth. However, the verification principle was soon seen to have problems. It was debated whether it applied to sentences, statements or propositions and how one separated out these different levels. The status of the principle was highly doubtful. If the verification principle was itself subjected to its own canon, then it failed the test. Thus it was literally meaningless. It could not be argued that the statement was true by definition, for it can be doubted or rejected without contradiction. The positivists tried to safeguard it as a recommendation for action or an assumed first principle, but this smacks of special pleading.

The principle also excluded areas which the positivist/empiricist wanted to include. Historical statements, such as 'Caesar crossed the Rubicon', could not be tested, for they were in the past. Likewise, and more seriously, all claims of a universal form could not be verified. This meant that all statements or general scientific laws could not be totally verified, for we never exhaust all possible sense-experiences and an exception may be waiting in the next sense-experience. Thus, in excluding religion, theology and metaphysics, historical and scientific statements were also ruled out.

This led to attempts to adapt the principle from a strong sense of verification to a weaker sense. This argued that a statement is meaningful if, and only if, we know how to verify it by sense-experience in principle. This weaker version seemed to pose less of a threat, for as long as some kind of verification was available, then this would satisfy the 'in principle' condition.

A. J. Ayer (1910–89) and R. Carnap (1891–1970) tended to move verification in the direction of testability and confirmability. Karl Popper (1902–94) stressed falsifiability.

Falsification principle

Following the model of natural science, Popper realized that universal statements could not be verified, but could be falsified by counter-examples. Indeed, the natural progression in science was to develop hypotheses with a view to testing them, by attempting to disprove them by one or more negative instances. In a sense, the more falsifiable the hypothesis, the more valuable it is likely to be. If no negative instances are found, then we may have confidence in the truth of the hypothesis. Built into this move is a recognition that both acceptance and rejection of hypotheses are incomplete and provisional. This procedure cannot establish the truth of scientific laws, and says nothing about non-scientific areas such as theology and metaphysics except that they are not science. The most that can be claimed for scientific laws by the method of falsification is probability, which is very far short of the certainty which was the initial aim of the logical positivist and empiricist.

Recent moves

While theology has continued to be attacked and defended on the basis of the verification and falsification principles, modern philosophy has tended to move away from strict verification to a much wider approach to linguistic and conceptual analysis. In philosophy of religion, much has been made of the 'Don't ask for the meaning, ask for the use' approach based on the later *Wittgenstein. This appears to allow religion and theology to function on their own terms, immune from external criteria or criticism. It is within the theological circle that meaning and truth are to be found. The Bible, however, is not afraid of seeing the Christian faith in terms of truth or falsity. Christians make claims for faith and offer evidence in support of their faith. Paul argues that if Christ did not rise from the dead, then Christianity is pointless and Christians are to be pitied. This would be a clear case of falsification. Christians need to develop appropriate criteria for truth and falsity, orthodoxy and *heresy, which will allow truth claims to be made and reinforce the spreading of the gospel and the defence of the faith.

See also: RELIGIOUS LANGUAGE; TRUTH.

Bibliography

A. J. Ayer, *Language, Truth and Logic* (London, ^{2}1946); K. Popper, *Logic of Scientific Discovery* (ET, London, 1959); F. Waismann, 'Verifiability', in A. Flew (ed.), *Logic and Language* (Oxford, 1951); J. Wisdom, *Philosophy and Psychoanalysis* (Oxford, 1953). See also Bibliography for *Logical positivism.

E. D. COOK

VERMIGLI, PETER MARTYR (PIETRO MARTIRE) (1499–1562)

This Italian Protestant Reformer was born in Florence and died in Zurich. The son of a shoemaker, he entered the Canons Regular of St Augustine of the Lateran Congregation at Fiesole in 1514 and was professed in 1518. His most formative years (1518–26) were spent at Padua University, where he taught himself Greek and received his doctorate; he later learned Hebrew at Bologna.

While Abbot of S. Pietro ad Aram in Naples (1537–40) he came under the influence of Juan de *Valdés, who introduced him to Protestant writings. Elected in 1541 Prior of S. Frediano at Lucca, a position of considerable importance, he initiated a series of far-reaching reforms, both educational and ecclesiastical; but, called to account for his actions, he chose to renounce his vows and fled to Zurich and the Protestant camp in 1542.

After five years with *Bucer at Strasbourg, where he expounded the OT and married an ex-nun from Metz, he was invited to England by *Cranmer in 1547 and was appointed Regius Professor of Divinity at Oxford and a canon of Christ Church. Here his lectures on 1 Corinthians provoked in May 1549 the public disputation on the Eucharist described in John Foxe's *Acts and Monuments* (see *Reformers, English). The following year he was involved in the vestiarian controversy. He assisted Cranmer in the revision of the Anglican liturgy (part of the 1552 Communion service is his), reform of the ecclesiastical laws and the formulation of the Forty-Two Articles (the statement on predestination is attributed to him). On Mary's accession he was allowed to return to Strasbourg.

In 1556 he was invited to Zurich, where he occupied the chair of Hebrew until his death. His last venture abroad was to attend the Colloquy of Poissy in 1561, when he spoke in Tuscan to persuade his fellow-Florentine, Catherine de Medici.

Vermigli influenced the Reformation's course in ways both hidden and apparent, for, unlike most of his exiled compatriots, he became, and remained, a bastion of biblical orthodoxy. He was the friend and confidant of *Bullinger and *Calvin, and a father in God to many of the Marian exiles from England – especially John *Jewel, who lived with him at Strasbourg and Zurich. Because of his calm, informed and balanced judgment, his opinion was sought on many issues of the day. The influence he exerted on Queen Elizabeth and the English Reformation settlement is attested but imponderable.

Deeply skilled in the three classical languages, he excelled in *patristic learning, while his *Aristotelian training at Padua made him a formidable controversialist. He was a voluminous writer and *erudite exegete*, his commentaries on Scripture remaining standard works of Protestant reference for generations. His major contribution to the Reformation was in the arena of *eucharistic doctrine, and his *Defensio* (against Stephen Gardiner) has been judged the weightiest treatise of the era on this subject. Calvin declared that 'the whole [doctrine of the Eucharist] was crowned by Peter Martyr, who left nothing more to be done'.

Vermigli taught that a *sacrament is a work of God from beginning to end, and consists of a dynamic *relatio* between two distinct realities rather than a given *quid*. In the Eucharist the two realities are the *fundamentum* (the bread and wine on the table) and the *terminus* (the body of Christ in heaven). The sacrament is created by the concurrence of three factors: Christ's historic institution, God's word in consecration, and the Holy Spirit's power in reception. Employing a subtle but consistent distinction, he maintained that the believer truly and spiritually (but not 'really' and corporeally) feeds on Christ's glorified flesh and blood in partaking of the consecrated elements. These suffer no change of *substantia*, yet become, not Christ's body and blood, but the sacrament of his body and blood. The *signa* of bread and wine are raised to the dignity of visible words of God by being transformed into the instrument of the Spirit. But *sacramentum est tantum in usu* ('the sacrament exists only in its use') means that the Eucharist is an event that happens rather than an object to be venerated or reserved, and it happens when it is received by faith: hence the *manducatio impiorum* ('eating by the ungodly') is sacramentally a non-event. But for believers there is a *duplex manducatio* ('twofold eating'): with their mouths they eat the outward symbols, yet by the same act with their spirits they eat the true body of Christ in heaven.

Bibliography

Works: *Life, Letters, and Sermons*, ed. J. P. Donnelly (Kirksville, MO, 1999); *The Peter Martyr Library*, eds. J. P. Donnelly *et al.* (Kirksville, 1994–).

Studies: S. Corda, *Veritas Sacramenti: A Study in Vermigli's Doctrine of the Lord's Supper* (Zurich, 1975); J. P. Donnelly, *Calvinism and Scholasticism in Vermigli's Doctrine of Man and Grace* (Leiden, 1976); J. P. Donnelly and R. M. Kingdon, *A Bibliography of the Works of Peter Martyr Vermigli* (Kirksville, 1990); G. Duffy and J. C. McLelland, *Life, Early Letters and Eucharistic Writings of Peter Martyr* (Oxford, 1989); R. M. Kingdon, *The Political Thought of Peter Martyr Vermigli: Selected Texts and Commentary* (Geneva,

1980); T. Kirby, E. Campi and F. A. James III (eds.), *A Companion to Peter Martyr Vermigli* (Leiden, 2009); J. C. McLelland (ed.), *Peter Martyr Vermigli and Italian Reform* (Waterloo, Ontario, 1980); P. M. J. McNair, *Peter Martyr in Italy: An Anatomy of Apostasy* (Oxford, 1967).

P. M. J. McNair

VICTORINES

The Victorines were a twelfth-century group of commentators, poets, exegetes and mystical writers who were part of the staff of the Abbey Church of St Victor in the suburbs of Paris. They lived in community and followed a collection of *ascetic instructions attributed to St *Augustine. The school was founded in 1108 by William of Champeaux (c. 1070–1121; teacher of *Abelard), and adopted its own Book of Rules under its first abbot Gilduin (1135–53). The Victorines had a widespread influence on communities and monasteries in France, Italy, Germany, England, Denmark and Ireland. Aiming at a balance between monastic life and devotion to scholarship, these priests served the student population of Paris and tried to create a synthesis of the new learning of the medieval schools with the traditional approach of the Fathers. These activities, they believed, should find their focus in contemplating and loving God.

The most famous representatives of the school were Adam of St Victor (c. 1110–c. 1180), a lyric poet and liturgist; Hugh of St Victor (c. 1096–1141), a biblical commentator who laid out a method of scriptural study in his *Didascalion*; Richard of St Victor (c. 1123–1173), a spiritual writer who emphasized the mystical meaning of Scripture; and Andrew of Wigmore (d. 1175), an exegete who concentrated on the literal study of the Bible.

Bibliography

F. Copleston, *A History of Philosophy*, vol. 2:1 (Westminster, 1950); M. Haren, *Medieval Thought* (New York, 1985); J. Leclerq et al., *A History of Christian Spirituality*, vol. 2 (London, 1968); B. Smalley, *The Study of the Bible in the Middle Ages* (Oxford, ²1952); M. Swanson, *The Twelfth-Century Renaissance* (Manchester, 1999).

R. G. Clouse

VICTORINUS (AFER), CAIUS MARIUS (fl. 350–365)

Victorinus was a Christian Neoplatonist from Africa (hence distinguished as 'Afer'). He became a famous rhetorician in Rome, and as a pagan wrote rhetorical and logical works (mostly lost), including translations of, or commentaries on, Aristotle, Cicero and the Neoplatonists Plotinus and Porphyry (see *Aristotelianism; *Platonism). He was thus an important link between Greek and Latin worlds of thought. His bold conversion to Christianity in mature life (c. 355) later impressed Augustine (*Confessions* VIII, ii. 3–v. 10), who had read his Neoplatonic translations. Victorinus lost his professorship under the pagan emperor Julian in 362.

His surviving Christian works comprise three against *Arianism (*To Candidus, on the Generation of the Divine Word; Against Arius; The Acceptance of Homoousios*), a commentary on Paul's Galatians, Ephesians and Philippians, and a few hymns. He also wrote against *Manichaeism and on Scripture. He was perhaps the first systematic theologian of the *Trinity (cf. P. Henry, *JTS* 1950, pp. 42–55), primarily in metaphysical rather than scriptural terms, and including a 'psychological trinitarianism' akin to Augustine's. His importance lies in his pioneering Christian-Neoplatonic synthesis, in which he stretched Neoplatonism in an attempt, which was not wholly successful, to accommodate the faith of Nicaea (see *Councils). Despite the obscure complexity of his thought, he blazed the trail for Christian Platonism in the West.

Bibliography

Trinitarian works in *Sources Chrétiennes* 68–69, ET in *FC* 69; Pauline commentary, A. Locher (ed.), *Bibliotheca Teubneriana* (Leipzig, 1972), no ET; R. A. Markus in *CHLGEMP*, pp. 329–340.

D. F. Wright

VINCENT OF LERINS, see CATHOLICITY

VIRGIN BIRTH

In accordance with popular usage, the term 'virgin birth' will be used in this article to refer to the virginal conception of Jesus, the belief that he was conceived by the Virgin *Mary

Virgin birth

without sexual intercourse. There is also, in the Catholic tradition, a later belief that Mary's virginity was physically preserved during the actual birth process – i.e. that the hymen was not broken. This belief is found in *Leo's *Tome*, which was officially accepted by the Council of Chalcedon. It has been questioned by at least some Roman Catholic scholars, such as Karl *Rahner.

The virgin birth is taught clearly in only two NT passages: Matt. 1:18–25 and Luke 1:26–38. Others are sometimes cited (such as Mark 6:3; John 1:13 – on which see below; Gal. 4:4) but there is no certain reference to the virgin birth in any of these latter passages. The paucity of references in the NT is sometimes given as an argument against the historicity of the doctrine. But it should be noted that the virgin birth is almost the only point in common between the two infancy narratives, a clear indication that it is based on an earlier, common tradition. It should also be noted that, in view of the gospel record, the alternative to the virgin birth is not a normal birth within wedlock (for which there is no evidence) but an illegitimate birth (which seems to be the charge in John 8:41 and which is countered in Matt. 1:18–25).

The virgin birth is common to all mainstream orthodox Christian confessions. In the early church it was questioned only by *Ebionites (who denied Jesus' deity) and by *docetists (who denied his true humanity). It was included in the early *creeds and is affirmed today in the Apostles' and Nicene Creeds. With the rise of *liberal theology it has increasingly come to be questioned. This is largely because the normative status of Scripture is denied, and sometimes also because the possibility of the miraculous is denied. Because of its inclusion in the creeds and because of confusion between the virgin birth and the incarnation, the doctrine of the virgin birth has often become a central point of controversy. It has thereby been given a prominence out of proportion to its place in the NT or its theological significance.

The NT teaches that Mary remained a virgin 'until she gave birth to a son' (Matt. 1:25). But in the following century the belief emerged that she remained perpetually a virgin, that her marriage with Joseph was never consummated. This view was opposed by some – notably *Tertullian and some of the fourth-century opponents of *asceticism. But the dominant majority view in the early church was that Mary remained a perpetual virgin and that Jesus' 'brothers' were either Joseph's children from a previous marriage or Jesus' cousins (*Jerome). This doctrine was not at first opposed by the Reformers. *Calvin reserved judgment on the question, and the strongly Protestant Geneva Bible (1560) repeatedly defends the doctrine. But more significant than the numerical support for this belief is the lack of early evidence for it and the dogmatic motivation behind it, namely an unbiblical belief that sexual intercourse is defiling.

In the popular mind the virgin birth is often confused with the *incarnation. This confusion has been encouraged by some of the literature on the subject. The doctrine of the incarnation states that the eternal Son, the second person of the Trinity, became man. The doctrine of the virgin birth states that this man Jesus did not have a human father. It does *not* state that God was his father. The virgin birth is not to be confused with pagan myths about gods mating with beautiful women. The virgin birth means that Jesus' conception was miraculous, that he had no human father. This is not to be confused with the belief that he was the eternal Son of God become man.

Granted that the virgin birth and the incarnation are distinct, do they logically entail one another? No. The virgin birth does not of itself prove the deity of Christ. *Arians (who deny Christ's deity), *adoptionists (who deny the incarnation) and Muslims have all traditionally believed in the virgin birth. The virgin birth is a supernatural conception which shows Jesus to be someone very special. It does not *prove* his deity. Conversely, while it can be argued that the incarnation required a supernatural birth, this does not necessarily mean a *virgin* birth. Scripture tells that Jesus was as a matter of fact conceived by a virgin. It never tells us that this was the only possible way for him to have been conceived.

What then is the relationship between the virgin birth and the incarnation? The virgin birth is not meant to be a biological explanation of the incarnation. It has sometimes been expounded in such terms, and it is at least partly for that reason that *Brunner and *Pannenberg both rejected the doctrine. The virgin birth is better seen, as by *Barth, as a sign pointing to the incarnation. It is fitting and congruous with the incarnation, to which it bears witness; Jesus' miraculous birth points to the fact that he was a unique person.

The virgin birth was criticized by J. A. T. *Robinson, among others, because it makes Jesus different from us, not truly human. (It is ironic that those who have the most to say about functional Christology often take diametrically opposed positions when it comes to Jesus' *humanity*.) In response, R. F. Aldwinkle has fairly stated that 'it is not the method by which a human being comes to be such which is decisive but the end product itself, namely a human being'. But there is a deeper issue here. The role of Christ requires that there should be both continuity and discontinuity between him and us; that he should be one of us (Heb. 2:10–18) and yet also different from us. Jesus is the second *Adam – one of the human race, yet inaugurating a new redeemed humanity. The virgin birth points to this combination of continuity and discontinuity.

Traditionally, it has often been held that the virgin birth is necessary for the sinlessness of Jesus Christ. This idea was introduced by some of the early Fathers (especially *Augustine) because of their beliefs about original *sin. Augustine held that lust is involved in all intercourse in fallen humanity. If this is so, then the virgin birth clearly protects Christ from being the product of sinful activity. But such a theory has no biblical basis. A modern variant of this argument is found in the claim that original sin is transmitted through the male line. This theory serves to explain how the virgin birth exempts Jesus from original sin, but there is no biblical basis for it.

Karl *Barth discerned in the virgin birth a denial of humanity's natural capacity for God, a favourite Barthian theme. According to this view, the significance of the virgin birth is the absence not of the sex act or of human lust, but of active human participation. Humanity is involved, but only as a 'non-willing, non-achieving, non-creative, non-sovereign, merely ready, merely receptive, virgin human being' (*CD* I.2, p. 191). Men rather than women are the active agents in the history of the world, and therefore the male must be set aside in the conception of Christ. This view is open to various objections. In addition to its sexist overtones, it appears to teach the total depravity of all males! But Barth is not without justice in applying the doctrine of the virgin birth to the realm of grace.

There is a variant reading of John 1:13 which affirms that Christ was 'born not of natural descent, nor of human decision or a husband's will, but born of God'. This is all but universally agreed not to be the original reading, but the verse is not without relevance. It is highly likely that John knew the tradition of the virgin birth, and it is possible that he was deliberately drawing a parallel between the virgin birth and regeneration. In conversion, as in the virgin birth, the initiative and the sovereignty lie with God.

Bibliography

T. Boslooper, *The Virgin Birth* (London, 1962); R. E. Brown, *The Virginal Conception and Bodily Resurrection of Jesus* (London, 1974); D. Edwards, *The Virgin Birth in History and Faith* (London, 1943); R. Gromacki, *The Virgin Birth* (Grand Rapids, 2002); A. N. S. Lane, 'The Rationale and Significance of the Virgin Birth', *Vox Evangelica* 10 (1977), pp. 48–64; J. G. Machen, *The Virgin Birth of Christ* (London, 1930); T. S. Perry and W. J. Abraham (eds.), *Mary for Evangelicals* (Downers Grove, 2006); H. von Campenhausen, *The Virgin Birth in the Theology of the Ancient Church* (London, 1964).

A. N. S. LANE

VISION OF GOD

The vision of God (*visio dei*), also called the beatific vision, is one of the classic theological definitions of the *eschatological goal of humanity.

The pagan world into which early Christianity spread also aspired to the vision of God in the form in which this was envisaged in the *Platonic tradition. This influenced the development of patristic and medieval thinking about the vision of God, with some unfortunate results. Instead of the context of personal fellowship with God in which the biblical notion of the vision belongs, Platonic influences promoted a more purely intellectualist and individualist understanding of the vision, as intellectual contemplation of eternal being, anticipated in this life in solitary *mystical ecstasy. With it came the Greek distinction between contemplation and action, which created a tension in medieval Christianity between the pursuit of the vision of God in the contemplative life, which required withdrawal from society, and the practice of neighbourly love in the active life. The Platonic form of the vision of God also tended to relativize the incarnation. Because the beatific vision was considered simply as the goal of monastic flight from the world, of *ascetic discipline and of all-too-Platonic forms of mysticism, the Reformers, followed by most Protestant theology, largely neglected the notion; but in doing so they neglected an important element in the eschatological hope of the NT and lost some of the valuable insights of medieval theology and spirituality.

In medieval Western theology the beatific vision was defined as the direct, intuitive, intellectual vision of the essence of God, whereas the Eastern church denied that God can be seen in his essence (see *Eastern Orthodox theology; *Hesychasm; *Iconoclastic controversies). The Council of Vienne (1311–12) and *scholastic theology insisted that the natural powers of the created intellect are incapable of the vision of God, which is a supernatural gift of God's grace to the faithful after death. Controversy over the views of Pope John XXII (1316–34) led to the decree of the Council of Florence (1439) to the effect that the beatific vision is already enjoyed by the redeemed in heaven before the last judgment.

Debate has taken place over whether or not the 'essence' of God can be seen (Benedict XII in the fourteenth century wrote of the saints 'who saw the essence of God'). The Council of Florence, however, went further and spoke with clarity about seeing the triune God, *as he is*, suggesting that God can be seen as he is *in himself* (*visio Dei per essentiam*), a thing impossible (theologians brought up God's incomprehensibility) for a mere creature and requiring the light of glory (*lumen gloriae*) to bring about. Western theologians (Thomas Aquinas) argued that in the beatific vision (*visio beata*) this essence could be seen; Gregory Palamas and the East argued that it could not. These discussions have included the twin discussion of the relationship of nature and grace, and the nature of the knowledge of God as analogical or univocal, both in this world and the world to come.

Further debate has also been waged over whether the *visio dei* is possible here on earth. The apostle Paul spoke of 'visions and revelations' and of being 'caught up to the third heaven' (2 Cor. 12:1–4).

The doctrine of the vision of God teaches that God himself is the ultimate goal of human life, that he will be known by the redeemed in heaven in an immediate relationship involving their whole persons, endlessly satisfying both the love of beauty and the love of truth, the object of all their attention and the source of all their joy. As Augustine (*City of God*, XXII.29) well recognized, the vision of God will not exclude but will include the corporate life of the redeemed and the reality of the new creation; for in the new creation all things and people will reflect God's glory, and he will be seen in all.

Bibliography

G. C. Berkouwer, *The Return of Christ* (Grand Rapids, 1972); V. Eossky, *The Vision of God* (London, 1963); A. E. Green, NCR II, pp. 186–193; K. E. Kirk, *The Vision of God* (London, 1931); J. Moltmann, *Theology and Joy* (London, 1973); J. Ratzinger, *Eschatology: Death and Eternal Life* (Washington, 1988).

D. W. H. THOMAS

VOCATION

There has been a subtle change in how vocation is understood recently. In the past, one might have started with a calling to a particular *ministry within the church (e.g. deacon and priest or evangelist and overseer) or perhaps to a particular role in society (e.g. a teacher or a medic/nurse). Contemporary theologians (from Karl Barth to Rowan Williams), however, are inclined to begin with the notion of a general calling to be human. *Baptism, Eucharist and Ministry* (the Lima Document) speaks of God calling 'the whole of humanity to become part of God's people' (p. 20). Such a statement comes out of a desire to work out exactly what it means to be *imago Dei. Yet, there is awareness that such a starting point needs careful nuancing, particularly given the ability of humans to indulge in illusions regarding their own omnipotence. Thus in the midst of the capacity for great glory (2 Cor. 3:18; cf. Irenaeus, *Adv. Haer* 20. 7), there is the acknowledgment of frailty, vulnerability and mortality.

This general vocation to fulfil the calling to be a human being leads into the specific calling that is given to baptized Christians. Generally speaking, Christian believers of all traditions see that it is *baptism rather than any other rite, for example ordination, which is foundational to understanding the particular calling that Christian people have to exercise in the world. Such a starting point comes from a rediscovery of the ministry of all believers (the *laos*), out of which particular ministries are given birth. For it is in baptism that the Christian is closely associated with the incarnation, death and resurrection of Jesus Christ. This identification which baptism brings with Christ in his *incarnation demonstrates the importance of the rite for shaping individual and corporate ministries within the body of Christ.

Thus, while Christians from the majority of denominations would affirm the sanctity of specific ministries, such roles and functions are rooted themselves in the general baptismal calling. This does not diminish particular roles or functions, but rather assumes that the voice of God can be heard by all Christians, and that the primary function of the priest, presbyter, elder or evangelist is to equip the rest of the church in its vocation to participate in the wider *missio Dei*. The Lima Document notes that relationship between those with specific public ministries and that of the laity is organic and interrelated. 'On the one hand, the community needs ordained ministers. Their presence reminds the community of divine initiative . . . On the other hand, the ordained ministry has no existence apart from the community' (pp. 21–22).

It is because of the rediscovery of the interrelatedness of ministers and people that there has been another shift in our understanding of vocation. Vocation is not restricted to the ecclesiastical arena, but, as David Ford has argued, encompasses the working out of the promise of baptism wherever the individual Christian is. Thus, while the rest of the world might have lost the sense of the sacred in its understanding of particular vocations, churches have been rediscovering that vocation is worked out in the workplace, at home or in education, just as much, and sometimes if not more so, than within the confines of the church. This was what the Protestant Reformers and their immediate successors had asserted, in contrast to the medieval tendency to restrict vocation to those called to priestly or monastic life, or to secular rule.

Bibliography

Faith and Order, *Baptism, Eucharist and Ministry*, Paper 111 (Geneva, 1982); D. Ford, *Self and Salvation: Being Transformed* (Cambridge, 1999); R. Williams, *On Christian Theology* (Oxford, 2000).

K. ELLIS

VOETIUS, GISBERTUS (1589–1676)

Gisbertus Voetius, a leading light of the Dutch Second Reformation, was born at Heusden, the Netherlands, to a prominent family of Westphalian descent and Reformed persuasion. He studied theology at the University of Leiden (1604–11), where he was influenced by Franciscus Gomarus, a staunch *Calvinist.

Voetius pastored at Vlijmen (1611–16) and at Heusden (1617–34). While at Heusden, he served as a delegate to the Synod of *Dort (1618–19), wrote influential scholastic works against *Arminianism, established himself as a writer of practical piety, assisted in the reformation at 's-Hertogenbosch, and developed the first comprehensive Protestant theology of *missions.

From 1634 to 1676, Voetius served at the Academy of Utrecht as professor of systematic theology, ethics and church polity. He also taught logic, metaphysics, and the Semitic languages Hebrew, Arabic and Syriac. For thirty-six years, he served as a preacher and pastor in addition to carrying a full teaching load.

Voetius's prolific writings include *Exercitia et Bibliotheca studiosi theologae* (1664; *The Exercises and Library of a Studious Theologian*), a comprehensive, 700-page introduction to theological literature and a four-year programme of theological study emphasizing that theology must be known and practised; *Selectarum disputationum theologicarum*, selections from theological debates; *Politicae Ecclesiasticae*, material on church polity that represents the ecclesiastical ideals of the Dutch Second Reformation; and *Te asketika sive Exercitia Pietatis* (1654; 'Ascetica' or the *Exercises of Godliness*), a detailed manual of piety in theory and practice.

As a polemical theologian, Voetius opposed the covenant theology of Johannes Cocceius, the rational philosophy of René *Descartes and the mystical subjectivism and separatism of Jean de Labadie.

Over time, a group of friends and students called the 'Utrecht circle' came to appreciate and support Voetius's convictions. By the time Voetius died on 1 November 1676, dedicated Voetians were in every university and ecclesiastical province of the Netherlands. Though he did not create a new theology, Voetius was a competent systematizer who influenced thousands. He was instrumental in training hundreds of ministers who followed him in striving to maintain harmonious union between orthodox doctrine and vital piety.

See also: REFORMED THEOLOGY.

Bibliography

Works: *Selectarum disputationum theologicarum*, 5 vols. (Amsterdam, 1648–69); *Politicae Ecclesiasticae*, 4 vols. (Amsterdam, 1663–76); *Reformed Dogmatics: Seventeenth-Century Reformed Theology Through the Writings of Wollebius, Voetius, and Turretin*, ed. and tr. J. W. Beardslee III (New York, 1965); *Spiritual Desertion*, with J. Hoornbeek, ed. M. E. Osterhaven, tr. J. Vriend and H. Boonstra (Grand Rapids, 2003).

Studies: J. R. Beeke, *Gisbertus Voetius: Toward a Reformed Marriage of Knowledge and Piety* (Grand Rapids, 1999); H. Hanko, 'Gijsbert Voetius: Defender of Orthodoxy', *The Standard Bearer* 72, 1996, pp. 229–232; T. A. McGahagan, 'Cartesianism in the Netherlands, 1639–1676: The New Science and the Calvinist Counter-Reformation' (PhD diss., University of Pennsylvania, 1976); J. van Oort, 'Augustine's Influence on the Preaching of Gisbertus Voetius', in *Collectanea Augustiniana*, vol. 2, ed. B. Bruning *et al.* (Louvain, 1990).

J. R. BEEKE

VOLTAIRE (FRANÇOIS-MARIE AROUET) (1694–1778)

The eighteenth century in Europe witnessed the release on a portentous scale of a blistering attack on traditional Christianity and its clerical representatives. Amongst the detractors none was more eloquent than Voltaire. A scintillating writer, able to represent with devastating skill much of his age's hostile discontent with the establishment, he conducted a passionate literary crusade in the cause of justice and humanity against the damaging superstitions and malpractices of the received faith. His authorship was prolific and wide-ranging in style and subject matter, and its unity can be variously described; but the religious question figures prominently in his productions. He early came under the influence of the English *deists, and this, together with continental sources, abetted the development of his own deism. Voltaire was not a systematic or profound philosopher or theologian, but he was effective enough to enjoy outstanding acclaim as a writer in his native France, and Europe generally, by the end of his turbulent life.

In Voltaire's writings, we meet the standard criticisms made in his day against Christianity's claims to be a revealed religion. The Bible was perceived to contain absurdities, contradictions, errors and immoralities and thus to be a shabby candidate for status as divine *revelation. Its depiction of God, especially in the OT, could be singularly unworthy of the supreme being. Yet Voltaire was neither *atheistic nor merely negative. His God was real, but freed from the tyrannous caprice of his usual representation; the atheistic *materialism of d'Holbach (1723–89) drew forth from Voltaire, late in his life, a defence of *theism. The appropriate substitute for revealed religion was natural religion, whereby the moral virtues of benevolence and fraternal love would resolve many of the social ills generated in Europe by erroneous belief.

However, Voltaire was no shallow optimist. In the wake of the Lisbon earthquake and in the course of the Seven Years War (1756–63), he grappled with the problem of suffering and earthly injustices. *Candide* (1759), his most widely known work, attacks (among other things) the philosophical optimism which holds this to be the best of all possible worlds. Less trenchant and less idealistic, perhaps, than his contemporary Jean-Jacques *Rousseau, Voltaire was not blinded by the promise of humanity to its perplexities. Ultimately only a vigorous struggle to change the world, not an essay in speculative *metaphysics, would achieve the desired ends.

Voltaire died, as he put it, 'worshipping God, not hating my enemies, loving my friends, detesting superstition'. This endeavour was undertaken resolutely outside the traditional framework. While debate about that framework continues, Voltaire's contribution will be neglected by many, but few who agree with him that 'never will twenty folio volumes produce a revolution; it is the portable little books of thirty sous which are to be feared' will underestimate it.

Bibliography

Works: *Complete Works*, ed. T. Besterman *et al.* (Geneva and Oxford, 1968 onwards).

Studies: T. Besterman, *Voltaire* (Oxford, 1976); N. Cronk (ed.), *The Cambridge Companion to Voltaire* (Cambridge, 2009); I. Davidson, *Voltaire: A Life* (London, 2010; rev. edn, 2012); H. Mason, *Voltaire* (London, 1975);

VOLUNTARISM

A theory or doctrine is voluntaristic when it gives explanatory emphasis to the *will at the expense, particularly, of the intellect or of moral character. For example, in discussions of the relation between morality and divine authority, certain writers (e.g. *Duns Scotus in the medieval period, and Samuel *Rutherford in the Puritan period), in an effort to do justice, as they see it, to divine sovereignty, have maintained that a principle is morally good or obligatory simply in virtue of the fact that God has willed it (and not because, say, it accords with God's moral nature). Thus Rutherford held that, had he so willed, God could have pardoned sin without an atonement. In criticism, it may be said that such a debate proceeds on too abstract and speculative (and perhaps too *anthropomorphic) a view of the divine nature. A voluntarist account of faith emphasizes the role of free will and of personal trust at the expense of the apprehension of and assent to truth, and is characteristic of *Arminianism but more especially of modern irrationalism.

Voluntarism is to be distinguished from voluntaryism, the idea that the Christian church is distinct from the state and that which church one joins and supports is a matter of personal choice.

Bibliography

Duns Scotus, *The Oxford Commentary on the Four Books of the Sentences*, II.xxxvii, tr. D. J. Walsh, in A. Hyman and J. J. Walsh (eds.), *Philosophy in the Middle Ages* (Indianapolis, 1973); J. Owen, *A Dissertation on Divine Justice* (1653), in *Works*, ed. W. H. Goold (1850–55; repr. London, 1965–68), vol. X; P. Quinn, *Divine Commands and Moral Requirements* (Oxford, 1978).

P. HELM

VOS, GEERHARDUS (1862–1947)

Born in the Netherlands, Vos was professor of biblical theology at Princeton Theological Seminary from 1893 to 1932.

Vos is important for his pioneering work in biblical theology, based on a conviction of the plenary inspiration and supreme authority of Scripture. He is among the first, and certainly the most gifted, in Protestant orthodox tradition to grasp the fundamental significance of the fact that God's special, redemptive revelation comes as an organically unfolding historical process, and to draw methodological (*hermeneutical) consequences from this fact. A controlling thrust of his life's work is that the Bible is not merely a collection of postulates about God, man, the world, etc., but that post-fall verbal *revelation is a function of redemption; revelation is invariably focused on, and patterned by, the ongoing history of God's redemptive acts which has its centre and consummation in Christ. An important effect of this stress on the historical, *covenantal character of biblical revelation has been to point the way toward maintaining a properly high view of *Scripture, without falling into the unduly intellectualistic understanding of Christian faith that has sometimes accompanied that view.

Bibliography

R. B. Gaffin, Jr (ed.), *Redemptive History and Biblical Interpretation: The Shorter Writings of Geerhardus Vos* (Philadelphia, 1980) – contains an account of Vos's life and complete bibliography.

R. B. GAFFIN, JR

WALDENSIANS

Waldensians (also called Waldenses or Vaudois) are adherents of a twelfth-century evangelical movement that began in the context of Catholicism, was rejected by successive popes, became schismatic and suffered severe persecution from church and state both before and after the Reformation. It survives to this day. Similar in style and inspiration to the *Franciscan movement a generation later, it was founded by Peter Waldo, a rich merchant of Lyons who in 1173 was moved by Christ's words in Matt. 19:21 to sell all he had and give to the poor. He caused the Vulgate NT to be translated into the vernacular, and from 1177 gathered round him men and women dedicated to obey and preach the gospel to the letter. Catholics said of them: 'They go about in twos, barefoot, in woollen clothes, owning nothing but holding all things in common like the apostles.'

Banned by Pope Lucius III in 1184 for unauthorized preaching, these 'Poor Men of Lyons' organized themselves into an alternative church that spread widely through Latin Christendom. Ministers (called *barbes*) were ordained as bishops, priests and deacons with vows of poverty, chastity and obedience. At first, they deviated little from Catholic orthodoxy, but later they forbade all swearing and military service, rejected *purgatory and indulgences (see *Merit), requiem masses and works performed by the living for the dead. Yet they kept the seven sacraments of Catholicism, celebrating the Eucharist once a year, practising auricular confession, doing penance and invoking Mary with certain saints. Women preached. Catholic repression was intense: in 1211 alone about eighty men and women disciples were burnt alive in Strasbourg.

In their biblicism, their evangelical lifestyle and their condemnation of the abuses and worldliness of medieval Catholicism, they were proto-Protestants, and at Chanforan in 1532 they made common cause with the Reformers, giving up the vestiges of Roman practice and adopting the Genevan doctrine of *predestination. Since then they have remained a *Protestant denomination, known in Italy as 'la Chiesa Evangelica Valdese'. After murderous opposition – such as the massacre of 1655 that provoked a sonnet by John Milton and intervention from Oliver Cromwell – they were granted religious freedom in 1848. Today they are a small community, located mostly in Italy and South America.

Bibliography

G. Audisio and C. Davison, *The Waldensian Dissent: Persecution and Survival, c.1170–c.1570* (Cambridge, 1999); E. Cameron, *The Reformation of the Heretics: The Waldenses of the Alps, 1480–1580* (Oxford, 1984); idem, *Waldenses: Rejections of Holy Church in Medieval Europe* (Oxford, 2000); M. D. Lambert, *Medieval Heresy: Popular Movements from Bogomil to Hus* (London, 1977); G. A. Left, *Heresy in the Later Middle Ages* (Manchester, 1967); *Storia dei Valdesi*: vol. 1, A. Molnar (1176–1532); vol. 2, A. A. Hugon (1532–1848); vol. 3, V. Vinay (1848–1978) (Turin, 1974–80); G. Tourn, *The Waldensians: The First 800 Years*, ET C. P. Merlino (Turin, 1980); idem, *You Are My Witness: The Waldensians Across 800 Years* (Torino, 1989).

P. M. J. McNair

WARFIELD, BENJAMIN BRECKINRIDGE (1851–1921)

Warfield was the last great theologian of the conservative Presbyterians at *Princeton Theological Seminary, New Jersey. His activity as a theologian coincided with the period when higher-critical views of *Scripture and evolutionary conceptions of religion were replacing evangelical convictions in most of America's major institutions of higher learning. Warfield distinguished himself as a scholarly defender of *Augustinian Calvinism, supernatural Christianity, and the inspiration of the Bible. Some of his views, especially on biblical inerrancy (see *Infallibility and inerrancy), continue to play an important role among evangelicals.

Warfield was born into a wealthy Virginia family and received his early education privately. He entered Princeton College in 1868, the year that James McCosh, last of the major proponents of the Scottish philosophy of *Common Sense, began his service as president. Warfield then studied at Princeton Seminary, where he came under the influence of the ageing Charles *Hodge. Warfield had pursued scientific interests avidly before deciding to train for the ministry, and he continued to be an eager amateur reader of scientific literature throughout his entire life. Perhaps for this reason, Warfield had less difficulty than many of his evangelical contemporaries in making peace with the scientific aspects of Charles Darwin's theory of evolution (see *Creation and evolution). He may also have been helped in this direction by the example of McCosh, who was both a forthright Calvinist and an unembarrassed theistic evolutionist. After graduating from seminary in 1876, Warfield married, travelled in Europe, served a brief pastorate in Baltimore, and was then called to teach NT at a Presbyterian seminary in Allegheny, Pennsylvania. In 1887 he succeeded Archibald Alexander Hodge (1823–86) as Professor of Didactic and Polemic Theology at Princeton.

Unlike several other Princeton theologians, Warfield was not an active churchman. His concerns were almost entirely intellectual and theological. His reserved personality, and perhaps the long years of care for his invalid wife, contributed to what his brother called 'a certain intellectual austerity, a loftiness and aloofness' (Ethelbert Warfield, 'Biographical Sketch', in *Works*, I, p. viii). Throughout his years at Princeton, Warfield wrote an incredible number of essays, reviews, pamphlets and monographs for both scholars and the laity. (He also regularly published hymns and poetry.) His scholarship was detailed and precise. He laboured to provide accurate summaries of his opponents, but could be astringent in pointing out their errors. Although he probably had the keenest intellect of any Old Princeton theologian, the nature of the times, especially with the growing diversification of academic life, gave his work a somewhat more fragmentary quality than that of his greatest predecessor, Charles Hodge. Warfield's primary contribution lay in three areas: the Bible, Calvinism and the nature of religious experience.

When higher-critical views of Scripture gained popularity in America, Warfield joined with other conservatives to define more exactly the divine inspiration and total truthfulness of Scripture. In 1881 he published with A. A. Hodge a famous essay on 'Inspiration' which set forth his position. Over the centuries, this piece argued, the Bible had received the most convincing demonstrations of its divine origin. The church's historic belief that the letter as well as the spirit of Scripture came from God was still a valid position. In this article, as in several other important essays, Warfield painstakingly investigated the Scriptures' testimony concerning themselves. His conclusion was that when the Bible spoke, God spoke. This 1881 essay placed somewhat greater emphasis on 'proofs' for Scripture than Charles Hodge had usually done, and it made more of the fact that the inspiration of Scripture (and its consequent freedom from error) applied, strictly considered, only to the original autographs of the text. But in general, Warfield was only restating in response to contemporary criticism the kind of confidence in Scripture that had once been commonplace in both Catholic and Protestant circles. In over 100 further writings on Scripture, Warfield drew attention repeatedly to the Bible's testimony about its own authority. He also asserted that terms like 'inerrancy' did not imply a mechanical process of inspiration. Warfield held rather that biblical inspiration involved a process of *concursus* whereby human actions and the working of the Holy Spirit coincided. This meant that historical study of the Bible was appropriate, just so long as such study did not presuppose an exclusively human origin for Scripture.

Warfield's convictions about the Bible had wide currency in his own day and have continued to be studied seriously in the present. Not so well known is his adherence to the theology of the *Reformation. When at the end of the century American Presbyterians debated whether to amend the *Westminster Confession (see *Reformed theology), Warfield responded with a series of careful studies on the meaning of that document. His own opinion never wavered: the Reformers of the sixteenth and seventeenth centuries had provided sound guidelines for the church. To tamper with these in favour of modern views of human betterment or divine immanence would be fatal. Warfield penned several careful monographs on the Confession, many penetrating studies of *Calvin's thought, and a number of academic treatises on figures in the early church (especially Augustine). All testified to his belief that the theological principles of these earlier periods were fully sufficient for the present. In 1904 he summed up the burden of these historical exercises: 'Calvinism is just religion in its purity. We have only, therefore, to conceive of religion in its purity, and that is Calvinism' (*Selected Shorter Writings*, I, p. 389).

Warfield's convictions on *religious experience were the product of his high view of Scripture and his fervent Calvinism. He saw two major opponents to orthodoxy in his day: the modernism which exalted the spirit of the age over Scripture and over confessional traditions, and the popular piety which treated Jesus as merely a motivational force and the Holy Spirit as a private possession for personal manipulation. Against the first tendency, Warfield tried to rebut efforts at grounding religion in evolutionary optimism or the *romantic sense of the self. Against the latter, he wrote tracts decrying the shallowness of modern *fundamentalism, and many works pricking the pretentions of '*perfectionism'. In all of these efforts, Warfield held to the objectivity of God's work. God had objectively given his word in Scripture. He had objectively given the church as the means to offer grace through preaching, prayer and the sacraments. Those who relied on inward subjectivity, whether of the right or the left, to find what God had offered objectively were deluding themselves as well as scorning the work of God.

Warfield ranks with his contemporaries, the Dutchmen Herman *Bavinck and Abraham *Kuyper, and the Scot James *Orr, as the greatest of modern conservative Calvinist theologians. His works are not popular with the theological community at large, nor are they taken too seriously by evangelicals, except where they refer to Scripture. Yet they remain a reservoir for those who, with Warfield, revere the work of God in Scripture and the history of the church and who value careful intellectual labour applied to an understanding of that work.

Bibliography

Works: *The Works of Benjamin B. Warfield*, 10 vols. (New York, 1927–32; repr. Grand Rapids, 1981); *Selected Shorter Writings of Benjamin B. Warfield*, ed. J. E. Meeter, 2 vols. (Philipsburg, 1970, 1973).
Studies: J. H. Gerstner, 'Warfield's Case for Biblical Inerrancy', in *God's Inerrant Word*, ed. J. Warwick Montgomery (Minneapolis, 1974); W. A. Hoffecker, 'Benjamin B. Warfield', in *Reformed Theology in America*, ed. D. F. Wells (Grand Rapids, 1985); J. E. Meeter and R. Nicole, *A Bibliography of Benjamin Breckinridge Warfield 1851–1921* (Nutley, 1974); T. F. Torrance, 'Review of Warfield's *Inspiration and Authority of the Bible*', *SJT* 7 (1954), pp. 104–108; F. Zaspel, *The Theology of B. B. Warfield* (Wheaton, 2010).

M. A. NOLL

WEALTH, see POVERTY AND WEALTH

WEBER, MAX (1864–1920)

A German sociologist, Max Weber, with Émile *Durkheim, is often called a founder of modern sociology. Bred in the German idealist milieu with its historical emphasis, he was particularly interested in social change and studied religion as a factor in such change. His most famous work in this context was *The Protestant Ethic and the Spirit of Capitalism* (1904–05; ET London, 1930), in which he argued that the this-worldly *asceticism of Calvinists (see *Reformed theology), which was a consequence of the doctrine of *predestination, was an important factor in the formation of capitalist societies. This study was explicitly directed against the economic determinism of *Marxist theory and initiated a debate which is not yet finished, particularly since the technological revolution has intensified interest in the Protestant work ethic.

Weber, however, was not consistent in his opposition to social determinism. In support of his thesis in *The Protestant Ethic*, he engaged in a series of studies of world religions which was left uncompleted when he died. The main contribution of his *Sociology of Religion* (1922) is considered to be the development of a system for classifying different types of religious leader in terms of their social significance (i.e. the type of person who would be attracted to a particular type of leader), and the sort of organization established by them. This last facet was developed by Weber's close friend, Ernst *Troeltsch.

Weber's influence is still very apparent in the *sociology of religion, which has persisted with his attempt to establish natural laws in the area of sociology while clinging to belief in human self-determination.

Bibliography

R. Bendix, *Max Weber* (London, 1960); S. Budd, *Sociologists and Religion* (London, 1973); J. Freund, *The Sociology of Max Weber* (London, 1968); P. Ghosh, *A Historian Reads Max Weber: Essays on the Protestant Ethic* (Wiesbaden, 2008); D. Käsler, *Max Weber: An Introduction to His Life and Work*, tr. P. Hurd (Chicago, 1988); J. Radkau, *Max Weber: A Biography* (London, 2009); R. Swedberg (ed.), *The Max Weber Dictionary* (Stanford, 2005); S. Turner (ed.), *The Cambridge Companion to Weber* (Cambridge, 2000).

D. A. HUGHES

WESLEY, CHARLES (1707–88)

Charles Wesley was co-founder of the Methodist movement and a great hymn writer. Son of the Anglican clergyman, Samuel Wesley, and the incomparable Susanna, educated at Westminster School in London and at Christ Church, Oxford, and ordained to the priesthood of the Church of England in 1735, he developed a passion for evangelical and sacramental renewal in the church.

Charles frequently led the way in many of the personal and institutional developments that revolved around the rising Evangelical Revival of the eighteenth century. He founded the so-called 'Holy Club' while a student at Oxford and experienced God's unconditional love in a 'religious experience' on 21 May 1738 that preceded the famous 'Aldersgate Experience' of his older brother *John, three days later. Charles's gift to the Revival and modern Christianity was the production of some 9,000 hymns and sacred poems through which the vast majority of people called Methodists learned theology. It is not too much to say that *Methodism was born in the song of this amazing hymn writer.

In the early years of the Revival, it was not uncommon for Wesley to preach in the open air to a spellbound crowd gathered by his rich voice singing one of his own hymns. The blossoming of his evangelical hymns began in 1739 with the advent of three successive editions of *Hymns and Sacred Poems*, jointly published with his brother John. But Charles also produced hymn collections on various themes, including the great festivals of the Christian year, the Trinity, families, times of trouble, and important theological topics such as 'God's everlasting love'. The 166 hymns in *Hymns on the Lord's Supper*, also a joint venture with John, demonstrated the centrality of the *Eucharist to their spirituality. Producing about 180 hymns per year until his death, Wesley's most important publication was the 1780 *A Collection of Hymns for the Use of the People Called Methodist*. For many years this hymn book provided the standard poetic explication of virtually every dimension of Methodist teaching. Charles's lyrical theology reflects the genius of a spirituality that united Anglican purity of intent with Puritan inward assurance, all within the larger context of the catholic Christian heritage and worked out in structures of accountable discipleship. His holistic vision of the Christian life linked warm-hearted piety and servant ministry among the poor. The concluding line of his famous hymn, 'Love Divine, All Loves Excelling', aptly describes his life and witness: 'lost in wonder, love, and praise.'

Bibliography

F. Baker, *Charles Wesley as Revealed by His Letters* (London, 1948); S T Kimbrough, Jr (ed.), *Charles Wesley: Poet and Theologian* (Nashville, 1992); K. Newport (ed.), *Charles Wesley: Life, Legacy, Literature* (Peterborough, 2007); J. E. Rattenbury, *The Evangelical Doctrines of Charles Wesley's Hymns* (London, 1941); idem, *The Eucharistic Hymns of John and Charles Wesley* (London, 1948); J. R. Tyson, *Charles Wesley* (Oxford, 1989).

P. W. CHILCOTE

WESLEY, JOHN (1703–91)

John Wesley was born in the rectory of Epworth, Lincolnshire, the fifteenth child of Samuel and Susannah Wesley. Together with his younger brother Charles (the hymnwriter), he gave leadership to the eighteenth-century Evangelical Revival and particularly to the Methodist movement.

Wesley was raised in a family with deep religious convictions. His grandfathers had distinguished themselves as *Puritan nonconformists. His father was educated in dissenting academies before deciding to return to the established church and attend Exeter College, Oxford. John's mother would have been an exceptional woman in any century.

John left home for school at Charterhouse in London when he was ten years old (1714), and went on to Christ Church, Oxford, in 1720 (BA, 1724; MA, 1727). He did not decide 'to make religion the business of his life' until 1725. This was his religious or moral conversion, and was no less real or important than his evangelical conversion thirteen years later. That same year he was ordained deacon, and the following year was elected fellow of Lincoln College. Through the influence of a 'religious friend' Wesley was guided to the writings of Thomas à Kempis (see *Imitation of Christ), Jeremy Taylor (1613–67) and later William Law. In the summer of 1727 he left Oxford to serve as his father's curate in Wroot, where he was ordained presbyter in 1728.

In 1729 he returned to Oxford at the request of Lincoln College and soon became spiritual leader of the small group of students his brother Charles had gathered. This band was called the 'Holy Club' by other students; later they were known as 'Methodists'. Together they studied the Greek NT, abridged numerous theological and devotional works, fasted twice a week, partook of the sacrament weekly and regularly visited those sick or imprisoned.

After their father's death in 1735, John and Charles left Oxford for Georgia. The two primary benefits of the brief mission came through contact with the German *Moravians and the new practice of giving special religious instruction to small groups of the most committed parishioners (men and women). Shortly after John's return to England in 1738 he met Peter Böhler, a Moravian minister who stressed the importance of *justification by faith alone, accompanied by an inner *assurance of salvation and victory over all known sin. Convinced by Böhler's arguments from Scripture, historic Christianity and the experience of several witnesses, Wesley began to seek and to preach justification by faith alone.

On 24 May 1738, at a small Moravian meeting in Aldersgate Street in London, Wesley felt his 'heart strangely warmed' while listening to the reading of Luther's preface to Romans. Modern scholars do not agree as to the exact nature of this evangelical experience, but history attests to the fact that nothing in Wesley was left untouched by it. The warmth of his evangelical experience was united with that of his brother Charles and another member of the Holy Club (George *Whitefield) to produce the flame of the Evangelical Revival and catch the attention of London, Bristol and the press.

The evangelical stress on a personal experience of salvation by faith alone was considered 'new doctrine' and unnecessary by most leaders of the Church of England (who maintained that a person was sufficiently saved by virtue of infant baptism). Established churches were soon closed to the Methodist preachers, forcing them into the open air. In April 1739 George Whitefield invited John to Bristol to organize the multitude of new converts among the Kingswood coal miners into small groups for Christian nurture and discipleship (one of Wesley's great talents).

The centre of Methodist theology was *love: the *love of God for all persons and the *grace of God available to all through faith in Jesus Christ alone for salvation.

This view of (prevenient) grace maintained that God reaches out to each person, offering a personal relationship and ensuring each one a valid opportunity to respond. Justification or saving faith was also a result of grace. *Conversion was understood as one experience with two inseparable parts: justification, in which the *righteousness of Christ was attributed (or imputed) to the believer; and the new birth or *regeneration, in which the Spirit began to produce (or impart) the righteousness of Christ. Sanctifying grace described the work of the Holy Spirit in the life of the believer between conversion and death. Wesley understood this activity to be both instantaneous and progressive. Because it is a work of grace received by faith alone, *sanctification could be instantaneous. Yet 'entire sanctification' was primarily understood as love for God and others. Therefore, sanctification was the infinite and dynamic love of God at work in a finite believer. In this sense, sanctification could never be a static state of 'absolute perfection' (which Wesley always denied), but rather must, in some sense, always be progressive (see *Perfection, perfectionism).

John Wesley's Methodism was more than just a theology. It was an understanding of the Christian life which stressed a joyful personal relationship with a loving Father. This relationship found expression through worship toward God and loving action toward others. Love for those who were lost meant 'offering them Christ' in *evangelism. Love for the poor meant social concern – homes for widows and orphans, free health clinics, help with food and clothing, schools and Sunday schools, etc. Love for the newly converted meant provision for discipleship – small nurture groups; opportunities to receive the sacrament of Communion when they were excluded from the parish church; books of hymns and sacred poems; Bible study notes; books of prayers; tracts; children's prayers, lessons and hymns; adult Christian literature (both theological and devotional); a monthly Christian magazine; in all over 400 different publications in his lifetime. Love for others in the Christian community meant honest attempts to put aside prejudice and focus on winning the lost (e.g. 'Letter to a Roman Catholic'), along with an *ecumenical willingness to appropriate genuine spiritual contributions from every tradition. Love for all nations caused Wesley to say 'the world is my parish'. His own evangelistic travels took him to Georgia, Germany, Wales, Ireland and Scotland. Wesley sent Methodist preachers to North America from 1769 onward, and, after the war with Britain, ordained them to continue their work on the frontier.

Wesley's personal efforts were formidable. During his fifty-two years as an itinerant, he averaged 4,000 miles annually, and preached more than 40,000 sermons in all. Yet the real genius of his work was in his ability to enlist, organize and develop the spiritual talents of others, both men and women. Through a growing structure of small groups, local leaders and travelling preachers, Wesley was able to maintain both the passion for evangelism and its fruit. He never lost sight of the need to nurture and disciple those newly won to Christ. In a real sense, John Wesley's Methodism was a revival of pastoral care and a product of *lay ministry (both male and female), as well as a response to evangelical theology and preaching. Through Wesley and Methodism, a viable Christian *spirituality was available to the masses of industrial labourers in eighteenth-century Britain.

See also: METHODISM.

Bibliography

Works: *Sermons*, ed. E. H. Sugden, 2 vols. (London, 1921); *Letters*, ed. J. Telford, 8 vols. (London, 1931); *Journal*, ed. N. Curnock, 8 vols. (London, 1938); *Works*, ed. T. Jackson, 14 vols. (Grand Rapids, 1975); *Works*, ed. F. Baker, A. C. Outler, R. P. Heitzenrater *et al.*, 18 vols. (Nashville, 1980–).

Studies: K. J. Collins, *The Theology of John Wesley* (Nashville, 2007); V. H. H. Green, *The Young Mr Wesley* (London, 1961); R. P. Heitzenrater, *The Elusive Mr Wesley*, 2 vols. (Nashville, 1984); H. Lindström, *John Wesley and Sanctification* (London, 1946); R. L. Maddox, *Responsible Grace: John Wesley's Practical Theology* (Nashville, 1994); R. L. Maddox and J. E. Vickers, *The Cambridge Companion to John Wesley* (Cambridge, 2010); T. C. Oden, *John Wesley's Teachings*, 3 vols. (Grand Rapids, 2012); A. C. Outler (ed.), *John Wesley* (New York, 1964); H. Rack, *Reasonable Enthusiast: John Wesley and the Rise of Methodism* (Philadelphia, 1989); M. Schmidt, *John Wesley: A Theological Biography*, 2 vols. in 3 (London and Nashville, 1962–73); R. G. Tuttle, *John Wesley: His Life and Theology* (Grand Rapids, 1978); L. Tyerman, *Life and Times of John Wesley*, 3 vols. (London, 1873); C. W. Williams, *John Wesley's Theology Today* (London, 1960).

T. R. ALBIN

WESLEYAN QUADRILATERAL

Albert C. Outler, a leading voice in the recovery of John *Wesley's stature as a serious theologian, coined this phrase to describe Wesley's theological method in an article written in 1972. He proposed that Wesley added a fourth factor, experience, to the Anglican triad of Scripture, tradition and reason enunciated by Richard *Hooker as the factors to be considered in constructing and justifying doctrine. Outler was not the first to recognize the four factors in Wesley's method, but his phrase brought the idea to prominence. It was widely accepted (particularly among American *Methodists) that this characterized Wesley's distinctive theological method, and certainly Wesley refers repeatedly to all of these, although never all four at one time.

Subsequently, however, there was considerable debate about what exactly is meant by 'tradition', 'reason' and 'experience' and how they relate to each other and to Scripture. John Cobb even argued that in the modern era, reason and experience had to be given the greater weight. William J. Abraham, who at first endorsed the quadrilateral as a fairly accurate analysis of Wesley's theological method, has now rejected it.

Randy L. Maddox presents a clearer formulation when he suggests that the quadrilateral 'could be more adequately described as a unilateral rule of Scripture within a trilateral hermeneutic of reason, tradition, and experience' (*Responsible Grace*, p. 46). Wesley undoubtedly followed the Reformation in holding to the authority of Scripture. For him, tradition, reason and experience were factors in the doctrinal interpretation of *Scripture, or could speak to corroborate the teaching of Scripture or determine questions that went beyond explicit scriptural teaching.

However inexact and fraught with questions these four terms may be (as Abraham argues), they are words used by Wesley. Their formulation as a so-called 'quadrilateral' should perhaps be seen as a first, helpful but (in the end) provisional and inadequate attempt to encapsulate Wesley's theological method. But it may also be questioned whether the consideration of these four factors is distinctive to Wesley.

Bibliography

W. J. Abraham, 'The Wesleyan Quadrilateral', in T. H. Runyon (ed.), *Wesleyan Theology Today: A Bicentenary Theological Consultation* (Nashville, 1985); *idem*, *Canon and Criterion in Christian Theology: From the Fathers to Feminism* (Oxford, 1998); R. Bauckham and B. Drewery (eds.), *Scripture, Tradition and Reason: A Study in the Criteria of Christian Doctrine* (Edinburgh, 1988); S. W. Gunter *et al.*, *Wesley and the Quadrilateral: Renewing the Conversation* (Nashville, 1997); S. J. Jones, *John Wesley's Conception and Use of Scripture* (Nashville, 1995); R. L. Maddox, *Responsible Grace: John Wesley's Practical Theology* (Nashville, 1994); A. C. Outler, 'The Wesleyan

Quadrilateral – in John Wesley', *Wesleyan Theological Journal* 20, 1985, pp. 7–18; D. A. Thorsen, *The Wesleyan Quadrilateral: Scripture, Tradition, Reason and Experience as a Model of Evangelical Theology* (Grand Rapids, 1990).

T. A. Noble

WESTCOTT, BROOKE FOSS (1825–1901)

Wescott was an English NT scholar and bishop, best known for his partnership at Cambridge (where he was Regius Professor of Divinity from 1870) with J. B. Lightfoot (1828–89) and F. J. A. Hort (1828–92) on an NT commentary based on a reliable Greek text. Although the project was not completed, Hort's introduction to the Westcott and Hort *New Testament in the Original Greek* (1881–2) remains a classic statement of the principles of textual criticism, and Westcott's commentaries on John (1880), the Johannine epistles (1883) and Hebrews (1889) are still valued for their spiritual insight and pioneering application of patristic exegesis, even if the text is sometimes over-translated. (Lightfoot produced his own equally famous commentaries on Galatians [1865], Philippians [1868] and Colossians with Philemon [1875], as well as critical editions of some of the *Apostolic Fathers – Clement of Rome, Ignatius and Polycarp.)

Less remembered now, but perhaps more significant at the time for the Church of England and the public's perception of her interests, was Westcott's concern for social issues. He was the first president of the Christian Social Union (founded 1889) and, like Lightfoot before him, was called from academic life to be Bishop of Durham (1890–1901). There he used his influence and administrative skills to mediate in the 1892 coal strike and developed an incarnational theology sharing much with the *Christian Socialism of F. D. Maurice in his sermons and addresses around the diocese.

Several of the Bishop Westcott Memorial Lectures deal with aspects of Westcott's thought.

Bibliography

S. Neill, *The Interpretation of the New Testament 1861–1961* (London, 1964); F. Olofsson, *Christus Redemptor et Consummator: A Study in the Theology of B. F. Westcott* (Uppsala, 1979).

P. N. Hillyer

WESTMINSTER CONFESSION AND STANDARDS

During the English Civil War between Charles I and Parliament, the Westminster Assembly was set up by Parliament to establish a 'covenanted uniformity' in theology and church government. It was to be 'an Assembly of learned, godly and judicious Divines', although it was not an ecclesiastical body but an advisory body for Parliament. The Westminster Assembly met from 1 July 1643 until 22 February 1648. It consisted of 121 ministers, plus ten from the House of Lords and twenty from the House of Commons, all of whom were full members of the Assembly. The Church of Scotland also sent representatives: four ministers and two elders. The chairman (the Prolocutor) was initially William Twisse, and after his death Charles Herle. The average attendance was around sixty to eighty at each session, although only about twenty played a significant part in the debates.

One of the earliest events in the life of the Assembly was the signing and approving of the Solemn League and Covenant. This was the document which committed the Scottish Parliament to support of the English Parliament in its struggle against Charles I. It also enshrined the principles of the National Covenant of 1638. The Assembly had begun by revising the *Thirty-Nine Articles, but on 12 October, shortly after signing and approving the Solemn League and Covenant, Parliament instructed the Assembly 'to consider among themselves of such a discipline and government as may be most agreeable to God's holy Word'. This took until almost the end of 1644 and resulted in two documents. The *Directory for the Publick Worship of God* was written in opposition to the liturgy then being used in the Church of England. It describes what should happen when the congregation gathers for worship, speaks about the public reading of Scripture, provides a sample prayer before the sermon, speaks about the preaching of the word and the prayer afterwards, then provides guidelines for the administration of the sacraments. It also gives instructions for the proper use of the Lord's day. Ministers are given help regarding the solemnization of marriage, the visitation of the sick, the burial of the dead, and guidelines for days of public fasting and of public thanksgiving. It concludes with some notes on the singing of psalms. The *Form of Presbyterial Church Government* contains instructions about the government of the church, not least regarding the duties of ministers, elders and deacons. It also deals with the various courts of the church, including presbyteries and assemblies. Finally, it explains the meaning of ordination and gives instructions for such ordinations.

The Assembly then turned their attention to preparing a confession of faith. The finished *Westminster Confession of Faith* (henceforth WCF) was presented to Parliament on 3 December 1646. They were required by Parliament to add notes and Scripture proofs, which they did, and the final version was presented to Parliament on 29 April 1647. The WCF consists of thirty-three chapters and represents a major codification of the developing *Reformed theology, which had its origins in the work of *Zwingli and *Calvin. Its chapters on the doctrine of God and the person and work of Christ place it firmly in the Nicaean and Chalcedonian tradition (see *Creeds). Its chapters on justification and sanctification follow the mainstream of the *Reformation. Its chapters on God's eternal decree, the fall of man, effectual calling and the perseverance of the saints reflect the Calvinistic tradition of the Reformation in which it is located, as do the chapters on the sacraments. Part of the significance of the WCF lies in the fact that it was the first confessional statement to fully expound federal theology (see *Covenant), following Archbishop Usher's *Irish Articles* which had already presented this theology in its 'seed form'. It also marks a significant change from earlier creeds and confessions in that the greater part of it is concerned with personal salvation and the *ordo salutis*.

When the WCF was finalized, it was shortly thereafter adopted and approved by the General Assembly of the Church of Scotland. In England it was of less permanent significance. The *Presbyterian Church was established in England on 13 October 1647, but Cromwell's army undermined this. Finally, in 1662, Charles II ejected the Presbyterian ministers, and that effectively spelled the end of Presbyterianism in England.

The Assembly then prepared the *Shorter Catechism*, presented on 5 November 1647, and the *Larger Catechism*, presented on 14 April 1648. These *catechisms provided a summary of the teaching of the WCF, especially for the education of the young.

Almost every Presbyterian church in the world either has (or used to have) the WCF as its principal subordinate standard of doctrine. It was also adopted by the original Synod in North America in 1729 and was later amended and revised in 1787.

See also: CONFESSIONS OF FAITH.

Bibliography

The Westminster Confession of Faith; W. Beveridge, *A Short History of the Westminster Assembly* (Greenville, 1993); S. W. Carruthers, *The Everyday Work of the Westminster Assembly* (Greenville, 1994); J. L. Duncan III (ed.), *The Westminster Confession into the 21st Century*, 2 vols. (Fearn, 2003, 2004); A. I. C. Heron, *The Westminster Confession in the Church Today* (Edinburgh, 1982).

A. T. B. McGOWAN

WHEATON DECLARATION

The Wheaton Declaration was issued by an ecumenical conference of evangelical missionaries who met at Wheaton College in Illinois on 9–16 April 1966. This 'Congress on the Church's Worldwide Mission', called by the Interdenominational Foreign Mission Association and the Evangelical Foreign Missions Association, attracted over 900 missionaries and national leaders, and was the largest evangelical gathering of the kind in North America to that date. The Congress's 'Declaration' called for greater cooperation and more research about evangelistic work. It also confessed that evangelicals had not applied biblical teaching to many of the great critical issues of the modern world, including *race relations, *family decay, war, social revolution and communism (see *Marxism and Christianity). On directly theological matters, it affirmed that the Bible, 'the only authoritative, inerrant Word of God', was the proper source of all missionary strategy. It denied that other *religions led truly to God (see *Christianity and other religions), while at the same time acknowledging that '*cultural accretions' sometimes compromised evangelical proclamation of the gospel. It reaffirmed the reality of eternal punishment (see *Eschatology) and repudiated the idea that all people would some day be redeemed (see *Universalism). And it warned about the danger of treating the Roman Catholic Church as a sister church. The Wheaton Congress helped pave the way for even larger international gatherings of evangelicals at Berlin (1966), *Lausanne (1974) and elsewhere.

Bibliography

H. Lindsell, 'Precedent-Setting in Missions Strategy', *CT*, 29 April 1966, p. 43; 'The Wheaton Declaration', *CT*, 13 May 1966, p. 48.

M. A. NOLL

WHITEFIELD, GEORGE (1714–70)

George Whitefield, the preacher and evangelist, was born at Gloucester, England. While an undergraduate at Oxford he was converted and experienced a call to the ministry of the Church of England. Following his ordination he preached his first sermon, which was said to have driven fifteen hearers mad. Tremendous congregations flooded the churches to hear him, but being denied the constant use of these buildings he resorted to the open air. Needing help, he influenced John (and Charles) *Wesley to undertake an outdoor ministry too. He preached twice and sometimes three times a day and proved able to make himself heard by crowds of 20,000; this was his manner of life from the age of twenty-two until he died at fifty-five.

Whitefield carried his message throughout most of the English-speaking world of that time. Important in this labour were his seven visits to America and fifteen to Scotland, together with his frequent ministry in Wales. He preached repeatedly in almost all the counties of England, founded two large churches in London and ministered regularly to the nobility at the home of Lady Huntingdon. At first he organized his followers into societies, and during his lifetime he was known as 'the leader and founder of *Methodism'.

Whitefield was drawn toward Calvinist theology (see *Reformed theology) even before his conversion and thereafter increased in his understanding of its doctrines. But John Wesley, in addressing a congregation of Whitefield's people, preached a severe sermon against *predestination. He published the sermon and Whitefield produced a reply. He wrote graciously, but Wesley was offended and broke off fellowship. Methodism was thereby divided into two branches, the Calvinistic (see *Calvinistic Methodism) and the *Arminian.

Whitefield sought to effect a reconciliation, but soon realized there was little hope of doing so as long as he remained at the head of his branch of the work. He determined to relinquish his leadership and allow Wesley to have first place. To the many who urged him to retain his prominence, he replied, 'Let the name of Whitefield perish, but Christ be glorified!' He became 'the servant of all', and throughout the rest of his life he helped any evangelical minister and especially assisted Wesley.

His ministry combined a clear declaration of the sovereignty of God with the free offer of salvation to all who would believe on Christ. A powerful urgency characterized his delivery; he often broke into copious tears as he pleaded with sinners. His major themes were the holiness of God and the sinfulness and helplessness of man, and justification through the *atonement of Christ. He was a man of holy life, and as Wesley suggested when preaching at his funeral, history records none 'who called so many myriads of sinners to repentance'.

Bibliography

Works: *The Works of the Rev. George Whitefield*, 6 vols. (London, 1771); *George Whitefield's Journals* (London, 1960); *George Whitefield's Letters* (Edinburgh, 1976).

Studies: A. Dallimore, *George Whitefield*, 2 vols. (Edinburgh and Westchester, 1970, 1980); F. Lambert, *'Pedlar in Divinity': George Whitefield and the Transatlantic Revivals, 1737–1770* (Princeton, 1994); H. S. Start, *The Divine Dramatist: George Whitefield and the Rise of Modern Evangelicalism* (Grand Rapids, 1991).

A. DALLIMORE

WHITEHEAD, A. N., see PROCESS THEOLOGY

WIESEL, ELIE (b. 1928)

Elie Wiesel is the most influential *Holocaust survivor in the world today. He was born in Sighet, North Transylvania (now part of Romania) on 30 September 1928. The Jews of Sighet were deported to Auschwitz-Birkenau in May 1944. Wiesel's mother and younger sister, Tzipora, were killed immediately on arrival. His father died in Buchenwald in January 1945 following a death march from Auschwitz. Wiesel was liberated on 11 April 1945. He later discovered his two elder sisters had also survived.

Wiesel decided against returning to Sighet. Initially he lived in France, then moved to the United States and became a naturalized American citizen in 1963. As the first chair of the United States Holocaust Memorial Council, Wiesel presided over the creation of an annual national commemoration of the Holocaust (the Days of Remembrance) in 1979, and the initial planning for the United States Holocaust Memorial Museum (which opened in 1993). His contributions to American public life were formally marked with the award of the Congressional Gold Medal (1985) and the Presidential Medal of Freedom (1992). International accolades include the Nobel Peace Prize (1986) and an honorary knighthood from the British government (2006).

Wiesel's work straddles different genres. Initially a journalist, he became a full-time writer in the mid 1960s and primarily writes in French. He has published novels, plays, a cantata, liturgies for Yom *hashoah* (Holocaust Remembrance Day, co-written with Albert Friedlander) and Passover, as well as numerous essays on biblical, Talmudic and Hasidic figures, recasting their stories in light of the Holocaust (e.g. portraying Isaac as the first survivor and Jeremiah as the first survivor-witness).

Wiesel insists he is not a theologian and maintains that there can be no theology either *about* or *after* Auschwitz. Nevertheless, he has profoundly influenced the development of Holocaust theology and contemporary *Jewish-Christian relations. Theologians cite Wiesel and his work, particularly *Night* (1958, ET 1960), as the authoritative testimonial voice on the subject of God and the deathcamps. Presented as an account of the impact of the Holocaust on his childhood faith, *Night* introduces the motif of the trial of God that dominates Wiesel's subsequent work. The text, and Wiesel's account of the public hanging of a young child (an account that can be read as a rewriting of the crucifixion) has inspired numerous Christian theologians (including Dorothee *Soelle, Jürgen *Moltmann and Paul Fiddes) to reflect on the theology of the cross and divine suffering (see *Impassibility of God and human suffering).

Bibliography

R. Franciosi (ed.), *Elie Wiesel: Interviews* (Jackson, 2002); C. Rittner (ed.), *Elie Wiesel: Between Memory and Hope* (New York, 1990); M. Sarot, 'Auschwitz, Morality and the Suffering of God', *Modern Theology* 7, 1991, pp. 135–152; E. Wiesel, *Night*, new tr. M. Wiesel (London, 2006).

I. WOLLASTON

WILL

It is a fundamental characteristic of human beings that they are capable of taking decisions about what they should do, and of carrying them out. According to Scripture such powers are an important part of the *imago Dei* ('image of God'). But what, more exactly, is the power to decide and how does it relate both to the divine will, and to the effects of *sin and divine *grace upon human nature?

Some have thought that the will is confined to the power to execute what the understanding believes that it is best, in all relevant circumstances, to do. The person expresses such preferences by appropriate mental acts, 'volitions', which bring about physical actions unless prevented by other circumstances (e.g. physical weakness or the compulsion of others). While some attribute to the will in this sense the power of acting against the understanding, what is sometimes called the power of contrary choice or the freedom of indifference, others have argued that such a theory is incoherent. *Augustine thought of the will in more dispositional terms, as the metaphysical and ethical directedness of human nature, as a set of preferences which, if not hindered by external factors, will express itself in actions of a certain character.

On either view there is a prima facie problem of reconciling the activity of the human will with the divine. Those who have attributed powers of contrary choice or self-determination to the human will have often attempted to effect such a reconciliation by limiting the scope of the divine decree in some respect, for example, by denying that God foreordains all human actions, while allowing that he foreknows them (see *Predestination). Others have rested content with maintaining that while God foreordains all human actions he is not the author of sin; either because, since sin is a deficiency,

God cannot be its author, or by holding that since to be free is to do what one wants to do, the occurrence of such wanting guarantees freedom and responsibility, whatever the exact nature and scope of the divine decree.

The question of the effects of sin upon human nature raises moral rather than metaphysical issues (see *Fall). No-one in the central Christian tradition has asserted that sin changes human nature into a nature of another kind. And yet if human beings are in bondage to sin, and cannot live in such a way as to please God by keeping his law, then divine grace is needed to renew them, and the question arises how divine renewal of such strength and depth can be efficacious if the human will is metaphysically free to resist and to reject it. So how the divine will in its savingly gracious operations harmonizes with the human will is a special case of the more general question of the relation between the human will and the divine will. Even if it is said that such divine grace constitutes a rescue, it is still nevertheless a rescue which does not violate the distinctive powers of human nature, but rather restores and redirects them. Such radical conclusions have been disputed by adopting less radical views of human need and of the divine provision.

Besides these metaphysical issues the effect of sin on the human will also raises ethical questions, particularly the question as to whether a person without grace is ethically free.

Discussion is sometimes confused because of a failure to distinguish the moral from the metaphysical dimension; at other times the biblical teaching on the bondage of the will to sin is resisted on the grounds that it is mistaken to make a distinction between the moral and the metaphysical. Rather, it is asserted that the power of contrary choice is the supreme moral value. But it is clear that according to Scripture redemption in principle secures the restoration of a particular ethical directedness lost at the fall. The *freedom that Christ brought is not so much an increase in the range of possible human powers, as a change in that range through release from the corrupting and enslaving power of sin.

In the history of Christian theology, *Augustinianism, both in its pre-Reformation and post-Reformation phases, has equally stressed the all-encompassing nature of the divine decree, and the bondage of the human will (*voluntas*) to sin, while still maintaining that God is not the author of sin, neither is violence done to the human will in gracious conversion. Those who, like Jonathan *Edwards, are in the Augustinian tradition, but who have adopted a non-Augustinian view of the will, have tried not altogether successfully to mitigate the consequences of this position for human responsibility by distinguishing between moral and natural ability and inability, arguing that while sin disables morally, it does not do so naturally.

One attempt to mediate between Augustinian and *Pelagian conceptions of the will has emphasized the idea of co-operation (sometimes called 'synergism') between the human and the divine will. But such a proposal is inherently unstable, being liable to lapse into a monergism of either the divine or the human will. It is not clear how, metaphysically, such a co-operation could be effected, nor is it easy to see how such a view could do justice to the biblical teaching already noted.

If, on the Augustinian view, the will is wholly dependent on the coming of enlivening grace, could it prepare itself for such a grace (see *Semi-Pelagianism)? Debate on 'preparationism' has been plagued by a lack of clarity over the central terms. Clearly, no consistent Augustinian could hold that a person might prepare himself to be renewed, for such preparation is encompassed in any renewal. But this is not to say that individuals may not, unknowingly, be prepared by grace for conversion, or that they ought to adopt a policy of total passivity when faced with the overtures of the gospel.

Bibliography

Augustine, *Enchiridion, Free Will, and Other Works*; D. and R. Basinger (eds.), *Predestination and Free Will: Four Views of Divine Sovereignty and Human Freedom* (Downers Grove, 1986); V. J. Bourke, *Will in Western Thought* (New York, 1964); J. Edwards, *The Freedom of the Will*, Works, vol. 1 (New Haven, 1957); J. Ellul, *The Ethics of Freedom* (London, 1976); A. Farrer, *The Freedom of the Will* (London, 1958); E. Gibson, *The Spirit of Medieval Philosophy* (London, 1936); E. Gilson, *The Christian Philosophy of St Augustine* (London, 1961); J. N. Lapsley (ed.), *The Concept of Willing* (Nashville, 1967); M. Luther, *The Bondage of the Will*, tr. J. I. Packer and O. R. Johnston (Cambridge, 1957); D. Müller, *NIDNTT* III, pp. 1015–1023.

P. HELM

WILLIAM OF OCKHAM
(1280/5–1349)

The English *scholastic theologian and philosopher William of Ockham joined the *Franciscan order and studied at Oxford. Following the usual programme in theology, he first lectured on the Bible and then on the Sentences of Peter *Lombard (probably 1317–19). Before he received his licence to teach, charges of heresy were brought against him by the chancellor of his university. Ockham was called to the papal court at Avignon in 1324 to defend himself. Articles of censure were drawn up, but the inquiry was never completed. While at Avignon, Ockham was drawn into his order's dispute with the pope concerning evangelical poverty. In 1328 he fled to Pisa where Emperor Lewis of Bavaria, an opponent of the pope, was residing. Excommunicated after leaving Avignon, Ockham stayed at the imperial court for the rest of his life. He died in Munich, probably of the Black Death.

Ockham's flight from Avignon divides his career: before, he was an academic, writing theological and philosophical works; after, he became a polemicist, defending his order and the emperor and condemning the pope for heresy and abuse of spiritual power.

The *Commentary on the Sentences* presents the most complete account of Ockham's thought, but he revised and edited only the first book (the *Ordinatio*). The other three books are available only in an unrevised 'report' (*Reportationes*). Also important is the *Summa Logicae*, since it is a more mature expression of his logic.

Ockham is the most important figure in the development of the 'modern way', the *nominalist or terminist movement, as opposed to the moderate realism of the 'ancient way' represented by such theologians as *Bonaventura, *Thomas Aquinas and *Duns Scotus. While some interpreters have held that Ockham was a destroyer who upset the careful balance between *faith and reason worked out by the earlier schoolmen, other interpreters have seen authentic Christian concern as the source of his position.

The root of his thought is an awareness that everything depends on *God as creator and conserver for both its existence and its place in creation. The logical implications of this dependence are worked out in his teaching that God has the power to conserve, destroy, create separately or differently everything found in experience or held on faith. This does not mean that Ockham distrusts the reliability of nature or God; rather, he accepts the regularities of nature and the constancy of moral norms, but shows the limitations of natural certainty in the light of God's omnipotence. This opposition to all necessity in creation is a Christian response to a natural *determinism that had become prominent in the arts faculty in Paris around 1270. So for Ockham, God is omnipotent and free, able to do everything that does not involve a logical contradiction, and the world is totally *contingent. True statements about finite things are contingent truths dependent on the divine will.

For Ockham, only individuals exist. The immediate awareness of individuals, intuitive knowledge, is the basis of knowledge of individuals. The objects of intuitive knowledge are not limited to material things, for there is intuitive knowledge of acts of desiring and will. Both sense-perception and introspection are sources of natural knowledge of reality. Through generalization other individuals of the same nature can be known, and this is the basis of the knowledge found in universal propositions.

Ockham insists that only propositions in the mode of possibility can be necessary. Hence it is not possible to infer the existence of what is not known, including the existence of God, from what is known. Where prior schoolmen had analysed diverse aspects of being, Ockham replaced such *metaphysical analyses with a logical analysis of the use of terms, their significative or non-significative role in propositions, and connections in arguments. Ockham does not deny the principle of causality or reduce it to the idea of regular sequence, but says we can discover the cause of an event only through experience. In general, Ockham rejects most of the metaphysical teachings of the earlier schoolmen.

In his political tracts, Ockham was mainly concerned with curbing the abuses that stemmed from the pope's claim to absolute power (*plenitudo potestatis*). He did not seek to subordinate either ecclesiastical or temporal power to the other, but wanted freedom from total ecclesiastical power. He sought to achieve this by restricting each power to its own sphere. True spiritual power is displayed in Christ, who renounced all possessions and attempts to make him a temporal king and lived on alms and exercised only a spiritual mission. Ockham made non-involvement in temporal matters the criterion of legitimate spiritual power; the pope errs when he claims temporal power where Christ refused to exercise such authority. Neither the pope, nor civil rulers, nor the clergy alone, but wise men who sincerely love justice and are guided by the gospel are competent to judge what is legitimate for the church.

See also: SCHOLASTICISM.

Bibliography

Works: *Predestination, God's Foreknowledge and Future Contingents*, tr. M. McCord Adams and N. Kretzmann (East Norwalk, 1969); *Ockham's Theory of Terms: Part I of the Summa Logicae*, tr. M. J. Loux (Notre Dame, 1974); *Ockham's Theory of Propositions: Part II of the Summa Logicae*, tr. A. J. Freddoso and H. Schuurman (Notre Dame, 1980); *Philosophical Writings*, ed. and tr. P. Boethner and S. F. Brown (Nashville, ²1989); *Quodlibetal Questions*, 2 vols., tr. A. J. Freddoso and F. G. Kelley (New Haven and London, 1991).

Studies: Standard histories of medieval philosophy contain an introductory account of Ockham's work. See also: M. McCord Adams, *William of Ockham*, 2 vols. (Notre Dame, 1987); J. P. Beckmann, *Ockham: Bibliographie, 1900–1990* (Hamburg, 1992); G. Left, *William of Ockham* (Manchester, 1975); A. S. McGrade, *The Political Thought of William of Ockham* (Cambridge, 1974); E. A. Moody, 'William of Ockham', in *EP* 8, pp. 306–317.

A. Vos

WILLIAMS, CHARLES WALTER STANSBY (1886–1945)

Charles Williams, the English novelist, poet, critic and lay theologian, grew up in St Albans and was educated at St Albans Grammar School, University College, London, and the Working Men's College, London. He worked as a proofreader and editor at the Oxford University Press from 1908 until his death. He produced seven novels, ten volumes of his own poetry (besides editing many others), six biographies, many verse plays (most of which were privately printed), four volumes of literary criticism, several volumes of theology (which are difficult to number, since some, e.g. *Religion and Love in Dante*, London, 1941, and *The Figure of Beatrice*, London, 1943, are as much literary criticism as theology), and one brief and idiosyncratic history of the church, *The Descent of the Dove* (London, 1939).

Williams is best remembered for his novels (e.g. *Descent into Hell*, London, 1937, and *All Hallows' Eve*, London, 1945), and his cycle of Arthurian poems, published in two volumes, *Taliessin Through Logres* (Oxford, 1938), and *The Region of the Summer Stars* (Oxford, 1944). In his fiction and poetry as well as in his essays, Williams expounds his 'theology of romantic love', the key idea deriving from Dante's vision of Beatrice as an image of beauty that beckoned him on to God, the perfection of all beauty. Williams stresses the notions of 'exchange', 'substitution' and 'coinherence', as summing up the law of 'the City' [of God]. An early interest in Rosicrucianism, and brief membership in the Order of the Golden Dawn, do not appear to have compromised his lifelong Anglican orthodoxy.

Bibliography

G. Cavaliero, *Charles Williams: Poet of Theology* (Grand Rapids, 1983); L. Glenn, *Charles W. S. Williams: A Checklist* (Kent, 1975); A. M. Hadfield, *Charles Williams: An Exploration of His Life and Work* (Oxford, 1983); T. Howard, *The Novels of Charles Williams* (Oxford, 1983); C. A. Huttar and P. J. Schakel (eds.), *The Rhetoric of Vision: Essays on Charles Williams* (London, 1996).

T. HOWARD

WILLIAMS, ROGER (c. 1603–83)

Roger Williams, a *Puritan dissenter, founded Rhode Island colony, a template for the separation of church and *state. Born in England, he attended Charterhouse and Cambridge, taking a degree in 1627. He migrated to Massachusetts in 1631, taught in Plymouth, and was pastor at Salem. He urged colonists to break from government-supported religion. True worship, he said, is never coerced, and civil officials should not enforce the first four commandments. Banished from Massachusetts in October 1635, he went into the wilderness and lived with Indians to avoid deportation to England. The Providence settlement was established on land purchased in 1636 from the Indians. A social covenant, worked out in 1638, governed only civic life. Religious dissenters flocked there, and

Williams secured the Rhode Island colony's charter in 1644. His foremost writings were *The Bloudy Tenent of Persecution* (1644), which advocated that none be persecuted for conscience's sake, and *The Bloody Tenent Yet More Bloody* (1652). He regarded ancient Israel's relationship with God as unique and a model for the church but not other nations. He rejected Episcopal, Presbyterian and Congregational systems, and in 1639 joined America's first Baptist congregation. Soon disappointed, he withdrew, claiming thereafter to be a 'Seeker' who awaited the reappearance of apostolic Christianity.

Bibliography

E. Gaustad, *Liberty of Conscience: Roger Williams in America* (Grand Rapids, 1991); W. C. Gilpin, *The Millenarian Piety of Roger Williams* (Chicago, 1979); P. Miller, *Roger Williams: His Contributions to the American Tradition* (Indianapolis, 1951).

S. INGERSOL

WILLIAMS, ROWAN (b. 1950)

The Most Reverend and Right Honourable Rowan Douglas Williams was the 104th Archbishop of Canterbury, as well as a noted theologian and poet. He was born in Swansea, Wales, on 14 June 1950 to a Welsh-speaking family. He was educated at Dynevor School, Swansea, and later attended Christ's College, Cambridge, reading theology. He received a DPhil from Wadham College, Oxford, in 1975, writing about twentieth-century Russian Orthodox theologian Vladimir *Lossky. He held a number of academic posts at Mirfield Theological College, the University of Cambridge, and Oxford University until in 1991 he was consecrated Bishop of Monmouth, then in 1999 Archbishop of Wales. In 2002 he was announced as the successor to George Carey as Archbishop of Canterbury. Williams stood down as Archbishop of Canterbury in 2012 in order to take up the position of Master of Magdalene College at Cambridge University.

Rowan Williams' theological publications are extensive, including historical works such as *Arius: Heresy and Tradition* and *Teresa of Avila* and theological works such as *On Christian Theology* and *The Wound of Knowledge*, which is a history of Christian *spirituality. He has also published socio-critical essays, works of poetry, reflections on icons and collections of sermons. His writing and sermons demonstrate an appreciation of the rich diversity of the Christian tradition. He eschews simple oppositions, arguing that the complexities and ambiguities to be found in fiction, drama and poetry are often more accurate accounts of cultural realities. Williams also has a highly nuanced approach to theological writing, reflecting a wide range of influences. These include his study of the early Church Fathers, Russian Orthodox theologians such as Sergei *Bulgakov and philosophers such as Gillian Rose (1947–95).

These diverse influences inform his belief that theology takes on celebratory, communicative and critical forms. None of these modes is dominant and must be continually considered in the light of Scripture, Christian tradition and experience. When Christians disagree, he advocates the practice of Christians reading the Bible together. Doctrinal themes, including creation, the incarnation and the Trinity, play an important role in his interpretation of ethical, political and social issues. Nevertheless, for Williams Christian orthodoxy is less a doctrine than a method of continually evaluating what we know of Jesus from the Christian life he initiated, and what in turn we learn of living a Christian life through the models put forth in Scripture. This way of thinking influences his approach to many ethical debates, including, most controversially, sexual ethics. In this context there is a tension between the thinking of Williams the theologian and Williams the church leader, which can be seen clearly by comparing his scholarly writing and his leadership as archbishop. For Williams, all human activity ought to be viewed in the light of the self-giving love of the Trinity, which models both giving and receiving.

Bibliography

Selected Works: *The Wound of Knowledge: Christian Spirituality from the New Testament to St. John of the Cross* (London, 1979); *Resurrection: Interpreting the Easter Gospel* (London, 1982); *The Truce of God* (London, 1983); *Arius: Heresy and Tradition* (London, 1987); *Teresa of Avila* (London, 1991); *Open to Judgement: Sermons and Addresses* (London, 1994); *Christ on Trial: How the Gospel Unsettles Our Judgement* (London, 2000); *Lost Icons: Reflection on Cultural Bereavement* (Edinburgh, 2000); *On Christian Theology* (Oxford, 2000); *Ponder These Things: Praying with Icons of the Virgin* (Norwich, 2002); *Writing in the Dust: Reflections on 11th September and Its Aftermath* (London, 2002); *Poems of Rowan Williams* (Newent, 2002).

Studies: M. Higton, *Difficult Gospel: The Theology of Rowan Williams* (London, 2004); T. Hobson, *Anarchy, Church and Utopia: Rowan Williams on Church* (London, 2005); R. Shortt, *Rowan Williams: An Introduction* (London, 2003).

J. P. MITCHELL

WINGREN, GUSTAF (1910–2000)

Gustaf Wingren succeeded Anders *Nygren as Professor of Systematic Theology (1951–77) at Lund in Sweden, and his work was in close dialogue both with that of his predecessor and, through him, with that of *Aulén. Of the three major Swedish theologians of the twentieth century, Wingren is the least well known, probably because his work is less richly dramatic and more cautious and corrective than that of Nygren and Aulén.

His published work is especially notable for its attempt to hold together the doctrines of *creation and redemption in a way which Protestant theology has traditionally found very difficult. His affirmation of creation and the moral law as starting points for Christian theology is intended to serve as a corrective to both Nygren's exclusive concentration on the descent-motif of *agape* and *Barth's Christocentrism and hostility to all talk of a relatively independent order of creation. In this way, he was enabled to give fuller weight to human reality outside the gospel. In *Christology, Wingren drew heavily on Nygren and *Irenaeus, but placed especial emphasis on the humanity of Jesus, the agent of salvation, once again underlining the significance of human action.

Bibliography

Works: *The Christian's Calling* (Edinburgh, 1958); *Theology in Conflict* (Edinburgh, 1958); *Man and Incarnation* (Edinburgh, 1959); *Creation and Law* (Edinburgh, 1961); *Gospel and Church* (Edinburgh, 1964).

Studies: B. Erling, 'Swedish Theology from Nygren to Wingren', *Religion in Life* 30, 1960–61, pp. 206–208; S. P. Schilling, *Contemporary Continental Theologians* (London, 1966).

J. B. WEBSTER

WISDOM IN EARLY CHRISTOLOGY

The concept of wisdom (*sophia*) in early Christian texts is a matter of current debate among scholars. The extent to which the few NT references to Christ in terms of wisdom echo OT and intertestamental references to wisdom is disputed, but the parallels should probably not be pressed too far. A number of texts in Jewish Wisdom literature appear to 'personify' the concept of wisdom; the nature and implications of this literary device have recently been re-evaluated.

The female personification of *Sophia* has been seen as an accident of gender in Hebrew and Greek grammar. However, in recent years some have sought to recover this feminine aspect of God, identifying a transformation in early Christian thinking from female *Sophia* to male Word (*Logos). The prologue to John's Gospel is seen as a strong example of this transformation, but the origin of the shift is debated by modern scholars. It has been noted that early Syriac Christianity found it easier to accommodate wisdom than Greek and Latin Christianity because the Semitic word for spirit is feminine, making it possible to identify the *Holy Spirit with *Sophia* and the mother of Christ. However, generally wisdom does not appear to have been regarded as a 'divine being' separate in some sense from Yahweh himself (cf. the personification of the 'name', 'glory', 'power' or 'arm' of the Lord), and the Christian doctrine of the pre-existence of Christ as the Son of God is not merely an adaptation of a supposed Jewish hypostatization of divine wisdom. The association of wisdom with Christ implied in certain NT passages emphasizes the link between creation and redemption.

In patristic *Christology the concept of wisdom, and in particular the wisdom passage in Prov. 8:22–31, becomes more prominent than in the NT. Although it is not typical of the Fathers in general, some writers identify wisdom with the Holy Spirit; for example, *Irenaeus, who understands wisdom to be pre-existent and collaborative in creation and salvation with the Word (*Against Heresies* 4.20.1–4). Theophilus of Antioch follows Irenaeus and, as the first to describe the Godhead as the Trinity, identifies the three persons as God, Word and Wisdom (*To Autolycus* 1.7; 2.15, 18). *Justin Martyr (*Dialogue with Trypho* 61, 129) quotes Prov. 8 as part of his argument that the Word (who is the divine Wisdom) is distinct yet inseparable from God. Athenagoras (*Embassy* 10) and *Tertullian (*Against Hermogenes* 18; 20; *Against Praxeas* 6–7) quote from Prov. 8 as part of a 'two-stage' history of the Logos: there is the Word immanent in the mind of God from all eternity and there is the Word expressed or sent forth for the purposes of creation.

*Origen (*On First Principles* 1.2.1–2) understands that wisdom in Prov. 8 refers to Christ, and by the time of the Arian controversy the idea that the OT wisdom passages spoke directly of Christ was so well established that Prov. 8:22–31, which in the LXX speaks of wisdom as 'created', 'established', 'made' and 'begotten', became a major storm centre. *Arius used this passage as one of his chief proof-texts and, in opposing his theology, *Athanasius provides the longest patristic commentary on Prov. 8.22 (*Against the Arians* 2.18–61, 72–82), asserting Christ's full divinity and identifying him as both the Word and the Wisdom of the Father (*Against the Arians* 1.16), as does *Augustine later (*On the Trinity* 2.14). After the Council of *Ephesus there was a tendency to link attributes of wisdom to *Mary as *Theotokos*, and aspects of the female symbolism for God were, in some traditions, channelled into the veneration of Mary.

Bibliography

J. D. G. Dunn, *Christology in the Making* (London, 1989); C. H. T. Fletcher-Louis, 'Wisdom Christology and the Parting of the Ways between Judaism and Christianity', in S. E. Porter and B. W. R. Pearson (eds.), *Christian-Jewish Relations through the Centuries*, JSNTS 192 (Sheffield, 2000); M. Hengel, *Studies in Early Christology* (London, 1998); G. M. Jantzen, *Power, Gender and Christian Mysticism* (Cambridge, 1995); B. Newman, 'The Transformations of Sophia', *Vox Benedictina* 11, 1994, pp. 33–57; T. E. Pollard, *Johannine Christology and the Early Church* (Cambridge, 1970); R. R. Ruether, *Goddesses and the Divine Feminine* (Los Angeles, 2005).

A. D. RICH

WISLØFF, CARL FREDRIK (1908–2004)

Born in Drammen, Norway, Wisløff graduated from the Free Faculty of Theology, Oslo, in 1931. In 1958 he defended his PhD thesis *Nattverd og Messe* at the University of Oslo (ET, *The Gift of Communion: Luther's Controversy with Rome on Eucharistic Sacrifice*, Minneapolis, 1964). Ordained in 1932, he became rector of the Practical Theology Department of the Free Faculty of Theology in 1940, and Professor of Church History in 1961.

Wisløff was one of the most outstanding representatives of evangelical Christianity in Scandinavia. A convinced *Lutheran, he also co-operated with evangelicals from different denominations, for instance in his collaboration on a new translation of the Bible into Norwegian. Wisløff's vigorous defence of the inspiration and authority of all *Scripture was a source of tension between him and colleagues. *Justification by *faith is one of the main themes in his theology.

Wisløff's paper on the *World Council of Churches (1952) gave Norwegian Christians guidelines for a critical attitude to the theological relativism advocated by the WCC. (The Norwegian Missionary Council withdrew from the International Missionary Council at the merger of the IMC and WCC in 1961.) Wisløff also strongly emphasized the *priesthood of all believers and urged freedom for Christian organizations and societies within the Church of Norway.

Wisløff was for many years a leading figure in the Norwegian Evangelical Student Movement and the International Fellowship of Evangelical Students. He was the author of more than thirty books, the best known being *Jeg vet på hvem jeg tror* (ET, *I Know in Whom I Believe*, Minneapolis, 1946), a *dogmatics translated into more than thirteen languages.

N. YRI

WITHERSPOON, JOHN (1723–94)

Witherspoon was a founder of American *Presbyterianism. Born in Gifford, Scotland, a minister's son, he received his MA and theology degrees from Edinburgh University. He was the pastor to several Church of Scotland congregations, including Paisley, for twenty-five years and became renowned through his writings. In 1768 he crossed the Atlantic to become the sixth president of the College of New Jersey (now Princeton University). The college prospered under his leadership, and he instilled in the curriculum and among American Presbyterians generally a respect for Scottish *common-sense philosophy. That philosophy's affinity for science and reasonable approach toward Christianity reoriented *Princeton theology from the pietistic theology of one of his predecessors, Jonathan *Edwards. Witherspoon tutored many students who became active in revolutionary politics, including James Madison, a key architect of the American Constitution and the United States' fourth president. Witherspoon served in the Continental Congress 1776–82 and was the only clergyman to sign the Declaration of Independence. The college suffered greatly during the war, and he spent the post-war years rebuilding it. In 1789, he moderated the opening sessions of the Presbyterian Church's First General Assembly, held in Philadelphia, and influenced the denomination's stances on doctrine, polity and worship.

Bibliography

'John Witherspoon', *Dictionary of American Biography*, vol. 20 (New York, 1943), pp. 435–438; J. J. A. Mackay, 'Witherspoon of Paisley and Princeton', *Theology Today* January 1962, pp. 473–481; M. Noll, 'John Witherspoon', in M. G. Toulouse and J. O. Duke (eds.), *Makers of Christian Theology in America* (Nashville, 1997), pp. 82–84; M. L. L. Stohlman, *John Witherspoon: Parson, Politician, Patriot* (Louisville and Westminster, 1976).

S. INGERSOL

WITTGENSTEIN, LUDWIG JOSEF JOHANN (1889–1951)

Wittgenstein explored two distinct philosophical approaches to the problem of language, meaning and logical necessity. His importance as a creative thinker extends not only to philosophy, but also less directly to theology, *hermeneutics and questions of method in the social sciences. He was deeply influenced by the intellectual and cultural climate of Vienna, where he was born, but in 1908 he moved to England to study engineering, and after 1930 taught philosophy at Cambridge for much of his remaining life. His passionate concern to understand the foundations on which any subsequent problem rested drove him from engineering to mathematics, from mathematics to logic, and from logic to the philosophy of logic, which he studied at Cambridge under Bertrand Russell (1872–1970). His earlier thought (roughly 1913–29) is dominated by the problem of logical necessity, the limits of language, and the nature of propositions. In his later thought (especially after 1933) he finds the foundation of language not in abstract logic but in the ongoing stream of human life in its varied forms.

Wittgenstein's earlier thought is available in his *Notebooks* and in the brief but rigorous *Tractatus Logico-Philosophicus*. This work begins by distinguishing things (or logical objects) from facts (or determinate states of affairs). A name may refer to a thing; but a proposition depicts a state of affairs. The combination of logical elements within an elementary proposition corresponds structurally with the combination of things which constitute facts, or states of affairs. Wittgenstein alludes to the proceedings of a Paris lawcourt, in which dolls and other models were set up in various formations to depict alleged states of affairs relating to a car accident. He comments, 'In the proposition a world is, as it were, put together experimentally' (*Notebooks*, p. 7). 'A proposition is a model of reality as we imagine it' (*Tractatus*, 4.01). 'A thought is a proposition with a sense' (4). Hence, if we could combine all fact-stating propositions within a single logical system, we could comprehensively describe the whole world, articulate all determinate thoughts and thus reach the very limits of language. His last proposition in the *Tractatus* reads: 'What we cannot speak about, we must pass over in silence' (7). Unlike Russell and A. J. Ayer (1910–89), Wittgenstein did not make this part of a positivist doctrine. Indeed, what could not be 'said' might still be profoundly important.

From 1929 onwards, however, Wittgenstein became increasingly aware that 'the crystalline purity' of the fact-stating language of the logician's classroom was 'a *preconceived* idea'; one which can only be removed 'by turning our whole examination round' (*Philosophical Investigations*, section 108). As a logician he had said, 'There *must* be . . .' But if we actually '*look* and *see*' (66), there comes before our eyes a wide *variety* of uses of language, each of which serves a concrete and particular situation. 'The speaking of language is part of an activity, or of a form of life' (23). Wittgenstein employed the term 'language-game' to draw attention to several points: that often (though not always) meaning depends on use; that meaning arises from the wholeness of language and 'the actions into which it is woven' (7); and that concepts change when there are changes in the situation in life which gives them their particular grammar. The richness and fruitfulness of this later angle of approach can be seen only when we follow Wittgenstein in attending to the concrete instances which he investigates. These are all language-uses which have significance for philosophy, but many also arise in theology and hermeneutics: understanding, meaning, intending, believing, thinking, fearing, expecting, loving and many more. The 'grammar' of *believing*, for example, cannot be separated from the speaker's own stance in life. Thus: 'If there were a verb meaning "to believe falsely", it would not have any significant first person present indicative.' Wittgenstein develops this approach further by examining the importance of shared practices and shared language-using behaviours. This has far-reaching consequences for the technical notion of 'private' language. Wittgenstein laid the foundation for work on language which we now take for granted, such as speech-act theory, and also re-enforced the importance of questions about community, context, and tradition, in hermeneutics and the social sciences.

See also: LOGICAL POSITIVISM; RELIGIOUS LANGUAGE.

Bibliography

Works: *Remarks on the Foundations of Mathematics* (Oxford, 1956); *Tractatus Logico-Philosophicus* (London, 1961); *Lectures and Conversations on Aesthetics, Psychology, and Religious Belief* (Oxford, 1966); *Philosophical Investigations* (Oxford, ³1967); *Zettel* (Oxford, 1967); *On Certainty* (Oxford, 1969).

Studies: A. C. Grayling, *Wittgenstein: A Very Short Introduction* (Oxford, 2001); A. Janik and S. Toulmin, *Wittgenstein's Vienna* (London, 1973); A. Kenny, *Wittgenstein* (London, 1975); N. Malcolm, *Ludwig Wittgenstein: A Memoir* (Oxford, 1958); R. Monk, *How to Read Wittgenstein* (Norton, MA, 2005); H. Morick (ed.), *Wittgenstein and the Problem of Other Minds* (New York, 1967); D. Pears, *Wittgenstein* (London, 1971); G. Pitcher, *The Philosophy of Wittgenstein* (Englewood Cliffs, 1964); R. Rhees, *Discussion of Wittgenstein* (London, 1970); Royal Institute of Philosophy Lecture VII: *Understanding Wittgenstein* (London, 1974); A. C. Thiselton, *The Two Horizons* (Exeter, 1980).

A. C. THISELTON

WOLLEBIUS, JOHANNES (1586–1629)

In 1611 Johannes Wollebius succeeded J. J. Grynaeus (1540–1617) as the cathedral preacher in Basle. In 1618 he succeeded Sebastian Beck (1583–1654) as professor of OT and he died of the plague at age forty-three. Wollebius' most famous work was his *Compendium of Christian Theology* (1626). Written in Latin, it became the theological textbook in Basle and elsewhere and was republished in English and Dutch, in several editions. The critical Latin edition appeared in 1935 and the modern critical English edition appeared in 1965.

The *Compendium* is a remarkable example of lucid brevity and a fair witness to *Dort-era *Reformed theology. Contrary to the caricature of Reformed orthodoxy drawn in earlier scholarship, the *Compendium* is trinitarian, *Protestant and federal (see *Covenant) in soteriology; its hermeneutic is Christ-centred. Employing, for example, Franciscus Junius' distinction between archetypal and ectypal theology, it witnesses to the methodological development of Reformed theology after *Calvin. Organized in two books, the *Compendium* is as concerned about ecclesiology and ethics as it is about predestination. In these characteristics it is typical of Reformed theology in Europe and Britain from Theodore *Beza to Peter *van Mastricht.

Bibliography

Works: *Christianae Theologiae Compendium*, ed. E. Bizer (Neukirchen, 1935).

Studies: J. W. Beardslee (ed.), *Reformed Dogmatics: J. Wollebius, G. Voetius, F. Turretin* (New York, 1965); E. P. Meijering, 'The Fathers in Reformed Orthodoxy. Systematic Theology: A. Polanus, J. Wolleb, and Francis Turretini', in I. Backus (ed.), *Reception of the Church Fathers in the West*, 2 vols. (Leiden, 1997); R. A. Muller, *Post-Reformation Reformed Dogmatics: The Rise and Development of Reformed Orthodoxy, ca. 1520 to ca. 1725* (Grand Rapids, ²2003); C. R. Trueman and R. S. Clark, *Protestant Scholasticism: Essays in Reassessment* (Carlisle, 1999).

R. S. CLARK

WOMAN, see ANTHROPLOGY;

FEMINIST THEOLOGY; WOMANIST THEOLOGY

WOMANIST THEOLOGY

Womanist theology surfaced in the US in the 1980s. The term 'womanist', coined by Alice Walker in her book *In Search of Our Mothers' Gardens: Womanist Prose*, derives from the black folk expression used of audacious adolescent girls, 'you acting womanish'. Womanism emerged amongst African-American women who found that early feminism reflected the circumstances of white middle-class women (e.g. by fighting for the right to work, whereas black American women had always had to work), while the Civil Rights Movement was aimed at African-American men. Similarly, womanist theology arose in criticism of feminist theologies that omitted analysis of the oppression of colour and *black theologies that omitted analysis of the oppression of women. Hence, womanist theology re-examines Christian beliefs, traditions, practices and texts from the perspective of African-American women, critiquing negative stereotypes and seeking empowerment. Pioneering and influential scholars in this area include: Delores Williams, Toinette Eugene, Katie Cannon, Renita Weems and Jacquelyn Grant. Womanist theologians are conscious of the social construction of black womanhood (that is, the negative and controlling stereotypes of black women as mammies, matriarchs, sexual sirens and welfare queens) and the triple oppressions of *gender, *race and class. Womanist theology is referred to as 'God-talk' and is inclusive of words and actions aimed at liberating black women from androcentrism and social domination. Methodological approaches vary, including: retrieving the stories of black women in the biblical narrative; exposing biblical texts and interpretations that degrade women of colour; employing a range of non-biblical sources, fictional and non-fictional.

Biblical interpretation

Womanist theology reinterprets texts against the background of *slavery and the experience of racism in order to eradicate negative portrayals of black women. While *feminist theologians re-read the story of Abram and Sarai (Gen. 16:1–16; 21:9–21) from Sarai's point of view, Weems and Williams make Hagar central. For Weems, Hagar is reconsidered as a symbol of the economic exploitation and racism that characterizes the history of black women in America. In addition, for Williams, Hagar's story is one of resistance and survival, accompanied by significant encounters with God.

God

Womanist theology is deeply dissatisfied with the traditional image of a white patriarchal God and encourages black women to find God in themselves. In *Sisters in the Wilderness*, Williams asks, 'who do you say God is?' She emphasizes God's wrath, love and forgiveness in respect of the exploitation of the poor (as found in Hosea), and draws attention to the Spirit's anointing of Mary. The prayer and music of Gospel churches is a useful resource in ascertaining the meaning of God as experienced by black women, revealing that little distinction is made between God and Jesus.

Christology

According to womanist theologians, the suffering of Jesus on the cross has been used to reinforce the subordination of black women; hence, a black female Christ has been developed as a necessary corrective. Womanist theologians focus on the humanness rather than maleness of Christ and refer to acts of liberation from oppression as Christ-like. In *White Women's Christ and Black Women's Jesus*, Grant argues that for black women Christ is a black woman; whereas K. B. Douglas argues that Christ can be seen in the faces of all persons who work towards liberation, including black men (and other women).

Ethics

As a moral theology, womanist theology promotes the portrayal of black women as agents in the continued struggle against the threefold oppressions of gender, race and class employing Christianity (and other religions) as tools and resources for change. Cannon argues, in *Black Womanist Ethics*, that black woman's moral reasoning has been left out of theological *ethics and, therefore, that theological ethics has provided ideological foundations for systems that corroborate the stereotyping and oppression of black women. Womanist ethics works towards an inclusive ethic that learns from black women's history, culture and traditions and takes seriously the lives and experiences of black women; hence, womanist ethics begins with oppression and the struggle to survive, rather than autonomy and free choice. Nevertheless, while highlighting black culture, womanist ethics is critical of female complicity in oppression and of sexist teaching and practices within the black church (including homophobia). Womanist ethics sees black women as theologically valuable active participants in the church and seeks an end to the sexist stereotypes that justify self-sacrifice and ignore domestic violence. In essence, womanist ethics views sin as oppression, and salvation as liberation; it is, therefore, inclusive of all groups of oppressed persons, retaining close connections with feminist, black, Asian and mujerista theologies (see *Liberation theology).

Womanist theologians have produced groundbreaking work revealing the hidden gender and racial bias in Christianity. In addition, womanist theology has shown that white women, while historically oppressed on the basis of gender, have participated in the oppression of black women, and black men, while historically oppressed on the basis of colour, have participated in the oppression of black women, although there is still work to be done concerning the oppression of poor African-Americans by affluent African-Americans. Tensions remain concerning engagement with 'malestream' theology and, as an experience-based ethic, womanist theological ethics risks being exclusive; nevertheless, the intention and aim of womanist theology is to be inclusive.

Bibliography

K. Baker-Fletcher and G. Baker-Fletcher, *My Sister, My Brother: Womanist and Xodus God-Talk* (New York, 1997); K. G. Cannon, *Katie's Canon: Womanism and the Soul of the Black Community* (New York, 1995); idem, *Black Womanist Ethics* (Atlanta, 1988); K. B. Douglas, *The Black Christ* (New York, 1994); idem, *Sexuality and the Black Church: A Womanist Perspective* (New York, 1999); T. M. Eugene, 'Moral Values and Black Womanists', *Journal of Religious Thought* 44, 1988, pp. 23–34; J. Grant (ed.), *Perspectives on Womanist Theology* (Atlanta, 1995); idem (ed.), *White Women's Christ and Black Women's Jesus: Feminist Christology and Womanist Response* (Atlanta, 1989); E. Townes (ed.), *A Troubling in My Soul: Womanist Perspectives on Evil and Suffering* (New York, 1994); idem (ed.), *Womanist Justice, Womanist Hope* (Atlanta, 1993); R. Weems, *Just a Sister Away: A Womanist Vision of Women's Relationships in the Bible* (San Diego, 1988); D. S. Williams, 'The Color of Feminism: Or Speaking the Black Woman's Tongue', *Journal of Religious Thought* 43, 1986, pp. 42–54; idem, *Sisters in the Wilderness: The Challenge of Womanist God-Talk* (New York, 1993).

E. McIntosh

WORK

Most people will spend the vast majority of their waking lives working at something, whether paid or unpaid. Not surprisingly, Scripture has plenty to say about how people ought to approach and carry out the perennial human task we call work. It instructs us that if we wish to eat we must work. Yet, it makes clear that toil and necessity are not all there is to life. Work is a gift and a blessing; it is even our co-mission with God. Its fruits are to be received with thankfulness and enjoyed. However, there also must be limits (*Sabbath) to our productive activity, manipulation of the earth and human consumption. Bound up with humanity's *fall, work too is subject to the curse, being tainted by the totalizing network of sin. Thus not all work is automatically good or sanctioned.

Nevertheless, Scripture also tells us that work has always been good for us and for *creation. It is necessary as a means of caring for ourselves, others, and even for the planet. It is also an arena within which personal and spiritual growth becomes possible. Thus, as we work with others and on creation, Scripture teaches us how to be honest, hard-working and diligent. It instructs us to promote and embody fairness and justice, especially for the weak and marginalized. It reorients us so that we can approach all of our work not simply for our own good but also for the good of others, the society and planet, and ultimately for God himself. In Scripture there are numerous lessons to be learnt about good and ethical work, work that is both pleasing to God and good for his creation.

And yet work is never really the primary theological matter or focal point for most biblical writers, if for any. The Scriptures address work and working life to be sure, but in most biblical texts this teaching is consequent, an application stemming from another theological or ethical point being made. Scripture as a whole simply does not intentionally offer something like a comprehensive theology of work.

Nevertheless, the church has always found it necessary to offer some exploratory reflection on work beyond Scripture, if simply practical teaching on the working life. She has wrestled with what Christians should and should not do as our work, as well as how we should conduct the work we undertake. And yet seldom has work itself been the subject or principal interest of the church's theological enquiry. Even *Luther, whom many credit with placing ordinary work on the theological agenda, was not chiefly concerned with the phenomenon of work itself. It was not for him a doctrine as was the theology of the cross. Luther does not offer a theology of work. Rather '*vocation' or calling was the doctrine he was expounding, and how and where our work (and everything else) found its place within our call to God, and thus Christian *discipleship.

Work itself has only recently in Christian theology come to be considered a 'doctrine' in its own right. Only since the mid-twentieth century have Christians sought specifically to understand work in terms of a theology of work. With the end of the Second World War and the need to rebuild Europe, Christian leaders sought to participate in the rebuilding process by showing how Christ and the Christian faith could play a vital role. They realized that European reconstruction itself hinged upon what people believed to be the goal, purposes, ways and ultimately the limitations of their work. As a resource the *WCC began developing what would eventually come to publication by Alan Richardson as *The Biblical Doctrine of Work*.

Likewise, French Catholic theologians around this same time began to query the possibility of theologies of 'secular realities' to aid in this rebuilding process. It is they who proposed the concept and laid the groundwork for what is now termed a 'theology of work'. Some scholars consider this theological turn to be the beginning of the process eventually culminating in the Second *Vatican Council. And, although the Council never produced a 'theology of work', most of its conclusions can be read as offering the necessary theological context and building materials for one. By 1981 Pope John Paul II offered the social encyclical *Laborem Exercens* (*On Human Work*) wholly devoted to the question of, and problems surrounding, human work. Although this is not a full-orbed theology of work (it is a pastoral letter teaching the faithful how to address what it identifies as *the* global social issue), it nevertheless offers the most comprehensive treatment of work itself officially sanctioned by the Vatican.

But what is a theology of work and how is this different from other Christian approaches to work and the working life? A theology of work is more than a summary of biblical teachings related to work, its products and practices. And it goes far beyond simply a Christian work ethic. It delves much deeper into the purposes, meaning, value and limitations of work than do most reflections offered within wider discussions like discipleship or justice. A Christian theology of work attempts to provide a comprehensive theological study, dogmatically reflecting on the nature and place of the phenomenon of work in God's universe; that is, in both human life and in the non-human creation. It is a theological exploration of work itself, undertaken by exploring work as the primary question, but with reference to the multitude of doctrines that theology has more traditionally expounded.

So why has a theology of work methodology only of late emerged within Christian theology? Why doesn't Scripture provide one as such? Why has the church only recently come to see work as a doctrine in its own right? It is primarily because work itself did not become an expressly theological problem (like the doctrine of the *Trinity did in the early church) until recently; that is, until the rise of industrial and post-industrial societies.

Until the industrial revolution there was nothing like work as we today know it and experience it sociologically and psychologically. The very concept of work was rather transparent. Work was universal, pervasive and a necessary part of life. But with few exceptions it was not the subject of careful philosophical let alone theological enquiry. The Greeks, with nobility generally, reasoned that labour should be limited to slaves or the masses. Yet by today's understanding of work, the 'philosopher kings' still worked by governing and engaging in the hard work of reasoning through political and social issues (philosophy).

Our contemporary, and now essentially globalized, conception of work grows out of our experiences in the Industrial Revolution with the rise of *capital and the subsequent rationalization of work and labour (see *Globalization). Adam Smith's economic and moral philosophy encapsulated these new more productive ways of working and organizing our working lives. Yet with the subsequent division of labour, a context arose where our daily work was increasingly disconnected from our lives around the home and family and eventually the village. Work became just another commodity that most of us would need to take to the 'job market' and sell to another. Our work and its products then belong to someone else, and thus become something other than an integrated expression of who we are and are becoming (e.g. a smith or shoemaker . . .). As Karl *Marx observed and explained, we become *alienated from our work and thus our very selves. We become disintegrated people, lost beings whose very personhood vanishes. We consequently fall, becoming lost in this new way of working. For Marx, the answer was to re-envision and reorganize work in such a way that our existence as producers is justified and thus we become able to save ourselves through our work.

It is therefore not surprising that contemporary work would become a specifically theological problem requiring a full doctrinal exposition. The need for salvation and justification has always led to theological proposals as to how God in Jesus Christ has undertaken this salvation for us. When work comes so close to theology that it offers an alternative soteriology, the church knows that the time has come to formulate a more comprehensive and specifically Christian theology of work.

Of course, a theology of 'works' is longstanding. The question of the relationship between our works (work of a particularly religious nature) and *salvation and *sanctification has been an enduring part of the theological landscape. We have been clear that our religious works are integrally related to, but in no way the basis or cause of, our salvation.

With the rise of new philosophical and sociological doctrines of work, such as the one offered by Marx, the church sees that the time has come to clarify where the theological problems lie in relation to this new working reality, and offer a carefully crafted theology of work prophetically appropriate for today's globalized world. It should by now likewise be obvious that any proposed theology of work, to be both comprehensive and compelling, will need to show how our ordinary work is integrally related to our salvation, and thus to the new creation, but not the cause or condition of it.

Bibliography

M. D. Chenu, *The Theology of Work* (Dublin, 1963); D. Cosden, *A Theology of Work: Work and the New Creation* (Carlisle, 2004); idem, *The Heavenly Good of Earthly Work* (Carlisle, 2006); L. Hardy, *The Fabric of This World* (Grand Rapids, 1990); *Laborem Exercens: Encyclical Letter of the Supreme Pontiff John Paul II on Human Work* (London, 1981); A. Larive, *After Sunday: A Theology of Work* (New York, 2004); A. Richardson, *The Biblical Doctrine of Work* (London, 1952); R. P. Stevens, *The Other Six Days* (Grand Rapids, 1999); M. Volf, *Work in the Spirit: Toward a Theology of Work* (Oxford, 1991).

D. T. COSDEN

WORLD COUNCIL OF CHURCHES

Four streams fed into the work of the World Council: Life and Work (1925), *Faith and Order (1927), the International Missionary Council (1921) and the World Council of Christian Education, which arose out of the World Sunday School Association of 1889. These emphases still spell out major thrusts in the council's work, and while ideally they represent complementary programmes, they sometimes seem to offer conflicting priorities. Further encouragement came from the Ecumenical Patriarch's appeal in 1920 for a 'League of Churches' to act as a permanent instrument of cooperation and fellowship.

In July 1937 representatives of Life and Work and Faith and Order met in London and agreed to merge to establish a World Council of Churches. A committee, meeting in Utrecht in 1938, set up a provisional committee for a World Council of Churches in process of formation, under the chairmanship of William *Temple (England) with W. A. Visser 't Hooft (Holland) as secretary. Their hopes for convoking a first assembly in 1941 were delayed by the outbreak of the Second World War until 1948 when 147 representatives from all the main ecclesiastical traditions, except the Roman Catholic Church, assembled in Amsterdam. The Council's original basis, reflecting language inherited from the World Alliance of YMCAs, spoke of 'a fellowship of churches which accept the Lord Jesus Christ as God and Saviour'. This was expanded at New Delhi in 1961 to incorporate scriptural authority and a trinitarian faith by adding the words 'according to the scriptures and therefore seek together to fulfil their common calling to the glory of the one God, Father, Son and Holy Spirit'.

Already facing ecclesiological questions consequent upon its foundation, the Council's Central Committee meeting in Toronto in 1950 adopted what has come to be known as the Toronto statement which emphatically denied any intentions of the Council aspiring to any churchly status and certainly not to operate as a super-church. Nor would it challenge the church claims of any of its member bodies, or demand that they recognize other members as fully churches, thereby affording confidence to its Orthodox members. Only churches are allowed membership, and the Council has no power to legislate on their behalf. Such actions as it takes, and statements that it issues, depend on their intrinsic truth and value for acceptance.

Faith and order issues remain important as the churches explore major convergences in belief and practice. Mission is no longer construed as the activity of sender nations working principally through a battery of missionary societies operating in 'receiver' countries. As *missio Dei*, *mission is now seen as the work of the whole people of God in every nation. Interfaith dialogue appears on the *ecumenical agenda with new urgency (see *Christianity and other religions). As over against the view that the Council is only concerned with the political dimension, it is active in the contemporary search for *spirituality. Discussions of the church as an inclusive community are essential for some churches but contentious for others. Traditional concern for social justice and peace are now supplemented by the promotion of a green agenda in the context of the biblical doctrine of *creation, whilst increasingly difficult ethical issues in biotechnology claim attention. Diakonia is a generic term describing the quite remarkable story of the Council's compassionate ministry.

The council brings together, not without difficulty, a wide diversity of Christian traditions, the principal being Orthodox, both Eastern and Oriental, Anglican, other Protestant, Pentecostal and African Instituted. Because of this it is difficult to discern a WCC theology as such, even though the staff and governing body members may develop policy documents within and across the Council's many programmes. For example, the very notion of a WCC theology would be anathema to the Orthodox, for they could not identify with anything other than an Orthodox theology. Within the council, tension sometimes emerges between those engaged in trying to work for greater unity amongst the churches and the articulation of theological convergences, and those who look to the Council to exercise leadership in applying theology in developing new ways of conceiving mission and of relating, prophetically, to injustice.

Notwithstanding the wide embrace of the Council, a number of major traditions do not belong. The Roman Catholic Church, which is often to be found in national and regional councils of churches, argues that its catholicity claims would be compromised if it were to join a worldwide fellowship of churches as just another member. Because of this the Council relates to the Vatican through a joint committee which discusses matters of mutual concern.

Many evangelicals find it difficult to relate to a body that does not comprehensively share all their doctrinal affirmations and is perceived by some to be over-concerned with political actions, whilst placing too little emphasis on evangelism. That said, evangelicals are divided on the issue, and there has always been an evangelical presence on the staff and in the governing bodies of the WCC. In like manner, the number of Pentecostal churches in membership of the World Council does not represent the movement's global strength. In recent years the WCC has initiated a series of meetings with these traditions involving both its own members and those outside.

The weight of council membership, now around 350 churches, has significantly moved towards the churches of the southern hemisphere and away from Europe and North America. Because the WCC is a council of churches, para-church bodies, though clearly crucial to worldwide Christian witness, are denied membership. Accordingly, since 1998 work has been taking place towards the establishment of a Global Christian Forum capable of overcoming all these deficiencies. It will bring together a broader spectrum of Christian organizations, but without any commitment in membership. Its first meeting took place in Limuru near Nairobi in November 2007.

Bibliography

J. Briggs, M. A. Oduyoye and G. Tsetsis (eds.), *A History of the Ecumenical Movement:*

Vol. 3, 1968–2000 (Geneva, 2004); M. van Elderen and M. Conway, *Introducing the World Council of Churches* (Geneva, 2001); G. Fackre, *Ecumenical Faith in Evangelical Perspective* (Grand Rapids, 1993); H. E. Fey (ed.), *A History of the Ecumenical Movement: Vol. 2, The Ecumenical Advance, 1948–1968* (Geneva, ²1986); N. Lossky et al. (eds.), *Dictionary of the Ecumenical Movement* (Geneva, ²2002); R. Rouse and S. Neill (eds.), *A History of the Ecumenical Movement: Vol. 1, 1517–1968* (Geneva, ³1986); G. Wainwright, *The Ecumenical Movement: Crisis and Opportunity for the Church* (Grand Rapids, 1983).

J. Briggs

WORSHIP

From the Old English *weorthscipe* ('worthiness', 'respect'), 'worship' means to ascribe worth to someone or something. In the broadest religious sense it can refer to the whole life of devotion to *God, which can encompass such diverse things as studying the sacred Scriptures, private prayer and the dedication of financial and material resources to God. More narrowly, 'worship' refers to the intentional corporate gathering of the church to hear the word of God and to respond with prayer, praise and thanksgiving.

More than just inspirational speech, worship involves an encounter with God, in which God empowers worshippers for lives of holiness and righteousness.

For many Protestants, the word 'liturgy' has become synonymous with 'worship'. Although often equated with 'a prescribed service order', the meaning of *liturgy is much deeper. The original Greek, *leitourgia*, refers to something done for or on behalf of the public, such as serving in a legislature or even paying taxes. 'Liturgy' implies that the worship gathering takes place on behalf of the world, insofar as the church offers the world's needs to God, and pleads for God's mercy on the world. Yet there is also the 'liturgy' of the church's going into the world on God's behalf to proclaim God's mercy and justice. Thus, 'liturgy' points to the worship gathering's relationship to both God and the world.

Why do Christians worship?

St Augustine said, 'you [God] have made us for yourself . . .' This means that humans, unlike other creatures, have the capacity to know that there is a Being whose powers and mode of existence utterly transcend ours. The experience of this One's presence evokes responses of awe, praise, confession of sin and human finitude, and service. Simply put, the awareness of God leads to the adoration of God.

But why do we worship with other persons? The reason is that we were created not only to be in communion with God's self, but also to be in communion with other humans (Gen. 2:19–25). We want to join with others in praising and adoring our Creator, because doing so enables us to be part of something greater than ourselves. Communal worship with others is a manifestation of the *image of God in humanity (Gen. 1:26–27), for Christians believe that God, as Trinity, is the ultimate communion of persons whose mutual interaction results in a great outpouring of love. In corporate worship, we manifest the divine image even as we experience the divine presence.

Therefore, the need to worship God and the need to be in communion with others are not in conflict. Indeed, when we gather with others to share our stories and our lives, to welcome each other into community, to experience the word of God as it challenges and upholds us, and to support one another in the response of faith, we experience the loving presence of God. Both the community and its liturgical actions mediate the presence of God to worshippers. In that case, worship is profoundly *incarnational in that it reflects God's self-manifestation in the human person of Jesus Christ.

What makes worship *Christian*?

Of course, worship is not something peculiar to Christians. What makes Christian worship distinctive is its *trinitarian* character, its affirmation that God is Father, Son and Holy Spirit. This affirmation is *liturgical* in that worship names the triune God in its acclamations, benedictions, prayers, songs and sacramental formulae (e.g. 'I baptize you in the name of the Father, and of the Son, and of the Holy Spirit'). When the church thus establishes the identity of the triune God, it places the worship under *this* God's power and authority and commits itself to the adoration and service of *this* God.

Christian worship is trinitarian in a *theological* sense, that is, with respect to its relationship to each person of the Trinity. Worship is offered *to* the first person of the Trinity, the Father (cf. John 17; Rom. 8:15), *through* the Son (cf. Heb. 7:23–25), *in the power of* the Holy Spirit (John 4:23–24; Rom. 8:15, 27; Eph. 5:18–20). This understanding is incarnated in the classic eucharistic prayers that address the Father, praising him for creation, Israel and the prophets; recall the saving work of the Son; and finally, ask the Father to send the Holy Spirit for the extension of his saving work into the eucharistic act. Many eucharistic prayers conclude with a trinitarian *doxology that summarizes the whole act of praise.

Ultimately, the trinitarian life of God that is modelled in worship will manifest itself in the lives of believers, through their mutual love and cooperation, as well as their common efforts to declare God's reconciliation to the world.

The basic shape of Christian worship

Worship throughout the universal church is diverse in ritual complexity, use of art, architecture and music, the piety of worshippers and styles of leadership. This diversity reflects the variety of theologies, histories and cultural contexts of churches. Yet a common shape for the Sunday service has emerged over the centuries: *gathering, word, meal* and *sending*.

In the *gathering* the church assembles in the presence and in the name of the triune God, making the transition from world to church. Typical acts include: (1) a call to worship, usually biblical words that bring the assembly before God; (2) a greeting (e.g. 'The Lord be with you') or trinitarian invocation ('In the name of the Father', etc.); (3) an opening prayer that invokes the presence of God and asks God to purify the hearts of worshippers (e.g. the Anglican 'collect for purity'); and (4) confession and pardon.

In the *word* God speaks to the church through the biblical readings and the sermon in order to convict of sin, call to repentance, promise forgiveness and exhort the assembly to holy living. Typically, a sermon bridges the biblical narrative and the listener's story so that the word becomes a living reality. Late-twentieth- and early twenty-first-century churches have utilized various non-sermonic means of proclaiming the word, such as plays, skits, dramatic readings, pantomimes and media presentations (e.g. video clips of motion pictures). The assembly responds to the word through professions of faith (a 'creed'), intercessory prayers for the church and world, and the Peace (an enacted sign of the wholeness and well-being that is salvation in Christ).

The *meal* begins with an offering of monetary gifts, symbolizing the self-offering of the assembly to God's service. The action may also include the presentation of the *eucharistic bread and wine as a way of affirming that the gifts of creation will be used by God for his saving purposes. The main act is the great thanksgiving in which the church gives thanks and praise to God over bread and cup for salvation in Jesus Christ. The faith-filled receiving of the eucharistic elements becomes an encounter with Christ himself, who offers forgiveness, peace and restoration. More than just a response to the word, the meal is truly a means of grace.

The *sending* serves as a transition from worship to the world. Sending rituals usually charge the assembly with faithful Christian living in the world, thereby making a connection to the assembly's mission. The ancient Latin dismissal *'Ite, misse est'* ('Go. You are sent.') demonstrates this link insofar as *'misse'* and 'mission' are from the same root word. Far from being a mere formality, then, the sending rite (especially the dismissal) challenges worshippers to enact the realities they have heard and experienced in worship.

Within the Sunday service, many Christians celebrate the rites of Christian initiation (i.e. baptism). The sacrament may take place within the *gathering*, as a reminder that baptism marks the beginning of the Christian life. Or it may be celebrated following the *word*, as a way of symbolizing how the candidate's acceptance of baptism, as well as the church's baptismal mission, are both responses to biblical imperatives. When celebrated within the Sunday service, baptism reminds the entire assembly of its baptismal death and resurrection with Christ – or, stated alternatively, its rebirth through water and the Holy Spirit.

For most, but not all, Christians, worship and sacraments will be borne along by song and other music. A 'gathering song' spiritually forms worshippers into a united body, just as it musically gathers the many voices into one for the praise of God. Songs also enable the assembly to proclaim the word of God and internalize its message, as well as envision a faith response to the word. Sending songs highlight and describe the church's mission in the world in light of the gospel. Many Christians affirm that music is far more than a decorative element in worship, but is actually God's gift to the church for the purpose of praising and glorifying him. As such, its primary purpose is to support the proclamation of the word and the celebration of the sacraments.

Challenges for today

Churches need to navigate between two extremes in worship. The first is *ritualism*, that is, a devotion to ancient rites and ceremonies for their own sake. While our worship must maintain continuity with that of previous generations because its basic pattern (or *ordo*) expresses the apostolic *kerygma*, the art, architecture, gestures, music and language of worship all need updating, reforming and enculturating in order to speak effectively to contemporary people (see *Asthetics).

Also to be avoided is a *pragmatism* that makes worship into something 'useful' (e.g. religious education, political indoctrination, evangelism, etc.). Such an approach risks exalting human agendas over divine truth and reducing the church to a mere instrument of the *missio Dei* at the expense of its identity as the elect of God who were chosen before the creation of the world.

Ultimately, worship must be God-centred *and* accessible to the people of the church.

Bibliography

R. P. Byars, *The Future of Protestant Worship: Beyond the Worship Wars* (Louisville, 2002); S. Chan, *Liturgical Theology: The Church as Worshiping Community* (Downers Grove, 2006); M. J. Dawn, *Reaching Out Without Dumbing Down: A Theology of Worship for the Turn-of-the-Century Culture* (Grand Rapids, 1995); G. W. Lathrop, *What Are the Essentials of Christian Worship?* (Minneapolis, 1994); T. G. Long, *Beyond the Worship Wars: Building Vital and Faithful Worship* (Washington DC, 2001); E. Underhill, *Worship* (New York, 1936); R. E. Webber, *The Worship Phenomenon* (Nashville, 1994).

J. A. TRUSCOTT

WRATH OF GOD

There are references to the wrath of God throughout Scripture, but it is difficult for many to reconcile it with the focus on the *love of God which comes to a climax in the profound assertion of 1 John 4:16: 'God is love.' The strong emphasis on God as a God of justice and vengeance, particularly in Western Christianity both in the medieval and early modern periods, produced a strong reaction. Many Christians in the modern era have consequently rejected the idea of a last judgment in which God would condemn anyone to eternal punishment in hell (see *Judgment of God), along with the belief that on the cross, Jesus 'propitiated' or turned aside the judgment and wrath of God by substituting himself as the innocent one in place of guilty humanity. This reaction against belief in the wrath of God was therefore a powerful reason for the development of *universalism (the belief that in the end all will be saved). The question whether it is legitimate to speak of the wrath of God therefore has wide implications for *eschatology, for the doctrine of the *atonement, and indeed for the doctrine of *God.

C. H. *Dodd, a leading NT scholar of the mid-twentieth century, proposed in his commentary on Romans that we should understand the wrath of God, not as a characteristic of God himself, but as a primitive attempt to conceptualize the 'inevitable process of cause and effect in a moral universe'. Dodd's proposal was opposed by NT scholars such as Leon Morris, R. V. G. Tasker and C. E. B. Cranfield.

Two theological questions arise: whether it is an *anthropomorphism to speak of the wrath of God, and whether it contradicts belief in the love of God. If 'wrath' or 'anger' is regarded as vindictive and spiteful petulance, then it is indeed incompatible with the Christian understanding of God. But if all our language of God is in fact drawn from the human context and so must be understood to apply analogically to God, then this concept too needs to be refined. God's anger should not be conceived as the same as the anger of sinful humanity.

Nor is anger necessarily contradictory to love. While sinful human anger can arise from selfishness and self-assertion, even humans can have righteous anger. Cranfield pointed out, for example, that a righteous opposition to apartheid not only could, but should, elicit anger against injustice. Morris argued that it was a necessary part of moral character to abhor *evil as well as to love good. God's wrath can be seen as arising out of his righteousness and indeed his love. As Hosea was deeply grieved by the unfaithfulness of his wife, so the Lord was deeply grieved by Israel's unfaithfulness precisely because he loved Israel. So parents may react with a deeply grieving anger when confronted by a child destroying himself through a foolish lifestyle of drugs and misuse of alcohol: their anger arises out of their love.

In some such way the concept of the wrath of God may be understood as arising out of God's love. As 1 John 4:16 declares, in himself God is love. Indeed Christians think of the triune God as an eternal fellowship of love. God's loving giving of himself to his creatures only takes the form of wrath when faced by our *sin. While the atonement therefore reveals God's wrath, meaning his inflexible opposition to sin, at the deepest level it reveals that he is love.

Bibliography

A. T. Hanson, *The Wrath of the Lamb* (London, 1957); L. Morris, *The Apostolic Preaching of the Cross* (London, ³1965); J. I. Packer, *Knowing God* (London, 1973); H. Schönweiss and H. C. Hahn, in *NIDNTT* I, pp. 105–113; R. V. G. Tasker, *The Biblical Doctrine of the Wrath of God* (London, 1951).

T. A. NOBLE

WRIGHT, N. T. (b. 1948)

A prolific author and erstwhile holder of various academic and ecclesiastical posts, N. T. (Tom) Wright, who was Bishop of Durham (2003–2010), has achieved towering status in both NT scholarship and the Anglican Communion. Whatever his final contributions to the church, Wright's publications – known for combining scholarly creativity with accessibility – ensure his position as one of the most important theological thinkers of the late twentieth and early twenty-first century. Amidst his various writing interests, most significant to date have been his work on Paul and *Jesus.

Paul

Alongside E. P. Sanders and J. D. G. Dunn, Wright is one of the most prominent figures within the so-called New Perspective on Paul. While there are significant differences between each of these three exegetes, Wright shares with them the conviction, discernible even in his 1980 doctoral thesis, that Paul's polemic against his opponents bore more on community self-definition than on any alleged legalism inherent in first-century Judaism. Against a virtually standard scholarly assumption of an early, low *Christology, Wright argues that the apostle's Messiah stands squarely within the framework of a modified Jewish monotheism; Messiah not only incorporates Israel but also embodies the culmination of Yahweh's creational purposes. Working on the premise that Paul and much of first-century Judaism saw itself in exile, Wright further argues that Paul's Messiah (as Israel) redeemed Israel from exile and thereby put an end to the law as well as the Jew-Gentile antagonisms which it engendered. Thus Wright sees Paul's controversy with the Judaizers concerning 'works of the law' more as an ecclesiological than a soteriological issue. Continued adherence to those practices by which Jews defined themselves (circumcision, dietary laws and calendrical observances) risked dividing the one, true people of God, who are to be marked off by their faith and confession that Jesus Christ is Lord. This marking off, which anticipates God's eschatological vindication of his people, is what Paul means by *justification. Understood this way, justification is not primarily about 'getting in' the covenant (conversion), but the appropriate means of identification that one is already in.

For Wright, the '*righteousness of God' (as it occurs, e.g. in Rom. 1:17) refers to God's own covenantal faithfulness and not, as *Luther would have it, a righteous status which God imputes to believers. Ultimately, the vindication of God's people depends on their incorporation into Christ. Whether this understanding of justification ultimately retains the effects of imputation, as classically understood, remains debated and in some quarters highly controversial. In his most recent writings on Paul, Wright has shown increasing interest in Paul's theological and political critique of Roman imperial ideology.

Jesus

Wright's most important treatments of Jesus can be found in the second and third volumes of his four-part *Christian Origins and the Question of God*. In the first volume of the series, Wright lays out his methodology of 'critical realism' for historical inquiry into Christian origins. Building on this in volume two, *Jesus and the Victory of God*, Wright argues that Jesus' ministry and teachings can best be explained as his taking on the vocation of prophet and Messiah, signalling the culmination of Israel's story, which includes the return from exile, the forgiveness of sins, the rebuilding of the temple and the in-gathering of the Gentiles. Along these lines, Jesus identifies himself as the Suffering Servant figure and in fact the embodiment of Israel's God who has returned to Zion. Wright works out his methods and results largely in response to the scepticism of the Jesus Seminar, whose influence peaked in the early 1990s. In volume three, *Resurrection of the Son of God*, Wright casts the notion of resurrection against the backdrop of second-temple Jewish (Pharisaical) understanding. Against various well-known explanations for the *resurrection, Wright argues that the early Christians' Easter belief is explicable on two facts: the sightings of the risen Lord and the empty tomb. These two facts in turn are explicable only by the fact of resurrection itself. By emphasizing Jesus as a Jewish figure, N. T. Wright takes his place in the 'Third Quest' of the *historical Jesus – a label coined by Wright himself.

Bibliography

Works: *Christian Origins and the Question of God: Vol. 1, The New Testament and the People of God* (London and Minneapolis, 1992); *Christian Origins and the Question of God: Vol. 2, Jesus and the Victory of God* (London and Minneapolis, 1996); *What Saint Paul Really Said: Was Paul of Tarsus the Real Founder of Christianity?* (Oxford and Grand Rapids, 1997); *Christian Origins and the Question of God: Vol. 3, The Resurrection of the Son of God* (London and Minneapolis, 2003); *Paul: In Fresh Perspective* (London and Minneapolis, 2005); *Simply Christian: Why Christianity Makes Sense* (London and New York, 2006); *Surprised by Hope* (New York, 2008); *How God Became King* (New York, 2013); *Christian Origins and the Question of God: Vol. 4, Paul and the Faithfulness of God* (London and Minneapolis, 2014).

N. PERRIN

WYCLIF, JOHN (c. 1329–84)

In his numerous books Wyclif discussed philosophy, politics and theology. His participation in contemporary political life was guided by the doctrine of 'dominion' which he expounded in *De dominio divino* (*Divine Lordship*, 1375) and *De civili dominio* (*Civil Lordship*, 1376). God is the supreme Lord, but he endowed humanity at creation with a derivative and conditional lordship over the world. Humanity is God's steward, but the *stewardship is entirely of grace and is forfeited if man falls into moral sin even though he may continue to hold possessions and exercise rule. But he who is in grace has a right to lordship even though he be destitute. In so far as the church is guilty of innumerable sins, it should forfeit its lordship and the state may strip it of its wealth.

The interest in Wyclif's theology centres upon its similarity to the thinking of the Protestant Reformers. The most striking resemblance is in his attitude to *Scripture. Scripture proceeds, as he puts it in *De veritate Sacrae Scripturae* (*The Truth of Sacred Scripture*), 'from the mouth of God'. It is the everlasting truth in written form and provides in essence all that needs to be known of law, ethics and philosophy. Scripture is superior in authority to the pope, the church and the teaching of the Church Fathers. It is the 'law of God' and its focus throughout is upon Christ. Wyclif's reverence for the Bible as the supreme authority for Christian thought and life is amply shown in his innumerable references to it, as well as in his resolve to have it translated into English and made available to the public at large.

Using the Bible as his standard, he launched an increasingly violent attack upon the wealth, power and decadence of the church. In *De ecclesia* (*The Church*, 1378) he explains that the members of the church are God's elect, for *predestination is the foundation of the church. But no-one, not even the pope, can be certain of his election, for the visible church includes the 'foreknown', that is the reprobate as well. But all true Christians have direct personal access to God and enjoy a common *priesthood. Wyclif lays heavy stress on moral character as a mark of the true Christian, and the immorality, the lust for temporal power and wealth amongst the clergy led him to call for the abolition of the monastic orders and the *papacy. By the same token he elevated the dignity of the true Christian layman to the extent of arguing that a priest was not necessary to administer Holy Communion.

He rejected the medieval doctrine of transubstantiation (see *Eucharist) and argued in *De Eucharistia* (*The Eucharist*, c. 1380) that the body of Christ is 'sacramentally concealed' in the elements. Similarly, he condemned indulgences (see *Merit) and the cult of the *saints, though reverence should be accorded to the Virgin *Mary.

Although Wyclif's thought was expressed in a typically medieval scholastic idiom, his teaching on Scripture and the primacy of preaching, as well as his condemnation of transubstantiation and his elevation of lay spirituality, justifies calling him 'the morning star of the Reformation', provided allowance be made for the greater clarity and sophistication of the Reformers' evangelical theology.

Bibliography

The works of Wyclif were published by the Wycliffe Society of London, 1843ff.; selections in ET, *LCC* 14, ed. M. Spinka, *Advocates of Reform* (London, 1953).
Studies: E. A. Block, *John Wyclif: Radical Dissenter* (San Diego, 1962); I. C. Levy (ed.), *A Companion to John Wyclif: Late Medieval Theologian* (Leiden, 2011); K. B. McFarlane, *John Wycliffe and the Beginnings of English Nonconformity* (London, 1952); J. Stacey, *Wyclif and Reform* (London, 1964); H. B. Workman, *John Wyclif*, 2 vols. (Oxford, 1926).

R. T. JONES

YALE SCHOOL

The term describes an influential approach to theology which flourished during the 1970s and 1980s at Yale Divinity School, most closely associated with H. *Frei and G. *Lindbeck and their students. Loosely inspired by *Barth, they united in opposing liberal revisionist views of Scripture and Christology by letting the biblical narratives speak on their own terms to identify both Jesus Christ and the church.

Frei's work on *hermeneutics shows that modern theologians, conservative and liberal alike, let extratextual theories about the nature and criteria of truth govern their interpretations of biblical narrative (*Eclipse of Biblical Narrative*). The truth of the Gospels was thought to refer either to the historical events behind the text or to existential human possibilities in front of the text (as P. *Ricœur and D. Tracy of the rival '*Chicago school' maintained). Eschewing general theories, Frei reads the Bible on its own terms as a realistic, history-like narrative that means just what it says and whose main purpose is to identify Jesus Christ as the one who is now living. He later revised his view and identified the literal sense with the consensus reading in the history of the church.

Lindbeck too criticizes liberal theology for being 'experiential-expressivist': for assuming that religious experience precedes formation in community. His '*postliberal' alternative appropriates Wittgenstein's insight that meaning is learned by participating in language games: Christians learn how to speak of God by participating in the form of life or culture of the church (hence his so-called 'cultural-linguistic' approach). Intratextuality means that the church takes its bearings from the biblical narrative; in what is perhaps his most oft-cited quote, Lindbeck says that 'it is the text . . . which absorbs the world, rather than the world the text' (*Nature of Doctrine*, p. 118).

Bibliography

H. Frei, *The Eclipse of Biblical Narrative: A Study of Eighteenth and Nineteenth Century Hermeneutics* (New Haven, 1974); idem, *Theology and Narrative*, ed. G. Hunsinger and W. Placher (Oxford, 1993); G. Lindbeck, *The Nature of Doctrine: Religion and Theology in a Postliberal Age* (Philadelphia, 1984); C. C. Pecknold, *Transforming Postliberal Theology: George Lindbeck, Pragmatism and Scripture* (London and New York, 2005); T. Phillips and D. Okholm (eds.), *The Nature of Confession: Evangelicals and Postliberals in Conversation* (Downers Grove, 1996); A. Vidu, *Postliberal Theological Method: A Critical Study* (Carlisle, 2005).

K. J. VANHOOZER

YODER, JOHN HOWARD (1927–97)

John Howard Yoder was a North American Mennonite theologian who made a case for the relevance of *Mennonite theology and ethics – and in particular its *pacifism – for the whole of the Christian church. In his early life he worked in France to reorganize the Mennonite church after the Second World War, overseeing children's homes and relief programmes. Subsequently he moved to Basel to study, where he was a student of Karl *Barth among others, and completed a PhD on the origin of Swiss Anabaptism. He served as professor at the University of Notre Dame and the Associated Mennonite Biblical Seminary, and in sabbaticals spent time in Argentina, where he encountered *liberation theology, and the Tantur Institute in Israel, prompting writings on the relationship between Christianity and *Judaism.

He was a prolific writer, publishing seventeen books and hundreds of articles.

Throughout his career Yoder sought to establish the radical social and political implications of Christian discipleship against those such as Reinhold *Niebuhr who argued that following the teaching of the NT was unrealistic in a fallen world. For Yoder this meant discarding the *Constantinian legacy of the church to rediscover a faithfulness to its origins in the person of Jesus Christ, unconditioned by expectations of the nation *state on its citizens. That the followers of Christ should be peaceful despite the many apparently urgent demands to be violent in pursuit or defence of their vision was fundamental to his vision of this discipleship. This pacifism was not based on the judgment that renouncing violence would be an effective means to peace and justice in the world, but on the understanding that it was a command of Christ to which Christians should be obedient. Yoder argued that Christians should relinquish responsibility for the 'direction of history' and place their hope not in the results of their own efforts but rather in God's power and promise to triumph over the forces of evil. He engaged broadly with those of very different opinions, including detailed argument on the implications of the just-war tradition for issues in modern warfare. Yoder saw the role of the *church in shaping the life of Christian disciples as crucial, but also sought to escape a merely sectarian vision by seeing the vocation of the church as service to the world, witnessing to the way of life to which all are ultimately called.

In 1992 a Mennonite denominational task force confronted Yoder with thirteen charges of sexual abuse against women, reporting the deep pain of the women who had given testimony. In response to the recommendations of the task force, the Indiana-Michigan Mennonite Conference suspended his ministerial credential and urged him to seek counselling and make restitution to the women he had abused. Yoder frequently acknowledged participating with women in sexual practices, characterizing the abuse as experimentation in Christian sexuality. It is likely that more than a hundred women were abused by Yoder from the mid-1970s over a period of two decades, although no legal charges were ever filed (Rachel Waltner Goossen, '"Defanging the Beast": Mennonite Responses to John Howard Yoder's Sexual Abuse', *MQR* 89, pp. 7–80).

Bibliography

Works: *The Priestly Kingdom: Social Ethics as Gospel* (Notre Dame, 1984); *The Politics of Jesus: Vicit Agnus Noster* (Grand Rapids, 1994); *The Royal Priesthood: Essays Ecclesiological and Ecumenical* (Grand Rapids, 1994); *When War Is Unjust: Being Honest in Just-War Thinking* (Maryknoll, ²1996).

Studies: C. A. Carter, *The Politics of the Cross: The Theology and Social Ethics of John Howard Yoder* (Grand Rapids, 2001); R. W. Goossen, '"Defanging the Beast": Mennonite Responses to John Howard Yoder's Sexual Abuse', *MQR* 89, January 2015, pp. 7–80; M. T. Nation, *John Howard Yoder: Mennonite Patience, Evangelical Witness, Catholic Convictions* (Grand Rapids, 2006).

D. L. CLOUGH

ZION

Zion (sometimes written 'Sion') is synonymous with Jerusalem in both OT and NT, but in post-biblical writing is often interpreted *eschatologically. Its theological importance depends less on geography and more on history. Today in Jerusalem, Mount Zion denotes the hilltop at the south-west corner of the Old City and is the site of the institution of the Eucharist at the Last Supper and the founding of the church at Pentecost, as well as the traditional tomb of King David.

Christianity (and Judaism) proclaim and claim Zion as the city of God and of 'the great king', and the setting and symbol of salvation in the end of days. Its meaning was extended from a designation for a specific site and a name for a city to an allusion to the entire land of Israel, a symbol of the historic fate of the people of Israel, and finally to a vision of universal redemption. Zion's multiple layers of meaning and its power to evoke a radically new era of reality are reflected in the use of the term by groups as diverse as Anabaptists who founded their Kingdom of New Zion in Münster in 1534, numerous churches (especially African and Protestant) who incorporate the word Zion in their name, the Church of the Latter-Day Saints (often called Mormons) for whom America is the land of Zion where the new Jerusalem will be established, and the founders of modern *Zionism such as Theodor Herzl.

Zion: the church

Thomas Aquinas's liturgical hymn *Lauda Sion* (Praise Sion) composed for the Mass of Corpus Christi demonstrates that whilst 'the great king' is Christ, Zion is *mater ecclesia*, the *church or body of Christ, the city of God on earth. As the place where the first church – the church of Jerusalem – was founded, it is the earthly mother of all churches. Zion is sometimes equated with *Mary, the virgin daughter of Zion who became the holy mother who enabled the incarnation. The Church Fathers and consequent theologians have applied the biblical praises and promises for the 'daughters of Zion' to Christians and Christianity.

The earthly Zion, Jerusalem, is often viewed with ambiguity. A strand of tradition denies it much importance, as, for example, in the story of Jesus' encounter with the Samaritan woman (John 4:1–42), or in Stephen's speech (Acts 7:1–53) before he was stoned. However, the notion of the incarnation bestows sacramental significance on tangible places, such as Zion, which are connected with Jesus' life, death, resurrection and ascension. Thus, the Emperor Constantine transformed Zion by major developments, including the building of the Church of the Holy Sepulchre and encouraging pilgrims to visit the holy city. Understood as sacred because it is the place where divinity and humanity encountered one another, pilgrims carried back relics to churches everywhere, thus constantly nourishing the bond with Zion. Henceforth, Christians made pilgrimages to 'The Holy Land': to sites linked to the life and ministry of Jesus, particularly in Jerusalem, Bethlehem and Galilee.

Paul displays special regard for the Jerusalem church as an important link between the Gentile church and Jewish Christianity but ultimately for Paul the true home of all Christians is not the 'present Jerusalem' but 'the Jerusalem on high' (Gal. 4:21–27). Jerusalem was increasingly spiritualized and transformed into a non-geographical eschatological 'heavenly' Jerusalem, identified with the true earthly manifestation of 'the city of God', the church. Thus every place where the Christian community gathers as the body of Christ becomes Zion.

In Christian theology today there is divergence of opinion about the significance of Zion as land. Walter Brueggemann argues that the subject of 'land' should become more central, and developed a theology of land. His view is in contrast to an earlier generation of scholars, such as W. D. Davies, who suggested that land was relatively unimportant and that Jesus paid little attention to the relationship between God, Israel and the land. Davies called this Christian de-emphasis on geographical specificity 'disenlandisement', pointing out that of the forty-seven references to Israel in the NT only three refer specifically to the land, while the overwhelming majority pertain to the Jewish people.

For contemporary Palestinian Christians, a theology of *liberation has developed out of a close association with land, although it is also influenced by a replacement theology, which has arisen from the experiences of Palestinian Christians living in Israel since 1948. Naim Ateek argues that before the creation of the state, the OT was considered an essential part of Christian Scripture, pointing and witnessing to Jesus, but since the creation of the state, some Jewish and Christian interpreters have read the OT largely as a Zionist text to such an extent that it has become almost repugnant to Palestinian Christians. In contrast, some evangelical Christians have proposed that the Jewish return to Zion from dispersion in over one hundred countries is the fulfilment of biblical prophecy. There are many manifestations of this position, particularly among the evangelical and charismatic sections of the church, and adherents are often called Christian Zionists (see *Dispensational theology). While it may appear to be a fairly clear-cut and unified theology, there are many subdivisions. Contemporary Roman Catholic theology is also ambivalent, but has been deeply influenced by *Nostra Aetate* in 1965 at the Second Vatican Council (and consequent papal documents on Catholic-Jewish relations in 1975, 1985, 1998 and 2001), the exchange of ambassadors in 1993 between the state of Israel and the Holy See and Pope John Paul II's pilgrimage to Israel in 2000.

Zion: the Jewish return

The centrality of Zion for Jews points to the common patrimony of *Judaism and Christianity, but this interrelatedness betrays rivalry conflicts. Ultimately, the dispute over the meaning of Zion as the city of God reflects rival claims to be the true Israel, or people of God.

Three thousand years ago, King David made Jerusalem the religious and national nucleus of the people of Israel so that Zion came to mean a city, a land and a people, whose historical existence is intimately linked with the metropolis, as a child is nurtured by its mother (cf. Isa. 66:10–13). Even when Titus destroyed the temple in AD 70 and Jews lost sovereignty over the sacred city, Jerusalem continued to serve as the pre-eminent symbol of a covenantal bond with the land of Israel. Fervent hope for a future ingathering of the exiles in a restored Jerusalem and the longing for Zion found expression in Jewish religious and communal life. Zionism took its name from the city.

Jews looked towards religious and political renewal in Zion (including, for Orthodox Jews, the restoration of the temple), and an idealized kingdom of David. Redemption was inconceivable without a return to Zion, as the spiritual centre of Jewish existence. Jewish liturgy remains permeated with a longing for Zion, which symbolizes the Jewish people's eschatological aspirations. The will to survive in the Diaspora generated Jewish messianic hopes of redemption, and Zion became a symbol of redress for all the wrongs which Jews had suffered. Thus, modern Zionism is in part the fusion of messianic fervour and the longing for Zion. Christian supporters in the early twentieth century, such as Arthur J. Balfour and Lloyd George, saw Zionism as fulfilment of an historical mission. In the aftermath of the *Holocaust, Zionism has become a pre-eminent part of Jewish theology and identity, even though Jews continue to argue passionately over its desired future course.

Bibliography
B. F. Batto and K. L. Roberts, *David and Zion* (Warsaw, 2004); P. W. L. Walker, *Jerusalem Past and Present in the Purposes of God* (Cambridge, 1992).

E. Kessler

ZIONISM
Zionism emerged as a political movement from within the liberal-humanist tradition of central and eastern Europe following the Napoleonic Wars. It differed, however, from other contemporary nationalist movements in so far as the Jews were landless as well as persecuted. The term 'Zionism' was coined in 1892 by Nathan Birnbaum, while a student in Vienna. In 1882 he had produced his first pamphlet opposing the idea of Jewish assimilation and in 1883 helped to found Kadimah, the first Jewish nationalist fraternity of students in Vienna. In 1885 he began to publish *Selbst-Emanzipation*, a journal dedicated to achieving Jewish emancipation. In the 1880s another Jewish philanthropic organization called Chovevei Zion was founded in Eastern Europe to promote a safe haven in Palestine for destitute and persecuted Jews. In 1893 Birnbaum published a booklet entitled *The National Rebirth of the Jewish People in Its Homeland as a Means of Solving the Jewish Problem*, in which he advocated more nationalistic ideas which Theodor Herzl was to expound later in *Der Judenstaat*, published in 1896.

Political Zionism
Herzl and Birnbaum articulated the deep longings of many Jewish people for their own homeland at the First Zionist Congress which Herzl convened in Basle in 1897. The secular and nationalist political Zionism of Herzl and Weizmann was opposed by the religious and philanthropic practical Zionism of Mizrahi and Ahad Ha'am who favoured a more gradual assimilation of Jews in Palestine where the rights of the indigenous Arabs would be respected. The former sought national revival, the latter national redemption, exposing the internal dualism if not inherent contradiction within Zionism, simultaneously a movement of national liberation but also one of territorial aggrandizement. Jews in Western Europe, North America and the Arab world were initially disinterested or opposed. Slowly, however, following the Germanic ethnocentric model of nationalism, Zionism became increasingly associated with ethnic identity and territorial expansion.

Messianic Zionism
The most recent form of Jewish Zionism to emerge is Messianic Zionism, associated with individuals like Rabbi Kook and Rabbi Kahne, the Gush Emunim movement, and Gershon Salomon and the Temple Mount Faithful. Religious Zionism developed from within the ultra-Orthodox subcultures of the 'Charedi Bible-belt' around Jerusalem following the 1967 Six Day War. The Charedim were the first to embrace a territorial form of mysticism rooted in the conquest narratives of the book of Joshua. Equating Arabs with the ancient Amaleks and, convinced they have a divinely ordained mandate to destroy the Palestinians, religious Zionists have been in the forefront of the confiscation of Palestinian land, attacks on Muslims and mosques and, in defiance of much

international opinion, the systematic expansion of the West Bank settlements, especially in cities such as Hebron and Bethlehem.

Christian Zionism

The largest and probably most influential form of Zionism is actually non-Jewish. Ironically, the Zionist vision was largely nurtured and shaped by Christians long before it was able to inspire widespread Jewish support. The term 'Christian Zionist' was probably first used by Theodor Herzl to describe Henri Dunant, the Swiss philanthropist and founder of the Red Cross. Dunant was one of only a handful of Gentiles to be invited to the First Zionist Congress. Proto-Christian Zionism arose as a movement in the 1820s, principally through the endeavours of Lewis Way, Edward Irving, John *Darby and the Albury Circle. Influential Christian leaders began to speculate on the imminent and literal fulfilment of promises made in the Hebrew Scriptures to the Jewish people. The belief that God would restore the Jews to Palestine as a Christian nation immediately before the return of Christ became a dominant belief and priority among Christian missions to the Jews. The Restorationist movement emerged as influential Christian ministers and politicians in Britain and the USA, such as Lord Shaftesbury, James Balfour, David Lloyd George and William Blackstone, became convinced that it was their destiny to facilitate the return of the Jews to Palestine. As more and more Jews emigrated to Palestine 'in unbelief' and the Zionist territorial enterprise emerged as a largely socialist and secular movement, Christians began to speculate that revival would follow their return rather than precede it.

The events of 1948 in the founding of the State of Israel and 1967 with the capture of the West Bank came to be seen by growing numbers of evangelicals as evidence of the fulfilment of biblical prophecy. Christian Zionist organizations claim a support base of between 50 and 100 million believers who believe it is their destiny to support Israel. They are also active politically in ensuring US foreign policy in the Middle East remains favourable toward Israel. Over 200 Christian Zionist organizations have been founded since 1980 to lobby the US government on behalf of Israel, fund the emigration of Jews to Palestine, adopt the West Bank Settlements, oppose peace negotiations, facilitate the rebuilding of the Jewish temple and so, they believe, speed the return of Christ (see *Dispensational theology; *Millennium).

Zionism as a political system should be distinguished from Judaism and from the traditional longings of the Jewish people to make *aliyah* and return to the land of their forefathers. The latter is not necessarily incompatible with the aspirations of the Palestinian people for self-determination or with international law.

See also: ZION.

Bibliography

K. Cragg, *Palestine: The Prize and Price of Zion* (London, 1997); T. Herzl, *A Jewish State* (London, 1896); W. Laqueur, *A History of Zionism* (London, 1972); M. Prior, *Zionism and the State of Israel: A Moral Inquiry* (London, 1999); H. M. Sachar, *A History of Israel from the Rise of Zionism to Our Time* (New York, 1998); A. Schlaim, *The Iron Wall* (London and New York, 2001); R. Sharif, *Non-Jewish Zionism: Its Roots in Western History* (London, 1983); S. Sizer, *Christian Zionism: Road-Map to Armageddon?* (Leicester, 2004); idem, *Zion's Christian Soldiers? The Bible, Israel and the Church* (Leicester, 2007); D. Vital, *The Origins of Zionism* (Oxford, 1975).

S. SIZER

ZIZIOULAS, JOHN D. (b. 1931)

John D. Zizioulas is one of the most important Orthodox theologians of the last century. Having studied at Athens and Harvard, he has devoted himself to the pursuit of Georges *Florovsky's call for a 'neo-patristic synthesis' in contemporary *Orthodox theology.

Although he has contributed to discussions of many issues, Zizioulas' most influential work is in the tightly interwoven doctrines of God, theological *anthropology, and ecclesiology (see *Church, doctrine of). Following the Greek Fathers, Zizioulas insists that the truly Christian doctrine of God is the doctrine of the *Trinity. The doctrine of the Trinity is 'a primordial ontological concept' . . . God 'has no ontological content, no true being, apart from communion' (*Being as Communion*, p. 17). This leads him to the conclusion that the divine substance is relational: 'love is not an emanation or "property" of the substance of God . . . but is *constitutive* of his substance, i.e. it is that which makes God what he is, the one God'

(*Being as Communion*, p. 46). Love is not an abstract attribute that is possessed by God; it is 'the *supreme ontological predicate*' (*Being as Communion*, p. 46). The divine persons have their being – are what and who they are – only in this communion of otherness and *love. Communion is an *ontological category; indeed, it is the ultimate ontological category. According to Zizioulas, God's own being is communion; God's own life is the life of love shared between the Father, Son and Holy Spirit.

And what is true of the divine persons is also true of creaturely persons made in the divine image. Human personhood is also relational, or it is nothing. It is not, however, merely relational in the abstract sense so common among various schools of *personalism in the twentieth century; rather, to be truly a human person is to be rightly related to the triune God. But a human person is only rightly related to the triune God (is only in communion with God) as that person is rightly related to the people of God. So for Zizioulas, theological anthropology and ecclesiology that are divorced from trinitarian theology are doomed from the beginning.

The thought of John Zizioulas strikes many theologians as being as promising as it is bold and provocative. He is not, however, without critics, and some important questions await reply: does Zizioulas read *existentialism into his patristic sources? Is his theology attentive enough to the salvation of the distinct person? Is his stout insistence on the radical freedom of God consistent with his fundamental thesis that 'Being Is Communion?' And is a Protestant appropriation of his thought possible – or even preferable?

Bibliography

Works: 'Human Capacity and Incapacity', *Scottish Journal of Theology* 28, 1975, pp. 401–448; 'On Being a Person: Towards an Ontology of Personhood', in C. Schwöbel and C. E. Gunton (eds.), *Persons, Divine and Human: King's College Essays in Theological Anthropology* (Edinburgh, 1991); *Being as Communion: Studies in Personhood and the Church* (Crestwood, 1993).

Studies: A. Papanikolaou, *Being with God: Trinity, Apophaticism, and Divine-Human Communion* (Notre Dame, 2006); M. Volf, *After Our Likeness: The Church as the Image of the Trinity* (Grand Rapids, 1998).

T. McCall

ZOROASTRIANISM AND CHRISTIANITY

Zoroastrianism, the Persian religion associated with Zoroaster, is an ancient and complex faith which has evolved through many stages. Its modern adherents, the Parsees (i.e. Persians), who are found mainly in the region of Bombay, India, though numbering only 100,000, exercise influence out of proportion to their numbers because of their cohesion, wealth and education. Their ancestors migrated to north-west India in the seventh and eighth centuries after the Muslim conquest of Iran. About 20,000 Zoroastrian Gabars are still left in Iran, concentrated in Tehran, Kirman and Yazd.

Numerous scholars have argued that Zoroastrianism influenced Judaism in the post-exilic period in the areas of demonology (see *Devil) and *eschatology. Others have seen parallels between the *dualism of Zoroastrianism and of the Dead Sea Scrolls. A few (e.g. J. R. Hinnells) have argued that the Zoroastrian concept of the *soshyant* ('saviour') influenced Christianity. To assess these claims one must consider the dates of the sources for our knowledge of Zoroastrian teachings.

The sources

Though many scholars have accepted the traditional date from Arabic sources that Zarathustra (Gk, Zoroaster) lived in the Achaemenid era (569–492 BC), a growing consensus has placed his *floruit* before 1000 BC because of the evidence of the *Gathas*, the seventeen hymns which are universally acknowledged to originate from the prophet.

The next oldest source is known collectively as the *Younger Avesta*. These texts may date from either before the Achaemenid era or mainly after it. Handed down orally for centuries, we have perhaps only one quarter of the originally extant traditions preserved. These are mainly works used in the various rituals.

The Zoroastrian works which deal with such subjects as cosmology, demonology and eschatology are written in Pahlavi (Middle Persian) and date from the ninth century, though they are believed to preserve traditions from the Sasanid era (AD 226–651), when Zoroastrianism was made the Iranian state religion. Of the fifty-five Pahlavi texts the two most important are: the *Bundahishn* (*The Creation*) and the *Denkard* (*Acts of Religion*), an encyclopaedia which includes a legendary life of Zoroaster.

Unfortunately, from the Parthian epoch (247 BC to AD 225), the crucial period for both Judaism and Christianity, almost no Persian text survives. Philosophers such as *Aristotle were interested in the Persian doctrines. Greek traditions placed Zoroaster 6,000 years before *Plato.

Teachings

The *Gathas* indicate that Zoroaster was concerned about the worship of Ahura Mazda ('The Wise Lord') and the care of 'cattle'. Though many have taken the latter in the literal sense, as in the closely related Hindu traditions, some scholars have argued that 'cattle' should be taken metaphorically for the good 'vision'. Whether Zoroaster's teachings were originally *monotheistic or *dualistic, with Angra Mainyu (Pahlavi Ahriman) as the primal evil being, is a matter of dispute among scholars. During the Sasanid period Zurvanism, a poorly attested heresy exalted Zurvan, the god of time, as the father of the twin spirits, Ahura Mazda and Angra Mainyu. The Parsees, who have been influenced by the West and Christianity, emphatically stress the monotheistic character of Ahura Mazda.

Man, who is naturally good, must choose between Angra Mainyu and Ahura Mazda. By choosing the side of truth instead of the lie, man can aid in the eventual triumph of Ahura Mazda. Man is saved according to his deeds. At the day of judgment he must cross the Cinvat Bridge, which expands for the righteous to pass into paradise, but contracts to a razor's edge for the wicked, who plunge into hell.

Ritual is very important to the Parsees. Prayer is constantly offered in the presence of a fire fed by sandalwood, and sacred texts are recited from memory. Parsees must wear the *sudreh* (a special shirt) and the *kusti* (a holy cord). When polluted they undergo purification with bull's urine in the *bareshnum* ceremony. Their dead are exposed to vultures in a Tower of Silence so as not to defile the sacred elements of earth, fire or water.

While the *Gathas* used the word *soshyant* to describe Zoroaster and his supporters as 'redeemers', the late Pahlavi texts speak of the coming of a future *Soshyant*, born of a virgin from the seed of Zoroaster which had been preserved in a lake. He will smite the demons, resurrect the dead and restore paradise.

While many parallels between *Judaism and Zoroastrianism may be noted, the very late sources which must be used to reconstruct the teachings of the latter cast considerable doubt on many alleged cases of Zoroastrian influence upon Judaism and Christianity. One demonstrable case of borrowing is the appearance of the demon Asmodeus in the book of Tobit, formed from the Iranian demon Aeshma.

Bibliography

K. Aryanpur, *Iranian Influence in Judaism and Christianity* (Tehran, 1973); M. Boyce, *A History of Zoroastrianism*, 2 vols. (Leiden, 1975, 1982); J. W. Boyd and D. A. Crosby, 'Is Zoroastrianism Dualistic or Monotheistic?', *JAAR* 47 (1979), pp. 557–588; J. Duchesne-Guillemin, 'The Religion of Ancient Iran', in C. J. Bleeker and G. Widengren (eds.), *Historia Religionum I: Religions of the Past* (Leiden, 1969); J. R. Hinnells, 'Christianity and the Mystery Cults', *Th* 71 (1968), pp. 20–25; *idem*, 'The Zoroastrian Doctrine of Salvation in the Roman World', in E. J. Sharpe and J. R. Hinnells (eds.), *Man and His Salvation* (Manchester, 1973); *idem*, 'Zoroastrian Saviour Imagery and Its Influences on the New Testament', *Numen* 16 (1969), pp. 161–185; S. Shaked, 'Iranian Influence on Judaism: First Century BCE to Second Century ACE', in W. D. Davies and L. Finkelstein (eds.), *The Cambridge History of Judaism, I: Introduction: The Persian Period* (Cambridge, 1984); R. E. Waterfield, *Christians in Persia* (New York, 1973); J. E. Whitehurst, 'The Zoroastrian Response to Westernization: A Case Study of the Parsis of Bombay', *JAAR* 37 (1969), pp. 224–236; D. Winston, 'The Iranian Component in the Bible, Apocrypha, and Qumran', *HR* 5 (1965–66), pp. 183–216.

E. M. YAMAUCHI

ZWINGLI, HULDRYCH (1484–1531)

Zwingli, the pioneer of the Swiss Reformation, was born at Wildhaus on 1 January 1484 and received his education at Basel, Berne and Vienna. He emerged with Renaissance enthusiasm, especially for *Erasmus, and perhaps some knowledge of Protestant doctrines of grace, acquired from Thomas Wyttenbach. Ordained in 1506, he became rector of Glarus, where he was a diligent pastor, effective preacher, affectionate colleague and industrious student. Chaplaincy service in the papal army brought him a pension but plunged him into opposition to the mercenary system. This caused tension in Glarus that led him to a new charge at Einsiedeln in 1516.

At Einsiedeln Zwingli ministered to the many pilgrims to the famous shrine of Mary. He enjoyed the resources of the Abbey library and had leisure to immerse himself in Erasmus' Greek NT (1516). The study of the original text gave him new insights into the gospel which were to affect all his future life, thought and work.

A vacancy at Zurich in 1519 opened the door to his reforming activity. Appointed people's priest in spite of opposition, he used the Great Minster pulpit for a systematic exposition of the NT, and later the OT. This preaching alerted both preacher and people to the wide gap between Scripture and contemporary belief and practice. A plague in 1519, which claimed Zwingli's brother and almost cost him his own life, added depth to his ministry. Quickly gathering adherents, he initiated the radical programme of reform which rapidly changed the ecclesiastical life of the city, the canton, and neighbouring cities such as Schaffhausen, Basel and Berne. Prominent changes included the ending of the Mass, the rejection of the *papacy and hierarchy, the suppression of the monasteries, the translation of the Bible and liturgy, the pruning of customs and practices according to Scripture, the improvement of theological training, the establishment of synodal ministry, enhancing the role of the *laity and the introduction of a tighter disciplinary system.

After 1525 Zwingli unfortunately found himself not only at odds with Roman Catholic adversaries but also embroiled with the *Anabaptists and *Lutherans. Controversies diverted resources and weakened the force of reform. The growing isolation of Zurich, the implacable hostility of the Swiss Forest Cantons and the possibility of Austrian intervention made the failure of the Marburg Colloquy (1529; see *Eucharist) a serious setback. The Forest Cantons caught Zurich unprepared at Kappel in October 1531, and Zwingli fell in the defeat which halted, although it did not reverse, the Reformation in German Switzerland.

Zwingli lived a busy life during the days of reform and reorganization, but he still found time to publish several important works. *The Clarity and Certainty of the Word of God* came out in 1522. In 1523 the *Sixty-Seven Theses*, for which he also composed a commentary, constituted the first Reformation *confession. To the same period belong the sermon *On Divine and Human Righteousness* and the essay *On the Canon of the Mass*. Perhaps his most significant theological treatise was his *Commentary on True and False Religion* (1525). The works *On Baptism* and *On the Lord's Supper* marked the beginning of the sacramental debates among the Reformers, each of them followed by further polemical treatises. In 1530 Zwingli published his Marburg address *The Providence of God*, and also prepared a statement, *Fidei Ratio*, for the Diet of Augsburg. In 1531 he wrote his very similar final work, *Exposition of the Faith*, in a vain effort to win over the king of France to the reforming cause.

Zwingli died prematurely, but not before he had launched the Reformation in Switzerland and helped to give it a distinctive stamp. Naturally he shared many of *Luther's concerns: *justification by faith, vernacular Bible translation, correction of abuses, biblical learning and the primacy of Scripture. He went beyond Luther, however, in radical application of the biblical rule. In a less autocratic society, he gave the city's councils a bigger voice as representatives of the church's laity. He devised a simpler liturgy. He acted more effectively to secure an educated ministry by the establishment of a theological college and by the so-called prophesyings at which pastors would study Scripture in the original tongues. He took sharper measures for *discipline, with a special body including lay delegates. He moved toward a *presbyterian system in taking over supervision from the distant bishop of Constance.

Theologically, too, Zwingli steered the Swiss churches into courses which would distinguish the Reformed family. Thus he gave a special emphasis to the primacy of Scripture as the rule of faith and conduct. The Berne Theses (1528) express his point that, as the church is born of God's word, so it can rule only on this basis. Sharing with Luther a firm belief in the efficacy of the word, he asserted with added strength that, although the word has instrinsic clarity, only illumination by the Holy Spirit enables us to pierce the thicket of misinterpretation and know and accept its saving truth. *Prayer is thus a *hermeneutical prerequisite.

In debate with the Anabaptists and Lutherans, Zwingli developed two important doctrines. As regards baptism, he turned to the *covenant theology of the OT, which in turn fed his strong views on election (see *Predestination) and controlled his understanding of church and society. He agreed with Luther in rejecting the eucharistic sacrifice, but saw in the Supper no necessary equation of sign and thing signified in virtue of the presence of Christ's humanity, which is now in fact at the right hand of the Father. Faith alone, he thought, perceives the presence and receives the benefits.

Zwingli is often depicted as a humanist Reformer with little theological perspicacity or spiritual profundity. Overdue reappraisals, however, have noted the crises at Einsiedeln and Zurich resulting from his problems with celibacy, his study of the NT, and his almost fatal sickness, which combined to give him an acute awareness of divine grace and divine over-ruling. He often adopts a rational style of argumentation, but closer analysis of his works reveals a sharper *trinitarian and *Christological focus. The eucharistic teaching initially suggests a weak memorialism, but it was clearly gaining in content as Zwingli came to appreciate the divine presence of Christ, the concept of the visible word and the role of the sacrament in the confirming of faith. Even what might often seem to be a compromise with *civil religion takes on a new aspect when set in the biblical context of covenant and election. If Zwingli did not himself develop all the emphases that characterize the Reformed churches, he sketched many of the outlines both practically and theologically. For this reason his brief and more localized ministry has a broad and lasting significance.

Bibliography

Works: ETs in G. W. Bromiley, *Zwingli and Bullinger* (London, 1953); E. J. Furcha and H. W. Pipkin, *Selected Writings of Huldrych Zwingli*, 2 vols. (Allison Park, 1984); S. M. Jackson, *Selected Works . . .* (New York, 1969[1901]); idem, *The Latin Works and the Correspondence . . .*, 3 vols. (New York and Philadelphia, 1912, 1922, 1929, repr. Durham, 1981–7).

Studies: E. J. Furcha and H. W. Pipkin (eds.), *Prophet, Pastor, Protestant: The Work of Huldrych Zwingli after Five Hundred Years* (Allison Park, 1984); V. Gäbler, *Huldrych Zwingli: His Life and Work* (Edinburgh, 1999); G. W. Locher, *Zwingli's Thought: New Perspectives* (Leiden, 1981); G. R. Potter, *Zwingli* (Cambridge, 1976); J. Rilliet, *Zwingli* (London, 1964); W. P. Stephens, *The Theology of Huldrych Zwingli* (Oxford, 1986); idem, *Zwingli: An Introduction to His Thought* (Oxford, 1992).

G. W. BROMILEY

Index of names

Abelard, P. 1–2, 79, 119, 316, 473, 530–531, 585, 623, 707, 734, 789, 801, 815, 881, 943
Adam of St Victor 943
Adorno, T. W. 8, 352
Adrienne von Speyr 95
Agricola, J. 43, 384, 507
Albertus Magnus 14–15, 63, 121, 264, 815
Alexander of Alexandria, Bishop 59, 74, 618
Alexander, A. 416, 705
Allen, R. 18
Althaus, P. 19
Altizer, T. 244, 690
Alves, R. 519
Ambrose 19–20, 69, 82–83, 85, 97, 108, 205, 234, 643–644, 655, 681, 732, 871
Ames, W. 20, 640, 666, 719–720, 729
Amyraut, M. 21–22, 120, 226
Anderson, G. 172, 756
Andrew of Wigmore 943
Anselm 26, 37–39, 50, 79, 86, 104, 111, 114, 150, 178, 218, 256, 273, 293, 309, 328, 355, 383–384, 423, 555, 562, 603, 672, 674–675, 736–737, 789, 801, 808, 815, 843, 845, 859, 881, 920
Antony of Egypt 68, 220, 590
Aphrahat 655, 883
Aristides 51, 664, 805
Aristotle 15, 41, 62–64, 86, 92, 126, 128, 264, 325, 377, 388, 444, 466, 563, 578, 588, 623, 631, 675, 681–682, 730, 749, 814–816, 848, 857, 859, 868, 880, 885, 903, 906, 908, 912, 918, 925, 943, 984
Arius 59–60, 74, 160, 176–177, 308, 397, 434, 549, 555, 618, 855, 965
Arminius, J. 64–65, 226, 267, 377, 382, 666, 701, 720, 859–860
Arnauld, A. 88, 463, 654
Arndt, J. 676
Asbury, F. 66, 565
Athanasius 16–17, 40, 48–49, 59–61, 69, 73–75, 78, 107–108, 115, 177, 241–242, 277, 308, 328, 334, 380, 384, 397, 422, 445, 549, 590, 618–619, 629, 655, 798, 808, 822, 856, 887, 895, 903, 916, 965
Athenagoras 51–52, 285, 664, 765, 965
Augustine 1, 3–4, 19, 25, 28, 31–32, 37–39, 41, 50, 69, 81–88, 97, 114–115, 128, 131, 142, 144, 146, 159, 167–169, 173, 184, 201, 211, 218, 225, 232, 234, 240, 251–253, 265–266, 295, 297–298, 316, 319, 322, 328–329, 335, 361, 363, 370, 375–376, 381, 390, 393, 398, 405, 407, 414, 422–423, 432, 436, 439, 462, 466, 475–476, 480–481, 483, 491, 530–531, 533–535, 548, 562, 571, 578–579, 583, 590, 595, 599, 621, 625, 643–645, 655, 657–658, 664, 666, 672, 675, 678–682, 684, 699–700, 711, 717–718, 726–727, 732, 736, 753, 757, 771, 778, 783–784, 797, 805, 808, 810, 833–835, 837, 841–842, 844, 850, 860, 867, 881, 887, 892–893, 896–899, 903, 905–906, 908, 912, 921, 923, 935, 941, 943, 945–946, 948, 951, 959, 965, 973
Aulén, G. 78, 88–89, 608, 624, 737, 801, 964
Aurelius, M. 483, 871
Austin, J. L. 195, 312, 763
Averroes 63, 92, 815–816, 906
Ayer, A. J. 293, 430, 528–529, 941, 966

Bacon, F. 417, 818
Bacon, R. 14, 350, 815, 881
Baillie, D. M. 93, 608
Baillie, J. 93–94, 132, 360, 608, 630, 681, 914
Baius, M. 87, 466
Balthasar, H. U. von 25, 36, 94–95, 211, 359, 366, 402, 551, 727, 773, 783, 836, 878
Bangs, N. 96, 568
Barclay, R. 722–723
Barclay, W. 102, 113, 547
Barlaam 404, 645
Barnes, E. W. 513–514, 585
Barth, K. 3–5, 19, 25–26, 37, 50, 73, 79, 88, 90–91, 95, 99, 103–106, 112, 115, 117–118, 120, 125, 128–129, 132, 139, 153, 158, 169, 179, 183, 197, 199, 206–207, 210–211, 226, 230–231, 236, 244–245, 254–257, 262, 270, 289, 298–299, 302, 311, 316, 319–321, 329, 333, 341, 346, 355, 359–360, 366, 370–371, 373, 385, 389, 402, 405–406, 423–424, 426–428, 439, 443, 449–450, 464–465, 475, 477–479, 482, 488–489, 492, 495, 499, 507, 514–515, 517, 519, 530, 533–535, 547, 595, 605, 608, 616, 621–622, 624, 629, 634, 639, 647–648, 673, 675, 678, 692, 699, 701, 708, 712–713, 728, 749–750, 761, 768–769, 772, 779, 781–782, 793, 807, 811–813, 827–828, 836, 843, 849, 851, 859, 866, 874, 885, 889, 892–893, 899, 902, 910, 912, 914–916, 919–920, 924, 936, 939, 944–946, 964, 978
Basil of Caesarea 52, 107–108, 277, 379, 422, 473, 655, 698, 826, 856, 916, 923
Basil the Great 60, 68–69, 107, 277, 403
Basilides of Alexandria 16, 260, 367
Bates, J. 834
Bauman, Z. 364, 692, 756
Baur, F. C. 186, 415, 517, 812, 871, 927–928
Bavinck, H. 108, 117, 310, 750, 885, 951
Bavinck, J. H. 108–109, 174, 758
Baxter, R. 109–110, 155, 406, 644, 721, 851, 859

Index of names

Baylor, M. G. 206
Beck, J. T. 110, 676
Bede 86, 114
Bellah, R. 189–190
Bellamy, J. 611
Bellarmine, R. 113, 466–467, 639
Belsham, T. 934
Benedict of Nursia 69, 114, 590
Bengel, J. A. 115, 193, 297, 677
Berdyayev, N. 793
Berengar 115–116
Berger, P. 478, 500, 832, 853–854
Berkeley, G. 116, 289, 292, 295, 435, 563, 591, 647
Berkhof, H. 117, 634
Berkhof, L. 117
Berkouwer, G. C. 73, 117–118, 310, 329, 634, 939
Bernard of Clairvaux 2, 14, 69, 86, 114–115, 119, 169, 188, 309–310, 347, 363, 408, 531, 555, 589–590, 599, 664–665, 682, 770, 805, 808, 839
Beza, T. 64, 120, 188, 200, 268, 329, 630, 665, 701, 719, 729, 747, 749, 888, 967
Biddle, J. 934
Biel, G. 87, 121, 225, 887
Biko, S. 122
Billings, J. T. 362
Birnbaum, N. 981
Blackham, H. J. 429
Bloch, E. 685
Bloesch, D. G. 125, 212, 310, 347
Blondel, M. 429, 584
Blyden, E. 121–122
Boardman, W. E. 406–407, 418
Boddy, A. A. 660
Boehme, J. 126, 508, 650, 676
Boethius 63, 126, 295, 681, 815, 881, 906, 912, 923
Boff, C. 127
Boff, L. 127, 182, 211, 351, 519–521, 685, 785
Bonaventura 14, 86, 127–128, 273, 350–351, 363, 450, 466, 599, 815, 961
Bonhoeffer, D. 70, 94, 103, 128–129, 168–170, 245, 279, 302, 359, 443, 600, 621, 673, 713, 765, 807, 859

Booth, C. 418, 665, 802, 806
Booth, W. 418, 665, 802–803
Borromeo, C. 743
Bossuet, J.-B. 129, 415
Boston, T. 130, 847
Boyce, J. P. 857
Bradwardine, T. 81, 87, 131, 381
Briggs, C. A. 131
Brightman, T. 47, 297, 572
Brown, W. A. 131–132
Browne, R. 204, 719
Bruner, F. D. 162, 662
Brunner, E. 98, 104, 132–133, 207, 256, 262, 279, 319, 361, 373, 492, 495, 514–515, 526, 581, 605, 608, 643, 807, 910, 936, 944
Bryan, W. J. 357
Buber, M. 132–133, 319–320, 341, 373
Bucer (Butzer), M. 133–134, 137, 185, 188, 199, 496, 538, 559, 599, 627–628, 747, 888, 942
Buchman, F. 594
Bukharev, F. 792
Bulgakov, M. 792
Bulgakov, S. 136–137, 278, 532, 793–794, 963
Bullinger, J. H. 98, 137–138, 199, 225, 394, 627, 630, 747, 749, 852, 937, 942
Bultmann, R. 50, 103, 138–139, 210, 215–216, 235, 245, 248–249, 254, 256–258, 262, 279, 319, 323, 361, 373, 393, 401, 411–412, 415–416, 443, 468, 478, 486, 488–489, 514–515, 519, 547, 601, 608, 624, 648, 708, 713, 768–769, 782, 803–804, 811, 819, 854–855, 882, 910, 919
Bunyan, J. 140–141, 719
Buren, P. van 244, 420
Bushnell, H. 141, 416, 787
Butler, J. 50, 141–142, 326, 546, 604, 939

Caesar Cremoninus 92
Cajetan, T. de V. C. 24, 265, 538, 909
Callistus 410–411
Calvin, J. 2, 21, 26, 41, 43, 72, 79, 81, 87, 89–90, 98–99, 105–106, 108, 120, 130, 134, 137, 143–147, 152, 156, 167, 169, 173, 181, 188, 199, 201–202, 225–226, 235, 242, 251, 253, 268, 294, 297, 323, 328–329, 332, 346, 361–362, 366, 384, 419, 423, 431, 437, 439, 443, 447, 450, 456, 477, 495–496, 500–501, 505, 507, 534, 559, 562, 604, 621, 626, 628, 630, 634, 639, 641–642, 665–666, 675, 678–679, 699–700, 702, 704, 711, 719, 737–740, 744, 746–750, 752, 758, 765–766, 779, 784, 799, 805–806, 808, 811, 813, 816, 818, 839–840, 851–852, 858–860, 868–869, 885, 888, 896–897, 915, 919–920, 928, 937, 942, 944, 951, 957, 967
Cameron, J. 21
Campbell, A. 149
Campbell, J. M. 149–151, 296, 893
Campbell, T. 149
Canisius, P. 157, 466, 744
Cappel, L. 21
Caputo, J. 302, 393, 690
Carnell, E. J. 50, 153–154, 357
Carroll, B. H. 858
Cassian, J. 69, 114, 590, 655, 664, 833
Cerinthus 367
Chalmers, T. 161, 297, 458, 693–694, 849
Channing, W. E. 934
Chao, J. 165
Chauncy, C. 774
Chemnitz, M. 162–163, 200, 345, 384–385, 541
Cho, Y. 663
Chrysippus 870
Chrysostom, J. 2, 43, 46, 78, 97, 115, 179–180, 225, 262, 277, 297, 405, 552, 627–628, 655, 919
Cisneros, F. X. de 741
Clarke, W. N. 191
Cleanthes 870
Clement of Alexandria 16, 50, 68, 96, 173, 191–192, 234, 251, 369, 565, 589–590, 643, 655, 664–665, 669, 680–681, 704, 757, 797, 805, 871

Index of names

Clement of Rome 57, 187, 400, 655, 956
Cobb, J. B. Jr 192, 568, 707–708, 955
Cocceius, J. 115, 130, 192–193, 226, 639, 677, 749, 947
Coleridge, S. T. 126, 193–194, 370, 386, 435, 458, 785–786
Columbanus 69
Comte, A. 122–124, 211, 429, 528, 687, 851, 853
Congar, Y. 203, 519, 783
Conn, H. 214
Conner, W. T. 858
Constans 60–61
Constantine 59–60, 68, 97, 166–167, 208, 265, 434, 440, 476, 505, 618, 643, 789, 791, 866, 896, 980
Constantius 60–61, 550
Contarini, G. 210, 559, 701, 742
Cotton, J. 220–221, 557–558, 721
Coxe, N. 226
Cranmer, T. 28, 43, 189, 199, 228, 431, 626, 712, 750–752, 806, 905, 942
Cremer, H. 235, 677
Croatto, J. S. 519
Cromwell, O. 109, 297, 492, 642, 721, 775, 896, 950, 957
Cudworth, R. 148
Culley, R. C. 873
Cullmann, O. 41, 197, 248, 298, 415, 445, 803
Cupitt, D. 624, 690, 829
Cyprian 54, 84, 97, 173, 240–241, 265, 509, 624, 655, 704, 718, 736, 757, 797, 808, 810, 880
Cyril of Alexandria 16–17, 46, 49, 160, 177, 219, 241–242, 277, 292, 433, 591–592, 609, 629, 634, 655, 788, 878
Cyril of Jerusalem 97, 155, 159, 887

Dabney, R. L. 242, 846
Dagg, J. L. 857
Dale, R. W. 188, 204, 347
Darby, J. N. 43, 47, 243, 259, 297–298, 356, 572, 660, 786, 982
Darwin, C. 53, 231–232, 417, 429, 617, 637, 709, 818, 950

D'Costa, G. 174, 758
Denney, J. 249, 347, 616
Derrida, J. 245–246, 249–250, 361, 393, 551, 571, 668, 689–690, 692, 764, 874
Descartes, R. 41, 148, 250, 269–270, 272, 292, 348, 363, 391, 393, 444, 527, 551, 556, 564, 603, 654, 668, 672, 688, 691, 730, 896, 947
Dewey, J. 163, 255, 361, 430
Dibelius, M. 139, 653
Dilthey, W. 258, 401, 777, 925
Diodore of Tarsus 45–46, 179
Dodd, C. H. 261–262, 298, 333, 412, 488, 608, 875, 975
Dominic 264
Dooyeweerd, H. 266, 310, 415, 750
Dostoevsky, F. M. 104, 257, 268–269, 319–320, 608
Drozdov, F. 343, 792
Dunant, H. 982
Dunn, J. D. G. 56, 162, 311, 468, 482, 568, 662, 976
Duns Scotus, J. 24, 86, 92, 121, 272–273, 328, 350, 371, 405, 449, 555, 672, 726–727, 762, 789, 816, 896, 949, 961
Dupuis, J. 172, 756
Durkheim, E. 34, 274, 301, 755, 832, 853, 952
Dwight, T. 611–612

Ebeling, G. 139, 279, 355, 599, 888
Edwards, J. 26, 73, 287–288, 297, 309, 354, 366, 406, 417, 435, 465, 475, 526, 561, 611–613, 675, 701, 722, 750, 760, 774, 842, 863, 870, 938, 960, 966
Einstein, A. 618, 682, 707, 901, 912
Eliade, M. 669, 755
Ellul, J. 288, 352, 851
Emerson, R. W. 289, 786
Engels, F. 152, 341, 435, 552–553, 775
Ephraim 883
Ephrem 655, 883
Episcopius, S. 65
Erasmus, D. 20, 87, 133, 137, 168–169, 228, 294, 328, 431, 539, 559, 627–628, 716, 744,

783, 816, 937, 984–985
Eriugena, J. S. 86, 115, 295, 600, 650, 655, 681–682, 732
Erskine, T. 295–296
Eugenius III, Pope 119
Eunomius 52, 61, 107, 371, 855
Eusebius of Caesarea 6, 16, 57, 59–60, 68, 78, 158, 208, 260, 275, 280, 308, 414, 483, 549, 618, 655, 684, 866
Eusebius of Nicomedia 59–60, 74, 549
Eutyches 160, 219, 222, 234, 510, 591–592

Faber, G. S. 47
Falwell, J. 357–358
Farel, W. 199, 332
Farmer, H. H. 333, 631
Farrer, A. M. 334, 361
Fee, G. 663
Feuerbach, L. A. 18, 42, 76, 299, 341, 429, 442, 553, 696, 812
Fichte, J. G. 342, 359–360, 391, 516
Finney, C. G. 100, 297, 310, 343, 416, 418, 547, 567, 665, 774, 802, 863
Fiorenza, E. S. 338, 344
Fletcher, J. 96, 100, 302, 566, 806
Florovsky, G. 345, 533, 570, 793, 814, 982
Ford, D. F. 475, 888, 947
Forsyth, P. T. 256, 346–347, 415, 478, 487, 878
Foucault, M. 91, 344, 348, 689–690, 692, 723, 874, 926
Fox, G. 125, 140, 722–723
Fox, M. 232–233
Francis of Assisi 349–350, 443, 460, 599, 861
Francke, A. H. 557, 676–677, 791
Frazer, J. 361, 755
Frei, H. 211, 354, 402, 602, 678, 687, 735, 888, 978
Freud, S. 76, 206, 341, 543, 689, 691, 881
Frith, J. 750–751
Fuller, A. 73, 226, 354, 433

Gadamer, H.-G. 210, 393, 401, 617, 926

989

Index of names

Galileo 92, 113, 377, 783–784, 818–819
Garvey, M. 121–122
Geertz, C. 238, 687, 735, 755
Gerhard, J. 541, 638, 676, 790
Gifford, A. 360, 605
Gill, J. 226, 354, 363, 433
Gilson, E. 361, 363, 816, 885, 909
Girard, R. 79–80, 212
Gladden, W. 849
Gogarten, F. 139, 256, 373, 514, 608, 910
González, J. L. 413, 520
Goodwin, T. 347, 373, 720–721
Gore, C. 186–187, 374, 487, 891–892
Gottschalk 86, 295, 375–376, 732
Grant, J. 124, 214, 968
Grégoire, H. 463
Gregory of Nazianzus 52, 107, 209, 370, 379, 421, 473, 799, 856, 916
Gregory of Nyssa 49, 52, 78, 107, 209, 247, 277, 295, 297, 327, 370–371, 379–380, 473, 543, 552, 655, 835, 856, 887, 916
Gregory of Palamas 404
Gregory of Rimini 87, 380–381
Gregory the Great 86, 97, 114, 159, 381, 436, 466, 590, 716
Gregory XIII, Pope 276, 743
Grenz, S. J. 214, 310, 313, 381–382, 690, 902
Gressmann, H. 415
Grosseteste, R. 14, 63
Grotius, H. 65, 79, 382, 506, 527, 629, 717, 913, 934
Guangxun, Ding 165
Gunkel, H. 415, 882
Gunton, C. E. 211, 347, 385–386, 494, 500, 583, 629
Gurney, J. J. 722
Gutiérrez, G. 172, 211, 216, 302, 386, 415, 518–522, 696, 785

Habermas, J. 210, 352
Hadow, J. 130
Hallesby, O. 387
Harmon, E. G., *see* White, E. 834

Harnack, A. von 84, 103–104, 131, 186, 233, 235, 256, 261–262, 299, 387, 398, 413, 468, 514–515, 517, 583–584, 591, 637, 711, 768, 781, 811
Hartshorne, C. 385, 632, 647, 707–708, 819, 859
Hauerwas, S. 63, 170, 183, 208, 211, 302, 361, 388, 495, 516, 603, 684, 735, 807
Hegel, G. W. F. 18, 91, 257, 298, 301, 323, 327, 341, 352, 359–360, 391–392, 415, 427, 435, 465, 489–490, 512, 514, 516, 553, 561, 564, 586, 605, 648, 650, 673, 696, 708–709, 713, 717, 786, 912, 918, 925
Heidegger, M. 138, 245, 248–249, 258, 316, 319, 392–393, 511–512, 515, 551, 631, 668, 691, 708, 727, 911, 926
Heim, K. 394
Henderson, A. 227–228
Henry, C. F. H. 310, 357, 395–396, 514, 762, 772
Herbert of Cherbury 396
Herrmann, W. 93, 103, 139, 178, 333, 403, 517, 781–782
Herzl, T. 979, 981–982
Hick, J. H. 111–112, 248, 293, 361, 404–405, 450, 515, 713, 877, 898, 936
Hilary of Poitiers 407–408
Hildegard of Bingen 233, 408, 475, 861
Hippolytus 6, 43, 201, 234, 251, 280, 307, 327, 367, 410–411, 575, 589, 704
Hodge, A. A. 417, 705, 735, 750, 950–951
Hodge, C. 329, 377, 416–417, 561, 705–706, 735, 750, 901–902, 910, 928, 950–951
Hoeksema, H. 433
Holl, K. 19, 419
Hooker, R. 154, 167, 187, 425–426, 502, 576, 681, 806, 955
Hopkins, S. 611
Horkheimer, M. 352
Hort, F. J. A. 193, 956
Howard, P. 594
Hromadka, J. L. 776
Hubmaier, B. 428, 869

Hügel, F. von 429, 584–585, 600, 929
Hugh of St Victor 681
Hume, D. 50, 142, 195, 218, 289, 291–292, 301, 429–431, 444, 484–485, 528, 563, 578–579, 605, 646, 668, 691, 734, 767, 846, 877, 898
Hus, J. 224, 432, 538, 712
Husserl, E. 249, 258, 393, 511, 551, 668–669, 911
Huxley, T. H. 14, 232, 429

Iavorsky, S. 790
Idowu, E. B. 10–11
Ignatius of Antioch 54, 56–57, 158, 176, 186, 201, 396, 552, 655
Ignatius of Loyola 437, 466, 600, 728, 742, 861–862
Ilarion 789–791
Irenaeus 3–4, 40, 43, 74, 78, 85, 89, 96, 158, 173, 176, 186, 225, 231, 234, 251, 259–260, 280, 296, 327–328, 366–369, 396–397, 410–411, 423, 446, 456–458, 571, 579, 651, 704, 711, 736, 753, 757, 766, 825, 886, 894, 898, 946, 964
Irving, E. 43, 47, 151, 296–297, 386, 423, 458–459, 786, 843, 893, 982
Iwashita, S. 464

James, W. 14, 163, 342, 361, 430, 462, 755, 761
Jansen, C. 87–88, 462
Jenkins, P. 900
Jenson, R. W. 212, 311, 385, 465, 692, 885–886, 913
Jerome 48, 69, 114, 158, 186, 206, 234, 465–466, 624, 655, 657, 659, 822, 924, 944
Jewel, J. 137, 471, 905, 942
Joachim of Fiore 47, 297, 472, 502, 531
John of Damascus 155, 277, 383, 419, 434, 436, 441, 460, 473–474, 874, 887
Julian of Eclanum 658
Julian of Norwich 479, 600, 861
Julian the Apostate 53, 789
Jüngel, E. 24, 106, 236–237, 479, 535, 713, 878

Index of names

Jung-Stilling, J. H. 791–792
Justin 50, 173, 367, 530, 571, 664, 680, 757
Justin Martyr 51, 201, 251, 296, 307, 367, 395, 436, 446, 480, 483, 552, 643, 704, 753, 770, 825, 964

Kähler, M. 110, 139, 347, 468, 484, 677
Kant, I. 7, 25, 50, 91, 111, 194, 218, 290, 293, 301, 318, 326, 341–342, 353, 359–360, 391–392, 435, 441, 444, 484–485, 516, 546, 561, 564, 571, 595, 603, 605, 623, 641, 668, 673–675, 688, 691, 713, 717, 735, 783, 786, 811–812, 841, 896, 898, 925
Kärkkäinen, V.-M. 663
Karlstadt, A. B. von 87, 436, 486, 538, 559, 597, 745
Käsemann, E. 139, 412, 486
Kato, B. 11
Keble, J. 31, 334, 487, 576, 786
Kepler, J. 820
Khomyakov, A. S. 792, 847
Kierkegaard, S. A. 4, 18, 50, 104, 132, 153, 256–257, 269–270, 319–320, 323, 326, 347, 393, 443, 489–490, 551, 608, 713, 878, 926
Kitamori, K. 71, 236, 464, 839, 878
Kittel, R. 415
Knox, J. 199, 496, 749, 752, 775, 821
Koyama, K. 464, 839
Kraemer, H. 174–175, 451, 497–498, 758–759
Kuhn, T. 653, 735
Küng, H. 36, 235, 482, 498–499, 515, 554, 704, 785
Kuyper, A. 8, 108, 117, 266, 275, 310, 377, 493, 499–500, 633, 678, 684, 694, 750, 851, 939, 951

LaCugna, C. M. 500
Ladd, G. E. 298, 804
Lash, N. 761
Law, W. 126, 443, 508, 862, 953
Leach, E. 873
Leech, K. 33
Leibniz, G. W. von 129, 250, 391–392, 509, 563–564, 673, 730, 787, 791–792, 816, 897
Leichuan, Wu 164–165
Leo the Great 510
Leo XIII, Pope 55, 64, 153, 350, 555, 583, 694, 785, 816, 909
Leontius of Byzantium 277, 433–434, 449, 474, 592, 716
Lessing, G. E. 291, 469, 511, 516, 565, 913
Lévinas, E. 689
Levi-Strauss, C. 873
Levshin, P. 791
Lewis, C. S. 26, 50, 334, 512–513, 543, 719
Lightfoot, J. B. 186, 927, 956
Lindbeck, G. 211, 261, 313, 516, 523, 678, 687–688, 735, 902, 926, 978
Lindsey, H. 43, 48, 298
Lindsey, T. 934
Lloyd-Jones, D. M. 73, 526, 722
Locke, J. 26, 289, 292, 326, 430–431, 435, 526–527, 563, 623, 668, 672, 674, 731, 734, 780, 913
Loisy, A. 387, 583–585
Lombard, P. 14–15, 81, 86, 97, 156, 272, 297–298, 380–381, 466, 530–531, 533, 659, 797, 815, 887, 906, 961
Lonergan, B. 467, 531–532, 551, 617, 816, 909, 917
Lossky, V. 53, 278, 532, 599, 793, 963
Lucaris, C. 200, 278, 790
Ludlow, J. M. F. 171
Lull, R. 460, 536–537
Luther, M. 3–4, 19, 43, 70, 72, 79, 81, 87, 89, 98, 121, 125, 130, 133–134, 137, 141, 143, 146, 152, 156, 163, 167, 169, 182, 189, 200, 206, 211, 225, 228, 235–236, 244, 251–252, 256–257, 265, 279, 294, 297, 307, 322–323, 325–326, 328, 341, 345, 384, 400, 405–406, 413, 419, 423, 428, 436, 443, 447, 456, 465, 480–482, 486, 495, 501–502, 504–507, 534, 537–542, 559, 562, 597, 600, 604, 608, 620, 628, 633–634, 638, 640–641, 651, 659, 665–667, 677, 684, 699–700, 704, 711–712, 714, 719, 737–740, 742, 744–745, 747–748, 751–752, 765, 771, 778–779, 782, 784, 801, 805, 808, 813, 816–818, 822–823, 839, 857, 859, 861–862, 867–868, 887–888, 909, 917–918, 930, 954, 970, 976, 985
Lyotard, J.-F. 689, 691–692

Macarius (Pseudo) 403, 543
Macchia, F. D. 663
MacDonald, G. 543
Machen, J. G. 544, 598, 705, 938
MacIntyre, A. C. 63, 544–545, 552, 684, 763
MacKay, D. M. 545–546
MacKinnon, D. M. 546, 735
Mackintosh, H. R. 93, 249, 487, 546–547, 914
Macquarrie, J. 248, 547, 713
Mahan, A. 418, 547–548
Mani 548–549
Marcel, G. 319, 361, 549
Marcellus of Ancyra 60–61, 549–550
Marcion 234, 260, 367, 387, 397, 457, 548, 550, 883, 894
Marion, J.-L. 361–362, 393, 551, 690, 692
Maritain, J. 363, 551, 816, 868, 909
Martineau, J. 150, 193, 934
Marx, K. 18, 53, 76, 152–153, 183, 298, 341, 352, 435–436, 552–554, 556, 694, 696, 775, 832, 851, 853, 868, 971
Mather, C. 557–558
Mather, I. 557, 870
Maurice, F. D. 153, 171, 193, 435, 500, 543, 776, 849, 956
Mauss, M. 361
Maximilia 593
Mbiti, J. 10–11, 123
McCosh, J. 705, 950
McGrath, A. E. 50, 230, 311, 481, 495, 690, 735, 772, 901
Mede, J. 297, 572
Melanchthon, P. 5, 81–82, 134, 137, 142, 163, 198, 200, 226, 345, 384–385, 393–394, 419, 431, 481, 505, 507, 538, 541, 559, 561, 627, 638, 640, 738–739, 805, 816, 852, 859, 888, 937

Index of names

Menzies, R. P. 663
Merton, T. 70, 563, 590, 600, 864
Metz, J. B. 355, 420, 519, 569
Meyendorff, J. 278, 434, 569
Míguez Bonino, J. 182, 519, 521, 568, 570, 685, 696
Milbank, J. 63, 211, 302, 361–362, 570–571, 726, 763, 849, 851
Miller, W. 834
Mingdao, Wang 165
Miyahira, N. 464
Moberly, R. C. 582
Mogila, P. 278, 790
Möhler, J. A. 586
Molinos, M. de 724
Moltmann, J. 71, 80, 181, 211–212, 236–237, 282, 299, 302, 361, 372, 415, 420, 424, 426–428, 445, 475, 519, 536, 586–588, 632, 647, 685, 699, 713, 770, 878, 899, 916, 936, 959
Montanus 549, 593
Moodie, T. D. 190
Moody, D. L. 48, 100, 418, 630, 858
More, H. 148
Mullins, E. Y. 102, 858
Müntzer, T. 22, 597, 745, 813, 897
Murray, A. 100, 274, 418, 597–598, 665
Murray, J. 226, 433, 598, 784
Musculus, W. 598–599

Nero, Emperor 43
Nesmelov, V. 792
Nestorius 17, 45, 160, 177, 222, 234, 241, 292, 555, 591, 609, 634, 884
Nevin, J. W. 416, 561, 787
Newbigin, J. E. L. 174, 212, 313, 364, 573, 581, 586, 615–616, 699, 758
Newman, J. H. 31–32, 50, 193, 199, 253, 263, 299–300, 374, 413, 576, 616–617, 783, 786, 826
Newton, I. 247, 291, 526, 618, 819, 912
Nicholas of Lyra 619–620

Niebuhr, H. R. 237, 494–495, 573, 608, 612, 620, 853, 861, 918
Niebuhr, R. 88, 153, 167, 361, 415, 493, 515, 554, 608, 620–621, 684, 848, 979
Nietzsche, F. 76, 91, 104, 125, 206, 244–245, 301, 319, 353, 490, 622, 689, 691–692, 695, 918, 926
Novak, M. 153, 500, 520
Novatian 624
Nowell, A. 156
Nygren, A. 88–89, 571, 599, 608, 624–625, 964

Ochino, B. 626, 933, 937
Oden, T. C. 627, 885
O'Donovan, O. 199, 206, 208, 211, 302, 311, 493, 505, 625, 684
Oecolampadius, J. 133, 538, 627–628, 740, 749
Oldham, J. H. 172, 284, 630, 848
Olevianus, C. 156, 226, 394, 630–631, 749, 888
Oman, J. W. 89–90, 333, 631
Origen 16, 59, 68, 97, 107, 148, 173, 191, 253, 280, 295–297, 308, 327, 334, 367, 380, 395, 400, 405, 433, 446, 465, 543, 552, 565, 589–590, 635–636, 643, 655, 657, 669, 680–681, 718, 736–737, 757, 770, 808, 825, 856, 874, 887, 912, 923, 935, 965
Orr, J. 232, 299, 327, 413, 637, 951
Osiander, A. 163, 228, 538, 559, 640–641, 779
Otto, R. 631, 641, 669, 782, 838
Owen, J. 79, 188, 386, 423, 640, 642–643, 720–721
Owen, R. 149, 171

Pachomius 68–69, 220, 664
Packer, J. I. 35, 79, 162, 311, 418, 644, 722, 905
Padilla, R. 216, 311, 521, 697
Pajon, C. 22
Palamas, G. 247, 278, 345, 371, 404, 569–570, 645, 946
Paley, W. 326, 604, 645–646, 819

Palmer, P. W. 96, 417–418, 567, 646, 665, 802
Panaetius 871
Panikkar, R. 410, 451
Pannenberg, W. 4, 24, 106, 212, 251, 271, 298–299, 323, 329, 381–382, 415, 424, 426–428, 449, 494, 533–534, 608, 628, 647–649, 709, 713, 767–768, 770, 782, 885, 944
Parham, C. F. 660
Park, E. A. 417, 611
Parker, T. 934
Pascal, B. 50, 77, 88, 326, 342, 347, 463, 595, 654, 731
Paschasius R. 86, 114–115, 295, 655, 732
Paul of Constantinople 61
Paul of Samosata 6, 308, 549, 804
Peckham, J. 156–157
Pelagius 84, 159, 328, 376, 480, 562, 657–658, 700
Pelikan, J. 198, 361, 413, 440, 658
Perkins, W. 20, 72, 156, 220, 595, 634, 640, 665–666, 719–720
Peterson, E. 685
Philo 26, 395, 400, 529–530, 588, 669–670, 680–681, 871, 903, 921
Pickstock, C. 570, 726
Pieris, A. 520
Pinnock, C. 35, 175, 311–313, 629, 677, 709, 759
Pius V, Pope 743
Pius IX, Pope 555, 652, 784, 939
Pius XII, Pope 284, 555, 652, 784
Placher, W. C. 678
Plantinga, A. 50, 112, 361, 671, 674, 678–679, 746–747, 896, 898
Plato 41, 62–63, 86, 148, 194, 334, 395, 400, 441, 444, 534, 563, 588, 623, 631, 669, 679–682, 727, 811, 848, 856, 892, 896–897, 912, 918, 984
Plotinus 83, 148, 316, 647, 650, 680–682, 877, 912, 943
Polanyi, M. 293, 312, 616, 682–683, 901, 915
Polkinghorne, J. 50, 361, 686

Index of names

Polycarp 43, 56–57, 186, 275, 456, 805, 956
Popper, K. 291, 528–529, 941
Porphyry 83, 125–126, 680, 798, 943
Posidonius 871
Praxeas 589
Preus, R. D. 638
Prisca 593
Prokopovich, F. 343, 790–791
Pseudo-Dionysius the Areopagite 26, 52–53, 111, 295, 403, 681, 692, 715–716, 917
Pusey, E. 31–32

Race, A. 172, 757
Rahner, K. 36, 95, 127, 211, 236, 263, 323, 355, 359, 424, 450, 467, 519, 551, 569, 599, 629, 727–728, 773, 783–784, 816, 879, 881, 909, 916, 936, 944
Ramm, B. 310, 728, 828
Ramsey, I. T. 302, 729, 764
Ramus, P. 109, 720, 729, 816
Rashdall, H. 585
Ratramnus 86, 114–115, 295, 375, 655, 732
Ratzinger, J. 181, 212, 413, 520, 523, 685, 732, 785
Rauschenbusch, W. 167, 298, 514–515, 554, 733, 849–850
Raven, C. E. 514, 733–734
Reid, T. 195, 671, 734, 747
Reimarus, H. S. 247, 511
Reitzenstein, R. 416
Remigius of Lyons 375
Richard of St Victor 169, 536, 943
Richardson, A. 608, 777, 970
Richardson, H. W. 190
Ricœur, P. 211, 329–330, 361, 442, 763–764, 777, 881, 901, 978
Ridley, N. 732, 750–751
Ritschl, A. 91, 93, 207, 262, 298, 326, 333, 346–347, 403, 435, 517, 547, 561, 637, 675–676, 711, 724, 781–782, 829, 843, 925, 927
Ro, Bong Rin 71
Roberts, J. D. 122–123, 520
Robinson, H. W. 220
Robinson, J. A. T. 50, 235, 245, 248, 341, 479, 515, 585, 782, 945
Robinson, J. M. 412
Rorty, R. 692
Roscelin 1, 623, 734
Rousseau, J.-J. 189–190, 291, 429, 787, 846, 914, 948
Ruether, R. R. 211, 213, 336–340, 787–788
Rufinus the Syrian 657
Russell, B. 292, 430, 528, 747, 966
Rutherford, S. 226–227, 794–795, 949
Ryle, G. 41, 292

Sabellius 397, 411, 549, 589
Saint-Cyran 463
Saiving, V. 337
Samosata, Paul of 6, 308, 549, 589, 804
Sanders, J. E. 175, 311, 313, 759, 859
Sartre, J.-P. 316, 319–320, 490, 549, 668
Sattler, M. 198, 813
Saturninus of Antioch 260, 367
Saussure. F. de 249, 873
Schaeffer, F. A. 7, 50, 190, 500, 809
Schaff, P. 198, 200, 234, 417, 561, 787
Schelling, F. W. J. 359–360, 391–392, 516, 673, 911
Schillebeeckx, E. 251, 265, 509, 798, 809–810
Schlatter, A. 207, 235, 257, 347, 677, 803, 810–811
Schleiermacher, F. D. E. 4, 26, 91, 103–104, 106, 132, 178, 191, 207, 253, 258, 262, 279, 298–299, 326, 333, 341, 398, 401, 416, 427, 442–443, 450, 485, 514–516, 547, 561, 586, 631, 639–641, 699, 701, 707, 711, 713, 761, 781–782, 786, 811–813, 843, 885, 888–889, 902, 911, 924–925, 935
Schmemann, A. 307, 569–570, 814
Schmitt, C. 685
Schwegler, A. 927
Schweitzer, A. 262, 298, 411, 676, 816–817
Schwenckfeld, C. 745, 817–818
Seerveld, C. 7–8
Seng, Kang Phee 165
Servetus, M. 398, 913, 933
Sheldon, C. 849
Shelton, J. B. 662
Sibbes, R. 220–221, 666, 720–721, 839–840
Siger of Brabant 92, 815–816
Simons, M. 22, 98, 560, 745, 840, 869, 897
Smith, A. 152, 694, 970
Smith, H. W. 406, 418
Smith, R. P. 406–407, 418, 665
Sobrino, J. 172, 444, 520–521, 686, 785, 847–848
Socinus, F. 398, 745, 852
Socinus, L. 745, 852
Socrates 49, 395, 444, 679–680
Soelle, D. 854–855, 959
Solovyov, V. 792–794
Song, C.-S. 71–72, 165
Spener, P. J. 193, 676–677, 806, 862, 888
Spinoza, Benedict (Baruch) de 250, 342, 359–360, 392, 563–564, 591, 650, 672, 730, 860–861, 913
Spurgeon, C. H. 249, 433, 526, 543, 722, 863–864
Staniloae, D. 278, 864–865
Staupitz, J. 81, 87
Stoddard, S. 870
Storkey, A. 849
Storr, V. F. 513–514
Strauss, D. F. 178, 516–517, 601, 776, 871–872, 927–928
Strong, A. H. 857–858, 872
Stronstad, R. 662
Suárez, F. de 24, 466–467, 772, 816
Swinburne, R. 41, 50, 671, 899
Symeon Stylites 884
Symeon the New Theologian 278, 403, 881

Takakura, T. 464
Tanner, K. 361–362, 767
Tareyev, M. 792
Tatian 51, 835, 871, 883
Tawney, R. H. 143, 172, 693, 776, 848, 851
Taylor, J. 154, 302, 595, 890, 953

Index of names

Taylor, M. C. 692
Taylor, N. W. 417, 611–612
Taylor, V. 412, 568, 875
Teilhard de Chardin, P. 467, 606, 647, 709, 734, 783, 890–891
Temple, W. 172, 183, 284, 361, 693, 848, 851, 891–892, 971
Teresa of Avila 443, 475, 599–600, 741, 861, 893–894
Tertullian 54, 85, 97, 176, 186, 201, 234, 240, 280, 296, 328, 367, 436, 446, 509, 550, 552, 565, 571, 575, 588–589, 594, 624, 643, 651, 655, 659, 684, 704, 718, 753, 765, 770, 797, 805, 808, 825, 835, 856, 871, 874, 894–895, 900, 921, 923, 944, 965
Theodore of Mopsuestia 45, 97, 177, 609
Theodore the Studite 434
Theodoret of Cyrrhus 45–46, 805, 884
Theodotus 6, 589
Theophilus of Antioch 52, 231, 964
Thielicke, H. 302, 904–905
Thomas Aquinas 3–4, 7, 14–15, 24, 26, 32, 50, 63–64, 79, 86, 92, 111–112, 121, 125, 128, 201, 206, 211, 230, 233, 253, 262, 264, 273, 300, 328, 350, 371, 377, 383, 388, 405, 436, 441, 446, 449, 466, 473, 495, 505, 531, 535, 537, 551, 555, 558, 562–564, 578, 595, 599, 603, 607, 620, 631, 645, 664, 672, 682, 700, 730, 762, 766, 771, 780, 783, 789, 797, 799, 805, 814–816, 825, 840, 845, 857, 859, 868, 874, 879, 885, 887, 892, 896, 904, 906–907, 909, 912, 939, 946, 961, 980
Thomas, M. M. 451
Thompson, J. L. 900
Thornwell, J. H. 909–910
Thurneysen, E. 104, 373, 910
Tikhon of Zadonsk 791
Tillich, P. 18, 50, 91, 111–112, 153, 207, 210, 235, 245, 319, 323, 355, 361, 393, 515, 517, 547, 608, 647, 681, 714, 762–763, 807, 881, 888, 902, 910–911, 917, 936
Tolstoy, L. 7–8, 644, 693, 792, 914
Tomlinson, D. 312
Torrance, T. F. 106, 150, 230, 311, 414, 618, 682, 735, 750, 878, 893, 901, 912, 914–917
Tracy, D. 210, 361, 917, 978
Troeltsch, E. 93, 248, 415, 429, 515, 613, 829–830, 853, 925, 952
Turner, M. M. B. 662
Turretin, F. 22, 79, 383, 639, 747, 750, 816, 928
Tyconius 83, 265, 571
Tylor, E. B. 34, 239
Tyndale, W. 738, 750–752, 801
Tyrrell, G. 387, 411, 429, 467, 584–585
Tzu, L. 889

Uchimura, K. 464
Underhill, E. 929
Ursinus, Z. 156, 225, 394, 631, 749, 888, 937

Valdés, J. de 933, 937, 942
Valentinus 16, 367–368
Van Mastricht, P. 639, 937–938, 967
Van Til, C. 266, 433, 809, 938–939
Vanhoozer, K. 170, 211, 310, 312–314, 689, 735, 763, 772, 903
Velichkovsky, P. 791
Vermigli, P. M. 747, 749, 888, 937, 941–942
Victorinus, C. M. 571, 681, 874, 943
Voetius, G. 937, 947
Volf, M. 181, 696
Voltaire 247, 291, 415, 429, 689, 787, 948
Vos, G. 117, 536, 598, 938, 949

Waldo, P. 949
Walker, A. 124, 968
Ward, G. 570, 726
Warfield, B. B. 117, 164, 200, 232, 288, 454, 544, 665, 705, 711, 750, 828, 938–939, 950–952
Weber, M. 18, 89, 143, 152, 274, 301, 613, 634, 755, 829–832, 853–854, 925, 952
Weiss, J. 298
Wells, D. 214
Wesley, C. 309, 568, 575, 806, 862, 952–953, 958
Wesley, J. 28, 43, 65–66, 73, 96, 100, 115, 126, 169, 208, 218, 297, 323, 377, 406, 417–419, 423–424, 508, 525, 543, 565–568, 646, 660, 665, 693, 698, 779, 802, 806, 846, 859, 862–863, 893, 901, 953–955, 958
Westcott, B. F. 171, 374, 681, 956
Weston, F. 33, 487
Whichcote, B. 148
White, E. 834–835
White, L. 281
Whitefield, G. 147–148, 309, 423, 526, 565, 954, 958
Whitehead, A. N. 111, 361, 497, 647, 681, 707–708, 819–820, 859
Wiesel, E. 420, 958–959
William of Champeaux 1, 734, 943
William of Ockham 1, 26, 87, 121, 350, 381, 405, 449, 672, 816, 881, 961–962
Williams, C. W. S. 512, 962
Williams, Roger 221, 913, 962–963
Williams, Rowan 570, 768–769, 946, 963
Wingren, G. 88, 964
Wisløff, C. F. 965
Witherspoon, J. 195, 705, 965–966
Wittgenstein, L. J. J. 250, 293, 312, 485, 508, 528, 617, 623, 687, 735, 763, 941, 966–967, 978
Wollebius, J. 967
Wolterstorff, N. 7–8, 111, 361, 453, 671, 746, 763, 912
Woods, G. F. 260
Wrede, W. 411
Wright, N. T. 299, 311, 313, 412, 448, 456, 482, 735, 770, 804, 976–977
Wyclif, J. 43, 115, 131, 432, 751, 977–978

Index of names

Yaozong, Wu 165
Yifan, Shen 165
Yoder, J. H. 170, 211, 302, 310, 359, 388, 493, 684, 712, 978–979
Yong, A. 311, 663

Yoshimitsu, Y. 464
Yu, Carver 165

Zeno 592, 653, 716, 870–871
Zinzendorf, N. von 676, 862

Zizioulas, J. 181, 211, 385, 414, 424, 916, 982–983
Zwingli, H. 98, 133, 137–138, 225, 307, 328, 428, 431, 437, 538, 540, 627–628, 700, 738, 740, 744–745, 747, 749, 841, 859, 888, 957, 984–986

Index of subjects

abortion 357
accommodation 2, 301–302, 818
Acts of Thomas 884
Adam 3–5
  last/second (Christ) 4
  sin of 4
adiaphora 5
adoptionism 6, 176, 280, 804
aesthetics 6–9
African Christian theology 9–12, 799
African Independent Churches, theology of 11–12
African theology (*see also* Black theology) 13
agape 534, 624, 848
agape meal 306
agnosticism 14
Albigenses 15
Alexandrian School 15–17, 177
alienation 17–18, 971
allegory 16
amillennialism, symbolic 572
Amyraldism 21–22
Anabaptist theology 22–24, 98, 428, 840
  and church discipline 185
  and church–state relations 897
Anabaptists 501, 740, 745, 813
analogy, of being (*analogia entis*) 24–25, 32, 371, 762
analytic theology 25–26
androcentrism 788
angels 26–27, 29–30, 112
Anglican Evangelical Group Movement 513
Anglicanism (*see also* Cranmer; Jewel; Keble) 27–30, 471
  and ministry 576
Anglican–Roman Catholic International Commission (ARCIC) 33, 181, 186, 497
Anglo-Catholic theology 28, 30–34, 374, 576
anhypostasia 433, 449
animism 34
annihilationism 34–35
anomoians/anhomoians (*see* heterousians) 61

anonymous Christianity 36, 728, 784
  and the fall 328
  and satisfaction 808
  and sin 383
anthropic principle 686
anthropocentrism 430
anthropology 39–42, 649
  and image of God 40–41
anthropomorphism 42
Antichrist 42–43
antinomianism 43–44, 322, 504, 507
Antioch
  Council of 60
  Fourth Creed 60
Antiochene School 45–46, 177
anti-Semitism 420, 476
aphthartodoketai 592
apocalyptic 46–48
apocalypticism 791
Apocryphon of John 368
Apollinarianism 40, 48–49, 397
apologetics 49–50, 153–154
apologists 51, 51–52
apophatic theology 52–53, 533
apostasy 53
apostle 54–56
Apostles' Creed 234–235
Apostolic Church 56–57
apostolic succession 54–55
Arab Christian thought (*see also* Islam and Christianity) 58
Arianism 19, 58–62, 74, 107, 176, 397, 619, 855
Aristotelianism 62–64, 92, 749
Arminianism (*see also* Synod of Dort) 64–66, 96, 268, 377, 566
  Wesleyan 65
ascension (heavenly session of Christ) 66–68
asceticism 68
  and monasticism 68–72, 180
assurance 65, 72–73, 667
Assyrian Church of the East 884
Athanasian Creed 234
atheism, practical 76–77
atonement 75, 77–80, 150, 212,

478, 568, 582, 629, 801
  and Abelard 1–2
  and Arminianism 65
  and evil 317
  and Forsyth 347
  and Gregory of Nyssa 380
  and incarnation 78
  and Islam 461
  and justification 79
  and legal justice 78
  and penal substitution 876
  and penalty 79
  and propitiation 78
  and reconciliation 78
  and satisfaction 79
  classic view 78, 89
  extent of 80–81
  governmental theory 65, 382
  limited 81, 749
  mystical views 78
  ransom theory 78
  subjective theory 79
  universal 80–81
Auburn Affirmation 598
Augsburg Confession 81–82, 198
Augustine
  and amillennialism 571
  and Christian Platonism 681–682
  and church–state relations 867
  and eschatology 297
  and evil 316, 897–898
  and faith 480
  and fatherhood of God 335
  and grace 376, 480, 562
  and history 414
  and Holy Spirit 422
  and image of God 439
  and joy 475
  and justification 481
  and kingdom of God 491
  and love 480
  and love of God 535–536
  and marriage 837
  and philosophy 672
  and political theology 684
  and predestination 480, 700, 833
  and sacraments 797

Index of subjects

Augustine (*cont.*)
  and sanctification 805
  and sexual differentiation 835
  and sin 4, 84, 480
  and sinlessness of Christ 844
  and the fall 328
  and vision of God 946
  and will 959
  City of God 85, 167, 297, 684, 867, 946
  Confessions 82–83
  The Trinity 85
Augustinianism 86–88, 842, 960
authority 89–91
  and Scripture 824
  divine 89–91
  human 89
  papal 896
autonomy 91–92, 291
Averroism 92
Azusa Street Mission 660

baptism 96–99, 201, 739, 753, 930, 946, 974
  and grace 376
  and Zwingli 985
  believers' 23, 97–98, 740, 745
  Eucharist and ministry 99, 186, 194, 285, 308, 325, 798, 946
  in the Spirit 99–101, 162, 660–661, 802
  infant 4, 97, 332, 736, 740, 753
Baptist confessions 200
Baptist Missionary Society 354
Baptist theology 101–102
  Particular (*see also* Fuller; Gill; Hall) 354
  Strict and Particular 433
Barmen Declaration 103, 183, 197
Barth, Karl
  and analogy 25, 371
  and assurance 73
  and atonement 79
  and autonomy 91
  and baptism 99
  and the Christian life 169
  and Christology 5, 105
  and church–state relations 866
  and conscience 206
  and covenant theology 226

  and creation 230–231
  and dialectical theology 255–257
  and doctrine of man 106
  and doubt 270
  and evil 316
  and the fall 329
  and hidden and revealed God 406
  and incarnation 179, 449
  and judgment 477–478
  and justification 482
  and law and gospel 507
  and love for God 534
  and love of God 533–535
  and natural theology 104, 231, 605
  and philosophy 673
  and predestination 701
  and resurrection of Christ 769
  and sanctification 807
  and Schleiermacher 812
  and Scripture 828
  and systematic theology 885
  and theonomy 91
  and time 912
  and Torrance 914–915
  and transfiguration of Christ 920
  and Trinity 106, 424, 533, 924
  and virgin birth 945
  and von Balthasar 95
  and Word of God 402, 699
beauty 94–95, 366
being (*see also* ontology) 110–112, 392, 549, 604
Belgic Confession 199
Benedictine tradition 114–115
Berlin Declaration 118–119
Bible Churchmen's Missionary Society 514
biblical theology 777, 949
biblicism, radical 12
black consciousness (*see also* black theology) 121–122
Black Consciousness Movement (South Africa) 122
Black Power 123
black theology 122–124, 520
black theology, and African theology 123
Black Theology Project 122, 124
'blackness' 123

blasphemy 125
Bonhoeffer and the Christian life 168
Brethren movement 243
Buddhism 134–136, 317

calling (*see also* vocation) 142–143
Calvin
  and accommodation 2
  and assurance 72
  and atonement 79, 81, 799
  and baptism 98, 147
  and catechisms 156
  and the Christian life 146, 169
  and Christology 145
  and church 739
  and church–state relations 147, 868, 897
  and covenant theology 225–226
  and doctrine of God 144
  and Eucharist 146, 307, 740
  and the fall 145, 173, 328
  and Holy Spirit 423
  and image of God 41, 145
  Institutes 144, 146, 738, 758, 888
  and justification 146, 737
  and knowledge of God 143–145, 495, 758
  and law 505, 739
  and ministry 146, 188
  and natural law 505
  and natural theology 604
  and offices of Christ 628
  and prayer 146
  and predestination 145–146, 700, 740
  and priesthood of all believers 704
  and repentance 146, 765
  and resurrection of Christ 766
  and providence 145
  and sanctification 146, 806
  and Scripture 143–145
  and *sensus divinitatis* 746
  and transfiguration of Christ 919–920
  and worship 146
Calvinism 377, 417, 749–750, 951
Calvinism, High 363

Index of subjects

Calvinistic Methodism 147–148
Cambridge Platonists 148–149
canon, and Scripture 182, 822
canon law 151, 282
capitalism 152–153
Caroline Divines 154–155
Carthage, Council of 657
casuistry 20, 155
cataphatic theology 716
Catechism of the Catholic Church (1992) 157
catechisms 155–157, 744
Catholic Apostolic Church 458
catholicity 158–159
cause 63
Celtic Christianity 159–160, 281
certainty 649
Chalcedon, Council of 160, 177, 222, 234, 277, 397, 422, 433, 448, 591
Chalcedonian Definition 46, 53, 234, 468
chance 715
charismatic movement/theology 161–162, 311, 424, 475, 501
charismatic renewal 577
Chicago School of Theology 163
Chicago Statement on Biblical Inerrancy (1978) 164, 454
Chicago Statement on Biblical Hermeneutics (1982) 164
Chicago/Lambeth Quadrilateral 29
China Inland Mission 283
Chinese theology 164–165
Christ
  and judgment 477
  and kingdom of God 314
  as last/second Adam 4
  as righteousness of God 778
  faith of 322
  human nature 843–844
  offices of 628–630
  sinlessness of 449, 843–844, 893, 945
  suffering of 447, 878
  union with see union with Christ
  uniqueness of 404, 451, 932
Christ-culture relationship, typology of 237, 239, 494
Christendom 166–168, 684, 866, 869

Christendom movement 167
Christendom, and post-Christendom 304
Christian life 168–170
Christian Social Union 171
Christian Socialism 171–172
Christianity and Islam 166, 460
Christianity and other religions (see also Kraemer) 172–175
Christian–Jewish relations 420, 477
Christification 891
Christology (see also Antiochene School; Apollinarianism; Docetism; Jesus; monarchianism; Novatian) 6, 16, 49, 74, 175, 176, 177–179, 241, 259, 855, 923
  and African theology 13
  and Apostolic Fathers 56
  and Barth 5, 105
  and Clement of Alexandria 191
  and Council of Chalcedon 160
  and Cyril of Alexandria 242
  and Eusebius of Caesarea 308
  and evangelism 314
  and Forsyth 347
  and Gregory of Nazianzus 379
  and Hilary of Poitiers 407
  and Holy Spirit 423
  and Irenaeus 457
  and John of Damascus 474
  and Leo the Great 510
  and models 583
  and non-Christian religions 36
  and Pannenberg 648
  and process theology 707
  and Reformers 738
  and Schleiermacher 812
  and Schwenckfeld 817
  and Sobrino 521, 848
  and wisdom 964
  and womanist theology 968
  Byzantine 178, 177
  Christ as mediator 558
  from below 629
  threefold office of Christ 79
  transcendental 728

church 180–184, 217, 240, 465, 497, 739, 818, 916
  and African theology 13
  and Anabaptists 23
  and Anglo-Catholic theology 33
  and Bucer 134
  and evangelism 314
  and family life 332
  and Holy Spirit 424
  and kingdom of God 491
  and Mennonite theology 560
  and Mercersburg theology 561
  and mission 183–184, 212
  and resurrection of Christ 767
  and Scripture 826
  and society 892
  and tradition 32
  apostolicity 182
  as communion/koinonia 181–182
  as family 331
  as sacrament 32
  as Zion 980
  branch theory 33
  catholicity 158, 182
  doctrine of 432, 752
  gathered 869
  holiness 182
  in Methodist theology 567–568
  invisible 158, 196, 712
  marks of 182, 703
  mega churches 713
  models of 573–574
  Moravian view 597
  new forms 577
  power of 961
  under communism 868
  unity of 182, 287
  visible 158, 196
church discipline 184–186
church government 186–189
  Presbyterian 703
Church of England 187
  and canon law 151
  and confirmation 202
Church of Scotland 188
Church of Scotland, Disruption (1843) 161
Church of the Nazarene 418
church praxis 182–183

999

Index of subjects

church–state relations (*see also* Constantine; theocracy) 183, 492, 505, 712, 745, 752
and Anabaptists 23
civil religion 189–190
collegiality and conciliarity 194–195
colonialism 364
common-sense philosophy 195, 612, 705, 747
communication of attributes (*communicatio idiomatum*) 178
communion of saints 182, 195–196
conceptualism 623
Concerned Evangelicals, Evangelical Witness in South Africa 866
conciliar fellowship 194
Conciliar movement 222
conciliarism 189
Concord, Book of 200, 346, 541
Concord, Formula of 200 5, 162, 345–346, 541, 638
Confessing Church 197
confessions and creeds 198
confessions of faith (*see also* Barmen Declaration; Lausanne Covenant) 197–200
confirmation 201–202, 509, 753
and Christianity 202–203
Congregational Federation 205
Congregational Union 204
Congregationalism 188, 204–205
congruism 701
conscience 205–207
Consensus Tigurinus 137, 199
conservative theology 207–208
Constance, Council of 222, 224
Constantinianism 308, 683
Constantinople, First Council of (381) 61, 208, 222
Constantinople, Second Council of (553) 222
Constantinople, Third Council of (680) 223
Constantinople, Fourth Council of (870) 223
Constantinople, Fifth Council of (880) 223
consumerism 209–210

contemplation, and revelation 95
contemporary theological trends 210–212
contextual theologies 213–214
contextualization 13, 70, 213, 215–217, 238, 452
contingency 217–218
contraception 785, 837
conventionalism 623
conversion 218–219, 753
Coptic Christianity 219–220
corporate personality 220
correlation, method of 515, 902, 911
cosmological argument 603
Cosmonomic Idea, philosophy of 266
councils 221–225
  ecumenical 222–223, 277
covenant 534–535, 778, 839
  and creation 230
  and grace 507
covenant theology 193, 225–227, 598, 639, 749, 930, 937, 985
Covenanters 227–228
creatio ex nihilo 230–231, 912
creation 229–231, 271, 300, 767, 858, 894, 964
creation (*see also* ecology) 715
  and covenant 230
  and evolution 231–232, 605
  and Moltmann 588
  and natural theology 231
  pluriformity in 275
  and resurrection of Christ 767
  and science 230
  and stewardship 231
  and Thomas Aquinas 908
creation-centred spirituality 232–233
creationism 232, 857
creeds 233–235, 712
creeds and confessions 702
creeds, and Ethiopian Orthodox Church 305
crisis theology *see* dialectical theology 255
cross 695
  and Anselm 38
  and Barth 236
  and Jüngel 236–237
  and Luther 235–236

and Moltmann 236, 587
theology of 235–237, 366, 406, 542
cult(s) 613, 853
cultural apologetics 809
culture 7–8, 238–240, 381, 620, 699, 861, 880
culture, and theology 237–239

Dalit theology 71
Dasein 393
death 243–244
death-of-God theology 244–245
deconstruction 245–246, 689, 692
deification 246–247
deism 247, 369, 604, 715, 948
deliverance *see* exorcism 321
democracy 621
democracy, religion of 163
demythologization 138–139, 248–249, 412, 488, 601, 803, 819
dependence, absolute 812
descent into hell 251
design argument [teleological] 431, 604, 646, 819
determinism [inc. scientific/ theological/philosophical] 251–252
devil 78
devil and demons (*see also* exorcism) 253–254, 321
dialectical theology 255–258, 910
Didache 57
différance 249
disciples 149
dispensational theology 258–259
dispensationalism 43, 258–259, 297–298, 357, 507, 572, 880
divine energies 371
divine light 404
Docetism 259–260, 397
doctrinal criticism 260
doctrine 260–261, 523, 929
  corruption of 253
  development of 252–253
  immutability of 253
dogma 262–263, 290
dominion 439
Donatism 83–84, 265–266, 398

1000

Index of subjects

Dort, Canons of 267–268, 666
Dort, Synod of 267–268, 639, 666
double effect, principle of 318
double-truth theory 92
doubt 269–270, 293
doubt, method of 1, 250, 269
doxology 270–271, 366
dualism 250, 271–272, 610, 680
Dutch Reformed theology 274–275
dynamic equivalence 216

Easter 275–276
Eastern Orthodox churches, and catechisms 157
Eastern Orthodox theology (*see also* hesychasm) 181, 277–279, 281
  and canon law 151
  and councils 221, 277
  and Eucharist 279, 307
  and the fall 279, 328
  and grace 378
  and Holy Spirit 278, 422–423
  and liturgy 525
  and Mary 555
  and Trinity 278, 923
  and World Council of Churches 279, 972
Ebionism 280
ecclesiology *see* church 521
eco-feminism 340
ecology 231, 280–282, 303, 708, 788
economy 282–283
ecumenical councils 234
ecumenical movement 283–286
ecumenical theology 212, 286–287, 499
  and ministry 577
ecumenism 263, 283
Eight-Fold Path 135
election *see* predestination 740, 859
election, and Augustine 84
emotivism 301
empiricism 289–290, 292–293, 300, 730
encounter, divine–human 333
enhypostasia 434, 449
Enlightenment 50, 174, 178, 262, 290–291, 312, 323, 352, 578, 688, 730, 746, 758

Enlightenment, and Romanticism 786
Ephesus, Council of 222, 292
episcopacy 186–187
epistemic justification 315
epistemology 292–293, 679, 908
Epistle of Barnabas 57
Erasmus, Desiderius, and Luther 294, 539
eros 534, 624
eschatology (*see also* amillennialism; dispensational theology; Joachimism; postmillennialism; premillennialism) 258, 296–299
  and Anabaptists 24
  and Moltmann 587
  and process theology 708
  and prophecy 193
  realized 298
essence of Christianity 299–300
essentialism and non-essentialism 623
Ethiopean Orthodox theology 305
ethics 106, 300–304, 595, 625
ethics, and womanist theology 968
Eucharist 19, 32–33, 305–308, 561, 698, 739–740, 747, 751, 814, 931, 974
  and Bucer 134
  and Council of Trent 921
  and Gregory of Nyssa 380
  and Luther 538, 540
  and Lutheranism 542
  and Schwenckfeld 817
  and Vermigli 942
  and Zwingli 538, 986
Eutychianism 397
Evangelical Fellowship of Congregational Churches 205
Evangelical Rationalists 745
Evangelical Revival 953–954
Evangelical Sisterhood of Mary 70
Evangelical Theological Society 310
evangelical theology 309–311, 375
  and process theology 708
  and society 851

  and spirituality 312, 863
  postconservative 312–313
evangelicals, and baptism 99
evangelicals, and World Council of Churches 972
evangelism 313–314, 746, 860
evidentialism 315–316, 746
evil 38, 272, 316–319, 404, 509, 675, 860, 877
evil (*see also* devils and demons; theodicy) 253
  and existence of God 317
  moral 316, 318, 898
  natural 316, 318, 898
evolution 357, 709, 891
evolution, theistic 232
evolutionary theology 734
exclusivism 173–174, 757–759
excommunication 377
existentialism 319–321
exorcism 321
experience, appeal to 163

faith 93, 168–169, 248, 319–320, 322–323, 326, 539, 938
  and history 323–324, 330, 415
  and history, and resurrection of Christ 768–769
  and Lutheranism 542, 930
  and reason 37–39, 104, 325–326, 462, 485, 649, 675, 730
  and revelation 118
  implicit 36
  rule of 322, 894, 900
  saving 324
  seeking understanding 756
  temporary 72
Faith and Order movement 284, 324–325
faithfulness 533–534
fall, the 281, 327–331, 438, 601, 607
  and immortality 445
falsification principle 764, 941
family 304, 330–332
fatalism 715
federal theology *see* covenant theology 226
federalism 226
fellowship (*see also* koinonia) 335–336

1001

Index of subjects

feminist theology (*see also*
  Schüssler Fiorenza)
  336–341, 402, 708, 787–788,
  799
feminist theology, and
  Christology 179
fideism 342, 674
filioque (*see also* Holy Spirit,
  procession of) 234, 277,
  398, 422, 645
Five Precepts 135
Florence, Council of 224, 651,
  946
forms, theory of 62, 680
foundationalism 315, 348–349,
  545, 746–747, 902
Fountain Trust 661
Franciscans 127–128, 349–351
Frankfurt Declaration 351–352
Franfurt School 352
free choice 546
Free Church of Scotland 161
Free Methodist Church 418
free will 860
free will, and suffering 318,
  878
freedom (*see also* grace) 39,
  352–353, 670
  and autonomy 353
  and Baptist theology 101–102
  and self-determination 353
  human 360
free-will defence 898
French Protestant Academy,
  Saumur 21
Fuller Seminary 310
functionalism 237
fundamental theology 355
fundamentalism 207, 310,
  356–358
fundamentalism, and
  evangelicals 357
Fundamentals 357

Gallican Confession 199
gender 304, 358–359, 969
gender roles 358–359
Genevan Confession 199
German idealism (*see also*
  Fichte) 359–360
ghosts 112
Gifford Lectures 360–361
gifts of the Spirit 161–162, 362,
  390
gift, theology of 361–362

Global Christian Forum 285,
  972
globalization 238, 303,
  364–365
glory of God 365–366, 702
glory, theology of 406
Gnesio-Lutherans 345
Gnosticism 176, 366–369, 396,
  457, 716
God 369–372
  and creation 271
  and gender terms 358
  and Hegel 392
  and process theology 707
  and womanist theology 968
  as pure act 111
  being of 111
  children of 856
  death of 244, 622
  doctrine of 63–64, 470, 632,
    738, 748
  essence and activities 404,
    645
  essence of 250, 874
  existence of (*see also*
    ontological argument)
    37, 218, 528, 654, 670,
    672, 679, 908
  existence of, and evil 317
  fatherhood of 334–335
  freedom of 273
  glory of 365–366
  hidden 405
  holiness of 372
  image of 3, 40–41, 438
  impassibility of 212, 372,
    445–447, 859, 878
  judgment of 477–478
  justice of 778
  knowledge of (*see also* hidden
    and revealed God) 75,
    106, 128, 341, 360, 405,
    485
  love of 372, 478, 533
  nature of 633, 679
  necessity of 112
  perfections of 371–372
  righteousness of 778, 781
  simplicity of 111, 371, 840
  suffering of 447, 479, 632
  union with 246
  vision of, *see* vision of God
    945
  will of 959–961
God–world relationship 588

gospel 374–375
  and culture 239
Gospel of Thomas 368
grace (*see also* Molinism) 119,
  320, 361, 376–378, 384,
  533–534, 566, 711, 751, 776,
  895, 954
  and Augustine 84, 700
  and election 64–65
  and nature 377, 879
  and paradox 93
  cheap 168
  common 378
  means of 376–377
  special 378
Ground of the Unity 596
Group Brotherhood 513
Guild of St Matthew 171
guilt, and forgiveness 383–385
guilt, original 842

Half-Way Covenant 870
Hasidism 133
healing 389–391, 662
Heidelberg Catechism 156,
  393–394, 937
hell (*see also* annihilationism)
  936
  descent into 251
Hellenization of Christianity
  261, 395
Helvetic Confession, First 137,
  199
Helvetic Confession, Second
  138, 199
heresy (*see also* blasphemy)
  396–398
hermeneutic circle 401
hermeneutics 216, 354,
  398–402, 777, 812, 824, 901
  and process theology 708
  deconstructionist 402
  feminist 402
  liberation 402
  postliberal 402
  Romantic 401
hermeneutics of suspicion 338,
  401–402, 764
hesychasm 403–404, 570, 645
heterousians 61
hidden and revealed God
  405–406
higher-life theology 406–407
Hinduism and Christianity
  408–410

Index of subjects

historical criticism 291
historical Jesus, quest for 139, 411–413, 468, 602, 817, 872, 976–977
historical relativism 925
historical theology 413–414
history (*see also* myth) 414–415, 648, 777
  and judgment of God 478
  and religion 511
  and society 85
  philosophy of 258
History-of-Religions School 415–416
holiness 802
holiness movement 356, 417–419, 567, 646, 665, 806
Holocaust (*see also* Wiesel, Elie) 419–421, 958
holy, experience of 641
Holy Saturday 95
Holy Spirit 421–424, 425, 696
  and Anabaptists 23
  and Athanasius 75
  and Basil of Caesarea 107
  and freedom 353
  and Gregory of Nazianzus 379
  and Moltmann 587
  and Owen 642
  and Trinity 162
  and wisdom 964
  procession of 39, 398, 645, 922–923
homoians 61
homoiousians 61
homoiousios 60
homoousios 60, 549, 855, 874
homosexuality 304, 358, 712, 837
Honest to God 248, 782
hope 426–427
  theology of 299, 427–428
House Churches 576
human personhood 983
human rights law 506
humanism 120, 429–430
  modern 430
  Renaissance 430–431
hymns 525, 953
hyper-Calvinism 432–433
hypostasis 433–434, 874

iconoclastic controversies 434–436, 441
idealism 435, 605, 786
  German 516
identity and sexuality 836
ideology 435–436
idolatry 436–437
image of God 438–440
images 440–441
imagination in theology 441–443
imitation of Christ 443–444
immaterialism 116, 444–445
immortality of the soul 680
immortality, conditional 35, 445
impassibility of God 446–448
imperialism 364
incarnation (*see also* Christology) 17, 74–75, 111, 178, 215, 448–450, 618, 929–930, 944–945
  and Anselm 38
  and Council of Chalcedon 160
  and *extra Calvinisticum* 449
  and images 441
  and *kenosis* 450
  and paradox 93
  and resurrection of Christ 765–766
  and truth 95
inclusivism 173–174, 757–759
Indian Christian theology 450–452
indigenization 70, 164, 213, 215
individualism 489–490
indulgences 537, 719
infallibility, papal 652
infralapsarianism 701
Intelligent Design 232
intermediate state 455–456
International Council on Biblical Inerrancy 164
International Missionary Council 284, 616
Inter-Varsity Fellowship 514
Iona Community 70
  and the fall 327
  and heresy 396
Islam 593
Islam and Christianity (*see also* Arab Christian thought) 459–461, 867
I–Thou relationship 133

Jansenism 88, 462–464, 466
Japanese theology 464
Jesuits 437, 463, 466–467, 742
Jesus 467–471
  and Judaism 472
  and kingdom of God 491
Jewish–Christian relations (*see also* supersessionism; Zion) 471–472
Joachimism 472–475, 572
Jubilee Group 33
Judaism 475–477, 592
  human 391, 717
  of God (*see also* annihilationism) 477–479, 718
Julianists 592
just-war theory 303, 644
justice, and righteousness 778
Justice, Peace and Integrity of Creation 282
justification 212, 285, 322, 480–482, 499, 562, 640, 751, 801, 921, 976
  and Luther 538–539
  and Lutheranism 542, 930
  and resurrection of Christ 766
  and sanctification 482, 805, 807
  and Schwenckfeld 817

karma 136, 409
kenosis 347
kenoticism 178, 487–488, 859
kerygma 488–489
Keswick Convention/movement 310, 407, 418–419, 665, 806
Kimbanguist Church, Zaire 12
kingdom of God 314, 490–493, 514
knowledge (*see also* epistemology) 154, 348, 485, 680, 961
  analysis of claims 673–674
  and foundationalism 348–349
  as warranted true belief 678
  ground of 359
  justification of claims 674
  mediated 391
knowledge of God *see* God, knowledge of; natural theology 76, 360, 493–495
koinonia 497

1003

Index of subjects

laity 29, 500–501
Landmark movement 858
language 116, 966–967
  metaphorical/figurative 763
  religious 670
  univocal 762–763
Lateran Councils 223–224, 425, 501–502
Latitudinarianism 502–503
Lausanne Committee for World Evangelization 503
Lausanne Congress 311
Lausanne Covenant (1974) 239, 503
law 383–384, 426, 504–506, 606, 907–908
  and gospel 482, 506–508, 542, 739
  biblical 44
  divine 44
  human 44
laws of nature 578, 618, 820
laying on of hands 508–509
lectio divina 590
legalism 504, 507
Leiden synopsis 509–510
Leo, Tome of 510
liberal evangelicalism 513–514
liberal theology 507, 514–516
liberalism 430
  German 516–518
liberalism and conservatism in theology 205, 544
liberation ethics 303
liberation theology 127, 172, 182–183, 211, 213, 386, 402, 518–522, 570, 685, 694, 785
Life and Work Movement 284
limbus 522–523
literary realism 354
liturgical theology 524
liturgy 32, 524–525
  and sacraments 797
  Anglican view 28
logic 63, 527–528
logical positivism 290, 293, 528–529, 564, 675, 764, 940
Logos 51–52, 74, 177, 191, 411, 529–530
logos endiathetos 52, 530
logos prophorikos 52, 530
logos spermatikos 51, 483, 529–530

London Bible College (now London School of Theology) 310
London Missionary Society 283
love, divine 89–90, 533–536
  and assurance 72
  and atonement 79
  and baptism 98
  and catechisms 156
  and the Christian life 169
  and Christology 540
  and church–state relations 538, 684
  and conscience 206
  and covenant theology 225
  and Erasmus 294, 539
  and Eucharist 307, 538, 540, 740, 747
  and faith 930
  and the fall 328
  and hidden and revealed God 405–406
  and image of God 3
  and imitation of Christ 443
  and justification 481–482, 506, 538–539
  and knowledge of God 495
  and law 505
  and law and gospel 506
  and Melanchthon 559
  and natural theology 604
  and priesthood of all believers 704, 739
  and repentance 765
  and revelation 771
  and righteousness 169, 538, 778–779
  and sanctification 805
  and Scripture 539–540
  and sin 384
  and theology of the cross 235–236
  and two kingdoms 867
  and vocation 970
  and Zwingli 538
Lutheran orthodoxy/scholasticism 637–639
Lutheran theology 200
  and church discipline 185
  and justification 482, 807
Lutheranism and Lutheran theology 507, 540–542, 747
Lyons, First Council of (1245) 224

Lyons, Second Council of (1274) 224

man, doctrine of 106
Manichaeism 82–83, 368, 398, 548–549
Marburg Colloquy 538
marriage 837
Marrow Controversy 130
Marrow of Theology 20, 719
martyrdom 68, 551–552, 878
Marxism 519–520, 552–554, 685, 793
Mary 554–556
  as Co-Redemptrix 556
  as mediatrix 555
  as mother of the church 556
  as *theotokos* 555
  Assumption of 555
  immaculate conception 273, 555, 784
materialism 76, 556–557
Medellín Conference 386, 518
mediation 558–559
Mennonite Church 560, 840
mental health/illness 389–390
Mercersburg theology 561
merit 481, 562
Messalians 543
metaphor 442
metaphorical theology 583
metaphysics 563–564, 675
metempsychosis 565
method, theological 531, 901–903
Methodism (*see also* Calvinistic Methodism) 565–569
Methodist Church in Great Britain 188
Methodist Episcopal Church in the USA 66, 96
Methodist Missionary Society 96
middle axioms 848
Middle Platonism 680
millennium 571–573
mind–body relation 271
ministry 573–577, 711
  and local church 574
  lay 576–577
  nineteenth-century developments 576–577
  threefold 186–187
minjung theology 71, 497

1004

Index of subjects

miracle 389, 431, 578–579, 872, 879, 927–928
missio Dei 287, 580, 611, 972
missiology (*see also* Allen; Kraemer) 23, 109, 212, 459, 579–582, 713, 972
 and apostleship 55–56
 and evangelism 580
 and Islam 461
 and Judaism 472
missionary movement 29
modalism 922
models 582–583
Modern Churchman's Union (now Modern Churchpeople's Union) 585
 Catholic 583–584
 English 585
modernity 585–586, 726
modernity (*see also* secularization) 831
Molinism 87, 466, 701
 and creation 588
 and Holy Spirit 587
 and love of God 536
 and Marxism 685
 and theology of cross 587
 and Trinity 587–588
monarchianism 588–589, 895
monastic theology 589–590
monasticism 68–70, 86–87, 664
monism 591
monophysitism 17, 219, 397, 591–592
monotheism 592–593
Montanism 593–594
Moral Majority 357
Moral Rearmament 594
moral theology 142, 467, 595–596
morality 320
Moravian theology 596–597, 862
motif-research 624
mysterium tremendum et facscinans 641
mystical theology 246, 533, 599–600, 931
mysticism 128, 169
myth 600–602, 872–873

Nag Hammadi library 367–368
narrative ethics 302

narrative theology 602–603, 763
Nation of Islam 122
National Association of Evangelicals 310
National Camp Meeting Association 418
National Covenant (Scotland) 227
natural law 300, 302, 504–505, 607, 780
natural philosophy 64
natural theology 605, 104–105, 494–495, 603–606, 674, 848
natural theology, and creation 231
naturalism 430
naturalism, evolutionary 77
naturalistic fallacy 301
nature 15, 606–607
nature, and grace 377, 495, 879
Neo-Kantianism 301
Neonomianism 110
neo-orthodoxy 262–263, 608
Neoplatonism 83, 295, 680, 715–716, 943
Neo-Thomism 909
Nestorianism 45–46, 397, 510
New Age (*see also* new religions and alternative spiritualities) 610–611
New England theology 611–612
New Haven theology 612–613
new religions 613–615, 756
New Theology 346
Nicaea, Creed of 397, 619
Nicaea, First Council of (325) 59–60, 176, 222, 397, 618–619
Nicaea, Second Council of (787) 223
Nicene Creed 209, 222, 234, 292, 397, 422, 523, 916
nominalism 121, 604, 622–623, 734, 961
non-realism 624
non-resistance 23
numinous 641

obedience 168–169, 625–626
obedience, wilful 23
Oberlin College 547
Odes of Solomon 883
ontological argument 37, 603

ontology (*see also* being) 631–632, 683
 of peace 571
 of violence 571
 trinitarian 571
open theism/openness theology 211, 311, 632–633, 677–678, 859
Orange, Second Council of 833
Oratory of Divine Love 741
ordination 509
ordo salutis 633–634
Oriental Orthodox theology 219, 592, 634–635
 and World Council of Churches 972
Orthodox Church of America 814
Orthodox Presbyterian Church 544
Orthodox theology, *Confession of Dositheus* 200
 and church discipline 185
ousia 433, 874
Oxford Movement 30–32, 487

pacifism/peace 303, 571, 643–644, 979
paleo-orthodoxy 627
panentheism 647, 708
Pannenberg, Wolfhart
 and faith 534
 and the fall 329
 and knowledge of God 494
 and Trinity 533
pantheism 370, 649–650
papacy 43, 466, 650–652, 961
paradigm 652–653
paradox in theology 93, 653–654
Parsees 983–984
patripassianism *see* Sabellianism 589
patristic theology (*see also* Christology) 211, 575, 627, 655–656
Pauline theology 976
Pelagianism 84, 131, 398, 480, 657–658, 841, 960
penance 456, 659
Pentecostal theology 183, 423–424, 501, 660–664
Pentecostalism 311, 356, 362, 579, 760
perfection, perfectionism 567, 664–665

1005

Index of subjects

perichoresis 335
perseverance 44, 566, 666–667
persona 895
personalism 667, 772
phenomenology 667–669
Philippist Lutherans 345
philosophy 266
   and 'theological turn' 551
   and theology 8, 126, 671–673
   modern 391
philosophy of religion 673–676
philosophy of theology 670–671, 716
phthartolatrai 592
pietism 262, 560, 676–677, 862, 888
Pilgrim Holiness Church 418
Platonism 679–681
   Christian 681–682
plerosis 347
pluralism 173–174, 304, 757–758
polemics 683
political ethics 303
political theology 569, 625, 683–686
polytheism 370, 686–687
poor, option for 521
positivism 301, 352, 687
post-foundationalist theology/ postfoundationalism 312, 678
postliberalism 170, 516, 602, 678, 687–688, 758, 978
   and hermeneutics 402
postmillennialism 297–298
   Protestant 572
postmodern ethics 302
postmodernism 340, 606, 610, 689, 691–693, 730
   and authority 90
   and systematic theology 688–690, 885
post-structuralism 764, 874
poverty and wealth 180, 693–695
power 695–696
pragmatism 697
praxis 521, 696–697
prayer 347, 403–404, 697–698
preaching, theology of 698–700, 974
predestination 64–65, 375, 406, 463, 700–702, 740, 834

premillennialism 297–298
   early church 571
   Protestant 572
Presbyterian Church in the United States (PCUSA) 909–910
Presbyterianism 188, 702–703
presuppositionalism 938–939
priesthood of all believers 703–705, 711–712, 739
Princeton theology 195, 416, 544, 705–706, 735, 750
Priscillianism 706
process theology 111, 192, 707–709, 819, 875
progress, idea of 709–710
propitiation 799
prosperity theology 390, 661, 710
Protestant principle 911
Protestantism 113, 711–714
   and Augustinianism 88
   and councils 222
providence 318, 714–715
punishment 717–718
purgatory 456, 537, 717–719, 751, 808
Puritan theology 719–722
   and church discipline 185
   and church–state relations 896
   and kingdom of God 492

Quakers (Society of Friends) 98, 722–723, 797
quandary ethics 388
queer theology 723, 836
quietism 129, 724

rabbinic theology 724–725
race 725–726, 969
Racovian Catechism 852
Radical Orthodoxy 211, 570, 726–727, 763, 849
Radical Reformation 98, 560, 712, 740, 744–746
Ramism 729
rationalism 292, 430, 517, 527, 691, 730–732, 888
Real, the 111–112
realism 623, 734–735
   common-sense 734
   critical 686, 735
   epistemological 734

   ontological 734
   semantic 734
reason 1, 290
   and faith 730
   and narrative 602
   and revelation 272, 731
   and theology 731–732
   and tradition 545
   and understanding 194
   limits of 293
rebaptism 735–736
reciprocity 588
redemption 736–737
Reformation theology 506, 737–741
   and confirmation 201
   and justification 507
   and law 507
   and ministry 575–576
   and poverty and wealth 694
   and society 850
Reformation, Catholic Counter- 741–744
Reformational Movement 851
Reformed epistemology 746–747
Reformed Orthodoxy 639–640, 937
Reformed theology (see also covenant theology) 748, 747–750, 501
   and church discipline 185
   and dogma 262
   and sacraments 797
   confessions 200
   English 750–752
   Scottish 752
regeneration 752–753, 938
reincarnation 409, 444, 565
relationality 588
relativism 754
religion 754–756
   and Hegel 392
   and history 511
religions, theology of 172, 174, 756–759
religious experience 194, 255, 293, 462, 674, 759–762, 929, 951
   and Islam 461
religious language 762–764, 908
religious studies 756
Remonstrant Articles 65, 267, 666

1006

Index of subjects

repentance, and conversion 218–219, 764–765
reprobation 700
Restorationism 55
resurrection of Christ 324, 648, 765–769, 977
  and immortality 445
  general 769–770
revealed theology 494
revelation (*see also* Scripture, doctrine of) 293, 405, 620, 648, 708, 770–773, 901, 949
  and contemplation 95
  and faith 118
  and reason 731
  and Scripture 823
  general 132, 293
  special 132, 293, 675
reverence for life 817
revival, theology of 310, 567, 774–775
revivals 309, 343
revolution, theology of 496, 775–777
righteousness 778–780
  active 538
  and justice 778
  distributive 779
  external or strange 539
  imputed 779
  infused 779
  of God *see* God, righteousness of 538
  passive 538
rights
  human 780–781
  natural 780–781
ritualism 31, 975
Roman Catholic Church
  and baptism 99
  and catechisms 157
  and charismatic movement 661
  and councils 221
Roman Catholic theology (*see also* fundamental theology; Mary; Modernism (Catholic); Vatican I; Vatican II) 55, 113, 118, 499, 783–785, 939
  and apostolic succession 55
  and canon law 151
  and catholicity 158
  and church 181

  and church government 187–188
  and church–state relations 868
  and dogma 263
  and justification 482, 807
  and liberation theology 685
  and Protestantism 714
  and World Council of Churches 972
Romanian Orthodox theology (*see also* Bulgakov) 500, 864
Romanticism, and hermeneutics 401, 785–787
Russian Orthodox theology 789, 788–794

Sabbath 795–796
Sabellianism 397, 589
sacralization/re-enchantment 833
sacraments 97, 170, 432, 481, 531, 712, 739, 784, 796–798, 803, 880–881
  and justification 481
sacrifice 798–799
saint (*see also* communion of saints) 800
salvation 242, 800–802
  and non-Christian religions 36
  history 803–804
  order of 806
Salvation Army 98, 418, 802–803
sanctification (*see also* Christian life) 417–418, 566, 598, 779, 804–807, 954
  and justification 482, 805, 807
  and resurrection of Christ 766–767
  entire 96, 418, 806
Satan 893
satisfaction 808–809
Savoy Declaration (1658) 200, 204
scepticism, philosophical 680
schism 84, 810
Schleiermacher and heresy 398
Schleitheim Confession 198, 813–814

scholasticism 14–15, 37, 86, 589, 814–816
science 266, 291
  and creation 230
  and Scripture 728
  and theology 304, 545–546, 679, 686, 768, 818–820
scientism 691
Scots Confession 199, 821
scriptural holiness 566
Scripture (*see also* accommodation) 676, 821–825, 948
  and Anabaptists 23
  and canon 182, 822–823
  and church 90, 826
  and historical criticism 401
  and history 323–324
  and imagination 442
  and Islam 461
  and Lutheranism 541–542
  and ministry 574–575
  and postconservative evangelicalism 312
  and Protestantism 711
  and revelation 28, 90, 216, 823, 825–827, 920
  and Zwingli 985
  authority of 90, 311, 326, 632, 737, 751, 824, 828, 951, 955, 977
  canonic principle 902
  doctrine of 827–828, 938
  fourfold sense 400
  in Reformation theology 400
  inerrancy 453–455
  infallibility 453–455, 705
  inspiration of 194, 453, 823–824, 951
  interpretation of (*see also* hermeneutics) 46, 51, 399–402, 619, 636, 689, 699, 738, 751, 819, 824
  allegorical 395, 399, 590
  figural 399
  grammatical 399
  literal 399
  spiritual 399
  New Testament authorship and dating 927
  sola Scriptura 118, 711, 824, 827
  trustworthiness 453
Sea of Faith movement 829
sect 853

1007

Index of subjects

sects 829–830
secular Christianity 830–831
secularity, theology of 129
secularization 831–833, 851, 853
Semi-Arians *see* homoiousians
Semi-Pelagianism 833–834
sensus divinitatis 747
Seventh-Day Adventism 834–835
Severans 592
sexuality (*see also* gender; queer theology) 30, 304, 835–837
shalom 644
Shepherd of Hermas 57
Shintoism 838–839
simplicity, divine 840–841
sin (*see also* temptation) 38, 598, 841–843, 960
   and suffering 877
   in Islam 460
   original 4, 20, 84, 841–842
sinlessness of Christ 843–844
slavery 29, 844–847, 910
   abolition of 845–847
   and world religions 845
   defence of 846
sobornost 794, 847
social ethics 712, 848–849
   and Methodism 567
Social Gospel (*see also* Rauschenbusch) 167, 170, 514, 849–850
society, theology of 850, 703, 850–852
Socinus and Socinianism 79, 398
sociology of religion 274, 853–854, 925, 952
Socratic method 680
sonship 855–856
sophia see wisdom in early Christology 137
soul 41, 112, 856–857
soul, pre-existence 856
Southern Baptist theology 857–858
sovereignty of God 858–860
spiritual warfare (*see also* angels; devil and demons) 254, 590
Spiritualists 745
spirituality (*see also* New Age; new religions and alternative spiritualities) 12, 347, 832, 861–864

apophatic 861
cataphatic 861
Celtic 160
state 691, 865–869
   and kingdom of God 491–492
   authority of 90
   Welfare State 693
stewardship 280–281, 606, 820, 869, 977
Stoics 529, 870–871
Stone-Campbell movement 149
structural analysis 873
structuralism 237, 873–874
Student Christian Movement 514
subordinationism 922
substance 874–875
substantia 895
substitution and representation 875–876
substitution, penal 629, 799, 801, 808, 876
suffering, human 212, 876–878, 948
   and bigger picture 877
   and free will 318, 877
   and sin 877
   and soul-making 877
supernatural 879
supersessionism 879–880
supralapsarianism 701
symbols 777, 880–881, 911
syncretism 451, 882–883
Syriac Christian theology 882–883
Syrian Christianity 883–884
Syrian Orthodox Church of Antioch 884
systematic theology 886, 885–886
   history of 886–889

Taizé Community 70
Taoism and Christianity 889–890
Tatian, *Diatessaron* 883
temptation 892–893
Tetrapolitan Confession 198–199
theism 686, 896–897
theodicy 80, 317–318, 509, 787, 897–899
theodramatics 442, 886, 902
theological aesthetics 94

theological exegesis 900
theology 903–904
   and foundationalism 348
   and reason 731–732
   and science 915
   ascetic 862
   from above 902
   from below 901–902
   from the side 902
   implicit 12
   mystical 862
   pragmatic 462
theonomy 91
theopaschitai 592
Thirty-Nine Articles 199, 905
Thomas Aquinas 906–907
   and analogy 371
   and Aristotelianism 63
   and atonement 79
   and church–state relations 868
   and conscience 206
   and creation 908
   and epistemology 908
   and existence of God 908
   and faith and reason 730, 908
   and image of God 3
   and impassibility of God 446
   and incarnation 449
   and merit 562
   and metaphysics 908
   and natural law 505, 908
   and perfection 664
   and philosophy 672
   and predestination 700
   and religious language 908
   and resurrection of Christ 766
   and revelation 771
   and sacraments 797
   and sanctification 805
   and the fall 328
   Summa Theologica 815, 885
Thomism and Neo-Thomism 264–265, 907–909
time and eternity 465, 912–913
toleration 746, 795, 913–914
tongues, gift of 162
Toronto experience 661
Tractarians 31
   and reason 545
   and Scripture 920
   catholic principle 903

Index of subjects

traducianism 856–857
tragedy 918
transcendental experience 727
transfiguration 919–920
transubstantiation 115–116, 377, 655
Trent, Council of 224, 384, 742, 808, 826, 920–921
  and grace 482
  and Scripture and tradition 826
Trinity 75, 211, 330, 370, 385, 427, 465, 571, 592, 699, 856, 921–924, 943
  and African Independent Churches 12
  and African theology 13
  and Apostolic Fathers 57
  and Augustine 85
  and Barth 106, 533
  and Basil of Caesarea 108
  and Cyril of Alexandria 241
  and Eusebius of Caesarea 308
  and fellowship 335–336
  and Gregory of Nazianzus 379
  and Gregory of Nyssa 379–380
  and Holy Spirit 424
  and hypostasis 923
  and Irenaeus 457
  and Islam 460
  and LaCugna 500
  and Moltmann 587–588
  and Origen 636
  and Owen 642
  and Pannenberg 533, 649
  and *persona* 923
  and Rahner 728
  and Schleiermacher 812
  and Tertullian 895
  and Torrance 916–917
  and truth 926
  and Unitarianism 934
  and worship 973
  and Zizioulas 982–983
tritheism 924
truth 38, 754, 925–927
  and incarnation 95
  and subjectivity 490
  coherence theory 926
  correspondence theory 925–926

indirect communication of 490
Tübingen School 516, 927–928
two kingdoms, doctrine of 684
Tyndale House, Cambridge 310

ultimate concern 911
union with Christ 929–931, 933
uniqueness of Christ 932–933
Unitarian Universalist Association 935
Unitarianism 398, 924, 933–935
United Reformed Church 188, 205
Universal Declaration of Human Rights [1948] 780–781
universalism 150, 935–936
utopia 436
Utrecht circle 947

Vatican Councils 939–940
Vatican I 188, 207, 224, 499, 651–652, 939
Vatican II 32, 181, 188, 194, 203, 207, 224, 284, 307, 355, 499, 554, 556, 652, 757, 781, 826, 939–940, 970
  and Scripture and tradition 826
  and church–state relations 868
  Dogmatic Constitution on the Church 554
verification 290
  and falsification 940–941
  eschatological 293
verification principle 528, 764, 940–941
via negativa 762
Victorines 943
Vienna Circle 528
Vienne, Council of 224, 946
Vineyard fellowship 661
virgin birth 544, 844, 943–945
virtue [and the virtues] 62–63, 388, 870, 909
vision of God 945–946
vocation (*see also* calling) 946–947
voluntarism 949

Waldensians 949–950
Wesley, John (*see also* Methodism)
  and assurance 73

and conversion 218, 862
and perfection 665
and sanctification 169, 417, 779, 806
and Whitefield 958
spirituality 862
theological method 955
Wesleyan Methodist Church 418
Wesleyan Quadrilateral 568, 955
Westminster Assembly 956–957
  Directory for the Publick Worship of God 956
  Form of Presbyterial Church Government 957
  Larger Catechism 156, 628, 957
  Shorter Catechism 157, 957
Westminster Confession 161, 198, 200, 325, 860, 951, 956–957
Westminster Theological Seminary 544, 598, 938
Wheaton Declaration 957–958
will 273, 959–960
  bondage of 960
  freedom of 273
Willowbank Report (1978) 239
wisdom 886
wisdom in early Christology 52, 137, 964–965
womanist theology 124, 214, 340, 968–969
women, ordination of 33, 338, 577, 704
work 969–971
World Council of Churches 118, 215, 279, 282, 284–286, 497, 616, 827, 965, 971–972
  Toronto statement 972
World Evangelical Fellowship (now World Evangelical Alliance) 285
World Missionary Conference (Edinburgh, 1910) 283
World's Evangelical Alliance 283, 285, 310
worship (*see also* doxology) 973–975
  and liturgy 973
  and pragmatism 975
  and ritualism 975
  freedom of 781
wrath of God 406, 975–976

1009

Index of subjects

Yale School 978

Zion 979–981
Zionism 133, 978, 981–982
  Christian 980, 982

Messianic 981
  political 981
Zoroastrianism 983–984
Zwingli, Huldrych 307
  and baptism 98, 985

and covenant theology 225, 985
and Eucharist 747, 986

Index of articles

Abelard, Peter 1
Accommodation 2
Adam 3
Adiaphora 5
Adoptionism 6
Aesthetics 6
African Christian theology 9
African Independent Churches, theology of 11
African theology: recent developments 13
Agnosticism 14
Albertus Magnus 14
Albigenses 15
Alexandrian School 15
Alienation 17
Allen, Roland 18
Althaus, Paul 19
Ambrose 19
Ames, William 20
Amyraldism 21
Anabaptist theology 22
Analogy 24
Analytic theology 25
Angels 26
Anglicanism 27
Anglo-Catholic theology 30
Animism 34
Annihilationism 34
Anonymous Christianity 36
Anselm 37
Anthropology 39
Anthropomorphism 42
Antichrist 42
Antinomianism 43
Antiochene School 45
Apocalyptic 46
Apollinarianism 48
Apologetics 49
Apologists 51
Apophatic theology 52
Apostasy 53
Apostle 54
Apostolic Fathers 56
Arab Christian thought 58
Arianism 58
Aristotelianism 62
Arminianism 64
Asbury, Francis 66
Ascension 66
Asceticism and monasticism 68

Asian Christian theology 70
Assurance 72
Athanasius 73
Atheism 76
Atonement 77
Atonement, extent of 80
Augsburg Confession 81
Augustine 82
Augustinianism 86
Aulén, Gustaf 88
Authority 89
Autonomy 91
Averroism 92

Baillie, Donald Macpherson 93
Baillie, John 93
Balthasar, Hans Urs von 94
Bangs, Nathan 96
Baptism 96
Baptism in the Spirit 99
Baptist theology 101
Barclay, William 102
Barmen Declaration 103
Barth, Karl 103
Basil of Caesarea 107
Bavinck, Herman 108
Bavinck, Johan Herman 108
Baxter, Richard 109
Beck, Johann Tobias 110
Being 110
Bellarmine, Robert 113
Benedict and the Benedictine tradition 114
Bengel, Johann Albrecht 115
Berengar 115
Berkeley, George 116
Berkhof, Hendrikus 117
Berkhof, Louis 117
Berkouwer, Gerrit Cornelis 117
Berlin Declaration 118
Bernard of Clairvaux 119
Beza, Theodore 120
Biel, Gabriel 121
Black consciousness 121
Black theology 122
Blasphemy 125
Bloesch, Donald G. 125
Boehme, Jacob 126
Boethius 126
Boff, Leonardo 127
Bonaventura 127

Bonhoeffer, Dietrich 128
Bossuet, Jacques-Bénigne 129
Boston, Thomas 130
Bradwardine, Thomas 131
Briggs, Charles Augustus 131
Brown, William Adams 131
Brunner, Emil 132
Buber, Martin 133
Bucer (Butzer), Martin 133
Buddhism and Christianity 134
Bulgakov, Sergei 136
Bullinger, Johann Heinrich 137
Bultmann, Rudolf 138
Bunyan, John 140
Bushnell, Horace 141
Butler, Joseph 141

Calling 142
Calvin, John 143
Calvinistic Methodism 147
Cambridge Platonists 148
Campbell, Alexander 149
Campbell, John McLeod 149
Canon law 151
Capitalism 152
Carnell, Edward John 153
Caroline Divines 154
Casuistry 155
Catechisms 155
Catholicity 158
Celtic Christianity 159
Chalcedon, Council of 160
Chalmers, Thomas 161
Charismatic Movement/theology 161
Chemnitz, Martin 162
Chicago School of Theology 163
Chicago Statement 164
Chinese theology 164
Christendom 166
Christian life 168
Christian Socialism 171
Christianity and other religions 172
Christology 175
Chrysostom, John 179
Church 180
Church discipline 184
Church government 186
Civil religion 189

1011

Index of articles

Clarke, William Newton 191
Clement of Alexandria 191
Cobb, John B. 192
Cocceius, Johannes 192
Coleridge, Samuel Taylor 193
Collegiality and conciliarity 194
Common-sense philosophy 195
Communion of saints 195
Confessing Church 197
Confessions of faith 197
Confirmation 201
Confucianism and Christianity 202
Congar, Yves 203
Congregationalism 204
Conscience 205
Conservative theology 207
Constantine 208
Constantinople, Council of 208
Consumerism 209
Contarini, Gasparo 210
Contemporary theological trends 210
Contextualization 215
Contextual theologies 213
Contingency 217
Conversion 218
Coptic Christianity 219
Corporate personality 220
Cotton, John 220
Councils 221
Covenanters 227
Covenant theology 225
Cranmer, Thomas 228
Creation 229
Creation and evolution 231
Creation-centred spirituality 232
Creeds 233
Cremer, Hermann 235
Cross, theology of the 235
Cultural theory and theology 237
Culture 238
Cyprian 240
Cyril of Alexandria 241

Dabney, Robert Lewis 242
Darby, John Nelson 243
Death 243
Death-of-God theology 244
Deconstruction 245
Deification 246
Deism 247

Demythologization 248
Denney, James 249
Derrida, Jacques 249
Descartes, René 250
Descent into hell 251
Determinism 251
Development of doctrine 252
Devils and demons 253
Dewey, John 255
Dialectical theology 255
Dilthey, Wilhelm 258
Dispensational theology 258
Docetism 259
Doctrinal criticism 260
Doctrine 260
Dodd, Charles Harold 261
Dogma 262
Dominic and the Dominicans 264
Donatism 265
Dooyeweerd, Herman 266
Dort, Canons of 267
Dort, Synod of 267
Dostoevsky, Fyodor Mikhailovich 268
Doubt 269
Doxology 270
Dualism 271
Duns Scotus, John 272
Durkheim, Emile 274
Dutch Reformed theology (South Africa) 274

Easter 275
Eastern Orthodox theology 277
Ebeling, Gerhard 279
Ebionism 280
Ecology 280
Economy 282
Ecumenical movement 283
Ecumenical theology 286
Edwards, Jonathan 287
Ellul, Jacques 288
Emerson, Ralph Waldo 289
Empiricism 289
Enlightenment, The 290
Ephesus, Council of 292
Epistemology 292
Erasmus, Desiderius 294
Eriugena, John Scotus 295
Erskine, Thomas 295
Eschatology 296
Essence of Christianity 299
Ethics 300
Ethiopian Orthodox theology 305

Eucharist 305
Eusebius of Caesarea 308
Evangelical theology 309
Evangelicalism, postconservative 312
Evangelism, theology of 313
Evidentialism 315
Evil 316
Existentialism 319
Exorcism 321

Faith 322
Faith and history 323
Faith and Order 324
Faith and reason 325
Fall 327
Family 330
Farel, William 332
Farmer, Herbert Henry 333
Farrer, Austin Marsden 334
Fatherhood of God 334
Fellowship 335
Feminist theology 336
Feuerbach, Ludwig Andreas 341
Fichte, Johann Gottlieb 342
Fideism 342
Filaret (Philaret) Drozdov 343
Finney, Charles Grandison 343
Fiorenza, Elisabeth Schüssler 344
Florovsky, Georges 345
Formula of Concord 345
Forsyth, Peter Taylor 346
Foucault, Michel 348
Foundationalism 348
Francis and the Franciscan tradition 349
Frankfurt Declaration 351
Frankfurt School 352
Freedom, Christian 352
Frei, Hans 354
Fuller, Andrew 354
Fundamental theology 355
Fundamentalism 356

Gender 358
German idealism 359
Gifford Lectures 360
Gift, theology of 361
Gifts of the Spirit 362
Gill, John 363
Gilson, Étienne 363
Globalization 364

Index of articles

Glory of God 365
Gnosticism 366
God 369
Gogarten, Friedrich 373
Goodwin, Thomas 373
Gore, Charles 374
Gospel 374
Gottschalk 375
Grace 376
Gregory of Nazianzus 379
Gregory of Nyssa 379
Gregory of Rimini 380
Gregory the Great 381
Grenz, Stanley J. 381
Grotius, Hugo 382
Guilt and forgiveness 383
Gunton, Colin Ewart 385
Gutiérrez, Gustavo 386

Hallesby, Ole 387
Harnack, Adolf 387
Hauerwas, Stanley 388
Healing 389
Hegel, Georg Wilhelm Friedrich 391
Heidegger, Martin 392
Heidelberg Catechism 393
Heim, Karl 394
Hellenization of Christianity 395
Henry, Carl F. H. 395
Herbert of Cherbury 396
Heresy 396
Hermeneutics 398
Herrmann, Wilhelm 403
Hesychasm 403
Hick, John Harwood 404
Hidden and revealed God 405
Higher-life theology 406
Hilary of Poitiers 407
Hildegard of Bingen 408
Hindusim and Christianity 408
Hippolytus 410
Historical Jesus, quest for 411
Historical theology 413
History 414
History-of-Religions School 415
Hodge, Charles 416
Holiness movements 417
Holl, Karl 419
Holocaust 419
Holy Spirit 421
Hooker, Richard 425
Hope 426

Hope, theology of 427
Hubmaier, Balthasar 428
Hügel, Friedrich von 429
Humanism (modern) 429
Humanism (Renaissance) 430
Hume, David 431
Hus, John 432
Hyper-Calvinism 432
Hypostasis 433

Iconoclastic controversies 434
Idealism 435
Ideology 435
Idolatry 436
Ignatius of Loyola 437
Image of God 438
Images 440
Imagination in theology 441
Imitation of Christ 443
Immortality 444
Impassibility of God and human suffering 445
Incarnation 448
Indian Christian theology 450
Infallibility and inerrancy of the Bible 453
Intermediate state 455
Irenaeus 456
Irving, Edward 458
Islam and Christianity 459

James, William 462
Jansenism 462
Japanese theology 464
Jenson, Robert W. 465
Jerome 465
Jesuit theology 466
Jesus 467
Jewel, John 471
Jewish-Christian relations 471
Joachimism 472
John of Damascus 473
Joy 474
Judaism and Christianity 475
Judgment of God 477
Julian of Norwich 479
Jüngel, Eberhard 479
Justification 480
Justin Martyr 483

Kähler, Martin 484
Kant, Immanuel 484
Karlstadt, Andreas Bodenstein von 486
Käsemann, Ernst 486

Keble, John 487
Kenoticism 487
Kerygma, kerygmatic theology 488
Kierkegaard, Søren Aabye 489
Kingdom of God 490
Knowledge of God 493
Knox, John 496
Koinonia 497
Korean theology 497
Kraemer, Hendrik 497
Küng, Hans 498
Kuyper, Abraham 499

LaCugna, Catherine Mowry 500
Laity 500
Lateran Councils 501
Latitudinarianism 502
Lausanne Covenant 503
Law 504
Law and gospel 506
Law, William 508
Laying on of hands 508
Leibniz, Gottfried von 509
Leiden Synopsis 509
Leo the Great 510
Lessing, Gotthold Ephraim 511
Levinas, Emmanuel 511
Lewis, Clive Staples 512
Liberal evangelicalism 513
Liberal theology 514
Liberalism, German 516
Liberation theology 518
Limbus 522
Lindbeck, George 523
Liturgical theology 524
Liturgy 524
Lloyd-Jones, David Martyn 526
Locke, John 526
Logical positivism 528
Logic in theology 527
Logos 529
Lombard, Peter 530
Lonergan, Bernard 531
Lossky, Vladimir 532
Love 533
Love of God 535
Lull, Raymond 536
Luther, Martin 537
Lutheranism and Lutheran theology 540

Macarius (Pseudo-) 543
MacDonald, George 543

Index of articles

Machen, John Gresham 544
MacIntyre, Alasdair Chambers 544
MacKay, Donald M. 545
MacKinnon, Donald M. 546
Mackintosh, Hugh Ross 546
Macquarrie, John 547
Mahan, Asa 547
Manichaeism 548
Marcel, Gabriel 549
Marcellus of Ancyra 549
Marcion 550
Marion, Jean-Luc 551
Maritain, Jacques 551
Martyrdom 551
Marxism and Christianity 552
Mary 554
Materialism 556
Mather, Cotton 557
Mather, Increase 557
Mediation 558
Melanchthon, Philipp 559
Mennonite theology 560
Mercersburg Theology 561
Merit 562
Merton, Thomas 563
Metaphysics 563
Metempsychosis 565
Methodism 565
Metz, Johannes Baptist 569
Meyendorff, John 569
Míguez Bonino, José 570
Milbank, John 570
Millennium 571
Ministry 573
Miracle 578
Missiology 579
Moberly, Robert Campbell 582
Models 582
Modernism (Catholic) 583
Modernism (English) 585
Modernity 585
Möhler, Johann Adam 586
Moltmann, Jürgen 586
Monarchianism 588
Monastic theology 589
Monism 591
Monophysitism 591
Monotheism 592
Montanism 593
Moral Rearmament 594
Moral theology 595
Moravian theology 596
Müntzer, Thomas 597
Murray, Andrew 597

Murray, John 598
Musculus, Wolfgang 598
Mystical theology 599
Myth 600

Narrative theology 602
Natural theology 603
Nature, theology of 606
Neo-orthodoxy 608
Nestorius 609
New Age 610
New England theology 611
New Haven theology 612
New religions 613
Newbigin, James Edward Lesslie 615
Newman, John Henry 616
Newton, Isaac 618
Nicaea, Council of 618
Nicholas of Lyra 619
Niebuhr, H. Richard 620
Niebuhr, Reinhold 621
Nietzsche, Friedrich 621
Nominalism 622
Non-realism 624
Novatian 624
Nygren, Anders 624

O'Donovan, Oliver 625
Obedience of Christ 625
Ochino, Bernardino 626
Oden, Thomas Clark 627
Oecolampadius, John 627
Offices of Christ 628
Oldham, Joseph Houldsworth 630
Olevianus, Caspar 630
Oman, John Wood 631
Ontology 631
Open theism/openness theology 632
Ordo salutis 633
Oriental Orthodox theology 634
Origen 635
Orr, James 637
Orthodoxy/Scholasticism, Lutheran 637
Orthodoxy/Scholasticism, Reformed 639
Osiander, Andreas 640
Otto, Rudolf 641
Owen, John 642

Pacifism/peace 643
Packer, James Innell 644

Palamas, Gregory 645
Paley, William 645
Palmer, Phoebe Worrall 646
Panentheism 647
Pannenberg, Wolfhart 647
Pantheism 649
Papacy 650
Paradigm 652
Paradox in theology 653
Pascal, Blaise 654
Paschasius Radbertus 655
Patristic theology 655
Pelagianism 657
Pelikan, Jaroslav 658
Penance 659
Pentecostal theology 660
Perfection, perfectionism 664
Perkins, William 665
Perseverance 666
Personalism 667
Phenomenology 667
Philo 669
Philosophical theology 670
Philosophy and theology 671
Philosophy of religion 673
Pietism 676
Pinnock, Clark 677
Placher, William 678
Plantinga, Alvin 678
Platonism 679
Platonism, Christian 681
Polanyi, Michael 682
Polemics 683
Political theology 683
Polkinghorne, John 686
Polytheism 686
Positivism 687
Postliberalism 687
Postmodern theology 688
Postmodernism 691
Poverty and wealth 693
Power 695
Praxis and orthopraxis 696
Prayer, theology of 697
Preaching, theology of 698
Predestination 700
Presbyterianism 702
Priesthood of all believers 704
Princeton theology 705
Priscillianism 706
Process theology 707
Progress, idea of 709
Prosperity theology 710
Protestantism 711
Providence 714

Index of articles

Pseudo-Dionysius the Areopagite 715
Punishment 717
Purgatory 718
Puritan theology 719

Quaker theology 722
Queer theology 723
Quietism 724

Rabbinic theology 724
Race 725
Radical Orthodoxy 726
Rahner, Karl 727
Ramm, Bernard 728
Ramsey, Ian Thomas 729
Ramus, Petrus 729
Rationalism 730
Ratramnus 732
Ratzinger, Joseph 732
Rauschenbusch, Walter 733
Raven, C. E. 733
Realism 734
Rebaptism 735
Redemption 736
Reformation theology 737
Reformation, Catholic Counter- 741
Reformation, Radical 744
Reformed epistemology 746
Reformed theology 747
Reformers, English 750
Reformers, Scottish 752
Regeneration 752
Relativism 754
Religion 754
Religions, theology of 756
Religious experience 759
Religious language 762
Repentance 764
Resurrection of Christ 765
Resurrection, general 769
Revelation 770
Revival, theology of 774
Revolution, theology of 775
Richardson, Alan 777
Ricœur, Paul 777
Righteousness 778
Rights, human 780
Ritschl, Albrecht 781
Robinson, John Arthur Thomas 782
Roman Catholic theology 783
Romanticism 785
Rousseau, Jean-Jacques 787

Ruether, Rosemary Radford 787
Russian Orthodox theology 788
Rutherford, Samuel 794

Sabbath 795
Sacrament 796
Sacrifice 798
Saint 800
Salvation 800
Salvation Army 802
Salvation-history 803
Samosata, Paul of 804
Sanctification 804
Satisfaction 808
Schaeffer, Francis August 809
Schillebeeckx, Edward 809
Schism 810
Schlatter, Adolf 810
Schleiermacher, Friedrich Daniel Ernst 811
Schleitheim Confession 813
Schmemann, Alexander 814
Scholasticism 814
Schweitzer, Albert 816
Schwenckfeld, Caspar 817
Science and theology 818
Scots Confession 821
Scripture 821
Scripture and tradition 825
Scripture, doctrine of 827
Sea of Faith Movement 829
Sects 829
Secular Christianity 830
Secularization 831
Semi-Pelagianism 833
Seventh-Day Adventism 834
Sexuality 835
Shintoism and Christianity 838
Sibbes, Richard 839
Simons, Menno 840
Simplicity, divine 840
Sin 841
Sinlessness of Christ 843
Slavery 844
Sobornost 847
Sobrino, Jon 847
Social ethics 848
Social Gospel 849
Society, theology of 850
Socinus and Socinianism 852
Sociology of religion 853
Soelle, Dorothee 854
Sonship 855

Soul, origin of 856
Southern Baptist theology 857
Sovereignty of God 858
Spinoza, Benedict (Baruch) de 860
Spirituality 861
Spurgeon, Charles Haddon 864
Staniloae, Dumitru 864
State 865
Stewardship 869
Stoddard, Solomon 870
Stoicism 870
Strauss, David Friedrich 871
Strong, Augustus Hopkins 872
Structuralism 873
Substance 874
Substitution and representation 875
Substitution, penal 876
Suffering 876
Supernatural 879
Supersessionism 879
Symbol 880
Symeon the New Theologian 881
Syncretism 882
Syriac Christian theology 882
Syrian Christianity 883
Systematic theology 885
Systematic theology, history of 886

Taoism and Christianity 889
Taylor, Jeremy 890
Teilhard de Chardin, Pierre 890
Temple, William 891
Temptation 892
Teresa of Avila 893
Tertullian 894
Theism 896
Theocracy 896
Theodicy 897
Theological exegesis 900
Theological method 901
Theology 903
Thielicke, Helmut 904
Thirty-Nine Articles 905
Thomas Aquinas 906
Thomism and Neo-Thomism 907
Thornwell, James Henley 909
Thurneysen, Eduard 910
Tillich, Paul 910
Time and eternity 912
Toleration 913

1015

Index of articles

Tolstoy, Leo 914
Torrance, Thomas Forsyth 914
Tracy, David 917
Tragedy 918
Transfiguration 919
Trent, Council of 920
Trinity 921
Tritheism 924
Troeltsch, Ernst 925
Truth 925
Tübingen School 927
Turretin, Francis 928

Underhill, Evelyn 929
Union with Christ 929
Uniqueness of Christ 932
Unitarianism 933
Universalism 935
Ursinus, Zacharias 937

Valdés, Juan de 937
Van Mastricht, Peter 937
Van Til, Cornelius 938
Vatican Councils 939
Verification and falsification 940
Vermigli, Peter Martyr 941
Victorines 943

Victorinus (Afer), Caius Marius 943
Virgin birth 943
Vision of God 945
Vocation 946
Voetius, Gisbertus 947
Voltaire 948
Voluntarism 949
Vos, Geerhardus 949

Waldensians 949
Warfield, Benjamin Breckinridge 950
Weber, Max 952
Wesley, Charles 952
Wesley, John 953
Wesleyan quadrilateral 955
Westcott, Brooke Foss 956
Westminster Confession and Standards 956
Wheaton Declaration 957
Whitefield, George 958
Wiesel, Elie 958
Will 959
William of Ockham 961
Williams, Charles Walter Stansby 962
Williams, Roger 962

Williams, Rowan 963
Wingren, Gustaf 964
Wisdom in early Christology 964
Wisløff, Carl Fredrik 965
Witherspoon, John 965
Wittgenstein, Ludwig Josef Johann 966
Wollebius, Johannes 967
Womanist theology 968
Work 969
World Council of Churches 971
Worship 973
Wrath of God 975
Wright, N. T. 976
Wyclif, John 977

Yale School 978
Yoder, John Howard 978

Zion 979
Zionism 981
Zizioulas, John D. 982
Zoroastrianism and Christianity 983
Zwingli, Huldrych 984